Education Statistics
of the United States
First Edition, 1999

Education

Statistics
of the United States

First Edition, 1999

Edited by Mark S. Littman and Deirdre A. Gaquin

Bernan Press
Washington, DC

ISBN: 0-89059-066-4

ISSN: 1524-394X

Book design and composition by Northeastern Graphic Services, Inc., Hackensack, NJ, and Automated Graphic Systems, Inc., White Plains, MD.

Printed in the United States of America on acid-free paper that meets the American National Standards Institute Z39-48 standard.

2000 1999   4 3 2 1

Bernan Press
1130 Connecticut Avenue, NW
Suite 675
Washington, DC 20036
email: info@bernan.com

Contents

Figures and Tables

PART B—EDUCATIONAL ATTAINMENT
Figures

Tables

Educational Attainment and Background or Family Characteristics

Educational Attainment, Employment, and Income

PART D—STATE- and COUNTY-LEVEL EDUCATION STATISTICS
Figures

Tables

Preface

Education Statistics is a new entry in the Bernan Press U.S. DataBook Series. This publication brings together education-related data from several sources, including the U.S. Bureau of the Census (Census) and the National Center for Education Statistics (NCES). The data presented in Parts A (school enrollment) and B (educational attainment) are no longer available in print form from Census. The data in Part D (school enrollment and financial data by county) have been tabulated for the first time here from computer files of the NCES.

Part A of this publication consists of the most recently available national school enrollment data from the U.S. Bureau of the Census, which relate to enrollment as of October 1996. Also included here are historical tables on school enrollment covering the entire half-century period from 1947 to 1996, when available.

Part B of this publication consists of national-level data on educational attainment, gauged by the highest grade of school completed and degrees received, from the March 1997 Current Population Survey.

Part C of this publication consists of a variety of state-level tables that can be compared with the other parts of this book. The tables were gleaned largely from the National Center for Education Statistics' *Digest of Education Statistics 1997*. However, some tables have been updated where more recent information has become available (e.g., private school enrollment figures presented here are more recent than those shown in the 1997 *Digest*).

Part D of this volume contains current education data tabulated for each county (or county equivalent) in the United States from the Common Core of Data (CCD) file for 1995–1996 collected by the National Center for Edu-

cation Statistics. There are over 14,700 regular public elementary and secondary school districts in the United States, with considerable variation in number and size among states. Most state local education agency boundaries are not coterminous with county boundaries. In fact, in only a handful of states are school districts coextensive with county boundaries. We have aggregated these education statistics for those users who are interested in education statistics at the county level. Data items presented include total enrollment, minority enrollment, number of schools by level, number of teachers, number of dropouts, percentage of students who are eligible for free lunches, and several indicators of school revenue and expenditures. We have appended certain geographic codes to these data (Federal Information Processing Standards (FIPS) and Beale codes) so users may more readily relate these data to their own data sets.

Sources and definitions important to each group of tables follow immediately after the last table in each part of this publication. Thus, sources and definitions of school enrollment topics from the October 1996 Current Population Survey (CPS) are provided after Part A, those from educational attainment topics from the March 1997 CPS are provided after Part B, and so on for NCES and Common Core of Data topics (Parts C and D).

Special thanks go to George Hall for his editorial direction, and to Mary Reynolds and Carletta Cutchember for their formatting work on the data tables. Also, thanks to Ben Shupe for his work on the figures, to the production staff at Bernan Press, and to statisticians at the U.S. Bureau of the Census and the National Center for Education Statistics for collecting much of the data contained in this book.

The school enrollment tables that follow include preprimary through college enrollment for the population 3 years old and over and are cross-classified by such characteristics as age, race/ethnicity and gender of student, whether enrolled in public or private school, and full- or part-time enrollment for college students, as well as family background characteristics such as labor force status of the mother, family income, educational attainment of the householder, and metropolitan/nonmetropolitan residence.

Not only are enrollment rates for usual school attendance ages high in the United States relative to those of much of the world's population, but enrollment rates are also higher at younger and older ages than has historically been the case in this country. This situation has been fueled by large preprimary enrollment for 3 and 4 year olds, by adults returning to college, and by proportionately larger numbers of women enrolling in college.

Over 70 million persons, representing more than one-fourth of the total population of the United States, were enrolled in "regular" schools in October 1996.[1] Not only does the country's student body include nearly half of the three and four year olds in the nation, but it also contains 5 percent of the population in their 30s and early 40s.

Enrollment in the prime school ages between 7 and 15 years old was nearly universal 50 years ago in the United States and has remained so, with over 99 percent of persons in these age groups enrolled in 1996. The largest proportionate enrollment increases have been at younger and older ages. Nearly five times the proportion of 3 and 4 year olds were enrolled in 1996 as in 1964 (the earliest year for which such data are available), and enrollment rates for 5 and 6 year olds have increased from 58 percent in1950 to 94 percent in 1996. In 1950, only about 29 percent of 18 and

---

[1]Enrollment in regular schools, according to the U.S. Census Bureau definition, is that which advances a person toward an elementary or high school diploma or college or professional degree. Included is enrollment in preprimary and kindergarten. Excluded is enrollment in schools outside the regular school system, including trade schools, business schools, and such schools as those for the mentally handicapped that do not advance students toward a "regular school degree."

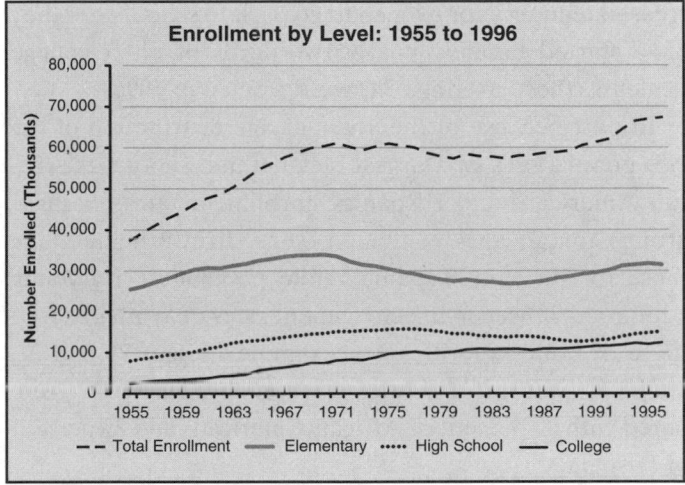

Source: U.S. Bureau of the Census.

19 year olds were enrolled in school—half of the comparable figure for 1996.

Below what have been traditional college attendance ages (in the 18- to 24-year-old range), males and females in the United States have had comparable enrollment rates for at least the past 50 years. This is not the custom in many countries, where enrollment rates for men far outstrip those for women. However, men in the United States have

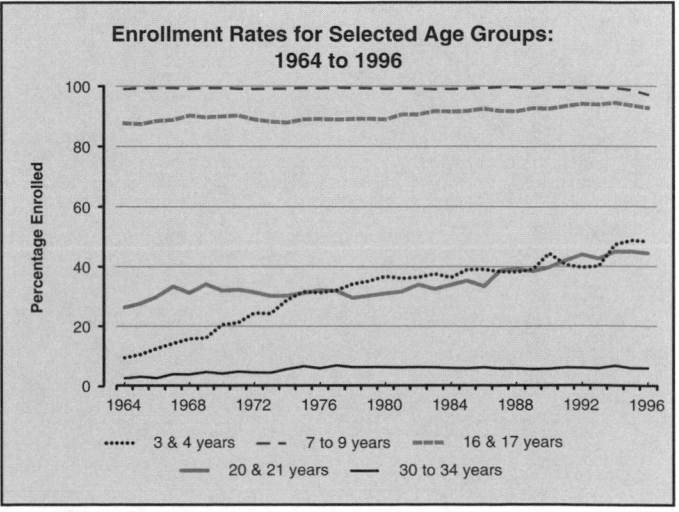

Source: U.S. Bureau of the Census.

historically had considerably higher enrollment rates at college ages than have women. For example, as late as 1960, nearly half of 18- and 19-year-old men were enrolled compared to about 30 percent of women. By 1996, however, women had caught up with men and were enrolled at higher rates than men in some older age groups. As a result of larger proportions of women being enrolled and an increased tendency for women to go back to school after they have started families, nearly two-thirds of older college students (those over age 34) were women in 1996.

In part because of the younger age distribution of the U.S. population's two largest racial/ethnic minorities, African Americans and Hispanics, enrollment rates for these groups for all ages combined were slightly higher than those for the non-Hispanic White population. By young adulthood, however, the enrollment rates of Whites exceed those of both minorities. For example, at ages 20 and 21, about 45 percent of Whites were enrolled in 1996, compared with 37 percent of African Americans and 25 percent of Hispanics.

Although a free public education in the United States through the 12th grade is universally available, some persons choose to send their elementary- and secondary-age children to private schools, either for religious training not offered in the public system or because they feel private education broadens the life chances of their children in some other way. About 11 percent of elementary school students and 8 percent of high school students attended private schools in 1996. At the college level, about 21 percent of enrollment was in private institutions, with more than one-third of enrollment in graduate programs at private universities. While college attendance in public settings is not free, enrollment in private colleges can be considerably more expensive than in public institutions: In the 1996–97 school year, annual tuition averaged about $3,000 at public 4-year colleges but nearly $13,000 at private colleges (see table C–59).

Approximately one of four persons enrolled in higher education in the United States in 1995 was classified as belonging to a minority.[2] This proportion has increased a few percentage points during the late 1990s. The largest fraction were African Americans (about 42 percent of total minority enrollment), followed by Hispanics, who represented about 31 percent of minority enrollment.

---

[2]Includes non-Hispanic Blacks, Hispanics, Asian and Pacific Islanders and American Indians/Alaskan Natives.

Table A-1. Enrollment Status of the Population 3 Years Old and Over, by Age, Sex, Race, Hispanic Origin, and Selected Educational Characteristics: October 1996

(Numbers in thousands. Civilian noninstitutional population.)

Age, sex, race and Hispanic origin	Population	Enrolled in school						Not enrolled in school					
		Total		Below college level[1]		In college		Total		High school graduate		Not high school graduate	
		Number	Percent	Number	Percent	Number	Percent	Number	Percent	Number	Percent	Number	Percent
ALL RACES													
Both sexes, 3 years old and over ...	253 175	70 297	27.8	55 070	21.8	15 226	6.0	182 879	72.2	144 450	57.1	38 428	15.2
3 to 34 years old	124 447	67 317	54.1	54 869	44.1	12 448	10.0	57 129	45.9	43 230	34.7	13 899	11.2
3 and 4 years old	8 193	3 959	48.3	3 959	48.3	—	—	4 234	51.7	—	—	4 234	51.7
5 and 6 years old	8 393	7 893	94.0	7 893	94.0	—	—	501	6.0	—	—	501	6.0
7 to 9 years old	11 905	11 577	97.2	11 577	97.2	—	—	329	2.8	—	—	329	2.8
10 to 13 years old	15 661	15 359	98.1	15 359	98.1	—	—	302	1.9	—	—	302	1.9
14 and 15 years old	7 750	7 598	98.0	7 586	97.9	13	0.2	152	2.0	—	—	152	2.0
16 and 17 years old	7 782	7 220	92.8	6 996	89.9	224	2.9	561	7.2	97	1.3	464	6.0
18 and 19 years old	7 376	4 539	61.5	1 229	16.7	3 309	44.9	2 837	38.5	1 897	25.7	940	12.8
20 and 21 years old	6 800	3 017	44.4	110	1.6	2 907	42.8	3 783	55.6	2 883	42.4	901	13.2
22 to 24 years old	10 495	2 605	24.8	54	0.5	2 551	24.3	7 890	75.2	6 584	62.7	1 306	12.4
25 to 29 years old	18 982	2 265	11.9	49	0.3	2 215	11.7	16 717	88.1	14 483	76.3	2 234	11.8
30 to 34 years old	21 111	1 286	6.1	58	0.3	1 228	5.8	19 824	93.9	17 287	81.9	2 538	12.0
35 years old and over	128 729	2 979	2.3	201	0.2	2 778	2.2	125 749	97.7	101 220	78.6	24 529	19.1
35 to 44 years old	43 281	1 935	4.5	125	0.3	1 810	4.2	41 346	95.5	36 462	84.3	4 883	11.3
45 to 54 years old	32 554	790	2.4	46	0.1	744	2.3	31 764	97.6	27 658	85.0	4 106	12.6
55 years old and over	52 894	254	0.5	29	0.1	225	0.4	52 639	99.5	37 099	70.1	15 540	29.4
Male, 3 years old and over	123 103	35 092	28.5	28 272	23.0	6 820	5.5	88 011	71.5	69 591	56.5	18 419	15.0
3 to 34 years old	62 510	33 993	54.4	28 186	45.1	5 807	9.3	28 517	45.6	21 302	34.1	7 215	11.5
3 and 4 years old	4 182	1 961	46.9	1 961	46.9	—	—	2 221	53.1	—	—	2 221	53.1
5 and 6 years old	4 320	4 052	93.8	4 052	93.8	—	—	268	6.2	—	—	268	6.2
7 to 9 years old	6 098	5 928	97.2	5 928	97.2	—	—	170	2.8	—	—	170	2.8
10 to 13 years old	7 957	7 794	98.0	7 794	98.0	—	—	163	2.0	—	—	163	2.0
14 and 15 years old	3 989	3 931	98.5	3 926	98.4	5	0.1	59	1.5	—	—	59	1.5
16 and 17 years old	4 012	3 738	93.2	3 645	90.9	92	2.3	274	6.8	48	1.2	227	5.7
18 and 19 years old	3 711	2 258	60.8	769	20.7	1 489	40.1	1 453	39.2	965	26.0	488	13.1
20 and 21 years old	3 268	1 436	43.9	56	1.7	1 379	42.2	1 832	56.1	1 374	42.1	458	14.0
22 to 24 years old	5 306	1 335	25.2	16	0.3	1 319	24.9	3 971	74.8	3 289	62.0	682	12.9
25 to 29 years old	9 295	1 058	11.4	20	0.2	1 038	11.2	8 237	88.6	7 095	76.3	1 141	12.3
30 to 34 years old	10 372	504	4.9	19	0.2	485	4.7	9 868	95.1	8 530	82.2	1 338	12.9
35 years old and over	60 593	1 099	1.8	85	0.1	1 013	1.7	59 494	98.2	48 290	79.7	11 205	18.5
35 to 44 years old	21 320	794	3.7	64	0.3	730	3.4	20 527	96.3	17 965	84.3	2 561	12.0
45 to 54 years old	15 852	235	1.5	15	0.1	219	1.4	15 617	98.5	13 667	86.2	1 951	12.3
55 years old and over	23 420	70	0.3	6	—	65	0.3	23 350	99.7	16 658	71.1	6 693	28.6
Female, 3 years old and over	130 073	35 205	27.1	26 799	20.6	8 406	6.5	94 868	72.9	74 859	57.6	20 009	15.4
3 to 34 years old	61 937	33 324	53.8	26 683	43.1	6 641	10.7	28 613	46.2	21 928	35.4	6 684	10.8
3 and 4 years old	4 011	1 998	49.8	1 998	49.8	—	—	2 012	50.2	—	—	2 012	50.2
5 and 6 years old	4 073	3 841	94.3	3 841	94.3	—	—	232	5.7	—	—	232	5.7
7 to 9 years old	5 807	5 649	97.3	5 649	97.3	—	—	158	2.7	—	—	158	2.7
10 to 13 years old	7 704	7 565	98.2	7 565	98.2	—	—	139	1.8	—	—	139	1.8
14 and 15 years old	3 761	3 668	97.5	3 660	97.3	8	0.2	93	2.5	—	—	93	2.5
16 and 17 years old	3 769	3 483	92.4	3 351	88.9	132	3.5	287	7.6	50	1.3	237	6.3
18 and 19 years old	3 665	2 281	62.2	460	12.6	1 821	49.7	1 384	37.8	932	25.4	452	12.3
20 and 21 years old	3 532	1 581	44.8	53	1.5	1 528	43.3	1 951	55.3	1 508	42.7	443	12.5
22 to 24 years old	5 189	1 270	24.5	38	0.7	1 233	23.8	3 919	75.5	3 295	63.5	624	12.0
25 to 29 years old	9 687	1 207	12.5	30	0.3	1 177	12.2	8 480	87.5	7 387	76.3	1 093	11.3
30 to 34 years old	10 738	782	7.3	39	0.4	743	6.9	9 956	92.7	8 757	81.6	1 200	11.2
35 years old and over	68 136	1 881	2.8	116	0.2	1 765	2.6	66 255	97.2	52 930	77.7	13 325	19.6
35 to 44 years old	21 960	1 141	5.2	61	0.3	1 080	4.9	20 819	94.8	18 497	84.2	2 322	10.6
45 to 54 years old	16 702	555	3.3	30	0.2	525	3.1	16 147	96.7	13 992	83.8	2 155	12.9
55 years old and over	29 473	184	0.6	24	0.1	160	0.5	29 289	99.4	20 442	69.4	8 847	30.0

See footnotes at end of table.

Table A-1. Enrollment Status of the Population 3 Years Old and Over, by Age, Sex, Race, Hispanic Origin, and Selected Educational Characteristics: October 1996 — Continued

(Numbers in thousands. Civilian noninstitutional population.)

Age, sex, race and Hispanic origin	Population	Enrolled in school						Not enrolled in school					
		Total		Below college level[1]		In college		Total		High school graduate		Not high school graduate	
		Number	Percent	Number	Percent	Number	Percent	Number	Percent	Number	Percent	Number	Percent
WHITE													
Both sexes, 3 years old and over ...	209 507	55 378	26.4	43 190	20.6	12 189	5.8	154 129	73.6	123 402	58.9	30 727	14.7
3 to 34 years old	99 199	52 987	53.4	43 052	43.4	9 934	10.0	46 212	46.6	35 144	35.4	11 069	11.2
3 and 4 years old	6 374	3 052	47.9	3 052	47.9	—	—	3 322	52.1	—	—	3 322	52.1
5 and 6 years old	6 558	6 215	94.8	6 215	94.8	—	—	342	5.2	—	—	342	5.2
7 to 9 years old	9 309	9 042	97.1	9 042	97.1	—	—	267	2.9	—	—	267	2.9
10 to 13 years old	12 359	12 133	98.2	12 133	98.2	—	—	226	1.8	—	—	226	1.8
14 and 15 years old	6 120	5 997	98.0	5 986	97.8	11	0.2	124	2.0	—	—	124	2.0
16 and 17 years old	6 118	5 680	92.8	5 524	90.3	156	2.6	438	7.2	70	1.1	369	6.0
18 and 19 years old	5 833	3 645	62.5	914	15.7	2 731	46.8	2 187	37.5	1 453	24.9	735	12.6
20 and 21 years old	5 410	2 428	44.9	66	1.2	2 362	43.7	2 982	55.1	2 307	42.6	676	12.5
22 to 24 years old	8 433	2 070	24.6	40	0.5	2 030	24.1	6 363	75.5	5 316	63.0	1 047	12.4
25 to 29 years old	15 436	1 741	11.3	38	0.2	1 704	11.0	13 695	88.7	11 849	76.8	1 846	12.0
30 to 34 years old	17 249	984	5.7	44	0.3	940	5.5	16 266	94.3	14 150	82.0	2 116	12.3
35 years old and over	110 308	2 392	2.2	138	0.1	2 254	2.0	107 917	97.8	88 258	80.0	19 658	17.8
35 to 44 years old	35 960	1 515	4.2	83	0.2	1 433	4.0	34 445	95.8	30 684	85.3	3 761	10.5
45 to 54 years old	27 701	668	2.4	38	0.1	631	2.3	27 032	97.6	23 912	86.3	3 120	11.3
55 years old and over	46 648	208	0.5	17	—	191	0.4	46 440	99.6	33 663	72.2	12 777	27.4
Male, 3 years old and over	102 625	27 663	27.0	22 210	21.6	5 453	5.3	74 962	73.0	60 053	58.5	14 909	14.5
3 to 34 years old	50 238	26 791	53.3	22 149	44.1	4 642	9.2	23 447	46.7	17 622	35.1	5 825	11.6
3 and 4 years old	3 268	1 519	46.5	1 519	46.5	—	—	1 749	53.5	—	—	1 749	53.5
5 and 6 years old	3 362	3 179	94.6	3 179	94.6	—	—	182	5.4	—	—	182	5.4
7 to 9 years old	4 775	4 627	96.9	4 627	96.9	—	—	147	3.1	—	—	147	3.1
10 to 13 years old	6 339	6 214	98.0	6 214	98.0	—	—	126	2.0	—	—	126	2.0
14 and 15 years old	3 139	3 096	98.6	3 091	98.5	5	0.2	43	1.4	—	—	43	1.4
16 and 17 years old	3 146	2 926	93.0	2 861	91.0	65	2.1	220	7.0	34	1.1	186	5.9
18 and 19 years old	2 953	1 799	60.9	576	19.5	1 223	41.4	1 155	39.1	773	26.2	382	12.9
20 and 21 years old	2 638	1 149	43.6	33	1.2	1 117	42.3	1 489	56.4	1 139	43.2	350	13.3
22 to 24 years old	4 306	1 095	25.4	16	0.4	1 079	25.1	3 211	74.6	2 669	62.0	543	12.6
25 to 29 years old	7 691	814	10.6	17	0.2	797	10.4	6 877	89.4	5 887	76.5	990	12.9
30 to 34 years old	8 620	372	4.3	15	0.2	357	4.1	8 248	95.7	7 121	82.6	1 127	13.1
35 years old and over	52 387	872	1.7	61	0.1	811	1.6	51 515	98.3	42 431	81.0	9 084	17.3
35 to 44 years old	17 945	612	3.4	43	0.2	568	3.2	17 333	96.6	15 329	85.4	2 004	11.2
45 to 54 years old	13 667	197	1.4	12	0.1	185	1.4	13 470	98.6	11 977	87.6	1 493	10.9
55 years old and over	20 775	63	0.3	6	—	58	0.3	20 712	99.7	15 125	72.8	5 587	26.9
Female, 3 years old and over	106 883	27 716	25.9	20 980	19.6	6 735	6.3	79 167	74.1	63 349	59.3	15 818	14.8
3 to 34 years old	48 961	26 196	53.5	20 904	42.7	5 292	10.8	22 765	46.5	17 522	35.8	5 244	10.7
3 and 4 years old	3 105	1 532	49.3	1 532	49.3	—	—	1 573	50.7	—	—	1 573	50.7
5 and 6 years old	3 196	3 036	95.0	3 036	95.0	—	—	160	5.0	—	—	160	5.0
7 to 9 years old	4 534	4 415	97.4	4 415	97.4	—	—	120	2.6	—	—	120	2.6
10 to 13 years old	6 020	5 919	98.3	5 919	98.3	—	—	100	1.7	—	—	100	1.7
14 and 15 years old	2 981	2 901	97.3	2 894	97.1	6	0.2	80	2.7	—	—	80	2.7
16 and 17 years old	2 972	2 754	92.7	2 662	89.6	91	3.1	218	7.4	36	1.2	183	6.2
18 and 19 years old	2 879	1 847	64.1	338	11.8	1 508	52.4	1 033	35.9	680	23.6	353	12.3
20 and 21 years old	2 772	1 279	46.1	33	1.2	1 246	44.9	1 494	53.9	1 168	42.1	325	11.7
22 to 24 years old	4 127	975	23.6	24	0.6	951	23.1	3 151	76.4	2 647	64.2	504	12.2
25 to 29 years old	7 745	927	12.0	21	0.3	906	11.7	6 818	88.0	5 962	77.0	856	11.1
30 to 34 years old	8 629	611	7.1	28	0.3	583	6.8	8 018	92.9	7 029	81.5	989	11.5
35 years old and over	57 921	1 520	2.6	77	0.1	1 443	2.5	56 402	97.4	45 827	79.1	10 575	18.3
35 to 44 years old	18 015	903	5.0	39	0.2	864	4.8	17 112	95.0	15 354	85.2	1 757	9.8
45 to 54 years old	14 034	471	3.4	26	0.2	446	3.2	13 562	96.6	11 935	85.1	1 627	11.6
55 years old and over	25 873	145	0.6	11	—	133	0.5	25 728	99.4	18 538	71.7	7 190	27.8

See footnotes at end of table.

Table A-1. Enrollment Status of the Population 3 Years Old and Over, by Age, Sex, Race, Hispanic Origin, and Selected Educational Characteristics: October 1996 — Continued

(Numbers in thousands. Civilian noninstitutional population.)

Age, sex, race and Hispanic origin	Population	Enrolled in school						Not enrolled in school					
		Total		Below college level[1]		In college		Total		High school graduate		Not high school graduate	
		Number	Percent	Number	Percent	Number	Percent	Number	Percent	Number	Percent	Number	Percent
BLACK													
Both sexes, 3 years old and over ...	32 121	10 851	33.8	8 950	27.9	1 901	5.9	21 271	66.2	15 179	47.3	6 091	19.0
3 to 34 years old	18 596	10 443	56.2	8 896	47.8	1 547	8.3	8 154	43.9	5 920	31.8	2 234	12.0
3 and 4 years old	1 377	687	49.9	687	49.9	—	—	690	50.1	—	—	690	50.1
5 and 6 years old	1 363	1 233	90.5	1 233	90.5	—	—	130	9.6	—	—	130	9.6
7 to 9 years old	1 946	1 895	97.4	1 895	97.4	—	—	50	2.6	—	—	50	2.6
10 to 13 years old	2 496	2 431	97.4	2 431	97.4	—	—	65	2.6	—	—	65	2.6
14 and 15 years old	1 211	1 197	98.9	1 196	98.7	2	0.2	14	1.2	—	—	14	1.2
16 and 17 years old	1 250	1 151	92.1	1 108	88.7	43	3.4	99	7.9	22	1.8	77	6.1
18 and 19 years old	1 161	613	52.8	268	23.1	345	29.7	548	47.2	373	32.1	175	15.1
20 and 21 years old	1 050	389	37.0	42	4.0	346	33.0	662	63.0	469	44.7	193	18.3
22 to 24 years old	1 426	300	21.0	8	0.6	292	20.5	1 126	79.0	913	64.0	213	14.9
25 to 29 years old	2 553	349	13.7	12	0.5	337	13.2	2 204	86.3	1 917	75.1	287	11.2
30 to 34 years old	2 762	197	7.1	14	0.5	182	6.6	2 566	92.9	2 226	80.6	340	12.3
35 years old and over	13 525	408	3.0	55	0.4	354	2.6	13 117	97.0	9 259	68.5	3 858	28.5
35 to 44 years old	5 327	289	5.4	37	0.7	253	4.7	5 037	94.6	4 193	78.7	844	15.8
45 to 54 years old	3 458	86	2.5	7	0.2	79	2.3	3 372	97.5	2 611	75.5	761	22.0
55 years old and over	4 740	32	0.7	10	0.2	22	0.5	4 708	99.3	2 455	51.8	2 253	47.5
Male, 3 years old and over	14 864	5 302	35.7	4 538	30.5	764	5.1	9 562	64.3	6 749	45.4	2 812	18.9
3 to 34 years old	8 927	5 159	57.8	4 514	50.6	644	7.2	3 768	42.2	2 684	30.1	1 084	12.1
3 and 4 years old	669	315	47.0	315	47.0	—	—	354	53.0	—	—	354	53.0
5 and 6 years old	708	638	90.1	638	90.1	—	—	70	9.9	—	—	70	9.9
7 to 9 years old	977	958	98.1	958	98.1	—	—	19	1.9	—	—	19	1.9
10 to 13 years old	1 254	1 218	97.2	1 218	97.2	—	—	35	2.8	—	—	35	2.8
14 and 15 years old	621	610	98.1	610	98.1	—	—	12	1.9	—	—	12	1.9
16 and 17 years old	636	596	93.7	579	91.0	17	2.7	40	6.3	9	1.4	31	4.9
18 and 19 years old	564	311	55.2	166	29.4	145	25.8	253	44.8	162	28.8	90	16.0
20 and 21 years old	2 895	178	6.1	16	0.6	162	5.6	2 718	93.9	2 311	79.8	407	14.1
22 to 24 years old	660	122	18.6	1	0.1	122	18.5	538	81.5	428	64.8	110	16.6
25 to 29 years old	1 129	145	12.8	3	0.3	142	12.6	984	87.2	884	78.3	100	8.9
30 to 34 years old	1 251	67	5.4	4	0.3	64	5.1	1 184	94.6	1 014	81.0	170	13.6
35 years old and over	5 937	143	2.4	23	0.4	120	2.0	5 793	97.6	4 065	68.5	1 728	29.1
35 to 44 years old	2 431	112	4.6	21	0.9	91	3.7	2 320	95.4	1 883	77.4	437	18.0
45 to 54 years old	1 557	27	1.7	3	0.2	25	1.6	1 530	98.3	1 166	74.9	364	23.4
55 years old and over	1 949	5	0.2	—	—	5	0.2	1 944	99.8	1 017	52.2	927	47.6
Female, 3 years old and over	17 258	5 549	32.2	4 413	25.6	1 136	6.6	11 709	67.9	8 430	48.9	3 279	19.0
3 to 34 years old	9 670	5 284	54.7	4 381	45.3	903	9.3	4 386	45.4	3 236	33.5	1 150	11.9
3 and 4 years old	709	373	52.6	373	52.6	—	—	336	47.4	—	—	336	47.4
5 and 6 years old	655	595	90.8	595	90.8	—	—	60	9.2	—	—	60	9.2
7 to 9 years old	969	937	96.7	937	96.7	—	—	32	3.3	—	—	32	3.3
10 to 13 years old	1 242	1 213	97.6	1 213	97.6	—	—	29	2.4	—	—	29	2.4
14 and 15 years old	590	588	99.6	586	99.3	2	0.3	2	0.4	—	—	2	0.4
16 and 17 years old	614	555	90.4	529	86.2	26	4.2	59	9.6	13	2.2	45	7.4
18 and 19 years old	597	302	50.5	103	17.2	199	33.4	296	49.5	211	35.3	85	14.2
20 and 21 years old	593	210	35.5	19	3.1	192	32.4	382	64.5	282	47.6	100	16.9
22 to 24 years old	766	178	23.2	8	1.0	170	22.2	588	76.8	485	63.3	103	13.5
25 to 29 years old	1 424	204	14.4	9	0.6	195	13.7	1 220	85.7	1 033	72.5	187	13.1
30 to 34 years old	1 511	129	8.6	11	0.7	119	7.9	1 382	91.4	1 212	80.2	170	11.2
35 years old and over	7 588	265	3.5	31	0.4	234	3.1	7 323	96.5	5 194	68.5	2 129	28.1
35 to 44 years old	2 895	178	6.1	16	0.6	162	5.6	2 718	93.9	2 311	79.8	407	14.1
45 to 54 years old	1 901	59	3.1	5	0.3	55	2.9	1 842	96.9	1 445	76.0	397	20.9
55 years old and over	2 791	28	1.0	10	0.4	17	0.6	2 764	99.0	1 438	51.5	1 326	47.5

See footnotes at end of table.

Table A-1.   Enrollment Status of the Population 3 Years Old and Over, by Age, Sex, Race, Hispanic Origin, and Selected Educational Characteristics: October 1996 — Continued

(Numbers in thousands. Civilian noninstitutional population.)

Age, sex, race and Hispanic origin	Population	Enrolled in school						Not enrolled in school					
		Total		Below college level[1]		In college		Total		High school graduate		Not high school graduate	
		Number	Percent	Number	Percent	Number	Percent	Number	Percent	Number	Percent	Number	Percent
HISPANIC ORIGIN[2]													
Both sexes, 3 years old and over	26 873	8 818	32.8	7 595	28.3	1 223	4.6	18 055	67.2	9 146	34.0	8 909	33.2
3 to 34 years old	17 050	8 570	50.3	7 531	44.2	1 039	6.1	8 481	49.7	4 174	24.5	4 307	25.3
3 and 4 years old	1 318	502	38.1	502	38.1	—	—	816	61.9	—	—	816	61.9
5 and 6 years old	1 328	1 188	89.5	1 188	89.5	—	—	140	10.6	—	—	140	10.6
7 to 9 years old	1 643	1 588	96.6	1 588	96.6	—	—	55	3.4	—	—	55	3.4
10 to 13 years old	2 173	2 122	97.6	2 122	97.6	—	—	51	2.4	—	—	51	2.4
14 and 15 years old	1 013	978	96.6	975	96.2	3	0.3	35	3.4	—	—	35	3.4
16 and 17 years old	971	862	88.7	842	86.7	19	2.0	110	11.3	5	0.5	105	10.8
18 and 19 years old	1 000	470	47.0	230	23.0	240	24.0	530	53.0	236	23.6	295	29.5
20 and 21 years old	965	244	25.3	31	3.2	213	22.1	721	74.7	350	36.3	370	38.4
22 to 24 years old	1 545	272	17.6	19	1.3	253	16.4	1 273	82.4	727	47.1	545	35.3
25 to 29 years old	2 524	217	8.6	19	0.8	198	7.8	2 307	91.4	1 406	55.7	901	35.7
30 to 34 years old	2 570	127	5.0	15	0.6	112	4.4	2 443	95.1	1 450	56.4	993	38.6
35 years old and over	9 823	248	2.5	64	0.7	184	1.9	9 574	97.5	4 972	50.6	4 602	46.9
35 to 44 years old	4 326	186	4.3	44	1.0	142	3.3	4 140	95.7	2 493	57.6	1 647	38.1
45 to 54 years old	2 337	43	1.9	12	0.5	31	1.3	2 294	98.2	1 265	54.1	1 029	44.0
55 years old and over	3 159	19	0.6	8	0.2	11	0.4	3 141	99.4	1 214	38.4	1 926	61.0
Male, 3 years old and over	13 462	4 437	33.0	3 908	29.0	529	3.9	9 025	67.0	4 707	35.0	4 318	32.1
3 to 34 years old	8 771	4 316	49.2	3 876	44.2	440	5.0	4 454	50.8	2 222	25.3	2 232	25.5
3 and 4 years old	637	252	39.6	252	39.6	—	—	385	60.5	—	—	385	60.5
5 and 6 years old	681	620	91.0	620	91.0	—	—	61	9.0	—	—	61	9.0
7 to 9 years old	823	785	95.4	785	95.4	—	—	38	4.6	—	—	38	4.6
10 to 13 years old	1 109	1 085	97.9	1 085	97.9	—	—	24	2.1	—	—	24	2.1
14 and 15 years old	522	511	98.0	508	97.4	3	0.6	10	2.0	—	—	10	2.0
16 and 17 years old	498	450	90.4	445	89.5	5	0.9	48	9.6	3	0.6	45	9.0
18 and 19 years old	506	237	46.8	139	27.5	98	19.3	269	53.2	115	22.7	154	30.5
20 and 21 years old	486	95	19.5	17	3.6	78	16.0	391	80.5	186	38.2	206	42.3
22 to 24 years old	823	133	16.2	9	1.1	124	15.1	690	83.8	393	47.8	297	36.1
25 to 29 years old	1 306	89	6.8	10	0.8	79	6.0	1 218	93.2	728	55.7	490	37.5
30 to 34 years old	1 379	59	4.3	6	0.4	54	3.9	1 320	95.7	797	57.8	523	37.9
35 years old and over	4 692	121	2.6	31	0.7	90	1.9	4 571	97.4	2 485	53.0	2 086	44.5
35 to 44 years old	2 159	102	4.7	21	1.0	80	3.7	2 057	95.3	1 253	58.1	804	37.2
45 to 54 years old	1 161	16	1.4	7	0.6	9	0.8	1 145	98.6	637	54.9	508	43.7
55 years old and over	1 372	3	0.2	3	0.2	—	—	1 369	99.8	595	43.3	774	56.5
Female, 3 years old and over	13 411	4 381	32.7	3 688	27.5	693	5.2	9 030	67.3	4 438	33.1	4 591	34.2
3 to 34 years old	8 280	4 254	51.4	3 655	44.1	599	7.2	4 026	48.6	1 951	23.6	2 075	25.1
3 and 4 years old	681	250	36.8	250	36.8	—	—	431	63.2	—	—	431	63.2
5 and 6 years old	647	568	87.8	568	87.8	—	—	79	12.2	—	—	79	12.2
7 to 9 years old	820	803	97.9	803	97.9	—	—	17	2.1	—	—	17	2.1
10 to 13 years old	1 064	1 036	97.4	1 036	97.4	—	—	28	2.6	—	—	28	2.6
14 and 15 years old	491	467	95.0	467	95.0	—	—	24	5.0	—	—	24	5.0
16 and 17 years old	474	411	86.9	397	83.7	15	3.1	62	13.2	2	0.4	60	12.7
18 and 19 years old	494	233	47.2	91	18.4	142	28.8	261	52.8	121	24.5	140	28.4
20 and 21 years old	479	149	31.1	13	2.8	136	28.4	330	68.9	165	34.4	165	34.5
22 to 24 years old	721	139	19.3	10	1.5	128	17.8	582	80.8	334	46.3	249	34.5
25 to 29 years old	1 218	128	10.5	9	0.8	119	9.8	1 089	89.5	677	55.6	412	33.8
30 to 34 years old	1 191	68	5.7	9	0.8	59	4.9	1 123	94.3	652	54.8	470	39.5
35 years old and over	5 131	127	2.5	33	0.6	95	1.8	5 004	97.5	2 487	48.5	2 517	49.1
35 to 44 years old	2 167	85	3.9	23	1.1	62	2.9	2 082	96.1	1 240	57.2	843	38.9
45 to 54 years old	1 176	27	2.3	5	0.5	22	1.8	1 149	97.7	628	53.4	522	44.4
55 years old and over	1 788	16	0.9	5	0.3	11	0.6	1 772	99.1	620	34.7	1 152	64.5

See footnotes at end of table.

Table A-1. Enrollment Status of the Population 3 Years Old and Over, by Age, Sex, Race, Hispanic Origin, and Selected Educational Characteristics: October 1996 — Continued

(Numbers in thousands. Civilian noninstitutional population.)

Age, sex, race and Hispanic origin	Population	Enrolled in school						Not enrolled in school					
		Total		Below college level[1]		In college		Total		High school graduate		Not high school graduate	
		Number	Percent	Number	Percent	Number	Percent	Number	Percent	Number	Percent	Number	Percent
MEXICAN ORIGIN[2]													
Both sexes, 3 years old and over	17 179	5 820	33.9	5 162	30.1	658	3.8	11 359	66.1	4 998	29.1	6 361	37.0
3 to 34 years old	11 490	5 691	49.5	5 119	44.6	572	5.0	5 799	50.5	2 486	21.6	3 313	28.8
3 and 4 years old	986	363	36.8	363	36.8	—	—	623	63.2	—	—	623	63.2
5 and 6 years old	970	863	89.0	863	89.0	—	—	107	11.0	—	—	107	11.0
7 to 9 years old	1 188	1 145	96.4	1 145	96.4	—	—	43	3.6	—	—	43	3.6
10 to 13 years old	1 436	1 400	97.5	1 400	97.5	—	—	36	2.5	—	—	36	2.5
14 and 15 years old	670	649	96.9	646	96.4	3	0.5	21	3.1	—	—	21	3.1
16 and 17 years old	597	513	86.0	504	84.5	9	1.5	84	14.0	3	0.4	81	13.6
18 and 19 years old	671	297	44.3	149	22.2	148	22.0	374	55.7	151	22.5	223	33.2
20 and 21 years old	677	148	21.9	18	2.7	130	19.3	528	78.1	240	35.4	289	42.7
22 to 24 years old	1 085	147	13.6	11	1.1	136	12.5	937	86.4	483	44.5	455	41.9
25 to 29 years old	1 661	106	6.4	17	1.0	89	5.4	1 555	93.6	846	50.9	710	42.7
30 to 34 years old	1 550	60	3.9	3	0.2	56	3.6	1 490	96.2	765	49.3	726	46.8
35 years old and over	5 689	129	2.3	42	0.8	87	1.5	5 560	97.7	2 511	44.1	3 049	53.6
35 to 44 years old	2 682	109	4.1	27	1.0	82	3.1	2 573	95.9	1 405	52.4	1 168	43.6
45 to 54 years old	1 392	14	1.0	10	0.7	4	0.3	1 378	99.0	643	46.2	734	52.8
55 years old and over	1 615	6	0.3	6	0.3	—	—	1 610	99.7	463	28.7	1 146	71.0
Male, 3 years old and over	8 844	2 976	33.7	2 690	30.4	286	3.2	5 868	66.4	2 671	30.2	3 197	36.2
3 to 34 years old	6 004	2 901	48.3	2 667	44.4	234	3.9	3 103	51.7	1 369	22.8	1 734	28.9
3 and 4 years old	439	165	37.5	165	37.5	—	—	275	62.5	—	—	275	62.5
5 and 6 years old	485	434	89.5	434	89.5	—	—	51	10.5	—	—	51	10.5
7 to 9 years old	605	576	95.3	576	95.3	—	—	28	4.7	—	—	28	4.7
10 to 13 years old	776	761	98.1	761	98.1	—	—	15	1.9	—	—	15	1.9
14 and 15 years old	356	349	98.2	346	97.2	3	0.9	7	1.9	—	—	7	1.9
16 and 17 years old	309	274	88.7	274	88.7	—	—	35	11.3	2	0.5	33	10.8
18 and 19 years old	336	146	43.5	90	26.9	56	16.6	190	56.5	69	20.6	121	35.9
20 and 21 years old	340	59	17.3	5	1.4	54	15.9	281	82.7	128	37.5	153	45.2
22 to 24 years old	589	76	12.9	6	1.0	70	11.9	513	87.1	264	44.9	249	42.3
25 to 29 years old	888	36	4.1	10	1.1	26	3.0	852	95.9	450	50.6	402	45.3
30 to 34 years old	882	25	2.8	—	—	25	2.8	858	97.2	457	51.8	401	45.4
35 years old and over	2 840	75	2.6	23	0.8	52	1.8	2 765	97.4	1 302	45.9	1 463	51.5
35 to 44 years old	1 407	64	4.6	13	0.9	51	3.6	143	95.4	737	52.4	606	43.1
45 to 54 years old	704	8	1.1	7	1.0	1	0.2	696	98.9	338	48.0	358	50.9
55 years old and over	729	3	0.4	3	0.4	—	—	726	99.6	227	31.2	499	68.4
Female, 3 years old and over	8 335	2 844	34.1	2 472	29.7	372	4.5	5 491	65.9	2 327	27.9	3 164	38.0
3 to 34 years old	5 486	2 790	50.9	2 453	44.7	337	6.2	2 696	49.1	1 117	20.4	1 578	28.8
3 and 4 years old	547	198	36.3	198	36.3	—	—	348	63.7	—	—	348	63.7
5 and 6 years old	485	429	88.5	429	88.5	—	—	56	11.5	—	—	56	11.5
7 to 9 years old	583	568	97.5	568	97.5	—	—	15	2.5	—	—	15	2.5
10 to 13 years old	661	639	96.7	639	96.7	—	—	22	3.3	—	—	22	3.3
14 and 15 years old	314	300	95.5	300	95.5	—	—	14	4.5	—	—	14	4.5
16 and 17 years old	288	239	83.0	230	79.9	9	3.1	49	17.0	1	0.3	48	16.6
18 and 19 years old	335	151	45.0	59	17.6	92	27.4	185	55.0	82	24.5	103	30.6
20 and 21 years old	337	90	26.6	13	3.9	76	22.6	247	73.4	112	33.3	135	40.1
22 to 24 years old	496	72	14.5	6	1.1	66	13.3	424	85.6	219	44.1	206	41.5
25 to 29 years old	773	70	9.0	7	0.9	63	8.1	703	91.0	396	51.2	307	39.8
30 to 34 years old	668	35	5.2	3	0.5	32	4.7	633	94.8	308	46.1	325	48.7
35 years old and over	2 849	54	1.9	19	0.7	35	1.2	2 795	98.1	1 209	42.4	1 586	55.7
35 to 44 years old	1 275	45	3.6	14	1.1	31	2.5	1 230	96.5	667	52.4	562	44.1
45 to 54 years old	687	6	0.9	3	0.4	3	0.5	681	99.1	306	44.5	376	54.7
55 years old and over	887	3	0.3	3	0.3	—	—	884	99.7	236	26.6	648	73.1

Source: October 1996 Current Population Survey, Education and Social Stratification Branch, U.S. Bureau of the Census

1. Includes nursery school, kindergarten, and grades 1 to 12.
2. May be of any race.

— Represents zero or rounds to zero.

Table A-2. Enrollment Status of the Population 3 Years Old and Over, by Age, Metropolitan Status, Race, Hispanic Origin, and Selected Educational Characteristics: October 1996

(Numbers in thousands. Civilian noninstitutional population.)

Age, metropolitan status, race and Hispanic origin	Population	Enrolled in school						Not enrolled in school					
		Total		Below college level[1]		In college		Total		High school graduate		Not high school graduate	
		Number	Percent	Number	Percent	Number	Percent	Number	Percent	Number	Percent	Number	Percent
ALL RACES													
Metropolitan Areas													
Total, 3 years old and over	203 035	56 898	28.0	43 953	21.7	12 945	6.4	146 137	72.0	117 031	57.6	29 106	14.3
3 and 4 years old	6 604	3 303	50.0	3 303	50.0	—	—	3 301	50.0	—	—	3 301	50.0
5 and 6 years old	6 812	6 408	94.1	6 408	94.1	—	—	404	5.9	—	—	404	5.9
7 to 13 years old	21 899	21 424	97.8	21 424	97.8	—	—	476	2.2	—	—	476	2.2
14 and 15 years old	6 170	6 053	98.1	6 040	97.9	13	0.2	117	1.9	—	—	117	1.9
16 and 17 years old	6 054	5 633	93.0	5 435	89.8	197	3.3	422	7.0	77	1.3	345	5.7
18 and 19 years old	5 806	3 630	62.5	930	16.0	2 700	46.5	2 175	37.5	1 449	25.0	726	12.5
20 and 21 years old	5 451	2 517	46.2	104	1.9	2 412	44.3	2 934	53.8	2 222	40.8	712	13.1
22 to 24 years old	8 514	2 263	26.6	46	0.5	2 218	26.1	6 251	73.4	5 230	61.4	1 021	12.0
25 to 29 years old	15 728	2 032	12.9	48	0.3	1 985	12.6	13 696	87.1	11 930	75.9	1 766	11.2
30 to 34 years old	17 357	1 116	6.4	38	0.2	1 078	6.2	16 241	93.6	14 190	81.8	2 051	11.8
35 to 44 years old	35 268	1 623	4.6	113	0.3	1 510	4.3	33 646	95.4	29 823	84.6	3 823	10.8
45 years and over	67 371	899	1.3	66	0.1	832	1.2	66 473	98.7	52 108	77.4	14 364	21.3
Metropolitan Areas - Central City													
Total, 3 years old and over	75 482	21 568	28.6	16 211	21.5	5 358	7.1	53 914	71.4	40 830	54.1	13 084	17.3
3 and 4 years old	2 600	1 220	46.9	1 220	46.9	—	—	1 380	53.1	—	—	1 380	53.1
5 and 6 years old	2 612	2 420	92.7	2 420	92.7	—	—	192	7.4	—	—	192	7.4
7 to 13 years old	8 085	7 893	97.6	7 893	97.6	—	—	192	2.4	—	—	192	2.4
14 and 15 years old	2 222	2 174	97.9	2 171	97.7	3	0.2	48	2.2	—	—	48	2.2
16 and 17 years old	2 151	1 964	91.3	1 894	88.0	70	3.3	188	8.7	29	1.4	159	7.4
18 and 19 years old	2 243	1 307	58.3	393	17.5	914	40.7	936	41.7	588	26.2	348	15.5
20 and 21 years old	2 342	1 030	44.0	53	2.3	977	41.7	1 312	56.0	932	39.8	380	16.2
22 to 24 years old	3 737	1 070	28.6	27	0.7	1 043	27.9	2 667	71.4	2 148	57.5	519	13.9
25 to 29 years old	6 827	1 017	14.9	23	0.3	994	14.6	5 809	85.1	4 908	71.9	901	13.2
30 to 34 years old	6 695	469	7.0	20	0.3	449	6.7	6 226	93.0	5 227	78.1	998	14.9
35 to 44 years old	12 257	628	5.1	51	0.4	577	4.7	11 629	94.9	9 823	80.2	1 805	14.7
45 years and over	23 711	374	1.6	44	0.2	330	1.4	23 337	98.4	17 175	72.4	6 162	26.0
Metropolitan Areas - Outside Central City													
Total, 3 years old and over	127 553	35 330	27.7	27 743	21.8	7 587	6.0	92 223	72.3	76 201	59.7	16 022	12.6
3 and 4 years old	4 004	2 082	52.0	2 082	52.0	—	—	1 922	48.0	—	—	1 922	48.0
5 and 6 years old	4 200	3 988	94.9	3 988	94.9	—	—	212	5.1	—	—	212	5.1
7 to 13 years old	13 814	13 530	98.0	13 530	98.0	—	—	284	2.1	—	—	284	2.1
14 and 15 years old	3 948	3 879	98.2	3 869	98.0	9	0.2	70	1.8	—	—	70	1.8
16 and 17 years old	3 903	3 669	94.0	3 542	90.8	127	3.3	234	6.0	48	1.2	187	4.8
18 and 19 years old	3 562	2 323	65.2	536	15.1	1 786	50.2	1 239	34.8	861	24.2	378	10.6
20 and 21 years old	3 109	1 486	47.8	51	1.6	1 436	46.2	1 622	52.2	1 290	41.5	332	10.7
22 to 24 years old	4 777	1 193	25.0	18	0.4	1 175	24.6	3 584	75.0	3 083	64.5	501	10.5
25 to 29 years old	8 901	1 015	11.4	24	0.3	991	11.1	7 886	88.6	7 022	78.9	864	9.7
30 to 34 years old	10 662	646	6.1	18	0.2	629	5.9	10 016	93.9	8 963	84.1	1 053	9.9
35 to 44 years old	23 012	995	4.3	62	0.3	933	4.1	22 017	95.7	20 000	86.9	2 017	8.8
45 years and over	43 661	525	1.2	22	0.1	503	1.2	43 136	98.8	34 934	80.0	8 202	18.8
Nonmetropolitan													
Total, 3 years old and over	50 140	13 398	26.7	11 117	22.2	2 282	4.6	36 742	73.3	27 419	54.7	9 322	18.6
3 and 4 years old	1 589	657	41.3	657	41.3	—	—	933	58.7	—	—	933	58.7
5 and 6 years old	1 581	1 485	93.9	1 485	93.9	—	—	96	6.1	—	—	96	6.1
7 to 13 years old	5 667	5 512	97.3	5 512	97.3	—	—	155	2.7	—	—	155	2.7

See footnotes at end of table.

Table A-2. Enrollment Status of the Population 3 Years Old and Over, by Age, Metropolitan Status, Race, Hispanic Origin, and Selected Educational Characteristics: October 1996 — Continued

(Numbers in thousands. Civilian noninstitutional population.)

Age, metropolitan status, race and Hispanic origin	Population	Enrolled in school						Not enrolled in school					
		Total		Below college level[1]		In college		Total		High school graduate		Not high school graduate	
		Number	Percent	Number	Percent	Number	Percent	Number	Percent	Number	Percent	Number	Percent
14 and 15 years old	1 580	1 546	97.8	1 546	97.8	—	—	34	2.2	—	—	34	2.2
16 and 17 years old	1 727	1 588	91.9	1 561	90.4	27	1.6	140	8.1	20	1.2	119	6.9
18 and 19 years old	1 570	909	57.9	300	19.1	609	38.8	661	42.1	447	28.5	214	13.6
20 and 21 years old	1 349	500	37.1	5	0.4	495	36.7	849	62.9	660	49.0	188	14.0
22 to 24 years old	1 981	342	17.3	8	0.4	333	16.8	1 639	82.7	1 354	68.4	285	14.4
25 to 29 years old	3 254	233	7.2	2	0.1	231	7.1	3 021	92.9	2 553	78.5	469	14.4
30 to 34 years old	3 754	170	4.5	20	0.5	150	4.0	3 583	95.5	3 097	82.5	486	13.0
35 to 44 years old	8 012	313	3.9	12	0.2	300	3.8	7 700	96.1	6 639	82.9	1 061	13.2
45 years and over	18 076	145	0.8	9	0.1	136	0.8	17 931	99.2	12 649	70.0	5 282	29.2
WHITE													
Metropolitan Areas													
Total, 3 years old and over	165 216	43 993	26.6	33 809	20.5	10 184	6.2	121 223	73.4	98 396	59.6	22 827	13.8
3 and 4 years old	5 039	2 511	49.8	2 511	49.8	—	—	2 528	50.2	—	—	2 528	50.2
5 and 6 years old	5 241	4 968	94.8	4 968	94.8			273	5.2	—		273	5.2
7 to 13 years old	16 867	16 509	97.9	16 509	97.9	—	—	358	2.1	—	—	358	2.1
14 and 15 years old	4 767	4 676	98.1	4 665	97.9	11	0.2	91	1.9	—	—	91	1.9
16 and 17 years old	4 666	4 338	93.0	4 204	90.1	134	2.9	328	7.0	50	1.1	278	6.0
18 and 19 years old	4 536	2 877	63.4	677	14.9	2 200	48.5	1 659	36.6	1 094	24.1	565	12.5
20 and 21 years old	4 265	1 995	46.8	60	1.4	1 935	45.4	2 270	53.2	1 739	40.8	532	12.5
22 to 24 years old	6 754	1 780	26.4	31	0.5	1 749	25.9	4 974	73.6	4 149	61.4	824	12.2
25 to 29 years old	12 594	1 535	12.2	36	0.3	1 499	11.9	11 058	87.8	9 593	76.2	1 466	11.6
30 to 34 years old	13 975	834	6.0	27	0.2	807	5.8	13 141	94.0	11 448	81.9	1 693	12.1
35 to 44 years old	28 806	1 233	4.3	74	0.3	1 159	4.0	27 573	95.7	24 679	85.7	2 895	10.1
45 years and over	57 705	736	1.3	46	0.1	691	1.2	56 969	98.7	45 645	79.1	11 324	19.6
Metropolitan Areas - Central City													
Total, 3 years old and over	52 749	13 981	26.5	10 237	19.4	3 743	7.1	38 769	73.5	30 016	56.9	8 753	16.6
3 and 4 years old	1 598	748	46.8	748	46.8	—	—	850	53.2	—	—	850	53.2
5 and 6 years old	1 707	1 600	93.8	1 600	93.8	—	—	106	6.2	—	—	106	6.2
7 to 13 years old	5 045	4 931	97.7	4 931	97.7	—	—	114	2.3	—	—	114	2.3
14 and 15 years old	1 432	1 395	97.5	1 392	97.2	3	0.2	37	2.6	—	—	37	2.6
16 and 17 years old	1 396	1 258	90.1	1 222	87.5	36	2.6	138	9.9	13	1.0	125	8.9
18 and 19 years old	1 448	853	58.9	222	15.3	631	43.6	596	41.1	358	24.8	237	16.4
20 and 21 years old	1 596	736	46.1	22	1.4	714	44.7	861	53.9	621	38.9	240	15.0
22 to 24 years old	2 673	766	28.7	16	0.6	751	28.1	1 907	71.3	1 534	57.4	373	14.0
25 to 29 years old	4 824	692	14.4	11	0.2	681	14.1	4 131	85.7	3 479	72.1	653	13.5
30 to 34 years old	4 614	310	6.7	13	0.3	297	6.4	4 304	93.3	3 573	77.5	730	15.8
35 to 44 years old	8 668	412	4.8	29	0.3	383	4.4	8 256	95.3	7 071	81.6	1 185	13.7
45 years and over	17 749	279	1.6	31	0.2	248	1.4	17 470	98.4	13 367	75.3	4 103	23.1
Metropolitan Areas - Outside Central City													
Total, 3 years old and over	112 466	30 012	26.7	23 571	21.0	6 441	5.7	82 454	73.3	68 379	60.8	14 074	12.5
3 and 4 years old	3 441	1 763	51.2	1 763	51.2	—	—	1 678	48.8	—	—	1 678	48.8
5 and 6 years old	3 534	3 367	95.3	3 367	95.3	—	—	167	4.7	—	—	167	4.7
7 to 13 years old	11 823	11 579	97.9	11 579	97.9	—	—	244	2.1	—	—	244	2.1
14 and 15 years old	3 335	3 280	98.4	3 273	98.1	8	0.2	55	1.6	—	—	55	1.6
16 and 17 years old	3 270	3 080	94.2	2 982	91.2	97	3.0	190	5.8	37	1.1	154	4.7
18 and 19 years old	3 088	2 025	65.6	455	14.8	1 569	50.8	1 063	34.4	735	23.8	328	10.6
20 and 21 years old	2 669	1 260	47.2	39	1.5	1 221	45.7	1 410	52.8	1 118	41.9	292	10.9
22 to 24 years old	4 080	1 014	24.9	16	0.4	998	24.5	3 067	75.2	2 615	64.1	451	11.1
25 to 29 years old	7 770	843	10.9	24	0.3	819	10.5	6 927	89.2	6 114	78.7	813	10.5
30 to 34 years old	9 361	524	5.6	14	0.2	510	5.5	8 837	94.4	7 874	84.1	963	10.3
35 to 44 years old	20 139	821	4.1	45	0.2	776	3.9	19 318	95.9	17 608	87.4	1 709	8.5
45 years and over	39 957	458	1.2	15	—	443	1.1	39 499	98.9	32 279	80.8	7 221	18.1

See footnotes at end of table.

Table A-2. Enrollment Status of the Population 3 Years Old and Over, by Age, Metropolitan Status, Race, Hispanic Origin, and Selected Educational Characteristics: October 1996 — Continued

(Numbers in thousands. Civilian noninstitutional population.)

Age, metropolitan status, race and Hispanic origin	Population	Enrolled in school						Not enrolled in school					
		Total		Below college level[1]		In college		Total		High school graduate		Not high school graduate	
		Number	Percent	Number	Percent	Number	Percent	Number	Percent	Number	Percent	Number	Percent
Nonmetropolitan													
Total, 3 years old and over	44 292	11 385	25.7	9 381	21.2	2 004	4.5	32 906	74.3	25 007	56.5	7 900	17.8
3 and 4 years old	1 335	541	40.5	541	40.5	—	—	794	59.5	—	—	794	59.5
5 and 6 years old	1 317	1 248	94.7	1 248	94.7	—	—	69	5.3	—	—	69	5.3
7 to 13 years old	4 801	4 666	97.2	4 666	97.2	—	—	135	2.8	—	—	135	2.8
14 and 15 years old	1 353	1 321	97.6	1 321	97.6	—	—	32	2.4	—	—	32	2.4
16 and 17 years old	1 452	1 342	92.4	1 319	90.9	22	1.5	110	7.6	20	1.4	91	6.2
18 and 19 years old	1 297	768	59.2	237	18.3	531	41.0	529	40.8	359	27.7	170	13.1
20 and 21 years old	1 145	433	37.8	5	0.5	427	37.3	712	62.2	568	49.6	144	12.6
22 to 24 years old	1 679	290	17.3	8	0.5	282	16.8	1 389	82.7	1 167	69.5	222	13.3
25 to 29 years old	2 843	206	7.3	2	0.1	204	7.2	2 637	92.8	2 256	79.4	381	13.4
30 to 34 years old	3 274	149	4.6	16	0.5	133	4.1	3 125	95.4	2 702	82.5	423	12.9
35 to 44 years old	7 154	282	4.0	9	0.1	274	3.8	6 871	96.1	6 005	83.9	866	12.1
45 years and over	16 643	140	0.8	9	0.1	131	0.8	16 503	99.2	11 930	71.7	4 574	27.5
BLACK													
Metropolitan Areas													
Total, 3 years old and over	27 659	9 352	33.8	7 637	27.6	1 715	6.2	18 308	66.2	13 375	48.4	4 933	17.8
3 and 4 years old	1 189	603	50.7	603	50.7	—	—	586	49.3	—	—	586	49.3
5 and 6 years old	1 178	1 062	90.2	1 062	90.2	—	—	115	9.8	—	—	115	9.8
7 to 13 years old	3 786	3 684	97.3	3 684	97.3	—	—	102	2.7	—	—	102	2.7
14 and 15 years old	1 046	1 032	98.7	1 030	98.5	2	0.2	14	1.3	—	—	14	1.3
16 and 17 years old	1 028	953	92.7	910	88.6	43	4.2	75	7.3	22	2.1	53	5.1
18 and 19 years old	941	503	53.5	224	23.8	280	29.7	438	46.5	302	32.1	136	14.5
20 and 21 years old	901	345	38.3	42	4.7	302	33.6	556	61.7	401	44.6	154	17.2
22 to 24 years old	1 175	257	21.9	8	0.7	249	21.2	918	78.1	758	64.5	159	13.6
25 to 29 years old	2 236	336	15.0	12	0.5	324	14.5	1 900	85.0	1 677	75.0	223	10.0
30 to 34 years old	2 396	186	7.8	10	0.4	176	7.3	2 210	92.2	1 929	80.5	281	11.7
35 to 44 years old	4 696	276	5.9	33	0.7	243	5.2	4 420	94.1	3 742	79.7	678	14.4
45 years and over	7 088	115	1.6	18	0.3	97	1.4	6 973	98.4	4 543	64.1	2 430	34.3
Metropolitan Areas - Central City													
Total, 3 years old and over	17 810	5 944	33.4	4 859	27.3	1 085	6.1	11 866	66.6	8 368	47.0	3 499	19.6
3 and 4 years old	797	388	48.7	388	48.7	—	—	409	51.3	—	—	409	51.3
5 and 6 years old	755	674	89.3	674	89.3	—	—	81	10.7	—	—	81	10.7
7 to 13 years old	2 452	2 379	97.0	2 379	97.0	—	—	73	3.0	—	—	73	3.0
14 and 15 years old	640	637	99.6	637	99.6	—	—	2	0.4	—	—	2	0.4
16 and 17 years old	608	563	92.7	532	87.5	31	5.2	44	7.3	16	2.6	29	4.8
18 and 19 years old	672	363	54.0	163	24.3	200	29.7	309	46.0	205	30.5	104	15.5
20 and 21 years old	612	220	35.9	30	5.0	190	31.0	392	64.1	266	43.5	126	20.6
22 to 24 years old	738	176	23.8	6	0.8	170	23.1	563	76.2	444	60.1	119	16.1
25 to 29 years old	1 461	220	15.0	12	0.8	208	14.2	1 242	85.0	1 054	72.1	187	12.8
30 to 34 years old	1 574	110	7.0	7	0.4	103	6.6	1 464	93.0	1 242	78.9	222	14.1
35 to 44 years old	150	44	29.3	—	—	44	29.3	106	70.7	68	45.2	38	25.5
45 years and over	4 718	66	1.4	10	0.2	56	1.2	4 652	98.6	2 954	62.6	1 697	36.0
Metropolitan Areas - Outside Central City													
Total, 3 years old and over	9 849	3 408	34.6	2 778	28.2	630	6.4	6 441	65.4	5 007	50.8	1 434	14.6
3 and 4 years old	392	214	54.7	214	54.7	—	—	177	45.3	—	—	177	45.3
5 and 6 years old	423	388	91.8	388	91.8	—	—	35	8.2	—	—	35	8.2
7 to 13 years old	1 334	1 305	97.9	1 305	97.9	—	—	29	2.1	—	—	29	2.1
14 and 15 years old	406	395	97.1	393	96.7	2	0.5	12	2.9	—	—	12	2.9
16 and 17 years old	420	390	92.8	378	90.0	11	2.7	30	7.2	6	1.5	24	5.7

See footnotes at end of table.

Table A-2. Enrollment Status of the Population 3 Years Old and Over, by Age, Metropolitan Status, Race, Hispanic Origin, and Selected Educational Characteristics: October 1996 — Continued

(Numbers in thousands. Civilian noninstitutional population.)

Age, metropolitan status, race and Hispanic origin	Population	Enrolled in school						Not enrolled in school					
		Total		Below college level[1]		In college		Total		High school graduate		Not high school graduate	
		Number	Percent	Number	Percent	Number	Percent	Number	Percent	Number	Percent	Number	Percent
18 and 19 years old	269	140	52.1	61	22.5	80	29.6	129	47.9	97	36.0	32	12.0
20 and 21 years old	288	125	43.3	12	4.1	113	39.2	163	56.7	135	46.8	29	9.9
22 to 24 years old	437	81	18.6	3	0.6	79	18.0	355	81.4	314	72.1	41	9.3
25 to 29 years old	775	116	15.0	—	—	116	15.0	659	85.0	623	80.4	36	4.6
30 to 34 years old	822	76	9.3	4	0.4	72	0.0	746	90.8	687	83.6	59	7.2
35 to 44 years old	1 913	129	6.7	13	0.7	116	6.0	1 785	93.3	1 556	81.3	229	12.0
45 years and over	2 371	49	2.1	8	0.3	41	1.7	2 322	97.9	1 589	67.0	733	30.9
Nonmetropolitan													
Total, 3 years old and over	4 462	1 499	33.6	1 313	29.4	186	4.2	2 963	66.4	1 804	40.4	1 159	26.0
3 and 4 years old	188	85	44.9	85	44.9	—	—	104	55.1	—	—	104	55.1
5 and 6 years old	186	171	92.0	171	92.0	—	—	15	8.0	—	—	15	8.0
7 to 13 years old	656	643	98.0	643	98.0	—	—	13	2.0	—	—	13	2.0
14 and 15 years old	165	165	100.0	165	100.0	—	—	—	—	—	—	—	—
16 and 17 years old	222	198	89.2	198	89.2	—	—	24	10.8	—	—	24	10.8
18 and 19 years old	220	110	49.9	44	20.2	65	29.6	110	50.1	71	32.3	39	17.8
20 and 21 years old	150	44	29.3	—	—	44	29.3	106	70.7	68	45.2	38	25.5
22 to 24 years old	251	43	17.1	—	—	43	17.1	208	82.9	155	61.6	54	21.4
25 to 29 years old	317	13	4.1	—	—	13	4.1	304	95.9	240	75.8	64	20.1
30 to 34 years old	366	10	2.8	4	1.0	7	1.8	356	97.2	297	81.1	59	16.1
35 to 44 years old	631	13	2.1	3	0.6	10	1.6	618	97.9	452	71.6	166	26.3
45 years and over	1 110	4	0.4	—	—	4	0.4	1 106	99.6	522	47.1	584	52.6
HISPANIC ORIGIN[2]													
Metropolitan Areas													
Total, 3 years old and over	24 381	7 969	32.7	6 811	27.9	1 158	4.8	16 412	67.3	8 393	34.4	8 018	32.9
3 and 4 years old	1 164	452	38.9	452	38.9	—	—	712	61.2	—	—	712	61.2
5 and 6 years old	1 182	1 057	89.4	1 057	89.4	—	—	125	10.6	—	—	125	10.6
7 to 13 years old	3 430	3 340	97.4	3 340	97.4	—	—	90	2.6	—	—	90	2.6
14 and 15 years old	909	876	96.3	872	95.9	3	0.4	34	3.7	—	—	34	3.7
16 and 17 years old	881	778	88.2	758	86.0	19	2.2	104	11.8	5	0.6	99	11.2
18 and 19 years old	911	424	46.5	201	22.1	222	24.4	488	53.5	229	25.2	258	28.3
20 and 21 years old	868	227	26.1	31	3.5	196	22.6	641	73.9	296	34.1	346	39.8
22 to 24 years old	1 374	259	18.8	17	1.2	242	17.6	1 116	81.2	623	45.3	493	35.9
25 to 29 years old	2 349	212	9.0	19	0.8	193	8.2	2 137	91.0	1 310	55.8	827	35.2
30 to 34 years old	2 381	117	4.9	8	0.3	109	4.6	2 264	95.1	1 349	56.6	916	38.5
35 to 44 years old	3 978	169	4.2	39	1.0	130	3.3	3 810	95.8	2 316	58.2	1 494	37.5
45 years and over	4 951	59	1.2	17	0.3	42	0.9	4 892	98.8	2 266	45.8	2 627	53.1
Metropolitan Areas - Central City													
Total, 3 years old and over	13 135	4 369	33.3	3 801	28.9	568	4.3	8 766	66.7	4 271	32.5	4 496	34.2
3 and 4 years old	587	229	39.0	229	39.0	—	—	358	61.0	—	—	358	61.0
5 and 6 years old	667	589	88.2	589	88.2	—	—	79	11.8	—	—	79	11.8
7 to 13 years old	1 869	1 828	97.8	1 828	97.8	—	—	41	2.2	—	—	41	2.2
14 and 15 years old	533	508	95.4	505	94.7	3	0.6	25	4.7	—	—	25	4.7
16 and 17 years old	524	459	87.5	453	86.4	6	1.1	65	12.5	4	0.8	61	11.7
18 and 19 years old	551	253	45.9	132	23.9	121	22.0	298	54.1	136	24.7	162	29.4
20 and 21 years old	436	108	24.7	12	2.8	95	21.9	328	75.3	157	36.0	171	39.3
22 to 24 years old	787	150	19.0	7	1.0	142	18.1	637	81.0	362	46.0	276	35.0
25 to 29 years old	1 275	94	7.4	8	0.6	86	6.7	1 181	92.7	724	56.8	457	35.8
30 to 34 years old	1 201	46	3.8	4	0.3	43	3.6	1 155	96.2	661	55.0	494	41.1
35 to 44 years old	2 014	80	4.0	22	1.1	58	2.9	1 934	96.0	1 112	55.2	822	40.8
45 years and over	2 693	27	1.0	13	0.5	14	0.5	2 665	99.0	1 115	41.4	1 550	57.6

See footnotes at end of table.

Table A-2. Enrollment Status of the Population 3 Years Old and Over, by Age, Metropolitan Status, Race, Hispanic Origin, and Selected Educational Characteristics: October 1996 — Continued

(Numbers in thousands. Civilian noninstitutional population.)

| Age, metropolitan status, race and Hispanic origin | Population | Enrolled in school | | | | | | Not enrolled in school | | | | | |
| | | Total | | Below college level[1] | | In college | | Total | | High school graduate | | Not high school graduate | |
		Number	Percent	Number	Percent	Number	Percent	Number	Percent	Number	Percent	Number	Percent
Metropolitan Areas - Outside Central City													
Total, 3 years old and over	11 246	3 600	32.0	3 010	26.8	590	5.3	7 645	68.0	4 123	36.7	3 523	31.3
3 and 4 years old	577	223	38.7	223	38.7	—	—	353	61.3	—	—	353	61.3
5 and 6 years old	514	468	91.0	468	91.0	—	—	46	9.0	—	—	46	9.0
7 to 13 years old	1 562	1 512	96.9	1 512	96.9	—	—	49	3.2	—	—	49	3.2
14 and 15 years old	376	367	97.7	367	97.7	—	—	9	2.3	—	—	9	2.3
16 and 17 years old	357	319	89.3	305	85.5	14	3.8	38	10.7	1	0.3	37	10.5
18 and 19 years old	361	171	47.5	70	19.4	101	28.1	190	52.6	93	25.9	96	26.7
20 and 21 years old	433	119	27.6	18	4.3	101	23.3	313	72.4	139	32.1	174	40.3
22 to 24 years old	588	109	18.6	9	1.5	100	17.0	478	81.4	261	44.5	217	37.0
25 to 29 years old	1 074	119	11.0	11	1.0	107	10.0	956	89.0	586	54.5	370	34.5
30 to 34 years old	1 180	71	6.0	4	0.4	67	5.7	1 109	94.0	688	58.3	422	35.7
35 to 44 years old	1 965	89	4.5	17	0.9	72	3.7	1 876	95.5	1 204	61.3	671	34.2
45 years and over	2 259	32	1.4	4	0.2	28	1.2	2 227	98.6	1 151	50.9	1 076	47.7
Nonmetropolitan													
Total, 3 years old and over	2 492	849	34.1	784	31.5	65	2.6	1 643	65.9	753	30.2	891	35.7
3 and 4 years old	154	50	32.5	50	32.5	—	—	104	67.5	—	—	104	67.5
5 and 6 years old	147	131	89.7	131	89.7	—	—	15	10.3	—	—	15	10.3
7 to 13 years old	386	369	95.7	369	95.7	—	—	16	4.3	—	—	16	4.3
14 and 15 years old	104	102	98.8	102	98.8	—	—	1	1.2	—	—	1	1.2
16 and 17 years old	90	84	93.1	84	93.1	—	—	6	6.9	—	—	6	6.9
18 and 19 years old	89	46	52.0	28	32.0	18	20.0	43	48.0	6	7.1	36	40.9
20 and 21 years old	96	17	17.6	—	—	17	17.6	79	82.4	55	56.7	25	25.7
22 to 24 years old	170	13	7.8	3	1.6	10	6.2	157	92.2	104	61.3	53	30.9
25 to 29 years old	174	5	2.6	—	—	5	2.6	170	97.4	96	54.8	74	42.6
30 to 34 years old	189	10	5.3	7	3.7	3	1.6	179	94.7	101	53.6	78	41.1
35 to 44 years old	348	18	5.1	5	1.6	12	3.5	330	94.9	177	50.9	153	44.0
45 years and over	545	3	0.5	3	0.5	—	—	542	99.5	213	39.1	329	60.3

Source: October 1996 Current Population Survey, Education and Social Stratification Branch, U.S. Bureau of the Census

1. Includes nursery school, kindergarten, and grades 1 to 12.
2. May be of any race.

— Represents zero or rounds to zero.

Table A-3. Enrollment Status of the Population 3 Years Old and Over, by Age, Metropolitan Status, Race, Hispanic Origin, and Selected Educational Characteristics: October 1996

(Numbers in thousands. Civilian noninstitutional population.)

Age, sex, race and Hispanic origin	Population	Total Number	Total Percent	Nursery	Kinder-garten	Elem. 1	Elem. 2	Elem. 3	Elem. 4	Elem. 5	Elem. 6	Elem. 7	Elem. 8
ALL RACES													
Both sexes	253 175	70 297	27.8	4 212	4 034	4 209	3 942	3 889	3 880	3 972	4 013	3 835	3 774
3 years old	4 045	1 506	37.2	1 458	48	—	—	—	—	—	—	—	—
4 years old	4 148	2 454	59.2	2 197	257	—	—	—	—	—	—	—	—
5 years old	4 185	3 835	91.7	492	3 129	202	12	—	—	—	—	—	—
6 years old	4 208	4 057	96.4	65	579	3 204	202	7	—	—	—	—	—
7 years old	4 066	3 972	97.7	—	22	726	2 963	236	13	—	—	2	1
8 years old	3 917	3 788	96.7	—	—	30	696	2 819	213	8	6	—	11
9 years old	3 922	3 817	97.3	—	—	46	61	757	2 761	165	15	4	2
10 years old	3 997	3 926	98.2	—	—	—	8	58	806	2 829	186	17	8
11 years old	3 926	3 824	97.4	—	—	—	—	11	77	867	2 629	200	21
12 years old	3 886	3 808	98.0	—	—	—	—	4	89	1 047	2 483	155
13 years old	3 852	3 801	98.7	—	—	—	—	4	10	98	998	2 477
14 years old	3 915	3 862	98.6	—	—	—	—	2	4	8	97	949
15 years old	3 835	3 737	97.4	—	—	—	—	—	—	—	16	116
16 years old	3 999	3 841	96.1	—	—	—	—	—	—	2	4	14
17 years old	3 783	3 379	89.3	—	—	—	—	—	—	—	3	6
18 years old	3 597	2 450	68.1	—	—	—	—	—	—	—	—	—
19 years old	3 779	2 088	55.3	—	—	—	—	—	—	—	—	—
20 years old	3 266	1 598	48.9	—	—	—	—	—	—	—	—	—
21 years old	3 533	1 418	40.1	—	—	—	—	—	—	—	—	—
22 years old	3 394	1 145	33.7	—	—	—	—	—	—	—	—	—
23 years old	3 420	819	24.0	—	—	—	—	—	—	—	—	—
24 years old	3 681	641	17.4	—	—	—	—	—	—	—	—	—
25 to 29 years old	18 982	2 265	11.9	—	—	—	—	—	—	—	3	—	—
30 to 34 years old	21 111	1 286	6.1	—	—	—	—	—	—	—	1	2	4
35 to 39 years old	22 373	1 138	5.1	—	—	—	—	—	—	—	8	2	4
40 to 44 years old	20 908	797	3.8	—	—	—	—	—	—	—	6	2	3
45 to 49 years old	18 466	531	2.9	—	—	—	—	—	—	—	2	—	—
50 to 54 years old	14 088	259	1.8	—	—	—	—	—	—	—	3	—	3
55 to 59 years old	11 233	107	1.0	—	—	—	—	—	—	—	—	3	—
60 to 64 years old	9 781	75	0.8	—	—	—	—	—	—	—	—	—	—
65 years and over	31 880	72	0.2	—	—	—	—	—	—	—	—	2	—
Male	123 103	35 092	28.5	2 069	2 126	2 196	2 042	1 950	2 020	2 064	2 043	1 905	1 914
3 years old	2 064	727	35.2	703	24	—	—	—	—	—	—	—	—
4 years old	2 118	1 234	58.3	1 096	139	—	—	—	—	—	—	—	—
5 years old	2 145	1 959	91.3	229	1 625	97	8	—	—	—	—	—	—
6 years old	2 175	2 093	96.2	41	331	1 618	98	4	—	—	—	—	—
7 years old	2 076	2 029	97.7	—	8	435	1 465	107	6	—	—	2	—
8 years old	2 017	1 958	97.1	—	—	15	429	1 395	105	5	3	—	2
9 years old	2 004	1 941	96.8	—	—	30	35	408	1 391	69	1	2	—
10 years old	2 062	2 027	98.3	—	—	—	6	34	457	1 429	83	6	2
11 years old	1 977	1 929	97.6	—	—	—	—	1	56	504	1 252	96	12
12 years old	1 937	1 887	97.4	—	—	—	—	2	47	629	1 125	59
13 years old	1 981	1 952	98.5	—	—	—	—	—	7	65	594	181
14 years old	2 016	1 998	99.1	—	—	—	—	2	3	1	64	567
15 years old	1 973	1 933	98.0	—	—	—	—	—	—	—	11	73
16 years old	2 082	2 017	96.9	—	—	—	—	—	—	2	—	11
17 years old	1 930	1 720	89.1	—	—	—	—	—	—	—	—	—
18 years old	1 809	1 233	68.2	—	—	—	—	—	—	—	—	—
19 years old	1 901	1 025	53.9	—	—	—	—	—	—	—	—	—
20 years old	1 568	728	46.4	—	—	—	—	—	—	—	—	—
21 years old	1 699	708	41.7	—	—	—	—	—	—	—	—	—
22 years old	1 779	613	34.4	—	—	—	—	—	—	—	—	—
23 years old	1 687	426	25.3	—	—	—	—	—	—	—	—	—
24 years old	1 840	296	16.1	—	—	—	—	—	—	—	—	—
25 to 29 years old	9 295	1 058	11.4	—	—	—	—	—	—	—	—	—

See footnotes at end of table.

Table A-3. Enrollment Status of the Population 3 Years Old and Over, by Age, Metropolitan Status, Race, Hispanic Origin, and Selected Educational Characteristics: October 1996 — Continued

(Numbers in thousands. Civilian noninstitutional population.)

Age, sex, race and Hispanic origin	Enrolled in school										Not enrolled in school	
	High school grades				College (years)						High school graduate	Not high school graduate
	1	2	3	4	1	2	3	4	5	6+		
ALL RACES												
Both sexes	4 052	3 934	3 662	3 662	3 671	3 571	2 672	2 390	1 007	1 915	144 450	38 428
3 years old	—	—	—	—	—	—	—	—	—	—	—	2 540
4 years old	—	—	—	—	—	—	—	—	—	—	—	1 694
5 years old	—	—	—	—	—	—	—	—	—	—	—	350
6 years old	—	—	—	—	—	—	—	—	—	—	—	151
7 years old	5	—	—	3	—	—	—	—	—	—	—	94
8 years old	4	—	—	—	—	—	—	—	—	—	—	130
9 years old	4	—	3	—	—	—	—	—	—	—	—	105
10 years old	2	11	—	—	—	—	—	—	—	—	—	71
11 years old	2	1	10	5	—	—	—	—	—	—	—	102
12 years old	17	3	11	—	—	—	—	—	—	—	—	78
13 years old	200	14	2	—	—	—	—	—	—	—	—	51
14 years old	2 590	199	1	11	—	—	—	—	—	—	—	53
15 years old	996	2 407	199	20	11	—	—	—	2	—	—	99
16 years old	191	1 041	2 329	238	21	—	—	—	3	—	9	149
17 years old	31	151	855	2 132	186	13	2	—	—	—	88	315
18 years old	6	47	163	790	1 316	120	7	2	1	—	695	452
19 years old	—	5	38	181	596	1 086	135	32	5	11	1 202	488
20 years old	3	11	2	59	231	537	668	72	3	13	1 240	428
21 years old	2	—	11	21	157	282	380	529	25	10	1 643	473
22 years old	6	—	3	12	119	180	210	474	79	63	1 831	418
23 years old	—	1	—	11	82	116	154	264	90	102	2 166	435
24 years old	—	3	2	15	59	116	89	155	99	102	2 587	453
25 to 29 years old	—	6	4	36	322	365	374	354	264	536	14 483	2 234
30 to 34 years old	3	8	9	31	197	245	217	152	142	275	17 287	2 538
35 to 39 years old	—	7	5	44	165	217	182	143	129	233	18 566	2 670
40 to 44 years old	2	9	9	25	80	130	123	110	83	215	17 897	2 214
45 to 49 years old	7	1	—	18	58	84	64	65	44	186	15 896	2 039
50 to 54 years old	5	—	—	5	31	24	36	28	28	95	11 762	2 066
55 to 59 years old	2	3	5	3	14	22	15	1	4	35	8 900	2 226
60 to 64 years old	4	—	—	3	10	23	2	6	6	21	7 443	2 262
65 years and over	—	5	—	—	17	12	14	4	2	16	20 756	11 052
Male	2 122	2 098	1 901	1 821	1 588	1 548	1 167	1 230	377	911	69 591	18 419
3 years old	—	—	—	—	—	—	—	—	—	—	—	1 338
4 years old	—	—	—	—	—	—	—	—	—	—	—	884
5 years old	—	—	—	—	—	—	—	—	—	—	—	186
6 years old	—	—	—	—	—	—	—	—	—	—	—	83
7 years old	2	—	—	3	—	—	—	—	—	—	—	48
8 years old	2	—	—	—	—	—	—	—	—	—	—	59
9 years old	2	—	3	—	—	—	—	—	—	—	—	63
10 years old	2	7	—	—	—	—	—	—	—	—	—	35
11 years old	2	1	2	2	—	—	—	—	—	—	—	48
12 years old	12	3	11	—	—	—	—	—	—	—	—	50
13 years old	95	7	2	—	—	—	—	—	—	—	—	29
14 years old	1 262	95	1	2	—	—	—	—	—	—	—	18
15 years old	565	1 182	93	4	5	—	—	—	—	—	—	40
16 years old	138	651	1 110	96	6	—	—	—	3	—	5	60
17 years old	21	97	552	996	84	—	—	—	—	—	43	167
18 years old	2	32	97	494	557	50	—	—	—	—	333	243
19 years old	—	—	29	115	316	472	64	23	—	7	632	245
20 years old	3	3	2	38	104	264	272	34	3	7	609	231
21 years old	2	—	5	3	78	139	206	263	9	2	765	226
22 years old	—	—	3	6	57	92	102	290	28	34	935	232
23 years old	—	1	—	—	38	51	79	152	56	49	1 055	205
24 years old	—	3	—	3	21	51	50	96	32	39	1 300	245
25 to 29 years old	—	2	3	14	136	159	163	163	110	307	7 095	1 141

See footnotes at end of table.

Table A-3. Enrollment Status of the Population 3 Years Old and Over, by Age, Metropolitan Status, Race, Hispanic Origin, and Selected Educational Characteristics: October 1996 — Continued

(Numbers in thousands. Civilian noninstitutional population.)

Age, sex, race and Hispanic origin	Population	Enrolled in school											
		Total		Nursery	Kinder-garten	Elementary grades							
		Number	Percent			1	2	3	4	5	6	7	8
30 to 34 years old	10 372	504	4.9	—	—	—	—	—	—	—	—	2	—
35 to 39 years old	11 020	494	4.5	—	—	—	—	—	—	—	6	2	4
40 to 44 years old	10 300	300	2.9	—	—	—	—	—	—	—	2	—	3
45 to 49 years old	9 026	161	1.8	—	—	—	—	—	—	—	—	—	—
50 to 54 years old	6 826	74	1.1	—	—	—	—	—	—	—	—	—	—
55 to 59 years old	5 412	29	0.5	—	—	—	—	—	—	—	—	—	—
60 to 64 years old	4 613	26	0.6	—	—	—	—	—	—	—	—	—	—
65 years and over	13 396	15	0.1	—	—	—	—	—	—	—	—	—	—
Female	130 073	35 205	27.1	2 143	1 908	2 013	1 900	1 939	1 860	1 908	1 970	1 930	1 860
3 years old	1 981	779	39.3	755	24	—	—	—	—	—	—	—	—
4 years old	2 030	1 219	60.1	1 101	118	—	—	—	—	—	—	—	—
5 years old	2 040	1 876	92.0	263	1 504	106	4	—	—	—	—	—	—
6 years old	2 033	1 965	96.6	23	248	1 586	103	4	—	—	—	—	—
7 years old	1 990	1 943	97.7	—	13	291	1 498	129	7	—	—	—	1
8 years old	1 900	1 830	96.3	—	—	14	267	1 424	108	3	2	—	9
9 years old	1 918	1 876	97.8	—	—	16	26	348	1 370	96	15	2	2
10 years old	1 935	1 899	98.2	—	—	—	2	24	349	1 401	103	11	6
11 years old	1 949	1 895	97.2	—	—	—	9	21	364	1 377	104	9
12 years old	1 949	1 921	98.6	—	—	—	—	2	42	418	1 358	96
13 years old	1 871	1 849	98.8	—	—	—	—	4	2	33	403	1 295
14 years old	1 899	1 864	98.2	—	—	—	—	—	1	7	33	382
15 years old	1 862	1 804	96.9	—	—	—	—	—	—	—	5	43
16 years old	1 917	1 824	95.2	—	—	—	—	—	—	—	4	3
17 years old	1 853	1 659	89.5	—	—	—	—	—	—	—	3	6
18 years old	1 788	1 217	68.1	—	—	—	—	—	—	—	—	—
19 years old	1 877	1 064	56.7	—	—	—	—	—	—	—	—	—
20 years old	1 698	871	51.3	—	—	—	—	—	—	—	—	—
21 years old	1 834	710	38.7	—	—	—	—	—	—	—	—	—
22 years old	1 615	532	32.9	—	—	—	—	—	—	—	—	—
23 years old	1 733	392	22.6	—	—	—	—	—	—	—	—	—
24 years old	1 841	346	18.8	—	—	—	—	—	—	—	—	—
25 to 29 years old	9 687	1 207	12.5	—	—	—	—	—	—	—	3	—
30 to 34 years old	10 738	782	7.3	—	—	—	—	—	—	—	1	—	4
35 to 39 years old	11 353	644	5.7	—	—	—	—	—	—	—	2	—
40 to 44 years old	10 608	497	4.7	—	—	—	—	—	—	—	4	2	—
45 to 49 years old	9 441	370	3.9	—	—	—	—	—	—	—	2	—
50 to 54 years old	7 262	185	2.6	—	—	—	—	—	—	—	3	—	3
55 to 59 years old	5 821	78	1.3	—	—	—	—	—	—	—	—	3	—
60 to 64 years old	5 168	49	0.9	—	—	—	—	—	—	—	—	—
65 years and over	18 484	57	0.3	—	—	—	—	—	—	—	—	2	—

White

Both sexes	209 507	55 378	26.4	3 284	3 163	3 279	3 106	2 954	3 112	3 121	3 140	3 017	2 962
3 years old	3 143	1 179	37.5	1 150	29	—	—	—	—	—	—	—	—
4 years old	3 230	1 872	58.0	1 697	175	—	—	—	—	—	—	—	—
5 years old	3 268	3 004	91.9	382	2 469	148	6	—	—	—	—	—	—
6 years old	3 290	3 211	97.6	55	481	2 511	162	2	—	—	—	—	1
7 years old	3 174	3 096	97.5	—	9	561	2 359	153	5	—	—	—	1
8 years old	2 994	2 892	96.6	—	—	18	546	2 165	142	4	3	—	11
9 years old	3 141	3 054	97.2	—	—	42	29	586	2 260	120	13	—	2
10 years old	3 156	3 098	98.2	—	—	—	4	40	643	2 252	130	10	8
11 years old	3 123	3 041	97.4	—	—	—	9	55	675	2 124	150	19
12 years old	3 038	2 980	98.1	—	—	—	3	60	805	988	98
13 years old	3 042	3 014	99.1	—	—	—	2	10	48	790	2 019
14 years old	3 104	3 058	98.5	—	—	—	2	1	7	55	718
15 years old	3 016	2 938	97.4	—	—	—	—	—	—	10	65
16 years old	3 106	2 990	96.3	—	—	—	—	—	2	2	14
17 years old	3 013	2 690	89.3	—	—	—	—	—	—	3	—

See footnotes at end of table.

Table A-3. Enrollment Status of the Population 3 Years Old and Over, by Age, Metropolitan Status, Race, Hispanic Origin, and Selected Educational Characteristics: October 1996 — Continued

(Numbers in thousands. Civilian noninstitutional population.)

| Age, sex, race and Hispanic origin | Enrolled in school | | | | | | | | | | Not enrolled in school | |
| | High school grades | | | | College (years) | | | | | | High school graduate | Not high school graduate |
	1	2	3	4	1	2	3	4	5	6+		
30 to 34 years old	—	2	3	12	46	88	86	66	47	152	8 530	1 338
35 to 39 years old	—	7	2	17	76	79	71	70	44	115	9 092	1 435
40 to 44 years old	—	5	9	6	35	44	38	48	23	87	8 873	1 127
45 to 49 years old	4	—	—	4	13	29	26	17	12	56	7 880	985
50 to 54 years old	5	—	—	3	8	8	7	2	5	35	5 787	965
55 to 59 years old	—	—	3	3	2	10	2	1	2	5	4 284	1 099
60 to 64 years old	—	—	—	—	4	6	—	4	2	11	3 507	1 079
65 years and over	—	—	—	—	2	6	—	—	—	6	8 866	4 515
Female	1 930	1 835	1 761	1 841	2 083	2 023	1 505	1 161	630	1 004	74 859	20 009
3 years old	—	—	—	—	—	—	—	—	—	—	—	1 202
4 years old	—	—	—	—	—	—	—	—	—	—	—	811
5 years old	—	—	—	—	—	—	—	—	—	—	—	164
6 years old	—	—	—	—	—	—	—	—	—	—	—	69
7 years old	3	—	—	—	—	—	—	—	—	—	—	47
8 years old	2	—	—	—	—	—	—	—	—	—	—	70
9 years old	1	—	—	—	—	—	—	—	—	—	—	42
10 years old	—	4	—	—	—	—	—	—	—	—	—	36
11 years old	—	—	8	3	—	—	—	—	—	—	—	54
12 years old	5	—	—	—	—	—	—	—	—	—	—	28
13 years old	104	7	—	—	—	—	—	—	—	—	—	22
14 years old	1 328	104	—	9	—	—	—	—	—	—	—	35
15 years old	401	1 226	106	16	6	—	—	—	2	—	—	58
16 years old	52	390	1 218	142	15	—	—	—	—	—	4	89
17 years old	10	54	333	1 136	102	13	2	—	—	—	45	149
18 years old	3	15	65	296	758	70	7	2	1	—	361	209
19 years old	—	5	10	66	280	614	71	9	5	5	570	243
20 years old	—	8	—	21	128	273	396	38	—	7	631	197
21 years old	—	—	6	18	79	143	173	266	16	8	878	246
22 years old	6	—	—	6	62	88	107	183	51	29	896	186
23 years old	—	—	—	11	43	65	75	112	34	53	1 111	230
24 years old	—	—	2	12	39	65	39	60	66	63	1 287	208
25 to 29 years old	—	4	1	22	186	205	212	191	155	229	7 387	1 093
30 to 34 years old	3	6	6	19	151	157	131	86	94	123	8 757	1 200
35 to 39 years old	—	—	2	27	89	138	110	73	85	118	9 474	1 235
40 to 44 years old	2	3	—	19	45	86	86	62	60	128	9 023	1 087
45 to 49 years old	4	1	—	14	45	56	38	48	31	130	8 016	1 054
50 to 54 years old	—	—	—	2	23	15	29	26	23	60	5 975	1 101
55 to 59 years old	2	3	2	—	12	11	13	—	2	30	4 616	1 127
60 to 64 years old	4	—	—	3	6	17	2	2	4	11	3 936	1 184
65 years and over	—	5	—	—	15	5	14	4	2	10	11 890	6 537
White												
Both sexes	3 206	3 123	2 851	2 871	2 864	2 821	2 189	1 987	815	1 512	123 402	30 727
3 years old	—	—	—	—	—	—	—	—	—	—	—	1 964
4 years old	—	—	—	—	—	—	—	—	—	—	—	1 358
5 years old	—	—	—	—	—	—	—	—	—	—	—	264
6 years old	—	—	—	—	—	—	—	—	—	—	—	79
7 years old	5	—	2	3	—	—	—	—	—	—	—	78
8 years old	4	—	—	—	—	—	—	—	—	—	—	102
9 years old	2	—	—	—	—	—	—	—	—	—	—	87
10 years old	—	11	—	—	—	—	—	—	—	—	—	58
11 years old	—	1	6	2	—	—	—	—	—	—	—	82
12 years old	14	3	9	—	—	—	—	—	—	—	—	58
13 years old	130	14	2	—	—	—	—	—	—	—	—	28
14 years old	2 117	146	1	11	—	—	—	—	—	—	—	46
15 years old	772	1 939	133	9	9	—	—	—	2	—	—	78
16 years old	116	822	1 879	139	14	—	—	—	3	—	4	111
17 years old	15	111	661	1 760	126	11	2	—	—	—	65	257

See footnotes at end of table.

Table A-3. Enrollment Status of the Population 3 Years Old and Over, by Age, Metropolitan Status, Race, Hispanic Origin, and Selected Educational Characteristics: October 1996 — Continued

(Numbers in thousands. Civilian noninstitutional population.)

| Age, sex, race and Hispanic origin | Population | Enrolled in school | | | | Elementary grades | | | | | | | |
| | | Total | | Nursery | Kinder-garten | 1 | 2 | 3 | 4 | 5 | 6 | 7 | 8 |
		Number	Percent										
18 years old	2 835	1 973	69.6	—	—	—	—	—	—	—	—	—	—
19 years old	2 998	1 672	55.8	—	—	—	—	—	—	—	—	—	—
20 years old	2 607	1 310	50.2	—	—	—	—	—	—	—	—	—	—
21 years old	2 803	1 118	39.9	—	—	—	—	—	—	—	—	—	—
22 years old	2 735	927	33.9	—	—	—	—	—	—	—	—	—	—
23 years old	2 705	642	23.7	—	—	—	—	—	—	—	—	—	—
24 years old	2 992	501	16.7	—	—	—	—	—	—	—	—	—	—
25 to 29 years old	15 436	1 741	11.3	—	—	—	—	—	—	—	—	—	—
30 to 34 years old	17 249	984	5.7	—	—	—	—	—	—	—	1	2	—
35 to 39 years old	18 528	902	4.9	—	—	—	—	—	—	—	2	2	—
40 to 44 years old	17 432	613	3.5	—	—	—	—	—	—	—	—	2	3
45 to 49 years old	15 629	446	2.9	—	—	—	—	—	—	—	2	—	—
50 to 54 years old	12 072	222	1.8	—	—	—	—	—	—	—	3	—	3
55 to 59 years old	9 697	88	0.9	—	—	—	—	—	—	—	—	3	—
60 to 64 years old	8 504	66	0.8	—	—	—	—	—	—	—	—	—	—
65 years and over	28 446	54	0.2	—	—	—	—	—	—	—	—	—	—
Male	102 625	27 663	27.0	1 638	1 655	1 705	1 593	1 493	1 621	1 637	1 593	1 515	1 529
3 years old	1 614	571	35.4	557	14	—	—	—	—	—	—	—	—
4 years old	1 655	949	57.3	858	91	—	—	—	—	—	—	—	—
5 years old	1 675	1 529	91.3	187	1 275	64	2	—	—	—	—	—	—
6 years old	1 687	1 651	97.8	36	269	1 267	76	2	—	—	—	—	—
7 years old	1 627	1 584	97.4	—	6	337	1 168	66	3	—	—	—	—
8 years old	1 535	1 486	96.8	—	—	10	325	1 080	65	1	—	—	2
9 years old	1 612	1 557	96.6	—	—	27	20	316	1 141	51	1	—	—
10 years old	1 618	1 595	98.5	—	—	—	2	29	369	1 127	56	4	2
11 years old	1 606	1 568	97.6	—	—	—	—	41	418	1 022	72	10
12 years old	1 541	1 499	97.3	—	—	—	—	—	34	481	929	34
13 years old	1 573	1 552	98.6	—	—	—	—	—	7	28	461	980
14 years old	1 592	1 576	99.0	—	—	—	—	2	—	—	39	441
15 years old	1 548	1 520	98.2	—	—	—	—	—	—	—	6	45
16 years old	1 596	1 544	96.8	—	—	—	—	—	—	2	—	11
17 years old	1 550	1 382	89.1	—	—	—	—	—	—	—	—	—
18 years old	1 441	996	69.1	—	—	—	—	—	—	—	—	—	—
19 years old	1 512	802	53.1	—	—	—	—	—	—	—	—	—	—
20 years old	1 246	565	45.3	—	—	—	—	—	—	—	—	—	—
21 years old	1 392	585	42.0	—	—	—	—	—	—	—	—	—	—
22 years old	1 444	501	34.7	—	—	—	—	—	—	—	—	—	—
23 years old	1 340	344	25.7	—	—	—	—	—	—	—	—	—	—
24 years old	1 523	249	16.4	—	—	—	—	—	—	—	—	—	—
25 to 29 years old	7 691	814	10.6	—	—	—	—	—	—	—	—	—	—
30 to 34 years old	8 620	372	4.3	—	—	—	—	—	—	—	—	2	—
35 to 39 years old	9 260	380	4.1	—	—	—	—	—	—	—	2	2	—
40 to 44 years old	8 685	232	2.7	—	—	—	—	—	—	—	—	—	3
45 to 49 years old	7 744	136	1.8	—	—	—	—	—	—	—	—	—	—
50 to 54 years old	5 923	61	1.0	—	—	—	—	—	—	—	—	—	—
55 to 59 years old	4 706	26	0.6	—	—	—	—	—	—	—	—	—	—
60 to 64 years old	4 062	26	0.7	—	—	—	—	—	—	—	—	—	—
65 years and over	12 007	10	0.1	—	—	—	—	—	—	—	—	—	—
Female	106 883	27 716	25.9	1 646	1 508	1 574	1 513	1 461	1 491	1 484	1 548	1 502	1 433
3 years old	1 530	609	39.8	594	15	—	—	—	—	—	—	—	—
4 years old	1 576	924	58.6	839	85	—	—	—	—	—	—	—	—
5 years old	1 593	1 476	92.6	195	1 194	83	4	—	—	—	—	—	—
6 years old	1 603	1 560	97.4	18	212	1 244	87	—	—	—	—	—	—
7 years old	1 547	1 512	97.7	—	3	224	1 192	87	2	—	—	—	1
8 years old	1 459	1 406	96.4	—	—	8	221	1 084	77	3	2	—	9
9 years old	1 529	1 497	97.9	—	—	15	9	270	1 120	69	12	—	2
10 years old	1 537	1 504	97.8	—	—	—	2	11	274	1 126	74	6	6

See footnotes at end of table.

Table A-3. Enrollment Status of the Population 3 Years Old and Over, by Age, Metropolitan Status, Race, Hispanic Origin, and Selected Educational Characteristics: October 1996 — Continued

(Numbers in thousands. Civilian noninstitutional population.)

| Age, sex, race and Hispanic origin | Enrolled in school | | | | | | | | | | Not enrolled in school | |
| | High school grades | | | | College (years) | | | | | | High school graduate | Not high school graduate |
	1	2	3	4	1	2	3	4	5	6+		
18 years old	2	33	93	632	1 115	95	3	—	1	—	501	361
19 years old	—	5	29	120	449	924	110	23	5	7	952	374
20 years old	3	8	2	36	196	425	583	54	—	4	969	329
21 years old	2	—	2	12	102	191	331	452	18	7	1 338	346
22 years old	6	—	3	12	70	133	183	401	69	51	1 495	313
23 years old	—	—	—	7	61	92	119	207	69	88	1 726	337
24 years old	—	3	2	6	49	86	75	133	70	77	2 095	396
25 to 29 years old	—	6	4	27	219	278	281	283	224	417	11 849	1 846
30 to 34 years old	3	5	9	23	148	184	174	130	111	193	14 150	2 116
35 to 39 years old	—	2	5	34	137	171	138	126	101	183	15 490	2 136
40 to 44 years old	—	9	6	17	57	99	85	92	72	169	15 194	1 625
45 to 49 years old	6	1	—	15	43	69	54	55	40	161	13 618	1 564
50 to 54 years old	5	—	—	2	29	17	33	20	24	86	10 294	1 556
55 to 59 years old	—	—	5	3	14	16	8	1	4	35	7 849	1 760
60 to 64 years old	4	—	—	—	10	27	2	6	2	19	6 604	1 834
65 years and over	—	3	—	—	15	7	8	4	2	16	19 209	9 183
Male	1 685	1 653	1 449	1 443	1 267	1 215	947	1 030	305	690	60 053	14 909
3 years old	—	—	—	—	—	—	—	—	—	—	—	1 043
4 years old	—	—	—	—	—	—	—	—	—	—	—	706
5 years old	—	—	—	—	—	—	—	—	—	—	—	146
6 years old	—	—	—	—	—	—	—	—	—	—	—	36
7 years old	2	—	—	3	—	—	—	—	—	—	—	43
8 years old	2	—	—	—	—	—	—	—	—	—	—	49
9 years old	1	—	—	—	—	—	—	—	—	—	—	56
10 years old	—	7	—	—	—	—	—	—	—	—	—	24
11 years old	—	1	2	2	—	—	—	—	—	—	—	38
12 years old	9	3	9	—	—	—	—	—	—	—	—	42
13 years old	67	7	2	—	—	—	—	—	—	—	—	22
14 years old	1 022	68	1	2	—	—	—	—	—	—	—	16
15 years old	469	939	52	4	—	—	—	—	—	—	—	27
16 years old	85	517	866	57	3	—	—	—	3	—	—	52
17 years old	11	69	409	834	59	—	—	—	—	—	34	134
18 years old	2	23	58	397	480	36	—	—	—	—	250	195
19 years old	—	—	26	70	236	400	50	15	—	7	523	187
20 years old	3	3	2	20	87	213	220	16	—	1	503	178
21 years old	2	—	32	—	66	96	187	223	5	2	635	172
22 years old	—	—	3	6	38	63	85	251	24	30	773	170
23 years old	—	—	—	—	30	42	64	122	44	41	840	155
24 years old	—	3	—	3	20	43	48	81	23	28	1 056	217
25 to 29 years old	—	2	3	11	94	114	125	144	92	227	5 887	990
30 to 34 years old	—	2	3	8	34	69	64	52	41	97	7 121	1 127
35 to 39 years old	—	2	2	14	70	65	52	58	28	83	7 704	1 176
40 to 44 years old	—	5	6	6	23	30	22	45	23	69	7 625	828
45 to 49 years old	4	—	—	3	6	23	19	17	12	53	6 863	745
50 to 54 years old	5	—	—	—	8	6	7	—	5	31	5 114	748
55 to 59 years old	—	—	3	3	2	8	2	1	2	5	3 788	891
60 to 64 years old	—	—	—	—	4	6	—	4	2	11	3 150	886
65 years and over	—	—	—	—	2	2	—	—	—	6	8 187	3 810
Female	1 521	1 469	1 402	1 428	1 597	1 605	1 242	958	511	823	63 349	15 818
3 years old	—	—	—	—	—	—	—	—	—	—	—	921
4 years old	—	—	—	—	—	—	—	—	—	—	—	652
5 years old	—	—	—	—	—	—	—	—	—	—	—	118
6 years old	—	—	—	—	—	—	—	—	—	—	—	42
7 years old	3	—	—	—	—	—	—	—	—	—	—	35
8 years old	2	—	—	—	—	—	—	—	—	—	—	53
9 years old	1	—	—	—	—	—	—	—	—	—	—	32
10 years old	—	4	—	—	—	—	—	—	—	—	—	34

See footnotes at end of table.

Table A-3. Enrollment Status of the Population 3 Years Old and Over, by Age, Metropolitan Status, Race, Hispanic Origin, and Selected Educational Characteristics: October 1996 — Continued

(Numbers in thousands. Civilian noninstitutional population.)

Age, sex, race and Hispanic origin	Population	Enrolled in school											
		Total		Nursery	Kinder-garten	Elementary grades							
		Number	Percent			1	2	3	4	5	6	7	8
11 years old	1 517	1 473	97.1	—	—	—	—	—	13	257	1 101	79	9
12 years old	1 496	1 480	98.9	—	—	—	—	—	2	26	324	1 059	64
13 years old	1 469	1 462	99.5	—	—	—	—	—	2	2	20	329	1 038
14 years old	1 512	1 483	98.0	—	—	—	—	—	—	1	7	16	277
15 years old	1 469	1 418	96.6	—	—	—	—	—	—	—	—	4	20
16 years old	1 510	1 446	95.8	—	—	—	—	—	—	—	—	2	3
17 years old	1 462	1 308	89.4	—	—	—	—	—	—	—	—	3	—
18 years old	1 394	977	70.1	—	—	—	—	—	—	—	—	—	—
19 years old	1 486	870	58.5	—	—	—	—	—	—	—	—	—	—
20 years old	1 361	745	54.7	—	—	—	—	—	—	—	—	—	—
21 years old	1 411	534	37.8	—	—	—	—	—	—	—	—	—	—
22 years old	1 292	426	33.0	—	—	—	—	—	—	—	—	—	—
23 years old	1 365	298	21.8	—	—	—	—	—	—	—	—	—	—
24 years old	1 470	252	17.1	—	—	—	—	—	—	—	—	—	—
25 to 29 years old	7 745	927	12.0	—	—	—	—	—	—	—	—	1	—
30 to 34 years old	8 629	611	7.1	—	—	—	—	—	—	—	1	—	—
35 to 39 years old	9 268	523	5.6	—	—	—	—	—	—	—	—	—	—
40 to 44 years old	8 747	381	4.4	—	—	—	—	—	—	—	—	2	—
45 to 49 years old	7 885	311	3.9	—	—	—	—	—	—	—	2	—	—
50 to 54 years old	6 149	161	2.6	—	—	—	—	—	—	—	3	—	3
55 to 59 years old	4 991	62	1.2	—	—	—	—	—	—	—	—	3	—
60 to 64 years old	4 442	39	0.9	—	—	—	—	—	—	—	—	—	—
65 years and over	16 440	44	0.3	—	—	—	—	—	—	—	—	—	—
Black													
Both sexes	32 121	10 851	33.8	702	634	697	621	719	588	645	641	615	644
3 years old	690	238	34.5	226	12	—	—	—	—	—	—	—	—
4 years old	688	449	65.3	389	60	—	—	—	—	—	—	—	—
5 years old	668	597	89.3	76	481	39	—	—	—	—	—	—	—
6 years old	695	636	91.6	10	74	520	28	4	—	—	—	—	—
7 years old	656	646	98.5	—	6	124	454	52	8	—	—	2	—
8 years old	703	678	96.5	—	—	11	117	505	37	4	3	—	—
9 years old	587	572	97.4	—	—	3	21	143	367	31	2	2	—
10 years old	640	628	98.0	—	—	—	—	15	152	417	37	5	—
11 years old	620	603	97.1	—	—	—	—	1	22	169	354	45	2
12 years old	636	620	97.4	—	—	—	—	—	1	22	188	357	49
13 years old	599	581	97.0	—	—	—	—	—	2	—	49	155	334
14 years old	604	601	99.6	—	—	—	—	—	—	1	—	39	207
15 years old	608	596	98.1	—	—	—	—	—	—	—	—	7	42
16 years old	653	620	95.0	—	—	—	—	—	—	—	—	3	—
17 years old	597	531	88.9	—	—	—	—	—	—	—	—	—	3
18 years old	573	348	60.7	—	—	—	—	—	—	—	—	—	—
19 years old	588	265	45.1	—	—	—	—	—	—	—	—	—	—
20 years old	493	182	36.9	—	—	—	—	—	—	—	—	—	—
21 years old	557	207	37.1	—	—	—	—	—	—	—	—	—	—
22 years old	467	129	27.7	—	—	—	—	—	—	—	—	—	—
23 years old	507	110	21.8	—	—	—	—	—	—	—	—	—	—
24 years old	451	60	13.4	—	—	—	—	—	—	—	3	—	—
25 to 29 years old	2 553	349	13.7	—	—	—	—	—	—	—	3	—	—
30 to 34 years old	2 762	197	7.1	—	—	—	—	—	—	—	—	—	4
35 to 39 years old	2 806	166	5.9	—	—	—	—	—	—	—	3	—	4
40 to 44 years old	2 520	123	4.9	—	—	—	—	—	—	—	2	—	—
45 to 49 years old	2 051	58	2.8	—	—	—	—	—	—	—	—	—	—
50 to 54 years old	1 407	29	2.1	—	—	—	—	—	—	—	—	—	—
55 to 59 years old	1 147	19	1.7	—	—	—	—	—	—	—	—	—	—
60 to 64 years old	973	3	0.3	—	—	—	—	—	—	—	—	—	—
65 years and over	2 620	10	0.4	—	—	—	—	—	—	—	—	—	—

Table A-3. Enrollment Status of the Population 3 Years Old and Over, by Age, Metropolitan Status, Race, Hispanic Origin, and Selected Educational Characteristics: October 1996 — Continued

(Numbers in thousands. Civilian noninstitutional population.)

Age, sex, race and Hispanic origin	Enrolled in school										Not enrolled in school	
	High school grades				College (years)						High school graduate	Not high school graduate
	1	2	3	4	1	2	3	4	5	6+		
11 years old	—	—	4	—	—	—	—	—	—	—	—	43
12 years old	5	—	—	—	—	—	—	—	—	—	—	16
13 years old	64	7	—	—	—	—	—	—	—	—	—	7
14 years old	1 095	78	81	9	—	—	—	—	—	—	—	30
15 years old	303	999	81	5	5	—	—	—	2	—	—	51
16 years old	30	305	1 013	82	11	—	—	—	—	—	4	60
17 years old	4	41	253	927	67	11	2	—	—	—	31	123
18 years old	—	—	10	35	235	58	3	—	1	—	251	166
19 years old	—	—	5	3	51	525	60	9	5	—	429	187
20 years old	—	—	5	—	16	212	363	38	—	2	465	151
21 years old	—	—	—	—	12	95	144	229	13	5	703	175
22 years old	—	6	—	—	6	70	97	150	45	20	723	143
23 years old	—	—	—	—	7	50	54	84	24	47	886	182
24 years old	—	—	—	2	3	43	27	53	47	49	1 039	180
25 to 29 years old	—	4	1	15	125	164	156	139	132	190	5 962	856
30 to 34 years old	3	3	6	15	115	115	110	78	70	96	7 029	989
35 to 39 years old	—	—	2	20	68	109	86	68	73	101	7 786	960
40 to 44 years old	—	3	—	11	34	69	64	47	49	100	7 569	797
45 to 49 years old	2	1	—	12	37	46	35	38	29	108	6 756	819
50 to 54 years old	—	—	—	2	21	11	26	20	19	55	5 180	809
55 to 59 years old	—	—	2	—	12	8	5	—	2	30	4 061	868
60 to 64 years old	4	—	—	—	6	17	2	2	—	8	3 454	948
65 years and over	—	3	—	—	12	5	8	4	2	10	11 022	5 373
Black												
Both sexes	613	602	571	657	556	485	281	271	109	199	15 179	6 091
3 years old	—	—	—	—	—	—	—	—	—	—	—	452
4 years old	—	—	—	—	—	—	—	—	—	—	—	239
5 years old	—	—	—	—	—	—	—	—	—	—	—	71
6 years old	—	—	—	—	—	—	—	—	—	—	—	59
7 years old	—	—	—	—	—	—	—	—	—	—	—	10
8 years old	—	—	—	—	—	—	—	—	—	—	—	25
9 years old	—	—	3	—	—	—	—	—	—	—	—	15
10 years old	2	—	—	—	—	—	—	—	—	—	—	13
11 years old	2	—	4	3	—	—	—	—	—	—	—	18
12 years old	3	—	—	—	—	—	—	—	—	—	—	16
13 years old	40	—	—	—	—	—	—	—	—	—	—	18
14 years old	324	29	—	—	—	—	—	—	—	—	—	2
15 years old	152	337	47	11	2	—	—	—	—	—	—	12
16 years old	65	183	291	75	3	—	—	—	—	—	5	28
17 years old	15	24	151	298	40	—	—	—	—	—	17	49
18 years old	3	11	57	137	131	9	—	—	—	—	153	72
19 years old	—	—	5	54	99	80	12	8	—	5	220	103
20 years old	—	3	—	21	26	69	38	15	—	9	221	90
21 years old	—	—	9	9	41	62	32	50	3	—	248	102
22 years old	—	—	—	—	33	22	11	50	6	6	245	93
23 years old	—	1	—	2	16	21	21	29	14	7	323	74
24 years old	—	—	—	5	2	19	5	16	8	5	345	46
25 to 29 years old	—	—	—	9	69	74	57	48	23	66	1 917	287
30 to 34 years old	—	3	—	7	47	46	30	6	27	26	2 226	340
35 to 39 years old	—	5	—	10	21	40	23	16	16	27	2 255	385
40 to 44 years old	2	—	3	7	10	20	31	13	5	30	1 938	459
45 to 49 years old	2	—	—	2	9	7	9	10	3	14	1 627	367
50 to 54 years old	—	—	—	3	2	6	3	8	2	4	984	394
55 to 59 years old	2	3	—	—	—	6	8	—	—	—	736	391
60 to 64 years old	—	—	—	3	—	—	—	—	—	—	634	335
65 years and over	—	2	—	—	2	2	3	—	—	—	1 084	1 526

See footnotes at end of table.

Table A-3. Enrollment Status of the Population 3 Years Old and Over, by Age, Metropolitan Status, Race, Hispanic Origin, and Selected Educational Characteristics: October 1996 — Continued

(Numbers in thousands. Civilian noninstitutional population.)

Age, sex, race and Hispanic origin	Population	Enrolled in school											
		Total		Nursery	Kinder-garten	Elementary grades							
		Number	Percent			1	2	3	4	5	6	7	8
Male	14 864	5 302	35.7	310	345	370	319	351	297	327	350	311	299
3 years old	327	104	31.9	101	3	—	—	—	—	—	—	—	—
4 years old	342	210	61.5	176	34	—	—	—	—	—	—	—	—
5 years old	346	312	90.2	28	262	—	—	—	—	—	—	—	—
6 years old	363	326	90.0	5	46	263	13	—	—	—	—	—	—
7 years old	322	319	99.2	—	—	77	210	26	3	—	—	2	—
8 years old	369	359	97.3	—	—	5	81	242	23	4	3	—	—
9 years old	286	280	97.9	—	—	3	15	76	172	12	—	—	—
10 years old	345	334	96.9	—	—	—	—	5	83	223	19	2	—
11 years old	294	284	96.5	—	—	—	—	1	14	76	168	20	2
12 years old	312	304	97.5	—	—	—	—	—	1	11	119	149	20
13 years old	303	296	97.9	—	—	—	—	—	—	—	36	109	133
14 years old	316	316	100.0	—	—	—	—	—	—	1	—	23	113
15 years old	306	294	96.2	—	—	—	—	—	—	—	—	5	27
16 years old	363	341	96.7	—	—	—	—	—	—	—	—	—	—
17 years old	284	255	89.9	—	—	—	—	—	—	—	—	—	—
18 years old	286	175	61.2	—	—	—	—	—	—	—	—	—	—
19 years old	277	136	49.0	—	—	—	—	—	—	—	—	—	—
20 years old	224	93	41.7	—	—	—	—	—	—	—	—	—	—
21 years old	233	85	36.4	—	—	—	—	—	—	—	—	—	—
22 years old	235	61	25.9	—	—	—	—	—	—	—	—	—	—
23 years old	226	42	18.5	—	—	—	—	—	—	—	—	—	—
24 years old	199	20	9.9	—	—	—	—	—	—	—	—	—	—
25 to 29 years old	1 129	145	12.8	—	—	—	—	—	—	—	—	—	—
30 to 34 years old	1 251	67	5.4	—	—	—	—	—	—	—	—	—	—
35 to 39 years old	1 279	80	6.3	—	—	—	—	—	—	—	3	—	4
40 to 44 years old	1 153	31	2.7	—	—	—	—	—	—	—	2	—	—
45 to 49 years old	931	18	1.9	—	—	—	—	—	—	—	—	—	—
50 to 54 years old	626	9	1.5	—	—	—	—	—	—	—	—	—	—
55 to 59 years old	501	3	0.5	—	—	—	—	—	—	—	—	—	—
60 to 64 years old	417	—	—	—	—	—	—	—	—	—	—	—	—
65 years and over	1 030	2	0.2	—	—	—	—	—	—	—	—	—	—
Female	17 258	5 549	32.2	392	289	327	302	369	291	318	291	304	345
3 years old	363	134	36.8	125	9	—	—	—	—	—	—	—	—
4 years old	346	239	69.1	213	26	—	—	—	—	—	—	—	—
5 years old	323	285	88.4	48	219	17	—	—	—	—	—	—	—
6 years old	332	310	93.2	5	28	257	16	4	—	—	—	—	—
7 years old	334	327	97.8	—	6	47	243	26	4	—	—	—	—
8 years old	334	319	95.5	—	—	6	36	263	14	—	—	—	—
9 years old	301	292	96.9	—	—	—	7	67	195	20	2	2	—
10 years old	295	294	99.4	—	—	—	—	10	69	194	18	3	—
11 years old	326	319	97.7	—	—	—	—	—	7	94	185	26	—
12 years old	325	316	97.4	—	—	—	—	—	—	11	69	208	28
13 years old	296	284	96.1	—	—	—	—	—	2	—	13	46	201
14 years old	288	286	99.2	—	—	—	—	—	—	—	—	17	94
15 years old	302	302	100.0	—	—	—	—	—	—	—	—	1	15
16 years old	300	279	93.0	—	—	—	—	—	—	—	—	3	—
17 years old	313	276	88.0	—	—	—	—	—	—	—	—	—	3
18 years old	287	173	60.3	—	—	—	—	—	—	—	—	—	—
19 years old	311	129	41.5	—	—	—	—	—	—	—	—	—	—
20 years old	269	88	33.0	—	—	—	—	—	—	—	—	—	—
21 years old	324	122	37.6	—	—	—	—	—	—	—	—	—	—
22 years old	232	68	29.4	—	—	—	—	—	—	—	—	—	—
23 years old	281	69	24.4	—	—	—	—	—	—	—	—	—	—
24 years old	253	41	16.1	—	—	—	—	—	—	—	—	—	—
25 to 29 years old	1 424	204	14.4	—	—	—	—	—	—	—	3	—	—
30 to 34 years old	1 511	129	8.6	—	—	—	—	—	—	—	—	—	4

See footnotes at end of table.

Table A-3. Enrollment Status of the Population 3 Years Old and Over, by Age, Metropolitan Status, Race, Hispanic Origin, and Selected Educational Characteristics: October 1996 — Continued

(Numbers in thousands. Civilian noninstitutional population.)

Age, sex, race and Hispanic origin	Enrolled in school										Not enrolled in school	
	High school grades				College (years)						High school graduate	Not high school graduate
	1	2	3	4	1	2	3	4	5	6+		
Male	316	325	323	294	194	197	105	128	40	99	6 749	2 812
3 years old	—	—	—	—	—	—	—	—	—	—	—	222
4 years old	—	—	—	—	—	—	—	—	—	—	—	132
5 years old	—	—	—	—	—	—	—	—	—	—	—	34
6 years old	—	—	—	—	—	—	—	—	—	—	—	36
7 years old	—	—	—	—	—	—	—	—	—	—	—	3
8 years old	—	—	—	—	—	—	—	—	—	—	—	10
9 years old	—	—	3	—	—	—	—	—	—	—	—	6
10 years old	2	—	—	—	—	—	—	—	—	—	—	11
11 years old	2	—	—	—	—	—	—	—	—	—	—	10
12 years old	3	—	—	—	—	—	—	—	—	—	—	8
13 years old	18	—	—	—	—	—	—	—	—	—	—	6
14 years old	165	14	—	—	—	—	—	—	—	—	—	—
15 years old	67	166	29	—	—	—	—	—	—	—	—	12
16 years old	50	114	153	23	1	—	—	—	—	—	5	7
17 years old	9	19	94	117	16	—	—	—	—	—	4	24
18 years old	—	7	35	82	48	4	—	—	—	—	68	43
19 years old	—	—	3	39	46	33	6	8	—	—	94	48
20 years old	—	—	—	18	9	28	18	15	—	5	83	48
21 years old	—	—	3	3	10	28	13	28	—	—	104	44
22 years old	—	—	—	—	11	12	4	27	3	4	119	55
23 years old	—	1	—	—	3	7	9	11	6	4	152	33
24 years old	—	—	—	—	1	6	2	11	—	1	157	22
25 to 29 years old	—	—	—	3	25	36	16	13	8	44	884	100
30 to 34 years old	—	—	—	4	12	14	14	1	6	15	1 014	170
35 to 39 years old	—	5	—	3	4	13	7	11	16	13	1 017	181
40 to 44 years old	—	—	3	—	—	6	9	—	—	11	865	256
45 to 49 years old	—	—	—	—	7	3	7	—	1	—	716	196
50 to 54 years old	—	—	—	3	—	2	—	2	—	2	450	168
55 to 59 years old	—	—	—	—	—	3	—	—	—	—	316	182
60 to 64 years old	—	—	—	—	—	—	—	—	—	—	253	164
65 years and over	—	—	—	—	—	2	—	—	—	—	447	581
Female	297	277	248	363	362	288	176	142	68	100	8 430	3 279
3 years old	—	—	—	—	—	—	—	—	—	—	—	229
4 years old	—	—	—	—	—	—	—	—	—	—	—	107
5 years old	—	—	—	—	—	—	—	—	—	—	—	37
6 years old	—	—	—	—	—	—	—	—	—	—	—	23
7 years old	—	—	—	—	—	—	—	—	—	—	—	7
8 years old	—	—	—	—	—	—	—	—	—	—	—	15
9 years old	—	—	—	—	—	—	—	—	—	—	—	9
10 years old	—	—	—	—	—	—	—	—	—	—	—	2
11 years old	—	—	4	3	—	—	—	—	—	—	—	8
12 years old	—	—	—	—	—	—	—	—	—	—	—	8
13 years old	22	—	—	—	—	—	—	—	—	—	—	12
14 years old	159	15	—	—	—	—	—	—	—	—	—	2
15 years old	85	170	18	11	2	—	—	—	—	—	—	—
16 years old	15	69	138	52	2	—	—	—	—	—	—	21
17 years old	7	5	57	180	24	—	—	—	—	—	13	24
18 years old	3	5	22	54	83	5	—	—	—	—	85	29
19 years old	—	—	3	15	53	47	7	—	—	5	126	56
20 years old	—	3	—	3	17	41	19	—	—	4	138	42
21 years old	—	—	6	6	31	34	19	23	3	—	144	58
22 years old	—	—	—	—	23	11	7	23	3	2	126	38
23 years old	—	—	—	2	13	14	12	18	8	2	171	42
24 years old	—	—	—	5	2	13	3	5	8	4	188	24
25 to 29 years old	—	—	—	7	44	38	40	35	16	22	1 033	187
30 to 34 years old	—	3	—	4	35	32	16	5	20	11	1 212	170

See footnotes at end of table.

Table A-3. Enrollment Status of the Population 3 Years Old and Over, by Age, Metropolitan Status, Race, Hispanic Origin, and Selected Educational Characteristics: October 1996 — Continued

(Numbers in thousands. Civilian noninstitutional population.)

| Age, sex, race and Hispanic origin | Population | Enrolled in school | | | | | | | | | | | |
| | | Total | | Nursery | Kinder-garten | Elementary grades | | | | | | | |
		Number	Percent			1	2	3	4	5	6	7	8
35 to 39 years old	1 528	86	5.6	—	—	—	—	—	—	—	—	—	—
40 to 44 years old	1 368	92	6.7	—	—	—	—	—	—	—	—	—	—
45 to 49 years old	1 121	39	3.5	—	—	—	—	—	—	—	—	—	—
50 to 54 years old	781	20	2.5	—	—	—	—	—	—	—	—	—	—
55 to 59 years old	646	17	2.6	—	—	—	—	—	—	—	—	—	—
60 to 64 years old	556	3	0.6	—	—	—	—	—	—	—	—	—	—
65 years and over	1 590	8	0.5	—	—	—	—	—	—	—	—	—	—
Hispanic origin													
Both sexes	26 873	8 818	32.8	533	602	595	511	590	562	584	540	524	535
3 years old	610	155	25.4	138	17	—	—	—	—	—	—	—	—
4 years old	708	347	49.1	294	53	—	—	—	—	—	—	—	—
5 years old	711	610	85.7	95	471	42	2	—	—	—	—	—	—
6 years old	617	579	93.8	6	61	463	49	—	—	—	—	—	—
7 years old	538	524	97.4	—	—	84	367	71	2	—	—	—	—
8 years old	556	537	96.5	—	—	3	90	405	38	1	—	—	—
9 years old	549	527	96.0	—	—	3	2	94	384	44	—	—	—
10 years old	582	567	97.4	—	—	—	2	16	117	396	36	—	1
11 years old	549	527	96.1	—	—	—	—	5	16	116	318	63	9
12 years old	512	502	98.1	—	—	—	—	—	20	162	283	26
13 years old	531	525	99.0	—	—	—	—	2	7	16	152	305
14 years old	507	493	97.2	—	—	—	—	2	—	1	13	165
15 years old	506	485	95.9	—	—	—	—	—	—	—	3	24
16 years old	509	476	93.6	—	—	—	—	—	—	2	—	4
17 years old	463	385	83.2	—	—	—	—	—	—	—	—	—
18 years old	466	249	53.4	—	—	—	—	—	—	—	—	—
19 years old	534	221	41.4	—	—	—	—	—	—	—	—	—
20 years old	478	145	30.3	—	—	—	—	—	—	—	—	—
21 years old	486	99	20.4	—	—	—	—	—	—	—	—	—
22 years old	526	137	26.1	—	—	—	—	—	—	—	—	—
23 years old	493	81	16.4	—	—	—	—	—	—	—	—	—
24 years old	525	54	10.3	—	—	—	—	—	—	—	—	—
25 to 29 years old	2 524	217	8.6	—	—	—	—	—	—	—	—	—
30 to 34 years old	2 570	127	5.0	—	—	—	—	—	—	—	2	—
35 to 39 years old	2 454	99	4.0	—	—	—	—	—	—	—	2	—
40 to 44 years old	1 872	88	4.7	—	—	—	—	—	—	4	2	—
45 to 49 years old	1 400	28	2.0	—	—	—	—	—	—	2	—	—
50 to 54 years old	938	15	1.6	—	—	—	—	—	—	—	—	—
55 to 59 years old	895	10	1.2	—	—	—	—	—	—	—	3	—
60 to 64 years old	679	—	—	—	—	—	—	—	—	—	—	—
65 years and over	1 585	8	0.5	—	—	—	—	—	—	—	—	—
Male	13 462	4 437	33.0	264	305	317	282	299	262	294	287	252	290
3 years old	302	73	24.2	67	6	—	—	—	—	—	—	—	—
4 years old	335	179	53.3	153	26	—	—	—	—	—	—	—	—
5 years old	348	304	87.4	43	241	21	—	—	—	—	—	—	—
6 years old	333	316	94.9	2	31	253	29	—	—	—	—	—	—
7 years old	283	276	97.7	—	—	37	207	33	—	—	—	—	—
8 years old	298	283	95.1	—	—	3	45	215	20	—	—	—	—
9 years old	242	225	93.0	—	—	3	—	41	168	13	—	—	1
10 years old	278	277	99.4	—	—	—	—	10	60	193	11	—	7
11 years old	288	280	97.1	—	—	—	—	—	77	157	29
12 years old	261	252	96.8	—	—	—	—	—	6	106	122	10
13 years old	282	277	98.1	—	—	—	—	—	5	11	83	155
14 years old	255	251	98.5	—	—	—	—	—	—	11	92
15 years old	267	260	97.5	—	—	—	—	—	—	3	22
16 years old	276	264	95.5	—	—	—	—	—	—	2	—	2
17 years old	221	186	84.2	—	—	—	—	—	—	—	—	—

See footnotes at end of table.

Table A-3. Enrollment Status of the Population 3 Years Old and Over, by Age, Metropolitan Status, Race, Hispanic Origin, and Selected Educational Characteristics: October 1996 — Continued

(Numbers in thousands. Civilian noninstitutional population.)

Age, sex, race and Hispanic origin	Enrolled in school										Not enrolled in school	
	High school grades				College (years)						High school graduate	Not high school graduate
	1	2	3	4	1	2	3	4	5	6+		
35 to 39 years old	—	—	—	7	17	27	16	5	—	15	1 238	204
40 to 44 years old	—	—	—	7	10	14	22	13	5	19	1 073	203
45 to 49 years old	2	—	—	2	2	5	2	10	3	14	911	171
50 to 54 years old	2	—	—	—	2	4	3	6	2	2	535	226
55 to 59 years old	—	3	—	—	—	3	8	—	2	—	420	209
60 to 64 years old	2	—	—	3	—	—	—	—	—	—	381	171
65 years and over	—	2	—	—	2	—	3	—	—	—	637	945
Hispanic origin												
Both sexes	516	541	458	503	356	318	192	183	71	102	9 146	8 909
3 years old	—	—	—	—	—	—	—	—	—	—	—	455
4 years old	—	—	—	—	—	—	—	—	—	—	—	361
5 years old	—	—	—	—	—	—	—	—	—	—	—	102
6 years old	—	—	—	—	—	—	—	—	—	—	—	39
7 years old	—	—	—	—	—	—	—	—	—	—	—	14
8 years old	—	—	—	—	—	—	—	—	—	—	—	19
9 years old	—	—	—	—	—	—	—	—	—	—	—	22
10 years old	—	—	—	—	—	—	—	—	—	—	—	15
11 years old	—	—	—	—	—	—	—	—	—	—	—	21
12 years old	6	—	5	—	—	—	—	—	—	—	—	10
13 years old	37	7	—	—	—	—	—	—	—	—	—	5
14 years old	280	28	—	4	—	—	—	—	—	—	—	14
15 years old	139	277	32	5	3	—	—	—	—	—	—	21
16 years old	31	166	233	36	4	—	—	—	—	—	—	32
17 years old	8	35	113	214	13	2	—	—	—	—	5	72
18 years old	—	5	32	112	91	9	—	—	—	—	83	134
19 years old	—	1	31	49	68	69	3	—	—	—	153	160
20 years old	3	8	—	9	37	59	23	5	—	—	161	173
21 years old	2	—	—	8	20	24	28	16	—	—	189	198
22 years old	3	—	—	6	15	25	27	46	10	6	217	172
23 years old	—	—	—	2	17	19	15	14	5	8	235	177
24 years old	—	—	2	6	6	4	10	12	7	5	275	196
25 to 29 years old	—	6	3	10	26	43	31	48	10	40	1 406	901
30 to 34 years old	3	—	—	10	15	24	35	15	11	12	1 450	993
35 to 39 years old	—	—	—	19	19	20	9	12	12	5	1 396	959
40 to 44 years old	—	7	6	4	10	12	7	10	15	10	1 097	687
45 to 49 years old	4	—	—	6	—	8	3	4	—	1	764	607
50 to 54 years old	—	—	—	—	6	—	1	—	—	8	500	422
55 to 59 years old	—	—	2	3	—	—	—	—	—	3	439	446
60 to 64 years old	—	—	—	—	—	—	—	—	—	—	277	402
65 years and over	—	—	—	—	4	—	—	—	—	4	498	1 079
Male	274	301	240	243	128	170	78	81	22	50	4 707	4 318
3 years old	—	—	—	—	—	—	—	—	—	—	—	229
4 years old	—	—	—	—	—	—	—	—	—	—	—	156
5 years old	—	—	—	—	—	—	—	—	—	—	—	44
6 years old	—	—	—	—	—	—	—	—	—	—	—	17
7 years old	—	—	—	—	—	—	—	—	—	—	—	6
8 years old	—	—	—	—	—	—	—	—	—	—	—	14
9 years old	—	—	—	—	—	—	—	—	—	—	—	17
10 years old	—	—	—	—	—	—	—	—	—	—	—	2
11 years old	—	—	—	—	—	—	—	—	—	—	—	8
12 years old	3	—	5	—	—	—	—	—	—	—	—	8
13 years old	19	5	—	—	—	—	—	—	—	—	—	5
14 years old	135	11	—	—	—	—	—	—	—	—	—	4
15 years old	78	141	9	3	3	—	—	—	—	—	—	7
16 years old	21	104	118	16	—	—	—	—	—	—	—	13
17 years old	8	26	54	94	5	—	—	—	—	—	3	32

See footnotes at end of table.

Table A-3. Enrollment Status of the Population 3 Years Old and Over, by Age, Metropolitan Status, Race, Hispanic Origin, and Selected Educational Characteristics: October 1996 — Continued

(Numbers in thousands. Civilian noninstitutional population.)

Age, sex, race and Hispanic origin	Population	Total		Nursery	Kinder-garten	Elementary grades							
		Number	Percent			1	2	3	4	5	6	7	8
18 years old	232	113	48.8	—	—	—	—	—	—	—	—	—	—
19 years old	273	123	45.1	—	—	—	—	—	—	—	—	—	—
20 years old	238	54	22.6	—	—	—	—	—	—	—	—	—	—
21 years old	249	41	16.6	—	—	—	—	—	—	—	—	—	—
22 years old	261	63	24.1	—	—	—	—	—	—	—	—	—	—
23 years old	271	46	16.8	—	—	—	—	—	—	—	—	—	—
24 years old	291	25	8.5	—	—	—	—	—	—	—	—	—	—
25 to 29 years old	1 306	89	6.8	—	—	—	—	—	—	—	—	—	—
30 to 34 years old	1 379	59	4.3	—	—	—	—	—	—	—	—	2	—
35 to 39 years old	1 214	46	3.8	—	—	—	—	—	—	—	—	2	—
40 to 44 years old	945	55	5.8	—	—	—	—	—	—	—	—	—	—
45 to 49 years old	686	12	1.7	—	—	—	—	—	—	—	—	—	—
50 to 54 years old	476	5	1.0	—	—	—	—	—	—	—	—	—	—
55 to 59 years old	404	3	0.7	—	—	—	—	—	—	—	—	—	—
60 to 64 years old	314	—	—	—	—	—	—	—	—	—	—	—	—
65 years and over	653	—	—	—	—	—	—	—	—	—	—	—	—
Female	13 411	4 381	32.7	270	297	278	230	291	299	291	254	273	245
3 years old	309	82	26.6	72	10	—	—	—	—	—	—	—	—
4 years old	373	168	45.2	142	27	—	—	—	—	—	—	—	—
5 years old	363	305	84.2	52	230	21	2	—	—	—	—	—	—
6 years old	285	263	92.5	4	30	209	20	—	—	—	—	—	—
7 years old	255	248	97.0	—	—	48	160	38	2	—	—	—	—
8 years old	258	254	98.1	—	—	—	45	190	18	1	—	—	—
9 years old	307	302	98.4	—	—	—	2	52	216	31	24	—	—
10 years old	304	290	95.6	—	—	—	2	5	57	203	161	—	—
11 years old	260	247	95.0	—	—	—	5	5	39	56	35	2
12 years old	251	250	99.5	—	—	—	—	—	14	5	161	16
13 years old	249	249	100.0	—	—	—	—	2	2	1	69	151
14 years old	253	242	96.0	—	—	—	—	—	—	—	3	73
15 years old	239	224	94.1	—	—	—	—	—	—	—	—	2
16 years old	232	213	91.5	—	—	—	—	—	—	—	—	2
17 years old	241	199	82.4	—	—	—	—	—	—	—	—	—
18 years old	234	135	58.0	—	—	—	—	—	—	—	—	—	—
19 years old	260	98	37.5	—	—	—	—	—	—	—	—	—	—
20 years old	241	91	37.9	—	—	—	—	—	—	—	—	—	—
21 years old	238	58	24.3	—	—	—	—	—	—	—	—	—	—
22 years old	265	74	28.0	—	—	—	—	—	—	—	—	—	—
23 years old	222	35	15.9	—	—	—	—	—	—	—	—	—	—
24 years old	234	29	12.5	—	—	—	—	—	—	—	—	—	—
25 to 29 years old	1 218	128	10.5	—	—	—	—	—	—	—	—	—	—
30 to 34 years old	1 191	68	5.7	—	—	—	—	—	—	—	—	—	—
35 to 39 years old	1 241	52	4.2	—	—	—	—	—	—	—	—	—	—
40 to 44 years old	927	33	3.5	—	—	—	—	—	—	—	4	2	—
45 to 49 years old	714	16	2.3	—	—	—	—	—	—	—	2	3	—
50 to 54 years old	462	10	2.3	—	—	—	—	—	—	—	—	—	—
55 to 59 years old	491	7	1.5	—	—	—	—	—	—	—	—	3	—
60 to 64 years old	364	—	—	—	—	—	—	—	—	—	—	—	—
65 years and over	932	8	0.9	—	—	—	—	—	—	—	—	—	—

See footnotes at end of table.

Table A-3. Enrollment Status of the Population 3 Years Old and Over, by Age, Metropolitan Status, Race, Hispanic Origin, and Selected Educational Characteristics: October 1996 — Continued

(Numbers in thousands. Civilian noninstitutional population.)

Age, sex, race and Hispanic origin	Enrolled in school										Not enrolled in school	
	High school grades				College (years)						High school graduate	Not high school graduate
	1	2	3	4	1	2	3	4	5	6+		
18 years old	—	5	17	56	29	6	—	—	—	—	36	83
19 years old	—	—	28	33	22	40	—	—	—	—	78	72
20 years old	3	—	—	9	15	19	5	—	—	—	88	96
21 years old	2	—	—	—	6	19	6	8	—	—	98	109
22 years old	—	—	—	6	11	10	8	19	6	—	103	95
23 years old	—	—	—	—	7	15	9	4	8	—	129	96
24 years old	—	—	—	3	1	4	5	4	3	—	161	105
25 to 29 years old	—	2	3	4	10	12	19	22	16	—	728	490
30 to 34 years old	—	—	—	4	1	18	18	8	5	—	797	523
35 to 39 years old	—	—	—	8	8	12	5	9	2	—	690	478
40 to 44 years old	—	5	6	—	10	12	3	8	4	—	564	326
45 to 49 years old	4	—	—	3	—	4	—	—	1	—	368	306
50 to 54 years old	—	—	—	—	—	—	—	—	5	—	269	201
55 to 59 years old	—	—	—	3	—	—	—	—	—	—	206	195
60 to 64 years old	—	—	—	—	—	—	—	—	—	—	146	168
65 years and over	—	—	—	—	—	—	—	—	—	—	242	411
Female	242	240	218	260	228	148	114	101	49	53	4 438	4 591
3 years old	—	—	—	—	—	—	—	—	—	—	—	226
4 years old	—	—	—	—	—	—	—	—	—	—	—	204
5 years old	—	—	—	—	—	—	—	—	—	—	—	57
6 years old	—	—	—	—	—	—	—	—	—	—	—	21
7 years old	—	—	—	—	—	—	—	—	—	—	—	8
8 years old	—	—	—	—	—	—	—	—	—	—	—	5
9 years old	—	—	—	—	—	—	—	—	—	—	—	5
10 years old	—	—	—	—	—	—	—	—	—	—	—	13
11 years old	—	—	—	—	—	—	—	—	—	—	—	13
12 years old	2	—	—	—	—	—	—	—	—	—	—	1
13 years old	18	2	—	4	—	—	—	—	—	—	—	—
14 years old	145	18	18	4	—	—	—	—	—	—	—	10
15 years old	61	137	23	2	—	—	—	—	—	—	—	14
16 years old	10	62	114	20	4	—	—	—	—	—	—	20
17 years old	—	9	60	120	8	2	—	—	—	—	2	40
18 years old	—	—	14	56	62	3	—	—	—	—	47	52
19 years old	—	1	3	16	45	29	3	—	—	—	74	89
20 years old	—	5	—	—	23	40	18	5	—	—	73	76
21 years old	—	—	—	8	14	5	22	8	—	—	91	89
22 years old	3	—	—	—	4	15	19	27	6	—	114	77
23 years old	—	—	—	2	10	4	7	10	2	—	106	81
24 years old	—	—	2	3	5	—	5	8	3	3	114	91
25 to 29 years old	—	4	—	5	16	31	12	26	10	24	677	412
30 to 34 years old	3	—	—	6	14	6	16	7	8	6	652	470
35 to 39 years old	—	—	—	11	12	8	4	4	12	3	707	482
40 to 44 years old	—	2	—	4	—	—	3	2	8	7	533	361
45 to 49 years old	—	—	—	3	—	4	3	4	—	—	396	301
50 to 54 years old	—	—	—	—	6	—	1	—	—	3	231	221
55 to 59 years old	—	—	2	—	—	—	—	—	—	3	233	251
60 to 64 years old	—	—	—	—	—	—	—	—	—	—	131	233
65 years and over	—	—	—	—	4	—	—	—	—	4	256	668

Source: October 1996 Current Population Survey, Education and Social Stratification Branch, U.S. Bureau of the Census

1. May be of any race.

— Represents zero or rounds to zero.

Table A-4. Preprimary School Enrollment of Persons 3 to 6 Years Old, by Residence, Mother's Labor Force Status and Education, Family Income, Race, and Hispanic Origin: October 1996

(Numbers in thousands. Civilian noninstitutional population.)

Metropolitan status, region, characteristics of the mother, family income, age, race and Hispanic origin	Population	Enrolled in nursery school						Enrolled in kindergarten						Enrolled in elementary school
		Total		Public		Private		Total		Public		Private		
		Total	Full day	Total	Full day	Total	Full day	Total	Full day	Total	Full day	Total	Full day	
ALL RACES														
3 to 6 Years Old														
Total children	16 586	4 212	1 796	1 868	831	2 344	964	4 012	2 096	3 332	1 693	680	403	3 628
Total metropolitan	13 416	3 480	1 530	1 476	680	2 003	850	3 246	1 595	2 635	1 222	610	373	2 985
Metropolitan areas of 1 million or more	9 085	2 381	1 005	965	422	1 416	583	2 203	1 049	1 776	781	426	268	2 069
Central city	3 395	794	404	424	213	371	192	792	454	611	327	182	127	804
Outside central city	5 690	1 586	601	541	210	1 045	391	1 410	595	1 166	454	245	141	1 265
Metropolitan areas of less than 1 million	4 332	1 099	524	512	257	587	267	1 043	546	859	441	184	106	916
Central city	1 817	458	228	209	105	248	123	421	209	337	160	84	49	371
Outside central city	2 514	641	296	303	152	339	144	622	338	522	281	100	57	545
Nonmetropolitan	3 170	732	266	392	152	341	114	766	501	696	471	70	29	643
3 and 4 Years Old														
Total children	8 193	3 655	1 548	1 540	690	2 115	858	304	143	201	87	103	56	—
Total metropolitan	6 604	3 054	1 332	1 227	569	1 826	763	249	117	162	63	87	54	—
Metropolitan areas of 1 million or more	4 474	2 111	890	825	366	1 286	524	200	83	135	43	66	40	—
Central city	1 681	693	355	359	180	334	175	102	41	64	18	38	23	—
Outside central city	2 793	1 418	536	466	186	952	349	98	42	71	25	28	17	—
Metropolitan areas of less than 1 million	2 130	942	442	402	203	540	239	49	34	27	20	22	14	—
Central city	919	400	202	168	85	232	116	25	12	15	8	10	5	—
Outside central city	1 211	543	240	234	117	308	123	24	22	12	12	12	10	—
Nonmetropolitan	1 589	602	216	313	121	289	95	55	26	40	24	15	2	—
Region:														
Northeast	1 439	752	254	256	101	496	153	61	33	44	23	17	10	—
Midwest	1 930	925	273	408	121	517	152	42	14	31	9	11	5	—
South	2 755	1 162	676	522	332	640	343	112	65	51	34	61	31	—
West	2 070	815	345	353	135	462	210	89	31	75	22	14	9	—
Labor force status of mother:														
Children living with mother	7 646	3 450	1 430	1 417	621	2 034	809	276	130	180	78	96	52	—
Mother in labor force	4 789	2 385	1 108	955	436	1 431	672	170	83	100	42	70	41	—
Employed	4 423	2 236	1 044	862	400	1 374	644	151	70	90	38	61	32	—
Fulltime	3 008	1 465	830	547	298	918	531	108	57	66	32	41	25	—
Parttime	1 416	771	214	315	101	456	113	43	13	24	6	19	7	—
Unemployed	366	150	64	93	36	57	28	19	13	10	4	9	9	—
Mother not in labor force	2 857	1 065	322	462	185	603	137	106	47	80	36	26	11	—
Children not living with mother	547	205	118	123	69	82	49	28	14	22	9	7	4	—
Education of mother:														
Children living with mother	7 646	3 450	1 430	1 417	621	2 034	809	276	130	180	78	96	52	—
Elementary: 0 to 8 years	440	99	48	92	42	7	5	24	6	21	6	2	—	—
High school: 9 to 11 years	902	271	128	216	106	55	22	37	23	35	22	2	2	—
High school graduate	2 471	956	367	536	229	420	138	75	32	47	19	28	14	—
College:														
Less than a bachelor's degree	2 190	1 092	466	374	152	719	314	101	39	57	19	43	21	—
Bachelor's degree or more	1 644	1 031	421	199	92	833	329	39	29	19	13	21	16	—
Family income:														
Less than $10,000	1 145	382	174	322	132	60	42	43	17	30	12	13	5	—
$10,000 to $14,999	642	242	100	166	56	76	45	19	7	9	4	9	3	—
$15,000 to $19,999	502	199	94	155	74	44	21	30	21	25	16	5	5	—
$20,000 to $24,999	754	282	148	158	102	123	46	38	10	31	8	7	2	—
$25,000 to $29,999	525	213	95	115	58	98	38	11	5	9	3	3	3	—
$30,000 to $34,999	494	196	94	87	44	109	50	21	10	15	7	7	3	—
$35,000 to $39,999	531	238	101	93	35	145	67	22	15	10	5	12	10	—
$40,000 to $49,999	806	372	150	110	47	262	103	16	6	11	6	5	—	—
$50,000 to $74,999	1 292	702	242	134	40	568	203	39	15	20	6	19	9	—
$75,000 and over	871	585	232	83	39	501	193	36	14	20	6	15	8	—
Not reported	630	245	116	117	64	127	52	29	23	21	15	8	8	—

See footnotes at end of table.

Table A-4. Preprimary School Enrollment of Persons 3 to 6 Years Old, by Residence, Mother's Labor Force Status and Education, Family Income, Race, and Hispanic Origin: October 1996 — Continued

(Numbers in thousands. Civilian noninstitutional population.)

Metropolitan status, region, characteristics of the mother, family income, age, race and Hispanic origin	Popula-tion	Enrolled in nursery school						Enrolled in kindergarten						Enrolled in elemen-tary school
		Total		Public		Private		Total		Public		Private		
		Total	Full day	Total	Full day	Total	Full day	Total	Full day	Total	Full day	Total	Full day	
5 Years Old														
Total children	4 185	492	223	290	127	202	96	3 129	1 648	2 652	1 359	477	289	214
Total metropolitan	3 376	388	190	228	108	159	82	2 533	1 241	2 108	977	425	264	187
Metropolitan areas of 1 million or more	2 286	250	110	134	53	115	57	1 698	806	1 400	617	297	188	152
Central city	825	93	45	61	30	32	15	594	347	476	264	118	82	64
Outside central city	1 462	157	65	73	23	84	42	1 103	459	924	353	179	106	88
Metropolitan areas of less than 1 million	1 090	138	80	94	55	44	25	835	435	707	360	128	75	35
Central city	451	50	24	37	20	13	4	330	164	272	126	58	38	15
Outside central city	639	88	56	57	35	31	21	505	271	436	234	69	37	20
Nonmetropolitan	808	105	33	62	19	43	14	596	407	544	382	52	25	28
Region:														
Northeast	706	52	21	17	8	34	13	532	279	429	207	103	72	69
Midwest	936	139	58	75	22	65	36	703	268	579	203	125	64	25
South	1 486	175	106	104	69	71	37	1 146	890	988	785	158	105	54
West	1 057	126	38	94	28	32	9	748	212	656	164	92	48	67
Labor force status of mother:														
Children living with mother	3 885	448	194	256	106	192	88	2 901	1 526	2 442	1 247	459	279	207
Mother in labor force	2 552	303	130	158	61	145	69	1 964	1 065	1 628	842	336	223	138
Employed	2 369	275	114	130	45	145	69	1 835	994	1 505	776	330	218	125
Fulltime	1 632	199	89	111	42	89	47	1 245	719	1 015	549	229	170	98
Parttime	737	75	26	19	3	56	22	590	275	490	227	100	48	27
Unemployed	183	28	15	28	15	—	—	129	71	123	66	6	6	13
Mother not in labor force	1 333	146	65	98	46	47	19	936	461	814	405	123	56	69
Children not living with mother	299	44	28	34	21	10	8	228	122	210	112	18	10	8
Education of mother:														
Children living with mother	3 885	448	194	256	106	192	88	2 901	1 526	2 442	1 247	459	279	207
Elementary: 0 to 8 years	227	33	17	28	15	5	2	142	66	137	64	5	2	4
High school: 9 to 11 years	410	42	22	38	22	4	—	295	171	293	169	2	2	22
High school graduate	1 225	150	57	103	31	46	25	889	512	811	456	77	56	81
College:														
Less than a bachelor's degree	1 238	134	53	62	26	71	27	964	467	774	366	190	101	49
Bachelor's degree or more	786	90	45	25	11	65	34	612	310	427	191	185	119	50
Family income:														
Less than $10,000	500	52	27	49	27	3	1	358	221	336	200	22	21	28
$10,000 to $14,999	357	33	16	28	15	4	—	264	144	256	140	8	4	13
$15,000 to $19,999	295	35	21	30	17	5	5	208	112	194	105	14	7	14
$20,000 to $24,999	376	55	16	39	10	17	6	260	146	234	133	27	12	29
$25,000 to $29,999	271	31	10	14	5	17	6	209	92	190	79	19	13	13
$30,000 to $34,999	247	10	6	6	3	4	3	204	109	173	90	31	18	3
$35,000 to $39,999	270	34	12	29	12	5	—	213	97	178	73	35	24	15
$40,000 to $49,999	380	61	23	30	5	31	18	277	150	233	128	44	22	22
$50,000 to $74,999	686	83	47	32	15	51	32	532	235	388	157	145	78	26
$75,000 and over	465	66	31	21	10	44	21	357	184	256	113	101	71	28
Not reported	338	33	12	13	7	20	5	247	158	214	140	33	18	24
WHITE														
3 to 6 Years Old														
Total children	12 931	3 284	1 251	1 314	488	1 969	763	3 155	1 524	2 588	1 207	567	318	2 828
Total metropolitan	10 279	2 663	1 059	1 006	390	1 657	669	2 517	1 134	2 018	844	499	290	2 299
Metropolitan areas of 1 million or more	6 821	1 787	662	624	209	1 163	453	1 662	717	1 321	513	341	204	1 574
Central city	2 056	467	204	208	71	259	132	482	246	352	161	129	85	526
Outside central city	4 765	1 320	459	416	138	904	321	1 180	471	969	352	211	119	1 049
Metropolitan areas of less than 1 million	3 458	876	396	382	181	494	215	855	417	697	331	158	86	724
Central city	1 249	303	142	120	54	183	88	300	136	237	101	63	35	270
Outside central city	2 210	573	255	262	127	311	127	555	281	460	230	95	51	454
Nonmetropolitan	2 652	621	192	308	98	313	94	638	390	570	363	68	27	530

See footnotes at end of table.

Table A-4. Preprimary School Enrollment of Persons 3 to 6 Years Old, by Residence, Mother's Labor Force Status and Education, Family Income, Race, and Hispanic Origin: October 1996 — Continued

(Numbers in thousands. Civilian noninstitutional population.)

Metropolitan status, region, characteristics of the mother, family income, age, race and Hispanic origin	Popula-tion	Enrolled in nursery school						Enrolled in kindergarten						Enrolled in elementary school
		Total		Public		Private		Total		Public		Private		
		Total	Full day	Total	Full day	Total	Full day	Total	Full day	Total	Full day	Total	Full day	
3 and 4 Years Old														
Total children	6 374	2 847	1 074	1 073	403	1 774	671	205	75	134	44	71	31	—
Total metropolitan	5 039	2 338	920	833	328	1 505	592	173	65	116	34	57	31	—
Metropolitan areas of 1 million or more	3 353	1 589	589	539	187	1 051	401	146	50	99	25	47	25	—
Central city	999	409	187	178	65	231	122	68	25	39	8	29	18	—
Outside central city	2 354	1 180	401	361	122	819	279	78	25	60	18	18	8	—
Metropolitan areas of less than 1 million	1 686	748	331	294	140	454	191	27	15	16	9	11	6	—
Central city	599	258	121	91	40	167	81	13	3	10	3	2	—	—
Outside central city	1 087	491	210	203	100	287	110	14	12	6	6	8	6	—
Nonmetropolitan	1 335	509	154	240	75	269	79	32	10	18	10	14		—
Region:														
Northeast	1 142	628	200	204	73	424	127	45	23	32	14	13	9	—
Midwest	1 548	728	178	274	59	454	120	20	—	17	—	3	—	—
South	1 981	835	432	315	177	520	255	66	31	25	16	42	15	—
West	1 703	656	264	280	94	376	170	73	21	60	13	13	0	—
Labor force status of mother:														
Children living with mother	6 041	2 722	1 014	1 012	380	1 710	634	192	73	123	41	69	31	—
Mother in labor force	3 727	1 828	764	651	256	1 177	507	106	38	61	17	45	20	—
Employed	3 532	1 745	740	610	246	1 136	495	102	36	59	17	43	18	—
Fulltime	2 313	1 091	561	371	168	719	393	67	27	44	16	24	11	—
Parttime	1 219	655	180	238	78	416	101	35	8	15	1	19	7	—
Unemployed	195	83	24	41	11	42	13	4	2	2	—	2	2	—
Mother not in labor force	2 314	894	251	361	124	533	127	85	35	62	24	24	11	—
Children not living with mother	332	125	60	61	23	64	37	13	2	10	2	2	—	—
Education of mother:														
Children living with mother	6 041	2 722	1 014	1 012	380	1 710	634	192	73	123	41	69	31	—
Elementary: 0 to 8 years	382	95	45	87	40	7	5	24	6	21	6	2	—	—
High school: 9 to 11 years	604	171	69	133	55	38	14	13	3	13	3	—	—	—
High school graduate	1 907	734	253	378	153	356	100	49	18	30	11	19	7	—
College:														
Less than a bachelor's degree	1 760	867	325	265	81	601	244	73	23	42	10	30	12	—
Bachelor's degree or more	1 388	856	322	148	51	708	271	34	24	17	12	17	12	—
Family income:														
Less than $10,000	587	167	62	145	45	22	16	20	3	15	3	5	—	—
$10,000 to $14,999	460	181	65	121	29	60	35	14	2	8	2	6	—	—
$15,000 to $19,999	400	165	77	131	61	34	17	19	13	15	8	5	5	—
$20,000 to $24,999	554	176	82	97	61	79	21	29	7	22	5	7	2	—
$25,000 to $29,999	455	182	76	102	44	81	31	6	6	—	—	—	—	—
$30,000 to $34,999	395	154	54	55	15	99	39	15	3	11	3	3	—	—
$35,000 to $39,999	450	190	69	71	26	119	43	17	10	10	5	7	5	—
$40,000 to $49,999	102	13	4	13	4	—	—	75	34	71	31	4	3	8
$50,000 to $74,999	1 139	631	221	130	38	501	183	30	11	14	2	17	9	—
$75,000 and over	791	529	198	66	26	463	172	30	11	18	4	12	7	—
Not reported	440	164	59	67	28	97	31	12	9	7	5	4	4	—
5 Years Old														
Total children	3 268	382	157	211	74	171	83	2 469	1 213	2 061	975	408	239	153
Total metropolitan	2 592	297	136	160	62	138	73	1 961	885	1 605	671	356	214	131
Metropolitan areas of 1 million or more	1 708	183	74	83	22	99	52	1 276	551	1 033	401	244	150	107
Central city	493	55	16	30	6	24	10	351	181	267	127	84	54	41
Outside central city	1 215	128	57	53	15	75	42	925	370	766	275	159	96	66
Metropolitan areas of less than 1 million	884	114	62	77	41	37	22	685	334	572	270	113	64	24
Central city	322	41	18	27	14	13	4	236	110	190	81	45	29	9
Outside central city	561	73	45	49	27	24	17	449	224	382	189	67	35	15
Nonmetropolitan	676	86	21	51	12	34	9	508	328	456	303	52	25	22
Region:														
Northeast	561	40	18	14	4	26	13	440	221	348	160	92	61	45

See footnotes at end of table.

Table A-4.   Preprimary School Enrollment of Persons 3 to 6 Years Old, by Residence, Mother's Labor Force Status and Education, Family Income, Race, and Hispanic Origin: October 1996 — Continued

(Numbers in thousands. Civilian noninstitutional population.)

Metropolitan status, region, characteristics of the mother, family income, age, race and Hispanic origin	Population	Enrolled in nursery school						Enrolled in kindergarten						Enrolled in elementary school
		Total		Public		Private		Total		Public		Private		
		Total	Full day	Total	Full day	Total	Full day	Total	Full day	Total	Full day	Total	Full day	
Midwest	777	126	48	63	14	63	34	577	200	467	146	109	54	18
South	1 060	123	61	68	35	55	26	814	617	695	541	120	77	45
West	870	94	31	67	21	27	9	638	175	550	128	87	47	46
Labor force status of mother:														
Children living with mother	3 069	358	144	196	69	162	75	2 312	1 139	1 922	910	390	229	148
Mother in labor force	1 956	225	91	110	34	115	57	1 526	763	1 252	586	275	177	99
Employed	1 854	212	87	97	30	115	57	1 451	729	1 181	556	271	174	92
Fulltime	1 219	149	64	83	30	66	34	937	494	755	366	182	129	67
Parttime	635	63	22	14	—	49	22	515	235	426	190	89	45	24
Unemployed	102	13	4	13	4	—	—	75	34	71	31	4	3	8
Mother not in labor force	1 113	132	53	86	35	47	18	786	376	671	324	115	52	49
Children not living with mother	199	24	13	15	5	9	8	156	74	138	64	18	10	5
Education of mother:														
Children living with mother	3 069	358	144	196	69	162	75	2 312	1 139	1 922	910	390	229	148
Elementary: 0 to 8 years	201	26	15	24	13	2	2	127	63	121	61	5	2	3
High school: 9 to 11 years	304	34	15	30	15	4	—	222	118	221	116	2	2	16
High school graduate	955	117	42	76	16	41	25	710	380	636	328	74	52	51
College:														
Less than a bachelor' degree	933	102	36	49	19	53	17	729	322	578	251	151	71	40
Bachelor's degree or more	676	78	37	17	7	62	31	525	257	367	155	158	102	39
Family income:														
Less than $10,000	294	25	9	24	9	2	—	211	121	194	105	16	16	16
$10,000 to $14,999	268	14	5	10	5	4	—	199	101	192	97	8	4	9
$15,000 to $19,999	227	29	16	27	14	2	2	169	91	157	86	12	5	4
$20,000 to $24,999	280	50	16	38	10	13	6	188	102	171	92	17	9	20
$25,000 to $29,999	221	23	7	13	4	10	3	175	73	156	60	19	13	9
$30,000 to $34,999	228	10	6	6	3	4	3	185	101	157	86	28	15	3
$35,000 to $39,999	217	27	6	22	6	5	—	169	70	140	52	29	18	14
$40,000 to $49,999	324	52	19	24	4	28	15	237	123	201	106	36	17	19
$50,000 to $74,999	583	66	33	22	6	44	27	462	185	338	124	123	61	21
$75,000 and over	410	58	31	17	10	41	21	318	158	224	94	94	64	20
Not reported	215	26	9	9	4	17	5	155	90	129	73	26	16	19
BLACK														
3 to 6 Years Old														
Total children	2 741	701	476	459	300	242	176	628	463	539	391	89	72	591
Total metropolitan	2 367	614	417	392	254	222	163	540	380	453	310	87	70	511
Metropolitan areas of 1 million or more	1 697	434	299	280	185	154	114	402	280	335	227	68	53	370
Central city	1 103	271	187	195	131	77	56	261	192	217	153	44	39	236
Outside central city	595	163	112	86	54	77	58	142	88	118	73	24	15	134
Metropolitan areas of less than 1 million	670	180	118	111	69	68	48	137	100	118	83	19	17	142
Central city	450	126	82	76	48	50	34	88	60	75	49	14	11	80
Outside central city	219	54	36	36	22	18	14	49	40	43	34	6	6	61
Nonmetropolitan	374	87	59	67	45	20	13	88	83	86	81	2	2	80
3 and 4 Years Old														
Total children	1 377	615	411	392	250	223	162	72	53	44	29	29	24	—
Total metropolitan	1 189	543	364	332	211	211	152	59	43	33	21	27	22	—
Metropolitan areas of 1 million or more	844	386	264	240	156	146	108	46	33	29	18	17	15	—
Central city	539	236	158	167	108	69	49	26	16	19	11	7	5	—
Outside central city	305	150	106	73	48	77	58	20	17	11	7	10	10	—
Metropolitan areas of less than 1 million	345	157	100	93	56	65	44	13	10	3	3	10	7	—
Central city	258	117	76	67	42	50	34	10	7	3	3	6	3	—
Outside central city	87	41	24	26	14	14	11	4	4	—	—	4	4	—
Nonmetropolitan	188	72	48	60	38	12	9	13	10	11	8	2	2	—
Region:														
Northeast	231	86	49	46	25	40	24	14	10	12	8	2	2	—
Midwest	326	164	82	119	55	45	26	22	14	14	9	8	5	—

See footnotes at end of table.

Table A-4. Preprimary School Enrollment of Persons 3 to 6 Years Old, by Residence, Mother's Labor Force Status and Education, Family Income, Race, and Hispanic Origin: October 1996 — Continued

(Numbers in thousands. Civilian noninstitutional population.)

Metropolitan status, region, characteristics of the mother, family income, age, race and Hispanic origin	Popula-tion	Enrolled in nursery school						Enrolled in kindergarten						Enrolled in elemen-tary school
		Total		Public		Private		Total		Public		Private		
		Total	Full day	Total	Full day	Total	Full day	Total	Full day	Total	Full day	Total	Full day	
South	682	299	236	197	151	103	85	37	28	18	12	19	16	—
West	139	65	44	31	18	34	26	—	—	—	—	—	—	—
Labor force status of mother:														
Children living with mother	1 197	548	362	340	213	208	149	57	42	33	23	24	19	—
Mother in labor force	833	438	299	254	154	184	145	48	35	26	16	21	19	—
Employed	673	376	260	207	129	169	131	34	25	20	13	14	12	—
Fulltime	527	302	238	143	110	159	128	26	20	11	8	14	12	—
Parttime	146	74	21	64	19	10	2	9	5	9	5	—	—	—
Unemployed	161	62	39	47	25	15	15	14	10	7	3	7	7	—
Mother not in labor force	364	110	63	85	59	25	4	10	7	7	7	3	—	—
Children not living with mother	180	67	49	52	37	14	12	15	11	11	6	4	4	—
Education of mother:														
Children living with mother	1 197	548	362	340	213	208	149	57	42	33	23	24	19	—
Elementary: 0 to 8 years	30	3	3	3	3	—	—	—	—	—	—	—	—	—
High school: 9 to 11 years	259	91	52	77	47	14	5	16	13	14	11	2	2	—
High school graduate	432	172	107	127	70	46	38	18	12	9	6	9	7	—
College:														
Less than a bachelor's degree	351	193	134	102	67	90	67	21	15	10	7	11	8	—
Bachelor's degree or more	126	90	67	31	26	59	41	2	2	—	—	2	2	—
Family income:														
Less than $10,000	500	199	109	164	84	35	25	19	13	11	8	8	5	—
$10,000 to $14,999	131	54	33	40	23	14	9	4	4	1	1	3	3	—
$15,000 to $19,999	75	23	12	15	9	8	3	5	3	5	3	—	—	—
$20,000 to $24,999	147	78	55	56	38	22	17	4	1	4	1	—	—	—
$25,000 to $29,999	46	15	14	8	8	7	6	5	5	2	2	3	3	—
$30,000 to $34,999	81	38	36	27	26	10	10	7	7	4	4	3	3	—
$35,000 to $39,999	66	41	32	17	8	23	23	5	5	—	—	5	5	—
$40,000 to $49,999	73	47	35	18	15	29	20	—	—	—	—	—	—	—
$50,000 to $74,999	77	39	20	2	—	37	20	2	—	2	—	—	—	—
$75,000 and over	34	27	22	14	10	13	12	5	2	2	2	2	—	—
Not reported	147	54	43	31	28	23	15	16	13	13	9	4	4	—
5 Years Old														
Total children	668	76	59	59	46	18	13	481	351	433	313	48	38	39
Total metropolitan	571	61	48	51	39	10	9	416	287	368	249	48	38	35
Metropolitan areas of 1 million or more	420	43	30	38	26	6	5	304	206	265	178	38	28	29
Central city	282	30	25	24	20	6	5	204	150	176	125	28	25	22
Outside central city	137	13	6	13	6	—	—	100	56	90	53	10	3	7
Metropolitan areas of less than 1 million	151	18	18	14	14	4	4	112	81	103	71	9	9	6
Central city	94	6	6	6	6	—	—	67	45	59	37	7	7	5
Outside central city	58	11	11	8	8	4	4	45	36	43	34	2	2	1
Nonmetropolitan	97	15	11	7	7	8	4	65	65	65	64	—	—	4
Region:														
Northeast	106	9	4	4	4	5	—	65	43	57	35	8	8	16
Midwest	123	12	8	10	6	2	2	97	55	84	45	13	10	7
South	371	47	44	36	33	11	11	284	243	258	224	27	19	9
West	69	9	3	9	3	—	—	35	10	35	10	—	—	7
Labor force status of mother:														
Children living with mother	580	61	48	45	35	17	13	417	308	369	269	48	38	37
Mother in labor force	431	49	37	32	24	16	12	318	238	274	204	44	34	30
Employed	364	35	25	18	13	16	12	277	211	232	177	44	34	25
Fulltime	305	27	22	15	10	12	12	236	185	202	153	34	31	22
Parttime	59	7	3	3	3	4	—	41	26	31	23	10	3	2
Unemployed	67	14	11	14	11	—	—	42	28	42	28	—	—	5
Mother not in labor force	149	13	11	12	11	1	1	99	69	95	65	4	4	7
Children not living with mother	88	15	11	14	11	1	—	64	44	64	44	—	—	2
Education of mother:														
Children living with mother	580	61	48	45	35	17	13	417	308	369	269	48	38	37

See footnotes at end of table.

Table A-4. Preprimary School Enrollment of Persons 3 to 6 Years Old, by Residence, Mother's Labor Force Status and Education, Family Income, Race, and Hispanic Origin: October 1996 — Continued

(Numbers in thousands. Civilian noninstitutional population.)

Metropolitan status, region, characteristics of the mother, family income, age, race and Hispanic origin	Popula-tion	Enrolled in nursery school						Enrolled in kindergarten						Enrolled in elemen-tary school
		Total		Public		Private		Total		Public		Private		
		Total	Full day	Total	Full day	Total	Full day	Total	Full day	Total	Full day	Total	Full day	
Elementary: 0 to 8 years	15	3	3	3	3	—	—	9	3	9	3	—	—	—
High school: 9 to 11 years	79	7	7	7	7	—	—	54	44	54	44	—	—	—
High school graduate	218	19	15	19	15	—	—	148	113	148	113	—	—	27
College:														
Less than a bachelor's degree	226	26	17	13	8	13	9	173	125	139	96	34	28	7
Bachelor's degree or more	41	6	6	2	2	4	4	32	23	18	14	14	10	3
Family income:														
Less than $10,000	186	23	18	22	18	2	1	136	96	131	91	5	5	12
$10,000 to $14,999	71	15	11	15	11	—	—	50	42	50	41	—	—	4
$15,000 to $19,999	48	6	6	3	3	2	2	30	21	28	19	2	2	4
$20,000 to $24,999	73	4	—	—	4	—	52	41	45	38	6	3	7	—
$25,000 to $29,999	32	3	3	1	1	2	2	22	10	22	10	—	—	5
$30,000 to $34,999	14	—	—	—	—	14	6	11	3	3	3	—	—	—
$35,000 to $39,999	41	6	6	6	6	—	—	32	21	27	15	6	6	1
$40,000 to $49,999	36	8	5	5	2	3	3	22	19	17	14	5	5	2
$50,000 to $74,999	61	8	8	3	3	5	5	43	30	29	21	14	9	4
$75,000 and over	12	—	—	—	—	—	—	12	12	8	8	4	4	—
Not reported	92	3	3	3	3	—	—	69	53	66	53	3	—	1

HISPANIC ORIGIN[1]

3 to 6 Years Old

Total children	2 646	533	243	403	173	130	71	602	290	539	245	63	45	556
Total metropolitan	2 345	480	210	359	144	121	65	525	254	469	209	56	45	503
Metropolitan areas of 1 million or more	1 692	332	144	233	90	99	55	398	201	351	163	46	38	352
Central city	907	171	80	132	50	39	30	212	119	184	94	28	25	210
Outside central city	785	161	64	100	39	60	25	186	82	168	69	18	13	141
Metropolitan areas of less than 1 million	653	148	65	126	55	22	11	128	53	118	46	10	7	151
Central city	347	59	27	48	21	11	6	78	32	74	27	4	4	87
Outside central city	305	89	38	78	33	11	5	49	21	44	18	5	3	65
Nonmetropolitan	301	53	34	44	28	9	5	76	36	70	36	7	—	53

3 and 4 Years Old

Total children	1 318	433	196	321	135	112	61	70	25	58	20	11	5	—
Total metropolitan	1 164	390	167	286	110	104	57	62	19	52	14	9	5	—
Metropolitan areas of 1 million or more	865	284	125	194	75	90	50	58	18	49	13	9	5	—
Central city	443	143	74	107	44	36	30	40	12	35	7	5	5	—
Outside central city	422	141	51	87	31	54	20	18	6	13	6	5	—	—
Metropolitan areas of less than 1 million	298	107	42	92	35	14	7	4	1	4	1	—	—	—
Central city	144	44	21	37	15	7	6	2	—	2	—	—	—	—
Outside central city	154	63	21	55	19	8	1	1	1	1	1	—	—	—
Nonmetropolitan	154	42	30	34	25	8	4	8	6	6	6	2	—	—
Region:														
Northeast	182	71	42	49	34	22	8	10	5	8	5	2	—	—
Midwest	99	37	18	26	9	11	9	14	—	14	—	—	—	—
South	375	139	74	87	44	52	30	8	6	6	6	2	—	—
West	662	187	62	159	47	28	15	38	14	31	10	7	5	—
Labor force status of mother:														
Children living with mother	1 230	398	184	300	133	98	51	67	25	56	20	11	5	—
Mother in labor force	605	227	116	157	73	70	42	24	5	19	5	4	—	—
Employed	553	211	113	141	71	70	42	22	5	17	5	4	—	—
Fulltime	419	146	80	89	45	56	34	17	3	13	3	4	—	—
Parttime	135	65	33	52	25	13	8	4	2	4	2	—	—	—
Unemployed	52	16	3	16	3	—	—	2	—	2	—	—	—	—
Mother not in labor force	625	172	68	143	59	28	9	43	20	37	15	7	5	—
Children not living with mother	88	34	13	20	2	14	10	2	—	2	—	—	—	—
Education of mother:														
Children living with mother	1 230	398	184	300	133	98	51	67	25	56	20	11	5	—
Elementary: 0 to 8 years	320	80	42	77	38	3	3	20	6	18	6	2	—	—

See footnotes at end of table.

Table A-4. Preprimary School Enrollment of Persons 3 to 6 Years Old, by Residence, Mother's Labor Force Status and Education, Family Income, Race, and Hispanic Origin: October 1996 — Continued

(Numbers in thousands. Civilian noninstitutional population.)

Metropolitan status, region, characteristics of the mother, family income, age, race and Hispanic origin	Population	Enrolled in nursery school						Enrolled in kindergarten						Enrolled in elementary school
		Total		Public		Private		Total		Public		Private		
		Total	Full day	Total	Full day	Total	Full day	Total	Full day	Total	Full day	Total	Full day	
High school: 9 to 11 years	297	68	27	68	27	—	—	12	5	12	5	—	—	—
High school graduate	304	100	55	87	48	13	6	11	4	9	4	2	—	—
College:														
Less than a bachelor's degree	212	105	38	57	19	48	19	19	7	14	2	5	5	—
Bachelor's degree or more	97	44	22	11	—	33	22	5	3	3	3	2	—	—
Family income:														
Less than $10,000	271	67	20	64	17	3	3	14	5	12	5	2	—	—
$10,000 to $14,999	178	58	23	51	17	7	6	7	—	—	—	—	—	—
$15,000 to $19,999	172	74	44	64	33	10	10	6	3	6	3	—	—	—
$20,000 to $24,999	144	43	27	37	27	5	—	12	4	9	4	2	—	—
$25,000 to $29,999	96	35	17	29	12	7	4	3	—	—	—	—	—	—
$30,000 to $34,999	60	11	3	11	3	—	—	8	3	8	3	—	—	—
$35,000 to $39,999	87	30	12	22	8	8	4	6	5	2	—	5	5	—
$40,000 to $49,999	77	20	6	5	—	15	6	3	3	3	3	—	—	—
$50,000 to $74,999	102	44	18	11	6	32	12	2	—	—	—	—	—	—
$75,000 and over	56	26	16	7	3	19	13	9	2	9	2	—	—	—
Not reported	75	25	12	18	8	6	4	—	—	—	—	—	—	—
5 Years Old														
Total children	711	95	45	76	36	18	9	471	242	422	204	49	38	44
Total metropolitan	624	86	43	68	34	17	8	411	211	367	173	44	38	39
Metropolitan areas of 1 million or more	442	48	19	39	15	10	5	295	161	261	130	34	31	32
Central city	236	28	6	25	6	3	—	150	94	127	73	24	20	19
Outside central city	206	20	13	13	9	7	5	145	68	134	57	11	11	14
Metropolitan areas of less than 1 million	182	38	24	30	20	8	4	116	50	106	43	10	7	6
Central city	111	16	6	11	6	4	—	71	30	67	26	4	4	6
Outside central city	72	22	18	18	14	4	4	44	20	39	17	5	3	—
Nonmetropolitan	87	9	2	8	1	1	1	60	30	56	30	5	—	5
Region:														
Northeast	111	4	2	2	2	2	—	81	71	62	51	19	19	16
Midwest	43	3	1	3	1	—	—	34	6	34	6	—	—	2
South	204	25	13	18	9	7	4	144	103	123	89	21	14	2
West	354	62	29	53	23	10	6	212	62	204	57	8	5	24
Labor force status of mother:														
Children living with mother	652	88	40	75	36	13	4	428	212	389	184	39	29	44
Mother in labor force	356	37	9	32	9	5	—	258	123	230	99	29	24	21
Employed	322	31	6	26	6	5	—	238	116	209	92	29	24	18
Fulltime	268	26	6	23	6	3	—	200	92	172	68	29	24	18
Parttime	54	5	—	3	—	2	—	38	24	38	24	—	—	—
Unemployed	34	6	3	6	3	—	20	7	20	7	—	—	3	—
Mother not in labor force	297	51	31	43	27	8	4	170	89	159	84	10	5	23
Children not living with mother	59	7	6	1	—	6	6	43	30	34	20	10	10	—
Education of mother:														
Children living with mother	652	88	40	75	36	13	4	428	212	389	184	39	29	44
Elementary: 0 to 8 years	163	24	13	24	13	—	—	109	51	104	49	5	2	2
High school: 9 to 11 years	149	26	15	22	15	4	—	89	47	89	47	—	—	16
High school graduate	163	28	9	19	5	9	4	98	45	94	40	5	5	9
College:														
Less than a bachelor's degree	145	10	4	10	4	—	—	108	48	87	34	21	14	9
Bachelor's degree or more	32	—	—	—	—	—	—	24	21	16	13	8	8	8
Family income:														
Less than $10,000	108	18	9	18	9	—	—	59	42	59	42	—	—	9
$10,000 to $14,999	147	12	6	12	6	—	—	98	39	93	37	5	2	4
$15,000 to $19,999	90	15	10	15	10	—	—	53	21	50	18	3	3	2
$20,000 to $24,999	99	24	4	19	3	5	1	59	35	59	35	—	—	8
$25,000 to $29,999	56	4	3	4	3	—	—	45	13	43	11	2	2	7
$30,000 to $34,999	41	2	2	—	—	2	2	31	20	26	20	5	—	—
$35,000 to $39,999	40	3	—	3	—	—	30	12	26	7	4	4	7	—
$40,000 to $49,999	34	4	4	—	4	—	4	26	14	21	9	5	5	—

See footnotes at end of table.

Table A-4. Preprimary School Enrollment of Persons 3 to 6 Years Old, by Residence, Mother's Labor Force Status and Education, Family Income, Race, and Hispanic Origin: October 1996 — Continued

(Numbers in thousands. Civilian noninstitutional population.)

Metropolitan status, region, characteristics of the mother, family income, age, race and Hispanic origin	Popula-tion	Enrolled in nursery school						Enrolled in kindergarten						Enrolled in elemen-tary school
		Total		Public		Private		Total		Public		Private		
		Total	Full day	Total	Full day	Total	Full day	Total	Full day	Total	Full day	Total	Full day	
$50,000 to $74,999	36	5	2	—	5	—	2	23	14	16	10	7	5	4
$75,000 and over	30	3	3	3	3	—	—	25	20	12	8	13	13	3
Not reported	30	5	3	3	3	2	—	22	12	17	7	5	5	—

Source: October 1996 Current Population Survey, Education and Social Stratification Branch, U.S. Bureau of the Census

1. May be of any race.

— Represents zero or rounds to zero.

Table A-5. Level of Enrollment Below College for Persons 3 to 24 Years Old, by Control of School, Metropolitan Status, Sex, Race and Hispanic Origin: October 1996

(Numbers in thousands. Civilian noninstitutional population.)

Metropolitan status, sex, race and Hispanic origin	Total			Nursery school			Kindergarten			Elementary school			High school		
	Total	Public	Private	Total	Public	Private	Total	Public	Private	Total	Public	Private	Total	Public	Private
ALL RACES															
Both sexes	54 762	47 203	7 559	4 212	1 868	2 344	4 034	3 353	680	31 467	28 116	3 351	15 049	13 865	1 184
Total metropolitan	43 689	37 132	6 557	3 480	1 476	2 003	3 265	2 654	610	25 041	22 143	2 898	11 903	10 858	1 045
Metropolitan areas of 1 million or more	29 271	24 650	4 621	2 381	965	1 416	2 222	1 795	426	16 809	14 785	2 024	7 859	7 105	755
Central city	10 569	8 832	1 737	795	424	371	796	614	182	6 216	5 334	882	2 762	2 460	302
Outside central city	18 702	15 818	2 884	1 586	541	1 045	1 426	1 181	245	10 593	9 451	1 141	5 097	4 645	453
Metropolitan areas of less than 1 million	14 418	12 482	1 936	1 099	512	587	1 043	859	184	8 232	7 357	875	4 044	3 754	290
Central city	5 503	4 682	820	458	209	248	421	337	84	3 137	2 764	373	1 487	1 372	116
Outside central city	8 915	7 800	1 115	641	303	339	622	522	100	5 095	4 593	502	2 556	2 382	174
Nonmetropolitan	11 073	10 071	1 002	732	392	341	769	699	70	6 426	5 973	453	3 146	3 007	139
Male	28 147	24 302	3 845	2 069	928	1 141	2 126	1 779	347	16 115	14 398	1 717	7 838	7 197	640
Total metropolitan	22 537	19 208	3 329	1 725	743	982	1 737	1 428	309	12 884	11 410	1 474	6 191	5 627	564
Metropolitan areas of 1 million or more	15 059	12 748	2 311	1 181	495	686	1 184	961	223	8 657	7 654	1 003	4 037	3 638	399
Central city	5 489	4 610	879	389	195	103	430	334	96	3 227	2 815	412	1 443	1 266	178
Outside central city	9 569	8 138	1 432	792	300	492	754	627	127	5 429	4 838	591	2 594	2 372	221
Metropolitan areas of less than 1 million	7 479	6 461	1 018	544	248	296	553	467	86	4 227	3 756	471	2 154	1 989	165
Central city	2 855	2 408	448	236	102	134	212	169	43	1 605	1 405	200	802	731	71
Outside central city	4 623	4 053	570	308	146	162	341	298	43	2 622	2 351	271	1 352	1 257	95
Nonmetropolitan	5 610	5 094	516	344	185	159	388	350	38	3 231	2 988	243	1 647	1 571	76
Female	26 614	22 900	3 714	2 143	940	1 203	1 908	1 575	333	15 352	13 718	1 634	7 211	6 668	543
Total metropolitan	21 151	17 924	3 228	1 755	733	1 022	1 527	1 226	301	12 157	10 733	1 424	5 712	5 232	480
Metropolitan areas of 1 million or more	14 212	11 902	2 310	1 200	470	730	1 037	834	203	8 152	7 132	1 020	3 822	3 467	356
Central city	5 080	4 222	858	406	228	178	366	281	85	2 989	2 519	470	1 319	1 194	125
Outside central city	9 132	7 681	1 452	794	241	552	671	554	118	5 163	4 613	550	2 504	2 273	231
Metropolitan areas of less than 1 million	6 939	6 022	918	555	264	291	490	392	98	4 005	3 601	404	1 890	1 765	125
Central city	2 647	2 275	373	221	107	114	209	168	41	1 532	1 359	173	685	640	45
Outside central city	4 292	3 747	545	334	156	177	281	224	57	2 473	2 242	231	1 204	1 125	80
Nonmetropolitan	5 463	4 977	486	388	207	181	381	348	32	3 195	2 985	210	1 499	1 436	63
WHITE															
Both sexes	42 971	36 483	6 489	3 284	1 314	1 969	3 163	2 596	567	24 667	21 763	2 905	11 857	10 809	1 048
Total metropolitan	33 626	28 088	5 538	2 663	1 006	1 657	2 523	2 024	499	19 279	16 818	2 461	9 162	8 240	921
Metropolitan areas of 1 million or more	21 893	18 072	3 821	1 787	624	1 163	1 668	1 327	341	12 589	10 931	1 658	5 850	5 190	660
Central city	6 176	4 891	1 285	467	208	259	484	354	129	3 638	2 980	657	1 588	1 348	240
Outside central city	15 717	13 182	2 536	1 320	416	904	1 184	973	211	8 952	7 951	1 001	4 262	3 842	420
Metropolitan areas of less than 1 million	11 733	10 016	1 717	876	382	494	855	697	158	6 690	5 887	803	3 312	3 050	262
Central city	3 976	3 291	685	303	120	183	300	237	63	2 268	1 929	339	1 105	1 006	100
Outside central city	7 757	6 725	1 032	573	262	311	555	460	95	4 422	3 958	464	2 207	2 045	162
Nonmetropolitan	9 345	8 394	951	621	308	313	641	572	68	5 388	4 944	444	2 695	2 569	126
Male	22 116	18 796	3 321	1 638	670	968	1 655	1 374	281	12 676	11 160	1 517	6 147	5 592	555
Total metropolitan	17 356	14 536	2 821	1 333	517	817	1 334	1 091	243	9 966	8 691	1 276	4 723	4 237	485
Metropolitan areas of 1 million or more	11 248	9 336	1 912	887	325	562	869	705	164	6 498	5 656	842	2 994	2 650	344
Central city	3 265	2 606	659	238	92	145	255	197	59	1 930	1 606	324	841	711	130
Outside central city	7 983	6 730	1 253	649	233	417	613	508	105	4 568	4 050	518	2 153	1 939	214
Metropolitan areas of less than 1 million	6 108	5 200	909	446	191	255	465	387	79	3 469	3 035	434	1 728	1 587	141
Central city	2 072	1 696	376	158	56	102	158	122	36	1 183	1 001	181	574	517	57
Outside central city	4 036	3 504	533	288	136	152	307	265	43	2 286	2 033	253	1 154	1 070	84
Nonmetropolitan	4 760	4 260	500	305	154	151	321	283	38	2 710	2 469	241	1 424	1 354	70
Female	20 855	17 687	3 168	1 646	644	1 002	1 508	1 222	286	11 991	10 603	1 388	5 710	5 218	492
Total metropolitan	16 270	13 553	2 717	1 329	489	840	1 188	933	256	9 313	8 128	1 185	4 439	4 003	436

See footnotes at end of table.

Table A-5. Level of Enrollment Below College for Persons 3 to 24 Years Old, by Control of School, Metropolitan Status, Sex, Race and Hispanic Origin: October 1996 — Continued

(Numbers in thousands. Civilian noninstitutional population.)

Metropolitan status, sex, race and Hispanic origin	Total			Nursery school			Kindergarten			Elementary school			High school		
	Total	Public	Private	Total	Public	Private	Total	Public	Private	Total	Public	Private	Total	Public	Private
Metropolitan areas of 1 million or more	10 645	8 736	1 909	899	299	600	799	622	177	6 091	5 275	816	2 855	2 540	315
Central city	2 911	2 285	626	229	116	113	228	158	71	1 707	1 374	333	746	637	109
Outside central city	7 734	6 452	1 282	670	183	487	571	465	106	4 384	3 901	483	2 109	1 903	206
Metropolitan areas of less than 1 million	5 625	4 816	808	430	191	240	389	310	79	3 221	2 852	369	1 584	1 463	121
Central city	1 904	1 595	309	145	64	81	142	115	28	1 085	928	158	531	489	43
Outside central city	3 720	3 221	499	285	126	159	247	195	52	2 136	1 925	211	1 053	975	78
Nonmetropolitan	4 585	4 134	451	316	154	162	320	290	30	2 678	2 476	203	1 271	1 214	56
BLACK															
Both sexes	8 870	8 123	746	702	459	243	634	545	89	5 156	4 839	317	2 378	2 281	97
Total metropolitan	7 564	6 851	712	614	392	223	546	459	87	4 369	4 058	311	2 034	1 942	92
Metropolitan areas of 1 million or more	5 505	4 931	574	435	280	154	409	341	68	3 186	2 906	281	1 475	1 404	72
Central city	3 615	3 265	350	272	195	77	262	219	44	2 121	1 941	180	959	910	49
Outside central city	1 890	1 666	224	163	86	77	147	122	24	1 065	964	101	516	494	22
Metropolitan areas of less than 1 million	2 059	1 920	138	180	111	68	137	118	19	1 183	1 153	31	559	538	20
Central city	1 196	1 103	93	126	76	50	88	75	14	688	671	17	294	281	12
Outside central city	863	818	45	54	36	18	49	43	6	495	482	14	265	257	8
Nonmetropolitan	1 306	1 272	34	87	67	20	88	86	2	787	781	6	344	339	5
Male	4 508	4 139	369	310	214	96	345	287	58	2 614	2 463	151	1 238	1 175	63
Total metropolitan	3 871	3 510	360	284	190	94	297	239	58	2 216	2 066	150	1 073	1 015	58
Metropolitan areas of 1 million or more	2 796	2 514	283	204	142	62	233	182	51	1 625	1 494	131	735	696	39
Central city	1 819	1 651	167	118	92	26	148	116	32	1 076	1 001	75	477	442	34
Outside central city	978	862	115	85	50	35	84	65	19	549	493	56	258	253	5
Metropolitan areas of less than 1 million	1 075	997	78	80	48	32	65	57	7	591	572	19	338	320	19
Central city	622	564	58	69	41	28	42	35	7	335	323	12	176	165	11
Outside central city	452	432	20	11	7	4	23	23	—	256	248	8	162	155	8
Nonmetropolitan	637	629	8	26	24	2	48	48	—	398	397	1	165	159	5
Female	4 362	3 984	378	392	245	147	289	258	31	2 541	2 375	166	1 140	1 106	34
Total metropolitan	3 693	3 341	352	330	202	129	249	220	29	2 153	1 992	161	960	927	34
Metropolitan areas of 1 million or more	2 709	2 417	292	231	139	93	176	159	17	1 561	1 411	150	740	708	32
Central city	1 796	1 613	183	154	103	51	114	103	12	1 045	940	105	483	468	15
Outside central city	913	804	109	78	35	42	62	57	5	515	471	45	257	240	17
Metropolitan areas of less than 1 million	984	924	60	99	63	36	73	61	12	592	581	11	220	219	1
Central city	573	539	35	57	34	22	47	40	6	353	348	5	118	116	1
Outside central city	411	385	26	43	29	14	26	21	6	239	233	6	102	102	—
Nonmetropolitan	669	643	26	61	43	18	40	38	2	388	383	5	179	179	—
HISPANIC ORIGIN															
Both sexes	7 497	6 927	570	533	403	130	602	539	63	4 427	4 146	281	1 935	1 839	96
Total metropolitan	6 728	6 197	532	480	359	121	525	469	56	3 985	3 724	261	1 738	1 645	93
Metropolitan areas of 1 million or more	4 908	4 477	432	332	233	99	398	351	46	2 908	2 700	208	1 270	1 192	78
Central city	2 753	2 478	275	171	132	39	212	184	28	1 613	1 470	143	758	692	65
Outside central city	2 155	1 999	156	161	100	60	186	168	18	1 296	1 230	65	512	500	12
Metropolitan areas of less than 1 million	1 820	1 720	100	148	126	22	128	118	10	1 077	1 024	53	467	452	15
Central city	1 001	941	60	59	48	11	78	74	4	599	564	35	264	255	10
Outside central city	819	779	40	89	78	11	49	44	5	478	459	19	203	198	5
Nonmetropolitan	769	730	39	53	44	9	76	70	7	442	422	19	198	194	3
Male	3 861	3 584	277	264	192	72	305	276	28	2 277	2 134	143	1 015	982	34
Total metropolitan	3 456	3 208	248	236	167	68	261	239	21	2 050	1 925	126	909	876	33
Metropolitan areas of 1 million or more	2 540	2 335	204	173	110	63	201	184	17	1 491	1 395	96	675	647	28
Central city	1 464	1 328	136	90	60	30	117	102	15	837	774	64	420	392	28

See footnotes at end of table.

Table A-5. Level of Enrollment Below College for Persons 3 to 24 Years Old, by Control of School, Metropolitan Status, Sex, Race and Hispanic Origin: October 1996 — Continued

(Numbers in thousands. Civilian noninstitutional population.)

Metropolitan status, sex, race and Hispanic origin	Total			Nursery school			Kindergarten			Elementary school			High school		
	Total	Public	Private	Total	Public	Private	Total	Public	Private	Total	Public	Private	Total	Public	Private
Outside central city	1 075	1 008	68	83	49	33	84	82	2	654	621	32	255	255	—
Metropolitan areas of less than 1 million	916	872	44	63	58	5	60	56	4	559	530	30	234	229	5
Central city	506	483	24	20	20	—	45	40	4	308	291	16	133	131	3
Outside central city	410	390	20	42	37	5	15	15	—	252	239	13	101	99	2
Nonmetropolitan	405	376	29	28	24	4	44	37	7	227	209	17	106	105	1
Female	3 636	3 343	293	270	211	58	297	262	34	2 150	2 012	138	920	858	63
Total metropolitan	3 273	2 989	284	245	192	53	265	230	34	1 935	1 799	136	829	769	60
Metropolitan areas of 1 million or more	2 368	2 141	227	159	123	36	197	168	29	1 417	1 305	112	595	545	50
Central city	1 289	1 150	139	81	72	9	95	82	13	775	696	79	338	300	38
Outside central city	1 079	991	88	78	51	27	102	86	16	642	609	33	257	245	12
Metropolitan areas of less than 1 million	904	848	56	86	69	17	68	63	5	518	494	24	233	223	10
Central city	495	459	36	39	28	11	34	34	—	291	273	18	131	124	7
Outside central city	409	389	20	47	41	6	34	29	5	226	221	6	102	99	3
Nonmetropolitan	364	354	10	25	20	5	32	32	—	215	213	2	92	89	3

Source: October 1996 Current Population Survey, Education and Social Stratification Branch, U.S. Bureau of the Census

1. May be of any race.

— Represents zero or rounds to zero.

Table A-6. Enrollment Status of Primary Family Members 3 to 17 Years Old, by Family Income, Level of Enrollment, Control of School, Sex, Race and Hispanic Origin: October 1996

(Numbers in thousands. Civilian noninstitutional population.)

Metropolitan status, sex, race and Hispanic origin	Total	Family income										
		Less than $10,000	$10,000 to $14,999	$15,000 to $19,999	$20,000 to $24,999	$25,000 to $29,999	$30,000 to $34,999	$35,000 to $39,999	$40,000 to $49,999	$50,000 to $74,999	$75,000 and over	Not reported
ALL RACES												
Both sexes 3 to 17 years old	57 985	6 425	4 377	3 331	4 307	3 776	3 692	3 657	5 658	9 938	7 803	5 023
Enrolled below college	52 006	5 418	3 844	2 930	3 720	3 380	3 322	3 299	5 123	9 172	7 390	4 409
Nursery school	4 143	427	268	236	330	253	208	267	439	784	650	280
Public	1 827	367	187	190	193	139	94	117	140	163	105	133
Private	2 316	60	81	47	137	114	114	151	300	621	545	147
Kindergarten	3 917	488	309	268	320	252	252	269	352	667	455	286
Public	3 264	453	288	247	282	228	214	218	293	480	321	239
Private	653	34	20	21	38	24	38	52	58	188	133	47
Elementary, 1 to 8 years	30 702	3 420	2 461	1 771	2 189	2 092	1 991	1 992	2 996	5 161	4 092	2 538
Public	27 385	3 268	2 370	1 646	2 068	1 920	1 803	1 788	2 650	4 383	3 248	2 241
Private	3 317	152	91	125	121	172	188	203	346	778	844	296
High school, 1 to 4 years	13 244	1 083	806	655	881	783	870	770	1 336	2 560	2 193	1 306
Public	12 174	1 059	778	623	834	743	824	717	1 262	2 332	1 785	1 217
Private	1 071	24	29	31	47	40	47	53	74	228	408	88
Enrolled in college	209	9	7	3	8	9	10	14	17	29	64	39
Not enrolled	5 770	998	526	399	579	387	360	344	518	737	349	575
3 to 14 years old	5 252	893	484	353	517	345	334	319	486	691	318	511
15 to 17 years old	518	105	42	46	62	41	26	25	32	46	32	63
High school graduate	73	7	4	8	11	11	1	3	4	11	4	10
Not high school graduate	445	98	38	38	51	30	25	21	29	34	28	53
Male, 3 to 17 years old	29 775	3 156	2 132	1 763	2 276	1 917	1 977	1 900	2 865	5 189	4 078	2 521
Enrolled below college	26 655	2 704	1 871	1 540	1 971	1 691	1 776	1 722	2 567	4 758	3 857	2 197
Nursery school	2 047	219	114	123	175	132	107	139	205	357	331	145
Public	918	177	87	97	112	69	43	64	60	70	62	75
Private	1 129	42	27	26	62	64	64	75	145	287	268	71
Kindergarten	2 062	251	157	138	185	112	140	157	186	335	250	150
Public	1 734	237	144	125	160	102	120	123	160	245	185	133
Private	328	14	14	13	25	9	21	34	26	90	66	17
Elementary, 1 to 8 years	15 751	1 699	1 160	937	1 147	1 057	1 064	1 040	1 510	2 673	2 183	1 281
Public	14 052	1 626	1 108	881	1 085	952	973	927	1 349	2 287	1 742	1 122
Private	1 699	73	53	56	63	105	91	113	161	386	441	159
High school, 1 to 4 years	6 795	535	440	343	464	390	465	386	667	1 392	1 093	620
Public	6 215	522	428	326	448	358	438	354	630	1 252	892	568
Private	580	14	13	17	16	32	27	32	37	140	201	52
Enrolled in college	89	3	—	—	5	4	6	6	2	10	35	18
Not enrolled	3 031	450	261	223	300	222	195	172	296	420	187	306
3 to 14 years old	2 746	405	240	200	268	193	176	158	272	386	168	281
15 to 17 years old	285	45	20	24	32	30	19	13	24	35	19	24
High school graduate	43	2	—	8	8	7	1	3	4	11	—	—
Not high school graduate	242	43	20	16	24	22	18	10	21	23	19	24
Female, 3 to 17 years old	28 210	3 269	2 245	1 568	2 031	1 859	1 714	1 757	2 792	4 749	3 725	2 502
Enrolled below college	25 351	2 714	1 973	1 389	1 748	1 689	1 546	1 576	2 556	4 414	3 533	2 212
Nursery school	2 096	209	154	113	155	120	101	128	234	427	319	134
Public	909	190	100	93	80	70	51	52	79	93	42	58
Private	1 187	19	54	21	75	50	50	76	155	334	277	76
Kindergarten	1 855	237	152	130	135	141	112	112	166	332	204	135
Public	1 530	216	145	122	123	126	95	94	134	235	136	106
Private	326	21	7	8	13	15	17	18	32	98	68	30
Elementary, 1 to 8 years	14 951	1 721	1 301	834	1 041	1 035	927	951	1 486	2 488	1 909	1 257
Public	13 333	1 642	1 262	765	983	968	830	861	1 301	2 096	1 505	1 119
Private	1 618	79	39	69	58	67	97	90	185	392	404	137
High school, 1 to 4 years	6 449	547	366	312	417	393	406	385	670	1 168	1 100	686
Public	5 958	538	350	298	386	385	385	363	632	1 080	893	649
Private	491	10	16	14	31	8	20	22	38	88	207	37
Enrolled in college	120	6	7	3	3	5	4	8	14	19	30	20
Not enrolled	2 739	548	265	176	279	164	165	172	222	316	163	269
3 to 14 years old	2 506	488	244	154	250	153	158	161	214	306	150	230
15 to 17 years old	233	60	21	22	30	12	7	11	8	11	13	39
High school graduate	30	6	4	—	3	4	—	1	—	—	4	10
Not high school graduate	203	54	18	22	27	8	7	11	8	11	9	29
WHITE												
Both sexes, 3 to 17 years old	45 531	3 580	3 004	2 361	3 194	3 047	2 943	3 142	4 954	8 627	7 051	3 628

See footnotes at end of table.

Table A-6. Enrollment Status of Primary Family Members 3 to 17 Years Old, by Family Income, Level of Enrollment, Control of School, Sex, Race and Hispanic Origin: October 1996 — Continued

(Numbers in thousands. Civilian noninstitutional population.)

Metropolitan status, sex, race and Hispanic origin	Total	Family income										
		Less than $10,000	$10,000 to $14,999	$15,000 to $19,999	$20,000 to $24,999	$25,000 to $29,999	$30,000 to $34,999	$35,000 to $39,999	$40,000 to $49,999	$50,000 to $74,999	$75,000 and over	Not reported
Enrolled below college	40 915	3 003	2 628	2 068	2 740	2 703	2 636	2 829	4 475	7 968	6 683	3 180
Nursery school	3 233	188	194	197	223	211	166	213	367	699	587	188
Public	1 283	166	130	162	132	121	62	89	112	149	84	75
Private	1 949	22	64	34	91	90	104	124	254	550	503	114
Kindergarten	3 070	277	230	202	235	216	222	218	302	585	407	176
Public	2 524	256	214	183	211	195	191	177	251	423	284	140
Private	546	22	16	19	24	22	31	41	50	162	123	36
Elementary, 1 to 8 years	24 095	1 952	1 670	1 211	1 650	1 645	1 595	1 722	2 659	4 442	3 676	1 872
Public	21 221	1 840	1 591	1 136	1 557	1 502	1 440	1 526	2 339	3 745	2 916	1 627
Private	2 874	112	78	75	93	143	155	196	320	698	760	245
High school, 1 to 4 years	10 517	587	534	459	633	631	653	676	1 148	2 242	2 013	943
Public	9 547	570	513	431	593	597	608	628	1 077	2 026	1 628	875
Private	970	16	21	28	40	33	45	48	71	216	384	68
Enrolled in college	146	2	7	3	5	5	7	10	8	23	51	25
Not enrolled	4 470	575	369	290	449	338	300	303	471	635	317	423
3 to 14 years old	4 083	516	339	256	403	306	280	282	442	599	292	368
15 to 17 years old	387	59	30	34	46	32	21	21	29	36	25	54
High school graduate	47	2	4	6	4	6	1	3	2	9	2	10
Not high school graduate	340	57	26	29	42	27	20	18	27	26	23	44
Male, 3 to 17 years old	23 442	1 768	1 485	1 251	1 693	1 529	1 586	1 641	2 512	4 499	3 651	1 827
Enrolled below college	21 005	1 510	1 295	1 095	1 457	1 332	1 418	1 488	2 247	4 131	3 449	1 584
Nursery school	1 619	93	92	110	128	101	88	112	170	328	304	93
Public	662	82	69	85	86	56	29	48	44	70	53	42
Private	957	12	23	25	42	45	60	64	127	258	251	51
Kindergarten	1 607	139	115	102	136	97	120	119	162	308	222	89
Public	1 340	131	104	91	123	87	102	96	141	229	161	75
Private	267	7	11	11	13	9	17	23	21	79	61	14
Elementary, 1 to 8 years	12 402	964	810	648	872	831	859	904	1 343	2 279	1 940	950
Public	10 903	908	764	612	823	747	782	791	1 192	1 932	1 536	815
Private	1 499	56	47	35	49	84	77	113	151	348	404	134
High school, 1 to 4 years	5 377	313	277	235	321	304	351	353	571	1 216	983	453
Public	4 855	302	272	220	308	278	325	323	538	1 076	800	414
Private	522	12	5	15	13	25	27	30	33	140	183	39
Enrolled in college	66	2	—	5	—	2	2	2	2	10	30	11
Not enrolled	2 371	256	191	156	232	197	165	150	263	357	172	231
3 to 14 years old	2 152	231	177	137	207	172	148	141	240	331	159	210
15 to 17 years old	218	25	14	19	25	25	17	10	23	26	14	21
High school graduate	29	2	—	5	4	5	1	3	2	9	—	—
Not high school graduate	189	24	14	14	21	20	16	7	21	17	14	21
Female, 3 to 17 years old	22 089	1 813	1 519	1 110	1 501	1 518	1 357	1 501	2 441	4 128	3 400	1 801
Enrolled below college	19 909	1 494	1 333	973	1 283	1 371	1 218	1 341	2 228	3 837	3 234	1 596
Nursery school	1 613	94	102	87	95	111	78	101	196	371	283	96
Public	621	84	61	77	46	65	34	41	69	79	31	33
Private	992	10	41	9	48	45	44	60	128	292	252	63
Kindergarten	1 463	139	115	101	99	119	102	99	139	277	185	87
Public	1 184	124	110	93	89	107	88	82	110	194	123	65
Private	278	14	5	8	10	12	14	17	29	83	62	22
Elementary, 1 to 8 years	11 693	988	859	563	778	814	736	818	1 316	2 163	1 736	923
Public	10 319	932	828	524	734	755	658	735	1 147	1 813	1 380	812
Private	1 375	56	31	39	43	59	78	83	169	350	355	111
High school, 1 to 4 years	5 140	273	257	223	312	327	302	323	576	1 026	1 030	491
Public	4 692	268	241	211	285	319	283	305	539	950	829	462
Private	448	5	16	13	27	8	19	17	38	76	201	29
Enrolled in college	80	—	7	3	—	—	4	7	5	13	22	14
Not enrolled	2 100	319	178	134	218	142	135	153	208	278	144	191
3 to 14 years old	1 931	285	162	119	196	134	131	141	202	269	133	158
15 to 17 years old	169	34	16	15	21	7	4	11	6	9	11	33
High school graduate	17	—	4	—	—	1	—	1	—	—	2	10
Not high school graduate	151	34	12	15	21	6	4	11	6	9	9	23

BLACK

	Total	Less than $10,000	$10,000 to $14,999	$15,000 to $19,999	$20,000 to $24,999	$25,000 to $29,999	$30,000 to $34,999	$35,000 to $39,999	$40,000 to $49,999	$50,000 to $74,999	$75,000 and over	Not reported
Both sexes, 3 to 17 years old	9 336	2 525	1 054	762	838	541	550	402	486	791	310	1 076
Enrolled below college	8 288	2 151	941	680	730	501	501	370	444	730	295	947
Nursery school	684	220	63	29	77	21	38	47	55	45	27	62
Public	449	185	49	18	53	11	27	24	23	5	14	39
Private	235	35	14	11	24	10	10	23	32	40	13	23

Table A-6. Enrollment Status of Primary Family Members 3 to 17 Years Old, by Family Income, Level of Enrollment, Control of School, Sex, Race and Hispanic Origin: October 1996 — Continued

(Numbers in thousands. Civilian noninstitutional population.)

Metropolitan status, sex, race and Hispanic origin	Total	Family income										
		Less than $10,000	$10,000 to $14,999	$15,000 to $19,999	$20,000 to $24,999	$25,000 to $29,999	$30,000 to $34,999	$35,000 to $39,999	$40,000 to $49,999	$50,000 to $74,999	$75,000 and over	Not reported
Kindergarten	616	194	66	40	60	23	21	37	29	46	17	82
Public	532	181	62	38	49	20	15	26	24	30	10	76
Private	83	13	4	2	11	3	6	11	5	16	7	6
Elementary, 1 to 8 years	151	15	6	16	13	18	13	—	6	27	16	22
Public	4 677	1 273	603	423	392	318	257	208	230	382	125	467
Private	314	34	12	30	22	22	33	4	19	52	44	41
High school, 1 to 4 years	1 998	430	197	158	179	118	152	73	110	205	82	294
Public	1 927	428	191	154	171	111	151	69	110	197	63	282
Private	71	2	6	3	8	7	2	5	—	8	19	12
Enrolled in college	45	7	—	—	3	4	4	—	9	5	5	9
Not enrolled	1 004	367	113	83	105	37	46	32	34	56	10	121
3 to 14 years old	899	326	105	75	94	28	41	29	32	49	3	117
15 to 17 years old	105	42	8	8	11	9	5	3	2	7	7	4
High school graduate	21	5	—	2	3	6	—	—	2	2	2	—
Not high school graduate	84	37	8	5	9	3	5	3	—	5	5	4
Male, 3 to 17 years old	4 716	1 241	481	413	446	294	297	199	250	389	183	522
Enrolled below college	4 193	1 076	434	366	396	274	265	179	225	352	172	454
Nursery school	307	116	22	7	33	14	15	20	24	12	14	31
Public	212	89	19	7	25	7	11	12	13	—	10	20
Private	95	27	3	—	—	7	4	8	11	12	4	11
Kindergarten	329	104	36	24	30	8	12	30	19	17	6	41
Public	276	98	34	22	22	8	9	19	14	8	4	38
Private	52	7	2	2	8	—	3	11	5	9	2	3
Elementary, 1 to 8 years	2 542	667	266	245	227	181	154	101	129	227	100	246
Public	2 391	651	261	230	214	163	141	101	123	199	84	224
Private	151	15	6	16	13	18	13	—	6	27	16	22
High school, 1 to 4 years	1 016	190	109	89	105	71	84	28	54	97	53	136
Public	974	188	103	88	102	65	84	28	54	96	40	127
Private	42	2	6	2	3	7	—	—	—	1	12	9
Enrolled in college	17	1	—	—	—	4	4	—	—	—	5	4
Not enrolled	505	164	47	47	51	17	29	20	25	36	6	64
3 to 14 years old	454	145	45	43	48	12	27	16	23	31	1	64
15 to 17 years old	52	19	3	5	3	5	2	3	2	5	5	—
High school graduate	9	—	—	2	—	3	—	—	2	2	—	—
Not high school graduate	43	19	3	2	3	2	2	3	—	3	5	—
Female, 3 to 17 years old	4 621	1 284	573	349	392	247	253	203	236	402	126	555
Enrolled below college	4 095	1 075	507	314	334	227	236	191	218	377	122	493
Nursery school	377	104	42	22	45	7	23	27	32	32	13	31
Public	237	96	31	11	28	4	17	12	10	5	5	19
Private	140	9	11	11	16	2	6	16	22	28	9	12
Kindergarten	287	90	30	16	29	15	9	7	10	29	10	41
Public	256	84	28	16	27	12	6	7	10	23	6	37
Private	31	6	2	—	—	3	3	—	—	—	4	4
Elementary, 1 to 8 years	2 449	640	348	208	186	159	136	111	120	207	69	263
Public	2 286	621	342	194	178	155	116	107	107	183	41	243
Private	163	19	6	14	9	4	19	4	14	25	28	19
High school, 1 to 4 years	982	240	88	68	74	46	68	46	56	109	29	158
Public	953	240	88	67	69	46	66	41	56	101	23	155
Private	29	—	—	2	5	—	2	5	—	7	6	3
Enrolled in college	28	6	—	—	3	—	—	—	9	5	—	5
Not enrolled	498	203	65	35	55	20	17	12	9	20	4	58
3 to 14 years old	445	181	60	32	46	16	14	12	9	18	2	53
15 to 17 years old	53	23	5	3	8	4	2	—	—	2	2	4
High school graduate	12	5	—	—	3	3	—	—	—	—	2	—
Not high school graduate	41	18	5	3	6	1	2	—	—	2	—	4
HISPANIC ORIGIN [1]												
Both sexes, 3 to 17 years old	8 161	1 522	1 315	887	919	644	486	437	513	552	340	546
Enrolled below college	6 995	1 241	1 143	760	777	567	433	384	437	481	321	451
Nursery school	520	81	66	93	66	39	11	34	23	49	29	30
Public	393	78	59	83	56	32	11	25	5	11	10	22
Private	127	3	7	10	9	7	—	8	18	38	19	8
Kindergarten	578	84	114	62	70	51	43	37	34	26	36	22
Public	520	82	104	59	67	48	38	28	30	23	23	17
Private	58	2	10	3	2	2	5	9	5	3	13	5
Elementary, 1 to 8 years	4 318	818	739	431	480	363	274	234	281	259	175	265

Table A-6. Enrollment Status of Primary Family Members 3 to 17 Years Old, by Family Income, Level of Enrollment, Control of School, Sex, Race and Hispanic Origin: October 1996 — Continued

(Numbers in thousands. Civilian noninstitutional population.)

Metropolitan status, sex, race and Hispanic origin	Total	Family income										
		Less than $10,000	$10,000 to $14,999	$15,000 to $19,999	$20,000 to $24,999	$25,000 to $29,999	$30,000 to $34,999	$35,000 to $39,999	$40,000 to $49,999	$50,000 to $74,999	$75,000 and over	Not reported
Public	4 041	797	721	406	474	324	246	210	255	237	140	231
Private	277	21	19	25	6	38	28	25	25	22	36	35
High school, 1 to 4 years	1 579	258	223	174	162	115	106	79	99	148	81	133
Public	1 490	255	208	163	157	111	103	77	90	138	58	129
Private	89	3	15	11	5	4	3	2	8	10	23	4
Enrolled in college	17	3	4	—	3	—	2	—	—	—	—	4
Not enrolled	1 149	279	168	127	138	77	50	54	76	71	19	91
3 to 14 years old	1 054	255	157	118	129	66	47	54	66	71	19	74
15 to 17 years old	95	23	11	10	10	11	4	—	10	—	—	17
High school graduate	4	2	1	—	1	—	—	—	—	—	—	—
Not high school graduate	91	22	10	9	9	11	4	—	10	—	—	17
Male, 3 to 17 years old	4 162	724	625	457	498	314	286	242	233	270	192	321
Enrolled below college	3 599	601	547	403	427	268	252	220	200	227	181	273
Nursery school	258	36	31	46	49	13	2	24	7	14	17	19
Public	187	35	29	36	43	6	2	16	—	—	6	14
Private	71	1	2	10	5	7	—	8	7	14	11	6
Kindergarten	299	48	49	28	40	23	30	18	17	16	19	11
Public	270	46	44	28	40	21	25	14	12	16	16	8
Private	28	2	5	—	2	—	5	4	5	—	3	2
Elementary, 1 to 8 years	2 227	383	374	228	253	185	155	134	131	121	94	167
Public	2 087	369	366	215	251	160	145	113	131	110	82	145
Private	139	14	8	13	3	25	10	21	—	11	12	22
High school, 1 to 4 years	815	134	93	101	86	46	64	44	45	75	51	76
Public	783	131	88	96	86	42	64	44	42	74	41	74
Private	33	3	4	5	—	4	—	—	2	1	11	2
Enrolled in college	8	—	—	—	3	—	2	—	—	—	—	2
Not enrolled	555	123	78	54	67	46	32	21	33	43	11	46
3 to 14 years old	503	112	72	54	58	41	29	21	24	43	11	37
15 to 17 years old	52	11	6	—	10	5	4	—	8	—	—	9
High school graduate	3	2	—	—	1	—	—	—	—	—	—	—
Not high school graduate	49	9	6	—	9	5	4	—	8	—	—	9
Female, 3 to 17 years old	3 999	798	689	430	421	331	199	196	281	282	148	225
Enrolled below college	3 396	639	595	357	350	300	181	164	237	254	141	178
Nursery school	261	45	197	47	17	26	9	10	16	35	12	11
Public	205	43	30	47	13	26	9	10	5	11	4	8
Private	56	2	4	—	4	—	—	—	11	23	8	2
Kindergarten	279	36	65	34	30	27	13	18	18	9	17	12
Public	249	36	60	31	28	27	13	14	18	6	8	9
Private	30	—	5	3	2	—	—	5	—	3	10	3
Elementary, 1 to 8 years	2 091	435	365	203	227	177	118	100	149	137	81	99
Public	1 953	428	354	192	224	164	101	96	124	126	57	86
Private	138	6	11	11	3	13	17	4	25	11	24	13
High school, 1 to 4 years	764	124	131	73	76	70	42	35	54	73	30	57
Public	708	124	120	67	71	70	39	33	48	64	18	55
Private	56	—	11	6	5	—	3	2	6	9	12	2
Enrolled in college	10	3	4	—	—	—	—	—	—	—	—	2
Not enrolled	594	156	90	73	71	31	18	32	43	28	8	45
3 to 14 years old	551	143	85	64	71	25	18	32	42	28	8	37
15 to 17 years old	43	13	5	9	—	6	—	—	2	—	—	8
High school graduate	1	—	1	—	—	—	—	—	—	—	—	—
Not high school graduate	42	13	4	9	—	6	—	—	2	—	—	8

Source: October 1996 Current Population Survey, Education and Social Stratification Branch, U.S. Bureau of the Census

1. May be of any race.

— Represents zero or rounds to zero.

Table A-7. Enrollment Status of Primary Family Members 3 to 17 Years Old, by Educational Attainment of Family Householder, Level of Enrollment, Control of School, Sex, Race and Hispanic Origin: October 1996

(Numbers in thousands. Civilian noninstitutional population.)

Level and control of school, sex, race and Hispanic origin	Total	Education completed by family householder					
		Elementary school		High school		College	
		0 to 4 years	5 to 8 years	9 to 11 years	Graduate	Less than a bachelor's degree	Bachelor's degree or more
ALL RACES							
Both sexes 3 to 17 years old	57 985	848	2 857	6 407	18 963	15 733	13 178
Enrolled below college	52 006	722	2 361	5 488	17 003	14 269	12 162
Nursery school	4 143	38	126	386	1 213	1 139	1 241
Public	1 827	32	111	311	692	412	270
Private	2 316	6	15	76	521	727	971
Kindergarten	3 917	53	166	456	1 225	1 129	889
Public	3 264	45	162	435	1 077	910	635
Private	653	8	4	21	148	219	253
Elementary, 1 to 8 years	30 702	441	1 507	3 407	10 250	8 328	6 769
Public	27 385	430	1 446	3 300	9 435	7 347	5 427
Private	3 317	11	61	106	816	980	1 343
High school, 1 to 4 years	13 244	189	562	1 240	4 315	3 674	3 264
Public	12 174	183	547	1 201	4 069	3 405	2 769
Private	1 071	7	16	39	246	268	495
Enrolled in college	209	—	9	17	47	54	82
Not enrolled	5 770	127	487	902	1 912	1 410	933
3 to 14 years old	5 252	104	417	792	1 727	1 311	900
15 to 17 years old	518	23	70	110	185	98	33
High school graduate	73	3	2	3	34	22	9
Not high school graduate	445	20	67	107	151	76	24
Male, 3 to 17 years old	29 775	432	1 428	3 308	9 752	8 083	6 772
Enrolled below college	26 655	366	1 180	2 858	8 750	7 276	6 225
Nursery school	2 047	21	59	167	650	538	613
Public	918	15	44	131	382	196	150
Private	1 129	6	15	35	269	341	463
Kindergarten	2 062	24	91	257	615	623	452
Public	1 734	19	89	245	542	506	333
Private	328	5	2	11	73	117	120
Elementary, 1 to 8 years	15 751	226	772	1 787	5 231	4 195	3 539
Public	14 052	221	724	1 731	4 844	3 669	2 863
Private	1 699	5	48	56	387	527	677
High school, 1 to 4 years	6 795	95	258	648	2 253	1 920	1 620
Public	6 215	95	251	633	2 118	1 766	1 353
Private	580	—	8	15	136	154	268
Enrolled in college	89	—	3	3	21	26	36
Not enrolled	3 031	66	245	447	981	781	511
3 to 14 years old	2 746	48	212	398	871	725	492
15 to 17 years old	285	19	33	49	109	55	19
High school graduate	43	3	2	—	17	13	7
Not high school graduate	242	16	31	49	92	42	12
Female, 3 to 17 years old	28 210	416	1 429	3 099	9 211	7 650	6 406
Enrolled below college	25 351	356	1 182	2 631	8 253	6 993	5 938
Nursery school	2 096	17	67	220	563	601	628
Public	909	17	67	179	310	216	120
Private	1 187	—	1	40	252	386	508
Kindergarten	1 855	29	75	199	610	505	436
Public	1 530	26	73	189	534	404	303
Private	326	3	2	9	76	102	134
Elementary, 1 to 8 years	14 951	215	735	1 620	5 019	4 132	3 230
Public	13 333	208	722	1 569	4 591	3 679	2 564
Private	1 618	7	13	51	428	454	666
High school, 1 to 4 years	6 449	94	304	592	2 062	1 754	1 644
Public	5 958	87	296	568	1 951	1 639	1 416
Private	491	7	8	24	110	114	227
Enrolled in college	120	—	6	14	26	28	46
Not enrolled	2 739	61	242	455	932	629	422

See footnotes at end of table.

Table A-7. Enrollment Status of Primary Family Members 3 to 17 Years Old, by Educational Attainment of Family Householder, Level of Enrollment, Control of School, Sex, Race and Hispanic Origin: October 1996 — Continued

(Numbers in thousands. Civilian noninstitutional population.)

Level and control of school, sex, race and Hispanic origin	Total	Education completed by family householder					
		Elementary school		High school		College	
		0 to 4 years	5 to 8 years	9 to 11 years	Graduate	Less than a bachelor's degree	Bachelor's degree or more
3 to 14 years old	2 506	57	205	394	856	586	408
15 to 17 years old	233	4	36	61	75	43	14
High school graduate	30	—	—	3	17	9	2
Not high school graduate	203	4	36	58	59	34	13
WHITE							
Both sexes, 3 to 17 years old	45 531	631	2 248	4 418	14 736	12 285	11 211
Enrolled below college	40 915	532	1 849	3 762	13 261	11 153	10 358
Nursery school	3 233	25	108	235	940	882	1 042
Public	1 283	25	93	186	497	275	208
Private	1 949	—	15	49	444	606	834
Kindergarten	3 070	38	144	301	951	878	758
Public	2 524	30	140	285	828	707	535
Private	546	8	4	16	123	172	223
Elementary, 1 to 8 years	24 095	326	1 158	2 372	7 981	6 466	5 793
Public	21 221	318	1 100	2 281	7 258	5 666	4 598
Private	2 874	7	58	91	724	800	1 195
High school, 1 to 4 years	10 517	144	439	854	3 388	2 927	2 765
Public	9 547	137	426	820	3 169	2 686	2 309
Private	970	7	14	33	220	241	455
Enrolled in college	146	—	6	12	35	36	57
Not enrolled	4 470	99	393	645	1 440	1 096	797
3 to 14 years old	4 083	76	337	563	1 310	1 028	768
15 to 17 years old	387	23	55	82	130	68	29
High school graduate	47	3	2	3	21	11	7
Not high school graduate	340	20	53	79	109	57	22
Male, 3 to 17 years old	23 442	312	1 146	2 262	7 676	6 291	5 755
Enrolled below college	21 005	268	964	1 943	6 898	5 658	5 274
Nursery school	1 619	11	52	110	515	408	523
Public	662	11	37	80	288	121	124
Private	957	—	15	29	227	287	399
Kindergarten	1 607	20	89	157	480	491	372
Public	1 340	14	87	148	422	403	265
Private	267	5	2	8	58	87	106
Elementary, 1 to 8 years	12 402	164	615	1 246	4 125	3 245	3 007
Public	10 903	162	570	1 194	3 791	2 800	2 385
Private	1 499	2	45	52	334	445	621
High school, 1 to 4 years	5 377	73	209	431	1 777	1 514	1 372
Public	4 855	73	204	420	1 654	1 379	1 125
Private	522	—	5	11	123	135	247
Enrolled in college	66	—	—	3	17	21	25
Not enrolled	2 371	44	181	316	761	612	456
3 to 14 years old	2 152	25	159	277	675	578	438
15 to 17 years old	218	19	22	39	86	34	19
High school graduate	29	3	2	—	13	4	7
Not high school graduate	189	16	20	39	73	30	12
Female, 3 to 17 years old	22 089	319	1 102	2 156	7 060	5 995	5 457
Enrolled below college	19 909	264	885	1 818	6 363	5 495	5 084
Nursery school	1 613	14	57	125	425	473	519
Public	621	14	56	105	208	154	84
Private	992	—	1	20	217	320	435
Kindergarten	1 463	18	55	144	471	388	386
Public	1 184	15	53	137	407	304	269
Private	278	3	2	8	64	84	117
Elementary, 1 to 8 years	11 693	161	543	1 126	3 856	3 221	2 786
Public	10 319	156	530	1 088	3 467	2 866	2 213
Private	1 375	5	13	39	389	355	574
High school, 1 to 4 years	5 140	71	230	422	1 611	1 413	1 393

See footnotes at end of table.

Table A-7. Enrollment Status of Primary Family Members 3 to 17 Years Old, by Educational Attainment of Family Householder, Level of Enrollment, Control of School, Sex, Race and Hispanic Origin: October 1996 — Continued

(Numbers in thousands. Civilian noninstitutional population.)

Level and control of school, sex, race and Hispanic origin	Total	Education completed by family householder					
		Elementary school		High school		College	
		0 to 4 years	5 to 8 years	9 to 11 years	Graduate	Less than a bachelor's degree	Bachelor's degree or more
Public	4 692	64	222	400	1 514	1 307	1 184
Private	448	7	8	22	97	106	209
Enrolled in college	80	—	6	8	18	16	32
Not enrolled	2 100	55	211	329	679	484	341
3 to 14 years old	1 931	51	178	286	635	450	330
15 to 17 years old	169	4	33	43	44	34	11
High school graduate	17	—	—	3	8	7	—
Not high school graduate	151	4	33	40	36	27	11
BLACK							
Both sexes, 3 to 17 years old	9 336	73	427	1 712	3 506	2 623	995
Enrolled below college	8 288	64	355	1 486	3 104	2 366	913
Nursery school	684	3	12	133	228	211	97
Public	449	3	12	110	172	109	43
Private	235	—	—	23	56	102	54
Kindergarten	616	11	14	123	232	181	55
Public	532	11	14	118	209	140	41
Private	83	—	—	5	23	42	14
Elementary, 1 to 8 years	151	—	3	2	49	70	27
Public	4 677	37	239	879	1 814	1 288	421
Private	314	2	3	11	77	141	80
High school, 1 to 4 years	1 998	12	87	341	753	545	260
Public	1 927	12	87	337	729	528	233
Private	71	—	—	4	24	17	26
Enrolled in college	45	—	3	5	6	17	13
Not enrolled	1 004	9	69	220	396	240	70
3 to 14 years old	899	9	58	201	346	217	68
15 to 17 years old	105	—	11	19	50	23	2
High school graduate	21	—	—	—	12	7	2
Not high school graduate	84	—	10	19	38	16	—
Male, 3 to 17 years old	4 716	32	206	907	1 706	1 380	485
Enrolled below college	4 193	27	152	792	1 520	1 247	455
Nursery school	307	—	6	49	107	107	38
Public	212	—	6	47	82	61	17
Private	95	—	—	2	25	46	21
Kindergarten	329	3	2	78	117	94	35
Public	276	3	2	75	102	66	28
Private	52	—	—	3	14	28	7
Elementary, 1 to 8 years	2 542	14	111	473	917	759	268
Public	2 391	14	108	471	868	689	241
Private	151	—	3	2	49	70	27
High school, 1 to 4 years	1 016	10	34	192	379	287	114
Public	974	10	34	188	366	274	102
Private	42	—	—	4	13	14	12
Enrolled in college	17	—	3	—	1	5	8
Not enrolled	505	5	51	115	185	127	22
3 to 14 years old	454	5	43	106	164	114	22
15 to 17 years old	52	—	8	9	21	14	—
High school graduate	9	—	—	—	4	5	—
Not high school graduate	43	—	8	9	17	9	—
Female, 3 to 17 years old	4 621	41	221	804	1 800	1 244	511
Enrolled below college	4 095	37	203	694	1 584	1 119	458
Nursery school	377	3	7	84	121	104	59
Public	237	3	7	63	90	49	26
Private	140	—	—	20	31	56	33
Kindergarten	287	7	12	45	115	88	20
Public	256	7	12	43	107	74	13
Private	31	—	—	2	8	14	7

See footnotes at end of table.

Table A-7. Enrollment Status of Primary Family Members 3 to 17 Years Old, by Educational Attainment of Family Householder, Level of Enrollment, Control of School, Sex, Race and Hispanic Origin: October 1996 — Continued

(Numbers in thousands. Civilian noninstitutional population.)

Level and control of school, sex, race and Hispanic origin	Total	Education completed by family householder					
		Elementary school		High school		College	
		0 to 4 years	5 to 8 years	9 to 11 years	Graduate	Less than a bachelor's degree	Bachelor's degree or more
Elementary, 1 to 8 years	2 449	25	131	417	974	670	233
Public	2 286	23	131	408	946	599	180
Private	163	2	—	9	28	71	53
High school, 1 to 4 years	982	3	53	149	374	258	146
Public	953	3	53	149	363	254	131
Private	29	—	—	—	11	3	15
Enrolled in college	28	—	—	5	5	12	5
Not enrolled	498	3	18	105	212	112	48
3 to 14 years old	445	3	15	95	183	103	46
15 to 17 years old	53	—	3	11	29	9	2
High school graduate	12	—	—	—	—	2	2
Not high school graduate	41	—	3	11	21	7	—
HISPANIC ORIGIN [1]							
Both sexes, 3 to 17 years old	8 161	600	1 630	1 787	2 132	1 393	618
Enrolled below college	6 995	506	1 359	1 452	1 888	1 251	539
Nursery school	520	25	76	99	158	95	66
Public	393	25	76	97	125	46	22
Private	127	—	—	2	32	49	44
Kindergarten	578	36	105	96	158	138	46
Public	520	28	102	93	148	117	31
Private	58	8	2	2	10	21	15
Elementary, 1 to 8 years	4 318	308	875	975	1 152	712	297
Public	4 041	298	854	955	1 070	627	236
Private	277	10	21	20	81	84	61
High school, 1 to 4 years	1 579	137	303	282	420	307	130
Public	1 490	131	297	268	401	293	101
Private	89	7	7	14	19	14	28
Enrolled in college	17	—	53	11	5	—	—
Not enrolled	1 149	94	269	325	239	142	80
3 to 14 years old	1 054	74	244	305	216	135	80
15 to 17 years old	95	20	25	20	23	7	—
High school graduate	4	—	2	—	2	—	—
Not high school graduate	91	20	23	20	21	7	—
Male, 3 to 17 years old	4 162	297	797	913	1 101	718	336
Enrolled below college	3 599	256	676	745	992	650	280
Nursery school	258	11	27	42	89	44	45
Public	187	11	27	40	68	23	18
Private	71	—	—	2	21	21	27
Kindergarten	299	18	65	42	84	76	13
Public	270	12	65	40	79	62	11
Private	28	5	—	2	5	14	2
Elementary, 1 to 8 years	2 227	160	443	515	603	358	149
Public	2 087	155	428	502	562	317	123
Private	139	5	14	13	41	41	26
High school, 1 to 4 years	815	67	141	146	216	172	73
Public	783	67	139	144	207	169	57
Private	33	—	2	2	9	3	16
Enrolled in college	8	—	—	3	5	—	—
Not enrolled	555	41	121	165	104	68	56
3 to 14 years old	503	25	108	158	94	62	56
15 to 17 years old	52	16	13	7	11	6	—
High school graduate	3	—	2	—	1	—	—
Not high school graduate	49	16	11	7	10	6	—
Female, 3 to 17 years old	3 999	303	833	874	1 031	675	283
Enrolled below college	3 396	250	683	706	896	601	259
Nursery school	261	14	49	57	69	51	21
Public	205	14	49	57	58	24	4

See footnotes at end of table.

Table A-7.   Enrollment Status of Primary Family Members 3 to 17 Years Old, by Educational Attainment of Family Householder, Level of Enrollment, Control of School, Sex, Race and Hispanic Origin: October 1996 — Continued

(Numbers in thousands. Civilian noninstitutional population.)

| Level and control of school, sex, race and Hispanic origin | Total | Education completed by family householder | | | | | |
| | | Elementary school | | High school | | College | |
		0 to 4 years	5 to 8 years	9 to 11 years	Graduate	Less than a bachelor's degree	Bachelor's degree or more
Private	56	—	—	—	11	28	17
Kindergarten	279	18	40	53	74	61	33
Public	249	15	37	53	69	54	20
Private	30	3	2	—	5	7	12
Elementary, 1 to 8 years	2 091	148	432	460	549	353	148
Public	1 953	143	425	453	509	310	113
Private	138	5	7	7	41	43	35
High school, 1 to 4 years	764	70	162	136	204	135	57
Public	708	63	158	124	194	124	45
Private	56	7	4	12	11	11	12
Enrolled in college	10	—	2	7	—	—	—
Not enrolled	594	53	148	160	134	74	24
3 to 14 years old	551	49	136	147	123	72	24
15 to 17 years old	43	4	13	13	12	2	—
High school graduate	1	—	—	—	1	—	—
Not high school graduate	42	4	13	13	11	2	—

Source: October 1996 Current Population Survey, Education and Social Stratification Branch, U.S. Bureau of the Census

1. May be of any race.

— Represents zero or rounds to zero.

Table A-8. Persons 15 to 24 Years Old Enrolled in Secondary School in Previous Year by Current Enrollment Status, Age, Sex, Race, Hispanic Origin, and Family Income (for Dependent Family Members):   October 1996

(Numbers in thousands. Civilian noninstitutional population.)

Age, family income, sex, race and Hispanic origin	Total	Current grade in which enrolled						Enrolled last year, not currently enrolled					
		8	9	10	11	12	College year 1 (Graduated this year)	Highest grade completed					
								Total	7 and 8	9	10	11	12 (Graduated this year)
ALL PERSONS													
All Races													
Both sexes, 15 to 24 year	15 304	135	1 197	3 662	3 597	3 468	1 674	1 570	60	94	138	253	1 025
15 years old	3 752	116	961	2 403	194	20	6	52	20	23	10	—	—
16 years old	3 918	14	191	1 041	2 329	238	14	92	21	26	34	8	4
17 years old	3 508	6	31	151	855	2 132	147	186	12	30	41	38	64
18 years old	2 751	—	9	6	7	3	3	1	2	8	26	117	451
19 years old	873	—	—	5	38	181	289	360	3	—	12	53	293
20 to 24 years old	503	—	9	15	19	115	67	277	5	7	16	38	212
Male, 15 to 24 years old	7 978	84	725	1 969	1 856	1 752	755	836	23	50	76	114	572
15 years old	1 932	73	560	1 182	88	4	1	23	6	15	2	—	—
16 years old	2 045	11	138	651	1 110	96	4	34	6	9	18	1	—
17 years old	1 812	—	21	97	522	996	65	111	8	18	27	22	34
18 years old	1 429	—	2	32	97	494	492	312	—	5	20	57	230
19 years old	502	—	—	—	29	115	151	207	3	—	3	20	181
20 to 24 years old	259	—	3	7	10	47	42	149	—	3	6	13	127
Female, 15 to 24 years ol	7 327	52	473	1 693	1 741	1 716	919	734	37	43	62	139	452
15 years old	1 820	43	401	1 222	106	16	5	29	14	8	8	—	—
16 years old	1 873	3	52	390	1 218	142	10	58	15	17	15	7	4
17 years old	1 696	6	10	54	333	1 136	82	75	3	12	14	16	30
18 years old	1 322	—	3	15	65	290	659	290	—	3	6	59	221
19 years old	372	—	—	5	10	66	138	153	—	—	9	32	112
20 to 24 years old	244	—	6	8	9	68	25	128	5	4	10	25	85
White													
Both sexes, 15 to 24 year	11 954	79	909	2 918	2 804	2 729	1 337	1 178	43	83	82	196	774
15 years old	2 958	65	767	1 936	133	9	6	41	15	23	4	—	—
16 years old	3 038	14	116	822	1 879	139	8	62	13	19	22	4	4
17 years old	2 792	—	15	111	661	1 760	100	145	7	27	29	33	49
18 years old	2 180	—	2	33	93	630	975	448	—	8	16	97	327
19 years old	652	—	—	5	29	120	219	278	3	—	5	41	229
20 to 24 years old	334	—	9	11	9	71	30	204	5	6	6	22	165
Male, 15 to 24 years old	6 272	56	566	1 555	1 418	1 387	603	686	18	46	50	102	471
15 years old	1 524	45	464	939	52	4	1	18	3	15	—	—	—
16 years old	1 566	11	85	517	866	57	1	29	5	8	14	1	—
17 years old	1 458	—	11	69	409	834	49	86	6	15	18	19	28
18 years old	1 155	—	2	23	58	397	421	253	—	5	15	52	181
19 years old	388	—	—	—	26	70	110	182	3	—	3	20	157
20 to 24 years old	180	—	3	6	7	27	20	117	—	2	—	9	105
Female, 15 to 24 years ol	5 683	22	343	1 363	1 386	1 342	734	492	25	37	32	94	303
15 years old	1 433	20	303	997	81	5	5	23	12	8	4	—	—
16 years old	1 472	3	30	305	1 013	82	7	32	7	11	7	3	4
17 years old	1 334	—	4	41	253	927	50	59	1	12	11	14	21
18 years old	1 025	—	—	10	35	233	553	194	—	3	1	44	146
19 years old	264	—	—	5	3	51	109	96	—	—	3	21	73
20 to 24 years old	154	—	6	5	2	44	10	87	5	4	6	13	60
Black													
Both sexes, 15 to 24 year	2 551	44	236	558	556	607	228	323	9	10	49	48	206
15 years old	586	42	152	336	41	11	—	5	3	—	2	—	—
16 years old	639	—	65	183	291	75	3	22	2	6	10	4	—
17 years old	552	3	15	24	151	298	31	30	5	3	10	2	10
18 years old	448	—	3	11	57	132	120	125	—	—	10	16	98
19 years old	188	—	—	0	5	54	51	77	—	—	7	12	59
20 to 24 years old	137	—	—	4	9	37	23	64	—	1	10	14	39

Table A-8. Persons 15 to 24 Years Old Enrolled in Secondary School in Previous Year by Current Enrollment Status, Age, Sex, Race, Hispanic Origin, and Family Income (for Dependent Family Members):   October 1996 — Continued

(Numbers in thousands. Civilian noninstitutional population.)

Age, family income, sex, race and Hispanic origin	Total	Current grade in which enrolled						Enrolled last year, not currently enrolled					
							College year 1 (Graduated this year)	Highest grade completed					
		8	9	10	11	12		Total	7 and 8	9	10	11	12 (Graduated this year)
Male, 15 to 24 years old	1 267	27	126	306	311	282	95	120	5	4	25	8	78
15 years old	289	27	67	166	23	—	—	5	3	—	2	—	—
16 years old	345	—	50	114	153	23	1	4	—	—	4	—	—
17 years old	260	—	9	19	94	117	7	14	2	3	7	—	2
18 years old	216	—	—	7	35	82	45	48	—	—	5	4	39
19 years old	92	—	—	—	3	39	26	24	—	—	—	—	24
20 to 24 years old	65	—	—	—	3	21	16	25	—	1	6	4	13
Female, 15 to 24 years ol	1 284	18	110	252	244	325	133	203	4	6	24	40	129
15 years old	298	15	85	169	18	11	—	—	—	—	—	—	—
16 years old	295	—	15	69	138	52	2	18	2	6	7	4	—
17 years old	291	3	7	5	57	180	24	16	2	—	3	2	8
18 years old	232	—	3	5	22	50	75	77	—	—	5	12	60
19 years old	96	—	—	—	3	15	25	53	—	—	7	12	35
20 to 24 years old	72	—	—	3	6	16	7	39	—	—	3	10	26
Hispanic Origin[1]													
Both sexes, 15 to 24 year	1 907	28	182	492	442	446	106	211	10	21	21	58	101
15 years old	481	24	137	277	32	5	—	5	5	—	—	—	—
16 years old	489	4	31	166	233	36	—	19	—	11	5	2	—
17 years old	400	—	8	35	113	214	10	19	—	5	3	7	3
18 years old	297	—	—	5	32	112	79	69	—	—	5	22	42
19 years old	149	—	—	1	31	49	14	53	3	—	2	17	32
20 to 24 years old	92	—	6	8	2	29	2	46	2	5	5	10	24
Male, 15 to 24 years old	1 004	24	108	278	226	218	34	116	6	7	8	39	56
15 years old	255	22	76	141	9	3	—	3	3	—	—	—	—
16 years old	268	2	21	104	118	16	—	6	—	6	—	—	—
17 years old	195	—	8	26	54	94	5	9	—	—	3	4	1
18 years old	144	—	—	5	17	56	25	41	—	—	4	20	17
19 years old	101	—	—	—	28	33	3	38	3	—	—	10	25
20 to 24 years old	41	—	3	3	—	15	2	19	—	1	—	5	12
Female, 15 to 24 years ol	903	4	74	214	216	228	72	96	4	14	14	18	46
15 years old	226	2	61	137	23	2	—	2	2	—	—	—	—
16 years old	221	2	10	62	114	20	—	12	—	5	5	2	—
17 years old	205	—	—	9	60	120	6	11	—	5	—	3	2
18 years old	153	—	—	—	14	56	55	28	—	—	1	2	25
19 years old	47	—	—	1	3	16	11	16	—	—	2	6	7
20 to 24 years old	51	—	3	5	2	14	—	27	2	4	5	5	11
DEPENDENT FAMILY MEMBERS													
All Races													
Both sexes, all incomes	14 211	135	1 158	3 526	3 456	3 269	1 504	1 163	47	68	108	167	773
Less than $10,000	1 279	35	154	360	306	244	59	121	8	19	18	12	64
$10,000 to $14,999	882	25	127	200	232	173	49	76	6	—	12	15	43
$15,000 to $19,999	733	9	73	211	159	163	45	73	6	—	15	12	40
$20,000 to $24,999	953	10	111	218	208	210	65	131	3	18	16	11	84
$25,000 to $29,999	900	5	73	230	200	204	82	105	5	9	—	31	61
$30,000 to $34,999	957	7	89	246	203	221	97	94	5	7	6	9	68
$35,000 to $39,999	758	5	63	213	189	146	85	57	3	4	—	6	44
$40,000 to $49,999	1 419	11	77	329	367	364	164	105	—	1	8	17	80
$50,000 to $74,999	2 594	8	156	597	656	671	333	173	—	3	10	27	134
$75,000 and over	2 272	3	128	530	588	558	359	107	—	4	14	5	84
Not reported	1 463	16	105	392	349	315	166	119	11	3	10	22	73
Male, all incomes	7 532	84	705	1 893	1 795	1 688	694	672	23	43	65	81	460
Less than $10,000	652	28	95	181	164	119	13	53	3	7	12	2	29
$10,000 to $14,999	469	7	77	121	113	88	25	37	—	—	5	9	23
$15,000 to $19,999	407	5	39	130	85	87	14	48	3	—	9	12	24
$20,000 to $24,999	516	7	66	133	125	87	26	72	—	12	11	3	46

Table A-8. Persons 15 to 24 Years Old Enrolled in Secondary School in Previous Year by Current Enrollment Status, Age, Sex, Race, Hispanic Origin, and Family Income (for Dependent Family Members):   October 1996 — Continued

(Numbers in thousands. Civilian noninstitutional population.)

Age, family income, sex, race and Hispanic origin	Total	Current grade in which enrolled						Enrolled last year, not currently enrolled					
		8	9	10	11	12	College year 1 (Graduated this year)	Highest grade completed					
								Total	7 and 8	9	10	11	12 (Graduated this year)
$25,000 to $29,999	467	4	49	105	97	110	42	62	3	8	—	18	33
$30,000 to $34,999	520	7	62	124	110	133	29	56	5	4	—	4	43
$35,000 to $39,999	428	5	33	120	109	71	41	48	3	4	—	3	37
$40,000 to $49,999	761	11	48	180	183	184	96	59	—	1	4	7	47
$50,000 to $74,999	1 440	—	110	340	362	361	158	109	—	3	7	10	90
$75,000 and over	1 162	1	68	273	284	304	161	72	—	4	12	3	53
Not reported	709	10	58	187	164	144	89	57	7	—	5	10	35
Female, all incomes	6 679	52	453	1 632	1 661	1 581	810	490	23	25	44	86	313
Less than $10,000	627	7	59	179	143	125	46	68	5	12	5	11	35
$10,000 to $14,999	413	18	51	78	119	84	23	39	6	—	7	6	19
$15,000 to $19,999	326	4	34	81	74	76	31	25	3	—	7	—	16
$20,000 to $24,999	437	4	45	85	82	123	38	60	3	6	5	8	38
$25,000 to $29,999	433	2	24	125	104	94	40	43	2	1	—	12	28
$30,000 to $34,999	437	—	27	122	93	88	68	39	—	3	6	5	25
$35,000 to $39,999	331	—	30	93	70	75	44	9	—	—	—	2	7
$40,000 to $49,999	658	—	29	149	185	180	68	46	—	—	4	9	33
$50,000 to $74,999	1 153	8	46	257	293	311	175	64	—	—	3	17	44
$75,000 and over	1 111	3	59	257	304	254	198	35	—	1	2	2	31
Not reported	754	6	48	205	185	170	77	62	5	3	5	12	37

White

Age, family income, sex, race and Hispanic origin	Total	8	9	10	11	12	College year 1 (Graduated this year)	Total	7 and 8	9	10	11	12 (Graduated this year)
Both sexes, all incomes	11 089	79	877	2 812	2 700	2 563	1 197	861	34	59	64	132	571
Less than $10,000	641	9	74	213	160	102	30	54	3	12	9	5	27
$10,000 to $14,999	565	7	69	153	161	101	25	51	6	—	5	6	33
$15,000 to $19,999	486	4	46	141	123	105	30	37	4	—	1	11	20
$20,000 to $24,999	702	10	81	162	144	171	41	94	3	18	16	8	50
$25,000 to $29,999	690	3	61	173	155	157	61	80	5	8	—	28	39
$30,000 to $34,999	732	7	65	206	129	173	78	74	3	7	—	9	55
$35,000 to $39,999	644	5	57	176	164	134	63	45	—	—	—	6	34
$40,000 to $49,999	325	—	16	104	55	63	60	27	—	3	—	5	18
$50,000 to $74,999	2 281	8	147	544	546	589	296	150	—	3	10	22	116
$75,000 and over	2 087	3	124	483	547	510	330	90	—	4	9	5	72
Not reported	1 064	12	82	281	246	224	125	96	11	3	8	18	55
Male, all incomes	5 899	56	550	1 500	1 371	1 332	551	539	18	40	41	73	367
Less than $10,000	344	9	57	114	90	42	9	24	3	5	4	2	12
$10,000 to $14,999	294	4	40	90	72	52	12	24	—	—	5	2	18
$15,000 to $19,999	277	2	22	81	77	55	7	31	3	—	—	11	18
$20,000 to $24,999	368	7	47	95	80	69	17	52	—	12	11	3	27
$25,000 to $29,999	357	3	40	72	74	86	29	53	3	8	—	18	24
$30,000 to $34,999	407	7	49	103	74	110	18	47	3	4	—	4	37
$35,000 to $39,999	366	5	33	103	90	70	26	37	—	4	—	3	30
$40,000 to $49,999	661	11	47	152	162	148	83	56	—	1	4	7	44
$50,000 to $74,999	1 254	—	104	309	285	317	139	100	—	3	7	10	80
$75,000 and over	1 047	1	65	250	252	273	142	65	—	4	7	3	51
Not reported	523	8	46	129	115	109	69	47	7	—	3	10	27
Female, all incomes	5 190	22	327	1 312	1 329	1 231	646	323	17	19	24	60	204
Less than $10,000	297	—	17	99	70	59	21	30	—	7	5	3	15
$10,000 to $14,999	271	3	29	62	89	49	13	26	6	—	—	5	16
$15,000 to $19,999	210	2	24	60	46	50	23	5	1	—	—	—	3
$20,000 to $24,999	334	4	34	66	64	102	24	41	3	6	5	5	23
$25,000 to $29,999	333	—	21	101	82	71	32	27	2	—	—	10	15
$30,000 to $34,999	325	—	16	104	55	63	60	27	—	3	—	5	18
$35,000 to $39,999	278	—	24	73	73	63	37	7	—	—	—	2	5
$40,000 to $49,999	535	—	24	127	163	150	36	35	—	—	2	7	26
$50,000 to $74,999	1 026	8	43	235	260	272	157	50	—	—	3	12	35
$75,000 and over	1 039	3	59	233	295	236	188	25	—	1	2	2	21
Not reported	541	3	36	152	131	115	56	49	5	3	5	9	28

See footnotes at end of table.

Table A-8. Persons 15 to 24 Years Old Enrolled in Secondary School in Previous Year by Current Enrollment Status, Age, Sex, Race, Hispanic Origin, and Family Income (for Dependent Family Members): October 1996 — Continued

(Numbers in thousands. Civilian noninstitutional population.)

Age, family income, sex, race and Hispanic origin	Total	Current grade in which enrolled						Enrolled last year, not currently enrolled					
		8	9	10	11	12	College year 1 (Graduated this year)	Total	Highest grade completed				
									7 and 8	9	10	11	12 (Graduated this year)
Black													
Both sexes, all incomes	2 387	44	231	540	526	583	215	247	9	9	37	26	167
Less than $10,000	571	25	73	129	123	136	24	62	2	8	9	7	35
$10,000 to $14,999	230	11	47	28	47	64	17	16	—	—	7	4	5
$15,000 to $19,999	199	5	24	55	28	46	12	28	2	—	10	—	16
$20,000 to $24,999	178	—	25	39	33	36	14	30	—	—	—	3	27
$25,000 to $29,999	173	2	12	42	34	41	16	25	—	1	—	2	22
$30,000 to $34,999	174	—	20	29	56	36	16	17	2	—	6	—	9
$35,000 to $39,999	94	—	5	33	20	8	15	13	3	—	—	—	10
$40,000 to $49,999	147	—	1	30	22	51	33	9	—	—	—	—	9
$50,000 to $74,999	218	—	2	37	70	64	27	18	—	—	—	5	13
$75,000 and over	80	—	—	18	15	27	8	11	—	—	5	—	6
Not reported	323	2	22	99	76	74	32	19	—	—	—	4	15
Male, all incomes	1 227	27	123	296	302	280	93	106	5	3	23	4	72
Less than $10,000	274	18	31	61	63	71	2	27	—	3	9	—	16
$10,000 to $14,999	120	3	26	19	27	28	10	6	—	—	—	4	2
$15,000 to $19,999	109	3	17	42	4	23	5	15	—	—	9	—	7
$20,000 to $24,999	103	—	16	31	25	17	2	11	—	—	—	—	11
$25,000 to $29,999	91	—	8	24	19	23	8	9	—	—	—	—	9
$30,000 to $34,999	88	—	12	14	32	13	11	5	2	—	—	—	2
$35,000 to $39,999	53	—	—	13	19	1	9	11	3	—	—	—	8
$40,000 to $49,999	63	—	—	15	10	27	10	2	—	—	—	—	2
$50,000 to $74,999	123	—	1	17	46	34	16	8	—	—	—	—	8
$75,000 and over	51	—	—	11	15	15	4	5	—	—	5	—	—
Not reported	150	2	12	49	41	28	12	6	—	—	—	—	6
Female, all incomes	1 160	18	108	244	224	303	123	141	4	6	14	22	95
Less than $10,000	297	6	42	69	60	65	22	34	2	5	—	7	20
$10,000 to $14,999	109	7	21	9	20	35	7	10	—	—	7	—	2
$15,000 to $19,999	89	2	8	13	24	23	7	13	2	—	2	—	9
$20,000 to $24,999	75	—	—	8	8	19	12	19	—	—	—	3	15
$25,000 to $29,999	81	2	4	18	15	18	8	16	—	1	—	2	13
$30,000 to $34,999	86	—	8	15	23	22	5	12	—	—	6	—	7
$35,000 to $39,999	41	—	5	20	1	7	6	2	—	—	—	—	2
$40,000 to $49,999	83	—	1	15	13	25	23	7	—	—	—	—	7
$50,000 to $74,999	95	—	2	19	24	30	11	9	—	—	—	5	4
$75,000 and over	30	—	—	8	—	12	4	6	—	—	—	—	6
Not reported	173	—	10	49	35	47	19	13	—	—	—	4	9
Hispanic Origin[1]													
Both sexes, all incomes	1 714	28	176	467	413	388	89	153	8	10	13	44	78
Less than $10,000	303	11	28	102	87	50	13	12	—	3	2	—	7
$10,000 to $14,999	234	—	35	58	74	48	5	13	—	—	—	5	8
$15,000 to $19,999	184	2	17	72	40	30	7	17	3	—	—	12	3
$20,000 to $24,999	187	—	28	36	45	39	6	32	—	4	8	5	14
$25,000 to $29,999	147	3	13	42	33	26	10	19	2	2	—	11	4
$30,000 to $34,999	119	3	13	25	11	52	5	10	—	—	—	—	10
$35,000 to $39,999	76	2	3	22	14	32	3	—	—	—	—	—	—
$40,000 to $49,999	98	—	5	27	24	22	5	14	—	—	—	3	11
$50,000 to $74,999	126	—	6	29	30	36	15	9	—	—	—	3	6
$75,000 and over	70	—	3	25	17	15	5	6	—	—	—	—	6
Not reported	170	6	25	30	37	38	13	20	3	—	3	5	9
Male, all incomes	940	24	104	264	216	201	31	99	6	6	8	32	46
Less than $10,000	162	9	19	54	52	23	1	3	—	—	—	—	3
$10,000 to $14,999	99	—	20	30	24	19	3	4	—	—	—	—	4
$15,000 to $19,999	119	2	9	39	31	21	—	17	3	—	—	12	3
$20,000 to $24,999	98	—	14	29	25	8	—	21	—	4	8	3	7
$25,000 to $29,999	69	3	8	21	9	11	2	15	—	2	—	8	4
$30,000 to $34,999	82	3	10	12	5	43	2	6	—	—	—	—	6
$35,000 to $39,999	50	2	—	17	12	19	—	—	—	—	—	—	—

Table A-8.   Persons 15 to 24 Years Old Enrolled in Secondary School in Previous Year by Current Enrollment Status, Age, Sex, Race, Hispanic Origin, and Family Income (for Dependent Family Members):   October 1996 — Continued

(Numbers in thousands. Civilian noninstitutional population.)

Age, family income, sex, race and Hispanic origin	Total	Current grade in which enrolled						Enrolled last year, not currently enrolled					
								Highest grade completed					
		8	9	10	11	12	College year 1 (Graduated this year)	Total	7 and 8	9	10	11	12 (Graduated this year)
$40,000 to $49,999	42	—	3	12	9	8	3	7	—	—	—	3	3
$50,000 to $74,999	69	—	3	13	22	18	7	6	—	—	—	3	3
$75,000 and over	49	—	—	23	8	9	5	3	—	—	—	—	3
Not reported	102	4	19	14	19	22	9	15	3	—	—	3	9
Female, all incomes	773	4	71	203	196	187	57	54	2	3	5	12	32
Less than $10,000	141	2	9	48	35	27	11	9	—	3	2	—	4
$10,000 to $14,999	135	—	16	27	51	29	2	9	—	—	—	5	4
$15,000 to $19,999	65	—	8	33	9	9	7	—	—	—	—	—	—
$20,000 to $24,999	90	—	14	8	20	31	6	11	—	—	1	3	7
$25,000 to $29,999	78	—	5	21	24	15	8	4	2	—	—	2	—
$30,000 to $34,999	37	—	3	14	5	9	3	3	—	—	—	—	3
$35,000 to $39,999	26	—	—	4	3	13	3	—	—	—	—	—	—
$40,000 to $49,999	56	—	2	15	15	14	3	8	—	—	—	—	8
$50,000 to $74,999	57	—	3	16	8	18	9	3	—	—	—	—	3
$75,000 and over	21	—	—	1	9	6	—	3	—	—	—	—	3
Not reported	68	2	6	16	18	17	5	5	—	—	3	2	—

Source: October 1996 Current Population Survey, Education and Social Stratification Branch, U.S. Bureau of the Census

1. May be of any race.

— Represents zero or rounds to zero.

Table A-9.   College Enrollment of the Population 15 Years Old and Over, by Attendance Status, Type and Control of School, Age, Sex, Race and Hispanic Origin: October 1996

(Numbers in thousands. Civilian noninstitutional population.)

Age, sex, race and Hispanic origin	Total population	Enrolled in school												
		Total		Enrolled below college	Total, enrolled in college	Undergraduate						Graduate		
						Two year college			Four year college					
		Number	Percent			Total	Full time	Part time	Total	Full time	Part time	Total	Full time	Part time
ALL RACES														
Both Sexes														
15 years old and over	205 108	27 647	13.5	12 421	15 226	4 174	2 209	1 965	8 130	6 325	1 806	2 922	1 305	1 617
15 to 17 years old	11 617	10 957	94.3	10 720	237	91	61	29	142	127	15	4	4	—
18 and 19 years old	7 376	4 539	61.5	1 229	3 309	1 132	934	198	2 161	2 008	152	17	14	3
20 and 21 years old	6 800	3 017	44.4	110	2 907	669	457	212	2 187	2 003	184	52	42	9
22 to 24 years old	10 495	2 605	24.8	54	2 551	515	271	244	1 502	1 244	258	534	420	114
25 to 29 years old	18 982	2 265	11.9	49	2 215	577	204	373	838	469	368	800	429	371
30 to 34 years old	21 111	1 286	6.1	58	1 228	345	111	234	466	206	260	417	141	276
35 years old and over	128 729	2 979	2.3	201	2 778	845	171	674	835	266	569	1 098	254	844
35 to 39 years old	22 373	1 138	5.1	70	1 068	324	69	255	383	150	232	362	114	248
40 to 44 years old	20 908	797	3.8	56	742	240	42	197	204	47	156	298	72	226
45 to 49 years old	18 466	531	2.9	29	501	141	37	104	130	37	93	230	45	186
50 to 54 years old	14 088	259	1.8	17	243	51	14	37	69	22	47	123	18	105
55 to 59 years old	11 233	107	1.0	16	92	30	7	24	22	2	20	39	3	36
60 to 64 years old	9 781	75	0.8	7	68	27	—	2	7	3	5	8	7	27
65 years and over	31 880	72	0.2	7	65	33	2	31	14	3	11	18	3	16
Public school, 15 years old and over	(X)	23 531	(X)	11 517	12 014	3 890	2 041	1 849	6 231	4 796	1 436	1 893	821	1 072
15 to 17 years old	(X)	10 127	(X)	9 936	191	86	56	29	104	91	13	2	2	—
18 and 19 years old	(X)	3 825	(X)	1 140	2 684	1 082	886	195	1 586	1 441	145	17	14	3
20 and 21 years old	(X)	2 412	(X)	103	2 309	630	428	202	1 660	1 512	148	20	20	—
22 to 24 years old	(X)	2 134	(X)	54	2 080	468	236	232	1 270	1 035	235	342	257	85
25 to 29 years old	(X)	1 748	(X)	43	1 705	524	183	342	655	361	294	525	272	253
30 to 34 years old	(X)	990	(X)	52	938	313	102	211	341	162	179	284	98	186
35 years old and over	(X)	2 296	(X)	189	2 107	787	150	638	616	194	422	703	158	545
35 to 39 years old	(X)	844	(X)	69	775	295	58	237	277	109	168	203	59	144
40 to 44 years old	(X)	620	(X)	54	567	224	37	187	159	33	126	184	40	144
45 years old and over	(X)	831	(X)	66	765	269	55	214	180	52	128	317	59	257
Private school, 15 years old and over	(X)	4 116	(X)	904	3 212	284	168	116	1 899	1 529	370	1 029	484	545
15 to 17 years old	(X)	830	(X)	784	46	5	5	—	38	36	2	3	3	—
18 and 19 years old	(X)	714	(X)	89	625	51	48	3	575	567	7	—	—	—
20 and 21 years old	(X)	604	(X)	6	598	39	29	11	527	491	36	32	22	9
22 to 24 years old	(X)	471	(X)	—	471	47	35	12	232	209	23	192	164	28
25 to 29 years old	(X)	517	(X)	6	511	53	21	32	183	109	74	275	157	118
30 to 34 years old	(X)	297	(X)	6	290	32	9	22	125	44	81	133	43	90
35 years old and over	(X)	683	(X)	11	672	58	21	37	219	72	147	395	96	299
35 to 39 years old	(X)	294	(X)	—	293	29	11	18	106	41	64	159	54	104
40 to 44 years old	(X)	177	(X)	2	175	16	6	10	44	14	30	115	32	83
45 years old and over	(X)	213	(X)	9	204	13	5	9	69	17	52	121	9	112
Male														
15 years old and over	98 529	13 360	13.6	6 540	6 820	1 752	974	778	3 781	3 058	724	1 288	650	638
15 to 17 years old	5 985	5 671	94.7	5 573	97	33	23	11	61	61	—	3	3	—
18 and 19 years old	3 711	2 258	60.8	769	1 489	526	427	100	956	907	48	7	7	—
20 and 21 years old	3 268	1 436	43.9	56	1 379	295	203	91	1 064	966	99	20	15	5
22 to 24 years old	5 306	1 335	25.2	16	1 319	238	137	100	842	719	123	239	201	38
25 to 29 years old	9 295	1 058	11.4	20	1 038	249	94	154	373	205	168	417	245	172
30 to 34 years old	10 372	504	4.9	19	485	118	24	94	168	84	83	199	69	130
35 years old and over	60 593	1 099	1.8	85	1 013	293	65	227	318	115	203	403	110	293
35 to 39 years old	11 020	494	4.5	39	455	123	30	93	173	64	108	159	52	107
40 to 44 years old	10 300	300	2.9	26	275	95	15	80	70	20	50	110	40	69
45 to 49 years old	9 026	161	1.8	8	153	39	14	24	46	20	27	68	8	61
50 to 54 years old	6 826	74	1.1	8	66	13	4	9	13	6	7	40	8	32
55 to 59 years old	5 412	29	0.5	6	23	10	—	10	7	—	7	7	—	7

See footnotes at end of table.

Table A-9. College Enrollment of the Population 15 Years Old and Over, by Attendance Status, Type and Control of School, Age, Sex, Race and Hispanic Origin: October 1996 — Continued

(Numbers in thousands. Civilian noninstitutional population.)

Age, sex, race and Hispanic origin	Total population	Total		Enrolled below college	Total, enrolled in college	Undergraduate						Graduate		
		Number	Percent			Two year college			Four year college			Total	Full time	Part time
						Total	Full time	Part time	Total	Full time	Part time			
60 to 64 years old	4 613	26	0.6	—	26	9	—	9	5	5	—	13	—	13
65 years and over	13 396	15	0.1	—	15	4	2	2	5	—	5	6	3	3
Public school, 15 years old and over	(X)	11 423	(X)	6 066	5 357	1 638	902	736	2 936	2 339	597	784	371	412
15 to 17 years old	(X)	5 235	(X)	5 158	77	31	20	11	46	46	—	—	—	—
18 and 19 years old	(X)	1 925	(X)	718	1 207	497	397	100	703	657	46	7	7	—
20 and 21 years old	(X)	1 152	(X)	53	1 098	281	197	84	813	732	81	5	5	—
22 to 24 years old	(X)	1 074	(X)	16	1 058	216	120	96	709	594	115	133	107	26
25 to 29 years old	(X)	815	(X)	20	795	226	85	141	302	159	143	267	150	117
30 to 34 years old	(X)	385	(X)	16	368	107	21	86	127	66	61	135	44	91
35 years old and over	(X)	837	(X)	83	754	280	62	218	236	85	151	237	59	178
35 to 39 years old	(X)	359	(X)	39	320	112	27	86	123	47	76	84	27	57
40 to 44 years old	(X)	235	(X)	24	212	94	15	79	54	14	40	63	22	42
45 years old and over	(X)	243	(X)	21	222	74	20	54	58	24	34	90	11	79
Private school, 15 years old and over	(X)	1 937	(X)	474	1 463	114	72	42	845	719	126	504	278	226
15 to 17 years old	(X)	436	(X)	415	21	3	3	—	15	15	—	3	3	—
18 and 19 years old	(X)	333	(X)	51	282	29	29	—	252	250	2	—	—	—
20 and 21 years old	(X)	284	(X)	3	281	14	7	8	251	234	18	16	10	5
22 to 24 years old	(X)	261	(X)	—	261	22	17	4	133	125	7	106	95	12
25 to 29 years old	(X)	243	(X)	—	243	22	9	13	71	46	25	149	94	55
30 to 34 years old	(X)	120	(X)	3	117	11	3	8	41	19	22	65	26	39
35 years old and over	(X)	262	(X)	2	260	12	3	9	82	30	52	166	51	115
35 to 39 years old	(X)	135	(X)	—	135	11	3	8	49	17	32	75	25	50
40 to 44 years old	(X)	65	(X)	2	63	1	—	1	15	6	10	47	19	28
45 years old and over	(X)	62	(X)	—	62	—	—	—	17	7	10	45	7	37
Female														
15 years old and over	106 579	14 287	13.4	5 881	8 406	2 423	1 235	1 187	4 349	3 267	1 082	1 634	655	979
15 to 17 years old	5 631	5 286	93.9	5 146	140	57	38	19	81	66	15	2	2	—
18 and 19 years old	3 665	2 281	62.2	460	1 821	606	507	98	1 205	1 101	104	10	7	3
20 and 21 years old	3 532	1 581	44.8	53	1 528	374	253	121	1 122	1 037	85	31	27	4
22 to 24 years old	5 189	1 270	24.5	38	1 233	277	134	143	660	525	135	295	219	76
25 to 29 years old	9 687	1 207	12.5	30	1 177	329	110	219	465	264	200	384	184	199
30 to 34 years old	10 738	782	7.3	39	743	227	87	139	299	121	177	218	72	146
35 years old and over	68 136	1 881	2.8	116	1 765	553	105	447	517	151	366	695	144	551
35 to 39 years old	11 353	644	5.7	31	613	200	39	161	210	86	124	203	62	141
40 to 44 years old	10 608	497	4.7	30	467	144	27	117	134	27	107	189	32	157
45 to 49 years old	9 441	370	3.9	22	348	103	23	80	84	17	67	162	37	125
50 to 54 years old	7 262	185	2.6	9	177	37	10	28	56	16	40	83	10	73
55 to 59 years old	5 821	78	1.3	10	68	21	7	14	16	2	13	32	3	29
60 to 64 years old	5 168	49	0.9	7	42	19	—	19	8	—	8	14	—	14
65 years and over	18 484	57	0.3	7	50	28	—	28	9	3	7	12	—	12
Public school, 15 years old and over	(X)	12 109	(X)	5 452	6 657	2 253	1 139	1 113	3 295	2 457	838	1 109	449	660
15 to 17 years old	(X)	4 892	(X)	4 777	114	55	36	19	58	45	13	2	2	—
18 and 19 years old	(X)	1 899	(X)	422	1 477	584	489	95	883	784	99	10	7	3
20 and 21 years old	(X)	1 261	(X)	50	1 211	349	231	118	847	780	67	15	15	—
22 to 24 years old	(X)	1 060	(X)	38	1 022	252	116	136	561	441	120	209	150	59
25 to 29 years old	(X)	933	(X)	24	909	298	98	201	353	202	151	258	122	136
30 to 34 years old	(X)	605	(X)	35	570	206	81	125	214	96	118	149	54	95
35 years old and over	(X)	1 459	(X)	106	1 353	507	88	419	380	109	271	466	99	367
35 to 39 years old	(X)	486	(X)	31	455	183	31	151	154	62	92	119	32	87
40 to 44 years old	(X)	385	(X)	30	355	130	22	108	105	19	86	121	18	102
45 years old and over	(X)	588	(X)	45	543	195	35	160	122	28	93	227	49	178
Private school, 15 years old and over	(X)	2 179	(X)	430	1 749	170	96	74	1 054	810	244	525	206	320
15 to 17 years old	(X)	395	(X)	369	25	2	2	—	23	21	2	—	—	—
18 and 19 years old	(X)	382	(X)	38	344	21	18	3	323	317	5	—	—	—
20 and 21 years old	(X)	320	(X)	3	317	25	22	3	275	257	18	16	12	4

See footnotes at end of table.

Table A-9.   College Enrollment of the Population 15 Years Old and Over, by Attendance Status, Type and Control of School, Age, Sex, Race and Hispanic Origin: October 1996 — Continued

(Numbers in thousands. Civilian noninstitutional population.)

Age, sex, race and Hispanic origin	Total population	Enrolled in school												
		Total		Enrolled below college	Total, enrolled in college	Undergraduate						Graduate		
		Number	Percent			Two year college			Four year college			Total	Full time	Part time
						Total	Full time	Part time	Total	Full time	Part time			
22 to 24 years old	(X)	210	(X)	—	210	25	18	7	100	84	15	86	69	17
25 to 29 years old	(X)	274	(X)	6	268	30	12	19	111	62	49	126	62	64
30 to 34 years old	(X)	177	(X)	4	173	20	7	14	85	26	59	68	17	51
35 years old and over	(X)	422	(X)	9	412	46	18	28	137	43	95	229	45	184
35 to 39 years old	(X)	159	(X)	—	158	18	7	10	57	24	33	84	30	54
40 to 44 years old	(X)	112	(X)	—	112	15	6	9	29	9	20	68	13	55
45 years old and over	(X)	151	(X)	9	142	13	5	9	52	10	42	77	2	75
WHITE														
Both Sexes														
15 years old and over	171 804	21 878	12.7	9 689	12 189	3 295	1 743	1 552	6 565	5 142	1 424	2 328	964	1 364
15 to 17 years old	9 134	8 618	94.4	8 451	167	66	44	22	97	84	13	4	4	—
18 and 19 years old	5 833	3 645	62.5	914	2 731	945	770	175	1 774	1 669	105	12	9	3
20 and 21 years old	5 410	2 428	44.9	66	2 362	515	347	168	1 819	1 670	149	29	22	7
22 to 24 years old	8 433	2 070	24.6	40	2 030	396	190	206	1 211	1 009	202	423	334	89
25 to 29 years old	15 436	1 741	11.3	38	1 704	418	164	255	644	347	297	641	312	329
30 to 34 years old	17 249	984	5.7	44	940	277	98	179	360	149	211	304	96	208
35 years old and over	110 308	2 392	2.2	138	2 254	678	131	548	661	214	447	915	186	729
35 to 39 years old	18 528	902	4.9	45	857	276	54	222	297	121	176	284	71	213
40 to 44 years old	17 432	613	3.5	37	576	170	32	138	164	34	130	241	57	184
45 to 49 years old	15 629	446	2.9	24	422	113	31	82	107	34	74	201	36	165
50 to 54 years old	12 072	222	1.8	13	209	45	12	33	54	17	37	110	16	94
55 to 59 years old	9 697	88	0.9	10	78	23	2	21	16	2	13	39	3	36
60 to 64 years old	8 504	66	0.8	4	62	27	—	27	13	5	8	21	—	21
65 years and over	28 446	54	0.2	3	51	24	—	24	9	—	9	18	3	16
Public school, 15 years old and over	(X)	18 480	(X)	8 914	9 566	3 070	1 616	1 454	4 968	3 858	1 109	1 529	606	923
15 to 17 years old	(X)	7 877	(X)	7 747	130	61	39	22	68	57	11	2	2	—
18 and 19 years old	9 260	380	4.1	23	357	107	26	81	138	60	78	111	18	94
20 and 21 years old	(X)	1 922	(X)	62	1 859	489	328	161	1 360	1 241	119	11	11	—
22 to 24 years old	(X)	1 687	(X)	40	1 648	361	166	195	1 013	831	182	274	204	70
25 to 29 years old	(X)	1 334	(X)	38	1 297	378	146	232	497	263	234	422	195	227
30 to 34 years old	(X)	757	(X)	41	717	252	90	162	251	110	141	214	64	149
35 years old and over	(X)	1 840	(X)	132	1 708	626	115	511	486	163	324	596	122	473
Private school, 15 years old and over	(X)	3 397	(X)	775	2 622	226	127	98	1 598	1 284	314	799	357	441
15 to 17 years old	(X)	741	(X)	705	37	5	5	—	29	27	2	3	3	—
18 and 19 years old	(X)	582	(X)	59	523	41	38	3	482	476	5	—	—	—
20 and 21 years old	(X)	506	(X)	3	503	26	19	8	459	428	30	18	12	7
22 to 24 years old	(X)	383	(X)	—	383	36	24	12	198	178	20	149	130	19
25 to 29 years old	(X)	407	(X)	—	407	40	18	22	147	84	63	219	117	102
30 to 34 years old	(X)	226	(X)	3	224	25	8	17	108	39	70	90	32	59
35 years old and over	(X)	551	(X)	5	546	53	16	37	175	51	124	319	64	255
Male														
15 years old and over	83 289	10 547	12.7	5 094	5 453	1 373	767	606	3 086	2 500	586	995	453	542
15 to 17 years old	4 694	4 446	94.7	4 377	69	30	19	11	37	37	—	3	3	—
18 and 19 years old	2 953	1 799	60.9	576	1 223	429	340	89	787	752	35	7	7	—
20 and 21 years old	2 638	1 149	43.6	33	1 117	230	159	71	877	794	83	9	7	2
22 to 24 years old	4 306	1 095	25.4	16	1 079	195	105	90	693	596	98	191	160	30
25 to 29 years old	7 691	814	10.6	17	797	170	71	100	307	158	149	320	167	153
30 to 34 years old	8 620	372	4.3	15	357	95	20	75	124	56	68	138	43	95
35 years old and over	52 387	872	1.7	61	811	223	52	171	260	106	153	328	67	262
35 to 39 years old	9 260	380	4.1	23	357	107	26	81	138	60	78	111	18	94
40 to 44 years old	8 685	232	2.7	20	212	60	11	49	60	18	42	92	33	59
45 to 49 years old	7 744	136	1.8	7	129	27	11	15	38	20	18	64	6	58
50 to 54 years old	5 923	61	1.0	5	56	11	4	7	10	3	7	35	8	28

See footnotes at end of table.

Table A-9.   College Enrollment of the Population 15 Years Old and Over, by Attendance Status, Type and Control of School, Age, Sex, Race and Hispanic Origin: October 1996 — Continued

(Numbers in thousands. Civilian noninstitutional population.)

Age, sex, race and Hispanic origin	Total population	Enrolled in school				Undergraduate						Graduate		
		Total		Enrolled below college	Total, enrolled in college	Two year college			Four year college			Total	Full time	Part time
		Number	Percent			Total	Full time	Part time	Total	Full time	Part time			
55 to 59 years old	4 706	26	0.6	6	21	7	—	7	7	—	7	7	—	7
60 to 64 years old	4 062	26	0.7	—	26	9	—	9	5	5	—	13	—	13
65 years and over	12 007	10	0.1	—	10	2	—	2	2	—	2	6	3	3
Public school, 15 years old and over	(X)	8 979	(X)	4 698	4 281	1 275	711	564	2 380	1 900	480	627	263	363
15 to 17 years old	(X)	4 068	(X)	4 013	55	27	16	11	28	28	—	—	—	—
18 and 19 years old	(X)	1 539	(X)	546	993	406	317	89	580	546	35	7	7	—
20 and 21 years old	(X)	923	(X)	33	890	220	156	63	670	602	68	—	—	—
22 to 24 years old	(X)	886	(X)	16	870	179	94	86	582	491	91	109	87	21
25 to 29 years old	(X)	620	(X)	17	603	148	61	86	240	114	127	215	108	108
30 to 34 years old	(X)	276	(X)	12	263	84	17	67	89	40	48	90	24	66
35 years old and over	(X)	667	(X)	61	606	211	49	162	190	79	111	205	37	168
Private school, 15 years old and over	(X)	1 569	(X)	396	1 172	98	56	42	706	600	106	368	190	178
15 to 17 years old	(X)	378	(X)	364	14	3	3	—	0	0	—	0	0	—
18 and 19 years old	(X)	260	(X)	29	230	24	24	—	207	207	—	—	—	—
20 and 21 years old	(X)	226	(X)	—	226	10	3	8	207	192	15	9	7	2
22 to 24 years old	(X)	209	(X)	—	209	16	12	4	111	105	7	82	73	9
25 to 29 years old	(X)	194	(X)	—	194	22	9	13	67	45	23	104	59	45
30 to 34 years old	(X)	97	(X)	3	94	11	2	8	35	16	19	48	20	28
35 years old and over	(X)	205	(X)	—	205	12	3	9	70	27	42	123	29	94
Female														
15 years old and over	88 515	11 330	12.8	4 595	6 735	1 922	977	946	3 480	2 642	838	1 333	511	822
15 to 17 years old	4 441	4 172	93.9	4 074	98	36	25	11	60	47	13	2	2	—
18 and 19 years old	2 879	1 847	64.1	338	1 508	516	430	85	987	917	70	5	3	3
20 and 21 years old	2 772	1 279	46.1	33	1 246	284	187	97	941	875	66	20	16	4
22 to 24 years old	4 127	975	23.6	24	951	201	85	116	518	413	105	232	174	59
25 to 29 years old	7 745	927	12.0	21	906	248	93	155	337	189	147	322	145	176
30 to 34 years old	8 629	611	7.1	28	583	182	78	104	236	93	143	166	52	113
35 years old and over	57 921	1 520	2.6	77	1 443	456	79	377	401	107	294	586	119	467
35 to 39 years old	9 268	523	5.6	22	500	168	27	141	159	61	98	173	54	120
40 to 44 years old	8 747	381	4.4	17	364	110	21	89	104	16	88	150	24	125
45 to 49 years old	7 885	311	3.9	17	293	87	20	67	70	14	56	137	30	107
50 to 54 years old	6 149	161	2.6	8	152	33	8	26	45	14	31	74	8	66
55 to 59 years old	4 991	62	1.2	5	57	16	2	14	9	2	7	32	3	29
60 to 64 years old	4 442	39	0.9	4	35	19	—	19	8	—	8	8	—	8
65 years and over	16 440	44	0.3	3	41	22	—	22	7	—	7	12	—	12
Public school, 15 years old and over	(X)	9 502	(X)	4 216	5 286	1 795	905	890	2 588	1 958	630	903	343	559
15 to 17 years old	(X)	3 808	(X)	3 733	75	34	23	11	39	29	11	2	2	—
18 and 19 years old	(X)	1 524	(X)	309	1 215	498	416	83	712	647	65	5	3	3
20 and 21 years old	(X)	999	(X)	30	969	269	171	97	690	639	50	11	11	—
22 to 24 years old	(X)	802	(X)	24	777	181	72	109	431	340	91	165	116	49
25 to 29 years old	(X)	714	(X)	21	693	230	85	146	257	150	107	206	87	119
30 to 34 years old	(X)	482	(X)	28	454	168	73	95	162	70	93	123	40	83
35 years old and over	(X)	1 173	(X)	71	1 102	415	66	349	296	84	213	390	85	306
Private school, 15 years old and over	(X)	1 829	(X)	379	1 450	127	71	56	892	684	208	430	167	263
15 to 17 years old	(X)	364	(X)	341	23	2	2	—	21	18	2	—	—	—
18 and 19 years old	(X)	322	(X)	30	293	18	15	3	275	270	5	—	—	—
20 and 21 years old	(X)	280	(X)	3	277	16	16	—	252	236	15	9	5	4
22 to 24 years old	(X)	174	(X)	—	174	20	12	7	87	73	14	67	58	10
25 to 29 years old	(X)	213	(X)	—	213	18	9	9	80	40	40	115	58	57
30 to 34 years old	(X)	130	(X)	—	130	14	5	9	73	23	50	43	12	30
35 years old and over	(X)	346	(X)	5	341	40	12	28	105	24	81	196	35	161

See footnotes at end of table.

Table A-9. College Enrollment of the Population 15 Years Old and Over, by Attendance Status, Type and Control of School, Age, Sex, Race and Hispanic Origin: October 1996 — Continued

(Numbers in thousands. Civilian noninstitutional population.)

Age, sex, race and Hispanic origin	Total population	Enrolled in school												
		Total		Enrolled below college	Total, enrolled in college	Undergraduate						Graduate		
						Two year college			Four year college					
		Number	Percent			Total	Full time	Part time	Total	Full time	Part time	Total	Full time	Part time
BLACK														
Both Sexes														
15 years old and over	24 335	4 002	16.5	2 102	1 901	580	289	292	1 013	731	281	308	159	149
15 to 17 years old	1 857	1 747	94.1	1 702	45	21	14	7	24	22	2	—	—	—
18 and 19 years old	1 161	613	52.8	268	345	98	82	16	242	213	29	5	5	—
20 and 21 years old	1 050	389	37.0	42	346	106	74	32	228	206	22	13	10	3
22 to 24 years old	1 426	300	21.0	8	292	59	47	11	186	146	40	47	36	10
25 to 29 years old	2 553	349	13.7	12	337	125	29	96	122	66	56	89	65	24
30 to 34 years old	2 762	197	7.1	14	182	60	10	50	69	38	31	53	15	38
35 years old and over	13 525	408	3.0	55	354	111	32	79	141	39	102	101	28	74
35 to 39 years old	2 806	166	5.9	22	144	35	12	23	66	19	47	43	20	23
40 to 44 years old	2 520	123	4.9	14	109	39	9	30	35	12	23	35	8	27
45 to 49 years old	2 051	58	2.8	4	53	18	2	16	18	2	16	17	—	17
50 to 54 years old	1 407	29	2.1	3	26	6	2	4	14	4	9	6	—	6
55 to 59 years old	1 147	19	1.7	5	14	7	4	3	7	—	7	—	—	—
60 to 64 years old	973	3	0.3	3	—	—	—	—	—	—	—	—	—	—
65 years and over	2 620	10	0.4	2	8	6	2	4	2	2	—	—	—	—
Public school, 15 years old and over	(X)	3 528	(X)	2 008	1 519	539	264	275	797	559	238	184	97	87
15 to 17 years old	(X)	1 650	(X)	1 650	40	21	14	7	19	18	2	—	—	—
18 and 19 years old	(X)	532	(X)	246	286	94	78	16	187	160	27	5	5	—
20 and 21 years old	(X)	318	(X)	39	278	94	65	28	178	159	19	7	7	—
22 to 24 years old	(X)	253	(X)	8	245	56	44	11	158	120	38	32	23	8
25 to 29 years old	(X)	273	(X)	6	267	113	26	87	98	49	49	57	43	14
30 to 34 years old	(X)	146	(X)	11	135	55	9	46	52	33	19	29	10	18
35 years old and over	(X)	316	(X)	48	267	107	27	79	106	20	85	55	9	46
Private school, 15 years old and over	(X)	475	(X)	93	381	42	24	17	215	172	43	124	62	62
15 to 17 years old	(X)	57	(X)	53	4	—	—	—	4	4	—	—	—	—
18 and 19 years old	(X)	80	(X)	22	59	4	4	—	55	53	2	—	—	—
20 and 21 years old	(X)	71	(X)	3	68	12	9	3	50	47	3	6	3	3
22 to 24 years old	(X)	47	(X)	—	47	3	3	—	29	26	2	15	13	2
25 to 29 years old	(X)	76	(X)	6	70	13	3	9	25	17	7	32	22	10
30 to 34 years old	(X)	51	(X)	4	47	6	1	5	17	5	12	24	5	19
35 years old and over	(X)	92	(X)	6	86	4	4	—	36	19	17	46	19	27
Male														
15 years old and over	10 940	1 857	17.0	1 093	764	229	119	110	396	311	84	140	94	46
15 to 17 years old	942	890	94.5	873	17	4	4	—	13	13	—	—	—	—
18 and 19 years old	564	311	55.2	166	145	43	36	6	103	93	10	—	—	—
20 and 21 years old	458	178	39.0	24	155	50	33	16	100	94	5	5	2	3
22 to 24 years old	660	122	18.6	1	122	16	16	—	87	69	18	19	19	—
25 to 29 years old	1 129	145	12.8	3	142	59	17	42	31	18	12	52	44	8
30 to 34 years old	1 251	67	5.4	4	64	19	4	15	23	19	3	22	8	14
35 years old and over	5 937	143	2.4	23	120	38	9	29	40	4	36	42	21	21
35 to 39 years old	1 279	80	6.3	15	65	14	4	10	22	—	22	29	18	11
40 to 44 years old	1 153	31	2.7	5	26	8	3	5	7	2	5	11	3	8
45 to 49 years old	931	18	1.9	—	18	9	—	9	9	—	9	1	—	1
50 to 54 years old	626	9	1.5	3	6	2	—	—	2	2	—	2	—	2
55 to 59 years old	501	3	0.5	—	3	3	—	—	3	—	—	—	—	—
60 to 64 years old	417	—	—	—	—	—	—	—	—	—	—	—	—	—
65 years and over	1 030	2	0.2	—	2	2	2	—	—	—	—	—	—	—
Public school, 15 years old and over	(X)	1 618	(X)	1 036	582	225	115	110	297	222	74	61	50	11
15 to 17 years old	(X)	851	(X)	838	13	4	4	—	9	9	—	—	—	—
18 and 19 years old	(X)	264	(X)	149	116	43	36	6	73	65	8	—	—	—

See footnotes at end of table.

Table A-9. College Enrollment of the Population 15 Years Old and Over, by Attendance Status, Type and Control of School, Age, Sex, Race and Hispanic Origin: October 1996 — Continued

(Numbers in thousands. Civilian noninstitutional population.)

Age, sex, race and Hispanic origin	Total population	Enrolled in school												
		Total		Enrolled below college	Total, enrolled in college	Undergraduate						Graduate		
						Two year college			Four year college					
		Number	Percent			Total	Full time	Part time	Total	Full time	Part time	Total	Full time	Part time
20 and 21 years old	(X)	134	(X)	21	114	46	29	16	66	60	5	2	2	—
22 to 24 years old	(X)	95	(X)	1	94	16	16	—	69	52	17	9	9	—
25 to 29 years old	(X)	114	(X)	3	111	59	17	42	29	18	12	22	22	—
30 to 34 years old	(X)	56	(X)	4	52	19	4	15	17	17	1	16	8	8
35 years old and over	(X)	105	(X)	21	83	38	9	29	33	2	32	12	9	3
Private school, 15 years old and over ..	(X)	239	(X)	57	182	4	4	—	99	89	10	79	44	35
15 to 17 years old	(X)	39	(X)	35	4	—	—	—	4	4	—	—	—	—
18 and 19 years old	(X)	47	(X)	17	30	—	—	—	30	28	2	—	—	—
20 and 21 years old	(X)	44	(X)	3	41	4	4	—	34	34	—	3	—	3
22 to 24 years old	(X)	28	(X)	—	28	—	—	—	18	17	1	10	10	—
25 to 29 years old	(X)	31	(X)	—	31	—	—	—	1	1	1	29	22	8
30 to 34 years old	(X)	12	(X)	—	12	—	—	—	5	3	3	6	—	6
35 years old and over	(X)	39	(X)	2	37	—	—	—	6	2	4	30	12	19
Female														
15 years old and over	13 395	2 145	16.0	1 009	1 136	351	169	182	617	420	197	168	65	103
15 to 17 years old	916	857	93.6	829	28	17	11	7	10	9	2	—	—	—
18 and 19 years old	597	302	50.5	103	199	55	45	10	139	120	19	5	5	—
20 and 21 years old	593	210	35.5	19	192	56	41	15	128	112	16	7	7	—
22 to 24 years old	766	178	23.2	8	170	42	31	11	99	77	22	28	18	10
25 to 29 years old	1 424	204	14.4	9	195	66	12	54	92	48	44	38	21	16
30 to 34 years old	1 511	129	8.6	11	119	42	7	35	46	19	27	31	7	24
35 years old and over	7 588	265	3.5	31	234	73	23	50	102	35	66	59	7	52
35 to 39 years old	1 528	86	5.6	7	79	20	8	12	44	19	25	15	2	13
40 to 44 years old	1 368	92	6.7	9	83	31	6	25	28	10	18	24	5	19
45 to 49 years old	1 121	39	3.5	4	35	9	2	7	9	2	7	16	—	16
50 to 54 years old	781	20	2.5	—	19	4	2	2	11	2	9	4	—	4
55 to 59 years old	646	17	2.6	5	11	4	4	—	7	—	7	—	—	—
60 to 64 years old	556	3	0.6	3	—	—	—	—	—	—	—	—	—	—
65 years and over	1 590	8	0.5	2	6	4	—	4	2	2	—	—	—	—
Public school, 15 years old and over	(X)	1 909	(X)	972	937	314	149	165	500	337	164	123	47	76
15 to 17 years old	(X)	839	(X)	812	28	17	11	7	10	9	2	—	—	—
18 and 19 years old	(X)	268	(X)	98	170	52	42	10	114	95	19	5	5	—
20 and 21 years old	(X)	183	(X)	19	165	48	36	12	112	99	13	4	4	—
22 to 24 years old	(X)	159	(X)	8	151	39	28	11	89	68	20	23	15	8
25 to 29 years old	(X)	159	(X)	3	156	53	9	44	68	31	37	35	21	14
30 to 34 years old	(X)	90	(X)	7	83	36	6	30	35	17	18	13	2	10
35 years old and over	(X)	211	(X)	27	184	68	18	50	72	19	54	44	—	44
Private school, 15 years old and over ..	(X)	236	(X)	37	199	38	21	17	116	83	33	45	18	27
15 to 17 years old	(X)	18	(X)	18	—	—	—	—	—	—	—	—	—	—
18 and 19 years old	(X)	34	(X)	5	29	4	4	—	25	25	—	—	—	—
20 and 21 years old	(X)	27	(X)	—	27	8	5	3	16	13	3	3	3	—
22 to 24 years old	(X)	19	(X)	—	19	3	3	—	11	9	2	5	3	2
25 to 29 years old	(X)	45	(X)	6	39	13	3	9	24	17	7	3	1	2
30 to 34 years old	(X)	39	(X)	4	35	6	1	5	12	2	9	18	5	13
35 years old and over	(X)	54	(X)	4	49	4	4	—	29	17	13	16	7	9
HISPANIC ORIGIN[1]														
Both Sexes														
15 years old and over	19 903	2 925	14.7	1 702	1 223	444	224	220	605	413	192	174	71	102
15 to 17 years old	1 477	1 346	91.2	1 324	23	10	10	—	12	8	4	—	—	—
18 and 19 years old	1 000	470	47.0	230	240	111	76	35	129	107	22	—	—	—
20 and 21 years old	965	244	25.3	31	213	102	69	33	111	88	23	—	—	—
22 to 24 years old	1 545	272	17.6	19	253	75	22	53	136	114	22	41	36	6

See footnotes at end of table.

Table A-9. College Enrollment of the Population 15 Years Old and Over, by Attendance Status, Type and Control of School, Age, Sex, Race and Hispanic Origin: October 1996 — Continued

(Numbers in thousands. Civilian noninstitutional population.)

Age, sex, race and Hispanic origin	Total population	Enrolled in school												
		Total		Enrolled below college	Total, enrolled in college	Undergraduate						Graduate		
						Two year college			Four year college					
		Number	Percent			Total	Full time	Part time	Total	Full time	Part time	Total	Full time	Part time
25 to 29 years old	2 524	217	8.6	19	198	47	14	34	100	60	39	51	21	30
30 to 34 years old	2 570	127	5.0	15	112	25	12	13	64	21	43	23	2	21
35 years old and over	9 823	248	2.5	64	184	73	21	53	52	14	38	59	13	46
35 to 39 years old	2 454	99	4.0	21	78	34	12	23	26	6	20	18	7	11
40 to 44 years old	1 872	88	4.7	23	64	24	3	21	15	6	9	25	6	19
45 to 49 years old	1 400	28	2.0	12	16	9	6	3	6	—	6	1	—	1
50 to 54 years old	938	15	1.6	—	15	2	—	2	5	2	3	8	—	8
55 to 59 years old	895	10	1.2	8	3	—	—	—	—	—	—	3	—	3
60 to 64 years old	679	—	—	—	—	—	—	—	—	—	—	—	—	—
65 years and over	1 585	8	0.5	—	8	4	—	4	—	—	—	4	—	4
Public school, 15 years old and over	(X)	2 660	(X)	1 629	1 031	403	198	205	502	340	162	126	38	88
15 to 17 years old	(X)	1 278	(X)	1 257	21	8	8	—	12	8	4	—	—	—
18 and 19 years old	(X)	438	(X)	226	212	106	71	35	106	85	22	—	—	—
20 and 21 years old	(X)	222	(X)	28	194	96	66	30	98	77	21	—	—	—
22 to 24 years old	(X)	214	(X)	19	195	64	17	47	111	94	18	20	18	3
25 to 29 years old	(X)	181	(X)	19	162	43	14	29	83	51	32	37	12	25
30 to 34 years old	(X)	110	(X)	15	95	23	9	13	50	12	38	23	2	21
35 years old and over	(X)	216	(X)	64	152	64	14	50	42	14	28	46	7	40
Private school, 15 years old and over	(X)	265	(X)	73	192	41	25	15	103	74	30	48	33	14
15 to 17 years old	(X)	69	(X)	67	2	2	2	—	—	—	—	—	—	—
18 and 19 years old	(X)	32	(X)	4	28	5	5	—	23	23	—	—	—	—
20 and 21 years old	(X)	22	(X)	2	19	6	3	2	14	11	2	—	—	—
22 to 24 years old	(X)	58	(X)	—	58	12	6	6	25	21	4	21	18	3
25 to 29 years old	(X)	35	(X)	—	35	4	—	4	17	9	8	14	9	5
30 to 34 years old	(X)	17	(X)	—	17	2	2	—	15	9	5	—	—	—
35 years old and over	(X)	32	(X)	—	32	9	6	3	10	—	10	12	6	6
Male														
15 years old and over	9 958	1 444	14.5	915	529	195	82	113	263	176	87	72	46	25
15 to 17 years old	765	710	92.9	703	8	6	6	—	2	2	—	—	—	—
18 and 19 years old	506	237	46.8	139	98	38	21	16	60	46	14	—	—	—
20 and 21 years old	486	95	19.5	17	78	37	26	11	41	31	10	—	—	—
22 to 24 years old	823	133	16.2	9	124	39	8	31	58	51	7	28	28	—
25 to 29 years old	1 306	89	6.8	10	79	23	7	16	40	26	13	16	10	6
30 to 34 years old	1 379	59	4.3	6	54	16	4	11	29	10	19	9	—	9
35 years old and over	4 692	121	2.6	31	90	37	10	27	33	9	24	19	9	11
35 to 39 years old	1 214	46	3.8	11	36	11	3	8	22	6	16	2	2	—
40 to 44 years old	945	55	5.8	11	44	22	3	19	11	3	8	11	6	5
45 to 49 years old	686	12	1.7	7	5	4	4	—	—	—	—	1	—	1
50 to 54 years old	476	5	1.0	—	5	—	—	—	—	—	—	5	—	5
55 to 59 years old	404	3	0.7	3	—	—	—	—	—	—	—	—	—	—
60 to 64 years old	314	—	—	—	—	—	—	—	—	—	—	—	—	—
65 years and over	653	—	—	—	—	—	—	—	—	—	—	—	—	—
Public school, 15 years old and over	(X)	1 353	(X)	893	461	178	73	105	232	152	80	51	25	25
15 to 17 years old	(X)	688	(X)	680	8	6	6	—	2	2	—	—	—	—
18 and 19 years old	(X)	229	(X)	139	90	35	19	16	55	41	14	—	—	—
20 and 21 years old	(X)	89	(X)	17	71	35	26	9	37	27	10	—	—	—
22 to 24 years old	(X)	104	(X)	9	95	31	4	27	51	44	7	13	13	—
25 to 29 years old	(X)	76	(X)	10	66	21	7	14	34	24	10	12	6	6
30 to 34 years old	(X)	53	(X)	6	47	13	2	11	25	6	19	9	—	9
35 years old and over	(X)	115	(X)	31	83	37	10	27	29	9	20	17	7	11
Private school, 15 years old and over	(X)	91	(X)	22	69	17	9	9	31	23	8	21	21	—
15 to 17 years old	(X)	22	(X)	22	—	—	—	—	—	—	—	—	—	—
18 and 19 years old	(X)	8	(X)	—	8	3	3	—	5	5	—	—	—	—
20 and 21 years old	(X)	6	(X)	—	6	2	—	2	4	4	—	—	—	—
22 to 24 years old	(X)	29	(X)	—	29	8	4	4	7	7	—	15	15	—

See footnotes at end of table.

Table A-9. College Enrollment of the Population 15 Years Old and Over, by Attendance Status, Type and Control of School, Age, Sex, Race and Hispanic Origin: October 1996 — Continued

(Numbers in thousands. Civilian noninstitutional population.)

Age, sex, race and Hispanic origin	Total population	Enrolled in school												
		Total		Enrolled below college	Total, enrolled in college	Undergraduate						Graduate		
						Two year college			Four year college					
		Number	Percent			Total	Full time	Part time	Total	Full time	Part time	Total	Full time	Part time
25 to 29 years old	(X)	12	(X)	—	12	2	—	2	6	3	3	4	4	—
30 to 34 years old	(X)	7	(X)	—	7	2	2	—	4	4	—	—	—	—
35 years old and over	(X)	6	(X)	—	6	—	—	—	4	—	4	2	2	—
Female														
15 years old and over	9 946	1 480	14.9	787	693	249	142	107	343	238	105	102	25	77
15 to 17 years old	712	636	89.3	621	15	5	5	—	10	6	4	—	—	—
18 and 19 years old	494	233	47.2	91	142	73	54	18	69	61	8	—	—	—
20 and 21 years old	479	149	31.1	13	136	65	43	22	71	58	13	—	—	—
22 to 24 years old	721	139	19.3	10	128	36	14	22	79	63	15	14	8	6
25 to 29 years old	1 218	128	10.5	9	119	24	7	17	60	34	26	35	11	24
30 to 34 years old	1 191	68	5.7	9	59	10	7	2	35	11	24	14	2	12
35 years old and over	5 131	127	2.5	33	95	36	11	25	19	5	14	39	4	35
35 to 39 years old	1 241	52	4.2	11	42	23	9	14	4	—	4	15	4	11
40 to 44 years old	927	33	3.5	12	20	2	—	—	3	2	1	15	—	15
45 to 49 years old	714	16	2.3	5	11	5	2	3	6	—	—	—	—	—
50 to 54 years old	462	10	2.3	—	10	2	—	2	5	2	3	3	—	3
55 to 59 years old	491	7	1.5	5	3	—	—	—	—	—	—	3	—	3
60 to 64 years old	364	—	—	—	—	—	—	—	—	—	—	—	—	—
65 years and over	932	8	0.9	—	8	4	—	4	—	—	—	4	—	4
Public school, 15 years old and over	(X)	1 307	(X)	737	570	225	125	100	270	187	83	75	12	63
15 to 17 years old	(X)	590	(X)	577	13	3	3	—	10	6	4	—	—	—
18 and 19 years old	(X)	209	(X)	87	122	70	52	18	52	44	8	—	—	—
20 and 21 years old	(X)	134	(X)	11	123	62	40	22	61	50	11	—	—	—
22 to 24 years old	(X)	110	(X)	10	100	32	12	20	61	49	11	7	5	3
25 to 29 years old	(X)	105	(X)	9	96	22	7	15	49	27	22	25	6	19
30 to 34 years old	(X)	58	(X)	9	48	10	7	2	25	6	18	14	2	12
35 years old and over	(X)	102	(X)	33	69	27	4	23	13	5	8	29	—	29
Private school, 15 years old and over	(X)	173	(X)	50	123	23	17	7	73	50	22	27	13	14
15 to 17 years old	(X)	46	(X)	44	2	2	2	—	—	—	—	—	—	—
18 and 19 years old	(X)	24	(X)	4	20	3	3	—	17	17	—	—	—	—
20 and 21 years old	(X)	15	(X)	2	13	3	3	—	10	7	2	—	—	—
22 to 24 years old	(X)	29	(X)	—	29	4	2	1	18	14	4	7	4	3
25 to 29 years old	(X)	23	(X)	—	23	2	—	2	11	7	4	10	5	5
30 to 34 years old	(X)	10	(X)	—	10	—	—	—	10	5	5	—	—	—
35 years old and over	(X)	26	(X)	—	26	9	6	3	6	—	6	10	4	6

Source: October 1996 Current Population Survey, Education and Social Stratification Branch, U.S. Bureau of the Census

1. May be of any race.

— Represents zero or rounds to zero.

(X) Data not available or not applicable.

Table A-10. Attendance Status of College Students 15 Years Old and Over, by Sex, Age, Year and Type of College, Race, and Hispanic Origin: October 1996

(Numbers in thousands. Civilian noninstitutional population.)

Year and type of college, age, race, and Hispanic origin	Both sexes			Male			Female		
	Total	Full time		Total	Full time		Total	Full time	
		Number	Percent		Number	Percent		Number	Percent
ALL RACES									
15 Years Old and Over									
Enrolled in college	15 226	9 839	64.6	6 820	4 681	68.6	8 406	5 157	61.4
1st year	3 671	2 540	69.2	1 588	1 177	74.1	2 083	1 364	65.5
2nd year	3 571	2 395	67.1	1 548	1 054	68.1	2 023	1 340	66.3
3rd year	2 672	1 796	67.2	1 167	820	70.3	1 505	975	64.8
4th year	2 390	1 803	75.4	1 230	980	79.7	1 161	823	70.9
5th year	1 007	446	44.4	377	182	48.2	630	265	42.1
6th year or higher	1 915	858	44.8	911	468	51.4	1 004	390	38.8
Two year college (1st to 4th year)	4 174	2 209	52.9	1 752	974	55.6	2 423	1 235	51.0
1st and 2nd year	3 552	1 981	55.8	1 528	890	58.2	2 023	1 091	53.9
3rd and 4th year	623	228	36.6	223	84	37.7	399	144	36.1
Four year college (1st to 4th year)	8 130	6 325	77.8	3 781	3 058	80.9	4 349	3 267	75.1
1st and 2nd year	3 691	2 954	80.0	1 607	1 341	83.5	2 083	1 612	77.4
3rd and 4th year	4 440	3 371	75.9	2 174	1 716	79.0	2 266	1 655	73.0
15 to 19 Years Old									
Enrolled in college	3 546	3 149	88.8	1 586	1 427	90.0	1 961	1 722	87.8
1st year	2 129	1 844	86.6	968	860	88.9	1 161	983	84.7
2nd year	1 219	1 121	91.9	522	476	91.1	697	645	92.5
3rd year	144	137	95.5	64	63	(B)	80	74	92.8
4th year	33	29	(B)	23	19	(B)	10	10	(B)
5th year	9	7	(B)	3	3	(B)	7	4	(B)
6th year or higher	11	11	(B)	7	7	(B)	5	5	(B)
Two year college (1st to 4th year)	1 223	995	81.4	560	450	80.3	663	546	82.4
1st and 2nd year	1 197	972	81.2	553	443	80.1	643	529	82.2
3rd and 4th year	26	23	(B)	7	7	(B)	19	17	(B)
Four year college (1st to 4th year)	2 303	2 136	92.8	1 017	968	95.3	1 286	1 168	90.8
1st and 2nd year	2 152	1 993	92.6	937	893	95.4	1 215	1 099	90.5
3rd and 4th year	151	143	94.5	80	75	93.7	71	68	(B)
20 to 24 Years Old									
Enrolled in college	5 458	4 438	81.3	2 698	2 242	83.1	2 760	2 196	79.5
1st year	648	403	62.2	298	197	66.2	350	206	58.7
2nd year	1 231	900	73.1	597	452	75.7	634	448	70.7
3rd year	1 500	1 299	86.6	710	600	84.6	791	698	88.3
4th year	1 493	1 374	92.0	835	776	93.0	659	597	90.7
5th year	295	216	73.2	129	103	80.0	167	113	68.0
6th year or higher	290	246	84.8	131	114	86.9	159	133	83.1
Two year college (1st to 4th year)	1 184	728	61.5	532	341	64.0	652	387	59.5
1st and 2nd year	971	605	62.4	431	291	67.4	539	315	58.4
3rd and 4th year	213	123	57.5	101	50	49.4	112	73	64.7
Four year college (1st to 4th year)	3 689	3 247	88.0	1 906	1 685	88.4	1 783	1 562	87.6
1st and 2nd year	909	697	76.8	463	358	77.3	446	339	76.1
3rd and 4th year	2 780	2 550	91.7	1 443	1 327	92.0	1 337	1 223	91.5
25 to 34 Years Old									
Enrolled in college	3 443	1 561	45.3	1 523	722	47.4	1 920	839	43.7

See footnotes at end of table.

Table A-10. Attendance Status of College Students 15 Years Old and Over, by Sex, Age, Year and Type of College, Race, and Hispanic Origin: October 1996 — Continued

(Numbers in thousands. Civilian noninstitutional population.)

Year and type of college, age, race, and Hispanic origin	Both sexes			Male			Female		
	Total	Full time		Total	Full time		Total	Full time	
		Number	Percent		Number	Percent		Number	Percent
1st year	519	208	40.1	182	83	45.4	337	126	37.3
2nd year	610	227	37.2	247	74	29.8	363	153	42.3
3rd year	591	265	44.8	249	123	49.3	342	142	41.6
4th year	507	290	57.3	229	128	56.0	277	162	58.3
5th year	406	141	34.6	157	48	30.3	249	93	37.4
6th year or higher	811	430	53.0	459	266	58.1	352	163	46.4
Two year college (1st to 4th year)	922	315	34.2	367	118	32.2	556	197	35.5
1st and 2nd year	759	258	34.0	306	96	31.5	452	161	35.6
3rd and 4th year	164	58	35.2	60	22	(B)	103	36	34.7
Four year college (1st to 4th year)	1 304	675	51.8	541	289	53.5	763	386	50.6
1st and 2nd year	370	178	48.0	123	60	48.8	247	118	47.6
3rd and 4th year	934	498	53.3	418	229	54.9	516	268	52.0
35 Years Old and Over									
Enrolled in college	2 778	691	24.9	1 013	291	28.7	1 765	400	22.7
1st year	376	86	22.8	140	37	26.1	235	49	20.8
2nd year	511	147	28.8	182	53	29.2	329	94	28.5
3rd year	437	94	21.6	145	34	23.6	292	60	20.6
4th year	357	110	30.9	143	56	39.5	214	54	25.2
5th year	296	83	28.0	89	28	32.1	207	54	26.2
6th year or higher	803	171	21.3	314	82	26.0	488	90	18.3
Two year college (1st to 4th year)	845	171	20.2	293	65	22.4	553	105	19.1
1st and 2nd year	626	146	23.4	237	60	25.2	388	87	22.3
3rd and 4th year	220	24	11.1	55	6	(B)	164	19	11.4
Four year college (1st to 4th year)	835	266	31.9	318	115	36.2	517	151	29.3
1st and 2nd year	261	86	33.0	85	30	35.4	176	56	31.9
3rd and 4th year	574	180	31.4	233	85	36.5	342	95	27.9
WHITE									
15 years old and over	12 189	7 849	64.4	5 453	3 719	68.2	6 735	4 129	61.3
1st year	2 864	2 008	70.1	1 267	943	74.4	1 597	1 065	66.7
2nd year	2 821	1 890	67.0	1 215	835	68.7	1 605	1 055	65.7
3rd year	2 189	1 499	68.5	947	677	71.5	1 242	822	66.2
4th year	1 987	1 488	74.9	1 030	812	78.8	958	677	70.7
5th year	815	351	43.1	305	132	43.4	511	219	42.9
6th year or higher	1 512	612	40.5	690	320	46.4	823	292	35.5
15 to 19 years old	2 898	2 581	89.1	1 292	1 158	89.6	1 606	1 424	88.7
20 to 24 years old	4 393	3 571	81.3	2 196	1 821	83.0	2 197	1 750	79.7
25 to 34 years old	2 644	1 166	44.1	1 154	515	44.6	1 490	651	43.7
35 years old and over	2 254	530	23.5	811	225	27.8	1 443	305	21.2
Two Year College (1st to 4th Year)									
15 years old and over	3 295	1 743	52.9	1 373	767	55.9	1 922	977	50.8
15 to 19 years old	1 011	814	80.6	459	359	78.3	552	455	82.5
20 to 24 years old	911	537	58.9	426	265	62.2	485	272	56.0
25 to 34 years old	695	262	37.6	265	90	34.1	430	171	39.8
35 years old and over	678	131	19.3	223	52	23.5	456	79	17.2
Four Year College (1st to 4th Year)									
15 years old and over	6 565	5 142	78.3	3 086	2 500	81.0	3 480	2 642	75.9
15 to 19 years old	1 871	1 753	93.7	824	789	95.8	1 047	964	92.1

See footnotes at end of table.

Table A-10. Attendance Status of College Students 15 Years Old and Over, by Sex, Age, Year and Type of College, Race, and Hispanic Origin: October 1996 — Continued

(Numbers in thousands. Civilian noninstitutional population.)

Year and type of college, age, race, and Hispanic origin	Both sexes			Male			Female		
	Total	Full time		Total	Full time		Total	Full time	
		Number	Percent		Number	Percent		Number	Percent
20 to 24 years old	3 030	2 678	88.4	1 571	1 390	88.5	1 459	1 289	88.3
25 to 34 years old	1 004	496	49.5	431	214	49.7	572	282	49.3
35 years old and over	661	214	32.3	260	106	41.0	401	107	26.7
BLACK									
15 years old and over	1 901	1 179	62.0	764	524	68.6	1 136	654	57.6
1st year	556	350	63.0	194	135	69.6	362	215	59.4
2nd year	485	320	66.1	197	126	63.8	288	195	67.6
3rd year	281	148	52.7	105	59	55.6	176	90	51.1
4th year	271	201	74.3	128	112	86.9	142	90	62.9
5th year	109	50	46.3	40	26	(B)	68	25	(B)
6th year or higher	199	109	54.5	99	68	68.6	100	41	40.5
15 to 19 years old	389	335	86.1	162	146	90.1	227	189	83.3
20 to 24 years old	638	520	81.5	276	234	84.6	362	286	79.1
25 to 34 years old	520	225	43.2	206	110	53.7	314	114	36.3
35 years old and over	354	99	28.0	120	34	28.4	234	65	27.8
Two Year College (1st to 4th Year)									
15 years old and over	580	289	49.7	229	119	52.1	351	169	48.2
15 to 19 years old	119	96	80.5	46	40	(B)	73	56	(B)
20 to 24 years old	165	122	73.9	66	50	(B)	99	72	73.1
25 to 34 years old	186	39	21.2	78	21	26.4	107	19	17.5
35 years old and over	111	32	28.7	38	9	(B)	73	23	(B)
Four Year College (1st to 4th Year)									
15 years old and over	1 013	731	72.2	396	311	78.7	617	420	68.1
15 to 19 years old	266	235	88.4	116	106	91.6	150	129	86.0
20 to 24 years old	414	352	85.1	187	163	87.5	228	189	83.0
25 to 34 years old	191	105	54.7	54	38	(B)	138	67	48.5
35 years old and over	141	39	27.9	40	4	(B)	102	35	34.7
HISPANIC ORIGIN [1]									
15 years old and over	1 223	708	57.9	529	303	57.3	693	405	58.4
1st year	356	207	58.1	128	61	47.9	228	145	63.8
2nd year	318	183	57.6	170	92	54.1	148	92	61.6
3rd year	192	123	64.2	78	46	58.7	114	77	68.0
4th year	183	123	67.6	81	58	71.1	101	66	64.8
5th year	71	24	(B)	22	15	(B)	49	9	(B)
6th year or higher	102	47	45.9	50	31	(B)	53	16	(B)
15 to 19 years old	263	202	76.8	106	75	71.3	157	126	80.5
20 to 24 years old	466	330	70.8	202	143	70.8	264	187	70.8
25 to 34 years old	310	129	41.8	132	57	43.4	178	72	40.6
35 years old and over	184	47	25.7	90	28	30.9	95	20	20.8
Two Year College (1st to 4th Year)									
15 years old and over	444	224	50.4	195	82	41.8	249	142	57.2
15 to 19 years old	121	86	71.2	44	27	(B)	78	59	76.2
20 to 24 years old	177	92	51.7	76	34	44.4	101	58	57.2
25 to 34 years old	72	25	(B)	39	11	(B)	34	14	(B)
35 years old and over	73	21	(B)	37	10	(B)	36	11	(B)

See footnotes at end of table.

Table A-10.   Attendance Status of College Students 15 Years Old and Over, by Sex, Age, Year and Type of College, Race, and Hispanic Origin: October 1996 — Continued

(Numbers in thousands. Civilian noninstitutional population.)

Year and type of college, age, race, and Hispanic origin	Both sexes			Male			Female		
	Total	Full time		Total	Full time		Total	Full time	
		Number	Percent		Number	Percent		Number	Percent
Four Year College (1st to 4th Year)									
15 years old and over	605	413	68.3	263	176	66.8	343	238	69.4
15 to 19 years old	141	115	81.6	62	48	(B)	79	67	84.6
20 to 24 years old	248	203	81.9	98	82	83.2	150	121	81.0
25 to 34 years old	164	81	49.6	69	36	(B)	95	45	47.4
35 years old and over	52	14	(B)	33	9	(B)	19	5	(B)

Source: October 1996 Current Population Survey, Education and Social Stratification Branch, U.S. Bureau of the Census

1. May be of any race.

(B) The base of the derived measure is less than 75,000.

Table A-11. Employment Status of High School and College Students 15 Years Old and Over, by Level of School, Type of College, Attendance Status, Age, Sex, Race and Hispanic Origin: October 1996

(Numbers in thousands. Civilian noninstitutional population.)

Age, level of enrollment, type of college, sex, race, and Hispanic origin	All students			Full time students			Part time students		
	Total	Employed		Total	Employed		Total	Employed	
		Full time	Part time		Full time	Part time		Full time	Part time
ALL RACES									
Both Sexes									
Enrolled in high school	12 212	353	3 114	12 212	353	3 114	—	—	—
15 years old	3 592	6	383	3 592	6	383	—	—	—
16 and 17 years old	6 967	104	2 307	6 967	104	2 307	—	—	—
18 and 19 years old	1 229	102	374	1 229	102	374	—	—	—
20 years old and over	424	142	51	424	142	51	—	—	—
Enrolled in college	15 226	5 101	4 509	9 839	1 319	3 648	5 388	3 782	860
15 to 17 years old	237	12	67	193	5	47	44	7	20
18 and 19 years old	3 309	327	1 231	2 956	180	1 095	353	147	136
20 and 21 years old	2 907	424	1 228	2 502	225	1 094	405	199	134
22 to 24 years old	2 551	711	925	1 936	297	785	615	414	140
25 to 29 years old	2 215	1 153	461	1 102	279	336	1 113	874	125
30 to 34 years old	1 228	702	242	458	128	144	770	574	98
35 years old and over	2 778	1 772	354	691	205	146	2 087	1 567	207
Two year college (1st to 4th year)	4 174	1 586	1 246	2 209	358	894	1 965	1 228	353
15 to 19 years old	1 223	177	555	995	96	456	227	80	99
20 to 24 years old	1 184	387	448	728	122	331	456	265	118
25 to 34 years old	922	521	155	315	86	89	607	435	66
35 years old and over	845	501	88	171	54	18	674	447	70
Four year college (1st to 4th year)	8 130	1 895	2 733	6 325	658	2 391	1 806	1 237	342
15 to 19 years old	2 303	161	740	2 136	87	686	167	73	54
20 to 24 years old	3 689	586	1 557	3 247	329	1 421	441	257	136
25 to 34 years old	1 304	640	327	675	168	223	629	472	104
35 years old and over	835	508	109	266	73	61	569	434	48
Fifth year of college or higher	2 922	1 620	529	1 305	303	364	1 617	1 317	165
15 to 19 years old	21	2	3	18	2	1	3	—	3
20 to 24 years old	586	163	148	462	72	128	123	91	20
25 to 34 years old	1 217	693	221	570	153	168	647	540	53
35 years old and over	1 098	764	156	254	78	67	844	686	89
Male									
Enrolled in high school	6 423	192	1 621	6 423	192	1 621	—	—	—
15 years old	1 844	3	212	1 844	3	212	—	—	—
16 and 17 years old	3 632	50	1 153	3 632	50	1 153	—	—	—
18 and 19 years old	769	59	239	769	59	239	—	—	—
20 years old and over	178	80	17	178	80	17	—	—	—
Enrolled in college	6 820	2 400	1 863	4 681	726	1 601	2 139	1 674	262
15 to 17 years old	97	4	23	86	4	15	11	1	8
18 and 19 years old	1 489	152	490	1 341	87	448	148	65	42
20 and 21 years old	1 379	219	528	1 184	118	462	195	101	66
22 to 24 years old	1 319	359	479	1 058	180	423	261	180	56
25 to 29 years old	1 038	577	208	544	155	161	494	422	47
30 to 34 years old	485	339	60	177	68	41	308	271	19
35 years old and over	1 013	748	74	291	115	50	723	634	25
Two year college (1st to 4th year)	1 752	754	467	974	190	359	778	564	108
15 to 19 years old	560	94	223	450	50	182	110	44	41
20 to 24 years old	532	192	194	341	73	148	192	120	47
25 to 34 years old	367	262	42	118	44	29	249	218	13
35 years old and over	293	206	7	65	23	1	227	183	6
Four year college (1st to 4th year)	3 781	900	1 191	3 058	373	1 061	724	527	130
15 to 19 years old	1 017	63	291	968	41	282	48	21	9
20 to 24 years old	1 906	318	748	1 685	188	680	221	130	68

See footnotes at end of table.

Table A-11. Employment Status of High School and College Students 15 Years Old and Over, by Level of School, Type of College, Attendance Status, Age, Sex, Race and Hispanic Origin: October 1996 — Continued

(Numbers in thousands. Civilian noninstitutional population.)

Age, level of enrollment, type of college, sex, race, and Hispanic origin	All students			Full time students			Part time students		
	Total	Employed		Total	Employed		Total	Employed	
		Full time	Part time		Full time	Part time		Full time	Part time
25 to 34 years old	541	296	116	289	96	75	251	200	41
35 years old and over	318	223	36	115	47	24	203	176	13
Fifth year of college or higher	1 288	746	205	650	164	181	638	582	24
15 to 19 years old	9	—	—	9	—	—	—	—	—
20 to 24 years old	259	68	65	216	37	58	43	32	7
25 to 34 years old	616	359	110	314	83	98	302	276	11
35 years old and over	403	318	31	110	44	25	293	275	6
Female									
Enrolled in high school	5 789	161	1 493	5 789	161	1 493	—	—	—
15 years old	1 747	3	170	1 747	3	170	—	—	—
16 and 17 years old	3 335	54	1 154	3 335	54	1 154	—	—	—
18 and 19 years old	460	43	135	460	43	135	—	—	—
20 years old and over	246	61	34	246	61	34	—	—	—
Enrolled in college	8 406	2 701	2 646	5 157	593	2 048	3 249	2 108	598
15 to 17 years old	140	8	44	106	2	32	33	6	12
18 and 19 years old	1 821	175	740	1 616	93	647	205	82	94
20 and 21 years old	1 528	206	700	1 317	108	632	210	98	68
22 to 24 years old	1 233	352	446	878	117	362	355	234	84
25 to 29 years old	1 177	575	253	558	124	175	619	451	79
30 to 34 years old	743	363	182	281	60	103	462	302	78
35 years old and over	1 765	1 024	280	400	90	97	1 365	934	183
Two year college (1st to 4th year)	2 423	832	780	1 235	168	535	1 187	663	245
15 to 19 years old	663	83	332	546	47	274	117	36	58
20 to 24 years old	652	195	254	387	49	183	264	146	71
25 to 34 years old	556	260	112	197	42	60	359	217	53
35 years old and over	553	294	81	105	30	17	447	264	64
Four year college (1st to 4th year)	4 349	995	1 542	3 267	285	1 330	1 082	710	212
15 to 19 years old	1 286	98	449	1 168	46	404	119	52	45
20 to 24 years old	1 783	268	809	1 562	141	741	220	128	69
25 to 34 years old	763	345	211	386	72	149	377	272	63
35 years old and over	517	284	73	151	26	37	366	258	36
Fifth year of college or higher	1 634	875	323	655	140	182	979	735	141
15 to 19 years old	12	2	3	9	2	1	3	—	3
20 to 24 years old	326	94	83	246	35	70	80	59	13
25 to 34 years old	601	334	112	256	69	70	345	264	42
35 years old and over	695	445	126	144	34	42	551	412	84
WHITE									
Both Sexes									
Enrolled in high school	9 569	296	2 751	9 569	296	2 751	—	—	—
15 years old	2 853	6	344	2 853	6	344	—	—	—
16 and 17 years old	5 503	92	2 019	5 503	92	2 019	—	—	—
18 and 19 years old	914	80	342	914	80	342	—	—	—
20 years old and over	300	118	46	300	118	46	—	—	—
Enrolled in college	12 189	4 164	3 866	7 849	1 068	3 162	4 340	3 096	705
15 to 17 years old	167	9	49	132	4	35	35	5	14
18 and 19 years old	2 731	272	1 116	2 449	151	999	282	121	117
20 and 21 years old	2 362	368	1 075	2 039	208	961	324	160	114
22 to 24 years old	2 030	598	785	1 532	250	677	498	348	108
25 to 29 years old	1 704	921	366	824	212	260	880	709	106
30 to 34 years old	940	527	197	342	85	117	598	442	80
35 years old and over	2 254	1 469	279	530	158	113	1 724	1 312	166
Two year college (1st to 4th year)	3 295	1 311	1 078	1 743	304	788	1 552	1 008	290

See footnotes at end of table.

Table A-11. Employment Status of High School and College Students 15 Years Old and Over, by Level of School, Type of College, Attendance Status, Age, Sex, Race and Hispanic Origin: October 1996 — Continued

(Numbers in thousands. Civilian noninstitutional population.)

Age, level of enrollment, type of college, sex, race, and Hispanic origin	All students			Full time students			Part time students		
	Total	Employed		Total	Employed		Total	Employed	
		Full time	Part time		Full time	Part time		Full time	Part time
15 to 19 years old	1 011	162	498	814	84	416	196	78	82
20 to 24 years old	911	348	372	537	113	273	374	234	98
25 to 34 years old	695	387	137	262	63	86	434	324	51
35 years old and over	678	415	71	131	43	12	548	372	59
Four year college (1st to 4th year)	6 565	1 496	2 377	5 142	526	2 097	1 424	970	280
15 to 19 years old	1 871	117	664	1 753	70	617	118	48	47
20 to 24 years old	3 030	496	1 363	2 678	292	1 256	351	204	107
25 to 34 years old	1 004	478	271	496	109	175	507	369	96
35 years old and over	661	405	79	214	56	49	447	350	29
Fifth year of college or higher	2 328	1 357	411	964	238	277	1 364	1 119	135
15 to 19 years old	16	2	3	13	2	1	3	—	3
20 to 24 years old	452	122	125	356	52	109	96	71	16
25 to 34 years old	945	584	154	408	126	116	537	458	39
35 years old and over	915	649	129	186	59	52	729	590	77
Male									
Enrolled in high school	5 019	169	1 421	5 019	169	1 421	—	—	—
15 years old	1 464	3	197	1 464	3	197	—	—	—
16 and 17 years old	2 848	48	989	2 848	48	989	—	—	—
18 and 19 years old	576	50	221	576	50	221	—	—	—
20 years old and over	132	68	13	132	68	13	—	—	—
Enrolled in college	5 453	1 990	1 602	3 719	601	1 392	1 734	1 389	210
15 to 17 years old	69	3	18	59	2	11	11	1	8
18 and 19 years old	1 223	134	451	1 099	77	413	124	57	39
20 and 21 years old	1 117	189	470	960	109	414	156	80	55
22 to 24 years old	1 079	308	416	861	152	373	218	157	44
25 to 29 years old	797	470	154	396	121	117	402	349	37
30 to 34 years old	357	253	44	119	42	29	238	212	15
35 years old and over	811	632	49	225	98	36	586	534	13
Two year college (1st to 4th year)	1 373	624	404	767	168	319	606	456	84
15 to 19 years old	459	91	197	359	47	159	100	44	38
20 to 24 years old	426	176	169	265	70	131	161	106	38
25 to 34 years old	906	451	212	428	91	143	478	360	69
35 years old and over	223	170	4	52	22	1	171	147	3
Four year college (1st to 4th year)	3 086	739	1 064	2 500	309	957	586	430	108
15 to 19 years old	824	45	273	789	32	264	35	13	9
20 to 24 years old	1 571	271	669	1 390	166	613	181	105	56
25 to 34 years old	431	236	97	214	68	58	217	169	39
35 years old and over	260	187	26	106	43	22	153	143	4
Fifth year of college or higher	995	627	134	453	124	116	542	503	18
15 to 19 years old	9	—	—	9	—	—	—	—	—
20 to 24 years old	199	50	48	167	24	43	33	26	5
25 to 34 years old	458	300	67	210	67	60	247	233	7
35 years old and over	328	276	19	67	33	13	262	243	6
Female									
Enrolled in high school	4 550	127	1 330	4 550	127	1 330	—	—	—
15 years old	1 388	3	147	1 388	3	147	—	—	—
16 and 17 years old	2 655	45	1 030	2 655	45	1 030	—	—	—
18 and 19 years old	338	30	120	338	30	120	—	—	—
20 years old and over	168	49	33	168	49	33	—	—	—
Enrolled in college	6 735	2 175	2 264	4 129	467	1 769	2 606	1 707	495
15 to 17 years old	98	6	31	74	2	24	24	4	6
18 and 19 years old	1 508	139	664	1 350	74	586	158	64	78
20 and 21 years old	1 246	179	605	1 078	99	546	167	80	58

See footnotes at end of table.

Table A-11. Employment Status of High School and College Students 15 Years Old and Over, by Level of School, Type of College, Attendance Status, Age, Sex, Race and Hispanic Origin: October 1996 — Continued

(Numbers in thousands. Civilian noninstitutional population.)

Age, level of enrollment, type of college, sex, race, and Hispanic origin	All students			Full time students			Part time students		
	Total	Employed		Total	Employed		Total	Employed	
		Full time	Part time		Full time	Part time		Full time	Part time
22 to 24 years old	951	290	369	671	98	305	280	192	64
25 to 29 years old	906	451	212	428	91	143	478	360	69
30 to 34 years old	583	274	153	223	44	88	360	230	65
35 years old and over	1 443	837	230	305	60	77	1 138	777	153
Two year college (1st to 4th year)	1 922	688	674	977	136	469	946	552	206
15 to 19 years old	552	71	301	455	37	257	97	34	44
20 to 24 years old	485	172	203	272	44	142	214	129	61
25 to 34 years old	430	200	103	171	35	58	259	165	45
35 years old and over	456	245	68	79	21	11	377	224	56
Four year college (1st to 4th year)	3 480	757	1 312	2 642	217	1 140	838	540	172
15 to 19 years old	1 047	72	391	964	38	353	83	35	38
20 to 24 years old	1 459	225	695	1 289	126	643	170	99	51
25 to 34 years old	572	241	175	282	41	117	290	200	57
35 years old and over	401	219	52	107	13	27	294	206	25
Fifth year of college or higher	1 333	730	270	511	114	160	822	616	117
15 to 19 years old	7	2	3	4	2	1	3	—	3
20 to 24 years old	252	72	76	189	27	66	63	44	11
25 to 34 years old	487	283	88	198	59	56	290	224	32
35 years old and over	586	373	110	119	26	38	467	347	72
BLACK									
Both Sexes									
Enrolled in high school	2 033	53	254	2 033	53	254	—	—	—
15 years old	546	—	27	546	—	27	—	—	—
16 and 17 years old	1 103	7	198	1 103	7	198	—	—	—
18 and 19 years old	268	22	25	268	22	25	—	—	—
20 years old and over	116	24	4	116	24	4	—	—	—
Enrolled in college	1 901	671	367	1 179	176	270	722	496	97
15 to 17 years old	45	3	13	36	1	8	9	2	5
18 and 19 years old	345	42	62	299	21	50	45	21	13
20 and 21 years old	346	44	83	290	17	69	56	27	14
22 to 24 years old	292	65	86	230	37	64	62	28	21
25 to 29 years old	337	169	55	161	40	43	176	128	12
30 to 34 years old	182	121	24	64	30	13	119	91	11
35 years old and over	354	227	44	99	29	23	255	199	21
Two year college (1st to 4th year)	580	200	106	289	36	60	292	164	46
15 to 19 years old	119	7	32	96	5	19	23	2	13
20 to 24 years old	165	19	49	122	8	35	43	11	14
25 to 34 years old	186	111	12	39	16	—	146	94	12
35 years old and over	111	63	13	32	7	6	79	56	7
Four year college (1st to 4th year)	1 013	308	206	731	103	167	281	205	39
15 to 19 years old	266	38	44	235	18	39	31	20	5
20 to 24 years old	414	61	114	352	28	93	62	33	21
25 to 34 years old	191	120	30	105	46	26	87	74	3
35 years old and over	141	89	18	39	12	9	102	77	9
Fifth year of college or higher	308	163	55	159	36	43	149	127	12
15 to 19 years old	5	—	—	5	—	—	—	—	—
20 to 24 years old	59	28	6	46	18	6	13	10	—
25 to 34 years old	142	59	37	81	8	29	62	51	8
35 years old and over	101	75	13	28	10	8	74	65	4
Male									
Enrolled in high school	1 052	23	140	1 052	23	140	—	—	—
15 years old	262	—	—	262	—	10	—	—	—

See footnotes at end of table.

Table A-11. Employment Status of High School and College Students 15 Years Old and Over, by Level of School, Type of College, Attendance Status, Age, Sex, Race and Hispanic Origin: October 1996 — Continued

(Numbers in thousands. Civilian noninstitutional population.)

Age, level of enrollment, type of college, sex, race, and Hispanic origin	All students			Full time students			Part time students		
	Total	Employed		Total	Employed		Total	Employed	
		Full time	Part time		Full time	Part time		Full time	Part time
16 and 17 years old	579	2	111	579	2	111	—	—	—
18 and 19 years old	166	9	15	166	9	15	—	—	—
20 years old and over	45	11	4	45	11	4	—	—	—
Enrolled in college	764	261	145	524	83	120	240	177	25
15 to 17 years old	17	1	5	17	1	5	—	—	—
18 and 19 years old	145	13	21	129	8	19	16	4	2
20 and 21 years old	155	22	28	130	9	24	25	13	4
22 to 24 years old	122	29	37	104	22	31	18	8	7
25 to 29 years old	142	70	33	80	16	26	62	53	6
30 to 34 years old	64	47	10	31	20	8	33	27	3
35 years old and over	120	79	11	34	7	8	86	72	3
Two year college (1st to 4th year)	229	92	35	119	15	22	110	78	13
15 to 19 years old	46	—	11	40	—	9	6	—	2
20 to 24 years old	66	10	17	50	3	13	16	8	4
25 to 34 years old	78	58	6	21	12	—	58	46	6
35 years old and over	38	24	—	9	—	—	29	24	—
Four year college (1st to 4th year)	396	107	70	311	48	60	84	59	10
15 to 19 years old	116	14	15	106	10	15	10	4	—
20 to 24 years old	187	31	42	163	18	35	23	13	7
25 to 34 years old	54	36	8	38	21	8	16	15	—
35 years old and over	40	27	5	4	—	2	36	27	3
Fifth year of college or higher	140	61	41	94	21	38	46	40	3
15 to 19 years old	—	—	—	—	—	—	—	—	—
20 to 24 years old	24	10	6	21	10	6	3	—	—
25 to 34 years old	74	22	29	52	3	26	22	19	3
35 years old and over	42	29	6	21	7	6	21	21	—
Female									
Enrolled in high school	981	30	113	981	30	113	—	—	—
15 years old	284	—	16	284	—	16	—	—	—
16 and 17 years old	524	5	87	524	5	87	—	—	—
18 and 19 years old	103	13	10	103	13	10	—	—	—
20 years old and over	71	12	—	71	12	—	—	—	—
Enrolled in college	1 136	411	222	654	92	149	482	318	72
15 to 17 years old	28	2	8	19	—	3	9	2	5
18 and 19 years old	199	30	41	170	13	31	29	17	10
20 and 21 years old	192	22	55	160	9	45	31	14	10
22 to 24 years old	170	35	49	126	15	34	44	20	15
25 to 29 years old	195	99	22	81	24	16	114	75	6
30 to 34 years old	119	74	14	33	10	5	86	64	9
35 years old and over	234	148	33	65	21	15	169	127	18
Two year college (1st to 4th year)	351	108	71	169	22	38	182	86	34
15 to 19 years old	73	7	21	56	5	10	17	2	10
20 to 24 years old	99	9	32	72	6	22	27	3	10
25 to 34 years old	107	52	6	19	4	—	89	48	6
35 years old and over	73	40	13	23	7	6	50	32	7
Four year college (1st to 4th year)	617	201	136	420	56	107	197	146	29
15 to 19 years old	150	24	29	129	8	24	21	16	5
20 to 24 years old	228	31	72	189	11	58	39	20	14
25 to 34 years old	138	84	22	67	25	18	71	59	3
35 years old and over	102	62	14	35	12	7	66	51	6
Fifth year of college or higher	168	101	14	65	15	5	103	86	10
15 to 19 years old	5	—	—	5	—	—	—	—	—
20 to 24 years old	35	18	—	25	8	—	10	10	—
25 to 34 years old	69	37	8	29	5	3	40	32	6
35 years old and over	59	46	6	7	2	2	52	44	4

See footnotes at end of table.

Table A-11. Employment Status of High School and College Students 15 Years Old and Over, by Level of School, Type of College, Attendance Status, Age, Sex, Race and Hispanic Origin: October 1996 — Continued

(Numbers in thousands. Civilian noninstitutional population.)

Age, level of enrollment, type of college, sex, race, and Hispanic origin	All students			Full time students			Part time students		
	Total	Employed		Total	Employed		Total	Employed	
		Full time	Part time		Full time	Part time		Full time	Part time
HISPANIC ORIGIN [1]									
Both Sexes									
Enrolled in high school	1 652	106	228	1 652	106	228	—	—	—
15 years old	454	—	26	454	—	26	—	—	—
16 and 17 years old	836	31	137	836	31	137	—	—	—
18 and 19 years old	230	26	46	230	26	46	—	—	—
20 years old and over	133	48	19	133	48	19	—	—	—
Enrolled in college	1 223	412	342	708	90	262	514	322	80
15 to 17 years old	23	—	—	18	—	—	4	—	—
18 and 19 years old	240	40	83	183	17	68	57	23	16
20 and 21 years old	213	35	100	158	12	79	56	23	21
22 to 24 years old	253	63	91	172	15	67	80	48	23
25 to 29 years old	190	101	43	95	22	33	103	78	10
30 to 34 years old	112	59	15	35	5	9	77	54	5
35 years old and over	184	114	10	47	18	6	137	96	4
Two year college (1st to 4th year)	444	156	125	224	27	94	220	129	32
15 to 19 years old	121	23	39	86	5	33	35	18	6
20 to 24 years old	177	58	71	92	8	48	86	50	23
25 to 34 years old	72	39	13	25	4	13	47	35	—
35 years old and over	73	37	2	21	10	—	53	27	2
Four year college (1st to 4th year)	605	172	195	413	51	156	192	122	39
15 to 19 years old	141	18	44	115	12	35	26	6	9
20 to 24 years old	248	37	114	203	19	96	45	18	19
25 to 34 years old	164	81	33	81	19	22	82	62	11
35 years old and over	52	36	3	14	—	3	38	36	—
Fifth year of college or higher	174	83	22	71	12	12	102	71	9
15 to 19 years old	—	—	—	—	—	—	—	—	—
20 to 24 years old	41	3	6	36	—	—	6	3	3
25 to 34 years old	74	40	11	23	5	6	51	36	5
35 years old and over	59	40	5	13	8	3	46	32	2
Male									
Enrolled in high school	880	71	134	880	71	134	—	—	—
15 years old	231	—	22	231	—	22	—	—	—
16 and 17 years old	441	19	63	441	19	63	—	—	—
18 and 19 years old	139	14	43	139	14	43	—	—	—
20 years old and over	69	39	6	69	39	6	—	—	—
Enrolled in college	529	192	158	303	41	119	226	151	39
15 to 17 years old	8	—	—	8	—	—	—	—	—
18 and 19 years old	98	20	45	67	8	34	30	13	11
20 and 21 years old	78	12	38	57	3	31	21	9	7
22 to 24 years old	124	27	47	86	6	35	38	21	13
25 to 29 years old	79	43	14	43	16	11	36	27	3
30 to 34 years old	54	33	8	14	2	2	39	31	5
35 years old and over	90	57	6	28	7	6	62	50	—
Two year college (1st to 4th year)	195	82	59	82	10	40	113	72	19
15 to 19 years old	44	7	23	27	—	16	16	7	6
20 to 24 years old	76	29	29	34	3	17	42	26	13
25 to 34 years old	39	26	7	11	4	7	28	22	—
35 years old and over	37	21	—	10	4	—	27	17	—
Four year college (1st to 4th year)	263	81	93	176	27	73	87	54	20
15 to 19 years old	62	13	22	48	8	17	14	6	5
20 to 24 years old	98	10	53	82	6	45	17	5	7

See footnotes at end of table.

Table A-11. Employment Status of High School and College Students 15 Years Old and Over, by Level of School, Type of College, Attendance Status, Age, Sex, Race and Hispanic Origin: October 1996 — Continued

(Numbers in thousands. Civilian noninstitutional population.)

Age, level of enrollment, type of college, sex, race, and Hispanic origin	All students			Full time students			Part time students		
	Total	Employed		Total	Employed		Total	Employed	
		Full time	Part time		Full time	Part time		Full time	Part time
25 to 34 years old	69	35	15	36	14	7	33	21	8
35 years old and over	33	22	3	9	—	3	24	22	—
Fifth year of college or higher	72	29	6	46	4	6	25	25	—
15 to 19 years old	—	—	—	—	—	—	—	—	—
20 to 24 years old	28	—	3	28	—	3	—	—	—
25 to 34 years old	25	15	—	10	—	—	15	15	—
35 years old and over	19	14	3	9	4	3	11	11	—
Female									
Enrolled in high school	772	35	94	772	35	94	—	—	—
15 years old	223	—	4	223	—	4	—	—	—
16 and 17 years old	395	13	73	395	13	73	—	—	—
18 and 19 years old	91	13	3	91	13	3	—	—	—
20 years old and over	64	9	13	64	9	13	—	—	—
Enrolled in college	693	220	185	405	49	143	288	171	41
15 to 17 years old	15	—	—	10	—	—	4	—	—
18 and 19 years old	142	20	39	116	9	34	26	11	5
20 and 21 years old	136	23	62	101	9	48	35	14	14
22 to 24 years old	128	36	43	86	10	33	42	26	11
25 to 29 years old	119	58	29	52	7	22	67	51	8
30 to 34 years old	59	27	7	20	4	7	38	23	—
35 years old and over	95	57	4	20	11	—	75	46	4
Two year college (1st to 4th year)	249	74	66	142	17	54	107	57	13
15 to 19 years old	78	15	17	59	5	17	18	11	—
20 to 24 years old	101	29	41	58	6	31	43	24	11
25 to 34 years old	34	13	6	14	—	6	20	13	—
35 years old and over	36	16	2	11	6	—	25	10	2
Four year college (1st to 4th year)	343	92	102	238	24	83	105	68	19
15 to 19 years old	79	4	22	67	4	17	12	—	5
20 to 24 years old	150	27	62	121	14	50	28	13	11
25 to 34 years old	95	46	19	45	6	16	50	40	3
35 years old and over	19	14	—	5	—	—	14	14	—
Fifth year of college or higher	102	54	16	25	—	6	77	46	9
15 to 19 years old	—	—	—	—	—	—	—	—	—
20 to 24 years old	14	3	3	8	—	—	6	3	3
25 to 34 years old	49	25	11	13	—	6	36	21	5
35 years old and over	39	26	2	4	—	—	35	22	2

Source: October 1996 Current Population Survey, Education and Social Stratification Branch, U.S. Bureau of the Census

1. May be of any race.

— Represents zero or rounds to zero.

NOTE: Persons enrolled in high school are assumed to be attending full-time

Table A-12. Population 15 Years Old and Over Enrolled in Vocational Courses, by Employment Status, Age, Sex, Race, and Hispanic Origin: October 1996

(Numbers in thousands. Civilian noninstitutional population.)

Selected characteristics, age, sex, race, and Hispanic origin	Total population			Employed						Not employed		In college and taking vocational courses
	Total	Vocational courses		Total		Full time		Part time		Total	Vocational courses	
		Number	Percent	Total	Vocational courses	Total	Vocational courses	Total	Vocational courses			
ALL RACES												
Male												
15 years old and over	98 529	1 916	1.9	69 366	1 593	62 833	1 435	6 533	158	29 163	323	363
15 to 19 years old	9 696	133	1.4	3 478	59	1 209	30	2 269	29	6 218	74	62
20 to 24 years old	8 574	257	3.0	6 506	191	5 312	151	1 194	40	2 068	66	115
25 to 34 years old	19 667	460	2.3	17 641	429	16 975	388	666	41	2 026	31	98
35 to 44 years old	21 320	507	2.4	19 179	465	18 723	454	456	10	2 142	42	58
45 to 64 years old	25 876	482	1.9	20 276	417	19 296	400	981	17	5 600	65	25
65 years old and over	13 396	78	0.6	2 287	32	1 318	12	968	20	11 109	46	5
Educational attainment:												
Not a high school graduate	22 090	129	0.6	10 021	89	7 767	83	2 254	6	12 072	40	2
High school graduate only	30 281	488	1.6	22 253	382	20 995	334	1 258	48	8 028	106	81
College, less than a bachelor's degree	23 903	689	2.9	18 477	568	16 430	495	2 047	74	5 426	121	207
College, bachelor's degree or more	22 253	611	2.8	18 616	554	17 641	523	974	31	3 637	57	73
Metropolitan status:												
Metropolitan	78 960	1 647	2.1	56 003	1 358	50 820	1 227	5 183	131	22 957	288	334
Central city	28 625	554	1.9	19 361	437	17 519	383	1 842	54	9 264	117	155
Outside central city	50 335	1 092	2.2	36 642	921	33 301	844	3 342	78	13 692	171	179
Nonmetropolitan	19 569	270	1.4	13 363	234	12 014	208	1 349	27	6 206	35	29
Region:												
Northeast	19 108	341	1.8	13 012	279	11 841	254	1 171	24	6 096	62	71
Midwest	23 263	458	2.0	17 010	413	15 218	373	1 792	39	6 252	46	69
South	34 340	587	1.7	24 054	463	21 910	408	2 143	55	10 286	124	121
West	21 819	530	2.4	15 290	438	13 864	399	1 426	39	6 529	91	101
15 to 24 years old												
Educational attainment:												
Not a high school graduate	8 306	44	0.5	2 918	23	1 200	20	1 718	3	5 387	21	—
High school graduate only	4 304	138	3.2	3 117	84	2 746	56	370	28	1 188	54	58
College, less than a bachelor's degree	4 728	193	4.1	3 194	133	1 894	98	1 299	36	1 534	60	112
College, bachelor's degree or more	931	15	1.6	755	10	680	7	75	3	176	5	7
Metropolitan status:												
Metropolitan	14 446	329	2.3	7 839	202	5 085	147	2 754	56	6 607	127	161
Central city	5 652	128	2.3	2 877	72	1 959	54	918	18	2 775	56	55
Outside central city	8 794	201	2.3	4 962	131	3 126	93	1 836	38	3 832	71	107
Nonmetropolitan	3 824	61	1.6	2 144	48	1 436	34	709	14	1 679	13	16
Region:												
Northeast	3 234	47	1.5	1 551	19	967	12	584	8	1 682	28	29
Midwest	4 353	105	2.4	2 621	83	1 575	68	1 046	15	1 732	21	32
South	6 435	146	2.3	3 512	88	2 430	62	1 082	25	2 923	59	76
West	4 248	92	2.2	2 300	60	1 549	38	751	21	1 948	32	40
Female												
15 years old and over	106579	2 246	2.1	59 593	1 570	45 691	1 187	13 902	383	46 985	676	466
15 to 19 years old	9 296	128	1.4	3 359	54	879	13	2 480	42	5 937	74	75
20 to 24 years old	8 721	300	3.5	5 676	171	4 015	101	1 661	70	3 045	129	146
25 to 34 years old	20 425	547	2.7	14 759	369	12 252	306	2 507	63	5 666	178	106
35 to 44 years old	21 960	606	2.8	16 568	484	13 520	368	3 049	116	5 392	123	78
45 to 64 years old	27 692	597	2.2	17 670	464	14 384	381	3 287	83	10 022	133	57
65 years old and over	18 484	68	0.4	1 560	28	642	18	918	9	16 923	40	3

See footnotes at end of table.

Table A-12. Population 15 Years Old and Over Enrolled in Vocational Courses, by Employment Status, Age, Sex, Race, and Hispanic Origin: October 1996 — Continued

(Numbers in thousands. Civilian noninstitutional population.)

Selected characteristics, age, sex, race, and Hispanic origin	Total population			Employed						Not employed		In college and taking vocational courses
	Total	Vocational courses		Total		Full time		Part time		Total	Vocational courses	
		Number	Percent	Total	Vocational courses	Total	Vocational courses	Total	Vocational courses			
Educational attainment:												
Not a high school graduate	23 300	176	0.8	6 384	50	3 839	29	2 544	21	16 916	125	13
High school graduate only	35 324	614	1.7	19 465	399	15 387	297	4 079	102	15 858	215	101
College, less than a bachelor's degree	27 820	848	3.1	18 607	643	13 781	468	4 826	175	9 213	205	260
College, bachelor's degree or more	20 135	608	3.0	15 137	478	12 685	394	2 453	84	4 998	131	92
Metropolitan status:												
Metropolitan	85 627	1 869	2.2	48 340	1 303	37 252	975	11 089	328	37 287	567	375
Central city	32 447	665	2.1	17 512	436	13 994	321	3 518	115	14 935	229	175
Outside central city	53 180	1 204	2.3	30 828	867	23 257	654	7 571	212	22 352	337	201
Nonmetropolitan	20 951	376	1.8	11 253	267	8 440	212	2 813	55	9 699	109	90
Region:												
Northeast	21 258	455	2.1	11 635	318	8 708	235	2 927	83	9 623	138	85
Midwest	24 750	451	1.8	14 603	336	10 633	256	3 970	80	10 147	115	97
South	37 789	733	1.9	20 884	511	16 976	393	3 909	118	16 904	222	125
West	22 781	607	2.7	12 470	405	9 374	304	3 096	101	10 311	202	158
15 to 24 years old												
Educational attainment:												
Not a high school graduate	7 528	66	0.9	2 143	23	533	12	1 610	11	5 386	43	13
High school graduate only	4 278	162	3.8	2 608	72	1 887	35	722	37	1 669	89	66
College, less than a bachelor's degree	5 034	167	3.3	3 324	106	1 667	42	1 657	64	1 710	61	127
College, bachelor's degree or more	1 178	34	2.9	960	25	807	25	153	—	217	9	15
Metropolitan status:												
Metropolitan	14 417	349	2.4	7 172	179	3 938	88	3 234	91	7 244	170	181
Central city	5 931	169	2.9	2 801	83	1 669	36	1 131	47	3 131	86	89
Outside central city	8 485	180	2.1	4 372	96	2 269	51	2 102	45	4 114	84	91
Nonmetropolitan	3 601	80	2.2	1 863	47	956	27	907	20	1 738	33	40
Region:												
Northeast	3 285	86	2.6	1 575	34	854	20	721	14	1 710	52	37
Midwest	4 201	98	2.3	2 379	64	1 130	36	1 249	28	1 822	34	46
South	6 467	144	2.2	3 062	78	1 846	34	1 216	43	3 405	66	75
West	4 064	100	2.5	2 020	50	1 065	23	955	27	2 044	50	63
WHITE												
Male												
15 years old and over	83 289	1 622	2.0	59 771	1 390	54 119	1 251	5 653	139	23 518	233	287
15 to 19 years old	7 647	110	1.4	3 039	53	1 029	27	2 010	26	4 609	56	48
20 to 24 years old	6 944	198	2.9	5 535	159	4 479	121	1 056	38	1 409	39	97
25 to 34 years old	16 311	365	2.2	14 852	338	14 367	308	485	31	1 459	26	74
35 to 44 years old	17 945	457	2.6	16 402	429	16 052	421	349	8	1 543	29	46
45 to 64 years old	22 435	423	1.9	17 849	380	16 995	362	853	17	4 587	43	20
65 years old and over	12 007	70	0.6	2 095	31	1 197	12	898	19	9 912	39	3
Educational attainment:												
Not a high school graduate	17 770	95	0.5	8 529	66	6 590	60	1 939	6	9 241	29	2
High school graduate only	25 614	405	1.6	19 026	338	17 938	290	1 088	48	6 588	67	61
College, less than a bachelor's degree	20 323	571	2.8	15 838	486	14 054	429	1 784	57	4 485	85	166
College, bachelor's degree or more	19 582	551	2.8	16 379	500	15 536	471	843	28	3 204	51	58
Metropolitan status:												
Metropolitan	65 678	1 374	2.1	47 557	1 166	43 169	1 054	4 388	112	18 121	208	258
Central city	20 800	362	1.7	14 724	308	13 298	273	1 426	35	6 075	54	100
Outside central city	44 878	1 012	2.3	32 833	858	29 871	781	2 962	78	12 045	153	158
Nonmetropolitan	17 611	249	1.4	12 214	224	10 949	197	1 265	27	5 397	25	29

See footnotes at end of table.

Table A-12. Population 15 Years Old and Over Enrolled in Vocational Courses, by Employment Status, Age, Sex, Race, and Hispanic Origin: October 1996 — Continued

(Numbers in thousands. Civilian noninstitutional population.)

Selected characteristics, age, sex, race, and Hispanic origin	Total population			Employed						Not employed		In college and taking vocational courses
	Total	Vocational courses		Total		Full time		Part time		Total	Vocational courses	
		Number	Percent	Total	Vocational courses	Total	Vocational courses	Total	Vocational courses			
Region:												
Northeast	16 342	281	1.7	11 313	238	10 278	218	1 035	20	5 029	43	46
Midwest	20 818	401	1.9	15 522	372	13 861	336	1 660	36	5 297	29	67
South	27 593	488	1.8	19 735	391	17 999	343	1 735	48	7 859	97	101
West	18 536	452	2.4	13 202	389	11 980	354	1 221	35	5 334	63	74
15 to 24 years old												
Educational attainment:												
Not a high school graduate	6 490	30	0.5	2 564	17	1 056	14	1 508	3	3 926	12	—
High school graduate only	3 449	115	3.3	2 639	78	2 298	49	341	28	811	37	46
College, less than a bachelor's degree	3 880	148	3.8	2 742	107	1 585	77	1 157	30	1 138	41	92
College, bachelor's degree or more	772	15	2.0	629	10	568	7	61	3	143	5	7
Female												
15 years old and over	88 515	1 849	2.1	49 791	1 355	37 346	1 042	12 445	313	38 724	494	370
15 to 19 years old	7 320	82	1.1	2 905	40	725	13	2 181	27	4 415	42	52
20 to 24 years old	6 899	232	3.4	4 716	144	3 294	85	1 422	59	2 183	89	116
25 to 34 years old	16 375	441	2.7	11 977	309	9 773	256	2 204	53	4 398	132	91
35 to 44 years old	18 015	513	2.9	13 661	425	10 840	325	2 821	100	4 354	89	68
45 to 64 years old	23 467	526	2.2	15 129	411	12 153	345	2 976	66	8 337	115	43
65 years old and over	16 440	54	0.3	1 401	26	561	18	841	8	15 038	28	—
Educational attainment:												
Not a high school graduate	18 411	137	0.7	5 162	46	2 989	28	2 172	18	13 249	91	10
High school graduate only	29 685	464	1.6	16 242	324	12 567	244	3 675	80	13 443	140	70
College, less than a bachelor's degree	23 269	717	3.1	15 517	550	11 180	403	4 337	147	7 752	167	211
College, bachelor's degree or more	17 151	530	3.1	12 870	435	10 610	367	2 260	68	4 281	96	79
Metropolitan status:												
Metropolitan	69 945	1 519	2.2	39 692	1 111	29 882	848	9 810	263	30 253	407	291
Central city	22 853	461	2.0	12 404	326	9 663	258	2 741	69	10 449	135	124
Outside central city	47 092	1 058	2.3	27 288	785	20 220	591	7 068	194	19 804	273	167
Nonmetropolitan	18 570	330	1.8	10 099	243	7 464	194	2 635	50	8 471	86	79
Region:												
Northeast	18 033	365	2.0	9 954	272	7 278	202	2 676	71	8 079	92	60
Midwest	21 810	401	1.8	13 074	316	9 359	242	3 715	74	8 737	85	89
South	29 413	566	1.9	16 147	407	12 842	318	3 304	89	13 266	159	89
West	19 259	517	2.7	10 617	360	7 867	281	2 750	79	8 642	157	132
15 to 24 years old												
Educational attainment:												
Not a high school graduate	5 892	52	0.9	1 866	21	447	12	1 419	9	4 026	31	10
High school graduate only	3 229	100	3.1	2 063	50	1 461	27	602	23	1 166	50	46
College, less than a bachelor's degree	4 109	133	3.2	2 855	90	1 414	36	1 441	55	1 253	42	102
College, bachelor's degree or more	989	29	3.0	837	23	696	23	141	—	152	7	10
BLACK												
Male												
15 years old and over	10 940	187	1.7	6 650	132	6 046	117	604	15	4 290	55	44
15 to 19 years old	1 505	8	0.5	317	4	140	3	177	1	1 188	4	1
20 to 24 years old	1 118	47	4.2	644	23	570	23	74	—	474	24	13
25 to 34 years old	2 380	62	2.6	1 955	58	1 817	47	138	10	425	5	20
35 to 44 years old	2 431	28	1.1	1 948	23	1 875	20	72	3	484	4	5

See footnotes at end of table.

Table A-12. Population 15 Years Old and Over Enrolled in Vocational Courses, by Employment Status, Age, Sex, Race, and Hispanic Origin: October 1996 — Continued

(Numbers in thousands. Civilian noninstitutional population.)

Selected characteristics, age, sex, race, and Hispanic origin	Total population			Employed						Not employed		In college and taking vocational courses
	Total	Vocational courses		Total		Full time		Part time		Total	Vocational courses	
		Number	Percent	Total	Vocational courses	Total	Vocational courses	Total	Vocational courses			
45 to 64 years old	2 475	38	1.5	1 660	25	1 565	25	94	—	815	13	5
65 years old and over	1 030	5	0.5	126	—	78	—	48	—	904	5	—
Educational attainment:												
Not a high school graduate	3 413	26	0.8	1 124	16	887	16	237	—	2 288	10	—
High school graduate only	3 729	44	1.2	2 581	28	2 449	28	132	—	1 148	16	6
College, less than a bachelor's degree	2 518	85	3.4	1 866	61	1 708	49	158	12	652	24	27
College, bachelor's degree or more	1 280	32	2.5	1 078	27	1 002	24	76	3	202	5	11
Metropolitan status:												
Metropolitan	9 431	175	1.9	5 774	126	5 228	111	546	15	3 657	49	44
Central city	5 854	131	2.2	3 357	91	3 050	76	307	15	2 496	40	31
Outside central city	3 577	44	1.2	2 416	35	2 178	35	238	—	1 161	8	13
Nonmetropolitan	1 510	13	0.8	876	6	818	6	58	—	633	7	—
Region:												
Northeast	2 006	36	1.8	1 187	25	1 099	21	88	4	819	12	22
Midwest	1 940	45	2.3	1 153	32	1 049	28	105	4	787	13	—
South	6 021	81	1.3	3 782	59	3 426	52	355	7	2 239	21	15
West	973	25	2.6	528	16	472	16	56	—	446	9	7
15 to 24 years old												
Educational attainment:												
Not a high school graduate	1 395	11	0.8	252	3	106	3	146	—	1 142	8	—
High school graduate only	684	12	1.8	393	5	369	5	24	—	291	7	4
College, less than a bachelor's degree	494	31	6.2	275	18	197	17	78	1	218	12	10
College, bachelor's degree or more	51	—	(X)	41	—	38	—	3	—	10	—	—
Female												
15 years old and over	13 395	269	2.0	7 253	141	6 269	101	983	40	6 142	128	57
15 to 19 years old	1 513	40	2.7	327	12	128	—	199	12	1 186	29	20
20 to 24 years old	1 359	44	3.2	712	16	552	8	160	8	647	28	15
25 to 34 years old	2 935	69	2.3	2 037	37	1 823	31	214	6	898	31	10
35 to 44 years old	2 895	64	2.2	2 149	46	2 008	36	141	10	747	18	4
45 to 64 years old	3 103	42	1.4	1 907	30	1 697	25	210	4	1 196	13	5
65 years old and over	1 590	9	0.6	121	—	61	—	60	—	1 469	9	3
Educational attainment:												
Not a high school graduate	3 828	32	0.9	904	5	645	1	260	4	2 924	28	3
High school graduate only	4 406	123	2.8	2 592	64	2 299	48	293	16	1 814	59	22
College, less than a bachelor's degree	3 518	83	2.4	2 442	59	2 102	41	340	19	1 076	24	29
College, bachelor's degree or more	1 643	30	1.8	1 314	13	1 224	11	90	1	329	17	2
Metropolitan status:												
Metropolitan	11 570	233	2.0	6 376	123	5 515	87	861	36	5 194	110	47
Central city	7 658	151	2.0	4 066	76	3 462	48	604	28	3 592	76	34
Outside central city	3 912	81	2.1	2 310	47	2 053	39	257	8	1 602	34	13
Nonmetropolitan	1 825	36	2.0	877	18	754	14	123	4	948	18	10
Region:												
Northeast	2 513	66	2.6	1 308	26	1 114	24	194	2	1 205	40	18
Midwest	2 355	41	1.7	1 204	19	1 019	12	185	7	1 151	22	6
South	7 433	135	1.8	4 178	85	3 669	59	509	26	3 255	50	32
West	1 094	27	2.4	562	11	467	6	95	5	532	15	1
15 to 24 years old												
Educational attainment:												
Not a high school graduate	1 298	12	1.0	199	2	66	—	134	2	1 099	11	3

See footnotes at end of table.

Table A-12. Population 15 Years Old and Over Enrolled in Vocational Courses, by Employment Status, Age, Sex, Race, and Hispanic Origin: October 1996 — Continued

(Numbers in thousands. Civilian noninstitutional population.)

Selected characteristics, age, sex, race, and Hispanic origin	Total population			Employed						Not employed		In college and taking vocational courses
	Total	Vocational courses		Total		Full time		Part time		Total	Vocational courses	
		Number	Percent	Total	Vocational courses	Total	Vocational courses	Total	Vocational courses			
High school graduate only	840	52	6.2	452	20	357	8	95	12	389	32	14
College, less than a bachelor's degree ..	642	18	2.7	319	6	190	—	128	6	323	11	15
College, bachelor's degree or more	91	2	2.6	69	—	66	—	3	—	22	2	2
HISPANIC ORIGIN [1]												
Male												
15 years old and over	9 958	174	1.8	7 289	137	6 773	121	516	17	2 668	37	40
15 to 19 years old	1 271	13	1.0	417	6	205	3	212	3	853	7	—
20 to 24 years old	1 310	41	3.1	1 032	32	915	29	117	3	277	9	17
25 to 34 years old	2 686	30	1.1	2 386	28	2 329	17	57	11	299	2	11
35 to 44 years old	2 159	62	2.9	1 920	54	1 874	54	45	—	239	8	10
45 to 64 years old	1 880	29	1.5	1 424	18	1 359	18	64	—	456	10	2
65 years old and over	653			110	—	90	—	20	—	543	—	—
Educational attainment:												
Not a high school graduate	4 708	38	0.8	2 956	28	2 739	28	217	—	1 752	10	—
High school graduate only	2 650	52	2.0	2 160	38	2 057	34	103	3	490	14	11
College, less than a bachelor's degree	1 722	59	3.4	1 423	47	1 252	33	171	13	299	12	25
College, bachelor's degree or more	878	25	2.9	750	25	725	25	25	—	128	—	4
Metropolitan status:												
Metropolitan	9 055	166	1.8	6 633	129	6 175	115	458	14	2 421	37	34
Central city	4 833	65	1.3	3 358	55	3 112	44	246	11	1 476	9	25
Outside central city	4 222	101	2.4	3 276	74	3 064	71	212	2	946	27	10
Nonmetropolitan	903	8	0.9	656	8	598	5	58	3	247	—	5
Region:												
Northeast	1 528	18	1.2	989	13	933	10	55	3	540	5	—
Midwest	769	12	1.6	596	12	548	7	48	5	172	—	7
South	3 354	39	1.2	2 515	27	2 298	24	216	3	839	12	14
West	4 307	104	2.4	3 190	85	2 993	80	197	5	1 117	19	18
15 to 24 years old												
Educational attainment:												
Not a high school graduate	1 566	14	0.9	676	10	524	10	152	—	890	4	—
High school graduate only	575	23	4.1	460	17	410	14	51	3	114	6	7
College, less than a bachelor's degree ..	382	16	4.3	278	10	158	7	120	3	104	6	10
College, bachelor's degree or more	57	—	(X)	36	—	29	—	6	—	22	—	—
Female												
15 years old and over	9 946	229	2.3	4 806	110	3 961	86	846	25	5 139	119	75
15 to 19 years old	1 207	33	2.8	293	12	139	5	153	7	914	22	30
20 to 24 years old	1 200	45	3.7	602	16	449	8	154	8	597	29	16
25 to 34 years old	2 408	67	2.8	1 415	30	1 225	26	190	4	993	37	19
35 to 44 years old	2 167	43	2.0	1 334	24	1 180	22	153	2	834	19	10
45 to 64 years old	2 032	36	1.8	1 075	28	921	25	153	3	957	8	—
65 years old and over	932	5	0.5	88	—	46	—	42	—	845	5	—
Educational attainment:												
Not a high school graduate	4 818	69	1.4	1 498	16	1 159	14	339	2	3 320	53	5
High school graduate only	2 541	65	2.6	1 450	31	1 272	26	178	5	1 091	34	24
College, less than a bachelor's degree	1 760	66	3.7	1 255	44	992	32	263	12	505	22	33
College, bachelor's degree or more	827	29	3.5	604	19	538	15	66	4	223	10	13
Metropolitan status:												
Metropolitan	9 090	221	2.4	4 393	110	3 640	85	753	25	4 697	111	72
Central city	4 919	100	2.0	2 200	51	1 831	38	369	14	2 718	49	41

See footnotes at end of table.

Table A-12.   Population 15 Years Old and Over Enrolled in Vocational Courses, by Employment Status, Age, Sex, Race, and Hispanic Origin: October 1996 — Continued

(Numbers in thousands. Civilian noninstitutional population.)

Selected characteristics, age, sex, race, and Hispanic origin	Total population			Employed						Not employed		In college and taking vocational courses
	Total	Vocational courses		Total		Full time		Part time		Total	Vocational courses	
		Number	Percent	Total	Vocational courses	Total	Vocational courses	Total	Vocational courses			
Outside central city	4 171	121	2.9	2 192	58	1 809	47	384	11	1 979	63	31
Nonmetropolitan	856	8	0.9	414	1	321	1	93	—	442	7	3
Region:												
Northeast	1 698	41	2.4	728	15	596	13	132	2	970	26	15
Midwest	672	18	2.7	330	7	285	4	45	3	342	11	13
South	3 430	74	2.2	1 714	35	1 454	25	260	11	1 717	39	20
West	4 145	96	2.3	2 035	53	1 626	44	408	8	2 110	43	28
15 to 24 years old												
Educational attainment:												
Not a high school graduate	1 369	24	1.8	297	5	167	2	130	2	1 072	19	5
High school graduate only	564	32	5.6	287	10	242	6	45	3	277	22	22
College, less than a bachelor's degree ..	424	22	5.2	272	13	146	4	126	9	152	9	20
College, bachelor's degree or more	49	—	(X)	39	—	34	—	6	—	10	—	—

Source: October 1996 Current Population Survey, Education and Social Stratification Branch, U.S. Bureau of the Census

1. May be of any race.

— Represents zero or rounds to zero.

Table A-13. Level of Enrollment of the Population 15 Years Old and Over, by Type of School, Attendance Status, Age, Sex, Marital Status, Race and Hispanic Origin: October 1996

(Numbers in thousands. Civilian noninstitutional population.)

Age, sex, marital status, race, and Hispanic origin	Enrolled in college												Not enrolled in school		
	Total	Full time	Undergraduate students						Graduate students		Enrolled in high school or below	Total	High school graduate	Not high school graduate
			Total	Full time	Two year college		Four year college		Total	Full time				
					Total	Full time	Total	Full time						
ALL RACES															
All Marital Statuses															
Both sexes, 15 years and over	15 226	9 839	12 305	8 534	4 174	2 209	8 130	6 325	2 922	1 305	12 421	177 461	144 450	33 010
15 to 17 years old	237	193	233	189	91	61	142	127	4	4	10 720	660	97	563
18 and 19 years old	3 309	2 956	3 293	2 943	1 132	934	2 161	2 008	17	14	1 229	2 837	1 897	940
20 and 21 years old	2 907	2 502	2 856	2 460	669	457	2 187	2 003	52	42	110	3 783	2 883	901
22 to 24 years old	2 551	1 936	2 017	1 516	515	271	1 502	1 244	534	420	54	7 890	6 584	1 306
25 to 34 years old	3 443	1 561	2 226	990	922	315	1 304	675	1 217	570	108	36 542	31 770	4 772
35 years old and over	2 778	691	1 680	437	845	171	835	266	1 098	254	201	125 749	101 220	24 529
Male, 15 years and over	6 820	4 681	5 533	4 031	1 752	974	3 781	3 058	1 288	650	6 540	85 169	69 591	15 578
15 to 17 years old	97	86	95	84	33	23	61	61	3	3	5 573	315	48	267
18 and 19 years old	1 489	1 341	1 482	1 334	526	427	956	907	7	7	769	1 453	965	488
20 and 21 years old	1 379	1 184	1 359	1 169	295	203	1 064	966	20	15	56	1 832	1 374	458
22 to 24 years old	1 319	1 058	1 080	857	238	137	842	719	239	201	16	3 971	3 289	682
25 to 34 years old	1 523	722	907	407	367	118	541	289	616	314	39	18 105	15 626	2 479
35 years old and over	1 013	291	610	180	293	65	318	115	403	110	85	59 494	48 290	11 205
Female, 15 years and over	8 406	5 157	6 772	4 502	2 423	1 235	4 349	3 267	1 634	655	5 881	92 291	74 859	17 432
15 to 17 years old	140	106	138	105	57	38	81	66	2	2	5 146	345	50	296
18 and 19 years old	1 821	1 616	1 811	1 609	606	507	1 205	1 101	10	7	460	1 384	932	452
20 and 21 years old	1 528	1 317	1 497	1 291	374	253	1 122	1 037	31	27	53	1 951	1 508	443
22 to 24 years old	1 233	878	937	659	277	134	660	525	295	219	38	3 919	3 295	624
25 to 34 years old	1 920	839	1 319	583	556	197	763	386	601	256	69	18 437	16 144	2 293
35 years old and over	1 765	400	1 070	257	553	105	517	151	695	144	116	66 255	52 930	13 325
Married, Spouse Present															
Both sexes, 15 years and over	3 670	1 232	2 320	844	1 040	262	1 280	581	1 350	389	240	108 084	91 076	17 008
15 to 17 years old	2	2	1	—	1	—	—	—	2	2	30	53	6	47
18 and 19 years old	43	25	43	25	20	8	22	17	—	—	22	267	171	96
20 and 21 years old	130	87	130	87	47	16	83	72	—	—	10	744	530	215
22 to 24 years old	304	202	246	166	71	29	175	137	58	36	12	2 473	2 004	469
25 to 34 years old	1 438	535	888	335	380	114	508	221	550	200	46	20 752	18 185	2 567
35 years old and over	1 753	381	1 013	230	522	95	492	134	740	151	121	83 795	70 181	13 614
Male, 15 years and over	1 562	543	942	329	391	82	551	247	620	214	103	55 107	45 911	9 196
15 to 17 years old	1	—	1	—	1	—	—	—	—	—	8	—	—	—
18 and 19 years old	9	3	9	3	8	2	1	1	—	—	8	71	48	23
20 and 21 years old	37	28	37	28	9	1	28	27	—	—	—	218	153	64
22 to 24 years old	150	103	122	77	36	9	86	68	29	25	6	1 021	797	224
25 to 34 years old	621	231	357	122	142	31	215	91	264	109	14	9 645	8 359	1 286
35 years old and over	743	179	417	99	196	39	221	60	327	80	67	44 152	36 553	7 598
Female, 15 years and over	2 108	689	1 378	515	649	181	729	334	730	175	137	52 977	45 165	7 812
15 to 17 years old	2	2	—	—	—	—	—	—	2	2	21	53	6	47
18 and 19 years old	34	22	34	22	12	5	21	16	—	—	15	196	123	73
20 and 21 years old	93	60	93	60	38	15	55	45	—	—	10	527	377	150
22 to 24 years old	154	100	124	89	35	20	89	69	30	11	6	1 452	1 207	245
25 to 34 years old	817	304	531	214	238	84	294	130	286	91	32	11 106	9 825	1 281
35 years old and over	1 009	202	596	131	326	57	271	74	413	72	54	39 643	33 627	6 016

See footnotes at end of table.

Table A-13. Level of Enrollment of the Population 15 Years Old and Over, by Type of School, Attendance Status, Age, Sex, Marital Status, Race and Hispanic Origin: October 1996 — Continued

(Numbers in thousands. Civilian noninstitutional population.)

Age, sex, marital status, race, and Hispanic origin	Enrolled in college										Enrolled in high school or below	Not enrolled in school		
	Total	Full time	Undergraduate students						Graduate students			Total	High school graduate	Not high school graduate
			Total	Full time	Two year college		Four year college		Total	Full time				
					Total	Full time	Total	Full time						
Never Married														
Both sexes, 15 years and over	10 300	8 103	9 029	7 311	2 636	1 800	6 393	5 512	1 271	791	12 025	32 639	26 390	6 249
15 to 17 years old	230	188	227	186	85	58	142	127	3	3	10 610	587	89	498
18 and 19 years old	3 256	2 920	3 239	2 906	1 102	917	2 137	1 989	17	14	1 206	2 530	1 708	823
20 and 21 years old	2 729	2 374	2 680	2 334	601	423	2 079	1 911	50	40	100	2 909	2 261	648
22 to 24 years old	2 163	1 684	1 698	1 310	404	230	1 294	1 079	465	374	39	4 931	4 235	697
25 to 34 years old	1 589	829	994	505	366	148	628	357	595	324	45	11 530	10 023	1 507
35 years old and over	334	107	192	70	78	22	114	48	142	37	25	10 150	8 074	2 076
Male, 15 years and over	4 949	3 997	4 349	3 600	1 224	852	3 125	2 747	599	397	6 387	18 087	14 538	3 549
15 to 17 years old	96	86	94	84	33	23	61	61	3	3	5 524	308	47	261
18 and 19 years old	1 476	1 334	1 469	1 327	517	423	953	904	7	7	761	1 378	917	461
20 and 21 years old	1 330	1 145	1 310	1 130	279	195	1 031	935	20	15	56	1 578	1 192	386
22 to 24 years old	1 145	942	938	769	187	124	751	646	207	173	10	2 793	2 381	412
25 to 34 years old	772	430	455	246	177	77	278	169	317	184	24	6 760	5 842	918
35 years old and over	129	59	84	43	32	11	52	32	45	16	10	5 269	4 158	1 111
Female, 15 years and over	5 351	4 106	4 679	3 711	1 412	947	3 267	2 764	672	395	5 638	14 552	11 852	2 700
15 to 17 years old	133	102	133	102	52	36	81	66	—	—	5 086	279	42	237
18 and 19 years old	1 780	1 587	1 770	1 579	586	494	1 184	1 085	10	7	445	1 152	790	362
20 and 21 years old	1 399	1 229	1 370	1 204	322	228	1 048	976	29	25	43	1 331	1 069	262
22 to 24 years old	1 018	741	760	540	216	107	543	433	259	201	29	2 138	1 853	285
25 to 34 years old	817	400	539	259	189	71	349	188	278	140	21	4 770	4 181	589
35 years old and over	204	47	108	27	46	11	62	15	96	21	14	4 881	3 916	965
Other Marital Status														
Both sexes, 15 years and over	1 257	503	956	379	498	147	458	232	301	125	156	36 738	26 984	9 754
15 to 17 years old	5	3	5	3	5	3	—	—	—	—	81	20	2	17
18 and 19 years old	11	11	11	11	9	9	2	2	—	—	—	39	18	21
20 and 21 years old	48	40	46	38	21	18	25	20	2	2	—	129	92	38
22 to 24 years old	84	50	74	39	40	12	33	28	10	10	3	486	345	141
25 to 34 years old	416	197	345	150	177	53	168	97	72	47	16	4 259	3 562	698
35 years old and over	692	203	475	137	246	53	230	84	217	66	55	31 804	22 965	8 839
Male, 15 years and over	310	142	242	103	137	40	105	63	69	39	49	11 976	9 142	2 833
15 to 17 years old	—	—	—	—	—	—	—	—	—	—	41	7	1	6
18 and 19 years old	4	4	4	4	2	2	2	2	—	—	—	3	—	3
20 and 21 years old	12	11	12	11	7	7	5	4	—	—	—	36	29	7
22 to 24 years old	24	13	20	10	15	4	5	5	4	4	—	157	111	47
25 to 34 years old	130	61	96	40	48	11	48	29	34	21	—	1 699	1 424	275
35 years old and over	141	52	110	38	65	16	45	22	31	14	8	10 073	7 578	2 495
Female, 15 years and over	946	362	714	276	361	108	353	169	232	86	106	24 762	17 842	6 920
15 to 17 years old	5	3	5	3	5	3	—	—	—	—	40	13	2	11
18 and 19 years old	8	8	8	8	8	8	—	—	—	—	—	36	18	18
20 and 21 years old	36	29	34	27	14	11	20	16	2	2	—	94	63	31
22 to 24 years old	61	37	54	30	26	8	28	22	7	7	3	329	235	94
25 to 34 years old	286	135	249	110	129	42	120	68	38	25	16	2 560	2 138	422
35 years old and over	551	151	365	99	181	37	185	62	186	51	47	21 731	15 387	6 344

See footnotes at end of table.

Table A-13. Level of Enrollment of the Population 15 Years Old and Over, by Type of School, Attendance Status, Age, Sex, Marital Status, Race and Hispanic Origin: October 1996 — Continued

(Numbers in thousands. Civilian noninstitutional population.)

Age, sex, marital status, race, and Hispanic origin	Enrolled in college										Enrolled in high school or below	Not enrolled in school		
	Total	Full time	Undergraduate students						Graduate students			Total	High school graduate	Not high school graduate
			Total	Full time	Two year college		Four year college		Total	Full time				
					Total	Full time	Total	Full time						
WHITE														
All Marital Statuses														
Both sexes, 15 years and over	12 189	7 849	9 861	6 885	3 295	1 743	6 565	5 142	2 328	964	9 689	149 926	123 402	26 524
15 to 17 years old	167	132	163	128	66	44	97	84	4	4	8 451	516	70	447
18 and 19 years old	2 731	2 449	2 719	2 440	945	770	1 774	1 669	12	9	914	2 187	1 453	735
20 and 21 years old	2 362	2 039	2 333	2 016	515	347	1 819	1 670	29	22	66	2 982	2 307	676
22 to 24 years old	2 030	1 532	1 607	1 199	396	190	1 211	1 009	423	334	40	6 363	5 316	1 047
25 to 34 years old	2 644	1 166	1 699	758	695	262	1 004	496	945	408	81	29 961	25 999	3 962
35 years old and over	2 254	530	1 339	344	678	131	661	214	915	186	138	107 917	88 258	19 658
Male, 15 years and over	5 453	3 719	4 459	3 266	1 373	767	3 086	2 500	995	453	5 094	72 741	60 053	12 688
15 to 17 years old	69	59	67	56	30	19	37	37	3	3	4 377	247	34	213
18 and 19 years old	1 223	1 099	1 216	1 092	429	340	787	752	7	7	576	1 155	773	382
20 and 21 years old	1 117	960	1 108	954	230	159	877	794	9	7	33	1 489	1 139	350
22 to 24 years old	1 079	861	889	701	195	105	693	596	191	160	16	3 211	2 669	543
25 to 34 years old	1 154	515	697	305	265	90	431	214	458	210	32	15 124	13 008	2 117
35 years old and over	811	225	483	159	223	52	260	106	328	67	61	51 515	42 431	9 084
Female, 15 years and over	6 735	4 129	5 402	3 619	1 922	977	3 480	2 642	1 333	511	4 595	77 185	63 349	13 836
15 to 17 years old	98	74	96	72	36	25	60	47	2	2	4 074	269	36	234
18 and 19 years old	1 508	1 350	1 503	1 347	516	430	987	917	5	3	338	1 033	680	353
20 and 21 years old	1 246	1 078	1 226	1 063	284	187	941	875	20	16	33	I 494	1 168	325
22 to 24 years old	951	671	719	498	201	85	518	413	232	174	24	3 151	2 647	504
25 to 34 years old	1 490	651	1 002	453	430	171	572	282	487	198	49	14 836	12 991	1 845
35 years old and over	1 443	305	857	186	456	79	401	107	586	119	77	56 402	45 827	10 575
Married, Spouse Present														
Both sexes, 15 years and over	3 089	998	1 981	729	884	222	1 097	507	1 108	270	204	95 848	81 099	14 749
15 to 17 years old	2	2	1	—	1	—	—	—	2	2	26	50	6	45
18 and 19 years old	41	24	41	24	20	8	21	16	—	—	19	237	141	96
20 and 21 years old	105	76	105	76	31	9	75	66	—	—	9	691	483	208
22 to 24 years old	277	184	221	148	62	23	159	125	56	35	11	2 250	1 806	444
25 to 34 years old	1 189	425	754	292	324	106	429	186	436	133	40	18 128	15 798	2 330
35 years old and over	1 474	289	859	189	446	76	413	114	615	100	100	74 492	62 865	11 627
Male, 15 years and over	1 272	411	787	280	320	69	467	210	485	131	82	48 803	40 863	7 940
15 to 17 years old	1	—	1	—	1	—	—	—	—	—	6			
18 and 19 years old	9	3	9	3	8	2	1	1	—	—	8	60	37	23
20 and 21 years old	32	28	32	28	4	1	28	27	—	—	—	208	147	61
22 to 24 years old	137	92	109	68	36	9	73	58	28	24	6	927	718	209
25 to 34 years old	478	163	283	96	107	26	176	70	195	68	11	8 466	7 297	1 169
35 years old and over	615	124	354	85	165	31	189	54	261	39	51	39 142	32 665	6 477
Female, 15 years and over	1 817	587	1 194	449	564	152	630	297	623	138	122	47 046	40 237	6 809
15 to 17 years old	2	2	—	—	—	—	—	—	2	2	20	50	6	45
18 and 19 years old	33	20	33	20	12	5	20	15	—	—	11	176	104	72
20 and 21 years old	74	48	74	48	27	9	46	39	—	—	9	483	336	147
22 to 24 years old	140	91	112	80	26	13	86	67	27	11	5	1 323	1 089	234
25 to 34 years old	711	261	471	196	217	80	253	116	240	65	28	9 662	8 502	1 161
35 years old and over	859	165	505	104	281	45	224	60	354	61	49	35 351	30 201	5 150

See footnotes at end of table.

Table A-13. Level of Enrollment of the Population 15 Years Old and Over, by Type of School, Attendance Status, Age, Sex, Marital Status, Race and Hispanic Origin: October 1996 — Continued

(Numbers in thousands. Civilian noninstitutional population.)

Age, sex, marital status, race, and Hispanic origin	Enrolled in college										Enrolled in high school or below	Not enrolled in school		
	Total	Full time	Undergraduate students						Graduate students			Total	High school graduate	Not high school graduate
			Total	Full time	Two year college		Four year college		Total	Full time				
					Total	Full time	Total	Full time						
Never Married														
Both sexes, 15 years and over	8 129	6 444	7 156	5 852	2 036	1 398	5 120	4 454	973	592	9 377	24 274	19 971	4 303
15 to 17 years old	160	128	157	125	60	41	97	84	3	3	8 360	448	62	386
18 and 19 years old	47	40	45	38	20	18	25	20	2	2	—	119	85	33
20 and 21 years old	2 210	1 923	2 183	1 903	464	319	1 719	1 583	27	20	57	2 173	1 738	434
22 to 24 years old	1 678	1 302	1 320	1 012	296	155	1 024	857	359	290	25	3 689	3 211	477
25 to 34 years old	1 152	595	699	357	254	115	445	241	453	239	29	8 417	7 378	1 039
35 years old and over	251	82	131	50	47	14	84	37	120	32	10	7 636	6 287	1 349
Male, 15 years and over	3 955	3 191	3 497	2 899	962	666	2 535	2 233	458	292	4 977	14 106	11 526	2 581
15 to 17 years old	69	59	66	56	29	19	37	37	3	3	4 341	241	34	207
18 and 19 years old	1 210	1 092	1 204	1 085	420	336	784	749	7	7	568	1 091	736	355
20 and 21 years old	1 073	921	1 064	915	220	151	844	764	9	7	33	1 245	962	283
22 to 24 years old	921	756	762	623	147	92	615	532	159	132	10	2 142	1 853	289
25 to 34 years old	581	308	341	180	128	61	213	119	240	128	21	5 243	4 546	697
35 years old and over	102	56	61	40	18	7	43	32	41	16	5	4 145	3 395	750
Female, 15 years and over	4 174	3 253	3 659	2 953	1 074	732	2 585	2 222	515	300	4 400	10 168	8 445	1 723
15 to 17 years old	91	69	91	69	31	22	60	47	—	—	4 019	207	28	179
18 and 19 years old	1 468	1 322	1 463	1 319	496	417	967	902	5	3	327	820	558	263
20 and 21 years old	1 138	1 002	1 120	988	245	168	875	820	18	14	24	928	776	152
22 to 24 years old	758	547	558	389	149	64	409	325	200	158	16	1 547	1 358	189
25 to 34 years old	570	287	358	177	125	54	232	123	212	111	8	3 174	2 833	342
35 years old and over	149	26	70	11	29	6	41	5	79	15	5	3 491	2 892	599
Other Marital Status														
Both sexes, 15 years and over	970	406	723	304	375	124	348	181	247	102	109	29 804	22 332	7 472
15 to 17 years old	5	3	5	3	5	3	—	—	—	—	66	18	2	16
18 and 19 years old	11	11	11	11	9	9	2	2	—	—	—	39	18	21
20 and 21 years old	47	40	45	38	20	18	25	20	2	2	—	119	85	33
22 to 24 years old	75	47	67	38	38	12	28	26	8	8	3	424	298	126
25 to 34 years old	303	146	246	110	117	40	129	69	57	36	12	3 415	2 822	593
35 years old and over	529	159	350	104	186	41	164	63	180	55	27	25 789	19 106	6 683
Male, 15 years and over	226	117	174	88	91	31	84	57	52	29	35	9 832	7 665	2 168
15 to 17 years old	—	—	—	—	—	—	—	—	—	—	30	7	1	6
18 and 19 years old	4	4	4	4	2	2	2	2	—	—	—	3	—	3
20 and 21 years old	12	11	12	11	7	7	5	4	—	—	—	36	29	7
22 to 24 years old	22	13	18	10	13	4	5	5	4	4	—	143	98	45
25 to 34 years old	95	44	72	30	29	4	43	26	22	14	—	1 416	1 165	250
35 years old and over	94	45	68	34	39	14	28	20	26	12	5	8 229	6 372	1 857
Female, 15 years and over	744	289	549	216	284	93	265	124	195	72	74	19 971	14 667	5 304
15 to 17 years old	5	3	5	3	5	3	—	—	—	—	36	12	2	10
18 and 19 years old	8	8	8	8	8	8	—	—	—	—	—	36	18	18
20 and 21 years old	35	29	33	27	13	11	20	16	2	2	—	83	56	27
22 to 24 years old	54	33	49	28	26	8	23	21	5	5	3	281	200	81
25 to 34 years old	208	102	174	80	87	36	86	44	35	22	12	1 999	1 657	343
35 years old and over	435	114	282	71	146	28	136	43	153	43	22	17 560	12 734	4 826

See footnotes at end of table.

Table A-13. Level of Enrollment of the Population 15 Years Old and Over, by Type of School, Attendance Status, Age, Sex, Marital Status, Race and Hispanic Origin: October 1996 — Continued

(Numbers in thousands. Civilian noninstitutional population.)

Age, sex, marital status, race, and Hispanic origin	Enrolled in college										Enrolled in high school or below	Not enrolled in school		
	Total	Full time	Undergraduate students						Graduate students			Total	High school graduate	Not high school graduate
			Total	Full time	Two year college		Four year college		Total	Full time				
					Total	Full time	Total	Full time						
BLACK														
All Marital Statuses														
Both sexes, 15 years and over	1 901	1 179	1 593	1 020	580	289	1 013	731	308	159	2 102	20 333	15 179	5 153
15 to 17 years old	45	36	45	36	21	14	24	22	—	—	1 702	110	22	88
18 and 19 years old	345	299	340	295	98	82	242	213	5	5	268	548	373	175
20 and 21 years old	346	290	334	280	106	74	228	206	13	10	42	662	469	193
22 to 24 years old	292	230	245	193	59	47	186	146	47	36	8	1 126	913	213
25 to 34 years old	520	225	377	144	186	39	191	105	142	81	26	4 770	4 143	627
35 years old and over	354	99	252	71	111	32	141	39	101	28	55	13 117	9 259	3 858
Male, 15 years and over	764	524	625	431	229	119	396	311	140	94	1 093	9 083	6 749	2 334
15 to 17 years old	17	17	17	17	4	4	13	13	—	—	873	52	9	43
18 and 19 years old	145	129	145	129	43	36	103	93	—	—	166	253	162	90
20 and 21 years old	155	130	149	128	50	33	100	94	5	2	24	279	187	92
22 to 24 years old	122	104	103	85	16	16	87	69	19	19	1	538	428	110
25 to 34 years old	206	110	132	58	78	21	54	38	74	52	6	2 168	1 898	270
35 years old and over	120	34	78	13	38	9	40	4	42	21	23	5 793	4 065	1 728
Female, 15 years and over	1 136	654	968	589	351	169	617	420	168	65	1 009	11 250	8 430	2 820
15 to 17 years old	28	19	28	19	17	11	10	9	—	—	829	59	13	45
18 and 19 years old	199	170	195	165	55	45	139	120	5	5	103	296	211	85
20 and 21 years old	192	160	184	153	56	41	128	112	7	7	19	382	282	100
22 to 24 years old	170	126	142	108	42	31	99	77	28	18	8	588	485	103
25 to 34 years old	314	114	245	86	107	19	138	67	69	29	20	2 601	2 245	356
35 years old and over	234	65	174	58	73	23	102	35	59	7	31	7 323	5 194	2 129
Married, Spouse Present														
Both sexes, 15 years and over	341	117	216	64	88	22	128	42	125	53	28	7 660	6 174	1 486
15 to 17 years old	—	—	—	—	—	—	—	—	—	—	—	2	—	2
18 and 19 years old	—	—	—	—	—	—	—	—	—	—	4	23	23	—
20 and 21 years old	17	5	17	5	10	2	6	3	—	—	—	30	26	4
22 to 24 years old	14	10	13	10	3	3	10	6	1	1	—	142	127	15
25 to 34 years old	145	55	92	26	37	6	56	21	53	29	6	1 583	1 453	130
35 years old and over	166	46	94	23	38	12	56	12	72	23	18	5 879	4 545	1 334
Male, 15 years and over	158	69	91	30	40	8	52	21	67	39	18	4 143	3 243	900
15 to 17 years old	—	—	—	—	—	—	—	—	—	—	—	—	—	—
18 and 19 years old	—	—	—	—	—	—	—	—	—	—	—	11	11	—
20 and 21 years old	5	—	5	—	5	—	—	—	—	—	—	6	3	4
22 to 24 years old	10	7	9	6	—	—	9	6	1	1	—	65	54	12
25 to 34 years old	78	36	49	18	26	5	23	13	29	18	3	776	710	66
35 years old and over	66	26	28	5	9	3	19	2	38	21	15	3 285	2 466	819
Female, 15 years and over	183	48	125	34	48	14	77	20	58	14	11	3 516	2 931	585
15 to 17 years old	—	—	—	—	—	—	—	—	—	—	—	2	—	2
18 and 19 years old	—	—	—	—	—	—	—	—	—	—	4	12	12	—
20 and 21 years old	11	5	11	5	5	2	6	3	—	—	—	24	24	—
22 to 24 years old	4	3	4	3	3	3	1	—	—	—	—	77	73	4
25 to 34 years old	68	19	44	8	11	—	32	7	24	12	3	807	743	64
35 years old and over	100	21	66	18	29	8	37	10	34	2	3	2 594	2 079	515

See footnotes at end of table.

Table A-13. Level of Enrollment of the Population 15 Years Old and Over, by Type of School, Attendance Status, Age, Sex, Marital Status, Race and Hispanic Origin: October 1996 — Continued

(Numbers in thousands. Civilian noninstitutional population.)

Age, sex, marital status, race, and Hispanic origin	Enrolled in college										Enrolled in high school or below	Not enrolled in school		
	Total	Full time	Undergraduate students						Graduate students			Total	High school graduate	Not high school graduate
			Total	Full time	Two year college		Four year college		Total	Full time				
					Total	Full time	Total	Full time						
Never Married														
Both sexes, 15 years and over	1 341	997	1 184	903	391	251	793	652	157	94	2 033	6 870	5 160	1 710
15 to 17 years old	45	36	45	36	21	14	24	22	—	—	1 688	106	22	84
18 and 19 years old	345	299	340	295	98	82	242	213	5	5	264	526	350	175
20 and 21 years old	330	285	317	275	95	72	222	203	13	10	42	621	437	185
22 to 24 years old	274	219	228	183	56	44	172	139	46	36	8	940	753	188
25 to 34 years old	284	137	207	96	99	30	108	66	77	41	16	2 464	2 063	401
35 years old and over	65	21	48	18	22	9	25	9	17	3	14	2 212	1 535	677
Male, 15 years and over	548	444	485	396	156	109	330	287	63	48	1 061	3 147	2 311	836
15 to 17 years old	17	17	17	17	4	4	13	13	—	—	862	52	9	43
18 and 19 years old	145	129	145	129	43	36	103	93	—	—	166	241	151	90
20 and 21 years old	149	130	144	128	44	33	100	94	5	2	24	273	184	89
22 to 24 years old	112	97	94	79	16	16	77	63	18	18	1	466	367	98
25 to 34 years old	106	67	71	40	41	16	30	24	35	27	4	1 151	966	185
35 years old and over	19	4	14	4	8	4	6	—	5	—	5	965	633	331
Female, 15 years and over	793	553	699	507	236	142	463	365	94	46	972	3 722	2 849	874
15 to 17 years old	28	19	28	19	17	11	10	9	—	—	825	55	13	41
18 and 19 years old	199	170	195	165	55	45	139	120	5	5	99	284	199	85
20 and 21 years old	180	155	173	148	51	39	122	109	7	7	19	349	253	96
22 to 24 years old	162	122	134	105	39	28	95	77	28	18	7	475	385	89
25 to 34 years old	178	70	136	56	59	14	78	42	41	14	13	1 313	1 096	217
35 years old and over	46	17	33	14	14	5	19	9	12	3	9	1 248	902	346
Other Marital Status														
Both sexes, 15 years and over	218	65	192	53	101	15	91	37	25	12	41	5 803	3 846	1 958
15 to 17 years old	—	—	—	—	—	—	—	—	—	—	15	2	—	2
18 and 19 years old	—	—	—	—	—	—	—	—	—	—	—	—	—	—
20 and 21 years old	—	—	—	—	—	—	—	—	—	—	—	10	6	4
22 to 24 years old	4	—	4	—	—	—	4	—	—	—	—	44	33	10
25 to 34 years old	90	32	78	22	50	4	28	18	13	10	4	723	628	96
35 years old and over	123	32	110	30	51	12	59	18	13	2	22	5 025	3 179	1 846
Male, 15 years and over	58	12	48	5	34	2	15	3	10	7	14	1 792	1 195	597
15 to 17 years old	—	—	—	—	—	—	—	—	—	—	11	—	—	—
18 and 19 years old	—	—	—	—	—	—	—	—	—	—	—	—	—	—
20 and 21 years old	—	—	—	—	—	—	—	—	—	—	—	—	—	—
22 to 24 years old	—	—	—	—	—	—	—	—	—	—	—	7	7	—
25 to 34 years old	22	7	13	—	12	—	—	—	10	7	—	242	222	20
35 years old and over	36	4	36	4	22	2	14	2	—	—	3	1 544	966	577
Female, 15 years and over	160	53	144	48	67	13	77	34	16	5	27	4 011	2 651	1 361
15 to 17 years old	—	—	—	—	—	—	—	—	—	—	4	2	—	2
18 and 19 years old	—	—	—	—	—	—	—	—	—	—	—	—	—	—
20 and 21 years old	—	—	—	—	—	—	—	—	—	—	—	10	6	4
22 to 24 years old	4	—	4	—	—	—	4	—	—	—	—	37	27	10
25 to 34 years old	68	25	65	22	38	4	27	18	3	3	4	481	405	76
35 years old and over	88	27	75	25	30	10	45	16	13	2	19	3 482	2 213	1 269

See footnotes at end of table.

Table A-13. Level of Enrollment of the Population 15 Years Old and Over, by Type of School, Attendance Status, Age, Sex, Marital Status, Race and Hispanic Origin: October 1996 — Continued

(Numbers in thousands. Civilian noninstitutional population.)

Age, sex, marital status, race, and Hispanic origin	Enrolled in college										Enrolled in high school or below	Not enrolled in school		
	Total	Full time	Undergraduate students						Graduate students			Total	High school graduate	Not high school graduate
			Total	Full time	Two year college		Four year college		Total	Full time				
					Total	Full time	Total	Full time						
HISPANIC ORIGIN [1]														
All Marital Statuses														
Both sexes, 15 years and over	1 223	708	1 049	637	444	224	605	413	174	71	1 702	16 979	9 146	7 833
15 to 17 years old	23	18	23	18	10	10	12	8	—	—	1 324	131	5	126
18 and 19 years old	240	183	240	183	111	76	129	107	—	—	230	530	236	295
20 and 21 years old	213	158	213	158	102	69	111	88	—	—	31	721	350	370
22 to 24 years old	253	172	211	137	75	22	136	114	41	36	19	1 273	727	545
25 to 34 years old	310	129	236	107	72	25	164	81	74	23	34	4 750	2 855	1 895
35 years old and over	184	47	125	34	73	21	52	14	59	13	64	9 574	4 972	4 602
Male, 15 years and over	529	303	458	257	195	82	263	176	72	46	915	8 513	4 707	3 806
15 to 17 years old	8	8	8	8	6	6	2	2	—	—	703	54	3	51
18 and 19 years old	98	67	98	67	38	21	60	46	—	—	139	269	115	154
20 and 21 years old	78	57	78	57	37	26	41	31	—	—	17	391	186	206
22 to 24 years old	124	86	97	59	39	8	58	51	28	28	9	690	393	297
25 to 34 years old	132	57	107	47	39	11	69	36	25	10	16	2 538	1 525	1 012
35 years old and over	90	28	70	19	37	10	33	9	19	9	31	4 571	2 485	2 086
Female, 15 years and over	693	405	591	380	249	142	343	238	102	25	787	8 465	4 438	4 027
15 to 17 years old	15	10	15	10	5	5	10	6	—	—	621	76	2	74
18 and 19 years old	142	116	142	116	73	54	69	61	—	—	91	261	121	140
20 and 21 years old	136	101	136	101	65	43	71	58	—	—	13	330	165	165
22 to 24 years old	128	86	115	78	36	14	79	63	14	8	10	582	334	249
25 to 34 years old	178	72	129	59	34	14	95	45	49	13	18	2 212	1 330	882
35 years old and over	95	20	55	15	36	11	19	5	39	4	33	5 004	2 487	2 517
Married, Spouse Present														
Both sexes, 15 years and over	292	96	207	78	86	24	120	53	85	18	97	9 897	5 478	4 418
15 to 17 years old	—	—	—	—	—	—	—	—	—	—	13	23	—	23
18 and 19 years old	8	5	8	5	—	—	8	5	—	—	10	68	28	39
20 and 21 years old	9	—	9	—	6	—	3	—	—	—	5	215	91	124
22 to 24 years old	33	22	26	18	7	3	18	15	8	5	8	526	290	236
25 to 34 years old	128	43	96	38	33	13	63	26	32	5	10	2 883	1 702	1 181
35 years old and over	113	25	68	17	39	9	28	9	45	8	50	6 183	3 367	2 816
Male, 15 years and over	139	47	109	36	45	10	64	26	30	12	40	5 138	2 872	2 266
15 to 17 years old	—	—	—	—	—	—	—	—	—	—	2	—	—	—
18 and 19 years old	—	—	—	—	—	—	—	—	—	—	2	17	8	10
20 and 21 years old	—	—	—	—	—	—	—	—	—	—	—	69	32	37
22 to 24 years old	17	10	12	6	4	—	8	6	5	5	3	267	160	108
25 to 34 years old	64	23	53	21	20	7	33	14	11	3	4	1 436	857	579
35 years old and over	58	13	43	9	20	3	23	6	15	4	29	3 348	1 816	1 533
Female, 15 years and over	153	48	98	42	41	15	56	28	55	6	57	4 759	2 606	2 153
15 to 17 years old	—	—	—	—	—	—	—	—	—	—	11	23	—	23
18 and 19 years old	8	5	8	5	—	—	8	5	—	—	8	50	21	29
20 and 21 years old	9	—	9	—	6	—	3	—	—	—	5	146	59	87
22 to 24 years old	16	12	13	12	3	3	10	9	3	—	5	258	130	128
25 to 34 years old	64	19	43	18	13	6	30	12	22	2	6	1 447	845	603
35 years old and over	55	12	25	8	19	5	6	2	30	4	22	2 835	1 552	1 283

See footnotes at end of table.

Table A-13. Level of Enrollment of the Population 15 Years Old and Over, by Type of School, Attendance Status, Age, Sex, Marital Status, Race and Hispanic Origin: October 1996 — Continued

(Numbers in thousands. Civilian noninstitutional population.)

Age, sex, marital status, race, and Hispanic origin	Enrolled in college										Enrolled in high school or below	Not enrolled in school		
	Total	Full time	Undergraduate students						Graduate students			Total	High school graduate	Not high school graduate
			Total	Full time	Two year college		Four year college		Total	Full time				
					Total	Full time	Total	Full time						
Never Married														
Both sexes, 15 years and over	817	570	743	519	306	178	438	340	74	51	1 579	4 004	2 202	1 802
15 to 17 years old	23	18	23	18	10	10	12	8	—	—	1 306	98	5	93
18 and 19 years old	230	176	230	176	109	74	121	103	—	—	220	452	207	245
20 and 21 years old	193	149	193	149	85	60	109	88	—	—	25	488	255	233
22 to 24 years old	213	150	179	119	61	19	118	100	34	31	11	666	403	263
25 to 34 years old	136	71	98	53	28	11	71	42	38	18	14	1 373	852	520
35 years old and over	22	6	20	3	13	3	7	—	3	3	2	927	479	448
Male, 15 years and over	345	234	310	202	130	63	180	139	35	32	869	2 333	1 251	1 083
15 to 17 years old	8	8	8	8	6	6	2	2	—	—	697	51	3	48
18 and 19 years old	98	67	98	67	38	21	60	46	—	—	137	252	107	145
20 and 21 years old	75	54	75	54	35	23	41	31	—	—	17	314	150	165
22 to 24 years old	103	76	80	53	31	8	50	45	23	23	6	374	211	163
25 to 34 years old	50	26	40	19	15	4	24	15	10	7	12	880	532	348
35 years old and over	12	3	9	—	6	—	3	—	3	3	—	462	248	214
Female, 15 years and over	472	336	434	317	175	115	258	201	38	19	710	1 671	952	719
15 to 17 years old	15	10	15	10	5	5	10	6	—	—	609	47	2	45
18 and 19 years old	132	109	132	109	71	52	61	57	—	—	83	200	100	100
20 and 21 years old	118	94	118	94	50	37	68	58	—	—	8	174	105	68
22 to 24 years old	110	74	99	66	31	11	69	55	11	8	5	292	192	99
25 to 34 years old	86	44	59	33	12	7	46	27	27	11	2	493	321	172
35 years old and over	11	3	11	3	7	3	4	—	—	—	2	465	231	234
Other Marital Status														
Both sexes, 15 years and over	114	43	99	41	52	21	47	19	15	2	26	3 078	1 465	1 613
15 to 17 years old	—	—	—	—	—	—	—	—	—	—	5	10	—	10
18 and 19 years old	2	2	2	2	2	2	—	—	—	—	—	10	—	10
20 and 21 years old	11	9	11	9	11	9	—	—	—	—	—	18	4	14
22 to 24 years old	7	—	7	—	7	—	—	—	—	—	—	81	34	47
25 to 34 years old	45	16	42	16	12	2	30	14	4	—	10	494	301	193
35 years old and over	49	16	38	14	21	9	17	5	11	2	11	2 464	1 125	1 339
Male, 15 years and over	45	22	39	19	20	9	19	11	6	2	6	1 043	585	458
15 to 17 years old	—	—	—	—	—	—	—	—	—	—	3	3	—	3
18 and 19 years old	—	—	—	—	—	—	—	—	—	—	—	—	—	—
20 and 21 years old	2	2	2	2	2	2	—	—	—	—	—	—	4	4
22 to 24 years old	4	—	4	—	4	—	—	—	—	—	—	49	23	26
25 to 34 years old	18	7	14	7	3	—	12	7	4	—	—	222	136	86
35 years old and over	20	12	18	10	10	6	8	3	2	2	3	760	421	339
Female, 15 years and over	69	21	60	21	32	13	28	9	9	—	20	2 035	880	1 155
15 to 17 years old	—	—	—	—	—	—	—	—	—	—	2	7	—	7
18 and 19 years old	2	2	2	2	2	2	—	—	—	—	—	10	—	10
20 and 21 years old	8	6	8	6	8	6	—	—	—	—	—	10	—	10
22 to 24 years old	2	—	2	—	2	—	—	—	—	—	—	33	11	21
25 to 34 years old	27	8	27	8	9	2	19	7	—	—	10	272	165	107
35 years old and over	29	4	20	4	11	2	9	2	9	—	9	1 703	704	999

Source: October 1996 Current Population Survey, Education and Social Stratification Branch, U.S. Bureau of the Census

1. May be of any race.

— Represents zero or rounds to zero.

Table A-14. Enrollment and Employment Status of Recent High School Graduates, 16 to 24 Years Old, by Type of School, Year of School, Attainment Level of Persons Not Enrolled, Sex, Race and Hispanic Origin: October 1996

(Numbers in thousands. Civilian noninstitutional population.)

College characteristics, employment status, race, and Hispanic origin	Both sexes			Male			Female		
	All graduates	Graduated from high school		All graduates	Graduated from high school		All graduates	Graduated from high school	
		This year	Earlier		This year	Earlier		This year	Earlier
ALL RACES									
All Persons									
Enrolled in college									
All students	8 916	1 729	7 187	4 256	779	3 477	4 660	950	3 710
1st year	2 694	1 668	1 025	1 238	753	484	1 456	915	541
2nd year	2 446	28	2 418	1 119	11	1 107	1 327	17	1 310
3rd year or higher	3 776	32	3 743	1 900	14	1 885	1 876	18	1 858
Full time students	7 531	1 589	5 942	3 654	720	2 934	3 878	870	3 008
1st year	2 197	1 541	656	1 042	701	341	1 155	839	316
2nd year	2 016	24	1 992	928	10	918	1 089	14	1 074
3rd year or higher	3 318	24	3 294	1 684	8	1 676	1 634	16	1 618
Two year college (1st to 4th year)									
All students	2 359	615	1 744	1 073	279	794	1 286	335	950
1st year	1 149	584	565	537	270	267	612	313	299
2nd year	970	23	948	429	9	419	542	13	528
3rd and 4th year	239	8	231	108	—	108	132	8	123
Full time students	1 703	526	1 178	783	239	544	920	286	633
1st year	843	501	342	402	231	171	441	270	171
2nd year	715	19	696	325	8	317	390	11	379
3rd and 4th year	146	6	140	57	—	57	89	6	83
Four year college (1st to 4th year)									
All students	5 952	1 108	4 844	2 914	496	2 418	3 038	612	2 426
1st year	1 545	1 085	460	701	483	218	844	601	242
2nd year	1 476	6	1 470	690	2	688	786	4	782
3rd and 4th year	2 932	17	2 914	1 523	11	1 513	1 408	7	1 402
Full time students	5 349	1 061	4 289	2 645	480	2 165	2 704	580	2 124
1st year	1 355	1 040	315	640	470	170	714	570	144
2nd year	1 302	6	1 296	603	2	600	699	4	695
3rd and 4th year	2 693	15	2 678	1 402	8	1 394	1 291	7	1 284
Not enrolled in college									
Total	11 528	931	10 530	5 705	518	5 158	5 823	413	5 372
Enrolled in vocational courses	324	44	280	169	26	143	155	19	136
Years of school completed:									
High school graduate only	6 714	884	5 773	3 434	494	2 915	3 280	390	2 858
Some college or more	4 813	46	4 757	2 270	24	2 244	2 543	22	2 514
Employed Persons									
Enrolled in college									
All students	4 882	676	4 206	2 239	286	1 953	2 643	390	2 253
1st year	1 239	645	595	548	275	273	691	370	321
2nd year	1 436	13	1 422	627	3	623	809	10	799
3rd year or higher	2 206	18	2 189	1 064	8	1 056	1 143	10	1 133

See footnotes at end of table.

Table A-14. Enrollment and Employment Status of Recent High School Graduates, 16 to 24 Years Old, by Type of School, Year of School, Attainment Level of Persons Not Enrolled, Sex, Race and Hispanic Origin: October 1996 — Continued

(Numbers in thousands. Civilian noninstitutional population.)

College characteristics, employment status, race, and Hispanic origin	Both sexes			Male			Female		
	All graduates	Graduated from high school		All graduates	Graduated from high school		All graduates	Graduated from high school	
		This year	Earlier		This year	Earlier		This year	Earlier
Full time students	3 706	562	3 144	1 728	242	1 486	1 977	320	1 657
1st year	830	541	289	388	236	152	441	305	136
2nd year	1 089	9	1 080	472	2	470	618	8	610
3rd year or higher	1 787	12	1 775	868	4	864	918	8	911
Two year college (1st to 4th year)									
All students	1 541	310	1 231	692	123	569	849	187	663
1st year	641	293	348	295	120	175	347	173	174
2nd year	713	10	702	308	3	305	405	7	397
3rd and 4th year	187	6	181	89	—	89	98	6	92
Full time students	994	235	759	448	92	356	546	143	403
1st year	385	225	160	181	90	91	204	135	69
2nd year	508	7	501	226	2	225	281	5	276
3rd and 4th year	102	4	98	40	—	40	61	4	58
Four year college (1st to 4th year)									
All students	3 027	361	2 666	1 413	159	1 255	1 613	202	1 411
1st year	598	351	247	254	155	99	344	196	148
2nd year	723	3	720	319	—	319	405	3	402
3rd and 4th year	1 706	7	1 699	841	4	837	865	3	862
Full time students	2 511	326	2 186	1 186	150	1 036	1 326	176	1 150
1st year	445	316	129	208	146	61	237	170	67
2nd year	582	3	579	245	—	245	337	3	334
3rd and 4th year	1 485	7	1 478	733	4	729	752	3	749
Not enrolled in college									
Total	9 073	549	8 498	4 825	319	4 492	4 248	231	4 007
Enrolled in vocational courses	217	23	194	122	14	108	95	9	86
Years of school completed:									
High school graduate only	4 897	517	4 360	2 762	304	2 446	2 135	213	1 914
Some college or more	4 176	33	4 138	2 064	15	2 045	2 113	18	2 093
WHITE									
All Persons									
Enrolled in college									
All students	7 231	1 377	5 854	3 466	619	2 847	3 765	758	3 007
1st year	2 132	1 331	801	1 002	602	400	1 131	730	401
2nd year	1 957	19	1 937	893	3	890	1 064	16	1 048
3rd year or higher	3 142	26	3 116	1 571	14	1 557	1 570	12	1 558
Full time students	6 119	1 275	4 844	2 969	574	2 396	3 150	701	2 449
1st year	1 742	1 242	501	835	564	272	907	678	229
2nd year	1 615	15	1 599	744	2	743	870	14	857
3rd year or higher	2 762	18	2 745	1 390	8	1 382	1 372	10	1 363
Two year college (1st to 4th year)									
All students	1 889	502	1 386	869	222	647	1 020	281	739
1st year	923	477	446	440	219	221	483	259	225
2nd year	769	17	752	345	3	341	424	13	411
3rd and 4th year	197	8	188	85	—	85	112	8	103

See footnotes at end of table.

Table A-14. Enrollment and Employment Status of Recent High School Graduates, 16 to 24 Years Old, by Type of School, Year of School, Attainment Level of Persons Not Enrolled, Sex, Race and Hispanic Origin: October 1996 — Continued

(Numbers in thousands. Civilian noninstitutional population.)

College characteristics, employment status, race, and Hispanic origin	Both sexes			Male			Female		
	All graduates	Graduated from high school		All graduates	Graduated from high school		All graduates	Graduated from high school	
		This year	Earlier		This year	Earlier		This year	Earlier
Full time students	1 339	429	910	621	188	433	718	241	478
1st year	649	410	239	312	186	126	336	224	113
2nd year	568	13	556	264	2	262	304	11	294
3rd and 4th year	122	6	116	45	—	45	77	6	71
Four year college (1st to 4th year)									
All students	4 876	868	4 009	2 389	393	1 995	2 488	474	2 013
1st year	1 209	854	356	562	383	179	647	471	176
2nd year	1 188	3	1 185	548	—	548	639	3	637
3rd and 4th year	2 479	11	2 468	1 278	11	1 268	1 201	—	1 200
Full time students	4 413	843	3 570	2 173	386	1 787	2 240	458	1 782
1st year	1 094	832	262	523	378	146	571	454	116
2nd year	1 047	3	1 044	481	—	481	566	3	563
3rd and 4th year	2 272	8	2 264	1 169	8	1 161	1 103	—	1 103
Not enrolled in college									
Total	9 189	716	8 430	4 633	432	4 182	4 556	283	4 247
Enrolled in vocational courses	237	31	206	133	26	107	104	5	98
Years of school completed:									
High school graduate only	5 188	674	4 475	2 751	411	2 325	2 436	263	2 150
Some college or more	4 002	42	3 954	1 882	22	1 858	2 119	20	2 097
Employed Persons									
Enrolled in college									
All students	4 238	584	3 654	1 977	256	1 722	2 261	328	1 933
1st year	1 061	555	506	501	245	256	560	310	250
2nd year	1 241	13	1 228	550	3	547	691	10	681
3rd year or higher	1 935	15	1 920	926	8	918	1 009	8	1 002
Full time students	3 266	499	2 768	1 546	222	1 323	1 721	277	1 444
1st year	736	481	255	361	217	145	375	264	111
2nd year	947	9	938	427	2	425	520	8	513
3rd year or higher	1 583	9	1 574	757	4	754	826	5	821
Two year college (1st to 4th year)									
All students	1 362	279	1 083	625	115	510	737	164	573
1st year	583	263	320	280	112	168	303	151	152
2nd year	618	10	608	274	3	271	344	7	337
3rd and 4th year	161	6	155	71	—	71	90	6	84
Full time students	880	216	664	408	86	321	472	129	343
1st year	349	206	143	170	85	85	179	121	58
2nd year	440	7	433	204	2	202	236	5	231
3rd and 4th year	91	4	87	33	—	33	58	4	54
Four year college (1st to 4th year)									
All students	2 626	299	2 327	1 254	137	1 117	1 373	163	1 210
1st year	479	292	186	221	133	88	258	160	98
2nd year	623	3	620	276	—	276	347	3	344
3rd and 4th year	1 524	4	1 520	756	4	752	768	—	767

See footnotes at end of table.

Table A-14. Enrollment and Employment Status of Recent High School Graduates, 16 to 24 Years Old, by Type of School, Year of School, Attainment Level of Persons Not Enrolled, Sex, Race and Hispanic Origin: October 1996 — Continued

(Numbers in thousands. Civilian noninstitutional population.)

College characteristics, employment status, race, and Hispanic origin	Both sexes			Male			Female		
	All graduates	Graduated from high school		All graduates	Graduated from high school		All graduates	Graduated from high school	
		This year	Earlier		This year	Earlier		This year	Earlier
Full time students	2 226	282	1 944	1 071	136	935	1 155	146	1 009
1st year	387	275	112	191	132	59	196	143	53
2nd year	508	3	505	223	—	223	285	3	282
3rd and 4th year	1 331	4	1 327	657	4	653	675	—	674
Not enrolled in college									
Total	7 524	463	7 035	4 031	284	3 732	3 493	179	3 303
Enrolled in vocational courses	169	18	151	95	14	81	74	3	71
Years of school completed:									
High school graduate only	3 983	434	3 529	2 312	271	2 030	1 671	164	1 499
Some college or more	3 540	29	3 506	1 718	13	1 702	1 822	16	1 804
BLACK									
All Persons									
Enrolled in college									
All students	1 008	230	778	434	95	339	574	135	439
1st year	377	228	149	140	95	45	237	133	104
2nd year	281	—	281	118	—	118	163	—	163
3rd year or higher	351	2	348	176	—	176	175	2	172
Full time students	843	203	640	375	83	292	468	120	348
1st year	298	200	98	118	83	35	180	117	63
2nd year	240	—	240	100	—	100	140	—	140
3rd year or higher	305	2	302	157	—	157	147	2	145
Two year college (1st to 4th year)									
All students	271	78	193	109	35	74	162	43	119
1st year	149	78	71	55	35	20	94	43	51
2nd year	108	—	108	41	—	41	67	—	67
3rd and 4th year	14	—	14	13	—	13	1	—	1
Full time students	212	64	148	86	28	58	126	35	90
1st year	126	64	63	49	28	20	78	35	42
2nd year	77	—	77	30	—	30	47	—	47
3rd and 4th year	8	—	8	7	—	7	1	—	1
Four year college (1st to 4th year)									
All students	55	—	55	20	—	20	35	—	35
1st year	227	150	78	85	60	25	142	90	53
2nd year	173	—	173	77	—	77	96	—	96
3rd and 4th year	273	2	271	139	—	139	134	2	131
Full time students	580	139	441	268	55	214	312	84	228
1st year	172	137	35	70	55	15	102	82	20
2nd year	163	—	163	70	—	70	93	—	93
3rd and 4th year	246	2	243	129	—	129	117	2	114
Not enrolled in college									
Total	1 792	186	1 591	793	74	711	999	111	880
Enrolled in vocational courses	69	13	56	29	—	29	40	13	28

See footnotes at end of table.

Table A-14. Enrollment and Employment Status of Recent High School Graduates, 16 to 24 Years Old, by Type of School, Year of School, Attainment Level of Persons Not Enrolled, Sex, Race and Hispanic Origin: October 1996 — Continued

(Numbers in thousands. Civilian noninstitutional population.)

College characteristics, employment status, race, and Hispanic origin	Both sexes			Male			Female		
	All graduates	Graduated from high school		All graduates	Graduated from high school		All graduates	Graduated from high school	
		This year	Earlier		This year	Earlier		This year	Earlier
Years of school completed:									
High school graduate only	1 270	185	1 075	569	74	487	701	110	587
Some college or more	522	1	516	224	—	224	298	1	292
Employed Persons									
Enrolled in college									
All students	388	74	315	151	25	127	237	49	188
1st year	126	71	55	31	25	7	95	47	48
2nd year	112	—	112	47	—	47	65	—	65
3rd year or higher	150	2	148	73	—	73	78	2	75
Full time students	263	50	213	113	17	96	150	33	117
1st year	64	48	16	19	17	2	45	31	14
2nd year	88	—	88	33	—	33	55	—	55
3rd year or higher	111	2	109	61	—	61	50	2	48
Two year college (1st to 4th year)									
All students	98	24	75	35	6	30	63	18	45
1st year	33	24	9	6	6	—	27	18	9
2nd year	55	—	55	20	—	20	35	—	35
3rd and 4th year	11	—	11	10	—	10	1	—	1
Full time students	63	13	50	21	3	18	42	10	32
1st year	18	13	4	3	3	—	15	10	4
2nd year	40	—	40	13	—	13	27	—	27
3rd and 4th year	6	—	6	5	—	5	1	—	1
Four year college (1st to 4th year)									
All students	256	50	206	100	19	81	156	31	125
1st year	93	48	46	26	19	7	67	28	39
2nd year	57	—	57	27	—	27	30	—	30
3rd and 4th year	106	2	103	47	—	47	59	2	56
Full time students	176	37	139	76	14	62	100	23	77
1st year	46	34	12	16	14	2	30	21	10
2nd year	48	—	48	20	—	20	28	—	28
3rd and 4th year	82	2	80	40	—	40	42	2	39
Not enrolled in college									
Total	1 160	76	1 084	558	27	530	602	48	554
Enrolled in vocational courses	38	6	32	23	—	23	15	6	10
Years of school completed:									
High school graduate only	764	75	689	369	27	341	395	47	348
Some college or more	396	1	395	189	—	189	207	1	206
HISPANIC ORIGIN [1]									
All Persons									
Enrolled in college									
All students	704	115	589	302	38	264	402	77	325
1st year	251	106	145	94	34	60	157	72	85
2nd year	212	7	205	113	2	111	99	6	93
3rd year or higher	241	2	239	95	2	92	146	—	146

See footnotes at end of table.

Table A-14. Enrollment and Employment Status of Recent High School Graduates, 16 to 24 Years Old, by Type of School, Year of School, Attainment Level of Persons Not Enrolled, Sex, Race and Hispanic Origin: October 1996 — Continued

(Numbers in thousands. Civilian noninstitutional population.)

College characteristics, employment status, race, and Hispanic origin	Both sexes			Male			Female		
	All graduates	Graduated from high school		All graduates	Graduated from high school		All graduates	Graduated from high school	
		This year	Earlier		This year	Earlier		This year	Earlier
Full time students	517	103	414	215	34	181	302	69	233
1st year	165	93	72	54	29	24	112	64	48
2nd year	142	7	135	72	2	70	70	6	65
3rd year or higher	210	2	207	89	2	87	120	—	120
Two year college (1st to 4th year)									
All students	283	73	210	114	22	93	169	52	117
1st year	151	66	85	59	20	39	92	46	46
2nd year	96	7	89	50	2	48	46	6	41
3rd and 4th year	36	—	36	5	—	5	30	—	30
Full time students	171	63	107	58	17	40	113	46	67
1st year	81	56	25	24	15	9	57	40	16
2nd year	62	7	54	31	2	29	31	6	26
3rd and 4th year	27	—	27	3	—	3	25	—	25
Four year college (1st to 4th year)									
All students	380	42	338	160	16	144	220	26	194
1st year	100	40	60	35	14	21	65	26	39
2nd year	116	—	116	63	—	63	53	—	53
3rd and 4th year	164	2	162	62	2	60	102	—	102
Full time students	311	40	271	130	16	113	181	23	158
1st year	84	37	47	30	14	16	55	23	31
2nd year	80	—	80	41	—	41	39	—	39
3rd and 4th year	146	2	144	59	2	56	88	—	88
Not enrolled in college									
Total	1 347	112	1 207	712	65	632	635	46	575
Enrolled in vocational courses	35	10	25	23	7	16	12	3	9
Years of school completed:									
High school graduate only	980	108	846	527	62	453	453	46	393
Some college or more	367	3	361	185	3	178	182	—	182
Employed Persons									
Enrolled in college									
All students	400	55	346	187	28	159	213	27	187
1st year	133	50	82	69	24	46	63	27	37
2nd year	117	2	115	64	2	62	52	—	52
3rd year or higher	151	2	149	53	2	51	98	—	98
Full time students	256	45	211	115	24	92	141	22	119
1st year	67	41	26	32	19	13	35	22	13
2nd year	67	2	65	35	2	33	32	—	32
3rd year or higher	122	2	119	48	2	45	74	—	74
Two year college (1st to 4th year)									
All students	180	33	147	85	17	68	95	16	79
1st year	95	31	63	48	15	33	46	16	31
2nd year	55	2	53	32	2	30	23	—	23
3rd and 4th year	31	—	31	5	—	5	26	—	26

See footnotes at end of table.

Table A-14. Enrollment and Employment Status of Recent High School Graduates, 16 to 24 Years Old, by Type of School, Year of School, Attainment Level of Persons Not Enrolled, Sex, Race and Hispanic Origin: October 1996 — Continued

(Numbers in thousands. Civilian noninstitutional population.)

College characteristics, employment status, race, and Hispanic origin	Both sexes			Male			Female		
	All graduates	Graduated from high school		All graduates	Graduated from high school		All graduates	Graduated from high school	
		This year	Earlier		This year	Earlier		This year	Earlier
Full time students	91	26	65	36	13	23	55	13	42
1st year	37	24	13	17	11	6	21	13	7
2nd year	29	2	27	17	2	15	12	—	12
3rd and 4th year	25	—	25	3	—	3	22	—	22
Four year college (1st to 4th year)									
All students	211	22	190	99	11	88	113	11	102
1st year	38	19	19	21	8	13	17	11	6
2nd year	62	—	62	32	—	32	30	—	30
3rd and 4th year	111	2	109	45	2	43	66	—	66
Full time students	162	19	143	76	11	66	86	9	77
1st year	30	17	13	16	8	8	14	9	6
2nd year	38	—	38	19	—	19	20	—	20
3rd and 4th year	94	2	91	42	2	40	52	—	52
Not enrolled in college									
Total	972	46	911	587	29	546	385	17	366
Enrolled in vocational courses	20	3	17	14	3	10	6	—	6
Years of school completed:									
High school graduate only	673	46	616	431	29	393	242	17	223
Some college or more	298	—	295	156	—	153	143	—	143

Source: October 1996 Current Population Survey, Education and Social Stratification Branch, U.S. Bureau of the Census

1. May be of any race.

— Represents zero or rounds to zero.

Table A-15. Enrollment Status of Primary Family Members 18 to 24 Years Old, by Family Income, Level of Enrollment, Type and Control of School, Attendance Status, Sex, Family Status, Race and Hispanic Origin: October 1996

(Numbers in thousands. Civilian noninstitutional population.)

Level and type of school, sex, family status, race, and Hispanic origin	Total	Family income										
		Less than $10,000	$10,000 to $14,999	$15,000 to $19,999	$20,000 to $24,999	$25,000 to $29,999	$30,000 to $34,999	$35,000 to $39,999	$40,000 to $49,999	$50,000 to $74,999	$75,000 and over	Not reported
ALL RACES												
Dependent Family Member												
Male	7 639	531	468	389	414	452	402	452	717	1 570	1 454	790
Enrolled	3 850	188	178	134	180	163	186	232	390	835	983	382
Below college	786	107	77	46	55	50	62	45	81	110	91	63
College	3 064	81	101	88	124	113	124	187	309	726	892	319
Full-time	2 671	70	76	58	113	98	111	162	274	637	787	285
Part-time	393	11	25	30	12	15	13	25	35	89	104	34
Two year college (1st to 4th year)	838	26	46	29	41	40	42	78	82	194	190	70
Full-time	628	25	33	16	36	36	32	58	61	140	135	56
Part-time	210	2	12	13	5	4	10	20	21	54	55	14
Four year college (1st to 4th year)	2 103	55	55	54	83	69	81	104	218	499	646	240
Full-time	1 947	46	42	40	76	58	78	99	208	469	609	222
Part-time	156	9	13	15	7	11	3	5	10	30	37	18
Fifth year of college or higher	123	—	—	5	1	4	2	5	9	33	56	9
Full-time	95	—	—	2	1	4	2	5	5	28	43	6
Part-time	28	—	—	3	—	—	—	—	4	5	13	3
Public college	2 470	73	85	74	104	105	100	171	237	592	680	250
Full-time	2 112	62	62	47	93	93	86	146	202	509	594	218
Part-time	358	11	23	27	12	11	13	25	35	83	86	32
Two year college (1st to 4th year)	805	23	43	25	41	40	42	72	82	183	186	68
Full-time	600	22	30	12	36	36	32	52	61	132	134	54
Part-time	204	2	12	13	5	4	10	20	21	51	52	14
Four year college (1st to 4th year)	1 590	50	43	46	63	60	56	96	146	384	467	178
Full-time	1 454	41	32	32	56	54	53	91	137	358	441	160
Part-time	136	9	11	15	7	7	3	5	10	27	26	18
Fifth year of college or higher	76	—	—	2	1	4	2	4	8	24	27	4
Full-time	58	—	—	2	1	4	2	4	4	19	19	4
Part-time	18	—	—	—	—	—	—	—	4	5	9	—
Not enrolled	3 789	343	291	255	235	289	216	221	327	734	472	408
Not high school graduate	887	176	120	112	65	91	35	31	47	84	11	115
High school graduate	2 902	167	171	143	169	197	181	190	280	650	461	293
No college	1 832	148	128	103	124	142	123	127	155	396	196	191
Less than a bachelor's degree	794	19	39	41	42	44	50	46	105	196	144	66
Bachelor's degree or more	276	—	4	—	3	10	8	17	19	58	121	36
Female	6 269	461	333	249	388	417	410	335	604	1 231	1 134	707
Enrolled	3 630	202	156	151	187	207	214	206	368	781	817	341
Below college	445	81	42	19	20	44	28	16	36	67	49	44
College	3 185	121	115	132	167	164	186	190	332	714	767	297
Full-time	2 750	109	105	94	143	139	151	167	265	636	689	251
Part-time	435	11	9	39	24	25	35	22	66	78	78	46
Two year college (1st to 4th year)	866	58	45	59	59	43	65	36	110	183	141	67
Full-time	653	53	36	39	41	27	44	26	78	153	107	51
Part-time	213	5	9	20	18	16	21	10	32	30	35	17
Four year college (1st to 4th year)	2 181	60	65	70	106	113	112	149	206	496	587	219
Full-time	1 994	53	65	54	100	103	97	140	182	453	555	191
Part-time	187	7	—	15	6	9	15	9	24	43	32	27
Fifth year of college or higher	137	3	4	3	2	8	10	5	16	35	39	12
Full-time	103	3	4	—	2	8	10	2	6	30	28	10
Part-time	35	—	—	3	—	—	—	3	10	5	11	2

See footnotes at end of table.

Table A-15. Enrollment Status of Primary Family Members 18 to 24 Years Old, by Family Income, Level of Enrollment, Type and Control of School, Attendance Status, Sex, Family Status, Race and Hispanic Origin: October 1996 — Continued

(Numbers in thousands. Civilian noninstitutional population.)

Level and type of school, sex, family status, race, and Hispanic origin	Total	Family income										
		Less than $10,000	$10,000 to $14,999	$15,000 to $19,999	$20,000 to $24,999	$25,000 to $29,999	$30,000 to $34,999	$35,000 to $39,999	$40,000 to $49,999	$50,000 to $74,999	$75,000 and over	Not reported
Public college	2 526	109	106	131	122	139	148	162	272	532	564	241
Full-time	2 130	98	97	92	97	116	117	140	214	464	497	198
Part-time	397	11	9	39	24	23	31	22	59	68	67	43
Two year college (1st to 4th year)	827	55	45	58	56	40	59	36	103	178	136	58
Full-time	622	50	36	39	38	26	41	26	71	148	102	45
Part-time	204	5	9	20	18	14	18	10	32	30	35	13
Four year college (1st to 4th year)	1 608	54	57	69	65	91	82	121	158	329	405	177
Full-time	1 444	48	57	54	59	81	69	112	139	294	381	149
Part-time	164	7	—	15	6	9	13	9	19	35	24	27
Fifth year of college or higher	91	—	4	3	—	8	7	5	11	24	23	6
Full-time	63	—	4	—	—	8	7	2	3	21	14	4
Part-time	28	—	3	—	—	—	—	3	8	3	9	2
Not enrolled	2 639	259	177	98	201	209	196	129	236	450	317	366
Not high school graduate	460	91	38	21	60	32	26	8	49	50	5	80
High school graduate	2 179	100	139	77	141	177	170	121	187	400	312	286
No college	1 301	119	95	56	113	125	106	59	119	223	131	155
Less than a bachelor's degree	616	39	39	21	22	46	47	53	51	125	73	100
Bachelor's degree or more	262	9	4	1	5	7	18	9	18	52	108	31
Married, Spouse Present												
Male	1 514	180	212	180	212	168	122	98	120	87	27	108
Enrolled	208	22	26	23	29	23	36	4	17	15	3	9
Below college	14	2	—	2	2	—	6	—	—	—	1	—
College	194	20	26	21	27	23	30	4	17	15	2	9
Full-time	131	20	21	18	25	17	8	3	3	9	2	4
Part-time	63	—	5	3	2	5	22	1	14	6	—	5
Two year college (1st to 4th year)	50	1	3	3	2	3	14	—	13	6	2	4
Full-time	10	1	3	1	—	—	—	—	3	—	2	—
Part-time	40	—	—	2	2	3	14	—	10	6	—	4
Four year college (1st to 4th year)	115	19	19	13	17	16	9	4	4	9	—	5
Full-time	96	10	14	12	17	13	5	3	—	9	—	4
Part-time	19	—	5	1	—	2	4	1	4	—	—	2
Fifth year of college or higher	29	1	4	5	8	4	7	—	—	—	—	—
Full-time	25	1	4	5	8	4	3	—	—	—	—	—
Part-time	4	—	—	—	—	—	4	—	—	—	—	—
Public college	158	15	25	14	22	18	19	4	17	15	—	9
Other Marital and Family Status												
Male	103	15	20	11	21	13	5	3	3	9	—	4
Part-time	55	—	5	3	2	5	14	1	14	6	—	5
Two year college (1st to 4th year)	43	1	3	3	2	3	10	—	13	6	—	4
Full-time	8	1	3	1	—	—	—	3	—	—	—	—
Part-time	35	—	—	2	2	3	10	—	10	6	—	4
Four year college (1st to 4th year)	102	14	19	9	17	11	9	4	4	9	—	5
Full-time	83	14	14	8	17	9	5	3	—	9	—	4
Part-time	19	—	5	1	—	2	4	1	4	—	—	2
Fifth year of college or higher	12	—	3	2	4	4	—	—	—	—	—	—
Full-time	12	—	3	2	4	4	—	—	—	—	—	—
Part-time	—	—	—	—	—	—	—	—	—	—	—	—
Not enrolled	1 307	158	186	157	183	145	85	94	102	72	23	99
Not high school graduate	308	99	46	27	37	36	11	4	7	3	4	36

See footnotes at end of table.

Table A-15.   Enrollment Status of Primary Family Members 18 to 24 Years Old, by Family Income, Level of Enrollment, Type and Control of School, Attendance Status, Sex, Family Status, Race and Hispanic Origin: October 1996 — Continued

(Numbers in thousands. Civilian noninstitutional population.)

Level and type of school, sex, family status, race, and Hispanic origin	Total	Family income										
		Less than $10,000	$10,000 to $14,999	$15,000 to $19,999	$20,000 to $24,999	$25,000 to $29,999	$30,000 to $34,999	$35,000 to $39,999	$40,000 to $49,999	$50,000 to $74,999	$75,000 and over	Not reported
High school graduate	998	59	141	130	146	110	75	90	96	69	19	64
No college	621	49	111	94	76	65	44	39	41	43	14	47
Less than a bachelor's degree	293	6	19	32	54	40	29	43	32	21	5	14
Bachelor's degree or more ...	84	3	11	4	16	5	2	9	23	6	—	4
Female	2 474	233	311	274	359	259	196	191	232	185	56	178
Enrolled	311	27	40	26	34	26	38	42	33	24	7	16
Below college	30	4	6	1	10	—	6	—	1	—	—	2
College	280	23	34	25	23	26	32	42	32	24	7	13
Full-time	181	16	22	21	13	13	26	27	17	15	5	7
Part-time	99	7	12	4	10	13	6	15	15	9	1	7
Two year college (1st to 4th year)	86	5	13	10	12	6	11	19	4	4	1	1
Full-time	40	5	5	8	5	1	8	9	—	—	—	—
Part-time	46	—	9	2	6	5	3	10	4	4	1	1
Four year college (1st to 4th year)	165	15	19	15	12	11	18	19	19	20	5	12
Full-time	130	11	16	13	8	6	15	18	17	15	5	7
Part-time	35	4	4	2	4	6	3	—	2	5	—	6
Fifth year of college or higher	30	2	2	—	—	9	3	4	9	—	—	—
Full-time	11	—	2	—	—	6	3	—	—	—	—	—
Part-time	19	2	—	—	—	3	—	4	9	—	—	—
Public college	244	19	34	23	18	22	27	40	21	20	7	13
Full-time	151	12	22	19	7	9	21	26	10	13	5	7
Part-time	93	7	12	4	10	13	6	15	11	7	1	7
Two year college (1st to 4th year)	81	5	13	10	9	6	11	18	4	4	1	1
Full-time	36	5	5	8	2	1	8	7	—	—	—	—
Part-time	46	—	9	2	6	5	3	10	4	4	1	1
Four year college (1st to 4th year)	137	11	19	13	9	7	14	19	11	16	5	12
Full-time	105	7	16	11	5	1	11	18	10	13	5	7
Part-time	31	4	4	2	4	6	3	—	1	2	—	6
Fifth year of college or higher	26	2	2	—	—	9	3	4	6	—	—	—
Full-time	11	—	2	—	—	6	3	—	—	—	—	—
Part-time	16	2	—	—	—	3	—	4	6	—	—	—
Not enrolled	2 163	206	271	248	326	233	158	150	199	162	49	163
Not high school graduate	463	100	96	50	69	48	15	18	12	7	2	48
High school graduate	19	4	—	3	2	—	5	—	—	—	—	5
No college	955	78	124	131	147	78	78	67	84	64	20	84
Less than a bachelor's degree	560	25	41	56	86	79	56	45	66	66	19	20
Bachelor's degree or more ...	186	3	10	12	25	27	10	19	37	24	8	11

Other Marital and Family Status

Level and type of school, sex, family status, race, and Hispanic origin	Total	Less than $10,000	$10,000 to $14,999	$15,000 to $19,999	$20,000 to $24,999	$25,000 to $29,999	$30,000 to $34,999	$35,000 to $39,999	$40,000 to $49,999	$50,000 to $74,999	$75,000 and over	Not reported
Male	428	86	66	45	26	33	40	23	22	29	14	43
Enrolled	97	25	8	9	4	5	5	4	9	5	10	13
Below college	4	1	—	—	—	—	—	—	—	—	—	3
College	93	24	8	9	4	5	5	4	9	5	10	10
Full-time	79	24	8	9	4	5	5	2	7	5	4	7
Part-time	14	—	—	—	—	—	—	2	2	—	6	3
Two year college (1st to 4th year)	22	4	—	3	2	—	5	—	3	—	—	5
Full-time	18	4	—	3	2	—	5	—	3	—	—	2
Part-time	3	—	—	—	—	—	—	—	—	—	—	3
Four year college (1st to 4th year)	64	15	8	6	2	5	—	4	6	5	7	5
Full-time	53	15	8	6	2	5	—	2	4	5	1	5
Part-time	10	—	—	—	—	—	—	2	2	—	6	—

See footnotes at end of table.

Table A-15. Enrollment Status of Primary Family Members 18 to 24 Years Old, by Family Income, Level of Enrollment, Type and Control of School, Attendance Status, Sex, Family Status, Race and Hispanic Origin: October 1996 — Continued

(Numbers in thousands. Civilian noninstitutional population.)

Level and type of school, sex, family status, race, and Hispanic origin	Total	Family income										
		Less than $10,000	$10,000 to $14,999	$15,000 to $19,999	$20,000 to $24,999	$25,000 to $29,999	$30,000 to $34,999	$35,000 to $39,999	$40,000 to $49,999	$50,000 to $74,999	$75,000 and over	Not reported
Fifth year of college or higher	7	4	—	—	—	—	—	—	—	—	3	—
Full-time	7	4	—	—	—	—	—	—	—	—	3	—
Part-time	—	—	—	—	—	—	—	—	—	—	—	—
Public college	80	19	8	9	2	5	5	4	6	5	7	10
Full-time	67	19	8	9	2	5	5	2	4	5	1	7
Part-time	14	—	—	—	—	—	—	—	2	—	6	3
Two year college (1st to 4th year)	19	4	—	3	2	—	5	—	—	—	—	5
Full-time	16	4	—	3	2	—	5	—	—	—	—	2
Part-time	3	—	—	—	—	—	—	—	—	—	—	3
Four year college (1st to 4th year)	61	15	8	6	—	5	—	4	6	5	7	5
Full-time	51	15	8	6	—	5	—	2	4	5	1	5
Part-time	10	—	—	—	—	—	—	2	2	—	6	—
Fifth year of college or higher	—	—	—	—	—	—	—	—	—	—	—	—
Full-time	—	—	—	—	—	—	—	—	—	—	—	—
Part-time	—	—	—	—	—	—	—	—	—	—	—	—
Not enrolled	331	61	58	36	22	28	35	19	13	24	5	30
Not high school graduate	85	28	27	6	2	5	3	4	—	3	—	7
High school graduate	247	33	31	31	20	23	32	15	13	21	5	24
No college	180	30	20	30	14	21	20	10	6	11	4	14
Less than a bachelor's degree	52	3	11	1	6	2	7	5	2	7	1	7
Bachelor's degree or more	16	—	—	—	—	—	5	—	5	3	—	2
Female	1 146	593	165	77	80	32	35	19	19	34	16	75
Enrolled	244	119	24	18	16	7	6	5	8	18	11	11
Below college	33	28	2	—	—	—	—	—	3	—	—	11
College	211	91	22	18	16	7	6	5	6	18	11	11
Full-time	156	79	12	8	8	4	6	5	6	11	8	10
Part-time	55	12	10	10	8	3	—	—	—	7	3	2
Two year college (1st to 4th year)	111	64	6	9	5	4	3	2	6	5	—	7
Full-time	80	53	—	3	2	4	3	2	6	2	—	6
Part-time	31	11	6	6	3	—	—	—	—	3	—	2
Four year college (1st to 4th year)	93	25	16	7	9	3	3	3	—	13	11	4
Full-time	69	24	12	2	3	—	3	3	—	9	8	4
Part-time	24	1	4	4	5	3	—	—	—	4	3	—
Fifth year of college or higher	8	2	—	3	2	—	—	—	—	—	—	—
Full-time	8	2	—	3	2	—	—	—	—	—	—	—
Part-time	—	—	—	—	—	—	—	—	—	—	—	—
Public college	188	75	18	18	16	7	6	2	6	18	11	11
Full-time	135	64	7	8	8	4	6	2	6	11	8	10
Part-time	53	11	10	10	8	3	—	—	—	7	3	2
Two year college (1st to 4th year)	100	53	6	9	5	4	3	2	6	5	—	7
Full-time	70	43	—	3	2	4	3	2	6	2	—	6
Part-time	29	9	6	6	3	—	—	—	—	3	—	2
Four year college (1st to 4th year)	81	20	11	7	9	3	3	—	—	13	11	4
Full-time	57	19	7	2	3	—	3	—	—	9	8	4
Part-time	24	1	4	4	5	3	—	—	—	4	3	—
Fifth year of college or higher	8	2	—	3	2	—	—	—	—	—	—	—
Full-time	8	2	—	3	2	—	—	—	—	—	—	—
Part-time	—	—	—	—	—	—	—	—	—	—	—	—
Not enrolled	901	474	141	59	64	25	29	15	11	15	6	64
Not high school graduate	344	239	55	4	5	3	10	4	—	5	2	16
High school graduate	558	235	86	55	58	22	18	11	11	10	4	48
No college	394	192	69	38	33	11	5	6	6	2	—	33

See footnotes at end of table.

Table A-15. Enrollment Status of Primary Family Members 18 to 24 Years Old, by Family Income, Level of Enrollment, Type and Control of School, Attendance Status, Sex, Family Status, Race and Hispanic Origin: October 1996 — Continued

(Numbers in thousands. Civilian noninstitutional population.)

Level and type of school, sex, family status, race, and Hispanic origin	Total	Family income										
		Less than $10,000	$10,000 to $14,999	$15,000 to $19,999	$20,000 to $24,999	$25,000 to $29,999	$30,000 to $34,999	$35,000 to $39,999	$40,000 to $49,999	$50,000 to $74,999	$75,000 and over	Not reported
Less than a bachelor's degree	123	41	15	10	22	6	6	2	5	5	4	7
Bachelor's degree or more	41	2	2	6	3	5	8	3	—	3	—	8
WHITE												
Dependent Family Member												
Male	5 971	257	274	269	301	334	315	359	610	1 336	1 307	609
Enrolled	3 092	78	110	84	128	127	135	181	336	721	881	312
Below college	573	36	50	31	39	40	51	39	76	89	85	36
College	2 519	42	60	53	90	87	84	142	259	632	796	275
Full-time	2 199	39	51	31	82	72	77	117	226	553	702	249
Part-time	320	3	8	22	8	15	7	25	33	79	94	26
Two year college (1st to 4th year)	668	13	29	21	30	36	25	57	66	165	174	50
Full-time	490	12	25	8	25	32	22	37	46	115	123	44
Part-time	178	2	4	13	5	4	4	20	20	50	51	6
Four year college (1st to 4th year)	1 745	28	31	32	59	47	58	80	185	436	573	216
Full-time	1 624	28	27	23	56	36	55	75	175	410	542	198
Part-time	121	1	4	9	3	11	3	5	10	26	31	18
Fifth year of college or higher	107	—	—	—	1	4	—	5	8	30	50	9
Full-time	85	—	—	—	1	4	—	5	4	28	37	6
Part-time	22	—	—	—	—	—	—	—	—	2	13	3
Public college	2 021	37	52	42	76	83	59	134	199	511	618	211
Full-time	1 727	34	44	20	68	72	52	109	165	437	539	187
Part-time	293	3	8	22	8	11	7	25	33	74	79	24
Two year college (1st to 4th year)	644	13	29	17	30	36	25	55	66	154	170	48
Full-time	472	12	25	5	25	32	22	35	46	107	122	42
Part-time	173	2	4	13	5	4	4	20	20	47	48	6
Four year college (1st to 4th year)	1 311	23	23	24	45	43	33	76	124	335	424	159
Full-time	1 205	23	19	15	42	36	30	71	115	311	402	141
Part-time	106	1	4	9	3	7	3	5	10	24	22	18
Fifth year of college or higher	66	—	—	—	1	4	—	4	8	22	24	4
Full-time	51	—	—	—	1	4	—	4	4	19	15	4
Part-time	15	—	—	—	—	—	—	—	4	2	9	—
Not enrolled	2 879	179	165	185	172	207	180	179	274	615	426	297
Not high school graduate	620	84	63	85	55	75	32	28	34	67	10	86
High school graduate	2 259	95	101	100	117	132	148	151	240	548	416	210
No college	1 393	85	69	65	83	99	104	100	137	329	181	142
Less than a bachelor's degree	640	10	29	35	31	29	41	35	89	166	132	45
Bachelor's degree or more	225	—	4	—	3	4	3	17	15	53	102	24
Female	4 774	225	178	162	280	308	294	270	506	1 057	1 019	476
Enrolled	2 853	90	84	99	139	152	155	160	300	674	756	243
Below college	314	28	29	14	18	31	18	16	24	59	49	28
College	2 538	62	55	85	121	121	137	144	276	615	707	216
Full-time	2 212	54	52	53	101	104	112	128	221	561	643	183
Part-time	327	8	3	31	20	18	25	16	55	54	64	32
Two year college (1st to 4th year)	686	37	22	44	51	35	43	35	102	149	126	43
Full-time	520	36	19	29	34	20	32	24	73	125	96	33
Part-time	166	1	3	16	17	16	11	10	29	23	30	10
Four year college (1st to 4th year)	1 765	25	33	40	70	82	92	108	161	441	550	164
Full-time	1 627	19	33	25	67	80	77	102	142	413	526	144
Part-time	139	7	—	15	3	2	15	6	19	28	25	20

See footnotes at end of table.

Table A-15.   Enrollment Status of Primary Family Members 18 to 24 Years Old, by Family Income, Level of Enrollment, Type and Control of School, Attendance Status, Sex, Family Status, Race and Hispanic Origin: October 1996 — Continued

(Numbers in thousands. Civilian noninstitutional population.)

Level and type of school, sex, family status, race, and Hispanic origin	Total	Family income										
		Less than $10,000	$10,000 to $14,999	$15,000 to $19,999	$20,000 to $24,999	$25,000 to $29,999	$30,000 to $34,999	$35,000 to $39,999	$40,000 to $49,999	$50,000 to $74,999	$75,000 and over	Not reported
Fifth year of college or higher	87	—	—	—	—	4	3	2	14	25	31	9
Full-time	65	—	—	—	—	4	3	2	6	22	22	6
Part-time	22	—	—	—	—	—	—	—	8	3	9	2
Public college	1 950	56	47	84	92	101	102	118	221	440	514	176
Full-time	1 651	48	44	52	72	86	81	102	174	391	458	143
Part-time	299	8	3	31	20	15	21	16	48	49	55	32
Two year college (1st to 4th year)	653	34	22	44	48	32	37	35	95	144	121	41
Full-time	492	33	19	28	31	19	29	24	67	121	91	31
Part-time	161	1	3	16	17	14	8	10	29	23	30	10
Four year college (1st to 4th year)	1 242	22	26	40	44	65	65	81	118	278	376	129
Full-time	1 123	15	26	24	40	63	52	75	104	255	359	109
Part-time	118	7	—	15	3	2	13	6	13	23	16	20
Fifth year of college or higher	55	—	—	—	—	4	—	2	8	18	17	6
Full time	35	—	—	—	—	4	—	2	2	15	8	4
Part-time	20	—	—	—	—	—	—	—	6	3	9	2
Not enrolled	1 921	134	94	63	141	156	139	109	206	384	263	233
Not high school graduate	338	55	21	18	44	27	19	8	44	38	5	59
High school graduate	1 584	79	74	45	96	129	120	101	162	346	258	174
No college	911	59	43	31	81	83	88	47	99	192	91	96
Less than a bachelor's degree	465	15	27	14	15	39	25	46	46	115	69	55
Bachelor's degree or more	208	4	3	1	—	7	7	9	18	40	97	22
Married, Spouse Present												
Male	1 381	160	196	154	206	160	98	84	106	84	24	108
Enrolled	189	18	26	20	29	20	31	4	14	15	3	9
Below college	14	2	—	2	2	—	6	—	—	—	1	—
College	175	16	26	18	27	20	25	4	14	15	2	9
Full-time	121	16	21	15	25	15	8	3	3	9	2	4
Part-time	54	—	5	3	2	5	17	1	11	6	—	5
Two year college (1st to 4th year)	45	1	3	3	2	3	9	—	13	6	2	4
Full-time	10	1	3	1	—	—	—	—	3	—	2	—
Part-time	34	—	—	2	2	3	9	—	10	6	—	4
Four year college (1st to 4th year)	103	15	19	10	—	13	9	4	1	9	—	5
Full-time	86	15	14	9	17	11	5	3	—	9	—	4
Part-time	16	—	5	1	—	2	4	1	1	—	—	2
Fifth year of college or higher	28	—	4	5	8	4	7	—	—	—	—	—
Full-time	24	—	4	5	8	4	3	—	—	—	—	—
Part-time	4	—	—	—	—	—	4	—	—	—	—	—
Not enrolled	1 192	142	170	134	177	140	67	81	91	70	21	99
Not high school graduate	290	91	46	23	36	34	7	4	7	3	4	36
High school graduate	902	51	124	111	141	107	59	77	85	66	17	64
No college	564	42	94	89	72	64	32	33	37	43	13	47
Less than a bachelor's degree	265	6	19	18	53	37	27	35	30	21	4	14
Bachelor's degree or more	73	3	11	4	16	5	—	9	18	3	—	4
Female	2 242	198	286	250	329	242	172	164	201	182	51	168
Enrolled	271	18	37	23	27	26	35	28	33	24	5	16
Below college	25	4	6	—	7	—	6	—	1	—	—	2
College	246	14	31	23	20	26	28	28	32	24	5	13
Full-time	160	13	19	21	10	13	23	17	17	15	5	7
Part-time	86	1	12	2	10	13	5	10	15	9	—	7
Two year college (1st to 4th year)	66	3	13	8	—	6	11	7	4	4	—	1
Full-time	27	3	5	8	2	1	8	1	—	—	—	—

See footnotes at end of table.

Table A-15.   Enrollment Status of Primary Family Members 18 to 24 Years Old, by Family Income, Level of Enrollment, Type and Control of School, Attendance Status, Sex, Family Status, Race and Hispanic Origin: October 1996 — Continued

(Numbers in thousands. Civilian noninstitutional population.)

Level and type of school, sex, family status, race, and Hispanic origin	Total	Family income										
		Less than $10,000	$10,000 to $14,999	$15,000 to $19,999	$20,000 to $24,999	$25,000 to $29,999	$30,000 to $34,999	$35,000 to $39,999	$40,000 to $49,999	$50,000 to $74,999	$75,000 and over	Not reported
Part-time	39	—	9	—	6	5	3	6	4	4	—	1
Four year college (1st to 4th year)	152	11	16	15	12	11	15	17	19	20	5	12
Full-time	121	10	13	13	8	6	12	16	17	15	5	7
Part-time	31	1	4	2	4	6	2	—	2	5	—	6
Fifth year of college or higher	27	—	2	—	—	9	3	4	9	—	—	—
Full-time	11	—	2	—	—	6	3	—	—	—	—	—
Part-time	16	—	—	—	—	3	—	4	9	—	—	—
Not enrolled	1 971	180	250	227	302	216	137	136	168	158	45	152
Not high school graduate	449	99	93	48	68	48	11	14	12	7	1	47
High school graduate	1 522	81	156	179	234	167	126	122	156	150	44	106
No college	839	58	111	121	125	72	63	63	67	62	18	80
Less than a bachelor's degree	506	20	35	45	84	72	54	44	52	66	18	15
Bachelor's degree or more	177	3	10	12	25	23	10	15	37	22	8	11
Other Marital and Family Status												
Male	287	46	50	35	13	24	28	20	10	21	13	29
Enrolled	57	12	8	5	2	—	—	4	5	5	10	6
Below college	3	—	—	—	—	—	—	—	—	—	—	3
College	54	12	8	5	2	—	—	4	5	5	10	3
Full-time	43	12	8	5	2	—	—	2	3	5	4	3
Part-time	10	—	—	—	—	—	—	2	2	—	6	—
Two year college (1st to 4th year)	9	4	—	3	—	—	—	—	3	—	—	—
Full-time	9	4	—	3	—	—	—	—	3	—	—	—
Part-time	—	—	—	—	—	—	—	—	—	—	—	—
Four year college (1st to 4th year)	41	8	8	2	2	—	—	4	2	5	7	3
Full-time	31	8	8	2	2	—	—	2	—	5	1	3
Part-time	10	—	—	—	—	—	—	2	2	—	6	—
Fifth year of college or higher	3	—	—	—	—	—	—	—	—	—	3	—
Full-time	3	—	—	—	—	—	—	—	—	—	3	—
Part-time	—	—	—	—	—	—	—	—	—	—	—	—
Not enrolled	230	34	42	30	11	24	28	16	5	16	3	23
Not high school graduate	66	19	19	6	2	4	3	4	—	3	—	7
High school graduate	165	15	23	24	9	19	26	12	5	13	3	16
No college	126	15	17	23	4	18	13	10	—	11	3	11
Less than a bachelor's degree	29	—	6	1	5	1	7	1	2	2	—	3
Bachelor's degree or more	9	—	—	—	—	—	5	—	2	—	—	2
Female	618	270	113	63	33	24	28	10	14	24	12	29
Enrolled	146	68	11	15	6	7	3	5	5	16	8	2
Below college	20	17	—	—	—	—	—	—	3	—	—	—
College	126	51	11	15	6	7	3	5	3	16	8	2
Full-time	89	43	4	5	3	4	3	5	3	9	8	2
Part-time	38	8	7	10	3	3	—	—	—	7	—	—
Two year college (1st to 4th year)	68	34	6	9	3	4	3	2	3	3	—	1
Full-time	42	27	—	3	—	4	3	2	3	—	—	1
Part-time	26	8	6	6	3	—	—	—	—	3	—	—
Four year college (1st to 4th year)	56	14	5	7	3	3	—	3	—	13	8	1
Full-time	44	14	4	2	3	—	—	3	—	9	8	1
Part-time	12	—	1	4	—	3	—	—	—	4	—	—
Fifth year of college or higher	2	2	—	—	—	—	—	—	—	—	—	—
Full-time	2	2	—	—	—	—	—	—	—	—	—	—
Part-time	—	—	—	—	—	—	—	—	—	—	—	—

See footnotes at end of table.

Table A-15. Enrollment Status of Primary Family Members 18 to 24 Years Old, by Family Income, Level of Enrollment, Type and Control of School, Attendance Status, Sex, Family Status, Race and Hispanic Origin: October 1996 — Continued

(Numbers in thousands. Civilian noninstitutional population.)

Level and type of school, sex, family status, race, and Hispanic origin	Total	Family income										
		Less than $10,000	$10,000 to $14,999	$15,000 to $19,999	$20,000 to $24,999	$25,000 to $29,999	$30,000 to $34,999	$35,000 to $39,999	$40,000 to $49,999	$50,000 to $74,999	$75,000 and over	Not reported
Not enrolled	472	202	102	47	27	17	25	5	8	8	4	27
Not high school graduate	183	113	41	4	3	3	10	—	—	—	—	9
High school graduate	289	89	61	43	24	14	15	5	8	8	4	18
No college	191	68	46	29	17	6	5	2	3	2	—	12
Less than a bachelor's degree	68	19	13	8	7	2	2	2	5	3	4	2
Bachelor's degree or more ...	31	2	2	6	—	5	8	—	—	3	—	4

BLACK

Dependent Family Member

Male	1 223	249	159	92	85	97	64	68	74	155	60	122
Enrolled	502	93	53	31	38	25	38	34	41	70	40	41
Below college	188	68	22	13	14	9	8	6	5	16	3	24
College	314	24	31	18	24	16	30	28	36	54	37	17
Full-time	268	16	17	10	20	16	28	28	36	49	34	14
Part-time	46	8	14	8	4	—	3	—	—	5	3	2
Two year college (1st to 4th year)	96	6	14	—	8	4	8	15	15	16	7	2
Full-time	78	6	5	—	8	4	6	15	15	12	7	—
Part-time	18	—	9	—	—	—	3	—	—	4	—	2
Four year college (1st to 4th year)	211	19	17	13	16	12	20	13	21	37	29	14
Full-time	185	11	12	8	12	12	20	13	21	37	27	14
Part-time	26	8	5	5	4	—	—	—	—	1	3	—
Fifth year of college or higher	7	—	—	5	—	—	2	—	1	—	—	—
Full-time	4	—	—	2	—	—	2	—	1	—	—	—
Part-time	3	—	—	3	—	—	—	—	—	—	—	—
Public college	250	24	26	15	18	12	30	20	30	42	16	17
Full-time	209	16	14	10	14	12	28	20	30	38	14	14
Part-time	41	8	12	5	4	—	3	—	—	4	3	2
Two year college (1st to 4th year)	92	6	14	—	8	4	8	11	15	16	7	2
Full-time	74	6	5	—	8	4	6	11	15	12	7	—
Part-time	18	—	9	—	—	—	3	—	—	4	—	2
Four year college (1st to 4th year)	154	19	12	13	9	8	20	9	15	25	9	14
Full-time	131	11	9	8	5	8	20	9	15	25	6	14
Part-time	23	8	3	5	4	—	—	—	—	—	3	—
Fifth year of college or higher	4	—	—	2	—	—	2	—	—	—	—	—
Full-time	4	—	—	2	—	—	2	—	—	—	—	—
Part-time	—	—	—	—	—	—	—	—	—	—	—	—
Not enrolled	721	156	106	61	47	72	26	34	33	85	20	82
Not high school graduate	225	88	48	22	—	13	3	3	9	8	—	21
High school graduate	496	68	58	39	37	59	23	31	24	76	20	61
No college	376	60	52	34	34	41	14	22	14	58	7	40
Less than a bachelor's degree	101	8	7	4	—	12	10	9	11	14	9	15
Bachelor's degree or more ...	20	—	—	—	—	6	—	—	—	5	4	5
Female	1 105	217	142	68	79	78	71	58	56	97	42	196
Enrolled	521	96	67	43	26	40	28	40	35	57	20	69
Below college	106	45	12	5	—	11	10	—	8	7	—	8
College	415	51	54	38	26	29	19	40	26	50	20	61
Full-time	356	51	49	31	26	25	16	33	24	35	14	51
Part-time	60	—	5	7	—	5	2	6	2	15	6	11
Two year college (1st to 4th year)	99	15	22	10	2	7	5	—	—	11	5	23
Full-time	73	15	16	5	2	7	2	—	—	5	3	17
Part-time	26	—	5	4	—	—	2	—	—	6	2	6

See footnotes at end of table.

Table A-15. Enrollment Status of Primary Family Members 18 to 24 Years Old, by Family Income, Level of Enrollment, Type and Control of School, Attendance Status, Sex, Family Status, Race and Hispanic Origin: October 1996 — Continued

(Numbers in thousands. Civilian noninstitutional population.)

Level and type of school, sex, family status, race, and Hispanic origin	Total	Family income										
		Less than $10,000	$10,000 to $14,999	$15,000 to $19,999	$20,000 to $24,999	$25,000 to $29,999	$30,000 to $34,999	$35,000 to $39,999	$40,000 to $49,999	$50,000 to $74,999	$75,000 and over	Not reported
Four year college (1st to 4th year)	285	33	28	25	22	22	9	37	24	31	15	38
Full-time	262	33	28	25	22	18	9	33	24	24	12	33
Part-time	24	—	—	—	—	5	—	3	—	7	4	5
Fifth year of college or higher	31	3	4	3	2	—	5	3	2	8	—	—
Full-time	21	3	4	—	2	—	5	—	—	6	—	—
Part-time	10	—	—	3	—	—	—	3	2	2	—	—
Public college	371	46	53	38	16	27	16	39	24	45	15	52
Full-time	320	46	48	31	16	22	14	33	22	35	9	44
Part-time	51	—	5	7	—	5	2	6	2	10	6	7
Two year college (1st to 4th year)	93	15	22	10	2	7	5	—	—	11	5	17
Full-time	70	15	16	5	2	7	2	—	—	5	3	14
Part-time	22	—	5	4	—	—	2	—	—	6	2	2
Four year college (1st to 4th year)	255	31	27	25	13	20	7	36	22	28	10	35
Full-time	234	31	27	25	13	15	7	33	22	24	6	30
Part-time	21	—	—	—	—	5	—	3	—	4	4	5
Fifth year of college or higher	24	—	4	3	—	—	5	3	2	6	—	—
Full-time	15	—	4	—	—	—	5	—	—	6	—	—
Part-time	8	—	—	3	—	—	—	3	2	—	—	—
Not enrolled	584	121	75	25	53	39	42	19	21	40	22	127
Not high school graduate	99	33	16	—	14	2	7	—	1	8	—	19
High school graduate	485	88	59	25	39	36	36	19	20	32	22	108
No college	331	59	47	22	27	33	12	12	18	25	19	56
Less than a bachelor's degree	125	24	12	4	6	3	17	7	2	3	3	44
Bachelor's degree or more	29	5	—	—	5	—	6	—	—	4	—	8
Married, Spouse Present												
Male	98	19	10	27	4	—	18	10	8	3	—	—
Enrolled	15	4	—	—	—	—	5	—	3	—	—	—
Below college	—	—	—	—	—	—	—	—	—	—	—	—
College	15	4	—	3	—	—	5	—	3	—	—	—
Full-time	7	4	—	3	—	—	—	—	—	—	—	—
Part-time	8	—	—	—	—	—	5	—	3	—	—	—
Two year college (1st to 4th year)	5	—	—	—	—	—	5	—	—	—	—	—
Full-time	—	—	—	—	—	—	—	—	—	—	—	—
Part-time	5	—	—	—	—	—	5	—	—	—	—	—
Four year college (1st to 4th year)	9	4	—	3	—	—	—	—	—	—	—	—
Full-time	6	4	—	3	—	—	—	—	—	—	—	—
Part-time	3	—	—	—	—	—	—	—	—	—	—	—
Fifth year of college or higher	1	1	—	—	—	—	—	—	—	—	—	—
Full-time	1	1	—	—	—	—	—	—	—	—	—	—
Part-time	—	—	—	—	—	—	—	—	—	—	—	—
Not enrolled	83	15	10	24	4	—	13	10	4	3	—	—
Not high school graduate	15	8	—	4	—	—	3	—	—	—	—	—
High school graduate	68	7	10	20	4	—	10	10	4	3	—	—
No college	44	7	10	5	4	—	10	5	3	—	—	—
Less than a bachelor's degree	20	—	—	14	—	—	—	4	2	—	—	—
Bachelor's degree or more	3	—	—	—	—	—	—	—	—	—	—	—
Female	131	25	13	13	20	6	13	8	22	2	—	9
Enrolled	19	6	3	—	7	—	1	3	—	—	—	—
Below college	4	—	—	—	4	—	—	—	—	—	—	—
College	15	5	3	—	3	—	1	3	—	—	—	—
Full-time	8	2	3	—	3	—	—	—	—	—	—	—

See footnotes at end of table.

Table A-15.   Enrollment Status of Primary Family Members 18 to 24 Years Old, by Family Income, Level of Enrollment, Type and Control of School, Attendance Status, Sex, Family Status, Race and Hispanic Origin: October 1996 — Continued

(Numbers in thousands. Civilian noninstitutional population.)

Level and type of school, sex, family status, race, and Hispanic origin	Total	Family income										
		Less than $10,000	$10,000 to $14,999	$15,000 to $19,999	$20,000 to $24,999	$25,000 to $29,999	$30,000 to $34,999	$35,000 to $39,999	$40,000 to $49,999	$50,000 to $74,999	$75,000 and over	Not reported
Part-time	7	3	—	—	—	—	—	3	—	—	—	—
Two year college (1st to 4th year)	8	2	—	—	3	—	—	3	—	—	—	—
Full-time	5	2	—	—	3	—	1	—	—	—	—	—
Part-time	3	—	—	—	—	—	—	3	—	—	—	—
Four year college (1st to 4th year)	7	3	3	—	—	—	1	—	—	—	—	—
Full-time	3	—	3	—	—	—	—	—	—	—	—	—
Part-time	4	3	—	—	—	—	1	—	—	—	—	—
Fifth year of college or higher	—	—	—	—	—	—	—	—	—	—	—	—
Full-time	—	—	—	—	—	—	—	—	—	—	—	—
Part-time	—	—	—	—	—	—	—	—	—	—	—	—
Not enrolled	112	19	10	13	13	6	12	5	22	2	—	9
Not high school graduate	4	—	—	—	—	—	—	3	—	—	—	—
High school graduate	108	19	10	13	13	6	12	2	22	2	—	9
No college	72	15	10	7	12	3	10	2	10	—	—	4
Less than a bachelor's degree	31	4	—	6	1	—	2	—	12	—	—	5
Bachelor's degree or more	5	—	—	—	—	3	—	—	—	2	—	—
Other Marital and Family Status												
Male	92	28	16	7	13	6	7	3	8	—	2	3
Enrolled	21	11	—	—	2	4	—	—	4	—	—	—
Below college	—	—	—	—	—	—	—	—	—	—	—	—
College	21	11	—	—	2	4	—	—	4	—	—	—
Full-time	21	11	—	—	2	4	—	—	4	—	—	—
Part-time	—	—	—	—	—	—	—	—	—	—	—	—
Two year college (1st to 4th year)	2	—	—	—	2	—	—	—	—	—	—	—
Full-time	2	—	—	—	2	—	—	—	—	—	—	—
Part-time	—	—	—	—	—	—	—	—	—	—	—	—
Four year college (1st to 4th year)	15	6	—	—	—	4	—	—	4	—	—	—
Full-time	15	6	—	—	—	4	—	—	4	—	—	—
Part-time	—	—	—	—	—	—	—	—	—	—	—	—
Fifth year of college or higher	4	4	—	—	—	—	—	—	—	—	—	—
Full-time	4	4	—	—	—	—	—	—	—	—	—	—
Part-time	—	—	—	—	—	—	—	—	—	—	—	—
Not enrolled	70	17	16	7	10	1	7	3	4	—	2	3
Not high school graduate	12	3	8	—	—	1	—	—	—	—	—	3
High school graduate	58	14	8	7	10	1	7	3	4	—	2	3
No college	46	12	3	7	10	1	7	—	4	—	1	3
Less than a bachelor's degree	12	3	5	—	1	—	—	3	—	—	1	—
Bachelor's degree or more	—	—	—	—	—	—	—	—	—	—	—	—
Female	482	309	50	11	42	8	7	10	3	7	5	31
Enrolled	91	49	13	3	10	—	3	—	3	2	3	5
Below college	13	11	2	—	—	—	—	—	—	—	—	—
College	78	38	11	3	10	—	3	—	3	2	3	5
Full-time	61	34	8	3	5	—	3	—	3	2	—	4
Part-time	17	4	3	—	5	—	—	—	—	—	3	2
Two year college (1st to 4th year)	38	30	—	—	2	—	—	—	—	2	—	2
Full-time	34	26	—	—	2	—	—	—	—	2	—	—
Part-time	5	3	—	—	—	—	—	—	—	—	—	2
Four year college (1st to 4th year)	34	8	11	—	5	—	3	—	—	—	3	3
Full-time	22	7	8	—	—	—	3	—	—	—	—	3
Part-time	12	1	3	—	5	—	—	—	—	—	3	—

See footnotes at end of table.

Table A-15.   Enrollment Status of Primary Family Members 18 to 24 Years Old, by Family Income, Level of Enrollment, Type and Control of School, Attendance Status, Sex, Family Status, Race and Hispanic Origin: October 1996 — Continued

(Numbers in thousands. Civilian noninstitutional population.)

Level and type of school, sex, family status, race, and Hispanic origin	Total	Family income										
		Less than $10,000	$10,000 to $14,999	$15,000 to $19,999	$20,000 to $24,999	$25,000 to $29,999	$30,000 to $34,999	$35,000 to $39,999	$40,000 to $49,999	$50,000 to $74,999	$75,000 and over	Not reported
Fifth year of college or higher	6	—	—	3	2	—	—	—	—	—	—	—
Full-time	6	—	—	3	2	—	—	—	—	—	—	—
Part-time	—	—	—	—	—	—	—	—	—	—	—	—
Not enrolled	391	260	37	8	32	8	4	10	—	6	2	25
Not high school graduate	152	123	13	—	2	—	—	4	—	5	2	3
High school graduate	239	137	24	8	30	8	4	6	—	1	—	23
No college	189	118	22	8	15	4	—	3	—	—	—	18
Less than a bachelor's degree	44	19	1	—	11	4	4	—	—	1	—	4
Bachelor's degree or more	7	—	—	—	3	1	—	3	—	—	—	—
HISPANIC ORIGIN[1]												
Dependent Family Member												
Male	978	143	117	119	86	81	63	68	53	91	58	99
Enrolled	363	40	50	32	26	19	26	41	30	38	34	25
Below college	146	33	26	11	10	17	15	12	10	—	3	9
College	217	8	24	22	16	2	11	29	20	38	32	16
Full-time	154	8	16	5	12	2	11	21	11	24	27	16
Part-time	63	—	8	16	4	—	—	7	9	14	5	—
Two year college (1st to 4th year)	85	2	14	11	9	2	5	11	9	20	3	—
Full-time	43	2	10	4	5	2	5	4	—	8	3	—
Part-time	43	—	4	7	4	—	—	7	9	11	—	—
Four year college (1st to 4th year)	125	6	10	11	6	—	6	14	11	18	29	14
Full-time	104	6	6	2	6	—	6	14	11	16	25	14
Part-time	21	—	4	9	—	—	—	—	—	2	5	—
Fifth year of college or higher	7	—	—	—	—	—	—	4	—	—	—	3
Full-time	7	—	—	—	—	—	—	4	—	—	—	3
Part-time	—	—	—	—	—	—	—	—	—	—	—	—
Public college	201	8	24	18	16	2	11	29	15	38	32	10
Full-time	138	8	16	2	12	2	11	21	6	24	27	10
Part-time	63	—	8	16	4	—	—	7	9	14	5	—
Two year college (1st to 4th year)	82	2	14	7	9	2	5	11	9	20	3	—
Full-time	39	2	10	—	5	2	5	4	—	8	3	—
Part-time	43	—	4	7	4	—	—	7	9	11	—	—
Four year college (1st to 4th year)	115	6	10	11	6	—	6	14	6	18	29	10
Full-time	95	6	6	2	6	—	6	14	6	16	25	10
Part-time	21	—	4	9	—	—	—	—	—	2	5	—
Fifth year of college or higher	4	—	—	—	1	—	—	4	—	—	—	—
Full-time	4	—	—	—	1	—	—	4	—	—	—	—
Part-time	—	—	—	—	—	—	—	—	—	—	—	—
Not enrolled	615	103	67	86	60	62	36	27	23	53	23	74
Not high school graduate	311	60	37	57	28	39	7	10	9	22	3	39
High school graduate	303	44	29	29	32	23	29	17	13	31	20	35
No college	209	40	15	18	24	16	19	5	13	16	12	31
Less than a bachelor's degree	80	3	14	11	7	6	11	10	—	15	—	2
Bachelor's degree or more	15	—	1	—	—	1	—	2	—	—	8	2
Female	724	131	81	44	67	78	58	30	51	73	38	73
Enrolled	355	50	46	35	23	34	26	22	12	47	29	31
Below college	82	20	24	1	8	4	4	—	2	8	3	8
College	273	31	22	34	15	30	22	22	10	40	26	23
Full-time	227	28	19	20	10	27	22	12	8	37	26	18
Part-time	46	2	3	14	6	2	—	10	2	2	—	5

See footnotes at end of table.

Table A-15. Enrollment Status of Primary Family Members 18 to 24 Years Old, by Family Income, Level of Enrollment, Type and Control of School, Attendance Status, Sex, Family Status, Race and Hispanic Origin: October 1996 — Continued

(Numbers in thousands. Civilian noninstitutional population.)

Level and type of school, sex, family status, race, and Hispanic origin	Total	Less than $10,000	$10,000 to $14,999	$15,000 to $19,999	$20,000 to $24,999	$25,000 to $29,999	$30,000 to $34,999	$35,000 to $39,999	$40,000 to $49,999	$50,000 to $74,999	$75,000 and over	Not reported
Two year college (1st to 4th year)	112	19	15	17	10	14	6	7	3	12	—	10
Full-time	87	19	12	9	4	12	6	3	3	12	—	8
Part-time	25	—	3	8	6	2	—	4	—	—	—	2
Four year college (1st to 4th year)	157	12	7	17	6	15	16	15	8	24	26	12
Full-time	136	10	7	11	6	15	16	9	5	22	26	10
Part-time	21	2	—	6	—	—	—	6	2	2	—	3
Fifth year of college or higher	4	—	—	—	—	—	—	—	—	4	—	—
Full-time	4	—	—	—	—	—	—	—	—	4	—	—
Part-time	—	—	—	—	—	—	—	—	—	—	—	—
Public college	222	26	22	34	11	20	12	22	5	28	23	19
Full-time	179	24	19	20	6	18	12	12	5	26	23	14
Part-time	44	2	3	14	6	2	—	10	—	2	—	5
Two year college (1st to 4th year)	106	16	15	17	10	14	6	7	3	9	—	10
Full-time	81	16	12	9	4	12	6	3	3	9	—	8
Part-time	25	—	3	8	6	2	—	4	—	—	—	2
Four year college (1st to 4th year)	116	10	7	17	2	6	7	15	3	19	23	9
Full-time	98	7	7	11	2	6	7	9	3	17	23	6
Part-time	19	2	—	6	—	—	—	6	—	2	—	3
Fifth year of college or higher	—	—	—	—	—	—	—	—	—	—	—	—
Full-time	—	—	—	—	—	—	—	—	—	—	—	—
Part-time	—	—	—	—	—	—	—	—	—	—	—	—
Not enrolled	369	81	35	9	44	44	32	8	38	26	9	42
Not high school graduate	127	45	12	—	19	16	—	—	11	1	—	23
High school graduate	242	36	23	9	25	29	32	8	28	25	9	19
No college	172	28	13	7	20	15	27	3	19	17	9	14
Less than a bachelor's degree	54	8	10	2	5	14	2	2	6	4	—	—
Bachelor's degree or more	16	—	—	—	—	—	3	2	3	4	—	5
Married, Spouse Present												
Male	373	85	67	47	42	20	17	11	23	16	7	38
Enrolled	22	—	—	2	10	2	7	—	—	—	—	—
Below college	5	—	—	—	—	—	3	—	—	—	—	—
College	17	—	—	—	10	2	4	—	—	—	—	—
Full-time	10	—	—	—	10	—	—	—	—	—	—	—
Part-time	7	—	—	—	—	2	4	—	—	—	—	—
Two year college (1st to 4th year)	4	—	—	—	—	—	4	—	—	—	—	—
Full-time	—	—	—	—	—	—	—	—	—	—	—	—
Part-time	4	—	—	—	—	—	4	—	—	—	—	—
Four year college (1st to 4th year)	8	—	—	—	6	2	—	—	—	—	—	—
Full-time	6	—	—	—	6	—	—	—	—	—	—	—
Part-time	2	—	—	—	—	2	—	—	—	—	—	—
Fifth year of college or higher	5	—	—	—	5	—	—	—	—	—	—	—
Full-time	5	—	—	—	5	—	—	—	—	—	—	—
Part-time	—	—	—	—	—	—	—	—	—	—	—	—
Not enrolled	350	85	67	45	32	17	10	11	23	16	7	38
Not high school graduate	151	64	25	12	10	8	3	—	3	—	4	22
High school graduate	199	21	41	33	22	10	7	11	19	16	2	16
No college	158	17	41	26	17	3	7	11	10	6	2	16
Less than a bachelor's degree	37	4	—	7	5	6	—	—	5	10	—	—
Bachelor's degree or more	4	—	—	—	—	—	—	—	4	—	—	—

See footnotes at end of table.

Table A-15. Enrollment Status of Primary Family Members 18 to 24 Years Old, by Family Income, Level of Enrollment, Type and Control of School, Attendance Status, Sex, Family Status, Race and Hispanic Origin: October 1996 — Continued

(Numbers in thousands. Civilian noninstitutional population.)

Level and type of school, sex, family status, race, and Hispanic origin	Total	Family income										
		Less than $10,000	$10,000 to $14,999	$15,000 to $19,999	$20,000 to $24,999	$25,000 to $29,999	$30,000 to $34,999	$35,000 to $39,999	$40,000 to $49,999	$50,000 to $74,999	$75,000 and over	Not reported
Female	504	84	101	66	78	24	34	16	21	24	3	54
Enrolled	52	6	12	—	11	3	9	—	3	—	—	7
Below college	18	4	3	—	3	—	6	—	—	—	—	2
College	33	2	9	—	8	3	3	—	3	—	—	5
Full-time	17	1	5	—	3	—	3	—	—	—	—	5
Part-time	17	1	4	—	5	3	—	—	3	—	—	5
Two year college (1st to 4th year)	9	—	4	—	2	—	3	—	—	—	—	—
Full-time	3	—	—	—	—	—	—	—	—	—	—	—
Part-time	6	—	4	—	2	—	—	—	—	—	—	—
Four year college (1st to 4th year)	21	2	5	—	6	3	—	—	—	—	—	5
Full-time	14	1	5	—	3	—	—	—	—	—	—	5
Part-time	7	1	—	—	3	3	—	—	—	—	—	—
Fifth year of college or higher	3	—	—	—	—	—	—	—	3	—	—	—
Full-time	—	—	—	—	—	—	—	—	—	—	—	—
Part-time	3	—	—	—	—	—	—	—	3	—	—	—
Not enrolled	452	79	89	66	66	21	24	16	18	24	3	46
Not high school graduate	242	55	59	26	43	6	3	9	8	5	—	29
High school graduate	210	24	30	41	23	15	21	7	10	18	3	18
No college	153	22	24	35	19	7	12	—	8	9	—	18
Less than a bachelor's degree	52	2	6	6	4	8	9	5	3	7	3	—
Bachelor's degree or more ...	5	—	—	—	—	—	—	3	—	2	—	—

Other Marital and Family Status

Male	121	20	25	22	3	10	19	1	7	—	—	14
Enrolled	11	3	2	—	—	—	—	—	3	—	—	3
Below college	3	—	—	—	—	—	—	—	—	—	—	3
College	8	3	2	—	—	—	—	—	3	—	—	—
Full-time	8	3	2	—	—	—	—	—	3	—	—	—
Part-time	—	—	—	—	—	—	—	—	—	—	—	—
Two year college (1st to 4th year)	6	3	—	—	—	—	—	—	3	—	—	—
Full-time	6	3	—	—	—	—	—	—	3	—	—	—
Part-time	—	—	—	—	—	—	—	—	—	—	—	—
Four year college (1st to 4th year)	2	—	2	—	—	—	—	—	—	—	—	—
Full-time	2	—	2	—	—	—	—	—	—	—	—	—
Part-time	—	—	—	—	—	—	—	—	—	—	—	—
Fifth year of college or higher	—	—	—	—	—	—	—	—	—	—	—	—
Full-time	—	—	—	—	—	—	—	—	—	—	—	—
Part-time	—	—	—	—	—	—	—	—	—	—	—	—
Not enrolled	110	17	23	22	3	10	19	1	4	—	—	11
Not high school graduate	43	14	14	6	2	1	2	—	—	—	—	4
High school graduate	67	3	9	17	1	9	17	1	4	—	—	7
No college	53	3	5	16	1	9	10	—	2	—	—	7
Less than a bachelor's degree	12	—	3	1	—	—	7	1	—	—	—	—
Bachelor's degree or more ...	2	—	—	—	—	—	—	—	2	—	—	—
Female	218	129	32	23	7	6	2	—	—	5	—	15
Enrolled	37	21	2	9	—	4	—	—	—	2	—	—
Below college	9	9	—	—	—	—	—	—	—	—	—	—
College	28	11	2	9	—	4	—	—	—	2	—	—
Full-time	18	10	—	3	—	4	—	—	—	2	—	—
Part-time	10	1	2	6	—	—	—	—	—	—	—	—

See footnotes at end of table.

Table A-15. Enrollment Status of Primary Family Members 18 to 24 Years Old, by Family Income, Level of Enrollment, Type and Control of School, Attendance Status, Sex, Family Status, Race and Hispanic Origin: October 1996 — Continued

(Numbers in thousands. Civilian noninstitutional population.)

Level and type of school, sex, family status, race, and Hispanic origin	Total	Family income										
		Less than $10,000	$10,000 to $14,999	$15,000 to $19,999	$20,000 to $24,999	$25,000 to $29,999	$30,000 to $34,999	$35,000 to $39,999	$40,000 to $49,999	$50,000 to $74,999	$75,000 and over	Not reported
Two year college (1st to 4th year)	25	11	2	9	—	4	—	—	—	—	—	—
Full-time	16	10	—	3	—	4	—	—	—	—	—	—
Part-time	10	1	2	6	—	—	—	—	—	—	—	—
Four year college (1st to 4th year)	2	—	—	—	—	—	—	—	—	2	—	—
Full-time	2	—	—	—	—	—	—	—	—	2	—	—
Part-time	—	—	—	—	—	—	—	—	—	—	—	—
Fifth year of college or higher	—	—	—	—	—	—	—	—	—	—	—	—
Full-time	—	—	—	—	—	—	—	—	—	—	—	—
Part-time	—	—	—	—	—	—	—	—	—	—	—	—
Not enrolled	181	108	29	15	7	2	2	—	—	2	—	15
Not high school graduate	105	74	13	3	2	—	2	—	—	—	—	10
High school graduate	76	34	17	12	4	2	—	—	—	2	—	4
No college	61	31	17	10	—	—	—	—	—	2	—	2
Less than a bachelor's degree	12	l	—	2	4	2	—	—	—	—	—	2
Bachelor's degree or more ...	2	2	—	—	—	—	—	—	—	—	—	—

Source: October 1996 Current Population Survey, Education and Social Stratification Branch, U.S. Bureau of the Census

1. May be of any race.

— Represents zero or rounds to zero.

Table A-16.   Families by Full Time Enrollment of Dependent Members 18 to 24 Years Old, by Family Income, Race, and Hispanic Origin: October 1996

(Numbers in thousands. Civilian noninstitutional population.)

Number of dependent members, enrollment status, race, and Hispanic origin	Total	Family income										
		Less than $10,000	$10,000 to $14,999	$15,000 to $19,999	$20,000 to $24,999	$25,000 to $29,999	$30,000 to $34,999	$35,000 to $39,999	$40,000 to $49,999	$50,000 to $74,999	$75,000 and over	Not reported
ALL RACES												
All families	71,088	5,904	5,142	4,161	5,182	4,892	4,656	4,569	6,882	12,050	9,834	7,816
No dependents 18 to 24 years old[1]	60,823	5,151	4,573	3,672	4,568	4,223	4,044	3,967	5,896	10,058	7,978	6,694
With dependents 18 to 24 years old[2]	10,265	754	569	489	614	670	611	602	986	1,992	1,855	1,122
None attending college full time	6,022	596	424	362	405	474	396	341	573	1,034	729	689
One or more attending college full time	4,244	158	145	127	210	196	216	262	414	958	1,126	433
One dependent 18 to 24 years old	8,420	651	469	421	531	577	512	500	817	1,560	1,444	938
Not attending college full time	5,219	519	356	323	357	420	347	296	505	881	625	590
Attending college full time	3,201	132	113	98	174	157	165	204	312	679	819	348
Two or more dependents 18 to 24 years old	1,845	103	100	68	83	93	100	102	169	431	411	184
None attending college full time	803	77	68	39	48	54	49	45	67	153	104	99
One attending college full time	535	19	20	23	19	27	32	30	45	143	138	40
Two or more attending college full time	507	7	12	6	17	12	19	28	57	135	169	45
WHITE												
All families	59,611	3,695	3,991	3,352	4,228	4,150	3,949	3,947	6,128	10,755	8,967	6,450
No dependents 18 to 24 years old[1]	51,541	3,308	3,650	3,004	3,770	3,652	3,475	3,464	5,290	9,029	7,285	5,613
With dependents 18 to 24 years old[2]	8,070	387	342	348	458	498	474	482	837	1,726	1,682	836
None attending college full time	4,591	303	254	268	301	355	318	279	490	880	651	492
One or more attending college full time	3,479	84	87	80	157	143	157	203	348	846	1,031	345
One dependent 18 to 24 years old	6,620	340	288	308	401	423	401	401	696	1,361	1,298	704
Not attending college full time	4,001	270	218	244	267	309	280	244	433	751	555	429
Attending college full time	2,619	71	70	63	134	114	121	157	263	609	742	275
Two or more dependents 18 to 24 years old	1,450	47	53	41	57	75	73	82	141	365	384	132
None attending college full time	590	34	36	24	34	45	38	36	56	129	96	63
One attending college full time	426	9	9	17	14	20	21	30	36	117	127	26
Two or more attending college full time	434	4	8	—	9	10	15	16	49	119	161	43
BLACK												
All families	8,646	1,926	930	647	739	558	509	467	540	859	429	1,043
No dependents 18 to 24 years old[1]	7,045	1,599	742	536	623	428	420	374	450	694	354	824
With dependents 18 to 24 years old[2]	1,600	327	188	111	116	130	88	93	91	164	75	219
None attending college full time	1,124	267	136	78	83	95	51	49	49	112	41	162
One or more attending college full time	476	59	51	33	33	34	37	43	42	53	33	57
One dependent 18 to 24 years old	1,321	275	149	91	97	115	72	75	76	129	63	178
Not attending college full time	944	225	109	64	70	89	41	40	44	95	37	130
Attending college full time	377	50	41	27	27	26	31	35	32	34	27	49
Two or more dependents 18 to 24 years old	280	52	38	20	19	15	16	17	15	36	11	40
None attending college full time	180	43	28	14	12	7	10	9	5	16	5	32
One attending college full time	67	10	11	6	2	6	6	—	5	10	2	8
Two or more attending college full time	33	—	—	—	4	2	—	8	5	9	4	—
HISPANIC ORIGIN [3]												
All families	6,929	1,205	1,010	706	690	572	445	366	435	540	354	606
No dependents 18 to 24 years old[1]	5,596	981	862	570	581	450	353	285	345	423	275	471
With dependents 18 to 24 years old[2]	1,333	224	148	135	109	122	92	80	91	117	79	136
None attending college full time	996	194	117	110	89	100	62	51	73	67	34	99
One or more attending college full time	337	31	31	25	20	23	29	29	17	50	45	36
One dependent 18 to 24 years old	1,063	198	123	113	79	95	64	58	75	82	70	105
Not attending college full time	826	172	96	96	68	81	57	42	58	45	34	79
Attending college full time	237	26	27	17	12	14	8	16	17	38	36	27
Two or more dependents 18 to 24 years old	270	26	25	22	30	27	27	22	16	35	9	30
None attending college full time	169	22	20	14	22	19	6	9	15	22	—	21
One attending college full time	71	2	4	8	5	6	13	11	—	7	7	7
Two or more attending college full time	30	2	—	—	4	3	8	2	1	6	2	3

Source: October 1996 Current Population Survey, Education and Social Stratification Branch, U.S. Bureau of the Census

1. Includes families with no member 18 to 24 years old and those in which the only member 18 to 24 years old are the family householder, or other members who are married, spouse present.
2. Excludes families in which the only members 18 to 24 years old are the family householders, or other members who are married, spouse present.
3. May be of any race.

— Represents zero or rounds to zero.

Table A-17. Enrollment Status of Dependent Family Members 18 to 24 Years Old, by Educational Attainment of Family Householder, Level of Enrollment, Attendance Status, Sex, Race, and Hispanic Origin: October 1996

(Numbers in thousands. Civilian noninstitutional population.)

Level and type of school, attendance status, sex, race, and Hispanic origin	Total	Elementary school		High school		College	
		0 to 4 years	5 to 8 years	9 to 11 years	Graduate	Less than a bachelor's degree	Bachelor's degree or more
ALL RACES							
Both sexes	13,908	299	856	1,444	4,524	3,601	3,185
Enrolled	7,479	88	292	466	2,100	2,103	2,430
Below college	1,231	38	93	160	472	287	180
College	6,248	50	199	306	1,627	1,816	2,249
Full time	5,420	32	152	242	1,396	1,546	2,052
Part time	828	18	47	64	232	270	197
Two year college (1st to 4th year)	1,704	20	60	123	522	577	402
Full time	1,282	12	38	85	408	433	308
Part time	422	9	23	38	114	144	94
Four year college (1st to 4th year)	4,284	30	131	176	1,062	1,194	1,691
Full time	3,941	21	109	153	954	1,080	1,624
Part time	343	9	22	23	108	114	67
Fifth year of college or higher	260	—	8	7	43	45	156
Full time	198	—	5	4	34	34	121
Part time	63	—	3	3	10	11	35
Not enrolled	6,429	210	564	977	2,424	1,498	756
Not high school graduate	1,348	109	247	388	362	179	62
High school graduate	5,081	102	316	589	2,062	1,318	693
No college	3,133	73	222	466	1,379	730	262
Less than a bachelor's degree	1,410	21	68	110	532	452	226
Bachelor's degree or more	538	8	26	12	151	136	205
Male	7,639	191	514	761	2,507	1,980	1,687
Enrolled	3,850	45	157	230	1,076	1,125	1,217
Below college	786	17	63	94	314	203	95
College	3,064	28	94	137	762	921	1,122
Full time	2,671	22	70	105	653	789	1,031
Part time	393	6	25	32	108	132	91
Two year college (1st to 4th year)	838	9	31	51	256	278	212
Full time	628	9	17	35	197	209	162
Part time	210	—	15	16	59	69	51
Four year college (1st to 4th year)	2,103	18	62	82	487	609	843
Full time	1,947	13	52	66	446	556	814
Part time	156	6	10	16	41	54	29
Fifth year of college or higher	123	—	1	4	18	34	66
Full time	95	—	1	4	11	24	56
Part time	28	—	—	—	8	9	11
Not enrolled	3,789	146	357	530	1,431	855	470
Not high school graduate	887	86	173	235	242	126	25
High school graduate	2,902	60	183	295	1,189	729	445
No college	1,832	48	135	239	812	426	173
Less than a bachelor's degree	794	9	32	49	309	242	153
Bachelor's degree or more	276	3	17	8	69	61	119
Female	6,269	108	342	683	2,017	1,621	1,499
Enrolled	3,630	43	135	236	1,024	979	1,212
Below college	445	21	30	67	158	84	85
College	3,185	23	105	169	866	895	1,127
Full time	2,750	10	82	137	742	757	1,021
Part time	435	12	23	33	124	137	106
Two year college (1st to 4th year)	866	11	29	72	266	298	190
Full time	653	2	21	49	211	224	146
Part time	213	9	8	22	55	75	44
Four year college (1st to 4th year)	2,181	11	68	94	575	584	848
Full time	1,994	8	57	87	508	524	810
Part time	187	4	12	7	67	61	38
Fifth year of college or higher	137	—	8	3	25	12	89
Full time	103	—	5	—	23	10	65

See footnotes at end of table.

Table A-17.   Enrollment Status of Dependent Family Members 18 to 24 Years Old, by Educational Attainment of Family Householder, Level of Enrollment, Attendance Status, Sex, Race, and Hispanic Origin: October 1996 — Continued

(Numbers in thousands. Civilian noninstitutional population.)

Level and type of school, attendance status, sex, race, and Hispanic origin	Total	Education completed by family householder					
		Elementary school		High school		College	
		0 to 4 years	5 to 8 years	9 to 11 years	Graduate	Less than a bachelor's degree	Bachelor's degree or more
Part time	35	—	3	3	2	2	24
Not enrolled	2,639	64	207	447	993	642	286
Not high school graduate	460	23	74	153	120	53	37
High school graduate	2,179	42	133	294	873	589	249
No college	1,301	24	88	228	568	304	90
Less than a bachelor's degree	616	12	36	62	223	210	73
Bachelor's degree or more	262	5	9	5	82	75	86
WHITE							
Both sexes	10,745	240	681	947	3,453	2,801	2,624
Enrolled	5,945	66	245	275	1,654	1,676	2,029
Below college	887	33	72	73	339	219	152
College	5,058	33	173	203	1,316	1,457	1,877
Full time	4,411	19	130	161	1,124	1,253	1,723
Part time	647	14	42	41	192	203	154
Two year college (1st to 4th year)	1,354	14	57	82	420	466	315
Full time	1,010	10	35	56	327	342	242
Part time	344	5	23	26	93	124	73
Four year college (1st to 4th year)	3,510	19	109	117	866	962	1,438
Full time	3,251	10	92	102	774	889	1,385
Part time	259	9	17	15	92	73	53
Fifth year of college or higher	193	—	6	4	30	29	124
Full time	149	—	3	4	23	23	97
Part time	44	—	3	—	8	6	27
Not enrolled	4,800	174	436	672	1,798	1,125	595
Not high school graduate	958	91	202	263	231	123	47
High school graduate	3,843	83	234	408	1,567	1,002	548
No college	2,304	65	167	318	1,008	539	207
Less than a bachelor's degree	1,105	14	45	80	432	358	177
Bachelor's degree or more	433	5	22	10	128	104	164
Male	5,971	151	431	522	1,939	1,547	1,381
Enrolled	3,092	34	144	143	854	896	1,020
Below college	573	17	55	38	223	153	87
College	2,519	17	89	106	631	744	933
Full time	2,199	11	64	82	540	641	860
Part time	320	6	25	24	91	102	73
Two year college (1st to 4th year)	668	7	28	45	206	216	166
Full time	490	7	14	29	160	157	123
Part time	178	—	15	16	46	59	43
Four year college (1st to 4th year)	1,745	10	60	57	409	499	710
Full time	1,624	4	50	49	371	462	688
Part time	121	6	10	8	38	37	22
Fifth year of college or higher	107	—	1	4	17	28	57
Full time	85	—	1	4	9	22	49
Part time	22	—	—	—	8	6	8
Not enrolled	2,879	116	286	379	1,085	651	361
Not high school graduate	620	70	140	153	161	81	15
High school graduate	2,259	46	146	227	924	570	346
No college	1,393	40	100	175	611	335	133
Less than a bachelor's degree	640	6	30	47	252	184	122
Bachelor's degree or more	225	—	17	5	61	51	91
Female	4,774	89	250	424	1,514	1,253	1,243
Enrolled	2,853	32	101	132	800	779	1,009
Below college	314	15	17	35	116	66	65
College	2,538	16	84	97	684	713	944
Full time	2,212	8	66	80	583	612	863
Part time	327	8	18	17	101	101	81

See footnotes at end of table.

Table A-17. Enrollment Status of Dependent Family Members 18 to 24 Years Old, by Educational Attainment of Family Householder, Level of Enrollment, Attendance Status, Sex, Race, and Hispanic Origin: October 1996 — Continued

(Numbers in thousands. Civilian noninstitutional population.)

Level and type of school, attendance status, sex, race, and Hispanic origin	Total	Elementary school		High school		College	
		0 to 4 years	5 to 8 years	9 to 11 years	Graduate	Less than a bachelor's degree	Bachelor's degree or more
Two year college (1st to 4th year)	686	7	29	37	214	249	149
Full time	520	2	21	27	167	185	119
Part time	166	5	8	10	47	65	31
Four year college (1st to 4th year)	1,765	9	49	60	457	463	728
Full time	1,627	6	42	53	403	427	697
Part time	139	4	7	7	54	36	31
Fifth year of college or higher	87	—	6	—	13	1	67
Full time	65	—	3	—	13	1	48
Part time	22	—	3	—	—	—	19
Not enrolled	1,921	58	149	292	714	474	234
Not high school graduate	338	20	62	111	70	42	32
High school graduate	1,584	37	87	182	643	432	202
No college	911	24	67	144	397	205	75
Less than a bachelor's degree	465	8	15	33	180	174	55
Bachelor's degree or more	200	5	6	5	67	53	73
BLACK							
Both sexes	2,328	11	116	464	876	582	280
Enrolled	1,023	2	21	182	330	304	184
Below college	314	—	—	31	87	122	74
College	729	2	6	97	216	246	163
Full time	623	2	6	74	187	209	146
Part time	106	—	—	23	29	37	17
Two year college (1st to 4th year)	195	—	—	36	64	59	36
Full time	151	—	—	24	50	55	23
Part time	43	—	—	12	14	4	14
Four year college (1st to 4th year)	496	2	6	57	143	171	118
Full time	447	2	6	49	129	143	117
Part time	50	—	—	8	14	28	1
Fifth year of college or higher	39	—	—	3	10	16	9
Full time	25	—	—	—	8	11	6
Part time	13	—	—	3	2	5	3
Not enrolled	1,305	9	95	282	545	278	96
Not high school graduate	324	6	37	108	116	50	7
High school graduate	981	3	58	174	430	228	89
No college	707	1	39	143	330	152	41
Less than a bachelor's degree	225	2	15	28	79	61	41
Bachelor's degree or more	49	—	4	2	21	15	7
Male	1,223	7	56	229	462	317	152
Enrolled	502	—	7	87	163	163	82
Below college	188	—	7	56	76	41	7
College	314	—	—	31	87	122	74
Full time	268	—	—	23	70	105	70
Part time	46	—	—	8	17	17	5
Two year college (1st to 4th year)	96	—	—	6	37	33	20
Full time	78	—	—	6	23	33	16
Part time	18	—	—	—	14	—	4
Four year college (1st to 4th year)	211	—	—	25	48	84	54
Full time	185	—	—	17	45	70	53
Part time	26	—	—	8	4	14	1
Fifth year of college or higher	7	—	—	—	2	5	1
Full time	4	—	—	—	2	2	1
Part time	3	—	—	—	—	3	—
Not enrolled	721	7	48	143	299	155	70
Not high school graduate	225	6	25	77	70	39	7
High school graduate	496	1	23	65	229	115	63
No college	376	1	23	63	178	78	33
Less than a bachelor's degree	101	—	—	—	42	32	26

See footnotes at end of table.

Table A-17. Enrollment Status of Dependent Family Members 18 to 24 Years Old, by Educational Attainment of Family Householder, Level of Enrollment, Attendance Status, Sex, Race, and Hispanic Origin: October 1996 — Continued

(Numbers in thousands. Civilian noninstitutional population.)

Level and type of school, attendance status, sex, race, and Hispanic origin	Total	Education completed by family householder					
		Elementary school		High school		College	
		0 to 4 years	5 to 8 years	9 to 11 years	Graduate	Less than a bachelor's degree	Bachelor's degree or more
Bachelor's degree or more	20	—	—	2	8	5	4
Female	1,105	4	60	234	414	265	128
Enrolled	521	2	13	95	167	141	102
Below college	106	—	7	30	38	18	14
College	415	2	6	66	129	124	88
Full time	356	2	6	51	118	104	76
Part time	60	—	—	15	12	20	12
Two year college (1st to 4th year)	99	—	—	30	27	26	16
Full time	73	—	—	18	27	22	7
Part time	26	—	—	12	—	4	10
Four year college (1st to 4th year)	285	2	6	33	95	86	64
Full time	262	2	6	33	85	73	64
Part time	24	—	—	—	10	14	—
Fifth year of college or higher	31	—	—	3	8	11	8
Full time	21	—	—	—	6	9	5
Part time	10	—	—	3	2	2	3
Not enrolled	584	2	47	139	247	123	26
Not high school graduate	99	—	12	31	46	11	—
High school graduate	485	2	35	108	201	112	26
No college	331	—	16	80	152	74	9
Less than a bachelor's degree	125	2	15	28	36	28	14
Bachelor's degree or more	29	—	4	—	12	10	3

HISPANIC ORIGIN[1]

Both sexes	1,702	216	384	315	424	223	140
Enrolled	718	61	139	104	192	125	97
Below college	228	33	56	31	71	23	14
College	490	28	83	73	121	102	83
Full time	380	14	61	52	108	77	69
Part time	109	14	22	21	13	25	14
Two year college (1st to 4th year)	197	9	40	39	61	22	26
Full time	129	5	27	22	50	12	14
Part time	68	5	14	17	11	10	12
Four year college (1st to 4th year)	282	19	42	34	57	77	54
Full time	241	10	33	30	55	61	51
Part time	42	9	8	4	2	15	2
Fifth year of college or higher	10	—	1	—	3	4	4
Full time	10	—	1	—	3	4	4
Part time	—	—	—	—	—	—	—
Not enrolled	984	155	245	211	232	99	43
Not high school graduate	438	82	134	130	71	18	2
High school graduate	546	73	111	81	160	80	40
No college	381	57	73	64	128	41	20
Less than a bachelor's degree	133	14	33	17	28	31	11
Bachelor's degree or more	31	3	6	—	5	9	9
Male	978	134	252	182	220	128	61
Enrolled	363	32	87	45	85	74	41
Below college	146	17	45	13	43	21	6
College	217	14	41	32	42	54	35
Full time	154	9	27	14	35	42	28
Part time	63	6	15	18	7	12	7
Two year college (1st to 4th year)	85	5	22	19	23	7	10
Full time	43	5	11	5	17	—	6
Part time	43	—	11	14	7	7	4
Four year college (1st to 4th year)	125	10	18	13	16	43	25
Full time	104	4	15	9	16	38	22
Part time	21	6	4	4	—	5	2

See footnotes at end of table.

Table A-17.   Enrollment Status of Dependent Family Members 18 to 24 Years Old, by Educational Attainment of Family Householder, Level of Enrollment, Attendance Status, Sex, Race, and Hispanic Origin: October 1996 — Continued

(Numbers in thousands. Civilian noninstitutional population.)

Level and type of school, attendance status, sex, race, and Hispanic origin	Total	Education completed by family householder					
		Elementary school		High school		College	
		0 to 4 years	5 to 8 years	9 to 11 years	Graduate	Less than a bachelor's degree	Bachelor's degree or more
Fifth year of college or higher	7	—	1	—	3	4	—
Full time	7	—	1	—	3	4	—
Part time	—	—	—	—	—	—	—
Not enrolled	615	103	165	138	135	54	21
Not high school graduate	311	63	89	89	61	10	—
High school graduate	303	40	76	48	74	44	21
No college	209	35	46	37	56	26	9
Less than a bachelor's degree	80	6	25	11	15	17	6
Bachelor's degree or more	15	—	6	—	3	—	6
Female	724	81	132	133	204	96	78
Enrolled	355	29	52	59	107	51	56
Below college	82	15	11	18	28	2	8
College	273	14	42	41	79	48	48
Full time	227	6	34	38	73	35	41
Part time	46	8	8	3	7	13	7
Two year college (1st to 4th year)	112	5	18	20	38	14	16
Full time	87	—	15	17	34	12	8
Part time	25	5	3	3	4	2	7
Four year college (1st to 4th year)	157	9	23	21	41	34	29
Full time	136	6	19	21	39	23	29
Part time	21	4	4	—	2	11	—
Fifth year of college or higher	4	—	—	—	—	—	4
Full time	4	—	—	—	—	—	4
Part time	—	—	—	—	—	—	—
Not enrolled	369	52	80	74	97	45	22
Not high school graduate	127	19	45	41	11	8	2
High school graduate	242	33	34	33	86	37	20
No college	172	22	27	27	71	14	12
Less than a bachelor's degree	54	8	8	6	13	14	5
Bachelor's degree or more	16	3	—	—	2	9	3

Source: October 1996 Current Population Survey, Education and Social Stratification Branch, U.S. Bureau of the Census

1. May be of any race.

— Represents zero or rounds to zero.

Table A-18.   College Enrollment This Year for High School Graduates 15 Years Old and Over, by Enrollment Status This Year, Attendance Status, Years of School Completed, Age, Sex, Race and Hispanic Origin: October 1996

(Numbers in thousands. Civilian noninstitutional population.)

Highest grade completed, age, sex, race, and Hispanic origin	Total	Not enrolled in 1996			Enrolled in college in 1996				
					Total		Enrolled full time in 1996		
		Total	Not enrolled in 1995	Enrolled in 1995	Total	Not enrolled in 1995	Enrolled in 1995	Total	Not enrolled in 1995
ALL RACES									
Both Sexes									
15 years old and over	159,548	144,450	138,469	5,981	15,098	3,212	11,886	9,761	1,302
High school graduate only	65,485	63,039	61,635	1,404	2,446	758	1,688	1,706	380
Some college, no degree	38,264	29,905	28,231	1,673	8,359	1,268	7,091	6,149	604
Associate degree	13,420	12,194	11,520	674	1,226	305	921	571	75
Bachelor's degree	29,034	26,724	25,185	1,539	2,310	697	1,613	1,076	213
Master's degree	9,016	8,405	7,884	520	611	135	477	211	21
Professional or doctorate degree	4,329	4,184	4,014	170	145	50	96	48	8
Enrolled in 2 year college (1st to 4th year)	4,174	—	—	—	4,174	1,303	2,872	2,209	498
Enrolled in 4 year college (1st to 4th year)	8,130	—	—	—	8,130	1,125	7,006	6,325	596
15 to 19 years old	5,477	1,994	1,020	974	3,483	332	3,151	3,101	248
High school graduate only	3,170	1,768	955	813	1,403	215	1,188	1,230	157
Some college, no degree	2,296	222	61	161	2,074	112	1,961	1,867	89
Bachelor's degree	11	4	3	1	7	5	2	4	—
Enrolled in 2 year college (1st to 4th year)	1,223	—	—	—	1,223	136	1,087	995	92
Enrolled in 4 year college (1st to 4th year)	2,303	—	—	—	2,303	207	2,096	2,136	165
20 to 24 years old	14,907	9,467	7,798	1,669	5,440	850	4,591	4,433	539
High school graduate only	5,352	4,889	4,677	212	463	192	271	298	116
Some college, no degree	7,456	3,094	2,320	774	4,362	543	3,819	3,659	353
Bachelor's degree	2,098	1,483	800	683	615	115	501	477	70
Enrolled in 2 year college (1st to 4th year)	1,184	—	—	—	1,184	401	783	728	225
Enrolled in 4 year college (1st to 4th year)	3,689	—	—	—	3,689	352	3,337	3,247	248
25 years old and over	139,164	132,990	129,652	3,338	6,174	2,030	4,144	2,227	515
High school graduate only	56,962	56,382	56,003	379	580	351	229	179	107
Some college, no degree	41,932	38,782	37,369	1,413	3,150	918	2,232	1,194	238
Bachelor's degree	40,270	37,825	36,280	1,545	2,445	761	1,684	854	170
Enrolled in 2 year college (1st to 4th year)	1,768	—	—	—	1,768	766	1,002	486	181
Enrolled in 4 year college (1st to 4th year)	2,268	—	—	—	2,268	616	1,651	1,019	209
Male									
15 years old and over	76,365	69,591	66,956	2,635	6,773	1,271	5,503	4,654	582
High school graduate only	30,231	29,155	28,429	726	1,075	315	760	796	182
Some college, no degree	18,154	14,324	13,582	742	3,830	501	3,329	2,908	264
Associate degree	5,730	5,202	4,982	220	528	129	399	281	42
Bachelor's degree	14,603	13,611	12,978	633	992	260	732	521	78
Master's degree	4,588	4,311	4,095	216	277	49	228	116	10
Professional or doctorate degree	3,059	2,987	2,889	98	72	17	55	33	6
Enrolled in 2 year college (1st to 4th year)	1,752	—	—	—	1,752	502	1,250	974	211
Enrolled in 4 year college (1st to 4th year)	3,781	—	—	—	3,781	473	3,308	3,058	292
15 to 19 years old	2,577	1,013	488	524	1,564	173	1,392	1,413	133
High school graduate only	1,536	912	467	445	624	114	510	567	89
Some college, no degree	1,034	96	18	78	938	56	882	844	42
Bachelor's degree	7	4	3	1	3	3	—	3	3
Enrolled in 2 year college (1st to 4th year)	560	—	—	—	560	63	496	450	45
Enrolled in 4 year college (1st to 4th year)	1,017	—	—	—	1,017	110	907	968	89
20 to 24 years old	7,357	4,663	3,839	825	2,693	353	2,340	2,242	248
High school graduate only	2,741	2,497	2,370	127	244	79	165	166	56
Some college, no degree	3,691	1,508	1,122	387	2,183	238	1,944	1,859	167
Bachelor's degree	925	659	347	311	266	35	231	217	25

See footnotes at end of table.

Table A-18. College Enrollment This Year for High School Graduates 15 Years Old and Over, by Enrollment Status This Year, Attendance Status, Years of School Completed, Age, Sex, Race and Hispanic Origin: October 1996 — Continued

(Numbers in thousands. Civilian noninstitutional population.)

Highest grade completed, age, sex, race, and Hispanic origin	Total	Not enrolled in 1996			Enrolled in college in 1996				
					Total			Enrolled full time in 1996	
		Total	Not enrolled in 1995	Enrolled in 1995	Total	Not enrolled in 1995	Enrolled in 1995	Total	Not enrolled in 1995
Enrolled in 2 year college (1st to 4th year)	532	—	—	—	532	144	388	341	83
Enrolled in 4 year college (1st to 4th year)	1,906	—	—	—	1,906	179	1,727	1,685	139
25 years old and over	66,431	63,915	62,629	1,286	2,516	745	1,771	999	201
High school graduate only	25,953	25,747	25,593	154	207	121	86	64	37
Some college, no degree	19,158	17,921	17,424	497	1,237	335	901	486	97
Bachelor's degree	21,319	20,247	19,612	635	1,072	288	784	449	66
Enrolled in 2 year college (1st to 4th year)	659	—	—	—	659	294	365	184	83
Enrolled in 4 year college (1st to 4th year)	905	—	—	—	905	200	705	432	71
Female									
15 years old and over	83,183	74,859	71,513	3,346	8,324	1,941	6,383	5,107	720
High school graduate only	35,254	33,884	33,206	678	1,371	443	928	910	198
Some college, no degree	20,110	15,581	14,649	932	4,529	767	3,763	3,241	340
Associate degree	7,690	6,992	6,538	454	698	176	522	290	34
Bachelor's degree	14,430	13,113	12,206	906	1,318	437	881	555	135
Master's degree	4,428	4,093	3,789	304	335	86	249	95	11
Professional or doctorate degree	1,270	1,197	1,125	72	73	32	41	15	3
Enrolled in 2 year college (1st to 4th year)	2,423	—	—	—	2,423	801	1,622	1,235	286
Enrolled in 4 year college (1st to 4th year)	4,349	—	—	—	4,349	652	3,698	3,267	304
15 to 19 years old	2,900	981	531	450	1,919	159	1,759	1,688	115
High school graduate only	1,634	856	488	367	778	100	678	663	68
Some college, no degree	1,262	126	43	83	1,136	56	1,080	1,023	47
Bachelor's degree	4	—	—	4	—	3	2	2	—
Enrolled in 2 year college (1st to 4th year)	663	—	—	—	663	72	590	546	47
Enrolled in 4 year college (1st to 4th year)	1,286	—	—	—	1,286	96	1,190	1,168	77
20 to 24 years old	7,550	4,803	3,959	844	2,747	497	2,250	2,191	291
High school graduate only	2,612	2,393	2,307	85	219	113	106	132	60
Some college, no degree	3,765	1,586	1,199	387	2,179	305	1,875	1,800	186
Bachelor's degree	1,173	824	453	372	349	79	270	259	46
Enrolled in 2 year college (1st to 4th year)	652	—	—	—	652	257	395	387	142
Enrolled in 4 year college (1st to 4th year)	1,783	—	—	—	1,783	173	1,610	1,562	109
25 years old and over	72,733	69,075	67,023	2,051	3,658	1,285	2,373	1,228	314
High school graduate only	31,009	30,636	30,410	226	373	230	143	115	70
Some college, no degree	22,773	20,861	19,945	916	1,913	582	1,331	708	141
Bachelor's degree	18,951	17,578	16,668	910	1,373	473	900	405	103
Enrolled in 2 year college (1st to 4th year)	1,108	—	—	—	1,108	472	637	302	98
Enrolled in 4 year college (1st to 4th year)	1,362	—	—	—	1,362	416	946	587	137
WHITE									
Both Sexes									
15 years old and over	135,511	123,402	118,462	4,941	12,109	2,540	9,569	7,805	1,000
High school graduate only	55,219	53,286	52,220	1,066	1,932	589	1,343	1,368	301
Some college, no degree	31,920	25,211	23,832	1,379	6,710	997	5,712	4,955	470
Associate degree	11,646	10,619	10,048	571	1,026	242	784	498	60
Bachelor's degree	25,153	23,283	21,937	1,346	1,869	567	1,302	822	154
Master's degree	7,758	7,298	6,861	437	460	104	357	131	10
Professional or doctorate degree	3,815	3,705	3,564	141	111	41	70	32	5
Enrolled in 2 year college (1st to 4th year)	3,295	—	—	—	3,295	1,014	2,281	1,743	391
Enrolled in 4 year college (1st to 4th year)	6,565	—	—	—	6,565	877	5,688	5,142	456

See footnotes at end of table.

Table A-18. College Enrollment This Year for High School Graduates 15 Years Old and Over, by Enrollment Status This Year, Attendance Status, Years of School Completed, Age, Sex, Race and Hispanic Origin: October 1996 — Continued

(Numbers in thousands. Civilian noninstitutional population.)

Highest grade completed, age, sex, race, and Hispanic origin	Total	Not enrolled in 1996			Enrolled in college in 1996				
		Total	Not enrolled in 1995	Enrolled in 1995	Total		Enrolled full time in 1996		
					Total	Not enrolled in 1995	Enrolled in 1995	Total	Not enrolled in 1995
15 to 19 years old	4,377	1,523	784	739	2,855	272	2,583	2,551	204
High school graduate only	2,484	1,342	733	609	1,142	167	975	1,009	124
Some college, no degree	1,882	176	48	129	1,706	100	1,606	1,538	77
Bachelor's degree	11	4	3	1	7	5	2	4	32
Enrolled in 2 year college (1st to 4th year)	1,011	—	—	—	1,011	116	895	814	78
Enrolled in 4 year college (1st to 4th year)	1,871	—	—	—	1,871	164	1,707	1,753	133
20 to 24 years old	12,006	7,623	6,234	1,389	4,384	664	3,719	3,571	405
High school graduate only	4,155	3,807	3,642	165	348	158	190	213	89
Some college, no degree	6,102	2,536	1,901	635	3,566	438	3,128	2,996	280
Bachelor's degree	1,749	1,280	691	589	470	69	401	363	36
Enrolled in 2 year college (1st to 4th year)	911	—	—	—	911	321	590	537	163
Enrolled in 4 year college (1st to 4th year)	3,030	—	—	—	3,030	280	2,749	2,678	200
25 years old and over	119,127	114,257	111,444	2,813	4,870	1,603	3,267	1,683	391
High school graduate only	48,579	48,137	47,846	292	442	264	178	147	88
Some college, no degree	35,582	33,117	31,931	1,187	2,465	702	1,762	918	172
Bachelor's degree	34,966	33,002	31,667	1,335	1,964	637	1,327	618	130
Enrolled in 2 year college (1st to 4th year)	1,374	—	—	—	1,374	578	796	392	150
Enrolled in 4 year college (1st to 4th year)	1,744	—	—	—	1,744	467	1,278	754	138
Male									
15 years old and over	65,474	60,053	57,834	2,220	5,420	1,018	4,403	3,706	472
High school graduate only	25,583	24,737	24,155	582	846	242	604	636	145
Some college, no degree	15,276	12,195	11,565	630	3,081	418	2,663	2,347	238
Associate degree	5,034	4,577	4,390	187	457	111	347	252	35
Bachelor's degree	12,799	12,019	11,469	550	780	196	585	377	52
Master's degree	4,012	3,807	3,622	185	205	37	168	73	—
Professional or doctorate degree	2,769	2,719	2,633	86	51	14	36	21	2
Enrolled in 2 year college (1st to 4th year)	1,373	—	—	—	1,373	395	978	767	178
Enrolled in 4 year college (1st to 4th year)	3,086	—	—	—	3,086	398	2,688	2,500	252
15 to 19 years old	2,084	807	378	430	1,277	145	1,131	1,150	112
High school graduate only	1,234	724	359	365	510	91	419	462	71
Some college, no degree	843	79	16	64	764	52	712	685	39
Bachelor's degree	7	4	3	1	3	3	—	3	3
Enrolled in 2 year college (1st to 4th year)	459	—	—	—	459	57	403	359	40
Enrolled in 4 year college (1st to 4th year)	824	—	—	—	824	90	734	789	73
20 to 24 years old	5,998	3,807	3,123	684	2,191	306	1,884	1,821	215
High school graduate only	2,199	2,011	1,906	105	188	65	123	121	43
Some college, no degree	3,034	1,236	914	322	1,798	217	1,581	1,534	158
Bachelor's degree	765	560	304	256	205	24	180	166	14
Enrolled in 2 year college (1st to 4th year)	426	—	—	—	426	124	302	265	68
Enrolled in 4 year college (1st to 4th year)	6,008	3,815	3,110	705	2,193	358	1,835	1,750	190
25 years old and over	57,392	55,439	54,333	1,106	1,953	566	1,387	735	145
High school graduate only	22,150	22,002	21,891	111	148	87	62	52	31
Some college, no degree	16,433	15,457	15,026	431	976	259	717	381	76
Bachelor's degree	18,809	17,980	17,416	564	829	220	609	302	38
Enrolled in 2 year college (1st to 4th year)	488	—	—	—	488	214	274	143	71
Enrolled in 4 year college (1st to 4th year)	724	—	—	—	724	157	567	334	48

See footnotes at end of table.

Table A-18. College Enrollment This Year for High School Graduates 15 Years Old and Over, by Enrollment Status This Year, Attendance Status, Years of School Completed, Age, Sex, Race and Hispanic Origin: October 1996 — Continued

(Numbers in thousands. Civilian noninstitutional population.)

Highest grade completed, age, sex, race, and Hispanic origin	Total	Not enrolled in 1996			Enrolled in college in 1996				
		Total	Not enrolled in 1995	Enrolled in 1995	Total		Enrolled full time in 1996		
					Total	Not enrolled in 1995	Enrolled in 1995	Total	Not enrolled in 1995
Female									
15 years old and over	70,037	63,349	60,628	2,721	6,688	1,522	5,166	4,099	528
High school graduate only	29,635	28,549	28,065	484	1,086	347	739	733	156
Some college, no degree	16,644	13,016	12,267	749	3,629	579	3,049	2,607	233
Associate degree	6,612	6,043	5,658	385	569	132	438	245	25
Bachelor's degree	12,353	11,264	10,468	796	1,089	371	718	444	102
Master's degree	3,746	3,491	3,239	252	255	66	189	59	9
Professional or doctorate degree	1,046	986	931	55	60	26	34	11	3
Enrolled in 2 year college (1st to 4th year)	1,922	—	—	—	1,922	619	1,303	977	213
Enrolled in 4 year college (1st to 4th year)	3,480	—	—	—	3,480	479	3,000	2,642	204
15 to 19 years old	2,293	715	406	309	1,578	126	1,452	1,402	92
High school graduate only	1,251	618	374	244	633	76	556	547	50
Some college, no degree	1,039	97	32	65	941	47	894	853	38
Bachelor's degree	4	—	—	—	4	3	2	2	—
Enrolled in 2 year college (1st to 4th year)	552	—	—	—	552	59	492	455	39
Enrolled in 4 year college (1st to 4th year)	1,047	—	—	—	1,047	74	973	964	60
20 to 24 years old	6,008	3,815	3,110	705	2,193	358	1,835	1,750	190
High school graduate only	1,956	1,796	1,736	60	160	93	67	91	46
Some college, no degree	3,068	1,300	988	313	1,768	220	1,547	1,462	122
Bachelor's degree	984	720	387	333	265	44	221	196	22
Enrolled in 2 year college (1st to 4th year)	485	—	—	—	485	197	289	272	95
Enrolled in 4 year college (1st to 4th year)	1,459	—	—	—	1,459	115	1,344	1,289	67
25 years old and over	61,736	58,818	57,111	1,707	2,917	1,037	1,880	947	246
High school graduate only	26,429	26,135	25,955	181	294	177	116	94	57
Some college, no degree	19,149	17,661	16,905	755	1,489	443	1,046	537	97
Bachelor's degree	16,157	15,022	14,251	771	1,135	417	718	316	93
Enrolled in 2 year college (1st to 4th year)	885	—	—	—	885	363	522	250	79
Enrolled in 4 year college (1st to 4th year)	1,020	—	—	—	1,020	310	711	420	00
BLACK									
Both Sexes									
15 years old and over	17,048	15,179	14,428	752	1,869	499	1,369	1,159	212
High school graduate only	8,104	7,752	7,478	274	353	128	224	219	60
Some college, no degree	4,793	3,715	3,477	239	1,078	231	847	749	111
Associate degree	1,230	1,098	1,032	66	132	47	84	37	8
Bachelor's degree	2,056	1,834	1,721	113	221	75	146	119	30
Master's degree	687	614	557	57	73	14	59	27	3
Professional or doctorate degree	178	166	163	3	12	4	8	8	—
Enrolled in 2 year college (1st to 4th year)	580	—	—	—	580	228	353	289	88
Enrolled in 4 year college (1st to 4th year)	1,013	—	—	—	1,013	196	817	731	99
15 to 19 years old	774	395	202	193	379	52	327	327	37
High school graduate only	535	360	192	167	176	42	134	144	27
Some college, no degree	239	35	10	25	204	11	193	183	11
Bachelor's degree	—	35	10	25	204	11	193	183	11
Enrolled in 2 year college (1st to 4th year)	119	—	—	—	119	18	101	96	13
Enrolled in 4 year college (1st to 4th year)	266	—	—	—	266	34	231	235	24
20 to 24 years old	2,011	1,382	1,199	183	629	137	492	516	104
High school graduate only	976	900	861	39	77	28	49	58	25

See footnotes at end of table.

Table A-18.   College Enrollment This Year for High School Graduates 15 Years Old and Over, by Enrollment Status This Year, Attendance Status, Years of School Completed, Age, Sex, Race and Hispanic Origin: October 1996 — Continued

(Numbers in thousands. Civilian noninstitutional population.)

Highest grade completed, age, sex, race, and Hispanic origin	Total	Not enrolled in 1996			Enrolled in college in 1996				
		Total	Not enrolled in 1995	Enrolled in 1995	Total		Enrolled full time in 1996		
					Total	Not enrolled in 1995	Enrolled in 1995	Total	Not enrolled in 1995
Some college, no degree	892	398	290	108	494	84	411	413	59
Bachelor's degree	143	85	48	36	58	26	32	45	20
Enrolled in 2 year college (1st to 4th year)	165	—	—	—	165	60	104	122	50
Enrolled in 4 year college (1st to 4th year)	414	—	—	—	414	59	355	352	42
25 years old and over	14,263	13,402	13,027	376	860	310	551	316	71
High school graduate only	6,592	6,492	6,425	67	100	59	41	18	8
Some college, no degree	4,892	4,380	4,209	172	512	184	328	189	49
Bachelor's degree	2,778	2,530	2,393	137	249	67	182	110	13
Enrolled in 2 year college (1st to 4th year)	297	—	—	—	297	149	147	71	25
Enrolled in 4 year college (1st to 4th year)	365	—	—	—	365	112	252	164	37
Male									
15 years old and over	7,504	6,749	6,477	272	755	165	589	515	60
High school graduate only	3,712	3,563	3,457	106	149	46	103	101	25
Some college, no degree	2,075	1,642	1,552	90	433	72	361	315	21
Associate degree	437	405	384	21	32	8	24	11	1
Bachelor's degree	940	839	797	41	102	36	65	64	10
Master's degree	256	226	212	14	31	3	28	16	3
Professional or doctorate degree	83	75	75	—	8	—	8	8	—
Enrolled in 2 year college (1st to 4th year)	229	—	—	—	229	80	148	119	28
Enrolled in 4 year college (1st to 4th year)	396	—	—	—	396	49	347	311	18
15 to 19 years old	328	171	95	76	157	22	135	141	17
High school graduate only	236	159	94	65	77	19	58	68	14
Some college, no degree	92	12	1	11	80	3	78	73	3
Bachelor's degree	—	—	—	—	—	—	—	—	—
Enrolled in 2 year college (1st to 4th year)	46	—	—	—	46	6	41	40	6
Enrolled in 4 year college (1st to 4th year)	116	—	—	—	116	16	100	106	11
20 to 24 years old	891	615	532	83	276	34	243	234	24
High school graduate only	439	403	390	13	36	12	24	28	11
Some college, no degree	401	182	129	52	220	17	203	188	8
Bachelor's degree	51	30	13	17	21	5	16	18	5
Enrolled in 2 year college (1st to 4th year)	66	—	—	—	66	19	47	50	14
Enrolled in 4 year college (1st to 4th year)	187	—	—	—	187	8	178	163	4
25 years old and over	6,284	5,964	5,850	114	321	110	211	140	20
High school graduate only	3,037	3,001	2,974	28	36	15	21	5	—
Some college, no degree	2,018	1,853	1,805	48	166	61	105	64	12
Bachelor's degree	1,229	1,110	1,071	38	119	34	85	70	8
Enrolled in 2 year college (1st to 4th year)	117	—	—	—	117	55	61	30	8
Enrolled in 4 year college (1st to 4th year)	103	—	—	—	103	24	79	52	3
Female									
15 years old and over	9,544	8,430	7,951	479	1,114	334	780	644	152
High school graduate only	4,392	4,189	4,020	168	204	83	121	118	35
Some college, no degree	2,718	2,074	1,925	149	644	159	485	434	90
Associate degree	793	693	648	45	100	39	61	27	7
Bachelor's degree	1,115	995	924	72	120	39	81	55	20
Master's degree	431	388	345	43	43	11	32	11	—
Professional or doctorate degree	95	91	88	3	4	4	—	—	—
Enrolled in 2 year college (1st to 4th year)	351	—	—	—	351	147	204	169	60
Enrolled in 4 year college (1st to 4th year)	617	—	—	—	617	147	470	420	81

See footnotes at end of table.

Table A-18. College Enrollment This Year for High School Graduates 15 Years Old and Over, by Enrollment Status This Year, Attendance Status, Years of School Completed, Age, Sex, Race and Hispanic Origin: October 1996 — Continued

(Numbers in thousands. Civilian noninstitutional population.)

Highest grade completed, age, sex, race, and Hispanic origin	Total	Not enrolled in 1996			Enrolled in college in 1996				
		Total	Not enrolled in 1995	Enrolled in 1995	Total			Enrolled full time in 1996	
					Total	Not enrolled in 1995	Enrolled in 1995	Total	Not enrolled in 1995
15 to 19 years old	446	224	107	117	222	30	191	186	21
High school graduate only	299	201	98	103	98	22	76	76	13
Some college, no degree	146	23	9	14	124	8	115	110	8
Bachelor's degree	—	—	—	—	—	—	—	—	—
Enrolled in 2 year college (1st to 4th year)	73	—	—	—	73	12	60	56	7
Enrolled in 4 year college (1st to 4th year)	150	—	—	—	150	18	131	129	14
20 to 24 years old	1,120	767	667	100	353	104	249	282	80
High school graduate only	538	497	471	26	41	16	25	30	14
Some college, no degree	491	216	161	55	275	67	208	225	51
Bachelor's degree	91	54	35	19	37	21	16	27	15
Enrolled in 2 year college (1st to 4th year)	99	—	—	—	99	41	58	72	36
Enrolled in 4 year college (1st to 4th year)	228	—	—	—	228	50	177	189	38
25 years old and over	7,979	7,439	7,177	262	540	200	340	177	51
High school graduate only	3,555	3,491	3,451	40	64	44	20	12	8
Some college, no degree	2,874	2,528	2,404	124	346	123	223	125	38
Bachelor's degree	1,550	1,420	1,322	98	129	32	97	39	5
Enrolled in 2 year college (1st to 4th year)	180	—	—	—	180	94	86	42	16
Enrolled in 4 year college (1st to 4th year)	262	—	—	—	262	88	173	112	34
HISPANIC ORIGIN [1]									
Both Sexes									
15 years old and over	10,333	9,146	8,765	381	1,187	260	927	689	100
High school graduate only	5,152	4,922	4,793	129	230	99	132	133	48
Some college, no degree	2,675	2,020	1,905	115	654	99	556	429	41
Associate degree	804	682	660	22	122	31	91	61	10
Bachelor's degree	1,229	1,093	1,008	85	136	25	111	55	—
Master's degree	290	261	241	20	29	—	29	9	—
Professional or doctorate degree	183	167	158	9	15	6	9	2	—
Enrolled in 2 year college (1st to 4th year)	444	—	—	—	444	141	303	224	60
Enrolled in 4 year college (1st to 4th year)	605	—	—	—	605	116	490	413	57
15 to 19 years old	489	241	153	87	248	40	209	190	28
High school graduate only	324	217	139	78	107	21	86	92	21
Some college, no degree	161	21	11	10	141	18	123	98	6
Bachelor's degree	3	3	3	—	—	—	—	—	—
Enrolled in 2 year college (1st to 4th year)	121	—	—	—	121	23	98	86	20
Enrolled in 4 year college (1st to 4th year)	141	—	—	—	141	26	116	115	17
20 to 24 years old	1,533	1,078	965	112	456	84	372	328	45
High school graduate only	789	737	714	24	51	27	24	24	17
Some college, no degree	642	275	223	53	366	54	313	274	28
Bachelor's degree	103	65	29	36	38	3	35	31	—
Enrolled in 2 year college (1st to 4th year)	177	—	—	—	177	56	121	92	21
Enrolled in 4 year college (1st to 4th year)	248	—	—	—	248	32	216	203	26
25 years old and over	8,310	7,828	7,646	181	483	137	346	171	27
High school graduate only	4,039	3,968	3,940	28	72	50	21	18	10
Some college, no degree	2,675	2,406	2,332	75	269	58	211	118	17
Bachelor's degree	1,596	1,454	1,375	79	142	28	114	36	—
Enrolled in 2 year college (1st to 4th year)	146	—	—	—	146	62	84	46	19
Enrolled in 4 year college (1st to 4th year)	252	—	—	—	252	84	168	115	31

See footnotes at end of table.

Table A-18.   College Enrollment This Year for High School Graduates 15 Years Old and Over, by Enrollment Status This Year, Attendance Status, Years of School Completed, Age, Sex, Race and Hispanic Origin: October 1996 — Continued

(Numbers in thousands. Civilian noninstitutional population.)

Highest grade completed, age, sex, race, and Hispanic origin	Total	Not enrolled in 1996			Enrolled in college in 1996				
		Total	Not enrolled in 1995	Enrolled in 1995	Total		Enrolled full time in 1996		
					Total	Not enrolled in 1995	Enrolled in 1995	Total	Not enrolled in 1995
Male									
15 years old and over	5,228	4,707	4,533	174	521	107	414	300	33
High school graduate only	2,632	2,547	2,488	59	84	37	47	37	10
Some college, no degree	1,341	1,032	982	50	309	49	260	189	19
Associate degree	378	318	306	12	60	17	42	32	5
Bachelor's degree	600	548	513	34	52	1	51	38	—
Master's degree	154	140	130	9	14	—	14	5	—
Professional or doctorate degree	124	122	113	9	2	2	—	—	—
Enrolled in 2 year college (1st to 4th year)	195	—	—	—	195	64	131	82	15
Enrolled in 4 year college (1st to 4th year)	263	—	—	—	263	48	214	176	22
15 to 19 years old	220	118	72	46	102	21	82	72	12
High school graduate only	137	110	67	43	27	6	21	25	6
Some college, no degree	80	4	1	3	76	15	61	47	6
Bachelor's degree	3	3	3	—	—	—	—	—	—
Enrolled in 2 year college (1st to 4th year)	44	—	—	—	44	9	34	27	6
Enrolled in 4 year college (1st to 4th year)	62	—	—	—	62	15	47	48	9
20 to 24 years old	779	579	528	51	200	28	172	143	12
High school graduate only	426	405	393	12	21	6	15	8	2
Some college, no degree	299	144	118	27	154	22	133	111	10
Bachelor's degree	54	30	17	12	24	—	24	24	—
Enrolled in 2 year college (1st to 4th year)	76	—	—	—	76	19	57	34	1
Enrolled in 4 year college (1st to 4th year)	98	—	—	—	98	11	87	82	11
25 years old and over	4,229	4,011	3,934	77	219	58	160	85	9
High school graduate only	2,069	2,032	2,029	4	36	25	11	4	2
Some college, no degree	1,340	1,202	1,169	33	138	30	108	62	7
Bachelor's degree	821	777	736	41	44	3	41	19	—
Enrolled in 2 year college (1st to 4th year)	75	—	—	—	75	36	39	21	8
Enrolled in 4 year college (1st to 4th year)	111	—	—	—	111	31	80	49	4
Female									
15 years old and over	5,105	4,438	4,232	207	666	153	513	389	66
High school graduate only	2,521	2,374	2,304	70	146	62	84	96	39
Some college, no degree	1,334	988	924	65	346	50	296	240	22
Associate degree	426	364	354	10	62	14	49	30	6
Bachelor's degree	630	545	495	51	84	24	60	17	—
Master's degree	136	122	111	11	14	—	14	4	—
Professional or doctorate degree	59	45	45	—	13	4	9	2	—
Enrolled in 2 year college (1st to 4th year)	249	—	—	—	249	77	172	142	46
Enrolled in 4 year college (1st to 4th year)	343	—	—	—	343	67	275	238	35
15 to 19 years old	269	123	82	41	146	19	127	118	16
High school graduate only	187	107	72	35	81	16	65	67	16
Some college, no degree	81	16	9	7	65	3	62	51	—
Bachelor's degree	—	—	—	—	—	—	—	—	—
Enrolled in 2 year college (1st to 4th year)	78	—	—	—	78	14	63	59	14
Enrolled in 4 year college (1st to 4th year)	79	—	—	—	79	11	68	67	8
20 to 24 years old	755	499	438	61	256	56	201	185	32
High school graduate only	363	332	321	11	30	21	9	15	15
Some college, no degree	343	131	105	26	212	32	180	163	18
Bachelor's degree	49	35	12	24	14	3	11	7	

See footnotes at end of table.

Table A-18.   College Enrollment This Year for High School Graduates 15 Years Old and Over, by Enrollment Status This Year, Attendance Status, Years of School Completed, Age, Sex, Race and Hispanic Origin: October 1996 — Continued

(Numbers in thousands. Civilian noninstitutional population.)

Highest grade completed, age, sex, race, and Hispanic origin	Total	Not enrolled in 1996			Enrolled in college in 1996				
		Total	Not enrolled in 1995	Enrolled in 1995	Total		Enrolled full time in 1996		
					Total	Not enrolled in 1995	Enrolled in 1995	Total	Not enrolled in 1995
Enrolled in 2 year college (1st to 4th year)	101	—	—	—	101	37	64	58	20
Enrolled in 4 year college (1st to 4th year)	150	—	—	—	150	21	129	121	14
25 years old and over	4,081	3,817	3,712	105	264	79	185	86	18
High school graduate only	1,970	1,935	1,911	24	35	25	10	14	8
Some college, no degree	1,336	1,205	1,163	42	131	28	103	56	10
Bachelor's degree	775	677	639	38	98	25	73	17	—
Enrolled in 2 year college (1st to 4th year)	70	—	—	—	70	26	45	25	11
Enrolled in 4 year college (1st to 4th year)	141	—	—	—	141	53	88	66	27

Source: October 1996 Current Population Survey, Education and Social Stratification Branch, U.S. Bureau of the Census

1. May bo of any raoo.

— Represents zero or rounds to zero.

Table A-19.   Families with Children 5 to 17 Years Old by Enrollment Status in Kindergarten to High School, by Control of School, Family Income, Metropolitan Status, Region, Type of Family Race and Hispanic Origin: October 1996

(Numbers in thousands. Civilian noninstitutional population.)

Family income, metropolitan status, region, family type, race, and Hispanic origin	All families	Families with at least one child 5 to 17 years old												
		Total	Families with at least one child enrolled in											
			Kindergarten to high school			Kindergarten			Elementary			High school		
			Total	Public	Private	Total	Public	Private	Total	Public	Private	Total	Public	Private
ALL RACES														
All family types														
All families	71,088	30,073	29,213	26,386	3,528	3,686	3,118	568	21,566	19,274	2,521	11,344	10,457	948
Family income:														
Less than $10,000	5,904	3,014	2,909	2,795	145	455	433	22	2,294	2,189	115	916	895	21
$10,000 to $14,999	5,142	2,127	2,074	2,007	96	284	275	9	1,609	1,557	65	696	672	27
$15,000 to $19,999	4,161	1,704	1,650	1,548	128	241	224	17	1,211	1,130	91	568	540	35
$20,000 to $24,999	5,182	2,100	2,014	1,912	145	279	252	27	1,529	1,444	105	735	695	40
$25,000 to $29,999	4,892	1,987	1,931	1,802	160	245	222	23	1,439	1,325	131	682	650	32
$30,000 to $34,999	4,656	1,994	1,952	1,773	212	234	202	32	1,395	1,253	154	748	704	44
$35,000 to $39,999	4,569	1,945	1,884	1,709	215	247	210	37	1,437	1,296	158	671	627	47
$40,000 to $49,999	6,882	3,018	2,944	2,687	324	338	287	51	2,209	1,976	255	1,157	1,101	64
$50,000 to $74,999	12,050	5,335	5,211	4,528	823	659	481	178	3,708	3,183	560	2,181	1,999	199
$75,000 and over	9,834	4,197	4,105	3,341	953	436	306	130	2,924	2,327	644	1,860	1,524	356
Not reported	7,816	2,653	2,539	2,284	328	268	226	42	1,810	1,595	243	1,128	1,051	82
Metropolitan status:														
Total metropolitan	56,477	24,016	23,350	20,854	3,108	2,987	2,472	515	17,239	15,234	2,196	9,012	8,211	850
Metropolitan areas of 1 million or more	37,304	16,075	15,627	13,899	2,188	2,022	1,668	353	11,590	10,190	1,539	5,963	5,382	619
Central city	12,569	5,654	5,479	4,762	878	674	544	130	4,179	3,572	667	2,045	1,808	252
Outside central city	24,735	10,421	10,148	9,137	1,310	1,348	1,124	224	7,411	6,618	872	3,919	3,574	367
Metropolitan areas of less than 1 million	19,173	7,941	7,723	6,955	920	965	804	161	5,649	5,044	657	3,049	2,830	231
Central city	7,309	3,046	2,956	2,609	393	374	305	69	2,154	1,894	272	1,125	1,032	98
Outside central city	11,863	4,895	4,767	4,347	526	591	499	93	3,495	3,150	385	1,924	1,798	133
Nonmetropolitan	14,612	6,057	5,863	5,532	420	699	646	53	4,327	4,040	325	2,332	2,245	98
Region:														
Northeast	13,666	5,635	5,472	4,797	869	609	479	130	4,054	3,543	589	2,139	1,875	285
Midwest	16,742	6,991	6,806	6,073	890	876	717	159	5,070	4,449	652	2,759	2,533	232
South	25,631	10,835	10,493	9,619	1,088	1,329	1,149	180	7,678	6,981	769	3,929	3,686	263
West	15,049	6,612	6,442	5,897	681	872	774	99	4,764	4,300	511	2,517	2,362	170
Married-couple families														
All families	55,049	21,529	20,956	18,652	2,876	2,720	2,225	495	15,590	13,710	2,058	8,293	7,554	790
Family income:														
Less than $10,000	2,250	787	765	730	53	125	113	12	590	553	44	275	266	9
$10,000 to $14,999	2,966	958	927	903	37	139	130	9	723	708	20	302	294	10
$15,000 to $19,999	2,781	910	883	826	71	159	148	12	681	632	52	270	256	17
$20,000 to $24,999	3,790	1,304	1,252	1,185	98	195	177	18	987	929	74	435	406	29
$25,000 to $29,999	3,649	1,315	1,286	1,192	110	182	161	21	989	904	91	448	424	24
$30,000 to $34,999	3,624	1,484	1,447	1,332	132	202	175	27	1,056	971	90	534	504	29
$35,000 to $39,999	3,821	1,597	1,551	1,415	173	202	169	33	1,204	1,096	123	569	527	45
$40,000 to $49,999	5,852	2,538	2,477	2,241	294	301	256	45	1,900	1,685	234	944	891	59
$50,000 to $74,999	10,915	4,793	4,699	4,071	762	609	443	167	3,368	2,884	519	1,978	1,812	183
$75,000 and over	9,314	4,008	3,919	3,193	904	416	298	118	2,805	2,236	616	1,771	1,448	341
Not reported	6,086	1,835	1,750	1,563	242	190	155	34	1,287	1,112	196	768	727	44
Metropolitan status:														
Total metropolitan	43,267	17,017	16,581	14,566	2,516	2,182	1,735	447	12,363	10,738	1,775	6,511	5,848	707
Metropolitan areas of 1 million or more	28,323	11,333	11,044	9,674	1,734	1,467	1,164	303	8,280	7,177	1,208	4,199	3,725	508
Central city	8,305	3,327	3,236	2,688	658	414	309	105	2,469	1,996	514	1,185	1,012	186
Outside central city	20,018	8,006	7,808	6,986	1,076	1,052	855	198	5,812	5,181	694	3,015	2,712	322

See footnotes at end of table.

Table A-19. Families with Children 5 to 17 Years Old by Enrollment Status in Kindergarten to High School, by Control of School, Family Income, Metropolitan Status, Region, Type of Family Race and Hispanic Origin: October 1996 — Continued

(Numbers in thousands. Civilian noninstitutional population.)

Family income, metropolitan status, region, family type, race, and Hispanic origin	All families	Families with at least one child 5 to 17 years old												
		Total	Families with at least one child enrolled in											
			Kindergarten to high school			Kindergarten			Elementary			High school		
			Total	Public	Private	Total	Public	Private	Total	Public	Private	Total	Public	Private
Metropolitan areas of less than 1 million	14,944	5,684	5,537	4,892	782	715	571	144	4,083	3,561	567	2,312	2,124	199
Central city	5,168	1,867	1,809	1,534	316	241	181	60	1,327	1,116	222	756	682	79
Outside central city	9,776	3,817	3,728	3,357	467	474	390	84	2,756	2,445	345	1,556	1,441	120
Nonmetropolitan	11,782	4,513	4,375	4,086	360	538	489	49	3,227	2,972	283	1,782	1,706	83
Region:														
Northeast	10,426	4,000	3,893	3,364	673	478	371	107	2,902	2,506	460	1,509	1,296	227
Midwest	13,407	5,288	5,148	4,520	756	677	532	145	3,827	3,296	548	2,161	1,957	209
South	19,509	7,398	7,176	6,478	876	908	747	161	5,252	4,692	623	2,788	2,596	208
West	11,707	4,844	4,738	4,290	570	657	575	82	3,608	3,216	427	1,835	1,705	146
Other families, female householder														
All families	12,196	6,850	6,637	6,224	519	783	731	52	4,907	4,585	360	2,400	2,273	138
Family income:														
Less than $10,000	3,207	2,037	1,967	1,890	90	312	302	10	1,570	1,505	69	571	559	13
$10,000 to $14,999	1,754	1,027	1,005	968	50	128	128	—	780	748	36	354	337	17
$15,000 to $19,999	1,082	680	658	620	50	59	54	5	459	434	32	270	256	18
$20,000 to $24,999	1,111	645	621	592	41	67	58	9	447	425	25	247	236	11
$25,000 to $29,999	891	536	513	487	30	50	48	2	365	344	28	182	174	8
$30,000 to $34,999	750	358	354	298	69	22	18	5	259	204	60	137	128	9
$35,000 to $39,999	506	237	232	202	30	27	22	5	177	153	24	70	68	2
$40,000 to $49,999	633	297	289	268	29	23	17	6	186	168	20	137	134	5
$50,000 to $74,999	692	313	295	263	35	26	25	2	199	174	25	108	96	12
$75,000 and over	296	109	106	86	25	12	8	4	65	51	14	50	40	11
Not reported	1,274	613	597	552	60	56	52	4	400	379	27	275	245	32
Metropolitan status:														
Total metropolitan	10,043	5,673	5,498	5,113	479	654	606	47	4,050	3,750	337	1,970	1,851	125
Metropolitan areas of 1 million or more	6,840	3,867	3,745	3,459	368	451	420	31	2,791	2,559	264	1,388	1,291	101
Central city	3,419	2,023	1,960	1,817	188	219	202	18	1,516	1,406	127	749	690	62
Outside central city	3,421	1,844	1,785	1,641	180	231	218	13	1,275	1,153	137	639	602	39
Metropolitan areas of less than 1 million	3,203	1,806	1,753	1,654	111	203	187	16	1,259	1,191	73	582	560	24
Central city	1,699	982	952	892	63	118	111	7	681	639	42	298	284	14
Outside central city	1,505	824	801	762	48	84	76	9	578	552	31	284	276	10
Nonmetropolitan	2,153	1,177	1,139	1,111	40	129	124	5	857	835	23	430	422	13
Region:														
Northeast	2,505	1,339	1,294	1,172	168	109	93	16	981	881	115	502	457	51
Midwest	2,493	1,317	1,284	1,190	116	162	148	15	983	903	89	433	413	20
South	4,778	2,822	2,734	2,605	159	343	329	14	2,032	1,937	104	942	900	46
West	2,420	1,372	1,325	1,257	75	168	161	7	911	865	52	523	502	20
WHITE														
All family types														
All families	59,611	23,868	23,175	20,729	3,034	2,972	2,477	495	17,016	15,052	2,141	8,986	8,180	856
Family income:														
Less than $10,000	3,695	1,746	1,679	1,603	100	262	244	18	1,328	1,254	80	500	485	15
$10,000 to $14,999	3,991	1,538	1,493	1,440	74	217	208	9	1,142	1,098	51	488	469	19
$15,000 to $19,999	3,352	1,225	1,182	1,111	89	180	169	11	838	787	58	397	371	30
$20,000 to $24,999	4,228	1,560	1,498	1,417	109	204	190	14	1,144	1,077	80	523	490	34
$25,000 to $29,999	4,150	1,567	1,523	1,415	134	215	192	23	1,139	1,043	108	536	507	29
$30,000 to $34,999	3,949	1,606	1,569	1,410	173	212	184	28	1,116	1,004	120	558	518	40

See footnotes at end of table.

Table A-19. Families with Children 5 to 17 Years Old by Enrollment Status in Kindergarten to High School, by Control of School, Family Income, Metropolitan Status, Region, Type of Family Race and Hispanic Origin: October 1996 — Continued

(Numbers in thousands. Civilian noninstitutional population.)

Family income, metropolitan status, region, family type, race, and Hispanic origin	All families	Families with at least one child 5 to 17 years old												
		Families with at least one child enrolled in												
		Total	Kindergarten to high school			Kindergarten			Elementary			High school		
			Total	Public	Private	Total	Public	Private	Total	Public	Private	Total	Public	Private
$35,000 to $39,999	3,947	1,653	1,605	1,438	207	205	172	33	1,210	1,073	154	584	541	45
$40,000 to $49,999	6,128	2,617	2,548	2,315	299	303	254	49	1,941	1,730	232	992	939	61
$50,000 to $74,999	10,755	4,646	4,538	3,925	735	596	440	156	3,226	2,759	493	1,887	1,711	189
$75,000 and over	8,967	3,772	3,690	2,998	862	400	278	123	2,603	2,076	569	1,703	1,388	335
Not reported	6,450	1,938	1,850	1,657	254	177	145	32	1,328	1,151	196	819	761	60
Metropolitan status:														
Total metropolitan	46,505	18,673	18,142	16,015	2,626	2,375	1,929	446	13,318	11,637	1,821	6,974	6,251	761
Metropolitan areas of 1 million or more	30,056	12,116	11,762	10,338	1,785	1,557	1,264	294	8,662	7,536	1,219	4,461	3,939	547
Central city	8,253	3,312	3,198	2,656	646	415	317	97	2,393	1,956	474	1,180	978	207
Outside central city	21,803	8,803	8,564	7,682	1,140	1,143	946	197	6,269	5,580	745	3,281	2,961	340
Metropolitan areas of less than 1 million	16,449	6,557	6,379	5,677	841	817	665	152	4,655	4,101	601	2,513	2,312	213
Central city	5,669	2,238	2,183	1,872	349	276	214	62	1,582	1,351	241	865	781	90
Outside central city	10,780	4,319	4,196	3,806	491	541	451	90	3,073	2,750	360	1,648	1,531	124
Nonmetropolitan	13,106	5,196	5,034	4,714	408	597	548	49	3,699	3,415	320	2,013	1,929	95
Region:														
Northeast	11,633	4,518	4,384	3,811	718	503	386	117	3,203	2,791	471	1,709	1,479	245
Midwest	14,852	6,004	5,838	5,185	797	740	597	142	4,323	3,760	590	2,392	2,184	211
South	20,276	7,862	7,615	6,876	924	977	834	143	5,511	4,919	648	2,853	2,634	239
West	12,851	5,484	5,338	4,858	596	752	659	93	3,979	3,583	432	2,032	1,884	161
Married-couple families														
All families	48,889	18,548	18,061	15,997	2,570	2,433	1,991	442	13,386	11,716	1,824	7,054	6,365	728
Family income:														
Less than $10,000	1,800	637	621	586	51	105	93	12	489	452	42	204	195	9
$10,000 to $14,999	2,549	787	764	745	26	126	117	9	582	570	15	246	241	5
$15,000 to $19,999	2,410	727	701	659	51	126	120	5	530	494	39	202	188	14
$20,000 to $24,999	3,329	1,089	1,053	997	80	179	167	12	830	781	61	342	318	25
$25,000 to $29,999	3,248	1,110	1,082	999	99	169	148	21	836	761	80	372	348	24
$30,000 to $34,999	3,157	1,225	1,193	1,086	119	188	165	23	877	801	81	398	373	25
$35,000 to $39,999	3,387	1,386	1,353	1,223	166	177	147	30	1,039	935	119	496	456	43
$40,000 to $49,999	5,318	2,256	2,199	1,983	274	277	232	45	1,700	1,504	216	828	777	56
$50,000 to $74,999	9,835	4,227	4,141	3,577	682	552	405	147	2,960	2,528	458	1,732	1,573	172
$75,000 and over	8,532	3,614	3,535	2,878	815	386	275	111	2,504	2,003	542	1,623	1,322	319
Not reported	5,323	1,491	1,420	1,264	205	148	121	26	1,040	887	171	611	576	35
Metropolitan status:														
Total metropolitan	37,826	14,437	14,067	12,284	2,218	1,938	1,541	397	10,453	9,035	1,544	5,423	4,809	646
Metropolitan areas of 1 million or more	24,296	9,362	9,123	7,947	1,482	1,276	1,017	259	6,820	5,887	1,013	3,406	2,973	455
Central city	6,150	2,309	2,249	1,808	522	318	235	84	1,705	1,336	401	779	629	154
Outside central city	18,146	7,053	6,874	6,139	959	957	783	175	5,115	4,551	612	2,628	2,343	301
Metropolitan areas of less than 1 million	13,530	5,075	4,943	4,337	737	663	524	139	3,633	3,148	531	2,016	1,836	191
Central city	4,413	1,573	1,528	1,272	293	210	155	55	1,107	912	205	636	564	77
Outside central city	9,117	3,502	3,415	3,065	443	453	369	84	2,527	2,235	326	1,380	1,272	114
Nonmetropolitan	11,063	4,112	3,994	3,713	352	494	450	45	2,933	2,681	280	1,631	1,556	82
Region:														
Northeast	9,355	3,471	3,374	2,897	596	425	320	105	2,487	2,143	398	1,302	1,108	201
Midwest	12,437	4,835	4,708	4,129	702	632	499	134	3,493	3,000	511	1,972	1,778	196
South	16,846	6,099	5,926	5,315	768	782	656	126	4,322	3,826	549	2,243	2,068	192
West	10,251	4,143	4,052	3,655	504	593	517	76	3,084	2,747	366	1,537	1,410	139

See footnotes at end of table.

Table A-19. Families with Children 5 to 17 Years Old by Enrollment Status in Kindergarten to High School, by Control of School, Family Income, Metropolitan Status, Region, Type of Family Race and Hispanic Origin: October 1996 — Continued

(Numbers in thousands. Civilian noninstitutional population.)

Family income, metropolitan status, region, family type, race, and Hispanic origin	All families	Total	Kindergarten to high school			Kindergarten			Elementary			High school		
			Total	Public	Private	Total	Public	Private	Total	Public	Private	Total	Public	Private
Other families, female householder														
All families	7,829	4,074	3,937	3,646	354	406	372	34	2,869	2,650	234	1,441	1,341	110
Family income:														
Less than $10,000	1,609	991	951	912	46	142	136	6	756	723	35	261	254	6
$10,000 to $14,999	1,159	670	648	619	38	78	78	—	504	477	27	216	203	14
$15,000 to $19,999	737	422	408	380	38	37	32	5	265	249	19	171	159	16
$20,000 to $24,999	696	364	348	328	23	18	16	2	252	238	14	143	134	9
$25,000 to $29,999	623	351	341	323	24	36	33	2	240	226	17	123	118	5
$30,000 to $34,999	561	255	251	208	45	20	15	5	176	143	36	91	81	9
$35,000 to $39,999	371	180	176	147	29	18	15	3	129	105	24	60	59	2
$40,000 to $49,999	509	281	277	260	36	16	12	4	208	181	31	143	139	4
$50,000 to $74,999	561	235	225	196	33	23	21	2	153	130	23	81	68	12
$75,000 and over	241	92	89	70	23	7	2	4	55	43	12	42	33	11
Not reported	799	307	300	280	30	16	14	2	202	193	10	157	138	21
Metropolitan status:														
Total metropolitan	6,321	3,276	3,167	2,903	315	334	305	30	2,283	2,084	211	1,159	1,068	97
Metropolitan areas of 1 million or more	4,188	2,134	2,052	1,865	231	216	198	18	1,473	1,332	151	786	708	83
Central city	1,584	829	792	712	98	71	64	6	576	525	53	345	297	49
Outside central city	2,605	1,305	1,259	1,153	133	145	134	11	897	808	98	442	411	33
Metropolitan areas of less than 1 million	2,133	1,142	1,115	1,038	84	119	107	12	810	752	60	373	360	14
Central city	964	543	535	488	48	58	52	6	388	353	35	177	170	8
Outside central city	1,168	599	580	550	36	61	54	6	422	399	25	195	190	7
Nonmetropolitan	1,508	799	770	743	39	72	67	5	587	566	22	282	273	13
Region:														
Northeast	1,709	829	801	722	103	62	55	6	596	535	65	306	275	38
Midwest	1,695	832	807	740	80	74	65	9	608	547	65	274	260	15
South	2,532	1,363	1,319	1,227	112	144	132	12	964	901	66	476	441	39
West	1,893	1,051	1,010	957	58	127	119	7	701	667	37	384	366	18
BLACK														
All family types														
All families	8,646	4,803	4,668	4,391	360	547	497	50	3,548	3,301	282	1,788	1,731	67
Family income:														
Less than $10,000	1,926	1,133	1,104	1,073	37	178	174	4	872	842	31	357	355	2
$10,000 to $14,999	930	475	469	455	18	57	57	—	377	368	12	162	156	5
$15,000 to $19,999	647	398	386	365	27	37	35	2	315	293	25	143	141	5
$20,000 to $24,999	739	420	399	385	29	61	52	9	303	294	19	150	144	6
$25,000 to $29,999	558	328	316	298	23	18	18	—	232	217	19	110	107	3
$30,000 to $34,999	509	281	277	260	36	16	12	4	208	181	31	143	139	4
$35,000 to $39,999	467	228	218	211	6	34	29	4	174	171	2	72	70	2
$40,000 to $49,999	540	292	292	275	17	25	22	3	204	186	17	115	115	—
$50,000 to $74,999	859	482	468	416	61	42	27	15	326	281	46	205	199	9
$75,000 and over	429	202	195	156	51	11	8	3	148	111	43	78	64	14
Not reported	1,043	564	543	497	54	69	63	6	388	356	37	251	240	14
Metropolitan status:														
Total metropolitan	7,490	4,139	4,027	3,750	360	473	423	50	3,062	2,815	282	1,540	1,482	67
Metropolitan areas of 1 million or more	5,343	3,019	2,942	2,709	311	355	312	43	2,258	2,040	252	1,120	1,076	54
Central city	3,424	1,936	1,883	1,740	190	217	192	25	1,479	1,343	156	684	654	37

See footnotes at end of table.

Table A-19. Families with Children 5 to 17 Years Old by Enrollment Status in Kindergarten to High School, by Control of School, Family Income, Metropolitan Status, Region, Type of Family Race and Hispanic Origin: October 1996 — Continued

(Numbers in thousands. Civilian noninstitutional population.)

Family income, metropolitan status, region, family type, race, and Hispanic origin	All families	Families with at least one child 5 to 17 years old												
		Families with at least one child enrolled in												
		Total	Kindergarten to high school			Kindergarten			Elementary			High school		
			Total	Public	Private	Total	Public	Private	Total	Public	Private	Total	Public	Private
Outside central city	1,919	1,083	1,059	969	121	139	120	18	779	697	96	436	422	17
Metropolitan areas of less than 1 million	2,147	1,120	1,085	1,041	49	118	111	7	804	775	31	419	407	13
Central city	1,332	665	635	608	30	79	74	5	474	457	19	196	189	6
Outside central city	815	455	450	433	19	39	37	2	329	318	11	224	218	6
Nonmetropolitan	1,156	664	641	641	—	74	74	—	486	486	—	248	248	—
Region:														
Northeast	1,568	905	877	794	125	85	74	11	703	623	96	351	325	33
Midwest	1,541	816	806	749	70	107	97	11	626	579	51	297	284	16
South	4,809	2,690	2,603	2,489	136	311	283	28	1,961	1,867	107	968	952	17
West	728	392	381	359	28	44	44	—	258	232	28	172	171	1
Married-couple families														
All families	3,995	1,906	1,846	1,695	191	160	130	30	1,412	1,276	150	810	776	43
Family income:														
Less than $10,000	314	97	97	97	2	16	16	—	63	63	2	44	44	—
$10,000 to $14,999	287	106	101	95	6	5	5	—	86	83	3	36	33	3
$15,000 to $19,999	245	118	116	108	11	14	12	2	102	94	8	48	48	2
$20,000 to $24,999	296	130	117	112	11	6	4	2	100	97	7	49	45	4
$25,000 to $29,999	282	144	144	136	8	6	6	—	103	95	8	52	52	—
$30,000 to $34,999	311	176	172	168	10	9	4	4	124	118	6	103	99	4
$35,000 to $39,999	306	160	149	144	5	20	17	3	122	120	2	60	58	2
$40,000 to $49,999	361	182	182	170	13	14	14	—	139	126	13	71	71	—
$50,000 to $74,999	687	377	372	326	52	37	24	13	265	226	39	166	161	9
$75,000 and over	373	188	181	142	51	6	4	3	137	100	43	73	59	14
Not reported	532	226	214	197	23	28	24	4	170	153	19	107	107	4
Metropolitan status:														
Total metropolitan	3,496	1,626	1,580	1,429	191	137	107	30	1,212	1,076	150	696	663	43
Metropolitan areas of 1 million or more	2,504	1,208	1,174	1,041	171	109	82	28	900	780	134	492	461	40
Central city	1,453	692	670	592	98	59	45	14	521	447	80	266	248	25
Outside central city	1,051	516	504	450	73	50	37	14	380	333	54	226	213	15
Metropolitan areas of less than 1 million	992	418	406	388	20	28	25	3	312	296	16	205	202	3
Central city	523	189	180	169	11	14	11	3	143	135	8	75	75	—
Outside central city	470	228	227	219	10	14	14	—	168	160	8	130	127	3
Nonmetropolitan	499	280	266	266	—	23	23	—	200	200	—	114	114	—
Region:														
Northeast	698	357	346	308	58	34	34	—	287	250	45	148	133	21
Midwest	712	328	326	295	36	24	19	5	248	219	28	139	132	10
South	2,235	1,073	1,032	962	82	88	63	25	772	717	62	461	451	10
West	349	147	141	130	15	14	14	—	105	90	15	62	61	1
Other families, female householder														
All families	3,916	2,526	2,455	2,342	151	346	328	18	1,872	1,775	117	850	827	24
Family income:														
Less than $10,000	1,476	973	944	913	35	160	156	4	765	735	29	279	277	2
$10,000 to $14,999	534	318	318	310	12	48	47	—	246	240	9	117	114	3
$15,000 to $19,999	324	248	241	231	13	17	17	—	190	180	13	96	93	3
$20,000 to $24,999	374	252	245	235	18	44	37	7	176	169	11	90	88	2
$25,000 to $29,999	220	160	148	139	14	10	10	—	113	106	11	49	46	3
$30,000 to $34,999	157	79	79	66	24	3	3	—	67	46	24	33	33	—
$35,000 to $39,999	124	52	52	50	2	9	7	2	43	43	—	7	7	—

See footnotes at end of table.

Table A-19. Families with Children 5 to 17 Years Old by Enrollment Status in Kindergarten to High School, by Control of School, Family Income, Metropolitan Status, Region, Type of Family Race and Hispanic Origin: October 1996 — Continued

(Numbers in thousands. Civilian noninstitutional population.)

Family income, metropolitan status, region, family type, race, and Hispanic origin	All families	Total	Kindergarten to high school Total	Public	Private	Kindergarten Total	Public	Private	Elementary Total	Public	Private	High school Total	Public	Private
$40,000 to $49,999	133	81	81	77	5	11	8	3	45	40	5	36	36	—
$50,000 to $74,999	112	66	58	56	2	3	3	—	37	35	2	24	24	—
$75,000 and over	37	8	8	8	—	4	4	—	6	6	—	4	4	—
Not reported	427	288	281	257	26	38	36	2	184	174	13	116	105	11
Metropolitan status:														
Total metropolitan	3,372	2,203	2,140	2,027	151	296	278	18	1,636	1,538	117	730	706	24
Metropolitan areas of 1 million or more	2,405	1,599	1,560	1,467	129	216	202	13	1,231	1,142	109	541	527	14
Central city	1,718	1,133	1,106	1,044	88	144	132	11	891	832	72	375	363	12
Outside central city	687	466	454	423	41	72	70	2	340	309	37	165	164	2
Metropolitan areas of less than 1 million	968	604	580	559	22	80	76	4	405	397	8	190	180	10
Central city	688	411	391	379	13	59	57	2	278	273	5	107	101	6
Outside central city	280	193	109	100	9	21	19	2	127	124	3	82	79	3
Nonmetropolitan	544	323	316	316	—	50	50	—	236	236	—	120	120	—
Region:														
Northeast	747	485	467	427	61	45	36	9	374	335	48	181	170	11
Midwest	726	448	441	415	34	82	76	6	345	327	22	143	138	6
South	2,156	1,410	1,367	1,332	45	196	194	3	1,028	999	35	446	440	7
West	287	183	181	169	11	23	23	—	125	114	11	80	80	—

HISPANIC ORIGIN[1]

All family types

All families	6,945	3,725	3,586	3,378	281	484	441	43	2,730	2,552	207	1,366	1,287	81
Family income:														
Less than $10,000	1,200	660	633	625	15	63	63	—	501	491	15	213	210	3
$10,000 to $14,999	1,023	587	572	555	26	97	91	6	435	426	13	206	193	13
$15,000 to $19,999	720	391	372	354	26	59	54	5	258	243	15	147	135	13
$20,000 to $24,999	713	405	379	377	11	58	58	—	295	293	7	145	141	4
$25,000 to $29,999	562	311	303	289	28	48	46	2	236	214	27	95	92	4
$30,000 to $34,999	460	240	235	210	28	31	28	3	180	162	21	90	86	4
$35,000 to $39,999	377	199	196	181	20	33	30	3	158	138	20	70	68	2
$40,000 to $49,999	404	224	216	203	18	28	26	3	179	171	13	88	83	5
$50,000 to $74,999	528	267	260	237	29	20	16	4	181	165	16	127	120	10
$75,000 and over	362	177	177	128	52	24	11	13	120	87	35	73	54	19
Not reported	597	266	243	219	29	22	17	5	186	162	25	111	106	4
Metropolitan status:														
Total metropolitan	6,306	3,364	3,234	3,041	261	424	384	40	2,454	2,286	193	1,232	1,154	78
Metropolitan areas of 1 million or more	4,743	2,469	2,372	2,217	206	312	281	31	1,806	1,671	153	879	815	64
Central city	2,461	1,337	1,290	1,189	139	159	137	22	956	871	101	503	449	54
Outside central city	2,282	1,132	1,082	1,028	67	153	144	9	850	800	53	376	366	10
Metropolitan areas of less than 1 million	1,562	895	863	824	55	112	103	9	648	616	40	353	339	14
Central city	897	509	496	469	34	69	66	3	366	343	26	202	190	11
Outside central city	666	386	366	355	21	43	37	6	282	273	13	151	149	2
Nonmetropolitan	640	361	352	337	20	59	56	3	277	266	13	134	133	3
Region:														
Northeast	1,134	570	548	498	72	68	51	17	411	381	42	216	184	34
Midwest	487	255	249	227	30	38	38	—	198	172	26	106	92	14
South	2,401	1,171	1,141	1,072	80	154	134	20	871	818	58	414	402	12
West	2,924	1,729	1,649	1,580	99	224	218	6	1,250	1,181	81	631	609	22

See footnotes at end of table.

Table A-19. Families with Children 5 to 17 Years Old by Enrollment Status in Kindergarten to High School, by Control of School, Family Income, Metropolitan Status, Region, Type of Family Race and Hispanic Origin: October 1996 — Continued

(Numbers in thousands. Civilian noninstitutional population.)

Family income, metropolitan status, region, family type, race, and Hispanic origin	All families	Families with at least one child 5 to 17 years old												
		Total	Families with at least one child enrolled in											
			Kindergarten to high school			Kindergarten			Elementary			High school		
			Total	Public	Private	Total	Public	Private	Total	Public	Private	Total	Public	Private
Married-couple families														
All families	4,852	2,594	2,504	2,347	217	354	324	31	1,958	1,819	163	948	882	68
Family income:														
Less than $10,000	503	234	227	227	3	21	21	—	189	189	3	74	70	3
$10,000 to $14,999	681	388	378	369	16	66	60	6	295	291	8	129	124	5
$15,000 to $19,999	495	265	249	236	19	48	46	3	186	172	13	84	74	10
$20,000 to $24,999	539	313	295	292	11	50	50	—	237	235	7	116	111	4
$25,000 to $29,999	431	241	235	229	18	38	36	2	193	180	17	71	67	4
$30,000 to $34,999	339	187	183	163	21	29	26	3	136	123	14	73	69	4
$35,000 to $39,999	329	171	167	152	20	23	20	3	141	121	20	61	59	2
$40,000 to $49,999	326	206	201	190	15	23	23	—	164	158	10	83	78	5
$50,000 to $74,999	480	249	244	221	29	20	16	4	171	154	16	123	115	10
$75,000 and over	333	163	163	124	42	17	11	5	113	83	34	73	54	19
Not reported	396	179	163	145	23	20	15	5	133	112	21	63	60	2
Metropolitan status:														
Total metropolitan	4,349	2,312	2,230	2,087	198	306	278	28	1,747	1,618	150	841	776	65
Metropolitan areas of 1 million or more	3,251	1,690	1,639	1,522	154	228	210	18	1,287	1,182	119	588	533	54
Central city	1,531	843	825	746	108	110	93	16	625	560	80	305	261	44
Outside central city	1,720	848	814	776	47	119	117	2	662	622	39	282	273	10
Metropolitan areas of less than 1 million	1,097	621	591	564	44	77	68	9	461	437	32	254	243	11
Central city	612	326	314	298	23	42	39	3	240	225	18	137	128	8
Outside central city	485	295	278	266	21	35	29	6	220	211	13	117	115	2
Nonmetropolitan	503	283	274	260	19	48	45	3	211	201	12	106	106	3
Region:														
Northeast	623	292	277	246	47	40	28	12	214	197	26	102	79	25
Midwest	345	186	185	165	26	29	29	—	149	126	23	78	64	14
South	1,766	849	822	770	58	115	100	15	632	595	41	316	304	12
West	2,117	1,267	1,221	1,166	86	170	166	4	963	901	73	453	434	18
Other families, female householder														
All families	1,546	921	889	853	50	102	97	5	656	623	38	341	328	13
Family income:														
Less than $10,000	617	400	383	375	12	43	43	—	299	290	12	124	124	—
$10,000 to $14,999	271	173	169	164	8	24	24	—	123	120	3	72	65	8
$15,000 to $19,999	144	94	92	87	7	6	4	2	54	52	2	47	44	3
$20,000 to $24,999	121	66	64	64	—	7	7	—	46	46	—	21	21	—
$25,000 to $29,999	76	52	52	48	6	9	9	—	31	25	6	21	21	—
$30,000 to $34,999	83	34	34	29	7	2	2	—	32	27	7	9	9	—
$35,000 to $39,999	25	16	16	16	—	4	4	—	10	10	—	8	8	—
$40,000 to $49,999	33	6	6	3	3	4	1	3	6	3	3	2	2	—
$50,000 to $74,999	36	13	11	11	—	—	—	—	8	8	—	3	3	—
$75,000 and over	12	4	4	2	2	—	—	—	4	2	2	—	—	—
Not reported	127	63	60	54	6	3	3	—	44	40	4	34	32	2
Metropolitan status:														
Total metropolitan	1,443	855	825	789	49	90	86	5	604	571	37	318	305	13
Metropolitan areas of 1 million or more	1,084	626	595	570	38	58	53	5	446	421	29	231	221	10
Central city	692	403	386	370	25	33	31	3	287	271	18	164	154	10
Outside central city	392	223	209	200	13	24	22	2	159	150	11	67	67	—

See footnotes at end of table.

Table A-19.   Families with Children 5 to 17 Years Old by Enrollment Status in Kindergarten to High School, by Control of School, Family Income, Metropolitan Status, Region, Type of Family Race and Hispanic Origin: October 1996 — Continued

(Numbers in thousands. Civilian noninstitutional population.)

Family income, metropolitan status, region, family type, race, and Hispanic origin	All families	Families with at least one child 5 to 17 years old												
		Total	Families with at least one child enrolled in											
			Kindergarten to high school			Kindergarten			Elementary			High school		
			Total	Public	Private	Total	Public	Private	Total	Public	Private	Total	Public	Private
Metropolitan areas of less than 1 million	359	230	230	219	11	33	33	—	158	150	8	86	83	3
Central city	232	150	150	139	11	25	25	—	102	94	8	57	54	3
Outside central city	127	80	80	80	—	8	8	—	56	56	—	30	30	—
Nonmetropolitan	103	66	65	64	1	11	11	—	53	52	1	23	23	—
Region:														
Northeast	407	238	233	218	22	25	22	3	180	167	15	92	83	9
Midwest	108	56	54	52	4	7	7	—	39	36	4	28	28	—
South	468	264	264	255	14	26	26	—	205	194	14	84	84	—
West	564	363	338	328	11	44	42	2	231	226	5	137	133	4

Source: October 1996 Current Population Survey, Education and Social Stratification Branch, U.S. Bureau of the Census

1. May be of any race.

— Represents zero or rounds to zero.

Table A-20. School Enrollment of Persons 3 to 34 Years Old, by Level and Control of School, Race and Hispanic Origin: October 1955 to 1996

(Numbers in thousands. Civilian noninstitutional population.)

	Total enrolled	Nursery school			Kindergarten			Elementary school			High school			College			College full-time
		Total	Public	Private	Total	Public	Private	Total	Public	Private	Total	Public	Private	Total	Public	Private	
ALL RACES																	
1996	67,311	4,212	1,868	2,344	4,034	3,353	681	31,476	28,112	3,364	15,140	13,956	1,184	12,449	9,906	2,543	9,148
1995	66,939	4,399	2,012	2,387	3,877	3,174	704	31,788	28,357	3,431	14,828	13,620	1,208	12,046	9,333	2,713	8,786
1994	66,427	4,259	1,940	2,319	3,863	3,278	585	31,487	28,109	3,378	14,521	13,453	1,068	12,298	9,536	2,762	8,813
1993 r	64,414	3,032	1,258	1,774	4,275	3,589	686	31,219	28,278	2,941	13,989	12,985	1,004	11,901	9,440	2,461	8,706
1993	62,730	3,018	1,230	1,788	4,180	3,499	681	30,604	27,688	2,914	13,522	12,542	977	11,409	9,031	2,374	8,308
1992	62,082	2,899	1,098	1,801	4,130	3,507	623	30,165	27,066	3,102	13,219	12,268	952	11,671	9,282	2,386	8,503
1991	61,276	2,933	1,094	1,839	4,152	3,531	621	29,591	26,632	2,958	13,010	12,069	945	11,589	9,078	2,511	8,461
1990	60,588	3,401	1,212	2,188	3,899	332	567	29,265	26,591	2,674	12,719	11,818	903	11,306	8,889	2,417	8,154
1989	59,236	2,877	971	1,906	3,868	3,293	575	28,637	25,897	2,740	12,786	11,980	806	11,066	8,576	2,490	7,905
1988	58,847	2,639	838	1,770	3,958	3,420	538	28,223	25,443	2,778	13,093	12,095	998	10,937	8,663	2,278	7,771
1987	58,691	2,587	848	1,739	4,018	3,423	595	27,524	24,760	2,765	13,647	12,577	1,070	10,915	8,556	2,361	7,560
1986	58,153	2,554	835	1,719	3,961	3,328	633	27,121	24,163	2,958	13,912	12,746	1,166	10,605	8,153	2,452	7,507
1985	58,014	2,491	854	1,637	3,815	3,221	594	26,866	23,803	3,063	13,979	12,764	1,215	10,863	8,379	2,483	7,720
1984	57,313	2,354	761	1,593	3,484	2,953	531	26,838	24,120	2,718	13,777	12,721	1,057	10,859	8,467	2,392	7,822
1983	57,745	2,350	809	1,541	3,361	2,706	656	27,198	24,203	2,994	14,010	12,792	1,218	10,825	8,185	2,640	7,711
1982	57,905	2,153	729	1,423	3,299	2,746	553	27,412	24,381	3,031	14,123	13,004	1,118	10,919	8,354	2,565	7,736
1981	58,390	2,058	663	1,396	3,161	2,616	545	27,795	24,758	3,037	14,642	13,523	1,119	10,734	8,159	2,576	7,569
1980	57,348	1,987	633	1,354	3,176	2,690	486	27,449	24,398	3,051	14,556	(NA)	(NA)	10,180	(NA)	(NA)	7,147
1979	57,854	1,869	636	1,233	3,025	2,593	432	27,865	24,756	3,109	15,116	13,994	1,122	9,978	7,699	2,280	7,010
1978	58,616	1,824	587	1,237	2,989	2,493	496	28,490	25,252	3,238	15,475	14,231	1,244	9,838	7,427	2,410	6,979
1977	60,013	1,618	562	1,056	3,191	2,665	526	29,234	25,983	3,251	15,753	14,505	1,248	10,217	7,925	2,292	7,196
1976	60,482	1,526	476	1,050	3,490	2,962	528	29,774	26,698	3,075	15,742	14,541	1,201	9,950	7,739	2,211	7,176
1975	60,969	1,748	574	1,174	3,393	2,851	542	30,446	27,166	3,279	15,683	14,503	1,180	9,697	7,704	1,994	7,105
1974	60,259	1,607	423	1,184	3,252	2,726	526	31,126	27,956	3,169	15,447	14,275	1,172	8,827	6,905	1,922	6,351
1973	59,392	1,324	400	924	3,074	2,582	493	31,469	28,201	3,268	15,347	14,162	1,184	8,179	6,224	1,955	6,089
1972	60,142	1,283	402	881	3,135	2,636	499	32,242	28,693	3,549	15,169	14,015	1,155	8,313	6,337	1,976	6,314
1971	61,106	1,066	317	749	3,263	2,689	574	33,507	29,829	3,678	15,183	14,057	1,126	8,087	6,271	1,816	6,204
1970	60,357	1,096	333	763	3,183	2,647	536	33,950	30,001	3,949	14,715	13,545	1,170	7,413	5,699	1,714	5,763
1969	59,913	860	245	615	3,276	2,682	594	33,788	29,825	3,964	14,553	13,400	1,153	7,435	5,439	1,995	5,810
1968	58,791	816	262	554	3,268	2,709	559	33,761	29,527	4,234	14,145	12,793	1,352	6,801	4,948	1,854	5,357
1967	57,656	713	230	484	3,312	2,678	635	33,440	28,877	4,562	13,790	12,498	1,292	6,401	4,540	1,861	4,976
1966	56,167	688	215	473	3,115	2,527	588	32,916	28,208	4,706	13,364	11,985	1,377	6,085	4,178	1,908	4,847
1965	54,701	520	127	393	3,057	2,439	618	32,474	27,596	4,878	12,975	11,517	1,457	5,675	3,840	1,835	4,414
1964	52,490	471	91	380	2,830	2,349	481	31,734	26,811	4,923	12,812	11,403	1,410	4,643	3,025	1,618	3,556
1963	50,356	(NA)	(NA)	(NA)	2,340	1,936	404	31,245	26,502	4,742	12,438	11,186	1,251	4,336	2,897	1,439	3,260
1962	48,704	(NA)	(NA)	(NA)	2,319	1,914	405	30,661	26,148	4,513	11,516	10,431	1,085	4,208	2,820	1,388	3,237
1961	47,708	(NA)	(NA)	(NA)	2,299	1,926	373	30,718	26,221	4,497	10,959	9,817	1,141	3,731	2,376	1,354	2,902
1960	46,260	(NA)	(NA)	(NA)	2,092	1,691	401	30,349	25,814	4,535	10,249	9,215	1,033	3,570	2,307	1,262	2,681
1959	44,370	(NA)	(NA)	(NA)	2,032	1,678	354	29,382	24,680	4,702	9,616	8,571	1,045	3,340	2,120	1,220	2,464
1958	42,900	(NA)	(NA)	(NA)	1,991	1,569	422	28,184	23,800	4,385	9,482	8,485	998	3,242	2,088	1,155	(NA)
1957	41,166	(NA)	(NA)	(NA)	1,824	1,471	353	27,248	23,076	4,172	8,956	8,059	897	3,138	2,054	1,084	(NA)
1956	39,353	(NA)	(NA)	(NA)	1,758	1,566	192	26,169	22,474	3,695	8,543	7,668	875	2,883	1,824	1,059	(NA)
1955	37,426	(NA)	(NA)	(NA)	1,628	1,365	263	25,458	22,078	3,379	7,961	7,181	780	2,379	1,515	864	(NA)
WHITE																	
1996	52,987	3,284	1,314	1,970	3,163	2,596	567	24,671	21,768	2,903	11,934	10,883	1,051	9,935	7,759	2,176	7,318
1995	52,862	3,553	1,435	2,118	3,032	2,440	592	24,934	21,989	2,945	11,521	10,482	1,039	9,814	7,592	2,222	7,146
1994	52,482	3,376	1,330	2,046	3,010	2,505	505	24,770	21,888	2,882	11,372	10,481	891	9,955	7,665	2,290	7,107
1993 r	51,034	2,434	851	1,583	3,323	2,730	593	24,637	22,078	2,559	10,960	10,124	836	9,685	7,695	1,990	6,996
1993	49,985	2,447	843	1,604	3,273	2,681	592	24,249	21,714	2,535	10,651	9,834	819	9,366	7,428	1,940	6,739
1992	49,713	2,387	785	1,602	3,256	2,727	529	23,932	21,213	2,718	10,480	9,648	833	9,658	7,653	2,001	6,985
1991	49,156	2,447	810	1,637	3,274	2,766	508	23,547	20,948	2,599	10,309	9,467	841	9,579	7,464	2,118	6,919
1990	48,897	2,830	869	1,961	3,081	2,609	472	23,343	20,984	2,359	10,177	9,370	807	9,466	7,411	2,056	6,776
1989	47,923	2,393	712	1,681	3,118	2,611	506	22,867	20,468	2,399	10,172	9,443	730	9,374	7,219	2,158	6,658
1988	47,672	2,234	651	1,583	3,192	2,722	471	22,541	20,086	2,455	10,462	9,571	890	9,245	7,302	1,940	6,488
1987	47,471	2,204	630	1,574	3,120	2,591	529	22,037	19,538	2,498	10,967	10,019	947	9,143	7,113	2,034	6,275
1986	47,267	2,144	601	1,543	3,161	2,589	572	21,761	19,090	2,671	11,259	10,229	1,030	8,943	6,821	2,122	6,253
1985	47,452	2,087	617	1,470	3,060	2,545	515	21,593	18,817	2,776	11,378	10,258	1,120	9,334	7,131	2,203	6,597
1984	46,941	1,915	543	1,372	2,788	2,319	469	21,730	19,282	2,449	11,240	10,266	974	9,269	7,163	2,105	6,672

See footnotes at end of table.

Table A-20. School Enrollment of Persons 3 to 34 Years Old, by Level and Control of School, Race and Hispanic Origin: October 1955 to 1996 — Continued

(Numbers in thousands. Civilian noninstitutional population.)

	Total enrolled	Nursery school			Kindergarten			Elementary school			High school			College			College full-time
		Total	Public	Private	Total	Public	Private	Total	Public	Private	Total	Public	Private	Total	Public	Private	
1983	47,423	1,932	563	1,369	2,769	2,181	588	22,054	19,340	2,714	11,425	10,339	1,086	9,242	6,949	2,293	6,532
1982	47,662	1,783	504	1,279	2,677	2,189	489	22,297	19,583	2,713	11,577	10,541	1,036	9,328	7,102	2,227	6,579
1981	48,169	1,685	447	1,238	2,597	2,130	467	22,663	19,924	2,739	12,062	11,035	1,027	9,162	6,906	2,256	6,452
1980	47,673	1,637	432	1,205	2,595	2,172	423	22,510	19,743	2,768	12,056	(NA)	(NA)	8,875	(NA)	(NA)	6,212
1979	48,225	1,537	428	1,110	2,437	2,069	368	22,959	20,174	2,785	12,583	11,549	1,033	8,709	6,672	2,037	6,058
1978	48,843	1,456	351	1,105	2,452	2,009	444	23,524	20,551	2,973	12,897	11,741	1,156	8,514	6,368	2,145	5,974
1977	50,151	1,314	372	942	2,611	2,153	458	24,262	21,312	2,950	13,152	11,980	1,172	8,812	6,743	2,069	6,165
1976	50,761	1,246	318	929	2,881	2,423	457	24,776	21,947	2,829	13,214	12,093	1,121	8,644	6,657	1,987	6,170
1975	51,430	1,432	392	1,040	2,845	2,363	483	25,412	22,351	3,059	13,224	12,112	1,112	8,516	6,724	1,792	6,183
1974	50,992	1,340	293	1,048	2,745	2,268	477	26,051	23,063	2,990	13,073	11,966	1,107	7,781	6,049	1,732	5,575
1973	50,617	1,087	242	845	2,584	2,139	445	26,531	23,506	3,025	13,091	11,967	1,124	7,324	5,550	1,773	5,408
1972	51,314	1,079	285	794	2,633	2,185	448	27,185	23,869	3,316	12,959	11,876	1,083	7,458	5,644	1,814	5,678
1971	52,081	888	225	664	2,735	2,207	527	28,187	24,720	3,466	12,998	11,937	1,061	7,273	5,624	1,650	5,560
1970	51,719	893	198	695	2,706	2,233	473	28,638	24,923	3,715	12,723	11,599	1,124	6,759	5,168	1,591	5,221
1969	51,465	676	136	539	2,803	2,289	515	28,572	24,803	3,768	12,588	11,502	1,085	6,827	4,967	1,860	5,307
1968	50,608	664	163	501	2,775	2,272	504	28,634	24,580	4,054	12,280	11,007	1,272	6,255	4,501	1,753	4,919
1967	49,721	564	134	429	2,840	2,254	587	28,415	24,044	4,371	11,997	10,769	1,228	5,905	4,155	1,750	4,604
1966	48,620	564	127	437	2,693	2,163	530	28,012	23,469	4,542	11,643	10,312	1,320	5,708	3,914	1,795	4,550
1965	47,451	451	93	358	2,648	2,086	562	27,679	22,976	4,703	11,356	9,961	1,395	5,317	3,568	1,749	4,111
1964	44,850	(NA)	(NA)	(NA)	2,157	1,795	362	27,099	22,381	4,718	11,257	9,898	1,359	4,338	2,798	1,540	(NA)
1963	43,815	(NA)	(NA)	(NA)	2,064	1,699	365	26,709	22,181	4,527	10,994	9,782	1,212	4,050	2,680	1,370	(NA)
1962	42,501	(NA)	(NA)	(NA)	2,025	1,667	358	26,272	21,922	4,350	10,270	9,217	1,053	3,934	2,620	1,314	(NA)
1961	42,498	(NA)	(NA)	(NA)	1,968	1,618	350	26,294	22,014	4,281	9,737	8,635	1,102	3,498	2,205	1,293	(NA)
1960	40,348	(NA)	(NA)	(NA)	1,849	1,485	364	26,035	21,696	4,339	9,122	8,124	999	3,342	2,126	1,215	(NA)
1959	38,857	(NA)	(NA)	(NA)	1,758	1,434	324	25,395	20,854	4,541	8,586	7,572	1,014	3,118	1,960	1,158	(NA)
1958	37,662	(NA)	(NA)	(NA)	1,769	1,383	386	24,380	20,178	4,203	8,484	7,501	982	3,030	1,928	1,101	(NA)
1957	36,132	(NA)	(NA)	(NA)	1,595	1,258	337	23,610	19,595	4,015	7,995	7,121	874	2,932	1,924	1,006	(NA)
1956	34,041	(NA)	(NA)	(NA)	1,544	1,364	180	22,740	19,186	3,554	7,670	6,825	845	2,687	1,704	983	(NA)
1955	32,929	(NA)	(NA)	(NA)	1,484	1,244	240	22,185	18,947	3,238	7,036	6,303	733	2,224	1,429	795	(NA)
BLACK																	
1996	10,447	702	459	243	634	545	89	5,161	4,839	322	2,399	2,298	101	1,551	1,253	298	1,080
1995	10,395	663	478	185	653	564	89	5,182	4,843	339	2,459	2,348	111	1,440	1,121	319	1,032
1994	10,337	721	513	208	662	603	59	5,077	4,702	375	2,400	2,282	118	1,477	1,201	276	1,046
1993 r	9,786	433	320	113	721	649	72	5,009	4,733	276	2,317	2,197	120	1,305	1,006	299	951
1993	9,470	414	307	107	687	618	69	4,865	4,599	266	2,244	2,128	115	1,261	973	288	914
1992	9,150	374	250	124	688	625	63	4,730	4,494	234	2,152	2,072	72	1,217	980	237	904
1991	9,031	360	244	117	676	598	79	4,672	4,445	229	2,100	2,044	56	1,220	1,004	217	900
1990	8,854	431	283	148	636	574	62	4,627	4,428	199	1,975	1,909	65	1,188	963	227	869
1989	8,707	366	216	150	601	557	44	4,528	4,296	232	2,069	2,027	42	1,139	932	208	833
1988	8,609	286	168	118	591	547	44	4,538	4,289	250	2,079	2,016	62	1,114	894	220	801
1987	8,712	277	164	113	699	658	41	4,402	4,206	194	2,140	2,056	84	1,193	977	218	852
1986	8,556	315	200	115	647	600	47	4,326	4,134	193	2,130	2,040	91	1,138	896	242	859
1985	8,444	332	212	120	625	562	63	4,307	4,131	175	2,131	2,068	63	1,049	860	190	767
1984	8,226	340	179	161	563	513	51	4,123	3,947	177	2,061	2,002	59	1,138	918	220	810
1983	8,199	326	215	111	476	427	48	4,153	3,964	189	2,143	2,057	86	1,102	858	245	806
1982	8,262	305	192	113	508	463	45	4,194	3,974	220	2,128	2,073	55	1,127	865	263	800
1981	8,350	284	182	102	474	412	62	4,291	4,087	204	2,168	2,102	65	1,133	898	235	815
1980	8,251	294	180	115	490	440	50	4,259	4,058	202	2,200	(NA)	(NA)	1,007	(NA)	(NA)	723
1979	8,317	278	185	95	497	443	54	4,296	4,053	243	2,245	2,171	74	1,002	814	188	748
1978	8,416	312	210	102	451	414	38	4,356	4,154	202	2,276	2,211	65	1,020	822	199	753
1977	8,564	250	171	78	496	447	50	4,387	4,166	221	2,327	2,269	59	1,103	916	187	803
1976	8,518	226	146	80	542	482	60	4,430	4,256	175	2,258	2,187	71	1,062	887	175	817
1975	8,400	276	171	105	468	426	42	4,509	4,344	165	2,199	2,140	59	948	782	166	742
1974	8,215	227	121	106	463	416	47	4,585	4,455	131	2,125	2,072	54	814	659	155	589
1973	7,834	210	146	64	423	391	32	4,473	4,277	196	2,044	1,988	56	685	537	147	536
1972	7,959	185	113	72	448	402	46	4,573	4,382	191	2,025	1,971	54	727	582	145	525
1971	8,179	151	90	61	464	422	42	4,877	4,712	165	2,006	1,951	55	680	532	148	534
1970	7,829	178	129	49	426	374	53	4,868	4,668	200	1,834	1,794	41	522	422	100	427
1969	7,680	170	102	68	425	361	64	4,785	4,633	151	1,808	1,751	57	492	372	120	401
1968	7,448	132	89	43	448	397	51	4,716	4,569	146	1,718	1,656	62	434	359	75	338

See footnotes at end of table.

Table A-20. School Enrollment of Persons 3 to 34 Years Old, by Level and Control of School, Race and Hispanic Origin: October 1955 to 1996 — Continued

(Numbers in thousands. Civilian noninstitutional population.)

	Total enrolled	Nursery school			Kindergarten			Elementary school			High school			College			College full-time
		Total	Public	Private	Total	Public	Private	Total	Public	Private	Total	Public	Private	Total	Public	Private	
1967	7,196	140	92	47	418	375	44	4,618	4,444	173	1,651	1,605	46	370	280	90	271
1966	7,547	125	88	37	420	364	56	4,904	4,739	165	1,721	1,673	48	282	(NA)	(NA)	210
1965	7,252	72	37	35	407	353	54	4,796	4,620	176	1,619	1,556	62	358	272	86	218
1964	6,807	(NA)	(NA)	(NA)	312	275	37	4,634	4,430	205	1,556	1,505	51	306	227	78	(NA)
1963	6,541	(NA)	(NA)	(NA)	276	237	39	4,536	4,321	215	1,444	1,404	39	286	217	69	(NA)
1962	6,203	(NA)	(NA)	(NA)	294	247	47	4,389	4,226	163	1,246	1,214	32	274	200	74	(NA)
1961	6,210	(NA)	(NA)	(NA)	331	308	23	4,424	4,207	216	1,222	1,182	39	233	171	61	(NA)
1960	5,910	(NA)	(NA)	(NA)	243	206	37	4,313	4,118	195	1,127	1,092	34	227	180	46	(NA)
1959	5,513	(NA)	(NA)	(NA)	274	244	30	3,987	3,826	161	1,030	999	31	222	160	62	(NA)
1958	5,238	(NA)	(NA)	(NA)	222	186	36	3,804	3,621	182	998	981	17	212	160	53	(NA)
1957	5,034	(NA)	(NA)	(NA)	229	213	16	3,638	3,483	155	961	939	22	206	132	74	(NA)
1956	4,712	(NA)	(NA)	(NA)	214	202	12	3,429	3,287	142	873	843	30	196	120	76	(NA)
1955	4,498	(NA)	(NA)	(NA)	144	121	23	3,273	3,131	142	926	878	48	155	86	69	(NA)
HISPANIC ORIGIN[1]																	
1996	8,569	533	403	130	602	539	63	4,428	4,149	279	1,967	1,871	96	1,039	879	160	660
1995	8,313	510	350	160	558	465	93	4,421	4,152	269	1,806	1,725	81	1,012	862	150	664
1994	7,947	400	278	122	559	516	43	4,148	3,835	313	1,856	1,766	90	982	852	130	570
1993 ʳ	7,651	231	169	62	639	576	63	4,027	3,779	248	1,722	1,653	69	1,029	872	157	686
1993	6,689	194	142	52	538	484	53	3,534	3,317	217	1,556	1,496	60	867	731	134	573
1992	6,598	209	139	70	554	493	60	3,525	3,271	252	1,494	1,435	59	813	710	104	487
1991	6,306	215	146	69	552	525	27	3,461	3,240	221	1,357	1,299	61	721	607	115	481
1990	6,072	242	153	88	475	446	29	3,301	3,107	197	1,437	1,374	64	617	515	100	380
1989	5,722	181	95	86	404	382	21	3,219	3,031	188	1,278	1,231	48	642	557	82	416
1988	5,588	151	111	40	461	445	16	3,160	2,954	207	1,163	1,113	49	654	592	60	414
1987	5,619	226	138	88	439	399	39	3,048	2,861	187	1,239	1,160	80	668	551	115	414
1986	5,513	179	114	65	465	421	44	2,995	2,787	208	1,197	1,116	81	677	540	137	418
1985	5,070	168	105	63	364	315	49	2,803	2,607	196	1,156	1,090	167	579	464	116	381
1984	4,284	117	78	39	293	267	26	2,384	2,218	166	966	909	57	524	433	91	356
1983	4,618	108	60	48	335	285	50	2,548	2,323	225	1,104	1,027	77	523	441	82	335
1982	4,478	83	46	37	329	291	37	2,501	2,276	225	1,072	995	77	493	398	96	312
1981	4,551	131	68	63	306	282	24	2,474	2,239	235	1,130	1,056	74	510	398	112	343
1980	4,263	146	70	75	263	234	30	2,363	2,134	228	1,048	(NA)	(NA)	443	(NA)	(NA)	294
1979	3,608	89	50	39	226	210	16	1,934	1,745	189	920	875	45	440	365	75	314
1978	3,455	87	47	39	231	198	33	1,893	1,704	188	868	825	43	377	315	62	231
1977	3,516	75	30	46	220	206	14	1,874	1,654	220	928	836	92	418	357	60	287
1976	3,623	68	38	30	262	242	20	1,934	1,768	165	932	867	65	427	354	73	297
1975	3,741	85	47	39	235	218	17	2,062	1,858	204	948	886	61	411	358	53	287
1974	3,620	85	37	48	225	207	18	2,040	1,780	260	916	858	59	354	297	57	247
1973	3,171	68	41	27	171	165	6	1,884	1,712	172	758	707	51	290	247	43	201
1972	3,257	61	43	18	241	227	14	1,879	1,705	173	834	784	50	242	213	29	178

Source: U.S. Bureau of the Census

1. May be of any race.

(NA) Not applicable or not available.

r = Revised, controlled to the 1990 census-based population estimates; previous 1993 data controlled to 1980 based population estimates

Data shown for 1966 and earlier years for the Black population are for Black and Other races combined.

Table A-21.   Percentage of Persons 3 to 34 Years Old Enrolled in School, by Age, Sex, Race, and Hispanic Origin: October 1947 to 1996

State	Total enrolled	Age										
		3 and 4 years	5 and 6 years	7 to 9 years	10 to 13 years	14 and 15 years	16 and 17 years	18 and 19 years	20 and 21 years	22 to 24 years	25 to 29 years	30 to 34 years
ALL RACES												
Total												
1996	54.1	48.3	94.0	97.2	98.1	98.0	92.8	61.5	44.4	24.8	11.9	6.1
1995	53.7	48.7	96.0	98.7	99.1	98.9	93.6	59.4	44.9	23.2	11.6	6.0
1994	53.3	47.3	96.7	99.3	99.4	98.8	94.4	60.2	44.9	24.1	10.8	6.7
1993r	51.9	40.1	95.3	99.5	99.5	98.9	93.9	61.4	42.6	23.5	10.2	5.9
1993	51.8	40.4	95.4	99.5	99.5	98.9	94.0	61.6	42.7	23.6	10.2	5.9
1992	51.4	39.7	95.5	99.4	99.4	99.1	94.1	61.4	44.0	23.7	9.8	6.1
1991	50.7	40.5	95.4	99.6	99.7	98.8	93.3	59.6	42.0	22.2	10.2	6.2
1990	50.2	44.4	96.5	99.7	99.6	99.0	92.5	57.3	39.7	21.0	9.7	5.8
1989	49.1	39.1	95.2	99.2	99.4	98.8	92.7	56.0	38.5	19.9	9.3	5.7
1988	48.7	38.2	96.0	99.6	99.7	98.9	91.6	55.7	39.1	18.3	8.3	5.9
1987	48.6	38.3	95.1	99.6	99.5	98.6	91.7	55.6	38.7	17.5	9.0	5.9
1986	48.5	39.0	95.3	99.3	99.1	98.9	92.5	55.2	33.4	18.2	9.1	6.3
1985	48.3	38.9	96.1	99.1	99.3	98.1	91.7	51.6	35.3	16.9	9.2	6.0
1984	47.9	36.3	94.5	99.0	99.4	97.8	91.5	50.1	33.9	17.3	9.1	6.1
1983	48.4	37.5	95.4	98.9	99.4	98.3	91.7	50.4	32.5	16.6	9.6	6.3
1982	48.6	36.4	95.0	99.2	99.1	98.5	90.6	47.8	34.0	16.8	9.6	6.4
1981	48.9	36.0	94.0	99.2	99.3	98.0	90.6	49.0	31.6	16.5	9.0	6.3
1980	49.7	36.7	95.7	99.1	99.4	98.2	89.0	46.4	31.0	16.3	9.3	6.4
1979	50.3	35.1	95.8	99.2	99.1	98.1	89.2	45.0	30.2	15.8	9.6	6.4
1978	51.2	34.2	95.3	99.3	99.0	98.4	89.1	45.4	29.5	16.3	9.4	6.4
1977	52.5	32.0	95.8	99.5	99.4	98.5	88.9	46.2	31.8	16.5	10.8	6.9
1976	53.1	31.3	95.5	99.2	99.2	98.2	89.1	46.2	32.0	17.1	10.0	6.0
1975	53.7	31.5	94.7	99.3	99.3	98.2	89.0	46.9	31.2	16.2	10.1	6.6
1974	53.6	28.8	94.2	99.1	99.5	97.9	87.9	43.1	30.2	15.1	9.6	5.7
1973	53.5	24.2	92.5	99.1	99.2	97.5	88.3	42.9	30.1	14.5	8.5	4.5
1972	54.9	24.4	91.9	99.0	99.3	97.6	88.9	46.3	31.4	14.8	8.6	4.6
1971	56.2	21.2	91.6	99.1	99.2	98.6	90.2	49.2	32.2	15.4	8.0	4.9
1970	56.4	20.5	89.5	99.3	99.2	98.1	90.0	47.7	31.9	14.9	7.5	4.2
1969	57.0	16.1	88.4	99.3	99.1	98.1	89.7	50.2	34.1	15.4	7.9	4.8
1968	56.7	15.7	87.6	99.1	99.1	98.0	90.2	50.4	31.2	13.8	7.0	3.9
1967	56.6	14.2	87.4	99.4	99.1	98.2	88.8	47.6	33.3	13.6	6.6	4.0
1966	56.1	12.5	85.1	99.3	99.3	98.6	88.5	47.2	29.9	13.2	6.5	2.7
1965	55.5	10.6	84.4	99.3	99.4	98.9	87.4	46.3	27.6	13.2	6.1	3.2
1964	54.5	9.5	83.3	99.0	99.0	98.6	87.7	41.6	26.3	9.9	5.2	2.6
1963	58.5	(NA)	82.7	99.4	99.3	98.4	87.1	40.9	25.0	11.4	4.9	2.5
1962	57.8	(NA)	82.2	99.2	99.3	98.0	84.3	41.8	23.0	10.3	5.0	2.6
1961	56.8	(NA)	81.7	99.4	99.3	97.6	83.6	38.0	21.5	8.4	4.4	2.0
1960	56.4	(NA)	80.7	99.6	99.5	97.8	82.6	38.4	19.4	8.7	4.9	2.4
1959	55.5	(NA)	80.0	99.4	99.4	97.5	82.9	36.8	18.8	8.6	5.1	2.2
1958	54.8	(NA)	80.4	99.5	99.5	96.9	80.6	37.6	13.4		5.7	2.2
1957	53.6	(NA)	78.6	99.5	99.5	97.1	80.5	34.9	14.0		5.5	1.8
1956	52.3	(NA)	77.6	99.4	99.2	96.9	78.4	35.4	12.8		5.1	1.9
1955	50.8	(NA)	78.1	99.2	99.2	95.9	77.4	31.5	11.1		4.2	1.6
1954	50.0	(NA)	77.3	99.2	99.5	95.8	78.0	32.4	11.2		4.1	1.5
1953	48.8	(NA)	55.7	99.4	99.4	96.5	74.7	31.2	11.1		2.9	1.7
1952	46.8	(NA)	54.7	98.7	98.9	96.2	73.4	28.7	9.5		2.6	1.1
1951	45.4	(NA)	54.5	99.0	99.2	94.8	75.1	26.3	8.3		2.5	(NA)
1950	44.2	(NA)	58.2	98.9	98.6	94.7	71.3	29.4	9.0		3.0	(NA)
1949	43.9	(NA)	59.3	98.5	98.7	93.5	69.5	25.3	9.2		3.8	1.1
1948	43.1	(NA)	56.0	98.3	98.0	92.7	71.2	26.9	9.7		2.6	0.9
1947	42.3	(NA)	58.0	98.4	98.6	91.6	67.6	24.3	10.2		3.0	1.0

See footnotes at end of table.

Table A-21.   Percentage of Persons 3 to 34 Years Old Enrolled in School, by Age, Sex, Race, and Hispanic Origin: October 1947 to 1996 — Continued

	Total enrolled	Age										
		3 and 4 years	5 and 6 years	7 to 9 years	10 to 13 years	14 and 15 years	16 and 17 years	18 and 19 years	20 and 21 years	22 to 24 years	25 to 29 years	30 to 34 years
Male												
1996	54.4	46.9	93.8	97.2	98.0	98.5	93.2	60.8	43.9	25.2	11.4	4.9
1995	54.3	49.4	95.3	98.9	99.1	99.0	94.5	59.5	44.7	22.8	11.0	5.4
1994	53.7	47.6	97.0	99.2	99.4	98.8	94.3	60.4	42.7	24.2	10.5	5.9
1993r	52.6	41.1	95.5	99.5	99.6	99.0	94.9	61.1	42.3	25.3	9.6	5.2
1993	52.6	41.5	95.5	99.5	99.6	99.0	95.0	61.6	42.6	25.5	9.6	5.2
1992	51.9	40.3	95.7	99.5	99.5	99.2	95.4	61.6	41.7	23.8	9.1	5.2
1991	51.5	39.9	95.0	99.7	99.8	99.1	93.7	59.8	41.8	24.0	10.6	5.6
1990	50.9	43.9	96.5	99.7	99.6	99.1	92.7	58.2	40.3	22.3	9.2	4.8
1989	49.7	38.8	95.1	99.3	99.2	99.2	93.2	56.6	37.3	20.4	9.3	5.0
1988	49.6	38.3	95.9	99.6	99.7	98.9	92.1	56.2	39.0	20.5	8.1	5.5
1987	49.9	40.0	95.7	99.7	99.7	98.7	92.3	57.9	41.2	18.7	9.1	5.0
1986	49.6	39.0	96.0	99.4	98.9	99.0	92.6	57.5	33.8	19.6	9.5	6.0
1985	49.2	36.7	95.3	99.0	99.2	98.3	92.4	52.2	36.5	18.8	9.4	5.6
1984	49.1	35.9	94.0	98.8	99.3	97.5	91.8	52.4	36.2	20.1	9.6	5.4
1983	49.7	38.1	95.1	98.8	99.3	98.4	91.8	50.4	35.2	19.4	10.7	5.8
1982	49.7	36.4	94.7	99.2	99.0	98.7	91.3	48.9	35.2	18.5	10.1	5.8
1981	50.2	36.8	94.2	98.9	99.2	98.2	90.7	50.5	32.1	19.2	9.6	5.6
1980	50.9	37.8	95.0	99.0	99.4	98.7	89.1	47.0	32.6	17.8	9.8	5.9
1979	51.8	34.6	96.3	99.0	98.9	98.3	90.8	46.6	31.6	17.6	10.4	6.0
1978	52.9	34.0	95.1	99.1	98.8	98.4	89.5	47.8	31.7	19.1	10.9	6.5
1977	54.3	32.1	94.7	99.5	99.2	98.7	90.0	48.4	34.6	19.7	12.6	7.1
1976	55.1	30.9	95.6	98.9	99.1	98.6	90.5	48.2	33.6	20.7	13.0	6.8
1975	56.0	30.6	94.3	99.2	98.9	98.4	90.7	49.9	35.3	20.0	13.1	7.7
1974	56.0	28.1	94.4	99.1	99.3	98.0	88.6	45.8	34.8	19.4	12.7	6.7
1973	56.1	24.5	92.2	99.0	99.2	97.9	89.4	47.9	34.4	19.1	11.8	5.6
1972	57.8	24.4	91.7	98.9	99.3	97.7	90.2	51.2	37.3	21.3	12.1	5.8
1971	59.3	20.0	90.9	99.0	98.8	98.7	91.7	55.4	38.9	23.3	11.9	6.3
1970	59.7	21.2	88.9	99.3	98.8	98.2	91.3	54.4	42.7	21.2	11.0	5.3
1969	60.5	15.5	87.7	99.0	98.9	98.1	91.6	59.4	46.5	22.9	11.4	5.9
1968	60.4	15.4	87.3	98.9	98.9	98.2	91.7	60.4	45.0	20.5	10.8	5.0
1967	60.0	14.2	86.6	99.4	98.9	98.3	91.0	56.3	44.3	21.0	9.9	5.4
1966	59.7	12.3	84.5	99.2	99.1	98.7	89.9	57.8	41.4	21.3	9.6	3.8
1965	58.8	10.2	84.4	99.3	99.3	99.0	88.0	55.6	37.6	21.1	9.4	4.5
1964	57.5	8.9	83.4	98.7	98.9	99.0	89.8	50.9	34.4	16.1	8.1	3.6
1963	62.3	(NA)	82.7	99.2	99.0	98.7	89.4	51.0	33.6	19.5	7.8	3.7
1962	61.7	(NA)	82.6	99.1	99.2	98.7	87.1	51.2	31.3	17.7	8.5	3.9
1961	60.4	(NA)	82.0	99.5	99.2	98.1	84.7	48.6	29.5	13.9	7.1	2.9
1960	60.0	(NA)	80.8	99.6	99.4	97.9	84.5	47.8	27.1	15.0	8.4	3.7
1959	59.1	(NA)	79.5	99.2	99.4	97.8	84.8	45.6	28.3	13.7	8.9	3.3
1958	58.7	(NA)	80.6	99.6	99.4	96.9	83.8	47.5	21.0		9.5	2.9
1957	57.5	(NA)	78.3	99.4	99.6	98.0	82.8	43.3	21.3		9.5	2.6
1956	56.3	(NA)	77.1	99.2	99.1	97.1	79.9	45.1	20.6		8.9	2.7
1955	54.9	(NA)	78.1	99.1	99.4	95.7	81.1	42.5	18.1		7.0	2.1
1954	54.0	(NA)	76.3	99.0	99.4	96.1	80.9	40.6	19.1		6.7	1.9
1953	50.2	(NA)	55.0	99.3	99.1	96.4	76.5	37.7	18.5		5.5	2.0
1952	49.4	(NA)	54.8	98.6	98.9	96.2	73.9	37.2	16.9		4.7	1.7
1951	56.8	(NA)	55.1	99.1	99.1	95.1	74.3	32.4	14.3		4.2	(NA)
1950	54.8	(NA)	56.8	98.8	98.7	95.2	72.8	35.7	14.3		5.9	(NA)
1949	45.8	(NA)	60.1	98.5	98.6	93.9	70.8	31.6	15.4		6.8	1.9
1948	44.8	(NA)	55.1	99.5	98.1	92.0	72.1	34.3	16.5		5.1	1.5
1947	44.3	(NA)	57.4	98.5	98.7	90.3	67.6	31.4	17.0		5.8	1.7

See footnotes at end of table.

Table A-21. Percentage of Persons 3 to 34 Years Old Enrolled in School, by Age, Sex, Race, and Hispanic Origin: October 1947 to 1996 — Continued

	Total enrolled	Age										
		3 and 4 years	5 and 6 years	7 to 9 years	10 to 13 years	14 and 15 years	16 and 17 years	18 and 19 years	20 and 21 years	22 to 24 years	25 to 29 years	30 to 34 years
Female												
1996	53.8	49.8	94.3	97.3	98.2	97.5	92.4	62.2	44.8	24.5	12.5	7.3
1995	53.2	48.1	96.8	98.5	99.1	98.8	92.6	59.2	45.1	23.6	12.2	6.5
1994	52.9	46.9	96.4	99.5	99.4	98.7	94.4	60.0	47.0	23.9	11.1	7.5
1993r	51.1	39.0	95.2	99.4	99.5	98.7	92.8	61.7	42.8	21.7	10.8	6.6
1993	51.0	39.3	95.2	99.4	99.5	98.7	92.9	61.7	42.9	21.8	10.8	6.6
1992	51.0	39.1	95.2	99.2	99.2	99.1	92.7	61.2	46.1	23.6	10.5	7.0
1991	49.9	41.1	95.8	99.5	99.6	98.4	92.8	59.4	42.2	20.4	9.8	6.8
1990	49.5	44.9	96.4	99.6	99.7	98.9	92.4	56.3	39.2	19.9	10.2	6.9
1989	48.4	39.5	95.2	99.2	99.6	98.4	92.2	55.5	39.7	19.5	9.3	6.4
1988	47.7	38.1	96.0	99.6	99.7	98.8	91.2	55.2	39.1	16.2	8.6	6.4
1987	47.4	36.6	94.5	99.5	99.2	98.4	91.1	53.4	36.4	16.5	9.0	6.7
1986	47.4	39.0	94.6	99.2	99.4	98.7	92.5	52.9	33.0	16.8	8.8	6.7
1985	47.4	41.2	97.0	99.2	99.4	97.9	90.9	51.0	34.1	15.1	9.1	6.4
1984	46.6	36.7	95.1	99.3	99.4	98.2	91.2	48.0	31.7	14.6	8.6	6.8
1983	47.0	36.9	95.8	99.0	99.5	98.2	91.6	50.3	29.9	13.9	8.5	6.7
1982	47.5	38.4	95.3	99.2	99.3	98.3	89.9	46.8	32.9	15.1	9.0	7.0
1981	47.7	35.2	93.8	99.5	99.4	97.7	90.5	47.5	31.2	13.9	8.4	6.9
1980	48.5	35.5	96.4	99.2	99.4	97.7	88.8	45.8	29.5	14.9	8.8	7.0
1979	49.0	35.6	95.2	99.4	99.4	97.9	87.6	43.4	28.9	14.1	8.8	6.7
1978	49.5	34.5	95.5	99.5	99.2	98.4	88.8	43.0	27.5	13.6	7.9	6.2
1977	50.7	32.0	96.9	99.5	99.6	98.3	87.7	44.0	29.1	13.6	9.1	6.7
1976	51.0	31.6	95.5	99.4	99.3	97.8	87.7	44.4	30.6	13.8	7.3	5.2
1975	51.5	32.4	95.2	99.5	99.6	98.0	87.2	44.2	27.4	12.6	7.2	5.6
1974	51.3	29.5	93.9	99.2	99.7	97.9	87.1	40.7	26.0	11.1	6.7	4.6
1973	50.9	23.8	92.9	99.3	99.2	97.1	87.2	38.2	26.3	10.2	5.4	3.6
1972	52.0	24.4	92.2	99.1	99.4	97.5	87.6	41.8	26.3	8.9	5.3	3.6
1971	53.2	22.4	92.3	99.2	99.5	98.5	88.7	43.4	26.8	8.4	4.4	3.6
1970	53.2	19.8	90.2	99.3	99.5	98.0	88.6	41.6	23.6	9.4	4.3	3.1
1969	53.6	16.8	89.1	99.6	99.4	98.2	87.7	41.8	25.3	9.1	4.6	3.8
1968	53.2	16.1	88.0	99.3	99.3	97.8	88.7	41.3	21.5	8.3	3.4	2.9
1967	53.3	14.1	88.2	99.5	99.3	98.2	86.7	40.3	24.9	7.4	3.6	2.8
1966	52.7	12.7	85.7	99.4	99.5	98.4	87.1	37.7	20.9	6.6	3.6	1.7
1965	52.3	10.9	84.4	99.3	99.5	98.7	86.9	37.7	19.5	6.5	3.1	2.1
1964	51.5	10.2	83.2	99.3	99.2	98.2	85.6	33.7	19.5	4.4	2.6	1.6
1963	54.9	(NA)	82.6	99.6	99.6	98.0	84.8	32.3	17.8	4.4	2.4	1.5
1962	54.0	(NA)	81.7	99.3	99.4	97.3	81.5	33.7	16.1	3.9	1.8	1.4
1961	53.4	(NA)	81.4	99.3	99.4	97.2	82.4	28.6	14.9	3.7	1.9	1.2
1960	52.8	(NA)	80.6	99.6	99.5	97.6	80.6	30.0	13.1	3.4	1.8	1.2
1959	52.0	(NA)	80.5	99.6	99.5	97.1	81.0	29.2	11.1	4.4	1.7	1.3
1958	51.0	(NA)	80.2	99.4	99.5	96.9	77.3	29.4		7.3	2.2	1.5
1957	50.0	(NA)	79.0	99.6	99.5	96.2	78.1	28.1		8.2	1.9	1.1
1956	48.7	(NA)	78.2	99.5	99.4	96.8	76.9	27.4		6.8	1.7	1.2
1955	47.0	(NA)	78.1	99.3	99.0	96.1	73.8	22.5		6.1	1.8	1.1
1954	46.3	(NA)	78.3	99.5	99.7	95.4	75.2	25.4		6.0	1.7	1.1
1953	43.0	(NA)	56.6	99.5	99.7	96.6	72.9	25.9		6.4	0.5	1.4
1952	41.9	(NA)	54.6	98.9	98.9	96.6	72.9	22.1		4.9	0.6	0.7
1951	49.1	(NA)	54.0	98.9	99.3	94.5	75.4	21.3		4.3	1.0	(NA)
1950	48.4	(NA)	59.5	99.0	98.4	94.3	69.8	24.3		4.6	0.4	(NA)
1949	39.2	(NA)	58.4	98.5	98.8	93.1	68.2	19.9		3.7	1.1	0.4
1948	38.4	(NA)	56.8	98.2	97.8	93.5	70.3	20.3		3.4	0.4	0.4
1947	38.0	(NA)	58.7	98.4	98.5	92.8	67.5	18.5		3.9	0.4	0.3

See footnotes at end of table.

Table A-21. Percentage of Persons 3 to 34 Years Old Enrolled in School, by Age, Sex, Race, and Hispanic Origin: October 1947 to 1996 — Continued

	Total enrolled	Age										
		3 and 4 years	5 and 6 years	7 to 9 years	10 to 13 years	14 and 15 years	16 and 17 years	18 and 19 years	20 and 21 years	22 to 24 years	25 to 29 years	30 to 34 years
WHITE												
Total												
1996	53.4	47.9	94.8	97.1	98.2	98.0	92.8	62.5	44.9	24.6	11.3	5.7
1995	53.2	49.6	96.2	98.9	99.0	98.8	93.7	59.3	46.2	23.1	11.5	5.5
1994	52.6	47.0	96.6	99.2	99.3	98.7	94.3	60.9	46.2	23.5	10.4	6.6
1993r	51.2	40.4	95.4	99.5	99.5	98.9	93.9	61.4	43.7	23.1	9.7	5.9
1993	51.1	40.8	95.5	99.5	99.5	98.9	94.1	61.7	44.0	23.3	9.8	5.9
1992	50.7	40.1	95.4	99.4	99.3	99.2	94.2	61.7	45.3	23.3	9.6	6.0
1991	50.0	41.3	95.3	99.6	99.7	98.7	93.3	59.7	43.2	21.7	9.9	6.0
1990	49.5	44.9	96.5	99.7	99.6	99.1	92.5	57.1	41.0	20.2	9.9	5.9
1989	48.4	39.4	95.2	99.2	99.4	98.8	92.3	56.4	39.5	20.0	9.4	5.6
1988	48.0	38.9	96.1	99.7	99.7	98.8	91.4	55.8	40.2	18.6	8.2	5.9
1987	47.7	38.2	94.8	99.6	99.4	98.5	91.8	55.3	39.6	17.3	8.7	5.7
1986	47.7	39.1	95.3	99.3	99.2	99.0	92.2	55.3	33.9	17.7	9.1	6.2
1985	47.8	38.6	96.4	99.3	99.3	98.1	91.6	52.4	36.1	17.0	9.2	5.9
1984	47.3	36.0	94.6	99.0	99.4	97.8	91.2	51.1	34.3	17.2	9.1	6.2
1983	47.7	37.6	95.7	98.9	99.3	98.4	91.4	50.9	33.4	16.4	9.4	6.1
1982	47.9	35.9	94.9	99.2	99.2	98.6	90.3	47.9	35.1	16.2	9.6	6.2
1981	48.2	35.6	93.9	99.3	99.3	98.1	90.4	48.5	32.6	16.2	8.5	6.1
1980	48.9	36.3	95.8	99.0	99.4	98.3	88.6	46.3	31.9	16.4	9.2	6.3
1979	49.6	33.9	95.8	99.2	99.2	98.2	89.0	44.5	31.1	15.7	9.7	6.3
1978	50.3	32.7	95.4	99.3	99.0	98.4	88.7	44.9	29.6	16.1	9.4	6.2
1977	51.6	31.1	95.6	99.5	99.4	98.5	88.5	45.5	31.8	16.3	10.6	6.6
1976	52.3	30.4	95.8	99.1	99.2	98.1	89.1	45.4	32.5	17.0	10.0	5.7
1975	53.1	30.9	94.8	99.4	99.3	98.3	89.3	46.5	31.8	16.8	10.0	6.6
1974	53.0	28.6	94.4	99.2	99.4	98.1	87.9	42.6	30.7	15.2	9.6	5.5
1973	53.1	23.2	93.0	99.1	99.3	97.6	88.3	43.4	31.3	14.6	8.7	4.5
1972	54.4	23.8	92.2	99.1	99.3	97.6	88.9	46.6	32.6	15.0	8.7	4.5
1971	55.8	20.9	91.9	99.1	99.2	98.7	90.5	49.4	32.7	15.9	8.1	4.8
1970	56.2	19.9	90.3	99.3	99.1	98.2	90.6	48.7	33.1	15.7	7.7	4.2
1969	56.8	15.1	89.2	99.4	99.2	98.2	90.2	50.9	35.4	16.2	8.2	5.0
1968	56.6	15.0	88.5	99.1	99.1	98.1	90.8	50.9	32.8	14.5	7.4	3.9
1967	56.5	13.3	88.2	99.5	99.2	98.5	89.5	48.4	34.7	14.1	6.7	4.1
1966	56.1	12.3	85.7	99.3	99.3	98.8	89.0	48.2	32.2	14.0	6.9	2.7
1965	55.5	10.3	85.3	99.4	99.4	99.0	87.8	47.1	29.4	14.1	6.5	3.2
1964	54.4	9.3	84.0	99.0	99.0	98.8	88.3	42.3	27.8	10.6	5.4	2.6
1963	58.4	(NA)	83.7	99.5	99.3	98.5	87.8	41.0	26.2	12.2	5.2	2.6
1962	57.9	(NA)	83.2	99.3	99.4	98.2	85.9	43.0	24.1	10.9	5.2	2.7
1961	56.9	(NA)	82.2	99.6	99.5	98.0	84.5	39.0	22.4	9.0	4.6	2.1
1960	56.4	(NA)	82.0	99.7	99.5	98.1	83.3	38.9	20.6	9.3	5.2	2.6
1959	55.5	(NA)	81.0	99.5	99.5	97.9	83.8	37.3	19.9	8.9	5.4	2.3
1958	54.9	(NA)	81.4	99.6		90.0		38.1	14.1		5.9	2.3
1957	53.7	(NA)	79.3	99.7		90.1		34.6	14.7		5.7	1.9
1956	52.5	(NA)	78.4	99.4		89.2		35.9	13.4		5.4	2.1
1955	50.8	(NA)	79.2	99.3		87.5		32.1	11.6		4.2	1.6
1954	50.2	(NA)	78.6	99.6		88.3		33.6	12.0		4.0	1.5
1953	46.6	(NA)	67.1	99.7		86.4		31.7	11.9		3.1	1.8
1952	45.4	(NA)	54.8	99.1		86.1		28.9	9.8		2.7	1.2
1951	52.8	(NA)	54.5	99.3		86.3		26.9	8.8		2.8	(NA)
1950	51.6	(NA)		89.0		84.4		30.5	9.5		3.0	(NA)
1949	42.6	(NA)		88.8		83.0		25.9	9.6		4.0	1.2
1948	41.8	(NA)		87.8		83.9		27.3	10.0		2.8	0.9
1947	41.2	(NA)		88.7		80.2		24.8	10.5		3.0	1.1

See footnotes at end of table.

Table A-21. Percentage of Persons 3 to 34 Years Old Enrolled in School, by Age, Sex, Race, and Hispanic Origin: October 1947 to 1996 — Continued

	Total enrolled	Age										
		3 and 4 years	5 and 6 years	7 to 9 years	10 to 13 years	14 and 15 years	16 and 17 years	18 and 19 years	20 and 21 years	22 to 24 years	25 to 29 years	30 to 34 years
Male												
1996	53.3	46.5	94.6	96.9	98.0	98.6	93.0	60.9	43.6	25.4	10.6	4.3
1995	53.5	49.6	95.5	99.0	99.0	98.8	94.2	59.4	46.3	22.7	11.3	5.0
1994	52.7	46.2	97.0	99.1	99.3	98.7	94.3	61.3	43.4	23.6	9.9	5.8
1993r	51.6	41.2	95.1	99.5	99.5	98.9	95.0	60.1	44.4	24.5	9.1	5.2
1993	51.6	41.7	95.2	99.5	99.5	99.0	95.1	60.6	44.8	24.9	9.1	5.2
1992	50.8	39.8	95.1	99.5	99.5	99.0	95.5	60.7	44.0	23.6	8.6	5.2
1991	50.4	40.6	94.9	99.7	99.8	98.9	94.2	58.4	42.4	23.3	10.0	5.4
1990	50.0	44.9	96.7	99.7	99.6	99.2	92.3	57.3	41.2	21.8	9.4	4.9
1989	48.9	38.7	95.4	99.3	99.2	99.3	92.6	57.3	39.3	20.4	9.3	5.0
1988	48.7	39.0	96.1	99.7	99.6	98.9	91.6	56.5	40.9	20.7	7.8	5.4
1987	48.8	39.8	95.2	99.6	99.7	98.8	92.5	57.3	42.1	18.4	8.6	5.0
1986	48.6	39.3	95.6	99.4	99.0	99.1	92.1	57.5	34.2	19.2	9.6	5.7
1985	48.5	37.3	95.7	99.3	99.2	98.2	92.5	51.9	37.2	19.0	9.5	5.4
1984	48.3	35.8	94.1	98.7	99.3	97.6	91.5	52.6	36.3	20.2	9.2	5.4
1983	48.9	38.2	95.1	98.8	99.3	98.3	91.6	50.7	36.6	19.2	10.4	5.6
1982	48.9	36.3	94.8	99.2	99.1	98.8	91.0	48.5	36.5	18.0	10.2	5.4
1981	49.2	36.8	94.3	99.1	99.2	98.3	90.5	49.2	33.3	19.1	9.1	5.5
1980	50.0	38.0	95.2	98.8	99.4	98.7	88.8	47.5	33.7	18.2	9.6	5.6
1979	50.7	33.5	96.3	99.0	99.0	98.3	90.3	46.1	32.2	17.6	10.5	5.9
1978	51.9	33.1	95.3	99.2	98.9	98.3	88.9	47.2	32.0	19.2	10.9	6.4
1977	53.3	31.7	94.3	99.6	99.3	98.7	89.5	47.7	34.7	19.4	12.6	6.8
1976	54.2	29.9	95.8	98.8	99.1	98.5	90.6	46.9	34.2	20.4	12.9	6.5
1975	55.4	30.8	94.3	99.2	99.0	98.5	91.0	49.6	36.3	20.5	13.1	7.5
1974	55.2	27.7	94.8	99.1	99.2	98.2	88.2	45.5	35.0	19.2	12.8	6.4
1973	55.6	23.5	92.7	99.0	99.3	98.0	89.4	48.4	35.7	19.6	12.1	5.4
1972	57.3	23.4	91.7	98.9	99.2	97.7	90.4	51.5	38.4	21.6	12.5	5.8
1971	59.0	20.1	91.2	99.0	98.9	98.9	92.0	55.9	39.7	24.6	12.1	6.2
1970	59.6	20.7	89.7	99.3	98.8	98.3	92.2	56.0	45.0	22.6	11.2	5.4
1969	60.5	14.5	88.5	99.1	98.9	98.2	92.2	60.9	48.9	24.2	12.2	6.2
1968	60.4	14.8	87.9	99.0	99.0	98.2	92.1	61.5	47.8	21.9	11.4	5.0
1967	60.0	13.6	87.5	99.5	99.0	98.5	91.4	57.2	46.9	22.0	10.5	5.4
1966	59.8	12.2	85.0	99.2	99.1	98.8	90.3	59.0	44.9	23.0	10.3	3.8
1965	59.0	10.4	84.8	99.3	99.3	99.1	88.6	56.6	39.9	23.3	10.0	4.5
1964	57.6	8.8	84.0	98.8	98.9	99.0	90.4	52.4	36.6	17.7	8.3	3.6
1963	62.3	(NA)	84.1	99.4	99.0	98.8	89.8	51.6	35.2	21.1	8.2	3.8
1962	61.9	(NA)	83.9	99.1	99.3	98.7	88.5	52.7	33.7	18.8	8.9	4.2
1961	60.4	(NA)	82.6	99.7	99.4	98.3	85.5	49.6	31.1	15.0	7.5	3.1
1960	60.3	(NA)	82.3	99.7	99.5	98.1	85.2	49.5	29.2	16.3	8.9	4.0
1959	59.2	(NA)	80.1	99.3	99.4	98.1	85.9	47.1	30.8	14.1	9.5	3.4
1958	58.8	(NA)	81.5	99.6		91.1		48.1	22.3		9.9	3.0
1957	57.7	(NA)	79.1	99.7		91.9		44.0	22.9		9.9	2.7
1956	56.5	(NA)	78.2	99.4		90.1		46.4	21.8		9.3	2.9
1955	54.9	(NA)	79.0	99.4		89.1		43.9	19.3		7.1	2.2
1954	54.3	(NA)	78.0	99.4		89.6		43.3	20.5		6.5	1.9
1953	50.5	(NA)	56.8	99.4		87.9		38.1	20.3		5.7	2.2
1952	49.4	(NA)	55.2	99.1		87.0		38.3	17.8		5.0	1.6
1951	56.8	(NA)	55.4	99.3		86.6		33.8	14.9		4.2	(NA)
1950	54.7	(NA)		88.6		85.0		37.3	14.6		5.9	(NA)
1949	45.9	(NA)		89.1		84.1		32.1	15.7		7.1	2.0
1948	45.3	(NA)		87.6		84.4		35.9	17.2		5.3	1.5
1947	44.4	(NA)		88.6		79.6		32.6	17.4		5.9	1.8

See footnotes at end of table.

Table A-21. Percentage of Persons 3 to 34 Years Old Enrolled in School, by Age, Sex, Race, and Hispanic Origin: October 1947 to 1996 — Continued

	Total enrolled	Age										
		3 and 4 years	5 and 6 years	7 to 9 years	10 to 13 years	14 and 15 years	16 and 17 years	18 and 19 years	20 and 21 years	22 to 24 years	25 to 29 years	30 to 34 years
Female												
1996	53.5	49.3	95.0	97.4	98.3	97.3	92.7	64.1	46.1	23.6	12.0	7.1
1995	52.9	49.6	96.9	98.8	99.1	98.8	93.3	59.2	46.0	23.6	11.7	6.0
1994	52.6	47.9	96.1	99.4	99.4	98.8	94.4	60.5	49.0	23.5	11.0	7.4
1993r	50.7	39.5	95.7	99.5	99.5	98.9	92.8	62.8	43.0	21.7	10.4	6.5
1993	50.6	39.9	95.8	99.5	99.5	98.9	93.0	62.9	43.3	21.8	10.4	6.5
1992	50.5	40.4	95.7	99.2	99.1	99.4	92.8	62.7	46.6	22.9	10.6	6.7
1991	49.5	42.0	95.7	99.5	99.6	98.5	92.5	60.9	43.9	20.2	9.7	6.7
1990	49.0	44.8	96.4	99.7	99.7	98.9	92.8	57.0	40.9	18.7	10.4	6.9
1989	47.8	40.2	94.9	99.2	99.6	98.1	92.1	55.6	39.7	19.6	9.6	6.3
1988	47.2	38.8	96.1	99.6	99.8	98.8	91.1	55.1	39.6	16.5	8.6	6.3
1987	46.7	36.4	94.4	99.5	99.2	98.3	91.0	53.3	37.3	16.2	8.7	6.4
1986	46.8	39.0	94.9	99.1	99.3	98.8	92.2	53.0	33.7	16.2	8.7	6.7
1985	47.0	39.9	97.1	99.3	99.3	97.9	90.8	52.9	35.0	15.0	9.0	6.4
1984	46.3	36.1	95.2	99.3	99.4	98.0	91.0	49.6	32.3	14.2	8.9	6.9
1983	46.6	36.0	96.5	99.0	99.4	98.4	91.2	51.1	30.5	13.6	8.5	6.7
1982	46.9	35.5	95.0	99.2	99.4	98.4	89.6	47.4	33.7	14.5	9.0	6.9
1981	47.1	34.3	93.5	99.5	99.4	97.8	90.4	47.8	31.9	13.4	7.9	6.7
1980	47.9	34.6	96.4	99.2	99.4	97.8	88.4	45.1	30.2	14.8	8.9	7.0
1979	48.4	34.4	95.3	99.5	99.5	98.1	87.7	43.0	30.0	13.9	9.0	6.7
1978	48.7	32.2	95.6	99.5	99.2	98.5	88.4	42.7	27.4	13.0	7.9	6.0
1977	49.9	30.5	96.9	99.5	99.6	98.4	87.4	43.4	29.0	13.3	8.8	6.3
1976	50.4	31.0	95.8	99.5	99.3	97.6	87.7	44.0	30.9	13.7	7.1	4.8
1975	50.9	30.9	95.3	99.5	99.6	98.1	87.5	43.5	27.5	12.2	7.0	5.7
1974	50.9	29.5	94.0	99.3	99.7	97.9	87.6	39.9	26.6	11.4	6.5	4.6
1973	50.5	22.9	93.2	99.3	99.3	97.1	87.3	38.7	27.4	9.9	5.4	3.6
1972	51.5	24.4	92.7	99.2	99.4	97.5	87.3	41.9	27.5	8.9	5.1	3.2
1971	52.6	21.7	92.6	99.3	99.5	98.4	88.9	43.2	27.0	8.1	4.3	3.5
1970	52.9	19.1	90.9	99.3	99.5	98.1	89.0	41.8	24.1	9.7	4.4	3.1
1969	53.2	15.8	89.8	99.6	99.5	98.2	88.2	41.8	25.8	9.4	4.5	3.7
1968	52.9	15.2	89.0	99.3	99.3	98.0	89.4	41.3	22.3	8.2	3.7	2.8
1967	53.0	13.1	89.0	99.6	99.4	98.5	87.4	41.0	25.6	7.5	3.3	2.9
1966	52.5	12.4	86.4	99.5	99.5	98.7	87.6	38.6	22.3	6.6	3.9	1.7
1965	52.2	10.3	85.7	99.4	99.5	98.9	87.0	38.3	20.9	6.3	3.2	2.0
1964	51.3	9.9	83.9	99.2	99.1	98.6	86.1	33.7	20.3	4.5	2.6	1.6
1963	54.7	(NA)	83.8	99.7	99.5	98.2	85.7	32.1	18.6	4.4	2.4	1.5
1962	54.0	(NA)	82.4	99.5	99.5	97.6	83.3	34.6	16.3	4.1	1.8	1.4
1961	53.4	(NA)	81.7	99.5	99.5	97.7	83.5	29.7	15.3	3.8	2.1	1.3
1960	52.7	(NA)	81.6	99.7	99.6	98.1	81.4	29.7	13.5	3.5	1.8	1.2
1959	52.0	(NA)	81.9	99.7	99.6	97.7	81.6	28.8	11.1	4.6	1.7	1.3
1958	51.1	(NA)	81.2	99.6		88.9		29.9		7.5	2.2	1.6
1957	49.8	(NA)	79.5	99.7		88.2		27.0		8.3	1.7	1.1
1956	48.6	(NA)	78.6	99.5		88.2		27.3		7.0	1.8	1.3
1955	46.9	(NA)	79.5	99.3		85.9		22.4		6.2	1.5	1.0
1954	46.4	(NA)	79.1	99.8		87.0		25.3		6.4	1.7	1.1
1953	42.9	(NA)	57.4	99.9		84.9		26.5		6.5	0.6	1.5
1952	41.7	(NA)	54.3	99.1		85.3		21.1		4.3	0.6	0.7
1951	49.0	(NA)	53.6	99.4		86.0		21.7		4.3	0.9	(NA)
1950	48.6	(NA)		89.4		83.7		24.2		4.8	0.4	(NA)
1949	39.4	(NA)		88.6		81.9		20.5		3.8	1.2	0.4
1948	38.4	(NA)		87.9		83.4		19.7		3.5	0.4	0.4
1947	38.1	(NA)		88.9		80.8		18.3		4.1	0.4	0.4

See footnotes at end of table.

Table A-21. Percentage of Persons 3 to 34 Years Old Enrolled in School, by Age, Sex, Race, and Hispanic Origin: October 1947 to 1996 — Continued

	Total enrolled	Age										
		3 and 4 years	5 and 6 years	7 to 9 years	10 to 13 years	14 and 15 years	16 and 17 years	18 and 19 years	20 and 21 years	22 to 24 years	25 to 29 years	30 to 34 years
BLACK												
Total												
1996	56.2	49.9	90.5	97.4	97.4	98.9	92.1	52.8	37.0	21.0	13.7	7.1
1995	56.1	47.5	95.5	97.7	99.2	99.0	92.9	57.4	37.4	19.9	10.0	7.8
1994	56.4	51.9	97.2	99.7	99.6	99.2	95.4	54.0	34.9	22.6	10.5	7.2
1993r	53.8	39.8	94.5	99.0	99.8	98.5	94.8	57.6	30.1	18.0	10.4	5.5
1993	53.6	39.8	94.6	99.0	99.8	98.5	94.7	57.7	30.0	18.1	10.4	5.5
1992	53.0	38.6	95.9	99.4	99.7	99.4	93.0	56.2	33.3	20.3	7.9	5.3
1991	52.5	37.2	95.8	99.6	100.0	99.1	91.7	55.6	30.0	18.2	8.7	6.5
1990	51.9	41.6	96.3	99.9	99.9	99.2	91.7	55.2	28.4	20.0	6.1	4.4
1989	51.3	38.9	94.9	99.0	99.4	99.4	93.7	50.2	30.7	17.2	6.4	4.9
1988	50.6	33.4	95.5	99.7	99.7	98.9	91.5	50.3	28.1	13.2	7.2	5.6
1987	51.7	36.8	95.8	99.7	99.8	98.3	91.5	53.2	28.7	15.0	9.3	6.0
1986	51.6	38.6	95.4	99.8	99.0	98.3	93.9	50.7	25.6	17.1	8.0	6.2
1985	50.9	42.7	95.7	98.4	99.5	97.9	91.7	44.1	27.7	13.7	7.5	5.9
1984	50.1	36.2	94.1	99.5	99.3	97.9	92.4	44.3	27.7	15.7	7.4	5.1
1983	50.8	36.2	94.7	99.1	99.7	97.8	92.6	46.1	23.4	15.6	7.4	6.5
1982	51.6	38.6	95.4	99.2	98.9	98.1	91.6	43.6	24.3	17.0	7.8	7.6
1981	52.5	36.7	94.5	98.8	99.4	97.1	91.3	48.2	23.4	14.7	8.4	7.0
1980	53.9	38.2	95.4	99.4	99.4	97.9	90.6	45.7	23.4	13.6	8.8	6.8
1979	55.0	40.8	96.0	99.4	98.7	97.4	90.8	46.6	23.7	15.0	7.9	6.8
1978	56.3	41.3	93.9	99.5	98.9	98.5	91.2	46.2	25.6	15.0	8.7	7.9
1977	57.7	35.2	96.5	99.3	99.0	98.8	90.8	48.3	29.5	15.2	11.3	9.0
1976	57.9	34.5	94.0	99.3	98.8	99.0	89.0	50.4	28.2	16.4	9.4	8.1
1975	57.7	33.5	94.3	99.3	99.2	97.4	86.9	47.1	27.1	14.2	9.4	7.1
1974	57.3	29.1	92.8	99.2	99.8	97.0	87.1	44.0	23.4	12.1	8.9	6.9
1973	55.8	28.9	89.9	99.2	99.0	96.7	87.7	37.8	20.5	12.4	6.1	5.0
1972	57.8	28.3	90.0	98.7	99.3	97.4	89.5	42.8	22.0	13.1	6.5	5.9
1971	58.6	21.5	89.8	99.0	98.8	98.4	89.2	46.6	27.3	11.4	6.2	5.2
1970	57.4	22.7	84.9	99.3	99.3	97.6	85.7	40.1	22.8	8.0	4.8	3.4
1969	57.8	21.2	84.1	98.8	99.1	97.9	85.8	44.5	23.3	8.6	4.3	3.4
1968	57.4	18.7	82.7	99.2	99.0	97.7	86.4	45.4	18.2	7.9	3.1	3.3
1967	56.8	17.7	82.2	99.1	98.7	86.1	84.1	40.7	21.2	7.2	5.0	2.4
1966	55.5	13.7	80.8	99.2	99.2	97.4	85.2	37.7	11.6	6.1	2.3	2.3
1965	55.6	11.8	79.1	98.9	99.3	98.1	83.9	39.6	12.8	6.2	2.1	2.4
1964	54.5	10.5	80.3	99.0	99.0	96.9	82.4	35.6	14.0	3.8	3.1	2.9
1963	58.8	(NA)	76.6	98.5	99.5	97.6	82.0	39.8	16.2	5.5	3.3	2.0
1962	57.1	(NA)	76.0	98.6	98.8	97.1	73.2	33.4	14.9	6.1	3.8	1.5
1961	56.8	(NA)	79.1	98.0	98.3	95.1	76.8	30.6	15.9	4.3	2.4	1.1
1960	55.9	(NA)	73.3	99.3	99.0	95.9	76.9	34.6	11.9	4.4	2.9	1.0
1959	55.1	(NA)	74.3	98.9	99.1	93.9	76.3	33.6	11.6	6.3	2.8	1.3
1958	54.0	(NA)	73.9	98.8		82.8		34.3	8.7		3.9	1.3
1957	53.5	(NA)	74.3	98.2		84.8		36.7	8.8		4.6	1.2
1956	51.5	(NA)	72.8	98.4		81.2		31.8	8.7		3.1	0.7
1955	50.7	(NA)	71.1	98.2		82.8		27.6	7.2		4.9	1.8
1954	48.6	(NA)	68.8	98.0		78.8		24.0	5.8		4.8	1.4
1953	45.5	(NA)	46.3	97.3		82.3		27.6	5.4		1.7	0.8
1952	46.4	(NA)	54.0	96.4		77.3				6.3		
1951	53.4	(NA)	54.9	97.3		77.1		20.8	6.2		2.7	(NA)
1950	51.2	(NA)	86.8			75.5		23.3	6.3		3.0	(NA)
1949	40.9	(NA)	83.7			69.5		20.0	6.2		1.8	0.5
1948	39.2	(NA)	80.1			66.8		24.6	6.3		1.5	0.6
1947	41.0	(NA)	84.8			71.9		20.2	6.9		2.5	0.5

See footnotes at end of table.

Table A-21. Percentage of Persons 3 to 34 Years Old Enrolled in School, by Age, Sex, Race, and Hispanic Origin: October 1947 to 1996 — Continued

	Total enrolled	3 and 4 years	5 and 6 years	7 to 9 years	10 to 13 years	14 and 15 years	16 and 17 years	18 and 19 years	20 and 21 years	22 to 24 years	25 to 29 years	30 to 34 years
Males												
1996	57.8	47.0	90.1	98.1	97.2	98.1	93.7	55.2	39.0	18.6	12.8	5.4
1995	58.3	51.5	94.7	98.2	99.5	99.6	95.2	59.1	36.1	20.3	6.1	6.7
1994	58.4	56.8	97.1	99.6	99.5	99.7	95.3	53.4	33.7	21.3	10.8	5.7
1993r	56.0	41.6	96.8	99.3	100.0	99.0	96.1	63.4	23.7	19.6	10.4	3.1
1993	55.8	41.7	96.9	99.3	100.0	99.0	96.0	63.6	23.9	19.6	10.3	3.1
1992	54.8	41.3	97.6	99.9	99.7	99.9	94.5	60.7	27.1	18.7	7.6	3.3
1991	54.5	35.2	95.4	99.8	100.0	100.0	90.4	62.2	30.1	19.3	8.6	4.8
1990	53.9	38.3	96.1	99.9	99.9	99.7	93.2	60.7	31.1	20.0	4.6	2.3
1989	52.6	40.2	92.9	98.9	98.8	99.3	95.6	51.0	23.2	15.5	5.5	3.2
1988	52.4	34.5	96.0	99.6	100.0	99.1	93.2	49.7	20.7	14.7	6.3	4.1
1987	54.0	39.0	97.4	100.0	99.8	98.1	91.8	58.7	30.3	15.5	8.4	3.4
1986	53.8	38.7	97.1	99.6	98.8	98.4	94.7	54.1	25.4	17.3	7.1	5.9
1985	52.6	34.6	94.6	98.2	99.1	98.2	91.8	49.5	29.7	13.2	6.9	5.7
1984	52.6	37.2	92.8	99.5	99.1	96.9	93.2	48.6	29.7	17.5	5.7	3.9
1983	52.9	37.1	95.8	98.9	99.4	98.4	91.8	46.6	23.5	17.2	9.1	6.6
1982	53.2	37.4	93.9	99.3	98.4	97.8	92.2	46.5	20.9	17.4	8.5	7.1
1981	54.5	34.8	94.5	98.5	99.2	97.3	92.1	51.9	20.6	14.7	8.4	5.6
1980	56.1	36.6	94.1	99.5	99.4	98.5	90.8	42.8	23.0	13.3	10.6	7.3
1979	57.8	40.4	96.6	99.0	98.4	98.5	94.6	48.0	26.9	14.6	8.1	6.3
1978	58.7	37.9	93.2	99.4	98.8	99.0	92.8	50.5	25.2	14.7	9.5	7.8
1977	60.3	32.4	96.0	99.1	98.6	99.0	92.5	50.5	31.0	18.5	12.1	9.2
1976	61.1	36.3	94.4	99.5	98.8	99.5	90.9	54.9	28.0	18.7	11.0	8.8
1975	60.3	29.5	94.6	99.3	99.0	97.6	88.2	49.9	28.7	14.7	11.8	8.6
1974	60.7	30.3	91.8	99.5	99.6	96.1	90.1	46.1	27.7	16.0	10.4	9.7
1973	58.6	29.2	89.0	99.2	99.1	96.9	89.0	43.5	24.5	13.9	6.9	6.5
1972	60.9	32.1	90.8	98.4	99.4	97.6	88.9	47.7	27.1	18.4	7.3	5.2
1971	60.4	19.0	88.7	99.1	98.1	97.7	90.0	50.7	31.3	12.9	8.5	6.4
1970	59.5	22.3	84.2	99.2	99.1	98.0	85.4	41.3	27.8	9.6	6.1	3.6
1969	60.0	21.3	83.1	98.3	98.9	98.0	87.4	49.5	28.4	10.7	2.8	2.9
1968	60.0	16.9	84.1	98.8	98.4	98.5	88.5	53.1	23.4	7.5	5.2	3.4
1967	59.2	17.0	81.0	99.0	98.3	96.5	86.7	48.6	24.5	9.0	3.5	3.5
1966	58.1	12.7	80.0	99.1	99.0	98.2	87.4	46.3	14.4	9.1	2.6	2.7
1965	57.7	9.5	81.0	99.3	99.4	98.7	82.2	47.5	18.5	4.3	2.6	2.3
1964	56.8	9.4	80.7	98.2	98.7	98.8	84.3	39.9	14.2	3.8	3.5	4.0
1963	61.9	(NA)	74.3	97.7	99.2	98.2	85.9	46.5	21.7	7.1	4.7	2.7
1962	60.4	(NA)	74.5	98.9	98.6	99.1	77.1	40.3	15.0	10.1	5.8	1.7
1961	60.0	(NA)	78.7	98.4	97.6	96.6	78.6	41.7	19.9	6.1	4.0	1.9
1960	58.3	(NA)	71.8	99.4	98.7	97.0	79.1	36.9	13.7	6.3	3.9	1.0
1959	58.0	(NA)	76.0	98.7	99.1	95.8	76.3	35.5	12.5	10.6	4.5	1.8
1958	58.0	(NA)	74.2	98.8		87.6		43.4	11.8		6.3	2.4
1957	55.9	(NA)	73.1	98.2		84.7		38.5	10.3		6.0	1.2
1956	54.3	(NA)	70.4	97.6		81.3		36.8	12.5		5.3	0.9
1955	54.4	(NA)	72.8	98.2		85.2		32.9	9.8		6.2	1.9
1954	52.0	(NA)	64.7	97.5		82.8		21.6	10.1		7.9	1.9
1953	47.8	(NA)	41.6	97.1		79.1		34.6	5.8		3.3	0.9
1952	49.7	(NA)	51.4	96.0		72.5			6.0			
1951	56.9	(NA)	52.8	98.0		74.9		23.6	9.0		4.3	(NA)
1950	56.0	(NA)		87.0		79.3		19.9	11.1		6.1	(NA)
1949	45.0	(NA)		83.1		68.8		26.1	11.8		3.3	1.1
1948	40.4	(NA)		78.9		63.9		24.0	10.5		2.5	1.4
1947	45.1	(NA)		84.6		72.6		20.7	12.3		5.1	0.8

See footnotes at end of table.

Table A-21.   Percentage of Persons 3 to 34 Years Old Enrolled in School, by Age, Sex, Race, and Hispanic Origin: October 1947 to 1996 — Continued

	Total enrolled	Age										
		3 and 4 years	5 and 6 years	7 to 9 years	10 to 13 years	14 and 15 years	16 and 17 years	18 and 19 years	20 and 21 years	22 to 24 years	25 to 29 years	30 to 34 years
Female												
1996	54.7	52.6	90.8	96.7	97.6	99.6	90.4	50.5	35.5	23.2	14.4	8.6
1995	54.1	43.6	96.3	97.2	99.0	98.3	90.4	55.9	38.5	19.5	13.0	8.7
1994	54.4	47.0	97.2	99.7	99.7	98.6	95.5	54.6	35.9	23.6	10.3	8.5
1993r	51.6	37.9	92.0	98.7	99.7	97.9	93.4	52.0	35.3	16.6	10.5	7.4
1993	51.6	37.8	92.1	98.7	99.7	97.9	93.4	51.9	35.1	16.7	10.5	7.5
1992	51.3	35.8	94.1	98.9	99.6	98.8	91.5	51.8	38.6	21.6	8.2	6.9
1991	50.6	39.5	96.1	99.5	100.0	98.2	93.1	49.4	29.9	17.3	8.8	7.9
1990	50.1	45.0	96.5	99.8	99.8	98.7	90.2	50.0	26.0	20.1	7.3	6.2
1989	50.1	37.6	97.1	99.2	99.9	99.5	91.7	49.4	37.3	18.6	7.1	6.3
1988	49.0	32.3	94.9	99.8	99.3	98.6	89.8	50.9	34.3	11.9	7.9	6.9
1987	49.6	34.4	94.1	99.3	99.7	98.6	91.2	48.2	27.4	14.6	10.0	8.1
1986	49.5	38.6	93.7	100.0	99.3	98.2	93.1	47.6	25.7	16.9	8.6	6.5
1985	49.4	50.2	97.1	98.7	99.9	97.6	91.6	39.0	26.0	14.1	7.9	6.1
1984	47.8	39.2	95.3	99.5	99.4	99.0	91.7	40.3	25.9	14.1	8.8	6.2
1983	48.8	35.2	93.6	99.3	100.0	97.1	93.4	45.7	23.3	14.2	6.0	6.5
1082	50.2	39.8	97.0	99.1	99.5	98.3	91.0	41.0	27.2	16.6	7.2	8.0
1981	50.6	38.7	94.4	99.1	99.6	97.0	90.5	44.9	25.7	14.7	8.4	8.1
1980	52.0	39.7	96.7	99.3	99.3	97.4	90.4	48.2	23.7	13.9	7.4	6.5
1979	52.5	41.2	95.5	99.7	99.0	96.4	87.1	45.4	21.1	15.3	7.7	7.3
1978	54.1	44.8	94.7	99.6	99.1	98.0	89.6	42.4	26.0	15.2	8.1	8.0
1977	55.4	38.1	97.0	99.4	99.4	98.5	89.1	46.3	28.2	12.6	10.7	8.9
1976	55.0	32.6	93.6	99.1	98.8	98.4	87.0	46.4	28.4	14.5	8.1	7.6
1975	55.3	37.6	93.9	99.3	99.4	97.2	85.6	44.7	25.8	13.8	7.5	5.9
1974	54.2	28.0	93.8	98.9	100.0	97.9	84.2	42.1	20.1	9.0	7.7	4.8
1973	53.3	28.5	90.9	99.2	98.9	96.5	86.4	32.8	17.3	11.1	5.5	3.8
1972	54.9	24.5	89.1	99.0	99.3	97.3	90.1	38.7	17.9	8.5	5.9	6.5
1971	56.9	24.1	90.9	98.9	99.4	99.0	88.4	43.1	24.1	10.1	4.2	4.2
1970	55.5	23.2	85.7	99.5	99.5	97.2	85.9	38.9	18.9	6.7	3.6	3.3
1969	55.8	21.1	85.0	99.4	99.2	97.7	84.3	40.1	19.6	6.9	5.5	3.7
1968	54.9	20.5	81.3	99.7	99.5	96.9	84.3	38.6	14.5	8.3	1.5	3.2
1967	54.6	18.5	83.4	99.2	99.0	95.8	81.6	34.0	18.5	5.6	6.1	1.5
1966	53.2	14.7	81.6	99.3	99.4	96.5	83.1	30.3	9.3	3.6	2.0	2.0
1965	53.6	14.1	77.3	98.6	99.2	97.6	85.6	32.5	8.0	7.8	1.7	2.4
1964	52.5	11.7	79.9	99.9	99.3	95.0	80.6	31.7	13.7	3.8	2.8	2.0
1963	58.0	(NA)	79.0	99.2	99.8	96.9	78.2	33.9	11.5	4.3	2.2	1.5
1962	54.1	(NA)	77.5	98.3	99.1	95.2	69.5	27.3	14.9	3.0	2.2	1.3
1961	53.8	(NA)	79.5	97.6	99.0	93.5	75.1	20.6	12.4	2.7	1.0	0.4
1960	53.7	(NA)	74.9	99.1	99.3	94.8	74.7	32.2	10.4	2.8	2.1	1.0
1959	52.4	(NA)	72.5	99.2	99.1	92.0	76.4	31.9	10.8	2.7	1.4	1.0
1958	50.3	(NA)	73.7	98.7		78.1		26.4	6.0		1.9	0.4
1957	51.3	(NA)	75.6	98.2		85.0		35.1	7.6		3.5	1.1
1956	49.0	(NA)	75.2	99.1		81.1		27.5	5.7		1.3	0.6
1955	47.4	(NA)	69.4	98.1		80.5		23.1	5.5		3.8	1.7
1954	45.6	(NA)	73.0	98.6		74.7		25.7	2.9		2.3	0.9
1953	43.5	(NA)	51.1	97.6		85.5		21.6	5.0		0.3	0.7
1952	43.6	(NA)	56.3	97.0		82.3			6.4			
1951	50.3	(NA)	57.1	96.5		79.2		17.9	4.3		1.5	(NA)
1950	47.0	(NA)		86.5		71.9		25.7	3.0		0.6	(NA)
1949	37.3	(NA)		84.5		70.0		14.5	1.9		0.7	(NA)
1948	38.2	(NA)		81.3		69.6		25.2	2.7		0.6	(NA)
1947	37.3	(NA)		84.9		71.3		19.9	2.5		0.3	0.3

See footnotes at end of table.

Table A-21. Percentage of Persons 3 to 34 Years Old Enrolled in School, by Age, Sex, Race, and Hispanic Origin: October 1947 to 1996 — Continued

	Total enrolled	Age										
		3 and 4 years	5 and 6 years	7 to 9 years	10 to 13 years	14 and 15 years	16 and 17 years	18 and 19 years	20 and 21 years	22 to 24 years	25 to 29 years	30 to 34 years
HISPANIC ORIGIN[1]												
Total												
1996	50.3	38.1	89.5	96.6	97.6	96.6	88.7	47.0	25.3	17.6	8.6	5.0
1995	49.7	36.9	93.9	98.5	99.2	98.9	88.2	46.1	27.1	15.6	7.1	4.7
1994	49.0	30.8	96.1	99.2	99.4	96.1	88.3	51.4	24.9	15.1	8.1	5.7
1993ʳ	48.6	26.8	93.6	99.6	99.2	97.6	88.1	50.0	31.8	13.8	7.7	5.1
1993	48.9	26.8	93.8	99.6	99.2	97.6	88.3	50.0	31.8	13.7	7.7	4.8
1992	49.2	28.8	96.0	99.5	99.1	98.8	87.2	53.7	30.1	14.5	6.7	6.0
1991	47.9	30.6	92.4	99.9	99.4	97.2	82.6	47.9	26.4	11.6	6.9	5.9
1990	47.4	29.8	94.8	99.6	99.2	99.0	85.4	44.1	27.2	9.9	6.3	3.1
1989	45.8	23.8	92.8	98.0	99.3	96.5	86.4	44.6	18.8	12.0	6.6	3.5
1988	46.0	24.5	95.7	99.6	99.8	98.8	78.8	44.1	16.7	12.1	5.8	6.2
1987	47.2	30.7	93.0	99.2	99.4	97.6	87.1	39.1	26.5	12.3	7.5	4.9
1986	48.2	28.8	93.7	99.4	99.3	97.2	84.0	46.0	21.4	13.7	9.2	5.6
1985	47.7	27.0	94.5	98.4	99.4	96.1	84.5	41.8	24.0	11.6	8.6	5.6
1984	47.7	24.2	93.9	98.7	99.4	94.9	85.7	39.9	28.1	11.3	6.6	7.5
1983	49.3	23.5	95.1	98.5	99.7	96.0	88.6	44.3	24.0	12.5	7.1	5.7
1982	49.4	21.8	92.2	98.7	98.8	96.9	85.5	39.2	22.7	10.4	8.2	4.4
1981	49.0	24.5	90.4	99.2	99.1	94.0	82.8	37.8	20.6	12.3	8.0	4.7
1980	49.8	28.5	94.5	98.4	99.7	94.3	81.8	37.8	19.5	11.7	6.9	4.1
1979	48.6	22.5	92.5	98.7	99.0	96.3	82.3	39.9	22.6	10.0	7.8	7.1
1978	48.3	22.5	91.4	99.5	98.0	95.2	83.0	35.7	16.8	11.8	8.0	4.1
1977	50.8	19.5	93.7	99.0	99.3	97.6	83.6	40.6	23.1	10.8	9.3	5.6
1976	51.8	22.2	95.0	97.5	99.1	95.4	81.3	45.2	24.0	14.8	7.9	2.7
1975	54.8	27.3	92.1	99.6	99.2	95.6	86.2	44.0	27.5	14.1	8.3	4.1
1974	54.3	25.3	92.1	98.8	99.2	96.1	78.3	45.2	23.2	11.3	6.7	2.2
1973	52.8	18.8	90.7	98.7	99.1	94.4	80.2	39.2	21.5	10.0	6.8	1.3
1972	53.0	20.5	90.0	98.7	99.1	96.7	83.9	41.4	17.0	9.9	5.2	3.5
Male												
1996	49.2	39.6	91.0	95.4	97.9	98.0	90.4	46.8	19.5	16.2	6.8	4.3
1995	49.1	40.8	93.6	98.8	98.8	98.4	88.4	47.4	24.8	14.8	5.6	4.5
1994	48.0	32.6	96.5	98.6	99.3	94.6	86.6	54.2	23.7	14.0	7.1	4.2
1993ʳ	46.6	26.9	93.4	99.8	98.8	96.9	88.7	47.8	31.6	13.0	5.5	5.4
1993	47.4	27.0	93.6	99.8	98.8	96.9	89.1	47.7	31.6	12.8	5.5	5.4
1992	47.9	24.9	96.5	100.0	99.2	98.1	89.2	52.6	24.3	13.8	5.3	3.5
1991	46.4	30.7	92.3	99.8	99.7	97.8	83.6	42.1	20.8	9.9	6.8	3.3
1990	47.1	27.3	95.6	99.5	99.0	99.1	85.5	40.7	21.7	11.2	4.6	4.0
1989	45.8	21.3	92.5	97.7	98.6	98.0	88.7	44.2	17.1	12.2	7.3	4.1
1988	46.2	27.9	96.7	99.2	100.0	98.1	80.9	44.7	21.6	12.5	4.5	5.0
1987	47.8	30.5	92.8	99.7	100.0	98.1	90.9	42.3	30.1	11.4	7.8	5.1
1986	47.3	29.4	93.0	100.0	99.4	96.8	85.0	45.8	19.2	13.0	9.1	4.4
1985	47.5	26.4	95.3	98.9	99.1	96.2	88.9	38.6	20.3	12.6	8.7	3.8
1984	48.6	20.0	93.6	98.2	100.0	95.7	85.1	38.8	27.5	12.3	8.2	4.0
1983	50.7	25.0	91.9	98.8	99.6	97.8	88.2	40.4	26.2	15.1	6.9	4.6
1982	50.4	25.2	90.3	99.6	98.4	96.8	87.8	39.7	21.6	11.2	10.8	3.1
1981	49.6	25.5	89.6	98.8	99.0	92.3	84.5	36.0	24.4	11.4	8.3	4.3
1980	49.9	30.1	94.0	97.7	99.4	96.7	81.5	36.9	21.4	10.7	6.8	6.2
1979	51.0	22.8	93.8	98.7	99.0	96.6	85.1	42.6	24.0	12.4	8.7	6.1
1978	50.5	22.6	93.2	99.1	97.8	94.0	80.4	40.0	18.1	13.6	9.5	4.4
1977	54.2	23.2	91.4	100.0	98.7	99.1	89.4	43.1	22.8	16.0	13.1	6.4
1976	55.0	22.1	94.6	97.4	98.5	97.3	85.5	46.3	27.1	18.6	11.4	5.6
1975	58.1	26.7	89.7	99.6	98.8	97.4	88.3	51.9	31.3	15.9	11.9	7.2
1974	56.0	23.5	93.1	98.3	98.5	97.9	78.6	46.8	22.3	14.5	8.4	7.4
1973	55.5	23.1	92.4	99.1	99.1	96.5	86.6	45.8	23.8	10.8	9.9	6.7
1972	54.7	20.4	90.3	98.8	99.1	98.1	87.8	40.5	20.0	13.9	5.8	2.5

See footnotes at end of table.

Table A-21. Percentage of Persons 3 to 34 Years Old Enrolled in School, by Age, Sex, Race, and Hispanic Origin: October 1947 to 1996 — Continued

	Total enrolled	Age										
		3 and 4 years	5 and 6 years	7 to 9 years	10 to 13 years	14 and 15 years	16 and 17 years	18 and 19 years	20 and 21 years	22 to 24 years	25 to 29 years	30 to 34 years
Female												
1996	51.4	36.8	87.8	97.9	97.4	95.0	86.9	47.2	31.1	19.3	10.5	5.7
1995	50.3	32.7	94.3	98.2	99.6	99.4	88.0	44.8	29.2	16.6	8.7	4.9
1994	50.2	28.9	95.7	99.8	99.4	97.6	90.2	48.6	26.4	16.5	9.1	7.3
1993ʳ	50.7	26.7	93.9	99.4	99.6	98.2	87.3	51.9	31.9	14.7	10.2	4.7
1993	50.6	26.7	93.9	99.4	99.6	98.2	87.4	51.9	32.0	14.5	10.2	4.8
1992	50.6	32.7	95.4	99.0	99.1	99.6	85.0	54.9	35.6	15.4	8.2	6.0
1991	49.5	30.5	92.6	100.0	99.2	96.6	81.5	53.7	32.0	13.6	7.0	5.9
1990	47.7	32.3	93.9	99.7	99.4	98.8	85.3	47.2	33.1	8.4	8.1	3.1
1989	45.9	26.5	93.3	98.3	100.0	95.1	83.7	45.0	20.8	11.9	5.8	3.5
1988	45.8	20.7	94.6	100.0	99.6	99.6	76.6	43.5	11.2	11.5	7.2	6.2
1987	46.5	30.8	93.2	98.7	98.9	97.1	82.6	36.2	22.0	13.2	7.3	4.9
1986	49.0	28.2	94.4	98.7	99.2	97.5	83.0	46.2	23.7	14.5	9.2	5.6
1985	47.9	27.7	93.7	98.0	99.7	96.0	80.0	44.7	27.4	10.4	8.6	5.6
1984	46.8	28.2	94.2	99.2	98.7	94.0	86.3	40.8	28.7	10.4	4.9	7.5
1983	48.0	22.0	98.3	98.1	99.8	94.1	89.1	47.6	21.7	10.1	7.4	5.7
1982	48.4	16.3	90.9	97.8	99.2	97.1	82.8	38.7	23.7	9.7	5.7	4.4
1981	48.4	23.4	91.3	99.6	99.3	95.7	80.8	39.4	16.8	13.1	7.7	4.7
1980	49.8	26.6	94.9	99.0	99.9	92.1	82.2	38.8	17.6	12.6	6.9	4.1
1979	46.3	22.3	91.1	98.7	98.9	95.9	79.5	37.1	21.5	7.8	7.0	7.1
1978	46.2	22.5	89.4	100.0	98.2	96.6	86.2	31.9	15.7	10.1	6.5	4.1
1977	47.6	15.8	96.3	97.9	99.9	95.9	77.4	38.5	23.4	6.2	5.9	5.6
1976	48.8	22.3	95.5	97.6	99.7	93.6	77.6	44.2	21.4	12.1	4.8	2.7
1975	51.7	27.9	94.4	99.5	99.7	93.8	84.0	37.1	24.3	12.5	5.3	4.1
1974	52.5	27.4	91.1	99.2	100.0	94.1	77.9	43.7	23.9	8.4	4.9	2.2
1973	50.1	14.0	88.9	98.3	99.1	92.5	74.9	32.9	19.4	9.2	3.9	1.3
1972	51.4	20.5	89.7	98.5	99.0	95.4	80.0	42.4	14.6	6.8	4.7	3.5

SOURCE: U.S. Bureau of the Census.

Data shown for 1966 and earlier years for the Black population are for Black and Other races combined.

1. May be of any race.

r = Revised, controlled to 1990 census-based population estimates; previous 1993 data controlled to 1980 based population estimates.

NOTE: Data for 1947 to 1953 exclude kindergarten. Nursery school was first collected in 1964.

(NA) Not applicable or not available.

Table A-22. Persons 6 to 17 Years Old Enrolled Below Modal Grade : 1971 to 1996

(Numbers in thousands. Civilian noninstitutional population.)

Race, Hispanic origin, and year	Percent below modal grade				Dropout rate for 15 to 17 years	Population in age group			
	6 to 8 years	9 to 11 years	12 to 14 years	15 to 17 years		6 to 8 years	9 to 11 years	12 to 14 years	15 to 17 years
ALL RACES									
Total									
1996	17.9	23.3	28.8	31.0	4.8	12,191	11,845	11,653	11,617
1995	17.5	25.6	30.8	32.8	4.1	11,728	11,812	11,582	11,401
1994	18.9	26.2	31.3	30.9	3.8	11,601	11,528	11,462	10,560
1993ʳ	18.7	28.1	31.0	32.3	3.8	11,363	11,283	10,981	10,247
1993	18.7	28.0	30.8	32.0	3.7	11,363	11,283	10,981	10,247
1992	19.4	21.1	30.9	30.5	3.6	11,260	11,183	10,723	10,114
1991	21.2	26.9	29.6	30.0	4.6	11,120	11,099	10,440	9,923
1990	21.5	27.6	31.0	30.1	4.7	11,015	10,914	10,152	9,912
1989	21.4	29.0	31.8	28.0	4.5	11,007	10,673	9,928	10,020
1988	20.4	28.4	28.7	26.2	5.1	10,906	10,350	9,869	10,379
1987	20.9	26.7	27.6	24.8	5.1	10,702	10,053	9,795	10,944
1986	19.2	26.5	27.3	25.8	4.9	10,389	9,959	9,908	11,149
1985	17.9	24.9	25.7	25.5	5.1	10,076	9,673	10,442	11,024
1984	16.6	23.9	27.0	24.6	5.3	9,707	9,594	10,858	10,711
1983	15.4	24.4	24.8	23.7	5.2	9,605	9,730	11,123	10,768
1982	16.6	22.8	23.9	23.0	5.4	9,492	10,169	10,989	11,131
1981	14.4	23.3	23.0	23.8	6.1	9,519	10,657	10,712	11,757
1980	14.3	20.3	22.6	22.5	6.6	9,350	10,681	10,537	11,835
1979	13.0	20.2	20.3	21.6	6.5	9,804	10,545	10,886	12,190
1978	12.4	19.5	19.2	21.8	6.5	10,246	10,448	11,391	12,346
1977	10.7	18.9	18.9	21.2	6.4	10,449	10,537	11,826	12,472
1976	10.6	18.1	19.8	22.2	6.3	10,334	10,872	12,137	12,550
1975	11.1	17.4	21.3	22.5	6.4	10,256	11,343	12,372	12,531
1974	10.3	17.8	21.7	21.6	7.1	10,343	11,789	12,415	12,566
1973	10.7	18.4	21.5	21.3	7.1	10,614	11,946	12,542	12,309
1972	10.7	19.6	21.9	22.3	6.6	11,119	12,152	12,451	12,283
1971	11.1	19.7	22.0	22.5	5.7	11,938	12,648	12,429	11,906
Male									
1996	20.7	26.0	33.9	36.9	4.5	6,268	6,043	5,934	5,985
1995	20.2	28.0	35.2	38.5	3.5	5,999	6,027	5,930	5,840
1994	21.1	28.0	35.6	35.7	3.9	5,894	6,026	5,874	5,640
1993ʳ	21.2	32.1	35.4	40.3	3.3	5,837	5,736	5,629	5,262
1993	21.1	32.0	35.0	38.7	3.1	5,837	5,736	5,629	5,262
1992	21.6	32.6	37.0	35.2	2.7	5,738	5,742	5,502	5,166
1991	24.0	30.7	34.7	35.5	4.3	5,674	5,704	5,343	5,085
1990	23.9	32.0	36.2	35.3	4.6	5,629	5,603	5,200	5,078
1989	25.1	32.9	36.7	33.4	4.3	5,632	5,472	5,088	5,151
1988	23.5	33.2	33.7	30.6	4.8	5,580	5,298	5,065	5,286
1987	23.7	31.8	31.8	29.2	4.6	5,496	5,147	5,036	5,535
1986	22.9	30.4	32.2	30.2	4.9	5,311	5,113	5,066	5,697
1985	20.6	28.3	29.0	30.2	4.9	5,159	4,946	5,340	5,623
1984	18.8	27.7	31.1	30.2	5.5	4,963	4,905	5,521	5,469
1983	17.8	28.7	30.3	28.5	5.3	4,913	4,974	5,690	5,463
1982	19.2	26.4	28.0	27.9	5.2	4,852	5,198	5,566	5,688
1981	17.2	27.9	25.6	28.1	6.2	4,866	5,447	5,510	5,914
1980	16.4	23.4	27.3	26.8	6.4	4,774	5,453	5,282	6,067
1979	15.5	23.4	24.1	27.4	5.9	5,004	5,379	5,555	6,174
1978	14.7	22.9	22.9	26.2	6.7	5,227	5,326	5,797	6,265
1977	12.5	22.4	22.6	25.3	6.1	5,327	5,371	6,044	6,297
1976	12.5	20.9	23.4	27.5	5.7	5,265	5,540	6,185	6,356
1975	12.6	21.2	25.8	26.8	5.7	5,223	5,782	6,336	6,309
1974	12.2	21.2	25.9	26.3	7.0	5,267	6,011	6,329	6,352
1973	12.8	20.8	25.2	26.4	6.8	5,403	6,082	6,397	6,215
1972	12.5	23.3	26.8	26.8	6.2	5,662	6,188	6,322	6,232
1971	13.5	22.8	26.1	27.2	5.0	6,088	6,440	6,293	6,019

See footnotes at end of table.

Table A-22. Persons 6 to 17 Years Old Enrolled Below Modal Grade : 1971 to 1996 — Continued

(Numbers in thousands. Civilian noninstitutional population.)

Race, Hispanic origin, and year	Percent below modal grade				Dropout rate for 15 to 17 years	Population in age group			
	6 to 8 years	9 to 11 years	12 to 14 years	15 to 17 years		6 to 8 years	9 to 11 years	12 to 14 years	15 to 17 years
Female									
1996	14.9	20.4	23.4	24.7	5.3	5,923	5,802	5,719	5,632
1995	14.6	23.1	26.0	26.7	4.4	5,728	5,786	5,653	5,552
1994	16.5	24.2	26.7	24.8	3.6	5,705	5,644	5,666	5,384
1993ʳ	16.3	24.0	26.4	26.4	4.4	5,526	5,545	5,353	4,984
1993	16.1	23.9	26.2	24.9	4.3	5,526	5,545	5,353	4,984
1992	17.1	23.5	24.6	25.6	4.5	5,523	5,441	5,220	4,947
1991	18.2	22.8	24.6	24.2	5.1	5,445	5,395	5,098	4,838
1990	19.1	23.2	25.7	24.7	4.7	5,387	5,312	4,951	4,834
1989	18.1	22.6	26.6	22.3	4.6	5,375	5,201	4,840	4,869
1988	17.3	23.6	23.4	21.7	5.4	5,327	5,052	4,803	5,093
1987	17.8	21.5	23.2	20.2	5.6	5,206	4,906	4,759	5,408
1986	15.2	22.4	22.1	21.1	4.9	5,078	4,846	4,842	5,452
1985	15.1	21.4	22.1	20.6	5.5	4,917	4,727	5,102	5,401
1984	14.2	19.8	22.9	18.7	5.1	4,744	4,689	5,337	5,242
1983	12.9	19.9	19.1	18.6	5.2	4,692	4,756	5,433	5,305
1982	13.8	19.0	19.7	17.9	5.7	4,640	4,971	5,423	5,443
1981	11.6	18.4	20.1	19.6	6.1	4,653	5,210	5,202	5,843
1980	12.1	17.0	17.8	18.0	6.7	4,576	5,228	5,255	5,768
1979	10.4	16.9	16.4	15.6	7.1	4,800	5,166	5,331	6,016
1978	10.1	16.0	15.3	17.2	6.4	5,019	5,122	5,594	6,081
1977	8.9	15.2	15.0	17.1	6.6	5,122	5,166	5,782	6,175
1976	8.6	15.1	16.0	16.8	7.0	5,069	5,332	5,952	6,194
1975	9.4	13.5	16.7	18.2	7.2	5,033	5,561	6,036	6,222
1974	8.3	14.4	17.4	16.8	7.1	5,076	5,778	6,086	6,214
1973	8.7	15.8	16.5	16.1	7.4	5,211	5,864	6,145	6,094
1972	8.9	15.7	17.0	17.7	7.1	5,457	5,964	6,129	6,051
1971	8.7	12.3	17.8	17.6	6.5	5,850	6,208	6,136	5,887
WHITE									
Total									
1996	18.1	22.6	27.6	30.1	4.9	9,458	9,420	9,184	9,135
1995	17.7	24.9	29.2	31.0	3.9	9,221	9,340	9,130	8,933
1994	19.4	25.8	30.1	29.6	3.7	9,087	9,261	9,121	8,668
1993ʳ	18.8	27.3	29.4	31.2	3.9	9,018	8,967	8,728	8,160
1993	18.7	27.2	29.2	29.7	3.6	9,074	9,017	8,783	8,159
1992	19.5	27.5	29.6	28.1	3.5	8,956	8,996	8,520	8,031
1991	21.3	25.7	27.7	27.2	4.7	8,874	8,840	8,328	7,903
1990	21.9	26.8	28.4	27.3	4.6	8,860	8,752	8,140	7,909
1989	22.4	26.8	29.9	25.7	4.6	8,858	8,527	7,994	8,026
1988	21.0	27.6	27.2	23.9	5.4	8,758	8,323	7,929	8,353
1987	21.1	25.9	26.0	22.7	5.1	8,606	8,117	7,846	8,887
1986	19.1	25.1	25.3	23.7	5.0	8,395	8,000	8,054	9,037
1985	18.0	23.3	23.3	23.0	5.3	8,136	7,840	8,429	9,045
1984	16.3	22.1	24.7	22.7	5.6	7,915	7,781	8,827	8,853
1983	15.5	22.4	23.1	21.1	5.4	7,821	7,906	9,152	8,831
1982	16.4	21.8	22.1	21.1	5.6	7,729	8,294	9,035	9,184
1981	14.7	22.2	21.0	21.6	6.1	7,782	8,741	8,813	9,762
1980	14.1	19.0	21.1	19.3	6.7	7,635	8,823	8,739	10,132
1979	12.9	18.4	18.5	19.4	6.5	8,041	8,747	9,026	10,239
1978	12.4	18.0	17.9	19.3	6.8	8,460	8,686	9,522	10,358
1977	10.6	17.7	17.5	19.3	6.6	8,675	8,771	9,918	10,510
1976	10.5	17.2	18.7	19.7	6.3	8,612	9,066	10,187	10,622
1975	11.0	16.0	20.0	20.4	6.3	8,566	9,486	10,466	10,583
1974	10.2	16.5	19.7	19.4	6.9	8,656	9,912	10,508	10,678
1973	10.6	17.3	19.9	19.1	7.0	8,929	10,117	10,704	10,481
1972	10.3	18.2	20.1	20.0	6.6	9,359	10,313	10,606	10,506
1971	10.5	18.3	20.4	19.9	5.5	9,988	10,692	10,682	10,231

See footnotes at end of table.

Table A-22. Persons 6 to 17 Years Old Enrolled Below Modal Grade : 1971 to 1996 — Continued

(Numbers in thousands. Civilian noninstitutional population.)

Race, Hispanic origin, and year	Percent below modal grade				Dropout rate for 15 to 17 years	Population in age group			
	6 to 8 years	9 to 11 years	12 to 14 years	15 to 17 years		6 to 8 years	9 to 11 years	12 to 14 years	15 to 17 years
Male									
1996	20.8	25.9	32.3	36.5	4.5	4,849	4,836	4,706	4,694
1995	20.5	28.0	33.4	36.5	3.8	4,727	4,797	4,680	4,592
1994	22.0	27.9	34.4	35.2	4.0	4,659	4,758	4,679	4,457
1993ʳ	21.4	31.8	33.8	37.6	3.2	4,625	4,601	4,476	4,178
1993	21.4	31.6	33.6	36.1	3.1	4,662	4,614	4,485	4,178
1992	21.5	31.8	35.8	32.4	2.8	4,602	4,607	4,359	4,115
1991	24.4	29.1	32.5	32.5	4.2	4,556	4,568	4,270	4,047
1990	24.6	31.3	33.3	32.6	4.8	4,555	4,482	4,186	4,054
1989	26.0	32.1	35.0	30.8	4.6	4,544	4,378	4,112	4,107
1988	24.7	32.8	32.2	28.8	5.1	4,493	4,272	4,062	4,281
1987	24.6	30.5	30.4	26.6	4.5	4,415	4,167	4,069	4,504
1986	22.9	28.9	30.1	27.9	5.2	4,307	4,108	4,125	4,624
1985	21.1	26.5	26.7	28.0	4.9	4,175	4,024	4,307	4,634
1984	18.1	25.8	28.7	28.1	5.8	4,061	3,994	4,501	4,542
1983	18.1	26.3	28.0	26.3	5.6	4,002	4,054	4,697	4,481
1982	19.3	26.2	26.2	26.1	5.3	3,956	4,260	4,591	4,711
1981	17.3	26.9	24.2	25.4	6.3	3,990	4,480	4,556	4,937
1980	16.3	21.9	25.7	23.9	6.7	3,907	4,517	4,399	5,066
1979	15.4	20.8	22.3	24.8	6.2	4,114	4,475	4,616	5,201
1978	14.7	21.2	22.0	23.1	7.2	4,328	4,441	4,843	5,287
1977	13.4	17.2	17.8	15.8	6.0	3,773	4,034	4,444	4,473
1976	12.6	20.2	22.1	24.8	5.6	4,402	4,632	5,200	5,398
1975	12.9	19.7	24.7	24.7	5.4	4,376	4,848	5,385	5,332
1974	12.1	19.5	23.7	23.8	7.0	4,422	5,066	5,383	5,402
1973	12.5	19.6	23.1	24.0	6.6	4,559	5,165	5,469	5,319
1972	12.2	21.9	24.6	24.3	6.1	4,778	5,266	5,410	5,340
1971	12.6	21.6	23.9	24.4	4.6	5,106	5,461	5,455	5,185
Female									
1996	15.3	19.2	22.7	23.2	5.3	4,609	4,583	4,477	4,441
1995	14.7	21.6	24.8	25.0	4.1	4,494	4,543	4,449	4,342
1994	16.7	23.5	25.7	23.6	3.4	4,427	4,504	4,443	4,212
1993ʳ	15.9	22.6	24.8	24.4	4.3	4,393	4,366	4,252	3,982
1993	15.8	22.5	24.6	23.1	4.2	4,412	4,404	4,298	3,982
1992	17.3	22.9	23.2	23.6	4.3	4,354	4,389	4,161	3,916
1991	18.1	22.1	22.6	21.5	5.2	4,318	4,272	4,058	3,856
1990	19.0	22.2	23.2	21.8	4.5	4,305	4,270	3,954	3,855
1989	18.6	21.3	24.5	20.3	4.7	4,314	4,149	3,882	3,919
1988	17.1	22.2	21.9	18.8	5.6	4,265	4,051	3,867	4,072
1987	17.3	21.0	21.3	18.7	5.8	4,191	3,950	3,777	4,383
1986	15.0	21.1	20.2	19.3	4.8	4,088	3,892	3,929	4,413
1985	14.8	19.9	19.7	17.6	5.7	3,961	3,816	4,122	4,411
1984	14.3	18.3	20.5	17.0	5.4	3,854	3,787	4,326	4,311
1983	12.7	18.3	17.9	15.8	5.2	3,819	3,852	4,455	4,350
1982	13.4	17.2	17.8	15.8	6.0	3,773	4,034	4,444	4,473
1981	11.9	17.3	17.6	17.6	5.9	3,792	4,261	4,257	4,825
1980	11.7	16.0	16.5	14.7	6.6	3,728	4,306	4,340	5,066
1979	10.3	15.8	14.5	13.8	6.9	3,927	4,272	4,410	5,038
1978	10.0	14.7	13.7	15.2	6.4	4,132	4,245	4,679	5,071
1977	8.5	14.1	13.7	14.9	6.8	4,239	4,287	4,839	5,185
1976	8.4	14.1	15.1	14.5	6.9	4,210	4,434	4,987	5,224
1975	9.1	12.2	15.1	16.0	7.1	4,190	4,638	5,081	5,251
1974	8.2	13.4	15.5	15.0	6.7	4,234	4,846	5,125	5,276
1973	8.5	14.8	16.5	14.0	7.4	4,370	4,952	5,235	5,162
1972	8.3	14.2	15.4	15.5	7.2	4,581	5,047	5,196	5,166
1971	8.4	14.9	16.6	15.2	6.3	4,882	5,231	5,227	5,046

See footnotes at end of table.

Table A-22. Persons 6 to 17 Years Old Enrolled Below Modal Grade : 1971 to 1996 — Continued

(Numbers in thousands. Civilian noninstitutional population.)

Race, Hispanic origin, and year	Percent below modal grade				Dropout rate for 15 to 17 years	Population in age group			
	6 to 8 years	9 to 11 years	12 to 14 years	15 to 17 years		6 to 8 years	9 to 11 years	12 to 14 years	15 to 17 years
BLACK									
Total									
1996	18.4	29.2	36.8	36.9	4.8	2,054	1,847	1,839	1,858
1995	16.8	31.1	38.3	41.3	4.1	1,909	1,890	1,822	1,851
1994	18.4	35.1	36.1	37.7	3.3	1,912	1,795	1,835	1,809
1993ʳ	20.0	33.6	34.8	45.1	3.6	1,767	1,763	1,747	1,641
1993	19.9	33.4	38.8	43.3	3.6	1,709	1,710	1,695	1,642
1992	20.6	28.7	38.0	40.6	4.2	1,761	1,635	1,686	1,621
1991	21.0	34.3	40.7	43.4	5.3	1,674	1,701	1,643	1,574
1990	21.9	33.1	46.1	42.9	5.2	1,645	1,712	1,574	1,571
1989	19.6	34.0	41.3	39.3	3.9	1,642	1,682	1,554	1,618
1988	18.6	33.1	37.6	38.4	4.7	1,680	1,629	1,545	1,637
1987	19.8	33.1	35.6	35.3	5.1	1,679	1,554	1,552	1,654
1986	12.7	34.6	38.5	38.3	4.6	1,611	1,542	1,530	1,692
1985	18.0	33.9	37.9	37.7	4.6	1,568	1,498	1,635	1,627
1984	17.9	32.3	38.1	34.6	4.1	1,446	1,440	1,052	1,530
1983	15.3	34.9	34.4	35.8	4.7	1,429	1,450	1,601	1,617
1982	17.2	27.1	32.5	32.6	4.6	1,765	1,874	1,953	1,947
1981	13.9	26.2	33.7	36.1	6.3	1,437	1,594	1,615	1,679
1980	14.9	27.8	30.5	37.6	5.1	1,460	1,606	1,568	1,728
1979	12.5	29.5	29.2	34.3	6.4	1,515	1,576	1,636	1,722
1978	12.6	27.8	26.6	35.4	5.7	1,557	1,523	1,664	1,764
1977	11.3	24.9	26.3	32.2	5.4	1,552	1,558	1,698	1,754
1976	10.5	23.2	26.1	35.6	6.7	1,493	1,633	1,724	1,726
1975	11.9	26.1	29.2	34.9	8.0	1,489	1,656	1,720	1,760
1974	11.6	26.2	33.2	34.4	8.2	1,509	1,684	1,750	1,682
1973	12.0	25.8	31.7	35.4	8.2	1,525	1,650	1,671	1,671
1972	13.2	30.5	33.1	37.3	6.6	1,585	1,638	1,691	1,636
1971	14.2	27.9	34.7	40.2	7.0	1,794	1,787	1,638	1,533
Male									
1996	21.3	30.4	45.1	43.2	4.5	1,054	925	931	943
1995	18.8	31.2	45.0	47.5	2.9	982	944	922	952
1994	19.4	30.3	39.9	39.8	3.2	951	928	928	898
1993ʳ	21.8	36.5	44.3	53.0	2.5	903	884	891	832
1993	21.6	36.5	44.2	51.8	2.5	864	857	867	832
1992	24.5	28.7	44.5	47.0	2.8	864	862	860	813
1991	22.9	39.6	46.2	50.6	5.4	846	878	839	798
1990	23.2	37.3	52.7	49.1	4.3	828	877	791	795
1989	21.7	38.8	44.8	46.7	2.8	831	858	785	828
1988	18.9	37.2	43.7	41.4	4.1	851	828	780	828
1987	21.6	41.1	39.7	42.3	4.9	861	779	802	818
1986	15.0	39.0	45.2	45.9	4.0	806	792	770	855
1985	19.5	38.2	41.4	40.3	5.4	778	775	830	816
1984	24.1	38.1	42.5	42.8	4.2	729	727	832	769
1983	16.8	42.0	43.1	40.6	4.4	721	723	808	799
1982	18.8	27.5	36.2	36.9	4.8	898	937	975	977
1981	17.7	34.2	33.3	42.4	5.4	723	811	814	832
1980	16.8	31.8	36.2	43.3	4.9	736	807	770	876
1979	14.7	37.3	33.8	43.6	4.0	762	796	828	853
1978	15.4	33.0	30.3	43.1	4.1	774	767	847	870
1977	12.1	29.8	31.1	35.3	4.8	776	782	858	868
1976	11.5	26.1	30.9	43.3	5.7	755	816	870	855
1975	12.8	30.7	32.5	40.2	7.6	743	849	845	879
1974	13.5	31.0	40.9	41.1	7.2	747	858	861	849
1973	14.1	29.5	38.0	42.0	8.5	752	831	837	824
1972	14.5	36.8	41.3	43.8	6.6	787	828	836	818
1971	18.1	30.9	38.5	47.6	7.4	890	900	810	757

See footnotes at end of table.

Table A-22. Persons 6 to 17 Years Old Enrolled Below Modal Grade : 1971 to 1996 — Continued

(Numbers in thousands. Civilian noninstitutional population.)

Race, Hispanic origin, and year	Percent below modal grade				Dropout rate for 15 to 17 years	Population in age group			
	6 to 8 years	9 to 11 years	12 to 14 years	15 to 17 years		6 to 8 years	9 to 11 years	12 to 14 years	15 to 17 years
Female									
1996	13.4	28.1	28.4	30.3	4.9	1,000	922	909	915
1995	14.8	23.6	30.9	34.6	5.3	928	946	901	898
1994	17.5	29.1	32.3	35.4	3.6	961	867	908	911
1993ʳ	18.0	30.8	33.1	36.6	4.7	864	879	856	809
1993	18.1	30.3	33.2	34.6	4.7	844	854	828	809
1992	16.7	28.7	31.2	34.2	5.6	897	773	826	808
1991	19.0	28.6	35.0	36.0	5.2	828	823	804	776
1990	20.7	28.7	39.3	36.6	6.1	817	835	783	776
1989	17.5	29.0	37.7	31.5	5.1	811	824	769	790
1988	18.2	28.8	31.4	35.2	5.3	829	801	765	809
1987	18.0	25.2	31.3	28.5	5.3	818	775	750	836
1986	10.4	30.0	31.7	30.2	5.3	805	750	760	837
1985	16.6	29.3	34.2	35.1	3.8	790	723	805	811
1984	11.5	26.4	33.5	26.3	4.0	716	715	820	767
1983	13.8	27.8	25.5	31.2	5.0	708	727	793	818
1982	15.5	26.7	28.7	28.1	4.3	867	937	978	970
1981	10.1	17.9	34.2	29.9	7.1	714	783	801	847
1980	12.8	23.8	25.1	31.7	5.3	724	799	798	852
1979	10.4	21.5	24.5	25.2	8.7	753	780	808	869
1978	9.8	22.6	22.6	27.9	7.2	783	756	817	894
1977	10.6	20.0	21.3	29.1	6.0	776	776	840	886
1976	9.5	20.3	21.2	28.1	7.7	738	817	854	871
1975	11.0	21.3	25.9	29.6	8.3	746	807	875	881
1974	9.7	21.3	25.8	27.5	9.2	762	826	889	833
1973	10.0	22.1	25.4	28.9	7.9	773	819	834	847
1972	11.9	24.1	25.1	30.9	6.6	798	810	855	818
1971	10.4	24.9	31.0	33.1	6.7	904	887	828	776
HISPANIC ORIGIN [1]									
Total									
1996	14.9	22.9	35.5	39.0	8.4	1,711	1,680	1,550	1,478
1995	14.4	26.1	38.5	43.6	7.4	1,597	1,628	1,496	1,373
1994	16.8	28.4	32.3	39.9	8.8	1,526	1,593	1,442	1,347
1993ʳ	18.9	29.2	33.2	42.2	8.2	1,390	1,255	1,204	1,225
1993	18.9	29.2	32.7	38.3	7.9	1,455	1,295	1,243	1,226
1992	16.2	25.3	34.3	39.9	8.1	1,272	1,371	1,141	1,110
1991	21.8	30.7	35.8	38.4	11.3	1,290	1,356	1,088	1,023
1990	21.5	34.8	37.7	39.8	9.0	1,270	1,230	1,095	1,062
1989	21.9	33.8	39.9	39.5	10.6	1,257	1,154	1,079	1,001
1988	23.2	37.0	45.0	36.8	13.7	1,248	1,107	1,052	953
1987	16.9	31.2	38.9	37.3	9.1	1,181	1,054	1,063	981
1986	19.1	33.3	42.5	35.5	11.0	1,067	1,119	1,025	1,018
1985	18.7	32.4	35.8	35.7	11.3	1,035	1,047	957	946
1984	20.2	32.7	34.7	38.5	10.7	901	829	806	816
1983	20.2	32.7	39.5	38.0	8.3	903	909	949	860
1982	21.9	32.6	37.3	37.0	10.9	923	875	924	883
1981	17.9	34.7	34.9	34.9	13.3	882	939	866	963
1980	20.8	26.1	34.8	35.8	12.6	881	949	863	889
1979	18.2	33.6	33.0	30.3	10.9	729	712	697	755
1978	19.8	29.1	33.6	37.8	12.3	723	684	666	751
1977	13.0	24.1	25.1	35.2	11.0	676	693	662	773
Male									
1996	13.5	25.8	40.5	45.1	6.8	914	808	798	764
1995	11.4	31.1	42.4	47.6	7.5	794	839	776	697
1994	16.4	27.5	36.3	45.1	11.4	778	845	721	676

See footnotes at end of table.

Table A-22.   Persons 6 to 17 Years Old Enrolled Below Modal Grade : 1971 to 1996 — Continued

(Numbers in thousands. Civilian noninstitutional population.)

Race, Hispanic origin, and year	Percent below modal grade				Dropout rate for 15 to 17 years	Population in age group			
	6 to 8 years	9 to 11 years	12 to 14 years	15 to 17 years		6 to 8 years	9 to 11 years	12 to 14 years	15 to 17 years
1993ʳ	19.1	35.1	37.2	50.4	7.6	722	612	618	658
1993	19.1	34.3	36.9	46.0	7.3	778	637	648	658
1992	15.6	27.2	42.5	46.2	6.8	636	687	602	576
1991	22.7	31.5	43.9	42.6	10.7	651	691	544	521
1990	22.2	36.4	40.2	43.8	9.0	676	616	590	564
1989	23.7	36.1	40.0	45.2	7.8	642	584	560	511
1988	26.9	42.0	53.8	40.5	12.4	676	566	470	523
1987	19.8	31.7	44.8	38.7	6.4	600	524	569	517
1986	22.2	38.0	49.3	37.8	10.8	544	555	535	471
1985	16.7	36.8	38.4	43.4	7.8	521	527	502	449
1984	18.3	35.7	33.1	42.8	10.0	443	420	423	432
1983	22.2	38.8	45.7	41.8	8.2	445	479	479	428
1982	23.1	36.4	39.1	43.4	10.1	428	426	466	477
1981	19.9	39.8	38.0	40.0	14.3	438	480	439	495
1980	22.5	29.9	40.5	40.7	13.5	418	481	415	445
1979	19.0	34.6	36.4	31.3	8.8	368	358	349	386
1978	23.5	29.9	33.9	37.3	13.6	388	335	339	413
1977	11.5	31.4	23.3	38.4	6.7	365	325	330	406
Female									
1996	16.6	20.3	30.4	32.4	10.4	798	871	753	712
1995	17.5	20.6	34.5	39.5	7.2	802	789	721	677
1994	17.2	29.2	28.5	34.9	6.1	748	747	722	671
1993ʳ	18.9	24.2	29.0	32.3	8.7	667	643	586	567
1993	18.7	24.3	28.3	29.3	8.6	678	658	597	567
1992	16.8	23.4	25.0	33.1	9.6	636	684	539	534
1991	20.8	29.8	27.6	34.1	12.0	639	665	544	502
1990	20.7	33.2	34.9	35.3	9.0	594	614	505	498
1989	20.0	31.4	39.7	33.5	13.5	615	570	519	490
1988	18.7	31.8	37.8	32.3	15.3	572	541	582	430
1987	13.8	30.8	32.2	35.8	12.1	581	530	494	464
1986	15.9	28.7	35.1	33.5	11.2	523	564	490	547
1985	20.8	27.9	33.0	28.8	14.5	514	520	455	497
1984	22.1	29.6	36.6	33.6	11.5	458	409	383	384
1983	18.1	25.8	33.2	34.3	8.3	458	430	470	432
1982	20.8	29.0	35.6	29.6	11.8	495	449	458	406
1981	16.0	29.4	31.6	29.5	12.2	444	459	427	468
1900	19.2	22.2	29.5	30.9	11.7	463	468	448	444
1979	17.5	32.5	29.6	29.3	13.0	361	354	348	369
1978	15.5	28.4	33.3	38.5	10.7	335	349	327	338
1977	14.8	17.7	26.8	31.6	15.8	311	368	332	367

Source: U.S. Bureau of the Census

1. May be of any race.

— Represents zero or rounds to zero.
r = Revised, controlled to the 1990 census-based population estimates; previous 1993 data controlled to 1980 based population estimates

Table A-23.   High School Dropout Rates by Gender, Grade, Race and Hispanic Origin: October 1967 to 1996

(Numbers in thousands. Civilian noninstitutional population.)

Year, grade, race and Hispanic origin	Both sexes			Male			Female		
	Total students	Dropouts	Dropout rate	Total students	Dropouts	Dropout rate	Total students	Dropouts	Drop
Total - Grades 10–12									
1996	10,249	485	4.7	5,175	240	4.6	5,072	244	
1995	10,106	544	5.4	5,161	297	5.8	4,946	247	
1994	9,922	497	5.0	5,048	249	4.9	4,873	247	
1993ʳ	9,430	404	4.3	4,787	211	4.4	4,640	192	
1993	9,021	382	4.2	4,570	199	4.4	4,452	183	
1992	8,939	384	4.3	4,580	175	3.8	4,357	207	
1991	8,612	348	4.0	4,380	167	3.8	4,231	180	
1990	8,679	347	4.0	4,356	177	4.1	4,323	170	
1989	8,974	404	4.5	4,519	203	4.5	4,453	199	
1988	9,590	461	4.8	4,960	256	5.2	4,628	206	
1987	9,802	403	4.1	4,921	215	4.4	4,879	187	
1986	9,829	421	4.3	4,910	213	4.3	4,917	208	
1985	9,704	504	5.2	4,831	259	5.4	4,874	245	
1984	10,041	507	5.0	4,986	268	5.4	5,054	238	
1983	10,331	535	5.2	5,130	294	5.7	5,200	241	
1982	10,611	577	5.4	5,310	305	5.7	5,301	271	
1981	10,868	639	5.9	5,379	322	6.0	5,487	316	
1980	10,891	658	6.0	5,445	362	6.6	5,448	296	
1979	11,136	744	6.7	5,479	369	6.7	5,658	377	
1978	11,116	743	6.7	5,558	415	7.5	5,558	328	
1977	11,300	734	6.5	5,657	392	6.9	5,643	342	
1976	10,996	644	5.9	5,534	360	6.5	5,463	285	
1975	11,033	639	5.8	5,485	296	5.4	5,548	343	
1974	11,026	742	6.7	5,421	402	7.4	5,605	340	
1973	10,851	683	6.3	5,407	370	6.8	5,444	313	
1972	10,664	659	6.2	5,305	317	6.0	5,358	341	
1971	10,451	562	5.4	5,193	297	5.7	5,258	266	
1970	10,281	588	5.7	5,145	288	5.6	5,138	302	
1969	10,212	551	5.4	5,069	273	5.4	5,142	278	
1968	9,814	506	5.2	4,831	247	5.1	4,983	259	
1967	9,350	486	5.2	4,605	237	5.1	4,745	249	
Total - Grade 10									
1996	3,691	94	2.5	1,906	50	2.6	1,784	43	
1995	3,552	88	2.5	1,823	40	2.2	1,728	47	
1994	3,474	76	2.2	1,793	45	2.5	1,681	31	
1993ʳ	3,265	86	2.6	1,696	52	3.1	1,567	33	
1993	3,139	81	2.6	1,627	50	3.1	1,513	31	
1992	3,197	81	2.5	1,657	37	2.2	1,539	43	
1991	3,132	105	3.4	1,571	46	2.9	1,561	59	
1990	3,215	90	2.8	1,660	43	2.6	1,555	47	
1989	3,071	99	3.2	1,567	56	3.6	1,504	43	
1988	3,308	112	3.4	1,716	63	3.7	1,592	49	
1987	3,492	106	3.0	1,818	45	2.5	1,674	61	
1986	3,555	119	3.3	1,820	56	3.1	1,734	63	
1985	3,491	143	4.1	1,797	74	4.1	1,695	69	
1984	3,415	135	4.0	1,735	76	4.4	1,680	59	
1983	3,468	129	3.7	1,755	70	4.0	1,713	59	
1982	3,540	144	4.1	1,792	69	3.9	1,747	74	
1981	3,735	144	3.9	1,816	65	3.6	1,918	78	
1980	3,817	166	4.3	1,957	95	4.9	1,861	71	
1979	3,920	217	5.5	1,985	102	5.1	1,934	114	
1978	3,878	185	4.8	1,943	96	4.9	1,935	89	
1977	3,970	177	4.5	2,021	96	4.8	1,949	81	
1976	3,914	145	3.7	1,960	79	4.0	1,955	67	
1975	3,983	183	4.6	2,017	87	4.3	1,967	97	
1974	3,901	223	5.7	1,951	122	6.3	1,949	101	
1973	3,899	210	5.4	1,930	112	5.8	1,969	98	

See footnotes at end of table.

Table A-23.   High School Dropout Rates by Gender, Grade, Race and Hispanic Origin: October 1967 to 1996 — Continued

(Numbers in thousands. Civilian noninstitutional population.)

Year, grade, race and Hispanic origin	Both sexes			Male			Female		
	Total students	Dropouts	Dropout rate	Total students	Dropouts	Dropout rate	Total students	Dropouts	Dropout rate
1972	3,868	203	5.2	1,940	106	5.5	1,928	97	5.0
1971	3,762	174	4.6	1,925	95	4.9	1,838	79	4.3
1970	3,686	186	5.0	1,865	90	4.8	1,822	97	5.3
1969	3,485	159	4.6	1,756	84	4.8	1,729	75	4.3
1968	3,615	151	4.2	1,849	75	4.1	1,767	76	4.3
1967	3,370	129	3.8	1,726	64	3.7	1,644	65	4.0
Total - Grade 11									
1996	3,606	138	3.8	1,828	76	4.2	1,778	62	3.5
1995	3,568	159	4.5	1,846	89	4.8	1,724	71	4.1
1994	3,587	132	3.7	1,864	61	3.3	1,722	70	4.1
1993ʳ	3,375	106	3.1	1,725	43	2.5	1,650	63	3.8
1993	3,218	100	3.1	1,643	40	2.4	1,575	60	3.8
1992	3,213	120	3.7	1,642	52	3.2	1,570	67	4.3
1991	3,083	101	3.3	1,598	42	2.6	1,484	58	3.9
1990	2,976	98	3.3	1,462	57	3.9	1,514	41	2.7
1989	3,302	125	3.8	1,683	67	4.0	1,618	57	3.5
1988	3,447	161	4.7	1,819	89	4.9	1,627	72	4.4
1987	3,566	122	3.4	1,766	71	4.0	1,800	51	2.8
1986	3,433	116	3.4	1,700	51	3.0	1,733	65	3.8
1985	3,274	139	4.2	1,618	70	4.3	1,656	69	4.2
1984	3,328	163	4.9	1,682	87	5.2	1,646	76	4.6
1983	3,601	162	4.5	1,825	87	4.8	1,775	75	4.2
1982	3,694	218	5.9	1,872	122	6.5	1,822	96	5.3
1981	3,787	262	6.9	1,937	144	7.4	1,850	118	6.4
1980	3,670	225	6.1	1,832	120	6.6	1,839	105	5.7
1979	3,718	229	6.2	1,840	102	5.5	1,879	128	6.8
1978	3,708	230	6.2	1,905	113	5.9	1,803	117	6.5
1977	3,832	244	6.4	1,964	133	6.8	1,867	110	5.9
1976	3,786	227	6.0	1,955	123	6.3	1,831	104	5.7
1975	3,596	230	6.4	1,828	103	5.6	1,767	126	7.1
1974	3,721	237	6.4	1,819	123	6.8	1,902	114	6.0
1973	3,631	237	6.5	1,877	126	6.7	1,754	111	6.3
1972	3,581	241	6.7	1,825	107	5.9	1,756	134	7.6
1971	3,585	185	5.2	1,772	82	4.6	1,811	103	5.7
1970	3,456	198	5.7	1,750	96	5.5	1,706	102	6.0
1969	3,489	190	5.4	1,779	100	5.6	1,710	90	5.3
1968	3,255	179	5.5	1,640	91	5.5	1,614	88	5.5
1967	3,068	169	5.5	1,557	76	4.9	1,511	93	6.2
Total - Grade 12									
1996	2,952	253	8.6	1,441	114	7.9	1,510	139	9.2
1995	2,986	297	9.9	1,492	168	11.3	1,494	129	8.6
1994	2,861	289	10.1	1,391	143	10.3	1,470	146	9.9
1993ʳ	2,790	212	7.6	1,366	116	8.5	1,423	96	6.7
1993	2,664	201	7.5	1,300	109	8.4	1,364	92	6.7
1992	2,529	183	7.2	1,281	86	6.7	1,248	97	7.8
1991	2,397	142	5.9	1,211	79	6.5	1,186	63	5.3
1990	2,488	159	6.4	1,234	77	6.2	1,254	82	6.5
1989	2,601	180	6.9	1,269	80	6.3	1,331	99	7.4
1988	2,835	188	6.6	1,425	104	7.3	1,409	85	6.0
1987	2,744	175	6.4	1,337	99	7.4	1,405	75	5.3
1986	2,841	186	6.5	1,390	106	7.6	1,450	80	5.5
1985	2,939	222	7.6	1,416	115	8.1	1,523	107	7.0
1984	3,298	209	6.3	1,569	105	6.7	1,728	103	6.0
1983	3,262	244	7.5	1,550	137	8.8	1,712	107	6.3
1982	3,377	215	6.4	1,646	114	6.9	1,732	101	5.8
1981	3,346	233	7.0	1,626	113	6.9	1,719	120	7.0
1980	3,404	267	7.8	1,656	147	8.9	1,748	120	6.9

See footnotes at end of table.

Table A-23.   High School Dropout Rates by Gender, Grade, Race and Hispanic Origin: October 1967 to 1996 — Continued

(Numbers in thousands. Civilian noninstitutional population.)

Year, grade, race and Hispanic origin	Both sexes			Male			Female		
	Total students	Dropouts	Dropout rate	Total students	Dropouts	Dropout rate	Total students	Dropouts	Dropout rate
1979	3,498	298	8.5	1,654	164	9.9	1,845	135	7.3
1978	3,530	328	9.3	1,710	206	12.0	1,820	122	6.7
1977	3,498	313	8.9	1,672	163	9.7	1,827	151	8.3
1976	3,296	272	8.3	1,619	158	9.8	1,677	114	6.8
1975	3,454	226	6.5	1,640	106	6.5	1,814	120	6.6
1974	3,404	282	8.3	1,651	157	9.5	1,754	125	7.1
1973	3,321	236	7.1	1,600	132	8.3	1,721	104	6.0
1972	3,215	215	6.7	1,540	104	6.8	1,674	110	6.6
1971	3,104	203	6.5	1,496	120	8.0	1,609	84	5.2
1970	3,139	204	6.5	1,530	102	6.7	1,610	103	6.4
1969	3,238	202	6.2	1,534	89	5.8	1,703	113	6.6
1968	2,944	176	6.0	1,342	81	6.0	1,602	95	5.9
1967	2,912	188	6.5	1,322	97	7.3	1,590	91	5.7
White - Grades 10–12									
1996	8,005	361	4.5	4,077	198	4.8	3,928	163	4.1
1995	7,926	402	5.1	4,079	220	5.4	3,849	183	4.8
1994	7,862	371	4.7	4,014	184	4.6	3,848	188	4.9
1993ʳ	7,442	306	4.1	3,790	157	4.1	3,654	150	4.1
1993	9,140	470	5.1	4,577	244	5.3	4,562	226	5.0
1992	7,077	292	4.1	3,646	140	3.8	3,430	151	4.4
1991	6,856	254	3.7	3,514	127	3.6	3,343	128	3.8
1990	6,984	266	3.8	3,522	144	4.1	3,462	122	3.5
1989	7,243	286	3.9	3,653	149	4.1	3,589	136	3.8
1988	7,727	362	4.7	4,016	203	5.1	3,712	161	4.3
1987	7,979	299	3.7	4,023	163	4.1	3,953	135	3.4
1986	8,011	333	4.2	4,007	168	4.2	4,007	166	4.1
1985	7,967	384	4.8	3,963	195	4.9	4,003	188	4.7
1984	8,221	410	5.0	4,119	220	5.3	4,101	190	4.6
1983	8,531	410	4.8	4,264	232	5.4	4,264	177	4.2
1982	8,769	444	5.1	4,381	231	5.3	4,390	214	4.9
1981	9,067	478	5.3	4,532	254	5.6	4,536	224	4.9
1980	9,177	517	5.6	4,624	294	6.4	4,554	224	4.9
1979	9,437	588	6.2	4,694	311	6.6	4,742	277	5.8
1978	9,360	574	6.1	4,747	329	6.9	4,611	244	5.3
1977	9,536	594	6.2	4,766	327	6.9	4,770	267	5.6
1976	9,362	532	5.7	4,708	297	6.3	4,654	235	5.0
1975	9,440	507	5.4	4,709	234	5.0	4,732	274	5.8
1974	9,403	566	6.0	4,650	326	7.0	4,754	241	5.1
1973	9,359	537	5.7	4,708	288	6.1	4,649	248	5.3
1972	9,173	520	5.7	4,588	247	5.4	4,583	272	5.9
1971	9,140	470	5.1	4,577	244	5.3	4,562	226	5.0
1970	8,959	449	5.0	4,496	212	4.7	4,462	237	5.3
1969	8,878	429	4.8	4,438	208	4.7	4,439	221	5.0
1968	8,580	387	4.5	4,246	190	4.5	4,331	196	4.5
1967	8,186	379	4.6	4,060	189	4.7	4,126	190	4.6
Black - Grades 10-12									
1996	1,704	107	6.3	803	37	4.6	901	70	7.8
1995	1,598	97	6.1	797	63	7.9	802	35	4.4
1994	1,559	96	6.1	763	50	6.5	795	45	5.7
1993ʳ	1,499	80	5.3	740	43	5.8	758	37	4.9
1993	1,447	78	5.4	724	41	5.7	722	36	5.0
1992	1,422	70	4.9	702	23	3.3	720	48	6.7
1991	1,366	85	6.3	85	38	5.5	683	48	7.0
1990	1,303	66	5.2	36	26	4.1	666	40	6.0
1989	1,384	106	7.7	684	47	6.9	701	60	8.6
1988	1,468	93	6.3	751	50	6.7	717	43	6.0
1987	1,463	93	6.4	730	45	6.2	732	47	6.4

See footnotes at end of table.

Table A-23. High School Dropout Rates by Gender, Grade, Race and Hispanic Origin: October 1967 to 1996 — Continued

(Numbers in thousands. Civilian noninstitutional population.)

Year, grade, race and Hispanic origin	Both sexes			Male			Female		
	Total students	Dropouts	Dropout rate	Total students	Dropouts	Dropout rate	Total students	Dropouts	Dropout rate
1986	1,449	68	4.7	711	34	4.8	737	34	4.6
1985	1,422	110	7.7	703	58	8.3	719	52	7.2
1984	1,524	88	5.8	711	44	6.2	813	43	5.3
1983	1,498	103	6.9	687	48	7.0	810	55	6.8
1982	1,553	121	7.8	786	71	9.0	767	50	6.5
1981	1,516	146	9.6	704	66	9.4	815	83	10.2
1980	1,496	124	8.3	714	57	8.0	781	66	8.5
1979	1,479	142	9.6	679	51	7.5	802	92	11.5
1978	1,542	160	10.4	706	78	11.0	835	81	9.7
1977	1,588	133	8.4	746	62	8.3	789	71	9.0
1976	1,449	105	7.2	729	62	8.5	721	45	6.2
1975	1,416	123	8.7	673	56	8.3	743	67	9.0
1974	1,441	167	11.6	679	73	10.8	761	93	12.2
1973	1,372	138	10.1	650	78	12.0	725	61	8.4
1972	1,373	133	9.7	644	65	10.1	756	68	9.0
1971	1,195	87	7.3	552	51	9.2	643	37	5.8
1970	1,192	133	11.2	587	74	12.6	606	60	9.9
1969	1,209	113	9.3	562	58	10.3	646	55	8.5
1968	1,123	113	10.1	523	52	9.9	600	61	10.2
1967	1,066	106	9.9	485	47	9.7	578	58	10.0
Hispanic Origin[1] - Grades 10–12									
1996	1,195	100	8.4	588	54	9.2	608	46	7.6
1995	1,251	145	11.6	644	70	10.9	608	76	12.5
1994	1,179	109	9.2	607	51	8.4	572	58	10.1
1993r	1,061	69	6.5	488	25	5.1	573	44	7.5
1993	943	60	6.4	436	21	4.8	508	39	7.7
1992	917	72	7.9	468	27	5.8	441	38	8.6
1991	809	59	7.3	396	41	10.4	417	20	4.8
1990	811	65	8.0	379	33	8.7	428	31	7.2
1989	762	59	7.7	394	30	7.6	366	28	7.7
1988	730	77	10.5	398	49	12.3	333	28	8.4
1987	769	43	5.6	380	19	5.0	389	24	6.2
1986	764	91	11.9	376	44	11.7	388	48	12.4
1985	729	71	9.7	333	31	9.3	396	39	9.8
1984	706	77	10.9	311	38	12.2	396	40	10.1
1983	691	68	9.8	351	48	13.7	340	21	6.2
1982	692	65	9.4	370	35	9.5	321	29	9.0
1981	717	77	10.7	350	37	10.6	367	40	10.9
1980	646	74	11.5	295	50	16.9	350	24	6.9
1979	593	58	9.8	295	30	10.2	298	27	9.1
1978	567	70	12.3	295	46	15.6	271	23	8.5
1977	627	50	8.0	341	35	10.3	287	15	5.2
1976	638	46	7.2	300	22	7.3	336	23	6.8
1975	614	67	10.9	317	32	10.1	294	34	11.6
1974	547	53	9.7	271	34	12.5	278	20	7.2
1973	499	50	10.0	240	19	7.9	259	31	12.0
1972	498	55	11.0	253	28	11.1	247	27	10.9

Source: U.S. Bureau of the Census

1. May be of any race.

— Represents zero or rounds to zero.

r = Revised, controlled to the 1990 census-based population estimates; previous 1993 data controlled to 1980 based population estimates

Table A-24.   Population 14 to 24 Years Old by High School Graduate Status, College Enrollment, Attainment, Gender, Race and Hispanic Origin: October 1967 to 1996

(Numbers in thousands. Civilian noninstitutional population.)

Year, race and Hispanic origin	Total	Population 18 to 24 years old					High school dropouts		High school graduates 14 to 24 years old		
		High school graduates		Percent						Percent	
		Total	Enrolled in college	High school graduates	Enrolled in college	Of high school graduates enrolled in college	Number	Percent	All graduates	Enrolled in college	Enrolled or completed some college
ALL RACES											
Total											
1996	24,671	20,131	8,767	81.6	35.5	43.5	3,147	12.8	20,465	44.0	67.1
1995	24,900	20,125	8,539	80.8	34.3	42.4	3,471	13.9	20,359	42.7	67.1
1994	25,254	20,581	8,729	81.5	34.6	42.4	3,365	13.3	20,779	42.7	66.9
1993r	25,522	20,844	8,630	81.7	33.8	41.4	3,349	13.1	21,060	41.6	65.3
1993	24,100	19,772	8,193	82.0	34.0	41.4	3,070	12.7	19,979	41.6	65.4
1992	24,278	19,921	8,343	82.1	34.4	41.9	3,083	12.7	20,194	42.3	65.6
1991	24,572	19,883	8,172	80.9	33.3	41.1	3,486	14.2	20,065	41.4	60.7
1990	24,852	20,311	7,964	82.3	32.0	39.1	3,379	13.6	20,571	39.6	58.9
1989	25,261	20,461	7,804	81.0	30.9	38.1	3,644	14.4	20,749	38.5	57.9
1988	25,733	20,900	7,791	81.2	30.3	37.3	3,749	14.6	21,204	37.6	57.4
1987	25,950	21,118	7,693	81.4	29.6	36.4	3,751	14.5	21,477	36.9	56.2
1986	26,512	21,768	7,477	82.1	28.2	34.3	3,687	13.9	22,086	34.8	55.0
1985	27,122	22,349	7,537	82.4	27.8	33.7	3,687	13.9	22,722	34.3	54.3
1984	28,031	22,870	7,591	81.6	27.1	33.2	4,142	14.8	23,252	33.7	53.0
1983	28,580	22,988	7,477	80.4	26.2	32.5	4,410	15.4	23,359	33.1	52.8
1982	28,846	23,291	7,678	80.7	26.6	33.0	4,500	15.6	23,708	33.5	52.7
1981	28,965	23,343	7,575	80.6	26.2	32.5	4,520	15.6	23,705	32.9	51.7
1980	28,957	23,413	7,400	80.9	25.6	31.6	4,515	15.6	23,856	32.1	51.1
1979	27,974	22,421	6,991	80.1	25.0	31.2	4,560	16.3	22,911	31.9	51.6
1978	27,647	22,309	6,995	80.7	25.3	31.4	4,388	15.9	22,759	31.9	51.4
1977	27,331	22,008	7,142	80.5	26.1	32.5	4,313	15.8	22,499	33.0	52.0
1976	26,919	21,677	7,181	80.5	26.7	33.1	4,276	15.9	22,158	33.7	53.4
1975	26,387	21,326	6,935	80.8	26.3	32.5	4,110	15.6	21,824	33.1	52.5
1974	25,670	20,725	6,316	80.7	24.6	30.5	4,070	15.9	21,267	31.2	51.3
1973	25,237	20,377	6,055	80.7	24.0	29.7	3,973	15.7	20,895	30.4	50.7
1972	24,579	19,618	6,257	79.8	25.5	31.9	4,068	16.6	20,107	32.6	52.9
1971	23,668	18,691	6,210	79.0	26.2	33.2	4,025	17.0	19,130	33.9	53.1
1970	22,552	17,768	5,805	78.8	25.7	32.7	3,908	17.3	18,218	33.5	52.3
1969	21,362	16,703	5,840	78.2	27.3	35.0	3,769	17.6	17,152	35.7	52.5
1968	20,562	15,683	5,356	76.3	26.0	34.2	3,929	19.1	16,165	35.2	51.5
1967	20,009	15,114	5,100	75.5	25.5	33.7	3,967	19.8	15,642	34.9	50.5
Male											
1996	12,285	9,815	4,187	80.0	34.1	42.6	1,628	13.2	9,960	43.0	65.6
1995	12,351	9,789	4,089	79.3	33.1	41.8	1,791	14.5	9,884	42.1	64.2
1994	12,557	9,970	4,152	79.4	33.1	41.6	1,804	14.4	10,051	41.9	64.9
1993r	12,712	10,142	4,237	79.8	33.3	41.8	1,745	13.7	10,229	42.0	63.9
1993	11,898	9,541	3,994	80.2	33.6	41.9	1,575	13.2	9,625	42.0	64.1
1992	11,965	9,576	3,912	80.0	32.7	40.9	1,617	13.5	9,706	41.3	64.1
1991	12,036	9,493	3,954	78.9	32.9	41.7	1,810	15.0	9,564	41.9	59.2
1990	12,134	9,778	3,922	80.6	32.3	40.1	1,689	13.9	9,894	40.5	58.0
1989	12,325	9,700	3,717	78.7	30.2	38.3	1,941	15.7	9,810	38.6	57.2
1988	12,491	9,832	3,770	78.7	30.2	38.3	1,950	15.6	9,947	38.5	56.5
1987	12,626	10,030	3,867	79.4	30.6	38.6	1,948	15.4	10,207	39.0	56.0
1986	12,921	10,338	3,702	80.0	28.7	35.8	1,924	14.9	10,465	36.2	54.4
1985	13,199	10,614	3,749	80.4	28.4	35.3	2,015	15.3	10,784	36.0	54.6
1984	13,744	10,914	3,929	79.4	28.6	36.0	2,184	15.9	11,052	36.4	53.6
1983	14,003	10,906	3,820	77.9	27.3	35.0	2,379	17.0	10,959	35.5	52.7
1982	14,083	11,120	3,837	79.0	27.2	34.5	2,329	16.5	11,295	35.0	53.0
1981	14,127	11,052	3,833	78.2	27.1	34.7	2,424	17.2	11,203	35.1	52.1

See footnotes at end of table.

Table A-24.   Population 14 to 24 Years Old by High School Graduate Status, College Enrollment, Attainment, Gender, Race and Hispanic Origin: October 1967 to 1996 — Continued

(Numbers in thousands. Civilian noninstitutional population.)

Year, race and Hispanic origin	Total	Population 18 to 24 years old					High school dropouts		High school graduates 14 to 24 years old		
		High school graduates		Percent						Percent	
		Total	Enrolled in college	High school graduates	Enrolled in college	Of high school graduates enrolled in college	Number	Percent	All graduates	Enrolled in college	Enrolled or completed some college
1980	14,107	11,125	3,717	78.9	26.3	33.4	2,390	16.9	11,309	33.7	51.4
1979	13,571	10,657	3,508	78.5	25.8	32.9	2,320	17.1	10,838	33.6	52.4
1978	13,385	10,614	3,621	79.3	27.1	34.1	2,200	16.4	10,789	34.5	52.6
1977	13,218	10,440	3,712	79.0	28.1	35.6	2,170	16.4	10,626	36.0	54.2
1976	13,012	10,312	3,673	79.2	28.2	35.6	2,109	16.2	10,492	36.0	55.7
1975	12,724	10,214	3,693	80.3	29.0	36.2	1,928	15.2	10,415	36.7	56.1
1974	12,315	9,835	3,411	79.9	27.7	34.7	1,958	15.9	10,073	35.3	55.6
1973	12,111	9,716	3,360	80.2	27.7	34.6	1,853	15.3	9,908	35.1	55.4
1972	11,712	9,247	3,534	79.0	30.2	38.2	1,898	16.2	9,461	38.8	59.0
1971	11,092	8,669	3,599	78.2	32.4	41.5	1,865	16.8	8,855	42.1	60.1
1970	10,385	8,087	3,331	77.9	32.1	41.2	1,746	16.8	8,279	41.8	59.2
1969	9,610	7,445	3,002	77.2	35.2	45.0	1,040	17.0	7,009	40.2	61.2
1968	9,251	6,864	3,152	74.2	34.1	45.9	1,777	19.2	8,038	46.7	61.1
1967	8,999	6,678	2,982	74.2	33.1	44.7	1,804	20.0	6,829	45.1	58.8
Female											
1996	12,386	10,317	4,582	83.3	37.0	44.4	1,519	12.3	10,507	44.9	68.6
1995	12,548	10,338	4,452	82.4	35.5	43.1	1,679	13.4	10,477	43.4	69.8
1994	12,696	10,611	4,576	83.6	36.0	43.1	1,561	12.3	10,729	43.4	68.7
1993r	12,810	10,702	4,393	83.5	34.3	41.0	1,604	12.5	10,831	41.3	66.6
1993	12,202	10,232	4,199	83.9	34.4	41.0	1,494	12.2	10,355	41.2	66.7
1992	12,313	10,344	4,429	84.0	36.0	42.8	1,466	11.9	10,486	43.3	66.9
1991	12,536	10,391	4,218	82.9	33.6	40.6	1,676	13.4	10,502	41.0	62.1
1990	12,718	10,533	4,042	82.8	31.8	38.4	1,690	13.3	10,676	38.7	59.8
1989	12,936	10,758	4,085	83.2	31.6	38.0	1,702	13.2	10,936	38.4	58.6
1988	13,242	11,068	4,021	83.6	30.4	36.3	1,799	13.5	11,257	36.8	58.2
1987	13,324	11,086	3,826	83.2	28.7	34.5	1,803	13.5	11,268	35.0	56.4
1986	13,591	11,430	3,775	84.1	27.8	33.0	1,751	12.9	11,623	33.5	55.5
1985	13,923	11,736	3,788	84.3	27.2	32.3	1,804	13.0	11,937	32.8	54.0
1984	14,287	11,956	3,662	83.7	25.6	30.6	1,958	13.7	12,199	31.3	52.4
1983	14,577	12,082	3,657	82.9	25.1	30.3	2,031	13.9	12,294	31.0	52.8
1982	14,763	12,171	3,841	82.4	26.0	31.6	2,171	14.7	12,411	32.1	52.4
1981	14,838	12,290	3,741	82.8	25.2	30.4	2,097	14.1	12,503	31.0	51.3
1980	14,851	12,287	3,682	82.7	24.8	30.0	2,124	14.3	12,547	30.6	50.8
1979	14,403	11,763	3,482	81.7	24.2	29.6	2,240	15.6	12,074	30.4	50.8
1978	14,262	11,694	3,373	82.0	23.7	28.8	2,188	15.3	11,969	29.6	50.3
1977	14,113	11,569	3,431	82.0	24.3	29.7	2,143	15.2	11,875	30.3	50.0
1976	13,907	11,365	3,508	81.7	25.2	30.9	2,168	15.6	11,666	31.6	51.4
1975	13,663	11,113	3,243	81.3	23.7	29.2	2,181	16.0	11,407	29.9	49.2
1974	13,355	10,889	2,905	81.5	21.8	26.7	2,112	15.8	11,194	27.4	47.5
1973	13,126	10,663	2,696	81.2	20.5	25.3	2,119	16.1	10,986	26.1	46.5
1972	12,867	10,371	2,724	80.6	21.2	26.3	2,170	16.9	10,644	27.0	47.4
1971	12,576	10,020	2,610	79.7	20.8	26.0	2,159	17.2	10,272	26.9	47.1
1970	12,167	9,680	2,474	79.6	20.3	25.6	2,163	17.8	9,908	26.3	46.6
1969	11,713	9,259	2,448	79.0	20.9	26.4	2,128	18.2	9,499	27.1	45.7
1968	11,311	8,820	2,205	78.0	19.5	25.0	2,150	19.0	9,072	25.9	44.4
1967	11,011	8,436	2,117	76.6	19.2	25.1	2,162	19.6	8,694	26.0	44.7
WHITE											
Total											
1996	19,676	16,199	7,123	82.3	36.2	44.0	2,458	12.5	16,436	44.3	68.4
1995	19,866	16,269	7,011	81.9	35.3	43.1	2,711	13.6	16,439	43.4	68.3

See footnotes at end of table.

Table A-24. Population 14 to 24 Years Old by High School Graduate Status, College Enrollment, Attainment, Gender, Race and Hispanic Origin: October 1967 to 1996 — Continued

(Numbers in thousands. Civilian noninstitutional population.)

Year, race and Hispanic origin	Total	Population 18 to 24 years old					High school dropouts		High school graduates 14 to 24 years old		
		High school graduates		Percent			Number	Percent	All graduates	Percent	
		Total	Enrolled in college	High school graduates	Enrolled in college	Of high school graduates enrolled in college				Enrolled in college	Enrolled or completed some college
1994	20,171	16,670	7,118	82.6	35.3	42.7	2,553	12.7	16,814	42.9	67.6
1993r	20,493	16,989	7,074	82.9	34.5	41.6	2,595	12.7	17,161	41.8	66.5
1993	19,430	16,196	6,763	83.4	34.8	41.8	2,369	12.2	16,361	41.9	66.7
1992	19,671	16,379	6,916	83.3	35.2	42.2	2,398	12.2	16,586	42.7	67.0
1991	19,980	16,324	6,813	81.7	34.1	41.7	2,845	14.2	16,467	42.0	62.3
1990	20,393	16,823	6,635	82.5	32.5	39.4	2,751	13.5	17,022	39.8	60.1
1989	20,825	17,089	6,631	82.1	31.8	38.8	2,926	14.1	17,329	39.1	58.9
1988	21,261	17,491	6,659	82.3	31.3	38.1	3,012	14.2	17,720	38.4	58.5
1987	21,493	17,689	6,483	82.3	30.2	36.6	3,042	14.2	17,982	37.1	56.8
1986	22,020	18,291	6,307	83.1	28.6	34.5	2,961	13.4	18,554	34.9	55.5
1985	22,632	18,916	6,500	83.6	28.7	34.4	3,050	13.5	19,229	35.0	55.3
1984	23,347	19,373	6,256	83.0	28.0	33.7	3,281	14.1	19,686	34.2	53.8
1983	23,899	19,643	6,463	82.2	27.0	32.9	3,428	14.3	19,948	33.5	53.4
1982	24,206	19,944	6,694	82.4	27.2	33.1	3,523	14.6	20,292	33.6	53.1
1981	24,486	20,123	6,549	82.2	26.7	32.5	3,590	14.7	20,439	33.0	52.1
1980	24,482	20,214	6,423	82.6	26.2	31.8	3,525	14.4	20,583	32.3	51.4
1979	23,895	19,616	6,120	82.1	25.6	31.2	3,571	14.9	20,033	31.8	51.7
1978	23,650	19,526	6,077	82.6	25.7	31.1	3,464	14.6	19,911	31.7	51.3
1977	23,430	19,291	6,209	82.3	26.5	32.2	3,445	14.7	19,712	32.6	52.1
1976	23,119	19,045	6,276	82.4	27.1	33.0	3,407	14.7	19,462	33.5	53.5
1975	22,703	18,883	6,116	83.2	26.9	32.4	3,149	13.9	19,298	33.0	52.7
1974	22,141	18,318	5,589	82.7	25.2	30.5	3,212	14.5	18,794	31.2	51.7
1973	21,766	18,023	5,438	82.8	25.0	30.2	3,085	14.2	18,470	30.8	51.6
1972	21,315	17,410	5,624	81.7	26.4	32.3	3,241	15.2	17,838	33.0	53.9
1971	20,533	16,593	5,594	81.3	27.2	33.5	3,156	15.4	17,087	34.2	54.1
1970	19,608	15,960	5,305	81.4	27.1	33.2	2,974	15.2	16,334	33.9	53.4
1969	18,606	15,031	5,347	80.8	28.7	35.6	2,915	15.7	15,383	36.2	53.5
1968	17,951	14,127	4,929	78.7	27.5	34.9	3,107	17.3	14,506	35.7	52.5
1967	17,500	13,657	4,708	78.0	26.9	34.5	3,141	17.9	14,022	35.2	51.4
Male											
1996	9,897	8,000	3,419	80.8	34.5	42.7	1,275	12.9	8,104	43.0	66.0
1995	9,980	8,001	3,398	80.2	34.0	42.5	1,430	14.3	8,067	42.7	65.3
1994	10,123	8,168	3,406	80.7	33.6	41.7	1,377	13.6	8,227	41.9	65.4
1993r	10,294	8,338	3,498	81.0	34.0	42.0	1,388	13.5	8,411	42.1	65.1
1993	9,653	7,807	3,284	80.9	34.0	42.1	1,429	14.8	7,978	42.6	61.4
1992	9,744	7,911	3,291	81.2	33.8	41.6	1,300	13.3	8,016	42.1	65.8
1991	9,896	7,843	3,270	79.3	33.0	41.7	1,520	15.4	7,899	41.9	59.9
1990	10,053	8,157	3,292	81.1	32.7	40.3	1,430	14.2	8,246	40.7	58.8
1989	10,240	8,177	3,223	79.9	31.5	39.4	1,572	15.4	8,271	39.7	58.5
1988	10,380	8,268	3,260	79.7	31.4	39.4	1,594	15.4	8,365	39.6	57.8
1987	10,549	8,498	3,289	80.6	31.2	38.7	1,593	15.1	8,647	39.2	56.4
1986	10,814	8,780	3,168	81.2	29.3	36.1	1,575	14.6	8,886	36.4	55.1
1985	11,108	9,077	3,254	81.7	29.3	35.8	1,637	14.7	9,229	36.6	55.5
1984	11,521	9,348	3,406	81.1	29.6	36.4	1,744	15.1	9,459	36.8	54.2
1983	11,787	9,411	3,335	79.8	28.3	35.4	1,865	15.8	9,534	35.9	53.5
1982	11,874	9,611	3,308	80.9	27.9	34.4	1,810	15.2	9,761	34.9	53.2
1981	12,040	9,619	3,340	79.9	27.7	34.7	1,960	16.3	9,754	35.1	52.8
1980	12,011	9,686	3,275	80.6	27.3	33.8	1,883	15.7	9,838	34.1	51.8
1979	11,721	9,457	3,104	80.7	26.5	32.8	1,830	15.6	9,615	33.4	52.7
1978	11,572	9,438	3,195	81.6	27.6	33.9	1,722	14.9	9,582	34.3	52.5
1977	11,445	9,263	3,286	80.9	28.7	35.5	1,779	15.5	9,422	35.8	54.5
1976	11,279	9,186	3,250	81.4	28.8	35.4	1,691	15.0	9,340	35.7	55.9
1975	11,050	9,139	3,326	82.7	30.1	36.4	1,490	13.5	9,310	36.9	56.6
1974	10,722	8,768	3,035	81.8	28.3	34.6	1,579	14.7	8,980	35.2	55.9

See footnotes at end of table.

Table A-24. Population 14 to 24 Years Old by High School Graduate Status, College Enrollment, Attainment, Gender, Race and Hispanic Origin: October 1967 to 1996 — Continued

(Numbers in thousands. Civilian noninstitutional population.)

Year, race and Hispanic origin	Total	Population 18 to 24 years old					High school dropouts		High school graduates 14 to 24 years old		
		High school graduates		Percent			Number	Percent	All graduates	Percent	
		Total	Enrolled in college	High school graduates	Enrolled in college	Of high school graduates enrolled in college				Enrolled in college	Enrolled or completed some college
1973	10,511	8,637	3,032	82.2	28.8	35.1	1,453	13.8	8,817	35.6	56.5
1972	10,212	8,278	3,195	81.1	31.3	38.6	1,506	14.7	8,462	39.2	60.1
1971	9,653	7,807	3,284	80.9	34.0	42.1	1,429	14.8	7,978	42.6	61.4
1970	9,053	7,324	3,096	80.9	34.2	42.3	1,297	14.3	7,496	42.9	60.9
1969	8,420	6,740	3,146	80.0	37.4	46.7	1,248	14.8	6,882	47.3	62.8
1968	8,084	6,221	2,949	77.0	36.5	47.4	1,401	17.3	6,372	48.1	62.7
1967	7,864	6,073	2,761	77.2	35.1	45.5	1,391	17.7	6,210	45.9	60.0
Female											
1996	9,778	8,200	3,705	83.9	37.9	45.2	1,182	12.1	8,333	45.6	70.7
1995	9,886	8,271	3,615	83.7	36.6	43.7	1,281	13.0	8,376	44.0	71.3
1994	10,048	8,503	3,714	84.6	37.0	43.7	1,175	11.7	8,588	43.9	69.7
1993r	10,199	8,651	3,576	84.8	35.1	41.3	1,207	11.8	8,750	41.5	67.9
1993	9,790	8,339	3,450	85.2	35.2	41.4	1,125	11.5	8,435	41.6	68.0
1992	9,928	8,468	3,625	85.3	36.5	42.8	1,098	11.1	8,569	43.2	68.1
1991	10,119	8,481	3,544	83.8	35.0	41.8	1,324	13.1	8,568	42.1	64.5
1990	10,340	8,666	3,344	83.8	32.3	38.6	1,322	12.8	8,775	38.9	61.4
1989	10,586	8,913	3,409	84.2	32.2	38.2	1,354	12.8	9,059	38.6	59.2
1988	10,881	9,223	3,399	84.8	31.2	36.9	1,418	13.0	9,355	37.3	59.1
1987	10,944	9,189	3,192	84.0	29.2	34.7	1,449	13.2	9,334	36.2	57.2
1986	11,205	9,509	3,139	84.9	28.0	33.0	1,388	12.4	9,667	33.6	55.8
1985	11,524	9,840	3,247	85.4	28.2	33.0	1,413	12.3	10,001	33.6	55.2
1984	11,826	10,026	3,120	84.8	26.4	31.1	1,535	13.0	10,089	31.8	53.4
1983	12,112	10,233	3,129	84.5	25.8	30.6	1,563	12.9	10,233	31.3	53.4
1982	12,332	10,333	3,285	83.8	26.6	31.8	1,713	13.0	10,530	32.3	52.9
1981	12,446	10,504	3,208	84.4	25.8	30.5	1,629	13.1	10,687	31.1	51.6
1980	12,471	10,528	3,147	84.4	25.2	29.9	1,642	13.2	10,749	30.6	50.9
1979	12,174	10,157	3,015	83.4	24.8	29.7	1,741	14.3	10,417	30.3	50.8
1978	12,078	10,088	2,882	83.5	23.9	28.6	1,742	14.4	10,327	29.3	50.3
1977	11,985	10,029	2,923	83.7	24.4	29.1	1,666	13.9	10,292	29.7	50.0
1976	11,840	9,860	3,026	83.3	25.6	30.7	1,717	14.5	10,118	31.4	51.3
1975	11,653	9,743	2,790	83.6	23.9	28.6	1,658	14.2	9,986	29.4	49.1
1974	11,419	9,551	2,555	83.6	22.4	26.8	1,633	14.3	9,811	27.5	47.8
1973	11,255	9,387	2,406	83.4	21.4	25.6	1,632	14.5	9,653	26.4	47.1
1972	11,103	9,132	2,428	82.2	21.9	26.6	1,735	15.6	9,377	27.4	48.3
1971	10,880	8,887	2,310	81.7	21.2	26.0	1,726	15.9	9,107	26.8	47.7
1970	10,555	8,634	2,209	81.8	20.9	25.6	1,675	15.9	8,837	26.3	47.2
1969	10,186	8,291	2,200	81.4	21.6	26.5	1,668	16.4	8,501	27.2	46.3
1968	9,866	7,906	1,980	80.1	20.1	25.0	1,706	17.3	8,135	26.0	45.1
1967	9,637	7,586	1,949	78.7	20.2	25.7	1,750	18.2	7,815	26.6	45.7
BLACK											
Total											
1996	3,637	2,738	983	75.3	27.0	35.9	581	16.0	2,805	36.6	54.6
1995	3,625	2,788	988	76.9	27.3	35.5	2	14.4	2,828	35.8	58.0
1994	3,661	2,818	1,001	77.0	27.3	35.5	568	15.5	2,859	36.3	59.2
1993r	3,666	2,747	897	74.9	24.5	32.8	0	16.4	2,771	32.8	54.0
1993	3,516	2,629	861	74.8	24.5	32.8	578	16.4	2,653	32.9	53.9
1992	3,521	2,625	886	74.6	25.2	33.8	575	16.3	2,668	34.3	53.3
1991	3,504	2,630	828	75.1	23.6	31.5	545	15.6	2,658	31.8	46.0
1990	3,520	2,710	894	77.0	25.4	33.0	530	15.1	2,759	33.7	48.0
1989	3,559	2,708	835	76.1	23.5	30.8	583	16.4	2,750	31.5	49.2

See footnotes at end of table.

Table A-24. Population 14 to 24 Years Old by High School Graduate Status, College Enrollment, Attainment, Gender, Race and Hispanic Origin: October 1967 to 1996 — Continued

(Numbers in thousands. Civilian noninstitutional population.)

Year, race and Hispanic origin	Total	Population 18 to 24 years old					High school dropouts		High school graduates 14 to 24 years old		
		High school graduates		Percent						Percent	
		Total	Enrolled in college	High school graduates	Enrolled in college	Of high school graduates enrolled in college	Number	Percent	All graduates	Enrolled in college	Enrolled or completed some college
1988	3,568	2,680	752	75.1	21.1	28.1	631	17.7	2,741	28.6	46.3
1987	3,603	2,739	823	76.0	22.8	30.0	611	17.0	2,790	30.6	48.1
1986	3,653	2,795	812	76.5	22.2	29.1	617	16.8	2,837	29.3	47.8
1985	3,716	2,810	734	75.6	19.8	26.1	655	17.6	2,848	26.5	43.8
1984	3,862	2,885	786	74.7	20.4	27.2	712	18.4	2,950	28.0	45.2
1983	3,865	2,740	741	70.9	19.2	27.0	832	21.5	2,790	27.7	45.0
1982	3,872	2,744	767	70.9	19.8	28.0	851	22.0	2,793	28.2	45.5
1981	3,778	2,678	750	70.9	19.9	28.0	821	21.7	2,718	28.7	44.8
1980	3,721	2,592	715	69.7	19.2	27.6	876	23.5	2,656	28.1	45.9
1979	3,510	2,356	696	67.1	19.8	29.5	895	25.5	2,415	30.6	48.4
1978	3,452	2,340	694	67.8	20.1	29.7	850	24.6	2,396	30.6	47.8
1977	3,387	2,286	721	67.5	21.3	31.5	808	23.9	2,342	32.4	46.9
1976	3,315	2,239	749	67.5	22.6	33.5	803	24.2	2,291	34.2	50.4
1975	3,213	2,081	665	64.8	20.7	32.0	877	27.3	2,149	32.6	48.1
1974	3,105	2,083	555	67.1	17.9	26.6	780	25.1	2,145	27.5	44.8
1973	3,114	2,079	498	66.8	16.0	24.0	826	26.5	2,139	25.0	41.6
1972	2,986	1,992	540	66.7	18.1	27.1	782	26.2	2,044	28.0	42.0
1971	2,866	1,789	522	62.4	18.2	29.2	825	28.8	1,833	30.0	42.3
1970	2,692	1,602	416	59.5	15.5	26.0	897	33.3	1,635	26.7	39.4
1969	2,542	1,497	407	58.9	16.0	27.2	828	32.6	1,547	27.5	40.1
1968	2,421	1,399	352	57.8	14.5	25.2	799	33.0	1,432	26.0	38.1
1967	2,283	1,276	297	55.9	13.0	23.3	788	34.5	1,316	23.7	35.0
Male											
1996	1,682	1,199	422	71.3	25.1	35.2	292	17.4	1,225	35.8	53.7
1995	1,660	1,247	430	75.1	25.9	34.4	235	14.2	1,262	35.1	56.2
1994	1,733	1,277	440	73.7	25.4	34.5	303	17.5	1,293	35.3	57.9
1993r	1,703	1,240	387	72.8	22.7	31.2	266	15.6	1,247	31.4	50.1
1993	1,659	1,207	379	72.8	22.8	31.4	258	15.6	1,214	31.5	50.0
1992	1,676	1,211	356	72.3	21.2	29.4	259	15.5	1,226	29.7	49.4
1991	1,635	1,174	378	71.8	23.1	32.2	252	15.4	1,188	32.4	47.0
1990	1,634	1,240	426	75.9	26.1	34.4	223	13.6	1,260	35.1	48.8
1989	1,654	1,195	324	72.2	19.6	27.1	307	18.6	1,207	27.5	45.8
1988	1,653	1,189	297	71.9	18.0	25.0	312	18.9	1,205	25.1	42.5
1987	1,666	1,188	377	71.3	22.6	31.7	312	18.7	1,209	32.3	48.0
1986	1,687	1,220	349	72.3	20.7	28.6	300	17.8	1,239	29.1	44.4
1985	1,720	1,244	345	72.3	20.1	27.7	323	18.8	1,258	28.2	43.6
1984	1,811	1,272	367	70.2	20.3	28.9	362	20.2	1,295	29.6	45.2
1983	1,807	1,202	331	66.5	18.3	27.5	435	24.1	1,228	27.9	43.6
1982	1,786	1,171	331	65.6	18.5	28.3	458	25.6	1,188	28.6	44.5
1981	1,730	1,154	325	66.7	18.8	28.2	419	24.2	1,165	28.5	42.3
1980	1,690	1,115	293	66.0	17.3	26.3	440	26.0	1,141	26.9	44.1
1979	1,577	973	304	61.7	19.3	31.2	457	29.0	988	32.0	46.7
1978	1,554	956	305	61.5	19.6	31.9	451	29.0	981	32.4	49.3
1977	1,528	970	309	63.5	20.2	31.9	369	24.1	991	33.0	47.6
1976	1,503	936	331	62.3	22.0	35.4	393	26.1	952	35.9	50.3
1975	1,451	897	294	61.8	20.3	32.8	404	27.8	923	33.4	50.5
1974	1,396	919	280	65.8	20.1	30.5	346	24.8	941	31.1	47.3
1973	1,434	952	266	66.4	18.5	27.9	371	25.9	962	28.4	44.2
1972	1,373	870	287	63.4	20.9	33.0	373	27.2	897	34.0	47.4
1971	1,318	769	262	58.3	19.9	34.1	416	31.6	783	34.9	45.8
1970	1,220	668	192	54.8	15.7	28.7	436	35.7	684	29.5	41.4
1969	1,141	631	202	55.3	17.7	32.0	383	33.6	653	32.5	44.6
1968	1,087	582	170	53.5	15.6	29.2	370	34.0	600	30.3	43.2
1967	1,032	525	167	50.9	16.2	31.8	397	38.5	539	32.3	41.6

See footnotes at end of table.

Table A-24. Population 14 to 24 Years Old by High School Graduate Status, College Enrollment, Attainment, Gender, Race and Hispanic Origin: October 1967 to 1996 — Continued

(Numbers in thousands. Civilian noninstitutional population.)

Year, race and Hispanic origin	Total	Population 18 to 24 years old					High school dropouts		High school graduates 14 to 24 years old		
		High school graduates		Percent						Percent	
		Total	Enrolled in college	High school graduates	Enrolled in college	Of high school graduates enrolled in college	Number	Percent	All graduates	Enrolled in college	Enrolled or completed some college
Female											
1996	1,956	1,539	561	78.7	28.7	36.4	288	14.7	1,580	37.3	55.3
1995	1,965	1,541	558	78.4	28.4	36.2	287	14.6	1,566	36.3	59.5
1994	1,928	1,542	561	80.0	29.1	36.4	265	13.7	1,567	37.1	60.3
1993r	1,965	1,508	511	76.7	26.0	33.9	337	17.2	1,526	34.1	57.2
1993	1,857	1,425	484	76.7	26.1	34.0	319	17.2	1,441	34.1	57.1
1992	1,845	1,417	531	76.8	28.8	37.5	315	17.1	1,446	38.2	56.6
1991	1,869	1,455	450	77.8	24.1	30.9	296	15.8	1,468	31.4	45.2
1990	1,886	1,468	467	77.8	24.8	31.8	306	16.2	1,498	32.4	47.3
1989	1,905	1,511	511	79.3	26.8	33.8	277	14.5	1,541	34.7	51.8
1988	1,915	1,492	455	77.9	23.8	30.5	318	16.6	1,538	31.3	49.2
1987	1,937	1,550	445	80.0	23.0	28.7	298	15.4	1,579	29.4	48.9
1986	1,966	1,574	462	80.1	23.5	29.4	306	15.6	1,598	29.3	50.4
1985	1,996	1,565	389	78.4	19.5	24.9	332	16.6	1,592	25.1	44.0
1984	2,052	1,613	419	78.6	20.4	26.0	349	17.0	1,655	26.8	45.1
1983	2,058	1,539	411	74.8	20.0	26.7	398	19.3	1,561	27.5	46.3
1982	2,086	1,572	436	75.4	20.9	27.7	393	18.8	1,604	27.9	46.3
1981	2,049	1,526	424	74.5	20.7	27.8	402	19.6	1,554	28.8	46.6
1980	2,031	1,475	422	72.6	20.8	28.6	436	21.5	1,511	29.1	47.4
1979	1,934	1,383	392	71.5	20.3	28.3	439	22.7	1,426	29.7	49.8
1978	1,897	1,384	390	73.0	20.6	28.2	398	21.0	1,415	29.3	46.7
1977	1,859	1,317	413	70.8	22.2	31.4	439	23.6	1,354	31.9	46.2
1976	1,813	1,302	417	71.8	23.0	32.0	410	22.6	1,338	32.9	50.3
1975	1,761	1,182	372	67.1	21.1	31.5	473	26.9	1,224	32.0	46.4
1974	1,709	1,167	277	68.3	16.2	23.7	434	25.4	1,207	24.8	42.9
1973	1,681	1,125	231	66.9	13.7	20.5	456	27.1	1,177	22.2	39.4
1972	1,613	1,123	253	69.6	15.7	22.5	408	25.3	1,150	23.2	37.9
1971	1,547	1,019	259	65.9	16.7	25.4	409	26.4	1,049	26.4	39.8
1970	1,471	935	225	63.6	15.3	24.1	461	31.3	955	24.7	39.3
1969	1,402	867	206	61.8	14.7	23.8	444	31.7	896	24.0	38.6
1968	1,334	819	183	61.4	13.7	22.3	430	32.2	834	22.9	35.9
1967	1,249	751	130	60.1	10.4	17.3	391	31.3	778	17.9	33.2
HISPANIC ORIGIN[1]											
Total											
1996	3,510	2,019	706	57.5	20.1	35.0	1,210	34.5	2,046	34.5	52.5
1995	3,603	2,112	745	58.6	20.7	35.3	1,250	34.7	2,142	35.7	55.8
1994	3,523	1,995	662	56.6	18.8	33.2	1,224	34.7	2,009	33.4	54.3
1993r	3,363	2,049	728	60.9	21.6	35.5	1,103	32.8	2,081	35.8	55.6
1993	2,772	1,682	602	60.7	21.7	35.8	907	32.7	1,712	36.0	55.8
1992	2,754	1,579	586	57.3	21.3	37.1	936	33.9	1,603	37.6	55.0
1991	2,874	1,498	516	52.1	18.0	34.4	1,139	39.6	1,519	34.6	47.6
1990	2,749	1,498	435	54.5	15.8	29.0	1,025	37.3	1,523	29.4	44.7
1989	2,818	1,576	453	55.9	16.1	28.7	1,062	37.7	1,600	29.4	43.6
1988	2,642	1,458	450	55.2	17.0	30.9	1,046	39.6	1,481	31.3	47.0
1987	2,592	1,597	455	61.6	17.6	28.5	849	32.8	1,612	28.7	44.0
1986	2,514	1,507	458	59.9	18.2	30.4	864	34.4	1,535	30.9	45.6
1985	2,221	1,396	375	62.9	16.9	26.9	700	31.5	1,419	27.6	46.7
1984	2,018	1,212	362	60.1	17.9	29.9	691	34.2	1,223	30.0	46.0
1983	2,025	1,110	349	54.8	17.2	31.4	759	37.5	1,134	32.3	48.4
1982r	2,001	1,153	337	57.6	16.8	29.2	740	37.0	1,173	30.0	47.3
1981	2,052	1,144	342	55.8	16.7	29.9	790	38.5	1,166	30.5	45.8

See footnotes at end of table.

Table A-24. Population 14 to 24 Years Old by High School Graduate Status, College Enrollment, Attainment, Gender, Race and Hispanic Origin: October 1967 to 1996 — Continued

(Numbers in thousands. Civilian noninstitutional population.)

Year, race and Hispanic origin	Total	Population 18 to 24 years old					High school dropouts		High school graduates 14 to 24 years old		
		High school graduates		Percent						Percent	
		Total	Enrolled in college	High school graduates	Enrolled in college	Of high school graduates enrolled in college	Number	Percent	All graduates	Enrolled in college	Enrolled or completed some college
1980	2,033	1,099	327	54.1	16.1	29.8	820	40.3	1,117	30.1	47.3
1979	1,754	968	292	55.2	16.6	30.2	687	39.2	1,001	31.2	45.7
1978	1,672	935	254	55.9	15.2	27.2	656	39.2	965	28.0	43.2
1977	1,609	880	277	54.7	17.2	31.5	622	38.7	900	32.4	43.8
1976	1,551	862	309	55.6	19.9	35.8	566	36.5	891	36.3	48.9
1975	1,446	832	295	57.5	20.4	35.5	505	34.9	849	36.5	50.8
1974	1,506	842	272	55.9	18.1	32.3	558	37.1	858	33.1	47.8
1973	1,285	709	206	55.2	16.0	29.1	500	38.9	732	30.3	43.0
1972	1,338	694	179	51.9	13.4	25.8	541	40.4	709	27.2	36.7
Male											
1996	1,815	994	300	54.8	16.5	30.2	657	36.2	1,005	30.6	48.8
1995	1,907	1,106	356	58.0	18.7	32.2	653	34.2	1,022	36.2	52.3
1994	1,896	1,021	312	53.8	16.5	30.6	685	36.1	1,026	30.7	52.7
1993r	1,710	1,005	338	58.8	19.8	33.6	591	34.6	1,023	33.7	51.2
1993	1,354	786	266	58.1	19.6	33.8	470	34.7	803	33.9	51.1
1992	1,384	720	247	52.0	17.8	34.3	531	38.4	736	34.8	52.2
1991	1,503	719	211	47.8	14.0	29.3	668	44.4	728	29.7	42.2
1990	1,403	753	214	53.7	15.3	28.4	559	39.8	770	29.4	46.5
1989	1,439	756	211	52.5	14.7	27.9	580	40.3	767	28.2	42.7
1988	1,375	724	228	52.7	16.6	31.5	553	40.2	736	32.2	48.3
1987	1,337	795	247	59.5	18.5	31.1	461	34.5	803	31.1	45.1
1986	1,339	769	233	57.4	17.4	30.3	499	37.3	776	30.5	44.4
1985	1,132	659	168	58.2	14.8	25.5	405	35.8	675	26.4	44.9
1984	956	549	154	57.4	16.1	28.1	338	35.4	554	28.2	45.7
1983	968	476	152	49.2	15.7	31.9	396	40.9	489	33.1	47.4
1982	944	519	141	55.0	14.9	27.2	347	36.8	525	28.0	44.8
1981	988	498	164	50.4	16.6	32.9	428	43.3	506	33.6	48.6
1980	1,012	518	160	51.2	15.8	30.9	431	42.6	521	31.1	49.5
1979	837	454	153	54.2	18.3	33.7	328	39.2	469	34.3	49.5
1978	781	420	126	53.8	16.1	30.0	313	40.1	438	30.4	46.3
1977	754	396	139	52.5	18.4	35.1	295	39.1	404	35.9	46.5
1976	701	378	150	53.9	21.4	39.7	253	36.1	403	39.8	51.8
1975	678	383	145	56.5	21.4	37.9	221	32.6	390	37.9	55.4
1974	720	390	141	54.2	19.6	36.2	279	38.8	401	36.7	51.4
1973	625	348	105	55.7	16.8	30.2	228	36.5	361	32.1	45.4
1972	609	301	92	49.4	15.1	30.6	253	41.5	309	32.0	44.3
Female											
1996	1,694	1,026	406	60.6	24.0	39.6	554	32.7	1,043	40.4	56.0
1995	1,696	1,011	389	59.6	22.9	38.4	598	35.4	1,022	38.6	59.6
1994	1,628	973	350	59.8	21.5	36.0	539	33.1	983	36.2	55.9
1993r	1,652	1,045	390	63.3	23.6	37.3	510	30.9	1,059	37.8	60.1
1993	1,418	895	336	63.1	23.7	37.5	439	31.0	907	38.0	60.4
1992	1,369	860	339	62.8	24.8	39.4	405	29.6	867	39.9	57.4
1991	1,372	780	305	56.9	22.2	39.1	473	34.5	791	39.2	52.5
1990	1,346	745	221	55.3	16.4	29.7	465	34.5	753	29.5	43.0
1989	1,377	823	244	59.8	17.7	29.6	482	35.0	836	30.5	44.5
1988	1,267	736	224	58.1	17.7	30.4	492	38.8	747	30.5	45.8
1987	1,256	801	208	63.8	16.6	26.0	387	30.8	808	26.4	43.2
1986	1,175	739	226	62.9	19.2	30.6	365	31.1	759	31.4	46.8
1985	1,091	734	205	67.3	18.8	27.9	295	27.0	743	28.4	48.0
1984	1,061	661	207	62.3	19.5	31.3	353	33.2	667	31.5	46.6
1983	1,057	634	198	60.0	18.7	31.2	363	34.3	644	31.8	49.7

See footnotes at end of table.

Table A-24. Population 14 to 24 Years Old by High School Graduate Status, College Enrollment, Attainment, Gender, Race and Hispanic Origin: October 1967 to 1996 — Continued

(Numbers in thousands. Civilian noninstitutional population.)

Year, race and Hispanic origin	Total	Population 18 to 24 years old					High school dropouts		High school graduates 14 to 24 years old		
		High school graduates		Percent						Percent	
		Total	Enrolled in college	High school graduates	Enrolled in college	Of high school graduates enrolled in college	Number	Percent	All graduates	Enrolled in college	Enrolled or completed some college
1982	1,056	634	196	60.0	18.6	30.9	393	37.2	648	31.8	49.2
1981	1,064	646	178	60.7	16.7	27.6	362	34.0	662	28.2	43.4
1980	1,021	579	165	56.7	16.2	28.5	389	38.1	595	29.1	45.4
1979	917	516	140	56.3	15.3	27.1	358	39.0	534	28.1	42.3
1978	891	516	128	57.9	14.4	24.8	343	38.5	528	25.8	40.0
1977	855	483	139	56.5	16.3	28.8	326	38.1	495	29.7	41.6
1976	850	483	160	56.8	18.8	33.1	313	36.8	489	33.5	46.5
1975	769	449	150	58.4	19.5	33.4	283	36.8	460	34.8	46.7
1974	786	451	129	57.4	16.4	28.6	280	35.6	459	29.2	43.4
1973	658	362	102	55.0	15.5	28.2	272	41.3	372	28.8	41.1
1972	728	394	88	54.1	12.1	22.3	288	39.6	402	23.6	31.1

Source: U.S. Bureau of the Census

1. May be of any race.

— Represents zero or rounds to zero.

r = Revised, controlled to the 1990 census-based population estimates; previous 1993 data controlled to 1980 based population estimates

Table A-25. Age Distribution of College Students 14 Years Old and Over, by Gender: October 1947 to 1996

State	All Students								Male				
	Total	14 to 17 years	18 and 19 years	20 and 21 years	22 to 24 years	25 to 29 years	30 to 34 years	35 years & over	Total	14 to 17 years	18 and 19 years	20 and 21 years	22 to 24 years
ALL RACES													
Total													
1996	15 226	237	3 309	2 907	2 551	2 215	1 228	2 778	6 820	97	1 489	1 379	1 319
1995	14 715	158	3 101	2 940	2 498	2 143	1 206	2 669	6 703	68	1 431	1 423	1 235
1994	15 022	150	3 051	3 028	2 650	2 026	1 393	2 725	6 764	65	1 416	1 414	1 322
1993 r	14 394	130	3 070	2 892	2 668	1 914	1 226	2 493	6 599	55	1 407	1 405	1 425
1993	13 898	123	2 926	2 734	2 533	1 867	1 227	2 488	6 324	52	1 337	1 312	1 345
1992	14 035	205	2 892	2 938	2 512	1 829	1 296	2 364	6 192	97	1 325	1 344	1 243
1991	14 057	132	2 929	2 939	2 304	1 983	1 302	2 468	6 439	49	1 326	1 390	1 238
1990	13 621	178	3 019	2 767	2 178	1 927	1 235	2 319	6 192	86	1 443	1 364	1 115
1989	13 180	183	3 066	2 570	2 168	1 889	1 192	2 112	5 950	73	1 422	1 228	1 067
1988	13 116	182	3 046	2 681	2 064	1 735	1 228	2 179	5 950	58	1 365	1 295	1 110
1987	12 719	239	3 045	2 642	2 006	1 826	1 159	1 802	6 030	116	1 483	1 350	1 034
1986	12 651	201	2 967	2 374	2 136	1 860	1 245	1 867	5 957	82	1 421	1 161	1 120
1985	12 524	262	2 907	2 616	2 014	1 884	1 180	1 661	5 906	131	1 349	1 313	1 087
1984	12 304	253	2 867	2 597	2 127	1 857	1 158	1 445	5 989	91	1 373	1 337	1 219
1983	12 320	260	2 940	2 495	2 042	1 921	1 167	1 495	6 010	108	1 340	1 310	1 170
1982	12 308	254	2 929	2 689	2 060	1 859	1 129	1 389	5 899	112	1 376	1 346	1 115
1981	12 127	232	3 044	2 545	1 986	1 717	1 211	1 393	5 825	96	1 450	1 239	1 144
1980	11 387	249	2 933	2 423	1 870	1 641	1 062	1 207	5 430	96	1 369	1 246	989
1979	11 380	311	2 844	2 353	1 794	1 679	996	1 402	5 480	129	1 341	1 192	975
1978	11 141	274	2 899	2 298	1 798	1 619	950	1 303	5 580	106	1 391	1 202	1 028
1977	11 546	274	2 913	2 430	1 799	1 809	992	1 329	5 889	112	1 396	1 280	1 036
1976	11 139	281	2 937	2 398	1 846	1 686	803	1 189	5 785	105	1 391	1 209	1 073
1975	10 880	293	2 943	2 313	1 679	1 616	853	1 183	5 911	128	1 426	1 256	1 011
1974	9 852	309	2 597	2 192	1 527	1 482	720	1 025	5 402	145	1 262	1 206	943
1973	8 966	295	2 517	2 073	1 465	1 278	551	787	5 048	121	1 293	1 130	937
1972	9 096	295	2 680	2 116	1 461	1 229	531	783	5 218	141	1 366	1 170	998
1971	8 087	284	2 726	1 997	1 487	1 067	527	(NA)	4 850	129	1 444	1 090	1 065
1970	7 413	260	2 594	1 857	1 354	939	410	(NA)	4 401	130	1 346	1 083	902
1969	7 435	242	2 601	1 945	1 294	918	435	(NA)	4 448	120	1 397	1 112	883
1968	6 801	281	2 501	1 826	1 029	790	373	(NA)	4 124	134	1 357	1 093	702
1967	6 401	239	2 286	1 816	998	707	356	(NA)	3 841	96	1 198	1 066	718
1966	6 085	254	2 440	1 472	987	679	254	(NA)	3 749	105	1 355	899	722
1965	5 675	264	2 215	1 326	940	614	316	(NA)	3 503	113	1 218	804	699
1964	4 643	291	1 616	1 287	670	523	256	(NA)	2 888	165	866	769	510
1963	4 336	180	1 504	1 212	717	482	241	(NA)	2 742	99	796	734	574
1962	4 208	233	1 612	996	630	486	251	(NA)	2 742	125	891	617	508
1961	3 731	213	1 470	892	507	437	212	(NA)	2 356	84	834	554	393
1960	3 570	222	1 299	790	509	491	259	(NA)	2 339	99	734	503	411
1959	3 340	210	1 175	739	489	503	224	(NA)	2 187	92	651	501	355
1958	3 242	167	1 114	1 221		534	206	(NA)	2 129	73	621	850	
1957	3 138	176	989	1 236		553	184	(NA)	2 028	77	538	827	
1956	2 883	167	934	1 105		494	183	(NA)	1 932	77	512	781	
1955	2 379	147	745	931		406	150	(NA)	1 579	57	432	647	
1950	2 175	180	733	939		324	(NA)	(NA)	1 474	74	395	692	
1947	2 311	188	620	1 088		321	94	(NA)	1 687	87	343	872	

See footnotes at end of table.

Table A-25.   Age Distribution of College Students 14 Years Old and Over, by Gender: October 1947 to 1996 — Continued

State	Male			Female							
	25 to 29 years	30 to 34 years	35 years & over	Total	14 to 17 years	18 and 19 years	20 and 21 years	22 to 24 years	25 to 29 years	30 to 34 years	35 years & over
ALL RACES											
Total											
1996	1 038	485	1 013	8 406	140	1 821	1 528	1 233	1 177	743	1 765
1995	1 008	553	985	8 013	90	1 671	1 518	1 263	1 135	653	1 684
1994	972	617	958	8 258	85	1 635	1 613	1 328	1 054	776	1 766
1993 ʳ	892	534	880	7 795	75	1 663	1 487	1 243	1 022	692	1 613
1993	872	534	873	7 574	71	1 588	1 422	1 189	995	693	1 616
1992	845	547	789	7 844	107	1 566	1 594	1 269	984	748	1 575
1991	1 018	587	832	7 618	83	1 603	1 549	1 066	965	715	1 636
1990	910	502	772	7 429	91	1 576	1 403	1 063	1 017	732	1 546
1989	926	517	716	7 231	110	1 643	1 342	1 100	964	675	1 396
1988	835	560	727	7 166	124	1 682	1 386	953	900	668	1 452
1987	921	500	625	6 689	123	1 562	1 292	972	905	659	1 176
1986	968	577	628	6 694	120	1 546	1 213	1 016	892	667	1 240
1985	942	522	561	6 618	129	1 559	1 303	926	941	658	1 100
1984	965	527	476	6 315	161	1 494	1 260	908	892	630	970
1983	1 055	521	506	6 310	153	1 600	1 185	872	865	645	989
1982	968	492	490	6 410	141	1 553	1 343	945	891	637	900
1981	909	533	453	6 303	136	1 594	1 305	842	808	677	940
1980	853	472	405	5 957	153	1 565	1 178	882	788	590	802
1979	893	463	487	5 900	183	1 503	1 161	818	786	533	914
1978	922	474	457	5 559	168	1 507	1 096	770	697	476	845
1977	1 035	511	520	5 657	162	1 517	1 151	763	774	481	809
1976	1 067	451	489	5 354	176	1 546	1 189	773	619	352	700
1975	1 025	496	569	4 969	164	1 517	1 058	668	590	357	614
1974	951	420	476	4 449	165	1 335	986	584	531	300	548
1973	867	329	371	3 918	174	1 224	944	528	411	222	416
1972	848	330	365	3 877	153	1 314	946	464	381	200	418
1971	787	334	(NA)	3 236	154	1 281	906	423	280	192	(NA)
1970	684	256	(NA)	3 013	130	1 248	774	452	255	154	(NA)
1969	671	265	(NA)	2 987	122	1 204	833	411	247	171	(NA)
1968	603	236	(NA)	2 677	147	1 144	733	328	187	138	(NA)
1967	524	239	(NA)	2 560	143	1 088	749	280	183	117	(NA)
1966	494	174	(NA)	2 337	149	1 085	573	265	185	80	(NA)
1965	458	211	(NA)	2 172	151	997	522	241	156	105	(NA)
1964	396	182	(NA)	1 755	126	750	518	160	127	74	(NA)
1963	365	174	(NA)	1 594	81	708	478	143	117	67	(NA)
1962	406	195	(NA)	1 466	108	721	379	122	80	56	(NA)
1961	337	154	(NA)	1 375	129	636	338	114	100	58	(NA)
1960	399	193	(NA)	1 231	123	565	287	98	92	66	(NA)
1959	422	166	(NA)	1 153	118	524	238	134	81	58	(NA)
1958	439	146	(NA)	1 113	94	493		371	95	60	(NA)
1957	459	127	(NA)	1 110	99	451		409	94	57	(NA)
1956	429	133	(NA)	951	90	422		324	65	50	(NA)
1955	337	107	(NA)	800	90	313		285	69	43	(NA)
1950	314	(NA)	(NA)	701	106	338		247	10	(NA)	(NA)
1947	301	84	(NA)	624	101	277		216	20	10	(NA)

See footnotes at end of table.

Table A-25.   Age Distribution of College Students 14 Years Old and Over, by Gender: October 1947 to 1996 — Continued

State	All Students								Male				
	Total	14 to 17 years	18 and 19 years	20 and 21 years	22 to 24 years	25 to 29 years	30 to 34 years	35years & over	Total	14 to 17 years	18 and 19 years	20 and 21 years	22 to 24 years
WHITE													
Total													
1996	12 189	167	2 731	2 362	2 030	1 704	940	2 254	5 453	70	1 223	1 117	1 079
1995	12 021	116	2 577	2 437	1 997	1 745	941	2 208	5 535	44	1 195	1 201	1 002
1994	12 222	101	2 568	2 459	2 091	1 592	1 143	2 267	5 524	44	1 212	1 140	1 054
1993 r	11 735	103	2 566	2 356	2 152	1 507	1 003	2 049	5 403	44	1 157	1 196	1 145
1993	11 434	98	2 456	2 243	2 064	1 490	1 015	2 068	5 222	41	1 103	1 120	1 090
1992	11 710	158	2 419	2 466	2 031	1 512	1 070	2 053	5 210	82	1 102	1 162	1 027
1991	11 686	104	2 487	2 449	1 877	1 598	1 063	2 107	5 304	41	1 112	1 146	1 012
1990	11 488	132	2 548	2 341	1 746	1 638	1 060	2 023	5 235	63	1 218	1 151	923
1989	11 243	147	2 648	2 170	1 813	1 611	986	1 868	5 136	63	1 253	1 070	900
1988	11 140	137	2 639	2 270	1 750	1 425	1 023	1 896	5 078	50	1 194	1 114	952
1987	10 731	194	2 564	2 254	1 665	1 483	985	1 584	5 104	97	1 260	1 156	873
1986	10 707	173	2 549	2 015	1 743	1 580	1 037	1 609	5 074	69	1 254	982	932
1985	10 781	229	2 539	2 257	1 704	1 590	1 014	1 448	5 103	120	1 176	1 137	941
1984	10 520	209	2 541	2 206	1 779	1 566	967	1 252	5 111	73	1 224	1 143	1 039
1983	10 565	214	2 597	2 161	1 705	1 603	961	1 324	5 162	87	1 197	1 149	989
1982	10 551	216	2 549	2 348	1 697	1 581	938	1 222	5 077	95	1 189	1 188	931
1981	10 353	197	2 639	2 239	1 671	1 390	1 027	1 190	5 010	86	1 259	1 104	977
1980	9 925	212	2 578	2 131	1 625	1 413	915	1 051	4 804	79	1 232	1 114	878
1979	9 956	256	2 498	2 079	1 543	1 474	859	1 247	4 823	110	1 192	1 058	854
1978	9 661	229	2 553	1 993	1 531	1 399	808	1 148	4 913	90	1 239	1 056	900
1977	9 962	227	2 579	2 099	1 531	1 550	827	1 149	5 156	91	1 272	1 124	890
1976	9 679	237	2 577	2 108	1 591	1 458	673	1 035	5 084	89	1 244	1 073	933
1975	9 546	252	2 613	2 042	1 461	1 410	737	1 031	5 263	111	1 283	1 134	909
1974	8 689	271	2 308	1 940	1 341	1 308	908	908	4 782	128	1 143	1 067	825
1973	8 014	253	2 281	1 865	1 292	1 152	481	690	4 218	111	1 177	1 017	838
1972	7 458	259	2 411	1 917	1 296	1 119	456	(NA)	4 395	120	1 242	1 062	891
1971	7 273	251	2 485	1 758	1 351	965	463	(NA)	4 407	117	1 328	964	992
1970	6 759	230	2 361	1 684	1 260	853	371	(NA)	4 066	117	1 251	995	850
1969	6 827	222	2 377	1 762	1 208	855	404	(NA)	4 146	110	1 298	1 021	827
1968	6 255	251	2 284	1 691	954	741	333	(NA)	3 843	117	1 262	1 021	666
1967	5 905	220	2 105	1 688	915	646	329	(NA)	3 560	88	1 097	998	666
1966	5 708	233	2 293	2 313		869		(NA)	3 536	93	1 281	1 541	
1965	5 317	233	2 074	2 139		871		(NA)	3 326	104	1 152	1 441	
1964	4 337	257	1 519	1 850		711		(NA)	2 720	147	823	1 226	
1963	4 050	171	1 391	1 817		671		(NA)	2 593	94	746	1 246	
1962	3 934	217	1 509	1 517		691		(NA)	2 586	120	836	1 066	
1961	3 498	204	1 388	1 296		10		(NA)	2 208	79	786	883	
1960	3 342	214	1 211	1 209		709		(NA)	2 214	97	691	859	
1959	3 118	193	1 101	1 134		690		(NA)	2 067	88	620	798	
1958	3 030	155	1 044	1 136		695		(NA)	1 999	68	577	802	
1957	2 932	161	921	1 165		685		(NA)	1 938	68	510	797	
1956	2 687	152	869	1 025		641		(NA)	1 808	68	474	733	
1955	2 224	125	715	880		504		(NA)	1 495	47	418	621	

See footnotes at end of table.

Table A-25. Age Distribution of College Students 14 Years Old and Over, by Gender: October 1947 to 1996 — Continued

State	Male			Female							
	25 to 29 years	30 to 34 years	35 years & over	Total	14 to 17 years	18 and 19 years	20 and 21 years	22 to 24 years	25 to 29 years	30 to 34 years	35 years & over
WHITE											
Total											
1996	797	357	811	6 735	97	1 508	1 246	951	906	583	1 443
1995	857	432	804	6 486	72	1 383	1 237	995	887	508	1 404
1994	749	512	815	6 698	57	1 357	1 320	1 037	844	631	1 453
1993 r	705	451	705	6 331	59	1 409	1 160	1 007	802	552	1 344
1993	699	457	711	6 212	57	1 353	1 123	974	791	558	1 357
1992	689	471	678	6 499	76	1 317	1 303	1 005	823	599	1 376
1991	809	480	703	6 382	63	1 375	1 304	865	789	583	1 404
1990	782	434	665	6 253	69	1 331	1 190	823	856	627	1 358
1989	789	438	623	6 107	84	1 395	1 101	913	822	548	1 245
1988	685	470	613	6 063	87	1 445	1 156	798	740	554	1 283
1987	740	436	541	5 627	97	1 304	1 097	791	743	550	1 044
1986	835	475	528	5 632	105	1 295	1 033	811	745	562	1 081
1985	812	449	468	5 679	110	1 363	1 120	764	778	565	979
1984	796	434	402	5 410	136	1 317	1 063	740	770	533	851
1983	875	421	444	5 404	127	1 400	1 012	717	720	540	800
1982	831	415	428	5 472	120	1 360	1 159	766	749	523	795
1981	745	448	391	5 342	111	1 380	1 134	694	646	578	799
1980	735	400	366	5 121	133	1 346	1 017	747	678	514	686
1979	788	398	423	5 131	146	1 306	1 021	688	686	461	823
1978	810	413	405	4 748	139	1 314	937	631	590	395	742
1977	907	433	439	4 806	135	1 307	975	641	643	394	711
1976	936	382	427	4 593	147	1 334	1 034	658	521	291	608
1975	911	426	489	4 284	141	1 330	908	552	500	311	542
1974	855	350	414	3 907	143	1 166	873	516	453	263	493
1973	789	286	(NA)	3 107	142	1 104	848	454	363	196	(NA)
1972	784	296	(NA)	3 061	138	1 169	855	404	334	160	(NA)
1971	712	293	(NA)	2 867	134	1 157	794	359	252	170	(NA)
1970	622	231	(NA)	2 693	113	1 110	689	410	231	140	(NA)
1969	637	252	(NA)	2 681	112	1 079	741	380	218	151	(NA)
1968	564	213	(NA)	2 412	134	1 022	670	288	177	120	(NA)
1967	494	217	(NA)	2 345	133	1 009	690	250	152	112	(NA)
1966		621	(NA)	2 172	140	1 012		772		248	(NA)
1965		629	(NA)	1 991	129	922		698		242	(NA)
1964		524	(NA)	1 617	110	696		624		187	(NA)
1963		507	(NA)	1 457	77	645		571		164	(NA)
1962		564	(NA)	1 348	97	673		451		127	(NA)
1961		460	(NA)	1 290	125	602		413		150	(NA)
1960		567	(NA)	1 128	117	520		350		142	(NA)
1959		561	(NA)	1 051	105	481		336		129	(NA)
1958		552	(NA)	1 031	87	467		334		143	(NA)
1957		563	(NA)	994	93	411		368		122	(NA)
1956		533	(NA)	879	84	395		292		108	(NA)
1955		409	(NA)	729	78	297		259		95	(NA)

See footnotes at end of table.

Table A-25.   Age Distribution of College Students 14 Years Old and Over, by Gender: October 1947 to 1996 — Continued

State	All Students								Male				
	Total	14 to 17 years	18 and 19 years	20 and 21 years	22 to 24 years	25 to 29 years	30 to 34 years	35years & over	Total	14 to 17 years	18 and 19 years	20 and 21 years	22 to 24 years
BLACK													
Total													
1996	1 901	45	345	346	292	337	182	354	764	17	145	155	122
1995	1 772	24	344	339	305	233	193	334	710	13	145	142	143
1994	1 800	36	310	347	344	256	184	323	745	16	132	161	147
1993 r	1 599	13	322	311	264	253	143	293	652	4	151	109	127
1993	1 545	13	311	297	253	245	141	284	636	4	148	107	124
1992	1 424	28	291	316	279	170	132	208	527	8	123	114	119
1991	1 477	18	303	302	223	216	157	257	629	7	137	138	103
1990	1 393	35	349	287	258	150	108	207	587	16	164	151	111
1989	1 287	32	302	290	243	156	119	146	480	8	126	104	94
1988	1 321	33	281	273	198	188	142	206	494	6	108	90	99
1987	1 351	32	341	264	218	220	121	155	587	13	154	124	99
1986	1 359	19	308	242	262	187	143	198	580	12	120	111	118
1985	1 263	21	259	274	201	183	112	213	552	10	121	140	84
1984	1 332	40	265	274	247	182	131	193	618	16	112	129	126
1983	1 273	31	258	242	241	179	151	171	560	12	93	112	126
1982	1 294	22	274	242	251	196	142	167	544	9	124	92	115
1981	1 335	31	306	232	212	219	132	203	566	7	133	92	100
1980	1 163	30	283	225	180	176	113	156	476	14	98	101	79
1979	1 156	43	279	224	193	150	112	155	498	12	110	110	84
1978	1 175	38	270	238	186	167	121	155	504	13	114	106	85
1977	1 284	37	269	262	190	210	136	180	571	18	90	115	104
1976	1 217	34	302	252	195	171	109	154	551	11	121	113	97
1975	1 099	34	260	237	168	151	97	152	523	14	111	107	76
1974	930	34	233	190	132	136	88	117	485	13	102	100	78
1973	781	37	194	164	140	89	60	97	358	7	96	93	77
1972	727	32	229	168	143	87	68	(NA)	384	18	102	91	94
1971	680	29	204	199	119	79	50	(NA)	363	11	94	106	62
1970	522	21	191	152	73	54	31	(NA)	253	10	73	81	38
1969	492	19	193	149	65	39	26	(NA)	236	10	86	75	41
1968	434	20	182	112	58	33	29	(NA)	221	12	83	61	26
1967	370	16	141	105	51	42	15	(NA)	199	7	78	57	32
1966	282	17	112		112	41		(NA)	154	10	47		72
1965	274	30	111		99	34		(NA)	126	8	52		47
1964	234	30	78		79	47		(NA)	120	16	35		36
1963	286	9	113		112	52		(NA)	149	5	50		62
1962	274	16	103		109	46		(NA)	156	5	55		59
1961	233	9	82		103	39		(NA)	148	5	48		64
1960	227	8	88		90	41		(NA)	125	2	43		55
1959	222	17	74		94	37		(NA)	120	4	31		58
1958	212	12	70		85	45		(NA)	130	5	44		48
1957	206	15	68		71	52		(NA)	90	9	28		30
1956	196	15	65		80	36		(NA)	124	9	38		48
1955	155	21	31		51	52		(NA)	84	9	15		25

See footnotes at end of table.

Table A-25.   Age Distribution of College Students 14 Years Old and Over, by Gender: October 1947 to 1996 — Continued

State	Male			Female							
	25 to 29 years	30 to 34 years	35 years & over	Total	14 to 17 years	18 and 19 years	20 and 21 years	22 to 24 years	25 to 29 years	30 to 34 years	35 years & over
BLACK											
Total											
1996	142	64	120	1 136	28	199	192	170	195	119	234
1995	65	80	122	1 062	11	199	197	162	168	113	212
1994	118	72	99	1 054	21	178	186	197	138	112	224
1993 r	118	36	107	947	9	172	202	137	135	107	186
1993	116	36	102	909	8	163	191	130	129	106	182
1992	73	37	54	897	21	168	202	161	97	95	154
1991	99	55	90	848	11	166	164	120	118	102	167
1990	52	26	65	807	19	185	136	146	98	82	141
1989	65	37	47	807	24	176	186	149	91	82	99
1988	75	48	68	827	27	173	183	99	113	94	138
1987	99	37	62	764	19	186	140	119	121	84	93
1986	81	64	74	779	7	187	131	144	106	79	124
1985	64	40	93	712	11	138	134	117	119	72	121
1984	99	62	74	714	24	153	145	121	83	69	119
1983	91	64	62	714	19	164	131	116	88	87	100
1982	91	51	62	750	12	150	150	136	105	92	105
1981	115	57	62	769	24	172	140	112	105	75	141
1980	92	53	39	686	16	185	124	101	84	60	116
1979	71	47	64	659	31	169	114	109	79	66	91
1978	82	52	52	671	25	155	133	102	85	68	103
1977	101	62	81	712	19	179	147	87	108	74	98
1976	90	57	62	665	23	181	139	97	81	52	92
1975	82	53	80	577	20	150	130	92	69	44	72
1974	70	60	62	448	22	131	91	55	66	28	55
1973	49	36	(NA)	325	30	97	71	63	40	24	(NA)
1972	49	30	(NA)	343	14	127	77	49	38	38	(NA)
1971	58	31	(NA)	317	18	109	93	57	21	19	(NA)
1970	33	19	(NA)	269	11	118	71	36	22	11	(NA)
1969	15	10	(NA)	256	9	108	74	24	25	17	(NA)
1968	27	13	(NA)	213	8	100	51	32	7	15	(NA)
1967	15	11	(NA)	171	9	63	48	19	27	4	(NA)
1966		25	(NA)	128	7	65		40		16	(NA)
1965		19	(NA)	148	22	59		52		15	(NA)
1964		33	(NA)	114	14	43		43		14	(NA)
1963		32	(NA)	137	4	63		50		20	(NA)
1962		37	(NA)	118	11	48		50		9	(NA)
1961		31	(NA)	85	4	34		39		8	(NA)
1960		25	(NA)	102	6	45		35		16	(NA)
1959		27	(NA)	102	13	43		36		10	(NA)
1958		33	(NA)	82	7	26		37		12	(NA)
1957		23	(NA)	116	6	40		41		29	(NA)
1956		29	(NA)	72	6	27		32		7	(NA)
1955		35	(NA)	71	12	16		26		17	(NA)

See footnotes at end of table.

Table A-25.   Age Distribution of College Students 14 Years Old and Over, by Gender: October 1947 to 1996 — Continued

State	All Students								Male				
	Total	14 to 17 years	18 and 19 years	20 and 21 years	22 to 24 years	25 to 29 years	30 to 34 years	35 years & over	Total	14 to 17 years	18 and 19 years	20 and 21 years	22 to 24 years
HISPANIC ORIGIN[1]													
Total													
1996	1 223	22	240	213	253	198	112	184	529	8	98	78	124
1995	1 207	20	264	245	236	153	97	193	568	14	121	111	124
1994	1 187	9	225	230	207	180	132	205	529	3	89	115	108
1993 [r]	1 169	17	222	299	207	178	106	139	539	7	81	154	103
1993	995	15	195	241	166	149	100	129	442	6	69	118	79
1992	918	17	230	200	156	124	90	102	388	9	93	80	74
1991	830	10	188	203	125	124	72	109	347	5	68	79	64
1990	748	13	148	188	99	109	59	130	364	12	70	80	64
1989	754	17	177	134	142	112	58	114	353	5	75	66	70
1988	747	13	203	110	137	118	73	93	355	9	75	76	77
1987	739	8	152	155	148	137	67	73	390	3	76	100	71
1986	794	16	171	146	141	164	67	89	377	4	92	67	74
1985	580	16	127	128	120	111	78	(NA)	279	10	44	53	71
1984	524	5	136	133	93	100	57	(NA)	231	2	42	63	49
1983	521	17	134	124	91	114	41	(NA)	253	10	41	61	50
1982	494	16	143	104	90	94	47	(NA)	216	6	52	47	42
1981	510	15	129	123	90	103	50	(NA)	258	6	57	68	39
1980	443	10	137	94	84	69	49	(NA)	222	2	68	52	34
1979	439	18	124	95	73	73	56	(NA)	225	8	67	43	43
1978	377	15	109	68	77	78	30	(NA)	196	7	53	30	43
1977	417	14	123	95	59	81	45	(NA)	224	6	54	45	40
1976	426	13	143	83	83	73	31	(NA)	223	3	69	39	42
1975	411	13	118	101	76	68	35	(NA)	218	3	53	52	40
1974	354	11	112	96	64	39	32	(NA)	195	6	55	44	42
1973	289	15	82	69	55	45	23	(NA)	168	11	39	37	29
1972	242	14	70	60	49	34	15	(NA)	126	7	28	35	29

See footnotes at end of table.

Table A-25.   Age Distribution of College Students 14 Years Old and Over, by Gender: October 1947 to 1996 — Continued

State	Male			Female							
	25 to 29 years	30 to 34 years	35 years & over	Total	14 to 17 years	18 and 19 years	20 and 21 years	22 to 24 years	25 to 29 years	30 to 34 years	35 years & over
HISPANIC ORIGIN[1]											
Total											
1996	79	54	90	693	15	142	136	128	119	59	95
1995	71	55	73	639	6	143	134	112	82	42	120
1994	73	55	86	659	6	136	119	99	106	78	119
1993 [r]	71	67	56	630	10	141	145	104	107	40	83
1993	57	63	51	553	9	126	123	87	93	38	78
1992	57	35	40	530	7	137	120	82	67	55	62
1991	64	30	37	483	5	120	124	61	59	42	72
1990	39	30	67	384	1	78	108	35	70	29	63
1989	63	31	42	401	11	103	69	72	49	27	71
1988	48	29	43	391	4	129	35	60	70	43	51
1987	77	42	21	349	5	76	56	76	60	25	51
1986	80	26	34	417	12	79	80	67	84	41	54
1985	72	29	(NA)	299	6	82	75	48	39	49	(NA)
1984	49	26	(NA)	292	3	94	70	43	51	31	(NA)
1983	74	17	(NA)	270	7	93	64	41	40	25	(NA)
1982	49	20	(NA)	278	10	91	57	48	45	27	(NA)
1981	55	33	(NA)	252	9	72	55	51	48	17	(NA)
1980	36	30	(NA)	221	8	63	42	50	33	20	(NA)
1979	39	25	(NA)	215	10	58	52	30	34	31	(NA)
1978	49	14	(NA)	181	8	56	38	34	29	16	(NA)
1977	56	23	(NA)	194	8	70	50	19	25	22	(NA)
1976	50	20	(NA)	203	9	74	45	41	23	11	(NA)
1975	45	25	(NA)	193	10	65	49	36	23	10	(NA)
1974	24	24	(NA)	157	5	56	51	22	15	8	(NA)
1973	32	20	(NA)	123	5	44	33	25	13	3	(NA)
1972	20	7	(NA)	117	7	43	25	20	14	8	(NA)

SOURCE: U.S. Bureau of the Census.

Data shown for 1966 and earlier years for the Black population are for Black and Other races combined.

1. May be of any race.

r = Revised, controlled to 1990 census-based population estimates; previous 1993 data controlled to 1980 based population estimates.

NOTE: Data for 1947 to 1953 exclude kindergarten. Nursery school was first collected in 1964.

(NA) Not applicable or not available.

Table A-26. College Enrollment of Students 14 to 34 Years Old, by Type of College, Attendance Status, Age and Sex: October 1970 to 1996

(Numbers in thousands. Civilian noninstitutional population.)

Year and type of college	All students Total	14 to 19 years	20 to 21 years	22 to 24 years	25 to 34 years	Public	Private	Male Total	Male Full-time	Male Part-time	Female Total	Female Full-time	Female Part-time
All Undergraduates													
1996	10,624	3,526	2,856	2,017	2,226	8,718	1,906	4,922	3,852	1,072	5,702	4,246	1,456
1995	10,315	3,251	2,881	2,033	2,150	8,221	2,094	4,867	3,749	1,118	5,450	4,062	1,388
1994	10,578	3,193	3,006	2,099	2,281	8,464	2,114	4,942	3,788	1,154	5,637	4,075	1,562
1993r	11,901	3,200	2,892	2,668	3,140	9,441	2,460	5,719	4,330	1,389	6,182	4,375	1,807
1993	9,874	3,045	2,721	2,020	2,088	8,029	1,846	4,681	3,637	1,044	5,193	3,830	1,362
1992	10,093	3,097	2,902	2,004	2,090	8,260	1,833	4,609	3,574	1,033	5,485	4,031	1,453
1991	9,840	3,061	2,902	1,757	2,120	7,953	1,887	4,661	3,598	1,063	5,179	3,871	1,308
1990	9,683	3,194	2,740	1,681	2,067	7,829	1,853	4,602	3,533	1,070	5,080	3,699	1,379
1989	9,357	3,250	2,529	1,658	1,921	7,483	1,874	4,357	3,347	1,011	5,000	3,628	1,372
1988	9,339	3,229	2,645	1,600	1,865	7,579	1,763	4,413	3,360	1,053	4,926	3,612	1,314
1987	9,228	3,283	2,585	1,512	1,848	7,416	1,810	4,550	3,394	1,158	4,677	3,293	1,384
1986	8,972	3,158	2,298	1,583	1,932	7,067	1,905	4,338	3,273	1,065	4,635	3,315	1,320
1985	9,114	3,169	2,586	1,475	1,884	7,211	1,903	4,385	3,402	984	4,728	3,452	1,276
1984	9,058	3,120	2,565	1,547	1,828	7,242	1,816	4,506	3,519	987	4,551	3,302	1,249
1983	9,012	3,200	2,464	1,475	1,873	7,014	1,998	4,488	3,417	1,071	4,525	3,314	1,211
1982	9,110	3,183	2,657	1,526	1,745	7,174	1,935	4,450	3,451	999	4,660	3,355	1,305
1981	9,053	3,276	2,511	1,458	1,808	7,035	2,018	4,443	3,397	1,046	4,610	3,343	1,266
1980	8,488	3,182	2,393	1,316	1,599	NA	NA	4,111	3,192	920	4,377	3,123	1,254
1979	8,287	3,156	2,308	1,297	1,526	6,541	1,746	4,106	3,163	943	4,183	3,051	1,132
1978	8,158	3,173	2,247	1,233	1,506	6,340	1,816	4,188	3,221	967	3,969	2,948	1,021
1977	8,408	3,184	2,376	1,206	1,640	6,683	1,724	4,372	3,304	1,068	4,027	3,002	1,025
1976	8,270	3,216	2,358	1,224	1,472	6,578	1,692	4,301	3,291	1,010	3,969	3,090	879
1975	8,108	3,237	2,255	1,072	1,546	6,598	1,510	4,393	3,394	999	3,715	2,902	813
1974	7,338	2,906	2,131	1,028	1,272	5,843	1,494	4,030	3,128	902	3,307	2,561	746
1973	6,794	2,812	2,031	924	1,028	5,279	1,516	3,791	3,035	756	3,004	2,423	581
1972	6,992	2,974	2,065	944	1,011	5,460	1,532	3,982	3,231	751	3,010	2,445	565
1971	6,895	3,008	1,936	1,019	931	5,472	1,423	4,017	3,240	777	2,878	2,348	530
1970	6,274	2,854	1,803	866	750	4,910	1,363	3,627	3,045	582	2,646	2,164	482
Two-Year College Students													
1996	3,329	1,223	669	515	922	3,103	226	1,459	909	551	1,870	1,130	740
1995	3,121	1,028	608	593	892	2,860	262	1,383	842	542	1,739	985	754
1994	3,318	1,063	623	621	1,011	3,014	304	1,439	869	570	1,879	1,046	833
1993r	3,502	1,131	745	648	978	3,260	243	1,556	978	578	1,141	805	805
1993	3,352	1,077	696	614	965	3,119	233	1,480	925	555	1,872	1,093	778
1992	3,442	1,084	789	581	988	3,206	236	1,447	877	569	1,995	1,139	856
1991	3,496	1,120	732	560	1,084	3,276	220	1,576	910	666	1,920	1,110	810
1990	3,190	1,059	689	475	967	2,972	218	1,412	808	605	1,777	984	792
1989	2,951	1,048	557	467	880	2,734	218	1,274	742	533	1,677	856	821
1988	3,175	1,134	665	497	879	NA	NA	1,383	810	573	1,792	963	829
1987	3,043	1,111	624	457	851	NA	NA	1,367	754	613	1,676	858	818
1986	2,831	1,023	506	427	875	NA	NA	1,294	717	577	1,538	786	752
1985	2,772	959	558	403	851	2,516	256	1,179	678	501	1,593	860	733
1984	2,756	994	525	442	795	2,496	260	1,333	812	521	1,422	766	656
1983	2,931	1,050	595	405	882	2,663	268	1,370	786	584	1,560	852	709
1982	3,011	1,088	604	494	826	2,750	260	1,359	832	527	1,652	905	747
1981	2,892	1,144	566	414	768	2,646	245	1,333	801	532	1,559	842	717
1980	2,666	1,080	450	417	721	NA	NA	1,195	739	456	1,472	759	713
1979	2,407	933	403	407	664	2,233	174	1,106	661	445	1,301	680	621
1978	2,453	966	427	391	670	2,247	206	1,214	679	535	1,239	664	575
1977	2,510	933	455	380	741	2,362	148	1,253	681	572	1,256	691	565
1976	2,435	907	444	367	718	2,282	153	1,272	734	538	1,163	696	467
1975	2,561	1,024	431	354	752	2,437	123	1,412	850	562	1,148	717	431
1974	2,072	834	369	305	565	1,917	154	1,172	709	463	899	528	371
1973	1,797	816	278	254	449	1,669	128	1,012	629	383	785	471	314
1972	1,910	883	334	267	426	1,816	94	1,125	770	355	785	484	301

See footnotes at end of table.

Table A-26. College Enrollment of Students 14 to 34 Years Old, by Type of College, Attendance Status, Age and Sex: October 1970 to 1996 — Continued

(Numbers in thousands. Civilian noninstitutional population.)

Year and type of college	Full-Time					Part-time				
	Total	14 to 19 years	20 to 21 years	22 to 24 years	25 to 34 years	Total	14 to 19 years	20 to 21 years	22 to 24 years	25 to 34 years
All Undergraduates										
1996	8,097	3,130	2,460	1,515	990	2,528	394	396	502	1,235
1995	7,811	2,902	2,462	1,444	1,004	2,504	349	419	589	1,147
1994	7,863	2,843	2,585	1,455	980	2,714	349	421	644	1,300
1993r	8,705	2,868	2,524	1,889	1,424	3,194	331	367	779	1,717
1993	7,467	2,732	2,380	1,429	927	2,407	314	342	590	1,161
1992	7,605	2,838	2,506	1,427	834	2,488	259	396	578	1,255
1991	7,469	2,809	2,534	1,248	878	2,371	252	368	509	1,242
1990	7,234	2,912	2,333	1,165	824	2,449	282	408	515	1,244
1989	6,973	2,989	2,209	1,122	655	2,383	260	321	536	1,266
1988	6,972	2,925	2,275	1,079	691	2,367	303	371	521	1,173
1987	6,685	2,892	2,179	1,005	610	2,543	391	406	507	1,238
1986	6,589	2,880	1,974	1,055	681	2,383	278	324	528	1,251
1985	6,854	2,900	2,237	1,017	701	2,259	269	349	457	1,184
1984	6,823	2,840	2,221	1,067	689	2,237	274	344	480	1,139
1983	6,729	2,895	2,124	993	718	2,282	305	340	482	1,153
1982	6,807	2,880	2,286	979	662	2,304	302	372	547	1,083
1981	6,740	2,983	2,157	986	613	2,312	293	353	471	1,195
1980	6,315	2,897	2,107	810	500	2,173	282	286	505	1,098
1979	6,225	2,892	1,994	814	525	2,062	264	314	483	1,001
1978	6,169	2,872	1,919	821	559	1,988	302	328	412	947
1977	6,304	2,855	2,075	775	598	2,104	329	301	431	1,042
1976	6,381	2,963	2,033	821	563	1,889	253	325	403	909
1975	6,296	2,987	1,958	696	655	1,812	250	297	376	891
1974	5,689	2,661	1,842	697	488	1,649	245	289	331	784
1973	5,460	2,629	1,801	630	398	1,334	183	230	294	630
1972	5,678	2,797	1,845	624	412	1,314	177	220	320	599
1971	5,588	2,801	1,729	700	357	1,307	207	207	319	574
1970	5,208	2,685	1,628	591	301	1,066	169	175	275	449
Two-Year College Students										
1996	2,038	995	457	271	315	1,291	227	212	244	607
1995	1,827	811	397	298	321	1,295	217	211	295	572
1994	1,916	848	407	319	341	1,402	214	216	302	670
1993r	2,119	891	515	348	365	1,382	240	230	300	613
1993	2,018	850	483	325	360	1,334	227	213	288	605
1992	2,017	897	528	287	304	1,425	187	261	294	683
1991	2,021	915	476	269	361	1,475	205	256	291	723
1990	1,793	847	408	227	310	1,397	212	281	247	657
1989	1,597	860	368	160	210	1,354	188	189	307	669
1988	1,773	926	410	209	227	1,402	207	256	288	651
1987	1,611	839	368	192	212	1,432	272	256	264	639
1986	1,503	814	296	170	223	1,328	209	210	257	652
1985	1,538	779	341	174	244	1,234	180	217	229	607
1984	1,579	812	330	190	247	1,177	182	195	252	548
1983	1,638	855	374	159	250	1,293	195	221	245	631
1982	1,737	883	381	214	260	1,274	206	223	280	566
1981	1,643	927	357	170	188	1,249	217	209	243	579
1980	1,498	884	287	160	167	1,168	195	163	256	554
1979	1,341	749	251	156	185	1,066	184	152	251	479
1978	1,343	778	243	157	167	1,110	190	184	234	503
1977	1,372	718	283	162	208	1,138	216	172	218	533
1976	1,430	764	261	177	228	1,005	143	183	190	490
1975	1,567	865	274	155	274	994	159	157	199	478
1974	1,237	702	233	151	152	835	132	136	154	413
1973	1,100	702	164	121	111	697	114	113	133	338
1972	1,255	772	223	134	126	655	111	111	133	300

See footnotes at end of table.

Table A-26.   College Enrollment of Students 14 to 34 Years Old, by Type of College, Attendance Status, Age and Sex: October 1970 to 1996 — Continued

(Numbers in thousands. Civilian noninstitutional population.)

Year and type of college	All students							Male			Female		
	Total	14 to 19 years	20 to 21 years	22 to 24 years	25 to 34 years	Public	Private	Total	Full-time	Part-time	Total	Full-time	Part-time
1971	1,830	928	307	263	331	1,726	105	1,087	726	361	743	473	270
1970	1,692	895	281	234	283	1,559	133	1,001	726	275	691	452	239
Graduate Students													
1996	1,824	21	52	534	1,217	1,190	634	885	540	345	939	511	428
1995	1,731	8	60	465	1,198	1,109	621	852	521	331	878	452	427
1994	1,719	9	21	551	1,138	1,072	647	865	528	337	854	420	434
1993r	1,576	3	14	537	1,022	1,037	539	792	489	303	783	399	399
1993	1,535	3	13	514	1,006	1,009	527	770	470	300	765	371	394
1992	1,578	—	36	508	1,035	1,021	557	795	511	284	784	388	396
1991	1,749	—	37	547	1,165	1,124	625	948	593	355	802	398	404
1990	1,621	2	27	497	1,095	1,058	563	818	494	324	803	426	375
1989	1,711	—	40	509	1,161	1,092	618	876	525	351	835	408	428
1988	1,598	—	36	464	1,098	1,084	515	810	443	368	788	357	432
1987	1,690	1	57	494	1,137	1,140	551	854	506	348	836	368	468
1986	1,633	—	44	530	1,057	1,087	545	910	540	370	723	376	347
1985	1,749	—	31	540	1,179	1,168	581	959	550	409	790	313	477
1984	1,802	—	32	580	1,190	1,225	576	1,007	612	395	794	387	407
1983	1,814	—	32	568	1,214	1,171	643	1,017	623	394	797	359	438
1982	1,810	1	32	535	1,244	1,180	630	960	568	392	850	362	488
1981	1,681	—	34	530	1,120	1,124	558	929	514	415	753	314	439
1980	1,692	2	31	554	1,104	NA	NA	914	500	414	777	332	445
1979	1,691	—	45	497	1,149	1,157	534	888	469	419	804	317	487
1978	1,681	—	51	565	1,063	1,087	594	935	477	458	745	334	411
1977	1,810	2	53	593	1,161	1,241	568	995	548	447	813	338	475
1976	1,680	—	40	622	1,017	1,161	519	994	542	452	686	254	432
1975	1,590	—	59	607	923	1,105	484	949	542	407	640	267	373
1974	1,490	—	61	499	930	1,061	428	897	457	440	593	205	388
1973	1,385	—	42	541	801	945	439	887	467	420	498	163	335
1972	1,320	1	52	517	749	877	443	872	481	391	450	155	295
1971	1,192	1	60	468	663	799	393	833	480	353	359	136	223
1970	1,140	—	54	488	599	789	351	774	432	342	366	123	243

See footnotes at end of table.

Table A-26.   College Enrollment of Students 14 to 34 Years Old, by Type of College, Attendance Status, Age and Sex: October 1970 to 1996 — Continued

(Numbers in thousands. Civilian noninstitutional population.)

Year and type of college	Full-Time					Part-time				
	Total	14 to 19 years	20 to 21 years	22 to 24 years	25 to 34 years	Total	14 to 19 years	20 to 21 years	22 to 24 years	25 to 34 years
1971	1,199	797	209	124	70	631	131	98	139	261
1970	1,177	786	197	114	80	515	109	84	120	203
Graduate Students										
1996	1,051	18	42	420	570	773	3	9	114	647
1995	974	8	43	352	571	756	—	17	112	627
1994	949	9	19	377	343	771	—	2	174	594
1993r	873	3	11	376	482	703	—	3	161	540
1993	841	3	10	358	469	694	—	3	156	536
1992	898	—	33	387	478	680	—	3	120	557
1991	992	—	29	423	539	757	—	8	124	626
1990	920	2	25	376	518	699	—	2	121	577
1989	932	—	33	375	525	779	—	7	135	637
1988	799	—	31	304	465	799	—	5	160	634
1987	874	1	52	343	477	816	—	5	151	660
1986	914	3	40	422	449	719	—	4	108	608
1985	861	—	27	385	449	887	—	4	155	728
1984	998	—	27	427	544	803	—	6	153	644
1983	982	—	32	420	530	833	—	—	148	685
1982	931	—	28	381	522	879	1	4	153	721
1981	828	—	28	355	447	854	—	6	175	673
1980	832	2	24	403	403	859	—	7	151	701
1979	786	—	32	358	395	906	—	13	139	754
1978	811	—	37	396	376	869	—	14	169	687
1977	886	2	43	382	459	922	—	10	211	702
1976	796	—	35	405	355	884	—	5	217	662
1975	809	—	43	382	386	780	—	16	225	537
1974	662	—	41	289	330	828	—	20	210	600
1973	630	—	33	350	248	755	—	9	191	553
1972	636	1	44	332	262	686	—	8	185	487
1971	616	1	57	299	261	576	—	3	169	402
1970	555	—	42	304	212	585	—	12	184	387

Source: U.S. Bureau of the Census

— Represents zero or rounds to zero.

r = Revised, controlled to the 1990 census-based population estimates; previous 1993 data controlled to 1980 based population estimates

Notes and Definitions: School Enrollment

Comparable tables to those published here were disseminated by the U.S. Census Bureau in the P-20 series of *Current Population Reports (CPR)* for most years between 1947 and 1994; the data were collected through the October Current Population Survey (CPS). Since that time the tables have not been available in printed form, but they are available on the U.S. Bureau of the Census website at <www.census.gov>. For information about the availability of earlier reports or data questions not addressed in this definitions section, contact the Education and Social Stratification Branch, Population Division, U.S. Bureau of the Census at (301) 457–2464.

Population coverage. The figures in this section for October 1996 are sample survey data and relate to the civilian noninstitutional population of the 50 states and the District of Columbia. The estimation procedure used for this survey involves the inflation of the weighted sample results to independent estimates of the civilian noninstitutional population of the United States by age, sex, race, and Hispanic origin. These independent estimates are based on civilian noninstitutional population counts from the decennial censuses and have been updated with statistics on births, deaths, immigration, and emigration statistics on the strength of the Armed Forces. Data published for 1972 through 1980 were based on independent population estimates derived by updating the 1970 decennial census counts. Data published for 1981 and 1993 were based on independent population estimates derived by updating the 1980 decennial census counts. Starting with the data collected in the October 1994 CPS, independent estimates were based on civilian noninstitutional population controls for age, race, and sex established by the 1990 decennial census and adjusted for an undercount of about 1.6 percent.

School enrollment. The school enrollment statistics from the current survey are based on replies to the interviewer's inquiry about whether the person was enrolled in regular school. Interviewers were instructed to count as enrolled anyone who had been enrolled at any time during the current term or school year in any type of public, parochial, or other private school in the regular school system. Such schools include nursery schools, kindergartens, elementary schools, high schools, colleges, universities, and professional schools. Attendance may be on either a full-time or part-time basis and during the day or night. Regular schooling is that which may advance a person toward an elementary or high school diploma, or a college, university, or professional school degree. Children enrolled in nursery schools and kindergarten are included in the enrollment figures for regular schools and are also shown separately.

Enrollment in schools that are not in the regular school system, such as trade schools, business colleges, and schools for the mentally handicapped, that do not advance students to regular school degrees, is not included.

Persons enrolled in classes that do not require physical presence in school, such as correspondence courses or other courses of independent study, and in training courses given directly on the job, are also excluded from the count of those enrolled in school, unless such courses are being counted for credit at a regular school.

Level of school. The statistics on level of school indicate the number of persons enrolled at each of five levels: nursery school, kindergarten, elementary school (1st to 8th grades), high school (9th to 12th grades), and college or professional school. The last group includes graduate students in colleges or universities. Persons enrolled in elementary, middle school, intermediate school, or junior school through the 8th grade are classified as being in elementary school. All persons enrolled in 9th through 12th grade are classified as being in high school.

Nursery school. A nursery school is defined as a group or class that is organized to provide educational experiences for children during the year or years preceding kindergarten. It includes instruction as an important and integral phase of its program of child care. Private homes in which essentially custodial care is provided are not considered nursery schools. Children attending nursery school are classified as attending during either part of the day or the full day. Part-day attendance refers to those who attend in the morning or in the afternoon, but not both. Full-day attendance refers to those who attend in both the morning and the afternoon.

Head Start. Children enrolled in Head Start programs or similar programs sponsored by local agencies to provide preschool education to young children are counted as being in nursery school.

Public or private school. In this report, a public school is defined as any educational institution operated by publicly elected or appointed school officials and supported by public funds. Private schools include educational institutions established and operated by religious bodies, as well as

Basic School Enrollment Supplement

(Questions included in the October CPS since 1967)
*= added since 1987 (year)

1. Is . . . attending or enrolled in regular school? (Regular school includes elementary school, high school, and schooling that leads to college or professional school degree.)
   - <1>   Yes
   - <2>   No (Go to 6)

2. Is . . . enrolled in public or private school?
   - <1>   Public
   - <2>   Private

3. What grade or year is . . . attending?
   - <1–12> Grades 1 through 12—elementary through high school (Skip to 7)
   - <21>   1st year of college (freshman)
   - <22>   2nd year of college (sophomore)
   - <23>   3rd year of college (junior)
   - <24>   4th year of college (senior)
   - <25>   1st year of graduate school
   - <26>   2nd year or higher of graduate school
   - <30>   College, no year reported

4. Is . . . attending college full-time or part-time?
   - <1>   Full-time
   - <2>   Part-time

5. Is this a 2-year or a 4-year college or university?
   - <1>   2-year college (community or junior college)
   - <2>   4-year college or university

6. Excluding (regular college courses and) on the job training, is . . . taking any business, vocational, technical, secretarial, trade, or correspondence courses? (1987)*
   - <1>   Yes
   - <2>   No

7. Was . . . attending or enrolled in a regular school or college in October 1995, that is, October of last year?
   - <1>   Yes
   - <2>   No   (Skip to 9)

8. What grade or year was . . . attending last year? (1989)*
   - <1–12> Grades 1 through 12 elementary through high school
   - <21>   1st year of college (freshman)
   - <22>   2nd year of college (sophomore)
   - <23>   3rd year of college (junior)
   - <24>   4th year of college (senior)
   - <25>   1st year of graduate school
   - <26>   2nd year or higher of graduate school
   - <30>   College, no year reported

9. INTERNAL CHECK ITEM A ENROLLED GRADE =
   1–12 (End questions)
   All others
   Age = 15–29   15–24 through 1995)
   - College graduate (Skip to 11)
   - High school graduate (Skip to 12)
   - Not high school graduate (Ask 10)
   Age = 30+ (End questions)

10. In what calendar year did . . . last attend regular school?
    - <1>   1996
    - <2>   1995 or before
    - <3>   Never attended
    —(Skip to 13)—

11. In what calendar year did . . . receive his/her most recent degree? (1993)*
    - <1>   1996
    - <2>   1995 or before

12. In what calendar year did . . . complete high school?
    - <1>   1996
    - <2>   1995 or before

13. Did . . . complete high school by means of an equivalency test, such as the GED? (1988)*
    - <1>   Yes
    - <2>   No

School Enrollment Supplement—Children's Items

1. Age = 0–2 (Go to next child)
   3–5 (Ask 2)   (Ask 3 through 1995)
   6–14 (Skip to 3)

2. Is . . . attending or enrolled in regular school, kindergarten, or elementary school? (1994)*
   - <1>   Yes (Skip to 4)
   - <2>   No   (End questions)

3. Is .. attending or enrolled in regular school?
   (Regular school includes nursery school, kindergarten, elementary school, and schooling that leads to a high school diploma or college degree.)
   - <1>   Yes (Ask 4)
   - <2>   No   (End questions)

4. Is . . . enrolled in public or private school?
   - <1>   Public
   - <2>   Private

5. What grade or year is . . . attending?
   (If nursery school or kindergarten, ask if full-day or part-day.)
   - <A>   Nursery (preschool, prekindergarten) full-day
   - <B>   Nursery (preschool, prekindergarten) part-day
   - <C>   Kindergarten full-day
   - <D>   Kindergarten part-day
   - <1–8> Grades 1 through 8—Elementary
   - <9–12> Grades 9 through 12—High school

those that are under other private control. In cases where enrollment was in a school or college that was both publicly and privately controlled or supported, enrollment was counted according to whether it was primarily public or private.

Modal grade. Enrolled persons are classified according to their relative progress in school, that is, whether the grade or year in which were enrolled was below, at, or above the modal (or typical) grade for persons of their age at the time of the survey. The modal grade is the year of school in which the largest proportion of students of a given age is enrolled.

Annual high school dropout rate. The annual high school dropout rate is an estimate of the proportion of students who drop out of school in a single year. This section briefly explains how the dropout rate is calculated. For further explanation and details of its derivation, see CPR series P-20, no. 413, "School Enrollment—Social and Economic Characteristics of Students: October 1983."

Annual dropout rates for a single grade (x) are estimated as the ratio of the number of persons who were enrolled in grade (x) in the year preceding the survey, did not complete grade (x), and are not currently enrolled to the number enrolled in grade (x) at the start of the year preceding this survey. Persons reported as enrolled last year but not currently enrolled are presented in table A-8 by the highest grade completed and are presumed to have dropped out of the succeeding grade (except those who graduated this year). Thus, individuals counted as 10th-grade dropouts are those not enrolled in school whose highest grade completed is the 9th grade (They include not only those persons who were enrolled in the 10th grade in the fall of the year preceding the survey and who left school without completing the year, but also those persons who finished the 9th grade in the spring preceding the survey and who were not enrolled at the survey date.) These estimates form the numerator of estimates of the annual grade specific dropout rate.

$$\text{Dropout from grade n} = \frac{\text{Not enrolled and highest grade completed} = n-1}{\text{Enrolled in grade } n+1 + \text{Not enrolled and highest grade completed} = n-1}$$

Persons currently enrolled in high school are presumed to have successfully completed and been enrolled in the preceding grade in the preceding year. Thus, those who

have successfully completed the 10th grade are enrolled in the 11th grade. Along with the persons who dropped out of that grade, they comprise the denominator of the estimate of the annual grade-specific dropout rate.

Dropped out of grade	Numerator	Denominator	
	Not currently enrolled and highest grade =	Current grade in which enrolled =	Not currently enrolled and highest grade =
10	9	11	9
11	10	12	10
12	11	College 1 + (not enrolled, completed 12 and graduated this year)	11

Since persons who completed the 12th grade cannot be presumed to enroll in college, the estimate of the number of persons enrolled in the 12th grade one year prior to the survey is constructed as the sum of the number of persons reported as having graduated from high school "this year" in table A-8 (both those enrolled in the first year of college and persons not currently enrolled whose highest grade completed is the 12th grade) and those persons not currently enrolled who were enrolled last year and whose highest grade completed is the 11th grade (dropouts).

The annual dropout rate for all grades during one year can be obtained by summing the components of the rates for the individual grades—in other words, those persons who were enrolled in the 10th, 11th, or 12th grade last year and who are not currently enrolled and do not have a diploma. The following chart shows the components of the annual dropout rate calculation for each grade.

In addition to the annual rate, two other estimates of dropouts are frequently used. The annual dropout rate is different from a "pool" (or status) measure such as the proportion of an age group who are high school dropouts (not enrolled in school, not high school graduates, shown in table A-1), which does not depend on when the individuals dropped out.

A third measure of dropouts is the cohort measure, most commonly from a longitudinal study, in which one calculates the proportion of a specific group of people enrolled in a specific year who had not received diplomas (and who were no longer in school) some years later—for example, the proportion of a cohort enrolled in 9th grade in year X who were not enrolled and had not received a diploma by year X+4.

College enrollment. The college enrollment statistics are based on replies to the interviewer's inquiry as to whether the person was attending of enrolled in college. Interviewers were instructed to count as enrolled anyone who had been enrolled at any time during the current term or school year, except those who have left for the remainder of the term. Thus, regular college enrollment includes those persons attending a four-year or two-year college, university, or professional school (such as medical or law school) in courses that may advance the student toward a recognized college or university degree (e.g., BA or MA). Attendance may be either full time or part time, during the day or night. The college student need not be working toward a degree, but he/she must be enrolled in a class for which credit would be applied toward a degree. See *School enrollment.*

Two-year and four-year colleges. College students were asked to report whether the college in which they were enrolled was a two-year college (junior or community college) or a four-year college or university. Students enrolled in the first four years were classified by the type of college they reported. Type of college is shown in tables for undergraduates only. Graduate students are shown as a separate group.

Revisions in processing and tabulations have resulted in data that are not strictly comparable to those published for earlier years. In tabulations for years prior to 1987, students in the fourth academic year of college were assumed to be in a four-year college or university regardless of the type of college they reported (74,000 fourth-year students were reported enrolled in two-year colleges in 1986 on the questionnaire but included in four-year colleges in the tabulations). Also, before 1987 type of college was not allocated for students who did not report college (about 250,000 students in the first to third year in 1986). Revised edit and allocation procedures for 1987 and 1988 increased the estimated number of college students, which also increased the numbers of persons reported in two-year and four-year colleges. The following table shows data for 1986 using both the revised and old processing and tabulation systems. The differences are due to procedural changes rather than real change.

Undergraduates (x 1000)	Revised	Old	Difference
14 to 34 years old	9,098	8,972	126
2-year college	3,087	2,831	256
4-year college	6,011	5,892	119
Type not reported	000	249	−249

Full-time and part-time attendance. College students were classified, in this report, according to whether they were attending school on a full-time or part-time basis. A student was regarded as attending college full time if he/she was taking 12 or more hours of classes during the average school week or part time if he/she was taking fewer than 12 hours of classes during the average school week.

School enrollment in year preceding current survey. Enrollment in regular school or college in October of the preceding year was queried for all persons (enrolled and not enrolled). In years before 1988, the question was asked only of persons who were not currently attending regular school or who were enrolled in college. In the tabulations of persons enrolled in secondary school in the previous year, persons currently enrolled in high school are assumed to have been enrolled the previous year.

Vocational school enrollment. Vocational school enrollment includes enrollment in business, vocational, technical, secretarial, trade, or correspondence courses that are not counted as regular school enrollment and are not for recreation or adult education classes. Courses counted as college enrollment also would not be included as vocational.

Comparability of enrollment data in previous years. Changes in the edit and tabulation packages used in processing the October CPS school enrollment supplement have caused some minor revisions in the estimates. The current edit and tabulation package began with 1987 data. The 1986 data, which were published in CPR series P-20, no. 429, were reprocessed with the rewritten programs in order to clarify comparability. The historical tables contain enrollment data in time series. In earlier editions of this report, in each table, there were two presentations for 1986. In this publication, only the revised 1986 data are shown in the historical tables.

Major changes in the data because of the 1987 edit revisions are as follows:

a. Among 14 and 15 year olds, an edit improvement allowed persons with enrollment data not reported who were previously automatically imputed "not enrolled" to be enrolled.

b. Revisions in tabulation of enrollment in the previous year simplifies calculation of an annual high school dropout rate.

c. Edit improvement caused increases in college enrollment estimates, most notable above age 24; this age group was largely ignored in earlier edits.

d. Type of college is fully allocated (discussed earlier).

e. Tabulations of type of college are available by race.

f. "Dependent family member" is defined consistently.

g. New data on employment status, vocational course enrollment, college retention and reentry, and families with children enrolled in public and private school are available.

In the series of reports on school enrollment for 1987 to 1992, race and Hispanic origin were erroneously tabulated for a small percentage of children 3 to 14 years old. Race and Hispanic origin of an adult in the household were attributed to the child, rather than using the child's reported characteristics. In the vast majority of cases, these characteristics were the same for family members, but for a small percentage of children, they were different. The correction made the following proportional changes in the numbers of children in each group: White (−0.5 percent), Black (+3.1 percent), Hispanic origin (−4.6 percent).

The historical tables show two sets of data for 1993. The data labeled 1993r were processed using population controls based on the 1990 census, adjusted for undercount. Compared with the data labeled 1993, which used population controls based on the 1980 census, the 1993r data show the effect of the change in population controls.

The change in 1994 from a paper-and-pencil survey to a computer-assisted survey had some effect on the data. Most notably, the enrollment question for children 3 to 5 years old was different from the question for older children—it included a reference to nursery school. In 1994, reported nursery school enrollment was significantly higher than in earlier years.

Age. The age classification is based on the age of the person at his/her last birthday.

Race. The population is divided into three groups on the basis of race—White, Black, and other races. The last category includes American Indians, Japanese, Chinese, other Asian and Pacific Islanders, and any other race except White and Black. In this report, the "other races" category is not shown separately.

Hispanic origin. Information on origin or descent was obtained by asking, "What is (this person's) origin or descent?" Responses generally refer to a person's perceived national or ethnic lineage and do not necessarily indicate the country of his/her birth or that of his/her parents' birth.

Persons of Hispanic origin are persons who reported themselves as Mexican American, Chicano, Mexican, Mexicano, Puerto Rican, Cuban, Central or South American, or other Hispanic origin. However, all persons who reported themselves as Mexican American, Chicano, Mexican, or Mexicano were combined into one category—Mexican. Persons of Hispanic origin may be of any race.

Marital status. The marital status category "married, spouse present," shown in this report, includes persons who are currently married and living with their spouse. The category "never married" is self-explanatory. The category "other marital status" includes persons who are separated, divorced, or widowed.

Household. A household consists of all the persons who occupy a housing unit. A house, an apartment or other group of rooms, or a single room, is regarded as a housing unit when it is occupied or intended for occupancy as separate living quarters, that is, when the occupants do not live and eat with any other persons in the structure and there is direct access from the outside through a common hall.

A household includes the related family members and all the unrelated persons, if any, such as lodgers, foster children, wards, or employees who share the housing unit. A person living alone in a housing unit or a group of unrelated persons sharing a housing unit as partners is also counted as a household. The count of households excludes group quarters.

Family. A family (also referred to in this publication as a primary family) is a group of two persons or more (one of whom is the householder) related by birth, marriage, or adoption and residing together; all such persons are considered members of one family.

Householder. The householder refers to the person (or one of the persons) in whose name the housing unit is owned or rented (maintained) or, if there is no such person, any adult member, excluding roomers, boarders, or paid employees. If the house is owned or rented jointly by a married couple, the householder may be either the husband or the wife. The person designated as the householder is the "reference person" to whom the relationship of all other household members, if any, is recorded.

Prior to 1980, the husband was always considered the householder in married-couple households. The number of householders is equal to the number of households. Also, the number of family householders is equal to the number of families.

Family householder. The family member who is also the householder (the person or one of the persons who maintain the household), or reference person, is the family householder.

Head versus householder. Beginning with the 1980 census, the Bureau of the Census discontinued the use of the terms "head of household" and "head of family." Instead, the terms "householder" and "family householder" were used. Recent social changes resulted in greater sharing of household responsibilities among the adult members and, therefore, made the term "head" inappropriate in the analysis of household and family data. Specifically, the bureau reconsidered its long-time practice of always classifying the husband as the reference person (head) when he and his wife are living together.

In this report, the term "householder" is used in the presentation of data that had previously been presented with the designation "head." The householder is the first adult household member listed on the questionnaire. The instructions call for listing first the person (or one of the persons) in whose name the home is owned or rented. If a home is owned jointly by a married couple, either the husband or the wife may be listed first, thereby becoming the reference person, or householder, to whom the relationship of other household members is to be recorded.

The practice of using the term "head of family" or "family head" to refer to the person maintaining the household was discontinued in CPS surveys conducted after the 1980 Census of Population. In surveys taken prior to the 1980 Census of Population, husbands in husband-wife families were always classified as "family head." Women were only "family heads" if no spouse was present. The person who maintains the household is now called the "family householder."

Dependent family member. In theory, a dependent family member is one who is financially dependent on the householder. In these data, a dependent family member is a primary family member, under 25 years old, who is an own child, brother/sister, or other relative (not parent) of the householder and is not "married, spouse present."

In analyses of data on college enrollment by family income for earlier years, persons who were primary family members, 18 to 24 years old, and not "married, spouse present" were often treated as dependent family members, although they were not labeled as such and included some householders (e.g., "other marital status" in table 13 of CPR series P-20, no. 429). The family income reported for dependent family members is presumed to be that of the parental family; for others, it is presumed to be that of the individual and his/her spouse. In table A-15, persons labeled "dependent family member" and "other marital and family status" combined are equivalent to persons labeled "other marital status" in table 13 of CPR series P-20, no. 429. Persons who are "other marital and family status" in this report are the family householders who are not "married, spouse present."

Educational attainment. Data on educational attainment are derived from a single question that asks, "What is the highest level of school . . . has completed, or the highest degree . . . has received?" Levels of completion beyond a high school degree are identified with specific categories, such as associate, bachelors, and masters. The question on educational attainment applies only to progress in "regular" schools. Such schools include public, private, and parochial elementary and high schools (both junior and senior), colleges, universities, and professional schools (whether day or night schools.) Thus, regular schooling is that which may advance a person toward an elementary school certificate, a high school diploma, or a college, university, or professional school degree. Schooling in other than regular schools is counted only if the credits obtained are regarded as transferable to schools in the regular school system.

The single educational attainment question now in use was introduced in the CPS beginning in January 1992 and is similar to that used in the 1990 Decennial Census of Population and Housing. Consequently, data on educational attainment from the 1994 CPS are not directly comparable to CPS data from years prior to 1992. The new question replaces the two-part question used in the CPS that asked respondents to report the highest grade they had attended and whether they had completed that grade.

Labor force status.

In the labor force. The definition of labor force and employment status relates to the population 15 years old and over. Persons are classified as being in the labor force if they were employed as civilians, unemployed, or in the Armed Forces during the survey week. Data tabulated from the October CPS are for the civilian population only.

Not in the labor force. All civilians who are not classified as employed or unemployed are defined as "not in the labor force."

Employed. Employed persons comprise (1) all civilians who, during the survey week that includes October 12, did any work at all as paid employees or in their own business or profession, on their own farm, or in a business operation owned by a member of the family and (2) all those who were not working but who had jobs or businesses from which they were temporarily absent because of illness, bad weather, vacation, or labor-management dispute, or because they were taking time off for personal reasons, whether or not they were paid by their employers for time off and whether or not they were seeking other jobs. Excluded from the employed group are persons whose only activity consisted of work around the house (such as own-home housework and painting or repairing their own home) or volunteer work for religious, charitable, and similar organizations.

Unemployed. Unemployed persons are those civilians who, during the survey week, had no employment but were available for work and (1) had engaged in any specific job-seeking activity within the past four weeks, such as registering at a public or private employment office, meeting with prospective employers, checking with friends or relatives, placing or answering advertisements, writing letters of application, or being on a union or professional register; (2) were waiting to be called back to a job from which they have been laid off; or (3) were waiting to report to a new wage or salary job within 30 days.

Full-time and part-time employment. Persons who worked 35 hours or more during the survey week and those who worked 1 to 34 hours but usually work full time are classified as employed full time. Part-time workers are persons who worked 1 to 34 hours during the survey week and usually work only 1 to 34 hours. Persons with a job but not at work during the survey week are classified according to whether they usually work full time or part time.

Family Income. In this report, family income is derived from a single question asked of the household respondent when a household first enters the sample and is updated on the one-year anniversary of entry. Income includes money income from jobs; net income from business, farm, or rent; pensions; dividends; interest; Social Security payment; and any other money income. The income of nonrelatives living in the household is excluded, but the income of all family members 14 years old and over, including those temporarily living away, is included. It should be noted that while characteristics of the person, such as age and marital status, and the composition of families refer to the date of the interview, family income statistics refer to receipts over a 12-month period starting 12 to 16 months prior to the interview.

The income tables include in the lowest income group those who were classified as having no income in the 12-month reference period and those reporting loss in net income from farm and nonfarm self-employment or in rental income.

The detailed income tables included a separate category ("not reported") for families for which no income information was obtained. In most other CPSs showing income data, the missing income data have been allocated.

The money income level of families shown in this report may be somewhat understated. Income data from the October control card are based on the respondent's estimate of total family money income in broad, fixed income intervals. Income data collected in the March supplement to the CPS are based on responses to 11 direct question asked about each person 15 years old and over and identify 23 different sources of income in the preceding calendar year. Previous research has shown that the use of broad income intervals to record money income tends to reduce the rate of nonresponse, while increasing the likelihood that the amounts reported will be significantly understated as compared with results from more detailed questions.

Metropolitan/nonmetropolitan residence. The population residing in Metropolitan Statistical Areas (MSAs) constitutes the metropolitan population. MSAs are defined by the Office of Management and Budget for use in the presentation of statistics by agencies of the federal government. An MSA is a geographic area consisting of a large population nucleus together with adjacent communities that have a high degree of economic and social integration with that nucleus. The definitions specify a boundary around each large city so as to include most or all of its suburbs. Entire counties form the MSA buildings blocks, except in New England, where cities and towns are used. The former term SMSA was changed to MSA in 1983.

An area qualifies for recognition as an MSA if (1) it includes a city of at least 50,000 population, or (2) it includes a Census Bureau–defined urbanized area of at least 50,000 with a total metropolitan population of at least 100,000 (75,000 in New England). In addition to the county containing the main city or urbanized area, an MSA may include other counties having strong commuting ties to the central county. If specified conditions are met, certain large MSAs are designated as consolidated MSAs (CMSAs) and divided into component primary MSAs (PMSAs).

Central cities. The largest city in each MSA is always designated a central city. There may be additional central cities if specified requirements, designed to identify places of central character within the MSA, are met. Although the largest central cities are generally included in the title of the MSA, there may be central cities that are not part of the title. The balance of the MSA outside the central city or cities often is regarded as equivalent to "suburbs."

In July 1985, the CPS began carrying the Metropolitan Statistical Area definitions announced by the Office of Management and Budget on June 30, 1984. Figures published from the CPS in the early 1980s and throughout most of the 1970s referred to metropolitan areas as defined on the basis of the 1970 census. Because there are important differences in the population classified as metropolitan using the 1970 and 1984 definitions, comparisons should be avoided.

Comparability of metropolitan estimates. A redesigned CPS sample based on the 1990 census began to be phased in during April 1994 and was completed in July 1995. During the phase-in, when part of the sample was based on the 1980 census and part was based on the 1990 census, estimates by metropolitan status had limited reliability. Estimates for 1994 by metropolitan status should be used cautiously or not at all. Although estimates in this report were based on population controls derived from the 1990 census, metropolitan definitions were based on the 1980 census, because phase-in of the new sample was in the early stages.

The recent CPS metropolitan estimates (since 1986) have been consistently higher than independent estimates of the metropolitan population prepared by the Census Bureau; the CPS nonmetropolitan estimates have been lower than the independent estimates. The apparent overestimation of metropolitan and underestimation of nonmetropolitan population in the CPS relative to the bureau's independent estimates should be taken into account when using the data.

Geographic regions. The four major regions of the United States for which data are presented represent groups of states as follows:

Northeast—Connecticut, Maine, Massachusetts, New Hampshire, New Jersey, New York, Pennsylvania, Rhode Island, and Vermont.

Midwest[1]—Illinois, Indiana, Iowa, Kansas, Michigan, Minnesota, Missouri, Nebraska, North Dakota, Ohio, South Dakota, and Wisconsin.

South—Alabama, Arkansas, Delaware, District of Columbia, Florida, Georgia, Kentucky, Louisiana, Maryland, Mississippi, North Carolina, Oklahoma, South Carolina, Tennessee, Texas, Virginia, and West Virginia.

West—Alaska, Arizona, California, Colorado, Hawaii, Idaho, Montana, Nevada, New Mexico, Oregon, Utah, Washington, and Wyoming.

Symbols. The following symbols are used throughout the tables:

-    Represents zero or rounds to zero.
- B   The base of the derived figure is less than 75,000.
- NA Not available or not applicable.

Rounding of estimates. Individual figures are rounded to the nearest thousand without being adjusted to group totals, which are independently rounded. With few exceptions, percentages are based on the rounded absolute numbers.

---

[1]Formerly North Central.

The tables that follow include data about years of school completed for persons 15 years old and over cross-classified by such characteristics as age, race/ethnicity, gender, marital status, labor force status, occupation, earnings, region, and metropolitan/nonmetropolitan residence.

Not only are people enrolling in school in greater proportions, as indicated in the previous section, but larger proportions are also *completing* higher levels of schooling than ever before in American history. In 1950, only one-third of the adult population in the United States were high school graduates. Only half of Americans were high school graduates as recently as the mid-1960s. By 1997, 82 percent of U.S. adults 25 years old and over (87 percent of those in their late 20s) were high school graduates. And this proportion has continued to increase in the 1990s despite some countervailing demographic trends (such as increased immigration from less developed countries with relatively lower education levels).

The United States has one of the highest proportions of its adult population with college experience compared with other industrialized countries. The proportion of people who have completed four years of college or more continued to grow into the 1990s for most but not all subgroups of the U.S. population. In 1950, only 6 percent of people 25 years old and over had completed four or more years of college. This proportion tripled by the early 1980s and reached 21 percent by 1990 and 24 percent in 1997. The continued growth in this percentage has been fueled by persons of nontraditional college age returning to college. For younger age groups (persons 25 to 29 years of age, for example), there has not been much change in the proportion completing four years of college or more in the past 20 years; the numbers fluctuated between 22 percent and 24 percent between 1977 and 1994. Since that time, the proportion of college graduates in this age group has increased to 28 percent. Reflecting enrollment and college completion at older ages, the percentage of persons 25 years old and over who completed four or more years of college increased steadily during this entire period, from 15 percent in 1977 to 22 percent by 1994, and reached 24 percent in 1996 and 1997.

The proportion completing college has historically been higher for men than for women, but recent changes portend a reversal of this tendency. For all age groups combined (25 years old and over), about 26 percent of men and 22 percent of women had completed four or more years of college by 1997. But for the youngest age group (25 to 29 years old), 29 percent of women had completed four or more years of college compared with 26 percent of men. A similar reversal by gender appears to have occurred for African Americans. For Hispanics, the proportion of college graduates was about the same for both young men and women.

Although there have been major improvements in educational attainment for African Americans as well as for persons of Hispanic origin, the education gap between these groups and the White population in the United States has not disappeared. In 1950, only 14 percent of African Americans were high school graduates, a figure that climbed to 75 percent by 1997. Even though this is considerably higher than the comparable proportion for Hispanics (55 percent in 1997), it remains below that for the non-Hispanic White population (86 percent of whom were high school graduates in 1997). However, at younger ages, the proportions of Whites and African Americans completing high school were indistinguishable in 1997, with nearly nine of ten persons in their late 20s graduating from high

FIGURE B-1

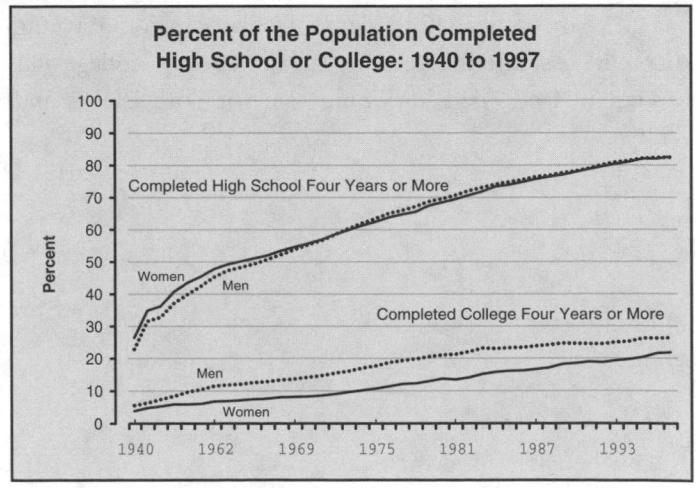

Source: U.S. Bureau of the Census.

FIGURE B-2

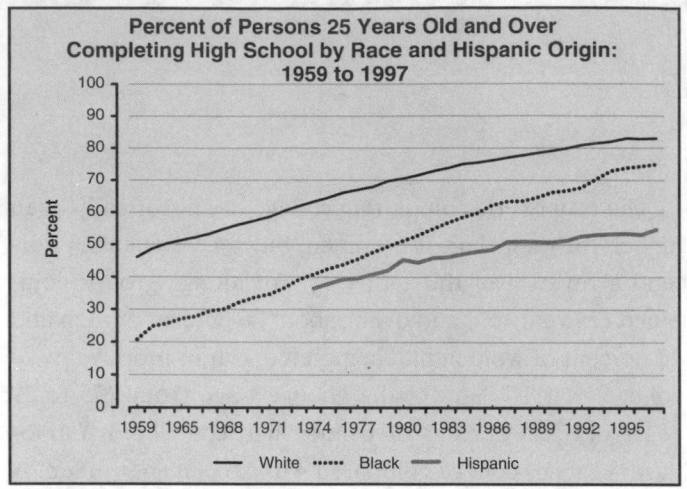

Percent of Persons 25 Years Old and Over
Completing High School by Race and Hispanic Origin:
1959 to 1997

— White   ••••• Black   — Hispanic

Source: U.S. Bureau of the Census.

FIGURE B-3

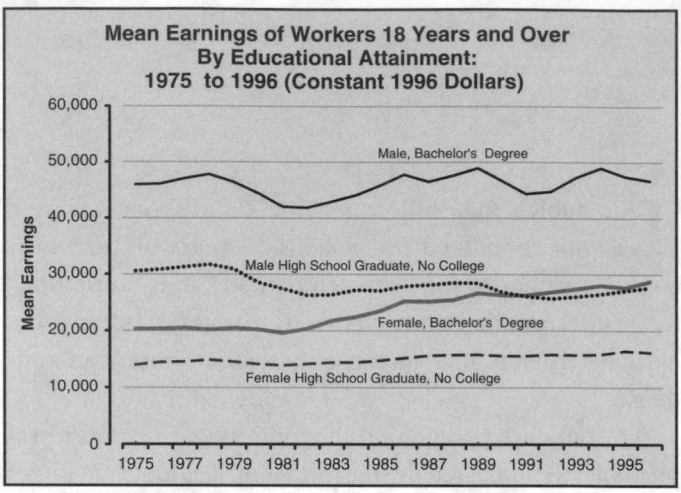

Mean Earnings of Workers 18 Years and Over
By Educational Attainment:
1975 to 1996 (Constant 1996 Dollars)

Source: U.S. Bureau of the Census.

school regardless of race. Hispanics, regardless of age, lag behind Whites and African Americans in terms of educational attainment.

The gap between the percentages of Blacks and Whites who have completed four or more years of college has actually widened in the past several decades, despite increased proportions of both Blacks and Whites who have graduated from college. In 1997, approximately twice the proportion of adult Whites as Blacks were college graduates (25 percent versus 13 percent, respectively). This gap was not smaller for those in their late twenties (29 versus 14 percent in 1997), and this was also the case for high school graduates. For young African-American women, the proportion completing four or more years of college has increased in the 1990s to 16 percent in 1997. There has been no clear trend this decade for African-American men in the 25- to 29-year-old age group. The proportion completing four or more years of college by 1997 was no higher than it was 20 years earlier (12 percent). The proportion of young Hispanics completing four or more years of college (11 percent in 1997) lagged behind that for both Blacks and Whites.

The economic returns on education have historically favored those with more education. The more education one has attained, the more one can expect to earn. The earnings gap between those with relatively low and relatively high educational attainment has not only widened in the past 20 years, but the earnings of some education groups have actually declined. For persons 18 years old and over with a high school diploma but no college, for example, mean earnings have declined for men from about $30,500 in 1975 to $27,600 in 1996 when inflation is taken into account (that is, in 1996 dollars in both years). For persons with a bachelor's degree, mean earnings increased for both men and women during this period, averaging $46,700 for men in 1996, up about $700 over 1975.[1]

---

[1] For women high school graduates, mean earnings have increased by about $2,000 during this period to reach $16,100 in 1996, but women are on average working more—both in terms of weeks per year and hours per day—now than they were in 1975. For women with a bachelor's degree, average earnings increased from $20,300 to $28,700 between 1975 and 1996.

Table B-1. Educational Attainment of Persons 15 Years Old and Over, by Age, Sex, Race, and Hispanic Origin: March 1997

(Numbers in thousands. Civilian noninstitutional population.)

Age, sex, race, and Hispanic origin	Total	None	Elementary			High School			
			1st-4th grade	5th-6th grade	7th-8th grade	9th grade	10th grade	11th grade	High school graduate
ALL RACES									
Both Sexes									
Total, 15 years and over	207 235	984	2 021	3 857	9 693	8 345	9 936	12 977	65 514
15 to 17 years	11 666	14	7	40	2 443	3 681	3 433	1 882	145
18 and 19 years	7 498	17	12	43	101	255	486	2 330	2 312
20 to 24 years	17 489	36	78	225	225	383	412	1 184	5 472
25 to 29 years	19 260	52	107	265	276	313	485	936	5 821
30 to 34 years	20 996	63	122	324	298	423	550	917	6 889
35 to 39 years	22 755	78	131	346	315	405	572	1 004	7 991
40 to 44 years	21 205	72	157	284	355	361	459	708	7 237
45 to 49 years	18 354	93	150	238	389	291	413	669	5 825
50 to 54 years	14 659	81	105	260	499	276	346	541	5 001
55 to 59 years	11 579	72	178	315	499	271	478	518	4 233
60 to 64 years	9 896	87	175	310	622	313	481	490	3 657
65 to 69 years	9 501	75	184	290	751	370	501	592	3 425
70 to 74 years	8 514	71	208	278	820	335	485	534	3 006
75 years and over	13 862	171	406	639	2 099	668	835	672	4 502
18 years and over	195 568	969	2 014	3 816	7 250	4 664	6 503	11 095	65 370
25 years and over	170 581	916	1 924	3 548	6 924	4 026	5 605	7 580	57 586
65 years and over	31 877	318	798	1 206	3 670	1 373	1 821	1 798	10 933
Male									
Total, 15 years and over	100 159	525	1 020	1 966	4 795	4 176	4 852	6 523	30 255
15 to 17 years	6 004	11	4	24	1 361	1 958	1 739	839	59
18 and 19 years	3 783	11	4	27	61	145	267	1 312	1 134
20 to 24 years	8 751	20	41	129	136	191	202	686	2 836
25 to 29 years	9 613	35	64	130	159	161	259	557	2 970
30 to 34 years	10 426	30	64	187	153	212	309	509	3 512
35 to 39 years	11 323	50	76	195	157	215	273	579	4 053
40 to 44 years	10 470	39	92	152	170	196	260	398	3 551
45 to 49 years	8 969	54	73	120	175	128	238	317	2 551
50 to 54 years	7 150	46	56	139	262	133	167	239	2 171
55 to 59 years	5 575	45	93	165	287	143	221	203	1 906
60 to 64 years	4 689	33	87	160	311	141	193	196	1 537
65 to 69 years	4 321	36	88	151	354	168	190	232	1 332
70 to 74 years	3 764	31	92	138	395	154	210	209	1 121
75 years and over	5 319	82	186	251	815	231	324	245	1 521
18 years and over	94 154	513	1 016	1 941	3 434	2 218	3 112	5 684	30 196
25 years and over	81 620	483	971	1 786	3 237	1 882	2 644	3 686	26 226
65 years and over	13 404	149	366	539	1 564	553	724	686	3 974
Female									
Total, 15 years and over	107 076	459	1 000	1 891	4 898	4 168	5 085	6 454	35 259
15 to 17 years	5 662	3	3	16	1 082	1 722	1 694	1 044	85
18 and 19 years	3 715	5	7	16	40	110	219	1 018	1 178
20 to 24 years	8 737	17	37	96	89	192	210	498	2 635
25 to 29 years	9 647	16	43	134	117	151	226	378	2 850
30 to 34 years	10 570	32	58	137	145	211	241	408	3 377
35 to 39 years	11 432	28	55	152	158	190	299	425	3 938
40 to 44 years	10 735	33	65	132	186	165	198	310	3 685
45 to 49 years	9 385	39	77	118	214	163	175	352	3 273
50 to 54 years	7 509	35	49	121	238	143	180	302	2 830
55 to 59 years	6 003	27	85	150	212	128	257	315	2 328
60 to 64 years	5 207	55	88	150	311	173	288	294	2 120
65 to 69 years	5 180	39	97	139	397	202	311	359	2 093
70 to 74 years	4 750	40	116	140	425	181	275	325	1 885
75 years and over	8 544	89	220	389	1 284	437	511	427	2 981

See footnotes at end of table.

Table B-1.   Educational Attainment of Persons 15 Years Old and Over, by Age, Sex, Race, and Hispanic Origin: March 1997 — Continued

(Numbers in thousands. Civilian noninstitutional population.)

Age, sex, race, and Hispanic origin	College							Percent	
	Some college, no degree	Associate Degree		Bachelor's degree	Master's degree	Professional degree	Doctorate degree	High school graduate or more	Bachelor's degree or more
		Occupational	Academic						
ALL RACES									
Both Sexes									
Total, 15 years and over	38 062	6 978	6 358	29 089	9 205	2 455	1 761	76.9	20.5
15 to 17 years	21	—	—	—	—	—	—	1.4	—
18 and 19 years	1 916	15	2	9	1	—	—	56.7	0.1
20 to 24 years	6 757	436	477	1 723	73	8	—	85.5	10.3
25 to 29 years	4 160	751	739	4 390	692	184	90	87.4	27.8
30 to 34 years	3 883	1 009	982	4 099	972	291	174	87.2	26.4
35 to 39 years	4 225	1 075	938	4 060	1 139	284	191	87.5	24.9
40 to 44 years	4 069	1 016	898	3 708	1 308	394	178	88.7	26.4
45 to 49 years	3 281	874	752	3 264	1 458	349	308	87.8	29.3
50 to 54 years	2 496	518	542	2 283	1 213	239	259	85.6	27.2
55 to 59 years	1 779	362	318	1 499	721	156	178	79.9	22.1
60 to 64 years	1 370	275	212	1 083	540	149	132	75.0	19.2
65 to 69 years	1 250	214	203	987	405	145	109	70.9	17.3
70 to 74 years	1 163	167	148	839	291	95	77	67.9	15.3
75 years and over	1 691	265	149	1 144	395	161	65	60.4	12.7
18 years and over	38 041	6 978	6 358	29 089	9 205	2 455	1 761	81.4	21.7
25 years and over	29 367	6 527	5 880	27 357	9 132	2 447	1 761	82.1	23.9
65 years and over	4 104	646	499	2 970	1 090	401	250	65.5	14.8
Male									
Total, 15 years and over	18 192	3 112	2 619	14 387	4 809	1 711	1 218	76.2	22.1
15 to 17 years	9	—	—	—	—	—	—	1.1	—
18 and 19 years	815	6	—	—	—	—	—	51.7	—
20 to 24 years	3 335	213	212	716	33	2	—	84.0	8.6
25 to 29 years	2 088	324	335	2 069	311	111	38	85.8	26.3
30 to 34 years	1 826	534	370	1 962	481	175	102	86.0	26.1
35 to 39 years	2 007	481	369	1 972	599	187	107	86.4	25.3
40 to 44 years	2 025	424	335	1 799	652	248	128	87.5	27.0
45 to 49 years	1 594	436	354	1 730	732	260	207	87.7	32.7
50 to 54 years	1 241	212	235	1 206	668	179	196	85.4	31.4
55 to 59 years	790	153	125	796	401	112	136	79.3	25.9
60 to 64 years	673	123	93	592	336	112	103	76.1	24.4
65 to 69 years	617	68	86	548	233	128	90	71.8	23.1
70 to 74 years	487	46	61	493	197	67	64	67.4	21.8
75 years and over	684	89	42	505	166	130	46	59.9	15.9
18 years and over	18 183	3 112	2 619	14 387	4 809	1 711	1 218	81.0	23.5
25 years and over	14 033	2 893	2 406	13 672	4 776	1 708	1 218	82.0	26.2
65 years and over	1 789	204	189	1 546	596	325	200	65.8	19.9
Female									
Total, 15 years and over	19 870	3 866	3 740	14 702	4 396	744	543	77.6	19.0
15 to 17 years	12	—	—	—	—	—	—	1.7	—
18 and 19 years	1 101	9	1	9	1	—	—	61.9	0.3
20 to 24 years	3 422	223	265	1 008	39	5	—	87.0	12.0
25 to 29 years	2 073	427	404	2 321	381	73	52	88.9	29.3
30 to 34 years	2 057	475	611	2 137	491	116	72	88.3	26.6
35 to 39 years	2 218	594	569	2 088	540	97	84	88.6	24.6
40 to 44 years	2 044	592	563	1 909	657	146	50	89.8	25.7
45 to 49 years	1 687	438	398	1 534	726	90	100	87.9	26.1
50 to 54 years	1 254	306	306	1 077	545	60	63	85.8	23.2
55 to 59 years	989	209	194	703	320	45	42	80.4	18.5
60 to 64 years	697	151	119	491	204	37	30	73.9	14.6
65 to 69 years	633	146	117	439	171	18	19	70.2	12.5
70 to 74 years	676	121	87	346	94	28	13	68.4	10.1
75 years and over	1 006	177	107	639	228	30	19	60.7	10.7

See footnotes at end of table.

**Table B-1.   Educational Attainment of Persons 15 Years Old and Over, by Age, Sex, Race, and Hispanic Origin: March 1997
— Continued**

(Numbers in thousands. Civilian noninstitutional population.)

Age, sex, race, and Hispanic origin	Total	None	Elementary			High School			
			1st-4th grade	5th-6th grade	7th-8th grade	9th grade	10th grade	11th grade	High school graduate
18 years and over	101 414	456	997	1 875	3 816	2 446	3 391	5 410	35 174
25 years and over	88 961	434	953	1 763	3 687	2 144	2 961	3 894	31 360
65 years and over	18 474	168	432	667	2 106	820	1 097	1 111	6 959
WHITE									
Both Sexes									
Total, 15 years and over	173 296	701	1 555	3 171	8 006	6 804	7 980	9 813	55 074
15 to 17 years	9 246	8	5	28	1 890	2 934	2 769	1 493	104
18 and 19 years	5 949	11	8	43	89	184	346	1 842	1 847
20 to 24 years	14 043	22	75	213	204	319	303	819	4 263
25 to 29 years	15 567	36	95	230	244	274	376	683	4 576
30 to 34 years	17 072	43	96	281	251	372	425	655	5 547
35 to 39 years	18 786	56	109	332	249	346	452	751	6 578
40 to 44 years	17 652	46	137	239	271	296	369	484	6 004
45 to 49 years	15 526	74	129	211	303	210	305	459	4 842
50 to 54 years	12 545	63	84	222	385	224	289	372	4 273
55 to 59 years	9 935	62	140	211	431	201	378	377	3 708
60 to 64 years	8 512	55	110	225	506	258	412	350	3 252
65 to 69 years	8 345	55	140	233	624	308	392	477	3 109
70 to 74 years	7 638	47	151	199	687	277	420	460	2 809
75 years and over	12 481	124	277	504	1 872	602	745	593	4 161
18 years and over	164 050	693	1 550	3 143	6 116	3 870	5 212	8 320	54 971
25 years and over	144 058	661	1 467	2 887	5 823	3 368	4 563	5 659	48 860
65 years and over	28 464	227	567	936	3 183	1 187	1 558	1 530	10 079
Male									
Total, 15 years and over	84 540	379	773	1 619	4 024	3 424	3 938	5 034	25 493
15 to 17 years	4 775	8	1	14	1 055	1 548	1 417	682	40
18 and 19 years	3 043	8	4	27	50	100	193	1 077	909
20 to 24 years	7 151	5	38	124	124	173	154	500	2 230
25 to 29 years	7 892	23	58	119	149	149	209	417	2 377
30 to 34 years	8 557	22	45	163	138	184	243	386	2 853
35 to 39 years	9 487	38	66	186	124	182	229	454	3 386
40 to 44 years	8 827	24	76	120	134	165	222	270	2 960
45 to 49 years	7 698	46	67	111	152	98	178	216	2 140
50 to 54 years	6 184	37	39	112	203	119	143	157	1 866
55 to 59 years	4 831	41	67	111	253	108	177	145	1 679
60 to 64 years	4 073	20	56	118	265	115	159	141	1 369
65 to 69 years	3 817	24	65	119	305	144	149	191	1 214
70 to 74 years	3 402	24	72	98	337	126	178	191	1 059
75 years and over	4 804	60	118	195	736	213	288	207	1 412
18 years and over	79 765	372	771	1 605	2 969	1 875	2 521	4 352	25 454
25 years and over	69 571	358	729	1 454	2 795	1 603	2 174	2 775	22 314
65 years and over	12 022	108	256	413	1 378	483	615	590	3 685
Female									
Total, 15 years and over	88 756	322	782	1 552	3 982	3 380	4 042	4 779	29 581
15 to 17 years	4 471	—	3	14	835	1 385	1 352	811	64
18 and 19 years	2 906	2	4	16	39	84	153	765	938
20 to 24 years	6 892	17	37	89	80	146	149	318	2 033
25 to 29 years	7 674	13	37	110	95	125	167	266	2 199
30 to 34 years	8 515	21	51	118	113	187	182	269	2 694
35 to 39 years	9 299	19	43	146	125	164	223	297	3 193
40 to 44 years	8 825	22	61	119	137	131	148	213	3 044
45 to 49 years	7 828	28	62	100	151	113	127	243	2 702
50 to 54 years	6 361	26	45	110	182	105	145	215	2 407
55 to 59 years	5 104	21	73	100	179	92	201	232	2 029

See footnotes at end of table.

Table B-1. Educational Attainment of Persons 15 Years Old and Over, by Age, Sex, Race, and Hispanic Origin: March 1997 — Continued

(Numbers in thousands. Civilian noninstitutional population.)

Age, sex, race, and Hispanic origin	College							Percent	
	Some college, no degree	Associate Degree		Bachelor's degree	Master's degree	Professional degree	Doctorate degree	High school graduate or more	Bachelor's degree or more
		Occupational	Academic						
18 years and over	19 858	3 866	3 740	14 702	4 396	744	543	81.9	20.1
25 years and over	15 335	3 634	3 473	13 685	4 356	739	543	82.2	21.7
65 years and over	2 315	443	310	1 424	493	76	51	65.3	11.1
WHITE									
Both Sexes									
Total, 15 years and over	31 798	5 995	5 439	25 231	8 004	2 178	1 547	78.1	21.3
15 to 17 years	16	—	—	—	—	—	—	1.3	—
18 and 19 years	1 555	15	2	7	1	—	—	57.6	0.1
20 to 24 years	5 503	377	425	1 452	60	8	—	86.1	10.8
25 to 29 years	3 286	625	640	3 741	532	152	78	87.6	28.9
30 to 34 years	3 085	835	815	3 507	796	233	131	87.6	27.3
35 to 39 years	3 373	912	754	3 504	964	244	161	87.8	25.9
40 to 44 years	3 347	877	773	3 172	1 139	348	152	89.6	27.3
45 to 49 years	2 820	789	641	2 829	1 311	317	286	89.1	30.5
50 to 54 years	2 215	446	469	1 970	1 083	219	232	86.9	27.9
55 to 59 years	1 557	306	284	1 331	638	153	158	81.9	23.0
60 to 64 years	1 234	231	181	959	477	137	124	77.5	19.9
65 to 69 years	1 130	185	188	912	375	127	89	73.3	18.0
70 to 74 years	1 094	149	141	779	258	91	77	70.7	15.8
75 years and over	1 584	248	126	1 067	371	148	59	62.2	13.2
18 years and over	31 782	5 995	5 438	25 231	8 004	2 178	1 547	82.4	22.5
25 years and over	24 724	5 603	5 012	23 771	7 943	2 170	1 547	83.0	24.6
65 years and over	3 809	582	455	2 758	1 003	367	225	67.7	15.3
Male									
Total, 15 years and over	15 349	2 728	2 313	12 655	4 206	1 540	1 064	77.3	23.0
15 to 17 years	9	—	—	—	—	—	—	1.0	—
18 and 19 years	668	6	—	—	—	—	—	52.1	—
20 to 24 years	2 751	195	198	627	29	2	—	84.4	9.2
25 to 29 years	1 644	286	313	1 792	227	95	34	85.8	27.2
30 to 34 years	1 470	453	319	1 698	384	131	68	86.2	26.7
35 to 39 years	1 651	424	302	1 685	502	172	88	86.5	25.8
40 to 44 years	1 696	382	306	1 590	557	219	107	88.6	28.0
45 to 49 years	1 390	390	310	1 515	655	239	192	88.7	33.8
50 to 54 years	1 117	182	210	1 044	618	163	173	86.9	32.3
55 to 59 years	690	127	110	728	363	109	123	81.3	27.4
60 to 64 years	614	104	76	528	301	106	100	78.5	25.4
65 to 69 years	542	60	75	509	228	115	75	73.9	24.3
70 to 74 years	456	35	60	454	179	67	64	69.8	22.5
75 years and over	650	83	33	484	162	122	40	62.1	16.8
18 years and over	15 340	2 728	2 312	12 655	4 206	1 540	1 064	81.9	24.4
25 years and over	11 920	2 527	2 114	12 028	4 177	1 538	1 064	82.9	27.0
65 years and over	1 648	178	169	1 447	570	304	178	68.0	20.8
Female									
Total, 15 years and over	16 449	3 267	3 126	12 575	3 798	637	483	78.8	19.7
15 to 17 years	7	—	—	—	—	—	—	1.6	—
18 and 19 years	886	9	1	7	1	—	—	63.4	0.3
20 to 24 years	2 752	182	227	825	31	5	—	87.9	12.5
25 to 29 years	1 642	339	328	1 948	305	57	44	89.4	30.7
30 to 34 years	1 615	382	496	1 809	412	102	63	88.9	28.0
35 to 39 years	1 721	487	452	1 819	462	73	73	89.0	26.1
40 to 44 years	1 651	495	467	1 582	582	129	44	90.6	26.5
45 to 49 years	1 430	399	331	1 314	656	78	93	89.5	27.4
50 to 54 years	1 098	263	258	926	465	56	59	87.0	23.7
55 to 59 years	867	179	174	603	275	44	36	82.4	18.8

See footnotes at end of table.

Table B-1. Educational Attainment of Persons 15 Years Old and Over, by Age, Sex, Race, and Hispanic Origin: March 1997 — Continued

(Numbers in thousands. Civilian noninstitutional population.)

Age, sex, race, and Hispanic origin	Total	None	Elementary			High School			
			1st-4th grade	5th-6th grade	7th-8th grade	9th grade	10th grade	11th grade	High school graduate
60 to 64 years	4 439	35	54	107	241	143	253	209	1 884
65 to 69 years	4 528	32	75	113	319	163	243	286	1 895
70 to 74 years	4 236	23	78	101	350	151	242	269	1 750
75 years and over	7 677	64	158	309	1 136	389	457	386	2 750
18 years and over	84 285	322	779	1 538	3 147	1 995	2 690	3 968	29 517
25 years and over	74 487	303	738	1 433	3 028	1 765	2 389	2 884	26 546
65 years and over	16 442	118	311	523	1 805	703	942	940	6 395

BLACK

Both Sexes

Age, sex, race, and Hispanic origin	Total	None	1st-4th grade	5th-6th grade	7th-8th grade	9th grade	10th grade	11th grade	High school graduate
Total, 15 years and over	24 627	138	303	444	1 312	1 179	1 561	2 730	8 222
15 to 17 years	1 855	7	2	10	441	571	492	296	30
18 and 19 years	1 192	6	—	—	12	57	111	398	390
20 to 24 years	2 500	15	—	4	15	50	85	302	967
25 to 29 years	2 613	11	5	9	4	31	77	223	1 031
30 to 34 years	2 737	10	12	19	33	32	103	235	1 043
35 to 39 years	2 876	11	10	3	44	32	101	234	1 115
40 to 44 years	2 539	13	9	26	71	33	70	198	981
45 to 49 years	2 076	9	11	8	65	62	95	193	784
50 to 54 years	1 448	4	10	16	92	45	45	146	532
55 to 59 years	1 184	5	27	70	50	59	94	133	401
60 to 64 years	982	8	34	58	83	50	66	129	302
65 to 69 years	906	10	31	45	104	56	91	108	247
70 to 74 years	664	6	37	67	109	51	56	69	151
75 years and over	1 046	23	114	109	190	50	75	66	248
18 years and over	22 772	131	301	434	871	608	1 069	2 434	8 192
25 years and over	19 072	110	301	429	845	500	872	1 733	6 835
65 years and over	2 616	39	183	221	403	157	221	243	646

Male

Age, sex, race, and Hispanic origin	Total	None	1st-4th grade	5th-6th grade	7th-8th grade	9th grade	10th grade	11th grade	High school graduate
Total, 15 years and over	11 113	96	180	242	621	576	715	1 276	3 750
15 to 17 years	929	4	2	8	242	327	231	106	10
18 and 19 years	594	3	—	—	11	35	66	196	186
20 to 24 years	1 144	15	—	3	11	10	33	163	469
25 to 29 years	1 186	8	2	3	1	7	35	120	492
30 to 34 years	1 228	4	9	11	10	17	54	105	512
35 to 39 years	1 335	8	5	3	27	16	36	118	544
40 to 44 years	1 148	8	9	15	34	13	37	120	481
45 to 49 years	942	6	5	5	17	28	52	93	340
50 to 54 years	645	4	8	15	50	13	21	70	229
55 to 59 years	524	3	21	49	26	28	39	53	161
60 to 64 years	424	8	23	31	27	24	32	49	117
65 to 69 years	372	9	19	26	43	20	30	37	80
70 to 74 years	273	3	17	30	56	25	26	18	48
75 years and over	369	15	60	42	66	13	24	28	81
18 years and over	10 183	93	178	234	379	249	484	1 170	3 740
25 years and over	8 446	75	178	230	357	205	385	812	3 085
65 years and over	1 014	27	96	99	166	59	79	84	209

Female

Age, sex, race, and Hispanic origin	Total	None	1st-4th grade	5th-6th grade	7th-8th grade	9th grade	10th grade	11th grade	High school graduate
Total, 15 years and over	13 514	42	123	202	692	603	846	1 453	4 472
15 to 17 years	925	3	—	2	200	245	261	190	20
18 and 19 years	598	3	—	—	—	22	46	202	203
20 to 24 years	1 364	—	—	1	4	41	52	139	498
25 to 29 years	1 427	3	3	5	4	24	42	103	539
30 to 34 years	1 509	6	3	8	23	15	49	130	531
35 to 39 years	1 541	3	5	—	17	16	65	116	571

See footnotes at end of table.

Table B-1. Educational Attainment of Persons 15 Years Old and Over, by Age, Sex, Race, and Hispanic Origin: March 1997 — Continued

(Numbers in thousands. Civilian noninstitutional population.)

Age, sex, race, and Hispanic origin	College							Percent	
	Some college, no degree	Associate Degree		Bachelor's degree	Master's degree	Professional degree	Doctorate degree	High school graduate or more	Bachelor's degree or more
		Occupational	Academic						
60 to 64 years	620	127	105	431	176	31	24	76.5	14.9
65 to 69 years	588	125	113	403	147	12	15	72.8	12.7
70 to 74 years	638	114	81	325	78	24	13	71.4	10.4
75 years and over	935	165	92	583	209	27	19	62.2	10.9
18 years and over	16 442	3 267	3 126	12 575	3 798	637	483	82.9	20.8
25 years and over	12 804	3 076	2 898	11 743	3 767	632	483	83.2	22.3
65 years and over	2 160	404	286	1 311	434	63	46	67.5	11.3

BLACK

Both Sexes

Total, 15 years and over	4 729	692	651	1 944	572	85	65	68.9	10.8
15 to 17 years	5	—	—	—	—	—	—	1.9	—
18 and 19 years	218	—	—	—	—	—	—	51.0	—
20 to 24 years	865	39	32	127	5	—	—	81.2	5.3
25 to 29 years	693	88	64	316	49	5	6	86.2	14.4
30 to 34 years	633	130	120	304	53	7	4	83.8	13.5
35 to 39 years	690	114	131	326	45	17	2	84.9	13.6
40 to 44 years	563	91	92	282	82	17	9	83.4	15.4
45 to 49 years	374	65	94	209	84	14	9	78.6	15.2
50 to 54 years	210	50	54	151	84	1	10	75.2	16.9
55 to 59 years	157	42	24	56	61	1	4	63.1	10.3
60 to 64 years	106	25	18	58	36	8	2	56.5	10.6
65 to 69 years	94	21	12	38	29	9	12	50.9	9.6
70 to 74 years	48	15	2	28	25	—	—	40.5	8.0
75 years and over	72	12	8	49	20	6	6	40.2	7.7
18 years and over	4 724	692	651	1 944	572	85	65	74.3	11.7
25 years and over	3 641	653	619	1 817	567	85	65	74.9	13.3
65 years and over	214	47	22	115	73	15	18	44.0	8.5

Male

Total, 15 years and over	2 103	244	219	800	203	52	36	66.6	9.8
15 to 17 years	—	—	—	—	—	—	—	1.1	—
18 and 19 years	97	—	—	—	—	—	—	47.7	—
20 to 24 years	384	10	9	37	—	—	—	79.5	3.2
25 to 29 years	331	29	16	113	25	5	—	85.2	12.1
30 to 34 years	275	50	38	115	23	5	2	82.9	11.8
35 to 39 years	298	41	44	171	18	4	2	84.1	14.6
40 to 44 years	243	19	21	100	29	13	4	79.3	12.8
45 to 49 years	166	38	37	108	34	11	2	78.2	16.5
50 to 54 years	95	15	20	74	22	1	9	72.0	16.3
55 to 59 years	69	21	10	20	23	—	2	58.4	8.6
60 to 64 years	45	13	14	26	11	5	—	54.4	10.0
65 to 69 years	59	2	10	17	5	6	7	50.3	9.5
70 to 74 years	20	8	—	10	11	—	—	35.6	7.6
75 years and over	21	—	—	9	2	3	6	32.8	5.3
18 years and over	2 103	244	219	800	203	52	36	72.6	10.7
25 years and over	1 622	234	210	763	203	52	36	73.5	12.5
65 years and over	100	10	10	35	19	9	13	39.9	7.5

Female

Total, 15 years and over	2 626	448	432	1 144	370	33	29	70.7	11.7
15 to 17 years	5	—	—	—	—	—	—	2.7	—
18 and 19 years	121	—	—	—	—	—	—	54.2	—
20 to 24 years	481	29	24	90	5	—	—	82.6	7.0
25 to 29 years	363	59	48	202	25	—	6	87.1	16.4
30 to 34 years	358	80	82	189	31	3	2	84.5	14.9
35 to 39 years	392	73	87	155	27	13	—	85.6	12.7

See footnotes at end of table.

Table B-1. Educational Attainment of Persons 15 Years Old and Over, by Age, Sex, Race, and Hispanic Origin: March 1997 — Continued

(Numbers in thousands. Civilian noninstitutional population.)

Age, sex, race, and Hispanic origin	Total	None	Elementary			High School			
			1st-4th grade	5th-6th grade	7th-8th grade	9th grade	10th grade	11th grade	High school graduate
40 to 44 years	1 391	5	—	10	37	20	33	78	500
45 to 49 years	1 134	4	6	4	48	33	44	100	444
50 to 54 years	803	—	2	1	43	32	24	76	303
55 to 59 years	660	2	6	21	24	32	54	80	240
60 to 64 years	558	1	10	28	56	26	34	79	185
65 to 69 years	534	1	13	18	61	36	61	70	167
70 to 74 years	392	4	20	37	52	25	30	51	103
75 years and over	677	8	55	66	123	36	51	38	167
18 years and over	12 589	38	123	200	492	358	585	1 263	4 452
25 years and over	10 626	35	123	199	487	295	487	922	3 750
65 years and over	1 603	12	87	122	237	98	142	159	437

HISPANIC ORIGIN [1]

Both Sexes

Age, sex, race, and Hispanic origin	Total	None	1st-4th grade	5th-6th grade	7th-8th grade	9th grade	10th grade	11th grade	High school graduate
Total, 15 years and over	20 700	451	1 102	2 151	1 683	1 584	1 338	1 899	5 022
15 to 17 years	1 597	2	5	14	359	473	453	271	17
18 and 19 years	1 034	13	8	39	30	84	101	324	259
20 to 24 years	2 592	16	60	208	130	187	115	310	735
25 to 29 years	2 778	24	93	226	141	179	142	257	791
30 to 34 years	2 717	28	93	278	156	191	119	207	724
35 to 39 years	2 453	31	107	325	145	101	93	163	704
40 to 44 years	1 935	19	128	215	145	88	76	121	545
45 to 49 years	1 355	36	96	169	105	54	52	63	336
50 to 54 years	1 105	45	62	178	111	64	43	43	271
55 to 59 years	937	53	112	121	83	57	43	49	229
60 to 64 years	682	31	77	133	75	44	36	25	145
65 to 69 years	560	51	84	72	67	30	27	30	114
70 to 74 years	432	37	80	80	59	14	18	20	62
75 years and over	524	65	96	93	77	19	20	15	91
18 years and over	19 103	449	1 097	2 137	1 324	1 111	886	1 628	5 005
25 years and over	15 476	420	1 029	1 890	1 164	840	669	995	4 011
65 years and over	1 516	152	260	245	203	63	65	65	267

Male

Age, sex, race, and Hispanic origin	Total	None	1st-4th grade	5th-6th grade	7th-8th grade	9th grade	10th grade	11th grade	High school graduate
Total, 15 years and over	10 627	236	536	1 122	896	847	685	1 025	2 492
15 to 17 years	886	2	1	9	228	270	235	136	3
18 and 19 years	540	11	4	24	15	45	58	187	116
20 to 24 years	1 445	7	33	127	90	112	62	189	371
25 to 29 years	1 498	12	55	124	100	103	79	138	427
30 to 34 years	1 406	13	43	158	79	91	59	121	390
35 to 39 years	1 254	23	66	179	61	57	37	90	371
40 to 44 years	998	9	69	111	69	49	41	62	264
45 to 49 years	660	20	47	83	52	21	21	34	159
50 to 54 years	559	27	30	84	49	41	23	15	130
55 to 59 years	418	39	54	52	36	26	24	17	84
60 to 64 years	323	8	32	61	33	13	18	11	68
65 to 69 years	229	23	31	32	27	9	9	10	49
70 to 74 years	204	17	31	43	26	2	5	8	31
75 years and over	207	24	38	36	31	8	15	4	31
18 years and over	9 741	234	534	1 114	668	577	451	889	2 490
25 years and over	7 755	216	497	963	563	420	331	513	2 003
65 years and over	640	65	100	111	84	19	28	23	110

Female

Age, sex, race, and Hispanic origin	Total	None	1st-4th grade	5th-6th grade	7th-8th grade	9th grade	10th grade	11th grade	High school graduate
Total, 15 years and over	10 073	215	566	1 020	788	737	653	874	2 529
15 to 17 years	711	—	3	5	131	203	218	135	14
18 and 19 years	494	2	4	15	15	39	43	136	143

See footnotes at end of table.

Table B-1.   Educational Attainment of Persons 15 Years Old and Over, by Age, Sex, Race, and Hispanic Origin: March 1997 — Continued

(Numbers in thousands. Civilian noninstitutional population.)

Age, sex, race, and Hispanic origin	College							Percent	
	Some college, no degree	Associate Degree		Bachelor's degree	Master's degree	Professional degree	Doctorate degree	High school graduate or more	Bachelor's degree or more
		Occupational	Academic						
40 to 44 years	321	73	71	182	53	4	5	86.9	17.5
45 to 49 years	208	27	57	101	49	2	7	79.0	14.1
50 to 54 years	115	35	33	77	62	—	1	77.9	17.4
55 to 59 years	89	21	14	36	38	1	2	66.7	11.6
60 to 64 years	61	13	5	32	24	3	2	58.1	11.0
65 to 69 years	35	19	2	21	23	3	4	51.3	9.7
70 to 74 years	27	7	2	18	14	—	—	43.9	8.2
75 years and over	51	12	8	40	18	3	—	44.3	9.1
18 years and over	2 621	448	432	1 144	370	33	29	75.7	12.5
25 years and over	2 019	419	409	1 054	364	33	29	76.0	13.9
65 years and over	113	37	12	80	55	7	4	46.5	9.1

HISPANIC ORIGIN [1]

Both Sexes

Age, sex, race, and Hispanic origin	Some college, no degree	Occupational	Academic	Bachelor's degree	Master's degree	Professional degree	Doctorate degree	High school graduate or more	Bachelor's degree or more
Total, 15 years and over	2 895	430	459	1 228	282	103	73	50.7	8.1
15 to 17 years	3	—	—	—	—	—	—	1.3	—
18 and 19 years	170	5	—	—	—	—	—	42.0	—
20 to 24 years	668	37	41	75	7	3	—	60.4	3.3
25 to 29 years	459	63	98	256	37	9	4	61.8	11.0
30 to 34 years	429	81	85	248	50	20	9	60.6	12.0
35 to 39 years	365	78	75	208	37	8	15	60.7	10.9
40 to 44 years	298	46	48	131	38	23	13	59.0	10.6
45 to 49 years	178	43	44	121	38	9	9	57.4	13.1
50 to 54 years	129	29	33	54	28	13	4	50.6	8.9
55 to 59 years	72	23	14	51	17	6	5	44.6	8.5
60 to 64 years	44	13	6	34	14	3	1	38.3	7.7
65 to 69 years	31	3	6	23	10	5	7	35.5	7.9
70 to 74 years	35	3	6	10	5	2	2	28.6	4.2
75 years and over	15	6	3	16	2	3	4	26.6	4.7
18 years and over	2 892	430	459	1 228	282	103	73	54.8	8.8
25 years and over	2 054	387	418	1 153	275	100	73	54.7	10.3
65 years and over	81	11	15	49	16	9	13	30.4	5.8

Male

Age, sex, race, and Hispanic origin	Some college, no degree	Occupational	Academic	Bachelor's degree	Master's degree	Professional degree	Doctorate degree	High school graduate or more	Bachelor's degree or more
Total, 15 years and over	1 495	197	227	591	174	59	44	49.7	8.2
15 to 17 years	2	—	—	—	—	—	—	0.5	—
18 and 19 years	75	4	—	—	—	—	—	36.1	—
20 to 24 years	374	15	21	42	4	—	—	57.2	3.2
25 to 29 years	235	31	50	125	13	6	—	59.2	9.6
30 to 34 years	218	31	39	120	29	10	5	59.9	11.7
35 to 39 years	177	31	35	89	23	5	11	59.1	10.2
40 to 44 years	161	27	26	63	26	14	7	58.9	11.0
45 to 49 years	74	19	26	71	23	6	5	57.9	15.8
50 to 54 years	78	15	16	17	20	10	2	51.7	8.8
55 to 59 years	30	9	3	24	12	4	5	40.9	10.9
60 to 64 years	32	10	4	21	10	—	1	45.3	10.0
65 to 69 years	9	2	3	6	9	5	4	38.1	10.6
70 to 74 years	24	3	3	7	2	—	1	34.9	4.9
75 years and over	8	1	—	7	1	—	3	24.4	5.3
18 years and over	1 494	197	227	591	174	59	44	54.2	8.9
25 years and over	1 045	179	205	548	170	59	44	54.9	10.6
65 years and over	42	6	6	20	12	5	8	32.6	7.1

Female

Age, sex, race, and Hispanic origin	Some college, no degree	Occupational	Academic	Bachelor's degree	Master's degree	Professional degree	Doctorate degree	High school graduate or more	Bachelor's degree or more
Total, 15 years and over	1 400	233	233	637	108	43	28	51.7	8.1
15 to 17 years	2	—	—	—	—	—	—	2.2	—
18 and 19 years	95	2	—	—	—	—	—	48.5	—

See footnotes at end of table.

Table B-1.   Educational Attainment of Persons 15 Years Old and Over, by Age, Sex, Race, and Hispanic Origin: March 1997 — Continued

(Numbers in thousands. Civilian noninstitutional population.)

Age, sex, race, and Hispanic origin	Total	None	Elementary			High School			
			1st-4th grade	5th-6th grade	7th-8th grade	9th grade	10th grade	11th grade	High school graduate
20 to 24 years	1 146	9	27	81	41	75	54	121	365
25 to 29 years	1 280	12	37	102	40	76	63	119	364
30 to 34 years	1 311	15	50	120	77	100	60	86	334
35 to 39 years	1 198	8	41	146	84	44	56	73	333
40 to 44 years	937	10	59	104	76	39	35	59	281
45 to 49 years	695	16	49	87	54	33	32	29	177
50 to 54 years	547	18	31	93	63	23	20	28	141
55 to 59 years	518	15	59	69	47	31	19	32	145
60 to 64 years	359	24	45	72	41	31	17	14	77
65 to 69 years	331	27	53	40	40	20	19	20	65
70 to 74 years	228	19	49	37	33	12	13	13	31
75 years and over	317	41	58	56	46	11	6	10	60
18 years and over	9 362	215	563	1 023	657	534	435	739	2 515
25 years and over	7 721	204	532	927	601	420	338	482	2 007
65 years and over	876	87	160	133	119	44	37	43	157

See footnotes at end of table.

Table B-1.   Educational Attainment of Persons 15 Years Old and Over, by Age, Sex, Race, and Hispanic Origin: March 1997 — Continued

(Numbers in thousands. Civilian noninstitutional population.)

Age, sex, race, and Hispanic origin	Some college, no degree	Associate Degree		Bachelor's degree	Master's degree	Professional degree	Doctorate degree	Percent	
		Occupational	Academic					High school graduate or more	Bachelor's degree or more
20 to 24 years	294	22	20	33	3	3	—	64.5	3.3
25 to 29 years	223	32	48	132	24	3	4	64.9	12.7
30 to 34 years	211	50	46	128	21	10	4	61.2	12.4
35 to 39 years	189	48	40	119	14	3	4	62.4	11.7
40 to 44 years	137	19	23	68	12	9	6	59.2	10.1
45 to 49 years	105	24	18	51	15	3	4	57.0	10.5
50 to 54 years	51	13	17	38	7	2	2	49.6	9.0
55 to 59 years	42	15	11	27	5	1	—	47.5	6.5
60 to 64 years	12	3	2	13	4	3	—	32.0	5.6
65 to 69 years	22	1	4	16	1	—	3	33.6	6.1
70 to 74 years	10	—	3	3	2	2	1	23.0	3.6
75 years and over	7	5	3	9	—	3	1	28.0	4.4
18 years and over	1 398	233	233	637	108	43	28	55.5	8.7
25 years and over	1 009	209	213	605	105	40	28	54.6	10.1
65 years and over	39	6	9	29	4	5	5	28.8	4.8

Source: March 1997 Current Population Survey, Education and Social Stratification Branch, U.S. Bureau of the Census.

1. May be of any race.

— Represents zero or rounds to zero.

Table B-2. Educational Attainment of Persons 15 Years Old and Over, by Single Year of Age, Sex, Race, and Hispanic Origin: March 1997

(Numbers in thousands. Civilian noninstitutional population.)

Age, sex, race, and Hispanic origin	Total	None	Elementary			High School			
			1st-4th grade	5th-6th grade	7th-8th grade	9th grade	10th grade	11th grade	High school graduate
ALL RACES									
Both Sexes									
Total, 15 years and over	207 235	984	2 021	3 857	9 693	8 345	9 936	12 977	65 514
15 to 17 years	11 666	14	7	40	2 443	3 681	3 433	1 882	145
15 years	3 854	5	4	32	1 886	1 576	313	24	14
16 years	3 908	7	1	7	440	1 734	1 514	189	14
17 years	3 905	3	2	1	117	371	1 607	1 669	116
18 years and over	195 568	969	2 014	3 816	7 250	4 664	6 503	11 095	65 370
18 and 19 years	7 498	17	12	43	101	255	486	2 330	2 312
18 years	3 674	12	7	16	58	152	315	1 777	820
19 years	3 824	6	4	27	43	103	171	553	1 492
20 years and over	188 070	953	2 002	3 773	7 149	4 409	6 017	8 764	63 058
20 to 24 years	17 489	36	78	225	225	383	412	1 184	5 472
20 years	3 597	12	10	42	49	62	84	307	1 155
21 years	3 536	11	8	31	19	111	106	269	1 120
22 years	3 291	5	15	50	43	71	83	217	955
23 years	3 413	5	16	49	60	60	79	217	1 118
24 years	3 652	4	29	53	54	79	60	174	1 125
25 years and over	170 581	916	1 924	3 548	6 924	4 026	5 605	7 580	57 586
25 to 29 years	19 260	52	107	265	276	313	485	936	5 821
25 years	3 769	4	23	40	55	70	71	230	1 153
26 years	3 994	7	21	58	40	62	119	181	1 274
27 years	3 730	8	18	48	61	52	113	155	1 065
28 years	3 882	21	28	58	50	58	102	182	1 206
29 years	3 885	11	17	61	70	72	81	188	1 122
30 to 34 years	20 996	63	122	324	298	423	550	917	6 889
30 years	4 005	10	23	63	44	81	90	176	1 340
31 years	4 006	19	18	55	44	77	80	173	1 358
32 years	4 298	12	26	73	67	75	113	179	1 396
33 years	4 135	12	30	69	81	66	139	177	1 339
34 years	4 462	9	25	64	62	124	129	211	1 457
35 to 39 years	22 755	78	131	346	315	405	572	1 004	7 991
35 years	4 513	11	24	70	55	71	114	210	1 591
36 years	4 727	22	39	57	82	94	139	221	1 655
37 years	4 520	16	15	72	52	66	92	211	1 537
38 years	4 589	14	26	69	62	91	121	176	1 664
39 years	4 406	16	27	78	63	83	107	186	1 544
40 to 44 years	21 205	72	157	284	355	361	459	708	7 237
40 years	4 525	18	18	81	63	80	107	171	1 512
41 years	4 555	5	65	53	74	72	100	162	1 661
42 years	4 114	19	21	64	86	85	98	131	1 398
43 years	4 134	13	26	40	57	63	81	133	1 317
44 years	3 877	17	27	47	74	61	74	111	1 349
45 to 49 years	18 354	93	150	238	389	291	413	669	5 825
45 years	3 821	12	30	60	76	56	70	122	1 248
46 years	3 692	22	23	48	64	58	72	149	1 166
47 years	3 635	19	44	51	94	52	101	147	1 085
48 years	3 546	11	28	32	80	57	66	130	1 133
49 years	3 660	29	25	47	75	68	103	121	1 194
50 to 54 years	14 659	81	105	260	499	276	346	541	5 001
50 years	3 638	24	37	70	100	55	59	130	1 154

See footnotes at end of table.

Table B-2. Educational Attainment of Persons 15 Years Old and Over, by Single Year of Age, Sex, Race, and Hispanic Origin: March 1997 — Continued

(Numbers in thousands. Civilian noninstitutional population.)

Age, sex, race, and Hispanic origin	Some college, no degree	Associate Degree		Bachelor's degree	Master's degree	Professional degree	Doctorate degree	Percent	
		Occupational	Academic					High school graduate or more	Bachelor's degree or more
ALL RACES									
Both Sexes									
Total, 15 years and over	38 062	6 978	6 358	29 089	9 205	2 455	1 761	76.9	20.5
15 to 17 years	21	—	—	—	—	—	—	1.4	—
15 years	—	—	—	—	—	—	—	0.4	—
16 years	2	—	—	—	—	—	—	0.4	—
17 years	19	—	—	—	—	—	—	3.5	—
18 years and over	38 041	6 978	6 358	29 089	9 205	2 455	1 761	81.4	21.7
18 and 19 years	1 916	15	2	9	1	—	—	56.7	0.1
18 years	515	2	—	2	—	—	—	36.4	—
19 years	1 402	13	2	8	1	—	—	76.3	0.2
20 years and over	36 125	6 963	6 357	29 080	9 205	2 455	1 761	82.4	22.6
20 to 24 years	6 757	436	477	1 723	73	8	—	85.5	10.3
20 years	1 778	56	28	14	—	—	—	84.3	0.4
21 years	1 646	53	98	63	2	—	—	84.3	1.8
22 years	1 322	84	135	297	11	3	—	85.3	9.4
23 years	984	130	83	591	18	2	—	85.7	17.9
24 years	1 027	113	133	758	42	2	—	87.6	22.0
25 years and over	29 367	6 527	5 880	27 357	9 132	2 447	1 761	82.1	23.9
25 to 29 years	4 160	751	739	4 390	692	184	90	87.4	27.8
25 years	889	154	138	830	85	17	12	86.9	25.0
26 years	888	152	142	904	96	30	19	87.8	26.3
27 years	808	142	113	955	144	35	14	87.8	30.8
28 years	811	131	181	813	171	53	17	87.2	27.1
29 years	763	172	166	888	197	48	29	87.1	29.9
30 to 34 years	3 883	1 009	982	4 099	972	291	174	87.2	26.4
30 years	805	231	220	753	184	54	21	88.1	24.7
31 years	746	174	146	861	170	41	44	88.3	27.8
32 years	796	186	201	901	192	62	18	87.3	27.3
33 years	745	158	209	774	220	63	53	86.1	26.9
34 years	790	260	205	811	206	71	38	86.0	25.2
35 to 39 years	4 225	1 075	938	4 060	1 139	284	191	87.5	24.9
35 years	839	206	200	813	199	60	51	87.7	24.9
36 years	864	209	206	782	261	50	45	86.2	24.1
37 years	822	269	181	862	217	75	33	88.4	26.3
38 years	873	199	198	812	226	40	19	87.8	23.9
39 years	827	193	153	791	236	59	43	87.3	25.6
40 to 44 years	4 069	1 016	898	3 708	1 308	394	178	88.7	26.4
40 years	898	229	172	801	267	77	31	88.1	26.0
41 years	845	194	204	755	246	77	42	88.3	24.6
42 years	800	172	149	729	266	66	29	87.7	26.5
43 years	827	209	193	755	289	81	49	90.0	28.4
44 years	699	212	179	667	240	93	28	89.4	26.5
45 to 49 years	3 281	874	752	3 264	1 458	349	308	87.8	29.3
45 years	656	187	194	700	278	53	78	88.8	29.0
46 years	671	195	127	689	269	78	62	88.2	29.7
47 years	669	145	172	602	317	90	46	86.0	29.0
48 years	662	178	116	629	299	74	51	88.6	29.7
49 years	623	169	143	644	295	54	70	87.2	29.1
50 to 54 years	2 496	518	542	2 283	1 213	239	259	85.6	27.2
50 years	662	131	156	634	293	50	85	87.0	29.2

See footnotes at end of table.

Table B-2. Educational Attainment of Persons 15 Years Old and Over, by Single Year of Age, Sex, Race, and Hispanic Origin: March 1997 — Continued

(Numbers in thousands. Civilian noninstitutional population.)

| Age, sex, race, and Hispanic origin | Total | None | Elementary | | | High School | | | |
			1st-4th grade	5th-6th grade	7th-8th grade	9th grade	10th grade	11th grade	High school graduate
51 years	2 739	15	24	43	110	55	58	112	930
52 years	2 687	10	20	47	110	70	51	89	914
53 years	2 777	11	20	58	80	50	105	118	955
54 years	2 817	21	4	42	99	47	73	93	1 048
55 to 59 years	11 579	72	178	315	499	271	478	518	4 233
55 years	2 569	6	48	59	112	54	105	125	869
56 years	2 479	10	36	57	99	51	101	99	945
57 years	2 175	23	25	62	122	43	88	93	770
58 years	2 249	7	42	75	73	52	78	93	862
59 years	2 107	25	26	62	93	70	107	108	788
60 to 64 years	9 896	87	175	310	622	313	481	490	3 657
60 years	2 034	17	26	53	95	59	83	105	780
61 years	2 061	19	44	61	144	49	108	94	740
62 years	1 976	13	44	52	123	80	90	82	764
63 years	2 029	25	36	70	122	57	116	134	707
04 years	1 798	13	24	74	138	68	84	75	666
65 years and over	31 877	318	798	1 206	3 670	1 373	1 821	1 798	10 933
65 to 69 years	9 501	75	184	290	751	370	501	592	3 425
65 years	1 826	11	27	54	126	79	76	99	652
66 years	1 958	19	35	38	133	78	115	122	750
67 years	2 007	17	49	71	141	77	116	143	712
68 years	1 879	11	55	51	194	63	107	135	631
69 years	1 830	17	19	76	157	72	87	93	680
70 to 74 years	8 514	71	208	278	820	335	485	534	3 006
70 years	1 863	17	41	57	191	64	134	104	635
71 years	1 749	17	34	33	143	80	83	114	636
72 years	1 699	15	56	51	125	71	108	110	635
73 years	1 664	9	35	70	185	54	86	133	541
74 years	1 539	14	41	67	175	66	74	74	559
75 years and over	13 862	171	406	639	2 099	668	835	672	4 502
Male									
Total, 15 years and over	100 159	525	1 020	1 966	4 795	4 176	4 852	6 523	30 255
15 to 17 years	6 004	11	4	24	1 361	1 958	1 739	839	59
15 years	1 977	3	2	18	1 004	794	133	13	10
16 years	2 029	6	1	5	287	956	700	67	4
17 years	1 998	3	—	1	69	208	907	759	46
18 years and over	94 154	513	1 016	1 941	3 434	2 218	3 112	5 684	30 196
18 and 19 years	3 783	11	4	27	61	145	267	1 312	1 134
18 years	1 856	6	—	8	31	77	179	1 006	346
19 years	1 927	5	4	19	30	68	88	306	788
20 years and over	90 371	502	1 012	1 914	3 373	2 073	2 846	4 372	29 062
20 to 24 years	8 751	20	41	129	136	191	202	686	2 836
20 years	1 741	11	2	27	26	34	47	181	562
21 years	1 754	5	7	12	17	48	63	158	577
22 years	1 628	2	11	28	20	35	28	148	473
23 years	1 741	1	4	34	40	34	38	110	605
24 years	1 887	1	18	27	33	40	26	89	619
25 years and over	81 620	483	971	1 786	3 237	1 882	2 644	3 686	26 226
25 to 29 years	9 613	35	64	130	159	161	259	557	2 970
25 years	1 976	2	14	21	47	39	35	152	648
26 years	1 885	4	7	27	25	40	68	97	624

See footnotes at end of table.

Table B-2. Educational Attainment of Persons 15 Years Old and Over, by Single Year of Age, Sex, Race, and Hispanic Origin: March 1997 — Continued

(Numbers in thousands. Civilian noninstitutional population.)

Age, sex, race, and Hispanic origin	Some college, no degree	College Associate Degree Occupational	College Associate Degree Academic	Bachelor's degree	Master's degree	Professional degree	Doctorate degree	Percent High school graduate or more	Percent Bachelor's degree or more
51 years	470	94	88	394	244	65	40	84.8	27.1
52 years	436	113	111	399	223	33	59	85.2	26.6
53 years	460	98	81	415	224	55	49	84.1	26.7
54 years	467	83	106	442	230	37	25	86.5	26.0
55 to 59 years	1 779	362	318	1 499	721	156	178	79.9	22.1
55 years	433	81	85	345	182	40	25	80.2	23.0
56 years	364	73	72	328	169	28	47	81.7	23.1
57 years	320	58	66	292	154	19	39	79.0	23.2
58 years	364	73	49	294	117	38	30	81.2	21.3
59 years	298	77	46	240	100	30	37	76.7	19.3
60 to 64 years	1 370	275	212	1 083	540	149	132	75.0	19.2
60 years	316	48	49	220	125	30	27	78.5	19.8
61 years	282	66	45	243	111	31	25	74.8	19.9
62 years	262	49	43	213	110	24	25	75.4	18.8
63 years	272	55	41	245	88	32	29	72.4	19.4
64 years	239	56	33	163	106	30	26	73.5	18.1
65 years and over	4 104	646	499	2 970	1 090	401	250	65.5	14.8
65 to 69 years	1 250	214	203	987	405	145	109	70.9	17.3
65 years	243	50	32	244	99	22	12	74.1	20.6
66 years	250	28	44	179	88	49	30	72.4	17.7
67 years	258	63	58	170	93	24	17	69.5	15.1
68 years	253	37	34	196	63	26	21	67.1	16.3
69 years	246	36	35	198	61	25	29	71.6	17.1
70 to 74 years	1 163	167	148	839	291	95	77	67.9	15.3
70 years	256	28	43	184	58	34	17	67.4	15.7
71 years	238	48	34	188	67	11	23	71.2	16.5
72 years	226	29	26	150	56	30	12	68.5	14.6
73 years	248	39	22	158	61	14	10	65.7	14.6
74 years	194	23	23	159	49	6	14	66.8	14.8
75 years and over	1 691	265	149	1 144	395	161	65	60.4	12.7
Male									
Total, 15 years and over	18 192	3 112	2 619	14 387	4 809	1 711	1 218	76.2	22.1
15 to 17 years	9	—	—	—	—	—	—	1.1	—
15 years	—	—	—	—	—	—	—	0.5	—
16 years	2	—	—	—	—	—	—	0.3	—
17 years	7	—	—	—	—	—	—	2.6	—
18 years and over	18 183	3 112	2 619	14 387	4 809	1 711	1 218	81.0	23.5
18 and 19 years	815	6	—	—	—	—	—	51.7	—
18 years	200	2	—	—	—	—	—	29.5	—
19 years	615	4	—	—	—	—	—	73.1	—
20 years and over	17 368	3 106	2 618	14 387	4 809	1 711	1 218	82.2	24.5
20 to 24 years	3 335	213	212	716	33	2	—	84.0	8.6
20 years	802	27	14	9	—	—	—	81.1	0.5
21 years	776	25	43	22	2	—	—	82.3	1.3
22 years	689	34	52	105	4	—	—	83.3	6.7
23 years	520	68	38	239	7	2	—	85.0	14.3
24 years	549	59	65	341	21	—	—	87.7	19.2
25 years and over	14 033	2 893	2 406	13 672	4 776	1 708	1 218	82.0	26.2
25 to 29 years	2 088	324	335	2 069	311	111	38	85.8	26.3
25 years	443	54	76	400	34	7	2	84.3	22.5
26 years	409	63	71	381	46	14	7	85.7	23.8

See footnotes at end of table.

Table B-2. Educational Attainment of Persons 15 Years Old and Over, by Single Year of Age, Sex, Race, and Hispanic Origin: March 1997 — Continued

(Numbers in thousands. Civilian noninstitutional population.)

Age, sex, race, and Hispanic origin	Total	None	Elementary			High School			
			1st-4th grade	5th-6th grade	7th-8th grade	9th grade	10th grade	11th grade	High school graduate
27 years	1 908	4	14	27	37	30	49	97	571
28 years	1 941	16	22	32	24	16	73	104	573
29 years	1 903	9	7	23	27	35	35	107	553
30 to 34 years	10 426	30	64	187	153	212	309	509	3 512
30 years	2 029	3	17	37	26	43	55	84	675
31 years	2 028	9	5	31	21	37	49	96	715
32 years	2 158	11	23	42	23	34	61	95	720
33 years	2 074	5	12	42	52	33	77	115	693
34 years	2 138	2	6	35	31	65	67	119	710
35 to 39 years	11 323	50	76	195	157	215	273	579	4 053
35 years	2 254	11	17	42	25	48	47	121	836
36 years	2 365	10	27	26	34	57	79	153	838
37 years	2 213	10	11	43	25	26	37	105	784
38 years	2 259	8	16	34	33	46	53	86	845
39 years	2 232	11	5	50	40	37	58	113	750
40 to 44 years	10 470	39	92	152	170	196	260	398	3 551
40 years	2 270	12	10	50	23	28	56	108	791
41 years	2 250	—	40	22	36	40	58	97	859
42 years	2 022	8	14	35	46	61	57	66	641
43 years	2 081	13	9	19	27	30	49	85	636
44 years	1 848	6	20	26	37	37	41	43	625
45 to 49 years	8 969	54	73	120	175	128	238	317	2 551
45 years	1 896	7	17	22	38	18	47	64	559
46 years	1 810	13	9	25	29	23	36	70	529
47 years	1 761	12	22	24	33	31	48	63	476
48 years	1 747	9	12	21	36	29	45	69	492
49 years	1 755	12	13	28	38	26	61	52	496
50 to 54 years	7 150	46	56	139	262	133	167	239	2 171
50 years	1 798	18	21	49	53	27	29	73	509
51 years	820	7	9	40	86	36	32	39	258
52 years	1 270	2	8	27	65	27	22	45	381
53 years	1 332	5	12	31	42	24	44	36	402
54 years	1 377	15	3	16	40	24	39	40	480
55 to 59 years	5 575	45	93	165	287	143	221	203	1 906
55 years	1 262	2	33	21	60	31	59	48	392
56 years	1 188	4	16	22	49	17	56	41	463
57 years	998	12	10	33	79	19	36	34	304
58 years	1 075	7	19	46	41	28	40	52	377
59 years	1 053	20	14	42	57	48	30	28	369
60 to 64 years	4 689	33	87	160	311	141	193	196	1 537
60 years	949	6	8	19	49	25	33	36	342
61 years	1 007	10	26	31	76	15	42	43	320
62 years	924	3	17	30	60	39	34	29	313
63 years	962	6	25	37	67	36	50	63	309
64 years	847	7	12	43	60	25	33	25	253
65 years and over	13 404	149	366	539	1 564	553	724	686	3 974
65 to 69 years	4 321	36	88	151	354	168	190	232	1 332
65 years	828	4	5	23	59	26	34	44	269
66 years	919	8	19	20	62	43	34	34	311
67 years	894	11	24	36	61	33	44	55	279
68 years	859	6	31	31	86	30	46	59	215
69 years	820	7	9	40	86	36	32	39	258
70 to 74 years	3 764	31	92	138	395	154	210	209	1 121
70 years	873	14	21	31	104	38	74	35	226
71 years	752	5	14	15	63	30	46	51	234
72 years	698	5	21	26	56	26	20	52	235
73 years	710	216	—	40	81	25	36	—	52 197

See footnotes at end of table.

Table B-2. Educational Attainment of Persons 15 Years Old and Over, by Single Year of Age, Sex, Race, and Hispanic Origin: March 1997 — Continued

(Numbers in thousands. Civilian noninstitutional population.)

| Age, sex, race, and Hispanic origin | Some college, no degree | College | | Bachelor's degree | Master's degree | Professional degree | Doctorate degree | Percent | |
| | | Associate Degree | | | | | | High school graduate or more | Bachelor's degree or more |
		Occupational	Academic						
27 years	428	64	59	446	56	20	5	86.5	27.6
28 years	413	55	68	420	84	37	5	85.3	28.1
29 years	394	88	60	421	90	34	18	87.2	29.6
30 to 34 years	1 826	534	370	1 962	481	175	102	86.0	26.1
30 years	395	126	82	354	87	30	14	86.9	23.9
31 years	365	77	51	447	86	26	13	87.7	28.2
32 years	392	107	81	419	96	37	16	86.6	26.3
33 years	336	77	80	366	110	39	36	83.8	26.6
34 years	338	146	76	376	102	43	23	84.8	25.4
35 to 39 years	2 007	481	369	1 972	599	187	107	86.4	25.3
35 years	383	83	94	392	96	34	26	86.2	24.3
36 years	386	87	61	398	148	32	28	83.6	25.6
37 years	394	125	73	413	101	51	14	88.3	26.1
38 years	408	89	75	401	124	29	13	87.8	25.1
39 years	436	98	66	368	131	41	27	85.9	25.4
40 to 44 years	2 025	424	335	1 799	652	248	128	87.5	27.0
40 years	434	94	61	399	144	36	25	87.4	26.6
41 years	397	83	76	344	112	55	31	87.0	24.1
42 years	418	73	60	342	136	41	24	85.8	26.8
43 years	435	90	70	386	150	45	38	88.9	29.7
44 years	340	84	69	328	109	71	12	88.6	28.1
45 to 49 years	1 594	436	354	1 730	732	260	207	87.7	32.7
45 years	335	87	106	372	129	46	47	88.7	31.4
46 years	349	82	64	358	127	48	46	88.6	32.0
47 years	320	87	77	302	174	61	30	86.7	32.2
48 years	329	90	43	348	130	62	32	87.3	32.7
49 years	261	90	63	349	171	43	52	86.9	35.0
50 to 54 years	1 241	212	235	1 206	668	179	196	85.4	31.4
50 years	312	53	58	341	153	40	61	85.0	33.1
51 years	108	9	8	104	33	25	25	69.5	22.9
52 years	223	54	50	182	119	20	45	84.6	28.8
53 years	225	33	36	221	133	46	44	85.5	33.3
54 years	232	25	53	234	129	30	18	87.2	29.8
55 to 59 years	790	153	125	796	401	112	136	79.3	25.9
55 years	198	42	37	197	99	27	16	79.8	26.8
56 years	172	25	23	153	82	21	44	82.7	25.2
57 years	125	31	28	137	101	17	32	77.6	28.7
58 years	152	35	14	161	59	25	20	78.3	24.6
59 years	144	21	23	149	60	22	25	77.2	24.3
60 to 64 years	673	123	93	592	336	112	103	76.1	24.4
60 years	131	27	21	129	80	21	21	81.4	26.5
61 years	134	28	21	149	66	28	17	75.9	25.9
62 years	134	23	18	120	71	14	20	77.1	24.3
63 years	125	23	16	107	46	27	24	70.5	21.3
64 years	148	22	18	87	72	22	20	75.8	23.8
65 years and over	1 789	204	189	1 546	596	325	200	65.8	19.9
65 to 69 years	617	68	86	548	233	128	90	71.8	23.1
65 years	125	13	16	127	52	20	10	76.3	25.2
66 years	130	7	22	107	57	42	22	76.0	24.8
67 years	128	23	24	96	47	19	13	70.7	19.7
68 years	125	16	15	113	44	22	20	66.3	23.1
69 years	108	9	8	104	33	25	25	69.5	22.9
70 to 74 years	487	46	61	493	197	67	64	67.4	21.8
70 years	122	9	22	110	36	21	10	63.7	20.3
71 years	99	19	5	101	47	2	19	70.1	22.6
72 years	79	2	14	87	35	28	12	70.5	23.1
73 years	98	8	6	84	45	11	10	64.7	21.2

See footnotes at end of table.

Table B-2. Educational Attainment of Persons 15 Years Old and Over, by Single Year of Age, Sex, Race, and Hispanic Origin: March 1997 — Continued

(Numbers in thousands. Civilian noninstitutional population.)

Age, sex, race, and Hispanic origin	Total	None	Elementary			High School			
			1st-4th grade	5th-6th grade	7th-8th grade	9th grade	10th grade	11th grade	High school graduate
74 years	732	6	20	25	90	34	35	20	229
75 years and over	5 319	82	186	251	815	231	324	245	1 521
Female									
Total, 15 years and over	107 076	459	1 000	1 891	4 898	4 168	5 085	6 454	35 259
15 to 17 years	5 662	3	3	16	1 082	1 722	1 694	1 044	85
15 years	1 877	2	1	15	882	781	180	11	5
16 years	1 879	1	—	2	153	778	814	122	10
17 years	1 907	—	2	—	48	163	700	910	70
18 years and over	101 414	456	997	1 875	3 816	2 446	3 391	5 410	35 174
18 and 19 years	3 715	5	7	16	40	110	219	1 018	1 178
18 years	1 819	5	7	8	27	74	136	771	474
19 years	1 896	—	—	8	13	35	83	248	704
20 years and over	97 699	450	990	1 859	3 776	2 336	3 172	4 392	33 996
20 to 24 years	8 737	17	37	96	89	192	210	498	2 635
20 years	1 856	1	8	14	24	28	37	126	593
21 years	1 781	6	1	19	1	63	43	111	543
22 years	1 663	2	5	22	23	36	55	69	481
23 years	1 672	4	12	15	20	26	41	107	513
24 years	1 765	3	11	26	21	39	35	85	505
25 years and over	88 961	434	953	1 763	3 687	2 144	2 961	3 894	31 360
25 to 29 years	9 647	16	43	134	117	151	226	378	2 850
25 years	1 793	2	9	18	8	30	36	78	505
26 years	2 109	3	14	31	15	21	51	84	650
27 years	1 822	4	4	21	24	22	64	57	493
28 years	1 941	5	5	26	27	42	30	78	634
29 years	1 982	2	11	38	43	36	45	81	569
30 to 34 years	10 570	32	58	137	145	211	241	408	3 377
30 years	2 067	7	6	26	18	39	35	91	665
31 years	1 978	10	13	24	23	41	30	77	643
32 years	2 140	1	3	32	44	40	52	84	676
33 years	2 061	6	17	27	30	32	62	63	646
34 years	2 324	7	19	29	31	59	62	93	747
35 to 39 years	11 432	28	55	152	158	190	299	425	3 938
35 years	2 259	—	6	28	30	23	67	89	755
36 years	2 362	11	12	31	48	36	60	68	817
37 years	2 307	6	3	29	27	40	55	106	753
38 years	2 330	6	11	35	30	44	68	90	819
39 years	2 174	5	22	29	23	46	49	73	794
40 to 44 years	10 735	33	65	132	186	165	198	310	3 685
40 years	2 255	6	8	31	40	52	51	63	721
41 years	2 305	5	25	31	38	32	42	65	801
42 years	2 092	11	7	28	40	24	41	65	757
43 years	2 053	—	17	21	30	34	32	49	682
44 years	2 029	11	7	21	37	23	33	68	724
45 to 49 years	9 385	39	77	118	214	163	175	352	3 273
45 years	1 925	5	13	38	38	38	23	58	689
46 years	1 882	8	14	23	35	34	36	79	637
47 years	1 874	7	23	27	61	21	52	84	609
48 years	1 799	2	15	12	43	28	21	61	641
49 years	1 904	17	12	18	37	42	42	69	697
50 to 54 years	7 509	35	49	121	238	143	180	302	2 830

See footnotes at end of table.

Table B-2.   Educational Attainment of Persons 15 Years Old and Over, by Single Year of Age, Sex, Race, and Hispanic Origin: March 1997 — Continued

(Numbers in thousands. Civilian noninstitutional population.)

Age, sex, race, and Hispanic origin	Some college, no degree	Associate Degree Occupational	Associate Degree Academic	Bachelor's degree	Master's degree	Professional degree	Doctorate degree	Percent High school graduate or more	Percent Bachelor's degree or more
74 years	89	8	14	111	35	4	13	68.5	22.1
75 years and over	684	89	42	505	166	130	46	59.9	15.9
Female									
Total, 15 years and over	19 870	3 866	3 740	14 702	4 396	744	543	77.6	19.0
15 to 17 years	12	—	—	—	—	—	—	1.7	—
15 years	—	—	—	—	—	—	—	0.2	—
16 years	—	—	—	—	—	—	—	0.5	—
17 years	12	—	—	—	—	—	—	4.3	—
18 years and over	19 858	3 866	3 740	14 702	4 396	744	543	81.9	20.1
18 and 19 years	1 101	9	1	9	1	—	—	61.9	0.3
18 years	315	—	—	2	—	—	—	43.4	0.1
19 years	786	9	1	8	1	—	—	79.6	0.4
20 years and over	18 757	3 857	3 738	14 692	4 396	744	543	82.6	20.9
20 to 24 years	3 422	223	265	1 008	39	5	—	87.0	12.0
20 years	977	29	14	5	—	—	—	87.2	0.3
21 years	870	28	55	41	—	—	—	86.3	2.3
22 years	633	50	84	192	7	3	—	87.2	12.2
23 years	464	62	45	352	11	—	—	86.5	21.7
24 years	478	54	68	417	21	2	—	87.5	25.0
25 years and over	15 335	3 634	3 473	13 685	4 356	739	543	82.2	21.7
25 to 29 years	2 073	427	404	2 321	381	73	52	88.9	29.3
25 years	446	100	61	430	50	10	10	89.9	27.9
26 years	479	90	71	523	50	16	12	89.6	28.5
27 years	380	77	54	509	88	16	8	89.2	34.0
28 years	398	76	113	393	87	16	12	89.1	26.2
29 years	369	84	105	467	107	14	10	87.1	30.2
30 to 34 years	2 057	475	611	2 137	491	116	72	88.3	26.6
30 years	411	105	138	399	97	24	7	89.3	25.5
31 years	381	97	95	413	85	15	31	89.0	27.5
32 years	404	79	120	482	95	26	2	88.1	28.3
33 years	409	81	129	408	110	24	17	88.5	27.1
34 years	453	114	130	435	104	28	15	87.1	25.0
35 to 39 years	2 218	594	569	2 088	540	97	84	88.6	24.6
35 years	456	123	106	420	104	27	25	89.3	25.5
36 years	479	122	145	384	113	18	17	88.7	22.5
37 years	428	144	108	449	116	24	19	88.5	26.4
38 years	465	110	124	411	102	11	6	87.8	22.7
39 years	390	95	87	423	105	17	17	88.6	25.8
40 to 44 years	2 044	592	563	1 909	657	146	50	89.8	25.7
40 years	464	135	112	402	123	41	6	88.9	25.4
41 years	448	111	129	411	133	22	11	89.7	25.1
42 years	383	98	88	387	130	26	5	89.6	26.2
43 years	392	119	124	369	139	35	11	91.1	27.0
44 years	358	128	110	339	131	21	16	90.1	25.0
45 to 49 years	1 687	438	398	1 534	726	90	100	87.9	26.1
45 years	321	100	88	327	149	7	31	88.9	26.8
46 years	323	113	62	331	142	29	16	87.8	27.5
47 years	349	58	95	300	143	29	16	85.3	26.0
48 years	333	88	73	282	168	12	19	89.8	26.7
49 years	362	79	80	295	125	12	18	87.5	23.6
50 to 54 years	1 254	306	306	1 077	545	60	63	85.8	23.2

See footnotes at end of table.

Table B-2. Educational Attainment of Persons 15 Years Old and Over, by Single Year of Age, Sex, Race, and Hispanic Origin: March 1997 — Continued

(Numbers in thousands. Civilian noninstitutional population.)

| Age, sex, race, and Hispanic origin | Total | None | Elementary | | | High School | | | |
			1st-4th grade	5th-6th grade	7th-8th grade	9th grade	10th grade	11th grade	High school graduate
50 years	1 841	6	16	21	47	28	31	56	645
51 years	1 366	9	11	28	48	23	25	66	530
52 years	1 417	8	12	20	45	43	30	44	533
53 years	1 445	6	8	27	38	26	61	82	553
54 years	1 440	6	1	26	59	23	34	53	569
55 to 59 years	6 003	27	85	150	212	128	257	315	2 328
55 years	1 307	4	15	37	52	23	46	77	477
56 years	1 292	7	20	35	50	34	45	58	481
57 years	1 177	11	15	29	42	24	52	59	466
58 years	1 174	—	23	29	32	24	38	41	485
59 years	1 054	5	12	20	36	23	76	80	419
60 to 64 years	5 207	55	88	150	311	173	288	294	2 120
60 years	1 085	11	17	34	47	34	50	69	439
61 years	1 053	9	18	29	69	34	66	51	419
62 years	1 053	10	28	23	63	41	57	54	451
63 years	1 067	19	12	32	55	21	65	71	398
64 years	949	6	12	31	79	43	50	50	413
65 years and over	18 474	168	432	667	2 106	820	1 097	1 111	6 959
65 to 69 years	5 180	39	97	139	397	202	311	359	2 093
65 years	998	7	22	31	67	53	42	54	383
66 years	1 039	11	16	18	71	35	81	87	439
67 years	1 114	6	25	35	80	44	71	88	433
68 years	1 020	5	24	20	108	34	62	76	416
69 years	1 009	10	10	35	71	36	54	54	422
70 to 74 years	4 750	40	116	140	425	181	275	325	1 885
70 years	990	3	20	26	86	26	60	69	409
71 years	997	11	19	17	80	51	38	63	403
72 years	1 002	10	35	25	69	44	88	58	400
73 years	954	7	20	30	104	29	51	81	343
74 years	807	8	22	42	85	32	39	54	330
75 years and over	8 544	89	220	389	1 284	437	511	427	2 981
WHITE									
Both Sexes									
Total, 15 years and over	173 296	701	1 555	3 171	8 006	6 804	7 980	9 813	55 074
15 to 17 years	9 246	8	5	28	1 890	2 934	2 769	1 493	104
15 years	3 041	3	1	22	1 497	1 268	221	16	13
16 years	3 113	5	1	5	329	1 394	1 233	141	3
17 years	3 092	—	2	1	63	271	1 315	1 336	88
18 years and over	164 050	693	1 550	3 143	6 116	3 870	5 212	8 320	54 971
18 and 19 years	5 949	11	8	43	89	184	346	1 842	1 847
18 years	2 911	9	4	16	49	102	225	1 448	650
19 years	3 038	2	4	27	40	82	122	393	1 197
20 years and over	158 100	683	1 542	3 100	6 027	3 686	4 865	6 478	53 123
20 to 24 years	14 043	22	75	213	204	319	303	819	4 263
20 years	2 835	3	10	41	37	53	63	197	852
21 years	2 806	7	8	31	16	80	90	174	869
22 years	2 628	2	15	46	43	57	54	161	724
23 years	2 751	5	16	48	57	60	52	154	861
24 years	3 023	4	26	47	51	68	43	133	957
25 years and over	144 058	661	1 467	2 887	5 823	3 368	4 563	5 659	48 860

See footnotes at end of table.

Table B-2. Educational Attainment of Persons 15 Years Old and Over, by Single Year of Age, Sex, Race, and Hispanic Origin: March 1997 — Continued

(Numbers in thousands. Civilian noninstitutional population.)

Age, sex, race, and Hispanic origin	College							Percent	
	Some college, no degree	Associate Degree		Bachelor's degree	Master's degree	Professional degree	Doctorate degree	High school graduate or more	Bachelor's degree or more
		Occupational	Academic						
50 years	350	78	97	292	140	10	24	88.9	25.3
51 years	221	46	49	167	109	21	12	84.6	22.7
52 years	213	59	61	217	104	13	14	85.7	24.6
53 years	235	65	46	193	91	9	5	82.8	20.7
54 years	235	58	54	208	101	7	7	86.0	22.4
55 to 59 years	989	209	194	703	320	45	42	80.4	18.5
55 years	235	40	48	148	83	14	9	80.6	19.4
56 years	192	48	49	175	87	7	3	80.7	21.1
57 years	195	27	38	156	53	3	8	80.2	18.6
58 years	213	38	35	134	58	13	10	83.9	18.3
59 years	154	56	23	91	40	8	13	76.2	14.3
60 to 64 years	697	151	119	491	204	37	30	73.9	14.6
60 years	185	21	28	91	44	10	6	75.9	13.9
61 years	148	37	24	94	45	3	7	73.8	14.1
62 years	127	26	25	93	40	10	5	73.9	14.1
63 years	146	33	26	137	41	6	5	74.2	17.8
64 years	91	34	16	76	33	9	6	71.5	13.1
65 years and over	2 315	443	310	1 424	493	76	51	65.3	11.1
65 to 69 years	633	146	117	439	171	18	19	70.2	12.5
65 years	118	37	16	117	47	2	2	72.3	16.8
66 years	120	21	22	72	31	8	9	69.3	11.4
67 years	130	40	33	74	46	4	3	68.5	11.5
68 years	128	21	19	83	20	4	1	67.8	10.6
69 years	138	27	27	94	28	—	3	73.2	12.4
70 to 74 years	676	121	87	346	94	28	13	68.4	10.1
70 years	134	19	21	74	23	13	7	70.6	11.8
71 years	139	29	29	87	20	9	4	72.0	11.9
72 years	147	26	11	63	21	2	1	67.0	8.7
73 years	151	30	16	74	16	2	—	66.4	9.7
74 years	105	15	9	49	14	2	2	65.2	8.2
75 years and over	1 006	177	107	639	228	30	19	60.7	10.7
WHITE									
Both Sexes									
Total, 15 years and over	31 798	5 995	5 439	25 231	8 004	2 178	1 547	78.1	21.3
15 to 17 years	16	—	—	—	—	—	—	1.3	—
15 years	—	—	—	—	—	—	—	0.4	—
16 years	2	—	—	—	—	—	—	0.2	—
17 years	14	—	—	—	—	—	—	3.3	—
18 years and over	31 782	5 995	5 438	25 231	8 004	2 178	1 547	82.4	22.5
18 and 19 years	1 555	15	2	7	1	—	—	57.6	0.1
18 years	405	2	—	2	—	—	—	36.4	0.1
19 years	1 150	13	2	6	1	—	—	77.9	0.2
20 years and over	30 228	5 980	5 437	25 223	8 004	2 178	1 547	83.3	23.4
20 to 24 years	5 503	377	425	1 452	60	8	—	86.1	10.8
20 years	1 506	47	21	7	—	—	—	85.8	0.2
21 years	1 358	48	97	24	2	—	—	85.5	0.9
22 years	1 078	68	119	245	11	3	—	85.6	9.8
23 years	778	113	73	517	13	2	—	85.7	19.3
24 years	783	100	113	660	35	2	—	87.7	23.1
25 years and over	24 724	5 603	5 012	23 771	7 943	2 170	1 547	83.0	24.6

See footnotes at end of table.

Table B-2. Educational Attainment of Persons 15 Years Old and Over, by Single Year of Age, Sex, Race, and Hispanic Origin: March 1997 — Continued

(Numbers in thousands. Civilian noninstitutional population.)

Age, sex, race, and Hispanic origin	Total	None	Elementary			High School			
			1st-4th grade	5th-6th grade	7th-8th grade	9th grade	10th grade	11th grade	High school graduate
25 to 29 years	15 567	36	95	230	244	274	376	683	4 576
25 years	3 013	4	20	38	51	63	48	157	911
26 years	3 217	7	21	58	37	50	92	134	976
27 years	3 015	5	15	38	55	51	84	115	835
28 years	3 127	824	—	57	36	45	76	132	949
29 years	3 195	11	15	38	65	65	75	145	905
30 to 34 years	17 072	43	96	281	251	372	425	655	5 547
30 years	3 341	10	11	55	36	74	81	128	1 065
31 years	3 245	9	16	51	39	75	62	141	1 085
32 years	3 492	9	19	58	51	64	83	121	1 138
33 years	3 358	9	27	57	68	54	102	119	1 071
34 years	3 635	6	23	59	58	105	98	146	1 187
35 to 39 years	18 786	56	109	332	249	346	452	751	6 578
35 years	3 671	5	18	67	54	63	84	164	1 294
36 years	3 906	15	33	54	82	80	107	182	1 383
37 years	3 716	13	13	69	35	59	74	149	1 269
38 years	3 748	9	24	66	44	64	97	128	1 337
39 years	3 744	13	22	77	54	74	90	148	1 296
40 to 44 years	17 652	46	137	239	271	296	369	484	6 004
40 years	3 780	17	17	66	55	64	99	109	1 243
41 years	3 740	5	60	50	61	60	72	116	1 363
42 years	3 454	10	20	45	63	69	74	95	1 156
43 years	3 462	5	22	34	43	53	55	91	1 109
44 years	3 217	8	17	44	49	49	69	74	1 132
45 to 49 years	15 526	74	129	211	303	210	305	459	4 842
45 years	3 268	7	27	59	63	40	63	90	1 061
46 years	3 060	21	23	39	53	40	39	104	938
47 years	2 996	14	33	36	66	30	67	94	891
48 years	3 059	11	23	32	61	47	54	98	952
49 years	3 141	20	23	44	61	52	82	73	999
50 to 54 years	12 545	63	84	222	385	224	289	372	4 273
50 years	3 161	18	24	61	72	49	50	81	986
51 years	2 301	12	18	34	87	45	49	75	795
52 years	2 295	8	20	47	87	63	48	74	760
53 years	2 365	6	19	44	62	33	78	76	828
54 years	2 422	19	3	37	76	35	65	66	903
55 to 59 years	9 935	62	140	211	431	201	378	377	3 708
55 years	2 201	6	33	40	89	38	65	100	765
56 years	2 131	8	35	40	79	38	82	62	842
57 years	1 862	15	22	47	106	40	75	64	680
58 years	1 927	7	30	47	69	27	64	73	740
59 years	1 815	25	20	37	89	58	90	79	680
60 to 64 years	8 512	55	110	225	506	258	412	350	3 252
60 years	1 749	14	17	42	72	46	67	68	684
61 years	1 789	7	35	46	125	41	95	58	659
62 years	1 692	13	19	49	100	61	73	64	686
63 years	1 763	11	17	42	99	54	110	102	634
64 years	1 518	10	21	46	109	57	67	58	590
65 years and over	28 464	227	567	936	3 183	1 187	1 558	1 530	10 079
Male									
Total, 15 years and over	84 540	379	773	1 619	4 024	3 424	3 938	5 034	25 493
15 to 17 years	4 775	8	1	14	1 055	1 548	1 417	682	40
15 years	1 564	3	—	10	807	630	96	10	8
16 years	1 609	5	1	3	217	761	571	48	—

See footnotes at end of table.

Table B-2. Educational Attainment of Persons 15 Years Old and Over, by Single Year of Age, Sex, Race, and Hispanic Origin: March 1997 — Continued

(Numbers in thousands. Civilian noninstitutional population.)

| Age, sex, race, and Hispanic origin | Some college, no degree | College | | | | | | Percent | |
| | | Associate Degree | | Bachelor's degree | Master's degree | Professional degree | Doctorate degree | High school graduate or more | Bachelor's degree or more |
		Occupational	Academic						
25 to 29 years	3 286	625	640	3 741	532	152	78	87.6	28.9
25 years	675	121	119	714	68	17	8	87.3	26.8
26 years	703	134	117	766	76	28	17	87.6	27.6
27 years	611	116	106	823	117	31	14	88.0	32.7
28 years	672	117	150	678	127	39	17	87.9	27.5
29 years	626	137	149	759	144	38	22	87.0	30.1
30 to 34 years	3 085	835	815	3 507	796	233	131	87.6	27.3
30 years	653	199	167	652	152	37	21	88.2	25.8
31 years	588	131	118	743	130	26	31	87.9	28.6
32 years	628	154	178	767	161	50	11	88.4	28.3
33 years	607	138	181	659	178	57	33	87.1	27.6
34 years	609	214	171	686	176	63	35	86.4	26.4
35 to 39 years	3 373	912	754	3 504	964	244	161	87.8	25.9
35 years	632	178	163	685	175	45	44	87.6	25.9
36 years	696	171	153	702	212	35	36	86.7	25.2
37 years	656	231	152	713	181	75	27	88.9	26.8
38 years	712	164	162	704	187	34	18	88.5	25.1
39 years	676	169	124	700	209	56	37	87.2	26.7
40 to 44 years	3 347	877	773	3 172	1 139	348	152	89.6	27.3
40 years	741	201	141	700	235	69	23	88.7	27.2
41 years	668	164	164	633	207	74	42	88.6	25.6
42 years	675	154	129	638	242	59	25	89.1	28.0
43 years	680	182	170	658	242	79	40	91.2	29.4
44 years	583	176	171	543	213	66	22	90.3	26.2
45 to 49 years	2 820	789	641	2 829	1 311	317	286	89.1	30.5
45 years	556	174	177	582	246	53	69	89.3	29.1
46 years	575	168	100	598	230	71	62	89.6	31.4
47 years	566	128	132	532	282	80	45	88.7	31.4
48 years	581	164	106	547	275	63	43	89.3	30.4
49 years	542	155	125	570	277	49	67	88.7	30.7
50 to 54 years	2 215	446	469	1 970	1 083	219	232	86.9	27.9
50 years	606	122	134	551	282	47	79	88.8	30.3
51 years	405	77	72	330	210	59	34	86.1	27.5
52 years	390	93	99	332	194	27	53	84.9	26.4
53 years	412	79	69	362	203	53	42	86.6	27.9
54 years	401	75	94	396	194	33	24	87.6	26.7
55 to 59 years	1 557	306	284	1 331	638	153	158	81.9	23.0
55 years	385	63	83	313	158	40	23	83.2	24.3
56 years	306	72	56	290	150	28	43	83.8	24.0
57 years	273	50	60	246	132	19	33	80.2	23.1
58 years	325	60	45	264	111	38	26	83.5	22.7
59 years	268	62	41	219	86	27	33	78.0	20.2
60 to 64 years	1 234	231	181	959	477	137	124	77.5	19.9
60 years	288	41	42	201	112	29	25	81.4	21.0
61 years	260	60	38	215	103	27	21	77.3	20.4
62 years	229	30	32	191	96	24	23	77.5	19.8
63 years	250	55	40	212	78	30	29	75.3	19.8
64 years	206	45	29	139	88	26	26	75.7	18.4
65 years and over	3 809	582	455	2 758	1 003	367	225	67.7	15.3
Male									
Total, 15 years and over	15 349	2 728	2 313	12 655	4 206	1 540	1 064	77.3	23.0
15 to 17 years	9	—	—	—	—	—	—	1.0	—
15 years	—	—	—	—	—	—	—	0.5	—
16 years	2	—	—	—	—	—	—	0.1	—

See footnotes at end of table.

Table B-2. Educational Attainment of Persons 15 Years Old and Over, by Single Year of Age, Sex, Race, and Hispanic Origin: March 1997 — Continued

(Numbers in thousands. Civilian noninstitutional population.)

Age, sex, race, and Hispanic origin	Total	None	Elementary			High School			
			1st-4th grade	5th-6th grade	7th-8th grade	9th grade	10th grade	11th grade	High school graduate
17 years	1 602	—	—	1	31	157	750	624	32
18 years and over	79 765	372	771	1 605	2 969	1 875	2 521	4 352	25 454
18 and 19 years	3 043	8	4	27	50	100	193	1 077	909
18 years	1 500	6	—	8	23	45	130	844	277
19 years	1 543	2	4	19	26	55	63	233	632
20 years and over	76 722	363	767	1 578	2 919	1 776	2 328	3 275	24 545
20 to 24 years	7 151	5	38	124	124	173	154	500	2 230
20 years	1 391	1	2	27	18	28	39	120	425
21 years	1 400	1	7	12	16	42	52	102	456
22 years	1 331	—	11	27	20	28	17	116	361
23 years	1 444	1	4	34	37	34	25	92	465
24 years	1 586	1	15	24	33	40	21	70	523
25 years and over	69 571	358	729	1 454	2 795	1 603	2 174	2 775	22 314
25 to 29 years	7 892	23	58	119	149	149	209	417	2 377
25 years	1 598	2	14	21	43	36	24	98	519
26 years	1 548	4	7	27	22	34	57	83	479
27 years	1 565	2	14	21	37	30	35	73	456
28 years	1 598	5	18	32	20	16	57	68	486
29 years	1 583	9	4	18	27	33	35	94	437
30 to 34 years	8 557	22	45	163	138	184	243	386	2 853
30 years	1 669	3	8	33	23	41	52	67	522
31 years	1 666	4	5	30	17	34	41	83	587
32 years	1 740	7	16	33	23	28	49	78	570
33 years	1 690	5	12	34	46	25	50	70	576
34 years	1 792	2	4	33	29	56	51	88	597
35 to 39 years	9 487	38	66	186	124	182	229	454	3 386
35 years	1 876	5	12	40	24	41	36	101	710
36 years	1 996	10	23	23	32	52	65	110	715
37 years	1 842	7	11	41	15	26	31	80	642
38 years	1 861	4	16	31	20	30	41	66	691
39 years	1 911	11	3	50	33	32	55	96	629
40 to 44 years	8 827	24	76	120	134	165	222	270	2 960
40 years	1 920	12	10	37	21	23	55	67	647
41 years	1 891	—	35	22	31	37	49	72	709
42 years	1 720	3	12	22	33	50	36	53	542
43 years	1 769	5	8	16	20	27	40	49	542
44 years	1 527	4	10	23	28	27	41	29	519
45 to 49 years	7 698	46	67	111	152	98	178	216	2 140
45 years	1 618	2	17	22	31	10	42	44	487
46 years	1 543	13	9	23	25	17	25	49	432
47 years	1 475	12	17	17	30	20	31	42	384
48 years	1 545	9	12	21	32	27	36	47	427
49 years	1 518	8	11	28	34	23	44	34	411
50 to 54 years	6 184	37	39	112	203	119	143	157	1 866
50 years	1 563	16	10	40	42	27	26	43	428
51 years	1 158	6	6	11	42	27	29	30	332
52 years	1 109	—	8	27	49	27	22	32	346
53 years	1 153	3	12	24	34	18	30	27	338
54 years	1 200	13	3	11	36	20	37	25	421
55 to 59 years	4 831	41	67	111	253	108	177	145	1 679
55 years	1 082	2	21	18	46	20	38	40	337
56 years	1 028	4	16	11	40	12	50	20	418
57 years	877	8	8	30	73	17	31	24	269
58 years	936	7	13	27	40	15	34	41	338
59 years	908	20	9	24	53	45	25	21	317

See footnotes at end of table.

Table B-2. Educational Attainment of Persons 15 Years Old and Over, by Single Year of Age, Sex, Race, and Hispanic Origin: March 1997 — Continued

(Numbers in thousands. Civilian noninstitutional population.)

| Age, sex, race, and Hispanic origin | Some college, no degree | College | | Bachelor's degree | Master's degree | Professional degree | Doctorate degree | Percent | |
| | | Associate Degree | | | | | | High school graduate or more | Bachelor's degree or more |
		Occupational	Academic						
17 years	7	—	—	—	—	—	—	2.4	—
18 years and over	15 340	2 728	2 312	12 655	4 206	1 540	1 064	81.9	24.4
18 and 19 years	668	6	—	—	—	—	—	52.1	—
18 years	164	2	—	—	—	—	—	29.6	—
19 years	505	4	—	—	—	—	—	73.9	—
20 years and over	14 671	2 722	2 312	12 655	4 206	1 540	1 064	83.0	25.4
20 to 24 years	2 751	195	198	627	29	2	—	84.4	9.2
20 years	689	23	14	4	—	—	—	83.0	0.3
21 years	631	25	43	10	2	—	—	83.3	0.8
22 years	580	27	52	90	4	—	—	83.6	7.1
23 years	430	66	33	213	7	2	—	84.3	15.4
24 years	423	54	56	310	16	—	—	87.2	20.6
25 years and over	11 920	2 527	2 114	12 028	4 177	1 538	1 064	82.9	27.0
25 to 29 years	1 644	286	313	1 792	227	95	34	85.8	27.2
25 years	329	51	69	358	25	7	2	85.1	24.5
26 years	336	57	66	320	36	12	6	84.8	24.2
27 years	325	60	54	387	45	20	5	86.5	29.2
28 years	328	53	63	359	58	28	5	86.4	28.2
29 years	325	66	60	368	63	29	15	86.1	30.0
30 to 34 years	1 470	453	319	1 698	384	131	68	86.2	26.7
30 years	338	105	65	312	70	15	14	86.4	24.6
31 years	287	61	49	381	63	17	6	87.1	28.1
32 years	290	94	73	363	79	27	9	86.6	27.5
33 years	279	68	66	319	88	32	19	85.6	27.2
34 years	277	124	66	323	84	39	20	85.3	26.0
35 to 39 years	1 651	424	302	1 685	502	172	88	86.5	25.8
35 years	293	77	79	321	82	31	24	86.1	24.4
36 years	324	83	43	352	117	24	22	84.2	25.8
37 years	327	107	63	348	82	51	10	88.5	26.7
38 years	340	78	64	341	103	25	12	88.9	25.8
39 years	367	80	53	322	118	41	20	85.3	26.2
40 to 44 years	1 696	382	306	1 590	557	219	107	88.6	28.0
40 years	371	88	58	360	118	36	16	88.3	27.7
41 years	329	67	62	298	97	52	31	87.0	25.3
42 years	342	71	58	312	128	38	20	87.8	29.0
43 years	360	80	61	356	128	45	29	90.6	31.5
44 years	294	76	67	264	86	47	11	89.4	26.7
45 to 49 years	1 390	390	310	1 515	655	239	192	88.7	33.8
45 years	285	80	100	301	109	46	41	89.6	30.7
46 years	301	73	53	319	111	46	46	89.5	33.9
47 years	264	75	61	281	159	53	29	88.5	35.4
48 years	309	79	40	303	120	54	27	88.0	32.6
49 years	230	83	55	311	155	40	49	88.0	36.6
50 to 54 years	1 117	182	210	1 044	618	163	173	86.9	32.3
50 years	291	49	51	298	148	37	58	87.0	34.6
51 years	221	40	32	191	127	41	21	86.9	32.9
52 years	205	40	43	148	110	14	39	85.2	28.0
53 years	211	30	31	196	119	44	37	87.2	34.3
54 years	188	23	53	211	114	26	18	87.9	30.8
55 to 59 years	690	127	110	728	363	109	123	81.3	27.4
55 years	183	29	35	183	88	26	16	82.9	28.9
56 years	139	25	23	135	75	21	39	85.1	26.4
57 years	106	29	24	125	90	17	26	78.3	29.4
58 years	139	27	11	149	53	25	18	81.1	26.1
59 years	123	17	18	136	56	20	24	78.4	26.0

See footnotes at end of table.

Table B-2. Educational Attainment of Persons 15 Years Old and Over, by Single Year of Age, Sex, Race, and Hispanic Origin: March 1997 — Continued

(Numbers in thousands. Civilian noninstitutional population.)

Age, sex, race, and Hispanic origin	Total	None	Elementary			High School			
			1st-4th grade	5th-6th grade	7th-8th grade	9th grade	10th grade	11th grade	High school graduate
60 to 64 years	4 073	20	56	118	265	115	159	141	1 369
60 years	815	6	5	15	33	19	20	19	307
61 years	888	2	21	22	69	9	41	28	284
62 years	811	3	12	30	52	32	24	26	278
63 years	855	1	8	27	64	34	47	48	275
64 years	704	7	10	25	47	22	28	20	224
65 years and over	12 022	108	256	413	1 378	483	615	590	3 685
Female									
Total, 15 years and over	88 756	322	782	1 552	3 982	3 380	4 042	4 779	29 581
15 to 17 years	4 471	—	3	14	835	1 385	1 352	811	64
15 years	1 477	—	1	13	690	638	125	6	5
16 years	1 504	—	—	2	112	633	662	93	3
17 years	1 490	—	2	—	32	114	565	713	57
18 years and over	84 285	322	779	1 538	3 147	1 995	2 690	3 968	29 517
18 and 19 years	2 906	2	4	16	39	84	153	765	938
18 years	1 411	2	4	8	26	57	94	605	373
19 years	1 495	—	—	8	13	27	59	161	565
20 years and over	81 378	319	775	1 522	3 108	1 911	2 537	3 202	28 579
20 to 24 years	6 892	17	37	89	80	146	149	318	2 033
20 years	1 444	1	8	13	19	25	24	77	427
21 years	1 406	6	1	19	—	38	38	71	413
22 years	1 296	2	5	19	23	29	38	45	363
23 years	1 307	4	12	14	20	26	27	63	396
24 years	1 438	3	11	23	18	28	22	63	434
25 years and over	74 487	303	738	1 433	3 028	1 765	2 389	2 884	26 546
25 to 29 years	7 674	13	37	110	95	125	167	266	2 199
25 years	1 415	2	6	17	8	27	24	59	392
26 years	1 669	3	14	31	15	16	36	50	497
27 years	1 450	3	1	17	17	21	49	42	379
28 years	1 529	3	5	24	16	29	19	64	463
29 years	1 611	2	11	21	38	33	40	51	468
30 to 34 years	8 515	21	51	118	113	187	182	269	2 694
30 years	1 672	7	3	22	12	32	29	61	543
31 years	1 579	5	11	22	22	41	20	58	498
32 years	1 752	1	3	26	28	36	34	43	568
33 years	1 668	3	14	23	22	29	52	49	495
34 years	1 843	4	19	26	29	49	47	59	589
35 to 39 years	9 299	19	43	146	125	164	223	297	3 193
35 years	1 795	—	6	26	30	21	48	63	585
36 years	1 910	5	9	31	30	35	41	52	668
37 years	1 874	6	2	27	20	33	42	69	627
38 years	1 887	6	8	34	24	34	56	62	645
39 years	1 833	218	—	27	21	42	35	—	52 667
40 to 44 years	8 825	22	61	119	137	131	148	213	3 044
40 years	1 860	5	7	28	33	41	44	43	596
41 years	1 849	5	25	29	31	23	23	44	654
42 years	1 734	7	7	23	30	19	37	42	614
43 years	1 693	—	14	18	22	26	15	41	567
44 years	1 690	5	7	21	21	22	28	44	612
45 to 49 years	7 828	28	62	100	151	113	127	243	2 702
45 years	1 651	5	10	37	32	31	21	46	575

See footnotes at end of table.

Table B-2. Educational Attainment of Persons 15 Years Old and Over, by Single Year of Age, Sex, Race, and Hispanic Origin: March 1997 — Continued

(Numbers in thousands. Civilian noninstitutional population.)

Age, sex, race, and Hispanic origin	Some college, no degree	Associate Degree		Bachelor's degree	Master's degree	Professional degree	Doctorate degree	Percent	
		Occupational	Academic					High school graduate or more	Bachelor's degree or more
60 to 64 years	614	104	76	528	301	106	100	78.5	25.4
60 years	119	23	14	119	76	21	19	85.7	28.8
61 years	128	28	18	134	61	26	16	78.3	26.6
62 years	126	12	17	104	64	14	20	78.1	24.8
63 years	118	23	14	103	42	26	24	73.2	22.8
64 years	123	18	13	69	59	20	20	77.5	23.8
65 years and over	1 648	178	169	1 447	570	304	178	68.0	20.8
Female									
Total, 15 years and over	16 449	3 267	3 126	12 575	3 798	637	483	78.8	19.7
15 to 17 years	7	—	—	—	—	—	—	1.6	—
15 years	—	—	—	—	—	—	—	0.3	—
16 years	—	—	—	—	—	—	—	0.2	—
17 years	7	—	—	—	—	—	—	4.3	—
18 years and over	16 442	3 267	3 126	12 575	3 798	637	483	82.9	20.8
18 and 19 years	886	9	1	7	1	—	—	63.4	0.3
18 years	241	—	—	2	—	—	—	43.6	0.1
19 years	645	9	1	6	1	—	—	82.1	0.4
20 years and over	15 556	3 258	3 125	12 568	3 798	637	483	83.6	21.5
20 to 24 years	2 752	182	227	825	31	5	—	87.9	12.5
20 years	818	24	8	3	—	—	—	88.5	0.2
21 years	727	23	55	14	—	—	—	87.6	1.0
22 years	498	42	68	155	7	3	—	87.6	12.7
23 years	348	47	40	303	6	—	—	87.2	23.7
24 years	360	46	57	351	18	2	—	88.3	25.8
25 years and over	12 804	3 076	2 898	11 743	3 767	632	483	83.2	22.3
25 to 29 years	1 642	339	328	1 948	305	57	44	89.4	30.7
25 years	345	71	50	356	43	10	6	89.9	29.3
26 years	366	77	51	445	40	16	11	90.1	30.7
27 years	286	56	51	436	72	11	8	89.7	36.4
28 years	343	64	86	320	69	11	12	89.5	26.9
29 years	301	71	89	392	80	9	7	87.9	30.3
30 to 34 years	1 615	382	496	1 809	412	102	63	88.9	28.0
30 years	315	93	102	340	82	22	7	90.0	27.0
31 years	302	70	69	362	67	9	25	88.7	29.3
32 years	338	59	105	404	82	22	2	90.2	29.1
33 years	328	70	116	340	89	24	14	88.5	28.0
34 years	332	89	105	363	92	24	15	87.4	26.8
35 to 39 years	1 721	487	452	1 819	462	73	73	89.0	26.1
35 years	339	101	84	364	93	14	20	89.2	27.4
36 years	372	88	110	350	95	11	13	89.4	24.6
37 years	329	124	90	365	98	24	17	89.3	26.9
38 years	372	86	98	363	84	9	6	88.1	24.5
39 years	309	89	70	377	92	15	17	89.2	27.3
40 to 44 years	1 651	495	467	1 582	582	129	44	90.6	26.5
40 years	370	114	83	340	117	33	6	89.2	26.7
41 years	339	97	101	334	110	22	11	90.3	25.8
42 years	333	82	71	326	115	21	5	90.5	27.0
43 years	319	102	108	302	114	33	11	92.0	27.2
44 years	289	101	104	279	126	19	11	91.2	25.8
45 to 49 years	1 430	399	331	1 314	656	78	93	89.5	27.4
45 years	271	94	77	281	137	7	28	89.0	27.4

See footnotes at end of table.

Table B-2. Educational Attainment of Persons 15 Years Old and Over, by Single Year of Age, Sex, Race, and Hispanic Origin: March 1997 — Continued

(Numbers in thousands. Civilian noninstitutional population.)

Age, sex, race, and Hispanic origin	Total	None	Elementary			High School			
			1st-4th grade	5th-6th grade	7th-8th grade	9th grade	10th grade	11th grade	High school graduate
46 years	1 517	7	14	16	28	23	14	55	507
47 years	1 522	2	16	19	36	10	36	52	507
48 years	1 514	2	11	12	29	20	18	50	524
49 years	1 624	12	12	17	27	29	38	39	589
50 to 54 years	6 361	26	45	110	182	105	145	215	2 407
50 years	1 598	2	14	21	31	23	24	38	558
51 years	1 143	6	11	23	44	18	20	45	463
52 years	1 186	8	12	20	38	35	26	42	413
53 years	1 211	3	7	20	28	15	48	49	491
54 years	1 222	6	1	26	40	14	28	41	482
55 to 59 years	5 104	21	73	100	179	92	201	232	2 029
55 years	1 119	4	12	22	43	18	27	60	428
56 years	1 102	5	19	29	38	26	33	42	424
57 years	985	7	14	16	33	23	45	40	411
58 years	991	—	17	20	29	13	31	32	402
59 years	907	5	11	14	36	13	66	50	363
60 to 64 years	4 439	35	54	107	241	143	253	209	1 884
60 years	934	8	12	27	40	27	48	49	377
61 years	901	4	14	24	56	32	54	30	375
62 years	881	10	7	19	49	30	49	38	408
63 years	909	10	9	16	35	20	62	54	358
64 years	814	3	12	22	61	35	39	38	366
65 years and over	16 442	118	311	523	1 805	703	942	940	6 395
BLACK									
Both Sexes									
Total, 15 years and over	24 627	138	303	444	1 312	1 179	1 561	2 730	8 222
15 to 17 years	1 855	7	2	10	441	571	492	296	30
15 years	609	2	2	10	298	224	64	8	—
16 years	603	2	—	—	99	262	201	31	8
17 years	643	3	—	—	45	85	227	256	22
18 years and over	22 772	131	301	434	871	608	1 069	2 434	8 192
18 and 19 years	1 192	6	—	—	12	57	111	398	390
18 years	570	3	—	—	8	38	68	258	129
19 years	622	3	—	—	3	20	43	140	261
20 years and over	21 580	125	301	434	859	550	957	2 036	7 802
20 to 24 years	2 508	15	—	4	15	50	85	302	967
20 years	574	9	—	—	10	3	16	89	248
21 years	531	3	—	—	1	28	6	83	199
22 years	483	2	—	1	—	10	27	47	177
23 years	505	—	—	1	3	—	24	54	218
24 years	416	—	—	2	1	9	12	29	124
25 years and over	19 072	110	301	429	845	500	872	1 733	6 835
25 to 29 years	2 613	11	5	9	4	31	77	223	1 031
25 years	561	—	—	—	1	2	14	67	201
26 years	568	—	—	—	—	12	19	42	257
27 years	500	3	3	4	1	—	22	33	178
28 years	534	8	—	1	—	13	22	43	211
29 years	450	—	2	4	2	3	—	38	184
30 to 34 years	2 737	10	12	19	33	32	103	235	1 043
30 years	542	—	4	7	3	6	6	40	227
31 years	504	3	—	—	3	—	14	24	208

See footnotes at end of table.

Table B-2.   Educational Attainment of Persons 15 Years Old and Over, by Single Year of Age, Sex, Race, and Hispanic Origin: March 1997 — Continued

(Numbers in thousands. Civilian noninstitutional population.)

Age, sex, race, and Hispanic origin	Some college, no degree	Associate Degree		Bachelor's degree	Master's degree	Professional degree	Doctorate degree	Percent	
		Occupational	Academic					High school graduate or more	Bachelor's degree or more
46 years	274	95	47	279	119	24	16	89.7	28.9
47 years	302	53	71	251	123	28	16	88.8	27.5
48 years	272	85	66	245	155	10	16	90.6	28.0
49 years	312	72	69	259	122	9	18	89.3	25.1
50 to 54 years	1 098	263	258	926	465	56	59	87.0	23.7
50 years	315	73	83	253	134	10	21	90.5	26.1
51 years	184	37	40	139	83	18	12	85.4	22.0
52 years	185	52	56	184	85	13	14	84.6	25.0
53 years	201	49	37	166	84	9	5	85.9	21.7
54 years	213	52	42	185	80	7	6	87.3	22.7
55 to 59 years	867	179	174	603	275	44	36	82.4	18.8
55 years	202	34	48	130	70	14	7	83.4	19.8
56 years	168	47	33	155	75	7	3	82.6	21.7
57 years	167	20	36	121	42	3	8	82.0	17.6
58 years	186	33	35	115	58	13	8	85.8	19.5
59 years	144	45	23	84	30	7	10	77.7	14.3
60 to 64 years	620	127	105	431	176	31	24	76.5	14.9
60 years	169	19	28	82	36	8	6	77.6	14.2
61 years	132	31	20	82	42	2	4	76.3	14.3
62 years	104	18	15	88	32	10	3	77.0	15.1
63 years	133	32	26	109	36	4	5	77.4	17.0
64 years	82	27	16	70	29	7	6	74.2	13.8
65 years and over	2 160	404	286	1 311	434	63	46	67.5	11.3
BLACK									
Both Sexes									
Total, 15 years and over	4 729	692	651	1 944	572	85	65	68.9	10.8
15 to 17 years	5	—	—	—	—	—	—	1.9	—
15 years	—	—	—	—	—	—	—	—	—
16 years	—	—	—	—	—	—	—	1.3	—
17 years	5	—	—	—	—	—	—	4.2	—
18 years and over	4 724	692	651	1 944	572	85	65	74.3	11.7
18 and 19 years	218	—	—	—	—	—	—	51.0	—
18 years	65	—	—	—	—	—	—	34.1	—
19 years	153	—	—	—	—	—	—	66.5	—
20 years and over	4 506	692	651	1 944	572	85	65	75.6	12.4
20 to 24 years	865	39	32	127	5	—	—	81.2	5.3
20 years	182	9	3	5	—	—	—	77.9	0.8
21 years	189	4	—	17	—	—	—	77.1	3.2
22 years	177	8	6	26	—	—	—	81.8	5.4
23 years	140	15	4	41	5	—	—	83.7	9.1
24 years	177	3	19	39	—	—	—	87.2	9.5
25 years and over	3 641	653	619	1 817	567	85	65	74.9	13.3
25 to 29 years	693	88	64	316	49	5	6	86.2	14.4
25 years	169	19	13	67	3	—	4	85.0	13.2
26 years	138	14	19	62	4	—	—	87.1	11.7
27 years	161	16	7	60	11	—	—	86.6	14.1
28 years	118	9	16	73	15	5	—	83.8	17.5
29 years	106	30	9	53	17	—	2	89.0	15.9
30 to 34 years	633	130	120	304	53	7	4	83.8	13.5
30 years	117	21	37	63	12	—	—	87.9	13.8
31 years	126	30	19	58	11	4	4	91.3	15.3

See footnotes at end of table.

Table B-2. Educational Attainment of Persons 15 Years Old and Over, by Single Year of Age, Sex, Race, and Hispanic Origin: March 1997 — Continued

(Numbers in thousands. Civilian noninstitutional population.)

Age, sex, race, and Hispanic origin	Total	None	Elementary			High School			
			1st-4th grade	5th-6th grade	7th-8th grade	9th grade	10th grade	11th grade	High school graduate
32 years	543	4	4	6	14	8	26	57	177
33 years	513	—	3	5	11	4	33	55	196
34 years	635	3	2	1	2	14	24	59	235
35 to 39 years	2 876	11	10	3	44	32	101	234	1 115
35 years	633	5	5	1	1	3	26	44	236
36 years	544	—	3	—	12	4	25	58	201
37 years	597	—	2	—	10	7	18	56	202
38 years	608	3	—	2	15	9	19	43	266
39 years	494	3	—	—	5	10	13	33	210
40 to 44 years	2 539	13	9	26	71	33	70	198	981
40 years	536	1	—	7	9	6	5	51	218
41 years	600	—	—	2	8	8	23	46	231
42 years	450	4	—	13	18	8	20	25	190
43 years	475	4	1	3	11	8	17	42	166
44 years	478	4	9	—	25	4	5	35	176
45 to 49 years	2 076	9	11	8	65	62	95	193	784
45 years	430	2	3	1	10	13	7	31	159
46 years	460	—	—	—	8	17	33	42	175
47 years	484	4	7	7	24	18	25	52	138
48 years	326	—	1	—	13	7	11	23	152
49 years	376	4	—	1	11	7	19	45	160
50 to 54 years	1 448	4	10	16	92	45	45	146	532
50 years	341	2	7	5	19	3	7	43	132
51 years	298	—	3	4	20	8	7	34	92
52 years	237	—	—	—	21	8	4	9	96
53 years	284	—	—	2	15	15	25	35	97
54 years	289	2	—	4	16	12	2	25	115
55 to 59 years	1 184	5	27	70	50	59	94	133	401
55 years	271	—	12	13	12	13	34	21	83
56 years	252	—	1	15	18	14	18	33	70
57 years	202	5	1	2	13	—	12	29	72
58 years	235	—	8	18	3	22	13	20	98
59 years	224	—	4	22	4	10	16	29	78
60 to 64 years	982	8	34	58	83	50	66	129	302
60 years	208	—	2	9	14	11	14	33	75
61 years	203	8	9	13	14	8	13	35	59
62 years	194	—	9	4	11	17	17	18	61
63 years	175	1	13	14	18	3	5	30	55
64 years	203	—	—	19	26	10	16	13	52
65 years and over	2 616	39	183	221	403	157	221	243	646
Male									
Total, 15 years and over	11 113	96	180	242	621	576	715	1 276	3 750
15 to 17 years	929	4	2	8	242	327	231	106	10
15 years	302	—	2	8	145	125	19	3	—
16 years	325	1	—	—	66	158	87	13	—
17 years	302	3	—	—	31	43	125	90	10
18 years and over	10 183	93	178	234	379	249	484	1 170	3 740
18 and 19 years	594	3	—	—	11	35	66	196	186
18 years	271	—	—	—	8	22	42	128	52
19 years	323	3	—	—	3	13	24	67	135
20 years and over	9 589	90	178	234	368	214	418	975	3 554
20 to 24 years	1 144	15	—	3	11	10	33	163	469

See footnotes at end of table.

Table B-2. Educational Attainment of Persons 15 Years Old and Over, by Single Year of Age, Sex, Race, and Hispanic Origin: March 1997 — Continued

(Numbers in thousands. Civilian noninstitutional population.)

| Age, sex, race, and Hispanic origin | College | | | | | | | Percent | |
| | Some college, no degree | Associate Degree | | Bachelor's degree | Master's degree | Professional degree | Doctorate degree | High school graduate or more | Bachelor's degree or more |
		Occupational	Academic						
32 years	128	26	19	60	11	3	—	78.2	13.8
33 years	112	17	20	49	8	—	—	78.3	11.1
34 years	151	35	24	74	11	—	—	83.6	13.4
35 to 39 years	690	114	131	326	45	17	2	84.9	13.6
35 years	174	20	30	76	7	3	—	86.4	13.6
36 years	133	24	38	27	11	8	—	81.2	8.5
37 years	139	33	17	98	15	1	—	84.6	19.0
38 years	118	23	29	77	3	3	—	85.0	13.5
39 years	126	15	17	50	9	3	2	87.2	12.8
40 to 44 years	563	91	92	282	82	17	9	83.4	15.4
40 years	123	23	23	58	10	2	—	85.3	13.0
41 years	139	15	35	65	25	3	—	85.4	15.4
42 years	93	14	14	38	11	2	—	80.4	11.4
43 years	118	18	17	43	24	—	4	82.1	14.8
44 years	91	21	3	78	13	11	5	83.2	22.4
45 to 49 years	374	65	94	209	84	14	9	78.6	15.2
45 years	90	10	16	72	10	—	6	84.3	20.1
46 years	81	18	19	41	26	—	—	78.2	14.5
47 years	90	17	39	32	24	7	—	71.9	13.1
48 years	55	8	3	26	17	5	4	83.1	15.8
49 years	57	11	16	38	7	2	—	77.5	12.7
50 to 54 years	210	50	54	151	84	1	10	75.2	16.9
50 years	44	7	17	49	5	1	—	74.6	15.9
51 years	53	12	11	29	25	—	—	74.4	18.1
52 years	21	10	12	34	19	—	4	82.8	24.1
53 years	37	13	7	22	10	—	4	67.2	12.8
54 years	54	8	7	17	24	—	2	78.5	15.0
55 to 59 years	157	42	24	56	61	1	4	63.1	10.3
55 years	29	10	3	16	23	—	2	60.9	14.9
56 years	44	—	12	13	12	—	2	60.7	10.6
57 years	32	5	2	15	15	—	—	69.4	14.6
58 years	28	12	3	6	4	—	—	63.9	4.2
59 years	25	15	5	6	8	1	—	61.7	6.8
60 to 64 years	106	25	18	58	36	8	2	56.5	10.6
60 years	21	6	7	6	9	1	—	59.9	7.7
61 years	17	6	2	12	5	3	—	50.6	9.4
62 years	29	9	4	5	8	—	2	61.2	8.2
63 years	13	—	1	17	5	—	—	52.1	12.7
64 years	26	4	5	18	9	4	—	58.3	15.3
65 years and over	214	47	22	115	73	15	18	44.0	8.5
Male									
Total, 15 years and over	2 103	244	219	800	203	52	36	66.6	9.8
15 to 17 years	—	—	—	—	—	—	—	1.1	—
15 years	—	—	—	—	—	—	—	—	—
16 years	—	—	—	—	—	—	—	—	—
17 years	—	—	—	—	—	—	—	3.3	—
18 years and over	2 103	244	219	800	203	52	36	72.6	10.7
18 and 19 years	97	—	—	—	—	—	—	47.7	—
18 years	19	—	—	—	—	—	—	26.0	—
19 years	79	—	—	—	—	—	—	65.9	—
20 years and over	2 006	244	219	800	203	52	36	74.2	11.4
20 to 24 years	384	10	9	37	—	—	—	79.5	3.2

See footnotes at end of table.

Table B-2. Educational Attainment of Persons 15 Years Old and Over, by Single Year of Age, Sex, Race, and Hispanic Origin: March 1997 — Continued

(Numbers in thousands. Civilian noninstitutional population.)

Age, sex, race, and Hispanic origin	Total	None	Elementary			High School			
			1st-4th grade	5th-6th grade	7th-8th grade	9th grade	10th grade	11th grade	High school graduate
20 years	239	9	—	—	8	—	5	48	104
21 years	265	3	—	—	—	3	2	49	97
22 years	206	2	—	1	—	7	11	30	76
23 years	223	—	—	—	3	—	11	19	118
24 years	210	—	—	2	—	—	4	17	74
25 years and over	8 446	75	178	230	357	205	385	812	3 085
25 to 29 years	1 186	8	2	3	1	7	35	120	492
25 years	269	—	—	—	1	—	8	48	99
26 years	232	—	—	—	—	7	6	11	133
27 years	240	2	—	3	—	—	8	20	86
28 years	242	6	—	—	—	—	14	32	77
29 years	203	—	2	—	—	—	—	8	97
30 to 34 years	1 228	4	9	11	10	17	54	105	512
30 years	229	—	4	4	—	—	1	12	120
31 years	233	—	—	—	3	—	4	9	110
32 years	260	4	4	2	—	4	12	18	98
33 years	246	—	—	5	6	4	26	41	86
34 years	260	—	2	—	2	9	11	25	98
35 to 39 years	1 335	8	5	3	27	16	36	118	544
35 years	283	5	5	1	1	1	10	21	105
36 years	230	—	—	—	—	2	10	42	89
37 years	281	—	—	—	7	—	6	25	112
38 years	285	3	—	2	13	8	8	18	127
39 years	256	—	—	—	5	5	3	13	111
40 to 44 years	1 148	8	9	15	34	13	37	120	481
40 years	257	—	—	5	1	2	—	39	123
41 years	258	—	—	—	6	—	9	25	119
42 years	205	4	—	7	11	8	20	10	80
43 years	217	4	1	3	7	—	9	34	76
44 years	210	—	9	—	9	4	—	12	83
45 to 49 years	942	6	5	5	17	28	52	93	340
45 years	205	2	—	—	5	8	5	20	64
46 years	201	—	—	—	5	6	10	19	80
47 years	233	—	5	4	1	11	13	21	70
48 years	117	—	—	—	3	—	8	16	53
49 years	187	4	—	1	4	3	15	17	74
50 to 54 years	645	4	8	15	50	13	21	70	229
50 years	170	2	5	5	9	—	3	29	66
51 years	139	—	3	3	19	4	5	15	44
52 years	80	—	—	—	14	—	—	7	19
53 years	116	—	—	2	5	5	12	6	49
54 years	139	2	—	4	4	4	2	13	51
55 to 59 years	524	3	21	49	26	28	39	53	161
55 years	130	—	12	3	9	9	16	7	42
56 years	98	—	—	10	6	5	7	17	24
57 years	76	3	—	2	5	—	4	10	28
58 years	104	—	4	16	1	10	6	11	27
59 years	116	—	4	18	4	3	5	8	39
60 to 64 years	424	8	23	31	27	24	32	49	117
60 years	94	—	2	3	8	4	13	16	25
61 years	87	8	5	8	4	6	2	15	21
62 years	75	—	4	—	2	8	10	3	26
63 years	67	—	12	9	3	2	2	13	25
64 years	101	—	—	10	10	4	5	3	19
65 years and over	1 014	27	96	99	166	59	79	84	209

See footnotes at end of table.

Table B-2. Educational Attainment of Persons 15 Years Old and Over, by Single Year of Age, Sex, Race, and Hispanic Origin: March 1997 — Continued

(Numbers in thousands. Civilian noninstitutional population.)

Age, sex, race, and Hispanic origin	College							Percent	
	Some college, no degree	Associate Degree		Bachelor's degree	Master's degree	Professional degree	Doctorate degree	High school graduate or more	Bachelor's degree or more
		Occupational	Academic						
20 years	57	4	—	5	—	—	—	70.8	1.9
21 years	103	—	—	7	—	—	—	78.1	2.7
22 years	75	4	—	—	—	—	—	75.0	—
23 years	58	2	—	13	—	—	—	85.6	5.8
24 years	92	—	9	12	—	—	—	88.9	5.8
25 years and over	1 622	234	210	763	203	52	36	73.5	12.5
25 to 29 years	331	29	16	113	25	5		85.2	12.1
25 years	85	—	5	23	—	—		78.8	8.5
26 years	47	3	3	21	1	—	—	89.8	9.5
27 years	80	3	5	29	3	—	—	85.8	13.3
28 years	66	—	2	30	10	5	—	78.8	18.7
29 years	52	22	—	10	11	—	—	95.1	10.5
30 to 34 years	275	50	38	115	23	5	2	82.9	11.8
30 years	37	14	12	22	4	—	—	91.1	11.2
31 years	63	9	—	27	3	4	2	93.4	15.5
32 years	75	7	7	23	6	—	—	83.3	11.4
33 years	48	6	11	9	5	—	—	66.8	5.5
34 years	52	14	8	34	5	—	—	81.2	15.2
35 to 39 years	298	41	44	171	18	4	2	84.1	14.6
35 years	75	2	11	41	3	—	—	84.2	15.7
36 years	51	3	13	11	7	1	—	76.3	8.4
37 years	54	17	3	54	5	—	—	86.8	20.8
38 years	55	5	11	35	—	3	—	82.4	13.2
39 years	63	14	7	30	3	—	2	89.9	13.9
40 to 44 years	243	19	21	100	29	13	4	79.3	12.8
40 years	47	2	1	30	8	—	—	81.8	14.6
41 years	50	8	11	18	9	3	—	84.7	11.6
42 years	52	1	2	7	—	2	—	70.4	4.3
43 years	58	7	7	7	2	—	4	74.0	5.9
44 years	35	1	—	38	10	9	—	83.8	27.1
45 to 49 years	166	38	37	108	34	11	2	78.2	16.5
45 years	45	4	5	42	2	—	2	80.0	22.4
46 years	40	8	8	16	9	—	—	80.1	12.7
47 years	53	12	16	7	12	7	—	76.4	11.3
48 years	7	7	—	16	4	2	—	76.9	19.9
49 years	22	6	8	26	7	2	—	77.3	18.7
50 to 54 years	95	15	20	74	22	1	9	72.0	16.3
50 years	18	2	7	22	1	1	—	68.8	13.4
51 years	28	4	2	13	—	—	—	65.2	9.9
52 years	2	5	7	20	4	—	4	74.3	34.2
53 years	9	2	4	12	5	—	4	73.7	18.4
54 years	38	2	—	7	12	—	1	79.9	14.2
55 to 59 years	69	21	10	20	23	—	2	58.4	8.6
55 years	5	8	3	4	11	—	—	56.4	11.7
56 years	21	—	—	4	—	—	2	53.4	6.6
57 years	14	2	—	3	5	—	—	68.0	10.2
58 years	11	8	3	3	4	—	—	53.2	6.4
59 years	17	4	5	6	3	—	—	63.4	7.6
60 to 64 years	45	13	14	26	11	5	—	54.4	10.0
60 years	10	3	7	2	—	—	—	49.9	1.7
61 years	6	—	—	8	3	3	—	46.3	14.9
62 years	8	5	1	5	4	—	—	64.1	12.0
63 years	—	—	1	—	—	—	—	(B)	(B)
64 years	22	4	5	12	5	2	—	68.5	18.9
65 years and over	100	10	10	35	19	9	13	39.9	7.5

See footnotes at end of table.

Table B-2. Educational Attainment of Persons 15 Years Old and Over, by Single Year of Age, Sex, Race, and Hispanic Origin: March 1997 — Continued

(Numbers in thousands. Civilian noninstitutional population.)

Age, sex, race, and Hispanic origin	Total	None	Elementary			High School			
			1st-4th grade	5th-6th grade	7th-8th grade	9th grade	10th grade	11th grade	High school graduate
Female									
Total, 15 years and over	13 514	42	123	202	692	603	846	1 453	4 472
15 to 17 years	925	3	—	2	200	245	261	190	20
15 years	306	2	—	2	153	99	45	5	—
16 years	278	1	—	—	33	104	115	18	8
17 years	341	—	—	—	14	42	101	166	12
18 years and over	12 589	38	123	200	492	358	585	1 263	4 452
18 and 19 years	598	3	—	—	—	22	46	202	203
18 years	299	3	—	—	—	16	26	130	77
19 years	299	—	—	—	—	7	20	72	126
20 years and over	11 991	35	123	200	491	336	539	1 061	4 248
20 to 24 years	1 364	—	—	1	4	41	52	139	498
20 years	334	—	—	—	2	3	11	41	144
21 years	266	—	—	—	1	25	3	34	102
22 years	276	—	—	—	—	3	16	17	101
23 years	282	—	—	1	—	—	14	35	101
24 years	206	—	—	—	1	9	8	12	51
25 years and over	10 626	35	123	199	487	295	487	922	3 750
25 to 29 years	1 427	3	3	5	4	24	42	103	539
25 years	292	—	—	—	—	2	6	19	102
26 years	336	—	—	—	—	5	13	31	124
27 years	260	1	3	—	1	—	14	12	92
28 years	292	2	—	1	—	13	8	11	134
29 years	247	—	—	4	2	3	—	30	87
30 to 34 years	1 509	6	3	8	23	15	49	130	531
30 years	313	—	—	3	3	6	6	27	106
31 years	271	3	—	—	—	—	10	15	98
32 years	283	—	—	4	14	4	14	39	79
33 years	266	—	3	—	5	—	7	14	110
34 years	375	3	—	1	—	4	13	34	137
35 to 39 years	1 541	3	5	—	17	16	65	116	571
35 years	350	—	—	—	—	2	16	24	131
36 years	314	—	3	—	11	2	15	16	112
37 years	316	—	2	—	3	7	12	31	90
38 years	323	—	—	—	3	1	12	25	138
39 years	238	3	—	—	—	5	10	20	99
40 to 44 years	1 391	5	—	10	37	20	33	78	500
40 years	279	1	—	3	7	4	5	12	95
41 years	342	—	—	2	3	8	15	21	112
42 years	245	—	—	5	6	1	—	15	110
43 years	258	—	—	—	5	8	9	8	90
44 years	267	4	—	—	15	—	5	22	93
45 to 49 years	1 134	4	6	4	48	33	44	100	444
45 years	225	—	3	1	5	5	2	11	95
46 years	258	—	—	—	3	11	22	23	95
47 years	252	4	3	3	23	7	12	31	68
48 years	209	—	1	—	11	7	3	7	100
49 years	190	—	—	—	7	4	4	28	86
50 to 54 years	803	—	2	1	43	32	24	76	303
50 years	170	—	2	—	11	3	4	14	66
51 years	159	—	—	1	2	3	3	19	48
52 years	156	—	—	—	7	8	4	2	78

See footnotes at end of table.

Table B-2. Educational Attainment of Persons 15 Years Old and Over, by Single Year of Age, Sex, Race, and Hispanic Origin: March 1997 — Continued

(Numbers in thousands. Civilian noninstitutional population.)

Age, sex, race, and Hispanic origin	Some college, no degree	College Associate Degree Occupational	College Associate Degree Academic	Bachelor's degree	Master's degree	Professional degree	Doctorate degree	Percent High school graduate or more	Percent Bachelor's degree or more
Female									
Total, 15 years and over	2 626	448	432	1 144	370	33	29	70.7	11.7
15 to 17 years	5	—	—	—	—	—	—	2.7	—
15 years	—	—	—	—	—	—	—	—	—
16 years	—	—	—	—	—	—	—	2.8	—
17 years	5	—	—	—	—	—	—	5.1	—
18 years and over	2 621	448	432	1 144	370	33	29	75.7	12.5
18 and 19 years	121	—	—	—	—	—	—	54.2	—
18 years	47	—	—	—	—	—	—	41.4	—
19 years	74	—	—	—	—	—	—	67.0	—
20 years and over	2 500	448	432	1 144	370	33	29	76.8	13.1
20 to 24 years	481	29	24	90	5	—	—	82.6	7.0
20 years	125	5	3	—	—	—	—	82.9	—
21 years	87	4	—	10	—	—	—	76.0	3.6
22 years	102	5	6	26	—	—	—	86.9	9.4
23 years	82	12	4	28	5	—	—	82.3	11.6
24 years	85	3	10	27	—	—	—	85.5	13.2
25 years and over	2 019	419	409	1 054	364	33	29	76.0	13.9
25 to 29 years	363	59	48	202	25	—	6	87.1	16.4
25 years	84	19	8	45	3	—	4	90.7	17.7
26 years	91	11	16	41	3	—	—	85.3	13.2
27 years	81	13	2	31	7	—	—	87.4	14.9
28 years	52	9	14	43	5	—	—	88.0	16.5
29 years	54	8	9	42	6	—	2	84.0	20.4
30 to 34 years	358	80	82	189	31	3	2	84.5	14.9
30 years	80	7	25	41	8	—	—	85.5	15.6
31 years	63	21	19	31	8	—	2	89.5	15.1
32 years	53	19	12	37	5	3	—	73.6	15.9
33 years	64	10	9	40	4	—	—	89.0	16.4
34 years	99	22	16	40	6	—	—	85.2	12.2
35 to 39 years	392	73	87	155	27	13	—	85.6	12.7
35 years	99	18	19	35	4	3	—	88.2	11.9
36 years	82	21	25	16	4	7	—	84.9	8.5
37 years	85	16	14	44	10	1	—	82.6	17.3
38 years	63	18	18	42	3	—	—	87.3	13.8
39 years	62	1	10	20	6	3	—	84.2	11.7
40 to 44 years	321	73	71	182	53	4	5	86.9	17.5
40 years	76	21	22	28	2	2	—	88.5	11.6
41 years	89	7	24	47	16	—	—	85.9	18.2
42 years	41	13	11	31	11	—	—	88.8	17.3
43 years	60	12	10	35	22	—	—	88.9	22.2
44 years	56	20	3	40	2	2	5	82.7	18.7
45 to 49 years	208	27	57	101	49	2	7	79.0	14.1
45 years	46	6	11	29	8	—	3	88.2	18.1
46 years	42	10	12	24	16	—	—	76.8	15.8
47 years	37	5	23	25	12	—	—	67.8	14.7
48 years	48	2	3	10	13	2	3	86.6	13.6
49 years	35	5	8	13	—	—	—	77.6	6.7
50 to 54 years	115	35	33	77	62	—	1	77.9	17.4
50 years	25	5	9	27	5	—	—	80.4	18.4
51 years	25	8	9	15	25	—	—	82.5	25.3
52 years	20	5	4	15	15	—	—	87.2	18.9

See footnotes at end of table.

Table B-2. Educational Attainment of Persons 15 Years Old and Over, by Single Year of Age, Sex, Race, and Hispanic Origin: March 1997 — Continued

(Numbers in thousands. Civilian noninstitutional population.)

Age, sex, race, and Hispanic origin	Total	None	Elementary			High School			
			1st-4th grade	5th-6th grade	7th-8th grade	9th grade	10th grade	11th grade	High school graduate
53 years	168	—	—	—	11	10	13	29	48
54 years	149	—	—	—	13	9	—	12	64
55 to 59 years	660	2	6	21	24	32	54	80	240
55 years	141	—	—	10	3	5	18	14	41
56 years	155	—	1	5	12	8	11	16	46
57 years	126	2	1	—	7	—	8	19	44
58 years	131	—	4	2	2	12	7	10	71
59 years	107	—	—	4	—	7	11	21	39
60 to 64 years	558	1	10	28	56	26	34	79	185
60 years	114	—	—	6	5	7	1	17	50
61 years	116	—	5	5	10	2	12	20	38
62 years	118	—	4	4	9	10	7	15	35
63 years	108	1	1	5	15	1	3	17	30
64 years	102	—	—	9	17	7	11	10	33
65 years and over	1 603	12	87	122	237	90	142	150	437
HISPANIC ORIGIN [1]									
Both Sexes									
Total, 15 years and over	20 700	451	1 102	2 151	1 683	1 584	1 338	1 899	5 022
15 to 17 years	1 597	2	5	14	359	473	453	271	17
15 years	515	1	1	8	251	191	59	4	—
16 years	496	1	1	5	76	218	161	34	—
17 years	585	—	2	1	32	64	232	233	17
18 years and over	19 103	449	1 097	2 137	1 324	1 111	886	1 628	5 005
18 and 19 years	1 034	13	8	39	30	84	101	324	259
18 years	492	9	4	15	14	48	58	201	97
19 years	542	5	4	25	15	36	43	123	162
20 years and over	18 068	436	1 089	2 097	1 295	1 027	784	1 304	4 746
20 to 24 years	2 592	16	60	208	130	187	115	310	735
20 years	530	3	7	39	14	37	25	90	158
21 years	504	3	8	27	15	48	43	60	150
22 years	517	5	15	48	30	32	15	55	136
23 years	487	3	14	47	35	34	17	53	135
24 years	554	3	17	47	36	36	16	51	157
25 years and over	15 476	420	1 029	1 890	1 164	840	669	995	4 011
25 to 29 years	2 778	24	93	226	141	179	142	257	791
25 years	607	4	20	37	29	39	21	64	186
26 years	604	1	21	52	22	37	37	50	189
27 years	528	4	14	45	32	30	34	49	139
28 years	531	6	22	56	25	28	32	49	145
29 years	507	8	15	37	33	44	19	45	131
30 to 34 years	2 717	28	93	278	156	191	119	207	724
30 years	533	6	11	57	24	45	17	41	134
31 years	571	3	16	50	16	47	30	51	172
32 years	579	4	18	59	36	26	22	39	162
33 years	505	9	25	57	42	23	24	32	132
34 years	528	6	23	55	38	50	26	44	123
35 to 39 years	2 453	31	107	325	145	101	93	163	704
35 years	511	1	19	63	27	12	18	40	150
36 years	552	12	34	55	45	33	25	36	156
37 years	451	9	14	67	21	15	21	36	121
38 years	487	4	22	67	27	24	10	33	142

See footnotes at end of table.

Table B-2. Educational Attainment of Persons 15 Years Old and Over, by Single Year of Age, Sex, Race, and Hispanic Origin: March 1997 — Continued

(Numbers in thousands. Civilian noninstitutional population.)

Age, sex, race, and Hispanic origin	Some college, no degree	Associate Degree		Bachelor's degree	Master's degree	Professional degree	Doctorate degree	Percent	
		Occupational	Academic					High school graduate or more	Bachelor's degree or more
53 years	29	11	4	10	5	—	—	62.8	9.0
54 years	16	6	7	10	13	—	1	77.3	15.8
55 to 59 years	89	21	14	36	38	1	2	66.7	11.6
55 years	24	2	—	12	12	—	2	65.0	17.7
56 years	22	—	12	9	11	—	—	65.3	13.1
57 years	18	3	2	12	10	—	—	70.3	17.2
58 years	17	4	—	3	—	—	—	72.5	2.5
59 years	8	11	—	—	5	1	—	60.0	5.9
60 to 64 years	61	13	5	32	24	3	2	58.1	11.0
60 years	11	2	—	4	9	1	—	68.1	12.6
61 years	11	6	2	4	2	—	—	53.9	5.4
62 years	21	4	3	—	5	—	2	59.3	5.8
63 years	13	—	—	17	5	—	—	60.2	20.6
64 years	4	—	—	6	4	2	—	48.2	11.8
65 years and over	113	37	12	80	55	7	4	46.5	9.1

HISPANIC ORIGIN [1]

Both Sexes

Age, sex, race, and Hispanic origin	Some college, no degree	Associate Degree		Bachelor's degree	Master's degree	Professional degree	Doctorate degree	Percent	
		Occupational	Academic					High school graduate or more	Bachelor's degree or more
Total, 15 years and over	2 895	430	459	1 228	282	103	73	50.7	8.1
15 to 17 years	3	—	—	—	—	—	—	1.3	—
15 years	—	—	—	—	—	—	—	—	—
16 years	—	—	—	—	—	—	—	—	—
17 years	3	—	—	—	—	—	—	3.4	—
18 years and over	2 892	430	459	1 228	282	103	73	54.8	8.8
18 and 19 years	170	5	—	—	—	—	—	42.0	—
18 years	44	2	—	—	—	—	—	29.1	—
19 years	126	3	—	—	—	—	—	53.7	—
20 years and over	2 722	424	459	1 228	282	103	73	55.5	9.3
20 to 24 years	668	37	41	75	7	3	—	60.4	3.3
20 years	152	2	—	4	—	—	—	59.4	0.7
21 years	128	10	8	3	2	—	—	59.7	0.9
22 years	145	8	9	15	1	3	—	61.2	3.7
23 years	111	9	12	17	—	—	—	58.2	3.5
24 years	133	8	12	36	4	—	—	63.3	7.2
25 years and over	2 054	387	418	1 153	275	100	73	54.7	10.3
25 to 29 years	459	63	98	256	37	9	4	61.8	11.0
25 years	87	17	29	61	8	3	—	64.5	11.9
26 years	103	13	12	56	8	3	—	63.7	11.1
27 years	91	11	17	57	3	2	—	60.6	11.6
28 years	89	15	21	36	7	—	1	59.1	8.2
29 years	88	7	19	47	11	1	3	60.4	12.2
30 to 34 years	429	81	85	248	50	20	9	60.6	12.0
30 years	100	17	31	38	6	5	2	62.5	9.7
31 years	91	14	9	54	16	2	—	62.5	12.5
32 years	117	19	14	46	10	7	—	64.7	10.9
33 years	50	19	21	55	12	4	3	58.4	14.5
34 years	71	13	11	55	6	2	4	53.9	12.8
35 to 39 years	365	78	75	208	37	8	15	60.7	10.9
35 years	86	16	16	50	7	4	3	65.1	12.5
36 years	65	15	14	50	7	—	8	57.0	11.7
37 years	73	20	11	30	8	4	—	59.5	9.4
38 years	68	17	17	44	11	—	—	61.6	11.5

See footnotes at end of table.

Table B-2. Educational Attainment of Persons 15 Years Old and Over, by Single Year of Age, Sex, Race, and Hispanic Origin: March 1997 — Continued

(Numbers in thousands. Civilian noninstitutional population.)

Age, sex, race, and Hispanic origin	Total	None	Elementary			High School			
			1st-4th grade	5th-6th grade	7th-8th grade	9th grade	10th grade	11th grade	High school graduate
39 years	452	4	19	73	25	17	19	19	135
40 to 44 years	1 935	19	128	215	145	88	76	121	545
40 years	434	2	16	61	30	15	23	30	125
41 years	447	3	58	45	29	15	13	30	123
42 years	357	3	19	36	37	22	12	12	105
43 years	373	4	21	35	24	14	16	29	103
44 years	324	6	13	39	25	22	12	20	88
45 to 49 years	1 355	36	96	169	105	54	52	63	336
45 years	315	2	25	48	24	7	12	9	67
46 years	289	8	20	36	23	10	2	18	81
47 years	228	5	19	33	19	13	14	10	63
48 years	252	9	19	23	16	10	15	20	60
49 years	270	12	14	29	23	14	9	7	65
50 to 54 years	1 105	45	62	178	111	64	43	43	271
50 years	280	16	17	45	32	9	10	10	66
51 years	224	7	12	31	23	11	7	12	69
52 years	222	6	15	34	24	13	8	13	46
53 years	183	1	14	35	16	10	8	2	45
54 years	197	15	3	31	16	20	11	6	44
55 to 59 years	937	53	112	121	83	57	43	49	229
55 years	203	2	27	25	19	11	11	13	51
56 years	213	6	28	30	12	13	15	10	64
57 years	161	13	19	19	18	12	4	7	33
58 years	177	7	25	26	17	8	4	8	36
59 years	183	25	13	20	18	13	9	11	44
60 to 64 years	682	31	77	133	75	44	36	25	145
60 years	135	10	14	25	9	8	7	2	31
61 years	126	3	22	18	17	9	5	7	25
62 years	143	9	19	32	19	10	6	3	26
63 years	139	7	7	25	19	8	12	8	32
64 years	137	3	15	33	11	9	6	5	31
65 years and over	1 516	152	260	245	203	63	65	65	267

See footnotes at end of table.

Table B-2. Educational Attainment of Persons 15 Years Old and Over, by Single Year of Age, Sex, Race, and Hispanic Origin: March 1997 — Continued

(Numbers in thousands. Civilian noninstitutional population.)

Age, sex, race, and Hispanic origin	Some college, no degree	Associate Degree		Bachelor's degree	Master's degree	Professional degree	Doctorate degree	Percent	
		Occupational	Academic					High school graduate or more	Bachelor's degree or more
39 years	72	10	16	33	4	—	3	60.6	9.0
40 to 44 years	298	46	48	131	38	23	13	59.0	10.6
40 years	75	8	6	26	10	3	2	59.0	9.6
41 years	63	10	16	31	5	3	2	56.9	9.4
42 years	36	7	8	35	16	5	4	60.2	16.6
43 years	78	9	9	21	4	5	1	61.6	8.2
44 years	46	12	10	18	3	6	3	57.8	9.4
45 to 49 years	178	43	44	121	38	9	9	57.4	13.1
45 years	48	4	18	38	7	2	3	59.5	16.0
46 years	44	11	2	25	6	3	—	59.6	11.8
47 years	20	3	5	15	6	1	4	50.8	11.3
48 years	35	8	7	15	12	—	2	55.2	11.6
49 years	32	16	11	28	7	3	—	60.3	13.9
50 to 54 years	129	29	33	54	28	13	4	50.6	8.9
50 years	35	9	5	16	6	2	1	50.4	9.0
51 years	20	4	8	10	6	3	—	53.4	8.5
52 years	29	4	6	10	11	1	2	48.9	11.0
53 years	24	7	9	7	1	2	1	52.7	6.0
54 years	22	5	4	12	3	4	—	47.9	9.7
55 to 59 years	72	23	14	51	17	6	5	44.6	8.5
55 years	15	6	3	13	3	4	—	46.8	9.9
56 years	10	1	5	12	2	—	4	46.0	8.2
57 years	16	7	4	9	—	—	—	42.9	5.7
58 years	12	6	2	14	10	—	1	45.8	14.3
59 years	20	3	—	3	2	2	—	40.6	4.1
60 to 64 years	44	13	6	34	14	3	1	38.3	7.7
60 years	10	2	—	6	8	3	1	45.3	13.7
61 years	7	—	3	8	3	—	—	36.2	8.8
62 years	8	3	—	8	—	—	—	31.9	6.0
63 years	15	—	1	3	2	—	—	38.3	4.1
64 years	4	8	2	8	—	—	—	40.0	6.3
65 years and over	81	11	15	49	16	9	13	30.4	5.8

Source: March 1997 Current Population Survey, Education and Social Stratification Branch, U.S. Bureau of the Census.

1. May be of any race.

— Represents zero or rounds to zero.

(B) Base less than 75,000.

Table B-3. Educational Attainment of Persons 15 Years Old and Over, by Marital Status, Age, Sex, Race, and Hispanic Origin: March 1997

(Numbers in thousands. Civilian noninstitutional population.)

Marital status, age, sex, race, and Hispanic origin	Total	Elementary		High School		College				Percent:	
		None-4th grade	5th-8th grade	9th-11th grade	High school graduate	Some college no degree	Associate degree	Bachelor's degree	Advanced degree	High school graduate or more	Bachelor's degree or more
ALL RACES											
Male											
15 to 17 years	6 004	15	1 385	4 536	59	9	—	—	—	1.1	—
Never married	5 940	15	1 369	4 499	49	9	—	—	—	1.0	—
Married, spouse present	12	—	—	8	4	—	—	—	—	(B)	(B)
Married, spouse absent	26	—	6	20	—	—	—	—	—	(B)	(B)
Separated	24	—	6	18	—	—	—	—	—	(B)	(B)
Widowed	4	—	3	1	—	—	—	—	—	(B)	(B)
Divorced	23	—	7	9	7	—	—	—	—	(B)	(B)
18 years and over	94 154	1 530	5 376	11 015	30 196	18 183	5 731	14 387	7 738	81.0	23.5
Never married	25 375	376	907	4 090	7 813	6 498	1 270	3 366	1 056	78.8	17.4
Married, spouse present	54 654	732	3 091	5 129	17 410	9 311	3 031	9 474	5 070	83.6	28.1
Married, spouse absent	3 232	187	357	489	1 026	505	178	319	170	68.0	15.1
Separated	1 956	70	135	349	700	322	111	181	89	71.7	13.8
Widowed	2 686	158	578	456	813	300	72	193	115	55.6	11.5
Divorced	8 208	77	442	850	3 135	1 569	579	1 036	521	83.3	19.0
18 to 24 years	12 535	76	353	2 802	3 970	4 150	432	716	36	74.2	6.0
Never married	10 953	68	251	2 509	3 293	3 818	360	624	31	74.2	6.0
Married, spouse present	1 249	7	67	220	547	273	56	75	5	76.5	6.4
Married, spouse absent	203	1	31	51	76	22	16	6	—	59.1	2.9
Separated	118	—	10	34	43	17	9	6	—	63.0	5.0
Widowed	2	—	—	—	2	—	—	—	—	(B)	(B)
Divorced	128	—	4	24	53	36	1	11	—	78.6	8.6
25 years and over	81 620	1 454	5 023	8 212	26 226	14 033	5 299	13 672	7 702	82.0	26.2
Never married	14 422	308	657	1 582	4 520	2 679	910	2 742	1 025	82.3	26.1
Married, spouse present	53 405	725	3 024	4 910	16 863	9 038	3 576	9 399	5 871	83.8	28.6
Married, spouse absent	3 029	186	326	439	950	483	162	313	170	68.6	16.0
Separated	1 838	70	125	315	657	305	102	175	89	72.2	14.4
Widowed	2 685	158	578	456	812	300	72	193	115	55.6	11.5
Divorced	8 079	77	438	826	3 082	1 532	579	1 025	521	83.4	19.1
25 to 34 years	20 040	194	629	2 008	6 482	3 913	1 564	4 031	1 218	85.9	26.2
Never married	8 102	85	263	825	2 456	1 662	561	1 756	494	85.5	27.8
Married, spouse present	9 866	68	268	922	3 173	1 879	845	2 058	654	87.3	27.5
Married, spouse absent	750	38	83	122	271	109	40	62	26	67.6	11.7
Separated	434	8	24	77	185	67	30	36	6	74.8	9.8
Widowed	31	—	—	4	19	2	2	4	—	(B)	(B)
Divorced	1 291	2	15	135	564	263	116	151	44	88.2	15.1
35 to 44 years	21 793	258	673	1 922	7 604	4 032	1 610	3 771	1 922	86.9	26.1
Never married	3 785	85	123	455	1 378	702	206	596	239	82.5	22.1
Married, spouse present	14 436	136	414	1 092	4 724	2 619	1 147	2 764	1 540	88.6	29.8
Married, spouse absent	953	31	64	140	366	173	59	85	35	75.4	12.7
Separated	658	14	14	112	270	136	37	49	26	78.7	11.3
Widowed	59	1	—	6	14	14	2	17	4	(B)	(B)
Divorced	2 561	5	72	229	1 121	525	196	310	103	88.0	16.1
45 to 54 years	16 119	229	695	1 222	4 722	2 835	1 238	2 935	2 242	86.7	32.1
Never married	1 393	62	82	141	369	190	115	265	169	79.5	31.2
Married, spouse present	11 638	112	456	762	3 365	2 048	898	2 196	1 800	88.6	34.3
Married, spouse absent	648	49	70	85	142	121	33	97	50	68.5	22.7
Separated	395	2	33	68	110	65	29	59	30	74.2	22.5
Widowed	156	3	14	22	46	31	10	21	10	74.8	19.6
Divorced	2 285	3	73	212	801	445	181	356	213	87.4	24.9
55 to 64 years	10 265	258	922	1 097	3 443	1 463	494	1 388	1 199	77.8	25.2
Never married	595	44	76	65	170	61	20	70	89	68.9	26.7
Married, spouse present	7 848	134	626	785	2 708	1 132	378	1 125	961	80.3	26.6
Married, spouse absent	357	36	44	58	99	35	11	45	30	61.3	20.9

See footnotes at end of table.

Table B-3.   Educational Attainment of Persons 15 Years Old and Over, by Marital Status, Age, Sex, Race, and Hispanic Origin: March 1997 — Continued

(Numbers in thousands. Civilian noninstitutional population.)

Marital status, age, sex, race, and Hispanic origin	Total	Elementary		High School		College				Percent:	
		None-4th grade	5th-8th grade	9th-11th grade	High school graduate	Some college no degree	Associate degree	Bachelor's degree	Advanced degree	High school graduate or more	Bachelor's degree or more
Separated	207	28	23	40	54	22	3	27	12	56.2	18.6
Widowed	331	13	60	54	106	40	21	23	14	61.5	11.1
Divorced	1 134	31	116	136	361	195	65	125	106	75.1	20.3
65 years and over	13 404	515	2 103	1 963	3 974	1 789	392	1 546	1 121	65.8	19.9
Never married	548	32	112	95	147	64	8	55	34	56.4	16.4
Married, spouse present	9 617	276	1 260	1 349	2 893	1 360	307	1 256	916	70.0	22.6
Married, spouse absent	322	31	66	34	72	46	20	23	29	59.3	16.3
Separated	143	18	32	18	38	15	3	4	15	52.4	13.3
Widowed	2 108	141	504	370	627	214	38	128	87	51.9	10.2
Divorced	809	35	162	115	235	105	20	82	55	61.4	17.0
Female											
15 to 17 years	5 662	6	1 098	4 460	85	12	—	—	—	1.7	—
Never married	5 570	5	1 079	4 398	79	10	—	—	—	1.6	—
Married, spouse present	40	2	5	31	—	2	—	—	—	(B)	(B)
Married, spouse absent	41	—	13	25	3	—	—	—	—	(B)	(B)
Separated	31	—	8	24	—	—	—	—	—	(B)	(B)
Widowed	2	—	2	—	—	—	—	—	—	(B)	(B)
Divorced	9	—	—	6	3	—	—	—	—	(B)	(B)
18 years and over	101 414	1 453	5 691	11 247	35 174	19 858	7 606	14 702	5 684	81.9	20.1
Never married	20 503	245	528	2 742	5 794	5 891	1 167	3 150	986	82.9	20.2
Married, spouse present	54 626	597	2 388	4 668	20 146	9 401	4 686	9 147	3 591	86.0	23.3
Married, spouse absent	4 122	109	365	728	1 404	773	275	339	128	70.8	11.3
Separated	3 018	72	259	544	1 068	585	206	203	81	71.0	9.4
Widowed	11 056	410	1 959	1 891	3 901	1 366	470	734	325	61.5	9.6
Divorced	11 107	92	451	1 219	3 928	2 426	1 007	1 332	653	84.1	17.9
18 to 24 years	12 452	67	242	2 247	3 813	4 524	498	1 017	45	79.5	8.5
Never married	9 571	36	108	1 753	2 728	3 806	322	792	27	80.2	8.6
Married, spouse present	2 321	27	113	360	873	562	158	211	17	78.5	9.8
Married, spouse absent	318	4	12	109	105	69	11	8	—	60.6	2.6
Separated	214	2	9	77	70	48	4	5	—	59.1	2.2
Widowed	21	—	—	—	14	7	—	—	—	(B)	(B)
Divorced	222	—	9	26	93	81	7	6	1	84.4	2.8
25 years and over	88 961	1 387	5 449	9 000	31 360	15 335	7 107	13 685	5 638	82.2	21.7
Never married	10 932	209	420	989	3 066	2 086	845	2 358	959	85.2	30.3
Married, spouse present	52 305	570	2 275	4 308	19 273	8 840	4 528	8 936	3 574	86.3	23.9
Married, spouse absent	3 804	105	352	619	1 299	704	264	331	128	71.7	12.1
Separated	2 804	70	250	467	999	536	202	199	81	71.9	10.0
Widowed	11 035	410	1 959	1 891	3 886	1 360	470	734	325	61.4	9.6
Divorced	10 885	92	442	1 193	3 835	2 345	1 000	1 326	652	84.1	18.2
25 to 34 years	20 217	150	534	1 615	6 228	4 130	1 917	4 458	1 186	88.6	27.9
Never married	5 778	59	133	499	1 513	1 250	441	1 473	410	88.0	32.6
Married, spouse present	11 761	84	351	789	3 694	2 214	1 209	2 702	718	89.6	29.1
Married, spouse absent	984	5	29	144	393	252	69	73	19	81.9	9.3
Separated	744	2	18	105	304	199	57	51	10	83.2	8.2
Widowed	77	—	3	18	27	13	4	9	2	72.4	14.3
Divorced	1 617	2	17	165	601	401	193	202	37	88.6	14.7
35 to 44 years	22 167	181	627	1 587	7 623	4 262	2 317	3 997	1 573	89.2	25.1
Never married	2 642	40	62	231	810	481	236	532	249	87.4	29.6
Married, spouse present	14 729	107	395	827	5 078	2 736	1 575	2 911	1 100	91.0	27.2
Married, spouse absent	1 256	17	84	192	438	257	113	113	42	76.7	12.3
Separated	1 023	11	71	168	357	223	86	83	25	75.6	10.5
Widowed	278	4	10	31	110	44	43	21	16	83.9	13.1
Divorced	3 262	13	76	306	1 187	744	350	420	166	87.9	17.9
45 to 54 years	16 894	200	691	1 315	6 103	2 942	1 448	2 611	1 584	86.9	24.8
Never married	1 192	36	63	103	338	197	111	195	148	83.0	28.8
Married, spouse present	11 296	113	391	763	4 282	1 892	962	1 804	1 089	88.8	25.6

See footnotes at end of table.

Table B-3. Educational Attainment of Persons 15 Years Old and Over, by Marital Status, Age, Sex, Race, and Hispanic Origin: March 1997 — Continued

(Numbers in thousands. Civilian noninstitutional population.)

Marital status, age, sex, race, and Hispanic origin	Total	Elementary		High School		College				Percent:	
		None-4th grade	5th-8th grade	9th-11th grade	High school graduate	Some college no degree	Associate degree	Bachelor's degree	Advanced degree	High school graduate or more	Bachelor's degree or more
Married, spouse absent	796	25	85	119	266	126	48	81	46	71.3	16.0
Separated	601	16	67	94	213	90	42	46	33	70.6	13.1
Widowed	650	10	45	98	236	105	65	57	33	76.4	13.9
Divorced	2 960	17	106	232	981	622	262	473	267	88.0	25.0
55 to 64 years	11 210	255	824	1 454	4 448	1 686	673	1 194	677	77.4	16.7
Never married	523	32	46	65	148	60	29	65	78	72.7	27.3
Married, spouse present ...	7 151	126	402	823	3 037	1 055	422	861	424	81.1	18.0
Married, spouse absent	366	27	65	87	103	29	13	30	12	51.1	11.4
Separated	273	21	46	70	84	14	9	17	11	49.6	10.3
Widowed	1 485	50	211	232	565	194	86	97	51	66.9	10.0
Divorced	1 685	20	100	247	594	348	123	141	112	78.2	15.0
65 years and over	18 474	601	2 774	3 028	6 959	2 315	753	1 424	620	65.3	11.1
Never married	797	41	116	92	257	98	28	93	74	68.8	20.9
Married, spouse present ...	7 369	141	735	1 106	3 183	943	360	657	243	73.1	12.2
Married, spouse absent	401	32	90	77	90	40	20	34	9	50.5	10.8
Separated	164	20	48	31	41	11	9	2	2	39.6	2.9
Widowed	8 545	347	1 690	1 512	2 948	1 003	272	550	223	58.5	9.0
Divorced	1 361	39	143	242	473	231	73	90	71	68.9	11.8

WHITE

Male

18 years and over	79 765	1 143	4 574	8 749	25 454	15 340	5 041	12 655	6 810	81.9	24.4
Never married	19 739	259	769	2 959	5 815	5 120	1 103	2 863	851	79.8	18.8
Married, spouse present ...	48 471	585	2 710	4 431	15 496	8 257	3 263	8 443	5 287	84.1	28.3
Married, spouse absent	2 365	137	281	336	742	376	117	250	124	68.1	15.8
Separated	1 368	45	95	225	476	227	79	145	75	73.3	16.1
Widowed	2 261	109	458	336	745	263	58	188	104	60.1	12.9
Divorced	6 929	54	355	687	2 656	1 324	499	911	444	84.2	19.6
18 to 24 years	10 194	56	325	2 196	3 139	3 420	399	627	31	74.7	6.5
Never married	8 794	47	228	1 940	2 551	3 129	332	542	26	74.8	6.5
Married, spouse present ...	1 107	7	62	194	471	244	53	71	5	76.2	6.8
Married, spouse absent	106	1	31	45	73	16	14	6	—	58.5	3.1
Separated	110	—	10	31	43	13	7	6	—	62.8	5.3
Widowed	2	—	—	—	2	—	—	—	—	(B)	(B)
Divorced	105	—	4	18	42	32	1	9	—	78.9	8.4
25 years and over	69 571	1 087	4 249	6 552	22 314	11 920	4 641	12 028	6 779	82.9	27.0
Never married	10 945	211	541	1 019	3 263	1 991	772	2 322	824	83.8	28.7
Married, spouse present ...	47 364	578	2 647	4 237	15 024	8 013	3 210	8 372	5 282	84.2	28.8
Married, spouse absent	2 179	136	251	291	669	360	103	244	124	68.9	16.9
Separated	1 258	45	85	194	433	214	72	139	75	74.2	17.0
Widowed	2 259	109	458	336	743	263	58	188	104	60.0	12.9
Divorced	6 825	54	351	668	2 615	1 292	499	902	444	84.3	19.7
25 to 34 years	16 449	147	570	1 587	5 230	3 114	1 371	3 490	940	86.0	26.9
Never married	6 112	58	237	554	1 762	1 213	477	1 460	350	86.1	29.6
Married, spouse present ...	8 724	65	249	835	2 798	1 634	760	1 842	542	86.8	27.3
Married, spouse absent	532	23	69	84	196	71	31	43	15	66.9	11.0
Separated	303	2	17	51	131	42	26	28	5	76.7	10.9
Widowed	23	—	—	—	16	2	—	4	—	(B)	(B)
Divorced	1 058	2	15	113	457	195	103	140	33	87.7	16.4
35 to 44 years	18 314	203	564	1 521	6 345	3 347	1 414	3 275	1 645	87.5	26.9
Never married	2 829	54	96	306	964	511	176	516	205	83.9	25.5
Married, spouse present ...	12 611	118	354	923	4 152	2 281	1 031	2 411	1 340	88.9	29.7
Married, spouse absent	663	26	51	95	246	125	38	64	17	74.0	12.3
Separated	443	14	10	72	174	92	26	38	17	78.3	12.5
Widowed	51	1	—	6	14	9	2	14	4	(B)	(B)
Divorced	2 159	4	62	190	969	421	167	269	78	88.1	16.0

See footnotes at end of table.

Table B-3. Educational Attainment of Persons 15 Years Old and Over, by Marital Status, Age, Sex, Race, and Hispanic Origin: March 1997 — Continued

(Numbers in thousands. Civilian noninstitutional population.)

Marital status, age, sex, race, and Hispanic origin	Total	Elementary		High School		College				Percent:	
		None–4th grade	5th–8th grade	9th–11th grade	High school graduate	Some college no degree	Associate degree	Bachelor's degree	Advanced degree	High school graduate or more	Bachelor's degree or more
45 to 54 years	13 882	189	578	911	4 006	2 506	1 092	2 560	2 040	87.9	33.1
Never married	1 099	51	58	60	285	159	99	231	156	84.6	35.2
Married, spouse present	10 206	82	398	614	2 923	1 816	808	1 926	1 639	89.3	34.9
Married, spouse absent	504	49	58	58	95	100	25	75	45	67.3	23.8
Separated	278	2	23	41	65	51	20	48	28	76.4	27.3
Widowed	134	3	12	13	43	25	7	21	10	79.1	23.0
Divorced	1 939	3	53	165	661	407	153	305	191	88.6	25.6
55 to 64 years	8 904	184	747	846	3 048	1 304	418	1 256	1 102	80.1	26.5
Never married	439	27	50	33	123	47	12	65	82	74.9	33.5
Married, spouse present	6 980	110	536	643	2 441	1 009	331	1 020	892	81.5	27.4
Married, spouse absent	257	20	36	29	74	29	4	38	27	66.8	25.3
Separated	142	17	19	17	37	19	—	22	12	62.8	23.7
Widowed	250	11	35	31	87	36	14	23	14	69.2	14.6
Divorced	978	15	90	111	324	183	57	111	88	78.0	20.3
65 years and over	12 022	364	1 790	1 689	3 685	1 648	347	1 447	1 052	68.0	20.8
Never married	466	22	100	66	129	61	8	49	32	59.8	17.2
Married, spouse present	8 843	203	1 111	1 223	2 711	1 273	280	1 173	870	71.3	23.1
Married, spouse absent	223	17	37	25	58	36	6	23	20	64.4	19.4
Separated	92	10	16	13	26	10	—	4	13	57.5	18.1
Widowed	1 801	93	411	286	583	191	35	126	76	56.1	11.2
Divorced	690	29	131	89	204	87	18	77	55	63.8	19.1
Female											
18 years and over	84 285	1 101	4 685	8 653	29 517	16 442	6 393	12 575	4 918	82.9	20.8
Never married	14 735	173	416	1 712	3 929	4 367	838	2 478	820	84.4	22.4
Married, spouse present	48 276	494	2 079	4 028	18 008	8 361	4 136	8 034	3 135	86.3	23.1
Married, spouse absent	2 653	83	218	457	884	477	188	250	96	71.4	13.0
Separated	1 873	57	149	310	644	351	145	149	68	72.4	11.6
Widowed	9 401	289	1 612	1 532	3 447	1 200	393	644	285	63.5	9.9
Divorced	9 220	61	361	923	3 249	2 037	837	1 170	582	85.4	19.0
18 to 24 years	9 798	60	224	1 615	2 971	3 638	419	833	37	80.6	8.9
Never married	7 283	29	98	1 206	2 012	3 017	255	644	22	81.7	9.1
Married, spouse present	2 064	27	108	308	780	501	147	179	14	78.5	9.4
Married, spouse absent	243	4	11	77	88	45	10	7	—	62.0	2.9
Separated	166	2	8	50	60	37	4	5	—	63.8	2.9
Widowed	10	—	—	—	10	—	—	—	—	(B)	(B)
Divorced	198	—	7	25	81	75	7	2	1	83.9	1.5
25 years and over	74 487	1 040	4 461	7 038	26 546	12 804	5 974	11 743	4 881	83.2	22.3
Never married	7 452	144	318	507	1 918	1 350	584	1 834	798	87.0	35.3
Married, spouse present	46 212	467	1 970	3 721	17 228	7 860	3 990	7 855	3 121	86.7	23.8
Married, spouse absent	2 409	79	207	379	796	432	177	243	96	72.4	14.1
Separated	1 707	55	141	259	584	314	141	144	68	73.3	12.4
Widowed	9 391	289	1 612	1 532	3 437	1 200	393	644	285	63.4	9.9
Divorced	9 022	61	354	898	3 167	1 963	830	1 167	582	85.4	19.4
25 to 34 years	16 189	122	436	1 197	4 893	3 256	1 545	3 757	983	89.2	29.3
Never married	3 930	36	101	249	921	830	304	1 162	326	90.2	37.9
Married, spouse present	10 199	79	296	698	3 200	1 932	1 031	2 357	606	89.5	29.0
Married, spouse absent	637	5	23	105	247	147	45	55	12	79.3	10.5
Separated	470	2	16	71	181	115	39	39	7	81.1	9.8
Widowed	66	—	2	15	24	12	2	9	2	(B)	(B)
Divorced	1 357	2	14	130	502	336	163	174	36	89.2	15.5
35 to 44 years	18 124	144	528	1 177	6 237	3 373	1 902	3 401	1 363	89.8	26.3
Never married	1 655	31	49	119	449	251	150	390	216	87.9	36.6
Married, spouse present	12 826	90	353	675	4 462	2 348	1 386	2 557	955	91.3	27.4
Married, spouse absent	766	16	59	122	250	147	68	72	30	74.2	13.4
Separated	621	11	47	106	204	125	54	55	20	73.7	12.0
Widowed	218	4	10	21	94	30	24	19	16	83.8	15.9

See footnotes at end of table.

Table B-3. Educational Attainment of Persons 15 Years Old and Over, by Marital Status, Age, Sex, Race, and Hispanic Origin: March 1997 — Continued

(Numbers in thousands. Civilian noninstitutional population.)

Marital status, age, sex, race, and Hispanic origin	Total	Elementary		High School		College				Percent:	
		None-4th grade	5th-8th grade	9th-11th grade	High school graduate	Some college no degree	Associate degree	Bachelor's degree	Advanced degree	High school graduate or more	Bachelor's degree or more
Divorced	2 660	4	56	239	982	596	274	363	146	88.8	19.1
45 to 54 years	14 189	161	543	948	5 109	2 528	1 252	2 240	1 408	88.4	25.7
Never married	842	31	44	46	220	143	79	152	127	85.6	33.2
Married, spouse present	9 961	93	335	629	3 770	1 708	862	1 575	989	89.4	25.7
Married, spouse absent	503	17	49	52	167	82	40	59	37	76.6	19.1
Separated	377	12	42	36	130	59	37	31	30	76.1	16.2
Widowed	458	7	31	53	180	71	49	44	22	80.0	14.3
Divorced	2 425	13	84	168	771	524	222	410	233	89.1	26.5
55 to 64 years	9 543	183	627	1 129	3 913	1 487	585	1 034	585	79.7	17.0
Never married	366	22	37	24	103	39	24	52	64	77.2	31.7
Married, spouse present	6 391	94	336	712	2 786	970	376	751	366	82.1	17.5
Married, spouse absent	232	24	27	53	59	26	6	27	9	55.3	15.8
Separated	164	18	18	39	48	11	4	17	9	54.1	15.5
Widowed	1 146	31	144	171	469	146	72	70	43	69.8	9.8
Divorced	1 408	11	83	169	496	304	107	134	104	81.3	16.9
65 years and over	16 442	430	2 328	2 586	6 395	2 160	690	1 311	543	67.5	11.3
Never married	660	24	86	68	226	87	27	77	65	72.9	21.5
Married, spouse present	6 835	110	651	1 006	3 011	902	334	616	205	74.2	12.0
Married, spouse absent	270	17	49	48	72	30	18	29	7	57.7	13.4
Separated	75	13	18	8	20	5	6	2	2	(B)	(B)
Widowed	7 503	247	1 424	1 272	2 669	940	246	503	202	60.8	9.4
Divorced	1 172	31	117	191	417	201	65	86	63	71.0	12.8

BLACK

Male

18 years and over	10 183	270	613	1 904	3 740	2 103	463	800	290	72.6	10.7
Never married	4 224	89	113	984	1 650	1 000	107	220	62	71.9	6.7
Married, spouse present	3 955	84	270	545	1 398	767	246	476	168	77.3	16.3
Married, spouse absent	659	35	47	139	251	113	25	31	19	66.5	7.5
Separated	508	13	38	116	201	90	23	21	7	67.2	5.5
Widowed	340	39	106	96	55	22	15	3	4	29.1	1.9
Divorced	1 006	22	77	140	386	201	70	71	38	76.2	10.8
18 to 24 years	1 738	18	25	502	655	482	19	37	—	68.6	2.1
Never married	1 585	18	21	468	578	452	16	32	—	68.1	2.0
Married, spouse present	120	—	5	23	67	20	2	3	—	76.6	2.3
Married, spouse absent	14	—	—	6	2	7	—	—	—	(B)	(B)
Separated	7	—	—	3	—	4	—	—	—	(B)	(B)
Widowed	—	—	—	—	—	—	—	—	—	(B)	(B)
Divorced	18	—	—	5	8	3	—	2	—	(B)	(B)
25 years and over	8 446	253	588	1 401	3 085	1 622	444	763	290	73.5	12.5
Never married	2 640	72	92	516	1 072	548	90	188	62	74.2	9.5
Married, spouse present	3 835	84	265	522	1 331	747	244	473	168	77.3	16.7
Married, spouse absent	644	35	47	133	248	106	25	31	19	66.6	7.7
Separated	501	13	38	113	201	86	23	21	7	67.4	5.6
Widowed	340	39	106	96	55	22	15	3	4	29.1	1.9
Divorced	988	22	77	134	378	199	70	68	38	76.3	10.8
25 to 34 years	2 414	23	25	338	1 004	605	132	228	59	84.0	11.9
Never married	1 389	14	11	242	576	346	47	125	28	80.8	11.0
Married, spouse present	698	—	6	47	284	181	65	93	22	92.4	16.5
Married, spouse absent	141	9	8	28	56	30	4	3	4	68.5	4.8
Separated	96	—	7	19	41	23	4	3	—	73.7	3.4
Widowed	8	—	—	3	3	—	2	—	—	(B)	(B)
Divorced	178	—	—	18	84	49	13	8	5	90.0	7.4
35 to 44 years	2 483	30	80	340	1 025	541	125	272	70	81.9	13.8
Never married	815	25	27	138	370	167	21	51	16	76.6	8.2
Married, spouse present	1 117	—	39	127	425	233	74	183	37	85.1	19.7

See footnotes at end of table.

Table B-3. Educational Attainment of Persons 15 Years Old and Over, by Marital Status, Age, Sex, Race, and Hispanic Origin: March 1997 — Continued

(Numbers in thousands. Civilian noninstitutional population.)

Marital status, age, sex, race, and Hispanic origin	Total	Elementary		High School		College				Percent:	
		None-4th grade	5th-8th grade	9th-11th grade	High school graduate	Some college no degree	Associate degree	Bachelor's degree	Advanced degree	High school graduate or more	Bachelor's degree or more
Married, spouse absent	231	5	5	42	114	43	7	13	3	77.6	6.6
Separated	198	—	4	40	92	43	7	9	3	77.8	6.0
Widowed	7	—	—	—	—	5	—	3	—	(B)	(B)
Divorced	313	—	10	32	117	93	23	23	15	86.7	12.1
45 to 54 years	1 587	22	86	278	569	261	109	182	79	75.7	16.4
Never married	240	7	20	79	68	28	14	13	11	55.6	9.8
Married, spouse present ...	948	14	45	125	333	180	60	132	58	80.6	20.1
Married, spouse absent	119	—	8	27	39	22	8	10	4	70.8	12.3
Separated	102	—	8	27	39	14	8	3	2	66.1	5.6
Widowed	15	—	—	9	3	1	3	—	—	(B)	(B)
Divorced	265	—	13	39	126	31	24	26	7	80.4	12.4
55 to 64 years	948	55	132	224	278	114	58	46	41	56.6	9.2
Never married	131	16	23	32	41	7	8	—	4	46.0	3.3
Married, spouse present ...	533	12	49	121	170	93	33	32	23	65.8	10.3
Married, spouse absent	85	11	8	28	25	3	3	5	3	45.4	8.7
Separated	56	5	4	22	17	1	3	5	—	(B)	(B)
Widowed	70	—	25	23	14	1	7	—	—	(B)	(B)
Divorced	128	16	26	20	28	9	8	9	11	50.8	16.3
65 years and over	1 014	123	264	221	209	100	20	35	40	39.9	7.5
Never married	65	9	10	25	17	—	—	—	3	(B)	(B)
Married, spouse present ...	538	58	126	101	119	60	12	33	28	46.9	11.5
Married, spouse absent	68	10	19	9	13	8	3	—	6	(B)	(B)
Separated	49	7	16	5	12	5	2	—	2	(B)	(B)
Widowed	238	39	81	60	36	16	2	—	4	24.4	1.6
Divorced	104	6	28	25	24	16	2	2	—	42.4	1.9
Female											
18 years and over	12 589	161	692	2 207	4 452	2 621	880	1 144	432	75.7	12.5
Never married	4 680	49	89	910	1 675	1 190	242	426	99	77.6	11.2
Married, spouse present ...	3 805	20	134	469	1 382	718	358	496	227	83.6	19.0
Married, spouse absent	1 235	11	120	239	467	254	68	55	20	70.0	6.0
Separated	1 017	7	97	210	385	213	52	38	13	69.1	5.1
Widowed	1 307	71	281	317	361	130	66	52	28	48.8	6.2
Divorced	1 563	11	67	271	567	329	145	115	58	77.6	11.0
18 to 24 years	1 963	3	5	502	701	602	53	90	5	74.0	4.9
Never married	1 733	3	4	454	614	537	43	72	5	73.4	4.5
Married, spouse present ...	146	—	—	27	59	36	9	15	—	81.4	10.1
Married, spouse absent	59	—	1	20	16	21	1	—	—	(B)	(B)
Separated	37	—	1	18	9	9	—	—	—	(B)	(B)
Widowed	5	—	—	—	4	2	—	—	—	(B)	(B)
Divorced	20	—	—	1	9	6	—	3	—	(B)	(B)
25 years and over	10 626	158	686	1 704	3 750	2 019	828	1 054	427	76.0	13.9
Never married	2 947	46	85	455	1 062	653	199	354	94	80.1	15.2
Married, spouse present ...	3 659	20	134	442	1 323	682	350	481	227	83.7	19.3
Married, spouse absent	1 176	11	119	219	451	233	68	55	20	70.3	6.3
Separated	980	7	96	192	376	205	52	38	13	69.9	5.3
Widowed	1 302	71	281	317	357	129	66	52	28	48.6	6.2
Divorced	1 543	11	67	270	557	322	145	111	58	77.4	11.0
25 to 34 years	2 936	16	40	362	1 071	721	269	391	67	85.8	15.6
Never married	1 513	16	19	234	538	370	89	203	45	82.2	16.4
Married, spouse present ...	899	—	13	62	318	206	129	152	18	91.7	19.0
Married, spouse absent	308	—	4	36	139	89	24	13	4	87.2	5.5
Separated	260	—	1	32	122	77	17	8	3	87.4	4.4
Widowed	9	—	1	3	2	—	2	—	—	(B)	(B)
Divorced	206	—	3	27	73	55	25	22	—	85.5	10.8
35 to 44 years	2 932	12	64	329	1 071	713	304	337	103	86.2	15.0
Never married	871	5	10	104	342	216	77	98	19	86.2	13.4

See footnotes at end of table.

Table B-3. Educational Attainment of Persons 15 Years Old and Over, by Marital Status, Age, Sex, Race, and Hispanic Origin: March 1997 — Continued

(Numbers in thousands. Civilian noninstitutional population.)

Marital status, age, sex, race, and Hispanic origin	Total	Elementary		High School		College				Percent:	
		None-4th grade	5th-8th grade	9th-11th grade	High school graduate	Some college no degree	Associate degree	Bachelor's degree	Advanced degree	High school graduate or more	Bachelor's degree or more
Married, spouse present ...	1 125	—	19	102	387	259	116	174	67	89.2	21.5
Married, spouse absent	408	1	24	57	166	101	30	22	5	79.7	6.8
Separated	347	—	24	51	131	92	25	19	5	78.3	6.9
Widowed	57	—	—	10	14	14	18	2	—	(B)	(B)
Divorced	472	5	10	56	162	122	63	40	12	84.9	11.1
45 to 54 years	1 937	12	96	308	746	323	153	178	121	78.5	15.5
Never married	300	4	17	55	112	41	31	30	11	74.8	13.4
Married, spouse present ...	797	6	19	90	321	141	66	85	68	85.6	19.3
Married, spouse absent	239	1	31	65	85	32	4	15	6	59.7	8.9
Separated	197	1	22	56	74	28	3	11	2	59.8	6.9
Widowed	147	—	13	37	38	31	16	6	5	65.6	8.0
Divorced	455	2	15	61	191	77	35	42	31	82.8	16.1
55 to 64 years	1 219	19	128	306	425	149	53	68	70	62.8	11.3
Never married	139	7	8	39	44	18	2	9	12	61.1	15.2
Married, spouse present ...	461	2	26	99	174	51	23	44	42	72.5	18.6
Married, spouse absent	112	1	23	33	43	2	7	1	3	49.6	2.9
Separated	98	1	21	30	36	2	5	—	3	46.9	2.8
Widowed	266	8	57	60	81	37	5	11	7	53.2	6.7
Divorced	241	1	15	76	84	41	15	2	8	61.9	4.2
65 years and over	1 603	99	359	399	437	113	49	80	66	46.5	9.1
Never married	124	14	30	23	27	8	—	14	8	46.2	18.1
Married, spouse present ...	377	12	57	89	124	23	15	26	31	57.9	15.0
Married, spouse absent	109	8	37	29	18	9	2	3	2	31.6	5.1
Separated	78	5	28	23	14	6	2	—	—	28.5	—
Widowed	823	62	210	207	222	46	26	33	16	41.7	6.0
Divorced	169	2	24	50	47	27	6	4	7	54.3	6.8
HISPANIC ORIGIN [1]											
Male											
18 years and over	9 741	768	1 781	1 916	2 490	1 494	424	591	278	54.2	8.9
Never married	3 482	152	476	905	887	672	136	200	54	56.0	7.3
Married, spouse present ...	4 030	403	942	709	1 277	601	215	342	191	55.6	11.0
Married, spouse absent	714	126	223	139	148	53	8	11	6	31.7	2.3
Separated	272	37	58	73	72	20	6	5	1	38.7	2.4
Widowed	146	41	54	14	22	8	5	—	1	25.2	1.1
Divorced	568	16	86	89	155	99	60	38	26	66.4	11.2
18 to 24 years	1 986	56	255	653	486	449	40	42	4	51.4	2.3
Never married	1 635	49	172	560	390	392	34	36	3	52.2	2.4
Married, spouse present ...	270	5	53	75	76	49	5	5	1	50.6	2.2
Married, spouse absent	60	1	26	17	12	2	—	—	—	(B)	(B)
Separated	17	—	5	8	2	2	—	—	—	(B)	(B)
Widowed	2	—	—	—	2	—	—	—	—	(B)	(B)
Divorced	19	—	3	2	7	6	—	2	—	(B)	(B)
25 years and over	7 755	712	1 526	1 263	2 003	1 045	384	548	274	54.9	10.6
Never married	1 847	103	304	346	498	280	101	164	51	59.3	11.6
Married, spouse present ...	4 561	428	888	695	1 201	612	210	337	190	55.9	11.6
Married, spouse absent	654	124	197	122	136	50	8	11	6	32.3	2.5
Separated	255	37	52	65	70	18	6	5	1	39.7	2.6
Widowed	145	41	54	14	20	8	5	—	1	24.4	1.1
Divorced	550	16	83	87	148	94	60	36	26	66.1	11.2
25 to 34 years	2 904	122	461	591	817	453	152	244	63	59.6	10.6
Never married	1 201	39	194	237	300	215	74	123	17	60.8	11.7
Married, spouse present ...	1 413	60	191	290	441	210	66	109	46	61.7	11.0
Married, spouse absent	192	23	69	39	45	9	1	7	—	32.0	3.7
Separated	52	2	14	14	15	1	1	4	—	(B)	(B)
Widowed	3	—	—	—	3	—	—	—	—	(B)	(B)
Divorced	94	—	7	24	28	19	10	5	—	66.7	5.5

See footnotes at end of table.

Table B-3. Educational Attainment of Persons 15 Years Old and Over, by Marital Status, Age, Sex, Race, and Hispanic Origin: March 1997 — Continued

(Numbers in thousands. Civilian noninstitutional population.)

Marital status, age, sex, race, and Hispanic origin	Total	Elementary		High School		College				Percent:	
		None-4th grade	5th-8th grade	9th-11th grade	High school graduate	Some college no degree	Associate degree	Bachelor's degree	Advanced degree	High school graduate or more	Bachelor's degree or more
35 to 44 years	2 253	167	420	337	635	337	119	152	86	59.0	10.6
Never married	445	26	57	82	167	44	16	33	20	62.8	11.8
Married, spouse present	1 437	118	299	197	353	238	73	104	56	57.2	11.1
Married, spouse absent	166	22	41	33	48	12	7	3	—	42.6	2.1
Separated	74	10	3	23	29	3	5	1	—	(B)	(B)
Widowed	4	1	—	—	2	1	—	—	—	(B)	(B)
Divorced	200	—	23	24	66	42	22	11	11	76.1	11.1
45 to 54 years	1 218	125	267	156	289	152	76	87	66	55.0	12.6
Never married	112	11	23	20	19	19	11	3	6	50.9	7.8
Married, spouse present	782	66	170	83	212	96	43	70	42	59.2	14.3
Married, spouse absent	160	47	47	34	13	14	—	—	5	20.0	3.1
Separated	52	2	19	17	6	8	—	—	—	(B)	(B)
Widowed	18	1	6	1	3	3	4	—	—	(B)	(B)
Divorced	146	—	20	17	42	20	19	15	12	74.4	18.8
55 to 64 years	741	132	182	110	152	61	26	45	33	42.8	10.5
Never married	57	17	16	5	7	1	—	6	4	(B)	(B)
Married, spouse present	515	87	123	73	115	38	18	36	25	45.0	12.0
Married, spouse absent	93	20	24	15	22	13	—	—	—	36.8	—
Separated	55	17	8	12	14	5	—	—	—	(B)	(B)
Widowed	21	6	4	5	1	3	—	—	1	(B)	(B)
Divorced	55	2	15	11	7	7	8	3	2	(B)	(B)
65 years and over	640	165	196	70	110	42	12	20	25	32.6	7.1
Never married	32	8	13	1	5	2	—	—	3	(B)	(B)
Married, spouse present	413	97	105	50	80	31	10	19	20	38.9	9.4
Married, spouse absent	42	12	16	1	9	3	—	—	1	(B)	(B)
Separated	24	6	8	—	7	2	—	—	1	(B)	(B)
Widowed	99	33	44	8	11	1	1	—	—	13.9	—
Divorced	54	15	18	10	5	6	—	2	—	(B)	(B)
Female											
18 years and over	9 362	778	1 680	1 708	2 515	1 398	466	637	180	55.5	8.7
Never married	2 360	109	252	518	682	509	101	148	41	62.7	8.0
Married, spouse present	4 879	400	961	781	1 308	659	257	398	116	56.1	10.5
Married, spouse absent	673	75	164	167	140	68	30	25	4	39.6	4.3
Separated	499	56	125	126	103	49	28	9	3	38.5	2.4
Widowed	575	146	173	85	115	23	7	19	6	29.6	4.3
Divorced	875	48	130	156	271	139	71	46	13	61.8	6.8
18 to 24 years	1 640	42	152	468	508	389	44	33	6	59.7	2.3
Never married	1 139	20	57	311	377	322	31	20	1	65.9	1.8
Married, spouse present	417	18	84	124	105	57	13	12	4	45.9	3.8
Married, spouse absent	63	4	10	24	19	5	—	1	—	(B)	(B)
Separated	32	2	6	9	11	3	—	—	—	(B)	(B)
Widowed	—	—	—	—	—	—	—	—	—	(B)	(B)
Divorced	22	—	1	10	7	5	—	—	—	(B)	(B)
25 years and over	7 721	736	1 528	1 240	2 007	1 009	421	605	174	54.6	10.1
Never married	1 221	89	195	208	304	187	70	129	39	59.8	13.8
Married, spouse present	4 462	382	877	657	1 203	602	243	386	111	57.1	11.2
Married, spouse absent	610	71	155	143	121	63	30	24	4	39.6	4.6
Separated	467	54	119	117	92	45	28	9	3	38.0	2.5
Widowed	575	146	173	85	115	23	7	19	6	29.6	4.3
Divorced	853	48	129	146	265	134	71	46	13	62.1	7.0
25 to 34 years	2 591	115	340	503	698	434	175	260	66	63.0	12.6
Never married	685	29	73	125	178	117	47	86	31	66.9	17.0
Married, spouse present	1 580	79	230	308	422	251	99	156	34	60.9	12.0
Married, spouse absent	159	5	25	42	44	25	7	12	—	55.1	7.4
Separated	109	2	18	27	29	23	7	4	—	56.7	3.3
Widowed	12	—	1	6	2	3	—	—	—	(B)	(B)

See footnotes at end of table.

Table B-3. Educational Attainment of Persons 15 Years Old and Over, by Marital Status, Age, Sex, Race, and Hispanic Origin: March 1997 — Continued

(Numbers in thousands. Civilian noninstitutional population.)

Marital status, age, sex, race, and Hispanic origin	Total	Elementary		High School		College				Percent:	
		None-4th grade	5th-8th grade	9th-11th grade	High school graduate	Some college no degree	Associate degree	Bachelor's degree	Advanced degree	High school graduate or more	Bachelor's degree or more
Divorced	155	2	10	22	52	39	23	6	1	77.6	4.4
35 to 44 years	2 135	118	410	304	614	326	129	187	47	61.0	11.0
Never married	269	15	48	54	77	42	6	23	3	56.3	9.8
Married, spouse present ...	1 343	83	273	129	387	217	81	137	37	63.9	13.0
Married, spouse absent	210	14	44	65	42	19	17	7	3	41.8	4.6
Separated	169	9	31	59	38	11	17	3	1	41.3	2.4
Widowed	27	2	4	8	8	3	—	1	—	(B)	(B)
Divorced	285	5	41	48	99	46	23	19	4	67.0	7.9
45 to 54 years	1 242	114	296	164	317	156	72	88	34	53.7	9.9
Never married	121	13	26	14	20	21	13	14	1	56.4	12.4
Married, spouse present ...	763	72	177	100	203	85	40	58	27	54.2	11.2
Married, spouse absent	117	17	42	19	20	10	5	1	2	32.7	2.2
Separated	97	12	36	16	17	9	4	1	2	33.2	2.6
Widowed	44	6	14	6	13	1	1	3	—	(B)	(B)
Divorced	198	6	36	26	62	39	12	13	4	65.4	8.8
55 to 64 years	877	142	229	144	222	54	31	40	14	41.1	6.2
Never married	81	13	25	8	17	7	3	5	2	42.7	8.2
Married, spouse present ...	475	78	119	68	134	31	13	22	9	44.1	6.4
Married, spouse absent	75	18	27	14	9	5	—	2	—	(B)	(B)
Separated	57	17	19	13	6	1	—	2	—	(B)	(B)
Widowed	108	25	33	17	23	3	2	5	—	30.3	4.6
Divorced	138	8	25	37	38	8	12	7	3	49.5	7.7
65 years and over	876	247	252	124	157	39	15	29	14	28.8	4.8
Never married	66	20	22	7	12	1	—	1	3	(B)	(B)
Married, spouse present ...	300	70	76	52	56	17	10	14	4	33.7	6.0
Married, spouse absent	50	17	17	4	6	4	—	3	—	(B)	(B)
Separated	34	14	14	1	3	2	—	—	—	(B)	(B)
Widowed	384	114	121	49	68	14	4	10	5	26.4	4.1
Divorced	76	27	17	12	14	3	1	1	1	26.5	3.2

Source: March 1997 Current Population Survey, Education and Social Stratification Branch, U.S. Bureau of the Census.

1. May be of any race.

— Represents zero or rounds to zero.

(B) Base less than 75,000.

Table B-4.   Educational Attainment of Persons 15 Years Old and Over, by Household Relationship, Age, Sex, Race, and Hispanic Origin: March 1997

(Numbers in thousands. Civilian noninstitutional population.)

Household relationship, age, sex, race, and Hispanic origin	Total	Elementary		High School		College				Percent:	
		None-4th grade	5th-8th grade	9th-11th grade	High school graduate	Some college no degree	Associate degree	Bachelor's degree	Advanced degree	High school graduate or more	Bachelor's degree or more
ALL RACES											
Male											
15 to 17 years	6 004	15	1 385	4 536	59	9	—	—	—	1.1	—
Householder	33	—	3	31	—	—	—	—	—	(B)	(B)
Family householder	28	—	2	27	—	—	—	—	—	(B)	(B)
Married, spouse present ..	5	—	—	5	—	—	—	—	—	(B)	(B)
Nonfamily householder	5	—	1	4	—	—	—	—	—	(B)	(B)
Living alone	—	—	—	—	—	—	—	—	—	(B)	(B)
Spouse	3	—	—	3	—	—	—	—	—	(B)	(B)
Other relative	5 804	15	1 329	4 400	51	9	—	—	—	1.0	—
Nonrelative	165	—	54	103	8	—	—	—	—	5.0	—
18 years and over	94 105	1 530	5 372	11 006	30 181	18 163	5 731	14 387	7 735	81.0	23.5
Householder	60 040	837	3 435	5 628	18 791	10 851	4 093	10 369	6 037	83.5	27.3
Family householder	46 338	638	2 597	4 342	14 822	8 116	3 146	7 832	4 844	83.6	27.4
Married, spouse present ..	42 514	548	2 333	3 786	13 446	7 417	2 925	7 432	4 628	84.3	28.4
Nonfamily householder	13 702	200	838	1 285	3 968	2 735	946	2 537	1 192	83.0	27.2
Living alone	10 442	163	729	1 020	2 973	1 996	710	1 854	995	81.7	27.3
Spouse	11 082	147	617	1 157	3 592	1 718	678	1 954	1 219	82.7	28.6
Other relative	17 290	433	938	3 534	5 878	4 406	678	1 195	228	71.6	8.2
Nonrelative	5 693	112	382	688	1 921	1 188	282	870	252	79.2	19.7
18 to 24 years	12 502	76	349	2 798	3 960	4 136	432	716	36	74.2	6.0
Householder	2 375	11	73	325	857	674	139	277	20	82.8	12.5
Family householder	1 190	3	52	227	491	282	54	73	7	76.2	6.7
Married, spouse present ..	827	2	40	133	365	183	43	56	5	78.8	7.3
Nonfamily householder	1 185	7	20	98	365	392	85	204	13	89.4	18.2
Living alone	565	6	14	46	157	202	49	85	7	88.4	16.2
Spouse	295	4	15	46	131	70	11	18	—	78.1	6.0
Other relative	8 514	45	189	2 179	2 600	2 997	239	256	9	71.7	3.1
Nonrelative	1 318	16	73	248	372	394	43	165	7	74.4	13.0
25 years and over	81 604	1 454	5 023	8 208	26 221	14 027	5 299	13 672	7 700	82.0	26.2
Householder	57 665	826	3 363	5 302	17 934	10 177	3 954	10 092	6 017	83.5	27.9
Family householder	45 148	634	2 545	4 115	14 331	7 834	3 093	7 759	4 837	83.8	27.9
Married, spouse present ..	41 687	546	2 293	3 652	13 080	7 234	2 882	7 376	4 623	84.4	28.8
Nonfamily householder	12 517	192	818	1 187	3 603	2 343	861	2 333	1 180	82.4	28.1
Living alone	9 877	158	715	974	2 816	1 794	661	1 769	989	81.3	27.9
Spouse	10 787	144	602	1 111	3 461	1 647	667	1 936	1 219	82.8	29.3
Other relative	8 777	388	749	1 355	3 278	1 410	439	939	219	71.6	13.2
Nonrelative	4 375	96	309	440	1 549	793	239	705	245	80.7	21.7
25 to 34 years	20 029	194	629	2 004	6 480	3 911	1 564	4 031	1 215	85.9	26.2
Householder	11 847	77	260	952	3 613	2 389	1 071	2 600	886	89.1	29.4
Family householder	8 313	65	204	759	2 666	1 645	767	1 679	529	87.6	26.6
Married, spouse present ..	7 280	40	165	600	2 293	1 435	687	1 568	492	88.9	28.3
Nonfamily householder	3 534	12	56	192	948	744	304	921	356	92.6	36.1
Living alone	2 235	7	29	107	607	458	189	585	252	93.6	37.5
Spouse	2 228	18	74	255	750	367	150	466	149	84.4	27.6
Other relative	3 976	65	193	589	1 496	777	225	560	72	78.7	15.9
Nonrelative	1 979	34	103	208	621	378	119	406	109	82.6	26.1
35 to 44 years	21 788	258	673	1 922	7 602	4 029	1 610	3 771	1 922	86.9	26.1
Householder	15 037	121	400	1 138	4 953	2 907	1 216	2 819	1 483	89.0	28.6
Family householder	12 033	108	333	902	3 947	2 265	1 005	2 223	1 250	88.8	28.9
Married, spouse present ..	11 032	95	295	762	3 513	2 091	936	2 132	1 208	89.6	30.3
Nonfamily householder	3 004	13	67	236	1 007	641	210	596	233	89.5	27.6
Living alone	2 380	13	45	182	774	517	163	478	209	89.9	28.9
Spouse	3 211	32	93	301	1 139	493	207	618	328	86.7	29.4
Other relative	2 306	73	100	380	1 007	397	126	167	57	76.0	9.7
Nonrelative	1 234	31	80	103	503	232	62	167	55	82.6	18.0

See footnotes at end of table.

Table B-4. Educational Attainment of Persons 15 Years Old and Over, by Household Relationship, Age, Sex, Race, and Hispanic Origin: March 1997 — Continued

(Numbers in thousands. Civilian noninstitutional population.)

Household relationship, age, sex, race, and Hispanic origin	Total	Elementary		High School		College				Percent:	
		None-4th grade	5th-8th grade	9th-11th grade	High school graduate	Some college no degree	Associate degree	Bachelor's degree	Advanced degree	High school graduate or more	Bachelor's degree or more
45 to 64 years	26 383	487	1 617	2 319	8 165	4 298	1 732	4 324	3 441	83.2	29.4
Householder	20 047	262	1 091	1 653	6 187	3 367	1 356	3 398	2 734	85.0	30.6
Family householder	16 539	207	895	1 299	5 231	2 729	1 081	2 800	2 296	85.5	30.8
Married, spouse present	15 503	181	817	1 187	4 905	2 561	1 026	2 646	2 180	85.9	31.1
Nonfamily householder	3 508	55	195	354	957	637	274	598	438	82.8	29.5
Living alone	2 947	33	166	305	788	522	240	509	385	82.9	30.3
Spouse	3 745	52	227	331	1 087	595	240	642	570	83.7	32.4
Other relative	1 695	151	228	259	535	192	83	180	68	62.4	14.6
Nonrelative	897	22	72	76	355	145	53	104	69	81.0	19.2
65 years and over	13 404	515	2 103	1 963	3 974	1 789	392	1 546	1 121	65.8	19.9
Householder	10 733	366	1 612	1 559	3 180	1 514	312	1 276	914	67.0	20.4
Family householder	8 262	254	1 113	1 155	2 488	1 194	240	1 057	761	69.5	22.0
Married, spouse present	7 872	229	1 015	1 104	2 369	1 147	232	1 031	743	70.2	22.5
Nonfamily householder	2 471	112	499	404	692	320	73	218	153	58.9	15.0
Living alone	2 014	105	474	381	647	207	60	107	143	68.5	14.7
Spouse	1 604	41	208	224	485	192	70	210	173	70.5	23.9
Other relative	800	99	229	128	240	45	5	33	22	43.1	6.9
Nonrelative	266	9	55	52	69	38	6	27	12	56.5	14.5
Female											
15 to 17 years	5 662	6	1 098	4 460	85	12	—	—	—	1.7	—
Householder	65	—	13	51	—	—	—	—	—	(B)	(B)
Family householder	55	—	7	48	—	—	—	—	—	(B)	(B)
Married, spouse present	2	—	—	2	—	—	—	—	—	(B)	(B)
Nonfamily householder	10	—	5	4	—	—	—	—	—	(B)	(B)
Living alone	3	—	—	2	—	—	—	—	—	(B)	(B)
Spouse	18	2	—	14	—	2	—	—	—	(B)	(B)
Other relative	5 370	3	1 046	4 237	75	9	—	—	—	1.6	—
Nonrelative	210	2	40	158	10	—	—	—	—	4.9	—
18 years and over	101 354	1 453	5 690	11 247	35 155	19 831	7 605	14 694	5 679	81.9	20.1
Householder	40 880	585	2 929	5 076	13 294	7 661	3 013	5 754	2 568	79.0	20.4
Family householder	23 820	291	1 368	3 049	8 213	4 671	1 919	3 072	1 236	80.2	18.1
Married, spouse present	11 082	105	475	1 024	3 613	2 026	970	2 027	843	85.5	25.9
Nonfamily householder	17 060	294	1 561	2 026	5 081	2 990	1 094	2 682	1 332	77.2	23.5
Living alone	14 958	282	1 503	1 892	4 545	2 495	926	2 156	1 159	75.4	22.2
Spouse	42 501	457	1 800	3 491	16 117	7 203	3 661	7 029	2 743	86.5	23.0
Other relative	13 409	340	796	2 201	4 154	3 995	617	1 130	177	75.1	9.7
Nonrelative	4 563	70	164	479	1 591	972	314	781	191	84.4	21.3
18 to 24 years	12 405	67	242	2 247	3 795	4 498	497	1 014	45	79.4	8.5
Householder	2 688	9	66	444	935	760	112	345	16	80.7	13.4
Family householder	1 691	9	62	394	675	413	57	78	3	72.5	4.8
Married, spouse present	499	2	25	98	182	121	23	48	—	74.9	9.7
Nonfamily householder	997	—	4	51	261	347	55	267	13	94.5	28.1
Living alone	516	—	2	27	139	169	23	149	7	94.3	30.2
Spouse	1 594	21	66	209	609	391	128	154	17	81.5	10.7
Other relative	6 770	31	81	1 390	1 793	2 932	193	338	11	77.8	5.2
Nonrelative	1 353	5	29	204	458	416	63	178	1	82.4	13.2
25 years and over	88 948	1 387	5 448	9 000	31 360	15 333	7 107	13 680	5 634	82.2	21.7
Householder	38 192	576	2 863	4 631	12 359	6 901	2 901	5 409	2 552	78.9	20.8
Family householder	22 129	282	1 306	2 655	7 539	4 258	1 862	2 994	1 233	80.8	19.1
Married, spouse present	10 584	103	450	926	3 431	1 906	946	1 979	843	86.0	26.7
Nonfamily householder	16 063	294	1 557	1 976	4 821	2 643	1 039	2 415	1 319	76.2	23.2
Living alone	14 442	282	1 501	1 865	4 406	2 326	902	2 007	1 153	74.7	21.9
Spouse	40 907	436	1 734	3 283	15 508	6 813	3 532	6 875	2 727	86.7	23.5
Other relative	6 639	309	715	811	2 361	1 063	424	792	165	72.4	14.4
Nonrelative	3 210	65	136	275	1 133	556	251	604	190	85.2	24.7
25 to 34 years	20 208	150	533	1 615	6 228	4 128	1 917	4 453	1 186	88.6	27.9
Householder	7 467	36	174	778	2 042	1 613	699	1 602	522	86.8	28.4

See footnotes at end of table.

Table B-4.   Educational Attainment of Persons 15 Years Old and Over, by Household Relationship, Age, Sex, Race, and Hispanic Origin: March 1997 — Continued

(Numbers in thousands. Civilian noninstitutional population.)

Household relationship, age, sex, race, and Hispanic origin	Total	Elementary		High School		College				Percent:	
		None-4th grade	5th-8th grade	9th-11th grade	High school graduate	Some college no degree	Associate degree	Bachelor's degree	Advanced degree	High school graduate or more	Bachelor's degree or more
Family householder	5 424	36	164	723	1 681	1 212	544	835	228	83.0	19.6
Married, spouse present	2 622	17	96	229	646	516	283	642	194	87.0	31.9
Nonfamily householder	2 043	—	10	55	361	401	155	767	294	96.8	51.9
Living alone	1 395	—	4	43	239	249	101	525	234	96.6	54.4
Spouse	8 852	66	237	534	2 923	1 638	908	2 024	523	90.6	28.8
Other relative	2 301	31	76	201	751	567	179	437	58	86.6	21.5
Nonrelative	1 588	17	46	102	512	309	130	389	82	89.6	29.7
35 to 44 years	22 167	181	627	1 587	7 623	4 262	2 317	3 997	1 573	89.2	25.1
Householder	8 786	58	237	785	2 840	1 795	934	1 480	657	87.7	24.3
Family householder	6 992	54	219	669	2 407	1 479	741	1 008	416	86.5	20.4
Married, spouse present	3 223	24	71	213	1 032	605	350	647	280	90.4	28.8
Nonfamily householder	1 793	4	18	115	433	315	193	472	242	92.3	39.8
Living alone	1 498	1	13	99	363	274	156	389	202	92.4	39.5
Spouse	11 346	78	312	590	3 980	2 106	1 211	2 252	817	91.4	27.1
Other relative	1 235	32	54	142	496	220	99	148	42	81.5	15.4
Nonrelative	800	12	24	70	307	142	73	117	56	86.7	21.6
45 to 64 years	28 104	455	1 515	2 769	10 551	4 628	2 121	3 806	2 261	83.1	21.6
Householder	11 265	162	683	1 248	3 740	2 059	852	1 537	984	81.4	22.4
Family householder	6 842	101	460	747	2 386	1 204	474	962	508	80.9	21.5
Married, spouse present	3 516	45	159	301	1 247	611	259	577	316	85.6	25.4
Nonfamily householder	4 423	61	222	501	1 354	855	378	575	477	82.3	23.8
Living alone	3 930	51	197	450	1 202	760	333	506	430	82.2	23.8
Spouse	14 664	173	593	1 254	5 963	2 310	1 110	2 065	1 196	86.2	22.2
Other relative	1 523	96	194	198	599	169	114	121	33	68.0	10.1
Nonrelative	652	25	45	69	249	90	45	82	47	78.7	19.8
65 years and over	18 469	601	2 774	3 028	6 959	2 315	753	1 424	615	65.3	11.0
Householder	10 675	321	1 769	1 820	3 737	1 434	415	790	389	63.4	11.0
Family householder	2 871	91	463	516	1 065	363	103	189	82	62.7	9.4
Married, spouse present	1 223	17	124	183	507	174	55	112	53	73.6	13.4
Nonfamily householder	7 804	230	1 306	1 304	2 672	1 071	313	601	307	63.6	11.6
Living alone	7 619	230	1 286	1 273	2 602	1 043	313	586	287	63.4	11.5
Spouse	6 045	120	593	905	2 642	759	303	534	190	73.2	12.0
Other relative	1 580	149	391	269	514	106	32	86	32	48.8	7.5
Nonrelative	170	11	21	34	66	16	3	15	5	61.1	11.6

WHITE

Male

Household relationship, age, sex, race, and Hispanic origin	Total	None-4th grade	5th-8th grade	9th-11th grade	High school graduate	Some college no degree	Associate degree	Bachelor's degree	Advanced degree	High school graduate or more	Bachelor's degree or more
18 years and over	79 733	1 143	4 571	8 740	25 446	15 329	5 041	12 655	6 808	81.9	24.4
Householder	52 595	648	2 983	4 708	16 521	9 553	3 631	9 245	5 306	84.1	27.7
Family householder	41 120	507	2 286	3 743	13 196	7 249	2 824	7 000	4 315	84.1	27.5
Married, spouse present	38 187	449	2 087	3 331	12 147	6 688	2 653	6 686	4 148	84.6	28.4
Nonfamily householder	11 476	141	697	965	3 326	2 304	807	2 245	991	84.3	28.2
Living alone	8 730	112	609	754	2 517	1 680	600	1 631	827	83.1	28.2
Spouse	9 484	105	515	944	3 064	1 449	589	1 699	1 119	83.5	29.7
Other relative	13 053	300	746	2 591	4 327	3 368	597	939	185	72.1	8.6
Nonrelative	4 601	90	327	497	1 533	960	223	772	198	80.1	21.1
25 years and over	69 555	1 087	4 249	6 548	22 310	11 915	4 641	12 028	6 777	82.9	27.0
Householder	50 548	638	2 910	4 428	15 810	8 965	3 501	9 009	5 287	84.2	28.3
Family householder	40 086	504	2 234	3 549	12 785	7 003	2 770	6 933	4 308	84.3	28.0
Married, spouse present	37 435	447	2 047	3 209	11 831	6 518	2 611	6 630	4 143	84.8	28.8
Nonfamily householder	10 462	134	676	879	3 024	1 962	731	2 076	979	83.9	29.2
Living alone	8 254	106	595	717	2 388	1 506	559	1 561	820	82.8	28.9
Spouse	9 242	101	504	912	2 952	1 391	581	1 683	1 119	83.6	30.3
Other relative	6 293	272	581	900	2 325	940	380	717	178	72.1	14.2
Nonrelative	3 472	77	253	308	1 224	618	180	619	193	81.6	23.4

See footnotes at end of table.

Table B-4. Educational Attainment of Persons 15 Years Old and Over, by Household Relationship, Age, Sex, Race, and Hispanic Origin: March 1997 — Continued

(Numbers in thousands. Civilian noninstitutional population.)

Household relationship, age, sex, race, and Hispanic origin	Total	Elementary		High School		College				Percent:	
		None-4th grade	5th-8th grade	9th-11th grade	High school graduate	Some college no degree	Associate degree	Bachelor's degree	Advanced degree	High school graduate or more	Bachelor's degree or more
Female											
18 years and over	84 256	1 101	4 684	8 653	29 505	16 437	6 392	12 571	4 914	82.9	20.8
Householder	32 407	421	2 308	3 673	10 490	6 040	2 415	4 866	2 193	80.2	21.8
Family householder	17 769	201	970	1 998	6 106	3 449	1 477	2 520	1 046	82.2	20.1
Married, spouse present	9 457	84	381	843	3 088	1 758	821	1 750	732	86.2	26.2
Nonfamily householder	14 638	220	1 338	1 675	4 384	2 590	938	2 346	1 147	77.9	23.9
Living alone	12 781	207	1 296	1 556	3 935	2 155	787	1 857	987	76.1	22.3
Spouse	38 036	384	1 610	3 067	14 596	6 481	3 278	6 222	2 398	86.7	22.7
Other relative	9 996	239	619	1 530	3 099	3 077	449	836	146	76.1	9.8
Nonrelative	3 817	56	146	382	1 320	839	250	646	176	84.7	21.6
25 years and over	74 477	1 040	4 460	7 038	26 546	12 802	5 974	11 740	4 877	83.2	22.3
Householder	30 471	412	2 248	3 408	9 827	5 489	2 326	4 579	2 182	80.1	22.2
Family householder	16 644	192	914	1 774	5 644	3 180	1 431	2 463	1 046	82.7	21.1
Married, spouse present	9 031	82	358	765	2 927	1 653	802	1 712	732	86.7	27.1
Nonfamily householder	13 827	220	1 334	1 633	4 183	2 310	895	2 116	1 137	76.9	23.5
Living alone	12 377	207	1 294	1 538	3 828	2 033	770	1 727	980	75.4	21.9
Spouse	36 584	364	1 548	2 880	14 043	6 125	3 156	6 084	2 384	86.9	23.1
Other relative	4 730	214	544	537	1 726	703	299	573	134	72.6	15.0
Nonrelative	2 692	51	120	213	950	485	193	504	175	85.7	25.2
BLACK											
Male											
18 years and over	10 176	270	613	1 904	3 740	2 096	463	800	290	72.6	10.7
Householder	5 062	131	355	759	1 750	971	332	522	243	75.4	15.1
Family householder	3 393	79	240	469	1 225	619	222	367	172	76.8	15.9
Married, spouse present	2 744	60	184	350	948	531	189	335	149	78.4	17.6
Nonfamily householder	1 669	52	115	290	525	352	109	154	71	72.6	13.5
Living alone	1 303	46	104	242	371	266	87	118	69	70.0	14.3
Spouse	1 125	21	75	181	422	214	56	136	19	75.4	13.8
Other relative	3 154	96	132	799	1 243	735	41	96	11	67.4	3.4
Nonrelative	836	21	51	165	325	176	34	47	17	71.6	7.6
25 years and over	8 446	253	588	1 401	3 085	1 622	444	763	290	73.5	12.5
Householder	4 836	131	355	719	1 633	916	332	508	243	75.1	15.5
Family householder	3 279	79	240	441	1 157	603	222	365	172	76.8	16.4
Married, spouse present	2 686	60	184	340	906	524	189	335	149	78.3	18.0
Nonfamily householder	1 558	52	115	278	476	313	109	143	71	71.4	13.7
Living alone	1 253	46	104	233	352	248	87	114	69	69.4	14.6
Spouse	1 074	21	72	166	404	205	54	133	19	75.8	14.2
Other relative	1 843	81	110	400	773	360	25	82	11	67.9	5.1
Nonrelative	693	19	51	116	275	141	34	40	17	73.2	8.2
Female											
18 years and over	12 564	161	692	2 207	4 446	2 601	880	1 144	432	75.6	12.5
Householder	7 014	100	504	1 279	2 419	1 367	511	590	244	73.1	11.9
Family householder	5 033	46	303	952	1 823	1 056	388	342	122	74.1	9.2
Married, spouse present	1 105	7	49	144	383	201	124	139	58	81.9	17.8
Nonfamily householder	1 981	54	201	327	596	310	122	248	122	70.6	18.7
Living alone	1 823	54	187	314	523	277	119	233	115	69.5	19.1
Spouse	2 615	13	81	316	961	493	230	353	169	84.3	19.9
Other relative	2 427	38	94	520	855	649	107	148	16	73.2	6.7
Nonrelative	508	11	13	91	211	92	32	53	3	77.3	11.2
25 years and over	10 626	158	686	1 704	3 750	2 019	828	1 054	427	76.0	13.9
Householder	6 401	100	502	1 125	2 185	1 213	493	544	239	73.0	12.2
Family householder	4 541	46	301	805	1 628	944	377	321	119	74.6	9.7
Married, spouse present	1 052	7	49	131	369	188	120	129	58	82.2	17.8

See footnotes at end of table.

Table B-4.   Educational Attainment of Persons 15 Years Old and Over, by Household Relationship, Age, Sex, Race, and Hispanic Origin: March 1997 — Continued

(Numbers in thousands. Civilian noninstitutional population.)

Household relationship, age, sex, race, and Hispanic origin	Total	Elementary		High School		College				Percent:	
		None-4th grade	5th-8th grade	9th-11th grade	High school graduate	Some college no degree	Associate degree	Bachelor's degree	Advanced degree	High school graduate or more	Bachelor's degree or more
Nonfamily householder	1 860	54	201	320	557	269	116	223	120	69.1	18.4
Living alone	1 745	54	187	306	503	248	116	216	115	68.6	19.0
Spouse	2 536	13	81	302	929	469	226	348	169	84.4	20.4
Other relative	1 337	34	92	219	492	290	78	115	16	74.1	9.8
Nonrelative	352	11	11	59	144	47	30	46	3	76.9	14.1
HISPANIC ORIGIN[1]											
Male											
18 years and over	9 723	768	1 778	1 908	2 488	1 489	424	591	278	54.2	8.9
Householder	4 838	421	877	776	1 266	701	239	388	170	57.1	11.5
Family householder	3 987	347	731	645	1 059	569	192	303	142	56.8	11.2
Married, spouse present	3 499	307	640	515	946	508	174	276	135	58.2	11.7
Nonfamily householder	851	75	146	131	207	132	48	85	28	58.7	13.3
Living alone	575	58	102	82	140	87	41	43	22	57.9	11.3
Spouse	1 051	95	226	184	272	123	40	58	52	51.9	10.5
Other relative	2 888	187	451	746	735	544	104	100	20	52.0	4.1
Nonrelative	946	64	223	201	214	122	40	44	36	48.3	8.5
25 years and over	7 746	712	1 526	1 259	2 001	1 042	384	548	274	54.9	10.6
Householder	4 504	413	824	681	1 175	642	230	371	168	57.4	12.0
Family householder	3 752	345	686	574	994	530	187	295	141	57.2	11.6
Married, spouse present	3 350	307	608	475	905	480	170	273	133	58.5	12.1
Nonfamily householder	751	67	138	107	181	112	44	76	27	58.5	13.7
Living alone	532	52	95	75	131	81	39	36	22	58.2	11.0
Spouse	981	91	216	172	245	109	40	57	52	51.2	11.1
Other relative	1 564	158	332	296	403	199	75	82	19	49.8	6.4
Nonrelative	696	50	154	111	178	91	39	38	35	54.7	10.5
Female											
18 years and over	9 359	778	1 679	1 708	2 515	1 397	466	637	180	55.5	8.7
Householder	3 357	292	628	714	837	432	169	222	61	51.3	8.5
Family householder	2 619	174	492	593	692	330	144	159	34	51.9	7.4
Married, spouse present	1 016	77	183	206	255	125	57	88	24	54.1	11.0
Nonfamily householder	738	118	135	120	146	102	25	63	27	49.3	12.3
Living alone	621	112	117	107	107	79	21	50	27	45.8	12.4
Spouse	3 600	298	704	516	991	500	191	309	90	57.8	11.1
Other relative	1 911	151	270	394	534	399	75	63	24	57.3	4.6
Nonrelative	491	36	77	84	152	65	30	43	4	59.8	9.5
25 years and over	7 720	736	1 527	1 240	2 007	1 009	421	605	174	54.6	10.1
Householder	3 034	283	593	614	717	384	167	217	60	50.9	9.1
Family householder	2 334	165	457	503	586	292	142	154	34	51.8	8.0
Married, spouse present	928	75	171	181	225	111	56	85	24	54.0	11.8
Nonfamily householder	701	118	135	111	130	92	25	63	26	47.9	12.7
Living alone	604	112	117	101	103	74	21	49	26	45.3	12.5
Spouse	3 355	287	655	447	928	469	183	300	86	58.6	11.5
Other relative	991	133	217	137	260	121	48	51	24	50.9	7.6
Nonrelative	341	33	63	42	102	36	24	37	4	59.4	11.9

Source: March 1997 Current Population Survey, Education and Social Stratification Branch, U.S. Bureau of the Census.

1. May be of any race.

— Represents zero or rounds to zero.

(B) Base less than 75,000.

Table B-5. Educational Attainment of Husband, by Educational Attainment of Wife for Married Couples, by Age of Husband, Race, and Hispanic Origin: March 1997

(Numbers in thousands. Civilian noninstitutional population.)

Education of husband, age, race, and Hispanic origin	All wives	Not high school graduate				High school graduate or more		College			
		Total	Elementary		High School	Total	High school graduate only	Some college no degree	Associate degree	Bachelor's degree	Advanced degree
			None - 4th grade	5th - 8th grade	9th - 11th grade						
ALL RACES											
18 Years and Over											
All husbands	54 654	7 686	599	2 393	4 694	46 968	20 140	9 403	4 686	9 147	3 591
Not high school graduate	8 953	4 703	520	1 713	2 470	4 249	3 098	677	220	191	63
Elementary: None to 4th grade	732	628	285	233	110	104	67	28	2	5	2
5th to 8th grade	3 091	1 936	175	1 085	675	1 155	879	158	63	41	13
High school: 9th to 11th grade	5 129	2 140	61	395	1 684	2 990	2 151	491	155	144	48
High school graduate	45 701	2 983	79	680	2 224	42 719	17 042	8 726	4 466	8 957	3 528
High School Graduate Only	17 410	2 062	55	512	1 495	15 348	10 360	2 419	1 201	1 069	299
College: Some, no degree	9 311	523	13	86	424	8 788	3 288	3 069	938	1 157	335
Associate degree	3 031	100	0	31	120	3 471	1 007	797	019	504	194
Bachelor's degree ...	9 474	178	1	27	149	9 296	1 733	1 665	987	3 966	946
Advanced degree	5 876	60	4	23	33	5 816	595	776	520	2 170	1 755
18 to 24 Years											
All husbands	1 249	270	10	47	213	979	475	320	93	84	8
Not high school graduate	294	174	10	40	124	120	92	20	—	4	4
Elementary: None to 4th grade	7	6	—	4	2	1	1	—	—	—	—
5th to 8th grade	67	53	7	28	17	14	9	5	—	—	—
High school: 9th to 11th grade	220	116	3	9	104	104	81	15	—	4	4
High school graduate	955	95	—	7	89	860	383	300	93	80	4
High School Graduate Only	547	81	—	7	75	465	304	114	32	16	—
College: Some, no degree	273	14	—	—	14	259	69	142	31	16	1
Associate degree	56	—	—	—	—	56	6	19	26	5	—
Bachelor's degree ...	75	—	—	—	—	75	4	26	4	38	2
Advanced degree	5	—	—	—	—	5	—	—	—	5	—
25 to 34 Years											
All husbands	9 866	1 070	61	263	745	8 796	3 184	1 886	959	2 183	584
Not high school graduate	1 258	647	46	188	413	611	392	150	39	19	12
Elementary: None to 4th grade	68	58	18	19	21	10	4	6	—	—	—
5th to 8th grade	268	187	20	106	60	81	58	14	7	3	—
High school: 9th to 11th grade	922	402	7	63	332	520	330	130	32	15	12
High school graduate	8 608	423	16	75	332	8 185	2 792	1 737	920	2 164	572
High School Graduate Only	3 173	288	13	49	226	2 884	1 857	453	280	229	65
College: Some, no degree	1 879	89	1	17	70	1 790	495	745	212	296	41
Associate degree	845	28	—	5	23	817	210	187	217	156	46
Bachelor's degree ...	2 058	11	1	2	8	2 047	196	301	181	1 183	186
Advanced degree	654	6	—	2	5	647	34	51	29	300	234
35 to 44 Years											
All husbands	14 436	1 432	112	477	843	13 004	4 851	2 728	1 517	2 945	963
Not high school graduate	1 642	841	100	340	401	800	554	146	51	38	12
Elementary: None to 4th grade	136	114	49	57	9	21	13	6	—	2	—
5th to 8th grade	414	308	39	193	76	106	66	25	6	7	2
High school: 9th to 11th grade	1 092	419	12	90	317	673	474	114	46	30	9
High school graduate	12 794	590	12	137	442	12 204	4 298	2 582	1 466	2 907	951
High School Graduate Only	4 724	405	8	101	295	4 319	2 658	768	384	417	91
College: Some, no degree	2 619	99	3	17	79	2 520	843	893	336	351	97
Associate degree	1 147	35	1	4	31	1 112	313	275	249	222	53
Bachelor's degree ...	2 764	35	—	6	30	2 728	391	486	332	1 238	281
Advanced degree	1 540	16	—	9	7	1 524	93	160	165	678	428

See footnotes at end of table.

Table B-5. Educational Attainment of Husband, by Educational Attainment of Wife for Married Couples, by Age of Husband, Race, and Hispanic Origin: March 1997 — Continued

(Numbers in thousands. Civilian noninstitutional population.)

Education of husband, age, race, and Hispanic origin	All wives	Not high school graduate				High school graduate or more		College			
		Total	Elementary		High School	Total	High school graduate only	Some college no degree	Associate degree	Bachelor's degree	Advanced degree
			None - 4th grade	5th - 8th grade	9th - 11th grade						
45 to 54 Years											
All husbands	11 638	1 174	99	351	725	10 463	4 262	1 984	1 099	2 001	1 117
Not high school graduate	1 330	639	85	237	317	691	525	85	33	36	12
Elementary: None to 4th grade	112	102	50	34	17	10	7	3	—	—	—
5th to 8th grade	456	273	30	154	89	183	148	23	7	4	1
High school: 9th to 11th grade	762	264	5	49	210	498	370	60	25	32	11
High school graduate	10 307	535	14	114	408	9 772	3 736	1 899	1 067	1 965	1 104
High School Graduate Only	3 365	359	9	88	262	3 006	2 078	408	256	204	61
College: Some, no degree	2 048	93	—	11	82	1 955	714	627	211	304	99
Associate degree	898	37	2	9	27	861	301	186	191	128	55
Bachelor's degree	2 196	36	—	3	33	2 160	476	419	246	731	288
Advanced degree	1 800	11	4	3	4	1 790	167	259	163	598	602
55 to 64 Years											
All husbands	7 848	1 325	136	384	806	6 523	3 232	1 232	513	999	547
Not high school graduate	1 544	771	118	255	398	772	578	119	41	28	7
Elementary: None to 4th grade	134	109	61	28	20	25	15	6	2	—	2
5th to 8th grade	626	344	42	167	135	282	218	36	19	7	1
High school: 9th to 11th grade	785	319	15	61	242	466	345	76	21	20	4
High school graduate	6 304	554	18	128	408	5 750	2 654	1 113	472	971	539
High School Graduate Only	2 708	410	9	106	295	2 297	1 664	343	140	107	44
College: Some, no degree	1 132	84	5	10	70	1 048	491	310	89	109	49
Associate degree	378	27	4	5	18	351	121	84	61	48	37
Bachelor's degree	1 125	23	—	6	18	1 102	274	210	99	412	107
Advanced degree	961	10	—	2	8	952	105	167	82	295	303
65 Years and Over											
All husbands	9 617	2 415	180	872	1 363	7 202	4 137	1 253	504	935	374
Not high school graduate	2 885	1 631	161	653	817	1 255	958	158	56	67	16
Elementary: None to 4th grade	276	239	106	92	41	37	27	7	—	3	—
5th to 8th grade	1 260	771	36	438	297	489	380	56	25	20	8
High school: 9th to 11th grade	1 349	621	19	123	479	729	551	96	31	43	8
High school graduate	6 732	784	20	219	546	5 948	3 179	1 094	448	868	358
High School Graduate Only	2 893	518	16	160	342	2 375	1 799	333	109	97	38
College: Some, no degree	1 360	144	4	31	109	1 216	676	352	59	81	47
Associate degree	307	33	—	9	24	274	116	46	75	35	2
Bachelor's degree	1 256	72	—	11	62	1 184	392	224	124	363	82
Advanced degree	916	17	—	8	9	899	196	140	82	293	188
WHITE											
18 Years and Over											
All husbands	48 471	6 657	496	2 107	4 054	41 814	18 057	8 378	4 139	8 067	3 172
Not high school graduate	7 725	4 035	439	1 509	2 087	3 691	2 724	587	183	158	38
Elementary: None to 4th grade	585	497	229	185	83	88	60	19	2	5	2
5th to 8th grade	2 710	1 698	164	965	569	1 011	787	140	47	29	9
High school: 9th to 11th grade	4 431	1 839	46	359	1 434	2 592	1 877	429	135	125	27
High school graduate	40 746	2 622	56	599	1 967	38 123	15 333	7 791	3 956	7 909	3 134
High School Graduate Only	15 496	1 820	36	454	1 329	13 676	9 264	2 164	1 056	928	263
College: Some, no degree	8 257	464	13	80	371	7 792	2 980	2 675	826	1 028	283
Associate degree	3 263	146	6	31	109	3 118	955	720	747	525	170
Bachelor's degree	8 443	150	1	15	133	8 293	1 575	1 508	840	3 514	856
Advanced degree	5 287	43	—	18	24	5 244	559	725	487	1 913	1 561

See footnotes at end of table.

Table B-5. Educational Attainment of Husband, by Educational Attainment of Wife for Married Couples, by Age of Husband, Race, and Hispanic Origin: March 1997 — Continued

(Numbers in thousands. Civilian noninstitutional population.)

Education of husband, age, race, and Hispanic origin	All wives	Not high school graduate				High school graduate or more		College			
		Total	Elementary		High School	Total	High school graduate only	Some college no degree	Associate degree	Bachelor's degree	Advanced degree
			None - 4th grade	5th - 8th grade	9th - 11th grade						
18 to 44 Years											
All husbands	22 442	2 446	170	719	1 557	19 995	7 468	4 291	2 267	4 597	1 373
Not high school graduate	2 807	1 476	146	522	808	1 331	900	278	84	50	19
Elementary: None to 4th grade	190	162	60	75	27	28	18	8	—	2	—
5th to 8th grade	665	493	66	300	127	173	120	37	10	4	2
High school: 9th to 11th grade	1 952	821	21	146	654	1 131	761	234	75	44	17
High school graduate	19 635	971	24	197	749	18 664	6 569	4 013	2 183	4 546	1 354
High School Graduate Only	7 421	694	18	147	529	6 727	4 229	1 164	611	585	138
College: Some, no degree	4 159	173	4	34	135	3 986	1 237	1 519	503	593	134
Associate degree	1 844	53	1	9	44	1 791	472	428	448	344	99
Bachelor's degree	4 324	36	1	2	33	4 288	520	719	448	2 180	422
Advanced degree	1 887	14	—	6	8	1 873	111	183	174	844	561
45 Years and Over											
All husbands	26 029	4 211	325	1 388	2 497	21 818	10 589	4 088	1 873	3 471	1 799
Not high school graduate	4 918	2 559	293	987	1 278	2 359	1 824	309	99	108	19
Elementary: None to 4th grade	395	335	170	109	56	60	42	11	2	3	2
5th to 8th grade	2 044	1 206	98	665	443	838	667	103	37	24	7
High school: 9th to 11th grade	2 479	1 017	26	212	780	1 461	1 115	195	61	80	9
High school graduate	21 111	1 652	32	402	1 218	19 459	8 765	3 778	1 773	3 363	1 780
High School Graduate Only	8 075	1 125	18	307	800	6 940	5 034	1 000	446	344	126
College: Some, no degree	4 098	291	9	46	237	3 806	1 743	1 156	323	435	149
Associate degree	1 419	92	5	22	66	1 327	484	292	299	181	71
Bachelor's degree	4 119	114	—	14	100	4 005	1 056	789	392	1 334	435
Advanced degree	3 400	29	—	13	16	3 372	448	541	313	1 069	1 000
BLACK											
18 Years and Over											
All husbands	3 955	648	23	133	492	3 306	1 443	732	390	513	229
Not high school graduate	899	440	22	110	308	460	309	73	31	26	21
Elementary: None to 4th grade	84	72	16	35	22	12	7	5	—	—	—
5th to 8th grade	270	155	3	59	93	115	74	17	12	9	4
High school: 9th to 11th grade	545	213	3	16	194	332	228	51	19	16	17
High school graduate	3 055	208	1	23	184	2 847	1 134	659	359	487	208
High School Graduate Only	1 398	146	1	16	129	1 252	768	224	124	104	32
College: Some, no degree	767	39	—	4	34	728	221	273	92	95	48
Associate degree	246	6	—	—	6	240	71	48	56	45	21
Bachelor's degree	476	10	—	3	7	466	62	91	79	177	57
Advanced degree	168	8	—	—	8	160	12	23	7	67	51
18 to 44 Years											
All husbands	1 935	190	—	15	175	1 745	704	460	228	304	50
Not high school graduate	247	105	—	9	95	143	101	24	6	7	4
Elementary: None to 4th grade	—	—	—	—	—	—	—	—	—	—	—
5th to 8th grade	50	24	—	6	18	26	10	7	3	6	—
High school: 9th to 11th grade	198	80	—	3	77	117	92	17	3	1	4
High school graduate	1 688	85	—	6	80	1 603	602	436	221	297	46
High School Graduate Only	776	53	—	3	50	723	420	148	77	62	16
College: Some, no degree	434	19	—	—	19	415	117	174	66	55	3
Associate degree	141	3	—	—	3	138	37	38	35	28	—
Bachelor's degree	278	7	—	3	4	271	24	68	39	119	21
Advanced degree	59	4	—	—	4	55	4	7	5	34	6

See footnotes at end of table.

Table B-5. Educational Attainment of Husband, by Educational Attainment of Wife for Married Couples, by Age of Husband, Race, and Hispanic Origin: March 1997 — Continued

(Numbers in thousands. Civilian noninstitutional population.)

Education of husband, age, race, and Hispanic origin	All wives	Not high school graduate				High school graduate or more			College		
		Total	Elementary		High School	Total	High school graduate only	Some college no degree	Associate degree	Bachelor's degree	Advanced degree
			None - 4th grade	5th - 8th grade	9th - 11th grade						
45 Years and Over											
All husbands	2 019	458	22	118	318	1 561	740	271	162	208	180
Not high school graduate	652	335	21	101	213	317	208	49	25	18	17
Elementary: None to 4th grade	84	72	16	35	22	12	7	5	—	—	—
5th to 8th grade	220	131	2	54	75	90	64	9	9	3	4
High school: 9th to 11th grade	347	132	3	13	117	215	137	34	15	15	13
High school graduate	1 367	123	1	18	104	1 244	531	223	137	190	163
High School Graduate Only	622	93	1	13	79	529	348	76	48	42	15
College: Some, no degree	334	20	—	4	16	314	104	99	26	40	45
Associate degree	105	3	—	—	3	102	33	9	22	17	20
Bachelor's degree ...	198	2	—	—	2	195	38	23	40	58	36
Advanced degree	109	4	—	—	4	105	8	16	2	32	46
HISPANIC ORIGIN [1]											
18 Years and Over											
All husbands	4 830	2 138	394	966	778	2 692	1 344	663	238	340	108
Not high school graduate	2 144	1 634	364	769	501	510	335	110	24	30	10
Elementary: None to 4th grade	433	386	188	152	46	48	29	13	2	2	2
5th to 8th grade	942	760	139	472	149	182	130	30	9	9	5
High school: 9th to 11th grade	769	489	37	146	306	280	177	67	14	19	4
High school graduate	2 686	504	30	196	278	2 182	1 008	553	214	310	97
High School Graduate Only	1 277	341	19	136	186	936	665	148	66	50	7
College: Some, no degree	661	103	8	37	58	559	194	246	42	67	9
Associate degree	215	25	2	12	11	190	40	66	52	27	5
Bachelor's degree ...	342	21	1	3	17	321	82	63	30	116	31
Advanced degree	191	14	—	9	5	177	27	30	24	51	45
18 to 44 Years											
All husbands	3 120	1 267	161	556	550	1 854	888	485	172	241	67
Not high school graduate	1 289	951	146	448	357	338	217	82	17	20	2
Elementary: None to 4th grade	183	163	60	75	28	20	13	5	—	2	—
5th to 8th grade	543	436	67	271	98	108	75	24	5	2	2
High school: 9th to 11th grade	562	352	19	102	230	210	130	53	12	16	—
High school graduate	1 831	316	15	108	193	1 515	670	404	155	221	65
High School Graduate Only	869	214	9	70	135	656	453	109	51	36	7
College: Some, no degree	497	76	3	27	45	422	142	187	35	50	8
Associate degree	144	11	1	3	8	133	25	46	35	23	4
Bachelor's degree ...	217	8	1	2	5	209	44	43	18	83	21
Advanced degree	103	7	—	6	1	96	6	19	17	29	25
45 Years and Over											
All husbands	1 710	872	233	410	229	839	456	178	66	99	40
Not high school graduate	855	683	218	321	144	172	118	29	7	10	8
Elementary: None to 4th grade	250	222	129	76	17	28	16	8	2	—	2
5th to 8th grade	398	324	71	201	51	74	55	6	4	7	3
High school: 9th to 11th grade	207	137	18	43	76	70	47	14	2	4	4
High school graduate	855	188	15	89	84	667	338	149	59	89	32
High School Graduate Only	408	127	9	66	52	280	212	39	15	14	—
College: Some, no degree	164	27	4	10	13	137	52	59	7	18	1
Associate degree	71	14	1	9	4	57	15	20	18	3	—
Bachelor's degree ...	125	13	—	1	12	112	38	20	12	32	10
Advanced degree	88	7	—	3	4	81	21	10	7	21	21

Source: March 1997 Current Population Survey, Education and Social Stratification Branch, U.S. Bureau of the Census.

1. May be of any race.

— Represents zero or rounds to zero.

Table B-6. Educational Attainment of Persons 16 Years Old and Over, by Labor Force Status, Age, Sex, Race, and Hispanic Origin: March 1997

(Numbers in thousands. Civilian noninstitutional population.)

Marital status, age, sex, race, and Hispanic origin	Total	Elementary		High School		College				Percent:	
		None-4th grade	5th-8th grade	9th-11th grade	High school graduate	Some college no degree	Associate degree	Bachelor's degree	Advanced degree	High school graduate or more	Bachelor's degree or more
ALL RACES											
Male											
Civilian labor force	72 329	726	2 806	8 202	23 063	13 976	4 912	12 220	6 425	83.8	25.8
16 and 17 years	1 501	1	106	1 351	37	5	—	—	—	2.8	—
18 to 24 years	9 271	51	280	1 813	3 293	2 806	366	632	31	76.9	7.1
25 years and over	61 557	673	2 419	5 038	19 733	11 165	4 546	11 588	6 395	86.8	29.2
25 to 29 years	8 702	77	267	851	2 686	1 883	622	1 897	420	86.3	26.6
30 to 34 years	9 489	66	303	850	3 187	1 666	844	1 892	680	87.2	27.1
35 to 44 years	19 753	200	596	1 529	6 833	3 688	1 481	3 593	1 833	88.2	27.5
45 to 54 years	14 376	151	525	966	4 065	2 585	1 134	2 807	2 143	88.6	34.4
55 to 64 years	6 947	131	484	603	2 311	1 037	362	1 068	952	82.5	29.1
65 years and over	2 289	48	245	240	651	306	103	331	366	76.7	30.4
Employed	68 026	664	2 526	7 007	21 607	13 226	4 752	11 931	6 314	85.0	26.8
16 and 17 years	1 146	—	55	1 056	30	5	—	—	—	3.1	—
18 to 24 years	8 196	46	243	1 439	2 931	2 546	350	611	31	78.9	7.8
25 years and over	58 683	617	2 228	4 512	18 646	10 675	4 402	11 320	6 284	87.5	30.0
25 to 29 years	8 149	77	234	737	2 462	1 781	592	1 859	406	87.1	27.8
30 to 34 years	9 011	58	274	726	3 003	1 602	827	1 853	667	88.3	28.0
35 to 44 years	18 806	185	537	1 345	6 450	3 523	1 453	3 505	1 806	89.0	28.2
45 to 54 years	13 846	135	496	894	3 888	2 485	1 092	2 736	2 120	89.0	35.1
55 to 64 years	6 659	115	457	574	2 208	993	337	1 044	931	82.8	29.7
65 years and over	2 213	47	229	235	634	290	101	322	354	76.9	30.6
Unemployed	4 302	62	280	1 195	1 456	750	159	289	111	64.3	9.3
16 and 17 years	355	1	51	295	7	—	—	—	—	2.0	—
18 to 24 years	1 075	5	38	374	362	260	16	21	—	61.3	2.0
25 years and over	2 873	56	192	526	1 087	490	144	268	111	73.1	13.2
25 to 29 years	553	—	33	114	223	102	30	37	14	73.4	9.3
30 to 34 years	478	8	29	124	183	64	17	39	13	66.3	10.8
35 to 44 years	947	15	58	184	383	165	28	88	28	72.9	12.2
45 to 54 years	530	16	29	72	177	100	42	72	24	78.1	18.0
55 to 64 years	288	16	27	29	103	44	26	24	21	75.2	15.5
65 years and over	76	1	15	5	17	16	2	8	12	71.9	26.3
Not in labor force	25 060	814	2 932	6 393	6 935	4 004	730	2 049	1 203	59.5	13.0
16 and 17 years	2 524	8	256	2 244	12	4	—	—	—	0.6	—
18 to 24 years	3 128	25	72	982	592	1 315	64	74	5	65.5	2.5
25 years and over	19 407	781	2 603	3 168	6 330	2 686	666	1 975	1 198	66.2	16.4
25 to 29 years	748	21	23	127	234	143	28	141	31	77.1	22.9
30 to 34 years	754	28	37	177	276	115	33	40	47	67.9	11.5
35 to 44 years	1 794	57	78	389	721	276	87	140	46	70.8	10.4
45 to 54 years	1 687	78	170	257	648	243	97	123	72	70.1	11.6
55 to 64 years	3 309	128	438	494	1 129	426	131	316	247	68.0	17.0
65 years and over	11 115	467	1 859	1 723	3 323	1 483	290	1 215	755	63.6	17.7
Female											
Civilian labor force	62 899	302	1 328	5 862	20 925	13 223	5 700	11 016	4 541	88.1	24.7
16 and 17 years	1 428	—	33	1 354	33	8	—	—	—	2.9	—
18 to 24 years	8 594	19	92	1 178	2 850	3 131	406	887	32	85.0	10.7
25 years and over	52 877	283	1 203	3 330	18 043	10 085	5 295	10 129	4 509	90.9	27.7
25 to 29 years	7 437	24	103	370	2 102	1 615	731	2 029	463	93.3	33.5
30 to 34 years	7 880	28	123	480	2 513	1 539	898	1 682	617	92.0	29.2
35 to 44 years	17 223	76	320	943	5 911	3 355	1 972	3 265	1 382	92.2	27.0
45 to 54 years	12 911	77	312	745	4 581	2 337	1 208	2 208	1 445	91.2	28.3
55 to 64 years	5 795	54	226	566	2 313	984	380	758	513	85.4	21.9
65 years and over	1 631	24	120	227	622	255	106	187	90	77.2	17.0
Employed	59 654	260	1 198	5 014	19 802	12 609	5 528	10 789	4 454	89.2	25.6
16 and 17 years	1 174	—	18	1 121	27	8	—	—	—	3.0	—

See footnotes at end of table.

Table B-6.   Educational Attainment of Persons 16 Years Old and Over, by Labor Force Status, Age, Sex, Race, and Hispanic Origin: March 1997 — Continued

(Numbers in thousands. Civilian noninstitutional population.)

Marital status, age, sex, race, and Hispanic origin	Total	Elementary		High School		College				Percent:	
		None-4th grade	5th-8th grade	9th-11th grade	High school graduate	Some college no degree	Associate degree	Bachelor's degree	Advanced degree	High school graduate or more	Bachelor's degree or more
18 to 24 years	7 764	19	74	937	2 533	2 924	382	863	32	86.7	11.5
25 years and over	50 716	241	1 106	2 956	17 242	9 676	5 146	9 926	4 422	91.5	28.3
25 to 29 years	6 999	17	89	285	1 958	1 503	703	1 989	455	94.4	34.9
30 to 34 years	7 491	26	108	411	2 373	1 466	867	1 641	598	92.7	29.9
35 to 44 years	16 487	63	284	807	5 641	3 222	1 911	3 201	1 357	93.0	27.6
45 to 54 years	12 534	66	292	697	4 419	2 279	1 191	2 166	1 424	91.6	28.6
55 to 64 years	5 629	48	217	535	2 245	967	369	748	500	85.8	22.2
65 years and over	1 575	21	115	220	606	240	104	181	87	77.3	17.0
Unemployed	3 245	42	131	849	1 123	615	172	227	87	68.5	9.7
16 and 17 years	254	—	15	233	6	—	—	—	—	2.3	—
18 to 24 years	830	—	19	241	317	206	24	24	—	68.7	2.9
25 years and over	2 161	42	98	374	800	408	148	203	87	76.2	13.4
25 to 29 years	438	7	14	84	144	112	28	40	8	75.9	11.0
30 to 34 years	389	2	15	68	140	73	31	41	19	78.1	15.4
35 to 44 years	735	13	36	136	270	133	60	63	25	75.0	11.9
45 to 54 years	377	11	20	48	161	58	17	42	20	79.2	16.6
55 to 64 years	166	7	9	31	68	17	11	10	13	71.6	13.8
65 years and over	56	2	5	7	17	15	1	6	2	(B)	(B)
Not in labor force	42 228	1 154	4 565	8 867	14 319	6 627	1 894	3 666	1 137	65.5	11.4
16 and 17 years	2 358	3	170	2 133	48	4	—	—	—	2.2	—
18 to 24 years	3 840	48	149	1 064	964	1 385	91	127	13	67.2	3.6
25 years and over	36 030	1 103	4 246	5 670	13 308	5 237	1 803	3 539	1 124	69.4	12.9
25 to 29 years	2 199	35	148	386	747	455	97	289	41	74.1	15.0
30 to 34 years	2 668	62	160	380	860	512	181	450	63	77.4	19.2
35 to 44 years	4 925	105	308	645	1 707	903	344	726	187	78.5	18.5
45 to 54 years	3 980	124	379	570	1 522	605	240	401	139	73.0	13.6
55 to 64 years	5 415	201	598	888	2 135	702	292	437	164	68.9	11.1
65 years and over	16 843	577	2 654	2 801	6 336	2 060	648	1 237	530	64.2	10.5

WHITE

Male

Civilian labor force	61 982	611	2 429	6 819	19 503	11 882	4 348	10 743	5 646	84.1	26.4
16 and 17 years	1 299	1	83	1 188	22	5	—	—	—	2.1	—
18 to 24 years	7 825	48	272	1 504	2 664	2 411	341	558	26	76.7	7.5
25 years and over	52 858	562	2 073	4 127	16 818	9 467	4 006	10 185	5 620	87.2	29.9
25 to 29 years	7 287	70	249	696	2 205	1 503	564	1 670	330	86.1	27.4
30 to 34 years	7 903	55	270	706	2 626	1 361	724	1 633	530	87.0	27.4
35 to 44 years	16 879	169	514	1 276	5 788	3 101	1 309	3 135	1 587	88.4	28.0
45 to 54 years	12 550	130	441	743	3 517	2 299	1 010	2 457	1 952	89.5	35.1
55 to 64 years	6 172	105	394	489	2 081	931	306	977	887	84.0	30.2
65 years and over	2 067	32	205	217	602	272	94	312	333	78.0	31.2
Employed	58 778	557	2 191	5 955	18 476	11 300	4 220	10 529	5 550	85.2	27.4
16 and 17 years	1 023	—	46	954	18	5	—	—	—	2.3	—
18 to 24 years	7 115	44	238	1 248	2 459	2 227	332	541	26	78.5	8.0
25 years and over	50 640	514	1 907	3 753	15 999	9 068	3 888	9 988	5 524	87.8	30.6
25 to 29 years	6 879	70	216	619	2 044	1 426	537	1 645	321	86.8	28.6
30 to 34 years	7 560	51	244	619	2 497	1 313	711	1 608	518	87.9	28.1
35 to 44 years	16 157	159	461	1 147	5 503	2 964	1 290	3 070	1 563	89.1	28.7
45 to 54 years	12 114	114	417	687	3 377	2 212	974	2 401	1 931	89.9	35.8
55 to 64 years	5 921	89	372	468	1 993	894	283	956	867	84.3	30.8
65 years and over	2 009	31	197	212	586	260	92	308	324	78.1	31.5
Unemployed	3 204	54	238	864	1 027	582	128	214	96	63.9	9.7
16 and 17 years	276	1	37	234	3	—	—	—	—	1.3	—
18 to 24 years	710	5	34	256	205	184	10	17	—	58.5	2.4
25 years and over	2 218	48	166	374	819	399	119	197	96	73.5	13.2
25 to 29 years	407	—	33	77	161	77	26	25	8	73.0	8.3
30 to 34 years	343	5	26	87	129	48	12	25	12	65.9	10.7
35 to 44 years	722	10	53	129	285	137	19	65	24	73.4	12.4
45 to 54 years	436	16	24	55	140	87	36	56	22	78.2	17.9

Table B-6. Educational Attainment of Persons 16 Years Old and Over, by Labor Force Status, Age, Sex, Race, and Hispanic Origin: March 1997 — Continued

(Numbers in thousands. Civilian noninstitutional population.)

Marital status, age, sex, race, and Hispanic origin	Total	Elementary		High School		College				Percent:	
		None-4th grade	5th-8th grade	9th-11th grade	High school graduate	Some college no degree	Associate degree	Bachelor's degree	Advanced degree	High school graduate or more	Bachelor's degree or more
55 to 64 years	251	16	22	21	88	38	23	22	21	76.5	16.9
65 years and over	58	1	8	5	16	12	2	4	9	(B)	(B)
Not in labor force	20 343	538	2 398	4 825	5 789	3 297	616	1 806	1 074	61.9	14.2
16 and 17 years	1 909	5	170	1 721	10	4	—	—	—	0.7	—
18 to 24 years	2 259	8	53	684	407	987	56	59	5	67.0	2.8
25 years and over	16 174	526	2 175	2 419	5 372	2 306	561	1 746	1 069	68.3	17.4
25 to 29 years	462	10	19	78	130	87	26	92	19	76.7	24.1
30 to 34 years	506	12	32	105	191	75	23	38	31	70.7	13.5
35 to 44 years	1 240	34	50	241	521	192	72	107	23	73.8	10.5
45 to 54 years	1 287	59	137	168	482	203	76	99	64	71.8	12.6
55 to 64 years	2 724	79	352	356	964	372	110	274	215	71.1	18.0
65 years and over	9 956	332	1 585	1 471	3 083	1 377	253	1 135	718	66.0	18.6
Female											
Civilian labor force	51 910	238	1 068	4 567	17 200	10 788	4 719	9 376	3 954	88.7	25.7
16 and 17 years	1 213	—	21	1 165	21	5	—	—	—	2.2	—
18 to 24 years	6 872	19	83	871	2 237	2 547	341	747	27	85.8	11.3
25 years and over	43 825	219	964	2 531	14 942	8 236	4 378	8 629	3 927	91.5	28.7
25 to 29 years	5 931	21	75	267	1 621	1 270	581	1 722	375	93.9	35.4
30 to 34 years	6 349	23	100	359	2 009	1 194	720	1 422	522	92.4	30.6
35 to 44 years	14 143	65	268	699	4 875	2 656	1 603	2 763	1 214	92.7	28.1
45 to 54 years	10 959	58	251	545	3 845	2 007	1 052	1 905	1 296	92.2	29.2
55 to 64 years	5 005	36	176	461	2 025	884	324	652	447	86.5	21.9
65 years and over	1 436	14	93	199	568	224	99	166	73	78.7	16.7
Employed	49 633	205	970	4 001	16 374	10 382	4 608	9 207	3 887	89.6	26.4
16 and 17 years	1 007	—	16	969	17	5	—	—	—	2.2	—
18 to 24 years	6 361	19	68	742	2 024	2 415	329	737	27	87.0	12.0
25 years and over	42 265	186	886	2 291	14 333	7 961	4 279	8 470	3 859	92.0	29.2
25 to 29 years	5 654	17	66	221	1 515	1 216	560	1 691	368	94.6	36.4
30 to 34 years	6 108	21	88	330	1 915	1 150	703	1 391	509	92.8	31.1
35 to 44 years	13 613	56	241	602	4 679	2 559	1 565	2 715	1 197	93.4	28.7
45 to 54 years	10 637	48	234	513	3 709	1 952	1 035	1 866	1 280	92.5	29.6
55 to 64 years	4 863	33	169	433	1 963	868	319	644	434	86.9	22.2
65 years and over	1 390	12	89	192	551	215	97	163	71	78.9	16.8
Unemployed	2 277	33	98	565	826	406	112	169	68	69.4	10.4
16 and 17 years	206	—	5	197	4	—	—	—	—	2.2	—
18 to 24 years	511	—	15	129	213	132	12	10	—	71.8	1.9
25 years and over	1 560	33	78	240	609	275	99	159	68	77.5	14.5
25 to 29 years	278	4	10	46	106	54	21	31	8	78.5	13.7
30 to 34 years	242	2	12	30	94	44	18	30	13	81.8	17.7
35 to 44 years	530	10	28	98	196	97	38	48	17	74.5	12.2
45 to 54 years	322	11	17	32	135	56	17	39	16	81.5	17.1
55 to 64 years	142	3	7	28	62	16	5	8	13	72.9	14.6
65 years and over	46	2	5	7	16	9	1	3	2	(B)	(B)
Not in labor force	35 321	865	3 764	6 861	12 366	5 645	1 668	3 192	960	67.5	11.8
16 and 17 years	1 781	2	126	1 614	38	2	—	—	—	2.2	—
18 to 24 years	2 911	41	141	740	734	1 084	75	86	10	68.3	3.3
25 years and over	30 628	822	3 497	4 507	11 594	4 559	1 592	3 106	950	71.2	13.2
25 to 29 years	1 735	29	130	291	577	369	86	224	28	74.0	14.6
30 to 34 years	2 153	49	130	280	681	415	155	387	55	78.7	20.5
35 to 44 years	3 970	79	259	478	1 357	716	299	636	147	79.5	19.7
45 to 54 years	3 227	103	292	403	1 265	521	200	333	111	75.3	13.8
55 to 64 years	4 537	146	451	668	1 887	603	261	383	138	72.1	11.5
65 years and over	15 005	416	2 234	2 387	5 827	1 936	591	1 144	470	66.4	10.8

See footnotes at end of table.

Table B-6. Educational Attainment of Persons 16 Years Old and Over, by Labor Force Status, Age, Sex, Race, and Hispanic Origin: March 1997 — Continued

(Numbers in thousands. Civilian noninstitutional population.)

Marital status, age, sex, race, and Hispanic origin	Total	Elementary		High School		College				Percent:	
		None-4th grade	5th-8th grade	9th-11th grade	High school graduate	Some college no degree	Associate degree	Bachelor's degree	Advanced degree	High school graduate or more	Bachelor's degree or more
BLACK											
Male											
Civilian labor force	7 110	64	259	1 122	2 762	1 583	383	695	241	79.7	13.2
16 and 17 years	162	—	18	136	8	—	—	—	—	5.0	—
18 to 24 years	1 071	—	8	250	492	273	15	34	—	75.9	3.1
25 years and over	5 877	64	233	737	2 262	1 310	369	661	241	82.4	15.3
25 to 29 years	975	2	1	118	394	293	44	96	27	87.6	12.6
30 to 34 years	1 027	7	18	108	430	246	78	114	27	87.0	13.7
35 to 44 years	1 985	9	54	200	835	454	113	256	64	86.8	16.1
45 to 54 years	1 263	12	65	198	423	230	91	164	79	78.2	19.3
55 to 64 years	498	19	63	101	152	70	39	27	27	63.3	10.8
65 years and over	128	14	33	12	29	17	4	4	16	54.0	15.9
Employed	6 208	64	225	820	2 412	1 443	358	653	233	82.1	14.3
16 and 17 years	90	—	7	79	5	—	—	—	—	5.1	—
18 to 24 years	752	—	5	140	355	210	9	34	—	80.8	4.5
25 years and over	5 365	64	213	601	2 052	1 233	349	620	233	83.6	15.9
25 to 29 years	852	2	1	85	336	269	41	92	27	89.7	13.9
30 to 34 years	916	7	15	74	390	230	73	100	27	89.5	13.8
35 to 44 years	1 817	9	50	155	756	433	107	246	61	88.2	16.9
45 to 54 years	1 186	12	60	182	394	219	88	153	77	78.6	19.4
55 to 64 years	474	19	60	93	147	65	36	25	27	63.5	10.9
65 years and over	120	14	27	12	29	17	4	4	14	55.6	14.9
Unemployed	902	—	34	302	350	140	26	42	8	62.7	5.5
16 and 17 years	71	—	11	57	4	—	—	—	—	(B)	(B)
18 to 24 years	319	—	3	110	136	64	6	—	—	64.5	—
25 years and over	512	—	20	136	210	77	19	42	8	69.6	9.7
25 to 29 years	123	—	—	33	57	24	3	5	—	73.1	3.8
30 to 34 years	111	—	3	34	40	16	4	14	—	66.9	12.7
35 to 44 years	169	—	3	46	80	21	6	10	3	70.9	7.7
45 to 54 years	77	—	5	16	29	11	3	11	2	72.7	17.0
55 to 64 years	24	—	3	7	5	5	2	2	—	(B)	(B)
65 years and over	8	—	6	—	—	—	—	—	3	(B)	(B)
Not in labor force	3 599	209	450	1 298	947	486	71	95	42	45.6	3.8
16 and 17 years	465	4	79	381	2	—	—	—	—	0.4	—
18 to 24 years	647	18	17	253	147	205	4	3	—	55.5	0.5
25 years and over	2 487	188	354	664	798	281	67	92	42	51.5	5.4
25 to 29 years	192	8	3	44	90	30	—	14	2	71.5	8.6
30 to 34 years	179	5	3	68	75	20	8	—	—	57.1	—
35 to 44 years	459	21	26	139	180	73	6	12	1	59.3	2.8
45 to 54 years	322	10	21	80	147	31	18	15	—	65.6	4.8
55 to 64 years	450	35	69	124	126	44	19	19	14	49.3	7.4
65 years and over	885	109	232	209	180	84	16	31	24	37.9	6.3
Female											
Civilian labor force	8 141	24	138	1 070	2 963	1 967	720	935	324	84.9	15.5
16 and 17 years	161	—	3	145	10	3	—	—	—	7.9	—
18 to 24 years	1 335	—	2	248	523	434	47	77	5	81.3	6.2
25 years and over	6 645	24	133	678	2 430	1 531	673	858	319	87.4	17.7
25 to 29 years	1 118	3	4	82	401	306	100	190	31	92.0	19.8
30 to 34 years	1 147	1	14	106	393	287	140	171	36	89.5	18.0
35 to 44 years	2 274	2	33	186	819	573	279	295	86	90.3	16.8
45 to 54 years	1 388	6	28	174	556	257	117	146	104	85.0	18.0
55 to 64 years	577	5	34	101	224	88	33	44	48	75.6	15.9
65 years and over	142	7	19	28	37	20	5	12	14	62.4	18.3
Employed	7 332	18	119	818	2 701	1 803	667	891	316	87.0	16.5
16 and 17 years	126	—	—	114	10	3	—	—	—	10.0	—

See footnotes at end of table.

Table B-6. Educational Attainment of Persons 16 Years Old and Over, by Labor Force Status, Age, Sex, Race, and Hispanic Origin: March 1997 — Continued

(Numbers in thousands. Civilian noninstitutional population.)

Marital status, age, sex, race, and Hispanic origin	Total	Elementary		High School		College				Percent:	
		None-4th grade	5th-8th grade	9th-11th grade	High school graduate	Some college no degree	Associate degree	Bachelor's degree	Advanced degree	High school graduate or more	Bachelor's degree or more
18 to 24 years	1 064	—	—	148	433	373	35	70	5	86.1	7.1
25 years and over	6 142	18	119	556	2 258	1 427	632	820	311	88.7	18.4
25 to 29 years	977	—	3	46	369	256	92	180	31	95.0	21.6
30 to 34 years	1 014	1	11	69	348	265	126	160	32	91.9	19.0
35 to 44 years	2 118	—	28	157	752	550	262	285	84	91.2	17.4
45 to 54 years	1 340	6	25	159	534	255	117	143	102	85.8	18.3
55 to 64 years	561	4	32	98	219	86	30	44	48	76.1	16.4
65 years and over	132	7	19	27	37	14	5	8	14	59.9	17.2
Unemployed	809	6	20	253	261	165	53	44	8	65.6	6.4
16 and 17 years	35	—	3	31	—	—	—	—	—	(B)	(B)
18 to 24 years	271	—	2	100	90	61	11	7	—	62.5	2.5
25 years and over	503	6	14	122	171	104	41	37	8	71.8	8.9
25 to 29 years	141	3	2	37	32	50	8	10	—	70.6	7.0
30 to 34 years	133	—	3	37	45	22	13	11	3	70.5	10.6
35 to 44 years	157	1	5	29	68	23	17	11	2	77.2	8.1
45 to 54 years	48	—	3	16	22	2	—	3	2	(B)	(B)
55 to 64 years	16	1	2	3	5	1	3	—	—	(B)	(B)
65 years and over	10	—	—	—	—	6	—	3	—	(B)	(B)
Not in labor force	5 043	139	600	1 682	1 509	655	155	198	106	52.0	6.0
16 and 17 years	458	1	43	401	10	2	—	—	—	2.7	—
18 to 24 years	625	3	3	255	179	168	6	10	—	58.2	1.6
25 years and over	3 960	134	553	1 027	1 321	484	148	187	106	56.7	7.4
25 to 29 years	307	3	5	86	138	57	6	12	—	69.4	4.0
30 to 34 years	352	8	17	88	139	71	18	12	—	68.0	3.5
35 to 44 years	649	10	30	142	252	137	25	38	15	71.8	8.1
45 to 54 years	549	6	68	134	191	65	36	33	17	62.2	9.1
55 to 64 years	642	14	94	205	201	62	20	24	22	51.3	7.3
65 years and over	1 461	93	340	371	400	93	45	68	51	45.0	8.2

HISPANIC ORIGIN [1]

Male

Marital status, age, sex, race, and Hispanic origin	Total	None-4th grade	5th-8th grade	9th-11th grade	High school graduate	Some college no degree	Associate degree	Bachelor's degree	Advanced degree	High school graduate or more	Bachelor's degree or more
Civilian labor force	8 129	529	1 435	1 635	2 111	1 269	381	517	252	55.7	9.5
16 and 17 years	178	1	26	148	3	—	—	—	—	1.6	—
18 to 24 years	1 547	45	217	466	409	341	30	35	4	52.9	2.5
25 years and over	6 404	482	1 192	1 021	1 699	928	351	482	248	57.9	11.4
25 to 29 years	1 372	62	209	285	393	215	80	111	18	59.5	9.4
30 to 34 years	1 295	51	208	240	374	204	62	111	44	61.4	11.9
35 to 44 years	2 039	159	401	293	543	310	112	140	80	58.2	10.8
45 to 54 years	1 081	100	241	131	251	138	73	83	64	56.4	13.6
55 to 64 years	510	89	111	65	108	48	22	36	30	47.9	13.0
65 years and over	107	21	22	7	29	12	3	1	12	53.5	12.4
Employed	7 385	477	1 291	1 405	1 929	1 182	354	505	241	57.0	10.1
16 and 17 years	115	—	13	100	3	—	—	—	—	2.5	—
18 to 24 years	1 337	40	196	373	355	308	26	35	4	54.4	2.9
25 years and over	5 932	437	1 083	932	1 572	875	328	470	237	58.7	11.9
25 to 29 years	1 261	62	186	262	358	202	68	105	18	59.5	9.7
30 to 34 years	1 221	47	194	214	350	201	62	111	42	62.7	12.5
35 to 44 years	1 869	148	354	263	504	284	110	134	71	59.1	11.0
45 to 54 years	1 020	86	232	126	235	131	63	83	64	56.5	14.4
55 to 64 years	465	74	100	61	100	44	22	36	29	49.7	14.0
65 years and over	96	19	17	7	25	12	3	1	12	55.3	13.9
Unemployed	744	52	143	231	182	86	27	12	12	42.8	3.1
16 and 17 years	63	1	14	48	—	—	—	—	—	(B)	(B)
18 to 24 years	210	5	21	93	54	33	4	—	—	43.5	—
25 years and over	471	46	109	90	128	53	23	12	12	48.2	4.9
25 to 29 years	111	—	22	23	36	13	12	6	—	59.5	5.5
30 to 34 years	74	5	14	27	24	4	—	—	2	(B)	(B)
35 to 44 years	170	10	47	30	40	26	2	6	9	48.1	8.4
45 to 54 years	61	14	8	5	16	7	10	—	—	(B)	(B)

See footnotes at end of table.

Table B-6. Educational Attainment of Persons 16 Years Old and Over, by Labor Force Status, Age, Sex, Race, and Hispanic Origin: March 1997 — Continued

(Numbers in thousands. Civilian noninstitutional population.)

| Marital status, age, sex, race, and Hispanic origin | Total | Elementary | | High School | | College | | | | Percent: | |
		None-4th grade	5th-8th grade	9th-11th grade	High school graduate	Some college no degree	Associate degree	Bachelor's degree	Advanced degree	High school graduate or more	Bachelor's degree or more
55 to 64 years	45	16	11	5	8	4	—	—	1	(B)	(B)
65 years and over	11	1	6	—	4	—	—	—	—	(B)	(B)
Not in labor force	2 128	241	420	783	356	210	36	62	19	32.1	3.8
16 and 17 years	405	1	48	355	—	2	—	—	—	0.4	—
18 to 24 years	420	11	39	187	66	101	10	7	—	43.7	1.7
25 years and over	1 304	230	334	242	290	108	26	55	19	38.2	5.7
25 to 29 years	108	5	16	35	24	17	2	9	—	48.3	8.4
30 to 34 years	98	4	28	31	14	12	4	4	—	35.3	4.1
35 to 44 years	199	8	19	43	89	23	4	10	2	64.3	5.8
45 to 54 years	135	25	27	24	36	13	3	5	1	43.6	4.7
55 to 64 years	231	43	71	44	44	13	4	9	3	31.7	5.0
65 years and over	532	145	173	63	81	29	9	19	13	28.4	6.0
Female											
Civilian labor force	5 380	212	625	886	1 661	1 003	369	488	136	68.0	11.6
16 and 17 years	122	—	4	110	8	—	—	—	—	6.4	—
18 to 24 years	930	17	52	198	346	260	34	23	1	71.3	2.6
25 years and over	4 328	195	569	578	1 307	743	335	465	135	69.0	13.9
25 to 29 years	825	21	45	114	260	171	73	113	28	78.2	17.0
30 to 34 years	836	23	89	131	236	150	79	103	25	71.0	15.4
35 to 44 years	1 445	64	221	179	452	256	94	141	37	67.9	12.3
45 to 54 years	773	46	136	84	218	118	63	78	30	65.6	14.0
55 to 64 years	381	31	65	57	125	39	25	28	11	59.7	10.2
65 years and over	68	10	13	13	17	9	1	3	3	(B)	(B)
Employed	4 877	176	558	739	1 500	952	346	472	134	69.8	12.4
16 and 17 years	80	—	2	74	4	—	—	—	—	6.0	—
18 to 24 years	782	17	39	144	287	241	32	21	1	74.4	2.8
25 years and over	4 015	159	517	521	1 209	711	314	452	132	70.2	14.6
25 to 29 years	756	17	39	92	241	165	67	107	28	80.4	17.8
30 to 34 years	781	21	77	122	220	140	75	103	23	71.9	16.2
35 to 44 years	1 329	51	198	160	413	246	88	135	37	69.2	13.0
45 to 54 years	730	36	131	79	204	113	60	76	30	66.3	14.5
55 to 64 years	356	26	60	55	115	37	24	28	11	60.3	10.9
65 years and over	63	8	12	13	15	9	—	3	3	(B)	(B)
Unemployed	503	36	67	147	160	51	23	16	2	50.2	3.5
16 and 17 years	42	—	2	36	3	—	—	—	—	(B)	(B)
18 to 24 years	148	—	13	54	59	19	1	2	—	55.0	1.4
25 years and over	313	36	52	57	99	32	22	14	2	53.7	5.1
25 to 29 years	69	4	6	21	19	6	6	6	—	(B)	(B)
30 to 34 years	55	2	12	9	16	9	4	—	2	(B)	(B)
35 to 44 years	116	13	23	19	38	10	7	6	—	52.4	5.1
45 to 54 years	43	9	5	5	14	5	3	2	—	(B)	(B)
55 to 64 years	25	5	5	2	10	2	1	—	—	(B)	(B)
65 years and over	5	2	—	—	1	—	1	—	—	(B)	(B)
Not in labor force	4 478	568	1 095	1 263	868	395	95	149	43	34.6	4.3
16 and 17 years	377	2	36	331	7	1	—	—	—	2.1	—
18 to 24 years	709	25	100	270	162	128	11	10	4	44.3	2.0
25 years and over	3 392	541	959	663	700	266	84	139	39	36.2	5.3
25 to 29 years	453	28	97	144	104	52	• 5	19	3	40.5	5.0
30 to 34 years	475	42	109	115	98	61	17	25	9	44.2	7.2
35 to 44 years	690	54	189	125	162	70	35	46	9	46.7	8.1
45 to 54 years	469	68	161	80	99	38	9	11	4	34.1	3.1
55 to 64 years	496	111	164	87	97	15	6	12	3	26.9	3.1
65 years and over	808	237	240	111	140	30	13	26	11	27.2	4.5

Source: March 1997 Current Population Survey, Education and Social Stratification Branch, U.S. Bureau of the Census.

1. May be of any race.

— Represents zero or rounds to zero.

(B) Base less than 75,000.

Table B-7. Educational Attainment of Persons 18 to 64 Years Old, by Occupation of Employed Person, Age, Sex, Race, and Hispanic Origin: March 1997

(Numbers in thousands. Civilian noninstitutional population.)

| Occupation, age, sex, race, and Hispanic origin | Total | Elementary | | High School | | College | | | | Percent: | |
		None-4th grade	5th-8th grade	9th-11th grade	High school graduate	Some college no degree	Associate degree	Bachelor's degree	Advanced degree	High school graduate or more	Bachelor's degree or more
ALL RACES											
Male											
18 to 24 years	8 196	46	243	1 439	2 931	2 546	350	611	31	78.9	7.8
Executive, administrative, and managerial	416	—	2	27	123	100	28	134	3	93.1	33.0
Professional specialty	512	—	—	8	48	203	33	201	17	98.4	42.7
Technicians and related support	257	—	—	11	59	111	34	41	3	95.9	16.8
Sales	1 051	—	8	158	319	444	41	81	—	84.2	7.7
Administrative support, including clerical	678	—	—	59	193	340	21	64	1	91.2	9.6
Private household	1	—	—	1	—	—	—	—	—	(B)	(B)
Other service	1 521	5	58	352	448	553	62	44	—	72.7	2.9
Farming, forestry, and fishing	325	8	61	96	93	48	16	2	1	49.3	1.0
Precision production, craft, and repair	1 161	24	49	193	583	229	60	22	2	77.1	2.0
Machine operators, assemblers, and inspectors	767	3	41	144	421	133	17	8	—	75.5	1.0
Transportation and material moving	448	1	8	82	190	146	11	10	—	79.7	2.1
Handlers, equipment cleaners, helpers, and laborers	1 059	6	16	307	454	240	28	5	4	69.0	0.8
25 to 64 years	56 471	571	1 999	4 277	18 012	10 384	4 301	10 998	5 929	87.9	30.0
Executive, administrative, and managerial	9 220	7	58	221	1 679	1 709	642	3 232	1 671	96.9	53.2
Professional specialty	7 965	—	15	43	414	650	501	2 979	3 362	99.3	79.6
Technicians and related support	1 675	—	8	32	271	429	355	456	122	97.6	34.5
Sales	6 190	20	64	204	1 657	1 463	484	1 975	323	95.3	37.1
Administrative support, including clerical	3 035	5	34	126	996	831	275	662	106	94.6	25.3
Private household	14	3	2	4	3	—	—	2	—	(B)	(B)
Other service	4 701	76	332	494	1 759	1 057	429	439	115	80.8	11.8
Farming, forestry, and fishing	1 906	184	272	240	675	257	94	139	45	63.5	9.7
Precision production, craft, and repair	11 123	89	512	1 289	5 237	2 249	994	647	104	83.0	6.8
Machine operators, assemblers, and inspectors	4 130	78	285	577	2 111	645	244	149	41	77.2	4.6
Transportation and material moving	4 101	20	243	645	2 091	716	193	179	14	77.9	4.7
Handlers, equipment cleaners, helpers, and laborers	2 411	87	172	402	1 119	378	90	139	25	72.6	6.8
25 to 34 years	17 160	136	508	1 463	5 466	3 383	1 419	3 713	1 073	87.7	27.9
Executive, administrative, and managerial	2 219	3	6	47	392	396	188	977	210	97.5	53.5
Professional specialty	2 437	—	5	11	129	229	175	1 177	711	99.4	77.5
Technicians and related support	602	—	1	10	64	187	113	194	32	98.1	37.5
Sales	1 855	7	15	52	511	471	155	600	43	96.0	34.7
Administrative support, including clerical	1 040	—	11	41	307	320	90	256	14	94.9	26.0
Private household	7	—	2	4	1	—	—	—	—	(B)	(B)
Other service	1 655	23	112	165	566	416	170	176	27	81.9	12.2
Farming, forestry, and fishing	562	37	95	101	181	69	29	42	8	58.5	8.8
Precision production, craft, and repair	3 266	22	104	486	1 502	635	345	158	16	81.3	5.3
Machine operators, assemblers, and inspectors	1 402	23	65	212	759	221	73	38	11	78.6	3.5
Transportation and material moving	1 155	4	42	155	608	245	52	47	2	82.6	4.3
Handlers, equipment cleaners, helpers, and laborers	960	16	51	179	445	193	28	47	—	74.4	4.9
35 to 44 years	18 806	185	537	1 345	6 450	3 523	1 453	3 505	1 806	89.0	28.2
Executive, administrative, and managerial	3 121	2	16	72	654	577	199	1 038	563	97.1	51.3
Professional specialty	2 506	—	1	18	157	189	159	1 002	980	99.3	79.1
Technicians and related support	643	—	3	8	115	157	165	140	54	98.3	30.2
Sales	1 922	10	8	76	557	431	155	588	97	95.1	35.6
Administrative support, including clerical	913	2	10	43	284	241	91	216	26	94.0	26.5
Private household	5	3	—	—	2	—	—	—	—	(B)	(B)
Other service	1 462	21	91	150	587	364	111	115	22	82.0	9.4
Farming, forestry, and fishing	593	56	43	72	249	96	32	39	6	71.2	7.6
Precision production, craft, and repair	4 127	24	177	384	2 046	874	352	235	35	85.8	6.5
Machine operators, assemblers, and inspectors	1 410	25	74	178	737	243	97	48	8	80.3	4.0

See footnotes at end of table.

Table B-7.   Educational Attainment of Persons 18 to 64 Years Old, by Occupation of Employed Person, Age, Sex, Race, and Hispanic Origin: March 1997 — Continued

(Numbers in thousands. Civilian noninstitutional population.)

Occupation, age, sex, race, and Hispanic origin	Total	Elementary		High School		College				Percent:	
		None-4th grade	5th-8th grade	9th-11th grade	High school graduate	Some college no degree	Associate degree	Bachelor's degree	Advanced degree	High school graduate or more	Bachelor's degree or more
Transportation and material moving	1 331	5	56	215	687	256	62	47	2	79.3	3.7
Handlers, equipment cleaners, helpers, and laborers	773	38	58	128	375	94	30	37	13	71.0	6.4
45 to 64 years	20 505	250	954	1 468	6 096	3 478	1 429	3 780	3 050	87.0	33.3
Executive, administrative, and managerial	3 879	2	37	101	633	736	255	1 218	898	96.4	54.5
Professional specialty	3 022	—	10	15	128	232	167	800	1 671	99.2	81.8
Technicians and related support	431	—	4	14	92	84	78	123	36	95.8	36.9
Sales	2 413	3	41	75	589	562	173	786	183	95.0	40.2
Administrative support, including clerical	1 081	2	14	42	405	270	93	190	66	94.7	23.6
Private household	2	—	—	—	—	—	—	2	—	(B)	(B)
Other service	1 584	32	129	178	605	277	147	148	67	78.6	13.6
Farming, forestry, and fishing	751	91	134	67	245	91	33	59	31	61.1	12.0
Precision production, craft, and repair	3 729	43	231	420	1 690	741	297	254	54	81.4	8.2
Machine operators, assemblers, and inspectors	1 318	30	146	187	615	181	74	62	23	72.5	6.4
Transportation and material moving	1 616	12	146	275	795	215	80	84	10	73.2	5.8
Handlers, equipment cleaners, helpers, and laborers	678	34	63	94	298	90	31	55	12	71.8	9.9
Female											
18 to 24 years	7 764	19	74	937	2 533	2 924	382	863	32	86.7	11.5
Executive, administrative, and managerial	500	—	2	19	81	157	37	199	5	95.8	40.7
Professional specialty	722	—	—	25	69	231	53	323	21	96.6	47.6
Technicians and related support	223	—	—	14	51	80	46	33	—	93.6	14.7
Sales	1 614	3	8	285	592	587	40	97	2	81.7	6.1
Administrative support, including clerical	1 948	—	3	130	606	948	112	147	2	93.2	7.7
Private household	139	4	9	34	50	29	10	2	—	66.0	1.8
Other service	1 872	2	18	290	707	735	62	55	2	83.4	3.1
Farming, forestry, and fishing	72	4	2	18	25	16	4	3	—	(B)	(B)
Precision production, craft, and repair	96	3	5	15	29	34	5	4	—	76.2	4.5
Machine operators, assemblers, and inspectors	372	3	22	66	207	63	9	—	—	75.4	0.1
Transportation and material moving	50	—	—	4	30	14	2	—	—	(B)	(B)
Handlers, equipment cleaners, helpers, and laborers	156	—	4	37	84	31	—	—	—	73.7	—
25 to 64 years	49 141	219	990	2 736	16 637	9 437	5 042	9 745	4 335	92.0	28.7
Executive, administrative, and managerial	7 469	2	27	139	1 818	1 661	750	2 210	863	97.8	41.1
Professional specialty	9 549	3	18	44	627	813	1 160	3 931	2 953	99.3	72.1
Technicians and related support	1 901	—	5	30	432	415	529	388	100	98.1	25.7
Sales	5 480	3	60	382	2 158	1 261	455	1 016	144	91.9	21.2
Administrative support, including clerical	11 926	9	54	355	5 330	3 230	1 361	1 420	168	96.5	13.3
Private household	502	23	72	84	197	85	13	27	—	64.2	5.4
Other service	7 082	80	349	924	3 419	1 270	489	481	69	80.9	7.8
Farming, forestry, and fishing	464	17	30	41	180	82	38	67	8	80.9	16.2
Precision production, craft, and repair	1 081	6	56	146	530	189	73	64	15	80.7	7.4
Machine operators, assemblers, and inspectors	2 574	60	267	440	1 359	258	105	75	9	70.2	3.2
Transportation and material moving	418	—	2	56	222	92	27	13	5	86.1	4.5
Handlers, equipment cleaners, helpers, and laborers	697	15	49	96	364	81	40	52	—	77.0	7.5
25 to 34 years	14 490	43	197	697	4 331	2 969	1 570	3 630	1 053	93.5	32.3
Executive, administrative, and managerial	2 090	2	4	17	420	450	216	814	168	98.9	47.0
Professional specialty	2 856	1	1	19	180	223	317	1 392	723	99.3	74.1
Technicians and related support	643	—	1	6	113	123	202	159	39	98.8	30.7
Sales	1 738	1	8	125	566	417	144	438	38	92.3	27.4
Administrative support, including clerical	3 386	1	12	82	1 264	992	445	533	56	97.2	17.4
Private household	100	6	20	14	36	15	—	10	—	60.8	10.4
Other service	2 279	13	53	248	1 055	520	171	199	22	86.2	9.7
Farming, forestry, and fishing	108	4	12	9	37	21	10	15	1	76.6	14.8
Precision production, craft, and repair	260	5	5	30	114	54	21	28	4	85.0	12.3

See footnotes at end of table.

Table B-7. Educational Attainment of Persons 18 to 64 Years Old, by Occupation of Employed Person, Age, Sex, Race, and Hispanic Origin: March 1997 — Continued

(Numbers in thousands. Civilian noninstitutional population.)

Occupation, age, sex, race, and Hispanic origin	Total	Elementary		High School		College				Percent:	
		None–4th grade	5th-8th grade	9th-11th grade	High school graduate	Some college no degree	Associate degree	Bachelor's degree	Advanced degree	High school graduate or more	Bachelor's degree or more
Machine operators, assemblers, and inspectors	692	9	66	104	354	103	25	29	2	74.1	4.5
Transportation and material moving	115	—	2	13	63	26	10	2	—	87.1	1.7
Handlers, equipment cleaners, helpers, and laborers	224	2	13	30	131	27	11	10	—	79.9	4.5
35 to 44 years	16 487	63	284	807	5 641	3 222	1 911	3 201	1 357	93.0	27.6
Executive, administrative, and managerial	2 607	—	8	48	657	565	273	748	308	97.8	40.5
Professional specialty	3 200	—	10	12	182	317	476	1 302	902	99.3	68.9
Technicians and related support	709	—	—	10	163	147	213	144	33	98.6	24.9
Sales	1 695	—	17	125	670	399	136	315	33	91.6	20.6
Administrative support, including clerical	4 024	4	13	122	1 792	1 103	510	426	54	96.5	11.9
Private household	170	6	15	25	79	33	7	6	—	73.2	3.7
Other service	2 218	20	88	239	1 107	404	179	159	22	84.3	8.1
Farming, forestry, and fishing	138	5	9	5	56	20	16	26	—	85.9	19.0
Precision production, craft, and repair	425	—	23	53	223	77	23	22	2	81.9	5.8
Machine operators, assemblers, and inspectors	902	26	83	122	506	83	55	26	—	74.3	2.9
Transportation and material moving	132	—	—	12	66	41	6	4	3	90.9	5.5
Handlers, equipment cleaners, helpers, and laborers	266	1	17	33	139	34	19	23	—	80.7	8.5
45 to 64 years	18 163	113	509	1 232	6 665	3 246	1 560	2 914	1 924	89.8	26.6
Executive, administrative, and managerial	2 771	—	14	73	741	647	261	647	387	96.8	37.3
Professional specialty	3 493	2	7	13	265	273	367	1 237	1 329	99.4	73.4
Technicians and related support	548	—	4	14	156	145	115	86	28	96.7	20.8
Sales	2 047	2	35	132	922	445	176	262	72	91.7	16.4
Administrative support, including clerical	4 517	4	29	150	2 274	1 134	407	461	58	96.0	11.5
Private household	232	12	38	46	83	37	6	11	—	59.1	4.6
Other service	2 585	47	209	437	1 257	346	140	124	25	73.2	5.8
Farming, forestry, and fishing	217	8	9	27	88	41	13	26	6	80.0	15.1
Precision production, craft, and repair	396	1	29	63	193	58	29	14	9	76.5	5.7
Machine operators, assemblers, and inspectors	980	25	118	214	499	73	25	20	7	63.6	2.7
Transportation and material moving	170	—	—	31	93	25	12	7	2	81.7	5.7
Handlers, equipment cleaners, helpers, and laborers	207	13	19	32	93	20	11	19	—	69.2	9.3

WHITE

Male

25 to 64 years	48 631	483	1 711	3 541	15 413	8 808	3 796	9 680	5 199	88.2	30.6
Executive, administrative, and managerial	8 416	5	49	197	1 542	1 546	610	2 945	1 522	97.0	53.1
Professional specialty	6 922	—	15	33	342	547	454	2 631	2 900	99.3	79.9
Technicians and related support	1 409	—	8	26	233	360	308	377	96	97.6	33.6
Sales	5 583	9	64	187	1 499	1 302	449	1 773	299	95.3	37.1
Administrative support, including clerical	2 385	5	31	101	810	593	213	545	88	94.3	26.5
Private household	7	—	2	—	3	—	—	2	—	(B)	(B)
Other service	3 615	64	262	367	1 293	806	368	361	94	80.8	12.6
Farming, forestry, and fishing	1 733	171	243	194	618	240	92	135	41	64.9	10.1
Precision production, craft, and repair	9 900	73	463	1 131	4 669	2 026	893	550	95	83.2	6.5
Machine operators, assemblers, and inspectors	3 367	66	232	453	1 770	527	172	118	30	77.7	4.4
Transportation and material moving	3 405	15	201	536	1 762	570	155	152	14	77.9	4.9
Handlers, equipment cleaners, helpers, and laborers	1 890	75	141	317	873	291	81	92	19	71.8	5.9

Female

25 to 64 years	40 874	174	797	2 098	13 782	7 746	4 181	8 307	3 789	92.5	29.6
Executive, administrative, and managerial	6 515	—	25	123	1 598	1 483	666	1 894	725	97.7	40.2
Professional specialty	8 295	3	16	32	537	680	984	3 415	2 627	99.4	72.8
Technicians and related support	1 581	—	2	22	369	355	434	330	69	98.5	25.2

See footnotes at end of table.

Table B-7. Educational Attainment of Persons 18 to 64 Years Old, by Occupation of Employed Person, Age, Sex, Race, and Hispanic Origin: March 1997 — Continued

(Numbers in thousands. Civilian noninstitutional population.)

Occupation, age, sex, race, and Hispanic origin	Total	Elementary		High School		College				Percent:	
		None-4th grade	5th-8th grade	9th-11th grade	High school graduate	Some college no degree	Associate degree	Bachelor's degree	Advanced degree	High school graduate or more	Bachelor's degree or more
Sales	4 710	3	56	316	1 845	1 093	383	880	133	92.0	21.5
Administrative support, including clerical	9 982	6	44	279	4 709	2 531	1 102	1 171	140	96.7	13.1
Private household	397	19	59	61	144	78	11	25	—	64.9	6.3
Other service	5 383	64	284	640	2 565	983	397	386	65	81.6	8.4
Farming, forestry, and fishing	449	15	30	40	175	80	38	62	8	80.9	15.6
Precision production, craft, and repair	876	6	46	122	420	153	54	59	15	80.1	8.5
Machine operators, assemblers, and inspectors	1 811	44	191	336	950	188	66	34	2	68.5	2.0
Transportation and material moving	333	—	2	42	184	70	17	13	5	86.7	5.7
Handlers, equipment cleaners, helpers, and laborers	543	13	40	85	288	51	29	37	—	74.6	6.7
BLACK											
Male											
25 to 64 years	5 246	50	186	589	2 023	1 216	345	615	219	84.3	15.9
Executive, administrative, and managerial	455	—	9	15	96	113	19	139	64	94.7	44.6
Professional specialty	438	—	—	10	54	80	30	151	113	97.7	60.4
Technicians and related support	166	—	—	6	23	59	41	34	2	96.2	22.0
Sales	309	8	—	11	87	101	24	71	5	93.7	24.9
Administrative support, including clerical	476	—	2	14	143	199	37	70	11	96.6	17.1
Private household	4	—	—	4	—	—	—	—	—	(B)	(B)
Other service	813	4	37	104	370	203	37	44	13	82.1	7.1
Farming, forestry, and fishing	100	7	19	32	35	7	—	—	—	41.5	
Precision production, craft, and repair	896	11	34	116	456	171	58	47	2	82.1	5.5
Machine operators, assemblers, and inspectors	574	2	25	112	266	88	59	14	7	75.8	3.8
Transportation and material moving	595	5	37	94	287	127	34	10	—	77.2	1.8
Handlers, equipment cleaners, helpers, and laborers	421	12	23	71	205	69	6	34	—	74.6	8.0
Female											
25 to 64 years	6 010	12	99	529	2 221	1 413	627	812	297	89.4	18.4
Executive, administrative, and managerial	594	—	—	12	141	151	60	152	79	97.9	38.7
Professional specialty	851	—	2	11	75	116	133	326	187	98.4	60.2
Technicians and related support	212	—	3	4	55	51	67	24	7	96.6	14.8
Sales	480	—	4	54	177	132	42	69	2	87.9	14.9
Administrative support, including clerical	1 557	—	7	60	512	594	201	164	20	95.7	11.8
Private household	81	—	10	20	45	3	2	—	—	62.1	
Other service	1 375	6	33	247	724	246	69	50	—	79.2	3.6
Farming, forestry, and fishing	8	2	—	—	6	—	—	—	—	(B)	(B)
Precision production, craft, and repair	142	—	4	14	76	33	15	—	—	86.8	0.3
Machine operators, assemblers, and inspectors	527	1	31	84	317	52	24	16	2	78.0	3.4
Transportation and material moving	76	—	—	12	37	16	11	—	—	—	—
Handlers, equipment cleaners, helpers, and laborers	106	3	5	9	57	19	3	10	—	84.1	9.6
HISPANIC ORIGIN[1]											
Male											
25 to 64 years	5 836	417	1 067	925	1 547	862	325	469	225	58.7	11.9
Executive, administrative, and managerial	452	3	21	24	88	103	44	112	57	89.4	37.4
Professional specialty	336	—	7	6	32	53	25	111	102	96.0	63.4
Technicians and related support	112	—	4	1	20	38	26	18	5	94.9	19.9
Sales	408	7	31	42	113	101	36	63	15	80.4	19.2
Administrative support, including clerical	297	2	19	28	106	69	29	40	5	83.7	15.2
Private household	2	—	2	—	—	—	—	—	—	(B)	(B)
Other service	887	50	222	159	251	101	33	52	18	51.3	7.9
Farming, forestry, and fishing	500	154	170	70	55	24	16	7	4	21.1	2.1

See footnotes at end of table.

Table B-7. Educational Attainment of Persons 18 to 64 Years Old, by Occupation of Employed Person, Age, Sex, Race, and Hispanic Origin: March 1997 — Continued

(Numbers in thousands. Civilian noninstitutional population.)

Occupation, age, sex, race, and Hispanic origin	Total	Elementary		High School		College				Percent:	
		None-4th grade	5th-8th grade	9th-11th grade	High school graduate	Some college no degree	Associate degree	Bachelor's degree	Advanced degree	High school graduate or more	Bachelor's degree or more
Precision production, craft, and repair	1 239	67	246	243	358	216	70	33	7	55.2	3.2
Machine operators, assemblers, and inspectors	687	60	158	133	232	56	28	14	8	49.1	3.2
Transportation and material moving	472	13	78	124	187	48	12	5	5	54.4	2.1
Handlers, equipment cleaners, helpers, and laborers	445	61	109	94	106	53	8	14	—	40.5	3.1
Female											
25 to 64 years	3 952	152	505	508	1 193	702	314	449	130	70.5	14.6
Executive, administrative, and managerial	414	—	11	19	111	98	48	99	28	92.9	30.7
Professional specialty	415	3	10	5	41	47	56	174	78	95.5	60.9
Technicians and related support	126	—	1	5	18	39	37	25	1	94.8	21.0
Sales	369	3	25	56	135	84	34	29	2	77.0	8.5
Administrative support, including clerical	864	4	16	63	344	271	78	78	10	90.4	10.1
Private household	160	19	47	30	34	22	3	6	—	40.4	3.7
Other service	836	55	161	159	289	100	39	29	5	55.2	4.1
Farming, forestry, and fishing	48	12	17	2	11	1	2	—	3	(B)	(B)
Precision production, craft, and repair	103	6	25	20	29	15	5	2	2	49.8	3.1
Machine operators, assemblers, and inspectors	493	40	161	117	148	19	3	5	—	35.5	1.1
Transportation and material moving	22	—	2	5	8	2	4	—	—	(B)	(B)
Handlers, equipment cleaners, helpers, and laborers	101	9	29	25	27	4	6	1	—	38.1	1.2

Source: March 1997 Current Population Survey, Education and Social Stratification Branch, U.S. Bureau of the Census.

1. May be of any race.

— Represents zero or rounds to zero.

(B) Base less than 75,000.

Table B-8. Income by Educational Attainment for Persons 18 Years Old and Over, by Age, Sex, Race and Hispanic Origin: March 1997

(Numbers in thousands. Civilian noninstitutional population.)

Income, standard error, age, sex, race, and Hispanic origin	Total	Not a high school graduate				High school graduate or more							
		Total	Elementary		High School	Total	High school graduate only	College					
			None - 4th grade	5th - 8th grade	9th - 11th grade			Some college no degree	Associate degree	Bachelor's degree	Master's degree	Professional degree	Doctorate degree

ALL RACES

Both Sexes

18 years and over	195 568	36 311	2 983	11 066	22 261	159 258	65 370	38 041	13 336	29 089	9 205	2 455	1 761
Without income	11 250	4 446	440	1 169	2 837	6 804	3 689	1 845	407	669	141	34	19
With income	184 318	31 864	2 543	9 897	19 424	152 454	61 681	36 196	12 929	28 420	9 065	2 421	1 742
Median income .. ($) ..	18 383	9 820	7 526	9 783	10 223	21 223	16 470	17 893	24 431	30 566	40 797	62 183	57 171
Standard error .. ($) ..	96	88	215	127	125	86	108	187	322	205	406	2 406	2 044
Mean income ..... ($) ..	26 172	13 228	10 016	12 892	13 820	28 877	20 874	23 844	28 172	37 970	50 677	92 129	72 337
Standard error .. ($) ..	143	167	297	205	250	167	169	300	427	400	996	4 060	2 882

Male

18 years and over, with income	90 449	16 316	1 408	5 070	9 838	74 133	29 109	17 535	5 625	14 204	4 742	1 704	1 215
Median income .. ($) ..	24 806	12 736	9 758	12 581	13 520	28 209	22 530	24 016	31 634	37 930	49 667	71 799	62 255
Standard error .. ($) ..	155	167	443	230	241	213	197	346	398	527	1 092	2 645	1 639
Mean income ..... ($) ..	33 795	16 677	11 901	16 173	17 620	37 563	27 247	30 557	36 160	47 763	63 478	102 210	81 271
Standard error .. ($) ..	253	301	476	333	463	298	317	534	861	674	1 723	4 770	3 832
Year-round, full-time workers	53 744	6 222	444	1 771	4 008	47 522	17 585	10 156	4 133	10 188	3 290	1 277	893
Median income .. ($) ..	33 573	20 134	15 565	18 135	21 341	36 060	29 071	32 232	36 461	45 153	60 390	85 963	71 227
Standard error .. ($) ..	267	262	516	648	314	152	325	257	416	516	1 001	3 317	3 362
Mean income ..... ($) ..	44 202	24 354	18 277	22 147	26 003	46 800	33 782	40 330	41 762	55 366	75 797	119 340	91 828
Standard error .. ($) ..	386	615	1 194	657	896	426	466	852	1 111	830	2 341	6 028	4 744
25 years and over, with income	79 423	13 811	1 341	4 798	7 671	65 612	25 510	13 756	5 210	13 510	4 709	1 702	1 215
Median income .. ($) ..	27 248	14 102	9 817	12 846	16 058	31 209	24 814	29 160	33 065	39 624	50 003	71 869	62 255
Standard error .. ($) ..	123	172	441	261	255	132	229	398	645	521	1 013	2 643	1 639
Mean income ..... ($) ..	36 830	18 279	12 025	16 535	20 464	40 735	29 218	35 923	37 654	49 147	63 748	102 309	81 271
Standard error .. ($) ..	283	349	491	349	579	330	355	659	896	702	1 734	4 774	3 832
Year-round, full-time workers	49 764	5 481	415	1 626	3 441	44 283	15 840	9 173	3 931	9 898	3 272	1 277	893
Median income .. ($) ..	35 622	21 100	15 865	19 120	22 717	37 331	30 709	34 845	37 131	45 846	60 508	85 963	71 227
Standard error .. ($) ..	150	253	518	674	414	152	184	456	435	458	945	3 317	3 362
Mean income ..... ($) ..	46 201	25 613	18 529	22 954	27 723	48 749	35 413	42 637	42 676	56 161	76 033	119 340	91 828
Standard error .. ($) ..	413	691	1 254	704	1 033	452	511	934	1 130	850	2 353	6 028	4 744
25 to 34 years, with income	19 354	2 569	166	577	1 826	16 785	6 268	3 804	1 540	3 983	770	280	140
Median income .. ($) ..	25 179	14 462	12 513	14 200	14 798	26 759	22 428	25 284	28 677	34 076	38 437	41 754	41 433
Standard error .. ($) ..	195	418	1 476	895	488	195	320	361	905	622	1 903	3 276	4 918
Mean income ..... ($) ..	29 418	16 456	12 840	17 079	16 589	31 402	24 622	29 299	33 015	39 072	42 285	55 800	47 495
Standard error .. ($) ..	369	370	984	872	430	416	443	972	1 956	925	1 506	3 702	3 486
Year-round, full-time workers	14 449	1 563	94	386	1 082	12 887	4 642	2 874	1 270	3 201	549	234	117
Median income .. ($) ..	28 962	17 597	15 451	16 496	18 815	30 597	25 759	27 870	30 812	37 327	44 496	47 380	45 008
Standard error .. ($) ..	356	498	856	634	687	196	257	586	494	603	1 103	3 813	6 721
Mean income ..... ($) ..	33 849	19 927	16 385	20 252	20 120	35 538	27 809	33 348	35 640	43 787	49 853	60 636	51 871
Standard error .. ($) ..	441	465	1 170	1 142	521	486	337	1 211	2 311	1 089	1 799	3 906	3 704
35 to 44 years, with income	21 181	2 628	232	634	1 761	18 553	7 383	3 948	1 582	3 736	1 233	435	236
Median income .. ($) ..	32 167	16 453	10 784	15 169	18 260	35 630	27 699	33 181	36 595	46 864	61 518	88 467	70 149
Standard error .. ($) ..	217	391	607	827	615	241	495	943	713	824	2 350	5 165	4 288
Mean income ..... ($) ..	41 614	20 103	12 486	17 429	22 072	44 661	31 647	37 527	39 252	56 782	77 684	127 902	89 391

See footnotes at end of table.

Table B-8.   Income by Educational Attainment for Persons 18 Years Old and Over, by Age, Sex, Race and Hispanic Origin: March 1997 — Continued

(Numbers in thousands. Civilian noninstitutional population.)

| Income, standard error, age, sex, race, and Hispanic origin | Total | Not a high school graduate | | | | High school graduate or more | | | | | | | | |
| | | Total | Elementary | | High School | Total | High school graduate only | College | | | | | | |
			None - 4th grade	5th - 8th grade	9th - 11th grade			Some college no degree	Associate degree	Bachelor's degree	Master's degree	Professional degree	Doctorate degree
Standard error .. ($) ..	605	918	2 017	918	1 295	671	707	960	980	1 581	4 713	10 728	8 202
Year-round, full-time workers	16 577	1 553	123	379	1 051	15 024	5 611	3 157	1 330	3 221	1 082	411	210
Median income .. ($) ..	36 957	21 232	13 795	18 968	23 254	39 125	31 506	36 575	39 181	50 703	65 892	90 634	72 155
Standard error .. ($) ..	236	459	940	1 124	748	449	284	476	975	529	1 397	4 227	4 435
Mean income ..... ($) ..	47 494	24 669	17 208	21 786	26 583	49 853	35 983	40 887	43 190	60 944	83 300	131 073	95 998
Standard error .. ($) ..	731	872	3 634	1 303	1 107	795	876	1 108	1 042	1 766	5 272	11 144	8 879
45 to 54 years, with income	15 748	2 028	220	644	1 164	13 720	4 568	2 801	1 216	2 910	1 383	439	403
Median income .. ($) ..	36 232	17 214	11 043	15 590	20 044	39 994	30 602	36 122	40 869	46 033	57 537	94 990	71 825
Standard error .. ($) ..	313	634	801	1 010	1 015	450	460	655	1 193	898	1 813	4 587	4 907
Mean income ..... ($) ..	47 295	23 014	13 426	18 867	27 118	50 884	36 655	42 770	41 878	56 967	74 809	136 016	88 273
Standard error .. ($) ..	820	1 612	991	919	2 739	901	1 300	1 474	1 184	1 684	3 379	12 726	6 415
Year-round, full-time workers	12 234	1 246	102	401	743	10 988	3 425	2 204	1 008	2 446	1 165	403	337
Median income .. ($) ..	41 481	23 213	18 019	20 870	25 292	43 895	34 829	40 661	44 754	50 506	61 872	95 801	77 060
Standard error .. ($) ..	310	794	1 964	1 042	803	680	729	622	1 365	918	2 039	4 239	4 536
Mean income ..... ($) ..	54 317	30 057	18 548	23 221	35 321	57 068	40 709	48 541	45 945	61 179	81 953	141 067	96 135
Standard error .. ($) ..	996	2 549	1 466	1 200	4 192	1 063	1 648	1 786	1 261	1 705	3 884	13 706	7 350
55 to 64 years, with income	9 966	2 144	238	881	1 026	7 823	3 360	1 430	480	1 359	731	224	239
Median income .. ($) ..	29 526	14 758	9 522	13 478	18 952	34 599	27 490	33 423	34 087	43 355	49 289	87 555	64 383
Standard error .. ($) ..	584	526	1 708	572	1 252	617	662	1 116	1 895	2 496	3 250	10 702	6 168
Mean income ..... ($) ..	41 079	19 827	12 673	16 361	24 460	46 903	32 347	49 207	45 585	55 667	60 780	107 370	91 631
Standard error .. ($) ..	927	850	1 148	718	1 612	1 136	774	4 044	5 721	2 170	2 964	9 748	11 458
Year-round, full-time workers	5 441	904	75	346	482	4 538	1 871	797	276	847	406	160	180
Median income .. ($) ..	39 563	23 779	18 924	19 633	27 741	43 195	35 954	42 284	46 905	54 687	63 459	97 759	74 571
Standard error .. ($) ..	669	1 337	2 111	1 647	1 167	1 065	677	2 150	1 825	4 025	2 464	644	9 762
Mean income ..... ($) ..	54 743	28 643	22 790	21 933	34 377	59 941	41 197	66 317	60 596	66 564	73 013	129 158	103 353
Standard error .. ($) ..	1 540	1 184	2 150	1 351	1 074	1 808	1 171	7 031	9 643	2 907	4 255	11 844	14 377
65 years and over, with income	13 173	4 442	485	2 062	1 895	8 731	3 932	1 772	392	1 523	591	324	197
Median income .. ($) ..	16 684	12 264	8 271	11 723	13 732	20 551	17 154	19 931	21 224	25 761	29 459	42 112	48 884
Standard error .. ($) ..	221	197	555	267	295	283	331	720	1 151	931	1 515	5 858	6 391
Mean income ..... ($) ..	24 302	15 347	10 573	15 454	16 451	28 858	21 828	25 029	26 622	36 007	40 415	58 933	68 720
Standard error .. ($) ..	381	339	507	582	451	532	484	739	1 505	1 616	2 564	4 629	8 652
Year-round, full-time workers	1 063	216	20	114	83	846	291	140	46	182	69	69	49
Median income .. ($) ..	42 836	25 877	(B)	25 995	26 871	48 203	36 117	38 104	(B)	59 324	(B)	(B)	(B)
Standard error .. ($) ..	2 086	1 717	(B)	4 237	3 102	2 303	1 530	4 317	(B)	4 383	(B)	(B)	(B)
Mean income ..... ($) ..	56 806	35 206	(B)	38 165	34 593	62 324	46 209	45 042	(B)	73 263	(B)	(B)	(B)
Standard error .. ($) ..	2 437	3 201	(B)	5 178	4 098	2 873	3 707	3 267	(B)	5 461	(B)	(B)	(B)
Female													
18 years and over with income	93 868	15 548	1 135	4 827	9 586	78 320	32 571	18 661	7 305	14 216	4 322	717	527
Median income .. ($) ..	13 379	7 373	6 592	7 399	7 511	15 691	12 052	13 521	19 742	24 376	33 113	41 970	42 431
Standard error .. ($) ..	104	67	171	107	125	107	100	206	374	352	737	2 353	1 968
Mean income ..... ($) ..	18 826	9 610	7 677	9 445	9 921	20 655	15 178	17 537	22 021	28 186	36 633	68 179	51 751
Standard error .. ($) ..	127	116	272	206	154	149	130	275	321	391	755	7 525	3 142
Year-round, full-time workers	36 419	2 745	143	645	1 956	33 674	12 426	7 483	3 685	7 121	2 224	413	322
Median income .. ($) ..	24 943	15 781	12 232	14 594	16 422	25 775	20 630	23 716	27 211	32 544	41 824	57 624	56 267

See footnotes at end of table.

Table B-8.   Income by Educational Attainment for Persons 18 Years Old and Over, by Age, Sex, Race and Hispanic Origin: March 1997 — Continued

(Numbers in thousands. Civilian noninstitutional population.)

| Income, standard error, age, sex, race, and Hispanic origin | Total | Not a high school graduate | | | | High school graduate or more | | | | | | | |
| | | Total | Elementary | | High School | Total | High school graduate only | College | | | | | |
			None - 4th grade	5th - 8th grade	9th - 11th grade			Some college no degree	Associate degree	Bachelor's degree	Master's degree	Professional degree	Doctorate degree
Standard error .. ($) ..	148	261	934	603	314	131	143	297	377	363	566	3 635	3 300
Mean income ..... ($) ..	30 117	17 713	13 615	16 939	18 268	31 128	23 131	27 722	30 124	38 752	47 487	95 476	66 300
Standard error .. ($) ..	269	316	968	704	369	288	220	590	434	622	1 147	12 476	4 401
25 years and over, with income	83 056	13 703	1 087	4 688	7 929	69 353	29 212	14 528	6 839	13 247	4 285	715	527
Median income .. ($) ..	14 682	7 895	6 652	7 459	8 544	17 052	12 702	16 255	20 460	25 192	33 302	42 059	42 431
Standard error .. ($) ..	111	104	176	124	147	114	152	232	343	291	779	2 409	1 968
Mean income ..... ($) ..	20 005	10 170	7 786	9 521	10 881	21 948	15 848	19 828	22 598	28 926	36 711	68 326	51 751
Standard error .. ($) ..	141	126	282	209	175	165	142	342	336	415	751	7 550	3 142
Year-round, full-time workers	33 549	2 501	133	617	1 751	31 048	11 363	6 582	3 468	6 689	2 213	413	322
Median income .. ($) ..	25 808	16 173	12 471	14 805	16 953	26 617	21 175	25 167	28 083	33 525	41 901	57 624	56 267
Standard error .. ($) ..	131	271	1 105	580	333	133	143	267	526	437	564	3 635	3 300
Mean income ..... ($) ..	31 183	18 189	13 996	17 052	18 909	32 230	23 822	29 179	30 857	39 604	47 589	95 476	66 300
Standard error .. ($) ..	289	335	1 014	706	398	309	234	661	448	655	1 152	12 476	4 401
25 to 34 years, with income	18 481	1 740	91	357	1 293	16 741	5 600	3 840	1 852	4 295	853	178	122
Median income .. ($) ..	16 384	7 455	6 695	6 294	8 063	17 779	12 682	15 260	20 140	25 066	28 480	41 272	30 756
Standard error .. ($) ..	225	281	747	465	393	245	301	429	656	398	856	3 826	4 691
Mean income ..... ($) ..	19 201	9 469	7 589	7 941	10 023	20 213	14 337	17 438	21 013	26 156	30 859	49 649	38 461
Standard error .. ($) ..	237	330	893	718	390	256	263	635	574	539	1 366	4 091	4 166
Year-round, full-time workers	9 481	489	18	94	378	8 991	2 717	1 945	1 030	2 612	476	126	86
Median income .. ($) ..	23 838	14 580	(B)	11 699	15 674	24 449	19 165	21 993	25 587	29 632	32 872	50 847	36 154
Standard error .. ($) ..	270	568	(B)	775	983	269	362	345	552	511	1 126	7 261	3 994
Mean income ..... ($) ..	27 181	16 815	(B)	15 161	17 424	27 745	20 243	25 037	27 967	33 184	39 869	58 005	46 688
Standard error .. ($) ..	373	716	(B)	2 009	771	389	304	1 135	742	713	2 020	4 855	4 880
35 to 44 years, with income	20 637	1 947	127	457	1 363	18 690	7 031	4 037	2 235	3 852	1 176	230	129
Median income .. ($) ..	18 447	8 809	7 464	9 395	8 768	20 152	15 601	18 351	22 488	27 530	36 122	45 790	43 815
Standard error .. ($) ..	288	345	773	652	441	219	277	480	750	744	963	7 513	4 083
Mean income ..... ($) ..	23 260	11 148	8 111	10 413	11 678	24 523	17 732	21 245	24 086	30 764	40 684	83 342	66 303
Standard error .. ($) ..	325	363	647	567	476	354	301	466	584	775	1 956	16 140	9 826
Year-round, full-time workers	11 094	728	40	179	509	10 366	3 842	2 206	1 312	2 091	702	127	85
Median income .. ($) ..	26 787	15 841	(B)	14 353	17 048	27 602	21 648	26 187	29 706	36 300	43 316	85 248	57 132
Standard error .. ($) ..	242	571	(B)	792	773	322	228	483	701	615	1 536	10 522	6 630
Mean income ..... ($) ..	32 639	18 038	(B)	15 840	19 305	33 665	24 398	29 643	31 210	42 913	51 671	121 865	86 614
Standard error .. ($) ..	526	585	(B)	848	755	558	407	636	685	1 135	2 868	27 526	13 507
45 to 54 years, with income	15 693	1 789	150	550	1 089	13 904	5 621	2 777	1 391	2 539	1 266	150	161
Median income .. ($) ..	19 046	9 026	7 805	7 169	10 541	20 900	15 802	20 004	23 360	29 363	39 515	50 992	48 644
Standard error .. ($) ..	284	483	863	387	442	265	318	527	1 003	807	848	4 476	2 872
Mean income ..... ($) ..	24 276	11 172	9 673	9 808	12 067	25 961	18 203	24 165	26 144	32 885	40 188	81 087	53 846
Standard error .. ($) ..	400	377	985	688	490	444	386	1 269	838	1 028	1 189	17 567	4 147
Year-round, full-time workers	8 709	665	39	188	438	8 044	3 123	1 661	843	1 461	744	105	107
Median income .. ($) ..	27 154	15 957	(B)	13 346	16 896	28 692	21 777	26 781	30 923	37 446	44 318	53 585	62 675
Standard error .. ($) ..	280	456	(B)	1 097	549	489	322	472	817	887	1 035	11 175	6 221
Mean income ..... ($) ..	33 255	17 879	(B)	16 364	18 644	34 525	24 954	32 677	33 297	43 306	49 436	98 376	66 237
Standard error .. ($) ..	635	692	(B)	1 368	838	680	518	2 019	1 003	1 473	1 465	24 528	4 672

See footnotes at end of table.

Table B-8. Income by Educational Attainment for Persons 18 Years Old and Over, by Age, Sex, Race and Hispanic Origin: March 1997 — Continued

(Numbers in thousands. Civilian noninstitutional population.)

| Income, standard error, age, sex, race, and Hispanic origin | Total | Not a high school graduate | | | | High school graduate or more | | | | | | | |
| | | Total | Elementary | | High School | Total | High school graduate only | College | | | | | |
			None - 4th grade	5th - 8th grade	9th - 11th grade			Some college no degree	Associate degree	Bachelor's degree	Master's degree	Professional degree	Doctorate degree
55 to 64 years, with income	10 220	2 069	176	662	1 231	8 151	4 125	1 585	615	1 163	512	81	70
Median income .. ($) ..	13 316	7 565	5 687	7 104	8 712	15 826	12 441	16 378	17 785	22 726	36 788	40 800	(B)
Standard error .. ($) ..	335	316	535	343	519	370	375	836	1 868	1 356	2 059	10 375	(B)
Mean income ..... ($) ..	19 029	10 348	6 923	9 706	11 183	21 232	16 238	20 057	21 419	29 375	37 964	48 361	(B)
Standard error .. ($) ..	327	324	833	559	432	393	414	660	1 218	1 523	1 637	9 219	(B)
Year-round, full-time workers	3 706	507	26	125	355	3 199	1 480	667	251	452	264	47	38
Median income .. ($) ..	25 080	17 627	(B)	18 721	17 401	26 580	21 959	26 942	27 196	36 579	44 149	(B)	(B)
Standard error .. ($) ..	431	985	(B)	1 515	1 536	421	374	1 060	1 692	1 661	2 457	(B)	(B)
Mean income ..... ($) ..	30 410	19 854	(B)	20 327	20 090	32 081	25 421	30 037	32 482	42 165	45 638	(B)	(B)
Standard error .. ($) ..	586	780	(B)	1 750	905	656	620	1 011	1 930	2 743	1 730	(D)	(B)
65 years and over, with income	18 026	6 158	543	2 662	2 953	11 867	6 834	2 289	746	1 398	479	76	45
Median income .. ($) ..	9 626	7 714	6 539	7 539	8 257	11 298	9 982	11 895	12 267	16 116	23 400	15 996	(B)
Standard error .. ($) ..	84	116	210	151	171	149	160	368	489	618	2 058	4 484	(B)
Mean income ..... ($) ..	13 938	9 709	7 502	9 475	10 325	16 132	12 975	15 918	16 435	24 806	26 852	62 758	(B)
Standard error .. ($) ..	250	182	346	277	275	363	234	521	833	1 711	1 446	34 652	(B)
Year-round, full-time workers	559	112	10	31	71	448	200	103	32	73	27	7	6
Median income .. ($) ..	27 070	17 297	(B)	(B)	(B)	31 109	28 237	27 463	(B)	(B)	(B)	(B)	(B)
Standard error .. ($) ..	1 393	1 746	(B)	(B)	(B)	1 937	2 043	3 651	(B)	(B)	(B)	(B)	(B)
Mean income ..... ($) ..	43 023	19 485	(B)	(B)	(B)	48 908	31 869	35 480	(B)	(B)	(B)	(B)	(B)
Standard error .. ($) ..	5 994	1 424	(B)	(B)	(B)	7 420	2 879	5 003	(B)	(B)	(B)	(B)	(B)
WHITE													
Both Sexes													
18 years and over	164 050	28 905	2 244	9 259	17 402	135 145	54 971	31 782	11 433	25 231	8 004	2 178	1 547
Without income	8 097	3 173	345	938	1 890	4 923	2 775	1 292	293	457	76	20	11
With income	155 953	25 731	1 899	8 321	15 511	130 222	52 196	30 491	11 140	24 774	7 928	2 158	1 536
Median income .. ($) ..	19 102	10 227	7 858	9 972	10 736	21 722	17 002	18 129	24 670	30 967	41 249	64 041	59 179
Standard error .. ($) ..	106	101	316	147	136	93	119	211	360	224	443	2 550	1 900
Mean income ..... ($) ..	26 990	13 684	10 152	13 100	14 430	29 619	21 474	24 217	28 572	38 842	51 476	91 171	73 190
Standard error .. ($) ..	156	200	361	226	305	181	189	311	482	446	1 064	3 983	2 858
Male													
18 years and over with income	77 506	13 471	1 053	4 342	8 075	64 036	24 783	14 964	4 972	12 547	4 167	1 539	1 064
Median income .. ($) ..	25 705	13 259	10 310	12 810	14 209	29 418	23 613	24 819	32 146	39 156	50 751	72 787	63 606
Standard error .. ($) ..	130	182	397	274	258	223	238	356	476	618	737	2 903	2 083
Mean income ..... ($) ..	35 079	17 275	12 274	16 392	18 402	38 824	28 264	31 478	36 967	49 125	64 572	102 890	81 832
Standard error .. ($) ..	279	355	588	361	553	325	351	583	959	746	1 820	4 929	3 758
Year-round, full-time workers	46 629	5 297	374	1 541	3 382	41 332	15 122	8 712	3 671	9 023	2 898	1 138	767
Median income .. ($) ..	34 768	20 142	15 172	18 285	21 400	36 748	29 868	33 043	36 918	46 102	60 944	87 597	72 596
Standard error .. ($) ..	276	289	664	685	355	164	301	581	461	472	843	3 050	2 491
Mean income ..... ($) ..	45 360	24 541	18 083	22 076	26 379	48 029	34 803	41 165	42 675	56 808	76 771	120 586	92 884
Standard error .. ($) ..	422	709	1 394	709	1 048	464	534	923	1 238	918	2 459	6 282	4 600
25 years and over, with income	68 256	11 355	1 004	4 082	6 269	56 901	21 871	11 765	4 590	11 937	4 138	1 536	1 064
Median income .. ($) ..	28 387	14 638	10 353	13 106	16 751	31 931	25 574	30 070	34 016	40 591	50 920	72 917	63 606

See footnotes at end of table.

Table B-8. Income by Educational Attainment for Persons 18 Years Old and Over, by Age, Sex, Race and Hispanic Origin: March 1997 — Continued

(Numbers in thousands. Civilian noninstitutional population.)

Income, standard error, age, sex, race, and Hispanic origin	Total	Not a high school graduate				High school graduate or more							
		Total	Elementary		High School	Total	High school graduate only	College					
			None - 4th grade	5th - 8th grade	9th - 11th grade			Some college no degree	Associate degree	Bachelor's degree	Master's degree	Professional degree	Doctorate degree
Standard error .. ($) ..	212	188	412	285	275	146	186	342	670	400	734	2 922	2 083
Mean income ..... ($) ..	38 159	18 970	12 378	16 798	21 440	41 989	30 190	36 972	38 552	50 544	64 842	103 001	81 832
Standard error .. ($) ..	311	414	605	380	696	359	391	717	1 000	778	1 830	4 935	3 758
Year-round, full-time workers	43 093	4 604	345	1 398	2 862	38 489	13 627	7 825	3 484	8 765	2 884	1 138	767
Median income ..($) ..	36 361	21 287	15 542	19 405	23 075	38 490	31 199	35 731	37 751	46 806	61 029	87 597	72 596
Standard error .. ($) ..	162	277	626	691	487	293	202	339	674	477	841	3 050	2 491
Mean income ..... ($) ..	47 510	26 023	18 369	22 998	28 422	50 081	36 528	43 729	43 644	57 640	76 961	120 586	92 884
Standard error .. ($) ..	452	808	1 483	768	1 226	493	585	1 016	1 262	941	2 470	6 282	4 600
25 to 34 years, with income	16 086	2 158	136	524	1 499	13 928	5 118	3 073	1 357	3 456	597	225	102
Median income ..($) ..	25 726	14 953	13 058	14 077	15 405	27 307	23 761	25 435	29 467	34 362	40 214	41 627	42 951
Standard error .. ($) ..	208	416	1 450	1 018	494	217	405	402	835		2 105	3 487	5 352
Mean income ..... ($) ..	30 131	16 914	13 818	16 434	17 362	32 179	25 382	29 967	33 905	39 607	43 757	54 830	47 595
Standard error .. ($) ..	398	390	1 016	767	483	450	345	1 061	2 192	1 035	1 778	4 295	4 278
Year-round, full-time workers	12 300	1 370	85	360	926	10 930	3 921	2 355	1 146	2 798	448	182	80
Median income ..($) ..	29 421	17 751	15 587	16 334	19 118	30 915	26 188	28 201	31 123	37 331	44 466	47 236	51 064
Standard error .. ($) ..	383	561	1 010	668	730	220	267	731	541	671	1 113	3 620	6 255
Mean income ..... ($) ..	34 268	19 895	16 665	19 042	20 524	36 070	28 395	33 622	36 583	44 290	50 443	60 313	53 824
Standard error .. ($) ..	488	472	1 285	940	581	540	376	1 295	2 553	1 213	2 071	4 617	4 650
35 to 44 years, with income	17 949	2 153	179	528	1 446	15 796	6 206	3 300	1 392	3 258	1 054	391	196
Median income ..($) ..	34 026	17 179	11 151	15 676	19 279	36 616	29 114	35 173	37 320	49 029	62 105	89 781	71 992
Standard error .. ($) ..	557	468	622	792	652	257	580	724	892	1 320	2 543	5 514	4 431
Mean income ..... ($) ..	43 417	21 262	13 075	18 196	23 394	46 436	33 062	38 604	40 144	58 971	78 650	131 863	94 711
Standard error .. ($) ..	670	1 103	2 574	1 066	1 554	738	824	818	1 079	1 773	4 955	11 672	9 535
Year-round, full-time workers	14 251	1 307	100	318	889	12 944	4 776	2 668	1 168	2 848	940	373	172
Median income ..($) ..	37 922	21 735	13 433	19 604	23 978	40 222	32 031	37 162	40 129	51 408	65 775	91 196	78 160
Standard error .. ($) ..	450	512	961	1 110	815	269	312	542	886	573	1 557	5 377	4 031
Mean income ..... ($) ..	48 934	25 473	17 121	22 573	27 451	51 303	37 203	41 347	44 238	62 666	83 494	133 567	102 975
Standard error .. ($) ..	797	1 014	4 437	1 521	1 280	865	1 014	875	1 148	1 962	5 461	12 027	10 427
45 to 54 years, with income	13 642	1 588	180	538	870	12 055	3 912	2 481	1 084	2 548	1 263	402	365
Median income ..($) ..	37 278	18 050	11 182	16 285	21 344	40 804	31 492	36 744	40 985	47 390	58 536	91 207	71 459
Standard error .. ($) ..	393	800	773	1 249	1 323	323	474	693	1 239	1 262	1 828	5 010	4 949
Mean income ..... ($) ..	49 077	24 365	13 627	19 754	29 430	52 332	37 098	43 804	42 289	59 062	75 425	130 634	90 320
Standard error .. ($) ..	900	2 032	1 101	1 060	3 618	974	1 464	1 640	1 265	1 882	3 545	12 375	7 022
Year-round, full-time workers	10 757	1 003	89	335	579	9 755	2 988	1 964	902	2 162	1 066	366	307
Median income ..($) ..	42 250	23 684	16 122	21 895	25 765	45 224	35 361	41 008	44 847	51 543	62 417	92 846	76 090
Standard error .. ($) ..	385	983	2 684	1 509	871	537	583	629	1 430	852	2 368	4 636	5 235
Mean income ..... ($) ..	55 818	31 082	17 762	24 246	37 083	58 361	42 096	49 603	46 095	63 330	82 456	135 687	97 963
Standard error .. ($) ..	1 084	3 143	1 603	1 386	5 343	1 143	1 873	1 982	1 352	1 889	4 067	13 393	8 031
55 to 64 years, with income	8 708	1 698	168	720	809	7 009	2 982	1 277	410	1 242	660	216	223
Median income ..($) ..	30 841	15 684	9 538	13 851	20 579	35 756	27 982	34 218	35 582	46 211	51 350	88 650	63 841
Standard error .. ($) ..	471	557	1 742	733	985	554	784	1 254	2 192	2 586	3 857	10 330	5 965
Mean income ..... ($) ..	43 012	20 828	12 356	16 573	26 378	48 387	33 352	51 054	48 215	57 527	62 664	109 321	82 503
Standard error .. ($) ..	1 010	1 035	1 422	782	1 989	1 208	847	4 511	6 658	2 308	3 195	10 033	7 000
Year-round, full-time workers	4 832	737	55	290	392	4 095	1 685	707	228	788	366	155	167
Median income ..($) ..	40 863	24 093	(B)	20 103	28 092	44 918	36 492	43 216	49 921	56 745	64 963	97 848	73 832

See footnotes at end of table.

Table B-8. Income by Educational Attainment for Persons 18 Years Old and Over, by Age, Sex, Race and Hispanic Origin: March 1997 — Continued

(Numbers in thousands. Civilian noninstitutional population.)

Income, standard error, age, sex, race, and Hispanic origin	Total	Not a high school graduate				High school graduate or more							
		Total	Elementary		High School	Total	High school graduate only	College					
			None - 4th grade	5th - 8th grade	9th - 11th grade			Some college no degree	Associate degree	Bachelor's degree	Master's degree	Professional degree	Doctorate degree
Standard error .. ($) ..	594	1 305	(B)	1 770	1 603	1 038	811	2 213	2 728	4 038	3 031	319	9 930
Mean income ..... ($)	56 525	29 214	(B)	21 480	35 771	61 437	42 115	69 637	65 932	67 755	75 060	131 932	90 553
Standard error .. ($) ..	1 648	1 386	(B)	1 415	2 227	1 904	1 273	7 891	11 594	3 062	4 595	12 102	8 028
65 years and over, with income	11 872	3 758	342	1 771	1 645	8 113	3 651	1 635	347	1 434	564	304	178
Median income .. ($) ..	17 268	12 680	8 670	11 976	14 189	20 850	17 459	20 214	21 512	26 105	29 506	44 324	48 451
Standard error .. ($) ..	223	221	645	289	323	283	360	761	1 332	910	1 519	5 439	5 598
Mean income ..... ($) ..	24 983	15 718	10 799	15 682	16 779	29 274	22 066	25 480	27 243	36 576	40 204	60 512	69 111
Standard error .. ($) ..	410	371	578	635	478	559	500	784	1 644	1 693	2 582	4 864	9 381
Year-round, full-time workers	952	187	16	95	76	765	257	131	39	170	64	62	42
Median income .. ($) ..	43 470	25 600	(B)	24 593	26 585	49 379	36 540	30 659	(D)	60 049	(D)	(D)	(D)
Standard error .. ($) ..	2 187	1 694	(B)	3 776	2 650	2 425	1 988	5 632	(B)	3 850	(B)	(B)	(B)
Mean income ..... ($) ..	57 673	35 074	(B)	39 582	32 134	63 194	46 701	46 014	(B)	74 001	(B)	(B)	(B)
Standard error .. ($) ..	2 623	3 559	(B)	6 110	3 897	3 066	3 972	3 431	(B)	5 695	(B)	(B)	(B)
Female													
18 years and over with income	78 447	12 261	846	3 979	7 436	66 186	27 413	15 526	6 168	12 227	3 760	620	472
Median income .. ($) ..	13 534	7 559	6 606	7 556	7 832	15 683	12 164	13 292	19 489	24 224	33 151	43 357	45 373
Standard error .. ($) ..	112	105	189	153	165	119	110	222	434	388	768	2 833	2 333
Mean income ..... ($) ..	18 998	9 738	7 507	9 508	10 116	20 714	15 336	17 219	21 806	28 291	36 965	62 064	53 699
Standard error .. ($) ..	128	132	290	229	177	148	144	206	345	430	841	6 159	3 451
Year-round, full-time workers	29 589	2 130	109	524	1 496	27 459	10 115	5 923	2 971	5 921	1 892	348	289
Median income .. ($) ..	25 363	15 616	11 467	13 841	16 427	26 178	21 045	23 983	27 564	33 131	41 965	61 027	58 850
Standard error .. ($) ..	146	300	710	632	345	147	159	333	499	461	601	5 060	3 183
Mean income ..... ($) ..	30 514	17 614	12 613	16 612	18 331	31 515	23 623	27 255	30 258	39 491	48 133	86 512	69 542
Standard error .. ($) ..	263	358	892	778	420	280	254	356	467	713	1 313	10 240	4 780
25 years and over, with income	69 864	10 897	804	3 850	6 243	58 967	24 775	12 184	5 772	11 418	3 729	617	472
Median income .. ($) ..	14 753	8 091	6 676	7 663	8 752	17 020	12 793	15 928	20 270	25 091	33 318	43 608	45 373
Standard error .. ($) ..	120	113	193	168	162	128	164	260	385	347	809	2 888	2 333
Mean income ..... ($) ..	20 121	10 275	7 636	9 602	11 029	21 940	15 969	19 364	22 384	29 003	37 041	62 210	53 699
Standard error .. ($) ..	141	143	301	233	198	162	156	246	361	456	836	6 182	3 451
Year-round, full-time workers	27 277	1 939	99	500	1 339	25 339	9 270	5 211	2 791	5 546	1 884	348	289
Median income .. ($) ..	26 253	16 021	11 632	14 136	16 942	27 052	21 611	25 410	28 544	34 111	42 031	61 027	58 850
Standard error .. ($) ..	148	315	760	622	373	149	160	291	549	450	615	5 060	3 183
Mean income ..... ($) ..	31 600	18 090	13 023	16 746	18 967	32 634	24 326	28 684	31 025	40 443	48 228	86 512	69 542
Standard error .. ($) ..	281	378	942	774	452	299	270	387	480	752	1 318	10 240	4 780
25 to 34 years, with income	14 813	1 280	66	279	934	13 533	4 381	3 044	1 495	3 642	711	154	105
Median income .. ($) ..	17 035	7 683	(B)	5 972	8 634	18 425	13 217	15 116	20 339	25 159	28 591	42 100	28 338
Standard error .. ($) ..	268	361	(B)	512	434	290	373	516	712	416	1 003	4 011	5 279
Mean income ..... ($) ..	19 645	9 857	(B)	7 659	10 738	20 571	14 849	17 028	20 488	26 550	31 066	51 340	39 489
Standard error .. ($) ..	245	417	(B)	850	499	262	317	398	585	614	1 530	4 639	4 784
Year-round, full-time workers	7 610	393	13	71	309	7 217	2 125	1 511	808	2 189	405	105	74
Median income .. ($) ..	24 619	14 641	(B)	(B)	16 049	25 177	20 045	22 366	25 859	30 100	32 880	56 264	(B)
Standard error .. ($) ..	290	794	(B)	(B)	1 101	229	360	473	598	511	1 063	6 701	(B)
Mean income ..... ($) ..	27 680	16 921	(B)	(B)	17 616	28 266	20 914	24 441	27 513	33 833	40 022	61 717	(B)
Standard error .. ($) ..	356	858	(B)	(B)	911	370	354	514	703	829	2 239	5 570	(B)

See footnotes at end of table.

Table B-8. Income by Educational Attainment for Persons 18 Years Old and Over, by Age, Sex, Race and Hispanic Origin: March 1997 — Continued

(Numbers in thousands. Civilian noninstitutional population.)

| Income, standard error, age, sex, race, and Hispanic origin | Total | Not a high school graduate | | | | High school graduate or more | | | | | | | |
| | | Total | Elementary | | High School | Total | High school graduate only | College | | | | | |
			None - 4th grade	5th - 8th grade	9th - 11th grade			Some college no degree	Associate degree	Bachelor's degree	Master's degree	Professional degree	Doctorate degree
35 to 44 years, with income	16 927	1 483	97	381	1 005	15 444	5 769	3 203	1 837	3 294	1 035	191	115
Median income .. ($) ..	18 617	8 774	7 268	9 545	8 615	20 297	15 814	17 896	22 340	26 835	36 061	47 726	47 077
Standard error .. ($) ..	347	399	855	672	525	230	325	580	769	639	1 053	7 428	6 557
Mean income .. ($) ..	23 373	10 907	8 227	10 278	11 405	24 570	18 012	21 326	23 951	30 120	40 887	71 879	69 609
Standard error .. ($) ..	339	385	789	578	516	366	344	553	635	834	2 179	12 902	10 930
Year-round, full-time workers	8 856	564	34	158	371	8 293	3 126	1 664	1 033	1 686	607	102	74
Median income .. ($) ..	27 235	15 498	(B)	14 081	16 977	28 262	22 087	26 502	29 906	36 571	42 597	88 152	(B)
Standard error .. ($) ..	288	630	(B)	737	957	390	255	636	775	765	1 582	9 585	(B)
Mean income .. ($) ..	33 198	17 873	(B)	15 274	19 548	34 239	24 846	30 442	31 403	43 729	52 227	105 639	(B)
Standard error .. ($) ..	546	680	(B)	809	931	577	466	798	727	1 285	3 262	22 080	(B)
45 to 54 years, with income	13 237	1 339	112	435	792	11 897	4 697	2 395	1 217	2 188	1 116	134	150
Median income .. ($) ..	19 159	8 748	7 475	7 355	10 357	20 861	15 724	19 641	22 914	29 803	39 558	50 498	49 988
Standard error .. ($) ..	306	541	754	549	571	286	361	561	1 066	809	900	4 194	5 491
Mean income .. ($) ..	24 183	10 534	8 541	9 492	11 389	25 720	17 854	22 201	26 140	33 186	40 509	81 897	55 503
Standard error .. ($) ..	387	388	824	736	498	422	406	566	913	1 125	1 305	19 509	4 232
Year-round, full-time workers	7 200	500	26	157	317	6 700	2 554	1 370	712	1 232	635	94	103
Median income .. ($) ..	27 530	15 389	(B)	12 503	16 642	29 178	21 934	26 733	31 191	38 148	44 289	52 768	62 852
Standard error .. ($) ..	440	598	(B)	922	646	534	348	528	982	1 009	1 018	8 576	5 747
Mean income .. ($) ..	33 394	16 981	(B)	16 084	17 753	34 619	25 138	30 121	33 746	44 054	50 282	99 846	66 492
Standard error .. ($) ..	604	699	(B)	1 590	749	640	600	702	1 121	1 641	1 668	27 135	4 704
55 to 64 years, with income	8 780	1 610	123	498	989	7 170	3 642	1 406	539	1 007	444	74	58
Median income .. ($) ..	13 589	7 627	5 491	7 072	8 754	15 725	12 560	16 002	17 816	22 907	36 425	(B)	(B)
Standard error .. ($) ..	358	377	720	383	585	370	434	819	2 069	1 946	2 917	(B)	(B)
Mean income .. ($) ..	19 489	10 567	7 033	9 828	11 379	21 492	16 511	19 942	21 275	30 413	38 193	(B)	(B)
Standard error .. ($) ..	368	378	1 034	617	509	434	458	706	1 320	1 721	1 822	(B)	(B)
Year-round, full-time workers	3 143	394	20	94	280	2 749	1 284	576	213	381	219	44	32
Median income .. ($) ..	25 471	18 096	(B)	19 317	17 497	26 829	22 152	26 462	28 302	37 692	46 231	(B)	(B)
Standard error .. ($) ..	489	1 224	(B)	1 711	1 730	500	446	1 048	1 874	2 355	2 119	(B)	(B)
Mean income .. ($) ..	31 120	20 390	(B)	20 439	20 801	32 656	25 897	30 005	33 177	43 653	46 425	(B)	(B)
Standard error .. ($) ..	667	886	(B)	1 594	1 103	740	692	1 104	2 106	3 200	1 968	(B)	(B)
65 years and over, with income	16 108	5 186	405	2 258	2 524	10 922	6 287	2 136	683	1 286	423	63	44
Median income .. ($) ..	9 919	8 036	6 656	7 808	8 608	11 496	10 206	12 105	12 278	16 452	24 561	(B)	(B)
Standard error .. ($) ..	90	123	235	178	184	152	179	379	480	608	2 527	(B)	(B)
Mean income .. ($) ..	14 146	10 039	7 576	9 700	10 738	16 096	13 150	16 193	16 503	24 870	27 327	(B)	(B)
Standard error .. ($) ..	217	208	373	313	316	299	247	551	873	1 781	1 571	(B)	(B)
Year-round, full-time workers	468	88	7	20	62	380	181	90	25	59	17	2	6
Median income .. ($) ..	28 405	19 774	(B)	(B)	(B)	31 718	29 233	28 955	(B)	(B)	(B)	(B)	(B)
Standard error .. ($) ..	1 681	2 028	(B)	(B)	(B)	2 282	1 892	4 345	(B)	(B)	(B)	(B)	(B)
Mean income .. ($) ..	40 717	20 691	(B)	(B)	(B)	45 378	32 815	37 092	(B)	(B)	(B)	(B)	(B)
Standard error .. ($) ..	4 451	1 718	(B)	(B)	(B)	5 404	3 130	5 643	(B)	(B)	(B)	(B)	(B)

See footnotes at end of table.

Table B-8. Income by Educational Attainment for Persons 18 Years Old and Over, by Age, Sex, Race and Hispanic Origin: March 1997 — Continued

(Numbers in thousands. Civilian noninstitutional population.)

| Income, standard error, age, sex, race, and Hispanic origin | Total | Not a high school graduate | | | | High school graduate or more | | | | | | | |
| | | Total | Elementary | | High School | Total | High school graduate only | College | | | | | |
			None - 4th grade	5th - 8th grade	9th - 11th grade			Some college no degree	Associate degree	Bachelor's degree	Master's degree	Professional degree	Doctorate degree
BLACK													
Both Sexes													
18 years and over	22 772	5 846	432	1 305	4 110	16 926	8 192	4 724	1 343	1 944	572	85	65
Without income	2 196	980	39	130	811	1 216	686	369	70	64	19	1	6
With income	20 577	4 866	392	1 174	3 299	15 710	7 506	4 355	1 273	1 880	553	84	59
Median income .. ($) ..	14 457	7 552	6 757	8 201	7 555	17 345	13 367	17 633	23 415	27 659	35 256	41 057	(B)
Standard error .. ($) ..	250	211	290	434	276	241	352	456	808	781	2 205	14 467	(B)
Mean income ..... ($) ..	19 687	11 009	9 160	11 502	11 053	22 375	17 281	22 623	24 792	31 474	36 809	106 184	(B)
Standard error .. ($) ..	378	266	601	586	324	483	451	1 209	785	1 062	1 785	35 702	(B)
Male													
18 years and over with income	9 069	2 258	250	562	1 446	6 811	3 408	1 898	437	783	201	51	33
Median income .. ($) ..	17 171	10 299	7 136	11 135	10 390	21 188	16 627	21 436	27 493	31 380	38 768	(B)	(B)
Standard error .. ($) ..	326	406	414	624	549	424	495	751	2 171	1 212	3 043	(B)	(B)
Mean income ..... ($) ..	23 253	13 601	10 246	14 464	13 845	26 454	21 148	25 754	29 990	35 161	41 527	(B)	(B)
Standard error .. ($) ..	648	473	768	1 064	595	839	885	1 635	1 491	1 597	3 927	(B)	(B)
Year-round, full-time workers	4 795	695	41	160	494	4 100	1 910	1 124	320	551	129	42	23
Median income .. ($) ..	27 149	20 375	(B)	17 008	21 220	29 353	24 930	29 828	31 751	36 787	40 157	(B)	(B)
Standard error .. ($) ..	379	818	(B)	2 096	867	798	673	1 073	1 101	1 655	2 259	(B)	(B)
Mean income ..... ($) ..	32 726	23 473	(B)	22 395	24 175	34 294	27 079	34 963	34 231	42 139	47 552	(B)	(B)
Standard error .. ($) ..	1 009	976	(B)	2 205	1 159	1 163	606	2 629	1 631	1 938	5 519	(B)	(B)
25 years and over, with income	7 796	1 947	235	550	1 162	5 848	2 864	1 533	418	748	201	51	33
Median income .. ($) ..	20 074	11 451	7 231	11 306	12 253	23 954	18 898	25 500	30 001	32 164	38 768	(B)	(B)
Standard error .. ($) ..	459	421	650	626	647	584	779	714	2 095	1 297	3 043	(B)	(B)
Mean income ..... ($) ..	25 502	14 833	10 484	14 679	15 785	29 054	23 142	29 489	30 709	36 088	41 527	(B)	(B)
Standard error .. ($) ..	743	517	807	1 081	671	962	1 035	1 983	1 518	1 644	3 927	(B)	(B)
Year-round, full-time workers	4 484	659	41	159	459	3 825	1 725	1 056	307	543	129	42	23
Median income .. ($) ..	28 287	20 537	(B)	17 052	21 589	30 454	26 054	30 536	31 884	37 107	40 157	(B)	(B)
Standard error .. ($) ..	845	803	(B)	2 101	983	367	700	736	1 233	1 702	2 259	(B)	(B)
Mean income ..... ($) ..	33 659	23 681	(B)	22 479	24 497	35 377	28 018	35 848	34 868	42 443	47 552	(B)	(B)
Standard error .. ($) ..	1 072	986	(B)	2 216	1 172	1 240	651	2 791	1 649	1 957	5 519	(B)	(B)
25 to 34 years, with income	2 167	288	16	22	251	1 878	913	557	126	224	47	10	2
Median income .. ($) ..	19 585	10 602	(B)	(B)	10 545	21 124	16 899	25 060	23 074	30 611	(B)	(B)	(B)
Standard error .. ($) ..	806	1 274	(B)	(B)	1 370	637	1 001	1 292	2 576	1 589	(B)	(B)	(B)
Mean income ..... ($) ..	23 114	13 496	(B)	(B)	12 501	24 591	21 609	24 788	23 924	32 105	(B)	(B)	(B)
Standard error .. ($) ..	1 187	1 408	(B)	(B)	1 081	1 344	2 481	1 488	2 015	2 137	(B)	(B)	(B)
Year-round, full-time workers	1 383	114	4	9	100	1 269	550	404	90	178	36	10	2
Median income .. ($) ..	25 756	17 332	(B)	(B)	17 542	26 373	22 183	27 484	25 798	33 529	(B)	(B)	(B)
Standard error .. ($) ..	526	1 745	(B)	(B)	1 841	552	830	1 042	3 565	2 903	(B)	(B)	(B)
Mean income ..... ($) ..	28 160	20 370	(B)	(B)	17 516	28 858	24 975	29 814	25 562	35 903	(B)	(B)	(B)
Standard error .. ($) ..	832	2 724	(B)	(B)	1 394	866	912	1 818	1 619	2 381	(B)	(B)	(B)
35 to 44 years, with income	2 295	368	30	78	260	1 927	956	511	122	269	45	17	6
Median income .. ($) ..	22 895	12 346	(B)	11 439	13 531	25 523	20 897	26 655	31 110	33 515	(B)	(B)	(B)

See footnotes at end of table.

Table B-8. Income by Educational Attainment for Persons 18 Years Old and Over, by Age, Sex, Race and Hispanic Origin: March 1997 — Continued

(Numbers in thousands. Civilian noninstitutional population.)

Income, standard error, age, sex, race, and Hispanic origin	Total	Not a high school graduate				High school graduate or more							
		Total	Elementary		High School	Total	High school graduate only	College					
			None - 4th grade	5th - 8th grade	9th - 11th grade			Some college no degree	Associate degree	Bachelor's degree	Master's degree	Professional degree	Doctorate degree
Standard error .. ($) ..	784	1 090	(B)	2 721	1 231	794	1 014	1 959	2 508	2 474	(B)	(B)	(B)
Mean income ..... ($) ..	27 824	13 318	(B)	12 850	13 984	30 595	23 522	33 562	32 355	41 244	(B)	(B)	(B)
Standard error .. ($) ..	1 471	824	(B)	1 715	1 013	1 725	929	5 493	2 178	3 441	(B)	(B)	(B)
Year-round, full-time workers	1 624	174	9	41	125	1 450	678	396	109	212	33	14	6
Median income .. ($) ..	28 302	17 350	(B)	(B)	18 100	30 651	25 859	32 230	31 754	37 192	(B)	(B)	(B)
Standard error .. ($) ..	1 399	1 462	(B)	(B)	1 722	688	1 196	1 759	1 923	2 689	(B)	(B)	(B)
Mean income ..... ($) ..	34 035	19 002	(B)	(B)	19 475	35 841	27 940	39 386	34 149	46 646	(B)	(B)	(B)
Standard error .. ($) ..	1 994	957	(B)	(B)	1 138	2 217	1 053	6 992	2 171	4 042	(B)	(B)	(B)
45 to 54 years, with													
income	1 496	363	22	77	265	1 132	526	252	99	175	56	12	11
Median income .. ($) ..	24 744	15 785	(B)	14 732	16 879	27 950	22 568	27 783	40 265	35 752	(B)	(B)	(B)
Standard error .. ($) ..	1 003	1 371	(B)	1 948	2 020	1 971	1 992	2 826	4 891	2 086	(B)	(B)	(B)
Mean income ..... ($) ..	32 056	18 990	(B)	15 303	20 615	36 247	26 206	34 026	38 600	37 263	(B)	(B)	(B)
Standard error .. ($) ..	2 422	1 380	(B)	1 502	1 802	3 139	2 891	2 429	4 227	2 780	(B)	(B)	(B)
Year-round, full-time workers	1 003	204	8	51	145	799	341	189	77	134	39	11	7
Median income .. ($) ..	33 219	22 416	(B)	(B)	24 024	35 972	29 315	35 164	45 681	40 039	(B)	(B)	(B)
Standard error .. ($) ..	1 729	1 308	(B)	(B)	1 490	934	2 278	2 871	3 986	2 354	(B)	(B)	(B)
Mean income ..... ($) ..	39 684	26 746	(B)	(B)	30 024	42 987	29 619	39 503	45 628	43 192	(B)	(B)	(B)
Standard error .. ($) ..	3 206	1 896	(B)	(B)	2 441	3 972	1 295	2 886	4 445	2 590	(B)	(B)	(B)
55 to 64 years, with													
income	875	361	53	119	190	513	264	112	51	45	34	5	2
Median income .. ($) ..	17 166	11 885	(B)	12 056	11 444	27 714	23 396	31 500	(B)	(B)	(B)	(B)	(B)
Standard error .. ($) ..	2 035	1 241	(B)	1 607	2 330	3 199	4 606	4 514	(B)	(B)	(B)	(B)	(B)
Mean income ..... ($) ..	23 193	15 872	(B)	14 071	17 361	28 347	24 403	34 394	(B)	(B)	(B)	(B)	(B)
Standard error .. ($) ..	1 095	1 141	(B)	1 880	1 678	1 576	1 891	3 304	(B)	(B)	(B)	(B)	(B)
Year-round, full-time workers	410	143	18	42	83	267	134	62	31	15	18	5	2
Median income .. ($) ..	31 178	22 315	(B)	(B)	26 959	33 244	32 037	(B)	(B)	(B)	(B)	(B)	(B)
Standard error .. ($) ..	690	3 237	(B)	(B)	1 881	1 921	1 197	(B)	(B)	(B)	(B)	(B)	(B)
Mean income ..... ($) ..	33 372	25 305	(B)	(B)	27 704	37 713	33 102	(B)	(B)	(B)	(B)	(B)	(B)
Standard error .. ($) ..	1 666	1 941	(B)	(B)	2 504	2 215	2 709	(B)	(B)	(B)	(B)	(B)	(B)
65 years and over, with													
income	963	566	115	255	197	397	205	100	20	35	19	8	10
Median income .. ($) ..	11 628	9 826	7 070	10 317	10 745	15 422	12 785	16 019	(B)	(B)	(B)	(B)	(B)
Standard error .. ($) ..	537	491	607	767	939	1 366	1 173	2 843	(B)	(B)	(B)	(B)	(B)
Mean income ..... ($) ..	17 255	13 171	8 900	14 198	14 331	23 082	18 711	17 897	(B)	(B)	(B)	(B)	(B)
Standard error .. ($) ..	1 038	981	844	1 690	1 659	1 994	2 535	1 812	(B)	(B)	(B)	(B)	(B)
Year-round, full-time workers	65	23	3	16	5	41	22	4	—	5	3	2	5
Median income .. ($) ..	(B)	(B)	(B)	(B)	(B)	(B)	(B)	(B)	(B)	(B)	(B)	(B)	(B)
Standard error .. ($) ..	(B)	(B)	(B)	(B)	(B)	(B)	(B)	(B)	(B)	(B)	(B)	(B)	(B)
Mean income ..... ($) ..	(B)	(B)	(B)	(B)	(B)	(B)	(B)	(B)	(B)	(B)	(B)	(B)	(B)
Standard error .. ($) ..	(B)	(B)	(B)	(B)	(B)	(B)	(B)	(B)	(B)	(B)	(B)	(B)	(B)
Female													
18 years and over with													
income	11 507	2 608	143	612	1 854	8 899	4 098	2 457	836	1 098	351	33	26
Median income .. ($) ..	12 143	6 685	6 171	6 705	6 737	15 494	11 362	15 607	21 079	26 302	33 242	(B)	(B)
Standard error .... ($) ..	243	141	445	228	191	291	300	534	1 088	742	2 501	(B)	(B)
Mean income .... ($) ..	16 877	8 765	7 258	8 779	8 876	19 254	14 067	20 203	22 078	28 844	34 106	(B)	(B)
Standard error .. ($) ..	438	259	903	486	319	554	353	1 728	865	1 403	1 630	(B)	(B)

See footnotes at end of table.

Table B-8.   Income by Educational Attainment for Persons 18 Years Old and Over, by Age, Sex, Race and Hispanic Origin: March 1997 — Continued

(Numbers in thousands. Civilian noninstitutional population.)

Income, standard error, age, sex, race, and Hispanic origin	Total	Not a high school graduate				High school graduate or more							
		Total	Elementary		High School	Total	High school graduate only	College					
			None - 4th grade	5th - 8th grade	9th - 11th grade			Some college no degree	Associate degree	Bachelor's degree	Master's degree	Professional degree	Doctorate degree
Year-round, full-time workers	5 091	446	11	67	368	4 645	1 835	1 307	529	708	236	18	12
Median income .. ($) ..	21 991	16 612	(B)	(B)	16 534	22 603	18 522	22 495	25 686	30 336	39 364	(B)	(B)
Standard error .. ($) ..	272	673	(B)	(B)	827	435	427	594	722	745	1 951	(B)	(B)
Mean income ..... ($) ..	26 573	18 246	(B)	(B)	18 188	27 373	20 599	30 163	27 524	34 667	40 617	(B)	(B)
Standard error .. ($) ..	886	844	(B)	(B)	951	965	425	3 160	977	1 716	1 705	(B)	(B)
25 years and over, with income	9 834	2 227	139	608	1 480	7 607	3 502	1 902	784	1 012	346	33	26
Median income .. ($) ..	13 810	7 047	6 166	6 713	7 371	16 993	12 228	18 231	21 570	26 835	33 842	(B)	(B)
Standard error .. ($) ..	360	151	466	228	249	301	351	511	1 076	758	2 475	(B)	(B)
Mean income ..... ($) ..	18 180	9 328	7 283	8 799	9 739	20 772	14 897	23 168	22 617	29 827	34 251	(B)	(B)
Standard error .. ($) ..	505	282	923	188	362	630	300	2 208	805	1 407	1 650	(D)	(D)
Year-round, full-time workers	4 656	405	11	67	328	4 250	1 658	1 150	501	678	234	18	12
Median income .. ($) ..	22 529	16 969	(B)	(B)	17 019	23 632	19 019	23 741	26 017	30 521	39 552	(B)	(B)
Standard error .. ($) ..	416	719	(B)	(B)	892	570	415	759	787	713	1 916	(B)	(B)
Mean income ..... ($) ..	27 444	18 737	(B)	(B)	18 788	28 274	21 180	31 781	28 039	34 973	40 776	(B)	(B)
Standard error .. ($) ..	962	912	(B)	(B)	1 047	1 048	451	3 575	1 009	1 785	1 714	(B)	(B)
25 to 34 years, with income	2 730	368	13	36	319	2 362	991	675	256	377	52	3	8
Median income .. ($) ..	13 769	6 380	(B)	(B)	6 404	15 517	11 352	16 349	19 274	24 904	(B)	(B)	(B)
Standard error .. ($) ..	497	440	(B)	(B)	511	467	581	743	1 951	1 545	(B)	(B)	(B)
Mean income ..... ($) ..	16 304	7 768	(B)	(B)	7 640	17 633	12 157	19 806	21 480	24 204	(B)	(B)	(B)
Standard error .. ($) ..	889	513	(B)	(B)	534	1 016	429	3 328	1 658	1 087	(B)	(B)	(B)
Year-round, full-time workers	1 373	58	1	8	49	1 315	473	379	154	265	34	3	6
Median income .. ($) ..	20 620	(B)	(B)	(B)	(B)	20 877	16 632	21 091	24 291	27 109	(B)	(B)	(B)
Standard error .. ($) ..	447	(B)	(B)	(B)	(B)	442	646	718	1 197	1 014	(B)	(B)	(B)
Mean income ..... ($) ..	23 680	(B)	(B)	(B)	(B)	23 985	17 401	27 686	26 765	27 984	(B)	(B)	(B)
Standard error .. ($) ..	1 662	(B)	(B)	(B)	(B)	1 734	553	5 810	2 143	1 039	(B)	(B)	(B)
35 to 44 years, with income	2 749	351	11	48	292	2 398	1 003	674	298	325	75	17	5
Median income .. ($) ..	17 606	7 843	(B)	(B)	7 905	18 999	14 370	20 055	24 361	30 925	29 407	(B)	(B)
Standard error .. ($) ..	511	758	(B)	(B)	815	507	837	956	1 830	1 598	8 669	(B)	(B)
Mean income ..... ($) ..	20 320	10 541	(B)	(B)	10 273	21 752	15 813	21 369	23 968	34 420	35 013	(B)	(B)
Standard error .. ($) ..	572	772	(B)	(B)	803	632	624	886	1 249	3 037	4 225	(B)	(B)
Year-round, full-time workers	1 684	111	—	14	97	1 573	573	454	221	250	58	11	5
Median income .. ($) ..	24 475	18 297	(B)	(B)	17 026	25 109	19 350	25 415	27 624	33 538	(B)	(B)	(B)
Standard error .. ($) ..	905	2 374	(B)	(B)	2 324	769	660	920	1 893	1 689	(B)	(B)	(B)
Mean income ..... ($) ..	27 340	18 836	(B)	(B)	18 243	27 941	21 790	27 178	28 556	38 528	(B)	(B)	(B)
Standard error .. ($) ..	759	1 444	(B)	(B)	1 452	800	824	933	1 166	3 691	(B)	(B)	(B)
45 to 54 years, with income	1 754	338	12	72	254	1 416	696	299	136	165	111	2	8
Median income .. ($) ..	18 442	9 189	(B)	(B)	11 099	21 243	16 186	22 828	23 156	30 004	43 812	(B)	(B)
Standard error .. ($) ..	892	1 382	(B)	(B)	1 239	866	758	2 201	2 160	1 985	2 561	(B)	(B)
Mean income ..... ($) ..	25 294	12 627	(B)	(B)	14 010	28 313	20 167	40 170	24 112	35 156	42 607	(B)	(B)
Standard error .. ($) ..	2 153	1 176	(B)	(B)	1 441	2 634	1 464	11 507	2 394	4 397	2 566	(B)	(B)
Year-round, full-time workers	1 103	116	6	9	102	986	437	238	97	118	95	—	1
Median income .. ($) ..	25 589	18 237	(B)	(B)	18 435	26 403	20 737	26 595	26 695	31 584	45 523	(B)	(B)
Standard error .. ($) ..	652	1 464	(B)	(B)	1 448	665	1 062	1 186	2 858	2 409	2 742	(B)	(B)
Mean income ..... ($) ..	32 880	21 883	(B)	(B)	21 797	34 179	23 837	47 822	29 270	40 181	44 250	(B)	(B)
Standard error .. ($) ..	3 243	2 566	(B)	(B)	2 823	3 607	986	14 332	2 558	5 517	2 445	(B)	(B)

See footnotes at end of table.

Table B-8. Income by Educational Attainment for Persons 18 Years Old and Over, by Age, Sex, Race and Hispanic Origin: March 1997 — Continued

(Numbers in thousands. Civilian noninstitutional population.)

| Income, standard error, age, sex, race, and Hispanic origin | Total | Not a high school graduate | | | | High school graduate or more | | | | | | | |
| | | Total | Elementary | | High School | Total | High school graduate only | College | | | | | |
			None - 4th grade	5th - 8th grade	9th - 11th grade			Some college no degree	Associate degree	Bachelor's degree	Master's degree	Professional degree	Doctorate degree
55 to 64 years, with													
income	1 061	358	15	114	229	703	385	141	45	68	58	4	4
Median income .. ($) ..	12 337	7 981	(B)	7 475	8 626	17 735	11 794	19 008	(B)	(B)	(B)	(B)	(B)
Standard error .. ($) ..	802	866	(B)	1 623	1 215	1 267	839	1 560	(B)	(B)	(B)	(B)	(B)
Mean income ... ($) ..	16 551	9 833	(B)	9 324	10 345	19 967	14 606	21 558	(B)	(B)	(B)	(B)	(B)
Standard error .. ($) ..	716	575	(B)	933	757	972	894	2 218	(B)	(B)	(B)	(B)	(B)
Year-round, full-time													
workers	429	97	—	26	71	332	160	73	22	39	37	1	—
Median income .. ($) ..	22 395	16 947	(B)	(B)	(B)	26 008	21 022	(B)	(B)	(B)	(B)	(B)	(B)
Standard error .. ($) ..	1 110	1 933	(B)	(B)	(B)	894	1 007	(B)	(B)	(B)	(B)	(B)	(B)
Mean income ..... ($) ..	26 101	16 932	(B)	(B)	(B)	28 767	22 652	(B)	(B)	(B)	(B)	(B)	(B)
Standard error .. ($) ..	1 146	918	(B)	(B)	(B)	1 360	1 344	(B)	(B)	(B)	(B)	(B)	(B)
65 years and over, with													
income	1 541	813	89	338	387	727	428	113	49	78	51	7	1
Median income .. ($) ..	7 231	6 708	6 224	6 682	6 831	8 785	7 893	8 007	(B)	12 945	(B)	(B)	(B)
Standard error .. ($) ..	145	171	613	246	256	585	582	1 139	(B)	2 282	(B)	(B)	(B)
Mean income ..... ($) ..	10 709	7 920	6 747	8 245	7 906	13 829	10 797	11 132	(B)	26 550	(B)	(B)	(B)
Standard error .. ($) ..	605	317	676	621	351	1 202	817	1 257	(B)	9 078	(B)	(B)	(B)
Year-round, full-time													
workers	67	23	4	10	9	44	15	6	5	5	10	3	—
Median income .. ($) ..	(B)	(B)	(B)	(B)	(B)	(B)	(B)	(B)	(B)	(B)	(B)	(B)	(B)
Standard error .. ($) ..	(B)	(B)	(B)	(B)	(B)	(B)	(B)	(B)	(B)	(B)	(B)	(B)	(B)
Mean income ..... ($) ..	(B)	(B)	(B)	(B)	(B)	(B)	(B)	(B)	(B)	(B)	(B)	(B)	(B)
Standard error .. ($) ..	(B)	(B)	(B)	(B)	(B)	(B)	(B)	(B)	(B)	(B)	(B)	(B)	(B)
HISPANIC ORIGIN [1]													
Both Sexes													
18 years and over	19 103	8 632	1 546	3 461	3 624	10 471	5 005	2 892	889	1 228	282	103	73
Without income	2 532	1 594	292	627	675	939	548	265	47	66	4	5	4
With income	16 570	7 038	1 254	2 834	2 949	9 532	4 457	2 627	843	1 162	277	98	68
Median income .. ($) ..	12 772	9 878	8 097	10 286	10 290	16 896	14 777	15 786	22 029	26 725	30 135	37 048	(B)
Standard error .. ($) ..	233	201	423	272	292	282	423	539	985	924	2 567	7 459	(B)
Mean income ..... ($) ..	17 929	11 926	10 112	12 296	12 343	22 360	17 688	20 940	24 448	31 810	37 869	69 938	(B)
Standard error .. ($) ..	383	219	515	337	343	636	413	1 343	1 468	2 487	3 703	25 400	(B)
Male													
18 years and over with													
income	9 032	4 010	708	1 642	1 660	5 022	2 348	1 413	408	576	173	59	44
Median income .. ($) ..	15 855	12 099	10 607	12 376	12 494	20 567	17 851	18 579	26 153	31 083	30 320	(B)	(B)
Standard error .. ($) ..	247	208	478	387	440	445	656	843	1 138	1 558	3 520	(B)	(B)
Mean income ..... ($) ..	21 339	14 529	12 255	15 131	14 903	26 776	21 326	25 610	30 002	38 058	39 596	(B)	(B)
Standard error .. ($) ..	596	328	831	500	502	1 021	607	2 415	2 697	4 757	3 569	(B)	(B)
Year-round, full-time													
workers	5 532	2 231	323	946	962	3 301	1 528	868	276	416	127	50	36
Median income .. ($) ..	21 286	16 190	14 549	16 155	16 782	26 269	22 569	25 673	31 588	36 846	34 711	(B)	(B)
Standard error .. ($) ..	312	297	755	475	441	421	740	923	1 770	2 117	5 588	(B)	(B)
Mean income ..... ($) ..	27 527	18 837	17 085	18 779	19 482	33 401	25 679	34 455	37 295	45 212	43 153	(B)	(B)
Standard error .. ($) ..	917	485	1 626	720	681	1 477	688	3 819	3 603	6 445	4 074	(B)	(B)
25 years and over, with													
income	7 376	3 251	660	1 436	1 156	4 125	1 926	1 013	373	539	169	59	44
Median income .. ($) ..	17 598	13 101	10 773	13 028	15 044	23 473	20 493	23 014	26 932	31 919	30 729	(B)	(B)

See footnotes at end of table.

Table B-8. Income by Educational Attainment for Persons 18 Years Old and Over, by Age, Sex, Race and Hispanic Origin: March 1997 — Continued

(Numbers in thousands. Civilian noninstitutional population.)

Income, standard error, age, sex, race, and Hispanic origin	Total	Not a high school graduate				High school graduate or more							
		Total	Elementary		High School	Total	High school graduate only	College					
			None - 4th grade	5th - 8th grade	9th - 11th grade			Some college no degree	Associate degree	Bachelor's degree	Master's degree	Professional degree	Doctorate degree
Standard error .. ($) ..	382	386	516	625	568	636	625	1 119	1 708	2 238	3 979	(B)	(B)
Mean income ..... ($) ..	23 691	15 782	12 599	15 857	17 503	29 925	23 359	31 037	31 613	39 368	40 090	(B)	(B)
Standard error .. ($) ..	717	385	884	557	646	1 222	695	3 311	2 898	5 065	3 626	(B)	(B)
Year-round, full-time workers	4 803	1 875	297	823	755	2 928	1 321	730	270	396	124	50	36
Median income .. ($) ..	22 662	16 935	15 059	16 854	17 995	27 356	24 402	27 369	31 531	37 481	35 563	(B)	(B)
Standard error .. ($) ..	476	310	781	485	819	574	811	1 077	1 691	2 480	5 801	(B)	(B)
Mean income ..... ($) ..	29 295	19 890	17 631	19 696	20 990	35 316	27 014	37 421	37 507	46 216	43 587	(B)	(B)
Standard error .. ($) ..	1 047	562	1 756	807	828	1 653	755	4 509	3 684	6 747	4 132	(B)	(B)
25 to 34 years, with income	2 754	1 072	115	418	538	1 682	795	434	149	241	42	16	5
Median income .. ($) ..	17 293	13 582	13 066	13 007	14 080	21 625	19 242	22 028	24 843	28 717	(B)	(B)	(D)
Standard error .. ($) ..	434	593	1 472	952	795	589	1 155	1 303	2 012	2 863	(B)	(B)	(B)
Mean income ..... ($) ..	21 910	15 118	13 574	14 910	15 610	26 239	20 956	31 385	26 506	31 366	(B)	(B)	(B)
Standard error .. ($) ..	1 084	473	1 037	738	712	1 725	746	6 248	2 262	2 233	(B)	(B)	(B)
Year-round, full-time workers	1 998	739	75	288	376	1 259	611	326	101	172	32	12	5
Median income .. ($) ..	20 965	15 816	14 927	15 462	16 266	25 198	21 544	25 904	26 967	34 946	(B)	(B)	(B)
Standard error .. ($) ..	478	441	1 413	819	614	666	766	1 159	2 074	3 616	(B)	(B)	(B)
Mean income ..... ($) ..	25 370	17 333	15 651	17 003	17 921	30 090	23 265	37 520	29 699	36 823	(B)	(B)	(B)
Standard error .. ($) ..	1 448	529	1 278	893	735	2 248	840	8 219	2 221	2 473	(B)	(B)	(B)
35 to 44 years, with income	2 144	860	152	405	304	1 283	599	331	116	150	49	19	18
Median income .. ($) ..	20 562	15 313	11 607	15 946	17 166	25 647	22 250	25 589	31 640	32 271	(B)	(B)	(B)
Standard error .. ($) ..	642	685	758	818	1 433	864	1 317	2 222	5 044	3 465	(B)	(B)	(B)
Mean income ..... ($) ..	26 410	17 857	14 004	18 185	19 347	32 143	26 061	29 615	32 981	49 079	(B)	(B)	(B)
Standard error .. ($) ..	1 475	958	3 225	1 365	1 163	2 340	1 618	2 178	3 355	17 232	(B)	(B)	(B)
Year-round, full-time workers	1 507	562	93	256	214	945	401	255	99	118	39	17	14
Median income .. ($) ..	25 009	18 282	13 647	18 860	21 175	30 477	26 790	29 096	36 257	37 451	(B)	(B)	(B)
Standard error .. ($) ..	829	1 196	991	1 480	1 438	1 117	1 427	2 173	4 049	6 291	(D)	(D)	(B)
Mean income ..... ($) ..	31 437	21 582	17 816	21 745	23 013	37 302	30 320	33 823	36 762	56 853	(B)	(B)	(B)
Standard error .. ($) ..	1 985	1 327	5 146	1 917	1 361	3 021	1 530	2 599	3 454	21 756	(B)	(B)	(B)
45 to 54 years, with income	1 179	524	118	257	149	655	281	149	73	86	43	16	7
Median income .. ($) ..	20 418	15 115	11 849	15 297	17 981	26 239	22 135	25 143	(B)	37 498	(B)	(B)	(B)
Standard error .. ($) ..	788	1 088	1 194	1 603	1 765	1 110	1 839	4 613	(B)	5 866	(B)	(B)	(B)
Mean income ..... ($) ..	26 759	17 810	13 494	17 856	21 146	33 925	24 963	31 125	(B)	44 515	(B)	(B)	(B)
Standard error .. ($) ..	1 712	1 038	1 280	1 340	2 540	2 883	1 799	3 164	(B)	5 730	(B)	(B)	(B)
Year-round, full-time workers	860	366	71	181	113	495	204	109	53	74	35	15	6
Median income .. ($) ..	23 986	17 969	(B)	17 610	19 838	31 593	25 985	34 546	(B)	(B)	(B)	(B)	(B)
Standard error .. ($) ..	1 304	1 062	(B)	1 454	1 676	1 658	1 309	3 754	(B)	(B)	(B)	(B)	(B)
Mean income ..... ($) ..	31 552	20 590	(B)	20 283	23 669	39 661	29 443	37 413	(B)	(B)	(B)	(B)	(B)
Standard error .. ($) ..	2 228	1 299	(B)	1 535	3 169	3 636	2 137	3 663	(B)	(B)	(B)	(B)	(B)
55 to 64 years, with income	698	394	122	173	98	304	147	57	23	43	22	4	7
Median income .. ($) ..	15 997	11 786	10 611	11 989	14 086	26 366	23 391	(B)	(B)	(B)	(B)	(B)	(B)
Standard error .. ($) ..	1 038	819	1 941	1 270	2 209	2 200	3 605	(B)	(B)	(B)	(B)	(B)	(B)
Mean income ..... ($) ..	24 889	15 110	12 710	14 377	19 393	37 567	25 977	(B)	(B)	(B)	(B)	(B)	(B)
Standard error .. ($) ..	3 017	1 183	1 638	1 415	3 371	6 558	2 623	(B)	(B)	(B)	(B)	(B)	(B)
Year-round, full-time workers	367	179	46	84	50	188	87	31	14	30	15	4	7
Median income .. ($) ..	25 310	18 244	(B)	16 465	(B)	32 350	28 520	(B)	(B)	(B)	(B)	(B)	(B)

See footnotes at end of table.

Table B-8.   Income by Educational Attainment for Persons 18 Years Old and Over, by Age, Sex, Race and Hispanic Origin: March 1997 — Continued

(Numbers in thousands. Civilian noninstitutional population.)

Income, standard error, age, sex, race, and Hispanic origin	Total	Not a high school graduate				High school graduate or more							
		Total	Elementary		High School	Total	High school graduate only	College					
			None - 4th grade	5th - 8th grade	9th - 11th grade			Some college no degree	Associate degree	Bachelor's degree	Master's degree	Professional degree	Doctorate degree
Standard error .. ($) ..	1 945	1 807	(B)	1 682	(B)	3 511	2 091	(B)	(B)	(B)	(B)	(B)	(B)
Mean income ..... ($) ..	36 192	23 051	(B)	19 988	(B)	48 752	31 888	(B)	(B)	(B)	(B)	(B)	(B)
Standard error .. ($) ..	5 469	2 069	(B)	2 325	(B)	10 280	3 640	(B)	(B)	(B)	(B)	(B)	(B)
65 years and over, with													
income	602	401	152	182	67	201	103	42	12	19	12	5	8
Median income .. ($) ..	10 332	8 862	7 556	9 093	(B)	15 165	14 302	(B)	(B)	(B)	(B)	(B)	(B)
Standard error .. ($) ..	613	458	695	523	(B)	1 733	2 001	(B)	(B)	(B)	(B)	(B)	(B)
Mean income ..... ($) ..	14 748	11 112	9 669	11 439	(B)	22 012	18 095	(B)	(B)	(B)	(B)	(B)	(B)
Standard error .. ($) ..	992	682	873	1 088	(B)	2 425	2 260	(B)	(B)	(B)	(B)	(B)	(B)
Year-round, full-time workers	70	28	12	15	1	42	19	9	2	3	3	2	4
Median income .. ($) ..	(B)	(B)	(B)	(B)	(B)	(B)	(B)	(B)	(B)	(B)	(B)	(B)	(B)
Standard error .. ($) ..	(B)	(B)	(B)	(B)	(B)	(B)	(B)	(B)	(B)	(B)	(B)	(B)	(B)
Mean income ..... ($) ..	(B)	(B)	(B)	(B)	(B)	(B)	(B)	(B)	(B)	(B)	(B)	(B)	(B)
Standard error .. ($) ..	(B)	(B)	(B)	(B)	(B)	(B)	(B)	(B)	(B)	(B)	(B)	(B)	(B)
Female													
18 years and over with													
income	7 538	3 028	546	1 192	1 289	4 510	2 109	1 215	434	586	104	38	24
Median income .. ($) ..	9 782	6 953	6 609	7 046	7 108	13 209	11 333	12 094	19 051	24 518	29 742	(B)	(B)
Standard error .. ($) ..	225	166	265	287	293	479	394	642	1 835	1 266	5 381	(B)	(B)
Mean income ..... ($) ..	13 842	8 480	7 333	8 392	9 046	17 443	13 637	15 509	19 226	25 660	34 994	(B)	(B)
Standard error .. ($) ..	435	225	406	327	396	697	511	645	1 147	1 439	7 856	(B)	(B)
Year-round, full-time workers	2 948	805	90	350	364	2 144	973	519	223	338	59	20	12
Median income .. ($) ..	19 296	13 304	11 180	12 766	14 541	21 973	18 145	21 251	24 668	31 939	(B)	(B)	(B)
Standard error .. ($) ..	546	502	731	674	747	398	848	785	1 359	1 364	(B)	(B)	(B)
Mean income ..... ($) ..	23 328	14 927	11 870	13 990	16 585	26 482	20 322	23 948	26 555	35 847	(B)	(B)	(B)
Standard error .. ($) ..	998	500	958	615	876	1 342	847	993	1 604	1 801	(B)	(B)	(B)
25 years and over, with													
income	6 337	2 621	518	1 113	990	3 715	1 696	895	400	560	101	38	24
Median income .. ($) ..	10 525	7 252	6 649	7 150	8 042	15 180	12 255	15 168	19 851	24 948	30 372	(B)	(B)
Standard error .. ($) ..	259	173	271	295	451	511	493	1 070	1 770	1 268	4 102	(B)	(B)
Mean income ..... ($) ..	14 883	8 877	7 420	8 540	10 017	19 121	14 731	17 847	19 670	25 953	35 722	(B)	(B)
Standard error .. ($) ..	510	249	423	344	477	832	609	789	1 215	1 495	8 029	(B)	(B)
Year-round, full-time workers	2 632	725	80	328	317	1 907	830	458	204	326	58	20	12
Median income .. ($) ..	20 328	13 647	11 318	13 201	14 910	22 926	19 681	22 087	25 035	32 254	(B)	(B)	(B)
Standard error .. ($) ..	399	531	780	723	919	572	837	1 028	1 361	1 369	(B)	(B)	(B)
Mean income ..... ($) ..	24 321	15 279	12 285	14 328	17 021	27 759	21 243	24 865	27 382	36 271	(B)	(B)	(B)
Standard error .. ($) ..	1 109	539	1 026	637	980	1 496	965	1 062	1 697	1 849	(B)	(B)	(B)
25 to 34 years, with													
income	2 064	632	58	206	368	1 432	582	382	168	241	42	12	6
Median income .. ($) ..	11 455	7 071	(B)	6 189	7 641	15 056	11 984	14 316	18 855	24 397	(B)	(B)	(B)
Standard error .. ($) ..	461	418	(B)	897	673	798	677	1 514	2 323	1 664	(B)	(B)	(B)
Mean income ..... ($) ..	14 528	8 412	(B)	6 803	9 592	17 228	13 323	15 851	19 185	24 040	(B)	(B)	(B)
Standard error .. ($) ..	584	530	(B)	585	818	779	707	1 000	1 837	1 813	(B)	(B)	(B)
Year-round, full-time workers	948	193	13	59	121	755	303	197	76	151	18	6	4
Median income .. ($) ..	20 020	13 327	(B)	(B)	14 968	21 489	17 327	20 207	25 209	28 341	(B)	(B)	(B)
Standard error .. ($) ..	669	918	(B)	(B)	1 335	486	1 424	1 009	2 689	1 940	(B)	(B)	(B)
Mean income ..... ($) ..	22 189	14 877	(B)	(B)	16 872	24 061	18 485	21 383	27 699	31 892	(B)	(B)	(B)
Standard error .. ($) ..	1 022	1 227	(B)	(B)	1 821	1 219	825	1 238	2 723	1 966	(B)	(B)	(B)

See footnotes at end of table.

Table B-8.   Income by Educational Attainment for Persons 18 Years Old and Over, by Age, Sex, Race and Hispanic Origin: March 1997 — Continued

(Numbers in thousands. Civilian noninstitutional population.)

Income, standard error, age, sex, race, and Hispanic origin	Total	Not a high school graduate				High school graduate or more							
		Total	Elementary		High School	Total	High school graduate only	College					
			None - 4th grade	5th - 8th grade	9th - 11th grade			Some college no degree	Associate degree	Bachelor's degree	Master's degree	Professional degree	Doctorate degree
35 to 44 years, with													
income	1 778	630	78	291	260	1 148	523	290	120	173	24	12	6
Median income .. ($) ..	11 856	8 898	8 526	9 759	8 069	15 670	12 883	16 507	20 522	25 692	(B)	(B)	(B)
Standard error .. ($) ..	401	542	1 151	828	861	1 025	1 058	3 194	2 944	(B)	(B)	(B)	(B)
Mean income ..... ($) ..	17 312	10 007	8 604	10 607	9 757	21 319	16 188	19 777	19 737	26 955	(B)	(B)	(B)
Standard error .. ($) ..	1 538	486	950	714	806	2 343	1 489	1 562	2 297	2 895	(B)	(B)	(B)
Year-round, full-time													
workers	903	266	31	139	96	637	295	151	68	97	16	8	1
Median income .. ($) ..	20 405	13 069	(B)	13 786	13 259	24 219	19 793	25 620	(B)	33 854	(B)	(B)	(B)
Standard error .. ($) ..	924	801	(B)	901	1 739	971	1 225	3 019	(B)	2 807	(B)	(B)	(B)
Mean income ..... ($) ..	26 048	14 714	(B)	14 870	15 472	30 777	23 152	27 792	(B)	37 822	(B)	(B)	(B)
Standard error .. ($)	2 907	743	(R)	930	1 451	4 067	2 364	1 954	(B)	3 606	(B)	(B)	(B)
45 to 54 years, with													
income	1 015	431	69	233	129	584	266	135	70	79	22	6	6
Median income .. ($) ..	12 167	8 393	(B)	7 360	10 624	17 044	13 973	16 945	(B)	32 063	(B)	(B)	(B)
Standard error .. ($) ..	756	860	(B)	939	1 086	1 178	1 596	2 126	(B)	5 168	(B)	(B)	(B)
Mean income ..... ($) ..	16 468	9 533	(B)	8 658	11 406	21 585	14 902	19 514	(B)	33 816	(B)	(B)	(B)
Standard error .. ($) ..	877	591	(B)	736	1 261	1 356	1 142	1 928	(B)	5 356	(B)	(B)	(B)
Year-round, full-time													
workers	500	159	19	84	56	341	139	81	41	52	17	3	6
Median income .. ($) ..	20 400	13 864	(B)	13 189	(B)	24 410	20 892	21 784	(B)	(B)	(B)	(B)	(B)
Standard error .. ($) ..	1 181	1 125	(B)	1 364	(B)	1 220	1 620	3 279	(B)	(B)	(B)	(B)	(B)
Mean income ..... ($) ..	25 096	14 906	(B)	13 617	(B)	29 850	21 531	24 678	(B)	(B)	(B)	(B)	(B)
Standard error .. ($) ..	1 403	882	(B)	901	(B)	1 865	1 502	2 529	(B)	(B)	(B)	(B)	(B)
55 to 64 years, with													
income	701	380	93	167	119	321	188	53	28	39	9	5	—
Median income .. ($) ..	9 039	6 688	5 575	6 316	8 673	14 885	12 711	(B)	(B)	(B)	(B)	(B)	(B)
Standard error .. ($) ..	963	500	874	821	1 408	2 436	1 927	(B)	(B)	(B)	(B)	(B)	(B)
Mean income ..... ($) ..	13 637	8 901	6 860	8 579	10 948	19 234	16 332	(B)	(B)	(B)	(B)	(B)	(B)
Standard error .. ($) ..	907	731	1 268	1 107	1 357	1 631	2 004	(B)	(B)	(B)	(B)	(B)	(B)
Year-round, full-time													
workers	252	96	14	45	37	157	80	25	18	24	6	3	—
Median income .. ($) ..	20 840	15 372	(B)	(B)	(B)	25 168	20 856	(B)	(B)	(B)	(B)	(B)	(B)
Standard error .. ($) ..	994	1 892	(B)	(B)	(B)	2 611	1 345	(B)	(B)	(B)	(B)	(B)	(B)
Mean income ..... ($) ..	23 629	17 026	(B)	(B)	(B)	27 672	22 340	(B)	(B)	(B)	(B)	(B)	(B)
Standard error .. ($) ..	1 503	1 731	(B)	(B)	(B)	1 993	1 932	(B)	(B)	(B)	(B)	(B)	(B)
65 years and over, with													
income	779	549	219	215	114	230	138	35	15	29	4	5	5
Median income .. ($) ..	6 928	6 524	6 370	6 442	7 122	9 227	9 500	(B)	(B)	(B)	(B)	(B)	(B)
Standard error .. ($) ..	220	224	325	355	645	933	1 469	(B)	(B)	(B)	(B)	(B)	(B)
Mean income ..... ($) ..	9 334	7 583	6 944	7 252	9 434	13 514	12 621	(B)	(B)	(B)	(B)	(B)	(B)
Standard error .. ($) ..	571	488	584	645	1 628	1 442	1 605	(B)	(B)	(B)	(B)	(B)	(B)
Year-round, full-time													
workers	29	11	3	1	7	18	13	3	—	1	—	—	—
Median income .. ($) ..	(B)	(B)	(B)	(B)	(B)	(B)	(B)	(B)	(B)	(B)	(B)	(B)	(B)
Standard error .. ($) ..	(B)	(B)	(B)	(B)	(B)	(B)	(B)	(B)	(B)	(B)	(B)	(B)	(B)
Mean income ..... ($) ..	(B)	(B)	(B)	(B)	(B)	(B)	(B)	(B)	(B)	(B)	(B)	(B)	(B)
Standard error .. ($) ..	(B)	(B)	(B)	(B)	(B)	(B)	(B)	(B)	(B)	(B)	(B)	(B)	(B)

Source: March 1997 Current Population Survey, Education and Social Stratification Branch, U.S. Bureau of the Census.

1. May be of any race.

— Represents zero or rounds to zero.

(B) Base less than 75,000.

Table B-9.   Earnings by Educational Attainment for Persons 18 Years Old and Over, by Age, Sex, Race and Hispanic Origin: March 1997

(Numbers in thousands. Civilian noninstitutional population.)

Earnings, standard error, age, sex, race, and Hispanic origin	Total	Not a high school graduate				High school graduate or more							
		Total	Elementary		High School	Total	High school graduate only	College					
			None - 4th grade	5th - 8th grade	9th - 11th grade			Some college no degree	Associate degree	Bachelor's degree	Master-'s degree	Professional degree	Doctorate degree

ALL RACES

Both Sexes

18 years and over, with													
earnings	138 703	17 075	1 030	4 126	11 919	121 628	45 908	29 427	10 983	24 028	7 671	2 101	1 509
Median earnings ..($) ...	21 272	11 684	10 964	12 098	11 591	22 853	18 544	18 792	25 527	31 230	41 037	63 539	56 958
Standard error ... ($) ...	81	126	373	217	167	136	165	228	265	184	330	2 452	2 140
Mean earnings .. ($) ...	28 106	15 011	12 475	15 050	15 216	29 945	22 154	23 937	28 514	38 112	50 162	94 038	72 464
Standard error ... ($) ...	176	286	617	353	387	195	209	341	472	436	1 111	4 500	3 144
Year round, full-time													
workers	90 143	8 966	587	2 415	5 963	81 178	30 003	17 631	7 819	17 306	5 514	1 689	1 215
Median earnings ..($) ...	28 326	17 514	14 075	16 444	18 877	30 266	24 026	26 792	30 834	37 008	46 876	75 112	62 099
Standard error ... ($) ...	176	225	581	308	320	91	183	182	242	217	422	2 345	1 557
Mean earnings .. ($) ...	36 539	21 387	16 172	19 489	22 669	38 212	28 121	33 148	34 467	45 856	60 217	107 458	80 000
Standard error ... ($) ...	248	432	943	459	614	269	281	526	614	541	1 455	5 399	3 618

Male

18 years and over, with													
earnings	73 955	10 583	724	2 745	7 114	63 372	23 966	15 112	5 096	12 562	4 089	1 498	1 049
Median earnings ..($) ...	26 397	14 112	11 873	14 322	14 451	29 595	24 045	24 162	31 679	37 897	50 108	72 005	62 263
Standard error ... ($) ...	122	268	405	461	364	267	255	406	342	624	1 054	2 502	2 051
Mean earnings .. ($) ...	34 705	17 826	13 741	17 279	18 453	37 523	27 642	30 057	35 484	46 702	62 145	102 913	81 492
Standard error ... ($) ...	291	440	816	479	622	329	364	574	920	720	1 913	5 204	4 203
Year round, full-time													
workers	53 739	6 221	444	1 771	4 007	47 518	17 582	10 156	4 133	10 188	3 290	1 277	893
Median earnings ..($) ...	32 159	19 608	14 782	17 425	20 944	35 173	27 820	31 505	35 497	42 520	55 922	78 144	66 159
Standard error ... ($) ...	114	335	623	489	314	139	347	242	365	574	1 154	2 320	1 571
Mean earnings .. ($) ...	42 077	23 457	17 249	20 881	25 283	44 515	32 521	38 491	39 873	52 354	70 859	112 873	86 436
Standard error ... ($) ...	372	605	1 194	578	890	410	450	800	1 088	806	2 278	5 901	4 626

18 to 24 years, with													
earnings	10 289	2 274	47	259	1 969	8 015	3 438	3 478	403	662	31	2	—
Median earnings ..($) ...	9 158	5 784	(B)	10 180	5 151	10 136	11 418	7 290	11 833	16 801	(B)	(B)	(B)
Standard error ... ($) ...	223	364	(B)	901	357	193	263	214	818	1 153	(B)	(B)	(B)
Mean earnings .. ($) ...	11 473	7 923	(B)	9 802	7 612	12 481	13 127	9 986	16 447	19 190	(B)	(B)	(B)
Standard error ... ($) ...	195	259	(B)	622	281	236	286	259	2 794	909	(B)	(B)	(B)
Year round, full-time													
workers	3 979	741	29	145	567	3 238	1 744	983	202	290	19	—	—
Median earnings ..($) ...	17 259	13 268	(B)	12 130	13 900	18 331	17 321	17 347	21 957	26 761	(B)	(B)	(B)
Standard error ... ($) ...	263	503	(B)	601	615	377	393	500	1 448	636	(B)	(B)	(B)
Mean earnings .. ($) ...	18 856	14 975	(B)	13 058	15 478	19 744	18 779	18 336	23 447	26 838	(B)	(B)	(B)
Standard error ... ($) ...	372	471	(B)	710	558	440	396	446	5 409	1 035	(B)	(B)	(B)

25 years and over, with													
earnings	63 666	8 309	678	2 486	5 145	55 357	20 528	11 634	4 693	11 900	4 058	1 495	1 049
Median earnings ..($) ...	30 306	16 506	12 067	15 173	18 140	32 051	26 313	30 346	33 067	40 089	50 240	72 052	62 263
Standard error ... ($) ...	116	211	433	407	429	120	174	236	730	460	884	2 499	2 051
Mean earnings .. ($) ...	38 459	20 537	13 957	18 057	22 602	41 149	30 073	36 058	37 120	48 234	62 416	103 055	81 492
Standard error ... ($) ...	331	547	854	519	836	369	417	720	960	753	1 926	5 209	4 203
Year round, full-time													
workers	49 760	5 480	415	1 626	3 440	44 280	15 838	9 172	3 931	9 898	3 272	1 277	893
Median earnings ..($) ...	34 463	20 636	15 109	18 336	22 206	36 312	30 090	33 293	36 072	43 780	56 076	78 144	66 159
Standard error ... ($) ...	305	253	620	715	341	138	217	607	361	813	1 063	2 320	1 571
Mean earnings .. ($) ...	43 934	24 604	17 429	21 577	26 900	46 326	34 034	40 652	40 719	53 102	71 071	112 873	86 436
Standard error ... ($) ...	398	680	1 255	619	1 027	436	494	877	1 105	826	2 290	5 901	4 626

25 to 34 years, with													
earnings	18 711	2 393	145	551	1 697	16 318	6 067	3 686	1 519	3 899	739	273	135

See footnotes at end of table.

Table B-9. Earnings by Educational Attainment for Persons 18 Years Old and Over, by Age, Sex, Race and Hispanic Origin: March 1997 — Continued

(Numbers in thousands. Civilian noninstitutional population.)

Earnings, standard error, age, sex, race, and Hispanic origin	Total	Not a high school graduate				High school graduate or more							
		Total	Elementary		High School	Total	High school graduate only	College					
			None - 4th grade	5th - 8th grade	9th - 11th grade			Some college no degree	Associate degree	Bachelor's degree	Master's degree	Professional degree	Doctorate degree
Median earnings ..($) ...	25 157	14 881	13 521	14 449	15 179	26 651	22 514	25 186	28 167	33 419	37 750	42 289	41 283
Standard error ... ($) ...	198	374	1 140	806	459	196	327	415	926	752	2 073	3 066	3 899
Mean earnings .. ($) ...	29 127	16 838	13 899	17 219	16 964	30 930	24 561	28 919	32 388	38 019	40 920	54 720	48 170
Standard error ... ($) ...	372	375	1 003	841	442	418	445	978	1 962	925	1 517	3 749	3 383
Year round, full-time workers ...	14 448	1 563	94	386	1 082	12 886	4 642	2 873	1 270	3 201	549	234	117
Median earnings ..($) ...	28 406	17 438	15 451	16 450	18 612	30 302	25 531	27 415	30 563	36 688	43 825	46 968	41 935
Standard error ... ($) ...	366	454	856	615	706	184	254	457	474	441	1 284	3 554	6 225
Mean earnings .. ($) ...	33 055	19 684	16 266	19 887	19 910	34 677	27 349	32 624	34 854	42 402	48 143	58 987	50 776
Standard error ... ($) ...	433	449	1 136	1 051	518	478	322	1 200	2 288	1 068	1 722	3 858	3 639
35 to 44 years, with earnings ...	20 064	2 318	191	577	1 550	17 746	6 923	3 756	1 528	3 658	1 217	435	229
Median earnings ..($) ...	32 462	17 268	11 590	15 867	19 262	35 715	28 410	33 556	36 114	46 158	59 500	81 315	66 640
Standard error ... ($) ...	336	387	582	629	626	223	582	1 093	645	795	2 462	4 751	3 653
Mean earnings .. ($) ...	41 533	20 978	13 495	17 268	23 282	44 218	31 949	37 068	38 680	55 039	74 411	121 535	89 226
Standard error ... ($) ...	618	1 013	2 433	747	1 450	679	735	940	920	1 578	4 710	10 464	8 318
Year round, full-time workers ...	16 577	1 553	123	379	1 051	15 024	5 611	3 157	1 330	3 221	1 082	411	210
Median earnings ..($) ...	36 368	20 949	13 531	18 804	22 820	37 954	31 088	36 140	37 726	50 126	62 079	85 077	68 854
Standard error ... ($) ...	225	476	989	1 223	715	500	273	408	967	991	2 030	5 212	4 713
Mean earnings .. ($) ...	45 840	24 074	16 879	20 747	26 116	48 090	35 138	39 630	41 558	58 497	79 119	124 647	93 329
Standard error ... ($) ...	714	841	3 644	867	1 110	777	868	1 054	963	1 740	5 212	10 849	8 891
45 to 54 years, with earnings ...	14 573	1 667	151	529	986	12 906	4 162	2 623	1 149	2 808	1 339	436	390
Median earnings ..($) ...	36 619	19 575	13 354	17 087	21 982	39 849	30 931	36 068	40 390	44 928	54 209	87 589	67 235
Standard error ... ($) ...	296	681	1 660	1 032	888	483	429	649	1 332	1 366	1 931	5 603	2 722
Mean earnings .. ($) ...	47 171	25 055	15 244	19 756	29 405	50 027	35 953	42 451	40 986	54 498	71 285	129 226	84 058
Standard error ... ($) ...	853	1 937	1 254	1 012	3 204	922	1 373	1 541	1 154	1 677	3 391	12 596	6 245
Year round, full-time workers ...	12 234	1 246	102	401	743	10 988	3 425	2 204	1 008	2 446	1 165	403	337
Median earnings ..($) ...	40 362	22 478	16 571	20 493	24 882	41 777	33 087	39 601	41 784	48 587	58 173	91 074	70 491
Standard error ... ($) ...	265	727	2 519	1 022	829	261	891	946	744	1 492	2 034	8 873	2 781
Mean earnings .. ($) ...	51 705	29 311	17 631	22 609	34 527	54 244	39 178	46 499	43 745	57 729	76 971	134 666	89 480
Standard error ... ($) ...	970	2 547	1 515	1 167	4 191	1 034	1 598	1 771	1 198	1 648	3 809	13 488	7 014
55 to 64 years, with earnings ...	7 486	1 303	133	533	637	6 183	2 556	1 132	368	1 121	587	203	215
Median earnings ..($) ...	30 742	19 965	12 620	15 852	25 200	33 267	29 630	31 383	32 855	36 913	45 807	83 127	62 204
Standard error ... ($) ...	323	915	1 559	775	1 309	1 134	875	694	2 434	2 282	4 364	9 668	5 672
Mean earnings .. ($) ...	41 855	23 364	15 235	18 010	29 539	45 751	32 380	47 545	44 860	51 347	53 001	106 852	90 196
Standard error ... ($) ...	1 105	1 284	1 638	1 017	2 401	1 297	854	4 537	7 345	2 352	3 037	10 333	12 400
Year round, full-time workers ...	5 439	904	75	346	482	4 536	1 869	797	276	847	406	160	180
Median earnings ..($) ...	36 336	22 554	16 593	18 949	27 416	39 638	33 470	39 084	40 928	49 652	58 622	99 302	68 188
Standard error ... ($) ...	409	1 048	1 416	1 653	1 075	794	1 389	1 858	3 843	2 361	3 020	4 963	6 652
Mean earnings .. ($) ...	49 916	27 244	20 102	20 887	32 926	54 433	38 032	59 390	55 129	59 580	63 652	121 601	97 005
Standard error ... ($) ...	1 419	1 128	2 223	1 298	1 770	1 667	1 030	6 273	9 583	2 768	3 413	11 825	14 133
65 years and over, with earnings ...	2 833	629	58	295	276	2 205	821	436	129	413	177	149	80
Median earnings ..($) ...	11 973	8 798	(B)	9 718	7 344	13 774	11 026	11 472	12 291	21 183	14 108	51 369	54 959
Standard error ... ($) ...	391	750	(B)	802	1 465	990	623	919	2 488	4 602	2 769	5 870	9 958
Mean earnings .. ($) ...	24 534	15 156	(B)	18 205	13 118	27 208	17 993	19 447	17 769	33 386	33 722	55 772	79 578
Standard error ... ($) ...	1 181	1 509	(B)	2 785	1 619	1 444	1 420	1 643	2 088	4 052	6 204	6 366	18 117
Year round, full-time workers ...	1 062	215	20	114	82	846	291	140	46	182	69	69	49
Median earnings ..($) ...	30 573	16 971	(B)	16 950	20 424	35 179	25 225	24 116	(B)	46 322	(B)	(B)	(B)
Standard error ... ($) ...	1 964	2 700	(B)	3 992	3 562	1 904	1 866	3 261	(B)	6 170	(B)	(B)	(B)
Mean earnings .. ($) ...	42 025	25 827	(B)	28 537	24 620	46 145	33 142	29 810	(B)	53 438	(B)	(B)	(B)
Standard error ... ($) ...	2 133	2 941	(B)	4 810	3 650	2 521	3 259	2 893	(B)	4 340	(B)	(B)	(B)

See footnotes at end of table.

Table B-9. Earnings by Educational Attainment for Persons 18 Years Old and Over, by Age, Sex, Race and Hispanic Origin: March 1997 — Continued

(Numbers in thousands. Civilian noninstitutional population.)

Earnings, standard error, age, sex, race, and Hispanic origin	Total	Not a high school graduate				High school graduate or more							
		Total	Elementary		High School	Total	High school graduate only	College					
			None-4th grade	5th-8th grade	9th-11th grade			Some college no degree	Associate degree	Bachelor's degree	Master's degree	Professional degree	Doctorate degree
Female													
18 years and over, with													
earnings	64 748	6 492	306	1 382	4 805	58 256	21 942	14 315	5 887	11 466	3 582	604	460
Median earnings ..($)	16 534	8 305	8 271	8 984	8 008	17 749	14 044	14 338	20 879	25 839	34 342	44 905	42 434
Standard error ... ($)	107	259	728	421	349	149	182	319	305	248	873	3 003	2 064
Mean earnings .. ($)	20 570	10 421	9 476	10 622	10 423	21 701	16 161	17 475	22 480	28 701	36 483	72 015	51 865
Standard error ... ($)	165	193	693	394	231	180	160	331	329	421	803	8 714	3 354
Year round, full-time workers	36 404	2 744	143	645	1 956	33 660	12 422	7 476	3 685	7 118	2 224	413	322
Median earnings ..($)	23 717	15 086	11 907	13 683	15 680	24 777	19 978	22 419	26 168	31 432	40 355	56 431	51 989
Standard error ... ($)	166	273	894	633	295	169	164	241	331	230	483	3 945	3 064
Mean earnings .. ($)	28 363	16 692	12 834	15 664	17 313	29 315	21 893	25 889	28 403	36 555	44 471	90 711	62 169
Standard error ... ($)	260	296	996	607	353	278	207	573	401	593	1 096	12 368	4 311
18 to 24 years, with													
earnings	9 504	1 382	26	95	1 260	8 122	3 024	3 706	442	916	34	—	—
Median earnings ..($)	6 744	3 640	(B)	5 465	3 468	7 422	7 418	6 210	11 036	16 357	(B)	(B)	(B)
Standard error ... ($)	129	220	(B)	896	230	163	288	184	851	824	(B)	(B)	(B)
Mean earnings .. ($)	9 226	5 348	(B)	6 595	5 248	9 886	9 054	8 318	12 300	17 184	(B)	(B)	(B)
Standard error ... ($)	159	279	(B)	919	296	178	234	222	633	691	(B)	(B)	(B)
Year round, full-time workers	2 870	244	10	28	206	2 626	1 063	901	218	432	11	—	—
Median earnings ..($)	15 269	11 371	(B)	(B)	11 599	15 663	13 790	14 545	16 989	23 534	(B)	(B)	(B)
Standard error ... ($)	269	427	(B)	(B)	451	274	446	436	803	872	(B)	(B)	(B)
Mean earnings .. ($)	17 002	12 214	(B)	(B)	12 512	17 447	15 219	16 481	16 985	24 967	(B)	(B)	(B)
Standard error ... ($)	321	614	(B)	(B)	652	343	448	564	784	1 080	(B)	(B)	(B)
25 years and over, with													
earnings	55 244	5 111	280	1 286	3 545	50 134	18 918	10 609	5 444	10 550	3 548	604	460
Median earnings ..($)	18 773	10 193	8 604	9 338	10 689	20 114	15 489	18 262	21 671	26 711	34 596	44 905	42 434
Standard error ... ($)	150	223	741	433	276	111	151	281	319	256	811	3 003	2 064
Mean earnings .. ($)	22 521	11 793	9 836	10 921	12 263	23 615	17 297	20 674	23 307	29 701	36 575	72 015	51 865
Standard error ... ($)	188	224	741	414	279	204	178	429	346	450	798	8 714	3 354
Year round, full-time workers	33 535	2 500	133	617	1 751	31 034	11 358	6 574	3 468	6 686	2 213	413	322
Median earnings ..($)	24 803	15 458	12 131	13 911	16 132	25 632	20 501	23 832	26 773	31 910	40 415	56 431	51 989
Standard error ... ($)	171	260	1 051	624	303	127	136	313	337	235	443	3 945	3 064
Mean earnings .. ($)	29 335	17 129	13 157	15 860	17 878	30 319	22 517	27 179	29 120	37 304	44 567	90 711	62 169
Standard error ... ($)	279	316	1 050	624	382	298	220	643	416	624	1 100	12 368	4 311
25 to 34 years, with													
earnings	15 929	1 163	50	238	875	14 766	4 765	3 337	1 678	3 908	797	167	114
Median earnings ..($)	17 842	8 264	(B)	7 002	8 820	18 897	13 688	16 233	20 546	25 355	28 640	41 582	32 324
Standard error ... ($)	250	484	(B)	737	617	255	321	354	628	314	935	3 355	4 338
Mean earnings .. ($)	20 173	10 276	(B)	8 869	10 765	20 952	15 041	17 741	21 683	26 854	30 718	48 816	39 707
Standard error ... ($)	255	428	(B)	974	495	270	284	700	584	541	1 369	3 338	4 303
Year round, full-time workers	9 478	489	18	93	378	8 989	2 717	1 943	1 030	2 612	476	126	86
Median earnings ..($)	22 941	14 137	(B)	11 387	14 969	23 583	18 463	21 215	25 018	28 741	31 919	49 799	36 154
Standard error ... ($)	289	629	(B)	669	770	289	387	314	630	558	655	6 932	3 994
Mean earnings .. ($)	26 119	16 241	(B)	14 654	16 826	26 657	19 526	23 738	27 020	32 013	38 416	53 956	45 722
Standard error ... ($)	360	697	(B)	1 955	751	376	295	1 117	730	685	1 947	3 862	4 953
35 to 44 years, with													
earnings	17 601	1 328	69	315	944	16 273	6 038	3 476	1 996	3 364	1 069	208	122
Median earnings ..($)	20 200	11 097	(B)	11 343	11 199	20 974	16 579	19 516	22 591	29 184	36 036	50 367	42 279
Standard error ... ($)	182	356	(B)	601	469	186	270	475	726	868	875	9 200	2 272
Mean earnings .. ($)	24 239	12 732	(B)	12 114	13 225	25 178	18 349	21 612	24 128	31 642	40 654	84 613	66 727
Standard error ... ($)	354	465	(B)	664	607	379	316	461	557	789	2 003	17 564	10 173

See footnotes at end of table.

Table B-9. Earnings by Educational Attainment for Persons 18 Years Old and Over, by Age, Sex, Race and Hispanic Origin: March 1997 — Continued

(Numbers in thousands. Civilian noninstitutional population.)

Earnings, standard error, age, sex, race, and Hispanic origin	Total	Not a high school graduate				High school graduate or more							
		Total	Elementary		High School	Total	High school graduate only	College					
			None - 4th grade	5th - 8th grade	9th - 11th grade			Some college no degree	Associate degree	Bachelor's degree	Master's degree	Professional degree	Doctorate degree
Year round, full-time workers	11 092	728	40	179	509	10 363	3 842	2 204	1 312	2 091	702	127	85
Median earnings ..($) ...	25 586	15 191	(B)	14 113	16 260	26 320	20 857	24 935	27 407	35 136	41 587	77 748	52 194
Standard error ... ($) ...	233	554	(B)	739	653	239	215	453	820	653	884	9 438	8 456
Mean earnings .. ($) ...	30 879	17 174	(B)	15 471	18 261	31 842	23 134	27 853	29 493	40 521	48 994	115 966	83 989
Standard error ... ($) ...	512	552	(B)	834	707	543	388	578	664	1 080	2 815	27 481	13 550
45 to 54 years, with earnings	13 226	1 200	76	330	794	12 026	4 708	2 372	1 232	2 244	1 174	150	147
Median earnings ..($) ...	20 810	11 331	10 432	10 044	11 905	21 954	17 136	21 256	23 237	29 350	38 433	48 816	47 288
Standard error ... ($) ...	233	388	1 732	793	466	240	288	469	1 220	789	1 123	6 115	1 808
Mean earnings .. ($) ...	25 204	12 660	11 605	11 664	13 175	26 457	19 336	24 951	25 719	32 039	38 610	75 602	52 522
Standard error ... ($) ...	438	477	1 621	882	598	475	415	1 443	805	1 014	1 059	17 369	3 761
Year round, full-time workers	8 706	665	39	188	438	8 041	3 123	1 660	843	1 458	744	105	107
Median earnings ..($) ...	26 227	15 616	(B)	13 090	16 385	27 157	21 155	25 813	29 617	35 089	41 655	53 585	53 993
Standard error ... ($) ...	258	419	(B)	1 049	486	264	305	411	1 126	982	512	8 841	6 994
Mean earnings .. ($) ...	31 222	17 212	(B)	15 713	18 007	32 381	23 833	30 666	31 248	40 113	45 441	94 147	60 740
Standard error ... ($) ...	612	678	(B)	1 304	829	656	503	2 003	909	1 359	1 261	24 222	4 116
55 to 64 years, with earnings	6 360	939	55	248	635	5 421	2 559	1 092	415	809	420	58	66
Median earnings ..($) ...	16 949	11 826	(B)	10 878	12 531	18 503	15 239	18 017	19 755	26 233	35 554	(B)	(B)
Standard error ... ($) ...	332	562	(B)	1 055	701	503	464	908	1 351	1 117	1 509	(B)	(B)
Mean earnings .. ($) ...	20 732	13 181	(B)	12 399	13 777	22 040	17 286	20 325	21 674	28 749	34 762	(B)	(B)
Standard error ... ($) ...	385	512	(B)	933	643	437	445	715	1 191	1 667	1 566	(B)	(B)
Year round, full-time workers	3 701	507	26	125	355	3 194	1 478	664	251	452	264	47	38
Median earnings ..($) ...	23 773	16 963	(B)	17 312	16 962	25 426	21 200	25 277	25 909	32 543	40 317	(B)	(B)
Standard error ... ($) ...	487	490	(B)	1 190	648	400	354	1 188	1 281	1 754	2 075	(B)	(B)
Mean earnings .. ($) ...	27 629	18 624	(B)	18 450	19 039	29 057	23 179	27 340	28 982	37 616	41 668	(B)	(B)
Standard error ... ($) ...	523	687	(B)	1 263	850	586	506	858	1 433	2 615	1 609	(B)	(B)
65 years and over, with earnings	2 128	480	30	166	206	1 647	840	332	123	226	00	20	10
Median earnings ..($) ...	6 928	5 583	(B)	4 693	5 894	7 336	6 891	7 041	8 867	7 565	12 248	(B)	(B)
Standard error ... ($) ...	290	590	(B)	864	716	404	454	946	1 770	1 101	8 077	(B)	(B)
Mean earnings .. ($) ...	14 559	7 988	(B)	7 692	7 931	16 476	11 194	10 939	13 524	30 233	21 598	(B)	(B)
Standard error ... ($) ...	1 639	640	(B)	1 270	725	2 102	873	971	1 837	8 737	3 368	(B)	(B)
Year round, full-time workers	558	112	10	31	71	446	198	103	32	73	27	7	6
Median earnings ..($) ...	20 973	13 037	(B)	(B)	(B)	23 976	21 063	21 645	(B)	(B)	(B)	(B)	(B)
Standard error ... ($) ...	922	1 191	(B)	(B)	(B)	1 506	1 418	1 941	(B)	(B)	(B)	(B)	(B)
Mean earnings .. ($) ...	35 170	13 449	(B)	(B)	(B)	40 624	25 878	20 477	(B)	(B)	(B)	(B)	(B)
Standard error ... ($) ...	5 948	1 116	(B)	(B)	(B)	7 380	2 732	1 672	(B)	(B)	(B)	(B)	(B)

WHITE

Both Sexes

18 years and over, with earnings	117 230	13 972	852	3 513	9 607	103 258	38 463	24 664	9 423	20 846	6 676	1 867	1 318
Median earnings ..($) ...	21 750	11 778	10 708	12 033	11 818	23 592	19 310	19 026	25 746	31 575	41 327	65 908	59 239
Standard error ... ($) ...	89	140	371	240	188	147	183	260	295	201	370	2 643	2 043
Mean earnings .. ($) ...	28 844	15 358	12 213	15 131	15 719	30 669	22 782	24 229	28 867	38 936	50 813	92 612	73 647
Standard error ... ($) ...	192	340	707	393	469	211	235	350	535	489	1 189	4 391	3 111
Year round, full-time workers	76 200	7 426	484	2 065	4 877	68 775	25 229	14 628	6 642	14 945	4 790	1 485	1 056
Median earnings ..($) ...	29 431	17 652	13 535	16 340	19 132	30 821	24 769	27 235	31 284	37 522	47 316	76 202	63 873
Standard error ... ($) ...	192	278	779	359	353	100	193	201	275	412	689	1 414	1 933
Mean earnings .. ($) ...	37 498	21 632	16 083	19 463	23 101	39 211	28 983	33 650	35 196	47 051	61 126	106 292	81 178
Standard error ... ($) ...	270	511	1 117	508	738	292	328	537	707	610	1 555	5 281	3 524

See footnotes at end of table.

Table B-9. Earnings by Educational Attainment for Persons 18 Years Old and Over, by Age, Sex, Race and Hispanic Origin: March 1997 — Continued

(Numbers in thousands. Civilian noninstitutional population.)

| Earnings, standard error, age, sex, race, and Hispanic origin | Total | Not a high school graduate | | | | High school graduate or more | | | | | | | |
| | | Total | Elementary | | High School | Total | High school graduate only | College | | | | | |
			None-4th grade	5th-8th grade	9th-11th grade			Some college no degree	Associate degree	Bachelor's degree	Master's degree	Professional degree	Doctorate degree
Male													
18 years and over, with													
earnings	63 532	8 899	607	2 377	5 915	54 634	20 329	12 911	4 507	11 065	3 569	1 345	907
Median earnings ..($)	27 075	14 302	11 743	14 285	14 833	30 457	25 086	24 918	32 061	39 305	50 773	75 015	64 569
Standard error ... ($)	131	300	400	528	376	136	203	390	379	765	542	2 514	2 160
Mean earnings .. ($)	35 821	18 246	13 798	17 351	19 063	38 683	28 591	30 847	36 222	48 014	63 113	103 490	82 615
Standard error ... ($)	320	514	941	526	737	359	405	625	1 025	800	2 026	5 384	4 118
Year round, full-time													
workers	46 624	5 296	374	1 541	3 381	41 328	15 119	8 712	3 671	9 023	2 898	1 138	767
Median earnings ..($)	32 996	19 700	14 452	17 487	21 044	35 783	28 754	31 958	35 894	44 024	56 834	80 239	66 844
Standard error ... ($)	324	352	758	565	343	149	386	270	402	862	1 400	2 417	1 858
Mean earnings .. ($)	43 141	23 681	17 346	20 830	25 681	45 635	33 489	39 309	40 729	53 604	71 604	113 895	87 281
Standard error ... ($)	406	700	1 399	628	1 042	446	516	865	1 213	892	2 386	6 128	4 468
18 to 24 years, with													
earnings	8 768	1 951	44	251	1 657	6 816	2 809	3 020	375	584	26	2	—
Median earnings ..($)	9 595	6 446	(B)	10 327	5 795	10 388	11 858	7 439	12 207	17 383	(B)	(B)	(B)
Standard error ... ($)	232	411	(B)	831	462	203	305	280	1 372	1 231	(B)	(B)	(B)
Mean earnings .. ($)	11 825	8 250	(B)	9 983	7 919	12 848	13 666	10 102	16 789	19 980	(B)	(B)	(B)
Standard error ... ($)	219	269	(B)	628	293	268	326	281	2 995	986	(B)	(B)	(B)
Year round, full-time													
workers	3 534	693	29	144	520	2 841	1 494	887	187	258	14	—	—
Median earnings ..($)	17 184	13 185	(B)	12 153	13 800	18 359	17 464	17 065	22 449	26 998	(B)	(B)	(B)
Standard error ... ($)	270	507	(B)	622	624	403	441	447	1 375	820	(B)	(B)	(B)
Mean earnings .. ($)	18 813	14 640	(B)	13 078	15 067	19 832	18 907	18 080	24 065	27 174	(B)	(B)	(B)
Standard error ... ($)	408	420	(B)	715	484	492	441	471	5 825	1 106	(B)	(B)	(B)
25 years and over, with													
earnings	54 765	6 947	563	2 126	4 258	47 817	17 520	9 891	4 132	10 482	3 543	1 343	907
Median earnings ..($)	30 951	16 732	11 906	15 266	18 759	33 066	26 915	30 944	34 162	40 742	50 892	75 061	64 569
Standard error ... ($)	127	240	429	451	484	323	182	264	826	347	540	2 510	2 160
Mean earnings .. ($)	39 662	21 054	14 029	18 219	23 400	42 366	30 984	37 181	37 986	49 575	63 380	103 649	82 615
Standard error ... ($)	363	644	992	576	998	401	460	785	1 074	837	2 039	5 390	4 118
Year round, full-time													
workers	43 090	4 603	345	1 398	2 861	38 487	13 625	7 825	3 484	8 765	2 884	1 138	767
Median earnings ..($)	35 424	20 873	14 876	18 597	22 476	36 947	30 572	34 779	36 524	45 150	56 957	80 239	66 844
Standard error ... ($)	147	272	764	760	425	148	190	550	393	600	1 436	2 417	1 858
Mean earnings .. ($)	45 137	25 042	17 570	21 626	27 612	47 540	35 088	41 716	41 626	54 383	71 773	113 895	87 281
Standard error ... ($)	435	798	1 489	679	1 220	474	566	952	1 235	914	2 397	6 128	4 468
25 to 34 years, with													
earnings	15 663	2 045	126	503	1 416	13 618	4 982	2 998	1 341	3 404	577	218	96
Median earnings ..($)	25 677	15 210	13 481	14 373	15 703	27 186	23 745	25 330	29 149	33 794	40 042	42 370	42 424
Standard error ... ($)	205	397	1 376	954	516	211	415	422	927	763	2 099	3 263	4 901
Mean earnings .. ($)	29 703	17 164	14 141	16 605	17 631	31 586	25 186	29 376	33 195	38 512	42 408	53 867	48 863
Standard error ... ($)	398	400	1 037	788	494	449	336	1 055	2 195	1 028	1 788	4 383	4 206
Year round, full-time													
workers	12 300	1 370	85	360	926	10 929	3 921	2 355	1 146	2 798	448	182	80
Median earnings ..($)	28 921	17 698	15 587	16 289	19 106	30 596	25 977	27 639	30 869	36 726	43 748	46 824	45 339
Standard error ... ($)	389	551	1 010	645	731	205	263	592	502	459	1 241	3 319	6 892
Mean earnings .. ($)	33 464	19 769	16 533	18 909	20 401	35 181	27 943	32 821	35 752	42 846	48 934	58 695	52 598
Standard error ... ($)	479	471	1 248	938	579	530	359	1 279	2 528	1 189	1 984	4 566	4 645
35 to 44 years, with													
earnings	17 141	1 956	160	492	1 304	15 185	5 867	3 155	1 342	3 198	1 044	390	189
Median earnings ..($)	34 431	17 630	11 407	16 081	20 045	36 534	29 692	35 182	36 775	47 546	59 645	82 276	69 600
Standard error ... ($)	547	562	628	687	698	239	536	652	705	1 467	2 414	6 202	5 056
Mean earnings .. ($)	43 031	21 684	13 430	17 713	24 193	45 781	33 174	38 063	39 603	56 960	74 698	125 989	95 342
Standard error ... ($)	680	1 187	2 869	833	1 706	745	853	795	1 011	1 768	4 923	11 374	9 722

See footnotes at end of table.

Table B-9. Earnings by Educational Attainment for Persons 18 Years Old and Over, by Age, Sex, Race and Hispanic Origin: March 1997 — Continued

(Numbers in thousands. Civilian noninstitutional population.)

Earnings, standard error, age, sex, race, and Hispanic origin	Total	Not a high school graduate				High school graduate or more							
		Total	Elementary		High School	Total	High school graduate only	College					
			None - 4th grade	5th - 8th grade	9th - 11th grade			Some college no degree	Associate degree	Bachelor's degree	Master's degree	Professional degree	Doctorate degree
Year round, full-time workers	14 251	1 307	100	318	889	12 944	4 776	2 668	1 168	2 848	940	373	172
Median earnings ..($) ...	37 115	21 530	13 109	19 468	23 590	39 512	31 656	36 692	38 939	50 675	61 884	85 734	75 268
Standard error ... ($) ...	243	509	972	1 205	814	522	303	446	1 250	481	1 935	5 503	5 666
Mean earnings ... ($) ...	47 244	24 830	16 759	21 347	26 984	49 508	36 367	40 255	42 539	60 057	78 916	127 765	100 307
Standard error ... ($) ...	780	978	4 447	990	1 283	846	1 005	846	1 059	1 933	5 387	11 693	10 482
45 to 54 years, with earnings	12 738	1 342	130	446	766	11 396	3 605	2 328	1 028	2 463	1 221	399	352
Median earnings ..($) ...	37 381	19 999	12 865	17 885	22 700	40 518	31 597	36 683	40 622	46 476	55 549	82 493	67 018
Standard error ... ($) ...	420	767	1 453	1 375	1 225	286	438	661	1 245	1 188	2 076	5 575	2 643
Mean earnings .. ($) ...	48 561	25 993	15 088	20 445	31 076	51 218	37 046	43 603	41 301	56 388	71 901	123 292	86 129
Standard error ... ($) ...	927	2 383	1 357	1 164	4 087	991	1 528	1 714	1 229	1 877	3 560	12 175	6 858
Year round, full-time workers	10 757	1 003	89	335	579	9 755	2 988	1 964	902	2 162	1 066	366	307
Median earnings ..($) ...	41 010	22 913	14 289	21 370	25 492	42 373	34 183	40 139	42 099	50 260	60 030	90 295	69 113
Standard error ... ($) ...	291	987	2 300	1 043	907	475	947	764	1 323	1 021	1 927	6 844	2 696
Mean earnings ... ($) ...	53 111	30 312	16 905	23 530	36 293	55 455	40 524	47 694	43 978	59 608	77 496	128 745	91 058
Standard error ... ($) ...	1 054	3 141	1 669	1 349	5 343	1 110	1 815	1 969	1 279	1 828	3 985	13 096	7 667
55 to 64 years, with earnings	6 656	1 068	104	442	521	5 589	2 300	1 017	311	1 031	532	196	202
Median earnings ..($) ...	31 168	20 323	11 847	16 019	25 331	34 673	29 546	31 647	35 076	39 873	47 246	84 524	61 663
Standard error ... ($) ...	361	807	1 344	855	1 307	1 087	999	758	3 186	2 806	4 315	9 506	7 274
Mean earnings .. ($) ...	43 092	23 892	14 796	17 941	30 769	46 759	32 916	49 375	47 527	52 771	54 266	108 613	79 601
Standard error ... ($) ...	1 180	1 531	1 980	1 125	2 888	1 361	926	5 033	8 653	2 499	3 276	10 645	7 370
Year round, full-time workers	4 830	737	55	290	392	4 093	1 683	707	228	788	366	155	167
Median earnings ..($) ...	37 185	23 184	(B)	19 470	27 484	40 629	34 283	40 167	45 672	50 710	60 543	8	66 915
Standard error ... ($) ...	536	1 234	(B)	1 786	1 451	522	1 478	1 645	4 551	1 934	2 898	8	6 465
Mean earnings .. ($) ...	51 426	27 852	(B)	20 597	34 038	55 668	38 740	62 337	59 740	60 570	65 330	124 151	84 731
Standard error ... ($) ...	1 509	1 324	(B)	1 417	2 102	1 745	1 118	7 042	11 541	2 916	3 672	12 106	7 702
65 years and over, with earnings	2 566	537	43	243	251	2 029	766	393	110	385	168	140	68
Median earnings ..($) ...	12 047	9 293	(B)	9 867	7 499	13 705	10 677	11 893	12 500	21 301	13 674	50 737	(B)
Standard error ... ($) ...	384	768	(B)	779	1 858	1 079	630	1 203	2 584	4 754	2 736	5 824	(B)
Mean earnings .. ($) ...	24 882	15 590	(B)	19 016	13 088	27 339	17 576	20 040	18 666	33 929	31 996	55 927	(B)
Standard error ... ($) ...	1 269	1 717	(B)	3 313	1 693	1 527	1 434	1 766	2 332	4 295	6 121	6 710	(B)
Year round, full-time workers	951	186	16	95	75	765	257	131	39	170	64	62	42
Median earnings ..($) ...	30 667	16 570	(B)	15 125	(B)	35 492	25 507	24 770	(B)	47 698	(B)	(B)	(B)
Standard error ... ($) ...	2 168	2 715	(B)	4 033	(B)	1 640	1 502	4 085	(B)	5 275	(B)	(B)	(B)
Mean earnings .. ($) ...	42 382	25 863	(B)	29 254	(B)	46 398	33 199	30 473	(B)	54 137	(B)	(B)	(B)
Standard error ... ($) ...	2 284	3 328	(B)	5 671	(B)	2 672	3 423	3 028	(B)	4 486	(B)	(B)	(B)
Female													
18 years and over, with earnings	53 697	5 073	245	1 136	3 692	48 624	18 134	11 753	4 916	9 781	3 107	523	411
Median earnings ..($) ...	16 568	8 242	7 322	8 815	8 080	17 783	14 165	13 932	20 731	25 759	34 025	46 110	45 460
Standard error ... ($) ...	121	281	688	437	385	170	209	341	332	276	969	3 277	2 540
Mean earnings .. ($) ...	20 590	10 290	8 276	10 488	10 362	21 664	16 270	16 959	22 122	28 667	36 687	64 618	53 862
Standard error ... ($) ...	161	210	626	444	251	175	178	219	348	467	903	7 005	3 681
Year round, full-time workers	29 576	2 129	109	524	1 496	27 447	10 111	5 915	2 971	5 921	1 892	348	289
Median earnings ..($) ...	24 166	14 893	11 041	13 208	15 690	25 137	20 272	22 661	26 345	31 638	40 424	59 566	55 174
Standard error ... ($) ...	179	330	781	621	336	142	150	309	385	248	466	3 268	2 572
Mean earnings .. ($) ...	28 603	16 536	11 765	15 442	17 269	29 539	22 246	25 315	28 357	37 065	45 079	81 401	64 989
Standard error ... ($) ...	250	335	966	703	397	266	239	310	423	676	1 262	10 058	4 703

See footnotes at end of table.

Table B-9. **Earnings by Educational Attainment for Persons 18 Years Old and Over, by Age, Sex, Race and Hispanic Origin: March 1997 — Continued**

(Numbers in thousands. Civilian noninstitutional population.)

Earnings, standard error, age, sex, race, and Hispanic origin	Total	Not a high school graduate				High school graduate or more							
		Total	Elementary		High School	Total	High school graduate only	College					
			None - 4th grade	5th - 8th grade	9th - 11th grade			Some college no degree	Associate degree	Bachelor's degree	Master's degree	Professional degree	Doctorate degree
18 to 24 years, with													
earnings	7 724	1 064	26	91	947	6 661	2 408	3 057	383	784	29	—	—
Median earnings ..($) ...	6 841	3 599	(B)	5 336	3 381	7 467	7 624	6 208	10 612	16 161	(B)	(B)	(B)
Standard error ... ($) ...	141	256	(B)	876	272	195	360	195	875	799	(B)	(B)	(B)
Mean earnings .. ($) ...	9 267	5 347	(B)	6 219	5 257	9 893	9 150	8 218	11 794	17 141	(B)	(B)	(B)
Standard error ... ($) ...	179	311	(B)	890	337	199	265	234	650	768	(B)	(B)	(B)
Year round, full-time													
workers	2 311	191	10	24	157	2 120	845	711	180	375	9	—	—
Median earnings ..($) ...	15 404	11 193	(B)	(B)	11 542	15 799	14 072	14 660	16 796	23 392	(B)	(B)	(B)
Standard error ... ($) ...	290	491	(B)	(B)	528	297	500	464	953	909	(B)	(B)	(B)
Mean earnings .. ($) ...	17 056	12 119	(B)	(B)	12 609	17 501	15 404	16 245	16 606	24 844	(B)	(B)	(B)
Standard error ... ($) ...	360	732	(B)	(B)	796	383	521	577	850	1 215	(B)	(B)	(B)
25 years and over, with													
earnings	45 973	4 009	219	1 046	2 745	41 964	15 726	8 695	4 533	8 997	3 079	523	411
Median earnings ..($) ...	18 878	10 017	7 605	9 230	10 607	20 199	15 572	18 014	21 581	26 672	34 250	46 110	45 460
Standard error ... ($) ...	172	261	764	451	314	123	168	325	348	286	921	3 277	2 540
Mean earnings .. ($) ...	22 492	11 601	8 595	10 858	12 124	23 533	17 360	20 033	22 994	29 671	36 773	64 618	53 862
Standard error ... ($) ...	183	243	679	472	299	197	197	266	366	500	896	7 005	3 681
Year round, full-time													
workers	27 265	1 938	99	499	1 339	25 327	9 266	5 204	2 791	5 546	1 884	348	289
Median earnings ..($) ...	25 187	15 295	11 166	13 494	16 135	25 955	20 792	24 088	27 017	32 150	40 476	59 566	55 174
Standard error ... ($) ...	141	306	846	611	349	142	151	341	386	253	447	3 268	2 572
Mean earnings .. ($) ...	29 582	16 972	12 090	15 687	17 814	30 547	22 870	26 555	29 113	37 892	45 170	81 401	64 989
Standard error ... ($) ...	267	357	1 035	725	427	284	254	335	437	714	1 267	10 058	4 703
25 to 34 years, with													
earnings	12 889	914	42	190	681	11 976	3 774	2 634	1 349	3 313	663	144	97
Median earnings ..($) ...	18 429	8 534	(B)	6 759	9 474	19 481	14 100	16 318	20 739	25 432	28 612	42 290	31 584
Standard error ... ($) ...	282	506	(B)	699	665	290	398	440	659	346	1 159	4 642	5 415
Mean earnings .. ($) ...	20 526	10 689	(B)	8 651	11 487	21 276	15 483	17 466	21 159	27 148	30 987	50 709	41 127
Standard error ... ($) ...	255	502	(B)	1 128	583	269	340	393	591	618	1 569	3 750	4 980
Year round, full-time													
workers	7 608	393	13	71	309	7 215	2 125	1 509	808	2 189	405	105	74
Median earnings ..($) ...	23 809	14 315	(B)	(B)	15 460	24 442	19 275	21 639	25 232	29 152	31 892	55 580	(B)
Standard error ... ($) ...	307	751	(B)	(B)	957	308	444	401	660	624	604	7 110	(B)
Mean earnings .. ($) ...	26 605	16 395	(B)	(B)	17 078	27 160	20 165	23 270	26 520	32 571	38 777	57 148	(B)
Standard error ... ($) ...	340	834	(B)	(B)	884	353	345	466	697	797	2 217	4 341	(B)
35 to 44 years, with													
earnings	14 491	1 034	62	274	699	13 457	4 989	2 754	1 639	2 849	942	175	108
Median earnings ..($) ...	20 258	11 022	(B)	11 291	11 171	21 013	16 715	19 055	22 333	28 515	36 000	51 985	44 000
Standard error ... ($) ...	197	382	(B)	591	530	202	318	606	663	1 009	1 014	9 156	4 376
Mean earnings .. ($) ...	24 228	12 307	(B)	11 753	12 848	25 144	18 500	21 553	23 810	31 129	40 991	72 605	70 698
Standard error ... ($) ...	362	465	(B)	647	627	385	358	544	585	847	2 233	13 657	11 357
Year round, full-time													
workers	8 854	564	34	158	371	8 290	3 125	1 662	1 033	1 686	607	102	74
Median earnings ..($) ...	25 822	15 019	(B)	13 882	16 306	26 615	21 124	24 933	27 669	35 380	41 403	85 169	(B)
Standard error ... ($) ...	271	600	(B)	725	725	275	234	531	1 018	746	928	7 739	(B)
Mean earnings .. ($) ...	31 269	16 887	(B)	14 886	18 301	32 247	23 408	28 391	29 497	41 209	49 728	99 049	(B)
Standard error ... ($) ...	527	630	(B)	788	855	557	444	722	693	1 212	3 210	21 872	(B)
45 to 54 years, with													
earnings	11 195	910	58	271	581	10 285	3 938	2 029	1 075	1 932	1 033	134	143
Median earnings ..($) ...	20 778	10 832	(B)	9 720	11 521	21 859	16 999	20 961	22 879	29 477	38 193	47 834	47 386
Standard error ... ($) ...	256	435	(B)	802	522	262	310	512	1 215	790	1 112	5 825	1 824
Mean earnings .. ($) ...	24 879	11 936	(B)	11 469	12 397	26 025	18 909	22 723	25 555	31 950	38 804	76 577	52 382
Standard error ... ($) ...	407	487	(B)	1 011	582	436	432	541	877	1 098	1 165	19 274	3 782
Year round, full-time													
workers	7 199	500	26	157	317	6 699	2 554	1 370	712	1 232	635	94	103
Median earnings ..($) ...	26 472	15 017	(B)	12 324	16 216	27 381	21 198	25 767	29 944	35 440	41 627	52 768	54 468
Standard error ... ($) ...	300	649	(B)	931	631	374	330	456	1 077	904	531	7 907	6 936

See footnotes at end of table.

Table B-9. Earnings by Educational Attainment for Persons 18 Years Old and Over, by Age, Sex, Race and Hispanic Origin: March 1997 — Continued

(Numbers in thousands. Civilian noninstitutional population.)

| Earnings, standard error, age, sex, race, and Hispanic origin | Total | Not a high school graduate | | | | High school graduate or more | | | | | | | |
| | | Total | Elementary | | High School | Total | High school graduate only | College | | | | | |
			None-4th grade	5th-8th grade	9th-11th grade			Some college no degree	Associate degree	Bachelor's degree	Master's degree	Professional degree	Doctorate degree
Mean earnings .. ($) ...	31 159	16 349	(B)	15 354	17 196	32 264	23 915	27 998	31 543	40 359	46 101	95 686	60 855
Standard error ... ($) ...	569	674	(B)	1 508	726	604	584	615	1 013	1 497	1 444	26 794	4 131
55 to 64 years, with													
earnings	5 493	753	43	189	521	4 740	2 245	970	356	696	363	55	54
Median earnings ..($) ...	16 795	11 731	(B)	11 172	12 239	18 154	15 252	17 344	20 095	26 670	34 730	(B)	(B)
Standard error ... ($) ...	342	621	(B)	1 420	735	580	471	946	1 437	1 346	1 717	(B)	(B)
Mean earnings .. ($) ...	20 859	13 273	(B)	12 779	13 830	22 064	17 423	19 965	21 675	29 157	34 281	(B)	(B)
Standard error ... ($) ...	429	603	(B)	1 143	746	482	490	770	1 262	1 893	1 745	(B)	(B)
Year round, full-time													
workers	3 138	394	20	94	280	2 744	1 282	573	213	381	219	44	32
Median earnings ..($) ...	24 079	17 077	(B)	17 963	16 964	25 480	21 316	24 693	26 499	33 514	41 941	(B)	(B)
Standard error ... ($) ...	553	660	(B)	1 570	784	470	399	1 361	1 807	1 903	2 639	(B)	(B)
Mean earnings .. ($) ...	28 076	19 206	(B)	19 275	19 575	29 348	23 450	27 326	29 245	38 378	41 903	(B)	(B)
Standard error ... ($) ...	596	843	(B)	1 587	1 036	662	559	953	1 484	3 057	1 849	(B)	(B)
65 years and over, with													
earnings	1 905	399	14	122	263	1 506	779	307	114	207	77	14	9
Median earnings ..($) ...	6 712	5 510	(B)	4 779	5 772	7 042	6 714	6 813	8 256	7 211	9 323	(B)	(B)
Standard error ... ($) ...	297	618	(B)	1 083	798	337	463	844	1 565	1 054	7 608	(B)	(B)
Mean earnings .. ($) ...	13 274	7 941	(B)	7 952	7 863	14 686	11 147	10 858	12 940	30 459	19 415	(B)	(B)
Standard error ... ($) ...	1 174	717	(B)	1 574	779	1 467	937	1 023	1 852	9 480	3 571	(B)	(B)
Year round, full-time													
workers	467	88	7	20	62	378	179	90	25	59	17	2	6
Median earnings ..($) ...	21 391	13 075	(B)	(B)	(B)	24 348	21 437	22 209	(B)	(B)	(B)	(B)	(B)
Standard error ... ($) ...	1 068	1 435	(B)	(B)	(B)	1 556	2 091	1 789	(B)	(B)	(B)	(B)	(B)
Mean earnings .. ($) ...	31 923	13 658	(B)	(B)	(B)	36 194	26 504	20 909	(B)	(B)	(B)	(B)	(B)
Standard error ... ($) ...	4 354	1 345	(B)	(B)	(B)	5 305	2 990	1 820	(B)	(B)	(B)	(B)	(B)
BLACK													
Both Sexes													
18 years and over, with													
earnings	15 255	2 383	87	401	1 895	12 871	5 844	3 674	1 109	1 655	471	73	46
Median earnings ..($) ...	17 622	10 939	12 163	12 322	10 526	19 482	15 612	18 896	24 016	28 707	37 194	(B)	(B)
Standard error ... ($) ...	276	379	2 253	974	440	317	315	545	1 053	1 026	1 735	(B)	(B)
Mean earnings .. ($) ...	21 978	13 110	13 468	14 462	12 807	23 620	18 722	23 148	25 220	31 955	37 592	(B)	(B)
Standard error ... ($) ...	485	434	1 688	1 036	494	566	554	1 390	799	1 080	1 830	(B)	(B)
Year round, full-time													
workers	9 886	1 141	52	227	862	8 745	3 745	2 431	849	1 259	365	60	35
Median earnings ..($) ...	23 740	17 272	(B)	16 804	17 664	25 022	20 777	24 462	26 537	31 736	39 579	(B)	(B)
Standard error ... ($) ...	371	474	(B)	747	736	325	313	659	608	623	1 580	(B)	(B)
Mean earnings .. ($) ...	28 378	20 399	(B)	19 830	20 800	29 419	23 095	30 715	28 869	36 762	41 268	(B)	(B)
Standard error ... ($) ...	657	644	(B)	1 376	759	736	368	2 044	839	1 268	2 081	(B)	(B)
Male													
18 years and over, with													
earnings	7 125	1 290	66	262	962	5 836	2 836	1 649	398	700	180	46	27
Median earnings ..($) ...	20 582	13 132	(B)	13 831	12 735	22 392	18 634	22 031	28 567	31 651	38 650	(B)	(B)
Standard error ... ($) ...	376	739	(B)	1 077	870	465	806	798	2 041	1 063	3 005	(B)	(B)
Mean earnings .. ($) ...	25 067	15 461	(B)	16 015	15 440	27 190	22 267	25 594	29 561	35 558	40 313	(B)	(B)
Standard error ... ($) ...	785	648	(B)	1 413	770	941	1 034	1 752	1 529	1 664	4 035	(B)	(B)
Year round, full-time													
workers	4 795	695	41	160	494	4 100	1 910	1 124	320	551	129	42	23
Median earnings ..($) ...	26 417	19 261	(B)	16 843	20 481	27 933	24 118	28 997	31 054	36 330	40 388	(B)	(B)
Standard error ... ($) ...	379	1 139	(B)	1 991	1 075	718	706	1 344	838	1 753	2 635	(B)	(B)
Mean earnings .. ($) ...	31 336	22 260	(B)	21 032	23 236	32 874	26 069	33 012	32 974	40 590	45 715	(B)	(B)
Standard error ... ($) ...	976	884	(B)	1 783	1 082	1 127	583	2 463	1 578	1 861	5 155	(B)	(B)

See footnotes at end of table.

Table B-9. Earnings by Educational Attainment for Persons 18 Years Old and Over, by Age, Sex, Race and Hispanic Origin: March 1997 — Continued

(Numbers in thousands. Civilian noninstitutional population.)

| Earnings, standard error, age, sex, race, and Hispanic origin | Total | Not a high school graduate | | | | High school graduate or more | | | | | | | |
| | | Total | Elementary | | High School | Total | High school graduate only | College | | | | | |
			None - 4th grade	5th - 8th grade	9th - 11th grade			Some college no degree	Associate degree	Bachelor's degree	Master's degree	Professional degree	Doctorate degree
18 to 24 years, with													
earnings	1 096	248	—	8	240	848	492	303	19	35	—	—	—
Median earnings ..($)	6 802	3 220	(B)	(B)	3 266	7 910	9 254	6 856	(B)	(B)	(B)	(B)	(B)
Standard error ... ($)	357	681	(B)	(B)	670	736	953	611	(B)	(B)	(B)	(B)	(B)
Mean earnings .. ($)	9 241	5 930	(B)	(B)	5 989	10 210	10 534	9 595	(B)	(B)	(B)	(B)	(B)
Standard error ... ($)	463	1 042	(B)	(B)	1 072	502	638	861	(B)	(B)	(B)	(B)	(B)
Year round, full-time													
workers	311	36	—	1	35	274	185	69	12	8	—	—	—
Median earnings ..($)	17 390	(B)	(B)	(B)	(B)	17 740	16 776	(B)	(B)	(B)	(B)	(B)	(B)
Standard error ... ($)	1 357	(B)	(B)	(B)	(B)	1 364	1 432	(B)	(B)	(B)	(B)	(B)	(B)
Mean earnings .. ($)	18 911	(B)	(B)	(B)	(B)	18 812	17 898	(B)	(B)	(B)	(B)	(B)	(B)
Standard error ... ($)	994	(B)	(B)	(B)	(B)	879	980	(B)	(B)	(B)	(B)	(B)	(B)
25 years and over, with													
earnings	6 030	1 042	66	254	722	4 988	2 344	1 346	379	666	180	46	27
Median earnings ..($)	23 275	15 581	(B)	14 152	16 307	25 489	21 376	25 890	29 748	32 413	38 650	(B)	(B)
Standard error ... ($)	515	525	(B)	1 050	669	447	567	798	1 906	1 530	3 005	(B)	(B)
Mean earnings .. ($)	27 944	17 731	(B)	16 392	18 583	30 077	24 729	29 193	30 356	36 921	40 313	(B)	(B)
Standard error ... ($)	910	713	(B)	1 438	878	1 083	1 227	2 102	1 557	1 700	4 035	(B)	(B)
Year round, full-time													
workers	4 484	659	41	159	459	3 825	1 725	1 056	307	543	129	42	23
Median earnings ..($)	27 108	19 460	(B)	16 884	20 781	29 507	25 195	30 148	31 177	36 681	40 388	(B)	(B)
Standard error ... ($)	385	1 103	(B)	2 002	1 188	738	676	977	822	1 752	2 635	(B)	(B)
Mean earnings .. ($)	32 197	22 404	(B)	21 107	23 489	33 883	26 945	33 776	33 564	40 909	45 715	(B)	(B)
Standard error ... ($)	1 038	885	(B)	1 791	1 084	1 202	626	2 616	1 597	1 878	5 155	(B)	(B)
25 to 34 years, with													
earnings	2 024	245	10	19	216	1 778	854	534	121	212	45	10	2
Median earnings ..($)	20 436	12 416	(B)	(B)	12 252	21 654	17 682	24 887	23 108	30 798	(B)	(B)	(B)
Standard error ... ($)	628	1 248	(B)	(B)	1 398	605	1 098	1 221	1 683	2 206	(B)	(B)	(B)
Mean earnings .. ($)	23 607	13 888	(B)	(B)	12 836	24 947	22 208	25 058	23 796	32 080	(B)	(B)	(B)
Standard error ... ($)	1 250	1 360	(B)	(B)	1 133	1 402	2 627	1 522	2 030	2 230	(B)	(B)	(B)
Year round, full-time													
workers	1 383	114	4	9	100	1 269	550	404	90	178	36	10	2
Median earnings ..($)	25 117	16 896	(B)	(B)	16 965	25 893	22 016	27 219	24 650	33 529	(B)	(B)	(B)
Standard error ... ($)	683	921	(B)	(B)	1 463	597	691	1 052	1 978	2 903	(B)	(B)	(B)
Mean earnings .. ($)	27 555	18 757	(B)	(B)	16 613	28 344	24 385	29 370	25 086	35 467	(B)	(B)	(B)
Standard error ... ($)	811	2 151	(B)	(B)	1 275	852	850	1 813	1 602	2 380	(B)	(B)	(B)
35 to 44 years, with													
earnings	2 029	264	9	61	195	1 765	844	471	122	259	45	17	6
Median earnings ..($)	24 570	15 721	(B)	(B)	16 037	26 448	22 468	27 716	30 761	33 965	(B)	(B)	(B)
Standard error ... ($)	812	830	(B)	(B)	907	829	1 067	2 679	2 617	2 777	(B)	(B)	(B)
Mean earnings .. ($)	29 228	15 813	(B)	(B)	16 252	31 236	24 661	33 311	31 040	41 099	(B)	(B)	(B)
Standard error ... ($)	1 557	956	(B)	(B)	1 106	1 770	960	5 573	2 130	3 435	(B)	(B)	(B)
Year round, full-time													
workers	1 624	174	9	41	125	1 450	678	396	109	212	33	14	6
Median earnings ..($)	27 135	17 021	(B)	(B)	17 269	30 015	25 136	31 674	31 399	37 143	(B)	(B)	(B)
Standard error ... ($)	989	899	(B)	(B)	1 067	1 123	1 103	1 567	1 494	2 853	(B)	(B)	(B)
Mean earnings .. ($)	32 710	18 562	(B)	(B)	18 906	34 409	27 026	36 935	33 003	45 228	(B)	(B)	(B)
Standard error ... ($)	1 893	939	(B)	(B)	1 109	2 105	1 026	6 558	2 090	3 931	(B)	(B)	(B)
45 to 54 years, with													
earnings	1 276	271	12	65	194	1 005	436	235	91	162	56	12	11
Median earnings ..($)	26 416	18 606	(B)	(B)	20 652	29 822	25 462	27 250	36 834	35 899	(B)	(B)	(B)
Standard error ... ($)	660	1 641	(B)	(B)	1 865	1 574	1 293	2 310	4 581	3 387	(B)	(B)	(B)
Mean earnings .. ($)	33 969	22 024	(B)	(B)	24 319	37 197	28 249	31 485	38 661	37 408	(B)	(B)	(B)
Standard error ... ($)	2 776	1 598	(B)	(B)	2 095	3 480	3 407	2 279	4 275	2 601	(B)	(B)	(B)
Year round, full-time													
workers	1 003	204	8	51	145	799	341	189	77	134	39	11	7
Median earnings ..($)	30 456	22 155	(B)	(B)	23 552	33 750	27 369	31 882	40 196	39 457	(B)	(B)	(B)
Standard error ... ($)	1 351	1 293	(B)	(B)	1 175	1 955	1 310	3 177	5 264	2 573	(B)	(B)	(B)

See footnotes at end of table.

Table B-9. Earnings by Educational Attainment for Persons 18 Years Old and Over, by Age, Sex, Race and Hispanic Origin: March 1997 — Continued

(Numbers in thousands. Civilian noninstitutional population.)

Earnings, standard error, age, sex, race, and Hispanic origin	Total	Not a high school graduate				High school graduate or more							
		Total	Elementary		High School	Total	High school graduate only	College					
			None-4th grade	5th-8th grade	9th-11th grade			Some college no degree	Associate degree	Bachelor's degree	Master's degree	Professional degree	Doctorate degree
Mean earnings .. ($) ...	37 723	26 068	(B)	(B)	29 112	40 699	28 322	35 912	43 105	41 006	(B)	(B)	(B)
Standard error ... ($) ...	3 181	1 866	(B)	(B)	2 418	3 946	1 264	2 497	4 420	2 375	(B)	(B)	(B)
55 to 64 years, with													
earnings	538	187	22	63	102	351	173	80	40	24	27	5	2
Median earnings ..($) ...	27 872	18 130	(B)	(B)	25 222	31 079	30 715	30 614	(B)	(B)	(B)	(B)	(B)
Standard error ... ($) ...	2 284	2 109	(B)	(B)	3 830	757	1 074	5 893	(B)	(B)	(B)	(B)	(B)
Mean earnings .. ($) ...	27 625	21 128	(B)	(B)	24 466	31 095	28 182	32 470	(B)	(B)	(B)	(B)	(B)
Standard error ... ($) ...	1 385	1 679	(B)	(B)	2 390	1 852	2 417	3 524	(B)	(B)	(B)	(B)	(B)
Year round, full-time workers	410	143	18	42	83	267	134	62	31	15	18	5	2
Median earnings ..($) ...	30 371	21 115	(B)	(B)	26 959	32 146	31 451	(B)	(B)	(B)	(B)	(B)	(B)
Standard error ... ($) ...	931	3 314	(B)	(B)	1 881	1 436	794	(B)	(B)	(B)	(B)	(B)	(B)
Mean earnings .. ($) ...	31 405	23 750	(B)	(B)	27 476	35 525	31 561	(R)	(R)	(R)	(R)	(B)	(B)
Standard error ... ($) ...	1 553	1 836	(B)	(B)	2 470	2 055	2 523	(B)	(B)	(B)	(B)	(B)	(B)
65 years and over, with													
earnings	163	74	13	46	15	89	36	26	5	9	7	2	5
Median earnings ..($) ...	8 392	(B)	(B)	(B)	(B)	14 427	(B)	(B)	(B)	(B)	(B)	(B)	(B)
Standard error ... ($) ...	2 363	(B)	(B)	(B)	(B)	5 562	(B)	(B)	(B)	(B)	(B)	(B)	(B)
Mean earnings .. ($) ...	19 668	(B)	(B)	(B)	(B)	25 214	(B)	(B)	(B)	(B)	(B)	(B)	(B)
Standard error ... ($) ...	3 649	(B)	(B)	(B)	(B)	5 963	(B)	(B)	(B)	(B)	(B)	(B)	(B)
Year round, full-time workers	65	23	3	16	5	41	22	4	—	5	3	2	5
Median earnings ..($) ...	(B)	(B)	(B)	(B)	(B)	(B)	(B)	(B)	(B)	(B)	(B)	(B)	(B)
Standard error ... ($) ...	(B)	(B)	(B)	(B)	(B)	(B)	(B)	(B)	(B)	(B)	(B)	(B)	(B)
Mean earnings .. ($) ...	(B)	(B)	(B)	(B)	(B)	(B)	(B)	(B)	(B)	(B)	(B)	(B)	(B)
Standard error ... ($) ...	(B)	(B)	(B)	(B)	(B)	(B)	(B)	(B)	(B)	(B)	(B)	(B)	(B)
Female													
18 years and over, with													
earnings	8 129	1 094	21	140	933	7 036	3 008	2 025	711	954	291	27	19
Median earnings ..($) ...	16 169	7 735	(R)	10 038	7 325	17 386	13 479	16 938	21 651	27 035	36 814	(B)	(B)
Standard error ... ($) ...	271	704	(B)	1 701	682	307	428	532	944	753	1 745	(B)	(B)
Mean earnings .. ($) ...	19 271	10 337	(B)	11 555	10 092	20 659	15 379	21 155	22 793	29 311	35 909	(B)	(B)
Standard error ... ($) ...	592	526	(B)	1 262	575	674	433	2 078	870	1 402	1 572	(B)	(B)
Year round, full-time workers	5 091	446	11	67	368	4 645	1 835	1 307	529	708	236	18	12
Median earnings ..($) ...	21 474	15 743	(B)	(B)	15 690	21 977	18 152	21 674	25 198	29 984	38 942	(B)	(B)
Standard error ... ($) ...	256	629	(B)	(B)	678	267	465	403	901	815	1 855	(B)	(B)
Mean earnings .. ($) ...	25 592	17 497	(B)	(B)	17 534	26 369	19 998	28 739	26 391	33 780	38 831	(B)	(B)
Standard error ... ($) ...	880	855	(B)	(B)	957	959	409	3 154	904	1 706	1 484	(B)	(B)
18 to 24 years, with													
earnings	1 340	254	—	—	254	1 086	511	457	43	69	5	—	—
Median earnings ..($) ...	6 192	3 749	(B)	(B)	3 749	7 095	6 431	7 150	(B)	(B)	(B)	(B)	(B)
Standard error ... ($) ...	386	467	(B)	(B)	467	454	657	746	(B)	(B)	(B)	(B)	(B)
Mean earnings .. ($) ...	9 135	5 491	(B)	(B)	5 491	9 988	8 645	9 784	(B)	(B)	(B)	(B)	(B)
Standard error ... ($) ...	449	793	(B)	(B)	793	513	586	870	(B)	(B)	(B)	(B)	(B)
Year round, full-time workers	435	40	—	—	40	395	177	157	29	30	2	—	—
Median earnings ..($) ...	13 926	(B)	(B)	(B)	(B)	14 289	12 557	13 220	(B)	(B)	(B)	(B)	(B)
Standard error ... ($) ...	1 046	(B)	(B)	(B)	(B)	1 096	1 012	1 416	(B)	(B)	(B)	(B)	(B)
Mean earnings .. ($) ...	16 665	(B)	(B)	(B)	(B)	17 047	14 698	17 465	(B)	(B)	(B)	(B)	(B)
Standard error ... ($) ...	911	(B)	(B)	(B)	(B)	992	1 028	1 984	(B)	(B)	(B)	(B)	(B)
25 years and over, with													
earnings	6 789	839	21	140	679	5 950	2 497	1 568	668	885	286	27	19
Median earnings ..($) ...	17 957	10 231	(B)	10 038	10 369	19 211	15 050	19 640	22 020	27 534	37 100	(B)	(B)
Standard error ... ($) ...	347	662	(B)	1 701	754	345	414	577	1 080	870	1 778	(B)	(B)
Mean earnings .. ($) ...	21 271	11 804	(B)	11 555	11 815	22 606	16 759	24 470	23 292	30 258	36 138	(B)	(B)

See footnotes at end of table.

Table B-9. Earnings by Educational Attainment for Persons 18 Years Old and Over, by Age, Sex, Race and Hispanic Origin: March 1997 — Continued

(Numbers in thousands. Civilian noninstitutional population.)

Earnings, standard error, age, sex, race, and Hispanic origin	Total	Not a high school graduate				High school graduate or more							
		Total	Elementary		High School	Total	High school graduate only	College				Professional degree	Doctorate degree
			None-4th grade	5th-8th grade	9th-11th grade			Some college no degree	Associate degree	Bachelor's degree	Master's degree		
Standard error ...($) ...	695	617	(B)	1 262	702	784	495	2 655	899	1 486	1 592	(B)	(B)
Year round, full-time workers	4 656	405	11	67	328	4 250	1 658	1 150	501	678	234	18	12
Median earnings ..($) ...	22 010	16 045	(B)	(B)	16 048	22 538	18 720	22 417	25 443	30 182	39 121	(B)	(B)
Standard error ...($) ...	262	621	(B)	(B)	666	465	454	602	833	793	1 813	(B)	(B)
Mean earnings .. ($) ...	26 427	17 953	(B)	(B)	18 102	27 235	20 564	30 282	26 849	34 079	38 972	(B)	(B)
Standard error ...($) ...	956	924	(B)	(B)	1 053	1 041	432	3 568	933	1 774	1 491	(B)	(B)
25 to 34 years, with													
earnings	2 250	185	1	19	164	2 065	787	610	239	369	49	3	8
Median earnings ..($) ...	15 579	5 674	(B)	(B)	5 490	16 370	12 758	16 360	19 111	24 583	(B)	(B)	(B)
Standard error ...($) ...	423	1 003	(B)	(B)	1 083	428	563	596	1 497	1 434	(B)	(B)	(B)
Mean earnings .. ($) ...	17 351	7 641	(B)	(B)	7 329	18 219	13 125	19 260	21 352	23 985	(B)	(B)	(B)
Standard error ...($) ...	1 054	923	(B)	(B)	933	1 140	472	3 658	1 607	1 063	(B)	(B)	(B)
Year round, full-time workers	1 373	58	1	8	49	1 315	473	379	154	265	34	3	6
Median earnings ..($) ...	20 325	(B)	(B)	(B)	(B)	20 541	16 154	20 516	23 667	26 820	(B)	(B)	(B)
Standard error ...($) ...	401	(B)	(B)	(B)	(B)	376	633	492	1 641	996	(B)	(B)	(B)
Mean earnings .. ($) ...	22 757	(B)	(B)	(B)	(B)	23 064	16 852	26 008	25 736	27 438	(B)	(B)	(B)
Standard error ...($) ...	1 649	(B)	(B)	(B)	(B)	1 720	541	5 783	1 950	999	(B)	(B)	(B)
35 to 44 years, with													
earnings	2 288	217	—	30	186	2 071	825	580	269	307	68	17	5
Median earnings ..($) ...	19 559	10 529	(B)	(B)	10 365	20 300	15 908	21 572	25 262	31 092	(B)	(B)	(B)
Standard error ...($) ...	519	1 329	(B)	(B)	1 245	548	587	1 068	1 770	1 926	(B)	(B)	(B)
Mean earnings .. ($) ...	21 878	12 415	(B)	(B)	11 898	22 869	17 054	22 323	24 675	34 067	(B)	(B)	(B)
Standard error ...($) ...	631	1 110	(B)	(B)	1 138	677	684	909	1 228	3 141	(B)	(B)	(B)
Year round, full-time workers	1 684	111	—	14	97	1 573	573	454	221	250	58	11	5
Median earnings ..($) ...	23 544	16 322	(B)	(B)	15 340	24 223	19 021	24 691	26 563	33 174	(B)	(B)	(B)
Standard error ...($) ...	1 048	3 015	(B)	(B)	1 831	1 012	679	1 003	1 106	1 627	(B)	(B)	(B)
Mean earnings .. ($) ...	26 379	18 279	(B)	(B)	17 612	26 951	21 293	26 080	27 412	37 152	(B)	(B)	(B)
Standard error ...($) ...	740	1 464	(B)	(B)	1 469	780	785	884	1 152	3 679	(B)	(B)	(B)
45 to 54 years, with													
earnings	1 455	221	6	28	187	1 233	581	265	121	152	110	2	1
Median earnings ..($) ...	20 943	13 272	(B)	(B)	13 804	22 608	18 025	24 097	22 910	30 794	41 780	(B)	(B)
Standard error ...($) ...	699	1 732	(B)	(B)	1 810	1 235	984	2 013	2 391	1 500	1 811	(B)	(B)
Mean earnings .. ($) ...	27 820	15 120	(B)	(B)	15 414	30 098	21 874	42 622	24 778	36 249	40 421	(B)	(B)
Standard error ...($) ...	2 555	1 654	(B)	(B)	1 851	2 985	1 628	12 898	2 300	4 605	2 352	(B)	(B)
Year round, full-time workers	1 103	116	6	9	102	986	437	238	97	118	95	—	1
Median earnings ..($) ...	25 181	17 026	(B)	(B)	17 071	25 936	20 753	25 667	25 863	31 371	42 701	(B)	(B)
Standard error ...($) ...	859	1 021	(B)	(B)	1 082	574	1 056	1 438	1 831	2 427	2 386	(B)	(B)
Mean earnings .. ($) ...	31 858	21 050	(B)	(B)	20 895	33 134	23 179	46 414	28 004	39 652	41 989	(B)	(B)
Standard error ...($) ...	3 236	2 582	(B)	(B)	2 836	3 599	940	14 345	2 260	5 489	2 034	(B)	(B)
55 to 64 years, with													
earnings	636	153	4	40	109	483	254	98	32	47	47	1	4
Median earnings ..($) ...	18 290	12 444	(B)	(B)	14 021	20 234	15 621	22 787	(B)	(B)	(B)	(B)	(B)
Standard error ...($) ...	1 033	1 831	(B)	(B)	1 924	1 116	2 262	2 948	(B)	(B)	(B)	(B)	(B)
Mean earnings .. ($) ...	19 980	12 884	(B)	(B)	13 253	22 223	16 489	22 794	(B)	(B)	(B)	(B)	(B)
Standard error ...($) ...	943	964	(B)	(B)	1 173	1 152	1 155	2 132	(B)	(B)	(B)	(B)	(B)
Year round, full-time workers	429	97	—	26	71	332	160	73	22	39	37	1	—
Median earnings ..($) ...	22 122	16 585	(B)	(B)	(B)	25 456	20 665	(B)	(B)	(B)	(B)	(B)	(B)
Standard error ...($) ...	910	1 662	(B)	(B)	(B)	1 273	931	(B)	(B)	(B)	(B)	(B)	(B)
Mean earnings .. ($) ...	24 823	16 424	(B)	(B)	(B)	27 264	21 790	(B)	(B)	(B)	(B)	(B)	(B)
Standard error ...($) ...	1 037	946	(B)	(B)	(B)	1 221	1 328	(B)	(B)	(B)	(B)	(B)	(B)
65 years and over, with													
earnings	162	64	9	23	32	98	50	15	7	10	11	3	1
Median earnings ..($) ...	9 649	(B)	(B)	(B)	(B)	12 164	(B)	(B)	(B)	(B)	(B)	(B)	(B)

See footnotes at end of table.

Table B-9. Earnings by Educational Attainment for Persons 18 Years Old and Over, by Age, Sex, Race and Hispanic Origin: March 1997 — Continued

(Numbers in thousands. Civilian noninstitutional population.)

| Earnings, standard error, age, sex, race, and Hispanic origin | Total | Not a high school graduate | | | | High school graduate or more | | | | | | | |
| | | Total | Elementary | | High School | Total | High school graduate only | College | | | | | |
			None - 4th grade	5th - 8th grade	9th - 11th grade			Some college no degree	Associate degree	Bachelor's degree	Master's degree	Professional degree	Doctorate degree
Standard error ... ($) ...	1 700	(B)	(B)	(B)	(B)	2 772	(B)	(B)	(B)	(B)	(B)	(B)	(B)
Mean earnings .. ($) ...	13 380	(B)	(B)	(B)	(B)	17 090	(B)	(B)	(B)	(B)	(B)	(B)	(B)
Standard error ... ($) ...	2 060	(B)	(B)	(B)	(B)	3 154	(B)	(B)	(B)	(B)	(B)	(B)	(B)
Year round, full-time workers	67	23	4	10	9	44	15	6	5	5	10	3	—
Median earnings ..($) ...	(B)	(B)	(B)	(B)	(B)	(B)	(B)	(B)	(B)	(B)	(B)	(B)	(B)
Standard error ... ($) ...	(B)	(B)	(B)	(B)	(B)	(B)	(B)	(B)	(B)	(B)	(B)	(R)	(B)
Mean earnings .. ($) ...	(B)	(B)	(B)	(B)	(B)	(B)	(B)	(B)	(B)	(B)	(B)	(B)	(B)
Standard error ... ($) ...	(B)	(B)	(B)	(B)	(B)	(B)	(B)	(B)	(B)	(B)	(B)	(B)	(B)
HISPANIC ORIGIN [1]													
Both Sexes													
18 years and over, with earnings	13 365	5 062	728	2 032	2 302	8 304	3 783	2 340	756	1 027	253	83	62
Median earnings ..($) ...	14 985	11 538	10 777	11 898	11 478	17 974	15 842	16 355	22 224	27 779	30 414	41 182	(B)
Standard error ... ($) ...	233	178	411	271	287	461	332	542	975	1 630	2 694	11 857	(B)
Mean earnings .. ($) ...	19 439	13 287	11 935	13 736	13 319	23 188	18 528	21 303	25 014	32 955	36 827	78 329	(B)
Standard error ... ($) ...	458	263	812	368	401	711	444	1 487	1 532	2 746	3 807	29 509	(B)
Year round, full-time workers	8 480	3 035	413	1 295	1 326	5 444	2 501	1 387	499	754	186	71	47
Median earnings ..($) ...	20 334	15 259	13 363	15 066	16 057	23 803	20 515	22 902	26 912	33 347	35 905	(B)	(B)
Standard error ... ($) ...	234	263	738	449	412	461	380	853	891	1 520	3 573	(B)	(B)
Mean earnings .. ($) ...	25 329	17 391	15 640	16 933	18 383	29 754	22 997	29 585	31 374	39 653	43 872	(B)	(B)
Standard error ... ($) ...	683	352	1 298	456	530	1 032	528	2 417	2 068	3 619	4 731	(B)	(B)
Male													
18 years and over, with earnings	7 975	3 382	517	1 382	1 483	4 594	2 116	1 303	384	531	163	55	41
Median earnings ..($) ...	16 581	12 733	11 831	13 287	12 872	21 112	18 482	19 079	26 095	31 475	29 471	(B)	(B)
Standard error ... ($) ...	244	364	467	662	588	446	821	921	1 158	1 675	3 031	(B)	(B)
Mean earnings .. ($) ...	21 870	14 986	13 461	15 441	15 094	26 938	21 593	25 795	29 693	38 130	36 370	(B)	(B)
Standard error ... ($) ...	657	347	1 092	477	529	1 094	628	2 599	2 730	5 090	3 371	(B)	(B)
Year round, full-time workers	5 532	2 231	323	946	962	3 301	1 528	868	276	416	127	50	36
Median earnings ..($) ...	21 076	16 084	14 309	16 029	16 730	25 793	22 349	25 008	30 864	36 332	34 668	(B)	(B)
Standard error ... ($) ...	309	295	770	460	443	420	665	995	1 787	1 766	4 904	(B)	(B)
Mean earnings .. ($) ...	26 817	18 424	16 790	18 133	19 258	32 490	25 173	33 503	36 042	43 668	40 999	(B)	(B)
Standard error ... ($) ...	904	440	1 623	569	651	1 462	667	3 806	3 452	6 384	3 751	(B)	(B)
18 to 24 years, with earnings	1 549	704	41	196	468	845	404	372	30	34	4	—	—
Median earnings ..($) ...	10 109	9 570	(B)	10 480	8 988	10 436	10 544	10 268	(B)	(B)	(B)	(B)	(B)
Standard error ... ($) ...	367	691	(B)	798	894	430	595	876	(B)	(B)	(B)	(B)	(B)
Mean earnings .. ($) ...	10 819	9 333	(B)	10 205	9 076	12 057	12 114	11 433	(B)	(B)	(B)	(B)	(B)
Standard error ... ($) ...	366	406	(B)	660	530	570	844	791	(B)	(B)	(B)	(B)	(B)
Year round, full-time workers	729	357	26	123	207	373	206	138	6	19	3	—	—
Median earnings ..($) ...	13 987	12 398	(B)	12 033	13 015	16 028	15 227	16 293	(B)	(B)	(B)	(B)	(B)
Standard error ... ($) ...	592	446	(B)	670	769	571	1 181	720	(B)	(B)	(B)	(B)	(B)
Mean earnings .. ($) ...	15 743	13 292	(B)	12 630	13 986	18 087	17 106	18 144	(B)	(B)	(B)	(B)	(B)
Standard error ... ($) ...	505	453	(B)	706	621	839	1 173	1 145	(B)	(B)	(B)	(B)	(B)
25 years and over, with earnings	6 426	2 678	476	1 186	1 015	3 748	1 712	931	353	497	159	55	41
Median earnings ..($) ...	19 217	14 527	12 083	14 496	15 850	24 296	21 234	23 711	26 864	32 259	30 093	(B)	(B)
Standard error ... ($) ...	500	478	539	741	508	634	622	1 281	1 468	2 260	3 435	(B)	(B)
Mean earnings .. ($) ...	24 535	16 472	13 920	16 304	17 866	30 294	23 832	31 545	31 153	39 554	36 902	(B)	(B)
Standard error ... ($) ...	800	411	1 173	534	686	1 318	721	3 577	2 915	5 414	3 423	(B)	(B)

See footnotes at end of table.

Table B-9. Earnings by Educational Attainment for Persons 18 Years Old and Over, by Age, Sex, Race and Hispanic Origin: March 1997 — Continued

(Numbers in thousands. Civilian noninstitutional population.)

Earnings, standard error, age, sex, race, and Hispanic origin	Total	Not a high school graduate				High school graduate or more							
		Total	Elementary		High School	Total	High school graduate only	College					
			None - 4th grade	5th - 8th grade	9th - 11th grade			Some college no degree	Associate degree	Bachelor's degree	Master-'s degree	Professional degree	Doctorate degree
Year round, full-time													
workers	4 803	1 875	297	823	755	2 928	1 321	730	270	396	124	50	36
Median earnings ..($) ...	22 363	16 810	14 804	16 692	17 891	26 875	23 959	26 731	30 799	36 922	35 281	(B)	(B)
Standard error ... ($) ...	377	308	809	468	811	414	783	896	1 784	2 436	5 002	(B)	(B)
Mean earnings .. ($) ...	28 498	19 400	17 310	18 955	20 706	34 323	26 433	36 396	36 226	44 615	41 455	(B)	(B)
Standard error ... ($) ...	1 032	507	1 754	632	790	1 636	733	4 496	3 529	6 684	3 799	(B)	(B)
25 to 34 years, with													
earnings	2 685	1 045	113	409	522	1 641	780	419	146	235	42	14	5
Median earnings ..($) ...	17 226	13 597	12 868	12 983	14 255	21 685	19 268	22 155	24 377	28 849	(B)	(B)	(B)
Standard error ... ($) ...	408	630	1 413	938	878	590	1 279	1 259	2 122	2 648	(B)	(B)	(B)
Mean earnings .. ($) ...	21 777	15 093	13 432	14 816	15 672	26 031	20 856	31 317	25 753	31 147	(B)	(B)	(B)
Standard error ... ($) ...	1 105	478	1 020	749	718	1 761	739	6 450	2 348	2 265	(B)	(B)	(B)
Year round, full-time													
workers	1 998	739	75	288	376	1 259	611	326	101	172	32	12	5
Median earnings ..($) ...	20 811	15 786	14 927	15 444	16 241	24 885	21 407	25 419	26 664	33 721	(B)	(B)	(B)
Standard error ... ($) ...	464	439	1 413	796	627	757	718	1 220	1 659	3 398	(B)	(B)	(B)
Mean earnings .. ($) ...	25 027	17 222	15 515	16 865	17 836	29 610	23 029	36 745	28 826	36 259	(B)	(B)	(B)
Standard error ... ($) ...	1 443	523	1 226	883	728	2 242	819	8 208	2 253	2 456	(B)	(B)	(B)
35 to 44 years, with													
earnings	2 015	823	149	389	285	1 192	543	311	111	142	49	19	18
Median earnings ..($) ...	21 017	15 559	11 538	16 008	17 499	26 190	23 397	25 879	32 058	33 957	(B)	(B)	(B)
Standard error ... ($) ...	619	555	758	726	1 491	793	1 364	1 785	4 961	3 467	(B)	(B)	(B)
Mean earnings .. ($) ...	26 543	17 550	13 978	17 357	19 687	32 748	26 779	30 201	33 705	49 466	(B)	(B)	(B)
Standard error ... ($) ...	1 526	855	3 281	948	1 167	2 466	1 636	2 239	3 362	18 110	(B)	(B)	(B)
Year round, full-time													
workers	1 507	562	93	256	214	945	401	255	99	118	39	17	14
Median earnings ..($) ...	24 713	17 985	13 568	18 558	21 116	30 241	26 659	27 920	35 896	37 218	(B)	(B)	(B)
Standard error ... ($) ...	822	1 197	1 050	1 536	1 385	1 437	1 281	2 468	4 080	4 650	(B)	(B)	(B)
Mean earnings .. ($) ...	30 638	20 794	17 764	20 241	22 760	36 497	29 897	33 052	36 349	55 417	(B)	(B)	(B)
Standard error ... ($) ...	1 949	1 118	5 143	1 137	1 319	2 992	1 493	2 583	3 444	21 624	(B)	(B)	(B)
45 to 54 years, with													
earnings	1 090	475	98	244	134	614	256	139	71	84	42	16	7
Median earnings ..($) ...	20 777	15 454	13 050	15 028	18 165	26 477	22 825	26 310	(B)	37 455	(B)	(B)	(B)
Standard error ... ($) ...	751	1 044	1 459	1 621	1 621	1 253	1 849	5 343	(B)	7 795	(B)	(B)	(B)
Mean earnings .. ($) ...	26 925	17 698	14 480	17 215	20 944	34 068	25 212	30 632	(B)	44 598	(B)	(B)	(B)
Standard error ... ($) ...	1 802	1 081	1 371	1 306	2 780	2 998	1 889	2 897	(B)	5 626	(B)	(B)	(B)
Year round, full-time													
workers	860	366	71	181	113	495	204	109	53	74	35	15	6
Median earnings ..($) ...	23 493	17 497	(B)	17 171	19 616	31 143	25 395	34 546	(B)	(B)	(B)	(B)	(B)
Standard error ... ($) ...	1 133	1 065	(B)	1 389	1 741	1 652	1 519	3 754	(B)	(B)	(B)	(B)	(B)
Mean earnings .. ($) ...	30 618	20 110	(B)	19 718	23 092	38 390	28 710	35 312	(B)	(B)	(B)	(B)	(B)
Standard error ... ($) ...	2 185	1 262	(B)	1 466	3 104	3 574	2 105	3 112	(B)	(B)	(B)	(B)	(B)
55 to 64 years, with													
earnings	521	274	89	118	67	247	108	51	22	35	20	4	7
Median earnings ..($) ...	19 336	14 386	12 089	12 827	(B)	27 527	26 596	(B)	(B)	(B)	(B)	(B)	(B)
Standard error ... ($) ...	1 805	1 559	1 912	1 685	(B)	2 275	2 324	(B)	(B)	(B)	(B)	(B)	(B)
Mean earnings .. ($) ...	27 288	16 957	14 322	15 873	(B)	38 779	29 060	(B)	(B)	(B)	(B)	(B)	(B)
Standard error ... ($) ...	3 884	1 503	2 060	1 944	(B)	7 852	3 126	(B)	(B)	(B)	(B)	(B)	(B)
Year round, full-time													
workers	367	179	46	84	50	188	87	31	14	30	15	4	7
Median earnings ..($) ...	24 466	17 917	(B)	16 015	(B)	31 303	27 049	(B)	(B)	(B)	(B)	(B)	(B)
Standard error ... ($) ...	1 847	1 817	(B)	2 173	(B)	3 763	1 946	(B)	(B)	(B)	(B)	(B)	(B)
Mean earnings .. ($) ...	34 308	22 416	(B)	19 623	(B)	45 674	30 932	(B)	(B)	(B)	(B)	(B)	(B)
Standard error ... ($) ...	5 356	1 913	(B)	2 323	(B)	10 120	3 500	(B)	(B)	(B)	(B)	(B)	(B)
65 years and over, with													
earnings	115	61	26	27	8	54	25	11	4	3	5	2	4
Median earnings ..($) ...	12 375	(B)	(B)	(B)	(B)	(B)	(B)	(B)	(B)	(B)	(B)	(B)	(B)
Standard error ... ($) ...	1 982	(B)	(B)	(B)	(B)	(B)	(B)	(B)	(B)	(B)	(B)	(B)	(B)

See footnotes at end of table.

Table B-9. Earnings by Educational Attainment for Persons 18 Years Old and Over, by Age, Sex, Race and Hispanic Origin: March 1997 — Continued

(Numbers in thousands. Civilian noninstitutional population.)

Earnings, standard error, age, sex, race, and Hispanic origin	Total	Not a high school graduate				High school graduate or more							
		Total	Elementary		High School	Total	High school graduate only	College					
			None - 4th grade	5th - 8th grade	9th - 11th grade			Some college no degree	Associate degree	Bachelor's degree	Master's degree	Professional degree	Doctorate degree
Mean earnings .. ($) ...	18 630	(B)	(B)	(B)	(B)	(B)	(B)	(B)	(B)	(B)	(B)	(B)	(B)
Standard error ... ($) ...	2 970	(B)	(B)	(B)	(B)	(B)	(B)	(B)	(B)	(B)	(B)	(B)	(B)
Year round, full-time workers	70	28	12	15	1	42	19	9	2	3	3	2	4
Median earnings ..($) ...	(B)	(B)	(B)	(B)	(B)	(B)	(B)	(B)	(B)	(B)	(B)	(B)	(B)
Standard error ... ($) ...	(B)	(B)	(B)	(B)	(B)	(B)	(B)	(B)	(B)	(B)	(B)	(B)	(B)
Mean earnings .. ($) ...	(B)	(B)	(B)	(B)	(B)	(B)	(B)	(B)	(B)	(B)	(B)	(B)	(B)
Standard error ... ($) ...	(B)	(B)	(B)	(B)	(B)	(B)	(B)	(B)	(B)	(B)	(B)	(B)	(B)
Female													
18 years and over, with earnings	5 390	1 680	211	651	819	3 710	1 667	1 037	372	495	90	28	21
Median earnings ..($) ...	12 074	8 799	7 685	9 490	8 349	15 010	12 461	12 503	20 088	25 945	31 595	(B)	(B)
Standard error ... ($) ...	233	421	802	532	864	485	479	822	1 378	1 066	4 363	(B)	(B)
Mean earnings .. ($) ...	15 841	9 867	8 188	10 114	10 103	18 545	14 635	15 659	20 192	27 407	37 660	(B)	(B)
Standard error ... ($) ...	578	332	649	459	547	816	577	664	1 191	1 503	8 816	(B)	(B)
Year round, full-time workers	2 948	804	90	349	364	2 144	973	519	223	338	59	20	12
Median earnings ..($) ...	18 689	12 836	11 134	12 418	13 982	21 452	17 510	20 908	23 389	31 477	(B)	(B)	(B)
Standard error ... ($) ...	557	480	703	611	705	362	697	694	1 631	1 126	(B)	(B)	(B)
Mean earnings .. ($) ...	22 536	14 525	11 533	13 684	16 075	25 541	19 582	23 031	25 588	34 709	(B)	(B)	(B)
Standard error ... ($) ...	987	486	962	608	844	1 329	832	897	1 542	1 743	(B)	(B)	(B)
18 to 24 years, with earnings	990	298	22	60	217	691	352	280	34	24	1	—	—
Median earnings ..($) ...	6 522	4 187	(B)	(B)	3 477	7 525	8 671	6 312	(B)	(B)	(B)	(B)	(B)
Standard error ... ($) ...	395	541	(B)	(B)	670	660	1 065	542	(B)	(B)	(B)	(B)	(B)
Mean earnings .. ($) ...	8 336	5 690	(B)	(B)	5 446	9 477	9 531	8 309	(B)	(B)	(B)	(B)	(B)
Standard error ... ($) ...	411	529	(B)	(B)	663	525	684	820	(B)	(B)	(B)	(B)	(B)
Year round, full-time workers	317	80	10	22	48	237	144	61	19	12	1	—	—
Median earnings ..($) ...	13 570	10 997	(B)	(B)	(B)	14 948	14 076	(B)	(B)	(B)	(B)	(B)	(B)
Standard error ... ($) ...	808	668	(R)	(R)	(R)	786	1 068	(B)	(B)	(B)	(B)	(B)	(B)
Mean earnings .. ($) ...	14 658	11 308	(B)	(B)	(B)	15 787	14 520	(B)	(B)	(B)	(B)	(B)	(B)
Standard error ... ($) ...	793	1 024	(B)	(B)	(B)	973	1 101	(B)	(B)	(B)	(B)	(B)	(B)
25 years and over, with earnings	4 400	1 381	189	591	602	3 019	1 314	757	338	472	88	28	21
Median earnings ..($) ...	13 695	9 783	7 921	9 913	10 360	17 079	14 146	16 386	20 515	26 454	31 860	(B)	(B)
Standard error ... ($) ...	455	400	853	556	598	485	748	1 027	1 220	1 086	4 251	(B)	(B)
Mean earnings .. ($) ...	17 529	10 770	8 451	10 481	11 781	20 622	16 003	18 376	20 864	27 967	38 015	(B)	(B)
Standard error ... ($) ...	695	374	697	490	668	984	695	795	1 265	1 557	8 940	(B)	(B)
Year round, full-time workers	2 631	724	80	327	317	1 907	830	458	204	326	58	20	12
Median earnings ..($) ...	19 917	13 258	11 261	12 850	14 392	22 198	19 010	21 669	23 914	31 746	(B)	(B)	(B)
Standard error ... ($) ...	495	528	746	692	775	386	971	689	1 665	1 169	(B)	(B)	(B)
Mean earnings .. ($) ...	23 484	14 880	11 906	14 037	16 505	26 752	20 457	23 879	26 342	35 094	(B)	(B)	(B)
Standard error ... ($) ...	1 098	523	1 036	629	942	1 483	947	950	1 634	1 791	(B)	(B)	(B)
25 to 34 years, with earnings	1 686	420	42	129	249	1 265	504	333	158	219	37	8	6
Median earnings ..($) ...	13 037	8 485	(B)	8 150	9 297	16 090	12 401	15 230	18 153	25 205	(B)	(B)	(B)
Standard error ... ($) ...	762	659	(B)	959	1 122	705	827	1 628	2 321	1 451	(B)	(B)	(B)
Mean earnings .. ($) ...	16 067	9 742	(B)	8 101	11 099	18 168	14 175	16 579	19 260	25 389	(B)	(B)	(B)
Standard error ... ($) ...	669	701	(B)	732	1 080	837	752	1 068	1 849	1 784	(B)	(B)	(B)
Year round, full-time workers	948	193	13	59	121	755	303	197	76	151	18	6	4
Median earnings ..($) ...	19 674	12 880	(B)	(B)	14 794	21 202	17 002	20 084	25 134	28 341	(B)	(B)	(B)
Standard error ... ($) ...	746	969	(B)	(B)	1 220	465	1 273	1 025	2 463	1 929	(B)	(B)	(B)
Mean earnings .. ($) ...	21 744	14 571	(B)	(B)	16 528	23 576	18 130	21 001	27 013	31 374	(B)	(B)	(B)
Standard error ... ($) ...	1 006	1 176	(B)	(B)	1 737	1 201	814	1 231	2 715	1 876	(B)	(B)	(B)

See footnotes at end of table.

Table B-9. Earnings by Educational Attainment for Persons 18 Years Old and Over, by Age, Sex, Race and Hispanic Origin: March 1997 — Continued

(Numbers in thousands. Civilian noninstitutional population.)

Earnings, standard error, age, sex, race, and Hispanic origin	Total	Not a high school graduate				High school graduate or more							
		Total	Elementary		High School	Total	High school graduate only	College					
			None - 4th grade	5th - 8th grade	9th - 11th grade			Some college no degree	Associate degree	Bachelor's degree	Master's degree	Professional degree	Doctorate degree
35 to 44 years, with													
earnings	1 432	465	59	222	184	967	433	257	96	144	22	10	6
Median earnings ..($) ...	13 872	10 314	(B)	11 314	9 398	17 736	14 942	17 162	20 904	27 336	(B)	(B)	(B)
Standard error ... ($) ...	762	560	(B)	803	1 107	1 092	1 197	2 310	1 446	2 721	(B)	(B)	(B)
Mean earnings .. ($) ...	19 089	10 901	(B)	11 782	10 459	23 023	17 779	19 735	21 793	29 145	(B)	(B)	(B)
Standard error ... ($) ...	1 873	572	(B)	785	1 011	2 734	1 711	1 473	2 386	3 022	(B)	(B)	(B)
Year round, full-time workers	903	266	31	139	96	637	295	151	68	97	16	8	1
Median earnings ..($) ...	19 743	12 786	(B)	13 669	12 458	23 197	19 315	25 137	(B)	32 710	(B)	(B)	(B)
Standard error ... ($) ...	962	716	(B)	883	1 441	1 136	1 166	2 873	(B)	2 576	(B)	(B)	(B)
Mean earnings .. ($) ...	25 196	14 298	(B)	14 594	14 809	29 742	22 248	26 633	(B)	36 873	(B)	(B)	(B)
Standard error ... ($) ...	2 900	722	(B)	903	1 417	4 061	2 357	1 732	(B)	3 560	(B)	(B)	(B)
45 to 54 years, with													
earnings	797	286	44	149	93	510	222	119	61	77	20	6	6
Median earnings ..($) ...	14 775	10 841	(B)	10 242	11 870	18 546	15 595	17 240	(B)	31 617	(B)	(B)	(B)
Standard error ... ($) ...	850	622	(B)	1 163	910	1 611	1 173	1 993	(B)	5 678	(B)	(B)	(B)
Mean earnings .. ($) ...	18 452	11 212	(B)	10 292	13 269	22 517	16 302	19 824	(B)	31 959	(B)	(B)	(B)
Standard error ... ($) ...	980	696	(B)	802	1 513	1 392	1 230	2 027	(B)	5 334	(B)	(B)	(B)
Year round, full-time workers	500	159	19	84	56	341	139	81	41	52	17	3	6
Median earnings ..($) ...	20 001	13 475	(B)	12 760	(B)	23 853	20 571	20 977	(B)	(B)	(B)	(B)	(B)
Standard error ... ($) ...	1 254	1 070	(B)	1 242	(B)	1 271	1 751	2 823	(B)	(B)	(B)	(B)	(B)
Mean earnings .. ($) ...	24 141	14 648	(B)	13 262	(B)	28 569	21 197	23 931	(B)	(B)	(B)	(B)	(B)
Standard error ... ($) ...	1 312	886	(B)	899	(B)	1 738	1 477	2 467	(B)	(B)	(B)	(B)	(B)
55 to 64 years, with													
earnings	401	166	31	73	62	235	131	39	24	30	8	3	—
Median earnings ..($) ...	14 269	10 401	(B)	(B)	(B)	20 290	15 261	(B)	(B)	(B)	(B)	(B)	(B)
Standard error ... ($) ...	1 430	1 445	(B)	(B)	(B)	2 153	2 342	(B)	(B)	(B)	(B)	(B)	(B)
Mean earnings .. ($) ...	17 349	12 246	(B)	(B)	(B)	20 968	16 900	(B)	(B)	(B)	(B)	(B)	(B)
Standard error ... ($) ...	1 147	1 270	(B)	(B)	(B)	1 628	1 679	(B)	(B)	(B)	(B)	(B)	(B)
Year round, full-time workers	252	96	14	45	37	157	80	25	18	24	6	3	—
Median earnings ..($) ...	20 535	14 706	(B)	(B)	(B)	23 988	20 649	(B)	(B)	(B)	(B)	(B)	(B)
Standard error ... ($) ...	1 259	1 774	(B)	(B)	(B)	2 421	1 738	(B)	(B)	(B)	(B)	(B)	(B)
Mean earnings .. ($) ...	22 658	16 613	(B)	(B)	(B)	26 360	21 184	(B)	(B)	(B)	(B)	(B)	(B)
Standard error ... ($) ...	1 414	1 754	(B)	(B)	(B)	1 843	1 737	(B)	(B)	(B)	(B)	(B)	(B)
65 years and over, with													
earnings	85	44	13	16	14	41	24	10	—	3	—	2	3
Median earnings ..($) ...	7 913	(B)	(B)	(B)	(B)	(B)	(B)	(B)	(B)	(B)	(B)	(B)	(B)
Standard error ... ($) ...	2 176	(B)	(B)	(B)	(B)	(B)	(B)	(B)	(B)	(B)	(B)	(B)	(B)
Mean earnings .. ($) ...	12 441	(B)	(B)	(B)	(B)	(B)	(B)	(B)	(B)	(B)	(B)	(B)	(B)
Standard error ... ($) ...	2 375	(B)	(B)	(B)	(B)	(B)	(B)	(B)	(B)	(B)	(B)	(B)	(B)
Year round, full-time workers	29	11	3	1	7	18	13	3	—	1	—	—	—
Median earnings ..($) ...	(B)	(B)	(B)	(B)	(B)	(B)	(B)	(B)	(B)	(B)	(B)	(B)	(B)
Standard error ... ($) ...	(B)	(B)	(B)	(B)	(B)	(B)	(B)	(B)	(B)	(B)	(B)	(B)	(B)
Mean earnings .. ($) ...	(B)	(B)	(B)	(B)	(B)	(B)	(B)	(B)	(B)	(B)	(B)	(B)	(B)
Standard error ... ($) ...	(B)	(B)	(B)	(B)	(B)	(B)	(B)	(B)	(B)	(B)	(B)	(B)	(B)

Source: March 1997 Current Population Survey, Education and Social Stratification Branch, U.S. Bureau of the Census.

1. May be of any race.

— Represents zero or rounds to zero.

(B) Base less than 75,000.

Table B-10. Educational Attainment of Persons 18 Years Old and Over, by Metropolitan and Nonmetropolitan Status, Age, Sex, Race, and Hispanic Origin: March 1997

(Numbers in thousands. Civilian noninstitutional population.)

Metropolitan status, age, sex, race, and Hispanic origin	Total	Elementary		High School		College				Percent:	
		None-4th grade	5th-8th grade	9th-11th grade	High school graduate	Some college no degree	Associate degree	Bachelor's degree	Advanced degree	High school graduate or more	Bachelor's degree or more
ALL RACES											
Both Sexes											
18 years and over	195 568	2 983	11 066	22 261	65 370	38 041	13 336	29 089	13 421	81.4	21.7
Metropolitan areas	157 482	2 407	8 107	16 862	50 424	31 451	10 840	25 483	11 908	82.6	23.7
Metropolitan areas											
1,000,000+	86 111	1 339	4 475	9 129	26 150	16 991	5 631	15 159	7 237	82.6	26.0
Central city	32 001	854	2 259	4 418	9 299	6 030	1 708	5 002	2 431	76.5	23.2
Balance of MSA	54 109	485	2 216	4 710	16 852	10 961	3 923	10 156	4 806	86.3	27.7
Metropolitan areas <											
1,000,000	71 371	1 068	3 632	7 734	24 274	14 461	5 208	10 324	4 670	82.6	21.0
Central city	26 573	476	1 432	3 021	8 366	5 575	1 807	3 977	1 919	81.5	22.2
Balance of MSA	44 798	592	2 200	4 713	15 908	8 886	3 401	6 347	2 751	83.2	20.3
Nonmetropolitan area	38 086	576	2 960	5 399	14 945	6 590	2 497	3 606	1 514	76.5	13.4
25 years and over	170 581	2 840	10 472	17 212	57 586	29 367	12 106	27 357	13 341	82.1	23.0
Metropolitan areas	137 382	2 295	7 632	12 901	44 498	24 173	10 104	23 940	11 839	83.4	26.0
Metropolitan areas											
1,000,000+	75 242	1 264	4 175	6 955	23 064	13 166	5 243	14 178	7 197	83.5	28.4
Central city	27 361	801	2 092	3 337	8 044	4 614	1 572	4 493	2 407	77.2	25.2
Balance of MSA	47 881	463	2 083	3 618	15 020	8 552	3 670	9 685	4 790	87.1	30.2
Metropolitan areas <											
1,000,000	62 140	1 032	3 457	5 946	21 434	11 008	4 861	9 762	4 641	83.2	23.2
Central city	22 693	464	1 333	2 255	7 161	4 157	1 680	3 741	1 903	82.1	24.9
Balance of MSA	39 447	568	2 124	3 691	14 273	6 851	3 181	6 021	2 738	83.8	22.2
Nonmetropolitan area	33 199	545	2 840	4 311	13 088	5 194	2 302	3 417	1 502	76.8	14.8
25 to 44 years	84 216	782	2 464	7 132	27 937	16 338	7 408	16 257	5 898	87.7	26.3
Metropolitan areas	69 309	679	2 057	5 484	21 646	13 707	6 035	14 392	5 309	88.1	28.4
Metropolitan areas											
1,000,000+	38 882	405	1 375	3 108	11 326	7 593	3 135	8 637	3 303	87.4	30.7
Central city	14 671	249	777	1 597	4 284	2 761	977	2 859	1 167	82.1	27.4
Balance of MSA	24 211	156	598	1 511	7 042	4 832	2 158	5 779	2 136	90.6	32.7
Metropolitan areas <											
1,000,000	30 427	274	681	2 376	10 320	6 114	2 900	5 755	2 006	89.1	25.5
Central city	11 461	110	310	971	3 548	2 396	1 059	2 236	831	87.9	26.8
Balance of MSA	18 966	164	371	1 405	6 772	3 718	1 842	3 519	1 175	89.0	24.7
Nonmetropolitan area	14 908	103	407	1 649	6 291	2 630	1 373	1 865	589	85.5	16.5
45 to 64 years	54 488	943	3 132	5 088	18 716	8 926	3 853	8 129	5 702	83.2	25.4
Metropolitan areas	43 453	759	2 244	3 655	14 333	7 182	3 166	7 093	5 021	84.7	27.9
Metropolitan areas											
1,000,000+	23 578	411	1 213	1 970	7 360	3 830	1 625	4 176	2 995	84.8	30.4
Central city	7 952	248	631	956	2 264	1 266	460	1 178	949	76.9	26.7
Balance of MSA	15 626	163	582	1 015	5 096	2 563	1 165	2 998	2 045	88.7	32.3
Metropolitan areas <											
1,000,000	19 875	348	1 032	1 684	6 972	3 353	1 542	2 918	2 026	84.6	24.9
Central city	6 727	135	392	585	2 145	1 134	455	1 072	810	83.5	28.0
Balance of MSA	13 148	213	640	1 099	4 828	2 219	1 087	1 846	1 216	85.2	23.3
Nonmetropolitan area	11 034	184	887	1 433	4 383	1 744	686	1 036	681	77.3	15.6
65 years and over	31 877	1 116	4 877	4 992	10 933	4 104	1 146	2 970	1 741	65.5	14.8
Metropolitan areas	24 620	858	3 331	3 762	8 519	3 284	902	2 455	1 509	67.7	16.1
Metropolitan areas											
1,000,000+	12 782	448	1 587	1 877	4 378	1 743	483	1 365	900	69.4	17.7
Central city	4 738	304	684	784	1 496	586	135	457	291	62.6	15.8
Balance of MSA	8 044	144	903	1 093	2 882	1 157	348	909	609	73.4	18.9
Metropolitan areas <											
1,000,000	11 838	410	1 744	1 885	4 141	1 540	419	1 089	609	65.9	14.3
Central city	4 504	219	631	698	1 468	627	167	433	262	65.6	15.4
Balance of MSA	7 334	191	1 113	1 187	2 674	913	252	656	348	66.0	13.7
Nonmetropolitan area	7 257	258	1 546	1 229	2 414	820	243	515	232	58.2	10.3

See footnotes at end of table.

Table B-10. Educational Attainment of Persons 18 Years Old and Over, by Metropolitan and Nonmetropolitan Status, Age, Sex, Race, and Hispanic Origin: March 1997 — Continued

(Numbers in thousands. Civilian noninstitutional population.)

Metropolitan status, age, sex, race, and Hispanic origin	Total	Elementary		High School		College				Percent:	
		None–4th grade	5th–8th grade	9th–11th grade	High school graduate	Some college no degree	Associate degree	Bachelor's degree	Advanced degree	High school graduate or more	Bachelor's degree or more
Male											
18 years and over	94 154	1 530	5 376	11 015	30 196	18 183	5 731	14 387	7 738	81.0	23.5
Metropolitan areas	75 914	1 185	3 917	8 402	23 097	15 066	4 618	12 682	6 947	82.2	25.9
Metropolitan areas											
1,000,000+	41 590	638	2 157	4 545	11 925	8 158	2 372	7 507	4 289	82.4	28.4
Central city	15 249	384	1 058	2 102	4 357	2 807	704	2 427	1 410	76.8	25.2
Balance of MSA	26 341	254	1 099	2 443	7 568	5 351	1 668	5 080	2 879	85.6	30.2
Metropolitan areas <											
1,000,000	34 325	546	1 760	3 857	11 173	6 908	2 247	5 175	2 659	82.0	22.8
Central city	12 461	223	623	1 380	3 786	2 636	780	1 978	1 056	82.1	24.3
Balance of MSA	21 864	323	1 137	2 478	7 387	4 273	1 467	3 197	1 603	82.0	22.0
Nonmetropolitan area	18 240	345	1 459	2 612	7 099	3 117	1 112	1 705	790	75.8	13.7
25 years and over	81 620	1 454	5 023	8 212	26 226	14 033	5 299	13 672	7 702	82.0	26.2
Metropolitan areas	65 795	1 129	3 636	6 200	20 065	11 539	4 275	12 033	6 917	83.3	28.8
Metropolitan areas											
1,000,000+	36 068	601	1 971	3 327	10 338	6 285	2 177	7 102	4 266	83.6	31.5
Central city	12 915	356	952	1 509	3 734	2 127	634	2 207	1 396	78.2	27.9
Balance of MSA	23 153	245	1 019	1 818	6 604	4 158	1 543	4 895	2 871	86.7	33.5
Metropolitan areas <											
1,000,000	29 727	528	1 665	2 873	9 727	5 254	2 098	4 931	2 651	83.0	25.5
Central city	10 570	217	567	961	3 222	1 957	730	1 861	1 054	83.5	27.6
Balance of MSA	19 157	311	1 097	1 912	6 505	3 297	1 368	3 070	1 597	82.7	24.4
Nonmetropolitan area	15 825	325	1 387	2 012	6 161	2 493	1 024	1 638	785	76.5	15.3
25 to 44 years	41 833	451	1 303	3 929	14 087	7 946	3 174	7 803	3 140	86.4	26.2
Metropolitan areas	34 515	385	1 105	3 038	10 889	6 694	2 568	6 947	2 890	86.9	28.5
Metropolitan areas											
1,000,000+	19 426	224	744	1 701	5 695	3 744	1 286	4 180	1 852	86.3	31.0
Central city	7 365	133	424	795	2 220	1 347	398	1 392	657	81.7	27.8
Balance of MSA	12 061	92	320	906	3 475	2 398	889	2 788	1 194	89.1	33.0
Metropolitan areas <											
1,000,000	15 090	160	361	1 337	5 194	2 950	1 281	2 768	1 039	87.7	25.2
Central city	5 624	54	159	466	1 761	1 182	504	1 077	422	87.9	26.7
Balance of MSA	9 466	106	203	871	3 433	1 768	778	1 690	616	87.5	24.4
Nonmetropolitan area	7 317	67	197	892	3 198	1 252	607	855	249	84.2	15.1
45 to 64 years	26 383	487	1 617	2 319	8 165	4 298	1 732	4 324	3 441	83.2	29.4
Metropolitan areas	21 000	363	1 118	1 668	6 193	3 431	1 390	3 786	3 051	85.0	32.6
Metropolitan areas											
1,000,000+	11 357	184	597	904	3 139	1 794	705	2 197	1 836	85.2	35.5
Central city	3 669	91	285	415	971	571	189	571	578	78.5	31.3
Balance of MSA	7 688	94	312	488	2 168	1 224	516	1 627	1 258	88.4	37.5
Metropolitan areas <											
1,000,000	9 643	179	521	764	3 054	1 637	685	1 588	1 215	84.8	29.1
Central city	3 171	63	165	252	941	516	195	566	474	84.9	32.8
Balance of MSA	6 472	116	356	513	2 113	1 121	490	1 022	741	84.8	27.2
Nonmetropolitan area	5 384	124	499	651	1 972	867	342	538	390	76.3	17.2
65 years and over	13 404	515	2 103	1 963	3 974	1 789	392	1 546	1 121	65.8	19.9
Metropolitan areas	10 280	381	1 413	1 494	2 983	1 414	318	1 301	976	68.0	22.1
Metropolitan areas											
1,000,000+	5 285	192	630	722	1 504	747	185	725	579	70.8	24.7
Central city	1 880	133	244	299	543	210	48	244	160	64.1	21.5
Balance of MSA	3 405	59	387	424	961	537	138	481	418	74.5	26.4
Metropolitan areas <											
1,000,000	4 995	189	782	772	1 479	668	132	576	397	65.1	19.5
Central city	1 775	101	243	244	520	260	32	219	157	66.9	21.2
Balance of MSA	3 220	89	539	528	959	408	100	357	240	64.1	18.5
Nonmetropolitan area	3 124	134	691	469	991	374	75	245	145	58.6	12.5

See footnotes at end of table.

Table B-10. Educational Attainment of Persons 18 Years Old and Over, by Metropolitan and Nonmetropolitan Status, Age, Sex, Race, and Hispanic Origin: March 1997 — Continued

(Numbers in thousands. Civilian noninstitutional population.)

Metropolitan status, age, sex, race, and Hispanic origin	Total	Elementary		High School		College				Percent:	
		None-4th grade	5th-8th grade	9th-11th grade	High school graduate	Some college no degree	Associate degree	Bachelor's degree	Advanced degree	High school graduate or more	Bachelor's degree or more
Female											
18 years and over	101 414	1 453	5 691	11 247	35 174	19 858	7 606	14 702	5 684	81.9	20.1
Metropolitan areas	81 567	1 223	4 190	8 460	27 327	16 386	6 221	12 801	4 960	83.0	21.8
Metropolitan areas 1,000,000+	44 521	701	2 318	4 584	14 226	8 833	3 259	7 651	2 949	82.9	23.8
Central city	16 752	470	1 201	2 316	4 941	3 223	1 004	2 575	1 021	76.2	21.5
Balance of MSA	27 769	231	1 117	2 267	9 284	5 610	2 255	5 076	1 928	87.0	25.2
Metropolitan areas < 1,000,000	37 046	521	1 872	3 877	13 101	7 553	2 962	5 149	2 012	83.1	19.3
Central city	14 112	253	809	1 641	4 580	2 939	1 028	2 000	863	80.8	20.3
Balance of MSA	22 934	269	1 063	2 235	8 522	4 613	1 934	3 150	1 149	84.4	18.7
Nonmetropolitan area	19 846	231	1 501	2 787	7 847	3 473	1 384	1 901	723	77.2	13.2
25 years and over	88 961	1 387	5 449	9 000	31 360	15 335	7 107	13 685	5 638	82.2	21.7
Metropolitan areas	71 587	1 167	3 996	6 701	24 434	12 634	5 829	11 907	4 921	83.4	23.5
Metropolitan areas 1,000,000+	39 174	663	2 203	3 628	12 726	6 880	3 066	7 076	2 931	83.4	25.5
Central city	14 446	445	1 140	1 828	4 311	2 487	938	2 286	1 011	76.4	22.8
Balance of MSA	24 728	218	1 064	1 800	8 416	4 393	2 128	4 790	1 920	87.5	27.1
Metropolitan areas < 1,000,000	32 413	503	1 792	3 072	11 707	5 753	2 763	4 831	1 990	83.4	21.0
Central city	12 123	246	765	1 294	3 938	2 200	950	1 880	849	81.0	22.5
Balance of MSA	20 290	257	1 027	1 779	7 769	3 553	1 813	2 951	1 141	84.9	20.2
Nonmetropolitan area	17 374	220	1 453	2 299	6 927	2 701	1 279	1 778	717	77.1	14.4
25 to 44 years	42 384	331	1 161	3 203	13 851	8 392	4 234	8 455	2 758	88.9	26.5
Metropolitan areas	34 793	294	951	2 446	10 757	7 013	3 468	7 445	2 418	89.4	28.3
Metropolitan areas 1,000,000+	19 456	181	631	1 407	5 631	3 848	1 849	4 458	1 451	88.6	30.4
Central city	7 305	116	353	802	2 064	1 414	579	1 467	509	82.6	27.1
Balance of MSA	12 150	64	279	605	3 567	2 434	1 269	2 991	942	92.2	32.4
Metropolitan areas < 1,000,000	15 337	113	320	1 039	5 127	3 165	1 619	2 987	967	90.4	25.8
Central city	5 837	55	151	505	1 788	1 215	555	1 159	409	87.8	26.9
Balance of MSA	9 500	58	169	534	3 339	1 950	1 064	1 828	558	92.0	25.1
Nonmetropolitan area	7 590	37	210	757	3 093	1 379	766	1 010	340	86.8	17.8
45 to 64 years	28 104	455	1 515	2 769	10 551	4 628	2 121	3 806	2 261	83.1	21.6
Metropolitan areas	22 454	396	1 126	1 987	8 140	3 751	1 776	3 308	1 970	84.4	23.5
Metropolitan areas 1,000,000+	12 221	226	615	1 067	4 222	2 035	919	1 978	1 158	84.4	25.7
Central city	4 283	157	346	540	1 294	696	271	607	372	75.6	22.9
Balance of MSA	7 939	69	269	526	2 928	1 339	648	1 371	787	89.1	27.2
Metropolitan areas < 1,000,000	10 232	169	511	920	3 918	1 716	857	1 330	811	84.4	20.9
Central city	3 556	73	226	333	1 203	618	260	506	336	82.2	23.7
Balance of MSA	6 676	96	285	587	2 715	1 098	597	823	475	85.5	19.4
Nonmetropolitan area	5 651	60	388	782	2 411	876	344	498	291	78.2	14.0
65 years and over	18 474	601	2 774	3 028	6 959	2 315	753	1 424	620	65.3	11.1
Metropolitan areas	14 340	477	1 918	2 268	5 536	1 869	584	1 154	533	67.5	11.8
Metropolitan areas 1,000,000+	7 497	256	957	1 155	2 874	997	298	640	321	68.4	12.8
Central city	2 858	171	441	486	953	377	88	212	130	61.6	12.0
Balance of MSA	4 639	85	516	669	1 921	620	210	428	191	72.6	13.3
Metropolitan areas < 1,000,000	6 843	221	961	1 113	2 663	873	287	514	212	66.5	10.6
Central city	2 729	118	388	455	948	367	134	215	105	64.8	11.7
Balance of MSA	4 114	103	574	659	1 715	505	152	299	108	67.5	9.9
Nonmetropolitan area	4 133	124	855	760	1 423	446	169	271	86	57.9	8.6

See footnotes at end of table.

Table B-10. Educational Attainment of Persons 18 Years Old and Over, by Metropolitan and Nonmetropolitan Status, Age, Sex, Race, and Hispanic Origin: March 1997 — Continued

(Numbers in thousands. Civilian noninstitutional population.)

Metropolitan status, age, sex, race, and Hispanic origin	Total	Elementary		High School		College				Percent:	
		None-4th grade	5th-8th grade	9th-11th grade	High school graduate	Some college no degree	Associate degree	Bachelor's degree	Advanced degree	High school graduate or more	Bachelor's degree or more
WHITE											
Both Sexes											
18 years and over	164 050	2 244	9 259	17 402	54 971	31 782	11 433	25 231	11 728	82.4	22.5
Metropolitan areas	129 922	1 820	6 668	12 962	41 485	25 735	9 132	21 824	10 296	83.5	24.7
Metropolitan areas 1,000,000+	68 203	1 004	3 621	6 590	20 476	13 290	4 591	12 553	6 079	83.6	27.3
Central city	21 290	583	1 673	2 538	5 779	3 918	1 135	3 762	1 903	77.5	26.6
Balance of MSA	46 913	421	1 947	4 052	14 697	9 372	3 456	8 791	4 176	86.3	27.6
Metropolitan areas < 1,000,000	61 719	816	3 047	6 373	21 010	12 445	4 541	9 271	4 217	83.4	21.9
Central city	20 890	337	1 096	2 223	6 423	4 389	1 378	3 403	1 642	82.5	24.2
Balance of MSA	40 829	479	1 951	4 150	14 587	8 056	3 162	5 868	2 575	83.9	20.7
Nonmetropolitan area	34 128	424	2 592	4 439	13 485	6 047	2 302	3 407	1 432	78.2	14.2
25 years and over	144 058	2 128	8 709	13 590	48 860	24 724	10 615	23 771	11 660	83.0	24.6
Metropolitan areas	114 031	1 729	6 230	9 989	36 912	19 897	8 508	20 528	10 239	84.3	27.0
Metropolitan areas 1,000,000+	60 032	946	3 345	5 059	18 201	10 389	4 274	11 774	6 044	84.4	29.7
Central city	18 329	544	1 526	1 914	5 023	3 014	1 042	3 383	1 884	78.3	28.7
Balance of MSA	41 702	402	1 819	3 145	13 178	7 375	3 232	8 391	4 160	87.1	30.1
Metropolitan areas < 1,000,000	54 000	782	2 885	4 931	18 711	9 509	4 234	8 754	4 195	84.1	24.0
Central city	17 910	327	1 008	1 652	5 560	3 256	1 280	3 197	1 631	83.3	27.0
Balance of MSA	36 089	455	1 877	3 278	13 151	6 253	2 954	5 557	2 565	84.5	22.5
Nonmetropolitan area	30 026	399	2 480	3 601	11 949	4 827	2 108	3 243	1 421	78.4	15.5
25 to 44 years	69 076	618	2 097	5 482	22 705	13 090	6 231	13 923	4 930	88.1	27.3
Metropolitan areas	55 845	520	1 746	4 172	17 159	10 698	4 996	12 173	4 381	88.5	29.6
Metropolitan areas 1,000,000+	30 092	318	1 158	2 259	8 469	5 658	2 512	7 078	2 640	87.6	32.3
Central city	9 617	181	639	954	2 505	1 660	642	2 158	878	81.6	31.6
Balance of MSA	20 474	137	520	1 305	5 963	3 997	1 870	4 920	1 762	90.4	32.6
Metropolitan areas < 1,000,000	25 753	202	587	1 914	8 690	5 041	2 484	5 094	1 741	89.5	26.5
Central city	8 733	74	256	690	2 605	1 761	789	1 873	684	88.3	29.3
Balance of MSA	17 019	128	331	1 223	6 085	3 280	1 695	3 221	1 057	90.1	25.1
Nonmetropolitan area	13 232	98	351	1 309	5 546	2 392	1 235	1 751	549	86.7	17.4
45 to 64 years	46 517	717	2 495	3 834	16 076	7 825	3 347	7 089	5 135	84.9	26.3
Metropolitan areas	36 490	582	1 768	2 665	11 994	6 180	2 706	6 104	4 491	86.3	29.0
Metropolitan areas 1,000,000+	19 019	308	928	1 354	5 842	3 171	1 343	3 470	2 604	86.4	31.9
Central city	5 242	162	432	499	1 336	883	304	846	781	79.2	31.0
Balance of MSA	13 776	146	496	855	4 506	2 288	1 038	2 624	1 823	89.1	32.3
Metropolitan areas < 1,000,000	17 472	274	840	1 311	6 152	3 009	1 364	2 634	1 888	86.1	25.9
Central city	5 363	100	283	376	1 674	937	348	928	717	85.8	30.7
Balance of MSA	12 109	173	557	935	4 478	2 073	1 016	1 706	1 170	86.2	23.8
Nonmetropolitan area	10 027	135	727	1 169	4 081	1 645	641	985	643	79.7	16.2
65 years and over	28 464	793	4 118	4 275	10 079	3 809	1 037	2 758	1 595	67.7	15.3
Metropolitan areas	21 696	627	2 717	3 152	7 759	3 019	805	2 251	1 367	70.1	16.7
Metropolitan areas 1,000,000+	10 921	321	1 259	1 446	3 891	1 560	419	1 226	801	72.3	18.6
Central city	3 470	201	455	461	1 182	471	95	379	225	67.8	17.4
Balance of MSA	7 451	119	804	984	2 709	1 089	324	847	576	74.4	19.1
Metropolitan areas < 1,000,000	10 775	307	1 458	1 706	3 868	1 459	386	1 025	566	67.8	14.8
Central city	3 814	153	468	586	1 280	558	144	395	229	68.3	16.4
Balance of MSA	6 961	154	989	1 120	2 588	900	243	630	337	67.5	13.9
Nonmetropolitan area	6 768	166	1 402	1 123	2 321	790	232	508	228	60.3	10.9

See footnotes at end of table.

Table B-10. Educational Attainment of Persons 18 Years Old and Over, by Metropolitan and Nonmetropolitan Status, Age, Sex, Race, and Hispanic Origin: March 1997 — Continued

(Numbers in thousands. Civilian noninstitutional population.)

Metropolitan status, age, sex, race, and Hispanic origin	Total	Elementary		High School		College				Percent:	
		None-4th grade	5th-8th grade	9th-11th grade	High school graduate	Some college no degree	Associate degree	Bachelor's degree	Advanced degree	High school graduate or more	Bachelor's degree or more
Male											
18 years and over	79 765	1 143	4 574	8 749	25 454	15 340	5 041	12 655	6 810	81.9	24.4
Metropolitan areas	63 281	891	3 282	6 592	18 990	12 465	3 983	11 026	6 052	83.0	27.0
Metropolitan areas 1,000,000+	33 298	483	1 786	3 337	9 254	6 457	1 991	6 359	3 631	83.2	30.0
Central city	10 431	256	812	1 244	2 717	1 876	496	1 916	1 116	77.8	29.1
Balance of MSA	22 866	228	974	2 094	6 537	4 581	1 495	4 443	2 515	85.6	30.4
Metropolitan areas < 1,000,000	29 983	408	1 496	3 255	9 736	6 008	1 992	4 667	2 421	82.8	23.6
Central city	9 997	148	485	1 053	2 944	2 148	612	1 706	902	83.1	26.1
Balance of MSA	19 986	260	1 011	2 202	6 792	3 861	1 380	2 961	1 518	82.6	22.4
Nonmetropolitan area	16 484	252	1 292	2 157	6 464	2 875	1 058	1 629	758	77.6	14.5
25 years and over	60 571	1 087	4 240	6 552	22 314	11 020	4 641	12 028	6 770	82.0	27.0
Metropolitan areas	55 113	849	3 022	4 878	16 604	9 601	3 672	10 461	6 026	84.1	29.9
Metropolitan areas 1,000,000+	29 046	457	1 615	2 438	8 084	5 008	1 815	6 017	3 611	84.5	33.1
Central city	8 905	239	721	876	2 348	1 435	440	1 743	1 103	79.4	32.0
Balance of MSA	20 141	218	894	1 562	5 736	3 574	1 375	4 275	2 508	86.7	33.7
Metropolitan areas < 1,000,000	26 067	392	1 407	2 440	8 519	4 592	1 857	4 443	2 415	83.7	26.3
Central city	8 481	145	434	717	2 529	1 577	574	1 604	902	84.7	29.6
Balance of MSA	17 585	248	973	1 723	5 991	3 016	1 283	2 839	1 513	83.3	24.7
Nonmetropolitan area	14 458	238	1 227	1 674	5 711	2 319	970	1 567	753	78.3	16.0
25 to 44 years	34 763	351	1 133	3 108	11 576	6 461	2 784	6 765	2 585	86.8	26.9
Metropolitan areas	28 131	288	944	2 378	8 675	5 318	2 210	5 957	2 359	87.2	29.6
Metropolitan areas 1,000,000+	15 231	174	625	1 261	4 257	2 858	1 077	3 510	1 468	86.5	32.7
Central city	5 011	94	356	483	1 335	864	279	1 105	497	81.4	32.0
Balance of MSA	10 220	80	270	778	2 922	1 995	798	2 405	971	89.0	33.0
Metropolitan areas < 1,000,000	12 900	115	319	1 117	4 419	2 460	1 133	2 447	891	88.0	25.9
Central city	4 398	34	135	358	1 325	906	397	905	339	88.0	28.3
Balance of MSA	8 502	81	184	759	3 093	1 554	736	1 542	553	88.0	24.6
Nonmetropolitan area	6 632	62	189	729	2 900	1 143	574	808	226	85.2	15.6
45 to 64 years	22 786	373	1 325	1 756	7 054	3 810	1 510	3 815	3 142	84.8	30.5
Metropolitan areas	17 889	287	919	1 228	5 213	2 996	1 186	3 299	2 760	86.4	33.9
Metropolitan areas 1,000,000+	9 294	143	485	621	2 504	1 492	580	1 853	1 616	86.6	37.3
Central city	2 508	58	206	208	589	413	127	430	476	81.2	36.2
Balance of MSA	6 786	85	279	413	1 915	1 080	452	1 423	1 140	88.5	37.8
Metropolitan areas < 1,000,000	8 595	144	434	607	2 710	1 504	606	1 447	1 144	86.2	30.1
Central city	2 584	44	121	156	748	447	152	494	422	87.6	35.5
Balance of MSA	6 011	100	313	451	1 962	1 057	454	952	723	85.6	27.9
Nonmetropolitan area	4 897	85	406	528	1 840	814	325	516	382	79.2	18.3
65 years and over	12 022	364	1 790	1 689	3 685	1 648	347	1 447	1 052	68.0	20.8
Metropolitan areas	9 093	274	1 159	1 272	2 715	1 286	276	1 205	906	70.3	23.2
Metropolitan areas 1,000,000+	4 521	140	505	555	1 324	658	158	655	527	73.5	26.1
Central city	1 386	88	159	184	425	158	34	207	130	68.9	24.4
Balance of MSA	3 135	53	346	371	899	499	124	447	397	75.5	26.9
Metropolitan areas < 1,000,000	4 571	134	654	717	1 391	628	118	550	379	67.1	20.3
Central city	1 500	67	179	204	455	224	25	205	142	70.1	23.1
Balance of MSA	3 071	67	475	513	936	404	94	345	238	65.6	19.0
Nonmetropolitan area	2 930	90	632	417	970	362	71	243	145	61.1	13.2

See footnotes at end of table.

Table B-10. Educational Attainment of Persons 18 Years Old and Over, by Metropolitan and Nonmetropolitan Status, Age, Sex, Race, and Hispanic Origin: March 1997 — Continued

(Numbers in thousands. Civilian noninstitutional population.)

Metropolitan status, age, sex, race, and Hispanic origin	Total	Elementary		High School		College				Percent:	
		None-4th grade	5th-8th grade	9th-11th grade	High school graduate	Some college no degree	Associate degree	Bachelor's degree	Advanced degree	High school graduate or more	Bachelor's degree or more
Female											
18 years and over	84 285	1 101	4 685	8 653	29 517	16 442	6 393	12 575	4 918	82.9	20.8
Metropolitan areas	66 642	929	3 385	6 371	22 495	13 270	5 149	10 798	4 244	84.0	22.6
Metropolitan areas 1,000,000+	34 905	521	1 835	3 252	11 222	6 833	2 600	6 194	2 448	83.9	24.8
Central city	10 858	327	861	1 294	3 062	2 042	639	1 846	787	77.1	24.3
Balance of MSA	24 047	194	973	1 958	8 160	4 792	1 961	4 348	1 661	87.0	25.0
Metropolitan areas < 1,000,000	31 736	408	1 551	3 118	11 274	6 437	2 549	4 604	1 796	84.0	20.2
Central city	10 894	189	611	1 170	3 480	2 241	767	1 697	740	81.9	22.4
Balance of MSA	20 843	219	940	1 949	7 794	4 196	1 782	2 907	1 056	85.1	19.0
Nonmetropolitan area	17 643	172	1 300	2 282	7 022	3 172	1 244	1 777	674	78.7	13.9
25 years and over	74 487	1 040	4 461	7 038	26 546	12 804	5 974	11 743	4 881	83.2	22.3
Metropolitan areas	58 919	879	3 208	5 111	20 308	10 296	4 836	10 067	4 213	84.4	24.2
Metropolitan areas 1,000,000+	30 985	489	1 730	2 621	10 117	5 380	2 459	5 757	2 433	84.4	26.4
Central city	9 425	305	805	1 038	2 674	1 579	602	1 640	780	77.2	25.7
Balance of MSA	21 561	185	925	1 582	7 442	3 801	1 857	4 117	1 653	87.5	26.8
Metropolitan areas < 1,000,000	27 933	390	1 478	2 490	10 191	4 916	2 377	4 310	1 780	84.4	21.8
Central city	9 429	183	574	935	3 031	1 679	706	1 593	728	82.1	24.6
Balance of MSA	18 504	207	904	1 555	7 160	3 237	1 671	2 718	1 052	85.6	20.4
Nonmetropolitan area	15 568	161	1 253	1 926	6 238	2 508	1 138	1 676	668	78.5	15.1
25 to 44 years	34 313	267	963	2 374	11 130	6 629	3 447	7 158	2 346	89.5	27.7
Metropolitan areas	27 714	231	801	1 794	8 483	5 380	2 786	6 216	2 022	89.8	29.7
Metropolitan areas 1,000,000+	14 861	144	533	997	4 212	2 799	1 435	3 568	1 172	88.7	31.9
Central city	4 606	88	283	471	1 171	796	363	1 053	381	81.7	31.1
Balance of MSA	10 255	57	250	527	3 041	2 003	1 072	2 515	790	91.9	32.2
Metropolitan areas < 1,000,000	12 853	87	268	797	4 272	2 581	1 351	2 648	850	91.0	27.2
Central city	4 336	40	121	333	1 280	855	392	969	346	88.6	30.3
Balance of MSA	8 517	47	147	464	2 991	1 725	959	1 679	505	92.3	25.6
Nonmetropolitan area	6 600	35	162	580	2 646	1 249	661	942	324	88.2	19.2
45 to 64 years	23 732	344	1 170	2 077	9 022	4 015	1 837	3 274	1 993	84.9	22.2
Metropolitan areas	18 602	294	849	1 437	6 781	3 184	1 521	2 805	1 731	86.1	24.4
Metropolitan areas 1,000,000+	9 725	165	443	733	3 338	1 679	763	1 617	988	86.2	26.8
Central city	2 735	104	226	291	747	470	177	416	304	77.3	26.3
Balance of MSA	6 990	61	217	442	2 591	1 209	586	1 201	683	89.7	27.0
Metropolitan areas < 1,000,000	8 877	130	406	704	3 443	1 505	758	1 188	743	86.0	21.8
Central city	2 780	56	163	220	926	490	195	434	296	84.2	26.2
Balance of MSA	6 097	74	243	484	2 517	1 016	562	754	448	86.9	19.7
Nonmetropolitan area	5 130	50	321	641	2 241	831	316	469	262	80.3	14.2
65 years and over	16 442	430	2 328	2 586	6 395	2 160	690	1 311	543	67.5	11.3
Metropolitan areas	12 603	354	1 558	1 880	5 044	1 733	529	1 046	460	69.9	12.0
Metropolitan areas 1,000,000+	6 400	180	754	891	2 567	902	261	571	274	71.5	13.2
Central city	2 084	113	296	277	757	313	61	171	95	67.0	12.8
Balance of MSA	4 316	67	458	614	1 810	589	200	400	179	73.6	13.4
Metropolitan areas < 1,000,000	6 204	173	804	989	2 477	830	268	475	187	68.3	10.7
Central city	2 314	86	290	382	825	334	119	190	87	67.2	12.0
Balance of MSA	3 890	87	514	607	1 652	496	149	285	99	68.9	9.9
Nonmetropolitan area	3 839	76	770	706	1 351	428	161	265	82	59.6	9.0

See footnotes at end of table.

Table B-10. Educational Attainment of Persons 18 Years Old and Over, by Metropolitan and Nonmetropolitan Status, Age, Sex, Race, and Hispanic Origin: March 1997 — Continued

(Numbers in thousands. Civilian noninstitutional population.)

Metropolitan status, age, sex, race, and Hispanic origin	Total	Elementary		High School		College				Percent:	
		None–4th grade	5th–8th grade	9th–11th grade	High school graduate	Some college no degree	Associate degree	Bachelor's degree	Advanced degree	High school graduate or more	Bachelor's degree or more

BLACK

Both Sexes

18 years and over	22 772	432	1 305	4 110	8 192	4 724	1 343	1 944	722	74.3	11.7
Metropolitan areas	19 655	318	995	3 292	7 011	4 342	1 208	1 808	681	76.6	12.7
Metropolitan areas 1,000,000+	12 790	163	582	2 159	4 520	2 870	730	1 275	492	77.3	13.8
Central city	8 157	136	430	1 663	2 922	1 702	418	617	269	72.7	10.9
Balance of MSA	4 633	27	152	496	1 598	1 167	313	658	222	85.4	19.0
Metropolitan areas < 1,000,000	6 864	155	413	1 133	2 491	1 472	477	533	190	75.2	10.5
Central city	4 293	96	249	681	1 578	909	320	332	128	76.1	10.7
Balance of MSA	2 571	59	164	452	913	563	158	200	61	73.7	10.2
Nonmetropolitan area	3 118	114	310	819	1 181	383	135	137	41	60.2	5.7
25 years and over	19 072	411	1 274	3 106	6 835	3 641	1 272	1 817	717	74.9	13.3
Metropolitan areas	16 585	303	971	2 490	5 918	3 387	1 137	1 702	676	77.3	14.3
Metropolitan areas 1,000,000+	10 816	151	566	1 644	3 831	2 248	692	1 192	492	78.2	15.6
Central city	6 868	124	414	1 275	2 490	1 330	392	574	269	73.6	12.3
Balance of MSA	3 948	27	152	368	1 342	918	300	618	222	86.1	21.3
Metropolitan areas < 1,000,000	5 769	153	405	846	2 087	1 139	444	511	185	75.7	12.1
Central city	3 619	93	240	516	1 308	721	297	316	126	76.5	12.2
Balance of MSA	2 150	59	164	330	779	418	147	195	59	74.3	11.8
Nonmetropolitan area	2 487	108	303	616	917	254	135	115	41	58.7	6.3
25 to 44 years	10 765	81	209	1 369	4 171	2 580	830	1 228	299	84.6	14.2
Metropolitan areas	9 463	78	165	1 081	3 555	2 416	728	1 153	287	86.0	15.2
Metropolitan areas 1,000,000+	6 146	42	115	709	2 248	1 596	427	807	204	85.9	16.4
Central city	3 740	29	72	553	1 445	916	235	377	113	82.5	13.1
Balance of MSA	2 406	13	42	155	803	679	192	430	91	91.3	21.6
Metropolitan areas < 1,000,000	3 318	37	50	373	1 307	821	302	346	83	86.1	12.0
Central city	2 049	22	28	236	777	508	207	220	50	86.0	13.2
Balance of MSA	1 269	14	22	136	530	313	95	126	33	86.4	12.5
Nonmetropolitan area	1 302	3	44	288	616	163	102	75	12	74.3	6.7
45 to 64 years	5 691	108	442	1 117	2 018	847	372	474	312	70.7	13.8
Metropolitan areas	4 896	74	312	876	1 781	779	347	442	286	74.2	14.9
Metropolitan areas 1,000,000+	3 246	43	180	556	1 192	521	223	310	220	76.0	16.3
Central city	2 074	38	143	420	766	321	123	157	107	71.0	12.7
Balance of MSA	1 172	5	38	136	426	200	100	153	113	84.7	22.7
Metropolitan areas < 1,000,000	1 650	31	131	319	589	259	124	131	66	70.8	11.9
Central city	1 025	17	83	180	387	163	76	70	48	72.6	11.5
Balance of MSA	626	14	48	139	202	96	48	62	18	67.9	12.7
Nonmetropolitan area	794	34	130	241	237	68	25	32	27	49.0	7.4
65 years and over	2 616	222	623	620	646	214	69	115	106	44.0	8.5
Metropolitan areas	2 225	151	495	533	582	191	61	108	104	47.0	9.5
Metropolitan areas 1,000,000+	1 424	66	271	379	391	131	43	75	68	49.7	10.0
Central city	1 054	57	199	302	279	93	35	40	50	47.0	8.5
Balance of MSA	370	9	72	77	112	38	8	35	18	57.3	14.3
Metropolitan areas < 1,000,000	801	85	223	154	191	60	19	33	36	42.3	8.6
Central city	545	54	129	100	144	50	14	26	28	48.1	9.8
Balance of MSA	256	31	94	54	47	10	5	8	8	29.9	6.0
Nonmetropolitan area	391	71	129	88	64	22	8	8	2	26.6	2.5

See footnotes at end of table.

Table B-10. Educational Attainment of Persons 18 Years Old and Over, by Metropolitan and Nonmetropolitan Status, Age, Sex, Race, and Hispanic Origin: March 1997 — Continued

(Numbers in thousands. Civilian noninstitutional population.)

Metropolitan status, age, sex, race, and Hispanic origin	Total	Elementary		High School		College				Percent:	
		None-4th grade	5th-8th grade	9th-11th grade	High school graduate	Some college no degree	Associate degree	Bachelor's degree	Advanced degree	High school graduate or more	Bachelor's degree or more
Male											
18 years and over	10 183	270	613	1 904	3 740	2 103	463	800	290	72.6	10.7
Metropolitan areas	8 797	192	476	1 512	3 223	1 932	428	753	282	75.2	11.8
Metropolitan areas 1,000,000+	5 803	92	275	1 011	2 127	1 309	267	514	208	76.3	12.4
Central city	3 567	71	185	752	1 345	737	151	221	105	71.7	9.1
Balance of MSA	2 236	21	89	259	783	571	116	293	103	83.5	17.7
Metropolitan areas < 1,000,000	2 994	100	201	501	1 095	623	162	239	73	73.2	10.4
Central city	1 793	62	110	278	686	339	117	144	56	74.9	11.2
Balance of MSA	1 201	38	91	222	409	284	45	95	17	70.7	9.3
Nonmetropolitan area	1 386	78	137	392	518	171	34	47	9	56.2	4.0
25 years and over	8 446	253	588	1 401	3 085	1 622	444	763	290	73.5	12.5
Metropolitan areas	7 367	181	457	1 106	2 713	1 498	410	721	282	76.3	13.6
Metropolitan areas 1,000,000+	4 861	84	260	756	1 785	1 023	256	489	208	77.4	14.3
Central city	2 946	63	170	557	1 133	568	144	206	105	73.2	10.6
Balance of MSA	1 915	21	89	199	652	455	112	283	103	83.8	20.2
Metropolitan areas < 1,000,000	2 506	97	197	350	928	475	153	232	73	74.3	12.2
Central city	1 520	59	106	208	572	270	111	137	56	75.4	12.7
Balance of MSA	986	38	91	141	356	205	43	95	17	72.5	11.4
Nonmetropolitan area	1 079	72	130	296	372	124	34	42	9	53.8	4.7
25 to 44 years	4 897	53	105	677	2 029	1 146	257	500	129	82.9	12.9
Metropolitan areas	4 358	51	100	532	1 783	1 069	231	469	123	84.3	13.6
Metropolitan areas 1,000,000+	2 883	28	70	364	1 159	720	138	315	88	84.0	14.0
Central city	1 705	16	41	264	723	397	90	137	39	81.2	10.3
Balance of MSA	1 177	12	29	100	437	324	49	178	49	88.0	19.3
Metropolitan areas < 1,000,000	1 475	23	30	168	623	349	93	154	35	85.0	12.8
Central city	862	14	16	88	360	196	73	92	23	86.3	13.4
Balance of MSA	613	9	14	80	263	152	20	62	12	83.2	12.1
Nonmetropolitan area	539	3	5	145	246	77	26	31	6	71.7	6.9
45 to 64 years	2 535	77	218	502	847	375	167	228	121	68.6	13.7
Metropolitan areas	2 156	46	145	393	735	339	161	219	118	72.9	15.6
Metropolitan areas 1,000,000+	1 444	23	83	255	499	239	104	149	91	75.0	16.6
Central city	857	18	58	188	317	128	43	59	46	69.2	12.2
Balance of MSA	587	5	25	67	182	111	61	90	46	83.5	23.1
Metropolitan areas < 1,000,000	712	22	63	138	236	100	57	70	27	68.7	13.6
Central city	436	15	35	85	156	50	36	38	22	69.0	13.6
Balance of MSA	276	8	28	53	81	49	21	32	5	68.1	13.6
Nonmetropolitan area	379	31	73	110	112	37	6	9	2	43.8	3.0
65 years and over	1 014	123	264	221	209	100	20	35	40	39.9	7.5
Metropolitan areas	853	84	212	180	195	90	18	33	40	44.2	8.6
Metropolitan areas 1,000,000+	535	32	107	137	127	63	14	26	29	48.3	10.2
Central city	384	28	72	105	94	43	12	11	21	46.7	8.1
Balance of MSA	151	4	35	32	33	21	2	15	8	52.3	15.5
Metropolitan areas < 1,000,000	318	52	105	43	68	27	4	8	11	37.2	6.0
Central city	222	30	55	35	57	24	2	7	11	45.7	8.4
Balance of MSA	97	22	50	8	12	3	2	1	—	17.6	0.6
Nonmetropolitan area	161	39	53	41	14	10	2	2	—	17.6	1.3

See footnotes at end of table.

Table B-10. Educational Attainment of Persons 18 Years Old and Over, by Metropolitan and Nonmetropolitan Status, Age, Sex, Race, and Hispanic Origin: March 1997 — Continued

(Numbers in thousands. Civilian noninstitutional population.)

Metropolitan status, age, sex, race, and Hispanic origin	Total	Elementary		High School		College				Percent:	
		None-4th grade	5th-8th grade	9th-11th grade	High school graduate	Some college no degree	Associate degree	Bachelor's degree	Advanced degree	High school graduate or more	Bachelor's degree or more
Female											
18 years and over	12 589	161	692	2 207	4 452	2 621	880	1 144	432	75.7	12.5
Metropolitan areas	10 857	126	519	1 780	3 789	2 410	780	1 055	400	77.7	13.4
Metropolitan areas 1,000,000+	6 987	70	307	1 148	2 393	1 561	464	761	283	78.2	14.9
Central city	4 591	64	245	911	1 577	965	267	397	164	73.4	12.2
Balance of MSA	2 397	6	63	237	815	596	197	364	119	87.3	20.2
Metropolitan areas < 1,000,000	3 870	55	212	632	1 396	849	316	294	116	76.8	10.6
Central city	2 500	34	139	402	892	570	203	188	72	77.0	10.4
Balance of MSA	1 370	21	73	230	504	279	113	105	44	76.3	10.9
Nonmetropolitan area	1 732	36	173	427	663	211	101	90	32	63.3	7.0
25 years and over	10 626	158	686	1 704	3 750	2 010	828	1 054	427	76.0	13.9
Metropolitan areas	9 218	123	514	1 384	3 205	1 889	727	981	395	78.1	14.9
Metropolitan areas 1,000,000+	5 954	67	306	888	2 046	1 225	436	702	283	78.8	16.6
Central city	3 922	61	243	719	1 357	762	248	368	164	73.9	13.6
Balance of MSA	2 032	6	63	169	690	463	188	334	119	88.3	22.3
Metropolitan areas < 1,000,000	3 263	55	208	496	1 159	664	291	279	111	76.7	11.9
Central city	2 099	34	135	308	736	451	186	179	70	77.3	11.8
Balance of MSA	1 165	21	73	188	423	213	104	100	42	75.7	12.1
Nonmetropolitan area	1 409	36	173	320	545	130	101	73	32	62.5	7.4
25 to 44 years	5 868	28	103	691	2 142	1 434	573	728	170	86.0	15.3
Metropolitan areas	5 106	28	65	549	1 772	1 347	497	683	164	87.4	16.6
Metropolitan areas 1,000,000+	3 263	14	45	344	1 089	875	288	492	116	87.7	18.6
Central city	2 035	12	32	289	722	519	145	240	74	83.6	15.5
Balance of MSA	1 228	1	13	55	367	356	143	252	41	94.3	23.8
Metropolitan areas < 1,000,000	1 843	14	20	204	683	472	209	192	48	87.1	13.0
Central city	1 187	8	12	148	417	312	134	128	27	85.8	13.1
Balance of MSA	656	6	8	56	267	160	74	63	21	80.3	12.0
Nonmetropolitan area	762	—	39	143	369	86	76	44	6	76.2	6.5
45 to 64 years	3 156	31	224	614	1 171	472	205	246	192	72.5	13.9
Metropolitan areas	2 740	28	166	483	1 046	441	186	223	167	75.3	14.3
Metropolitan areas 1,000,000+	1 802	20	97	302	693	282	119	162	129	76.8	16.1
Central city	1 217	20	85	232	449	192	80	99	61	72.4	13.1
Balance of MSA	585	—	13	70	244	90	39	63	68	85.9	22.4
Metropolitan areas < 1,000,000	938	8	69	181	353	159	67	61	39	72.4	10.7
Central city	589	2	48	95	231	113	41	32	26	75.3	9.9
Balance of MSA	349	6	21	86	121	46	27	29	13	67.7	11.9
Nonmetropolitan area	416	3	58	131	126	31	19	23	24	53.8	11.4
65 years and over	1 603	99	359	399	437	113	49	80	66	46.5	9.1
Metropolitan areas	1 372	67	283	353	387	101	43	74	63	48.8	10.0
Metropolitan areas 1,000,000+	889	34	164	242	264	68	29	49	39	50.5	9.9
Central city	670	29	127	198	185	50	23	29	29	47.2	8.7
Balance of MSA	219	5	37	44	79	18	6	20	10	60.7	13.5
Metropolitan areas < 1,000,000	483	33	119	111	123	33	14	25	24	45.7	10.3
Central city	323	24	74	65	88	27	11	18	17	49.7	10.8
Balance of MSA	159	9	44	46	35	7	3	7	8	37.5	9.3
Nonmetropolitan area	231	32	76	46	50	12	6	5	2	32.8	3.3

See footnotes at end of table.

Table B-10. Educational Attainment of Persons 18 Years Old and Over, by Metropolitan and Nonmetropolitan Status, Age, Sex, Race, and Hispanic Origin: March 1997 — Continued

(Numbers in thousands. Civilian noninstitutional population.)

Metropolitan status, age, sex, race, and Hispanic origin	Total	Elementary		High School		College				Percent:	
		None-4th grade	5th-8th grade	9th-11th grade	High school graduate	Some college no degree	Associate degree	Bachelor's degree	Advanced degree	High school graduate or more	Bachelor's degree or more
HISPANIC ORIGIN [1]											
Both Sexes											
18 years and over	19 103	1 546	3 461	3 624	5 005	2 892	889	1 228	457	54.8	8.8
Metropolitan areas	17 431	1 338	3 146	3 270	4 564	2 688	816	1 174	434	55.5	9.2
Metropolitan areas 1,000,000+	11 544	829	2 131	2 226	2 996	1 758	530	777	296	55.1	9.3
Central city	6 066	522	1 260	1 307	1 535	818	202	307	115	49.1	7.0
Balance of MSA	5 478	308	871	918	1 461	940	328	470	181	61.7	11.9
Metropolitan areas < 1,000,000	5 887	508	1 015	1 045	1 569	930	286	397	138	56.4	9.1
Central city	3 131	225	497	595	844	521	161	209	78	57.9	9.2
Balance of MSA	2 756	283	518	450	725	408	125	188	59	54.6	9.0
Nonmetropolitan area	1 672	208	316	354	440	204	73	53	23	47.5	4.6
25 years and over	15 476	1 449	3 054	2 503	4 011	2 054	805	1 153	448	54.7	10.3
Metropolitan areas	14 158	1 259	2 782	2 267	3 670	1 914	736	1 104	426	55.4	10.8
Metropolitan areas 1,000,000+	9 429	777	1 884	1 585	2 399	1 299	471	722	293	55.0	10.8
Central city	4 887	486	1 122	908	1 236	575	167	281	113	48.5	8.1
Balance of MSA	4 542	291	762	678	1 162	724	304	441	180	61.9	13.7
Metropolitan areas < 1,000,000	4 729	483	898	682	1 272	615	265	381	133	56.4	10.9
Central city	2 517	220	430	406	699	335	146	203	78	58.1	11.2
Balance of MSA	2 212	263	468	276	572	280	119	178	55	54.5	10.5
Nonmetropolitan area	1 318	189	272	236	340	140	69	49	22	47.1	5.4
25 to 44 years	9 882	522	1 631	1 736	2 763	1 551	575	843	262	60.6	11.2
Metropolitan areas	9 066	444	1 492	1 570	2 526	1 443	530	808	253	61.3	11.7
Metropolitan areas 1,000,000+	6 053	295	1 046	1 092	1 638	967	326	526	163	59.8	11.4
Central city	3 116	173	632	618	861	431	111	222	68	54.3	9.3
Balance of MSA	2 938	122	414	474	777	535	216	304	95	65.6	13.6
Metropolitan areas < 1,000,000	3 013	149	446	478	888	477	204	282	90	64.4	12.4
Central city	1 581	63	200	286	471	259	109	143	51	65.3	12.2
Balance of MSA	1 432	86	246	192	417	218	95	139	40	63.5	12.5
Nonmetropolitan area	816	79	139	166	237	107	44	35	9	53.0	5.3
45 to 64 years	4 079	514	975	574	981	423	204	261	147	49.4	10.0
Metropolitan areas	3 706	436	877	531	896	395	181	254	136	50.2	10.5
Metropolitan areas 1,000,000+	2 471	253	563	390	595	281	125	166	99	51.2	10.7
Central city	1 265	141	335	236	292	127	49	46	38	43.7	6.7
Balance of MSA	1 206	112	228	153	303	154	76	119	62	59.1	15.0
Metropolitan areas < 1,000,000	1 235	183	314	141	301	114	56	88	36	48.3	10.1
Central city	643	67	151	74	178	63	35	50	24	54.6	11.5
Balance of MSA	591	116	164	67	123	51	21	38	12	41.4	8.5
Nonmetropolitan area	373	78	98	43	85	28	23	7	11	41.5	5.0
65 years and over	1 516	412	448	194	267	81	26	49	39	30.4	5.8
Metropolitan areas	1 386	380	412	166	248	76	25	42	37	30.8	5.7
Metropolitan areas 1,000,000+	905	229	275	103	166	51	20	31	30	32.9	6.7
Central city	507	171	155	53	83	16	7	13	7	25.0	3.9
Balance of MSA	398	57	120	50	83	35	13	19	23	43.0	10.3
Metropolitan areas < 1,000,000	481	151	138	63	82	24	5	11	7	26.9	3.7
Central city	293	89	79	46	49	13	2	10	3	26.6	4.6
Balance of MSA	188	62	59	17	33	12	3	1	4	27.3	2.4
Nonmetropolitan area	130	33	36	28	19	5	1	7	2	26.1	6.6

See footnotes at end of table.

Table B-10. Educational Attainment of Persons 18 Years Old and Over, by Metropolitan and Nonmetropolitan Status, Age, Sex, Race, and Hispanic Origin: March 1997 — Continued

(Numbers in thousands. Civilian noninstitutional population.)

Metropolitan status, age, sex, race, and Hispanic origin	Total	Elementary		High School		College				Percent:	
		None-4th grade	5th-8th grade	9th-11th grade	High school graduate	Some college no degree	Associate degree	Bachelor's degree	Advanced degree	High school graduate or more	Bachelor's degree or more
Male											
18 years and over	9 741	768	1 781	1 916	2 490	1 494	424	591	278	54.2	8.9
Metropolitan areas	8 843	635	1 605	1 727	2 264	1 400	380	567	264	55.1	9.4
Metropolitan areas											
1,000,000+	5 896	388	1 097	1 200	1 479	926	240	385	180	54.5	9.6
Central city	3 069	221	651	693	752	409	99	164	80	49.0	7.9
Balance of MSA	2 827	167	446	507	727	517	142	221	100	60.4	11.4
Metropolitan areas <											
1,000,000	2 947	247	508	528	785	474	140	182	84	56.5	9.0
Central city	1 517	102	237	289	404	263	76	94	51	58.6	9.6
Balance of MSA	1 430	145	271	239	381	211	63	88	33	54.2	8.5
Nonmetropolitan area	898	133	176	189	225	94	44	23	13	44.5	4.1
25 years and over	7 755	712	1 526	1 203	2 003	1 045	384	548	274	54.9	10.8
Metropolitan areas	7 048	590	1 384	1 139	1 827	980	342	525	262	55.8	11.2
Metropolitan areas											
1,000,000+	4 719	361	939	795	1 197	683	211	353	179	55.6	11.3
Central city	2 417	204	563	441	629	275	81	144	79	50.0	9.2
Balance of MSA	2 301	157	376	354	568	407	130	208	100	61.4	13.4
Metropolitan areas <											
1,000,000	2 330	229	444	344	630	297	131	172	83	56.3	10.9
Central city	1 183	97	197	190	331	156	69	91	51	59.1	12.0
Balance of MSA	1 146	132	247	153	299	141	61	81	31	53.5	9.8
Nonmetropolitan area	707	122	142	124	176	65	42	23	12	45.0	5.0
25 to 44 years	5 156	290	881	928	1 452	790	270	396	150	59.3	10.6
Metropolitan areas	4 703	237	800	836	1 327	738	242	379	144	60.2	11.1
Metropolitan areas											
1,000,000+	3 172	156	571	575	866	510	147	255	93	59.0	11.0
Central city	1 641	85	357	313	466	203	55	117	45	54.0	9.9
Balance of MSA	1 531	70	214	262	400	306	92	137	49	64.3	12.2
Metropolitan areas <											
1,000,000	1 531	82	229	261	462	229	95	124	51	62.7	11.4
Central city	757	34	96	136	232	123	45	61	31	64.9	12.1
Balance of MSA	774	48	133	125	230	106	49	63	20	60.5	10.7
Nonmetropolitan area	453	52	81	92	124	52	28	17	6	50.2	5.0
45 to 64 years	1 960	257	449	265	441	213	102	132	99	50.4	11.8
Metropolitan areas	1 762	208	401	241	398	201	88	129	95	51.8	12.7
Metropolitan areas											
1,000,000+	1 182	119	256	183	269	148	56	84	68	52.8	12.9
Central city	563	51	145	104	133	62	22	17	30	46.8	8.3
Balance of MSA	619	68	111	80	136	86	34	67	38	58.3	17.0
Metropolitan areas <											
1,000,000	580	89	145	58	130	53	32	45	27	49.6	12.4
Central city	289	27	56	38	75	26	22	27	19	58.3	15.9
Balance of MSA	290	63	89	20	54	28	11	18	8	40.8	8.9
Nonmetropolitan area	198	49	48	24	43	12	14	3	4	38.4	3.7
65 years and over	640	165	196	70	110	42	12	20	25	32.6	7.1
Metropolitan areas	583	145	183	62	101	40	12	17	23	33.2	6.9
Metropolitan areas											
1,000,000+	364	87	113	37	62	25	8	14	18	35.1	8.9
Central city	213	68	61	24	31	10	4	10	5	27.9	7.0
Balance of MSA	152	19	52	13	31	15	4	4	13	45.2	11.4
Metropolitan areas <											
1,000,000	219	58	70	25	39	15	4	3	5	29.9	3.7
Central city	137	36	45	17	24	8	2	3	1	28.4	3.3
Balance of MSA	82	22	25	8	15	7	1	—	4	32.5	4.3
Nonmetropolitan area	56	20	13	8	9	1	—	3	2	(B)	(B)

See footnotes at end of table.

Table B-10. Educational Attainment of Persons 18 Years Old and Over, by Metropolitan and Nonmetropolitan Status, Age, Sex, Race, and Hispanic Origin: March 1997 — Continued

(Numbers in thousands. Civilian noninstitutional population.)

Metropolitan status, age, sex, race, and Hispanic origin	Total	Elementary		High School		College				Percent:	
		None-4th grade	5th-8th grade	9th-11th grade	High school graduate	Some college no degree	Associate degree	Bachelor's degree	Advanced degree	High school graduate or more	Bachelor's degree or more
Female											
18 years and over	9 362	778	1 680	1 708	2 515	1 398	466	637	180	55.5	8.7
Metropolitan areas	8 588	703	1 541	1 543	2 300	1 288	437	607	170	55.9	9.0
Metropolitan areas 1,000,000+	5 648	442	1 034	1 026	1 516	832	290	392	116	55.7	9.0
Central city	2 997	300	608	614	782	409	104	143	35	49.2	6.0
Balance of MSA	2 651	141	425	411	734	423	186	249	81	63.1	12.4
Metropolitan areas < 1,000,000	2 940	261	507	517	784	456	146	215	54	56.3	9.1
Central city	1 614	123	260	306	440	258	85	115	27	57.3	8.8
Balance of MSA	1 327	138	247	211	344	198	62	100	27	55.0	9.5
Nonmetropolitan area	773	75	139	165	215	110	29	30	10	50.9	5.1
25 years and over	7 721	736	1 528	1 240	2 007	1 009	421	605	174	54.6	10.1
Metropolitan areas	7 110	669	1 398	1 128	1 843	934	394	579	164	55.1	10.4
Metropolitan areas 1,000,000+	4 711	416	945	790	1 202	616	260	370	113	54.3	10.3
Central city	2 470	281	559	467	607	300	86	137	34	47.1	6.9
Balance of MSA	2 241	134	386	324	595	317	174	233	79	62.4	13.9
Metropolitan areas < 1,000,000	2 399	253	453	338	642	318	134	209	51	56.4	10.8
Central city	1 333	123	232	216	368	178	77	112	27	57.2	10.4
Balance of MSA	1 066	130	221	122	273	140	58	97	24	55.5	11.3
Nonmetropolitan area	611	67	130	112	164	75	27	26	10	49.5	5.8
25 to 44 years	4 726	233	750	808	1 311	760	304	447	112	62.1	11.8
Metropolitan areas	4 363	206	692	734	1 199	705	288	429	109	62.6	12.3
Metropolitan areas 1,000,000+	2 881	139	475	517	772	457	179	271	70	60.7	11.8
Central city	1 474	88	275	305	395	228	55	105	23	54.7	8.7
Balance of MSA	1 407	52	200	213	377	229	124	166	47	67.0	15.2
Metropolitan areas < 1,000,000	1 482	67	217	217	427	248	109	158	39	66.2	13.3
Central city	824	30	103	150	240	136	63	82	20	65.7	12.4
Balance of MSA	658	37	113	67	187	112	46	76	19	66.9	14.5
Nonmetropolitan area	363	26	58	74	112	56	16	18	3	56.5	5.7
45 to 64 years	2 119	256	526	309	539	210	102	129	48	48.5	8.3
Metropolitan areas	1 944	228	477	290	497	194	93	124	41	48.8	8.5
Metropolitan areas 1,000,000+	1 289	135	307	206	326	133	69	81	32	49.7	8.8
Central city	702	90	190	133	159	65	27	29	8	41.1	5.3
Balance of MSA	587	44	117	74	167	68	42	52	23	59.9	12.9
Metropolitan areas < 1,000,000	655	93	169	84	171	61	24	43	10	47.1	8.0
Central city	354	41	94	37	103	38	14	23	5	51.5	8.0
Balance of MSA	301	53	75	47	69	23	10	20	4	42.0	8.1
Nonmetropolitan area	175	28	49	18	42	16	9	4	7	45.0	6.4
65 years and over	876	247	252	124	157	39	15	29	14	28.8	4.8
Metropolitan areas	803	235	230	104	147	35	13	25	14	29.2	4.8
Metropolitan areas 1,000,000+	541	142	162	66	103	26	12	17	12	31.5	5.3
Central city	294	103	94	29	52	6	3	2	3	22.9	1.7
Balance of MSA	247	39	68	37	51	20	8	15	9	41.7	9.6
Metropolitan areas < 1,000,000	262	93	68	38	43	9	1	8	2	24.4	3.8
Central city	156	53	34	39	26	4	—	7	2	25.1	5.8
Balance of MSA	106	40	33	8	17	5	1	1	—	23.3	0.9
Nonmetropolitan area	73	12	23	20	10	4	1	4	—	(B)	(B)

Source: March 1997 Current Population Survey, Education and Social Stratification Branch, U.S. Bureau of the Census.

1. May be of any race.

— Represents zero or rounds to zero.

(B) Base less than 75,000.

Table B-11. Educational Attainment of Persons 18 Years Old and Over, by Metropolitan and Nonmetropolitan Residence, and Region March 1997

(Numbers in thousands. Civilian noninstitutional population.)

Residence and region	Total	Elementary		High School		College				Percent:	
		None-4th grade	5th-8th grade	9th-11th grade	High school graduate	Some college no degree	Associate degree	Bachelor's degree	Advanced degree	High school graduate or more	Bachelor's degree or more
NORTHEAST											
18 years and over	38 509	512	2 050	4 363	13 517	6 150	2 483	6 255	3 178	82.0	24.5
Metropolitan areas	34 434	496	1 802	3 907	11 738	5 579	2 169	5 814	2 929	82.0	25.4
Metropolitan areas											
1,000,000+	19 197	324	1 029	2 173	6 263	3 065	1 026	3 531	1 786	81.6	27.7
Central city	7 792	256	673	1 294	2 291	1 220	305	1 174	579	71.5	22.5
Balance of MSA	11 405	68	356	878	3 972	1 845	722	2 357	1 207	88.6	31.2
Metropolitan areas <											
1,000,000	15 238	172	774	1 734	5 475	2 514	1 143	2 283	1 143	82.4	22.5
Central city	3 761	78	311	611	1 359	513	241	430	218	73.4	17.2
Balance of MSA	11 477	94	462	1 123	4 116	2 001	902	1 854	925	85.4	24.2
Nonmetropolitan area	4 074	16	248	456	1 779	571	314	440	250	82.3	16.9
MIDWEST											
18 years and over	45 209	247	2 081	4 628	16 889	8 733	3 285	6 521	2 825	84.6	20.7
Metropolitan areas	33 659	206	1 274	3 296	11 853	6 775	2 448	5 405	2 401	85.8	23.2
Metropolitan areas											
1,000,000+	19 979	149	780	2 068	6 653	4 018	1 358	3 417	1 536	85.0	24.8
Central city	6 647	95	363	962	2 224	1 281	343	921	458	78.6	20.8
Balance of MSA	13 332	54	418	1 106	4 430	2 737	1 015	2 495	1 078	88.2	26.8
Metropolitan areas <											
1,000,000	13 680	57	494	1 229	5 199	2 758	1 091	1 988	865	87.0	20.9
Central city	5 476	40	222	619	1 882	1 059	399	832	423	83.9	22.9
Balance of MSA	8 204	17	272	610	3 317	1 699	692	1 156	442	89.1	19.5
Nonmetropolitan area	11 550	41	807	1 331	5 037	1 957	837	1 117	424	81.1	13.3
SOUTH											
18 years and over	68 902	1 216	4 438	8 978	23 089	13 228	4 228	9 273	4 452	78.8	19.9
Metropolitan areas	52 049	816	2 845	6 054	16 801	10 507	3 342	7 842	3 842	81.3	22.4
Metropolitan areas											
1,000,000+	23 398	298	1 222	2 680	7 162	4 778	1 416	3 829	2 012	82.0	25.0
Central city	7 829	174	519	1 117	2 415	1 502	349	1 156	597	76.9	22.4
Balance of MSA	15 569	125	703	1 562	4 747	3 276	1 067	2 673	1 415	84.6	26.3
Metropolitan areas <											
1,000,000	28 651	517	1 623	3 375	9 639	5 729	1 925	4 013	1 830	80.8	20.4
Central city	11 063	237	567	1 192	3 427	2 370	689	1 720	859	81.9	23.3
Balance of MSA	17 589	280	1 055	2 182	6 213	3 359	1 236	2 293	971	80.0	18.6
Nonmetropolitan area	16 853	400	1 593	2 923	6 288	2 721	887	1 431	610	70.8	12.1
WEST											
18 years and over	42 948	1 008	2 497	4 293	11 874	9 931	3 340	7 040	2 966	81.8	23.3
Metropolitan areas	37 339	889	2 185	3 605	10 032	8 590	2 880	6 422	2 736	82.1	24.5
Metropolitan areas											
1,000,000+	23 537	568	1 443	2 209	6 072	5 130	1 831	4 382	1 903	82.1	26.7
Central city	9 733	329	704	1 044	2 369	2 027	711	1 751	797	78.7	26.2
Balance of MSA	13 804	239	739	1 164	3 702	3 103	1 120	2 631	1 106	84.5	27.1
Metropolitan areas <											
1,000,000	13 802	322	742	1 396	3 961	3 460	1 049	2 040	833	82.2	20.8
Central city	6 274	120	331	599	1 698	1 633	478	995	419	83.3	22.5
Balance of MSA	7 528	201	411	797	2 263	1 827	571	1 044	414	81.3	19.4
Nonmetropolitan area	5 609	119	312	688	1 841	1 341	460	618	231	80.1	15.1

Source: March 1997 Current Population Survey, Education and Social Stratification Branch, U.S. Bureau of the Census.

— Represents zero or rounds to zero.

Table B-12.   Educational Attainment of Persons 18 Years Old and Over, by Age, Sex, Race, and Hispanic Origin, for Regions and Divisions: March 1997

(Numbers in thousands. Civilian noninstitutional population.)

Age, sex, race, Hispanic origin, region, and division	Total	Elementary		High School		College				Percent:	
		None-4th grade	5th-8th grade	9th-11th grade	High school graduate	Some college no degree	Associate degree	Bachelor's degree	Advanced degree	High school graduate or more	Bachelor's degree or more
NORTHEAST											
All Races											
Both sexes											
18 years and over	38 509	512	2 050	4 363	13 517	6 150	2 483	6 255	3 178	82.0	24.5
18 to 24 years	4 477	26	85	868	1 322	1 616	172	381	8	78.1	8.7
25 years and over	34 031	486	1 965	3 495	12 195	4 534	2 311	5 874	3 170	82.5	26.6
25 to 34 years	7 715	54	160	586	2 584	1 175	675	1 893	588	89.6	32.2
35 to 44 years	8 592	65	175	621	3 025	1 362	705	1 767	872	90.0	30.7
45 to 54 years	6 604	68	261	484	2 334	908	511	1 107	932	87.7	30.9
55 to 64 years	4 428	98	300	563	1 796	481	215	529	445	78.3	22.0
65 years and over	6 692	201	1 069	1 242	2 456	609	206	577	332	62.5	13.6
Males											
18 years and over	18 247	233	949	2 124	6 102	2 991	1 034	3 043	1 770	81.9	26.4
18 to 24 years	2 252	13	59	514	633	813	74	144	3	74.0	6.5
25 years and over	15 995	221	890	1 611	5 469	2 177	960	2 900	1 768	83.0	29.2
25 to 34 years	3 728	26	92	338	1 305	545	285	861	276	87.8	30.5
35 to 44 years	4 230	36	90	330	1 478	662	288	880	467	89.2	31.8
45 to 54 years	3 209	40	137	217	1 018	446	222	594	536	87.7	35.2
55 to 64 years	2 113	24	152	244	814	241	89	264	286	80.1	26.0
65 years and over	2 715	95	418	482	855	283	77	301	204	63.3	18.6
Females											
18 years and over	20 261	279	1 101	2 239	7 415	3 160	1 449	3 211	1 408	82.1	22.8
18 to 24 years	2 225	13	26	355	689	803	97	237	6	82.3	10.9
25 years and over	18 036	265	1 075	1 884	6 727	2 357	1 352	2 974	1 402	82.1	24.3
25 to 34 years	3 988	28	68	248	1 280	630	390	1 032	313	91.4	33.7
35 to 44 years	4 362	29	84	291	1 548	700	418	887	406	90.7	29.6
45 to 54 years	3 395	28	124	267	1 316	462	289	514	396	87.6	26.8
55 to 64 years	2 315	75	148	319	982	240	126	265	160	76.6	18.4
65 years and over	3 976	105	651	760	1 601	326	129	276	128	61.9	10.2
White											
Both sexes											
18 years and over	32 804	359	1 669	3 393	11 633	5 163	2 190	5 540	2 857	83.5	25.6
18 to 24 years	3 691	18	63	637	1 106	1 356	159	342	8	80.5	9.5
25 years and over	29 113	341	1 606	2 755	10 526	3 807	2 031	5 197	2 848	83.8	27.6
25 to 34 years	6 289	28	112	396	2 123	917	573	1 649	492	91.5	34.0
35 to 44 years	7 190	49	131	461	2 527	1 114	608	1 535	766	91.1	32.0
45 to 54 years	5 704	54	202	344	1 998	760	476	1 009	861	89.5	32.8
55 to 64 years	3 854	57	239	440	1 606	444	190	460	418	80.9	22.8
65 years and over	6 075	153	922	1 115	2 272	572	185	545	311	64.0	14.1
Black											
Both sexes											
18 years and over	4 347	93	283	867	1 556	834	241	349	123	71.4	10.9
18 to 24 years	644	8	18	209	178	207	11	14	—	63.6	2.2
25 years and over	3 702	85	265	658	1 378	627	231	334	123	72.8	12.4
25 to 34 years	1 015	19	30	163	376	229	76	98	25	79.1	12.1
35 to 44 years	1 037	11	35	135	413	211	77	124	32	82.6	15.0
45 to 54 years	711	4	40	131	273	130	33	62	38	75.4	14.0
55 to 64 years	430	14	41	111	164	27	25	32	17	61.4	11.2
65 years and over	509	37	119	118	152	30	20	19	12	46.1	6.2

See footnotes at end of table.

Table B-12. Educational Attainment of Persons 18 Years Old and Over, by Age, Sex, Race, and Hispanic Origin, for Regions and Divisions: March 1997 — Continued

(Numbers in thousands. Civilian noninstitutional population.)

Age, sex, race, Hispanic origin, region, and division	Total	Elementary		High School		College				Percent:	
		None-4th grade	5th-8th grade	9th-11th grade	High school graduate	Some college no degree	Associate degree	Bachelor's degree	Advanced degree	High school graduate or more	Bachelor's degree or more
Hispanic origin[1]											
Both sexes											
18 years and over	3 122	194	521	676	893	438	123	204	73	55.4	8.9
18 to 24 years	564	18	46	195	131	141	17	18	—	54.1	3.1
25 years and over	2 557	177	475	481	762	297	106	186	73	55.7	10.1
25 to 34 years	824	23	86	157	269	130	44	94	21	67.7	13.9
35 to 44 years	691	31	91	136	233	98	30	51	21	62.6	10.4
45 to 54 years	426	13	107	79	119	40	21	25	22	53.3	10.9
55 to 64 years	356	39	91	86	95	20	6	14	6	39.5	5.5
65 years and over	260	72	99	23	46	9	5	3	3	25.4	2.3
MIDWEST											
All Races											
Both sexes											
18 years and over	45 209	247	2 081	4 628	16 889	8 733	3 285	6 521	2 825	84.6	20.7
18 to 24 years	5 704	9	64	1 019	1 792	2 096	273	431	21	80.9	7.9
25 years and over	39 505	238	2 017	3 609	15 098	6 637	3 012	6 090	2 804	85.2	22.5
25 to 34 years	9 117	23	116	645	3 051	1 790	870	2 082	540	91.4	28.8
35 to 44 years	10 221	40	151	693	4 028	1 896	990	1 671	754	91.4	23.7
45 to 54 years	7 528	50	173	474	2 860	1 324	631	1 236	782	90.8	26.8
55 to 64 years	5 010	30	313	521	2 280	667	252	532	416	82.8	18.9
65 years and over	7 628	96	1 264	1 277	2 879	961	269	569	312	65.4	11.6
Males											
18 years and over	21 611	131	1 001	2 241	7 747	4 176	1 416	3 257	1 641	84.4	22.7
18 to 24 years	2 810	6	31	536	893	1 018	127	194	5	79.6	7.1
25 years and over	18 801	125	970	1 705	6 854	3 159	1 289	3 063	1 636	85.1	25.0
25 to 34 years	4 551	19	67	363	1 550	848	393	1 032	279	90.1	28.8
35 to 44 years	5 006	21	93	351	1 989	928	425	797	401	90.7	23.9
45 to 54 years	3 666	28	74	246	1 248	624	298	666	482	90.5	31.3
55 to 64 years	2 431	13	177	230	1 036	305	94	308	270	82.8	23.8
65 years and over	3 147	44	559	515	1 031	453	80	260	204	64.5	14.8
Females											
18 years and over	23 597	116	1 081	2 386	9 142	4 556	1 869	3 264	1 183	84.8	18.8
18 to 24 years	2 894	3	33	482	899	1 078	146	237	16	82.1	8.7
25 years and over	20 704	113	1 048	1 904	8 244	3 478	1 723	3 027	1 167	85.2	20.3
25 to 34 years	4 566	4	50	282	1 501	941	478	1 051	261	92.7	28.7
35 to 44 years	5 215	19	58	341	2 038	967	564	874	353	92.0	23.5
45 to 54 years	3 862	22	99	228	1 612	700	333	570	299	91.0	22.5
55 to 64 years	2 579	17	136	291	1 244	362	159	224	146	82.8	14.4
65 years and over	4 481	51	705	763	1 849	508	189	309	108	66.1	9.3
White											
Both sexes											
18 years and over	40 219	206	1 854	3 826	15 225	7 609	2 984	6 008	2 507	85.4	21.2
18 to 24 years	4 915	6	61	822	1 543	1 825	256	386	16	81.9	8.2
25 years and over	35 304	200	1 794	3 003	13 682	5 783	2 728	5 622	2 491	85.8	23.0
25 to 34 years	7 932	19	103	506	2 687	1 478	791	1 910	437	92.1	29.6
35 to 44 years	9 067	37	112	590	3 612	1 616	895	1 531	673	91.8	24.3
45 to 54 years	6 729	35	156	382	2 567	1 179	582	1 125	702	91.5	27.2
55 to 64 years	4 502	30	263	422	2 086	603	206	506	384	84.1	19.8
65 years and over	7 074	79	1 158	1 103	2 730	906	253	550	295	66.9	11.9

See footnotes at end of table.

Table B-12.   Educational Attainment of Persons 18 Years Old and Over, by Age, Sex, Race, and Hispanic Origin, for Regions and Divisions: March 1997 — Continued

(Numbers in thousands. Civilian noninstitutional population.)

Age, sex, race, Hispanic origin, region, and division	Total	Elementary		High School		College				Percent:	
		None-4th grade	5th-8th grade	9th-11th grade	High school graduate	Some college no degree	Associate degree	Bachelor's degree	Advanced degree	High school graduate or more	Bachelor's degree or more
Black											
Both sexes											
18 years and over	3 954	31	174	667	1 435	953	247	310	138	78.0	11.3
18 to 24 years	591	3	—	147	210	194	12	24	—	74.7	4.1
25 years and over	3 364	28	174	520	1 224	759	234	286	138	78.6	12.6
25 to 34 years	907	4	7	105	316	277	60	103	36	87.2	15.3
35 to 44 years	934	—	21	87	368	249	88	91	31	88.4	13.1
45 to 54 years	620	7	14	81	243	124	38	73	39	83.5	18.2
55 to 64 years	419	—	38	93	163	61	36	8	20	68.7	6.6
65 years and over	484	17	93	154	136	49	12	12	12	45.5	4.9
Hispanic origin[1]											
Both sexes											
18 years and over	1 363	77	244	273	395	214	54	72	35	56.4	7.9
18 to 24 years	284	2	39	84	71	74	8	4	1	56.0	1.9
25 years and over	1 079	75	205	189	323	139	46	68	34	56.6	9.5
25 to 34 years	415	11	60	83	135	59	19	34	15	63.1	11.8
35 to 44 years	362	22	66	61	116	47	19	23	6	58.8	8.2
45 to 54 years	167	18	39	23	37	27	7	6	10	51.7	9.2
55 to 64 years	78	9	21	13	24	5	—	4	1	44.7	6.9
65 years and over	59	15	19	9	11	1	—	1	2	(B)	(B)
SOUTH											
All Races											
Both sexes											
18 years and over	68 902	1 216	4 438	8 978	23 089	13 228	4 228	9 273	4 452	78.8	19.9
18 to 24 years	8 978	46	190	1 962	3 001	2 945	237	562	36	75.5	6.7
25 years and over	59 924	1 170	4 248	7 016	20 089	10 283	3 992	8 711	4 416	79.3	21.9
25 to 34 years	14 017	91	385	1 478	4 622	2 863	1 115	2 674	790	86.1	24.7
35 to 44 years	15 245	140	452	1 480	5 476	2 785	1 288	2 501	1 123	86.4	23.8
45 to 54 years	11 710	147	626	1 198	3 906	1 989	847	1 722	1 275	83.2	25.6
55 to 64 years	7 627	231	858	1 097	2 567	1 144	383	803	545	71.3	17.7
65 years and over	11 325	562	1 927	1 763	3 517	1 503	359	1 011	684	62.5	15.0
Males											
18 years and over	32 894	660	2 174	4 465	10 575	6 148	1 811	4 562	2 499	77.8	21.5
18 to 24 years	4 459	31	102	1 086	1 560	1 326	121	219	13	72.7	5.2
25 years and over	28 435	629	2 072	3 379	9 014	4 822	1 690	4 343	2 486	78.6	24.0
25 to 34 years	6 812	48	213	823	2 225	1 366	486	1 230	420	84.1	24.2
35 to 44 years	7 522	89	208	828	2 765	1 318	504	1 226	585	85.0	24.1
45 to 54 years	5 675	76	327	591	1 683	973	419	910	695	82.5	28.3
55 to 64 years	3 603	141	474	470	1 046	523	169	443	338	69.9	21.7
65 years and over	4 824	275	850	667	1 295	643	112	534	448	62.8	20.4
Females											
18 years and over	36 009	556	2 264	4 513	12 514	7 080	2 418	4 711	1 953	79.6	18.5
18 to 24 years	4 520	15	88	876	1 440	1 618	116	344	23	78.3	8.1
25 years and over	31 489	541	2 176	3 637	11 074	5 461	2 302	4 368	1 930	79.8	20.0
25 to 34 years	7 206	43	172	655	2 396	1 497	629	1 444	370	87.9	25.2
35 to 44 years	7 724	51	244	652	2 711	1 467	784	1 275	538	87.7	23.5
45 to 54 years	6 035	71	298	607	2 223	1 016	428	812	579	83.8	23.1
55 to 64 years	4 024	90	384	627	1 521	621	214	361	206	72.6	14.1
65 years and over	6 501	286	1 077	1 095	2 222	860	247	476	237	62.2	11.0

See footnotes at end of table.

Table B-12. Educational Attainment of Persons 18 Years Old and Over, by Age, Sex, Race, and Hispanic Origin, for Regions and Divisions: March 1997 — Continued

(Numbers in thousands. Civilian noninstitutional population.)

Age, sex, race, Hispanic origin, region, and division	Total	Elementary		High School		College				Percent:	
		None-4th grade	5th-8th grade	9th-11th grade	High school graduate	Some college no degree	Associate degree	Bachelor's degree	Advanced degree	High school graduate or more	Bachelor's degree or more
White											
Both sexes											
18 years and over	54 772	895	3 558	6 482	18 096	10 540	3 437	7 945	3 819	80.0	21.5
18 to 24 years	6 555	40	178	1 303	2 080	2 251	195	477	31	76.8	7.8
25 years and over	48 217	855	3 380	5 180	16 016	8 289	3 242	7 468	3 787	80.5	23.3
25 to 34 years	10 632	79	341	1 063	3 303	2 141	860	2 225	619	86.1	26.8
35 to 44 years	11 890	103	358	1 051	4 193	2 093	1 033	2 094	964	87.3	25.7
45 to 54 years	9 485	115	480	815	3 106	1 682	682	1 480	1 125	85.1	27.5
55 to 64 years	6 367	163	666	796	2 225	987	339	720	470	74.5	18.7
65 years and over	9 843	395	1 535	1 455	3 188	1 385	328	948	609	65.6	15.8
Black											
Both sexes											
18 years and over	12 437	287	801	2 324	4 559	2 380	695	1 007	384	72.6	11.2
18 to 24 years	2 181	6	12	607	854	600	28	69	5	71.4	3.4
25 years and over	10 256	281	789	1 718	3 704	1 779	668	938	379	72.8	12.8
25 to 34 years	2 880	12	24	381	1 196	635	230	342	59	85.5	13.9
35 to 44 years	2 926	32	88	393	1 175	624	221	309	86	82.5	13.5
45 to 54 years	1 939	22	123	355	734	272	153	170	111	74.2	14.4
55 to 64 years	1 109	60	170	292	297	141	35	60	54	52.9	10.2
65 years and over	1 401	155	384	296	302	108	29	57	70	40.4	9.0
Hispanic origin[1]											
Both sexes											
18 years and over	6 352	540	1 042	1 033	1 738	970	299	529	201	58.8	11.5
18 to 24 years	1 101	32	85	310	355	252	29	33	6	61.2	3.5
25 years and over	5 251	508	956	724	1 383	718	270	495	196	58.3	13.2
25 to 34 years	1 755	64	217	306	511	288	119	197	52	66.5	14.2
35 to 44 years	1 370	74	209	181	405	220	79	140	62	66.1	14.7
45 to 54 years	830	76	188	77	207	118	47	87	31	58.9	14.2
55 to 64 years	607	112	165	70	128	45	21	45	23	42.0	11.1
65 years and over	689	182	177	89	133	48	5	27	28	35.0	8.0
WEST											
All Races											
Both sexes											
18 years and over	42 948	1 008	2 497	4 293	11 874	9 931	3 340	7 040	2 966	81.8	23.3
18 to 24 years	5 827	62	255	1 201	1 670	2 017	249	358	15	73.9	6.4
25 years and over	37 121	946	2 242	3 092	10 204	7 914	3 091	6 682	2 951	83.1	25.9
25 to 34 years	9 406	175	501	915	2 453	2 216	820	1 840	486	83.1	24.7
35 to 44 years	9 901	194	523	715	2 698	2 252	944	1 829	745	85.5	26.0
45 to 54 years	7 171	165	326	381	1 726	1 556	697	1 481	838	87.8	32.3
55 to 64 years	4 410	154	275	371	1 247	858	318	718	470	81.9	26.9
65 years and over	6 233	258	616	710	2 080	1 031	312	813	413	74.6	19.7
Males											
18 years and over	21 402	505	1 252	2 184	5 772	4 868	1 469	3 525	1 827	81.6	25.0
18 to 24 years	3 013	26	160	667	884	993	109	159	15	71.7	5.8
25 years and over	18 389	479	1 091	1 517	4 888	3 875	1 360	3 366	1 812	83.2	28.2
25 to 34 years	4 949	100	257	484	1 402	1 154	401	908	244	83.0	23.3
35 to 44 years	5 035	112	282	412	1 372	1 125	394	868	469	84.0	26.6
45 to 54 years	3 569	86	157	168	773	792	299	766	528	88.5	36.3
55 to 64 years	2 117	81	119	153	547	395	143	374	305	83.3	32.1
65 years and over	2 718	101	276	300	793	409	124	450	266	75.1	26.3

See footnotes at end of table.

Table B-12.   Educational Attainment of Persons 18 Years Old and Over, by Age, Sex, Race, and Hispanic Origin, for Regions and Divisions: March 1997 — Continued

(Numbers in thousands. Civilian noninstitutional population.)

Age, sex, race, Hispanic origin, region, and division	Total	Elementary		High School		College				Percent:	
		None-4th grade	5th-8th grade	9th-11th grade	High school graduate	Some college no degree	Associate degree	Bachelor's degree	Advanced degree	High school graduate or more	Bachelor's degree or more
Females											
18 years and over	21 546	503	1 245	2 109	6 102	5 063	1 871	3 515	1 139	82.1	21.6
18 to 24 years	2 814	36	95	534	786	1 024	140	199	—	76.4	7.1
25 years and over	18 732	467	1 150	1 575	5 316	4 039	1 731	3 316	1 139	83.0	23.8
25 to 34 years	4 457	75	244	431	1 051	1 063	420	932	242	83.2	26.3
35 to 44 years	4 867	82	240	303	1 326	1 127	550	961	276	87.1	25.4
45 to 54 years	3 601	79	169	213	952	764	398	716	310	87.2	28.5
55 to 64 years	2 293	73	156	217	700	463	174	344	165	80.5	22.2
65 years and over	3 514	158	340	411	1 287	622	188	362	147	74.2	14.5
White											
Both sexes											
18 years and over	36 255	784	2 177	3 701	10 017	8 470	2 823	5 738	2 546	81.6	22.8
18 to 24 years	4 831	53	247	1 049	1 381	1 626	208	254	13	72.1	5.5
25 years and over	31 424	731	1 930	2 652	8 636	6 845	2 615	5 483	2 533	83.1	25.5
25 to 34 years	7 786	144	450	820	2 009	1 834	692	1 463	375	81.9	23.6
35 to 44 years	8 291	159	490	595	2 250	1 896	780	1 516	604	85.0	25.6
45 to 54 years	6 153	146	282	318	1 445	1 412	605	1 185	760	87.9	31.6
55 to 64 years	3 723	117	205	316	1 043	756	268	604	414	82.9	27.4
65 years and over	5 472	167	503	602	1 889	946	270	715	380	76.8	20.0
Black											
Both sexes											
18 years and over	2 034	21	47	253	642	557	160	279	76	84.3	17.5
18 to 24 years	284	4	1	43	114	82	21	20	—	83.3	6.9
25 years and over	1 750	17	46	210	529	475	139	259	76	84.4	19.2
25 to 34 years	548	3	3	51	187	186	36	77	6	89.5	15.0
35 to 44 years	518	—	—	55	141	170	43	85	24	89.4	21.1
45 to 54 years	253	—	4	19	66	58	38	55	13	90.7	26.8
55 to 64 years	208	—	11	34	79	35	14	15	22	78.5	17.4
65 years and over	223	14	27	52	57	26	8	27	12	58.4	17.7
Hispanic origin[1]											
Both sexes											
18 years and over	8 265	735	1 655	1 642	1 979	1 271	414	423	148	51.2	6.9
18 to 24 years	1 676	45	237	532	438	371	31	20	3	51.4	1.3
25 years and over	6 589	689	1 418	1 110	1 542	900	383	403	145	51.2	8.3
25 to 34 years	2 501	139	436	549	600	411	145	180	41	55.0	8.8
35 to 44 years	1 965	159	464	263	495	297	119	125	44	54.9	8.6
45 to 54 years	1 038	132	230	140	244	123	73	59	37	51.6	9.3
55 to 64 years	577	115	135	85	127	46	30	22	17	42.0	6.9
65 years and over	509	144	153	73	77	23	16	17	6	27.3	4.6
NEW ENGLAND											
All Races											
Both sexes											
18 years and over	10 020	118	441	1 012	3 335	1 600	753	1 773	988	84.3	27.6
25 years and over	8 897	117	427	823	2 982	1 185	713	1 666	984	84.6	29.8
25 to 34 years	2 023	6	39	140	639	305	183	546	164	90.8	35.1
35 to 44 years	2 360	12	27	163	769	362	229	509	289	91.5	33.8
45 to 64 years	2 789	49	119	201	958	330	230	465	437	86.7	32.3
65 years and over	1 726	50	241	319	616	188	71	146	95	64.6	14.0
Male											
18 years and over	4 840	59	204	532	1 541	795	299	848	562	83.6	29.1

See footnotes at end of table.

Table B-12. Educational Attainment of Persons 18 Years Old and Over, by Age, Sex, Race, and Hispanic Origin, for Regions and Divisions: March 1997 — Continued

(Numbers in thousands. Civilian noninstitutional population.)

Age, sex, race, Hispanic origin, region, and division	Total	Elementary		High School		College				Percent:	
		None-4th grade	5th-8th grade	9th-11th grade	High school graduate	Some college no degree	Associate degree	Bachelor's degree	Advanced degree	High school graduate or more	Bachelor's degree or more
25 years and over	4 252	59	194	425	1 371	567	279	795	562	84.1	31.9
25 to 34 years	965	1	21	86	329	146	62	240	79	88.8	33.1
35 to 44 years	1 181	5	15	101	399	158	100	243	160	89.8	34.2
45 to 64 years	1 348	25	60	95	417	167	95	234	256	86.6	36.3
65 years and over	758	28	98	142	227	95	22	78	67	64.6	19.1
Female											
18 years and over	5 180	59	237	480	1 794	805	453	926	426	85.0	26.1
25 years and over	4 645	58	232	398	1 611	619	434	870	423	85.2	27.8
25 to 34 years	1 058	5	18	54	310	159	120	305	85	92.7	36.9
35 to 44 years	1 179	7	12	61	370	204	130	266	129	93.2	33.5
45 to 64 years	1 441	24	59	106	542	163	135	231	181	86.9	28.6
65 years and over	967	22	143	176	389	92	49	68	28	64.7	9.9
25 years and over	8 897	117	427	823	2 982	1 185	713	1 666	984	84.6	29.8
White	8 333	100	400	728	2 810	1 091	670	1 602	932	85.3	30.4
Black	422	7	19	82	148	85	34	34	13	74.4	11.0
Hispanic origin[1]	309	18	48	58	102	22	22	25	14	60.1	12.6
MIDDLE ATLANTIC											
All Races											
Both sexes											
18 years and over	28 488	394	1 609	3 351	10 182	4 550	1 731	4 481	2 191	81.2	23.4
25 years and over	25 134	369	1 539	2 672	9 213	3 349	1 598	4 208	2 186	81.8	25.4
25 to 34 years	5 693	48	121	446	1 945	869	492	1 347	424	89.2	31.1
35 to 44 years	6 232	53	148	458	2 256	999	476	1 258	584	89.4	29.6
45 to 64 years	8 243	117	442	846	3 172	1 059	495	1 172	940	83.0	25.6
65 years and over	4 966	150	828	923	1 840	421	135	431	237	61.7	13.5
Male											
18 years and over	13 407	175	745	1 592	4 561	2 195	735	2 196	1 209	81.3	25.4
25 years and over	11 743	162	696	1 186	4 097	1 611	681	2 104	1 206	82.6	28.2
25 to 34 years	2 763	26	71	252	976	399	222	621	197	87.4	29.6
35 to 44 years	3 049	31	76	229	1 079	504	188	637	307	89.0	30.9
45 to 64 years	3 974	39	229	366	1 415	520	216	624	565	84.1	29.9
65 years and over	1 957	67	320	340	627	188	54	223	137	62.9	18.4
Female											
18 years and over	15 081	219	864	1 759	5 621	2 354	996	2 286	982	81.2	21.7
25 years and over	13 391	207	843	1 486	5 116	1 738	917	2 104	980	81.1	23.0
25 to 34 years	2 930	23	50	194	969	470	270	726	228	90.9	32.6
35 to 44 years	3 183	22	72	229	1 177	496	288	621	277	89.8	28.2
45 to 64 years	4 269	79	213	480	1 756	539	279	548	375	81.9	21.6
65 years and over	3 009	84	508	583	1 213	233	80	208	100	61.0	10.2
25 years and over	25 134	369	1 539	2 672	9 213	3 349	1 598	4 208	2 186	81.8	25.4
White	20 780	242	1 206	2 027	7 716	2 717	1 361	3 596	1 916	83.3	26.5
Black	3 280	78	246	576	1 230	542	196	300	111	72.6	12.5
Hispanic origin[1]	2 248	159	427	423	660	275	84	161	59	55.1	9.8
EAST NORTH CENTRAL											
All Races											
Both sexes											
18 years and over	31 906	194	1 416	3 281	12 297	6 206	2 139	4 401	1 971	84.7	20.0
25 years and over	27 861	187	1 365	2 570	11 012	4 712	1 958	4 102	1 953	85.2	21.7

See footnotes at end of table.

Table B-12. Educational Attainment of Persons 18 Years Old and Over, by Age, Sex, Race, and Hispanic Origin, for Regions and Divisions: March 1997 — Continued

(Numbers in thousands. Civilian noninstitutional population.)

Age, sex, race, Hispanic origin, region, and division	Total	Elementary		High School		College				Percent:	
		None-4th grade	5th-8th grade	9th-11th grade	High school graduate	Some college no degree	Associate degree	Bachelor's degree	Advanced degree	High school graduate or more	Bachelor's degree or more
25 to 34 years	6 470	18	75	479	2 289	1 242	559	1 398	410	91.2	28.0
35 to 44 years	7 156	27	116	452	2 944	1 359	659	1 101	498	91.7	22.3
45 to 64 years	8 888	64	328	718	3 729	1 424	566	1 209	851	87.5	23.2
65 years and over	5 347	78	846	921	2 051	687	174	395	194	65.5	11.0
Male											
18 years and over	15 246	100	664	1 591	5 588	3 035	905	2 226	1 136	84.6	22.1
25 years and over	13 244	95	637	1 207	4 962	2 284	825	2 105	1 131	85.4	24.4
25 to 34 years	3 245	16	43	265	1 168	588	248	702	214	90.0	28.2
35 to 44 years	3 476	14	69	236	1 422	644	273	548	268	90.8	23.5
45 to 64 years	4 308	30	161	342	1 655	691	247	665	517	87.6	27.4
65 years and over	2 215	34	363	364	716	361	56	189	132	65.6	14.5
Female											
18 years and over	16 660	94	753	1 689	6 709	3 171	1 234	2 175	835	84.8	18.1
25 years and over	14 616	92	728	1 364	6 051	2 428	1 133	1 997	822	85.1	19.3
25 to 34 years	3 224	2	32	214	1 120	654	310	696	196	92.3	27.7
35 to 44 years	3 680	13	47	216	1 521	715	386	552	230	92.5	21.3
45 to 64 years	4 580	34	166	376	2 074	733	319	543	334	87.4	19.2
65 years and over	3 132	43	483	558	1 335	326	118	206	62	65.4	8.6
25 years and over	27 861	187	1 365	2 570	11 012	4 712	1 958	4 102	1 953	85.2	21.7
White	24 520	162	1 188	2 106	9 827	4 008	1 750	3 757	1 721	85.9	22.3
Black	2 775	16	146	423	1 061	631	179	204	114	78.9	11.5
Hispanic origin[1]	865	63	167	144	253	120	36	50	31	56.8	9.4
WEST NORTH CENTRAL											
All Races											
Both sexes											
18 years and over	13 303	53	665	1 347	4 592	2 527	1 146	2 120	854	84.5	22.4
25 years and over	11 644	51	652	1 039	4 085	1 924	1 054	1 988	850	85.0	24.4
25 to 34 years	2 647	5	42	166	762	547	312	684	130	92.0	30.7
35 to 44 years	3 065	13	35	240	1 084	537	330	570	256	90.6	27.0
45 to 64 years	3 650	16	158	276	1 411	566	317	559	347	87.7	24.8
65 years and over	2 281	18	418	356	828	273	95	175	118	65.3	12.8
Male											
18 years and over	6 366	30	337	650	2 159	1 141	511	1 031	505	84.0	24.1
25 years and over	5 557	30	333	498	1 893	874	465	958	505	84.5	26.3
25 to 34 years	1 306	3	24	98	382	260	145	330	64	90.4	30.2
35 to 44 years	1 531	7	23	115	567	284	152	249	134	90.5	25.0
45 to 64 years	1 789	10	90	134	629	238	144	309	236	86.9	30.4
65 years and over	931	10	196	151	315	92	24	71	72	61.6	15.3
Female											
18 years and over	6 938	22	328	697	2 433	1 385	634	1 089	348	84.9	20.7
25 years and over	6 087	21	320	540	2 193	1 050	589	1 030	345	85.5	22.6
25 to 34 years	1 342	2	18	68	380	287	167	354	65	93.5	31.3
35 to 44 years	1 534	6	12	125	517	253	178	321	122	90.7	28.9
45 to 64 years	1 861	6	68	142	782	329	173	250	111	88.4	19.4
65 years and over	1 350	8	222	205	514	181	71	104	46	67.8	11.1
25 years and over	11 644	51	652	1 039	4 085	1 924	1 054	1 988	850	85.0	24.4
White	10 784	38	605	897	3 855	1 775	978	1 866	770	85.7	24.4
Black	589	12	27	97	164	128	55	82	24	77.0	18.1
Hispanic origin[1]	214	12	38	45	70	19	10	18	3	55.6	9.6

See footnotes at end of table.

Table B-12. Educational Attainment of Persons 18 Years Old and Over, by Age, Sex, Race, and Hispanic Origin, for Regions and Divisions: March 1997 — Continued

(Numbers in thousands. Civilian noninstitutional population.)

Age, sex, race, Hispanic origin, region, and division	Total	Elementary		High School		College				Percent:	
		None-4th grade	5th-8th grade	9th-11th grade	High school graduate	Some college no degree	Associate degree	Bachelor's degree	Advanced degree	High school graduate or more	Bachelor's degree or more
SOUTH ATLANTIC											
All Races											
Both sexes											
18 years and over	35 846	462	1 958	4 673	11 954	6 571	2 422	5 156	2 649	80.2	21.8
25 years and over	31 392	445	1 911	3 776	10 436	5 120	2 273	4 806	2 625	80.5	23.7
25 to 34 years	7 152	39	163	759	2 294	1 356	601	1 457	482	86.6	27.1
35 to 44 years	7 727	47	158	764	2 786	1 309	709	1 343	610	87.5	25.3
45 to 64 years	10 274	135	632	1 284	3 427	1 597	720	1 407	1 072	80.0	24.1
65 years and over	6 240	224	958	969	1 929	857	243	598	461	65.5	17.0
Male											
18 years and over	17 293	265	988	2 420	5 495	3 040	1 043	2 538	1 502	78.8	23.4
25 years and over	15 049	250	963	1 901	4 667	2 420	963	2 391	1 493	79.3	25.8
25 to 34 years	3 530	26	94	450	1 082	696	259	655	269	83.8	26.2
35 to 44 years	3 865	32	84	478	1 414	634	267	638	319	84.6	24.7
45 to 64 years	4 990	88	359	599	1 470	738	351	776	609	79.0	27.8
65 years and over	2 664	104	427	374	700	353	86	322	297	66.1	23.3
Female											
18 years and over	18 553	197	970	2 253	6 459	3 531	1 379	2 618	1 147	81.6	20.3
25 years and over	16 343	195	948	1 875	5 769	2 699	1 310	2 415	1 132	81.5	21.7
25 to 34 years	3 622	13	69	309	1 213	661	342	802	213	89.2	28.0
35 to 44 years	3 861	15	75	285	1 371	675	442	705	292	90.3	25.8
45 to 64 years	5 284	47	273	685	1 957	860	369	631	463	81.0	20.7
65 years and over	3 576	120	531	596	1 229	503	156	276	164	65.1	12.3
25 years and over	31 392	445	1 911	3 776	10 436	5 120	2 273	4 806	2 625	80.5	23.7
White	24 692	259	1 422	2 638	8 126	4 082	1 841	4 093	2 232	82.5	25.6
Black	5 956	169	453	1 079	2 148	955	384	537	231	71.4	12.9
Hispanic origin[1]	1 978	105	291	261	493	307	136	256	128	66.8	19.4
EAST SOUTH CENTRAL											
All Races											
Both sexes											
18 years and over	12 026	195	1 002	1 689	4 264	2 166	712	1 368	631	76.0	16.6
25 years and over	10 474	189	953	1 317	3 767	1 636	683	1 301	629	76.5	18.4
25 to 34 years	2 370	14	43	237	876	477	216	403	105	87.6	21.4
35 to 44 years	2 680	16	80	283	1 022	445	233	399	201	85.9	22.4
45 to 64 years	3 397	52	354	436	1 263	507	186	361	239	75.2	17.7
65 years and over	2 027	107	476	362	606	208	48	138	83	53.4	10.9
Male											
18 years and over	5 602	116	472	787	1 949	1 019	281	639	338	75.5	17.4
25 years and over	4 819	110	445	591	1 674	773	271	617	338	76.2	19.8
25 to 34 years	1 114	3	17	111	443	209	79	206	47	88.3	22.7
35 to 44 years	1 253	13	37	146	476	219	96	171	95	84.3	21.2
45 to 64 years	1 574	35	189	212	502	248	83	172	133	72.3	19.4
65 years and over	877	58	203	122	253	97	13	67	64	56.3	14.9
Female											
18 years and over	6 424	79	530	901	2 315	1 147	431	728	293	76.5	15.9
25 years and over	5 655	79	508	726	2 093	863	412	684	290	76.8	17.2
25 to 34 years	1 256	11	26	126	433	267	137	197	59	87.0	20.3
35 to 44 years	1 427	3	43	137	546	227	137	228	107	87.2	23.5

See footnotes at end of table.

Table B-12. Educational Attainment of Persons 18 Years Old and Over, by Age, Sex, Race, and Hispanic Origin, for Regions and Divisions: March 1997 — Continued

(Numbers in thousands. Civilian noninstitutional population.)

Age, sex, race, Hispanic origin, region, and division	Total	Elementary		High School		College				Percent:	
		None–4th grade	5th–8th grade	9th–11th grade	High school graduate	Some college no degree	Associate degree	Bachelor's degree	Advanced degree	High school graduate or more	Bachelor's degree or more
45 to 64 years	1 823	16	165	224	761	258	103	189	106	77.7	16.2
65 years and over	1 150	49	274	239	352	111	35	70	20	51.1	7.8
25 years and over	10 474	189	953	1 317	3 767	1 636	683	1 301	629	76.5	18.4
White	8 406	121	783	986	3 017	1 324	526	1 102	547	77.5	19.6
Black	1 980	65	170	323	726	298	156	173	69	71.8	12.2
Hispanic origin[1]	61	11	7	—	11	7	11	11	4	(B)	(B)

WEST SOUTH CENTRAL

All Races

Both sexes

18 years and over	21 031	559	1 478	2 616	6 872	4 490	1 094	2 750	1 172	77.9	18.6
25 years and over	18 058	536	1 384	1 922	5 885	3 527	1 037	2 604	1 162	78.7	20.9
25 to 34 years	4 496	38	179	482	1 451	1 030	299	814	203	84.4	22.6
35 to 44 years	4 839	77	214	434	1 668	1 030	346	759	312	85.0	22.1
45 to 64 years	5 665	191	498	575	1 784	1 029	324	757	509	77.7	22.3
65 years and over	3 058	230	493	432	982	439	68	275	140	62.2	13.6

Male

18 years and over	9 999	279	714	1 257	3 131	2 089	486	1 385	659	77.5	20.4
25 years and over	8 567	269	664	887	2 673	1 628	456	1 335	655	78.8	23.2
25 to 34 years	2 168	19	102	262	701	461	149	369	104	82.3	21.8
35 to 44 years	2 404	44	87	203	874	465	141	417	172	86.1	24.5
45 to 64 years	2 713	93	253	250	757	510	154	405	292	78.0	25.7
65 years and over	1 283	113	221	171	341	193	12	145	87	60.7	18.0

Female

18 years and over	11 032	280	764	1 359	3 741	2 401	608	1 365	513	78.2	17.0
25 years and over	9 491	267	720	1 036	3 212	1 899	580	1 269	507	78.7	18.7
25 to 34 years	2 328	19	77	220	750	569	150	445	98	86.4	23.3
35 to 44 years	2 435	33	127	231	794	565	205	342	140	84.0	19.8
45 to 64 years	2 951	98	244	325	1 027	519	170	352	217	77.4	19.3
65 years and over	1 776	118	272	260	641	246	56	130	53	63.4	10.3
25 years and over	18 058	536	1 384	1 922	5 885	3 527	1 037	2 604	1 162	78.7	20.9
White	15 118	475	1 175	1 556	4 873	2 883	874	2 273	1 009	78.8	21.7
Black	2 319	47	166	316	830	527	127	227	79	77.2	13.2
Hispanic origin[1]	3 212	392	659	462	880	404	123	229	64	52.9	9.1

MOUNTAIN

All Races

Both sexes

18 years and over	11 875	162	563	1 215	3 645	2 942	893	1 741	714	83.7	20.7
25 years and over	10 085	146	518	833	3 102	2 320	811	1 645	709	85.2	23.3
25 to 34 years	2 493	24	100	228	701	660	232	449	99	85.9	22.0
35 to 44 years	2 629	26	99	170	825	637	273	446	153	88.8	22.8
45 to 64 years	3 165	47	141	236	918	695	244	543	341	86.6	27.9
65 years and over	1 799	49	178	198	658	329	63	207	117	76.4	18.0

Male

18 years and over	5 847	92	276	604	1 778	1 390	411	865	430	83.4	22.2
25 years and over	4 943	85	254	385	1 480	1 110	381	821	426	85.4	25.2
25 to 34 years	1 276	15	47	114	382	333	121	213	51	86.2	20.7
35 to 44 years	1 337	22	56	94	426	308	129	210	92	87.1	22.6
45 to 64 years	1 510	24	63	95	391	331	110	287	209	87.9	32.9

See footnotes at end of table.

Table B-12. Educational Attainment of Persons 18 Years Old and Over, by Age, Sex, Race, and Hispanic Origin, for Regions and Divisions: March 1997 — Continued

(Numbers in thousands. Civilian noninstitutional population.)

Age, sex, race, Hispanic origin, region, and division	Total	Elementary		High School		College				Percent:	
		None-4th grade	5th-8th grade	9th-11th grade	High school graduate	Some college no degree	Associate degree	Bachelor's degree	Advanced degree	High school graduate or more	Bachelor's degree or more
65 years and over	820	24	88	82	281	139	22	111	73	76.4	22.5
Female											
18 years and over	6 028	70	287	611	1 867	1 552	482	877	284	84.0	19.2
25 years and over	5 142	62	264	447	1 622	1 210	430	824	284	85.0	21.5
25 to 34 years	1 217	9	53	114	319	327	111	235	48	85.5	23.3
35 to 44 years	1 292	5	42	76	399	329	144	237	61	90.5	23.0
45 to 64 years	1 655	23	78	141	526	364	134	256	132	85.3	23.4
65 years and over	978	25	90	116	377	190	41	96	44	76.4	14.3
25 years and over	10 085	146	518	833	3 102	2 320	811	1 645	709	85.2	23.3
White	9 273	105	461	745	2 861	2 131	757	1 539	675	85.9	23.9
Black	293	12	14	39	83	87	20	33	6	78.0	13.3
Hispanic origin[1]	1 541	95	297	262	443	230	100	83	30	57.6	7.3
PACIFIC											
All Races											
Both sexes											
18 years and over	31 073	846	1 934	3 078	8 229	6 989	2 447	5 299	2 252	81.1	24.3
25 years and over	27 036	799	1 724	2 260	7 102	5 593	2 279	5 036	2 242	82.3	26.9
25 to 34 years	6 914	151	401	686	1 752	1 557	588	1 391	387	82.1	25.7
35 to 44 years	7 272	168	424	545	1 873	1 615	671	1 383	593	84.4	27.2
45 to 64 years	8 416	272	460	516	2 055	1 719	771	1 657	967	85.2	31.2
65 years and over	4 434	209	438	512	1 423	702	248	605	295	73.8	20.3
Male											
18 years and over	15 555	413	976	1 580	3 994	3 478	1 058	2 660	1 396	80.9	26.1
25 years and over	13 446	395	837	1 132	3 408	2 765	979	2 545	1 386	82.4	29.2
25 to 34 years	3 673	85	210	370	1 021	821	280	695	193	81.9	24.2
35 to 44 years	3 698	90	226	318	946	817	265	659	377	82.8	28.0
45 to 64 years	4 176	143	213	227	929	857	332	852	624	86.0	35.4
65 years and over	1 898	77	188	218	512	270	102	330	102	74.6	28.0
Female											
18 years and over	15 518	433	958	1 498	4 235	3 511	1 388	2 638	856	81.4	22.5
25 years and over	13 590	405	887	1 128	3 694	2 828	1 301	2 492	856	82.2	24.6
25 to 34 years	3 240	66	191	317	731	735	308	697	194	82.3	27.5
35 to 44 years	3 574	78	198	227	927	798	407	724	216	85.9	26.3
45 to 64 years	4 239	129	247	289	1 126	862	439	804	343	84.3	27.0
65 years and over	2 536	133	250	295	910	432	147	266	103	73.3	14.6
25 years and over	27 036	799	1 724	2 260	7 102	5 593	2 279	5 036	2 242	82.3	26.9
White	22 151	627	1 469	1 907	5 774	4 714	1 858	3 944	1 858	81.9	26.2
Black	1 457	6	32	171	446	387	119	226	70	85.7	20.3
Hispanic origin[1]	5 049	594	1 120	848	1 099	669	283	321	115	49.2	8.6

Source: March 1997 Current Population Survey, Education and Social Stratification Branch, U.S. Bureau of the Census.

1. May be of any race.

— Represents zero or rounds to zero.

Table B-13. Educational Attainment of Persons 25 Years Old and Over, for States: March 1997

(Numbers in thousands. Civilian noninstitutional population.)

State	Total population	High school graduate or more		Completed Bachelor's degree or more	
		Percent	1.6* (s. e.) [1]	Percent	1.6* (s. e.) [1]
Alabama	2 773	77.6	2.0	19.3	1.9
Alaska	384	92.1	1.5	27.5	2.5
Arizona	2 875	82.6	1.8	19.5	1.9
Arkansas	1 593	76.9	2.0	14.6	1.7
California	20 229	80.7	0.8	27.5	0.9
Colorado	2 381	87.6	1.6	28.9	2.2
Connecticut	2 183	84.0	2.0	30.0	2.4
Delaware	474	84.4	2.2	26.8	2.7
District of Columbia	372	80.3	2.3	33.7	2.7
Florida	9 850	81.4	1.0	21.7	1.1
Georgia	4 685	78.8	1.8	22.3	1.9
Hawaii	764	83.7	2.2	22.5	2.5
Idaho	734	85.7	1.7	19.4	1.9
Illinois	7 427	84.4	1.1	25.0	1.3
Indiana	3 753	81.9	1.9	16.2	1.8
Iowa	1 830	86.7	1.7	21.7	2.1
Kansas	1 578	88.1	1.6	27.5	2.2
Kentucky	2 487	75.4	2.1	17.6	1.9
Louisiana	2 641	75.7	2.1	18.1	1.9
Maine	837	85.8	1.9	20.0	2.2
Maryland	3 275	84.7	2.0	32.2	2.6
Massachusetts	4 059	85.9	1.3	33.5	1.7
Michigan	6 061	86.0	1.1	21.0	1.3
Minnesota	2 951	87.9	1.6	28.3	2.2
Mississippi	1 654	77.5	2.1	20.9	2.0
Missouri	3 404	80.1	2.1	22.9	2.2
Montana	562	88.6	1.5	25.2	2.0
Nebraska	1 044	86.0	1.7	21.3	2.0
Nevada	1 082	85.4	2.0	19.9	2.2
New Hampshire	774	85.1	2.1	27.0	2.7
New Jersey	5 284	84.8	1.1	28.5	1.4
New Mexico	1 057	78.0	2.0	23.6	2.1
New York	11 826	80.0	0.9	25.8	1.0
North Carolina	4 755	78.4	1.6	22.6	1.6
North Dakota	391	82.6	1.9	20.5	2.0
Ohio	7 224	86.2	1.0	21.5	1.2
Oklahoma	2 110	85.2	1.6	20.5	1.8
Oregon	2 085	84.7	1.8	24.3	2.2
Pennsylvania	8 024	82.4	1.1	22.9	1.2
Rhode Island	667	77.5	2.2	25.7	2.3
South Carolina	2 327	77.3	2.4	19.2	2.2
South Dakota	446	85.6	1.7	20.1	2.0
Tennessee	3 560	76.1	2.1	17.1	1.9
Texas	11 714	78.5	1.0	22.4	1.1
Utah	1 087	89.5	1.6	26.7	2.3
Vermont	377	84.4	2.3	23.7	2.7
Virginia	4 416	81.3	1.9	28.0	2.2
Washington	3 573	88.8	1.7	26.1	2.4
West Virginia	1 239	77.3	1.8	14.7	1.5
Wisconsin	3 395	87.1	1.6	22.4	2.0
Wyoming	307	91.3	1.4	22.2	2.1

Note: Population values shown in this table are derived from the CPS sample, and may not match independently-derived estimates of the population.

1. The value of 1.6 times the standard error [1.6*(s.e.)], added to and subtracted from the estimated percentage, yields the 90-percent confidence interval. For further details of calculation and interpretation, see appendix B, Source and Accuracy of the Estimates.

Table B-14. Educational Attainment of Persons 18 Years Old and Over, by Age, Sex, Race, and Hispanic Origin for the 25 Largest States: March 1997

(Numbers in thousands. Civilian noninstitutional population.)

Age, sex, race, Hispanic origin, and state	Total population	High school graduate or more		Completed Bachelor's degree or more	
		Percent	1.6* (s. e.) [1]	Percent	1.6* (s. e.) [1]
Alabama					
18 years and over	3 150	76.6	1.9	17.6	1.7
18 to 24 years	377	69.5	5.9	4.6	2.7
25 to 44 years	1 237	87.9	2.3	24.4	3.1
45 to 64 years	945	78.5	3.3	20.0	3.3
65 years and over	591	54.4	5.1	7.7	2.7
25 years and over	2 773	77.6	2.0	19.3	1.9
Male	1 267	78.4	2.9	19.0	2.8
Female	1 506	76.9	2.7	19.6	2.6
White	2 076	81.1	2.2	21.5	2.3
Black	683	66.6	4.8	12.4	3.4
Hispanic origin[2]	14	(B)	(B)	(B)	(B)
Arizona					
18 years and over	3 371	80.6	1.8	17.0	1.7
18 to 24 years	496	69.1	5.4	2.9	2.0
25 to 44 years	1 473	82.4	2.6	18.3	2.6
45 to 64 years	819	82.9	3.4	24.2	3.9
65 years and over	583	82.5	4.1	15.9	3.9
25 years and over	2 875	82.6	1.8	19.5	1.9
Male	1 385	82.9	2.6	21.4	2.9
Female	1 490	82.3	2.6	17.7	2.6
White	2 622	83.3	1.9	19.8	2.0
Black	115	74.7	11.2	15.5	9.3
Hispanic origin[2]	634	54.8	5.4	7.4	2.9
California					
18 years and over	23 222	79.5	0.8	24.9	0.8
18 to 24 years	2 992	71.6	2.4	7.6	1.4
25 to 44 years	10 810	81.1	1.1	27.0	1.3
45 to 64 years	6 089	83.4	1.4	31.7	1.8
65 years and over	3 331	74.4	2.2	21.3	2.1
25 years and over	20 229	80.7	0.8	27.5	0.9
Male	10 083	81.2	1.1	30.2	1.3
Female	10 146	80.2	1.2	24.8	1.3
White	16 342	79.7	0.9	26.2	1.0
Black	1 329	85.1	3.0	20.5	3.5
Hispanic origin[2]	4 795	49.5	2.3	8.8	1.3
Florida					
18 years and over	11 037	80.9	1.0	20.2	1.0
18 to 24 years	1 187	76.6	3.2	8.0	2.1
25 to 44 years	4 285	85.8	1.4	21.9	1.7
45 to 64 years	3 078	81.8	1.8	24.9	2.0
65 years and over	2 486	73.4	2.3	17.3	2.0
25 years and over	9 850	81.4	1.0	21.7	1.1
Male	4 711	80.8	1.5	25.1	1.7
Female	5 139	82.0	1.4	18.6	1.4
White	8 609	83.3	1.1	22.8	1.2
Black	1 055	64.7	4.1	9.6	2.5
Hispanic origin[2]	1 502	65.7	3.4	17.1	2.7

See footnotes at end of table.

Table B-14. Educational Attainment of Persons 18 Years Old and Over, by Age, Sex, Race, and Hispanic Origin for the 25 Largest States: March 1997 — Continued

(Numbers in thousands. Civilian noninstitutional population.)

Age, sex, race, Hispanic origin, and state	Total population	High school graduate or more		Completed Bachelor's degree or more	
		Percent	1.6* (s. e.) [1]	Percent	1.6* (s. e.) [1]
Georgia					
18 years and over	5 448	78.6	1.7	20.1	1.7
18 to 24 years	763	77.0	4.7	6.2	2.7
25 to 44 years	2 421	85.3	2.2	26.6	2.8
45 to 64 years	1 504	78.9	3.2	20.6	3.2
65 years and over	760	58.0	5.5	12.0	3.6
25 years and over	4 685	78.8	1.8	22.3	1.9
Male	2 288	77.6	2.7	22.3	2.7
Female	2 397	79.9	2.5	22.4	2.6
White	3 236	82.6	2.1	26.0	2.4
Black	1 351	70.5	4.1	12.7	3.0
Hispanic origin[2]	92	85.6	12.0	27.6	15.2
Illinois					
18 years and over	8 564	83.5	1.0	23.0	1.1
18 to 24 years	1 137	77.7	3.1	9.9	2.2
25 to 44 years	3 665	89.3	1.3	28.5	1.9
45 to 64 years	2 453	86.2	1.8	26.4	2.2
65 years and over	1 309	67.4	3.3	12.6	2.3
25 years and over	7 427	84.4	1.1	25.0	1.3
Male	3 479	83.5	1.6	28.1	1.9
Female	3 948	85.3	1.4	22.3	1.7
White	6 208	84.8	1.1	26.2	1.4
Black	991	81.9	3.3	12.0	2.8
Hispanic origin[2]	519	54.0	5.9	8.2	3.2
Indiana					
18 years and over	4 310	81.9	1.8	15.2	1.7
18 to 24 years	557	81.6	5.0	8.4	3.6
25 to 44 years	1 780	90.5	2.1	19.1	2.8
45 to 64 years	1 187	82.4	3.3	17.4	3.3
65 years and over	786	61.5	5.3	7.8	2.9
25 years and over	3 753	81.9	1.9	16.2	1.8
Male	1 797	84.4	2.6	17.0	2.7
Female	1 956	79.6	2.8	15.4	2.5
White	3 463	82.2	2.0	16.1	1.9
Black	247	74.3	9.0	7.5	5.4
Hispanic origin[2]	73	(B)	(B)	(B)	(B)
Kentucky					
18 years and over	2 874	75.3	2.0	15.7	1.7
18 to 24 years	386	75.0	5.5	3.0	2.2
25 to 44 years	1 254	86.0	2.4	21.1	2.9
45 to 64 years	747	74.0	4.0	14.9	3.2
65 years and over	486	50.3	5.6	12.7	3.7
25 years and over	2 487	75.4	2.1	17.6	1.9
Male	1 155	75.0	3.2	19.7	2.9
Female	1 332	75.7	2.9	15.8	2.5
White	2 323	75.0	2.2	17.9	2.0
Black	150	80.4	8.6	9.6	6.4
Hispanic origin[2]	15	(B)	(B)	(B)	(B)

See footnotes at end of table.

Table B-14.　Educational Attainment of Persons 18 Years Old and Over, by Age, Sex, Race, and Hispanic Origin for the 25 Largest States:　March 1997 — Continued

(Numbers in thousands.　Civilian noninstitutional population.)

Age, sex, race, Hispanic origin, and state	Total population	High school graduate or more		Completed Bachelor's degree or more	
		Percent	1.6* (s. e.) [1]	Percent	1.6* (s. e.) [1]
Louisiana					
18 years and over	3 105	75.2	2.0	16.1	1.7
18 to 24 years	464	72.3	5.3	4.2	2.4
25 to 44 years	1 295	83.0	2.6	19.7	2.8
45 to 64 years	862	75.4	3.7	20.1	3.5
65 years and over	483	56.3	5.7	10.6	3.6
25 years and over	2 641	75.7	2.1	18.1	1.9
Male	1 268	75.3	3.1	20.1	2.8
Female	1 372	76.0	2.9	16.4	2.5
White	1 900	79.5	2.3	21.7	2.4
Black	695	65.3	4.9	8.9	2.9
Hispanic origin[2]	51	(B)	(B)	(B)	(B)
Maryland					
18 years and over	3 767	84.5	1.9	28.4	2.3
18 to 24 years	491	83.3	5.4	3.4	2.6
25 to 44 years	1 701	90.0	2.3	33.2	3.6
45 to 64 years	994	88.1	3.3	35.2	4.8
65 years and over	580	63.4	6.4	24.0	5.7
25 years and over	3 275	84.7	2.0	32.2	2.6
Male	1 544	84.3	3.0	34.5	3.9
Female	1 731	85.1	2.7	30.1	3.5
White	2 394	85.6	2.3	35.1	3.1
Black	756	79.9	5.0	15.5	4.5
Hispanic origin[2]	119	63.8	14.9	32.0	14.5
Massachusetts					
18 years and over	4 611	85.5	1.2	31.1	1.6
18 to 24 years	552	82.8	3.8	14.2	3.5
25 to 44 years	2 082	90.7	1.5	39.7	2.5
45 to 64 years	1 236	86.7	2.3	35.5	3.2
65 years and over	741	70.7	3.9	12.5	2.9
25 years and over	4 059	85.9	1.3	33.5	1.7
Male	1 960	85.5	1.9	35.0	2.5
Female	2 100	86.2	1.8	32.0	2.4
White	3 788	86.7	1.3	34.0	1.8
Black	171	74.2	8.4	13.3	6.5
Hispanic origin[2]	132	63.9	10.5	10.3	6.6
Michigan					
18 years and over	7 006	85.3	1.0	18.9	1.2
18 to 24 years	944	80.7	3.2	5.2	1.8
25 to 44 years	2 847	92.3	1.2	23.2	2.0
45 to 64 years	2 015	88.9	1.7	22.1	2.3
65 years and over	1 199	66.1	3.4	14.0	2.5
25 years and over	6 061	86.0	1.1	21.0	1.3
Male	2 868	85.4	1.6	23.0	1.9
Female	3 193	86.5	1.5	19.2	1.7
White	5 215	86.9	1.2	21.9	1.4
Black	705	79.3	4.0	11.4	3.1
Hispanic origin[2]	132	65.2	10.9	10.0	6.8

See footnotes at end of table.

Table B-14. Educational Attainment of Persons 18 Years Old and Over, by Age, Sex, Race, and Hispanic Origin for the 25 Largest States: March 1997 — Continued

(Numbers in thousands. Civilian noninstitutional population.)

Age, sex, race, Hispanic origin, and state	Total population	High school graduate or more		Completed Bachelor's degree or more	
		Percent	1.6* (s. e.) [1]	Percent	1.6* (s. e.) [1]
Minnesota					
18 years and over	3 358	87.1	1.5	25.8	2.0
18 to 24 years	406	81.2	5.1	7.8	3.5
25 to 44 years	1 537	93.6	1.6	32.0	3.1
45 to 64 years	976	89.6	2.6	31.3	3.9
65 years and over	438	64.4	6.0	8.5	3.5
25 years and over	2 951	87.9	1.6	28.3	2.2
Male	1 438	86.6	2.4	31.8	3.2
Female	1 513	89.2	2.1	24.9	2.9
White	2 807	87.8	1.6	28.1	2.2
Black	84	93.9	7.3	27.2	13.6
Hispanic origin[2]	69	(B)	(B)	(B)	(B)
Missouri					
18 years and over	3 860	79.6	1.9	21.2	2.0
18 to 24 years	456	75.8	6.0	8.2	3.9
25 to 44 years	1 604	86.7	2.6	27.7	3.4
45 to 64 years	1 058	83.3	3.4	21.6	3.8
65 years and over	742	61.5	5.4	14.4	3.9
25 years and over	3 404	80.1	2.1	22.9	2.2
Male	1 583	80.5	3.0	24.2	3.2
Female	1 821	79.8	2.8	21.8	2.9
White	2 971	82.1	2.1	23.7	2.3
Black	355	67.1	8.0	14.1	5.9
Hispanic origin[2]	47	(B)	(B)	(B)	(B)
New Jersey					
18 years and over	5 990	84.2	1.1	26.2	1.3
18 to 24 years	705	79.8	3.5	9.1	2.5
25 to 44 years	2 577	92.6	1.2	33.7	2.1
45 to 64 years	1 690	86.2	1.9	29.0	2.5
65 years and over	1 017	62.6	3.5	14.5	2.5
25 years and over	5 284	84.8	1.1	28.5	1.4
Male	2 525	85.1	1.6	32.5	2.1
Female	2 759	84.5	1.6	24.9	1.9
White	4 339	85.2	1.2	28.4	1.6
Black	652	79.7	3.8	15.6	3.5
Hispanic origin[2]	536	64.3	5.0	13.7	3.6
New York					
18 years and over	13 542	79.2	0.9	23.6	0.9
18 to 24 years	1 716	74.1	2.6	8.4	1.7
25 to 44 years	5 690	86.1	1.1	29.5	1.5
45 to 64 years	3 917	81.0	1.6	26.8	1.8
65 years and over	2 219	62.5	2.6	14.3	1.9
25 years and over	11 826	80.0	0.9	25.8	1.0
Male	5 476	81.2	1.3	27.9	1.5
Female	6 350	79.0	1.3	23.9	1.3
White	9 356	82.3	1.0	27.7	1.2
Black	1 870	68.6	2.8	11.6	2.0
Hispanic origin[2]	1 571	52.0	3.3	8.7	1.9

See footnotes at end of table.

Table B-14. Educational Attainment of Persons 18 Years Old and Over, by Age, Sex, Race, and Hispanic Origin for the 25 Largest States: March 1997 — Continued

(Numbers in thousands. Civilian noninstitutional population.)

Age, sex, race, Hispanic origin, and state	Total population	High school graduate or more		Completed Bachelor's degree or more	
		Percent	1.6* (s. e.) [1]	Percent	1.6* (s. e.) [1]
North Carolina					
18 years and over	5 459	78.3	1.5	21.0	1.5
18 to 24 years	704	77.6	4.2	10.8	3.2
25 to 44 years	2 304	86.3	1.9	26.1	2.5
45 to 64 years	1 596	77.8	2.8	20.9	2.7
65 years and over	855	58.0	4.6	16.1	3.4
25 years and over	4 755	78.4	1.6	22.6	1.6
Male	2 305	76.6	2.4	24.2	2.4
Female	2 450	80.1	2.2	21.0	2.2
White	3 708	79.8	1.8	24.8	1.9
Black	914	74.1	4.2	13.7	3.3
Hispanic origin[2]	85	54.7	15.5	17.8	11.9
Ohio					
18 years and over	8 250	85.7	1.0	19.7	1.1
18 to 24 years	1 026	82.5	3.0	7.1	2.1
25 to 44 years	3 576	92.0	1.2	25.3	1.9
45 to 64 years	2 190	89.2	1.7	24.2	2.4
65 years and over	1 458	67.3	3.2	8.3	1.9
25 years and over	7 224	86.2	1.0	21.5	1.2
Male	3 458	86.5	1.5	25.5	1.9
Female	3 766	85.9	1.5	17.9	1.6
White	6 425	87.2	1.1	22.0	1.3
Black	704	76.2	4.4	12.4	3.4
Hispanic origin[2]	77	60.1	15.3	13.4	10.7
Pennsylvania					
18 years and over	8 957	82.2	1.0	21.3	1.1
18 to 24 years	933	70.8	3.3	7.4	2.1
25 to 44 years	3 659	92.0	1.1	29.1	1.9
45 to 64 years	2 636	83.8	1.8	21.6	2.0
65 years and over	1 730	60.1	2.9	11.8	1.9
25 years and over	8 024	82.4	1.1	22.9	1.2
Male	3 742	83.0	1.5	25.7	1.8
Female	4 282	81.9	1.5	20.5	1.5
White	7 085	83.3	1.1	23.8	1.3
Black	758	76.2	4.1	12.2	3.2
Hispanic origin[2]	141	55.0	11.1	7.0	5.7
South Carolina					
18 years and over	2 749	77.3	2.2	17.3	2.0
18 to 24 years	422	77.3	5.6	6.8	3.3
25 to 44 years	1 140	87.0	2.7	20.7	3.3
45 to 64 years	825	73.8	4.2	20.0	3.8
65 years and over	362	54.8	7.1	12.9	4.8
25 years and over	2 327	77.3	2.4	19.2	2.2
Male	1 094	76.2	3.5	21.0	3.4
Female	1 233	78.4	3.2	17.7	3.0
White	1 717	81.3	2.6	22.6	2.7
Black	598	66.1	5.6	10.0	3.5
Hispanic origin[2]	19	(B)	(B)	(B)	(B)

See footnotes at end of table.

Table B-14. Educational Attainment of Persons 18 Years Old and Over, by Age, Sex, Race, and Hispanic Origin for the 25 Largest States: March 1997 — Continued

(Numbers in thousands. Civilian noninstitutional population.)

Age, sex, race, Hispanic origin, and state	Total population	High school graduate or more		Completed Bachelor's degree or more	
		Percent	1.6* (s. e.) [1]	Percent	1.6* (s. e.) [1]
Tennessee					
18 years and over	4 040	75.6	2.0	15.9	1.7
18 to 24 years	479	72.4	6.1	6.6	3.4
25 to 44 years	1 748	87.7	2.4	20.4	2.9
45 to 64 years	1 137	73.1	3.9	15.3	3.2
65 years and over	675	51.0	5.8	11.5	3.7
25 years and over	3 560	76.1	2.1	17.1	1.9
Male	1 645	75.0	3.2	19.0	2.9
Female	1 916	77.0	2.9	15.5	2.5
White	2 924	75.0	2.4	18.0	2.1
Black	600	80.9	5.1	11.1	4.1
Hispanic origin[2]	19	(B)	(B)	(B)	(B)
Texas					
18 years and over	13 659	77.6	1.0	19.8	0.9
18 to 24 years	1 945	71.9	2.8	4.5	1.3
25 to 44 years	6 258	83.6	1.3	23.9	1.5
45 to 64 years	3 661	77.7	1.9	23.9	1.9
65 years and over	1 795	62.1	3.1	14.0	2.2
25 years and over	11 714	78.5	1.0	22.4	1.1
Male	5 560	78.1	1.5	24.6	1.6
Female	6 154	78.9	1.4	20.4	1.4
White	10 079	77.4	1.1	22.5	1.1
Black	1 245	83.9	3.0	16.9	3.1
Hispanic origin[2]	3 125	52.4	2.6	9.0	1.5
Virginia					
18 years and over	5 024	81.4	1.8	26.2	2.0
18 to 24 years	608	82.1	5.0	13.0	4.4
25 to 44 years	2 141	89.8	2.1	31.9	3.2
45 to 64 years	1 528	77.0	3.4	25.8	3.6
65 years and over	748	65.5	5.5	21.4	4.8
25 years and over	4 416	81.3	1.9	28.0	2.2
Male	2 138	78.5	2.8	30.9	3.2
Female	2 279	83.8	2.5	25.4	2.9
White	3 351	83.2	2.1	30.3	2.5
Black	902	71.7	5.1	15.0	4.0
Hispanic origin[2]	119	73.6	13.7	27.8	14.0
Washington					
18 years and over	4 115	87.5	1.7	22.9	2.2
18 to 24 years	542	79.1	5.8	1.9	1.9
25 to 44 years	1 822	90.1	2.3	25.0	3.4
45 to 64 years	1 246	90.9	2.7	30.3	4.3
65 years and over	505	79.1	6.0	19.5	5.8
25 years and over	3 573	88.8	1.7	26.1	2.4
Male	1 769	88.0	2.6	27.6	3.5
Female	1 804	89.6	2.4	24.6	3.4
White	3 285	89.0	1.8	26.2	2.5
Black	67	(B)	(B)	(B)	(B)
Hispanic origin[2]	137	37.9	14.6	4.6	6.3

See footnotes at end of table.

Table B-14. Educational Attainment of Persons 18 Years Old and Over, by Age, Sex, Race, and Hispanic Origin for the 25 Largest States: March 1997 — Continued

(Numbers in thousands. Civilian noninstitutional population.)

Age, sex, race, Hispanic origin, and state	Total population	High school graduate or more		Completed Bachelor's degree or more	
		Percent	1.6* (s. e.) [1]	Percent	1.6* (s. e.) [1]
Wisconsin					
18 years and over	3 775	87.1	1.5	21.1	1.8
18 to 24 years	380	86.3	4.9	9.6	4.2
25 to 44 years	1 756	94.3	1.5	25.9	2.9
45 to 64 years	1 044	90.2	2.6	22.2	3.6
65 years and over	595	60.9	5.6	12.4	3.8
25 years and over	3 395	87.1	1.6	22.4	2.0
Male	1 641	88.0	2.2	24.9	3.0
Female	1 754	86.4	2.3	20.1	2.7
White	3 210	87.8	1.6	22.9	2.1
Black	127	77.1	11.0	9.8	7.8
Hispanic origin[2]	64	(B)	(B)	(B)	(B)

Note: Based on population estimates of states as of July 1, 1986. Population values shown in this table are derived from the CPS sample, and may not match independently-derived estimates of the population.

1. The value of 1.6 times the standard error [1.6*(s.e.)], added to and subtracted from the estimated percentage, yields the 90-percent confidence interval. For further details of calculation and interpretation, see appendix B, Source and Accuracy of the Estimates.

2. Persons of Hispanic origin may be of any race.

(B) Base less than 75,000.

Table B-15. Years of School Completed by People 25 Years Old and Over, by Age and Sex: Selected Years 1940 to 1997

(Numbers in thousands. Civilian noninstitutional population.)

Age, sex, and years	Total	Years of school completed						Median
		Elementary		High School		College		
		0 to 4 years	5 to 8 years	1 to 3 years	4 years	1 to 3 years	4 years or more	
25 YEARS OLD AND OVER								
Both Sexes								
1997	170 581	2 840	10 472	17 211	57 586	41 774	40 697	(NA)
1996	168 323	3 027	10 595	17 102	56 559	41 372	39 668	(NA)
1995	166 438	3 074	10 873	16 566	56 450	41 249	38 226	(NA)
1994	164 512	3 156	11 359	16 925	56 515	40 014	36 544	(NA)
1993	162 826	3 380	11 747	17 067	57 589	37 451	35 590	(NA)
1992	160 827	3 449	11 989	17 672	57 860	35 520	34 337	(NA)
1991	158 694	3 803	13 046	17 379	61 272	29 170	34 026	12.7
1990	156 538	3 833	13 758	17 461	60 119	28 075	33 291	12.7
1989	154 155	3 861	14 061	17 719	59 336	26 614	32 565	12.7
1988	151 635	3 714	14 550	17 847	58 940	25 799	30 787	12.7
1987	149 144	3 640	15 301	17 417	57 669	25 479	29 637	12.7
1986	146 606	3 894	15 672	17 484	56 338	24 729	28 489	12.6
1985	143 524	3 873	16 020	17 553	54 866	23 405	27 808	12.6
1984	140 794	3 884	16 258	17 433	54 073	22 281	26 862	12.6
1983	138 020	4 119	16 714	17 681	52 060	21 531	25 915	12.6
1982	135 526	4 119	17 232	18 006	51 426	20 692	24 050	12.6
1981	132 899	4 358	17 868	18 041	49 915	20 042	22 674	12.5
1980	130 409	4 390	18 426	18 086	47 934	19 379	22 193	12.5
1979	125 295	4 324	18 504	17 579	45 915	18 393	20 579	12.5
1978	123 019	4 445	19 309	18 175	44 381	17 379	19 332	12.4
1977	120 870	4 509	19 567	18 318	43 602	16 247	18 627	12.4
1976	118 848	4 601	19 912	18 204	43 157	15 477	17 496	12.4
1975	116 897	4 912	20 633	18 237	42 353	14 518	16 244	12.3
1974	115 005	5 106	21 200	18 274	41 460	13 665	15 300	12.3
1973	112 866	5 100	21 838	18 420	40 448	12 831	14 228	12.3
1972	111 133	5 124	22 503	18 855	39 171	12 117	13 364	12.2
1971	110 627	5 574	24 029	18 601	38 029	11 782	12 612	12.2
1970	109 310	5 747	24 519	18 682	37 134	11 164	12 062	12.2
1969	107 750	6 014	24 976	18 527	36 133	10 564	11 535	12.1
1968	106 469	6 248	25 467	18 724	34 603	10 254	11 171	12.1
1967	104 864	6 400	26 178	18 647	33 173	9 914	10 550	12.0
1966	103 876	6 705	26 478	18 859	32 391	9 235	10 212	12.0
1965	103 245	6 982	27 063	18 617	31 703	9 139	9 742	11.8
1964	102 421	7 295	27 551	18 419	30 728	9 085	9 345	11.7
1962	100 664	7 826	28 438	17 751	28 477	9 170	9 002	11.4
1960	99 465	8 303	31 218	19 140	24 440	8 747	7 617	10.6
1959	97 478	7 816	28 490	17 520	26 219	7 888	7 734	11.0
1957	95 630	8 561	29 316	16 951	24 832	6 985	7 172	10.6
1952	88 358	8 004	30 274	15 228	21 074	6 714	6 118	10.1
1950	87 484	9 491	31 617	14 817	17 625	6 246	5 272	9.3
1947	82 578	8 611	32 308	13 487	16 926	5 533	4 424	9.0
1940	74 776	10 105	34 413	11 182	10 552	4 075	3 407	8.6
Male								
1997	81 620	1 454	5 023	8 212	26 226	19 332	21 374	(NA)
1996	80 339	1 537	5 067	7 930	25 649	19 301	20 854	(NA)
1995	79 463	1 598	5 231	7 691	25 378	18 933	20 631	(NA)
1994	78 539	1 669	5 427	7 789	25 404	18 544	19 705	(NA)
1993	77 644	1 709	5 594	7 821	25 766	17 521	19 234	(NA)
1992	76 579	1 737	5 726	8 085	25 774	16 631	18 627	(NA)
1991	75 487	2 018	6 299	7 887	27 189	13 720	18 373	12.8
1990	74 421	2 004	6 557	8 000	26 426	13 271	18 164	12.8
1989	73 225	1 956	6 659	8 076	25 897	12 725	17 913	12.8

See footnotes at end of table.

Table B-15. Years of School Completed by People 25 Years Old and Over, by Age and Sex: Selected Years 1940 to 1997 – Continued

(Numbers in thousands. Civilian noninstitutional population.)

| Age, sex, and years | Total | Years of school completed | | | | | | Median |
| | | Elementary | | High School | | College | | |
		0 to 4 years	5 to 8 years	1 to 3 years	4 years	1 to 3 years	4 years or more	
1988	71 911	1 852	6 849	8 247	25 638	12 057	17 268	12.7
1987	70 677	1 794	7 259	7 909	24 998	12 062	16 654	12.7
1986	69 503	1 978	7 446	7 872	24 260	11 856	16 091	12.7
1985	67 756	1 947	7 629	7 783	23 552	11 164	15 682	12.7
1984	66 350	1 945	7 688	7 837	22 990	10 678	15 211	12.7
1983	65 004	2 103	7 750	7 867	22 048	10 310	14 926	12.7
1982	63 764	2 074	7 987	7 960	21 749	10 020	13 974	12.6
1981	62 509	2 141	8 322	8 084	21 019	9 734	13 208	12.6
1980	61 389	2 212	8 627	8 046	20 080	9 593	12 832	12.6
1979	58 986	2 190	8 785	7 636	19 250	9 100	12 025	12.6
1978	57 922	2 230	9 195	7 821	18 620	8 657	11 398	12.5
1977	56 917	2 296	9 330	7 969	18 290	8 104	10 926	12.5
1976	55 902	2 371	9 463	7 923	18 048	7 699	10 397	12.5
1975	55 036	2 568	9 760	7 985	17 769	7 274	9 679	12.4
1974	54 167	2 637	10 186	7 966	17 488	6 756	9 135	12.4
1073	53 007	2 598	10 488	8 120	17 011	6 376	8 473	12.3
1972	52 351	2 634	10 854	8 413	16 424	5 972	8 055	12.3
1971	52 357	2 933	11 703	8 264	16 008	5 798	7 653	12.2
1970	51 784	3 031	11 925	8 355	15 571	5 580	7 321	12.2
1969	51 031	3 095	12 182	8 398	15 177	5 263	6 917	12.1
1968	50 510	3 261	12 407	8 564	14 613	4 945	6 721	12.1
1967	49 756	3 417	12 736	8 463	14 015	4 755	6 372	12.0
1966	49 410	3 614	12 992	8 611	13 672	4 342	6 180	11.8
1965	49 242	3 774	13 308	8 529	13 334	4 370	5 923	11.7
1964	48 975	3 959	13 467	8 537	12 902	4 394	5 714	11.5
1962	48 283	4 213	13 927	8 399	11 932	4 315	5 497	11.1
1960	47 997	4 522	15 562	8 988	10 175	4 127	4 626	10.3
1959	47 041	4 257	14 039	8 326	10 870	3 801	4 765	10.7
1957	46 208	4 610	14 634	8 003	10 230	3 347	4 359	10.3
1952	42 368	4 396	14 876	7 048	8 760	3 164	3 480	9.7
1950	42 627	5 074	15 852	6 974	7 511	2 888	3 008	9.0
1947	40 483	4 615	16 086	6 535	7 353	2 625	2 478	8.9
1940	37 463	5 550	17 639	5 333	4 507	1 824	2 021	8.6
Female								
1997	88 961	1 387	5 450	8 999	31 360	22 442	19 323	(NA)
1996	87 984	1 491	5 528	9 171	30 911	22 071	18 813	(NA)
1995	86 975	1 476	5 642	8 874	31 072	22 317	17 594	(NA)
1994	85 973	1 487	5 932	9 135	31 111	21 470	16 838	(NA)
1993	85 181	1 672	6 154	9 246	31 823	19 930	16 357	(NA)
1992	84 248	1 712	6 263	9 587	32 086	18 889	15 709	(NA)
1991	83 207	1 784	6 747	9 491	34 083	15 449	15 652	12.7
1990	82 116	1 829	7 200	9 462	33 693	14 806	15 126	12.7
1989	80 930	1 904	7 402	9 643	33 440	13 888	14 652	12.6
1988	79 724	1 862	7 700	9 599	33 303	13 741	13 519	12.6
1987	78 467	1 846	8 042	9 508	32 671	13 417	12 983	12.6
1986	77 102	1 916	8 226	9 612	32 078	12 874	12 399	12.6
1985	75 768	1 926	8 390	9 770	31 314	12 242	12 126	12.6
1984	74 444	1 939	8 571	9 596	31 083	11 603	11 651	12.6
1983	73 016	2 015	8 964	9 814	30 012	11 220	10 990	12.5
1982	71 762	2 045	9 245	10 046	29 677	10 673	10 076	12.5
1981	70 390	2 217	9 545	9 957	28 896	10 309	9 466	12.5
1980	69 020	2 178	9 800	10 040	27 854	9 786	9 362	12.4
1979	66 309	2 133	9 720	9 945	26 665	9 293	8 554	12.4
1978	65 097	2 214	10 114	10 353	25 761	8 721	7 934	12.4
1977	63 953	2 213	10 236	10 349	25 312	8 142	7 701	12.4
1976	62 946	2 230	10 449	10 281	25 109	7 779	7 098	12.3
1975	61 861	2 344	10 871	10 252	24 584	7 243	6 565	12.3
1974	60 838	2 469	11 015	10 308	23 972	6 910	6 165	12.3

See footnotes at end of table.

**Table B-15.   Years of School Completed by People 25 Years Old and Over, by Age and Sex: Selected Years 1940 to 1997
— Continued**

(Numbers in thousands. Civilian noninstitutional population.)

| Age, sex, and years | Total | Years of school completed | | | | | | Median |
| | | Elementary | | High School | | College | | |
		0 to 4 years	5 to 8 years	1 to 3 years	4 years	1 to 3 years	4 years or more	
1973	59 799	2 502	11 350	10 300	23 437	6 454	5 755	12.2
1972	58 782	2 490	11 649	10 442	22 746	6 145	5 309	12.2
1971	58 270	2 641	12 327	10 339	22 021	5 984	4 959	12.2
1970	57 527	2 716	12 595	10 327	21 563	5 584	4 743	12.1
1969	56 719	2 919	12 796	10 131	20 955	5 301	4 619	12.1
1968	55 959	2 987	13 060	10 160	19 991	5 309	4 450	12.1
1967	55 107	2 985	13 439	10 185	19 157	5 162	4 178	12.0
1966	54 467	3 090	13 488	10 246	18 719	4 892	4 032	12.0
1965	54 004	3 207	13 753	10 085	18 369	4 767	3 820	12.0
1964	53 447	3 333	14 086	9 881	17 825	4 686	3 629	11.8
1962	52 381	3 613	14 511	9 352	16 545	4 855	3 505	11.6
1960	51 468	3 781	15 656	10 151	14 267	4 620	2 991	10.9
1959	50 437	3 559	14 451	9 194	15 349	4 087	2 969	11.2
1957	49 422	3 951	14 682	8 948	14 602	3 638	2 813	10.9
1952	45 990	3 608	15 398	8 180	12 314	3 550	2 638	10.4
1950	44 857	4 417	15 824	7 843	10 114	3 358	2 264	9.6
1947	42 095	3 996	16 222	6 952	9 573	2 908	1 946	8.9
1940	37 313	4 554	16 773	5 849	6 044	2 251	1 386	8.7

25 to 34 YEARS OLD

Both Sexes

Age, sex, and years	Total	0 to 4 years	5 to 8 years	1 to 3 years	4 years	1 to 3 years	4 years or more	Median
1997	40 256	334	1 163	3 624	12 710	11 524	10 892	(NA)
1996	40 919	418	1 169	3 780	13 087	11 624	10 841	(NA)
1995	41 388	394	1 264	3 667	14 061	11 659	10 342	(NA)
1994	41 946	367	1 297	4 057	14 483	11 913	9 829	(NA)
1993	41 864	382	1 223	3 894	15 036	11 361	9 968	(NA)
1992	42 493	433	1 250	4 071	16 021	10 860	9 861	(NA)
1991	42 905	465	1 322	4 178	17 503	9 283	10 153	12.9
1990	43 240	505	1 413	4 041	17 635	9 320	10 326	12.9
1989	43 240	446	1 352	4 013	17 901	9 072	10 454	12.9
1988	42 953	430	1 308	4 095	17 887	9 076	10 155	12.9
1987	42 635	390	1 360	3 995	17 539	9 157	10 196	12.9
1986	42 053	387	1 359	3 797	17 311	9 104	10 094	12.9
1985	40 858	362	1 328	3 703	16 748	8 980	9 737	12.9
1984	40 173	404	1 371	3 638	16 431	8 555	9 771	12.9
1983	39 342	376	1 324	3 664	15 804	8 567	9 605	12.9
1982	38 703	337	1 371	3 598	15 893	8 304	9 200	12.9
1981	37 828	337	1 428	3 665	15 419	8 198	8 782	12.9
1980	36 615	362	1 424	3 571	14 481	7 942	8 836	12.9
1979	34 053	370	1 381	3 452	13 338	7 415	8 096	12.9
1978	33 120	325	1 459	3 515	12 993	7 008	7 821	12.9
1977	32 284	269	1 383	3 715	12 845	6 398	7 676	12.8
1976	31 148	247	1 508	3 619	12 920	5 813	7 041	12.8
1975	30 092	313	1 644	3 743	12 544	5 403	6 443	12.7
1974	28 972	352	1 654	3 763	12 362	5 056	5 785	12.7
1973	27 793	333	1 850	3 915	12 194	4 454	5 047	12.6
1972	26 517	285	1 791	3 981	11 635	4 090	4 734	12.6
1971	25 545	327	2 011	3 986	11 232	3 822	4 169	12.6
1970	24 865	329	1 937	4 251	10 929	3 491	3 926	12.5
1969	24 072	359	2 086	4 140	10 592	3 202	3 693	12.5
1968	23 285	350	2 246	4 129	10 157	2 989	3 413	12.5
1967	22 388	319	2 293	4 017	9 645	2 946	3 169	12.5
1966	22 023	430	2 208	4 158	9 546	2 647	3 037	12.4
1965	21 980	543	2 437	4 058	9 500	2 561	2 880	12.4
1964	21 997	502	2 591	4 176	9 370	2 529	2 830	12.4
1962	22 130	597	2 936	4 371	8 815	2 552	2 859	12.4
1960	22 821	709	3 738	5 135	8 166	2 572	2 499	12.4

See footnotes at end of table.

Table B-15. Years of School Completed by People 25 Years Old and Over, by Age and Sex: Selected Years 1940 to 1997 – Continued

(Numbers in thousands. Civilian noninstitutional population.)

Age, sex, and years	Total	Years of school completed						Median
		Elementary		High School		College		
		0 to 4 years	5 to 8 years	1 to 3 years	4 years	1 to 3 years	4 years or more	
1959	22 922	761	3 348	4 741	8 979	2 398	2 480	12.3
1957	23 437	750	3 971	4 965	8 927	2 275	2 351	12.2
1952	23 138	844	4 362	4 898	8 620	2 220	2 052	12.2
1950	23 626	1 147	5 308	5 050	7 660	2 198	1 252	11.9
1947	22 627	1 015	5 523	4 997	7 630	1 908	1 378	11.9
1940	21 339	1 377	7 676	4 553	4 702	1 554	1 288	10.0
Male								
1997	20 039	193	629	2 007	6 482	5 477	5 249	(NA)
1996	20 390	225	601	2 055	6 701	5 536	5 274	(NA)
1995	20 589	229	708	1 930	7 176	5 373	5 174	(NA)
1994	20 873	230	716	2 134	7 408	5 510	4 873	(NA)
1993	20 856	237	679	1 986	7 604	5 308	5 041	(NA)
1992	21 125	231	682	2 057	8 113	5 116	4 927	(NA)
1991	21 319	270	694	2 095	8 810	4 441	5 009	12.9
1990	21 462	295	759	2 153	8 649	4 392	5 215	12.9
1989	21 461	251	698	2 129	8 659	4 391	5 335	12.9
1988	21 277	237	651	2 227	8 569	4 273	5 319	12.9
1987	21 142	223	698	2 030	8 544	4 384	5 263	12.9
1986	20 956	227	715	1 887	8 359	4 488	5 279	12.9
1985	20 184	194	700	1 823	7 955	4 433	5 080	12.9
1984	19 876	231	721	1 739	7 798	4 238	5 150	12.9
1983	19 438	213	659	1 724	7 351	4 284	5 207	13.0
1982	19 090	182	659	1 654	7 380	4 162	5 053	13.0
1981	18 625	176	733	1 679	6 991	4 185	4 863	13.0
1980	18 051	198	699	1 639	6 393	4 166	4 957	13.0
1979	16 719	197	695	1 476	5 852	3 862	4 637	13.0
1978	16 263	154	717	1 526	5 701	3 698	4 471	13.1
1977	15 863	134	672	1 625	5 634	3 403	4 396	13.0
1976	15 266	134	724	1 566	5 672	3 085	4 087	12.9
1975	14 776	177	815	1 605	5 508	2 915	3 757	12.9
1974	14 222	211	859	1 617	5 491	2 672	3 372	12.8
1973	13 638	204	966	1 760	5 363	2 416	2 927	12.7
1972	13 030	157	927	1 796	5 150	2 191	2 809	12.7
1971	12 596	170	1 092	1 771	5 049	2 005	2 506	12.6
1970	12 236	189	1 063	1 896	4 833	1 842	2 412	12.6
1969	11 788	204	1 121	1 849	4 652	1 719	2 241	12.6
1968	11 381	193	1 192	1 880	4 473	1 505	2 136	12.5
1967	10 876	170	1 209	1 814	4 187	1 522	1 973	12.5
1966	10 701	241	1 162	1 839	4 191	1 374	1 894	12.5
1965	10 693	325	1 240	1 802	4 188	1 316	1 822	12.5
1964	10 729	297	1 344	1 962	4 008	1 306	1 812	12.4
1962	10 762	334	1 569	2 008	3 700	1 309	1 842	12.4
1960	11 184	420	2 026	2 441	3 356	1 316	1 624	12.2
1959	11 226	416	1 822	2 238	3 682	1 256	1 658	12.3
1957	11 368	423	2 097	2 446	3 542	1 181	1 556	12.2
1952	10 936	502	2 202	2 268	3 458	1 118	1 268	12.1
1950	11 454	631	2 705	2 426	3 250	1 117	1 037	11.5
1947	10 894	544	2 665	2 494	3 337	993	738	11.7
1940	10 521	779	3 932	2 220	2 049	692	744	9.7
Female								
1997	20 217	149	533	1 615	6 227	6 047	5 643	(NA)
1996	20 528	195	569	1 734	6 386	6 090	5 568	(NA)
1995	20 800	165	556	1 738	6 885	6 286	5 170	(NA)
1994	21 073	138	581	1 923	7 075	6 404	4 953	(NA)
1993	21 007	143	543	1 907	7 432	6 054	4 928	(NA)

See footnotes at end of table.

Table B-15.   Years of School Completed by People 25 Years Old and Over, by Age and Sex: Selected Years 1940 to 1997 – Continued

(Numbers in thousands. Civilian noninstitutional population.)

| Age, sex, and years | Total | Years of school completed | | | | | | Median |
| | | Elementary | | High School | | College | | |
		0 to 4 years	5 to 8 years	1 to 3 years	4 years	1 to 3 years	4 years or more	
1992	21 368	203	567	2 014	7 908	5 744	4 933	(NA)
1991	21 586	195	629	2 085	8 693	4 841	5 143	12.9
1990	21 779	209	653	1 889	8 986	4 927	5 112	12.9
1989	21 777	195	654	1 885	9 242	4 681	5 119	12.9
1988	21 675	193	657	1 869	9 319	4 801	4 836	12.9
1987	21 494	168	662	1 965	8 995	4 772	4 932	12.9
1986	21 097	160	644	1 910	8 952	4 616	4 813	12.9
1985	20 673	168	627	1 880	8 794	4 547	4 657	12.9
1984	20 297	173	649	1 904	8 634	4 319	4 621	12.9
1983	19 903	161	665	1 941	8 452	4 285	4 398	12.9
1982	19 614	155	713	1 942	8 512	4 140	4 148	12.8
1981	19 203	161	698	1 986	8 427	4 013	3 918	12.8
1980	18 565	164	725	1 932	8 087	3 777	3 879	12.8
1979	17 334	173	685	1 977	7 486	3 553	3 460	12.8
1978	16 857	172	742	1 989	7 292	3 311	3 351	12.6
1977	16 421	136	710	2 088	7 212	2 995	3 280	12.7
1976	15 882	112	784	2 054	7 248	2 731	2 954	12.7
1975	15 316	135	833	2 139	7 037	2 489	2 686	12.6
1974	14 750	142	796	2 145	6 871	2 383	2 413	12.6
1973	14 155	129	884	2 154	6 830	2 037	2 121	12.6
1972	13 487	128	862	2 184	6 485	1 899	1 926	12.5
1971	12 950	156	919	2 212	6 183	1 816	1 663	12.5
1970	12 629	140	876	2 355	6 096	1 648	1 512	12.5
1969	12 285	155	965	2 291	5 941	1 481	1 451	12.4
1968	11 904	157	1 053	2 246	5 684	1 484	1 278	12.4
1967	11 512	149	1 084	2 200	5 458	1 426	1 195	12.4
1966	11 322	186	1 047	2 319	5 355	1 273	1 134	12.4
1965	11 284	218	1 197	2 256	5 310	1 244	1 060	12.4
1964	11 269	202	1 248	2 216	5 362	1 221	1 018	12.4
1962	11 368	263	1 367	2 363	5 115	1 243	1 017	12.3
1960	11 637	289	1 712	2 694	4 810	1 256	875	12.2
1959	11 696	345	1 526	2 503	5 297	1 142	822	12.3
1957	12 069	327	1 874	2 519	5 385	1 094	795	12.2
1952	12 202	342	2 160	2 630	5 162	1 102	784	12.2
1950	12 172	516	2 603	2 624	4 410	1 081	714	12.1
1947	11 733	471	2 858	2 503	4 293	915	640	12.0
1940	10 818	598	3 744	2 333	2 653	862	544	10.3

35 to 54 YEARS OLD

Both Sexes

1997	76 973	867	2 686	6 045	26 054	20 684	20 635	(NA)
1996	74 661	968	2 710	5 803	24 924	20 105	20 152	(NA)
1995	73 028	927	2 561	5 664	24 070	19 926	19 878	(NA)
1994	71 049	987	2 680	5 415	23 804	19 210	18 956	(NA)
1993	68 845	942	2 486	5 538	23 927	17 984	17 970	(NA)
1992	66 594	899	2 608	5 845	23 442	16 658	17 144	(NA)
1991	64 351	995	3 057	5 522	24 815	13 348	16 614	12.9
1990	62 499	980	3 104	5 529	24 434	12 553	15 899	12.9
1989	60 494	999	3 315	5 800	23 334	11 627	15 417	12.9
1988	58 555	958	3 272	5 889	23 049	11 017	14 369	12.8
1987	56 650	842	3 398	5 656	22 820	10 523	13 409	12.8
1986	55 170	896	3 614	5 769	22 151	10 110	12 629	12.8
1985	53 697	899	3 639	5 978	21 600	9 217	12 363	12.8
1984	52 297	893	3 754	6 158	21 290	8 702	11 500	12.7
1983	50 956	973	4 044	6 313	20 788	8 045	10 795	12.7
1982	49 722	963	4 320	6 657	20 445	7 580	9 756	12.6
1981	48 680	1 038	4 531	6 773	20 032	7 115	9 181	12.6
1980	48 124	1 034	4 676	7 063	19 584	6 943	8 822	12.6

See footnotes at end of table.

Table B-15. Years of School Completed by People 25 Years Old and Over, by Age and Sex: Selected Years 1940 to 1997 – Continued

(Numbers in thousands. Civilian noninstitutional population.)

Age, sex, and years	Total	Years of school completed						Median
		Elementary		High School		College		
		0 to 4 years	5 to 8 years	1 to 3 years	4 years	1 to 3 years	4 years or more	
1979	47 437	1 030	4 895	7 132	19 488	6 655	8 237	12.5
1978	46 921	1 107	5 262	7 590	19 012	6 286	7 667	12.5
1977	46 409	1 192	5 445	7 781	18 781	6 013	7 196	12.5
1976	46 271	1 245	5 729	7 671	18 893	5 957	6 776	12.5
1975	46 193	1 296	5 942	7 765	19 010	5 673	6 506	12.4
1974	46 217	1 293	6 244	7 896	19 038	5 375	6 372	12.4
1973	45 910	1 344	6 519	8 001	18 651	5 318	6 076	12.4
1972	45 956	1 367	7 004	8 521	18 400	5 074	5 589	12.3
1971	46 294	1 439	7 588	8 393	18 334	5 082	5 460	12.3
1970	46 319	1 461	7 935	8 555	18 200	4 875	5 294	12.3
1969	46 255	1 644	8 313	8 586	17 773	4 749	5 190	12.3
1968	46 396	1 654	8 698	8 838	17 362	4 642	5 200	12.2
1967	46 321	1 771	9 036	9 138	16 906	4 525	4 947	12.2
1966	46 313	1 837	9 528	9 309	16 605	4 230	4 805	12.1
1965	46 296	1 827	9 812	9 266	16 359	4 384	4 647	12.1
1964	46 089	1 905	10 259	9 289	15 760	4 397	4 482	12.1
1962	45 287	2 181	10 795	8 938	14 668	4 452	4 253	12.0
1960	44 742	2 424	12 536	9 502	12 517	4 123	3 639	11.3
1959	43 989	2 303	11 657	8 719	13 244	3 715	3 709	11.8
1957	42 645	2 658	12 349	8 384	12 041	3 248	3 360	11.3
1952	39 014	2 606	13 274	7 348	9 374	3 148	2 802	10.5
1950	38 432	3 404	14 420	6 976	7 262	2 878	2 516	9.7
1947	36 717	3 203	15 184	6 311	6 715	2 622	2 221	9.0
1940	33 845	4 549	16 270	4 972	4 217	1 836	1 540	8.6
Male								
1997	37 912	486	1 370	3 143	12 326	9 713	10 870	(NA)
1996	36 596	520	1 319	2 877	11 749	9 514	10 526	(NA)
1995	35 994	529	1 368	2 781	11 223	9 305	10 784	(NA)
1994	34 998	545	1 383	2 621	11 009	9 073	10 369	(NA)
1993	33 751	478	1 316	2 660	10 983	8 624	9 687	(NA)
1992	32 619	472	1 368	2 750	10 670	7 968	9 389	(NA)
1991	31 460	530	1 624	2 612	11 092	6 430	9 169	13.0
1990	30 623	527	1 658	2 573	10 790	6 169	8 905	13.0
1989	29 597	504	1 762	2 628	10 235	5 719	8 749	13.0
1988	28 645	498	1 725	2 654	10 100	5 327	8 340	12.9
1987	27 680	412	1 801	2 617	9 781	5 173	7 895	12.9
1986	26 925	475	1 919	2 699	9 393	5 013	7 426	12.9
1985	26 181	501	1 928	2 726	9 210	4 502	7 314	12.9
1984	25 460	506	2 014	2 831	8 926	4 257	6 929	12.8
1983	24 796	548	2 108	2 862	8 795	3 884	6 601	12.8
1982	24 164	530	2 302	2 989	8 609	3 757	5 977	12.7
1981	23 646	572	2 425	3 112	8 431	3 519	5 588	12.7
1980	23 373	590	2 492	3 202	8 278	3 442	5 370	12.7
1979	22 976	545	2 612	3 194	8 232	3 306	5 090	12.6
1978	22 719	609	2 779	3 377	8 001	3 136	4 817	12.6
1977	22 445	661	2 889	3 554	7 822	3 000	4 520	12.5
1976	22 403	730	3 004	3 473	7 904	2 969	4 323	12.5
1975	22 358	763	3 100	3 510	7 952	2 879	4 153	12.5
1974	22 367	733	3 286	3 532	8 004	2 730	4 081	12.6
1973	22 166	716	3 413	3 586	7 836	2 714	3 901	12.4
1972	22 200	749	3 674	3 917	7 663	2 564	3 631	12.4
1971	22 474	849	3 985	3 823	7 674	2 578	3 567	12.3
1970	22 475	834	4 208	3 876	7 612	2 555	3 390	12.3
1969	22 420	889	4 359	4 012	7 427	2 456	3 277	12.3
1968	22 521	931	4 487	4 160	7 324	2 364	3 257	12.2
1967	22 482	1 000	4 700	4 270	7 143	2 244	3 128	12.2
1966	22 508	1 085	4 886	4 455	6 990	2 029	3 063	12.1

See footnotes at end of table.

Table B-15.   Years of School Completed by People 25 Years Old and Over, by Age and Sex: Selected Years 1940 to 1997 – Continued

(Numbers in thousands. Civilian noninstitutional population.)

Age, sex, and years	Total	Years of school completed						Median
		Elementary		High School		College		
		0 to 4 years	5 to 8 years	1 to 3 years	4 years	1 to 3 years	4 years or more	
1965	22 534	1 081	5 076	4 462	6 815	2 161	2 937	12.1
1964	22 457	1 158	5 226	4 416	6 657	2 212	2 789	12.2
1962	22 081	1 235	5 545	4 359	6 202	2 142	2 598	11.9
1960	21 919	1 397	6 415	4 579	5 364	1 957	2 206	11.1
1959	21 511	1 350	5 781	4 329	5 604	1 827	2 250	11.5
1957	20 873	1 491	6 293	3 987	5 195	1 558	1 972	11.0
1952	18 888	1 466	6 512	3 462	4 040	1 518	1 576	10.3
1950	18 896	1 834	7 338	3 339	3 151	1 271	1 403	9.6
1947	18 165	1 678	7 765	3 102	2 907	1 168	1 258	8.6
1940	17 127	2 480	8 458	2 388	1 798	819	917	8.5
Female								
1997	39 061	381	1 319	2 902	13 726	10 969	9 766	(NA)
1996	38 065	449	1 301	2 924	13 174	10 592	9 623	(NA)
1995	37 034	396	1 192	2 881	12 846	10 623	9 096	(NA)
1994	36 051	443	1 298	2 792	12 795	10 140	8 587	(NA)
1993	35 093	462	1 169	2 877	12 944	9 358	8 283	(NA)
1992	33 975	427	1 240	3 096	12 770	8 687	7 756	(NA)
1991	32 891	464	1 431	2 910	13 723	6 919	7 443	12.8
1990	31 876	454	1 448	2 955	13 643	6 383	6 997	12.8
1989	30 898	498	1 552	3 171	13 099	5 908	6 669	12.8
1988	29 908	462	1 547	3 234	12 949	5 689	6 029	12.7
1987	28 969	430	1 598	3 039	13 038	5 349	5 513	12.7
1986	28 244	420	1 694	3 071	12 759	5 098	5 202	12.7
1985	27 516	398	1 710	3 252	12 391	4 715	5 049	12.7
1984	26 838	389	1 740	3 331	12 364	4 444	4 570	12.6
1983	26 161	427	1 935	3 450	11 993	4 161	4 193	12.6
1982	25 555	433	2 017	3 666	11 833	3 827	3 778	12.6
1981	25 034	467	2 105	3 661	11 599	3 605	3 595	12.5
1980	24 751	444	2 186	3 862	11 307	3 501	3 452	12.5
1979	24 461	486	2 282	3 935	11 258	3 353	3 147	12.5
1978	24 202	497	2 483	4 212	11 012	3 149	2 849	12.5
1977	23 964	534	2 557	4 227	10 959	3 014	2 678	12.4
1976	23 868	517	2 721	4 198	10 989	2 988	2 455	12.4
1975	23 835	533	2 842	4 256	11 058	2 793	2 352	12.4
1974	23 850	559	2 956	4 364	11 033	2 647	2 290	12.4
1973	23 744	628	3 106	4 415	10 815	2 603	2 174	12.3
1972	23 756	618	3 330	4 604	10 736	2 509	1 958	12.3
1971	23 821	590	3 604	4 570	10 660	2 505	1 894	12.3
1970	23 845	629	3 728	4 679	10 588	2 318	1 903	12.3
1969	23 834	755	3 953	4 575	10 349	2 293	1 913	12.3
1968	23 874	725	4 212	4 676	10 038	2 281	1 943	12.2
1967	23 839	773	4 334	4 868	9 762	2 282	1 819	12.2
1966	23 806	752	4 644	4 853	9 615	2 200	1 741	12.2
1965	23 765	746	4 735	4 803	9 545	2 223	1 712	12.2
1964	23 632	748	5 033	4 871	9 103	2 183	1 691	12.1
1962	23 206	946	5 250	4 579	8 466	2 310	1 655	12.1
1960	22 823	1 027	6 121	4 923	7 153	2 166	1 433	11.6
1959	22 478	953	5 876	4 390	7 640	1 888	1 459	12.0
1957	21 772	1 167	6 056	4 397	6 846	1 690	1 388	11.5
1952	20 126	1 140	6 762	3 886	5 334	1 630	1 226	10.7
1950	19 536	1 570	7 082	3 637	4 111	1 607	1 113	9.7
1947	18 552	1 525	7 419	3 209	3 808	1 454	963	9.3
1940	16 718	2 070	7 812	2 584	2 419	1 017	623	8.7

See footnotes at end of table.

**Table B-15.   Years of School Completed by People 25 Years Old and Over, by Age and Sex: Selected Years 1940 to 1997
– Continued**

(Numbers in thousands. Civilian noninstitutional population.)

Age, sex, and years	Total	Years of school completed						Median
		Elementary		High School		College		
		0 to 4 years	5 to 8 years	1 to 3 years	4 years	1 to 3 years	4 years or more	
55 YEARS OLD AND OVER								
Both Sexes								
1997	53 352	1 628	6 622	7 543	18 823	9 565	9 169	(NA)
1996	52 742	1 642	6 716	7 520	18 549	9 642	8 677	(NA)
1995	52 022	1 755	7 048	7 232	18 320	9 662	8 005	(NA)
1994	51 516	1 802	7 382	7 454	18 228	8 890	7 761	(NA)
1993	52 117	2 058	8 038	7 637	18 626	8 106	7 652	(NA)
1992	51 740	2 118	8 133	7 756	18 397	8 005	7 332	(NA)
1991	51 439	2 341	8 668	7 675	18 954	6 540	7 258	12.6
1990	50 798	2 349	9 239	7 893	18 050	6 202	7 064	12.3
1989	50 421	2 412	9 395	7 907	18 102	5 914	6 693	12.3
1988	50 128	2 325	9 969	7 860	18 004	5 705	6 263	12.3
1987	49 858	2 408	10 544	7 766	17 310	5 799	6 033	12.2
1986	49 383	2 611	10 699	7 917	16 876	5 515	5 767	12.2
1985	48 969	2 612	11 052	7 872	16 516	5 208	5 708	12.2
1984	48 324	2 584	11 131	7 636	16 353	5 026	5 593	12.2
1983	47 723	2 769	11 348	7 703	15 470	4 915	5 514	12.1
1982	47 102	2 818	11 541	7 751	15 091	4 807	5 095	12.1
1981	46 391	2 983	11 909	7 600	14 464	4 721	4 711	12.0
1980	45 670	2 994	12 326	7 451	13 869	4 494	4 535	12.0
1979	43 806	2 924	12 230	6 999	13 088	4 321	4 245	12.0
1978	42 977	3 013	12 593	7 069	12 376	4 086	3 843	11.6
1977	42 176	3 047	12 740	6 823	11 977	3 835	3 754	11.3
1976	41 429	3 107	12 674	6 915	11 346	3 709	3 677	11.1
1975	40 613	3 303	13 045	6 730	10 798	3 442	3 295	10.8
1974	39 817	3 461	13 302	6 615	10 060	3 233	3 145	10.4
1973	39 163	3 424	13 467	6 504	9 604	3 060	3 105	10.2
1972	38 659	3 471	13 706	6 351	9 136	2 952	3 042	10.0
1971	38 787	3 808	14 430	6 225	8 463	2 878	2 982	9.6
1970	38 126	3 957	14 647	5 877	8 005	2 797	2 843	9.2
1969	37 424	4 012	14 576	5 801	7 768	2 615	2 653	9.1
1968	36 789	4 244	14 522	5 760	7 085	2 624	2 558	8.9
1967	36 155	4 310	14 849	5 495	6 622	2 443	2 434	8.7
1966	35 540	4 438	14 742	5 392	6 240	2 358	2 370	8.6
1965	34 969	4 612	14 814	5 293	5 844	2 194	2 215	8.5
1964	34 335	4 888	14 701	4 954	5 598	2 159	2 033	8.3
1962	33 247	5 048	14 707	4 442	4 994	2 166	1 890	8.1
1960	31 902	5 169	14 944	4 503	3 757	2 051	1 479	8.5
1959	30 567	4 752	13 485	4 060	3 996	1 775	1 545	8.1
1957	29 548	5 153	12 996	3 602	3 864	1 462	1 461	8.0
1952	26 206	4 554	12 638	2 982	3 080	1 346	1 264	7.7
1950	25 427	4 940	11 947	2 791	2 704	1 170	1 005	8.3
1947	23 234	4 393	11 601	2 179	2 581	1 003	825	7.5
1940	19 592	4 178	10 467	1 656	1 633	685	579	8.2
Male								
1997	23 668	773	3 026	3 060	7 417	4 139	5 255	(NA)
1996	23 352	795	3 058	2 998	7 198	4 254	5 055	(NA)
1995	22 881	839	3 153	2 980	6 980	4 254	4 675	(NA)
1994	22 669	894	3 327	3 037	6 987	3 962	4 462	(NA)
1993	23 038	992	3 595	3 174	7 178	3 587	4 508	(NA)
1992	22 836	1 033	3 676	3 277	6 991	3 549	4 312	(NA)
1991	22 708	1 217	3 980	3 183	7 287	2 850	4 193	12.4
1990	22 337	1 182	4 141	3 274	6 986	2 707	4 046	12.4
1989	22 167	1 202	4 198	3 317	7 003	2 616	3 829	12.3

See footnotes at end of table.

Table B-15. Years of School Completed by People 25 Years Old and Over, by Age and Sex: Selected Years 1940 to 1997 – Continued

(Numbers in thousands. Civilian noninstitutional population.)

| Age, sex, and years | Total | Years of school completed | | | | | | Median |
| | | Elementary | | High School | | College | | |
		0 to 4 years	5 to 8 years	1 to 3 years	4 years	1 to 3 years	4 years or more	
1988	21 989	1 117	4 471	3 366	6 968	2 455	3 609	12.3
1987	21 855	1 160	4 762	3 261	6 673	2 504	3 496	12.3
1986	21 622	1 275	4 813	3 286	6 509	2 355	3 385	12.2
1985	21 391	1 252	5 001	3 234	6 387	2 229	3 289	12.2
1984	21 014	1 209	4 951	3 270	6 265	2 185	3 132	12.2
1983	20 769	1 343	4 986	3 282	5 906	2 141	3 117	12.1
1982	20 508	1 362	5 026	3 313	5 759	2 102	2 946	12.1
1981	20 237	1 394	5 165	3 292	5 597	2 032	2 758	12.0
1980	19 967	1 424	5 436	3 206	5 409	1 986	2 506	11.9
1979	19 292	1 446	5 479	2 964	5 167	1 935	2 301	11.8
1978	18 939	1 467	5 701	2 919	4 919	1 824	2 110	11.4
1977	18 608	1 502	5 770	2 787	4 835	1 700	2 011	11.2
1976	18 233	1 507	5 733	2 884	4 473	1 646	1 989	11.0
1975	17 903	1 628	5 845	2 871	4 308	1 480	1 768	10.5
1974	17 579	1 693	6 042	2 817	3 993	1 356	1 682	10.1
1973	17 263	1 678	6 111	2 774	3 811	1 245	1 645	9.9
1972	17 120	1 728	6 252	2 698	3 612	1 215	1 614	9.6
1971	17 288	1 913	6 629	2 668	3 285	1 214	1 579	9.1
1970	17 074	2 011	6 655	2 583	3 127	1 182	1 516	9.0
1969	16 822	2 003	6 701	2 536	3 099	1 086	1 397	8.8
1968	16 609	2 137	6 728	2 523	2 816	1 078	1 328	8.7
1967	16 398	2 247	6 827	2 379	2 685	989	1 271	8.5
1966	16 201	2 288	6 944	2 317	2 491	939	1 223	8.3
1965	16 015	2 368	6 992	2 265	2 331	893	1 164	8.2
1964	15 789	2 504	6 897	2 159	2 237	876	1 113	8.1
1962	15 440	2 644	6 813	2 032	2 030	864	1 057	8.0
1960	14 895	2 704	7 121	1 969	1 453	853	796	8.4
1959	14 304	2 491	6 436	1 759	1 584	718	857	7.9
1957	13 967	2 696	6 244	1 570	1 493	608	831	7.7
1952	12 544	2 428	6 162	1 318	1 262	528	636	7.5
1950	12 277	2 609	5 808	1 209	1 111	500	569	8.2
1947	11 424	2 393	5 656	939	1 109	464	482	7.3
1940	9 815	2 293	5 249	724	660	313	361	8.1
Female								
1997	29 684	855	3 596	4 483	11 407	5 427	3 916	(NA)
1996	29 390	848	3 659	4 523	11 350	5 387	3 623	(NA)
1995	29 142	915	3 894	4 255	11 340	5 410	3 330	(NA)
1994	28 848	909	4 054	4 419	11 242	4 926	3 298	(NA)
1993	29 080	1 066	4 442	4 462	11 447	4 519	3 149	(NA)
1992	28 904	1 084	4 456	4 478	11 409	4 455	3 021	(NA)
1991	28 729	1 125	4 687	4 495	11 667	3 690	3 066	12.3
1990	28 461	1 167	5 098	4 619	11 063	3 495	3 019	12.3
1989	28 255	1 211	5 195	4 587	11 099	3 300	2 863	12.3
1988	28 139	1 208	5 498	4 495	11 034	3 250	2 655	12.3
1987	28 004	1 248	5 782	4 504	10 637	3 294	2 539	12.2
1986	27 762	1 336	5 886	4 630	10 367	3 160	2 382	12.2
1985	27 578	1 360	6 052	4 638	10 129	2 979	2 420	12.2
1984	27 309	1 377	6 183	4 363	10 086	2 843	2 459	12.2
1983	26 954	1 428	6 364	4 423	9 567	2 774	2 398	12.1
1982	26 593	1 458	6 511	4 435	9 330	2 705	2 150	12.1
1981	26 152	1 589	6 742	4 308	8 868	2 690	1 954	12.0
1980	25 703	1 571	6 889	4 245	8 460	2 509	2 030	12.0
1979	24 514	1 474	6 750	4 034	7 920	2 389	1 944	12.0
1978	24 038	1 545	6 889	4 149	7 457	2 263	1 733	11.6
1977	23 568	1 546	6 972	4 034	7 141	2 135	1 742	11.0
1976	23 196	1 602	6 942	4 029	6 871	2 063	1 690	11.0
1975	22 710	1 675	7 198	3 858	6 490	1 962	1 527	10.9
1974	22 238	1 762	7 261	3 799	6 068	1 880	1 463	10.7

See footnotes at end of table.

Table B-15. Years of School Completed by People 25 Years Old and Over, by Age and Sex: Selected Years 1940 to 1997 – Continued

(Numbers in thousands. Civilian noninstitutional population.)

Age, sex, and years	Total	Years of school completed						Median
		Elementary		High School		College		
		0 to 4 years	5 to 8 years	1 to 3 years	4 years	1 to 3 years	4 years or more	
1973	21 900	1 746	7 359	3 729	5 790	1 814	1 461	10.5
1972	21 539	1 743	7 455	3 654	5 526	1 737	1 425	10.3
1971	21 500	1 896	7 805	3 556	5 179	1 665	1 402	9.9
1970	21 052	1 946	7 993	3 292	4 879	1 615	1 327	9.5
1969	20 601	2 009	7 878	3 264	4 669	1 526	1 255	9.4
1968	20 180	2 106	7 795	3 237	4 269	1 544	1 229	9.2
1967	19 756	2 063	8 021	3 117	3 937	1 454	1 164	8.9
1966	19 339	2 152	7 797	3 074	3 749	1 419	1 147	8.9
1965	18 955	2 243	7 821	3 026	3 514	1 300	1 048	8.7
1964	18 546	2 383	7 805	2 794	3 360	1 282	920	8.5
1962	17 807	2 404	7 894	2 410	2 964	1 302	833	8.3
1960	17 007	2 465	7 823	2 534	2 304	1 198	683	8.6
1959	16 263	2 261	7 049	2 301	2 412	1 057	688	8.3
1957	15 581	2 457	6 752	2 032	2 371	854	630	8.2
1952	13 662	2 126	6 476	1 664	1 818	818	628	7.9
1950	13 150	2 331	6 139	1 582	1 593	670	436	8.4
1947	11 810	2 000	5 945	1 240	1 472	539	343	7.6
1940	9 777	1 886	5 217	932	973	372	219	8.3

Source: 1947 and 1952 to 1997 March Current Population Survey (noninstitutional population, excluding members of the Armed Forces living in barracks), 1950 Census of Population and 1940 Census of Population (resident population).

(NA) Not available or not applicable.

Table B-16. Percent of People 25 Years Old and Over Who Have Completed High School or College, by Race, Sex, and Hispanic Origin: Selected Years 1940 to 1997

(Numbers in thousands. Civilian noninstitutional population.)

Age, sex, and years	All races			White			Black			Hispanic origin [1]		
	Total	Male	Female	Total	Male	Female	Total	Male	Female	Total	Male	Female
25 YEARS OLD AND OVER												
Completed 4 Years of High School or more												
1997	82.1	82.0	82.2	83.0	82.9	83.2	74.9	73.5	76.0	54.7	54.9	54.6
1996	81.7	81.9	81.6	82.8	82.7	82.8	74.3	74.3	74.2	53.1	53.0	53.3
1995	81.7	81.7	81.6	83.0	83.0	83.0	73.8	73.4	74.1	53.4	52.9	53.8
1994	80.9	81.0	80.7	82.0	82.1	81.9	72.9	71.7	73.8	53.3	53.4	53.2
1993	80.2	80.5	80.0	81.5	81.8	81.3	70.4	69.6	71.1	53.1	52.9	53.2
1992	79.4	79.7	79.2	80.9	81.1	80.7	67.7	67.0	68.2	52.6	53.7	51.5
1991	78.4	78.5	78.3	79.9	79.8	79.9	66.7	66.7	66.7	51.3	51.4	51.2
1990	77.6	77.7	77.5	79.1	79.1	79.0	66.2	65.8	66.5	50.8	50.3	51.3
1989	76.9	77.2	76.6	78.4	78.6	78.2	64.6	64.2	65.0	50.9	51.0	50.7
1988	76.2	76.4	76.0	77.7	77.7	77.6	63.5	63.7	63.4	51.0	52.0	50.0
1987	75.6	76.0	75.3	77.0	77.3	76.7	63.4	63.0	63.7	50.9	51.8	50.0
1986	74.7	75.1	74.4	76.2	76.5	75.9	62.3	61.5	63.0	48.5	49.2	47.8
1985	73.9	74.4	73.5	75.5	76.0	75.1	59.8	58.4	60.8	47.9	48.5	47.4
1984	73.3	73.7	73.0	75.0	75.4	74.6	58.5	57.1	59.7	47.1	48.6	45.7
1983	72.1	72.7	71.5	73.8	74.4	73.3	56.8	56.5	57.1	46.2	48.6	44.2
1982	71.0	71.7	70.3	72.8	73.4	72.3	54.9	55.7	54.3	45.9	48.1	44.1
1981	69.7	70.3	69.1	71.6	72.1	71.2	52.9	53.2	52.6	44.5	45.5	43.6
1980	68.6	69.2	68.1	70.5	71.0	70.1	51.2	51.1	51.3	45.3	46.4	44.1
1979	67.7	68.4	67.1	69.7	70.3	69.2	49.4	49.2	49.5	42.0	42.3	41.7
1978	65.9	66.8	65.2	67.9	68.6	67.2	47.6	47.9	47.3	40.8	42.2	39.6
1977	64.9	65.6	64.4	67.0	67.5	66.5	45.5	45.6	45.4	39.6	42.3	37.2
1976	64.1	64.7	63.5	66.1	66.7	65.5	43.8	42.3	45.0	39.3	41.4	37.3
1975	62.5	63.1	62.1	64.5	65.0	64.1	42.5	41.6	43.3	37.9	39.5	36.7
1974	61.2	61.6	60.9	63.3	63.6	63.0	40.8	39.9	41.5	36.5	38.3	34.9
1973	59.8	60.0	59.6	61.9	62.1	61.7	39.2	38.2	40.1	(NA)	(NA)	(NA)
1972	58.2	58.2	58.2	60.4	60.3	60.5	36.6	35.7	37.2	(NA)	(NA)	(NA)
1971	56.4	56.3	56.6	58.6	58.4	58.8	34.7	33.8	35.4	(NA)	(NA)	(NA)
1970	55.2	55.0	55.4	57.4	57.2	57.6	33.7	32.4	34.8	(NA)	(NA)	(NA)
1969	54.0	53.6	54.4	56.3	55.7	56.7	32.3	31.9	32.6	(NA)	(NA)	(NA)
1968	52.6	52.0	53.2	54.9	54.3	55.5	30.1	28.9	31.0	(NA)	(NA)	(NA)
1967	51.1	50.5	51.7	53.4	52.8	53.8	29.5	27.1	31.5	(NA)	(NA)	(NA)
1966	49.9	49.0	50.8	52.2	51.3	53.0	27.8	25.8	29.5	(NA)	(NA)	(NA)
1965	49.0	48.0	49.9	51.3	50.2	52.2	27.2	25.8	28.4	(NA)	(NA)	(NA)
1964	48.0	47.0	48.9	50.3	49.3	51.2	25.7	23.7	27.4	(NA)	(NA)	(NA)
1962	46.3	45.0	47.5	48.7	47.4	49.9	24.8	23.2	26.2	(NA)	(NA)	(NA)
1959	43.7	42.2	45.2	46.1	44.5	47.7	20.7	19.6	21.6	(NA)	(NA)	(NA)
1957	41.6	39.7	43.3	43.2	41.1	45.1	18.4	16.9	19.7	(NA)	(NA)	(NA)
1952	38.8	36.9	40.5	(NA)	(NA)	(NA)	15.0	14.0	15.7	(NA)	(NA)	(NA)
1950	34.3	32.6	36.0	(NA)	(NA)	(NA)	13.7	12.5	14.7	(NA)	(NA)	(NA)
1947	33.1	31.4	34.7	35.0	33.2	36.7	13.6	12.7	14.5	(NA)	(NA)	(NA)
1940	24.5	22.7	26.3	26.1	24.2	28.1	7.7	6.9	8.4	(NA)	(NA)	(NA)
Completed 4 Years of College or more												
1997	23.9	26.2	21.7	24.6	27.0	22.3	13.3	12.5	13.9	10.3	10.6	10.1
1996	23.6	26.0	21.4	24.3	26.9	21.8	13.6	12.4	14.6	9.3	10.3	8.3
1995	23.0	26.0	20.2	24.0	27.2	21.0	13.2	13.6	12.9	9.3	10.1	8.4
1994	22.2	25.1	19.6	22.9	26.1	20.0	12.9	12.8	13.0	9.1	9.6	8.6
1993	21.9	24.8	19.2	22.6	25.7	19.7	12.2	11.9	12.4	9.0	9.5	8.5
1992	21.4	24.3	18.6	22.1	25.2	19.1	11.9	11.9	12.0	9.3	10.2	8.5
1991	21.4	24.3	18.8	22.2	25.4	19.3	11.5	11.4	11.6	9.7	10.0	9.4
1990	21.3	24.4	18.4	22.0	25.3	19.0	11.3	11.9	10.8	9.2	9.8	8.7
1989	21.1	24.5	18.1	21.8	25.4	18.5	11.8	11.7	11.9	9.9	11.0	8.8
1988	20.3	24.0	17.0	20.9	25.0	17.3	11.2	11.1	11.4	10.1	12.3	8.1
1987	19.9	23.6	16.5	20.5	24.5	16.9	10.7	11.0	10.4	8.6	9.7	7.5

See footnotes at end of table.

Table B-16. Percent of People 25 Years Old and Over Who Have Completed High School or College, by Race, Sex, and Hispanic Origin: Selected Years 1940 to 1997 — Continued

(Numbers in thousands. Civilian noninstitutional population.)

Age, sex, and years	All races			White			Black			Hispanic origin [1]		
	Total	Male	Female	Total	Male	Female	Total	Male	Female	Total	Male	Female
1986	19.4	23.2	16.1	20.1	24.1	16.4	10.9	11.2	10.7	8.4	9.5	7.4
1985	19.4	23.1	16.0	20.0	24.0	16.3	11.1	11.2	11.0	8.5	9.7	7.3
1984	19.1	22.9	15.7	19.8	23.9	16.0	10.4	10.4	10.4	8.2	9.5	7.0
1983	18.8	23.0	15.1	19.5	24.0	15.4	9.5	10.0	9.2	7.9	9.2	6.8
1982	17.7	21.9	14.0	18.5	23.0	14.4	8.8	9.1	8.5	7.8	9.6	6.2
1981	17.1	21.1	13.4	17.8	22.2	13.8	8.2	8.2	8.2	7.7	9.7	5.9
1980	17.0	20.9	13.6	17.8	22.1	14.0	7.9	7.7	8.1	7.9	9.7	6.2
1979	16.4	20.4	12.9	17.2	21.4	13.3	7.9	8.3	7.5	6.7	8.2	5.3
1978	15.7	19.7	12.2	16.4	20.7	12.6	7.2	7.3	7.1	7.0	8.6	5.7
1977	15.4	19.2	12.0	16.1	20.2	12.4	7.2	7.0	7.4	6.2	8.1	4.4
1976	14.7	18.6	11.3	15.4	19.6	11.6	6.6	6.3	6.8	6.1	8.6	4.0
1975	13.9	17.6	10.6	14.5	18.4	11.0	6.4	6.7	6.2	6.3	8.3	4.6
1974	13.3	16.9	10.1	14.0	17.7	10.6	5.5	5.7	5.3	5.5	7.1	4.0
1973	12.6	16.0	9.6	13.1	16.8	9.9	6.0	5.9	6.0	(NA)	(NA)	(NA)
1972	12.0	15.4	9.0	12.6	16.2	9.4	5.1	5.5	4.8	(NA)	(NA)	(NA)
1971	11.4	14.6	8.5	12.0	15.5	8.9	4.5	4.7	4.3	(NA)	(NA)	(NA)
1970	11.0	14.1	8.2	11.6	15.0	8.6	4.5	4.6	4.4	(NA)	(NA)	(NA)
1909	10.7	13.8	8.1	11.2	14.3	8.5	4.8	4.8	4.5	(NA)	(NA)	(NA)
1968	10.5	13.3	8.0	11.0	14.1	8.3	4.3	3.7	4.8	(NA)	(NA)	(NA)
1967	10.1	12.8	7.6	10.6	13.6	7.9	4.0	3.4	4.4	(NA)	(NA)	(NA)
1966	9.8	12.5	7.4	10.4	13.3	7.7	3.8	3.9	3.7	(NA)	(NA)	(NA)
1965	9.4	12.0	7.1	9.9	12.7	7.3	4.7	4.9	4.5	(NA)	(NA)	(NA)
1964	9.1	11.7	6.8	9.6	12.3	7.1	3.9	4.5	3.4	(NA)	(NA)	(NA)
1962	8.9	11.4	6.7	9.5	12.2	7.0	4.0	3.9	4.0	(NA)	(NA)	(NA)
1959	8.1	10.3	6.0	8.6	11.0	6.2	3.3	3.8	2.9	(NA)	(NA)	(NA)
1957	7.6	9.6	5.8	8.0	10.1	6.0	2.9	2.7	3.0	(NA)	(NA)	(NA)
1952	7.0	8.3	5.8	(NA)	(NA)	(NA)	2.4	2.0	2.7	(NA)	(NA)	(NA)
1950	6.2	7.3	5.2	(NA)	(NA)	(NA)	2.3	2.1	2.4	(NA)	(NA)	(NA)
1947	5.4	6.2	4.7	5.7	6.6	4.9	2.5	2.4	2.6	(NA)	(NA)	(NA)
1940	4.6	5.5	3.8	4.9	5.9	4.0	1.3	1.4	1.2	(NA)	(NA)	(NA)
25 to 34 YEARS OLD												
Completed 4 Years of High School or More												
1997	87.4	85.8	88.9	87.6	85.8	89.4	86.2	85.2	87.1	61.8	59.2	64.9
1996	87.3	86.5	88.1	87.5	86.3	88.8	85.6	87.2	84.2	61.1	59.7	62.9
1995	86.8	86.3	87.4	87.4	86.6	88.2	86.5	88.1	85.1	57.1	55.7	58.7
1994	86.1	84.5	87.6	86.5	84.7	88.3	84.1	82.9	85.0	60.3	58.0	63.0
1993	86.7	86.0	87.4	87.3	86.1	88.5	82.8	85.0	80.9	60.9	58.3	64.0
1992	86.3	86.1	86.5	87.0	86.5	87.6	80.9	82.5	79.5	60.9	61.1	60.6
1991	85.4	84.9	85.8	85.8	85.1	86.6	81.7	83.5	80.1	56.7	56.4	57.1
1990	85.7	84.4	87.0	86.3	84.6	88.1	81.7	81.5	81.8	58.2	56.6	59.9
1989	85.5	84.4	86.5	86.0	84.8	87.1	82.2	80.6	83.6	61.0	61.0	61.0
1988	85.7	84.4	87.0	86.5	84.8	88.2	80.7	80.6	80.7	62.0	59.4	65.0
1987	86.0	85.5	86.4	86.3	85.6	87.0	83.3	84.8	82.1	59.8	58.6	61.0
1986	86.1	85.9	86.4	86.5	85.6	87.4	83.4	86.5	80.6	59.1	58.2	60.0
1985	86.1	85.9	86.4	86.8	86.4	87.3	80.6	80.8	80.4	60.9	58.6	63.1
1984	85.9	85.6	86.3	86.9	86.8	87.0	78.9	75.9	81.5	58.6	56.8	60.2
1983	86.0	86.0	86.0	86.9	86.9	86.9	79.4	78.9	79.8	58.3	57.8	58.9
1982	86.2	86.3	86.1	86.9	87.0	86.8	80.9	80.5	81.3	60.9	60.7	61.2
1981	86.3	86.5	86.1	87.6	87.6	87.6	77.3	78.4	76.4	59.8	59.1	60.4
1980	85.4	85.4	85.5	86.9	86.8	87.0	76.6	74.8	78.1	58.6	58.3	58.8
1979	85.6	86.3	84.9	87.0	87.7	86.4	74.8	73.9	75.4	57.0	55.5	58.5
1978	85.3	86.0	84.6	86.3	86.8	85.8	77.3	78.5	76.3	56.6	58.5	54.7
1977	85.4	86.6	84.2	86.8	87.6	86.0	74.4	77.5	72.0	58.1	62.1	54.8
1976	84.7	86.0	83.5	85.9	87.3	84.6	73.8	72.5	74.9	58.1	57.6	58.4
1975	83.1	84.5	81.8	84.4	85.7	83.2	71.0	72.2	70.1	51.7	51.1	52.1
1974	81.9	83.1	80.8	83.4	84.1	82.7	68.2	71.1	66.0	52.5	55.1	49.9
1973	80.2	80.6	79.8	82.0	82.4	81.6	64.2	63.1	64.9	(NA)	(NA)	(NA)
1972	79.8	80.5	79.2	81.5	82.3	80.8	64.1	61.8	66.2	(NA)	(NA)	(NA)
1971	77.2	78.1	76.4	79.5	80.8	78.3	57.5	54.1	60.7	(NA)	(NA)	(NA)

See footnotes at end of table.

Table B-16. Percent of People 25 Years Old and Over Who Have Completed High School or College, by Race, Sex, and Hispanic Origin: Selected Years 1940 to 1997 — Continued

(Numbers in thousands. Civilian noninstitutional population.)

Age, sex, and years	All races			White			Black			Hispanic origin [1]		
	Total	Male	Female	Total	Male	Female	Total	Male	Female	Total	Male	Female
1970	75.4	76.6	74.2	77.8	79.2	76.4	56.2	54.5	57.9	(NA)	(NA)	(NA)
1969	74.7	75.6	73.8	77.0	77.5	76.6	55.8	59.8	52.3	(NA)	(NA)	(NA)
1968	73.2	73.7	72.7	75.3	75.5	75.0	55.8	58.1	53.6	(NA)	(NA)	(NA)
1967	72.5	72.1	72.9	74.8	74.3	75.3	53.4	51.7	55.0	(NA)	(NA)	(NA)
1966	71.0	70.9	71.2	73.8	73.2	74.4	47.9	48.9	47.0	(NA)	(NA)	(NA)
1965	70.3	70.5	70.1	72.8	72.7	72.8	50.3	50.3	50.4	(NA)	(NA)	(NA)
1964	69.2	68.8	69.5	72.1	71.8	72.4	45.0	41.6	47.9	(NA)	(NA)	(NA)
1962	65.9	65.8	66.1	69.2	69.2	69.3	41.6	38.9	43.8	(NA)	(NA)	(NA)
1959	63.9	63.9	64.0	67.2	66.9	67.4	39.5	40.6	38.6	(NA)	(NA)	(NA)
1957	60.2	57.9	62.4	63.3	60.7	65.7	31.6	27.4	35.2	(NA)	(NA)	(NA)
1952	57.1	55.3	58.7	(NA)	(NA)	(NA)	28.1	27.9	28.3	(NA)	(NA)	(NA)
1950	52.8	50.6	55.0	(NA)	(NA)	(NA)	23.6	21.3	25.5	(NA)	(NA)	(NA)
1947	51.4	49.4	53.3	54.9	52.9	56.8	22.3	19.6	24.7	(NA)	(NA)	(NA)
1940	38.1	36.0	40.1	41.2	38.9	43.4	12.3	10.6	13.6	(NA)	(NA)	(NA)

Completed 4 Years of High School or More

1997	27.8	26.3	29.3	28.9	27.2	30.7	14.4	12.1	16.4	11.0	9.6	10.1
1996	27.1	26.1	28.2	28.1	27.2	29.1	14.6	12.4	16.4	10.0	10.2	9.8
1995	24.7	24.5	24.9	26.0	25.4	26.6	15.3	17.2	13.6	8.9	7.8	10.1
1994	23.3	22.5	24.0	24.2	23.6	24.8	13.7	11.7	15.4	8.0	6.6	9.8
1993	23.7	23.4	23.9	24.7	24.4	25.1	13.2	12.6	13.8	8.3	7.1	9.8
1992	23.6	23.2	24.0	25.0	24.2	25.7	11.3	12.0	10.6	9.5	8.8	10.3
1991	23.2	23.0	23.4	24.6	24.1	25.0	11.0	11.5	10.6	9.2	8.1	10.4
1990	23.2	23.7	22.8	24.2	24.2	24.3	13.4	15.1	11.9	8.1	7.3	9.1
1989	23.4	23.9	22.9	24.4	24.8	24.0	12.7	12.0	13.3	10.1	9.6	10.6
1988	22.5	23.2	21.9	23.5	24.0	22.9	12.2	12.6	11.9	11.4	12.1	10.6
1987	22.0	22.3	21.7	23.0	23.3	22.8	11.4	11.6	11.1	8.7	9.2	8.2
1986	22.4	22.9	21.9	23.5	24.1	22.9	11.8	10.1	13.3	9.0	8.9	9.1
1985	22.2	23.1	21.3	23.2	24.2	22.2	11.5	10.3	12.6	11.1	10.9	11.2
1984	21.9	23.2	20.7	23.1	24.3	21.9	11.6	12.9	10.5	10.6	9.6	11.6
1983	22.5	23.9	21.1	23.4	25.0	21.8	12.9	13.1	12.8	10.4	9.6	11.1
1982	21.7	23.3	20.2	22.7	24.5	20.9	12.6	11.8	13.2	9.7	10.7	8.7
1981	21.3	23.1	19.6	22.4	24.3	20.5	11.6	12.1	11.1	7.5	8.6	6.5
1980	22.5	24.0	21.0	23.7	25.5	22.0	11.6	10.5	12.5	7.7	8.4	6.9
1979	23.1	25.6	20.5	24.3	27.1	21.5	12.4	13.3	11.7	7.3	7.9	6.8
1978	23.3	26.0	20.6	24.5	27.6	21.4	11.8	10.7	12.6	9.6	9.6	9.7
1977	24.0	27.0	21.1	25.3	28.5	22.1	12.6	12.8	12.4	6.7	7.2	6.4
1976	23.7	27.5	20.1	24.6	28.7	20.6	13.0	12.0	13.6	7.4	10.3	4.8
1975	21.9	25.1	18.7	22.8	26.3	19.4	10.7	11.4	10.1	8.8	10.0	7.3
1974	20.7	23.9	17.6	22.0	25.3	18.8	7.9	8.8	7.2	5.7	7.2	4.6
1973	19.0	21.6	16.4	19.9	22.8	17.0	8.1	7.1	8.8	(NA)	(NA)	(NA)
1972	19.0	22.0	16.0	19.9	23.1	16.7	8.3	7.1	9.4	(NA)	(NA)	(NA)
1971	16.9	20.1	13.8	17.9	21.3	14.6	6.4	6.4	6.5	(NA)	(NA)	(NA)
1970	16.4	20.0	12.9	17.3	21.3	13.3	7.3	6.7	8.0	(NA)	(NA)	(NA)
1969	16.0	19.4	12.8	17.0	20.6	13.4	6.7	8.1	5.5	(NA)	(NA)	(NA)
1968	14.7	18.0	11.6	15.6	19.1	12.3	5.3	5.3	5.3	(NA)	(NA)	(NA)
1967	14.6	17.2	12.1	15.5	18.3	12.7	5.4	4.2	6.3	(NA)	(NA)	(NA)
1966	14.0	16.8	11.3	14.7	17.9	11.8	5.9	5.4	6.4	(NA)	(NA)	(NA)
1965	12.4	15.6	9.5	13.0	16.4	9.8	6.8	7.3	6.8	(NA)	(NA)	(NA)
1964	12.8	16.6	9.2	13.6	17.5	9.9	5.5	7.5	3.9	(NA)	(NA)	(NA)
1962	13.1	17.2	9.2	14.3	18.7	10.0	4.2	5.7	3.0	(NA)	(NA)	(NA)
1959	11.1	14.8	7.6	11.9	15.9	8.1	4.6	5.6	3.7	(NA)	(NA)	(NA)
1957	10.4	13.5	7.5	11.1	14.5	7.8	4.1	3.3	5.0	(NA)	(NA)	(NA)
1952	10.1	13.8	6.7	(NA)	(NA)	(NA)	4.6	3.2	5.8	(NA)	(NA)	(NA)
1950	7.7	9.6	5.9	(NA)	(NA)	(NA)	2.9	2.4	3.2	(NA)	(NA)	(NA)
1947	5.6	5.8	5.4	5.9	6.2	5.7	2.8	2.6	2.9	(NA)	(NA)	(NA)
1940	5.9	6.9	4.9	6.4	7.5	5.3	1.6	1.5	1.7	(NA)	(NA)	(NA)

Source: 1947 and 1952 to 1997 March Current Population Survey (noninstitutional population, excluding members of the Armed Forces living in barracks), 1950 Census of Population and 1940 Census of Population (resident population).

1. Persons of Hispanic origin may be of any race.

(NA) Not available or not applicable.

Table B-17.   Mean Earnings of Workers 18 Years Old and Over, by Educational Attainment, Race, Hispanic Origin, and Gender: 1975 to 1996

(Numbers in thousands. Civilian noninstitutional population.)

Earnings year	Total				Not a high school graduate				High school graduate			
	Mean Earnings (1996 Constant Dollars)	Mean Earnings (Current Dollars)	Number with earnings	Standard error	Mean Earnings (1996 Constant Dollars)	Mean Earnings (Current Dollars)	Number with earnings	Standard error	Mean Earnings (1996 Constant Dollars)	Mean Earnings (Current Dollars)	Number with earnings	Standard error
ALL RACES												
Total												
1996	28 106	28 106	168 703	176	15 011	15 011	17 075	286	22 154	22 154	45 908	209
1995	27 583	26 792	136 221	164	14 427	14 013	16 990	201	22 064	21 431	44 546	225
1994	27 370	25 852	135 096	153	14 501	13 697	16 479	288	21 437	20 248	44 614	170
1993	26 791	24 674	133 119	148	13 920	12 820	16 575	237	21 089	19 422	44 779	162
1992	25 975	23 227	130 860	99	14 325	12 809	16 612	152	20 954	18 737	45 340	110
1991	25 726	22 332	130 371	93	14 530	12 613	17 553	153	21 036	18 261	46 508	104
1990	26 162	21 793	130 080	91	15 104	12 582	18 698	115	21 392	17 820	51 977	95
1989	27 096	21 414	129 094	92	15 490	12 242	19 137	112	22 262	17 594	51 846	100
1900	20 005	20 000	127 504	88	15 708	11 889	19 635	118	22 215	16 750	51 297	98
1987	26 264	19 016	124 874	83	16 331	11 824	19 748	133	22 014	15 939	50 815	91
1986	25 982	18 149	122 757	72	16 038	11 203	19 665	149	21 645	15 120	50 104	77
1985	25 053	17 181	120 651	67	15 640	10 726	19 692	133	21 081	14 457	49 674	74
1984	24 287	16 083	118 183	57	15 681	10 384	20 206	130	20 980	13 893	48 452	68
1983	23 845	15 137	115 095	(NA)	15 521	9 853	20 020	(NA)	20 548	13 044	47 560	(NA)
1982	23 333	14 351	113 451	52	15 262	9 387	20 789	101	20 421	12 560	46 584	64
1981	23 516	13 624	113 301	48	16 151	9 357	22 296	110	20 901	12 109	47 332	59
1980	24 116	12 665	111 919	45	16 842	8 845	23 028	95	21 543	11 314	46 795	54
1979	25 491	11 795	110 826	43	18 197	8 420	23 783	75	22 960	10 624	45 497	50
1978	26 018	10 812	106 436	41	18 672	7 759	23 787	71	23 665	9 834	43 510	49
1977	25 599	9 887	103 119	35	18 295	7 066	24 854	60	23 336	9 013	41 696	41
1976	25 314	9 180	100 510	32	18 530	6 720	25 035	57	23 143	8 393	40 570	39
1975	24 941	8 552	97 881	31	18 076	6 198	24 916	53	22 873	7 843	39 827	38
Male												
1996	34 705	34 705	73 955	291	17 826	17 826	10 583	440	27 642	27 642	23 966	364
1995	34 233	33 251	72 634	275	17 243	16 748	10 312	296	27 111	26 333	23 473	349
1994	33 971	32 087	72 246	251	17 609	16 633	9 981	457	26 508	25 038	23 418	286
1993	33 191	30 568	71 183	244	16 229	14 946	10 151	233	26 030	23 973	23 388	259
1992	31 814	28 448	71 138	158	16 701	14 934	10 335	212	25 697	22 978	23 610	173
1991	31 673	27 494	70 145	148	17 344	15 056	10 679	187	26 107	22 663	24 110	163
1990	32 609	27 164	70 218	151	17 996	14 991	11 412	155	26 864	22 378	26 753	158
1989	34 195	27 025	69 798	155	18 634	14 727	11 774	150	28 480	22 508	26 469	172
1988	33 613	25 344	69 006	146	19 299	14 551	11 993	163	28 490	21 481	26 080	166
1987	33 169	24 015	67 951	138	20 088	14 544	12 117	188	28 126	20 364	25 981	150
1986	33 008	23 057	67 189	120	19 617	13 703	12 208	217	27 848	19 453	25 562	131
1985	31 822	21 823	66 439	111	19 137	13 124	12 137	185	27 086	18 575	25 496	125
1984	30 885	20 452	65 005	92	19 292	12 775	12 325	170	27 206	18 016	24 827	116
1983	30 206	19 175	63 816	89	18 986	12 052	12 376	160	26 352	16 728	24 449	108
1982	29 663	18 244	63 489	85	18 719	11 513	12 868	144	26 275	16 160	24 059	107
1981	30 279	17 542	63 547	79	20 140	11 668	13 701	146	27 445	15 900	24 435	101
1980	31 193	16 382	62 825	73	21 025	11 042	14 273	129	28 566	15 002	24 023	92
1979	33 347	15 430	62 464	70	22 969	10 628	14 711	102	30 941	14 317	23 318	87
1978	34 061	14 154	60 586	67	23 809	9 894	14 550	93	31 736	13 188	22 650	85
1977	33 368	12 888	59 441	56	23 144	8 939	15 369	81	31 308	12 092	21 846	70
1976	32 877	11 923	58 419	52	23 499	8 522	15 634	79	30 853	11 189	21 499	65
1975	32 345	11 091	57 297	49	22 873	7 843	15 613	71	30 549	10 475	21 347	64
Female												
1996	20 570	20 570	64 748	165	10 421	10 421	6 492	193	16 161	16 161	21 942	160
1995	19 987	19 414	63 587	144	10 079	9 790	6 678	208	16 442	15 970	21 073	263
1994	19 781	18 684	62 850	143	9 728	9 189	6 498	165	15 833	14 955	21 195	149

See footnotes at end of table.

Table B-17.   Mean Earnings of Workers 18 Years Old and Over, by Educational Attainment, Race, Hispanic Origin, and Gender: 1975 to 1996 — Continued

(Numbers in thousands. Civilian noninstitutional population.)

Earnings year	Some college/associate degree				Bachelor's Degree				Advanced Degree			
	Mean Earnings (1996 Constant Dollars)	Mean Earnings (Current Dollars)	Number with earnings	Standard error	Mean Earnings (1996 Constant Dollars)	Mean Earnings (Current Dollars)	Number with earnings	Standard error	Mean Earnings (1996 Constant Dollars)	Mean Earnings (Current Dollars)	Number with earnings	Standard error
ALL RACES												
Total												
1996	25 181	25 181	40 410	279	38 112	38 112	24 028	436	61 317	61 317	11 281	1 204
1995	24 567	23 862	40 142	245	38 072	36 980	23 285	463	58 340	56 667	11 258	490
1994	23 531	22 226	40 135	193	39 409	37 224	22 712	491	59 399	56 105	11 155	961
1993	23 387	21 539	39 429	173	38 135	35 121	21 815	425	60 576	55 789	10 521	1 140
1992	23 336	20 867	37 339	109	36 490	32 629	21 091	288	54 408	48 652	10 479	571
1991	23 674	20 551	35 732	116	36 084	31 323	20 475	275	53 036	46 039	10 103	571
1990	24 842	20 694	28 993	165	37 349	31 112	18 128	300	49 769	41 458	12 285	488
1989	25 629	20 255	28 078	161	38 891	30 736	17 767	304	51 902	41 019	12 265	506
1988	25 287	19 066	27 217	171	37 592	28 344	17 308	286	50 033	37 724	12 109	458
1987	24 935	18 054	26 404	156	37 179	26 919	16 497	289	49 678	35 968	11 411	447
1986	24 441	17 073	26 113	135	37 952	26 511	15 788	251	49 800	34 787	11 087	393
1985	23 840	16 349	25 402	127	36 275	24 877	15 373	238	47 987	32 909	10 510	367
1984	22 555	14 936	24 463	107	34 841	23 072	14 653	191	45 593	30 192	10 410	281
1983	22 440	14 245	23 208	(NA)	33 919	21 532	13 929	(NA)	44 633	28 333	10 377	(NA)
1982	21 955	13 503	22 602	105	32 960	20 272	13 425	181	43 761	26 915	10 051	272
1981	22 743	13 176	21 759	101	32 806	19 006	12 579	173	43 637	25 281	9 336	266
1980	23 628	12 409	21 384	97	34 417	18 075	12 175	171	44 381	23 308	8 535	254
1979	24 587	11 377	21 174	90	35 689	16 514	11 751	163	47 273	21 874	8 621	251
1978	24 924	10 357	20 121	85	36 797	15 291	11 001	159	48 545	20 173	8 017	248
1977	24 874	9 607	18 905	76	36 783	14 207	10 357	136	49 392	19 077	7 309	222
1976	24 302	8 813	17 786	76	35 938	13 033	10 132	120	49 389	17 911	6 985	218
1975	24 462	8 388	16 917	70	35 965	12 332	9 764	121	48 776	16 725	6 457	206
Male												
1996	31 426	31 426	20 208	488	46 702	46 702	12 562	720	74 406	74 406	6 636	1 792
1995	30 732	29 851	19 918	433	47 473	46 111	12 251	802	71 643	69 588	6 679	1 570
1994	29 258	27 636	19 859	324	48 995	46 278	12 324	796	70 967	67 032	6 663	1 422
1993	28 898	26 614	19 532	301	47 232	43 499	11 810	669	74 075	68 221	6 302	1 756
1992	28 696	25 660	18 768	169	44 776	40 039	11 353	456	65 225	58 324	6 344	837
1991	29 197	25 345	18 076	183	44 333	38 484	11 126	432	62 724	54 449	6 154	837
1990	31 356	26 120	14 844	288	46 699	38 901	9 807	505	59 744	49 768	7 402	751
1989	32 335	25 555	14 384	278	48 958	38 692	9 737	510	63 448	50 144	7 434	777
1988	31 601	23 827	14 019	285	47 622	35 906	9 466	479	60 581	45 677	7 449	689
1987	31 464	22 781	13 433	268	46 513	33 677	9 286	472	59 583	43 140	7 134	663
1986	31 185	21 784	13 502	229	47 780	33 376	8 908	406	59 891	41 836	7 009	583
1985	30 181	20 698	13 385	208	45 835	31 433	8 794	386	57 989	39 768	6 627	548
1984	28 485	18 863	12 818	178	44 100	29 203	8 387	301	54 068	35 804	6 648	403
1983	28 437	18 052	12 261	187	42 910	27 239	8 010	295	52 985	33 635	6 719	388
1982	27 816	17 108	12 103	172	41 880	25 758	7 865	285	52 206	32 109	6 594	390
1981	29 119	16 870	11 784	168	42 035	24 353	7 393	273	51 906	30 072	6 235	376
1980	30 220	15 871	11 663	158	44 442	23 340	7 132	272	53 022	27 846	5 733	360
1979	31 804	14 716	11 781	145	46 426	21 482	6 889	260	57 078	26 411	5 765	358
1978	32 203	13 382	11 352	137	47 794	19 861	6 611	250	58 414	24 274	5 422	351
1977	32 087	12 393	10 848	122	47 088	18 187	6 341	210	58 995	22 786	5 038	311
1976	31 369	11 376	10 282	122	46 088	16 714	6 135	186	58 464	21 202	4 868	301
1975	31 511	10 805	9 851	112	45 956	15 758	5 960	188	57 371	19 672	4 526	283
Female												
1996	18 933	18 933	20 202	406	28 701	28 701	11 466	421	42 625	42 625	4 646	1 333
1995	18 492	17 962	20 224	213	27 634	26 841	11 034	341	38 930	37 813	4 578	702
1994	17 922	16 928	20 276	199	28 038	26 483	10 388	463	42 248	39 905	4 493	1 040

See footnotes at end of table.

Table B-17. Mean Earnings of Workers 18 Years Old and Over, by Educational Attainment, Race, Hispanic Origin, and Gender: 1975 to 1996 — Continued

(Numbers in thousands. Civilian noninstitutional population.)

Earnings year	Total				Not a high school graduate				High school graduate			
	Mean Earnings (1996 Constant Dollars)	Mean Earnings (Current Dollars)	Number with earnings	Standard error	Mean Earnings (1996 Constant Dollars)	Mean Earnings (Current Dollars)	Number with earnings	Standard error	Mean Earnings (1996 Constant Dollars)	Mean Earnings (Current Dollars)	Number with earnings	Standard error
1993	19 436	17 900	61 937	141	10 274	9 462	6 425	482	15 686	14 446	21 391	174
1992	19 174	17 145	60 451	96	10 413	9 311	6 277	178	15 800	14 128	21 730	117
1991	18 800	16 320	60 226	91	10 158	8 818	6 875	161	15 578	13 523	22 398	109
1990	18 599	15 493	59 862	86	10 574	8 808	7 286	169	15 589	12 986	25 224	103
1989	18 738	14 809	59 296	84	10 462	8 268	7 363	167	15 776	12 468	25 377	98
1988	18 347	13 833	58 558	84	10 227	7 711	7 642	165	15 726	11 857	25 217	100
1987	18 023	13 049	56 923	80	10 364	7 504	7 631	171	15 620	11 309	24 834	100
1986	17 485	12 214	55 568	67	10 177	7 109	7 457	169	15 183	10 606	24 542	78
1985	16 759	11 493	54 212	63	10 024	6 874	7 555	179	14 749	10 115	24 178	76
1984	16 222	10 742	53 178	56	10 033	6 644	7 881	203	14 438	9 561	23 625	69
1983	15 928	10 111	51 279	(NA)	9 912	6 292	7 644	(NA)	14 409	9 147	23 111	(NA)
1982	15 288	9 403	49 962	50	9 645	5 932	7 921	123	14 170	8 715	22 525	66
1981	14 877	8 619	49 754	44	9 792	5 673	8 595	165	13 917	8 063	22 897	57
1980	15 060	7 909	49 094	42	10 021	5 263	8 755	134	14 134	7 423	22 772	53
1979	15 342	7 099	48 362	38	10 460	4 840	9 072	106	14 568	6 741	22 179	48
1978	15 392	6 396	45 850	35	10 581	4 397	9 237	111	14 901	6 192	20 860	46
1977	15 027	5 804	43 678	30	10 439	4 032	9 485	86	14 561	5 624	19 850	39
1976	14 816	5 373	42 091	28	10 266	3 723	9 401	76	14 449	5 240	19 071	37
1975	14 488	4 968	40 584	26	10 026	3 438	9 303	75	14 004	4 802	18 480	34

White

Total

Earnings year	Total				Not a high school graduate				High school graduate			
1996	28 844	28 844	117 230	192	15 358	15 358	13 972	340	22 782	22 782	38 463	235
1995	28 370	27 556	115 636	181	14 654	14 234	13 869	234	22 808	22 154	37 802	261
1994	28 263	26 696	114 586	173	14 759	13 941	13 119	350	22 139	20 911	37 562	196
1993	27 623	25 440	113 342	165	14 301	13 171	13 480	283	21 627	19 918	37 826	166
1992	26 764	23 932	112 120	106	14 754	13 193	13 494	174	21 544	19 265	38 692	123
1991	26 493	22 998	111 843	103	14 877	12 914	14 041	178	21 618	18 766	39 769	115
1990	26 891	22 401	111 972	101	15 333	12 773	14 799	126	21 917	18 257	44 635	105
1989	27 881	22 035	111 243	102	16 011	12 654	15 628	124	22 790	18 011	44 726	111
1988	27 343	20 616	110 159	97	16 228	12 236	16 042	129	22 790	17 183	44 399	107
1987	27 069	19 599	108 407	93	17 267	12 502	16 165	145	22 567	16 339	44 235	99
1986	26 767	18 698	106 384	79	16 613	11 605	16 094	134	22 209	15 514	43 593	84
1985	25 823	17 709	104 818	75	16 208	11 115	16 149	118	21 603	14 815	43 347	81
1984	24 986	16 546	103 022	62	16 206	10 732	16 559	113	21 555	14 274	42 547	74
1983	24 505	15 556	101 035	(NA)	16 130	10 239	16 568	(NA)	21 041	13 357	42 007	(NA)
1982	24 010	14 767	99 488	57	15 802	9 719	17 132	95	20 899	12 854	41 157	70
1981	24 212	14 027	99 510	53	16 807	9 737	18 298	105	21 326	12 355	42 080	64
1980	24 830	13 040	98 358	49	18 552	9 743	18 925	86	21 943	11 524	41 600	58
1979	26 269	12 155	97 544	47	19 077	8 827	19 504	80	22 543	10 431	40 458	54
1978	26 796	11 135	94 002	44	19 576	8 135	19 516	83	24 113	10 020	38 915	53
1977	26 386	10 191	91 254	37	19 198	7 415	20 492	65	23 750	9 173	37 521	44
1976	26 110	9 469	89 099	35	19 352	7 018	20 625	62	23 601	8 559	36 523	41
1975	25 708	8 815	86 894	33	18 776	6 438	20 696	57	23 345	8 005	35 799	41

Male

Earnings year	Total				Not a high school graduate				High school graduate			
1996	35 821	35 821	63 532	320	18 246	18 246	8 899	514	28 591	28 591	20 329	405
1995	35 288	34 276	62 520	298	17 535	17 032	8 660	338	28 278	27 467	19 982	403
1994	35 246	33 292	62 029	283	17 823	16 835	8 133	547	27 659	26 125	19 833	330
1993	34 441	31 719	61 356	270	16 608	15 295	8 430	265	26 908	24 781	19 835	264
1992	33 007	29 515	60 919	174	17 238	15 414	8 487	241	26 665	23 844	20 259	192
1991	32 850	28 516	60 770	163	17 855	15 499	8 720	211	27 043	23 475	20 765	179
1990	33 739	28 105	61 067	167	18 390	15 319	9 084	168	27 773	23 135	23 088	174
1989	35 445	28 013	60 877	171	19 254	15 217	9 805	165	29 471	23 291	23 029	191
1988	34 728	26 184	60 221	160	19 819	14 943	10 008	175	29 465	22 216	22 707	181

See footnotes at end of table.

Table B-17.   Mean Earnings of Workers 18 Years Old and Over, by Educational Attainment, Race, Hispanic Origin, and Gender: 1975 to 1996 — Continued

(Numbers in thousands. Civilian noninstitutional population.)

Earnings year	Some college/associate degree				Bachelor's Degree				Advanced Degree			
	Mean Earnings (1996 Constant Dollars)	Mean Earnings (Current Dollars)	Number with earnings	Standard error	Mean Earnings (1996 Constant Dollars)	Mean Earnings (Current Dollars)	Number with earnings	Standard error	Mean Earnings (1996 Constant Dollars)	Mean Earnings (Current Dollars)	Number with earnings	Standard error
1993	17 976	16 555	19 897	155	27 397	25 232	10 005	441	40 405	37 212	4 281	986
1992	17 919	16 023	18 571	138	26 830	23 991	9 738	272	37 815	33 814	4 135	594
1991	18 020	15 643	17 657	141	26 268	22 802	9 348	258	37 934	32 929	3 948	594
1990	18 009	15 002	14 149	154	26 330	21 933	8 321	270	34 648	28 862	4 883	459
1989	18 585	14 688	13 694	155	26 684	21 089	8 030	264	34 135	26 977	4 831	469
1988	18 580	14 009	13 198	179	25 486	19 216	7 842	253	33 170	25 010	4 660	451
1987	18 173	13 158	12 971	155	25 161	18 217	7 211	261	33 153	24 004	4 277	447
1986	17 220	12 029	12 611	133	25 229	17 623	6 880	233	32 457	22 672	4 078	367
1985	16 775	11 504	12 017	134	23 497	16 114	6 579	207	30 916	21 202	3 883	334
1984	16 028	10 614	11 645	110	22 448	14 865	6 266	193	30 617	20 275	3 762	313
1983	15 723	9 981	10 947	(NA)	21 752	13 808	5 919	(NA)	29 290	18 593	3 658	(NA)
1982	15 199	9 348	10 499	108	20 342	12 511	5 560	167	27 655	17 009	3 457	272
1981	15 208	8 811	9 975	98	19 650	11 384	5 186	156	27 008	15 647	3 101	264
1980	15 720	8 256	9 721	99	20 237	10 628	5 043	152	26 700	14 022	2 802	241
1979	15 539	7 190	9 393	89	20 475	9 474	4 862	137	27 483	12 717	2 856	231
1978	15 500	6 441	8 769	79	20 233	8 408	4 390	128	27 922	11 603	2 595	222
1977	15 162	5 856	8 057	69	20 514	7 923	4 016	115	28 087	10 848	2 271	191
1976	14 617	5 301	7 504	70	20 358	7 383	3 997	102	28 526	10 345	2 117	199
1975	14 637	5 019	7 066	62	20 307	6 963	3 804	98	28 633	9 818	1 931	187

White

Total

Earnings year	Some college/associate degree				Bachelor's Degree				Advanced Degree			
1996	25 511	25 511	34 087	293	38 936	38 936	20 846	489	61 779	61 779	9 861	1 230
1995	25 068	24 349	33 850	264	38 825	37 711	20 203	503	58 739	57 054	9 914	1 040
1994	23 978	22 648	34 006	218	40 227	37 996	19 917	551	59 790	56 475	9 981	1 020
1993	23 805	21 924	33 728	193	38 922	35 846	18 922	469	61 852	56 964	9 386	1 241
1992	23 884	21 357	32 014	120	37 007	33 092	18 555	312	55 186	49 347	9 363	611
1991	24 207	21 013	30 973	127	36 676	31 837	18 035	301	53 565	46 498	9 019	611
1990	25 324	21 095	25 105	182	37 966	31 626	15 993	328	50 309	41 908	11 049	522
1989	26 164	20 678	24 212	177	39 562	31 266	15 723	331	52 650	41 610	10 952	546
1988	25 709	19 384	23 643	187	38 311	28 886	15 221	314	50 570	38 129	10 854	489
1987	25 227	18 265	23 083	171	38 315	27 741	14 624	317	49 964	36 175	10 300	477
1986	24 868	17 371	22 653	146	38 740	27 061	14 055	271	50 484	35 265	9 987	422
1985	24 353	16 701	22 131	138	37 003	25 376	13 670	261	48 705	33 401	9 522	391
1984	22 949	15 197	21 451	117	35 445	23 472	13 056	207	46 081	30 515	9 409	298
1983	22 820	14 486	20 452	(NA)	34 521	21 914	12 577	(NA)	44 946	28 532	9 430	(NA)
1982	22 436	13 799	19 967	114	33 754	20 760	12 103	195	43 965	27 040	9 127	286
1981	23 171	13 424	19 102	112	33 467	19 389	11 450	185	44 125	25 564	8 582	280
1980	24 139	12 677	18 888	106	35 101	18 434	11 067	183	44 682	23 466	7 876	267
1979	25 013	11 574	18 835	98	36 217	16 758	10 807	172	47 729	22 085	7 940	266
1978	25 277	10 504	18 022	91	37 211	15 463	10 171	168	49 407	20 531	7 376	265
1977	25 298	9 771	16 968	82	37 444	14 462	9 534	144	50 066	19 337	6 739	235
1976	24 701	8 958	16 127	82	36 616	13 279	9 325	127	50 056	18 153	6 498	230
1975	24 862	8 525	15 423	75	36 737	12 597	8 955	129	49 345	16 920	6 021	217

Male

Earnings year	Some college/associate degree				Bachelor's Degree				Advanced Degree			
1996	32 238	32 238	17 418	534	48 014	48 014	11 065	800	75 481	75 481	5 821	1 871
1995	31 430	30 529	17 136	451	48 404	47 016	10 851	852	72 227	70 155	5 891	1 634
1994	29 898	28 240	17 091	361	50 368	47 575	10 992	880	71 599	67 629	5 979	1 504
1993	29 639	27 297	16 959	334	48 324	44 505	10 452	722	76 007	70 000	5 680	1 914
1992	29 509	26 387	16 335	187	45 731	40 893	10 118	488	66 349	59 329	5 720	890
1991	30 055	26 090	15 873	198	45 557	39 547	9 893	468	63 655	55 257	5 519	890
1990	32 222	26 841	13 003	317	47 754	39 780	8 770	546	60 485	50 385	6 731	798
1989	33 227	26 260	12 582	303	50 175	39 654	8 750	553	64 571	51 031	6 710	831
1988	32 444	24 462	12 277	310	48 591	36 637	8 467	521	61 249	46 181	6 762	728

See footnotes at end of table.

Table B-17.   Mean Earnings of Workers 18 Years Old and Over, by Educational Attainment, Race, Hispanic Origin, and Gender: 1975 to 1996 — Continued

(Numbers in thousands. Civilian noninstitutional population.)

Earnings year	Total				Not a high school graduate				High school graduate			
	Mean Earnings (1996 Constant Dollars)	Mean Earnings (Current Dollars)	Number with earnings	Standard error	Mean Earnings (1996 Constant Dollars)	Mean Earnings (Current Dollars)	Number with earnings	Standard error	Mean Earnings (1996 Constant Dollars)	Mean Earnings (Current Dollars)	Number with earnings	Standard error
1987	34 388	24 898	59 468	152	21 136	15 303	10 132	202	29 021	21 012	22 682	162
1986	34 203	23 892	58 932	131	20 282	14 168	10 239	183	28 815	20 128	22 392	143
1985	32 961	22 604	58 385	122	19 801	13 579	10 163	158	28 001	19 203	22 357	136
1984	31 975	21 174	57 362	100	20 006	13 248	10 280	148	28 210	18 681	21 989	125
1983	31 210	19 812	56 641	96	19 806	12 573	10 387	140	27 223	17 281	21 733	117
1982	30 663	18 859	56 364	92	19 433	11 952	10 816	129	27 091	16 662	21 436	116
1981	31 313	18 141	56 397	86	20 875	12 094	11 523	142	28 225	16 352	21 809	109
1980	32 265	16 945	55 772	79	21 972	11 539	11 937	114	29 289	15 382	21 453	99
1979	34 516	15 971	55 556	76	24 047	11 127	12 291	109	30 075	13 916	20 834	94
1978	35 199	14 627	54 113	72	24 926	10 358	12 141	103	32 569	13 534	20 328	91
1977	34 510	13 329	53 174	60	24 250	9 366	12 903	86	32 045	12 377	19 773	74
1976	34 033	12 342	52 312	56	24 450	8 867	13 117	85	31 703	11 497	19 446	69
1975	33 386	11 448	51 510	53	23 652	8 110	13 191	77	31 281	10 726	19 361	69

Female

Earnings year	Total				Not a high school graduate				High school graduate			
1996	20 590	20 590	53 697	161	10 290	10 290	5 073	210	16 270	16 270	18 134	178
1995	20 227	19 647	53 117	164	9 865	9 582	5 208	239	16 674	16 196	17 820	304
1994	20 022	18 912	52 557	163	9 761	9 220	4 987	192	15 963	15 078	17 729	168
1993	19 575	18 028	51 986	154	10 450	9 624	5 050	606	15 806	14 557	17 991	174
1992	19 335	17 289	51 200	106	10 544	9 428	5 007	207	15 917	14 233	18 434	129
1991	18 928	16 431	51 060	98	9 996	8 677	5 321	174	15 691	13 621	18 999	118
1990	18 678	15 559	50 905	94	10 474	8 725	5 715	186	15 643	13 031	21 547	113
1989	18 739	14 810	50 366	91	10 550	8 338	5 823	182	15 698	12 406	21 697	107
1988	18 438	13 902	49 938	93	10 275	7 747	6 034	184	15 803	11 915	21 692	110
1987	18 177	13 161	48 939	89	10 770	7 798	6 033	190	15 774	11 421	21 553	110
1986	17 532	12 247	47 452	72	10 197	7 123	5 855	181	15 233	10 641	21 201	84
1985	16 849	11 555	46 433	70	10 107	6 931	5 986	172	14 789	10 142	20 990	82
1984	16 206	10 732	45 660	61	9 988	6 614	6 279	175	14 438	9 561	20 558	74
1983	15 952	10 126	44 394	(NA)	9 951	6 317	6 181	(NA)	14 414	9 150	20 274	(NA)
1982	15 314	9 419	43 124	55	9 586	5 896	6 316	135	14 168	8 714	19 721	72
1981	14 924	8 646	43 113	48	9 885	5 727	6 775	148	13 902	8 054	20 271	61
1980	15 092	7 926	42 586	45	12 710	6 675	6 988	127	14 119	7 415	20 147	57
1979	15 355	7 105	41 988	41	10 609	4 909	7 213	110	14 547	6 731	19 624	51
1978	15 396	6 398	39 889	38	10 771	4 476	7 375	138	14 862	6 176	18 587	49
1977	15 038	5 808	38 080	32	10 608	4 097	7 589	95	14 509	5 604	17 748	41
1976	14 843	5 383	36 787	31	10 445	3 788	7 508	86	14 377	5 214	17 077	40
1975	14 529	4 982	35 384	28	10 207	3 500	7 505	80	13 999	4 800	16 438	36

Black

Total

Earnings year	Total				Not a high school graduate				High school graduate			
1996	21 978	21 978	15 255	485	13 110	13 110	2 383	434	18 722	18 722	5 844	554
1995	21 143	20 537	14 847	374	13 339	12 956	2 389	437	17 576	17 072	5 453	315
1994	20 933	19 772	14 754	274	13 451	12 705	2 290	463	17 411	16 446	5 596	276
1993	20 211	18 614	14 315	316	12 015	11 065	2 352	370	17 505	16 122	5 521	584
1992	19 477	17 416	13 836	210	12 388	11 077	2 451	345	17 066	15 260	5 379	249
1991	19 364	16 809	13 865	197	12 957	11 248	2 860	335	17 349	15 060	5 512	264
1990	19 960	16 627	13 731	186	13 426	11 184	2 853	298	17 760	14 794	6 049	213
1989	20 336	16 072	13 600	177	12 737	10 066	2 883	266	18 490	14 613	5 894	206
1988	20 316	15 318	13 356	191	13 531	10 202	2 970	343	18 349	13 835	5 760	236
1987	19 524	14 136	13 023	171	13 778	9 976	3 015	264	17 765	12 862	5 699	224
1986	19 318	13 494	12 729	167	13 407	9 365	3 028	282	17 574	12 276	5 470	190
1985	18 848	12 926	12 427	153	13 293	9 116	3 009	275	17 193	11 791	5 223	192
1984	18 124	12 002	11 948	131	13 176	8 725	3 127	292	16 433	10 882	4 927	170
1983	17 799	11 299	11 296	(NA)	12 393	7 867	3 035	(NA)	16 630	10 557	4 692	(NA)
1982	17 254	10 612	11 081	124	12 680	7 799	3 188	227	16 726	10 287	4 591	161
1981	17 463	10 117	11 088	109	12 980	7 520	3 514	208	17 250	9 994	4 388	159

See footnotes at end of table.

Table B-17.   Mean Earnings of Workers 18 Years Old and Over, by Educational Attainment, Race, Hispanic Origin, and Gender: 1975 to 1996 — Continued

(Numbers in thousands. Civilian noninstitutional population.)

Earnings year	Some college/associate degree				Bachelor's Degree				Advanced Degree			
	Mean Earnings (1996 Constant Dollars)	Mean Earnings (Current Dollars)	Number with earnings	Standard error	Mean Earnings (1996 Constant Dollars)	Mean Earnings (Current Dollars)	Number with earnings	Standard error	Mean Earnings (1996 Constant Dollars)	Mean Earnings (Current Dollars)	Number with earnings	Standard error
1987	32 195	23 310	11 771	295	48 154	34 865	8 384	510	59 998	43 440	6 499	702
1986	31 928	22 303	11 846	248	49 064	34 273	8 041	437	60 813	42 480	6 413	618
1985	30 972	21 240	11 831	224	46 902	32 165	7 970	416	58 849	40 358	6 064	580
1984	29 211	19 344	11 387	193	44 972	29 781	7 624	321	54 695	36 219	6 081	423
1983	28 967	18 388	10 974	202	43 677	27 726	7 379	309	53 530	33 981	6 168	409
1982	28 569	17 571	10 822	186	42 930	26 404	7 242	302	52 462	32 266	6 047	406
1981	29 866	17 303	10 448	184	43 053	24 943	6 824	289	52 466	30 396	5 794	393
1980	31 062	16 313	10 400	171	45 324	23 803	6 618	286	53 298	27 991	5 363	373
1979	32 510	15 043	10 572	157	47 081	21 785	6 464	271	57 584	26 645	5 395	374
1978	32 701	13 589	10 350	146	48 333	20 085	6 205	263	59 283	24 635	5 088	369
1977	32 770	12 657	9 853	131	47 953	18 521	5 941	219	59 790	23 093	4 704	325
1976	32 031	11 616	9 394	130	46 863	16 995	5 765	194	59 258	21 490	4 589	314
1975	32 162	11 028	9 096	119	46 892	16 079	5 587	197	57 913	19 858	4 275	295
Female												
1996	18 482	18 482	16 669	185	28 667	28 667	9 781	467	42 049	42 049	4 041	1 202
1995	18 543	18 011	16 714	246	27 711	26 916	9 352	383	38 982	37 864	4 022	709
1994	17 996	16 998	16 915	225	27 736	26 198	8 925	525	42 153	39 816	4 002	1 113
1993	17 905	16 490	16 769	168	27 320	25 161	8 470	501	40 162	36 988	3 705	967
1992	18 023	16 116	15 679	149	26 547	23 738	8 437	295	37 659	33 675	3 643	635
1991	18 060	15 677	15 100	155	25 886	22 471	8 140	276	37 655	32 687	3 500	635
1990	17 913	14 922	12 102	165	26 080	21 725	7 223	294	34 446	28 694	4 318	486
1989	18 524	14 640	11 630	170	26 244	20 741	6 973	272	33 796	26 709	4 242	510
1988	18 433	13 898	11 366	198	25 424	19 169	6 754	274	32 924	24 824	4 092	488
1987	17 976	13 015	11 312	167	25 096	18 170	6 240	289	32 807	23 753	3 801	482
1986	17 127	11 964	10 807	140	24 935	17 418	6 014	245	31 953	22 320	3 574	397
1985	16 752	11 488	10 300	148	23 160	15 883	5 700	229	30 916	21 202	3 458	357
1984	15 862	10 504	10 064	119	22 073	14 617	5 432	209	30 341	20 092	3 328	332
1983	15 704	9 969	9 478	(NA)	21 525	13 664	5 198	(NA)	28 718	18 230	3 262	(NA)
1982	15 179	9 336	9 145	117	20 083	12 352	4 861	181	27 281	16 779	3 080	287
1981	15 086	8 740	8 654	107	19 325	11 196	4 626	167	26 794	15 523	2 788	279
1980	15 654	8 221	8 488	108	19 892	10 447	4 449	159	26 294	13 809	2 513	253
1979	15 420	7 135	8 263	96	20 045	9 275	4 343	145	26 842	12 420	2 545	243
1978	15 262	6 342	7 672	85	19 807	8 231	3 966	131	27 443	11 404	2 288	235
1977	14 950	5 774	7 115	73	20 066	7 750	3 593	123	27 587	10 655	2 035	203
1976	14 477	5 250	6 733	74	20 025	7 262	3 560	109	27 936	10 131	1 909	207
1975	14 366	4 926	6 327	65	19 895	6 822	3 368	105	28 370	9 728	1 746	199
Black												
Total												
1996	23 628	23 628	4 783	1 084	31 955	31 955	1 655	1 080	48 731	48 731	590	5 269
1995	22 468	21 824	4 727	885	30 542	29 666	1 684	876	48 032	46 654	595	3 603
1994	20 783	19 631	4 610	573	32 754	30 938	1 679	907	51 509	48 653	579	3 282
1993	20 486	18 867	4 279	413	32 523	29 953	1 638	1 015	44 758	41 221	525	2 456
1992	20 934	18 719	4 054	338	30 706	27 457	1 429	819	46 342	41 439	523	1 885
1991	20 563	17 850	3 581	327	29 525	25 630	1 383	709	43 778	38 002	528	1 885
1990	21 859	18 209	3 004	411	31 750	26 448	1 217	745	39 570	32 962	607	1 461
1989	21 998	17 385	3 008	340	32 085	25 357	1 121	779	41 427	32 740	694	1 422
1988	22 229	16 760	2 802	443	31 418	23 689	1 204	702	40 852	30 802	621	1 346
1987	21 396	15 491	2 617	363	28 735	20 805	1 097	608	40 279	29 163	596	1 411
1986	21 106	14 743	2 662	423	30 640	21 403	1 004	810	39 372	27 503	564	1 130
1985	20 130	13 805	2 615	348	29 941	20 533	1 046	579	38 271	26 246	535	1 254
1984	19 465	12 890	2 396	277	29 190	19 330	937	551	36 351	24 072	561	884
1983	19 575	12 426	2 206	(NA)	27 106	17 207	828	(NA)	37 029	23 506	535	(NA)
1982	18 078	11 119	2 067	271	24 636	15 152	747	494	37 329	22 959	488	1 162
1981	19 774	11 456	2 078	255	25 178	14 587	708	457	33 595	19 463	398	788

See footnotes at end of table.

Table B-17.   Mean Earnings of Workers 18 Years Old and Over, by Educational Attainment, Race, Hispanic Origin, and Gender: 1975 to 1996 — Continued

(Numbers in thousands. Civilian noninstitutional population.)

Earnings year	Total				Not a high school graduate				High school graduate			
	Mean Earnings (1996 Constant Dollars)	Mean Earnings (Current Dollars)	Number with earnings	Standard error	Mean Earnings (1996 Constant Dollars)	Mean Earnings (Current Dollars)	Number with earnings	Standard error	Mean Earnings (1996 Constant Dollars)	Mean Earnings (Current Dollars)	Number with earnings	Standard error
1980	21 107	11 085	5 576	170	16 035	8 421	2 054	291	22 017	11 563	2 119	260
1979	18 845	8 720	10 856	97	13 883	6 424	3 776	187	18 852	8 723	4 267	135
1978	19 206	7 981	10 420	91	14 241	5 918	3 841	160	19 617	8 152	3 944	133
1977	18 825	7 271	10 014	70	13 997	5 406	3 946	126	19 556	7 553	3 604	116
1976	18 519	6 716	9 744	66	14 626	5 304	4 008	127	18 765	6 805	3 515	95
1975	18 052	6 190	9 368	57	14 550	4 989	3 922	116	18 318	6 281	3 495	83

Male

Earnings year	Total				Not a high school graduate				High school graduate			
1996	25 067	25 067	7 125	785	15 461	15 461	1 290	648	22 267	22 267	2 836	1 034
1995	24 581	23 876	7 090	718	15 316	14 877	1 280	652	20 090	19 514	2 812	443
1994	23 942	22 614	7 009	445	16 922	15 984	1 191	770	19 615	18 527	2 818	413
1993	22 919	21 108	6 833	518	14 196	13 074	1 305	574	20 270	18 668	2 775	903
1992	21 559	19 278	6 822	342	14 159	12 661	1 457	510	18 987	16 978	2 683	382
1991	21 435	18 607	6 830	284	18 102	15 714	1 624	423	19 989	17 352	2 731	382
1990	22 639	18 859	6 781	300	15 643	13 031	1 563	430	20 463	17 046	3 013	332
1989	22 912	18 108	6 654	283	14 965	11 827	1 614	355	21 078	16 658	2 848	328
1988	23 584	17 782	6 593	326	16 498	12 439	1 671	529	21 678	16 345	2 795	404
1987	22 335	16 171	6 505	283	16 434	11 899	1 711	375	20 441	14 800	2 769	374
1986	22 105	15 441	6 326	256	16 102	11 248	1 691	409	20 348	14 214	2 666	294
1985	21 774	14 932	6 237	254	15 751	10 802	1 716	396	20 008	13 721	2 572	308
1984	20 477	13 560	5 899	212	15 427	10 216	1 780	374	18 698	12 382	2 339	280
1983	20 147	12 789	5 707	205	14 326	9 094	1 768	339	18 834	11 956	2 312	265
1982	19 841	12 203	5 535	203	14 882	9 153	1 798	340	19 433	11 952	2 213	268
1981	20 604	11 937	5 651	174	15 994	9 266	1 925	318	20 549	11 905	2 191	261
1980	21 107	11 085	5 576	170	16 035	8 421	2 054	291	22 017	11 563	2 119	260
1979	22 483	10 403	5 581	157	17 155	7 938	2 138	278	23 042	10 662	2 087	225
1978	23 225	9 651	5 350	147	17 863	7 423	2 156	233	23 749	9 869	1 982	219
1977	22 551	8 710	5 220	110	17 212	6 648	2 230	187	24 162	9 332	1 770	184
1976	22 035	7 991	5 156	105	18 392	6 670	2 289	187	22 214	8 056	1 766	155
1975	21 992	7 541	4 864	89	18 560	6 364	2 247	173	22 885	7 847	1 684	138

Female

Earnings year	Total				Not a high school graduate				High school graduate			
1996	19 271	19 271	8 129	592	10 337	10 337	1 094	526	15 379	15 379	3 008	433
1995	18 001	17 485	7 757	277	11 056	10 739	1 108	544	14 900	14 473	2 641	433
1994	18 210	17 200	7 745	326	9 687	9 150	1 099	423	15 174	14 333	2 777	356
1993	17 738	16 336	7 481	371	9 297	8 562	1 048	388	14 713	13 550	2 746	730
1992	17 451	15 605	7 014	241	9 792	8 756	995	376	15 153	13 550	2 696	312
1991	17 355	15 065	7 034	231	10 542	9 151	1 237	524	14 757	12 810	2 781	301
1990	17 345	14 449	6 950	221	10 739	8 946	1 290	402	15 078	12 560	3 036	269
1989	17 869	14 122	6 946	215	9 904	7 827	1 269	403	16 071	12 701	3 046	255
1988	17 130	12 916	6 763	203	9 715	7 325	1 299	391	15 211	11 469	2 965	255
1987	16 720	12 106	6 518	193	10 292	7 452	1 304	360	15 234	11 030	2 930	256
1986	16 565	11 571	6 403	215	9 998	6 984	1 337	375	14 937	10 434	2 804	244
1985	15 900	10 904	6 190	170	10 031	6 879	1 293	366	14 462	9 918	2 651	233
1984	15 829	10 482	6 049	157	10 199	6 754	1 347	464	14 387	9 527	2 588	201
1983	15 403	9 778	5 589	(NA)	9 694	6 154	1 267	(NA)	14 488	9 197	2 380	(NA)
1982	14 672	9 024	5 546	141	9 832	6 047	1 390	279	14 206	8 737	2 378	186
1981	14 197	8 225	5 437	129	9 328	5 404	1 589	252	13 960	8 088	2 197	183
1980	14 631	7 684	(NA)	121	8 921	4 685	(NA)	242	14 296	7 508	(NA)	164
1979	14 998	6 940	5 275	112	9 613	4 448	1 638	232	14 839	6 866	2 180	154
1978	14 966	6 219	5 070	104	9 609	3 993	1 685	212	15 442	6 417	1 962	149
1977	14 768	5 704	4 794	84	9 820	3 793	1 716	158	15 113	5 837	1 834	142
1976	14 568	5 283	4 588	74	9 613	3 486	1 719	162	15 279	5 541	1 749	108
1975	13 800	4 732	4 504	68	9 172	3 145	1 675	140	14 071	4 825	1 811	96

See footnotes at end of table.

Table B-17. Mean Earnings of Workers 18 Years Old and Over, by Educational Attainment, Race, Hispanic Origin, and Gender: 1975 to 1996 — Continued

(Numbers in thousands. Civilian noninstitutional population.)

Earnings year	Some college/associate degree				Bachelor's Degree				Advanced Degree			
	Mean Earnings (1996 Constant Dollars)	Mean Earnings (Current Dollars)	Number with earnings	Standard error	Mean Earnings (1996 Constant Dollars)	Mean Earnings (Current Dollars)	Number with earnings	Standard error	Mean Earnings (1996 Constant Dollars)	Mean Earnings (Current Dollars)	Number with earnings	Standard error
1980	23 598	12 393	964	417	29 735	15 616	283	739	38 006	19 960	353	1 026
1979	21 385	9 895	1 826	237	29 117	13 473	622	534	39 294	18 182	366	872
1978	21 721	9 026	1 689	230	30 971	12 870	557	544	36 280	15 076	389	573
1977	21 544	8 321	1 578	182	28 708	11 088	532	342	38 187	14 749	354	494
1976	20 215	7 331	1 370	184	28 487	10 331	547	314	41 398	15 013	305	696
1975	21 033	7 212	1 193	170	27 627	9 473	517	280	35 967	12 333	241	433
Male												
1996	26 365	26 365	2 047	1 442	35 558	35 558	700	1 664	65 981	65 981	253	11 509
1995	27 639	26 846	2 047	1 948	37 090	36 026	659	1 815	58 875	57 186	293	6 801
1994	25 142	23 748	1 959	844	36 073	34 073	758	1 628	55 930	52 829	281	5 010
1993	23 599	21 734	1 804	691	38 163	35 147	721	1 811	51 437	47 372	228	4 974
1992	25 382	22 697	1 796	527	34 656	30 989	643	1 489	54 762	48 968	244	3 719
1991	23 671	20 548	1 570	542	30 038	26 075	650	966	50 603	43 927	255	3 719
1990	25 392	21 152	1 372	708	35 379	29 471	564	1 291	46 943	39 104	269	2 888
1989	25 627	20 253	1 352	566	34 788	27 493	515	1 201	48 292	38 166	326	2 655
1988	25 551	19 265	1 311	818	37 807	28 506	533	1 220	48 346	36 452	283	2 650
1987	24 973	18 081	1 250	612	32 243	23 345	482	1 091	47 060	34 073	294	2 545
1986	24 937	17 419	1 226	693	33 516	23 412	480	1 161	44 456	31 054	263	2 035
1985	23 936	16 415	1 230	628	34 731	23 818	477	1 072	46 584	31 947	243	2 484
1984	22 591	14 960	1 106	471	33 201	21 986	424	961	42 121	27 893	250	1 670
1983	23 808	15 113	996	500	32 089	20 370	363	1 033	40 117	25 466	268	1 470
1982	21 016	12 926	953	458	28 710	17 658	319	861	43 008	26 452	253	2 006
1981	23 716	13 740	1 002	432	28 694	16 624	327	776	36 389	21 082	205	1 197
1980	23 598	12 393	964	417	29 735	15 616	283	739	44 454	23 346	156	1 986
1979	25 871	11 971	931	384	34 926	16 161	259	1 071	45 583	21 092	166	1 673
1978	26 945	11 197	770	409	38 525	16 009	260	944	43 516	18 083	181	1 031
1977	25 951	10 023	799	300	33 601	12 978	234	641	42 423	16 385	188	808
1976	23 957	8 688	726	300	33 768	12 246	233	597	49 246	17 859	143	1 388
1975	24 804	8 505	599	267	33 007	11 318	213	572	40 012	13 720	121	702
Female												
1996	21 581	21 581	2 736	1 555	29 311	29 311	954	1 402	35 785	35 785	337	1 542
1995	18 516	17 985	2 679	429	26 332	25 577	1 025	768	37 665	36 585	304	1 616
1994	17 563	16 589	2 651	472	30 021	28 356	921	946	47 237	44 618	297	4 220
1993	18 218	16 778	2 475	495	28 085	25 865	917	1 073	39 616	36 485	296	1 862
1992	17 393	15 553	2 256	440	27 479	24 572	786	821	39 032	34 902	281	1 272
1991	18 136	15 743	2 010	400	29 070	25 235	733	912	37 401	32 467	273	1 272
1990	18 888	15 734	1 632	466	28 615	23 837	653	827	33 702	28 074	338	1 265
1989	19 036	15 044	1 656	411	29 787	23 541	606	1 017	35 344	27 933	368	1 290
1988	19 307	14 557	1 491	419	26 343	19 862	671	804	34 579	26 072	338	1 094
1987	18 125	13 123	1 367	412	25 987	18 815	615	668	33 677	24 383	302	1 062
1986	17 836	12 459	1 436	516	28 004	19 562	524	1 129	34 930	24 400	301	1 149
1985	16 752	11 488	1 385	347	25 925	17 779	569	569	31 354	21 502	292	1 003
1984	16 785	11 115	1 290	318	25 874	17 134	513	618	31 712	21 000	311	860
1983	16 092	10 215	1 210	(NA)	23 217	14 738	465	(NA)	33 930	21 539	267	(NA)
1982	15 566	9 574	1 114	315	21 599	13 284	428	576	31 214	19 198	235	1 077
1981	16 103	9 329	1 076	285	22 161	12 839	381	527	30 626	17 743	193	1 011
1980	16 269	8 544	(NA)	266	23 590	12 389	(NA)	568	32 899	17 278	197	951
1979	16 717	7 735	895	273	24 972	11 555	363	504	34 073	15 766	200	785
1978	17 343	7 207	919	248	24 358	10 122	297	598	29 982	12 459	208	585
1977	17 026	6 576	779	203	24 866	9 604	298	347	33 389	12 896	166	524
1976	15 996	5 801	644	199	24 569	8 910	314	321	34 471	12 501	162	465
1975	17 230	5 908	594	211	23 856	8 180	304	258	31 887	10 934	120	505

See footnotes at end of table.

Table B-17.   Mean Earnings of Workers 18 Years Old and Over, by Educational Attainment, Race, Hispanic Origin, and Gender: 1975 to 1996 — Continued

(Numbers in thousands. Civilian noninstitutional population.)

Earnings year	Total				Not a high school graduate				High school graduate			
	Mean Earnings (1996 Constant Dollars)	Mean Earnings (Current Dollars)	Number with earnings	Standard error	Mean Earnings (1996 Constant Dollars)	Mean Earnings (Current Dollars)	Number with earnings	Standard error	Mean Earnings (1996 Constant Dollars)	Mean Earnings (Current Dollars)	Number with earnings	Standard error
Hispanic origin [1]												
Total												
1996	19 439	19 439	13 365	458	13 287	13 287	5 062	263	18 528	18 528	3 783	444
1995	18 801	18 262	12 434	428	13 454	13 068	4 784	305	18 874	18 333	3 594	1 070
1994	19 658	18 568	12 035	478	14 539	13 733	4 686	944	18 340	17 323	3 444	401
1993	18 570	17 102	11 644	344	12 869	11 852	4 425	263	18 015	16 591	3 367	419
1992	18 815	16 824	10 171	252	13 236	11 836	3 962	273	18 692	16 714	2 991	425
1991	18 777	16 300	10 006	237	13 058	11 335	3 906	230	18 595	16 142	3 045	344
1990	19 139	15 943	9 729	222	12 446	10 368	3 929	210	18 507	15 417	3 282	297
1989	19 883	15 714	9 570	234	14 551	11 500	3 985	222	18 855	14 901	3 188	296
1900	19 904	15 007	9 220	245	14 049	11 045	3 824	240	19 453	14 607	2 953	315
1987	20 296	14 695	8 817	250	15 139	10 961	3 457	272	19 278	13 958	2 982	342
1986	19 409	13 558	8 393	205	14 167	9 896	3 379	237	19 167	13 389	2 835	300
1985	19 131	13 120	7 840	195	14 518	9 956	3 223	257	19 020	13 044	2 661	297
1984	19 002	12 583	7 349	228	14 604	9 671	3 129	293	19 417	12 858	2 457	343
1983	18 748	11 901	6 222	(NA)	14 923	9 473	2 674	(NA)	19 025	12 077	2 030	(NA)
1982	18 384	11 307	5 914	221	13 817	8 498	2 583	283	18 761	11 539	1 967	317
1981	18 766	10 872	5 930	194	14 922	8 645	2 648	255	19 066	11 046	1 966	304
1980	19 159	10 062	5 723	197	15 460	8 119	2 649	284	19 388	10 182	1 824	309
1979	19 986	9 248	5 545	175	16 604	7 683	2 533	272	20 181	9 338	1 812	272
1978	20 358	8 460	4 898	169	17 177	7 138	2 345	305	20 484	8 512	1 554	258
1977	20 094	7 761	4 752	130	16 951	6 547	2 306	205	20 917	8 079	1 461	226
1976	19 526	7 081	4 303	128	16 501	5 984	2 107	199	20 902	7 580	1 309	215
1975	19 152	6 567	4 078	124	15 929	5 462	2 028	198	19 712	6 759	1 293	183
Male												
1996	21 870	21 870	7 975	657	14 986	14 986	3 382	347	21 593	21 593	2 116	628
1995	20 912	20 312	7 337	544	15 210	14 774	3 140	347	21 499	20 882	2 039	1 467
1994	22 538	21 288	7 117	754	17 315	16 355	3 111	1 409	20 822	19 667	1 937	557
1993	21 130	19 460	6 957	526	14 737	13 572	2 928	357	20 375	18 765	1 954	566
1992	21 071	18 842	6 034	365	14 888	13 313	2 633	366	21 647	19 357	1 665	662
1991	21 330	18 516	5 932	316	15 129	13 133	2 548	263	21 406	18 582	1 705	471
1990	21 992	18 320	5 745	332	15 824	13 182	2 562	276	21 728	18 100	1 812	455
1989	22 886	18 087	5 641	352	16 661	13 167	2 632	265	22 243	17 579	1 711	452
1988	23 020	17 357	5 477	361	17 024	12 836	2 517	316	23 138	17 446	1 621	475
1987	23 546	17 048	5 248	372	17 711	12 823	2 281	369	23 168	16 774	1 616	523
1986	22 367	15 624	5 037	305	16 122	11 262	2 262	313	22 831	15 948	1 546	476
1985	22 300	15 293	4 702	285	17 018	11 671	2 111	342	22 751	15 602	1 491	464
1984	22 587	14 957	4 344	344	17 277	11 441	2 022	385	23 804	15 763	1 319	549
1983	22 472	14 265	3 577	324	17 884	11 353	1 678	400	22 974	14 584	1 074	549
1982	21 924	13 484	3 480	339	16 435	10 108	1 622	392	22 572	13 883	1 083	488
1981	22 529	13 052	3 504	292	18 032	10 447	1 686	342	23 324	13 513	1 037	489
1980	23 440	12 310	3 401	303	18 708	9 825	1 707	394	24 959	13 108	961	526
1979	24 490	11 332	3 269	268	20 300	9 393	1 615	378	25 316	11 714	952	448
1978	25 203	10 473	2 915	258	21 263	8 836	1 498	427	26 326	10 940	815	426
1977	24 998	9 655	2 833	198	21 210	8 192	1 460	281	26 890	10 386	776	372
1976	24 230	8 787	2 571	195	20 516	7 440	1 321	272	26 582	9 640	712	345
1975	23 803	8 162	2 456	189	19 671	6 745	1 287	268	24 923	8 546	691	289
Female												
1996	15 841	15 841	5 390	578	9 867	9 867	1 680	332	14 635	14 635	1 667	577
1995	15 762	15 310	5 096	685	10 099	9 809	1 644	565	15 432	14 989	1 555	1 541
1994	15 490	14 631	4 918	404	9 061	8 559	1 576	304	15 153	14 313	1 508	546

See footnotes at end of table.

Table B-17.   Mean Earnings of Workers 18 Years Old and Over, by Educational Attainment, Race, Hispanic Origin, and Gender: 1975 to 1996 — Continued

(Numbers in thousands. Civilian noninstitutional population.)

Earnings year	Some college/associate degree				Bachelor's Degree				Advanced Degree			
	Mean Earnings (1996 Constant Dollars)	Mean Earnings (Current Dollars)	Number with earnings	Standard error	Mean Earnings (1996 Constant Dollars)	Mean Earnings (Current Dollars)	Number with earnings	Standard error	Mean Earnings (1996 Constant Dollars)	Mean Earnings (Current Dollars)	Number with earnings	Standard error
Hispanic origin [1]												
Total												
1996	22 209	22 209	3 096	1 185	32 955	32 955	1 027	2 746	49 873	49 873	398	7 497
1995	20 511	19 923	2 856	904	31 506	30 602	866	1 678	46 959	45 612	334	3 004
1994	22 276	21 041	2 723	693	30 877	29 165	844	1 337	54 945	51 898	337	6 534
1993	20 677	19 043	2 728	548	32 964	30 359	799	3 355	48 899	45 034	325	4 169
1992	22 118	19 778	2 242	446	31 604	28 260	702	1 272	52 266	46 736	274	2 871
1991	22 029	19 123	2 080	456	30 669	26 623	665	1 249	46 257	40 154	311	2 871
1990	23 056	19 206	1 534	540	30 855	25 703	601	1 208	45 707	38 075	382	2 477
1989	23 670	18 707	1 513	608	35 628	28 157	535	1 519	49 693	39 273	349	2 861
1988	24 007	18 101	1 511	716	31 493	23 745	596	1 134	44 886	33 843	340	3 064
1987	23 340	16 899	1 400	524	31 912	23 105	644	1 139	47 530	34 413	335	3 055
1986	23 654	16 523	1 411	584	32 507	22 707	471	1 248	40 536	28 316	295	1 822
1985	22 336	15 318	1 226	513	30 444	20 878	458	1 104	41 350	28 357	273	1 843
1984	21 684	14 359	1 116	622	30 087	19 924	381	1 226	39 757	26 327	265	2 222
1983	21 063	13 371	976	(NA)	28 311	17 972	320	(NA)	38 362	24 352	222	(NA)
1982	21 312	13 108	873	546	29 569	18 186	303	1 463	45 797	28 167	186	2 784
1981	22 389	12 971	834	516	27 814	16 114	320	1 174	41 567	24 082	161	2 557
1980	22 642	11 891	808	558	29 849	15 676	283	1 267	41 719	21 910	157	2 623
1979	22 003	10 181	768	458	32 288	14 940	240	1 315	39 491	18 273	190	1 780
1978	23 042	9 575	661	446	33 654	13 985	213	1 195	41 711	17 333	125	1 903
1977	21 158	8 172	656	333	32 550	12 572	210	864	43 135	16 660	118	1 753
1976	19 997	7 252	592	333	30 999	11 242	177	887	38 605	14 000	118	1 667
1975	20 864	7 154	474	351	30 835	10 573	173	796	45 950	15 756	111	1 994
Male												
1996	26 682	26 682	1 687	2 101	38 130	38 130	531	5 090	49 307	49 307	259	6 300
1995	22 826	22 171	1 475	978	36 146	35 109	466	2 695	52 302	50 802	215	4 151
1994	25 956	24 517	1 410	855	35 781	33 797	450	2 185	64 431	60 858	210	10 036
1993	24 341	22 417	1 444	859	40 777	37 554	438	5 974	56 941	52 441	194	6 150
1992	25 758	23 033	1 193	596	37 385	33 430	164	1 957	59 992	53 645	194	4 216
1991	25 314	21 974	1 131	693	36 517	31 699	356	1 729	52 845	45 873	193	4 216
1990	26 861	22 376	852	831	37 796	31 485	314	1 966	56 997	47 479	205	4 339
1989	28 310	22 374	810	996	41 461	32 767	292	2 536	62 112	49 088	196	4 778
1988	28 689	21 631	811	1 205	35 724	26 935	333	1 807	54 266	40 916	194	4 602
1987	26 814	19 414	758	773	36 713	26 581	383	1 782	53 885	39 014	211	4 410
1986	28 166	19 675	778	962	39 264	27 427	274	1 975	46 580	32 538	176	2 705
1985	26 492	18 168	678	771	36 051	24 723	267	1 723	47 873	32 831	155	2 792
1984	26 066	17 261	611	1 014	35 993	23 835	223	1 878	46 401	30 727	168	3 231
1983	26 191	16 626	514	864	34 516	21 911	170	2 111	45 180	28 680	141	2 681
1982	25 299	15 560	495	845	36 689	22 565	153	2 632	56 052	34 474	125	3 995
1981	26 637	15 432	489	785	33 142	19 201	177	1 928	47 672	27 619	114	3 427
1980	27 288	14 331	451	890	36 605	19 224	167	1 986	46 921	24 642	114	3 439
1979	26 991	12 489	441	714	40 896	18 923	142	2 113	46 030	21 299	118	2 619
1978	27 782	11 545	393	665	40 664	16 898	127	1 861	49 818	20 702	82	2 730
1977	25 694	9 924	391	501	39 326	15 189	120	1 420	49 258	19 025	85	2 291
1976	24 384	8 843	342	508	37 639	13 650	114	1 299	44 627	16 184	81	2 339
1975	25 684	8 807	279	536	37 566	12 881	113	1 142	52 468	17 991	86	2 535
Female												
1996	16 856	16 856	1 409	581	27 407	27 407	495	1 503	50 960	50 960	139	17 662
1995	18 038	17 521	1 380	1 542	26 086	25 338	399	1 722	37 326	36 255	118	3 079
1994	18 325	17 309	1 313	1 081	25 268	23 867	393	1 272	39 457	37 269	127	4 428

See footnotes at end of table.

Table B-17.   Mean Earnings of Workers 18 Years Old and Over, by Educational Attainment, Race, Hispanic Origin, and Gender: 1975 to 1996 — Continued

(Numbers in thousands. Civilian noninstitutional population.)

Earnings year	Total				Not a high school graduate				High school graduate			
	Mean Earnings (1996 Constant Dollars)	Mean Earnings (Current Dollars)	Number with earnings	Standard error	Mean Earnings (1996 Constant Dollars)	Mean Earnings (Current Dollars)	Number with earnings	Standard error	Mean Earnings (1996 Constant Dollars)	Mean Earnings (Current Dollars)	Number with earnings	Standard error
1993	14 769	13 602	4 687	329	9 217	8 489	1 498	297	14 750	13 584	1 413	595
1992	15 522	13 880	4 137	304	9 968	8 913	1 330	334	14 981	13 396	1 326	435
1991	15 055	13 069	4 072	273	5 540	4 809	1 358	307	15 025	13 043	1 339	380
1990	15 025	12 516	3 984	254	6 114	5 093	1 367	309	14 536	12 109	1 470	354
1989	15 572	12 307	3 929	266	10 447	8 256	1 353	401	14 930	11 799	1 477	365
1988	15 349	11 573	3 749	290	10 076	7 597	1 307	349	14 966	11 284	1 332	392
1987	15 516	11 234	3 569	286	10 152	7 350	1 176	354	14 678	10 627	1 366	417
1986	14 970	10 457	3 356	231	10 207	7 130	1 117	338	14 772	10 319	1 289	332
1985	14 385	9 865	3 138	236	9 768	6 699	1 112	367	14 267	9 784	1 170	327
1984	13 817	9 150	3 005	252	9 722	6 438	1 107	436	14 334	9 492	1 138	380
1983	13 711	8 704	2 645	(NA)	9 932	6 305	996	(NA)	14 589	9 261	956	(NA)
1982	13 324	8 195	2 434	233	9 399	5 781	961	373	14 093	8 668	884	374
1981	13 330	7 723	2 426	215	9 469	5 486	962	364	14 313	8 292	929	342
1980	12 891	6 770	2 322	199	9 574	5 028	942	358	13 182	6 923	863	287
1979	13 518	6 255	2 276	184	10 103	4 675	918	347	14 497	6 708	860	286
1978	13 238	5 501	1 983	173	9 951	4 135	847	377	14 039	5 834	739	273
1977	12 852	4 964	1 919	137	9 598	3 707	846	276	14 152	5 466	685	236
1976	12 541	4 548	1 732	132	9 753	3 537	786	273	14 129	5 124	597	229
1975	12 109	4 152	1 622	122	9 429	3 233	741	277	13 730	4 708	602	209

See footnotes at end of table.

Table B-17.   Mean Earnings of Workers 18 Years Old and Over, by Educational Attainment, Race, Hispanic Origin, and Gender: 1975 to 1996 — Continued

(Numbers in thousands. Civilian noninstitutional population.)

Earnings year	Some college/associate degree				Bachelor's Degree				Advanced Degree			
	Mean Earnings (1996 Constant Dollars)	Mean Earnings (Current Dollars)	Number with earnings	Standard error	Mean Earnings (1996 Constant Dollars)	Mean Earnings (Current Dollars)	Number with earnings	Standard error	Mean Earnings (1996 Constant Dollars)	Mean Earnings (Current Dollars)	Number with earnings	Standard error
1993	16 559	15 250	1 284	609	23 483	21 627	361	1 258	36 919	34 001	131	4 391
1992	17 978	16 076	1 049	669	24 782	22 160	322	1 343	38 639	34 551	110	3 141
1991	18 110	15 721	948	564	23 951	20 791	309	1 377	35 390	30 721	117	3 141
1990	18 301	15 245	682	629	23 262	19 378	287	1 331	32 633	27 184	177	1 824
1989	18 324	14 482	703	629	28 618	22 617	243	1 379	33 784	26 700	153	2 265
1988	18 584	14 012	700	662	26 137	19 707	263	1 171	32 420	24 444	146	3 675
1987	19 238	13 929	642	688	24 865	18 003	261	1 033	36 717	26 584	124	3 436
1986	18 106	12 648	633	547	23 108	16 142	197	1 165	31 596	22 071	119	2 096
1985	17 193	11 791	548	639	22 606	15 503	191	1 098	32 780	22 480	118	2 173
1984	16 382	10 848	505	619	21 752	14 404	158	1 310	28 248	18 706	97	2 355
1983	15 359	9 750	462	(NA)	21 278	13 507	150	(NA)	26 492	16 817	81	(NA)
1982	16 090	9 896	378	605	22 306	13 719	150	1 235	24 785	15 244	61	2 247
1981	16 368	9 483	345	563	21 217	12 292	143	1 101	26 759	15 503	47	2 767
1980	16 772	8 808	357	576	20 123	10 568	116	1 177	27 930	14 668	43	2 935
1979	15 277	7 069	327	482	19 813	9 168	98	1 001	28 771	13 313	72	1 905
1978	16 089	6 686	268	507	23 304	9 684	86	1 098	26 249	10 908	43	1 872
1977	14 468	5 588	265	367	23 514	9 082	90	691	27 364	10 569	33	2 119
1976	13 994	5 075	250	373	18 982	6 884	63	826	25 418	9 218	37	1 425
1975	13 969	4 790	195	376	18 157	6 226	60	805	23 526	8 067	25	1 536

Source: March 1997 Current Population Survey, Education and Social Stratification Branch, U.S. Bureau of the Census.

1. May be of any race.

— Represents zero or rounds to zero.

(NA) Data not available or not applicable.

Notes and Definitions

Comparable tables to those published here in Part B were disseminated by the Census Bureau in the P-20 series of *Current Population Reports* for most years between 1947 and 1993. These tables have not been available in printed form since that time but are available on the Census Bureau's website at www.census.gov. We have included some tables here covering this entire historical period, including earnings by education attainment shown in both current dollars and 1996 dollars. In the historical data series, data prior to 1992 are not strictly comparable to those after that date. Before 1992, questions on degrees received were not asked in the Current Population Survey, and thus educational attainment was gauged only through years of school completed. For information about the availability of earlier reports or data questions not addressed in this definitions section, contact the Education and Social Stratification Branch, Population Division, U.S. Bureau of the Census at (301) 457–2464.

Age. Age classification is based on the age of the person at his/her last birthday. The adult universe (i.e., population of marriageable age) is composed of persons 15 years old and over for March supplement data and for CPS labor force data.

Annuities. See *Income.*

Armed Forces. Armed Forces members enumerated in off-base housing or on base with their families are included in the CPS data file in March. In addition to demographic and family data, supplemental data on income and work experience for Armed Forces members are included.

Civilian labor force. See *Labor Force.*

Class of worker. This term refers to the broad classification of the person's employer. In the March file, these broad classifications for current jobs are private, government, self-employed, without pay, and never worked. Private and government workers are considered "wage and salary workers"; this classification scheme includes self-employed, incorporated persons with "private" workers. For the longest job held last year, this class of workers scheme includes private; government by level/federal, state, and local; self-employed incorporated; self-employed unincorporated or farm; and without pay. The wage and salary category for longest job held includes private, government (all levels), and self-employed incorporated.

Dividends. See *Income.*

Duration of unemployment. Duration of unemployment represents the length of time (through the current survey week) during which persons classified as unemployed are continuously looking for work. For persons on layoff, duration of unemployment represents the number of full weeks since the termination of their most recent employment. A period of two weeks or more during which a person is employed or ceased looking for work is considered to break the continuity of the present period of seeking work. Average duration is an arithmetic mean computed from a distribution by single weeks of unemployment.

Earners, number of. The file includes all persons 15 years old and over in the household with $1 or more in wages and salaries, or $1 or more of a loss in net income from farm or nonfarm self-employment during the preceding year.

Education. See *Level of School Completed/Degree received.*

Employed. See *Labor Force.*

Energy Assistance Program. The Low-Income Home Energy Assistance Program provides financial assistance to qualified households to help their members pay heating costs. The program is funded by the federal government and administered by the states under broad guidelines. In some states, a household may automatically be eligible for this program if the household receives (1) Aid to Families with Dependent Children, (2) food stamps, (3) Supplemental Security Income (SSI), and (4) certain veterans' benefits.

The energy assistance questions were asked for the first time in 1982. Questions asked in the March 1989 survey included (1) recipient since October 1, 1988, and (2) total amount received during the reference period.

Family. A family is a group of two or more persons (one of whom is the householder) residing together and related by birth, marriage, or adoption. All such persons (including related subfamily members) are considered as members of one family. Beginning with the 1980 CPS, unrelated subfamilies (referred to in the past as secondary families) are no longer included in the count of families, nor are the members of unrelated subfamilies included in the count of family members.

Family household. A family household is a household maintained by a family (as defined above) and may include among the household members any unrelated persons (unrelated subfamily members and/or unrelated individuals) who may be residing there. The number of family households is equal to the number of families. The count of family household members differs from the count of family members, however, in that the family household members include all persons living in the household, whereas family members include only the householder and his/her relatives. See *Family*.

Farm self-employment new income. The term is defined as net money income (gross receipts minus operating expenses) from the operation of a farm by a person on his own account as an owner, as a renter, or as a sharecropper. Gross receipts include the value of all products sold, government crop loans, money received from the rental of farm equipment to others, and incidental receipts from the sale of wood, sand, gravel, etc.

Operating expenses include the cost of feed, fertilizer, seed, and other farming supplies; cash wages paid to farm hands; depreciation charges; case rent; interest on farm mortgages; farm building repairs; farm taxes (not state and federal income taxes); etc. The value of fuel, food, or other farm products used for household living is not included as part of net income. Inventory changes are considered in determining net income only when they are accounted for in replies based on income tax returns or other official records that reflect inventory changes.

Food stamps. The Food Stamp Act of 1977 was enacted for the purpose of increasing the food purchasing power of eligible households through the use of coupons to purchase food. The Food and Nutrition Service of the U.S. Department of Agriculture (USDA) administers the Food Stamp Program through state and local welfare offices. The Food Stamp Program is the major national income support program that provides benefits to all low-income and low-resource households regardless of household characteristics (e.g., sex, age, disability, etc.). The questions on participation in the Food Stamp Program in the March CPS were designed to identify households in which one or more of the current members received food stamps during the previous calendar year. Once a food stamp household was identified, a question was asked to determine the number of current household members covered by food stamps during the previous calendar year. Questions were also asked about the number of months food stamps were received during the previous calendar year and the total face value of all food stamps received during that period.

Full-time worker. Persons on full-time schedules include persons working 35 hours or more, persons who worked 1 to 34 hours for noneconomic reasons (e.g., illness) and usually work full time, and persons "with a job but not at work" who usually work full time.

Group health insurance coverage. Civilian persons 15 years old and over who worked in the previous calendar year and who participated in group health insurance plans provided by the employer or union were asked whether part or all of the health insurance premiums were paid for by the union or employer and the extent of persons covered.

Additional questions were asked to determine whether sample persons were covered by any other type of health insurance plan. These items are intended to measure retirees covered by continuing employer-provided coverage and persons who purchase coverage on their own.

Group quarters. Group quarters are noninstitutional living arrangements for groups not living in conventional housing units or for groups living in housing units containing nine or more persons unrelated to the person in charge.

Head versus householder. Beginning with the March 1980 CPS, the Bureau of the Census discontinued the use of the terms "head of household" and "head of family." Instead, the terms "householder" and "family householder" are used.

Highest grade of school attended. See *Level of School Completed/Degree received*.

Hispanic origin. Persons of Hispanic origin in this file are determined on the basis of a question that asked for self-identification of the person's origin or descent. Respondents are asked to select their origin (or the origin of some other household member) from a "flash card" listing ethnic origins. Persons of Hispanic origin, in particular, are those who indicated that their origin was Mexican American, Chicano, Mexican, Mexicano, Puerto Rican, Cuban, Central or South American, or other Hispanic.

Hours of work. Hours of work statistics relate to the actual number of hours worked during the survey week. For example, a person who normally works 40 hours a week but who is off on the Veterans Day holiday is reported as working 32 hours even though he or she is paid for the holiday.

For persons working in more than one job, the figures relate to the actual number of hours worked during the survey week. However, all the hours are credited to the major job.

Household. A household consists of all the persons who occupy a house, an apartment, or other group of rooms or a room that constitutes a housing unit. A group of rooms or a single room is regarded as a housing unit when it is occupied as separate living quarters, that is, when the occupants do not live and eat with any other person in the structure and when there is direct access from the outside or through a common hall. The count of households excludes persons living in group quarters such as rooming houses, military barracks, and institutions. Inmates of institutions (mental hospitals, rest homes, correctional institutions, etc.) are not included in the survey.

Householder. The householder refers to the person (or one of the persons) in whose name the housing unit is owned or rented (maintained) or, if there is no such person, any adult member, excluding roomers, boarders, or paid employees. If the house is owned or rented jointly by a married couple, the householder may be either the husband or the wife. The person designated as the householder in the file is the "reference person" on the CPS-260 control card to whom the relationship of all other household members, if any, is recorded.

Householder with no other relatives in household. A householder who has no relatives living in the household. This is the entry for a person living alone. Another example is the designated householder of an apartment shared by two or more unrelated individuals.

Householder with other relatives (including spouse) in household. The person designated as householder if he/she has one or more relatives (including a spouse) living in the household.

Income. For each person in the sample who is 15 years old and over, questions are asked on the amount of money income received in the preceding calendar year from each of the following sources: (1) money wages or salary; (2) net income from nonfarm self-employment; (3) net income from farm self-employment; (4) Social Security or railroad retirement; (5) Supplemental Security Income; (6) public assistance or welfare payments; (7) interest (on savings or bonds); (8) dividends, income from estates or trusts, or net rental income; (9) veterans' payment or unemployment and workers' compensation; (10) private pensions or government employee pensions; (11) alimony or child support, regular contributions from persons not living in the household, and other periodic income.

Although income statistics refer to receipts during the preceding year, the characteristics of the person, such as age, labor force status, etc., and the composition of households refer to the time of the survey. The income of the household does not include amounts received by persons who are members of the household during all or part of the income year if these persons no longer reside in the household at the time of enumeration. However, household income does include amounts reported by persons who did not reside in the household during the income year but who were members of the household at the time of enumeration.

Data on consumer income collected in the CPS by the Bureau of the Census cover money income received (exclusive of certain money receipts such as capital gains) before payments for personal income taxes, Social Security, unions dues, Medicare deductions, etc. Also, money income does not reflect the fact that some households receive part of their income in the form of nonmoney transfers such as food stamps, health benefits, subsidized housing, and energy assistance; that many farm households receive nonmoney income in the form of rent-free housing and goods produced and consumed on the farm; or that nonmoney income received by some nonfarm residents often takes the form of the use of business transportation and facilities or full or partial contributions for retirement programs, medical and educational expenses, etc. These elements should be considered when comparing income levels. Moreover, readers should be aware that for many different reasons there is a tendency in household surveys for respondents to underreport their income. From an analysis of independently derived income estimates, it has been determined that wages and salaries tend to be much better reported than such income types as public assistance, Social Security, and net income from interest, dividends, rents, etc.

Income Sources

Wages and salary. Money wages or salary is defined as total money earnings received for work performed by a person acting as an employee during the income year. It includes wages, salary, Armed Forces pay, commissions, tips, piece-rate payments, and cash bonuses earned before deductions are made for taxes, bonds, pensions, union dues, etc. Earnings for self-employed incorporated businesses are considered wages and salary.

Nonfarm self-employment. Net income from nonfarm self-employment is net money income (gross receipts minus expenses) from one's own business, professional enterprise, or partnership. Gross receipts include the value of all goods sold and services rendered. Expenses include costs of goods purchased, rent, heat, light, power, depreciation charges, wages and salaries paid, business taxes (not personal income taxes), etc. In general, inventory changes are considered in determining net income because replies based on income tax returns or other official records do reflect inventory changes. However, when values of inventory changes are not reported, net income figures exclusive of inventory changes are accepted. The value of salable merchandise consumed by the proprietors of retail stores is not included as part of net income.

Farm self-employment. Net income from farm self-employment is net money income (gross receipts minus operating expenses) from the operation of a farm by a person on his own account as an owner, as a renter, or as a sharecropper. Gross receipts include the value of all products sold, government crop loans, money received from the rental of farm equipment to others, and incidental receipts from the sale of wood, sand, gravel, etc.

Operating expenses include cost of feed, fertilizer, seed, and other farming supplies, cash wages paid to farm hands, depreciation charges, cash rent, interest on farm mortgages, farm building repairs, farm taxes (not state and federal income taxes), etc. The value of fuel, food, or other farm products used for family living is not included as part of net income. In general, inventory changes are considered in determining net income only when they are accounted for in replies based on income tax returns or other official records that reflect inventory changes; otherwise, inventory changes are not taken into account.

Social Security. Social Security includes Social Security pensions and survivors' benefits and permanent disability insurance payments made by the Social Security Administration prior to deductions for medical insurance and railroad retirement insurance checks from the U.S. government. Medicare reimbursements are not included.

Supplemental Security Income. Supplemental Security Income includes payments made by federal, state, and local welfare agencies to low-income persons who are (1) aged (65 years old and over), (2) blind, or (3) disabled.

Public assistance. Public assistance or welfare payments include public assistance payments such as Aid to Families with Dependent Children and general assistance.

Interest and dividends. Interest, dividends, income from estates or trusts, net rental income, and royalties include dividends from stockholdings or membership in associations; interest on savings or bonds; periodic receipts from estates or trust funds; net income from rental of a house, store, or other property to others; receipts from boarders or lodgers; and net royalties.

Unemployment compensation, workers' compensation, and veterans payments. Unemployment compensation, workers' compensation, or veterans payments include: (1) unemployment compensation received from government insurance agencies or private companies during periods of unemployment and any strike benefits received from union funds; (2) money paid periodically by the Veterans Administration (VA) to disabled members of the Armed Forces or to survivors of deceased veterans, subsistence allowances paid to veterans for education and on-the-job training, as well as so-called "refunds" paid to ex-serviceman as GI insurance premiums; and (3) workers' compensation received periodically from public or private insurance companies for injuries incurred at work. The cost of this insurance must have been paid by the employer and not by the person.

Private and government pensions and annuities. Many employers and unions have established pension programs for their employees so that on retirement the employee will receive regular income to replace his/her earnings. Many of these programs also provide income to an employee if he/she becomes severely disabled or to his/her survivors if the employee dies. Other types of retirement income include annuities and paid-up life insurance policies. Some people purchase annuities that yield a set amount over a certain number of years. Other people may convert their paid-up life insurance policy into an annuity after they retire.

Alimony and child support. Alimony is money received periodically from a former spouse following a divorce or separation. Child support is money received from a parent for the support of his or her children following a divorce or legal separation. Money received from relatives other than the parent or from friends is not considered child support.

Receipts not counted as income. Receipts from the following sources are not included as income: (1) money received from the sale of property, such as stocks, bonds, a house, or a car (unless the person is engaged in the business of selling such property, in which case the net proceeds are counted as income from self-employment); (2) withdrawals of bank deposits; (3) money borrowed; (4) tax refunds; (5) gifts; and (6) lump-sum inheritances of insurance payments.

Industry, occupation, and class of worker

Current job (basic data). For the employed, current job is the job held in the reference week (the week before the survey). Persons with two or more jobs are classified in the job at which the worker spends the most hours during the reference week. The unemployed are classified according to their latest full-time job lasting two or more weeks or by the job (either full time or part time) from which they were on layoff. The occupation/industry classification system for the 1990 Census of Population was used to code CPS data beginning with the January 1992 file.

Longest job (supplement data). Longest job applies to the job held longest during the preceding year for persons who worked that year, without regard to their current employment status.

Job seekers. All unemployed persons who made specific efforts to find a job sometime during the four-week period preceding the survey week.

Keeping house. Persons are classified as keeping house if they engage in their own housework. This is one of the "not in labor force" classifications; the employment status recode (ESR) equals 4.

LFSR (Labor force status recode). This classification is available for each civilian 15 years old and over according to his/her responses to the monthly (basic) labor force items in March.

Labor force. Persons are classified as being in the labor force if they are employed, unemployed, or in the Armed Forces during the survey week. The "civilian labor force" includes all civilians classified as employed or unemployed. The file includes labor force data for civilians age 15 and over. However, the official definition of the civilian labor force is age 16 and over.

  Employed. Employed persons comprise (1) all civilians who, during the survey week, did any work at all as paid employees or in their own business or profession, or on their own farm, or who worked 15 hours or more as unpaid workers on a farm or a business operated by a member of the family; and (2) all those who have jobs but who are not working because of illness, bad weather, vacation, or labor-management dispute, or because they are taking time off for personal reasons, whether or not they are seeking other jobs. Each employed person is counted only once. Those persons who held more than one job are counted in the job at which they worked the greatest number of hours during the survey week. If they worked an equal number of hours at more than one job, they are counted at the job they have held the longest.

  Unemployed. Unemployed persons are those civilians who, during the survey week, have no employment but are available for work and (1) have engaged in any specific job-seeking activity within the past four weeks such as registering at a public or private employment office, meeting with prospective employers, checking with friends or relatives, placing or answering advertisements, writing letters of application, or being on a union or professional register; (2) are waiting to be called back to a job from which they had been laid off; or (3) are waiting to report to a new wage or salary job within 30 days. The unemployed include job leavers, job losers, new job entrants, and job reentrants.

  Job leavers. Persons who quit or otherwise terminate their employment voluntarily and immediately begin looking for work.

  Job Losers. Persons whose employment ends involuntarily and who immediately begin looking for work, and those persons who are already on layoff.

  New job entrants. Persons who never worked at a full-time job lasting two weeks or longer.

  Job reentrants. Persons who previously worked at a full-time job lasting two weeks or longer but who are out of the labor force prior to beginning to look for work.

  Not in labor force. All civilians 15 years old and over who are not classified as employed or unemployed. These persons are further classified as being engaged in a major activity such as keeping house, going to school, unable to work because of long-term physical or mental illness, and other. The "other" group includes, for the most part, retired persons. Persons who report doing unpaid work in a family farm or business for less than 15 hours are also classified as not in the labor force.

For persons not in the labor force, questions on previous work experience, intentions to seek work again, desire for a job at the time of interview, and reasons for not looking for work are asked only in those households that are in the fourth and eighth months of the sample, that is, the "outgoing" groups—those that had been in the sample for three previous months and would not be in it for the subsequent month.

Finally, it should be noted that the unemployment rate represents the number of unemployed persons as a percentage of the civilian labor force 16 years old and over. This measure can also be computed for groups within the labor force classified by sex, age, marital status, race, etc. The job loser, job leaver, reentrant, and new entrant rates are each calculated as a percentage of the civilian labor force 16 years old and over; the sum of the rates for the four groups thus equals the total unemployment rate.

Layoff. A person who is unemployed but expects to be called back to a specific job is considered to be laid off. If he/she expects to be called back within 30 days, it is considered a temporary layoff; otherwise, it is an indefinite layoff.

Level of school completed/Degree received. These data changed in the March 1992 file. A new question, "What is the highest level of school ... has completed or the highest degree ... has received?" replaced the old "highest grade attended" and "year completed" questions. The new question provides more accurate data on the degree status of college students. Educational attainment applies only to progress in "regular" schools. Such schools include graded public, private, and parochial elementary and high schools (both junior and senior high), colleges, universities, and professional schools, whether day schools or night schools. Thus, regular schooling is that which may advance a person toward an elementary school certificate or high school diploma, or a college, university, or professional school degree. Schooling in other than regular schools is counted only if the credits obtained are regarded as transferable to a school in the regular school system.

Looking for work. A person who is trying to get work or trying to establish a business or profession.

Marital status. The marital status classification identifies four major categories: single (never married), married, widowed, and divorced. These terms refer to the marital status at the time of enumeration.

The category "married" is further divided into "married, civilian spouse present," "married, Armed Forces spouse present," "married, spouse absent" "married, Armed Forces spouse absent," and "separated." A person is classified as "married, spouse present" if the husband or wife is reported as a member of the household even though he or she may be temporarily absent on business or on vacation, visiting, in a hospital, etc., at the time of the enumeration. Persons reported as "separated" included those with legal separations, those living apart with intentions of obtaining a divorce, and other persons permanently or temporarily estranged from their spouses because of marital discord.

For the purpose of this file, the group "other marital status" includes "widowed and divorced," "separated," and "other married, spouse absent."

Medicaid. The Medicaid program is designed to provide medical assistance to needy families with dependent children and to aged, blind, or permanently and totally disabled individuals whose incomes and resources are insufficient to meet the costs of necessary medical services. The program is administered by state agencies through grants from the Health Care Financing Administration of the Department of Health and Human Services. Funding for medical assistance payments consists of a combination of federal, state, and, in some cases, local funds.

Medicaid is a categorical program with complex eligibility rules that vary from state to state. There are two basic groups of eligible individuals: the categorically eligible and the medically needy. The major categorically eligible groups are all Aid to Families with Dependent Children (AFDC) recipients and most Supplemental Security Income recipients. Other categorically eligible groups are (1) those who meet basic state cash assistance eligibility rules; aged, blind, disabled, or needy single parents with children; and, in some states, needy unemployed parents who have children but who are not currently receiving money payments; and (2) needy persons who meet categorical eligibility standards but are institutionalized for medical reasons (e.g., low-income elderly persons in nursing homes). However, such institutionalized persons are not included in the CPS universe and, therefore, are not reflected in these statistics.

In roughly one-half of the states, coverage is extended to the medically needy or persons meeting categorical age, sex, or disability criteria whose money incomes and assets exceed eligibility levels for cash assistance but are not sufficient to meet the cost of medical care. In such states, qualifying income and asset levels are usually above those set for cash assistance. Families with large medical expenses relative to their incomes and assets may also meet medically needy eligibility standards in these states.

The Medicaid question on the March CPS attempted to identify all persons who were covered by Medicaid at any time during the previous calendar year. The term "covered" means enrolled in the Medicaid program, that is, had a Medicaid medical assistance card or incurred medical bills that were paid for by Medicaid. In order to be counted, the person did not have to receive medical care paid for by Medicaid.

After data collection and creation of an initial microdata file, further refinements were made to assign Medicaid coverage to children. In this procedure, all children under 21 years old in families were assumed to be covered by Medicaid if either the householder or spouse reported being covered by Medicaid (this procedure was required mainly because the Medicaid coverage question was asked only for persons 15 years old and over). All adult AFDC recipients and their children, and SSI recipients living in states that legally require Medicaid coverage of all SSI recipients, were also assigned coverage.

Medicare. The Medicare program is designed to provide medical care for the aged and disabled. The Basic Hospital Insurance Plan (Part A) is designed to provide basic protection against hospital costs and related posthospital services. This plan also covers many persons under 65 years old who receive Social Security or railroad retirement benefits based on long-term disability. Part A is financed jointly by employers and employees through Social Security payroll deductions. Qualified persons 65 years old and over who are not otherwise eligible for Part A benefits may pay premiums directly to obtain this coverage. The Medical Insurance Plan (Part B) is a voluntary plan that builds on the hospital insurance protection provided by the basic plan. It provides insurance protection covering physicians' and surgeons' services and a variety of medical and other health services received either in hospitals or on an ambulatory basis. It is financed through monthly premium payments by each enrollee and is subsidized by federal general revenue funds.

The Medicare question on the March CPS attempted to identify all persons 15 years old and over who were covered by Medicare at any time during the previous calendar year. The term "covered" means enrolled in the Medicare program. In order to be counted, the person did not necessarily have to receive medical care paid for by Medicare.

Mobility status. The population of the United States 15 years old and over is classified according to mobility status on the basis of a comparison between the place of residence of each individual at the time of the March CPS and that person's place of residence in March of the previous year.

Nonmovers are all persons who are living in the same house at the end of the period as at the beginning of the period. Movers are all persons who are living in a different house at the end of the period than at the beginning of the period. Movers from abroad include all persons, either citizens or aliens, whose place of residence is outside the United States at the beginning of the period, that is, in an outlying area under the jurisdiction of the United States or in a foreign country. The mobility status for children is fully allocated from the mother if she is in the household; otherwise, it is allocated from the householder.

Never worked. A person who has never held a full-time civilian job lasting two consecutive weeks or longer.

Nonfamily householder. A nonfamily householder (formerly called a primary individual) is a person maintaining a household while living alone or with nonrelatives only.

Nonfarm self-employment net income. The term is defined as net money income (gross receipts minus expenses) from an individual's own business, professional enterprise, or partnership. Gross receipts include the value of all goods sold and services rendered. Expenses include costs of goods purchased, rent, heat, light, electricity, depreciation charges, wages and salaries paid, business taxes (not personal income taxes), etc. In general, inventory changes are considered in determining net income, and replies based on income tax returns or other official records do reflect inventory changes; however, when values of inventory changes are not reported, net income figures exclusive of inventory changes are accepted. The value of salable merchandise consumed by the proprietors of retail stores is not included as part of net income.

Nonworker. A person who did not do any work in the calendar year preceding the survey.

Nonrelative of householder with no own relatives in household. A nonrelative of the household who has no relatives of his or her own in the household. This category includes such nonrelatives as a ward, a lodger, a servant, or a hired hand who has no relatives of his or her own living with him or her in the household.

Nonrelative of householder with no own relatives (including spouse) in household. Any household member who is not related to the householder but has relatives of his or her own in the household; for example, a lodger, his or her spouse, and their son.

Other relative of householder. Any relative of the householder other than his or her spouse, child (including natural, adopted, foster, or stepchild), sibling, or parent; for example, grandson, daughter-in-law, etc.

Own child. A child related by birth, marriage, or adoption to the family householder.

Part-time work. Persons who work between 1 and 34 hours are designated as working part time in the current job held during the reference week. For the March supplement, a person is classified as having worked part time during the preceding calendar year if he or she worked less than 35 hours per week in a majority of the weeks in which he or she worked during the year. Conversely, the person is classified as having worked full time if he or she worked 35 hours or more per week during a majority of the weeks in which he or she worked.

Pension plan. The pension plan question on the March CPS attempted to identify whether pension plan coverage was available through an employer or union and whether the employee was included. This information was collected for civilian persons 15 years old and over who worked during the previous calendar year.

Population coverage. Population coverage includes the civilian population of the United States plus approximately 820,000 members of the Armed Forces in the United States living off post or with their families on post but excludes all other members of the Armed Forces. This file excludes inmates or institutions. The labor force and work experience data are not collected for Armed Forces members.

Poverty. Families and unrelated individuals are classified as being above or below the poverty level using a poverty index adopted by a federal interagency committee in 1969 and slightly modified in 1981.

The modified index provides a range of income cutoffs or "poverty thresholds" adjusted to take into account family size, number of children, and age of the family householder or unrelated individual; prior to 1981, adjustments were also made on the basis of farm-nonfarm residence and sex of the householder. The impact of these revisions on the poverty estimates is minimal at the national level. The poverty cutoffs are updated every year to reflect changes in the Consumer Price Index. For a detailed explanation of the poverty definition, see *Current Population Reports*, series

P-60, no. 154, "Money Income and Poverty Status of Persons in the United States: 1988."

Public assistance. See *Income*.

Public or other subsidized housing. Participation in public housing is determined by two factors: program eligibility and the availability of housing. Income standards for initial and continuing occupancy vary by local housing authority, although the limits are constrained by federal guidelines. Rental charges—which, in turn, define net benefits—are set by a federal statute not to exceed 30 percent of net monthly money income. A recipient unit can be either a family of two or more related persons or an individual who is handicapped, elderly, or displaced by urban renewal or natural disaster.

There are some programs through which housing assistance is provided to low-income families and individuals living in public or privately owned dwellings. Two of the more common types of programs in which federal, state, and local funds are used to subsidize private sector housing are rent supplement and interest reduction plans. Under a rent supplement plan the difference between the "fair market" rent and the rent charged to the tenant is paid to the owner by a government agency. Under an interest reduction program, the amount of interest paid on the mortgage by the owner is reduced so that subsequent savings can be passed along to low-income tenants in the form of lower rent charges.

There were two questions dealing with public and low-cost housing on the March CPS supplement questionnaire. The first question identified residence in a housing unit owned by a public agency. The second question identified beneficiaries who were not living in public housing projects but who were paying lower rent due to a government subsidy. These questions differ from other questions covering noncash benefits in that they establish current recipiency status in March of the current year rather than recipiency status during the previous year.

Race. The population is divided into five groups on the basis of race—White, Black, American Indian/Aleut Eskimo, Asian or Pacific Islander, and other races—beginning with March 1989. The last category includes any other race except the four mentioned. In most of the published tables, "other races" are shown in total population.

Related children. Related children in a family include own children and all other children in the household who are related to the householder by birth, marriage, or adoption.

For each type of family unit identified in the CPS, the count of own children under 18 years old is limited to single (never married) children; however, "own children under 25" and "own children of any age" include all children regardless of marital status. The totals include never-married children living away from home in college dormitories.

Related subfamily. A related subfamily is a married couple with or without children, or one parent with one or more own single (never married) children under 18 years old, living in a household and related to, but not including, the householder or spouse. The most common example of a related subfamily is a young married couple sharing the home of the husband's or wife's parents. The number of related subfamilies is not included in the number of families.

School lunches. The National School Lunch Program is designed to assist states in providing a school lunch for all children at moderate cost. The National School Lunch Act of 1946 was further amended in 1970 to provide free and reduced-price school lunches for children of needy families. The program is administered by the Food and Nutrition Service of the U.S. Department of Agriculture (USDA) through state education agencies or through regional USDA nutrition services for nonprofit private schools. The program is funded by a combination of federal funds and matching state funds.

All students eating lunches prepared at participating schools pay less than the total cost of the lunches. Some students pay the "full established" price for lunch (which itself is subsidized), while others pay a reduced price for lunch and still others receive a free lunch. Program regulations require students receiving free lunches to live in households with incomes below 125 percent of the official poverty level. Those students receiving a reduced-price school lunch (10 to 20 cents per meal) live in households with incomes between 125 percent and 195 percent of the official poverty level. The data in this file, however, do not distinguish between recipiency or free and reduced-price school lunches.

The questions on the March CPS provided a very limited amount of data for the school lunch program. Questions concerning the school lunch program were designed to identify the number of members 5 to 18 years old in households who "usually" ate a hot lunch. This criterion defined the universe of household members usually receiving this noncash benefit. This was followed by a question to identify the number of members receiving free or reduced-price lunches.

Self-employed. Self-employed persons are those who work for profit or fees in their own business, profession, or trade or operate a farm.

Stretches of unemployment. A continuous stretch is one that is not interrupted by the person getting a job or leaving the labor market to go to school, to keep house, etc. A period of two weeks or more during which a person is employed or ceased looking for work is considered to break the continuity of the period of seeking work.

Total money income. The term is defined as the arithmetic sum of money wages and salaries, net income from self-employment, and income other than earnings. The total income of a household is the arithmetic sum of the amounts received by all income recipients in the household. Total person's income is the sum of the amounts from the individual income types. Total family income is the sum of the total person's income for each family member.

Unable to work. A person is classified as unable to work because of long-term physical or mental illness, lasting six months or longer.

Unemployed. See *Labor Force.*

Unemployed compensation. See *Income.*

Unpaid family workers. Unpaid family workers are persons without pay for 15 hours a week or more on a farm or in a business operated by a member of the household to whom they are related by birth or marriage.

Unrelated individuals. Unrelated individuals are persons of any age (other than inmates of institutions) who are not living with any relatives. An unrelated individual may be (1) a nonfamily householder living alone or with nonrelatives only; (2) a roomer, boarder, or resident employee with no relatives in the household; or (3) a group quarters member who has no relatives living with him/her. Thus, a widow who occupies her house alone or with one or more other persons not related to her, a roomer not related to anyone else in the housing unit, a maid living as a member of her employer's household but with no relatives in the household, and a resident staff member in a hospital living apart from any relatives are all examples of unrelated individuals.

Persons living with relatives in group quarters were formerly considered as members of families. However, the number of such unrelated subfamilies is so small that persons in these unrelated subfamilies are included in the count of secondary individuals.

Veteran status. If a person served at any time during the four major wars of this century, the code for the most recent wartime service is entered.

Wage and salary workers. Wage and salary workers receive wages, salary, commission, tips, or pay in kind from a private employer or from a governmental unit. Also included are persons who are self-employed in an incorporated business. See *Income*.

Weeks worked in the income year. Persons are classified according to the number of different weeks, during the preceding calendar year, in which they did any civilian work for pay or profit (including paid vacations and sick leave) or worked without pay on a family-operated farm or business.

Workers. See *Labor force—Employed*.

Work experience. Those persons who, during the preceding calendar year, did not work for pay or profit or worked without pay on a family-operated farm or business at any time during the year, on a part-time or full-time basis.

Year-round full-time workers. A year-round full-time worker is one who usually worked 35 hours or more per week for 50 weeks or more during the preceding calendar year.

GLOSSARY: Geographic Concepts

Geographic division. An area composed of contiguous states, with Alaska and Hawaii also included in one of the divisions. (A state is one of the 51 major political units in the United States.) The nine geographic divisions have been largely unchanged for the presentation of summary statistics since the 1910 census.

   Regions. There are four regions: Northeast, Midwest (formerly North Central), West, and South. States and divisions within regions are presented below.

NORTHEAST REGION

New England Division	**Middle Atlantic Division**
Connecticut	New Jersey
Maine	New York
Massachusetts	Pennsylvania
New Hampshire	
Rhode Island	
Vermont	

MIDWEST REGION[1]

East North Central Division	**West North Central Division**
Illinois	Iowa
Indiana	Kansas
Michigan	Minnesota
Ohio	Missouri
Wisconsin	Nebraska
North Dakota	
South Dakota	

WEST REGION

Mountain Division	**Pacific Division**
Arizona	Alaska
Colorado	California
Idaho	Hawaii
Montana	Oregon
Nevada	Washington
Wyoming	
New Mexico	

SOUTH REGION

East South Central Division	**West South Central Division**
Alabama	Arkansas
Kentucky	Louisiana
Mississippi	Oklahoma
Tennessee	Texas
South Atlantic Division	
Delaware	
District of Columbia	
Florida	
Georgia	
Maryland	
North Carolina	
South Carolina	
Virginia	
West Virginia	

[1]The Midwest Region was designated as the North Central Region until June 1964.

Even though the U.S. population as a whole continued to increase in the 1980s and 1990s, total school enrollment (including college) in the United States did not again reach the level it had attained in 1971 until 20 years later, bottoming out about 1980. This apparent contradiction was not due to declining enrollment rates but to the baby boom population bulge (the large number of births that occurred between 1946 and 1963), the smaller number of children on average born to the baby boom generation, as well as the overall aging of the population as life expectancy increased for most groups. Average daily attendance in public elementary and secondary schools in the United States dropped from about 42 million to 38 million during the 1970s, with most (but not all) states experiencing declines. Many schools were closed, torn down, or sold for private use. By the mid-1990s, however, total enrollment was once again approaching 1970 levels, with most states experiencing enrollment increases during the 1990s. Only West Vir-

ginia and Mississippi have had declines in average daily attendance since 1990. In most states, the number of teachers in the 1990s has increased as well, with the exception of Maine and West Virginia (see table C-14).

Within the United States, there is considerable variation by region and state in enrollment patterns, eventual educational attainment, and spending on education. In terms of years of school completed, for example, anywhere between 92 percent (in Alaska) and 75 percent (in Kentucky) of people 25 years and over were at least high school graduates. The economic well-being of a state's population is at least in part reflected by overall educational attainment figures. States in which average earnings are relatively low and poverty rates relatively high also tend to have relatively low education attainment levels among their adult populations. The correlation is far from perfect, however, and some areas with relatively low proportions of high school graduates have high levels of college graduates. This

FIGURE C-1

Percent of Persons 25 Years Old and Over Who Were High School Graduates or More by State: March 1997

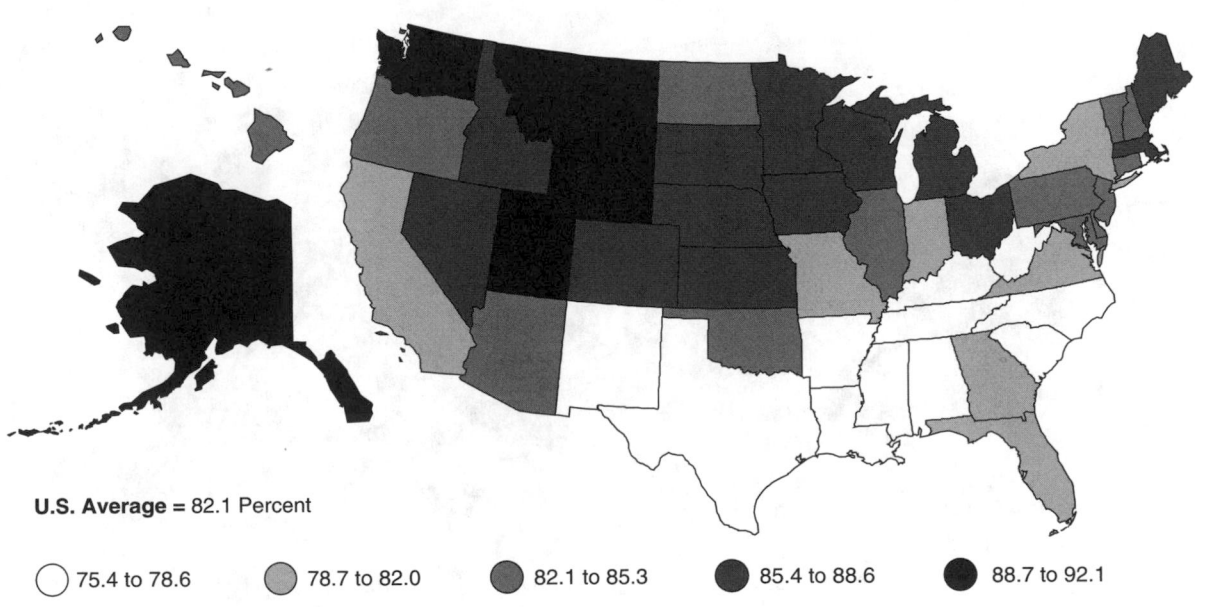

U.S. Average = 82.1 Percent

○ 75.4 to 78.6　　● 78.7 to 82.0　　● 82.1 to 85.3　　● 85.4 to 88.6　　● 88.7 to 92.1

Source: U.S. Bureau of the Census.

is a common pattern in some large cities. For example, the District of Columbia has a relatively high proportion of high school dropouts among its population when compared to states, but it also has the highest proportion of college graduates among its adult population (about a third) when compared to states. Washington, D.C. also has twice the national average proportion of persons with graduate or professional degrees.

Education is one of the largest single expenditures for states and local governments and averaged about a third of all expenditures for these governments in the 1990s. Approximately 70 percent of these expenditures were on public elementary and secondary education, with most of the remainder on higher education. Per capita expenditures on education averaged about $1,300 in 1992–93. They ranged from a high of about $2,440 in Alaska to a low of $960 in Tennessee.

Teacher salaries, a large fraction of educational expenditures, have increased over the entire period since the 1970s by about 18 percent (in constant dollars) but have shown little change during the 1990s. About a fourth of the states have actually experienced decreases in public school teacher salaries (in real terms) during the 1990s (see table C-17).

School size for elementary grades varies considerably by state. The average size of regular elementary schools in the United States was about 480 students in 1995–96 (see table C-24). States with relatively large rural populations had considerably smaller average school sizes, with Nebraska, Montana, and the Dakotas having average sizes under 200. Florida had the largest average elementary school size (nearly 800), and several states averaged over 600 pupils per elementary school (California, Georgia, Hawaii, and New York).

Secondary schools are typically larger than elementary schools, averaging about 770 students in 1995–96. Again, there is considerable difference among states. Two have average secondary school sizes under 200 (Montana and South Dakota), while several have an average size over 1,000 students (Arizona, California, Florida, Georgia, Hawaii, Maryland, Nevada, Utah, and Virginia).

Each year during the 1990s, more than 2 million young adults graduated from public high schools. While the number has increased about 5 percent during the 1990s, it is still below the peak reached about 1980 (see table C-26). Western states have typically had large increases in the number of high school graduates in the 1990s, while the picture is mixed elsewhere, with many Southern states ex-

FIGURE C-2

Average Annual Salary of Teachers In Public Elementary and Secondary Schools by State: 1995-1996

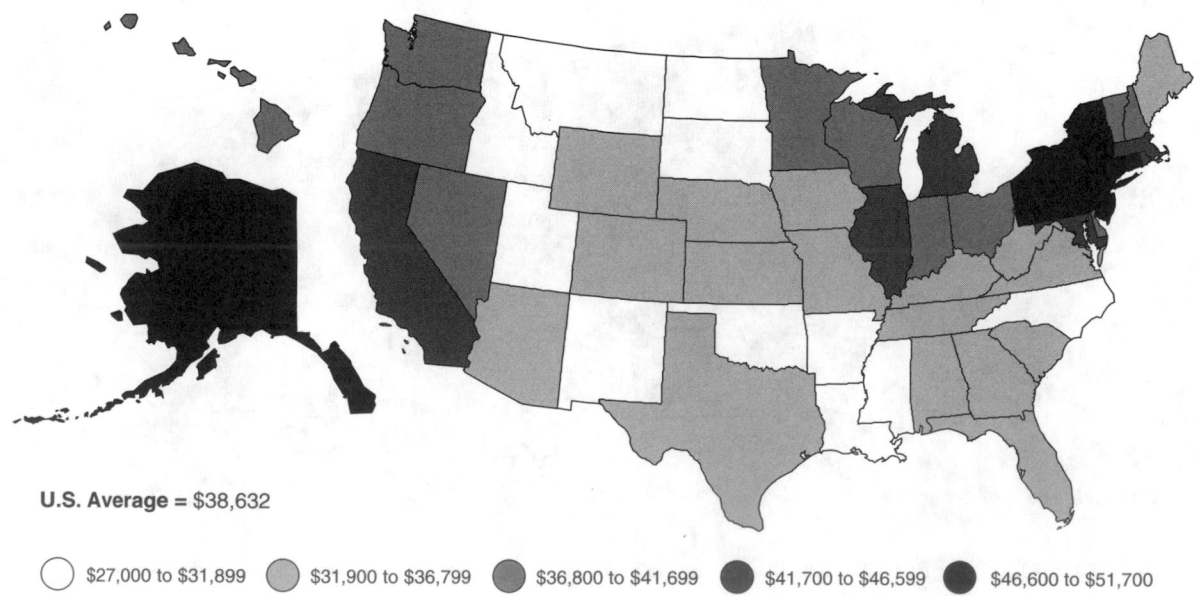

U.S. Average = $38,632

○ $27,000 to $31,899   ◐ $31,900 to $36,799   ● $36,800 to $41,699   ● $41,700 to $46,599   ● $46,600 to $51,700

Source: National Education Association.

periencing declines in the number of annual high school graduates (including Alabama, Georgia, Mississippi, North Carolina, Tennessee, and West Virginia).

Thirty states reported the number of high school dropouts in 1994–95 to the National Center for Education Statistics. There are several ways of gauging what constitutes "dropping out," since one can quit school one year and reenroll the next year or at some later point in life. Using the percent of 9th through 12th graders who dropped out as the indicator, about 4 percent of reporting states' high school student bodies dropped out during the 1994–95 school year. Nevada had the highest proportion dropping out (about 10 percent), while several states had 3 percent or fewer of their high school students drop out of school during 1994–95 (including North Dakota, Texas, Iowa, Maine, Louisiana, and Massachusetts).

Table C-1. Educational Attainment of Persons 25 years Old and Over, by State: April 1990

State	Number of persons 25 years old and over	Percent distribution of population, by highest level of education attained						
		Less than 9th grade	9th to 12th grade, no diploma	High school graduate	Some college, no degree	Associate degree	Bachelor's degree	Graduate or professional degree
United States	158 868 436	10.4	14.4	30.0	18.7	6.2	13.1	7.2
Alabama	2 545 969	13.7	19.4	29.4	16.8	5.0	10.1	5.5
Alaska	323 429	5.1	8.2	28.7	27.6	7.2	15.0	8.0
Arizona	2 301 177	9.0	12.3	26.1	25.4	6.8	13.3	7.0
Arkansas	1 496 150	15.2	18.4	32.7	16.6	3.7	8.9	4.5
California	18 695 499	11.2	12.6	22.3	22.6	7.9	15.3	8.1
Colorado	2 107 072	5.6	10.0	26.5	24.0	6.9	18.0	9.0
Connecticut	2 198 963	8.4	12.4	29.5	15.9	6.6	16.2	11.0
Delaware	428 499	7.2	15.3	32.7	16.9	6.5	13.7	7.7
District of Columbia	409 131	9.6	17.3	21.2	15.6	3.1	16.1	17.2
Florida	8 887 168	9.5	16.1	30.1	19.4	6.6	12.0	6.3
Georgia	4 023 420	12.0	17.1	29.6	17.0	5.0	12.9	6.4
Hawaii	709 820	10.1	9.8	28.7	20.1	8.3	15.8	7.1
Idaho	601 292	7.4	12.9	30.4	24.2	7.5	12.4	5.3
Illinois	7 293 930	10.3	13.5	30.0	19.4	5.8	13.6	7.5
Indiana	3 489 470	8.5	15.8	38.2	16.6	5.3	9.2	6.4
Iowa	1 776 798	9.2	10.7	38.5	17.0	7.7	11.7	5.2
Kansas	1 565 936	7.7	11.0	32.8	21.9	5.4	14.1	7.0
Kentucky	2 333 833	19.0	16.4	31.8	15.2	4.1	8.1	5.5
Louisiana	2 536 994	14.7	17.0	31.7	17.2	3.3	10.5	5.6
Maine	795 613	8.8	12.4	37.1	16.1	6.9	12.7	6.1
Maryland	3 122 665	7.9	13.7	28.1	18.6	5.2	15.6	10.9
Massachusetts	3 962 223	8.0	12.0	29.7	15.8	7.2	16.6	10.6
Michigan	5 842 642	7.8	15.5	32.3	20.4	6.7	10.9	6.4
Minnesota	2 770 562	8.6	9.0	33.0	19.0	8.6	15.6	6.3
Mississippi	1 538 997	15.6	20.1	27.5	16.9	5.2	9.7	5.1
Missouri	3 291 579	11.6	14.5	33.1	18.4	4.5	11.7	6.1
Montana	507 851	8.1	10.9	33.5	22.1	5.6	14.1	5.7
Nebraska	996 049	8.0	10.2	34.7	21.1	7.1	13.1	5.9
Nevada	789 638	6.0	15.2	31.5	25.8	6.2	10.1	5.2
New Hampshire	713 894	6.7	11.2	31.7	18.0	8.1	16.4	7.9
New Jersey	5 166 233	9.4	13.9	31.1	15.5	5.2	16.0	8.8
New Mexico	922 590	11.4	13.5	28.7	20.9	5.0	12.1	8.3
New York	11 818 569	10.2	15.0	29.5	15.7	6.5	13.2	9.9
North Carolina	4 253 494	12.7	17.3	29.0	16.8	6.8	12.0	5.4
North Dakota	396 550	15.0	8.3	28.0	20.5	10.0	13.5	4.5
Ohio	6 924 764	7.9	16.4	36.3	17.0	5.3	11.1	5.9
Oklahoma	1 995 424	9.8	15.6	30.5	21.3	5.0	11.8	6.0
Oregon	1 855 369	6.2	12.3	28.9	25.0	6.9	13.6	7.0
Pennsylvania	7 872 932	9.4	15.9	38.6	12.9	5.2	11.3	6.6
Rhode Island	658 956	11.1	16.9	29.5	15.0	6.3	13.5	7.8
South Carolina	2 167 590	13.6	18.1	29.5	15.8	6.3	11.2	5.4
South Dakota	430 500	13.4	9.5	33.7	18.8	7.4	12.3	4.9
Tennessee	3 139 066	16.0	17.0	30.0	16.9	4.2	10.5	5.4
Texas	10 310 605	13.5	14.4	25.6	21.1	5.2	13.9	6.5
Utah	897 321	3.4	11.5	27.2	27.9	7.8	15.4	6.8
Vermont	357 245	8.7	10.6	34.6	14.7	7.2	15.4	8.9
Virginia	3 974 814	11.2	13.7	26.6	18.5	5.5	15.4	9.1
Washington	3 126 390	5.5	10.7	27.9	25.0	7.9	15.9	7.0
West Virginia	1 171 766	16.8	17.3	36.6	13.2	3.8	7.5	4.8
Wisconsin	3 094 226	9.5	11.9	37.1	16.7	7.1	12.1	5.6
Wyoming	277 769	5.7	11.2	33.2	24.2	6.9	13.1	5.7

SOURCE: U.S. Department of Commerce, Bureau of the Census, 1990 Decennial Census. Published as Table 11 in *Digest of Education Statistics* 1997.

NOTE: Because of rounding, detail may not add to 100.0 percent.

Table C-2. Educational Attainment of Persons 25 Years Old and Over, by State and Race/Ethnicity: April 1990

State	Percent with high school diploma or higher						Percent with bachelor's degree or higher					
	Total	White[1]	Black[1]	Hispanic[2]	Asian/ Pacific Islander[1]	American Indian or Alaskan Native[1]	Total	White[1]	Black[1]	Hispanic[2]	Asian/ Pacific Islander[1]	American Indian or Alaskan Native[1]
United States	75.2	77.9	63.1	49.8	77.5	65.5	20.3	21.5	11.4	9.2	36.6	9.3
Alabama	66.9	70.3	54.6	73.8	78.9	64.9	15.7	17.3	9.3	20.1	43.7	11.6
Alaska	86.6	91.1	88.2	80.4	75.4	63.1	23.0	26.8	14.1	14.6	20.5	4.1
Arizona	78.7	82.4	75.1	51.7	80.2	52.1	20.3	22.2	14.3	6.9	37.5	4.6
Arkansas	66.3	68.6	51.5	59.1	66.4	65.4	13.3	14.1	8.4	11.1	24.6	9.8
California	76.2	81.1	75.6	45.0	77.2	71.4	23.4	25.4	14.8	7.1	34.1	11.1
Colorado	84.4	86.1	80.8	58.3	78.3	73.9	27.0	28.3	17.1	8.6	32.1	12.1
Connecticut	79.2	80.9	67.0	53.5	81.9	68.9	27.2	28.5	12.3	12.1	50.8	12.5
Delaware	77.5	80.3	63.2	60.1	86.1	62.0	21.4	23.0	10.6	16.5	55.9	10.2
District of Columbia	73.1	93.1	63.8	52.6	80.2	66.3	33.3	69.0	15.3	24.0	50.9	17.7
Florida	74.4	77.0	56.4	57.2	77.8	68.2	18.3	19.3	9.8	14.2	33.6	11.5
Georgia	70.9	74.9	58.6	66.2	77.5	71.6	19.3	21.8	11.0	20.5	38.6	12.5
Hawaii	80.1	89.3	94.2	73.9	74.7	84.4	22.9	30.2	15.2	10.3	19.4	17.7
Idaho	79.7	80.9	82.8	43.4	80.3	68.1	17.7	18.0	15.8	6.6	27.6	7.2
Illinois	76.2	79.1	65.2	45.0	83.9	71.4	21.0	22.4	11.4	8.0	40.8	13.4
Indiana	75.6	76.5	65.4	62.6	85.8	65.0	15.6	17.6	9.3	10.8	53.1	8.4
Iowa	80.1	80.3	70.1	61.2	76.1	67.6	16.0	16.7	12.8	13.7	47.3	9.7
Kansas	81.3	82.4	71.0	58.1	73.6	75.4	21.1	21.7	11.6	10.1	39.9	10.8
Kentucky	64.6	64.7	61.7	74.0	77.9	59.8	13.6	13.9	7.7	18.9	44.2	8.0
Louisiana	68.3	74.2	53.1	67.6	68.1	49.1	16.1	18.7	9.1	16.6	31.4	5.5
Maine	78.8	78.9	87.6	83.8	74.3	69.9	18.8	18.8	22.3	23.6	44.9	7.7
Maryland	78.4	80.8	70.6	70.3	84.8	73.4	26.5	28.9	16.1	25.2	50.3	19.7
Massachusetts ...	80.0	81.2	70.0	52.0	74.1	71.1	27.2	27.7	17.0	13.6	44.9	14.9
Michigan	76.8	78.6	64.9	60.9	83.3	67.8	17.4	18.1	10.1	11.6	54.1	7.6
Minnesota	82.4	82.8	76.2	71.1	69.7	68.2	21.8	21.9	17.5	17.2	33.5	7.7
Mississippi	64.3	71.7	47.3	67.7	68.2	57.4	14.7	17.2	8.8	17.1	35.1	8.1
Missouri	73.9	74.9	65.1	71.0	81.5	65.1	17.8	18.3	11.2	18.0	47.3	11.0
Montana	81.0	81.7	80.9	66.4	78.5	68.1	19.8	20.3	18.4	10.9	32.1	7.9
Nebraska	81.8	82.4	73.2	60.0	80.0	69.0	18.9	19.2	12.4	9.4	39.5	8.8
Nevada	78.8	80.9	70.8	53.7	74.1	69.8	15.3	15.9	9.0	7.0	21.9	8.0
New Hampshire	82.2	82.2	86.1	78.2	82.7	65.9	24.4	24.2	25.7	25.5	26.1	16.0
New Jersey	76.7	78.6	67.0	53.0	86.8	66.0	24.9	25.8	13.6	10.0	57.1	14.8
New Mexico	75.1	78.6	74.7	59.6	80.8	58.2	20.4	23.4	14.2	8.7	38.7	5.8
New York	76.7	78.5	64.7	50.4	72.4	65.2	23.1	25.3	12.6	9.3	38.7	13.4
North Carolina	70.0	73.1	58.1	71.0	77.9	51.5	17.4	19.3	9.5	17.9	39.3	7.9
North Dakota	76.7	76.9	95.9	75.2	83.7	64.3	18.1	18.3	17.1	15.9	37.8	8.3
Ohio	75.7	76.9	64.6	63.3	83.5	65.3	17.0	17.6	9.1	14.2	53.2	8.3
Oklahoma	74.6	75.7	70.1	55.9	76.1	68.1	17.8	18.7	12.0	10.5	34.7	10.8
Oregon	81.5	82.3	75.0	53.0	79.4	71.0	20.6	20.8	9.1	10.1	32.3	8.3
Pennsylvania	74.7	75.9	63.5	52.2	77.1	67.8	17.9	18.5	10.0	11.8	45.2	12.0
Rhode Island	72.0	73.0	65.9	46.8	59.6	64.5	21.3	21.8	12.7	8.9	30.6	8.3
South Carolina ...	68.3	73.6	53.3	71.8	77.4	62.5	16.6	19.8	7.6	19.8	34.4	10.9
South Dakota	77.1	77.8	82.2	71.3	74.3	62.5	17.2	17.6	24.1	13.4	33.1	6.8
Tennessee	67.1	68.2	59.4	71.5	79.3	63.1	16.0	16.7	10.2	21.9	42.6	10.5
Texas	72.1	76.2	66.1	44.6	79.1	70.9	20.3	22.6	12.0	7.3	41.3	13.9
Utah	85.1	86.2	77.0	61.0	80.7	59.3	22.3	22.7	15.9	9.1	29.4	6.4
Vermont	80.8	80.8	82.9	84.7	87.1	66.8	24.3	24.2	30.5	28.2	52.1	11.1
Virginia	75.2	78.3	60.3	70.5	82.1	70.7	24.5	27.0	11.1	22.4	40.2	14.7
Washington	83.8	85.0	81.2	56.7	77.3	72.3	22.9	23.3	15.4	11.0	30.2	9.1
West Virginia	66.0	66.0	64.7	70.3	88.8	57.9	12.3	12.2	10.9	17.6	63.3	6.5
Wisconsin	78.6	79.6	61.3	54.1	71.5	66.8	17.7	18.1	8.3	10.0	40.4	5.5
Wyoming	83.0	83.9	81.2	59.3	77.5	68.2	18.8	19.3	9.5	4.8	28.6	6.2

SOURCE: U.S. Department of Commerce, Bureau of the Census, 1990 Decennial Census. Published as Table 12 in *Digest of Education Statistics* 1997.

1. Includes people of Hispanic origin.
2. Persons of Hispanic origin may be of any race.

NOTE: Because of rounding, detail may not add to 100.0 percent.

Table C-3. Educational Attainment of Persons 25 Years Old and Over, for the 25 Largest States: March 1995

State	Number of persons 25 years old and over (in thousands)			Percent high school graduate or more						Percent completed bachelor's or higher degree					
	Total	Male	Female	Total		Male		Female		Total		Male		Female	
Alabama	2 701	1 277	1 424	74.4	(2.4)	75.2	(3.4)	73.7	(3.3)	28.3	(2.0)	21.0	(3.2)	13.9	(2.6)
Arizona	2 584	1 268	1 315	82.3	(2.0)	81.2	(3.0)	83.4	(2.8)	30.4	(2.1)	22.3	(3.2)	15.9	(2.7)
California	19 887	9 716	10 171	79.6	(0.8)	80.6	(1.2)	78.6	(1.2)	38.3	(0.9)	27.6	(1.3)	21.0	(1.2)
Florida	9 497	4 430	5 066	82.8	(1.0)	83.5	(1.4)	82.2	(1.3)	36.0	(1.1)	26.0	(1.6)	18.7	(1.4)
Georgia	4 583	2 174	2 408	78.1	(2.1)	77.9	(3.1)	78.4	(2.9)	35.7	(2.2)	24.7	(3.2)	20.9	(2.9)
Illinois	7 423	3 476	3 947	82.3	(1.1)	82.7	(1.6)	82.0	(1.5)	39.4	(1.3)	27.9	(1.9)	21.7	(1.7)
Indiana	3 589	1 667	1 921	81.6	(2.2)	81.2	(3.3)	82.0	(3.0)	27.5	(2.1)	19.7	(3.3)	14.6	(2.7)
Kentucky	2 447	1 157	1 290	76.7	(2.3)	78.5	(3.3)	75.1	(3.2)	31.4	(2.2)	22.8	(3.3)	16.3	(2.8)
Louisiana	2 614	1 257	1 357	75.8	(2.5)	76.0	(3.6)	75.6	(3.5)	32.1	(2.3)	23.1	(3.5)	17.3	(3.1)
Maryland	3 368	1 622	1 746	82.0	(2.1)	82.4	(3.1)	81.7	(3.0)	41.4	(2.5)	29.0	(3.6)	23.9	(3.3)
Massachusetts	3 961	1 878	2 083	85.8	(1.0)	86.4	(1.5)	85.3	(1.4)	51.2	(1.4)	35.4	(2.0)	30.0	(1.8)
Michigan	6 000	2 824	3 176	83.7	(1.1)	83.4	(1.6)	84.0	(1.5)	33.3	(1.2)	23.7	(1.8)	18.1	(1.5)
Minnesota	2 867	1 428	1 439	88.4	(1.8)	89.2	(2.5)	87.6	(2.6)	40.8	(2.5)	28.6	(3.6)	24.4	(3.4)
Missouri	3 367	1 637	1 730	82.2	(2.2)	82.3	(3.1)	82.2	(3.0)	34.4	(2.3)	24.3	(3.5)	19.7	(3.1)
New Jersey	5 168	2 485	2 683	85.4	(1.0)	86.5	(1.4)	84.4	(1.4)	43.9	(1.3)	30.9	(1.9)	25.1	(1.7)
New York	11 818	5 414	6 404	82.5	(0.8)	82.7	(1.2)	82.3	(1.1)	42.5	(0.9)	29.9	(1.5)	23.3	(1.2)
North Carolina	4 604	2 139	2 465	76.3	(1.1)	74.2	(1.7)	78.2	(1.5)	33.0	(1.1)	23.0	(1.7)	18.6	(1.4)
Ohio	6 980	3 219	3 761	83.4	(1.1)	83.3	(1.6)	83.4	(1.4)	31.7	(1.1)	22.3	(1.7)	17.4	(1.5)
Pennsylvania	7 916	3 776	4 140	81.5	(1.1)	80.3	(1.6)	82.5	(1.5)	32.5	(1.1)	23.0	(1.7)	18.2	(1.5)
South Carolina	2 300	1 096	1 204	74.3	(2.1)	73.3	(3.1)	75.2	(2.9)	28.5	(1.9)	19.7	(2.8)	16.9	(2.5)
Tennessee	3 337	1 508	1 829	77.4	(2.1)	75.3	(3.3)	79.1	(2.8)	28.6	(2.0)	19.7	(3.0)	16.3	(2.6)
Texas	11 262	5 464	5 798	76.2	(1.2)	76.4	(1.7)	76.0	(1.6)	34.9	(1.1)	25.1	(1.7)	19.0	(1.5)
Virginia	4 320	2 103	2 217	82.7	(1.8)	81.7	(2.6)	83.7	(2.4)	41.0	(2.1)	29.3	(3.1)	22.8	(2.8)
Washington	3 329	1 627	1 702	91.4	(1.5)	91.5	(2.1)	91.3	(2.1)	42.8	(2.3)	31.9	(3.5)	21.3	(3.0)
Wisconsin	3 182	1 545	1 638	86.6	(1.8)	86.8	(2.5)	86.3	(2.5)	31.7	(2.1)	21.6	(3.0)	19.7	(2.9)

SOURCE: U.S. Department of Commerce, Bureau of the Census, Current Population Reports, Educational Attainment in the United States: March 1995. Published as Table 13 in *Digest of Education Statistics* 1997.

NOTE: Because of rounding, detail may not add to totals. Standard errors appear in parentheses.

Table C-4.   Estimated Total and School-Age Resident Populations, by State: 1970 to 1996

State	1970[2]		1980[2]		1985[3]		1990[2]		1994[3]		1995[3]		1996[3]	
	Total, all ages	5 to 17-year-olds	Total, all ages	5 to 17-year-olds	Total, all ages	5 to 17-year-olds	Total, all ages	5 to 17-year-olds	Total, all ages	5 to 17-year-olds	Total, all ages	5 to 17-year-olds	Total, all ages	5 to 17-year-olds
United States	203 302	52 540	226 546	47 407	237 924	44 782	248 710	45 166	260 372	48 155	262 890	48 974	265 284	49 762
Alabama	3 444	934	3 894	866	3 973	798	4 041	774	4 215	774	4 246	778	4 273	780
Alaska	303	88	402	92	532	112	550	117	601	134	603	135	607	135
Arizona	1 775	486	2 718	578	3 184	601	3 665	686	4 092	781	4 305	795	4 428	807
Arkansas	1 923	498	2 286	496	2 327	461	2 351	455	2 455	469	2 485	478	2 510	484
California	19 971	4 999	23 668	4 681	26 441	4 752	29 760	5 337	31 362	5 831	31 565	5 969	31 878	6 132
Colorado	2 210	589	2 890	592	3 209	599	3 294	607	3 663	692	3 748	709	3 823	728
Connecticut	3 032	768	3 108	638	3 201	549	3 287	520	3 273	555	3 271	565	3 274	575
Delaware	548	148	594	125	618	113	666	114	708	124	717	125	725	126
District of Columbia	757	164	638	109	635	88	607	80	568	74	555	76	543	75
Florida	6 791	1 609	9 746	1 789	11 351	1 792	12 938	2 011	13 965	2 319	14 184	2 392	14 400	2 467
Georgia	4 588	1 223	5 463	1 231	5 963	1 195	6 478	1 230	7 063	1 335	7 209	1 370	7 353	1 401
Hawaii	770	204	965	198	1 040	194	1 108	196	1 173	209	1 179	212	1 184	215
Idaho	713	200	944	213	994	223	1 007	228	1 136	252	1 166	255	1 189	258
Illinois	11 110	2 859	11 427	2 401	11 400	2 192	11 431	2 095	11 734	2 168	11 790	2 206	11 847	2 241
Indiana	5 195	1 386	5 490	1 200	5 459	1 087	5 544	1 056	5 750	1 066	5 797	1 079	5 841	1 089
Iowa	2 825	743	2 914	604	2 830	543	2 777	525	2 832	538	2 843	539	2 852	537
Kansas	2 249	573	2 364	468	2 427	452	2 478	472	2 550	503	2 564	505	2 572	507
Kentucky	3 221	844	3 661	800	3 695	745	3 685	703	3 826	708	3 857	710	3 884	710
Louisiana	3 645	1 041	4 206	969	4 408	937	4 220	890	4 315	896	4 338	901	4 351	906
Maine	994	260	1 125	243	1 163	222	1 228	223	1 238	228	1 239	228	1 243	228
Maryland	3 924	1 038	4 217	895	4 413	788	4 781	803	5 000	882	5 039	905	5 072	927
Massachusetts	5 689	1 407	5 737	1 153	5 881	989	6 016	940	6 042	995	6 071	1 015	6 092	1 031
Michigan	8 882	2 450	9 262	2 067	9 076	1 824	9 295	1 754	9 486	1 812	9 538	1 845	9 594	1 865
Minnesota	3 806	1 051	4 076	865	4 184	796	4 375	828	4 572	907	4 615	920	4 658	931
Mississippi	2 217	635	2 521	599	2 588	576	2 573	550	2 668	548	2 696	551	2 716	552
Missouri	4 678	1 183	4 917	1 008	5 000	941	5 117	944	5 275	996	5 319	1 013	5 359	1 027
Montana	694	197	787	167	822	167	799	163	857	176	870	177	879	177
Nebraska	1 485	389	1 570	324	1 585	305	1 578	309	1 626	324	1 639	327	1 652	329
Nevada	489	127	800	160	951	166	1 202	204	1 464	262	1 533	277	1 603	293
New Hampshire ...	738	189	921	196	997	182	1 109	194	1 135	212	1 148	217	1 162	220
New Jersey	7 171	1 797	7 365	1 528	7 566	1 340	7 730	1 265	7 906	1 354	7 950	1 385	7 988	1 415
New Mexico	1 017	311	1 303	303	1 438	304	1 515	320	1 659	353	1 690	359	1 713	365
New York	18 241	4 358	17 558	3 552	17 792	3 173	17 990	3 000	18 197	3 131	18 191	3 174	18 185	3 220
North Carolina	5 084	1 323	5 882	1 254	6 254	1 175	6 629	1 147	7 079	1 249	7 202	1 285	7 323	1 321
North Dakota	618	175	653	136	677	133	639	127	640	128	642	128	644	127
Ohio	10 657	2 820	10 798	2 307	10 735	2 090	10 847	2 012	11 097	2 064	11 134	2 078	11 173	2 089
Oklahoma	2 559	640	3 025	622	3 271	635	3 146	609	3 254	639	3 275	646	3 301	653
Oregon	2 092	534	2 633	525	2 673	504	2 842	521	3 094	575	3 149	586	3 204	597
Pennsylvania	11 801	2 925	11 864	2 376	11 771	2 079	11 882	1 996	12 058	2 093	12 060	2 114	12 056	2 133
Rhode Island	950	225	947	186	969	163	1 003	159	996	167	992	170	990	172
South Carolina	2 591	720	3 122	703	3 303	663	3 487	663	3 643	674	3 667	680	3 699	684
South Dakota	666	187	691	147	698	139	696	144	724	153	730	153	732	153
Tennessee	3 926	1 002	4 591	972	4 715	903	4 877	882	5 175	928	5 247	944	5 320	958
Texas	11 199	3 002	14 229	3 137	16 273	3 318	16 987	3 437	18 434	3 725	18 801	3 792	19 128	3 870
Utah	1 059	312	1 461	350	1 643	418	1 723	457	1 910	487	1 958	490	2 000	490
Vermont	445	118	511	109	530	100	563	102	581	109	585	110	589	111
Virginia	4 651	1 197	5 347	1 114	5 715	1 039	6 187	1 060	6 550	1 133	6 615	1 156	6 675	1 177
Washington	3 413	881	4 132	826	4 400	816	4 867	893	5 351	1 008	5 448	1 030	5 533	1 051
West Virginia	1 744	442	1 950	414	1 907	383	1 793	337	1 822	320	1 825	318	1 826	315
Wisconsin	4 418	1 203	4 706	1 011	4 748	908	4 892	927	5 084	992	5 122	1 001	5 160	1 006
Wyoming	332	92	470	101	500	108	454	101	476	103	479	103	481	102

SOURCE: U.S. Department of Commerce, Bureau of the Census, Current Population Reports, Series P-25, No. 1095. Published as table 17 in *Digest of Education Statistics* 1997.

1. Includes Armed Forces residing in each state.
2. As of April 1.
3. Estimates as of July 1.

NOTE: Because of rounding, detail may not add to totals.

Table C-5.   Direct General Expenditures of State and Local Governments for all Functions and for Education, by Level and State: 1992-93

(In millions of dollars)

| State | Total direct general expenditures[1] | Education expenditures | | | | | | | |
| | | Total | Elementary and secondary education | | | Higher education | | | Other education[3] |
			Total	Current expenditure	Capital outlay[2]	Total	Current expenditure	Capital outlay[2]	
United States	$1 026 806	$342 287	$240 310	$218 208	$22 102	$88 109	$79 160	$8 949	$13 869
Alabama	13 754	4 441	2 530	2 320	210	1 577	1 416	160	334
Alaska	6 021	1 464	1 089	957	131	324	269	55	51
Arizona	14 195	5 129	3 463	2 702	760	1 503	1 371	132	163
Arkansas	7 209	2 792	1 714	1 583	131	859	733	126	218
California	134 571	39 425	26 530	24 892	1 639	11 494	10 353	1 141	1 401
Colorado	14 460	4 935	3 291	2 934	357	1 527	1 406	121	117
Connecticut	15 771	4 746	3 777	3 539	238	778	754	24	192
Delaware	3 063	1 160	681	632	48	396	382	14	83
District of Columbia	4 472	720	621	582	39	100	95	4	(NA)
Florida	50 431	14 879	11 160	9 754	1 405	3 193	2 699	494	526
Georgia	24 241	8 005	5 942	5 350	592	1 713	1 559	154	350
Hawaii	6 370	1 447	834	744	90	591	503	89	22
Idaho	3 458	1 281	837	756	82	390	348	41	54
Illinois	42 975	14 522	10 243	9 341	902	3 589	3 246	343	690
Indiana	19 966	7 478	4 923	4 391	532	2 248	2 001	247	308
Iowa	10 772	4 076	2 552	2 327	225	1 351	1 250	101	173
Kansas	9 017	3 615	2 392	2 194	198	1 098	1 003	95	125
Kentucky	12 399	4 170	2 595	2 430	165	1 243	1 077	166	331
Louisiana	16 533	4 941	3 372	3 189	183	1 302	1 223	79	267
Maine	4 790	1 615	1 187	1 094	92	369	330	38	60
Maryland	18 452	6 629	4 497	4 163	334	1 815	1 575	240	318
Massachusetts	25 822	6 655	4 972	4 819	153	1 331	1 260	71	352
Michigan	37 642	14 814	1 024	9 255	999	4 174	3 845	328	386
Minnesota	21 693	7 193	5 065	4 567	497	1 818	1 656	162	310
Mississippi	7 946	2 783	1 802	1 673	129	831	742	89	150
Missouri	15 230	5 510	4 104	3 688	416	1 205	1 130	75	202
Montana	3 104	1 146	810	770	40	264	248	16	72
Nebraska	5 803	2 368	1 606	1 464	142	686	637	49	76
Nevada	5 588	1 626	1 191	999	191	399	337	62	36
New Hampshire	4 258	1 381	1 016	973	42	319	299	20	46
New Jersey	36 406	12 667	10 020	9 414	606	2 305	2 094	211	342
New Mexico	6 548	2 295	1 403	1 248	155	811	745	66	82
New York	107 595	30 300	23 471	21 812	1 659	5 589	4 864	725	1 240
North Carolina	23 108	8 583	5 382	4 890	492	2 866	2 556	309	336
North Dakota	2 557	963	548	506	41	366	333	32	49
Ohio	39 443	13 902	9 842	9 371	470	3 497	2 858	639	563
Oklahoma	10 269	3 955	2 721	2 528	193	1 084	1 014	71	150
Oregon	12 417	4 484	3 098	2 893	205	1 232	1 129	102	154
Pennsylvania	45 942	16 902	12 448	11 440	1 008	3 421	3 133	288	1 034
Rhode Island	4 494	1 338	929	895	34	309	288	21	100
South Carolina	12 493	4 343	2 900	2 675	225	1 258	1 128	130	185
South Dakota	2 430	868	613	554	59	211	191	19	45
Tennessee	15 657	4 874	3 172	2 932	240	1 512	1 342	170	191
Texas	61 780	24 138	17 153	14 131	3 022	6 420	5 900	520	565
Utah	6 320	2 659	1 626	1 422	205	932	830	103	101

See footnotes at end of table.

Table C-5.   Direct General Expenditures of State and Local Governments for all Functions and for Education, by Level and State: 1992-93 — Continued

(In millions of dollars)

State	Total direct general expenditures[1]	Education expenditures							
		Total	Elementary and secondary education			Higher education			Other education[3]
			Total	Current expenditure	Capital outlay[2]	Total	Current expenditure	Capital outlay[2]	
Vermont	$2 257	$887	$550	$537	$13	$278	$257	$21	$59
Virginia	21 991	8 311	5 713	5 235	478	2 192	2 020	172	405
Washington	24 989	8 570	5 951	4 647	1 304	2 249	1 937	312	369
West Virginia	6 349	2 409	1 699	1 519	180	572	530	42	138
Wisconsin	21 353	8 012	5 431	4 930	501	2 268	2 042	227	312
Wyoming	2 402	881	594	548	47	252	223	29	34

SOURCE: U.S. Department of Commerce, Bureau of the Census, unpublished data. Published as table 35 in *Digest of Education Statistics* 1997.

1. Includes state and local government expenditures for education services, social services and income maintenance, transportation, public safety, environment and housing, governmental administration, interest on general debt, and other general expenditures. Includes intergovernmental expenditure to the federal government.
2. Includes outlays for 'other education'.
3. Includes assistance and subsidies to individuals and private institutions for elementary, secondary, and higher education, as well as miscellaneous education expenditures.

NOTE: Current expenditure data in this table differ from figures appearing in other tables because of slightly varying definitions used in the Governmental Finances and Common Core of Data surveys. Because of rounding, details may not add to totals.

(NA) Not applicable or not available.

Table C-6. Direct General Expenditures Per Capita of State and Local Governments for All Functions and for Education, by Level and State: 1992-93

(In millions of dollars)

| State | Total direct general expenditures[1] | Education expenditures | | | | | | | |
| | | Total | | Elementary and secondary education | | Higher education | | Other education[2] | |
		Amount per capita	As a percent of all functions	Amount per capita	As a percent of all functions[2]	Amount per capita	As a percent of all functions	Amount per capita[2]	As a percent of all functions[3]
United States	$3 981	$1 327	33.3	$932	23.4	$342	8.6	$54	1.4
Alabama	3 285	1 061	32.3	604	18.4	377	11.5	80	2.4
Alaska	10 052	2 444	24.3	1 818	18.1	541	5.4	86	0.9
Arizona	3 607	1 303	36.1	880	24.4	382	10.6	41	1.1
Arkansas	2 974	1 152	38.7	707	23.8	355	11.9	90	3.0
California	4 312	1 263	29.3	850	19.7	368	8.5	45	1.0
Colorado	4 055	1 384	34.1	923	22.8	428	10.6	33	0.8
Connecticut	4 813	1 448	30.1	1 152	23.9	237	4.9	58	1.2
Delaware	4 375	1 657	37.9	972	22.2	565	12.9	119	2.7
District of Columbia	7 724	1 244	16.1	1 072	13.9	172	2.2	(NA)	(NA)
Florida	3 687	1 088	29.5	816	22.1	233	6.3	38	1.0
Georgia	3 505	1 157	33.0	859	24.5	248	7.1	51	1.4
Hawaii	5 435	1 235	22.7	712	13.1	505	9.3	18	0.3
Idaho	3 146	1 166	37.0	762	24.2	355	11.3	49	1.6
Illinois	3 674	1 242	33.8	876	23.8	307	8.4	59	1.6
Indiana	3 495	1 309	37.5	862	24.7	393	11.3	54	1.5
Iowa	3 828	1 448	37.8	907	23.7	480	12.5	62	1.6
Kansas	3 563	1 428	40.1	945	26.5	434	12.2	49	1.4
Kentucky	3 272	1 100	33.6	685	20.9	328	10.0	87	2.7
Louisiana	3 849	1 150	29.9	785	20.4	303	7.9	62	1.6
Maine	3 866	1 304	33.7	958	24.8	298	7.7	48	1.3
Maryland	3 716	1 335	35.9	906	24.4	366	9.8	64	1.7
Massachusetts	4 295	1 107	25.8	827	19.3	221	5.2	59	1.4
Michigan	3 972	1 563	39.4	1 082	27.2	440	11.1	41	1.0
Minnesota	4 802	1 592	33.2	1 121	23.3	402	8.4	69	1.4
Mississippi	3 006	1 053	35.0	682	22.7	314	10.5	57	1.9
Missouri	2 910	1 053	36.2	784	26.9	230	7.9	38	1.3
Montana	3 700	1 366	36.9	965	26.1	314	8.5	86	2.3
Nebraska	3 611	1 473	40.8	999	27.7	427	11.8	47	1.3
Nevada	4 023	1 171	29.1	857	21.3	287	7.1	26	0.6
New Hampshire	3 785	1 228	32.4	903	23.9	284	7.5	41	1.1
New Jersey	4 621	1 608	34.8	1 272	27.5	293	6.3	43	0.9
New Mexico	4 052	1 420	35.1	868	21.4	502	12.4	51	1.2
New York	5 913	1 665	28.2	1 290	21.8	307	5.2	68	1.2
North Carolina	3 327	1 236	37.1	775	23.3	413	12.4	48	1.5
North Dakota	4 026	1 516	37.7	862	21.4	576	14.3	78	1.9
Ohio	3 556	1 253	35.2	887	25.0	315	8.9	51	1.4
Oklahoma	3 178	1 224	38.5	842	26.5	336	10.6	46	1.5
Oregon	4 096	1 479	36.1	1 022	24.9	406	9.9	51	1.2
Pennsylvania	3 813	1 403	36.8	1 033	27.1	284	7.4	86	2.2
Rhode Island	4 494	1 338	29.8	929	20.7	309	6.9	100	2.2
South Carolina	3 429	1 192	34.8	796	23.2	345	10.1	51	1.5
South Dakota	3 399	1 214	35.7	857	25.2	295	8.7	62	1.8
Tennessee	3 071	956	31.1	622	20.3	296	9.7	37	1.2
Texas	3 426	1 339	39.1	951	27.8	356	10.4	31	0.9
Utah	3 398	1 430	42.1	874	25.7	501	14.8	54	1.6

See footnotes at end of table.

Table C-6.   Direct General Expenditures Per Capita of State and Local Governments for All Functions and for Education, by Level and State: 1992-93 — Continued

(In millions of dollars)

State	Total direct general expenditures[1]	Education expenditures							
		Total		Elementary and secondary education		Higher education		Other education[2]	
		Amount per capita	As a percent of all functions	Amount per capita	As a percent of all functions[2]	Amount per capita	As a percent of all functions	Amount per capita[2]	As a percent of all functions[3]
Vermont	$3 919	$1 540	39.3	$955	24.4	$482	12.3	$103	2.6
Virginia	3 388	1 280	37.8	880	26.0	338	10.0	62	1.8
Washington	4 755	1 631	34.3	1 132	23.8	428	9.0	70	1.5
West Virginia	3 488	1 324	37.9	933	26.8	314	9.0	76	2.2
Wisconsin	4 238	1 590	37.5	1 078	25.4	450	10.6	62	1.5
Wyoming	5 112	1 874	36.7	1 265	24.7	537	10.5	72	1.4

SOURCE: U.S. Department of Commerce, Bureau of the Census, unpublished data. Published as table 36 in *Digest of Education Statistics* 1997.

1. Includes state and local government expenditures for education services, social services and income maintenance, transportation, public safety, environment and housing, governmental administration, interest on general debt, and other general expenditures. Includes intergovernmental expenditure to the federal government.
2. Includes assistance and subsidies to individuals and private institutions for elementary, secondary, and higher education, as well as miscellaneous education expenditures.

NOTE: Per capita amounts are based on population figures as of July 1, 1993, and are computed on the basis of amounts rounded to the nearest thousand. Because of rounding, details may not add to totals.

(NA) Not applicable or not available.

Table C-7. Enrollment in Public Elementary and Secondary Schools, by Level and State: Fall 1981 to Fall 1996

(Numbers in thousands. Civilian noninstitutional population.)

State or other area	Fall 1981 Total	Fall 1982 Total	Fall 1983 Total	Fall 1984 Total	Fall 1985 Total	Fall 1986 Total	Fall 1987 Total	Fall 1988 Total	Fall 1989 Total	Fall 1990 Total	Fall 1991 Total	Fall 1992 Total
United States	40 044 093	39 565 610	39 252 308	39 208 252	39 421 961	39 753 172	40 008 213	40 188 690	40 542 707	41 216 683	42 046 878	42 823 312
Alabama	743 448	724 037	721 901	712 586	730 460	733 735	729 234	724 751	723 743	721 806	722 004	731 634
Alaska[3]	90 858	89 413	98 206	104 599	107 345	107 848	106 869	106 481	109 280	113 903	118 680	122 487
Arizona	507 199	510 296	506 682	530 062	548 252	534 538	572 421	574 890	607 615	639 853	656 980	673 477
Arkansas	437 121	432 565	432 120	432 668	433 410	437 438	437 036	436 387	434 960	436 286	438 518	441 490
California	4 046 156	4 065 486	4 089 017	4 151 110	4 255 554	4 377 989	4 488 398	4 618 120	4 771 978	4 950 474	5 107 145	5 254 844
Colorado	544 174	545 209	542 196	545 427	550 642	558 415	560 236	560 081	562 755	574 213	593 030	612 635
Connecticut[5]	505 386	486 470	477 585	468 145	462 026	468 847	465 465	460 637	461 560	469 123	481 050	488 476
Delaware	95 072	92 646	91 406	91 767	92 901	94 410	95 659	96 678	97 808	99 658	102 196	104 321
District of Columbia	94 975	91 105	88 843	87 397	87 092	85 612	86 435	84 792	81 301	80 694	80 618	80 937
Florida	1 487 721	1 484 734	1 495 543	1 524 107	1 562 283	1 607 320	1 664 774	1 720 930	1 789 925	1 861 592	1 932 131	1 981 407
Georgia	1 056 117	1 053 689	1 050 859	1 062 315	1 079 594	1 096 425	1 110 947	1 107 994	1 126 535	1 151 687	1 177 569	1 207 186
Hawaii	162 805	162 024	162 241	163 860	164 169	164 640	166 160	167 488	169 493	171 708	174 747	177 448
Idaho	204 524	202 973	206 352	208 080	208 669	208 391	212 444	214 615	214 932	220 840	225 680	231 668
Illinois	1 924 084	1 880 289	1 853 316	1 834 355	1 826 478	1 825 185	1 811 446	1 794 916	1 797 355	1 821 407	1 848 166	1 873 567
Indiana	1 025 172	999 542	984 384	972 659	966 106	966 780	964 129	960 994	954 165	954 525	956 988	960 630
Iowa	516 216	504 983	497 287	491 011	485 332	481 286	480 826	478 200	478 486	483 652	491 363	494 839
Kansas	409 909	407 074	405 222	405 347	410 229	416 091	421 112	426 596	430 864	437 034	445 390	451 536
Kentucky	658 350	651 084	647 414	644 421	643 833	642 778	642 696	637 627	630 688	636 401	646 024	655 041
Louisiana	782 053	784 027	800 193	800 941	788 349	795 188	793 093	786 683	783 025	784 757	794 128	797 985
Maine	216 293	211 986	209 753	207 537	206 101	211 752	211 817	212 902	213 775	215 149	216 400	216 453
Maryland	721 841	699 201	683 491	673 840	671 560	675 747	683 797	688 947	698 806	715 176	736 238	751 850
Massachusetts	947 037	908 984	878 844	859 391	844 330	833 918	825 320	823 428	825 588	834 314	846 155	859 948
Michigan	1 724 787	1 674 697	1 635 963	1 609 448	1 602 747	1 597 154	1 589 287	1 582 785	1 576 785	1 584 431	1 593 561	1 603 610
Minnesota	733 741	715 190	705 236	701 697	705 140	711 134	721 481	726 950	739 553	756 374	773 571	793 724
Mississippi	471 615	468 294	467 744	466 058	471 195	498 639	505 550	503 326	502 020	502 417	504 127	506 668
Missouri	818 705	802 535	795 453	793 793	795 107	800 606	802 060	806 639	807 934	816 558	842 965	859 357
Montana	153 435	152 335	153 646	154 412	153 869	153 327	152 207	152 191	151 265	152 974	155 779	160 011
Nebraska	273 340	269 009	266 998	265 599	265 819	267 139	268 100	269 434	270 920	274 081	279 552	282 414
Nevada	151 339	151 104	150 442	151 633	154 948	161 239	168 353	176 474	186 834	201 316	211 810	222 974
New Hampshire	163 827	160 197	159 030	158 614	160 974	163 717	166 045	169 413	171 696	172 785	177 138	181 247
New Jersey	1 199 643	1 172 520	1 147 841	1 129 223	1 116 194	1 107 467	1 092 982	1 080 871	1 076 005	1 089 646	1 109 796	1 130 560
New Mexico	268 091	268 632	269 711	272 478	277 551	281 943	287 229	292 425	296 057	301 881	308 667	315 668
New York	2 783 017	2 718 678	2 674 818	2 645 811	2 621 378	2 607 719	2 594 070	2 573 715	2 565 841	2 598 337	2 643 993	2 689 686
North Carolina	1 108 960	1 096 815	1 089 606	1 088 724	1 086 165	1 085 248	1 085 976	1 083 156	1 080 744	1 086 871	1 097 598	1 114 083
North Dakota	117 708	117 078	117 213	118 711	118 570	118 703	119 004	118 809	117 816	117 825	118 376	118 734
Ohio	1 898 501	1 860 245	1 827 300	1 805 440	1 793 965	1 793 508	1 793 431	1 778 544	1 764 410	1 771 089	1 783 767	1 795 199
Oklahoma	582 572	593 825	591 389	589 690	592 327	593 183	584 212	580 426	578 580	579 087	588 263	597 096
Oregon	457 165	448 184	447 109	446 884	447 527	449 307	455 895	461 752	472 394	472 394	498 614	510 122
Pennsylvania	1 839 015	1 783 969	1 737 952	1 701 880	1 683 221	1 674 161	1 668 542	1 659 714	1 655 279	1 667 834	1 692 797	1 717 613
Rhode Island	143 414	139 959	136 412	134 610	133 949	134 690	134 800	134 585	133 585	135 729	138 813	142 144	143 798
South Carolina	609 158	608 518	604 553	602 718	606 643	611 629	614 921	615 774	616 177	622 112	627 470	640 464
South Dakota	125 657	123 897	123 060	123 314	124 291	125 458	126 817	126 910	127 329	129 164	131 576	134 573
Tennessee	838 297	828 264	822 057	817 212	813 753	818 073	823 783	821 580	819 660	824 595	833 651	855 231
Texas	2 935 547	2 985 659	2 989 796	3 040 305	3 131 705	3 209 515	3 236 787	3 283 707	3 328 514	3 382 887	3 464 371	3 541 769
Utah	355 554	370 183	378 208	390 141	403 305	415 994	423 386	431 119	438 554	446 652	456 430	463 870

See footnotes at end of table.

Table C-7. Enrollment in Public Elementary and Secondary Schools, by Level and State: Fall 1981 to Fall 1996 — Continued

(Numbers in thousands. Civilian noninstitutional population.)

State or other area	Fall 1981 Total	Fall 1982 Total	Fall 1983 Total	Fall 1984 Total	Fall 1985 Total	Fall 1986 Total	Fall 1987 Total	Fall 1988 Total	Fall 1989 Total	Fall 1990 Total	Fall 1991 Total	Fall 1992 Total
Vermont	93 183	91 454	90 416	90 089	90 157	92 112	92 755	93 381	94 779	95 762	97 137	98 558
Virginia	989 548	975 727	966 110	965 222	968 104	975 135	979 417	982 393	985 346	998 601	1 016 204	1 031 925
Washington ..	750 188	739 215	736 239	741 177	749 706	761 428	775 755	790 918	810 232	839 709	869 327	896 475
West Virginia	377 772	375 115	371 251	362 941	357 923	351 837	344 236	335 912	327 540	322 389	320 249	318 296
Wisconsin	804 262	784 830	774 646	767 542	768 234	767 819	772 363	774 857	782 905	797 621	814 671	829 415
Wyoming	99 541	101 665	99 254	101 261	102 779	100 955	98 455	97 793	97 172	98 226	102 074	100 313
Outlying areas												
American Samoa	9 896	(NA)	10 124	(NA)	(NA)	11 055	11 248	11 764	12 258	12 463	13 365	13 994
Guam	25 084	25 676	26 249	(NA)	26 043	25 676	25 936	26 041	26 493	26 391	28 334	30 077
Northern Marianas	5 300	(NA)	4 499	4 841	(NA)	(NA)	5 819	6 079	6 101	6 449	7 096	8 086
Puerto Rico ...	721 419	708 794	701 925	692 923	686 914	679 489	672 837	661 693	651 225	644 734	642 392	637 034
Virgin Islands	25 525	25 699	26 126	26 122	25 448	24 435	24 020	23 492	21 193	21 750	22 346	22 887

See footnotes at end of table.

Table C-7. Enrollment in Public Elementary and Secondary Schools, by Level and State: Fall 1981 to Fall 1996 — Continued

(Numbers in thousands. Civilian noninstitutional population.)

State or other area	Fall 1993			Fall 1994			Fall 1995			Estimated Fall 1996[1]
	Total	Kindergarten to grade 8	Grades 9 to 12	Total	Kindergarten to grade 8[2]	Grades 9 to 12	Total	Kindergarten to grade 8[2]	Grades 9 to 12	Total
United States	43 464 916	31 504 032	11 960 884	44 111 482	31 898 249	12 213 233	44 840 481	32 340 501	12 499 980	45 228 526
Alabama	734 288	535 637	198 651	736 531	535 246	201 285	746 149	539 309	206 840	741 933
Alaska[3]	125 948	93 601	32 347	127 057	93 719	33 338	127 618	93 434	34 184	126 015
Arizona	709 453	526 412	183 041	737 424	542 904	194 520	743 566	548 526	195 040	[4] 749 759
Arkansas	444 271	317 713	126 558	447 565	319 282	128 283	453 257	322 440	130 817	457 076
California	5 327 231	3 903 137	1 424 094	5 407 475	3 955 868	1 451 607	5 536 406	4 041 224	1 495 182	5 535 312
Colorado	625 062	459 930	165 132	640 521	469 755	170 766	656 279	478 881	177 398	673 438
Connecticut[5]	496 298	368 632	127 666	506 824	375 638	131 186	517 935	384 274	133 661	523 054
Delaware	105 547	76 617	28 930	106 813	76 819	29 994	108 461	77 028	31 433	[6] 110 549
District of Columbia	80 678	61 434	19 244	80 450	62 126	18 324	79 802	61 836	17 966	[4] 79 159
Florida	2 040 763	1 515 194	525 569	2 111 188	1 569 666	541 522	2 176 222	1 613 510	562 712	[6] 2 240 283
Georgia	1 235 304	910 425	324 879	1 270 948	934 650	336 298	1 311 126	965 707	345 419	1 321 239
Hawaii	180 410	131 638	48 772	183 795	133 675	50 120	187 180	135 671	51 509	188 485
Idaho	236 774	166 999	69 775	240 448	168 887	71 561	243 097	169 556	73 541	[6] 245 252
Illinois	1 893 078	1 356 329	536 749	1 916 172	1 368 041	548 131	1 943 623	1 390 475	553 148	1 961 299
Indiana	965 633	679 066	286 567	969 022	678 970	290 052	977 263	684 348	292 915	984 610
Iowa	498 519	348 006	150 513	500 440	345 865	154 575	502 343	343 997	158 346	504 511
Kansas	457 614	329 708	127 906	460 838	329 211	131 627	463 008	328 701	134 307	465 140
Kentucky	655 265	467 315	187 950	657 642	467 005	190 637	659 821	468 242	191 579	663 071
Louisiana	800 560	587 490	213 070	797 933	583 892	214 041	797 366	580 348	217 018	[6] 777 570
Maine	216 995	156 528	60 467	212 601	155 903	56 698	213 569	156 016	57 553	[6] 218 560
Maryland	772 638	569 497	203 141	790 938	580 903	210 035	805 544	590 155	215 389	818 947
Massachusetts	877 726	645 518	232 208	893 727	658 507	235 220	915 007	674 588	240 419	[4] 936 794
Michigan	1 599 377	1 159 968	439 409	1 614 784	1 170 251	444 533	1 641 456	1 191 671	449 785	1 662 100
Minnesota	810 233	576 980	233 253	821 693	581 426	240 267	835 166	586 080	249 086	836 700
Mississippi	505 907	368 688	137 219	505 962	366 846	139 116	506 272	366 186	140 086	[6] 504 168
Missouri	866 378	622 171	244 207	878 541	628 286	250 255	889 881	635 771	254 110	883 327
Montana	163 009	116 668	46 341	164 341	116 748	47 593	165 547	116 403	49 144	166 909
Nebraska	285 097	203 426	81 671	287 100	203 055	84 045	289 744	203 022	86 722	292 121
Nevada	235 800	175 054	60 746	250 747	185 336	65 411	265 041	195 892	69 149	[6] 282 131
New Hampshire ..	185 360	136 211	49 149	189 319	138 851	50 468	194 171	141 721	52 450	[6] 194 581
New Jersey ...	1 151 307	843 526	307 781	1 174 206	862 331	311 875	1 197 381	880 350	317 031	[4] 1 221 013
New Mexico ..	322 292	226 287	96 005	327 248	229 168	98 080	329 640	229 239	100 401	330 522
New York	2 733 813	1 920 609	813 204	2 766 208	1 949 245	816 963	2 813 230	1 980 208	833 022	2 825 000
North Carolina	1 133 231	828 171	305 060	1 156 767	847 463	309 304	1 183 090	871 320	311 770	[6] 1 199 962
North Dakota	119 127	84 127	35 000	119 288	83 419	35 869	119 100	82 333	36 767	[6] 118 427
Ohio	1 807 319	1 290 197	517 122	1 814 290	1 295 289	519 001	1 836 015	1 297 313	538 702	1 841 095
Oklahoma	604 076	441 094	162 982	609 718	442 607	167 111	616 393	445 780	170 613	620 379
Oregon	516 611	368 141	148 470	521 945	371 967	149 978	527 914	375 966	151 948	[6] 537 783
Pennsylvania	1 744 082	1 233 113	510 969	1 764 946	1 243 983	520 963	1 787 533	1 256 621	530 912	1 807 250
Rhode Island	145 676	107 047	38 629	147 487	107 913	39 574	149 799	109 815	39 984	151 181
South Carolina	643 696	466 951	176 745	648 725	468 850	179 875	645 586	463 305	182 281	648 980
South Dakota	142 825	102 281	40 544	143 482	101 805	41 677	144 685	101 491	43 194	[6] 142 910
Tennessee	866 557	630 015	236 542	881 425	640 604	240 821	893 770	650 601	243 169	891 101
Texas	3 608 262	2 681 053	927 209	3 677 171	2 720 623	956 548	3 748 167	2 757 273	990 894	3 809 186
Utah	471 365	329 926	141 439	474 675	328 482	146 193	477 121	327 790	149 331	[6] 478 085

See footnotes at end of table.

Table C-7.   Enrollment in Public Elementary and Secondary Schools, by Level and State: Fall 1981 to Fall 1996 — Continued

(Numbers in thousands. Civilian noninstitutional population.)

State or other area	Fall 1993			Fall 1994			Fall 1995			Estimated Fall 1996[1]
	Total	Kindergarten to grade 8	Grades 9 to 12	Total	Kindergarten to grade 8[2]	Grades 9 to 12	Total	Kindergarten to grade 8[2]	Grades 9 to 12	Total
Vermont	102 755	74 828	27 927	104 533	75 590	28 943	105 565	75 227	30 338	106 607
Virginia	1 045 471	767 347	278 124	1 060 809	774 319	286 490	1 079 854	787 945	291 909	[6] 1 096 093
Washington ..	915 952	660 424	255 528	938 314	673 107	265 207	956 572	680 009	276 563	[6] 971 903
West Virginia	314 383	215 784	98 599	310 511	212 808	97 703	307 112	211 008	96 104	[6] 303 441
Wisconsin	844 001	595 717	248 284	860 581	601 215	259 366	870 175	602 964	267 211	[6] 884 738
Wyoming	100 899	71 402	29 497	100 314	70 130	30 184	99 859	68 931	30 928	[6] 98 777
Outlying areas American										
Samoa	14 484	10 974	3 510	14 445	11 054	3 391	14 576	11 207	3 369	[4] 14 708
Guam	30 920	23 153	7 767	32 185	24 189	7 996	32 960	24 877	8 083	[4] 33 754
Northern Marianas	8 188	6 380	1 808	8 429	6 559	1 870	8 809	6 825	1 984	[6] 8 253
Puerto Rico ...	631 460	464 117	167 343	621 121	455 653	165 468	627 620	460 585	167 035	613 009
Virgin Islands	22 752	16 706	6 046	23 126	16 659	6 467	22 737	16 342	6 395	22 146

SOURCE: U.S. Department of Education, National Center for Education Statistics, Common Core of Data surveys. Published as table 40 in *Digest of Education Statistics* 1997.

1. Data estimated by state education agencies.
2. Includes a relatively small number of prekindergarten students.
3. Beginning in 1983, data include students enrolled in public schools on federal bases and other special arrangements.
4. Data estimated by the National Center for Education Statistics.
5. Beginning in 1986, data include state vocational/technical schools.
6. Actual data.

(NA) Not applicable or not available.

Table C-8. Enrollment in Public Elementary and Secondary Schools, by Grade and State: Fall 1995

(Numbers in thousands. Civilian noninstitutional population.)

State or other area	Total, all levels	Prekindergarten through grade 8 and elementary unclassified							
		Total	Prekindergarten[1]	Kindergarten	Grade 1	Grade 2	Grade 3	Grade 4	Grade 5
United States	44 840 481	32 340 501	636 846	3 536 227	3 670 903	3 507 022	3 444 740	3 430 583	3 437 943
Alabama	746 149	539 309	[2]9 324	59 739	61 694	57 452	57 732	56 486	57 142
Alaska	127 618	93 434	2 419	10 567	10 444	10 352	10 030	10 222	10 112
Arizona	743 566	548 526	4 027	61 420	64 215	61 418	59 828	60 202	59 894
Arkansas	453 257	322 440	1 525	36 731	36 369	34 257	33 621	33 955	34 875
California	5 536 406	4 041 224	[2]69 182	472 334	466 167	453 020	435 380	428 553	424 838
Colorado	656 279	478 881	10 472	50 316	52 767	51 786	52 030	52 783	52 646
Connecticut	517 935	384 274	8 093	44 148	45 969	43 030	42 010	41 365	40 650
Delaware	108 461	77 028	670	7 775	8 579	8 721	8 425	8 527	8 362
District of Columbia	79 802	61 836	5 387	7 736	7 931	6 533	6 063	5 852	5 332
Florida	2 176 222	1 613 510	51 123	176 767	180 182	175 891	172 039	173 169	175 358
Georgia	1 311 126	965 707	22 621	111 462	110 955	105 752	103 936	103 072	102 516
Hawaii	187 180	135 671	609	16 562	16 013	15 546	15 106	14 867	14 489
Idaho	243 097	169 556	1 665	17 750	18 260	18 285	17 952	17 640	18 626
Illinois	1 943 623	1 390 475	45 947	151 485	154 534	149 128	142 500	142 660	142 836
Indiana	977 263	684 348	4 901	73 833	80 279	74 964	71 585	72 356	73 101
Iowa	502 343	343 997	5 957	37 629	36 107	35 029	34 884	36 431	37 204
Kansas	463 008	328 701	3 209	33 925	35 538	35 037	35 100	36 004	36 596
Kentucky	659 821	468 242	20 290	45 038	47 250	45 845	56 613	46 834	48 572
Louisiana	797 366	580 348	19 440	61 323	63 719	59 414	59 552	61 315	61 232
Maine	213 569	156 016	821	16 826	17 250	17 003	16 568	17 419	17 397
Maryland	805 544	590 155	19 092	63 232	67 348	65 055	63 940	62 207	61 814
Massachusetts	915 007	674 588	14 792	79 163	79 565	75 647	73 380	71 800	71 606
Michigan	1 641 456	1 191 671	8 870	141 238	134 513	125 809	124 197	122 266	123 894
Minnesota	835 166	586 080	8 340	63 896	63 268	62 511	62 564	64 545	65 191
Mississippi	506 272	366 186	1 083	39 632	42 510	39 015	37 304	38 004	38 332
Missouri	889 881	635 771	16 225	68 513	69 659	67 080	66 928	68 159	68 889
Montana	165 547	116 403	519	12 214	12 519	12 279	12 535	12 899	13 200
Nebraska	289 744	203 022	3 853	22 282	21 748	21 082	21 210	21 886	22 351
Nevada	265 041	195 892	1 631	22 074	23 301	22 368	21 752	21 784	21 253
New Hampshire	194 171	141 721	1 357	8 859	17 973	16 601	16 566	16 275	16 480
New Jersey	1 197 381	880 350	9 301	93 978	102 521	95 581	91 352	88 686	86 889
New Mexico	329 640	229 239	3 426	24 329	26 152	24 703	24 395	24 200	24 407
New York	2 813 230	1 980 208	32 087	216 112	231 136	218 744	209 174	203 089	200 446
North Carolina	1 183 090	871 320	9 013	100 525	101 945	96 229	92 552	90 795	90 445
North Dakota	119 100	82 333	551	8 573	8 824	8 678	8 590	9 017	9 201
Ohio	1 836 015	1 297 313	18 997	141 589	148 354	140 090	138 135	138 942	140 465
Oklahoma	616 393	445 780	5 470	48 635	54 178	46 642	46 456	47 407	48 073
Oregon	527 914	375 966	855	39 875	41 952	40 802	40 790	41 721	42 083
Pennsylvania	1 787 533	1 256 621	3 502	134 584	146 077	139 562	136 887	137 850	135 565
Rhode Island	149 799	109 815	531	10 947	13 868	12 343	12 053	11 596	11 439
South Carolina	645 586	463 305	[2]8 067	39 964	55 944	51 837	50 451	50 860	51 338
South Dakota	144 685	101 491	1 475	10 609	10 700	10 365	10 675	10 937	11 234
Tennessee	893 770	650 601	[2]11 168	73 962	76 015	69 266	67 326	67 705	67 859
Texas	3 748 167	2 757 273	133 754	281 708	303 928	294 298	291 993	292 191	293 834
Utah	477 121	327 790	3 455	34 645	34 857	34 782	33 937	34 598	34 976
Vermont	105 565	75 227	1 111	7 953	8 371	8 067	8 200	8 287	8 327
Virginia	1 079 854	787 945	3 111	87 618	89 183	83 414	82 713	82 797	83 955
Washington	956 572	680 009	5 984	73 581	75 721	73 810	73 888	75 186	75 599
West Virginia	307 112	211 008	3 499	22 577	22 875	21 610	21 991	22 178	22 478
Wisconsin	870 175	602 964	18 045	62 859	64 574	63 141	64 541	65 427	66 577
Wyoming	99 859	68 931	(NA)	7 135	7 102	7 148	7 311	7 577	7 965

See footnotes at end of table.

Table C-8. Enrollment in Public Elementary and Secondary Schools, by Grade and State: Fall 1995 — Continued

(Numbers in thousands. Civilian noninstitutional population.)

State or other area	Total, all levels	Prekindergarten through grade 8 and elementary unclassified							
		Total	Prekindergarten[1]	Kindergarten	Grade 1	Grade 2	Grade 3	Grade 4	Grade 5
Outlying areas									
American Samoa	14 576	11 207	1 458	1 162	1 189	1 142	1 181	1 089	1 052
Guam	32 960	24 877	962	2 961	2 994	2 856	2 739	2 722	2 549
Northern Marianas ...	8 809	6 825	560	598	781	781	805	683	667
Puerto Rico	627 620	460 585	255	44 566	54 545	50 423	49 531	49 762	49 863
Virgin Islands	22 737	16 342	(NA)	1 638	1 647	1 654	1 717	1 655	1 712

See footnotes at end of table.

Table C-8.   Enrollment in Public Elementary and Secondary Schools, by Grade and State: Fall 1995 — Continued

(Numbers in thousands. Civilian noninstitutional population.)

State or other area	Prekindergarten through grade 8 and elementary unclassified				Grades 9 through 12 and secondary unclassified					
	Grade 6	Grade 7	Grade 8	Elementary unclassified	Total	Grade 9	Grade 10	Grade 11[2]	Grade 12	Secondary unclassified
United States	3 395 307	3 422 290	3 356 338	502 302	12 499 980	3 704 455	3 237 391	2 826 023	2 487 135	244 976
Alabama	58 704	61 122	59 914	(NA)	206 840	65 299	53 780	46 780	40 981	(NA)
Alaska	9 870	9 845	9 573	(NA)	34 184	10 263	9 045	7 765	7 111	(NA)
Arizona	58 281	58 829	56 407	4 005	195 040	59 346	52 654	43 547	39 197	296
Arkansas	35 104	37 023	36 696	2 284	130 817	37 005	35 209	30 566	27 083	954
California	413 776	409 978	399 039	68 957	1 495 182	437 974	396 020	343 419	287 428	30 341
Colorado	51 856	52 282	51 180	763	177 398	52 472	47 128	41 751	35 480	567
Connecticut	39 468	38 253	37 320	3 968	133 661	39 380	34 797	31 198	28 282	4
Delaware	8 520	8 883	8 566	(NA)	31 433	10 112	8 325	6 785	6 211	(NA)
District of Columbia	4 980	5 052	4 749	2 221	17 966	5 159	4 896	3 700	2 972	1 239
Florida	174 079	171 381	163 521	(NA)	562 712	182 980	154 030	126 183	99 519	(NA)
Georgia	103 015	102 287	100 091	(NA)	345 419	117 429	90 117	74 137	63 736	(NA)
Hawaii	14 617	14 022	13 793	47	51 509	16 277	13 274	11 442	10 478	38
Idaho	19 392	19 857	20 129	(NA)	73 541	20 195	19 349	17 904	16 093	(NA)
Illinois	138 679	133 484	132 678	56 544	553 148	149 289	139 115	122 384	107 244	35 116
Indiana	74 734	77 279	78 278	3 038	292 915	83 436	76 232	67 902	62 659	2 686
Iowa	37 117	38 833	38 715	6 091	158 346	41 385	39 680	36 861	34 565	5 855
Kansas	36 534	37 317	36 782	2 659	134 307	38 484	35 290	31 064	28 491	978
Kentucky	49 131	51 000	50 091	7 578	191 579	56 572	49 429	43 614	38 797	3 167
Louisiana	60 647	62 873	57 918	12 915	217 018	68 655	55 225	47 422	40 663	5 053
Maine	17 280	17 206	16 771	1 475	57 553	16 007	14 636	13 773	12 670	467
Maryland	61 099	60 747	58 835	6 786	215 389	64 468	54 286	47 345	42 974	6 316
Massachusetts	69 122	67 176	65 724	6 613	240 419	68 623	62 856	57 029	51 911	(NA)
Michigan	120 347	120 121	118 996	51 420	449 785	129 820	112 588	99 551	87 840	19 986
Minnesota	64 439	65 677	65 649	(NA)	249 086	67 226	64 478	59 589	57 793	(NA)
Mississippi	38 737	41 223	39 809	10 537	140 086	43 241	35 552	28 587	25 741	6 965
Missouri	67 847	69 368	66 493	6 610	254 110	72 575	66 804	59 378	52 939	2 414
Montana	13 153	13 407	13 342	336	49 144	13 921	12 569	11 635	10 897	122
Nebraska	22 777	22 817	23 016	(NA)	86 722	23 813	23 184	20 450	19 275	(NA)
Nevada	20 616	20 449	19 970	694	69 149	19 661	18 773	16 553	14 143	19
New Hampshire	15 805	15 798	15 487	520	52 450	15 420	13 597	12 387	10 996	50
New Jersey	84 950	83 920	81 997	61 175	317 031	84 649	76 042	70 493	65 647	20 200
New Mexico	25 300	26 434	25 893	(NA)	100 401	29 164	24 981	20 195	17 078	8 983
New York	197 470	199 440	194 347	78 163	833 022	235 320	205 305	178 043	142 841	71 513
North Carolina	88 925	89 747	88 056	23 088	311 770	100 505	82 512	69 100	59 653	(NA)
North Dakota	9 270	9 770	9 859	(NA)	36 767	9 927	9 377	8 950	8 513	(NA)
Ohio	137 737	141 979	142 469	8 556	538 702	159 777	138 771	125 275	114 879	(NA)
Oklahoma	48 683	49 709	49 012	1 515	170 613	49 992	45 289	38 997	35 733	602
Oregon	41 735	42 449	42 141	1 563	151 948	42 438	39 326	36 420	33 202	562
Pennsylvania	133 770	137 376	136 069	15 379	530 912	150 460	134 653	121 885	111 050	12 864
Rhode Island	11 586	11 515	11 032	2 905	39 984	11 922	10 530	9 113	8 263	156
South Carolina	51 322	52 214	51 308	(NA)	182 281	60 808	48 165	38 508	34 800	(NA)
South Dakota	11 143	11 583	11 654	1 116	43 194	12 176	11 388	10 090	9 116	424
Tennessee	66 227	68 309	66 513	16 251	243 169	74 398	64 144	55 308	49 319	(NA)
Texas	288 502	292 190	284 875	(NA)	990 894	335 819	255 132	213 714	186 229	(NA)
Utah	35 877	36 693	38 090	5 880	149 331	37 941	38 485	36 487	32 006	4 412
Vermont	8 553	8 352	8 006	(NA)	30 338	8 125	7 465	6 909	6 507	1 332
Virginia	82 996	81 619	81 254	29 285	291 909	86 779	76 045	66 764	62 204	117
Washington	75 313	75 875	75 052	(NA)	276 563	78 514	73 402	65 035	59 612	(NA)
West Virginia	22 825	24 521	25 089	1 365	96 104	26 261	24 769	22 052	21 844	1 178
Wisconsin	65 289	66 723	65 788	(NA)	267 211	74 700	70 262	64 458	57 791	(NA)
Wyoming	8 108	8 283	8 302	(NA)	30 928	8 293	8 430	7 526	6 679	(NA)

See footnotes at end of table.

Table C-8. Enrollment in Public Elementary and Secondary Schools, by Grade and State: Fall 1995 — Continued

(Numbers in thousands. Civilian noninstitutional population.)

State or other area	Prekindergarten through grade 8 and elementary unclassified				Grades 9 through 12 and secondary unclassified					
	Grade 6	Grade 7	Grade 8	Elementary unclassified	Total	Grade 9	Grade 10	Grade 11[2]	Grade 12	Secondary unclassified
Outlying areas										
American Samoa	1 042	941	951	(NA)	3 369	915	837	796	756	65
Guam	2 384	2 342	2 368	(NA)	8 083	2 862	2 122	1 666	1 433	(NA)
Northern Marianas ...	642	712	596	(NA)	1 984	575	536	406	467	(NA)
Puerto Rico	47 978	51 731	48 934	12 997	167 035	45 673	44 939	38 184	32 535	5 704
Virgin Islands	1 577	2 285	1 607	850	6 395	1 774	1 629	1 251	1 102	639

SOURCE: U.S. Department of Education, National Center for Education Statistics, Common Core of Data surveys. Published as table 41 in *Digest of Education Statistics* 1997.

1. Data include imputations for nonrespondents.
2. Includes imputations for underreporting.

(NA) Not applicable or not available.

Table C-9. Average Daily Attendance in Public Elementary and Secondary Schools, by State: 1969-70 to 1994-95

State or other area	1969-70	1979-80	1980-81	1985-86	1989-90	1990-91	1992-93	1993-94	1994-95
United States	41 934 376	38 288 911	37 703 744	36 523 103	37 799 296	38 426 543	39 570 462	40 146 393	40 720 763
Alabama	777 123	711 432	701 925	686 716	683 833	682 524	694 078	696 071	687 047
Alaska	72 489	79 945	83 745	98 535	98 213	102 585	110 797	112 869	113 874
Arizona	391 526	481 905	476 149	494 504	557 252	573 140	610 558	631 450	658 084
Arkansas	414 158	423 610	417 080	408 601	403 025	408 145	413 076	416 479	420 229
California[1]	4 418 423	4 044 736	4 014 917	4 245 090	4 893 341	5 065 647	5 066 708	5 108 907	5 198 308
Colorado	500 388	513 475	508 750	507 876	519 419	521 899	568 158	579 682	594 019
Connecticut	618 881	507 362	501 085	452 058	439 524	450 808	468 992	465 487	481 742
Delaware	120 819	94 058	89 609	84 936	89 838	91 052	95 660	97 247	98 793
District of Columbia	138 600	91 576	85 773	76 241	71 468	69 092	71 201	70 079	71 446
Florida	1 312 693	1 464 461	1 389 487	1 442 921	1 646 583	1 714 394	1 818 011	1 873 199	1 927 172
Georgia	1 019 427	989 433	988 612	1 004 799	1 054 097	1 075 728	1 125 385	1 148 319	1 181 724
Hawaii	168 140	151 563	151 713	151 174	157 360	160 193	165 851	169 779	169 254
Idaho	170 920	189 199	190 144	198 141	203 987	209 085	217 933	223 489	225 986
Illinois	2 084 844	1 770 435	1 765 357	1 604 265	1 587 733	1 618 101	1 685 678	1 709 915	1 734 175
Indiana	1 111 043	983 444	944 424	870 463	884 568	888 177	897 799	899 585	900 017
Iowa	624 403	510 081	501 403	454 341	450 224	456 614	467 788	477 916	478 285
Kansas	470 296	382 019	374 451	371 655	388 986	397 609	408 689	410 862	413 699
Kentucky	647 970	619 868	614 676	577 190	569 795	569 713	579 446	578 020	572 952
Louisiana	776 555	727 601	715 844	732 230	727 125	720 551	722 626	732 202	730 148
Maine	225 146	211 400	207 554	198 358	195 089	196 229	200 462	199 125	199 387
Maryland	785 989	686 336	664 866	592 383	620 617	637 370	668 778	687 455	701 594
Massachusetts	1 056 207	935 960	950 675	745 991	763 231	770 802	796 897	810 028	831 918
Michigan	1 991 235	1 758 427	1 711 139	1 481 068	1 446 996	1 452 700	1 467 900	1 474 413	1 492 653
Minnesota	864 595	748 606	710 836	669 385	699 001	714 072	744 567	756 725	770 549
Mississippi	524 623	454 401	446 515	448 117	476 048	474 029	473 262	471 367	470 974
Missouri	906 132	777 269	756 536	714 230	729 693	733 680	759 529	778 605	794 177
Montana	162 664	144 608	141 641	138 829	135 406	138 341	144 718	146 849	148 325
Nebraska	314 516	270 524	263 797	250 975	254 754	257 587	267 975	267 931	268 732
Nevada	113 421	134 995	138 481	143 941	173 149	185 755	204 440	217 681	229 862
New Hampshire	140 203	154 187	150 316	147 561	154 915	156 579	172 376	175 968	179 892
New Jersey	1 322 124	1 140 111	1 121 272	1 029 797	997 561	1 016 159	1 053 135	1 079 653	1 102 565
New Mexico	259 997	253 453	240 496	252 892	290 245	291 215	304 661	310 610	314 822
New York	3 099 192	2 530 289	2 475 055	2 276 842	2 244 110	2 278 531	2 347 468	2 404 426	2 388 973
North Carolina	1 104 295	1 072 150	1 055 651	1 014 795	1 012 274	1 012 613	1 035 258	1 051 295	1 071 640
North Dakota	141 961	118 986	111 759	108 947	109 659	109 691	111 174	111 770	111 502
Ohio	2 246 282	1 849 283	1 801 914	1 660 718	1 584 735	1 603 025	1 594 191	1 609 855	1 627 984
Oklahoma	560 993	548 065	542 800	553 370	543 170	548 387	560 744	566 155	570 381
Oregon	436 736	418 593	417 009	401 476	419 771	431 806	452 509	455 492	458 107
Pennsylvania	2 169 225	1 808 630	1 754 782	1 560 746	1 524 839	1 542 077	1 588 514	1 609 125	1 629 877
Rhode Island	163 205	139 195	135 096	122 109	125 934	129 856	134 736	135 016	136 229
South Carolina	600 292	569 612	580 132	558 716	569 029	573 138	581 775	586 178	608 699
South Dakota	158 543	124 934	121 663	118 269	119 823	121 403	126 916	127 550	128 335
Tennessee	836 010	806 696	797 237	762 225	761 766	767 738	786 146	796 744	806 895
Texas	2 432 420	2 608 817	2 647 288	2 923 741	3 075 333	3 085 648	3 237 958	3 306 297	3 364 830
Utah	287 405	312 813	323 048	379 249	408 917	417 609	432 781	439 484	442 617
Vermont	97 772	95 045	90 884	85 875	87 832	88 901	96 121	97 550	98 608
Virginia	995 580	955 105	938 794	904 347	989 197	1 011 513	1 049 901	1 065 071	1 079 496
Washington	764 735	710 929	704 655	696 372	755 141	781 371	833 641	850 813	870 163
West Virginia	372 278	353 264	351 823	330 145	301 947	300 067	294 202	291 238	287 937
Wisconsin	880 609	770 554	743 505	694 351	711 466	731 088	765 184	769 717	782 395
Wyoming	81 293	89 471	91 381	95 547	91 277	92 506	94 109	94 650	93 691
Outlying areas									
American Samoa	(NA)	(NA)	(NA)	10 816	11 448	12 272	14 150	14 094	14 000
Guam	20 315	(NA)	22 343	23 220	23 883	25 330	30 417	31 711	31 779
Northern Marianas	(NA)	(NA)	(NA)	4 921	6 809	6 062	7 334	7 278	7 351
Puerto Rico	(NA)	656 709	671 661	636 268	597 436	597 418	548 067	588 484	547 561
Virgin Islands	(NA)	(NA)	23 312	23 811	18 924	19 984	20 624	20 381	20 339

SOURCE: U.S. Department of Education, National Center for Education Statistics, Revenues and Expenditures for Public Elementary and Secondary Education; Statistics of State School Systems; and Common Core of Data survey. Published as table 44 in *Digest of Education Statistics* 1997.

1. Data for California are not strictly comparable with those for other states because California's attendance figures through 1990-91 include excused absences.

(NA) Not applicable or not available.

Table C-10. Enrollment in Public Elementary and Secondary Schools, by Race or Ethnicity and State: Fall 1986 and Fall 1995

State or other area	Percent distribution, fall 1986						Percent distribution, fall 1995					
	Total	White[1]	Black[1]	Hispanic	Asian or Pacific Islander	American Indian/ Alaskan Native	Total	White[1]	Black[1]	Hispanic	Asian or Pacific Islander	American Indian/ Alaskan Native
United States	100.0	70.4	16.1	9.9	2.8	0.9	100.0	64.8	16.8	13.5	3.7	1.1
Alabama	100.0	62.0	37.0	0.1	0.4	0.5	100.0	62.1	36.0	0.5	0.6	0.7
Alaska	100.0	65.7	4.3	1.7	3.3	25.1	100.0	63.7	4.6	2.7	4.4	24.5
Arizona	100.0	62.2	4.0	26.4	1.3	6.1	100.0	56.9	4.3	30.0	1.7	7.2
Arkansas	100.0	74.7	24.2	0.4	0.6	0.2	100.0	73.9	23.6	1.5	0.7	0.4
California	100.0	53.7	9.0	27.5	9.1	0.7	100.0	40.4	8.8	38.7	11.2	0.9
Colorado	100.0	78.7	4.5	13.7	2.0	1.0	100.0	72.5	5.5	18.4	2.5	1.1
Connecticut	100.0	77.2	12.1	8.9	1.5	0.2	100.0	72.0	13.5	11.8	2.4	0.3
Delaware	100.0	68.3	27.7	2.5	1.4	0.2	100.0	64.7	29.4	4.0	1.7	0.2
District of Columbia	100.0	4.0	91.1	3.9	0.9	0.1	100.0	4.0	87.6	7.0	1.4	(2)
Florida	100.0	65.4	23.7	9.5	1.2	0.2	100.0	57.5	25.3	15.3	1.8	0.2
Georgia	100.0	60.7	37.9	0.6	0.8	(2)	100.0	58.2	37.8	2.2	1.6	0.1
Hawaii	100.0	23.5	2.3	2.2	71.7	0.3	100.0	22.9	2.6	4.9	69.3	0.4
Idaho	100.0	92.6	0.3	4.9	0.8	1.3	100.0	88.4	0.6	8.4	1.2	1.3
Illinois	100.0	69.8	18.7	9.2	2.3	0.1	100.0	63.6	21.1	12.2	3.0	0.1
Indiana	100.0	88.7	9.0	1.7	0.5	0.1	100.0	85.6	11.1	2.3	0.8	0.2
Iowa	100.0	94.6	3.0	0.9	1.2	0.3	100.0	92.7	3.3	2.1	1.5	0.4
Kansas	100.0	85.6	7.6	4.4	1.9	0.6	100.0	82.6	8.5	6.0	1.8	1.1
Kentucky	100.0	89.2	10.2	0.1	0.5	(2)	100.0	89.1	9.8	0.4	0.6	0.1
Louisiana	100.0	56.5	41.3	0.8	1.1	0.3	100.0	51.0	46.0	1.1	1.3	0.5
Maine	100.0	98.3	0.5	0.2	0.8	0.2	100.0	97.3	0.8	0.4	0.9	0.6
Maryland	100.0	59.7	35.3	1.7	3.1	0.2	100.0	57.5	35.0	3.3	3.8	0.3
Massachusetts	100.0	83.7	7.4	6.0	2.8	0.1	100.0	78.5	8.2	9.3	3.8	0.2
Michigan	100.0	76.4	19.0	1.8	1.2	0.8	100.0	76.4	18.4	2.7	1.5	1.0
Minnesota	100.0	93.9	2.1	0.9	1.7	1.5	100.0	87.4	4.8	2.0	3.9	1.9
Mississippi	100.0	43.9	55.5	0.1	0.4	0.1	100.0	47.7	51.0	0.3	0.6	0.4
Missouri	100.0	83.4	14.9	0.7	0.8	0.2	100.0	81.7	16.1	1.0	1.0	0.2
Montana	100.0	92.7	0.3	0.9	0.5	5.5	100.0	87.5	0.5	1.4	0.8	9.8
Nebraska	100.0	91.4	4.4	2.4	0.8	1.0	100.0	87.2	5.9	4.4	1.3	1.4
Nevada	100.0	77.4	9.6	7.5	3.2	2.3	100.0	66.5	9.8	17.2	4.5	1.9
New Hampshire	100.0	98.0	0.7	0.5	0.8	0.1	100.0	96.7	0.9	1.2	1.1	0.2
New Jersey	100.0	69.1	17.4	10.7	2.7	0.1	100.0	62.5	18.5	13.5	5.4	0.2
New Mexico	100.0	43.1	2.3	45.1	0.8	8.7	100.0	39.5	2.4	46.8	1.0	10.4
New York	100.0	68.4	16.5	12.3	2.7	0.2	100.0	56.9	20.2	17.4	5.0	0.4
North Carolina	100.0	68.4	28.9	0.4	0.6	1.7	100.0	64.6	30.7	1.9	1.3	1.5
North Dakota	100.0	92.4	0.6	1.1	0.8	5.0	100.0	90.8	0.8	1.1	0.8	6.6
Ohio	100.0	83.1	15.0	1.0	0.7	0.1	100.0	82.2	15.3	1.4	1.0	0.1
Oklahoma	100.0	79.0	7.8	1.6	1.0	10.6	100.0	69.4	10.5	3.9	1.3	15.0
Oregon	100.0	89.8	2.2	3.9	2.4	1.7	100.0	85.3	2.6	6.8	3.4	2.0
Pennsylvania	100.0	84.4	12.6	1.8	1.2	0.1	100.0	80.6	14.0	3.5	1.8	0.1
Rhode Island	100.0	87.9	5.6	3.7	2.4	0.3	100.0	78.9	7.0	10.3	3.3	0.5
South Carolina	100.0	54.6	44.5	0.2	0.6	0.1	100.0	56.3	42.1	0.7	0.8	0.2
South Dakota	100.0	90.6	0.5	0.6	0.7	7.6	100.0	83.7	0.9	0.7	0.7	13.9
Tennessee	100.0	76.5	22.6	0.2	0.6	(2)	100.0	75.3	23.1	0.7	0.8	0.1
Texas	100.0	51.0	14.4	32.5	2.0	0.2	100.0	46.4	14.3	36.7	2.3	0.3
Utah	100.0	93.7	0.4	3.0	1.5	1.5	100.0	90.4	0.7	5.3	2.2	1.4
Vermont	100.0	98.4	0.3	0.2	0.6	0.6	100.0	97.3	0.7	0.4	1.0	0.6
Virginia	100.0	72.6	23.7	1.0	2.6	0.1	100.0	66.6	26.5	3.2	3.5	0.2
Washington	100.0	84.5	4.2	3.8	5.1	2.3	100.0	78.3	4.7	7.8	6.5	2.6
West Virginia	100.0	95.9	3.7	0.1	0.3	(2)	100.0	95.2	4.0	0.3	0.4	0.1
Wisconsin	100.0	86.6	8.9	1.9	1.7	1.0	100.0	83.2	9.4	3.3	2.8	1.3
Wyoming	100.0	90.7	0.9	5.9	0.6	1.9	100.0	89.3	1.0	6.1	0.8	2.7

See footnotes at end of table.

Table C-10. Enrollment in Public Elementary and Secondary Schools, by Race or Ethnicity and State: Fall 1986 and Fall 1995 — Continued

State or other area	Percent distribution, fall 1986						Percent distribution, fall 1995					
	Total	White[1]	Black[1]	Hispanic	Asian or Pacific Islander	American Indian/ Alaskan Native	Total	White[1]	Black[1]	Hispanic	Asian or Pacific Islander	American Indian/ Alaskan Native
Outlying areas												
American Samoa	(NA)	(NA)	(NA)	(NA)	(NA)	(NA)	100.0	(NA)	(NA)	(NA)	100.0	(NA)
Guam	(NA)	(NA)	(NA)	(NA)	(NA)	(NA)	100.0	6.7	1.3	0.5	91.5	(NA)
Northern Marianas	(NA)	(NA)	(NA)	(NA)	(NA)	(NA)	100.0	0.7	(NA)	(NA)	99.3	(NA)
Puerto Rico	(NA)	(NA)	(NA)	(NA)	(NA)	(NA)	100.0	(NA)	(NA)	100.0	(NA)	(NA)
Virgin Islands	(NA)	(NA)	(NA)	(NA)	(NA)	(NA)	100.0	0.9	84.5	14.3	0.4	(NA)

SOURCE: U.S. Department of Education, National Center for Education Statistics, Revenues and Expenditures for Public Elementary and Secondary Education; Statistics of State School Systems; and Common Core of Data survey. Published as table 45 in *Digest of Education Statistics* 1997.

1. Excludes persons of Hispanic origin.
2. Less than 0.05 percent.

NOTE: The 1986-87 data were derived from the 1986 Elementary and Secondary School Civil Rights sample survey of public school districts. Because of rounding, details may not add to totals.

(NA) Not applicable or not available.

Table C-11. State Legislation on Gifted and Talented Programs and Number and Percent of Students Receiving Services in Public Elementary and Secondary Schools, by State; 1993-94 and 1995-96

State or other area	State-mandated gifted and talented programs 1995-1996[1]	Discretionary state-supported gifted and talented programs 1995-96[2]	Gifted and talented students receiving services 1993-94	Gifted and talented students as a percent of enrollment 1993-94
Alabama	X		16 522	2.4
Alaska	X		4 696	4.0
Arizona	X		39 200	—
Arkansas	X		34 710	8.0
California		X	290 000	5.0
Colorado		X	—	—
Connecticut	X		16 871	3.5
Delaware		X	—	5.0
District of Columbia	—	—	—	9.0
Florida	X		74 572	3.5
Georgia	—	—	—	5.0
Hawaii	X		18 000	11.0
Idaho	X		—	1.3
Illinois	X		166 234	5.0
Indiana		X	85 192	8.9
Iowa	X		—	4.0
Kansas	X		—	0.1
Kentucky	X		52 600	5.0
Louisiana	X		24 000	3.2
Maine	X		10 100	5.0
Maryland		X	90 222	12.0
Massachusetts		X	—	—
Michigan		X	225 154	14.0
Minnesota		X	55 467	7.2
Mississippi	X		21 678	4.3
Missouri		X	24 877	5.0
Montana	X		—	—
Nebraska	X		18 600	10.0
Nevada		X	8 343	2.0
New Hampshire		X	—	—
New Jersey	—	—	—	—
New Mexico	X		—	—
New York	X		135 000	6.0
North Carolina	X		88 450	8.0
North Dakota		X	1 107	1.0
Ohio	X		244 670	13.0
Oklahoma	X		61 082	10.0
Oregon	X		—	8.5
Pennsylvania	X		79 756	4.6
Rhode Island		X	—	3.5-5.0
South Carolina	X		52 000	10.0
South Dakota		X	6 515	4.4
Tennessee	X		18 626	2.0
Texas	X		248 769	7.0
Utah	X		—	—
Vermont	—	—	—	—
Virginia	X		121 598	9.2
Washington		X	38 781	1.5
West Virginia	X		—	3.5
Wisconsin	X		—	15.0
Wyoming		X	—	3.0
Guam	X		—	—

SOURCE: Council of State Directors of Programs for the Gifted, The 1994 and 1996 State of the States Gifted and Talented Education Reports. Published as table 54 in *Digest of Education Statistics* 1997.

1. Mandate requiring identification of and/or services for gifted/talented students.
2. No mandate requiring identification of or services for gifted/talented students.
3. Grades 2 through 6 only.
4. Data for 1991-92.

— Represents zero or rounds to zero.

Table C-12. Number of Children Served under Individuals with Disabilities Education Act and Chapter 1 of the Education Consolidation and Improvement Act, State Operated Programs, by Age Group and State: 1990-91 to 1995-96

State	Birth to age 21				Percent of students that are disabled 1995-96[1]	Ages 0 to 5				Percent change, birth to 21, 1990-91 to 1995-96
	1990-91	1993-94	1994-95	1995-96		1990-91	1993-94	1994-95	1995-96	
United States	4 761 742	5 308 660	5 377 868	5 573 350	12.4	440 661	578 225	518 746	544 436	17.0
Alabama	94 945	99 760	99 171	98 266	13.2	7 498	9 161	8 498	8 594	3.5
Alaska	14 745	18 006	17 552	17 604	13.8	1 813	2 633	2 068	2 015	19.4
Arizona	57 235	69 530	72 443	76 089	10.2	4 936	7 685	7 277	7 880	32.9
Arkansas	47 835	53 187	52 637	53 880	11.9	5 274	6 972	6 901	7 520	12.6
California	469 282	533 807	544 018	565 670	10.2	40 489	52 061	51 990	54 795	20.5
Colorado	57 102	66 343	68 037	69 850	10.6	4 894	6 985	6 753	7 153	22.3
Connecticut	64 562	71 863	73 792	76 123	14.7	6 142	7 875	6 961	7 338	17.9
Delaware	14 294	15 196	15 424	15 624	14.4	1 579	1 953	2 010	1 905	9.3
District of Columbia	6 290	6 994	6 627	7 058	8.8	411	600	338	387	12.2
Florida	236 013	286 772	294 608	310 184	14.3	16 387	29 879	25 177	27 080	31.4
Georgia	101 997	123 143	129 212	135 042	10.3	7 333	11 869	12 789	13 314	32.4
Hawaii	13 169	15 348	15 137	16 029	8.6	1 273	1 890	1 199	1 306	21.7
Idaho	22 017	23 571	22 868	23 826	9.8	3 129	3 657	2 980	3 091	8.2
Illinois	239 185	250 829	250 524	257 427	13.2	26 122	27 985	24 258	25 432	7.6
Indiana	114 643	127 961	128 576	133 962	13.7	8 937	12 874	11 065	12 261	16.9
Iowa	60 695	63 373	64 028	65 952	13.1	6 329	6 633	5 673	5 838	8.7
Kansas	45 212	50 438	51 661	53 602	11.6	4 308	6 421	5 856	6 135	18.6
Kentucky	79 421	80 539	80 687	82 887	12.6	11 008	13 668	14 009	14 683	4.4
Louisiana	73 663	86 931	88 711	91 059	11.4	7 541	11 083	9 658	9 588	23.6
Maine	27 987	29 350	30 562	31 870	14.9	2 895	2 873	3 220	3 553	13.9
Maryland	91 940	97 998	96 771	100 863	12.5	10 409	12 018	9 052	9 486	9.7
Massachusetts	154 616	160 275	156 670	157 196	17.2	17 014	21 163	14 267	14 241	1.7
Michigan	166 927	181 251	182 833	188 768	11.5	14 963	19 748	17 664	18 241	13.1
Minnesota	80 896	90 850	93 975	98 311	11.8	10 529	12 725	10 758	10 781	21.5
Mississippi	60 934	64 153	65 490	66 804	13.2	5 704	5 896	6 449	6 607	9.6
Missouri	101 955	114 008	116 826	121 407	13.6	4 889	9 108	7 975	8 395	19.1
Montana	17 204	18 401	17 679	18 364	11.1	1 934	2 131	1 635	1 766	6.7
Nebraska	32 761	37 203	38 026	39 201	13.5	2 961	3 728	3 311	3 304	19.7
Nevada	18 440	25 242	26 363	28 202	10.6	1 742	3 215	2 900	3 166	52.9
New Hampshire	19 658	23 354	23 754	25 150	13.0	2 077	2 561	1 996	2 165	27.9
New Jersey	181 319	190 003	191 912	197 062	16.5	17 190	18 025	15 942	16 639	8.7
New Mexico	36 037	43 474	45 364	47 578	14.4	2 247	3 631	4 116	4 563	32.0
New York	307 458	365 697	374 361	394 104	14.0	26 353	46 243	45 009	47 972	28.2
North Carolina	123 126	136 513	139 513	147 078	12.4	10 700	15 042	15 133	16 671	19.5
North Dakota	12 504	12 440	12 176	12 355	10.4	1 374	1 336	1 119	1 169	-1.2
Ohio	205 440	219 875	223 640	227 529	12.4	12 487	16 347	18 193	18 204	10.8
Oklahoma	65 653	73 130	70 809	71 728	11.6	5 359	6 627	4 970	5 312	9.3
Oregon	55 149	63 212	59 363	65 022	12.3	3 581	5 859	4 774	6 097	17.9
Pennsylvania	219 428	211 422	207 436	211 711	11.8	23 156	24 312	19 715	20 680	-3.5
Rhode Island	21 076	23 582	23 693	25 072	16.7	2 112	2 798	2 131	2 333	19.0
South Carolina	77 765	81 930	82 626	86 522	13.4	8 346	10 571	9 904	10 319	11.3
South Dakota	14 987	15 907	15 755	15 512	10.7	2 366	2 518	2 227	2 176	3.5
Tennessee	104 898	119 146	123 753	126 461	14.1	7 536	11 799	9 825	10 151	20.6
Texas	350 636	411 917	420 540	441 543	11.8	30 955	38 059	30 647	32 262	25.9
Utah	47 747	51 950	51 218	52 463	11.0	4 565	5 256	4 568	4 861	9.9
Vermont	12 263	10 513	10 718	11 242	10.6	1 200	1 232	1 184	1 215	-8.3
Virginia	113 971	131 599	136 166	141 759	13.1	11 791	14 271	12 746	13 284	24.4
Washington	85 395	101 254	104 483	106 890	11.2	11 409	14 392	12 830	12 565	25.2
West Virginia	43 135	44 528	45 315	46 487	15.1	3 630	5 298	4 461	4 842	7.8
Wisconsin	86 930	102 412	102 215	106 413	12.2	12 213	15 648	13 070	13 545	22.4
Wyoming	11 202	12 480	12 150	12 549	12.6	1 571	1 911	1 495	1 556	12.0

SOURCE: U.S. Department of Education, National Center for Education Statistics, Revenues and Expenditures for Public Elementary and Secondary Education; Statistics of State School Systems; and Common Core of Data survey. Published as table 55 in *Digest of Education Statistics* 1997.

1. Percent based on the enrollment in public schools, prekindergarten through 12th grade.

NOTE: Individuals with Disabilities Education Act (IDEA), formerly known as the Education of the Handicapped Act, now extends the right to a free and appropriate education to 3- to 5-year-old disabled children.

Table C-13. Private Elementary and Secondary Schools, Enrollment, FTE Teachers, and High School Graduates, by State: United States, 1995-96

State or other area	Number of schools	Enrollment	Teachers	High school graduates, 1994-95
United States	27 686	5 032 200	361 909	245 543
Alabama	287	66 958	4 814	3 581
Alaska	65	6 113	530	178
Arizona	296	44 134	3 070	2 221
Arkansas	245	27 454	2 081	1 081
California	3 470	629 344	41 073	26 353
Colorado	342	48 977	3 843	1 928
Connecticut	355	70 605	6 381	5 166
Delaware	112	25 528	1 878	1 436
District of Columbia	84	17 468	1 852	1 242
Florida	1 284	253 831	19 093	10 151
Georgia	525	97 807	8 282	5 075
Hawaii	127	34 541	2 532	2 603
Idaho	77	9 210	607	380
Illinois	1 470	300 981	18 617	14 681
Indiana	661	99 258	6 653	4 055
Iowa	274	49 461	3 309	2 601
Kansas	265	39 306	2 623	1 621
Kentucky	382	67 181	4 581	3 242
Louisiana	647	147 147	9 849	7 457
Maine	134	16 896	1 531	1 759
Maryland	606	125 092	10 142	6 235
Massachusetts	655	12 569	11 068	8 561
Michigan	1 034	189 065	11 550	8 805
Minnesota	570	8 647	5 835	3 373
Mississippi	18	5 016	3 447	3 174
Missouri	775	126 985	9 162	5 894
Montana	88	8 458	673	356
Nebraska	279	41 320	2 695	1 783
Nevada	63	12 251	711	381
New Hampshire	[2] 10	22 633	2 101	1 730
New Jersey	914	207 275	15 585	12 030
New Mexico	194	22 893	1 756	947
New York	1 997	466 239	35 328	25 489
North Carolina	542	81 437	6 990	3 144
North Dakota	55	7 321	523	381
Ohio	1 071	255 277	15 085	12 639
Oklahoma	135	24 653	2 014	1 296
Oregon	[2] 410	43 501	3 431	2 042
Pennsylvania	1 894	346 800	23 085	18 138
Rhode Island	128	23 543	1 941	1 354
South Carolina	282	50 162	3 943	2 378
South Dakota	93	10 056	724	436
Tennessee	504	80 701	6 388	4 427
Texas	1 593	229 353	19 042	8 767
Utah	[2] 97	12 840	1 013	590
Vermont	84	9 669	977	1 081
Virginia	493	86 507	7 723	4 463
Washington	504	74 890	5 132	2 998
West Virginia	135	13 241	1 113	698
Wisconsin	961	143 231	9 312	5 119
Wyoming	37	2 272	221	24

SOURCE: U. S. Department of Education, National Center for Education Statistics, Private School Survey, 1995– 96. Published as Table 17 in Private School Universe Survey, 1995-96, *Statistical Analysis Report NCES 98-229*, issued March 1998.

1. NCES employed an area frame sample to account for noninclusion of schools at the national level. However, caution should be exercised in interpreting state by state characteristics since the samples were not designed to represent the states.
2. The coefficient of variation for this estimate is larger than 25 percent. The standard error for this estimate is presented in the corresponding table in appendix A of the report indicated below.

Table C-14. Public Elementary and Secondary Teachers, by Level and State: Fall 1991 to Fall 1996

State or other area	Fall 1991	Fall 1992	Fall 1993	Fall 1994[1]				Fall 1995[1]				Estimated, 1996[2]
				Total	Elementary	Secondary	Unclassified	Total	Elementary	Secondary	Unclassified	
United States	2 432 243	2 458 956	2 503 901	2 551 875	1 419 749	911 671	220 455	2 598 220	1 428 852	952 189	217 179	[3] 2 637 846
Alabama	40 480	41 961	43 003	42 791	24 170	18 423	198	44 056	24 935	19 121	(NA)	[4] 42 492
Alaska	7 118	7 282	7 193	7 205	4 666	2 539	(NA)	7 379	4 780	2 599	(NA)	7 644
Arizona	33 978	36 076	37 493	38 132	27 595	10 537	(NA)	38 017	27 518	10 499	(NA)	[3] 39 315
Arkansas	25 785	26 017	26 014	26 181	13 884	12 160	137	26 449	13 882	12 370	197	29 194
California	224 000	218 566	221 787	225 016	142 810	58 586	23 620	230 849	145 601	60 743	24 505	228 028
Colorado	33 093	33 419	33 661	34 894	18 008	16 886	(NA)	35 388	17 998	17 390	(NA)	35 900
Connecticut	34 383	34 193	34 526	35 316	20 745	9 340	5 231	36 070	21 230	9 445	5 395	36 800
Delaware	6 095	6 252	6 380	6 416	3 215	3 201	(NA)	6 463	3 205	3 258	(NA)	6 642
District of Columbia	6 346	6 064	6 056	6 110	3 497	2 173	440	5 305	3 083	1 815	407	[3] 5 398
Florida	109 939	107 590	110 653	110 674	48 150	40 893	21 631	114 938	50 660	42 745	21 533	[4] 120 450
Georgia	63 816	66 942	74 172	77 914	56 211	21 703	(NA)	79 480	40 888	38 592	(NA)	81 683
Hawaii	9 451	10 083	10 111	10 240	5 770	4 425	45	10 500	5 843	4 616	41	10 675
Idaho	11 626	11 827	12 007	12 582	6 388	6 018	176	12 784	6 505	6 122	157	13 059
Illinois	110 153	111 461	110 874	110 830	66 462	28 619	15 749	113 538	67 972	29 208	16 358	115 859
Indiana	54 509	54 552	55 107	55 496	27 527	25 251	2 718	55 821	28 257	24 881	2 683	56 412
Iowa	31 395	31 403	31 616	31 726	18 662	11 973	1 091	32 318	19 151	12 063	1 104	32 549
Kansas	29 324	29 753	30 283	30 579	14 823	12 763	2 993	30 729	14 752	12 878	3 099	30 750
Kentucky	37 571	37 868	37 324	38 784	27 054	11 730	(NA)	39 120	27 422	11 698	(NA)	39 235
Louisiana	46 170	46 904	46 913	47 599	26 916	12 176	8 507	46 980	27 691	19 289	(NA)	48 047
Maine	15 416	15 375	15 344	15 404	10 524	4 880	(NA)	15 392	10 553	4 839	(NA)	14 458
Maryland	43 616	44 495	44 171	46 565	25 792	20 773	(NA)	47 819	24 999	22 820	(NA)	47 005
Massachusetts	55 963	57 225	58 766	60 489	22 342	29 922	8 225	62 710	23 121	30 891	8 698	[3] 65 863
Michigan	82 967	82 301	80 267	80 522	34 846	36 701	8 975	83 179	36 406	38 200	8 573	84 200
Minnesota	44 903	45 050	46 956	46 958	23 980	22 948	30	46 971	23 979	22 983	9	47 600
Mississippi	28 111	27 829	28 376	28 866	15 071	8 864	4 931	28 997	15 047	9 070	4 880	29 237
Missouri	52 643	52 984	54 860	56 606	29 054	26 782	770	57 951	29 386	27 817	748	59 222
Montana	9 883	10 135	9 949	10 079	7 009	3 070	(NA)	10 076	6 974	3 102	(NA)	10 110
Nebraska	19 069	19 323	19 616	19 774	11 368	8 406	(NA)	20 028	11 452	8 506	70	[4] 20 109
Nevada	11 409	11 953	12 579	13 414	6 784	5 058	1 572	13 878	7 057	5 210	1 611	[4] 764
New Hampshire	11 464	11 654	11 972	12 109	8 158	3 951	(NA)	12 346	8 447	3 899	(NA)	12 394
New Jersey	80 515	83 057	84 564	85 258	47 280	26 439	11 539	86 706	48 359	26 362	11 985	[3] 90 703
New Mexico	17 498	17 912	18 404	19 025	11 265	4 342	3 418	19 398	11 311	4 518	3 569	[4] 19 608
New York	171 914	176 375	179 413	182 273	91 408	63 928	26 937	181 559	92 550	62 355	26 654	185 063
North Carolina	65 326	66 630	69 421	71 592	42 480	24 700	4 412	73 201	42 990	25 795	4 416	73 839
North Dakota	7 733	7 794	7 755	7 796	5 223	2 573	(NA)	7 501	5 061	2 440	(NA)	7 706
Ohio	103 372	106 233	107 444	109 085	72 005	36 912	168	107 347	71 376	35 718	253	104 583
Oklahoma	37 650	38 433	39 031	39 406	18 735	16 517	4 154	39 364	18 582	16 601	4 181	39 350
Oregon	26 745	26 634	26 488	26 208	14 128	8 484	3 596	26 680	13 889	8 981	3 810	26 757
Pennsylvania	100 475	100 912	101 302	102 988	46 918	43 798	12 272	104 921	47 975	44 455	12 491	106 400
Rhode Island	9 709	10 069	9 823	10 066	4 597	4 090	1 379	10 482	4 540	4 477	1 465	10 586
South Carolina	37 115	37 295	38 620	39 437	26 820	12 617	(NA)	39 922	27 122	12 800	(NA)	40 640
South Dakota	8 868	8 767	9 557	9 985	6 098	2 738	1 149	9 641	5 889	2 676	1 076	9 474
Tennessee	43 062	43 566	46 066	47 406	33 039	12 795	1 572	53 403	37 969	13 939	1 495	51 369
Texas	219 192	219 385	224 830	234 213	116 999	85 987	31 227	240 371	118 881	88 843	32 647	[2] 47 526
Utah	18 305	19 191	19 053	19 524	9 041	8 056	2 427	20 039	9 162	8 390	2 487	[4] 20 224
Vermont	7 031	7 521	7 330	7 566	3 131	2 952	1 483	7 676	3 129	2 969	1 578	7 952
Virginia	64 537	68 181	70 859	72 505	44 246	28 259	(NA)	74 731	46 225	28 506	(NA)	80 896
Washington	42 931	44 295	45 524	46 439	24 077	18 247	4 115	46 907	24 423	18 501	3 983	[4] 47 479
West Virginia	20 997	20 961	21 029	21 024	10 212	7 244	3 568	21 073	10 600	6 788	3 685	20 642
Wisconsin	52 028	53 387	52 822	54 054	37 235	16 819	(NA)	55 033	36 808	17 015	1 210	55 296
Wyoming	6 564	5 821	6 537	6 754	3 331	3 423	(NA)	6 734	3 217	3 391	126	6 700

See footnotes at end of table.

Table C-14. Public Elementary and Secondary Teachers, by Level and State: Fall 1991 to Fall 1996 — Continued

State or other area	Fall 1991	Fall 1992	Fall 1993	Fall 1994[1]				Fall 1995[1]				Estimated, 1996[2]
				Total	Elementary	Secondary	Unclassified	Total	Elementary	Secondary	Unclassified	
Outlying areas												
American Samoa	671	725	656	698	484	196	18	728	521	192	15	[3] 754
Guam	1 499	1 628	1 644	1 826	870	784	172	1 802	801	825	176	[3] 1 893
Northern Marianas ...	430	425	431	406	224	182	(NA)	422	240	182	(NA)	[4] 421
Puerto Rico	37 291	38 381	39 816	39 933	22 001	14 617	3 315	39 328	21 680	14 386	3 262	39 748
Virgin Islands	1 581	1 595	1 570	1 528	757	703	68	1 622	731	814	77	1 636

SOURCE: U.S. Department of Education, National Center for Education Statistics, Revenues and Expenditures for Public Elementary and Secondary Education; Statistics of State School Systems; and Common Core of Data survey. Published as table 65 in *Digest of Education Statistics* 1997.

1. Data have been revised from previously published figures.
2. Data estimated by state education agencies.
3. Data imputed by the National Center for Education Statistics based on previous year's data.
4. Actual preliminary count by state.

NOTE: Distribution of elementary and secondary teachers determined by reporting units. Teachers reported in full-time equivalents.

(NA) Not applicable or not available.

Table C-15. Teachers, Enrollment, and Pupil-teacher Ratios in Public Elementary and Secondary Schools, by State: Fall 1990 to Fall 1995

State or other area	Pupil-teacher ratio, fall 1990	Pupil-teacher ratio, fall 1991	Pupil-teacher ratio, fall 1992	Fall 1993			Fall 1994			Fall 1995		
				Teachers	Enrollment	Pupil-teacher ratio	Teachers	Enrollment	Pupil-teacher ratio	Teachers	Enrollment	Pupil-teacher ratio
United States	17.2	17.3	17.4	2 503 901	43 464 916	17.4	2 551 875	44 111 482	17.3	2 598 220	44 840 481	17.3
Alabama	19.9	17.8	17.4	43 003	734 288	17.1	42 791	736 531	17.2	44 056	746 149	16.9
Alaska	17.0	16.7	16.8	7 193	125 948	17.5	7 205	127 057	17.6	7 379	127 618	17.3
Arizona	19.4	19.3	18.7	37 493	709 453	18.9	38 132	737 424	19.3	38 017	743 566	19.6
Arkansas	16.8	17.0	17.0	26 014	444 271	17.1	26 181	447 565	17.1	26 449	453 257	17.1
California	22.8	22.8	24.0	221 787	5 327 231	24.0	225 016	5 407 475	24.0	230 849	5 536 406	24.0
Colorado	17.8	17.9	18.3	33 661	625 062	18.6	34 894	640 521	18.4	35 388	656 279	18.5
Connecticut	13.5	14.0	14.3	34 526	496 298	14.4	35 316	506 824	14.4	36 070	517 935	14.4
Delaware	16.7	16.8	16.7	6 380	105 547	16.5	6 416	106 813	16.6	6 463	108 461	16.8
District of Columbia ..	13.6	12.7	13.3	6 056	80 678	13.3	6 110	80 450	13.2	5 305	79 802	15.0
Florida	17.2	17.6	18.4	110 653	2 040 763	18.4	110 674	2 111 188	19.1	114 938	2 176 222	18.9
Georgia	18.3	18.5	18.0	74 172	1 235 304	16.7	77 914	1 270 948	16.3	79 480	1 311 126	16.5
Hawaii	18.9	18.5	17.6	10 111	180 410	17.8	10 240	183 795	17.9	10 500	187 180	17.8
Idaho	19.6	19.4	19.6	12 007	236 774	19.7	12 582	240 448	19.1	12 784	243 097	19.0
Illinois	16.7	16.8	16.8	110 874	1 893 078	17.1	110 830	1 916 172	17.3	113 538	1 943 623	17.1
Indiana	17.4	17.6	17.6	55 107	965 633	17.5	55 496	969 022	17.5	55 821	977 263	17.5
Iowa	15.6	15.7	15.8	31 616	498 519	15.8	31 726	500 440	15.8	32 318	502 343	15.5
Kansas	15.0	15.2	15.2	30 283	457 614	15.1	30 579	460 838	15.1	30 729	463 008	15.1
Kentucky	17.3	17.2	17.3	37 324	655 265	17.6	38 784	657 642	17.0	39 120	659 821	16.9
Louisiana	17.3	16.6	17.0	46 913	800 560	17.1	47 599	797 933	16.8	46 980	797 366	16.6
Maine	13.9	14.0	14.1	15 344	216 995	14.1	15 404	212 601	13.8	15 392	213 569	13.9
Maryland	16.8	16.9	16.9	44 171	772 638	17.5	46 565	790 938	17.0	47 819	805 544	16.8
Massachusetts	15.4	15.1	15.0	58 766	877 726	14.9	60 489	893 727	14.8	62 710	915 007	14.6
Michigan	19.8	19.2	19.5	80 267	1 599 377	19.9	80 522	1 614 784	20.1	83 179	1 641 456	19.7
Minnesota	17.4	17.2	17.6	46 956	810 233	17.3	46 958	821 693	17.5	46 971	835 166	17.8
Mississippi	17.9	17.9	18.2	28 376	505 907	17.8	28 866	505 962	17.5	28 997	506 272	17.5
Missouri	15.6	16.0	16.2	54 860	866 378	15.8	56 606	878 541	15.5	57 951	889 881	15.4
Montana	15.9	15.8	15.8	9 949	163 009	16.4	10 079	164 341	16.3	10 076	165 547	16.4
Nebraska	14.6	14.7	14.6	19 616	285 097	14.5	19 774	287 100	14.5	20 028	289 744	14.5
Nevada	19.4	18.6	18.7	12 579	235 800	18.7	13 414	250 747	18.7	13 878	265 041	19.1
New Hampshire	16.2	15.5	15.6	11 972	185 360	15.5	12 109	189 319	15.6	12 346	194 171	15.7
New Jersey	13.6	13.8	13.6	84 564	1 151 307	13.6	85 258	1 174 206	13.8	86 706	1 197 381	13.8
New Mexico	18.1	17.6	17.6	18 404	322 292	17.5	19 025	327 248	17.2	19 398	329 640	17.0
New York	14.7	15.4	15.2	179 413	2 733 813	15.2	182 273	2 766 208	15.2	181 559	2 813 230	15.5
North Carolina	16.9	16.8	16.7	69 421	1 133 231	16.3	71 592	1 156 767	16.2	73 201	1 183 090	16.2
North Dakota	15.5	15.3	15.2	7 755	119 127	15.4	7 796	119 288	15.3	7 501	119 100	15.9
Ohio	17.2	17.3	16.9	107 444	1 807 319	16.8	109 085	1 814 290	16.6	107 347	1 836 015	17.1
Oklahoma	15.6	15.6	15.5	39 031	604 076	15.5	39 406	609 718	15.5	39 364	616 393	15.7
Oregon	18.0	18.6	19.2	26 488	516 611	19.5	26 208	521 945	19.9	26 680	527 914	19.8
Pennsylvania	16.6	16.8	17.0	101 302	1 744 082	17.2	102 988	1 764 946	17.1	104 921	1 787 533	17.0
Rhode Island	14.6	14.6	14.3	9 823	145 676	14.8	10 066	147 487	14.7	10 482	149 799	14.3
South Carolina	16.8	16.9	17.2	38 620	643 696	16.7	39 437	648 725	16.4	39 922	645 586	16.2
South Dakota	15.2	14.8	15.3	9 557	142 825	14.9	9 985	143 482	14.4	9 641	144 685	15.0
Tennessee	19.2	19.4	19.6	46 066	866 557	18.8	47 406	881 425	18.6	53 403	893 770	16.7
Texas	15.4	15.8	16.1	224 830	3 608 262	16.0	234 213	3 677 171	15.7	240 371	3 748 167	15.6
Utah	25.0	24.9	24.2	19 053	471 365	24.7	19 524	474 675	24.3	20 039	477 121	23.8
Vermont	13.2	13.8	13.1	7 330	102 755	14.0	7 566	104 533	13.8	7 676	105 565	13.8
Virginia	15.7	15.7	15.1	70 859	1 045 471	14.8	72 505	1 060 809	14.6	74 731	1 079 854	14.4
Washington	20.1	20.2	20.2	45 524	915 952	20.1	46 439	938 314	20.2	46 907	956 572	20.4
West Virginia	15.0	15.3	15.2	21 029	314 383	14.9	21 024	310 511	14.8	21 073	307 112	14.6
Wisconsin	16.2	15.7	15.5	52 822	844 001	16.0	54 054	860 581	15.9	55 033	870 175	15.8
Wyoming	14.5	15.6	17.2	6 537	100 899	15.4	6 754	100 314	14.9	6 734	99 859	14.8
Outlying areas												
American Samoa	18.8	19.9	19.3	656	14 484	22.1	698	14 445	20.7	728	14 576	20.0
Guam	17.1	18.9	18.5	1 644	30 920	18.8	1 826	32 185	17.6	1 802	32 960	18.3
Northern Marianas ...	15.5	16.5	19.0	431	8 188	19.0	406	8 429	20.8	422	8 809	20.9
Puerto Rico	18.8	17.2	16.6	39 816	631 460	15.9	39 933	621 121	15.6	39 328	627 620	16.0
Virgin Islands	13.8	14.1	14.3	1 570	22 752	14.5	1 528	23 126	15.1	1 622	22 737	14.0

SOURCE: U.S. Department of Education, National Center for Education Statistics, Revenues and Expenditures for Public Elementary and Secondary Education; Statistics of State School Systems; and Common Core of Data survey. Published as table 66 in *Digest of Education Statistics* 1997.

NOTE: Some data have been revised from previously published figures. Teachers reported in full-time equivalents.

Table C-16. Highest Degree Earned and Number of Years Teaching Experience for Teachers in Public Elementary and Secondary Schools, by State: 1993-94

State or other area	Total[1]	Percent of teachers, by highest degree[2]				Percent of teachers, by years of full-time teaching			
		Bachelor's	Master's	Education specialist	Doctor's	Less than 3	3 to 9	10 to 20	Over 20
United States	2 561 294	52.0	42.0	4.6	0.7	9.7	25.5	35.0	29.8
Alabama	44 791	38.5	52.6	7.8	0.7	11.1	22.0	42.2	24.7
Alaska	8 152	59.0	35.3	4.2	(3)	8.0	29.3	42.7	20.0
Arizona	37 600	51.4	43.3	4.0	0.7	13.1	29.1	38.1	19.8
Arkansas	30 621	64.9	32.5	1.8	0.5	9.2	27.3	40.2	23.3
California	209 032	58.6	32.6	6.8	1.0	9.8	27.8	31.8	30.7
Colorado	35 723	46.5	49.4	2.5	0.5	9.4	26.1	38.7	25.7
Connecticut	35 465	19.6	62.4	15.7	1.4	6.4	19.8	35.5	38.3
Delaware	7 027	46.0	48.3	5.1	(NA)	7.7	24.1	36.2	32.0
District of Columbia	5 185	41.2	54.4	2.4	2.0	10.8	14.7	30.6	43.9
Florida	106 535	57.2	37.0	3.3	1.4	8.7	29.4	37.8	24.0
Georgia	74 907	48.9	42.5	7.7	(3)	13.3	28.3	35.6	22.8
Hawaii	11 137	47.8	21.7	27.5	1.0	16.2	28.1	22.0	33.7
Idaho	12 166	74.4	21.7	2.6	0.6	12.4	33.3	33.7	20.6
Illinois	111 511	49.7	46.1	3.4	0.5	9.0	25.1	30.8	35.1
Indiana	57 732	21.4	72.9	4.9	(NA)	5.6	24.7	37.1	32.6
Iowa	35 861	67.3	31.3	1.2	(3)	10.1	23.3	32.1	34.5
Kansas	31 164	53.5	42.8	2.3	1.1	12.3	28.2	35.2	24.3
Kentucky	41 571	23.4	56.8	18.7	0.8	9.5	26.8	32.9	30.8
Louisiana	48 948	60.5	31.2	6.9	0.5	9.7	29.8	35.1	25.5
Maine	15 658	68.4	28.4	1.6	(3)	7.0	28.7	37.4	26.9
Maryland	43 862	43.3	49.6	6.2	0.6	11.7	23.6	32.4	32.4
Massachusetts	58 416	38.8	54.8	3.9	0.9	8.4	17.1	33.6	41.0
Michigan	83 288	46.6	48.1	4.7	0.6	7.4	21.5	29.4	41.9
Minnesota	44 150	63.4	33.6	2.6	(3)	13.0	20.0	33.0	34.0
Mississippi	29 851	56.3	37.5	4.3	(3)	10.5	22.8	39.8	26.9
Missouri	62 454	54.3	42.4	2.2	0.6	10.6	26.9	37.2	25.3
Montana	12 851	71.3	26.0	1.8	0.5	11.1	27.5	39.0	22.5
Nebraska	20 411	61.5	36.0	1.9	(3)	10.1	24.4	39.0	26.5
Nevada	12 822	50.5	42.8	5.7	0.6	12.0	33.2	35.0	19.8
New Hampshire	12 299	60.2	35.9	2.6	0.7	10.6	26.8	38.2	24.4
New Jersey	83 935	56.2	37.4	4.8	1.0	5.8	21.1	34.6	38.5
New Mexico	19 265	53.2	43.6	2.2	(3)	12.5	32.5	33.9	21.1
New York	178 701	25.0	68.1	5.3	1.5	10.3	23.9	29.7	36.1
North Carolina	72 305	61.8	35.0	1.2	0.5	9.7	26.6	38.8	25.0
North Dakota	8 404	79.3	18.0	1.6	(NA)	12.1	27.2	37.7	23.0
Ohio	111 518	53.2	41.8	3.1	(3)	6.8	23.2	38.6	31.4
Oklahoma	42 220	56.9	39.5	3.2	(3)	10.4	27.0	41.2	21.5
Oregon	25 706	51.5	43.1	4.0	0.8	7.4	27.0	39.6	26.0
Pennsylvania	114 571	46.7	45.6	6.9	(3)	6.9	18.3	33.0	41.8
Rhode Island	9 217	40.1	53.3	5.7	1.0	7.2	21.9	28.6	42.3
South Carolina	39 623	48.8	43.4	5.6	0.7	10.5	25.1	42.3	22.1
South Dakota	10 579	75.1	23.2	1.5	(NA)	10.4	28.6	37.3	23.8
Tennessee	47 662	51.2	42.0	4.8	1.2	12.4	22.9	35.5	29.2
Texas	223 800	69.7	26.8	1.8	0.9	12.1	30.1	37.5	20.4
Utah	19 884	70.6	23.5	4.2	(3)	12.7	32.8	36.1	18.3
Vermont	7 327	49.4	47.5	2.1	(NA)	12.3	25.3	34.4	28.0
Virginia	64 937	64.4	31.3	2.4	0.5	10.5	26.0	37.5	26.1
Washington	48 452	56.3	37.5	3.6	1.0	10.8	30.1	32.2	26.9
West Virginia	21 473	41.7	53.1	4.3	(NA)	4.4	21.6	42.7	31.4
Wisconsin	62 958	59.3	38.1	1.7	0.6	9.1	24.7	29.5	36.7
Wyoming	7 567	71.3	26.5	1.4	(3)	9.4	22.6	41.6	26.5

SOURCE: U.S. Department of Education, National Center for Education Statistics, 'Schools and Staffing Survey, 1993-94.' Published as table 68 in *Digest of Education Statistics* 1997.

1. Data are based on a head count of all teachers rather than on the number of full-time equivalent teachers appearing in other tables.
2. Teachers with less than a bachelor's degree are not shown.
3. Less than 0.05 percent.

NOTE: Excludes prekindergarten teachers. Details may not add to totals due to rounding or item nonresponse.

(NA) Not applicable or not available.

Table C-17.   Estimated Average Annual Salary of Teachers in Public Elementary and Secondary Schools, by State: 1969-70 to 1996-97

State	Current dollars							Constant 1996-97 Dollars[1]						Percent change, 1979-80 to 1996-97 in constant dollars
	1969-70	1979-80	1989-90	1993-94	1994-95	1995-96	1996-97	1969-70	1979-80	1989-90	1993-94	1994-95[2]	1995-96	
United States	$8 626	$15 970	$31 367	$35 733	$36 609	[2]$37 560	[2]$38 509	$36 287	$32 689	$39 256	$38 834	$38 678	$38 632	17.8
Alabama	6 818	13 060	24 828	28 705	31 144	31 313	32 549	28 681	26 733	31 072	31 196	32 904	32 206	21.8
Alaska	10 560	27 210	43 153	47 512	47 951	[2]49 620	[2]50 647	44 423	55 696	54 006	51 636	50 661	51 036	0.0
Arizona	8 711	15 054	29 402	31 800	32 175	[2]507	[2]33 350	36 644	30 814	36 796	34 560	33 993	33 411	8.2
Arkansas	6 307	12 299	22 352	28 098	28 934	29 322	[2]29 975	26 532	25 175	27 973	30 537	30 569	30 159	19.1
California	10 315	18 020	37 998	40 264	41 078	42 259	[2]43 474	43 392	36 885	47 554	43 759	43 399	43 465	17.9
Colorado	7 761	16 205	30 758	33 826	34 571	35 364	[2]36 175	32 648	33 170	38 493	36 762	36 525	36 373	9.1
Connecticut	9 262	16 229	40 461	49 769	50 045	50 254	50 426	38 962	33 219	50 637	54 089	52 873	51 688	51.8
Delaware	9 015	16 148	33 377	37 469	39 076	40 533	41 436	37 923	33 054	41 771	40 721	41 284	41 689	25.4
District of Columbia	10 285	22 190	38 402	42 543	43 700	43 700	[2]45 012	43 266	45 421	48 060	46 236	46 170	44 947	0.0
Florida	8 412	14 149	28 803	31 944	32 588	33 330	33 881	35 387	28 962	36 047	34 717	34 430	34 281	17.0
Georgia	7 276	13 853	28 006	30 712	32 291	34 002	36 042	30 608	28 356	35 049	33 378	34 116	34 972	27.1
Hawaii	9 453	19 920	32 047	36 564	38 518	35 807	35 842	39 766	40 774	40 106	39 738	40 695	36 829	0.0
Idaho	6 890	13 611	23 861	27 756	29 783	30 891	31 818	28 984	27 860	29 862	30 165	31 466	31 772	14.2
Illinois	9 569	17 601	32 794	39 387	39 431	40 919	42 679	40 254	36 028	41 041	42 806	41 659	42 086	18.5
Indiana	8 833	15 599	30 902	35 712	36 785	37 675	38 575	37 158	31 930	38 674	38 812	38 864	38 750	20.8
Iowa	8 355	15 203	26 747	30 760	31 511	32 372	33 275	35 147	31 119	33 474	33 430	33 292	33 296	6.9
Kansas	7 612	13 690	28 744	33 914	34 652	35 134	35 837	32 021	28 022	35 973	36 858	36 610	36 136	27.9
Kentucky	6 953	14 520	26 292	31 625	32 257	33 080	[2]33 950	29 249	29 721	32 904	34 370	34 080	34 024	14.2
Louisiana	7 028	13 760	24 300	26 095	26 461	26 800	28 347	29 565	28 166	30 411	28 360	27 956	27 565	0.6
Maine	7 572	13 071	26 881	30 996	31 972	32 869	[2]33 800	31 853	26 755	33 641	33 686	33 779	33 807	26.3
Maryland	9 383	17 558	36 319	39 453	40 661	41 160	41 148	39 471	35 940	45 453	42 877	42 959	42 334	14.5
Massachusetts	8 764	17 253	34 712	39 023	40 795	42 264	43 806	36 868	35 315	43 442	42 410	43 100	43 470	24.0
Michigan	9 826	19 663	37 072	44 856	41 895	[2]44 796	[2]44 251	41 335	40 248	46 395	48 749	44 263	46 074	9.9
Minnesota	8 658	15 912	32 190	35 440	35 948	[2]36 937	[2]37 975	36 422	32 570	40 286	38 516	37 980	37 991	16.6
Mississippi	5 798	11 850	24 292	25 153	26 818	27 692	27 720	24 390	24 256	30 401	27 336	28 334	28 482	14.3
Missouri	7 799	13 682	27 094	30 319	31 189	33 341	[2]34 342	32 808	28 006	33 908	32 951	32 952	34 292	22.6
Montana	7 606	14 537	25 081	28 200	28 785	29 364	[2]29 950	31 996	29 756	31 389	30 648	30 412	30 202	0.7
Nebraska	7 375	13 516	25 522	29 564	30 922	31 496	31 768	31 024	27 666	31 940	32 130	32 670	32 395	14.8
Nevada	9 215	16 295	30 590	33 955	34 836	36 167	37 340	38 765	33 354	38 283	36 902	36 805	37 199	11.9
New Hampshire ..	7 771	13 017	28 986	34 121	34 720	35 792	[2]36 867	32 690	26 645	36 276	37 083	36 682	36 813	38.4
New Jersey	9 130	17 161	35 676	44 693	46 087	47 910	[2]49 349	38 407	35 127	44 648	48 572	48 692	49 277	40.5
New Mexico	7 796	14 887	24 756	27 202	28 493	29 074	29 715	32 795	30 472	30 982	29 563	30 103	29 904	0.0
New York	10 336	19 812	38 925	45 772	47 612	48 115	49 560	43 480	40 553	48 714	49 745	50 303	49 488	22.2
North Carolina	7 494	14 117	27 883	29 728	30 793	30 411	[2]31 225	31 525	28 896	34 895	32 308	32 533	31 279	8.1
North Dakota	6 696	13 263	23 016	25 506	26 327	26 969	27 711	28 168	27 148	28 804	27 720	27 815	27 738	2.1
Ohio	8 300	15 269	31 218	35 673	36 802	37 835	38 831	34 916	31 254	39 069	38 769	38 882	38 914	24.2
Oklahoma	6 882	13 107	23 070	27 009	28 172	28 404	29 270	28 950	26 829	28 872	29 353	29 764	29 214	9.1
Oregon	8 818	16 266	30 840	37 713	38 555	39 706	40 900	37 095	33 295	38 596	40 986	40 734	40 839	22.8
Pennsylvania	8 858	16 515	33 338	42 411	44 510	46 087	47 429	37 263	33 805	41 722	46 092	47 025	47 402	40.3
Rhode Island	8 776	18 002	36 057	39 261	40 729	[2]184	[2]43 019	36 918	36 848	45 125	42 669	43 031	43 363	16.7
South Carolina	6 927	13 063	27 217	29 566	30 279	31 622	32 659	29 140	26 739	34 062	32 132	31 990	32 524	22.1
South Dakota	6 403	12 348	21 300	25 259	25 994	26 346	26 764	26 936	25 275	26 657	27 451	27 463	27 098	5.9
Tennessee	7 050	13 972	27 052	30 514	32 477	33 126	33 789	29 657	28 600	33 855	33 162	34 312	34 071	18.1
Texas	7 255	14 132	27 496	30 529	31 223	32 000	32 644	30 520	28 927	34 411	33 179	32 988	32 913	12.8
Utah	7 644	14 909	23 686	27 706	29 082	30 588	31 750	32 156	30 517	29 643	30 111	30 726	31 461	4.0

See footnotes at end of table.

Table C-17.   Estimated Average Annual Salary of Teachers in Public Elementary and Secondary Schools, by State: 1969-70 to 1996-97 — Continued

State	Current dollars							Constant 1996-97 Dollars[1]						Percent change, 1979-80 to 1996-97 in constant dollars
	1969-70	1979-80	1989-90	1993-94	1994-95	1995-96	1996-97	1969-70	1979-80	1989-90	1993-94	1994-95[2]	1995-96	
Vermont	$7 968	$12 484	$29 012	$34 517	$35 406	$36 295	[2] $37 200	$33 519	$25 554	$36 308	$37 513	$37 407	$37 330	45.6
Virginia	8 070	14 060	30 938	33 009	33 987	34 792	[2] 35 837	33 948	28 780	38 719	35 874	35 908	35 785	24.5
Washington	9 225	18 820	30 457	35 863	36 151	37 853	37 860	38 807	38 523	38 117	38 976	38 194	38 933	0.0
West Virginia	7 650	13 710	22 842	30 549	31 944	32 155	33 159	32 181	28 063	28 586	33 200	33 749	33 072	18.2
Wisconsin	8 963	16 006	31 921	35 990	37 746	38 182	[2] 38 950	37 705	32 775	39 949	39 114	39 879	39 271	18.9
Wyoming	8 232	16 012	28 141	30 952	31 285	31 571	31 721	34 630	32 775	35 218	33 638	33 053	32 472	0.0

SOURCE: National Education Association, Estimates of School Statistics; and unpublished data. (Latest edition 1996-97. Copyright 1997 by the National Education Association.) Published as table 78 in *Digest of Education Statistics* 1997.

1. Based on the Consumer Price Index prepared by the Bureau of Labor Statistics, U.S. Department of Labor. Price index does not account for different rates of change in the cost of living among states.
2. Estimated by the National Education Association.

NOTE: Some data have been revised from previously published figures.

Table C-18.   Average Annual Salary of Instructional Staff[1] in Public Elementary and Secondary Schools, by State: 1939-40 to 1996-97

State	Current dollars									Constant 1996-97 dollars[2]				
	1939-40	1949-50	1959-60	1969-70	1979-80	1989-90	1994-95	1995-96	1996-97	1969-70	1979-80	1989-90	1994-95	1995-96
United States	$1 441	$3 010	$5 174	$9 047	$16 715	$32 638	[3]$38 441	[3]$39 451	[3]$40 580	$38 058	$34 214	$40 846	$40 613	$40 577
Alabama	744	2 111	4 002	6 954	13 338	26 200	32 597	32 459	33 744	29 253	27 302	32 789	34 439	33 385
Alaska	(NA)	(NA)	6 859	10 993	27 697	[3] 195	[3] 48 929	[3] 50 516	[3] 52 033	46 244	56 693	54 016	51 694	51 957
Arizona	1 544	3 556	5 590	8 975	16 180	33 592	[3] 41 325	[3] 42 870	[3] 44 157	37 755	33 119	42 040	43 660	44 093
Arkansas	584	1 801	3 295	6 461	12 704	23 296	30 103	30 607	[3] 31 526	27 180	26 004	29 155	31 804	31 480
California	2 351	(NA)	[3] 6 600	10 950	18 626	[3] 39 309	[3] 42 538	[3] 44 027	[3] 45 349	46 063	38 126	49 195	44 942	45 283
Colorado	1 393	2 821	4 997	8 105	16 840	31 832	35 712	36 353	[3] 37 445	34 095	34 470	39 837	37 730	37 390
Connecticut	1 861	3 558	6 008	9 597	16 989	41 888	51 770	51 951	52 067	40 372	34 775	52 422	54 696	53 433
Delaware	1 684	3 273	[3] 5 800	9 387	16 845	34 620	40 668	42 177	43 085	39 488	34 480	43 327	42 966	43 380
District of														
Columbia	2 350	3 920	6 280	10 700	23 027	43 637	39 663	39 663	[3] 40 854	45 012	47 134	54 611	41 904	40 795
Florida	1 012	2 958	5 080	8 785	14 875	30 275	33 617	34 411	34 983	36 956	30 448	37 889	35 517	35 393
Georgia	770	1 963	[4] 3 904	7 520	14 547	29 541	33 963	35 786	37 933	31 634	29 776	36 970	35 882	36 807
Hawaii	(NA)	(NA)	5 390	9 600	20 436	32 956	37 319	37 057	36 986	40 384	41 831	41 244	39 428	38 114
Idaho	1 057	2 481	4 216	7 081	14 110	24 758	31 063	32 285	33 277	29 788	28 882	30 984	32 818	33 206
Illinois	1 700	3 458	[5] 819	9 789	18 271	33 912	40 855	42 411	44 235	41 179	37 399	42 440	43 164	43 621
Indiana	1 433	3 401	5 542	9 239	16 256	31 905	37 922	38 832	39 998	38 866	33 275	39 929	40 065	39 940
Iowa	1 017	2 420	[3] 4 030	8 779	15 776	27 619	32 622	33 529	34 480	36 931	32 292	34 565	34 466	34 486
Kansas	1 014	2 628	[3] 4 450	7 811	14 513	30 154	36 709	37 626	38 379	32 858	29 707	37 737	38 784	38 700
Kentucky	826	1 936	3 327	7 325	15 350	27 482	34 232	33 115	[3] 34 109	30 814	31 420	34 394	36 167	34 060
Louisiana	1 006	2 983	4 978	7 264	14 020	25 036	27 631	28 167	[3] 29 013	30 558	28 698	31 332	29 192	28 971
Maine	894	2 115	3 694	8 059	13 743	27 831	33 050	33 994	[3] 35 015	33 902	28 131	34 830	34 918	34 964
Maryland	1 642	3 594	5 557	9 885	18 308	37 520	42 300	42 958	42 988	41 583	37 475	46 956	44 690	44 184
Massachusetts ..	2 037	3 338	[6] 5 545	9 347	18 900	40 175	49 860	52 663	[3] 54 244	39 320	38 687	50 279	52 678	54 166
Michigan	1 576	3 420	5 654	10 125	20 682	[3] 37 286	[3] 48 507	[3] 50 764	[3] 52 288	42 593	42 334	46 663	51 248	52 212
Minnesota	1 276	3 013	5 275	9 250	16 654	33 340	37 145	[3] 37 680	[3] 38 811	38 912	34 089	41 725	39 244	38 755
Mississippi	559	1 416	3 314	5 959	12 274	25 079	27 764	28 712	28 648	25 068	25 124	31 386	29 333	29 531
Missouri	1 159	2 581	4 536	8 064	14 543	28 166	32 725	33 870	[3] 34 887	33 923	29 768	35 250	34 574	34 836
Montana	1 184	2 962	[3] 4 425	7 875	15 080	29 526	30 052	30 908	[3] 31 836	33 128	30 867	36 952	31 750	31 790
Nebraska	829	2 292	3 876	7 633	14 236	27 024	32 803	34 023	35 045	32 110	29 140	33 820	34 657	34 994
Nevada	1 557	3 209	5 693	9 615	17 290	31 970	36 553	37 879	39 179	40 447	35 391	40 010	38 619	38 960
New														
Hampshire ...	1 258	2 712	4 455	8 016	13 508	[3] 29 798	[3] 39 564	42 188	[3] 489	33 721	27 650	37 292	41 800	43 392
New Jersey	2 093	3 511	5 871	9 650	18 851	37 485	48 463	50 435	[3] 51 949	40 595	38 586	46 912	51 202	51 874
New Mexico	1 144	3 215	5 382	10 021	15 406	25 790	28 866	[3] 29 389	[3] 30 271	42 155	31 535	32 276	30 497	30 228
New York	2 604	3 706	6 537	11 240	20 400	40 000	48 500	48 754	50 218	47 283	41 757	50 060	51 241	50 145
North Carolina ...	946	2 688	4 178	7 762	14 445	28 952	32 070	31 622	[3] 32 571	32 652	29 568	36 233	33 882	32 524
North Dakota	745	2 324	3 695	6 840	13 684	23 788	26 515	27 153	27 905	28 774	28 010	29 770	28 013	27 928
Ohio	1 587	3 088	5 124	8 594	16 100	32 467	37 988	39 038	40 087	36 152	32 955	40 632	40 135	40 152
Oklahoma	1 014	2 736	4 659	7 257	13 500	23 944	29 129	30 584	31 000	30 528	27 633	29 966	30 775	31 457
Oregon	1 333	3 323	5 535	9 200	16 996	32 100	39 800	40 980	[3] 42 210	38 702	34 789	40 173	42 049	42 149
Pennsylvania	1 640	3 006	5 308	8 899	17 060	34 110	45 456	47 087	48 500	37 435	34 920	42 688	48 025	48 430
Rhode Island	1 809	3 294	[7] 5 499	9 030	18 425	36 704	41 464	[3] 42 900	[3] 44 188	37 986	37 714	45 935	43 807	44 124
South Carolina ..	743	1 891	3 450	7 069	13 670	28 453	31 748	33 155	34 219	29 737	27 981	35 609	33 542	34 101
South Dakota	807	2 064	3 725	7 200	13 010	22 120	26 037	27 354	27 767	30 288	26 630	27 683	27 508	28 134
Tennessee	862	2 302	3 929	7 187	14 193	27 949	33 724	34 412	35 093	30 234	29 052	34 978	35 630	35 394
Texas	1 079	3 122	4 708	7 598	14 729	28 549	33 164	33 861	35 217	31 962	30 149	35 729	35 038	34 827
Utah	1 394	3 103	5 096	8 049	17 403	24 591	30 145	31 780	33 000	33 860	35 622	30 775	31 849	32 687
Vermont	981	2 348	4 466	8 225	13 300	29 012	36 375	37 054	[3] 38 167	34 600	27 224	36 308	38 431	38 111
Virginia	899	2 328	4 312	8 364	14 655	31 656	34 828	35 535	[3] 36 602	35 185	29 998	39 617	36 796	36 549
Washington	1 706	3 487	25 643	9 792	19 735	31 828	37 807	39 594	39 591	41 192	40 396	39 832	39 944	40 724
West Virginia	1 170	2 425	3 952	7 954	14 395	23 842	33 070	33 266	34 360	33 460	29 465	29 838	34 939	34 246
Wisconsin	1 379	3 007	[8] 4 870	9 150	16 335	32 445	38 952	39 212	[3] 40 389	38 491	33 436	40 605	41 153	40 331
Wyoming	1 169	2 798	4 937	8 496	16 830	29 047	32 181	32 493	32 626	35 740	34 450	36 352	34 000	33 420

See footnotes at end of table.

**Table C-18. Average Annual Salary of Instructional Staff[1] in Public Elementary and Secondary Schools, by State: 1939-40 to 1996-97
— Continued**

State	Current dollars									Constant 1996-97 dollars[2]				
	1939-40	1949-50	1959-60	1969-70	1979-80	1989-90	1994-95	1995-96	1996-97	1969-70	1979-80	1989-90	1994-95	1995-96
Outlying areas														
American														
Samoa	(NA)	(NA)	$852	$5 130	(NA)	(NA)	(NA)	(NA)	(NA)	$21 580	(NA)	(NA)	(NA)	(NA)
Guam	(NA)	(NA)	4 107	7 800	(NA)	(NA)	(NA)	(NA)	(NA)	32 812	(NA)	(NA)	(NA)	(NA)
Northern														
Marianas	(NA)	(NA)	9 2 360	(NA)	(NA)	(NA)	(NA)	(NA)	(NA)	(NA)	(NA)	(NA)	(NA)	(NA)
Puerto Rico	(NA)	(NA)	3 407	(NA)	(NA)	(NA)	(NA)	(NA)	(NA)	(NA)	(NA)	(NA)	(NA)	(NA)

SOURCE: U.S. Department of Education, National Center for Education Statistics, Statistics of State School Systems; National Education Association, Estimates of School Statistics; (Latest edition 1996-97. Copyright 1997 by the National Education Association.) Published as table 80 in *Digest of Education Statistics 1997.*

1. Includes supervisors, principals, classroom teachers, and other instructional staff.
2. Based on the Consumer Price Index prepared by the Bureau of Labor Statistics, U.S. Department of Labor. Price index does not account for different rates of change in the cost of living among states.
3. Estimated by National Education Association.
4. Excludes kindergarten teachers.
5. Includes administrators.
6. Includes clerical assistants to instructional personnel.
7. Includes attendance personnel.
8. Excludes vocational schools not operated as part of the regular public school system.
9. Median salary.

NOTE: Some data have been revised from previously published figures.

Table C-19. Staff Employed in Public School Systems, by Type of Assignment and State: Fall 1995

State	Total	School district staff			School staff						Student support staff	Other support services staff
		Officials and administrators	Administrative support staff	Instruction coordinators	Principals and assistant principals	School and library support staff	Teachers	Instructional aides	Guidance	Librarians		
United States[1]	4 994 358	49 315	144 842	33 683	120 629	237 389	2 598 220	494 289	87 528	50 862	142 655	1 034 946
Alabama	83 256	428	1 039	980	2 221	2 768	44 056	6 657	1 684	1 259	468	21 696
Alaska[2]	15 022	294	549	112	436	886	7 379	1 751	225	147	819	2 424
Arizona	75 931	428	641	182	1 611	6 123	38 017	9 613	1 050	737	7 312	10 217
Arkansas	49 178	554	583	179	1 460	1 646	26 449	3 523	1 223	952	387	12 222
California[3]	444 014	2 155	19 920	4 685	10 335	28 571	230 849	56 822	5 115	896	9 989	74 677
Colorado	67 447	846	2 211	775	1 749	4 749	35 388	5 919	1 080	700	1 608	12 422
Connecticut	66 133	955	1 611	453	1 823	3 246	36 070	7 520	1 116	672	3 239	9 428
Delaware	11 869	87	388	58	399	472	6 463	861	215	122	498	2 306
District of Columbia	9 410	402	290	144	305	442	5 305	327	217	143	53	1 782
Florida	237 721	1 739	12 267	812	5 964	12 110	114 938	24 111	4 794	2 560	7 147	51 279
Georgia[4]	165 058	2 127	3 488	691	3 754	6 423	79 480	21 709	2 476	1 987	2 699	40 224
Hawaii	16 841	141	263	438	483	704	10 500	937	540	287	512	2 036
Idaho	21 814	114	443	210	661	876	12 784	1 914	520	185	381	3 726
Illinois	209 036	3 292	5 114	1 656	5 132	9 984	113 538	21 137	2 823	1 941	6 503	37 916
Indiana	116 363	928	496	1 368	2 818	7 872	55 821	14 421	1 720	1 021	1 650	28 248
Iowa	62 075	519	756	382	1 762	4 465	32 318	6 083	1 331	662	2 192	11 605
Kansas	57 265	1 253	961	74	1 671	2 487	30 729	4 760	1 087	972	2 298	10 973
Kentucky	84 425	1 170	2 188	434	1 906	3 147	39 120	10 916	1 282	1 173	2 093	20 996
Louisiana	93 070	265	689	1 026	2 379	2 907	46 980	10 026	2 610	1 172	2 248	22 768
Maine	29 413	448	660	113	853	1 393	15 392	3 776	600	238	1 049	4 891
Maryland	87 868	720	719	701	2 647	3 765	47 819	7 318	1 830	1 043	1 443	19 863
Massachusetts	113 154	991	5 788	1 065	2 166	3 073	62 710	12 867	2 090	611	1 860	19 933
Michigan	177 495	2 250	3 264	497	5 079	7 890	83 179	14 318	2 871	1 450	6 704	49 993
Minnesota	74 891	1 288	1 735	487	1 589	3 316	46 971	6 088	902	986	2 863	8 666
Mississippi	60 855	906	1 433	418	1 493	2 110	28 997	8 758	824	750	2 221	12 945
Missouri	120 621	638	4 578	1 244	2 579	8 189	57 951	7 228	2 593	1 368	1 758	32 495
Montana[4,5]	18 586	156	469	155	489	907	10 076	1 938	403	348	68	3 577
Nebraska	37 894	612	684	236	953	1 479	20 028	3 578	755	575	996	7 998
Nevada	23 742	184	489	101	680	1 340	13 878	1 489	498	241	605	4 237
New Hampshire	23 143	360	455	144	479	812	12 346	3 519	620	281	447	3 680
New Jersey	163 069	1 680	6 826	1 305	4 383	8 393	86 706	13 936	3 150	1 781	8 767	26 142
New Mexico	40 124	435	1 887	553	859	2 694	19 398	4 574	645	259	1 039	7 781
New York	355 723	2 737	23 774	1 263	6 878	7 110	181 559	28 001	5 456	2 998	8 720	87 227
North Carolina[4]	140 204	1 285	2 977	720	3 993	5 794	73 201	22 287	2 976	2 176	2 720	22 075
North Dakota	13 804	435	164	54	394	475	7 501	1 471	248	183	364	2 515
Ohio	194 579	5 242	9 467	353	971	12 597	107 347	10 092	3 219	1 628	1 252	42 411
Oklahoma[4]	83 802	533	94	590	1 456	5 754	39 364	7 186	1 390	902	12 589	13 944
Oregon	51 458	874	1 315	341	1 622	3 410	26 680	6 381	1 229	612	997	7 997
Pennsylvania	198 087	1 344	7 175	1 594	4 087	9 840	104 921	14 831	3 676	2 202	9 904	38 513
Rhode Island	16 517	148	426	78	361	804	10 482	1 458	309	75	378	1 998
South Carolina[4,5]	74 859	264	1 830	467	2 224	3 537	39 922	7 558	1 517	1 097	2 494	13 949
South Dakota[4]	18 126	268	400	148	473	878	9 641	2 302	354	202	269	3 191
Tennessee	98 948	918	2 297	761	4 654	4 572	53 403	9 992	1 456	1 386	2 927	16 582
Texas	462 661	2 580	2 451	1 100	11 251	18 644	240 371	43 046	8 219	4 252	3 679	127 068
Utah	37 385	109	715	465	926	2 098	20 039	5 037	596	291	369	6 740
Vermont	15 640	152	278	294	411	719	7 676	2 931	332	216	1 668	963
Virginia[2]	137 546	1 760	1 739	1 483	3 535	5 627	74 731	12 072	3 111	1 950	3 147	28 391
Washington[2,4]	91 322	1 015	2 540	841	2 501	4 760	46 907	8 582	1 758	1 263	3 695	17 460
West Virginia	38 645	279	1 896	322	1 095	366	21 073	2 957	611	357	886	8 803
Wisconsin	95 105	842	2 276	1 090	2 353	4 463	55 033	8 361	1 925	1 416	4 005	13 341
Wyoming	13 164	165	144	41	326	702	6 734	1 350	257	137	676	2 632

See footnotes at end of table.

Table C-19.   Staff Employed in Public School Systems, by Type of Assignment and State: Fall 1995 — Continued

| State | Total | School district staff | | | School staff | | | | | | | Student support staff | Other support services staff |
		Officials and administrators	Administrative support staff	Instruction coordinators	Principals and assistant principals	School and library support staff	Teachers	Instructional aides	Guidance	Librarians			
Outlying areas													
American Samoa	1 417	30	38	26	60	81	728	15	19	6		48	366
Guam	3 728	15	288	18	62	40	1 802	476	80	30		146	771
Northern Marianas ...	1 054	9	88	17	30	54	422	216	28	4		75	111
Puerto Rico	69 731	314	111	618	1 382	4 738	39 328	(NA)	886	865		1 995	19 494
Virgin Islands	3 421	36	322	21	86	106	1 622	298	86	46		431	367

SOURCE: U.S. Department of Education, National Center for Education Statistics, Common Core of Data survey; and unpublished estimates. Published as table 83 in *Digest of Education Statistics* 1997.

1. Includes imputations for undercounts in designated states.
2. Includes imputation for instruction coordinators.
3. Includes imputation for prekindergarten teachers.
4. Includes imputation for support staff.
5. Includes imputation for instruction aides.

NOTE: Some data have been revised from previously published figures.

Table C-20. Staff and Teachers in Public Elementary and Secondary Schools, by State: Fall 1989 to Fall 1995

State	Teachers as a percent of staff				Fall 1993			Fall 1994[1]			Fall 1995		
	Fall 1989	Fall 1990	Fall 1991	Fall 1992	Staff	Teachers	Teachers as a percent of staff	Staff	Teachers	Teachers as a percent of staff	Staff	Teachers	Teachers as a percent of staff
United States[2]	53.2	53.4	53.3	52.2	4 808 080	2 503 901	52.1	4 904 757	2 551 875	52.0	4 994 358	2 598 220	52.0
Alabama	50.0	48.7	49.4	[3]53.2	[3]80 923	[3]43 003	53.1	81 544	[3]42 791	[3]52.5	83 256	44 056	52.9
Alaska	48.3	50.3	50.9	49.2	15 689	7 193	45.8	15 150	7 205	[3]47.6	[3]15 022	7 379	[3]49.1
Arizona	52.7	52.0	51.9	50.4	74 679	37 493	50.2	74 540	38 132	51.2	75 931	38 017	50.1
Arkansas	51.8	52.2	49.9	53.2	50 502	26 014	51.5	50 201	26 181	52.2	49 178	26 449	53.8
California	50.7	51.7	52.2	[3]51.1	[3]431 093	[3]221 787	[3]51.4	436 140	[3]225 016	[3]51.6	444 014	[3]230 849	[3]52.0
Colorado	52.7	52.6	52.9	52.9	62 927	33 661	53.5	64 985	34 894	53.7	67 447	35 388	52.5
Connecticut	55.5	56.3	56.8	53.7	62 014	34 526	55.7	64 742	35 316	54.5	66 133	36 070	54.5
Delaware	54.8	55.2	55.5	54.9	11 640	6 380	54.8	11 759	6 416	54.6	11 869	6 463	54.5
District of Columbia	57.0	58.3	57.0	57.4	10 591	6 056	57.2	10 507	6 110	58.2	9 410	5 305	56.4
Florida	50.5	49.8	50.0	49.5	226 911	110 653	48.8	226 975	110 674	48.8	237 721	114 938	48.3
Georgia	48.8	48.9	48.0	[3]46.9	[3]156 005	74 172	[3]47.5	[3]161 390	77 914	[3]48.3	[3]165 058	79 480	[3]48.2
Hawaii	60.2	59.9	60.7	56.9	18 292	10 111	55.3	16 567	10 240	61.8	16 841	10 500	62.3
Idaho	62.4	62.3	62.4	60.4	19 983	12 007	60.1	21 194	12 582	59.4	21 814	12 784	58.6
Illinois	56.6	56.7	55.9	55.9	198 862	110 874	55.8	204 413	110 830	54.2	209 036	113 538	54.3
Indiana	50.9	50.7	50.1	48.7	113 892	55 107	48.4	115 441	55 496	48.1	116 363	55 821	48.0
Iowa	53.4	53.0	52.1	52.2	60 267	31 616	52.5	60 469	31 726	52.5	62 075	32 318	52.1
Kansas	57.3	56.8	56.8	54.9	55 783	30 283	54.3	56 790	30 579	53.8	57 265	30 729	53.7
Kentucky	50.1	49.5	48.7	47.8	81 279	37 324	45.9	81 720	38 784	47.5	84 425	39 120	46.3
Louisiana	49.9	49.8	69.6	50.9	93 197	46 913	50.3	96 124	47 599	49.5	93 070	46 980	50.5
Maine	57.8	57.3	56.9	53.1	28 865	15 344	53.2	29 264	15 404	52.6	29 413	15 392	52.3
Maryland	54.4	53.9	54.6	55.0	82 753	44 171	53.4	84 699	46 565	55.0	87 868	47 819	54.4
Massachusetts	56.7	57.2	56.5	56.5	104 196	58 766	56.4	108 281	60 489	55.9	113 154	62 710	55.4
Michigan	46.9	46.4	46.6	47.3	169 283	80 267	47.4	164 766	80 522	48.9	177 495	83 179	46.9
Minnesota	56.5	56.2	57.4	56.9	74 859	46 956	62.7	74 914	46 958	62.7	74 891	46 971	62.7
Mississippi	49.0	48.3	47.5	48.1	59 853	28 376	47.4	60 708	28 866	47.5	60 855	28 997	47.6
Missouri	50.6	50.6	52.3	48.4	112 810	54 860	48.6	116 974	56 606	48.4	120 621	57 951	48.0
Montana	[4]76.8	[4]76.4	[4]75.6	[3]54.0	[3]18 717	9 949	[3]53.2	[3]18 452	10 079	[3]54.6	[3]18 586	10 076	[3]54.2
Nebraska	55.4	53.4	55.0	54.2	[3]36 832	19 616	[3]53.3	37 144	19 774	53.2	37 894	20 028	52.9
Nevada	[4]89.0	[4]89.4	[4]86.8	[3]55.7	22 418	12 579	56.1	23 098	13 414	58.1	23 742	13 878	58.5
New Hampshire	51.4	51.8	56.0	54.8	21 913	11 972	54.6	22 336	12 109	54.2	23 143	12 346	53.3
New Jersey	54.3	54.2	54.2	54.8	160 202	84 564	52.8	161 586	85 258	52.8	163 069	86 706	53.2
New Mexico	50.2	50.3	50.7	51.5	36 694	18 404	50.2	39 016	19 025	48.8	40 124	19 398	48.3
New York	50.6	50.9	50.8	51.3	353 603	179 413	50.7	356 386	182 273	51.1	355 723	181 559	51.0
North Carolina	51.6	51.2	51.7	[3]51.5	133 059	69 421	52.2	[3]137 791	71 592	[3]52.0	[3]140 204	73 201	[3]52.2
North Dakota	55.3	54.5	56.9	56.5	13 780	7 755	56.3	13 919	7 796	56.0	13 804	7 501	54.3
Ohio	54.0	54.0	53.1	52.9	201 828	107 444	53.2	200 141	109 085	54.5	194 579	107 347	55.2
Oklahoma	54.2	54.2	54.0	53.3	73 067	39 031	53.4	[3]78 270	39 406	[3]50.3	[3]83 802	39 364	47.0
Oregon	53.1	53.2	53.0	51.5	50 392	26 488	52.6	50 377	26 208	52.0	51 458	26 680	51.8
Pennsylvania	55.4	52.5	52.7	52.7	190 885	101 302	53.1	193 696	102 988	53.2	198 087	104 921	53.0
Rhode Island	61.7	60.2	62.8	63.6	15 442	9 823	63.6	15 438	10 066	65.2	16 517	10 482	63.5
South Carolina	57.4	56.0	55.7	55.6	[3]71 433	38 620	[3]54.1	[3]74 196	39 437	[3]53.2	[3]74 859	39 922	[3]53.3
South Dakota	58.0	56.3	60.1	55.9	17 201	9 557	55.6	[3]17 989	9 985	[3]55.5	[3]18 126	9 641	[3]53.2
Tennessee	49.8	49.4	51.0	50.2	[3]92 349	46 066	[3]49.9	96 281	47 406	49.2	98 948	53 403	54.0
Texas	59.9	66.0	65.0	52.2	433 102	224 830	51.9	450 462	234 213	52.0	462 661	240 371	52.0
Utah	56.2	55.2	55.0	55.1	35 301	19 053	54.0	36 186	19 524	54.0	37 385	20 039	53.6
Vermont	57.3	53.6	50.5	50.2	[3]14 928	7 330	[3]49.1	15 337	7 566	49.3	15 640	7 676	49.1
Virginia	51.7	49.0	[5]49.4	[5]53.8	130 033	70 859	54.5	133 485	[3]72 505	[3]54.3	137 546	[3]74 731	[3]54.3
Washington	55.5	55.1	55.0	54.4	87 734	45 524	51.9	[3]90 438	46 439	[3]51.3	[3]91 322	46 907	[3]51.4
West Virginia	54.9	54.9	54.5	54.5	38 486	21 029	54.6	38 481	21 024	54.6	38 645	21 073	54.5
Wisconsin	59.0	58.1	59.0	57.9	88 640	52 822	59.6	100 996	54 054	53.5	95 105	55 033	57.9
Wyoming	49.9	53.1	50.0	50.6	12 893	6 537	50.7	12 999	6 754	52.0	13 164	6 734	51.2

See footnotes at end of table.

Table C-20.   Staff and Teachers in Public Elementary and Secondary Schools, by State: Fall 1989 to Fall 1995 — Continued

State	Teachers as a percent of staff				Fall 1993			Fall 1994[1]			Fall 1995		
	Fall 1989	Fall 1990	Fall 1991	Fall 1992	Staff	Teachers	Teachers as a percent of staff	Staff	Teachers	Teachers as a percent of staff	Staff	Teachers	Teachers as a percent of staff
Outlying areas													
American Samoa	53.1	52.6	52.5	53.7	1 339	656	49.0	1 340	698	52.1	1 417	728	51.4
Guam ....:......	54.3	52.6	50.6	46.3	3 839	1 644	42.8	4 730	1 826	38.6	3 728	1 802	48.3
Northern Marianas	52.0	51.1	47.5	38.8	1 101	431	39.1	1 051	406	38.6	1 054	422	40.0
Puerto Rico	53.5	55.4	54.9	56.7	68 005	39 816	58.5	68 868	39 933	58.0	69 731	39 328	56.4
Virgin Islands	48.0	48.0	48.1	47.6	3 324	1 570	47.2	[4] 3 193	1 528	47.9	3 421	1 622	47.4

SOURCE: U.S. Department of Education, National Center for Education Statistics, Common Core of Data survey; and unpublished estimates. Published as table 85 in *Digest of Education Statistics* 1997.

1. Some data have been revised from previously published figures.
2. U.S. totals include imputations for underreporting and nonreporting states.
3. Includes imputations for underreporting.
4. Support staff underreported.
5. Data estimated by the National Center for Education Statistics.

NOTE: Some data have been revised from previously published figures.

Table C-21. Staff, Enrollment, and Pupil-Staff Ratios in Public Elementary and Secondary Schools, By State: Fall 1989 to Fall 1995

State	Pupil-staff ratio				Fall 1993			Fall 1994[1]			Fall 1995		
	Fall 1989	Fall 1990	Fall 1991	Fall 1992	Staff	Enrollment	Pupil-staff ratio	Staff	Enrollment	Pupil-staff ratio	Staff	Enrollment	Pupil-staff ratio
United States	[2]9.1	[2]9.2	[2]9.2	[2]9.1	[2]4 808 080	43 464 916	[2]9.0	[2]4 904 757	[2]44 111 482	[2]9.0	[2]4 994 358	[2]44 840 481	[2]9.0
Alabama	9.1	9.7	8.8	[3]9.3	[3]80 923	734 288	[3]9.1	[3]81 544	736 531	[3]9.0	83 256	746 149	[3]9.0
Alaska	8.1	8.5	8.5	8.3	15 689	125 948	8.0	[3]15 150	127 057	[3]8.4	[3]15 022	127 618	[3]8.4
Arizona	10.0	10.1	10.0	9.4	74 679	709 453	9.5	74 540	737 424	9.9	75 931	743 566	9.8
Arkansas	8.8	8.8	8.5	9.0	50 502	444 271	8.8	50 201	447 565	8.9	49 178	453 257	9.2
California	11.4	11.8	11.9	[3]12.3	[3]431 093	5 327 231	[3]12.4	[3]436 140	5 407 475	[3]12.4	[3]444 014	5 536 406	[3]12.5
Colorado	9.3	9.3	9.5	9.8	62 927	625 062	9.9	64 985	640 521	9.9	67 447	656 279	9.7
Connecticut	7.4	7.6	8.0	7.7	62 014	496 298	8.0	64 742	506 824	7.8	66 133	517 935	7.8
Delaware	9.0	9.2	9.3	9.2	11 640	105 547	9.1	11 759	106 813	9.1	11 869	108 461	9.1
District of Columbia	7.7	7.9	7.2	7.7	10 591	80 678	7.6	10 507	80 450	7.7	9 410	79 802	8.5
Florida	8.7	8.6	8.8	9.1	226 911	2 040 763	9.0	226 975	2 111 188	9.3	237 721	2 176 222	9.2
Georgia	8.9	8.9	8.9	[3]8.5	[3]156 005	1 235 304	[3]7.9	[3]161 390	1 270 948	[3]7.9	[3]165 058	1 311 126	[3]7.9
Hawaii	11.5	11.3	11.2	10.0	18 292	180 410	9.9	16 567	183 795	11.1	16 841	187 180	11.1
Idaho	12.5	12.2	12.1	11.8	19 983	236 774	11.8	21 194	240 448	11.3	21 814	243 097	11.1
Illinois	9.6	9.5	9.4	9.4	198 862	1 893 078	9.5	204 413	1 916 172	9.4	209 036	1 943 623	9.3
Indiana	8.9	8.8	8.8	8.6	113 892	965 633	8.5	115 441	969 022	8.4	116 363	977 263	8.4
Iowa	8.4	8.3	8.1	8.2	60 267	498 519	8.3	60 469	500 440	8.3	62 075	502 343	8.1
Kansas	8.6	8.5	8.6	8.3	55 783	457 614	8.2	56 790	460 838	8.1	57 265	463 008	8.1
Kentucky	8.8	8.6	8.4	8.3	81 279	655 265	8.1	81 720	657 642	8.0	84 425	659 821	7.8
Louisiana	8.8	8.6	[4]12.0	8.7	93 197	800 560	8.6	96 124	797 933	8.3	93 070	797 366	8.6
Maine	8.1	8.0	8.0	7.5	28 865	216 995	7.5	29 264	212 601	7.3	29 413	213 569	7.3
Maryland	9.1	9.1	9.2	9.3	82 753	772 638	9.3	84 699	790 938	9.3	87 868	805 544	9.2
Massachusetts	7.9	8.8	8.5	8.5	104 196	877 726	8.4	108 281	893 727	8.3	113 154	915 007	8.1
Michigan	9.2	9.2	8.9	9.2	169 283	1 599 377	9.4	164 766	1 614 784	9.8	177 495	1 641 456	9.2
Minnesota	9.7	9.8	9.9	10.0	74 859	810 233	10.8	74 914	821 693	11.0	74 891	835 166	11.2
Mississippi	8.9	8.6	8.5	8.8	59 853	505 907	8.5	60 708	505 962	8.3	60 855	506 272	8.3
Missouri	8.0	7.9	8.4	[3]7.9	112 810	866 378	7.7	116 974	878 541	7.5	120 621	889 881	7.4
Montana	[4]12.1	[4]12.2	[4]11.9	[3]8.5	[3]18 717	163 009	[3]8.7	[3]18 452	164 341	[3]8.9	[3]18 586	165 547	[3]8.9
Nebraska	8.1	7.8	8.1	[3]7.9	[3]36 832	285 097	[3]7.7	37 144	287 100	7.7	37 894	289 744	7.6
Nevada	[4]18.1	[4]17.3	[4]16.1	[3]10.4	22 418	235 800	10.5	23 098	250 747	10.9	23 742	265 041	11.2
New Hampshire	8.4	8.4	8.6	8.5	21 913	185 360	8.5	22 336	189 319	8.5	23 143	194 171	8.4
New Jersey	7.3	7.4	7.5	7.5	160 202	1 151 307	7.2	161 586	1 174 206	7.3	163 069	1 197 381	7.3
New Mexico	9.2	9.1	8.9	9.1	36 694	322 292	8.8	39 016	327 248	8.4	40 124	329 640	8.2
New York	7.4	7.5	7.8	7.8	353 603	2 733 813	7.7	356 386	2 766 208	7.8	355 723	2 813 230	7.9
North Carolina	8.8	8.7	8.7	[3]8.6	133 059	1 133 231	8.5	[3]137 791	1 156 767	[3]8.4	[3]140 204	1 183 090	[3]8.4
North Dakota	8.3	8.5	8.7	8.6	13 780	119 127	8.6	13 919	119 288	8.6	13 804	119 100	8.6
Ohio	9.4	9.3	9.2	8.9	201 828	1 807 319	9.0	200 141	1 814 290	9.1	194 579	1 836 015	9.4
Oklahoma	8.8	8.4	8.4	8.3	73 067	604 076	8.3	[3]78 270	609 718	[3]7.8	[3]840	616 393	[3]7.4
Oregon	9.8	9.6	9.9	9.9	50 392	516 611	10.3	50 377	521 945	10.4	51 458	527 914	10.3
Pennsylvania	8.7	8.7	8.9	9.0	190 885	1 744 082	9.1	193 696	1 764 946	9.1	198 087	1 787 533	9.0
Rhode Island	8.9	8.8	9.2	9.1	15 442	145 676	9.4	15 438	147 487	9.6	16 517	149 799	9.1
South Carolina	9.7	9.4	9.4	9.5	[3]71 433	643 696	[3]9.0	[3]74 196	648 725	[3]8.7	[3]74 859	645 586	[3]8.6
South Dakota	9.0	8.5	8.9	8.6	17 201	142 825	8.3	[3]17 989	143 482	[3]8.0	[3]18 126	144 685	[3]8.0
Tennessee	9.5	9.5	9.9	9.9	[3]92 349	866 557	[3]9.4	96 281	881 425	[3]9.2	98 948	893 770	[3]9.0
Texas	10.0	10.2	10.3	8.4	433 102	3 608 262	8.3	450 462	3 677 171	8.2	462 661	3 748 167	8.1
Utah	14.0	13.8	13.7	13.3	35 301	471 365	13.4	36 186	474 675	13.1	37 385	477 121	12.8
Vermont	7.9	7.1	7.0	6.6	[3]14 928	102 755	[3]6.9	15 337	104 533	6.8	15 640	105 565	6.7
Virginia	8.2	7.7	[5]7.8	8.1	130 033	1 045 471	8.0	[3]798	1 060 809	[3]7.9	[3]137 546	1 079 854	[3]7.9
Washington	11.2	11.1	11.1	11.0	87 734	915 952	10.4	[3]90 438	938 314	[3]10.4	[3]91 322	956 572	[3]10.5
West Virginia	8.3	8.2	8.3	8.3	38 486	314 383	8.2	38 481	310 511	8.1	38 645	307 112	7.9
Wisconsin	9.4	9.4	9.2	9.0	88 640	844 001	9.5	100 996	860 581	8.5	95 105	870 175	9.1
Wyoming	7.2	7.7	7.8	8.7	12 893	100 899	7.8	12 999	100 314	7.7	13 164	99 859	7.6

See footnotes at end of table.

Table C-21.   Staff, Enrollment, and Pupil-Staff Ratios in Public Elementary and Secondary Schools, By State: Fall 1989 to Fall 1995 — Continued

State	Pupil-staff ratio				Fall 1993			Fall 1994[1]			Fall 1995		
	Fall 1989	Fall 1990	Fall 1991	Fall 1992	Staff	Enrollment	Pupil-staff ratio	Staff	Enrollment	Pupil-staff ratio	Staff	Enrollment	Pupil-staff ratio
Outlying areas													
American Samoa ...	9.9	9.9	10.5	10.4	1 339	14 484	10.8	1 340	14 445	10.8	1 417	14 576	10.3
Guam	8.9	9.0	9.6	8.6	3 839	30 920	8.1	4 730	32 185	6.8	3 728	32 960	8.8
Northern Marianas	8.9	7.9	7.8	7.4	1 101	8 188	7.4	1 051	8 429	8.0	1 054	8 809	8.4
Puerto Rico	10.4	10.4	9.5	9.4	68 005	631 460	9.3	[4] 68 868	621 121	[4] 9.0	69 731	627 620	9.0
Virgin Islands	6.4	6.6	6.8	6.8	3 324	22 752	6.8	[4] 3 193	23 126	[4] 7.2	3 421	22 737	6.6

SOURCE: U.S. Department of Education, National Center for Education Statistics, Common Core of Data survey; and unpublished estimates. Published as table 86 in *Digest of Education Statistics* 1997.

1. Some data have been revised from previously published figures.
2. U.S. totals include imputations for underreporting and nonreporting states.
3. Includes imputations for underreporting.
4. Support staff underreported.
5. Data estimated by the National Center for Education Statistics.

NOTE: Some data have been revised from previously published figures.

Table C-22.   Number and Percentage of Public Elementary and Secondary Education Agencies, by State and Type of Agency: 1995-96

State or other area	Total agencies	Regular school districts, including supervisory union components		Regional education service agencies and supervisory union administrative centers		State-operated agencies		Federally operated and other agencies	
		Number	Percent	Number	Percent	Number	Percent	Number	Percent
United States	16 410	14 883	90.7	1 185	7.2	197	1.2	145	0.9
Alabama	131	127	96.9	—	—	1	0.8	3	2.3
Alaska	56	56	100.0	—	—	—	—	—	—
Arizona	242	227	93.8	5	2.1	1	0.4	9	3.7
Arkansas	335	314	93.7	17	5.1	4	1.2	—	—
California	1 067	1 006	94.3	58	5.4	3	0.3	—	—
Colorado	194	176	90.7	18	9.3	—	—	—	—
Connecticut	179	166	92.7	6	3.4	4	2.2	3	1.7
Delaware	22	19	86.4	—	—	3	13.6	—	—
District of Columbia	1	1	100.0	—	—	—	—	—	—
Florida	74	67	90.5	—	—	1	1.4	6	8.1
Georgia	184	181	98.4	—	—	—	—	3	1.6
Hawaii	1	1	100.0	—	—	—	—	—	—
Idaho	113	112	99.1	—	—	1	0.9	—	—
Illinois	1 038	916	88.2	86	8.3	5	0.5	31	3.0
Indiana	327	295	90.2	28	8.6	3	0.9	1	0.3
Iowa	421	390	92.6	15	3.6	15	3.6	1	0.2
Kansas	304	304	100.0	—	—	—	—	—	—
Kentucky	258	176	68.2	—	—	80	31.0	2	0.8
Louisiana	72	66	91.7	—	—	5	6.9	1	1.4
Maine	329	285	86.6	42	12.8	1	0.3	1	0.3
Maryland	24	24	100.0	—	—	—	—	—	—
Massachusetts	464	353	76.1	85	18.3	1	0.2	25	5.4
Michigan	695	633	91.1	57	8.2	4	0.6	1	0.1
Minnesota	489	419	85.7	67	13.7	3	0.6	—	—
Mississippi	165	153	92.7	—	—	11	6.7	1	0.6
Missouri	542	536	98.9	—	—	2	0.4	4	0.7
Montana	561	481	85.7	77	13.7	3	0.5	—	—
Nebraska	799	680	85.1	112	14.0	7	0.9	—	—
Nevada	18	17	94.4	—	—	1	5.6	—	—
New Hampshire	247	178	72.1	69	27.9	—	—	—	—
New Jersey	620	608	98.1	12	1.9	—	—	—	—
New Mexico	89	89	100.0	—	—	—	—	—	—
New York	757	719	95.0	38	5.0	—	—	—	—
North Carolina	123	119	96.7	—	—	2	1.6	2	1.6
North Dakota	289	243	84.1	38	13.1	3	1.0	5	1.7
Ohio	790	661	83.7	102	12.9	3	0.4	24	3.0
Oklahoma	551	551	100.0	—	—	—	—	—	—
Oregon	258	248	96.1	7	2.7	2	0.8	1	0.4
Pennsylvania	614	501	81.6	101	16.4	12	2.0	—	—
Rhode Island	37	36	97.3	—	—	1	2.7	—	—
South Carolina	106	95	89.6	11	10.4	—	—	—	—
South Dakota	218	177	81.2	17	7.8	5	2.3	19	8.7
Tennessee	140	140	100.0	—	—	—	—	—	—
Texas	1 044	1 044	100.0	—	—	—	—	—	—
Utah	47	40	85.1	5	10.6	2	4.3	—	—
Vermont	344	284	82.6	60	17.4	—	—	—	—
Virginia	165	141	85.5	22	13.3	—	—	2	1.2
Washington	305	296	97.0	9	3.0	—	—	—	—
West Virginia	57	55	96.5	—	—	2	3.5	—	—
Wisconsin	446	428	96.0	16	3.6	2	0.4	—	—
Wyoming	58	49	84.5	5	8.6	4	6.9	—	—

See footnotes at end of table.

Table C-22.   Number and Percentage of Public Elementary and Secondary Education Agencies, by State and Type of Agency: 1995-96 — Continued

State or other area	Total agencies	Regular school districts, including supervisory union components		Regional education service agencies and supervisory union administrative centers		State-operated agencies		Federally operated and other agencies	
		Number	Percent	Number	Percent	Number	Percent	Number	Percent
Department of Defense Overseas Schools	12	—	—	—	—	—	—	12	100.0
Outlying areas									
American Samoa	1	1	100.0	—	—	—	—	—	—
Guam	1	1	100.0	—	—	—	—	—	—
Northern Marianas	1	1	100.0	—	—	—	—	—	—
Puerto Rico	1	1	100.0	—	—	—	—	—	—
Virgin Islands	1	1	100.0	—	—	—	—	—	—

SOURCE: U.S. Department of Education, National Center for Education Statistics, Common Core of Data survey. Published as table 91 in *Digest of Education Statistics* 1997.

1. Data are based on a head count of all teachers rather than on the number of full-time equivalent teachers appearing in other tables.

NOTE: Excludes prekindergarten teachers. Details may not add to totals due to rounding or item nonresponse.

— Represents zero or rounds to zero.

Table C-23. Public Elementary and Secondary Schools, by Type and State: 1990-91 to 1995-96

State	Total, all schools, 1990-91	Total, all schools, 1993-94	Total, all schools, 1994-95	Number of schools, 1995-96			Combined elementary/secondary[3]				Other[4]	Alternatives[5]	Special education[5]
				Total	Elementary[1]	Secondary[2]	Total	Prekindergarten, kindergarten or 1st grade to grade 12	Other schools ending with grade 12	Other combined schools			
United States	84 538	85 393	86 221	87 125	61 165	20 997	2 796	1 505	662	629	2 167	3 243	1 992
Alabama	1 297	1 294	1 309	1 319	864	298	154	119	15	20	3	18	17
Alaska	498	496	498	495	186	87	208	161	4	43	14	36	3
Arizona	1 049	1 133	1 136	1 133	817	240	15	4	9	2	61	43	16
Arkansas	1 098	1 070	1 073	1 098	674	414	7	6	0	1	3	0	0
California	7 913	7 734	7 821	7 876	5 750	1 866	182	110	41	31	78	756	127
Colorado	1 344	1 419	1 460	1 486	1 034	356	22	5	7	10	74	102	9
Connecticut	985	1 000	1 045	1 045	763	188	26	2	3	21	68	54	18
Delaware	173	177	182	181	120	42	19	14	1	4	0	2	28
District of Columbia ..	181	173	175	186	126	41	2	0	0	2	17	7	11
Florida	2 516	2 615	2 733	2 760	1 914	443	346	194	77	75	57	262	104
Georgia	1 734	1 755	1 767	1 763	1 383	307	73	17	43	13	0	19	8
Hawaii	235	241	242	246	186	44	16	5	5	6	0	1	4
Idaho	582	603	608	618	384	209	18	10	2	6	7	45	14
Illinois	4 239	4 195	4 195	4 142	3 061	898	32	24	4	4	151	44	240
Indiana	1 915	1 912	1 912	1 924	1 406	448	34	13	15	6	36	33	44
Iowa	1 588	1 556	1 554	1 556	1 075	443	28	6	21	1	10	26	18
Kansas	1 477	1 482	1 491	1 487	1 048	426	9	2	4	3	4	18	1
Kentucky	1 400	1 372	1 374	1 402	1 002	360	3	0	1	2	37	49	8
Louisiana	1 533	1 459	1 459	1 470	1 006	319	119	91	16	12	26	56	39
Maine	747	706	733	726	550	158	14	9	3	2	4	0	2
Maryland	1 220	1 271	1 263	1 276	1 038	213	20	9	5	6	5	27	47
Massachusetts	1 842	1 791	1 831	1 850	1 465	336	27	18	6	3	22	29	7
Michigan	3 313	3 356	3 432	3 748	2 514	811	92	40	34	18	331	135	159
Minnesota	1 590	2 083	2 100	2 157	1 190	686	92	26	27	39	189	513	108
Mississippi	972	1 009	1 018	1 011	571	314	75	62	10	3	51	35	0
Missouri	2 199	2 217	2 234	2 256	1 447	627	30	4	18	8	152	61	67
Montana	900	900	899	894	532	361	0	0	0	0	1	3	2
Nebraska	1 506	1 427	1 419	1 411	1 010	354	26	11	7	8	21	0	63
Nevada	354	407	421	423	313	96	9	2	6	1	5	23	12
New Hampshire	439	461	458	460	357	98	5	3	0	2	0	0	0
New Jersey	2 272	2 287	2 295	2 279	1 770	427	7	1	4	2	75	0	79
New Mexico	681	709	715	721	536	178	3	1	2	0	4	25	14
New York	4 010	4 082	4 130	4 149	2 972	940	145	85	37	23	92	65	83
North Carolina	1 955	1 958	1 968	1 985	1 538	393	44	20	9	15	10	48	27
North Dakota	663	640	623	613	352	224	4	1	2	1	33	0	31
Ohio	3 731	3 818	3 812	3 865	2 694	948	130	49	24	57	93	10	34
Oklahoma	1 880	1 820	1 824	1 830	1 216	604	0	0	0	0	10	0	15
Oregon	1 199	1 219	1 213	1 216	913	252	46	31	8	7	5	35	15
Pennsylvania	3 260	3 193	3 190	3 182	2 350	788	30	9	12	9	14	10	11
Rhode Island	309	311	308	310	249	57	2	2	0	0	2	3	4
South Carolina	1 097	1 094	1 094	1 095	795	289	11	4	5	2	0	18	11
South Dakota	802	777	827	824	506	301	2	1	1	0	15	11	15
Tennessee	1 543	1 523	1 554	1 563	1 133	338	53	36	6	11	39	14	17
Texas	5 991	6 324	6 465	6 638	4 515	1 721	402	208	101	93	0	345	221
Utah	714	718	728	735	476	227	10	5	2	3	22	40	24
Vermont	397	400	394	384	271	55	17	12	5	0	41	1	60
Virginia	1 811	1 828	1 851	1 889	1 384	394	20	3	13	4	91	60	48
Washington	1 936	2 030	2 064	2 124	1 315	534	105	49	30	26	170	122	81
West Virginia	1 015	907	883	877	624	209	29	11	2	16	15	12	12
Wisconsin	2 018	2 032	2 030	2 037	1 486	518	33	10	15	8	0	18	9
Wyoming	415	409	411	410	284	117	0	0	0	0	9	9	5

See footnotes at end of table.

Table C-23. Public Elementary and Secondary Schools, by Type and State: 1990-91 to 1995-96 — Continued

| State | Total, all schools, 1990-91 | Total, all schools, 1993-94 | Total, all schools, 1994-95 | Total | Elemen-tary[1] | Secon-dary[2] | Combined elementary/secondary[3] | | | | Other[4] | Alterna-tives[5] | Special education[5] |
							Total	Prekinder-garten, kindergarten or 1st grade to grade 12	Other schools ending with grade 12	Other combined schools			
Department of Defense Overseas Schools	(NA)	(NA)	(NA)	171	116	41	14	11	2	1	0	0	0
Outlying areas													
American Samoa	30	31	31	31	24	6	0	0	0	0	1	0	1
Guam	35	35	35	35	30	5	0	0	0	0	0	0	1
Northern Marianas	26	25	25	24	20	4	0	0	0	0	0	0	0
Puerto Rico	1 619	1 584	1 566	1 561	972	359	191	2	1	188	39	10	22
Virgin Islands	33	32	32	34	23	10	1	0	0	1	0	0	0

SOURCE: U.S. Department of Education, National Center for Education Statistics, Common Core of Data survey. Published as Table 96 in *Digest of Education Statistics* 1997

1. Includes schools beginning with grade 6 or below and with no grade higher than 8.
2. Includes schools with no grade lower than 7.
3. Includes schools beginning with grade 6 or below and ending with grade 9 or above.
4. Includes special education, alternative, and other schools not classified by grade span.
5. Schools are included under elementary, secondary, combined, or other as appropriate.

NOTE: Some data have been revised from previously published figures.

(NA) Not applicable or not available.

Table C-24. Public Elementary Schools, by Grade Span and Average School Size, by State: 1995-96

State or other area	Total, all elementary schools	Total, all regular elementary schools[1]	Schools, by grade span						All elementary schools	Regular elementary schools[1]
			Prekindergarten, kindergarten, or 1st grade to grades 3 or 4	Prekindergarten, kindergarten, or 1st grade to grade 5	Prekindergarten, kindergarten, or 1st grade to grade 6[1]	Prekindergarten, kindergarten, or 1st grade to grade 8[2]	Grades 4, 5, or 6, to 6, 7, or 8	Other grade spans		
United States	61 165	56 697	4 944	19 885	15 996	4 503	10 205	5 632	476	481
Alabama	864	853	87	244	199	74	173	87	490	496
Alaska	186	184	4	28	100	17	19	18	371	374
Arizona	817	800	45	182	267	153	111	59	587	593
Arkansas	674	673	89	64	361	6	87	67	394	391
California	5 750	5 708	176	1 769	2 331	547	715	212	620	623
Colorado	1 034	1 034	34	470	250	15	195	70	431	431
Connecticut	763	761	83	297	140	40	141	62	469	469
Delaware	120	112	40	14	8	1	29	28	560	593
District of Columbia	126	125	8	11	89	5	8	5	419	420
Florida	1 914	1 861	24	1 174	222	32	356	106	782	798
Georgia	1 383	1 381	33	736	115	23	279	197	657	658
Hawaii	186	185	1	32	123	8	17	5	627	630
Idaho	384	382	32	76	172	17	52	35	370	371
Illinois	3 061	2 963	344	539	628	714	454	382	423	433
Indiana	1 406	1 395	63	584	421	36	229	73	442	445
Iowa	1 075	1 066	130	311	264	20	212	138	288	290
Kansas	1 048	1 041	77	311	260	134	167	99	287	288
Kentucky	1 002	992	58	404	225	104	181	30	418	422
Louisiana	1 006	982	113	288	212	75	207	111	498	501
Maine	550	550	82	89	87	107	89	96	261	261
Maryland	1 038	998	19	580	168	18	193	60	547	562
Massachusetts	1 465	1 456	217	450	275	76	242	205	430	431
Michigan	2 514	2 475	224	947	574	66	442	261	434	436
Minnesota	1 190	1 044	144	231	462	34	157	162	426	474
Mississippi	571	571	78	83	156	52	112	90	518	518
Missouri	1 447	1 446	98	475	375	108	258	133	388	389
Montana	532	531	29	76	252	63	44	68	188	189
Nebraska	1 010	972	61	107	492	164	55	131	168	174
Nevada	313	306	11	128	87	19	43	25	586	597
New Hampshire ...	357	357	57	74	78	47	66	35	373	373
New Jersey	1 770	1 764	270	432	297	261	306	204	456	457
New Mexico	536	525	27	192	158	4	98	57	404	409
New York	2 972	2 970	278	932	793	75	521	373	611	611
North Carolina	1 538	1 519	81	696	198	112	334	117	537	542
North Dakota	352	352	15	26	227	42	20	22	192	192
Ohio	2 694	2 682	329	773	784	86	480	242	428	429
Oklahoma	1 216	1 207	53	346	215	297	203	102	338	339
Oregon	913	894	56	372	189	87	160	49	377	383
Pennsylvania	2 350	2 350	296	817	624	61	393	159	483	483
Rhode Island	249	248	34	75	70	4	36	30	406	406
South Carolina	795	791	89	333	89	21	197	66	540	542
South Dakota	506	502	31	108	137	87	77	66	183	184
Tennessee	1 133	1 132	108	322	227	226	177	73	511	511
Texas	4 515	4 414	473	1 667	770	96	979	530	551	559
Utah	476	474	8	90	325	2	36	15	547	548
Vermont	271	252	21	20	122	61	18	29	240	254
Virginia	1 384	1 380	80	697	178	2	270	157	528	529
Washington	1 315	1 276	64	422	478	58	190	103	451	461
West Virginia	624	622	58	186	234	36	83	27	294	295
Wisconsin	1 486	1 477	97	535	363	105	252	134	373	374
Wyoming	284	283	15	70	125	5	42	27	209	209

See footnotes at end of table.

Table C-24.   Public Elementary Schools, by Grade Span and Average School Size, by State: 1995-96 — Continued

State or other area	Total, all elementary schools	Total, all regular elementary schools[1]	Schools, by grade span						All elementary schools	Regular elementary schools[1]
			Prekindergarten, kindergarten, or 1st grade to grades 3 or 4	Prekindergarten, kindergarten, or 1st grade to grade 5	Prekindergarten, kindergarten, or 1st grade to grade 6[1]	Prekindergarten, kindergarten, or 1st grade to grade 8[2]	Grades 4, 5, or 6, to 6, 7, or 8	Other grade spans		
Department of Defense Overseas Schools	116	116	6	25	59	11	14	1	488	488
Outlying areas American Samoa	24	24	0	1	0	21	1	1	467	467
Guam	30	29	0	21	0	0	6	3	843	849
Northern Marianas	20	20	0	0	10	0	0	10	274	274
Puerto Rico	972	971	98	27	755	5	39	48	304	305
Virgin Islands	23	23	0	0	23	0	0	0	505	505

SOURCE: U.S. Department of Education, National Center for Education Statistics, Common Core of Data survey. Published as table 97 in *Digest of Education Statistics* 1997.

1. Excludes special education and alternative schools.
2. Average for schools reporting enrollment data.

NOTE: Includes schools beginning with grade 6 or below and with no grade higher than 8. Excludes schools not reported by grade level, such as some special education schools for the disabled.

Table C-25. Public Secondary Schools, by Grade Span and Average School Size, by State: 1995-96

State	Total, all secondary schools	Total, all regular secondary schools[1]	Schools, by grade span							Vocational schools[2]	Average of students per school[3]	
			Grades 7 to 8 and 7 to 9	Grades 7 to 12	Grades 8 to 12	Grades 9 to 12	Grades 10 to 12	Other spans ending with grade 12	Other grade spans		All secondary schools	Regular secondary schools[1]
United States	20 997	18 090	3 743	3 158	463	11 321	847	141	1 324	890	703	771
Alabama	298	284	34	78	10	154	11	1	10	3	708	736
Alaska	87	72	14	22	3	40	2	0	6	5	453	520
Arizona	240	218	67	8	2	152	8	0	3	6	1 008	1 067
Arkansas	414	414	77	214	1	47	59	0	16	0	447	447
California	1 866	1 256	426	99	44	1 117	103	10	67	0	960	1 352
Colorado	356	306	55	66	2	205	13	2	13	7	588	657
Connecticut	188	166	30	7	1	147	1	0	2	18	778	820
Delaware	42	34	10	2	0	30	0	0	0	5	930	989
District of Columbia	41	39	18	0	0	22	1	0	0	1	569	580
Florida	443	314	28	44	16	258	24	18	55	40	1 159	1 561
Georgia	307	288	22	9	26	244	2	0	4	1	1 146	1 204
Hawaii	44	41	10	9	2	20	0	0	3	0	1 367	1 462
Idaho	209	164	46	37	1	92	20	1	12	0	470	583
Illinois	898	836	219	33	9	588	9	3	37	27	701	730
Indiana	448	408	70	105	2	231	8	1	31	26	809	833
Iowa	443	418	70	103	2	249	16	0	3	0	408	425
Kansas	426	420	67	64	3	274	12	3	3	0	377	381
Kentucky	360	316	41	56	7	208	9	1	38	12	625	689
Louisiana	319	282	62	50	12	181	6	2	6	10	764	821
Maine	158	131	22	13	1	91	2	0	29	27	506	506
Maryland	213	185	27	5	3	167	2	2	7	11	1 080	1 176
Massachusetts	336	275	41	45	16	223	4	2	5	45	789	842
Michigan	811	706	113	120	18	473	21	6	60	48	671	724
Minnesota	686	446	87	241	39	199	59	24	37	12	457	670
Mississippi	314	229	44	42	9	106	15	3	95	85	672	672
Missouri	627	557	60	205	9	262	18	1	72	59	527	535
Montana	361	357	185	0	0	173	2	0	1	0	181	182
Nebraska	354	353	40	219	2	81	11	0	1	0	334	335
Nevada	96	74	16	17	4	53	1	0	5	3	844	1 023
New Hampshire	98	98	24	0	0	72	2	0	0	0	580	580
New Jersey	427	382	70	37	10	254	3	2	51	44	887	936
New Mexico	178	156	41	27	2	93	7	0	8	0	624	695
New York	940	858	134	195	14	499	26	1	71	24	946	968
North Carolina	393	360	53	23	3	282	16	1	15	8	882	940
North Dakota	224	217	19	150	5	32	7	1	10	7	242	242
Ohio	948	854	172	143	31	498	16	3	85	83	724	738
Oklahoma	604	601	123	0	0	377	82	4	18	0	333	335
Oregon	252	237	43	25	6	171	4	0	3	0	684	718
Pennsylvania	788	701	113	176	18	346	47	8	80	83	855	860
Rhode Island	57	52	14	3	0	38	1	0	1	2	850	907
South Carolina	289	230	35	23	9	159	6	1	56	43	836	892
South Dakota	301	293	112	0	0	182	3	0	4	3	173	174
Tennessee	338	301	57	38	4	200	11	0	28	27	876	918
Texas	1 721	1 393	309	198	34	977	36	31	136	21	679	821
Utah	227	190	80	30	11	45	50	2	9	2	917	1 073
Vermont	55	54	6	24	0	25	0	0	0	0	611	621
Virginia	394	322	39	15	43	227	9	0	61	49	981	1 041
Washington	534	415	121	54	18	271	40	5	25	8	640	786
West Virginia	209	170	47	23	3	81	17	0	38	34	622	650
Wisconsin	518	506	89	61	6	342	15	2	3	0	580	592
Wyoming	117	111	41	0	2	63	10	0	1	1	347	360

See footnotes at end of table.

Table C-25. Public Secondary Schools, by Grade Span and Average School Size, by State: 1995-96 — Continued

State	Total, all secondary schools	Total, all regular secondary schools[1]	Schools, by grade span							Vocational schools[2]	Average of students per school[3]	
			Grades 7 to 8 and 7 to 9	Grades 7 to 12	Grades 8 to 12	Grades 9 to 12	Grades 10 to 12	Other spans ending with grade 12	Other grade spans		All secondary schools	Regular secondary schools[1]
Department of Defense Overseas Schools	41	41	3	26	0	12	0	0	0	0	475	475
Outlying areas												
American Samoa	6	5	0	0	0	6	0	0	0	1	551	600
Guam	5	5	0	0	0	5	0	0	0	0	1 617	1 617
Northern Marianas	4	4	1	2	0	1	0	0	0	0	803	803
Puerto Rico	359	332	168	29	0	3	136	0	23	27	643	656
Virgin Islands	10	9	5	0	0	4	0	0	1	1	1 136	1 136

SOURCE: U.S. Department of Education, National Center for Education Statistics, Common Core of Data survey. Published as table 98 in *Digest of Education Statistics* 1997.

1. Excludes vocational, special education, and alternative schools.
2. Vocational schools are included under appropriate grade span.
3. Average for schools reporting enrollment data.

NOTE: Includes schools with no grade lower than 7. Excludes schools not reported by grade level, such as some special education schools for the disabled.

Table C-26. Public High School Graduates, by State: 1969-70 to 1996-97

State or other area	1969-70	1979-80	1980-81	1985-86	1990-91	1992-93	1993-94[1]	1994-95	Estimated 1995-96	Estimated 1996-97	Percent change, 1990-91 to 1996-97
United States	2 588 639	2 747 678	2 725 285	2 382 616	2 234 893	2 233 241	2 220 849	2 273 541	[2] 2 292 626	[2] 2 357 649	5.5
Alabama	45 286	45 190	44 894	39 620	39 042	36 007	34 447	36 268	[3] 35 043	35 253	-9.7
Alaska	3 297	5 223	5 343	5 464	5 458	5 535	5 747	5 765	5 709	6 376	16.8
Arizona	22 040	28 633	28 416	27 533	31 282	31 747	31 799	30 989	[4] 31 014	[4] 31 826	1.7
Arkansas	26 068	29 052	29 577	26 227	25 668	25 655	24 990	24 636	24 628	24 874	-3.1
California	260 908	249 217	242 172	229 026	234 164	249 320	253 083	255 200	262 441	265 400	13.3
Colorado	30 312	36 804	35 897	32 621	31 293	31 839	31 867	32 409	[3] 32 607	34 688	10.8
Connecticut	34 755	37 683	38 369	33 571	27 290	26 799	26 330	26 445	[3] 26 445	26 560	-2.7
Delaware	6 985	7 582	7 349	5 791	5 223	5 492	5 230	5 234	[3] 5 609	5 822	11.5
District of Columbia[5] ...	4 980	4 959	4 848	3 875	3 369	3 136	3 207	2 974	[4] 2 928	[4] 2 956	-12.3
Florida	70 478	87 324	88 755	83 029	87 419	89 428	88 032	89 827	89 242	96 070	9.9
Georgia	56 859	61 621	62 963	59 082	60 088	57 602	56 356	56 660	[3] 57 797	59 421	-1.1
Hawaii	10 407	11 493	11 472	9 958	8 974	8 854	9 369	9 407	9 993	10 143	13.0
Idaho	12 296	13 187	12 679	12 059	11 961	12 974	13 281	14 198	[3] 14 667	15 562	30.1
Illinois	126 864	135 579	136 795	114 319	103 329	103 628	102 126	105 164	[3] 104 626	107 766	4.3
Indiana	69 984	73 143	73 381	59 817	57 892	57 559	54 650	56 058	56 575	57 720	-0.3
Iowa	44 063	43 445	42 635	34 279	28 593	30 677	30 247	31 268	[3] 31 689	32 479	13.6
Kansas	33 394	30 890	29 397	25 587	24 414	24 720	25 319	26 125	[3] 25 803	26 450	8.3
Kentucky	37 473	41 203	41 714	37 288	35 835	36 361	38 454	37 626	37 245	37 453	4.5
Louisiana	43 641	46 297	46 199	39 965	33 489	33 682	34 822	36 480	36 881	[4] 36 128	7.9
Maine	14 003	15 445	15 554	13 006	13 151	12 103	11 384	11 501	[3] 13 470	13 250	0.8
Maryland	46 462	54 270	54 050	46 700	39 014	39 523	39 091	41 387	[3] 41 785	42 482	8.9
Massachusetts	63 865	73 802	74 831	60 360	50 216	48 321	47 453	47 679	[4] 48 451	[4] 50 482	0.5
Michigan	121 000	124 316	124 372	101 042	88 234	85 302	83 385	84 628	84 300	90 600	2.7
Minnesota	60 480	64 908	64 166	51 988	46 474	48 002	47 514	49 354	50 300	52 500	13.0
Mississippi	29 653	27 586	28 083	25 134	23 665	23 597	23 379	23 837	23 040	23 185	-2.0
Missouri	55 315	62 265	60 359	49 204	46 928	46 864	46 566	48 862	48 870	49 986	6.5
Montana	11 520	12 135	11 634	9 761	9 013	9 389	9 601	10 134	10 234	10 645	18.1
Nebraska	21 280	22 410	21 411	17 845	16 500	17 569	17 072	17 969	[3] 18 591	20 682	25.3
Nevada	5 449	8 473	9 069	8 784	9 370	9 042	9 485	10 038	10 374	11 257	20.1
New Hampshire	8 516	11 722	11 552	10 648	10 059	10 065	9 933	10 145	9 478	9 353	-7.0
New Jersey	86 498	94 564	93 168	78 781	67 003	67 134	66 125	67 403	[4] 68 222	[4] 70 798	5.7
New Mexico	16 060	18 424	17 915	15 468	15 157	15 172	14 892	14 928	[3] 15 446	15 871	4.7
New York	190 000	204 064	198 465	162 165	133 562	132 963	132 708	132 401	134 500	137 420	2.9
North Carolina	68 886	70 862	69 395	65 865	62 792	60 460	57 738	59 540	[3] 56 770	58 000	-7.6
North Dakota	11 150	9 928	9 924	7 610	7 573	7 310	7 522	7 817	[3] 7 967	8 063	6.5
Ohio	142 248	144 169	143 503	119 561	107 484	109 200	107 700	109 418	102 755	103 755	-3.5
Oklahoma	36 293	39 305	38 875	34 452	33 007	30 542	31 872	33 319	32 843	30 628	-7.2
Oregon	32 236	29 939	28 729	26 286	24 597	26 301	26 338	26 713	[3] 27 093	27 200	10.6
Pennsylvania	151 014	146 458	144 645	122 871	104 770	103 715	101 958	104 146	108 520	112 920	7.8
Rhode Island	10 146	10 864	10 719	8 908	7 744	7 640	7 450	7 826	7 693	7 695	-0.6
South Carolina	34 940	38 697	38 347	34 500	32 999	31 297	30 603	30 680	34 300	35 800	8.5
South Dakota	11 757	10 689	10 385	7 870	7 127	7 952	8 442	8 355	[3] 8 671	9 385	31.7
Tennessee	49 000	49 845	50 648	43 263	44 847	44 166	40 643	43 556	[3] 43 556	43 902	-2.1
Texas	139 046	171 449	171 665	161 150	174 306	160 546	163 191	170 322	171 321	175 996	1.0
Utah	18 395	20 035	19 886	19 774	22 219	24 197	26 407	27 670	27 819	30 248	36.1
Vermont	6 095	6 733	6 424	5 794	5 212	5 215	5 414	5 871	[4] 5 885	[4] 6 048	16.0
Virginia	58 562	66 621	67 126	63 113	58 441	56 948	56 140	58 260	[3] 59 633	61 388	5.0
Washington	50 425	50 402	50 046	45 805	42 514	45 262	47 235	49 294	50 670	53 843	26.6
West Virginia	26 139	23 369	23 580	21 870	21 064	20 228	19 884	20 131	[3] 20 531	19 947	-5.3
Wisconsin	66 753	69 332	67 743	58 340	49 340	50 027	48 371	51 735	52 710	55 473	12.4
Wyoming	5 363	6 072	6 161	5 587	5 728	6 174	5 997	5 889	[3] 5 886	5 900	3.0

See footnotes at end of table.

Table C-26. Public High School Graduates, by State: 1969-70 to 1996-97 — Continued

State or other area	1969-70	1979-80	1980-81	1985-86	1990-91	1992-93	1993-94[1]	1994-95	Estimated 1995-96	Estimated 1996-97	Percent change, 1990-91 to 1996-97
Outlying areas											
American Samoa	[6]367	(NA)	(NA)	608	597	712	738	695	[4]696	[4]702	17.6
Guam	972	(NA)	(NA)	840	1 014	912	985	987	[4]1 003	[4]1 027	1.3
Northern Marianas	(NA)	(NA)	(NA)	(NA)	273	245	328	319	[3]322	288	5.5
Puerto Rico	24 917	(NA)	(NA)	31 597	29 329	29 064	27 718	29 747	[3]29 875	30 003	2.3
Virgin Islands	[6]432	(NA)	(NA)	1 044	981	927	886	995	940	935	-4.7

SOURCE: U.S. Department of Education, National Center for Education Statistics, Common Core of Data surveys. Published as table 100 in *Digest of Education Statistics* 1997.

1. Revised from previously published data.
2. National total includes estimates for nonreporting states.
3. Actual count.
4. Data imputed by the National Center for Education Statistics based on previous year's data.
5. Beginning in 1985-86, graduates from adult programs are excluded.
6. Data are for 1970-71.

NOTE: Data include graduates of regular day school programs, but exclude graduates of other programs and persons receiving high school equivalency certificates. They also exclude graduates of subcollegiate departments of institutions of higher education, federal schools for American Indians and on federal installations, and residential schools for disabled children. Some data have been revised from previously published figures. All 1995-96 and 1996-97 data are state estimates unless otherwise indicated.

(NA) Not applicable or not available.

Table C-27. High School Graduates and Dropouts in Public Elementary and Secondary Schools, by Race or Ethnicity and State: 1994-95

State	High school graduates, by race/ethnicity						Percent of 9th to 12th graders who dropped out during 1994-95					
	Total	White[1]	Black[1]	Hispanic	Asian or Pacific Islander	American Indian/ Alaskan Native	Total	White[1]	Black[1]	Hispanic	Asian or Pacific Islander	American Indian/ Alaskan Native
United States	2 252 064	1 637 556	288 032	212 101	92 659	21 716	(NA)	(NA)	(NA)	(NA)	(NA)	(NA)
Alabama	36 268	24 816	10 637	131	251	433	6.2	5.8	7.1	6.6	3.0	1.6
Alaska	5 765	4 054	230	123	248	1 110	(NA)	(NA)	(NA)	(NA)	(NA)	(NA)
Arizona	30 989	20 094	1 135	7 047	769	1 944	(NA)	(NA)	(NA)	(NA)	(NA)	(NA)
Arkansas	24 636	18 883	5 279	194	206	74	4.9	4.0	7.8	9.5	4.8	4.5
California	255 200	120 488	18 864	76 557	37 029	2 262	4.4	2.8	7.9	6.5	2.4	4.8
Colorado	32 409	25 584	1 396	4 195	990	244	(NA)	(NA)	(NA)	(NA)	(NA)	(NA)
Connecticut	26 445	20 965	2 774	1 940	707	59	4.9	3.3	8.8	12.9	2.8	2.6
Delaware	5 234	3 712	1 247	135	128	12	4.6	4.0	5.8	7.5	3.0	1.2
District of Columbia ..	2 946	94	2 646	152	54	0	10.6	10.9	10.6	15.4	10.0	0.0
Florida	89 827	55 815	18 501	12 882	2 458	171	(NA)	(NA)	(NA)	(NA)	(NA)	(NA)
Georgia	56 660	36 600	18 273	658	1 063	66	9.0	8.2	10.3	13.1	5.6	9.4
Hawaii	3 162	1 811	171	456	693	31	4.9	3.7	5.1	5.6	4.2	8.3
Idaho	14 198	13 323	41	548	169	117	(NA)	(NA)	(NA)	(NA)	(NA)	(NA)
Illinois	105 164	77 181	15 411	8 263	4 089	220	(NA)	(NA)	(NA)	(NA)	(NA)	(NA)
Indiana	56 058	50 011	4 597	991	421	38	4.6	4.3	6.9	6.8	1.3	5.8
Iowa	31 268	29 654	580	403	562	69	3.4	3.3	7.0	9.2	3.0	10.6
Kansas	26 125	22 648	1 587	1 096	594	200	5.0	4.3	9.4	12.1	4.7	7.4
Kentucky[2]	37 588	33 795	2 923	146	249	475	(NA)	(NA)	(NA)	(NA)	(NA)	(NA)
Louisiana	36 766	21 788	13 803	404	644	127	3.5	2.3	5.0	8.1	3.1	2.4
Maine	11 501	11 253	65	41	93	49	3.3	3.4	3.8	4.8	2.4	5.9
Maryland	41 387	25 662	12 354	1 223	2 068	80	(NA)	(NA)	(NA)	(NA)	(NA)	(NA)
Massachusetts	47 679	39 844	3 278	2 699	1 804	54	3.5	2.6	7.2	9.2	3.0	5.2
Michigan	84 628	70 216	10 558	1 634	1 454	766	(NA)	(NA)	(NA)	(NA)	(NA)	(NA)
Minnesota	49 354	45 539	1 051	690	1 571	503	5.2	4.0	20.6	15.8	7.6	20.4
Mississippi	23 837	12 513	11 033	35	182	74	6.4	6.1	7.1	5.4	6.3	9.9
Missouri	48 862	42 386	5 420	404	564	88	7.1	6.1	13.3	9.9	4.6	9.0
Montana	10 134	9 250	33	145	74	632	(NA)	(NA)	(NA)	(NA)	(NA)	(NA)
Nebraska	17 969	16 574	608	445	236	106	4.5	3.5	12.8	13.2	8.2	16.1
Nevada	10 038	7 590	761	1 035	521	131	10.3	8.8	11.8	17.2	9.0	12.8
New Hampshire[3]	10 145	9 794	87	113	132	19	(NA)	(NA)	(NA)	(NA)	(NA)	(NA)
New Jersey	67 403	46 742	9 868	6 766	3 932	95	(NA)	(NA)	(NA)	(NA)	(NA)	(NA)
New Mexico	14 928	6 611	313	6 235	232	1 537	8.5	6.4	9.5	10.9	6.7	8.6
New York	132 401	92 226	18 885	12 910	7 949	431	4.1	2.5	6.8	8.1	3.3	5.3
North Carolina	59 540	41 076	16 266	496	914	788	(NA)	(NA)	(NA)	(NA)	(NA)	(NA)
North Dakota	7 817	7 345	66	53	67	286	2.5	(NA)	(NA)	(NA)	(NA)	(NA)
Ohio	96 992	87 263	7 475	1 043	1 112	99	5.3	4.5	9.8	11.6	3.9	9.9
Oklahoma	33 804	24 644	2 852	852	551	4 905	(NA)	(NA)	(NA)	(NA)	(NA)	(NA)
Oregon	26 483	23 777	274	1 081	941	410	7.1	6.4	10.9	17.6	5.4	10.7
Pennsylvania	104 146	89 993	9 860	1 966	2 271	56	4.1	2.9	10.2	12.2	3.3	8.8
Rhode Island	7 826	6 759	428	348	259	32	4.6	4.0	7.4	9.5	4.1	2.7
South Carolina[3]	30 680	18 424	11 748	147	312	49	(NA)	(NA)	(NA)	(NA)	(NA)	(NA)
South Dakota	8 355	7 646	34	43	69	563	(NA)	(NA)	(NA)	(NA)	(NA)	(NA)
Tennessee	41 319	33 490	7 165	178	463	23	(NA)	(NA)	(NA)	(NA)	(NA)	(NA)
Texas	170 322	95 072	20 286	49 375	5 189	400	2.7	1.8	3.5	3.6	4.2	3.6
Utah	27 670	26 053	90	736	560	231	3.5	(NA)	(NA)	(NA)	(NA)	(NA)
Vermont	5 867	5 730	24	30	53	30	(NA)	(NA)	(NA)	(NA)	(NA)	(NA)
Virginia	58 260	41 640	12 469	1 407	2 654	90	(NA)	(NA)	(NA)	(NA)	(NA)	(NA)
Washington[2]	48 254	39 188	1 816	2 319	3 959	972	(NA)	(NA)	(NA)	(NA)	(NA)	(NA)
West Virginia	20 131	19 221	698	60	124	28	4.2	4.2	5.3	1.1	1.0	7.5
Wisconsin	51 735	47 354	2 030	942	967	442	(NA)	(NA)	(NA)	(NA)	(NA)	(NA)
Wyoming	5 889	5 365	42	329	58	95	6.7	5.9	19.0	13.0	2.7	17.4

See footnotes at end of table.

Table C-27. High School Graduates and Dropouts in Public Elementary and Secondary Schools, by Race or Ethnicity and State: 1994-95 — Continued

State	High school graduates, by race/ethnicity						Percent of 9th to 12th graders who dropped out during 1994-95					
	Total	White[1]	Black[1]	Hispanic	Asian or Pacific Islander	American Indian/ Alaskan Native	Total	White[1]	Black[1]	Hispanic	Asian or Pacific Islander	American Indian/ Alaskan Native
Outlying areas												
American Samoa	695	0	0	0	695	0	(NA)	(NA)	(NA)	(NA)	(NA)	(NA)
Guam	(NA)	(NA)	(NA)	(NA)	(NA)	(NA)	(NA)	(NA)	(NA)	(NA)	(NA)	(NA)
Northern Marianas ...	319	0	0	0	319	0	(NA)	(NA)	(NA)	(NA)	(NA)	(NA)
Puerto Rico	29 747	0	0	29 747	0	0	(NA)	(NA)	(NA)	2.2	(NA)	(NA)
Virgin Islands	(NA)	(NA)	(NA)	(NA)	(NA)	(NA)	(NA)	(NA)	(NA)	(NA)	(NA)	(NA)

SOURCE: U.S. Department of Education, National Center for Education Statistics, Common Core of Data survey; and unpublished data. Published as table 101 in *Digest of Education Statistics* 1997.

1. Excludes persons of Hispanic origin.
2. Estimates provided by state education agencies.
3. Racial/ethnic distribution estimated by NCES based on 12th grade racial/ethnic distribution reported by state.

NOTE: Because data for some graduates are not available by race, totals differ from figures reported elsewhere.

(NA) Not applicable or not available.

Table C-28. Average Proficiency in Reading for 4th Graders in public schools,[1] by selected characteristics, region, and state: 1994

State	Average	Race/ethnicity						Sex		Parental education[2]			
		White	Black	Hispanic	Asian	Pacific Islander	American Indian	Male	Female	Did not finish high school	Graduated high school	Some education after high school	Graduated college
United States	212	223	186	188	231	216	200	207	218	188	206	222	222
Region													
Northeast	212	224	184	191	(3)	(3)	(3)	207	216	(3)	202	222	221
Southeast	208	219	188	184	(3)	(3)	(3)	202	215	186	207	222	216
Central	218	225	182	199	(3)	(3)	(3)	212	225	(3)	215	221	226
West	212	222	186	186	5 226	(3)	(3)	207	217	188	201	221	223
State													
Alabama	208	220	188	178	(3)	(3)	(3)	203	213	197	201	217	217
Arizona	206	220	183	188	(3)	(3)	181	201	211	189	200	219	218
Arkansas	209	218	183	192	(3)	(3)	(3)	204	213	196	203	221	215
California	197	211	182	174	211	5 213	(3)	194	200	166	191	207	207
Colorado	213	222	191	193	(3)	(3)	204	209	218	192	213	220	222
Connecticut	222	234	190	190	(3)	(3)	(3)	218	226	204	209	234	231
Delaware	206	215	188	190	(3)	(3)	(3)	200	212	185	202	217	214
Florida	205	218	183	189	(3)	(3)	(3)	199	210	187	195	219	212
Georgia	207	222	185	184	(3)	(3)	(3)	201	212	185	199	219	217
Hawaii	201	219	189	185	219	191	(3)	194	208	192	194	215	208
Indiana	220	225	193	201	(3)	(3)	(3)	216	223	198	216	230	229
Iowa	223	225	5 186	204	(3)	(3)	(3)	219	227	211	219	232	229
Kentucky	212	215	190	196	(3)	(3)	(3)	206	217	195	212	222	218
Louisiana	197	213	180	175	(3)	(3)	(3)	193	200	188	196	209	200
Maine	228	229	(3)	218	(3)	(3)	(3)	225	231	214	225	237	236
Maryland	210	223	185	197	232	(3)	(3)	205	214	195	202	215	217
Massachusetts	223	231	199	194	5 201	(3)	(3)	221	226	206	212	230	232
Minnesota	218	222	173	202	(3)	(3)	196	214	223	(3)	212	220	229
Mississippi	202	220	187	181	(3)	(3)	(3)	196	207	192	199	213	207
Missouri	217	223	192	200	(3)	(3)	212	213	221	199	216	227	225
Montana[4]	222	226	(3)	208	(NA)	(NA)	203	218	227	211	219	227	230
Nebraska[4]	220	224	5 190	205	(3)	(3)	202	216	224	(3)	215	232	231
New Hampshire[4]	223	224	(3)	213	(3)	(3)	(3)	218	229	207	220	236	231
New Jersey	219	231	193	200	237	(3)	(3)	216	222	193	209	225	230
New Mexico	205	219	196	196	(3)	(3)	185	201	208	188	200	220	215
New York	212	226	191	193	230	(3)	(3)	207	216	196	208	224	220
North Carolina	214	225	193	189	(3)	(3)	5 201	209	220	195	204	226	223
North Dakota	225	228	(3)	212	(3)	(3)	5 197	221	230	(3)	217	232	233
Pennsylvania[4]	215	224	180	187	(3)	(3)	(3)	211	220	187	210	221	224
Rhode Island[4]	220	226	197	195	203	(3)	(3)	215	225	203	217	230	228
South Carolina	203	219	184	182	(3)	(3)	(3)	199	208	189	193	216	213
Tennessee[4]	213	220	188	196	(3)	(3)	(3)	208	217	200	213	225	219
Texas	212	227	191	198	(3)	(3)	(3)	210	214	195	207	224	222
Utah	217	221	(3)	199	(3)	(3)	195	213	222	(3)	211	225	226
Virginia	213	224	192	206	(3)	(3)	(3)	208	219	196	207	220	221

See footnotes at end of table.

Table C-28.   Average Proficiency in Reading for 4th Graders in public schools,[1] by selected characteristics, region, and state: 1994 — Continued

State	Average	Race/ethnicity						Sex		Parental education[2]			
		White	Black	Hispanic	Asian	Pacific Islander	American Indian	Male	Female	Did not finish high school	Graduated high school	Some education after high school	Graduated college
Washington	213	217	198	190	220	208	207	209	217	197	209	216	223
West Virginia	213	215	202	192	(3)	(3)	(3)	208	218	196	213	226	221
Wisconsin[4]	224	228	197	203	(3)	(3)	(3)	221	227	212	223	228	233
Wyoming	221	224	(3)	209	(3)	(3)	[5]210	218	224	203	215	230	228
Department of Defense Overseas Schools	218	224	205	211	222	215	210	213	223	(3)	209	226	223
Guam	181	192	171	171	180	183	(3)	172	190	164	176	189	185

SOURCE: U.S. Department of Education, National Center for Education Statistics, National Assessment of Educational Progress, NAEP 1994 Reading Report Card for the Nation and the States, prepared by Educational Testing Service. Published as table 111 in *Digest of Education Statistics* 1997.

1. As measured by the National Assessment of Educational Progress (NAEP). Forty-one states and Guam participated in the test, but the sample size in two states was insufficient to permit a reliable estimate.
2. Parents' highest level of education. Data not shown for students who did not know parents' level of education.
3. Sample size is insufficient to permit a reliable estimate.
4. Did not satisfy one or more of the guidelines for school sample participation rates. Data are subject to appreciable nonresponse bias.
5. The nature of the sample does not allow accurate determination of the variability of this value.

NOTE: These test scores are from the National Assessment of Educational Progress (NAEP). The NAEP scores have been evaluated at certain performance levels. A score of 300 implies an ability to find, understand, summarize, and explain relatively complicated literary and informational material. A score of 250 implies an ability to search for specific information, interrelate ideas, and make generalizations about literature, science, and social studies materials. A score of 200 implies an ability to understand, combine ideas, and make inferences based on short uncomplicated passages about specific or sequentially related information. A score of 150 implies an ability to follow brief written directions and carry out simple, discrete reading tasks. Scale ranges from 0 to 500. Excludes states not participating in the survey. Some data have been revised from previously published figures.

(NA) Not applicable or not available.

Table C-29. Average Proficiency in Mathematics Content Areas for 8th Graders in Public Schools, by Region and State: 1996

State	Average proficiency		Percent attaining mathematics achievement levels [1]								Percent of students by highest level of education attained by parents [2]							
			Below basic		Basic or above[3]		Proficient or above[4]		Advanced or above[5]		Did not finish high school		Graduated high school		Some education after high school		Graduated college	
United States	271	(1.1)	38	(1.1)	62	(1.1)	24	(1.1)	4	(0.5)	8	(0.5)	23	(0.8)	19	(0.8)	39	(1.4)
Region																		
Northeast	277	(3.1)	33	(3.1)	67	(3.1)	27	(3.7)	5	(1.9)	(NA)	(NA)	(NA)	(NA)	(NA)	(NA)	(NA)	(NA)
Southeast	266	(2.6)	44	(3.2)	56	(3.2)	18	(1.8)	3	(0.6)	(NA)	(NA)	(NA)	(NA)	(NA)	(NA)	(NA)	(NA)
Central	277	(3.1)	31	(3.4)	69	(3.4)	29	(2.5)	5	(1.0)	(NA)	(NA)	(NA)	(NA)	(NA)	(NA)	(NA)	(NA)
West	269	(2.2)	41	(2.2)	59	(2.2)	22	(1.9)	3	(0.6)	(NA)	(NA)	(NA)	(NA)	(NA)	(NA)	(NA)	(NA)
State																		
Alabama	257	(2.1)	55	(2.6)	45	(2.6)	12	(1.8)	1	(0.4)	10	(0.8)	30	(1.5)	15	(0.8)	37	(2.1)
Alaska	278	(1.8)	32	(2.3)	68	(2.3)	30	(1.6)	7	(1.1)	4	(0.7)	19	(1.1)	20	(1.1)	43	(1.5)
Arizona	268	(1.6)	43	(1.9)	57	(1.9)	18	(1.2)	2	(0.3)	9	(0.9)	18	(1.1)	21	(1.0)	38	(1.8)
Arkansas	262	(1.5)	48	(1.8)	52	(1.8)	13	(1.0)	2	(0.4)	10	(0.8)	30	(1.6)	19	(1.0)	30	(1.4)
California	263	(1.9)	49	(2.1)	51	(2.1)	17	(1.5)	3	(0.5)	10	(0.8)	17	(0.8)	16	(1.0)	38	(1.7)
Colorado	276	(1.1)	33	(1.3)	67	(1.3)	25	(1.3)	3	(0.5)	6	(0.6)	19	(0.9)	20	(0.8)	45	(1.5)
Connecticut	280	(1.1)	30	(1.4)	70	(1.4)	31	(1.5)	5	(0.6)	5	(0.6)	19	(0.9)	17	(0.8)	51	(1.3)
Delaware	267	(0.9)	45	(1.3)	55	(1.3)	19	(1.0)	3	(0.6)	5	(0.5)	27	(1.2)	19	(0.9)	38	(1.2)
District of Columbia	233	(1.3)	80	(1.2)	20	(1.2)	5	(0.8)	1	(0.3)	7	(0.6)	28	(1.1)	18	(0.9)	33	(1.3)
Florida	264	(1.8)	46	(2.1)	54	(2.1)	17	(1.3)	2	(0.4)	8	(0.7)	23	(1.1)	18	(0.9)	40	(1.6)
Georgia	262	(1.6)	49	(2.0)	51	(2.0)	16	(1.8)	2	(0.5)	8	(0.7)	27	(1.4)	18	(1.0)	39	(2.0)
Hawaii	262	(1.0)	49	(1.5)	51	(1.5)	16	(0.9)	2	(0.4)	4	(0.5)	26	(1.1)	16	(0.8)	38	(1.0)
Indiana	276	(1.4)	32	(2.0)	68	(2.0)	24	(1.7)	3	(0.5)	7	(0.7)	30	(1.2)	21	(1.1)	36	(1.4)
Iowa	284	(1.3)	22	(1.4)	78	(1.4)	31	(1.8)	4	(0.6)	5	(0.5)	24	(1.6)	19	(0.9)	46	(1.7)
Kentucky	267	(1.1)	44	(1.6)	56	(1.6)	16	(1.2)	1	(0.3)	13	(0.8)	31	(0.9)	17	(0.8)	30	(1.3)
Louisiana	252	(1.6)	62	(2.0)	38	(2.0)	7	(1.1)	0	(0.2)	9	(0.7)	33	(1.0)	19	(0.8)	30	(1.3)
Maine	284	(1.3)	23	(1.5)	77	(1.5)	31	(1.7)	6	(0.7)	5	(0.5)	23	(0.9)	21	(1.1)	44	(1.6)
Maryland	270	(2.1)	43	(2.2)	57	(2.2)	24	(2.3)	5	(1.0)	5	(0.6)	24	(1.3)	17	(1.0)	45	(1.6)
Massachusetts	278	(1.7)	32	(2.3)	68	(2.3)	28	(1.8)	5	(0.8)	6	(0.6)	18	(1.0)	15	(0.8)	51	(1.7)
Michigan	277	(1.8)	33	(2.1)	67	(2.1)	28	(1.8)	4	(0.8)	5	(0.5)	22	(1.5)	21	(0.9)	42	(1.6)
Minnesota	284	(1.3)	25	(1.5)	75	(1.5)	34	(1.8)	6	(0.8)	3	(0.3)	21	(1.1)	19	(1.1)	50	(1.6)
Mississippi	250	(1.2)	64	(1.3)	36	(1.3)	7	(0.8)	0	(0.2)	11	(0.6)	29	(1.1)	15	(0.7)	36	(1.2)
Missouri	273	(1.4)	36	(2.0)	64	(2.0)	22	(1.4)	2	(0.5)	8	(0.6)	27	(1.0)	19	(0.9)	37	(1.6)
Montana	283	(1.3)	25	(1.7)	75	(1.7)	32	(1.5)	5	(0.5)	6	(0.8)	21	(1.1)	20	(1.2)	48	(1.5)
Nebraska	283	(1.0)	24	(1.1)	76	(1.1)	31	(1.5)	5	(0.7)	6	(0.7)	19	(1.5)	18	(1.2)	49	(2.4)
New Mexico	262	(1.2)	49	(1.6)	51	(1.6)	14	(1.1)	2	(0.3)	11	(0.9)	25	(1.1)	19	(1.0)	34	(1.3)
New York	270	(1.7)	39	(2.0)	61	(2.0)	22	(1.5)	3	(0.5)	6	(0.6)	20	(1.1)	17	(1.0)	45	(1.5)
North Carolina	268	(1.4)	44	(1.8)	56	(1.8)	20	(1.3)	3	(0.6)	7	(0.5)	24	(1.1)	20	(0.9)	40	(1.5)
North Dakota	284	(0.9)	23	(1.2)	77	(1.2)	33	(1.5)	4	(0.7)	3	(0.4)	19	(1.0)	16	(0.7)	55	(1.2)
Oregon	276	(1.5)	33	(1.7)	67	(1.7)	26	(1.6)	4	(0.7)	7	(0.6)	18	(0.9)	20	(1.0)	44	(1.7)
Rhode Island	269	(0.9)	40	(1.6)	60	(1.6)	20	(1.3)	3	(0.4)	8	(0.5)	22	(0.9)	17	(0.7)	40	(0.9)
South Carolina	261	(1.5)	52	(1.7)	48	(1.7)	14	(1.2)	2	(0.4)	9	(0.7)	28	(1.1)	17	(0.9)	37	(1.4)
Tennessee	263	(1.4)	47	(1.8)	53	(1.8)	15	(1.3)	2	(0.3)	10	(0.7)	32	(1.4)	19	(0.8)	31	(1.6)
Texas	270	(1.4)	41	(1.8)	59	(1.8)	21	(1.5)	3	(0.4)	13	(1.1)	21	(1.0)	15	(1.0)	38	(2.0)
Utah	277	(1.0)	30	(1.5)	70	(1.5)	24	(1.3)	3	(0.4)	3	(0.4)	17	(0.8)	18	(0.8)	53	(1.3)
Vermont	279	(1.0)	28	(1.7)	72	(1.7)	27	(1.4)	4	(0.6)	5	(0.5)	25	(1.1)	16	(0.9)	49	(1.4)
Virginia	270	(1.6)	42	(2.0)	58	(2.0)	21	(1.2)	3	(0.4)	8	(0.8)	26	(1.1)	16	(0.9)	42	(1.7)
Washington	276	(1.3)	33	(1.6)	67	(1.6)	26	(1.2)	4	(0.7)	6	(0.6)	16	(0.9)	21	(0.8)	46	(1.4)
West Virginia	265	(1.0)	46	(1.6)	54	(1.6)	14	(0.9)	1	(0.4)	11	(0.8)	33	(0.9)	19	(0.8)	30	(1.1)

See footnotes at end of table.

Table C-29. Average Proficiency in Mathematics Content Areas for 8th Graders in Public Schools, by Region and State: 1996 — Continued

State	Average proficiency	Percent attaining mathematics achievement levels [1]				Percent of students by highest level of education attained by parents [2]			
		Below basic	Basic or above [3]	Proficient or above [4]	Advanced or above [5]	Did not finish high school	Graduated high school	Some education after high school	Graduated college
Wisconsin	283 (1.5)	25 (2.0)	75 (2.0)	32 (2.0)	5 (0.8)	5 (0.7)	26 (1.1)	21 (0.9)	40 (1.6)
Wyoming	275 (0.9)	32 (1.2)	68 (1.2)	22 (1.0)	2 (0.6)	5 (0.5)	21 (0.9)	20 (0.8)	44 (1.2)
Outlying areas Guam	239 (1.7)	71 (1.6)	29 (1.6)	6 (0.8)	0 (NA)	2 (0.6)	21 (1.5)	22 (1.7)	43 (2.1)

SOURCE: U.S. Department of Education, National Center for Education Statistics, National Assessment of Educational Progress, NAEP 1996 Mathematics Report Card for the Nation and the States, prepared by Educational Testing Service. Published as table 120 in *Digest of Education Statistics* 1997.

1. Achievement levels are in development status.
2. Excludes students who responded "I don't know" to the question about educational level of parents.
3. This level denotes partial mastery of prerequisite knowledge and skills that are fundamental for proficient work at the 8th grade.
4. This level represents solid academic performance for 8th graders. Students reaching this level have demonstrated competency over challenging subject matter, including subject-matter knowledge, application of such knowledge to real-world situations, and analytical skills appropriate to the subject matter.
5. This level signifies superior performance.

NOTE: These test scores are from the National Assessment of Educational Progress (NAEP). Forty-four states, the District of Columbia, and one outlying area participated in the 1996 Trial State Assessment of 8th graders. Results are not shown for states with a school participation rate of less than 70 percent. Scale ranges from 0 to 500. Standard errors appear in parentheses.

(NA) Not applicable or not available.

Table C-30. Average Proficiency in Mathematics Content Areas for 4th Graders in Public Schools, by Regions and State: 1996

State	Average proficiency		Percent attaining mathematics achievement levels [1]								Percent of students by highest level of education attained by parents [2]							
			Below basic		Basic or above [3]		Proficient or above [4]		Advanced or above [5]		Did not finish high school		Graduated high school		Some education after high school		Graduated college	
United States	224	(1.0)	36	(1.4)	64	(1.4)	21	(1.0)	2	(0.3)	4	(0.4)	13	(0.7)	7	(0.4)	37	(1.3)
Region																		
Northeast	228	(2.0)	30	(2.9)	70	(2.9)	26	(1.6)	3	(0.9)	(NA)	(NA)	(NA)	(NA)	(NA)	(NA)	(NA)	(NA)
Southeast	218	(1.9)	45	(2.9)	55	(2.9)	16	(2.4)	2	(0.8)	(NA)	(NA)	(NA)	(NA)	(NA)	(NA)	(NA)	(NA)
Central	231	(2.9)	25	(2.6)	75	(2.6)	27	(2.1)	2	(0.6)	(NA)	(NA)	(NA)	(NA)	(NA)	(NA)	(NA)	(NA)
West	220	(1.7)	42	(2.8)	58	(2.8)	18	(1.7)	2	(0.5)	(NA)	(NA)	(NA)	(NA)	(NA)	(NA)	(NA)	(NA)
State																		
Alabama	212	(1.2)	52	(2.0)	48	(2.0)	11	(1.1)	1	(0.2)	7	(0.8)	19	(1.0)	9	(0.7)	35	(1.6)
Alaska	224	(1.3)	35	(2.0)	65	(2.0)	21	(1.2)	2	(0.5)	3	(0.5)	10	(0.9)	8	(0.7)	34	(1.5)
Arizona	218	(1.7)	43	(2.4)	57	(2.4)	15	(1.6)	1	(0.4)	5	(0.5)	11	(0.9)	9	(0.6)	34	(1.7)
Arkansas	216	(1.5)	46	(2.2)	54	(2.2)	13	(1.4)	1	(0.3)	6	(0.6)	20	(1.0)	9	(0.7)	31	(1.3)
California	209	(1.8)	54	(2.4)	46	(2.4)	11	(1.5)	1	(0.4)	4	(0.6)	9	(0.7)	7	(0.6)	32	(1.4)
Colorado	226	(1.0)	33	(1.6)	67	(1.6)	22	(1.3)	2	(0.3)	3	(0.4)	10	(0.7)	10	(0.6)	42	(1.6)
Connecticut	232	(1.1)	25	(1.5)	75	(1.5)	31	(1.7)	3	(0.5)	3	(0.4)	9	(0.6)	8	(0.6)	47	(1.3)
Delaware	215	(0.6)	46	(1.1)	54	(1.1)	16	(1.2)	1	(0.4)	3	(0.4)	13	(0.8)	8	(0.7)	37	(1.0)
District of Columbia	187	(1.1)	80	(0.8)	20	(0.8)	5	(0.5)	1	(0.4)	4	(0.4)	15	(0.6)	6	(0.4)	42	(1.0)
Florida	216	(1.2)	45	(1.7)	55	(1.7)	15	(1.1)	1	(0.2)	4	(0.6)	12	(1.0)	7	(0.6)	38	(1.5)
Georgia	215	(1.5)	47	(2.1)	53	(2.1)	13	(1.3)	1	(0.3)	6	(0.6)	17	(0.9)	7	(0.6)	36	(1.6)
Hawaii	215	(1.5)	47	(1.6)	53	(1.6)	16	(1.1)	2	(0.4)	2	(0.3)	12	(0.7)	6	(0.5)	39	(1.2)
Indiana	229	(1.0)	28	(1.7)	72	(1.7)	24	(1.6)	2	(0.5)	4	(0.4)	19	(1.0)	9	(0.9)	37	(1.8)
Iowa	229	(1.1)	26	(1.4)	74	(1.4)	22	(1.4)	1	(0.4)	3	(0.4)	16	(0.9)	9	(0.7)	36	(1.7)
Kentucky	220	(1.1)	40	(1.8)	60	(1.8)	16	(1.1)	1	(0.3)	9	(0.9)	19	(1.1)	8	(0.7)	31	(1.2)
Louisiana	209	(1.1)	56	(1.8)	44	(1.8)	8	(0.9)	0	(0.2)	6	(0.6)	19	(1.1)	9	(0.7)	35	(1.4)
Maine	232	(1.0)	25	(1.4)	75	(1.4)	27	(1.4)	3	(0.6)	3	(0.4)	13	(0.9)	9	(0.6)	39	(1.8)
Maryland	221	(1.6)	41	(1.8)	59	(1.8)	22	(1.7)	3	(0.7)	3	(0.4)	13	(0.9)	7	(0.6)	45	(1.6)
Massachusetts	229	(1.4)	29	(1.8)	71	(1.8)	24	(1.9)	2	(0.5)	2	(0.3)	10	(0.7)	8	(0.6)	48	(1.9)
Michigan	226	(1.3)	32	(1.8)	68	(1.8)	23	(1.5)	2	(0.5)	4	(0.5)	14	(1.0)	8	(0.7)	38	(1.5)
Minnesota	232	(1.1)	24	(1.5)	76	(1.5)	29	(1.5)	3	(0.5)	2	(0.3)	11	(0.8)	7	(0.6)	42	(1.5)
Mississippi	208	(1.2)	58	(1.9)	42	(1.9)	8	(0.9)	0	(0.2)	7	(0.6)	19	(1.0)	7	(0.5)	35	(1.3)
Missouri	225	(1.1)	34	(1.7)	66	(1.7)	20	(1.3)	1	(0.3)	4	(0.5)	16	(0.9)	9	(0.7)	36	(1.6)
Montana	228	(1.2)	29	(1.9)	71	(1.9)	22	(1.6)	1	(0.4)	3	(0.4)	11	(0.8)	11	(0.8)	40	(1.5)
Nebraska	228	(1.2)	30	(1.6)	70	(1.6)	24	(1.4)	2	(0.3)	3	(0.4)	13	(0.9)	9	(0.7)	41	(1.2)
Nevada	218	(1.3)	43	(1.8)	57	(1.8)	14	(1.2)	1	(0.3)	4	(0.6)	12	(0.7)	8	(0.6)	34	(1.2)
New Jersey	227	(1.5)	32	(2.1)	68	(2.1)	25	(1.7)	3	(0.7)	3	(0.5)	12	(1.1)	7	(0.6)	46	(2.0)
New Mexico	214	(1.8)	49	(2.4)	51	(2.4)	13	(1.2)	1	(0.3)	6	(0.6)	15	(0.8)	11	(0.9)	35	(1.3)
New York	223	(1.2)	36	(1.8)	64	(1.8)	20	(1.2)	2	(0.4)	4	(0.4)	10	(0.8)	6	(0.6)	43	(1.6)
North Carolina	224	(1.2)	36	(1.6)	64	(1.6)	21	(1.3)	2	(0.4)	5	(0.6)	12	(0.8)	7	(0.6)	42	(1.7)
North Dakota	231	(1.2)	25	(1.9)	75	(1.9)	24	(1.3)	2	(0.5)	2	(0.3)	11	(0.7)	8	(0.8)	47	(1.4)
Oregon	223	(1.4)	35	(2.2)	65	(2.2)	21	(1.3)	2	(0.5)	4	(0.5)	11	(0.8)	7	(0.5)	38	(1.5)
Pennsylvania	226	(1.2)	32	(1.8)	68	(1.8)	20	(1.5)	1	(0.3)	(NA)	(NA)	(NA)	(NA)	(NA)	(NA)	(NA)	(NA)
Rhode Island	220	(1.4)	39	(2.0)	61	(2.0)	17	(1.3)	1	(0.3)	5	(0.4)	12	(0.9)	7	(0.5)	40	(1.3)
South Carolina	213	(1.3)	52	(2.0)	48	(2.0)	12	(1.3)	1	(0.3)	5	(0.5)	16	(1.0)	7	(0.8)	38	(1.2)
Tennessee	219	(1.4)	42	(2.0)	58	(2.0)	17	(1.5)	1	(0.3)	6	(0.6)	19	(0.9)	8	(0.6)	36	(1.5)
Texas	229	(1.4)	31	(1.9)	69	(1.9)	25	(1.5)	3	(0.5)	6	(0.5)	11	(0.8)	7	(0.5)	38	(1.6)
Utah	227	(1.2)	31	(1.6)	69	(1.6)	23	(1.3)	2	(0.4)	2	(0.3)	10	(0.7)	8	(0.6)	41	(1.7)
Vermont	225	(1.2)	33	(2.1)	67	(2.1)	23	(1.1)	3	(0.5)	3	(0.4)	12	(0.9)	7	(0.7)	44	(1.4)

See footnotes at end of table.

Table C-30. Average Proficiency in Mathematics Content Areas for 4th Graders in Public Schools, by Regions and State: 1996 — Continued

State	Average proficiency		Percent attaining mathematics achievement levels [1]								Percent of students by highest level of education attained by parents [2]							
			Below basic		Basic or above [3]		Proficient or above [4]		Advanced or above [5]		Did not finish high school		Graduated high school		Some education after high school		Graduated college	
Virginia	223	(1.4)	38	(2.2)	62	(2.2)	19	(1.5)	2	(0.5)	5	(0.7)	15	(1.0)	7	(0.7)	41	(1.8)
Washington	225	(1.2)	33	(1.8)	67	(1.8)	21	(1.2)	1	(0.2)	2	(0.3)	9	(0.7)	8	(0.6)	38	(1.5)
West Virginia	223	(1.0)	37	(1.6)	63	(1.6)	19	(1.2)	2	(0.5)	7	(0.7)	21	(0.9)	9	(0.7)	35	(1.4)
Wisconsin	231	(1.0)	26	(1.2)	74	(1.2)	27	(1.3)	3	(0.6)	2	(0.5)	13	(1.0)	8	(0.8)	38	(1.6)
Wyoming	223	(1.4)	36	(1.7)	64	(1.7)	19	(1.2)	1	(0.3)	4	(0.5)	12	(0.7)	8	(0.5)	38	(1.2)
Guam	188	(1.3)	77	(1.4)	23	(1.4)	3	(0.5)	0	(NA)	5	(0.7)	14	(1.0)	5	(0.6)	36	(1.4)

SOURCE: U.S. Department of Education, National Center for Education Statistics, National Assessment of Educational Progress, NAEP 1996 Mathematics Report Card for the Nation and the States, prepared by Educational Testing Service. Published as table 121 in *Digest of Education Statistics* 1997.

1. Achievement levels are in development status.
2. Excludes students who responded "I don't know" to the question about educational level of parents.
3. This level denotes partial mastery of prerequisite knowledge and skills that are fundamental for proficient work at the 4th grade.
4. This level represents solid academic mastery for 4th graders. Students reaching this level have demonstrated competency over challenging subject matter, including subject-matter knowledge, application of such knowledge to real-world situations, and analytical skills appropriate to the subject matter.
5. This level signifies superior performance.

NOTE: These test scores are from the National Assessment of Educational Progress (NAEP). Forty-seven states, the District of Columbia, and one outlying area participated in the 1996 Trial State Assessment of 4th graders. Results are not shown for states with a school participation rate of less than 70 percent. Scale ranges from 0 to 500. Standard errors appear in parentheses.

(NA) Not applicable or not available.

Table C-31. Selected Characteristics of 8th Grade Students in Public Schools, by Region and State: 1992[1]

State	Math units required for graduation	Year of revision of state guides with NCTM standards[2]	Length of school year		Passing test in math required for graduation in 1993	Percent of students with 4 or more hours of math instruction each week	Percent of students reporting					
			1989	1992			Spending 30 minutes or more on math homework each day	Spending 1 or 2 hours on all homework each day	Spending more than 2 hours on all homework each day	Positive attitudes towards math[3]	Both parents living at home	Watching 6 or more hours of television each day
Total	(NA)	(NA)	(NA)	(NA)	(NA)	32	64	59	8	59	75	13
Region												
Northeast	(NA)	(NA)	(NA)	(NA)	(NA)	35	59	62	8	56	75	14
Southeast	(NA)	(NA)	(NA)	(NA)	(NA)	37	65	56	7	59	71	17
Central	(NA)	(NA)	(NA)	(NA)	(NA)	24	63	65	6	63	79	11
West	(NA)	(NA)	(NA)	(NA)	(NA)	30	68	56	10	56	75	12
State												
Alabama	2	1989	175	175	YES	60	65	59	7	62	72	20
Alaska	2	Devel.,1994	(NA)	180	NO	(NA)	(NA)	(NA)	(NA)	(NA)	(NA)	(NA)
Arizona	2	1992	175	175	NO	34	65	56	5	54	76	9
Arkansas	3	1993	178	178	NO	42	61	56	7	60	75	20
California	2	1991	180	180	NO	43	67	63	10	56	74	10
Colorado	(4)	1994	180	(5)	NO	27	65	61	7	58	77	7
Connecticut	3	Devel.,1995	180	180	NO	21	61	70	9	59	79	11
Delaware	2	Devel.,1994	180	180	NO	30	57	62	5	63	73	17
District of Columbia	3	1993	190	180	NO	52	63	63	10	73	45	31
Florida	3	Devel.,1994	180	180	YES	40	62	57	7	61	71	15
Georgia	3	1992	180	180	YES	56	65	59	7	66	71	18
Hawaii	3	Devel.,1994	183	180	YES	34	68	55	11	54	75	22
Idaho	2	1994	180	180	NO	28	63	57	5	56	83	7
Illinois	2	Devel.,1994	180	180	NO	(NA)	(NA)	(NA)	(NA)	(NA)	(NA)	(NA)
Indiana	2	1991	180	180	NO	32	62	60	6	61	78	9
Iowa	(4)	1987	180	180	NO	20	61	63	4	63	83	7
Kansas	2	1991	(NA)	180	NO	(NA)	(NA)	(NA)	(NA)	(NA)	(NA)	(NA)
Kentucky	3	1993	175	175	NO	47	61	54	6	57	78	13
Louisiana	3	Devel.,1994	180	180	YES	54	62	61	10	63	71	20
Maine	2	Devel.,1994	(NA)	175	NO	12	66	70	8	61	81	8
Maryland	3	1985	180	180	YES	45	60	65	7	61	73	17
Massachusetts	(4)	1994	(NA)	180	NO	28	67	70	9	57	77	8
Michigan	3	Devel.,1994	180	180	YES	39	67	61	7	60	75	13
Minnesota	1	Devel.,1994	175	175	NO	41	64	59	5	57	85	5
Mississippi	2	1993	(NA)	180	YES	60	68	60	8	67	70	21
Missouri	2	1990	(NA)	174	NO	44	66	60	6	60	77	12
Montana	2	Devel.,1995	180	180	NO	(NA)	(NA)	(NA)	(NA)	(NA)	(NA)	(NA)
Nebraska	(4)	Devel.,1994	(5)	(5)	NO	25	69	61	5	60	81	8
Nevada	2	1993	(NA)	180	YES	(NA)	(NA)	(NA)	(NA)	(NA)	(NA)	(NA)
New Hampshire	2	1993	180	180	NO	38	62	68	9	58	81	7
New Jersey	3	1993	180	180	YES	28	62	68	10	62	78	13
New Mexico	3	1992	180	180	YES	26	65	56	7	56	75	11
New York	2	1992	180	180	YES	20	54	66	9	62	75	15
North Carolina	2	1993	180	180	YES	52	64	64	7	65	73	16
North Dakota	2	1990	180	180	NO	44	70	63	6	55	85	5
Ohio	2	1993	182	182	YES	26	62	62	6	62	74	12
Oklahoma	2	Devel.,1994	175	175	NO	37	69	59	7	58	78	11
Oregon	2	None	175	(5)	NO	(NA)	(NA)	(NA)	(NA)	(NA)	(NA)	(NA)
Pennsylvania	3	Devel.,1994	180	180	NO	24	58	63	4	59	79	9
Rhode Island	2	1993	180	180	NO	43	62	67	7	56	78	9
South Carolina	3	Devel.,1995	(NA)	180	YES	59	61	61	7	70	73	17
South Dakota	2	1991	(NA)	175	NO	(NA)	(NA)	(NA)	(NA)	(NA)	(NA)	(NA)
Tennessee	2	1991	(NA)	180	YES	60	67	62	6	58	73	14
Texas	3	1993	175	175	YES	38	67	57	8	61	75	12
Utah	2	Devel.,1994	(NA)	180	NO	28	62	56	5	55	85	5

See footnotes at end of table.

Table C-31.   Selected Characteristics of 8th Grade Students in Public Schools, by Region and State: 1992[1] — Continued

State	Math units required for graduation	Year of revision of state guides with NCTM standards[2]	Length of school year		Passing test in math required for graduation in 1993	Percent of students with 4 or more hours of math instruction each week	Percent of students reporting					
			1989	1992			Spending 30 minutes or more on math homework each day	Spending 1 or 2 hours on all homework each day	Spending more than 2 hours on all homework each day	Positive attitudes towards math[3]	Both parents living at home	Watching 6 or more hours of television each day
Vermont	(6)	1988	(NA)	175	NO	(NA)	(NA)	(NA)	(NA)	(NA)	(NA)	(NA)
Virginia	2	Devel.,1994	180	180	YES	38	65	63	7	63	77	15
Washington	2	1992	(NA)	180	NO	(NA)	(NA)	(NA)	(NA)	(NA)	(NA)	(NA)
West Virginia	2	Devel.,1995	180	180	YES	40	57	55	5	58	78	13
Wisconsin	2	1990	180	180	NO	32	59	61	5	59	80	8
Wyoming	(4)	(NA)	175	175	NO	24	60	55	5	58	81	8
Outlying areas												
Guam	(NA)	(NA)	(NA)	(NA)	(NA)	28	68	47	12	50	79	20
Virgin Islands	(NA)	(NA)	(NA)	180	(NA)	31	61	47	11	75	56	32

SOURCE: U.S. Department of Education, National Center for Education Statistics, National Assessment of Educational Progress, The State of Mathematics Achievement, by Educational Testing Service; and Council of Chief State School Officers, State Education Indicators. Published as table 122 in *Digest of Education* 1997.

1. Data are for 1992 unless otherwise specified.
2. Standards recommended by the National Council of Teachers of Mathematics.
3. Percent of students agreeing or strongly agreeing with positive statements about mathematics.
4. Local board determines.
5. No statewide policy.
6. 5 units of math and science combined.

(NA) Not applicable or not available.

Table C-32. Average Proficiency in Science for 8th Graders in Public Schools, by Selected Characteristics and State: 1996

State	Average	Race/ethnicity					Sex		Parental education[1]			
		White	Black	Hispanic	Asian	American Indian	Male	Female	Did not finish high school	Graduated high school	Some education after high school	Graduated college
United States	148	159	120	127	150	148	149	148	131	140	155	157
State												
Alabama	139	151	117	107	(2)	(2)	138	139	130	129	145	147
Alaska[3]	153	162	(2)	137	152	129	155	150	(2)	141	155	163
Arizona	145	157	124	129	(2)	121	147	143	121	136	151	158
Arkansas[3]	144	154	116	122	(2)	(2)	147	142	129	136	150	154
California	138	156	121	121	148	(2)	140	136	118	129	144	153
Colorado	155	162	142	135	155	142	156	153	133	142	157	163
Connecticut	155	165	121	122	163	(2)	156	155	129	140	155	167
Delaware	142	152	122	116	(2)	(2)	143	140	121	135	146	151
District of Columbia	113	(2)	112	98	(2)	(2)	113	113	106	107	120	121
Florida	142	155	119	129	(2)	(2)	144	140	127	132	148	150
Georgia	142	155	122	128	(2)	(2)	144	139	127	129	145	153
Hawaii	135	146	128	121	138	(2)	135	135	119	120	139	147
Indiana	153	158	125	139	(2)	(2)	154	152	139	144	156	162
Iowa[3]	158	160	131	140	(2)	(2)	159	157	141	150	160	165
Kentucky	147	151	127	113	(2)	(2)	148	147	130	143	151	158
Louisiana	132	148	113	104	(2)	(2)	136	129	123	128	141	136
Maine	163	164	(2)	141	(2)	(2)	165	161	141	153	164	171
Maryland[3]	145	160	124	121	161	(2)	146	145	126	136	147	153
Massachusetts	157	163	126	126	152	(2)	159	154	134	145	156	166
Michigan[3]	153	161	122	134	(2)	(2)	156	150	137	144	156	161
Minnesota	159	162	130	134	152	(2)	161	157	137	151	161	165
Mississippi	133	149	119	105	(2)	(2)	134	132	125	126	142	138
Missouri	151	158	120	130	(2)	(2)	152	150	136	144	156	159
Montana[3]	162	166	(2)	147	(2)	139	164	160	139	155	164	168
Nebraska	157	161	130	134	(2)	(2)	160	155	133	148	161	165
New Mexico	141	159	(2)	130	(2)	126	143	139	119	131	147	154
New York[3]	146	161	120	116	155	(2)	148	143	123	138	147	157
North Carolina	147	157	126	123	(2)	136	149	145	126	134	150	158
North Dakota	162	164	(2)	137	(2)	137	163	161	148	157	160	167
Oregon	155	158	(2)	133	157	142	157	153	137	143	157	164
Rhode Island	149	155	130	118	142	(2)	150	148	123	141	154	160
South Carolina[3]	139	153	122	122	(2)	(2)	141	136	125	127	145	148
Tennessee	143	151	117	104	(2)	(2)	144	142	127	135	149	154
Texas	145	161	127	129	157	(2)	147	143	128	137	152	157
Utah	156	159	(2)	133	143	(2)	159	154	129	147	156	162
Vermont[3]	157	159	(2)	136	(2)	(2)	158	156	132	146	157	167
Virginia	149	158	126	132	165	(2)	150	148	127	136	152	161
Washington	150	156	127	125	149	130	152	147	128	141	154	158
West Virginia	147	149	127	122	(2)	(2)	148	147	130	142	152	156
Wisconsin[3]	160	165	115	141	(2)	(2)	161	158	140	155	161	169
Wyoming	158	161	(2)	140	(2)	138	159	156	139	150	159	165
Department of Defense Overseas Schools	155	164	140	146	156	(2)	157	154	(2)	144	159	158
Guam	120	138	(2)	106	122	(2)	120	120	106	113	130	128

SOURCE: U.S. Department of Education, National Center for Education Statistics, National Assessment of Educational Progress, NAEP 1996 Science Report Card for the Nation and the States, prepared by Educational Testing Service. Published as table 125 in *Digest of Education* 1997.

1. Parents' highest level of education. Data not shown for students who did not know parents' level of education.
2. Sample size is insufficient to permit a reliable estimate.
3. Did not satisfy one or more of the guidelines for school sample participation rates. Data are subject to appreciable nonresponse bias.

NOTE: These test scores are from the National Assessment of Educational Progress (NAEP). The NAEP scores have been evaluate at certain performance levels. A score of 300 implies an ability to find, understand, summarize, and explain relatively complicated literary and informational material. A score of 250 implies an ability to search for specific information, interrelate ideas, and make generalizations about literature, science, and social studies materials. A score of 200 implies an ability to understand, combine ideas, and make inferences based on short uncomplicated passages about specific or sequentially related information. A score of 150 implies an ability to follow brief written directions and carry out simple, discrete reading tasks. Scale ranges from 0 to 500. Excludes states not participating in the survey. Some data have been revised from previously published figures.

Table C-33. Scholastic Assessment Test [1] Score Averages, by State: 1974-75 to 1994-95

State	1974-75 Verbal	1974-75 Mathematical	1980-81 Verbal	1980-81 Mathematical	1985-86 Verbal	1985-86 Mathematical	1990-91 Verbal	1990-91 Mathematical	1992-93 Verbal	1992-93 Mathematical	1993-94 Verbal	1993-94 Mathematical	1994-95 Verbal	1994-95 Mathematical	Percent of graduates taking SAT, 1994-95
United States	434	472	424	466	431	475	422	474	424	478	423	479	428	482	41
Alabama	426	457	457	488	476	514	476	515	480	526	482	529	491	538	8
Alaska	461	481	449	486	445	479	439	481	438	477	434	477	445	489	47
Arizona	496	525	476	514	466	509	442	490	444	497	443	496	448	496	27
Arkansas	482	510	477	510	482	519	482	523	478	519	477	518	482	523	6
California	435	473	426	475	423	481	415	482	415	484	413	482	417	485	45
Colorado	479	515	467	513	466	514	453	506	454	509	456	513	462	518	29
Connecticut	442	471	430	463	440	474	429	468	430	474	426	472	431	477	81
Delaware	439	476	429	470	442	475	428	464	429	465	428	464	429	468	68
District of Columbia	(NA)	(NA)	(NA)	(NA)	413	439	405	435	405	441	406	443	412	445	53
Florida	441	474	424	463	426	469	416	466	416	466	413	466	420	469	48
Georgia	397	427	390	426	402	440	400	444	399	445	398	446	406	448	65
Hawaii	414	478	390	464	403	477	405	478	401	478	401	480	407	482	57
Idaho	493	524	486	523	475	512	463	505	465	507	461	508	468	511	15
Illinois	460	510	459	508	466	519	471	535	475	541	478	546	488	560	13
Indiana	418	463	406	451	415	459	408	457	409	460	410	466	415	467	58
Iowa	523	568	515	566	519	576	515	578	520	583	506	574	516	583	5
Kansas	503	540	502	542	498	544	493	546	494	548	494	550	503	557	9
Kentucky	470	507	474	509	483	519	473	520	476	522	474	523	477	522	11
Louisiana	456	491	461	494	474	507	476	518	481	527	481	530	486	535	9
Maine	437	471	426	465	434	466	421	458	422	463	420	463	427	469	68
Maryland	436	471	423	461	436	475	429	475	431	478	429	479	430	479	64
Massachusetts	434	469	422	462	436	473	426	470	427	476	426	475	430	477	80
Michigan	451	498	456	508	462	514	461	519	469	528	472	537	484	549	11
Minnesota	506	552	486	539	482	540	480	543	489	556	495	562	506	579	9
Mississippi	477	503	473	502	485	516	477	520	481	521	485	528	496	540	4
Missouri	465	500	462	504	476	519	476	526	481	532	485	537	495	550	9
Montana	500	547	485	539	485	541	464	518	459	516	463	523	473	536	21
Nebraska	459	507	489	537	493	549	481	543	479	544	482	543	494	556	9
Nevada	465	497	445	487	445	485	435	484	432	488	429	484	434	483	30
New Hampshire	449	485	439	479	450	485	440	481	442	487	438	486	444	491	70
New Jersey	424	454	414	450	424	465	417	469	419	473	418	475	420	478	70
New Mexico	486	516	474	510	489	527	474	522	478	525	475	528	485	530	11
New York	441	484	427	471	427	471	413	468	416	471	416	472	419	473	74
North Carolina	399	428	391	427	399	436	400	444	406	453	405	455	411	454	60
North Dakota	510	554	494	544	508	556	502	571	518	583	497	559	515	592	5
Ohio	456	499	457	500	460	503	450	496	454	505	456	510	460	515	23
Oklahoma	480	514	485	526	487	521	476	521	482	530	482	537	491	536	9
Oregon	440	468	431	469	444	486	439	483	441	492	436	491	448	499	51
Pennsylvania	430	470	421	459	429	465	417	459	418	460	417	462	419	461	70
Rhode Island	432	469	415	452	432	466	421	459	419	464	420	462	425	463	70
South Carolina	382	412	374	406	395	431	395	437	396	442	395	443	401	443	58
South Dakota	523	561	519	561	531	567	496	551	502	558	483	548	505	563	5
Tennessee	477	511	475	514	486	521	487	528	486	531	488	535	497	543	12
Texas	431	467	415	455	419	458	411	463	413	472	412	474	419	474	47
Utah	516	553	511	548	506	541	494	537	500	549	509	558	513	563	4
Vermont	439	476	427	467	442	474	424	466	426	467	427	472	429	472	68
Virginia	431	463	424	461	435	473	424	466	425	469	424	469	428	468	65
Washington	489	522	472	517	461	502	433	480	435	486	434	488	443	494	48
West Virginia	462	502	458	495	462	502	441	485	439	485	439	482	448	484	17
Wisconsin	492	544	477	533	478	536	481	542	485	551	487	557	501	572	9
Wyoming	506	548	478	528	484	534	466	514	463	507	459	521	476	525	10

SOURCE: College Entrance Examination Board, 'College-Bound Seniors: 1995 Profile of SAT Program Test Takers,' (Copyright @ 1995 by the College Entrance Examination Board. All rights reserved.) Published as table 133 in *Digest of Education Statistics* 1997.

1. Formerly known as the Scholastic Aptitude Test.
2. Based on the number of high school graduates in 1995 as projected by the Western Interstate Commission for Higher Education and the number of 1995 seniors who took the SAT.

NOTE: Possible scores on each part of the SAT range from 200 to 800. Rankings of states based on SAT scores alone are invalid because of the varying proportions of students in each state taking the tests.

(NA) Not applicable or not available.

Table C-34. Ages for Compulsory School Attendance, Special Education Services for Students, Policies for Kindergarten Programs, and Year-Round Schools, by State: 1997 and 1995

State or other area	Compulsory attendance 1997	Compulsory special education services, 1997[1]	Year-round schools, 1995		Provision of kindergarten education, 1995			
			Has policy on year-round schools	Has districts with year-round schools	School districts required to offer		Attendance required	
					Half day	Full day	Half day	Full day
Alabama	7 to 16	3 to 21		X		X		
Alaska	[2] 7 to 16	3 to 21		X				
Arizona	[3] 6 to 16	3 to 21	X	X	X		X	
Arkansas	5 to 17	3 to 21	X	X		X		X
California	6 to 18	3 to 21	X	X	X			
Colorado	7 to 16	[4] 3 to 20		X				
Connecticut	7 to 16	3 to 20			X			
Delaware	5 to 17	3 to 20			X			
District of Columbia	5 to 18	[5] 3 to 21				X		X
Florida	6 to 16	3 to 20	X	X		X		X
Georgia	7 to 16	3 to 21			X		X	
Hawaii	[6] 6 to 18	3 to 20		X				
Idaho	7 to 16	3 to 20	X	X				
Illinois	7 to 16	3 to 20	X	X	X			
Indiana	[7] 7 to 18	3 to 21		X	X			
Iowa	6 to 16	3 to 19						
Kansas	7 to 16	3 to 20						
Kentucky	[8] 6 to 16	3 to 20		X	X			
Louisiana	7 to 17	3 to 21						
Maine	7 to 17	2 to 21						
Maryland	5 to 17	3 to 19			X			
Massachusetts	6 to 16	3 to 21			X			
Michigan	6 to 16	Birth to 20						
Minnesota	[9] 7 to 16	3 to 19	X	X	X			
Mississippi	6 to 17	3 to 20		X		X		
Missouri	7 to 16	3 to 20		X	X		X	
Montana	[10] 7 to 16	3 to 18		X	X			
Nebraska	7 to 16	3 to 19	X					
Nevada	7 to 17	3 to 21		X	X			
New Hampshire	6 to 16	3 to 20						
New Jersey	6 to 16	3 to 21						
New Mexico	5 to 18	3 to 21		X	X		X	
New York	[11] 6 to 16	3 to 21	X	X				
North Carolina	7 to 16	3 to 20	X	X				
North Dakota	7 to 16	3 to 20			X	X	X	X
Ohio	6 to 18	3 to 21		X	X		X	
Oklahoma	5 to 18	3 to 21	X	X	X			
Oregon	7 to 18	3 to 21		X	X			
Pennsylvania	8 to 17	3 to 20			X			
Rhode Island	6 to 16	[4] 3 to 21			X		X	
South Carolina	[12] 5 to 17	3 to 21		X	X		X	
South Dakota	6 to 16	3 to 21	X	X	X	X		
Tennessee	7 to 17	3 to 21		X	X		X	
Texas	6 to 17	3 to 21	X	X	X	X		
Utah	6 to 18	3 to 21	X	X	X		X	

See footnotes at end of table.

Table C-34. Ages for Compulsory School Attendance, Special Education Services for Students, Policies for Kindergarten Programs, and Year-Round Schools, by State: 1997 and 1995

State or other area	Compulsory attendance 1997	Compulsory special education services, 1997[1]	Year-round schools, 1995		Provision of kindergarten education, 1995			
			Has policy on year-round schools	Has districts with year-round schools	School districts required to offer		Attendance required	
					Half day	Full day	Half day	Full day
Vermont	7 to 16	3 to 21						
Virginia	5 to 18	2 to 21		X	X		X	X
Washington	[13]8 to 18	3 to 20		X				
West Virginia	6 to 16	3 to 20	X		X			
Wisconsin	[14]6 to 18	[4]3 to 20			X			
Wyoming	7 to 16	[4]3 to 20			X			

SOURCE: U.S. Department of Education, Office of Special Education and Rehabilitative Services, The Eighteenth Annual Report to Congress on the Implementation of The Individuals with Disabilities Education Act, 1996; National Association of State Directors of Special Education, Inc., unpublished data; Education Commission of the States, 'Clearinghouse Notes,' March 1997; and Council of Chief State School Officers, State Education Policies on Student Attendance and Use of Time: 1995. Published as table 152 in *Digest of Education Statistics* 1997.

1. Most states have an upper age limit whereby education is provided up to a certain age or completion of secondary school, whichever comes first.
2. Ages 7 to 16 or high school graduation.
3. Ages 6 to 16 or tenth grade completion.
4. Upper age limit for eligibility has been updated for 1997.
5. State has established two points in the program year by which children must be 3 years of age to be eligible for services.
6. Students over the age of 16 may withdraw with the approval of a principal and student's guardians, and if an alternative education program exists.
7. From age 7 until student (1) graduates; (2) between age 16 to 18 and meets requirements for exit interview before graduation; or (3) reaches 18. Withdrawal before 18 requires parent/guardian and principal written permission.
8. Must have parental signature for leaving school between ages 16 to 18.
9. Age 18 takes effect in 2000.
10. Age 16 or completion of eighth grade.
11. Ages 6 to 17 for New York City and Buffalo.
12. Permits parental waiver of kindergarten at age 5.
13. Or can exit if age 16 or older, has a useful occupation, has met graduation requirements or has a certificate of education competency.
14. Ages 6 to 18 or high school graduation.

Table C-35. State Requirements for High School Graduation, in Carnegie Units: 1993 and 1996

State	1993 All courses	1996 All courses	1996 English/language arts	Social studies	Mathematics	Science	Physical education/health	Electives	Other courses	First graduating class to which these requirements apply	Notes
Alabama Standard	22	24	4.0	4.0	4.0	4.0	1.5	5.5	1 (.5 fine arts; .5 computer applications)	2000	Students must become computer literate through related coursework.
Alaska	21	21	4.0	3.0	2.0	2.0	1.0	9.0	NA	NA	NA
Arizona	20	20	4.0	2.5	2.0	2.0	0.0	8.0	1.5 (.5 free enterprise, 1 fine arts)	1996	State board is required to adopt competency tests for graduation in reading, writing and mathematics (1996). Social studies requirement includes 1 unit in world history and geography; 1.5 units in U.S. and Arizona Constitutions and Arizona history.[1]
Arkansas Technical postsecondary preparatory	20	21	4.0	2.0	3.0	3.0	1.0	3.0	5 (.5 oral communications; 1 vocational/technical; .5 fine arts; seniors take at least 3 academic courses)	1997	Science requirements include 1 unit in life science and 1 unit in physical science. Physical education requirement includes .5 unit in health and safety and .5 unit in physical education. Physical education cannot exceed 1 unit.[2]
College preparatory	NA	21	4.0	3.0	3.0	3.0	1.0	3.0	4 (.5 oral communication; .5 fine arts; seniors take at least 3 academic courses)	1988	Science requirements include 1 unit in life science and 1 unit in physical science. Physical education requirement includes .5 unit in health and safety and .5 unit in physical education. Physical education cannot exceed 1 unit.[1,2]
California Standard	13	13	3.0	3.0	2.0	2.0	2.0	NA	1 (includes foreign language or American Sign Language or visual and performing arts)	1989	Social studies requirement includes 1 unit in U.S. history and geography, 1 unit in world history, culture and geography, .5 unit American government, and .5 unit economics. Science requirement includes 1 unit in biological and 1 unit in physical science.[3]
Colorado	NA	(1)	(1)	(1)	(1)	(1)	(1)	(1)	NA	NA	(1,3)
Connecticut	20	20	4.0	3.0	3.0	2.0	1.0	1.0	6	1988	Electives could be in arts or vocational education.
Delaware Standard (1997, 98)	19	19	4.0	3.0	2.0	2.0	1.5	6.5	NA	1997	Physical education requirement includes .5 unit in health and 1 unit in physical education.
Standard (1999)	NA	20	4.0	3.0	2.0	2.0	1.5	6.5	1 (computer literacy); students must become computer literate through formal class or related coursework.	1999	Physical education requirement includes .5 unit in health and 1 unit in physical education.
Standard (2000)	NA	22	4.0	3.0	3.0	3.0	1.5	NA	7.5 (1 computer literacy; students must become computer literate through formal class or related coursework; 3 Career Pathway[4]; 3.5 additional academic coursework).	2000	Physical education requirement includes .5 unit in health and 1 unit in physical education.

See footnotes at end of table.

Table C-35. State Requirements for High School Graduation, in Carnegie Units: 1993 and 1996 — Continued

State	1993	1996	1996							First graduating class to which these requirements apply	Notes
			Subject areas								
	All courses	All courses	English/ language arts	Social studies	Mathe-matics	Science	Physical education/ health	Elec-tives	Other courses		
District of Columbia	24	24	4.0	3.5	3.0	3.0	1.5	3.5	5 (2 foreign language; 1 life skills; 1 career/vocational; .5 fine arts; .5 music)	1996	D.C. requires 100 hours of community service without credit.
Florida	24	24	4.0	2.5	3.0	3.0	1.0	9.0	1.5 (.5 economics; 1 practical arts or exploratory career education)	NA	Social studies requirement includes 1 unit in American history, 1 unit in world history and .5 unit in American government. Two science units must have a laboratory component. The physical education requirement includes .5 unit in life management skills and .5 units in physical education.[1,2]
Georgia Standard	21	21	4.0	3.0	3.0	3.0	1.0	6.0	1 (computor technology and/or fine arts and/or vocational education and/or junior ROTC)	1997	Students who completed 4 units of vocational education in addition to requirements receive a state seal of endorsement. Mathematics requirement includes 1 unit in algebra.[1,2]
Advanced	21	21	4.0	3.0	3.0	3.0	1.0	4.0	3 (2 foreign language; 1 fine arts, vocational education, computer technology, or ROTC)	NA	([1,2])
Hawaii Standard	22	22	4.0	4.0	3.0	3.0	2.0	6.0	NA	1997	Physical education includes 1 unit in health and guidance and 1 unit in physical education. 10th grade students take the Hawaii State Test of Essential Competencies (HSTEC).
Recognition diploma	NA	24	4.0	4.0	3.0	3.0	2.0	6.0	2 (foreign language, performing/fine arts, or vocational education)	1997	Physical education requirement includes 1 unit in health and guidance and 1 unit in physical education. 10th grade students take Hawaii State of Essential Competencies (HSTEC).
Idaho	21	21	4.0	2.0	2.0	2.0	1.5	6.0	3.5 (.5 reading; .5 speech; .5 consumer education; 2 humanities. Practical arts may substitute for 1 of the 2 units in the humanities)	1997	State requires a C average, demonstrated competency in core curriculum on a junior class competency test or adherence to a local district's achievement plan for graduation. History requirement includes 1 unit in U.S. history and 1 unit in American government. Both science units must include a laboratory component. The physical education requirement includes .5 unit in health and 1 unit in physical education.
Illinois	16	16	3.0	2.0	2.0	1.0	4.5	2.2	1.25 (1 from music, art, foreign language which includes American Sign Language, or vocational education; .25 from consumer education)	1995	1 year of mathematics may be computer technology. Social studies requirement includes 1 unit in U.S. history or .5 unit in U.S. history and .5 unit in American government. Physical education requirement includes .5 unit in health education.[2]
Indiana Standard	20	20	4.0	2.0	2.0	2.0	1.5	8.0	NA	1989	State does not use standard Carnegie units. Tenth grade exit exam begins with the class of 1999-2000.[1]

See footnotes at end of table.

Table C-35. State Requirements for High School Graduation, in Carnegie Units: 1993 and 1996 — Continued

State	1993 All courses	1996 All courses	1996 Subject areas							First graduating class to which these requirements apply	Notes
			English/ language arts	Social studies	Mathematics	Science	Physical education/ health	Electives	Other courses		
Academic honors	24	24	4.0	3.0	4.0	4.0	1.0	4.0	3 or 4 in foreign language (3 years of 1 language or 2 years in 2 languages)	1990	State does not use standard Carnegie units. Tenth grade exit exam begins with the class of 1999-2000.[1]
Iowa	NA	NA	NA	1.5	NA	NA	NA	NA	NA	NA	All students must participate in physical education unless they qualify under certain exceptions. Social studies requirement includes 1 unit in U.S. history and .5 unit in American government.[1,3]
Kansas	21	21	4.0	3.0	2.0	2.0	1.0	9.0	NA	NA	Students are required to take a course in Kansas history or government (consisting of a minimum of 9 weeks and 1,800 minutes) in grades 7-12. English/language arts requirement includes 3 units in English. Social studies requirement includes 1 unit in American history and .5 unit in American government.[1]
Kentucky Standard	20	20	4.0	2.0	3.0	2.0	1.0	8.0	NA	1987	Social studies requirement includes 1 unit in U.S. history. The physical education requirement includes .5 unit in health and .5 unit in physical education.
Commonwealth	22	22	5.0	2.0	3.0	2.0	1.0	8.0	1 foreign language in advanced placement	1993	Completion of 1 exam in at least 3 of the advanced placement classes (science or mathematics, foreign language and English) is required. Physical education requirement includes .5 unit in health and .5 unit in physical education.
Louisiana Standard	23	23	4.0	3.0	3.0	3.0	2.0	7.5	.5 computer literacy	1987	With an ACT score of 29 or above, 3.5 GPA or above with no semester grade lower than a B, and no unexcused absences or suspensions, students may receive a Scholar Program Seal on their diploma.[1,2]
Regents program	24	24	4.0	3.5	3.0	3.0	2.0	4.5	4 (3 foreign language; 1 fine arts)	1983	([1,2])
Maine	16	16	4.0	2.0	2.0	2.0	1.5	3.5	1 fine arts	1989	Social studies requirement includes 1 unit in American history and 1 unit in American government. One science unit must include a laboratory component. Students must pass computer proficiency standards.[1]
Maryland	21	21	4.0	3.0	3.0	2.0	1.0	5.0	3 (1 fine arts; 1 industrial arts/technology education, home economics, vocational education, or computer studies; and 1 community service)	1997	([1])

See footnotes at end of table.

Table C-35. State Requirements for High School Graduation, in Carnegie Units: 1993 and 1996 — Continued

State	1993 All courses	1996 All courses	1996 English/ language arts	Social studies	Mathe- matics	Science	Physical education/ health	Elec- tives	Other courses	First graduating class to which these require- ments apply	Notes
Massachusetts	NA	NA	NA	1.0	NA	NA	4.0	NA	NA	NA	American history is required.[1,2,3]
Michigan	NA	NA	NA	NA	NA	NA	NA	NA	NA	1993	A competency exam is optional for students wanting an endorsed diploma. Students must receive instruction on U.S. and Michigan history and take a semester of civics.[3]
Minnesota	20	NA	NA	NA	NA	NA	NA	NA	NA	2000	[1,2]
Mississippi	18	18	4.0	2.0	2.0	2.0	NA	8.0	NA	1989	One science unit must include a laboratory component.
Missouri Standard	22	22	3.0	2.0	2.0	2.0	1.0	10.0	2 (1 practical arts; 1 fine arts)	1988	Local districts may add to the requirements.
College preparatory certificate	24	24	4.0	3.0	3.0	2.0	1.0	9.0	2 (1 practical arts; 1 fine arts)	1988	Social studies requirement includes 1 unit in American history. One science unit must include a laboratory component. Of the 9 elective units, 3 core electives are selected from foreign language, English, social studies, mathematics, science or fine arts. A GPA of 3.0 and SAT of 1014 or enhanced ACT of 21 is required.
Montana	20	20	4.0	2.0	2.0	2.0	1.0	7.0	2 (1 fine arts; 1 vocational/practical arts)	1989	NA
Nebraska	NA	NA	NA	NA	NA	NA	NA	NA	NA	1991	The state does not use standard Carnegie units.[3]
Nevada	22	22	4.0	2.0	2.0	2.0	2.5	8.5	1.5 (1 arts and humanities; .5 computer literacy)	1992	Computer literacy course requirement may be waived by demonstration of competency. Social studies requirement includes 1 unit in American government and 1 unit American history. Physical education requirement includes .5 unit in health and 2 units in physical education.[1,2]
New Hampshire	20	20	4.0	2.0	2.0	2.0	1.2	7.0	1.5 (.5 arts; .5 computer education; .5 basic business and economics)	1989	The social studies requirement includes 1 unit in U.S. and New Hampshire history and 1 elective unit. Science requirement includes 1 unit in physical and 1 unit in biological science. Physical education requirement includes .25 unit in health and 1 unit in physical education.[3]
New Jersey	22	22	4.0	3.0	3.0	2.0	4.0	4.0	1.5 (1 fine, practical, or performing arts; .5 career education)	1990	110 credit hours are required for graduation. (The state does not use standard Carnegie units.) Social studies requirement includes 2 units in U.S. history and 1 unit in world history/cultures. Science unit may be either natural or physical science.[1,2]

See footnotes at end of table.

Table C-35. State Requirements for High School Graduation, in Carnegie Units: 1993 and 1996 — Continued

State	1993	1996	1996							First graduating class to which these require-ments apply	Notes
			Subject areas								
	All courses		English/ language arts	Social studies	Mathe-matics	Science	Physical education/ health	Elec-tives	Other courses		
New Mexico	23	23	4.0	3.0	3.0	2.0	1.0	9.0	1 communication skills	1990	One science unit must have a laboratory component. Social studies requirement includes government and economics, world history and geography, and U.S. history and geography. [2]
New York Standard	18	20	NA	4.0	NA	NA	2.5	2.0	4 (1 art and/or music; 3 second language)	1989	Social studies requirement includes U.S. history and government.[2]
Regents diploma	18	18	4.0	4.0	2.0	2.0	2.5	3.0	1 (foreign language, art and/or music, occupational, technical or home economics education)	2000	Physical education requirement includes .5 unit in health and 2 physical education. Physical education courses may not be included toward the 18.5 units required for graduation. One science credit must include a laboratory component. The 3 to 5 elective units are chosen from a specified sequence of courses.[2]
North Carolina Standard	20	20	4.0	2.0	2.0	2.0	1.0	9.0	NA	1987	One science class must include a laboratory component.[2]
Scholars program	22	22	4.0	3.0	3.0	3.0	1.0	4.0	4 (2 foreign language; 2 additional credits from English, mathematics, science, social science, or foreign language)	1994	One science class must include a laboratory component.[2]
North Dakota	17	17	4.0	3.0	2.0	2.0	1.0	5.0	NA	1994	The social studies requirement includes 1 unit in world history and geography. A unit of higher level foreign language may be substituted for the fourth unit of English.[3]
Ohio	18	18	3.0	2.0	2.0	1.0	1.0	9.0	3 (total units in a subject area other than language arts/English must be taken to complete a 'minor')	1988	([1,2])
Oklahoma Standard	20	21	4.0	2.0	3.0	2.0	0.0	8.0	2 (1 fine/performing arts; 1 citizenship skills)	2000	([1])
College preparatory	15	15	4.0	2.0	3.0	2.0	0.0	NA	4 (3 units chosen from foreign language, computer science, English, mathematics, history, sociology, science, speech, or psychology; 1 unit from economics, geography, government or non-Western culture)	1996	([1])

See footnotes at end of table.

Table C-35. State Requirements for High School Graduation, in Carnegie Units: 1993 and 1996 — Continued

State	1993 All courses	1996 All courses	English/ language arts	Social studies	Mathe- matics	Science	Physical education/ health	Elec- tives	Other courses	First graduating class to which these require- ments apply	Notes
Oregon	22	22	3.0	3.5	2.0	2.0	2.0	8.0	1 (.5 career development; 1 applied arts, fine arts, or foreign language)	1988	Students receive an honors diploma for a GPA of 3.5 or higher.
Pennsylvania	21	21	4.0	3.0	3.0	3.0	1.0	5.0	2 credits in arts, humanities or computer science	1989	Students must achieve 52 state academic performances and locally developed outcomes.
Rhode Island											
Standard	16	16	4.0	2.0	2.0	2.0	NA	6.0	NA	1989	NA
College preparatory	18	18	4.0	2.0	3.0	2.0	NA	4.0	3 (2 credits in foreign language; .5 computer; .5 arts)	NA	NA
South Carolina											
Technical preparatory	20	24	4.0	3.0	4.0	3.0	1.0	3.0	6 (4 credits in occupational specialty; 2 in foreign language)	2000	Students must complete an occupational specialty program consisting of four sequential units of instruction in a career major. Students must demonstrate keyboarding proficiency and computer literacy before high school graduation. The social studies requirement includes 1 world history or geography; 1 unit in U.S. history; .5 unit in U.S. government and .5 unit in economics.[2]
Dual Path	22	24	4.0	4.0	4.0	4.0	1.0	1.0	6 (4 occupational specialty; 2 foreign language)	2000	Social studies requirement includes 1 unit in world history; 1 unit in world geography; 1 unit in U.S. history; .5 unit in U.S. government; and .5 unit in economics.[2]
College preparatory	NA	24	4.0	4.0	4.0	4.0	1.0	4.0	3 credits in foreign language	NA	Proficiency in computer keyboarding/computer literacy is required for graduation. Social studies requirement includes 1 unit in world history; 1 unit in world geography; 1 unit in U.S. history; .5 unit in U.S. government; and .5 unit in economics.[2]
South Dakota	20	20	4.0	3.0	2.0	2.0	NA	8.0	1 (.5 computer studies; .5 fine arts)	1989	Language arts/English requirement includes 1.5 units in writing, .5 unit in American literature, .5 unit in literature and .5 unit in speech. Social studies requirement includes 1 unit in U.S. history, .5 unit in U.S. government and .5 unit in geography. Both science units must include a laboratory.
Tennessee											
Technical preparatory	20	20	4.0	3.0	3.0	3.0	1.0	2.0	4 (program of study focusing on a particular technical area)	1989	Exit exam with no passing standards is required before graduation; it is used to assess readiness for workplace or higher education.
University preparatory	20	20	4.0	3.0	3.0	3.0	1.0	3.0	3 (2 in foreign language; 1 fine art)	1989	Exit exam with no passing standards is required before graduation; it is used to assess readiness for workplace or higher education.

See footnotes at end of table.

Table C-35. State Requirements for High School Graduation, in Carnegie Units: 1993 and 1996 — Continued

State	1993 All courses	1996 All courses	1996 Subject areas English/ language arts	Social studies	Mathe-matics	Science	Physical education/ health	Elec-tives	Other courses	First graduating class to which these require-ments apply	Notes
Texas											
Standard (1998)	21	22	4.0	2.0	3.0	2.0	2.0	7.0	2 (.5 economics/free enterprise; .5 speech; 1 technology application)	1998	Physical education requirement includes .5 unit in health and 1.5 units in physical education.[2]
Standard (2000)	22	24	4.0	4.0	3.0	3.0	2.0	3.0	5 (3 foreign language; 1 technology application; 1 fine arts)	2000	Students must choose one of the three-credit additional options for electives. College Board advanced placement and International Baccalaureate courses may be substituted for requirements in appropriate proficiency areas to receive dual credits for college coursework. Physical education requirement includes .5 unit in health and 1.5 units in physical education. Social studies requirement includes economics.
Utah	24	24	3.0	3.0	2.0	2.0	2.0	9.5	2.5 (1.5 arts; 1 applied technical education or occupational preparation)	1988	Students may accumulate credits more quickly than peers and be eligible to receive a Centennial Scholarship for Early Graduation to be applied to college tuition.[1,3]
Vermont	14	14	4.0	3.0	0.0	0.0	1.5	NA	1 arts	1989	A total of 5 credits are required in mathematics and science.
Virginia											
Standard	21	21	4.0	3.0	2.0	2.0	2.0	6.0	2 (1 additional mathematics or science; 1 fine or practical arts)	1989	([2])
Advanced studies	23	23	4.0	3.0	3.0	3.0	2.0	4.0	4 (3 foreign language; 1 fine or practical arts)	NA	([2])
Washington	19	19	3.0	2.5	2.0	2.0	2.0	5.5	2 (1 occupational education; 1 fine/visual or performing arts)	1991	([1])
West Virginia											
Standard (1989)	21	21	4.0	3.0	2.0	2.0	2.0	8.0	NA	1989	Electives must be from applied arts, fine or performing arts, or a foreign language.
Standard (2002)	21	21	4.0	3.0	2.0	2.0	2.0	7.0	1 art, music, theater or dance	2002	NA
Wisconsin	13	22	4.0	3.0	2.0	2.0	2.0	NA	NA	1989	Grades 9-12 need 1.5 units of physical education and grades 7-12 need .5 unit of health.[1,3]
Wyoming	18	18	4.0	3.0	2.0	2.0	NA	5.0	NA	1997	NA

SOURCE: Education Commission of the States, Clearinghouse Notes, 'Minimum High School Graduation Requirements' November 1996. Published as table 155 in Digest of Education 1997.

1. State allows dual credit for college coursework.
2. Minimum competency test is required.

3. Local boards determine at least some requirements.
4. A Career Pathway is a planned program of sequenced or specialized courses designed to develop knowledge and skills in a particular career area. Students may use the Additional Academic Coursework (visual and performing arts, foreign language and/or vocational technical education coursework, including Junior ROTC) as an option, to pursue individual academic interests. The credits in these two categories will eventually replace the elective credits.

NOTE: Local school districts frequently have other graduation requirements in addition to state requirements.

NA Not applicable or not available.

Table C-36. Revenues for Public Elementary and Secondary Schools, by Source and State: 1994-95

(Amounts in thousands of dollars)

State	Total	Federal		State		Local and intermediate		Private[1]	
		Amount	Percent of total	Amount	Percent of total	Amount	Percent of total	Amount	Percent of total
United States	$273 137 899	$18 581 511	6.8	$127 719 673	46.8	$119 538 243	43.8	$7 298 472	2.7
Alabama	3 541 876	343 927	9.7	2 161 685	61.0	766 020	21.6	270 244	7.6
Alaska	1 207 000	129 911	10.8	815 286	67.5	234 263	19.4	27 541	2.3
Arizona	3 783 285	354 242	9.4	1 664 966	44.0	1 673 192	44.2	90 886	2.4
Arkansas	2 175 109	199 163	9.2	1 266 778	58.2	605 499	27.8	103 669	4.8
California	28 891 301	2 751 519	9.5	15 670 329	54.2	10 127 054	35.1	342 399	1.2
Colorado	3 679 162	193 865	5.3	1 578 428	42.9	1 788 285	48.6	118 585	3.2
Connecticut	4 431 602	177 446	4.0	1 748 802	39.5	2 375 694	53.6	129 660	2.9
Delaware	745 036	53 885	7.2	479 319	64.3	199 689	26.8	12 143	1.6
District of Columbia	701 300	66 716	9.5	0	(NA)	631 028	90.0	3 556	0.5
Florida	12 805 853	971 277	7.6	6 286 323	49.1	5 067 892	39.6	480 362	3.8
Georgia	6 965 472	512 456	7.4	3 530 615	50.7	2 785 137	40.0	137 265	2.0
Hawaii	1 177 915	86 882	7.4	1 062 296	90.2	6 307	0.5	22 429	1.9
Idaho	1 088 596	84 012	7.7	666 387	61.2	318 671	29.3	19 527	1.8
Illinois	12 016 320	780 212	6.5	3 361 268	28.0	7 605 409	63.3	260 431	2.2
Indiana	6 362 528	306 971	4.8	3 391 558	53.3	2 472 119	38.9	191 880	3.0
Iowa	2 881 176	151 225	5.2	1 381 238	47.9	1 182 483	41.0	166 230	5.8
Kansas	2 883 345	152 757	5.3	1 655 905	57.4	1 002 034	34.8	72 648	2.5
Kentucky	3 240 926	301 243	9.3	2 132 169	65.8	782 230	24.1	25 283	0.8
Louisiana	3 837 862	458 344	11.9	1 999 368	52.1	1 281 012	33.4	99 138	2.6
Maine	1 400 439	79 403	5.7	670 517	47.9	635 247	45.4	15 272	1.1
Maryland	5 559 604	279 464	5.0	2 059 241	37.0	3 049 831	54.9	171 068	3.1
Massachusetts	6 549 468	352 760	5.4	2 376 538	36.3	3 668 716	56.0	151 453	2.3
Michigan	11 925 311	734 290	6.2	8 023 133	67.3	2 937 025	24.6	230 863	1.9
Minnesota	5 606 567	247 964	4.4	2 939 545	52.4	2 210 175	39.4	208 884	3.7
Mississippi	2 099 795	310 249	14.8	1 185 185	56.4	532 021	25.3	72 340	3.4
Missouri	4 891 384	317 002	6.5	1 892 112	38.7	2 481 121	50.7	201 149	4.1
Montana	915 392	91 912	10.0	453 778	49.6	331 846	36.3	37 857	4.1
Nebraska	1 797 785	104 608	5.8	582 430	32.4	1 002 900	55.8	107 847	6.0
Nevada	1 370 529	67 369	4.9	412 904	30.1	837 374	61.1	52 883	3.9
New Hampshire	1 149 673	35 169	3.1	83 611	7.3	1 004 110	87.3	26 782	2.3
New Jersey	11 485 382	383 016	3.3	4 361 977	38.0	6 433 765	56.0	306 623	2.7
New Mexico	1 695 358	199 231	11.8	1 261 807	74.4	196 841	11.6	37 480	2.2
New York	24 889 904	1 196 994	4.8	10 127 462	40.7	13 330 601	53.6	234 847	0.9
North Carolina	5 940 519	443 701	7.5	3 867 413	65.1	1 463 703	24.6	165 702	2.8
North Dakota	592 481	73 400	12.4	249 273	42.1	238 440	40.2	31 367	5.3
Ohio	11 024 539	714 840	6.5	4 410 699	40.0	5 433 715	49.3	465 286	4.2
Oklahoma	2 767 709	260 760	9.4	1 644 176	59.4	715 199	25.8	147 575	5.3
Oregon	3 294 014	224 139	6.8	1 521 760	46.2	1 442 103	43.8	106 011	3.2
Pennsylvania	13 271 164	746 601	5.6	5 325 072	40.1	6 943 281	52.3	256 210	1.9
Rhode Island	1 080 260	59 458	5.5	437 494	40.5	571 698	52.9	11 609	1.1
South Carolina	3 450 203	299 232	8.7	1 598 971	46.3	1 399 989	40.6	152 010	4.4
South Dakota	691 685	69 162	10.0	183 552	26.5	418 328	60.5	20 643	3.0
Tennessee	3 908 306	348 729	8.9	1 855 784	47.5	1 443 757	36.9	260 036	6.7
Texas	19 678 883	1 511 000	7.7	7 908 524	40.2	9 712 168	49.4	547 191	2.8
Utah	1 940 247	133 543	6.9	1 054 222	54.3	645 245	33.3	107 237	5.5
Vermont	753 905	34 424	4.6	224 941	29.8	476 096	63.2	18 445	2.4
Virginia	6 456 380	368 102	5.7	2 052 415	31.8	3 813 487	59.1	222 376	3.4
Washington	5 976 441	357 615	6.0	4 103 287	68.7	1 330 433	22.3	185 106	3.1
West Virginia	1 940 425	156 555	8.1	1 234 701	63.6	520 036	26.8	29 134	1.5
Wisconsin	5 985 761	262 315	4.4	2 460 520	41.1	3 139 562	52.5	123 364	2.1
Wyoming	632 720	42 453	6.7	303 908	48.0	275 412	43.5	10 947	1.7

See footnotes at end of table.

Table C-36.   Revenues for Public Elementary and Secondary Schools, by Source and State: 1994-95 — Continued

(Amounts in thousands of dollars)

State	Total	Federal		State		Local and intermediate		Private[1]	
		Amount	Percent of total	Amount	Percent of total	Amount	Percent of total	Amount	Percent of total
Outlying areas									
American Samoa	$45 151	$37 858	83.8	$6 987	15.5	$190	0.4	$116	0.3
Guam	171 866	17 132	10.0	0	(NA)	153 269	89.2	1 465	0.9
Northern Marianas	44 122	11 663	26.4	32 321	73.3	54	0.1	85	0.2
Puerto Rico	1 641 580	474 419	28.9	1 166 632	71.1	218	(2)	311	(2)
Virgin Islands	142 961	25 435	17.8	0	(NA)	117 441	82.1	85	0.1

SOURCE: U.S. Department of Education, National Center for Education Statistics, Common Core of Data survey. Published as table 159 in *Digest of Education Statistics* 1997.

1. Includes revenues from gifts, and tuition and fees from patrons.
2. Less than .05 percent.

NOTE: Excludes revenues for state education agencies. Because of rounding, details may not add to totals.

(NA) Not applicable or not available.

Table C-37.   Funds and Staff for State Education Agencies[1], by Source of Funding and State: 1992-93

State	Funds retained for state administration, by source in thousands				Total state administration funds per student	State education agency (FTE) staff, by source of funds for position			
	Total	Federal (core actitivies)[2]	Percent federal	State and local		Total FTE staff	Federally supported (core activites)[2]	State and local supported	Students per state FTE staff
United States	$1 966 453	$526 847	26.8	$1 439 606	46	28 626	7 054	21 572	1 496
Alabama	52 111	13 007	25.0	39 103	71	1 006	127	879	727
Alaska	38 461	5 046	13.1	33 414	314	503	44	460	244
Arizona	19 315	7 460	38.6	11 856	29	362	175	187	1 862
Arkansas	17 561	4 204	23.9	13 356	40	290	74	216	1 522
California	148 989	52 316	35.1	96 673	28	1 898	419	1 479	2 768
Colorado	21 361	5 991	28.0	15 370	35	223	90	133	2 750
Connecticut	139 733	11 433	8.2	128 300	286	2 005	196	1 809	244
Delaware	10 949	2 578	23.5	8 371	105	128	44	84	817
District of Columbia	(NA)	(NA)	(NA)	(NA)	(NA)	(NA)	(NA)	(NA)	(NA)
Florida	56 310	25 470	45.2	30 840	28	688	323	366	2 878
Georgia	58 632	9 918	16.9	48 714	49	935	147	788	1 291
Hawaii	(NA)	(NA)	(NA)	(NA)	(NA)	(NA)	(NA)	(NA)	(NA)
Idaho	7 346	2 938	40.0	4 408	32	104	45	59	2 224
Illinois	42 854	22 092	51.6	20 762	23	746	317	429	2 511
Indiana	29 220	7 339	25.1	21 880	30	309	132	177	3 109
Iowa	20 589	9 582	46.5	11 007	42	226	106	120	2 192
Kansas	12 701	5 422	42.7	7 279	28	199	83	116	2 269
Kentucky	49 745	6 202	12.5	43 542	76	859	105	754	763
Louisiana	35 978	13 015	36.2	22 963	45	573	254	320	1 393
Maine	17 356	4 248	24.5	13 109	80	207	90	117	1 046
Maryland	42 343	8 737	20.6	33 606	56	556	126	430	1 351
Massachusetts	30 191	13 557	44.9	16 633	35	368	173	195	2 337
Michigan	53 743	15 656	29.1	38 088	34	844	256	588	1 899
Minnesota	23 730	9 072	38.2	14 658	30	416	129	287	1 908
Mississippi	40 892	5 703	13.9	35 190	81	724	144	580	700
Missouri	42 860	8 708	20.3	34 152	50	1 448	132	1 317	593
Montana	8 070	3 490	43.2	4 581	50	137	52	85	1 168
Nebraska	20 624	5 018	24.3	15 607	73	398	75	323	710
Nevada	5 305	2 643	49.8	2 662	24	90	47	42	2 491
New Hampshire	7 889	2 662	33.7	5 226	44	157	60	97	1 154
New Jersey	65 111	25 857	39.7	39 254	58	1 001	326	675	1 129
New Mexico	10 398	3 753	36.1	6 645	33	216	67	149	1 461
New York	181 649	47 866	26.4	133 783	68	2 565	567	1 998	1 049
North Carolina	49 298	13 990	28.4	35 308	44	796	144	652	1 399
North Dakota	5 683	3 187	56.1	2 496	48	93	52	41	1 277
Ohio	32 879	14 741	44.8	18 139	18	511	242	269	3 513
Oklahoma	32 178	8 347	25.9	23 831	54	499	98	401	1 196
Oregon	61 178	15 822	25.9	45 357	120	418	58	360	1 221
Pennsylvania	72 979	19 746	27.1	53 233	42	1 134	237	897	1 515
Rhode Island	13 705	4 347	31.7	9 358	95	152	59	93	948
South Carolina	87 109	9 130	10.5	77 979	136	946	105	841	677
South Dakota	7 419	3 988	53.8	3 430	55	102	42	60	1 324
Tennessee	36 778	10 525	28.6	26 253	43	456	100	356	1 876
Texas	59 560	18 321	30.8	41 238	17	1 013	358	654	3 498
Utah	25 763	6 092	23.6	19 671	56	364	62	302	1 273

See footnotes at end of table.

Table C-37.   Funds and Staff for State Education Agencies[1], by Source of Funding and State: 1992-93 — Continued

State	Funds retained for state administration, by source in thousands				Total state administration funds per student	State education agency (FTE) staff, by source of funds for position			
	Total	Federal (core actitivies)[2]	Percent federal	State and local		Total FTE staff	Federally supported (core activites)[2]	State and local supported	Students per state FTE staff
Vermont	$7 348	$2 672	36.4	$4 675	75	143	65	78	689
Virginia	29 236	9 830	33.6	19 406	28	371	102	270	2 781
Washington	19 472	6 843	35.1	12 629	22	253	88	165	3 542
West Virginia	21 188	5 069	23.9	16 119	67	403	113	289	790
Wisconsin	87 883	11 377	12.9	76 506	106	692	179	512	1 199
Wyoming	4 782	1 837	38.4	2 945	48	100	25	75	1 003

SOURCE: U.S. General Accounting Office, Education Finance, Extent of Federal Funding in State Education Agencies; and U.S. Department of Education, National Center for Education Statistics, Common Core of Data survey. Published as table 161 in *Digest of Education Statistics* 1997.

1. Excludes funds for schools and school districts.
2. Core education activities include: Chapter 1; Chapter 2; Special Education; Child Nutrition; Vocational Education; Adult Education; AIDS Education; Civil Rights Act; and Homeless Education Programs.
3. Excludes District of Columbia and Hawaii.
4. Excludes State Teacher Retirement Program.

NOTE: Because of rounding, details may not add to totals.

(NA) Not applicable or not available.

Table C-38.   Expenditures for Instruction in Public Elementary and Secondary Schools, by Subfunction and State: 1993-94 and 1994-95

(In thousands of dollars)

State	1993-94					
	Total	Salaries	Employee benefits	Purchased services[2]	Supplies	Tuition and other
United States	$141 620 474	$103 506 419	$27 456 084	$3 421 355	$5 507 720	$1 728 895
Alabama	1 757 077	1 329 103	317 861	5 505	87 994	16 613
Alaska	517 200	370 381	84 893	20 562	21 311	20 053
Arizona	1 680 405	1 404 486	207 938	13 704	28 531	25 745
Arkansas	1 116 796	862 527	194 647	17 569	32 663	9 390
California	15 028 418	10 535 742	3 275 864	417 732	534 495	264 585
Colorado	1 815 426	1 403 567	280 586	54 564	69 799	6 909
Connecticut	2 501 019	1 949 504	435 277	37 744	64 920	13 574
Delaware	399 147	279 411	94 677	6 374	14 897	3 788
District of Columbia	351 028	251 437	73 230	7 967	5 558	12 835
Florida	5 970 755	4 016 237	1 336 262	361 131	196 670	60 455
Georgia	3 473 765	2 571 602	712 847	33 534	151 782	4 000
Hawaii	615 270	443 179	123 385	19 218	27 938	1 551
Idaho	543 377	389 041	120 933	8 960	23 999	444
Illinois	6 064 603	4 697 555	905 583	105 297	235 412	120 755
Indiana	3 121 188	2 309 246	673 493	32 707	100 174	5 569
Iowa	1 558 177	1 115 162	263 334	62 452	107 452	9 777
Kansas	1 345 121	1 069 472	187 192	11 579	71 444	5 434
Kentucky	1 768 270	1 427 161	269 831	88	71 170	20
Louisiana	1 967 293	1 459 276	403 272	16 167	84 227	4 352
Maine	808 608	550 050	166 324	22 399	26 660	43 175
Maryland	2 890 997	1 992 747	658 207	73 927	80 822	85 295
Massachusetts	3 398 730	2 461 875	385 677	267 298	98 610	185 269
Michigan	5 691 574	4 139 256	1 259 843	77 832	193 110	21 533
Minnesota	2 757 594	2 033 003	538 195	68 805	98 115	19 476
Mississippi	1 066 080	821 115	166 575	16 477	56 697	5 215
Missouri	2 415 629	1 840 689	329 085	43 996	191 915	9 945
Montana	514 036	369 489	97 938	13 156	31 205	2 247
Nebraska	941 392	700 536	159 735	21 827	37 875	21 419
Nevada	654 996	491 876	132 187	4 662	25 270	1 000
New Hampshire	646 681	467 975	100 808	13 691	21 158	43 050
New Jersey	6 260 952	4 527 397	1 183 042	45 473	212 716	292 324
New Mexico	775 050	570 209	148 257	7 981	43 549	5 054
New York	14 884 460	10 895 343	3 302 335	340 172	344 180	2 429
North Carolina	3 161 009	2 383 123	588 767	45 782	140 203	3 134
North Dakota	320 294	234 827	58 894	8 274	15 493	2 806
Ohio	5 717 214	4 170 324	1 158 036	94 873	224 924	69 057
Oklahoma	1 572 751	1 199 978	269 447	19 719	81 967	1 641
Oregon	1 708 679	1 133 552	427 436	50 290	88 577	8 823
Pennsylvania	7 144 739	4 753 300	1 609 574	479 975	212 470	89 420
Rhode Island	659 748	461 270	147 798	16 235	13 146	21 300
South Carolina	1 651 858	1 251 017	312 363	22 422	64 858	1 197
South Dakota	360 621	262 590	57 153	10 549	20 787	9 542
Tennessee	2 125 274	1 635 375	372 014	39 428	72 376	6 080
Texas	9 602 153	7 492 386	1 197 000	156 463	719 546	36 758
Utah	1 013 630	662 696	230 024	14 387	47 072	59 451
Vermont	419 909	295 898	79 058	14 198	12 934	17 822
Virginia	3 275 030	2 487 274	621 527	43 510	117 838	4 881
Washington	2 921 122	2 066 990	639 335	85 052	109 654	20 091
West Virginia	1 034 956	723 919	262 282	10 065	38 524	166
Wisconsin	3 285 249	2 300 226	768 388	49 266	115 175	52 194
Wyoming	345 120	246 023	67 675	10 316	19 854	1 252

See footnotes at end of table.

Table C-38. Expenditures for Instruction in Public Elementary and Secondary Schools, by Subfunction and State: 1993-94 and 1994-95 — Continued

(In thousands of dollars)

State	1994-95[1]					
	Total	Salaries	Employee benefits	Purchased services[2]	Supplies	Tuition and other
United States	$150 521 920	$109 680 814	$29 184 690	$3 819 015	$5 762 374	$2 075 027
Alabama	1 906 471	1 446 029	335 738	5 645	99 824	19 236
Alaska	574 167	413 346	100 477	18 210	21 512	20 622
Arizona	1 811 054	1 500 416	238 820	16 435	31 128	24 256
Arkansas	1 144 389	868 482	206 954	23 230	35 930	9 793
California	15 549 692	11 038 093	3 262 337	424 379	536 517	288 366
Colorado	1 970 908	1 508 701	306 238	67 936	80 563	7 470
Connecticut	2 721 552	2 004 391	463 152	50 246	64 845	138 919
Delaware	431 618	297 607	103 254	7 194	15 843	7 719
District of Columbia	336 543	239 594	65 979	5 251	3 556	22 163
Florida	6 395 934	4 283 275	1 422 087	408 034	209 508	73 030
Georgia	3 779 713	2 799 934	770 839	39 991	164 184	4 763
Hawaii	636 952	457 861	127 015	18 255	32 471	1 352
Idaho	602 232	430 919	130 741	11 204	28 940	428
Illinois	6 367 082	4 797 408	1 061 451	120 542	265 284	122 397
Indiana	3 262 523	2 417 230	697 094	35 344	107 345	5 510
Iowa	1 623 942	1 160 673	277 271	56 959	116 398	12 641
Kansas	1 387 198	1 108 730	193 070	12 294	67 297	5 807
Kentucky	1 787 624	1 423 656	291 715	94	72 140	19
Louisiana	2 071 476	1 544 288	415 405	19 349	87 321	5 113
Maine	859 560	570 803	190 981	24 493	27 895	45 388
Maryland	3 127 996	2 130 372	729 842	86 737	88 971	92 074
Massachusetts	3 994 523	2 691 297	728 275	254 433	111 466	209 053
Michigan	6 228 315	4 328 190	1 569 832	84 022	210 776	35 495
Minnesota	2 946 240	2 160 089	579 243	78 764	105 214	22 929
Mississippi	1 197 868	891 328	216 101	18 628	65 880	5 931
Missouri	2 597 027	1 969 708	355 700	53 142	207 753	10 724
Montana	525 617	379 161	101 394	11 080	31 900	2 082
Nebraska	997 580	732 361	178 023	24 370	40 341	22 484
Nevada	706 132	528 908	144 432	4 552	27 143	1 097
New Hampshire	679 046	498 773	97 439	16 606	21 773	44 455
New Jersey	6 467 203	4 715 340	1 128 758	51 960	232 132	339 014
New Mexico	837 029	618 787	158 931	8 022	45 294	5 995
New York	15 636 396	11 525 744	3 387 241	358 939	361 933	2 539
North Carolina	3 387 680	2 556 856	623 633	48 461	155 787	2 942
North Dakota	328 461	240 567	60 009	8 896	16 378	2 610
Ohio	5 960 083	4 362 651	1 182 673	103 167	235 248	76 343
Oklahoma	1 662 373	1 266 325	261 121	26 166	97 571	11 190
Oregon	1 776 148	1 193 420	412 583	59 993	99 712	10 441
Pennsylvania	7 460 973	5 049 611	1 591 109	512 608	224 403	83 241
Rhode Island	669 274	470 133	150 373	11 784	14 302	22 683
South Carolina	1 727 214	1 298 160	320 509	27 097	80 175	1 274
South Dakota	376 116	272 643	59 785	11 243	22 634	9 811
Tennessee	2 285 884	1 740 065	395 947	38 603	104 857	6 413
Texas	10 753 150	8 517 213	1 268 868	294 413	606 632	66 025
Utah	1 089 195	706 401	250 913	16 429	46 339	69 112
Vermont	434 933	306 881	77 637	15 984	13 596	20 835
Virginia	3 483 576	2 640 491	671 729	48 638	118 633	4 085
Washington	3 075 785	2 156 923	670 680	101 440	124 646	22 096
West Virginia	1 090 056	766 359	280 057	11 134	32 343	163
Wisconsin	3 441 286	2 400 781	800 389	55 545	129 411	55 160
Wyoming	358 131	253 841	70 846	11 073	20 630	1 741

See footnotes at end of table.

Table C-38. Expenditures for Instruction in Public Elementary and Secondary Schools, by Subfunction and State: 1993-94 and 1994-95 — Continued

(In thousands of dollars)

| State | 1993-94 | | | | | |
	Total	Salaries	Employee benefits	Purchased services[2]	Supplies	Tuition and other
Outlying areas						
American Samoa	$11 582	$8 612	$1 336	$316	$1 090	$229
Guam	86 713	72 705	13 292	75	385	255
Northern Marianas	29 959	19 199	4 620	2 234	3 660	247
Puerto Rico	972 817	798 483	114 161	9 683	20 961	29 529
Virgin Islands	68 548	55 140	10 763	525	604	1 515

See footnotes at end of table.

Table C-38.   Expenditures for Instruction in Public Elementary and Secondary Schools, by Subfunction and State: 1993-94 and 1994-95 — Continued

(In thousands of dollars)

State	1994-95[1]					
	Total	Salaries	Employee benefits	Purchased services[2]	Supplies	Tuition and other
Outlying areas						
American Samoa	$11 796	$8 900	$1 386	$236	$1 065	$211
Guam	79 336	65 432	13 237	83	424	161
Northern Marianas	35 613	21 718	6 259	3 678	3 551	407
Puerto Rico	1 093 038	903 531	127 031	11 148	20 234	31 094
Virgin Islands	69 349	55 563	11 042	572	652	1 520

SOURCE: U.S. Department of Education, National Center for Education Statistics, Common Core of Data surveys. Published as table 164 in *Digest of Education Statistics* 1997.

1. Preliminary data.
2. Includes purchased professional services of teachers or others who provide instruction for students and travel for instructional staff.

NOTE: Excludes expenditures for state education agencies. Because of rounding, details may not add to totals. Some 1993-94 data have been revised from previously published figures.

Table C-39. Current Expenditures for Public Elementary and Secondary Education, by State: 1969-70 to 1996-97

(In thousands of dollars)

State	1969-70	1979-80	1980-81	1984-85	1985-86	1986-87	1987-88	1988-89
United States	$34 217 773	$86 984 142	$94 321 093	$126 337 491	$137 164 965	$146 364 922	$157 097 951	$173 098 906
Alabama	422 730	1 146 713	1 393 137	1 590 856	1 761 154	1 775 997	1 873 390	2 188 020
Alaska	81 374	377 947	476 368	754 967	818 219	769 015	756 577	739 020
Arizona	281 941	949 753	1 075 362	1 436 844	1 649 832	1 836 908	2 002 395	2 143 148
Arkansas	235 083	666 949	709 394	1 005 347	1 085 943	1 118 904	1 211 156	1 319 370
California	3 831 595	9 172 158	9 936 642	13 477 768	15 040 898	16 512 668	17 402 063	19 417 178
Colorado	369 218	1 243 049	1 369 883	1 868 058	2 018 579	2 129 964	2 172 563	2 324 625
Connecticut	588 710	1 227 892	1 440 881	2 117 798	2 144 094	2 414 708	2 748 567	2 984 542
Delaware	108 747	269 108	270 439	353 191	391 558	418 116	440 631	479 327
District of Columbia	141 138	298 448	295 155	387 918	406 910	441 135	489 357	584 035
Florida	961 273	2 766 468	3 336 657	4 589 068	5 092 668	5 650 083	6 288 977	7 245 515
Georgia	599 371	1 608 028	1 688 714	2 629 681	2 979 980	3 254 786	3 549 038	4 006 069
Hawaii	141 324	351 889	395 038	521 692	575 456	576 749	608 264	643 319
Idaho	103 107	313 927	352 912	467 532	492 092	513 011	532 274	570 013
Illinois	1 896 067	4 579 355	4 773 179	5 662 354	6 066 390	6 463 564	6 923 298	7 655 153
Indiana	809 105	1 851 292	1 898 194	2 696 072	2 851 080	3 106 616	3 330 525	3 779 468
Iowa	527 086	1 186 659	1 337 504	1 599 674	1 644 359	1 708 440	1 859 173	1 925 623
Kansas	362 593	830 133	958 281	1 315 469	1 423 225	1 486 814	1 568 041	1 712 260
Kentucky	353 265	1 054 459	1 096 472	1 384 722	1 434 962	1 583 158	1 741 799	1 918 741
Louisiana	503 217	1 303 902	1 767 692	2 191 478	2 333 748	2 260 393	2 289 241	2 468 307
Maine	155 907	385 492	401 355	599 189	688 673	760 446	839 860	921 931
Maryland	721 794	1 783 056	1 937 159	2 446 771	2 634 209	2 845 404	3 128 165	3 505 018
Massachusetts	907 341	2 638 734	2 794 762	3 139 486	3 403 505	3 744 131	4 098 062	4 516 604
Michigan	1 799 945	4 642 847	5 196 249	5 735 303	6 184 767	6 427 556	6 913 261	7 492 267
Minnesota	781 243	1 786 768	1 900 322	2 461 571	2 637 722	2 818 390	2 981 209	3 282 296
Mississippi	262 760	756 018	716 878	1 023 720	1 058 301	1 112 535	1 221 560	1 365 846
Missouri	642 030	1 504 988	1 643 258	2 106 539	2 277 576	2 515 846	2 747 234	3 096 666
Montana	127 176	358 118	380 092	538 245	567 901	583 861	590 226	592 454
Nebraska	231 612	581 615	629 017	870 019	911 983	948 149	995 235	1 105 009
Nevada	87 273	281 901	287 752	397 254	495 147	513 014	555 272	628 657
New Hampshire	101 370	295 400	340 518	473 151	522 604	589 850	677 507	733 240
New Jersey	1 343 564	3 638 533	3 648 914	4 697 534	5 735 895	6 099 473	6 621 860	7 309 147
New Mexico	183 736	515 451	560 213	784 442	808 036	865 789	916 305	975 552
New York	4 111 839	8 760 500	9 259 948	12 681 301	13 686 039	14 724 687	16 073 392	17 127 596
North Carolina	676 193	1 880 862	2 112 417	2 674 774	2 991 747	3 193 337	3 424 194	3 892 971
North Dakota	97 895	228 483	254 197	365 341	379 470	374 941	385 427	431 814
Ohio	1 639 805	3 836 576	4 149 858	5 504 161	5 856 999	6 114 426	6 446 903	7 484 434
Oklahoma	339 105	1 055 844	1 193 373	1 575 467	1 740 981	1 707 396	1 692 283	1 833 743
Oregon	403 844	1 126 812	1 292 624	1 560 242	1 662 372	1 747 125	1 944 657	2 123 241
Pennsylvania	1 912 644	4 584 320	4 955 115	6 660 369	6 750 520	7 176 886	7 679 986	8 579 546
Rhode Island	145 443	362 046	395 389	525 824	569 935	608 318	663 800	747 852
South Carolina	367 689	997 984	1 006 088	1 556 552	1 708 603	1 814 160	1 932 502	2 118 732
South Dakota	109 375	238 332	242 215	338 800	360 832	368 266	389 436	428 014
Tennessee	473 226	1 319 303	1 429 938	1 836 012	1 990 889	2 167 026	2 352 183	2 668 341
Texas	1 518 181	4 997 689	5 310 181	8 996 476	9 642 812	10 152 521	10 791 854	11 761 447
Utah	179 981	518 251	587 648	813 817	906 484	932 740	974 666	1 043 759
Vermont	78 921	189 811	224 901	313 026	346 164	378 264	456 992	485 226
Virginia	704 677	1 881 519	2 045 412	2 845 540	3 183 707	3 444 952	3 793 475	4 151 050
Washington	699 984	1 825 782	1 791 477	2 565 957	2 702 652	2 808 636	3 005 980	3 209 992
West Virginia	249 404	678 386	754 889	1 090 514	1 164 882	1 229 069	1 231 966	1 202 486
Wisconsin	777 288	1 908 523	2 035 879	2 655 729	2 893 797	3 086 878	3 318 247	3 688 311
Wyoming	69 584	226 067	271 153	453 874	488 616	489 825	466 921	491 930

See footnotes at end of table.

Table C-39. Current Expenditures for Public Elementary and Secondary Education, by State: 1969-70 to 1996-97 — Continued

(In thousands of dollars)

State	1989-90[1]	1990-91	1991-92	1992-93	1993-94[1]	1994-95	Estimated 1995-96[2]	Estimated 1996-97[2]
United States	$188 229 359	$202 037 752	$211 210 190	$220 948 052	$231 542 764	$243 844 646	[3] $258 922 087	[3] $274 065 348
Alabama	2 275 233	2 475 216	2 465 523	2 610 514	2 809 713	3 026 287	3 169 728	3 459 903
Alaska	828 051	854 499	931 869	967 765	1 002 515	1 020 675	1 051 296	1 082 834
Arizona	2 258 660	2 469 543	2 599 586	2 753 504	2 911 304	3 144 540	[4] 3 331 835	[4] 3 549 233
Arkansas	1 404 545	1 510 092	1 656 201	1 703 621	1 782 645	1 873 595	[5] 1 496 991	1 541 900
California	21 485 782	22 748 218	23 696 863	24 219 792	25 140 639	25 949 033	27 521 544	30 273 699
Colorado	2 451 833	2 642 850	2 754 087	2 919 916	2 954 793	3 232 976	3 315 190	[4] 3 593 903
Connecticut	3 444 520	3 540 411	3 665 505	3 739 497	3 943 891	4 247 327	4 321 000	4 471 000
Delaware	520 953	543 933	572 152	600 161	643 915	694 473	[5] 748 655	[4] 783 317
District of Columbia	639 983	647 901	677 422	670 677	713 427	666 938	[4] 695 279	[4] 728 611
Florida	8 228 531	9 045 710	9 314 079	9 661 012	10 331 896	11 019 735	11 469 259	12 019 783
Georgia	4 505 962	4 804 225	4 856 583	5 273 143	5 643 843	6 136 689	[5] 7 781 018	8 247 879
Hawaii	700 012	827 579	884 591	946 074	998 143	1 028 729	960 400	982 000
Idaho	627 794	708 045	760 440	804 231	859 088	951 350	[5] 1 042 161	1 090 031
Illinois	8 125 493	8 932 538	9 244 655	9 942 737	10 076 889	10 640 279	12 181 620	12 547 068
Indiana	4 074 578	4 379 142	4 544 829	4 797 946	5 064 685	5 243 761	5 559 000	5 837 000
Iowa	2 004 742	2 136 561	2 356 196	2 459 141	2 527 434	2 622 510	2 743 145	2 873 445
Kansas	1 848 302	1 938 012	2 028 440	2 224 080	2 325 247	2 406 580	[5] 2 492 762	2 567 544
Kentucky	2 134 011	2 480 363	2 709 623	2 823 134	2 952 119	2 988 892	3 460 737	3 557 638
Louisiana	2 838 283	3 023 690	3 188 024	3 199 919	3 309 018	3 475 926	[5] 3 461 971	3 531 211
Maine	1 048 195	1 070 965	1 121 360	1 217 418	1 208 411	1 281 706	1 271 792	1 322 663
Maryland	3 894 644	4 240 862	4 362 679	4 556 266	4 783 023	5 083 380	4 926 216	5 323 364
Massachusetts	4 760 390	4 906 828	5 035 973	5 281 067	5 637 337	6 062 303	[4] 6 522 008	[4] 7 054 231
Michigan	8 025 621	8 545 805	9 156 501	9 532 994	9 816 830	10 440 206	0	11 039 483
Minnesota	3 474 398	3 740 820	3 936 695	4 135 284	4 328 093	4 622 930	4 857 100	4 975 400
Mississippi	1 472 710	1 510 552	1 536 295	1 600 752	1 725 386	1 921 480	[5] 1 998 743	2 098 680
Missouri	3 288 738	3 487 786	3 611 613	3 710 426	3 981 614	4 275 217	4 172 801	4 405 644
Montana	641 345	719 963	751 710	785 159	822 015	844 257	861 142	878 365
Nebraska	1 233 431	1 297 643	1 381 290	1 430 039	1 513 971	1 594 928	1 658 725	1 749 955
Nevada	712 898	864 379	962 800	1 035 623	1 099 685	1 186 132	1 286 767	1 415 231
New Hampshire	821 671	890 116	927 625	972 963	1 007 129	1 053 966	1 184 025	1 251 854
New Jersey	8 119 336	8 897 612	9 660 899	9 915 482	10 448 096	10 776 982	11 548 068	12 440 741
New Mexico	1 020 148	1 134 156	1 212 189	1 240 310	1 323 459	1 443 789	1 823 809	2 125 111
New York	18 090 978	19 514 583	19 781 384	20 898 267	22 059 949	22 989 629	23 748 287	24 531 980
North Carolina	4 342 826	4 605 384	4 660 027	4 930 823	5 145 416	5 440 426	5 845 439	6 169 266
North Dakota	459 391	460 581	491 293	511 095	522 377	532 398	561 849	578 704
Ohio	7 994 379	8 407 428	9 124 731	9 173 393	9 612 678	10 030 956	10 396 689	11 000 000
Oklahoma	1 905 332	2 107 513	2 268 958	2 442 320	2 680 113	2 763 721	2 951 191	3 039 727
Oregon	2 297 944	2 453 934	2 626 803	2 849 009	2 852 723	2 948 539	3 028 000	3 247 000
Pennsylvania	9 496 788	10 087 322	10 371 796	10 944 392	11 236 417	11 587 027	12 300 000	13 020 000
Rhode Island	801 908	823 655	865 898	934 815	990 094	1 017 554	1 071 151	1 103 286
South Carolina	2 322 618	2 494 254	2 564 949	2 690 009	2 790 878	2 920 230	2 920 230	3 173 705
South Dakota	447 074	481 304	518 156	553 005	584 894	612 825	624 379	665 026
Tennessee	2 790 808	2 903 209	2 859 755	3 139 223	3 305 579	3 540 682	4 264 551	4 570 746
Texas	12 763 954	13 695 327	14 709 628	15 121 655	16 193 722	17 572 269	19 658 698	20 944 470
Utah	1 130 135	1 235 916	1 296 723	1 376 319	1 511 205	1 618 047	1 739 255	1 833 122
Vermont	546 901	599 018	606 410	616 212	643 828	665 559	706 280	753 516
Virginia	4 621 071	4 958 213	4 993 480	5 228 326	5 441 384	5 750 318	6 062 752	6 672 808
Washington	3 550 819	3 906 471	4 259 048	4 679 698	4 892 690	5 138 931	5 613 481	5 790 558
West Virginia	1 316 637	1 473 640	1 503 980	1 626 005	1 663 868	1 758 557	1 763 439	1 825 159
Wisconsin	3 929 920	4 292 434	4 597 004	4 954 900	5 170 343	5 422 264	5 435 968	5 732 554
Wyoming	509 084	521 549	545 870	547 938	558 353	577 144	580 000	595 000

See footnotes at end of table.

Table C-39.   Current Expenditures for Public Elementary and Secondary Education, by State: 1969-70 to 1996-97 — Continued

(In thousands of dollars)

State	1969-70	1979-80	1980-81	1984-85	1985-86	1986-87	1987-88	1988-89
Outlying areas								
American Samoa	(NA)	(NA)	(NA)	$13 348	$14 997	$19 497	$20 186	$22 314
Guam	$16 652	(NA)	(NA)	58 815	78 545	78 278	76 359	94 368
Northern Marianas	(NA)	(NA)	(NA)	9 394	12 556	15 714	19 694	16 118
Puerto Rico	(NA)	(NA)	$713 000	856 743	842 827	872 050	935 392	1 030 387
Virgin Islands	(NA)	(NA)	(NA)	(NA)	76 751	97 585	89 217	111 750

See footnotes at end of table.

Table C-39.   Current Expenditures for Public Elementary and Secondary Education, by State: 1969-70 to 1996-97 — Continued

(In thousands of dollars)

State	1989-90[1]	1990-91	1991-92	1992-93	1993-94[1]	1994-95	Estimated 1995-96[2]	Estimated 1996-97[2]
Outlying areas								
American Samoa	$21 838	$24 946	$26 972	$23 636	$25 161	$28 643	$30 372	$32 377
Guam	101 130	116 406	132 494	161 477	160 797	157 913	173 721	187 947
Northern Marianas	20 476	26 822	32 498	38 784	32 824	38 427	42 499	50 953
Puerto Rico	1 045 407	1 142 863	1 207 235	1 295 452	1 360 762	1 501 485	1 646 313	1 658 302
Virgin Islands	128 065	119 950	121 660	120 510	120 556	122 094	135 291	140 299

SOURCE: U.S. Department of Education, National Center for Education Statistics, Statistics of State School Systems; and Common Core of Data surveys. Published as table 165 in *Digest of Education Statistics* 1997.

1. Data revised from previously published figures.
2. Data estimated by state education agencies.

NOTE: Beginning in 1980-81, expenditures for state administration are excluded. Because of rounding, details may not add to totals.

(NA) Not applicable or not available.

Table C-40. Total Expenditures for Public Elementary and Secondary Education, by Function and State: 1994-95

(In thousands)

State	Total expenditures							
		Current expenditures for elementary and secondary programs						
				Student services				
	Total	Current expenditures for public schools	Instruction	Total	Students[3]	Instructional[4]	General administration	School administration
United States	$278 965 657	$243 844 646	$150 521 920	$82 355 354	$11 679 338	$9 654 714	$5 731 462	$14 149 344
Alabama	3 372 114	3 026 287	1 906 471	887 965	95 915	101 461	67 361	178 661
Alaska	1 208 525	1 020 675	574 167	414 601	46 112	59 776	59 146	62 651
Arizona	4 071 643	3 144 540	1 811 054	1 122 492	136 819	101 247	127 861	172 402
Arkansas	2 094 833	1 873 595	1 144 389	601 518	80 417	81 129	69 890	108 937
California	29 070 435	25 949 033	15 549 692	9 299 207	1 389 412	1 184 061	157 603	1 988 240
Colorado	3 867 788	3 232 976	1 970 908	1 138 810	134 882	105 180	95 407	212 746
Connecticut	4 501 537	4 247 327	2 721 552	1 308 873	205 801	125 781	85 815	230 445
Delaware	776 034	694 473	431 618	234 509	35 208	10 054	8 607	39 851
District of Columbia	706 728	666 938	336 543	301 372	68 249	35 583	24 128	35 772
Florida	13 756 867	11 019 735	6 395 934	4 085 932	493 124	621 024	124 221	751 327
Georgia	7 394 767	6 136 689	3 770 713	1 980 420	243 585	308 258	92 699	390 256
Hawaii	1 185 571	1 028 729	636 952	328 578	56 477	47 903	8 317	61 235
Idaho	1 110 948	951 350	602 232	304 596	47 883	27 869	22 736	57 616
Illinois	12 102 804	10 640 279	6 367 082	3 913 546	598 430	414 320	346 332	567 303
Indiana	6 297 458	5 243 761	3 262 523	1 746 052	220 704	150 548	97 521	286 489
Iowa	2 876 604	2 622 510	1 623 942	869 366	151 650	111 906	93 466	136 484
Kansas	2 651 153	2 406 580	1 387 198	901 603	122 448	96 919	97 200	163 849
Kentucky	3 228 465	2 988 892	1 787 624	1 048 826	114 995	94 131	116 323	192 833
Louisiana	3 811 767	3 475 926	2 071 476	1 092 851	129 617	134 672	79 512	191 691
Maine	1 402 024	1 281 706	859 560	375 712	37 206	35 897	25 281	71 727
Maryland	5 616 288	5 083 380	3 127 996	1 714 032	204 542	205 561	28 724	407 145
Massachusetts	6 255 672	6 062 303	3 994 523	1 867 028	280 004	193 981	154 586	262 665
Michigan	11 864 469	10 440 206	6 228 315	3 905 033	646 546	440 927	216 139	621 034
Minnesota	5 829 727	4 622 930	2 946 240	1 490 265	150 969	244 948	120 037	211 671
Mississippi	2 158 879	1 921 480	1 197 868	573 685	67 952	75 608	57 872	104 056
Missouri	4 970 915	4 275 217	2 597 027	1 491 719	177 983	172 595	135 644	250 535
Montana	917 118	844 257	525 617	283 019	38 085	28 041	28 878	44 106
Nebraska	1 858 791	1 594 928	997 580	464 411	61 438	52 704	59 617	80 733
Nevada	1 382 856	1 186 132	706 132	439 092	44 003	34 017	19 791	85 859
New Hampshire	1 165 598	1 053 966	679 046	337 455	57 185	29 372	37 333	59 972
New Jersey	11 785 829	10 776 982	6 467 203	3 962 515	711 455	343 400	333 877	616 362
New Mexico	1 675 685	1 443 789	837 029	527 597	109 502	62 194	38 770	73 534
New York	26 273 275	22 989 629	15 636 396	6 716 673	920 036	515 478	532 921	967 188
North Carolina	6 206 915	5 440 426	3 387 680	1 700 284	275 299	203 004	109 618	360 519
North Dakota	585 046	532 398	328 461	158 320	15 055	11 342	26 664	24 667
Ohio	11 711 711	10 030 956	5 960 083	3 696 226	494 237	491 446	256 871	600 742
Oklahoma	3 064 964	2 763 721	1 662 373	932 702	146 932	80 318	111 885	153 770
Oregon	3 327 032	2 948 539	1 776 148	1 071 438	144 181	140 178	64 919	186 509
Pennsylvania	13 135 222	11 587 027	7 460 973	3 674 151	520 141	360 427	323 749	531 342
Rhode Island	1 059 316	1 017 554	669 274	319 313	63 298	35 542	23 123	51 408
South Carolina	3 353 682	2 920 230	1 727 214	1 007 017	188 416	164 710	50 323	185 744
South Dakota	695 692	612 825	376 116	203 434	25 030	20 853	18 149	34 923
Tennessee	4 027 607	3 540 682	2 285 884	1 063 138	107 096	184 306	77 382	193 446
Texas	20 352 717	17 572 269	10 753 150	5 793 863	818 794	756 747	657 189	983 347
Utah	2 050 021	1 618 047	1 089 195	433 062	46 035	59 045	16 309	91 455
Vermont	727 870	665 559	434 933	209 344	39 133	20 037	19 726	43 535
Virginia	6 637 550	5 750 318	3 483 576	1 959 196	276 456	310 885	63 440	343 478
Washington	6 172 350	5 138 931	3 075 785	1 824 722	324 236	248 340	137 716	258 070
West Virginia	1 945 379	1 758 557	1 090 056	564 738	56 646	47 696	45 205	103 189
Wisconsin	6 030 769	5 422 264	3 441 286	1 816 370	227 651	255 756	152 683	282 766
Wyoming	638 647	577 144	358 131	198 676	32 069	17 539	12 896	35 055

See footnotes at end of table.

Table C-40.   Total Expenditures for Public Elementary and Secondary Education, by Function and State: 1994-95 — Continued

(In thousands)

State	Total expenditures							
	Current expenditures for elementary and secondary programs					Other current expenditures[1]	Capital outlay[2]	Interest on school debt
	Student services			Food services	Enterprise operations[5]			
	Operation and maintenance	Student transportation	Other support services					
United States	$24 543 091	$9 889 137	$6 708 268	$10 266 321	$701 051	$5 148 505	$24 453 851	$5 518 655
Alabama	257 876	125 387	61 304	231 851	0	55 454	247 086	43 287
Alaska	149 321	35 338	2 258	27 454	4 453	5 636	157 651	24 563
Arizona	355 175	121 234	107 755	169 981	41 012	26 014	725 588	175 501
Arkansas	160 194	71 079	29 872	112 852	14 837	11 060	165 941	44 237
California	2 703 051	728 475	1 148 364	1 096 200	3 934	493 215	2 529 013	99 174
Colorado	288 364	91 328	210 903	112 961	10 297	8 237	458 354	168 220
Connecticut	390 086	180 164	90 782	124 397	92 505	66 132	86 860	101 217
Delaware	66 400	40 603	33 785	28 347	0	20 661	52 594	8 306
District of Columbia	100 787	14 673	22 179	26 953	2 071	9 183	27 400	3 206
Florida	1 284 882	461 045	350 308	537 869	0	398 246	2 077 463	261 424
Georgia	541 410	236 703	167 517	372 965	3 583	245 749	899 069	113 260
Hawaii	109 945	20 932	23 769	63 199	0	33 858	94 706	28 277
Idaho	88 963	44 129	15 399	44 522	0	1 699	134 626	23 273
Illinois	1 176 403	488 953	321 805	359 650	0	387 113	835 313	240 099
Indiana	571 228	296 455	123 106	235 186	0	40 278	644 345	369 075
Iowa	230 119	83 499	62 242	118 903	10 299	15 714	209 806	28 574
Kansas	267 158	99 645	54 384	117 778	0	3 238	186 381	54 954
Kentucky	310 055	178 019	42 470	152 442	0	7 540	167 857	64 176
Louisiana	301 605	198 378	57 375	262 485	49 114	22 939	219 307	93 594
Maine	124 030	59 747	21 824	46 432	3	15 461	69 977	34 880
Maryland	508 935	258 942	100 184	161 657	79 695	20 811	458 718	53 379
Massachusetts	607 195	260 916	107 680	200 752	0	22 046	56 327	114 995
Michigan	1 106 729	443 303	430 355	306 858	0	396 602	779 103	248 558
Minnesota	374 231	246 818	141 593	186 425	0	206 489	832 894	167 414
Mississippi	161 563	79 374	27 260	149 321	606	12 975	189 219	35 206
Missouri	414 091	252 573	88 297	186 472	0	72 886	527 098	95 714
Montana	88 928	36 971	18 010	35 335	286	3 446	58 245	11 170
Nebraska	137 977	45 967	25 975	61 069	71 868	1 895	234 277	27 691
Nevada	124 105	52 440	78 878	40 907	0	7 831	126 517	62 377
New Hampshire	95 545	47 868	10 180	37 465	0	3 853	80 403	27 376
New Jersey	1 187 881	542 987	226 552	305 128	42 136	155 678	713 452	139 717
New Mexico	151 975	72 478	19 144	69 589	9 575	9 795	199 753	22 348
New York	2 112 752	1 135 476	532 822	636 560	0	891 267	1 911 244	481 135
North Carolina	452 060	202 679	97 104	352 461	0	34 895	602 044	129 550
North Dakota	47 023	24 086	9 483	26 159	19 459	4 271	41 158	7 218
Ohio	976 449	267 937	608 545	372 258	2 390	693 248	709 604	277 903
Oklahoma	281 658	89 730	68 410	146 101	22 545	10 678	271 306	19 259
Oregon	283 418	117 678	134 554	98 931	2 023	9 784	304 585	64 124
Pennsylvania	1 191 240	464 772	282 480	442 456	9 448	284 200	994 217	269 779
Rhode Island	86 956	47 007	11 979	28 967	0	6 645	17 978	17 140
South Carolina	265 137	91 002	61 685	175 774	10 225	61 754	293 549	78 150
South Dakota	59 110	24 625	20 743	31 867	1 408	1 194	69 492	12 181
Tennessee	326 088	128 713	46 107	191 660	0	16 785	395 526	74 614
Texas	1 956 723	485 709	135 354	993 076	32 180	87 311	2 148 179	544 958
Utah	147 363	45 359	27 497	91 662	4 128	48 035	337 844	46 095
Vermont	53 494	22 184	11 236	19 129	2 154	3 502	49 269	9 540
Virginia	604 534	253 327	107 077	221 934	85 611	110 016	631 622	145 594
Washington	530 680	206 454	119 226	165 327	73 097	24 984	785 663	222 772
West Virginia	174 973	113 597	23 432	103 652	111	28 917	141 023	16 882
Wisconsin	493 584	229 896	174 034	164 608	0	47 641	455 293	105 571
Wyoming	63 640	22 485	14 992	20 336	0	1 643	48 913	10 947

See footnotes at end of table.

Table C-40.   Total Expenditures for Public Elementary and Secondary Education, by Function and State: 1994-95 — Continued

(In thousands)

State	Total expenditures							
	Total	Current expenditures for elementary and secondary programs						
		Current expenditures for public schools	Instruction	Student services				
				Total	Students[3]	Instructional[4]	General administration	School administration
Outlying areas								
American Samoa	$34 511	$28 643	$11 796	$11 453	$3 314	$2 397	$471	$1 568
Guam	158 302	157 913	79 336	68 478	19 120	4 585	2 207	9 681
Northern Marianas	41 546	38 427	35 613	0	0	0	0	0
Puerto Rico	1 551 369	1 501 485	1 093 038	219 007	34 985	0	94 633	15 904
Virgin Islands	137 020	122 094	69 349	45 951	6 171	7 677	9 289	6 801

See footnotes at end of table.

Table C-40.   Total Expenditures for Public Elementary and Secondary Education, by Function and State: 1994-95 — Continued

(In thousands)

State	Total expenditures							
	Current expenditures for elementary and secondary programs					Other current expenditures[1]	Capital outlay[2]	Interest on school debt
	Student services			Food services	Enterprise operations[5]			
	Operation and maintenance	Student transportation	Other support services					
Outlying areas								
American Samoa	$1 614	$834	$1 254	$5 394	$0	$2 901	$2 967	$0
Guam	16 199	10 608	6 078	10 099	0	169	219	0
Northern Marianas	0	0	0	2 814	0	261	2 858	0
Puerto Rico	38 081	34 259	1 144	189 440	0	20 351	28 709	824
Virgin Islands	7 020	3 214	5 780	6 731	64	1 485	13 441	0

SOURCE: U.S. Department of Education, National Center for Education Statistics, Common Core of Data survey. Published as table 166 in *Digest of Education Statistics* 1997.

1. Includes expenditures for adult education, community colleges, private school programs funded by local and state education agencies, and community services.
2. Includes expenditures for property and for building and alterations completed by school district staff or contractors..
3. Includes expenditures for health, attendance, and speech pathology services.
4. Includes expenditures for curriculum development, staff training, libraries, and media and computer centers.
5. Includes expenditures for operations funded by sales of products or services (e.g., school bookstore or computer time).

NOTE: Excludes expenditures for state education agencies. Because of rounding, details may not add to totals.

Table C-41. Current Expenditure per Pupil in Average Daily Attendance in Public Elementary and Secondary Schools, by State: 1959-60 to 1994-95

State	Unadjusted dollars													
	1959-60	1969-70	1979-80	1980-81	1985-86	1986-87	1987-88	1988-89	1989-90	1990-91	1991-92	1992-93	1993-94	1994-95
United States	$375	$816	$2 272	$2 502	$3 756	$3 970	$4 240	$4 645	$4 980	$5 258	$5 421	$5 584	$5 767	$5 988
Alabama	241	544	1 612	1 985	2 565	2 573	2 718	3 197	3 327	3 627	3 616	3 761	4 037	4 405
Alaska	546	1 123	4 728	5 688	8 304	8 010	7 971	7 716	8 431	8 330	8 450	8 735	8 882	8 963
Arizona	404	720	1 971	2 258	3 336	3 544	3 744	3 902	4 053	4 309	4 381	4 510	4 611	4 778
Arkansas	225	568	1 574	1 701	2 658	2 733	2 989	3 273	3 485	3 700	4 031	4 124	4 280	4 459
California	[2] 424	867	2 268	2 475	3 543	3 728	3 840	4 135	4 391	4 491	4 746	4 780	4 921	4 992
Colorado	396	738	2 421	2 693	3 975	4 147	4 220	4 521	4 720	5 064	5 172	5 139	5 097	5 443
Connecticut	436	951	2 420	2 876	4 743	5 435	6 230	6 857	7 837	7 853	8 012	7 973	8 473	8 817
Delaware	456	900	2 861	3 018	4 610	4 825	5 017	5 422	5 799	5 974	6 093	6 274	6 621	7 030
District of Columbia	431	1 018	3 259	3 441	5 337	5 742	6 132	7 850	8 955	9 377	9 549	9 419	10 180	9 335
Florida	318	732	1 889	2 401	3 529	3 794	4 092	4 563	4 997	5 276	5 243	5 314	5 516	5 718
Georgia	253	588	1 625	1 708	2 966	3 181	3 434	3 852	4 275	4 466	4 419	4 686	4 915	5 193
Hawaii	325	841	2 322	2 604	3 807	3 787	3 919	4 121	4 448	5 166	5 420	5 704	5 879	6 078
Idaho	290	603	1 659	1 856	2 484	2 585	2 667	2 833	3 078	3 386	3 556	3 690	3 844	4 210
Illinois	438	909	2 587	2 704	3 781	4 106	4 369	4 906	5 118	5 520	5 670	5 898	5 893	6 136
Indiana	369	728	1 882	2 010	3 275	3 556	3 794	4 284	4 606	4 930	5 074	5 344	5 630	5 826
Iowa	368	844	2 326	2 668	3 619	3 770	4 124	4 285	4 453	4 679	5 096	5 257	5 288	5 483
Kansas	348	771	2 173	2 559	3 829	3 933	4 076	4 443	4 752	4 874	5 007	5 442	5 659	5 817
Kentucky	233	545	1 701	1 784	2 486	2 733	3 011	3 347	3 745	4 354	4 719	4 872	5 107	5 217
Louisiana	372	648	1 792	2 469	3 187	3 069	3 138	3 317	3 903	4 196	4 352	4 428	4 519	4 761
Maine	283	692	1 824	1 934	3 472	3 850	4 258	4 744	5 373	5 458	5 652	6 073	6 069	6 428
Maryland	393	918	2 598	2 914	4 447	4 777	5 201	5 758	6 275	6 654	6 679	6 813	6 958	7 245
Massachusetts	409	859	2 819	2 940	4 562	5 145	5 471	5 972	6 237	6 366	6 408	6 627	6 959	7 287
Michigan	415	904	2 640	3 037	4 176	4 353	4 692	5 150	5 546	5 883	6 268	6 494	6 658	6 994
Minnesota	425	904	2 387	2 673	3 941	4 180	4 386	4 755	4 971	5 239	5 409	5 554	5 720	6 000
Mississippi	206	501	1 664	1 605	2 362	2 350	2 548	2 861	3 094	3 187	3 245	3 382	3 660	4 080
Missouri	344	709	1 936	2 172	3 189	3 472	3 786	4 263	4 507	4 754	4 830	4 885	5 114	5 383
Montana	411	782	2 476	2 683	4 091	4 194	4 246	4 293	4 736	5 204	5 319	5 425	5 598	5 692
Nebraska	337	736	2 150	2 384	3 634	3 756	3 943	4 360	4 842	5 038	5 263	5 336	5 651	5 935
Nevada	430	769	2 088	2 078	3 440	3 440	3 623	3 871	4 117	4 653	4 926	5 066	5 052	5 160
New Hampshire	347	723	1 916	2 265	3 542	3 933	4 457	4 807	5 304	5 685	5 790	5 644	5 723	5 859
New Jersey	388	1 016	3 191	3 254	5 570	5 953	6 564	7 549	8 139	8 756	9 317	9 415	9 677	9 774
New Mexico	363	707	2 034	2 329	3 195	3 558	3 691	3 473	3 515	3 895	3 765	4 071	4 261	4 586
New York	562	1 327	3 462	3 741	6 011	6 497	7 151	7 663	8 062	8 565	8 527	8 902	9 175	9 623
North Carolina	237	612	1 754	2 001	2 948	3 129	3 368	3 874	4 290	4 548	4 554	4 763	4 894	5 077
North Dakota	367	690	1 920	2 275	3 483	3 437	3 519	3 952	4 189	4 199	4 441	4 597	4 674	4 775
Ohio	365	730	2 075	2 303	3 527	3 673	3 998	4 686	5 045	5 245	5 694	5 754	5 971	6 162
Oklahoma	311	604	1 926	2 199	3 146	3 099	3 093	3 379	3 508	3 843	4 076	4 355	4 734	4 845
Oregon	448	925	2 692	3 100	4 141	4 337	4 789	5 182	5 474	5 683	5 913	6 296	6 263	6 436
Pennsylvania	409	882	2 535	2 824	4 325	4 616	4 989	5 597	6 228	6 541	6 613	6 890	6 983	7 109
Rhode Island	413	891	2 601	2 927	4 667	4 985	5 329	6 064	6 368	6 343	6 546	6 938	7 333	7 469
South Carolina	220	613	1 752	1 734	3 058	3 214	3 408	3 736	4 082	4 352	4 436	4 624	4 761	4 797
South Dakota	347	690	1 908	1 991	3 051	3 097	3 249	3 585	3 731	3 965	4 173	4 357	4 586	4 775
Tennessee	238	566	1 635	1 794	2 612	2 827	3 068	3 491	3 664	3 782	3 692	3 993	4 149	4 388
Texas	332	624	1 916	2 006	3 298	3 409	3 608	3 877	4 150	4 438	4 632	4 670	4 898	5 222
Utah	322	626	1 657	1 819	2 390	2 415	2 454	2 588	2 764	2 960	3 040	3 180	3 439	3 656
Vermont	344	807	1 997	2 475	4 031	4 399	5 207	5 481	6 227	6 738	6 671	6 411	6 600	6 750
Virginia	274	708	1 970	2 179	3 520	3 780	4 149	4 539	4 672	4 902	4 878	4 980	5 109	5 327
Washington	420	915	2 568	2 542	3 881	3 964	4 164	4 359	4 702	5 000	5 271	5 614	5 751	5 906
West Virginia	258	670	1 920	2 146	3 528	3 784	3 858	3 883	4 360	4 911	5 078	5 527	5 713	6 107
Wisconsin	413	883	2 477	2 738	4 168	4 523	4 747	5 266	5 524	5 871	6 139	6 475	6 717	6 930
Wyoming	450	856	2 527	2 967	5 114	5 201	5 051	5 375	5 577	5 638	5 812	5 822	5 899	6 160

See footnotes at end of table.

Table C-41. Current Expenditure per Pupil in Average Daily Attendance in Public Elementary and Secondary Schools, by State: 1959-60 to 1994-95 — Continued

State	Constant 1994-95 dollars[1]													
	1959-60	1969-70	1979-80	1980-81	1985-86	1986-87	1987-88	1988-89	1989-90	1990-91	1991-92	1992-93	1993-94	1994-95
United States	$1 920	$3 249	$4 401	$4 344	$5 191	$5 369	$5 505	$5 764	$5 899	$5 905	$5 900	$5 892	$5 933	$5 988
Alabama	1 234	2 166	3 123	3 446	3 545	3 479	3 529	3 967	3 941	4 073	3 935	3 969	4 152	4 405
Alaska	2 797	4 470	9 159	9 877	11 478	10 831	10 349	9 576	9 987	9 355	9 196	9 218	9 137	8 963
Arizona	2 066	2 867	3 818	3 921	4 612	4 793	4 861	4 843	4 801	4 839	4 767	4 759	4 743	4 778
Arkansas	1 153	2 260	3 050	2 953	3 674	3 696	3 881	4 062	4 128	4 156	4 386	4 352	4 403	4 459
California	[2] 2 170	3 453	4 393	4 297	4 897	5 040	4 986	5 132	5 201	5 044	5 165	5 045	5 062	4 992
Colorado	2 028	2 938	4 690	4 675	5 494	5 608	5 479	5 610	5 591	5 687	5 628	5 424	5 243	5 443
Connecticut	2 232	3 788	4 689	4 993	6 556	7 349	8 090	8 511	9 283	8 821	8 720	8 414	8 715	8 817
Delaware	2 333	3 584	5 543	5 240	6 372	6 524	6 515	6 730	6 869	6 710	6 630	6 621	6 811	7 030
District of Columbia	2 207	4 055	6 314	5 975	7 377	7 765	7 962	9 743	10 607	10 532	10 392	9 940	10 472	9 335
Florida	1 626	2 916	3 660	4 170	4 878	5 130	5 313	5 663	5 920	5 926	5 706	5 608	5 674	5 718
Georgia	1 297	2 341	3 149	2 966	4 099	4 302	4 459	4 781	5 064	5 016	4 809	4 945	5 056	5 193
Hawaii	1 661	3 347	4 498	4 521	5 261	5 121	5 088	5 114	5 269	5 802	5 898	6 020	6 048	6 078
Idaho	1 483	2 402	3 215	3 223	3 433	3 496	3 463	3 516	3 646	3 803	3 870	3 894	3 954	4 210
Illinois	2 244	3 621	5 011	4 695	5 227	5 552	5 672	6 088	6 062	6 200	6 170	6 225	6 062	6 136
Indiana	1 887	2 899	3 647	3 490	4 527	4 808	4 926	5 317	5 456	5 538	5 521	5 640	5 791	5 826
Iowa	1 882	3 361	4 507	4 632	5 003	5 098	5 354	5 318	5 275	5 255	5 546	5 548	5 440	5 483
Kansas	1 780	3 070	4 210	4 444	5 293	5 318	5 293	5 514	5 628	5 474	5 449	5 743	5 822	5 817
Kentucky	1 193	2 171	3 296	3 097	3 436	3 696	3 909	4 154	4 436	4 890	5 135	5 142	5 254	5 217
Louisiana	1 904	2 580	3 472	4 288	4 405	4 150	4 075	4 117	4 624	4 713	4 737	4 673	4 649	4 761
Maine	1 447	2 757	3 533	3 358	4 799	5 205	5 529	5 887	6 364	6 130	6 151	6 409	6 243	6 428
Maryland	2 010	3 656	5 033	5 059	6 146	6 460	6 753	7 146	7 434	7 473	7 268	7 190	7 157	7 245
Massachusetts	2 093	3 421	5 462	5 104	6 306	6 957	7 104	7 412	7 388	7 150	6 974	6 994	7 159	7 287
Michigan	2 125	3 599	5 115	5 273	5 772	5 887	6 092	6 391	6 570	6 607	6 821	6 854	6 849	6 994
Minnesota	2 177	3 598	4 624	4 642	5 447	5 652	5 695	5 901	5 888	5 884	5 886	5 861	5 883	6 000
Mississippi	1 054	1 994	3 223	2 788	3 264	3 178	3 308	3 550	3 665	3 579	3 532	3 569	3 765	4 080
Missouri	1 761	2 821	3 751	3 771	4 408	4 694	4 915	5 290	5 339	5 339	5 256	5 155	5 260	5 383
Montana	2 103	3 113	4 798	4 659	5 654	5 672	5 513	5 327	5 611	5 845	5 789	5 726	5 758	5 692
Nebraska	1 725	2 932	4 165	4 140	5 023	5 078	5 120	5 411	5 735	5 658	5 728	5 632	5 813	5 935
Nevada	2 203	3 064	4 046	3 608	4 755	4 651	4 704	4 804	4 877	5 226	5 361	5 346	5 197	5 160
New Hampshire	1 777	2 879	3 712	3 933	4 895	5 319	5 787	5 966	6 283	6 385	6 301	5 957	5 887	5 859
New Jersey	1 984	4 046	6 183	5 650	7 699	8 050	8 523	9 369	9 641	9 834	10 140	9 936	9 955	9 774
New Mexico	1 856	2 815	3 940	4 045	4 416	4 811	4 793	4 310	4 163	4 374	4 097	4 296	4 383	4 586
New York	2 875	5 283	6 708	6 496	8 308	8 786	9 285	9 511	9 549	9 619	9 280	9 395	9 438	9 623
North Carolina	1 214	2 438	3 399	3 474	4 075	4 230	4 373	4 808	5 082	5 108	4 956	5 026	5 035	5 077
North Dakota	1 877	2 746	3 720	3 949	4 814	4 648	4 570	4 904	4 962	4 716	4 833	4 852	4 808	4 775
Ohio	1 869	2 907	4 019	3 999	4 875	4 967	5 191	5 816	5 976	5 891	6 197	6 073	6 142	6 162
Oklahoma	1 594	2 407	3 732	3 817	4 349	4 190	4 016	4 194	4 155	4 316	4 436	4 596	4 870	4 845
Oregon	2 295	3 682	5 215	5 382	5 723	5 864	6 218	6 432	6 485	6 383	6 435	6 644	6 442	6 436
Pennsylvania	2 096	3 511	4 911	4 903	5 978	6 242	6 478	6 947	7 377	7 347	7 197	7 271	7 183	7 109
Rhode Island	2 116	3 548	5 039	5 082	6 451	6 741	6 919	7 526	7 543	7 124	7 124	7 322	7 543	7 469
South Carolina	1 126	2 439	3 394	3 011	4 227	4 346	4 425	4 636	4 835	4 888	4 827	4 880	4 898	4 797
South Dakota	1 775	2 747	3 696	3 457	4 217	4 188	4 218	4 449	4 420	4 453	4 541	4 598	4 717	4 775
Tennessee	1 219	2 254	3 169	3 114	3 610	3 823	3 984	4 333	4 340	4 247	4 018	4 214	4 268	4 388
Texas	1 701	2 485	3 712	3 483	4 559	4 610	4 684	4 812	4 916	4 985	5 041	4 928	5 038	5 222
Utah	1 651	2 493	3 210	3 158	3 304	3 265	3 186	3 212	3 274	3 324	3 309	3 356	3 537	3 656
Vermont	1 761	3 214	3 869	4 297	5 572	5 949	6 761	6 802	7 376	7 568	7 259	6 765	6 789	6 750
Virginia	1 404	2 818	3 817	3 783	4 866	5 112	5 387	5 634	5 534	5 505	5 309	5 255	5 255	5 327
Washington	2 152	3 645	4 976	4 414	5 364	5 360	5 406	5 410	5 570	5 615	5 736	5 924	5 915	5 906
West Virginia	1 323	2 667	3 721	3 726	4 877	5 117	5 009	4 819	5 165	5 165	5 516	5 526	5 833	5 877	6 107
Wisconsin	2 114	3 515	4 799	4 754	5 761	6 115	6 164	6 536	6 543	6 594	6 681	6 834	6 910	6 930
Wyoming	2 305	3 408	4 895	5 152	7 068	7 033	6 559	6 671	6 607	6 332	6 325	6 144	6 068	6 160

See footnotes at end of table.

Table C-41. Current Expenditure per Pupil in Average Daily Attendance in Public Elementary and Secondary Schools, by State: 1959-60 to 1994-95 — Continued

State	Unadjusted dollars													
	1959-60	1969-70	1979-80	1980-81	1985-86	1986-87	1987-88	1988-89	1989-90	1990-91	1991-92	1992-93	1993-94	1994-95
Outlying areas														
American Samoa ...	(NA)	(NA)	(NA)	(NA)	$1 387	$1 846	$1 908	$1 988	$1 908	$2 033	$2 085	$1 670	$1 785	$2 046
Guam	$236	$820	(NA)	(NA)	3 383	3 344	3 295	4 067	4 234	4 596	5 231	5 309	5 071	4 969
Northern Marianas	(NA)	(NA)	(NA)	(NA)	2 552	3 099	3 366	2 414	3 007	4 425	5 247	5 288	4 510	5 227
Puerto Rico	106	(NA)	(NA)	(NA)	1 325	1 384	1 504	1 692	1 750	1 913	2 162	2 364	2 312	2 742
Virgin Islands	271	(NA)	(NA)	(NA)	3 223	4 277	4 036	5 281	6 767	6 002	5 935	5 843	5 915	6 003

See footnotes at end of table.

Table C-41.   Current Expenditure per Pupil in Average Daily Attendance in Public Elementary and Secondary Schools, by State: 1959-60 to 1994-95 — Continued

State	Constant 1994-95 dollars[1]													
	1959-60	1969-70	1979-80	1980-81	1985-86	1986-87	1987-88	1988-89	1989-90	1990-91	1991-92	1992-93	1993-94	1994-95
Outlying areas														
American Samoa ...	(NA)	(NA)	(NA)	(NA)	$1 916	$2 497	$2 478	$2 468	$2 260	$2 283	$2 269	$1 763	$1 836	$2 046
Guam	$1 210	$3 264	(NA)	(NA)	4 676	4 522	4 279	5 048	5 016	5 161	5 692	5 602	5 216	4 969
Northern Marianas	(NA)	(NA)	(NA)	(NA)	3 527	4 190	4 370	(NA)	3 562	4 969	5 710	5 581	4 639	5 227
Puerto Rico	544	(NA)	(NA)	(NA)	1 831	1 872	1 953	2 100	2 073	2 149	2 352	2 494	2 379	2 742
Virgin Islands	1 385	(NA)	(NA)	(NA)	4 455	5 784	5 241	6 555	8 016	6 741	6 459	6 166	6 085	6 003

SOURCE: U.S. Department of Education, National Center for Education Statistics, Statistics of State School Systems; and Common Core of Data surveys. Published as table 168 in *Digest of Education Statistics* 1997.

1. Based on the Consumer Price Index, prepared by the Bureau of Labor Statistics, U.S. Department of Labor, adjusted to a school-year basis. These data do not reflect differences in inflation rates from state to state.
2. Estimated by the National Center for Education Statistics.

NOTE: Beginning in 1980-81, state administration expenditures are excluded. Beginning in 1988-89, extensive changes were made in the data collection procedures. Some data have been revised from previously published figures.

(NA) Not applicable or not available.

Table C-42. Total First-Time Freshmen Enrolled in Institutions of Higher Education, by Attendance Status, Sex, Control of Institution, and State: Fall 1992 to Fall 1995

State	Fall 1992	Fall 1993	Fall 1994	Fall 1995[1] Total	Full-time Total	Full-time Men	Full-time Women	Part-time Total	Part-time Men	Part-time Women	Public institutions	Private institutions
United States	2 184 113	2 160 710	2 133 205	2 168 831	1 646 812	767 185	879 627	522 019	233 867	288 152	1 686 431	482 400
Alabama	42 604	41 812	41 542	37 166	31 562	14 198	17 364	5 604	2 406	3 198	32 879	4 287
Alaska	2 584	2 700	1 835	1 880	1 564	740	824	316	116	200	1 770	110
Arizona	31 358	36 671	32 753	37 049	22 769	11 167	11 602	14 280	5 992	8 288	33 317	3 732
Arkansas	18 680	17 406	16 378	16 924	14 838	6 515	8 323	2 086	848	1 238	14 268	2 656
California	252 762	250 810	258 687	272 715	149 633	70 140	79 493	123 082	58 678	64 404	242 622	30 093
Colorado	33 359	31 353	31 001	32 775	24 070	11 989	12 081	8 705	4 049	4 656	28 597	4 178
Connecticut	22 490	21 489	21 259	21 268	16 611	7 718	8 893	4 657	1 749	2 908	12 846	8 422
Delaware	7 227	7 361	6 921	8 092	5 915	2 502	3 413	2 177	849	1 328	6 354	1 738
District of Columbia	8 427	8 954	9 706	9 077	7 921	3 150	4 771	1 156	423	733	666	8 411
Florida	72 311	71 351	71 318	72 722	53 386	24 941	28 445	19 336	8 282	11 054	57 040	15 682
Georgia	56 389	59 784	58 991	59 829	47 798	20 923	26 875	12 031	4 608	7 423	47 808	12 021
Hawaii	9 461	9 752	10 309	9 524	6 493	2 949	3 544	3 031	1 394	1 637	7 659	1 865
Idaho	10 960	11 069	10 646	10 103	8 663	4 060	4 603	1 440	606	834	7 061	3 042
Illinois	116 967	112 542	111 309	109 483	73 639	35 197	38 442	35 844	16 194	19 650	86 201	23 282
Indiana	50 147	49 111	48 059	51 071	42 687	20 316	22 371	8 384	3 542	4 842	36 654	14 417
Iowa	36 730	35 922	35 229	35 097	29 377	14 200	15 177	5 720	2 220	3 500	26 574	8 523
Kansas	25 453	25 304	24 641	29 083	19 544	9 823	9 721	9 539	3 989	5 550	26 466	2 617
Kentucky	29 738	31 334	28 983	29 024	25 575	11 205	14 370	3 449	1 483	1 966	23 022	6 002
Louisiana	31 810	30 160	30 951	31 412	28 400	12 358	16 042	3 012	1 264	1 748	26 809	4 603
Maine	8 765	8 751	8 149	8 273	7 371	3 540	3 831	902	289	613	5 271	3 002
Maryland	32 133	31 675	31 647	32 993	23 809	10 749	13 060	9 184	3 716	5 468	28 362	4 631
Massachusetts	64 751	68 316	65 768	64 892	55 057	25 029	30 028	9 835	3 646	6 189	30 325	34 567
Michigan	88 744	87 025	83 697	76 360	55 364	25 375	29 989	20 996	9 095	11 901	61 438	14 922
Minnesota	50 869	43 794	43 783	46 794	35 920	17 413	18 507	10 874	4 613	6 261	37 165	9 629
Mississippi	25 960	26 223	25 862	26 602	23 001	10 488	12 513	3 601	1 294	2 307	24 857	1 745
Missouri	39 886	40 868	38 544	39 610	32 820	14 827	17 993	6 790	2 982	3 808	26 585	13 025
Montana	6 413	6 950	6 819	7 473	6 599	3 264	3 335	874	361	513	6 516	957
Nebraska	17 362	15 943	16 616	16 147	13 769	6 677	7 092	2 378	1 016	1 362	12 991	3 156
Nevada	4 620	5 367	6 939	6 799	3 563	1 617	1 946	3 236	1 427	1 809	6 673	126
New Hampshire	11 316	11 659	11 373	11 789	9 889	4 418	5 471	1 900	746	1 154	6 219	5 570
New Jersey	44 932	44 971	43 063	45 308	37 835	17 771	20 064	7 473	3 190	4 283	36 209	9 099
New Mexico	11 818	13 358	13 864	12 104	7 431	3 456	3 975	4 673	2 028	2 645	11 474	630
New York	158 380	157 350	155 922	151 682	135 432	62 009	73 423	16 250	6 980	9 270	92 134	59 548
North Carolina	55 075	52 857	51 346	51 706	45 432	20 218	25 214	6 274	2 879	3 395	38 634	13 072
North Dakota	8 813	8 322	8 122	8 386	7 556	4 042	3 514	830	359	471	7 468	918
Ohio	92 902	90 190	88 585	89 510	72 960	33 783	39 177	16 550	7 210	9 340	66 140	23 370
Oklahoma	30 296	30 252	29 627	28 474	19 948	9 498	10 450	8 526	3 611	4 915	25 458	3 016
Oregon	22 930	23 293	23 321	20 562	15 977	7 615	8 362	4 585	2 297	2 288	17 032	3 530
Pennsylvania	113 070	100 372	98 488	101 053	86 253	40 778	45 475	14 800	5 998	8 802	60 478	40 575
Rhode Island	12 813	13 106	12 645	12 745	11 258	5 465	5 793	1 487	601	886	5 571	7 174
South Carolina	30 185	30 070	28 577	29 036	24 775	10 951	13 824	4 261	1 838	2 423	22 947	6 089
South Dakota	6 513	6 691	6 607	6 378	5 759	2 674	3 085	619	227	392	5 076	1 302
Tennessee	35 721	35 341	34 180	36 628	32 542	14 824	17 718	4 086	1 635	2 451	25 592	11 036
Texas	127 584	129 921	127 586	131 905	95 676	45 706	49 970	36 229	16 528	19 701	112 347	19 558
Utah	23 536	24 465	24 383	24 041	19 223	8 882	10 341	4 818	2 532	2 286	18 683	5 358
Vermont	6 274	6 347	6 132	6 506	5 658	2 706	2 952	848	266	582	3 784	2 722
Virginia	45 011	43 820	45 272	46 533	40 174	18 098	22 076	6 359	2 795	3 564	35 162	11 371
Washington	68 649	70 476	68 613	73 255	44 022	20 968	23 054	29 233	13 866	15 367	67 822	5 433
West Virginia	17 029	15 727	15 928	15 880	13 900	6 597	7 303	1 980	720	1 260	13 087	2 793
Wisconsin	47 271	47 351	46 479	49 201	39 420	18 328	21 092	9 781	4 102	5 679	40 597	8 604
Wyoming	4 686	4 858	4 814	4 626	3 914	1 900	2 014	712	253	459	4 435	191

See footnotes at end of table.

Table C-42. Total First-Time Freshmen Enrolled in Institutions of Higher Education, by Attendance Status, Sex, Control of Institution, and State: Fall 1992 to Fall 1995 — Continued

State	Fall 1992	Fall 1993	Fall 1994	Fall 1995[1]								Public institutions	Private institutions
				Total	Full-time			Part-time					
					Total	Men	Women	Total	Men	Women			
U.S. Service Schools	10 349	10 116	9 936	11 286	4 060	3 428	632	7 226	6 075	1 151	11 286	(NA)
Outlying areas	35 409	41 759	30 573	38 692	35 379	14 296	21 083	3 313	1 411	1 902	17 390	21 302
American Samoa	989	967	948	943	702	360	342	241	134	107	943	(NA)
Federated States of Micronesia	409	235	410	354	314	163	151	40	22	18	354	(NA)
Guam	709	1 490	956	478	303	104	199	175	77	98	478	(NA)
Marshall Islands	139	166	22	(NA)	(NA)	(NA)	(NA)	(NA)	(NA)	(NA)	(NA)	(NA)
Northern Marianas ...	173	455	440	153	101	40	61	52	24	28	153	(NA)
Palau	24	24	13	14	13	3	10	1		1	14	(NA)
Puerto Rico	32 664	38 057	27 408	36 343	33 593	13 540	20 053	2 750	1 139	1 611	15 041	21 302
Virgin Islands	302	365	376	407	353	86	267	54	15	39	407	(NA)

SOURCE: U.S. Department of Education, National Center for Education Statistics, Integrated Postsecondary Education Data System, 'Fall Enrollment' surveys. Published as table 182 in *Digest of Education Statistics* 1997.

1. Preliminary data.

(NA) Not applicable or not available.

Table C-43. Total Fall Enrollment in Institutions of Higher Education, by State: 1970 to 1995

State	Fall 1970	Fall 1975	Fall 1980	Fall 1985	Fall 1990	Fall 1991	Fall 1992	Fall 1993	Fall 1994	Fall 1995	Percent changes, 1990 to 1995
United States	8 580 887	11 184 859	12 096 895	12 247 055	13 818 637	14 358 953	14 487 359	14 304 803	14 278 790	14 261 781	3.2
Alabama	103 936	164 700	164 306	179 343	218 589	224 331	230 537	233 525	229 511	225 612	3.2
Alaska	9 471	13 998	21 296	27 479	29 833	30 793	30 902	30 638	28 798	29 348	-1.6
Arizona	109 619	173 542	202 716	216 854	264 148	272 971	274 671	272 300	274 932	273 981	3.7
Arkansas	52 039	65 547	77 607	77 958	90 425	94 340	97 578	99 262	96 294	98 180	8.6
California	1 257 245	1 787 932	1 790 993	1 650 439	1 808 740	2 024 274	1 978 003	1 836 349	1 835 791	1 817 042	0.5
Colorado	123 395	149 814	162 916	161 314	227 131	235 108	241 352	239 805	241 295	242 739	6.9
Connecticut	124 700	148 491	159 632	159 348	168 604	165 824	165 874	162 300	159 990	157 695	-6.5
Delaware	25 260	32 389	32 939	31 883	42 004	42 988	42 763	43 528	44 197	44 307	5.5
District of Columbia	77 158	84 190	86 675	78 201	79 551	77 353	81 202	81 565	77 256	77 277	-2.9
Florida	235 525	344 267	411 891	451 392	588 086	611 781	618 285	623 403	634 237	637 303	8.4
Georgia	126 511	173 585	184 159	196 826	251 786	277 023	293 606	302 844	308 587	314 712	25.0
Hawaii	36 562	46 671	47 181	49 937	56 436	57 302	61 162	62 871	64 322	63 198	12.0
Idaho	34 567	39 075	43 018	42 668	51 881	55 397	57 798	58 768	60 393	59 566	14.8
Illinois	452 146	584 089	644 245	678 689	729 246	753 297	748 805	734 089	731 420	717 854	-1.6
Indiana	192 668	213 820	247 253	250 567	284 832	290 301	296 912	294 685	292 276	289 615	1.7
Iowa	108 902	121 678	140 449	152 897	170 515	171 024	172 805	172 797	172 450	173 835	1.9
Kansas	102 485	120 833	136 605	141 359	163 733	167 699	169 419	170 135	170 603	177 643	8.5
Kentucky	98 591	125 253	143 066	141 724	177 852	187 958	188 322	187 332	182 577	178 858	0.6
Louisiana	120 728	153 213	160 058	177 176	186 840	197 438	204 379	201 987	203 567	203 935	9.1
Maine	34 134	40 443	43 264	52 201	57 186	57 178	57 977	56 294	56 724	56 547	-1.1
Maryland	149 607	205 570	225 526	231 649	259 700	267 931	268 399	268 005	266 214	266 310	2.5
Massachusetts	303 809	384 485	418 415	421 175	417 833	419 381	422 976	420 127	416 505	413 794	-1.0
Michigan	392 726	496 405	520 131	507 293	569 803	568 491	560 773	568 210	551 307	548 339	-3.8
Minnesota	160 788	184 756	206 691	221 162	253 789	255 054	272 920	268 118	289 300	280 816	10.6
Mississippi	73 967	99 962	102 364	101 180	122 883	125 350	123 754	122 408	120 884	122 600	0.2
Missouri	183 930	223 115	234 421	241 146	289 899	297 154	296 617	297 062	293 810	291 536	0.6
Montana	30 062	30 843	35 177	35 958	35 876	37 821	39 644	39 557	40 095	42 674	18.9
Nebraska	66 915	74 705	89 488	97 769	112 831	113 648	122 603	115 523	116 000	115 718	2.6
Nevada	13 669	30 187	40 455	43 656	61 728	62 664	63 877	63 947	64 085	67 826	9.9
New Hampshire	29 400	41 030	46 794	52 283	59 510	63 718	63 924	64 043	62 847	64 327	8.1
New Jersey	216 121	297 114	321 610	297 658	324 286	334 641	343 232	343 029	335 480	333 831	2.9
New Mexico	44 461	51 944	58 283	68 295	85 500	93 507	99 276	101 460	101 881	102 405	19.8
New York	806 479	1 005 063	992 237	1 000 098	1 048 286	1 056 487	1 064 822	1 062 924	1 057 841	1 041 566	-0.6
North Carolina	171 925	251 786	287 537	327 288	352 138	371 968	383 453	371 280	369 386	372 030	5.6
North Dakota	31 495	29 743	34 069	37 939	37 878	38 739	40 470	40 316	40 184	40 399	6.7
Ohio	376 267	436 052	489 145	514 745	557 690	569 326	573 183	562 402	549 304	540 275	-3.1
Oklahoma	110 155	146 613	160 295	169 173	173 221	183 536	187 846	183 342	185 174	180 676	4.3
Oregon	122 177	145 281	157 458	137 967	165 741	167 107	167 415	165 834	164 447	167 145	0.8
Pennsylvania	411 044	470 536	507 716	533 198	604 060	620 036	626 904	621 228	611 174	617 759	2.3
Rhode Island	45 898	64 479	66 869	69 927	78 273	79 112	79 165	77 407	74 718	74 100	-5.3
South Carolina	69 518	133 023	132 476	131 902	159 302	164 907	171 443	174 302	173 070	174 125	9.3
South Dakota	30 639	30 260	32 761	32 772	34 208	36 332	37 596	38 166	37 764	36 695	7.3
Tennessee	135 103	181 435	204 581	194 845	226 238	238 042	242 970	244 936	242 966	245 962	8.7
Texas	442 225	624 390	701 391	769 692	901 437	917 443	938 526	942 178	954 495	952 525	5.7
Utah	81 687	87 323	93 987	103 994	121 303	130 419	133 083	138 139	146 196	147 324	21.5
Vermont	22 209	29 095	30 628	31 416	36 398	37 436	37 377	36 415	35 409	35 065	-3.7
Virginia	151 915	244 671	280 504	292 416	353 442	356 325	354 172	348 535	354 149	355 919	0.7
Washington	183 544	227 168	303 603	231 553	263 384	274 760	275 556	279 845	284 662	285 819	8.5
West Virginia	63 153	78 619	81 973	76 659	84 790	88 602	90 252	88 852	87 741	86 034	1.5
Wisconsin	202 058	240 701	269 086	275 069	299 774	308 986	307 902	309 036	303 861	300 223	0.1
Wyoming	15 220	18 078	21 147	24 204	31 326	32 118	31 548	30 702	30 682	30 176	-3.7

See footnotes at end of table.

Table C-43.   Total Fall Enrollment in Institutions of Higher Education, by State: 1970 to 1995 — Continued

State	Fall 1970	Fall 1975	Fall 1980	Fall 1985	Fall 1990	Fall 1991	Fall 1992	Fall 1993	Fall 1994	Fall 1995	Percent changes, 1990 to 1995
U.S. Service Schools	17 079	36 897	49 808	54 719	48 692	53 532	53 329	52 998	51 939	88 451	81.7
Outlying areas	67 237	104 270	137 749	164 890	164 618	168 771	169 759	172 989	170 686	183 657	11.6
American Samoa	(NA)	689	976	758	1 219	1 267	1 295	1 264	1 249	1 232	1.1
Federated States of Micronesia	(NA)	(NA)	(NA)	(NA)	975	837	1 028	1 148	1 374	1 296	32.9
Guam	2 719	3 800	3 217	4 601	4 741	5 016	4 845	5 843	6 449	6 010	26.8
Marshall Islands	(NA)	(NA)	(NA)	(NA)	(NA)	(NA)	374	386	424	418	-9.0
Northern Marianas ...	(NA)	(NA)	(NA)	318	661	847	796	1 261	1 253	959	45.1
Palau	(NA)	(NA)	(NA)	(NA)	491	355	445	436	403	351	-28.5
Puerto Rico	63 073	97 517	131 184	155 917	154 065	157 733	158 120	159 709	156 439	170 337	10.6
Trust Territory of the Pacific	(NA)	185	224	724	(NA)	(NA)	(NA)	(NA)	(NA)	(NA)	-9.0
Virgin Islands	1 445	2 079	2 148	2 572	2 466	2 716	2 856	2 942	3 095	3 054	23.8

SOURCE: U.S. Department of Education, National Center for Education Statistics, Higher Education General Information Survey (HEGIS), 'Fall Enrollment in Colleges and Universities' surveys; and Integrated Postsecondary Education Data System (IPEDS), 'Fall Enrollment' surveys. Published as table 190 in *Digest of Education Statistics* 1997.

1. Preliminary data.
2. Some data revised from previously published figures.

(NA) Not applicable or not available.

Table C-44. Total Fall Enrollment in Public Institutions of Higher Education, by State: 1970 to 1995

State	Fall 1970	Fall 1975	Fall 1980	Fall 1985	Fall 1990	Fall 1991	Fall 1992	Fall 1993	Fall 1994	Fall 1995[1]	Percent changes, 1990 to 1995
United States	6 428 134	8 834 508	9 457 394	9 479 273	10 844 717	11 309 563	11 384 567	11 189 088	11 133 680	11 092 374	2.3
Alabama	87 884	145 698	143 674	158 688	195 939	202 311	206 287	210 094	206 546	203 165	3.7
Alaska	8 563	13 218	20 561	26 510	27 792	29 019	29 037	28 708	27 631	28 368	2.1
Arizona	107 315	168 666	194 034	202 036	248 213	253 631	255 907	246 754	252 184	254 530	2.5
Arkansas	43 599	56 127	66 068	66 123	78 645	82 152	85 829	87 942	85 601	87 067	10.7
California	1 123 529	1 617 558	1 599 838	1 444 207	1 594 710	1 804 654	1 748 649	1 604 158	1 582 837	1 564 230	-1.9
Colorado	108 562	136 370	145 598	142 031	200 653	206 645	212 427	209 932	209 717	210 312	4.8
Connecticut	73 391	93 567	97 788	98 616	109 556	107 321	107 786	105 446	102 450	100 539	-8.2
Delaware	21 151	27 082	28 325	27 933	34 252	35 311	35 313	35 771	36 322	36 204	5.7
District of Columbia	12 194	15 159	13 900	12 080	11 990	11 422	11 578	10 608	10 599	9 663	-19.4
Florida	189 450	287 745	334 349	362 241	489 081	506 342	511 226	518 480	528 024	530 607	8.5
Georgia	101 900	142 593	140 158	148 956	196 413	218 924	233 078	239 755	243 855	248 682	26.6
Hawaii	32 963	43 278	43 269	43 246	45 728	45 682	49 605	50 618	51 646	50 198	9.8
Idaho	27 072	31 298	34 491	33 666	41 315	44 149	46 607	47 524	48 994	48 986	18.6
Illinois	315 634	444 458	491 274	520 224	551 333	571 249	566 614	549 745	545 958	530 248	-3.8
Indiana	136 739	159 453	189 224	193 833	223 953	228 378	234 624	231 259	228 270	224 705	0.4
Iowa	68 390	83 572	97 454	109 765	117 834	120 360	122 841	122 267	122 017	122 396	3.9
Kansas	88 215	107 761	121 987	127 220	149 117	152 349	153 399	154 016	152 798	160 449	7.6
Kentucky	77 240	105 265	114 884	110 836	147 095	155 773	157 838	156 160	151 575	148 808	1.2
Louisiana	101 127	132 054	136 703	153 173	158 290	168 822	177 373	173 950	175 112	174 873	10.5
Maine	25 405	31 092	31 878	33 188	41 500	40 928	40 846	39 819	39 188	38 195	-8.0
Maryland	118 988	176 544	195 051	198 992	220 783	228 638	227 987	226 666	223 692	222 857	0.9
Massachusetts	116 127	173 564	183 765	185 602	186 035	180 559	183 119	181 461	179 799	176 777	-5.0
Michigan	339 625	436 655	454 147	434 270	487 359	486 301	473 322	483 145	466 758	462 390	-5.1
Minnesota	130 567	148 630	162 379	173 984	199 211	199 753	212 158	207 131	227 015	217 249	9.1
Mississippi	64 968	89 919	90 661	90 704	109 038	111 386	109 911	109 373	108 398	110 600	1.4
Missouri	132 540	158 196	165 179	168 829	200 093	203 125	198 610	197 821	191 859	189 993	-5.0
Montana	27 287	27 798	31 178	32 032	31 865	33 453	33 765	34 326	34 927	37 435	17.5
Nebraska	51 454	61 240	73 509	81 202	94 614	94 692	103 196	95 782	95 877	95 599	1.0
Nevada	13 576	30 010	40 280	43 368	61 242	61 985	63 192	63 229	63 271	66 683	8.9
New Hampshire	15 979	24 205	24 119	26 669	32 163	34 518	35 255	35 571	34 988	36 069	12.1
New Jersey	145 373	227 764	247 028	237 297	261 601	270 728	278 385	278 361	272 420	271 069	3.6
New Mexico	40 795	47 605	55 077	66 059	83 403	89 853	94 901	98 093	97 073	97 220	16.6
New York	449 437	613 842	563 251	563 251	616 884	605 898	606 308	604 989	604 433	588 491	-4.6
North Carolina	123 761	201 288	228 154	267 044	285 405	305 473	315 518	303 556	303 649	303 099	6.2
North Dakota	30 192	27 954	31 709	34 802	34 690	35 218	36 783	36 644	36 639	36 810	6.1
Ohio	281 099	336 931	381 765	379 164	427 613	436 292	437 027	429 756	417 566	409 818	-4.2
Oklahoma	91 438	124 372	137 188	146 827	151 073	160 166	164 728	160 901	161 748	158 026	4.6
Oregon	108 483	129 785	140 102	119 612	144 427	144 451	144 902	143 352	141 027	143 617	-0.6
Pennsylvania	232 982	287 436	292 499	300 523	343 478	354 435	359 856	351 747	342 065	339 928	-1.0
Rhode Island	25 527	32 311	35 052	35 389	42 350	42 503	43 264	40 833	39 376	38 653	-8.7
South Carolina	47 101	107 690	107 683	105 854	131 134	137 012	145 580	148 933	148 514	148 706	13.4
South Dakota	23 936	21 925	24 328	23 339	26 596	28 888	30 346	31 427	30 980	29 693	11.6
Tennessee	98 897	139 526	156 835	147 951	175 049	186 441	192 302	194 225	191 425	193 136	10.3
Texas	365 522	542 212	613 552	677 192	802 314	816 554	832 458	834 696	843 002	836 851	4.3
Utah	49 588	56 536	59 598	69 426	86 108	94 802	96 958	100 271	108 593	110 560	28.4
Vermont	12 536	17 145	17 984	18 844	20 910	21 485	21 397	21 001	20 505	20 470	-2.1
Virginia	123 279	215 253	246 500	250 754	291 286	298 107	297 522	293 810	293 165	293 127	0.6
Washington	162 718	202 531	276 028	201 532	227 632	238 345	238 763	241 813	244 772	246 635	8.3
West Virginia	51 363	68 117	71 228	66 531	74 108	78 215	79 284	77 500	76 120	74 857	1.0
Wisconsin	170 374	210 535	235 179	238 735	253 529	260 082	256 890	256 669	250 246	245 770	-3.1
Wyoming	15 220	18 078	21 121	24 204	30 623	31 251	30 687	30 002	30 015	29 420	-3.9

See footnotes at end of table.

Table C-44.   Total Fall Enrollment in Public Institutions of Higher Education, by State: 1970 to 1995 — Continued

State	Fall 1970	Fall 1975	Fall 1980	Fall 1985	Fall 1990	Fall 1991	Fall 1992	Fall 1993	Fall 1994	Fall 1995[1]	Percent changes, 1990 to 1995
U.S. Service Schools[2]	17 079	36 897	49 808	54 719	48 692	53 532	53 329	52 998	51 939	88 451	81.7
Outlying areas	46 680	59 923	60 692	65 411	66 244	66 074	66 702	69 115	70 917	77 050	16.3
American Samoa	(NA)	689	976	758	1 219	1 267	1 295	1 264	1 249	1 232	1.1
Federated States of Micronesia	(NA)	(NA)	(NA)	(NA)	975	837	1 028	1 148	1 374	1 296	32.9
Guam	2 719	3 800	3 217	4 601	4 741	5 016	4 845	5 843	6 449	6 010	26.8
Marshall Islands	(NA)	(NA)	(NA)	(NA)	(NA)	(NA)	374	386	424	418	-9.0
Northern Marianas ...	(NA)	(NA)	(NA)	318	661	847	796	1 261	1 253	959	45.1
Palau	(NA)	(NA)	(NA)	(NA)	491	355	445	436	403	351	-28.5
Puerto Rico	42 516	53 170	54 127	56 438	55 691	55 036	55 063	55 835	56 670	63 730	14.4
Trust Territory of the Pacific	(NA)	185	224	724	(NA)	(NA)	(NA)	(NA)	(NA)	(NA)	-9.0
Virgin Islands	1 445	2 079	2 148	2 572	2 466	2 716	2 856	2 942	3 095	3 054	23.8

SOURCE: U.S. Department of Education, National Center for Education Statistics, Higher Education General Information Survey (HEGIS), 'Fall Enrollment in Colleges and Universities' surveys; and Integrated Postsecondary Education Data System (IPEDS), 'Fall Enrollment' surveys. Published as table 191 in *Digest of Education Statistics* 1997.

1. Preliminary data.
2. Some data revised from previously published figures.

(NA) Not applicable or not available.

Table C-45. Total Fall Enrollment in Private Institutions of Higher Education, by State: 1970 to 1995

State	Fall 1970	Fall 1975	Fall 1980	Fall 1985	Fall 1990	Fall 1991	Fall 1992	Fall 1993	Fall 1994	Fall 1995	Percent changes, 1990 to 1995
United States	2 152 753	2 350 351	2 639 501	2 767 782	2 973 920	3 049 390	3 102 792	3 115 715	3 145 110	3 169 407	6.6
Alabama	16 052	19 002	20 632	20 655	22 650	22 020	24 250	23 431	22 965	22 447	-0.9
Alaska	908	780	735	969	2 041	1 774	1 865	1 930	1 167	980	-52.0
Arizona	2 304	4 876	8 682	14 818	15 935	19 340	18 764	25 546	22 748	19 451	22.1
Arkansas	8 440	9 420	11 539	11 835	11 780	12 188	11 749	11 320	10 693	11 113	-5.7
California	133 716	170 374	191 155	206 232	214 030	219 620	229 354	232 191	252 954	252 812	18.1
Colorado	14 833	13 444	17 318	19 283	26 478	28 463	28 925	29 873	31 578	32 427	22.5
Connecticut	51 309	54 924	61 844	60 732	59 048	58 503	58 088	56 854	57 540	57 156	-3.2
Delaware	4 109	5 307	4 614	3 950	7 752	7 677	7 450	7 757	7 875	8 103	4.5
District of Columbia	64 964	69 031	72 775	66 121	67 561	65 931	69 624	70 957	66 657	67 614	0.1
Florida	46 075	56 522	77 542	89 151	99 005	105 439	107 059	104 923	106 213	106 696	7.8
Georgia	24 611	30 992	44 001	47 870	55 373	58 099	60 528	63 089	64 732	66 030	19.2
Hawaii	3 599	3 393	3 912	6 691	10 708	11 620	11 557	12 253	12 676	13 000	21.4
Idaho	7 495	7 777	8 527	9 002	10 566	11 248	11 191	11 244	11 399	10 580	0.1
Illinois	136 512	139 631	152 971	158 465	177 913	182 048	182 191	184 344	185 462	187 606	5.4
Indiana	55 929	54 367	58 029	56 734	60 879	61 923	62 288	63 426	64 006	64 820	6.5
Iowa	40 512	38 106	42 995	43 132	52 681	50 664	49 964	50 530	50 433	51 439	-2.4
Kansas	14 270	13 072	14 618	14 139	14 616	15 350	16 020	16 119	17 805	17 194	17.6
Kentucky	21 351	19 988	28 182	30 888	30 757	32 185	30 484	31 172	31 002	30 050	-2.3
Louisiana	19 601	21 159	23 355	24 003	28 550	28 616	27 006	28 037	28 455	29 062	1.8
Maine	8 729	9 351	11 386	19 013	15 686	16 250	17 131	16 475	17 536	18 352	17.0
Maryland	30 619	29 026	30 475	32 657	38 917	39 293	40 412	41 339	42 522	43 453	11.7
Massachusetts	187 682	210 921	234 650	235 573	231 798	238 822	239 857	238 666	236 706	237 017	2.3
Michigan	53 101	59 750	65 984	73 023	82 444	82 190	87 451	85 065	84 549	85 949	4.3
Minnesota	30 221	36 126	44 312	47 178	54 578	55 301	60 762	60 987	62 285	63 567	16.5
Mississippi	8 999	10 043	11 703	10 476	13 845	13 964	13 843	13 035	12 486	12 090	-12.7
Missouri	51 390	64 919	69 242	72 317	89 806	94 029	98 007	99 241	101 951	101 543	13.1
Montana	2 775	3 045	3 999	3 926	4 011	4 368	5 879	5 231	5 168	5 239	30.6
Nebraska	15 461	13 465	15 979	16 567	18 217	18 956	19 407	19 741	20 123	20 119	10.4
Nevada	93	177	175	288	486	679	685	718	814	1 143	135.2
New Hampshire	13 421	16 825	22 675	25 614	27 347	29 200	28 669	28 472	27 859	28 258	3.3
New Jersey	70 748	69 350	74 582	60 361	62 685	63 913	64 847	64 668	63 060	62 762	0.1
New Mexico	3 666	4 339	3 206	2 236	2 097	3 654	4 375	3 367	4 808	5 185	147.3
New York	357 042	391 221	428 986	436 847	431 402	450 589	458 514	457 935	453 408	453 075	5.0
North Carolina	48 164	50 498	59 383	60 244	66 733	66 495	67 935	67 724	65 737	68 931	3.3
North Dakota	1 303	1 789	2 360	3 137	3 188	3 521	3 687	3 672	3 545	3 589	12.6
Ohio	95 168	99 121	107 380	135 581	130 077	133 034	136 156	132 646	131 738	130 457	0.3
Oklahoma	18 717	22 241	23 107	22 346	22 148	23 370	23 118	22 441	23 426	22 650	2.3
Oregon	13 694	15 496	17 356	18 355	21 314	22 656	22 513	22 482	23 420	23 528	10.4
Pennsylvania	178 062	183 100	215 217	232 675	260 582	265 601	267 048	269 481	268 609	277 831	6.6
Rhode Island	20 371	32 168	31 817	34 538	35 923	36 609	35 901	36 574	35 342	35 447	-1.3
South Carolina	22 417	25 333	24 793	26 048	28 168	27 895	25 863	25 369	24 556	25 419	-9.8
South Dakota	6 703	8 335	8 433	9 433	7 612	7 444	7 250	6 739	6 784	7 002	-8.0
Tennessee	36 206	41 909	47 746	46 894	51 189	51 601	50 668	50 711	51 541	52 826	3.2
Texas	76 703	82 178	87 839	92 500	99 123	100 889	106 068	107 482	111 493	115 674	16.7
Utah	32 099	30 787	34 389	34 568	35 195	35 617	36 125	37 868	37 603	36 764	4.5

See footnotes at end of table.

Table C-45.   Total Fall Enrollment in Private Institutions of Higher Education, by State: 1970 to 1995 — Continued

State	Fall 1970	Fall 1975	Fall 1980	Fall 1985	Fall 1990	Fall 1991	Fall 1992	Fall 1993	Fall 1994	Fall 1995	Percent changes, 1990 to 1995
Vermont	9 673	11 950	12 644	12 572	15 488	15 951	15 980	15 414	14 904	14 595	-5.8
Virginia	28 636	29 418	34 004	41 662	62 156	58 218	56 650	54 725	60 984	62 792	1.0
Washington	20 826	24 637	27 575	30 021	35 752	36 415	36 793	38 032	39 890	39 184	9.6
West Virginia	11 790	10 502	10 745	10 128	10 682	10 387	10 968	11 352	11 621	11 177	4.6
Wisconsin	31 684	30 166	33 907	36 334	46 245	48 904	51 012	52 367	53 615	54 453	17.7
Wyoming	(NA)	(NA)	26	(NA)	703	867	861	700	667	756	7.5
U.S, Service Schools[2]	20 557	44 347	77 057	99 479	98 374	102 697	103 057	103 874	99 769	106 607	8.4
Puerto Rico	20 557	44 347	77 057	99 479	98 374	102 697	103 057	103 874	99 769	106 607	8.4

SOURCE: U.S. Department of Education, National Center for Education Statistics, Higher Education General Information Survey (HEGIS), 'Fall Enrollment in Colleges and Universities' surveys; and Integrated Postsecondary Education Data System (IPEDS), 'Fall Enrollment' surveys. Published as table 192 in *Digest of Education Statistics* 1997.

1. Preliminary data.
2. Some data revised from previously published figures.

(NA) Not applicable or not available.

Table C-46.   Total Fall Enrollment in All Institutions of Higher Education, by Attendance Status, Sex, and State: 1994 and 1995

State	Total	Fall 1994[1] Full-time Men	Full-time Women	Part-time Men	Part-time Women	Total	Fall 1995[2] Full-time Men	Full-time Women	Part-time Men	Part-time Women
United States	14 278 790	3 855 183	4 282 593	2 516 715	3 624 299	14 261 781	3 807 392	4 321 410	2 535 147	3 597 832
Alabama	229 511	69 230	82 660	33 045	44 576	225 612	68 713	83 031	31 064	42 804
Alaska	28 798	5 668	6 788	6 161	10 181	29 348	5 424	6 559	6 444	10 921
Arizona	274 932	63 697	64 013	60 773	86 449	273 981	61 685	64 369	61 226	86 701
Arkansas	96 294	30 261	36 712	11 093	18 228	98 180	30 077	37 101	11 626	19 376
California	1 835 791	412 716	450 914	421 148	551 013	1 817 042	408 376	458 540	410 267	539 859
Colorado	241 295	63 265	65 091	48 463	64 476	242 739	62 892	65 994	48 117	65 736
Connecticut	159 990	39 144	42 766	30 283	47 797	157 695	38 877	43 222	29 623	45 973
Delaware	44 197	11 521	14 411	7 533	10 732	44 307	11 287	14 252	7 576	11 192
District of Columbia	77 256	22 470	26 610	12 646	15 530	77 277	22 706	27 643	11 807	15 121
Florida	634 237	142 547	159 592	136 851	195 247	637 303	142 368	162 172	135 424	197 339
Georgia	308 587	92 709	110 110	42 371	63 397	314 712	93 962	115 663	40 920	64 167
Hawaii	64 322	16 061	19 169	12 871	16 221	63 198	16 175	19 166	12 030	15 827
Idaho	60 393	19 255	21 103	7 908	12 127	59 566	19 013	21 136	7 706	11 711
Illinois	731 420	178 957	193 474	145 279	213 710	717 854	174 969	193 430	141 323	208 132
Indiana	292 276	92 089	97 935	41 063	61 189	289 615	90 941	98 818	41 298	58 558
Iowa	172 450	58 901	61 720	19 478	32 351	173 835	58 553	62 170	19 478	33 634
Kansas	170 603	48 013	49 915	28 114	44 561	177 643	47 394	50 144	31 446	48 659
Kentucky	182 577	53 533	65 836	22 407	40 801	178 858	52 229	65 429	22 025	39 175
Louisiana	203 567	64 832	79 536	21 798	37 401	203 935	64 292	79 971	21 820	37 852
Maine	56 724	15 014	17 035	8 032	16 643	56 547	14 632	16 920	7 978	17 017
Maryland	266 214	57 746	66 913	54 678	86 877	266 310	57 822	68 689	54 075	85 724
Massachusetts	416 505	123 189	138 072	60 797	94 447	413 794	121 670	140 343	59 062	92 719
Michigan	551 307	130 298	148 247	112 668	160 094	548 339	127 404	146 846	113 756	160 333
Minnesota	289 300	77 477	84 168	53 571	74 084	280 816	74 919	83 181	51 380	71 336
Mississippi	120 884	40 937	49 527	11 282	19 138	122 690	41 390	50 577	11 219	19 504
Missouri	293 810	79 571	87 509	50 435	76 295	291 536	77 858	88 270	49 402	76 006
Montana	40 095	15 246	15 508	3 798	5 543	42 674	15 967	16 789	3 991	5 927
Nebraska	116 000	32 353	34 308	19 706	29 633	115 718	32 125	34 529	20 327	28 737
Nevada	64 085	10 186	11 011	18 044	24 844	67 826	10 196	11 524	19 787	26 319
New Hampshire	62 847	18 376	21 513	8 470	14 488	64 327	18 307	21 598	9 070	15 352
New Jersey	335 480	81 351	91 263	65 599	97 267	333 831	81 944	92 990	63 695	95 202
New Mexico	101 881	23 684	27 696	20 075	30 426	102 405	23 306	28 210	19 900	30 989
New York	1 057 841	311 858	363 375	144 142	238 466	1 041 566	301 712	363 252	142 426	234 176
North Carolina	369 386	104 943	130 290	54 140	80 013	372 030	105 756	132 332	54 248	79 694
North Dakota	40 184	16 426	15 439	3 585	4 734	40 399	16 462	15 756	3 480	4 701
Ohio	549 304	160 869	181 175	87 286	119 974	540 275	157 392	180 152	84 648	118 083
Oklahoma	185 174	52 979	57 218	30 890	44 087	180 676	51 848	56 218	30 422	42 188
Oregon	164 447	45 748	46 680	31 295	40 724	167 145	43 214	46 067	33 792	44 072
Pennsylvania	611 174	186 827	199 592	91 629	133 126	617 759	186 435	201 884	91 493	137 947
Rhode Island	74 718	22 796	24 221	10 770	16 931	74 100	22 522	24 308	10 642	16 628
South Carolina	173 070	49 154	58 332	24 356	41 228	174 125	48 980	60 159	23 666	41 320
South Dakota	37 764	12 950	14 538	3 717	6 559	36 695	12 586	14 021	3 610	6 478
Tennessee	242 966	72 240	83 777	35 384	51 565	245 962	73 010	86 590	35 318	51 044
Texas	954 495	250 851	263 609	192 609	247 426	952 525	248 597	267 274	189 578	247 076
Utah	146 196	48 699	47 148	24 669	25 680	147 324	49 018	48 685	24 854	24 767
Vermont	35 409	11 434	12 461	3 684	7 830	35 065	11 238	12 739	3 599	7 489
Virginia	354 149	92 054	107 374	63 443	91 278	355 919	91 570	108 894	63 394	92 061
Washington	284 662	81 419	90 980	45 744	66 519	285 819	81 914	93 836	44 585	65 484
West Virginia	87 741	29 373	31 215	9 381	17 772	86 034	28 848	30 935	9 191	17 060
Wisconsin	303 861	85 012	95 951	49 305	73 593	300 223	84 279	97 288	48 088	70 568
Wyoming	30 682	8 669	8 886	4 793	8 334	30 176	8 532	9 068	4 543	8 033

See footnotes at end of table.

Table C-46.   Total Fall Enrollment in All Institutions of Higher Education, by Attendance Status, Sex, and State: 1994 and 1995 — Continued

State	Fall 1994[1]					Fall 1995[2]				
	Total	Full-time		Part-time		Total	Full-time		Part-time	
		Men	Women	Men	Women		Men	Women	Men	Women
U.S. Service Schools[2]	51 939	20 585	9 207	9 453	12 694	88 451	16 006	2 676	58 708	11 061
Outlying areas	170 686	49 427	76 346	19 016	25 897	183 657	53 526	83 879	18 544	27 708
American Samoa	1 249	433	438	222	156	1 232	428	436	217	151
Federated States of Micronesia	1 374	449	422	316	187	1 296	518	447	150	181
Guam	6 449	1 174	1 770	1 645	1 860	6 010	989	1 597	1 567	1 857
Marshall Islands	424	92	76	147	109	418	89	75	146	108
Northern Marianas	1 253	148	202	425	478	959	203	253	188	315
Palau	403	198	136	34	35	351	143	125	31	52
Puerto Rico	156 439	46 580	72 315	15 769	21 775	170 337	50 834	79 876	15 798	23 829
Virgin Islands	3 095	353	987	458	1 297	3 054	322	1 070	447	1 215

SOURCE: U.S. Department of Education, National Center for Education Statistics, Integrated Postsecondary Education Data System (IPEDS), 'Fall Enrollment' survey. Published as table 193 in *Digest of Education Statistics* 1997.

1. Revised from previously published data.
2. Preliminary data.

Table C-47. Total Fall Enrollment in Public Institutions of Higher Education, by Attendance Status, Sex, and State: 1994 and 1995

State	Fall 1994[1]					Fall 1995[2]				
	Total	Full-time		Part-time		Total	Full-time		Part-time	
		Men	Women	Men	Women		Men	Women	Men	Women
United States	11 133 680	2 813 226	3 137 594	2 116 842	3 066 018	11 092 374	2 769 745	3 155 556	2 137 890	3 029 183
Alabama	206 546	60 804	71 839	31 510	42 393	203 165	60 666	72 704	29 366	40 429
Alaska	27 631	5 367	6 318	5 995	9 951	28 368	5 171	6 201	6 290	10 706
Arizona	252 184	53 487	55 865	58 995	83 837	254 530	52 572	57 142	59 849	84 967
Arkansas	85 601	25 767	31 632	10 681	17 521	87 067	25 493	31 866	11 145	18 563
California	1 582 837	323 244	356 573	388 424	514 596	1 564 230	319 499	362 281	378 663	503 787
Colorado	209 717	52 922	55 323	42 777	58 695	210 312	52 690	55 717	42 163	59 742
Connecticut	102 450	21 556	24 035	21 546	35 313	100 539	21 063	23 818	21 226	34 432
Delaware	36 322	9 961	12 534	5 874	7 953	36 204	9 713	12 429	5 897	8 165
District of Columbia	10 599	1 651	2 093	2 804	4 051	9 663	1 444	2 015	2 482	3 722
Florida	528 024	105 949	124 501	119 118	178 456	530 607	105 794	126 880	118 165	179 768
Georgia	243 855	68 164	81 927	36 659	57 105	248 682	68 441	86 296	36 366	57 579
Hawaii	51 646	12 600	15 202	9 809	14 035	50 198	12 419	14 997	9 392	13 390
Idaho	48 994	14 930	15 440	7 481	11 143	48 986	14 759	15 562	7 443	11 222
Illinois	545 958	120 292	130 610	117 878	177 178	530 248	116 061	128 965	114 352	170 870
Indiana	228 270	66 120	72 001	37 294	52 855	224 795	65 085	71 868	37 579	50 263
Iowa	122 017	41 780	42 084	14 724	23 429	122 396	41 636	42 672	14 870	23 218
Kansas	152 798	41 950	42 874	26 354	41 620	160 449	41 551	43 254	29 814	45 830
Kentucky	151 575	42 852	52 976	19 789	35 958	148 808	42 192	53 218	19 316	34 082
Louisiana	175 112	55 288	67 727	18 522	33 575	174 873	54 727	68 616	18 188	33 342
Maine	39 188	10 588	10 479	6 748	11 373	38 195	10 024	10 288	6 646	11 237
Maryland	223 692	47 252	54 760	47 011	74 669	222 857	46 869	56 092	46 512	73 384
Massachusetts	179 799	44 675	50 704	32 804	51 616	176 777	43 528	50 097	32 004	51 148
Michigan	466 758	109 531	120 876	98 338	138 013	462 390	106 872	119 925	98 467	137 126
Minnesota	227 015	58 482	59 576	46 968	61 989	217 249	55 886	58 199	43 815	59 349
Mississippi	108 398	37 258	44 200	10 041	16 899	110 600	37 592	45 524	9 988	17 496
Missouri	191 859	49 912	56 907	32 007	53 033	189 993	48 618	56 455	31 883	53 037
Montana	34 927	13 835	13 378	3 191	4 523	37 435	14 596	14 638	3 320	4 881
Nebraska	95 877	25 633	26 008	18 119	26 117	95 599	25 462	26 147	18 694	25 296
Nevada	63 271	9 938	10 756	17 939	24 638	66 683	9 790	11 031	19 698	26 164
New Hampshire	34 988	10 169	12 204	4 715	7 900	36 069	10 016	11 947	5 461	8 645
New Jersey	272 420	62 691	72 201	55 501	82 027	271 069	63 116	73 508	53 991	80 454
New Mexico	97 073	21 890	25 679	19 779	29 725	97 220	21 459	25 789	19 638	30 334
New York	604 433	165 600	200 641	88 732	149 460	588 491	158 869	197 894	87 647	144 081
North Carolina	303 649	79 562	101 016	50 051	73 020	303 099	79 417	101 777	49 422	72 483
North Dakota	36 639	15 137	13 620	3 447	4 435	36 810	15 101	13 936	3 371	4 402
Ohio	417 566	117 887	135 467	67 350	96 862	409 818	115 135	133 907	65 403	95 373
Oklahoma	161 748	43 443	47 988	28 561	41 756	158 026	42 828	47 622	27 747	39 829
Oregon	141 027	37 290	37 211	29 039	37 487	143 617	34 837	36 319	31 503	40 958
Pennsylvania	342 565	104 923	112 304	49 492	75 846	339 928	104 724	113 496	47 661	74 047
Rhode Island	39 376	8 302	11 100	7 127	12 847	38 653	8 123	11 040	6 919	12 571
South Carolina	148 514	39 912	46 905	22 928	38 769	148 706	39 600	48 272	22 148	38 686
South Dakota	30 980	11 139	11 643	3 045	5 153	29 693	10 710	11 159	2 858	4 966
Tennessee	191 425	51 302	61 486	32 341	46 296	193 136	51 586	63 275	32 233	46 042
Texas	843 002	208 779	223 409	178 286	232 528	836 851	205 744	225 376	174 241	231 490
Utah	108 593	32 052	30 885	22 471	23 185	110 560	32 939	32 010	22 957	22 654
Vermont	20 505	6 216	6 614	2 478	5 197	20 470	6 094	6 749	2 464	5 163
Virginia	293 165	73 308	82 383	55 892	81 582	293 127	73 170	83 865	55 091	81 001
Washington	244 772	68 791	75 747	40 628	59 606	246 635	69 018	78 010	40 335	59 272
West Virginia	76 120	25 514	25 794	8 620	16 192	74 857	25 009	25 724	8 542	15 582
Wisconsin	250 246	68 941	76 009	42 713	62 583	245 770	68 248	77 247	41 414	58 861
Wyoming	30 015	8 005	8 883	4 793	8 334	29 420	7 783	9 061	4 543	8 033

See footnotes at end of table.

Table C-47.   Total Fall Enrollment in Public Institutions of Higher Education, by Attendance Status, Sex, and State: 1994 and 1995 — Continued

State	Fall 1994[1]					Fall 1995[2]				
	Total	Full-time		Part-time		Total	Full-time		Part-time	
		Men	Women	Men	Women		Men	Women	Men	Women
U.S. Service Schools[2]	51 939	20 585	9 207	9 453	12 694	88 451	16 006	2 676	58 708	11 061
Outlying areas	70 917	20 386	32 001	7 297	11 233	77 050	22 397	36 464	6 978	11 211
American Samoa	1 249	433	438	222	156	1 232	428	436	217	151
Federated States of Micronesia	1 374	449	422	316	187	1 296	518	447	150	181
Guam	6 449	1 174	1 770	1 645	1 860	6 010	989	1 597	1 567	1 857
Marshall Islands	424	92	76	147	109	418	89	75	146	108
Northern Marianas	1 253	148	202	425	478	959	203	253	188	315
Palau	403	198	136	34	35	351	143	125	31	52
Puerto Rico	56 670	17 539	27 970	4 050	7 111	63 730	19 705	32 461	4 232	7 332
Virgin Islands	3 095	353	987	458	1 297	3 054	322	1 070	447	1 215

SOURCE: U.S. Department of Education, National Center for Education Statistics, Integrated Postsecondary Education Data System (IPEDS), 'Fall Enrollment' surveys. Published as table 194 in *Digest of Education Statistics* 1997.

1. Revised from previously published data.
2. Preliminary data.

Table C-48. Total Fall Enrollment in Private Institutions of Higher Education, by Attendance Status, Sex, and State: 1994 and 1995

State	Fall 1994[1]					Fall 1995[2]				
	Total	Full-time		Part-time		Total	Full-time		Part-time	
		Men	Women	Men	Women		Men	Women	Men	Women
United States	3 145 110	1 041 957	1 144 999	399 873	558 281	3 169 407	1 037 647	1 165 854	397 257	568 649
Alabama	22 965	8 426	10 821	1 535	2 183	22 447	8 047	10 327	1 698	2 375
Alaska	1 167	301	470	166	230	980	253	358	154	215
Arizona	22 748	10 210	8 148	1 778	2 612	19 451	9 113	7 227	1 377	1 734
Arkansas	10 693	4 494	5 080	412	707	11 113	4 584	5 235	481	813
California	252 954	89 472	94 341	32 724	36 417	252 812	88 877	96 259	31 604	36 072
Colorado	31 578	10 343	9 768	5 686	5 781	32 427	10 202	10 277	5 954	5 994
Connecticut	57 540	17 588	18 731	8 737	12 484	57 156	17 814	19 404	8 397	11 541
Delaware	7 875	1 560	1 877	1 659	2 779	8 103	1 574	1 823	1 679	3 027
District of Columbia	66 657	20 819	24 517	9 842	11 479	67 614	21 262	25 628	9 325	11 399
Florida	106 213	36 598	35 091	17 733	16 791	106 696	36 574	35 292	17 259	17 571
Georgia	64 732	24 545	28 183	5 712	6 292	66 030	25 521	29 367	4 554	6 588
Hawaii	12 676	3 461	3 967	3 062	2 186	13 000	3 756	4 169	2 638	2 437
Idaho	11 399	4 325	5 663	427	984	10 580	4 254	5 574	263	489
Illinois	185 462	58 665	62 864	27 401	36 532	187 606	58 908	64 465	26 971	37 262
Indiana	64 006	25 969	25 934	3 769	8 334	64 820	25 856	26 950	3 719	8 295
Iowa	50 433	17 121	19 636	4 754	8 922	51 439	16 917	19 498	4 608	10 416
Kansas	17 805	6 063	7 041	1 760	2 941	17 194	5 843	6 890	1 632	2 829
Kentucky	31 002	10 681	12 860	2 618	4 843	30 050	10 037	12 211	2 709	5 093
Louisiana	28 455	9 544	11 809	3 276	3 826	29 062	9 565	11 355	3 632	4 510
Maine	17 536	4 426	6 556	1 284	5 270	18 352	4 608	6 632	1 332	5 780
Maryland	42 522	10 494	12 153	7 667	12 208	43 453	10 953	12 597	7 563	12 340
Massachusetts	236 706	78 514	87 368	27 993	42 831	237 017	78 142	90 246	27 058	41 571
Michigan	84 549	20 767	27 371	14 330	22 081	85 949	20 532	26 921	15 289	23 207
Minnesota	62 285	18 995	24 592	6 603	12 095	63 567	19 033	24 982	7 565	11 987
Mississippi	12 486	3 679	5 327	1 241	2 239	12 090	3 798	5 053	1 231	2 008
Missouri	101 951	29 659	30 602	18 428	23 262	101 543	29 240	31 815	17 519	22 969
Montana	5 168	1 411	2 130	607	1 020	5 239	1 371	2 151	671	1 046
Nebraska	20 123	6 720	8 300	1 587	3 516	20 119	6 663	8 382	1 633	3 441
Nevada	814	248	255	105	206	1 143	406	493	89	155
New Hampshire	27 859	8 207	9 309	3 755	6 588	28 258	8 291	9 651	3 609	6 707
New Jersey	63 060	18 660	19 062	10 098	15 240	62 762	18 828	19 482	9 704	14 748
New Mexico	4 808	1 794	2 017	296	701	5 185	1 847	2 421	262	655
New York	453 408	146 258	162 734	55 410	89 006	453 075	142 843	165 358	54 779	90 095
North Carolina	65 737	25 381	29 274	4 089	6 993	68 931	26 339	30 555	4 826	7 211
North Dakota	3 545	1 289	1 819	138	299	3 589	1 361	1 820	109	299
Ohio	131 738	42 982	45 708	19 936	23 112	130 457	42 257	46 245	19 245	22 710
Oklahoma	23 426	9 536	9 230	2 329	2 331	22 650	9 020	8 596	2 675	2 359
Oregon	23 420	8 458	9 469	2 256	3 237	23 528	8 377	9 748	2 289	3 114
Pennsylvania	268 609	81 904	87 288	42 137	57 280	277 831	81 711	88 388	43 832	63 900
Rhode Island	35 342	14 494	13 121	3 643	4 084	35 447	14 399	13 268	3 723	4 057
South Carolina	24 556	9 242	11 427	1 428	2 459	25 419	9 380	11 887	1 518	2 634
South Dakota	6 784	1 811	2 895	672	1 406	7 002	1 876	2 862	752	1 512
Tennessee	51 541	20 938	22 291	3 043	5 269	52 826	21 424	23 315	3 085	5 002
Texas	111 493	42 072	40 200	14 323	14 898	115 674	42 853	41 898	15 337	15 586
Utah	37 603	16 647	16 263	2 198	2 495	36 764	16 079	16 675	1 897	2 113

See footnotes at end of table.

Table C-48. Total Fall Enrollment in Private Institutions of Higher Education, by Attendance Status, Sex, and State: 1994 and 1995 — Continued

State	Fall 1994[1]					Fall 1995[2]				
	Total	Full-time		Part-time		Total	Full-time		Part-time	
		Men	Women	Men	Women		Men	Women	Men	Women
Vermont	14 904	5 218	5 847	1 206	2 633	14 595	5 144	5 990	1 135	2 326
Virginia	60 984	18 746	24 991	7 551	9 696	62 792	18 400	25 029	8 303	11 060
Washington	39 890	12 628	15 233	5 116	6 913	39 184	12 896	15 826	4 250	6 212
West Virginia	11 621	3 859	5 421	761	1 580	11 177	3 839	5 211	649	1 478
Wisconsin	53 615	16 071	19 942	6 592	11 010	54 453	16 031	20 041	6 674	11 707
Wyoming	667	664	3	(NA)	(NA)	756	749	7	(NA)	(NA)
Puerto Rico	99 769	29 041	44 345	11 719	14 664	106 607	31 129	47 415	11 566	16 497

SOURCE: U.S. Department of Education, National Center for Education Statistics, Integrated Postsecondary Education Data System (IPEDS), 'Fall Enrollment' surveys. Published as table 195 in *Digest of Education Statistics* 1997.

1. Preliminary data.

(NA) Not applicable or not available.

Table C-49.   Total Fall Enrollment in Institutions of Higher Education, by Control, Type of Institution, and State: 1994 and 1995

State	Fall 1994[1]				Fall 1995[2]			
	Public 4-year	Public 2-year	Private 4-year	Private 2-year	Public 4-year	Public 2-year	Private 4-year	Private 2-year
United States	5 825 213	5 308 467	2 923 867	221 243	5 814 545	5 277 829	2 954 707	214 700
Alabama	126 079	80 467	21 609	1 356	126 508	76 657	21 949	498
Alaska	27 037	594	828	339	27 556	812	776	204
Arizona	101 418	150 766	21 819	929	101 718	152 812	18 562	889
Arkansas	64 540	21 061	10 347	346	62 809	24 258	10 667	446
California	483 332	1 099 505	239 288	13 666	490 231	1 073 999	238 755	14 057
Colorado	132 748	76 969	28 224	3 354	132 616	77 696	28 804	3 623
Connecticut	57 867	44 583	55 767	1 773	57 711	42 828	55 594	1 562
Delaware	24 966	11 356	7 875	(NA)	24 540	11 664	8 103	(NA)
District of Columbia	10 599	(NA)	66 657	(NA)	9 663	(NA)	67 614	(NA)
Florida	201 242	326 782	101 233	4 980	206 961	323 646	101 265	5 431
Georgia	157 391	86 464	58 559	6 173	160 425	88 257	61 480	4 550
Hawaii	23 741	27 905	12 676	(NA)	23 345	26 853	13 000	(NA)
Idaho	41 629	7 365	2 988	8 411	41 449	7 537	2 308	8 272
Illinois	194 489	351 469	179 359	6 103	192 532	337 716	183 336	4 270
Indiana	186 586	41 684	60 357	3 649	184 184	40 611	61 331	3 489
Iowa	65 617	56 400	49 042	1 391	65 841	56 555	50 324	1 115
Kansas	86 285	66 513	16 888	917	86 770	73 679	16 316	878
Kentucky	106 259	45 316	26 496	4 506	105 529	43 279	27 382	2 668
Louisiana	147 110	28 002	27 251	1 204	147 920	26 953	27 884	1 178
Maine	31 899	7 289	15 664	1 872	31 275	6 920	16 437	1 915
Maryland	112 250	111 442	41 381	1 141	113 738	109 119	42 267	1 186
Massachusetts	101 796	78 003	222 237	14 469	101 814	74 963	228 964	8 053
Michigan	258 107	208 651	82 086	2 463	258 996	203 394	83 304	2 645
Minnesota	119 233	107 782	57 897	4 388	117 188	100 061	59 410	4 157
Mississippi	57 507	50 891	11 431	1 055	58 847	51 753	11 278	812
Missouri	117 361	74 498	96 085	5 866	117 871	72 122	96 946	4 597
Montana	30 604	4 323	4 395	773	31 412	6 023	4 319	920
Nebraska	58 007	37 870	19 698	425	58 081	37 518	19 575	544
Nevada	31 333	31 938	787	27	30 831	35 852	1 116	27
New Hampshire	26 315	8 673	24 011	3 848	26 497	9 572	24 227	4 031
New Jersey	136 654	135 766	59 079	3 981	137 829	133 240	58 045	4 717
New Mexico	50 800	46 273	4 157	651	49 819	47 401	4 231	954
New York	345 202	259 231	424 708	28 700	335 728	252 763	425 065	28 010
North Carolina	156 445	147 204	63 203	2 534	157 414	145 685	67 448	1 483
North Dakota	28 301	8 338	3 299	246	28 396	8 414	3 334	255
Ohio	267 719	149 847	117 273	14 465	262 036	147 782	117 115	13 342
Oklahoma	97 271	64 477	20 768	2 658	95 387	62 639	20 621	2 029
Oregon	62 651	78 376	23 252	168	63 056	80 561	23 359	169
Pennsylvania	231 347	111 218	220 321	48 288	233 433	106 495	220 269	57 562
Rhode Island	23 375	16 001	33 211	2 131	22 764	15 889	33 021	2 426
South Carolina	87 374	61 140	23 070	1 486	87 813	60 893	24 124	1 295
South Dakota	30 783	197	6 573	211	29 484	209	6 769	233
Tennessee	114 151	77 274	48 722	2 819	115 042	78 094	50 388	2 438
Texas	423 647	419 355	105 376	6 117	417 431	419 420	109 724	5 950
Utah	79 554	29 039	36 405	1 198	80 088	30 472	35 505	1 259
Vermont	15 873	4 632	14 717	187	15 835	4 635	14 394	201
Virginia	162 432	130 733	56 440	4 544	164 782	128 345	57 917	4 875
Washington	85 523	159 249	37 781	2 109	86 080	160 555	36 950	2 234
West Virginia	68 912	7 208	10 768	853	67 877	6 980	10 391	786
Wisconsin	142 998	107 248	51 809	1 806	139 192	106 578	52 744	1 709
Wyoming	12 022	17 993	(NA)	667	11 361	18 059	(NA)	756

See footnotes at end of table.

Table C-49. Total Fall Enrollment in Institutions of Higher Education, by Control, Type of Institution, and State: 1994 and 1995 — Continued

State	Fall 1994[1]				Fall 1995[2]			
	Public 4-year	Public 2-year	Private 4-year	Private 2-year	Public 4-year	Public 2-year	Private 4-year	Private 2-year
U.S. Service Schools	18 832	33 107	(NA)	(NA)	18 840	69 611	(NA)	(NA)
Outlying areas	57 588	13 329	87 311	12 458	62 568	14 482	97 712	8 895
American Samoa	(NA)	1 249	(NA)	(NA)	(NA)	1 232	(NA)	(NA)
Federated States of Micronesia	(NA)	1 374	(NA)	(NA)	(NA)	1 296	(NA)	(NA)
Guam	4 064	2 385	(NA)	(NA)	3 654	2 356	(NA)	(NA)
Marshall Islands	(NA)	424	(NA)	(NA)	(NA)	418	(NA)	(NA)
Northern Marianas	(NA)	1 253	(NA)	(NA)	(NA)	959	(NA)	(NA)
Palau	(NA)	403	(NA)	(NA)	(NA)	351	(NA)	(NA)
Puerto Rico	50 429	6 241	87 311	12 458	55 860	7 870	97 712	8 895
Virgin Islands	3 095	(NA)	(NA)	(NA)	3 054	(NA)	(NA)	(NA)

SOURCE: U.S. Department of Education, National Center for Education Statistics, Integrated Postsecondary Education Data System (IPEDS), 'Fall Enrollment' surveys. Published as table 196 in *Digest of Education Statistics* 1997.

1. Revised from previously published data.
2. Preliminary data.

(NA) Not applicable or not available.

Table C-50. Total Fall Enrollment in Institutions of Higher Education, by Level of Enrollment and State: 1993 to 1995

State	Fall 1993[1]				Fall 1994[1]				Fall 1995[2]		
	Total	Under-graduate	First professional	Graduate	Total	Under-graduate	First professional	Graduate	Under-graduate	First professional	Graduate
United States	14 304 803	12 323 959	292 431	1 688 413	14 278 790	12 262 608	294 713	1 721 469	12 231 719	297 592	1 732 470
Alabama	233 525	208 019	3 520	21 986	229 511	202 408	3 834	23 269	198 050	4 139	23 423
Alaska	30 638	29 047	(NA)	1 591	28 798	27 189	(NA)	1 609	27 657	(NA)	1 691
Arizona	272 300	239 657	2 720	29 923	274 932	241 290	1 549	32 093	242 113	1 561	30 307
Arkansas	99 262	90 123	1 705	7 434	96 294	87 197	1 705	7 392	88 460	1 702	8 018
California	1 836 349	1 628 210	35 331	172 808	1 835 791	1 624 924	35 340	175 527	1 605 825	35 547	175 670
Colorado	239 805	200 368	3 183	36 254	241 295	201 110	3 206	36 979	201 005	3 130	38 604
Connecticut	162 300	128 063	3 309	30 928	159 990	125 939	3 394	30 657	124 063	3 416	30 216
Delaware	43 528	37 913	1 403	4 212	44 197	38 296	1 333	4 568	38 177	1 289	4 841
District of Columbia	81 565	47 666	8 732	25 167	77 256	43 623	8 819	24 814	43 365	9 068	24 844
Florida	623 403	554 662	8 693	60 048	634 237	562 961	8 653	62 623	564 635	9 284	63 384
Georgia	302 844	259 718	8 970	34 156	308 587	263 604	9 595	35 388	267 900	10 060	36 752
Hawaii	62 871	54 512	516	7 843	64 322	55 850	495	7 977	54 901	498	7 799
Idaho	58 768	51 651	509	6 608	60 393	51 783	559	8 051	51 978	529	7 059
Illinois	734 089	621 576	16 817	95 696	731 420	617 549	17 173	96 698	601 745	17 368	98 741
Indiana	294 685	255 747	5 470	33 468	292 276	252 801	5 513	33 962	249 847	5 339	34 429
Iowa	172 797	149 762	6 580	16 455	172 450	149 331	6 650	16 469	151 082	6 568	16 185
Kansas	170 135	148 164	2 129	19 842	170 603	148 046	2 075	20 482	155 852	2 074	19 717
Kentucky	187 332	163 460	4 946	18 926	182 577	158 177	4 512	19 888	153 840	4 647	20 371
Louisiana	201 987	171 195	6 071	24 721	203 567	172 561	6 102	24 904	171 941	6 129	25 865
Maine	56 294	50 391	663	5 240	56 724	50 274	667	5 783	49 730	681	6 136
Maryland	268 005	223 272	3 900	40 833	266 214	220 535	4 173	41 506	218 536	4 410	43 364
Massachusetts	420 127	329 593	13 421	77 113	416 505	323 868	13 283	79 354	319 541	13 450	80 803
Michigan	568 210	490 372	11 361	66 477	551 307	474 357	10 681	66 269	470 493	10 719	67 127
Minnesota	268 118	231 090	7 082	29 946	289 300	251 649	5 838	31 813	242 048	6 085	32 683
Mississippi	122 408	109 959	1 779	10 670	120 884	108 003	1 895	10 986	109 298	1 759	11 633
Missouri	297 062	251 661	10 050	35 351	293 810	247 484	10 208	36 118	242 876	9 370	39 290
Montana	39 557	35 945	223	3 389	40 095	36 414	235	3 446	39 113	236	3 325
Nebraska	115 523	101 048	3 159	11 316	116 000	100 482	3 219	12 299	100 107	3 165	12 446
Nevada	63 947	57 227	202	6 518	64 085	57 103	218	6 764	60 398	211	7 217
New Hampshire	64 043	54 884	484	8 675	62 847	53 154	724	8 969	54 114	702	9 511
New Jersey	343 029	293 162	6 512	43 355	335 480	286 020	6 588	42 872	284 552	6 611	42 668
New Mexico	101 460	88 301	649	12 510	101 881	88 643	625	12 613	88 793	635	12 977
New York	1 062 024	865 052	27 393	170 479	1 057 841	856 719	27 707	173 415	841 352	27 783	172 431
North Carolina	371 280	331 937	6 196	33 147	369 386	327 812	6 525	35 049	329 893	6 663	35 474
North Dakota	40 316	37 226	497	2 593	40 184	37 016	483	2 685	37 183	447	2 769
Ohio	562 402	484 422	12 304	65 676	549 304	471 266	12 321	65 717	461 524	12 500	66 251
Oklahoma	183 342	157 413	3 349	22 580	185 174	159 288	3 582	22 304	154 949	3 481	22 246
Oregon	165 834	146 370	4 013	15 451	164 447	144 583	3 559	16 305	147 444	3 653	16 048
Pennsylvania	621 228	524 312	15 190	81 726	611 174	513 257	15 462	82 455	520 371	15 626	81 762
Rhode Island	77 407	67 598	324	9 485	74 718	64 743	655	9 320	64 072	820	9 208
South Carolina	174 302	149 183	2 470	22 649	173 070	148 120	2 369	22 581	148 808	2 423	22 894
South Dakota	38 166	33 573	516	4 077	37 764	33 281	512	3 971	32 160	637	3 898
Tennessee	244 936	214 249	5 451	25 236	242 966	211 374	5 766	25 826	213 842	5 619	26 501
Texas	942 178	822 359	17 017	102 802	954 495	832 145	19 194	103 156	830 381	19 463	102 681
Utah	138 139	125 984	1 247	10 908	146 196	132 211	1 250	12 735	134 319	1 253	11 752
Vermont	36 415	31 228	885	4 302	35 409	30 459	898	4 052	30 488	890	3 687
Virginia	348 535	296 858	6 396	45 281	354 149	300 598	6 419	47 132	300 612	6 461	48 846
Washington	279 845	254 630	3 285	21 930	284 662	257 746	3 307	23 609	259 928	3 596	22 295
West Virginia	88 852	75 138	1 413	12 301	87 741	74 844	1 384	11 513	73 845	1 397	10 792
Wisconsin	309 036	274 280	3 509	31 247	303 861	269 548	3 568	30 745	267 273	3 605	29 345
Wyoming	30 702	27 713	224	2 765	30 682	27 771	232	2 679	27 620	225	2 331

See footnotes at end of table.

Table C-50.   Total Fall Enrollment in Institutions of Higher Education, by Level of Enrollment and State: 1993 to 1995
— Continued

State	Fall 1993[1]				Fall 1994[1]				Fall 1995[2]		
	Total	Under-graduate	First professional	Graduate	Total	Under-graduate	First professional	Graduate	Under-graduate	First professional	Graduate
U.S. Service Schools	52 998	48 016	663	4 319	51 939	47 202	659	4 078	83 620	668	4 163
Outlying areas	172 989	158 854	3 256	10 879	170 686	155 093	2 691	12 902	168 107	2 890	12 660
American Samoa	1 264	1 264	(NA)	(NA)	1 249	1 249	(NA)	(NA)	1 232	(NA)	(NA)
Federated States of Micronesia	1 148	1 148	(NA)	(NA)	1 374	1 374	(NA)	(NA)	1 296	(NA)	(NA)
Guam	5 843	5 522	(NA)	321	6 449	6 052	(NA)	397	5 644	(NA)	366
Marshall Islands	386	386	(NA)	(NA)	424	424	(NA)	(NA)	418	(NA)	(NA)
Northern Marianas ...	1 261	1 261	(NA)	(NA)	1 253	1 253	(NA)	(NA)	959	(NA)	(NA)
Palau	436	436	(NA)	(NA)	403	403	(NA)	(NA)	351	(NA)	(NA)
Puerto Rico	159 709	146 164	3 256	10 289	156 439	141 543	2 691	12 205	155 430	2 890	12 017
Virgin Islands	2 942	2 673	(NA)	269	3 095	2 795	(NA)	300	2 777	(NA)	277

SOURCE: U.S. Department of Education, National Center for Education Statistics, Integrated Postsecondary Education Data System (IPEDS), 'Fall Enrollment' surveys. Published as table 197 in *Digest of Education Statistics* 1997.

1. Revised from previously published data.
2. Preliminary data.

(NA) Not applicable or not available.

Table C-51. Total Fall Enrollment in Institutions of Higher Education, by Control, Level of Enrollment, and State: 1995 [1]

State	Public					Private				
	Undergraduate			First professional	Graduate	Undergraduate			First professional	Graduate
	Total	4-year	2-year			Total	4-year	2-year		
United States	9 903 626	4 626 228	5 277 398	115 072	1 073 676	2 328 093	2 113 393	214 700	182 520	658 794
Alabama	179 073	102 416	76 657	2 282	21 810	18 977	18 479	498	1 857	1 613
Alaska	26 878	26 066	812	(NA)	1 490	779	575	204	(NA)	201
Arizona	228 108	75 296	152 812	1 561	24 861	14 005	13 116	889	(NA)	5 446
Arkansas	77 654	53 396	24 258	1 702	7 711	10 806	10 360	446	(NA)	307
California	1 461 528	387 529	1 073 999	7 866	94 836	144 297	130 240	14 057	27 681	80 834
Colorado	179 961	102 265	77 696	1 784	28 567	21 044	17 421	3 623	1 346	10 037
Connecticut	84 780	41 952	42 828	1 161	14 598	39 283	37 721	1 562	2 255	15 618
Delaware	32 707	21 043	11 664	(NA)	3 497	5 470	5 470	(NA)	1 289	1 344
District of Columbia	9 179	9 179	(NA)	(NA)	484	34 186	34 186	(NA)	9 068	24 360
Florida	486 639	162 993	323 646	3 411	40 557	77 996	72 565	5 431	5 873	22 827
Georgia	217 773	129 516	88 257	3 076	27 833	50 127	45 577	4 550	6 984	8 919
Hawaii	43 651	16 798	26 853	453	6 094	11 250	11 250	(NA)	45	1 705
Idaho	41 777	34 240	7 537	529	6 680	10 201	1 929	8 272	(NA)	379
Illinois	479 731	142 015	337 716	4 397	46 120	122 014	117 744	4 270	12 971	52 621
Indiana	193 364	152 753	40 611	3 529	27 902	56 483	52 994	3 489	1 810	6 527
Iowa	106 854	50 299	56 555	2 811	12 731	44 228	43 113	1 115	3 757	3 454
Kansas	140 376	66 697	73 679	2 005	18 068	15 476	14 598	878	69	1 649
Kentucky	128 633	85 354	43 279	2 990	17 185	25 207	22 539	2 668	1 657	3 186
Louisiana	151 350	124 397	26 953	2 631	20 892	20 591	19 413	1 178	3 498	4 973
Maine	34 057	27 137	6 920	286	3 852	15 673	13 758	1 915	395	2 284
Maryland	194 618	85 499	109 119	3 593	24 646	23 918	22 732	1 186	817	18 718
Massachusetts	157 775	82 812	74 963	423	18 579	161 766	153 713	8 053	13 027	62 224
Michigan	397 593	194 199	203 394	6 615	58 182	72 900	70 255	2 645	4 104	8 945
Minnesota	198 113	98 052	100 061	2 612	16 524	43 935	39 778	4 157	3 473	16 159
Mississippi	99 430	47 677	51 753	1 212	9 958	9 868	9 056	812	547	1 675
Missouri	169 460	97 338	72 122	2 441	18 092	73 416	68 819	4 597	6 929	21 198
Montana	34 020	27 997	6 023	236	3 179	5 093	4 173	920	(NA)	146
Nebraska	83 346	45 828	37 518	1 345	10 908	16 761	16 217	544	1 820	1 538
Nevada	59 581	23 729	35 852	211	6 891	817	790	27	(NA)	326
New Hampshire	32 122	22 550	9 572	(NA)	3 947	21 992	17 961	4 031	702	5 564
New Jersey	240 280	107 040	133 240	3 593	27 196	44 272	39 555	4 717	3 018	15 472
New Mexico	84 537	37 136	47 401	635	12 048	4 256	3 302	954	(NA)	929
New York	523 666	270 903	252 763	4 760	60 065	317 686	289 676	28 010	23 023	112 366
North Carolina	272 390	126 705	145 685	2 604	28 105	57 503	56 020	1 483	4 059	7 369
North Dakota	33 726	25 312	8 414	447	2 637	3 457	3 202	255	(NA)	132
Ohio	355 683	208 332	147 351	7 722	46 413	105 841	92 499	13 342	4 778	19 838
Oklahoma	137 601	74 962	62 639	2 045	18 380	17 348	15 319	2 029	1 436	3 866
Oregon	130 049	49 488	80 561	1 200	12 368	17 395	17 226	169	2 453	3 680
Pennsylvania	297 548	191 053	106 495	4 416	37 964	222 823	165 261	57 562	11 210	43 798
Rhode Island	33 619	17 730	15 889	15	5 019	30 453	28 027	2 426	805	4 189
South Carolina	125 825	64 932	60 893	1 876	21 005	22 983	21 688	1 295	547	1 889
South Dakota	25 660	25 451	209	533	3 500	6 500	6 267	233	104	398
Tennessee	170 622	92 528	78 094	2 749	19 765	43 220	40 782	2 438	2 870	6 736
Texas	744 492	325 072	419 420	9 829	82 530	85 889	79 939	5 950	9 634	20 151
Utah	101 576	71 104	30 472	785	8 199	32 743	31 484	1 259	468	3 553
Vermont	18 559	13 924	4 635	377	1 534	11 929	11 728	201	513	2 153
Virginia	248 866	120 521	128 345	4 376	39 885	51 746	46 871	4 875	2 085	8 961
Washington	231 917	71 362	160 555	1 831	12 887	28 011	25 777	2 234	1 765	9 408
West Virginia	63 108	56 128	6 980	1 397	10 352	10 737	9 951	786	(NA)	440
Wisconsin	223 287	116 709	106 578	1 827	20 656	43 986	42 277	1 709	1 778	8 689
Wyoming	26 864	8 805	18 059	225	2 331	756	(NA)	756	(NA)	(NA)

See footnotes at end of table.

**Table C-51. Total Fall Enrollment in Institutions of Higher Education, by Control, Level of Enrollment, and State: 1995 [1]
— Continued**

State	Public					Private				
	Undergraduate			First professional	Graduate	Undergraduate			First professional	Graduate
	Total	4-year	2-year			Total	4-year	2-year		
U.S. Service Schools	83 620	14 009	69 611	668	4 163	(NA)	(NA)	(NA)	(NA)	(NA)
Outlying areas	70 515	56 033	14 482	1 114	5 421	97 592	88 697	8 895	1 776	7 239
American Samoa	1 232	(NA)	1 232	(NA)	(NA)	(NA)	(NA)	(NA)	(NA)	(NA)
Federated States of Micronesia	1 296	(NA)	1 296	(NA)	(NA)	(NA)	(NA)	(NA)	(NA)	(NA)
Guam	5 644	3 288	2 356	(NA)	366	(NA)	(NA)	(NA)	(NA)	(NA)
Marshall Islands	418	(NA)	418	(NA)	(NA)	(NA)	(NA)	(NA)	(NA)	(NA)
Northern Marianas ...	959	(NA)	959	(NA)	(NA)	(NA)	(NA)	(NA)	(NA)	(NA)
Palau	351	(NA)	351	(NA)	(NA)	(NA)	(NA)	(NA)	(NA)	(NA)
Puerto Rico	57 838	49 968	7 870	1 114	4 778	97 592	88 697	8 895	1 776	7 239
Virgin Islands	2 777	2 777	(NA)	(NA)	277	(NA)	(NA)	(NA)	(NA)	(NA)

SOURCE: U.S. Department of Education, National Center for Education Statistics, Integrated Postsecondary Education Data System (IPEDS), 'Fall Enrollment' surveys. Published as table 198 in *Digest of Education Statistics* 1997.

1. Preliminary data.

(NA) Not applicable or not available.

Table C-52. Full-Time-Equivalent Fall Enrollment in Institutions of Higher Education, by Control, Type of Institution, and State: 1993 to 1995

State	Public 4-year			Public 2-year			Private 4-year			Public 4-year		
	1993[1]	1994[1]	1995[2]	1993	1994	1995[2]	1993	1994	1995[2]	1993	1994	1995[2]
United States	4765983	4749524	4757223	3046411	3034872	2994592	2354938	2387817	2415621	184 083	175 859	167 520
Alabama	105 089	103 200	104 189	56 950	56 255	54 564	19 224	19 485	19 533	1 750	1 231	450
Alaska	18 072	17 810	17 823	253	244	326	1 004	622	588	238	303	167
Arizona	78 324	82 558	83 010	76 627	76 262	76 822	22 320	19 129	16 658	1 077	929	889
Arkansas	55 685	54 540	53 057	14 074	13 281	15 177	9 599	9 666	9 975	951	346	349
California	417 202	413 527	421 100	577 405	575 613	563 047	178 651	199 213	199 346	13 271	12 344	12 886
Colorado	104 399	104 474	104 521	40 444	40 104	40 332	18 942	21 477	21 702	3 867	3 121	3 442
Connecticut	45 083	43 582	43 441	22 805	22 303	21 322	42 414	43 398	43 831	1 163	1 188	1 157
Delaware	20 946	20 982	20 533	6 349	6 529	6 705	5 182	5 232	5 298	(NA)	(NA)	(NA)
District of Columbia	6 583	6 495	5 950	(NA)	(NA)	(NA)	56 151	53 802	55 068	(NA)	(NA)	(NA)
Florida	147 729	155 232	160 046	180 327	179 177	176 817	79 769	80 234	80 301	4 454	4 884	5 123
Georgia	126 594	128 563	132 111	54 825	55 739	56 843	50 329	52 189	55 179	5 685	5 319	4 132
Hawaii	19 311	19 437	19 158	16 025	16 692	16 222	9 287	9 485	9 916	(NA)	(NA)	(NA)
Idaho	31 449	32 237	32 161	5 007	5 218	5 265	2 141	2 252	1 998	8 522	8 280	8 122
Illinois	163 884	161 500	159 900	191 411	190 046	183 337	130 625	141 160	144 744	5 019	5 421	3 784
Indiana	151 282	147 844	146 709	23 954	24 279	23 310	53 004	53 673	54 658	2 953	2 997	2 866
Iowa	58 156	57 556	57 870	39 833	39 735	39 829	40 644	40 905	41 377	1 930	1 212	926
Kansas	73 783	71 257	71 592	36 132	37 568	39 813	12 663	14 166	13 756	819	784	735
Kentucky	88 286	87 211	86 774	30 565	29 039	28 227	22 256	22 331	22 965	4 618	4 153	2 361
Louisiana	123 798	124 883	125 563	17 155	17 595	17 057	23 050	23 195	23 442	602	985	754
Maine	24 035	23 461	22 812	4 593	4 549	4 369	11 545	11 945	12 364	1 506	1 602	1 655
Maryland	85 869	86 578	87 997	59 917	58 471	57 419	28 575	29 393	30 193	870	937	1 032
Massachusetts	79 000	78 686	78 616	48 436	47 035	44 938	184 779	184 199	189 336	9 592	9 506	5 997
Michigan	209 703	205 800	206 495	114 289	108 182	103 720	62 076	61 100	61 116	1 971	1 614	1 728
Minnesota	91 811	89 990	88 696	55 659	67 471	62 765	46 201	47 395	48 406	3 833	3 521	3 263
Mississippi	51 147	50 417	51 561	41 568	40 669	41 384	9 928	9 425	9 400	1 107	960	722
Missouri	97 160	95 401	94 930	44 231	41 935	40 677	69 802	71 773	73 005	5 150	4 934	3 939
Montana	26 678	26 857	27 724	2 992	3 294	4 607	3 556	3 652	3 597	571	529	600
Nebraska	48 511	47 248	47 537	18 634	20 129	19 711	16 285	16 682	16 627	443	338	403
Nevada	21 318	21 963	21 806	13 807	13 855	15 191	559	598	967	25	27	27
New Hampshire	21 763	21 962	21 960	5 316	5 025	5 136	18 876	18 603	18 845	3 108	2 952	3 122
New Jersey	103 462	102 204	103 600	83 472	81 003	81 176	45 114	44 308	44 052	3 435	3 295	3 851
New Mexico	41 227	39 973	39 186	25 099	25 126	25 717	2 214	3 550	3 671	566	651	954
New York	268 270	272 066	265 171	182 769	180 543	175 517	343 641	339 369	339 528	27 827	26 016	25 311
North Carolina	131 718	132 091	132 949	91 489	91 727	91 106	58 064	56 789	60 326	2 538	2 241	1 327
North Dakota	25 257	25 055	25 147	6 592	6 642	6 792	3 094	3 038	3 091	264	242	249
Ohio	228 303	223 580	219 518	92 358	88 888	87 324	95 266	95 994	96 059	10 381	9 586	8 909
Oklahoma	77 877	78 501	77 450	38 250	38 063	37 142	17 652	18 138	17 675	1 948	2 459	1 909
Oregon	52 787	52 916	53 445	46 522	44 748	42 866	19 345	19 949	20 115	182	163	158
Pennsylvania	200 053	198 056	200 590	67 024	64 045	61 233	179 371	179 269	179 812	29 184	28 926	32 634
Rhode Island	18 836	18 015	17 634	8 696	8 524	8 490	29 658	28 720	28 583	2 025	1 930	2 149
South Carolina	71 698	71 132	71 984	37 219	37 571	37 475	21 103	20 849	21 694	1 748	1 343	1 200
South Dakota	26 215	25 822	24 753	171	158	172	5 336	5 384	5 487	128	143	143
Tennessee	94 910	93 976	95 789	47 353	46 958	46 996	43 144	44 083	45 903	2 846	2 425	2 018
Texas	339 313	339 801	337 321	233 900	237 787	237 117	86 388	87 907	91 399	4 875	5 987	5 641
Utah	58 244	61 636	62 683	17 260	18 453	19 369	33 985	33 661	33 170	1 085	1 079	1 146
Vermont	13 415	13 765	13 715	2 479	1 834	1 885	12 729	12 390	12 301	161	163	178
Virginia	136 339	136 115	138 030	68 650	67 688	66 674	42 023	46 742	46 992	3 698	3 744	4 016
Washington	76 501	77 461	78 111	96 449	101 499	103 132	29 432	30 620	30 744	1 988	1 938	2 063
West Virginia	56 628	55 841	55 159	4 840	4 930	4 792	8 860	9 349	9 104	944	846	776
Wisconsin	123 700	122 297	121 755	65 297	59 860	58 958	40 082	41 269	41 724	1 665	1 598	1 501
Wyoming	9 976	10 116	9 752	11 364	11 318	11 430	(NA)	(NA)	(NA)	700	667	756

See footnotes at end of table.

Table C-52. Full-Time-Equivalent Fall Enrollment in Institutions of Higher Education, by Control, Type of Institution, and State: 1993 to 1995 — Continued

State	Public 4-year			Public 2-year			Private 4-year			Public 4-year		
	1993[1]	1994[1]	1995[2]	1993	1994	1995[2]	1993	1994	1995[2]	1993	1994	1995[2]
U.S. Service Schools	18 604	17 854	17 849	19 575	19 413	24 297	(NA)	(NA)	(NA)	(NA)	(NA)	(NA)
Outlying areas	48 931	49 518	54 519	9 021	9 886	11 238	77 146	73 595	81 801	11 393	10 161	7 806
American Samoa	(NA)	(NA)	(NA)	1 007	998	988	(NA)	(NA)	(NA)	(NA)	(NA)	(NA)
Federated States of Micronesia	(NA)	(NA)	(NA)	743	1 040	1 076	(NA)	(NA)	(NA)	(NA)	(NA)	(NA)
Guam	2 908	3 159	2 787	912	1 049	1 032	(NA)	(NA)	(NA)	(NA)	(NA)	(NA)
Marshall Islands	(NA)	(NA)	(NA)	374	254	249	(NA)	(NA)	(NA)	(NA)	(NA)	(NA)
Northern Marianas ...	(NA)	(NA)	(NA)	653	653	625	(NA)	(NA)	(NA)	(NA)	(NA)	(NA)
Palau	(NA)	(NA)	(NA)	377	357	296	(NA)	(NA)	(NA)	(NA)	(NA)	(NA)
Puerto Rico	44 107	44 321	49 679	4 955	5 535	6 972	77 146	73 595	81 801	11 393	10 161	7 806
Virgin Islands	1 916	2 038	2 053	(NA)	(NA)	(NA)	(NA)	(NA)	(NA)	(NA)	(NA)	(NA)

SOURCE: U.S. Department of Education, National Center for Education Statistics, Integrated Postsecondary Education Data System (IPEDS), 'Fall Enrollment' surveys. Published as table 201 in *Digest of Education Statistics* 1997.

1. Revised from previously published data.
2. Preliminary data.

(NA) Not applicable or not available.

Table C-53. Residence and Migration of All Freshmen Students[1] in Institutions of Higher Education, by State: Fall 1994

State	Students enrolled in institutions located in the state[2]	Student residents of state — Attending college in any state[3]	Student residents of state — Attending college in home state[4]	Ratio of students remaining to— Students enrolled (col. 4/ col. 2)	Ratio of students remaining to— Student residents (col.4/ col.3)	Migration of students — Out of (col.3 - column 4)	Migration of students — Into column 2 - column 4	Migration of students — Net (column 8 - column 7)
	2	3	4	5	6	7	8	9
United States	2 111 310	2 074 870	1 746 637	0.83	0.84	328 233	364 673	[5] 36 440
Alabama	41 542	36 857	34 230	0.82	0.93	2 627	7 312	4 685
Alaska	1 761	2 988	1 487	0.84	0.50	1 501	274	-1 227
Arizona	32 753	28 930	26 320	0.80	0.91	2 610	6 433	3 823
Arkansas	16 178	15 728	13 454	0.83	0.86	2 274	2 724	450
California	255 308	254 428	235 856	0.92	0.93	18 572	19 452	880
Colorado	32 113	29 359	24 109	0.75	0.82	5 250	8 004	2 754
Connecticut	21 524	25 887	14 699	0.68	0.57	11 188	6 825	-4 363
Delaware	6 921	5 523	4 074	0.59	0.74	1 449	2 847	1 398
District of Columbia	9 706	3 873	2 339	0.24	0.60	1 534	7 367	5 833
Florida	70 212	67 826	57 316	0.82	0.85	10 510	12 896	2 386
Georgia	58 991	56 829	49 857	0.85	0.88	6 972	9 134	2 162
Hawaii	10 279	10 314	8 320	0.81	0.81	1 994	1 959	-35
Idaho	10 646	9 770	7 738	0.73	0.79	2 032	2 908	876
Illinois	110 396	120 051	102 114	0.92	0.85	17 937	8 282	-9 655
Indiana	48 059	42 524	37 023	0.77	0.87	5 501	11 036	5 535
Iowa	35 229	31 425	27 737	0.79	0.88	3 688	7 492	3 804
Kansas	24 641	22 760	20 340	0.83	0.89	2 420	4 301	1 881
Kentucky	28 604	27 210	24 091	0.84	0.89	3 119	4 513	1 394
Louisiana	30 897	29 129	25 413	0.82	0.87	3 716	5 484	1 768
Maine	8 102	9 325	5 893	0.73	0.63	3 432	2 209	-1 223
Maryland	32 734	35 441	24 962	0.76	0.70	10 479	7 772	-2 707
Massachusetts	65 768	55 975	42 892	0.65	0.77	13 083	22 876	9 793
Michigan	83 446	84 143	76 823	0.92	0.91	7 320	6 623	-697
Minnesota	37 991	38 095	29 384	0.77	0.77	8 711	8 607	-104
Mississippi	25 862	24 510	22 349	0.86	0.91	2 161	3 513	1 352
Missouri	38 302	35 660	29 961	0.78	0.84	5 699	8 341	2 642
Montana	6 819	7 218	5 225	0.77	0.72	1 993	1 594	-399
Nebraska	16 616	16 499	13 883	0.84	0.84	2 616	2 733	117
Nevada	6 939	6 403	4 746	0.68	0.74	1 657	2 193	536
New Hampshire	11 373	9 306	5 569	0.49	0.60	3 737	5 804	2 067
New Jersey	43 063	63 725	39 376	0.91	0.62	24 349	3 687	-20 662
New Mexico	13 864	14 298	12 059	0.87	0.84	2 239	1 805	-434
New York	155 799	157 630	131 641	0.84	0.84	25 989	24 158	-1 831
North Carolina	51 346	42 659	39 256	0.76	0.92	3 403	12 090	8 687
North Dakota	8 122	7 048	5 544	0.68	0.79	1 504	2 578	1 074
Ohio	88 460	86 809	75 746	0.86	0.87	11 063	12 714	1 651
Oklahoma	29 345	28 797	26 032	0.89	0.90	2 765	3 313	548
Oregon	23 321	21 992	18 209	0.78	0.83	3 783	5 112	1 329
Pennsylvania	97 982	91 568	76 826	0.78	0.84	14 742	21 156	6 414
Rhode Island	12 645	7 958	5 524	0.44	0.69	2 434	7 121	4 687
South Carolina	28 532	26 626	23 547	0.83	0.88	3 079	4 985	1 906
South Dakota	6 600	6 038	4 543	0.69	0.75	1 495	2 057	562
Tennessee	33 870	31 499	26 715	0.79	0.85	4 784	7 155	2 371
Texas	127 166	124 774	114 927	0.90	0.92	9 847	12 239	2 392
Utah	24 383	19 396	18 096	0.74	0.93	1 300	6 287	4 987
Vermont	6 132	4 628	2 603	0.42	0.56	2 025	3 529	1 504
Virginia	45 272	41 227	33 012	0.73	0.80	8 215	12 260	4 045
Washington	68 604	65 507	60 346	0.88	0.92	5 161	8 258	3 097
West Virginia	15 799	13 816	11 725	0.74	0.85	2 091	4 074	1 983
Wisconsin	46 479	45 339	39 109	0.84	0.86	6 230	7 370	1 140
Wyoming	4 814	4 646	3 597	0.75	0.77	1 049	1 217	168

See footnotes at end of table.

Table C-53. Residence and Migration of All Freshmen Students[1] in Institutions of Higher Education, by State: Fall 1994 — Continued

State	Students enrolled in institutions located in the state[2]	Student residents of state		Ratio of students remaining to—		Migration of students		
		Attending college in any state[3]	Attending college in home state[4]	Students enrolled (col. 4/ col. 2)	Student residents (col.4/ col.3)	Out of (col.3 - column 4)	Into column 2 - column 4	Net (column 8 - column 7)
	2	3	4	5	6	7	8	9
State unknown[5]	(NA)	24 904	(NA)	(NA)	(NA)	24 904	(NA)	-24 904
Outlying areas	29 493	30 958	28 474	0.97	0.92	2 484	1 019	-1 465
American Samoa	(NA)	53	(NA)	(NA)	(NA)	53	(NA)	-53
Federated States of Micronesia	410	1 322	409	1.00	0.31	913	1	-912
Guam	956	191	14	0.01	0.07	177	942	765
Marshall Islands	22	34	18	0.82	0.53	16	4	-12
Northern Marianas	440	450	440	1.00	0.98	10	(NA)	-10
Palau	13	19	13	1.00	0.68	6	(NA)	-6
Puerto Rico	27 276	28 121	27 221	1.00	0.97	900	55	-845
Virgin Islands	376	768	359	0.95	0.47	409	17	-392
Foreign countries	(NA)	34 975	(NA)	(NA)	(NA)	34 975	(NA)	-34 975

SOURCE: U.S. Department of Education, National Center for Education Statistics, Integrated Postsecondary Education Data System (IPEDS), 'Residence of First-Time Students' survey, 1994. Published as table 203 in *Digest of Education Statistics* 1997.

1. Students who are enrolled at the reporting institution for the first time.
2. All of the new students reported by the institutions in that state; i.e., all in-migrants and 'remaining' students.
3. All students living in a particular state when admitted to an institution in any state. Students may be enrolled in any state.
4. Students who attend institutions in their home state.
5. Includes students coming to U.S. colleges from foreign countries and the outlying areas.
6. Students are reported in 'state unknown' when an institution is unable to determine the student's home state.

NOTE: Data for U.S. Service Schools are included in state totals. Some data revised from previously published figures.

(NA) Not applicable or not available.

Table C-54. Total Fall Enrollment in Institutions of Higher Education, by Race/Ethnicity of Student and by State: 1992 to 1995

| State | 1995[1] | | | | | | | | Minority enrollment, by race/ethnicity | | | |
| | Total | White, non-Hispanic | Percent minority[2] | | | | | Non-resident alien | 1992[3] | 1993[3] | 1994[3] | 1995 |
			Total	Black, non-Hispanic	Hispanic	Asian/ Pacific Islander	American Indian/ Alaskan Native					
United States	14 261 781	10 311 243	3 496 174	1 473 672	1 093 839	797 359	131 304	454 364	22.5	23.5	24.6	25.3
Alabama	225 612	163 372	57 663	52 311	1 718	2 326	1 308	4 577	23.7	24.8	25.5	26.1
Alaska	29 348	23 211	5 534	1 004	796	879	2 855	603	18.3	18.6	18.7	19.3
Arizona	273 981	200 052	66 658	8 776	38 691	8 578	10 613	7 271	22.2	23.8	24.0	25.0
Arkansas	98 180	78 663	17 163	14 432	737	1 121	873	2 354	16.8	17.2	17.1	17.9
California	1 817 042	905 116	832 127	138 218	357 893	314 877	21 139	79 799	40.5	44.0	46.3	47.9
Colorado	242 739	195 023	42 071	8 421	22 483	8 146	3 021	5 645	15.8	16.4	16.9	17.7
Connecticut	157 695	126 335	25 763	11 879	7 735	5 610	539	5 597	14.2	15.1	16.3	16.9
Delaware	44 307	35 299	8 071	6 018	793	1 064	196	937	16.0	16.9	18.0	18.6
District of Columbia	77 277	37 346	31 906	24 429	3 015	4 248	214	8 025	44.0	44.0	45.4	46.1
Florida	637 303	426 419	191 314	83 432	86 064	18 927	2 891	19 570	27.5	28.4	29.5	31.0
Georgia	314 712	215 506	91 064	77 418	4 659	8 143	844	8 142	26.4	27.0	29.0	29.7
Hawaii	63 198	16 781	40 643	1 238	1 362	37 787	256	5 774	69.6	69.9	70.6	70.8
Idaho	59 566	54 535	3 740	390	1 683	874	793	1 291	5.5	6.1	6.1	6.4
Illinois	717 854	509 044	190 803	90 674	58 244	39 477	2 408	18 007	25.6	26.1	26.9	27.3
Indiana	289 615	250 483	30 578	17 980	6 277	5 233	1 088	8 554	9.8	10.2	10.5	10.9
Iowa	173 835	154 375	12 419	4 878	2 792	4 034	715	7 041	6.2	6.6	7.2	7.4
Kansas	177 643	149 727	21 926	9 419	5 856	4 043	2 608	5 990	10.7	11.0	11.5	12.8
Kentucky	178 858	159 762	15 977	12 089	1 150	2 083	655	3 119	8.2	8.6	8.9	9.1
Louisiana	203 935	135 074	62 880	53 002	4 634	4 120	1 124	5 981	29.7	30.2	31.4	31.8
Maine	56 547	53 241	2 712	620	359	875	858	594	4.4	3.3	3.7	4.8
Maryland	266 310	177 612	79 438	57 579	6 209	14 590	1 060	9 260	27.3	28.5	30.0	30.9
Massachusetts	413 794	322 092	67 405	23 079	18 102	24 513	1 711	24 297	14.4	15.2	16.5	17.3
Michigan	548 339	440 026	91 310	59 893	11 593	15 320	4 504	17 003	15.3	16.2	16.8	17.2
Minnesota	280 816	250 123	24 305	7 975	3 985	9 514	2 831	6 388	6.8	7.5	8.0	8.9
Mississippi	122 690	82 685	38 027	35 884	654	1 051	438	1 978	29.8	30.6	31.2	31.5
Missouri	291 536	246 071	38 051	25 493	4 653	6 405	1 500	7 414	12.6	12.9	13.2	13.4
Montana	42 674	36 924	4 729	146	484	337	3 762	1 021	12.9	11.5	11.5	11.4
Nebraska	115 718	104 352	8 784	3 408	2 268	2 216	892	2 582	7.2	7.0	7.4	7.8
Nevada	67 826	51 988	13 929	3 715	5 135	4 004	1 075	1 000	18.7	18.0	19.5	21.1
New Hampshire	64 327	59 885	3 280	1 056	950	1 017	257	1 162	5.4	4.9	4.6	5.2
New Jersey	333 831	230 349	92 089	39 273	30 764	21 105	947	11 393	24.8	25.6	27.4	28.6
New Mexico	102 405	57 229	43 383	2 593	32 067	1 694	7 029	1 793	39.8	40.9	41.8	43.1
New York	1 041 566	690 917	306 102	135 813	99 972	66 543	3 774	44 547	26.9	28.1	29.8	30.7
North Carolina	372 030	277 844	88 486	73 185	4 438	7 074	3 789	5 700	22.6	23.2	24.1	24.2
North Dakota	40 399	35 871	2 968	343	247	302	2 076	1 560	7.3	7.5	7.8	7.6
Ohio	540 275	452 802	71 511	50 853	7 831	10 782	2 045	15 962	12.1	12.7	13.2	13.6
Oklahoma	180 676	137 276	35 256	13 147	4 180	4 092	13 837	8 144	17.7	18.7	19.9	20.4
Oregon	167 145	139 202	21 555	2 980	6 306	9 683	2 586	6 388	10.6	11.6	12.2	13.4
Pennsylvania	617 759	516 552	84 254	51 269	11 171	20 463	1 351	16 953	12.5	12.5	13.2	14.0
Rhode Island	74 100	62 824	8 773	3 200	2 709	2 593	271	2 503	10.2	11.0	11.4	12.3
South Carolina	174 125	127 856	43 352	39 088	1 550	2 232	482	2 917	23.7	23.8	24.7	25.3
South Dakota	36 695	32 509	3 189	293	178	264	2 454	997	7.5	6.8	8.6	8.9
Tennessee	245 962	198 271	42 824	36 165	2 346	3 563	750	4 867	17.1	17.3	17.7	17.8
Texas	952 525	590 137	336 140	93 660	195 377	42 311	4 792	26 248	32.4	33.4	35.1	36.3
Utah	147 324	132 566	9 416	904	3 821	3 088	1 603	5 342	5.9	6.6	6.5	6.6
Vermont	35 065	32 242	2 033	477	481	676	399	790	4.0	3.9	4.8	5.9
Virginia	355 919	264 430	83 662	56 981	8 080	17 231	1 370	7 827	21.3	22.4	23.6	24.0
Washington	285 819	228 386	48 472	10 599	10 197	22 451	5 225	8 961	14.8	15.7	16.9	17.5
West Virginia	86 034	79 347	4 961	3 395	469	900	197	1 726	5.4	5.6	5.9	5.9
Wisconsin	300 223	265 457	27 864	12 670	6 283	6 452	2 459	6 902	8.7	9.1	9.4	9.5
Wyoming	30 176	27 517	2 212	254	1 269	236	453	447	7.3	6.7	6.9	7.4

See footnotes at end of table.

Table C-54. Total Fall Enrollment in Institutions of Higher Education, by Race/Ethnicity of Student and by State: 1992 to 1995 — Continued

| State | 1995[1] | | | | | | | | Minority enrollment, by race/ethnicity | | | |
| | Total | White, non-Hispanic | Percent minority[2] | | | | | Non-resident alien | 1992[3] | 1993[3] | 1994[3] | 1995 |
			Total	Black, non-Hispanic	Hispanic	Asian/ Pacific Islander	American Indian/ Alaskan Native					
U.S. Service Schools ...	88 451	70 537	17 402	11 674	3 129	2 212	387	512	21.1	21.6	22.0	19.8
Outlying areas	183 657	764	181 939	2 647	170 385	8 889	18	954	99.5	99.4	99.5	99.6
American Samoa	1 232	0	1 232	0	0	1 232	0	0	100.0	100.0	100.0	100.0
Federated States of Micronesia	1 296	0	1 295	0	0	1 295	0	1	100.0	100.0	100.0	100.0
Guam	6 010	527	4 978	38	41	4 890	9	505	89.5	89.3	90.0	90.4
Marshall Islands	418	0	407	0	0	407	0	11	100.0	99.7	100.0	100.0
Northern Marianas	959	58	673	0	2	671	0	228	89.5	92.1	92.3	92.1
Palau	351	0	351	0	0	351	0	0	100.0	100.0	100.0	100.0
Puerto Rico	170 337	20	170 252	12	170 224	11	5	65	100.0	99.9	100.0	100.0
Virgin Islands	3 054	159	2 751	2 597	118	32	4	144	91.3	91.7	92.5	94.5

SOURCE: U.S. Department of Education, National Center for Education Statistics, Integrated Postsecondary Education Data System (IPEDS), 'Fall Enrollment' surveys. Published as table 210 in *Digest of Education Statistics* 1997.

1. Preliminary data.
2. Percent minority based on U.S. citizen enrollment (total enrollment less enrollment of nonresident aliens).
3. Data revised from previously published figures.

NOTE: Because of adjustments to underreported and nonreported racial/ethnic data, figures are slightly different from corresponding data in other tables.

Table C-55.   Staff and Student/Staff Ratios in Institutions of Higher Education, by Type and Control of Institution and by State: Fall 1993

State	Full-time-equivalent staff				Full-time-equivalent faculty				Full-time-equivalent students per FTE staff				Full-time-equivalent students per FTE faculty				Full-time-equivalent faculty as a percent			
	Public		Private		Public		Private		Public		Private		Public		Private		Public		Private	
	4-year	2-year	4-year	2-year	4-year	2-year	4-year	2-year	4-year	2-year	4-year	2-year	4-year	2-year	4-year	2-year	4-year	2-year	4-year	2-year
United States ..	1 109 789	324 958	637 622	22 312	314 502	156 035	189 227	9 055	4.3	9.4	3.7	8.3	15.2	19.5	12.4	20.3	28.3	48.0	29.7	40.6
Alabama	32 656	5 338	3 947	267	6 878	2 856	1 377	105	3.2	10.7	4.9	6.5	15.3	19.9	14.0	16.7	21.1	53.5	34.9	39.3
Alaska	3 122	29	209	31	991	9	77	11	5.8	(NA)	4.8	7.8	18.2	(NA)	13.1	20.8	31.7	(NA)	36.7	37.5
Arizona	17 912	6 376	1 540	128	4 352	2 820	703	48	4.4	12.0	14.5	8.4	18.0	27.2	31.7	22.3	24.3	44.2	45.7	37.7
Arkansas	14 197	1 520	1 886	70	3 791	717	635	36	3.9	9.3	5.1	13.6	14.7	19.6	15.1	26.4	26.7	47.1	33.7	51.5
California	91 480	46 908	44 282	1 983	29 363	23 003	13 960	731	4.6	12.3	4.0	6.7	14.2	25.1	12.8	18.1	32.1	49.0	31.5	36.9
Colorado	20 415	4 260	3 720	406	7 633	2 184	1 326	176	5.1	9.5	5.1	9.5	13.7	18.5	14.3	22.0	37.4	51.3	35.6	43.2
Connecticut	10 598	2 723	14 722	238	3 092	1 482	4 920	89	4.3	8.4	2.9	4.9	14.6	15.4	8.6	13.1	29.2	54.4	33.4	37.3
Delaware	4 340	786	609	(NA)	992	297	236	(NA)	4.8	8.1	8.5	(NA)	21.1	21.3	21.9	(NA)	22.9	37.9	38.8	(NA)
District of Columbia	1 509	(NA)	26 456	(NA)	601	(NA)	5 605	(NA)	4.4	(NA)	2.1	(NA)	11.0	(NA)	10.0	(NA)	39.8	(NA)	21.2	(NA)
Florida	31 694	22 487	18 174	712	9 067	9 602	5 811	334	4.7	8.0	4.4	6.3	16.3	18.8	13.7	13.3	28.6	42.7	32.0	46.9
Georgia	30 490	7 542	14 352	673	7 593	3 735	4 103	300	4.2	7.3	3.5	8.5	16.7	14.7	12.3	19.0	24.9	49.5	28.6	44.6
Hawaii	4 903	1 505	1 216	(NA)	1 787	771	489	(NA)	3.9	10.6	7.6	(NA)	10.8	20.8	19.0	(NA)	36.5	51.2	40.3	(NA)
Idaho	5 681	640	374	874	2 082	281	171	372	5.5	7.8	5.7	9.7	15.1	17.8	12.5	22.9	36.7	44.0	45.8	42.5
Illinois	43 829	19 673	38 784	703	11 200	9 219	11 439	316	3.7	9.7	3.6	8.3	14.6	20.8	12.2	18.4	25.6	46.9	29.5	44.9
Indiana	33 476	3 711	12 212	240	9 940	1 828	3 749	102	4.5	6.5	4.3	12.3	15.2	13.1	14.1	29.0	29.7	49.3	30.7	42.4
Iowa	16 981	4 645	7 852	270	3 926	1 995	2 772	88	3.4	8.6	5.2	7.2	14.8	20.0	14.7	21.9	23.1	42.9	35.3	32.7
Kansas	15 759	4 739	2 407	185	4 705	2 198	955	73	4.7	7.6	5.3	4.4	15.7	16.4	13.3	11.2	29.9	46.4	39.7	39.6
Kentucky	20 157	2 677	4 457	413	5 833	1 570	1 598	161	4.4	11.4	5.0	11.2	15.1	19.5	13.9	28.7	28.9	58.7	35.8	39.0
Louisiana	16 702	1 509	6 259	66	5 674	853	1 906	31	7.4	11.4	3.7	9.1	21.8	20.1	12.1	19.3	34.0	56.5	30.5	47.1
Maine	5 097	600	2 860	113	1 475	296	822	58	4.7	7.7	4.0	13.3	16.3	15.5	14.1	26.2	28.9	49.4	28.7	51.0
Maryland	19 968	7 671	12 572	155	6 678	3 305	3 524	52	4.3	7.8	2.3	5.6	12.9	18.1	8.1	16.7	33.4	43.1	28.0	33.6
Massachusetts	18 285	5 486	55 034	1 247	5 165	2 617	14 103	495	4.3	8.8	3.4	7.7	15.3	18.5	13.1	19.4	28.2	47.7	25.6	39.7
Michigan	50 871	10 844	10 245	316	13 805	5 212	3 593	118	4.1	10.5	6.1	6.2	15.2	21.9	17.3	16.7	27.1	48.1	35.1	37.4
Minnesota	22 409	5 474	8 693	410	5 527	3 089	3 247	203	4.1	10.2	5.3	9.3	16.6	18.0	14.2	18.9	24.7	56.4	37.4	49.4
Mississippi	14 675	4 682	1 525	168	3 389	2 461	533	60	3.5	8.9	6.5	6.6	15.1	16.9	18.6	18.4	23.1	52.6	35.0	35.8
Missouri	22 494	4 723	18 095	721	7 531	2 211	5 588	321	4.3	9.4	3.9	7.1	12.9	20.0	12.5	16.0	33.5	46.8	30.9	44.5
Montana	4 790	444	668	92	1 550	201	227	33	5.6	6.7	5.3	6.2	17.2	14.9	15.7	17.3	32.4	45.2	34.0	36.0
Nebraska	12 424	2 158	3 904	139	3 291	887	1 421	45	3.9	8.6	4.2	3.2	14.7	21.0	11.5	9.8	26.5	41.1	36.4	32.7
Nevada	3 999	1 598	74	13	1 329	973	21	5	5.3	8.6	7.6	1.9	16.0	14.2	27.3	5.0	33.2	60.9	27.8	38.8
New Hampshire	3 879	834	5 145	265	1 233	548	1 530	102	5.6	6.4	3.7	11.7	17.6	9.7	12.3	30.5	31.8	65.7	29.7	38.4
New Jersey	27 779	8 188	11 854	371	6 914	3 373	3 442	139	3.7	10.2	3.8	9.3	15.0	24.7	13.1	24.6	24.9	41.2	29.0	37.6
New Mexico	12 122	2 992	405	43	2 817	1 309	166	20	3.4	8.4	5.5	13.0	14.6	19.2	13.3	27.7	23.2	43.7	41.0	47.0
New York	53 411	20 521	112 837	2 741	17 549	9 667	30 835	1 142	5.0	8.9	3.0	10.2	15.3	18.9	11.1	24.4	32.9	47.1	27.3	41.7
North Carolina	32 803	14 468	26 042	510	8 428	7 983	5 292	211	4.0	6.3	2.2	5.0	15.6	11.5	11.0	12.0	25.7	55.2	20.3	41.4
North Dakota	5 752	916	373	175	1 911	395	172	36	4.4	7.2	8.3	1.5	13.2	16.7	18.0	7.3	33.2	43.1	46.1	20.6
Ohio	49 726	9 961	19 099	889	13 916	4 847	6 978	432	4.6	9.3	5.0	11.7	16.4	19.1	13.7	24.0	28.0	48.7	36.5	48.6
Oklahoma	15 388	4 367	3 491	635	4 619	1 757	1 260	168	5.1	8.8	5.1	3.1	16.9	21.8	14.0	11.6	30.0	40.2	36.1	26.5
Oregon	15 169	6 836	3 909	23	4 894	3 098	1 533	8	3.5	6.8	4.9	7.9	10.8	15.0	12.6	22.8	32.3	45.3	39.2	34.6
Pennsylvania	51 345	7 583	51 886	3 207	15 180	4 034	16 216	1 131	3.9	8.8	3.5	9.1	13.2	16.6	11.1	25.8	29.6	53.2	31.3	35.3
Rhode Island	3 522	666	7 078	197	1 091	285	1 970	100	5.3	13.0	4.2	(NA)	17.3	30.5	15.1	(NA)	31.0	42.8	27.8	(NA)
South Carolina	19 962	4 985	4 103	217	5 369	2 278	1 362	80	3.6	7.5	5.1	8.1	13.4	16.3	15.5	21.8	26.9	45.7	33.2	37.0
South Dakota	4 181	30	997	24	1 482	13	382	14	6.3	5.8	5.3	5.2	17.7	13.5	14.0	8.9	35.4	42.6	38.3	59.1
Tennessee	22 325	4 728	17 842	348	6 428	2 240	4 330	166	4.3	10.0	2.4	8.2	14.8	21.1	10.0	17.2	28.8	47.4	24.3	47.5
Texas	80 362	28 794	21 879	535	19 876	13 895	6 801	234	4.2	8.1	3.9	9.1	17.1	16.8	12.7	20.8	24.7	48.3	31.1	43.7
Utah	11 894	1 506	4 351	131	3 343	556	1 647	69	4.9	11.5	7.8	8.3	17.4	31.0	20.6	15.7	28.1	36.9	37.9	52.9

See footnotes at end of table.

Table C-55.   Staff and Student/Staff Ratios in Institutions of Higher Education, by Type and Control of Institution and by State: Fall 1993 — Continued

State	Full-time-equivalent staff				Full-time-equivalent faculty				Full-time-equivalent students per FTE staff				Full-time-equivalent students per FTE faculty				Full-time-equivalent faculty as a percent			
	Public		Private		Public		Private		Public		Private		Public		Private		Public		Private	
	4-year	2-year	4-year	2-year	4-year	2-year	4-year	2-year	4-year	2-year	4-year	2-year	4-year	2-year	4-year	2-year	4-year	2-year	4-year	2-year
Vermont	3 437	459	3 069	151	1 131	235	954	99	3.9	5.4	4.1	1.1	11.9	10.5	13.3	1.6	32.9	51.3	31.1	65.0
Virginia	35 868	4 759	10 123	664	9 025	2 015	3 347	322	3.8	14.4	4.2	5.6	15.1	34.1	12.6	11.5	25.2	42.3	33.1	48.5
Washington	24 149	8 823	5 645	215	6 066	4 074	2 374	95	3.2	10.9	5.2	9.2	12.6	23.7	12.4	20.9	25.1	46.2	42.0	44.3
West Virginia	10 454	530	1 623	56	3 744	233	576	17	5.4	9.1	5.5	16.8	15.1	20.8	15.4	54.4	35.8	43.9	35.5	30.8
Wisconsin	26 118	10 643	8 744	130	7 798	5 826	3 153	62	4.7	6.1	4.6	12.8	15.9	11.2	12.7	26.7	29.9	54.7	36.1	48.0
Wyoming	2 848	1 533	(NA)	150	805	700	(NA)	43	3.5	7.4	(NA)	4.7	12.4	16.2	(NA)	16.3	28.3	45.7	(NA)	28.7
U.S. Service Schools	6 383	88	(NA)	(NA)	1 643	(NA)	(NA)	(NA)	2.9	222	(NA)	(NA)	11.3	(NA)	(NA)	(NA)	25.7	(NA)	(NA)	(NA)
Outlying areas	11 297	1 680	6 926	1 206	3 740	684	2 711	438	4.3	5.1	11.1	9.5	13.1	12.6	28.5	26.0	33.1	40.7	39.1	36.3
American Samoa	(NA)	180	(NA)	(NA)	(NA)	98	(NA)	(NA)	(NA)	5.6	(NA)	(NA)	(NA)	10.3	(NA)	(NA)	(NA)	54.4	(NA)	(NA)
Federated States of Micronesia	(NA)	83	(NA)	(NA)	(NA)	42	(NA)	(NA)	(NA)	9.0	(NA)	(NA)	(NA)	17.7	(NA)	(NA)	(NA)	50.6	(NA)	(NA)
Guam	591	325	(NA)	(NA)	222	152	(NA)	(NA)	4.9	2.8	(NA)	(NA)	13.1	6.0	(NA)	(NA)	37.6	46.8	(NA)	(NA)
Marshall Islands	(NA)	31	(NA)	(NA)	(NA)	8	(NA)	(NA)	(NA)	(NA)	(NA)	(NA)	(NA)	(NA)	(NA)	(NA)	(NA)	25.7	(NA)	(NA)
Northern Marianas	(NA)	181	(NA)	(NA)	(NA)	73	(NA)	(NA)	(NA)	3.6	(NA)	(NA)	(NA)	8.9	(NA)	(NA)	(NA)	40.4	(NA)	(NA)
Palau	(NA)	116	(NA)	(NA)	(NA)	43	(NA)	(NA)	(NA)	3.2	(NA)	(NA)	(NA)	8.7	(NA)	(NA)	(NA)	37.2	(NA)	(NA)
Puerto Rico	10 222	764	6 926	1 206	3 397	268	2 711	438	4.3	6.5	11.1	9.5	13.0	18.5	28.5	26.0	33.2	35.0	39.1	36.3
Virgin Islands	484	(NA)	(NA)	(NA)	121	(NA)	(NA)	(NA)	4.0	(NA)	(NA)	(NA)	15.8	(NA)	(NA)	(NA)	25.0	(NA)	(NA)	(NA)

SOURCE: U.S. Department of Education, National Center for Education Statistics, Integrated Postsecondary Education Data System (IPEDS), 'Fall Staff, 1993' and 'Fall Enrollment' surveys. Published as table 224 in *Digest of Education Statistics* 1997.

NOTE: Data include imputations for nonrespondent institutions.

(NA) Not applicable or not available.

Table C-56.   Average Salary of Full-time Instructional Faculty on 9-Month Contracts in Institutions of Higher Education, by Type and Control of Institution and by State: 1995-96

State	All instituitions	Public institutions					Private institutions				
		Total	4-year institutions			2-year	Total	4-year institutions			2-year
			Total	University	Other 4-year			Total	University	Other 4-year	
United States	$49 309	$48 837	$51 172	$55 068	$48 566	$43 295	$50 466	$50 819	$65 405	$44 504	$31 915
Alabama	40 505	41 450	43 580	47 854	40 872	36 364	35 431	35 594	(NA)	35 594	24 809
Alaska	49 036	49 646	49 594	49 685	49 531	56 164	37 489	37 489	(NA)	37 489	(NA)
Arizona	50 841	51 255	52 809	55 301	44 966	48 231	39 682	39 682	(NA)	39 682	(NA)
Arkansas	38 782	39 378	41 299	47 001	39 502	31 125	36 037	36 748	(NA)	36 748	16 052
California	57 716	57 320	60 674	70 350	58 876	52 789	59 328	59 716	74 410	52 233	33 405
Colorado	47 874	47 745	50 262	56 009	45 562	35 652	48 763	48 763	53 584	43 665	(NA)
Connecticut	59 253	59 018	61 635	67 363	56 188	51 143	59 524	60 090	77 086	53 141	33 576
Delaware	55 148	55 378	57 693	59 944	45 399	42 950	53 092	53 092	(NA)	53 092	(NA)
District of Columbia	56 994	51 610	51 610	(NA)	51 610	(NA)	57 758	57 758	59 352	44 266	(NA)
Florida	45 677	45 609	50 487	54 649	47 864	39 594	45 944	46 125	57 361	42 076	27 245
Georgia	45 188	45 297	47 318	52 580	46 014	36 167	44 883	45 385	67 915	39 120	29 695
Hawaii	51 470	51 937	56 477	57 741	48 292	44 244	46 540	46 540	(NA)	46 540	(NA)
Idaho	42 271	42 604	43 446	47 733	41 495	36 646	41 196	37 910	(NA)	37 910	42 721
Illinois	51 065	49 527	49 976	53 824	46 548	48 796	53 818	54 091	71 189	43 184	30 610
Indiana	47 351	47 006	49 176	51 805	43 809	34 662	48 101	48 324	68 842	42 239	29 925
Iowa	46 113	49 686	55 947	58 998	47 591	35 726	40 149	40 109	51 045	38 644	45 578
Kansas	41 497	43 372	46 436	48 886	41 003	35 716	30 603	31 003	(NA)	31 003	24 510
Kentucky	41 791	43 418	46 269	52 345	42 650	33 107	35 949	36 106	(NA)	36 106	27 036
Louisiana	40 689	39 037	39 929	46 288	38 298	31 745	48 104	48 133	54 380	37 270	46 619
Maine	43 075	41 823	43 946	47 438	41 987	33 378	46 393	46 966	(NA)	46 966	28 818
Maryland	49 835	48 994	51 395	57 592	48 264	44 772	52 861	52 923	68 457	45 004	24 267
Massachusetts	56 498	48 720	52 530	60 364	49 430	39 963	60 944	61 270	69 753	52 094	35 083
Michigan	52 555	54 677	55 244	61 133	50 274	52 722	41 843	42 067	44 205	41 805	26 714
Minnesota	46 617	47 873	52 284	62 922	46 711	41 664	43 613	43 803	(NA)	43 803	36 427
Mississippi	39 565	40 004	43 367	45 722	41 882	35 808	36 152	37 077	(NA)	37 077	22 701
Missouri	44 993	45 438	47 125	55 872	45 419	39 479	44 113	44 424	58 456	36 649	33 675
Montana	38 784	39 737	41 120	42 742	37 603	30 952	32 029	31 834	(NA)	31 834	34 981
Nebraska	43 443	44 599	48 000	54 734	43 255	33 692	39 726	39 726	46 658	35 985	(NA)
Nevada	49 235	49 338	52 010	55 724	49 758	43 284	29 688	29 688	(NA)	29 688	(NA)
New Hampshire	48 438	46 856	49 817	52 205	45 604	34 956	50 547	51 242	(NA)	51 242	24 508
New Jersey	60 408	60 796	64 539	73 263	61 394	52 283	59 408	59 540	71 701	49 817	39 947
New Mexico	42 565	42 715	46 635	49 071	39 650	31 257	39 443	39 443	(NA)	39 443	(NA)
New York	55 764	55 594	58 182	62 285	57 527	50 933	55 938	56 393	66 589	49 800	29 601
North Carolina	45 065	46 299	48 732	56 948	45 296	30 638	42 206	42 516	60 020	35 977	32 711
North Dakota	35 303	36 104	37 259	37 983	35 580	31 232	29 709	31 298	(NA)	31 298	22 297
Ohio	48 468	50 008	52 784	54 168	47 857	40 886	45 025	45 134	64 920	42 989	24 138
Oklahoma	40 798	41 046	42 958	48 109	38 836	35 038	39 807	40 286	51 464	35 457	25 039
Oregon	44 272	44 002	45 646	47 983	42 832	42 091	45 278	45 278	(NA)	45 278	(NA)
Pennsylvania	53 987	55 481	56 830	60 944	54 526	48 206	52 196	52 742	69 693	47 251	28 934
Rhode Island	52 805	50 493	53 509	57 683	46 702	41 379	54 585	54 585	(NA)	54 585	(NA)
South Carolina	40 820	41 813	46 655	52 582	40 494	31 510	36 544	36 682	(NA)	36 682	30 294
South Dakota	35 982	37 139	37 274	38 096	36 101	24 834	31 858	31 943	(NA)	31 943	24 000
Tennessee	44 431	44 940	48 112	54 072	46 011	34 743	43 278	43 586	66 150	35 055	27 747
Texas	45 164	44 294	46 992	53 063	41 883	39 331	48 938	49 130	58 942	41 439	24 942
Utah	45 437	43 796	45 919	50 097	39 301	35 147	49 268	49 540	50 420	38 275	33 089
Vermont	43 171	45 068	45 068	48 168	37 379	(NA)	41 430	42 640	(NA)	42 640	20 024
Virginia	47 365	48 405	51 675	56 288	48 691	38 142	43 894	44 204	(NA)	44 204	26 614
Washington	45 703	45 774	51 202	54 727	45 381	38 753	45 421	45 421	(NA)	45 421	(NA)
West Virginia	39 793	40 667	41 323	47 507	38 401	31 816	35 038	35 038	(NA)	35 038	(NA)
Wisconsin	48 332	49 578	51 246	62 321	47 325	47 064	42 805	42 805	54 746	39 066	(NA)
Wyoming	39 998	39 998	47 216	47 216	(NA)	32 766	(NA)	(NA)	(NA)	(NA)	(NA)

See footnotes at end of table.

Table C-56. Average Salary of Full-time Instructional Faculty on 9-Month Contracts in Institutions of Higher Education, by Type and Control of Institution and by State: 1995-96 — Continued

State	All instituitions	Public institutions					Private institutions				
		Total	4-year institutions			2-year	Total	4-year institutions			2-year
			Total	University	Other 4-year			Total	University	Other 4-year	
U.S. Service Schools	$61 758	$61 758	$61 758	(NA)	$61 758	(NA)	(NA)	(NA)	(NA)	(NA)	(NA)
Outlying areas	31 663	33 248	33 796	$34 217	33 495	$31 026	$19 633	$19 633	(NA)	$19 633	(NA)
American Samoa	32 522	32 522	(NA)	(NA)	(NA)	32 522	(NA)	(NA)	(NA)	(NA)	(NA)
Federated States of											
Micronesia	26 884	26 884	(NA)	(NA)	(NA)	26 884	(NA)	(NA)	(NA)	(NA)	(NA)
Guam	47 021	47 021	51 273	(NA)	51 273	42 964	(NA)	(NA)	(NA)	(NA)	(NA)
Marshall Islands	14 722	14 722	(NA)	(NA)	14 722	(NA)	(NA)	(NA)	(NA)	(NA)	(NA)
Northern Marianas ...	32 321	32 321	(NA)	(NA)	(NA)	32 321	(NA)	(NA)	(NA)	(NA)	(NA)
Palau	15 143	15 143	(NA)	(NA)	(NA)	15 143	(NA)	(NA)	(NA)	(NA)	(NA)
Puerto Rico	30 321	32 059	32 334	34 217	30 743	29 577	19 633	19 633	(NA)	19 633	(NA)
Virgin Islands	45 452	45 452	45 452	(NA)	45 452	(NA)	(NA)	(NA)	(NA)	(NA)	(NA)

SOURCE: U.S. Department of Education, National Center for Education Statistics, Integrated Postsecondary Education Data System (IPEDS), 'Salaries, Tenure, and Fringe Benefits of Full-Time Instructional Faculty, 1995-96' survey. Published as table 236 in *Digest of Education Statistics* 1997.

NOTE: Data include imputations for nonrespondent institutions.

(NA) Not applicable or not available.

Table C-57. Institutions of Higher Education and Branches, by Type, Control of Institution, and State: 1995-96

State	Total	Public 4-year institutions						Public 2-year	Private 4-year institutions						Public 2-year
		Total	Research[1]	Doctoral[2]	Masters[3]	Baccalaureate[4]	Other 4-year[5]		Total	Research[1]	Doctoral[2]	Masters[3]	Baccalaureate[4]	Other 4-year[5]	
United States	3 706	608	85	66	278	114	65	1 047	1 636	40	49	293	633	621	415
Alabama	82	18	2	2	13	1	0	35	18	0	0	4	10	4	11
Alaska	9	3	0	1	2	0	0	1	3	0	0	1	1	1	2
Arizona	45	5	2	1	1	0	1	18	18	0	0	2	6	10	4
Arkansas	38	10	1	0	6	2	1	16	10	0	0	1	8	1	2
California	349	31	9	1	19	0	2	107	169	3	9	35	26	96	42
Colorado	59	14	2	3	2	5	2	16	20	0	1	3	4	12	9
Connecticut	42	7	1	0	4	1	1	12	19	1	0	7	6	5	4
Delaware	9	2	1	0	1	0	0	3	4	0	0	2	1	1	0
District of Columbia	18	1	0	0	1	0	0	0	17	3	2	3	1	8	0
Florida	114	9	3	3	3	0	0	29	59	1	2	11	22	23	17
Georgia	120	19	2	1	12	1	3	54	37	1	2	2	21	11	10
Hawaii	17	3	1	0	0	2	0	7	7	0	0	2	1	4	0
Idaho	12	4	1	1	1	1	0	2	4	0	0	0	3	1	2
Illinois	169	12	3	2	7	0	0	49	95	2	3	15	28	47	13
Indiana	78	14	2	3	7	2	0	14	40	1	0	6	22	11	10
Iowa	59	3	2	0	1	0	0	17	36	0	0	5	25	6	3
Kansas	54	10	2	1	4	1	2	21	21	0	0	5	13	3	2
Kentucky	61	8	1	1	6	0	0	14	29	0	0	4	17	8	10
Louisiana	36	14	1	3	9	0	1	6	13	1	0	3	4	5	3
Maine	33	8	0	1	1	5	1	6	13	0	1	1	7	4	6
Maryland	57	13	1	1	9	1	1	20	21	1	0	4	6	10	3
Massachusetts	116	15	1	1	8	2	3	17	73	6	3	12	25	27	11
Michigan	109	15	3	2	10	0	0	30	56	0	2	6	22	26	8
Minnesota	106	11	1	0	6	4	0	51	36	0	1	4	16	15	8
Mississippi	46	9	2	1	3	2	1	22	12	0	0	2	5	5	3
Missouri	101	13	1	3	6	2	1	17	57	2	0	9	18	28	14
Montana	28	6	0	2	3	1	0	13	7	0	0	0	4	3	2
Nebraska	35	7	1	0	4	1	1	11	15	0	0	2	9	4	2
Nevada	10	2	0	1	1	0	0	4	3	0	0	0	1	2	1
New Hampshire	30	5	0	1	2	2	0	7	14	0	2	2	6	4	4
New Jersey	61	14	1	2	7	3	1	19	21	1	2	5	7	6	7
New Mexico	35	6	2	0	3	0	1	18	9	0	0	1	5	3	2
New York	310	42	3	3	19	8	9	47	169	8	9	29	44	79	52
North Carolina	121	16	2	1	9	3	1	58	42	1	1	7	26	7	5
North Dakota	21	6	0	2	1	3	0	9	5	0	0	1	1	3	1
Ohio	156	24	4	6	1	11	2	37	68	1	1	11	32	23	27
Oklahoma	45	14	2	0	6	4	2	15	11	0	1	4	3	3	5
Oregon	45	8	2	1	2	1	2	14	22	0	0	4	9	9	1
Pennsylvania	217	45	3	2	16	21	3	20	101	3	3	19	45	31	51
Rhode Island	12	2	1	0	1	0	0	1	8	1	0	1	2	4	1
South Carolina	59	12	2	0	6	3	1	21	22	0	0	2	17	3	4
South Dakota	21	8	0	1	2	2	3	1	10	0	0	0	8	2	2
Tennessee	76	10	1	3	5	0	1	14	42	1	0	5	24	12	10
Texas	179	40	4	6	22	2	6	67	58	1	3	14	21	19	14
Utah	17	5	2	0	1	2	0	5	4	1	0	2	1	0	3
Vermont	22	5	1	0	2	2	0	1	14	0	0	3	9	2	2
Virginia	89	15	3	3	6	3	0	24	39	0	0	13	19	7	11
Washington	64	8	2	0	5	1	0	29	24	0	0	11	2	11	3
West Virginia	28	13	1	0	1	9	2	3	10	0	0	3	6	1	2
Wisconsin	66	13	2	0	11	0	0	17	31	0	1	5	14	11	5
Wyoming	9	1	1	0	0	0	0	7	0	0	0	0	0	0	1

See footnotes at end of table.

Table C-57. Institutions of Higher Education and Branches, by Type, Control of Institution, and State: 1995-96 — Continued

State	Total	Public 4-year institutions						Public 2-year	Private 4-year institutions						Public 2-year
		Total	Research[1]	Doctoral[2]	Masters[3]	Bacca-laureate[4]	Other 4-year[5]		Total	Research[1]	Doctoral[2]	Masters[3]	Bacca-laureate[4]	Other 4-year[5]	
U.S. Service Schools	11	10	0	0	0	0	10	1	0	0	0	0	0	0	0
Outlying areas	74	13	0	1	4	4	4	14	37	0	0	6	19	12	10
American Samoa	1	0	0	0	0	0	0	1	0	0	0	0	0	0	0
Federated States of Micronesia	2	1	0	0	1	0	0	1	0	0	0	0	0	0	0
Guam	1	0	0	0	0	0	0	1	0	0	0	0	0	0	0
Marshall Islands ..	5	0	0	0	0	0	0	5	0	0	0	0	0	0	0
Northern Marianas	1	0	0	0	0	0	0	1	0	0	0	0	0	0	0
Palau	1	0	0	0	0	0	0	1	0	0	0	0	0	0	0
Puerto Rico	61	10	0	1	1	4	4	4	37	0	0	6	19	12	10
Virgin Islands	2	2	0	0	2	0	0	0	0	0	0	0	0	0	0

SOURCE: U.S. Department of Education, National Center for Education Statistics, Integrated Postsecondary Education Data System (IPEDS), 'Institutional Characteristics, 1995-96' survey. Published as table 242 in *Digest of Education Statistics* 1997.

1. Research instititutions are commited to graduate education through the doctorate, give high priority to research and receive more than $15.5 million in federal research funds annual.
2. Offer a full range of baccalaureate programs and are committed to eduation through the doctorate. They award at least 40 doctoral degrees annually in 5 or more disciplines.
3. Offer a full range of baccalaureate programs and are committed to education through the master's degree. The award at least 20 masters degrees per year.
4. Primarily undergraduate colleges with major emphasis on baccalaureate degrees.
5. Other specialized 4-year institutions awarding degrees primarily in single fields of study, such as medicine, business, fine arts, theology and engineering. Also, includes some institutions which have 4-year programs, but have not reported sufficient data to identify program category.

NOTE: New institutions which do not have sufficient data to report by detailed level are included under 'other 4-year' or 2-year depending on level reported by institution.

Table C-58. Degrees Awarded by Institutions of Higher Education, by Control, Level of Degree, and State: 1994-95

State	Public					Private				
	Associate degrees	Bachelor's degrees	First professional degrees	Master's degrees	Doctor's degrees (Ph.D., Ed.D., etc.)	Associate degrees	Bachelor's degrees	First professional degrees	Master's degrees	Doctor's degrees (Ph.D., Ed.D., etc.)
United States	451 539	776 670	29 871	224 152	28 917	88 152	383 464	45 929	173 477	15 529
Alabama	7 176	16 821	591	5 540	435	659	3 103	372	443	3
Alaska	834	1 428	(NA)	386	19	126	98	(NA)	77	(NA)
Arizona	5 886	13 877	445	4 850	787	923	2 298	(NA)	1 648	(NA)
Arkansas	2 416	7 141	482	1 982	155	76	1 482	(NA)	59	(NA)
California	53 982	83 300	2 200	18 187	2 847	6 521	26 414	6 583	19 878	2 520
Colorado	5 126	16 054	463	4 531	666	1 858	3 875	370	2 580	122
Connecticut	4 009	7 368	310	2 384	265	791	6 604	610	4 035	442
Delaware	934	3 552	(NA)	738	139	207	914	418	364	30
District of Columbia	73	542	(NA)	120	(NA)	132	6 485	2 467	6 487	474
Florida	34 286	30 885	942	8 449	961	6 447	14 039	1 552	6 344	692
Georgia	7 193	19 302	692	6 705	712	1 950	7 010	1 369	1 939	222
Hawaii	2 109	3 156	121	1 070	155	278	1 344	39	450	11
Idaho	1 140	3 870	167	934	80	3 041	365	(NA)	143	(NA)
Illinois	24 273	30 170	1 103	9 858	1 358	2 853	22 100	3 257	13 629	1 492
Indiana	7 918	20 941	948	5 648	1 013	2 145	9 312	537	1 949	139
Iowa	7 608	9 429	554	2 540	667	583	7 992	981	938	19
Kansas	6 482	11 522	572	3 748	450	479	3 072	19	602	(NA)
Kentucky	4 937	11 576	739	3 676	284	1 509	2 994	388	543	113
Louisiana	2 879	14 880	711	3 933	373	490	3 040	969	1 413	126
Maine	1 710	3 491	79	730	40	735	2 402	101	223	2
Maryland	8 186	15 864	808	4 658	587	446	4 044	193	4 333	290
Massachusetts	8 333	12 510	99	3 264	379	4 475	27 769	3 557	18 012	1 904
Michigan	19 578	33 837	1 493	13 720	1 493	3 118	10 480	1 003	1 740	55
Minnesota	8 623	15 996	682	3 508	685	3 593	8 072	856	2 252	204
Mississippi	5 340	8 602	346	2 227	340	179	1 733	146	394	59
Missouri	6 075	15 656	663	3 805	341	2 853	12 275	1 633	6 550	378
Montana	1 162	3 880	78	836	66	167	474	(NA)	21	(NA)
Nebraska	3 014	6 961	368	1 839	249	351	3 144	457	413	6
Nevada	1 379	3 291	54	895	77	32	80	(NA)	2	(NA)
New Hampshire	2 000	3 839	(NA)	684	51	1 530	3 556	193	1 578	61
New Jersey	12 012	18 138	906	4 846	584	843	6 489	764	3 415	469
New Mexico	3 199	5 582	172	2 218	285	78	781	(NA)	220	(NA)
New York	41 340	41 447	1 171	13 560	1 375	13 331	52 102	6 465	31 166	2 599
North Carolina	13 195	22 583	709	5 645	750	912	9 738	987	1 785	272
North Dakota	1 682	3 812	187	595	84	56	628	(NA)	33	(NA)
Ohio	17 030	32 988	1 901	10 421	1 644	3 153	16 600	1 168	4 966	547
Oklahoma	6 568	12 480	602	3 595	347	443	2 827	353	1 333	67
Oregon	5 488	9 219	321	2 705	430	325	3 698	583	1 209	63
Pennsylvania	12 801	31 872	1 200	8 742	1 283	7 768	31 155	2 742	10 895	1 119
Rhode Island	1 579	3 334	4	898	108	2 311	5 644	72	1 143	187
South Carolina	5 435	11 573	539	4 102	365	730	3 603	75	423	26
South Dakota	488	3 474	124	931	58	346	819	13	76	5
Tennessee	5 658	13 209	704	4 366	452	1 063	7 254	732	1 827	213
Texas	23 210	54 752	2 577	17 075	2 355	2 590	15 296	2 198	5 665	372
Utah	5 390	7 757	218	1 663	272	422	6 784	155	1 382	86
Vermont	664	2 323	90	384	53	647	2 268	(NA)	707	1
Virginia	8 941	23 265	1 172	8 381	1 048	1 941	7 841	645	2 325	29
Washington	18 210	16 843	453	3 610	651	892	4 985	456	4 337	36
West Virginia	2 124	7 349	358	2 140	159	716	1 307	(NA)	128	(NA)
Wisconsin	8 396	19 868	526	5 043	833	866	7 075	451	1 403	74
Wyoming	1 491	1 777	70	396	63	172	(NA)	(NA)	(NA)	(NA)

See footnotes at end of table.

Table C-58.   Degrees Awarded by Institutions of Higher Education, by Control, Level of Degree, and State: 1994-95 — Continued

State	Public					Private				
	Associate degrees	Bachelor's degrees	First professio-nal degrees	Master's degrees	Doctor's degrees (Ph.D., Ed.D., etc.)	Associate degrees	Bachelor's degrees	First professio-nal degrees	Master's degrees	Doctor's degrees (Ph.D., Ed.D., etc.)
U.S. Service Schools	11 977	3 284	157	1 391	44	(NA)	(NA)	(NA)	(NA)	(NA)
Outlying areas	2 075	6 417	267	737	32	2 328	7 885	390	1 062	35
American Samoa	419	(NA)	(NA)	(NA)	(NA)	(NA)	(NA)	(NA)	(NA)	(NA)
Federated States of Micronesia	163	(NA)	(NA)	(NA)	(NA)	(NA)	(NA)	(NA)	(NA)	(NA)
Guam	48	295	(NA)	45	(NA)	(NA)	(NA)	(NA)	(NA)	(NA)
Marshall Islands	40	(NA)	(NA)	(NA)	(NA)	(NA)	(NA)	(NA)	(NA)	(NA)
Northern Marianas	180	(NA)	(NA)	(NA)	(NA)	(NA)	(NA)	(NA)	(NA)	(NA)
Palau	21	(NA)	(NA)	(NA)	(NA)	(NA)	(NA)	(NA)	(NA)	(NA)
Puerto Rico	1 148	5 927	267	628	32	2 328	7 885	390	1 062	35
Virgin Islands	56	195	(NA)	64	(NA)	(NA)	(NA)	(NA)	(NA)	(NA)

SOURCE: U.S. Department of Education, National Center for Education Statistics, Integrated Postsecondary Education Data System (IPEDS), 'Completions' survey. Published as table 245 in *Digest of Education Statistics* 1997.

1. Includes degrees which require at least 6 years of college work for completion (including at least 2 years of preprofessional training). See Definitions for details.

NOTE: New institutions which do not have sufficient data to report by detailed level are included under 'other 4-year' or 2-year depending on level reported by institution.

(NA) Not applicable or not available.

Table C-59. Average Undergraduate Tuition and Fees and Room and Board Rates Paid by Students in Institutions of Higher Education, by Control of Institution and by State: 1995-96 and 1996-97

State	Public 4-year, 1995-96		Public 4-year, 1996-97[1]				Private 4-year, 1995-96		Private 4-year, 1996-97[1]				Public 2-year, tuition only (in-state)	
	Total	Tuition (in-state)	Total	Tuition (in-state)	Room	Board	Total	Tuition	Total	Tuition (in-state)	Room	Board	1995-96	1996-97[1]
United States	$7 014	$2 848	$7 331	$2 986	$2 212	$2 133	$17 612	$12 243	$18 476	$12 920	$2 885	$2 670	$1 239	$1 283
Alabama	5 735	2 239	6 008	2 363	1 811	1 834	11 636	7 580	12 182	8 023	1 852	2 307	1 316	1 358
Alaska	6 663	2 488	6 896	2 552	2 407	1 937	12 568	7 996	12 681	8 108	1 843	2 729	2 120	1 850
Arizona	5 996	1 926	6 307	2 009	2 361	1 937	11 290	7 008	12 122	7 811	2 077	2 234	764	782
Arkansas	5 055	2 028	5 398	2 255	1 669	1 474	10 157	6 553	10 764	7 012	1 560	2 193	912	941
California	8 209	2 664	8 324	2 731	3 038	2 556	20 040	13 905	20 987	14 650	3 287	3 050	361	371
Colorado	7 030	2 472	7 319	2 562	2 124	2 632	17 188	11 899	18 329	12 189	2 649	3 491	1 340	1 403
Connecticut	8 755	3 850	9 251	4 105	2 741	2 405	22 954	16 601	23 956	17 495	3 751	2 710	1 646	1 722
Delaware	8 512	4 003	8 896	4 180	2 530	2 185	11 450	7 285	12 800	7 674	2 785	2 341	1 266	1 330
District of Columbia	(NA)	1 118	(NA)	1 502	(NA)	(NA)	21 406	14 734	22 432	15 457	4 140	2 834	(NA)	(NA)
Florida	6 251	1 766	6 574	1 789	2 455	2 330	15 130	10 447	16 020	11 099	2 517	2 403	1 103	1 151
Georgia	5 690	2 104	6 499	2 244	2 138	2 117	15 215	10 221	16 459	10 973	3 060	2 427	1 060	1 110
Hawaii	(NA)	1 578	(NA)	2 298	(NA)	(NA)	11 610	6 230	14 102	6 492	2 950	4 660	524	780
Idaho	5 306	1 678	5 673	1 973	1 585	2 115	15 258	11 806	15 760	12 256	1 374	2 131	991	1 045
Illinois	7 841	3 355	8 192	3 525	2 130	2 538	16 671	11 649	17 649	12 424	2 814	2 412	1 232	1 290
Indiana	7 388	3 038	8 120	3 200	1 993	2 926	16 853	12 621	17 707	13 268	2 052	2 386	1 928	2 331
Iowa	5 945	2 564	6 174	2 655	1 771	1 748	15 878	11 894	16 559	12 394	1 913	2 252	1 785	1 840
Kansas	5 688	2 116	5 898	2 223	1 780	1 894	12 345	8 605	13 052	9 180	1 622	2 250	1 133	1 244
Kentucky	5 454	2 162	5 455	2 241	1 437	1 777	11 267	7 564	12 063	8 134	1 824	2 105	1 124	1 211
Louisiana	5 503	2 221	5 623	2 230	1 506	1 887	17 313	12 081	18 509	13 002	2 778	2 729	1 026	1 054
Maine	7 899	3 424	8 252	3 639	2 286	2 328	22 003	16 338	22 469	16 802	2 780	2 887	2 376	2 558
Maryland	8 731	3 575	9 177	3 848	2 826	2 503	21 076	14 561	22 014	15 365	3 622	3 028	1 969	2 103
Massachusetts	8 770	4 262	9 039	4 266	2 526	2 248	23 353	16 430	24 391	17 248	3 919	3 224	2 361	2 342
Michigan	8 189	3 895	8 648	3 986	2 115	2 546	13 425	9 259	14 037	9 683	2 157	2 196	1 527	1 578
Minnesota	6 734	3 229	7 131	3 539	2 063	1 530	17 177	12 864	17 980	13 633	2 122	2 225	2 050	2 219
Mississippi	5 416	2 459	5 528	2 497	1 482	1 549	9 965	6 835	10 480	7 226	1 656	1 599	941	952
Missouri	6 768	3 024	7 179	3 230	2 152	1 798	14 160	9 611	14 937	10 169	2 303	2 464	1 252	1 283
Montana	7 803	2 369	6 497	2 488	1 856	2 152	11 049	7 540	11 862	8 022	1 661	2 179	1 516	1 600
Nebraska	5 503	2 189	5 722	2 269	1 477	1 976	13 201	9 409	13 808	9 859	1 860	2 089	1 132	1 224
Nevada	7 400	1 686	7 690	1 814	3 191	2 684	(NA)	7 388	13 380	7 780	3 300	2 300	974	1 002
New Hampshire	8 730	4 445	9 126	4 644	2 711	1 770	20 984	14 965	21 447	15 863	3 178	2 406	2 410	2 784
New Jersey	9 118	3 972	9 668	4 269	3 228	2 171	19 753	13 579	20 998	14 388	3 437	3 174	1 880	1 947
New Mexico	5 299	1 940	5 427	2 016	1 528	1 883	14 251	9 717	15 256	10 356	2 322	2 578	674	689
New York	8 971	3 715	9 298	3 797	3 053	2 448	20 910	13 909	21 538	14 559	3 889	3 090	2 426	2 519
North Carolina	5 119	1 641	5 437	1 841	1 802	1 794	15 334	10 916	16 357	11 682	2 221	2 455	581	581
North Dakota	5 641	2 247	5 921	2 381	1 058	2 483	9 924	7 020	10 429	7 419	1 294	1 715	1 697	1 783
Ohio	8 157	3 606	8 480	3 834	2 535	2 111	17 186	12 425	17 914	12 989	2 429	2 496	2 266	2 323
Oklahoma	4 296	1 848	5 079	1 936	1 284	1 859	11 615	7 700	11 525	7 579	1 709	2 237	1 253	1 262
Oregon	7 395	3 246	7 986	3 407	1 890	2 689	18 841	13 856	19 878	14 766	2 387	2 725	1 342	1 524
Pennsylvania	9 138	4 731	9 509	4 994	2 314	2 201	19 894	14 131	20 860	14 908	3 068	2 883	1 906	2 012
Rhode Island	9 453	3 861	9 652	3 907	3 044	2 700	22 015	15 340	22 465	15 644	3 751	3 071	1 726	1 736
South Carolina	6 964	3 096	7 235	3 206	2 109	1 921	13 464	9 669	14 177	10 253	1 900	2 024	1 066	1 114
South Dakota	5 613	2 644	5 831	2 727	1 293	1 811	13 111	9 184	13 749	9 624	1 628	2 497	3 430	3 430
Tennessee	5 373	1 989	5 498	2 051	1 728	1 719	13 953	9 745	14 885	10 387	2 314	2 184	1 022	1 046
Texas	5 471	1 824	5 904	2 022	1 979	1 902	13 022	8 848	13 686	9 385	2 044	2 258	768	788
Utah	5 389	2 006	5 557	2 010	1 527	2 020	7 366	2 940	7 677	3 073	1 436	3 167	1 390	1 392

See footnotes at end of table.

Table C-59.   Average Undergraduate Tuition and Fees and Room and Board Rates Paid by Students in Institutions of Higher Education, by Control of Institution and by State: 1995-96 and 1996-97 — Continued

State	Public 4-year, 1995-96		Public 4-year, 1996-97[1]				Private 4-year, 1995-96		Private 4-year, 1996-97[1]				Public 2-year, tuition only (in-state)	
	Total	Tuition (in-state)	Total	Tuition (in-state)	Room	Board	Total	Tuition	Total	Tuition (in-state)	Room	Board	1995-96	1996-97[1]
Vermont	$10 657	$5 922	$11 366	$6 538	$3 161	$1 667	$21 589	$15 646	$22 748	$16 378	$3 554	$2 816	$2 370	$2 516
Virginia	8 207	3 917	8 451	3 962	2 302	2 187	15 032	10 614	15 761	11 149	2 159	2 453	1 433	1 465
Washington	7 129	2 792	7 313	2 928	2 234	2 151	17 956	13 147	18 597	13 794	2 543	2 261	1 370	1 445
West Virginia	6 119	2 020	6 348	2 088	2 086	2 174	14 412	10 185	15 213	10 805	1 965	2 444	1 319	1 376
Wisconsin	5 839	2 614	6 072	2 747	1 775	1 550	15 732	11 629	16 888	12 492	1 940	2 457	1 835	1 942
Wyoming	5 429	2 005	6 016	2 144	1 596	2 276	(NA)	(NA)	(NA)	(NA)	(NA)	(NA)	948	1 046

SOURCE: U.S. Department of Education, National Center for Education Statistics, Integrated Postsecondary Education Data System (IPEDS), 'Fall Enrollment' and 'Institutional Characteristics' surveys.   Published as table 313 in *Digest of Education Statistics* 1997.

1. Preliminary data based on fall 1995 enrollments.

NOTE: Data are for the entire academic year and are average charges. Tuition and fees were weighted by the number of full-time-equivalent undergraduates in 1995, but are not adjusted to reflect student residency. Room and board are based on full-time students. Because of rounding, details may not add to totals.

(NA) Not applicable or not available.

Table C-60. State Awards for Need-based[1] Undergraduate Scholarship and Grant Programs, by State: 1983-84 to 1995-96

(In millions)

State	1983-84	1985-86	1987-88	1988-89	1989-90	1990-91	1991-92	1992-93[2]	1993-94[2]	1994-95[2]	1995-96[2]	Percent change, 1983-84 to 1995-96[3]
United States	$1 024 206	$1 222 112	$1 377 996	$1 423 743	$1 529 421	$1 658 221	$1 781 820	$1 923 720	$2 195 993	$2 421 952	$2 435 687	138.0
Alabama	1 731	2 242	2 260	2 196	2 984	2 878	2 183	2 271	2 283	2 281	2 142	24.0
Alaska	189	241	240	234	228	464	475	470	454	444	430	128.0
Arizona	2 027	2 401	3 222	3 508	3 420	3 318	2 278	2 437	3 476	3 482	2 291	13.0
Arkansas	2 226	4 108	3 759	3 903	3 946	3 885	4 742	6 319	7 701	8 907	10 765	384.0
California	86 031	112 373	118 819	129 264	153 045	161 642	172 852	151 379	207 969	232 067	235 582	174.0
Colorado	7 341	9 282	9 327	9 395	10 349	11 276	12 380	14 812	16 480	18 252	21 076	187.0
Connecticut	9 371	11 095	14 650	21 149	19 915	20 580	20 595	20 805	20 641	20 690	20 372	117.0
Delaware	548	756	807	829	956	1 066	906	1 121	1 270	1 033	1 188	117.0
District of Columbia	759	1 106	1 106	1 075	1 069	947	978	1 015	1 022	1 022	939	24.0
Florida	12 515	14 819	15 245	16 522	20 134	24 729	29 279	29 628	31 277	36 824	34 822	178.0
Georgia	3 683	4 510	4 599	5 197	4 607	5 070	5 084	4 951	26 853	5 147	4 757	29.0
Hawaii	493	604	563	598	726	612	632	724	748	732	400	1.0
Idaho	378	509	343	348	346	350	483	580	634	779	763	102.0
Illinois	104 384	122 300	135 880	143 373	171 361	183 508	184 753	203 532	214 809	244 352	256 872	146.0
Indiana	20 380	26 448	45 408	35 692	41 874	46 756	[4] 50 441	55 814	55 814	67 742	68 340	235.0
Iowa	20 263	22 379	25 960	30 050	32 467	35 586	34 654	34 067	34 718	35 642	38 953	92.0
Kansas	4 664	5 609	5 337	5 540	6 478	6 462	6 587	6 894	9 060	9 802	9 526	104.0
Kentucky	7 886	8 758	12 161	12 522	12 605	19 866	16 996	20 520	20 619	25 517	26 215	232.0
Louisiana	1 693	2 003	1 880	1 947	2 786	3 827	4 446	5 125	6 374	6 429	6 580	289.0
Maine	477	809	1 418	1 408	1 877	4 802	5 002	5 200	5 170	5 787	6 988	1365.0
Maryland	5 459	6 859	8 737	12 841	14 800	15 607	16 253	20 828	23 713	24 571	30 350	456.0
Massachusetts	25 655	43 466	61 600	62 443	50 844	46 000	23 690	45 989	45 059	61 850	54 565	113.0
Michigan	30 753	57 645	70 099	75 467	70 721	68 918	78 116	75 469	79 735	81 340	84 154	174.0
Minnesota	46 600	45 486	63 300	68 293	58 136	74 656	81 322	83 170	102 920	97 920	92 069	98.0
Mississippi	1 015	1 288	1 230	1 251	1 243	1 136	1 131	1 244	1 255	1 248	1 175	16.0
Missouri	8 766	9 645	8 394	10 234	10 796	11 078	10 142	11 097	11 124	11 913	12 233	40.0
Montana	353	440	419	420	415	383	414	418	401	419	393	11.0
Nebraska	860	1 093	1 094	1 052	1 276	2 192	2 370	2 613	2 686	2 726	3 114	262.0
Nevada	327	414	352	352	[4] 352	321	326	341	342	342	2 595	694.0
New Hampshire ...	536	660	810	886	918	770	825	1 253	840	1 425	765	43.0
New Jersey	47 980	65 173	70 298	76 204	84 347	87 054	100 220	118 868	135 251	159 683	132 383	176.0
New Mexico	695	1 461	4 107	5 024	5 601	6 479	[4] 7 293	8 295	9 266	13 886	14 629	2005.0
New York	327 320	363 949	372 363	355 192	382 655	428 358	504 195	554 803	618 849	636 704	625 711	91.0
North Carolina	3 974	4 440	4 559	4 489	3 046	2 519	2 908	3 163	14 436	13 774	16 659	319.0
North Dakota	635	808	490	976	1 242	1 177	1 475	2 162	2 036	1 996	1 898	199.0
Ohio	41 974	45 000	49 200	50 865	53 848	54 600	57 275	66 000	77 940	91 225	86 053	105.0
Oklahoma	6 561	8 242	10 245	9 861	11 591	11 871	12 612	13 286	13 405	13 325	13 642	108.0
Oregon	8 546	9 514	9 959	10 108	10 092	11 809	12 023	12 606	12 903	13 761	13 651	60.0
Pennsylvania	83 474	96 800	110 992	118 986	132 344	142 389	158 092	173 214	188 751	218 604	232 020	178.0
Rhode Island	6 745	7 856	8 138	8 967	9 917	9 522	9 141	9 586	6 500	6 340	5 741	-15.0
South Carolina	12 588	15 146	16 346	17 810	18 150	17 901	16 800	17 105	16 795	17 297	18 622	48.0
South Dakota	440	624	516	506	504	468	480	587	589	589	562	28.0
Tennessee	6 700	9 434	12 591	11 977	12 977	13 487	12 793	13 723	16 755	18 313	18 811	181.0
Texas	21 438	19 033	22 705	22 266	24 784	24 135	27 385	27 467	29 102	29 102	40 768	90.0
Utah	1 538	1 131	1 133	1 081	1 091	1 001	1 034	1 115	1 132	1 129	1 197	-22.0

See footnotes at end of table.

Table C-60. State Awards for Need-based[1] Undergraduate Scholarship and Grant Programs, by State: 1983-84 to 1995-96 — Continued

(In millions)

State	1983-84	1985-86	1987-88	1988-89	1989-90	1990-91	1991-92	1992-93[2]	1993-94[2]	1994-95[2]	1995-96[2]	Percent change, 1983-84 to 1995-96[3]
Vermont	$7 039	$7 724	$8 414	$9 264	$11 137	$10 184	$11 019	$11 120	$11 167	$11 788	$11 865	69.0
Virginia	4 075	4 415	4 414	8 062	7 966	7 351	4 892	6 654	6 408	53 885	59 568	1362.0
Washington	7 530	8 827	12 425	12 858	13 925	21 095	23 527	23 571	46 617	53 369	56 573	651.0
West Virginia	4 376	5 167	5 189	5 204	5 217	5 559	5 781	5 868	5 802	6 761	8 132	86.0
Wisconsin	23 011	27 816	34 653	35 842	38 072	42 365	42 324	44 216	46 592	49 511	46 470	102.0
Wyoming	204	204	240	212	[4] 241	[4] 212	216	225	250	225	219	7.0

SOURCE: National Association of State Scholarship and Grant Programs, Annual Survey Report, (1983-84 to 1994-95) and National Association of State Student Grant and Aid Programs, Annual Survey Report (1995-96). Published as table 323 in *Digest of Education Statistics* 1997.

1. In 1987-88, 1988-89, 1989-90, 1990-91, 1991-92, 1992-93, 1993-94, 1994-95, and 1995-96 need-based aid to undergraduates comprised 81.0, 78.2, 76.8, 77.4, 74.7, 75.7, 75.7, 77.5, and 84.4 percent of all aid, respectively, compared with non-need-based aid or other types of aid to all undergraduate and graduate students. This table excludes loans.
2. Estimated.
3. Changes may reflect introduction of new programs or discontinuation of existing programs.
4. Data are estimated based on prior year's report.

NOTE: Some data have been revised from previously published figures. Because of rounding, details may not add to totals.

Table C-61.   Current-fund Revenue of Public Institutions of Higher Education, by State: 1980-81 to 1994-95

(In thousands)

State	1980-81	1985-86	1988-89	1989-90	1990-91	1991-92	1992-93	1993-94	1994-95[1]	Percent change, 1989-90 to 1994-95
United States	$43 195 617	$65 004 632	$81 927 371	$88 911 433	$94 904 506	$102 202 890	$108 186 484	$112 968 097	$119 312 493	34.2
Alabama	889 121	1 401 693	1 743 168	1 926 148	2 131 005	2 296 665	2 521 938	2 614 224	2 805 154	45.6
Alaska	159 446	221 837	244 857	270 926	291 826	304 857	323 740	342 624	344 877	27.3
Arizona	719 835	1 049 493	1 353 468	1 483 996	1 596 710	1 655 873	1 677 711	1 834 035	1 931 523	30.2
Arkansas	350 597	539 185	716 105	781 375	818 079	920 699	995 482	1 036 610	1 113 954	42.6
California	5 906 729	8 739 396	11 022 341	11 776 298	12 281 700	13 628 928	14 262 239	13 868 703	14 558 144	23.6
Colorado	747 040	1 085 076	1 371 303	1 390 413	1 483 901	1 594 541	1 714 698	1 803 735	1 914 233	37.7
Connecticut	378 527	578 866	788 194	833 154	889 831	940 067	976 380	1 020 170	1 148 389	37.8
Delaware	168 522	251 677	324 853	354 322	388 635	433 186	446 768	471 017	496 696	40.2
District of Columbia	66 138	84 144	98 240	96 906	95 729	100 038	98 170	99 749	103 770	7.1
Florida	1 202 788	1 810 090	2 510 894	2 812 644	2 944 935	3 049 921	3 202 499	3 411 727	3 584 085	27.4
Georgia	765 826	1 267 472	1 648 753	1 794 990	1 953 866	2 042 825	2 268 331	2 494 263	2 760 323	53.8
Hawaii	219 633	316 246	384 775	433 164	497 495	579 805	594 752	628 043	651 282	50.4
Idaho	169 274	235 507	290 303	320 119	359 710	396 173	416 359	456 107	492 918	54.0
Illinois	1 809 981	2 560 241	3 067 687	3 370 011	3 566 406	3 659 328	3 924 599	4 100 967	4 360 136	29.4
Indiana	1 094 560	1 701 421	2 083 416	2 302 583	2 494 029	2 767 477	2 882 592	3 009 908	3 080 345	33.8
Iowa	784 950	1 109 681	1 529 907	1 653 221	1 775 267	1 827 776	1 930 399	2 014 244	2 106 504	27.4
Kansas	594 104	864 119	1 047 219	1 174 759	1 219 129	1 297 129	1 350 052	1 469 872	1 553 593	32.2
Kentucky	671 414	943 068	1 194 424	1 283 778	1 450 958	1 565 021	1 576 644	1 656 119	1 778 568	38.5
Louisiana	735 374	1 055 941	1 180 464	1 301 127	1 447 772	1 553 258	1 821 190	1 844 187	1 968 669	51.3
Maine	157 370	222 624	317 636	352 024	373 770	375 512	384 730	398 639	400 426	13.7
Maryland	818 850	1 144 230	1 515 369	1 638 822	1 777 841	1 745 479	1 913 029	1 984 038	2 074 521	26.6
Massachusetts	582 873	1 075 348	1 365 350	1 429 770	1 457 142	1 525 943	1 639 854	1 491 921	1 586 319	10.9
Michigan	2 094 394	3 071 172	3 992 084	4 322 956	4 648 488	5 127 892	5 329 224	5 529 883	5 798 882	34.1
Minnesota	894 236	1 373 436	1 880 373	1 916 297	2 080 637	2 261 978	2 363 483	2 494 341	2 671 566	39.4
Mississippi	543 209	734 813	903 637	956 300	1 005 448	1 054 530	1 150 201	1 215 602	1 443 162	50.9
Missouri	717 626	1 032 685	1 289 742	1 416 556	1 517 071	1 566 480	1 698 594	1 805 266	1 978 783	39.7
Montana	123 933	181 462	197 605	227 403	258 189	334 243	349 102	362 905	385 984	69.7
Nebraska	390 372	554 814	699 859	787 282	870 289	941 062	989 156	1 033 731	1 124 836	42.9
Nevada	113 298	184 883	243 208	286 719	336 841	368 245	392 258	412 884	484 276	68.9
New Hampshire	131 000	100 462	255 940	275 121	304 315	324 186	348 839	373 498	391 619	42.3
New Jersey	917 143	1 446 098	2 065 233	2 253 830	2 413 530	2 610 949	2 745 100	2 920 767	3 106 652	37.8
New Mexico	334 392	473 716	786 667	858 989	944 248	1 056 819	1 125 366	1 190 519	1 316 934	53.3
New York	2 519 437	3 830 119	4 772 942	5 014 789	5 424 379	5 616 604	6 117 555	6 574 152	6 887 321	37.3
North Carolina	1 146 931	1 857 124	2 295 295	2 480 396	2 650 124	2 873 684	3 113 193	3 299 213	3 521 601	42.0
North Dakota	196 267	286 550	327 293	365 089	377 960	411 293	431 464	431 381	467 926	28.2
Ohio	1 828 079	2 824 411	3 561 646	3 871 477	4 184 621	4 484 576	4 628 902	4 895 812	4 976 134	28.5
Oklahoma	588 936	873 446	902 463	997 781	1 072 967	1 190 393	1 209 863	1 257 552	1 300 779	30.4
Oregon	647 391	899 709	1 128 211	1 242 595	1 358 244	1 523 505	1 615 882	1 687 205	1 816 031	46.1
Pennsylvania	1 575 104	2 473 794	3 262 178	3 511 535	3 692 745	4 153 483	4 262 533	4 423 633	4 684 460	33.4
Rhode Island	156 451	213 859	270 500	291 376	292 404	308 383	325 003	329 277	344 171	18.1
South Carolina	630 966	957 771	1 216 468	1 333 941	1 502 709	1 629 876	1 733 468	1 924 747	1 997 203	49.7
South Dakota	127 839	147 699	169 210	184 954	198 583	219 751	241 536	260 907	260 853	41.0
Tennessee	675 770	1 104 118	1 435 262	1 556 416	1 634 491	1 672 605	1 839 384	1 961 312	2 053 495	31.9
Texas	2 858 725	4 558 275	5 204 122	5 777 100	6 015 609	6 664 828	7 126 068	7 688 388	8 123 435	40.6
Utah	431 294	686 817	870 334	960 027	1 020 836	1 160 882	1 224 127	1 307 681	1 402 962	46.1
Vermont	127 337	191 559	244 836	267 178	281 526	298 524	305 477	316 905	329 679	23.4
Virginia	1 159 453	1 876 151	2 486 637	2 736 307	2 902 939	3 041 850	3 176 437	3 323 028	3 483 691	27.3
Washington	998 146	1 445 849	1 809 540	1 966 838	2 188 366	2 355 445	2 539 934	2 744 035	2 877 386	46.3
West Virginia	318 915	385 170	447 533	502 436	563 796	608 294	631 619	666 268	693 159	38.0
Wisconsin	1 228 414	1 761 927	2 191 795	2 343 203	2 487 501	2 629 388	2 775 635	2 954 564	3 033 547	29.5
Wyoming	140 520	208 595	224 602	237 093	251 760	271 290	270 515	278 270	293 209	23.7

See footnotes at end of table.

Table C-61. Current-fund Revenue of Public Institutions of Higher Education, by State: 1980-81 to 1994-95 — Continued

(In thousands)

State	1980-81	1985-86	1988-89	1989-90	1990-91	1991-92	1992-93	1993-94	1994-95[1]	Percent change, 1989-90 to 1994-95
U.S. Service Schools[2]	$586 095	$920 790	$993 422	$1 188 896	$1 128 158	$1 181 348	$1 204 411	$1 253 468	$1 248 328	5.0
Outlying areas	242 380	451 734	515 558	573 106	557 655	665 323	704 076	589 470	750 676	31.0
American Samoa	1 305	2 413	3 060	3 585	3 939	4 057	4 428	4 610	4 817	34.3
Federated States of Micronesia	(NA)	(NA)	1 789	1 842	2 063	2 078	3 453	3 932	6 517	253.8
Guam	14 291	31 139	39 282	50 411	61 667	70 658	74 928	68 198	71 873	42.6
Marshall Islands	(NA)	(NA)	(NA)	(NA)	(NA)	3 798	1 111	2 176	1 633	(NA)
Northern Marianas ...	(NA)	1 350	748	791	1 458	1 715	2 462	3 511	12 174	1440.0
Palau	(NA)	(NA)	3 643	4 038	4 100	3 948	5 133	4 762	4 083	1.1
Puerto Rico	213 012	392 194	441 449	487 133	428 768	518 747	581 128	468 739	615 912	26.4
Trust Territory of the Pacific	1 669	5 681	(NA)	(NA)	(NA)	(NA)	(NA)	(NA)	(NA)	(NA)
Virgin Islands	12 103	18 957	25 587	25 307	55 659	60 322	31 432	33 542	33 668	33.0

SOURCE: U.S. Department of Education, National Center for Education Statistics, Higher Education General Information Survey (HEGIS), 'Financial Statistics of Institutions of Higher Education' surveys; and Integrated Postsecondary Education Data System (IPEDS), 'Finance' surveys. Published as table 329 in *Digest of Education Statistics* 1997.

1. Preliminary data.
2. Data revised from previously published figures.

NOTE: Because of rounding, details may not add to totals.

(NA) Not applicable or not available.

Table C-62. Current-fund Revenue of Public Institutions of Higher Education, by Source of Funds and State: 1994-95 [1]

(In thousands)

State	Total	Tuition and fees	Federal appropriations, grants, and contracts[2]	State appropriations, grants, and contracts	Local appropriations, grants, and contracts	Private gifts, grants, and contracts	Endowment income	Auxiliary enterprises	Hospitals	Educational activites and other
United States	$119 312 493	$21 908 104	$13 191 843	$42 854 681	$4 756 884	$4 737 529	$693 313	$11 373 646	$12 527 982	$7 268 511
Alabama	2 805 154	394 846	288 564	932 269	12 827	108 873	20 115	196 402	688 581	162 677
Alaska	344 877	44 282	53 125	183 183	1 484	8 751	4 424	20 965	0	28 663
Arizona	1 931 523	417 437	289 468	677 981	207 387	94 965	4 951	172 181	0	67 154
Arkansas	1 113 954	157 945	88 617	428 995	4 836	28 841	1 561	91 823	262 342	48 995
California	14 558 144	1 925 425	1 488 730	5 136 791	1 436 249	467 666	93 966	977 893	1 786 356	1 245 068
Colorado	1 914 233	529 501	361 312	513 024	31 058	93 448	7 550	242 308	21 697	114 336
Connecticut	1 148 389	240 963	73 453	483 674	3	28 729	29	85 554	188 246	47 738
Delaware	496 696	168 566	45 589	144 038	6 404	18 424	19 594	63 401	0	30 680
District of Columbia	103 770	10 834	7 198	0	76 822	509	745	686	0	6 976
Florida	3 584 085	630 396	334 083	1 945 909	9 406	170 314	451	339 537	0	153 988
Georgia	2 760 323	421 658	259 024	1 353 550	24 990	142 696	3 383	234 879	243 834	76 310
Hawaii	651 282	49 393	118 703	400 248	866	15 809	1 907	55 564	0	8 792
Idaho	492 918	81 763	40 966	233 307	10 199	24 009	8 520	61 439	0	32 540
Illinois	4 360 136	785 264	411 547	1 526 511	415 509	128 261	4 540	439 042	290 289	359 172
Indiana	3 080 345	667 290	245 079	997 241	2 485	131 184	8 592	505 492	337 027	185 956
Iowa	2 106 504	306 259	291 733	644 529	28 206	67 431	1 189	211 661	408 107	147 390
Kansas	1 553 593	270 928	136 406	534 983	123 932	35 890	33 176	126 387	205 404	86 487
Kentucky	1 778 568	308 502	126 816	723 541	6 689	43 558	10 457	140 923	254 025	164 056
Louisiana	1 968 669	361 178	131 191	722 746	4 842	52 884	3 788	215 840	233 197	243 002
Maine	400 426	95 166	37 732	170 016	54	14 937	2 409	52 293	0	27 819
Maryland	2 074 521	533 817	231 506	746 749	135 183	84 204	5 402	245 288	0	92 372
Massachusetts	1 586 319	489 187	146 036	657 970	7 640	47 221	2 901	169 164	6 253	59 947
Michigan	5 798 882	1 324 433	576 638	1 549 814	270 342	280 757	31 474	789 543	693 849	282 031
Minnesota	2 671 566	452 163	281 445	944 101	12 140	204 456	10 967	228 265	349 949	188 079
Mississippi	1 443 162	211 749	167 756	577 021	33 999	41 484	917	154 065	193 866	62 305
Missouri	1 978 783	445 292	116 570	672 581	70 403	77 159	11 273	191 918	225 693	167 896
Montana	385 984	83 962	65 963	127 456	5 349	14 694	260	55 565	0	32 736
Nebraska	1 124 836	143 020	123 956	376 415	55 893	54 094	3 656	116 648	207 068	44 087
Nevada	484 276	74 680	52 260	245 977	6 989	27 855	1 468	46 037	0	29 010
New Hampshire	391 619	158 519	37 003	85 739	2 200	17 933	2 178	72 833	0	15 214
New Jersey	3 106 652	638 453	200 184	1 178 646	166 050	93 456	11 405	236 490	412 290	169 677
New Mexico	1 316 934	111 777	248 072	435 562	45 947	60 926	12 343	91 238	232 906	78 162
New York	6 887 321	1 353 229	511 853	2 936 415	400 559	268 175	16 413	411 486	821 039	168 152
North Carolina	3 521 601	395 357	410 645	1 719 471	80 338	160 493	24 455	568 919	0	161 922
North Dakota	467 926	90 081	69 312	152 737	10 617	9 330	2 647	84 185	13 076	35 941
Ohio	4 976 134	1 316 933	338 914	1 496 777	106 878	210 032	43 812	469 762	772 301	220 725
Oklahoma	1 300 779	212 190	182 377	588 246	16 827	46 596	2 463	206 153	0	45 927
Oregon	1 816 031	310 600	263 044	480 700	108 039	83 535	5 226	166 731	311 672	86 484
Pennsylvania	4 684 460	1 337 745	504 383	1 185 305	86 983	187 252	37 900	476 893	679 862	188 138
Rhode Island	344 171	113 798	40 573	123 733	0	4 928	0	47 155	0	13 984
South Carolina	1 997 203	349 249	177 590	632 927	25 902	73 937	2 718	182 026	492 824	60 029
South Dakota	260 853	61 618	35 396	104 922	17	8 661	1 038	31 226	0	17 974
Tennessee	2 053 495	316 665	177 565	867 689	14 391	91 514	14 222	173 029	304 376	94 043
Texas	8 123 435	1 173 143	833 823	3 444 421	337 615	343 462	140 806	548 766	269 625	1 031 775
Utah	1 402 962	185 596	178 645	414 059	26 961	39 222	10 343	111 192	256 821	180 124
Vermont	329 679	141 177	39 285	47 322	114	26 386	4 785	37 632	0	32 979
Virginia	3 483 691	759 433	304 650	920 807	27 942	169 963	30 181	445 412	755 757	69 546
Washington	2 877 386	512 285	472 037	988 475	19 136	141 288	11 783	353 953	246 295	132 135
West Virginia	693 159	175 146	66 256	326 596	2 012	18 004	0	84 271	0	20 874
Wisconsin	3 033 547	527 641	361 851	945 078	261 078	145 071	16 156	230 519	306 372	239 782
Wyoming	293 209	40 987	37 985	128 346	15 093	20 514	2 768	38 853	0	8 662

See footnotes at end of table.

Table C-62.   Current-fund Revenue of Public Institutions of Higher Education, by Source of Funds and State: 1994-95[1] — Continued

(In thousands)

State	Total	Tuition and fees	Federal appropriations, grants, and contracts[2]	State appropriations, grants, and contracts	Local appropriations, grants, and contracts	Private gifts, grants, and contracts	Endowment income	Auxiliary enterprises	Hospitals	Educational activites and other
U.S. Service Schools	$1 248 328	$583	$1 108 932	$0	$0	$7 667	$0	$74 163	$56 982	$0
Outlying areas	750 676	75 136	65 845	548 747	19 394	8 397	750	12 892	0	19 515
American Samoa	4 817	81	2 114	2 622	0	0	0	0	0	0
Federated States of Micronesia	6 517	3 061	299	50	2 470	70	8	506	0	53
Guam	71 873	6 947	7 095	39 743	11 761	896	509	2 759	0	2 162
Marshall Islands	1 633	521	697	313	0	11	12	67	0	11
Northern Marianas ...	12 174	2 357	3 020	6 388	146	0	0	38	0	225
Palau	4 083	781	522	1 993	0	0	0	598	0	189
Puerto Rico	615 912	56 847	47 348	480 551	2 680	5 807	0	6 148	0	16 532
Virgin Islands	33 668	4 542	4 750	17 087	2 336	1 613	220	2 777	0	343

SOURCE: U.S. Department of Education, National Center for Education Statistics, Integrated Postsecondary Education Data System (IPEDS), 'Finance' survey. Published as table 330 in *Digest of Education Statistics* 1997.

1. Preliminary data.
2. Includes independent operations (federally funded research and development centers).

NOTE: Because of rounding, details may not add to totals.

Table C-63. Current-fund Expenditures of Public Institutions of Higher Education, by State: 1980-81 to 1994-95

(In thousands)

State	1980-81	1985-86	1988-89	1989-90	1990-91	1991-92	1992-93	1993-94	1994-95[1]	Percent change, 1989-90 to 1994-95
United States	$42 279 806	$63 193 853	$78 945 618	$85 770 530	$92 961 093	$98 847 180	$104 570 101	$109 309 541	$115 464 975	34.6
Alabama	839 366	1 324 774	1 669 401	1 831 657	2 054 798	2 189 029	2 428 620	2 510 081	2 648 077	44.6
Alaska	158 700	224 042	240 913	268 057	289 606	306 218	322 620	336 405	336 584	25.6
Arizona	691 481	1 017 203	1 317 954	1 446 388	1 586 891	1 620 019	1 621 716	1 754 682	1 854 180	28.2
Arkansas	340 621	528 831	692 970	751 336	797 291	878 783	976 735	1 002 908	1 070 668	42.5
California	5 775 482	8 515 440	10 182 106	11 230 941	12 023 304	12 910 152	13 537 367	13 244 130	13 899 338	23.8
Colorado	738 363	1 057 558	1 331 091	1 374 188	1 452 137	1 546 642	1 670 921	1 760 679	1 862 438	35.5
Connecticut	367 850	562 696	774 179	811 282	886 846	957 627	981 286	1 026 593	1 134 014	39.8
Delaware	158 332	229 377	314 003	342 119	367 012	396 947	416 699	442 488	469 085	37.1
District of Columbia[2]	71 791	80 764	93 710	99 120	97 556	99 535	98 826	97 072	99 351	(3)
Florida	1 170 305	1 782 180	2 443 879	2 766 267	2 896 046	2 988 794	3 179 353	3 408 957	3 549 470	28.3
Georgia	754 060	1 255 964	1 622 707	1 769 744	1 929 993	2 015 816	2 227 608	2 453 100	2 728 682	54.2
Hawaii	222 718	312 248	379 799	424 473	498 307	575 337	602 346	613 356	653 303	53.9
Idaho	100 044	238 438	289 148	314 398	353 561	391 441	409 167	445 463	473 733	50.7
Illinois	1 780 403	2 571 409	3 015 395	3 310 763	3 528 967	3 644 740	3 877 243	4 053 858	4 293 437	29.7
Indiana	1 064 395	1 602 203	2 005 740	2 186 604	2 391 173	2 643 997	2 671 055	2 858 990	2 967 184	35.7
Iowa	767 590	1 092 542	1 491 442	1 617 626	1 734 476	1 776 217	1 899 159	1 981 068	2 051 631	26.8
Kansas	579 857	848 602	1 028 578	1 131 558	1 190 573	1 262 215	1 329 587	1 429 200	1 495 926	32.2
Kentucky	673 775	898 718	1 143 612	1 236 680	1 400 529	1 514 985	1 516 017	1 577 584	1 663 738	34.5
Louisiana	716 702	1 039 177	1 172 325	1 286 648	1 439 415	1 541 126	1 800 188	1 835 151	1 909 675	48.4
Maine	153 658	216 737	315 700	344 435	355 074	362 905	375 090	387 991	391 269	13.6
Maryland	795 100	1 064 430	1 389 900	1 522 145	1 684 341	1 674 918	1 829 812	1 940 403	1 997 636	31.2
Massachusetts	553 019	980 585	1 306 814	1 357 588	1 435 063	1 474 589	1 605 121	1 496 856	1 557 225	14.7
Michigan	2 053 795	2 946 336	3 745 488	4 076 519	4 416 914	4 741 682	4 925 759	5 095 422	5 395 757	32.4
Minnesota	876 632	1 324 691	1 809 757	1 802 133	2 012 225	2 219 016	2 286 336	2 459 437	2 624 464	45.6
Mississippi	539 222	706 380	864 611	922 574	978 366	1 012 544	1 102 806	1 200 196	1 358 795	47.3
Missouri	687 643	999 869	1 237 603	1 349 451	1 453 608	1 501 166	1 582 746	1 694 484	1 836 878	36.1
Montana	121 894	182 102	198 475	218 231	254 175	320 876	337 189	350 943	376 618	72.6
Nebraska	378 928	537 858	676 527	762 480	848 778	916 814	968 407	1 004 263	1 076 670	41.2
Nevada	111 347	180 107	240 711	281 018	330 592	363 306	377 786	415 785	447 901	59.4
New Hampshire	134 391	183 959	247 686	259 157	281 542	307 217	335 575	360 833	371 554	43.4
New Jersey	903 169	1 406 490	1 968 859	2 165 562	2 309 968	2 489 088	2 630 533	2 809 931	2 982 535	37.7
New Mexico	325 960	456 600	751 405	828 157	896 299	1 010 859	1 069 497	1 142 903	1 278 741	54.4
New York	2 519 104	3 802 602	4 732 811	5 058 750	5 605 621	5 681 964	6 096 863	6 481 594	6 922 118	36.8
North Carolina	1 128 383	1 799 173	2 238 155	2 420 825	2 581 156	2 770 977	3 002 915	3 192 215	3 406 215	40.7
North Dakota	192 046	288 214	319 583	357 832	367 959	408 219	419 268	432 190	456 730	27.6
Ohio	1 784 754	2 718 408	3 494 228	3 726 135	4 084 840	4 359 943	4 389 408	4 640 316	4 907 686	31.7
Oklahoma	583 174	844 829	887 293	973 213	1 057 248	1 158 696	1 177 061	1 214 084	1 263 002	29.8
Oregon	642 411	880 696	1 116 966	1 219 341	1 329 794	1 484 621	1 560 699	1 623 771	1 756 424	44.0
Pennsylvania	1 544 586	2 392 145	3 147 180	3 390 869	3 602 685	3 904 332	4 004 062	4 240 094	4 506 833	32.9
Rhode Island	158 365	213 253	270 411	287 194	292 199	303 606	330 038	331 359	344 457	19.9
South Carolina	617 963	951 848	1 179 216	1 324 647	1 475 074	1 595 552	1 702 419	1 766 671	1 817 631	37.2
South Dakota	124 103	149 092	169 308	184 153	197 853	217 756	240 061	259 120	252 443	37.1
Tennessee	665 885	1 081 052	1 411 226	1 519 680	1 585 614	1 621 202	1 776 066	1 911 953	2 042 171	34.4
Texas	2 736 276	4 375 082	5 166 389	5 604 164	5 959 584	6 370 847	6 982 016	7 414 174	7 817 433	39.5
Utah	405 314	669 714	835 250	914 771	993 625	1 116 845	1 174 239	1 260 797	1 354 017	48.0
Vermont	122 708	188 112	241 314	260 371	274 746	294 045	298 626	306 100	316 455	21.5
Virginia	1 143 755	1 825 156	2 431 539	2 682 902	2 812 109	2 939 683	3 072 851	3 301 020	3 414 167	27.3
Washington	993 171	1 399 780	1 779 855	1 922 673	2 157 074	2 278 549	2 486 455	2 639 504	2 807 168	46.0
West Virginia	317 482	376 293	451 503	493 825	548 802	582 453	609 447	650 642	674 664	36.6
Wisconsin	1 208 396	1 754 395	2 159 069	2 307 325	2 469 260	2 596 853	2 726 350	2 872 001	2 941 034	27.5
Wyoming	126 082	203 307	212 813	227 131	240 216	265 048	260 592	271 396	294 334	29.6

See footnotes at end of table.

Table C-63.   Current-fund Expenditures of Public Institutions of Higher Education, by State: 1980-81 to 1994-95 — Continued

(In thousands)

State	1980-81	1985-86	1988-89	1989-90	1990-91	1991-92	1992-93	1993-94	1994-95[1]	Percent change, 1989-90 to 1994-95
U.S. Service Schools[2]	$592 454	$912 393	$739 019	$805 430	$1 150 209	$1 241 392	$1 267 497	$1 309 330	$1 313 438	63.1
Outlying areas	268 310	451 370	494 087	543 925	516 958	574 988	654 292	662 130	727 524	33.8
American Samoa	1 609	1 092	2 642	2 879	3 187	3 228	3 356	3 416	3 483	21.0
Federated States of Micronesia	(NA)	(NA)	1 789	1 842	3 777	3 765	3 294	3 520	5 056	174.5
Guam	16 100	31 310	38 488	48 954	57 645	67 220	71 917	66 913	81 148	65.8
Marshall Islands	(NA)	(NA)	(NA)	(NA)	(NA)	3 588	1 298	1 527	1 237	(NA)
Northern Marianas ...	(NA)	1 350	950	1 003	2 798	3 194	2 505	3 214	12 366	1133.5
Palau	(NA)	(NA)	3 513	3 870	3 837	3 687	4 485	3 476	3 667	0.0
Puerto Rico	237 319	394 046	424 125	460 897	385 511	434 032	536 917	546 575	586 910	27.3
Trust Territory of the Pacific	1 447	5 992	(NA)	(NA)	(NA)	(NA)	(NA)	(NA)	(NA)	(NA)
Virgin Islands	11 835	17 580	22 580	24 480	60 202	56 274	30 520	33 489	33 656	37.5

SOURCE: U.S. Department of Education, National Center for Education Statistics, Higher Education General Information Survey (HEGIS), 'Financial Statistics of Institutions of Higher Education' surveys; and Integrated Postsecondary Education Data System (IPEDS), 'Finance' surveys. Published as table 346 in *Digest of Education Statistics* 1997.

1. Preliminary data.
2. Data revised from previously published figures.
3. Change of less than .05 percent.

NOTE: Because of rounding, details may not add to totals.

(NA) Not applicable or not available.

Table C-64. Current-fund Expenditures and Educational and General Expenditures of Private Institutions of Higher Education, by State: 1985-86 to 1994-95

(In thousands)

State	Current-fund expenditures					Educational and general expenditures				
	1985-86	1991-92	1992-93	1993-94	1994-95[1]	1985-86	1991-92	1992-93	1993-94	1994-95[1]
United States	$34 341 889	$57 341 982	$60 670 938	$64 041 076	$67 503 635	$25 255 003	$43 012 623	$45 766 989	$48 885 124	$51 984 234
Alabama	186 596	263 052	286 584	299 982	310 329	164 093	229 670	252 259	265 046	273 268
Alaska	10 171	18 454	22 693	23 199	19 825	9 106	15 851	18 687	18 140	15 631
Arizona	52 887	94 564	106 478	118 954	130 973	48 600	86 087	100 150	111 414	122 573
Arkansas	70 755	118 373	124 091	130 253	140 758	56 492	98 442	103 347	108 969	118 323
California	3 644 031	5 957 016	6 171 590	6 419 322	6 841 207	2 275 958	3 836 270	4 051 762	4 366 131	4 630 342
Colorado	160 193	305 244	306 824	327 275	342 407	142 218	269 386	279 956	297 087	312 444
Connecticut	836 949	1 376 756	1 437 827	1 527 283	1 608 612	733 144	1 224 643	1 280 969	1 363 083	1 441 297
Delaware	29 569	27 215	29 293	31 836	32 995	26 501	24 741	26 575	29 040	30 471
District of Columbia	1 307 377	2 100 279	2 307 943	2 386 469	2 533 943	803 566	1 246 366	1 311 616	1 375 811	1 463 154
Florida	723 270	1 386 602	1 510 855	1 561 498	1 672 960	553 391	1 089 712	1 193 708	1 234 246	1 329 012
Georgia	696 734	1 371 887	1 514 055	1 683 308	1 798 384	429 639	886 314	981 355	1 122 545	1 188 358
Hawaii	32 553	41 760	91 016	95 803	100 596	25 323	36 124	72 609	76 909	81 060
Idaho	49 768	82 255	87 532	95 011	98 011	37 736	65 018	72 006	82 923	86 269
Illinois	2 729 672	4 366 966	4 694 688	4 778 173	5 103 123	1 495 654	2 544 490	2 698 324	2 936 263	3 186 567
Indiana	530 163	889 004	941 404	1 000 966	1 073 603	426 813	736 784	782 734	831 223	895 861
Iowa	353 753	595 007	634 046	676 124	701 059	292 291	501 547	534 230	573 136	595 823
Kansas	105 193	147 336	157 139	171 402	180 052	87 719	126 939	136 036	149 127	157 710
Kentucky	194 873	304 780	315 147	330 341	348 262	159 293	255 870	263 722	275 986	291 198
Louisiana	353 433	629 158	673 080	739 368	624 279	221 928	397 191	439 834	459 780	523 694
Maine	133 778	210 328	223 573	238 196	250 032	106 912	176 530	187 523	199 895	210 350
Maryland	896 251	1 550 526	1 622 871	1 729 558	1 797 362	562 773	1 048 953	1 133 491	1 217 678	1 299 953
Massachusetts	3 544 867	5 580 304	5 850 688	6 116 367	6 416 410	2 817 687	4 600 897	4 874 439	5 122 411	5 430 455
Michigan	447 436	738 699	789 175	826 746	855 969	384 533	651 408	696 518	730 458	759 066
Minnesota	521 441	776 325	812 893	800 291	859 388	443 972	654 953	678 472	679 001	732 714
Mississippi	64 054	110 325	115 789	123 506	129 945	55 252	96 217	101 895	108 547	115 582
Missouri	904 573	1 645 969	1 666 001	1 769 749	1 897 323	713 411	1 306 990	1 347 644	1 453 221	1 579 030
Montana	22 349	33 238	39 500	44 193	50 343	18 565	28 567	33 873	38 509	44 086
Nebraska	161 066	269 968	287 540	303 472	319 962	138 929	242 660	258 485	271 942	290 697
Nevada	2 448	5 971	5 490	6 768	8 194	2 448	5 127	4 666	5 998	7 294
New Hampshire	264 440	432 080	455 312	487 785	507 227	230 657	374 323	395 395	426 736	442 671
New Jersey	714 733	1 082 717	1 167 222	1 208 726	1 252 185	540 245	863 322	926 131	980 224	1 022 274
New Mexico	22 196	46 252	33 162	40 520	42 331	19 678	39 813	28 659	35 079	37 509
New York	5 596 257	9 003 453	9 536 982	10 157 945	10 653 695	4 572 405	7 401 300	7 837 705	8 315 046	8 721 147
North Carolina	837 291	1 911 631	2 008 628	2 166 337	2 329 951	592 910	1 255 073	1 313 943	1 417 518	1 515 305
North Dakota	18 853	34 323	33 758	36 380	37 350	15 860	29 719	28 821	31 776	32 912
Ohio	976 303	1 613 085	1 696 377	1 807 756	1 905 659	833 879	1 403 786	1 486 111	1 586 086	1 673 414
Oklahoma	178 905	256 332	266 152	286 118	298 275	149 565	220 403	230 661	248 299	263 719
Oregon	171 604	287 800	307 280	334 424	365 448	149 289	256 162	275 352	299 529	327 566
Pennsylvania	3 155 505	5 452 687	5 667 740	6 008 469	6 246 550	2 033 015	3 521 644	3 802 781	4 115 506	4 386 385
Rhode Island	315 651	559 922	590 911	636 510	667 901	261 616	476 062	504 274	545 057	575 255
South Carolina	196 271	274 300	293 819	318 200	333 278	154 496	225 437	245 689	268 292	282 443
South Dakota	51 675	71 462	63 406	66 315	69 866	44 726	63 351	56 780	59 358	62 863
Tennessee	686 514	1 199 755	1 226 183	1 352 769	1 410 990	440 308	785 347	827 801	894 506	955 718
Texas	993 824	1 633 787	1 716 860	1 833 288	1 955 975	855 445	1 460 510	1 540 238	1 653 269	1 764 618
Utah	183 060	317 586	454 442	458 878	492 298	110 880	257 271	313 342	317 681	333 683

See footnotes at end of table.

Table C-64. Current-fund Expenditures and Educational and General Expenditures of Private Institutions of Higher Education, by State: 1985-86 to 1994-95 — Continued

(In thousands)

State	Current-fund expenditures					Educational and general expenditures				
	1985-86	1991-92	1992-93	1993-94	1994-95[1]	1985-86	1991-92	1992-93	1993-94	1994-95[1]
Vermont	$150 689	$287 261	$300 593	$269 666	$288 223	$126 299	$250 999	$261 364	$232 565	$250 310
Virginia	387 455	706 344	748 902	807 849	874 960	313 055	607 724	645 752	702 430	766 327
Washington	227 211	401 261	435 993	475 565	513 782	189 575	345 756	375 031	413 941	448 823
West Virginia	73 716	114 586	129 367	143 742	172 925	60 900	98 830	112 959	126 231	153 757
Wisconsin	373 533	651 420	702 292	775 629	827 317	326 254	585 465	633 564	701 051	746 036
Wyoming	(NA)	6 578	9 752	12 788	11 142	(NA)	6 578	7 752	10 426	9 219
Outlying areas	198 653	284 662	306 098	337 721	360 203	189 080	267 789	290 189	320 304	343 782
Puerto Rico	198 653	284 662	306 098	337 721	360 203	189 080	267 789	290 189	320 304	343 782

SOURCE: U.S. Department of Education, National Center for Education Statistics, Higher Education General Information Survey (HEGIS), 'Financial Statistics of Institutions of Higher Education' survey; and Integrated Postsecondary Education Data System (IPEDS), 'Finance' surveys. Published as table 348 in *Digest of Education Statistics* 1997.

1. Preliminary data.

NOTE: Because of rounding, details may not add to totals.

(NA) Not applicable or not available.

Table C-65. Participants in Adult Basic and Secondary Education Programs, by Level of Enrollment and State: Fiscal Years 1980, 1990, and 1995

State	1980				1990			1995		
		Level of enrollment				Level of enrollment			Level of enrollment	
	Total	Adult basic education	Adult secondary education	Ungraded	Total	Adult basic education[1]	Adult secondary education	Total	Adult basic education[1]	Adult secondary education
United States	2 018 906	915 936	531 663	571 307	3 535 970	2 435 649	1 100 321	3 875 452	2 948 302	927 150
Alabama	51 599	36 726	12 372	2 501	40 177	32 984	7 193	56 488	45 193	11 295
Alaska	5 667	2 200	2 188	1 279	5 067	4 267	800	7 906	6 203	1 703
Arizona	9 996	9 968	22	6	33 805	24 915	8 890	52 656	40 002	12 654
Arkansas	8 583	7 308	1 275	(NA)	29 065	17 103	11 962	42 457	24 344	18 113
California	267 625	60 385	(NA)	207 240	1 021 227	753 282	267 945	1 088 044	1 057 257	30 787
Colorado	9 381	4 295	2 644	2 442	12 183	9 877	2 306	14 851	11 020	3 831
Connecticut	21 889	8 882	4 805	8 202	46 434	25 560	20 874	26 170	15 766	10 404
Delaware	1 797	1 110	503	184	2 662	2 348	314	3 884	3 391	493
District of Columbia	25 214	4 928	6 502	13 784	19 586	12 631	6 955	9 138	6 656	2 482
Florida	467 162	100 958	184 568	181 636	419 429	249 339	170 090	474 651	302 990	171 661
Georgia	50 820	26 734	17 008	7 078	60 580	40 622	19 950	92 022	64 079	27 943
Hawaii	16 457	16 457	(NA)	(NA)	52 012	31 766	20 246	61 664	36 988	24 676
Idaho	12 851	8 915	3 010	926	11 171	9 180	1 991	9 828	7 467	2 361
Illinois	76 456	59 314	17 142	(NA)	87 121	69 770	17 351	94 808	80 122	14 686
Indiana	20 882	18 127	2 660	95	44 166	27 138	17 028	38 102	26 170	11 932
Iowa	25 851	16 928	5 153	3 770	41 507	30 470	11 037	40 510	28 961	11 549
Kansas	14 405	3 687	7 436	3 282	10 274	9 191	1 083	13 762	10 679	3 083
Kentucky	27 800	6 147	4 735	16 918	28 090	20 406	7 684	30 352	23 207	7 145
Louisiana	16 046	12 608	2 485	953	40 039	20 941	19 098	46 087	24 663	21 424
Maine	5 327	3 029	942	1 356	14 964	6 620	8 344	15 687	7 050	8 637
Maryland	34 572	23 421	6 043	5 108	41 230	36 244	4 986	30 677	21 692	8 985
Massachusetts	20 420	10 241	5 044	5 135	34 220	28 140	6 080	15 014	11 828	3 186
Michigan	40 973	29 945	(NA)	11 028	194 178	80 206	113 972	164 075	69 014	95 061
Minnesota	10 826	8 627	877	1 322	45 648	33 190	12 458	36 350	26 556	9 794
Mississippi	14 317	10 340	2 918	1 059	18 957	15 834	3 123	22 857	17 660	5 197
Missouri	33 292	27 206	3 732	2 354	31 815	27 274	4 541	34 804	29 882	4 922
Montana	3 525	1 795	978	752	6 071	3 962	2 109	6 545	4 044	2 501
Nebraska	7 514	5 152	2 362	(NA)	6 158	5 349	809	7 616	6 974	642
Nevada	3 063	845	82	2 136	17 262	7 270	9 992	16 359	4 556	11 803
New Hampshire	4 844	2 657	1 625	562	7 198	5 073	2 125	6 223	3 309	2 914
New Jersey	35 770	17 152	6 790	11 828	64 080	46 526	17 554	37 500	29 410	8 090
New Mexico	13 102	3 590	5 147	4 365	30 236	18 069	12 167	35 080	20 628	14 452
New York	94 574	57 217	20 002	17 355	156 611	125 893	30 718	209 390	165 892	43 498
North Carolina	84 252	33 854	46 679	3 719	109 740	71 698	38 042	120 945	83 673	37 272
North Dakota	2 810	1 963	538	309	3 587	2 500	1 087	3 270	2 329	941
Ohio	50 056	42 421	7 635	(NA)	95 476	79 527	15 949	110 305	91 221	19 084
Oklahoma	14 701	6 983	5 697	2 021	24 307	19 131	5 176	32 778	26 621	6 157
Oregon	27 645	10 690	12 594	4 361	37 075	24 915	12 160	40 800	22 875	17 925
Pennsylvania	29 477	19 246	6 436	3 795	52 444	40 108	12 336	52 176	37 497	14 679
Rhode Island	5 844	2 266	1 357	2 221	7 347	5 874	1 473	6 182	4 829	1 353
South Carolina	69 659	27 959	35 165	6 535	81 200	37 117	44 083	108 041	46 644	61 397
South Dakota	4 067	2 080	1 109	878	3 184	2 458	726	4 518	3 624	894
Tennessee	26 268	17 079	3 244	5 945	41 721	39 604	2 117	51 054	39 019	12 035
Texas	157 349	94 245	51 126	11 978	218 747	145 067	73 680	207 921	159 983	47 938
Utah	18 541	3 756	14 785	(NA)	24 841	6 003	18 838	30 302	11 147	19 155
Vermont	4 583	3 990	(NA)	593	4 808	4 452	356	4 800	4 434	366
Virginia	21 525	10 480	3 804	7 241	31 649	30 005	1 644	33 786	24 920	8 866
Washington	16 286	7 245	3 894	5 147	31 776	25 336	6 440	44 728	39 061	5 667
West Virginia	14 628	9 743	3 672	1 213	21 186	14 227	[2] 6 959	26 232	18 912	7 320
Wisconsin	16 158	14 185	1 973	(NA)	61 081	45 116	15 965	78 544	60 162	18 382
Wyoming	2 457	857	905	695	3 578	2 071	[2] 1 507	4 370	2 912	1 458

See footnotes at end of table.

Table C-65.   Participants in Adult Basic and Secondary Education Programs, by Level of Enrollment and State: Fiscal Years 1980, 1990, and 1995 — Continued

State	1980				1990			1995		
	Total	Level of enrollment			Total	Level of enrollment		Total	Level of enrollment	
		Adult basic education	Adult secondary education	Ungraded		Adult basic education[1]	Adult secondary education		Adult basic education[1]	Adult secondary education
Outlying areas										
American Samoa	313	252	61	(NA)	(NA)	(NA)	(NA)	(NA)	(NA)	(NA)
Northern Marianas ...	(NA)	(NA)	(NA)	(NA)	(NA)	(NA)	(NA)	430	246	184
Guam	1 346	612	471	263	1 311	414	2	2 034	632	1 402
Puerto Rico	30 164	17 844	9 010	3 310	28 436	28 436	(NA)	68 394	32 943	35 451
Trust Territories of the Pacific	3 753	2 138	699	916	(NA)	(NA)	(NA)	(NA)	(NA)	(NA)
Virgin Islands	3 500	1 002	859	1 639	1 653	1 215	438	2 285	965	1 320

SOURCE: U.S. Department of Education, National Center for Education Statistics, 'Women and Minority Groups Make Up Largest Segment of Adult Basic and Secondary Education Programs;' and Office of Vocational and Adult Education, Division of Adult Education and Literacy,'Adult Education Program Facts, Program Year 1990-1991,' and 'Adult Education Program Facts Program Year 1995-96.' Published as table 355 in *Digest of Education Statistics* 1997.

1. Includes English as a second language.
2. Estimated.

(NA) Not applicable or not available.

Table C-66. Number of Noncollegiate Institutions Offering Postsecondary Education, by Control and State: 1993-94, 1994-95, and 1995-96

State	1993-94			1994-95					1995-96				
	Total	Public	Private	Total	Public	Private			Total	Public	Private		
						Total	Nonprofit	Proprietary			Total	Nonprofit	Proprietary
United States	6 737	527	6 210	6 558	538	6 020	1 214	4 806	6 256	534	5 722	1 171	4 551
Alabama	76	10	66	71	8	63	8	55	63	7	56	7	49
Alaska	32	3	29	31	3	28	5	23	31	3	28	5	23
Arizona	125	4	121	124	4	120	16	104	113	4	109	16	93
Arkansas	82	20	62	76	19	57	9	48	69	16	53	8	45
California	1 126	32	1 094	1 041	35	1 006	230	776	997	35	962	225	737
Colorado	138	8	130	146	8	138	21	117	143	6	137	22	115
Connecticut	100	1	99	105	1	104	21	83	97	2	95	20	75
Delaware	15	1	14	14	1	13	2	11	12	1	11	2	9
District of Columbia	24	1	23	21	1	20	9	11	19	1	18	8	10
Florida	341	40	301	339	40	299	56	243	333	39	294	54	240
Georgia	102	4	98	104	4	100	15	85	101	5	96	16	80
Hawaii	29	1	28	26	1	25	4	21	22	1	21	3	18
Idaho	26	1	25	25	1	24	1	23	24	1	23	1	22
Illinois	304	12	202	285	11	274	56	218	264	10	254	56	198
Indiana	117	8	109	114	7	107	13	94	108	8	100	14	86
Iowa	72	0	72	66	0	66	17	49	62	0	62	16	46
Kansas	62	14	48	62	13	49	11	38	53	10	43	7	36
Kentucky	112	21	91	113	22	91	7	84	105	23	82	6	76
Louisiana	165	49	116	150	49	101	9	92	141	51	90	9	81
Maine	21	0	21	23	0	23	8	15	24	1	23	8	15
Maryland	135	0	135	122	0	122	21	101	112	0	112	20	92
Massachusetts ...	159	13	146	162	12	150	44	106	160	12	148	42	106
Michigan	247	6	241	282	6	276	44	232	264	6	258	43	215
Minnesota	89	14	75	88	5	83	18	65	79	4	75	16	59
Mississippi	52	0	52	49	0	49	4	45	38	0	38	3	35
Missouri	168	30	138	170	31	139	25	114	159	31	128	24	104
Montana	45	5	40	43	4	39	9	30	36	0	36	8	28
Nebraska	50	0	50	51	0	51	8	43	50	0	50	8	42
Nevada	46	0	46	47	0	47	1	46	57	0	57	1	56
New Hampshire	25	0	25	22	0	22	2	20	18	0	18	2	16
New Jersey	176	10	166	166	10	156	37	119	161	12	149	33	116
New Mexico	46	3	43	45	4	41	6	35	38	3	35	6	29
New York	353	15	338	337	26	311	118	193	343	31	312	115	197
North Carolina	81	4	77	81	4	77	8	69	74	4	70	7	63
North Dakota	19	0	19	19	0	19	6	13	17	0	17	5	12
Ohio	312	52	260	303	54	249	60	189	290	55	235	56	179
Oklahoma	95	34	61	111	33	78	5	73	108	33	75	4	71
Oregon	109	0	109	99	0	99	9	90	94	1	93	11	82
Pennsylvania	347	19	328	352	30	322	100	222	345	31	314	103	211
Rhode Island	28	0	28	28	0	28	9	19	29	0	29	9	20
South Carolina ...	60	2	58	56	2	54	11	43	57	1	56	11	45
South Dakota	17	5	12	17	5	12	5	7	16	5	11	4	7
Tennessee	143	30	113	139	29	110	20	90	135	29	106	17	89
Texas	382	6	376	360	7	353	37	316	350	6	344	38	306
Utah	43	6	37	42	6	36	2	34	39	5	34	2	32
Vermont	13	3	10	13	3	10	4	6	10	0	10	4	6
Virginia	148	11	137	144	11	133	32	101	139	12	127	31	96
Washington	111	5	106	107	5	102	13	89	104	5	99	12	87
West Virginia	70	19	51	73	18	55	14	41	71	19	52	13	39
Wisconsin	90	4	86	86	5	81	24	57	74	5	69	20	49
Wyoming	9	1	8	8	0	8	0	8	8	0	8	0	8

See footnotes at end of table.

Table C-66.   Number of Noncollegiate Institutions Offering Postsecondary Education, by Control and State: 1993-94, 1994-95, and 1995-96 — Continued

| State | 1993-94 | | | 1994-95 | | | | | 1995-96 | | | | |
| | Total | Public | Private | Total | Public | Private | | | Total | Public | Private | | |
						Total	Nonprofit	Proprietary			Total	Nonprofit	Proprietary
Outlying areas ...	95	5	90	84	6	78	16	62	84	6	78	14	64
American Samoa	0	0	0	0	0	0	0	0	0	0	0	0	0
Guam	1	0	1	0	0	0	0	0	0	0	0	0	0
Northern Marianas	0	0	0	0	0	0	0	0	0	0	0	0	0
Palau	0	0	0	0	0	0	0	0	0	0	0	0	0
Puerto Rico	94	5	89	84	6	78	16	62	84	6	78	14	64
Virgin Islands	0	0	0	0	0	0	0	0	0	0	0	0	0

SOURCE: U.S. Department of Education, National Center for Education Statistics, Integrated Postsecondary Education Data System (IPEDS), 'Institutional Characteristics' surveys. Published as table 356 in *Digest of Education Statistics* 1997.

Table C-67. U.S. Department of Education Obligations for Major Programs, by State or Other Area: Fiscal Year 1996

(In thousands)

State	Total	Grants for the disadvantaged[1]	Block grants to states for school improvement[2]	School assistance in federally affected areas	Vocational and adult education[4]	Education for the handicapped[5]	Bilingual education[6]	Indian education	Higher and continuing education[7]	Student financial assistance[8]	Public library programs[9]	Rehabilitation services[10]	Goals 2000[11]
United States	$23 169 044	$5 877 908	$1 014 622	$621 707	$1 324 769	$3 144 751	$186 524	$50 180	$1 037 480	$7 275 673	$122 624	$2 191 920	$320 885
Alabama	401 419	104 932	16 386	3 822	25 534	55 413	214	1 205	39 758	99 388	2 343	46 370	6 054
Alaska	115 798	22 498	4 974	50 357	4 984	10 390	1 016	5 715	2 456	4 618	899	7 862	29
Arizona	410 975	87 262	15 136	67 929	20 932	40 807	7 185	5 864	7 282	117 446	1 982	33 596	5 554
Arkansas	221 201	64 679	9 837	889	15 057	29 434	100	101	14 102	57 400	1 328	28 204	69
California	2 517 806	691 965	111 557	52 700	140 435	344 881	66 018	3 494	74 588	765 436	13 004	210 819	42 909
Colorado	254 932	57 264	12 210	6 140	16 096	41 004	2 129	321	11 759	75 903	1 564	26 538	4 004
Connecticut	181 800	45 962	9 703	5 411	12 061	42 656	1 754	21	6 326	39 105	1 660	17 077	66
Delaware	63 584	14 308	4 974	67	5 253	9 124	160	0	4 636	15 357	562	7 874	1 267
District of Columbia	369 884	17 857	4 874	1 515	4 363	4 756	716	0	198 518	123 567	570	11 595	1 552
Florida	979 634	252 802	43 463	11 227	61 095	172 852	8 532	40	26 151	279 772	5 548	103 138	15 014
Georgia	517 636	143 475	25 677	6 058	37 781	71 144	606	0	35 400	123 752	2 790	81 852	9 129
Hawaii	86 306	16 056	4 974	17 414	6 247	10 427	1 550	0	6 736	13 863	1 007	8 005	26
Idaho	102 623	22 888	4 975	3 230	6 904	14 720	747	213	3 351	30 615	650	11 252	3 076
Illinois	864 739	266 003	44 193	9 063	51 880	133 309	5 639	68	31 564	235 991	4 497	82 230	303
Indiana	420 921	92 514	19 058	538	30 439	68 549	301	8	12 979	143 409	2 324	44 122	6 681
Iowa	225 630	42 509	9 446	124	14 669	33 610	615	88	12 268	79 920	1 440	24 582	6 359
Kansas	213 163	49 909	9 092	9 759	12 565	28 661	989	281	10 230	66 239	1 369	20 909	3 160
Kentucky	351 966	109 184	15 497	966	23 672	47 360	275	0	14 596	91 289	1 626	41 842	5 659
Louisiana	476 701	156 947	21 338	5 346	27 048	48 661	2 011	405	25 631	131 605	2 630	47 287	7 793
Maine	102 845	24 459	4 974	2 443	6 495	16 700	743	112	5 203	26 410	899	12 840	1 567
Maryland	319 999	72 257	15 573	8 962	19 462	53 545	1 116	129	18 429	90 689	2 209	32 511	5 118
Massa- chusetts	525 798	103 185	20 499	3 904	23 859	91 048	3 951	61	18 676	202 189	2 522	42 540	13 366
Michigan	762 383	261 032	39 009	5 025	46 088	99 024	990	2 081	24 918	189 009	4 166	77 117	13 926
Minnesota	333 882	69 899	15 731	4 632	20 569	56 709	2 158	1 880	13 750	98 648	2 490	36 874	10 541
Mississippi	316 673	102 740	13 511	3 356	17 571	34 158	100	184	18 073	86 539	1 207	34 041	5 191
Missouri	418 419	98 868	18 601	6 040	26 773	60 645	1 008	35	13 893	129 487	2 152	48 134	12 782
Montana	113 558	21 422	4 974	20 219	5 751	9 946	1 606	1 604	7 064	29 748	685	8 949	1 590
Nebraska	152 432	20 470	5 542	6 728	8 170	19 935	500	342	4 528	60 934	829	14 419	2 024
Nevada	69 984	15 994	5 026	3 047	6 515	15 190	413	409	1 777	10 214	927	9 142	1 330
New Hampshire	73 135	13 604	4 974	986	6 208	13 074	412	0	2 729	20 196	652	8 984	1 315
New Jersey	476 660	118 721	24 258	11 571	29 886	99 695	2 086	97	13 214	120 798	3 103	44 273	8 959
New Mexico	223 086	49 780	7 619	36 628	9 840	24 248	4 303	4 327	8 541	56 231	1 181	17 726	2 663
New York	1 896 975	515 108	71 682	17 716	73 572	214 036	27 341	958	39 106	810 531	7 661	118 750	513
North Carolina	486 613	111 143	22 433	7 820	38 172	77 113	875	1 785	35 211	121 617	2 801	67 496	147
North Dakota ..	92 451	14 559	4 974	14 665	5 278	7 230	1 464	859	4 165	28 220	597	7 813	2 626
Ohio	969 863	247 970	41 853	3 537	55 788	126 415	829	6	21 717	338 348	4 762	99 296	29 341
Oklahoma	317 729	69 293	12 460	18 309	18 847	37 096	7 715	9 493	16 285	88 959	1 600	33 192	4 480
Oregon	216 654	66 750	10 675	2 516	14 935	33 291	2 289	1 071	8 061	45 714	1 430	26 047	3 876
Pennsylvania ..	927 378	258 813	42 383	2 611	54 771	125 741	1 668	0	24 468	310 111	5 196	101 323	294
Rhode Island ..	95 837	17 931	4 974	2 492	6 416	13 187	630	0	2 681	35 950	742	7 965	2 868
South Carolina	317 256	75 967	13 344	5 562	22 092	49 661	129	21	19 326	85 433	2 027	38 894	4 800
South Dakota ..	149 118	16 314	4 974	13 497	5 355	9 196	1 881	1 755	3 628	82 700	513	7 866	1 439
Tennessee	401 598	100 063	18 114	2 067	28 832	63 771	283	0	22 784	106 456	2 231	50 489	6 509
Texas	1 710 624	515 462	77 550	26 965	100 123	223 335	13 402	143	48 108	514 630	6 897	156 266	27 741
Utah	183 397	28 066	7 820	5 934	12 736	30 149	850	592	7 109	67 321	1 023	19 294	2 502

See footnotes at end of table.

Table C-67.   U.S. Department of Education Obligations for Major Programs, by State or Other Area: Fiscal Year 1996 — Continued

(In thousands)

State	Total	Grants for the disadvantaged[1]	Block grants to states for school improvement[2]	School assistance in federally affected areas	Vocational and adult education[4]	Education for the handicapped[5]	Bilingual education[6]	Indian education	Higher and continuing education[7]	Student financial assistance[8]	Public library programs[9]	Rehabilitation services[10]	Goals 2000[11]
Vermont	$68 681	$13 469	$4 974	$10	$5 106	$8 194	$274	$82	$4 259	$22 633	$552	$7 878	$1 250
Virginia	457 917	84 425	19 420	29 334	30 343	73 577	628	10	23 651	143 359	3 014	50 156	0
Washington	400 936	94 508	17 813	21 761	22 930	57 742	2 514	2 597	15 319	120 064	2 176	37 335	6 177
West Virginia	179 339	57 100	7 753	16	11 636	23 449	45	0	8 275	42 450	1 237	21 738	5 641
Wisconsin	409 962	101 937	18 972	6 474	25 106	57 479	981	1 435	16 147	127 609	2 306	44 808	6 707
Wyoming	61 614	13 287	4 974	5 460	4 977	7 562	595	287	3 046	13 002	532	6 605	1 287
Indian tribe setaside	70 234	0	6 763	0	12 311	35 848	0	0	0	0	2 540	10 572	2 200
Undistributed	389 922	22 843	1 120	67 549	2 812	0	0	0	2 138	292 717	7	735	0
Outlying areas													
American Samoa	7 670	0	1 328	0	349	3 096	194	0	614	822	89	819	358
Federated States of Micronesia	852	0	0	0	100	0	450	0	0	0	0	0	302
Guam	16 300	0	3 092	0	720	7 415	510	0	1 577	1 316	124	1 352	195
Marshall Islands	203	0	0	0	100	0	0	0	0	0	0	0	103
Northern Marianas	4 899	0	756	0	344	2 254	107	0	79	489	87	680	103
Palau	1 204	0	2	0	100	662	0	0	0	0	57	202	182
Puerto Rico	652 497	213 443	24 209	1 181	25 864	49 534	490	0	18 104	258 262	1 516	50 104	9 791
Trust Territories of the Pacific	798	0	0	0	0	0	0	0	798	0	0	0	0
Virgin Islands	14 954	0	2 552	137	847	6 045	352	0	1 618	1 194	87	1 742	380

SOURCE: U.S. Department of Education, National Center for Education Statistics, based on unpublished tabulations from the Office of Management and Budget; and U.S. Department of Commerce, Bureau of the Census, Federal Expenditures by State for Fiscal Year 1996. Published as table 363 in *Digest of Education Statistics* 1997.

1. Title I, formerly called Chapter 1, Education Consolidation and Improvement Act of 1981, includes Grants to Local Education Agencies, Migrant Education--Basic State Grants, Program for Neglected and Delinquent Children, Capital Expenses, and Even Start--State Educational Agencies.
2. Title VI, formerly called Chapter 2 Education Consolidation and Improvement Act of 1981, includes Eisenhower Professional Development Grants, Drug-Free Schools and Communities--State Grants, Education for Homeless Children and Youth, and Innovative Education Program Strategies.
3. Impact Aid--Basic Support Payments and Impact Aid--Payments for Children with Disabilities.
4. Includes Vocational Education--Basic Grants to States, Tech-Prep Education, and Adult Education-State Grant Program.
5. Includes Special Education--Grants to States, Preschool Grants, Special Education--Grants for Infants and Families with Disabilities, and Education of Children with Disabilities.
6. Includes Emergency Immigrant Education Program and Bilingual Education State Grants.
7. Includes Institutional Aid to Strengthen Higher Education Institutions serving significant numbers of low-income students, Other Special Programs for the Disadvantaged, Cooperative Education, Fund for the Improvement of Postsecondary Education, Fellowships and Scholarships, and annual interest subsidy grants for facilities construction.
8. Includes Pell Grants, State Student Incentive Grants, and Guaranteed Student Loan interest subsidies.
9. Includes Public Library Services, Public Library Construction and Technology Enhancement, and Interlibrary Cooperation and Resource Sharing.
10. Includes Rehabilitation Services--Vocational Rehabilitation Grants to States, Supported Employment Services for Individuals with Severe Disabilities, Rehabilitation Services--Client Assistance Program, Independent Living--State Grants, and Program of Protection and Advocacy of Individual Rights.
11. Includes State and Local Education Systemic Improvement Grants.
NOTE: Data reflect revisions to figures in the Budget of the United States Government, Fiscal Year 1998. To the extent possible, data represent obligations rather than outlays. Because of the exclusion of certain programs, totals in this table are lower than those reported in other tables. Because of rounding, details may not add to totals.

Table C-68. Appropriations for Title I and Title VI, Elementary and Secondary Education Act (ESEA) [1] of 1994, by State or Other Area: 1995-96 and 1996-97

(In thousands)

State	Title I total, school year 1995-96 [2]	Title I,[3] for school year 1996-97 [4]							Title VI [5]	
		Total	Total local education grants	Basic grants	Concentration grants	Neglected and delinquent children	Migrant children	Other [6]	1995 appropriation for 1995-96	1996 appropriation for 1996-97
	2	3	4	5	6	7	8	9	10	11
Total [7]	$7 214 160	$7 215 249	$6 730 348	$5 985 839	$677 241	$39 311	$305 474	$140 116	$347 250	$273 075
Alabama	128 941	128 784	123 588	109 394	14 194	765	2 558	1 872	5 329	4 220
Alaska	25 363	25 348	14 768	13 670	1 098	161	9 935	484	1 724	1 365
Arizona	106 404	105 959	96 885	85 076	11 808	735	6 774	1 566	5 445	4 312
Arkansas	78 984	78 937	73 881	65 500	8 380	404	3 491	1 161	3 208	2 541
California	832 630	830 700	718 895	636 279	82 616	4 016	91 622	16 166	40 033	31 703
Colorado	69 756	69 894	65 437	59 862	5 575	159	3 276	1 023	4 794	3 797
Connecticut	55 664	55 932	51 796	48 447	3 348	859	2 163	1 114	3 813	3 020
Delaware	16 551	17 074	15 782	14 235	1 546	198	412	682	1 724	1 365
District of Columbia	21 109	21 703	19 946	17 571	2 375	892	193	672	1 724	1 365
Florida	304 566	306 097	276 157	247 458	28 699	1 498	24 005	4 437	15 759	12 480
Georgia	173 817	175 799	167 492	150 082	17 410	1 150	4 765	2 393	9 204	7 289
Hawaii	19 809	19 751	19 148	17 446	1 702	108	0	495	1 724	1 365
Idaho	27 062	27 055	21 593	19 900	1 693	115	4 817	530	1 725	1 366
Illinois	327 812	327 388	318 070	285 475	32 595	1 768	1 716	5 835	14 853	11 763
Indiana	113 142	113 324	107 837	100 226	7 611	795	2 835	1 856	7 303	5 784
Iowa	52 168	52 283	50 647	47 861	2 786	271	299	1 066	3 709	2 937
Kansas	59 694	59 938	51 974	48 392	3 582	614	6 466	884	3 469	2 748
Kentucky	133 099	132 963	123 216	109 224	13 992	668	7 000	2 079	4 855	3 845
Louisiana	194 266	192 972	186 947	164 131	22 816	677	1 908	3 440	6 150	4 870
Maine	29 510	29 334	25 261	23 586	1 675	158	3 359	557	1 724	1 365
Maryland	88 441	88 763	85 552	78 783	6 769	1 220	266	1 724	6 055	4 795
Massachusetts	125 630	125 917	119 706	109 564	10 141	769	2 728	2 714	6 858	5 431
Michigan	319 510	319 188	301 328	271 510	29 818	1 034	11 873	4 952	12 492	9 893
Minnesota	85 678	85 557	81 130	75 273	5 857	235	2 326	1 867	6 259	4 957
Mississippi	127 060	126 428	122 733	108 047	14 686	297	1 344	2 054	3 760	2 978
Missouri	117 658	117 408	113 470	102 300	11 169	687	825	2 426	6 872	5 442
Montana	26 271	26 226	24 891	22 243	2 648	116	703	516	1 724	1 365
Nebraska	30 947	34 365	30 504	28 535	1 969	246	2 667	947	2 233	1 768
Nevada	19 502	19 543	18 392	16 698	1 693	171	485	495	1 789	1 417
New Hampshire	16 629	16 648	15 774	14 758	1 017	257	96	521	1 724	1 365
New Jersey	145 617	145 386	138 216	127 101	11 114	2 418	949	3 803	9 260	7 333
New Mexico	61 206	61 052	58 411	51 299	7 112	349	1 244	1 049	2 451	1 941
New York	629 845	627 760	605 122	541 515	63 607	2 532	5 707	14 399	21 432	16 973
North Carolina	135 690	136 057	129 098	118 883	10 215	885	4 222	1 852	8 535	6 759
North Dakota	17 786	17 773	16 649	14 956	1 693	51	516	557	1 724	1 365
Ohio	307 509	307 328	297 225	266 368	30 857	2 156	1 814	6 134	14 183	11 232
Oklahoma	85 716	85 198	82 401	73 140	9 261	293	1 288	1 216	4 402	3 486
Oregon	79 138	79 527	66 217	60 750	5 467	985	11 274	1 050	3 930	3 112
Pennsylvania	316 544	315 880	301 176	273 857	27 319	725	5 532	8 447	14 376	11 385
Rhode Island	22 023	21 939	20 774	18 736	2 038	307	153	706	1 724	1 365
South Carolina	93 744	93 480	90 762	81 526	9 236	866	568	1 284	4 647	3 680
South Dakota	19 973	19 921	18 688	16 964	1 724	98	605	531	1 724	1 365
Tennessee	123 584	123 385	120 850	106 841	14 009	640	99	1 796	6 375	5 049
Texas	627 277	625 538	571 097	504 863	66 234	1 497	43 794	9 150	25 634	20 300
Utah	34 138	34 293	32 272	30 208	2 064	385	1 132	504	3 361	2 661
Vermont	16 338	16 327	14 806	13 789	1 017	107	910	503	1 724	1 365
Virginia	102 077	102 822	99 659	91 983	7 676	838	777	1 548	7 768	6 151
Washington	113 253	113 398	97 894	90 095	7 799	812	13 142	1 550	6 944	5 499
West Virginia	70 712	70 426	69 048	60 868	8 180	270	100	1 008	2 200	1 742
Wisconsin	125 832	125 368	121 420	113 634	7 785	1 032	646	2 270	6 827	5 406
Wyoming	16 283	16 270	15 455	14 355	1 100	155	171	489	1 724	1 365

See footnotes at end of table.

Table C-68. Appropriations for Title I and Title VI, Elementary and Secondary Education Act (ESEA) [1] of 1994, by State or Other Area: 1995-96 and 1996-97 — Continued

(In thousands)

State	Title I total, school year 1995-96[2]	Title I,[3] for school year 1996-97[4]							Title VI[5]	
		Total	Total local education grants	Basic grants	Concentration grants	Neglected and delinquent children	Migrant children	Other[6]	1995 appropriation for 1995-96	1996 appropriation for 1996-97
	2	3	4	5	6	7	8	9	10	11
Other activities										
Bureau of Indian Affairs	$41 324	$41 609	$41 609	$0	$0	$0	$0	$0	$0	$0
Migrant coordination activities	6 000	5 999	0	0	0	0	5 999	0	0	0
Even Start Migrant, Indian, and Territory setaside	5 101	8 600	3 500	3 500	0	0	0	5 100	0	0
Even Start Evaluation/Technical Assistance	1 400	1 374	0	0	0	0	0	1 374	0	0
Even Start/State Literacy Initiative	1 000	0	0	0	0	0	0	0	0	0
Competitive grants	5 000	5 000	5 000	0	0	0	0	0	0	0
Outlying areas										
American Samoa	4 998	4 978	4 978	0	0	0	0	0	417	330
Guam	4 866	4 846	4 846	0	0	0	0	0	974	771
Northern Marianas	2 372	2 362	2 362	0	0	0	0	0	238	188
Puerto Rico	261 631	261 604	249 546	219 080	30 465	868	3 924	7 266	5 839	4 624
Virgin Islands	8 510	8 474	8 474	0	0	0	0	0	802	635

SOURCE: U.S. Department of Education, Budget Service, Elementary, Secondary, and Vocational Education Analysis Division; and unpublished data. Published as table 365 in *Digest of Education Statistics* 1997.

1. Elementary and Secondary Education Act was most recently revised through the Improving America's Schools Act (IASA) of 1994.
2. Data are based on fiscal year 1996 budget authorizations. Excludes $3,664,000 for evaluation and studies.
3. Formerly Chapter 1.
4. Data are based on fiscal year 1997 budget authorizations. Excludes $3,359,000 for evaluation and studies.
5. Formerly Chapter 2.
6. Includes capital expenses, and Even Start grants.
7. Total includes other activities and outlying areas.

NOTE: Column 3 total includes columns 4, 7, 8, and 9. Columns 5 and 6 are subset totals of column 4. Because of rounding, details may not add to totals.

Table C-69. Federal Science and Engineering Obligations to Colleges and Universities, by Agency and State: Fiscal Year 1995 [1]

(In thousands)

State	Total	Department of Agriculture	Department of Defense	Department of Education	Department of Energy	Environmental Protection Agency	Department of Health and Human Services	National Aeronautics and Space Administration	National Science Foundation	Other[2]
United States	$18 536 982	$943 630	$2 197 104	$187 934	$3 238 361	$164 464	$7 036 182	$1 878 496	$2 397 153	$493 658
Alabama	237 819	25 747	14 852	4 006	3 059	2 097	124 659	41 208	17 206	4 985
Alaska	33 093	3 709	1 230	341	49	128	1 885	11 457	8 985	5 309
Arizona	273 616	10 080	20 915	4 117	6 194	4 729	69 946	40 053	112 973	4 609
Arkansas	55 215	23 112	3 542	3 540	60	305	18 009	1 588	3 855	1 204
California	3 918 612	36 462	216 956	22 010	994 525	15 439	959 125	1 224 557	411 462	38 076
Colorado	359 221	14 876	22 523	4 679	9 804	3 076	130 445	23 301	129 580	20 937
Connecticut	257 255	6 794	9 693	880	11 203	287	199 312	2 237	22 588	4 261
Delaware	39 375	7 255	10 323	2 529	846	623	4 387	751	8 143	4 518
District of Columbia	190 663	1 764	32 931	4 499	3 092	746	83 648	9 511	11 370	43 102
Florida	300 639	22 162	35 986	5 239	12 346	2 862	127 713	21 819	56 266	16 246
Georgia	338 027	29 775	87 057	3 680	15 464	5 537	124 514	21 080	34 736	16 184
Hawaii	65 870	7 156	6 328	1 115	3 164	200	18 010	8 810	14 368	6 719
Idaho	20 487	9 050	245	984	0	802	3 143	603	2 898	2 762
Illinois	1 122 329	28 224	53 192	8 744	620 509	2 114	258 619	13 206	127 546	10 175
Indiana	213 025	23 434	20 573	1 998	15 830	533	91 941	5 334	50 164	3 218
Iowa	188 579	26 273	4 948	1 697	31 836	3 500	92 068	6 518	15 466	6 273
Kansas	78 346	13 978	1 707	5 346	3 659	5 247	33 067	2 837	11 254	1 251
Kentucky	86 452	23 591	1 120	2 088	5 249	1 312	39 233	1 550	11 568	741
Louisiana	140 148	18 395	11 774	1 334	19 225	5 997	54 452	5 767	12 238	10 966
Maine	19 184	8 661	493	1 156	220	284	2 735	295	3 467	1 873
Maryland	934 277	16 519	420 387	3 482	16 121	4 725	337 742	47 268	41 337	46 696
Massachusetts	1 214 730	15 164	453 517	4 133	90 617	9 098	386 153	63 414	172 166	20 468
Michigan	454 417	26 384	29 777	4 381	12 710	16 734	241 400	28 929	79 453	14 649
Minnesota	237 093	21 671	13 922	2 594	5 588	2 334	138 156	3 617	40 735	8 476
Mississippi	76 768	31 027	5 971	1 718	8 265	1 011	14 635	2 052	8 892	3 197
Missouri	275 337	26 369	8 605	3 851	4 929	695	202 697	5 875	20 934	1 382
Montana	36 546	11 933	1 143	1 406	1 598	706	4 706	1 998	11 357	1 699
Nebraska	60 153	17 218	1 845	706	669	103	21 970	1 999	12 109	3 534
Nevada	28 140	4 598	174	373	4 229	1 437	5 507	1 177	7 910	2 735
New Hampshire	70 103	4 422	2 802	488	1 260	695	36 076	10 912	9 994	3 454
New Jersey	357 376	14 720	31 521	2 537	132 831	8 844	92 433	7 658	55 205	11 627
New Mexico	681 628	8 661	53 249	3 462	542 141	663	27 181	26 488	18 641	1 142
New York	1 444 689	30 349	70 397	9 980	370 375	5 052	699 480	25 790	220 955	12 311
North Carolina	539 050	37 937	30 346	5 336	11 522	12 989	338 884	10 137	55 046	36 853
North Dakota	40 871	14 169	320	634	11 027	1 098	4 949	709	6 579	1 386
Ohio	399 785	23 185	55 135	6 678	6 951	6 755	222 176	21 922	43 556	13 427
Oklahoma	77 956	17 880	6 730	1 886	3 692	1 158	20 000	7 111	14 939	4 560
Oregon	189 259	24 069	21 350	5 973	9 686	6 725	73 661	5 855	29 809	12 131
Pennsylvania	863 724	33 151	168 002	12 408	22 859	4 808	483 956	19 038	110 855	8 647
Rhode Island	82 196	9 432	11 476	0	2 743	766	23 744	3 457	21 108	9 470
South Carolina	104 214	16 378	8 129	1 580	16 954	550	32 165	2 537	14 745	11 176
South Dakota	17 614	7 657	0	318	0	0	1 884	1 397	5 991	367
Tennessee	237 484	26 281	14 958	2 656	30 633	1 746	131 091	7 792	20 113	2 214
Texas	759 487	40 574	107 466	7 802	25 697	9 412	421 628	41 796	93 668	11 444
Utah	160 674	9 302	34 587	2 753	5 845	1 048	71 827	10 030	23 665	1 617
Vermont	39 893	7 652	776	1 587	534	410	25 187	324	3 374	49
Virginia	342 053	22 282	27 340	6 020	98 838	1 305	110 745	24 892	34 583	16 048
Washington	400 270	25 562	43 299	2 718	21 071	1 039	225 007	12 961	52 141	16 472
West Virginia	78 699	8 672	2 142	755	3 945	3 910	8 276	19 204	30 234	1 561
Wisconsin	308 406	24 059	13 306	7 593	17 452	2 164	167 911	14 704	51 721	9 496
Wyoming	16 988	5 480	734	237	1 213	477	1 144	975	5 798	930

See footnotes at end of table.

Table C-69.   Federal Science and Engineering Obligations to Colleges and Universities, by Agency and State: Fiscal Year 1995 [1]
— Continued

(In thousands)

State	Total	Department of Agriculture	Department of Defense	Department of Education	Department of Energy	Environmental Protection Agency	Department of Health and Human Services	National Aeronautics and Space Administation	National Science Foundation	Other[2]
Outlying areas	$69 147	$20 375	$1 310	$1 907	$32	$189	$26 900	$3 996	$13 407	$1 031
American Samoa	1 311	1 305	0	6	0	0	0	0	0	0
Guam	4 256	2 326	356	102	0	0	779	0	536	157
Puerto Rico	57 796	12 325	898	1 782	32	189	24 916	3 996	12 871	787
Trust Territories of the Pacific	2 584	2 445	0	17	0	0	122	0	0	0
Virgin Islands	3 200	1 974	56	0	0	0	1 083	0	0	87

SOURCE: National Science Foundation, Federal Support to Universities, Colleges, and Nonprofit Institutions, Fiscal Year 1995.   Published as table 366 in *Digest of Education Statistics* 1997.

1. Dollars reflect actual obligations during the fiscal year regardless of when the funds were actually spent by a recipient institution. Data include obligations to federally funded research and development centers administered by colleges and universities.
2. Includes U.S. Department of Commerce, U.S. Department of Housing and Urban Development, U.S. Department of the Interior, Agency for International Development, U.S. Department of Labor, U.S. Department of Transportation, and Nuclear Regulatory Commission.

NOTE: Total includes loans to individuals, such as the Federal Family Education Loan Program sponsored by the U.S. Department of Education, and federal training and development activities, as well as funds allocated to state agencies, even though the final recipient of such funds is known to be an academic institution. Tuition support programs such as Pell grants are included in these figures.

Table C-70. U.S. Department of Agriculture Obligations for Child Nutrition Programs, by State or Other Area: Fiscal Years 1995 and 1996

(In thousands)

State	Total, fiscal year 1995	Fiscal year 1996								
		Total	Special milk	School lunch[1]	School breakfast	State administrative expenses	Commodities and cash in lieu of commodities[2]	Child and adult care	Summer food service	Nutrition education and training
Total	$8 362 921	$8 527 590	$18 918	$4 761 006	$1 122 062	$99 900	$704 826	$1 552 637	$258 245	$9 995
Alabama	161 661	162 114	38	94 864	20 661	1 953	14 187	26 420	3 837	153
Alaska	21 225	22 384	6	13 267	1 896	405	1 306	5 428	14	63
Arizona	141 671	152 469	182	82 327	21 683	1 755	10 263	31 541	4 563	155
Arkansas	97 920	100 111	29	54 953	16 877	1 475	9 374	15 177	2 139	87
California	996 563	1 069 307	842	622 015	159 967	11 678	73 076	178 151	22 471	1 106
Colorado	86 904	89 243	130	45 177	7 416	1 296	7 924	25 522	1 647	130
Connecticut	62 948	65 571	497	36 008	7 891	857	6 537	11 314	2 359	108
Delaware	22 619	23 224	45	9 847	2 557	424	1 476	8 012	802	63
District of Columbia	21 964	23 245	13	14 144	3 174	349	1 270	2 523	1 710	63
Florida	414 622	433 007	140	263 025	65 564	4 412	30 200	46 118	23 104	443
Georgia	273 973	289 944	41	167 320	52 136	2 836	26 364	32 408	8 582	258
Hawaii	33 551	35 625	8	21 879	4 778	483	3 715	4 386	313	63
Idaho	32 162	32 386	216	20 213	3 165	501	2 871	4 637	690	63
Illinois	299 757	313 903	2 673	183 187	27 305	3 529	25 704	57 048	14 036	422
Indiana	124 866	126 965	319	72 251	14 890	1 561	14 494	21 720	1 532	199
Iowa	74 481	77 341	172	41 414	6 723	1 007	10 977	16 104	842	102
Kansas	91 398	91 049	140	40 296	9 030	931	7 650	32 046	863	92
Kentucky	136 412	143 730	113	82 423	25 780	1 642	15 352	15 079	3 209	133
Louisiana	234 257	239 544	58	127 668	38 045	3 061	18 814	44 965	6 760	173
Maine	32 865	34 389	129	16 211	3 018	494	2 881	10 788	805	63
Maryland	116 514	120 036	385	62 026	12 532	1 542	10 338	30 119	2 925	169
Massachusetts	133 231	145 662	512	71 609	16 301	1 823	13 696	37 404	4 121	196
Michigan	211 255	223 117	947	117 182	26 108	2 593	20 334	51 251	4 367	334
Minnesota	150 547	153 856	1 072	59 204	10 252	2 423	12 650	65 298	2 788	169
Mississippi	150 102	152 096	10	88 614	27 609	1 831	11 596	18 826	3 502	109
Missouri	148 563	148 921	438	79 777	20 501	1 871	12 951	29 389	3 810	183
Montana	25 591	27 096	46	13 054	2 327	742	2 658	7 783	424	63
Nebraska	58 413	60 179	224	24 393	3 531	993	6 545	23 780	649	63
Nevada	27 796	31 112	134	18 211	4 737	471	2 932	3 368	1 195	63
New Hampshire	18 296	19 190	235	10 288	1 914	476	2 941	2 947	326	63
New Jersey	152 008	159 973	960	96 525	13 216	1 745	15 870	24 751	6 649	258
New Mexico	91 372	94 822	6	42 136	11 354	1 780	4 461	29 554	5 469	63
New York	583 279	599 469	1 162	341 610	77 361	6 331	44 110	88 827	39 457	610
North Carolina	225 646	231 740	132	126 905	37 136	2 613	22 031	39 170	3 519	234
North Dakota	25 104	25 613	67	9 724	1 399	531	2 628	10 843	359	63
Ohio	244 491	246 381	932	138 759	28 519	2 909	25 889	44 535	4 452	386
Oklahoma	118 610	122 854	79	64 997	18 270	1 687	10 830	24 714	2 156	121
Oregon	83 270	88 585	214	40 246	10 356	1 194	7 256	27 876	1 338	106
Pennsylvania	245 960	251 751	834	149 758	27 261	2 724	23 282	33 162	14 334	396
Rhode Island	19 677	21 961	128	13 186	1 693	404	2 129	3 079	1 280	63
South Carolina	144 621	148 417	33	82 795	25 896	1 569	12 623	17 780	7 589	131
South Dakota	28 021	29 023	47	14 603	2 617	470	3 143	7 117	964	63
Tennessee	160 606	164 136	39	92 083	25 089	1 916	15 921	24 367	4 541	179
Texas	742 563	776 792	106	452 187	125 733	8 795	62 203	108 988	18 046	735
Utah	73 008	73 697	74	32 496	4 095	1 158	6 385	27 430	1 969	89
Vermont	14 196	15 150	101	6 841	1 578	344	1 422	4 538	263	63
Virginia	151 544	152 677	237	89 199	21 586	1 152	14 121	23 014	3 155	213
Washington	135 961	140 536	262	73 030	16 914	1 830	11 374	34 205	2 733	188
West Virginia	60 502	59 791	47	32 626	11 357	774	4 694	8 664	1 567	63
Wisconsin	108 580	115 045	1 575	62 239	6 316	1 418	17 100	24 001	2 211	185
Wyoming	14 831	15 382	12	7 310	1 227	339	1 606	4 742	83	63

See footnotes at end of table.

Table C-70.   U.S. Department of Agriculture Obligations for Child Nutrition Programs, by State or Other Area: Fiscal Years 1995 and 1996 — Continued

(In thousands)

State	Total, fiscal year 1995	Fiscal year 1996								
		Total	Special milk	School lunch[1]	School breakfast	State administrative expenses	Commodities and cash in lieu of commodities[2]	Child and adult care	Summer food service	Nutrition education and training
Administrative costs ...	$6 755	$6 396	$0	$0	$0	$0	$6 396	$0	$0	$0
Department of Defense dependents schools	5 942	5 566	0	4 759	0	0	807	0	0	0
Outlying areas										
American Samoa	63	63	0	0	0	0	0	0	0	63
Guam	4 483	4 769	0	2 808	856	223	531	291	0	60
Northern Marianas ...	72	63	0	0	0	0	0	0	0	63
Puerto Rico	159 370	165 018	0	108 313	25 182	1 671	10 006	14 980	4 735	132
Trust Territory of the Pacific	152	57	0	0	0	0	54	0	0	3
Virgin Islands	6 617	5 583	3	3 629	209	241	563	525	350	63
Undistributed[3]	353 492	199 464	2 074	119 394	8 474	638	0	65 934	6 641	0

SOURCE: U.S. Department of Agriculture, Food and Nutrition Service, Budget Division, unpublished data. Published as table 369 in Digest of Education Statistics 1997.

1. Special Meal Assistance program is combined with 'School Lunch' program.
2. Commodities are based on preliminary food orders for fiscal year 1996.
3. Undistributed amount reflects the difference between preliminary state earnings reports and federal obligations as of September 30, 1996.

NOTE: Data are based on obligations as reported September 30, 1996. Negative amounts occur when program receipts exceed the obligations. Because of rounding, details may not add to totals.

Table C-71. U.S. Department of Health and Human Services Allocations for Head Start and Enrollment in Head Start, by State or Other Area: Fiscal Years 1993 to 1996

State	1993		1994		1995		1996	
	Head Start allocations (in thousands)	Head Start enrollment[1]	Head Start allocations (in thousands)	Head Start enrollment[2]	Head Start allocations (in thousands)	Head Start enrollment[3]	Head Start allocations (in thousands)	Head Start enrollment[4]
Total	$2 683 158	713 943	$3 215 946	740 493	$3 402 946	750 696	$3 438 268	752 077
Alabama	46 937	14 106	54 282	14 525	57 542	14 552	58 265	14 429
Alaska	5 316	1 143	6 295	1 209	6 534	1 209	6 748	1 299
Arizona	35 503	9 189	44 416	9 846	47 208	10 029	47 617	9 818
Arkansas	26 337	8 792	30 719	9 065	32 681	9 244	33 153	9 193
California	305 180	67 684	371 227	70 995	392 331	72 650	392 965	72 606
Colorado	25 505	7 672	31 787	8 118	35 757	8 576	36 364	8 647
Connecticut	22 066	5 561	26 061	5 660	27 022	5 625	27 382	5 567
Delaware	5 265	1 455	5 815	1 455	6 027	1 574	6 239	1 455
District of Columbia	11 631	2 841	12 854	2 841	14 329	2 913	14 530	3 339
Florida	92 741	25 333	118 976	27 398	125 508	27 623	127 325	27 535
Georgia	66 499	18 594	81 974	19 445	85 792	19 523	86 596	19 563
Hawaii	8 882	2 183	9 939	2 260	10 312	2 226	10 981	2 517
Idaho	8 329	1 850	9 574	1 912	10 009	1 841	10 043	1 869
Illinois	117 770	30 268	139 137	30 537	148 120	31 579	148 915	31 817
Indiana	37 979	11 107	46 558	11 730	48 871	11 739	49 804	11 817
Iowa	20 111	5 758	23 430	5 946	25 539	6 199	25 968	6 178
Kansas	17 885	5 389	22 095	5 793	24 772	6 158	25 129	6 074
Kentucky	45 318	13 791	54 364	14 071	58 383	14 267	58 935	14 447
Louisiana	62 996	18 677	75 876	19 344	78 691	19 344	79 596	19 344
Maine	11 011	3 361	12 610	3 439	13 118	3 439	13 734	10 816
Maryland	32 073	8 338	38 810	8 509	42 023	8 874	42 461	8 915
Massachusetts	49 615	10 929	57 264	10 794	61 129	10 990	61 742	3 466
Michigan	107 451	29 960	126 686	30 701	132 990	30 936	135 349	31 198
Minnesota	30 823	8 167	36 930	8 576	38 281	8 576	38 812	8 641
Mississippi	83 560	24 036	92 012	24 110	95 493	24 150	97 001	24 081
Missouri	45 641	13 592	55 979	14 063	58 752	14 064	59 241	14 035
Montana	8 211	2 226	9 563	2 304	9 772	2 304	10 048	2 304
Nebraska	12 322	3 465	14 342	3 644	15 456	3 764	15 890	3 800
Nevada	6 341	1 593	8 017	1 793	8 315	1 793	8 213	1 823
New Hampshire	4 895	1 131	5 699	1 156	6 379	1 232	6 558	1 235
New Jersey	63 902	12 773	71 189	12 898	74 610	13 016	75 151	13 085
New Mexico	18 954	6 055	24 241	6 397	27 269	6 821	27 731	6 587
New York	181 968	37 829	215 678	39 062	226 840	39 491	228 243	40 365
North Carolina	54 263	15 296	66 643	15 695	71 603	16 161	72 594	16 002
North Dakota	5 666	1 653	6 723	1 738	6 966	1 738	7 206	1 874
Ohio	110 420	32 567	133 913	33 919	139 497	34 215	141 607	33 919
Oklahoma	32 274	10 625	39 073	11 165	40 705	11 165	41 397	11 165
Oregon	21 782	4 431	27 080	4 638	29 086	4 698	29 460	4 695
Pennsylvania	99 688	24 866	119 354	25 672	126 251	26 149	127 086	26 198
Rhode Island	8 328	2 380	10 060	2 476	10 453	2 434	10 549	2 567
South Carolina	33 063	9 709	40 772	10 142	44 021	10 415	44 540	10 164
South Dakota	6 629	1 894	7 985	2 025	8 258	2 025	8 480	2 258
Tennessee	47 993	13 859	58 610	14 380	61 630	14 213	62 163	14 291
Texas	172 536	49 110	213 394	51 521	223 309	51 925	224 923	52 107
Utah	13 208	3 822	15 832	4 028	18 145	4 334	18 219	4 201
Vermont	5 339	1 260	5 957	1 271	7 636	1 486	7 811	1 531
Virginia	39 440	10 650	46 411	10 993	48 896	11 147	49 706	11 028
Washington	37 558	7 799	45 968	8 260	53 385	8 803	52 311	8 878
West Virginia	22 303	6 317	26 014	6 402	27 626	6 522	28 125	6 515
Wisconsin	40 956	11 247	49 461	11 953	52 633	12 171	54 013	12 283
Wyoming	4 149	1 245	4 925	1 323	5 099	1 313	5 195	1 279

See footnotes at end of table.

Table C-71. **U.S. Department of Health and Human Services Allocations for Head Start and Enrollment in Head Start, by State or Other Area: Fiscal Years 1993 to 1996 — Continued**

State	1993		1994		1995		1996	
	Head Start allocations (in thousands)	Head Start enrollment[1]	Head Start allocations (in thousands)	Head Start enrollment[2]	Head Start allocations (in thousands)	Head Start enrollment[3]	Head Start allocations (in thousands)	Head Start enrollment[4]
Migrant programs	$108 011	33 886	$130 409	35 063	$138 802	35 243	$139 438	35 117
American Indian/Alaskan Native programs	74 800	17 973	90 793	18 738	95 130	18 821	96 836	19 071
Special projects	(NA)	(NA)	76	(NA)	(NA)	(NA)	(NA)	(NA)
Outlying areas								
Puerto Rico	113 047	31 306	127 066	32 145	132 423	32 118	134 072	31 744
Pacific Territories	7 613	5 779	9 019	5 849	9 309	5 849	9 541	5 849
Virgin Islands	5 074	1 421	6 009	1 501	6 228	1 430	6 267	1 446

SOURCE: U.S. Department of Health and Human Services, Office of Human Development Services. Published as table 370 in *Digest of Education Statistics* 1997.

1. The distribution of enrollment by age was: 6 percent were 5 years old and over; 64 percent were 4-year-olds; 27 percent were 3-year-olds; and 3 percent were under 3 years of age. Handicapped children accounted for 13.2 percent in Head Start programs. The racial/ethnic composition was: American Indian/Alaskan Native, 4 percent; Hispanic, 24 percent; black, 36 percent; white, 33 percent; and Asian, 3 percent.
2. The distribution of enrollment by age was: 6 percent were 5 years old and over; 64 percent were 4-year-olds; 27 percent were 3-year-olds; and 3 percent were under 3 years of age. Handicapped children accounted for 13.0 percent in Head Start programs. The racial/ethnic composition was: American Indian/Alaskan Native, 4 percent; Hispanic, 24 percent; black, 36 percent; white, 33 percent; and Asian, 3 percent.
3. The distribution of enrollment by age was: 7 percent were 5 years old and over; 61 percent were 4-year-olds; 28 percent were 3-year-olds; and 4 percent were under 3 years of age. Handicapped children accounted for 13.1 percent in Head Start programs. The racial/ethnic composition was: American Indian/Alaskan Native, 4 percent; Hispanic, 25 percent; black, 36 percent; white, 33 percent; and Asian, 3 percent.
4. The distribution of enrollment by age was: 6 percent were 5 years old and over; 62 percent were 4-year-olds; 29 percent were 3-year-olds; and 4 percent were under 3 years of age. Handicapped children accounted for 12.8 percent in Head Start programs. The racial/ethnic composition was: American Indian/Alaskan Native, 3.5 percent; Hispanic, 25.2 percent; black, 36 percent; white, 32.3 percent; and Asian, 3 percent.
NOTE: Because of rounding, details may not add to totals.

(NA) Not applicable or not available.

Table C-72. Average Eighth Grade Mathematics Scores by Content Areas, and Average Time Spent Studying Out of School, by Country: 1994-95

State	Average percent correct by content areas						
	Mathematics overall	Fractions and number sense	Geometry	Algebra	Data representation, and probability	Measurement	Proportionality
International average percent correct	55 (0.1)	58 (0.1)	56 (0.1)	52 (0.2)	62 (0.1)	51 (0.1)	45 (0.2)
Australia[1]	58 (0.9)	61 (0.9)	57 (1.0)	55 (1.0)	67 (0.8)	54 (1.0)	47 (0.9)
Austria[1]	62 (0.8)	66 (0.8)	57 (1.0)	59 (0.8)	68 (0.8)	62 (1.0)	49 (0.9)
Belgium (Flemish)	66 (1.4)	71 (1.2)	64 (1.5)	63 (1.7)	73 (1.3)	60 (1.3)	53 (1.8)
Belgium (French)[1]	59 (0.9)	62 (1.0)	58 (1.0)	53 (1.1)	68 (1.0)	56 (1.0)	48 (0.9)
Bulgaria[1]	60 (1.2)	60 (1.4)	65 (1.3)	62 (1.5)	62 (1.1)	54 (1.6)	47 (1.5)
Canada	59 (0.5)	64 (0.6)	58 (0.6)	54 (0.7)	69 (0.5)	51 (0.7)	48 (0.7)
Colombia[1]	29 (0.8)	31 (0.9)	29 (0.9)	28 (0.9)	37 (1.0)	25 (1.5)	23 (0.9)
Cyprus	48 (0.5)	50 (0.6)	47 (0.6)	48 (0.7)	53 (0.6)	44 (0.9)	40 (0.7)
Czech Republic	66 (1.1)	69 (1.1)	66 (1.1)	65 (1.3)	68 (0.9)	62 (1.2)	52 (1.3)
Denmark[1]	52 (0.7)	53 (0.9)	54 (0.9)	45 (0.7)	67 (0.9)	49 (1.0)	41 (0.8)
England[1]	53 (0.7)	54 (0.8)	54 (1.0)	49 (0.9)	66 (0.7)	50 (0.9)	41 (1.1)
France	61 (0.8)	64 (0.8)	66 (0.8)	54 (1.0)	71 (0.8)	57 (0.9)	49 (0.9)
Germany[1]	54 (1.1)	58 (1.1)	51 (1.4)	48 (1.3)	64 (1.2)	51 (1.1)	42 (1.3)
Greece[1]	49 (0.7)	53 (0.8)	51 (0.7)	46 (0.8)	56 (0.8)	43 (0.9)	39 (1.1)
Hong Kong	70 (1.4)	72 (1.4)	73 (1.5)	70 (1.5)	72 (1.3)	65 (1.7)	62 (1.4)
Hungary	62 (0.7)	65 (0.8)	60 (0.8)	63 (0.9)	66 (0.7)	56 (0.8)	47 (0.9)
Iceland	50 (1.1)	54 (1.2)	51 (1.4)	40 (1.3)	63 (1.1)	45 (1.4)	38 (1.4)
Iran, Islamic Republic	38 (0.6)	39 (0.6)	43 (0.8)	37 (0.8)	41 (0.6)	29 (1.2)	36 (0.8)
Ireland	59 (1.2)	65 (1.2)	51 (1.3)	53 (1.3)	69 (1.1)	53 (1.3)	51 (1.2)
Israel[1]	57 (1.3)	60 (1.4)	57 (1.4)	61 (1.6)	63 (1.3)	48 (1.6)	43 (1.6)
Japan	73 (0.4)	75 (0.4)	80 (0.4)	72 (0.6)	78 (0.4)	67 (0.5)	61 (0.5)
Korea	72 (0.5)	74 (0.5)	75 (0.6)	69 (0.6)	78 (0.6)	66 (0.7)	62 (0.6)
Kuwait[1]	30 (0.7)	27 (0.8)	38 (1.0)	30 (1.0)	38 (1.0)	23 (1.0)	21 (0.7)
Latvia (Latvian-speaking schools)	51 (0.8)	53 (0.9)	57 (0.8)	51 (0.9)	56 (0.8)	47 (0.9)	39 (0.9)
Lithuania[1]	48 (0.9)	51 (1.0)	53 (1.1)	47 (1.2)	52 (1.0)	43 (0.9)	35 (0.9)
Netherlands[1]	60 (1.6)	62 (1.6)	59 (1.8)	53 (1.6)	72 (1.7)	57 (1.6)	51 (1.9)
New Zealand	54 (1.0)	57 (1.1)	54 (1.1)	49 (1.1)	66 (1.0)	48 (1.2)	42 (1.0)
Norway	54 (0.5)	58 (0.6)	51 (0.6)	45 (0.7)	66 (0.6)	51 (0.6)	40 (0.6)
Portugal	43 (0.7)	44 (0.7)	44 (0.8)	40 (0.8)	54 (0.7)	39 (0.7)	32 (0.8)
Romania[1]	49 (1.0)	48 (1.0)	52 (0.9)	52 (1.3)	49 (1.0)	48 (1.1)	42 (1.2)
Russian Federation ..	60 (1.3)	62 (1.2)	63 (1.4)	63 (1.5)	60 (1.2)	56 (1.5)	48 (1.5)
Scotland[1]	52 (1.3)	53 (1.3)	52 (1.4)	46 (1.5)	65 (1.3)	48 (1.6)	40 (1.4)
Singapore	79 (0.9)	84 (0.8)	76 (1.0)	76 (1.1)	79 (0.8)	77 (1.0)	75 (1.0)
Slovak Republic	62 (0.8)	66 (0.8)	63 (0.8)	62 (0.9)	62 (0.7)	60 (0.9)	49 (1.0)
Slovenia[1]	61 (0.7)	63 (0.7)	60 (0.9)	61 (0.8)	66 (0.7)	59 (0.9)	49 (0.8)
South Africa[1]	24 (1.1)	26 (1.4)	24 (1.0)	23 (1.1)	26 (1.2)	18 (1.1)	21 (0.9)
Spain	51 (0.5)	52 (0.5)	49 (0.6)	54 (0.8)	60 (0.7)	44 (0.7)	40 (0.8)
Sweden	56 (0.7)	62 (0.8)	48 (0.7)	44 (0.9)	70 (0.7)	56 (0.9)	44 (0.9)
Switzerland[1]	62 (0.6)	67 (0.7)	60 (0.8)	53 (0.7)	72 (0.7)	61 (0.8)	52 (0.7)
Thailand[1]	57 (1.4)	60 (1.5)	62 (1.3)	53 (1.7)	63 (1.1)	50 (1.4)	51 (1.5)
United States	53 (1.1)	59 (1.1)	48 (1.2)	51 (1.2)	65 (1.1)	40 (1.1)	42 (1.1)

See footnotes at end of table.

Table C-72. Average Eighth Grade Mathematics Scores by Content Areas, and Average Time Spent Studying Out of School, by Country: 1994-95 — Continued

State	Distribution of daily out-of-school study time in all subjects, with mean mathematics scores															
	Less than 1 hour				At least 1, but less than 2 hours				At least 2, but less than 3 hours				More than 3 hours			
	Percent		Mean score		Percent		Mean score		Percent		Mean score		Percent		Mean score	
International average percent correct	(NA)	(NA)	(NA)	(NA)	(NA)	(NA)	(NA)	(NA)	(NA)	(NA)	(NA)	(NA)	(NA)	(NA)	(NA)	(NA)
Australia[1]	15	(0.9)	486	(5.7)	46	(1.0)	541	(4.4)	22	(0.6)	543	(5.2)	17	(0.7)	532	(4.8)
Austria[1]	9	(0.8)	524	(6.7)	46	(1.3)	551	(4.1)	21	(0.9)	544	(4.5)	24	(1.2)	528	(5.3)
Belgium (Flemish)	2	(0.4)	(2)	(NA)	25	(1.3)	552	(8.9)	28	(1.1)	592	(5.9)	45	(1.6)	560	(4.6)
Belgium (French)[1]	7	(0.8)	466	(7.4)	32	(1.0)	543	(4.6)	21	(1.3)	544	(5.5)	40	(1.5)	519	(4.5)
Bulgaria[1]	(NA)	(NA)	(NA)	(NA)	(NA)	(NA)	(NA)	(NA)	(NA)	(NA)	(NA)	(NA)	(NA)	(NA)	(NA)	(NA)
Canada	14	(1.2)	514	(5.6)	47	(1.1)	538	(2.8)	18	(0.7)	534	(3.7)	21	(1.1)	511	(3.6)
Colombia[1]	2	(0.4)	(2)	(NA)	17	(1.1)	394	(5.2)	20	(1.2)	389	(3.6)	61	(1.9)	390	(3.5)
Cyprus	9	(0.5)	442	(5.8)	19	(0.7)	475	(3.9)	26	(0.8)	491	(4.0)	46	(0.9)	475	(2.9)
Czech Republic	13	(1.1)	551	(7.1)	57	(1.1)	571	(5.1)	17	(0.9)	568	(8.2)	13	(0.8)	542	(7.6)
Denmark[1]	39	(1.6)	517	(4.4)	39	(1.4)	508	(3.8)	13	(0.8)	479	(4.1)	9	(0.7)	468	(6.9)
England[1]	(NA)	(NA)	(NA)	(NA)	(NA)	(NA)	(NA)	(NA)	(NA)	(NA)	(NA)	(NA)	(NA)	(NA)	(NA)	(NA)
France	8	(0.7)	505	(8.0)	33	(1.2)	545	(3.6)	28	(1.0)	547	(4.5)	31	(1.2)	537	(3.7)
Germany[1]	14	(1.1)	476	(6.7)	51	(1.2)	521	(4.3)	18	(1.0)	524	(7.0)	17	(0.9)	498	(5.0)
Greece[1]	6	(0.6)	450	(7.4)	14	(0.7)	483	(5.2)	21	(0.7)	485	(3.9)	59	(1.2)	491	(3.3)
Hong Kong	13	(1.0)	539	(9.3)	32	(0.9)	586	(6.6)	25	(0.9)	607	(6.1)	30	(1.1)	604	(7.2)
Hungary	4	(0.4)	483	(11.3)	33	(1.1)	536	(5.0)	22	(0.9)	541	(5.2)	41	(1.3)	545	(3.7)
Iceland	5	(1.0)	450	(12.0)	46	(1.7)	501	(5.1)	25	(1.3)	489	(5.4)	23	(1.4)	477	(7.3)
Iran, Islamic Republic	1	(0.2)	(2)	(NA)	5	(0.5)	428	(5.6)	12	(1.0)	436	(4.8)	82	(1.3)	431	(2.4)
Ireland	5	(0.6)	465	(8.8)	29	(1.0)	517	(5.3)	40	(1.1)	547	(5.5)	26	(1.2)	533	(5.7)
Israel[1]	5	(0.6)	539	(10.9)	36	(2.2)	546	(6.3)	26	(1.5)	521	(6.8)	33	(2.1)	502	(6.3)
Japan	13	(0.8)	578	(5.3)	39	(0.8)	607	(2.6)	20	(0.6)	609	(4.0)	28	(1.0)	612	(2.7)
Korea	15	(0.9)	582	(4.9)	32	(1.1)	604	(3.5)	25	(0.8)	607	(4.0)	29	(1.2)	628	(4.3)
Kuwait[1]	3	(0.6)	358	(10.3)	13	(1.5)	401	(5.5)	19	(1.3)	397	(5.1)	65	(1.8)	392	(2.0)
Latvia (Latvian-speaking schools)	4	(0.5)	467	(9.4)	35	(1.1)	507	(4.4)	32	(1.2)	497	(4.9)	29	(1.2)	487	(3.4)
Lithuania[1]	5	(0.6)	453	(9.4)	39	(1.4)	487	(3.9)	28	(1.0)	481	(4.6)	28	(1.4)	474	(5.4)
Netherlands[1]	3	(0.9)	492	(16.2)	54	(1.7)	539	(9.0)	27	(1.7)	562	(7.0)	16	(0.8)	524	(6.0)
New Zealand	12	(0.9)	472	(5.6)	51	(1.2)	519	(4.7)	21	(1.0)	518	(6.1)	17	(0.9)	495	(5.6)
Norway	6	(0.5)	481	(6.8)	50	(1.2)	514	(2.9)	24	(0.9)	510	(3.6)	21	(0.9)	483	(3.6)
Portugal	3	(0.3)	458	(8.1)	41	(1.1)	463	(3.1)	18	(0.7)	455	(3.3)	38	(1.2)	448	(3.0)
Romania[1]	9	(0.7)	459	(10.4)	16	(1.0)	464	(7.0)	15	(0.7)	481	(5.4)	60	(1.6)	494	(4.2)
Russian Federation ..	4	(0.5)	493	(10.3)	33	(1.1)	538	(5.3)	25	(1.0)	538	(5.2)	38	(1.4)	544	(6.9)
Scotland[1]	17	(1.4)	461	(4.8)	54	(1.2)	506	(5.7)	17	(1.0)	517	(8.6)	12	(0.8)	503	(7.4)
Singapore	2	(0.3)	(2)	(NA)	7	(0.4)	642	(8.0)	13	(0.6)	652	(6.6)	78	(0.9)	643	(4.9)
Slovak Republic	6	(0.5)	549	(8.3)	46	(0.9)	556	(3.9)	25	(0.7)	548	(4.4)	23	(1.0)	532	(4.1)
Slovenia[1]	5	(0.5)	551	(9.8)	36	(1.0)	561	(4.1)	21	(0.8)	537	(4.8)	37	(1.1)	523	(3.4)
South Africa[1]	(NA)	(NA)	(NA)	(NA)	(NA)	(NA)	(NA)	(NA)	(NA)	(NA)	(NA)	(NA)	(NA)	(NA)	(NA)	(NA)
Spain	3	(0.4)	443	(5.5)	26	(1.0)	490	(3.1)	18	(0.9)	495	(3.3)	53	(1.3)	487	(2.4)
Sweden	7	(0.6)	496	(6.9)	55	(1.2)	528	(3.1)	17	(0.8)	525	(4.3)	21	(0.9)	503	(4.2)
Switzerland[1]	4	(0.3)	523	(7.9)	44	(1.2)	556	(3.4)	19	(0.8)	548	(5.1)	33	(1.1)	536	(4.0)
Thailand[1]	3	(0.3)	495	(11.9)	26	(1.0)	514	(5.4)	18	(0.7)	515	(5.7)	54	(1.5)	531	(6.6)
United States	17	(1.1)	471	(7.2)	42	(0.9)	514	(4.2)	17	(0.7)	507	(5.5)	24	(0.8)	498	(5.9)

SOURCE: International Association for the Evaluation of Educational Achievement, Mathematics Achievement in the Middle School Years: IEA's Third International Mathematics and Science Study, 1997. Published as table 395 in *Digest of Education Statistics* 1997.

1. Countries not meeting all International Association for the Evaluation of Educational Achievement's sampling specifications.
2. Insufficient data.

(NA) Not applicable or not available.

Table C-73. Average Eighth Grade Science Scores by Content Areas, and Average Time Spent Studying Out of School, by Country: 1994-95

State	Average percent correct by content area											
	Overall science scores		Earth science		Life science		Physics		Chemistry		Environmental issues and the nature of science	
International average percent correct	56	(0.1)	55	(0.1)	59	(0.1)	55	(0.1)	51	(0.2)	53	(0.2)
Australia[1]	60	(0.7)	57	(0.8)	63	(0.8)	60	(0.7)	54	(0.9)	62	(1.0)
Austria[1]	61	(0.7)	62	(0.8)	65	(0.7)	62	(0.7)	58	(1.1)	55	(0.9)
Belgium (Flemish) ..	60	(1.1)	62	(1.2)	64	(1.1)	61	(1.1)	51	(1.3)	58	(1.5)
Belgium (French)[1] ..	50	(0.7)	50	(0.9)	55	(0.9)	51	(0.7)	41	(0.8)	46	(1.0)
Bulgaria[1]	62	(1.0)	58	(1.2)	64	(1.0)	60	(1.0)	65	(1.7)	59	(1.5)
Canada	59	(0.5)	58	(0.6)	62	(0.6)	59	(0.4)	52	(0.7)	61	(0.7)
Colombia[1]	39	(0.8)	37	(0.8)	44	(0.9)	37	(0.8)	32	(1.0)	40	(1.1)
Cyprus	47	(0.4)	46	(0.6)	49	(0.5)	46	(0.4)	45	(0.6)	46	(0.8)
Czech Republic	64	(0.8)	63	(1.2)	69	(0.8)	64	(0.7)	60	(1.2)	59	(1.1)
Denmark[1]	51	(0.6)	49	(0.7)	56	(0.7)	53	(0.7)	41	(0.8)	47	(1.0)
England[1]	61	(0.6)	59	(0.8)	64	(0.8)	62	(0.6)	55	(0.8)	65	(1.0)
France	54	(0.6)	55	(0.8)	56	(0.8)	54	(0.5)	47	(0.9)	53	(0.9)
Germany[1]	58	(1.0)	57	(1.0)	63	(1.1)	57	(1.0)	54	(1.3)	51	(1.3)
Greece[1]	52	(0.5)	49	(0.6)	54	(0.6)	53	(0.5)	51	(0.5)	51	(1.0)
Hong Kong	58	(1.0)	54	(1.0)	61	(1.0)	58	(0.9)	55	(1.0)	55	(1.3)
Hungary	61	(0.6)	60	(0.8)	65	(0.7)	60	(0.6)	60	(0.8)	53	(0.8)
Iceland	52	(0.9)	50	(1.2)	58	(1.0)	53	(0.9)	42	(0.8)	49	(1.0)
Iran, Islamic Republic	47	(0.6)	45	(0.6)	49	(0.6)	48	(0.7)	52	(0.8)	39	(1.1)
Ireland	58	(0.9)	61	(1.0)	60	(1.1)	56	(0.8)	54	(1.0)	60	(1.1)
Israel[1]	57	(1.1)	55	(1.1)	61	(1.1)	57	(1.1)	53	(1.5)	52	(1.6)
Japan	65	(0.3)	61	(0.4)	71	(0.4)	67	(0.3)	61	(0.5)	60	(0.7)
Korea	66	(0.3)	63	(0.5)	70	(0.4)	65	(0.5)	63	(0.6)	64	(0.8)
Kuwait[1]	43	(0.9)	43	(1.0)	45	(1.1)	43	(0.7)	40	(1.5)	39	(1.3)
Latvia (Latvian-speaking schools)	50	(0.6)	48	(0.8)	53	(0.7)	51	(0.7)	48	(0.8)	47	(1.0)
Lithuania[1]	49	(0.7)	46	(0.9)	52	(0.9)	51	(0.7)	48	(0.9)	40	(1.0)
Netherlands[1]	62	(1.0)	61	(1.4)	67	(1.4)	63	(0.9)	52	(0.9)	65	(1.6)
New Zealand	58	(0.8)	56	(0.9)	60	(1.0)	58	(0.7)	53	(1.1)	59	(1.2)
Norway	58	(0.4)	61	(0.6)	61	(0.5)	57	(0.4)	49	(0.6)	55	(0.8)
Portugal	50	(0.6)	50	(0.7)	53	(0.6)	48	(0.5)	50	(0.9)	45	(0.8)
Romania[1]	50	(0.8)	49	(1.0)	55	(1.0)	49	(0.8)	46	(1.0)	42	(1.0)
Russian Federation	58	(0.8)	58	(0.8)	62	(0.7)	57	(0.9)	57	(1.3)	50	(0.8)
Scotland[1]	55	(1.0)	52	(1.0)	57	(1.1)	57	(0.8)	51	(1.3)	57	(1.4)
Singapore	70	(1.0)	65	(1.1)	72	(1.0)	69	(0.8)	69	(1.2)	74	(1.1)
Slovak Republic	59	(0.6)	60	(0.7)	60	(0.6)	61	(0.6)	57	(0.8)	53	(0.9)
Slovenia[1]	62	(0.5)	64	(0.7)	65	(0.6)	61	(0.6)	56	(0.9)	59	(0.9)
South Africa[1]	27	(1.3)	26	(1.1)	27	(1.3)	27	(1.4)	26	(1.4)	26	(1.3)
Spain	56	(0.4)	57	(0.5)	58	(0.5)	55	(0.4)	51	(0.7)	53	(0.6)
Sweden	59	(0.6)	62	(0.7)	63	(0.7)	57	(0.5)	56	(0.7)	52	(0.8)
Switzerland[1]	56	(0.5)	58	(0.6)	59	(0.6)	58	(0.5)	50	(0.7)	51	(0.8)
Thailand[1]	57	(0.9)	56	(1.0)	66	(0.9)	54	(0.7)	43	(1.2)	62	(1.1)
United States	58	(1.0)	58	(1.0)	63	(1.1)	56	(0.8)	53	(1.2)	61	(1.0)

See footnotes at end of table.

Table C-73. Average Eighth Grade Science Scores by Content Areas, and Average Time Spent Studying Out of School, by Country: 1994-95 — Continued

State	Distribution of daily out-of-school study time in all subjects, with mean science scores							
	Less than 1 hour		At least 1, but less than 2 hours		At least 2, but less than 3 hours		More than 3 hours	
	Percent	Mean score	Percent	Mean score	Percent	Mean score	Percent	Mean score
International average percent correct	(NA) (NA)	(NA) (NA)	(NA) (NA)	(NA) (NA)	(NA) (NA)	(NA) (NA)	(NA) (NA)	(NA) (NA)
Australia[1]	15 (0.9)	505 (6.9)	46 (1.0)	556 (4.1)	22 (0.6)	22 (0.6)	17 (0.7)	546 (5.0)
Austria[1]	9 (0.8)	551 (9.9)	46 (1.3)	563 (4.8)	21 (0.9)	21 (0.9)	24 (1.2)	553 (4.8)
Belgium (Flemish)	2 (0.4)	(2) (NA)	25 (1.3)	545 (5.0)	28 (1.1)	28 (1.1)	45 (1.6)	547 (3.6)
Belgium (French)[1]	7 (0.8)	428 (6.9)	32 (1.0)	481 (4.7)	21 (1.3)	21 (1.3)	40 (1.5)	467 (4.0)
Bulgaria[1]	(NA) (NA)	(NA) (NA)	(NA) (NA)	(NA) (NA)	(NA) (NA)	(NA) (NA)	(NA) (NA)	(NA) (NA)
Canada	14 (1.2)	524 (6.1)	47 (1.1)	541 (2.8)	18 (0.7)	18 (0.7)	21 (1.1)	517 (3.6)
Colombia[1]	2 (0.4)	(2) (NA)	17 (1.1)	421 (5.3)	20 (1.2)	20 (1.2)	61 (1.9)	413 (5.8)
Cyprus	9 (0.5)	430 (7.0)	19 (0.7)	468 (4.4)	26 (0.8)	26 (0.8)	46 (0.9)	466 (2.9)
Czech Republic	13 (1.1)	558 (9.0)	57 (1.1)	579 (3.9)	17 (0.9)	17 (0.9)	13 (0.8)	560 (6.4)
Denmark[1]	39 (1.6)	494 (4.4)	39 (1.4)	479 (4.1)	13 (0.8)	13 (0.8)	9 (0.7)	457 (6.8)
England[1]	(NA) (NA)	(NA) (NA)	(NA) (NA)	(NA) (NA)	(NA) (NA)	(NA) (NA)	(NA) (NA)	(NA) (NA)
France	8 (0.7)	481 (6.8)	33 (1.2)	497 (3.3)	28 (1.0)	28 (1.0)	31 (1.2)	499 (3.4)
Germany[1]	14 (1.1)	505 (8.2)	51 (1.2)	541 (4.6)	18 (1.0)	18 (1.0)	17 (0.9)	525 (6.5)
Greece[1]	6 (0.6)	473 (4.8)	14 (0.7)	497 (5.0)	21 (0.7)	21 (0.7)	59 (1.2)	502 (2.5)
Hong Kong	13 (1.0)	489 (7.3)	32 (0.9)	519 (4.7)	25 (0.9)	25 (0.9)	30 (1.1)	534 (5.2)
Hungary	4 (0.4)	519 (10.0)	33 (1.1)	553 (4.4)	22 (0.9)	22 (0.9)	41 (1.3)	557 (3.0)
Iceland	5 (1.0)	470 (8.7)	46 (1.7)	505 (5.6)	25 (1.3)	25 (1.3)	23 (1.4)	488 (7.5)
Iran, Islamic Republic	1 (0.2)	(2) (NA)	5 (0.5)	476 (6.0)	12 (1.0)	12 (1.0)	82 (1.3)	471 (2.7)
Ireland	5 (0.6)	475 (9.0)	29 (1.0)	529 (5.4)	40 (1.1)	40 (1.1)	26 (1.2)	550 (4.9)
Israel[1]	5 (0.6)	532 (13.5)	36 (2.2)	555 (7.7)	26 (1.5)	26 (1.5)	33 (2.1)	505 (5.2)
Japan	13 (0.8)	551 (4.4)	39 (0.8)	573 (2.2)	20 (0.6)	20 (0.6)	28 (1.0)	577 (2.4)
Korea	15 (0.9)	544 (5.0)	32 (1.1)	564 (2.9)	25 (0.8)	25 (0.8)	29 (1.2)	581 (3.7)
Kuwait[1]	3 (0.6)	400 (10.4)	13 (1.5)	436 (7.8)	19 (1.3)	19 (1.3)	65 (1.8)	431 (3.4)
Latvia (Latvian-speaking schools)	4 (0.5)	468 (8.5)	35 (1.1)	492 (4.1)	32 (1.2)	32 (1.2)	29 (1.2)	481 (3.0)
Lithuania[1]	5 (0.6)	457 (9.1)	39 (1.4)	484 (4.5)	28 (1.0)	28 (1.0)	28 (1.4)	472 (4.7)
Netherlands[1]	3 (0.9)	519 (17.1)	54 (1.7)	559 (6.1)	27 (1.7)	27 (1.7)	16 (0.8)	545 (5.7)
New Zealand	12 (0.9)	488 (7.6)	51 (1.2)	536 (4.6)	21 (1.0)	21 (1.0)	17 (0.9)	516 (5.7)
Norway	6 (0.5)	501 (7.3)	50 (1.2)	533 (2.5)	24 (0.9)	24 (0.9)	21 (0.9)	516 (3.7)
Portugal	3 (0.3)	465 (8.8)	41 (1.1)	488 (2.9)	18 (0.7)	18 (0.7)	38 (1.2)	474 (2.8)
Romania[1]	9 (0.7)	460 (11.7)	16 (1.0)	468 (7.0)	15 (0.7)	15 (0.7)	60 (1.6)	499 (5.2)
Russian Federation	4 (0.5)	511 (10.1)	33 (1.1)	542 (4.4)	25 (1.0)	25 (1.0)	38 (1.4)	543 (4.6)
Scotland[1]	17 (1.4)	470 (5.3)	54 (1.2)	526 (5.1)	17 (1.0)	17 (1.0)	12 (0.8)	532 (6.5)
Singapore	2 (0.3)	(2) (NA)	7 (0.4)	604 (8.4)	13 (0.6)	13 (0.6)	78 (0.9)	607 (5.4)
Slovak Republic	6 (0.5)	551 (7.1)	46 (0.9)	552 (3.7)	25 (0.7)	25 (0.7)	23 (1.0)	536 (4.7)
Slovenia[1]	5 (0.5)	559 (9.2)	36 (1.0)	580 (3.5)	21 (0.8)	21 (0.8)	37 (1.1)	544 (3.3)
South Africa[1]	(NA) (NA)	(NA) (NA)	(NA) (NA)	(NA) (NA)	(NA) (NA)	(NA) (NA)	(NA) (NA)	(NA) (NA)
Spain	3 (0.4)	482 (7.9)	26 (1.0)	522 (2.8)	18 (0.9)	18 (0.9)	53 (1.3)	516 (2.2)
Sweden	7 (0.6)	520 (6.0)	55 (1.2)	544 (3.2)	17 (0.8)	17 (0.8)	21 (0.9)	523 (4.9)
Switzerland[1]	4 (0.3)	500 (8.3)	44 (1.2)	530 (3.1)	19 (0.8)	19 (0.8)	33 (1.1)	514 (3.5)
Thailand[1]	3 (0.3)	510 (8.8)	26 (1.0)	520 (4.0)	18 (0.7)	18 (0.7)	54 (1.5)	532 (4.1)
United States	17 (1.1)	507 (9.5)	42 (0.9)	548 (4.1)	17 (0.7)	17 (0.7)	24 (0.8)	533 (5.7)

SOURCE: International Association for the Evaluation of Educational Achievement, Science Achievement in the Middle School Years: IEA's Third International Mathematics and Science Study, 1997. Published as table 397 in *Digest of Education Statistics* 1997.

1. Countries not meeting all International Association for the Evaluation of Educational Achievement's sampling specifications.
2. Insufficient data.

(NA) Not applicable or not available.

Table C-74. Reading Literacy Test Scores of 9-year-olds: Selected Countries, 1992

State	Grade tested	Mean age	Overall mean score (s.e.)[1]		Narrative[2] 1st quartile	Narrative[2] mean score (s.e)[1]		Narrative[2] 3rd quartile	Expository[3] mean score (s.e.)[1]		Documents[4] mean score (s.e.)[1]	
Finland	3	9.7	569	(3.4)	508	568	(3.0)	602	569	(3.1)	569	(4.0)
United States	4	10.0	547	(2.8)	476	553	(3.1)	619	538	(2.6)	550	(2.7)
Sweden	3	9.8	539	(2.8)	466	536	(2.6)	592	542	(2.7)	539	(3.2)
France	4	10.1	531	(4.0)	467	532	(4.1)	580	533	(4.1)	527	(3.9)
Italy	4	9.9	529	(4.3)	468	533	(4.0)	576	538	(4.0)	517	(4.9)
New Zealand	5	10.0	528	(3.3)	452	534	(3.5)	594	531	(3.1)	521	(3.3)
Norway	3	9.8	524	(2.6)	455	525	(2.8)	576	528	(2.3)	519	(2.8)
Iceland[5]	3	9.8	518	(0.0)	448	518	(0.0)	571	517	(0.0)	519	(0.0)
Hong Kong	4	10.0	517	(3.9)	431	494	(4.1)	548	503	(3.4)	554	(4.2)
Singapore	3	9.3	515	(1.0)	450	521	(1.1)	567	519	(1.0)	504	(1.0)
Switzerland	3	9.7	511	(2.7)	438	506	(2.6)	566	507	(2.7)	522	(2.8)
Ireland	4	9.3	509	(3.6)	445	518	(3.7)	571	514	(3.2)	495	(3.8)
Belgium[6]	4	9.8	507	(3.2)	439	510	(3.3)	558	505	(2.8)	506	(3.5)
Greece	4	9.3	504	(3.7)	447	514	(3.8)	567	511	(3.6)	488	(3.8)
Spain	4	10.0	504	(2.5)	429	497	(2.4)	543	505	(2.3)	509	(2.7)
Germany (former West)	3	9.4	503	(3.0)	421	491	(2.8)	543	497	(2.9)	520	(3.2)
Canada[7]	3	8.9	500	(3.0)	437	502	(3.5)	566	499	(2.7)	500	(2.8)
Germany (former East)	3	9.5	499	(4.3)	414	482	(4.2)	531	493	(3.6)	522	(5.0)
Hungary	3	9.3	499	(3.1)	437	496	(2.9)	541	493	(3.1)	509	(3.5)
Slovenia	3	9.7	498	(2.6)	435	502	(2.7)	570	489	(2.5)	503	(2.5)
Netherlands	3	9.2	485	(3.6)	426	494	(3.3)	539	480	(3.4)	481	(3.9)
Cyprus	4	9.8	481	(2.3)	421	492	(2.4)	548	475	(2.3)	476	(2.1)
Portugal	4	10.4	478	(3.6)	419	483	(3.3)	532	480	(3.0)	471	(4.5)
Denmark	3	9.8	475	(3.5)	386	463	(3.4)	539	467	(3.5)	496	(3.6)
Trinidad/Tobago	4	9.6	451	(3.4)	383	455	(3.6)	502	458	(3.4)	440	(3.3)
Indonesia	4	10.8	394	(3.0)	351	402	(2.8)	436	411	(3.2)	369	(3.0)
Venezuela	4	10.1	383	(3.4)	322	378	(3.2)	426	396	(3.3)	374	(3.7)

SOURCE: International Association for the Evaluation of Educational Achievement, How in the World Do Students Read?, 1992. Published as table 403 in *Digest of Education Statistics* 1997.

1. s.e.=standard error.
2. Narrative prose is continuous text in which the writer's aim is to tell a story.
3. Expository prose is continuous text designed to describe factual information to the reader.
4. Documents are structured information presented in the form of charts, tables, maps, graphs, lists, or sets of instructions
5. Iceland tested all students, therefore standard errors are not applicable.
6. Only French-speaking students were tested.
7. British Columbia only.

Table C-75.   Number of Bachelor's Degree Recipients per 100 Persons of the Theoretical Age of Graduation, [1] **by Sex: Selected Countries, 1989 to 1994**

State	Men and women					Men					Women				
	1989	1990	1991	1992	1994	1989	1990	1991	1992	1994	1989	1990	1991	1992	1994
Australia	20.8	(NA)	24.4	26.3	31.5	19.3	(NA)	21.6	22.0	25.4	22.3	(NA)	27.3	30.8	37.9
Austria	6.7	2.0	7.8	(NA)	(NA)	7.7	8.7	8.5	7.8	(NA)	5.6	7.0	7.0	5.2	(NA)
Belgium	(NA)	(NA)	13.3	(NA)	(NA)	(NA)	(NA)	15.0	(NA)	(NA)	(NA)	(NA)	11.5	(NA)	(NA)
Canada	30.2	31.8	33.3	32.2	30.2	26.9	27.6	28.2	26.9	25.5	33.5	36.0	38.7	37.7	35.1
Denmark	12.9	15.0	16.5	22.1	[2] 20.2	11.5	13.2	14.4	17.6	[2] 16.1	14.4	16.8	18.7	26.9	[2] 24.6
Finland	(NA)	(NA)	(NA)	6.5	7.5	(NA)	(NA)	(NA)	(NA)	9.3	(NA)	(NA)	(NA)	(NA)	5.5
France	13.9	14.9	16.3	(NA)	(NA)	13.8	14.7	14.9	(NA)	(NA)	14.0	15.1	17.7	(NA)	(NA)
Germany[3]	13.2	12.9	13.3	(NA)	(NA)	16.1	15.7	15.9	(NA)	(NA)	10.1	10.0	10.6	(NA)	(NA)
Ireland	16.3	17.5	16.0	17.4	[2] 22.8	(NA)	16.9	15.8	17.7	[2] 22.3	(NA)	18.2	16.2	17.1	[2] 23.4
Italy	(NA)	(NA)	(NA)	(NA)	0.8	(NA)	(NA)	(NA)	(NA)	0.5	(NA)	(NA)	(NA)	(NA)	1.0
Japan	(NA)	21.8	23.7	23.4	23.4	(NA)	30.9	33.5	32.3	31.2	(NA)	12.3	13.7	14.1	15.3
Netherlands	10.2	8.0	8.3	17.8	[2] 17.4	12.3	9.4	9.6	17.6	[2] 17.2	7.9	6.5	6.9	18.0	[2] 17.6
New Zealand	15.7	15.1	16.1	18.0	[2] 21.9	16.4	15.7	16.5	17.7	[2] 19.9	15.0	14.6	15.8	18.3	[2] 24.0
Norway	(NA)	(NA)	(NA)	19.4	17.6	(NA)	(NA)	(NA)	14.8	12.5	(NA)	(NA)	(NA)	24.2	22.9
Portugal	(NA)	(NA)	(NA)	(NA)	1.8	(NA)	(NA)	(NA)	(NA)	1.2	(NA)	(NA)	(NA)	(NA)	2.4
Spain	(NA)	(NA)	(NA)	8.0	[2] 8.6	(NA)	(NA)	(NA)	5.8	[2] 6.8	(NA)	(NA)	(NA)	10.4	[2] 10.4
Sweden	13.1	12.2	12.5	11.4	6.9	11.1	10.5	11.0	9.6	4.8	15.1	14.0	14.2	13.3	9.1
Switzerland	7.7	7.8	7.6	(NA)	(NA)	10.1	10.3	9.8	(NA)	(NA)	5.3	5.1	5.4	(NA)	(NA)
Turkey	6.3	6.5	6.5	6.0	[2] 7.1	7.9	8.2	8.2	7.4	[2] 8.8	4.7	4.7	4.7	4.4	[2] 5.4
United Kingdom	(NA)	(NA)	(NA)	20.4	27.0	(NA)	(NA)	(NA)	21.1	26.5	(NA)	(NA)	(NA)	19.7	27.5
United States	27.8	28.1	28.1	27.4	31.8	26.1	25.9	25.3	24.7	28.4	29.6	30.5	31.0	30.3	35.2

SOURCE: Organization for Economic Cooperation and Development, Education at a Glance, 1996. Published as table 405 in *Digest of Education Statistics* 1997.

1. In most countries the theoretical age of graduation was 22 or 23. The range was from 21 to 25. The number of bachelor's degree recipients may be of any age.
2. Data for 1993.
3. Data for 1989 are for the former West Germany.

(NA) Not applicable or not available.

Table C-76. Public Education Expenditures per Student, by Level of Student: Selected Countries, 1985 to 1993

(In constant 1993 dollars)

State	Primary					Secondary					Higher education				
	1985	1990	1991	1992	1993	1985	1990	1991	1992	1993	1985	1990	1991	1992	1993
Austria	$3 554	$3 632	$3 791	$4 130	$4 291	$4 061	$4 771	$4 965	$6 612	$6 721	$6 753	$6 560	$6 834	$5 994	$8 642
Belgium	2 299	2 195	2 273	2 462	2 953	5 437	4 949	5 305	5 304	5 373	7 310	6 363	6 615	6 787	6 380
Denmark	3 677	4 579	4 665	4 346	4 745	5 196	5 459	5 706	5 088	6 175	8 826	8 582	8 153	6 911	8 045
France	(NA)	(NA)	2 749	2 987	3 154	(NA)	(NA)	4 923	5 593	5 685	(NA)	(NA)	5 050	6 200	6 033
Germany[2]	(NA)	(NA)	(NA)	3 069	2 815	(NA)	(NA)	(NA)	4 388	6 481	(NA)	(NA)	(NA)	(NA)	7 902
Japan	(NA)	(NA)	(NA)	3 636	3 960	(NA)	(NA)	(NA)	4 017	4 356	(NA)	(NA)	(NA)	12 205	7 556
Ireland	1 363	1 472	1 636	1 823	1 882	2 346	2 475	2 640	2 853	3 031	5 327	5 693	5 927	7 488	7 076
Norway	3 505	3 995	4 122	4 614	(NA)	4 961	5 307	5 704	6 386	(NA)	8 092	8 887	8 917	8 981	8 343
Portugal	1 369	1 989	2 239	(NA)	2 581	1 811	(NA)	2 508	(NA)	2 491	3 844	(NA)	6 536	(NA)	5 667
Spain	1 482	1 854	1 974	2 091	2 293	2 058	2 787	2 896	3 234	3 033	1 964	3 250	3 440	3 883	3 835
Sweden[1]	(NA)	5 429	5 803	4 985	4 917	(NA)	6 480	7 039	6 231	5 651	(NA)	8 929	9 083	7 333	12 693
Switzerland[1]	(NA)	(NA)	5 779	3 667	5 835	(NA)	(NA)	6 963	(NA)	7 024	(NA)	(NA)	15 577	13 286	15 731
Turkey	(NA)	(NA)	599	(NA)	832	(NA)	(NA)	535	(NA)	587	(NA)	(NA)	2 965	(NA)	2 696
United Kingdom	2 406	2 984	2 964	3 213	3 295	3 979	5 664	4 514	4 521	4 494	(NA)	(NA)	10 207	10 680	8 241
United States	4 495	5 380	5 492	5 768	5 492	5 440	6 742	6 866	6 664	6 541	10 527	12 373	12 521	12 236	14 607

SOURCE: Organization for Economic Cooperation and Development, Education at a Glance, 1996; and unpublished data. Published as table 408 in *Digest of Education Statistics* 1997.

1. Change in definition in 1992.
2. Data for 1985 are for the former West Germany.

NOTE: Data adjusted to U.S. dollars using the purchasing-power-parity (PPP) index. The data used in calculating expenditure per student include only the expenditure for educational institutions. Public subsidies for students' living expenses are excluded. The figures include public expenditures per student in public and private institutions.

(NA) Not applicable or not available.

Table C-77. Public Expenditures for Education as a Percentage of Gross Domestic Product, by Level of Education: Selected Countries, 1985 to 1993

State	All levels[1]							Primary education					
	1985	1988	1989	1990	1991	1992	1993	1985	1988	1989	1990	1991	1993
Australia	6.0	5.5	(NA)	(NA)	4.6	4.5	4.9	1.8	1.6	(NA)	(NA)	1.5	1.6
Austria	5.7	5.5	5.3	5.2	5.4	(NA)	5.3	1.0	1.0	0.9	0.9	1.0	1.0
Belgium	6.4	5.6	5.7	5.2	(NA)	(NA)	5.6	1.1	1.0	0.9	0.9	(NA)	1.1
Denmark	6.2	6.4	6.4	6.2	6.1	6.2	6.7	1.7	1.7	1.7	1.7	1.7	1.5
Germany[2]	4.6	4.3	(NA)	(NA)	4.1	3.7	4.5	0.6	0.6	(NA)	(NA)	0.5	0.7
Ireland	5.9	5.6	5.3	5.2	5.4	5.7	5.2	1.7	1.6	1.6	1.5	1.6	1.5
Italy	4.7	4.9	5.0	5.2	(NA)	(NA)	5.0	1.2	1.1	1.2	1.1	(NA)	1.1
Japan	(NA)	(NA)	(NA)	(NA)	(NA)	3.6	3.7	(NA)	(NA)	(NA)	(NA)	(NA)	1.4
Luxembourg	(NA)	6.0	5.8	(NA)	(NA)	(NA)	(NA)	(NA)	2.1	2.0	(NA)	(NA)	(NA)
New Zealand	(NA)	5.2	6.3	(NA)	5.8	(NA)	6.0	(NA)	1.4	1.7	(NA)	1.5	1.7
Norway	5.6	6.4	6.5	6.4	6.8	(NA)	7.6	1.7	1.9	1.8	1.6	1.7	1.7
Portugal	(NA)	(NA)	4.8	4.8	5.5	5.2	5.3	2.1	2.3	2.1	2.1	2.2	1.9
Spain	3.6	3.9	4.2	4.4	4.5	4.2	4.5	1.2	1.1	1.1	1.0	1.0	1.0
Sweden	(NA)	5.9	5.5	5.7	6.1	6.7	6.7	(NA)	2.2	2.0	2.0	2.2	2.0
Switzerland	5.1	5.1	(NA)	(NA)	5.4	(NA)	5.6	2.9	2.8	(NA)	(NA)	1.4	1.6
Turkey	(NA)	(NA)	(NA)	(NA)	4.0	(NA)	3.3	(NA)	(NA)	(NA)	(NA)	1.9	1.7
United Kingdom	5.3	5.0	4.9	5.1	4.9	4.1	4.7	1.2	1.3	1.3	1.3	1.3	1.6
United States	5.0	5.2	5.1	5.6	5.7	5.7	5.1	1.5	1.7	1.8	1.8	1.8	1.8

State	Secondary education						Higher education						
	1985	1988	1989	1990	1991	1993	1985	1988	1989	1990	1991	1992	1993
Australia	2.1	1.9	(NA)	(NA)	1.5	2.1	1.8	1.8	(NA)	(NA)	1.5	1.8	1.1
Austria	2.8	2.7	2.6	2.5	2.6	2.5	1.0	1.1	1.1	1.1	1.1	(NA)	1.1
Belgium	3.0	2.5	2.5	2.3	(NA)	2.6	1.0	0.9	0.9	0.9	(NA)	(NA)	1.0
Denmark	2.8	2.9	2.9	2.7	2.7	2.9	1.2	1.3	1.3	1.3	1.3	1.3	1.3
Germany[2]	2.2	2.0	(NA)	(NA)	1.9	2.3	1.0	1.0	(NA)	(NA)	0.9	1.0	0.9
Ireland	2.4	2.3	2.2	2.1	2.2	2.2	0.9	1.0	1.0	1.0	1.1	1.4	1.0
Italy	2.0	2.2	2.3	2.2	(NA)	2.4	0.6	0.8	0.7	1.0	(NA)	(NA)	0.8
Japan	(NA)	(NA)	(NA)	(NA)	(NA)	1.6	(NA)	(NA)	(NA)	(NA)	(NA)	0.3	0.4
Luxembourg	(NA)	2.5	2.4	(NA)	(NA)	(NA)	(NA)	0.2	0.2	(NA)	(NA)	(NA)	(NA)
New Zealand	(NA)	1.2	1.5	(NA)	1.3	2.7	(NA)	1.6	1.8	(NA)	2.0	(NA)	1.2
Norway	2.7	2.9	2.8	2.7	2.8	2.7	0.8	1.0	1.1	1.2	1.3	(NA)	1.5
Portugal	1.2	1.4	1.6	1.6	2.0	1.9	0.6	0.8	0.9	0.9	0.9	0.9	0.8
Spain	1.8	2.1	2.2	2.3	2.4	2.4	0.4	0.6	0.6	0.7	0.8	0.9	0.8
Sweden	0.0	2.5	2.4	2.5	2.7	2.6	(NA)	1.0	0.9	1.1	1.1	1.0	1.5
Switzerland	1.3	1.3	(NA)	(NA)	2.4	2.5	1.0	1.0	(NA)	(NA)	1.2	(NA)	1.2
Turkey	(NA)	(NA)	(NA)	(NA)	1.0	0.8	(NA)	(NA)	(NA)	(NA)	1.0	(NA)	0.8
United Kingdom	2.2	2.3	2.2	2.3	2.2	2.3	1.1	0.9	0.9	0.9	1.0	0.1	0.7
United States	1.9	1.9	1.9	2.0	2.0	1.9	1.3	1.4	1.2	1.5	1.5	1.6	1.2

SOURCE: Organization for Economic Cooperation and Development, Education at a Glance, 1996; and unpublished data. Published as table 409 in *Digest of Education Statistics* 1997.

1. Includes primary, secondary, and higher education not classified by level of education.
2. Data before 1990 are for the former West Germany.

(NA) Not applicable or not available.

Notes and Definitions: Education Characteristics by States

The tables in Part C were gleaned largely from the National Center for Education Statistics' *Digest of Education Statistics 1997*. Some of the tables have been updated where more recent information has become available. For example, private school enrollment figures presented here are more recent than those shown in the 1997 *Digest*. Many publications of the National Center for Education Statistics are available on the website at http://nces.ed.gov.

Academic support. This category of college expenditures includes those for support services that are an integral part of the institution's primary missions of instruction, research, or public service. It includes expenditures for libraries, galleries, audio/visual services, academic administration, personnel development, and course and curriculum development.

Achievement test. An examination that measures the extent to which a person has acquired certain information or mastered certain skills, usually as a result of specific instruction.

Administrative support staff. Personnel dealing with salary, benefits, supplies, and contractual fees for the office of the principal, full-time department chairpersons, and graduation expenses.

Agriculture. Courses designed to improve competencies in agricultural occupations. Included is the study of agricultural production, supplies, mechanization and products, agricultural science, forestry, and related services.

American College Testing Program (ACT). The ACT assessment program measures educational development and readiness to pursue college-level coursework in English, mathematics, natural science, and social studies. Student performance on the tests does not reflect innate ability and is influenced by a student's educational preparedness.

Appropriation (federal funds). Budget authority provided through the congressional appropriation process that permits federal agencies to incur obligations to make payments.

Appropriation (institutional revenues). An amount (other than a grant or contract) received from or made available to an institution through an act of a legislative body.

Associate degree. A degree granted for the successful completion of a subbaccalaureate program of studies, usually requiring at least two years (or equivalent) of full-time college-level study. This includes degrees granted in a cooperative or work-study program.

Auxiliary enterprises. This category includes those essentially self-supporting operations that exist to furnish a service to students, faculty, or staff and that charge a fee that is directly related to, although not necessarily equal to, the cost of the service. Examples are residence halls, food services, college stores, and intercollegiate athletics.

Average daily attendance (ADA). The aggregate attendance of a school during a reporting period (normally a school year) divided by the number of days school is in session during this period. Only days on which the pupils are under the guidance and direction of teachers should be considered days in session.

Average daily membership (ADM). The aggregate membership of a school during a reporting period (normally a school year) divided by the number of days school is in session during this period. Only days on which the pupils are under the guidance and direction of teachers should be considered as days in session. The average daily membership for groups of schools having varying lengths of terms is the average of the average daily memberships obtained for individual schools.

Bachelor's degree. A degree granted for the successful completion of a baccalaureate program of studies, usually requiring at least four years (or equivalent) of full-time college-level study. This includes degrees granted in a cooperative or work-study program.

Books. Nonperiodical printed publications bound in hard or soft covers or in loose-leaf format, of at least 49 pages, exclusive of the cover pages; juvenile nonperiodical publications of any length found in hard or soft covers.

Budget authority (BA). Authority provided by law to enter into obligations that will result in immediate or future outlays. It may be classified by the period of availability (one-year, multiple-year, no-year), by the timing of congressional action (current or permanent), or by the manner of determining the amount available (definite or indefinite).

Business. Program of instruction that prepares individuals for a variety of activities in planning, organizing, directing, and controlling business office systems and procedures.

Carnegie unit. A standard of measurement that represents one credit for the completion of a one-year course.

Catholic school. A private school over which a Roman Catholic church group exercises some control or provides some form of subsidy. Catholic schools for the most part include those operated or supported by a parish, a group of parishes, a diocese, or a Catholic religious order.

Central cities. The largest cities, with 50,000 or more inhabitants, in a Metropolitan Statistical Area (MSA). A smaller city within an MSA may also qualify if it has at least 25,000 inhabitants or has a population of one-third or more of that of the largest city and a minimum population of 25,000. An exception occurs where two cities have contiguous boundaries and constitute, for economic and social purposes, a single community of at least 50,000, the smaller of which must have a population of at least 15,000.

Class size. The membership of a class at a given date.

Classroom teacher. A staff member assigned the professional activities of instructing pupils in self-contained classes or courses or in classroom situations. Usually expressed in full-time equivalents.

Cohort. A group of individuals that have a statistical factor in common; for example, a year of birth.

College. A postsecondary school that offers general or liberal arts education, usually leading to an associate, bachelor's, master's, doctor's, or first-professional degree. Junior colleges and community colleges are included under this terminology.

Combined elementary and secondary school. A school that encompasses instruction at both the elementary and the secondary levels. It includes schools starting with grade 6 or below and ending with grade 9 or above.

Computer science. A group of instructional programs that describes computer and information science, including computer programming, data processing, and information systems.

Constant dollars. Dollar amounts that have been adjusted by means of price and cost indexes to eliminate the inflationary factor and allow direct comparison across years.

Consumer, personal, and miscellaneous services. A group of instructional programs that describes the fundamental skills a person is normally thought to need in order to function productively in society. Some examples are child development, consumer education, and family relations.

Consumer Price Index (CPI). This price index measures the average change in the cost of a fixed market basket of goods and services purchased by consumers.

Consumption. That portion of income that is spent on the purchase of goods and services rather than being saved.

Control of institutions. A classification of institutions of elementary/secondary or higher education by whether the institution is operated by publicly elected or appointed officials (public control) or by privately elected or appointed officials and derives its major source of funds from private sources (private control).

Credit. The unit of value, awarded for successful completion of certain instruction in relation to the total requirements for a diploma, certificate, or degree. Credits are frequently expressed in terms such as "Carnegie units," "semester credit hours," and "quarter credit hours."

Current dollars. Dollars amounts that have not been adjusted to compensate for inflation.

Current expenditures (elementary/secondary). The expenditures for operating local public schools, excluding capital outlay and interest on school debt. These expenditures include such items as salaries for school personnel, fixed charges, student transportation, school books and materials, and energy costs. Beginning in 1980–81, expenditures for state administration are excluded.

Current expenditures per pupil in average daily attendance. Current expenditures for the regular school term divided by the average daily attendance of full-time pupils (or full-time equivalency of pupils) during the term. See also *Current expenditures* and *Average daily attendance.*

Current-fund expenditures (higher education). Money spent to meet current operating costs, including salaries, wages, utilities, student services, public services, research libraries, scholarships and fellowships, auxiliary enterprises, hospitals, and independent operations. It excludes loans, capital expenditures, and investments.

Current-fund revenues (higher education). Money received during the current fiscal year from revenue that can be used to pay obligations currently due, and surpluses reappropriated for the current fiscal year.

Current Population Survey. See *Guide to sources.*

Disposable personal income. Current income received by persons less their contributions for Social Security insurance, personal tax, and nontax payments. It is the income available to persons for spending and saving. Nontax payments include passport fees, fines and penalties, donations, and tuition and fees paid to schools and hospitals operated mainly by the government. See also *Personal income.*

Doctor's degree. An earned degree carrying the title of doctor. The doctor of philosophy degree (Ph.D.) is the highest academic degree and requires mastery within a field of knowledge and demonstrated ability to perform scholarly research. Other doctorates are awarded for fulfilling specialized requirements in professional fields such as education (Ed.D.), musical arts (D.M.A.), business administration (D.B.A.), and engineering (D.Eng. or D.E.S.). Many doctor's degrees in academic and professional fields require an earned master's degree as a prerequisite. First-professional degrees, such as M.D. and D.D.S., are not included under this heading.

Educational and general expenditures. The sum of current funds expenditures on instruction, research, public service, academic support, student services, institutional support, operation and maintenance of plant, and awards from restricted and unrestricted funds.

Educational attainment. The highest grade of regular school attended and completed.

Elementary education/programs. Learning experiences concerned with the knowledge, skills, appreciations, attitudes, and behavioral characteristics that are considered to be needed by all pupils in terms of their awareness of life within our culture and the world of work and that normally may be achieved during the elementary school years (usually kindergarten through grade 8 or kindergarten through grade 6), as defined by applicable state laws and regulations.

Elementary school. A school classified as elementary by the state and local practice and composed of any span of grades not above grade 8. A preschool or kindergarten school is included under this heading only if it is an integral part of an elementary school or a regularly established school system.

Elementary/secondary school. As reported in this publication, this category includes only regular schools (i.e., schools that are part of state and local school systems and also most not-for-profit private elementary/secondary schools, both religiously affiliated and nonsectarian). Schools not reported include subcollegiate departments of institutions of higher education, residential schools for exceptional children, federal schools for American Indians, and federal schools on military posts and other federal installations.

Employment. Civilian, noninstitutional persons who (1) worked during any part of the survey week as paid employees; worked in their own business, profession, or farm or worked 15 hours or more as unpaid workers in a family-owned enterprise; or (2) were not working but had jobs or businesses from which they were temporarily absent due to illness, bad weather, vacation, labor-management dispute, or personal reasons whether or not they were seeking another job.

Endowment. A trust fund set aside to provide a perpetual source of revenue from proceeds of the endowment investment. Endowment funds are often created by donations from benefactors of an institution who may designate the use of the endowment revenue. Normally, institutions or their representatives manage the investments, but they are not permitted to spend the endowment fund itself, only the proceeds from the investments. Typical uses of endowments would be an endowed chair for a particular department or for a scholarship fund. Endowment totals tabulated in this book also include funds functioning as endowments, such as funds left over from the previous year and placed with the endowment investments by the institution. These funds may be withdrawn by the institution and spent as current funds at any time. Endowments are evaluated by two different measures, book value and market value. Book value is the purchase price of the endowment investment. Market value is the current worth of the endowment investment. Thus, the book value of a stock held in an endowment fund would be the purchase price of the stock. The market value of the stock would be its selling price as of a given day.

Engineering. Instructional programs that describe the mathematical and natural science knowledge gained by study, experience, and practice and applied with judgment to develop ways to utilize the materials and forces of nature economically for the benefit of mankind. It includes programs that prepare individuals to support and assist engineers and similar professionals.

English. A group of instructional programs that describes the English language arts, including composition, creative writing, and the study of literature.

Enrollment. The total number of students registered in a given school unit at a given time, generally in the fall of a year.

Expenditures. Charges incurred, whether paid or unpaid, that are presumed to benefit the current fiscal year. For elementary/secondary schools, these include all charges for current outlays plus capital outlays and interest on school debt. For institutions of higher education, these include current outlay plus capital outlays. For government, these include charges net of recoveries and other correcting transactions other than for retirement of debt, investment in securities, extension of credit, or as agency transactions. Government expenditures include only external transactions, such as the provision of perquisites or other payments in kind. Aggregates for groups of governments exclude intergovernmental transactions among the governments.

Expenditures per pupil. Charges incurred for a particular period of time divided by a student unit of measure, such as average daily attendance or average daily membership.

Extracurricular activities. Activities that are not part of the required curriculum and that take place outside of the regular course of study. As used here, they include both school-sponsored (e.g., varsity athletics, drama and debate clubs) and community-sponsored (e.g., hobby clubs and youth organizations such as the Junior Chamber of Commerce or Boy Scouts) activities.

Family. A group of two or more persons (one of whom is the householder) related by birth, marriage, or adoption and residing together. All such persons (including related subfamily members) are considered as members of one family.

Federal funds. Amounts collected and used by the federal government for the general purposes of the government. There are four types of federal fund accounts: the general fund, special funds, public enterprise funds, and intragovernmental funds. The major federal fund is the general fund, which is derived from general taxes and borrowing. Federal funds also include certain earmarked collections, such as those generated by and used to finance a continuing cycle of business-type operations.

Federal sources. Federal appropriations, grants, and contracts and federally funded research and development centers (FFRDCs). Federally subsidized student loans and Pell Grants are not included.

First-professional degree. A degree that signifies both completion of the academic requirements for beginning practice in a given profession and a level of professional skill beyond that normally required for a bachelor's degree. This degree usually is based on a program requiring at least two academic years of work prior to entrance and a total of at least six academic years of work to complete the degree program, including both prior-required college work and the professional program itself. By NCES definition, first-professional degrees are awarded in the fields of dentistry (D.D.S. or D.M.D.), medicine (M.D.), optometry (O.D.), osteopathic medicine (D.O.), pharmacy (D.Phar.), podiatric medicine (D.P.M.), veterinary medicine (D.V.M.), chiropractic (D.C. or D.C.M.), law (J.D.), and theological professions (M.Div. or M.H/L.).

First-professional enrollment. The number of students enrolled in a professional school or program that requires at least two years of academic college work for entrance and a total of at least six years for a degree. By NCES definition, first-professional enrollment includes only students in certain programs. See *First-professional degree* for a list of programs.

Fiscal year. The yearly accounting period for the federal government, which begins on October 1 and ends on the following September 30. The fiscal year is designated by the calendar year in which it ends; for example, fiscal year 1988 begins on October 1, 1987, and ends on September 30, 1988. (From fiscal year 1844 to fiscal year 1976, the fiscal year began on July 1 and ended on the following June 30.)

Foreign languages. A group of instructional programs that describes the structure and use of language that is common or indigenous to people of the same community or nation, the same geographical area, or the same cultural traditions. Programs cover such features as sound, literature, syntax, phonology, semantics, sentences, prose, and verse, as well as the development of skills and attitudes used in communicating and evaluating thoughts and feelings through oral and written language.

Full-time enrollment. The number of students enrolled in higher education courses with a total credit load equal to at least 75 percent of the normal full-time course load.

Full-time equivalent (FTE) enrollment. For institutions of higher education, enrollment of full-time students, plus the full-time equivalent of part-time students. The full-time equivalent of the part-time students is estimated using different factors depending on the type and control of institution and level of student.

Full-time instructional faculty. Those members of the instruction/research staff who are employed full time as defined by the institution, including faculty with release time for research and faculty on sabbatical leave. Full-time counts exclude faculty who are employed to teach fewer than two semesters, three quarters, two trimesters, or two four-month sessions; replacements for faculty on sabbatical leave or those on leave without pay; faculty for preclinical and clinical medicine; faculty who are donating their services; faculty who are members of military organizations and paid on a different pay scale from civilian employees; academic officers whose primary duties are administrative; and graduate students who assist in the instruction of courses.

Full-time worker. In educational institutions, an employee whose position requires him or her to be on the job on school days throughout the school year at least the number of hours the schools are in session. For higher education, a member of an educational institution's staff who is employed full time.

General administration support services. Salary, benefits, supplies, and contractual fees for boards of education staff and executive administration. They exclude state administration.

General Education Development (GED) program. Academic instruction to prepare persons to take the high school equivalency examination. See *GED recipient.*

GED recipient. A person who has obtained certification of high school equivalency by meeting state requirements and passing an approved exam, which is intended to provide an appraisal of the person's achievement or performance in the broad subject matter areas usually required for high school graduation.

General program. A program of study designed to prepare students for the common activities of a citizen, family member, and work. A general program of studies may include instruction in both academic and vocational areas.

Government appropriation. An amount (other than a grant or contract) received from or made available to an institution through an act of a legislative body.

Government grant or contract. Revenues from a government agency for a specific research project or other program.

Graduate. An individual who has received formal recognition for the successful completion of a prescribed program of studies.

Graduate enrollment. The number of students who hold the bachelor's or first-professional degree, or the equivalent, and who are working toward a master's or doctor's degree. First-professional students are counted separately. These enrollment data measure those students who are registered at a particular time during the fall. At some institutions, graduate enrollment also includes students who are in postbaccalaureate classes but not in degree programs. In specified tables, graduate enrollment includes all students in regular graduate programs and all students in postbaccalaureate classes but not in degree programs (unclassified postbaccalaureate students).

Graduate Record Examination (GRE). Multiple-choice examinations administered by the Educational Testing Service and taken by college students who are intending to attend certain graduate schools. The tests are offered in a variety of subject areas. Ordinarily, a student will take only the exam that applies to the intended field of study.

Graduation. Formal recognition given an individual for the successful completion of a prescribed program of studies.

Gross domestic product (GDP). The total national output of goods and services valued at market prices. GDP can be viewed in terms of expenditure categories, which include purchases of goods and services by consumers and government, gross private domestic investment, and net exports of goods and services. The goods and services included are largely those bought for final use (excluding illegal transactions) in the market economy. A number of inclusions, however, represent imputed values, the most important of which is rental value of owner-occupied housing. GDP, in this broad context, measures the output attributable to the factors of production_labor and property_supplied by U.S. residents.

Handicapped. Those children evaluated as having any of the following impairments who, because of these impairments, need special education and related services. (These definitions apply specifically to data from the U.S. Office of Special Education and Rehabilitative Services presented in this publication.)

Deaf. Having a hearing impairment that is so severe that the student is impaired in processing linguistic information through hearing (with or without amplification) and that adversely affects educational performance.

Deaf-blind. Having concomitant hearing and visual impairments that cause such severe communication and other developmental and educational problems that the student cannot be accommodated in special education programs for solely deaf or solely blind students.

Hard of hearing. Having a hearing impairment, whether permanent or fluctuating, that adversely affects the student's educational performance but that is not included under the definition of "deaf" in this section.

Mentally retarded. Having significantly subaverage general intellectual functioning, existing concurrently with defects in adaptive behavior and manifested during the developmental period, that adversely affects the child's educational performance.

Multihandicapped. Having concomitant impairments (such as mentally retarded-blind, mentally retarded-orthopedically impaired, etc.), the combination of which causes such severe educational problems that the student cannot be accommodated in special education programs solely for one of the impairments. The term does not include deaf-blind students but does include those students who are severely or profoundly mentally retarded.

Orthopedically impaired. Having a severe orthopedic impairment that adversely affects a student's educational performance. The term includes impairment resulting from congenital anomaly, disease, or other causes.

Other health impaired. Having limited strength, vitality, or alertness due to chronic or acute health problems such as a heart condition, tuberculosis, rheumatic fever, nephritis, asthma, sickle cell anemia, hemophilia, epilepsy, lead poisoning, leukemia, or diabetes that adversely affects the student's educational performance.

Seriously emotionally disturbed. Exhibiting one or more of the following characteristics over a long period of time, to a marked degree, and adversely affecting educational performance: an inability to learn that cannot be explained by intellectual, sensory, or health factors; an inability to build or maintain satisfactory interpersonal relationships with peers and teachers; inappropriate types of behavior or feelings under normal circumstances; a general pervasive mood of unhappiness or depression; or a tendency to develop physical symptoms or fears associated with personal or school problems. This term does not include children who are socially maladjusted unless they also display one or more of the listed characteristics.

Special learning disabled. Having a disorder in one or more of the basic psychological processes involved in understanding or in using spoken or written language that may manifest itself in an imperfect ability to listen, think, speak, read, write, spell, or do mathematical calculations. The term includes such conditions as perceptual handicaps, brain injury, minimal brain dysfuction, dyslexia, and developmental aphasia. The term does not include children who have learning problems that are primarily the result of visual, hearing, or environmental, cultural, or economic disadvantage.

Speech impaired. Having a communication disorder, such as stuttering, impaired articulation, language impairment, or voice impairment, that adversely affects the student's educational performance.

Visually handicapped. Having a visual impairment that, even with correction, adversely affects the student's educational performance. The term includes partially seeing and blind children.

Higher education. Study beyond secondary school at an institution that offers programs terminating in an associate, baccalaureate, or higher degree.

Higher education institutions (alternative classification)

Doctoral-rating. Characterized by a significant level and breadth of activity in commitment to doctoral-level education as measured by the number of doctorate recipients and the diversity in doctoral-level program offerings.

Comprehensive. Characterized by diverse postbaccalaureate programs (including first-professional) but not engaged in significant doctoral-level education.

General baccalaureate. Characterized by primary emphasis on general undergraduate, baccalaureate-level education. Not significantly engaged in postbaccalaureate education.

Specialized. Baccalaureate or postbaccalaureate institution emphasizing one area (plus closely related specialties), such as business or engineering. The programmatic emphasis is measured by the percentage of degrees granted in the program area.

2-year. Conferring at least 75 percent of its degrees and awards for work below the bachelor's level.

New. These institutions, though not necessarily newly organized, are new additions to the Higher Education General Information Survey universe. When degree and award data become available, they will be classified.

Higher education institutions (traditional classification)

4-year institution. An institution legally authorized to offer and offering at least a four-year program of college-level studies wholly or principally creditable toward a baccalaureate degree. In some tables, a further division between universities and other four-year institutions is made. A university is a postsecondary institution that typically comprises one or more graduate professional schools (see also *University*). For purposes of trend comparisons within this table, the selection of universities has been held constant for all tabulations after 1982. "Other 4-year institutions" include the rest of the nonuniversity four-year institutions.

2-year institution. An institution legally authorized to offer and offering at least a two-year program of college-level studies that terminates in an associate degree or is principally creditable toward a baccalaureate degree. The category also includes some institutions that have less than a two-year program but were designated as institutions of higher education in the Higher Education General Information Survey.

Higher Education Price Index. A price index that measures average changes in the prices of goods and services purchased by colleges and universities through current-fund education and general expenditures (excluding expenditures for sponsored research and auxiliary enterprises).

High school. A secondary school offering the final years of high school work necessary for graduation, usually including grades 10, 11, and 12 (in a 6–3-3 plan) or grades 9, 10, 11, and 12 (in a 6-2-4 plan).

High school program. A program of studies designed to prepare students for their postsecondary education and occupation. Three types of programs are usually distinguished: academic, vocational, and general. An academic program is designed to prepare students for continued study at a college or university. A vocational program is designed to prepare students for employment in one or more semiskilled, skilled, or technical occupations. A general program is designed to provide students with the understanding and competence to function effectively in a free society and usually represents a mixture of academic and vocational components.

Historically black colleges and universities. Accredited institutions of higher education established prior to 1964 with the principal mission of educating Black Americans. Federal regulations (20 USC 1061 (2)) allow for certain exceptions to the founding date.

Household. All the persons who occupy a housing unit. A house, apartment, other group of rooms, or single room is regarded as a housing unit when it is occupied or intended for occupancy as separate living quarters, that is, when the occupants do not live and eat with any other persons in the structure, and there is direct access from the outside or through a common hall.

Housing unit. A house, an apartment, a mobile home, a group of rooms, or a single room that is occupied as separate living quarters.

Imaginative writing. This type of writing can take a variety of forms, such as stories, poems, plays, or lyrics. It represents a special approach to sharing experiences and understanding the world and ourselves. In this form of writing, special attention is given to rhythm and tone; the use of anecdotes; the presence of metaphors and similes; shifts in plots; and the unexpected use of words, phrases, or punctuation.

Income tax. Taxes levied on net income, that is, on gross income less certain deductions permitted by law. These taxes can be levied on individuals or on corporations or unincorporated businesses where the income is taxed distinctly from individual income.

Independent operations. A group of self-supporting activities under control of a college or university. For purposes of financial surveys conducted by the National Center for Education Statistics, this category is composed principally of Federal Funded Research and Development Centers (FFRDCs).

Informative writing. This type of writing is used to share information and to convey messages, directions, and ideas.

It often involves reporting or retelling events or experiences that have already occurred.

Institutional support. The category of higher education expenditures that includes day-to-day operational support for colleges, excluding expenditures for physical plant operations. Examples of institutional support include general administrative services, executive direction and planning, legal and fiscal operations, and community relations.

Instruction. The category including expenditures of the college, schools, departments, and other instructional divisions of higher education institutions and expenditures for departmental research and public service that are not separately budgeted. This category includes expenditures for both credit and noncredit activities and excludes expenditures for academic administration where the primary function is administration (e.g., academic deans).

Instruction (elementary and secondary). Instruction encompasses all activities dealing directly with the interaction between teachers and students. Teaching may be provided for students in a school classroom, in another location such as a home or hospital, and in other learning situations such as those involving co-curricular activities. Instruction may be provided through some other approved medium such as television, radio, telephone, and correspondence. Instruction expenditures included salaries, employee benefits, purchase services, supplies, and tuition to private schools.

Instructional staff. Full-time equivalent number of positions, not the number of different individuals occupying the positions during the school year. In local schools, the category includes all public elementary and secondary (junior and senior high) day-school positions that are in the nature of teaching or in the improvement of the teaching-learning situation. It also includes consultants or supervisors of instruction, principals, teachers, guidance personnel, librarians, psychological personnel, and other instructional staff. It excludes administrative staff, attendance personnel, clerical personnel, and junior college staff.

Instructional support services. Salary, benefits, supplies, and contractual fees for staff providing instructional improvement, education media (library and audiovisual), and other instructional support services.

Junior high school. A separately organized and administered secondary school intermediate between the elementary and senior high schools, usually including grades 7, 8, and 9 (in a 6–3-3 plan) or grades 7 and 8 (in a 6–2-4 plan).

Labor force. Persons employed as civilians, unemployed (but looking for work), or in the Armed Forces during the survey week. The "civilian labor force" comprises all civilians classified as employed or unemployed.

Land-grant colleges. The first Morrill Act, in 1862, facilitated the establishment of colleges through grants of land or funds in lieu of land. The second Morrill Act, in 1890, provided for money grants and for the establishment of Black land-grant colleges and universities in those states with dual systems of higher education.

Local education agency. See *School district.*

Mandatory transfer. A transfer of current funds that must be made in order to fulfill a binding legal obligation of the institution. Included under mandatory transfers are debt service provisions relating to academic and administrative buildings, including (1) amounts set aside for debt retirement and interest and (2) required provisions for renewal and replacement of buildings to the extent that these are not financed from other funds.

Master's degree. A degree awarded for successful completion of a program generally requiring one or two years of full-time college-level study beyond the bachelor's degree. One type of master's degree, including the Master of Arts degree, or M.A., and the Master of Science degree, or M.S., is awarded in the liberal arts and sciences for advanced scholarship in a subject field or discipline and demonstrated ability to perform scholarly research. A second type of master's degree is awarded for the completion of a professionally oriented program, for example, an M.Ed. in education, an M.B.A. in business administration, an M.F.A. in fine arts, an M.M. in music, an M.S.W. in social work, and an M.P.A. in public administration. A third type of master's degree is awarded in professional fields for study beyond the first-professional degree, for example, the Master of Laws (L.L.M.) and Master of Science in various medical specializations.

Mathematics. A group of instruction programs that describes the science of numbers and their operations, interrelations, combinations, generalizations, and abstractions and of space configurations and their structure, measurement, transformations, and generalizations.

Mean test score. The score obtained by dividing the sum of the scores of all individuals in a group by the number of individuals in that group.

Metropolitan population. The population residing in Metropolitan Statistical Areas (MSAs). See *Metropolitan Statistical Area (MSA)*.

Metropolitan Statistical Area (MSA). A large population nucleus and the nearby communities that have a high degree of economic and social integration within that nucleus. Each MSA consists of one or more entire counties (or county equivalents) that meet specified standards pertaining to population, commuting ties, and metropolitan character. In New England, towns and cities, rather than counties, are the basic units. MSAs are designated by the Office of Management and Budget. An MSA includes a city and, generally, its entire urban area and the remainder of the county or counties in which the urban area is located. An MSA also includes such additional outlying counties that meet specified criteria relating to metropolitan character and level of commuting of workers into the central city or counties. Specified criteria governing the definition of MSAs recognized before 1980 are published in *Standard Metropolitan Statistical Areas: 1997*, issued by the Office of Management and Budget. New MSAs were designated when 1980 counts showed that they met one or both of the following criteria:

1. Included a city with a population of at least 50,000 within their corporate limits, or
2. Included a Census Bureau-defined urbanized area (which must have a population of at least 50,000) and a total MSA population of at least 100,000 (or, in New England, 75,000).

Migration. Geographic mobility involving a change of usual residence between clearly defined geographic units, that is, between counties, states, or regions.

Minimum-competency testing. Measuring the acquisition of competence or skills to or beyond a certain specified standard.

National Assessment of Education Programs (NAEP). See *Guide to sources*.

Newly qualified teacher. Persons who (1) first became eligible for a teaching license during the period of the study referenced or who were teaching at the time of the survey but were not certified or eligible for a teaching license, and (2) had never held full-time, regular teaching positions (as opposed to substitute) prior to completing the requirements for the degree that brought them into the survey.

Nonmetropolitan residence group. The population residing outside a Metropolitan Statistical Area. See *Metropolitan Statistical Area (MSA)*.

Nonresident alien. A person who is not a citizen of the United States and who is in this country on a temporary basis and does not have the right to remain indefinitely.

Nonsupervisory instructional staff. Persons such as curriculum specialists, counselors, librarians, remedial specialists, and others possessing education certification but not responsible for day-to-day teaching of the same group of pupils.

Normal school. A normal school was an institution that was engaged primarily in the preparation of teachers for positions in elementary and secondary schools. Prior to 1900, normal schools were often secondary schools with teacher training programs. During the early 20th century, normal schools gradually developed into higher education institutions.

Obligations. Amounts of orders placed, contracts awarded, services received, or similar legally binding commitments made by federal agencies during a given period that will require outlays during the same or some future period.

Occupational home economics. Courses of instruction emphasizing the acquisition of competencies needed for getting and holding a job or preparing for advancement in an occupational area using home economics knowledge and skills.

Occupied housing unit. Separate living quarters with occupants currently inhabiting the unit.

Off-budget federal entities. Organizational entities, federally owned in whole or in part, whose transactions belong in the budget under current budget accounting concepts but that have been excluded from the budget totals under provisions of law.

Operation and maintenance services. Salary, benefits, supplies, and contractual fees for supervision of operations and maintenance, building operation (heating, lighting, ventilation, repair, and replacement), care and upkeep of grounds and equipment, vehicle operations and maintenance (other than student transportation), security, and other operations and maintenance services.

Other support services. Salary, benefits, supplies, and contractual fees for business support services, central support services, and other support services not otherwise classified.

Other support services staff. All staff not reported in other categories. This group includes media personnel, social workers, bus drivers, security personnel, cafeteria workers, and other staff.

Outlays. The value of checks issued, interest accrued on the public debt, or other payments made, net of refunds and reimbursements.

Part-time enrollment. The number of students enrolled in higher education courses with a total credit load less than 75 percent of the normal full-time credit load.

Per capita income. Income computed for every man, woman, and child in a particular group. It is derived by dividing the total income of a particular group by the total population in that group.

Personal income. Current income received by persons from all sources minus their personal contributions for social insurance. Classified as "persons" are individuals (including owners of unincorporated firms), nonprofit institutions serving individuals, private trust funds, and private noninsured welfare funds. Personal income includes transfers (payments not resulting from current production) from government and business such as Social Security benefits and military pensions but excludes transfers among persons.

Persuasive writing. This type of writing attempts to bring about some action or change. Its primary purpose is to influence others. It is concerned with the positions, beliefs, and attitudes of the readers.

Physical plant assets. The values of land, buildings, and equipment owned, rented, or utilized by colleges. Assets exclude those plant values that are a part of endowment or other capital fund investments in real estate and construction in progress.

Postbaccalaureate enrollment. The number of graduate and first-professional students working toward advanced degrees and of students enrolled in graduate-level classes but not enrolled in degree programs. See also *Graduate enrollment* and *First-professional enrollment*.

Postsecondary education. The provision of formal instructional programs with a curriculum designed primarily for students who have completed the requirements for a high school diploma or equivalent. This category includes programs of an academic, vocational, and continuing professional education purpose and excludes avocational and adult basic education programs.

Private school or institution. A school or institution that is controlled by an individual or agency other than a state, a subdivision of a state, or the federal government; that is usually supported primarily by other than public funds; and the operation of whose program rests with other than publicly elected or appointed officials.

Property tax. The sum of money collected from a tax levied against the value of property.

Proprietary institution. An educational institution that is under private control but whose profits derive from revenues subject to taxation.

Public school or institution. A school or institution controlled and operated by publicly elected or appointed officials and deriving its primary support from public funds.

Pupil-teacher ratio. The enrollment of pupils at a given period of time divided by the full-time equivalent number of classroom teachers serving these pupils during the same period.

Racial/ethnic group. Classification indicating general racial or ethnic heritage based on self-identification, as in data collected by the Bureau of the Census, or on observer identification, as in data collected by the Office for Civil Rights. These categories are in accordance with the Office of Management and Budget standard classification scheme presented below.

> **White.** A person having origins in any of the original peoples of Europe, North Africa, or the Middle East; normally excludes persons of Hispanic origin except for tabulations produced by the Bureau of the Census, which are noted accordingly in this volume.
>
> **Black.** A person having origins in any of the Black racial groups in Africa; normally excludes persons of Hispanic origin except for tabulations produced by the Bureau of the Census, which are noted accordingly in this volume.
>
> **Hispanic.** A person of Mexican, Puerto Rican, Cuban, Central or South American, or other Spanish culture or origin, regardless of race.
>
> **Asian or Pacific Islander.** A person having origins in any of the original peoples of the Far East, Southeast

Asia, the Indian subcontinent, or the Pacific Islands. The area includes, for example, China, India, Japan, Korea, the Philippine Islands, and Samoa.

American Indian or Alaska Native. A person having origins in any of the original peoples of North America and maintaining cultural identification through tribal affiliation or community recognition.

Remedial education. Instruction for a student lacking those reading, writing, or math skills necessary to perform college-level work at the level required by the attending institution.

Resident population. The civilian population and Armed Forces personnel residing within the United States. It excludes Armed Forces personnel residing overseas.

Revenue. All funds received from external sources, net of refunds, and correcting transactions. Noncash transactions such as receipt of services, commodities, or other receipts in kind are excluded, as are funds received from the issuance of debt, liquidation of investments, and nonroutine sale of property.

Salary. The total amount regularly paid or stipulated to be paid to an individual, before deductions, for personal services rendered while on the payroll of a business or organization.

Sales and services. Revenues derived from the sales of goods or services that are incidental to the conduct of instruction, research, or public service. Examples include film rentals, scientific and literary publications, testing services, university presses, and dairy products.

Sales tax. Tax imposed on the sale and consumption of goods and services. It can be imposed either as a general tax on the retail price of all goods and services sold or as a tax on the sale of selected goods and services.

Scholarships and fellowships. This category of college expenditures applies only to money given in the form of outright grants and trainee stipends to individuals enrolled in formal coursework, either for credit or not. Aid to students in the form of tuition or fee remissions is included. College work-study funds are excluded and are reported under the program in which the student is working. In the tabulations in this volume, Pell Grants are not included in this expenditure category.

School. A division of the school system consisting of students in one or more grades or other identifiable groups and organized to give instruction of a defined type. One school may share a building with another school, or one school may be housed in several buildings.

School administration support services. Salary, benefits, supplies, and contractual fees for the office of the principal, full-time department chairpersons, and graduate expenses.

School climate. The social system and culture of the school, including the organizational structure of the school and values and expectations within it.

School district. An educational agency at the local level that exists primarily to operate public schools or to contract for public school services. Synonyms are "local basic administrative unit" and "local education agency."

Science. The body of related courses concerned with knowledge of the physical and biological world and with the processes of discovering and validating this knowledge.

Secondary instructional level. The general level of instruction provided for pupils in secondary schools (generally covering grades 7 through 12 or 9 through 12) and any instruction of a comparable nature and difficulty provided for adults and youth beyond the age of compulsory school attendance.

Secondary school. A school comprising any span of grades beginning with the next grade following an elementary or middle school (usually 7, 8, or 9) and ending with or below grade 12. Both junior high schools and senior high schools are included.

Senior high school. A secondary school offering the final years of high school work necessary for graduation.

Serial volumes. Publications issued in successive parts, usually at regular intervals, and, as a rule, intended to be continued indefinitely. Serials include periodicals, newspapers, annuals, memoirs, proceedings, and transactions of societies.

Social studies. A group of instructional programs that describes the substantive portions of behavior, past and present activities, interactions, and organizations of people associated for religious, benevolent, cultural, scientific, political, patriotic, or other purposes.

Socioeconomic status (SES). For the High School and Beyond Study and the National Longitudinal Study of the High School Class of 1972, the SES index is a composite of five equally weighted, standardized components: father's education, mother's education, family income, father's occupation, and household items. The terms high, middle, and low SES refer to the upper, middle two, and lower quartiles of the weighted SES composite index distribution.

Special education. Direct instructional activities or special learning experiences designed primarily for students identified as having exceptionalities in one or more aspects of the cognitive process or as being underachievers in relation to general level or model of their overall abilities. Such services usually are directed at students with the following conditions: (1) physically handicapped; (2) emotionally handicapped; (3) culturally different, including compensatory education; (4) mentally retarded; and (5) students with learning disabilities. Programs for the mentally gifted and talented are also included in some special education programs. See also *Handicapped.*

Standardized test. A test composed of a systematic sampling of behavior, administered and scored according to specific instructions, capable of being interpreted in terms of adequate norms, and for which there are data on reliability and validity.

Standardized test performance. The weighted distributions of composite scores from standardized tests used to group students according to performance.

Standard Metropolitan Statistical Area (SMSA). *See Metropolitan Statistical Area (MSA).*

Student. An individual for whom instruction is provided in an educational program under the jurisdiction of a school, school system, or other educational institution. No distinction is made between the terms "student" and "pupil," though "student" may refer to one receiving instruction at any level while "pupil" refers only to one attending school at the elementary or secondary level. A student may receive instruction in a school facility or in another location, such as at home or in a hospital. Instruction may be provided by direct student-teacher interaction or by some other approved medium such as television, radio, telephone, and correspondence.

Student support services. Salary, benefits, supplies, and contractual fees for staff providing attendance and social work, guidance, health and psychological services, speech pathology, audiology, and other support to students.

Subject-matter club. Organizations that are formed around a shared interest in a particular area of study and whose primary activities promote that interest. Examples of such organizations are math, science, business, and history clubs.

Supervisory staff. Principals, assistant principals, and supervisors of instruction. The term does not include superintendents or assistant superintendents.

Tax base. The collective value of objects, assets, and income components against which a tax is levied.

Tax expenditures. Losses of tax revenue attributable to provisions of the federal income tax laws that allow a special exclusion, exemption, or deduction from gross income or that provide a special credit, preferential rate of tax, or a deferral of tax liability affecting individual or corporate income tax liabilities.

Technical education. A program of vocational instruction that ordinarily includes the study of the science and mathematics underlying a technology, as well as the methods, skills, and materials commonly used and the services performed in the technology. Technical education prepares individuals for positions—such as draftsman or lab technician—in the occupational area between the skilled craftsman and the professional person.

Total expenditure per pupil in average daily attendance. All expenditures allocable to per-pupil costs divided by average daily attendance. These allocable expenditures include current expenditures for regular school programs, interest on school debt, and capital outlay. Beginning in 1980–81, expenditures for state administration are excluded and expenditures for other programs (summer schools, community colleges, and private schools) are included.

Trade and industrial occupations. The branch of vocational education that is concerned with preparing persons for initial employment or with updating or retraining workers in a wide range of trade and industrial occupations. Such occupations are skilled or semiskilled and are concerned with laying out, designing, producing, processing, assembling, testing, maintaining, servicing, or repairing any product or commodity.

Transcript. An official list of all courses taken by a student at a school or college showing the final grade received for each course, with definitions of the various grades given at the institution.

Trust funds. Amounts collected and used by the federal government for carrying out specific purposes and programs according to terms of a trust agreement or statute, such as the Social Security and unemployment trust funds. Trust fund receipts that are not anticipated to be used in the immediate future are generally invested in interest-bearing government securities and earn interest for the trust fund.

Tuition and fees. A payment or charge for instruction or compensation for services, privileges, or the use of equipment, books, or other goods.

Unclassified students. Students who are not candidates for a degree or other formal award, although they are taking higher education courses for credit in regular classes with other students.

Unadjusted dollars. See *Current dollars*.

Undergraduate students. Students registered at an institution of higher education who are working in a program leading to a baccalaureate degree or other formal award below the baccalaureate, such as an associate degree.

Unemployed. Civilians who had no employment but were available for work and, (1) had engaged in any specific job-seeking activity within the past four years, (2) were waiting to be called back to a job from which they had been laid off, or (3) were waiting to report to a new wage or salary job within 30 days.

U.S. Service Schools. These institutions of higher education are controlled by the U.S. Department of Defense and the U.S. Department of Transportation. The ten institutions counted in the NCES surveys of higher education institu-

tions included the Air Force Institute of Technology, Community College of the Air Force, Naval Postgraduate School, Uniformed Services University of the Health Sciences, U.S. Air Force Academy, U.S. Army Command and General Staff College, U.S. Coast Guard Academy, U.S. Merchant Marine Academy, U.S. Military Academy, and U.S. Naval Academy.

University. An institution of higher education that consists of a liberal arts college, a diverse graduate program, and usually two or more professional schools or faculties and that is empowered to confer degrees in various fields of study. For purposes of maintaining trend data in this publication, the selection of university institutions has not been revised since 1982.

Visual and performing arts. A group of instructional programs that generally describes the historic development, aesthetic qualities, and creative processes of the visual and performing arts.

Vocational education. Organized educational programs, services, and activities that are directly related to the preparation of individuals for paid or unpaid employment or for additional preparation for a career, that requires other than a baccalaureate or advanced degree.

Vocational home economics. Vocational courses of instruction emphasizing the acquisition of competencies needed for getting and holding a job or preparing for advancement in an occupational area using home economics knowledge or skills.

Geographic region

(1) One of four regions used by the Bureau of Economic Analysis of the U.S. Department of Commerce, the National Assessment of Education Progress, and the National Education Association, as follows (the National Education Association designated the Central region as Middle region in its classification).

Northeast	Southeast
Connecticut	Alabama
Delaware	Arkansas
District of Columbia	Florida
Maine	Georgia
Maryland	Kentucky
Massachusetts	Louisiana
New Hampshire	Mississippi
New Jersey	North Carolina
New York	South Carolina
Pennsylvania	Tennessee
Rhode Island	Virginia
Vermont	West Virginia

Central (Middle)

Illinois
Indiana
Iowa
Kansas
Michigan
Minnesota
Missouri
Nebraska
North Dakota
Ohio
South Dakota
Wisconsin

West

Alaska	
Arizona	Oregon
California	Texas
Colorado	Utah
Hawaii	Washington
Idaho	Wyoming
Montana	
Nevada	
New Mexico	
Oklahoma	

(2) One of the regions or divisions (in parentheses) used by the U.S. Bureau of the Census in Current Population Survey tabulations as follows:

Northeast	Midwest
(New England)	*(East North Central)*
Maine	Ohio
New Hampshire	Indiana
Vermont	Illinois
Massachusetts	Michigan
Rhode Island	Wisconsin
Connecticut	
(Middle Atlantic)	*(West North Central)*
New York	Minnesota
New Jersey	Iowa
Pennsylvania	Missouri
	North Dakota
	South Dakota
	Nebraska
	Kansas

South	West
(South Atlantic)	*(Mountain)*
Delaware	Montana
Maryland	Idaho
District of Columbia	Wyoming
Virginia	Colorado
West Virginia	New Mexico
North Carolina	Arizona
South Carolina	Utah
Georgia	Nevada
Florida	
(East South Central)	*(Pacific)*
Kentucky	Washington
Tennessee	Oregon
Alabama	California
Mississippi	Alaska
	Hawaii
(West South Central)	
Arkansas	
Louisiana	
Oklahoma	
Texas	

This section presents a variety of public elementary and secondary school education statistics aggregated for each county (or county equivalent—see definitions section) in the United States for the 1995–96 school year, the latest year for which such information is available. For comparison purposes, similar data are also shown for each state and for the United States as a whole. In only a handful of states are public school district (also known as local education agency) boundaries coextensive with county boundaries. Yet other local government data and demographic information are readily available at such geographic detail. We have tabulated these education data by county for those users who desire a more complete set of information at this geographic level and for those who wish to compare across states.

The nation's approximately 3,100 counties and equivalents vary enormously both in physical size and population. Not surprisingly, their public school populations also vary. Several have fewer than 100 public school students (includ-

ing the three Texas counties of Loving, Kenedy, and King). At the other extreme, counties such as Los Angeles, California (with 1.5 million public school students), or the combined boroughs of New York City, or Cook, Illinois, and Harris, Texas, have more public school elementary and secondary students than many whole states. The median number of students in public elementary and secondary schools in the 1995–96 school year was about 4,200 for counties (that is, half of the counties in the United States had more students and half had fewer students).

The median number of school districts per county is two. About a third of counties had only one school district. There is no perfect correlation between population or county physical size and number of school districts. Some very large counties (in terms of population) have only one school district (for example Dade County, Florida), while some counties that are not among the nation's most populous have very large numbers of school districts (e.g., Tulare, California with 50). Cook County, Illinois, has more

FIGURE D-1

Minorities as a Percent of Total Public Elementary And Secondary School Enrollment: 1995-1996

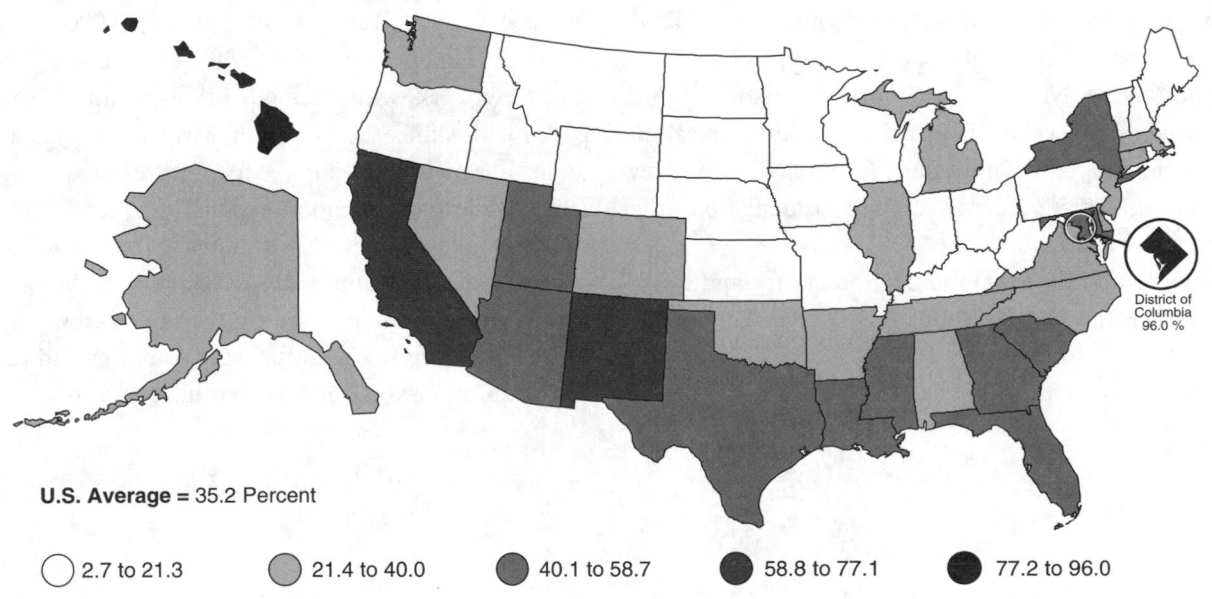

U.S. Average = 35.2 Percent

○ 2.7 to 21.3   ● 21.4 to 40.0   ● 40.1 to 58.7   ● 58.8 to 77.1   ● 77.2 to 96.0

Source: National Center for Education Statistics, Common Core of Data, 1995-1996.

FIGURE D-2

Educational Expenditures per Pupil: 1995-1996

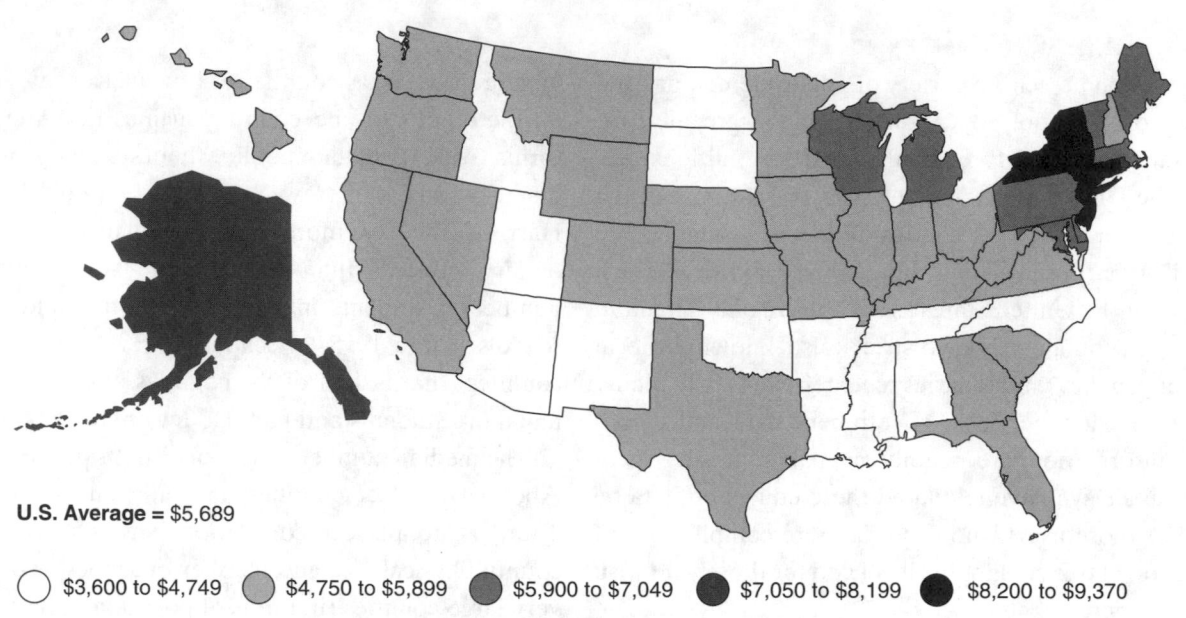

U.S. Average = $5,689

◯ $3,600 to $4,749　　◯ $4,750 to $5,899　　◯ $5,900 to $7,049　　● $7,050 to $8,199　　● $8,200 to $9,370

school districts than any other county, with 151. Eighteen *states* have fewer school districts than Cook County.

In the United States as a whole, minority students (that is, African American, Hispanic, Asian, or American Indian) represented about 35 percent of the public school student body in 1995–96. In five states, minority students were actually the majority (California, Hawaii, Mississippi, New Mexico, and Texas). In approximately one out of every eight counties throughout the country, minority students were the majority of the public school student body. On the other hand, several New England states have student bodies composed of fewer than 5 percent minorities. And about one out of three counties nationally had this relatively low proportion (under 5 percent) of their student body that were minority group members.

There were about 85,000 public elementary and secondary schools in the United States in 1995–96. The median number of schools for counties in the country was about 12, about half of which were elementary schools and the re-

mainder middle or high schools. There were 2.6 million teachers in these schools. The median pupil-teacher ratio was about 16 nationally (that is, 16 students for every teacher) and varied from a high of 24 in California and Utah to a low of 14 in seven states (Nebraska, Connecticut, Maine, Rhode Island, New Jersey, Vermont, and Virginia).

Expenditures per pupil vary enormously across the country. The U.S. average was about $5,600 in 1996 per pupil, with a median for counties of $4,900. States with relatively high per-pupil expenditures included New Jersey and New York, with averages of $9,400 and $9,300, compared with states such as Utah, Mississippi, Alabama, and Tennessee, with per-pupil expenditures under $4,000 in 1996. While the per capita expenditures for counties tend to be relatively high or low statewide, there is nevertheless considerable variation between counties in the same state. Variations between counties in the same state of $1,000 or more in per-pupil expenditures are common, and variations of several thousand dollars occur in several states.

Because the following state- and county-level tables (D-1 and D-2) are designed to be viewed as facing pages, please turn to page 520 for the beginning of table D-1.

Table D-1. School and Student Characteristics by State

State code	State	Population, 1996		School districts, 1995–1996	Level of schools, 1995–1996				Level of students, 1995–1996				Characteristics of students, 1995–1996		
		Total persons	Percent age 5–17		Number of schools	Percent			Number of students	Percent			Percent with IEP[1]	Percent free-lunch eligible	Percent minority
						Primary	Middle	High		Primary	Middle	High			
		1	2	3	4	5	6	7	8	9	10	11	12	13	14
00	UNITED STATES	265 283 783	18.8	14 367	85 102	59.3	17.1	18.7	44 840 481	50.7	19.5	26.7	NA	NA	35.2
01	ALABAMA	4 273 084	18.3	127	1 316	51.2	16.9	19.3	746 149	43.5	16.8	25.2	13.2	NA	37.8
02	ALASKA	607 007	22.2	55	479	34.9	6.9	14.0	127 618	47.5	13.0	23.9	13.8	23.8	36.2
04	ARIZONA	4 428 068	18.2	214	1 079	65.3	16.6	15.8	743 566	56.6	17.5	25.4	9.7	NA	43.5
05	ARKANSAS	2 509 793	19.3	311	1 095	52.9	15.8	29.3	453 257	48.6	19.8	27.9	10.5	35.5	26.4
06	CALIFORNIA	31 878 234	19.2	999	7 875	63.8	14.7	17.4	5 536 406	54.0	18.0	25.8	10.3	47.3	59.6
08	COLORADO	3 822 676	19.0	176	1 418	59.1	17.8	20.3	656 279	50.9	21.5	26.5	10.1	22.4	27.5
09	CONNECTICUT	3 274 238	17.6	166	976	63.1	18.1	16.0	517 935	53.1	20.7	25.4	13.4	24.6	27.8
10	DELAWARE	724 842	17.4	19	181	48.6	23.2	17.7	108 461	40.7	28.3	28.9	12.0	29.3	35.3
11	DISTRICT OF COLUMBIA	543 213	13.9	1	185	63.2	14.6	12.4	79 802	61.8	15.7	17.9	8.9	69.4	96.0
12	FLORIDA	14 399 985	17.1	67	2 689	57.6	15.4	13.4	2 176 222	51.0	20.2	21.0	13.1	37.2	42.6
13	GEORGIA	7 353 225	19.0	180	1 763	62.1	17.9	15.9	1 311 126	51.0	20.0	25.2	10.0	37.2	41.8
15	HAWAII	1 183 723	18.2	1	246	68.7	11.4	12.6	187 180	54.9	13.3	26.5	8.2	15.5	77.2
16	IDAHO	1 189 251	21.7	112	611	53.8	16.5	24.7	243 097	47.9	22.3	27.4	9.7	23.4	10.9
17	ILLINOIS	11 846 544	18.9	905	4 125	62.4	17.2	15.6	1 943 623	55.4	15.1	26.9	4.3	NA	36.2
18	INDIANA	5 840 528	18.6	292	1 863	63.1	16.2	18.6	977 263	49.3	18.3	30.8	13.6	22.2	14.4
19	IOWA	2 851 792	18.8	383	1 551	54.9	19.0	23.9	502 343	46.4	20.2	31.2	12.9	19.8	7.3
20	KANSAS	2 572 150	19.7	304	1 485	58.7	16.6	24.0	463 008	51.1	19.7	28.7	11.4	31.7	17.6
21	KENTUCKY	3 883 723	18.3	176	1 368	59.2	17.0	20.5	659 821	48.6	20.4	30.8	NA	NA	10.9
22	LOUISIANA	4 350 579	20.8	66	1 470	54.0	19.0	17.1	797 366	47.9	19.8	25.6	13.4	50.1	48.9
23	MAINE	1 243 316	18.4	228	697	64.6	17.5	15.4	213 569	49.9	21.3	26.7	13.4	24.3	2.7
24	MARYLAND	5 071 604	18.3	24	1 276	66.2	17.5	14.0	805 544	52.6	20.6	25.7	12.4	25.7	42.4
25	MASSACHUSETTS	6 092 352	16.9	248	1 831	66.0	16.3	15.8	915 007	52.8	18.8	26.0	17.1	NA	21.5
26	MICHIGAN	9 594 350	19.4	593	3 455	59.4	16.8	18.5	1 641 456	50.4	19.7	27.2	4.0	25.6	23.5
27	MINNESOTA	4 657 758	20.0	383	1 958	52.4	13.1	28.7	835 166	48.9	18.5	30.6	NA	19.0	12.6
28	MISSISSIPPI	2 716 115	20.3	153	888	50.0	19.1	19.7	506 272	44.3	19.0	24.2	13.2	54.5	52.3
29	MISSOURI	5 358 692	19.2	525	2 072	56.4	16.3	23.9	889 881	48.5	19.6	29.7	15.4	NA	18.2
30	MONTANA	879 372	20.1	465	893	54.1	26.1	19.6	165 547	49.6	20.4	29.3	11.1	23.2	12.5
31	NEBRASKA	1 652 093	19.9	653	1 390	68.4	7.2	22.5	289 744	52.1	14.6	32.7	13.8	20.6	13.0
32	NEVADA	1 603 163	18.3	17	419	64.0	14.3	17.9	265 041	52.5	20.7	25.7	10.6	32.7	33.1
33	NEW HAMPSHIRE	1 162 481	19.0	164	460	62.6	20.4	16.1	194 171	51.0	22.5	24.6	13.0	12.4	3.4
34	NEW JERSEY	7 987 933	17.7	582	2 278	63.6	17.1	13.4	1 197 381	53.1	17.8	25.7	5.4	24.3	37.5
35	NEW MEXICO	1 713 407	21.3	89	721	59.2	20.8	17.9	329 640	49.1	23.0	26.7	14.3	NA	60.6
36	NEW YORK	18 184 774	17.7	709	4 148	58.8	16.5	17.7	2 813 230	50.2	18.6	26.9	12.4	NA	43.1
37	NORTH CAROLINA	7 322 870	18.0	119	1 975	60.1	20.8	16.5	1 183 090	51.2	21.8	25.7	12.4	30.3	35.4
38	NORTH DAKOTA	643 539	19.8	234	573	57.9	6.8	34.0	119 100	51.2	12.3	33.8	10.2	20.2	10.4
39	OHIO	11 172 782	18.7	611	3 704	59.1	18.4	18.7	1 836 015	48.6	19.5	29.1	3.9	NA	17.8
40	OKLAHOMA	3 300 902	19.8	548	1 821	54.6	18.8	25.4	616 393	51.8	21.5	24.3	11.6	36.1	30.6
41	OREGON	3 203 735	18.6	233	1 216	61.8	16.9	16.9	527 914	48.6	21.2	28.2	10.8	23.2	14.8
42	PENNSYLVANIA	12 056 112	17.7	500	3 113	62.5	16.9	19.1	1 787 533	48.4	19.6	29.6	10.5	NA	19.4
44	RHODE ISLAND	990 225	17.4	36	309	68.0	17.2	13.6	149 799	51.0	21.6	27.2	16.5	26.7	21.1
45	SOUTH CAROLINA	3 698 746	18.5	95	1 052	55.7	23.2	18.8	645 586	46.1	25.0	28.1	11.3	39.7	43.3
46	SOUTH DAKOTA	732 405	20.9	173	818	51.5	23.7	22.6	144 685	48.4	21.9	29.2	11.3	NA	16.2
47	TENNESSEE	5 319 654	18.0	138	1 515	62.8	15.8	16.7	893 770	52.1	16.9	27.5	14.2	NA	25.1
48	TEXAS	19 128 261	20.2	1 044	6 638	52.1	20.7	19.2	3 748 167	49.3	22.7	25.1	11.6	40.3	53.6
49	UTAH	2 000 494	24.5	40	735	59.6	16.2	18.8	477 121	50.1	22.6	24.9	11.0	19.8	9.7
50	VERMONT	588 654	18.9	251	362	69.9	6.6	13.5	105 565	54.6	9.2	29.6	9.8	20.2	2.7
51	VIRGINIA	6 675 451	17.6	132	1 781	62.3	17.7	16.5	1 079 854	49.1	21.4	28.2	13.0	25.5	33.4
53	WASHINGTON	5 532 939	19.0	296	1 949	57.6	16.6	19.9	956 572	50.6	20.2	26.2	NA	NA	21.6
54	WEST VIRGINIA	1 825 754	17.3	55	842	64.1	16.3	14.7	307 112	47.8	20.5	28.3	15.1	39.8	4.8
55	WISCONSIN	5 159 795	19.5	426	2 037	60.3	17.2	20.9	870 175	49.3	18.9	30.3	12.2	20.2	16.8
56	WYOMING	481 400	21.2	49	401	59.1	21.9	18.7	99 859	48.4	23.9	27.1	11.3	19.4	10.6

1. IEP = Individual Education Program. See notes and definitions at end of this section.

Table D-1. School and Student Characteristics by State — Continued

State	Staff and students, 1995–1996						Revenues, fiscal 1996				Current expenditures, fiscal 1996		
	Number of teachers	Pupil/ Teacher ratio	Number of graduates	Dropouts grades 9–12 (percent)	Local school non-teaching staff	Central admin. staff	Total revenue ($1000)	Percent of revenue from			Amount	Amount per pupil	Percent for instruc- tion
								Federal Gov't	State gov't	Local gov't			
	15	16	17	18	19	20	21	22	23	24	25	26	27
UNITED STATES	2 598 220	17.3	2 362 195	NA	2 255 826	351 301	287 702 844	6.6	47.5	45.5	255 079 736	5689	61.7
ALABAMA	44 056	17.0	39 836	6.2	38 437	5 650	3 771 940	9.2	61.3	29.5	3 240 364	4343	62.7
ALASKA	7 379	17.0	5 775	NA	6 913	1 285	1 183 127	11.1	66.1	22.8	1 045 022	8189	56.6
ARIZONA	38 017	20.0	31 046	NA	37 713	7 360	4 151 421	9.0	44.1	42.9	3 327 969	4476	57.7
ARKANSAS	26 449	17.0	29 376	4.9	22 636	3 129	2 204 845	8.5	60.0	31.4	1 994 748	4401	62.4
CALIFORNIA	230 849	24.0	303 539	4.4	191 520	40 362	30 858 564	8.9	55.8	35.4	27 334 639	4937	59.8
COLORADO	35 388	19.0	32 985	NA	29 307	6 161	3 804 992	5.3	43.8	50.9	3 360 529	5121	61.6
CONNECTICUT	36 070	14.0	26 491	4.8	28 160	4 838	4 786 247	3.7	38.0	58.3	4 366 123	8430	63.7
DELAWARE	6 463	17.0	5 577	4.6	5 088	904	822 226	6.7	66.6	26.7	726 241	6696	61.6
DISTRICT OF COLUMBIA	5 305	15.0	3 061	10.6	3 486	889	675 409	8.1	—	91.9	679 106	8510	49.3
FLORIDA	114 938	19.0	93 064	NA	112 759	18 119	13 214 948	7.4	48.6	44.0	11 480 359	5275	58.1
GEORGIA	79 480	16.0	59 736	9.0	81 748	9 632	7 627 823	6.8	51.9	41.3	6 629 646	5056	62.1
HAWAII	10 500	18.0	9 980	4.9	6 039	1 548	1 201 888	7.8	89.8	2.4	1 040 682	5560	62.6
IDAHO	12 784	19.0	14 300	NA	8 783	1 524	1 179 927	7.1	64.3	28.6	1 019 594	4194	63.1
ILLINOIS	113 538	17.0	105 164	NA	88 259	14 825	12 290 140	6.1	27.3	66.6	10 727 091	5519	60.2
INDIANA	55 821	18.0	57 036	4.6	59 470	10 568	6 191 534	5.2	54.3	39.8	5 493 653	5621	62.1
IOWA	32 318	16.0	31 681	3.4	29 431	5 314	3 033 687	5.1	49.0	45.6	2 753 425	5481	61.4
KANSAS	30 729	15.0	26 125	5.0	25 335	3 742	2 948 036	5.4	57.3	33.0	2 488 077	5374	57.9
KENTUCKY	39 120	17.0	37 626	NA	42 795	5 086	3 492 890	8.3	65.3	26.4	3 171 493	4807	61.2
LOUISIANA	46 980	17.0	36 480	3.5	46 720	6 130	3 934 998	12.1	50.3	37.6	3 545 832	4447	59.2
MAINE	15 392	14.0	11 745	3.3	13 400	2 003	1 451 987	5.6	47.0	47.5	1 313 759	6151	67.2
MARYLAND	47 819	17.0	41 841	NA	39 739	6 616	5 695 850	4.9	38.2	56.9	5 311 207	6593	61.4
MASSACHUSETTS	62 710	15.0	47 679	3.5	44 690	5 987	6 772 855	4.7	38.3	57.0	6 435 458	7033	66.4
MICHIGAN	83 179	20.0	87 090	NA	91 176	11 720	12 698 697	6.1	66.8	27.0	11 137 877	6785	59.1
MINNESOTA	46 971	18.0	49 354	5.1	25 312	4 612	5 939 765	4.3	58.2	35.6	4 844 879	5801	63.9
MISSISSIPPI	28 997	17.0	25 532	6.4	29 925	3 679	2 225 798	13.7	57.8	28.5	2 000 321	3951	62.3
MISSOURI	57 951	15.0	48 862	7.0	58 803	10 647	5 263 003	6.0	40.2	53.4	4 531 192	5092	61.1
MONTANA	10 076	16.0	10 134	NA	8 133	1 395	941 538	9.9	48.6	32.1	868 892	5249	62.3
NEBRASKA	20 028	14.0	18 065	4.4	17 089	2 280	1 876 494	5.6	31.6	62.1	1 648 104	5688	62.4
NEVADA	13 878	19.0	10 982	10.3	9 588	1 931	1 554 888	4.5	32.0	63.5	1 296 629	4892	59.3
NEW HAMPSHIRE	12 346	16.0	10 145	NA	10 458	1 123	1 217 104	3.3	7.0	89.7	1 114 540	5740	65.1
NEW JERSEY	86 706	14.0	67 403	NA	69 702	13 386	11 882 657	3.4	38.6	58.0	11 208 558	9361	60.5
NEW MEXICO	19 398	17.0	15 179	8.5	18 496	3 783	1 783 804	12.2	73.9	13.9	1 517 517	4604	57.5
NEW YORK	181 559	15.0	136 436	4.1	151 846	13 498	25 849 431	5.8	39.7	54.1	23 522 461	8361	67.8
NORTH CAROLINA	73 201	16.0	60 717	NA	64 997	9 392	6 154 971	7.2	64.5	28.3	5 582 994	4719	62.3
NORTH DAKOTA	7 501	16.0	7 817	2.5	5 898	755	618 322	11.5	42.1	45.2	557 043	4677	61.0
OHIO	107 347	17.0	109 418	5.3	75 389	11 923	11 794 089	6.3	40.7	52.9	10 408 022	5669	59.6
OKLAHOMA	39 364	16.0	33 319	NA	44 611	7 219	2 856 688	9.3	59.3	29.4	2 804 088	4549	59.9
OREGON	26 680	20.0	29 830	7.1	23 477	4 599	3 366 831	6.5	54.1	37.8	3 056 801	5790	60.6
PENNSYLVANIA	104 921	17.0	104 146	4.1	86 729	13 610	14 047 905	5.5	39.8	54.2	12 374 073	6922	64.0
RHODE ISLAND	10 482	14.0	7 830	4.6	5 692	1 149	1 138 171	5.1	41.5	53.4	1 094 185	7304	66.6
SOUTH CAROLINA	39 922	16.0	32 683	NA	33 893	5 619	3 697 232	8.3	52.9	38.8	3 085 495	4779	59.0
SOUTH DAKOTA	9 641	15.0	8 491	NA	8 023	1 363	717 005	9.8	29.7	59.3	610 640	4220	60.7
TENNESSEE	53 403	17.0	45 355	NA	43 025	9 299	4 142 148	8.6	47.9	43.4	3 728 486	4172	63.8
TEXAS	240 371	16.0	170 322	2.7	224 378	25 501	21 689 792	7.2	42.9	49.6	18 801 462	5016	61.4
UTAH	20 039	24.0	29 551	3.5	16 653	3 111	2 066 218	6.7	58.6	34.8	1 719 782	3604	67.0
VERMONT	7 676	14.0	5 989	NA	7 572	1 281	773 448	4.7	27.8	67.5	684 864	6488	64.9
VIRGINIA	74 731	14.0	59 644	NA	60 944	9 641	6 826 448	5.3	31.1	63.6	5 969 608	5528	60.3
WASHINGTON	46 907	20.0	49 379	NA	41 777	7 352	6 327 993	5.8	68.0	26.2	5 367 559	5611	60.1
WEST VIRGINIA	21 073	15.0	20 648	4.2	15 686	1 782	1 990 094	8.0	63.0	28.9	1 806 004	5881	62.1
WISCONSIN	55 033	16.0	51 735	NA	37 789	7 100	6 304 318	4.3	42.9	52.8	5 670 826	6517	63.3
WYOMING	6 734	15.0	5 996	6.7	6 337	879	662 660	6.2	51.3	35.2	581 817	5826	62.0

Table D-2. School and Student Characteristics by County

State/County code	County	County type[1]	Population, 1996		Number of school districts, 1995–1996	Level of schools, 1995–1996				Level of students, 1995–1996				Characteristics of students, 1995–1996		
			Total persons	Percent age 5–17		Number of schools	Percent Primary	Middle	High	Number of students	Percent Primary	Middle	High	Percent with IEP[2]	Percent free-lunch eligible	Percent minority
		1	1	2	3	4	5	6	7	8	9	10	11	12	13	14
01000	**ALABAMA**															
01001	Autauga, AL	2	40 061	20.7	1	10	40.0	20.0	20.0	7 821	34.3	24.0	23.3	12.1	NA	25.1
01003	Baldwin, AL	2	123 023	18.2	1	34	58.8	26.5	14.7	20 648	42.1	29.7	28.2	14.4	NA	18.8
01005	Barbour, AL	6	26 475	20.1	2	12	66.7	8.3	25.0	5 033	53.5	15.0	31.4	9.7	NA	61.6
01007	Bibb, AL	6	18 142	20.8	1	8	50.0	25.0	25.0	3 656	44.3	12.8	42.9	18.1	NA	28.7
01009	Blount, AL	2	43 392	18.0	2	11	27.3	9.1	18.2	7 622	20.7	5.0	14.3	12.4	NA	4.7
01011	Bullock, AL	6	11 188	20.2	1	4	75.0	—	25.0	1 989	59.5	—	40.5	11.0	NA	99.7
01013	Butler, AL	7	21 530	21.4	1	6	33.3	16.7	16.7	4 173	36.3	23.3	20.4	15.3	NA	60.2
01015	Calhoun, AL	3	113 511	18.2	5	33	51.5	12.1	21.2	19 665	40.2	9.3	29.5	13.0	NA	27.4
01017	Chambers, AL	5	36 748	18.5	2	14	50.0	28.6	21.4	5 721	48.1	24.9	27.0	12.1	NA	57.2
01019	Cherokee, AL	6	21 170	17.4	1	7	14.3	14.3	14.3	3 794	19.0	10.3	12.5	19.0	NA	8.7
01021	Chilton, AL	6	35 323	19.1	1	9	22.2	11.1	22.2	6 257	29.4	11.8	21.4	19.1	NA	17.1
01023	Choctaw, AL	9	15 714	21.0	1	7	57.1	14.3	28.6	2 719	61.2	8.4	30.4	12.4	NA	67.2
01025	Clarke, AL	7	27 982	21.5	2	10	40.0	20.0	30.0	5 603	40.8	20.0	24.1	12.2	NA	58.6
01027	Clay, AL	9	13 544	17.9	1	7	42.9	—	42.9	2 635	46.4	—	39.1	9.9	NA	24.3
01029	Cleburne, AL	6	13 445	18.2	1	6	66.7	—	33.3	2 488	54.1	—	45.9	21.5	NA	7.2
01031	Coffee, AL	4	41 910	18.0	3	16	50.0	18.8	18.8	8 429	47.1	14.9	24.0	11.4	NA	26.8
01033	Colbert, AL	3	52 490	16.8	4	23	47.8	26.1	26.1	8 761	45.3	21.1	33.7	14.1	NA	24.7
01035	Conecuh, AL	7	14 112	19.9	1	7	71.4	14.3	14.3	2 386	56.0	14.0	30.0	19.7	NA	72.1
01037	Coosa, AL	8	11 444	17.7	1	5	80.0	—	20.0	1 851	72.0	—	28.0	15.4	NA	45.9
01039	Covington, AL	7	37 263	17.9	3	15	40.0	20.0	26.7	6 950	39.4	15.2	26.2	17.9	NA	17.3
01041	Crenshaw, AL	6	13 514	18.9	1	3	—	—	—	2 415	—	—	—	14.0	NA	36.9
01043	Cullman, AL	6	73 274	17.8	2	19	26.3	5.3	5.3	12 060	12.6	6.0	6.6	12.2	NA	1.9
01045	Dale, AL	3	49 167	19.0	3	16	43.8	25.0	25.0	7 822	37.2	26.7	30.4	14.3	NA	32.6
01047	Dallas, AL	4	47 362	22.1	2	23	69.6	13.0	17.4	9 888	52.2	15.3	32.6	12.8	NA	80.9
01049	De Kalb, AL	6	57 165	18.3	2	16	37.5	6.3	6.3	9 883	16.7	8.2	8.3	13.1	NA	16.6
01051	Elmore, AL	2	58 460	18.3	2	14	42.9	21.4	35.7	10 753	52.8	15.3	31.9	15.4	NA	27.3
01053	Escambia, AL	6	35 620	19.0	2	14	42.9	21.4	28.6	6 443	41.3	25.6	29.3	12.2	NA	41.9
01055	Etowah, AL	3	102 129	17.7	3	38	55.3	18.4	23.7	16 552	47.3	19.1	29.8	15.1	NA	21.4
01057	Fayette, AL	6	17 944	18.5	1	6	33.3	16.7	33.3	2 936	42.0	17.0	28.1	13.1	NA	17.4
01059	Franklin, AL	6	29 253	17.4	2	10	10.0	20.0	10.0	5 624	13.9	16.8	11.9	11.4	NA	7.2
01061	Geneva, AL	6	24 618	17.7	2	13	38.5	30.8	30.8	4 330	47.4	24.2	28.5	14.1	NA	19.6
01063	Greene, AL	8	9 947	23.7	1	4	50.0	—	25.0	2 182	38.0	—	26.9	11.4	NA	99.9
01065	Hale, AL	6	16 288	22.3	1	7	28.6	—	28.6	3 470	21.5	—	17.8	15.6	NA	75.3
01067	Henry, AL	6	15 232	19.0	1	6	33.3	33.3	33.3	2 842	45.9	24.0	30.1	13.4	NA	51.6
01069	Houston, AL	3	83 778	19.3	2	25	56.0	16.0	12.0	15 521	37.6	15.0	22.7	15.7	NA	35.7
01071	Jackson, AL	6	50 428	18.5	2	23	47.8	17.4	8.7	9 336	33.5	15.3	15.4	11.2	NA	16.2
01073	Jefferson, AL	2	661 927	17.1	10	194	55.2	21.1	18.0	112 513	45.8	21.3	27.0	12.9	NA	49.6
01075	Lamar, AL	9	15 591	18.1	1	3	—	—	—	2 957	—	—	—	11.8	NA	16.8
01077	Lauderdale, AL	3	83 593	16.8	2	22	40.9	9.1	13.6	13 594	34.1	0.2	17.9	12.1	NA	15.3
01079	Lawrence, AL	3	33 037	18.7	1	13	38.5	7.7	38.5	6 281	41.7	8.7	35.4	13.9	NA	39.0
01081	Lee, AL	4	95 038	15.4	3	26	57.7	19.2	23.1	15 764	49.3	22.2	28.5	12.3	NA	38.3
01083	Limestone, AL	2	59 844	17.5	2	16	50.0	6.3	6.3	10 455	25.3	6.6	7.9	10.4	NA	16.7
01085	Lowndes, AL	8	12 811	24.2	1	8	50.0	25.0	25.0	2 969	42.2	21.2	36.6	19.0	NA	99.4
01087	Macon, AL	6	23 563	18.5	1	8	62.5	12.5	12.5	4 280	46.5	9.0	30.1	8.6	NA	94.3
01089	Madison, AL	2	270 309	16.5	2	64	62.5	17.2	14.1	42 293	51.8	17.8	25.0	12.5	NA	33.0
01091	Marengo, AL	7	23 430	21.3	3	11	18.2	27.3	18.2	4 922	21.6	23.9	13.7	11.4	NA	69.9
01093	Marion, AL	7	30 718	17.4	2	14	42.9	14.3	42.9	5 516	48.4	16.7	34.9	13.0	NA	4.6
01095	Marshall, AL	4	79 159	17.4	4	28	46.4	21.4	21.4	14 174	43.3	21.6	25.2	11.8	NA	4.4
01097	Mobile, AL	2	395 952	19.7	1	88	63.6	17.0	15.9	65 400	49.8	19.9	28.0	14.0	NA	50.8
01099	Monroe, AL	7	23 874	21.8	1	11	27.3	18.2	27.3	5 180	26.7	18.7	24.3	9.3	NA	53.4
01101	Montgomery, AL	2	216 434	18.7	2	58	55.2	22.4	13.8	35 641	52.9	21.0	20.2	11.8	NA	68.7
01103	Morgan, AL	3	106 942	18.2	3	36	69.4	11.1	16.7	19 182	53.0	14.1	29.1	14.8	NA	16.3
01105	Perry, AL	7	12 717	22.3	1	6	33.3	33.3	33.3	2 450	38.7	32.7	28.6	13.8	NA	98.2
01107	Pickens, AL	6	20 864	20.2	1	9	44.4	11.1	33.3	3 954	41.5	9.3	34.2	13.7	NA	65.4
01109	Pike, AL	6	28 464	17.5	2	8	50.0	12.5	25.0	4 746	51.7	11.5	26.2	16.3	NA	55.4
01111	Randolph, AL	7	20 073	18.7	2	8	25.0	25.0	12.5	3 865	17.9	22.0	11.5	12.0	NA	33.0
01113	Russell, AL	2	51 439	18.1	2	17	70.6	17.6	11.8	8 752	49.2	24.3	26.5	10.1	NA	50.4
01115	St. Clair, AL	2	59 218	18.5	2	17	41.2	17.6	23.5	10 124	40.9	17.4	26.2	12.4	NA	11.5
01117	Shelby, AL	2	130 165	18.5	1	28	46.4	25.0	17.9	18 086	45.9	24.4	23.3	14.2	NA	13.6
01119	Sumter, AL	7	16 174	21.8	1	6	66.7	—	33.3	2 878	69.7	—	30.3	16.1	NA	99.6
01121	Talladega, AL	4	76 369	19.9	3	28	46.4	21.4	21.4	13 907	39.6	19.2	24.9	11.8	NA	43.1
01123	Tallapoosa, AL	6	39 810	18.1	2	10	30.0	20.0	20.0	7 231	34.0	16.0	24.3	11.7	NA	37.6
01125	Tuscaloosa, AL	3	158 779	16.7	2	46	60.9	15.2	15.2	25 505	51.5	18.2	23.5	12.8	NA	41.0
01127	Walker, AL	6	69 686	18.2	2	28	57.1	14.3	25.0	11 732	56.1	10.9	29.7	14.5	NA	10.6

1. County type code is from the Economic Research Service of the USDA. See notes and definitions at the end of this section.   2. IEP = Individual Education Program. See notes and definitions at the end of this section.

Table D-2. School and Student Characteristics by County — Continued

County	Number of teachers	Pupil/ teacher ratio	Number of graduates	Dropouts grades 9–12 (percent)	Local school non-teaching staff	Central admin. staff	Total revenue ($1000)	Federal Gov't	State Gov't	Local Gov't	Amount	Amount per pupil	Percent for instruction
	15	16	17	18	19	20	21	22	23	24	25	26	27
ALABAMA													
Autauga, AL	383	20.4	385	6.5	316	12	31 827	8.9	67.2	23.9	24 867	3 286	61.2
Baldwin, AL	1 216	17.0	1 025	7.5	982	60	93 379	7.1	59.0	33.9	78 232	3 919	62.3
Barbour, AL	318	15.8	234	7.4	273	27	24 202	12.3	67.4	20.3	22 348	4 454	60.3
Bibb, AL	199	18.4	182	6.3	165	11	14 917	12.9	74.9	12.2	13 612	3 846	62.1
Blount, AL	393	19.4	436	5.5	343	17	30 537	8.1	74.6	17.3	27 079	3 649	61.8
Bullock, AL	100	19.9	72	3.9	132	14	8 712	19.0	70.3	10.7	8 320	4 219	56.4
Butler, AL	237	17.6	250	8.9	214	19	18 120	14.9	73.0	12.1	16 676	3 878	60.6
Calhoun, AL	1 039	18.9	1 190	6.6	996	56	81 975	9.4	71.3	19.2	76 050	3 876	59.6
Chambers, AL	338	16.9	283	6.0	297	23	26 215	10.6	67.7	21.7	25 174	4 378	62.2
Cherokee, AL	212	17.9	254	6.8	196	10	16 620	8.8	71.4	19.8	15 173	4 085	60.2
Chilton, AL	355	17.6	364	7.1	289	20	26 068	8.7	74.6	16.7	24 228	3 890	61.1
Choctaw, AL	173	15.7	210	5.2	178	12	13 730	13.2	70.0	16.8	13 069	4 462	62.5
Clarke, AL	334	16.8	345	2.5	292	22	23 893	12.7	74.4	12.9	22 152	3 902	58.7
Clay, AL	158	16.7	150	6.9	129	6	10 648	9.5	77.3	13.3	10 305	3 939	63.1
Cleburne, AL	130	19.1	134	3.0	137	8	10 417	10.0	76.1	13.8	9 294	3 800	60.8
Coffee, AL	493	17.1	533	5.7	392	30	37 490	9.8	67.6	22.6	33 661	3 996	61.3
Colbert, AL	529	16.6	522	5.0	458	40	46 948	9.3	59.0	31.7	41 619	4 814	58.7
Conecuh, AL	140	17.0	108	3.6	143	13	11 172	13.8	72.1	14.1	10 137	4 256	60.9
Coosa, AL	94	19.8	101	4.6	110	6	7 752	13.0	74.8	12.3	7 423	4 002	58.6
Covington, AL	423	16.4	406	5.4	307	24	30 468	11.0	69.4	19.7	27 031	3 915	64.3
Crenshaw, AL	141	17.2	170	5.7	111	10	9 977	13.3	75.2	11.6	9 487	3 983	62.6
Cullman, AL	648	18.6	771	6.0	549	40	53 745	9.7	63.9	26.5	45 819	3 842	61.6
Dale, AL	465	16.8	485	5.3	397	25	33 778	11.1	71.1	17.9	33 077	4 187	59.2
Dallas, AL	575	17.2	474	6.0	617	39	41 493	17.2	71.4	11.4	39 117	3 854	60.4
De Kalb, AL	558	17.7	639	5.8	460	28	41 536	9.4	71.0	19.6	37 286	3 770	62.9
Elmore, AL	564	19.1	566	1.8	470	26	40 440	9.1	72.8	18.1	35 820	3 460	62.3
Escambia, AL	365	17.7	386	6.9	404	24	29 886	11.0	65.1	23.9	26 838	4 165	60.1
Etowah, AL	960	17.2	926	5.2	756	64	69 748	9.9	72.6	17.5	66 541	4 021	62.5
Fayette, AL	161	18.2	173	7.0	135	11	12 062	8.5	76.2	15.2	11 623	4 037	60.6
Franklin, AL	327	17.2	317	1.4	251	24	24 602	10.4	70.4	19.3	22 821	4 110	61.8
Geneva, AL	261	16.6	250	6.2	271	11	18 155	9.8	72.4	17.8	16 772	3 881	62.8
Greene, AL	122	17.9	132	2.1	147	10	11 733	19.1	65.7	15.2	10 107	4 504	55.9
Hale, AL	195	17.8	191	3.7	184	12	15 306	17.1	72.0	10.9	14 152	4 031	58.6
Henry, AL	165	17.2	161	4.6	179	11	12 600	11.4	72.2	16.4	12 234	4 334	60.7
Houston, AL	854	18.2	859	4.9	843	62	72 509	10.4	62.2	27.3	69 061	4 289	61.2
Jackson, AL	537	17.4	546	6.3	514	22	42 899	9.3	67.2	23.5	39 478	4 289	56.8
Jefferson, AL	6 955	16.2	6 026	5.8	5 396	434	547 684	8.3	59.0	32.7	509 692	4 447	60.3
Lamar, AL	157	18.9	201	4.7	140	13	13 482	7.9	70.3	21.7	11 252	3 762	59.8
Lauderdale, AL	826	16.5	819	4.9	627	39	80 768	6.3	48.8	44.9	58 130	4 323	61.3
Lawrence, AL	348	18.0	342	4.2	365	11	27 301	11.5	66.9	21.6	25 582	4 142	60.7
Lee, AL	944	16.7	764	6.1	788	52	85 764	6.2	50.8	43.1	65 286	4 273	59.9
Limestone, AL	607	17.2	559	7.1	495	28	51 524	5.8	58.8	35.4	43 786	4 281	62.8
Lowndes, AL	163	18.2	141	5.7	166	20	14 397	26.8	64.3	8.9	13 922	4 750	55.6
Macon, AL	251	17.1	209	3.2	240	17	22 379	20.1	58.4	21.5	20 390	4 781	59.2
Madison, AL	2 614	16.2	2 198	6.6	2 104	74	206 928	6.3	58.2	35.5	188 594	4 558	60.8
Marengo, AL	292	16.9	330	2.2	247	18	22 579	14.7	68.3	16.9	20 599	4 221	60.2
Marion, AL	323	17.1	348	3.9	215	15	22 274	8.1	74.5	17.4	19 923	3 620	62.9
Marshall, AL	812	17.5	770	8.3	727	47	62 980	7.5	67.5	25.0	57 701	4 136	60.1
Mobile, AL	3 560	18.4	3 333	8.7	3 089	243	274 190	13.7	66.7	19.7	245 589	3 799	63.6
Monroe, AL	290	17.8	295	6.7	266	12	21 615	10.5	72.6	17.0	19 609	3 731	64.9
Montgomery, AL	2 159	16.5	1 501	4.9	1 631	88	145 754	11.6	69.0	19.5	135 131	3 889	61.6
Morgan, AL	1 248	15.4	1 074	6.1	1 064	92	98 408	5.8	57.4	36.9	92 236	4 871	58.2
Perry, AL	139	17.7	120	5.8	143	11	11 910	20.2	68.7	11.1	10 955	4 527	56.8
Pickens, AL	214	18.5	205	2.0	242	16	17 265	14.7	73.9	11.5	15 806	4 001	60.7
Pike, AL	297	16.0	260	4.6	277	22	22 962	16.4	63.2	20.3	21 293	4 406	60.3
Randolph, AL	216	17.9	217	6.0	174	13	18 274	8.1	62.5	29.5	14 965	3 913	59.2
Russell, AL	490	17.9	380	8.5	590	28	41 185	14.5	63.8	21.7	36 673	4 269	58.7
St. Clair, AL	522	19.4	497	7.9	417	21	39 025	9.8	70.6	19.6	34 419	3 543	62.3
Shelby, AL	1 030	17.6	962	5.2	895	59	83 868	5.2	60.7	34.1	73 513	4 136	60.8
Sumter, AL	164	17.6	180	5.3	226	15	14 885	16.8	66.0	17.2	13 645	4 761	60.0
Talladega, AL	784	17.7	798	6.1	773	44	63 847	10.4	66.5	23.1	57 511	4 098	59.1
Tallapoosa, AL	416	17.4	383	7.4	286	19	30 990	7.4	67.5	25.1	27 713	3 910	63.4
Tuscaloosa, AL	1 627	15.7	1 318	7.1	1 284	81	122 329	8.8	64.1	27.1	110 840	4 416	62.6
Walker, AL	705	16.6	668	7.6	662	42	57 506	9.7	62.4	27.9	50 952	4 332	60.4

Items 15–27

Table D-2. School and Student Characteristics by County

State/County code	County	County type[1]	Population, 1996 Total persons	Percent age 5-17	Number of school districts, 1995-1996	Level of schools, 1995-1996 Number of schools	Percent Primary	Middle	High	Level of students, 1995-1996 Number of students	Percent Primary	Middle	High	Characteristics of students, 1995-1996 Percent with IEP[2]	Percent free-lunch eligible	Percent minority
			1	2	3	4	5	6	7	8	9	10	11	12	13	14
	ALABAMA—Con.															
01129	Washington, AL	8	17 341	21.4	1	10	40.0	10.0	20.0	3 803	28.1	6.9	18.2	8.6	NA	43.0
01131	Wilcox, AL	9	13 515	24.7	1	7	57.1	28.6	14.3	2 799	51.7	16.7	31.6	13.5	NA	99.1
01133	Winston, AL	6	23 602	17.4	2	7	28.6	—	28.6	4 534	35.8	—	28.1	14.7	NA	0.5
02000	**ALASKA**															
02013	Aleutians East Borough, AK	NA	2 304	18.1	1	6	—	—	—	392	—	—	—	20.2	9.2	85.5
02016	Aleutians West Census Area, AK	NA	4 984	11.0	3	5	20.0	—	20.0	613	43.9	—	20.2	12.1	6.9	59.9
02020	Anchorage, AK	3	250 505	20.3	1	80	68.8	8.8	13.8	46 697	58.3	13.4	26.2	14.4	14.6	31.1
02050	Bethel, AK	7	15 655	29.4	3	43	18.6	4.7	14.0	4 309	27.6	2.1	14.6	13.1	59.2	93.3
02060	Bristol Bay, AK	NA	1 322	19.1	2	11	54.5	—	9.1	972	32.5	—	11.2	13.4	42.8	85.3
02070	Dillingham, AK	NA	4 430	26.8	1	2	50.0	—	—	516	56.4	—	—	16.1	24.8	80.6
02090	Fairbanks North Star, AK	5	84 061	21.5	2	35	57.1	14.3	20.0	16 877	54.4	15.8	25.8	13.1	17.7	25.3
02100	Haines, AK	9	2 170	20.3	1	5	40.0	20.0	20.0	439	46.0	16.9	35.1	15.7	—	23.0
02110	Juneau, AK	5	29 756	20.4	2	10	50.0	20.0	10.0	6 882	38.6	18.9	22.8	11.5	6.2	28.8
02122	Kenai Peninsula, AK	5	47 131	23.7	1	38	39.5	10.5	21.1	10 314	46.2	15.1	29.5	12.9	19.1	13.8
02130	Ketchikan Gateway, AK	7	14 517	21.1	1	8	50.0	12.5	25.0	2 890	53.7	14.3	28.5	10.1	11.4	28.1
02150	Kodiak Island, AK	7	15 082	21.6	1	16	25.0	6.3	6.3	2 910	42.1	18.1	25.1	13.7	16.2	41.5
02164	Lake and Peninsula Borough, AK	NA	1 701	28.6	1	15	—	—	—	558	—	—	—	14.3	45.3	90.0
02170	Matanuska-Susitna, AK	6	52 500	25.6	1	28	53.6	10.7	21.4	12 338	46.7	19.3	29.4	13.4	20.3	11.2
02180	Nome, AK	7	8 908	28.5	2	18	5.6	—	11.1	2 508	16.3	—	12.2	16.3	43.7	90.3
02185	North Slope, AK	NA	7 110	27.0	1	10	10.0	10.0	10.0	2 133	37.3	10.9	8.6	8.0	11.4	92.2
02188	Northwest Arctic Borough, AK	NA	6 552	31.5	1	13	15.4	7.7	7.7	2 075	27.6	4.9	7.1	13.9	50.6	97.4
02201	Prince of Wales-Outer Ketchikan, AK	NA	7 187	24.4	5	22	18.2	4.5	18.2	1 531	36.6	6.4	18.4	18.9	27.3	53.6
02220	Sitka, AK	NA	8 510	22.7	2	9	33.3	11.1	22.2	2 084	39.7	18.4	35.3	11.9	18.4	41.9
02231	Skagway-Yakutat-Angoon, AK	NA	NA	NA	5	13	15.4	—	15.4	957	25.9	—	20.7	16.0	28.4	55.6
02240	Southeast Fairbanks, AK	NA	5 721	26.3	1	9	11.1	—	—	552	2.7	—	—	18.1	25.4	48.7
02261	Valdez-Cordova, AK	7	10 391	21.0	4	21	33.3	4.8	19.0	2 132	54.1	6.5	28.4	12.8	7.6	26.0
02270	Wade Hampton, AK	9	6 693	32.3	3	14	7.1	—	7.1	2 365	4.7	—	1.6	13.9	50.2	98.9
02280	Wrangell-Petersburg, AK	7	6 998	21.9	3	8	37.5	25.0	37.5	1 497	51.3	20.8	27.9	15.0	10.9	33.5
02290	Yukon-Koyukuk, AK	NA	6 008	29.5	7	40	15.0	—	5.0	2 465	12.0	—	2.6	15.6	24.2	72.6
04000	**ARIZONA**															
04001	Apache, AZ	5	69 087	29.2	11	34	55.9	20.6	20.6	16 105	44.1	21.5	27.1	8.5	NA	82.3
04003	Cochise, AZ	4	110 358	19.7	22	54	64.8	14.8	18.5	21 161	49.2	21.4	29.3	11.8	NA	48.2
04005	Coconino, AZ	5	112 260	22.0	6	34	64.7	11.8	23.5	20 064	52.4	16.6	31.0	11.0	NA	50.5
04007	Gila, AZ	4	47 338	18.7	8	23	47.8	26.1	26.1	8 562	46.9	23.0	30.1	15.7	NA	38.5
04009	Graham, AZ	7	30 780	23.5	7	16	50.0	18.8	25.0	6 182	48.5	21.4	29.7	8.0	NA	41.7
04011	Greenlee, AZ	7	9 330	25.1	6	10	50.0	10.0	30.0	2 259	58.3	0.2	41.3	6.1	NA	47.7
04012	La Paz, AZ	7	14 497	18.1	6	10	70.0	10.0	20.0	3 099	49.6	23.2	27.2	10.2	NA	56.6
04013	Maricopa, AZ	0	2 611 327	17.7	57	478	69.2	14.0	13.6	408 307	60.2	15.4	24.1	9.0	NA	38.8
04015	Mohave, AZ	2	126 294	15.5	14	36	69.4	19.4	11.1	19 074	59.2	23.0	17.8	12.0	NA	16.7
04017	Navajo, AZ	5	92 086	26.9	11	45	48.9	31.1	20.0	20 913	48.2	25.2	26.6	10.8	NA	57.8
04019	Pima, AZ	2	767 873	16.9	15	188	65.4	18.6	13.3	118 741	51.8	21.3	26.3	10.5	NA	48.4
04021	Pinal, AZ	1	135 376	20.3	20	53	58.5	22.6	18.9	25 228	52.4	21.1	26.5	12.2	NA	53.2
04023	Santa Cruz, AZ	6	36 952	23.2	6	17	64.7	17.6	17.6	8 448	51.3	23.1	25.6	5.8	NA	91.5
04025	Yavapai, AZ	4	139 368	15.2	19	46	65.2	15.2	19.6	20 087	54.2	18.5	27.3	10.4	NA	13.9
04027	Yuma, AZ	3	125 142	20.5	9	35	71.4	14.3	14.3	25 368	57.4	12.5	30.1	8.8	NA	69.7
05000	**ARKANSAS**															
05001	Arkansas, AR	7	21 046	20.6	3	12	41.7	33.3	25.0	3 777	38.5	33.9	27.6	9.3	38.5	34.9
05003	Ashley, AR	7	24 543	21.0	3	14	50.0	28.6	21.4	4 941	40.2	36.2	23.6	10.5	39.7	38.6
05005	Baxter, AR	7	36 382	14.7	3	11	45.5	27.3	27.3	5 039	36.4	36.9	26.8	9.2	30.3	0.8
05007	Benton, AR	3	125 956	18.1	7	38	57.9	23.7	18.4	22 008	53.5	25.1	21.5	9.0	21.7	8.6
05009	Boone, AR	7	31 906	18.2	6	17	52.9	11.8	35.3	5 833	46.9	18.4	34.6	9.3	26.1	0.7
05011	Bradley, AR	7	11 617	19.3	2	6	33.3	33.3	33.3	2 316	34.8	34.9	30.3	7.9	43.0	44.5
05013	Calhoun, AR	9	5 714	19.6	1	2	50.0	—	50.0	897	52.7	—	47.3	13.9	36.8	31.1
05015	Carroll, AR	7	22 492	17.9	3	6	50.0	—	50.0	3 675	53.3	—	46.7	10.9	26.0	3.8
05017	Chicot, AR	7	15 130	23.7	3	9	33.3	33.3	33.3	3 091	42.6	22.1	35.3	9.0	74.7	77.8
05019	Clark, AR	7	22 087	16.4	2	8	37.5	37.5	25.0	3 339	33.5	43.8	22.7	12.3	37.1	37.1
05021	Clay, AR	7	17 588	17.1	3	8	50.0	12.5	37.5	3 040	49.5	10.4	40.1	12.7	35.5	0.2
05023	Cleburne, AR	6	22 447	16.4	5	11	45.5	9.1	45.5	3 428	50.5	11.3	38.2	9.4	29.9	0.4
05025	Cleveland, AR	8	8 337	19.7	3	6	50.0	—	50.0	1 519	52.1	—	47.9	10.8	33.8	20.5
05027	Columbia, AR	7	25 469	19.1	6	14	42.9	14.3	42.9	4 937	38.8	30.0	31.2	9.3	40.9	47.0
05029	Conway, AR	6	19 885	20.1	3	10	50.0	20.0	30.0	3 602	42.6	30.5	26.9	15.0	30.7	22.4
05031	Craighead, AR	5	76 155	17.9	8	30	50.0	23.3	26.7	12 799	51.2	21.8	27.1	10.9	28.3	11.1

1. County type code is from the Economic Research Service of the USDA. See notes and definitions at the end of this section.   2. IEP = Individual Education Program. See notes and definitions at the end of this section.

Table D-2. School and Student Characteristics by County — Continued

County	Staff and students, 1995–1996						Revenues, fiscal 1995				Current expenditures, fiscal 1995		
	Number of teachers	Pupil/ teacher ratio	Number of graduates	Dropouts grades 9–12 (percent)	Local school non-teaching staff	Central admin. staff	Total revenue ($1000)	Percent of Revenue from			Amount	Amount per pupil	Percent for instruction
								Federal Gov't	State Gov't	Local Gov't			
	15	16	17	18	19	20	21	22	23	24	25	26	27
ALABAMA—Con.													
Washington, AL	231	16.5	262	2.6	233	12	16 095	10.8	68.4	20.7	16 042	4 272	59.8
Wilcox, AL	169	16.6	162	6.4	165	14	13 808	19.8	64.5	15.6	12 642	4 510	55.8
Winston, AL	266	17.0	284	3.9	226	14	19 902	7.5	71.5	20.9	18 282	4 058	59.5
ALASKA													
Aleutians East Borough, AK	36	11.0	29	NA	25	7	6 360	25.8	57.2	17.0	6 123	16 684	48.1
Aleutians West Census Area, AK	46	13.3	31	NA	48	12	11 124	30.4	45.0	24.5	9 258	15 508	39.5
Anchorage, AK	2 322	20.1	2 158	NA	1 716	654	335 193	8.2	65.8	26.0	295 087	6 192	50.3
Bethel, AK	388	11.1	167	NA	322	92	67 963	18.8	75.2	6.0	57 691	13 838	50.6
Bristol Bay, AK	74	13.1	20	NA	75	23	14 035	19.8	62.0	18.2	13 902	14 406	49.0
Dillingham, AK	39	13.1	25	NA	26	6	6 631	16.3	58.2	25.5	6 325	12 475	59.8
Fairbanks North Star, AK ..	901	18.7	688	NA	639	170	120 960	11.9	63.4	24.7	121 154	7 043	53.6
Haines, AK	29	15.3	23	NA	20	4	3 876	3.8	56.7	39.5	3 377	8 157	57.5
Juneau, AK	287	23.9	268	NA	228	72	43 196	3.7	58.4	37.9	41 302	7 688	52.7
Kenai Peninsula, AK	600	17.2	503	NA	399	120	90 866	3.3	55.6	41.1	81 720	8 058	50.8
Ketchikan Gateway, AK	148	19.6	145	NA	99	19	18 775	4.0	56.1	39.9	18 715	6 514	55.9
Kodiak Island, AK	165	17.6	142	NA	135	25	21 268	15.6	65.3	19.1	22 151	7 838	55.3
Lake and Peninsula Borough, AK	39	14.2	18	NA	58	16	12 075	15.8	58.9	25.3	8 795	15 566	42.6
Matanuska-Susitna, AK.....	687	18.0	648	NA	405	119	90 405	3.4	73.1	23.5	86 254	7 142	51.1
Nome, AK	184	13.7	99	NA	286	28	38 619	21.5	67.3	11.2	32 161	13 159	50.2
North Slope, AK	157	13.0	83	NA	299	55	44 810	10.1	23.3	66.5	43 089	20 766	38.6
Northwest Arctic Borough, AK	129	16.0	59	NA	185	40	24 611	19.8	71.4	8.8	25 018	12 803	48.0
Prince of Wales-Outer Ketchikan, AK	110	13.9	69	NA	104	31	18 966	24.4	65.6	10.0	16 339	11 077	56.7
Sitka, AK...........................	123	16.9	133	NA	72	16	13 744	6.5	56.6	36.9	12 498	6 837	57.1
Skagway-Yakutat- Angoon, AK	80	12.0	46	NA	80	16	12 957	24.8	58.6	16.6	11 502	12 302	54.8
Southeast Fairbanks, AK ..	39	14.1	24	NA	30	8	10 231	11.9	84.2	3.9	6 978	13 092	46.5
Valdez-Cordova, AK..........	137	15.6	121	NA	123	26	23 960	4.6	67.8	27.6	20 337	9 244	53.2
Wade Hampton, AK	157	15.1	56	NA	204	38	29 723	31.5	61.5	7.0	25 718	11 335	48.3
Wrangell-Petersburg, AK...	95	15.8	90	NA	75	13	13 573	8.4	67.1	24.5	11 943	7 888	57.4
Yukon-Koyukuk, AK	187	13.2	100	NA	223	53	43 147	14.8	71.4	13.8	39 468	16 024	49.5
ARIZONA													
Apache, AZ.......................	947	17.0	697	NA	1 183	55	112 804	37.3	36.8	25.9	88 648	5 754	51.5
Cochise, AZ......................	1 167	18.1	738	NA	1 116	61	102 871	12.9	56.7	30.5	87 714	4 124	56.8
Coconino, AZ....................	1 079	18.6	1 003	NA	1 060	37	112 037	17.5	38.1	44.4	91 856	4 496	56.3
Gila, AZ	489	17.5	425	NA	456	32	51 533	15.7	40.4	43.9	39 948	4 410	55.6
Graham, AZ	314	19.7	345	NA	266	23	28 168	13.6	69.6	16.7	23 200	3 863	58.8
Greenlee, AZ....................	131	17.2	78	NA	105	13	12 075	4.2	21.1	74.7	9 915	4 368	51.6
La Paz, AZ	177	17.5	137	NA	189	14	17 373	21.7	42.9	35.4	14 555	4 689	53.2
Maricopa, AZ.....................	20 451	20.0	17 000	NA	18 234	504	2 146 580	6.6	41.8	51.6	1 736 991	4 166	58.7
Mohave, AZ......................	977	19.5	754	NA	919	46	91 911	7.6	36.9	55.5	73 915	3 648	59.3
Navajo, AZ........................	1 095	19.1	827	NA	1 148	50	122 840	20.4	40.4	27.1	91 410	4 700	53.3
Pima, AZ...........................	6 091	19.5	5 017	NA	6 327	246	614 550	9.2	46.9	43.9	509 854	4 251	55.4
Pinal, AZ	1 364	18.5	864	NA	1 360	61	126 860	13.1	51.2	35.7	106 310	4 300	54.4
Santa Cruz, AZ.................	424	19.9	349	NA	370	13	46 583	10.7	52.1	37.2	34 628	4 006	53.9
Yavapai, AZ......................	1 056	19.0	869	NA	897	55	97 296	5.9	40.6	53.5	81 051	4 002	55.4
Yuma, AZ..........................	1 190	21.3	1 178	NA	1 382	72	131 735	12.7	57.4	29.9	111 583	4 086	53.9
ARKANSAS													
Arkansas, AR	229	16.5	273	3.6	188	14	15 464	11.5	59.6	28.9	15 623	4 032	63.1
Ashley, AR........................	284	17.4	278	5.4	256	13	20 697	10.4	63.9	25.6	19 961	4 020	63.0
Baxter, AR........................	270	18.7	283	3.0	221	14	20 969	9.5	53.4	37.1	19 643	3 999	62.0
Benton, AR.......................	1 099	20.0	1 021	2.1	1 028	65	87 671	5.5	49.8	44.7	76 131	3 759	62.6
Boone, AR	339	17.2	349	2.2	292	19	27 331	7.5	63.0	29.5	24 998	4 316	61.0
Bradley, AR	147	15.7	170	3.5	132	9	10 662	12.5	66.8	20.7	10 143	4 283	63.9
Calhoun, AR	52	17.2	53	NA	46	3	3 869	9.6	53.9	36.5	3 740	4 000	63.6
Carroll, AR........................	207	17.8	219	1.0	171	10	14 078	7.2	60.7	32.1	13 333	3 711	63.9
Chicot, AR	191	16.2	124	4.1	168	18	16 521	18.8	60.7	20.5	14 682	4 620	61.6
Clark, AR	201	16.6	176	1.5	160	9	18 518	13.6	55.7	30.7	17 781	4 995	58.3
Clay, AR	177	17.2	175	2.7	159	11	12 079	10.1	65.6	24.3	11 480	3 805	64.9
Cleburne, AR.....................	208	16.5	201	2.2	162	9	14 199	7.5	57.7	34.8	13 374	4 020	64.9
Cleveland, AR	97	15.6	95	3.6	77	7	6 892	13.4	63.6	23.0	6 855	4 501	63.8
Columbia, AR	299	16.5	297	3.4	211	12	19 625	10.3	64.0	25.7	19 928	3 972	65.5
Conway, AR	206	17.5	202	2.7	81	8	18 878	10.2	58.2	31.6	18 566	5 252	55.2
Craighead, AR...................	749	17.1	656	3.8	596	37	54 172	7.8	59.6	32.6	49 923	4 033	64.5

Table D-2. School and Student Characteristics by County

State/County code	County	County type[1]	Population, 1996		Number of school districts, 1995–1996	Level of schools, 1995–1996				Level of students, 1995–1996				Characteristics of students, 1995–1996		
			Total persons	Percent age 5–17		Number of schools	Percent			Number of students	Percent			Percent with IEP[2]	Percent free-lunch eligible	Percent minority
							Primary	Middle	High		Primary	Middle	High			
			1	2	3	4	5	6	7	8	9	10	11	12	13	14
	ARKANSAS—Con.															
05033	Crawford, AR	3	49 074	21.5	5	20	55.0	20.0	25.0	9 981	45.8	26.5	27.6	12.6	30.8	5.4
05035	Crittenden, AR	1	49 604	22.9	5	26	53.8	26.9	19.2	10 680	48.6	28.0	23.3	10.9	52.3	62.2
05037	Cross, AR	6	19 363	22.6	3	10	60.0	10.0	30.0	4 137	48.3	17.1	34.5	10.0	45.1	35.5
05039	Dallas, AR	7	9 335	19.7	3	8	50.0	12.5	37.5	1 862	48.9	17.3	33.8	16.3	43.0	50.5
05041	Desha, AR	7	15 513	23.4	4	10	50.0	10.0	40.0	4 070	54.7	12.2	33.1	11.0	53.3	58.1
05043	Drew, AR	7	17 863	20.7	2	7	42.9	28.6	28.6	3 315	39.5	29.7	30.8	10.1	36.4	35.1
05045	Faulkner, AR	2	73 909	18.9	6	26	57.7	19.2	23.1	13 078	48.6	26.8	24.6	11.5	20.8	10.9
05047	Franklin, AR	6	16 453	19.9	5	11	45.5	9.1	45.5	3 482	53.5	10.8	35.7	10.2	27.0	1.9
05049	Fulton, AR	9	10 708	17.5	3	6	50.0	—	50.0	1 723	53.7	—	46.3	11.7	38.9	0.3
05051	Garland, AR	4	82 038	15.8	7	23	47.8	21.7	30.4	12 601	45.6	25.0	29.4	10.1	31.4	14.7
05053	Grant, AR	6	15 463	19.9	2	7	42.9	28.6	28.6	4 277	41.5	34.7	23.7	10.1	22.5	3.4
05055	Greene, AR	7	35 037	18.4	4	15	53.3	20.0	26.7	6 220	41.7	19.4	38.9	12.2	28.6	1.0
05057	Hempstead, AR	6	22 064	20.4	4	10	40.0	20.0	40.0	4 452	45.8	26.9	27.3	9.7	46.9	45.9
05059	Hot Spring, AR	6	28 242	19.4	5	14	50.0	14.3	35.7	5 679	46.5	18.4	35.1	11.1	32.3	14.7
05061	Howard, AR	7	13 882	20.7	4	10	40.0	20.0	40.0	3 125	41.6	27.3	31.1	8.8	34.0	29.6
05063	Independence, AR	7	33 003	19.6	7	21	52.4	14.3	33.3	6 006	44.7	22.5	32.7	13.1	29.7	4.9
05065	Izard, AR	9	12 794	15.7	4	8	50.0	—	50.0	2 029	55.1	—	44.9	12.2	40.8	0.4
05067	Jackson, AR	7	18 485	19.3	3	9	55.6	11.1	33.3	3 013	53.3	11.7	35.0	12.5	41.4	25.6
05069	Jefferson, AR	3	83 007	20.6	7	39	53.8	30.8	15.4	18 834	44.3	36.1	19.6	8.2	39.8	62.6
05071	Johnson, AR	7	20 898	18.3	4	10	40.0	20.0	40.0	3 796	43.2	23.7	33.1	9.8	31.1	4.8
05073	Lafayette, AR	8	9 231	20.8	3	6	50.0	—	50.0	1 782	55.4	—	44.6	10.2	55.9	54.9
05075	Lawrence, AR	7	17 436	18.0	6	14	50.0	7.1	42.9	3 445	50.0	7.4	42.6	14.3	37.8	1.0
05077	Lee, AR	6	12 802	24.3	1	4	50.0	25.0	25.0	2 166	54.9	17.9	27.2	8.9	85.8	88.0
05079	Lincoln, AR	8	14 309	17.5	3	7	42.9	14.3	42.9	2 201	44.6	21.1	34.3	11.7	49.7	46.4
05081	Little River, AR	6	13 333	21.2	2	6	33.3	33.3	33.3	2 382	40.2	30.8	29.0	10.1	32.9	31.4
05083	Logan, AR	6	21 188	20.1	4	9	44.4	11.1	44.4	3 704	51.7	8.2	40.0	10.7	36.1	2.3
05085	Lonoke, AR	2	47 583	22.3	5	20	55.0	20.0	25.0	9 889	41.3	29.8	28.9	10.6	21.9	12.0
05087	Madison, AR	8	13 094	19.7	3	7	42.9	14.3	42.9	2 673	49.2	17.5	33.3	8.8	33.4	2.8
05089	Marion, AR	9	14 298	16.6	3	6	50.0	—	50.0	2 306	53.9	—	46.1	10.4	38.0	0.9
05091	Miller, AR	3	38 950	20.9	4	16	56.3	18.8	25.0	7 336	48.2	22.3	29.6	10.3	37.6	32.9
05093	Mississippi, AR	4	50 606	22.6	6	27	51.9	25.9	22.2	10 522	45.8	25.7	28.5	13.2	53.8	49.4
05095	Monroe, AR	7	10 381	21.7	3	6	50.0	—	50.0	2 179	51.6	—	48.4	10.1	64.0	57.6
05097	Montgomery, AR	9	8 448	17.2	3	6	50.0	—	50.0	1 402	54.3	—	45.7	11.1	36.7	2.2
05099	Nevada, AR	7	10 067	20.7	3	7	42.9	14.3	42.9	2 028	43.6	17.7	38.8	12.2	43.5	37.5
05101	Newton, AR	9	7 966	21.3	4	8	50.0	—	50.0	1 443	52.3	—	47.7	13.1	50.7	0.8
05103	Ouachita, AR	7	28 374	19.9	4	15	46.7	26.7	26.7	6 110	38.7	32.9	28.4	9.2	40.8	50.8
05105	Perry, AR	8	9 312	19.0	3	6	50.0	—	50.0	1 819	52.8	—	47.2	15.5	32.4	1.9
05107	Phillips, AR	7	27 906	25.1	5	15	46.7	20.0	33.3	6 402	43.5	25.6	30.9	11.6	69.1	77.6
05109	Pike, AR	9	10 485	19.4	4	10	50.0	—	50.0	2 210	54.5	—	45.5	13.4	30.2	7.8
05111	Poinsett, AR	6	24 720	19.5	5	13	46.2	15.4	38.5	5 073	53.2	9.6	37.2	12.5	41.1	12.5
05113	Polk, AR	7	19 336	19.2	5	12	50.0	8.3	41.7	3 688	48.9	12.6	38.6	9.6	43.4	5.2
05115	Pope, AR	5	51 326	19.1	5	19	52.6	21.1	26.3	9 636	42.4	25.8	31.8	9.4	27.8	5.7
05117	Prairie, AR	8	9 273	19.1	3	6	50.0	—	50.0	1 604	54.6	—	45.4	8.7	32.2	21.1
05119	Pulaski, AR	2	352 303	18.7	6	111	69.4	15.3	9.0	54 644	56.0	20.9	11.2	10.0	38.5	53.1
05121	Randolph, AR	7	17 742	19.1	4	10	50.0	10.0	40.0	2 994	54.1	15.9	30.0	10.9	37.2	2.0
05123	St. Francis, AR	6	28 348	24.4	3	14	57.1	21.4	21.4	6 477	43.6	24.6	31.8	10.1	61.4	66.0
05125	Saline, AR	2	74 555	20.5	5	21	57.1	19.0	23.8	11 837	47.3	28.4	24.3	9.4	14.4	3.7
05127	Scott, AR	6	10 775	18.2	1	3	33.3	33.3	33.3	1 711	42.3	31.4	26.2	7.7	35.7	2.9
05129	Searcy, AR	9	7 728	18.3	4	8	50.0	—	50.0	1 463	53.2	—	46.8	9.8	41.3	1.8
05131	Sebastian, AR	3	105 827	18.8	6	39	69.2	12.8	17.9	18 381	54.4	20.0	25.6	11.6	28.6	20.3
05133	Sevier, AR	6	14 754	19.8	3	8	50.0	12.5	37.5	2 973	50.8	13.7	35.5	8.2	38.7	20.5
05135	Sharp, AR	7	16 467	16.7	4	9	44.4	11.1	44.4	3 104	47.0	11.3	41.7	12.2	40.0	0.7
05137	Stone, AR	9	10 877	18.4	3	6	50.0	—	50.0	1 886	52.2	—	47.8	12.7	43.6	1.2
05139	Union, AR	5	46 036	20.0	9	25	56.0	8.0	36.0	8 992	49.5	13.4	37.1	11.1	38.8	43.0
05141	Van Buren, AR	8	15 325	17.2	5	11	45.5	9.1	45.5	2 341	45.9	15.0	39.1	10.6	44.4	1.7
05143	Washington, AR	3	134 984	17.9	9	46	56.5	21.7	21.7	23 821	50.2	25.2	24.5	9.7	21.9	8.1
05145	White, AR	4	61 954	18.7	9	27	44.4	22.2	33.3	11 174	51.5	20.5	28.0	10.9	28.9	5.2
05147	Woodruff, AR	7	9 203	21.6	3	6	50.0	—	50.0	1 764	53.7	—	46.3	10.5	58.8	44.8
05149	Yell, AR	7	19 000	18.6	6	14	50.0	7.1	42.9	3 734	53.3	10.3	36.3	12.0	35.4	7.5
06000	**CALIFORNIA**															
06001	Alameda, CA	0	1 328 139	17.3	21	310	64.5	15.8	15.8	199 979	54.3	18.9	25.5	10.7	35.8	63.2
06003	Alpine, CA	9	1 232	19.0	1	3	100.0	—	—	174	100.0	—	—	22.4	52.3	44.3
06005	Amador, CA	6	33 315	15.0	2	12	50.0	16.7	25.0	4 834	49.7	18.1	28.0	12.0	20.0	10.8
06007	Butte, CA	3	192 507	18.2	16	67	61.2	16.4	17.9	34 612	55.0	15.7	25.7	12.0	39.6	24.4
06009	Calaveras, CA	6	38 437	19.2	5	22	45.5	9.1	27.3	7 396	47.9	13.5	26.4	10.4	31.1	10.4
06011	Colusa, CA	6	18 223	23.5	5	19	26.3	10.5	47.4	4 160	43.1	19.8	34.7	10.5	61.1	55.7
06013	Contra Costa, CA	0	881 490	18.7	19	214	58.9	15.9	21.0	142 904	50.5	21.4	26.3	11.7	26.9	41.5

1. County type code is from the Economic Research Service of the USDA. See notes and definitions at the end of this section.   2. IEP = Individual Education Program. See notes and definitions at the end of this section.

Table D-2. School and Student Characteristics by County — Continued

County	Number of teachers	Pupil/ teacher ratio	Number of graduates	Dropouts grades 9–12 (percent)	Local school non-teaching staff	Central admin. staff	Total revenue ($1000)	Federal Gov't	State Gov't	Local Gov't	Amount	Amount per pupil	Percent for instruction
	15	16	17	18	19	20	21	22	23	24	25	26	27
ARKANSAS—Con.													
Crawford, AR	579	17.2	484	1.7	475	18	41 989	8.1	69.7	22.2	38 674	3 957	65.3
Crittenden, AR	642	16.6	485	8.8	521	28	44 819	13.1	66.8	20.0	42 824	4 002	65.2
Cross, AR	259	16.0	252	5.6	208	14	17 358	12.0	66.9	21.1	16 489	3 902	63.6
Dallas, AR	124	15.0	115	6.7	108	7	8 657	9.3	67.8	22.8	7 853	4 090	66.1
Desha, AR	256	15.9	248	6.6	231	14	18 618	11.8	64.8	23.4	17 448	4 269	62.5
Drew, AR	201	16.5	211	3.4	152	12	18 234	14.6	61.0	24.4	16 618	5 080	60.2
Faulkner, AR	728	18.0	710	1.7	496	27	54 776	5.2	66.3	28.5	48 540	3 837	63.6
Franklin, AR	207	16.8	199	1.6	149	10	16 925	14.3	58.8	26.9	16 114	4 644	59.2
Fulton, AR	107	16.1	120	1.9	89	7	7 572	9.2	69.0	21.8	7 017	4 033	63.0
Garland, AR	675	18.7	648	4.3	599	36	51 868	8.3	49.5	42.2	49 123	4 075	62.9
Grant, AR	226	19.0	231	1.7	198	12	17 917	6.6	70.3	23.1	15 862	3 818	63.7
Greene, AR	354	17.6	352	1.6	321	12	27 574	8.2	68.2	23.6	26 412	4 215	64.6
Hempstead, AR	262	17.0	227	2.0	261	12	19 762	11.7	66.1	22.2	19 029	4 269	63.3
Hot Spring, AR	342	16.6	338	3.6	176	18	23 963	7.6	66.6	25.7	23 222	4 094	64.0
Howard, AR	196	15.9	193	3.4	52	7	13 368	7.7	63.9	28.4	12 498	4 032	66.1
Independence, AR	373	16.1	371	2.7	251	17	28 383	6.6	58.7	34.8	26 554	4 454	63.4
Izard, AR	134	15.1	104	NA	124	7	10 448	11.1	64.2	24.8	9 789	5 072	62.8
Jackson, AR	190	15.9	200	4.7	199	10	13 140	11.0	63.1	26.0	13 691	4 425	62.3
Jefferson, AR	1 027	18.3	917	5.9	976	50	79 862	15.0	58.5	26.6	77 453	4 633	63.3
Johnson, AR	222	17.1	203	3.2	166	9	15 402	10.3	67.5	22.2	14 266	3 878	66.1
Lafayette, AR	123	14.4	101	4.7	118	8	8 251	11.4	59.4	29.2	8 103	4 687	63.0
Lawrence, AR	221	15.6	195	1.4	185	13	16 261	9.6	69.4	21.0	15 818	4 631	64.8
Lee, AR	124	17.4	127	5.9	142	12	11 675	21.0	62.3	16.7	10 122	4 432	61.7
Lincoln, AR	131	16.8	126	3.6	126	7	9 020	11.7	60.4	18.0	9 601	4 429	60.0
Little River, AR	152	15.7	166	2.7	138	19	10 004	9.2	52.1	38.7	10 570	4 370	62.6
Logan, AR	212	17.5	182	4.7	166	13	15 457	9.9	67.3	22.7	14 185	3 933	66.7
Lonoke, AR	546	18.1	481	2.9	441	26	39 962	8.1	70.6	21.3	35 718	3 720	65.0
Madison, AR	151	17.7	125	5.4	153	5	10 725	7.9	71.5	20.6	9 598	3 720	63.7
Marion, AR	133	17.3	123	1.7	121	6	10 868	7.8	56.0	36.2	8 667	3 908	62.1
Miller, AR	485	15.1	443	3.6	389	14	34 328	9.7	63.7	26.6	31 775	4 198	64.8
Mississippi, AR	635	16.6	532	10.1	596	33	49 424	15.1	66.1	18.8	45 813	4 302	63.0
Monroe, AR	138	15.8	112	4.9	127	8	9 613	17.4	62.8	19.9	9 340	4 222	61.8
Montgomery, AR	90	15.5	82	1.2	83	6	6 247	18.9	56.3	24.8	5 746	3 963	64.1
Nevada, AR	127	16.0	139	1.1	125	8	8 827	9.3	63.6	27.1	8 368	4 201	63.1
Newton, AR	98	14.8	104	3.2	114	10	7 402	12.4	70.9	16.8	7 034	4 788	61.9
Ouachita, AR	364	16.8	390	2.7	373	19	29 626	10.5	65.7	23.8	28 068	4 551	61.6
Perry, AR	108	16.9	96	1.7	104	5	8 166	10.0	70.5	19.4	7 587	4 375	63.1
Phillips, AR	396	16.2	291	6.7	421	15	30 921	18.0	64.6	17.3	30 175	4 658	61.0
Pike, AR	155	14.3	125	2.1	133	8	8 446	9.6	63.2	27.2	8 301	4 263	65.5
Poinsett, AR	316	16.0	260	3.0	260	18	23 581	13.7	65.8	20.5	22 514	4 439	63.3
Polk, AR	220	16.7	208	2.4	163	12	15 192	12.2	65.5	22.3	14 271	3 926	64.1
Pope, AR	544	17.7	525	4.2	458	19	38 536	7.9	53.6	38.4	37 474	3 997	66.2
Prairie, AR	104	15.5	94	5.7	94	5	6 404	8.7	61.3	30.0	6 610	4 088	63.7
Pulaski, AR	3 437	15.9	2 907	9.2	1 908	139	314 118	7.4	51.3	41.3	290 656	5 378	59.6
Randolph, AR	182	16.5	202	2.1	158	9	13 365	8.5	65.0	26.5	11 837	4 017	64.6
St. Francis, AR	369	17.6	385	0.6	380	28	29 081	14.7	68.7	16.5	28 661	4 355	60.5
Saline, AR	611	19.4	580	4.0	429	25	46 169	5.1	71.2	23.8	42 167	3 602	66.6
Scott, AR	100	17.1	110	4.0	100	6	6 910	18.4	65.9	15.8	6 466	3 837	60.7
Searcy, AR	92	15.9	42	1.2	84	6	6 622	10.1	70.8	19.1	6 165	4 308	63.3
Sebastian, AR	1 034	17.8	1 090	5.8	805	55	78 795	7.4	55.8	36.8	77 507	4 291	64.3
Sevier, AR	171	17.4	125	1.9	141	13	13 564	13.4	63.5	23.1	13 084	4 612	63.3
Sharp, AR	103	30.1	196	1.9	168	9	12 899	10.0	67.3	22.7	12 232	3 990	64.0
Stone, AR	111	17.0	100	1.2	95	8	8 208	11.1	69.9	19.0	7 317	3 955	63.7
Union, AR	562	16.0	461	6.6	456	31	38 098	10.0	60.3	29.6	37 807	4 082	64.2
Van Buren, AR	127	18.5	137	1.8	142	10	10 613	10.0	62.8	27.1	9 895	4 149	62.3
Washington, AR	1 201	19.8	1 180	3.7	1 047	53	103 562	7.0	58.9	34.1	93 216	4 092	64.5
White, AR	652	17.1	631	2.4	493	34	49 220	10.3	65.5	24.1	45 319	4 149	62.9
Woodruff, AR	119	14.8	114	5.9	106	6	7 918	14.9	63.7	21.4	7 430	4 110	62.8
Yell, AR	222	16.8	187	4.8	173	12	16 312	12.2	64.3	23.5	14 386	3 880	63.8
CALIFORNIA													
Alameda, CA	8 491	23.6	9 625	4.3	5 830	903	1 122 955	6.3	52.8	40.9	946 725	4 852	62.8
Alpine, CA	12	15.0	—	NA	14	2	2 507	31.0	43.2	25.8	1 860	10 629	54.1
Amador, CA	191	25.3	245	1.4	155	18	22 305	3.3	28.6	68.1	20 599	4 328	60.2
Butte, CA	1 541	22.5	1 677	4.8	1 441	224	187 141	16.4	49.5	34.1	173 851	5 285	66.3
Calaveras, CA	380	19.4	439	2.5	267	56	56 863	3.4	35.5	61.1	40 853	5 600	62.8
Colusa, CA	219	19.0	228	1.9	188	31	24 541	12.2	53.8	34.0	22 389	5 634	61.1
Contra Costa, CA	6 020	23.7	7 402	2.5	4 081	612	751 200	4.8	45.3	49.9	644 473	4 654	64.1

Table D-2. School and Student Characteristics by County

State/ County code	County	County type[1]	Population, 1996		Number of school districts, 1995–1996	Level of schools, 1995–1996				Level of students, 1995–1996				Characteristics of students, 1995–1996		
			Total persons	Percent age 5–17		Number of schools	Percent			Number of students	Percent			Percent with IEP[2]	Percent free-lunch eligible	Percent minority
							Primary	Middle	High		Primary	Middle	High			
			1	2	3	4	5	6	7	8	9	10	11	12	13	14
	CALIFORNIA—Con.															
06015	Del Norte, CA	7	26 947	20.6	2	13	61.5	7.7	15.4	5 332	58.2	13.9	26.3	11.4	41.8	27.0
06017	El Dorado, CA	1	151 706	20.2	16	56	53.6	19.6	21.4	28 632	50.3	18.8	28.4	11.4	23.7	14.0
06019	Fresno, CA	2	751 272	23.0	36	257	63.4	14.0	17.9	170 190	57.4	15.1	24.6	11.2	55.2	67.6
06021	Glenn, CA	6	26 202	23.2	11	23	43.5	13.0	39.1	6 188	50.2	19.8	27.7	NA	50.6	42.0
06023	Humboldt, CA	5	123 023	19.8	34	77	68.8	6.5	19.5	22 170	60.7	9.3	27.8	12.3	37.5	22.2
06025	Imperial, CA	4	142 651	24.3	17	57	52.6	15.8	26.3	32 285	54.9	16.7	27.1	9.2	55.7	85.0
06027	Inyo, CA	7	18 433	18.5	8	18	44.4	16.7	27.8	3 481	51.3	15.1	29.0	13.0	28.1	30.7
06029	Kern, CA	2	622 729	22.8	48	221	58.4	18.6	19.9	136 677	52.5	19.1	27.2	10.0	51.2	53.2
06031	Kings, CA	4	113 351	22.4	15	47	53.2	19.1	23.4	23 816	53.7	19.1	25.7	9.7	52.6	59.5
06033	Lake, CA	6	55 261	18.1	8	31	38.7	19.4	38.7	10 214	44.7	27.2	27.3	12.5	52.9	20.6
06035	Lassen, CA	6	31 431	18.5	11	24	45.8	16.7	29.2	5 511	55.2	13.1	29.8	NA	32.4	14.8
06037	Los Angeles, CA	0	9 127 751	18.9	82	1 677	67.1	14.4	15.7	1 508 589	53.8	18.3	25.3	9.3	58.5	78.6
06039	Madera, CA	2	110 481	22.6	11	49	59.2	10.2	24.5	23 360	58.6	12.6	23.7	12.7	52.7	56.2
06041	Marin, CA	0	233 230	14.0	20	69	60.9	14.5	20.3	27 350	50.3	20.7	27.2	14.3	13.5	22.9
06043	Mariposa, CA	8	15 869	17.4	2	15	53.3	6.7	20.0	2 741	58.4	12.3	24.7	10.5	26.7	11.5
06045	Mendocino, CA	4	83 298	21.1	13	55	47.3	9.1	36.4	15 878	51.8	16.4	30.8	15.8	42.9	25.4
06047	Merced, CA	3	192 311	25.2	21	77	55.8	20.8	22.1	47 462	51.1	21.0	27.2	11.1	62.6	64.2
06049	Modoc, CA	7	9 693	21.6	4	16	43.8	6.3	31.3	2 363	52.1	12.1	31.6	13.9	44.7	27.7
06051	Mono, CA	7	10 497	17.6	3	13	46.2	7.7	30.8	1 882	57.8	14.9	24.7	15.5	29.7	21.2
06053	Monterey, CA	2	339 047	20.6	26	104	59.6	17.3	18.3	63 752	54.7	18.8	23.4	10.2	51.0	68.5
06055	Napa, CA	0	116 512	17.5	6	42	66.7	9.5	19.0	18 340	55.4	15.1	28.9	12.5	32.9	31.6
06057	Nevada, CA	4	89 016	19.0	11	38	57.9	15.8	23.7	13 457	42.3	24.9	32.4	10.3	21.0	7.2
06059	Orange, CA	0	2 636 888	18.1	28	513	67.4	14.8	15.4	424 862	53.9	16.7	27.7	9.3	35.9	54.2
06061	Placer, CA	1	213 227	20.1	20	81	53.1	18.5	19.8	44 246	49.7	18.8	26.0	10.0	19.0	15.4
06063	Plumas, CA	6	20 597	20.0	1	18	50.0	5.6	38.9	3 655	50.1	6.8	35.4	11.8	36.7	13.5
06065	Riverside, CA	0	1 417 425	20.8	25	322	60.2	16.8	17.7	269 265	53.2	18.3	25.0	11.0	48.1	53.9
06067	Sacramento, CA	0	1 117 275	19.8	17	313	66.8	11.8	14.1	195 258	57.8	14.9	24.9	11.4	42.4	47.5
06069	San Benito, CA	6	44 503	23.1	12	22	68.2	13.6	9.1	9 624	59.7	13.9	24.8	11.6	35.8	57.5
06071	San Bernardino, CA	0	1 598 358	22.7	34	415	66.0	16.6	15.2	335 978	55.5	17.9	24.8	10.5	44.3	56.9
06073	San Diego, CA	0	2 655 463	18.4	44	544	67.8	14.5	14.5	438 201	54.3	18.5	25.4	10.4	46.3	53.3
06075	San Francisco, CA	0	735 315	12.1	2	114	66.7	14.9	14.9	62 830	47.8	20.2	29.0	10.8	63.6	86.9
06077	San Joaquin, CA	2	533 392	22.2	18	152	70.4	9.9	13.2	106 277	60.3	12.2	24.6	10.1	48.5	57.9
06079	San Luis Obispo, CA	3	229 437	16.9	13	71	59.2	15.5	21.1	35 171	51.8	18.4	28.6	11.2	29.1	24.5
06081	San Mateo, CA	0	686 909	16.0	24	159	66.7	17.6	15.7	89 850	52.6	20.0	27.4	10.3	27.4	58.3
06083	Santa Barbara, CA	2	385 573	17.2	24	100	66.0	13.0	20.0	60 027	56.7	16.5	26.2	11.2	38.9	55.0
06085	Santa Clara, CA	0	1 599 604	17.6	34	348	66.1	17.0	15.5	243 514	52.0	20.5	26.1	10.1	31.6	61.4
06087	Santa Cruz, CA	0	237 821	17.9	12	61	63.9	16.4	16.4	38 416	53.0	19.1	26.9	12.2	37.0	47.0
06089	Shasta, CA	3	161 740	21.2	26	71	59.2	16.9	19.7	30 418	47.8	20.6	30.3	12.4	41.6	15.2
06091	Sierra, CA	8	3 409	19.9	2	10	40.0	10.0	30.0	899	49.2	13.7	30.8	NA	30.9	9.1
06093	Siskiyou, CA	7	44 193	21.2	30	44	61.4	6.8	29.5	8 552	54.1	14.5	30.2	13.7	44.2	19.6
06095	Solano, CA	0	365 536	21.5	7	94	62.8	16.0	18.1	67 792	53.7	19.9	25.2	11.9	27.9	51.0
06097	Sonoma, CA	0	420 872	18.5	41	147	63.9	13.6	17.7	68 661	54.2	19.3	23.3	11.4	26.0	25.3
06099	Stanislaus, CA	2	415 786	22.9	30	130	65.4	16.2	16.2	88 917	54.1	18.2	26.5	12.5	44.3	44.5
06101	Sutter, CA	3	75 650	21.4	13	35	60.0	8.6	20.0	15 020	55.3	14.9	26.8	13.2	47.2	40.9
06103	Tehama, CA	6	54 108	21.1	19	32	65.6	12.5	15.6	11 065	55.6	15.0	28.6	10.7	47.2	21.1
06105	Trinity, CA	6	13 418	20.7	12	21	57.1	—	28.6	2 537	69.0	—	28.8	NA	51.2	16.2
06107	Tulare, CA	2	349 922	24.8	50	142	62.7	16.2	18.3	82 459	57.6	15.9	26.2	12.2	60.7	63.6
06109	Tuolumne, CA	6	52 196	17.7	13	24	54.2	—	25.0	8 140	68.8	—	29.0	12.0	34.1	10.7
06111	Ventura, CA	0	714 733	20.5	21	183	65.6	16.4	15.3	124 253	52.3	19.9	26.9	10.1	35.2	48.3
06113	Yolo, CA	0	149 925	18.3	6	50	54.0	16.0	24.0	25 107	50.9	24.3	22.9	10.4	39.7	43.8
06115	Yuba, CA	3	60 905	23.1	6	33	54.5	15.2	15.2	13 564	50.4	22.9	22.8	13.4	67.9	42.2
08000	**COLORADO**															
08001	Adams, CO	0	309 928	21.0	7	101	64.4	18.8	12.9	53 174	50.7	22.5	24.9	11.1	23.3	33.4
08003	Alamosa, CO	7	14 300	21.2	2	8	37.5	25.0	37.5	2 825	33.9	36.2	29.8	9.5	41.6	49.7
08005	Arapahoe, CO	0	455 035	19.8	8	129	69.0	16.3	14.0	87 041	48.5	23.3	27.9	11.3	13.1	24.0
08007	Archuleta, CO	9	7 953	21.4	1	3	33.3	33.3	33.3	1 479	53.6	16.8	29.5	9.2	23.7	22.5
08009	Baca, CO	9	4 491	18.7	5	11	45.5	9.1	45.5	930	54.5	7.7	37.7	7.5	33.2	10.0
08011	Bent, CO	9	5 478	21.1	2	5	40.0	20.0	40.0	1 038	52.3	16.6	31.1	9.5	44.1	36.3
08013	Boulder, CO	0	258 234	16.6	2	81	60.5	19.8	16.0	42 020	48.8	21.3	29.5	10.3	11.9	17.9
08015	Chaffee, CO	7	14 672	17.7	2	7	28.6	28.6	28.6	2 232	46.4	19.4	32.4	8.2	21.3	10.0
08017	Cheyenne, CO	9	2 323	22.8	2	5	40.0	20.0	20.0	498	43.0	22.5	19.1	9.0	21.9	9.0
08019	Clear Creek, CO	8	8 448	19.1	1	6	50.0	16.7	33.3	1 385	57.0	15.6	27.4	9.9	11.8	5.8
08021	Conejos, CO	9	7 869	25.6	3	10	40.0	20.0	40.0	2 041	48.3	17.8	33.9	7.0	53.1	55.2
08023	Costilla, CO	9	3 567	20.7	2	5	40.0	20.0	40.0	744	51.7	9.5	38.7	10.1	66.8	83.2
08025	Crowley, CO	8	4 200	16.0	1	2	50.0	—	50.0	644	58.7	—	41.3	10.4	55.9	31.8

1. County type code is from the Economic Research Service of the USDA. See notes and definitions at the end of this section. 2. IEP = Individual Education Program. See notes and definitions at the end of this section.

Table D-2. School and Student Characteristics by County — Continued

County	Staff and students, 1995–1996						Revenues, fiscal 1995				Current expenditures, fiscal 1995		
	Number of teachers	Pupil/ teacher ratio	Number of graduates	Dropouts grades 9–12 (percent)	Local school non-teaching staff	Central admin. staff	Total revenue ($1000)	Percent of Revenue from			Amount	Amount per pupil	Percent for instruction
								Federal Gov't	State Gov't	Local Gov't			
	15	16	17	18	19	20	21	22	23	24	25	26	27
CALIFORNIA—Con.													
Del Norte, CA	231	23.0	227	5.1	252	24	25 184	10.8	60.3	28.9	24 226	4 587	64.9
El Dorado, CA	1 224	23.4	1 392	2.2	1 014	139	143 257	6.3	53.5	40.2	127 812	4 497	62.3
Fresno, CA	7 130	23.9	7 517	5.0	6 178	972	930 777	11.4	61.1	27.5	804 797	4 870	60.6
Glenn, CA	294	21.0	291	4.6	275	39	36 278	9.3	57.8	32.9	33 443	5 497	60.0
Humboldt, CA	1 037	21.4	1 140	5.0	1 000	126	120 699	8.9	57.4	33.6	106 847	5 717	64.5
Imperial, CA	1 366	23.6	1 477	2.9	1 465	178	195 643	10.6	62.8	26.5	157 409	4 915	63.3
Inyo, CA	174	20.0	211	2.1	157	36	26 296	8.8	26.9	64.3	22 062	6 408	59.6
Kern, CA	5 690	24.0	6 404	4.6	5 053	836	740 908	9.5	56.9	33.6	644 463	4 884	59.9
Kings, CA	1 001	23.8	1 089	2.5	980	132	124 235	10.7	64.7	24.6	111 973	4 831	63.1
Lake, CA	462	22.1	459	3.8	421	54	58 653	9.4	55.0	35.6	49 221	4 827	60.3
Lassen, CA	265	20.8	279	2.0	229	41	34 549	6.0	57.3	36.7	29 907	5 592	60.2
Los Angeles, CA	58 876	25.6	67 091	6.6	48 873	6 702	8 129 291	10.1	59.4	30.5	6 952 034	4 761	64.1
Madera, CA	980	23.8	1 059	6.0	895	152	125 043	9.4	57.9	32.7	109 430	4 763	57.4
Marin, CA	1 352	20.2	1 540	1.6	1 011	185	182 699	3.7	20.6	75.7	167 679	6 326	63.5
Mariposa, CA	123	22.3	139	3.7	126	18	14 629	4.9	34.8	60.3	14 163	5 207	58.5
Mendocino, CA	808	19.7	910	4.5	777	88	116 608	7.7	48.5	43.8	88 890	5 669	63.7
Merced, CA	1 963	24.2	2 236	3.5	2 248	234	259 694	15.2	63.0	21.9	234 884	5 063	64.0
Modoc, CA	133	17.8	127	0.9	124	19	17 132	7.8	58.4	33.8	16 373	7 085	57.8
Mono, CA	97	19.4	85	5.7	68	9	11 884	5.0	24.2	70.8	11 344	6 438	60.5
Monterey, CA	2 737	23.3	2 643	3.9	2 190	353	367 644	12.7	47.0	40.3	313 246	5 113	61.6
Napa, CA	803	22.8	921	0.9	609	94	94 925	5.6	33.3	61.1	84 865	4 780	63.7
Nevada, CA	603	22.3	755	3.1	478	62	66 859	3.9	45.6	50.5	62 808	4 720	65.1
Orange, CA	16 435	25.9	22 080	2.7	13 244	1 699	1 998 146	6.0	42.1	51.9	1 804 586	4 377	63.1
Placer, CA	1 890	23.4	2 231	2.4	1 463	185	233 656	3.3	44.5	52.2	108 217	4 460	64.0
Plumas, CA	142	25.7	238	2.1	154	14	22 969	11.3	34.9	53.8	19 359	5 027	60.2
Riverside, CA	10 561	25.5	11 622	3.2	8 576	1 221	1 342 998	7.2	62.2	30.6	1 160 298	4 501	62.1
Sacramento, CA	7 925	24.6	8 464	4.6	7 249	1 123	1 005 247	8.7	60.8	30.5	908 357	4 805	61.1
San Benito, CA	393	24.5	405	1.5	310	64	47 179	6.2	55.2	38.6	40 982	4 519	64.1
San Bernardino, CA	13 385	25.1	14 525	3.9	10 475	1 464	1 641 340	6.9	67.1	25.9	1 442 824	4 405	62.6
San Diego, CA	18 002	24.3	20 464	3.9	14 917	2 331	2 297 143	7.8	48.0	44.3	2 044 755	4 802	61.0
San Francisco, CA	2 906	21.6	3 423	5.0	1 956	293	457 217	7.7	36.6	55.6	371 527	6 057	68.2
San Joaquin, CA	4 451	23.9	4 386	3.0	3 446	423	524 920	9.2	60.7	30.2	473 229	4 566	63.3
San Luis Obispo, CA	1 559	22.6	1 683	2.0	1 242	211	206 778	3.9	26.0	70.0	163 038	4 842	61.6
San Mateo, CA	4 021	22.3	4 798	2.5	2 755	506	507 445	5.6	24.0	70.4	464 597	5 343	60.9
Santa Barbara, CA	2 545	23.6	2 655	3.1	2 148	347	313 058	8.4	39.6	52.0	285 357	4 935	63.1
Santa Clara, CA	10 172	23.9	12 541	3.2	7 845	1 307	1 385 841	7.3	33.9	58.7	1 208 229	5 149	62.4
Santa Cruz, CA	1 569	24.5	1 770	3.8	1 396	233	201 774	7.6	47.0	45.4	176 650	4 730	61.7
Shasta, CA	1 298	23.4	1 516	4.5	1 315	162	163 984	6.6	52.0	41.4	147 182	5 031	62.5
Sierra, CA	53	16.9	47	2.2	48	7	6 119	3.5	61.5	35.0	6 171	7 312	64.8
Siskiyou, CA	459	18.6	472	4.6	398	64	53 209	12.2	57.4	30.5	50 127	5 767	60.7
Solano, CA	2 939	23.1	3 220	2.4	1 928	352	324 124	7.3	62.0	30.7	294 797	4 426	65.3
Sonoma, CA	2 933	23.4	3 201	2.4	2 241	350	366 745	4.1	43.6	52.4	321 800	4 863	65.1
Stanislaus, CA	3 730	23.8	4 207	4.0	2 737	451	445 900	8.9	54.0	37.0	403 040	4 585	64.1
Sutter, CA	678	22.2	720	4.1	521	82	78 691	9.8	56.8	33.4	72 554	5 037	60.7
Tehama, CA	518	21.3	548	1.7	410	75	60 769	8.7	57.3	33.9	55 246	5 104	62.4
Trinity, CA	144	17.6	158	1.2	175	27	16 930	7.5	64.2	28.3	17 654	7 076	61.1
Tulare, CA	3 492	23.6	3 627	4.0	3 155	467	454 312	14.1	61.6	24.3	386 153	4 810	63.9
Tuolumne, CA	352	23.1	478	1.6	258	50	40 313	3.8	43.6	52.6	37 528	4 645	63.4
Ventura, CA	4 794	25.9	6 469	3.4	3 678	520	614 735	6.5	48.4	45.1	536 868	4 480	61.6
Yolo, CA	1 134	22.1	1 277	3.6	919	149	123 344	7.2	51.5	41.3	112 261	4 652	61.9
Yuba, CA	576	23.5	486	4.2	496	77	73 040	15.8	62.7	21.5	66 319	4 952	61.8
COLORADO													
Adams, CO	2 693	19.7	2 423	NA	2 129	271	294 704	4.7	50.6	44.7	241 096	4 655	60.5
Alamosa, CO	167	16.9	157	NA	122	17	19 743	23.0	50.3	26.7	15 833	5 629	59.9
Arapahoe, CO	4 524	19.2	4 643	NA	3 708	632	513 989	3.5	42.8	53.7	444 437	5 221	61.0
Archuleta, CO	72	20.7	56	NA	44	5	7 817	3.7	33.7	62.7	5 872	4 412	57.9
Baca, CO	88	10.6	53	NA	59	10	6 546	2.4	53.1	44.5	5 675	6 115	54.1
Bent, CO	72	14.5	58	NA	53	10	6 165	6.8	64.4	28.8	5 468	5 350	54.7
Boulder, CO	2 231	18.8	2 201	NA	1 653	197	240 349	4.2	28.2	67.7	208 337	5 064	59.7
Chaffee, CO	149	15.0	143	NA	107	11	12 325	7.7	50.0	42.3	11 225	5 088	63.3
Cheyenne, CO	47	10.6	28	NA	32	7	3 770	1.5	22.9	75.6	3 215	6 292	55.5
Clear Creek, CO	75	18.5	72	NA	78	8	8 516	2.4	26.6	71.0	6 961	4 997	57.2
Conejos, CO	127	16.1	137	NA	90	11	10 946	8.8	73.3	17.9	9 123	4 557	62.8
Costilla, CO	50	15.0	44	NA	37	8	4 780	12.3	20.8	66.9	3 931	5 506	54.1
Crowley, CO	39	16.6	42	NA	30	5	3 371	9.6	65.5	24.9	2 670	4 349	56.3

Table D-2.   School and Student Characteristics by County

State/ County code	County	County type[1]	Population, 1996		Number of school districts, 1995–1996	Level of schools, 1995–1996				Level of students, 1995–1996				Characteristics of students, 1995–1996		
			Total persons	Percent age 5–17		Number of schools	Percent			Number of students	Percent			Percent with IEP[2]	Percent free-lunch eligible	Percent minority
							Primary	Middle	High		Primary	Middle	High			
			1	2	3	4	5	6	7	8	9	10	11	12	13	14
	COLORADO—Con.															
08027	Custer, CO	8	3 062	20.8	1	2	50.0	—	50.0	425	52.0	—	48.0	6.8	26.1	2.6
08029	Delta, CO	7	25 563	18.5	1	15	46.7	26.7	26.7	4 758	40.2	30.5	29.3	12.2	30.6	15.7
08031	Denver, CO	0	497 840	15.2	1	111	71.2	16.2	11.7	64 322	55.9	21.0	22.9	11.1	50.6	72.9
08033	Dolores, CO	9	1 677	20.6	1	3	33.3	33.3	33.3	347	46.7	21.3	32.0	9.2	15.3	12.7
08035	Douglas, CO	1	111 647	21.9	1	34	70.6	14.7	11.8	22 032	54.7	20.2	24.9	8.4	2.0	6.5
08037	Eagle, CO	7	30 525	17.5	1	10	50.0	30.0	20.0	3 865	51.7	25.9	22.3	7.5	15.3	27.8
08039	Elbert, CO	8	16 209	23.8	5	12	41.7	16.7	41.7	3 056	42.5	26.2	31.3	10.0	8.1	6.4
08041	El Paso, CO	2	472 924	19.8	15	159	62.9	17.0	18.9	84 262	50.9	22.9	26.0	10.2	18.9	25.5
08043	Fremont, CO	6	41 694	16.0	3	14	57.1	14.3	28.6	6 332	59.8	11.1	29.0	8.1	24.8	11.4
08045	Garfield, CO	7	36 499	20.0	3	20	45.0	30.0	25.0	8 475	48.1	27.1	24.8	7.3	13.0	13.9
08047	Gilpin, CO	8	3 725	17.7	1	2	50.0	—	50.0	364	54.7	—	45.3	14.3	9.3	1.9
08049	Grand, CO	9	9 536	19.4	2	8	50.0	25.0	25.0	1 758	47.6	25.4	27.0	9.7	12.2	5.3
08051	Gunnison, CO	7	12 148	15.2	1	8	50.0	37.5	12.5	1 703	36.5	37.0	26.5	8.2	8.3	5.3
08053	Hinsdale, CO	9	666	15.2	1	1	100.0	—	—	39	100.0	—	—	2.6	7.7	5.1
08055	Huerfano, CO	6	6 564	19.7	2	7	42.9	14.3	42.9	1 166	47.4	16.8	35.8	10.2	47.9	54.0
08057	Jackson, CO	9	1 521	18.7	1	2	50.0	—	50.0	327	53.5	—	46.5	11.6	28.7	11.0
08059	Jefferson, CO	0	492 528	19.3	1	135	67.4	14.8	13.3	85 392	55.6	17.0	25.9	8.5	9.9	13.4
08061	Kiowa, CO	9	1 646	22.7	2	5	40.0	20.0	20.0	389	50.9	13.1	20.8	11.3	17.2	3.9
08063	Kit Carson, CO	7	7 218	21.6	5	12	41.7	16.7	41.7	1 680	47.4	19.7	32.9	10.1	24.1	11.9
08065	Lake, CO	7	6 212	20.0	2	5	40.0	—	60.0	1 316	70.7	—	29.3	9.7	21.3	37.2
08067	La Plata, CO	7	39 453	19.1	3	21	42.9	28.6	23.8	6 824	41.6	26.9	29.1	8.6	17.3	19.1
08069	Larimer, CO	3	221 725	18.7	3	70	67.1	20.0	11.4	36 078	51.3	24.6	23.9	10.4	14.2	16.2
08071	Las Animas, CO	7	14 485	19.0	6	16	50.0	12.5	37.5	2 506	48.9	17.0	34.1	8.5	46.9	52.6
08073	Lincoln, CO	8	5 578	16.0	3	6	50.0	—	16.7	952	51.7	—	4.2	12.7	20.2	5.8
08075	Logan, CO	7	18 021	20.0	4	15	53.3	6.7	40.0	3 488	48.2	18.3	33.5	12.5	26.7	15.2
08077	Mesa, CO	5	108 371	20.1	3	41	53.7	19.5	22.0	19 390	46.0	23.5	29.4	10.9	33.7	13.6
08079	Mineral, CO	9	681	12.9	1	2	50.0	—	50.0	129	64.3	—	35.7	9.3	17.1	2.3
08081	Moffat, CO	7	12 086	24.2	1	8	75.0	12.5	12.5	2 815	38.1	32.5	29.3	13.3	13.9	9.2
08083	Montezuma, CO	7	21 999	23.1	4	20	65.0	15.0	15.0	4 824	54.0	17.1	27.0	9.6	30.9	27.3
08085	Montrose, CO	7	29 601	21.0	2	17	52.9	23.5	17.6	5 751	47.1	30.2	21.7	10.2	25.3	18.1
08087	Morgan, CO	6	24 788	21.7	5	16	50.0	18.8	31.3	5 229	50.8	20.6	28.6	9.9	33.4	33.2
08089	Otero, CO	6	20 901	21.5	7	21	42.9	23.8	33.3	4 505	45.9	22.2	31.9	8.5	46.5	48.5
08091	Ouray, CO	9	3 140	18.8	2	5	40.0	20.0	40.0	521	48.4	15.0	36.7	6.1	8.8	2.1
08093	Park, CO	8	11 602	20.7	2	8	50.0	25.0	25.0	2 136	49.0	22.8	28.2	10.5	12.4	6.4
08095	Phillips, CO	9	4 340	19.8	2	4	50.0	—	50.0	987	69.7	—	30.3	10.7	21.1	11.2
08097	Pitkin, CO	7	13 489	11.4	1	3	33.3	33.3	33.3	1 224	40.4	32.9	26.6	7.5	—	6.9
08099	Prowers, CO	7	13 689	23.3	4	13	53.8	7.7	30.8	3 080	49.5	15.7	28.5	8.4	36.7	35.6
08101	Pueblo, CO	3	131 217	19.7	2	50	58.0	24.0	16.0	22 977	47.0	23.3	28.1	8.8	36.3	48.0
08103	Rio Blanco, CO	9	6 348	22.9	2	6	33.3	33.3	33.3	1 638	44.3	24.6	31.1	7.0	14.9	6.2
08105	Rio Grande, CO	7	11 319	22.6	3	11	45.5	18.2	27.3	2 702	48.0	19.7	29.9	7.1	37.7	48.9
08107	Routt, CO	7	16 975	18.7	3	10	40.0	30.0	30.0	2 894	46.8	25.2	28.0	10.6	5.5	3.6
08109	Saguache, CO	9	5 784	23.6	3	9	33.3	22.2	33.3	1 123	49.3	20.9	26.5	7.5	65.0	65.3
08111	San Juan, CO	9	564	24.8	1	2	50.0	—	50.0	114	57.0	—	43.0	9.6	—	13.2
08113	San Miguel, CO	9	5 208	16.1	2	5	40.0	20.0	40.0	850	60.0	13.6	26.4	8.5	6.9	4.4
08115	Sedgwick, CO	9	2 651	19.1	2	4	50.0	—	50.0	497	52.3	—	47.7	7.6	30.6	17.3
08117	Summit, CO	9	17 896	14.2	1	6	66.7	16.7	16.7	2 274	50.6	23.5	25.9	8.0	3.8	3.9
08119	Teller, CO	6	18 717	21.5	2	7	57.1	14.3	28.6	3 600	47.2	21.7	31.2	11.1	11.0	5.8
08121	Washington, CO	9	4 673	20.4	5	10	50.0	—	50.0	1 060	63.0	—	37.0	10.7	28.2	7.5
08123	Weld, CO	3	152 189	20.8	13	64	51.6	21.9	23.4	25 947	49.6	27.1	23.0	10.1	32.1	35.0
08125	Yuma, CO	7	9 284	22.2	2	10	40.0	20.0	40.0	1 924	34.9	29.9	35.2	11.3	23.9	8.6
09000	**CONNECTICUT**															
09001	Fairfield, CT	2	833 761	17.3	25	207	68.6	16.9	13.5	123 515	56.3	18.5	25.1	11.5	23.1	33.3
09003	Hartford, CT	0	831 694	17.4	32	250	62.8	15.6	13.2	134 203	53.0	19.8	24.5	14.1	25.6	35.7
09005	Litchfield, CT	4	180 339	18.2	24	61	63.9	16.4	19.7	27 204	53.5	20.3	26.2	12.9	12.6	4.7
09007	Middlesex, CT	1	148 143	17.0	15	69	36.2	21.7	40.6	30 451	34.5	19.4	46.1	15.3	21.0	19.7
09009	New Haven, CT	2	794 672	17.3	27	220	67.7	18.6	12.7	116 524	54.6	22.5	22.8	13.9	30.1	30.3
09011	New London, CT	2	250 735	18.2	22	91	64.8	22.0	13.2	38 525	56.0	23.1	21.0	13.9	19.7	15.3
09013	Tolland, CT	1	130 265	17.8	15	44	54.5	22.7	20.5	20 084	45.9	26.6	27.4	12.6	12.1	6.5
09015	Windham, CT	4	104 629	20.4	18	34	61.8	20.6	17.6	16 696	54.4	23.5	22.1	16.4	25.8	12.5
10000	**DELAWARE**															
10001	Kent, DE	3	122 244	19.1	7	42	57.1	21.4	16.7	24 472	43.7	28.0	27.5	11.7	26.8	30.3
10003	New Castle, DE	2	471 417	17.0	8	102	48.0	25.5	26.5	63 440	38.8	30.3	28.5	11.0	28.4	38.7
10005	Sussex, DE	6	131 181	17.3	7	37	40.5	18.9	24.3	20 549	42.7	22.8	31.9	15.4	33.2	30.8

1. County type code is from the Economic Research Service of the USDA. See notes and definitions at the end of this section.   2. IEP = Individual Education Program. See notes and definitions at the end of this section.

Table D-2. School and Student Characteristics by County — Continued

County	Staff and students, 1995–1996						Revenues, fiscal 1995				Current expenditures, fiscal 1995		
	Number of teachers	Pupil/ teacher ratio	Number of graduates	Dropouts grades 9–12 (percent)	Local school non-teaching staff	Central admin. staff	Total revenue ($1000)	Percent of Revenue from			Amount	Amount per pupil	Percent for instruction
								Federal Gov't	State Gov't	Local Gov't			
	15	16	17	18	19	20	21	22	23	24	25	26	27
COLORADO—Con.													
Custer, CO	29	14.9	20	NA	19	3	2 539	8.1	22.6	69.3	2 046	4 990	56.5
Delta, CO	263	18.1	260	NA	221	15	26 561	5.4	51.0	43.5	23 270	5 099	54.5
Denver, CO	3 270	19.7	2 721	NA	3 290	340	391 829	8.4	28.0	63.7	351 373	5 598	59.9
Dolores, CO	23	15.4	30	NA	21	5	2 165	6.4	44.2	49.4	1 962	5 910	47.8
Douglas, CO	1 213	18.2	972	NA	876	104	155 302	1.4	28.4	70.2	96 160	4 798	55.5
Eagle, CO	237	16.3	136	NA	202	27	28 766	3.4	0.1	96.5	20 353	5 790	58.6
Elbert, CO	185	16.5	130	NA	161	22	17 219	1.6	57.6	40.8	13 214	4 833	57.2
El Paso, CO	4 537	18.6	4 136	NA	3 314	510	435 520	6.0	54.4	39.6	375 449	4 560	61.2
Fremont, CO	367	17.3	334	NA	275	26	30 225	6.5	61.3	32.2	26 381	4 330	62.7
Garfield, CO	479	17.7	359	NA	310	37	61 766	2.1	28.1	69.8	38 206	4 743	59.3
Gilpin, CO	30	12.3	25	NA	22	3	3 203	2.8	29.1	68.1	2 200	6 304	50.7
Grand, CO	115	15.3	121	NA	79	13	10 895	6.8	4.4	88.9	8 484	5 199	60.5
Gunnison, CO	116	14.7	79	NA	68	11	8 823	6.7	14.3	79.1	8 236	4 914	64.3
Hinsdale, CO	5	8.7	—	NA	5	2	588	3.4	6.1	90.5	507	13 342	49.9
Huerfano, CO	79	14.8	88	NA	65	9	7 370	7.3	31.9	60.8	5 838	5 126	55.5
Jackson, CO	24	13.8	24	NA	17	2	2 222	6.6	37.0	56.3	1 802	5 545	58.4
Jefferson, CO	3 986	21.4	4 411	NA	3 545	399	541 438	2.6	39.0	58.4	466 601	5 554	51.2
Kiowa, CO	35	11.2	28	NA	21	3	2 767	1.1	34.2	64.7	2 317	5 911	51.4
Kit Carson, CO	135	12.4	119	NA	96	11	10 660	4.3	52.8	42.8	9 334	5 630	53.6
Lake, CO	92	14.2	75	NA	82	15	12 756	17.0	36.0	47.0	10 097	8 586	54.4
La Plata, CO	431	15.8	350	NA	375	40	43 654	5.5	22.8	71.7	35 284	5 354	55.8
Larimer, CO	1 746	20.7	2 015	NA	1 518	203	185 698	4.6	42.1	53.3	157 635	4 413	60.9
Las Animas, CO	176	14.2	160	NA	104	19	16 937	6.5	56.0	37.4	14 518	5 852	50.0
Lincoln, CO	64	15.0	47	NA	40	8	8 647	18.5	42.1	39.3	6 767	7 199	66.0
Logan, CO	231	15.1	228	NA	154	19	20 029	5.3	58.0	36.7	16 958	5 029	57.6
Mesa, CO	1 079	18.0	1 083	NA	799	127	93 245	6.3	58.8	34.9	83 797	4 387	62.0
Mineral, CO	15	8.9	8	NA	4	3	1 217	1.3	31.0	67.7	957	8 250	63.0
Moffat, CO	150	18.7	145	NA	136	14	15 780	5.9	2.9	91.2	13 937	4 895	57.9
Montezuma, CO	277	17.4	255	NA	220	34	27 904	9.6	42.9	47.6	22 629	4 904	61.8
Montrose, CO	321	17.9	304	NA	254	28	31 219	7.0	55.1	37.9	24 857	4 367	56.1
Morgan, CO	338	15.5	265	NA	248	33	29 922	8.1	42.8	49.1	26 940	5 232	58.7
Otero, CO	318	14.2	277	NA	232	38	28 946	10.3	65.7	24.0	23 979	5 316	59.8
Ouray, CO	45	11.6	35	NA	24	4	3 801	2.6	43.1	54.3	2 972	5 839	59.7
Park, CO	124	17.2	103	NA	110	11	11 742	2.6	41.5	55.9	9 479	4 635	55.0
Phillips, CO	65	15.3	66	NA	48	6	8 656	18.3	37.4	44.3	6 794	7 137	54.0
Pitkin, CO	85	14.4	72	NA	46	7	10 325	0.8	1.5	97.8	8 045	6 721	60.2
Prowers, CO	198	15.6	168	NA	128	20	20 238	12.5	55.0	32.5	16 637	5 458	62.7
Pueblo, CO	1 190	19.2	1 079	NA	909	160	119 732	9.2	55.5	35.4	110 336	4 850	61.3
Rio Blanco, CO	89	18.4	94	NA	66	14	11 997	6.3	20.9	72.8	9 925	6 138	54.4
Rio Grande, CO	171	15.8	137	NA	109	20	14 513	6.7	61.1	32.2	12 296	4 766	61.0
Routt, CO	186	15.6	180	NA	114	14	19 240	5.4	8.0	86.6	15 756	5 517	57.2
Saguache, CO	92	12.2	45	NA	60	8	6 942	5.7	61.2	33.1	5 730	5 134	62.4
San Juan, CO	11	10.4	5	NA	3	3	1 064	4.6	33.3	62.1	830	8 925	57.6
San Miguel, CO	59	14.5	29	NA	37	10	7 173	2.3	14.5	83.1	4 985	6 342	55.7
Sedgwick, CO	45	11.1	50	NA	31	4	3 408	4.2	51.0	44.8	3 002	6 028	55.3
Summit, CO	150	15.2	98	NA	111	17	19 311	1.4	1.7	96.9	12 705	5 890	63.5
Teller, CO	186	19.3	194	NA	139	19	18 828	2.2	49.7	48.1	15 992	4 715	58.2
Washington, CO	95	11.1	63	NA	58	12	8 225	3.0	45.0	52.0	6 576	6 441	52.9
Weld, CO	1 432	18.1	1 180	NA	1 160	170	145 592	8.7	44.9	46.4	119 665	4 729	62.1
Yuma, CO	154	12.5	123	NA	91	10	12 283	6.6	38.1	55.3	10 010	5 241	55.7
CONNECTICUT													
Fairfield, CT	8 094	15.3	6 538	3.1	6 205	781	1 109 086	3.4	22.7	73.8	1 030 962	8 546	64.4
Hartford, CT	8 713	15.4	6 516	7.2	6 492	927	1 139 125	3.6	38.8	57.6	1 058 054	8 177	66.4
Litchfield, CT	1 830	14.9	1 390	5.5	1 517	188	241 566	1.7	34.6	63.7	197 491	7 401	63.5
Middlesex, CT	2 454	12.4	2 662	2.5	1 659	226	200 829	2.1	29.1	68.8	166 335	7 988	65.2
New Haven, CT	7 368	15.8	5 472	5.3	5 827	670	1 040 920	4.0	42.1	53.8	928 474	7 959	66.0
New London, CT	2 658	14.5	1 940	5.3	2 366	274	350 692	2.8	46.1	51.1	295 782	7 869	65.7
Tolland, CT	1 411	14.2	1 112	3.7	1 143	125	185 117	1.6	45.5	52.9	154 722	7 543	67.3
Windham, CT	1 219	13.7	861	7.9	1 528	163	164 081	3.6	61.8	34.7	128 050	7 437	65.6
DELAWARE													
Kent, DE	1 460	16.8	1 142	4.0	1 061	119	169 052	11.2	71.8	17.0	146 196	6 027	61.8
New Castle, DE	3 656	17.4	3 093	4.6	2 887	320	491 867	5.0	59.6	35.4	423 520	6 786	62.3
Sussex, DE	1 274	16.1	1 055	4.2	924	95	141 196	5.7	68.2	26.1	125 498	6 231	61.5

Table D-2. School and Student Characteristics by County

State/County code	County	County type[1]	Population, 1996		Number of school districts, 1995–1996	Level of schools, 1995–1996				Level of students, 1995–1996				Characteristics of students, 1995–1996		
			Total persons	Percent age 5–17		Number of schools	Percent			Number of students	Percent			Percent with IEP[2]	Percent free-lunch eligible	Percent minority
							Primary	Middle	High		Primary	Middle	High			
			1	2	3	4	5	6	7	8	9	10	11	12	13	14
11000	**DISTRICT OF COLUMBIA**															
11001	District of Columbia	0	543 213	13.9	1	185	63.2	14.6	12.4	79 802	61.8	15.7	17.9	8.9	66.3	96.0
12000	**FLORIDA**															
12001	Alachua, FL	3	196 525	17.2	2	43	55.8	16.3	14.0	30 108	47.7	21.6	23.1	13.7	37.5	42.3
12003	Baker, FL	6	20 556	25.0	1	6	50.0	16.7	—	4 635	49.4	24.5	—	13.6	36.5	17.7
12005	Bay, FL	3	144 637	20.3	1	35	62.9	17.1	11.4	25 228	49.8	22.8	24.7	16.3	34.6	19.1
12007	Bradford, FL	6	24 130	19.1	1	9	55.6	11.1	22.2	4 119	51.6	19.2	26.2	18.3	41.2	23.7
12009	Brevard, FL	2	453 998	17.1	1	82	62.2	15.9	11.0	65 451	57.5	21.1	14.6	14.7	24.3	20.1
12011	Broward, FL	0	1 438 228	15.6	1	191	61.8	16.2	13.6	208 359	51.0	20.2	23.9	10.8	31.6	51.0
12013	Calhoun, FL	8	12 217	20.9	1	5	40.0	20.0	20.0	2 279	41.9	13.7	18.3	15.3	39.1	17.9
12015	Charlotte, FL	3	130 426	12.5	1	21	47.6	19.0	19.0	15 593	44.9	24.7	17.0	14.1	30.5	13.0
12017	Citrus, FL	4	109 389	14.2	1	18	50.0	22.2	16.7	13 924	48.4	23.6	26.5	18.9	36.4	8.4
12019	Clay, FL	2	128 912	23.4	1	27	63.0	18.5	14.8	24 875	55.4	21.7	22.0	16.4	17.1	13.4
12021	Collier, FL	3	188 187	15.6	1	37	54.1	13.5	10.8	26 334	51.4	15.9	23.7	15.4	33.7	35.6
12023	Columbia, FL	6	49 291	22.6	1	12	50.0	8.3	—	9 137	43.6	7.4	—	13.4	45.2	27.4
12025	Dade, FL	0	2 076 175	17.7	1	316	63.3	14.9	16.1	333 809	52.7	20.5	23.5	9.4	52.9	85.8
12027	De Soto, FL	6	25 253	18.8	1	9	44.4	22.2	—	4 508	52.8	23.2	—	14.4	52.6	38.0
12029	Dixie, FL	9	12 352	19.7	1	4	25.0	25.0	—	2 271	21.8	24.0	—	24.6	51.7	11.6
12031	Duval, FL	2	721 139	19.9	1	154	65.6	14.3	10.4	123 910	52.9	22.5	19.2	15.4	38.3	45.2
12033	Escambia, FL	2	277 634	19.7	1	71	59.2	18.3	12.7	45 215	49.3	22.3	25.8	13.7	45.6	38.9
12035	Flagler, FL	2	42 142	15.6	1	5	60.0	20.0	—	5 361	46.7	24.1	—	16.6	32.0	21.6
12037	Franklin, FL	7	10 271	18.9	1	4	50.0	—	—	1 668	43.3	—	—	16.4	51.9	19.5
12039	Gadsden, FL	3	43 787	23.6	1	19	42.1	5.3	36.8	8 657	41.0	11.9	28.8	13.6	67.1	91.2
12041	Gilchrist, FL	8	12 871	20.2	1	4	50.0	—	—	2 529	47.6	—	—	15.4	41.7	6.4
12043	Glades, FL	8	7 851	20.1	1	5	60.0	—	—	1 102	52.2	—	—	9.8	45.8	50.7
12045	Gulf, FL	6	13 327	18.8	1	8	50.0	12.5	37.5	2 279	55.9	10.0	34.1	11.9	39.9	21.0
12047	Hamilton, FL	9	12 288	23.0	1	8	37.5	12.5	12.5	2 360	51.9	15.0	2.0	13.6	53.3	54.1
12049	Hardee, FL	6	20 130	23.5	1	9	66.7	—	11.1	5 325	53.6	—	22.5	13.6	35.6	52.9
12051	Hendry, FL	6	29 821	24.1	1	11	36.4	—	—	7 064	32.0	—	—	12.1	49.6	54.9
12053	Hernando, FL	0	121 266	14.9	1	17	52.9	23.5	11.8	15 393	47.3	28.1	16.4	13.9	35.6	13.4
12055	Highlands, FL	6	74 836	15.2	1	15	46.7	20.0	—	10 758	41.6	23.3	—	16.4	46.1	34.8
12057	Hillsborough, FL	0	897 522	18.7	1	161	65.2	14.3	9.3	143 192	55.6	16.3	18.8	12.9	41.5	43.0
12059	Holmes, FL	7	18 174	20.1	1	8	25.0	12.5	12.5	3 759	34.5	10.7	0.9	11.9	47.5	4.1
12061	Indian River, FL	4	96 490	15.4	1	19	63.2	5.3	10.5	13 647	48.2	6.8	25.7	15.7	34.8	25.2
12063	Jackson, FL	6	44 728	20.3	1	15	33.3	6.7	13.3	7 976	40.1	10.0	1.2	16.2	42.3	34.9
12065	Jefferson, FL	6	13 260	21.5	1	5	60.0	20.0	20.0	2 126	44.5	28.6	26.9	16.6	63.2	69.3
12067	Lafayette, FL	9	6 237	20.0	1	3	33.3	—	—	1 052	45.6	—	—	12.3	39.5	15.5
12069	Lake, FL	1	186 631	15.8	1	40	47.5	22.5	15.0	24 827	49.7	21.7	25.3	14.7	34.9	24.3
12071	Lee, FL	2	380 001	15.3	1	69	52.2	17.4	13.0	50 676	50.0	22.4	13.5	13.9	34.8	27.8
12073	Leon, FL	3	215 593	17.9	3	48	54.2	16.7	10.4	32 868	48.4	20.9	18.8	17.6	21.1	41.0
12075	Levy, FL	8	30 296	19.7	1	12	33.3	25.0	16.7	5 734	41.2	17.3	17.2	15.2	48.7	21.0
12077	Liberty, FL	8	6 542	19.2	1	4	75.0	—	—	1 242	57.1	—	—	17.5	41.9	15.8
12079	Madison, FL	7	17 513	21.1	1	9	44.4	22.2	—	3 434	45.8	23.1	—	18.1	59.7	59.8
12081	Manatee, FL	2	232 285	14.8	1	59	59.3	10.2	5.1	31 792	64.1	11.7	0.3	15.7	35.9	29.0
12083	Marion, FL	3	230 068	17.6	1	46	58.7	15.2	13.0	35 508	52.2	20.5	25.7	14.6	42.7	28.1
12085	Martin, FL	2	112 527	13.9	1	21	52.4	14.3	14.3	14 348	52.2	20.6	24.7	14.2	25.4	22.7
12087	Monroe, FL	4	80 730	13.0	1	13	61.5	7.7	15.4	9 508	62.6	9.5	14.0	14.2	28.6	26.7
12089	Nassau, FL	2	52 079	21.7	1	17	47.1	5.9	5.9	9 579	47.6	7.0	14.0	14.0	24.5	13.4
12091	Okaloosa, FL	3	165 873	20.3	1	36	58.3	16.7	13.9	29 454	44.7	22.0	25.8	10.9	21.8	19.5
12093	Okeechobee, FL	6	30 894	21.4	1	10	60.0	10.0	10.0	6 456	58.5	14.8	24.7	16.6	46.3	29.2
12095	Orange, FL	0	758 980	18.6	1	153	59.5	15.7	13.1	123 091	49.6	22.9	25.9	12.5	32.6	47.7
12097	Osceola, FL	1	135 812	19.7	1	30	43.3	26.7	20.0	25 633	45.0	23.7	27.2	12.8	33.0	39.4
12099	Palm Beach, FL	2	992 840	14.9	2	130	61.5	16.2	16.9	132 215	51.0	21.7	24.0	13.1	30.4	45.0
12101	Pasco, FL	0	311 556	14.1	1	45	57.8	13.3	11.1	41 668	48.6	17.4	13.8	15.7	35.5	11.0
12103	Pinellas, FL	0	868 887	13.9	1	144	55.6	17.4	18.1	101 998	49.5	23.7	24.0	16.9	30.8	24.6
12105	Polk, FL	2	440 954	19.0	1	116	53.4	17.2	18.1	72 693	50.0	22.0	25.0	11.7	44.1	31.8
12107	Putnam, FL	6	69 704	20.5	1	19	47.4	21.1	10.5	12 935	49.0	21.7	13.6	13.4	54.5	35.7
12109	St. Johns, FL	2	106 503	17.6	2	32	50.0	25.0	15.6	16 007	45.4	23.9	13.1	16.2	18.9	15.6
12111	St. Lucie, FL	2	174 728	17.9	1	34	58.8	14.7	8.8	27 044	52.9	18.7	13.3	13.0	42.8	39.4
12113	Santa Rosa, FL	2	108 186	21.5	1	29	48.3	13.8	17.2	19 762	46.4	17.8	20.3	12.1	24.7	8.2
12115	Sarasota, FL	2	296 518	12.4	1	36	55.6	16.7	16.7	31 035	48.0	20.4	24.4	16.7	25.3	16.2
12117	Seminole, FL	0	335 868	20.2	1	55	56.4	18.2	10.9	54 587	48.2	23.1	23.1	11.0	20.0	27.6
12119	Sumter, FL	6	35 948	18.2	1	10	50.0	20.0	—	5 767	49.1	26.1	—	13.8	54.0	31.5
12121	Suwannee, FL	7	30 901	22.2	1	8	37.5	12.5	25.0	5 690	35.3	20.1	23.2	13.2	37.7	21.6
12123	Taylor, FL	7	18 173	21.7	1	8	50.0	12.5	—	3 889	53.7	19.8	—	14.3	45.1	28.0
12125	Union, FL	8	12 451	18.7	1	4	25.0	—	50.0	2 189	39.1	—	28.1	15.2	34.9	20.9

1. County type code is from the Economic Research Service of the USDA. See notes and definitions at the end of this section.   2. IEP = Individual Education Program. See notes and definitions at the end of this section.

Table D-2. School and Student Characteristics by County — Continued

| County | Staff and students, 1995–1996 | | | | | | Revenues, fiscal 1995 | | | | Current expenditures, fiscal 1995 | | |
| | Number of teachers | Pupil/ teacher ratio | Number of graduates | Dropouts grades 9–12 (percent) | Local school non-teaching staff | Central admin. staff | Total revenue ($1000) | Percent of Revenue from | | | Amount | Amount per pupil | Percent for instruction |
								Federal Gov't	State Gov't	Local Gov't			
	15	16	17	18	19	20	21	22	23	24	25	26	27
DISTRICT OF COLUMBIA													
District of Columbia	4 273	18.7	3 061	11.2	3 269	836	700 111	9.4	—	90.6	666 938	8 290	50.5
FLORIDA													
Alachua, FL	1 652	18.2	1 177	NA	1 876	324	170 870	9.5	56.4	34.1	136 647	4 743	53.3
Baker, FL..........................	231	20.1	206	NA	233	44	25 139	6.7	76.9	16.3	21 096	4 540	51.4
Bay, FL.............................	1 463	17.2	1 084	NA	1 342	190	142 139	7.4	60.0	32.7	119 751	4 828	61.3
Bradford, FL......................	248	16.6	170	NA	157	19	23 191	8.0	70.4	21.6	18 944	4 603	54.9
Brevard, FL.......................	3 719	17.6	3 012	NA	3 059	369	347 200	6.1	52.5	41.3	299 696	4 640	60.0
Broward, FL.......................	9 870	21.1	8 222	NA	8 219	809	1 317 698	5.9	50.2	43.9	1 024 098	5 140	55.7
Calhoun, FL.......................	137	16.6	131	NA	105	23	11 926	9.1	75.1	15.8	10 650	4 655	59.0
Charlotte, FL......................	839	18.6	802	NA	899	127	95 539	5.1	28.4	66.5	77 411	5 129	55.6
Citrus, FL..........................	825	16.9	666	NA	771	161	79 094	6.4	42.2	51.4	65 019	4 793	54.1
Clay, FL............................	1 306	19.0	1 216	NA	992	193	118 889	5.2	66.6	28.2	99 554	4 176	56.4
Collier, FL.........................	1 461	18.0	968	NA	1 481	204	194 726	7.3	15.9	76.8	149 122	5 928	59.1
Columbia, FL......................	502	18.2	339	NA	514	67	46 758	9.3	70.3	20.4	41 337	4 656	59.6
Dade, FL...........................	16 565	20.2	14 587	NA	13 356	1 950	2 183 071	8.4	53.1	38.5	1 844 088	5 734	58.9
De Soto, FL.......................	241	18.7	152	NA	248	48	26 394	10.5	64.5	24.9	23 131	5 280	53.5
Dixie, FL...........................	142	16.0	72	NA	158	30	13 886	10.1	74.2	15.7	11 812	5 304	51.2
Duval, FL..........................	6 096	20.3	4 607	NA	4 645	754	670 683	7.4	56.2	36.3	560 115	4 615	57.1
Escambia, FL	2 621	17.3	2 225	NA	2 442	383	253 872	9.4	64.5	26.1	219 741	4 909	55.2
Flagler, FL.........................	310	17.3	238	NA	360	65	39 838	3.8	33.5	62.7	26 646	5 411	52.4
Franklin, FL........................	106	15.7	66	NA	80	18	9 699	9.6	54.3	36.1	8 449	5 180	58.0
Gadsden, FL......................	472	18.3	324	NA	553	59	48 928	16.5	69.8	13.7	43 066	4 993	52.4
Gilchrist, FL.......................	138	18.3	112	NA	121	25	13 784	6.6	76.5	16.9	11 985	5 051	53.7
Glades, FL.........................	65	17.0	42	NA	54	13	7 340	12.2	46.2	41.6	6 092	5 584	54.8
Gulf, FL.............................	139	16.4	157	NA	130	19	13 885	6.5	55.1	38.4	12 048	5 322	56.3
Hamilton, FL......................	149	15.8	142	NA	198	30	16 545	10.0	55.4	34.6	14 703	6 178	50.7
Hardee, FL	282	18.9	173	NA	374	66	30 778	12.9	60.6	26.5	26 734	5 698	56.3
Hendry, FL........................	361	19.6	304	NA	465	58	41 383	10.6	57.8	31.5	34 772	5 148	54.5
Hernando, FL.....................	807	19.1	682	NA	744	103	85 365	6.1	47.6	46.2	68 469	4 613	53.5
Highlands, FL.....................	569	18.9	359	NA	623	93	65 317	7.9	54.6	37.4	55 129	5 269	53.6
Hillsborough, FL	8 439	17.0	5 886	NA	7 951	1 075	886 056	9.1	56.1	34.8	747 392	5 393	56.8
Holmes, FL........................	223	16.9	197	NA	200	17	19 562	9.6	72.3	18.0	17 652	4 772	58.5
Indian River, FL.................	739	18.5	512	NA	662	89	87 570	5.0	27.0	67.9	67 084	5 096	54.6
Jackson, FL.......................	492	16.2	446	NA	526	57	48 071	9.6	75.0	15.4	37 709	4 679	56.3
Jefferson, FL	124	17.1	105	NA	162	26	12 583	10.7	71.5	17.8	11 252	5 255	53.2
Lafayette, FL......................	72	14.6	49	NA	65	11	6 150	9.7	71.1	19.3	5 170	5 005	49.7
Lake, FL............................	1 285	19.3	1 059	NA	1 293	160	128 117	7.3	54.2	38.4	103 787	4 395	54.9
Lee, FL..............................	2 697	18.8	2 142	NA	2 335	351	321 370	6.0	30.2	63.9	263 842	5 340	52.1
Leon, FL............................	1 768	18.6	1 295	NA	1 903	373	193 931	6.5	56.5	37.1	153 838	5 045	54.8
Levy, FL............................	312	18.4	214	NA	370	43	36 440	6.7	59.2	34.1	26 987	4 952	55.5
Liberty, FL.........................	71	17.5	61	NA	60	13	7 324	7.1	78.1	14.8	5 628	4 714	53.0
Madison, FL.......................	190	18.1	135	NA	190	30	18 326	12.5	71.9	15.6	16 778	4 995	56.8
Manatee, FL	1 677	19.0	1 125	NA	1 826	176	202 089	6.4	41.4	52.2	150 071	4 862	57.8
Marion, FL.........................	1 936	18.3	1 462	NA	2 038	247	190 458	8.2	59.1	32.7	161 565	4 749	57.3
Martin, FL..........................	763	18.8	614	NA	859	126	98 665	4.6	17.8	77.6	76 592	5 609	55.2
Monroe, FL........................	560	17.0	359	NA	615	71	64 793	7.8	19.1	73.1	54 154	5 773	56.6
Nassau, FL........................	480	20.0	404	NA	543	47	48 741	5.5	58.5	36.0	40 645	4 321	55.7
Okaloosa, FL.....................	1 598	18.4	1 724	NA	1 501	166	151 343	8.0	60.4	31.6	125 243	4 314	58.5
Okeechobee, FL.................	332	19.4	239	NA	414	47	47 244	8.3	74.8	17.0	31 451	4 988	56.8
Orange, FL........................	6 646	18.5	5 323	NA	7 060	1 197	745 661	6.5	42.7	50.9	580 058	4 888	52.2
Osceola, FL.......................	1 255	20.4	1 205	NA	1 275	237	143 661	4.6	51.1	44.3	109 225	4 508	53.7
Palm Beach, FL..................	7 356	18.0	5 645	NA	6 526	871	926 775	5.7	29.0	65.4	691 125	5 420	63.3
Pasco, FL..........................	2 318	18.0	1 778	NA	2 172	343	240 850	7.1	57.6	35.3	196 456	4 897	53.9
Pinellas, FL........................	5 643	18.1	4 668	NA	5 513	812	658 123	6.0	45.8	48.2	525 942	5 148	58.8
Polk, FL............................	4 105	17.7	3 096	NA	4 175	334	379 653	8.7	59.3	32.0	331 874	4 655	55.9
Putnam, FL........................	674	19.2	508	NA	853	93	70 253	9.6	59.8	30.6	59 176	4 626	54.3
St. Johns, FL.....................	868	18.4	721	NA	1 195	171	102 124	4.4	43.6	52.0	72 290	4 965	53.6
St. Lucie, FL......................	1 913	14.1	962	NA	1 680	225	159 712	7.9	45.7	46.4	132 888	5 069	55.3
Santa Rosa, FL	1 092	18.1	897	NA	774	90	99 827	7.4	64.4	28.2	83 693	4 411	58.5
Sarasota, FL......................	1 716	18.1	1 531	NA	1 738	201	251 644	3.7	20.3	76.1	178 513	5 866	54.5
Seminole, FL......................	2 823	19.3	2 570	NA	2 137	245	286 340	3.8	51.9	44.2	227 657	4 266	59.5
Sumter, FL.........................	307	18.8	235	NA	376	46	30 682	9.1	69.0	21.9	26 546	4 713	55.2
Suwannee, FL	292	19.5	304	NA	300	45	39 060	6.6	77.3	16.1	26 880	4 820	54.7
Taylor, FL..........................	207	18.8	147	NA	268	32	22 462	14.0	57.8	28.2	18 340	4 884	54.1
Union, FL..........................	123	17.8	82	NA	132	19	11 868	6.8	78.3	14.8	10 269	4 904	52.6

Table D-2. School and Student Characteristics by County

State/County code	County	County type[1]	Population, 1996		Number of school districts, 1995–1996	Level of schools, 1995–1996				Level of students, 1995–1996				Characteristics of students, 1995–1996		
			Total persons	Percent age 5–17		Number of schools	Percent Primary	Middle	High	Number of students	Percent Primary	Middle	High	Percent with IEP[2]	Percent free-lunch eligible	Percent minority
			1	2	3	4	5	6	7	8	9	10	11	12	13	14
	FLORIDA—Con.															
12127	Volusia, FL	2	414 322	15.4	1	71	60.6	11.3	9.9	56 740	51.7	20.2	19.3	14.4	33.3	24.1
12129	Wakulla, FL	8	18 105	23.2	1	6	50.0	16.7	16.7	4 270	45.4	24.6	24.8	17.1	29.7	14.4
12131	Walton, FL	6	35 255	18.8	1	9	44.4	—	22.2	5 233	46.1	—	26.2	13.6	44.6	14.2
12133	Washington, FL	6	19 212	20.2	2	10	20.0	30.0	20.0	3 433	47.4	18.5	19.3	15.2	40.0	24.7
13000	**GEORGIA**															
13001	Appling, GA	7	16 333	22.4	1	6	66.7	16.7	16.7	3 516	46.7	24.2	29.1	13.4	43.8	32.3
13003	Atkinson, GA	9	7 022	22.1	1	3	66.7	—	33.3	1 533	67.1	—	32.9	7.6	71.9	38.5
13005	Bacon, GA	7	10 344	22.4	1	3	66.7	—	—	2 176	47.5	—	—	12.5	41.4	26.1
13007	Baker, GA	8	3 686	22.1	1	1	100.0	—	—	433	100.0	—	—	16.4	82.0	73.9
13009	Baldwin, GA	4	41 947	17.4	1	9	66.7	22.2	11.1	6 361	50.9	22.8	26.3	11.6	46.7	60.8
13011	Banks, GA	8	11 918	19.6	1	4	50.0	25.0	25.0	1 901	50.7	23.8	25.5	11.3	39.9	5.4
13013	Barrow, GA	1	37 407	19.5	1	10	70.0	20.0	10.0	6 871	54.7	23.0	22.4	12.8	24.3	14.9
13015	Bartow, GA	1	66 293	19.2	2	18	66.7	16.7	11.1	12 995	53.5	20.0	19.9	11.2	25.8	12.7
13017	Ben Hill, GA	7	17 322	22.6	1	4	50.0	25.0	25.0	3 704	48.9	23.5	27.6	8.1	47.9	43.8
13019	Berrien, GA	7	15 784	20.0	1	4	50.0	25.0	25.0	2 944	50.8	24.3	24.9	12.2	42.8	18.6
13021	Bibb, GA	2	155 573	19.1	1	40	77.5	10.0	10.0	25 066	61.6	13.8	24.0	9.1	56.3	67.1
13023	Bleckley, GA	6	10 930	19.3	1	3	33.3	33.3	33.3	2 283	42.6	29.4	28.0	12.3	36.9	31.5
13025	Brantley, GA	9	13 048	22.4	1	5	60.0	20.0	20.0	2 826	49.5	24.4	26.1	13.8	42.6	5.7
13027	Brooks, GA	7	15 820	21.6	1	4	50.0	25.0	25.0	2 722	50.9	24.4	24.7	11.0	71.2	67.9
13029	Bryan, GA	2	22 286	23.8	1	6	66.7	—	—	5 092	49.7	—	—	7.3	29.0	17.9
13031	Bulloch, GA	6	49 328	17.0	1	13	53.8	23.1	15.4	8 325	52.0	15.9	26.1	10.5	44.9	40.3
13033	Burke, GA	6	21 542	23.9	1	5	60.0	20.0	20.0	4 898	48.3	23.7	28.0	7.0	66.6	69.3
13035	Butts, GA	6	16 583	18.9	1	4	50.0	25.0	25.0	3 124	51.2	23.7	25.1	9.7	38.1	42.4
13037	Calhoun, GA	8	4 844	21.9	1	2	50.0	—	—	1 070	47.4	—	—	11.3	75.3	80.9
13039	Camden, GA	6	42 798	20.3	1	10	70.0	20.0	10.0	8 608	54.1	23.5	22.4	9.5	26.8	27.1
13043	Candler, GA	7	8 676	20.1	1	3	33.3	33.3	33.3	1 722	54.1	24.4	21.4	10.2	53.0	45.4
13045	Carroll, GA	1	79 307	19.5	2	20	50.0	15.0	20.0	14 639	49.9	16.9	23.4	13.9	34.3	23.2
13047	Catoosa, GA	2	48 541	19.0	1	12	66.7	16.7	16.7	8 526	49.8	22.8	27.4	8.9	23.3	1.7
13049	Charlton, GA	8	9 293	22.0	1	4	50.0	25.0	25.0	1 984	40.6	19.6	39.8	10.6	44.9	35.0
13051	Chatham, GA	2	226 961	18.7	1	44	63.6	20.5	13.6	35 860	50.6	22.4	25.2	9.9	51.2	64.6
13053	Chattahoochee, GA	2	16 137	20.3	1	1	100.0	—	—	439	100.0	—	—	21.0	56.5	35.3
13055	Chattooga, GA	7	22 953	18.4	2	9	55.6	22.2	22.2	4 200	55.8	15.5	28.7	12.7	31.5	11.7
13057	Cherokee, GA	1	121 496	18.8	1	27	70.4	11.1	14.8	20 893	60.5	15.0	24.3	11.2	12.0	4.5
13059	Clarke, GA	3	90 602	14.7	1	20	65.0	20.0	15.0	11 316	51.2	21.8	27.0	10.4	51.2	61.6
13061	Clay, GA	9	3 360	21.8	1	1	100.0	—	—	369	100.0	—	—	12.5	92.4	90.5
13063	Clayton, GA	0	202 427	19.7	1	44	61.4	22.7	15.9	40 562	50.3	23.9	25.8	8.2	37.0	54.8
13065	Clinch, GA	7	6 582	22.1	1	2	50.0	—	50.0	1 459	66.0	—	34.0	18.9	56.5	41.3
13067	Cobb, GA	0	538 832	17.7	2	95	64.2	20.0	14.7	89 087	49.4	23.5	27.1	10.5	15.5	24.8
13069	Coffee, GA	7	33 188	21.8	1	10	80.0	—	10.0	7 260	66.8	—	24.4	12.6	51.9	38.0
13071	Colquitt, GA	7	38 960	21.1	1	13	76.9	15.4	7.7	8 238	49.3	23.8	26.9	10.2	49.4	39.0
13073	Columbia, GA	2	86 173	22.1	1	20	60.0	25.0	15.0	17 523	47.3	24.1	28.6	7.2	14.6	17.9
13075	Cook, GA	7	14 351	20.8	1	3	33.3	33.3	33.3	2 929	50.9	22.4	26.7	9.2	51.0	42.1
13077	Coweta, GA	1	76 295	19.9	1	19	68.4	21.1	10.5	13 484	52.7	23.1	24.2	11.9	26.2	27.9
13079	Crawford, GA	8	10 514	20.3	1	2	50.0	—	—	1 868	49.1	—	—	11.2	44.6	34.0
13081	Crisp, GA	6	20 643	22.3	1	5	40.0	40.0	20.0	4 605	33.4	38.5	28.0	9.5	62.2	59.3
13083	Dade, GA	2	14 486	19.1	1	5	60.0	20.0	20.0	2 433	50.1	23.9	25.9	7.5	32.7	0.9
13085	Dawson, GA	8	13 016	19.6	1	4	50.0	25.0	25.0	2 083	51.0	23.7	25.3	11.0	34.4	0.2
13087	Decatur, GA	6	26 529	22.4	1	9	55.6	22.2	11.1	5 929	40.1	22.5	28.2	8.9	54.7	52.8
13089	De Kalb, GA	0	589 796	16.9	2	115	74.8	6.1	18.3	90 123	60.7	7.8	31.2	8.5	41.9	81.9
13091	Dodge, GA	7	17 936	18.9	1	4	50.0	25.0	25.0	3 474	51.4	21.7	26.8	8.3	47.0	34.9
13093	Dooly, GA	6	10 416	22.5	1	4	50.0	25.0	25.0	1 839	48.8	23.3	27.9	8.3	76.9	80.7
13095	Dougherty, GA	3	96 581	22.2	1	26	57.7	26.9	15.4	18 027	49.1	23.3	27.6	9.9	54.6	76.2
13097	Douglas, GA	0	84 463	20.3	1	21	61.9	23.8	9.5	15 536	49.4	23.1	18.0	12.3	20.3	16.1
13099	Early, GA	6	12 149	22.4	1	3	33.3	33.3	33.3	2 751	49.2	22.6	28.2	9.5	64.5	62.3
13101	Echols, GA	9	2 325	22.5	1	1	—	—	—	659	—	—	—	9.1	41.7	20.9
13103	Effingham, GA	2	33 363	22.9	1	9	77.8	11.1	11.1	7 179	48.9	24.2	27.0	10.0	23.4	17.0
13105	Elbert, GA	6	19 286	19.5	1	6	66.7	16.7	16.7	3 962	49.5	23.0	27.5	10.5	46.8	42.2
13107	Emanuel, GA	7	21 030	22.6	1	8	62.5	12.5	12.5	5 017	48.8	15.7	20.4	10.9	59.0	46.6
13109	Evans, GA	8	9 519	21.6	1	3	33.3	33.3	33.3	1 907	52.1	24.2	23.7	12.0	56.3	46.3
13111	Fannin, GA	9	17 745	16.8	1	5	60.0	20.0	20.0	3 065	47.2	24.6	28.3	10.1	34.9	0.9
13113	Fayette, GA	1	81 891	21.6	1	21	61.9	19.0	19.0	16 725	44.6	24.7	30.7	9.5	5.1	13.3
13115	Floyd, GA	4	84 422	17.2	2	27	66.7	11.1	14.8	14 345	55.3	14.8	18.4	11.0	32.5	23.4
13117	Forsyth, GA	1	69 127	17.9	1	15	53.3	20.0	20.0	10 342	53.0	22.3	23.9	10.4	13.6	2.1
13119	Franklin, GA	8	18 184	17.1	1	5	60.0	20.0	20.0	3 385	50.8	23.1	26.1	15.6	33.6	15.0
13121	Fulton, GA	0	718 336	17.0	2	157	66.9	17.2	15.9	116 547	52.5	22.0	25.4	12.4	51.6	72.0

1. County type code is from the Economic Research Service of the USDA. See notes and definitions at the end of this section.   2. IEP = Individual Education Program. See notes and definitions at the end of this section.

Table D-2. School and Student Characteristics by County — Continued

County	Staff and students, 1995–1996						Revenues, fiscal 1995				Current expenditures, fiscal 1995		
	Number of teachers	Pupil/ teacher ratio	Number of graduates	Dropouts grades 9–12 (percent)	Local school non-teaching staff	Central admin. staff	Total revenue ($1000)	Percent of Revenue from			Amount	Amount per pupil	Percent for instruction
								Federal Gov't	State Gov't	Local Gov't			
	15	16	17	18	19	20	21	22	23	24	25	26	27
FLORIDA—Con.													
Volusia, FL	3 417	16.6	2 585	NA	3 298	363	324 580	5.5	48.0	46.5	269 017	4 845	57.1
Wakulla, FL	217	19.7	180	NA	220	35	30 856	4.3	82.1	13.6	18 276	4 503	52.1
Walton, FL	294	17.8	266	NA	345	45	31 289	7.9	42.8	49.4	24 627	4 801	57.6
Washington, FL	206	16.7	167	NA	216	45	24 520	10.6	71.0	18.5	18 807	6 041	56.8
GEORGIA													
Appling, GA	237	14.9	210	5.5	262	21	17 974	9.2	46.9	43.9	17 477	5 037	64.1
Atkinson, GA	87	17.6	64	11.6	90	13	6 356	14.1	71.1	14.9	6 301	4 289	60.0
Bacon, GA	139	15.7	101	13.7	133	11	9 160	10.3	72.8	17.0	9 014	4 162	60.2
Baker, GA	38	11.4	—	NA	47	7	3 362	10.8	46.2	43.1	3 082	7 882	53.5
Baldwin, GA	380	16.7	278	6.3	439	17	32 209	8.3	64.1	27.7	30 206	4 654	60.2
Banks, GA	104	18.3	86	9.1	100	8	8 249	8.4	57.2	34.4	7 351	4 198	59.6
Barrow, GA	416	16.5	252	10.2	374	29	32 157	6.1	59.6	34.3	30 193	4 574	63.2
Bartow, GA	839	15.5	476	10.2	833	50	64 748	4.9	52.5	42.6	58 322	4 747	59.8
Ben Hill, GA	239	15.5	175	8.0	201	14	23 574	7.0	69.9	23.1	15 950	4 346	66.2
Berrien, GA	193	15.3	150	9.3	183	20	14 970	15.0	67.6	17.5	13 426	4 685	56.4
Bibb, GA	1 466	17.1	917	12.8	1 584	137	129 493	9.7	55.5	34.8	119 702	4 812	60.2
Bleckley, GA	150	15.3	119	12.8	156	13	10 048	9.4	71.5	19.0	9 815	4 546	61.7
Brantley, GA	181	15.6	122	10.2	179	14	11 784	9.2	71.6	19.2	10 773	4 029	61.0
Brooks, GA	167	16.3	103	13.4	159	17	13 005	15.8	63.7	20.4	12 365	4 609	60.1
Bryan, GA	284	17.9	223	7.6	296	18	22 071	6.3	69.7	24.1	18 841	3 891	59.7
Bulloch, GA	525	15.9	389	11.9	501	37	39 739	8.3	61.2	30.5	36 035	4 497	61.0
Burke, GA	276	17.7	221	11.9	348	18	28 648	10.2	27.0	62.8	22 705	4 739	59.2
Butts, GA	172	18.2	135	11.0	168	16	13 991	8.3	64.0	27.6	13 010	4 337	58.6
Calhoun, GA	73	14.7	62	4.1	86	10	5 927	12.5	69.3	18.2	5 756	4 817	58.0
Camden, GA	478	18.0	283	11.4	542	38	37 439	7.3	66.2	26.5	33 813	4 170	59.1
Candler, GA	109	15.9	93	11.9	108	9	8 146	10.8	70.4	18.8	7 621	4 661	62.4
Carroll, GA	846	17.3	665	9.6	1 096	78	73 857	6.8	63.6	29.6	67 938	4 778	62.1
Catoosa, GA	480	17.8	450	8.8	479	24	38 181	5.3	67.4	27.3	34 971	4 226	60.6
Charlton, GA	123	16.1	78	15.6	105	14	9 227	9.5	64.6	25.9	8 326	4 167	58.4
Chatham, GA	2 072	17.3	1 630	5.5	2 622	175	213 447	7.4	43.5	49.1	194 233	5 480	61.8
Chattahoochee, GA	35	12.5	—	NA	39	7	2 735	17.2	67.6	15.2	2 428	5 700	59.1
Chattooga, GA	273	15.4	199	11.9	242	20	21 852	6.8	69.4	23.8	18 503	4 474	63.3
Cherokee, GA	1 205	17.3	867	6.7	1 023	69	102 539	3.0	55.4	41.6	88 040	4 469	62.0
Clarke, GA	756	15.0	490	13.2	784	58	75 199	7.2	50.5	42.3	62 085	5 596	59.6
Clay, GA	31	11.9	—	NA	44	3	2 582	17.4	63.4	19.2	2 309	5 936	57.6
Clayton, GA	2 329	17.4	1 619	13.0	3 066	174	202 817	5.3	51.3	43.5	186 317	4 759	58.7
Clinch, GA	98	14.9	66	9.9	97	9	7 838	10.2	61.9	27.9	7 204	5 055	59.9
Cobb, GA	5 303	16.8	4 319	4.3	4 217	363	437 946	2.0	46.8	51.2	412 619	4 773	64.9
Coffee, GA	453	16.0	315	11.5	444	35	35 378	9.4	65.4	25.2	32 315	4 690	60.5
Colquitt, GA	504	16.3	345	8.0	551	36	39 981	8.9	70.3	20.7	35 517	4 455	61.2
Columbia, GA	957	18.3	915	2.8	1 050	50	79 932	3.4	57.1	39.5	67 878	4 010	64.1
Cook, GA	174	16.8	122	10.6	205	12	17 102	8.4	72.7	18.8	12 565	4 396	60.0
Coweta, GA	780	17.3	538	12.7	838	33	72 505	5.1	53.9	40.9	57 327	4 516	62.3
Crawford, GA	111	16.8	95	13.5	120	11	9 225	8.9	67.7	23.4	8 754	4 686	61.4
Crisp, GA	278	16.6	206	7.2	333	25	24 895	11.5	69.4	19.1	21 452	4 663	63.0
Dade, GA	146	16.7	129	10.5	152	25	11 937	6.5	70.9	22.6	10 572	4 493	59.8
Dawson, GA	145	14.4	87	10.6	134	17	11 150	4.9	49.2	45.9	10 281	5 077	56.7
Decatur, GA	371	16.0	321	11.7	316	26	26 203	11.0	69.3	19.7	24 324	4 074	64.1
De Kalb, GA	5 388	16.7	4 318	7.8	5 602	383	533 167	4.7	40.1	55.1	500 424	5 792	66.2
Dodge, GA	212	16.4	188	8.9	224	17	16 374	10.6	73.2	16.2	15 391	4 587	63.7
Dooly, GA	124	14.8	67	12.3	149	9	10 651	13.3	63.0	23.7	10 069	5 817	61.8
Dougherty, GA	971	18.6	812	14.0	2 079	205	105 016	13.3	59.2	27.5	92 068	5 091	57.8
Douglas, GA	950	16.4	784	8.9	846	70	77 816	4.1	56.2	39.6	68 119	4 538	61.1
Early, GA	168	16.4	153	10.4	161	10	13 381	12.3	62.2	25.6	12 281	4 613	62.9
Echols, GA	43	15.3	33	8.6	47	8	4 591	5.4	76.5	18.1	3 091	4 683	61.5
Effingham, GA	407	17.6	308	10.2	460	21	31 689	6.1	63.0	30.9	27 667	4 092	63.2
Elbert, GA	240	16.5	189	9.5	207	17	17 689	9.6	69.5	20.9	18 020	4 563	60.8
Emanuel, GA	294	17.1	250	9.5	297	27	25 118	12.4	72.2	15.4	22 173	4 478	59.9
Evans, GA	123	15.5	91	9.3	84	11	10 802	9.1	78.2	12.7	7 392	3 921	62.1
Fannin, GA	182	16.9	149	11.3	178	17	15 270	10.4	64.6	25.0	13 425	4 472	60.9
Fayette, GA	1 088	15.4	951	5.4	767	54	91 162	1.8	46.1	52.0	70 905	4 427	67.1
Floyd, GA	945	15.2	612	7.9	788	77	75 696	5.9	54.6	39.5	70 675	4 932	59.5
Forsyth, GA	603	17.2	435	6.8	614	40	51 043	3.2	43.0	53.8	44 067	4 771	60.4
Franklin, GA	218	15.6	156	5.9	216	12	14 904	7.7	63.1	29.3	14 487	4 452	64.1
Fulton, GA	7 180	16.2	4 702	9.3	6 355	702	871 913	5.8	28.5	65.7	731 740	6 493	56.6

Table D-2.   School and Student Characteristics by County

State/County code	County	County type[1]	Population, 1996 Total persons	Population, 1996 Percent age 5–17	Number of school districts, 1995–1996	Level of schools, 1995–1996 Number of schools	Percent Primary	Percent Middle	Percent High	Level of students, 1995–1996 Number of students	Percent Primary	Percent Middle	Percent High	Characteristics of students, 1995–1996 Percent with IEP[2]	Percent free-lunch eligible	Percent minority
			1	2	3	4	5	6	7	8	9	10	11	12	13	14
	GEORGIA—Con.															
13123	Gilmer, GA	8	16 868	18.2	1	5	60.0	20.0	20.0	3 082	50.1	24.1	25.8	7.2	35.0	2.4
13125	Glascock, GA	9	2 429	17.9	1	1	—	—	—	475	—	—	—	13.9	37.9	13.1
13127	Glynn, GA	5	65 608	18.5	1	15	60.0	20.0	20.0	11 356	48.5	23.7	27.8	11.2	35.0	39.3
13129	Gordon, GA	6	39 369	19.6	2	12	58.3	25.0	16.7	7 609	53.2	22.6	24.2	12.5	25.7	6.2
13131	Grady, GA	6	21 454	20.8	1	7	71.4	—	14.3	4 599	55.1	—	27.1	9.3	50.1	42.2
13133	Greene, GA	6	13 010	23.0	1	4	75.0	—	25.0	2 538	53.8	—	46.2	13.8	71.5	79.0
13135	Gwinnett, GA	0	478 001	19.2	2	74	59.5	18.9	18.9	86 290	50.3	23.2	26.2	8.9	10.8	19.6
13137	Habersham, GA	7	30 794	17.2	1	10	70.0	10.0	10.0	5 381	49.3	12.5	26.1	11.9	23.3	8.8
13139	Hall, GA	6	113 033	18.2	2	30	63.3	20.0	16.7	19 982	49.0	25.8	25.2	9.7	28.3	23.1
13141	Hancock, GA	9	9 023	23.4	1	3	66.7	—	—	1 814	46.5	—	—	9.2	74.5	99.2
13143	Haralson, GA	6	23 871	18.9	2	8	62.5	12.5	12.5	4 652	54.4	14.1	17.2	11.2	33.3	6.9
13145	Harris, GA	2	21 303	18.7	1	5	60.0	20.0	20.0	3 532	51.6	22.9	25.5	10.4	35.7	28.3
13147	Hart, GA	6	21 005	17.9	1	8	62.5	12.5	25.0	3 374	48.1	23.2	28.7	12.4	34.8	29.6
13149	Heard, GA	8	9 855	21.1	1	4	75.0	—	—	1 942	60.6	—	—	13.1	43.8	17.7
13151	Henry, GA	1	90 969	19.4	1	20	60.0	20.0	15.0	15 754	47.3	26.6	25.4	9.1	16.1	14.8
13153	Houston, GA	2	101 384	20.1	1	27	55.6	22.2	18.5	19 331	44.7	23.5	29.0	9.1	29.2	33.5
13155	Irwin, GA	7	8 871	20.9	1	3	33.3	33.3	33.3	1 839	45.6	25.9	28.5	13.1	50.1	41.8
13157	Jackson, GA	6	35 230	19.1	3	13	53.8	15.4	23.1	6 604	49.8	19.4	22.7	14.1	36.8	10.6
13159	Jasper, GA	8	9 556	20.4	1	3	66.7	—	—	1 747	47.5	—	—	12.7	56.2	45.7
13161	Jeff Davis, GA	7	12 612	20.5	1	4	50.0	25.0	25.0	2 668	46.7	24.6	28.7	10.0	40.3	21.6
13163	Jefferson, GA	8	17 860	22.2	1	6	50.0	33.3	16.7	3 876	51.2	22.5	26.3	11.5	66.1	75.2
13165	Jenkins, GA	7	8 471	21.1	1	3	66.7	—	—	1 778	48.8	—	—	9.1	54.4	54.8
13167	Johnson, GA	9	8 252	21.5	1	3	66.7	—	—	1 524	49.9	—	—	12.5	61.7	53.7
13169	Jones, GA	2	22 330	20.1	1	4	50.0	25.0	25.0	4 416	47.8	24.0	28.2	7.1	28.1	28.7
13171	Lamar, GA	6	14 029	19.2	1	2	50.0	—	—	2 477	49.9	—	—	8.6	47.7	42.4
13173	Lanier, GA	9	6 610	21.3	1	2	50.0	—	—	1 352	46.8	—	—	9.6	53.8	33.4
13175	Laurens, GA	6	43 342	20.8	2	14	50.0	28.6	21.4	9 087	49.9	20.5	29.5	8.5	50.4	46.8
13177	Lee, GA	3	20 705	24.6	1	5	60.0	20.0	20.0	4 890	46.5	26.1	27.4	6.5	21.1	18.0
13179	Liberty, GA	4	59 063	20.1	1	11	63.6	18.2	18.2	10 874	49.4	24.0	26.5	5.3	34.7	62.0
13181	Lincoln, GA	8	8 026	19.8	1	2	50.0	—	—	1 569	49.9	—	—	13.1	47.5	46.2
13183	Long, GA	9	8 151	20.6	1	1	—	—	—	1 636	—	—	—	7.9	51.1	36.2
13185	Lowndes, GA	5	83 982	20.1	2	18	55.6	33.3	11.1	15 884	42.9	31.5	25.7	9.2	40.0	45.7
13187	Lumpkin, GA	7	17 286	17.6	1	4	50.0	25.0	25.0	2 893	51.1	23.0	26.0	12.0	28.1	3.9
13189	McDuffie, GA	2	21 474	21.3	1	6	50.0	33.3	16.7	4 459	36.4	37.6	26.0	9.1	47.8	47.8
13191	McIntosh, GA	9	9 592	20.4	1	2	50.0	—	—	1 689	50.4	—	—	6.5	57.1	55.8
13193	Macon, GA	6	13 141	23.6	1	7	42.9	14.3	28.6	2 523	40.7	17.4	30.1	6.7	72.3	82.1
13195	Madison, GA	3	24 192	19.2	1	6	66.7	16.7	16.7	4 330	49.2	23.6	27.2	13.8	31.0	10.2
13197	Marion, GA	8	6 345	20.7	1	2	50.0	—	50.0	1 774	53.3	—	46.7	9.5	52.8	50.7
13199	Meriwether, GA	6	22 944	21.3	1	9	55.6	11.1	22.2	4 209	50.8	10.7	30.7	13.1	58.2	64.9
13201	Miller, GA	9	6 144	20.7	1	2	50.0	—	—	1 287	49.9	—	—	12.7	50.2	43.9
13205	Mitchell, GA	6	20 990	24.0	2	5	40.0	20.0	20.0	4 736	37.0	18.3	26.0	11.1	66.1	68.0
13207	Monroe, GA	6	19 368	19.8	1	4	50.0	25.0	25.0	3 660	47.6	23.3	29.2	11.8	35.1	36.8
13209	Montgomery, GA	9	7 700	19.9	1	2	50.0	—	—	1 274	50.2	—	—	10.0	52.5	37.0
13211	Morgan, GA	6	14 171	20.0	1	4	50.0	25.0	25.0	2 640	47.0	24.7	28.3	12.5	40.1	39.4
13213	Murray, GA	7	30 777	20.5	1	8	62.5	25.0	12.5	6 001	51.3	24.2	24.5	8.2	30.4	2.0
13215	Muscogee, GA	2	183 394	19.1	1	50	68.0	18.0	14.0	33 117	53.8	18.2	27.9	8.8	47.6	61.0
13217	Newton, GA	1	52 709	19.8	1	13	61.5	15.4	7.7	9 223	52.6	16.3	16.2	12.6	37.7	31.6
13219	Oconee, GA	3	22 410	20.5	1	5	60.0	20.0	20.0	4 571	47.6	24.1	28.3	9.4	15.6	10.1
13221	Oglethorpe, GA	8	10 899	18.6	1	3	33.3	33.3	33.3	1 987	49.3	24.5	26.2	15.2	37.9	31.9
13223	Paulding, GA	1	64 072	19.8	1	14	64.3	21.4	14.3	11 256	54.1	23.1	22.8	9.0	18.2	5.9
13225	Peach, GA	2	23 529	20.3	1	5	60.0	20.0	20.0	4 478	56.9	16.3	26.8	7.2	49.9	55.8
13227	Pickens, GA	1	17 570	17.7	1	4	50.0	25.0	25.0	3 220	51.1	23.8	25.2	7.1	30.1	2.5
13229	Pierce, GA	7	15 270	21.3	1	4	50.0	25.0	25.0	3 048	36.6	17.8	45.6	10.8	44.4	15.5
13231	Pike, GA	8	11 702	19.4	1	4	25.0	50.0	—	2 363	33.7	37.5	—	6.9	25.4	22.4
13233	Polk, GA	6	35 370	19.1	1	11	54.5	27.3	18.2	6 826	50.5	24.2	25.3	8.5	37.9	22.6
13235	Pulaski, GA	6	8 268	19.9	1	3	33.3	33.3	33.3	1 707	46.0	22.8	31.1	11.5	56.8	48.3
13237	Putnam, GA	6	16 511	19.0	1	3	33.3	33.3	33.3	2 369	48.3	25.9	25.8	11.9	49.7	53.5
13239	Quitman, GA	9	2 463	18.7	1	1	100.0	—	—	260	100.0	—	—	18.1	92.3	90.0
13241	Rabun, GA	9	13 013	15.8	1	4	50.0	25.0	25.0	1 898	32.3	25.7	41.9	9.6	29.7	1.6
13243	Randolph, GA	7	7 989	22.4	1	2	50.0	—	—	1 984	44.0	—	—	8.4	78.8	83.6
13245	Richmond, GA	2	193 784	19.1	1	56	66.1	17.9	14.3	36 359	50.5	22.0	26.0	5.7	54.9	67.0
13247	Rockdale, GA	1	65 219	20.5	1	15	60.0	20.0	20.0	12 530	46.8	24.6	28.6	8.9	17.0	16.2
13249	Schley, GA	9	3 763	20.8	1	1	100.0	—	—	484	100.0	—	—	11.4	60.5	39.5
13251	Screven, GA	6	14 286	21.3	1	3	33.3	33.3	33.3	3 291	49.1	21.5	29.4	11.2	55.9	56.5
13253	Seminole, GA	6	9 252	19.7	1	2	50.0	—	—	1 982	48.4	—	—	6.8	61.0	52.8
13255	Spalding, GA	1	57 713	20.2	1	16	75.0	18.8	6.3	10 391	49.9	23.9	26.2	8.9	44.1	58.5

1. County type code is from the Economic Research Service of the USDA. See notes and definitions at the end of this section.   2. IEP = Individual Education Program. See notes and definitions at the end of this section.

Table D-2. School and Student Characteristics by County — Continued

County	Staff and students, 1995–1996						Revenues, fiscal 1995				Current expenditures, fiscal 1995		
	Number of teachers	Pupil/ teacher ratio	Number of graduates	Dropouts grades 9–12 (percent)	Local school non-teaching staff	Central admin. staff	Total revenue ($1000)	Percent of Revenue from			Amount	Amount per pupil	Percent for instruction
								Federal Gov't	State Gov't	Local Gov't			
	15	16	17	18	19	20	21	22	23	24	25	26	27
GEORGIA—Con.													
Gilmer, GA	175	17.6	130	10.7	200	16	16 893	6.0	63.2	30.8	13 248	4 423	61.2
Glascock, GA	33	14.4	24	8.8	21	5	5 032	3.7	78.4	17.9	1 971	3 974	60.6
Glynn, GA	703	16.2	500	10.0	899	136	66 056	6.6	47.3	46.1	58 739	5 276	60.3
Gordon, GA	461	16.5	332	14.5	465	33	36 205	5.7	60.5	33.8	33 664	4 783	57.2
Grady, GA	304	15.2	201	14.0	286	24	21 158	10.2	71.0	18.9	19 822	4 267	62.6
Greene, GA	149	17.0	125	11.5	156	13	14 209	12.3	57.8	29.9	13 448	5 284	57.3
Gwinnett, GA	4 967	17.4	4 037	4.2	3 784	250	451 886	2.2	44.3	53.5	380 602	4 648	64.5
Habersham, GA	325	16.6	287	11.7	320	23	28 465	4.9	60.6	34.6	24 696	4 612	61.0
Hall, GA	1 228	16.3	813	9.8	978	69	98 666	6.0	54.3	39.7	86 855	4 527	63.3
Hancock, GA	106	17.1	109	4.6	108	24	8 614	9.7	66.5	23.8	8 842	4 432	58.1
Haralson, GA	274	17.0	204	12.3	271	38	20 690	7.0	70.4	22.6	19 212	4 354	64.0
Harris, GA	208	17.0	182	8.2	237	17	19 237	6.4	49.1	44.5	14 744	4 399	62.4
Hart, GA	208	16.2	222	7.0	212	13	16 084	7.6	59.4	32.9	15 333	4 699	63.6
Heard, GA	120	16.2	56	11.2	141	10	8 865	9.9	56.3	33.8	8 563	4 710	61.8
Henry, GA	897	17.6	605	8.1	903	45	75 695	2.9	50.8	46.3	62 589	4 375	62.4
Houston, GA	1 226	15.8	1 072	6.2	1 019	60	97 350	6.0	60.3	33.7	86 921	4 726	60.8
Irwin, GA	135	13.6	85	8.4	142	12	10 650	9.4	68.2	22.3	9 170	4 925	61.8
Jackson, GA	416	15.9	308	13.5	366	31	32 683	6.9	62.2	30.9	29 458	4 569	60.7
Jasper, GA	111	15.7	102	3.6	143	11	9 287	9.3	58.5	32.2	8 466	4 770	58.0
Jeff Davis, GA	167	16.0	134	7.4	161	14	12 016	7.9	68.6	23.4	11 304	4 295	60.8
Jefferson, GA	239	16.2	180	7.6	245	14	21 898	11.4	73.1	15.5	15 693	4 183	59.7
Jenkins, GA	112	15.9	80	8.3	111	14	8 883	11.9	75.9	12.2	7 818	4 503	59.3
Johnson, GA	106	14.3	96	12.7	84	9	7 945	13.1	68.1	18.7	6 891	4 507	58.9
Jones, GA	224	19.7	190	9.6	212	18	17 082	7.2	70.0	22.8	14 790	3 527	63.3
Lamar, GA	146	16.9	101	13.6	126	10	11 499	8.6	63.7	27.7	10 479	4 377	56.9
Lanier, GA	86	15.7	75	8.1	81	15	6 436	12.0	70.9	17.1	6 161	4 615	55.7
Laurens, GA	556	16.3	480	7.8	551	31	45 003	9.7	65.8	24.5	42 217	4 777	62.3
Lee, GA	238	20.5	233	1.7	267	19	19 246	5.1	73.4	21.6	18 003	3 858	61.5
Liberty, GA	626	17.4	478	5.1	744	25	49 891	26.6	58.2	15.2	45 364	4 344	59.0
Lincoln, GA	93	16.9	73	8.7	109	6	7 763	10.4	67.3	22.4	6 849	4 621	60.9
Long, GA	93	17.6	34	4.9	95	7	8 895	7.3	75.7	17.0	4 947	3 421	61.1
Lowndes, GA	940	16.9	702	14.3	884	70	68 822	9.4	67.6	22.9	66 027	4 237	61.8
Lumpkin, GA	178	16.3	117	11.1	154	14	12 684	6.4	60.1	33.6	12 168	4 355	62.9
McDuffie, GA	268	16.7	237	12.5	265	11	20 613	10.2	67.0	22.8	18 972	4 203	61.2
McIntosh, GA	114	14.8	64	8.4	99	17	8 836	11.2	59.9	28.9	7 720	4 486	57.4
Macon, GA	164	15.4	134	7.3	182	14	14 238	13.0	57.7	29.3	11 747	4 530	59.6
Madison, GA	245	17.7	189	8.7	260	16	17 523	8.8	70.4	20.8	17 289	4 178	63.4
Marion, GA	99	17.9	105	7.2	124	10	7 766	9.2	69.4	21.4	7 042	4 222	60.8
Meriwether, GA	271	15.5	187	9.6	281	22	21 307	11.6	68.7	19.7	19 799	4 712	59.0
Miller, GA	86	15.0	82	9.3	80	10	6 853	11.9	63.0	25.2	6 018	4 784	62.2
Mitchell, GA	301	15.7	238	9.8	299	31	24 047	11.9	69.2	18.9	20 610	4 330	62.5
Monroe, GA	219	16.7	159	10.7	234	13	17 910	6.7	39.5	53.8	15 915	4 488	60.8
Montgomery, GA	79	16.1	57	10.0	88	9	7 627	9.1	75.8	15.0	5 304	4 352	60.1
Morgan, GA	177	15.0	142	8.4	174	14	13 516	8.7	56.3	35.0	13 842	5 243	61.1
Murray, GA	362	16.6	214	14.2	353	21	25 742	6.7	65.4	27.9	23 770	4 125	63.0
Muscogee, GA	1 911	17.3	1 532	8.4	2 071	264	183 840	9.2	54.9	35.9	166 562	5 123	58.3
Newton, GA	569	16.2	344	6.6	497	25	44 962	6.9	57.1	35.9	41 082	4 676	60.6
Oconee, GA	257	17.8	226	4.8	286	20	21 292	3.4	65.5	31.1	17 426	3 983	60.7
Oglethorpe, GA	135	14.7	98	8.8	110	9	9 519	8.2	69.4	22.5	8 969	4 630	62.6
Paulding, GA	650	17.3	430	9.5	535	33	47 880	3.8	61.8	34.4	42 767	4 159	62.6
Peach, GA	285	15.7	205	6.7	202	10	19 967	10.4	67.0	22.6	18 668	4 173	59.9
Pickens, GA	202	16.0	144	11.7	252	17	14 945	6.2	58.8	35.0	14 861	4 783	63.6
Pierce, GA	175	17.4	167	11.7	179	13	14 904	8.7	71.1	20.2	12 594	4 163	60.2
Pike, GA	124	19.1	110	5.2	140	13	9 597	6.7	64.6	28.7	8 466	3 845	56.1
Polk, GA	397	17.2	293	15.4	373	23	29 306	7.9	71.3	20.8	27 818	4 126	65.1
Pulaski, GA	121	14.1	110	5.3	99	12	8 267	10.4	69.0	20.6	8 415	4 991	61.0
Putnam, GA	149	15.9	91	6.4	167	11	12 115	10.1	50.6	39.3	11 495	4 948	62.6
Quitman, GA	23	11.3	—	NA	31	4	2 105	14.1	63.5	22.4	1 872	7 899	58.4
Rabun, GA	118	16.2	109	10.5	132	14	10 332	6.6	36.5	56.8	9 490	5 174	58.7
Randolph, GA	139	14.3	109	10.4	157	10	9 352	14.7	71.3	14.0	9 674	5 348	60.0
Richmond, GA	2 065	17.6	1 622	12.4	2 243	156	177 058	9.1	56.4	34.4	161 914	4 508	60.7
Rockdale, GA	758	16.5	688	4.9	766	45	67 100	3.6	48.1	48.3	61 654	4 985	59.3
Schley, GA	31	15.6	—	NA	46	5	2 989	10.9	60.4	28.7	2 417	5 165	57.2
Screven, GA	209	15.8	173	9.8	217	19	15 031	11.8	66.4	21.8	14 501	4 577	60.2
Seminole, GA	118	16.8	101	1.5	109	10	13 494	7.6	78.3	14.1	8 205	4 010	59.3
Spalding, GA	602	17.3	409	13.8	631	41	54 397	7.4	66.4	26.2	54 598	5 267	63.8

Table D-2. School and Student Characteristics by County

State/County code	County	County type[1]	Population, 1996 Total persons	Population, 1996 Percent age 5–17	Number of school districts, 1995–1996	Level of schools, 1995–1996 Number of schools	Percent Primary	Percent Middle	Percent High	Level of students, 1995–1996 Number of students	Percent Primary	Percent Middle	Percent High	Percent with IEP[2]	Percent free-lunch eligible	Percent minority
			1	2	3	4	5	6	7	8	9	10	11	12	13	14
	GEORGIA—Con.															
13257	Stephens, GA	7	25 246	17.1	1	6	66.7	16.7	16.7	4 221	50.6	23.3	26.1	11.4	32.3	17.6
13259	Stewart, GA	8	5 532	20.6	1	2	50.0	—	—	914	44.4	—	—	9.4	83.5	94.5
13261	Sumter, GA	6	30 668	21.4	1	7	42.9	28.6	28.6	5 700	44.5	27.6	27.9	8.1	65.5	72.5
13263	Talbot, GA	8	6 865	20.3	1	1	—	—	—	954	—	—	—	13.5	80.7	94.9
13265	Taliaferro, GA	9	1 861	20.4	1	1	100.0	—	—	161	100.0	—	—	9.3	82.6	94.4
13267	Tattnall, GA	7	18 728	17.9	1	4	75.0	—	25.0	3 386	75.2	—	24.8	8.6	57.1	43.0
13269	Taylor, GA	8	8 189	20.7	1	2	50.0	—	—	1 809	49.6	—	—	7.2	60.0	55.0
13271	Telfair, GA	7	11 662	20.8	1	3	66.7	—	—	2 216	49.2	—	—	8.0	54.1	47.7
13273	Terrell, GA	6	11 092	21.9	1	3	66.7	—	—	2 091	51.1	—	—	14.1	71.3	95.6
13275	Thomas, GA	6	41 908	21.0	2	10	60.0	20.0	20.0	8 890	50.3	23.4	26.2	11.3	49.8	51.3
13277	Tift, GA	7	36 850	20.9	1	10	60.0	30.0	10.0	7 566	43.6	36.4	20.0	11.7	43.5	43.5
13279	Toombs, GA	7	25 463	21.9	2	8	50.0	25.0	25.0	5 199	51.0	18.7	30.3	8.7	48.8	40.1
13281	Towns, GA	9	7 990	12.6	1	1	—	—	—	904	—	—	—	12.8	27.0	—
13283	Treutlen, GA	7	5 903	20.9	1	2	50.0	—	—	1 358	49.8	—	—	7.7	54.7	42.1
13285	Troup, GA	4	58 568	20.1	1	17	58.8	23.5	11.8	11 279	47.5	25.1	24.4	13.7	42.5	41.0
13287	Turner, GA	7	9 003	23.1	1	5	40.0	20.0	20.0	2 025	29.7	23.9	23.9	8.2	65.3	60.9
13289	Twiggs, GA	2	9 873	22.5	1	4	75.0	—	—	2 013	51.3	—	—	7.1	66.3	58.9
13291	Union, GA	9	14 923	16.1	1	5	20.0	20.0	40.0	2 280	42.3	22.7	30.4	11.9	35.0	0.2
13293	Upson, GA	7	26 923	18.5	1	4	50.0	25.0	25.0	5 032	48.1	23.3	28.6	10.3	40.0	35.0
13295	Walker, GA	2	61 163	18.8	2	18	66.7	16.7	11.1	10 008	49.2	19.6	23.5	9.5	29.6	5.2
13297	Walton, GA	1	49 307	19.9	2	12	58.3	16.7	16.7	9 524	52.2	19.5	21.3	10.2	29.6	23.4
13299	Ware, GA	7	35 568	19.8	1	10	60.0	20.0	10.0	6 711	46.9	21.1	26.2	11.8	47.0	38.1
13301	Warren, GA	8	6 001	20.0	1	2	50.0	—	—	1 146	55.6	—	—	12.6	77.1	92.8
13303	Washington, GA	7	19 910	21.3	1	6	66.7	16.7	16.7	3 832	48.8	24.5	26.6	7.4	60.2	69.9
13305	Wayne, GA	7	24 636	21.2	1	8	50.0	37.5	12.5	5 117	39.0	34.8	26.2	6.7	43.7	28.6
13307	Webster, GA	8	2 242	20.5	1	1	100.0	—	—	361	100.0	—	—	8.6	57.1	48.8
13309	Wheeler, GA	9	4 933	21.0	1	2	50.0	—	—	1 030	49.1	—	—	11.2	62.3	46.2
13311	White, GA	9	16 140	16.8	1	4	50.0	25.0	25.0	2 792	51.0	21.3	27.7	10.8	27.1	4.2
13313	Whitfield, GA	4	80 296	19.0	2	26	53.8	26.9	15.4	14 960	49.8	25.1	24.7	8.9	28.6	17.1
13315	Wilcox, GA	9	7 320	21.0	1	3	66.7	—	33.3	1 347	69.4	—	30.6	9.0	54.9	44.8
13317	Wilkes, GA	6	10 583	19.6	1	4	50.0	25.0	25.0	2 160	47.0	24.2	28.8	14.1	53.9	58.2
13319	Wilkinson, GA	8	10 801	21.6	1	4	50.0	25.0	25.0	2 015	51.7	22.8	25.6	11.0	50.6	61.3
13321	Worth, GA	6	22 003	21.9	1	5	60.0	20.0	20.0	4 635	47.2	24.9	27.9	8.3	50.7	41.6
15000	**HAWAII**															
15001	Hawaii, HI	5	138 422	21.1	(3)NA	(3)NA	(3)NA	(3)NA	(3)NA	(3)NA	(3)NA	(3)NA	(3)NA	(3)NA	(3)NA	(3)NA
15003	Honolulu, HI	2	871 766	17.5	(3)1	(3)246	(3)68.7	(3)11.8	(3)12.6	(3)187 190	(3)54.9	(3)13.5	(3)26.5	(3)8.2	(3)15.5	(3)77.1
15005	Kalawao, HI	NA	87	1.1	(3)NA	(3)NA	(3)NA	(3)NA	(3)NA	(3)NA	(3)NA	(3)NA	(3)NA	(3)NA	(3)NA	(3)NA
15007	Kauai, HI	5	56 435	19.9	(3)NA	(3)NA	(3)NA	(3)NA	(3)NA	(3)NA	(3)NA	(3)NA	(3)NA	(3)NA	(3)NA	(3)NA
15009	Maui, HI	5	117 013	19.2	(3)NA	(3)NA	(3)NA	(3)NA	(3)NA	(3)NA	(3)NA	(3)NA	(3)NA	(3)NA	(3)NA	(3)NA
16000	**IDAHO**															
16001	Ada, ID	2	260 057	19.8	3	76	65.8	17.1	15.8	47 818	51.5	24.0	24.5	9.2	13.3	NA
16003	Adams, ID	9	3 891	20.0	2	4	50.0	—	50.0	673	52.9	—	47.1	11.1	21.8	NA
16005	Bannock, ID	5	73 608	23.1	2	35	57.1	20.0	17.1	15 558	51.3	24.1	24.4	11.9	20.2	NA
16007	Bear Lake, ID	7	6 534	27.0	1	6	66.7	16.7	16.7	1 848	42.9	26.2	31.0	8.9	24.7	NA
16009	Benewah, ID	8	8 982	21.5	1	4	50.0	25.0	25.0	1 347	47.3	20.5	32.2	11.4	28.3	NA
16011	Bingham, ID	7	41 366	28.3	5	29	55.2	24.1	20.7	11 501	43.8	26.3	29.9	9.0	28.6	NA
16013	Blaine, ID	7	16 975	18.2	1	9	44.4	22.2	22.2	2 852	37.8	27.9	24.5	10.6	12.2	NA
16015	Boise, ID	8	4 864	20.2	3	7	57.1	—	42.9	1 084	59.8	—	40.2	7.8	25.2	NA
16017	Bonner, ID	6	33 976	20.5	1	15	60.0	13.3	26.7	6 167	51.6	15.9	32.5	7.1	26.2	NA
16019	Bonneville, ID	5	79 670	24.8	3	36	66.7	16.7	16.7	19 010	48.8	24.6	26.5	9.8	17.9	NA
16021	Boundary, ID	9	9 823	23.7	1	6	66.7	16.7	16.7	1 736	51.3	15.7	33.1	7.6	28.0	NA
16023	Butte, ID	9	3 126	26.7	1	4	50.0	25.0	25.0	691	43.1	20.4	36.5	10.1	24.0	NA
16025	Camas, ID	9	860	22.6	1	2	50.0	—	50.0	210	74.8	—	25.2	10.0	17.6	NA
16027	Canyon, ID	7	112 530	22.0	8	45	51.1	17.8	24.4	21 277	52.8	23.3	23.9	10.9	34.3	NA
16029	Caribou, ID	7	7 398	28.6	3	11	54.5	18.2	27.3	2 105	43.1	19.6	37.2	9.9	18.9	NA
16031	Cassia, ID	7	21 482	26.5	1	14	57.1	14.3	28.6	5 397	39.9	29.3	30.8	8.2	27.2	NA
16033	Clark, ID	9	830	21.6	1	2	50.0	—	50.0	225	49.8	—	50.2	12.0	23.1	NA
16035	Clearwater, ID	7	9 373	19.1	1	11	45.5	27.3	27.3	1 728	48.3	18.7	33.0	10.0	23.5	NA
16037	Custer, ID	9	4 311	21.9	2	7	71.4	—	28.6	999	56.3	—	43.7	11.4	16.6	NA
16039	Elmore, ID	6	23 894	20.5	3	14	64.3	14.3	21.4	4 985	55.8	21.8	22.4	9.2	24.2	NA
16041	Franklin, ID	7	10 515	28.9	2	6	50.0	16.7	33.3	2 939	53.8	13.3	32.9	6.3	24.4	NA
16043	Fremont, ID	7	11 594	27.9	1	7	57.1	14.3	28.6	2 612	43.5	19.4	37.2	11.4	31.3	NA
16045	Gem, ID	6	14 129	20.0	1	9	66.7	11.1	22.2	2 827	41.1	29.2	29.7	9.7	28.1	NA
16047	Gooding, ID	7	13 335	22.1	5	11	27.3	18.2	36.4	3 076	38.8	19.0	31.2	13.7	30.5	NA

1. County type code is from the Economic Research Service of the USDA. See notes and definitions at the end of this section.   2. IEP = Individual Education Program. See notes and definitions at the end of this section.   3. Hawaii, Kalawao, Kauai, and Maui Counties included with Honolulu County.

Table D-2. School and Student Characteristics by County — Continued

County	Staff and students, 1995–1996						Revenues, fiscal 1995					Current expenditures, fiscal 1995		
								Percent of Revenue from						
	Number of teachers	Pupil/ teacher ratio	Number of graduates	Dropouts grades 9–12 (percent)	Local school non-teaching staff	Central admin. staff	Total revenue ($1000)	Federal Gov't	State Gov't	Local Gov't	Amount	Amount per pupil	Percent for instruction
	15	16	17	18	19	20	21	22	23	24	25	26	27
GEORGIA—Con.													
Stephens, GA	275	15.4	224	15.2	234	18	22 639	6.6	61.4	32.0	19 762	4 700	61.3
Stewart, GA	62	14.7	50	5.3	72	11	5 485	13.7	61.4	24.9	4 814	5 624	54.6
Sumter, GA	331	17.2	298	11.3	381	30	19 624	8.3	66.7	25.0	18 494	3 115	58.2
Talbot, GA	62	15.4	47	8.8	68	7	5 043	15.7	58.7	25.6	4 722	5 110	56.7
Taliaferro, GA	12	13.4	—	NA	20	2	1 427	15.3	38.3	46.4	1 136	6 927	47.4
Tattnall, GA	211	16.0	148	10.8	196	14	15 057	10.8	70.9	18.4	13 793	4 296	61.1
Taylor, GA	110	16.4	71	10.3	123	12	8 027	11.6	71.3	17.0	7 192	4 174	62.1
Telfair, GA	149	14.9	115	8.5	147	11	11 506	11.3	69.2	19.5	10 319	4 621	61.9
Terrell, GA	148	14.1	104	1.6	130	19	11 557	12.6	63.2	24.1	10 216	4 971	61.0
Thomas, GA	510	17.4	417	11.8	555	41	44 591	10.2	68.9	20.9	41 608	4 735	62.8
Tift, GA	439	17.2	385	12.6	433	30	33 209	9.9	69.7	20.4	30 650	4 030	63.4
Toombs, GA	319	16.3	259	6.0	263	31	23 158	10.6	67.7	21.7	21 420	4 150	62.2
Towns, GA	56	16.1	53	11.9	61	4	4 173	8.4	50.9	40.6	4 019	4 717	62.9
Treutlen, GA	84	16.1	56	3.4	76	13	7 974	8.3	81.3	10.4	5 589	4 209	61.0
Troup, GA	744	15.2	453	7.6	740	38	58 958	7.6	56.3	36.1	53 593	4 838	57.4
Turner, GA	145	14.0	94	12.3	130	14	13 134	10.6	74.0	15.4	9 790	4 792	62.5
Twiggs, GA	128	15.7	82	9.7	139	18	10 856	11.3	58.2	30.4	9 863	4 951	55.2
Union, GA	138	16.5	130	13.7	138	12	11 014	10.4	63.2	26.4	10 213	4 646	61.8
Upson, GA	287	17.5	279	9.1	299	19	25 583	7.2	69.0	23.8	20 160	4 043	63.9
Walker, GA	607	16.5	466	13.2	541	45	49 155	6.4	65.4	28.2	43 772	4 384	61.3
Walton, GA	561	17.0	356	9.6	464	34	39 691	6.5	63.3	30.1	35 065	3 950	63.2
Ware, GA	428	15.7	356	10.4	380	30	39 117	8.2	70.4	21.5	34 800	5 131	61.2
Warren, GA	65	17.6	52	12.2	84	6	6 159	14.9	62.5	22.6	5 203	4 447	56.9
Washington, GA	226	17.0	184	16.1	172	21	20 754	9.6	53.2	37.2	18 345	4 762	53.3
Wayne, GA	290	17.7	296	9.2	353	25	23 435	8.7	62.3	29.0	20 711	4 231	61.8
Webster, GA	21	17.2	—	NA	34	2	2 019	12.3	63.4	24.3	1 774	5 475	53.3
Wheeler, GA	69	14.9	63	9.9	65	7	5 997	12.2	71.0	16.8	4 951	4 826	58.4
White, GA	162	17.2	126	9.2	170	17	16 926	3.9	60.8	35.3	12 276	4 598	62.4
Whitfield, GA	901	16.6	670	10.5	854	74	80 095	5.6	54.3	40.2	75 415	5 184	59.7
Wilcox, GA	86	15.7	81	10.2	57	16	7 197	11.0	73.0	16.0	6 307	4 590	61.2
Wilkes, GA	147	14.7	131	3.1	133	13	10 970	10.3	62.1	27.6	10 131	4 667	59.2
Wilkinson, GA	132	15.3	107	10.5	140	12	10 946	8.3	57.8	33.8	10 130	5 083	59.8
Worth, GA	256	18.1	191	6.8	343	29	22 833	10.6	69.8	19.5	18 496	4 093	60.1
HAWAII													
Hawaii, HI	(1)NA	(1)NA	(1)NA	(1)NA	(1)NA	(1)NA	(1)NA	(1)NA	(1)NA	(1)NA	(1)NA	(1)NA	(1)NA
Honolulu, HI	(1)10 421	(1)18.0	(1)9 980	(1)4.8	(1)5 500	(1)843	(1)1 173 579	(1)7.0	(1)90.5	(1)2.4	(1)1 028 730	(1)5 595	(1)61.9
Kalawao, HI	(1)NA	(1)NA	(1)NA	(1)NA	(1)NA	(1)NA	(1)NA	(1)NA	(1)NA	(1)NA	(1)NA	(1)NA	(1)NA
Kauai, HI	(1)NA	(1)NA	(1)NA	(1)NA	(1)NA	(1)NA	(1)NA	(1)NA	(1)NA	(1)NA	(1)NA	(1)NA	(1)NA
Maui, HI	(1)NA	(1)NA	(1)NA	(1)NA	(1)NA	(1)NA	(1)NA	(1)NA	(1)NA	(1)NA	(1)NA	(1)NA	(1)NA
IDAHO													
Ada, ID	2 434	19.6	2 624	NA	1 513	147	212 709	4.5	54.6	40.9	183 334	3 949	64.8
Adams, ID	47	14.3	36	NA	23	5	3 732	9.9	68.1	22.0	3 426	5 076	66.8
Bannock, ID	767	20.3	948	NA	524	46	67 036	8.6	67.5	23.9	61 269	3 924	63.2
Bear Lake, ID	94	19.7	108	NA	67	6	7 362	5.1	70.5	24.4	6 516	3 547	55.5
Benewah, ID	72	18.8	91	NA	51	4	6 244	9.1	61.5	29.5	5 672	4 246	59.5
Bingham, ID	582	19.8	741	NA	377	31	49 087	9.1	70.5	20.4	43 048	3 691	63.2
Blaine, ID	182	15.7	148	NA	99	9	18 376	2.4	18.2	79.4	14 438	5 160	68.2
Boise, ID	75	14.5	39	NA	45	6	5 831	15.1	52.8	32.1	4 974	5 360	53.0
Bonner, ID	314	19.6	344	NA	204	20	25 426	7.8	53.8	38.4	23 015	3 749	59.2
Bonneville, ID	946	20.1	1 236	NA	651	50	81 414	5.7	67.4	26.9	71 088	3 734	63.6
Boundary, ID	94	18.5	104	NA	69	10	7 950	10.2	63.7	26.1	7 183	3 975	62.8
Butte, ID	43	15.9	58	NA	31	3	3 635	6.7	72.5	20.7	3 471	4 889	64.3
Camas, ID	17	12.6	13	NA	10	2	1 412	6.2	65.8	28.0	1 224	5 856	63.7
Canyon, ID	1 095	19.4	1 137	NA	731	68	94 689	8.8	64.1	27.0	78 050	3 720	65.2
Caribou, ID	125	16.9	185	NA	83	7	10 949	4.6	60.4	35.0	9 315	4 173	65.5
Cassia, ID	280	19.3	325	NA	189	13	22 612	7.7	68.6	23.7	20 459	3 710	63.3
Clark, ID	18	12.8	16	NA	6	3	1 280	8.0	64.5	27.5	1 215	5 352	63.1
Clearwater, ID	103	16.8	113	NA	73	5	8 956	10.6	63.2	26.3	8 075	4 585	59.9
Custer, ID	62	16.2	60	NA	44	6	4 962	6.8	63.2	30.0	4 610	4 772	59.8
Elmore, ID	285	17.5	219	NA	148	12	22 344	17.8	64.3	17.9	19 800	3 998	64.3
Franklin, ID	148	19.9	201	NA	92	7	11 292	6.6	77.1	16.3	10 425	3 547	65.7
Fremont, ID	138	18.9	183	NA	96	5	11 152	9.4	68.2	22.4	10 700	4 003	62.3
Gem, ID	145	19.6	131	NA	95	6	11 294	8.3	69.1	22.6	10 329	3 742	65.7
Gooding, ID	169	18.2	173	NA	98	11	13 006	7.4	71.6	21.0	11 321	3 945	62.7

1. Hawaii, Kalawao, Kauai, and Maui Counties included with Honolulu County.

Table D-2.   School and Student Characteristics by County

State/County code	County	County type[1]	Population, 1996		Number of school districts, 1995–1996	Level of schools, 1995–1996				Level of students, 1995–1996				Characteristics of students, 1995–1996		
			Total persons	Percent age 5–17		Number of schools	Percent			Number of students	Percent			Percent with IEP[2]	Percent free-lunch eligible	Percent minority
							Primary	Middle	High		Primary	Middle	High			
			1	2	3	4	5	6	7	8	9	10	11	12	13	14

	IDAHO—Con.															
16049	Idaho, ID	7	14 924	20.4	2	12	50.0	8.3	33.3	2 631	54.4	6.9	35.5	9.4	25.5	NA
16051	Jefferson, ID	7	18 903	29.5	3	14	50.0	28.6	21.4	5 785	44.7	28.6	26.7	7.3	25.6	NA
16053	Jerome, ID	7	17 339	23.1	2	8	37.5	25.0	25.0	3 911	30.3	26.7	23.7	8.6	35.1	NA
16055	Kootenai, ID	4	95 535	19.1	5	35	57.1	14.3	28.6	16 847	50.1	22.0	27.9	8.3	15.2	NA
16057	Latah, ID	7	33 173	15.7	5	18	55.6	5.6	33.3	4 773	51.0	15.1	29.2	10.6	14.7	NA
16059	Lemhi, ID	7	8 098	20.2	2	7	28.6	28.6	28.6	1 524	27.3	34.6	29.1	10.8	21.7	NA
16061	Lewis, ID	9	4 002	20.2	3	7	42.9	14.3	42.9	1 251	43.6	18.2	38.2	11.9	34.6	NA
16063	Lincoln, ID	9	3 777	22.9	3	4	25.0	—	25.0	878	25.9	—	24.9	11.8	40.2	NA
16065	Madison, ID	7	23 458	22.7	2	16	50.0	25.0	18.8	5 921	32.5	38.3	28.7	9.1	23.6	NA
16067	Minidoka, ID	7	20 756	26.2	1	11	45.5	27.3	18.2	5 295	39.4	36.7	23.2	10.4	36.7	NA
16069	Nez Perce, ID	5	36 670	17.6	3	14	57.1	14.3	21.4	5 902	50.2	21.6	24.0	9.2	18.9	NA
16071	Oneida, ID	9	3 871	24.9	1	3	66.7	—	33.3	1 030	49.5	—	50.5	9.5	22.2	NA
16073	Owyhee, ID	8	10 012	23.9	4	12	41.7	8.3	33.3	2 471	52.0	6.7	40.8	10.5	42.7	NA
16075	Payette, ID	7	19 957	21.5	3	11	27.3	36.4	36.4	4 226	42.3	30.5	27.3	9.2	30.8	NA
16077	Power, ID	7	8 234	25.9	3	5	40.0	20.0	20.0	1 882	34.6	29.9	27.2	13.3	37.4	NA
16079	Shoshone, ID	7	14 024	19.7	4	14	57.1	14.3	28.6	2 750	44.0	22.6	33.4	12.0	31.7	NA
16081	Teton, ID	9	5 168	23.3	1	4	50.0	25.0	25.0	1 169	48.6	22.6	28.8	10.6	18.7	NA
16083	Twin Falls, ID	5	60 403	21.6	8	31	45.2	22.6	25.8	12 204	49.0	23.3	24.6	9.6	25.4	NA
16085	Valley, ID	9	7 988	19.9	2	7	42.9	14.3	42.9	1 704	52.2	11.6	36.2	12.0	18.0	NA
16087	Washington, ID	7	9 836	21.4	3	8	37.5	25.0	37.5	2 165	34.5	30.8	34.7	9.1	34.0	NA
17000	**ILLINOIS**															
17001	Adams, IL	5	67 816	19.2	6	28	50.0	17.9	21.4	12 046	35.5	32.0	23.4	3.8	NA	7.4
17003	Alexander, IL	7	10 228	20.4	3	8	37.5	25.0	25.0	2 013	50.7	19.5	22.1	7.7	NA	57.7
17005	Bond, IL	6	17 069	17.0	2	8	50.0	25.0	25.0	2 527	58.7	12.0	29.3	2.1	NA	5.9
17007	Boone, IL	2	37 389	20.9	3	14	78.6	7.1	14.3	6 646	60.5	12.3	27.2	3.1	NA	13.1
17009	Brown, IL	9	6 400	15.8	1	3	66.7	—	33.3	799	63.8	—	36.2	3.5	NA	0.8
17011	Bureau, IL	7	35 739	20.2	16	29	69.0	6.9	24.1	6 606	58.7	9.8	31.5	3.6	NA	6.8
17013	Calhoun, IL	8	5 011	18.2	2	5	40.0	20.0	40.0	774	46.5	19.1	34.4	2.8	NA	0.3
17015	Carroll, IL	7	16 907	19.2	5	18	38.9	33.3	27.8	3 381	44.8	26.8	28.4	2.2	NA	4.4
17017	Cass, IL	6	13 284	19.8	3	13	46.2	30.8	23.1	2 199	50.8	19.6	29.6	4.0	NA	1.6
17019	Champaign, IL	3	167 392	15.9	16	60	65.0	16.7	18.3	23 916	52.8	18.3	29.0	3.1	NA	25.0
17021	Christian, IL	6	34 730	18.9	5	21	52.4	19.0	28.6	5 841	50.9	18.9	30.2	2.8	NA	1.2
17023	Clark, IL	6	17 571	17.2	3	11	36.4	36.4	27.3	3 160	48.7	21.6	29.7	1.2	NA	0.7
17025	Clay, IL	7	14 397	19.5	3	11	45.5	27.3	27.3	2 738	47.7	23.3	29.0	2.1	NA	0.9
17027	Clinton, IL	1	35 368	20.5	12	20	70.0	15.0	15.0	5 720	63.3	12.1	24.6	1.8	NA	2.6
17029	Coles, IL	5	51 186	16.0	5	28	67.9	14.3	10.7	8 009	48.1	20.6	28.7	6.6	NA	4.7
17031	Cook, IL	0	5 096 540	18.1	151	1 192	74.3	11.3	10.7	763 254	63.5	8.8	26.0	4.1	NA	65.1
17033	Crawford, IL	7	21 071	18.2	4	10	40.0	20.0	20.0	3 821	46.0	20.6	10.4	1.5	NA	2.3
17035	Cumberland, IL	9	11 169	21.0	2	7	42.9	28.6	28.6	2 081	50.4	19.5	30.1	0.8	NA	0.5
17037	De Kalb, IL	1	82 703	16.2	11	38	50.0	21.1	23.7	14 601	44.9	23.6	28.9	2.8	NA	9.0
17039	De Witt, IL	6	16 795	19.4	2	10	50.0	30.0	20.0	3 366	44.4	26.6	29.0	2.0	NA	3.4
17041	Douglas, IL	6	19 799	21.4	4	11	36.4	27.3	36.4	3 293	50.0	17.9	32.1	1.2	NA	4.0
17043	Du Page, IL	0	859 310	18.7	49	234	64.5	21.4	9.8	142 039	48.9	21.5	28.7	2.5	NA	18.9
17045	Edgar, IL	6	20 106	19.6	5	16	62.5	12.5	25.0	3 898	55.7	13.2	31.1	1.7	NA	0.9
17047	Edwards, IL	9	7 129	18.7	1	3	66.7	—	33.3	1 127	67.1	—	32.9	3.5	NA	1.2
17049	Effingham, IL	7	33 337	21.9	5	20	70.0	5.0	25.0	6 502	53.2	14.5	32.3	1.2	NA	1.1
17051	Fayette, IL	6	21 362	18.7	5	15	40.0	20.0	26.7	3 532	46.7	15.9	27.7	4.4	NA	0.7
17053	Ford, IL	6	14 164	19.7	5	7	28.6	42.9	28.6	2 640	35.9	31.7	32.3	3.7	NA	1.2
17055	Franklin, IL	7	40 948	18.3	12	21	57.1	14.3	28.6	6 874	61.7	8.2	30.1	6.1	NA	0.3
17057	Fulton, IL	6	38 650	18.8	11	32	50.0	21.9	25.0	7 814	48.0	20.4	31.3	3.7	NA	1.4
17059	Gallatin, IL	8	6 753	17.8	1	3	33.3	33.3	33.3	1 036	49.5	22.4	28.1	5.0	NA	0.7
17061	Greene, IL	6	15 733	19.6	3	8	50.0	12.5	25.0	2 621	58.3	9.0	21.9	3.9	NA	0.6
17063	Grundy, IL	1	35 712	21.0	13	21	57.1	19.0	19.0	8 383	43.7	18.7	33.1	2.0	NA	3.8
17065	Hamilton, IL	7	8 622	18.4	1	8	75.0	12.5	12.5	1 501	55.3	13.6	31.1	6.6	NA	0.8
17067	Hancock, IL	7	21 205	19.7	8	24	37.5	25.0	29.2	4 363	49.0	17.5	32.5	3.8	NA	1.1
17069	Hardin, IL	9	5 068	18.6	1	3	33.3	33.3	33.3	861	50.9	15.7	33.4	0.1	NA	2.3
17071	Henderson, IL	9	8 526	19.6	2	5	40.0	20.0	40.0	1 352	56.4	12.8	30.8	3.3	NA	2.1
17073	Henry, IL	2	51 807	20.6	9	26	57.7	11.5	30.8	10 147	58.4	8.5	33.1	2.9	NA	4.7
17075	Iroquois, IL	6	31 625	19.8	12	33	42.4	24.2	24.2	5 992	42.7	27.4	28.4	4.7	NA	6.5
17077	Jackson, IL	5	61 154	14.4	9	25	56.0	24.0	16.0	8 211	48.8	21.3	29.6	6.6	NA	22.7
17079	Jasper, IL	7	10 635	21.4	1	11	54.5	36.4	—	2 053	43.6	22.6	—	3.1	NA	0.9
17081	Jefferson, IL	7	39 090	19.5	19	28	64.3	10.7	14.3	7 363	58.8	9.5	26.9	6.7	NA	12.3
17083	Jersey, IL	1	21 308	20.3	1	8	75.0	12.5	12.5	3 273	47.6	19.7	32.6	4.0	NA	0.5
17085	Jo Daviess, IL	6	21 783	20.1	7	20	55.0	30.0	25.0	4 084	44.7	21.8	21.6	3.6	NA	0.8
17087	Johnson, IL	9	12 954	14.8	6	8	62.5	12.5	25.0	1 851	63.9	6.1	30.0	1.2	NA	1.0

1. County type code is from the Economic Research Service of the USDA. See notes and definitions at the end of this section.   2. IEP = Individual Education Program. See notes and definitions at the end of this section.

ID (Idaho, ID)–IL (Johnson, IL)

Table D-2. School and Student Characteristics by County — Continued

County	Staff and students, 1995–1996						Revenues, fiscal 1995				Current expenditures, fiscal 1995		
	Number of teachers	Pupil/ teacher ratio	Number of graduates	Dropouts grades 9–12 (percent)	Local school non-teaching staff	Central admin. staff	Total revenue ($1000)	Percent of Revenue from			Amount	Amount per pupil	Percent for instruction
								Federal Gov't	State Gov't	Local Gov't			
	15	16	17	18	19	20	21	22	23	24	25	26	27
IDAHO—Con.													
Idaho, ID	152	17.3	162	NA	105	8	13 672	17.8	64.1	18.1	12 060	4 561	63.3
Jefferson, ID	282	20.5	363	NA	196	14	23 146	7.3	72.9	19.8	19 574	3 375	64.8
Jerome, ID	193	20.3	209	NA	123	11	16 125	8.8	67.5	23.7	13 667	3 557	62.8
Kootenai, ID	846	19.9	927	NA	539	47	70 013	5.9	54.6	39.5	62 391	3 821	64.1
Latah, ID	294	16.2	316	NA	194	25	27 138	4.6	54.1	41.3	23 444	4 906	63.3
Lemhi, ID	85	18.0	95	NA	62	9	6 761	10.3	65.0	24.7	5 645	3 817	62.4
Lewis, ID	81	15.5	76	NA	50	7	6 986	13.8	63.1	23.1	6 097	5 043	59.6
Lincoln, ID	65	13.5	66	NA	38	6	4 895	7.7	73.2	19.1	4 505	5 006	63.0
Madison, ID	296	20.0	471	NA	201	15	23 722	6.4	74.6	19.1	20 681	3 472	64.3
Minidoka, ID	277	19.1	314	NA	174	12	20 772	9.0	72.1	18.9	18 280	3 410	63.7
Nez Perce, ID	341	17.3	354	NA	239	28	32 505	6.7	45.5	47.9	29 438	5 005	61.6
Oneida, ID	56	18.3	71	NA	31	3	4 317	5.5	72.8	21.7	3 831	3 858	67.3
Owyhee, ID	147	16.8	136	NA	115	15	12 125	10.3	69.4	20.3	10 845	4 265	62.1
Payette, ID	218	19.4	232	NA	151	12	17 995	8.7	66.2	25.1	15 011	3 656	63.9
Power, ID	112	16.9	117	NA	66	9	10 391	9.1	51.0	39.9	9 358	4 866	61.3
Shoshone, ID	178	15.4	175	NA	130	14	15 485	13.3	58.8	27.9	14 856	5 367	61.4
Teton, ID	63	18.6	72	NA	34	3	4 605	5.7	65.8	28.6	4 342	3 705	64.2
Twin Falls, ID	635	19.2	676	NA	365	37	49 936	7.6	68.5	23.9	44 170	3 704	61.1
Valley, ID	99	17.2	116	NA	56	6	10 322	14.2	32.3	53.5	7 961	4 719	63.9
Washington, ID	125	17.4	119	NA	81	7	9 554	9.0	69.3	21.7	8 574	4 095	63.3
ILLINOIS													
Adams, IL	032	19.0	088	NA	013	22	53 807	7.5	51.0	41.0	49 622	4 514	54.8
Alexander, IL	126	16.0	108	NA	90	7	11 288	10.4	74.5	15.1	9 501	5 043	55.3
Bond, IL	138	18.3	159	NA	111	3	12 128	3.9	61.5	34.6	9 404	3 763	57.9
Boone, IL	336	19.8	346	NA	325	11	30 724	2.2	32.4	65.4	21 776	3 471	59.9
Brown, IL	51	15.8	56	NA	38	1	3 773	4.9	55.4	39.7	3 127	3 880	56.3
Bureau, IL	456	14.5	363	NA	298	19	35 397	3.7	47.5	48.8	30 519	4 635	61.2
Calhoun, IL	58	13.5	53	NA	52	2	4 113	5.9	61.0	33.1	3 733	4 958	58.7
Carroll, IL	212	15.9	232	NA	147	5	17 312	5.0	46.3	48.7	14 759	4 382	60.6
Cass, IL	160	13.8	151	NA	121	5	11 359	5.3	60.4	34.3	9 823	4 324	62.7
Champaign, IL	1 520	15.7	1 425	NA	1 092	44	130 784	6.2	35.4	58.4	105 453	4 507	62.7
Christian, IL	328	17.8	387	NA	271	7	29 081	4.3	55.0	40.8	22 839	3 910	58.1
Clark, IL	186	17.0	194	NA	133	3	13 316	4.6	64.4	31.0	11 570	3 754	59.2
Clay, IL	186	14.7	158	NA	155	5	13 665	7.8	64.1	28.1	11 655	4 287	61.9
Clinton, IL	291	19.7	290	NA	228	13	25 642	3.9	55.9	40.2	21 418	3 748	62.3
Coles, IL	473	16.9	480	NA	449	29	38 221	4.9	50.0	45.1	34 278	4 449	62.8
Cook, IL	43 703	17.5	36 686	NA	37 118	2 075	5 750 046	7.2	24.3	68.5	4 755 799	6 336	58.8
Crawford, IL	232	16.5	246	NA	187	8	17 737	3.9	46.5	49.6	15 292	4 002	54.2
Cumberland, IL	124	16.7	130	NA	87	2	8 866	4.5	65.4	30.1	7 750	3 746	60.0
De Kalb, IL	845	17.3	813	NA	683	32	73 737	2.3	29.5	68.2	60 753	4 394	61.1
De Witt, IL	220	15.3	201	NA	195	4	22 122	2.4	17.2	80.4	17 003	5 063	64.9
Douglas, IL	214	15.4	193	NA	107	5	15 784	4.6	41.1	54.3	13 463	4 122	60.4
Du Page, IL	7 872	18.0	8 478	NA	6 647	331	947 855	1.2	12.9	85.9	785 524	5 709	61.2
Edgar, IL	256	15.2	244	NA	203	9	19 279	5.2	53.3	41.5	16 505	4 285	60.1
Edwards, IL	65	17.5	83	NA	49	2	5 621	3.1	58.0	38.9	4 382	3 820	59.2
Effingham, IL	365	17.8	373	NA	281	13	28 033	4.0	55.1	40.9	23 836	3 769	60.6
Fayette, IL	203	17.4	212	NA	177	6	16 223	5.2	60.0	33.0	12 628	3 814	56.7
Ford, IL	148	17.8	168	NA	87	3	14 447	2.8	40.6	56.6	11 201	4 308	58.1
Franklin, IL	414	16.6	451	NA	268	11	34 630	7.5	68.1	24.4	30 804	4 495	65.0
Fulton, IL	526	14.9	547	NA	419	15	41 978	5.6	53.4	41.0	35 338	4 489	58.9
Gallatin, IL	69	15.0	56	NA	65	1	6 279	7.2	53.8	39.1	4 829	4 679	63.6
Greene, IL	175	14.9	194	NA	127	3	12 189	6.2	65.2	28.5	11 333	4 265	62.6
Grundy, IL	424	19.8	533	NA	283	18	47 199	1.3	15.0	83.6	36 308	4 752	55.8
Hamilton, IL	89	16.8	70	NA	86	4	8 135	8.2	65.0	26.8	6 875	4 748	59.4
Hancock, IL	294	14.9	296	NA	230	13	22 691	4.0	54.4	41.6	17 899	4 128	61.3
Hardin, IL	61	14.0	73	NA	42	1	4 820	9.1	75.0	15.9	4 654	5 092	62.2
Henderson, IL	91	14.9	69	NA	92	2	6 945	5.4	51.0	43.6	5 595	4 284	58.9
Henry, IL	567	17.9	688	NA	390	15	46 927	4.4	56.3	39.3	39 070	3 827	61.6
Iroquois, IL	376	15.9	341	NA	304	17	31 284	4.0	45.2	50.8	23 415	4 040	57.4
Jackson, IL	495	16.6	464	NA	410	25	46 931	7.2	57.1	35.7	37 629	4 598	59.6
Jasper, IL	119	17.2	140	NA	127	4	9 488	4.7	39.0	56.3	8 979	4 311	57.4
Jefferson, IL	415	17.7	446	NA	387	32	34 307	8.3	59.0	32.7	30 196	4 329	60.4
Jersey, IL	175	18.7	214	NA	147	5	14 739	3.9	60.7	35.4	13 113	4 045	57.6
Jo Daviess, IL	256	16.0	261	NA	195	8	19 969	2.8	34.7	62.6	16 348	4 166	60.5
Johnson, IL	110	16.9	101	NA	89	6	8 916	6.1	64.3	29.5	7 624	4 217	60.1

Table D-2. School and Student Characteristics by County

State/ County code	County	County type[1]	Population, 1996 Total persons	Population, 1996 Percent age 5-17	Number of school districts, 1995-1996	Level of schools, 1995-1996 Number of schools	Percent Primary	Percent Middle	Percent High	Level of students, 1995-1996 Number of students	Percent Primary	Percent Middle	Percent High	Percent with IEP[2]	Percent free-lunch eligible	Percent minority
			1	2	3	4	5	6	7	8	9	10	11	12	13	14
	ILLINOIS—Con.															
17089	Kane, IL	0	370 361	21.6	12	136	69.1	16.9	11.0	86 339	55.0	18.2	26.2	3.7	NA	31.5
17091	Kankakee, IL	3	101 949	21.1	14	47	59.6	17.0	14.9	18 892	46.6	21.0	26.2	5.9	NA	31.1
17093	Kendall, IL	1	47 894	22.7	6	19	42.1	36.8	21.1	8 951	41.8	28.1	30.1	2.4	NA	9.8
17095	Knox, IL	4	55 936	18.1	7	31	58.1	19.4	16.1	8 970	45.2	21.9	30.1	3.9	NA	10.6
17097	Lake, IL	0	582 983	19.8	48	189	61.9	24.9	9.5	108 354	48.7	23.6	25.9	3.5	NA	25.4
17099	La Salle, IL	4	109 462	19.2	31	52	71.2	9.6	15.4	17 720	56.0	11.2	31.2	4.8	NA	7.5
17101	Lawrence, IL	7	15 865	18.2	2	12	75.0	8.3	16.7	2 764	57.1	12.8	30.1	2.0	NA	2.1
17103	Lee, IL	7	35 959	19.3	6	19	47.4	21.1	21.1	5 771	47.9	19.9	25.4	3.5	NA	5.2
17105	Livingston, IL	6	40 597	18.6	14	25	64.0	8.0	24.0	8 357	57.2	9.6	29.3	5.2	NA	3.5
17107	Logan, IL	6	31 499	17.4	9	18	61.1	11.1	11.1	4 584	50.9	8.4	29.3	4.5	NA	3.6
17109	McDonough, IL	5	34 152	14.5	5	16	43.8	25.0	31.3	4 457	43.3	18.3	38.4	5.6	NA	5.5
17111	McHenry, IL	0	230 555	20.9	20	62	58.1	21.0	19.4	38 143	52.9	19.7	27.3	3.3	NA	6.9
17113	McLean, IL	3	139 133	17.4	12	57	61.4	15.8	21.1	23 559	54.4	15.4	27.5	3.2	NA	11.6
17115	Macon, IL	3	115 416	19.5	9	53	60.4	18.9	17.0	20 343	52.1	16.4	27.9	2.8	NA	23.9
17117	Macoupin, IL	6	48 994	19.9	9	31	51.6	19.4	29.0	10 230	53.4	17.6	29.1	3.4	NA	1.6
17119	Madison, IL	0	256 007	19.0	17	99	61.6	20.2	13.1	44 488	46.1	22.3	29.4	5.9	NA	13.2
17121	Marion, IL	7	42 295	20.1	15	34	50.0	23.5	17.6	8 691	42.8	22.5	33.2	5.5	NA	6.9
17123	Marshall, IL	6	12 789	19.5	2	7	57.1	14.3	28.6	1 762	59.9	8.2	31.9	3.3	NA	2.2
17125	Mason, IL	6	16 820	19.8	3	9	33.3	33.3	33.3	3 637	43.6	26.9	29.4	5.7	NA	1.1
17127	Massac, IL	7	15 336	18.5	2	12	66.7	16.7	16.7	2 635	58.2	11.0	30.8	5.4	NA	8.4
17129	Menard, IL	3	12 359	20.9	3	12	41.7	33.3	25.0	2 770	38.7	32.5	28.8	1.8	NA	1.0
17131	Mercer, IL	6	17 605	20.5	3	12	41.7	33.3	25.0	3 743	43.4	26.9	29.7	2.4	NA	1.0
17133	Monroe, IL	1	25 358	19.9	4	12	41.7	25.0	25.0	4 430	46.1	16.9	29.8	2.4	NA	1.8
17135	Montgomery, IL	6	31 059	19.0	5	22	50.0	27.3	22.7	5 671	47.0	23.6	29.3	2.5	NA	1.5
17137	Morgan, IL	4	36 252	18.3	6	25	64.0	12.0	20.0	6 031	53.9	15.5	29.4	4.3	NA	7.6
17139	Moultrie, IL	6	14 319	19.9	3	7	57.1	—	42.9	1 979	64.9	—	35.1	NA	NA	0.4
17141	Ogle, IL	2	50 107	20.7	11	31	58.1	19.4	16.1	10 084	49.5	19.8	24.9	2.3	NA	5.4
17143	Peoria, IL	2	183 337	19.5	17	79	51.9	21.5	15.2	28 353	51.5	18.3	28.1	7.5	NA	33.1
17145	Perry, IL	7	21 498	19.9	5	9	55.6	22.2	22.2	3 095	35.3	32.0	32.7	4.5	NA	4.5
17147	Piatt, IL	6	16 357	19.8	5	15	40.0	26.7	33.3	3 441	47.7	23.1	29.3	1.2	NA	0.6
17149	Pike, IL	7	17 251	18.8	5	15	40.0	26.7	33.3	3 096	43.3	26.3	30.5	5.4	NA	0.4
17151	Pope, IL	9	4 735	18.2	1	2	50.0	—	50.0	671	71.5	—	28.5	NA	NA	1.0
17153	Pulaski, IL	9	7 348	22.2	3	6	33.3	16.7	33.3	1 797	62.3	5.3	31.2	5.2	NA	46.7
17155	Putnam, IL	9	5 715	19.5	1	4	50.0	25.0	25.0	1 066	48.5	22.1	29.4	1.1	NA	5.3
17157	Randolph, IL	6	34 240	18.6	7	17	47.1	17.6	29.4	5 147	53.4	12.7	33.6	4.1	NA	6.5
17159	Richland, IL	7	16 747	19.5	2	9	44.4	33.3	11.1	2 934	35.3	32.1	6.0	4.6	NA	1.7
17161	Rock Island, IL	2	148 640	19.0	11	59	62.7	15.3	11.9	24 904	48.5	17.0	29.5	5.5	NA	23.1
17163	St. Clair, IL	0	264 419	21.0	28	99	65.7	17.2	14.1	47 210	57.8	15.3	25.0	6.3	NA	43.6
17165	Saline, IL	7	26 476	18.5	4	12	41.7	25.0	33.3	4 614	55.4	15.3	29.3	8.0	NA	6.1
17167	Sangamon, IL	3	191 771	18.8	16	110	37.3	12.7	11.8	41 481	36.8	13.4	18.3	7.1	NA	34.6
17169	Schuyler, IL	7	7 702	19.4	1	4	50.0	25.0	25.0	1 229	33.0	21.2	45.8	3.0	NA	0.2
17171	Scott, IL	9	5 615	19.7	2	5	40.0	20.0	40.0	1 103	60.6	7.1	32.4	7.2	NA	0.5
17173	Shelby, IL	6	22 660	19.5	9	22	45.5	18.2	31.8	4 585	49.1	19.2	31.1	2.0	NA	1.0
17175	Stark, IL	8	6 402	19.7	2	6	50.0	16.7	33.3	1 302	59.0	15.9	25.1	2.5	NA	1.1
17177	Stephenson, IL	4	49 167	19.2	6	24	45.8	29.2	20.8	8 220	42.8	28.1	28.8	4.1	NA	14.5
17179	Tazewell, IL	2	128 366	20.0	20	53	58.5	26.4	13.2	21 634	41.7	24.9	30.0	4.0	NA	2.0
17181	Union, IL	7	18 079	17.5	7	16	50.0	25.0	25.0	3 609	59.0	13.9	27.2	2.3	NA	4.1
17183	Vermilion, IL	4	85 260	19.7	13	43	51.2	23.3	20.9	15 421	48.4	20.0	26.0	4.3	NA	18.1
17185	Wabash, IL	7	12 681	20.1	2	5	80.0	—	20.0	2 314	66.7	—	33.3	7.1	NA	0.9
17187	Warren, IL	7	18 901	19.7	5	16	50.0	18.8	31.3	3 448	54.0	11.1	34.9	3.6	NA	3.9
17189	Washington, IL	6	15 204	20.0	7	10	80.0	—	20.0	2 447	62.0	—	38.0	3.0	NA	0.4
17191	Wayne, IL	7	17 049	18.6	8	15	73.3	6.7	20.0	3 034	65.3	4.6	30.2	2.7	NA	0.4
17193	White, IL	6	15 840	17.8	3	11	45.5	18.2	27.3	3 102	43.6	21.2	33.3	6.6	NA	1.4
17195	Whiteside, IL	4	60 225	20.5	12	34	58.8	17.6	20.6	11 479	52.2	14.2	28.1	4.4	NA	11.4
17197	Will, IL	0	427 818	22.1	32	118	61.0	24.6	10.2	67 906	49.6	21.3	25.3	4.5	NA	24.4
17199	Williamson, IL	5	60 764	17.9	6	27	66.7	11.1	22.2	9 674	55.9	14.3	29.8	7.0	NA	4.8
17201	Winnebago, IL	2	264 873	19.2	11	82	68.3	14.6	12.2	42 988	55.5	18.9	24.5	4.2	NA	26.0
17203	Woodford, IL	2	34 798	22.0	9	25	52.0	24.0	20.0	7 771	49.2	19.4	26.4	2.2	NA	1.2
18000	**INDIANA**															
18001	Adams, IN	2	32 686	22.5	3	11	45.5	27.3	27.3	5 280	37.8	23.9	38.3	11.2	12.0	4.2
18003	Allen, IN	2	310 803	19.5	4	85	64.7	18.8	14.1	49 666	48.5	19.9	29.5	12.2	23.8	23.1
18005	Bartholomew, IN	4	68 441	18.2	2	18	72.2	11.1	16.7	11 495	55.5	14.2	30.4	14.9	16.0	5.5
18007	Benton, IN	8	9 669	20.2	1	6	66.7	—	33.3	2 130	49.8	—	50.2	16.9	17.4	3.0
18009	Blackford, IN	6	14 134	17.9	1	8	62.5	25.0	12.5	2 384	44.7	26.5	28.8	17.7	21.1	0.6
18011	Boone, IN	1	42 453	19.2	3	14	64.3	14.3	21.4	7 629	49.9	17.7	32.4	10.7	8.3	1.2

1. County type code is from the Economic Research Service of the USDA. See notes and definitions at the end of this section.   2. IEP = Individual Education Program. See notes and definitions at the end of this section.

Table D-2. School and Student Characteristics by County — Continued

County	Staff and students, 1995–1996						Revenues, fiscal 1995					Current expenditures, fiscal 1995		
								Percent of Revenue from						
	Number of teachers	Pupil/ teacher ratio	Number of graduates	Dropouts grades 9–12 (percent)	Local school non-teaching staff	Central admin. staff	Total revenue ($1000)	Federal Gov't	State Gov't	Local Gov't	Amount	Amount per pupil	Percent for instruction
	15	16	17	18	19	20	21	22	23	24	25	26	27
ILLINOIS—Con.													
Kane, IL	4 317	20.0	4 478	NA	3 612	157	446 487	3.6	27.9	68.6	375 269	4 540	62.3
Kankakee, IL	1 062	17.8	1 042	NA	846	53	99 289	7.7	50.8	41.5	86 283	4 766	62.4
Kendall, IL	469	19.1	501	NA	330	16	45 971	1.1	27.1	71.8	37 151	4 264	60.8
Knox, IL	524	17.1	594	NA	390	16	45 139	6.1	51.4	42.5	35 469	4 019	62.2
Lake, IL	6 279	17.3	5 687	NA	4 818	325	732 465	2.6	18.3	79.1	590 748	5 757	57.8
La Salle, IL	1 125	15.8	1 117	NA	837	59	100 127	4.0	36.4	59.6	87 959	5 095	57.9
Lawrence, IL	184	15.0	200	NA	130	5	13 838	6.9	69.6	23.5	11 865	4 227	60.8
Lee, IL	343	16.8	329	NA	224	8	29 229	3.0	43.7	53.3	24 162	4 191	59.7
Livingston, IL	517	16.2	487	NA	326	14	41 892	3.1	45.4	51.5	35 322	4 477	60.4
Logan, IL	273	16.8	260	NA	194	12	22 055	4.6	37.0	58.5	18 798	4 514	59.1
McDonough, IL	301	14.8	299	NA	267	9	24 317	4.3	50.7	45.0	19 897	4 309	57.9
McHenry, IL	1 982	19.2	2 102	NA	1 683	65	177 836	2.2	23.4	74.4	161 358	4 423	62.2
McLean, IL	1 399	16.8	1 313	NA	1 011	46	119 443	3.2	30.5	66.3	96 279	4 468	59.1
Macon, IL	991	20.5	1 197	NA	840	55	93 666	6.0	53.5	40.5	79 320	3 994	53.9
Macoupin, IL	559	18.3	691	NA	398	13	48 554	4.9	62.3	32.7	39 036	3 864	59.7
Madison, IL	2 311	19.2	2 552	NA	1 728	74	210 886	6.1	46.9	47.0	181 712	4 195	57.9
Marion, IL	477	18.2	384	NA	434	19	40 582	6.5	62.9	30.6	33 796	3 936	59.3
Marshall, IL	124	14.2	34	NA	94	3	9 074	3.1	43.1	53.8	7 933	4 559	62.6
Mason, IL	244	14.9	241	NA	143	4	19 769	5.6	52.4	42.0	16 870	4 644	58.6
Massac, IL	149	17.7	175	NA	140	3	12 782	5.4	56.6	38.0	11 421	4 278	58.5
Menard, IL	156	17.8	157	NA	125	3	13 435	3.6	50.3	46.1	9 799	3 613	59.2
Mercer, IL	231	16.2	251	NA	172	3	16 880	4.0	60.4	35.6	14 572	3 879	58.7
Monroe, IL	242	18.3	248	NA	129	6	23 323	25.2	34.0	40.8	15 401	3 859	60.3
Montgomery, Il	305	18.6	302	NA	252	8	29 090	5.1	52.2	42.6	22 553	4 095	56.3
Morgan, IL	384	15.7	353	NA	334	20	28 814	3.9	43.1	53.1	25 282	4 182	59.0
Moultrie, IL	128	15.5	119	NA	83	3	9 739	3.7	47.2	49.2	7 814	3 925	59.9
Ogle, IL	633	15.9	591	NA	465	26	66 701	1.6	30.5	68.0	51 038	5 153	63.1
Peoria, IL	1 640	17.3	1 776	NA	1 442	62	172 176	7.3	42.8	49.9	134 735	4 708	57.3
Perry, IL	197	15.8	249	NA	128	6	16 001	6.1	60.0	33.9	13 294	4 283	62.0
Piatt, IL	210	16.4	203	NA	112	5	16 929	2.3	25.3	72.4	14 372	4 256	56.1
Pike, IL	235	13.2	191	NA	139	6	16 081	7.4	57.7	34.9	14 317	4 484	62.9
Pope, IL	47	14.4	41	NA	37	1	3 519	6.5	73.0	20.5	3 278	4 856	61.8
Pulaski, IL	117	15.4	102	NA	113	12	9 245	11.6	76.7	11.7	8 509	4 693	61.8
Putnam, IL	57	18.7	63	NA	41	7	5 394	3.4	23.8	72.8	4 337	4 146	56.8
Randolph, IL	313	16.5	397	NA	207	11	25 479	4.6	52.1	43.3	21 966	4 235	60.8
Richland, IL	184	15.9	162	NA	143	6	13 294	5.8	66.5	27.7	11 616	3 993	57.9
Rock Island, IL	1 390	17.9	1 390	NA	1 082	47	140 547	6.8	41.7	51.5	109 029	4 446	63.1
St. Clair, IL	2 515	18.8	2 663	NA	1 812	75	252 864	10.5	56.7	32.8	218 357	4 623	60.8
Saline, IL	271	17.0	325	NA	228	10	23 023	6.5	65.1	28.4	20 404	4 398	63.0
Sangamon, IL	2 068	20.1	1 669	NA	1 701	99	158 054	5.6	39.8	54.6	133 409	4 742	53.4
Schuyler, IL	81	15.2	73	NA	69	2	5 736	5.9	62.5	31.6	5 441	4 549	63.6
Scott, IL	74	15.0	73	NA	68	2	5 558	4.3	59.1	36.6	4 993	4 623	61.3
Shelby, IL	305	15.1	309	NA	212	9	22 643	3.7	57.0	39.4	18 640	4 128	60.5
Stark, IL	100	13.0	91	NA	57	2	7 526	3.5	48.8	47.7	5 964	4 484	59.9
Stephenson, IL	465	17.7	482	NA	411	11	40 644	4.2	47.3	48.4	38 184	4 727	54.5
Tazewell, IL	1 239	17.5	1 336	NA	904	54	107 417	3.7	43.1	53.1	90 289	4 394	61.7
Union, IL	219	16.5	205	NA	156	6	17 810	7.9	65.3	26.8	14 980	4 222	60.2
Vermilion, IL	983	15.7	870	NA	722	37	83 997	5.8	55.5	38.7	68 877	4 554	60.2
Wabash, IL	137	16.9	191	NA	111	4	11 511	4.0	60.7	35.3	10 733	4 654	62.8
Warren, IL	230	15.0	209	NA	139	9	17 900	5.2	53.9	40.9	14 621	4 197	61.8
Washington, IL	126	19.4	163	NA	89	7	11 382	2.9	51.4	45.7	9 518	3 974	57.4
Wayne, IL	200	15.1	215	NA	159	8	15 696	5.6	64.6	29.8	13 052	4 228	61.7
White, IL	199	15.6	191	NA	188	3	16 221	8.0	60.2	31.8	14 331	4 623	60.4
Whiteside, IL	671	17.1	753	NA	449	19	56 471	3.8	46.0	50.2	48 257	4 446	61.1
Will, IL	3 269	20.8	3 819	NA	2 503	148	366 223	3.0	28.7	68.3	300 201	4 620	57.4
Williamson, IL	463	20.9	502	NA	360	15	42 821	6.3	55.5	38.2	34 460	3 562	60.7
Winnebago, IL	2 512	17.1	2 117	NA	2 333	139	247 173	4.6	37.4	58.0	230 791	5 455	58.7
Woodford, IL	487	15.9	556	NA	316	11	38 892	2.8	48.0	49.2	32 983	4 209	61.8
INDIANA													
Adams, IN	287	18.4	391	3.7	146	20	32 102	5.6	52.3	42.2	24 869	4 796	58.0
Allen, IN	2 665	18.6	2 925	3.7	1 565	107	326 008	4.2	47.7	48.2	268 003	5 460	61.8
Bartholomew, IN	674	17.0	730	3.9	354	19	76 587	5.0	47.5	47.5	63 661	5 698	64.7
Benton, IN	137	15.5	164	3.1	62	5	14 206	1.7	49.1	49.2	11 931	5 440	58.1
Blackford, IN	155	15.4	200	3.6	77	9	13 911	4.5	62.3	33.2	12 847	5 375	65.2
Boone, IN	404	18.9	454	1.9	231	21	45 333	2.0	50.4	47.7	33 789	4 520	59.0

Table D-2. School and Student Characteristics by County

State/County code	County	County type[1]	Population, 1996		Number of school districts, 1995–1996	Level of schools, 1995–1996				Level of students, 1995–1996				Characteristics of students, 1995–1996		
			Total persons	Percent age 5–17		Number of schools	Percent			Number of students	Percent			Percent with IEP[2]	Percent free-lunch eligible	Percent minority
							Primary	Middle	High		Primary	Middle	High			
		1	2		3	4	5	6	7	8	9	10	11	12	13	14
INDIANA—Con.																
18013	Brown, IN	8	15 485	17.9	1	6	66.7	16.7	16.7	2 482	52.1	16.8	31.2	14.4	14.7	1.6
18015	Carroll, IN	6	19 643	18.9	2	6	50.0	16.7	33.3	2 909	50.5	14.2	35.3	11.6	12.6	1.6
18017	Cass, IN	6	38 829	19.2	3	13	53.8	15.4	30.8	7 065	48.5	13.1	38.4	14.8	20.4	3.8
18019	Clark, IN	2	92 530	18.7	3	30	63.3	13.3	20.0	14 349	50.4	15.8	30.8	14.6	25.7	10.9
18021	Clay, IN	3	26 491	18.8	1	10	60.0	10.0	20.0	4 764	46.3	12.8	33.9	16.1	19.1	0.3
18023	Clinton, IN	3	32 876	19.8	4	13	61.5	7.7	30.8	6 361	51.5	11.6	36.9	10.4	17.2	4.0
18025	Crawford, IN	8	10 559	20.1	1	6	83.3	—	16.7	1 935	55.1	—	44.9	15.7	35.2	—
18027	Daviess, IN	7	28 760	20.5	3	13	69.2	7.7	15.4	4 504	53.8	9.2	23.2	17.3	22.4	1.1
18029	Dearborn, IN	1	45 236	20.6	3	14	57.1	21.4	21.4	8 493	47.8	19.8	32.4	15.1	15.9	0.8
18031	Decatur, IN	6	25 105	21.0	2	10	50.0	20.0	30.0	4 445	43.4	14.6	42.0	12.8	11.8	0.6
18033	De Kalb, IN	2	38 272	20.7	3	14	64.3	7.1	21.4	7 359	46.6	12.0	36.8	11.6	9.4	1.1
18035	Delaware, IN	3	118 600	15.7	8	40	60.0	15.0	22.5	17 955	45.4	20.7	30.7	15.6	27.1	11.1
18037	Dubois, IN	7	39 088	19.6	4	18	61.1	16.7	22.2	7 252	47.2	19.0	33.8	10.8	6.7	1.0
18039	Elkhart, IN	3	168 941	19.5	7	52	69.2	15.4	15.4	30 508	54.8	17.5	27.7	14.7	18.6	13.3
18041	Fayette, IN	7	26 237	19.8	1	10	80.0	10.0	10.0	4 449	51.9	16.1	32.1	19.4	30.3	2.1
18043	Floyd, IN	2	70 746	19.0	1	18	77.8	11.1	11.1	11 312	52.7	14.7	32.5	14.2	24.1	7.3
18045	Fountain, IN	6	18 207	18.6	3	7	42.9	14.3	42.9	3 331	51.5	7.7	40.8	13.5	16.2	1.0
18047	Franklin, IN	6	21 530	21.5	1	5	60.0	20.0	20.0	2 816	55.7	13.0	31.3	17.2	21.9	0.2
18049	Fulton, IN	7	20 223	19.1	2	6	50.0	16.7	33.3	2 785	47.8	17.9	34.3	10.1	12.4	1.6
18051	Gibson, IN	6	32 058	18.5	4	14	71.4	7.1	21.4	5 478	57.5	10.7	31.8	13.6	13.8	2.9
18053	Grant, IN	4	73 469	17.7	4	28	64.3	21.4	14.3	11 897	46.4	24.7	28.9	11.7	25.7	14.1
18055	Greene, IN	6	32 942	18.4	5	13	46.2	15.4	38.5	6 014	55.6	6.7	37.6	12.9	20.9	0.5
18057	Hamilton, IN	0	147 719	20.2	6	39	61.5	17.9	12.8	26 942	46.8	24.8	25.7	11.5	4.5	3.4
18059	Hancock, IN	1	52 000	20.4	4	18	55.6	22.2	22.2	9 571	47.5	19.3	33.2	17.2	6.7	0.5
18061	Harrison, IN	2	33 349	20.8	3	15	46.7	26.7	26.7	6 055	38.1	26.6	35.4	14.5	17.5	0.7
18063	Hendricks, IN	1	89 343	20.1	6	29	62.1	17.2	20.7	16 161	48.6	19.6	31.8	10.7	5.8	0.9
18065	Henry, IN	6	49 135	18.0	5	23	60.9	13.0	26.1	8 731	52.2	15.2	32.6	18.0	20.3	1.7
18067	Howard, IN	3	84 126	19.1	5	27	70.4	11.1	18.5	14 461	57.0	12.3	30.7	16.2	21.7	10.6
18069	Huntington, IN	2	37 024	19.8	1	11	72.7	18.2	9.1	6 870	51.3	17.3	31.4	11.1	11.6	1.2
18071	Jackson, IN	7	40 467	19.5	4	15	60.0	13.3	26.7	6 568	44.8	20.6	34.6	12.8	17.9	2.1
18073	Jasper, IN	6	28 368	21.0	2	8	50.0	25.0	25.0	4 852	43.0	23.7	33.2	14.2	14.4	2.5
18075	Jay, IN	6	21 733	19.1	1	10	70.0	20.0	10.0	4 022	53.2	15.5	31.4	15.7	22.3	1.0
18077	Jefferson, IN	6	31 039	18.2	2	12	66.7	16.7	16.7	4 871	49.0	21.2	29.7	19.4	22.6	2.0
18079	Jennings, IN	7	26 747	19.6	1	8	75.0	12.5	12.5	4 630	54.6	16.0	29.4	16.2	21.3	1.7
18081	Johnson, IN	0	104 280	19.5	7	32	59.4	18.8	18.8	18 724	49.8	20.7	29.3	11.0	10.1	1.6
18083	Knox, IN	5	39 667	16.6	3	15	66.7	13.3	20.0	6 418	52.2	17.4	30.4	15.2	25.2	1.8
18085	Kosciusko, IN	6	69 932	20.1	4	28	64.3	17.9	17.9	14 384	50.9	19.0	30.1	11.1	12.8	3.6
18087	Lagrange, IN	8	32 103	24.1	3	14	57.1	21.4	21.4	6 332	47.5	22.0	30.4	11.5	10.3	3.0
18089	Lake, IN	0	479 940	20.3	16	149	66.4	16.1	14.1	85 849	46.8	19.0	29.2	11.4	32.3	45.2
18091	La Porte, IN	4	109 604	18.2	7	39	66.7	15.4	15.4	17 907	46.4	23.6	28.9	13.8	17.9	14.7
18093	Lawrence, IN	6	45 361	18.5	2	19	57.9	26.3	10.5	7 593	46.1	23.8	29.7	12.0	23.7	1.6
18095	Madison, IN	3	132 782	17.8	5	42	66.7	14.3	19.0	20 812	50.9	15.6	33.5	15.9	26.4	11.0
18097	Marion, IN	0	817 525	17.2	13	198	67.7	19.2	9.1	124 250	50.6	23.3	25.4	13.5	34.7	36.6
18099	Marshall, IN	6	45 173	20.2	5	15	60.0	6.7	33.3	7 960	52.7	10.4	36.9	12.0	16.7	5.1
18101	Martin, IN	7	10 581	19.6	2	5	40.0	20.0	40.0	1 963	40.2	13.7	46.2	15.3	24.4	0.2
18103	Miami, IN	6	32 686	20.4	4	18	61.1	16.7	22.2	7 728	51.3	15.0	33.7	14.1	19.6	5.7
18105	Monroe, IN	3	116 176	12.9	2	24	70.8	12.5	16.7	13 440	52.6	17.3	30.2	11.4	17.5	7.7
18107	Montgomery, IN	6	36 349	17.9	3	19	68.4	15.8	15.8	6 407	49.7	21.1	29.1	15.8	15.9	1.7
18109	Morgan, IN	1	63 244	20.2	4	23	65.2	17.4	17.4	11 149	46.9	20.3	32.7	13.0	12.9	5.3
18111	Newton, IN	8	14 611	21.3	2	8	75.0	—	25.0	2 846	52.5	—	47.5	13.5	18.3	3.8
18113	Noble, IN	6	41 449	20.8	3	16	62.5	18.8	18.8	7 789	50.6	21.6	27.8	9.7	14.6	5.3
18115	Ohio, IN	1	5 490	18.9	1	2	50.0	—	50.0	1 030	69.1	—	30.9	13.4	14.1	0.8
18117	Orange, IN	7	19 221	19.3	3	6	50.0	—	50.0	3 493	53.3	—	46.7	15.4	31.3	1.7
18119	Owen, IN	6	20 158	19.2	1	5	60.0	20.0	20.0	3 132	46.7	23.9	29.4	13.6	21.6	0.3
18121	Parke, IN	6	16 339	17.4	3	7	57.1	—	42.9	2 626	55.6	—	44.4	16.8	21.8	0.4
18123	Perry, IN	7	19 210	19.0	3	8	50.0	12.5	37.5	3 490	47.2	13.2	39.6	11.3	17.8	0.2
18125	Pike, IN	8	12 569	17.6	1	4	75.0	—	—	2 115	48.5	—	—	15.7	24.6	0.6
18127	Porter, IN	1	142 363	20.3	8	46	63.0	15.2	19.6	25 666	43.5	20.7	35.4	12.3	10.1	5.3
18129	Posey, IN	2	26 505	19.9	3	11	54.5	18.2	18.2	4 880	45.2	19.8	29.3	17.4	14.8	1.7
18131	Pulaski, IN	9	13 103	20.3	2	5	40.0	20.0	40.0	2 617	49.7	14.9	35.5	13.1	17.3	1.2
18133	Putnam, IN	6	33 451	17.0	4	16	56.3	12.5	25.0	6 772	48.2	13.6	34.3	16.0	16.1	1.7
18135	Randolph, IN	6	27 530	18.9	4	14	50.0	14.3	35.7	5 163	47.2	13.8	39.0	16.7	17.7	1.4
18137	Ripley, IN	6	26 932	20.6	4	10	40.0	20.0	40.0	5 219	46.5	12.1	41.4	12.0	15.9	0.5
18139	Rush, IN	6	18 285	20.5	1	6	66.7	16.7	16.7	2 881	50.4	17.0	32.6	14.2	16.1	1.0
18141	St. Joseph, IN	3	257 740	17.6	5	66	69.7	13.6	13.6	38 957	53.6	16.0	30.1	15.1	29.3	23.9
18143	Scott, IN	2	22 652	20.1	2	9	55.6	22.2	22.2	4 173	46.6	23.0	30.4	13.4	30.7	0.9

1. County type code is from the Economic Research Service of the USDA. See notes and definitions at the end of this section. 2. IEP = Individual Education Program. See notes and definitions at the end of this section.

Table D-2. School and Student Characteristics by County — Continued

County	Staff and students, 1995–1996						Revenues, fiscal 1995				Current expenditures, fiscal 1995		
	Number of teachers	Pupil/ teacher ratio	Number of graduates	Dropouts grades 9–12 (percent)	Local school non-teaching staff	Central admin. staff	Total revenue ($1000)	Percent of Revenue from			Amount	Amount per pupil	Percent for instruction
								Federal Gov't	State Gov't	Local Gov't			
	15	16	17	18	19	20	21	22	23	24	25	26	27
INDIANA—Con.													
Brown, IN	126	19.7	161	5.8	83	10	14 864	2.5	56.0	41.5	11 728	4 846	58.7
Carroll, IN	160	18.2	184	5.0	83	7	19 110	2.2	48.4	49.3	13 090	4 556	60.4
Cass, IN	476	14.8	470	4.2	303	15	50 663	5.2	48.4	46.4	37 869	5 396	62.4
Clark, IN	809	17.7	878	4.7	505	42	101 309	4.5	55.9	39.7	76 873	5 351	62.5
Clay, IN	260	18.3	300	4.1	158	11	30 123	3.9	55.6	40.5	22 304	4 745	64.6
Clinton, IN	363	17.5	380	3.7	184	19	38 385	4.9	55.4	39.7	31 008	4 901	61.5
Crawford, IN	93	20.8	117	7.3	50	3	10 612	5.6	67.4	27.0	8 538	4 532	63.4
Daviess, IN	229	19.7	266	6.1	108	10	28 171	7.6	51.4	41.0	23 164	5 298	63.2
Dearborn, IN	444	19.1	560	2.4	260	20	51 554	3.9	56.5	39.6	41 048	4 913	61.6
Decatur, IN	249	17.8	324	5.0	124	9	25 905	3.0	57.3	39.7	21 414	4 759	61.4
De Kalb, IN	416	17.7	556	6.9	195	24	45 436	6.5	49.9	43.6	38 565	5 246	60.4
Delaware, IN	1 060	16.9	1 160	5.5	561	47	122 514	5.9	54.5	39.7	98 542	5 722	58.9
Dubois, IN	353	20.5	487	2.2	200	25	50 394	3.3	41.1	55.6	38 751	5 436	63.3
Elkhart, IN	1 620	18.8	1 558	7.0	956	70	202 729	3.9	43.5	52.7	156 672	5 290	60.6
Fayette, IN	270	16.5	253	7.6	275	20	42 154	7.1	43.1	49.8	33 054	7 195	63.6
Floyd, IN	579	19.5	561	5.9	421	23	72 479	7.1	51.8	41.1	60 742	5 463	63.2
Fountain, IN	208	16.0	204	3.0	100	11	19 374	3.9	57.1	39.0	15 720	4 804	62.3
Franklin, IN	143	19.7	189	7.3	65	7	17 008	2.3	65.4	32.4	12 791	4 608	57.6
Fulton, IN	147	18.9	173	2.7	68	9	17 269	2.7	51.9	45.4	12 792	4 705	62.7
Gibson, IN	333	16.4	350	3.7	195	15	38 470	4.8	45.3	49.9	32 097	6 101	59.3
Grant, IN	693	17.2	686	2.8	385	49	80 473	6.7	57.1	36.3	66 264	5 540	60.8
Greene, IN	342	17.6	353	3.0	151	18	36 340	5.8	59.6	34.5	30 814	5 176	64.5
Hamilton, IN	1 527	17.6	1 466	2.5	731	81	178 994	1.5	39.3	59.2	129 496	5 024	61.6
Hancock, IN	553	17.3	649	2.0	296	39	60 860	3.3	49.7	47.0	45 567	4 873	61.4
Harrison, IN	321	18.9	364	3.2	187	17	38 215	4.1	57.5	38.4	28 383	4 734	61.3
Hendricks, IN	857	18.9	1 027	2.0	447	39	100 884	1.4	49.6	49.0	75 508	4 825	59.6
Henry, IN	517	16.9	545	4.2	338	81	58 729	5.7	57.8	36.5	46 043	5 332	62.6
Howard, IN	864	16.7	898	2.8	514	47	98 024	6.1	47.8	46.1	81 362	5 690	62.1
Huntington, IN	376	18.3	400	4.2	214	14	39 449	3.6	56.7	39.7	32 967	4 757	65.2
Jackson, IN	341	19.2	492	4.2	185	12	37 254	3.3	56.3	40.5	30 199	4 640	62.7
Jasper, IN	264	18.4	307	4.2	156	9	28 780	2.3	41.5	56.1	23 704	5 018	60.5
Jay, IN	239	16.9	237	3.6	144	12	23 958	6.7	60.1	33.1	20 055	4 958	61.3
Jefferson, IN	283	17.2	503	7.5	142	14	36 934	6.7	48.3	44.9	30 678	6 284	63.7
Jennings, IN	216	21.4	257	4.4	127	5	24 993	2.4	67.7	29.8	19 482	4 278	59.7
Johnson, IN	919	20.4	1 155	2.6	564	64	118 657	2.9	47.7	49.4	88 566	4 858	61.1
Knox, IN	364	17.6	368	4.1	203	19	39 184	5.6	58.8	35.6	31 410	4 899	61.1
Kosciusko, IN	778	18.5	846	4.5	431	46	92 945	3.3	46.8	49.9	70 331	4 925	61.5
Lagrange, IN	348	18.2	345	4.9	178	12	37 532	3.9	51.8	44.3	28 872	4 576	61.1
Lake, IN	4 410	19.5	5 159	3.7	2 657	259	609 489	5.6	55.9	38.5	487 509	5 660	60.4
La Porte, IN	1 030	17.4	1 074	5.1	593	39	120 049	4.1	52.2	43.7	96 889	5 307	62.3
Lawrence, IN	389	19.5	457	6.3	251	14	47 732	4.3	53.4	42.3	38 332	5 123	60.2
Madison, IN	1 228	17.0	1 328	4.2	557	55	133 631	5.4	60.4	34.2	112 171	5 327	63.9
Marion, IN	6 943	17.9	5 697	6.7	4 076	335	947 385	5.2	50.0	44.8	724 065	5 892	61.4
Marshall, IN	403	19.8	459	4.3	233	27	52 211	4.2	46.2	49.5	40 250	5 074	60.0
Martin, IN	102	19.3	145	2.8	46	8	11 577	4.8	64.7	30.5	9 374	4 773	62.6
Miami, IN	421	18.3	503	4.8	247	24	49 495	5.3	64.5	30.2	38 298	4 981	60.8
Monroe, IN	720	18.7	732	5.5	505	24	85 338	3.6	44.7	51.7	66 632	5 034	59.6
Montgomery, IN	407	15.7	372	4.3	203	58	46 383	5.1	42.2	52.7	34 681	5 560	59.4
Morgan, IN	608	18.3	702	7.1	277	24	62 402	3.2	61.2	35.6	49 399	4 481	62.4
Newton, IN	159	17.9	167	5.1	74	8	17 396	3.1	53.2	43.7	13 413	4 728	56.7
Noble, IN	405	19.2	408	4.3	289	14	45 387	2.8	52.6	44.6	34 527	4 524	62.0
Ohio, IN	48	21.4	74	3.8	33	2	5 112	2.4	73.8	23.8	4 255	4 188	66.4
Orange, IN	170	20.6	208	3.7	97	13	22 152	4.7	56.9	38.3	16 897	4 895	62.3
Owen, IN	174	18.1	169	4.1	88	7	16 957	3.8	67.4	28.9	13 967	4 637	65.5
Parke, IN	160	16.4	184	5.8	70	9	16 560	3.6	56.4	40.1	12 786	4 782	58.0
Perry, IN	193	18.1	238	3.3	82	8	19 935	3.8	65.7	30.5	16 754	4 769	63.3
Pike, IN	119	17.7	129	6.8	57	7	12 366	4.8	42.8	52.4	10 637	5 131	64.3
Porter, IN	1 407	18.2	1 902	2.2	739	64	178 906	2.8	44.9	52.4	137 899	5 463	59.7
Posey, IN	294	16.6	318	3.5	142	18	35 726	3.3	34.1	62.5	29 590	6 110	60.4
Pulaski, IN	140	18.7	171	3.2	81	9	15 637	7.2	48.6	44.2	12 845	4 910	59.3
Putnam, IN	365	18.5	354	3.6	214	29	45 002	3.4	56.4	40.2	32 137	4 927	56.9
Randolph, IN	307	16.8	343	5.0	167	23	30 333	5.1	60.5	34.5	25 522	5 001	61.1
Ripley, IN	279	18.7	322	3.3	154	18	33 377	4.0	53.9	42.1	26 641	5 220	59.2
Rush, IN	160	18.1	199	8.2	59	8	17 626	3.7	52.4	43.9	13 039	4 482	59.1
St. Joseph, IN	2 178	17.9	2 083	4.9	1 288	75	264 589	4.3	54.2	41.5	201 766	5 204	62.9
Scott, IN	216	19.4	250	5.4	127	30	24 207	6.1	65.7	28.2	20 329	5 016	61.6

Table D-2. School and Student Characteristics by County

State/ County code	County	County type[1]	Population, 1996		Number of school districts, 1995–1996	Level of schools, 1995–1996				Level of students, 1995–1996				Characteristics of students, 1995–1996		
			Total persons	Percent age 5–17		Number of schools	Percent			Number of students	Percent			Percent with IEP[2]	Percent free-lunch eligible	Percent minority
							Primary	Middle	High		Primary	Middle	High			
			1	2	3	4	5	6	7	8	9	10	11	12	13	14
	INDIANA—Con.															
18145	Shelby, IN	1	42 951	19.5	5	16	50.0	12.5	31.3	7 893	47.0	17.7	34.9	12.8	14.1	2.0
18147	Spencer, IN	8	20 540	19.8	2	9	66.7	11.1	22.2	3 861	49.5	10.0	40.5	10.0	14.0	1.9
18149	Starke, IN	6	23 399	20.2	3	9	44.4	22.2	33.3	4 483	48.0	19.2	32.8	13.8	25.0	2.5
18151	Steuben, IN	6	30 831	18.4	3	10	50.0	20.0	30.0	4 854	47.1	21.4	31.5	10.3	13.5	1.3
18153	Sullivan, IN	6	20 115	17.8	2	11	63.6	9.1	27.3	3 623	57.4	9.2	33.5	15.3	21.7	0.1
18155	Switzerland, IN	8	8 380	19.8	1	3	66.7	—	33.3	1 552	51.9	—	48.1	17.1	29.8	1.0
18157	Tippecanoe, IN	3	138 324	14.7	3	32	62.5	25.0	12.5	18 226	47.7	22.2	30.2	15.3	15.4	8.0
18159	Tipton, IN	3	16 453	19.2	2	6	50.0	16.7	33.3	2 913	45.5	16.2	38.3	12.5	11.4	1.8
18161	Union, IN	8	7 345	20.5	1	4	50.0	25.0	25.0	1 618	43.2	24.0	32.8	13.9	18.0	0.4
18163	Vanderburgh, IN	2	167 716	16.5	1	38	52.6	28.9	18.4	23 713	46.9	23.3	29.8	16.7	30.2	15.3
18165	Vermillion, IN	3	16 791	18.4	2	7	57.1	14.3	28.6	2 993	44.7	17.0	38.3	14.2	22.5	0.5
18167	Vigo, IN	3	106 389	16.5	1	30	66.7	20.0	13.3	16 971	48.0	23.6	28.4	15.8	28.1	8.5
18169	Wabash, IN	7	34 661	18.8	3	16	56.3	12.5	31.3	6 453	48.8	11.8	39.4	15.7	13.8	2.0
18171	Warren, IN	8	8 188	18.3	1	4	75.0	—	25.0	1 306	55.2	—	44.8	16.2	17.4	0.2
18173	Warrick, IN	2	50 070	20.7	1	15	66.7	13.3	20.0	8 971	52.3	14.3	33.4	13.8	12.7	1.4
18175	Washington, IN	6	26 689	20.2	3	9	44.4	22.2	33.3	4 681	46.0	18.6	35.4	15.1	23.1	0.3
18177	Wayne, IN	5	72 017	18.2	5	29	62.1	17.2	17.2	12 217	48.9	17.6	33.4	17.1	27.2	8.0
18179	Wells, IN	2	26 651	20.1	3	9	44.4	22.2	33.3	5 260	44.5	22.5	33.0	10.5	9.8	1.6
18181	White, IN	6	25 081	19.8	4	15	66.7	6.7	20.0	5 612	49.6	11.3	29.5	14.4	14.1	1.8
18183	Whitley, IN	2	29 863	20.3	2	9	66.7	11.1	11.1	5 089	52.4	10.1	22.2	11.5	7.9	1.2
19000	**IOWA**															
19001	Adair, IA	8	8 224	18.5	3	6	50.0	16.7	16.7	1 292	50.7	10.3	23.4	12.1	23.2	0.9
19003	Adams, IA	9	4 494	17.3	2	4	50.0	25.0	25.0	765	54.8	14.8	30.5	15.3	24.4	0.3
19005	Allamakee, IA	7	14 002	20.0	3	10	50.0	20.0	30.0	2 764	49.6	23.2	27.2	14.9	20.8	1.4
19007	Appanoose, IA	7	13 616	18.8	3	12	58.3	16.7	25.0	2 524	34.9	27.5	37.7	15.6	34.5	1.5
19009	Audubon, IA	7	6 894	18.2	2	5	40.0	20.0	40.0	1 209	38.4	16.3	45.3	9.8	17.3	1.3
19011	Benton, IA	6	24 510	20.2	4	15	60.0	20.0	20.0	4 176	54.4	14.8	30.9	11.8	15.8	1.1
19013	Black Hawk, IA	3	122 806	18.7	6	41	61.0	17.1	17.1	18 250	47.4	22.0	29.3	17.3	28.4	18.3
19015	Boone, IA	6	25 875	17.8	5	17	58.8	17.6	23.5	4 207	49.8	18.2	32.1	12.4	12.7	1.4
19017	Bremer, IA	6	23 280	18.9	7	25	56.0	20.0	20.0	5 793	43.2	18.9	32.5	11.2	12.4	1.1
19019	Buchanan, IA	6	21 175	22.8	3	15	60.0	20.0	20.0	3 452	47.7	22.5	29.8	14.2	17.2	1.5
19021	Buena Vista, IA	7	19 862	18.8	5	20	45.0	30.0	20.0	3 894	36.9	29.1	28.4	12.6	27.1	12.8
19023	Butler, IA	8	15 781	19.9	6	12	50.0	16.7	16.7	2 526	47.6	14.1	21.1	13.3	15.8	0.9
19025	Calhoun, IA	9	11 478	18.2	5	14	42.9	28.6	28.6	2 664	44.3	23.7	32.0	9.2	18.9	1.1
19027	Carroll, IA	7	21 536	21.5	4	11	36.4	18.2	45.5	3 239	40.8	23.6	35.6	11.7	18.5	1.1
19029	Cass, IA	6	14 930	19.0	2	13	61.5	7.7	23.1	3 238	48.8	9.9	28.8	14.1	22.2	1.9
19031	Cedar, IA	6	17 809	19.9	5	15	40.0	26.7	33.3	3 718	42.5	24.7	32.8	8.7	13.7	1.7
19033	Cerro Gordo, IA	5	46 584	17.9	5	21	52.4	23.8	23.8	7 404	43.9	25.5	30.7	13.1	19.1	6.1
19035	Cherokee, IA	7	13 477	20.1	4	16	50.0	31.3	18.8	2 790	37.4	34.4	28.2	12.0	14.9	2.2
19037	Chickasaw, IA	7	13 493	21.1	3	7	42.9	14.3	42.9	2 414	45.7	13.0	41.3	9.8	14.7	1.4
19039	Clarke, IA	6	8 255	19.2	2	5	40.0	20.0	40.0	1 820	53.4	13.0	33.6	15.9	27.8	1.0
19041	Clay, IA	7	17 598	19.9	3	11	63.6	18.2	18.2	3 095	50.2	17.9	32.0	12.4	16.8	2.3
19043	Clayton, IA	9	18 893	20.8	5	15	40.0	26.7	33.3	3 765	36.2	23.2	40.6	11.4	21.0	0.8
19045	Clinton, IA	4	50 471	19.6	6	27	59.3	18.5	22.2	9 101	44.3	22.9	32.8	12.5	18.7	5.1
19047	Crawford, IA	7	16 503	20.5	4	11	45.5	27.3	18.2	2 670	42.5	19.6	29.7	13.7	26.3	2.7
19049	Dallas, IA	2	33 900	20.5	8	23	47.8	26.1	26.1	7 649	48.8	22.5	28.7	11.7	13.9	4.2
19051	Davis, IA	7	8 447	19.8	1	3	33.3	33.3	33.3	1 330	35.3	31.4	33.3	12.0	22.9	0.6
19053	Decatur, IA	9	8 232	16.9	3	8	37.5	25.0	37.5	1 387	43.6	14.5	41.9	21.3	35.8	2.3
19055	Delaware, IA	6	18 506	22.5	3	11	63.6	9.1	27.3	3 811	46.5	17.4	36.1	9.3	17.5	1.2
19057	Des Moines, IA	5	42 564	18.9	4	24	54.2	25.0	20.8	7 532	43.1	24.4	32.5	15.7	21.2	9.3
19059	Dickinson, IA	7	15 725	17.8	4	10	40.0	20.0	30.0	2 857	39.0	24.3	29.8	12.6	14.5	1.9
19061	Dubuque, IA	3	88 201	20.0	2	26	69.2	11.5	19.2	12 610	46.6	15.3	38.1	17.0	19.0	3.3
19063	Emmet, IA	7	11 114	20.5	2	8	50.0	25.0	25.0	2 226	27.6	36.4	35.9	11.9	23.6	5.1
19065	Fayette, IA	6	22 061	19.3	5	16	62.5	6.3	31.3	4 453	52.1	9.3	38.6	11.9	20.1	1.7
19067	Floyd, IA	7	16 538	19.4	3	9	66.7	—	22.2	3 121	59.3	—	29.8	13.5	24.4	2.0
19069	Franklin, IA	7	11 017	19.0	3	11	63.6	9.1	27.3	2 098	47.1	15.8	37.1	8.4	19.0	6.7
19071	Fremont, IA	9	7 918	19.7	4	8	50.0	—	37.5	1 684	49.5	—	31.4	13.5	19.7	0.8
19073	Greene, IA	7	10 120	18.3	3	9	55.6	11.1	33.3	2 056	48.7	16.7	34.6	12.5	21.4	1.7
19075	Grundy, IA	8	12 340	19.0	3	12	41.7	16.7	33.3	2 748	43.1	11.2	32.2	12.4	13.0	1.9
19077	Guthrie, IA	8	11 420	18.9	4	11	45.5	18.2	36.4	2 343	47.2	11.8	40.9	12.1	20.9	0.7
19079	Hamilton, IA	7	16 102	18.7	4	12	50.0	25.0	16.7	3 116	39.6	21.1	22.7	10.8	18.0	3.1
19081	Hancock, IA	7	12 152	21.0	4	11	45.5	18.2	36.4	2 066	43.5	20.5	36.1	12.1	17.5	1.5
19083	Hardin, IA	7	18 682	18.9	6	14	42.9	21.4	28.6	3 680	42.4	19.2	29.0	10.3	20.7	3.1
19085	Harrison, IA	6	15 230	19.8	5	14	50.0	14.3	35.7	3 361	50.8	11.4	37.9	15.0	23.3	1.1
19087	Henry, IA	7	19 867	18.4	5	14	64.3	7.1	28.6	3 810	47.3	13.5	39.2	12.1	15.4	3.8

1. County type code is from the Economic Research Service of the USDA. See notes and definitions at the end of this section. 2. IEP = Individual Education Program. See notes and definitions at the end of this section.

Table D-2. School and Student Characteristics by County — Continued

County	Staff and students, 1995–1996						Revenues, fiscal 1995					Current expenditures, fiscal 1995		
								Percent of Revenue from						
	Number of teachers	Pupil/ teacher ratio	Number of graduates	Dropouts grades 9–12 (percent)	Local school non-teaching staff	Central admin. staff	Total revenue ($1000)	Federal Gov't	State Gov't	Local Gov't	Amount	Amount per pupil	Percent for instruction
	15	16	17	18	19	20	21	22	23	24	25	26	27
INDIANA—Con.													
Shelby, IN	403	19.6	498	2.9	214	18	46 997	3.2	53.5	43.3	36 519	4 680	63.6
Spencer, IN	201	19.2	260	2.3	107	6	22 850	2.4	44.6	53.0	18 474	4 858	62.4
Starke, IN	249	18.0	234	7.8	137	16	26 455	3.9	58.9	37.2	20 707	4 644	59.8
Steuben, IN	271	17.9	280	3.5	130	13	32 447	4.9	41.5	53.6	24 873	5 234	59.5
Sullivan, IN	224	16.2	271	4.7	87	6	24 809	3.2	44.7	52.1	19 189	5 311	64.0
Switzerland, IN	83	18.7	98	3.4	40	3	8 722	7.3	70.9	21.8	8 101	5 054	56.7
Tippecanoe, IN	998	18.3	1 079	3.3	488	37	129 757	2.9	41.2	55.9	93 597	5 241	60.8
Tipton, IN	167	17.5	229	4.8	92	8	18 425	2.3	54.5	43.2	14 168	4 782	58.9
Union, IN	86	18.7	103	1.1	37	5	8 314	1.6	61.8	36.6	6 257	4 248	62.8
Vanderburgh, IN	1 399	17.0	1 280	6.8	805	37	156 030	6.2	49.9	43.9	133 752	5 649	63.1
Vermillion, IN	194	15.5	216	6.2	84	7	19 953	5.6	42.3	52.2	15 816	5 174	60.7
Vigo, IN	967	17.6	960	7.3	578	26	104 257	6.2	53.8	40.0	82 627	4 894	60.6
Wabash, IN	354	18.2	440	3.9	230	15	43 819	4.5	51.1	44.4	34 583	5 363	63.3
Warren, IN	83	15.8	93	2.3	37	4	7 426	4.3	56.0	39.7	6 768	5 222	58.1
Warrick, IN	462	19.4	654	4.8	143	17	52 077	2.1	45.1	52.8	41 871	4 646	64.4
Washington, IN	237	19.8	262	5.6	126	16	27 525	6.3	61.1	32.7	22 173	4 830	63.3
Wayne, IN	618	19.8	738	4.6	534	75	79 064	5.1	57.8	37.1	62 256	5 049	62.4
Wells, IN	288	18.3	337	3.9	126	13	33 932	3.3	49.8	46.9	27 141	5 129	60.6
White, IN	311	18.1	380	2.8	162	20	35 097	2.4	44.8	52.8	25 551	4 583	59.7
Whitley, IN	264	19.3	344	2.7	141	24	31 143	2.7	54.6	42.7	24 275	4 872	61.2
IOWA							*						
Adair, IA	89	14.6	91	1.4	80	8	7 727	4.4	40.2	55.4	6 360	4 934	62.4
Adams, IA	53	14.5	55	1.3	42	6	4 497	5.8	39.6	54.6	3 809	4 928	63.9
Allamakee, IA	179	15.5	228	0.8	132	11	15 039	4.5	50.1	45.5	12 963	4 563	67.4
Appanoose, IA	186	13.6	138	7.4	129	10	14 617	6.4	53.7	40.0	12 555	5 038	66.4
Audubon, IA	96	12.6	72	1.3	80	9	7 451	4.3	43.4	52.3	5 755	4 776	61.3
Benton, IA	284	14.7	273	4.0	238	16	24 447	3.2	50.6	46.2	19 479	4 704	64.1
Black Hawk, IA	1 125	16.2	1 113	4.6	807	34	125 554	6.4	46.2	47.4	114 004	6 103	63.3
Boone, IA	293	14.3	266	3.5	218	17	24 835	2.5	48.7	48.8	20 114	4 869	64.4
Bremer, IA	374	15.5	407	1.1	229	22	31 912	2.9	51.3	45.8	26 869	4 577	63.6
Buchanan, IA	226	15.3	245	4.0	145	10	19 356	5.1	51.3	43.6	14 989	4 306	65.8
Buena Vista, IA	274	14.2	279	2.8	179	18	24 289	4.5	45.1	50.4	19 467	4 956	65.0
Butler, IA	189	13.4	156	1.0	114	16	17 555	3.0	45.4	51.6	12 970	4 706	61.8
Calhoun, IA	227	11.7	203	1.3	161	15	16 564	3.7	46.9	49.4	14 254	5 113	63.1
Carroll, IA	223	14.5	225	1.6	211	15	18 437	4.4	43.2	52.4	16 057	4 912	62.6
Cass, IA	217	14.9	201	2.7	174	15	18 952	3.6	45.4	51.0	14 935	4 590	65.2
Cedar, IA	269	13.8	289	1.5	200	17	20 417	2.8	44.5	52.7	17 392	4 765	65.8
Cerro Gordo, IA	500	14.8	477	4.5	348	22	50 558	6.1	39.5	54.3	45 241	6 061	55.9
Cherokee, IA	205	13.6	178	3.2	147	14	16 136	2.9	48.3	48.8	13 583	4 784	65.6
Chickasaw, IA	152	15.9	171	1.9	113	12	13 052	3.2	48.3	48.5	11 090	4 691	68.7
Clarke, IA	116	15.7	98	2.9	90	7	9 637	5.8	50.8	43.4	7 893	4 477	62.9
Clay, IA	207	15.0	207	2.1	164	10	18 347	3.1	49.6	47.3	14 462	4 643	66.9
Clayton, IA	254	14.8	289	1.4	174	18	34 200	10.2	31.7	58.1	29 565	7 863	41.3
Clinton, IA	568	16.0	600	5.7	488	30	53 335	3.0	53.0	44.0	46 470	4 988	65.1
Crawford, IA	197	13.6	189	1.2	157	15	15 740	5.1	47.3	47.6	13 151	4 736	65.4
Dallas, IA	501	15.3	376	3.1	378	27	42 379	2.3	45.8	52.0	33 233	4 561	64.5
Davis, IA	103	13.0	87	5.4	82	5	7 847	5.7	53.3	41.0	6 660	4 872	64.6
Decatur, IA	115	12.1	100	0.9	95	9	9 482	5.9	49.8	44.3	7 757	5 284	60.0
Delaware, IA	235	16.2	233	3.3	197	10	19 785	4.3	51.4	44.3	16 807	4 464	65.9
Des Moines, IA	501	15.0	467	3.3	404	17	48 432	5.6	45.8	48.6	42 715	5 573	59.9
Dickinson, IA	187	15.3	226	0.8	162	14	16 771	3.0	30.9	66.1	13 611	4 736	65.3
Dubuque, IA	800	15.8	902	1.8	734	22	70 529	4.2	48.8	47.0	62 464	5 018	63.6
Emmet, IA	157	14.2	148	0.9	127	8	18 517	8.4	36.8	54.8	15 013	6 649	51.2
Fayette, IA	283	15.7	330	2.1	189	17	25 704	4.5	50.4	45.0	22 106	4 883	65.6
Floyd, IA	235	13.3	231	2.2	170	10	18 668	4.5	48.5	47.0	15 751	4 904	65.9
Franklin, IA	137	15.4	176	2.6	117	9	10 630	3.1	43.7	53.3	9 435	4 758	63.9
Fremont, IA	137	12.3	143	3.7	93	12	9 753	4.6	43.8	51.6	8 288	4 901	65.4
Greene, IA	160	12.9	133	1.2	108	11	12 522	4.1	44.9	51.0	10 565	5 166	63.4
Grundy, IA	204	13.5	220	1.4	114	18	17 282	2.2	43.9	53.9	13 332	4 853	61.7
Guthrie, IA	190	12.4	211	2.1	127	13	13 497	4.0	45.1	50.9	11 428	4 830	62.6
Hamilton, IA	217	14.4	219	2.7	181	13	18 210	3.1	42.7	54.2	15 389	4 928	62.3
Hancock, IA	165	12.5	157	1.3	113	12	12 699	3.2	42.9	54.0	10 850	5 044	64.7
Hardin, IA	264	14.0	262	2.9	173	20	21 985	3.9	45.5	50.7	19 072	5 124	67.3
Harrison, IA	231	14.5	264	2.3	171	18	19 305	4.3	48.6	47.1	16 118	4 816	63.3
Henry, IA	267	14.3	265	3.6	189	17	21 681	2.6	50.3	47.1	17 800	4 502	66.1

Table D-2. School and Student Characteristics by County

State/ County code	County	County type[1]	Population, 1996		Number of school districts, 1995–1996	Level of schools, 1995–1996				Level of students, 1995–1996				Characteristics of students, 1995–1996		
			Total persons	Percent age 5–17		Number of schools	Percent			Number of students	Percent			Percent with IEP[2]	Percent free-lunch eligible	Percent minority
							Primary	Middle	High		Primary	Middle	High			
			1	2	3	4	5	6	7	8	9	10	11	12	13	14
	IOWA—Con.															
19089	Howard, IA	7	9 766	19.8	2	8	62.5	12.5	25.0	2 219	52.1	12.1	35.8	11.9	19.4	0.9
19091	Humboldt, IA	7	10 431	18.7	3	8	50.0	25.0	25.0	1 920	49.3	24.6	26.1	14.2	15.6	0.7
19093	Ida, IA	8	8 109	20.4	2	9	44.4	22.2	33.3	1 587	42.3	26.3	31.3	11.3	19.3	1.1
19095	Iowa, IA	8	15 381	18.3	5	10	50.0	10.0	40.0	2 759	45.1	7.7	47.2	13.9	12.5	2.9
19097	Jackson, IA	6	20 057	20.7	5	14	50.0	14.3	28.6	3 719	43.4	15.4	30.9	12.4	18.7	0.9
19099	Jasper, IA	6	35 470	19.1	6	20	50.0	20.0	30.0	6 404	48.5	18.0	33.6	13.9	13.2	1.9
19101	Jefferson, IA	7	16 901	17.6	1	7	71.4	14.3	14.3	2 149	47.0	24.1	29.0	14.3	16.2	3.1
19103	Johnson, IA	3	101 609	13.8	5	29	69.0	10.3	20.7	12 780	55.2	14.8	30.0	10.6	11.2	11.3
19105	Jones, IA	6	20 593	18.9	5	15	40.0	33.3	26.7	3 390	33.4	31.6	35.0	12.1	19.1	1.1
19107	Keokuk, IA	9	11 594	19.3	4	10	50.0	10.0	40.0	2 553	58.8	2.6	38.7	13.9	19.9	0.7
19109	Kossuth, IA	7	18 021	20.9	6	14	50.0	28.6	21.4	2 714	38.9	30.2	30.9	17.3	19.1	1.7
19111	Lee, IA	5	38 879	18.9	4	17	52.9	23.5	23.5	6 467	42.2	25.1	32.7	14.7	24.2	7.1
19113	Linn, IA	3	179 411	18.1	11	72	58.3	18.1	19.4	31 237	46.7	21.6	30.7	12.6	16.3	7.8
19115	Louisa, IA	8	12 017	20.3	4	10	50.0	20.0	30.0	3 030	55.7	8.6	35.7	10.0	24.1	13.8
19117	Lucas, IA	6	9 054	18.1	2	7	57.1	14.3	28.6	1 572	45.9	18.8	35.3	14.2	27.5	1.1
19119	Lyon, IA	6	11 962	22.2	4	10	40.0	30.0	30.0	2 268	47.4	18.7	33.9	11.8	16.9	1.4
19121	Madison, IA	6	13 663	20.6	3	11	36.4	36.4	27.3	2 864	40.9	26.1	33.0	13.2	14.6	0.6
19123	Mahaska, IA	7	21 757	19.0	3	12	58.3	25.0	16.7	3 299	51.2	23.4	25.3	11.7	23.1	2.3
19125	Marion, IA	6	31 359	19.1	5	20	55.0	15.0	25.0	5 707	45.3	15.2	30.5	11.9	15.1	2.5
19127	Marshall, IA	5	38 868	18.4	3	16	56.3	25.0	18.8	6 626	42.1	27.0	30.9	13.5	24.0	8.8
19129	Mills, IA	6	14 054	21.1	4	9	55.6	11.1	22.2	2 663	52.1	11.5	29.4	13.5	18.6	1.2
19131	Mitchell, IA	7	11 130	19.4	2	7	28.6	42.9	28.6	1 902	31.9	35.1	33.0	13.5	16.7	0.7
19133	Monona, IA	6	9 981	18.4	4	11	45.5	18.2	36.4	1 829	36.9	13.9	49.2	14.4	23.1	1.3
19135	Monroe, IA	7	8 113	19.2	1	6	66.7	16.7	16.7	1 369	36.6	32.0	31.4	15.1	26.6	2.8
19137	Montgomery, IA	6	11 908	18.4	3	10	50.0	20.0	20.0	2 118	38.0	24.5	25.1	14.3	19.9	0.6
19139	Muscatine, IA	4	41 158	20.6	3	17	70.6	11.8	17.6	7 722	49.9	16.8	33.3	13.3	23.2	17.7
19141	O'Brien, IA	7	15 030	20.0	3	10	50.0	20.0	30.0	3 041	45.3	21.6	33.1	15.1	18.7	2.0
19143	Osceola, IA	7	7 095	20.0	1	4	50.0	25.0	25.0	1 033	37.0	31.2	31.8	14.9	13.1	3.4
19145	Page, IA	7	16 784	18.9	5	15	40.0	26.7	26.7	3 045	32.2	27.9	32.9	12.5	19.0	2.2
19147	Palo Alto, IA	7	10 136	20.1	4	13	46.2	23.1	30.8	2 035	38.7	23.8	37.5	15.0	23.3	1.6
19149	Plymouth, IA	6	24 482	21.7	5	19	42.1	31.6	26.3	4 594	43.8	24.3	31.9	9.4	12.1	2.1
19151	Pocahontas, IA	9	9 001	18.9	2	9	44.4	22.2	33.3	1 429	48.8	20.4	30.9	12.1	23.2	1.8
19153	Polk, IA	2	354 150	17.5	10	118	66.9	16.1	13.6	59 660	50.1	21.7	24.3	11.9	19.8	15.0
19155	Pottawattamie, IA	2	84 939	19.7	9	41	56.1	19.5	22.0	16 724	50.7	17.7	29.4	14.2	25.0	4.0
19157	Poweshiek, IA	7	18 975	18.3	3	10	50.0	20.0	30.0	3 278	44.2	24.5	31.4	11.9	13.7	2.7
19159	Ringgold, IA	9	5 345	17.9	3	5	60.0	—	20.0	1 033	48.8	—	42.4	21.6	36.0	0.6
19161	Sac, IA	9	11 986	19.6	5	11	45.5	18.2	36.4	2 383	53.2	11.7	35.0	11.6	25.1	0.9
19163	Scott, IA	2	157 353	20.2	4	57	68.4	15.8	12.3	28 333	47.2	21.5	30.7	11.7	23.3	17.5
19165	Shelby, IA	6	13 065	20.3	4	13	46.2	23.1	30.8	2 813	44.1	24.7	31.2	11.6	22.4	1.2
19167	Sioux, IA	7	31 191	21.9	5	15	46.7	20.0	33.3	4 315	43.9	19.9	36.1	11.8	16.8	2.5
19169	Story, IA	4	74 610	14.2	7	30	56.7	20.0	23.3	11 121	47.5	21.1	31.3	10.6	11.8	8.2
19171	Tama, IA	6	17 678	19.4	6	12	58.3	16.7	25.0	3 132	49.4	17.8	32.8	13.8	20.2	11.7
19173	Taylor, IA	9	7 186	19.4	4	6	66.7	—	16.7	1 353	53.4	—	19.1	14.6	28.1	4.4
19175	Union, IA	7	12 613	19.4	2	10	50.0	20.0	30.0	2 228	32.6	29.7	37.7	13.7	28.6	1.3
19177	Van Buren, IA	9	7 807	18.7	3	8	50.0	12.5	25.0	1 453	46.4	13.6	33.0	11.7	27.6	0.6
19179	Wapello, IA	5	35 766	17.4	3	19	68.4	10.5	21.1	6 593	52.0	13.0	35.0	17.7	28.7	3.4
19181	Warren, IA	2	39 386	20.8	5	20	45.0	25.0	30.0	7 720	39.4	27.9	32.7	12.8	9.7	1.9
19183	Washington, IA	6	20 706	19.3	3	13	46.2	30.8	23.1	3 477	43.3	34.1	22.6	12.3	16.7	4.1
19185	Wayne, IA	9	6 847	17.1	3	7	42.9	14.3	42.9	1 281	54.7	8.4	36.9	11.7	32.7	1.2
19187	Webster, IA	5	39 014	18.7	3	17	64.7	17.6	17.6	5 965	43.9	25.7	30.4	15.4	23.2	7.4
19189	Winnebago, IA	7	11 984	18.7	4	11	45.5	27.3	27.3	3 013	41.7	25.1	33.2	13.0	14.2	2.9
19191	Winneshiek, IA	7	20 963	17.7	3	10	40.0	30.0	30.0	2 901	34.4	27.9	37.7	14.0	14.3	1.5
19193	Woodbury, IA	3	102 580	20.4	7	45	62.2	15.6	17.8	18 422	45.6	22.0	29.3	14.0	23.7	17.5
19195	Worth, IA	9	7 865	18.3	2	6	66.7	—	33.3	1 178	52.8	—	47.2	11.8	21.5	2.3
19197	Wright, IA	7	14 327	17.6	4	16	50.0	25.0	25.0	3 161	46.3	22.6	31.1	13.1	19.3	3.3
20000	**KANSAS**															
20001	Allen, KS	7	14 645	20.8	3	11	54.5	18.2	27.3	2 843	50.7	18.5	30.8	15.3	42.0	6.5
20003	Anderson, KS	6	8 054	20.1	2	9	77.8	—	22.2	1 480	58.9	—	41.1	10.6	39.5	2.4
20005	Atchison, KS	6	16 234	21.7	2	13	69.2	15.4	15.4	2 527	43.0	26.8	30.2	16.1	43.1	11.5
20007	Barber, KS	9	5 484	20.3	2	7	42.9	28.6	28.6	1 211	42.5	28.3	29.1	9.6	31.7	2.7
20009	Barton, KS	7	28 097	20.1	4	18	55.6	22.2	22.2	5 250	48.4	20.5	31.1	12.4	37.9	11.6
20011	Bourbon, KS	7	15 159	19.0	2	6	50.0	16.7	33.3	2 695	49.4	21.2	29.5	8.9	40.3	6.1
20013	Brown, KS	7	10 965	20.6	2	6	33.3	33.3	33.3	2 034	36.7	30.7	32.6	15.7	40.2	15.0
20015	Butler, KS	2	59 226	21.6	9	38	60.5	15.8	23.7	12 675	51.1	19.6	29.4	11.0	20.4	4.7
20017	Chase, KS	9	2 886	18.7	1	3	33.3	33.3	33.3	584	35.8	34.4	29.8	9.9	38.7	2.4
20019	Chautauqua, KS	9	4 379	17.5	2	4	50.0	—	50.0	751	71.2	—	28.8	11.1	49.9	9.3

1. County type code is from the Economic Research Service of the USDA. See notes and definitions at the end of this section. 2. IEP = Individual Education Program. See notes and definitions at the end of this section.

Table D-2. School and Student Characteristics by County — Continued

County	Staff and students, 1995–1996						Revenues, fiscal 1995					Current expenditures, fiscal 1995		
	Number of teachers	Pupil/ teacher ratio	Number of graduates	Dropouts grades 9–12 (percent)	Local school non-teaching staff	Central admin. staff	Total revenue ($1000)	Percent of Revenue from			Amount	Amount per pupil	Percent for instruction
								Federal Gov't	State Gov't	Local Gov't			
	15	16	17	18	19	20	21	22	23	24	25	26	27

IOWA—Con.

County	15	16	17	18	19	20	21	22	23	24	25	26	27
Howard, IA	154	14.4	184	1.4	105	8	12 957	4.5	44.5	51.1	11 195	4 897	65.9
Humboldt, IA	133	14.5	133	2.6	88	8	11 345	2.8	43.2	54.0	9 710	5 000	66.3
Ida, IA	130	12.2	105	1.6	82	8	9 349	3.5	44.0	52.5	8 130	4 972	67.2
Iowa, IA	183	15.1	168	1.1	123	14	18 448	2.7	41.6	55.7	15 026	4 802	64.5
Jackson, IA	275	13.5	278	4.4	206	21	21 794	4.3	52.0	43.7	19 254	5 204	67.5
Jasper, IA	414	15.5	450	1.4	314	20	36 307	2.9	51.9	45.2	31 070	4 881	64.5
Jefferson, IA	140	15.4	120	3.7	120	5	11 084	3.4	46.6	50.0	9 702	4 765	62.0
Johnson, IA	730	17.5	731	2.5	567	29	70 882	2.5	41.1	56.4	60 082	4 981	62.8
Jones, IA	241	14.1	284	4.5	200	15	20 464	3.6	50.4	46.1	16 988	4 737	63.7
Keokuk, IA	197	13.0	160	2.2	106	13	14 423	3.9	44.1	52.0	11 822	4 725	67.7
Kossuth, IA	212	12.8	164	0.8	166	14	17 464	3.9	37.2	58.9	14 954	5 494	67.5
Lee, IA	422	15.3	398	9.5	399	15	35 548	4.4	53.8	41.7	31 406	4 761	70.2
Linn, IA	1 817	17.2	1 960	2.2	1 662	71	243 166	5.8	34.3	59.9	199 415	6 453	49.7
Louisa, IA	205	14.8	186	5.8	143	15	17 529	5.0	43.8	51.2	14 468	4 956	67.1
Lucas, IA	124	12.7	85	6.3	80	8	8 811	4.7	54.7	40.6	7 523	4 687	69.7
Lyon, IA	156	14.5	183	0.9	94	13	12 990	3.8	48.1	48.2	10 502	4 505	67.7
Madison, IA	209	13.7	195	1.7	136	12	16 476	3.3	49.7	47.0	13 097	4 599	63.5
Mahaska, IA	216	15.3	214	4.3	147	9	18 843	3.8	53.3	42.9	15 602	4 594	67.0
Marion, IA	384	14.9	357	3.1	250	17	30 468	3.2	51.2	45.6	26 163	4 648	65.2
Marshall, IA	392	16.9	420	2.0	443	15	43 657	7.1	45.5	47.4	37 794	5 788	56.6
Mills, IA	163	16.4	155	2.8	223	9	14 921	4.3	45.8	49.9	13 074	5 054	61.9
Mitchell, IA	134	14.2	128	44.6	96	6	10 827	3.0	44.5	52.5	9 267	4 880	66.7
Monona, IA	139	13.1	135	2.9	105	11	10 412	5.2	44.5	50.2	9 019	4 988	65.6
Monroe, IA	07	15.7	09	0.5	57	4	7 475	4.9	55.0	40.1	8 005	4 592	65.2
Montgomery, IA	139	15.2	128	3.3	100	10	12 092	4.1	49.7	46.2	9 899	4 641	64.0
Muscatine, IA	465	16.6	482	7.8	359	13	44 765	4.1	50.8	45.1	37 832	4 782	70.2
O'Brien, IA	213	14.3	230	1.4	174	11	24 660	5.6	33.0	61.4	22 388	7 408	57.6
Osceola, IA	61	17.0	67	1.3	40	3	5 927	3.5	42.1	54.4	4 429	4 250	65.6
Page, IA	227	13.4	232	3.0	169	13	17 902	4.4	47.9	47.7	14 492	4 663	67.6
Palo Alto, IA	164	12.4	186	1.6	128	14	12 911	4.3	40.8	54.9	10 970	5 297	66.5
Plymouth, IA	298	15.4	282	1.9	183	21	24 447	3.5	44.3	52.2	20 226	4 523	64.5
Pocahontas, IA	119	12.0	104	0.2	74	6	8 539	3.6	46.3	50.2	7 365	5 302	67.0
Polk, IA	3 724	16.0	3 075	3.8	2 971	107	359 832	3.9	44.0	52.1	303 598	5 289	64.1
Pottawattamie, IA	962	17.4	903	3.2	711	41	102 005	5.5	49.0	45.5	77 713	4 748	64.5
Poweshiek, IA	236	13.9	216	1.2	161	11	17 272	3.2	47.1	49.7	14 723	4 582	66.5
Ringgold, IA	88	11.8	53	1.9	75	8	6 998	6.3	44.3	49.4	5 765	5 343	61.5
Sac, IA	180	13.2	148	2.5	129	15	14 045	4.0	48.0	48.0	11 609	4 750	64.8
Scott, IA	1 771	16.0	1 628	4.6	1 406	38	183 442	4.9	43.7	51.4	161 445	5 692	58.6
Shelby, IA	205	13.7	170	1.7	149	14	15 589	4.7	49.0	46.3	13 172	4 764	63.0
Sioux, IA	295	14.6	296	0.3	183	18	25 255	3.8	44.1	52.2	19 699	4 494	63.3
Story, IA	663	16.8	690	1.7	497	37	66 174	2.3	42.8	54.9	54 352	4 889	67.9
Tama, IA	226	13.8	202	3.2	168	15	18 315	4.3	48.7	47.0	15 888	5 018	64.6
Taylor, IA	97	14.0	70	4.6	86	9	8 422	5.1	49.7	45.2	6 471	4 865	62.5
Union, IA	157	14.2	181	5.1	128	10	17 656	9.6	38.6	51.8	15 783	6 965	49.2
Van Buren, IA	104	14.0	103	4.9	107	10	8 635	5.3	53.1	41.5	7 201	4 797	62.3
Wapello, IA	384	17.2	413	5.7	322	17	46 258	7.8	42.8	49.4	42 181	6 327	52.1
Warren, IA	513	15.0	445	5.7	403	30	41 032	2.1	54.6	43.4	35 768	4 640	65.2
Washington, IA	235	14.8	250	4.5	192	12	20 534	5.8	48.1	46.1	17 608	4 905	60.7
Wayne, IA	109	11.7	96	1.3	64	9	7 489	5.7	45.6	48.8	6 513	5 295	64.5
Webster, IA	412	14.5	363	4.9	366	16	46 657	7.1	39.1	53.8	40 630	6 679	53.0
Winnebago, IA	219	13.8	207	3.4	161	19	17 157	2.4	45.8	51.8	14 790	4 922	67.8
Winneshiek, IA	184	15.7	214	0.4	134	11	17 816	3.1	45.5	51.4	15 029	5 156	61.9
Woodbury, IA	1 183	15.6	1 036	3.1	803	38	106 089	6.7	46.3	47.0	95 221	5 218	61.9
Worth, IA	89	13.2	90	1.4	66	6	6 710	3.4	43.4	53.2	5 698	4 629	64.1
Wright, IA	219	14.4	239	1.9	130	14	18 374	3.0	42.6	54.4	15 615	4 775	64.7

KANSAS

County	15	16	17	18	19	20	21	22	23	24	25	26	27
Allen, KS	181	15.7	182	6.5	137	14	16 430	5.2	69.7	25.1	13 805	4 725	58.1
Anderson, KS	112	13.3	63	3.5	67	7	9 136	4.2	65.8	30.0	7 712	5 300	54.1
Atchison, KS	180	14.0	177	4.6	140	14	16 571	7.0	66.1	26.9	14 616	5 718	57.8
Barber, KS	93	13.0	67	1.7	55	9	7 358	3.8	60.9	35.3	6 349	5 417	53.1
Barton, KS	354	14.9	341	4.8	270	25	30 581	4.5	63.6	31.9	26 730	5 022	57.5
Bourbon, KS	183	14.7	164	8.7	137	10	13 827	7.2	70.8	22.0	12 199	4 557	65.5
Brown, KS	133	15.3	118	3.0	103	9	12 181	5.8	69.4	24.8	10 282	5 144	57.0
Butler, KS	781	16.2	716	3.1	779	51	70 243	3.5	66.2	30.2	61 083	4 885	59.4
Chase, KS	48	12.1	30	7.5	36	5	3 806	5.0	67.1	27.9	3 562	6 027	52.2
Chautauqua, KS	58	13.0	35	4.9	46	3	5 001	5.6	72.9	21.5	4 174	5 805	57.1

Table D-2. School and Student Characteristics by County

State/County code	County	County type[1]	Population, 1996		Number of school districts, 1995–1996	Level of schools, 1995–1996				Level of students, 1995–1996				Characteristics of students, 1995–1996		
			Total persons	Percent age 5–17		Number of schools	Percent Primary	Middle	High	Number of students	Percent Primary	Middle	High	Percent with IEP[2]	Percent free-lunch eligible	Percent minority
			1	2	3	4	5	6	7	8	9	10	11	12	13	14
	KANSAS—Con.															
20021	Cherokee, KS	6	22 505	20.2	4	19	63.2	10.5	21.1	3 935	59.9	10.5	29.1	8.9	43.7	4.8
20023	Cheyenne, KS	9	3 220	18.7	2	5	40.0	20.0	40.0	648	50.0	6.3	43.7	9.6	38.6	1.5
20025	Clark, KS	9	2 382	19.5	2	5	40.0	20.0	40.0	553	60.9	8.7	30.4	9.9	28.9	3.6
20027	Clay, KS	7	9 319	19.4	1	9	55.6	22.2	22.2	1 777	39.9	27.3	32.8	9.1	34.4	3.2
20029	Cloud, KS	7	10 247	17.2	2	9	55.6	11.1	33.3	1 707	39.5	13.9	46.6	14.8	42.1	1.2
20031	Coffey, KS	7	8 743	21.1	3	11	45.5	9.1	45.5	2 050	55.9	12.9	31.2	12.7	28.2	2.4
20033	Comanche, KS	9	2 072	17.8	1	4	50.0	—	50.0	414	56.3	—	43.7	15.7	33.8	2.4
20035	Cowley, KS	4	37 055	20.0	5	25	72.0	8.0	20.0	7 049	47.8	20.4	31.7	10.9	36.6	13.6
20037	Crawford, KS	4	36 337	17.5	5	19	63.2	10.5	26.3	6 149	51.9	16.3	31.8	9.8	36.3	4.5
20039	Decatur, KS	9	3 521	19.1	2	4	50.0	—	50.0	715	53.3	—	46.7	10.1	27.3	1.3
20041	Dickinson, KS	7	19 856	19.8	5	21	47.6	23.8	28.6	4 403	42.5	25.0	32.5	8.2	32.1	4.1
20043	Doniphan, KS	8	7 766	19.7	5	11	45.5	9.1	45.5	1 691	61.4	2.3	36.3	11.2	36.1	4.7
20045	Douglas, KS	3	89 899	15.1	3	33	66.7	21.2	12.1	12 174	53.7	24.6	21.7	12.8	27.6	16.2
20047	Edwards, KS	9	3 471	19.4	2	6	50.0	16.7	33.3	642	40.0	20.1	39.9	9.7	35.4	12.0
20049	Elk, KS	8	3 393	15.6	2	5	60.0	—	40.0	816	55.9	—	44.1	20.7	52.2	3.6
20051	Ellis, KS	7	26 186	19.6	3	15	66.7	13.3	20.0	4 351	47.5	22.6	30.0	12.1	23.5	3.4
20053	Ellsworth, KS	9	6 372	17.9	2	11	36.4	36.4	27.3	1 515	39.1	30.1	30.8	14.3	31.7	3.4
20055	Finney, KS	5	35 545	24.3	2	21	66.7	19.0	14.3	8 260	52.1	23.1	24.7	10.4	39.0	47.1
20057	Ford, KS	5	29 309	20.9	3	14	64.3	14.3	14.3	5 793	50.3	20.3	26.1	9.8	43.0	38.8
20059	Franklin, KS	6	23 565	20.8	4	16	62.5	6.3	31.3	4 819	54.3	12.5	33.2	11.3	29.3	4.8
20061	Geary, KS	5	26 341	19.0	1	18	77.8	11.1	5.6	6 754	58.1	21.2	20.0	10.6	56.6	50.0
20063	Gove, KS	9	3 089	20.7	3	7	42.9	14.3	42.9	780	50.0	6.7	43.3	11.0	16.8	0.6
20065	Graham, KS	9	3 260	20.5	2	6	50.0	16.7	33.3	643	44.2	21.3	34.5	12.7	42.8	7.8
20067	Grant, KS	7	7 697	26.4	1	5	60.0	20.0	20.0	1 801	49.1	24.0	26.9	9.5	40.8	36.9
20069	Gray, KS	9	5 527	24.4	4	8	50.0	12.5	37.5	1 174	57.8	2.6	39.7	9.2	23.7	8.5
20071	Greeley, KS	9	1 754	22.7	1	2	50.0	—	50.0	357	68.9	—	31.1	14.6	28.3	10.9
20073	Greenwood, KS	6	8 090	18.0	3	9	55.6	11.1	33.3	1 340	56.1	12.5	31.4	15.9	37.4	3.1
20075	Hamilton, KS	9	2 296	19.8	1	2	50.0	—	50.0	465	54.0	—	46.0	12.5	35.5	20.0
20077	Harper, KS	7	6 524	19.1	2	5	60.0	—	40.0	1 317	70.3	—	29.7	11.4	41.3	4.9
20079	Harvey, KS	2	31 302	20.5	5	21	61.9	14.3	23.8	5 877	45.2	23.5	31.2	12.3	30.3	14.1
20081	Haskell, KS	9	3 922	24.3	2	5	40.0	20.0	40.0	877	58.3	9.8	31.9	7.8	35.3	28.6
20083	Hodgeman, KS	9	2 231	20.7	2	4	50.0	—	50.0	448	66.3	—	33.7	11.8	21.2	4.2
20085	Jackson, KS	6	11 978	21.6	3	9	44.4	22.2	33.3	2 358	45.9	24.0	30.1	12.7	29.2	9.9
20087	Jefferson, KS	8	17 514	21.0	6	19	36.8	31.6	26.3	4 452	42.9	19.8	30.0	12.4	24.2	2.3
20089	Jewell, KS	9	4 011	18.3	3	9	33.3	33.3	33.3	705	45.5	20.3	34.2	10.1	34.2	2.0
20091	Johnson, KS	0	408 341	19.5	6	127	70.1	16.5	12.6	68 685	54.1	19.9	25.8	10.6	9.7	8.2
20093	Kearny, KS	9	4 216	24.6	2	6	33.3	33.3	33.3	1 234	58.0	15.8	26.2	9.4	34.3	31.8
20095	Kingman, KS	6	8 545	20.7	2	7	57.1	—	42.9	1 608	68.7	—	31.3	13.2	33.9	2.2
20097	Kiowa, KS	9	3 571	19.9	2	6	50.0	16.7	33.3	563	66.8	3.2	30.0	11.2	35.9	5.0
20099	Labette, KS	7	22 869	19.9	4	18	66.7	11.1	22.2	4 573	56.3	12.6	31.1	8.7	37.6	11.0
20101	Lane, KS	9	2 211	20.6	2	5	40.0	20.0	40.0	507	33.9	31.2	34.9	12.6	24.1	1.2
20103	Leavenworth, KS	1	69 904	20.4	6	32	53.1	28.1	18.8	12 236	49.6	24.6	25.8	10.9	21.7	16.7
20105	Lincoln, KS	9	3 388	18.7	2	4	50.0	—	50.0	618	48.7	—	51.3	12.0	32.8	1.5
20107	Linn, KS	8	8 974	19.9	3	11	63.6	9.1	27.3	2 086	57.9	7.7	34.4	11.2	35.0	1.2
20109	Logan, KS	9	3 113	20.4	2	6	50.0	16.7	33.3	676	45.1	20.1	34.8	17.3	33.1	1.6
20111	Lyon, KS	5	34 384	19.8	3	19	63.2	15.8	21.1	6 496	46.5	24.1	29.4	11.9	38.7	19.9
20113	McPherson, KS	7	27 548	20.2	5	18	55.6	16.7	27.8	5 361	49.6	19.0	31.4	11.7	20.2	4.3
20115	Marion, KS	6	12 898	18.5	5	14	42.9	21.4	35.7	2 572	53.8	14.1	32.1	14.5	31.3	3.4
20117	Marshall, KS	7	11 286	19.7	4	14	57.1	—	42.9	2 558	47.3	—	52.7	12.8	28.8	1.2
20119	Meade, KS	9	4 436	20.7	2	4	50.0	—	50.0	623	72.1	—	27.9	14.3	31.8	7.4
20121	Miami, KS	1	25 933	21.1	3	13	53.8	23.1	23.1	4 435	41.6	28.6	29.7	10.1	26.2	3.6
20123	Mitchell, KS	7	7 096	20.6	2	8	62.5	—	37.5	1 521	61.4	—	38.6	13.4	31.0	1.6
20125	Montgomery, KS	5	37 414	19.1	4	18	50.0	27.8	22.2	6 469	44.6	23.6	31.8	10.0	39.1	17.7
20127	Morris, KS	9	6 340	19.2	1	5	80.0	—	20.0	1 198	71.7	—	28.3	10.8	34.1	2.5
20129	Morton, KS	9	3 315	23.5	2	5	40.0	20.0	40.0	786	47.2	24.4	28.4	5.4	28.1	16.8
20131	Nemaha, KS	9	10 389	21.4	3	9	44.4	11.1	44.4	1 960	54.5	11.8	33.7	10.7	28.3	1.1
20133	Neosho, KS	7	16 893	19.2	2	13	61.5	7.7	30.8	3 220	56.3	14.6	29.1	12.4	38.0	4.8
20135	Ness, KS	9	3 663	21.0	4	8	50.0	—	50.0	750	53.2	—	46.8	8.3	26.3	0.9
20137	Norton, KS	7	5 762	16.6	3	8	37.5	25.0	37.5	1 106	51.4	17.1	31.5	11.1	31.7	2.6
20139	Osage, KS	6	16 726	20.8	5	15	53.3	13.3	33.3	3 269	62.1	7.7	30.3	11.7	31.0	3.9
20141	Osborne, KS	9	4 606	17.4	1	3	33.3	33.3	33.3	531	60.3	16.0	23.7	14.5	32.8	1.7
20143	Ottawa, KS	9	5 815	19.6	2	7	57.1	—	42.9	1 347	71.6	—	28.4	12.0	27.1	2.4
20145	Pawnee, KS	7	7 470	19.7	2	11	54.5	27.3	18.2	1 398	41.4	25.6	33.0	10.9	31.3	8.4
20147	Phillips, KS	7	6 194	18.8	3	7	42.9	14.3	42.9	1 177	47.8	19.4	32.8	9.0	31.7	1.1
20149	Pottawatomie, KS	6	17 908	21.9	4	16	62.5	6.3	31.3	3 782	56.2	9.5	34.3	13.5	26.5	3.3
20151	Pratt, KS	7	9 746	19.9	2	6	50.0	16.7	33.3	1 825	47.8	20.7	31.6	10.4	25.4	5.6

1. County type code is from the Economic Research Service of the USDA. See notes and definitions at the end of this section.   2. IEP = Individual Education Program. See notes and definitions at the end of this section.

Table D-2. School and Student Characteristics by County — Continued

County	Staff and students, 1995–1996						Revenues, fiscal 1995				Current expenditures, fiscal 1995		
	Number of teachers	Pupil/ teacher ratio	Number of graduates	Dropouts grades 9–12 (percent)	Local school non-teaching staff	Central admin. staff	Total revenue ($1000)	Percent of Revenue from			Amount	Amount per pupil	Percent for instruction
								Federal Gov't	State Gov't	Local Gov't			
	15	16	17	18	19	20	21	22	23	24	25	26	27
KANSAS—Con.													
Cherokee, KS	269	14.6	270	7.5	189	19	23 555	6.6	70.8	22.6	20 282	5 105	54.6
Cheyenne, KS	57	11.3	52	2.4	44	2	4 971	3.5	62.3	34.2	4 385	6 468	55.6
Clark, KS	44	12.7	36	0.6	42	4	4 009	2.3	54.4	43.4	3 632	6 568	51.7
Clay, KS	125	14.2	123	2.9	111	4	11 074	5.9	63.3	30.8	9 581	5 428	59.3
Cloud, KS	134	12.7	116	1.3	120	9	11 423	3.4	69.9	26.7	10 580	6 294	60.7
Coffey, KS	156	13.2	125	2.0	124	15	30 833	1.8	18.1	80.1	12 980	6 464	56.4
Comanche, KS	41	10.1	36	2.9	31	8	4 189	4.1	45.7	50.2	3 842	8 832	58.3
Cowley, KS	472	14.9	430	*4.3	434	37	43 592	4.7	61.3	34.0	36 827	5 245	57.8
Crawford, KS	332	18.5	374	6.1	443	31	41 067	6.0	68.1	25.9	36 018	5 753	63.1
Decatur, KS	62	11.5	59	1.3	44	3	4 954	3.9	69.3	26.7	4 459	6 034	54.8
Dickinson, KS	299	14.7	271	3.4	206	23	25 213	4.4	70.4	25.2	21 842	4 978	56.6
Doniphan, KS	142	11.9	90	1.3	102	12	11 567	4.6	75.3	20.2	9 882	5 946	54.4
Douglas, KS	821	14.8	149	5.1	717	54	69 808	4.5	50.2	45.3	60 948	5 135	60.1
Edwards, KS	58	11.0	46	4.4	49	4	4 832	4.4	61.1	34.5	4 102	6 234	54.6
Elk, KS	66	12.3	54	4.2	89	6	6 431	6.1	73.3	20.6	5 586	6 796	57.9
Ellis, KS	333	13.1	251	3.2	281	25	27 157	4.0	59.6	36.5	25 103	5 791	59.9
Ellsworth, KS	120	12.6	105	1.1	90	8	10 046	3.1	56.2	40.7	8 974	6 109	54.6
Finney, KS	499	16.5	346	14.7	455	34	46 006	4.5	52.0	43.6	38 286	4 731	53.0
Ford, KS	342	16.9	287	10.3	216	25	27 490	5.8	63.0	31.3	22 807	4 028	59.3
Franklin, KS	322	15.0	295	3.3	182	20	26 881	4.1	69.7	26.2	23 100	4 829	60.0
Geary, KS	408	16.6	255	10.0	377	33	34 390	18.7	65.9	15.4	32 908	4 590	54.1
Gove, KS	75	10.4	47	0.4	57	8	5 916	2.6	67.1	30.3	5 139	7 049	61.5
Graham, KS	61	10.6	51	1.9	40	4	4 798	4.0	67.2	28.8	4 537	7 056	61.9
Grant, KS	122	14.7	88	3.5	90	7	15 488	3.4	5.7	90.9	8 890	5 074	58.9
Gray, KS	90	13.1	82	1.1	71	10	9 566	2.7	57.9	39.4	7 437	6 027	51.9
Greeley, KS	35	10.2	25	0.9	19	4	2 682	2.6	46.7	50.7	2 195	5 916	55.4
Greenwood, KS	107	12.6	86	2.5	84	8	9 462	4.6	67.5	27.9	8 389	6 317	59.5
Hamilton, KS	35	13.3	18	0.7	21	4	3 426	3.1	24.6	72.3	2 797	6 415	53.3
Harper, KS	108	12.2	89	4.6	64	7	7 950	4.8	67.1	28.2	7 119	5 472	54.5
Harvey, KS	374	15.7	359	5.2	316	29	35 430	4.4	67.0	28.6	31 305	5 229	53.8
Haskell, KS	75	11.6	72	3.1	50	8	8 733	2.4	16.3	81.3	5 848	6 630	52.1
Hodgeman, KS	44	10.3	32	0.8	47	3	3 534	3.3	62.8	34.0	3 033	6 608	60.4
Jackson, KS	176	13.4	151	2.4	135	24	16 210	4.6	74.6	20.8	14 558	6 232	62.2
Jefferson, KS	295	15.1	259	2.7	203	39	27 209	3.1	76.3	20.6	23 574	5 406	54.3
Jewell, KS	68	10.3	49	NA	48	7	5 629	3.7	70.4	25.9	5 102	7 037	48.6
Johnson, KS	4 428	15.5	3 922	3.4	3 193	271	425 373	1.9	38.6	59.4	348 489	5 192	61.0
Kearny, KS	89	13.9	71	4.3	72	6	11 305	2.5	8.1	89.4	7 152	6 139	56.7
Kingman, KS	131	12.3	124	3.4	80	6	9 717	3.7	52.9	43.4	8 250	5 134	56.8
Kiowa, KS	63	8.9	62	2.4	38	7	5 622	3.2	48.3	48.5	4 591	6 702	49.7
Labette, KS	283	16.2	286	4.1	205	16	23 987	5.7	72.2	22.0	20 671	4 513	58.1
Lane, KS	48	10.5	46	1.9	24	5	4 084	2.6	57.6	39.8	3 294	6 298	54.9
Leavenworth, KS	768	15.9	631	3.9	547	51	65 896	11.8	62.7	25.6	58 386	4 710	57.3
Lincoln, KS	57	10.8	55	0.5	42	3	4 763	2.9	65.1	32.0	3 902	6 324	56.3
Linn, KS	142	14.7	148	2.8	92	10	13 364	4.5	40.1	55.4	11 647	5 979	55.7
Logan, KS	64	10.6	63	0.9	53	7	5 479	4.3	58.7	37.0	4 842	7 100	55.1
Lyon, KS	408	15.2	376	4.2	350	27	38 981	5.6	66.9	27.5	34 319	5 537	59.8
McPherson, KS	368	14.6	335	3.6	262	33	32 619	3.4	61.3	35.2	27 663	5 275	56.1
Marion, KS	196	13.1	161	2.9	128	15	16 434	3.3	72.5	24.1	13 804	5 422	55.7
Marshall, KS	202	12.7	184	3.1	182	14	17 127	4.2	72.1	23.8	15 143	5 745	61.8
Meade, KS	52	12.0	35	0.6	33	6	4 967	2.6	36.4	61.0	4 179	6 988	51.8
Miami, KS	274	16.2	269	4.7	310	18	30 375	4.0	61.1	34.9	24 544	5 572	61.4
Mitchell, KS	123	12.4	106	2.1	103	7	11 551	3.9	64.2	31.9	10 475	7 136	59.6
Montgomery, KS	401	16.1	381	6.3	242	26	31 319	6.2	67.8	26.1	27 989	4 299	58.3
Morris, KS	90	13.3	70	1.5	69	4	6 573	4.3	68.1	27.6	5 632	4 893	60.2
Morton, KS	69	11.4	57	5.4	62	6	8 463	3.0	17.0	80.0	5 496	7 213	61.2
Nemaha, KS	149	13.1	148	1.1	94	12	13 054	5.0	69.8	25.2	11 679	5 940	55.9
Neosho, KS	224	14.4	211	4.4	106	34	16 944	5.4	70.3	24.4	14 657	4 477	60.8
Ness, KS	81	9.3	58	1.8	44	8	6 296	2.6	56.0	41.4	5 512	7 253	54.4
Norton, KS	102	10.8	94	2.0	55	7	7 599	3.8	73.1	23.0	6 676	5 903	57.7
Osage, KS	233	14.1	223	3.2	134	20	19 951	4.6	74.6	20.8	16 943	5 142	54.1
Osborne, KS	44	12.1	36	2.4	26	3	3 377	4.6	75.9	19.5	2 964	5 499	56.7
Ottawa, KS	99	13.6	89	2.4	61	5	8 544	3.2	73.0	23.7	7 178	5 349	54.2
Pawnee, KS	104	13.5	105	4.3	118	15	10 943	4.4	59.8	35.8	10 312	7 141	60.3
Phillips, KS	103	11.5	83	2.3	112	16	10 683	4.6	71.0	24.4	10 209	8 644	59.5
Pottawatomie, KS	304	12.4	265	2.7	215	23	30 986	3.0	45.0	52.1	22 700	5 928	59.1
Pratt, KS	119	15.4	124	4.9	81	10	10 391	3.6	64.0	32.4	8 766	4 801	59.1

Table D-2. School and Student Characteristics by County

State/County code	County	County type[1]	Population, 1996		Number of school districts, 1995–1996	Level of schools, 1995–1996				Level of students, 1995–1996				Characteristics of students, 1995–1996		
			Total persons	Percent age 5–17		Number of schools	Percent			Number of students	Percent			Percent with IEP[2]	Percent free-lunch eligible	Percent minority
							Primary	Middle	High		Primary	Middle	High			
			1	2	3	4	5	6	7	8	9	10	11	12	13	14
KANSAS—Con.																
20153	Rawlins, KS	9	3 249	20.7	2	4	50.0	—	50.0	604	61.4	—	38.6	11.7	40.2	4.0
20155	Reno, KS	4	62 901	19.0	6	38	63.2	21.1	15.8	11 026	54.0	17.0	29.0	13.4	35.2	9.7
20157	Republic, KS	7	6 253	17.0	3	8	37.5	25.0	37.5	1 139	43.2	23.9	32.9	18.8	33.9	1.2
20159	Rice, KS	7	10 044	20.2	4	14	42.9	28.6	28.6	2 021	46.8	22.5	30.7	14.7	40.5	7.4
20161	Riley, KS	5	64 716	15.0	3	17	70.6	11.8	17.6	7 614	56.8	14.8	28.4	11.1	29.8	15.7
20163	Rooks, KS	9	5 849	20.1	3	7	42.9	14.3	42.9	1 151	63.7	3.9	32.4	13.7	34.8	2.3
20165	Rush, KS	9	3 537	17.2	2	8	50.0	25.0	25.0	747	43.9	22.4	33.7	11.8	39.4	2.1
20167	Russell, KS	7	7 658	17.8	2	10	60.0	10.0	30.0	1 451	49.8	19.7	30.5	14.5	40.5	3.9
20169	Saline, KS	5	51 782	19.5	3	24	58.3	25.0	16.7	8 678	49.7	20.3	29.9	12.5	33.1	11.5
20171	Scott, KS	7	5 029	21.9	1	4	50.0	25.0	25.0	1 164	45.0	25.7	29.3	11.3	29.7	7.7
20173	Sedgwick, KS	2	422 437	19.9	10	155	63.9	18.1	16.1	72 067	48.9	23.6	27.0	10.9	33.4	28.1
20175	Seward, KS	7	20 002	22.9	2	13	69.2	15.4	15.4	5 017	55.3	19.8	25.0	6.5	46.0	46.9
20177	Shawnee, KS	3	164 938	19.3	5	63	69.8	17.5	11.1	26 790	49.3	22.0	26.4	12.6	40.3	24.2
20179	Sheridan, KS	9	2 760	21.8	1	2	50.0	—	50.0	481	64.9	—	35.1	10.4	26.0	0.2
20181	Sherman, KS	7	6 733	19.4	1	5	60.0	20.0	20.0	1 301	55.4	16.6	28.0	13.3	36.5	14.8
20183	Smith, KS	9	4 741	17.4	2	4	50.0	—	50.0	852	50.7	—	49.3	10.7	30.8	0.5
20185	Stafford, KS	9	5 129	18.7	3	7	42.9	14.3	42.9	1 189	51.8	5.9	42.3	14.9	39.4	7.9
20187	Stanton, KS	9	2 297	23.2	1	5	60.0	20.0	20.0	579	52.8	15.7	31.4	7.4	40.2	27.6
20189	Stevens, KS	7	5 347	23.1	2	5	40.0	20.0	20.0	1 281	52.5	13.1	24.2	6.6	28.5	22.2
20191	Sumner, KS	6	26 901	22.0	7	21	47.6	19.0	33.3	4 913	49.7	20.3	30.0	11.7	31.0	6.4
20193	Thomas, KS	7	8 326	21.2	3	8	37.5	25.0	37.5	1 651	46.0	22.8	31.3	8.8	28.3	3.1
20195	Trego, KS	9	3 440	20.6	1	2	50.0	—	50.0	647	67.7	—	32.3	12.3	31.4	1.4
20197	Wabaunsee, KS	8	6 664	20.4	2	9	66.7	11.1	22.2	1 349	63.6	4.6	31.8	14.3	26.6	3.9
20199	Wallace, KS	9	1 812	21.7	2	4	50.0	—	50.0	412	65.0	—	35.0	7.3	34.0	6.3
20201	Washington, KS	9	6 738	19.2	4	13	53.8	7.7	38.5	1 363	55.5	6.5	38.0	11.2	37.8	0.9
20203	Wichita, KS	9	2 725	23.9	1	4	50.0	25.0	25.0	586	49.7	16.2	34.1	9.4	32.8	23.5
20205	Wilson, KS	7	10 353	19.5	3	10	50.0	20.0	30.0	2 230	47.6	14.5	37.8	9.9	43.0	2.6
20207	Woodson, KS	9	3 980	18.4	1	2	50.0	—	50.0	638	69.0	—	31.0	13.4	35.7	1.6
20209	Wyandotte, KS	0	153 427	20.7	4	69	62.3	21.7	15.9	29 113	47.0	26.4	26.6	12.3	54.8	54.7
21000	**KENTUCKY**															
21001	Adair, KY	7	16 460	17.9	1	6	66.7	16.7	16.7	2 623	46.4	22.0	31.6	NA	NA	3.1
21003	Allen, KY	7	15 844	18.4	1	4	25.0	50.0	25.0	2 854	29.9	41.6	28.5	NA	NA	2.0
21005	Anderson, KY	6	17 734	18.5	1	5	60.0	20.0	20.0	3 080	48.4	22.8	28.9	NA	NA	3.5
21007	Ballard, KY	9	8 252	16.9	1	3	33.3	33.3	33.3	1 429	53.0	16.5	30.4	NA	NA	4.2
21009	Barren, KY	7	36 255	17.6	3	15	66.7	13.3	20.0	6 599	50.3	17.7	32.0	NA	NA	8.1
21011	Bath, KY	8	10 143	17.9	1	5	60.0	20.0	20.0	1 844	37.9	31.8	30.4	NA	NA	2.0
21013	Bell, KY	7	30 193	19.6	3	19	63.2	15.8	21.1	5 912	44.5	22.6	32.9	NA	NA	2.9
21015	Boone, KY	0	72 926	20.2	2	21	57.1	19.0	23.8	12 509	47.0	21.7	31.3	NA	NA	2.1
21017	Bourbon, KY	2	19 199	18.5	2	9	55.6	22.2	22.2	3 555	44.6	25.9	29.5	NA	NA	11.1
21019	Boyd, KY	2	50 263	16.7	3	19	63.2	10.5	21.1	8 323	47.7	18.4	33.6	NA	NA	2.9
21021	Boyle, KY	7	26 945	17.6	2	11	63.6	18.2	18.2	4 450	49.0	20.6	30.4	NA	NA	12.6
21023	Bracken, KY	8	8 237	18.5	2	5	40.0	20.0	40.0	1 552	40.1	24.4	35.6	NA	NA	1.7
21025	Breathitt, KY	9	15 640	21.1	2	9	55.6	22.2	22.2	3 023	50.4	18.9	30.7	NA	NA	0.3
21027	Breckinridge, KY	9	16 901	19.1	2	9	77.8	—	22.2	3 119	66.0	—	34.0	NA	NA	4.6
21029	Bullitt, KY	2	57 161	21.1	1	18	50.0	22.2	22.2	10 041	45.4	25.1	29.0	NA	NA	1.0
21031	Butler, KY	9	11 701	19.2	1	7	57.1	14.3	14.3	2 421	46.6	22.7	28.5	NA	NA	1.2
21033	Caldwell, KY	6	13 290	16.9	1	4	50.0	25.0	25.0	2 152	45.1	25.1	29.8	NA	NA	8.6
21035	Calloway, KY	7	32 579	13.6	2	9	44.4	22.2	22.2	4 596	40.9	27.5	30.9	NA	NA	5.3
21037	Campbell, KY	0	87 233	18.2	7	29	55.2	13.8	27.6	13 124	51.4	13.2	35.1	NA	NA	2.5
21039	Carlisle, KY	9	5 309	17.4	1	3	33.3	33.3	33.3	890	46.3	25.4	28.3	NA	NA	2.7
21041	Carroll, KY	6	9 516	19.3	1	5	20.0	40.0	20.0	1 794	31.0	39.3	29.4	NA	NA	2.7
21043	Carter, KY	2	26 328	19.5	1	12	58.3	16.7	25.0	5 086	43.6	23.5	32.9	NA	NA	0.4
21045	Casey, KY	9	14 512	19.0	1	8	75.0	12.5	12.5	2 453	52.1	17.2	30.7	NA	NA	0.6
21047	Christian, KY	3	65 445	17.3	1	17	64.7	17.6	17.6	9 017	48.6	23.8	27.7	NA	NA	37.6
21049	Clark, KY	2	31 604	18.2	1	12	66.7	16.7	16.7	5 372	45.3	25.6	29.1	NA	NA	7.5
21051	Clay, KY	9	22 736	22.0	1	11	81.8	9.1	9.1	4 561	55.3	17.6	27.1	NA	NA	1.6
21053	Clinton, KY	9	9 269	17.9	1	3	33.3	33.3	33.3	1 544	30.5	40.1	29.4	NA	NA	0.3
21055	Crittenden, KY	7	9 400	17.5	1	5	60.0	20.0	20.0	1 572	50.1	18.4	31.5	NA	NA	1.1
21057	Cumberland, KY	9	6 977	16.6	1	3	33.3	33.3	33.3	1 188	46.8	27.1	26.1	NA	NA	5.2
21059	Daviess, KY	3	90 818	18.9	2	34	58.8	14.7	11.8	14 642	43.6	26.4	29.1	NA	NA	8.2
21061	Edmonson, KY	9	11 076	19.1	1	4	50.0	25.0	25.0	1 893	45.0	24.5	30.5	NA	NA	0.8
21063	Elliott, KY	8	6 584	21.2	1	4	75.0	—	25.0	1 349	52.6	—	47.4	NA	NA	—
21065	Estill, KY	6	15 494	19.5	1	8	62.5	25.0	12.5	2 786	37.8	33.5	28.8	NA	NA	0.4
21067	Fayette, KY	2	239 942	15.1	1	55	60.0	21.8	12.7	32 880	47.8	23.8	27.5	NA	NA	26.1
21069	Fleming, KY	7	13 161	18.1	1	6	66.7	16.7	16.7	2 416	50.8	16.7	32.5	NA	NA	2.6

1. County type code is from the Economic Research Service of the USDA. See notes and definitions at the end of this section.   2. IEP = Individual Education Program. See notes and definitions at the end of this section.

Table D-2. School and Student Characteristics by County — Continued

County	Staff and students, 1995–1996						Revenues, fiscal 1995					Current expenditures, fiscal 1995		
	Number of teachers	Pupil/ teacher ratio	Number of graduates	Dropouts grades 9–12 (percent)	Local school non-teaching staff	Central admin. staff	Total revenue ($1000)	Percent of Revenue from			Amount	Amount per pupil	Percent for instruction
								Federal Gov't	State Gov't	Local Gov't			
	15	16	17	18	19	20	21	22	23	24	25	26	27
KANSAS—Con.													
Rawlins, KS	56	10.8	38	1.4	51	6	4 615	3.3	71.9	24.8	4 300	7 203	58.9
Reno, KS	730	15.1	601	4.9	514	54	62 362	4.5	60.7	34.8	54 799	4 917	53.3
Republic, KS	96	11.9	74	2.1	64	9	8 233	4.1	70.0	26.0	7 433	6 463	57.4
Rice, KS	167	12.1	103	1.9	139	13	14 683	5.5	64.1	30.4	12 700	6 385	56.2
Riley, KS	475	16.0	477	3.5	396	31	45 722	6.4	61.5	32.1	38 826	5 012	58.8
Rooks, KS	104	11.1	85	0.8	59	9	8 206	4.1	61.1	34.8	7 206	6 159	55.6
Rush, KS	64	11.7	47	0.4	52	5	5 299	3.8	61.6	34.6	4 871	6 495	52.7
Russell, KS	126	11.6	108	2.7	87	8	9 171	5.2	56.4	38.4	8 448	5 979	56.3
Saline, KS	548	15.8	481	5.3	428	38	50 325	6.4	59.7	33.9	44 853	5 200	60.7
Scott, KS	82	14.3	68	3.2	54	5	6 529	3.2	60.8	36.0	5 796	4 988	61.0
Sedgwick, KS	4 182	17.2	3 825	6.9	3 293	352	391 810	5.3	58.5	36.3	354 860	5 026	58.0
Seward, KS	318	15.8	215	8.0	292	20	26 895	6.3	57.8	36.0	22 791	4 690	63.1
Shawnee, KS	1 698	15.8	1 478	7.4	1 555	113	160 182	5.3	58.4	36.3	143 670	5 287	55.2
Sheridan, KS	44	10.9	43	0.6	35	4	3 590	4.4	65.0	30.6	3 275	6 590	58.7
Sherman, KS	94	13.8	68	3.0	89	8	7 942	5.0	62.0	33.0	6 968	5 526	58.7
Smith, KS	70	12.3	64	0.4	46	6	5 879	4.3	70.4	25.3	4 992	5 745	59.4
Stafford, KS	89	13.4	64	3.2	65	7	8 025	3.6	56.2	40.2	6 719	5 904	54.0
Stanton, KS	43	13.4	40	2.5	89	4	4 768	1.8	7.2	91.0	3 622	6 366	55.7
Stevens, KS	93	13.8	79	3.1	78	9	15 606	2.1	6.1	91.8	7 988	6 275	54.9
Sumner, KS	325	15.1	308	2.1	255	27	27 574	3.7	74.3	22.1	24 316	5 090	59.7
Thomas, KS	137	12.1	119	3.3	106	17	10 703	4.1	64.1	31.8	9 121	5 331	59.4
Trego, KS	55	11.7	49	2.4	32	5	4 703	3.7	66.1	30.2	4 090	6 169	57.8
Wabaunsee, KS	104	13.0	77	1.6	87	6	8 634	3.5	72.7	23.8	7 716	5 954	54.1
Wallace, KS	41	10.0	32	1.7	35	5	3 418	4.3	62.4	33.3	2 821	6 576	55.0
Washington, KS	125	10.9	126	2.0	79	10	10 154	4.6	65.0	30.4	9 342	6 854	56.8
Wichita, KS	43	13.6	46	1.0	38	2	4 234	3.8	60.4	35.8	3 613	5 913	49.5
Wilson, KS	157	14.2	131	4.2	117	10	14 074	4.7	72.0	23.3	11 823	5 421	55.4
Woodson, KS	47	13.6	49	4.0	36	3	4 050	4.0	71.5	24.5	3 735	5 668	50.5
Wyandotte, KS	1 767	16.5	1 341	7.6	1 755	134	182 137	8.6	62.6	28.8	162 365	5 542	56.9
KENTUCKY													
Adair, KY	173	15.2	162	NA	189	29	14 391	11.9	72.3	15.8	13 858	5 336	60.0
Allen, KY	152	18.8	177	NA	172	16	13 821	7.4	75.4	17.2	12 002	4 255	55.3
Anderson, KY	173	17.8	168	NA	176	14	12 143	11.2	66.5	22.3	10 772	3 538	60.9
Ballard, KY	80	17.9	114	NA	93	7	8 109	8.2	70.4	21.4	7 328	5 061	62.0
Barren, KY	412	16.0	384	NA	411	40	37 397	6.5	60.1	33.3	31 614	4 841	59.6
Bath, KY	120	15.3	106	NA	133	17	10 491	13.5	71.5	15.0	10 452	5 607	59.0
Bell, KY	403	14.7	356	NA	441	30	35 478	12.9	69.4	17.7	34 174	5 674	55.2
Boone, KY	694	18.0	684	NA	187	16	60 909	3.8	53.3	43.0	50 655	4 172	59.2
Bourbon, KY	228	15.6	245	NA	264	25	20 745	10.7	64.7	24.6	20 272	5 608	57.4
Boyd, KY	500	16.6	520	NA	567	47	41 198	9.8	63.9	26.3	35 086	4 172	58.7
Boyle, KY	285	15.6	269	NA	283	30	24 736	8.9	62.3	28.8	22 957	5 145	58.8
Bracken, KY	93	16.7	94	NA	96	11	7 633	10.5	72.8	16.8	6 976	4 559	63.3
Breathitt, KY	206	14.7	168	NA	271	24	17 967	14.7	71.6	13.8	17 253	5 675	59.8
Breckinridge, KY	191	16.4	221	NA	246	24	19 021	14.4	64.5	21.1	17 722	5 715	55.3
Bullitt, KY	542	18.5	554	NA	614	35	47 772	5.8	70.4	23.8	42 615	4 288	58.5
Butler, KY	146	16.5	150	NA	148	20	12 367	9.6	75.5	14.9	10 880	4 498	58.9
Caldwell, KY	137	15.8	129	NA	134	14	11 148	8.2	72.2	19.5	9 772	4 575	59.0
Calloway, KY	268	17.2	305	NA	315	24	26 343	15.5	62.4	22.0	25 905	5 619	63.3
Campbell, KY	810	16.2	692	NA	693	64	68 393	6.7	61.4	31.9	61 359	4 708	59.1
Carlisle, KY	55	16.1	53	NA	50	4	4 438	9.7	69.4	20.9	4 023	4 598	64.3
Carroll, KY	116	15.5	123	NA	147	15	10 557	12.2	59.1	28.8	10 777	5 848	54.7
Carter, KY	312	16.3	327	NA	382	22	25 013	8.6	77.7	13.7	22 861	4 456	55.3
Casey, KY	171	14.4	155	NA	189	27	14 170	13.4	72.4	14.2	13 695	5 392	56.4
Christian, KY	534	16.9	492	NA	606	48	48 983	11.9	69.1	18.9	46 666	5 096	57.5
Clark, KY	311	17.3	349	NA	356	22	26 862	8.8	63.5	27.7	23 987	4 513	61.0
Clay, KY	307	14.9	228	NA	399	25	26 749	14.9	75.4	9.8	25 709	5 638	56.7
Clinton, KY	100	15.4	101	NA	116	17	9 885	17.7	64.8	17.6	10 305	6 465	53.5
Crittenden, KY	97	16.3	95	NA	121	17	8 030	8.3	71.9	19.8	7 572	4 759	58.8
Cumberland, KY	79	15.0	66	NA	85	12	6 513	10.9	73.3	15.8	5 951	5 060	56.8
Daviess, KY	875	16.7	858	NA	1 148	84	82 448	8.9	64.6	26.5	70 800	4 834	58.0
Edmonson, KY	114	16.6	137	NA	129	11	10 016	10.8	74.2	15.0	9 866	5 279	51.8
Elliott, KY	97	14.0	82	NA	115	9	9 281	11.1	68.7	20.2	8 187	6 078	56.8
Estill, KY	193	14.4	143	NA	177	27	15 455	10.8	76.5	12.8	14 760	5 294	53.3
Fayette, KY	2 092	15.7	1 666	NA	2 403	237	195 811	5.5	46.9	47.6	177 563	5 374	60.1
Fleming, KY	147	16.4	175	NA	138	21	12 985	12.5	72.3	15.2	11 987	4 968	64.6

Table D-2. School and Student Characteristics by County

State/County code	County	County type[1]	Population, 1996 Total persons	Population, 1996 Percent age 5–17	Number of school districts, 1995–1996	Level of schools, 1995–1996 Number of schools	Percent Primary	Percent Middle	Percent High	Level of students, 1995–1996 Number of students	Percent Primary	Percent Middle	Percent High	Percent with IEP[2]	Percent free-lunch eligible	Percent minority
			1	2	3	4	5	6	7	8	9	10	11	12	13	14
	KENTUCKY—Con.															
21071	Floyd, KY	7	43 744	20.9	1	20	70.0	5.0	20.0	8 144	64.9	5.3	29.6	NA	NA	0.5
21073	Franklin, KY	4	46 410	16.9	2	13	53.8	15.4	23.1	6 892	46.8	22.2	30.3	NA	NA	10.5
21075	Fulton, KY	7	7 794	18.1	2	4	50.0	—	50.0	1 467	61.8	—	38.2	NA	NA	33.7
21077	Gallatin, KY	1	6 409	19.6	1	3	33.3	33.3	33.3	1 247	50.0	25.7	24.2	NA	NA	2.6
21079	Garrard, KY	6	13 251	17.1	1	5	60.0	20.0	20.0	2 149	55.7	17.2	27.1	NA	NA	4.2
21081	Grant, KY	1	19 269	20.6	2	7	57.1	14.3	28.6	4 031	54.4	13.4	32.2	NA	NA	0.9
21083	Graves, KY	7	35 601	17.2	2	14	64.3	14.3	14.3	5 787	60.4	9.7	29.7	NA	NA	7.6
21085	Grayson, KY	7	22 910	18.8	1	7	57.1	14.3	14.3	4 052	52.7	15.5	31.6	NA	NA	1.1
21087	Green, KY	9	10 582	16.9	1	5	60.0	20.0	20.0	1 722	44.7	22.5	32.8	NA	NA	4.2
21089	Greenup, KY	2	37 183	19.0	3	19	57.9	21.1	21.1	6 790	39.5	24.5	35.9	NA	NA	1.4
21091	Hancock, KY	8	8 750	21.2	1	5	60.0	20.0	20.0	1 606	44.6	25.0	30.4	NA	NA	1.8
21093	Hardin, KY	4	89 404	19.7	3	30	53.3	23.3	20.0	15 644	42.7	25.4	31.8	NA	NA	19.7
21095	Harlan, KY	7	35 411	20.9	2	19	63.2	10.5	26.3	6 814	55.3	10.0	34.7	NA	NA	3.7
21097	Harrison, KY	6	17 170	19.2	1	6	66.7	16.7	16.7	3 137	44.7	24.3	31.0	NA	NA	4.5
21099	Hart, KY	9	16 328	18.7	1	6	83.3	—	16.7	2 302	59.2	—	40.8	NA	NA	5.4
21101	Henderson, KY	2	44 444	18.8	1	17	82.4	11.8	5.9	7 649	53.0	25.1	21.9	NA	NA	9.7
21103	Henry, KY	8	14 581	17.7	2	8	50.0	25.0	25.0	2 593	45.0	26.5	28.5	NA	NA	6.2
21105	Hickman, KY	9	5 306	16.0	2	2	50.0	—	50.0	867	54.8	—	45.2	NA	NA	14.0
21107	Hopkins, KY	7	46 545	18.5	2	20	55.0	20.0	20.0	8 145	49.3	21.1	29.4	NA	NA	9.5
21109	Jackson, KY	8	12 832	20.8	1	5	60.0	20.0	20.0	2 444	46.2	23.5	30.3	NA	NA	0.7
21111	Jefferson, KY	2	673 040	16.9	2	151	59.6	17.2	20.5	93 448	46.5	22.4	30.9	NA	NA	33.1
21113	Jessamine, KY	2	35 426	19.2	1	8	62.5	25.0	12.5	6 239	48.6	24.2	27.3	NA	NA	4.9
21115	Johnson, KY	7	24 147	20.2	2	12	58.3	16.7	25.0	4 821	51.9	16.3	31.8	NA	NA	0.6
21117	Kenton, KY	0	145 597	18.7	5	42	57.1	16.7	19.0	21 694	50.5	20.0	29.0	NA	NA	6.1
21119	Knott, KY	9	18 214	21.7	1	11	72.7	—	27.3	3 422	69.7	—	30.3	NA	NA	1.4
21121	Knox, KY	7	31 514	20.3	2	13	69.2	—	30.8	5 446	65.1	—	34.9	NA	NA	1.1
21123	Larue, KY	7	12 760	18.1	1	6	50.0	16.7	16.7	2 271	37.3	32.6	29.5	NA	NA	6.1
21125	Laurel, KY	7	49 185	20.0	2	16	68.8	12.5	12.5	8 951	48.2	23.4	28.2	NA	NA	1.3
21127	Lawrence, KY	8	15 468	20.7	1	5	60.0	20.0	20.0	2 763	46.4	23.3	30.3	NA	NA	0.4
21129	Lee, KY	9	7 906	18.7	1	4	50.0	25.0	25.0	1 466	46.2	26.8	27.0	NA	NA	0.1
21131	Leslie, KY	9	13 523	21.8	1	8	75.0	12.5	12.5	2 621	54.7	14.3	31.1	NA	NA	0.3
21133	Letcher, KY	7	26 744	21.5	2	19	63.2	15.8	21.1	5 155	58.5	8.7	32.8	NA	NA	1.0
21135	Lewis, KY	8	13 516	20.4	1	6	66.7	16.7	16.7	2 532	54.6	23.3	22.1	NA	NA	0.5
21137	Lincoln, KY	7	21 781	18.9	1	9	77.8	11.1	11.1	3 907	55.9	16.4	27.8	NA	NA	3.3
21139	Livingston, KY	9	9 290	16.3	1	6	66.7	16.7	16.7	1 471	53.4	15.9	30.7	NA	NA	0.2
21141	Logan, KY	7	25 902	18.9	2	14	42.9	42.9	14.3	4 606	42.7	27.4	29.9	NA	NA	11.5
21143	Lyon, KY	9	7 849	11.6	2	2	50.0	—	50.0	952	52.6	—	47.4	NA	NA	3.8
21145	McCracken, KY	5	64 940	17.4	2	18	55.6	22.2	22.2	10 243	48.6	21.7	29.7	NA	NA	17.4
21147	McCreary, KY	9	16 583	21.9	1	10	60.0	20.0	10.0	3 483	48.0	23.1	28.7	NA	NA	0.1
21149	McLean, KY	8	9 756	18.0	1	5	60.0	20.0	20.0	1 709	44.1	23.3	32.6	NA	NA	0.4
21151	Madison, KY	2	64 297	15.9	2	20	50.0	25.0	20.0	9 592	47.3	23.7	28.8	NA	NA	6.8
21153	Magoffin, KY	9	13 804	22.7	1	9	66.7	22.2	11.1	2 841	45.7	22.6	31.7	NA	NA	—
21155	Marion, KY	7	17 001	20.1	1	7	57.1	28.6	14.3	2 891	42.3	21.9	35.9	NA	NA	8.9
21157	Marshall, KY	7	29 683	16.3	1	11	54.5	27.3	18.2	5 155	43.0	21.8	35.2	NA	NA	0.4
21159	Martin, KY	9	12 658	23.0	1	10	60.0	20.0	20.0	2 891	43.7	23.4	32.9	NA	NA	0.2
21161	Mason, KY	6	16 891	18.2	1	5	20.0	40.0	40.0	2 813	31.2	40.0	28.8	NA	NA	12.5
21163	Meade, KY	6	27 522	22.2	1	9	77.8	11.1	11.1	4 330	51.5	16.9	31.6	NA	NA	5.6
21165	Menifee, KY	9	5 483	20.0	1	3	66.7	—	33.3	1 042	55.4	—	44.6	NA	NA	0.6
21167	Mercer, KY	6	20 412	17.5	3	9	33.3	22.2	33.3	3 445	41.4	25.4	32.5	NA	NA	5.9
21169	Metcalfe, KY	9	9 369	17.7	1	5	60.0	20.0	20.0	1 652	45.6	23.2	31.2	NA	NA	2.3
21171	Monroe, KY	7	11 314	17.6	1	5	60.0	20.0	20.0	2 125	44.7	24.6	30.7	NA	NA	4.8
21173	Montgomery, KY	6	20 492	19.2	1	6	50.0	16.7	33.3	3 648	43.4	24.9	31.7	NA	NA	5.1
21175	Morgan, KY	9	13 420	18.6	1	8	62.5	12.5	12.5	2 403	39.6	27.5	31.2	NA	NA	0.5
21177	Muhlenberg, KY	7	31 857	18.8	1	13	61.5	15.4	15.4	5 481	51.7	16.6	31.7	NA	NA	5.0
21179	Nelson, KY	6	34 332	20.8	2	13	53.8	30.8	15.4	5 869	41.5	25.7	32.8	NA	NA	9.5
21181	Nicholas, KY	8	6 942	18.5	1	2	50.0	—	50.0	1 290	69.3	—	30.7	NA	NA	0.4
21183	Ohio, KY	6	21 826	19.4	1	8	75.0	12.5	12.5	4 101	53.3	16.3	30.4	NA	NA	1.5
21185	Oldham, KY	2	42 287	21.1	1	11	54.5	18.2	27.3	7 418	45.3	24.8	29.9	NA	NA	3.4
21187	Owen, KY	8	9 905	19.4	1	5	40.0	20.0	20.0	1 829	44.9	24.3	30.2	NA	NA	2.0
21189	Owsley, KY	9	5 481	19.2	1	2	50.0	—	50.0	942	54.0	—	46.0	NA	NA	0.5
21191	Pendleton, KY	1	13 757	20.3	1	4	50.0	25.0	25.0	2 709	54.4	15.9	29.6	NA	NA	0.9
21193	Perry, KY	7	31 199	21.1	2	17	70.6	5.9	23.5	6 489	62.0	7.3	30.8	NA	NA	3.4
21195	Pike, KY	7	73 389	20.6	2	34	67.6	2.9	23.5	13 402	58.5	2.9	38.5	NA	NA	0.8
21197	Powell, KY	6	12 409	21.3	1	5	60.0	20.0	20.0	2 664	44.0	26.5	29.5	NA	NA	1.4
21199	Pulaski, KY	7	55 065	17.6	3	18	55.6	22.2	22.2	9 319	45.3	25.5	29.1	NA	NA	2.1
21201	Robertson, KY	9	2 209	17.2	1	2	50.0	—	50.0	366	57.4	—	42.6	NA	NA	0.8

1. County type code is from the Economic Research Service of the USDA. See notes and definitions at the end of this section.   2. IEP = Individual Education Program. See notes and definitions at the end of this section.

Table D-2. School and Student Characteristics by County — Continued

County	Staff and students, 1995–1996						Revenues, fiscal 1995					Current expenditures, fiscal 1995		
	Number of teachers	Pupil/ teacher ratio	Number of graduates	Dropouts grades 9–12 (percent)	Local school non-teaching staff	Central admin. staff	Total revenue ($1000)	Percent of Revenue from			Amount	Amount per pupil	Percent for instruction
								Federal Gov't	State Gov't	Local Gov't			
	15	16	17	18	19	20	21	22	23	24	25	26	27
KENTUCKY—Con.													
Floyd, KY	534	15.3	468	NA	606	42	48 531	10.5	63.8	25.7	46 129	5 594	56.2
Franklin, KY	419	16.4	422	NA	369	33	33 756	5.2	62.7	32.2	30 307	4 323	60.9
Fulton, KY	108	13.6	86	NA	118	15	8 812	14.3	66.4	19.4	8 856	5 800	58.0
Gallatin, KY	74	16.9	56	NA	88	11	5 774	7.0	71.1	21.9	5 791	4 958	57.6
Garrard, KY	136	15.8	118	NA	153	10	11 051	9.9	68.1	22.0	9 684	4 600	55.7
Grant, KY	228	17.6	198	NA	241	20	20 475	9.5	66.5	24.0	18 058	4 874	56.3
Graves, KY	318	18.2	344	NA	399	26	28 483	8.8	69.2	22.0	24 981	4 363	56.6
Grayson, KY	233	17.4	246	NA	257	19	20 612	9.3	70.3	20.3	18 077	4 491	60.9
Green, KY	104	16.6	126	NA	138	8	9 144	6.9	67.6	25.5	7 864	4 463	59.3
Greenup, KY	397	17.1	515	NA	429	38	35 209	7.5	66.3	26.2	32 617	4 753	58.9
Hancock, KY	101	16.0	108	NA	104	11	7 326	8.1	66.5	25.4	6 651	4 207	57.3
Hardin, KY	912	17.2	955	NA	1 052	104	80 862	7.8	69.7	22.6	73 589	4 689	58.9
Harlan, KY	483	14.1	443	NA	557	36	38 416	12.7	75.6	11.8	39 038	5 606	56.8
Harrison, KY	193	16.3	186	NA	183	19	16 194	7.7	72.3	20.0	14 499	4 591	56.2
Hart, KY	154	14.9	145	NA	147	13	11 886	12.4	72.4	15.2	10 530	4 512	56.4
Henderson, KY	422	18.1	424	NA	110	19	40 234	6.2	63.8	30.0	36 099	4 687	58.0
Henry, KY	155	16.7	146	NA	289	20	13 674	11.3	65.4	23.3	12 638	4 948	56.2
Hickman, KY	58	15.1	50	NA	60	6	4 603	8.6	68.8	22.7	4 326	4 978	58.6
Hopkins, KY	484	16.8	562	NA	565	55	44 325	8.9	66.5	24.7	40 518	4 918	56.9
Jackson, KY	167	14.7	135	NA	37	9	14 185	13.8	74.9	11.3	13 788	5 621	52.3
Jefferson, KY	5 559	16.8	5 279	NA	6 060	788	558 559	7.6	49.6	42.8	513 716	5 478	62.2
Jessamine, KY	358	17.4	348	NA	371	32	28 917	5.8	65.3	29.0	24 187	3 960	63.1
Johnson, KY	316	15.2	289	NA	369	26	27 814	9.9	73.2	16.9	25 135	5 077	56.0
Kenton, KY	1 229	17.7	1 180	NA	1 266	103	112 458	6.3	59.7	34.0	101 755	4 751	57.4
Knott, KY	230	14.9	199	NA	262	22	21 941	12.0	65.6	22.5	19 143	5 555	55.9
Knox, KY	373	14.6	299	NA	343	31	32 247	14.3	71.9	13.8	31 223	5 685	55.2
Larue, KY	140	16.2	123	NA	156	18	11 341	7.5	74.7	17.8	9 865	4 310	56.3
Laurel, KY	507	17.6	519	NA	699	47	45 605	10.4	72.4	17.2	42 277	4 719	57.0
Lawrence, KY	183	15.1	211	NA	198	13	14 679	11.1	74.0	14.9	13 349	4 861	57.2
Lee, KY	88	16.6	70	NA	97	13	8 675	14.0	74.6	11.4	7 740	5 181	61.9
Leslie, KY	177	14.8	178	NA	195	17	16 755	11.3	70.3	18.4	14 868	5 511	60.5
Letcher, KY	320	16.1	380	NA	388	34	32 598	10.6	66.1	23.2	29 815	5 590	56.8
Lewis, KY	159	15.9	146	NA	194	12	13 554	10.4	74.7	14.9	12 638	5 027	56.3
Lincoln, KY	256	15.3	250	NA	361	27	22 468	12.9	70.7	16.4	21 738	5 592	59.8
Livingston, KY	88	16.8	100	NA	105	8	7 581	11.7	64.5	23.7	6 755	4 506	57.1
Logan, KY	283	16.3	298	NA	314	21	25 736	8.8	65.9	25.4	24 653	5 295	59.7
Lyon, KY	55	17.3	68	NA	54	5	7 767	13.8	70.8	15.4	7 530	7 730	61.1
McCracken, KY	578	17.7	602	NA	577	52	52 074	11.7	62.6	25.7	48 940	4 784	58.5
McCreary, KY	232	15.0	163	NA	352	23	21 307	14.8	76.6	8.7	20 484	5 834	61.1
McLean, KY	110	15.5	119	NA	105	8	8 564	9.3	68.1	22.6	8 180	4 761	60.2
Madison, KY	581	16.5	589	NA	600	44	49 626	9.3	67.5	23.1	44 424	4 633	59.3
Magoffin, KY	201	14.2	152	NA	264	15	16 247	13.1	79.0	8.0	15 159	5 132	55.4
Marion, KY	193	15.0	212	NA	226	15	17 039	10.3	68.9	20.8	15 518	5 323	62.8
Marshall, KY	294	17.6	262	NA	249	11	22 716	8.1	64.9	27.0	20 049	3 946	59.8
Martin, KY	182	15.9	185	NA	237	16	15 347	12.8	68.1	19.2	14 912	5 034	55.9
Mason, KY	185	15.2	179	NA	183	18	13 987	10.1	62.7	27.3	12 155	4 354	60.8
Meade, KY	242	17.9	243	NA	204	14	19 677	7.1	75.9	17.0	16 561	3 967	59.9
Menifee, KY	69	15.1	55	NA	72	8	5 487	10.9	68.5	20.6	5 202	5 186	54.7
Mercer, KY	210	16.4	211	NA	209	20	17 667	6.9	66.7	26.4	15 655	4 613	59.6
Metcalfe, KY	111	14.9	105	NA	134	10	9 183	12.2	69.0	18.8	9 115	5 606	59.1
Monroe, KY	153	13.9	119	NA	196	16	12 219	11.5	72.1	16.4	11 822	5 627	55.9
Montgomery, KY	234	15.6	249	NA	313	25	21 113	10.7	68.4	20.8	19 024	5 172	64.0
Morgan, KY	171	14.1	128	NA	204	16	14 492	11.6	73.9	14.5	13 626	5 645	62.2
Muhlenberg, KY	378	14.5	368	NA	349	31	27 834	7.8	64.8	27.4	25 263	4 467	58.8
Nelson, KY	332	17.7	364	NA	295	25	29 956	7.4	62.6	30.0	26 550	4 584	56.9
Nicholas, KY	76	16.9	92	NA	89	10	7 604	21.0	64.5	14.5	6 238	4 828	54.5
Ohio, KY	245	16.7	233	NA	324	24	20 864	8.8	71.7	19.6	18 220	4 509	58.9
Oldham, KY	420	17.6	505	NA	454	44	37 158	4.4	58.5	37.1	30 150	4 077	61.5
Owen, KY	114	16.0	96	NA	25	2	9 872	7.9	72.2	20.0	9 204	4 967	57.4
Owsley, KY	71	13.2	55	NA	118	7	7 657	25.0	64.8	10.1	8 390	8 365	56.6
Pendleton, KY	149	18.2	160	NA	178	11	14 826	7.5	70.5	22.0	12 952	4 802	60.6
Perry, KY	427	15.2	228	NA	536	36	39 020	10.6	68.0	21.4	34 912	5 176	57.4
Pike, KY	876	15.3	914	NA	810	53	72 529	9.3	72.1	18.5	72 672	5 212	57.9
Powell, KY	156	17.1	148	NA	202	26	13 935	10.4	78.1	11.6	12 914	4 886	56.1
Pulaski, KY	576	16.2	504	NA	229	21	54 227	8.3	71.0	20.7	45 137	4 798	59.2
Robertson, KY	23	16.3	17	NA	27	4	1 951	9.5	72.3	18.2	1 856	5 071	56.4

Table D-2. School and Student Characteristics by County

State/County code	County	County type[1]	Population, 1996		Number of school districts, 1995–1996	Level of schools, 1995–1996				Level of students, 1995–1996				Characteristics of students, 1995–1996		
			Total persons	Percent age 5–17		Number of schools	Percent			Number of students	Percent			Percent with IEP[2]	Percent free-lunch eligible	Percent minority
							Primary	Middle	High		Primary	Middle	High			
			1	2	3	4	5	6	7	8	9	10	11	12	13	14
	KENTUCKY—Con.															
21203	Rockcastle, KY	6	15 627	18.9	1	5	60.0	20.0	20.0	2 987	48.1	23.7	28.2	NA	NA	0.5
21205	Rowan, KY	7	21 768	14.5	1	8	62.5	25.0	12.5	3 153	44.1	25.3	30.6	NA	NA	1.7
21207	Russell, KY	9	16 401	16.8	1	7	57.1	14.3	28.6	2 789	54.0	17.1	28.8	NA	NA	1.0
21209	Scott, KY	2	28 565	19.3	1	10	60.0	30.0	10.0	5 100	46.0	25.3	28.6	NA	NA	7.4
21211	Shelby, KY	6	28 227	17.8	1	9	44.4	33.3	22.2	4 617	42.3	28.3	29.4	NA	NA	12.7
21213	Simpson, KY	6	16 084	18.5	1	5	40.0	40.0	20.0	2 947	39.1	31.5	29.5	NA	NA	14.3
21215	Spencer, KY	8	8 649	19.3	1	2	50.0	—	50.0	1 667	55.4	—	44.6	NA	NA	1.4
21217	Taylor, KY	7	22 712	17.5	2	7	42.9	28.6	28.6	4 025	48.2	21.9	29.8	NA	NA	6.8
21219	Todd, KY	8	11 225	18.5	1	4	50.0	25.0	25.0	1 998	48.0	25.7	26.3	NA	NA	14.0
21221	Trigg, KY	8	11 857	16.4	1	3	33.3	33.3	33.3	1 848	47.3	23.5	29.2	NA	NA	17.1
21223	Trimble, KY	8	7 246	18.5	1	4	50.0	25.0	25.0	1 327	46.9	24.0	29.0	NA	NA	0.5
21225	Union, KY	6	16 508	21.9	1	5	60.0	20.0	20.0	2 807	41.3	24.1	34.7	NA	NA	10.9
21227	Warren, KY	5	85 545	17.1	2	30	60.0	13.3	23.3	13 744	53.2	16.3	30.4	NA	NA	13.5
21229	Washington, KY	7	10 815	19.1	1	5	80.0	—	20.0	1 791	57.3	—	42.7	NA	NA	12.1
21231	Wayne, KY	7	18 703	19.4	2	11	27.3	27.3	36.4	3 617	40.3	29.9	29.4	NA	NA	2.7
21233	Webster, KY	6	13 524	19.0	2	8	62.5	—	37.5	2 657	67.6	—	32.4	NA	NA	6.2
21235	Whitley, KY	7	35 668	19.4	3	16	62.5	12.5	25.0	7 186	52.7	16.9	30.4	NA	NA	0.7
21237	Wolfe, KY	9	7 363	21.3	1	5	60.0	20.0	20.0	1 394	42.0	25.6	32.4	NA	NA	0.2
21239	Woodford, KY	2	22 040	18.3	1	6	66.7	16.7	16.7	3 839	53.1	16.6	30.2	NA	NA	8.1
22000	**LOUISIANA**															
22001	Acadia, LA	2	57 590	22.9	1	25	64.0	16.0	16.0	10 917	50.8	18.8	24.7	13.6	53.0	28.8
22003	Allen, LA	6	23 892	19.0	1	10	30.0	10.0	30.0	4 551	43.5	11.1	22.4	11.4	45.3	25.3
22005	Ascension, LA	2	67 958	23.3	1	18	50.0	27.8	16.7	14 275	45.6	26.8	27.6	16.8	36.9	32.2
22007	Assumption, LA	6	22 681	23.2	1	12	41.7	41.7	8.3	4 976	42.6	31.2	24.2	10.5	57.7	45.2
22009	Avoyelles, LA	6	40 433	20.9	1	12	50.0	25.0	25.0	7 651	48.6	24.1	27.3	10.9	65.3	40.8
22011	Beauregard, LA	6	31 771	21.0	1	11	27.3	18.2	9.1	6 546	24.2	19.2	14.2	13.5	32.3	18.2
22013	Bienville, LA	6	16 676	20.0	1	9	33.3	—	22.2	3 037	33.8	—	21.1	10.6	67.0	60.8
22015	Bossier, LA	2	91 811	20.6	1	30	46.7	26.7	26.7	18 741	49.0	23.1	27.9	11.3	32.0	31.9
22017	Caddo, LA	2	245 095	20.4	1	74	66.2	14.9	16.2	49 578	54.0	16.9	28.6	14.1	48.0	61.6
22019	Calcasieu, LA	3	178 881	21.0	1	59	59.3	18.6	18.6	34 163	49.1	20.7	27.3	14.4	35.0	31.9
22021	Caldwell, LA	8	10 189	21.1	1	6	66.7	16.7	—	2 127	54.2	15.5	—	11.8	50.7	23.5
22023	Cameron, LA	8	8 733	21.6	1	7	42.9	—	14.3	2 111	30.8	—	17.0	19.7	27.2	6.3
22025	Catahoula, LA	7	11 155	22.2	1	9	44.4	11.1	33.3	2 317	46.1	15.7	34.6	9.9	53.8	37.4
22027	Claiborne, LA	6	17 185	18.3	1	9	22.2	22.2	22.2	3 029	33.2	20.7	19.4	17.3	59.4	64.1
22029	Concordia, LA	7	20 854	22.6	1	11	36.4	36.4	18.2	4 442	33.9	30.4	23.8	9.2	61.4	50.9
22031	De Soto, LA	6	23 428	21.4	1	9	22.2	11.1	22.2	5 434	45.2	7.9	18.3	10.1	32.0	56.4
22033	East Baton Rouge, LA	2	395 914	19.6	5	127	52.0	13.4	13.4	62 522	46.1	21.8	26.6	17.8	44.6	63.7
22035	East Carroll, LA	7	9 154	26.0	1	6	50.0	16.7	16.7	2 065	53.9	16.9	19.5	9.2	82.7	89.5
22037	East Feliciana, LA	6	20 833	21.1	1	5	40.0	20.0	20.0	3 066	31.5	14.3	13.4	9.2	69.3	75.4
22039	Evangeline, LA	7	34 281	22.6	1	15	40.0	6.7	13.3	7 122	38.8	5.3	18.2	14.7	64.1	39.4
22041	Franklin, LA	7	22 078	22.7	1	12	33.3	8.3	16.7	4 688	31.0	9.7	17.0	10.2	60.9	45.2
22043	Grant, LA	8	18 591	21.3	1	9	44.4	22.2	22.2	3 691	52.9	15.4	22.2	7.9	48.5	18.2
22045	Iberia, LA	4	71 685	22.9	1	33	63.6	24.2	9.1	15 701	52.4	25.8	18.5	16.3	53.1	43.2
22047	Iberville, LA	6	30 929	21.0	1	8	37.5	12.5	25.0	5 453	40.1	16.7	19.4	11.3	67.0	71.4
22049	Jackson, LA	6	15 492	21.1	1	9	44.4	11.1	22.2	2 956	31.1	12.2	16.7	11.8	43.8	35.8
22051	Jefferson, LA	0	455 043	19.2	1	83	66.3	18.1	10.8	56 021	51.6	23.5	23.9	15.1	51.3	52.7
22053	Jefferson Davis, LA	6	31 753	22.6	1	14	42.9	14.3	21.4	6 707	43.7	13.0	23.1	13.4	47.9	26.2
22055	Lafayette, LA	2	181 851	20.3	1	41	58.5	24.4	17.1	31 915	46.5	24.7	28.8	14.5	39.7	35.9
22057	Lafourche, LA	3	87 772	21.4	1	28	50.0	39.3	10.7	16 323	43.6	36.2	20.2	16.4	44.6	26.4
22059	La Salle, LA	7	13 840	20.4	1	9	44.4	33.3	22.2	2 947	42.6	29.1	28.3	9.4	34.3	13.3
22061	Lincoln, LA	4	42 302	16.8	1	17	52.9	17.6	23.5	7 164	47.6	16.9	27.6	7.9	42.8	49.4
22063	Livingston, LA	2	82 900	23.0	1	34	50.0	20.6	20.6	18 252	45.9	21.3	27.1	10.5	30.5	6.9
22065	Madison, LA	7	12 997	25.1	1	8	25.0	12.5	12.5	3 316	42.2	10.3	13.2	11.7	64.1	83.9
22067	Morehouse, LA	6	31 969	22.7	1	16	75.0	12.5	12.5	5 997	54.8	15.1	30.1	12.1	60.5	65.1
22069	Natchitoches, LA	6	38 173	21.9	2	16	62.5	18.8	12.5	7 972	55.1	12.6	13.7	13.2	52.4	53.9
22071	Orleans, LA	0	476 625	19.5	1	121	66.1	12.4	19.8	85 484	58.6	12.1	29.1	11.8	70.2	94.3
22073	Ouachita, LA	3	147 302	21.2	2	51	66.7	17.6	15.7	29 187	57.2	15.6	27.1	10.3	46.9	49.0
22075	Plaquemines, LA	1	25 848	22.7	1	8	12.5	25.0	—	5 275	13.1	15.1	—	3.7	42.2	38.1
22077	Pointe Coupee, LA	6	23 200	22.2	1	8	75.0	—	25.0	3 657	55.9	—	44.1	6.6	68.6	66.8
22079	Rapides, LA	3	126 290	21.1	2	55	52.7	20.0	18.2	24 850	44.9	21.2	27.4	13.3	48.3	42.9
22081	Red River, LA	8	9 746	22.3	1	5	20.0	20.0	20.0	2 104	30.3	17.7	16.3	11.2	66.5	58.2
22083	Richland, LA	6	20 892	22.8	1	12	50.0	25.0	25.0	4 280	51.2	22.5	26.2	16.0	62.0	56.0
22085	Sabine, LA	7	23 741	20.3	1	12	33.3	8.3	25.0	4 846	40.4	7.3	18.3	13.2	52.6	44.8
22087	St. Bernard, LA	0	66 641	19.4	1	17	58.8	23.5	17.6	9 555	50.2	20.3	29.4	16.6	41.4	16.8
22089	St. Charles, LA	0	47 031	22.0	1	19	57.9	31.6	10.5	9 973	45.7	27.5	26.8	14.9	35.6	35.9

1. County type code is from the Economic Research Service of the USDA. See notes and definitions at the end of this section.   2. IEP = Individual Education Program. See notes and definitions at the end of this section.

Table D-2.   School and Student Characteristics by County — Continued

County	Staff and students, 1995–1996						Revenues, fiscal 1995					Current expenditures, fiscal 1995		
	Number of teachers	Pupil/ teacher ratio	Number of graduates	Dropouts grades 9–12 (percent)	Local school non-teaching staff	Central admin. staff	Total revenue ($1000)	Percent of Revenue from			Amount	Amount per pupil	Percent for instruction
								Federal Gov't	State Gov't	Local Gov't			
	15	16	17	18	19	20	21	22	23	24	25	26	27
KENTUCKY—Con.													
Rockcastle, KY	184	16.3	159	NA	227	19	16 148	11.3	74.9	13.7	15 215	5 207	57.9
Rowan, KY	200	15.7	187	NA	212	17	17 326	10.0	70.8	19.2	15 994	5 120	57.7
Russell, KY	188	14.8	133	NA	270	15	15 395	11.5	67.7	20.8	14 371	5 134	63.3
Scott, KY	309	16.5	286	NA	257	14	34 161	5.4	44.8	49.8	24 381	4 894	57.1
Shelby, KY	265	17.5	267	NA	290	22	23 708	5.8	64.0	30.2	19 267	4 477	57.7
Simpson, KY	174	16.9	160	NA	216	26	16 011	10.2	63.2	26.6	17 457	6 061	54.3
Spencer, KY	106	15.8	75	NA	116	11	8 690	9.1	71.9	18.9	8 115	5 202	58.4
Taylor, KY	257	15.7	243	NA	267	30	20 583	8.7	70.3	21.0	18 102	4 511	58.7
Todd, KY	114	17.6	112	NA	156	13	10 001	10.4	75.2	14.4	9 251	4 828	56.3
Trigg, KY	119	15.5	123	NA	114	16	9 050	11.9	70.5	17.6	8 862	4 772	59.4
Trimble, KY	72	18.5	70	NA	108	8	6 996	11.7	61.8	26.5	6 482	5 029	56.7
Union, KY	187	15.0	208	NA	221	22	15 822	8.1	67.8	24.1	14 764	5 247	57.5
Warren, KY	814	16.9	821	NA	719	39	70 183	7.1	61.8	31.1	60 494	4 444	57.8
Washington, KY	109	16.4	117	NA	111	9	8 815	10.6	72.4	17.0	8 475	4 772	60.4
Wayne, KY	234	15.4	169	NA	328	26	21 098	11.6	70.1	18.4	19 273	5 432	56.9
Webster, KY	167	16.0	185	NA	187	19	14 084	7.5	67.2	25.3	12 521	4 679	56.3
Whitley, KY	433	16.6	411	NA	274	38	39 499	10.7	72.3	17.0	35 728	5 020	55.9
Wolfe, KY	97	14.4	73	NA	126	8	8 772	13.2	75.6	11.2	8 120	5 884	57.8
Woodford, KY	209	18.3	197	NA	238	32	18 648	6.8	57.3	36.0	16 523	4 276	61.4
LOUISIANA													
Acadia, LA	619	17.6	461	1.5	658	32	43 055	16.3	62.8	20.8	39 328	3 592	58.7
Allen, LA	282	16.1	247	3.2	280	11	19 662	13.2	62.9	23.9	19 080	4 177	56.8
Ascension, LA	860	16.6	763	1.6	840	23	68 382	8.9	45.9	45.2	62 154	4 401	61.2
Assumption, LA	303	16.4	209	1.5	311	20	23 197	15.0	60.1	24.9	22 017	4 346	59.4
Avoyelles, LA	409	18.7	383	2.7	343	23	31 900	16.1	66.2	17.7	29 429	3 776	58.8
Beauregard, LA	394	16.6	368	1.0	434	19	32 030	8.4	55.8	35.8	28 134	4 291	57.9
Bienville, LA	192	15.9	161	0.7	208	14	16 770	11.9	50.5	37.5	14 466	4 498	55.2
Bossier, LA	1 021	18.4	906	2.5	982	58	89 709	8.8	58.6	32.6	74 609	4 025	58.3
Caddo, LA	2 858	17.3	2 314	5.1	3 114	159	234 385	11.4	52.8	35.8	217 204	4 378	60.8
Calcasieu, LA	2 031	16.8	1 785	2.6	2 034	93	160 694	8.8	47.9	43.3	138 904	4 028	58.9
Caldwell, LA	129	16.5	90	10.8	139	15	9 667	14.2	61.7	24.1	8 762	4 219	61.9
Cameron, LA	142	14.9	99	0.9	156	13	12 051	6.4	44.6	49.0	12 402	5 994	53.5
Catahoula, LA	158	14.7	136	2.9	150	12	11 459	12.9	64.4	22.7	10 783	4 487	55.9
Claiborne, LA	195	15.5	142	0.7	198	10	13 287	14.8	62.6	22.5	12 995	4 297	58.0
Concordia, LA	270	16.5	148	2.1	270	18	19 585	15.1	60.8	24.1	19 083	4 400	56.2
De Soto, LA	341	15.9	245	1.1	331	14	30 595	10.6	49.4	40.0	24 501	4 461	55.7
East Baton Rouge, LA	4 006	15.6	3 016	2.6	3 673	103	301 526	10.6	51.2	38.2	292 498	4 759	60.0
East Carroll, LA	116	17.8	97	7.7	138	12	9 594	21.9	61.4	16.6	8 961	4 189	57.8
East Feliciana, LA	187	16.4	154	8.8	171	14	15 078	14.7	59.6	25.8	12 590	3 828	56.2
Evangeline, LA	444	16.1	343	0.9	465	33	30 550	16.9	65.9	17.2	28 477	3 962	59.3
Franklin, LA	307	15.3	216	7.0	251	16	19 545	16.0	67.6	16.4	19 432	4 160	60.9
Grant, LA	227	16.3	150	7.1	216	14	15 778	13.4	71.1	15.5	14 478	3 836	54.2
Iberia, LA	943	16.7	613	2.6	879	31	75 267	12.4	56.6	31.1	65 761	4 133	59.6
Iberville, LA	336	16.2	247	4.2	347	17	34 230	11.6	40.8	47.6	28 555	5 235	54.8
Jackson, LA	202	14.6	165	2.3	161	12	14 191	9.1	61.1	29.7	12 992	4 246	59.9
Jefferson, LA	3 326	16.8	2 276	4.3	3 377	102	350 237	8.5	38.6	52.9	275 276	4 847	62.5
Jefferson Davis, LA	392	17.1	393	1.4	387	23	31 334	12.8	58.8	28.5	28 200	4 137	56.9
Lafayette, LA	1 763	18.1	1 433	0.7	1 411	67	140 178	10.7	49.9	39.5	120 402	3 904	62.8
Lafourche, LA	1 002	16.3	832	2.6	798	20	69 077	12.4	62.1	25.5	64 124	3 876	60.1
La Salle, LA	172	17.1	138	1.8	141	11	12 789	11.6	62.0	26.4	11 795	3 990	58.5
Lincoln, LA	456	15.7	325	14.4	340	15	32 398	9.8	52.6	37.6	29 439	4 095	61.2
Livingston, LA	979	18.6	849	1.0	783	38	69 966	8.1	65.9	26.0	63 171	3 513	62.5
Madison, LA	150	22.2	170	5.4	170	12	12 467	19.4	67.0	13.6	11 499	3 495	56.7
Morehouse, LA	345	17.4	293	8.9	356	13	27 454	16.5	57.2	26.3	24 415	3 963	57.7
Natchitoches, LA	524	15.2	293	3.8	492	26	35 360	15.5	60.4	24.1	32 644	4 228	60.7
Orleans, LA	3 855	22.2	3 267	6.4	3 651	148	401 791	15.4	50.4	34.2	375 127	4 361	62.6
Ouachita, LA	1 716	17.0	790	5.2	1 670	84	125 692	12.7	55.1	32.1	113 456	3 924	63.6
Plaquemines, LA	306	17.2	223	2.4	295	22	28 617	10.7	35.4	53.9	24 030	4 630	56.5
Pointe Coupee, LA	213	17.2	139	1.1	221	15	19 095	15.0	52.2	32.8	16 401	4 396	53.2
Rapides, LA	1 556	16.0	1 224	0.9	1 380	30	123 151	11.3	53.2	35.5	112 210	4 536	59.1
Red River, LA	132	15.9	71	NA	145	8	9 324	17.4	56.7	26.0	9 113	4 409	55.3
Richland, LA	271	15.8	203	7.0	268	17	20 041	14.0	62.2	23.8	17 601	3 976	63.0
Sabine, LA	293	16.5	212	5.0	346	21	20 962	13.1	62.9	24.0	19 829	4 228	58.0
St. Bernard, LA	551	17.3	508	3.8	512	23	43 808	11.0	55.7	33.3	41 010	4 312	59.3
St. Charles, LA	624	16.0	499	2.3	574	35	66 267	5.8	33.0	61.2	57 010	5 806	60.9

KY (Rockcastle, KY)–LA (St. Charles, LA)

Table D-2.   School and Student Characteristics by County

State/County code	County	County type[1]	Population, 1996		Number of school districts, 1995–1996	Level of schools, 1995–1996				Level of students, 1995–1996				Characteristics of students, 1995–1996		
			Total persons	Percent age 5–17		Number of schools	Percent			Number of students	Percent			Percent with IEP[2]	Percent free-lunch eligible	Percent minority
							Primary	Middle	High		Primary	Middle	High			
		1	2	3	4	5	6	7	8	9	10	11	12	13	14
	LOUISIANA—Con.															
22091	St. Helena, LA	8	9 748	22.5	1	3	33.3	33.3	33.3	1 646	44.8	29.4	25.8	14.2	74.1	91.3
22093	St. James, LA	1	20 959	22.6	1	12	58.3	25.0	16.7	4 267	52.0	17.8	30.1	10.5	60.8	69.5
22095	St. John the Baptist, LA	1	42 260	24.0	1	13	69.2	15.4	15.4	7 211	62.0	12.0	26.1	4.1	61.7	69.0
22097	St. Landry, LA	2	82 955	22.9	1	37	67.6	10.8	18.9	17 566	56.2	12.1	26.4	13.1	61.7	54.0
22099	St. Martin, LA	2	46 239	23.0	1	17	41.2	41.2	17.6	9 187	37.8	35.3	26.9	14.4	58.0	46.8
22101	St. Mary, LA	4	57 425	23.0	1	26	50.0	26.9	15.4	11 822	40.9	27.3	26.1	15.1	56.9	50.3
22103	St. Tammany, LA	0	178 483	21.8	1	48	47.9	35.4	14.6	31 947	39.1	33.4	27.4	18.2	22.6	16.2
22105	Tangipahoa, LA	4	94 273	22.2	1	35	48.6	25.7	22.9	18 209	43.6	26.6	29.7	11.0	58.9	45.6
22107	Tensas, LA	9	6 883	23.9	1	6	33.3	16.7	33.3	1 539	28.2	17.5	23.9	19.3	81.6	78.2
22109	Terrebonne, LA	3	102 097	23.2	1	42	52.4	31.0	16.7	22 194	44.3	30.3	25.4	13.1	44.3	35.2
22111	Union, LA	6	21 607	20.2	1	10	30.0	10.0	10.0	4 043	30.0	10.5	13.5	3.2	50.2	42.5
22113	Vermilion, LA	6	51 299	22.2	1	20	55.0	15.0	20.0	9 733	47.7	20.7	26.9	15.2	44.3	23.7
22115	Vernon, LA	5	54 546	17.7	1	18	38.9	5.6	22.2	11 320	43.3	6.6	21.2	10.5	32.9	30.9
22117	Washington, LA	6	43 315	21.4	2	21	57.1	19.0	14.3	8 710	43.4	18.0	24.5	14.5	68.9	43.4
22119	Webster, LA	2	42 690	19.7	1	22	50.0	13.6	18.2	8 409	50.5	9.4	20.7	10.9	39.1	42.3
22121	West Baton Rouge, LA	2	20 616	21.3	1	11	45.5	27.3	27.3	4 156	41.4	27.7	30.9	10.6	49.4	49.1
22123	West Carroll, LA	9	12 191	21.4	1	8	50.0	—	12.5	2 770	35.3	—	15.9	11.6	50.5	22.6
22125	West Feliciana, LA	8	12 964	15.4	1	4	75.0	—	25.0	2 347	59.6	—	40.4	0.5	0.3	46.3
22127	Winn, LA	7	16 824	19.3	1	8	25.0	25.0	12.5	3 306	24.4	24.8	17.3	13.1	49.8	37.2
23000	**MAINE**															
23001	Androscoggin, ME	3	101 754	18.6	12	44	56.8	22.7	15.9	17 036	48.4	22.5	26.1	14.7	26.3	2.7
23003	Aroostook, ME	5	78 113	18.9	24	56	62.5	8.9	23.2	14 432	48.1	9.9	32.1	12.4	32.7	3.6
23005	Cumberland, ME	3	251 087	16.7	17	93	55.9	25.8	17.2	38 324	45.4	28.5	26.1	12.0	17.8	4.5
23007	Franklin, ME	6	29 200	19.4	4	18	61.1	16.7	16.7	5 457	46.8	20.7	28.0	14.2	29.0	1.2
23009	Hancock, ME	6	49 500	17.3	30	39	79.5	7.7	12.8	8 433	66.2	8.5	25.3	14.0	21.2	1.4
23011	Kennebec, ME	4	116 214	18.7	20	56	64.3	19.6	16.1	19 133	49.7	21.5	28.8	13.6	22.5	1.8
23013	Knox, ME	7	37 487	17.6	9	22	63.6	13.6	13.6	4 824	46.7	20.9	27.1	11.9	20.4	1.4
23015	Lincoln, ME	9	31 303	18.5	14	24	79.2	8.3	12.5	6 374	70.2	9.0	20.8	15.5	21.9	1.2
23017	Oxford, ME	6	53 797	19.3	8	40	70.0	12.5	15.0	10 791	54.8	17.2	27.9	14.6	28.3	1.1
23019	Penobscot, ME	3	144 989	18.1	26	90	60.0	24.4	13.3	25 612	47.1	23.3	27.4	12.9	26.5	2.5
23021	Piscataquis, ME	6	18 329	20.0	5	21	66.7	19.0	9.5	3 505	41.7	32.7	19.3	13.4	34.6	0.9
23023	Sagadahoc, ME	6	35 508	18.6	7	20	70.0	15.0	15.0	7 035	56.5	16.8	26.7	14.7	13.5	3.1
23025	Somerset, ME	7	52 507	20.7	8	39	66.7	17.9	12.8	9 910	49.4	21.1	27.0	14.1	32.6	1.4
23027	Waldo, ME	6	35 822	19.9	6	26	73.1	11.5	11.5	5 244	53.2	19.1	25.5	17.4	35.3	1.4
23029	Washington, ME	7	36 224	19.3	24	38	76.3	2.6	15.8	5 966	63.4	2.8	25.3	14.8	38.5	8.4
23031	York, ME	4	171 482	18.8	15	71	60.6	23.9	15.5	31 691	46.9	27.5	25.6	13.1	18.6	2.0
24000	**MARYLAND**															
24001	Allegany, MD	3	73 037	17.3	1	25	52.0	12.0	20.0	11 300	41.0	17.2	30.6	13.4	34.7	3.9
24003	Anne Arundel, MD	0	465 582	18.6	1	111	71.2	16.2	10.8	71 383	51.1	22.4	26.2	13.4	11.4	21.3
24005	Baltimore, MD	0	717 859	16.3	1	158	65.8	18.4	15.8	101 564	51.5	22.9	25.6	12.1	19.6	29.5
24009	Calvert, MD	1	66 779	21.9	1	17	58.8	29.4	11.8	13 496	49.8	25.5	24.7	11.4	11.8	18.1
24011	Caroline, MD	6	29 189	19.8	1	9	55.6	22.2	11.1	5 521	50.4	23.0	17.0	14.7	31.7	22.6
24013	Carroll, MD	1	143 648	20.2	1	33	60.6	21.2	15.2	25 408	49.7	23.2	26.8	13.3	6.7	3.8
24015	Cecil, MD	2	79 475	21.1	1	27	63.0	18.5	18.5	14 640	51.8	20.7	27.5	15.2	17.9	6.9
24017	Charles, MD	1	113 557	22.6	1	31	58.1	22.6	16.1	20 966	46.6	24.2	29.2	12.6	18.5	29.8
24019	Dorchester, MD	7	29 988	17.5	1	12	58.3	16.7	16.7	5 216	51.5	22.0	26.2	13.3	38.6	42.2
24021	Frederick, MD	1	179 327	20.0	1	49	59.2	24.5	16.3	32 766	50.4	23.8	25.8	12.4	10.6	10.7
24023	Garrett, MD	8	29 445	21.7	1	17	70.6	11.8	11.8	5 190	48.2	23.0	28.7	14.0	33.8	0.5
24025	Harford, MD	0	209 121	20.4	1	51	62.7	15.7	21.6	36 820	51.2	23.1	25.7	12.2	12.1	15.9
24027	Howard, MD	0	224 483	19.3	1	56	57.1	26.8	14.3	37 547	49.2	23.5	27.1	11.0	7.4	25.1
24029	Kent, MD	6	18 889	16.2	1	8	50.0	37.5	12.5	2 863	43.9	29.9	26.1	11.9	27.4	29.1
24031	Montgomery, MD	0	816 999	17.3	1	181	69.6	16.6	12.2	120 291	52.0	20.7	26.8	11.2	16.9	44.2
24033	Prince George's, MD	0	773 810	18.3	1	179	72.1	15.1	12.3	122 415	56.3	15.8	27.8	9.7	31.6	81.5
24035	Queen Anne's, MD	1	38 024	18.5	1	11	54.5	27.3	18.2	6 271	50.0	24.4	25.6	12.7	14.8	14.4
24037	St. Mary's, MD	4	82 655	21.4	1	24	66.7	16.7	12.5	13 950	50.2	22.9	26.8	13.4	21.1	23.3
24039	Somerset, MD	7	24 266	15.4	1	11	63.6	18.2	18.2	3 277	47.9	22.6	29.5	12.1	46.4	46.0
24041	Talbot, MD	6	32 381	15.8	1	9	66.7	11.1	22.2	4 427	51.3	18.3	30.4	12.6	22.2	27.4
24043	Washington, MD	3	127 278	17.3	1	44	61.4	18.2	15.9	19 824	49.6	22.8	25.4	14.5	23.3	8.0
24045	Wicomico, MD	5	79 253	18.8	1	21	71.4	9.5	19.0	13 796	60.2	12.2	27.6	11.4	29.3	36.5
24047	Worcester, MD	7	41 158	16.8	1	12	50.0	25.0	25.0	6 633	43.9	29.2	26.9	10.4	30.0	32.7
24510	Baltimore city, MD	0	675 401	18.0	1	180	69.4	15.6	11.1	109 980	58.2	18.6	19.5	15.9	65.2	85.7

1. County type code is from the Economic Research Service of the USDA. See notes and definitions at the end of this section.   2. IEP = Individual Education Program. See notes and definitions at the end of this section.

Table D-2. School and Student Characteristics by County — Continued

County	Staff and students, 1995–1996						Revenues, fiscal 1995				Current expenditures, fiscal 1995		
	Number of teachers	Pupil/ teacher ratio	Number of graduates	Dropouts grades 9–12 (percent)	Local school non-teaching staff	Central admin. staff	Total revenue ($1000)	Percent of Revenue from			Amount	Amount per pupil	Percent for instruction
								Federal Gov't	State Gov't	Local Gov't			
	15	16	17	18	19	20	21	22	23	24	25	26	27
LOUISIANA—Con.													
St. Helena, LA	98	16.8	70	4.8	115	13	7 602	21.2	68.0	10.8	7 506	4 400	52.7
St. James, LA	269	15.9	228	3.2	296	22	24 879	10.4	42.0	47.6	23 270	5 126	51.9
St. John the Baptist, LA	408	17.7	278	0.4	372	27	37 549	11.6	45.6	42.7	33 316	4 666	62.0
St. Landry, LA	1 045	16.8	726	1.8	1 073	48	71 749	15.0	66.3	18.6	67 996	3 850	60.1
St. Martin, LA	526	17.5	391	6.0	457	25	40 133	13.7	61.9	24.3	35 409	3 857	60.9
St. Mary, LA	665	17.8	577	1.3	695	36	56 360	14.1	50.3	35.6	49 868	4 183	55.9
St. Tammany, LA	1 990	16.1	1 203	3.8	1 812	62	156 554	6.3	53.5	40.3	139 254	4 434	61.7
Tangipahoa, LA	1 094	16.6	895	4.8	1 023	28	84 446	13.3	54.1	32.6	67 772	3 763	60.7
Tensas, LA	106	14.5	73	2.2	128	12	7 409	25.0	61.4	13.5	7 006	4 426	59.3
Terrebonne, LA	1 101	20.2	1 890	3.1	900	41	81 374	13.1	59.2	27.7	73 857	3 344	61.2
Union, LA	228	17.7	219	1.4	251	9	15 602	13.5	68.1	18.4	14 343	3 640	56.7
Vermilion, LA	580	16.8	480	1.7	487	28	46 938	11.3	51.4	37.3	40 083	4 070	61.3
Vernon, LA	697	16.2	518	0.2	741	21	56 304	24.3	58.3	17.4	51 576	4 455	59.6
Washington, LA	545	16.0	413	4.8	527	24	40 173	15.0	64.2	20.9	37 619	4 252	61.8
Webster, LA	486	17.3	386	4.3	421	15	33 392	12.6	64.0	23.4	30 900	3 604	58.9
West Baton Rouge, LA	215	19.4	187	3.9	217	13	19 475	10.3	46.8	42.9	17 197	4 217	55.4
West Carroll, LA	184	15.1	136	5.4	120	10	10 946	13.1	70.7	16.2	10 439	3 810	61.0
West Feliciana, LA	154	15.2	83	2.3	184	17	12 589	13.4	53.3	33.3	11 362	5 107	58.2
Winn, LA	203	16.3	131	5.5	227	14	16 126	12.7	59.5	27.8	15 001	4 502	59.0
MAINE													
Androscoggin, ME	1 071	15.9	928	5.1	1 035	44	108 519	5.6	53.1	41.3	99 089	5 682	66.4
Aroostook, ME	938	15.4	1 055	1.1	1 019	44	101 329	8.9	61.5	29.6	90 332	6 165	63.3
Cumberland, ME	2 433	15.7	1 911	3.3	2 344	103	266 874	4.0	32.5	63.5	239 486	6 391	64.5
Franklin, ME	352	15.5	361	1.4	333	12	34 620	5.0	46.5	48.5	31 499	5 757	63.4
Hancock, ME	621	13.6	438	3.0	520	23	72 798	4.1	41.5	54.4	50 059	5 992	65.6
Kennebec, ME	1 250	15.3	1 209	2.4	1 283	51	122 548	4.8	50.5	44.7	108 161	5 795	65.9
Knox, ME	347	13.9	307	2.3	292	15	32 872	4.8	28.0	67.2	29 648	6 123	64.8
Lincoln, ME	455	14.0	295	3.4	470	19	49 802	4.3	32.0	63.7	42 724	6 725	68.8
Oxford, ME	668	16.2	571	6.5	699	27	70 641	5.4	46.9	47.7	62 902	5 943	63.8
Penobscot, ME	1 626	15.8	1 491	3.2	1 449	61	168 274	5.4	51.0	43.6	146 715	5 760	66.1
Piscataquis, ME	194	18.0	130	2.2	233	8	23 929	6.8	58.5	34.7	21 293	6 131	67.7
Sagadahoc, ME	435	16.2	396	3.5	419	18	47 211	4.1	41.5	54.3	41 589	5 949	65.6
Somerset, ME	607	16.3	551	3.2	665	22	64 071	6.2	53.7	40.1	59 362	6 044	67.0
Waldo, ME	337	15.6	263	4.8	396	14	36 709	7.2	52.4	40.4	31 022	5 936	63.9
Washington, ME	452	13.2	376	5.0	418	23	50 473	15.0	47.4	37.6	42 709	7 049	62.6
York, ME	1 957	16.2	1 579	2.9	1 810	64	196 075	3.8	42.2	54.1	177 163	5 665	66.8
MARYLAND													
Allegany, MD	688	16.4	763	NA	471	36	69 880	8.4	53.1	38.5	66 725	5 903	59.9
Anne Arundel, MD	3 839	18.6	4 020	NA	2 861	154	490 992	3.5	33.1	63.5	435 691	6 172	58.3
Baltimore, MD	6 048	16.8	5 459	NA	4 448	284	681 565	4.0	31.6	64.3	635 453	6 404	55.3
Calvert, MD	643	21.0	668	NA	519	34	84 775	3.3	37.3	59.4	74 486	5 811	61.5
Caroline, MD	292	18.9	296	NA	287	23	31 648	6.9	54.4	38.7	29 214	5 522	58.4
Carroll, MD	1 359	18.7	1 478	NA	896	67	167 636	2.9	40.5	56.7	142 817	5 826	60.5
Cecil, MD	850	17.2	761	NA	575	41	94 714	4.0	49.3	46.7	81 239	5 698	59.9
Charles, MD	1 084	19.3	1 173	NA	785	57	150 314	3.5	40.9	55.6	125 259	6 134	56.4
Dorchester, MD	291	17.9	277	NA	183	22	33 044	9.0	50.0	41.1	31 218	6 044	58.9
Frederick, MD	1 877	17.5	1 807	NA	1 468	102	226 270	2.8	38.1	59.2	182 070	5 752	61.1
Garrett, MD	359	14.5	275	NA	255	17	32 521	8.5	52.4	39.1	30 903	6 055	59.6
Harford, MD	2 193	16.8	1 849	NA	1 494	88	215 258	3.9	45.8	50.4	203 426	5 658	61.7
Howard, MD	2 257	16.6	2 088	NA	1 544	102	275 308	1.7	28.7	69.6	249 871	6 917	60.2
Kent, MD	173	16.6	132	NA	136	15	19 612	6.1	36.9	57.0	18 340	6 564	58.4
Montgomery, MD	6 812	17.7	6 825	NA	6 684	187	1 057 931	2.8	18.0	79.2	914 754	7 813	63.9
Prince George's, MD	6 675	18.3	6 788	NA	5 852	325	816 911	5.0	41.8	53.2	776 806	6 557	58.4
Queen Anne's, MD	355	17.7	334	NA	212	31	45 881	4.8	34.6	60.7	36 523	6 067	59.3
St. Mary's, MD	779	17.9	672	NA	518	48	86 755	6.5	43.4	50.1	82 815	6 167	59.0
Somerset, MD	196	16.7	175	NA	163	24	22 727	11.3	51.9	36.8	21 548	6 453	56.2
Talbot, MD	265	16.7	241	NA	193	23	28 195	4.6	21.7	73.7	25 037	5 769	67.2
Washington, MD	1 190	16.7	1 081	NA	739	57	127 603	6.0	46.4	47.5	113 388	5 812	61.6
Wicomico, MD	823	16.8	696	NA	594	41	80 522	5.6	52.6	41.8	75 801	5 552	61.9
Worcester, MD	390	17.0	414	NA	352	29	43 528	5.6	16.8	77.6	41 062	6 377	59.3
Baltimore city, MD	6 047	18.2	3 569	NA	3 681	282	696 533	11.3	57.8	30.9	670 933	5 915	65.2

Table D-2.   School and Student Characteristics by County

State/ County code	County	County type [1]	Population, 1996 — Total persons	Population, 1996 — Percent age 5–17	Number of school districts, 1995–1996	Level of schools, 1995–1996 — Number of schools	Percent Primary	Percent Middle	Percent High	Level of students, 1995–1996 — Number of students	Percent Primary	Percent Middle	Percent High	Percent with IEP [2]	Percent free-lunch eligible	Percent minority
			1	2	3	4	5	6	7	8	9	10	11	12	13	14
25000	**MASSACHUSETTS**															
25001	Barnstable, MA	3	201 970	15.6	18	57	61.4	19.3	19.3	31 575	52.0	20.4	27.6	14.2	NA	7.8
25003	Berkshire, MA	3	134 788	17.7	18	56	64.3	10.7	21.4	21 400	51.2	16.3	30.0	18.3	NA	6.0
25005	Bristol, MA	2	513 899	18.7	27	167	67.1	17.4	14.4	84 075	49.7	21.3	27.9	16.1	NA	10.7
25007	Dukes, MA	9	13 259	17.2	6	7	85.7	—	14.3	2 312	75.4	—	24.6	17.5	NA	7.6
25009	Essex, MA	0	686 774	17.7	37	217	70.0	13.8	15.7	108 626	56.1	17.3	25.4	16.2	NA	22.1
25011	Franklin, MA	4	71 209	18.8	20	39	74.4	7.7	15.4	12 107	55.8	9.2	27.8	19.6	NA	5.0
25013	Hampden, MA	2	442 194	19.0	19	137	65.0	18.2	16.1	72 964	50.7	21.4	27.9	18.0	NA	35.5
25015	Hampshire, MA	2	149 610	15.2	19	58	60.3	19.0	20.7	20 923	45.6	24.0	30.4	17.7	NA	10.5
25017	Middlesex, MA	0	1 412 561	15.5	60	377	67.4	17.2	14.3	193 896	52.7	19.8	25.8	17.9	NA	17.9
25019	Nantucket, MA	7	7 267	14.7	1	3	33.3	33.3	33.3	1 093	52.2	24.5	23.3	13.4	NA	5.2
25021	Norfolk, MA	0	637 388	15.7	34	180	65.0	17.2	17.2	90 377	52.2	19.8	27.0	16.9	NA	11.5
25023	Plymouth, MA	1	456 820	20.0	29	136	64.7	17.6	14.7	79 224	53.9	19.6	20.3	15.4	NA	12.7
25025	Suffolk, MA	0	645 068	14.6	8	149	67.1	15.4	14.8	76 491	55.7	15.6	27.8	19.6	NA	75.7
25027	Worcester, MA	2	719 545	18.2	53	248	62.1	16.9	16.1	119 944	52.1	17.2	24.0	17.0	NA	15.3
26000	**MICHIGAN**															
26001	Alcona, MI	9	10 799	16.1	1	2	50.0	—	50.0	1 032	51.9	—	48.1	1.9	31.4	0.5
26003	Alger, MI	7	9 971	18.7	4	7	42.9	14.3	28.6	1 733	39.2	19.6	35.9	2.6	22.2	13.7
26005	Allegan, MI	2	99 019	22.1	10	41	58.5	17.1	24.4	17 359	46.9	18.8	34.3	3.5	14.2	6.7
26007	Alpena, MI	7	30 746	20.3	1	13	76.9	7.7	7.7	5 896	49.9	16.5	32.0	2.0	24.5	2.1
26009	Antrim, MI	9	20 595	19.3	6	14	42.9	14.3	21.4	4 128	43.3	13.8	19.6	2.2	21.1	3.2
26011	Arenac, MI	8	16 268	20.5	3	6	50.0	—	33.3	3 284	45.9	—	38.7	2.7	29.5	3.5
26013	Baraga, MI	9	8 472	18.9	3	6	50.0	16.7	33.3	1 528	42.8	6.7	50.5	3.1	27.4	28.1
26015	Barry, MI	6	53 145	20.9	3	15	46.7	26.7	26.7	8 067	39.6	31.2	29.1	3.5	14.3	2.4
26017	Bay, MI	2	110 824	19.7	5	43	53.5	11.6	14.0	17 484	44.4	22.3	30.9	4.9	26.1	8.8
26019	Benzie, MI	9	14 037	17.7	2	6	66.7	—	33.3	2 404	57.5	—	42.5	1.5	27.6	7.5
26021	Berrien, MI	3	161 434	20.1	16	74	60.8	17.6	20.3	29 311	51.9	18.4	29.4	4.8	33.2	29.8
26023	Branch, MI	6	42 991	20.6	3	16	56.3	18.8	25.0	6 891	44.3	22.3	33.4	5.0	18.4	2.5
26025	Calhoun, MI	2	140 112	19.7	11	68	55.9	25.0	14.7	25 340	47.7	26.3	24.2	4.7	28.4	19.9
26027	Cass, MI	6	50 050	20.3	4	20	50.0	25.0	25.0	7 623	44.7	27.8	27.5	4.5	27.5	16.1
26029	Charlevoix, MI	7	23 503	19.8	5	11	27.3	27.3	27.3	4 413	38.6	25.2	26.6	4.4	16.4	5.7
26031	Cheboygan, MI	7	22 993	19.7	4	12	50.0	16.7	25.0	3 960	48.1	16.6	28.9	5.5	23.9	1.8
26033	Chippewa, MI	7	37 289	17.6	6	20	55.0	10.0	25.0	5 809	44.3	15.4	28.6	4.6	27.3	25.6
26035	Clare, MI	7	28 618	19.4	3	14	35.7	21.4	42.9	5 585	43.6	28.4	28.0	7.2	39.9	1.8
26037	Clinton, MI	2	62 239	21.7	6	28	50.0	25.0	21.4	9 688	40.0	27.3	32.2	4.3	9.1	3.8
26039	Crawford, MI	9	13 671	19.4	1	4	50.0	25.0	25.0	2 250	39.3	32.9	27.7	2.9	34.7	2.0
26041	Delta, MI	7	39 047	20.7	6	22	59.1	9.1	18.2	7 408	47.4	11.1	30.1	3.3	21.0	7.5
26043	Dickinson, MI	7	27 285	19.5	4	10	40.0	20.0	10.0	5 110	32.1	15.7	13.9	4.2	15.2	1.8
26045	Eaton, MI	2	99 562	21.0	9	37	54.1	21.6	18.9	16 533	43.1	25.1	31.0	4.0	10.4	3.6
26047	Emmet, MI	7	27 870	19.6	4	13	53.8	15.4	23.1	4 887	43.8	18.6	27.5	1.8	18.0	6.1
26049	Genesee, MI	2	436 128	20.9	21	154	60.4	17.5	18.2	83 674	49.7	21.3	27.8	4.5	30.6	32.4
26051	Gladwin, MI	6	24 615	19.7	2	9	33.3	33.3	33.3	4 007	38.5	31.0	30.5	3.4	26.9	2.2
26053	Gogebic, MI	7	17 704	16.9	5	10	50.0	—	30.0	2 908	43.7	—	45.2	4.4	29.9	5.1
26055	Grand Traverse, MI	7	72 072	20.1	3	25	76.0	12.0	8.0	12 792	50.8	24.4	21.7	6.0	18.0	4.0
26057	Gratiot, MI	6	39 978	20.5	6	19	52.6	15.8	31.6	8 375	45.9	19.7	34.4	5.6	23.2	6.4
26059	Hillsdale, MI	6	45 887	21.1	8	20	50.0	5.0	40.0	7 909	52.9	6.9	34.9	4.9	21.7	1.9
26061	Houghton, MI	7	36 230	16.9	9	20	50.0	10.0	25.0	6 176	45.9	10.1	25.9	3.4	25.5	2.9
26063	Huron, MI	7	35 281	20.3	18	32	62.5	9.4	25.0	6 777	46.7	14.1	37.1	3.1	22.1	6.0
26065	Ingham, MI	2	285 737	17.7	12	108	64.8	19.4	14.8	49 500	47.7	24.8	27.2	5.2	23.9	28.0
26067	Ionia, MI	6	60 378	21.2	9	31	64.5	16.1	16.1	12 239	51.2	18.1	30.0	5.3	18.0	3.7
26069	Iosco, MI	7	24 761	19.0	4	17	47.1	29.4	17.6	6 948	49.0	23.7	21.7	5.5	30.4	3.0
26071	Iron, MI	9	13 121	16.8	26	27	66.7	3.7	14.8	4 618	65.4	7.9	18.6	1.1	15.7	35.8
26073	Isabella, MI	4	57 118	17.6	3	17	58.8	11.8	23.5	6 705	50.7	16.1	32.4	4.4	20.1	8.4
26075	Jackson, MI	3	154 563	19.0	12	55	58.2	14.5	25.5	25 049	53.6	16.1	27.8	3.7	25.3	12.4
26077	Kalamazoo, MI	2	229 008	17.8	9	76	55.3	19.7	19.7	34 223	50.0	22.1	26.8	3.6	23.4	21.5
26079	Kalkaska, MI	9	15 325	22.2	3	13	53.8	15.4	30.8	3 085	46.8	23.9	29.3	3.1	29.5	2.2
26081	Kent, MI	2	536 103	20.2	20	207	64.3	13.5	15.0	97 165	53.1	19.0	23.8	7.0	21.6	24.6
26083	Keweenaw, MI	9	2 010	15.1	1	1	100.0	—	—	8	100.0	—	—	NA	—	—
26085	Lake, MI	9	9 874	18.7	1	4	50.0	25.0	25.0	814	52.5	23.0	24.6	6.9	74.6	35.1
26087	Lapeer, MI	1	85 479	22.7	5	31	54.8	19.4	22.6	14 766	47.1	20.3	31.9	2.8	12.3	4.2
26089	Leelanau, MI	9	18 430	18.8	4	6	33.3	—	16.7	2 569	35.7	—	17.9	1.8	16.2	12.8
26091	Lenawee, MI	1	97 133	21.1	12	43	44.2	25.6	25.6	18 393	42.2	23.8	29.2	3.4	14.7	11.2
26093	Livingston, MI	1	137 616	21.4	5	35	57.1	20.0	20.0	23 089	46.9	23.8	28.6	3.7	5.2	3.3
26095	Luce, MI	9	6 180	20.2	1	4	50.0	25.0	25.0	1 275	46.4	24.5	29.1	3.7	32.9	6.3
26097	Mackinac, MI	7	11 096	19.3	6	10	50.0	10.0	20.0	1 879	58.6	0.2	23.4	2.5	27.7	43.6
26099	Macomb, MI	0	734 625	17.6	21	210	65.2	18.1	14.8	117 255	51.5	21.4	25.7	4.4	11.2	6.4

1. County type code is from the Economic Research Service of the USDA. See notes and definitions at the end of this section.   2. IEP = Individual Education Program. See notes and definitions at the end of this section.

Table D-2. School and Student Characteristics by County — Continued

County	Staff and students, 1995–1996						Revenues, fiscal 1995				Current expenditures, fiscal 1995		
	Number of teachers	Pupil/ teacher ratio	Number of graduates	Dropouts grades 9–12 (percent)	Local school non-teaching staff	Central admin. staff	Total revenue ($1000)	Percent of Revenue from			Amount	Amount per pupil	Percent for instruction
								Federal Gov't	State Gov't	Local Gov't			
	15	16	17	18	19	20	21	22	23	24	25	26	27
MASSACHUSETTS													
Barnstable, MA	NA	NA	1 596	3.1	1 304	291	267 263	2.6	17.7	79.7	189 480	6 119	63.4
Berkshire, MA	NA	NA	1 243	2.9	1 231	190	189 525	2.5	31.1	66.3	137 060	6 464	64.5
Bristol, MA	NA	NA	4 874	4.1	4 118	774	593 942	3.9	29.2	66.8	492 973	5 977	63.8
Dukes, MA	NA	NA	108	2.6	120	25	29 622	1.7	12.3	86.0	19 476	8 926	64.3
Essex, MA	NA	NA	5 358	3.6	4 538	894	832 244	4.3	31.8	63.9	645 904	6 115	65.4
Franklin, MA	NA	NA	645	4.3	801	125	100 391	2.9	33.1	64.1	75 705	6 409	61.6
Hampden, MA	NA	NA	3 415	5.9	4 276	517	559 896	5.7	43.6	50.7	453 113	6 300	64.1
Hampshire, MA	NA	NA	1 150	2.5	1 037	245	171 044	2.3	25.1	72.5	124 728	6 005	62.5
Middlesex, MA	NA	NA	10 914	2.2	8 773	1 685	1 620 150	2.9	24.6	72.6	1 301 173	6 850	64.6
Nantucket, MA	NA	NA	48	1.6	67	13	9 274	1.8	15.1	83.1	8 549	8 204	63.0
Norfolk, MA	NA	NA	5 236	1.3	3 958	664	748 070	2.0	27.7	70.3	562 306	6 379	64.6
Plymouth, MA	NA	NA	3 906	3.0	3 041	637	578 337	2.8	21.3	75.9	443 497	5 733	65.2
Suffolk, MA	NA	NA	3 264	7.4	4 190	855	693 199	6.7	29.9	63.5	575 902	7 830	62.5
Worcester, MA	NA	NA	5 922	3.3	5 252	931	933 947	3.4	31.1	65.5	689 499	5 908	65.3
MICHIGAN													
Alcona, MI	62	16.8	74	NA	87	3	7 758	6.1	40.0	54.0	6 097	6 128	63.7
Alger, MI	102	17.0	130	NA	70	11	10 925	6.0	65.1	28.9	9 087	5 250	60.4
Allegan, MI	876	19.8	1 159	NA	776	41	114 756	4.3	66.3	29.5	95 492	5 520	58.7
Alpena, MI	295	20.0	451	NA	276	15	34 164	7.2	66.4	26.5	31 471	5 472	55.5
Antrim, MI	238	17.3	224	NA	216	16	26 142	3.2	50.8	46.0	22 255	5 533	62.3
Arenac, MI	158	20.8	206	NA	130	8	17 504	7.3	70.8	21.9	15 364	4 704	63.4
Baraga, MI	85	18.1	119	NA	73	9	9 508	12.3	66.5	21.2	8 052	5 256	62.0
Barry, MI	421	10.2	460	NA	404	10	40 070	4.0	76.0	19.5	41 000	5 019	60.1
Bay, MI	770	22.7	1 260	NA	741	31	118 082	7.0	63.0	29.9	105 220	6 216	56.9
Benzie, MI	116	20.7	111	NA	125	6	12 623	4.8	51.2	44.0	11 817	5 031	63.3
Berrien, MI	1 595	18.4	1 489	NA	1 598	104	203 045	8.0	64.1	27.9	182 911	6 265	55.0
Branch, MI	315	21.9	411	NA	335	16	46 840	6.6	66.2	27.2	40 974	6 289	57.9
Calhoun, MI	1 406	18.0	1 315	NA	1 253	80	205 208	6.0	65.6	28.4	172 290	6 939	54.5
Cass, MI	393	19.4	393	NA	359	25	45 169	7.8	69.5	22.6	41 057	5 573	54.1
Charlevoix, MI	237	18.6	247	NA	216	20	37 129	4.5	49.7	45.8	32 094	7 278	55.5
Cheboygan, MI	205	19.3	257	NA	203	15	27 742	8.5	53.4	38.1	24 667	6 251	54.7
Chippewa, MI	330	17.6	345	NA	275	29	40 361	9.8	65.2	25.0	34 460	6 020	57.2
Clare, MI	280	20.0	348	NA	271	15	35 787	9.1	61.4	29.5	30 711	5 768	60.9
Clinton, MI	480	20.2	695	NA	416	31	60 151	3.0	80.8	16.1	55 403	5 857	58.3
Crawford, MI	NA	NA	100	NA	—	—	12 109	4.8	57.3	37.9	10 556	4 809	60.9
Delta, MI	384	19.3	545	NA	358	32	50 817	7.4	69.8	22.8	45 155	5 801	60.2
Dickinson, MI	266	19.2	383	NA	182	13	37 393	7.2	59.4	33.4	29 712	5 743	60.3
Eaton, MI	887	18.6	1 071	NA	859	49	113 079	3.6	71.8	24.5	95 677	5 857	57.9
Emmet, MI	172	28.3	307	NA	217	19	32 553	2.3	48.3	49.4	28 268	5 515	63.0
Genesee, MI	4 059	20.6	4 132	NA	4 438	199	632 281	8.0	68.5	23.6	553 005	6 796	55.3
Gladwin, MI	205	19.6	284	NA	222	9	21 718	6.8	69.3	24.0	19 367	4 985	60.2
Gogebic, MI	176	16.5	190	NA	148	20	21 745	9.1	61.2	29.7	19 079	6 574	59.1
Grand Traverse, MI	655	19.5	757	NA	691	31	93 129	6.5	55.2	38.3	85 026	6 741	52.3
Gratiot, MI	375	22.3	508	NA	483	33	62 325	7.0	70.7	22.4	52 265	6 383	55.3
Hillsdale, MI	413	19.1	421	NA	550	24	49 727	5.1	73.5	21.4	44 735	5 694	60.9
Houghton, MI	332	18.6	427	NA	234	25	37 833	6.3	70.8	22.9	32 273	5 358	58.7
Huron, MI	354	19.1	471	NA	255	26	43 354	5.5	63.8	30.6	36 587	5 664	60.0
Ingham, MI	2 597	19.1	2 715	NA	3 159	169	444 880	5.0	60.6	34.4	357 680	7 279	54.3
Ionia, MI	622	19.7	772	NA	572	35	79 906	4.3	70.0	25.7	64 745	5 410	59.0
Iosco, MI	315	22.1	383	NA	281	21	39 531	13.4	58.0	28.6	36 794	5 978	59.9
Iron, MI	243	19.0	168	NA	231	34	14 661	6.1	66.2	27.8	12 659	5 504	56.6
Isabella, MI	382	17.6	497	NA	373	28	46 933	4.3	70.9	24.8	38 774	5 955	63.2
Jackson, MI	1 238	20.2	1 336	NA	1 214	66	184 899	5.0	64.8	30.2	158 369	6 455	55.4
Kalamazoo, MI	1 895	18.1	1 745	NA	1 973	93	258 092	5.1	62.3	32.6	210 620	6 311	60.2
Kalkaska, MI	166	18.6	237	NA	187	9	17 885	5.1	48.5	46.5	14 810	5 002	59.1
Kent, MI	4 600	21.1	4 301	NA	4 996	257	736 344	5.1	60.1	34.8	575 192	6 414	57.7
Keweenaw, MI	1	8.0	—	NA	3	—	100	—	27.0	73.0	62	5 636	53.2
Lake, MI	88	9.3	34	NA	137	6	5 776	9.4	45.3	45.3	5 739	6 551	62.6
Lapeer, MI	636	23.2	862	NA	592	28	89 518	3.9	73.8	22.3	80 071	5 594	59.8
Leelanau, MI	150	17.2	141	NA	163	10	15 907	3.9	44.9	51.3	14 076	5 619	61.5
Lenawee, MI	881	20.9	1 085	NA	758	55	129 261	4.4	69.1	26.4	117 632	6 480	55.2
Livingston, MI	1 076	21.5	1 329	NA	955	69	163 117	3.1	64.8	32.1	133 171	5 952	56.7
Luce, MI	70	18.3	77	NA	58	5	7 190	9.7	62.8	27.5	6 418	5 218	64.6
Mackinac, MI	120	15.6	130	NA	103	14	12 686	7.2	48.4	44.3	10 923	5 758	61.0
Macomb, MI	5 437	21.6	6 618	NA	5 943	305	949 844	3.2	65.8	30.9	798 306	6 982	57.6

Table D-2. School and Student Characteristics by County

State/County code	County	County type[1]	Population, 1996 Total persons	Percent age 5–17	Number of school districts, 1995–1996	Level of schools, 1995–1996 Number of schools	Percent Primary	Middle	High	Level of students, 1995–1996 Number of students	Percent Primary	Middle	High	Percent with IEP[2]	Percent free-lunch eligible	Percent minority
			1	2	3	4	5	6	7	8	9	10	11	12	13	14
	MICHIGAN—Con.															
26101	Manistee, MI	7	22 902	17.8	4	14	57.1	14.3	14.3	3 787	43.3	17.6	22.6	3.7	30.8	8.9
26103	Marquette, MI	5	62 017	19.5	10	30	66.7	13.3	16.7	11 112	50.2	16.0	31.8	3.8	17.6	4.6
26105	Mason, MI	7	27 725	19.6	4	16	62.5	12.5	25.0	5 132	48.7	18.6	32.7	5.7	27.6	4.4
26107	Mecosta, MI	7	38 460	17.7	3	15	60.0	13.3	26.7	6 722	51.9	13.9	34.2	7.4	28.7	10.0
26109	Menominee, MI	7	24 551	20.3	4	13	53.8	7.7	30.8	4 399	43.6	13.3	37.0	3.9	20.4	1.3
26111	Midland, MI	2	80 669	20.4	5	32	59.4	18.8	18.8	14 076	52.6	22.9	24.5	4.8	16.0	5.6
26113	Missaukee, MI	9	13 607	22.4	2	6	50.0	16.7	16.7	2 394	46.1	13.4	16.2	2.9	28.7	0.9
26115	Monroe, MI	1	140 488	21.5	9	47	59.6	21.3	19.1	24 364	48.7	23.5	27.9	4.3	14.1	5.2
26117	Montcalm, MI	6	58 969	21.2	7	36	47.2	16.7	25.0	13 766	44.6	25.2	29.1	5.5	23.3	3.3
26119	Montmorency, MI	9	9 868	18.1	2	3	33.3	—	33.3	1 263	26.1	—	21.3	1.7	27.6	1.0
26121	Muskegon, MI	2	164 913	20.5	12	72	56.9	15.3	18.1	33 007	49.3	21.2	24.6	5.8	30.2	23.1
26123	Newaygo, MI	6	44 285	21.7	5	20	40.0	30.0	30.0	9 468	41.8	29.5	28.7	3.2	30.3	7.4
26125	Oakland, MI	0	1 162 098	18.0	28	341	61.9	18.8	14.1	179 352	49.5	22.6	26.4	3.9	12.2	17.1
26127	Oceana, MI	8	24 379	22.2	4	17	52.9	11.8	17.6	4 248	43.3	18.0	22.8	4.5	34.8	20.0
26129	Ogemaw, MI	7	20 790	20.0	1	5	40.0	20.0	20.0	2 978	45.0	21.4	30.9	2.9	29.7	1.4
26131	Ontonagon, MI	9	8 405	17.9	3	7	57.1	—	42.9	1 497	54.1	—	45.9	2.7	29.5	2.5
26133	Osceola, MI	9	22 047	22.6	4	15	46.7	13.3	26.7	5 770	42.5	15.3	23.3	3.4	32.7	2.4
26135	Oscoda, MI	9	8 775	17.4	2	4	50.0	—	50.0	1 396	56.5	—	43.5	3.0	33.5	0.9
26137	Otsego, MI	7	21 343	21.4	3	10	50.0	20.0	20.0	4 450	34.9	30.1	27.5	3.2	17.4	2.3
26139	Ottawa, MI	2	215 064	21.5	12	74	66.2	12.2	17.6	36 200	51.6	18.7	28.5	3.2	10.2	12.3
26141	Presque Isle, MI	7	14 407	19.7	3	8	50.0	12.5	37.5	2 292	41.8	5.3	52.9	2.3	25.9	0.8
26143	Roscommon, MI	7	22 847	15.9	2	10	50.0	20.0	20.0	4 220	41.5	28.5	28.7	4.0	38.0	1.6
26145	Saginaw, MI	2	211 808	20.8	15	85	58.8	17.6	18.8	37 414	47.7	22.7	28.4	6.0	32.9	39.1
26147	St. Clair, MI	0	155 636	20.7	7	56	55.4	21.4	21.4	27 422	45.9	24.7	28.6	5.1	18.1	6.5
26149	St. Joseph, MI	6	60 977	21.4	9	35	62.9	14.3	22.9	11 896	48.2	20.4	31.4	3.6	18.7	6.2
26151	Sanilac, MI	8	42 440	21.4	7	22	40.9	18.2	31.8	8 875	41.6	22.4	34.9	3.1	21.2	3.5
26153	Schoolcraft, MI	7	8 653	19.4	1	5	80.0	—	—	1 283	42.9	—	—	5.4	32.9	15.5
26155	Shiawassee, MI	4	72 333	21.8	8	35	54.3	17.1	25.7	14 702	50.9	16.8	32.0	4.2	14.3	2.6
26157	Tuscola, MI	6	57 837	21.9	9	32	43.8	21.9	31.3	12 504	42.2	22.2	33.8	4.7	21.1	4.2
26159	Van Buren, MI	2	75 308	21.9	12	42	52.4	21.4	26.2	17 298	48.0	21.3	30.7	4.3	28.5	17.3
26161	Washtenaw, MI	0	295 149	15.6	11	80	60.0	21.3	15.0	41 023	49.0	24.0	26.2	3.2	16.2	22.6
26163	Wayne, MI	0	2 039 819	19.5	37	568	65.1	16.0	13.9	350 298	56.8	15.8	25.0	5.2	41.3	55.2
26165	Wexford, MI	7	28 789	21.3	3	14	50.0	14.3	21.4	5 863	46.4	22.2	30.2	4.7	25.9	2.1
27000	**MINNESOTA**															
27001	Aitkin, MN	9	13 715	18.6	3	7	57.1	—	42.9	2 424	51.9	—	48.1	NA	34.4	5.5
27003	Anoka, MN	0	282 139	22.7	7	90	56.7	14.4	18.9	60 705	48.8	23.5	25.9	NA	10.4	6.7
27005	Becker, MN	6	29 161	22.4	6	14	64.3	—	35.7	5 135	52.7	—	47.3	NA	28.5	10.9
27007	Beltrami, MN	7	38 274	22.9	4	23	56.5	8.7	17.4	8 372	47.6	18.3	30.4	NA	35.3	27.4
27009	Benton, MN	3	33 336	22.2	2	8	37.5	37.5	25.0	5 179	34.4	34.7	30.8	NA	14.6	1.2
27011	Big Stone, MN	9	5 839	19.4	3	6	50.0	—	33.3	1 437	46.5	—	51.3	NA	28.6	1.9
27013	Blue Earth, MN	5	54 199	17.6	4	28	50.0	21.4	25.0	10 740	46.8	20.5	31.8	NA	16.7	4.7
27015	Brown, MN	7	27 262	20.6	4	13	53.8	15.4	30.8	4 675	51.1	15.7	33.2	NA	14.9	4.0
27017	Carlton, MN	6	30 426	21.8	7	17	52.9	—	41.2	6 626	57.2	—	41.4	NA	20.3	8.2
27019	Carver, MN	1	61 415	21.7	6	23	47.8	17.4	34.8	10 141	48.5	21.7	29.8	NA	6.7	4.1
27021	Cass, MN	9	25 329	20.9	4	12	41.7	8.3	50.0	3 264	47.8	8.1	44.1	NA	43.7	33.1
27023	Chippewa, MN	7	13 132	20.9	4	11	45.5	9.1	36.4	2 877	43.2	18.7	29.0	NA	18.2	3.8
27025	Chisago, MN	1	38 123	23.5	3	14	35.7	28.6	35.7	7 240	41.2	28.6	30.1	NA	13.3	1.9
27027	Clay, MN	3	51 848	19.1	5	22	45.5	18.2	31.8	9 532	44.7	22.5	32.5	NA	20.9	11.3
27029	Clearwater, MN	9	8 254	22.6	2	6	33.3	33.3	33.3	1 882	44.7	14.2	41.0	NA	35.4	12.0
27031	Cook, MN	9	4 688	18.2	1	4	75.0	—	25.0	722	53.5	—	46.5	NA	9.4	10.1
27033	Cottonwood, MN	7	12 321	20.2	5	12	58.3	8.3	33.3	3 017	50.5	3.8	45.7	NA	22.8	6.8
27035	Crow Wing, MN	7	50 634	20.5	4	21	57.1	9.5	28.6	10 174	46.6	21.6	28.3	NA	21.7	2.5
27037	Dakota, MN	0	326 016	21.5	10	120	55.8	16.7	23.3	66 755	53.1	19.0	22.6	NA	8.0	8.1
27039	Dodge, MN	6	16 855	23.6	2	8	50.0	12.5	37.5	2 730	42.5	20.4	37.1	NA	10.4	1.8
27041	Douglas, MN	7	30 459	20.8	6	20	60.0	5.0	30.0	7 761	49.4	14.3	36.2	NA	19.5	1.3
27043	Faribault, MN	7	16 405	20.8	5	12	50.0	25.0	25.0	2 938	43.6	22.4	34.0	NA	18.2	6.0
27045	Fillmore, MN	8	20 860	21.2	5	13	38.5	23.1	38.5	3 586	42.9	21.8	35.4	NA	19.4	1.2
27047	Freeborn, MN	7	31 972	19.6	4	14	50.0	21.4	28.6	5 283	46.9	27.4	25.7	NA	20.0	6.8
27049	Goodhue, MN	6	42 366	21.4	7	19	52.6	5.3	31.6	8 042	51.0	10.9	37.5	NA	11.9	4.2
27051	Grant, MN	9	6 154	19.7	3	7	57.1	—	42.9	1 629	49.5	—	50.5	NA	20.8	1.7
27053	Hennepin, MN	0	1 058 746	16.6	34	348	55.2	14.9	23.3	161 428	51.7	21.2	25.7	NA	23.3	26.3
27055	Houston, MN	3	19 226	21.4	4	9	44.4	—	55.6	3 629	49.4	—	50.6	NA	14.1	1.7
27057	Hubbard, MN	9	16 406	21.1	3	9	44.4	11.1	44.4	2 946	40.4	23.2	36.4	NA	31.3	6.6
27059	Isanti, MN	1	29 017	24.2	3	8	37.5	25.0	25.0	5 865	36.5	25.8	25.5	NA	17.1	2.5
27061	Itasca, MN	6	43 392	22.4	4	26	53.8	11.5	26.9	8 481	42.3	23.3	34.2	NA	24.4	7.8

1. County type code is from the Economic Research Service of the USDA. See notes and definitions at the end of this section.   2. IEP = Individual Education Program. See notes and definitions at the end of this section.

Table D-2. School and Student Characteristics by County — Continued

County	Staff and students, 1995–1996						Revenues, fiscal 1995				Current expenditures, fiscal 1995		
	Number of teachers	Pupil/ teacher ratio	Number of graduates	Dropouts grades 9–12 (percent)	Local school non-teaching staff	Central admin. staff	Total revenue ($1000)	Percent of Revenue from			Amount	Amount per pupil	Percent for instruction
								Federal Gov't	State Gov't	Local Gov't			
	15	16	17	18	19	20	21	22	23	24	25	26	27
MICHIGAN—Con.													
Manistee, MI	203	18.6	225	NA	171	12	23 680	8.3	60.1	31.5	21 475	5 665	58.1
Marquette, MI	593	18.7	812	NA	509	31	79 873	8.2	66.8	25.0	68 675	5 662	61.2
Mason, MI	288	17.8	306	NA	259	16	38 639	6.1	52.9	41.0	33 507	6 496	57.6
Mecosta, MI	329	20.5	422	NA	287	14	45 490	7.3	62.8	29.9	39 493	6 242	59.4
Menominee, MI	248	17.7	319	NA	201	17	26 558	5.5	72.9	21.6	23 482	5 407	61.3
Midland, MI	757	18.6	882	NA	769	41	108 750	3.6	54.0	42.5	93 091	6 764	57.9
Missaukee, MI	119	20.1	157	NA	131	18	13 086	5.6	70.1	24.2	11 635	4 810	61.4
Monroe, MI	1 165	20.9	1 639	NA	1 154	61	172 861	3.9	55.8	40.4	152 754	6 382	54.5
Montcalm, MI	724	19.0	719	NA	709	37	86 208	6.3	73.1	20.6	76 350	5 698	58.5
Montmorency, MI	68	18.6	72	NA	69	6	7 204	7.6	51.9	40.5	6 519	5 501	57.6
Muskegon, MI	1 722	19.2	1 936	NA	1 722	108	238 065	7.1	70.0	22.9	203 673	6 353	56.2
Newaygo, MI	473	20.0	496	NA	531	34	69 460	7.5	71.1	21.4	55 109	6 075	60.4
Oakland, MI	9 159	19.6	10 092	NA	9 807	740	1 634 567	3.4	56.6	40.0	1 356 173	7 730	55.8
Oceana, MI	209	20.3	217	NA	242	14	25 956	10.0	67.1	22.9	22 449	5 570	61.0
Ogemaw, MI	148	20.2	151	NA	162	9	15 072	7.7	64.4	27.9	13 775	4 832	59.9
Ontonagon, MI	98	15.3	99	NA	64	8	9 210	7.1	66.1	26.8	8 580	5 724	59.0
Osceola, MI	279	20.7	321	NA	274	18	31 587	6.5	72.7	20.8	28 109	5 042	60.2
Oscoda, MI	78	17.9	69	NA	70	5	7 644	7.5	55.2	37.3	6 593	4 673	63.1
Otsego, MI	236	18.9	279	NA	224	16	26 715	3.4	50.2	46.5	23 125	5 243	60.9
Ottawa, MI	1 858	19.5	1 957	NA	1 721	87	267 443	3.3	57.7	38.9	207 591	5 905	61.5
Presque Isle, MI	120	19.1	179	NA	93	11	12 177	6.0	63.7	30.3	10 800	4 783	60.1
Roscommon, MI	219	19.3	241	NA	270	16	29 304	8.7	45.8	45.5	25 171	6 230	58.8
Saginaw, MI	1 882	19.9	1 985	NA	1 900	117	263 742	8.4	69.7	21.9	226 770	6 247	55.7
St. Clair, MI	1 398	19.6	1 681	NA	1 331	51	189 539	6.2	61.8	33.0	160 666	6 068	60.4
St. Joseph, MI	642	18.5	662	NA	660	44	73 821	5.3	70.3	24.4	66 256	5 569	57.5
Sanilac, MI	448	19.8	636	NA	388	29	53 394	5.6	71.7	22.7	47 400	5 430	58.8
Schoolcraft, MI	72	17.8	89	NA	64	4	7 712	7.2	65.0	27.7	6 775	5 228	58.6
Shiawassee, MI	749	19.6	959	NA	620	48	95 523	3.9	75.1	21.0	83 027	5 690	60.2
Tuscola, MI	638	19.6	812	NA	648	33	80 307	6.5	75.0	18.5	72 747	5 978	60.3
Van Buren, MI	878	19.7	1 035	NA	868	56	117 213	7.3	63.5	29.2	101 215	6 001	58.6
Washtenaw, MI	2 065	19.9	2 125	NA	2 120	103	373 271	3.4	52.5	44.0	292 418	7 313	54.9
Wayne, MI	15 621	22.4	15 429	NA	22 139	2 062	2 729 628	7.1	70.2	22.8	2 376 989	7 002	61.6
Wexford, MI	283	20.7	337	NA	217	21	40 322	6.2	64.8	29.0	33 714	5 907	56.1
MINNESOTA													
Aitkin, MN	149	16.3	137	1.3	44	3	15 930	5.5	55.9	38.6	13 146	5 478	61.7
Anoka, MN	823	73.7	3 073	5.6	706	61	381 472	2.7	58.5	38.8	331 895	5 601	62.6
Becker, MN	310	16.6	323	2.4	76	6	31 886	6.4	63.0	30.6	27 503	5 328	65.2
Beltrami, MN	503	16.6	358	5.7	441	28	59 371	11.4	64.6	24.0	51 906	6 396	67.5
Benton, MN	284	18.2	313	1.2	181	12	35 633	4.0	59.4	36.6	27 196	5 327	65.5
Big Stone, MN	87	16.5	120	0.6	21	2	9 181	4.7	61.3	34.0	8 133	5 679	66.4
Blue Earth, MN	572	18.8	725	4.0	309	27	64 579	3.5	57.8	38.7	53 967	5 042	65.8
Brown, MN	279	16.8	311	1.8	147	16	27 851	2.9	60.2	36.9	23 605	5 137	65.9
Carlton, MN	385	17.2	490	3.6	145	17	42 848	5.4	65.9	28.7	35 653	5 403	65.2
Carver, MN	610	16.6	670	1.5	369	14	72 301	3.4	49.5	47.2	55 930	6 017	65.9
Cass, MN	172	19.0	196	10.4	17	5	32 139	8.4	32.1	59.5	27 013	8 261	60.8
Chippewa, MN	187	15.4	213	5.0	74	11	24 709	5.8	50.3	43.9	19 697	6 870	71.7
Chisago, MN	342	21.2	427	3.8	131	21	44 195	3.4	68.2	28.4	36 125	5 011	65.1
Clay, MN	361	26.4	549	1.8	25	—	59 698	4.7	69.7	25.6	48 829	5 168	68.1
Clearwater, MN	109	17.3	97	2.2	67	8	12 929	6.8	59.5	33.7	10 300	5 444	65.6
Cook, MN	43	16.9	47	7.1	—	—	4 644	5.5	26.5	68.0	4 027	5 672	65.8
Cottonwood, MN	169	17.8	211	1.0	82	6	21 579	4.0	50.4	45.7	17 989	6 045	66.9
Crow Wing, MN	289	35.3	662	7.1	70	4	65 215	4.8	47.3	47.9	54 152	5 440	68.9
Dakota, MN	3 386	19.7	3 383	4.7	1 883	169	427 429	2.2	48.0	49.8	348 006	5 433	66.0
Dodge, MN	144	18.9	184	2.1	47	4	22 971	1.5	48.4	50.1	12 642	4 691	66.5
Douglas, MN	420	18.5	482	4.5	36	6	49 405	4.7	56.9	38.4	40 430	5 189	68.0
Faribault, MN	180	16.3	214	2.2	92	5	24 244	3.5	46.9	49.6	20 831	7 069	72.0
Fillmore, MN	241	14.9	273	1.2	116	10	22 302	5.6	70.4	24.0	20 027	5 557	66.4
Freeborn, MN	303	17.5	358	6.2	—	—	31 368	4.1	65.5	30.4	28 439	5 325	65.9
Goodhue, MN	465	17.3	494	3.7	256	19	55 115	2.8	39.9	57.3	42 559	5 317	66.7
Grant, MN	100	16.4	110	0.9	61	7	9 880	5.7	57.3	37.0	8 390	5 892	62.5
Hennepin, MN	5 177	31.2	8 120	7.6	3 346	329	1 270 033	3.8	35.7	60.4	1 059 442	6 737	63.4
Houston, MN	200	18.2	248	2.0	93	5	21 611	2.9	69.5	27.5	18 221	5 248	66.9
Hubbard, MN	181	16.3	168	2.8	63	5	16 945	5.7	55.9	38.5	14 743	5 123	62.6
Isanti, MN	298	19.7	343	7.9	157	8	33 989	4.8	69.1	26.0	28 882	5 115	69.3
Itasca, MN	210	40.4	609	3.4	117	16	61 830	5.4	49.7	44.9	53 840	6 345	67.5

Table D-2. School and Student Characteristics by County

State/County code	County	County type[1]	Population, 1996		Number of school districts, 1995–1996	Level of schools, 1995–1996				Level of students, 1995–1996				Characteristics of students, 1995–1996		
			Total persons	Percent age 5–17		Number of schools	Percent Primary	Middle	High	Number of students	Percent Primary	Middle	High	Percent with IEP[2]	Percent free-lunch eligible	Percent minority
			1	2	3	4	5	6	7	8	9	10	11	12	13	14
	MINNESOTA—Con.															
27063	Jackson, MN	7	11 718	20.8	4	9	44.4	22.2	33.3	2 056	50.1	18.4	31.5	NA	18.8	4.9
27065	Kanabec, MN	6	13 838	23.3	2	6	33.3	16.7	50.0	2 863	35.2	17.3	47.5	NA	24.4	3.1
27067	Kandiyohi, MN	7	41 324	21.6	3	20	45.0	20.0	35.0	7 881	39.7	30.7	29.7	NA	24.5	12.3
27069	Kittson, MN	9	5 419	19.3	3	9	44.4	22.2	33.3	1 217	42.2	18.3	39.4	NA	18.7	3.9
27071	Koochiching, MN	7	15 858	19.8	3	10	50.0	—	50.0	2 597	49.1	—	50.9	NA	19.9	4.5
27073	Lac qui Parle, MN	9	8 228	20.3	4	5	60.0	—	40.0	1 897	43.4	—	56.6	NA	18.3	3.0
27075	Lake, MN	6	10 707	18.9	1	6	50.0	16.7	33.3	2 227	41.7	13.3	45.0	NA	15.4	1.3
27077	Lake of the Woods, MN	9	4 598	19.8	1	2	50.0	—	50.0	864	54.4	—	45.6	NA	35.4	0.8
27079	Le Sueur, MN	6	24 715	22.5	6	24	29.2	12.5	20.8	3 942	42.2	11.0	40.7	NA	18.3	4.3
27081	Lincoln, MN	9	6 687	21.3	4	5	40.0	—	60.0	1 117	38.3	—	61.7	NA	26.8	0.4
27083	Lyon, MN	7	24 791	21.2	8	21	47.6	14.3	38.1	6 449	46.6	10.5	42.9	NA	18.7	6.1
27085	McLeod, MN	6	33 636	21.6	8	23	56.5	13.0	21.7	6 443	48.8	18.4	32.5	NA	7.9	4.1
27087	Mahnomen, MN	9	5 144	25.9	2	7	57.1	—	42.9	1 538	50.7	—	49.3	NA	52.1	54.5
27089	Marshall, MN	8	10 563	23.1	5	12	50.0	8.3	41.7	2 031	46.3	4.5	49.2	NA	25.1	5.9
27091	Martin, MN	7	22 462	20.4	4	9	55.6	11.1	33.3	2 896	36.0	19.1	44.9	NA	23.8	3.7
27093	Meeker, MN	6	21 463	22.5	3	10	40.0	30.0	30.0	5 239	35.8	30.0	34.2	NA	16.2	2.8
27095	Mille Lacs, MN	6	20 312	22.3	4	13	38.5	15.4	38.5	6 166	46.4	17.5	34.8	NA	21.1	6.0
27097	Morrison, MN	6	30 528	24.3	5	14	50.0	7.1	42.9	6 227	44.7	14.0	41.3	NA	29.6	1.6
27099	Mower, MN	4	37 151	19.7	5	19	52.6	5.3	31.6	6 153	61.0	2.4	36.1	NA	19.1	3.9
27101	Murray, MN	9	9 609	21.2	2	5	60.0	—	40.0	1 606	51.5	—	48.5	NA	18.0	1.6
27103	Nicollet, MN	7	29 846	19.8	2	9	33.3	11.1	55.6	2 439	48.1	12.7	39.2	NA	10.1	3.1
27105	Nobles, MN	7	20 060	20.3	5	12	50.0	8.3	33.3	3 721	48.0	17.2	33.5	NA	21.7	14.2
27107	Norman, MN	8	7 753	21.2	4	7	57.1	—	42.9	1 567	51.5	—	48.5	NA	27.2	10.4
27109	Olmsted, MN	3	113 182	19.9	6	41	63.4	9.8	22.0	20 412	50.0	17.2	32.5	NA	13.8	10.3
27111	Otter Tail, MN	7	53 889	20.2	12	29	44.8	6.9	44.8	11 072	41.6	15.6	42.0	NA	21.6	3.0
27113	Pennington, MN	7	13 564	20.8	2	6	33.3	16.7	50.0	2 638	41.2	21.6	37.2	NA	21.5	4.0
27115	Pine, MN	6	23 331	22.4	3	8	50.0	—	50.0	3 540	52.1	—	47.9	NA	25.8	2.8
27117	Pipestone, MN	7	10 124	21.3	3	9	55.6	11.1	33.3	2 204	55.6	17.6	26.8	NA	21.5	4.4
27119	Polk, MN	3	32 433	21.5	8	22	54.5	—	40.9	6 683	47.9	—	43.8	NA	26.4	11.8
27121	Pope, MN	6	11 051	21.3	1	1	100.0	—	—	122	100.0	—	—	NA	23.0	3.3
27123	Ramsey, MN	0	484 484	17.8	9	202	57.4	12.9	23.3	82 742	53.4	19.3	24.3	NA	29.9	32.0
27125	Red Lake, MN	9	4 342	23.2	3	6	50.0	—	50.0	1 007	43.1	—	56.9	NA	32.9	3.5
27127	Redwood, MN	7	16 878	21.4	8	17	52.9	17.6	29.4	3 513	45.4	19.6	35.0	NA	18.9	5.4
27129	Renville, MN	7	17 075	21.3	5	6	50.0	—	33.3	1 659	56.4	—	40.4	NA	16.5	10.1
27131	Rice, MN	4	52 888	19.8	4	18	44.4	22.2	22.2	8 100	40.5	30.3	26.7	NA	14.5	5.7
27133	Rock, MN	6	9 948	22.2	2	4	50.0	—	25.0	1 880	39.7	—	10.5	NA	16.7	3.9
27135	Roseau, MN	9	16 215	22.7	4	15	46.7	20.0	33.3	3 951	48.1	16.4	35.5	NA	16.2	5.1
27137	St. Louis, MN	3	196 414	19.0	12	86	47.7	14.0	31.4	31 572	44.0	18.3	37.0	NA	19.8	6.7
27139	Scott, MN	1	72 813	22.6	5	22	40.9	31.8	22.7	11 390	41.1	31.3	27.4	NA	7.3	2.6
27141	Sherburne, MN	1	55 401	24.1	3	17	52.9	23.5	23.5	11 166	50.2	26.3	23.5	NA	7.9	2.5
27143	Sibley, MN	8	14 652	21.6	2	7	42.9	14.3	28.6	1 425	44.6	30.2	24.5	NA	15.1	7.8
27145	Stearns, MN	3	126 990	21.6	12	49	51.0	16.3	26.5	25 329	43.8	18.7	36.8	NA	15.2	2.6
27147	Steele, MN	7	31 567	21.6	3	12	50.0	16.7	33.3	6 335	45.9	18.8	35.3	NA	13.2	5.5
27149	Stevens, MN	7	10 197	18.3	4	8	50.0	—	50.0	1 839	46.8	—	53.2	NA	16.8	3.4
27151	Swift, MN	7	10 857	20.3	2	4	50.0	—	50.0	1 512	59.2	—	40.8	NA	18.8	3.1
27153	Todd, MN	6	24 128	24.3	6	14	50.0	7.1	42.9	5 021	44.8	9.3	45.9	NA	33.7	1.6
27155	Traverse, MN	9	4 298	20.4	2	4	50.0	—	25.0	752	51.5	—	34.3	NA	28.3	11.3
27157	Wabasha, MN	6	20 752	21.7	4	8	50.0	—	50.0	4 133	52.1	—	47.9	NA	13.4	2.0
27159	Wadena, MN	7	13 126	21.6	3	6	50.0	—	50.0	1 861	51.5	—	48.5	NA	39.4	0.9
27161	Waseca, MN	7	17 998	22.3	3	11	45.5	18.2	36.4	4 322	41.9	23.5	34.7	NA	15.8	3.2
27163	Washington, MN	0	185 074	22.9	4	55	65.5	16.4	16.4	33 737	54.3	21.6	24.2	NA	6.9	4.2
27165	Watonwan, MN	7	11 600	21.2	3	7	42.9	14.3	42.9	2 281	37.6	14.3	48.1	NA	27.1	19.5
27167	Wilkin, MN	6	7 381	21.4	3	6	33.3	—	50.0	1 571	14.7	—	39.4	NA	19.8	5.0
27169	Winona, MN	4	48 411	18.7	3	20	55.0	15.0	30.0	6 655	45.2	18.8	35.9	NA	16.6	5.6
27171	Wright, MN	1	80 757	24.5	10	29	48.3	20.7	31.0	17 036	47.8	18.2	33.9	NA	10.4	1.8
27173	Yellow Medicine, MN	7	11 559	20.8	2	8	50.0	12.5	25.0	2 329	50.9	9.9	38.8	NA	24.4	7.2
28000	**MISSISSIPPI**															
28001	Adams, MS	7	34 726	20.3	1	6	66.7	16.7	16.7	5 658	57.2	15.9	26.9	8.7	69.6	77.1
28003	Alcorn, MS	7	32 755	18.3	2	15	53.3	20.0	26.7	5 713	45.3	19.3	35.4	16.5	35.3	16.5
28005	Amite, MS	9	13 564	21.0	1	3	66.7	—	33.3	1 943	68.7	—	31.3	8.4	81.1	82.0
28007	Attala, MS	6	18 437	19.4	2	9	44.4	22.2	33.3	3 685	42.6	24.8	32.6	16.1	58.6	56.8
28009	Benton, MS	8	8 025	21.8	1	4	25.0	25.0	25.0	1 339	32.9	15.9	20.5	16.3	75.2	63.7
28011	Bolivar, MS	5	41 113	23.5	6	21	52.4	14.3	28.6	9 446	50.7	13.0	32.9	15.3	76.8	85.7
28013	Calhoun, MS	9	14 997	18.6	1	8	50.0	12.5	37.5	2 725	60.3	9.7	30.0	17.4	53.5	43.3
28015	Carroll, MS	9	10 009	20.1	1	4	50.0	—	50.0	1 188	54.4	—	45.6	5.8	76.2	80.1

1. County type code is from the Economic Research Service of the USDA. See notes and definitions at the end of this section.   2. IEP = Individual Education Program. See notes and definitions at the end of this section.

Table D-2. School and Student Characteristics by County — Continued

County	Staff and students, 1995–1996						Revenues, fiscal 1995				Current expenditures, fiscal 1995		
	Number of teachers	Pupil/ teacher ratio	Number of graduates	Dropouts grades 9–12 (percent)	Local school non-teaching staff	Central admin. staff	Total revenue ($1000)	Percent of Revenue from			Amount	Amount per pupil	Percent for instruction
								Federal Gov't	State Gov't	Local Gov't			
	15	16	17	18	19	20	21	22	23	24	25	26	27
MINNESOTA—Con.													
Jackson, MN	130	15.8	155	3.4	87	3	12 851	4.1	52.1	43.8	11 213	5 329	66.0
Kanabec, MN	158	18.1	149	5.7	66	2	16 193	4.4	73.0	22.6	13 489	4 782	66.1
Kandiyohi, MN	486	16.2	468	8.0	279	11	50 409	3.8	61.1	35.1	43 138	5 943	68.1
Kittson, MN	93	13.1	98	1.4	17	4	9 345	2.6	38.3	59.1	7 428	6 099	62.6
Koochiching, MN	163	15.9	192	3.3	102	14	16 067	4.5	58.7	36.8	14 759	5 622	63.3
Lac qui Parle, MN	103	18.3	178	0.4	83	5	12 452	4.8	61.2	33.9	11 744	6 162	68.1
Lake, MN	120	18.6	158	3.6	62	4	14 965	3.3	57.2	39.6	12 571	5 597	62.4
Lake of the Woods, MN	53	16.4	36	2.0	28	2	5 430	3.5	60.5	36.0	4 323	5 068	59.7
Le Sueur, MN	271	14.5	247	2.8	127	12	28 794	4.7	57.5	37.8	25 292	6 826	68.9
Lincoln, MN	74	15.2	123	0.7	—	5	8 226	4.5	59.6	36.0	6 678	5 952	65.4
Lyon, MN	296	21.8	504	2.2	198	12	50 590	10.0	45.4	44.6	43 482	6 684	61.0
McLeod, MN	244	26.4	436	5.6	209	15	38 111	2.4	65.5	32.1	31 880	5 034	64.7
Mahnomen, MN	112	13.8	113	10.1	79	6	11 317	14.5	66.9	18.6	10 378	6 730	65.1
Marshall, MN	107	19.1	154	1.9	118	8	18 908	6.9	42.7	50.4	15 822	6 879	57.5
Martin, MN	39	74.3	216	1.9	6	2	18 872	2.8	59.0	38.2	14 856	5 313	64.2
Meeker, MN	288	18.2	363	2.1	112	9	33 959	3.0	67.6	29.5	28 604	4 911	64.9
Mille Lacs, MN	348	17.7	351	2.4	125	10	37 563	4.5	67.2	28.3	31 145	5 110	64.5
Morrison, MN	371	16.8	471	0.8	193	23	42 081	5.9	69.3	24.8	38 096	5 993	67.8
Mower, MN	358	17.2	361	7.4	46	3	42 797	4.7	57.1	38.1	34 443	5 691	62.4
Murray, MN	104	15.5	110	0.4	56	4	10 137	5.6	60.6	33.8	9 438	5 932	64.3
Nicollet, MN	87	28.2	165	1.7	67	5	20 119	7.8	51.1	41.1	17 018	6 890	59.5
Nobles, MN	81	45.9	261	5.5	35	5	25 417	4.0	57.0	39.0	22 344	6 028	65.4
Norman, MN	71	21.9	130	1.2	94	4	11 223	5.3	56.8	37.9	9 716	6 065	66.8
Olmsted, MN	034	21.0	1 188	2.8	37	5	140 807	3.1	45.6	51.3	126 610	6 290	57.4
Otter Tail, MN	666	16.6	765	5.7	345	30	89 881	4.5	45.8	49.7	77 837	7 281	51.8
Pennington, MN	153	17.2	154	1.5	112	12	20 736	6.7	64.9	28.3	15 708	5 945	66.1
Pine, MN	195	18.2	213	5.8	98	11	21 095	4.5	66.1	29.4	17 883	5 089	63.2
Pipestone, MN	136	16.2	115	2.0	132	6	13 869	6.3	57.6	36.1	12 363	5 522	71.7
Polk, MN	270	24.8	463	2.8	67	5	40 945	4.4	65.1	30.5	35 215	5 334	66.3
Pope, MN	9	13.6	—	NA	6	1	1 056	4.1	61.8	34.1	917	8 651	73.4
Ramsey, MN	1 167	70.9	3 939	8.8	758	71	592 539	5.6	46.3	48.1	515 938	6 455	64.6
Red Lake, MN	71	14.2	100	NA	40	4	6 897	5.9	64.9	29.2	5 730	5 651	61.4
Redwood, MN	211	16.6	229	2.0	78	8	21 088	4.0	50.9	45.1	17 194	5 451	66.8
Renville, MN	44	37.7	125	2.8	23	—	11 937	5.6	51.3	43.1	10 170	5 040	64.7
Rice, MN	280	29.0	474	5.3	113	10	53 454	3.2	60.7	36.0	45 474	5 801	66.3
Rock, MN	88	21.4	149	1.0	18	5	11 352	4.4	63.1	32.6	9 448	4 078	67.3
Roseau, MN	131	30.2	245	0.8	139	8	25 390	3.4	68.0	28.5	18 802	5 143	63.7
St. Louis, MN	1 760	17.9	2 156	4.6	892	84	225 807	4.6	63.0	32.4	188 764	5 940	62.4
Scott, MN	512	22.2	645	1.0	246	17	67 912	1.8	58.1	40.1	58 568	5 204	64.8
Sherburne, MN	637	17.5	535	3.2	272	20	70 098	1.8	56.8	41.4	55 725	5 253	65.5
Sibley, MN	84	16.9	108	7.6	—	—	9 605	5.9	58.2	35.9	8 142	5 862	69.8
Stearns, MN	632	40.1	1 697	1.6	211	17	157 915	4.1	61.0	34.9	130 710	5 139	67.5
Steele, MN	96	65.8	420	3.4	47	3	34 424	3.2	62.6	34.2	31 567	5 078	63.3
Stevens, MN	116	15.8	165	0.9	9	1	12 581	5.3	57.7	37.0	10 331	5 495	68.1
Swift, MN	88	17.2	92	2.5	21	—	10 827	4.6	64.2	31.2	7 864	5 310	68.2
Todd, MN	307	16.3	401	3.3	64	5	38 361	6.0	66.0	28.0	32 071	6 513	69.0
Traverse, MN	54	14.1	34	0.6	53	2	4 847	5.1	55.1	39.8	4 428	5 857	64.0
Wabasha, MN	246	16.8	288	1.4	—	—	24 046	2.6	67.0	30.4	19 975	4 868	66.0
Wadena, MN	120	15.5	125	1.0	18	3	11 784	6.2	72.0	21.8	9 382	5 055	67.6
Waseca, MN	267	16.2	322	2.9	37	3	27 589	4.9	59.2	35.8	23 101	5 226	66.2
Washington, MN	1 600	21.1	1 876	3.6	1 277	69	202 032	2.0	53.2	44.8	162 713	5 013	65.7
Watonwan, MN	121	18.8	164	3.2	63	5	13 456	5.1	61.0	33.9	12 047	5 431	66.4
Wilkin, MN	108	14.6	133	2.0	29	2	9 820	5.2	54.6	40.1	8 920	5 537	66.8
Winona, MN	400	16.6	432	5.6	204	19	40 863	5.2	61.4	33.4	36 636	5 594	68.1
Wright, MN	925	18.4	986	2.3	512	40	108 989	3.3	55.4	41.3	87 811	5 334	66.4
Yellow Medicine, MN	126	18.5	164	1.5	32	6	14 578	4.2	59.7	36.1	12 213	5 416	66.5
MISSISSIPPI													
Adams, MS	273	20.7	359	5.5	365	43	25 410	17.8	48.7	33.5	22 797	4 099	59.5
Alcorn, MS	358	16.0	343	6.3	309	24	26 023	11.4	60.1	28.6	23 276	4 003	66.6
Amite, MS	113	17.3	102	5.2	112	13	8 694	20.3	56.7	23.0	8 398	4 121	58.9
Attala, MS	196	18.8	173	7.4	218	20	15 004	15.3	55.8	28.9	13 396	3 729	59.7
Benton, MS	80	16.8	82	8.2	101	10	5 708	21.7	63.3	15.0	5 770	4 098	58.1
Bolivar, MS	523	18.1	467	5.2	543	61	38 620	22.8	59.4	17.9	36 326	3 797	60.7
Calhoun, MS	158	17.3	165	4.8	155	18	11 707	13.8	64.5	21.7	10 563	3 883	59.9
Carroll, MS	70	16.9	63	8.7	71	7	5 556	18.5	52.8	28.7	5 006	4 103	59.6

Table D-2.   School and Student Characteristics by County

State/County code	County	County type [1]	Population, 1996		Number of school districts, 1995–1996	Level of schools, 1995–1996				Level of students, 1995–1996				Characteristics of students, 1995–1996		
			Total persons	Percent age 5–17		Number of schools	Percent			Number of students	Percent			Percent with IEP [2]	Percent free-lunch eligible	Percent minority
							Primary	Middle	High		Primary	Middle	High			
			1	2	3	4	5	6	7	8	9	10	11	12	13	14
	MISSISSIPPI—Con.															
28017	Chickasaw, MS	7	18 320	20.6	3	7	28.6	28.6	28.6	3 758	32.4	29.2	24.1	13.0	58.1	59.0
28019	Choctaw, MS	9	9 285	22.0	1	4	50.0	—	25.0	1 926	42.7	—	26.7	9.0	58.4	46.7
28021	Claiborne, MS	8	11 521	20.4	1	3	33.3	33.3	33.3	2 221	44.5	25.0	30.5	10.4	84.6	99.7
28023	Clarke, MS	7	17 860	20.7	2	6	50.0	16.7	33.3	3 406	47.4	20.1	32.5	15.1	53.5	48.6
28025	Clay, MS	7	21 746	22.0	2	9	44.4	22.2	22.2	4 353	42.7	36.6	19.4	13.7	70.0	78.1
28027	Coahoma, MS	7	31 645	24.1	3	21	61.9	19.0	14.3	7 043	53.2	25.3	21.1	14.9	79.0	86.1
28029	Copiah, MS	6	28 558	21.2	2	7	42.9	14.3	28.6	5 328	49.6	6.8	25.1	12.0	73.3	74.8
28031	Covington, MS	7	17 441	21.8	1	6	33.3	16.7	16.7	3 650	23.4	13.8	14.2	15.2	59.2	50.4
28033	De Soto, MS	1	87 823	20.0	1	17	52.9	23.5	23.5	15 907	50.8	18.7	30.6	13.4	21.1	17.5
28035	Forrest, MS	5	73 054	17.9	4	19	52.6	26.3	21.1	11 902	49.0	25.1	26.0	16.1	52.1	46.6
28037	Franklin, MS	9	8 270	20.9	1	4	50.0	25.0	25.0	1 891	48.0	25.6	26.3	14.1	59.5	51.1
28039	George, MS	6	18 599	21.7	1	7	57.1	28.6	14.3	3 851	42.8	29.8	27.4	11.7	39.2	13.4
28041	Greene, MS	8	11 797	21.0	1	5	60.0	20.0	20.0	1 964	48.7	22.0	29.3	15.3	59.2	26.9
28043	Grenada, MS	7	22 455	20.3	1	5	40.0	40.0	20.0	4 399	38.3	37.0	24.6	12.5	51.9	55.9
28045	Hancock, MS	2	38 304	19.2	2	8	62.5	12.5	25.0	5 947	46.5	9.9	43.6	11.6	53.1	13.3
28047	Harrison, MS	2	176 613	18.8	6	48	60.4	22.9	12.5	30 050	53.4	25.9	20.2	15.8	43.1	34.1
28049	Hinds, MS	2	250 381	19.1	7	76	57.9	21.1	14.5	44 522	45.4	25.6	26.2	9.1	58.2	77.7
28051	Holmes, MS	6	21 408	24.8	2	10	50.0	10.0	30.0	4 838	50.6	11.6	27.5	10.4	92.9	97.1
28053	Humphreys, MS	7	11 465	25.1	1	3	33.3	33.3	33.3	2 578	34.9	43.3	21.8	9.0	93.6	95.2
28055	Issaquena, MS	9	1 664	22.3	NA	NA	NA	NA	NA	NA	NA	NA	NA	NA	NA	NA
28057	Itawamba, MS	7	21 076	17.3	2	7	28.6	14.3	14.3	3 644	31.6	13.3	11.9	17.2	33.2	9.4
28059	Jackson, MS	2	128 267	21.0	4	44	56.8	25.0	13.6	25 043	48.8	29.0	19.8	13.2	34.4	29.2
28061	Jasper, MS	9	17 410	22.3	2	7	28.6	28.6	28.6	3 253	31.6	27.1	23.4	13.4	72.6	76.0
28063	Jefferson, MS	9	8 545	25.1	1	4	25.0	50.0	25.0	1 879	35.9	32.2	31.9	13.7	94.9	99.9
28065	Jefferson Davis, MS	9	13 949	22.4	1	4	50.0	—	25.0	2 702	50.1	—	20.8	16.7	90.4	81.3
28067	Jones, MS	5	63 447	19.5	3	23	65.2	13.0	17.4	11 892	54.3	8.6	36.6	14.6	50.6	40.8
28069	Kemper, MS	9	10 378	21.2	1	4	50.0	25.0	25.0	1 561	42.7	28.6	28.7	12.2	79.2	91.7
28071	Lafayette, MS	7	33 515	15.1	3	8	37.5	12.5	25.0	5 038	50.5	13.8	34.1	18.5	44.3	44.6
28073	Lamar, MS	7	34 843	21.0	2	7	28.6	—	14.3	7 138	10.5	—	5.6	11.8	28.2	13.7
28075	Lauderdale, MS	5	76 987	19.5	2	20	40.0	35.0	10.0	14 156	30.7	28.5	14.8	16.2	47.3	51.3
28077	Lawrence, MS	9	12 873	21.9	1	5	60.0	20.0	20.0	2 552	51.0	19.4	29.6	10.4	58.0	44.6
28079	Leake, MS	6	19 403	20.3	1	7	28.6	14.3	28.6	3 142	32.7	19.0	23.0	12.2	68.1	62.2
28081	Lee, MS	5	73 357	19.3	3	24	45.8	29.2	16.7	14 347	44.5	22.9	24.9	16.2	37.3	33.5
28083	Leflore, MS	7	36 907	22.5	2	14	57.1	21.4	21.4	7 488	47.7	20.7	31.6	15.7	84.9	89.1
28085	Lincoln, MS	7	31 490	20.8	2	10	20.0	30.0	10.0	5 952	16.7	26.6	12.1	13.0	50.2	41.3
28087	Lowndes, MS	5	61 203	20.1	3	24	50.0	25.0	20.0	11 530	49.4	22.9	20.3	9.0	49.8	57.3
28089	Madison, MS	2	68 273	19.9	2	13	53.8	23.1	15.4	11 281	43.4	23.6	23.7	10.9	49.9	60.4
28091	Marion, MS	7	26 093	22.4	2	7	28.6	28.6	14.3	4 880	21.1	14.9	11.9	17.7	63.5	43.1
28093	Marshall, MS	6	32 233	20.8	2	9	44.4	11.1	22.2	5 359	40.8	14.1	19.9	12.7	78.2	75.0
28095	Monroe, MS	7	37 922	20.2	3	15	40.0	26.7	20.0	6 646	32.1	21.0	22.1	12.9	48.2	42.0
28097	Montgomery, MS	7	12 413	20.5	2	6	50.0	16.7	33.3	2 283	59.0	11.2	29.8	14.0	65.0	66.4
28099	Neshoba, MS	7	27 043	21.7	3	12	66.7	8.3	25.0	5 662	57.1	2.3	40.6	10.5	49.6	53.9
28101	Newton, MS	7	21 455	19.7	3	6	33.3	16.7	33.3	3 798	37.4	11.1	28.3	15.4	50.8	44.1
28103	Noxubee, MS	9	12 414	23.5	1	5	60.0	20.0	20.0	2 460	46.3	25.1	28.6	4.8	88.5	99.9
28105	Oktibbeha, MS	7	39 303	15.8	2	13	30.8	30.8	15.4	5 711	27.1	28.9	23.8	11.7	60.3	71.4
28107	Panola, MS	7	32 615	22.5	2	9	66.7	11.1	22.2	6 631	61.8	14.1	24.1	13.5	70.8	69.0
28109	Pearl River, MS	6	44 359	20.5	3	14	50.0	28.6	21.4	8 226	44.1	25.0	30.9	11.7	46.2	19.0
28111	Perry, MS	9	11 874	22.6	2	6	66.7	—	16.7	2 506	62.5	—	19.2	13.1	53.6	31.7
28113	Pike, MS	7	38 093	21.9	3	14	50.0	28.6	21.4	7 357	42.9	27.7	29.4	11.8	66.2	63.4
28115	Pontotoc, MS	7	24 518	19.1	2	6	33.3	16.7	16.7	4 788	21.6	9.9	11.4	12.8	31.3	18.7
28117	Prentiss, MS	7	24 011	17.9	3	12	33.3	16.7	25.0	4 865	39.9	13.3	17.2	17.4	40.4	18.6
28119	Quitman, MS	9	9 888	23.6	1	4	75.0	—	25.0	1 791	72.8	—	27.2	13.0	93.6	97.0
28121	Rankin, MS	2	102 411	19.9	4	28	46.4	14.3	14.3	18 169	38.9	20.3	17.6	12.3	26.6	21.6
28123	Scott, MS	6	25 194	20.9	2	10	20.0	30.0	20.0	5 744	27.0	24.4	15.1	13.3	60.2	50.7
28125	Sharkey, MS	9	6 814	26.0	1	4	50.0	25.0	25.0	1 818	49.3	22.6	28.1	10.9	91.2	94.8
28127	Simpson, MS	6	25 221	21.1	1	7	42.9	28.6	28.6	4 340	46.5	27.4	26.1	12.4	61.8	50.4
28129	Smith, MS	8	15 069	20.1	1	4	25.0	—	—	3 092	14.5	—	—	11.2	46.0	31.0
28131	Stone, MS	6	12 670	20.0	1	4	50.0	25.0	25.0	2 583	48.0	24.7	27.3	14.9	46.4	26.4
28133	Sunflower, MS	7	36 266	20.2	3	15	46.7	33.3	20.0	6 877	51.2	27.7	21.1	11.8	84.9	93.3
28135	Tallahatchie, MS	9	15 033	23.2	2	7	57.1	14.3	28.6	3 111	50.0	21.3	28.7	14.8	83.2	82.4
28137	Tate, MS	6	22 842	20.7	2	8	62.5	—	37.5	4 716	57.8	—	42.2	18.4	48.6	46.4
28139	Tippah, MS	7	20 751	19.1	2	9	33.3	11.1	22.2	4 257	32.1	13.7	19.8	14.8	43.0	22.7
28141	Tishomingo, MS	6	18 430	16.4	1	6	50.0	16.7	—	3 181	39.5	11.0	—	15.1	35.3	4.6
28143	Tunica, MS	8	8 043	26.3	1	4	25.0	50.0	25.0	1 986	32.5	40.0	27.4	10.8	87.9	98.4
28145	Union, MS	7	23 117	18.8	2	8	25.0	12.5	12.5	4 497	19.8	13.4	11.6	13.6	32.7	18.5
28147	Walthall, MS	9	14 414	22.8	1	5	40.0	—	20.0	2 968	38.1	—	31.4	15.7	72.6	63.5

1. County type code is from the Economic Research Service of the USDA. See notes and definitions at the end of this section.   2. IEP = Individual Education Program. See notes and definitions at the end of this section.

Table D-2. School and Student Characteristics by County — Continued

County	Staff and students, 1995–1996						Revenues, fiscal 1995				Current expenditures, fiscal 1995		
	Number of teachers	Pupil/ teacher ratio	Number of graduates	Dropouts grades 9–12 (percent)	Local school non-teaching staff	Central admin. staff	Total revenue ($1000)	Percent of Revenue from			Amount	Amount per pupil	Percent for instruction
								Federal Gov't	State Gov't	Local Gov't			
	15	16	17	18	19	20	21	22	23	24	25	26	27
MISSISSIPPI—Con.													
Chickasaw, MS	215	17.5	217	5.8	195	22	15 246	14.4	64.9	20.7	14 120	3 626	63.3
Choctaw, MS	108	17.8	83	6.1	127	8	8 189	15.5	68.7	15.7	7 415	3 911	59.6
Claiborne, MS	114	19.5	126	9.2	133	18	11 397	15.4	46.0	38.6	10 609	4 833	63.9
Clarke, MS	181	18.8	178	6.9	195	21	13 865	14.0	58.3	27.7	12 259	3 616	59.7
Clay, MS	243	17.9	218	5.1	240	25	16 638	17.0	62.1	20.9	15 679	3 546	60.9
Coahoma, MS	408	17.2	306	6.8	404	40	28 193	21.6	62.5	15.9	26 967	3 711	61.6
Copiah, MS	282	18.9	249	5.1	270	30	19 987	19.3	55.9	24.8	19 125	3 660	57.8
Covington, MS	208	17.5	200	4.2	216	19	14 028	14.2	65.8	20.0	13 222	3 570	64.5
De Soto, MS	811	19.6	762	7.3	753	39	58 646	6.9	58.0	35.0	47 175	3 085	61.4
Forrest, MS	759	15.7	606	5.0	697	88	55 149	13.2	53.9	32.9	49 592	4 171	61.9
Franklin, MS	100	18.9	86	3.3	110	8	8 094	19.6	59.2	21.2	7 875	4 241	64.3
George, MS	210	18.4	193	3.3	210	15	12 613	13.3	66.6	20.1	11 953	3 163	65.0
Greene, MS	114	17.2	124	2.1	124	15	7 867	18.2	68.0	13.7	7 136	3 564	60.6
Grenada, MS	232	19.0	198	12.7	272	22	17 215	13.6	54.6	31.8	15 425	3 715	60.0
Hancock, MS	310	19.2	249	9.9	305	32	24 924	13.2	50.0	36.9	22 232	3 826	58.9
Harrison, MS	1 638	18.3	1 405	9.5	1 717	153	129 560	14.5	50.6	34.9	121 496	4 063	62.6
Hinds, MS	2 423	18.4	2 098	7.8	2 847	277	210 963	11.7	45.2	43.2	182 015	4 153	60.1
Holmes, MS	243	19.9	250	4.2	282	26	19 155	26.2	59.1	14.8	17 943	3 697	59.4
Humphreys, MS	119	21.8	89	6.0	170	20	11 307	23.5	48.6	27.9	9 462	3 750	58.7
Issaquena, MS	NA	NA	NA	NA	NA	NA	NA	NA	NA	NA	NA	NA	NA
Itawamba, MS	213	17.1	219	3.9	186	12	14 431	11.2	67.6	21.2	12 886	3 618	64.9
Jackson, MS	1 350	18.6	1 371	5.8	1 490	139	106 831	9.9	51.7	38.4	97 377	3 890	62.4
Jasper, MS	184	17.6	196	6.2	201	28	13 550	17.9	56.2	25.9	12 792	3 932	58.4
Jefferson, MS	107	17.6	103	8.0	111	19	8 361	21.9	59.1	18.9	8 149	4 170	66.4
Jefferson Davis, MS	168	16.1	163	8.5	169	15	11 948	19.6	59.5	20.9	11 525	4 112	61.1
Jones, MS	684	17.4	640	4.4	650	62	50 063	15.7	58.8	25.5	47 542	3 983	63.2
Kemper, MS	87	18.0	79	12.4	108	12	7 268	21.1	60.1	18.7	7 002	4 246	59.7
Lafayette, MS	306	16.5	277	5.8	291	23	21 498	12.6	59.6	27.8	19 966	4 004	63.1
Lamar, MS	406	17.6	372	2.6	354	22	25 416	9.0	63.6	27.4	22 807	3 274	64.6
Lauderdale, MS	820	17.3	832	3.1	767	81	59 924	13.5	57.7	28.9	55 426	3 845	63.6
Lawrence, MS	145	17.6	149	4.5	172	19	10 752	15.3	59.9	24.8	10 010	3 773	62.7
Leake, MS	178	17.6	189	8.8	183	16	12 372	18.3	62.4	19.2	11 695	3 652	62.1
Lee, MS	809	17.7	666	6.8	748	63	65 233	9.0	51.6	39.5	55 407	3 912	64.3
Leflore, MS	420	17.8	380	8.3	427	53	33 831	20.4	53.5	26.1	30 809	4 062	60.0
Lincoln, MS	329	18.1	388	4.3	352	29	24 979	13.6	57.4	29.0	23 069	3 856	62.8
Lowndes, MS	651	17.7	654	7.6	638	48	51 007	12.3	51.6	36.0	43 959	3 885	60.7
Madison, MS	567	19.9	453	4.9	565	44	46 601	14.6	49.5	35.9	36 976	3 377	62.8
Marion, MS	288	16.9	254	3.0	299	30	21 599	16.2	60.3	23.5	19 102	3 864	62.2
Marshall, MS	287	18.7	258	9.7	296	30	20 336	19.4	63.3	17.3	19 781	3 651	58.5
Monroe, MS	374	17.8	343	7.0	333	30	26 676	14.0	61.0	25.0	24 936	3 767	65.1
Montgomery, MS	140	16.3	107	5.3	137	15	10 126	16.1	60.2	23.7	9 339	4 092	62.9
Neshoba, MS	357	15.8	308	5.7	411	42	15 862	17.4	62.6	20.0	14 284	3 423	67.2
Newton, MS	213	17.8	216	5.7	209	21	17 639	13.2	56.6	30.3	14 894	3 936	61.4
Noxubee, MS	121	20.3	125	6.6	179	15	9 493	24.3	59.4	16.3	9 282	3 731	58.4
Oktibbeha, MS	358	16.0	323	6.5	361	37	26 610	15.9	53.3	30.9	24 870	4 378	64.0
Panola, MS	340	19.5	350	10.0	416	32	26 131	19.0	60.2	20.8	25 477	3 819	59.9
Pearl River, MS	441	18.7	430	5.7	518	48	30 391	11.9	62.3	25.8	28 650	3 539	62.7
Perry, MS	148	16.9	158	6.2	153	18	10 964	17.8	61.5	20.8	10 112	4 003	64.4
Pike, MS	410	18.0	532	5.5	396	44	30 598	16.9	58.3	24.8	27 780	3 729	63.1
Pontotoc, MS	243	19.7	243	2.4	233	20	16 852	10.8	69.2	20.0	16 079	3 384	64.5
Prentiss, MS	296	16.4	266	5.8	263	28	20 700	12.0	65.6	22.4	19 150	3 937	63.0
Quitman, MS	97	18.5	93	9.7	108	18	8 011	28.6	54.6	16.8	7 656	4 138	56.4
Rankin, MS	928	19.6	956	4.9	920	62	66 399	7.8	58.7	33.5	57 558	3 251	63.8
Scott, MS	304	18.9	274	8.8	300	29	22 712	16.3	62.1	21.7	20 435	3 627	64.5
Sharkey, MS	100	18.2	97	4.9	121	17	8 357	23.9	52.9	23.1	7 928	4 383	58.9
Simpson, MS	224	19.4	238	6.4	218	23	17 239	14.8	60.1	25.1	14 776	3 342	64.5
Smith, MS	173	17.9	173	5.7	164	11	12 712	12.8	56.7	30.4	11 002	3 574	64.9
Stone, MS	151	17.1	125	8.8	142	14	10 086	14.2	62.0	23.8	8 968	3 502	66.5
Sunflower, MS	370	18.6	299	8.1	359	46	26 200	22.1	58.7	19.2	23 866	3 426	60.9
Tallahatchie, MS	174	17.9	140	7.8	200	24	12 502	22.6	57.4	20.1	11 979	3 806	58.8
Tate, MS	261	18.1	251	8.6	251	27	18 395	14.6	68.3	17.0	16 747	3 537	63.3
Tippah, MS	239	17.8	218	6.1	206	16	16 964	13.0	67.8	19.2	15 264	3 610	64.0
Tishomingo, MS	179	17.8	183	6.5	158	8	13 180	13.0	64.2	22.8	11 767	3 732	64.2
Tunica, MS	98	20.3	92	5.7	137	20	10 520	22.6	43.4	34.0	8 859	4 461	52.2
Union, MS	238	18.9	230	5.6	227	18	17 743	9.7	66.2	24.1	16 540	3 698	62.8
Walthall, MS	175	16.9	199	6.9	181	13	11 782	19.0	62.6	18.4	11 067	3 654	66.6

Table D-2. School and Student Characteristics by County

State/ County code	County	County type[1]	Population, 1996		Number of school districts, 1995–1996	Level of schools, 1995–1996				Level of students, 1995–1996				Characteristics of students, 1995–1996		
			Total persons	Percent age 5–17		Number of schools	Percent			Number of students	Percent			Percent with IEP[2]	Percent free-lunch eligible	Percent minority
							Primary	Middle	High		Primary	Middle	High			
			1	2	3	4	5	6	7	8	9	10	11	12	13	14
	MISSISSIPPI—Con.															
28149	Warren, MS	4	49 047	21.5	1	14	71.4	14.3	14.3	9 587	55.2	17.2	27.7	11.7	49.9	56.8
28151	Washington, MS	5	66 115	23.8	4	24	58.3	16.7	16.7	13 479	45.3	17.1	21.8	12.8	78.7	86.4
28153	Wayne, MS	7	20 003	22.3	1	6	66.7	16.7	16.7	4 171	55.5	18.5	26.0	16.3	62.0	50.7
28155	Webster, MS	9	10 437	19.5	1	4	50.0	—	—	2 063	41.4	—	—	14.4	46.6	31.7
28157	Wilkinson, MS	9	9 294	21.1	1	3	66.7	—	33.3	1 819	57.4	—	42.6	11.4	88.3	99.9
28159	Winston, MS	7	19 442	21.3	1	6	16.7	33.3	16.7	3 737	22.4	29.1	20.6	14.6	61.8	64.1
28161	Yalobusha, MS	7	12 212	19.7	2	5	60.0	—	40.0	2 325	55.1	—	44.9	16.3	61.6	57.2
28163	Yazoo, MS	6	25 295	22.8	2	9	66.7	11.1	22.2	4 960	61.6	11.8	26.6	10.6	82.9	81.3
29000	**MISSOURI**															
29001	Adair, MO	7	24 501	15.1	3	10	60.0	10.0	30.0	3 017	47.6	19.5	32.9	13.8	23.5	1.9
29003	Andrew, MO	3	15 270	20.8	3	10	60.0	20.0	20.0	2 825	49.7	19.9	30.4	10.9	29.5	1.3
29005	Atchison, MO	9	7 291	17.6	3	6	50.0	—	50.0	1 191	52.6	—	47.4	20.4	27.4	1.4
29007	Audrain, MO	6	23 385	20.2	3	9	55.6	11.1	33.3	3 687	48.7	16.4	34.9	13.3	33.9	10.5
29009	Barry, MO	7	32 325	19.2	7	15	46.7	13.3	40.0	6 201	55.0	12.4	32.6	11.6	37.5	3.1
29011	Barton, MO	6	11 829	20.1	3	8	37.5	25.0	37.5	2 225	42.2	24.2	33.6	12.2	24.3	2.2
29013	Bates, MO	6	15 608	19.9	7	13	53.8	—	46.2	2 955	59.4	—	40.6	11.9	34.6	1.8
29015	Benton, MO	9	16 050	16.8	3	10	50.0	20.0	30.0	2 539	45.4	19.4	35.2	14.8	39.9	0.9
29017	Bollinger, MO	9	11 361	19.7	4	9	55.6	—	44.4	1 992	54.1	—	45.9	10.5	26.9	2.6
29019	Boone, MO	3	125 676	16.4	6	39	59.0	17.9	17.9	19 476	49.2	26.0	21.9	13.6	20.0	17.3
29021	Buchanan, MO	3	82 066	19.2	4	36	58.3	13.9	16.7	14 039	54.6	15.1	29.2	11.9	37.2	0.1
29023	Butler, MO	7	40 217	19.9	3	15	73.3	6.7	20.0	6 740	58.3	12.2	29.5	12.0	46.9	9.1
29025	Caldwell, MO	8	8 589	19.6	8	14	57.1	14.3	28.6	1 774	49.2	16.6	34.3	17.5	37.2	0.6
29027	Callaway, MO	6	36 036	19.4	4	14	57.1	14.3	28.6	4 754	52.3	17.2	30.5	19.4	32.7	7.0
29029	Camden, MO	7	32 552	16.5	4	12	50.0	16.7	33.3	4 877	38.2	28.5	33.3	11.6	29.5	1.4
29031	Cape Girardeau, MO	5	65 719	17.9	5	23	60.9	21.7	17.4	9 381	44.9	30.3	24.8	12.9	23.2	10.2
29033	Carroll, MO	6	10 273	20.2	5	11	45.5	9.1	45.5	1 889	45.4	9.5	45.1	13.6	19.2	2.4
29035	Carter, MO	9	6 187	20.9	2	4	50.0	—	50.0	1 395	53.4	—	46.6	14.1	50.7	0.4
29037	Cass, MO	1	75 665	21.7	10	31	51.6	16.1	25.8	14 157	45.3	22.5	31.8	11.5	18.5	3.9
29039	Cedar, MO	7	13 012	17.8	2	7	42.9	28.6	28.6	2 295	46.1	23.7	30.2	11.8	20.3	1.5
29041	Chariton, MO	9	8 818	19.6	4	8	50.0	—	50.0	1 465	51.3	—	48.7	11.1	21.3	4.6
29043	Christian, MO	2	44 871	21.7	7	23	47.8	21.7	30.4	8 365	46.6	22.6	30.8	11.4	21.6	1.3
29045	Clark, MO	9	7 499	21.1	4	8	62.5	—	37.5	1 443	52.1	—	47.9	12.1	29.6	0.3
29047	Clay, MO	0	170 447	18.9	6	54	59.3	20.4	14.8	29 184	44.7	26.8	28.0	12.7	16.5	6.8
29049	Clinton, MO	1	18 115	21.1	3	10	40.0	20.0	30.0	3 183	42.4	23.0	34.1	13.3	27.7	4.8
29051	Cole, MO	4	68 185	18.7	4	22	63.6	18.2	18.2	10 806	45.3	27.7	27.1	15.4	22.7	8.8
29053	Cooper, MO	6	15 947	18.3	6	14	50.0	14.3	35.7	2 531	46.8	16.0	37.3	14.8	27.6	9.8
29055	Crawford, MO	6	21 754	20.7	3	9	33.3	33.3	33.3	3 583	43.7	27.8	28.5	13.1	34.4	0.2
29057	Dade, MO	8	7 919	18.9	4	8	50.0	—	50.0	1 437	58.0	—	42.0	10.0	40.2	1.2
29059	Dallas, MO	8	14 728	20.4	1	4	50.0	25.0	25.0	2 044	38.1	32.1	29.8	11.0	20.8	0.6
29061	Daviess, MO	9	7 814	20.6	5	10	50.0	—	40.0	1 291	51.9	—	38.1	13.7	37.4	0.8
29063	De Kalb, MO	8	11 037	15.3	4	8	50.0	—	50.0	1 441	55.2	—	44.8	11.5	16.8	1.7
29065	Dent, MO	7	14 054	20.7	5	8	62.5	25.0	12.5	2 575	51.9	27.0	21.1	12.5	34.3	1.7
29067	Douglas, MO	6	12 235	20.2	3	5	60.0	20.0	20.0	1 900	45.9	27.3	26.8	12.7	41.4	1.7
29069	Dunklin, MO	7	32 991	20.5	7	18	50.0	11.1	38.9	6 031	50.7	12.3	37.0	14.7	14.6	16.1
29071	Franklin, MO	1	89 485	21.3	10	37	59.5	18.9	18.9	16 163	47.5	22.2	30.2	15.4	15.5	1.8
29073	Gasconade, MO	6	14 615	18.6	2	9	33.3	44.4	22.2	3 127	40.3	29.3	30.4	11.0	16.5	0.4
29075	Gentry, MO	8	6 887	18.7	3	7	42.9	14.3	42.9	1 340	47.0	11.3	41.6	17.0	39.2	2.2
29077	Greene, MO	2	223 873	17.2	8	77	64.9	19.5	15.6	34 832	47.0	23.5	29.5	11.9	23.4	5.8
29079	Grundy, MO	7	10 238	18.1	5	8	62.5	12.5	25.0	1 723	52.7	18.1	29.2	10.7	41.0	0.3
29081	Harrison, MO	7	8 317	17.5	5	12	58.3	—	41.7	1 557	53.4	—	46.6	12.5	42.8	1.6
29083	Henry, MO	6	21 051	18.6	7	13	61.5	7.7	30.8	3 372	51.9	11.7	36.4	13.1	14.5	2.5
29085	Hickory, MO	9	8 493	15.3	4	10	40.0	20.0	40.0	1 866	52.2	8.9	38.9	12.5	48.0	1.1
29087	Holt, MO	8	5 658	19.1	3	6	50.0	—	50.0	962	53.0	—	47.0	14.6	36.8	1.2
29089	Howard, MO	6	9 708	18.8	3	7	42.9	14.3	28.6	1 621	46.3	12.3	26.7	16.0	18.6	9.0
29091	Howell, MO	7	34 972	20.0	8	15	66.7	13.3	20.0	6 939	53.5	15.0	31.5	14.1	40.1	1.8
29093	Iron, MO	9	10 931	21.0	4	9	44.4	22.2	33.3	2 486	46.8	19.6	33.6	13.6	31.0	3.3
29095	Jackson, MO	0	646 341	18.6	12	194	61.9	17.0	14.9	102 547	50.7	21.6	24.7	12.5	30.3	38.8
29097	Jasper, MO	3	97 965	19.3	7	44	65.9	18.2	13.6	17 513	47.8	27.1	24.9	NA	31.5	4.8
29099	Jefferson, MO	1	188 863	22.0	11	52	51.9	28.8	17.3	34 726	49.4	24.8	25.7	13.9	19.0	1.6
29101	Johnson, MO	6	46 491	17.8	7	24	45.8	20.8	25.0	7 790	41.3	28.5	29.0	15.7	21.6	10.3
29103	Knox, MO	9	4 309	18.0	1	2	50.0	—	50.0	668	53.3	—	46.7	14.8	43.0	0.9
29105	Laclede, MO	6	29 804	20.2	4	10	50.0	30.0	20.0	5 360	41.3	35.0	23.7	13.3	10.9	1.5
29107	Lafayette, MO	1	32 259	19.9	6	16	43.8	18.8	37.5	5 839	49.7	15.9	34.4	16.2	22.4	5.4
29109	Lawrence, MO	6	32 396	20.2	6	17	52.9	11.8	29.4	5 836	50.2	10.4	32.5	12.8	29.2	1.6
29111	Lewis, MO	7	10 121	18.0	2	5	60.0	—	40.0	1 777	54.4	—	45.6	13.7	32.0	5.4

1. County type code is from the Economic Research Service of the USDA. See notes and definitions at the end of this section.   2. IEP = Individual Education Program. See notes and definitions at the end of this section.

Table D-2. School and Student Characteristics by County — Continued

County	Staff and students, 1995–1996						Revenues, fiscal 1995				Current expenditures, fiscal 1995		
	Number of teachers	Pupil/ teacher ratio	Number of graduates	Dropouts grades 9–12 (percent)	Local school non-teaching staff	Central admin. staff	Total revenue ($1000)	Percent of Revenue from			Amount	Amount per pupil	Percent for instruction
								Federal Gov't	State Gov't	Local Gov't			
	15	16	17	18	19	20	21	22	23	24	25	26	27
MISSISSIPPI—Con.													
Warren, MS	547	17.5	536	9.7	650	57	42 870	11.7	49.0	39.3	38 565	4 018	61.3
Washington, MS	713	18.9	850	4.8	841	78	56 016	22.4	55.5	22.1	52 969	3 860	62.2
Wayne, MS	235	17.8	237	5.5	264	17	16 022	18.9	62.3	18.8	15 231	3 664	65.3
Webster, MS	105	19.7	137	3.1	121	7	8 473	12.5	62.4	25.0	7 409	3 550	64.0
Wilkinson, MS	92	19.8	58	9.5	115	14	8 493	21.3	49.2	29.5	7 440	4 161	55.0
Winston, MS	212	17.6	255	8.7	211	20	15 452	17.8	60.3	21.9	14 859	3 958	62.5
Yalobusha, MS	132	17.6	147	8.6	134	20	9 239	16.7	66.7	16.6	8 592	3 584	60.7
Yazoo, MS	296	16.7	223	11.1	325	31	21 832	20.6	56.1	23.3	20 054	3 956	60.3
MISSOURI													
Adair, MO	203	14.9	202	4.4	108	43	15 555	9.3	37.0	53.8	12 986	4 300	60.2
Andrew, MO	201	14.0	201	4.1	119	28	12 520	6.0	47.3	46.7	11 240	3 918	64.7
Atchison, MO	106	11.3	84	3.0	55	13	6 187	5.9	33.7	60.4	5 483	4 528	65.1
Audrain, MO	245	15.0	278	4.4	194	47	18 683	7.3	39.0	53.7	15 688	4 178	62.0
Barry, MO	393	15.8	337	6.7	239	48	28 029	8.4	44.3	47.2	21 748	3 544	64.9
Barton, MO	147	15.1	138	5.7	73	22	9 664	4.9	41.4	53.6	8 363	3 771	63.9
Bates, MO	217	13.6	177	6.5	124	28	13 240	7.5	40.3	52.3	11 276	3 845	61.9
Benton, MO	159	16.0	151	4.4	86	18	10 441	8.8	38.4	52.9	9 289	3 851	62.8
Bollinger, MO	131	15.2	124	6.9	76	21	8 356	8.7	52.0	39.3	7 137	3 556	58.1
Boone, MO	1 263	15.4	1 097	8.7	666	238	97 950	5.4	34.3	60.3	85 844	4 585	62.3
Buchanan, MO	906	15.5	790	5.2	547	105	65 126	8.7	39.7	51.6	60 292	4 282	64.6
Butler, MO	399	16.9	405	11.2	293	64	31 189	11.9	45.1	42.9	26 321	3 807	63.5
Caldwell, MO	151	11.8	106	3.4	80	21	9 243	6.9	44.2	48.9	7 822	4 392	59.2
Callaway, MO	337	14.1	286	6.5	224	47	24 252	5.2	35.3	59.5	19 918	4 212	59.6
Camden, MO	309	15.8	278	4.4	291	49	22 905	7.0	30.3	62.7	18 992	4 070	62.0
Cape Girardeau, MO	576	16.3	566	7.0	331	73	40 991	6.7	32.0	61.4	35 201	3 830	64.9
Carroll, MO	152	12.4	143	5.0	76	29	9 928	7.3	40.5	52.2	9 115	4 725	62.8
Carter, MO	99	14.1	101	7.0	65	12	6 884	9.8	58.5	31.8	5 886	4 073	63.2
Cass, MO	873	16.2	884	3.8	448	142	66 491	4.6	41.2	54.2	55 090	3 947	62.0
Cedar, MO	148	15.5	134	7.8	88	21	9 542	7.9	45.0	47.1	8 525	3 891	60.1
Chariton, MO	118	12.4	115	2.1	64	16	7 245	7.8	30.0	62.2	6 610	4 494	63.0
Christian, MO	540	15.5	465	5.4	278	49	34 005	4.8	52.4	42.8	27 877	3 449	64.3
Clark, MO	120	12.0	89	4.1	68	17	6 847	8.2	43.8	48.0	6 180	4 319	63.5
Clay, MO	1 756	16.6	1 599	10.7	933	233	145 315	3.4	29.8	66.8	125 972	4 395	64.1
Clinton, MO	224	14.2	202	5.8	108	27	14 334	5.5	45.4	49.1	13 025	4 132	65.3
Cole, MO	693	15.6	707	4.5	364	103	52 686	4.8	30.5	64.6	46 641	4 375	65.4
Cooper, MO	186	13.6	168	4.2	99	29	13 439	5.8	41.8	52.4	11 061	4 355	60.7
Crawford, MO	216	16.6	188	8.4	140	25	14 006	7.3	44.8	47.9	12 263	3 547	65.1
Dade, MO	107	13.5	94	1.4	61	15	6 499	6.1	45.5	48.4	5 594	3 869	60.1
Dallas, MO	118	17.4	106	8.9	80	17	8 809	9.0	47.8	43.1	7 401	3 651	61.7
Daviess, MO	125	10.3	79	5.5	65	18	7 495	8.9	44.4	46.7	6 486	4 914	61.9
De Kalb, MO	117	12.3	87	5.2	79	17	6 736	6.8	47.2	46.0	6 036	4 218	60.6
Dent, MO	177	14.6	143	7.9	101	24	12 330	8.9	44.3	46.8	9 748	3 777	65.4
Douglas, MO	121	15.8	90	6.5	66	12	8 426	10.7	50.8	38.5	6 672	3 545	63.1
Dunklin, MO	425	14.2	375	5.7	253	58	29 121	13.5	44.8	41.6	24 598	4 060	64.2
Franklin, MO	949	17.0	872	6.4	800	127	72 428	5.4	36.0	58.6	62 872	4 006	62.3
Gasconade, MO	196	16.0	202	4.5	106	23	12 798	4.4	40.5	55.1	11 493	3 832	64.4
Gentry, MO	111	12.0	80	3.2	63	16	6 477	7.5	43.6	48.9	5 842	4 340	64.4
Greene, MO	2 054	17.0	2 008	7.7	1 352	263	154 645	5.7	35.3	58.9	139 338	4 006	62.3
Grundy, MO	134	12.9	112	6.8	107	16	8 870	7.4	41.2	51.3	7 741	4 364	62.5
Harrison, MO	145	10.8	111	2.5	86	28	9 058	8.6	40.2	51.2	8 005	5 175	64.3
Henry, MO	242	13.9	215	4.5	145	35	16 178	7.6	40.9	51.4	14 090	4 241	65.6
Hickory, MO	139	13.4	105	2.4	101	17	8 603	7.9	46.5	45.6	7 212	3 982	60.0
Holt, MO	85	11.3	70	1.3	39	11	4 787	7.2	32.2	60.6	4 447	4 676	62.3
Howard, MO	126	12.9	112	4.6	67	18	7 528	6.1	43.0	50.9	6 624	4 135	59.8
Howell, MO	431	16.1	357	5.6	275	58	32 036	10.8	48.2	41.1	25 269	3 823	66.6
Iron, MO	176	14.1	154	8.1	105	25	13 035	9.2	36.2	54.6	10 787	4 332	61.7
Jackson, MO	6 651	15.4	4 871	7.8	4 333	1 087	757 907	5.8	43.8	50.4	651 135	6 417	54.8
Jasper, MO	1 059	16.5	991	9.6	813	192	78 226	7.6	41.7	50.7	67 628	3 965	64.3
Jefferson, MO	1 914	18.1	1 772	7.8	948	216	143 874	4.0	42.2	53.8	127 159	3 701	65.5
Johnson, MO	508	15.3	425	5.4	316	66	34 936	10.4	43.0	46.6	29 682	3 867	61.7
Knox, MO	51	13.2	41	4.9	33	6	3 836	13.4	36.9	49.7	3 108	4 702	56.2
Laclede, MO	310	17.3	289	8.0	250	44	23 349	7.4	47.3	45.4	19 120	3 652	66.5
Lafayette, MO	393	14.9	384	5.1	192	50	28 046	7.3	41.3	51.4	24 339	4 152	64.6
Lawrence, MO	373	15.6	358	5.4	276	48	24 645	7.2	49.4	43.3	21 439	3 755	63.5
Lewis, MO	126	14.1	130	3.4	68	17	8 567	7.3	46.4	46.3	7 505	4 259	65.4

Table D-2. School and Student Characteristics by County

State/County code	County	County type[1]	Population, 1996 Total persons	Percent age 5–17	Number of school districts, 1995–1996	Number of schools	Percent Primary	Percent Middle	Percent High	Number of students	Percent Primary	Percent Middle	Percent High	Percent with IEP[2]	Percent free-lunch eligible	Percent minority
			1	2	3	4	5	6	7	8	9	10	11	12	13	14
	MISSOURI—Con.															
29113	Lincoln, MO	1	34 119	22.1	4	14	50.0	21.4	28.6	6 246	53.1	17.6	29.3	13.8	23.1	2.4
29115	Linn, MO	7	14 007	18.9	5	12	41.7	16.7	41.7	2 924	46.1	18.7	35.2	13.1	34.2	1.2
29117	Livingston, MO	7	14 306	18.9	3	9	55.6	22.2	22.2	2 431	39.3	27.4	33.3	16.0	17.1	2.2
29119	McDonald, MO	8	19 030	20.4	1	7	85.7	—	14.3	3 079	73.6	—	26.4	10.7	48.3	5.6
29121	Macon, MO	7	15 159	19.3	6	12	50.0	8.3	25.0	2 626	45.2	13.7	31.6	14.6	36.6	4.2
29123	Madison, MO	9	11 379	19.6	2	6	50.0	16.7	33.3	2 128	47.5	19.7	32.8	9.6	25.3	0.1
29125	Maries, MO	9	8 208	19.6	2	5	40.0	20.0	40.0	1 552	48.8	15.5	35.6	10.2	39.4	1.4
29127	Marion, MO	5	27 841	20.7	3	13	53.8	23.1	23.1	5 286	41.7	28.8	29.6	12.6	28.3	7.1
29129	Mercer, MO	9	4 004	17.9	2	4	50.0	—	50.0	711	50.8	—	49.2	12.2	35.7	0.4
29131	Miller, MO	7	22 321	21.1	5	13	38.5	23.1	38.5	5 094	44.0	23.7	32.3	12.5	31.6	1.4
29133	Mississippi, MO	7	13 629	22.5	2	9	44.4	33.3	22.2	2 740	40.2	23.1	36.7	13.5	30.9	33.5
29135	Moniteau, MO	6	13 047	21.4	6	11	63.6	9.1	27.3	2 443	51.7	11.5	36.8	14.3	21.0	2.0
29137	Monroe, MO	9	8 872	21.0	5	10	50.0	20.0	30.0	1 873	44.3	21.9	33.8	13.7	31.4	6.5
29139	Montgomery, MO	8	11 825	19.8	2	9	55.6	22.2	11.1	2 112	40.8	22.2	23.9	13.1	26.6	4.5
29141	Morgan, MO	9	17 592	17.1	2	7	42.9	28.6	28.6	2 066	48.8	23.4	27.7	14.0	45.5	2.2
29143	New Madrid, MO	7	20 611	22.9	4	12	58.3	8.3	33.3	3 822	58.7	8.3	33.0	14.9	51.5	28.1
29145	Newton, MO	3	47 751	19.7	5	18	55.6	22.2	22.2	7 745	49.8	26.5	23.7	9.4	34.9	5.2
29147	Nodaway, MO	6	21 030	17.2	7	16	43.8	12.5	37.5	3 235	40.3	18.4	35.6	15.6	25.6	0.6
29149	Oregon, MO	9	10 095	18.6	4	8	50.0	—	50.0	1 893	52.2	—	47.8	12.1	49.5	1.0
29151	Osage, MO	9	12 396	21.4	3	8	50.0	12.5	37.5	1 635	43.1	8.0	48.9	16.4	27.2	0.3
29153	Ozark, MO	9	9 629	18.5	5	10	50.0	10.0	30.0	1 765	50.7	6.2	20.3	14.8	46.6	0.5
29155	Pemiscot, MO	7	21 666	23.6	8	20	45.0	15.0	30.0	4 606	47.6	14.7	31.5	20.2	20.3	39.0
29157	Perry, MO	7	17 433	21.5	2	4	50.0	25.0	25.0	2 571	36.6	27.2	36.3	22.3	28.6	0.2
29159	Pettis, MO	7	36 767	19.6	6	16	62.5	6.3	31.3	6 096	50.7	16.3	33.1	14.5	38.8	7.2
29161	Phelps, MO	7	37 848	17.9	4	11	54.5	18.2	27.3	6 615	45.1	23.8	31.1	14.4	32.9	4.6
29163	Pike, MO	6	16 169	20.8	4	12	58.3	16.7	25.0	3 009	47.6	18.6	33.9	10.6	19.4	7.5
29165	Platte, MO	0	67 251	19.5	4	22	59.1	18.2	18.2	11 476	46.6	21.9	31.3	12.4	12.2	7.0
29167	Polk, MO	6	25 148	18.7	6	15	40.0	13.3	40.0	4 698	44.0	16.6	39.1	14.1	34.9	1.4
29169	Pulaski, MO	7	34 334	21.2	6	22	50.0	22.7	22.7	7 730	47.5	23.1	28.9	14.3	41.9	21.8
29171	Putnam, MO	9	5 049	17.2	1	2	50.0	—	50.0	882	54.1	—	45.9	10.3	—	—
29173	Ralls, MO	9	8 905	20.9	1	5	60.0	20.0	20.0	941	52.2	15.4	32.4	16.6	27.4	3.8
29175	Randolph, MO	6	23 793	19.1	5	15	53.3	20.0	26.7	3 862	48.4	19.3	32.2	15.1	36.5	8.0
29177	Ray, MO	1	22 660	21.6	5	12	41.7	16.7	41.7	3 853	41.1	25.2	33.7	11.7	19.3	3.3
29179	Reynolds, MO	9	6 699	20.6	4	8	50.0	—	37.5	1 361	50.1	—	45.8	16.1	40.3	2.6
29181	Ripley, MO	9	13 626	20.6	4	7	57.1	14.3	28.6	2 491	53.0	15.3	31.8	10.1	50.2	0.5
29183	St. Charles, MO	0	255 066	21.8	5	47	59.6	23.4	17.0	42 878	49.9	21.3	28.7	14.4	11.9	5.4
29185	St. Clair, MO	9	9 100	18.0	4	7	57.1	—	42.9	1 555	54.1	—	45.9	12.7	33.2	0.4
29186	Ste. Genevieve, MO	6	16 853	21.3	1	4	50.0	25.0	25.0	2 188	42.6	24.3	33.0	13.9	31.3	0.7
29187	St. Francois, MO	6	53 843	19.5	5	21	47.6	23.8	23.8	10 025	43.5	25.6	30.7	14.9	30.7	1.2
29189	St. Louis, MO	0	1 003 807	18.2	24	244	63.5	17.6	15.6	151 011	46.8	19.9	30.5	15.3	19.4	35.9
29195	Saline, MO	7	22 922	19.3	8	16	68.8	6.3	18.8	3 933	45.6	19.9	32.0	16.5	39.8	9.7
29197	Schuyler, MO	9	4 376	18.0	1	3	33.3	33.3	33.3	819	54.2	17.6	28.2	14.2	43.8	0.5
29199	Scotland, MO	9	4 800	18.3	2	3	66.7	—	33.3	827	55.1	—	44.9	16.3	4.5	—
29201	Scott, MO	5	40 241	21.6	7	20	60.0	10.0	30.0	7 757	50.7	16.1	33.2	10.7	35.7	16.3
29203	Shannon, MO	9	7 976	19.8	2	4	50.0	—	50.0	878	60.9	—	39.1	15.9	38.0	—
29205	Shelby, MO	9	6 845	19.5	2	6	50.0	16.7	33.3	1 309	44.9	17.3	37.8	15.0	25.4	1.1
29207	Stoddard, MO	7	29 625	19.4	7	17	47.1	5.9	41.2	5 688	52.9	9.1	37.8	12.2	29.8	1.8
29209	Stone, MO	8	25 875	16.6	5	12	41.7	16.7	41.7	4 111	46.6	17.3	36.1	12.1	40.8	1.3
29211	Sullivan, MO	9	6 648	17.0	3	6	50.0	—	50.0	948	52.1	—	47.9	12.2	39.8	0.8
29213	Taney, MO	6	33 271	15.9	7	15	53.3	20.0	26.7	5 437	52.7	18.1	29.3	11.6	28.6	2.1
29215	Texas, MO	9	22 385	20.8	7	15	46.7	20.0	33.3	4 479	44.3	16.0	39.7	14.1	36.4	1.1
29217	Vernon, MO	7	19 285	20.0	5	13	53.8	7.7	38.5	3 455	45.6	19.6	34.8	12.7	14.9	1.2
29219	Warren, MO	1	22 873	20.4	2	7	28.6	42.9	28.6	3 454	37.3	33.8	28.9	12.3	17.4	5.3
29221	Washington, MO	6	22 315	22.7	4	10	60.0	20.0	20.0	4 008	51.2	18.2	30.6	13.0	46.3	1.5
29223	Wayne, MO	9	12 842	18.2	2	6	50.0	16.7	33.3	2 149	39.4	15.4	45.1	15.6	41.7	0.4
29225	Webster, MO	2	27 601	21.7	4	12	41.7	25.0	33.3	4 180	41.4	26.4	32.2	12.9	29.2	0.6
29227	Worth, MO	9	2 335	18.6	1	2	50.0	—	50.0	500	51.8	—	48.2	11.6	45.0	—
29229	Wright, MO	6	19 241	21.4	5	13	46.2	15.4	30.8	4 023	48.0	20.3	31.5	13.3	40.9	1.4
29510	St. Louis city, MO	0	351 565	18.4	1	106	66.0	19.8	10.4	41 711	56.6	20.7	22.1	15.1	74.6	81.5
30000	**MONTANA**															
30001	Beaverhead, MT	7	9 144	20.0	9	13	69.2	15.4	15.4	1 810	46.6	21.7	31.7	9.0	14.2	3.5
30003	Big Horn, MT	6	12 308	27.3	9	17	58.8	23.5	17.6	2 633	54.7	19.4	25.9	13.1	51.8	68.4
30005	Blaine, MT	9	7 114	25.1	12	20	55.0	25.0	20.0	1 637	53.8	16.1	30.1	11.2	46.8	55.5
30007	Broadwater, MT	9	4 012	21.6	1	3	33.3	33.3	33.3	809	52.7	16.3	31.0	11.7	17.9	5.3
30009	Carbon, MT	8	9 248	20.6	13	23	43.5	30.4	26.1	1 688	43.0	22.3	34.7	9.4	18.2	2.5

1. County type code is from the Economic Research Service of the USDA. See notes and definitions at the end of this section.   2. IEP = Individual Education Program. See notes and definitions at the end of this section.

Table D-2. School and Student Characteristics by County — Continued

County	Staff and students, 1995–1996						Revenues, fiscal 1995				Current expenditures, fiscal 1995		
								Percent of Revenue from					
	Number of teachers	Pupil/ teacher ratio	Number of graduates	Dropouts grades 9–12 (percent)	Local school non-teaching staff	Central admin. staff	Total revenue ($1000)	Federal Gov't	State Gov't	Local Gov't	Amount	Amount per pupil	Percent for instruction
	15	16	17	18	19	20	21	22	23	24	25	26	27
MISSOURI—Con.													
Lincoln, MO	337	18.5	309	6.3	172	36	24 454	5.8	42.3	51.9	20 815	3 430	66.4
Linn, MO	217	13.5	198	4.1	97	30	14 941	6.1	48.7	45.2	12 527	4 327	65.6
Livingston, MO	148	16.4	187	4.1	79	24	12 551	8.7	41.2	50.0	11 111	4 511	68.0
McDonald, MO	181	17.0	106	11.9	86	20	11 579	11.2	49.8	39.0	9 397	3 200	66.7
Macon, MO	190	13.8	203	2.5	118	32	13 510	7.5	42.5	50.0	11 410	4 314	64.5
Madison, MO	128	16.7	137	7.4	67	15	8 329	8.6	48.6	42.9	7 482	3 503	61.0
Maries, MO	103	15.1	96	4.1	53	16	6 826	7.2	45.3	47.4	5 675	3 761	62.9
Marion, MO	343	15.4	322	9.1	208	63	24 022	8.8	41.4	49.8	21 024	3 928	63.9
Mercer, MO	61	11.6	49	1.3	31	9	4 144	5.5	35.3	59.3	3 348	5 027	58.2
Miller, MO	306	16.6	254	5.0	179	50	23 740	7.0	34.5	58.5	19 458	3 940	62.4
Mississippi, MO	192	14.3	160	8.3	190	21	13 714	13.2	42.7	44.1	11 961	4 316	67.4
Moniteau, MO	174	14.1	149	5.3	107	20	11 082	5.4	41.8	52.8	9 312	3 834	62.4
Monroe, MO	140	13.3	140	3.2	103	17	9 217	7.8	39.6	52.7	7 993	4 218	62.2
Montgomery, MO	145	14.5	135	9.2	89	26	9 340	6.6	40.5	53.0	8 377	3 995	63.3
Morgan, MO	145	14.3	112	8.0	98	19	9 735	8.4	31.2	60.4	8 018	3 991	63.8
New Madrid, MO	271	14.1	251	6.8	173	38	20 005	12.9	39.6	47.5	17 841	4 675	61.8
Newton, MO	429	18.1	408	7.5	264	58	30 220	7.3	46.8	45.9	24 590	3 274	62.3
Nodaway, MO	264	12.2	262	2.4	166	42	19 184	7.8	35.4	56.8	16 246	4 920	61.7
Oregon, MO	154	12.3	142	4.3	89	16	9 164	10.7	54.2	35.0	7 987	4 257	64.0
Osage, MO	126	12.9	160	2.7	81	18	8 465	5.7	39.4	55.0	6 887	4 171	60.0
Ozark, MO	141	12.5	137	2.7	172	21	8 907	10.1	50.7	39.2	7 551	4 165	62.4
Pemiscot, MO	329	14.0	270	6.3	164	52	23 177	14.3	48.5	37.2	20 881	4 475	64.2
Perry, MO	153	16.8	379	6.3	90	29	11 441	7.6	36.2	56.2	10 137	4 114	60.2
Pettis, MO	407	15.0	394	7.0	263	54	27 182	7.1	43.2	49.8	24 644	3 983	63.4
Phelps, MO	383	17.3	381	7.1	240	68	32 751	11.4	44.6	44.0	26 213	4 159	66.4
Pike, MO	209	14.4	194	4.9	136	32	15 576	10.6	32.9	56.5	12 714	4 275	64.4
Platte, MO	692	16.6	713	3.2	369	102	62 445	3.3	25.5	71.2	54 969	4 891	62.4
Polk, MO	314	15.0	268	4.5	216	38	20 174	8.6	52.2	39.2	17 345	3 793	61.1
Pulaski, MO	525	14.7	418	4.8	309	79	37 395	19.0	49.3	31.6	34 566	4 459	63.5
Putnam, MO	59	14.9	53	3.2	42	7	4 314	6.5	45.2	48.3	3 916	4 496	64.8
Ralls, MO	69	13.6	65	6.6	31	8	4 135	5.6	41.0	53.4	3 377	3 679	62.3
Randolph, MO	280	13.8	271	10.9	218	39	20 427	7.7	35.5	56.9	16 819	4 200	63.3
Ray, MO	258	15.0	251	6.6	104	36	17 195	5.0	46.1	48.9	15 230	4 025	64.0
Reynolds, MO	112	12.1	93	3.2	81	18	7 628	10.0	31.7	58.3	6 545	4 892	60.7
Ripley, MO	154	16.2	138	7.5	122	17	11 095	13.1	54.6	32.3	9 049	3 696	65.5
St. Charles, MO	2 521	17.0	2 276	4.2	1 209	513	208 582	3.3	31.2	65.5	184 265	4 478	64.5
St. Clair, MO	122	12.7	103	4.0	55	16	7 212	8.5	45.0	46.4	6 408	4 137	62.0
Ste. Genevieve, MO	135	16.3	140	4.1	86	16	9 963	5.6	26.9	67.5	8 658	4 001	61.9
St. Francois, MO	598	16.8	596	8.5	396	104	43 286	8.8	46.6	44.6	36 945	3 678	60.2
St. Louis, MO	9 997	15.1	8 642	5.6	7 148	1 871	1 021 583	3.9	25.1	71.0	931 614	6 225	61.7
Saline, MO	289	13.6	276	6.3	140	36	19 795	7.1	41.8	51.1	16 583	4 205	65.9
Schuyler, MO	59	13.9	43	5.2	30	8	4 004	7.9	46.8	45.3	3 281	4 096	62.8
Scotland, MO	62	13.3	45	2.5	38	6	4 348	7.3	40.1	52.7	3 498	4 351	68.2
Scott, MO	465	16.7	494	5.4	273	63	34 478	8.9	43.9	47.1	26 617	3 416	65.6
Shannon, MO	69	12.8	52	5.0	37	10	4 718	17.7	51.9	30.4	3 795	4 235	64.1
Shelby, MO	96	13.7	95	3.5	60	13	6 542	6.5	39.1	54.4	5 649	4 280	64.6
Stoddard, MO	367	15.5	381	4.8	199	41	24 541	7.4	43.4	49.2	20 470	3 593	63.9
Stone, MO	284	14.5	221	6.1	153	40	19 389	7.6	43.3	49.1	16 808	4 226	63.1
Sullivan, MO	77	12.3	77	5.9	49	12	5 115	6.9	43.7	49.4	4 406	4 774	59.8
Taney, MO	355	15.3	258	7.9	198	50	28 748	7.9	29.1	63.0	20 090	3 831	60.4
Texas, MO	310	14.4	299	5.8	170	37	21 404	9.6	53.3	37.1	17 828	3 896	63.4
Vernon, MO	228	15.2	198	5.2	151	34	16 641	8.6	43.7	47.8	14 590	4 301	63.5
Warren, MO	221	15.6	204	6.6	140	32	14 723	6.8	34.6	58.6	12 830	3 705	61.3
Washington, MO	253	15.8	226	6.1	226	35	18 188	11.0	46.8	42.2	14 564	3 691	60.6
Wayne, MO	142	15.2	120	7.3	86	18	9 975	10.9	51.3	37.8	8 239	3 861	63.9
Webster, MO	263	15.9	264	7.7	152	32	18 233	7.4	51.0	41.6	15 196	3 624	63.7
Worth, MO	38	13.1	24	1.9	22	4	2 306	9.8	44.2	46.1	2 057	4 414	62.0
Wright, MO	269	14.9	231	6.2	139	38	19 141	11.4	52.9	35.7	15 709	3 988	65.5
St. Louis city, MO	3 152	13.2	1 151	23.9	2 825	519	377 166	10.8	43.6	45.6	309 688	7 543	54.4
MONTANA													
Beaverhead, MT	109	16.7	108	NA	14	3	9 220	4.6	53.0	42.4	8 371	4 645	68.5
Big Horn, MT	181	14.5	130	NA	22	10	19 279	38.7	37.6	23.7	18 615	7 387	59.1
Blaine, MT	126	13.0	96	NA	17	4	11 998	24.6	47.3	28.1	11 018	6 714	57.7
Broadwater, MT	50	16.2	61	NA	6	1	3 674	6.0	48.6	45.4	3 348	4 233	66.8
Carbon, MT	136	12.4	129	NA	17	5	10 151	4.9	54.8	40.3	9 755	5 765	63.1

Table D-2. School and Student Characteristics by County

State/ County code	County	County type[1]	Population, 1996		Number of school districts, 1995–1996	Level of schools, 1995–1996				Level of students, 1995–1996				Characteristics of students, 1995–1996		
			Total persons	Percent age 5–17		Number of schools	Percent			Number of students	Percent			Percent with IEP[2]	Percent free-lunch eligible	Percent minority
							Primary	Middle	High		Primary	Middle	High			
			1	2	3	4	5	6	7	8	9	10	11	12	13	14
	MONTANA—Con.															
30011	Carter, MT	9	1 489	18.6	8	10	70.0	20.0	10.0	228	62.7	12.7	24.6	6.6	26.8	4.8
30013	Cascade, MT	3	81 087	19.4	14	43	62.8	20.9	16.3	15 178	47.4	23.3	29.2	10.4	23.0	11.8
30015	Chouteau, MT	8	5 361	21.0	13	17	52.9	23.5	23.5	1 128	50.0	18.2	31.8	9.2	19.1	1.3
30017	Custer, MT	7	12 285	20.7	12	20	80.0	10.0	10.0	2 309	50.1	14.6	35.3	10.9	13.5	4.9
30019	Daniels, MT	9	2 136	20.3	3	9	33.3	33.3	33.3	446	47.5	16.6	35.9	12.8	11.4	6.5
30021	Dawson, MT	7	9 085	20.5	7	10	60.0	20.0	20.0	1 831	45.0	23.1	31.9	10.0	18.2	2.5
30023	Deer Lodge, MT	7	10 093	17.5	2	6	50.0	33.3	16.7	1 765	38.8	29.2	32.1	9.9	16.5	5.7
30025	Fallon, MT	9	2 992	21.8	3	8	37.5	37.5	25.0	752	34.3	32.6	33.1	7.3	14.9	1.1
30027	Fergus, MT	7	12 697	19.6	14	24	50.0	25.0	25.0	2 483	51.9	17.4	30.8	11.0	18.6	2.9
30029	Flathead, MT	5	71 253	20.8	23	53	50.9	39.6	9.4	13 676	46.5	28.1	25.4	9.9	17.9	3.5
30031	Gallatin, MT	5	60 565	17.0	21	39	59.0	25.6	15.4	9 260	51.5	20.0	28.6	8.6	11.1	3.7
30033	Garfield, MT	9	1 410	22.8	10	12	75.0	16.7	8.3	276	52.9	11.6	35.5	6.2	7.6	0.7
30035	Glacier, MT	7	12 675	27.8	6	14	64.3	21.4	14.3	3 339	43.6	32.7	23.6	11.5	47.5	71.4
30037	Golden Valley, MT	8	984	20.8	2	6	33.3	33.3	33.3	232	51.7	14.2	34.1	14.7	34.5	2.6
30039	Granite, MT	9	2 585	19.1	4	7	42.9	28.6	28.6	532	50.8	14.7	34.6	10.2	25.4	0.6
30041	Hill, MT	7	17 730	22.7	12	21	52.4	23.8	23.8	3 725	48.8	21.8	29.4	11.1	32.6	33.2
30043	Jefferson, MT	9	9 668	22.3	8	12	50.0	33.3	16.7	1 955	54.9	19.2	25.9	8.2	12.1	4.5
30045	Judith Basin, MT	8	2 278	18.9	5	11	45.5	27.3	27.3	471	54.4	13.6	32.1	7.4	26.8	1.3
30047	Lake, MT	7	24 921	22.2	12	22	50.0	27.3	22.7	4 831	44.0	28.4	27.5	11.3	39.3	40.6
30049	Lewis and Clark, MT	5	53 345	19.9	11	30	70.0	16.7	13.3	10 323	46.7	23.2	30.1	10.5	14.3	5.7
30051	Liberty, MT	9	2 311	20.9	5	8	50.0	25.0	25.0	544	54.8	14.3	30.9	6.8	4.8	—
30053	Lincoln, MT	7	18 833	22.1	10	16	62.5	18.8	18.8	3 876	49.0	19.6	31.4	10.5	27.6	4.2
30055	McCone, MT	9	2 055	22.3	7	13	38.5	30.8	30.8	1 148	53.9	16.5	29.6	9.4	19.9	2.4
30057	Madison, MT	9	6 773	19.0	4	6	50.0	33.3	16.7	350	32.3	31.7	36.0	12.9	13.7	3.7
30059	Meagher, MT	8	1 798	19.6	4	5	60.0	20.0	20.0	323	49.2	21.1	29.7	9.6	25.1	6.2
30061	Mineral, MT	9	3 719	22.5	6	9	33.3	33.3	33.3	935	49.1	17.9	33.0	12.1	28.0	4.9
30063	Missoula, MT	5	88 523	18.2	14	44	52.3	36.4	11.4	14 508	48.9	22.8	28.3	10.4	21.5	6.0
30065	Musselshell, MT	8	4 675	20.2	5	7	42.9	28.6	28.6	916	49.6	18.6	31.9	14.1	20.6	5.6
30067	Park, MT	7	16 143	18.1	10	15	60.0	20.0	20.0	2 487	48.0	22.0	30.0	10.8	21.0	2.5
30069	Petroleum, MT	9	533	19.7	1	3	33.3	33.3	33.3	117	47.9	14.5	37.6	6.8	32.5	—
30071	Phillips, MT	9	5 025	23.1	8	16	50.0	25.0	25.0	1 084	48.2	18.0	33.8	11.3	21.3	16.1
30073	Pondera, MT	7	6 344	22.6	9	17	47.1	29.4	23.5	1 568	48.3	21.6	30.0	10.1	32.1	26.6
30075	Powder River, MT	9	1 930	20.4	7	8	75.0	12.5	12.5	439	51.9	13.9	34.2	12.3	14.1	4.6
30077	Powell, MT	7	7 115	15.7	8	9	77.8	11.1	11.1	1 208	57.7	14.2	28.1	11.7	20.2	4.7
30079	Prairie, MT	9	1 392	18.8	1	3	33.3	33.3	33.3	251	44.2	16.7	39.0	10.4	18.3	6.0
30081	Ravalli, MT	7	33 586	20.3	8	22	40.9	31.8	27.3	6 349	49.2	19.8	30.9	11.4	21.2	3.4
30083	Richland, MT	7	10 313	23.1	10	15	46.7	26.7	26.7	2 304	51.9	15.5	32.6	9.7	18.3	3.5
30085	Roosevelt, MT	7	11 065	25.6	12	22	31.8	40.9	27.3	2 938	46.1	28.5	25.4	16.0	54.0	64.9
30087	Rosebud, MT	7	10 457	28.0	11	17	47.1	29.4	23.5	2 592	50.5	19.2	30.4	15.0	36.7	40.9
30089	Sanders, MT	9	10 140	21.4	12	16	50.0	25.0	25.0	1 963	54.9	14.3	30.8	8.0	33.4	9.2
30091	Sheridan, MT	9	4 363	19.4	7	13	38.5	30.8	30.8	911	47.4	17.0	35.6	8.6	15.3	6.5
30093	Silver Bow, MT	5	34 634	17.7	5	14	78.6	14.3	7.1	5 916	56.6	15.1	28.3	13.8	20.9	7.3
30095	Stillwater, MT	8	7 653	20.2	13	18	44.4	27.8	27.8	1 606	50.7	16.0	33.3	14.3	13.9	3.2
30097	Sweet Grass, MT	9	3 437	19.1	6	7	71.4	14.3	14.3	596	54.9	13.3	31.9	11.4	18.3	0.5
30099	Teton, MT	8	6 371	22.0	11	17	47.1	29.4	23.5	1 396	53.6	16.1	30.3	9.0	17.8	3.4
30101	Toole, MT	7	4 918	21.5	4	10	60.0	20.0	20.0	1 131	53.1	17.7	29.2	9.7	15.6	5.3
30103	Treasure, MT	8	866	21.8	1	3	33.3	33.3	33.3	162	47.5	17.9	34.6	7.4	27.8	5.6
30105	Valley, MT	7	8 363	20.8	8	18	33.3	38.9	27.8	1 619	37.6	29.3	33.0	11.6	21.2	15.4
30107	Wheatland, MT	9	2 420	20.0	6	8	50.0	25.0	25.0	478	51.9	14.4	33.7	12.1	22.0	0.2
30109	Wibaux, MT	9	1 146	21.4	1	3	33.3	33.3	33.3	224	51.8	16.5	31.7	11.6	28.6	—
30111	Yellowstone, MT	3	125 966	19.5	19	61	67.2	19.7	13.1	22 291	55.1	15.8	29.1	13.3	19.2	9.8
30113	Yellowstone National Park (part), MT	NA	40	12.5	NA	NA	NA	NA	NA	NA	NA	NA	NA	NA	NA	NA
31000	**NEBRASKA**															
31001	Adams, NE	5	29 698	18.0	13	34	73.5	2.9	11.8	4 901	54.9	10.1	33.7	15.1	16.5	5.9
31003	Antelope, NE	9	7 453	22.6	9	16	50.0	6.3	25.0	1 310	53.2	0.2	44.3	9.6	22.0	0.7
31005	Arthur, NE	9	428	18.5	5	5	80.0	—	20.0	82	47.6	—	52.4	7.3	—	—
31007	Banner, NE	9	859	22.5	1	2	50.0	—	50.0	221	51.1	—	48.9	5.9	23.5	5.4
31009	Blaine, NE	9	651	22.1	1	2	50.0	—	50.0	177	43.5	—	56.5	5.1	25.4	0.6
31011	Boone, NE	9	6 536	20.7	11	15	73.3	—	26.7	1 336	51.2	—	48.8	11.5	21.6	0.7
31013	Box Butte, NE	7	12 984	24.8	7	13	76.9	7.7	15.4	2 908	44.4	20.0	35.7	10.9	16.4	12.4
31015	Boyd, NE	9	2 746	20.4	3	7	57.1	—	42.9	619	47.5	—	52.5	14.1	33.0	1.0
31017	Brown, NE	9	3 637	20.2	8	12	75.0	16.7	8.3	689	50.9	18.0	31.1	11.2	18.3	2.9
31019	Buffalo, NE	5	40 037	18.7	14	31	71.0	3.2	25.8	7 282	53.9	9.7	36.4	14.8	19.0	7.1
31021	Burt, NE	8	7 944	20.5	5	11	63.6	9.1	27.3	1 708	53.5	5.4	41.0	14.6	20.7	3.6
31023	Butler, NE	6	8 623	21.3	11	15	80.0	—	20.0	1 330	60.8	—	39.2	16.5	15.3	1.8

1. County type code is from the Economic Research Service of the USDA. See notes and definitions at the end of this section.   2. IEP = Individual Education Program. See notes and definitions at the end of this section.

Table D-2. School and Student Characteristics by County — Continued

County	Staff and students, 1995–1996						Revenues, fiscal 1995					Current expenditures, fiscal 1995		
	Number of teachers	Pupil/ teacher ratio	Number of graduates	Dropouts grades 9–12 (percent)	Local school non-teaching staff	Central admin. staff	Total revenue ($1000)	Federal Gov't	State Gov't	Local Gov't		Amount	Amount per pupil	Percent for instruction
	15	16	17	18	19	20	21	22	23	24		25	26	27
MONTANA—Con.														
Carter, MT	22	10.2	12	NA	2	1	1 628	3.1	39.4	57.6		1 526	7 131	61.3
Cascade, MT	858	17.7	912	NA	101	29	70 563	8.5	56.8	34.7		68 000	4 513	67.2
Chouteau, MT	90	12.5	86	NA	11	3	7 709	4.3	40.2	55.5		7 084	6 280	59.9
Custer, MT	152	15.2	188	NA	22	4	11 406	8.2	59.7	32.1		10 678	4 702	64.1
Daniels, MT	42	10.6	35	NA	7	2	3 389	2.9	48.2	48.9		3 342	7 234	58.4
Dawson, MT	118	15.5	125	NA	13	3	10 434	6.8	52.7	40.5		9 432	5 171	60.1
Deer Lodge, MT	92	19.1	118	NA	15	3	7 596	7.9	57.5	34.7		8 136	4 692	61.0
Fallon, MT	63	12.0	53	NA	7	2	5 845	2.9	47.0	50.1		5 350	7 259	62.5
Fergus, MT	166	15.0	157	NA	19	6	14 872	5.9	53.5	40.6		13 535	5 666	62.1
Flathead, MT	728	18.8	841	NA	102	16	65 556	6.1	51.4	42.4		60 226	4 522	65.1
Gallatin, MT	522	17.7	518	NA	71	17	47 611	4.8	47.7	47.6		40 689	4 444	61.4
Garfield, MT	27	10.4	32	NA	2	1	1 795	3.5	55.3	41.2		1 775	6 121	61.1
Glacier, MT	226	14.8	137	NA	29	8	22 415	27.7	42.8	29.5		20 368	6 256	59.2
Golden Valley, MT	24	9.7	15	NA	2	1	1 628	3.4	43.7	52.9		1 523	7 084	62.8
Granite, MT	38	13.9	50	NA	4	1	3 301	6.4	47.3	46.3		3 256	5 942	63.9
Hill, MT	228	16.3	211	NA	29	9	23 400	20.5	46.7	32.9		21 246	5 748	58.7
Jefferson, MT	117	16.7	101	NA	16	4	9 675	2.4	47.3	50.3		8 516	4 508	62.3
Judith Basin, MT	45	10.6	31	NA	5	1	3 263	4.5	45.9	49.6		3 182	6 520	62.8
Lake, MT	299	16.2	273	NA	44	7	26 500	19.3	49.2	31.5		24 545	5 127	63.3
Lewis and Clark, MT	581	17.8	640	NA	71	12	50 712	5.4	53.0	41.6		47 270	4 542	65.4
Liberty, MT	49	11.2	31	NA	6	2	3 663	2.7	44.7	52.6		3 568	6 326	62.1
Lincoln, MT	231	16.8	262	NA	26	6	19 262	7.0	59.9	33.2		18 718	4 786	65.3
McCone, MT	79	14.6	61	NA	10	2	6 819	5.3	43.9	50.8		6 233	5 610	60.9
Madison, MT	28	12.7	30	NA	4	1	2 529	4.2	40.9	54.9		2 382	6 845	58.6
Meagher, MT	27	12.1	24	NA	3	1	2 035	4.9	37.0	58.1		1 782	5 433	58.5
Mineral, MT	64	14.5	66	NA	9	3	6 206	9.2	48.4	42.4		5 657	6 279	65.8
Missoula, MT	821	17.7	836	NA	115	17	80 845	6.9	46.2	47.0		70 710	4 873	61.6
Musselshell, MT	58	15.8	63	NA	7	2	4 610	6.3	60.8	32.9		4 635	5 237	64.2
Park, MT	161	15.4	169	NA	19	5	14 679	8.3	47.7	44.0		12 806	5 002	63.3
Petroleum, MT	12	9.8	9	NA	2	—	852	3.4	50.0	46.6		844	7 153	49.1
Phillips, MT	94	11.6	101	NA	12	4	7 918	8.8	46.2	45.0		7 517	6 809	60.0
Pondera, MT	111	14.2	91	NA	14	4	13 684	37.8	37.0	25.2		9 824	6 417	57.6
Powder River, MT	35	12.6	35	NA	4	1	3 091	5.5	44.3	50.2		2 782	6 485	57.7
Powell, MT	80	15.1	67	NA	9	2	6 901	11.5	50.0	38.5		6 523	5 599	61.8
Prairie, MT	19	13.6	18	NA	2	1	1 610	6.6	43.3	50.1		1 520	5 984	63.4
Ravalli, MT	344	18.4	362	NA	48	9	28 649	6.8	58.5	34.7		25 864	4 293	63.5
Richland, MT	145	15.8	190	NA	21	5	13 788	6.4	51.5	42.1		12 595	5 353	60.9
Roosevelt, MT	213	13.8	124	NA	27	10	22 359	31.7	39.6	28.7		19 511	6 709	57.3
Rosebud, MT	195	13.3	168	NA	30	9	21 677	16.0	35.6	48.4		18 855	6 839	58.8
Sanders, MT	126	15.6	152	NA	17	4	10 904	7.8	51.4	40.8		10 362	5 171	59.8
Sheridan, MT	76	11.9	82	NA	9	4	6 562	5.6	52.2	42.2		6 505	7 094	59.7
Silver Bow, MT	305	19.4	313	NA	36	10	30 876	6.2	47.4	46.5		29 818	5 074	60.8
Stillwater, MT	107	15.0	117	NA	14	5	9 297	3.6	51.6	44.8		8 629	5 600	63.2
Sweet Grass, MT	44	13.6	45	NA	4	1	3 635	1.7	47.3	51.0		3 200	5 415	67.3
Teton, MT	106	13.1	84	NA	13	3	7 933	3.7	53.9	42.4		7 312	5 318	66.3
Toole, MT	78	14.5	85	NA	11	3	6 082	6.6	48.5	44.9		6 316	5 502	62.4
Treasure, MT	17	9.6	18	NA	2	1	1 451	8.0	35.6	56.4		1 396	7 546	58.5
Valley, MT	139	11.7	89	NA	18	4	11 226	9.2	40.7	50.1		10 878	6 769	59.7
Wheatland, MT	36	13.2	30	NA	4	1	3 023	4.8	49.4	45.8		2 872	6 176	60.4
Wibaux, MT	19	11.5	28	NA	3	1	1 389	5.8	54.6	39.6		1 481	5 900	57.7
Yellowstone, MT	1 236	18.0	1 325	NA	175	41	114 109	5.9	50.3	43.8		106 405	4 822	62.2
Yellowstone National Park (part), MT	NA	NA	NA	NA	NA	NA	NA	NA	NA	NA		NA	NA	NA
NEBRASKA														
Adams, NE	332	14.8	322	4.6	215	51	33 818	6.4	24.2	69.4		30 340	6 453	69.9
Antelope, NE	110	11.9	101	0.5	88	22	11 284	6.5	26.5	67.0		9 834	7 665	62.2
Arthur, NE	15	5.5	13	NA	3	2	940	0.1	15.3	84.6		843	8 184	67.5
Banner, NE	18	12.0	14	NA	17	3	1 566	4.2	13.8	82.1		1 354	6 637	51.6
Blaine, NE	19	9.1	13	NA	11	2	1 519	5.9	21.7	72.4		1 342	7 713	59.8
Boone, NE	114	11.7	85	0.2	72	13	8 847	4.0	22.6	73.4		7 297	5 617	68.1
Box Butte, NE	191	15.2	246	1.3	136	14	16 021	5.8	44.6	49.6		13 333	4 497	67.4
Boyd, NE	61	10.1	50	2.0	46	7	4 040	5.8	47.7	46.5		3 618	6 060	66.5
Brown, NE	60	11.4	41	1.9	34	8	5 589	4.3	23.8	71.9		4 728	6 842	65.1
Buffalo, NE	479	15.2	514	3.9	357	50	44 437	5.0	25.3	69.6		37 247	5 292	68.2
Burt, NE	123	13.9	105	2.8	95	14	10 135	3.9	30.3	65.8		8 494	5 047	64.7
Butler, NE	107	12.5	82	2.5	80	12	8 202	3.5	18.4	78.1		6 667	5 097	66.3

Table D-2.   School and Student Characteristics by County

State/ County code	County	County type[1]	Population, 1996		Number of school districts, 1995– 1996	Level of schools, 1995–1996				Level of students, 1995–1996				Characteristics of students, 1995–1996		
			Total persons	Percent age 5–17		Number of schools	Percent			Number of students	Percent			Percent with IEP[2]	Percent free-lunch eligible	Percent minority
							Primary	Middle	High		Primary	Middle	High			
			1	2	3	4	5	6	7	8	9	10	11	12	13	14
	NEBRASKA—Con.															
31025	Cass, NE	2	23 478	21.1	7	20	55.0	15.0	30.0	3 534	40.5	20.2	39.3	15.1	15.8	3.3
31027	Cedar, NE	9	9 936	22.7	5	11	45.5	9.1	45.5	1 881	53.6	3.2	43.2	11.6	24.7	0.9
31029	Chase, NE	9	4 265	21.7	5	8	62.5	12.5	25.0	1 117	62.3	4.6	33.1	14.7	23.6	3.6
31031	Cherry, NE	7	6 433	20.3	28	31	83.9	9.7	6.5	1 162	54.1	14.2	31.7	9.9	22.4	5.8
31033	Cheyenne, NE	7	9 690	20.5	7	16	56.3	18.8	25.0	2 054	43.2	26.3	30.4	13.6	16.9	5.0
31035	Clay, NE	9	7 209	20.9	6	11	54.5	—	45.5	1 575	51.3	—	48.7	19.9	16.4	2.8
31037	Colfax, NE	7	10 388	20.0	12	16	75.0	—	25.0	2 158	60.9	—	39.1	11.8	20.2	14.1
31039	Cuming, NE	7	10 126	20.8	5	11	54.5	9.1	36.4	1 672	50.1	3.8	46.1	16.6	22.8	4.7
31041	Custer, NE	7	12 228	20.6	17	26	73.1	3.8	23.1	2 389	51.1	8.9	40.1	9.4	18.9	0.9
31043	Dakota, NE	3	18 528	22.2	3	11	63.6	18.2	18.2	3 442	43.3	33.4	23.3	13.3	23.6	24.6
31045	Dawes, NE	7	9 086	18.4	14	18	77.8	5.6	16.7	1 616	36.9	19.8	43.3	17.3	20.9	10.3
31047	Dawson, NE	7	23 126	21.1	20	35	77.1	5.7	17.1	5 070	54.3	16.6	29.1	12.1	25.2	22.2
31049	Deuel, NE	9	2 068	19.9	2	5	60.0	—	40.0	554	59.7	—	40.3	9.7	23.6	7.9
31051	Dixon, NE	8	6 337	20.6	3	6	50.0	—	50.0	826	53.5	—	46.5	10.7	20.9	1.2
31053	Dodge, NE	4	35 022	19.3	17	32	78.1	3.1	18.8	6 356	52.7	16.1	31.2	15.6	18.2	1.8
31055	Douglas, NE	2	438 835	19.3	12	154	71.4	13.0	13.6	74 575	54.1	18.0	27.6	13.9	24.0	25.1
31057	Dundy, NE	9	2 387	19.7	1	3	66.7	—	33.3	391	66.8	—	33.2	14.3	18.7	1.0
31059	Fillmore, NE	9	6 871	20.2	9	15	53.3	—	40.0	1 379	49.8	—	47.5	13.9	13.4	3.3
31061	Franklin, NE	9	3 868	16.9	4	6	66.7	—	33.3	574	55.4	—	44.6	15.2	24.9	0.3
31063	Frontier, NE	9	3 220	20.9	3	6	50.0	—	50.0	729	53.2	—	46.8	16.5	22.4	2.2
31065	Furnas, NE	9	5 556	18.7	3	8	62.5	—	37.5	1 357	53.7	—	46.3	11.6	18.6	2.6
31067	Gage, NE	6	22 903	17.8	6	15	53.3	6.7	33.3	3 415	47.0	18.4	34.2	15.0	16.5	2.4
31069	Garden, NE	9	2 242	16.5	6	6	66.7	—	33.3	458	68.3	—	31.7	8.5	31.2	0.7
31071	Garfield, NE	9	2 081	19.6	7	7	85.7	—	14.3	417	49.2	—	50.8	14.6	17.3	1.4
31073	Gosper, NE	9	2 256	19.0	2	3	66.7	—	33.3	228	51.8	—	48.2	16.7	11.0	5.3
31075	Grant, NE	9	749	19.6	6	6	83.3	—	16.7	242	44.6	—	55.4	7.4	13.6	0.4
31077	Greeley, NE	9	2 969	23.8	4	8	50.0	—	50.0	709	49.8	—	50.2	13.8	37.4	3.5
31079	Hall, NE	5	51 485	21.0	12	31	77.4	9.7	12.9	9 459	55.8	17.7	26.5	14.5	22.5	13.6
31081	Hamilton, NE	7	9 245	21.8	4	8	50.0	12.5	37.5	1 733	51.5	19.2	29.3	12.1	14.4	1.4
31083	Harlan, NE	9	3 755	18.4	2	3	66.7	—	33.3	409	51.6	—	48.4	11.7	19.3	0.7
31085	Hayes, NE	9	1 136	20.8	1	2	50.0	—	50.0	161	48.4	—	51.6	9.9	29.8	7.5
31087	Hitchcock, NE	9	3 401	22.6	3	6	50.0	—	50.0	576	45.0	—	55.0	15.8	23.4	2.3
31089	Holt, NE	7	12 163	22.0	30	34	85.3	—	14.7	2 312	56.0	—	44.0	11.0	21.2	1.3
31091	Hooker, NE	9	707	18.5	1	2	50.0	—	50.0	233	45.1	—	54.9	10.7	30.0	0.9
31093	Howard, NE	9	6 444	21.4	5	8	62.5	—	37.5	1 579	57.3	—	42.7	15.1	27.2	1.8
31095	Jefferson, NE	7	8 454	18.2	4	9	55.6	—	44.4	1 981	50.4	—	49.6	13.9	17.3	2.0
31097	Johnson, NE	8	4 604	18.6	5	9	55.6	11.1	33.3	963	46.9	1.7	51.4	17.3	18.2	6.5
31099	Kearney, NE	7	6 648	19.6	3	8	37.5	12.5	37.5	1 378	38.0	25.8	35.9	14.0	11.2	3.3
31101	Keith, NE	7	8 643	21.2	7	13	69.2	7.7	15.4	1 602	44.6	19.9	35.1	15.2	15.4	6.3
31103	Keya Paha, NE	9	1 002	20.8	7	7	85.7	—	14.3	175	59.4	—	40.6	5.7	21.1	0.6
31105	Kimball, NE	6	4 056	19.9	1	4	50.0	25.0	25.0	760	47.9	23.0	29.1	9.2	23.8	8.8
31107	Knox, NE	9	9 387	19.8	7	14	50.0	—	50.0	2 082	50.0	—	50.0	13.7	40.5	10.3
31109	Lancaster, NE	3	231 765	17.1	11	70	70.0	15.7	12.9	35 030	53.7	19.5	26.7	14.1	17.1	10.5
31111	Lincoln, NE	5	33 619	22.0	12	28	67.9	7.1	25.0	6 200	48.0	17.2	34.8	15.8	19.2	9.2
31113	Logan, NE	9	894	24.9	1	2	50.0	—	50.0	210	45.7	—	54.3	13.8	25.7	—
31115	Loup, NE	9	698	20.5	1	2	50.0	—	50.0	156	47.4	—	52.6	13.5	32.7	0.6
31117	McPherson, NE	9	565	22.3	6	6	66.7	16.7	16.7	113	59.3	4.4	36.3	8.8	—	—
31119	Madison, NE	5	34 702	20.5	14	31	74.2	6.5	16.1	6 677	51.5	17.6	30.9	11.5	16.6	10.7
31121	Merrick, NE	7	8 149	20.8	5	11	54.5	9.1	36.4	1 600	49.5	17.2	33.3	14.7	15.1	3.4
31123	Morrill, NE	9	5 376	21.0	5	7	71.4	—	28.6	1 158	55.2	—	44.8	8.5	32.6	16.9
31125	Nance, NE	9	4 293	21.2	6	8	62.5	12.5	25.0	887	61.6	0.3	38.1	13.1	25.0	3.2
31127	Nemaha, NE	7	7 878	18.3	5	14	57.1	7.1	14.3	1 407	46.0	19.5	32.9	10.2	14.4	1.8
31129	Nuckolls, NE	9	5 376	20.0	4	8	62.5	—	37.5	937	48.3	—	51.7	18.7	20.3	1.7
31131	Otoe, NE	6	14 515	19.5	13	20	75.0	5.0	20.0	2 740	50.6	13.7	35.7	14.9	11.3	2.6
31133	Pawnee, NE	9	3 261	16.7	3	6	50.0	—	50.0	674	52.2	—	47.8	16.6	27.9	1.5
31135	Perkins, NE	9	3 250	22.7	3	5	60.0	—	40.0	677	61.0	—	39.0	11.1	15.1	6.4
31137	Phelps, NE	7	9 995	20.2	8	15	66.7	6.7	20.0	2 044	50.1	16.9	32.3	18.8	11.9	2.6
31139	Pierce, NE	9	7 945	21.3	7	11	72.7	—	27.3	1 546	47.9	—	52.1	10.9	17.6	1.6
31141	Platte, NE	7	30 755	22.7	11	28	82.1	3.6	14.3	5 015	48.6	17.5	33.8	15.2	13.4	6.2
31143	Polk, NE	9	5 581	20.7	4	9	44.4	11.1	44.4	1 204	49.8	6.1	44.0	11.9	13.5	2.3
31145	Red Willow, NE	7	11 448	20.1	7	17	70.6	5.9	17.6	2 230	51.3	17.9	12.1	17.2	19.0	3.8
31147	Richardson, NE	7	9 689	17.9	5	11	54.5	9.1	36.4	1 743	49.6	13.4	36.9	13.2	24.3	4.1
31149	Rock, NE	9	1 807	22.5	8	8	87.5	—	12.5	377	64.7	—	35.3	14.9	21.8	0.8
31151	Saline, NE	6	12 988	18.7	7	11	63.6	—	36.4	2 691	51.8	—	48.2	12.1	12.8	4.9
31153	Sarpy, NE	2	116 271	23.3	4	39	69.2	15.4	12.8	18 284	54.8	19.4	25.7	12.0	10.4	11.6
31155	Saunders, NE	6	19 135	21.2	19	28	71.4	7.1	21.4	3 053	55.1	10.3	34.7	14.7	15.8	1.9

1. County type code is from the Economic Research Service of the USDA. See notes and definitions at the end of this section.   2. IEP = Individual Education Program. See notes and definitions at the end of this section.

Table D-2.   School and Student Characteristics by County — Continued

County	Staff and students, 1995–1996						Revenues, fiscal 1995				Current expenditures, fiscal 1995		
	Number of teachers	Pupil/ teacher ratio	Number of graduates	Dropouts grades 9–12 (percent)	Local school non-teaching staff	Central admin. staff	Total revenue ($1000)	Percent of Revenue from			Amount	Amount per pupil	Percent for instruction
								Federal Gov't	State Gov't	Local Gov't			
	15	16	17	18	19	20	21	22	23	24	25	26	27
NEBRASKA—Con.													
Cass, NE	249	14.2	242	2.4	184	36	21 753	5.6	27.8	66.6	18 767	5 411	64.1
Cedar, NE	147	12.8	118	1.2	114	18	11 085	6.1	31.2	62.7	9 585	5 142	66.6
Chase, NE	92	12.2	86	1.1	60	11	8 099	2.8	16.1	81.1	6 880	6 159	67.0
Cherry, NE	103	11.3	59	3.6	64	8	7 372	5.7	34.0	60.2	5 899	5 107	67.2
Cheyenne, NE	159	12.9	142	2.3	142	22	15 149	5.2	27.7	67.1	13 783	6 639	64.1
Clay, NE	145	10.9	113	2.9	95	16	12 230	4.9	21.0	74.0	10 827	6 801	67.6
Colfax, NE	155	13.9	139	3.3	116	16	11 518	4.6	33.9	61.5	9 961	4 721	69.7
Cuming, NE	128	13.1	115	1.5	88	15	10 634	4.9	20.2	74.9	9 094	5 586	67.5
Custer, NE	193	12.4	186	0.7	168	23	16 972	3.9	25.6	70.6	14 039	5 740	66.9
Dakota, NE	204	16.9	183	3.9	144	15	16 928	7.8	44.6	47.7	13 765	4 069	65.4
Dawes, NE	115	14.1	198	17.1	80	14	9 193	4.7	47.4	47.9	7 482	5 171	67.6
Dawson, NE	345	14.7	287	5.8	209	39	29 573	4.1	31.6	64.2	25 241	5 162	69.7
Deuel, NE	56	9.9	14	1.1	21	6	3 566	3.0	14.5	82.5	3 272	7 067	66.5
Dixon, NE	70	11.9	56	3.9	47	8	5 173	4.7	47.4	47.9	4 262	5 354	66.9
Dodge, NE	413	15.4	426	3.6	294	54	37 226	5.7	31.2	63.1	35 223	5 537	67.5
Douglas, NE	4 656	16.0	4 072	6.9	4 071	517	472 892	5.6	32.2	62.2	394 932	5 396	63.2
Dundy, NE	33	12.0	32	NA	35	4	2 935	2.6	16.9	80.5	2 463	6 127	62.9
Fillmore, NE	130	10.6	83	0.9	94	24	11 239	2.6	15.6	81.8	9 509	7 166	66.9
Franklin, NE	58	10.0	43	2.4	37	6	4 541	4.3	14.5	81.2	4 030	7 021	66.6
Frontier, NE	62	11.8	47	0.5	59	10	5 506	3.8	15.9	80.3	4 971	7 011	59.4
Furnas, NE	112	12.2	96	0.7	87	13	10 603	2.6	21.5	75.9	9 115	6 742	68.3
Gage, NE	245	13.9	211	3.9	151	32	22 557	4.8	32.7	62.4	19 273	5 707	62.8
Garden, NE	46	10.0	32	0.7	26	8	4 125	3.2	21.2	75.6	3 535	7 442	65.1
Garfield, NE	37	11.3	28	1.4	25	4	2 001	0.4	40.5	50.1	2 000	5 504	68.0
Gosper, NE	22	10.2	21	2.7	19	3	1 917	3.0	16.3	80.6	1 530	5 953	64.5
Grant, NE	25	9.6	12	1.1	12	3	1 906	1.9	20.2	77.9	1 726	6 988	68.5
Greeley, NE	69	10.3	62	1.2	54	10	5 143	5.7	37.0	57.4	4 517	6 248	64.3
Hall, NE	588	16.1	619	5.5	366	72	57 373	5.0	34.8	60.1	48 798	5 185	72.0
Hamilton, NE	122	14.2	102	1.8	82	13	10 451	3.5	15.7	80.8	8 954	5 314	67.5
Harlan, NE	30	13.6	25	0.8	21	4	2 360	7.8	34.9	57.2	2 021	5 116	63.8
Hayes, NE	20	8.1	13	NA	19	2	1 829	3.1	12.7	84.2	1 558	9 386	59.4
Hitchcock, NE	61	9.5	39	NA	46	5	5 413	6.5	24.8	68.7	4 917	8 641	64.2
Holt, NE	199	11.6	182	1.2	112	18	14 215	5.1	36.6	58.3	11 919	5 104	67.6
Hooker, NE	22	10.5	18	NA	19	2	1 751	3.8	18.0	78.1	1 487	6 020	63.6
Howard, NE	116	13.6	104	2.4	76	12	9 574	3.7	34.5	61.8	8 652	5 651	66.1
Jefferson, NE	148	13.4	150	3.0	114	17	13 429	3.2	22.5	74.4	11 767	5 811	66.1
Johnson, NE	85	11.4	65	2.7	59	10	6 526	3.9	34.8	61.3	5 683	5 643	62.8
Kearney, NE	102	13.5	103	0.7	79	14	9 196	2.7	12.1	85.2	7 709	5 770	64.1
Keith, NE	116	13.9	117	3.6	83	17	12 898	7.7	23.3	68.9	11 268	6 566	66.2
Keya Paha, NE	21	8.5	18	4.2	6	2	1 259	5.2	26.0	68.9	1 038	5 831	64.7
Kimball, NE	54	14.0	40	3.2	47	8	4 356	4.9	13.5	81.6	4 320	5 814	66.3
Knox, NE	179	11.6	160	1.8	123	25	13 509	11.1	33.4	55.5	11 957	5 802	63.6
Lancaster, NE	2 354	14.9	1 915	6.0	1 908	424	230 314	5.3	26.3	68.4	192 169	5 548	66.8
Lincoln, NE	425	14.6	406	4.3	232	55	35 582	4.7	37.7	57.6	31 111	4 989	68.2
Logan, NE	21	10.2	14	1.3	19	2	1 704	5.0	22.1	72.9	1 535	7 525	58.8
Loup, NE	18	8.6	12	NA	14	3	1 234	4.2	23.0	72.8	1 005	6 979	60.0
McPherson, NE	14	8.2	5	NA	4	2	892	4.5	18.2	77.4	679	6 723	74.4
Madison, NE	435	15.4	455	2.1	317	60	36 117	4.6	34.3	61.2	30 261	4 511	68.8
Merrick, NE	125	12.8	113	2.2	80	15	11 129	3.4	27.5	69.1	8 939	5 705	66.1
Morrill, NE	82	14.1	72	1.4	66	10	8 044	6.1	33.1	60.9	6 319	5 279	63.9
Nance, NE	67	13.3	71	2.5	52	8	4 837	5.0	41.3	53.6	4 315	4 827	64.5
Nemaha, NE	100	14.0	93	0.7	66	13	10 006	5.2	28.2	66.7	8 942	6 619	63.1
Nuckolls, NE	81	11.6	80	0.9	53	11	6 702	3.3	35.3	61.4	6 213	6 596	67.9
Otoe, NE	203	13.5	185	5.5	170	18	15 959	3.1	30.4	66.4	13 274	4 927	71.3
Pawnee, NE	58	11.6	48	0.9	46	8	4 692	5.5	31.2	63.3	4 067	6 200	64.3
Perkins, NE	59	11.6	47	2.1	48	8	5 038	3.6	14.5	81.9	4 855	7 203	65.9
Phelps, NE	157	13.0	130	1.6	111	28	15 145	5.9	15.6	78.5	13 725	7 089	69.4
Pierce, NE	113	13.6	109	0.9	74	14	9 482	3.4	34.0	62.5	7 243	4 697	64.0
Platte, NE	321	15.6	349	4.4	252	49	32 094	7.8	23.1	69.1	29 047	5 886	67.2
Polk, NE	99	12.2	89	1.1	75	15	8 380	3.5	15.1	81.4	7 336	6 018	62.9
Red Willow, NE	177	12.6	160	3.7	132	17	14 595	3.7	35.5	60.9	12 948	5 994	66.8
Richardson, NE	130	13.4	113	3.1	78	14	11 238	4.7	37.2	58.1	9 102	5 186	64.9
Rock, NE	40	9.5	36	0.8	16	4	2 579	3.6	21.2	75.1	2 233	5 653	66.5
Saline, NE	177	15.2	172	1.4	131	24	15 294	3.9	30.5	65.6	15 291	5 863	69.4
Sarpy, NE	1 054	17.4	1 110	2.6	835	153	99 160	10.6	45.4	44.0	97 609	5 460	68.3
Saunders, NE	225	13.6	177	2.2	163	26	18 244	4.1	27.3	68.6	15 855	5 200	67.4

Table D-2.   School and Student Characteristics by County

State/ County code	County	County type[1]	Population, 1996		Number of school districts, 1995–1996	Level of schools, 1995–1996				Level of students, 1995–1996				Characteristics of students, 1995–1996		
			Total persons	Percent age 5–17		Number of schools	Percent			Number of students	Percent			Percent with IEP[2]	Percent free-lunch eligible	Percent minority
							Primary	Middle	High		Primary	Middle	High			
		1	1	2	3	4	5	6	7	8	9	10	11	12	13	14
	NEBRASKA—Con.															
31157	Scotts Bluff, NE	5	36 679	21.8	12	26	69.2	7.7	19.2	7 105	50.6	18.0	31.1	12.1	30.6	28.3
31159	Seward, NE	6	16 194	19.8	4	13	69.2	7.7	23.1	2 909	41.7	15.8	42.5	14.9	12.6	2.5
31161	Sheridan, NE	9	6 645	22.0	29	32	84.4	6.3	9.4	1 369	55.6	10.4	34.0	12.7	24.9	15.5
31163	Sherman, NE	9	3 574	21.7	5	9	66.7	11.1	22.2	692	34.8	25.6	39.6	14.9	29.5	1.2
31165	Sioux, NE	9	1 509	20.7	10	10	80.0	10.0	10.0	175	66.3	1.7	32.0	9.7	—	1.1
31167	Stanton, NE	9	6 195	23.8	6	7	85.7	—	14.3	527	55.2	—	44.8	10.6	16.5	3.2
31169	Thayer, NE	9	6 418	19.0	6	14	57.1	7.1	35.7	1 181	45.6	3.8	50.6	12.2	16.3	1.7
31171	Thomas, NE	9	824	24.9	2	3	66.7	—	33.3	139	44.6	—	55.4	11.5	36.7	0.7
31173	Thurston, NE	8	7 274	25.2	5	11	54.5	—	45.5	2 023	59.1	—	40.9	22.7	50.1	53.8
31175	Valley, NE	9	4 850	19.6	6	8	75.0	—	25.0	800	49.1	—	50.9	12.0	18.6	3.1
31177	Washington, NE	2	18 175	21.0	5	11	63.6	9.1	27.3	3 317	36.3	14.9	48.8	12.7	8.1	1.2
31179	Wayne, NE	7	9 517	17.3	7	14	57.1	7.1	21.4	1 786	44.2	17.1	36.3	9.2	14.9	3.3
31181	Webster, NE	9	4 037	18.0	3	6	50.0	—	50.0	785	49.2	—	50.8	14.5	15.8	1.7
31183	Wheeler, NE	9	957	20.6	1	3	66.7	—	33.3	162	48.8	—	51.2	7.4	40.7	—
31185	York, NE	7	14 707	19.8	5	13	38.5	23.1	38.5	2 275	44.4	14.7	40.9	17.1	12.9	2.1
32000	**NEVADA**															
32001	Churchill, NV	6	21 792	21.2	1	8	62.5	12.5	25.0	4 470	57.2	16.1	26.7	14.9	32.4	20.9
32003	Clark, NV	2	1 048 717	18.1	1	197	64.5	14.7	15.2	166 767	50.8	22.6	24.9	10.2	NA	39.3
32005	Douglas, NV	7	35 745	19.1	1	11	45.5	27.3	27.3	7 090	52.8	25.3	21.9	9.5	21.4	12.7
32007	Elko, NV	5	43 567	24.2	2	27	66.7	7.4	25.9	10 026	59.7	7.6	32.7	9.9	23.4	25.8
32009	Esmeralda, NV	9	1 180	18.2	1	3	100.0	—	—	124	100.0	—	—	13.7	53.2	16.9
32011	Eureka, NV	9	1 577	19.2	1	3	66.7	—	33.3	308	55.8	—	44.2	17.2	31.5	12.3
32013	Humboldt, NV	7	16 453	23.2	1	15	66.7	13.3	20.0	3 844	45.1	28.0	26.9	9.8	23.0	25.8
32015	Lander, NV	7	6 815	26.1	1	6	50.0	16.7	33.3	1 639	51.7	21.2	27.2	12.6	15.9	20.0
32017	Lincoln, NV	8	3 903	27.0	1	9	44.4	22.2	33.3	1 109	41.9	16.0	42.1	9.6	38.4	9.9
32019	Lyon, NV	6	27 357	20.5	1	15	46.7	26.7	26.7	5 426	41.1	31.2	27.7	14.3	36.1	16.3
32021	Mineral, NV	7	6 064	21.0	1	4	75.0	—	25.0	1 160	70.0	—	30.0	15.6	32.3	32.3
32023	Nye, NV	2	26 062	18.1	1	16	62.5	6.3	31.3	4 528	54.3	15.2	30.6	12.1	37.5	16.3
32027	Pershing, NV	9	4 708	21.3	1	4	50.0	25.0	25.0	967	53.1	24.1	22.9	18.9	32.4	29.3
32029	Storey, NV	8	2 917	17.3	1	4	50.0	25.0	25.0	480	49.0	21.0	30.0	16.0	NA	3.8
32031	Washoe, NV	2	298 787	17.0	1	79	69.6	13.9	11.4	47 572	58.5	15.4	25.6	10.6	26.9	25.9
32033	White Pine, NV	7	10 282	19.9	1	8	62.5	12.5	25.0	1 976	49.6	21.0	29.4	10.5	NA	16.6
32510	Carson City city, NV	4	47 237	16.6	1	10	70.0	20.0	10.0	7 694	48.1	23.0	29.0	13.9	27.9	21.3
33000	**NEW HAMPSHIRE**															
33001	Belknap, NH	6	51 466	19.9	7	26	61.5	19.2	19.2	9 096	51.1	22.8	26.1	13.7	15.6	1.4
33003	Carroll, NH	6	38 240	18.3	11	26	65.4	15.4	19.2	8 644	62.8	12.6	24.6	11.2	19.5	1.3
33005	Cheshire, NH	4	71 531	18.8	9	27	66.7	18.5	14.8	9 150	51.3	21.2	27.4	11.2	14.6	1.7
33007	Coos, NH	7	33 531	19.5	10	23	47.8	26.1	26.1	4 291	42.1	26.0	31.9	11.2	20.5	0.7
33009	Grafton, NH	5	78 329	17.8	30	55	61.8	16.4	21.8	14 612	51.7	16.3	32.0	11.6	14.4	2.3
33011	Hillsborough, NH	2	354 196	19.1	31	116	59.5	24.1	14.7	65 572	48.8	25.8	23.0	13.0	11.1	5.5
33013	Merrimack, NH	4	125 085	19.1	14	44	65.9	20.5	13.6	18 556	51.2	26.2	22.6	13.1	13.0	1.8
33015	Rockingham, NH	2	262 893	19.3	28	67	67.2	17.9	13.4	38 151	53.7	18.3	24.2	12.0	7.3	3.1
33017	Strafford, NH	2	107 344	17.9	13	38	65.8	18.4	15.8	17 087	50.8	23.0	26.1	15.7	16.6	2.9
33019	Sullivan, NH	7	39 866	19.6	11	38	63.2	23.7	10.5	9 012	47.0	25.8	20.6	13.9	15.1	1.3
34000	**NEW JERSEY**															
34001	Atlantic, NJ	2	235 447	17.2	24	74	62.2	20.3	10.8	38 862	56.6	17.3	23.5	4.4	30.3	43.1
34003	Bergen, NJ	0	846 498	15.6	76	267	62.5	15.0	16.5	111 146	51.1	16.1	29.5	4.2	9.3	29.4
34005	Burlington, NJ	0	410 931	19.3	42	128	60.2	22.7	14.1	64 281	46.9	23.6	26.1	7.8	13.2	25.3
34007	Camden, NJ	0	506 420	20.2	38	156	68.6	16.0	10.9	86 293	53.4	19.1	23.5	7.4	28.3	39.8
34009	Cape May, NJ	2	98 252	16.9	17	32	56.3	18.8	12.5	15 278	49.1	20.5	25.1	7.0	22.5	14.7
34011	Cumberland, NJ	3	135 943	20.1	16	53	69.8	18.9	7.5	25 118	52.3	22.6	18.0	8.0	43.4	49.3
34013	Essex, NJ	0	755 089	18.4	23	217	67.7	14.7	12.9	117 776	58.7	14.4	24.6	4.9	47.5	69.9
34015	Gloucester, NJ	0	244 203	20.8	28	80	61.3	16.3	15.0	43 170	50.7	18.0	23.7	6.0	14.8	15.5
34017	Hudson, NJ	0	550 789	16.5	13	100	73.0	5.0	15.0	75 483	69.8	2.2	26.2	6.2	55.3	76.9
34019	Hunterdon, NJ	1	118 737	18.4	30	46	63.0	15.2	10.9	19 342	55.3	16.0	26.0	3.2	3.1	4.5
34021	Mercer, NJ	2	330 226	17.2	11	89	62.9	16.9	11.2	50 694	45.6	24.1	26.1	7.2	23.5	43.0
34023	Middlesex, NJ	0	702 458	16.2	25	175	62.3	19.4	12.6	96 087	49.2	22.5	25.1	4.9	17.6	39.2
34025	Monmouth, NJ	0	591 182	18.7	52	167	59.9	19.8	14.4	92 557	50.4	20.7	26.6	4.4	14.4	21.6
34027	Morris, NJ	0	449 218	17.6	40	148	60.1	20.9	14.9	64 982	47.6	23.0	27.7	4.0	5.9	16.8
34029	Ocean, NJ	0	474 102	17.3	29	94	62.8	17.0	14.9	68 328	51.0	20.1	26.6	5.1	14.0	10.7
34031	Passaic, NJ	0	464 833	18.1	21	119	70.6	14.3	11.8	68 394	58.9	13.7	24.4	4.1	42.1	56.3
34033	Salem, NJ	1	67 540	20.4	15	33	51.5	21.2	12.1	12 260	44.1	21.0	24.6	6.9	21.8	24.9
34035	Somerset, NJ	0	269 902	16.3	19	70	58.6	24.3	12.9	34 020	48.9	25.3	23.9	3.2	9.2	25.6

1. County type code is from the Economic Research Service of the USDA. See notes and definitions at the end of this section.   2. IEP = Individual Education Program. See notes and definitions at the end of this section.

Table D-2.   School and Student Characteristics by County — Continued

County	Staff and students, 1995–1996						Revenues, fiscal 1995				Current expenditures, fiscal 1995		
	Number of teachers	Pupil/ teacher ratio	Number of graduates	Dropouts grades 9–12 (percent)	Local school non-teaching staff	Central admin. staff	Total revenue ($1000)	Percent of Revenue from			Amount	Amount per pupil	Percent for instruction
								Federal Gov't	State Gov't	Local Gov't			
	15	16	17	18	19	20	21	22	23	24	25	26	27
NEBRASKA—Con.													
Scotts Bluff, NE	446	15.9	445	5.4	361	56	38 253	7.4	44.6	48.0	34 021	4 816	68.1
Seward, NE	195	14.9	211	2.3	169	21	20 515	4.6	18.4	77.0	17 614	6 148	61.5
Sheridan, NE	124	11.1	99	1.7	79	13	8 838	5.5	42.8	51.7	7 272	5 110	70.5
Sherman, NE	61	11.4	40	4.1	40	6	4 565	5.0	25.2	69.7	4 145	6 114	68.3
Sioux, NE	25	6.9	8	NA	8	2	1 425	0.4	22.8	76.8	1 231	6 801	69.0
Stanton, NE	41	12.9	29	3.1	23	5	3 601	2.9	34.2	62.8	2 675	5 214	67.3
Thayer, NE	112	10.6	94	NA	60	15	9 529	2.8	20.8	76.4	8 343	6 953	66.8
Thomas, NE	16	8.7	11	2.0	15	2	1 273	4.9	19.1	76.0	1 120	8 296	67.0
Thurston, NE	175	11.5	107	5.3	124	25	13 296	25.8	41.4	32.7	11 190	5 706	61.3
Valley, NE	65	12.3	74	2.5	49	9	5 507	4.7	20.9	74.4	4 573	5 681	67.8
Washington, NE	196	16.9	228	3.0	169	20	17 581	2.7	32.6	64.7	15 091	4 550	64.7
Wayne, NE	134	13.3	123	1.3	75	19	13 714	3.7	27.2	69.1	11 853	6 911	70.1
Webster, NE	66	12.0	61	NA	38	7	5 184	3.7	29.4	67.0	4 552	5 806	66.3
Wheeler, NE	19	8.6	20	NA	12	2	1 404	4.4	14.5	81.1	1 405	8 515	60.0
York, NE	176	13.0	183	2.0	142	23	16 279	2.8	18.9	78.3	13 683	6 122	66.9
NEVADA													
Churchill, NV	246	18.1	225	10.1	190	18	25 710	6.7	54.8	38.5	23 024	5 293	63.1
Clark, NV	8 078	20.6	6 541	11.3	5 011	446	834 032	5.0	28.2	66.8	716 702	4 584	58.6
Douglas, NV	383	18.5	314	3.1	326	27	42 244	3.4	38.0	58.7	35 836	5 097	59.3
Elko, NV	570	17.6	456	5.8	342	16	54 249	4.4	39.4	56.2	48 698	5 134	60.3
Esmeralda, NV	11	11.3	—	NA	13	3	1 294	5.1	55.8	39.1	1 287	11 000	51.9
Eureka, NV	30	10.4	14	NA	26	4	7 288	1.4	—	98.6	4 252	15 406	54.4
Humboldt, NV	223	17.2	177	5.8	173	11	23 018	4.2	35.1	60.7	10 044	5 090	61.9
Lander, NV	95	17.3	83	9.4	61	4	8 988	4.4	50.0	45.6	8 741	5 739	64.1
Lincoln, NV	80	13.9	84	0.7	72	4	8 480	5.8	78.7	15.5	7 684	6 812	66.5
Lyon, NV	310	17.5	270	6.4	247	15	32 210	4.7	58.9	36.4	27 720	5 399	56.1
Mineral, NV	67	17.4	72	7.2	40	5	6 619	14.2	57.3	28.6	6 690	5 612	59.6
Nye, NV	262	17.3	227	6.8	191	18	26 269	4.4	43.5	52.2	21 878	5 247	59.3
Pershing, NV	60	16.1	35	2.3	57	5	6 809	4.7	48.2	47.0	5 604	6 325	64.2
Storey, NV	36	13.3	32	13.2	26	4	4 431	1.7	54.3	44.0	3 741	7 068	54.7
Washoe, NV	2 454	19.4	2 000	8.3	1 841	168	230 344	4.3	19.2	76.5	207 036	4 525	62.2
White Pine, NV	104	19.1	114	6.6	90	8	11 949	2.7	50.0	47.3	10 313	5 781	58.9
Carson City city, NV	428	18.0	342	5.8	384	18	43 776	4.1	33.2	62.7	37 098	5 034	60.8
NEW HAMPSHIRE													
Belknap, NH	813	11.2	602	NA	561	—	56 778	3.3	5.5	91.2	52 553	5 844	60.5
Carroll, NH	580	14.9	431	NA	511	—	63 074	3.0	5.7	91.3	51 709	6 172	64.9
Cheshire, NH	621	14.7	596	NA	583	—	60 963	3.1	9.9	87.0	53 396	5 848	62.9
Coos, NH	302	14.2	341	NA	256	—	26 571	4.8	18.3	76.9	22 820	5 346	62.3
Grafton, NH	1 068	13.7	1 009	NA	910	—	104 482	2.2	8.1	89.8	87 694	6 275	62.1
Hillsborough, NH	3 976	16.5	3 964	NA	2 809	—	384 589	3.1	4.4	92.5	348 490	5 468	64.1
Merrimack, NH	1 140	16.3	1 294	NA	1 058	—	112 471	2.9	10.5	86.6	97 266	5 386	59.6
Rockingham, NH	2 469	15.4	2 229	NA	1 849	—	228 906	2.6	4.6	92.8	206 739	6 037	66.2
Strafford, NH	1 037	16.5	1 032	NA	863	—	101 976	2.9	11.9	85.2	87 506	5 251	65.2
Sullivan, NH	602	15.0	559	NA	580	—	58 135	3.3	10.6	86.0	52 433	5 964	64.5
NEW JERSEY													
Atlantic, NJ	2 618	14.8	2 140	NA	2 308	330	371 255	3.7	38.2	58.2	314 325	8 446	55.0
Bergen, NJ	7 671	14.5	7 284	NA	5 404	935	1 197 149	1.7	12.6	85.7	1 084 619	10 024	59.3
Burlington, NJ	4 349	14.8	3 672	NA	4 378	554	597 569	3.5	43.6	52.9	537 289	8 340	56.0
Camden, NJ	5 728	15.1	4 738	NA	5 707	668	817 472	4.1	54.2	41.7	739 457	8 625	56.5
Cape May, NJ	1 160	13.2	714	NA	974	145	160 492	3.2	29.8	67.0	133 823	9 044	57.7
Cumberland, NJ	1 773	14.2	1 265	NA	1 627	197	229 577	5.6	67.2	27.3	204 441	8 228	57.6
Essex, NJ	8 135	14.5	5 709	NA	7 230	1 069	1 287 379	4.4	52.8	42.8	1 175 119	10 024	54.9
Gloucester, NJ	2 735	15.8	2 421	NA	2 329	373	375 706	2.9	52.0	45.0	313 819	7 577	57.1
Hudson, NJ	4 946	15.3	3 587	NA	3 800	585	682 666	6.2	51.1	42.7	625 136	8 572	59.9
Hunterdon, NJ	1 390	13.9	1 095	NA	1 075	154	187 298	1.4	21.2	77.4	169 313	9 209	56.4
Mercer, NJ	3 571	14.2	2 612	NA	3 095	431	537 798	3.1	36.7	60.1	470 429	9 485	55.4
Middlesex, NJ	6 538	14.7	5 670	NA	4 765	691	942 753	2.4	26.4	71.2	826 139	8 805	59.0
Monmouth, NJ	6 303	14.7	5 857	NA	4 542	718	881 645	3.0	31.3	65.7	781 919	8 697	57.6
Morris, NJ	4 620	14.1	4 346	NA	3 717	554	694 810	1.6	19.1	79.3	634 055	10 103	56.9
Ocean, NJ	4 380	15.6	3 890	NA	3 719	518	612 068	2.6	37.0	60.4	527 921	8 018	57.4
Passaic, NJ	4 611	14.8	3 517	NA	3 570	539	665 261	4.9	46.9	48.3	600 308	8 979	60.8
Salem, NJ	852	14.4	658	NA	739	110	116 397	4.6	54.2	41.2	100 716	8 334	55.5
Somerset, NJ	2 441	13.9	1 926	NA	1 747	292	378 592	1.5	17.4	81.1	326 992	9 303	56.6

Table D-2. School and Student Characteristics by County

State/County code	County	County type[1]	Population, 1996 — Total persons	Population, 1996 — Percent age 5–17	Number of school districts, 1995–1996	Level of schools, 1995–1996 — Number of schools	Percent — Primary	Percent — Middle	Percent — High	Level of students, 1995–1996 — Number of students	Percent — Primary	Percent — Middle	Percent — High	Characteristics of students, 1995–1996 — Percent with IEP[2]	Percent free-lunch eligible	Percent minority
			1	2	3	4	5	6	7	8	9	10	11	12	13	14
	NEW JERSEY—Con.															
34037	Sussex, NJ	1	141 308	21.0	26	45	64.4	13.3	17.8	25 640	55.2	14.4	27.6	4.7	5.9	4.4
34039	Union, NJ	0	497 281	16.5	24	145	60.7	21.4	12.4	71 251	52.1	19.8	26.8	4.9	32.0	50.9
34041	Warren, NJ	1	97 574	18.7	24	40	67.5	12.5	15.0	16 419	57.8	12.7	27.0	4.5	12.0	5.9
35000	**NEW MEXICO**															
35001	Bernalillo, NM	2	526 614	18.6	1	122	64.8	18.9	14.8	88 891	48.3	22.2	29.4	16.2	NA	55.2
35003	Catron, NM	9	2 657	20.6	2	6	66.7	—	33.3	516	54.1	—	45.9	11.6	NA	28.9
35005	Chaves, NM	5	62 564	22.6	4	32	56.3	21.9	18.8	13 147	53.6	18.2	28.2	15.8	NA	55.9
35006	Cibola, NM	6	25 473	25.3	1	11	63.6	18.2	9.1	3 999	50.2	15.6	7.7	10.6	NA	73.5
35007	Colfax, NM	7	13 867	21.2	4	16	37.5	37.5	25.0	2 753	32.7	35.1	32.3	16.5	NA	57.4
35009	Curry, NM	5	47 753	22.1	4	27	63.0	14.8	22.2	10 481	57.6	22.3	20.1	12.8	NA	44.8
35011	De Baca, NM	9	2 358	18.9	1	3	33.3	33.3	33.3	471	45.9	24.0	30.1	15.4	NA	39.5
35013	Dona Ana, NM	3	163 849	21.8	3	58	60.3	20.7	12.1	35 129	49.1	24.4	26.2	13.7	NA	75.0
35015	Eddy, NM	5	53 358	22.5	3	28	67.9	17.9	10.7	11 651	46.0	27.2	26.8	12.3	NA	49.2
35017	Grant, NM	7	30 700	22.4	2	14	64.3	14.3	21.4	6 260	45.6	22.1	32.3	15.8	NA	59.8
35019	Guadalupe, NM	9	4 195	22.3	2	7	42.9	28.6	28.6	1 037	45.3	21.6	33.1	16.1	NA	93.4
35021	Harding, NM	9	946	20.9	2	4	50.0	—	50.0	188	50.0	—	50.0	19.7	NA	49.5
35023	Hidalgo, NM	7	6 328	24.9	2	8	37.5	37.5	25.0	1 476	42.5	28.7	28.7	16.0	NA	58.0
35025	Lea, NM	5	56 634	24.7	5	36	58.3	25.0	16.7	13 353	50.0	29.2	20.8	12.4	NA	51.7
35027	Lincoln, NM	7	15 362	18.9	5	16	43.8	25.0	31.3	3 464	41.9	28.3	29.8	14.9	NA	41.8
35028	Los Alamos, NM	3	18 212	19.8	1	7	71.4	14.3	14.3	3 715	51.8	16.2	32.0	16.5	NA	15.5
35029	Luna, NM	6	23 089	21.7	1	11	63.6	27.3	9.1	5 417	48.7	30.7	20.6	8.4	NA	77.1
35031	McKinley, NM	5	67 754	27.9	2	36	61.1	13.9	25.0	15 943	48.5	19.3	32.1	13.9	NA	90.1
35033	Mora, NM	8	4 798	21.4	2	6	50.0	—	33.3	968	61.9	—	32.3	14.8	NA	91.5
35035	Otero, NM	4	55 881	21.7	3	21	66.7	19.0	14.3	10 222	53.9	19.2	27.0	13.4	NA	40.1
35037	Quay, NM	7	10 291	20.5	4	13	46.2	15.4	38.5	2 273	40.8	21.6	37.5	15.3	NA	49.5
35039	Rio Arriba, NM	6	37 580	22.9	4	29	69.0	17.2	13.8	7 131	60.2	16.1	23.6	10.9	NA	92.8
35041	Roosevelt, NM	7	18 700	20.7	4	14	42.9	21.4	35.7	3 829	35.2	31.5	33.3	12.6	NA	41.6
35043	Sandoval, NM	2	83 264	22.6	4	24	58.3	29.2	12.5	11 202	57.5	28.4	14.1	14.9	NA	56.1
35045	San Juan, NM	5	102 508	27.3	4	47	57.4	25.5	14.9	24 805	45.7	29.3	24.9	15.2	NA	56.7
35047	San Miguel, NM	6	28 703	21.4	3	19	63.2	21.1	15.8	6 027	49.6	22.9	27.5	11.4	NA	90.0
35049	Santa Fe, NM	3	119 011	18.4	2	31	71.0	19.4	9.7	15 185	55.5	19.1	25.5	12.0	NA	67.4
35051	Sierra, NM	6	10 953	14.0	1	5	40.0	40.0	20.0	1 810	34.3	39.4	26.2	14.2	NA	38.5
35053	Socorro, NM	7	16 155	22.5	2	9	44.4	33.3	22.2	2 677	35.7	35.4	28.9	13.5	NA	71.9
35055	Taos, NM	7	25 985	20.8	4	22	54.5	27.3	18.2	5 468	40.2	35.1	24.8	12.2	NA	80.2
35057	Torrance, NM	8	13 584	24.0	3	12	50.0	25.0	25.0	5 777	55.6	18.4	26.1	17.8	NA	36.9
35059	Union, NM	9	4 067	20.6	2	7	42.9	28.6	28.6	982	42.5	25.5	32.1	14.0	NA	38.7
35061	Valencia, NM	2	60 214	22.4	2	20	55.0	30.0	15.0	12 363	46.4	28.4	25.2	12.5	NA	63.8
36000	**NEW YORK**															
36001	Albany, NY	2	296 087	16.1	14	68	66.2	14.7	17.6	40 680	51.9	18.7	28.7	12.7	21.0	21.2
36003	Allegany, NY	7	51 282	20.0	13	20	30.0	5.0	15.0	9 261	26.7	4.3	15.4	8.8	30.1	1.6
36005	Bronx, NY	0	1 193 775	20.0	[3]NA	[3]NA	[3]NA	[3]NA	[3]NA	[3]NA	[3]NA	[3]NA	[3]NA	[3]NA	[3]NA	[3]NA
36007	Broome, NY	2	201 533	17.1	13	58	60.3	19.0	17.2	34 794	50.2	20.2	23.1	12.3	26.2	8.6
36009	Cattaraugus, NY	4	85 680	21.3	15	36	52.8	8.3	27.8	18 754	46.6	11.6	31.2	12.5	26.4	7.4
36011	Cayuga, NY	2	82 062	19.9	8	26	42.3	26.9	23.1	13 786	42.4	23.0	26.8	10.5	19.1	5.9
36013	Chautauqua, NY	3	140 800	19.4	19	58	53.4	13.8	24.1	26 214	46.8	14.6	28.0	11.2	28.3	8.9
36015	Chemung, NY	3	93 282	19.2	4	23	69.6	13.0	17.4	15 338	57.3	13.8	29.0	15.2	24.7	8.7
36017	Chenango, NY	6	52 121	21.1	10	26	50.0	15.4	23.1	10 734	47.2	16.0	25.5	15.1	28.3	2.2
36019	Clinton, NY	5	80 537	18.7	9	32	65.6	9.4	15.6	13 900	53.0	7.6	21.3	14.3	20.3	3.3
36021	Columbia, NY	6	63 613	18.4	7	21	47.6	19.0	28.6	9 967	41.4	22.2	28.3	14.2	21.8	9.8
36023	Cortland, NY	4	48 573	19.1	5	16	68.8	—	31.3	8 080	60.9	—	39.1	13.3	24.6	2.5
36025	Delaware, NY	6	47 287	19.4	13	23	30.4	13.0	13.0	8 464	24.2	13.5	15.0	13.6	26.4	3.0
36027	Dutchess, NY	2	262 675	17.8	15	73	60.3	19.2	20.5	43 233	49.9	20.5	29.6	12.6	14.4	18.9
36029	Erie, NY	0	954 021	17.5	31	222	60.8	16.2	20.3	145 199	54.2	16.7	26.5	11.7	29.5	25.2
36031	Essex, NY	6	37 789	18.1	11	15	20.0	6.7	13.3	5 155	26.0	4.8	14.7	11.8	27.1	1.3
36033	Franklin, NY	7	49 335	19.1	8	24	62.5	8.3	25.0	9 908	50.6	11.3	34.1	14.6	29.2	9.9
36035	Fulton, NY	4	53 965	20.4	8	24	54.2	16.7	20.8	10 416	45.7	18.3	29.9	12.5	24.1	3.2
36037	Genesee, NY	1	61 206	20.1	8	22	50.0	13.6	36.4	11 299	50.5	11.4	38.0	10.9	17.7	4.3
36039	Greene, NY	6	47 291	17.3	6	17	47.1	17.6	23.5	7 318	49.2	12.7	26.9	11.9	19.7	6.3
36041	Hamilton, NY	8	5 232	17.3	7	7	42.9	—	—	721	9.3	—	—	9.0	19.0	1.0
36043	Herkimer, NY	2	65 968	19.7	12	27	51.9	7.4	33.3	12 826	48.9	6.7	38.7	12.5	25.3	1.9
36045	Jefferson, NY	5	113 844	19.9	12	38	55.3	13.2	18.4	20 723	38.9	19.6	26.6	12.0	28.8	11.4
36047	Kings, NY	0	2 273 966	19.6	[3]1	[3]1 107	[3]59.6	[3]17.3	[3]11.8	[3]1 047 489	[3]51.0	[3]19.0	[3]25.5	[3]11.8	[3]NA	[3]83.5
36049	Lewis, NY	6	27 799	23.4	5	14	50.0	14.3	35.7	5 383	50.1	12.1	37.8	7.1	28.9	1.5
36051	Livingston, NY	1	65 898	18.4	9	20	50.0	10.0	35.0	11 177	49.7	9.4	35.8	18.5	17.9	3.7

1. County type code is from the Economic Research Service of the USDA. See notes and definitions at the end of this section.   2. IEP = Individual Education Program. See notes and definitions at the end of this section.   3. Bronx, New York, Queens, and Richmond Counties included with Kings County.

Table D-2. School and Student Characteristics by County — Continued

County	Staff and students, 1995–1996						Revenues, fiscal 1995				Current expenditures, fiscal 1995		
	Number of teachers	Pupil/ teacher ratio	Number of graduates	Dropouts grades 9–12 (percent)	Local school non-teaching staff	Central admin. staff	Total revenue ($1000)	Percent of Revenue from			Amount	Amount per pupil	Percent for instruction
								Federal Gov't	State Gov't	Local Gov't			
	15	16	17	18	19	20	21	22	23	24	25	26	27
NEW JERSEY—Con.													
Sussex, NJ	1 794	14.3	1 541	NA	1 152	177	243 968	2.0	39.4	58.5	220 149	8 723	56.6
Union, NJ	4 909	14.5	3 858	NA	3 872	622	716 075	3.4	31.5	65.1	640 067	9 236	57.6
Warren, NJ	1 202	13.7	903	NA	791	142	161 003	2.2	37.4	60.4	135 462	8 505	58.6
NEW MEXICO													
Bernalillo, NM	5 495	16.2	4 273	12.1	3 957	653	449 417	7.1	77.2	15.8	373 790	4 200	60.9
Catron, NM	39	13.4	36	3.0	41	6	3 978	12.6	72.9	14.5	3 271	6 389	48.1
Chaves, NM	731	18.0	652	7.9	810	752	58 188	9.9	82.4	7.8	50 564	3 866	60.8
Cibola, NM	230	17.4	199	5.5	224	22	18 836	20.5	72.9	6.6	15 864	4 021	54.4
Colfax, NM	170	16.2	159	3.6	122	19	16 012	8.0	79.9	12.1	12 962	4 669	55.6
Curry, NM	597	17.5	463	7.8	519	49	45 444	11.5	77.5	11.0	39 417	3 716	60.1
De Baca, NM	36	13.1	25	3.5	25	4	2 827	8.8	85.3	5.9	2 522	5 116	52.1
Dona Ana, NM	1 986	17.7	1 342	11.9	1 873	154	168 377	12.5	75.9	11.6	138 431	3 979	56.3
Eddy, NM	653	17.8	600	2.8	491	43	57 872	10.8	73.1	16.0	46 822	3 909	58.0
Grant, NM	365	17.2	351	3.3	260	30	29 782	10.8	80.9	8.2	25 704	4 135	58.2
Guadalupe, NM	73	14.3	58	3.9	79	14	6 964	11.5	79.1	9.4	5 928	5 484	50.3
Harding, NM	20	9.5	11	1.6	14	4	1 952	5.1	87.2	7.7	1 608	9 189	44.2
Hidalgo, NM	96	15.3	64	2.8	86	12	8 139	8.1	80.5	11.3	6 952	4 998	51.7
Lea, NM	729	18.3	648	3.3	553	59	60 914	9.4	72.5	18.1	50 696	3 788	58.7
Lincoln, NM	207	16.8	138	6.8	162	22	17 843	9.5	84.2	6.3	16 584	4 804	55.9
Los Alamos, NM	264	14.1	230	2.4	243	35	24 392	33.0	53.6	13.3	22 686	6 146	58.4
Luna, NM	288	18.8	254	11.9	232	27	22 215	14.0	78.6	7.4	18 608	3 476	60.9
McKinley, NM	915	17.4	777	6.8	1 042	91	83 355	34.2	54.4	11.4	61 749	3 944	53.9
Mora, NM	64	15.1	56	1.1	82	14	9 375	13.8	59.8	26.3	5 512	5 132	49.7
Otero, NM	563	18.2	493	1.4	469	51	45 179	13.2	77.7	9.1	39 232	3 822	56.7
Quay, NM	154	14.8	111	16.9	119	20	12 678	10.5	78.9	10.6	10 582	4 691	56.4
Rio Arriba, NM	412	17.3	277	11.3	382	51	41 352	15.7	70.6	13.6	33 237	4 636	50.8
Roosevelt, NM	231	16.6	180	6.5	232	30	19 260	11.2	77.2	11.6	16 573	4 256	55.3
Sandoval, NM	634	17.7	267	10.6	495	54	61 710	13.4	71.0	15.7	46 422	4 229	54.9
San Juan, NM	1 417	17.5	1 246	5.8	1 580	129	123 312	18.4	63.4	18.3	95 846	3 909	57.8
San Miguel, NM	337	17.9	277	8.4	374	30	34 925	15.3	75.4	9.4	25 911	4 127	52.3
Santa Fe, NM	849	17.9	654	12.8	768	110	75 911	8.5	71.8	19.7	59 024	3 928	57.4
Sierra, NM	100	18.2	75	11.6	123	75	8 647	9.6	76.3	14.0	7 261	4 041	56.8
Socorro, NM	157	17.0	159	3.7	146	17	13 637	15.6	73.9	10.5	11 289	4 241	53.7
Taos, NM	294	18.6	298	5.5	303	51	33 083	22.5	70.4	7.1	25 447	4 766	52.3
Torrance, NM	330	17.5	251	7.1	242	18	28 671	5.9	83.3	10.8	23 859	4 470	54.2
Union, NM	75	13.1	57	3.2	48	5	6 434	6.7	82.5	10.8	5 827	5 815	50.4
Valencia, NM	633	19.5	498	3.1	760	53	55 584	10.1	78.8	11.0	45 229	3 745	54.1
NEW YORK													
Albany, NY	2 663	15.3	2 164	2.2	2 548	472	355 232	4.1	29.3	66.6	321 758	8 268	63.9
Allegany, NY	670	13.8	608	3.0	464	80	81 362	4.8	70.7	24.4	68 970	7 366	65.3
Bronx, NY	[1]NA	[1]NA	[1]NA	[1]NA	[1]NA	[1]NA	[1]NA	[1]NA	[1]NA	[1]NA	[1]NA	[1]NA	[1]NA
Broome, NY	2 322	15.0	1 890	2.4	2 274	449	278 894	3.5	44.6	51.8	252 812	7 352	64.7
Cattaraugus, NY	1 370	13.7	1 109	2.2	1 235	187	149 336	4.9	65.1	30.0	131 962	7 445	66.8
Cayuga, NY	852	16.2	802	2.4	751	147	103 201	2.9	62.7	34.3	94 417	7 047	65.7
Chautauqua, NY	1 707	15.4	1 570	2.6	1 256	238	213 180	4.9	58.4	36.7	192 675	7 351	66.7
Chemung, NY	990	15.5	892	6.3	1 076	200	123 145	5.2	59.2	35.6	113 173	7 651	64.1
Chenango, NY	851	12.6	657	2.9	841	165	100 275	3.2	63.1	33.8	79 049	7 627	63.8
Clinton, NY	1 075	12.9	829	4.0	990	160	126 089	6.3	60.2	33.5	116 821	8 263	67.1
Columbia, NY	685	14.5	512	3.9	616	84	95 080	3.8	40.8	55.5	85 403	8 602	64.8
Cortland, NY	541	14.9	495	4.0	514	88	69 209	3.5	64.3	32.2	61 799	7 486	67.2
Delaware, NY	676	12.5	545	2.3	575	128	75 131	3.3	53.4	43.4	67 086	7 973	64.6
Dutchess, NY	2 779	15.6	2 386	2.8	2 410	486	373 743	2.2	36.5	61.3	348 946	8 298	64.2
Erie, NY	9 578	15.2	8 063	2.7	7 631	1 596	1 271 366	4.3	49.5	46.1	1 158 854	8 195	66.3
Essex, NY	409	12.6	312	1.9	325	53	47 722	3.7	38.2	58.2	43 571	8 616	66.5
Franklin, NY	703	14.1	560	3.5	703	121	83 410	4.9	61.8	33.3	76 320	7 978	66.9
Fulton, NY	750	13.9	529	3.8	676	132	95 218	3.6	67.0	29.5	76 441	7 426	68.0
Genesee, NY	756	15.0	698	1.8	568	96	93 011	2.8	56.5	40.7	85 360	7 619	68.8
Greene, NY	481	15.2	493	3.7	379	73	64 967	3.2	39.3	57.5	59 149	8 167	64.2
Hamilton, NY	87	8.3	43	0.5	65	16	11 639	2.9	13.9	83.1	10 062	13 956	65.7
Herkimer, NY	938	13.7	764	1.5	754	148	107 411	4.1	62.7	33.2	92 321	7 393	67.3
Jefferson, NY	1 419	14.6	1 173	3.2	1 204	208	163 182	6.1	65.6	28.3	143 174	7 220	66.3
Kings, NY	[1]54 591	[1]19.2	[1]35 026	[1]7.0	[1]45 399	[1]6 100	[1]8 025 686	[1]10.6	[1]40.8	[1]48.6	[1]7 788 536	[1]7 617	[1]71.2
Lewis, NY	331	16.2	358	2.5	263	47	43 008	1.2	67.2	31.6	37 770	6 979	65.3
Livingston, NY	892	12.5	629	2.7	750	147	91 832	2.8	58.6	38.5	79 173	7 537	66.5

1. Bronx, New York, Queens, and Richmond Counties included with Kings County.

Table D-2. School and Student Characteristics by County

State/ County code	County	County type[1]	Population, 1996		Number of school districts, 1995–1996	Level of schools, 1995–1996				Level of students, 1995–1996				Characteristics of students, 1995–1996		
			Total persons	Percent age 5–17		Number of schools	Percent Primary	Percent Middle	Percent High	Number of students	Percent Primary	Percent Middle	Percent High	Percent with IEP[2]	Percent free-lunch eligible	Percent minority
			1	2	3	4	5	6	7	8	9	10	11	12	13	14
	NEW YORK—Con.															
36053	Madison, NY	2	71 508	19.4	11	31	54.8	12.9	22.6	13 420	45.8	15.3	29.1	11.8	17.9	2.3
36055	Monroe, NY	0	721 996	18.1	20	176	65.3	17.0	15.9	122 015	53.1	20.7	24.7	12.1	24.4	30.5
36057	Montgomery, NY	2	51 894	18.8	5	18	55.6	16.7	27.8	8 420	48.0	20.9	31.0	10.4	27.9	11.9
36059	Nassau, NY	0	1 303 389	16.6	57	303	65.3	16.5	18.2	188 474	51.7	18.6	29.8	11.0	9.8	28.0
36061	New York, NY	0	1 533 774	12.3	[3]NA	[3]NA	[3]NA	[3]NA	[3]NA	[3]NA	[3]NA	[3]NA	[3]NA	[3]NA	[3]NA	[3]NA
36063	Niagara, NY	0	221 219	18.9	10	60	60.0	21.7	18.3	36 704	46.4	21.8	31.8	10.9	21.1	13.1
36065	Oneida, NY	2	236 437	18.2	16	75	61.3	17.3	20.0	39 391	52.2	20.1	26.1	12.4	27.4	10.9
36067	Onondaga, NY	2	466 675	18.2	19	127	62.2	19.7	15.7	79 803	51.7	22.4	25.0	13.4	24.4	18.3
36069	Ontario, NY	1	99 634	18.9	10	30	46.7	20.0	26.7	18 698	46.4	19.7	28.4	15.9	14.9	6.2
36071	Orange, NY	2	324 422	20.5	19	89	61.8	16.9	19.1	59 607	51.4	20.0	26.9	11.8	20.2	22.7
36073	Orleans, NY	1	44 979	20.2	6	16	43.8	25.0	31.3	9 483	48.4	21.2	30.4	16.5	20.8	8.0
36075	Oswego, NY	2	125 446	21.3	10	44	61.4	13.6	20.5	26 600	51.1	17.9	28.6	12.6	22.4	2.3
36077	Otsego, NY	6	61 470	18.0	12	23	39.1	8.7	21.7	10 249	33.8	7.1	22.9	10.5	23.6	2.6
36079	Putnam, NY	1	90 983	18.9	6	19	57.9	21.1	21.1	14 175	47.0	27.3	25.7	12.4	5.0	5.8
36081	Queens, NY	0	1 980 643	15.6	[3]NA	[3]NA	[3]NA	[3]NA	[3]NA	[3]NA	[3]NA	[3]NA	[3]NA	[3]NA	[3]NA	[3]NA
36083	Rensselaer, NY	2	155 098	17.9	13	45	60.0	15.6	20.0	23 898	49.6	19.6	26.0	14.4	21.3	8.8
36085	Richmond, NY	0	398 748	18.5	[3]NA	[3]NA	[3]NA	[3]NA	[3]NA	[3]NA	[3]NA	[3]NA	[3]NA	[3]NA	[3]NA	[3]NA
36087	Rockland, NY	0	278 136	19.9	10	64	54.7	26.6	15.6	38 772	43.5	25.8	30.1	12.9	13.3	35.4
36089	St. Lawrence, NY	5	114 759	19.4	18	43	51.2	9.3	27.9	20 427	44.9	11.8	31.0	13.0	29.0	2.2
36091	Saratoga, NY	2	194 837	19.3	12	53	60.4	18.9	20.8	34 155	50.8	23.7	25.5	11.1	10.0	3.3
36093	Schenectady, NY	2	147 599	16.9	6	41	65.9	19.5	14.6	21 529	51.4	20.9	27.7	12.7	21.1	16.0
36095	Schoharie, NY	2	33 012	19.0	6	13	38.5	15.4	23.1	5 842	38.7	13.8	26.8	13.2	25.4	2.5
36097	Schuyler, NY	8	19 108	20.8	2	6	50.0	16.7	33.3	2 408	44.0	19.2	36.8	6.9	24.0	1.3
36099	Seneca, NY	6	32 530	19.7	4	12	50.0	16.7	25.0	5 505	41.1	16.4	30.6	13.5	18.9	3.6
36101	Steuben, NY	4	99 201	20.8	15	42	54.8	9.5	21.4	20 276	43.5	12.2	29.3	13.4	27.6	2.8
36103	Suffolk, NY	0	1 356 896	18.7	73	331	62.5	19.6	15.7	229 309	50.0	22.3	26.8	14.2	15.4	21.3
36105	Sullivan, NY	6	70 346	18.6	11	25	48.0	12.0	28.0	12 096	46.1	13.7	30.0	15.5	31.5	21.9
36107	Tioga, NY	2	52 520	21.5	6	20	55.0	15.0	30.0	10 049	46.7	16.6	36.7	9.9	23.5	1.9
36109	Tompkins, NY	5	96 152	15.0	8	30	50.0	20.0	23.3	13 773	43.2	22.3	30.4	14.1	19.1	11.2
36111	Ulster, NY	4	167 082	17.3	11	50	64.0	16.0	18.0	28 113	52.3	16.7	30.7	13.0	20.9	13.2
36113	Warren, NY	3	61 490	19.0	9	22	45.5	18.2	27.3	11 270	42.9	21.3	29.8	11.9	19.4	2.1
36115	Washington, NY	3	60 777	19.6	12	23	52.2	4.3	26.1	11 493	45.5	3.3	28.8	16.1	21.2	2.2
36117	Wayne, NY	1	94 324	20.9	11	35	48.6	20.0	28.6	18 925	48.0	17.7	32.0	14.7	17.0	8.3
36119	Westchester, NY	0	893 412	16.0	49	248	57.7	16.9	17.7	126 628	52.1	19.7	25.3	13.2	21.2	41.8
36121	Wyoming, NY	6	44 357	20.2	5	11	54.5	9.1	36.4	6 162	48.9	10.1	40.9	10.8	17.4	2.3
36123	Yates, NY	6	24 300	20.0	2	6	50.0	16.7	33.3	3 192	48.2	17.1	34.7	13.2	22.4	2.3
37000	**NORTH CAROLINA**															
37001	Alamance, NC	3	116 514	16.2	2	30	60.0	20.0	20.0	18 461	51.2	23.1	25.8	12.8	24.6	30.1
37003	Alexander, NC	2	30 192	19.1	1	10	70.0	20.0	10.0	4 978	57.5	24.3	18.2	10.7	17.0	9.4
37005	Alleghany, NC	9	9 849	17.0	1	4	75.0	—	25.0	1 476	68.6	—	31.4	13.4	28.8	3.4
37007	Anson, NC	6	24 302	19.9	1	8	62.5	25.0	12.5	4 461	45.1	21.5	33.3	15.4	49.9	63.3
37009	Ashe, NC	9	23 792	17.0	1	8	50.0	—	37.5	3 504	52.5	—	47.1	11.4	31.1	1.2
37011	Avery, NC	9	15 626	17.8	1	9	77.8	11.1	11.1	2 455	57.4	14.7	27.9	17.0	37.3	1.8
37013	Beaufort, NC	6	44 027	19.9	1	14	50.0	21.4	21.4	7 806	44.8	22.0	25.7	15.1	38.3	44.3
37015	Bertie, NC	9	20 722	22.4	1	9	66.7	22.2	11.1	4 003	46.2	24.4	29.4	8.2	62.1	79.8
37017	Bladen, NC	6	30 330	20.7	1	14	42.9	21.4	21.4	5 674	46.1	17.2	23.1	11.5	47.2	52.2
37019	Brunswick, NC	3	63 225	17.7	1	13	46.2	23.1	30.8	9 294	46.1	28.2	25.7	10.6	38.0	27.1
37021	Buncombe, NC	3	191 800	16.7	2	43	58.1	23.3	18.6	28 819	48.1	24.4	27.5	12.9	26.1	13.8
37023	Burke, NC	2	80 986	18.0	1	22	63.6	18.2	13.6	13 237	50.1	23.1	26.2	14.6	21.9	15.3
37025	Cabarrus, NC	0	113 165	18.0	2	28	64.3	17.9	17.9	19 828	51.4	22.5	26.1	12.9	20.2	19.4
37027	Caldwell, NC	2	74 683	17.7	1	23	65.2	17.4	17.4	11 849	54.4	19.2	26.4	12.5	25.1	8.5
37029	Camden, NC	8	6 523	18.1	1	3	33.3	33.3	33.3	1 204	28.6	40.8	30.6	10.1	25.2	23.2
37031	Carteret, NC	6	58 773	16.9	1	14	50.0	28.6	21.4	8 345	44.7	27.2	28.2	14.6	28.7	14.5
37033	Caswell, NC	8	21 585	18.0	1	6	66.7	16.7	16.7	3 451	55.9	16.1	28.0	13.3	33.9	47.0
37035	Catawba, NC	2	129 104	18.1	3	39	56.4	17.9	20.5	21 143	54.7	17.8	27.0	13.1	19.5	18.4
37037	Chatham, NC	2	43 870	16.3	1	13	61.5	15.4	23.1	6 651	60.5	14.1	25.4	12.1	24.3	33.4
37039	Cherokee, NC	7	21 934	18.1	1	10	60.0	10.0	20.0	3 473	52.9	6.4	28.6	15.9	39.3	5.6
37041	Chowan, NC	7	14 099	19.7	1	4	50.0	25.0	25.0	2 608	48.7	23.8	27.5	10.0	45.9	52.8
37043	Clay, NC	9	8 132	18.9	1	3	33.3	33.3	33.3	1 238	35.7	34.2	30.1	9.9	25.5	1.7
37045	Cleveland, NC	4	91 381	18.4	3	26	65.4	15.4	15.4	16 217	51.5	22.5	25.8	14.9	28.8	31.7
37047	Columbus, NC	6	51 975	21.0	2	23	52.2	26.1	17.4	10 443	53.3	19.4	27.1	11.7	53.9	48.0
37049	Craven, NC	5	86 352	19.5	1	21	66.7	19.0	14.3	14 793	52.1	21.0	26.9	12.1	33.1	38.9
37051	Cumberland, NC	2	284 800	20.5	1	72	69.4	16.7	12.5	51 148	51.1	22.8	25.9	9.7	36.4	52.4
37053	Currituck, NC	1	16 766	19.2	1	6	83.3	—	16.7	2 979	73.4	—	26.6	13.9	24.1	13.7
37055	Dare, NC	7	26 803	16.3	1	8	37.5	25.0	25.0	4 192	43.1	20.8	22.3	10.6	16.9	6.5
37057	Davidson, NC	2	137 395	18.1	3	37	48.6	27.0	18.9	23 021	46.2	25.2	24.2	12.6	21.8	14.7

1. County type code is from the Economic Research Service of the USDA. See notes and definitions at the end of this section.   2. IEP = Individual Education Program. See notes and definitions at the end of this section.   3. Bronx, New York, Queens, and Richmond Counties included with Kings County.

Table D-2.   School and Student Characteristics by County — Continued

County	Staff and students, 1995–1996						Revenues, fiscal 1995				Current expenditures, fiscal 1995		
	Number of teachers	Pupil/ teacher ratio	Number of graduates	Dropouts grades 9–12 (percent)	Local school non-teaching staff	Central admin. staff	Total revenue ($1000)	Percent of Revenue from			Amount	Amount per pupil	Percent for instruction
								Federal Gov't	State Gov't	Local Gov't			
	15	16	17	18	19	20	21	22	23	24	25	26	27
NEW YORK—Con.													
Madison, NY	894	15.0	731	2.4	913	179	105 565	3.4	59.5	37.1	95 161	7 353	66.5
Monroe, NY	7 923	15.4	5 867	3.6	7 143	1 429	1 110 487	4.0	40.6	55.4	979 289	8 355	65.2
Montgomery, NY	573	14.7	492	4.1	342	76	75 726	5.1	59.7	35.2	65 316	7 754	66.4
Nassau, NY	12 907	14.6	12 342	1.0	10 147	2 864	2 202 569	1.5	17.2	81.3	2 053 667	11 204	63.4
New York, NY	(1)NA	(1)NA	(1)NA	(1)NA	(1)NA	(1)NA	(1)NA	(1)NA	(1)NA	(1)NA	(1)NA	(1)NA	(1)NA
Niagara, NY	2 284	16.1	2 097	1.9	1 482	309	321 277	3.9	52.4	43.7	294 831	8 111	67.5
Oneida, NY	2 542	15.5	2 197	3.7	2 111	406	342 541	4.1	56.2	39.7	304 182	7 626	65.9
Onondaga, NY	5 378	14.8	3 940	2.8	5 370	891	675 712	4.4	47.2	48.4	604 890	7 689	65.7
Ontario, NY	1 406	13.3	1 006	2.6	1 275	253	156 554	3.0	49.6	47.4	137 835	7 699	66.9
Orange, NY	3 788	15.7	3 160	3.7	3 186	691	505 333	2.8	46.5	50.7	460 525	8 055	64.6
Orleans, NY	767	12.4	486	2.3	599	132	64 933	4.3	62.4	33.3	58 062	6 712	68.3
Oswego, NY	1 749	15.2	1 477	4.6	1 713	291	219 972	3.1	53.2	43.6	199 476	7 705	64.8
Otsego, NY	712	14.4	632	1.7	612	93	92 595	2.8	60.6	36.6	76 360	7 511	66.3
Putnam, NY	940	15.1	776	2.2	870	126	153 628	1.0	23.2	75.8	144 061	10 229	67.6
Queens, NY	(1)NA	(1)NA	(1)NA	(1)NA	(1)NA	(1)NA	(1)NA	(1)NA	(1)NA	(1)NA	(1)NA	(1)NA	(1)NA
Rensselaer, NY	1 639	14.6	1 366	4.3	1 444	299	206 029	3.8	50.0	46.3	187 545	8 083	63.4
Richmond, NY	(1)NA	(1)NA	(1)NA	(1)NA	(1)NA	(1)NA	(1)NA	(1)NA	(1)NA	(1)NA	(1)NA	(1)NA	(1)NA
Rockland, NY	2 614	14.8	2 630	1.3	2 295	574	471 242	2.3	21.4	76.3	442 417	11 732	64.6
St. Lawrence, NY	1 452	14.1	1 304	2.5	1 099	230	169 161	4.3	65.1	30.6	151 283	7 722	67.3
Saratoga, NY	2 097	16.3	2 062	2.1	1 733	334	294 056	3.0	42.5	54.5	266 088	7 884	67.3
Schenectady, NY	1 317	16.3	1 195	3.9	1 193	212	187 876	3.7	41.4	54.9	169 744	7 938	65.8
Schoharie, NY	392	14.9	361	3.3	330	54	57 085	3.3	64.1	32.7	47 519	8 261	66.4
Schuyler, NY	151	15.9	173	2.9	123	23	23 712	3.8	64.8	31.5	20 534	8 464	65.1
Seneca, NY	370	14.9	313	4.1	318	54	45 237	3.7	59.3	37.0	39 504	7 276	64.9
Steuben, NY	1 468	13.8	1 230	4.0	1 298	243	182 843	3.9	65.9	30.2	155 924	7 990	66.9
Suffolk, NY	15 102	15.2	14 329	2.1	11 987	3 218	2 590 874	2.1	33.4	64.5	2 427 876	10 946	66.2
Sullivan, NY	914	13.2	588	4.1	803	167	116 754	3.5	42.3	54.2	106 136	9 256	66.6
Tioga, NY	629	16.0	581	2.6	568	88	75 888	3.3	64.3	32.4	69 215	6 856	64.3
Tompkins, NY	977	14.1	727	2.6	1 026	167	123 246	4.6	41.7	53.7	110 931	8 296	65.2
Ulster, NY	1 834	15.3	1 555	3.0	1 616	346	260 696	2.5	34.5	63.0	239 865	8 749	65.7
Warren, NY	753	15.0	698	2.5	612	114	101 042	2.9	38.7	58.5	89 174	8 026	68.0
Washington, NY	943	12.2	675	4.2	928	182	89 112	3.9	59.5	36.5	80 309	7 341	68.3
Wayne, NY	1 305	14.5	1 009	3.1	1 205	193	165 350	2.8	56.2	41.0	143 089	7 625	66.0
Westchester, NY	8 782	14.4	6 720	1.5	7 243	1 837	1 559 207	2.3	18.2	79.5	1 428 122	11 867	64.4
Wyoming, NY	406	15.2	386	2.0	265	47	48 390	3.1	64.6	32.3	44 344	7 125	68.6
Yates, NY	223	14.3	207	3.2	226	29	26 770	4.8	48.2	47.0	23 128	7 152	67.7
NORTH CAROLINA													
Alamance, NC	1 124	16.4	920	NA	906	36	94 221	6.1	61.0	32.9	80 149	4 473	61.0
Alexander, NC	277	18.0	271	NA	259	7	23 229	8.0	71.2	20.8	21 568	4 344	61.2
Alleghany, NC	115	12.8	89	NA	90	7	9 393	8.2	70.6	21.2	8 666	5 824	61.6
Anson, NC	327	13.6	246	NA	246	13	23 283	9.4	69.2	21.5	21 851	4 918	60.2
Ashe, NC	233	15.0	219	NA	197	9	18 695	8.5	71.0	20.4	17 656	5 032	61.4
Avery, NC	180	13.6	139	NA	157	9	14 511	8.3	67.9	23.8	13 278	5 391	59.1
Beaufort, NC	527	14.8	557	NA	408	22	41 649	9.6	67.7	22.7	38 613	4 870	61.3
Bertie, NC	245	16.3	201	NA	225	13	21 646	12.9	70.9	16.2	20 074	4 984	55.5
Bladen, NC	373	15.2	373	NA	349	12	29 785	12.5	68.5	19.0	28 445	5 099	60.1
Brunswick, NC	597	15.8	472	NA	429	16	48 378	7.3	61.2	31.6	43 445	4 817	60.1
Buncombe, NC	1 768	16.3	1 480	NA	1 647	41	162 759	6.7	59.2	34.1	145 847	5 055	62.4
Burke, NC	875	15.1	706	NA	796	24	67 912	5.8	65.1	29.1	60 207	4 628	63.6
Cabarrus, NC	1 208	16.4	997	NA	975	20	94 379	6.2	65.6	28.3	85 913	4 483	64.6
Caldwell, NC	746	15.9	595	NA	667	17	64 064	5.5	71.5	23.0	52 346	4 491	63.0
Camden, NC	89	13.5	66	NA	84	6	9 216	5.5	78.1	16.3	6 561	5 387	56.6
Carteret, NC	534	15.6	459	NA	463	16	43 157	6.9	61.5	31.6	38 558	4 701	62.8
Caswell, NC	218	15.8	181	NA	223	11	18 957	7.2	68.2	24.6	16 964	4 924	59.3
Catawba, NC	1 305	16.2	1 099	NA	1 074	32	106 233	5.3	64.3	30.4	97 166	4 679	65.3
Chatham, NC	395	16.8	308	NA	371	10	32 085	5.2	65.9	28.9	30 550	4 779	58.7
Cherokee, NC	234	14.8	222	NA	236	5	18 506	9.7	71.5	18.7	16 717	4 800	64.1
Chowan, NC	169	15.4	174	NA	169	11	14 810	7.8	68.9	23.4	13 462	5 095	59.8
Clay, NC	82	15.1	87	NA	61	3	6 823	6.1	78.5	15.4	6 328	5 191	61.3
Cleveland, NC	1 015	16.0	862	NA	907	29	86 343	7.7	62.5	29.8	75 746	4 766	62.8
Columbus, NC	668	15.6	624	NA	599	26	52 581	12.6	69.9	17.5	49 776	4 715	61.5
Craven, NC	922	16.0	674	NA	698	21	76 083	11.3	67.6	21.1	66 828	4 589	61.4
Cumberland, NC	3 086	16.6	2 621	NA	2 670	38	233 227	11.6	66.2	22.1	219 673	4 394	62.4
Currituck, NC	220	13.5	127	NA	175	19	17 631	5.2	59.9	34.9	15 960	5 372	60.1
Dare, NC	299	14.0	195	NA	240	9	24 669	4.5	55.0	40.5	21 443	5 415	60.0
Davidson, NC	1 440	16.0	1 245	NA	1 100	33	102 362	6.5	71.3	22.2	99 946	4 453	62.7

1. Bronx, New York, Queens, and Richmond Counties included with Kings County.

Table D-2. School and Student Characteristics by County

State/ County code	County	County type[1]	Population, 1996		Number of school districts, 1995–1996	Level of schools, 1995–1996				Level of students, 1995–1996				Characteristics of students, 1995–1996		
			Total persons	Percent age 5–17		Number of schools	Percent			Number of students	Percent			Percent with IEP[2]	Percent free-lunch eligible	Percent minority
							Primary	Middle	High		Primary	Middle	High			
			1	2	3	4	5	6	7	8	9	10	11	12	13	14
	NORTH CAROLINA— Con.															
37059	Davie, NC	2	30 243	18.5	1	9	55.6	33.3	11.1	4 832	43.4	29.9	26.7	12.9	13.1	11.7
37061	Duplin, NC	6	42 802	20.2	1	15	53.3	20.0	26.7	8 303	61.3	11.0	27.7	10.0	44.7	47.8
37063	Durham, NC	2	197 352	16.3	3	50	56.0	20.0	14.0	29 962	48.7	20.8	27.4	14.2	31.0	59.3
37065	Edgecombe, NC	3	56 166	21.1	1	15	53.3	20.0	20.0	8 033	49.2	22.2	27.9	12.5	44.7	60.9
37067	Forsyth, NC	2	284 207	16.5	1	58	56.9	22.4	17.2	40 895	50.9	21.8	26.5	12.1	26.9	41.2
37069	Franklin, NC	2	42 872	18.5	1	10	60.0	10.0	30.0	6 767	62.2	8.0	29.8	11.4	37.7	45.8
37071	Gaston, NC	0	182 623	19.0	1	53	62.3	22.6	13.2	29 334	56.7	23.3	19.8	13.2	24.5	21.2
37073	Gates, NC	8	9 911	19.2	1	6	33.3	50.0	16.7	1 947	32.7	40.3	27.1	11.4	37.6	46.8
37075	Graham, NC	9	7 616	19.0	1	3	33.3	33.3	33.3	1 250	56.7	15.6	27.7	16.2	38.4	11.6
37077	Granville, NC	6	41 622	18.1	1	12	58.3	25.0	16.7	7 141	45.4	27.7	26.9	11.6	32.3	43.9
37079	Greene, NC	8	17 660	19.6	1	4	25.0	50.0	25.0	2 862	30.3	41.8	28.0	18.0	49.4	60.7
37081	Guilford, NC	2	379 201	16.5	1	92	67.4	17.4	15.2	57 211	52.0	20.9	27.1	12.5	27.0	42.8
37083	Halifax, NC	4	57 183	20.7	3	23	60.9	21.7	13.0	11 017	49.5	20.3	24.1	11.1	55.4	72.7
37085	Harnett, NC	6	79 052	18.7	1	22	59.1	27.3	13.6	13 887	48.0	27.3	24.7	12.2	34.5	34.8
37087	Haywood, NC	6	50 387	15.8	1	15	60.0	20.0	20.0	7 401	50.1	23.0	26.9	12.8	25.6	3.1
37089	Henderson, NC	6	77 940	16.0	1	20	55.0	20.0	20.0	10 931	47.8	23.3	28.3	12.0	23.7	10.3
37091	Hertford, NC	6	22 447	20.6	1	6	50.0	33.3	16.7	4 382	40.0	32.8	27.2	9.6	61.0	75.7
37093	Hoke, NC	6	28 471	22.9	1	10	60.0	20.0	20.0	5 809	51.4	22.9	25.7	14.2	49.4	68.4
37095	Hyde, NC	9	5 413	20.4	1	4	50.0	—	25.0	760	48.4	—	40.0	15.4	57.8	48.2
37097	Iredell, NC	4	106 383	18.1	2	32	62.5	21.9	15.6	17 483	49.9	23.5	26.6	13.4	21.4	24.2
37099	Jackson, NC	7	29 668	15.8	1	6	66.7	—	16.7	3 586	63.4	—	25.4	14.2	28.8	9.9
37101	Johnston, NC	2	98 289	18.5	1	27	48.1	29.6	14.8	16 809	45.3	24.5	23.3	12.5	27.0	27.4
37103	Jones, NC	8	9 501	20.1	1	6	66.7	16.7	16.7	1 642	54.0	20.7	25.3	13.5	55.0	54.6
37105	Lee, NC	6	47 483	19.4	1	13	69.2	15.4	15.4	8 242	51.8	23.8	24.5	9.7	28.1	38.4
37107	Lenoir, NC	4	59 355	20.1	1	19	47.4	31.6	15.8	10 451	40.6	30.1	28.5	12.7	39.9	54.6
37109	Lincoln, NC	1	56 235	18.7	1	16	62.5	18.8	12.5	9 558	48.9	24.2	17.1	11.8	20.3	13.8
37111	McDowell, NC	6	38 057	18.3	1	11	72.7	18.2	9.1	6 151	56.0	23.8	20.1	11.3	22.6	6.5
37113	Macon, NC	7	27 114	15.0	1	11	63.6	9.1	9.1	3 741	38.2	20.9	24.6	13.6	26.4	2.6
37115	Madison, NC	3	18 242	16.9	1	8	75.0	12.5	12.5	2 552	45.8	23.7	30.5	14.3	37.3	0.8
37117	Martin, NC	6	26 438	20.2	1	13	53.8	15.4	30.8	5 027	55.3	14.5	30.2	13.2	44.2	57.8
37119	Mecklenburg, NC	0	597 589	17.4	1	126	61.9	23.0	11.9	89 544	54.1	22.3	21.1	9.7	29.5	46.5
37121	Mitchell, NC	9	14 719	16.7	1	7	57.1	28.6	14.3	2 347	41.6	30.8	27.6	13.8	40.1	1.4
37123	Montgomery, NC	7	24 144	19.9	1	8	50.0	25.0	25.0	4 278	47.2	24.7	28.1	13.4	39.2	42.6
37125	Moore, NC	6	68 483	17.3	1	18	61.1	22.2	11.1	10 329	52.9	19.7	19.2	12.8	30.4	30.8
37127	Nash, NC	3	87 991	19.3	1	27	59.3	25.9	14.8	17 867	52.3	28.9	18.8	11.1	39.9	57.8
37129	New Hanover, NC	3	143 513	17.3	1	30	66.7	20.0	13.3	21 180	49.3	22.8	27.9	11.9	26.9	31.7
37131	Northampton, NC	9	21 180	19.1	1	10	60.0	20.0	20.0	3 941	49.5	23.5	27.0	12.8	61.7	80.3
37133	Onslow, NC	3	144 533	17.1	1	28	50.0	28.6	21.4	20 489	47.7	25.2	27.0	9.8	29.4	31.4
37135	Orange, NC	2	108 795	14.3	2	19	57.9	26.3	10.5	13 627	49.8	22.9	27.0	13.2	16.3	27.0
37137	Pamlico, NC	9	12 188	18.2	1	4	50.0	25.0	25.0	2 099	43.7	28.2	28.1	14.8	36.6	35.6
37139	Pasquotank, NC	7	34 036	19.9	1	10	70.0	20.0	10.0	6 275	54.8	19.6	25.7	11.8	44.9	50.1
37141	Pender, NC	8	36 601	18.1	1	11	45.5	27.3	18.2	5 730	51.3	20.7	27.4	13.5	39.2	38.9
37143	Perquimans, NC	9	10 913	18.5	1	4	50.0	25.0	25.0	1 964	46.2	23.8	30.0	12.8	51.4	42.8
37145	Person, NC	6	32 793	18.1	1	11	72.7	18.2	9.1	5 523	49.8	22.8	27.4	13.6	31.1	38.5
37147	Pitt, NC	3	119 064	18.3	1	30	60.0	20.0	16.7	19 298	52.7	19.4	27.2	13.8	36.1	51.5
37149	Polk, NC	8	16 226	14.4	1	6	66.7	16.7	16.7	2 173	65.1	9.0	25.9	12.3	23.9	12.3
37151	Randolph, NC	2	117 455	18.0	2	30	63.3	20.0	16.7	19 208	54.1	20.9	25.0	13.6	19.6	11.4
37153	Richmond, NC	7	45 665	20.2	1	17	41.2	47.1	5.9	8 299	40.4	40.4	18.5	12.4	43.7	43.8
37155	Robeson, NC	4	113 169	23.0	1	41	56.1	26.8	17.1	23 482	49.4	26.2	24.4	12.9	59.4	76.7
37157	Rockingham, NC	4	89 575	17.8	1	25	64.0	20.0	16.0	14 343	50.3	22.6	26.8	16.7	25.6	27.5
37159	Rowan, NC	1	121 785	17.7	1	28	60.7	21.4	17.9	18 808	48.2	23.8	28.0	12.8	23.5	25.0
37161	Rutherford, NC	6	59 723	18.5	1	23	60.9	26.1	13.0	10 049	50.6	21.7	27.8	12.8	30.0	17.2
37163	Sampson, NC	6	50 675	20.3	2	19	52.6	21.1	26.3	9 715	53.4	18.4	28.2	14.2	41.1	47.0
37165	Scotland, NC	7	35 404	22.7	1	14	57.1	28.6	7.1	7 399	48.7	22.6	27.5	12.6	46.1	56.1
37167	Stanly, NC	6	54 850	18.3	2	19	73.7	5.3	21.1	9 376	64.9	5.3	29.8	14.3	22.9	20.0
37169	Stokes, NC	2	42 062	19.2	1	15	66.7	20.0	13.3	6 707	47.6	22.4	30.0	13.6	19.3	7.5
37171	Surry, NC	6	65 848	17.6	3	21	57.1	19.0	23.8	10 797	52.8	17.5	29.7	14.3	20.6	9.3
37173	Swain, NC	9	12 008	19.1	1	5	40.0	20.0	20.0	1 674	52.3	15.2	28.8	17.0	41.0	21.7
37175	Transylvania, NC	6	27 499	16.9	1	7	57.1	14.3	28.6	3 911	49.7	17.9	32.3	11.1	21.7	7.4
37177	Tyrrell, NC	9	3 820	21.1	1	2	50.0	—	—	807	46.0	—	—	14.9	51.2	51.2
37179	Union, NC	1	102 372	20.4	1	30	53.3	16.7	20.0	18 303	50.9	23.0	25.5	13.3	23.7	22.9
37181	Vance, NC	6	41 312	19.9	1	14	71.4	14.3	14.3	7 519	61.7	13.9	24.4	11.4	51.0	65.1
37183	Wake, NC	2	534 075	16.8	1	97	64.9	20.6	13.4	81 438	51.9	22.9	25.2	12.4	16.7	31.5
37185	Warren, NC	8	18 039	18.8	1	7	57.1	28.6	14.3	3 184	42.1	28.6	29.2	11.5	57.6	80.2
37187	Washington, NC	7	13 956	21.0	1	4	25.0	25.0	25.0	2 721	33.7	25.4	23.0	15.0	51.3	68.2
37189	Watauga, NC	7	40 357	13.4	1	9	88.9	—	11.1	4 882	70.9	—	29.1	13.3	19.5	2.6

1. County type code is from the Economic Research Service of the USDA. See notes and definitions at the end of this section.   2. IEP = Individual Education Program. See notes and definitions at the end of this section.

Table D-2.   School and Student Characteristics by County — Continued

County	Staff and students, 1995–1996						Revenues, fiscal 1995					Current expenditures, fiscal 1995		
	Number of teachers	Pupil/ teacher ratio	Number of graduates	Dropouts grades 9–12 (percent)	Local school non-teaching staff	Central admin. staff	Total revenue ($1000)	Percent of Revenue from			Amount	Amount per pupil	Percent for instruction
								Federal Gov't	State Gov't	Local Gov't			
	15	16	17	18	19	20	21	22	23	24	25	26	27
NORTH CAROLINA— Con.													
Davie, NC	307	15.7	281	NA	289	8	24 644	4.8	67.1	28.1	22 670	4 755	60.8
Duplin, NC	536	15.5	411	NA	416	14	47 614	8.7	71.4	20.0	35 434	4 292	62.6
Durham, NC	2 294	13.1	1 637	NA	2 726	72	160 507	5.5	55.8	38.7	155 746	5 589	58.8
Edgecombe, NC	509	15.8	486	NA	444	30	40 111	10.5	68.6	20.9	38 025	4 679	61.2
Forsyth, NC	2 939	13.9	2 163	NA	1 873	60	212 585	5.2	59.5	35.3	205 687	5 200	62.9
Franklin, NC	428	15.8	307	NA	331	14	32 535	9.8	67.7	22.5	29 963	4 528	59.8
Gaston, NC	1 808	16.2	1 460	NA	1 190	49	135 051	6.5	70.8	22.7	128 783	4 408	65.3
Gates, NC	123	15.8	110	NA	128	10	10 693	7.8	71.9	20.3	9 995	5 244	58.9
Graham, NC	97	12.9	78	NA	102	6	7 957	11.8	72.8	15.4	7 210	5 796	57.9
Granville, NC	440	16.2	318	NA	390	17	34 682	8.0	66.3	25.7	32 140	4 640	60.5
Greene, NC	187	15.3	157	NA	172	11	15 563	12.1	70.0	17.9	14 616	5 256	58.8
Guilford, NC	3 543	16.1	3 078	NA	3 234	52	318 460	5.4	58.6	36.0	297 907	5 350	61.1
Halifax, NC	700	15.7	513	NA	678	41	58 485	12.0	66.2	21.9	53 875	4 946	60.6
Harnett, NC	803	17.3	615	NA	690	19	68 615	7.5	64.7	27.8	57 153	4 290	64.0
Haywood, NC	490	15.1	377	NA	389	14	39 146	7.3	65.8	26.9	36 945	5 099	61.5
Henderson, NC	672	16.3	579	NA	520	21	54 504	5.6	63.0	31.4	48 801	4 579	64.9
Hertford, NC	265	16.5	228	NA	231	15	22 732	12.7	65.8	21.5	20 804	4 691	59.5
Hoke, NC	360	16.1	215	NA	324	13	25 929	12.4	73.8	13.7	25 225	4 422	61.2
Hyde, NC	73	10.4	53	NA	67	9	6 291	9.5	71.6	18.9	5 936	7 485	60.5
Iredell, NC	1 072	16.3	851	NA	857	26	87 176	5.5	64.0	30.5	79 046	4 635	62.0
Jackson, NC	243	14.8	169	NA	209	11	19 926	8.3	64.6	27.0	17 917	5 184	63.4
Johnston, NC	1 068	15.7	860	NA	929	17	83 968	5.5	67.9	26.6	72 642	4 517	62.0
Jones, NC	115	14.3	95	NA	100	7	9 577	11.7	72.1	16.2	9 047	5 501	54.5
Lee, NC	495	16.7	394	NA	447	14	41 446	7.8	62.5	29.8	36 500	4 499	62.9
Lenoir, NC	674	15.5	571	NA	569	16	55 049	10.0	68.2	21.8	49 878	4 799	62.9
Lincoln, NC	554	17.3	443	NA	455	18	45 245	5.7	67.8	26.6	40 606	4 445	63.8
McDowell, NC	370	16.6	332	NA	321	17	29 011	6.7	72.8	20.5	27 973	4 565	63.7
Macon, NC	255	14.7	192	NA	212	10	22 368	6.9	58.2	34.9	18 102	4 992	62.0
Madison, NC	186	13.7	157	NA	199	10	13 825	9.5	75.5	15.0	13 236	5 219	58.4
Martin, NC	378	13.3	335	NA	325	13	27 160	11.6	66.1	22.4	26 167	5 205	62.2
Mecklenburg, NC	5 248	17.1	4 055	NA	4 695	88	458 342	6.7	60.3	33.1	445 564	5 180	61.5
Mitchell, NC	151	15.5	124	NA	142	9	12 572	7.7	75.3	17.0	11 329	4 768	60.0
Montgomery, NC	275	15.6	229	NA	231	14	21 890	9.8	68.5	21.7	19 722	4 679	62.4
Moore, NC	653	15.8	545	NA	524	18	50 146	7.5	65.1	27.4	47 594	4 758	60.9
Nash, NC	1 101	16.2	896	NA	988	28	98 689	8.4	56.6	35.0	80 623	4 569	62.9
New Hanover, NC	1 361	15.6	1 168	NA	1 169	21	108 750	6.8	61.5	31.7	98 121	4 709	62.1
Northampton, NC	244	16.2	209	NA	206	11	21 112	12.7	66.1	21.3	18 637	4 723	57.4
Onslow, NC	1 169	17.5	1 024	NA	1 077	17	85 004	8.9	73.0	18.1	80 014	3 957	62.5
Orange, NC	924	14.7	704	NA	832	35	82 339	3.7	52.2	44.2	71 682	5 375	63.3
Pamlico, NC	149	14.1	140	NA	116	8	11 515	9.3	76.0	14.7	11 213	5 167	61.5
Pasquotank, NC	376	16.7	270	NA	265	18	31 629	9.1	66.5	24.4	28 670	4 600	60.6
Pender, NC	351	16.3	266	NA	313	12	26 966	9.3	67.5	23.3	25 645	4 741	59.0
Perquimans, NC	118	16.6	109	NA	126	10	11 757	11.5	70.4	18.1	10 664	5 474	56.2
Person, NC	377	14.6	285	NA	302	12	28 290	8.9	63.7	27.4	26 203	4 877	62.6
Pitt, NC	1 183	16.3	985	NA	1 006	31	91 537	9.0	67.6	23.5	86 808	4 536	62.3
Polk, NC	175	12.4	101	NA	120	10	14 077	5.3	62.2	32.5	11 825	5 647	62.2
Randolph, NC	1 143	16.8	966	NA	1 160	28	90 017	5.7	67.3	27.0	80 840	4 327	62.9
Richmond, NC	508	16.3	405	NA	404	13	41 076	9.6	69.7	20.8	37 185	4 500	63.8
Robeson, NC	1 443	16.3	1 185	NA	1 316	35	109 558	13.4	71.2	15.3	105 600	4 498	62.8
Rockingham, NC	881	16.3	809	NA	693	26	70 228	7.1	70.3	22.6	65 698	4 568	63.0
Rowan, NC	1 151	16.3	962	NA	1 016	18	84 552	6.5	72.0	21.5	82 103	4 499	63.9
Rutherford, NC	624	16.1	509	NA	627	16	58 298	7.3	58.4	34.4	47 111	4 708	63.4
Sampson, NC	599	16.2	594	NA	497	26	46 483	10.6	69.9	19.5	44 750	4 720	61.1
Scotland, NC	524	14.1	386	NA	415	18	37 413	10.1	66.1	23.7	36 123	4 905	61.9
Stanly, NC	559	16.8	491	NA	500	17	44 758	6.3	74.2	19.4	42 239	4 579	63.7
Stokes, NC	440	15.2	342	NA	326	11	33 126	5.5	67.7	26.8	31 054	4 707	60.6
Surry, NC	687	15.7	664	NA	575	24	54 426	6.2	67.9	25.9	50 386	4 720	62.4
Swain, NC	134	12.5	96	NA	99	10	10 212	15.1	69.0	16.0	9 138	5 462	62.1
Transylvania, NC	258	15.2	263	NA	189	10	20 919	6.8	62.4	30.8	18 627	4 688	61.8
Tyrrell, NC	60	13.5	36	NA	61	5	6 801	7.1	75.8	17.1	5 023	6 465	56.3
Union, NC	1 118	16.4	918	NA	938	33	87 142	5.3	65.6	29.1	78 755	4 477	62.7
Vance, NC	455	16.5	381	NA	563	20	40 139	9.8	61.5	28.7	34 960	4 762	59.7
Wake, NC	5 165	15.8	3 798	NA	3 867	88	479 473	3.6	49.9	46.4	357 563	4 648	61.9
Warren, NC	207	15.4	173	NA	163	15	17 764	13.2	67.0	19.8	16 034	5 139	57.1
Washington, NC	192	14.2	169	NA	138	9	15 639	9.5	73.5	17.0	13 847	5 110	63.0
Watauga, NC	334	14.6	273	NA	262	12	24 106	5.5	70.7	23.8	23 003	4 767	64.1

Items 15–27

Table D-2. School and Student Characteristics by County

State/County code	County	County type[1]	Population, 1996		Number of school districts, 1995–1996	Level of schools, 1995–1996				Level of students, 1995–1996				Characteristics of students, 1995–1996		
			Total persons	Percent age 5–17		Number of schools	Percent			Number of students	Percent			Percent with IEP[2]	Percent free-lunch eligible	Percent minority
							Primary	Middle	High		Primary	Middle	High			
			1	2	3	4	5	6	7	8	9	10	11	12	13	14
	NORTH CAROLINA— Con.															
37191	Wayne, NC	3	111 581	19.2	1	27	51.9	25.9	22.2	18 908	48.7	22.7	28.6	11.8	36.0	47.0
37193	Wilkes, NC	7	61 884	18.3	1	21	71.4	9.5	19.0	9 942	58.7	13.5	27.7	13.9	26.3	7.5
37195	Wilson, NC	4	67 809	20.3	1	23	60.9	26.1	13.0	12 174	47.8	25.0	27.2	12.5	42.1	57.4
37197	Yadkin, NC	2	34 161	16.9	1	10	80.0	—	20.0	5 296	74.2	—	25.8	14.5	18.6	10.4
37199	Yancey, NC	8	16 380	17.0	1	9	66.7	22.2	11.1	2 457	48.6	22.5	28.9	13.7	31.1	1.3
38000	**NORTH DAKOTA**															
38001	Adams, ND	9	2 841	18.8	2	3	66.7	—	33.3	526	66.2	—	33.8	9.9	21.7	1.0
38003	Barnes, ND	7	12 114	17.7	5	11	54.5	9.1	36.4	2 133	51.2	18.0	30.8	10.4	19.9	1.7
38005	Benson, ND	9	6 905	25.0	7	11	54.5	—	45.5	1 517	63.0	—	37.0	10.0	60.1	57.0
38007	Billings, ND	9	1 129	25.0	1	3	100.0	—	—	117	100.0	—	—	13.7	28.2	2.6
38009	Bottineau, ND	7	7 538	19.4	5	10	50.0	10.0	40.0	1 352	39.2	14.1	46.7	14.6	21.8	1.7
38011	Bowman, ND	9	3 303	21.0	3	6	50.0	—	50.0	758	55.3	—	44.7	7.3	22.8	0.7
38013	Burke, ND	9	2 469	19.4	3	6	50.0	—	50.0	487	43.3	—	56.7	11.5	23.6	1.4
38015	Burleigh, ND	3	65 681	20.1	12	37	75.7	10.8	13.5	11 393	53.3	23.3	23.4	9.4	13.3	6.7
38017	Cass, ND	3	113 343	17.6	9	46	63.0	15.2	21.7	18 490	52.3	21.9	25.6	9.1	11.8	5.2
38019	Cavalier, ND	9	5 270	19.2	5	9	44.4	11.1	44.4	930	48.9	10.9	40.2	9.6	18.2	1.5
38021	Dickey, ND	9	5 676	18.8	2	5	60.0	—	40.0	1 008	51.4	—	48.6	11.2	19.4	4.6
38023	Divide, ND	9	2 523	16.9	1	2	50.0	—	50.0	460	48.0	—	52.0	5.0	18.0	1.5
38025	Dunn, ND	9	3 751	22.3	4	6	66.7	—	33.3	656	58.5	—	41.5	7.9	24.8	12.2
38027	Eddy, ND	9	2 876	18.9	2	4	50.0	—	50.0	613	51.1	—	48.9	13.2	25.9	13.9
38029	Emmons, ND	8	4 443	19.0	5	8	62.5	—	37.5	806	55.8	—	44.2	13.8	30.0	0.4
38031	Foster, ND	9	3 866	19.9	1	2	50.0	—	50.0	719	64.5	—	35.5	8.9	17.1	2.5
38033	Golden Valley, ND	9	1 932	23.6	2	3	66.7	—	33.3	485	43.5	—	56.5	6.4	42.9	3.7
38035	Grand Forks, ND	3	71 450	17.7	7	31	64.5	9.7	22.6	12 248	56.5	9.8	30.6	10.5	16.2	9.6
38037	Grant, ND	8	3 114	19.7	3	6	50.0	16.7	33.3	472	53.2	10.8	36.0	6.4	37.1	5.1
38039	Griggs, ND	9	2 984	18.9	3	5	40.0	20.0	40.0	694	35.9	11.7	52.4	6.5	26.1	1.6
38041	Hettinger, ND	9	2 982	18.8	3	6	50.0	—	50.0	669	48.1	—	51.9	9.3	32.7	1.0
38043	Kidder, ND	8	2 997	21.1	5	8	50.0	—	50.0	618	48.7	—	51.3	6.6	29.0	1.1
38045	La Moure, ND	9	4 970	20.4	5	11	54.5	—	45.5	1 184	46.8	—	53.2	6.1	25.1	0.9
38047	Logan, ND	9	2 443	18.4	2	5	60.0	—	40.0	526	53.4	—	46.6	9.7	19.2	0.8
38049	McHenry, ND	9	6 161	20.5	6	12	50.0	—	50.0	1 317	52.1	—	47.9	9.9	28.9	2.1
38051	McIntosh, ND	9	3 642	15.5	4	8	50.0	—	50.0	672	47.3	—	52.7	7.1	29.0	0.9
38053	McKenzie, ND	9	5 851	23.6	7	13	69.2	7.7	23.1	1 203	55.4	4.2	40.3	10.7	30.7	23.4
38055	McLean, ND	8	9 897	22.2	8	16	50.0	—	50.0	2 357	46.9	—	53.1	9.5	22.8	11.2
38057	Mercer, ND	7	9 548	23.2	4	10	40.0	20.0	40.0	2 292	39.5	22.3	38.2	10.7	9.9	5.0
38059	Morton, ND	3	24 422	22.7	9	19	63.2	5.3	31.6	5 194	50.0	12.6	37.4	10.9	20.8	4.2
38061	Mountrail, ND	9	6 753	22.8	4	9	44.4	11.1	44.4	1 703	54.6	7.3	38.1	13.3	33.5	43.9
38063	Nelson, ND	8	3 905	17.4	2	7	57.1	14.3	28.6	878	49.4	17.9	32.7	11.3	27.6	0.6
38065	Oliver, ND	8	2 234	25.4	1	2	50.0	—	50.0	412	46.1	—	53.9	12.1	10.4	2.9
38067	Pembina, ND	9	8 741	20.6	7	15	46.7	6.7	46.7	2 046	55.9	8.1	36.0	8.9	16.1	6.5
38069	Pierce, ND	7	4 718	19.7	2	4	50.0	—	50.0	868	42.9	—	57.1	9.8	21.9	2.0
38071	Ramsey, ND	7	12 455	19.1	4	11	54.5	9.1	36.4	2 543	36.8	29.0	34.2	10.7	30.0	19.0
38073	Ransom, ND	8	5 794	19.4	5	10	50.0	20.0	30.0	1 293	37.2	28.7	34.1	10.4	12.9	2.3
38075	Renville, ND	9	2 843	21.2	3	6	50.0	—	50.0	786	45.4	—	54.6	16.0	21.0	2.9
38077	Richland, ND	6	18 162	19.4	8	16	50.0	12.5	37.5	3 451	45.3	17.4	37.3	11.0	16.5	7.3
38079	Rolette, ND	9	14 029	27.9	6	12	50.0	8.3	41.7	3 433	54.0	10.6	35.3	7.5	38.1	77.8
38081	Sargent, ND	9	4 441	20.2	3	7	57.1	—	42.9	885	53.9	—	46.1	10.3	11.9	2.7
38083	Sheridan, ND	9	1 859	17.3	2	4	50.0	—	50.0	239	51.0	—	49.0	14.2	29.3	1.7
38085	Sioux, ND	9	4 095	31.6	4	8	50.0	—	37.5	1 163	52.1	—	37.1	14.3	76.4	93.7
38087	Slope, ND	9	827	23.5	3	3	100.0	—	—	38	100.0	—	—	7.9	—	2.6
38089	Stark, ND	7	22 694	21.6	5	14	64.3	7.1	28.6	4 065	50.0	13.0	36.9	8.6	23.1	2.4
38091	Steele, ND	8	2 277	19.5	2	4	50.0	—	50.0	387	53.7	—	46.3	7.0	19.9	0.3
38093	Stutsman, ND	7	21 338	19.0	6	18	61.1	5.6	33.3	3 541	46.3	14.8	38.9	13.0	20.7	2.9
38095	Towner, ND	9	3 209	19.1	4	6	50.0	—	50.0	645	54.7	—	45.3	9.3	25.6	4.0
38097	Traill, ND	8	8 706	18.9	4	10	50.0	10.0	40.0	1 846	47.8	10.2	42.0	5.7	12.8	4.4
38099	Walsh, ND	6	12 799	19.9	8	17	52.9	11.8	35.3	2 503	41.6	22.9	35.4	11.1	21.9	9.1
38101	Ward, ND	5	59 734	19.5	11	36	63.9	8.3	22.2	10 632	53.3	9.7	20.4	11.6	17.5	8.6
38103	Wells, ND	9	5 271	17.9	5	9	55.6	—	44.4	1 095	63.4	—	36.6	9.9	21.6	1.0
38105	Williams, ND	7	20 534	22.1	7	23	65.2	8.7	26.1	4 330	49.4	13.6	37.0	10.1	18.8	10.3
39000	**OHIO**															
39001	Adams, OH	6	28 093	21.8	1	10	40.0	10.0	50.0	5 460	46.7	7.7	45.7	2.5	35.7	0.8
39003	Allen, OH	3	108 440	19.8	9	40	50.0	25.0	25.0	19 596	44.9	23.4	31.7	4.1	20.7	18.8
39005	Ashland, OH	4	51 372	20.0	4	21	52.4	23.8	23.8	8 051	43.6	23.9	32.5	2.8	14.5	1.7
39007	Ashtabula, OH	1	102 207	20.0	7	42	64.3	16.7	19.0	18 644	52.9	15.8	31.3	3.6	27.5	7.0

1. County type code is from the Economic Research Service of the USDA. See notes and definitions at the end of this section.   2. IEP = Individual Education Program. See notes and definitions at the end of this section.

Table D-2. School and Student Characteristics by County — Continued

County	Staff and students, 1995–1996						Revenues, fiscal 1995				Current expenditures, fiscal 1995		
	Number of teachers	Pupil/ teacher ratio	Number of graduates	Dropouts grades 9–12 (percent)	Local school non-teaching staff	Central admin. staff	Total revenue ($1000)	Percent of Revenue from			Amount	Amount per pupil	Percent for instruction
								Federal Gov't	State Gov't	Local Gov't			
	15	16	17	18	19	20	21	22	23	24	25	26	27
NORTH CAROLINA— Con.													
Wayne, NC	1 139	16.6	992	NA	1 031	21	86 778	11.3	70.6	18.1	82 786	4 471	63.3
Wilkes, NC	604	16.5	522	NA	531	15	55 084	6.1	62.0	31.8	46 450	4 698	62.3
Wilson, NC	776	15.7	601	NA	679	28	60 548	10.2	64.7	25.0	55 956	4 662	65.0
Yadkin, NC	315	16.8	253	NA	316	9	26 755	6.4	65.5	28.1	23 765	4 629	59.5
Yancey, NC	170	14.5	145	NA	159	7	13 588	8.5	73.0	18.4	12 809	5 291	59.1
NORTH DAKOTA													
Adams, ND	37	14.2	35	0.6	29	5	3 009	5.1	39.3	55.6	2 490	4 569	55.3
Barnes, ND	119	18.0	164	1.5	78	10	11 584	7.1	43.0	49.9	9 944	4 589	63.2
Benson, ND	117	13.0	63	11.2	105	21	6 606	21.7	43.3	35.0	5 801	5 226	58.4
Billings, ND	17	6.9	—	NA	13	1	1 466	6.0	5.3	88.7	1 511	11 992	49.7
Bottineau, ND	94	14.5	100	1.2	78	9	8 716	7.0	40.1	52.9	7 305	5 218	60.0
Bowman, ND	53	14.3	58	0.4	41	5	4 207	6.3	40.0	53.8	3 870	5 079	61.0
Burke, ND	45	10.9	46	0.5	29	5	3 058	6.9	43.1	50.0	2 821	5 510	60.5
Burleigh, ND	608	18.7	692	2.3	513	33	50 783	8.3	42.6	49.1	44 380	3 943	65.8
Cass, ND	1 036	17.9	1 085	3.0	706	65	97 938	4.9	35.6	59.5	79 492	4 349	65.1
Cavalier, ND	74	12.5	80	1.2	48	7	5 577	5.4	36.7	58.0	5 082	5 494	55.1
Dickey, ND	57	17.6	72	0.9	42	5	5 293	6.2	41.7	52.1	4 390	4 408	57.4
Divide, ND	30	15.5	35	NA	24	3	2 332	5.4	40.1	54.5	2 176	4 730	53.8
Dunn, ND	56	11.8	41	0.5	43	6	4 960	28.6	32.5	38.9	4 118	6 092	56.7
Eddy, ND	39	15.9	41	1.0	17	4	3 196	9.4	43.6	47.1	3 008	5 090	58.3
Emmons, ND	59	13.7	70	0.4	53	8	4 896	8.4	40.4	51.1	4 380	5 348	56.7
Foster, ND	42	17.1	50	1.5	20	2	3 030	0.1	45.1	40.0	2 070	5 600	61.1
Golden Valley, ND	38	12.7	31	0.5	32	5	2 836	6.4	41.4	52.2	2 788	5 382	52.8
Grand Forks, ND	714	17.2	752	1.3	486	41	66 865	13.7	35.7	50.6	47 506	3 876	67.0
Grant, ND	45	10.6	35	1.4	26	7	3 160	7.0	45.4	47.6	2 967	5 818	52.9
Griggs, ND	51	13.7	55	0.4	33	5	4 428	5.5	36.2	58.3	3 746	5 146	53.2
Hettinger, ND	49	13.6	56	NA	48	4	4 165	8.2	40.9	50.9	3 883	5 874	56.9
Kidder, ND	55	11.3	50	1.8	36	8	4 467	7.0	35.4	57.6	3 502	5 446	56.2
La Moure, ND	82	14.4	86	0.2	54	10	7 883	5.3	33.5	61.2	5 624	4 698	56.8
Logan, ND	44	11.9	45	0.6	20	5	2 901	9.1	47.2	43.7	2 548	5 275	56.4
McHenry, ND	91	14.4	107	NA	62	10	7 162	11.1	43.4	45.5	6 022	4 474	56.5
McIntosh, ND	48	14.1	51	0.5	36	6	3 635	8.6	40.4	50.9	3 485	5 233	57.8
McKenzie, ND	106	11.4	57	1.2	103	14	10 736	31.1	27.2	41.8	8 731	7 151	54.3
McLean, ND	160	14.0	191	1.2	112	24	11 722	7.1	46.9	46.0	10 335	4 239	56.4
Mercer, ND	136	16.9	153	0.7	85	10	14 544	3.5	33.9	62.6	10 319	4 382	58.4
Morton, ND	273	19.1	371	4.2	260	20	22 583	8.5	50.2	41.3	19 785	3 903	60.7
Mountrail, ND	122	13.9	116	4.4	95	12	8 464	22.6	42.9	34.5	7 735	4 518	60.2
Nelson, ND	58	15.2	74	0.3	50	5	4 948	6.1	38.5	55.4	4 650	5 272	53.6
Oliver, ND	24	17.5	28	0.6	20	3	1 934	4.9	45.0	50.1	1 814	4 446	59.2
Pembina, ND	141	14.6	123	0.8	84	13	12 251	5.2	41.5	53.4	9 836	4 903	61.3
Pierce, ND	62	14.0	77	0.3	35	2	4 242	5.9	46.7	47.4	3 557	4 056	60.4
Ramsey, ND	166	15.3	183	1.6	151	17	14 018	10.4	43.7	46.0	11 710	4 647	57.5
Ransom, ND	80	16.1	95	0.5	51	7	5 619	4.6	44.3	51.1	5 105	4 071	57.1
Renville, ND	58	13.5	69	0.4	44	6	4 094	7.8	44.8	47.3	3 700	4 568	55.6
Richland, ND	199	17.4	194	2.3	189	20	17 781	5.7	43.0	51.3	15 173	4 620	62.9
Rolette, ND	272	12.6	170	8.7	248	28	23 475	52.2	30.5	17.4	15 990	4 926	61.1
Sargent, ND	55	16.2	62	NA	34	6	4 091	3.3	41.4	55.3	3 642	4 425	55.8
Sheridan, ND	26	9.2	16	NA	17	3	1 551	6.1	44.4	49.5	1 538	5 717	61.7
Sioux, ND	108	10.8	60	8.0	85	15	4 735	46.6	41.3	12.1	4 410	7 362	62.1
Slope, ND	4	9.5	—	NA	3	1	425	23.5	33.6	42.8	261	6 366	60.9
Stark, ND	196	20.7	292	1.9	172	17	18 239	10.7	48.0	41.3	16 404	3 984	62.6
Steele, ND	35	11.2	31	0.9	17	2	2 409	3.5	34.5	62.1	2 061	5 326	54.9
Stutsman, ND	218	16.2	251	2.7	166	18	17 888	6.6	49.1	44.3	15 583	4 246	63.9
Towner, ND	48	13.4	51	1.5	33	5	3 447	6.1	40.5	53.4	3 096	4 734	57.3
Traill, ND	116	16.0	127	0.5	65	11	10 680	4.0	37.3	58.7	8 856	4 795	58.1
Walsh, ND	149	16.8	187	1.4	115	13	15 674	8.0	40.8	51.2	13 027	5 115	63.5
Ward, ND	640	16.6	655	4.3	440	26	53 424	16.0	42.6	41.4	44 482	4 259	59.3
Wells, ND	77	14.3	63	0.6	54	9	6 141	8.7	41.0	50.3	5 624	5 188	54.9
Williams, ND	276	15.7	284	4.1	166	18	22 958	10.4	42.2	47.4	20 676	4 732	60.6
OHIO													
Adams, OH	347	15.8	178	5.0	234	26	26 467	8.6	39.4	52.0	24 864	4 646	57.4
Allen, OH	1 018	19.2	1 093	6.9	761	121	111 094	8.1	43.1	48.8	106 651	5 393	58.4
Ashland, OH	417	19.3	561	4.0	288	35	49 432	4.6	37.1	58.3	43 708	5 364	63.5
Ashtabula, OH	913	20.4	1 090	7.2	731	102	98 193	7.5	49.4	43.2	93 106	5 042	60.2

Table D-2. School and Student Characteristics by County

State/County code	County	County type[1]	Population, 1996		Number of school districts, 1995–1996	Level of schools, 1995–1996				Level of students, 1995–1996				Characteristics of students, 1995–1996		
			Total persons	Percent age 5–17		Number of schools	Percent			Number of students	Percent			Percent with IEP[2]	Percent free-lunch eligible	Percent minority
							Primary	Middle	High		Primary	Middle	High			
			1	2	3	4	5	6	7	8	9	10	11	12	13	14
	OHIO—Con.															
39009	Athens, OH	4	61 162	15.4	5	23	52.2	26.1	21.7	9 587	48.2	20.7	31.1	3.2	21.2	3.9
39011	Auglaize, OH	3	47 059	21.2	6	21	52.4	14.3	28.6	9 445	47.2	16.8	34.1	3.9	9.0	1.3
39013	Belmont, OH	3	70 022	17.7	7	31	51.6	25.8	19.4	10 278	38.8	24.7	31.6	5.0	19.4	3.3
39015	Brown, OH	1	39 358	21.2	5	16	50.0	18.8	25.0	8 085	50.6	14.5	31.4	2.7	21.8	1.2
39017	Butler, OH	0	323 579	19.0	9	79	65.8	19.0	13.9	53 414	51.1	24.7	24.0	3.6	15.1	8.0
39019	Carroll, OH	2	28 522	20.4	2	10	60.0	20.0	20.0	4 139	48.6	14.9	36.5	4.7	21.1	1.3
39021	Champaign, OH	6	37 910	19.5	5	16	50.0	18.8	31.3	7 531	49.9	14.3	35.8	3.4	11.2	3.8
39023	Clark, OH	2	147 472	18.8	7	49	57.1	18.4	20.4	25 991	52.4	18.0	28.7	3.3	23.4	13.0
39025	Clermont, OH	0	169 670	21.2	9	44	50.0	22.7	22.7	28 911	45.3	22.7	31.9	4.0	13.2	1.8
39027	Clinton, OH	6	38 645	20.1	4	17	58.8	17.6	23.5	8 430	53.2	17.5	29.3	2.4	19.5	2.9
39029	Columbiana, OH	2	111 406	19.6	11	41	51.2	22.0	24.4	18 811	38.3	21.4	31.6	3.6	17.9	2.3
39031	Coshocton, OH	6	36 131	20.0	3	16	75.0	6.3	18.8	6 656	57.4	7.0	35.5	4.4	16.5	2.3
39033	Crawford, OH	3	47 290	19.4	6	28	57.1	21.4	21.4	8 589	41.9	22.4	35.8	2.7	20.0	1.8
39035	Cuyahoga, OH	0	1 401 552	17.0	31	344	61.9	18.9	14.2	200 683	48.3	21.5	28.1	4.9	6.2	45.5
39037	Darke, OH	6	54 259	20.3	7	25	48.0	24.0	28.0	9 711	45.0	18.7	36.3	3.4	11.9	1.4
39039	Defiance, OH	4	40 059	21.3	5	20	60.0	15.0	25.0	7 721	46.1	17.0	36.9	4.7	9.0	11.9
39041	Delaware, OH	1	83 245	20.1	4	19	57.9	21.1	21.1	12 404	48.6	22.9	28.5	2.9	7.9	2.9
39043	Erie, OH	4	78 913	19.2	7	31	51.6	25.8	19.4	14 677	43.6	24.1	32.2	4.4	19.9	15.2
39045	Fairfield, OH	1	119 182	20.0	8	40	52.5	27.5	20.0	20 998	47.5	24.5	28.1	2.4	11.8	2.2
39047	Fayette, OH	6	28 395	19.3	2	16	68.8	18.8	12.5	5 447	55.7	14.3	30.0	4.3	10.8	2.4
39049	Franklin, OH	0	1 013 724	17.3	16	296	57.4	17.9	13.5	160 454	46.9	19.6	25.0	2.8	4.6	28.0
39051	Fulton, OH	2	41 180	21.7	7	24	45.8	25.0	29.2	9 434	43.9	24.3	31.8	5.0	11.0	7.0
39053	Gallia, OH	6	32 820	19.8	2	11	72.7	9.1	9.1	5 763	58.2	4.4	15.8	4.0	31.9	4.3
39055	Geauga, OH	1	86 054	20.6	7	33	51.5	12.1	21.2	12 506	49.1	17.3	33.0	3.7	5.4	3.0
39057	Greene, OH	2	139 936	18.9	7	39	61.5	17.9	17.9	24 301	52.4	21.0	26.5	4.0	11.8	9.5
39059	Guernsey, OH	7	40 509	19.8	3	17	70.6	11.8	17.6	6 528	53.2	15.3	31.6	5.0	14.7	3.2
39061	Hamilton, OH	0	857 616	18.4	22	208	66.8	15.4	13.5	129 680	53.4	15.7	25.8	4.0	5.6	37.1
39063	Hancock, OH	4	68 562	19.4	8	31	54.8	19.4	25.8	11 627	46.1	18.8	35.1	4.8	10.5	5.6
39065	Hardin, OH	6	31 629	18.9	6	21	57.1	14.3	28.6	6 354	48.5	15.0	36.4	3.5	13.6	1.1
39067	Harrison, OH	6	16 001	19.4	2	11	54.5	9.1	36.4	3 069	47.4	2.9	49.8	6.3	29.1	4.0
39069	Henry, OH	6	29 901	21.2	4	13	53.8	15.4	23.1	5 418	46.3	14.0	32.8	3.6	9.1	9.1
39071	Highland, OH	6	39 388	20.2	5	20	65.0	10.0	25.0	8 096	52.8	9.2	38.1	2.4	17.3	2.4
39073	Hocking, OH	6	28 413	19.4	1	10	80.0	10.0	10.0	4 188	45.1	24.6	30.3	2.7	23.1	1.1
39075	Holmes, OH	7	36 786	25.1	2	17	70.6	11.8	11.8	4 811	58.4	13.3	24.8	4.2	14.4	0.5
39077	Huron, OH	4	59 563	21.2	7	33	63.6	15.2	21.2	11 904	52.4	13.2	34.4	4.4	17.0	5.1
39079	Jackson, OH	7	32 352	20.5	3	17	58.8	23.5	11.8	6 104	40.6	25.4	24.6	3.5	12.1	0.8
39081	Jefferson, OH	3	77 037	17.8	5	32	62.5	21.9	9.4	12 453	47.9	20.8	15.8	4.7	23.4	9.2
39083	Knox, OH	6	51 702	18.5	5	18	61.1	11.1	27.8	8 263	44.0	18.4	37.6	3.2	14.1	1.4
39085	Lake, OH	0	223 301	18.1	9	67	55.2	16.4	16.4	35 397	47.5	21.3	29.1	4.4	4.1	3.8
39087	Lawrence, OH	2	64 258	20.4	7	27	51.9	22.2	25.9	12 099	48.0	20.6	31.4	3.2	34.2	3.2
39089	Licking, OH	0	137 584	19.1	10	57	56.1	26.3	17.5	23 847	46.8	23.6	29.6	2.8	15.3	2.8
39091	Logan, OH	6	45 606	20.3	4	17	52.9	17.6	23.5	7 579	44.0	21.1	34.7	2.7	16.6	3.7
39093	Lorain, OH	0	281 231	20.1	14	97	51.5	20.6	18.6	46 044	46.2	21.1	31.7	4.1	20.7	19.8
39095	Lucas, OH	2	452 691	18.8	8	113	68.1	14.2	15.0	69 337	54.9	14.9	28.4	4.2	33.2	31.4
39097	Madison, OH	1	41 184	17.6	4	20	60.0	20.0	20.0	7 012	47.6	22.7	29.7	3.2	13.3	3.9
39099	Mahoning, OH	2	260 107	18.1	14	85	54.1	21.2	21.2	40 988	42.7	23.1	32.3	4.4	31.1	25.3
39101	Marion, OH	4	65 323	19.1	5	30	56.7	26.7	16.7	12 189	48.8	21.2	29.9	3.3	3.6	5.5
39103	Medina, OH	1	138 943	21.1	7	47	63.8	17.0	14.9	26 621	51.6	18.9	29.4	4.0	6.5	1.9
39105	Meigs, OH	6	23 938	20.2	3	18	72.2	—	16.7	4 194	50.2	—	34.3	3.8	45.3	1.1
39107	Mercer, OH	7	40 890	22.4	6	22	50.0	22.7	27.3	10 055	51.5	15.8	32.6	4.7	3.5	1.0
39109	Miami, OH	2	96 941	19.6	9	42	50.0	23.8	21.4	17 990	47.8	19.9	31.8	3.1	12.0	4.2
39111	Monroe, OH	6	15 268	19.3	1	10	60.0	—	40.0	3 139	61.7	—	38.3	2.5	36.6	0.2
39113	Montgomery, OH	2	566 312	17.6	16	153	64.7	19.0	12.4	87 150	51.9	20.6	25.6	4.1	8.4	30.4
39115	Morgan, OH	8	14 599	21.5	1	8	75.0	12.5	12.5	2 702	47.7	22.2	30.1	3.6	33.2	5.8
39117	Morrow, OH	6	30 481	21.6	4	15	46.7	20.0	26.7	5 541	44.8	14.6	35.4	2.7	17.1	0.7
39119	Muskingum, OH	4	84 349	19.6	6	38	60.5	23.7	15.8	16 552	46.4	23.6	30.0	3.5	9.5	5.7
39121	Noble, OH	8	12 134	21.2	2	4	50.0	—	50.0	2 559	69.8	—	30.2	5.3	23.6	0.1
39123	Ottawa, OH	6	40 535	18.6	6	22	63.6	13.6	22.7	6 808	48.1	17.8	34.1	4.5	12.4	5.9
39125	Paulding, OH	6	20 344	22.2	3	9	55.6	11.1	33.3	4 251	49.9	10.4	39.7	5.7	4.2	3.9
39127	Perry, OH	6	33 834	21.5	4	14	50.0	21.4	21.4	6 687	48.2	20.5	20.3	2.9	28.3	0.6
39129	Pickaway, OH	1	52 727	17.4	4	22	68.2	13.6	18.2	9 397	55.3	14.5	30.1	2.1	17.8	1.1
39131	Pike, OH	7	27 156	21.5	4	12	41.7	25.0	25.0	5 776	47.8	20.6	23.1	3.8	37.5	1.6
39133	Portage, OH	2	149 571	18.3	11	50	54.0	22.0	24.0	24 358	45.1	23.0	32.0	3.5	15.7	4.5
39135	Preble, OH	6	42 633	20.4	6	16	37.5	25.0	25.0	8 261	36.8	21.3	26.1	2.4	14.2	0.6
39137	Putnam, OH	6	35 199	23.0	9	23	47.8	13.0	39.1	7 645	51.6	7.9	40.6	3.7	7.8	5.5
39139	Richland, OH	3	128 151	19.0	9	49	57.1	20.4	18.4	22 617	47.8	22.8	26.7	2.7	7.3	12.0

1. County type code is from the Economic Research Service of the USDA. See notes and definitions at the end of this section.   2. IEP = Individual Education Program. See notes and definitions at the end of this section.

OH (Athens, OH)–OH (Richland, OH)

Table D-2. School and Student Characteristics by County — Continued

County	Staff and students, 1995–1996						Revenues, fiscal 1995				Current expenditures, fiscal 1995		
	Number of teachers	Pupil/ teacher ratio	Number of graduates	Dropouts grades 9–12 (percent)	Local school non-teaching staff	Central admin. staff	Total revenue ($1000)	Percent of Revenue from			Amount	Amount per pupil	Percent for instruction
								Federal Gov't	State Gov't	Local Gov't			
	15	16	17	18	19	20	21	22	23	24	25	26	27
OHIO—Con.													
Athens, OH	536	17.9	550	5.1	405	61	58 221	8.6	52.3	39.1	54 792	5 705	56.9
Auglaize, OH	433	21.8	602	2.3	349	52	43 783	4.6	43.9	51.5	39 425	4 238	61.8
Belmont, OH	591	17.4	804	2.5	429	74	56 264	7.7	51.6	40.7	52 938	5 051	61.3
Brown, OH	397	20.4	452	6.1	346	34	43 638	5.2	57.4	37.4	36 536	4 576	57.8
Butler, OH	2 851	18.7	2 728	5.8	2 299	317	295 308	5.3	39.7	55.0	268 735	5 080	59.5
Carroll, OH	193	21.5	303	1.7	126	22	17 018	6.1	56.2	37.7	16 784	4 089	60.3
Champaign, OH	411	18.3	419	5.7	305	45	36 111	3.7	46.7	49.6	33 661	4 480	59.8
Clark, OH	1 379	18.8	1 538	8.2	1 032	145	138 493	7.1	49.5	43.5	131 449	5 019	58.5
Clermont, OH	1 471	19.7	1 502	6.0	1 024	118	162 472	3.8	40.2	56.0	134 212	4 671	57.4
Clinton, OH	419	20.1	502	2.9	315	43	43 591	6.1	50.6	43.4	37 752	4 536	58.3
Columbiana, OH	966	19.5	1 523	3.7	761	116	117 514	6.0	49.8	44.2	98 528	5 236	59.3
Coshocton, OH	325	20.5	406	4.2	321	33	35 855	5.5	35.4	59.1	33 876	5 113	57.7
Crawford, OH	477	18.0	590	5.4	448	66	46 559	4.8	43.4	51.8	43 988	5 111	58.0
Cuyahoga, OH	12 018	16.7	7 285	6.7	9 883	1 617	1 529 181	6.3	33.8	59.9	1 380 135	6 953	57.5
Darke, OH	565	17.2	532	3.7	343	51	47 137	4.2	50.1	45.7	45 582	4 641	61.0
Defiance, OH	406	19.0	532	5.7	271	34	37 717	3.6	44.1	52.3	36 215	4 684	61.5
Delaware, OH	700	17.7	662	4.0	538	56	74 970	2.3	30.6	67.1	65 263	5 509	59.6
Erie, OH	831	17.7	905	4.4	626	103	106 337	4.3	32.4	63.3	97 306	6 696	56.8
Fairfield, OH	1 110	18.9	1 234	3.3	728	135	112 530	3.2	43.4	53.3	103 933	5 069	59.3
Fayette, OH	285	19.1	345	2.8	212	29	25 327	6.5	50.3	43.2	23 421	4 272	56.7
Franklin, OH	8 939	17.9	7 646	8.2	6 612	1 075	1 093 217	5.5	29.8	64.7	949 716	5 922	56.8
Fulton, OH	453	20.8	577	4.1	355	50	48 206	2.9	41.6	55.5	44 691	4 853	58.5
Gallia, OH	294	19.6	303	5.1	220	24	33 396	10.1	40.5	49.5	30 969	5 394	60.7
Geauga, OH	686	18.2	702	3.1	553	90	81 785	2.4	29.3	68.3	72 570	5 938	55.9
Greene, OH	1 260	19.3	1 474	5.1	964	147	134 267	5.0	41.4	53.5	127 475	5 274	60.0
Guernsey, OH	360	18.1	367	6.1	309	43	37 025	7.3	46.2	46.5	29 731	4 508	58.3
Hamilton, OH	6 950	18.7	3 730	2.8	5 046	935	882 426	7.4	30.9	61.6	801 018	6 194	60.0
Hancock, OH	676	17.2	693	3.8	515	68	68 318	3.1	33.5	63.4	61 861	5 403	59.6
Hardin, OH	326	19.5	430	2.6	281	30	30 478	6.1	49.4	44.4	28 934	4 537	61.3
Harrison, OH	192	16.0	261	1.9	147	18	16 357	7.7	43.9	48.4	14 666	4 742	58.3
Henry, OH	278	19.5	338	4.9	210	35	43 466	11.7	38.4	49.9	38 531	7 157	53.5
Highland, OH	390	20.7	470	4.7	301	41	36 534	6.1	61.0	33.0	33 354	4 162	57.3
Hocking, OH	171	24.5	308	4.3	177	22	19 646	7.0	49.3	43.8	16 633	4 065	56.3
Holmes, OH	279	17.2	285	2.7	200	15	23 914	7.9	40.3	51.9	20 887	4 338	59.0
Huron, OH	581	20.5	736	3.7	400	72	59 115	4.8	47.6	47.6	54 855	4 636	59.4
Jackson, OH	285	21.4	383	3.9	231	43	28 838	10.1	58.0	31.9	27 217	4 518	59.7
Jefferson, OH	675	18.5	938	2.9	523	70	73 239	7.6	40.5	51.9	65 545	5 143	61.0
Knox, OH	427	19.3	561	3.8	298	51	47 968	5.8	42.0	52.2	43 905	5 323	59.2
Lake, OH	1 901	18.6	2 094	4.2	1 520	292	247 881	2.8	26.2	71.0	229 204	6 545	57.6
Lawrence, OH	636	19.0	725	4.6	523	63	68 615	10.8	67.1	22.0	59 305	4 917	58.3
Licking, OH	1 337	17.8	1 334	4.4	1 023	147	124 675	4.5	43.2	52.4	116 545	4 910	57.5
Logan, OH	408	18.6	492	4.4	318	38	48 403	5.0	38.5	56.5	42 700	5 306	58.7
Lorain, OH	2 599	17.7	2 858	5.5	1 709	295	304 718	5.6	39.8	54.5	279 848	6 067	57.9
Lucas, OH	4 250	16.3	3 466	8.7	3 085	488	446 731	7.1	37.4	55.5	412 509	5 972	58.5
Madison, OH	328	21.4	413	4.2	266	29	41 851	3.7	40.8	55.4	37 505	5 390	54.5
Mahoning, OH	2 261	18.1	2 538	5.1	1 866	254	253 163	7.2	47.1	45.7	238 834	5 823	58.5
Marion, OH	642	19.0	643	4.7	420	58	65 821	5.7	50.4	43.9	63 236	5 218	61.5
Medina, OH	1 418	18.8	1 729	3.4	965	143	160 342	2.8	34.2	63.1	143 549	5 493	60.5
Meigs, OH	252	16.7	243	4.5	167	19	23 490	10.5	54.0	35.6	20 189	4 701	57.9
Mercer, OH	486	20.7	654	1.1	413	47	48 254	4.4	48.8	46.8	45 025	4 576	63.1
Miami, OH	865	20.8	832	5.7	656	104	97 555	4.5	40.8	54.7	93 334	5 155	60.2
Monroe, OH	175	17.9	258	2.7	164	18	17 114	8.2	39.4	52.4	17 847	5 558	58.8
Montgomery, OH	4 895	17.8	3 470	6.6	3 694	648	569 800	7.6	37.2	55.2	528 943	6 077	58.0
Morgan, OH	154	17.6	—	9.0	113	9	13 277	9.3	58.6	32.1	13 251	4 932	60.1
Morrow, OH	292	19.0	397	4.4	222	23	25 966	6.2	54.7	39.1	24 167	4 387	57.2
Muskingum, OH	848	19.5	941	4.0	702	93	94 466	7.0	50.7	42.3	87 119	5 253	57.8
Noble, OH	128	20.1	150	3.0	109	14	12 832	6.0	45.5	48.5	10 378	4 102	58.2
Ottawa, OH	372	18.3	464	3.7	350	31	47 282	2.7	25.3	72.0	41 854	6 109	58.6
Paulding, OH	234	18.1	263	4.8	171	17	21 184	3.9	52.2	43.9	20 133	4 678	59.7
Perry, OH	344	19.4	370	4.2	264	44	35 646	7.3	59.4	33.4	31 832	4 782	54.2
Pickaway, OH	468	20.1	528	4.2	346	39	48 202	4.0	40.8	55.2	42 389	4 563	59.0
Pike, OH	276	21.0	332	7.3	261	31	32 536	10.3	64.1	25.7	28 043	4 790	56.1
Portage, OH	1 339	18.2	1 456	4.7	1 039	166	141 830	3.4	43.1	53.4	131 209	5 404	58.9
Preble, OH	445	18.6	474	3.4	326	39	41 608	4.7	47.4	48.0	38 847	4 763	58.0
Putnam, OH	424	18.0	556	1.6	302	42	39 337	4.8	51.8	43.4	33 935	4 420	59.7
Richland, OH	1 357	16.7	1 334	3.7	974	153	139 296	5.1	41.4	53.5	126 768	5 636	58.6

Table D-2.   School and Student Characteristics by County

State/ County code	County	County type[1]	Population, 1996		Number of school districts, 1995–1996	Level of schools, 1995–1996				Level of students, 1995–1996				Characteristics of students, 1995–1996		
			Total persons	Percent age 5–17		Number of schools	Percent			Number of students	Percent			Percent with IEP[2]	Percent free-lunch eligible	Percent minority
							Primary	Middle	High		Primary	Middle	High			
			1	2	3	4	5	6	7	8	9	10	11.	12	13	14
	OHIO—Con.															
39141	Ross, OH.......................	4	74 407	18.5	7	28	53.6	21.4	25.0	12 230	44.3	19.5	36.2	2.9	22.1	4.3
39143	Sandusky, OH	4	62 732	20.7	5	23	65.2	13.0	21.7	11 786	52.6	16.4	31.0	4.5	18.1	13.3
39145	Scioto, OH	4	80 905	20.4	10	37	51.4	18.9	29.7	14 970	49.6	18.1	32.2	3.2	39.4	2.4
39147	Seneca, OH	5	60 368	21.3	7	28	64.3	7.1	25.0	10 276	51.0	8.0	35.2	6.1	16.4	6.9
39149	Shelby, OH	6	46 837	21.9	8	24	54.2	8.3	25.0	8 956	46.5	13.8	29.9	4.6	10.8	3.2
39151	Stark, OH	2	374 406	18.3	17	121	66.9	18.2	12.4	65 217	48.3	21.1	23.9	4.5	16.9	11.7
39153	Summit, OH	2	530 571	17.6	17	150	62.7	20.7	16.0	83 876	46.3	24.0	29.5	4.4	21.7	21.1
39155	Trumbull, OH	2	227 069	18.5	20	86	55.8	18.6	23.3	37 418	45.7	19.9	33.8	3.3	21.8	11.3
39157	Tuscarawas, OH.............	4	87 803	19.3	8	38	63.2	15.8	21.1	15 714	46.1	19.9	34.0	4.4	14.5	1.2
39159	Union, OH......................	6	37 396	19.5	3	14	57.1	21.4	21.4	5 565	44.3	24.9	30.8	4.1	4.0	1.2
39161	Van Wert, OH.................	6	30 426	20.4	3	16	56.3	18.8	18.8	4 550	48.4	11.9	38.4	4.0	11.0	3.7
39163	Vinton, OH.....................	9	12 068	20.8	1	7	71.4	14.3	14.3	2 489	57.5	14.6	27.8	3.8	32.5	0.4
39165	Warren, OH....................	1	134 791	19.2	8	40	52.5	27.5	20.0	22 459	45.0	27.0	28.0	3.7	7.7	1.7
39167	Washington, OH.............	3	63 827	19.1	6	28	71.4	7.1	21.4	11 325	54.2	8.9	37.0	2.4	10.4	1.9
39169	Wayne, OH....................	4	108 556	20.6	10	49	55.1	20.4	22.4	19 093	48.5	20.6	29.9	4.6	13.1	3.6
39171	Williams, OH..................	7	37 950	20.7	7	20	40.0	25.0	35.0	7 471	39.9	25.3	34.7	4.5	6.3	3.7
39173	Wood, OH......................	2	117 546	18.3	9	47	61.7	19.1	19.1	18 518	50.6	18.1	31.2	3.9	9.8	5.2
39175	Wyandot, OH.................	7	22 718	20.2	3	11	72.7	—	27.3	4 121	62.9	—	37.1	3.6	5.4	1.5
40000	**OKLAHOMA**															
40001	Adair, OK.......................	6	19 914	23.0	12	19	68.4	10.5	21.1	4 812	64.3	11.5	24.3	13.7	59.1	68.9
40003	Alfalfa, OK.....................	8	6 155	16.1	3	9	44.4	22.2	33.3	932	55.4	16.5	28.1	10.5	29.8	5.0
40005	Atoka, OK......................	7	13 250	20.0	7	14	57.1	14.3	28.6	2 274	61.7	12.5	25.8	12.8	59.2	28.0
40007	Beaver, OK....................	9	6 013	22.0	5	9	55.6	—	44.4	1 310	68.8	—	31.2	9.2	26.3	14.3
40009	Beckham, OK.................	7	18 552	21.3	5	16	43.8	25.0	31.3	3 828	45.9	32.6	21.5	10.6	38.1	12.9
40011	Blaine, OK.....................	6	10 748	20.5	4	11	36.4	27.3	36.4	2 334	54.9	18.3	26.8	11.4	45.3	30.4
40013	Bryan, OK......................	6	33 920	18.8	8	24	50.0	16.7	33.3	6 392	55.1	17.0	27.9	9.7	48.7	28.5
40015	Caddo, OK.....................	6	30 663	20.8	12	34	38.2	26.5	35.3	6 684	49.1	24.5	26.4	11.3	53.4	41.1
40017	Canadian, OK.................	2	83 342	22.9	10	36	63.9	16.7	16.7	17 300	51.7	20.9	21.6	8.2	14.7	12.8
40019	Carter, OK.....................	5	44 280	20.7	9	30	50.0	23.3	26.7	8 998	50.2	21.7	28.1	13.7	39.6	28.9
40021	Cherokee, OK.................	6	37 879	20.2	12	20	70.0	15.0	15.0	6 688	61.3	21.7	17.0	11.3	57.6	61.2
40023	Choctaw, OK..................	7	15 250	21.1	7	15	53.3	13.3	33.3	3 119	57.1	14.4	28.4	10.1	61.3	41.1
40025	Cimarron, OK.................	9	3 087	21.4	4	7	57.1	—	42.9	695	68.8	—	31.2	10.9	41.3	26.5
40027	Cleveland, OK................	2	194 687	19.8	6	64	65.6	18.8	10.9	35 563	49.9	26.4	18.6	11.6	20.0	19.9
40029	Coal, OK........................	9	6 162	20.6	4	8	50.0	12.5	37.5	1 181	54.7	14.1	31.2	12.4	45.5	34.7
40031	Comanche, OK...............	3	111 171	21.0	11	63	73.0	11.1	15.9	23 341	58.4	21.6	20.0	8.9	35.0	41.0
40033	Cotton, OK.....................	6	6 879	19.4	3	7	42.9	14.3	42.9	1 247	54.4	14.3	31.4	13.1	30.7	19.8
40035	Craig, OK.......................	6	14 440	17.6	5	14	35.7	28.6	35.7	2 866	48.5	23.8	27.7	8.8	37.5	50.9
40037	Creek, OK......................	2	65 469	21.0	15	39	53.8	20.5	25.6	12 858	52.1	22.3	25.6	11.1	34.2	22.2
40039	Custer, OK.....................	7	25 937	19.9	5	19	36.8	36.8	26.3	5 108	37.0	36.4	26.6	9.0	38.6	25.3
40041	Delaware, OK.................	6	33 141	18.1	9	18	55.6	16.7	27.8	6 092	55.8	17.5	26.8	10.8	47.5	48.8
40043	Dewey, OK.....................	9	5 112	20.2	4	11	36.4	27.3	36.4	1 221	50.9	23.1	26.0	13.7	29.3	9.7
40045	Ellis, OK........................	9	4 185	21.0	4	9	44.4	11.1	44.4	844	58.5	9.2	32.2	11.0	32.8	8.1
40047	Garfield, OK...................	3	57 312	19.7	8	32	59.4	15.6	25.0	10 285	57.4	18.9	23.7	11.6	30.2	15.8
40049	Garvin, OK.....................	6	26 733	19.7	8	23	43.5	26.1	30.4	5 614	51.9	21.8	26.3	12.8	35.5	19.2
40051	Grady, OK......................	6	44 896	21.5	12	34	41.2	32.4	26.5	8 565	44.3	31.8	24.0	10.6	29.6	14.8
40053	Grant, OK.......................	8	5 546	18.6	4	8	50.0	—	50.0	1 154	71.1	—	28.9	8.8	24.4	4.0
40055	Greer, OK.......................	7	6 750	14.9	2	6	33.3	33.3	33.3	1 048	54.8	25.4	19.8	11.9	43.7	23.2
40057	Harmon, OK...................	7	3 592	21.6	1	3	33.3	33.3	33.3	774	45.1	25.5	29.5	10.2	51.8	45.2
40059	Harper, OK.....................	9	3 781	20.2	2	6	33.3	33.3	33.3	820	44.9	21.3	33.8	11.2	28.7	5.2
40061	Haskell, OK....................	6	11 283	19.9	5	10	50.0	10.0	40.0	2 179	55.6	13.8	30.7	12.1	47.5	33.5
40063	Hughes, OK....................	7	13 077	19.1	6	15	40.0	20.0	40.0	2 576	46.3	25.4	28.3	14.4	52.3	32.2
40065	Jackson, OK...................	5	29 990	21.3	6	20	55.0	15.0	30.0	6 286	55.3	24.8	19.8	7.1	32.6	31.5
40067	Jefferson, OK.................	9	6 724	19.3	4	10	40.0	30.0	30.0	1 378	54.1	23.1	22.7	12.3	41.7	17.9
40069	Johnston, OK.................	7	10 458	20.2	7	13	53.8	7.7	38.5	2 120	62.1	10.0	27.9	13.5	60.0	33.2
40071	Kay, OK..........................	5	47 285	19.6	8	28	60.7	21.4	17.9	9 190	49.0	27.6	23.4	11.0	33.1	23.3
40073	Kingfisher, OK...............	6	13 471	21.9	6	15	40.0	20.0	40.0	3 141	47.5	20.9	31.6	12.0	29.4	12.3
40075	Kiowa, OK......................	6	10 859	20.3	4	11	45.5	18.2	36.4	2 018	48.7	16.8	34.5	11.9	50.8	25.4
40077	Latimer, OK...................	7	10 235	20.7	4	9	44.4	11.1	44.4	1 957	59.6	13.3	27.1	13.4	54.4	32.7
40079	Le Flore, OK..................	6	46 037	20.8	17	38	44.7	21.1	34.2	9 709	52.5	18.7	28.9	11.9	43.2	30.2
40081	Lincoln, OK....................	6	30 945	21.6	9	24	41.7	25.0	33.3	5 679	46.6	24.4	28.9	10.6	37.0	18.1
40083	Logan, OK......................	2	30 940	20.2	4	13	46.2	23.1	30.8	4 533	37.3	32.6	30.2	11.5	39.5	20.6
40085	Love, OK........................	9	8 637	19.6	4	8	50.0	12.5	37.5	1 584	58.8	13.5	27.7	10.0	35.5	21.4
40087	McClain, OK...................	2	25 475	21.5	7	19	36.8	31.6	31.6	5 236	46.6	26.1	27.3	11.0	25.8	21.6
40089	McCurtain, OK................	7	34 754	22.2	15	33	54.5	21.2	24.2	7 652	55.3	17.0	27.7	11.3	54.6	38.0
40091	McIntosh, OK.................	7	18 556	17.9	6	15	46.7	26.7	26.7	3 344	41.3	34.6	24.1	13.3	59.7	35.6

1. County type code is from the Economic Research Service of the USDA. See notes and definitions at the end of this section.   2. IEP = Individual Education Program. See notes and definitions at the end of this section.

Table D-2. School and Student Characteristics by County — Continued

County	Staff and students, 1995–1996						Revenues, fiscal 1995				Current expenditures, fiscal 1995		
	Number of teachers	Pupil/ teacher ratio	Number of graduates	Dropouts grades 9–12 (percent)	Local school non-teaching staff	Central admin. staff	Total revenue ($1000)	Percent of Revenue from			Amount	Amount per pupil	Percent for instruction
								Federal Gov't	State Gov't	Local Gov't			
	15	16	17	18	19	20	21	22	23	24	25	26	27
OHIO—Con.													
Ross, OH	575	21.3	714	5.0	516	59	77 256	7.0	48.2	44.8	67 139	5 430	58.7
Sandusky, OH	591	19.9	803	3.9	442	66	68 917	5.9	43.8	50.3	63 144	5 351	60.5
Scioto, OH	799	18.7	819	5.4	571	83	83 849	9.3	65.1	25.6	79 096	5 287	58.3
Seneca, OH	487	21.1	663	3.9	426	62	53 443	4.9	47.5	47.6	50 363	4 879	59.1
Shelby, OH	447	20.0	576	3.8	371	61	43 177	3.7	42.2	54.2	39 602	4 374	59.7
Stark, OH	3 670	17.8	3 934	4.3	2 630	429	365 064	5.9	42.4	51.7	343 279	5 304	60.5
Summit, OH	4 964	16.9	4 538	6.1	3 764	1 193	526 357	7.3	35.4	57.2	473 469	5 618	58.5
Trumbull, OH	2 001	18.7	2 317	4.3	1 544	231	234 388	4.8	39.5	55.7	222 680	5 951	54.9
Tuscarawas, OH	802	19.6	1 013	4.0	558	88	85 872	5.9	44.5	49.6	75 034	4 768	60.4
Union, OH	303	18.3	158	5.2	187	28	31 631	2.9	28.2	68.9	28 775	5 290	60.6
Van Wert, OH	255	17.8	299	3.4	187	19	30 272	4.4	42.3	53.3	27 654	6 059	59.2
Vinton, OH	126	19.8	140	4.5	103	14	10 575	9.2	64.5	26.4	10 158	4 139	60.6
Warren, OH	1 171	19.2	1 178	4.6	851	118	121 215	2.9	38.8	58.2	106 227	4 871	58.3
Washington, OH	597	19.0	807	3.5	419	64	60 256	5.7	38.6	55.6	56 302	4 978	58.6
Wayne, OH	964	19.8	1 191	3.5	763	95	114 093	5.4	40.1	54.5	101 422	5 304	58.5
Williams, OH	363	20.6	465	5.7	310	56	39 180	3.3	43.4	53.3	35 891	4 881	60.2
Wood, OH	924	20.0	1 108	3.1	672	107	120 725	4.4	35.0	60.6	114 682	6 266	58.7
Wyandot, OH	182	22.7	298	2.7	165	22	19 118	4.2	47.6	48.2	17 977	4 416	61.9
OKLAHOMA													
Adair, OK	336	14.3	220	NA	331	68	26 437	20.2	67.5	12.4	25 973	5 262	58.4
Alfalfa, OK	76	12.3	59	NA	65	8	5 282	4.9	47.3	47.8	5 275	5 954	61.0
Atoka, OK	166	13.7	152	NA	183	27	11 786	13.2	69.2	17.6	11 371	4 972	59.8
Beaver, OK	104	12.5	83	NA	90	18	7 767	4.3	44.7	51.0	7 834	6 045	57.9
Beckham, OK	270	14.2	225	NA	195	29	17 182	7.8	63.3	28.8	16 862	4 390	65.9
Blaine, OK	170	13.8	136	NA	154	22	13 280	10.9	56.0	33.1	11 552	4 901	62.6
Bryan, OK	431	14.8	347	NA	412	57	30 272	11.4	65.9	22.7	28 974	4 522	61.6
Caddo, OK	477	14.0	383	NA	432	71	34 354	15.2	60.0	24.8	32 785	4 856	61.7
Canadian, OK	994	17.4	913	NA	854	133	72 237	3.7	62.6	33.8	63 899	3 747	61.9
Carter, OK	559	16.1	482	NA	560	98	42 873	9.0	62.6	28.4	40 330	4 468	60.1
Cherokee, OK	479	14.0	317	NA	403	67	34 123	18.6	64.4	17.0	32 049	4 912	64.3
Choctaw, OK	221	14.1	179	NA	192	39	15 999	14.2	69.8	16.1	15 260	4 869	60.4
Cimarron, OK	65	10.7	55	NA	71	11	4 573	5.8	55.3	38.9	4 349	6 151	62.1
Cleveland, OK	2 187	16.3	1 939	NA	1 568	306	157 345	4.5	64.0	31.5	142 986	4 029	61.8
Coal, OK	85	13.9	93	NA	71	16	6 088	11.4	59.2	29.4	5 614	4 714	59.3
Comanche, OK	1 368	17.1	1 166	NA	1 691	202	104 228	11.2	65.0	23.8	101 024	4 376	57.9
Cotton, OK	87	14.4	80	NA	81	19	6 003	8.0	65.6	26.4	5 733	4 539	59.6
Craig, OK	187	15.3	169	NA	164	29	13 710	8.5	59.9	31.7	12 168	4 364	60.4
Creek, OK	774	16.6	697	NA	663	121	56 968	7.2	66.4	26.4	51 823	4 029	59.9
Custer, OK	373	13.7	282	NA	283	47	24 965	9.5	58.1	32.4	23 339	4 561	62.3
Delaware, OK	402	15.1	299	NA	334	64	29 007	13.4	60.0	26.6	27 270	4 655	60.1
Dewey, OK	102	12.0	101	NA	105	16	8 036	5.4	55.3	39.3	7 570	6 042	62.3
Ellis, OK	71	12.0	76	NA	60	13	5 411	4.5	54.6	40.8	5 083	5 724	61.6
Garfield, OK	676	15.2	586	NA	536	97	48 667	7.4	58.4	34.1	44 928	4 353	63.2
Garvin, OK	375	15.0	328	NA	296	54	26 117	7.5	66.0	26.5	24 081	4 244	63.9
Grady, OK	545	15.7	465	NA	456	93	38 135	6.3	64.7	29.0	34 316	4 031	62.8
Grant, OK	89	12.9	67	NA	91	14	6 412	3.7	40.6	55.7	5 710	5 382	63.8
Greer, OK	72	14.0	63	NA	59	10	5 420	9.4	63.3	27.2	5 109	5 040	60.0
Harmon, OK	56	13.9	51	NA	57	7	4 090	13.0	64.5	22.4	3 973	4 991	72.0
Harper, OK	67	12.2	63	NA	69	9	5 007	3.5	46.7	49.9	5 124	6 226	60.0
Haskell, OK	143	15.2	143	NA	108	20	10 494	10.7	66.4	23.0	10 072	4 667	64.0
Hughes, OK	168	15.3	170	NA	171	23	13 791	15.6	62.1	22.3	12 893	5 060	56.9
Jackson, OK	397	15.8	343	NA	316	46	29 028	11.8	64.5	23.6	26 695	4 370	63.8
Jefferson, OK	105	13.2	90	NA	94	19	7 266	7.2	68.1	24.7	6 776	4 928	62.9
Johnston, OK	151	14.1	112	NA	141	22	10 929	14.4	63.5	22.1	10 025	4 827	64.7
Kay, OK	545	16.9	539	NA	560	99	41 117	7.5	57.6	34.9	38 686	4 196	61.3
Kingfisher, OK	219	14.4	227	NA	188	28	16 528	6.0	47.8	46.1	14 499	4 525	62.5
Kiowa, OK	159	12.7	162	NA	140	25	12 187	10.1	63.1	26.8	11 043	4 983	59.4
Latimer, OK	130	15.1	119	NA	119	19	9 425	13.1	59.3	27.6	9 585	4 829	59.0
Le Flore, OK	638	15.2	557	NA	522	100	46 130	11.5	66.3	22.2	42 783	4 483	63.5
Lincoln, OK	365	15.6	372	NA	259	56	25 460	7.8	66.4	25.8	23 537	4 096	62.5
Logan, OK	311	14.6	261	NA	279	39	21 941	8.5	62.5	29.0	20 249	4 418	59.6
Love, OK	110	14.5	91	NA	101	19	7 462	7.3	67.0	25.7	7 104	4 516	63.0
McClain, OK	328	16.0	335	NA	258	40	22 323	7.5	66.5	26.1	20 459	3 919	65.4
McCurtain, OK	537	14.2	495	NA	502	85	39 381	11.8	67.5	20.7	36 681	4 744	59.7
McIntosh, OK	230	14.5	190	NA	215	36	17 204	16.2	63.0	20.8	15 526	4 540	59.6

Table D-2. School and Student Characteristics by County

State/County code	County	County type[1]	Population, 1996		Number of school districts, 1995–1996	Level of schools, 1995–1996				Level of students, 1995–1996				Characteristics of students, 1995–1996		
			Total persons	Percent age 5–17		Number of schools	Percent			Number of students	Percent			Percent with IEP[2]	Percent free-lunch eligible	Percent minority
							Primary	Middle	High		Primary	Middle	High			
			1	2	3	4	5	6	7	8	9	10	11	12	13	14
OKLAHOMA—Con.																
40093	Major, OK	6	7 758	20.6	4	10	40.0	20.0	40.0	1 774	46.1	20.7	33.2	16.7	22.3	4.5
40095	Marshall, OK	6	11 869	17.3	2	6	33.3	33.3	33.3	2 141	45.7	25.0	29.2	9.4	43.6	30.9
40097	Mayes, OK	6	36 565	20.3	8	22	54.5	22.7	22.7	6 862	52.6	22.2	25.2	10.7	36.7	38.8
40099	Murray, OK	7	12 400	19.7	2	7	28.6	42.9	28.6	2 397	37.1	34.3	28.6	9.1	47.8	26.4
40101	Muskogee, OK	4	69 298	20.7	11	38	57.9	15.8	26.3	13 982	52.0	20.0	28.1	10.5	41.8	48.0
40103	Noble, OK	7	11 239	20.3	4	9	44.4	11.1	44.4	2 365	56.7	14.0	29.3	13.9	35.3	15.4
40105	Nowata, OK	6	9 846	19.0	4	10	40.0	20.0	40.0	2 039	53.2	16.1	30.7	11.4	42.2	32.6
40107	Okfuskee, OK	6	11 358	19.8	7	15	46.7	13.3	40.0	2 314	57.5	15.3	27.2	12.6	57.1	43.8
40109	Oklahoma, OK	2	630 531	18.9	15	201	67.2	17.9	13.9	105 614	52.2	23.3	24.3	12.5	39.4	37.5
40111	Okmulgee, OK	6	37 821	20.1	11	26	50.0	19.2	30.8	7 214	52.7	19.6	27.6	10.7	45.7	40.2
40113	Osage, OK	2	42 503	20.9	13	26	50.0	23.1	26.9	4 855	56.4	19.3	24.3	15.9	44.2	43.5
40115	Ottawa, OK	6	30 310	18.2	8	25	52.0	20.0	28.0	5 815	54.9	18.8	26.3	10.5	43.3	43.7
40117	Pawnee, OK	6	16 043	20.4	3	9	55.6	22.2	22.2	2 609	49.8	22.0	28.1	11.5	38.6	24.8
40119	Payne, OK	4	64 219	15.8	7	28	60.7	17.9	21.4	10 267	49.3	25.2	25.5	12.5	30.0	17.0
40121	Pittsburg, OK	7	43 101	18.7	14	33	60.6	6.1	30.3	8 410	64.8	8.6	20.8	16.0	44.2	32.9
40123	Pontotoc, OK	6	34 822	18.9	9	25	52.0	16.0	32.0	6 832	55.7	21.9	22.5	12.9	46.7	34.4
40125	Pottawatomie, OK	2	61 682	20.5	14	37	54.1	16.2	29.7	12 260	53.3	17.7	29.0	10.7	38.3	25.9
40127	Pushmataha, OK	7	11 586	19.2	6	13	53.8	15.4	30.8	2 414	56.5	14.9	28.6	10.4	61.1	39.9
40129	Roger Mills, OK	9	3 721	21.6	4	9	44.4	11.1	44.4	803	60.1	9.6	30.3	11.2	45.3	17.4
40131	Rogers, OK	2	63 536	21.3	10	31	45.2	32.3	22.6	12 019	45.5	26.8	27.7	10.7	22.4	32.7
40133	Seminole, OK	6	24 960	20.4	10	24	50.0	12.5	37.5	5 027	58.5	13.3	28.1	12.4	55.1	41.1
40135	Sequoyah, OK	3	36 581	21.4	13	25	56.0	16.0	28.0	7 956	57.4	15.5	27.1	12.5	51.6	41.8
40137	Stephens, OK	4	43 336	19.9	8	28	57.1	17.9	25.0	8 413	52.3	17.6	30.1	9.1	31.5	13.6
40139	Texas, OK	7	17 322	21.9	9	22	54.5	13.6	31.8	3 326	57.4	13.1	29.5	7.9	29.1	21.5
40141	Tillman, OK	6	9 634	21.8	4	10	50.0	10.0	40.0	2 061	58.4	15.1	26.5	12.2	50.6	43.2
40143	Tulsa, OK	2	531 596	18.8	15	173	64.8	23.1	13.3	98 067	49.1	25.8	21.1	12.3	28.6	29.3
40145	Wagoner, OK	2	53 389	22.9	4	14	42.9	28.6	28.6	5 602	41.1	33.9	25.0	14.2	39.8	35.3
40147	Washington, OK	4	47 423	19.3	4	19	52.6	21.1	21.1	8 775	46.3	23.6	18.7	10.2	26.0	20.0
40149	Washita, OK	7	11 698	20.8	5	11	45.5	9.1	45.5	2 215	67.3	7.4	25.3	10.4	40.5	9.8
40151	Woods, OK	7	8 516	16.2	3	10	50.0	20.0	30.0	1 474	43.6	26.6	29.9	14.8	27.2	5.0
40153	Woodward, OK	7	18 667	21.6	4	16	56.3	18.8	25.0	3 784	44.3	27.3	28.4	11.2	27.1	11.2
41000	**OREGON**															
41001	Baker, OR	7	16 410	19.3	4	13	53.8	15.4	15.4	3 069	43.7	20.2	28.4	13.4	28.6	3.6
41003	Benton, OR	4	75 926	16.5	4	27	55.6	22.2	14.8	10 231	42.0	25.8	29.1	10.0	13.0	8.6
41005	Clackamas, OR	0	324 043	19.7	14	103	66.0	18.4	13.6	52 768	52.9	18.7	27.3	10.9	11.4	8.3
41007	Clatsop, OR	6	35 132	18.9	5	14	57.1	14.3	21.4	5 431	48.9	18.5	29.5	11.0	20.6	7.6
41009	Columbia, OR	1	42 969	21.3	5	27	59.3	18.5	22.2	8 933	49.4	19.5	31.1	10.4	13.3	6.3
41011	Coos, OR	5	63 036	18.7	6	31	64.5	16.1	19.4	10 817	47.6	20.4	32.0	12.7	30.5	14.2
41013	Crook, OR	7	16 615	20.0	1	6	66.7	16.7	16.7	3 007	48.2	23.3	28.5	9.8	20.9	5.4
41015	Curry, OR	7	21 038	15.0	7	11	54.5	18.2	27.3	3 388	46.0	24.3	29.6	10.9	28.8	10.3
41017	Deschutes, OR	5	98 524	19.0	5	31	64.5	19.4	16.1	16 934	44.9	24.5	30.6	10.6	18.4	4.1
41019	Douglas, OR	4	101 076	19.8	15	51	51.0	19.6	23.5	17 786	47.5	22.3	28.1	12.1	31.6	5.9
41021	Gilliam, OR	9	1 948	20.1	2	4	50.0	—	50.0	391	64.7	—	35.3	10.7	16.4	7.4
41023	Grant, OR	9	7 973	20.0	5	9	22.2	22.2	11.1	1 630	25.0	18.1	20.4	13.4	25.0	2.1
41025	Harney, OR	7	7 075	20.3	10	13	69.2	15.4	15.4	1 449	36.0	33.1	30.9	13.3	25.5	11.4
41027	Hood River, OR	6	19 338	19.9	1	9	55.6	22.2	11.1	3 601	44.8	22.1	27.4	10.7	31.7	30.7
41029	Jackson, OR	3	168 609	18.6	9	55	63.6	18.2	16.4	27 952	49.9	20.5	29.5	10.8	24.0	10.4
41031	Jefferson, OR	7	16 360	21.6	4	11	54.5	18.2	18.2	3 195	40.3	32.5	26.1	9.1	42.9	52.4
41033	Josephine, OR	4	72 182	17.9	2	26	61.5	19.2	15.4	11 599	46.6	23.7	29.6	8.6	41.1	8.1
41035	Klamath, OR	5	62 502	19.7	3	29	62.1	10.3	17.2	11 388	49.5	12.0	27.9	12.0	34.5	18.0
41037	Lake, OR	7	7 303	20.7	6	7	57.1	—	—	1 694	36.5	—	—	9.2	17.4	9.1
41039	Lane, OR	2	306 862	18.0	16	120	63.3	19.2	15.8	48 467	46.0	24.0	29.3	11.7	24.2	9.3
41041	Lincoln, OR	7	45 041	17.2	1	18	55.6	16.7	22.2	7 131	52.2	15.5	29.7	11.9	26.7	12.6
41043	Linn, OR	4	102 217	19.6	12	56	71.4	14.3	14.3	18 290	51.4	19.0	29.6	11.5	24.7	6.7
41045	Malheur, OR	7	28 425	22.5	9	22	63.6	9.1	18.2	5 889	53.0	16.1	27.1	11.4	42.7	36.2
41047	Marion, OR	2	260 919	19.4	23	103	64.1	17.5	15.5	48 123	46.9	23.2	28.9	10.3	22.8	19.5
41049	Morrow, OR	9	9 229	22.8	1	7	42.9	14.3	28.6	2 089	45.5	17.5	29.2	9.7	34.9	25.6
41051	Multnomah, OR	0	624 903	16.2	12	167	63.5	17.4	14.4	89 497	50.0	22.1	26.5	10.2	7.9	24.3
41053	Polk, OR	2	58 501	19.9	4	20	55.0	15.0	15.0	6 236	42.7	22.5	29.1	12.3	23.1	15.9
41055	Sherman, OR	9	1 825	20.1	1	4	75.0	—	25.0	424	70.8	—	29.2	16.0	12.3	6.6
41057	Tillamook, OR	6	24 098	17.6	3	13	69.2	7.7	23.1	3 855	55.4	9.6	34.9	12.8	23.6	8.4
41059	Umatilla, OR	4	64 547	20.7	10	34	52.9	17.6	23.5	12 446	50.8	19.7	26.7	10.8	29.2	23.9
41061	Union, OR	7	25 012	20.8	6	17	58.8	5.9	23.5	4 709	47.0	10.4	32.3	12.4	26.8	4.3
41063	Wallowa, OR	9	7 495	19.9	4	8	62.5	—	25.0	1 518	54.0	—	25.4	11.6	25.2	3.8
41065	Wasco, OR	7	23 093	20.2	8	14	57.1	14.3	21.4	3 925	46.6	18.0	29.3	13.1	29.5	17.0
41067	Washington, OR	0	383 603	19.2	13	101	66.3	17.8	14.9	63 601	49.2	23.9	26.0	10.1	13.7	17.2

1. County type code is from the Economic Research Service of the USDA. See notes and definitions at the end of this section.   2. IEP = Individual Education Program. See notes and definitions at the end of this section.

Table D-2. School and Student Characteristics by County — Continued

County	Staff and students, 1995–1996						Revenues, fiscal 1995				Current expenditures, fiscal 1995		
	Number of teachers	Pupil/ teacher ratio	Number of graduates	Dropouts grades 9–12 (percent)	Local school non-teaching staff	Central admin. staff	Total revenue ($1000)	Percent of Revenue from			Amount	Amount per pupil	Percent for instruction
								Federal Gov't	State Gov't	Local Gov't			
	15	16	17	18	19	20	21	22	23	24	25	26	27
OKLAHOMA—Con.													
Major, OK	126	14.1	115	NA	135	16	9 248	5.0	57.4	37.6	8 420	4 741	60.6
Marshall, OK	139	15.4	123	NA	116	19	10 710	9.6	53.0	37.4	8 676	4 098	62.7
Mayes, OK	443	15.5	428	NA	344	57	32 610	9.4	63.7	26.9	29 317	4 279	62.3
Murray, OK	137	17.5	158	NA	158	16	10 985	10.5	66.2	23.2	9 868	4 208	62.6
Muskogee, OK	880	15.9	736	NA	653	125	70 277	11.6	57.9	30.5	61 924	4 406	59.3
Noble, OK	164	14.4	124	NA	149	25	14 425	10.0	37.1	52.8	11 669	4 949	60.4
Nowata, OK	133	15.3	109	NA	121	20	9 799	9.9	65.4	24.7	9 087	4 648	61.9
Okfuskee, OK	160	14.4	157	NA	167	26	12 742	15.8	62.7	21.5	11 970	5 294	63.4
Oklahoma, OK	6 356	16.6	5 253	NA	7 441	880	504 119	8.2	55.0	36.8	446 356	4 252	59.9
Okmulgee, OK	461	15.7	369	NA	385	69	34 247	14.1	66.0	19.9	31 543	4 425	61.1
Osage, OK	345	14.1	254	NA	310	54	24 009	11.4	63.8	24.8	23 043	4 779	59.3
Ottawa, OK	379	15.3	377	NA	329	52	27 821	13.0	64.1	22.9	25 501	4 421	61.4
Pawnee, OK	165	15.8	128	NA	161	23	11 799	9.6	64.6	25.8	10 641	4 074	60.6
Payne, OK	620	16.5	579	NA	655	103	51 428	9.5	57.6	32.9	45 745	4 500	57.2
Pittsburg, OK	525	16.0	487	NA	480	81	41 505	12.1	63.9	24.0	37 673	4 585	59.8
Pontotoc, OK	468	14.6	394	NA	512	65	33 278	11.5	63.0	25.6	30 431	4 353	63.0
Pottawatomie, OK	764	16.1	712	NA	628	111	58 097	10.7	65.6	23.7	52 241	4 322	62.1
Pushmataha, OK	173	14.0	141	NA	140	25	12 690	12.2	70.7	17.1	11 669	4 717	60.1
Roger Mills, OK	88	9.2	57	NA	84	15	7 044	10.3	43.3	46.4	6 297	7 755	59.8
Rogers, OK	703	17.1	657	NA	616	106	51 911	5.6	56.2	38.2	46 078	3 981	60.1
Seminole, OK	365	13.8	283	NA	313	52	27 638	14.3	61.8	23.9	26 017	5 003	60.9
Sequoyah, OK	528	15.1	437	NA	441	70	39 638	15.1	66.8	18.1	36 621	4 589	59.5
Stephens, OK	530	15.9	503	NA	469	77	37 085	6.5	68.9	24.7	34 795	4 491	60.9
Texas, OK	243	13.7	236	NA	195	38	18 775	5.0	54.8	40.2	18 203	4 842	59.9
Tillman, OK	155	13.3	107	NA	123	24	9 948	10.8	67.6	21.7	9 788	4 735	60.9
Tulsa, OK	5 687	17.2	4 816	NA	5 915	1 066	475 152	6.1	51.9	41.9	413 195	4 246	55.6
Wagoner, OK	366	15.3	308	NA	287	46	24 936	8.4	68.9	22.7	23 051	4 023	62.6
Washington, OK	522	16.8	520	NA	470	94	43 394	3.9	53.8	42.3	36 488	4 172	60.0
Washita, OK	154	14.4	135	NA	155	28	11 165	8.1	59.2	32.7	10 592	4 754	60.7
Woods, OK	115	12.8	95	NA	112	18	9 573	6.5	46.2	47.3	8 683	5 584	59.7
Woodward, OK	268	14.1	231	NA	198	37	17 909	5.4	63.5	31.0	17 267	4 533	64.7
OREGON													
Baker, OR	182	16.9	168	5.2	201	13	19 679	7.0	54.7	38.3	18 286	5 884	58.6
Benton, OR	481	21.3	657	5.1	407	70	60 621	4.2	43.7	52.0	54 085	5 248	59.9
Clackamas, OR	2 456	21.5	3 109	5.0	2 040	239	316 933	3.6	43.2	53.2	282 262	5 467	62.1
Clatsop, OR	279	19.5	356	5.6	233	27	32 402	4.3	36.8	58.9	30 931	5 780	61.6
Columbia, OR	485	18.4	547	4.1	370	40	53 227	3.5	35.8	60.8	48 168	5 522	60.6
Coos, OR	528	20.5	673	5.2	465	46	61 873	6.9	52.8	40.3	57 391	5 191	57.6
Crook, OR	160	18.8	182	5.5	122	15	17 613	7.8	47.6	44.7	14 546	4 755	65.1
Curry, OR	182	18.6	187	5.6	157	18	18 992	10.3	32.9	56.8	17 537	5 292	61.9
Deschutes, OR	791	21.4	926	5.4	754	95	103 862	7.4	34.9	57.8	89 399	5 307	62.8
Douglas, OR	958	18.6	1 067	6.7	755	97	108 705	10.6	49.8	39.6	102 784	5 728	56.7
Gilliam, OR	31	12.8	30	1.7	25	6	3 860	1.9	32.9	65.2	3 094	8 477	60.0
Grant, OR	112	14.5	99	1.2	98	10	12 641	23.9	39.9	36.2	10 136	6 327	59.7
Harney, OR	99	14.0	113	4.2	86	10	10 595	13.2	53.8	33.0	9 519	6 414	59.1
Hood River, OR	209	17.2	194	7.6	141	15	24 665	8.4	46.6	45.0	20 601	5 803	63.5
Jackson, OR	1 332	21.0	1 669	7.4	1 010	140	151 493	5.3	47.2	47.6	140 078	5 091	64.1
Jefferson, OR	107	17.1	146	8.2	172	18	23 213	10.2	47.8	33.1	10 161	6 644	60.7
Josephine, OR	566	20.5	643	9.0	462	35	66 850	7.3	51.0	41.6	57 872	5 015	63.3
Klamath, OR	582	19.6	644	6.0	734	57	67 892	13.0	48.9	38.1	60 098	5 281	64.4
Lake, OR	93	18.2	96	2.1	72	18	10 484	14.5	41.4	44.1	9 243	5 795	61.1
Lane, OR	2 343	20.7	2 893	7.7	2 123	222	280 515	7.5	46.4	46.1	255 041	5 274	62.4
Lincoln, OR	355	20.1	412	7.9	372	39	41 469	8.4	23.6	68.1	40 394	5 788	58.7
Linn, OR	920	19.9	982	5.1	953	75	100 977	7.7	52.7	39.6	93 703	5 243	60.2
Malheur, OR	358	16.4	370	5.5	324	31	35 564	9.8	67.1	23.1	32 945	5 730	64.5
Marion, OR	2 272	21.2	2 722	8.7	2 035	304	279 272	5.9	54.7	39.4	242 002	5 462	62.0
Morrow, OR	131	16.0	113	6.0	144	7	12 950	5.4	49.7	44.9	12 189	6 004	61.0
Multnomah, OR	4 587	19.5	4 809	9.4	3 580	461	620 615	6.4	44.7	48.9	568 305	6 273	60.6
Polk, OR	331	18.8	373	6.1	293	33	36 117	5.4	57.0	37.7	31 662	5 154	65.5
Sherman, OR	33	12.7	35	3.2	25	3	3 712	1.3	52.1	46.6	3 228	7 686	50.0
Tillamook, OR	229	16.8	290	3.9	221	22	23 683	7.3	30.2	62.5	21 711	5 614	58.5
Umatilla, OR	709	17.5	660	8.3	566	60	77 637	6.2	61.7	32.1	64 621	5 139	60.0
Union, OR	279	16.9	379	4.2	200	25	26 945	4.9	61.4	33.7	24 622	5 200	63.0
Wallowa, OR	91	16.7	89	1.3	48	5	9 020	4.5	43.1	52.4	8 535	5 597	65.1
Wasco, OR	215	18.3	236	6.1	198	25	31 500	8.4	55.4	36.2	26 284	6 587	58.0
Washington, OR	2 932	21.7	3 337	6.8	2 370	217	345 802	3.7	41.5	54.7	314 050	5 111	60.9

Table D-2. School and Student Characteristics by County

State/County code	County	County type[1]	Population, 1996		Number of school districts, 1995-1996	Level of schools, 1995-1996				Level of students, 1995-1996				Characteristics of students, 1995-1996		
			Total persons	Percent age 5-17		Number of schools	Percent Primary	Middle	High	Number of students	Percent Primary	Middle	High	Percent with IEP[2]	Percent free-lunch eligible	Percent minority
			1	2	3	4	5	6	7	8	9	10	11	12	13	14
	OREGON—Con.															
41069	Wheeler, OR	9	1 658	16.8	3	4	25.0	—	25.0	280	20.7	—	14.3	7.1	36.4	4.3
41071	Yamhill, OR	1	78 248	21.2	7	31	54.8	22.6	22.6	13 778	47.4	19.9	32.7	11.7	21.8	12.7
42000	**PENNSYLVANIA**															
42001	Adams, PA	6	84 921	18.9	6	24	50.0	25.0	25.0	13 744	46.0	25.7	28.4	10.9	NA	6.0
42003	Allegheny, PA	0	1 296 037	15.7	43	315	62.2	18.4	17.8	170 020	47.5	21.9	29.6	10.0	NA	22.1
42005	Armstrong, PA	6	73 872	18.8	5	30	56.7	13.3	30.0	12 230	46.8	13.5	39.7	11.9	NA	1.3
42007	Beaver, PA	0	187 009	17.9	15	60	55.0	21.7	23.3	29 017	46.0	21.6	32.4	9.7	NA	10.0
42009	Bedford, PA	6	49 322	19.5	5	23	65.2	8.7	21.7	8 552	49.6	10.4	37.0	11.1	NA	1.2
42011	Berks, PA	2	352 353	17.4	18	101	63.4	18.8	17.8	59 965	51.7	19.1	29.2	8.6	NA	16.8
42013	Blair, PA	3	131 450	18.9	7	37	64.9	13.5	21.6	21 166	49.3	20.7	30.0	11.6	NA	2.8
42015	Bradford, PA	6	62 352	20.7	7	33	66.7	12.1	21.2	12 195	46.9	16.1	37.0	10.8	NA	1.8
42017	Bucks, PA	0	578 715	19.1	14	123	65.9	21.1	10.6	85 559	51.3	22.7	23.1	11.3	NA	8.9
42019	Butler, PA	1	167 732	18.9	7	44	70.5	9.1	15.9	27 074	52.4	13.4	25.1	10.4	NA	1.9
42021	Cambria, PA	3	158 500	18.2	13	41	48.8	19.5	29.3	21 763	42.3	21.4	32.8	11.8	NA	4.1
42023	Cameron, PA	7	5 745	18.9	1	3	33.3	33.3	33.3	1 179	32.0	25.4	42.7	11.8	NA	1.8
42025	Carbon, PA	2	58 783	17.5	7	21	42.9	23.8	28.6	8 830	47.2	21.3	31.0	11.5	NA	3.1
42027	Centre, PA	3	131 489	13.6	4	28	75.0	10.7	14.3	14 088	48.6	17.8	33.6	7.1	NA	5.8
42029	Chester, PA	0	410 744	18.4	14	91	59.3	23.1	15.4	59 386	49.4	24.9	23.6	8.6	NA	13.7
42031	Clarion, PA	7	42 205	18.2	7	19	57.9	5.3	36.8	7 999	49.4	2.8	47.8	12.3	NA	0.8
42033	Clearfield, PA	6	79 640	19.4	8	36	66.7	11.1	22.2	15 997	49.8	13.8	36.5	10.3	NA	0.8
42035	Clinton, PA	6	37 130	18.3	1	15	73.3	—	20.0	5 560	47.0	—	46.0	12.3	NA	0.6
42037	Columbia, PA	2	64 079	16.7	7	23	56.5	13.0	30.4	11 846	44.3	19.0	36.8	11.1	NA	2.5
42039	Crawford, PA	4	89 175	19.9	3	23	60.9	4.3	34.8	12 354	51.5	7.5	41.0	12.5	NA	3.2
42041	Cumberland, PA	2	207 042	16.8	10	70	62.9	20.0	14.3	51 522	31.5	16.7	20.7	NA	NA	9.3
42043	Dauphin, PA	2	246 807	17.5	11	70	62.9	17.1	20.0	38 190	52.5	19.7	27.8	10.9	NA	32.4
42045	Delaware, PA	0	547 592	17.0	15	100	67.0	18.0	15.0	68 301	49.6	22.1	28.3	10.2	NA	24.3
42047	Elk, PA	7	35 141	19.6	3	10	50.0	20.0	30.0	4 711	44.6	19.2	36.2	12.8	NA	1.3
42049	Erie, PA	2	280 570	19.7	13	77	59.7	19.5	19.5	43 036	46.5	20.6	30.0	12.6	NA	12.3
42051	Fayette, PA	1	145 628	18.9	6	44	65.9	20.5	13.6	21 837	52.1	20.5	27.3	14.1	NA	6.1
42053	Forest, PA	9	4 942	20.5	1	4	50.0	—	50.0	807	54.3	—	45.7	14.7	NA	0.6
42055	Franklin, PA	4	127 035	18.7	6	41	73.2	12.2	12.2	18 290	48.3	24.3	25.6	11.3	NA	8.1
42057	Fulton, PA	8	14 435	20.5	4	7	42.9	—	42.9	2 657	55.0	—	43.5	7.3	NA	2.4
42059	Greene, PA	6	42 054	19.4	5	17	64.7	5.9	23.5	6 863	46.6	10.6	33.4	16.6	NA	1.5
42061	Huntingdon, PA	6	44 977	17.8	4	20	75.0	5.0	20.0	6 666	51.5	8.9	39.6	12.0	NA	3.0
42063	Indiana, PA	6	90 073	18.4	7	23	52.2	13.0	34.8	13 801	47.5	14.4	38.1	9.9	NA	2.1
42065	Jefferson, PA	7	46 624	19.7	4	18	72.2	5.6	22.2	7 518	50.3	7.4	42.3	12.3	NA	0.9
42067	Juniata, PA	8	21 793	19.8	1	12	75.0	8.3	16.7	3 432	47.3	14.1	38.6	7.8	NA	1.3
42069	Lackawanna, PA	2	213 323	16.6	11	49	63.3	12.2	22.4	27 652	47.7	17.7	34.2	11.6	NA	4.7
42071	Lancaster, PA	2	450 834	19.5	17	124	66.9	18.5	12.9	66 335	52.8	20.1	26.7	10.4	NA	15.1
42073	Lawrence, PA	4	95 780	18.1	10	31	54.8	12.9	32.3	16 187	43.5	14.8	41.7	10.5	NA	7.3
42075	Lebanon, PA	2	117 179	18.5	6	34	64.7	17.6	17.6	17 814	47.6	23.0	29.4	9.1	NA	9.4
42077	Lehigh, PA	2	297 802	16.8	9	68	63.2	22.1	14.7	42 499	47.2	27.5	25.3	8.6	NA	21.5
42079	Luzerne, PA	2	321 309	16.2	12	72	65.3	12.5	20.8	41 926	49.0	12.8	35.7	9.8	NA	3.2
42081	Lycoming, PA	3	119 083	18.9	8	40	65.0	15.0	20.0	20 455	48.4	18.5	33.1	12.3	NA	7.1
42083	McKean, PA	7	48 156	18.5	5	16	56.3	12.5	31.3	7 983	51.0	10.8	38.2	11.8	NA	1.6
42085	Mercer, PA	3	122 155	18.0	12	40	45.0	22.5	30.0	19 568	41.3	16.0	39.0	11.7	NA	9.8
42087	Mifflin, PA	6	47 006	18.6	1	14	64.3	21.4	14.3	6 362	47.8	23.7	28.6	12.8	NA	2.0
42089	Monroe, PA	6	119 581	18.5	4	30	63.3	20.0	16.7	23 630	45.5	26.0	28.6	10.7	NA	11.7
42091	Montgomery, PA	0	708 782	16.5	21	140	63.6	19.3	16.4	91 066	48.3	24.0	27.0	10.7	NA	16.8
42093	Montour, PA	6	18 044	18.1	2	7	57.1	14.3	14.3	2 904	46.4	24.4	26.2	6.9	NA	5.6
42095	Northampton, PA	2	257 719	17.3	9	60	61.7	21.7	15.0	39 647	47.1	27.4	25.5	10.0	NA	15.2
42097	Northumberland, PA	4	95 897	17.5	6	32	62.5	18.8	18.8	14 506	47.5	21.9	30.5	8.3	NA	2.4
42099	Perry, PA	2	43 727	20.5	6	14	42.9	14.3	28.6	7 934	46.6	13.1	37.8	13.2	NA	3.6
42101	Philadelphia, PA	0	1 478 002	17.9	1	256	66.8	16.4	13.3	210 503	52.2	17.3	26.9	10.5	NA	79.6
42103	Pike, PA	1	38 139	18.2	1	6	50.0	33.3	16.7	4 079	43.0	31.9	25.1	5.1	NA	4.1
42105	Potter, PA	7	17 103	21.2	5	9	44.4	—	44.4	3 403	45.8	—	37.0	10.3	NA	1.7
42107	Schuylkill, PA	4	152 630	16.7	12	39	56.4	15.4	28.2	20 601	46.7	17.2	36.1	9.9	NA	2.0
42109	Snyder, PA	7	38 034	18.9	2	14	71.4	7.1	21.4	5 652	48.1	15.8	36.1	11.5	NA	2.4
42111	Somerset, PA	3	80 517	19.1	11	35	60.0	8.6	31.4	13 341	51.4	11.2	37.4	10.4	NA	0.9
42113	Sullivan, PA	8	6 145	18.5	1	3	66.7	—	33.3	971	51.0	—	49.0	12.6	NA	1.1
42115	Susquehanna, PA	8	42 002	20.4	6	14	50.0	7.1	42.9	8 976	54.2	2.4	43.4	12.4	NA	1.7
42117	Tioga, PA	6	41 510	19.6	3	16	50.0	6.3	43.8	7 235	49.1	9.4	41.5	8.5	NA	1.6
42119	Union, PA	6	40 826	15.9	2	10	50.0	30.0	20.0	4 463	38.2	34.2	27.5	7.4	NA	3.6
42121	Venango, PA	4	58 820	20.1	5	31	71.0	12.9	16.1	11 347	50.2	17.6	32.2	13.0	NA	2.0
42123	Warren, PA	6	44 624	19.2	1	21	71.4	4.8	23.8	7 201	44.8	13.9	41.3	12.6	NA	0.9

1. County type code is from the Economic Research Service of the USDA. See notes and definitions at the end of this section.   2. IEP = Individual Education Program. See notes and definitions at the end of this section.

Table D-2. School and Student Characteristics by County — Continued

County	Staff and students, 1995–1996						Revenues, fiscal 1995				Current expenditures, fiscal 1995		
	Number of teachers	Pupil/ teacher ratio	Number of graduates	Dropouts grades 9–12 (percent)	Local school non-teaching staff	Central admin. staff	Total revenue ($1000)	Percent of Revenue from			Amount	Amount per pupil	Percent for instruction
								Federal Gov't	State Gov't	Local Gov't			
	15	16	17	18	19	20	21	22	23	24	25	26	27
OREGON—Con.													
Wheeler, OR	26	10.9	32	2.7	18	7	2 801	12.0	40.6	47.3	2 394	8 674	56.0
Yamhill, OR	683	20.2	889	8.0	604	49	85 111	6.1	53.2	40.7	71 684	4 954	61.3
PENNSYLVANIA													
Adams, PA	718	19.1	800	2.9	527	65	125 903	7.4	34.8	57.8	112 311	8 327	62.1
Allegheny, PA	9 988	17.0	10 654	3.0	8 274	820	1 528 189	5.1	29.6	65.3	1 298 961	7 737	61.7
Armstrong, PA	721	17.0	805	1.9	506	58	91 965	3.9	46.0	50.0	77 458	6 621	61.9
Beaver, PA	1 611	18.0	1 928	2.2	1 219	113	204 511	5.4	47.6	47.0	174 620	6 051	62.6
Bedford, PA	487	17.5	644	2.6	372	44	53 988	6.5	55.6	38.0	46 222	5 410	62.8
Berks, PA	3 228	18.6	3 211	3.6	2 888	290	443 162	4.7	31.4	63.9	374 794	6 400	62.3
Blair, PA	1 109	19.1	1 404	3.1	978	115	135 965	7.0	53.3	39.7	112 040	5 269	62.2
Bradford, PA	723	16.9	719	3.6	524	49	79 072	6.0	55.9	38.1	71 866	5 904	62.7
Bucks, PA	4 508	19.0	5 158	2.0	3 560	330	738 212	2.1	22.8	75.1	641 475	7 659	66.1
Butler, PA	1 411	19.2	1 771	2.9	851	93	163 023	2.7	44.7	52.6	138 913	5 228	64.4
Cambria, PA	1 288	16.9	1 734	2.3	853	89	176 716	8.4	50.8	40.8	146 332	6 858	60.0
Cameron, PA	66	18.0	41	2.3	66	4	6 737	2.3	51.9	45.7	6 034	5 431	66.6
Carbon, PA	489	18.1	544	3.3	440	51	64 564	3.4	38.1	58.5	51 525	6 121	62.9
Centre, PA	831	17.0	894	2.0	766	77	103 044	6.0	32.1	61.9	94 635	6 863	60.1
Chester, PA	3 373	17.6	3 395	2.3	2 481	271	507 220	2.8	22.2	75.0	434 394	7 597	62.2
Clarion, PA	463	17.3	547	2.1	330	29	66 557	8.9	53.6	37.5	54 950	6 835	61.3
Clearfield, PA	913	17.5	1 057	3.2	640	66	98 967	5.7	55.6	38.7	86 537	5 417	63.9
Clinton, PA	374	14.9	361	3.0	276	22	40 370	5.4	47.3	47.3	36 938	6 597	68.0
Columbia, PA	692	17.1	770	2.7	570	61	75 202	3.6	46.6	50.8	62 661	5 686	63.3
Crawford, PA	716	17.2	738	2.0	485	29	82 609	6.2	52.9	40.9	67 298	5 503	62.3
Cumberland, PA	2 130	24.2	2 263	2.4	1 729	179	268 446	3.6	30.5	65.8	232 852	6 670	62.1
Dauphin, PA	2 384	16.0	2 001	5.3	1 913	184	281 207	3.6	32.7	63.7	234 867	6 349	64.3
Delaware, PA	3 838	17.8	3 981	2.9	3 095	340	570 484	3.1	25.5	71.4	495 564	7 408	64.5
Elk, PA	272	17.3	344	4.1	166	10	31 574	2.7	46.4	51.0	26 198	5 553	63.1
Erie, PA	2 261	19.0	2 652	3.0	1 786	156	309 717	7.1	45.4	47.5	259 839	6 048	62.7
Fayette, PA	1 080	20.2	1 469	3.6	811	72	140 242	8.7	59.4	31.9	115 383	5 280	63.2
Forest, PA	49	16.4	53	1.3	50	4	6 818	3.7	32.7	63.6	5 112	6 496	58.6
Franklin, PA	994	18.4	1 144	3.9	771	100	115 963	3.2	41.3	55.5	94 950	5 309	63.6
Fulton, PA	159	16.7	181	2.6	106	14	18 934	5.4	52.2	42.4	14 862	5 701	63.2
Greene, PA	420	16.3	505	3.6	239	27	51 615	6.7	45.0	48.3	43 448	6 243	60.4
Huntingdon, PA	397	16.8	457	2.4	283	35	42 495	5.7	55.0	39.3	37 397	5 643	63.2
Indiana, PA	776	17.8	979	2.2	523	64	104 332	7.2	53.0	39.9	88 792	6 365	61.2
Jefferson, PA	430	17.5	533	2.7	321	31	49 612	5.2	54.1	40.7	41 998	5 889	61.4
Juniata, PA	172	19.9	248	2.3	105	10	16 900	5.6	58.6	35.7	15 703	4 542	64.1
Lackawanna, PA	1 504	18.4	1 750	3.5	1 001	94	204 463	5.2	41.6	53.2	180 849	6 672	63.4
Lancaster, PA	3 624	18.3	3 670	3.8	2 778	262	487 422	5.4	30.6	64.0	399 230	6 114	63.3
Lawrence, PA	861	18.8	993	2.7	651	77	103 070	3.8	55.1	41.2	82 898	5 404	67.2
Lebanon, PA	985	18.1	1 115	2.5	809	109	116 823	2.9	38.0	59.2	97 819	5 548	63.9
Lehigh, PA	2 156	19.7	2 548	3.0	1 877	181	312 881	4.0	28.6	67.4	267 702	6 412	65.1
Luzerne, PA	2 228	18.8	2 699	2.9	1 424	180	305 669	5.6	39.2	55.1	265 889	6 487	65.2
Lycoming, PA	1 147	17.8	1 138	3.8	900	81	139 525	5.8	45.4	48.8	123 099	6 022	64.6
McKean, PA	450	17.8	534	3.5	332	37	66 474	8.5	49.3	42.2	57 008	7 065	64.6
Mercer, PA	1 095	17.9	1 230	2.3	911	86	149 199	9.5	49.0	41.5	128 313	6 592	65.6
Mifflin, PA	384	16.6	381	5.7	236	15	50 937	14.5	49.9	35.6	48 671	7 702	54.2
Monroe, PA	1 268	18.6	1 228	2.7	1 101	82	158 050	2.9	23.9	73.2	122 623	5 508	61.1
Montgomery, PA	5 380	16.9	5 139	2.3	4 455	530	834 811	2.3	18.4	79.3	736 625	8 283	62.2
Montour, PA	165	17.7	163	3.3	113	12	19 857	6.3	40.1	53.6	17 537	6 195	70.4
Northampton, PA	2 122	18.7	2 183	4.1	1 712	121	281 475	3.8	29.9	66.3	250 654	6 496	63.5
Northumberland, PA	806	18.0	917	4.1	613	50	85 689	4.9	54.0	41.1	74 248	5 119	65.1
Perry, PA	436	18.2	474	3.2	311	41	47 248	3.3	52.4	44.3	39 215	5 102	63.1
Philadelphia, PA	10 900	19.3	8 446	12.5	9 622	2 141	1 389 214	11.8	49.3	39.0	1 065 286	5 104	61.7
Pike, PA	234	17.5	164	1.1	154	16	30 113	3.0	21.4	75.5	23 728	6 231	64.3
Potter, PA	191	17.8	221	3.2	134	13	21 791	2.6	53.9	43.5	18 007	5 189	61.5
Schuylkill, PA	1 070	19.3	1 350	2.8	741	90	151 693	6.1	46.3	47.6	120 627	5 869	59.6
Snyder, PA	334	16.9	382	2.8	250	22	33 881	4.3	44.3	51.5	30 269	5 357	65.7
Somerset, PA	754	17.7	913	1.7	599	67	86 263	6.5	53.9	39.6	67 918	5 070	63.3
Sullivan, PA	67	14.4	63	NA	54	7	7 265	4.4	37.1	58.6	6 677	6 711	59.4
Susquehanna, PA	517	17.4	553	2.7	351	41	54 384	4.3	56.1	39.6	48 807	5 498	62.9
Tioga, PA	460	15.7	448	2.4	288	33	44 649	5.8	53.4	40.7	39 224	5 420	64.3
Union, PA	251	17.8	238	2.7	191	19	51 831	21.6	34.2	44.2	50 251	11 491	47.7
Venango, PA	628	18.1	789	4.4	519	35	76 743	5.1	56.0	38.9	60 350	5 266	62.3
Warren, PA	413	17.4	446	2.5	301	37	40 928	3.9	52.1	43.9	37 125	5 214	63.5

Table D-2. School and Student Characteristics by County

State/ County code	County	County type[1]	Population, 1996 Total persons	Percent age 5–17	Number of school districts, 1995–1996	Level of schools, 1995–1996 Number of schools	Percent Primary	Middle	High	Level of students, 1995–1996 Number of students	Percent Primary	Middle	High	Characteristics of students, 1995–1996 Percent with IEP[2]	Percent free-lunch eligible	Percent minority
			1	2	3	4	5	6	7	8	9	10	11	12	13	14
	PENNSYLVANIA—Con.															
42125	Washington, PA	0	206 708	17.5	15	62	56.5	19.4	24.2	30 851	47.1	18.5	34.3	10.9	NA	5.7
42127	Wayne, PA	6	44 718	18.9	3	16	56.3	25.0	18.8	9 092	46.7	24.9	28.4	11.9	NA	2.8
42129	Westmoreland, PA	0	376 297	17.1	17	101	60.4	21.8	17.8	57 516	47.2	22.4	30.5	10.2	NA	4.7
42131	Wyoming, PA	2	29 362	21.0	2	8	62.5	12.5	25.0	5 079	43.2	23.1	33.7	9.4	NA	1.3
42133	York, PA	2	368 332	18.1	17	98	64.3	18.4	16.3	54 600	47.8	24.8	27.2	11.4	NA	11.6
44000	**RHODE ISLAND**															
44001	Bristol, RI	2	49 213	16.8	2	18	61.1	27.8	11.1	6 885	37.3	35.0	27.7	17.5	11.3	2.1
44003	Kent, RI	2	162 185	17.6	4	47	68.1	19.1	12.8	23 559	51.3	19.6	29.1	16.6	14.2	4.3
44005	Newport, RI	4	82 746	17.8	6	30	70.0	16.7	13.3	11 738	45.5	28.1	26.3	17.2	15.8	11.5
44007	Providence, RI	2	577 906	17.2	18	176	69.3	15.3	13.6	87 977	53.2	19.8	26.8	16.2	36.3	31.9
44009	Washington, RI	2	118 175	18.0	7	38	63.2	18.4	15.8	19 640	48.9	23.4	27.1	16.7	10.4	5.2
45000	**SOUTH CAROLINA**															
45001	Abbeville, SC	6	24 275	18.0	1	9	55.6	11.1	33.3	3 807	53.8	12.8	33.4	14.1	43.4	46.0
45003	Aiken, SC	2	133 130	19.2	1	36	52.8	27.8	19.4	24 373	46.5	24.4	29.1	9.5	33.8	35.0
45005	Allendale, SC	7	11 471	20.8	1	5	60.0	20.0	20.0	2 235	54.9	16.6	28.5	11.9	84.0	90.3
45007	Anderson, SC	2	156 558	17.6	5	46	56.5	26.1	17.4	25 780	42.3	28.3	29.3	10.9	25.3	22.5
45009	Bamberg, SC	7	16 702	21.0	2	9	33.3	44.4	22.2	3 124	35.8	36.1	28.1	17.5	69.9	75.6
45011	Barnwell, SC	6	21 640	21.5	3	9	33.3	33.3	33.3	4 932	44.3	25.7	30.0	14.3	41.2	50.0
45013	Beaufort, SC	5	102 735	16.5	1	20	65.0	15.0	20.0	14 179	48.2	24.9	26.9	9.3	40.3	50.0
45015	Berkeley, SC	2	132 502	22.2	1	35	51.4	25.7	22.9	26 068	43.9	27.0	29.1	7.9	36.2	37.2
45017	Calhoun, SC	8	13 724	19.0	1	5	60.0	20.0	20.0	2 121	46.5	24.8	28.7	15.4	76.9	81.8
45019	Charleston, SC	2	277 721	16.9	1	71	62.0	22.5	15.5	43 485	51.6	23.3	25.1	11.2	46.9	60.4
45021	Cherokee, SC	2	48 003	18.6	1	18	72.2	16.7	11.1	8 358	52.8	23.3	24.0	9.3	35.5	30.9
45023	Chester, SC	6	33 488	19.5	1	9	33.3	33.3	22.2	6 571	47.2	19.4	23.1	12.4	47.3	52.0
45025	Chesterfield, SC	6	39 794	19.6	1	16	50.0	25.0	25.0	7 854	44.0	23.6	32.4	11.5	47.5	43.3
45027	Clarendon, SC	6	29 406	20.9	3	11	36.4	36.4	27.3	6 083	37.2	29.3	33.5	12.4	69.4	68.3
45029	Colleton, SC	6	36 893	20.9	1	13	53.8	30.8	15.4	6 950	37.1	34.8	28.1	11.9	56.3	57.2
45031	Darlington, SC	4	65 319	20.4	1	21	47.6	38.1	14.3	11 033	36.2	32.7	31.1	13.0	52.0	53.8
45033	Dillon, SC	6	29 574	22.7	3	12	41.7	33.3	25.0	6 462	35.9	38.7	25.4	9.5	64.8	60.2
45035	Dorchester, SC	2	84 920	20.3	2	22	50.0	27.3	18.2	17 634	39.7	30.6	21.1	9.1	27.4	32.7
45037	Edgefield, SC	2	19 051	20.0	1	7	57.1	28.6	14.3	4 046	48.8	25.5	25.7	10.8	51.5	57.4
45039	Fairfield, SC	6	22 305	20.4	1	7	57.1	28.6	14.3	3 663	40.6	30.3	29.1	14.8	58.6	81.7
45041	Florence, SC	3	123 365	20.4	5	36	55.6	25.0	19.4	22 997	46.1	23.8	30.1	10.9	49.3	53.6
45043	Georgetown, SC	6	51 555	21.4	1	18	50.0	22.2	27.8	10 708	47.1	20.0	32.9	12.0	49.7	57.9
45045	Greenville, SC	2	345 173	17.0	1	88	63.6	18.2	15.9	54 638	47.5	24.2	28.2	12.4	24.4	28.8
45047	Greenwood, SC	5	62 789	17.8	3	20	55.0	25.0	20.0	11 362	45.7	23.7	30.6	11.9	36.4	41.4
45049	Hampton, SC	7	19 098	22.5	2	10	60.0	20.0	20.0	4 320	49.1	19.6	31.3	10.5	67.0	71.0
45051	Horry, SC	3	163 856	16.8	1	33	57.6	21.2	21.2	25 476	47.6	21.1	31.3	13.1	44.2	30.3
45053	Jasper, SC	8	16 365	22.1	1	4	50.0	25.0	25.0	2 956	56.7	17.1	26.2	11.8	72.1	81.7
45055	Kershaw, SC	6	47 279	19.6	1	16	50.0	25.0	25.0	9 301	33.1	33.0	33.9	10.3	32.9	35.9
45057	Lancaster, SC	6	57 164	18.8	1	17	52.9	23.5	23.5	10 621	50.0	22.2	27.7	8.8	33.1	35.3
45059	Laurens, SC	6	61 614	17.9	2	16	56.3	31.3	12.5	9 044	49.8	24.4	25.8	12.6	40.5	39.3
45061	Lee, SC	6	18 537	22.2	1	7	42.9	28.6	28.6	3 380	32.7	37.2	30.1	9.3	77.4	90.1
45063	Lexington, SC	2	195 606	18.8	5	52	53.8	26.9	19.2	40 643	47.0	26.1	26.9	11.0	20.7	17.4
45065	McCormick, SC	8	9 432	18.1	1	3	33.3	33.3	33.3	1 347	37.9	31.3	30.8	12.5	54.2	78.5
45067	Marion, SC	6	34 895	22.8	4	14	50.0	21.4	28.6	7 123	41.8	24.1	34.1	14.4	61.8	71.6
45069	Marlboro, SC	7	29 770	20.5	1	8	75.0	12.5	12.5	5 694	58.1	13.5	28.4	9.1	64.2	64.7
45071	Newberry, SC	6	34 268	17.8	1	15	53.3	26.7	20.0	5 760	36.1	32.2	31.7	14.8	43.5	49.2
45073	Oconee, SC	6	62 643	17.6	1	21	57.1	23.8	19.0	9 874	44.3	25.2	30.5	13.2	28.6	13.4
45075	Orangeburg, SC	4	87 324	19.9	9	32	53.1	21.9	21.9	16 657	40.9	26.0	30.2	13.7	68.3	76.4
45077	Pickens, SC	2	103 983	15.8	1	24	62.5	20.8	16.7	15 306	50.9	24.8	24.4	10.1	19.9	10.2
45079	Richland, SC	2	292 601	17.0	4	83	48.2	25.3	16.9	43 763	45.5	23.0	27.8	11.4	41.8	68.3
45081	Saluda, SC	6	16 843	19.1	1	4	50.0	25.0	25.0	2 228	46.8	24.2	29.0	17.5	48.8	47.0
45083	Spartanburg, SC	2	242 962	17.3	8	65	60.0	26.2	13.8	39 165	49.5	25.2	25.3	11.3	30.4	29.7
45085	Sumter, SC	3	107 161	19.7	2	25	64.0	20.0	16.0	19 095	47.8	26.5	25.7	11.8	52.1	60.7
45087	Union, SC	6	30 709	17.9	1	10	50.0	20.0	30.0	5 243	42.7	24.4	32.9	11.7	41.9	40.8
45089	Williamsburg, SC	6	37 244	23.7	1	13	53.8	23.1	23.1	6 909	44.4	22.7	32.9	17.1	78.6	90.8
45091	York, SC	2	147 299	18.0	4	37	67.6	18.9	13.5	25 335	48.0	24.3	27.7	9.2	24.9	27.7
46000	**SOUTH DAKOTA**															
46003	Aurora, SD	9	3 038	22.9	4	11	27.3	27.3	27.3	731	44.9	12.6	27.6	6.6	NA	8.3
46005	Beadle, SD	7	18 149	19.4	5	24	54.2	20.8	20.8	3 444	44.4	24.3	29.9	12.8	NA	3.5
46007	Bennett, SD	9	3 379	27.9	2	7	71.4	14.3	14.3	816	66.8	11.0	22.2	9.7	NA	66.1
46009	Bon Homme, SD	9	7 032	18.5	3	15	46.7	33.3	20.0	1 589	53.4	16.6	30.0	13.4	NA	3.0

1. County type code is from the Economic Research Service of the USDA. See notes and definitions at the end of this section.   2. IEP = Individual Education Program. See notes and definitions at the end of this section.

Table D-2. School and Student Characteristics by County — Continued

County	Staff and students, 1995–1996						Revenues, fiscal 1995				Current expenditures, fiscal 1995		
	Number of teachers	Pupil/ teacher ratio	Number of graduates	Dropouts grades 9–12 (percent)	Local school non-teaching staff	Central admin. staff	Total revenue ($1000)	Percent of Revenue from			Amount	Amount per pupil	Percent for instruction
								Federal Gov't	State Gov't	Local Gov't			
	15	16	17	18	19	20	21	22	23	24	25	26	27
PENNSYLVANIA—Con.													
Washington, PA	1 782	17.3	2 120	2.6	1 322	118	249 196	5.4	42.5	52.0	203 546	6 650	63.3
Wayne, PA	488	18.6	545	3.3	316	25	65 930	3.6	30.7	65.7	52 638	5 887	59.9
Westmoreland, PA	2 936	19.6	3 970	2.8	2 077	209	396 162	4.4	42.8	52.7	334 336	5 867	63.1
Wyoming, PA	278	18.3	332	2.3	177	15	33 564	4.2	48.0	47.8	29 195	5 815	64.0
York, PA	2 912	18.7	3 013	4.2	2 151	248	345 921	2.9	36.2	60.9	279 431	5 369	63.9
RHODE ISLAND													
Bristol, RI	532	12.9	394	4.5	257	24	49 821	3.5	34.0	62.5	48 071	7 030	70.0
Kent, RI	1 766	13.3	1 432	4.3	924	99	178 773	3.2	34.4	62.3	173 124	7 323	67.8
Newport, RI	905	13.0	704	2.5	445	53	97 938	7.6	27.5	64.9	89 487	7 694	66.2
Providence, RI	5 839	15.1	4 216	5.4	3 016	401	612 161	6.0	46.6	47.4	562 924	6 591	67.0
Washington, RI	1 441	13.6	1 084	3.2	742	75	151 653	2.4	28.8	68.8	139 515	7 308	65.6
SOUTH CAROLINA													
Abbeville, SC	244	15.6	230	NA	31	5	20 115	8.7	50.6	40.8	17 458	4 619	59.7
Aiken, SC	1 297	18.8	1 237	NA	177	18	116 655	7.9	50.9	41.3	97 720	3 959	61.0
Allendale, SC	160	14.0	130	NA	19	3	12 830	15.7	49.9	34.4	11 265	4 900	56.6
Anderson, SC	1 530	16.9	1 455	NA	184	32	123 164	6.9	52.2	40.9	109 477	4 235	60.1
Bamberg, SC	203	15.4	179	NA	26	5	17 053	13.7	55.1	31.3	14 673	4 635	57.5
Barnwell, SC	318	15.5	291	NA	33	10	25 525	11.6	56.8	31.7	21 526	4 285	59.2
Beaufort, SC	890	15.9	631	NA	105	16	85 415	7.1	25.4	67.6	66 677	4 717	56.4
Berkeley, SC	1 436	18.2	1 303	NA	176	32	120 856	10.9	57.6	31.5	106 871	3 899	57.0
Calhoun, SC	144	14.0	101	NA	20	3	12 042	12.7	40.3	47.0	10 975	5 219	59.2
Charleston, SC	2 694	16.1	1 756	NA	309	44	234 126	10.1	42.3	47.6	196 759	4 405	59.8
Cherokee, SC	502	16.7	393	NA	67	7	43 894	7.8	46.1	46.1	38 591	4 622	62.6
Chester, SC	409	16.1	334	NA	48	6	35 232	8.6	50.3	41.1	29 803	4 453	60.9
Chesterfield, SC	487	16.1	432	NA	66	7	39 275	9.3	54.2	36.5	35 001	4 425	57.7
Clarendon, SC	356	17.1	391	NA	40	10	28 697	14.1	60.0	25.9	24 792	3 967	59.0
Colleton, SC	462	15.1	387	NA	57	14	35 564	11.0	50.7	38.3	32 875	4 664	58.5
Darlington, SC	775	14.2	632	NA	94	15	64 390	9.6	44.0	46.4	54 347	4 747	60.1
Dillon, SC	379	17.1	327	NA	47	13	29 575	14.3	62.4	23.3	27 436	4 161	57.4
Dorchester, SC	995	17.7	823	NA	112	15	80 506	6.5	54.7	38.8	71 014	4 038	63.7
Edgefield, SC	261	15.5	202	NA	38	6	22 593	11.7	49.6	38.7	18 581	4 523	57.3
Fairfield, SC	278	13.2	183	NA	38	10	28 854	9.2	26.8	64.1	23 039	6 044	55.4
Florence, SC	1 353	17.0	1 304	NA	159	34	110 464	11.3	54.9	33.8	94 973	4 046	58.7
Georgetown, SC	724	14.8	578	NA	91	8	68 000	8.4	37.0	54.6	53 765	4 958	58.2
Greenville, SC	3 226	16.9	2 804	NA	389	43	273 846	6.2	44.7	49.1	232 604	4 302	59.2
Greenwood, SC	735	15.5	553	NA	84	18	57 663	7.9	48.8	43.3	51 586	4 536	57.7
Hampton, SC	309	14.0	207	NA	37	8	24 380	13.3	51.9	34.8	21 850	4 972	56.8
Horry, SC	1 621	15.7	1 258	NA	185	21	145 144	7.8	35.0	57.2	122 782	4 862	59.6
Jasper, SC	192	15.4	108	NA	22	3	15 249	12.9	53.4	33.7	12 337	4 074	54.6
Kershaw, SC	517	18.0	506	NA	70	9	47 384	7.9	47.8	44.3	40 345	4 352	54.9
Lancaster, SC	636	16.7	489	NA	84	7	51 730	8.1	53.1	38.8	45 177	4 237	59.1
Laurens, SC	515	17.5	384	NA	72	13	41 545	9.7	56.8	33.6	36 578	4 051	58.7
Lee, SC	181	18.7	157	NA	26	4	17 097	18.0	61.2	20.8	15 060	4 359	54.7
Lexington, SC	2 563	15.9	2 075	NA	316	45	226 536	4.7	43.3	52.1	187 162	4 697	58.5
McCormick, SC	88	15.3	62	NA	13	5	8 844	23.4	45.4	31.3	7 293	5 323	50.8
Marion, SC	448	15.9	418	NA	58	15	36 097	13.9	59.7	26.4	31 317	4 238	59.9
Marlboro, SC	376	15.2	221	NA	39	7	28 370	13.4	57.6	29.0	25 496	4 401	59.2
Newberry, SC	359	16.0	309	NA	52	7	34 598	8.3	45.3	46.3	28 038	4 796	57.1
Oconee, SC	644	15.3	700	NA	88	11	58 077	6.5	34.1	59.4	49 873	5 090	58.7
Orangeburg, SC	1 090	15.3	913	NA	127	32	93 054	12.0	49.4	38.7	78 405	4 727	57.5
Pickens, SC	880	17.4	659	NA	110	12	70 930	5.8	50.2	44.1	62 001	4 094	65.5
Richland, SC	2 969	14.7	1 962	NA	368	56	244 644	8.0	39.3	52.8	214 106	5 170	58.7
Saluda, SC	147	15.2	115	NA	17	3	11 716	11.1	56.6	32.3	10 483	4 674	62.0
Spartanburg, SC	2 533	15.5	1 798	NA	292	45	214 955	6.2	42.8	51.0	179 658	4 636	61.7
Sumter, SC	1 097	17.4	861	NA	130	15	95 721	12.6	55.0	32.5	77 814	4 017	59.2
Union, SC	351	14.9	225	NA	41	4	26 462	10.1	53.6	36.3	23 442	4 405	62.0
Williamsburg, SC	412	16.8	319	NA	55	10	36 936	17.5	55.1	27.4	31 356	4 424	56.8
York, SC	1 476	17.2	1 281	NA	180	30	146 219	4.9	36.0	59.1	113 973	4 592	60.5
SOUTH DAKOTA													
Aurora, SD	66	11.0	52	NA	48	5	3 412	7.6	30.7	61.7	3 028	4 860	59.9
Beadle, SD	234	14.7	218	NA	167	17	17 090	6.1	35.4	58.5	15 584	4 479	62.0
Bennett, SD	72	11.3	33	NA	71	10	3 623	23.6	30.8	45.6	3 197	5 311	67.1
Bon Homme, SD	104	15.2	111	NA	73	5	7 771	7.2	30.5	62.3	6 616	4 304	59.7

Table D-2. School and Student Characteristics by County

State/ County code	County	County type[1]	Population, 1996		Number of school districts, 1995–1996	Level of schools, 1995–1996				Level of students, 1995–1996				Characteristics of students, 1995–1996		
			Total persons	Percent age 5–17		Number of schools	Percent			Number of students	Percent			Percent with IEP[2]	Percent free-lunch eligible	Percent minority
							Primary	Middle	High		Primary	Middle	High			
			1	2	3	4	5	6	7	8	9	10	11	12	13	14
	SOUTH DAKOTA—Con.															
46011	Brookings, SD	7	26 394	16.6	5	16	43.8	25.0	31.3	4 360	46.4	21.7	31.8	9.2	NA	4.2
46013	Brown, SD	5	35 829	19.0	6	24	50.0	25.0	25.0	5 759	52.0	23.5	24.6	12.1	NA	7.6
46015	Brule, SD	9	5 541	25.7	2	9	55.6	22.2	22.2	1 375	39.0	28.7	32.4	7.9	NA	18.3
46017	Buffalo, SD	9	1 805	34.1	NA	NA	NA	NA	NA	NA	NA	NA	NA	NA	NA	NA
46019	Butte, SD	6	9 039	21.1	2	9	44.4	33.3	22.2	2 022	42.0	29.2	28.8	10.2	NA	6.7
46021	Campbell, SD	9	1 893	18.2	2	6	33.3	33.3	33.3	317	47.3	20.5	32.2	11.0	NA	0.3
46023	Charles Mix, SD	9	9 395	24.4	5	18	44.4	27.8	27.8	2 177	54.8	17.1	28.1	9.5	NA	40.1
46025	Clark, SD	9	4 373	21.2	2	7	42.9	28.6	28.6	879	53.2	15.8	30.9	10.4	NA	3.5
46027	Clay, SD	7	13 639	14.4	2	7	42.9	28.6	28.6	1 622	34.6	31.8	33.5	10.3	NA	9.0
46029	Codington, SD	7	25 099	21.2	5	20	50.0	25.0	25.0	4 865	49.5	17.3	33.3	9.4	NA	3.2
46031	Corson, SD	9	4 269	29.1	5	11	45.5	27.3	27.3	959	64.4	11.2	24.4	18.9	NA	68.8
46033	Custer, SD	8	6 828	21.4	3	10	60.0	10.0	20.0	1 268	48.7	18.3	32.3	10.6	NA	6.2
46035	Davison, SD	7	17 769	19.9	3	14	50.0	21.4	21.4	3 382	41.5	24.9	33.2	10.8	NA	4.3
46037	Day, SD	9	6 567	20.1	5	13	38.5	30.8	30.8	1 430	50.9	18.0	31.1	9.4	NA	12.9
46039	Deuel, SD	9	4 578	19.7	1	4	50.0	25.0	25.0	673	44.1	25.1	30.8	11.6	NA	1.0
46041	Dewey, SD	9	5 772	30.2	4	17	52.9	23.5	23.5	2 115	61.2	13.9	24.9	13.2	NA	80.5
46043	Douglas, SD	9	3 577	22.1	2	6	33.3	33.3	33.3	520	40.2	29.6	30.2	9.2	NA	1.7
46045	Edmunds, SD	9	4 394	19.8	3	11	45.5	27.3	27.3	746	46.8	17.7	35.5	11.1	NA	1.5
46047	Fall River, SD	7	7 164	19.3	3	11	45.5	27.3	27.3	1 374	40.7	26.1	33.2	12.4	NA	12.7
46049	Faulk, SD	9	2 581	19.2	2	6	33.3	33.3	33.3	460	49.1	16.5	34.3	10.0	NA	0.9
46051	Grant, SD	7	8 054	22.6	3	8	37.5	37.5	25.0	1 634	43.7	23.4	32.9	11.4	NA	1.8
46053	Gregory, SD	9	5 125	21.5	3	10	40.0	30.0	30.0	1 130	44.6	21.9	33.5	9.1	NA	9.8
46055	Haakon, SD	9	2 514	27.6	2	13	69.2	15.4	15.4	695	47.2	16.5	36.3	6.0	NA	4.0
46057	Hamlin, SD	9	5 359	21.4	4	11	36.4	27.3	27.3	1 362	49.2	20.8	28.9	9.5	NA	1.8
46059	Hand, SD	9	4 143	21.1	2	6	66.7	16.7	16.7	688	54.8	15.4	29.8	10.3	NA	—
46061	Hanson, SD	9	2 942	23.5	2	8	50.0	25.0	25.0	550	43.1	24.0	32.9	10.4	NA	—
46063	Harding, SD	9	1 559	22.5	1	8	75.0	12.5	12.5	364	59.1	12.1	28.8	6.9	NA	—
46065	Hughes, SD	7	15 531	22.0	3	13	61.5	23.1	15.4	3 311	50.7	29.1	20.3	11.7	NA	17.9
46067	Hutchinson, SD	9	8 129	18.8	4	20	55.0	25.0	20.0	1 872	55.6	17.8	26.6	12.1	NA	3.0
46069	Hyde, SD	9	1 648	19.7	2	6	33.3	33.3	33.3	840	44.0	20.1	35.8	5.6	NA	61.2
46071	Jackson, SD	9	2 909	27.2	2	7	57.1	14.3	28.6	790	70.1	7.1	22.8	7.7	NA	64.3
46073	Jerauld, SD	9	2 310	20.3	2	7	42.9	28.6	28.6	551	36.1	27.9	35.9	11.4	NA	0.9
46075	Jones, SD	9	1 262	20.0	1	4	50.0	25.0	25.0	301	55.1	16.3	28.6	11.6	NA	5.6
46077	Kingsbury, SD	9	5 877	19.5	3	9	33.3	33.3	33.3	1 077	45.9	18.8	35.3	9.8	NA	0.5
46079	Lake, SD	6	10 656	19.7	4	15	46.7	26.7	26.7	2 274	44.3	24.1	31.6	8.3	NA	1.4
46081	Lawrence, SD	6	22 371	20.3	3	12	41.7	25.0	16.7	3 965	33.3	32.5	30.2	9.2	NA	6.2
46083	Lincoln, SD	3	18 377	22.6	3	15	40.0	40.0	20.0	3 285	45.1	24.9	30.0	12.4	NA	2.3
46085	Lyman, SD	9	3 849	25.4	2	8	50.0	25.0	25.0	729	49.7	22.1	28.3	8.0	NA	51.9
46087	McCook, SD	8	5 808	20.5	4	13	38.5	30.8	30.8	1 111	41.9	22.1	36.1	14.1	NA	0.7
46089	McPherson, SD	9	2 950	16.9	2	9	55.6	22.2	22.2	550	56.7	11.6	31.6	9.8	NA	1.6
46091	Marshall, SD	9	4 699	20.1	3	9	33.3	33.3	33.3	898	54.0	15.5	30.5	9.8	NA	4.9
46093	Meade, SD	6	22 592	24.3	2	21	81.0	9.5	9.5	3 314	46.0	24.7	29.3	8.7	NA	5.4
46095	Mellette, SD	9	2 023	27.7	2	9	77.8	11.1	11.1	506	60.9	16.8	22.3	14.4	NA	66.8
46097	Miner, SD	9	3 014	19.9	2	5	60.0	20.0	20.0	638	55.2	14.9	29.9	14.3	NA	0.6
46099	Minnehaha, SD	3	138 221	19.1	9	62	58.1	17.7	16.1	24 259	49.3	22.2	27.4	12.4	NA	7.4
46101	Moody, SD	8	6 608	22.8	3	9	44.4	22.2	33.3	1 782	31.9	22.2	45.8	7.5	NA	40.3
46103	Pennington, SD	3	87 145	20.1	5	47	63.8	21.3	14.9	18 696	46.9	25.4	27.7	9.4	NA	17.1
46105	Perkins, SD	9	3 647	19.7	3	13	61.5	23.1	15.4	788	51.6	16.6	31.7	10.2	NA	6.7
46107	Potter, SD	9	2 983	21.7	2	9	55.6	22.2	22.2	581	35.1	24.6	40.3	8.3	NA	2.2
46109	Roberts, SD	9	9 857	22.9	5	17	41.2	29.4	29.4	2 471	47.4	22.5	30.1	10.7	NA	44.6
46111	Sanborn, SD	9	2 759	20.2	2	8	50.0	25.0	25.0	649	46.2	20.3	33.4	12.0	NA	0.5
46113	Shannon, SD	7	11 837	33.5	6	13	69.2	15.4	15.4	3 555	68.8	8.7	22.4	6.9	NA	99.3
46115	Spink, SD	7	7 746	19.8	6	18	38.9	27.8	27.8	1 649	52.5	17.2	29.4	11.3	NA	2.4
46117	Stanley, SD	9	2 961	23.8	1	7	71.4	14.3	14.3	606	46.0	22.8	31.2	11.4	NA	12.0
46119	Sully, SD	9	1 593	22.2	2	7	57.1	14.3	14.3	427	53.4	12.9	29.3	10.8	NA	2.1
46121	Todd, SD	9	9 246	33.6	2	15	66.7	20.0	13.3	2 834	52.5	25.2	22.3	8.5	NA	93.4
46123	Tripp, SD	7	6 861	22.4	2	15	73.3	13.3	13.3	1 405	49.8	20.2	30.0	10.7	NA	18.5
46125	Turner, SD	8	8 630	20.3	5	15	33.3	33.3	33.3	1 626	51.0	16.7	32.3	13.8	NA	1.8
46127	Union, SD	8	11 644	22.0	5	15	33.3	33.3	33.3	2 558	41.2	26.5	32.2	13.0	NA	1.7
46129	Walworth, SD	7	5 784	19.2	2	7	42.9	28.6	28.6	1 105	47.2	22.9	29.9	10.5	NA	16.8
46135	Yankton, SD	7	20 848	19.0	3	13	53.8	23.1	23.1	3 741	51.8	15.8	32.4	10.3	NA	3.6
46137	Ziebach, SD	9	2 230	32.3	2	6	33.3	33.3	33.3	635	54.3	14.6	31.0	8.2	NA	84.4

1. County type code is from the Economic Research Service of the USDA. See notes and definitions at the end of this section.   2. IEP = Individual Education Program. See notes and definitions at the end of this section.

Table D-2. School and Student Characteristics by County — Continued

County	Staff and students, 1995–1996						Revenues, fiscal 1995				Current expenditures, fiscal 1995		
	Number of teachers	Pupil/ teacher ratio	Number of graduates	Dropouts grades 9–12 (percent)	Local school non-teaching staff	Central admin. staff	Total revenue ($1000)	Percent of Revenue from			Amount	Amount per pupil	Percent for instruction
								Federal Gov't	State Gov't	Local Gov't			
	15	16	17	18	19	20	21	22	23	24	25	26	27
SOUTH DAKOTA—Con.													
Brookings, SD	279	15.6	280	NA	202	12	22 546	3.8	27.1	69.2	18 739	4 296	65.2
Brown, SD	382	15.1	360	NA	270	21	30 289	5.0	24.2	70.8	26 615	4 742	60.6
Brule, SD	102	13.4	97	NA	51	4	6 596	13.2	21.0	65.8	5 833	4 202	66.8
Buffalo, SD	NA	NA	NA	NA	NA	NA	NA	NA	NA	NA	NA	NA	NA
Butte, SD	122	16.5	108	NA	91	3	8 360	11.0	34.8	54.2	7 598	3 861	61.8
Campbell, SD	28	11.5	20	NA	20	2	1 914	7.6	35.8	56.5	1 743	5 587	55.5
Charles Mix, SD	170	12.8	116	NA	151	7	8 865	19.9	31.5	48.6	8 634	4 617	62.9
Clark, SD	60	14.7	51	NA	45	4	3 760	8.0	17.8	74.2	3 564	4 159	58.4
Clay, SD	105	15.5	126	NA	71	4	8 999	5.7	26.6	67.6	7 888	4 692	63.6
Codington, SD	285	17.1	296	NA	196	15	21 026	4.5	19.9	75.6	18 728	3 896	63.4
Corson, SD	86	11.2	45	NA	73	6	5 426	35.8	38.1	26.1	5 162	6 311	62.4
Custer, SD	88	14.4	70	NA	96	12	6 287	11.6	23.1	65.3	5 637	4 343	66.8
Davison, SD	224	15.1	234	NA	141	6	17 551	5.9	39.8	54.3	16 097	4 751	62.2
Day, SD	109	13.2	99	NA	76	7	7 483	9.1	37.0	53.8	6 870	5 026	60.5
Deuel, SD	41	16.6	48	NA	36	2	2 917	8.8	22.9	68.3	2 587	3 884	58.1
Dewey, SD	140	15.1	96	NA	140	24	4 968	33.9	31.7	34.4	5 055	5 718	67.8
Douglas, SD	41	12.6	41	NA	28	2	2 458	8.7	36.4	54.9	2 355	4 511	57.9
Edmunds, SD	67	11.1	53	NA	27	2	3 889	8.6	21.9	69.5	3 843	5 151	61.4
Fall River, SD	100	13.7	91	NA	74	6	7 266	10.1	39.3	50.7	6 697	4 867	60.8
Faulk, SD	32	14.4	48	NA	24	2	2 688	8.3	16.7	75.0	2 622	5 440	61.2
Grant, SD	111	14.7	121	NA	66	4	8 143	5.2	16.1	78.6	7 329	4 442	60.3
Gregory, SD	78	14.5	93	NA	90	7	5 758	11.6	40.3	48.2	5 283	4 543	59.6
Haakon, SD	51	13.5	53	NA	28	2	3 174	6.5	19.2	74.3	2 989	4 307	65.5
Hamlin, SD	96	14.1	105	NA	100	6	6 683	7.0	25.7	67.3	5 466	4 254	59.6
Hand, SD	54	12.8	62	NA	37	3	4 466	6.9	23.5	69.6	3 654	5 176	62.2
Hanson, SD	46	12.0	41	NA	52	3	2 835	9.1	34.3	56.6	2 629	4 771	61.4
Harding, SD	33	11.0	24	NA	13	1	1 808	10.7	14.8	74.4	1 826	5 115	64.3
Hughes, SD	209	15.9	199	NA	171	11	15 180	5.9	27.1	67.0	13 375	4 360	66.5
Hutchinson, SD	127	14.7	115	NA	87	5	9 500	7.9	29.8	62.3	8 349	4 508	61.2
Hyde, SD	71	11.9	44	NA	27	1	1 786	8.4	18.9	72.7	1 585	4 516	61.8
Jackson, SD	76	10.4	24	NA	60	6	2 155	16.9	26.7	56.4	2 065	4 780	64.4
Jerauld, SD	52	10.6	53	NA	34	2	3 423	7.1	38.1	54.8	3 010	5 226	65.1
Jones, SD	24	12.4	18	NA	8	1	1 437	6.7	17.0	76.3	1 310	4 746	60.5
Kingsbury, SD	79	13.6	67	NA	53	3	5 440	5.6	28.1	66.3	4 809	4 528	61.2
Lake, SD	149	15.3	152	NA	108	8	10 517	5.3	26.3	68.4	9 624	4 304	65.8
Lawrence, SD	268	14.8	286	NA	187	36	18 699	5.4	15.5	79.1	15 327	3 884	65.9
Lincoln, SD	198	16.6	190	NA	145	7	14 330	3.9	33.0	63.1	12 395	3 878	62.9
Lyman, SD	66	11.1	40	NA	49	6	2 324	11.7	15.2	73.1	2 593	6 483	57.7
McCook, SD	85	13.1	98	NA	50	5	5 769	6.6	32.9	60.5	5 315	4 885	59.5
McPherson, SD	45	12.3	44	NA	31	2	3 168	8.5	17.0	74.5	3 038	5 387	61.7
Marshall, SD	67	13.4	60	NA	41	3	4 585	7.6	24.9	67.5	4 122	4 711	61.0
Meade, SD	216	15.3	178	NA	124	8	15 154	8.1	29.9	62.1	13 470	4 056	66.0
Mellette, SD	49	10.3	28	NA	38	2	3 091	31.8	36.4	31.8	3 108	6 395	63.3
Miner, SD	45	14.2	40	NA	26	2	2 978	7.8	27.2	65.1	2 689	4 235	63.9
Minnehaha, SD	1 439	16.9	1 333	NA	1 250	256	125 286	4.9	18.0	77.1	106 182	4 482	62.2
Moody, SD	128	13.9	165	NA	96	11	6 287	9.0	29.9	61.1	5 413	4 067	61.2
Pennington, SD	1 147	16.3	846	NA	766	77	85 433	12.3	28.1	59.6	79 255	4 256	62.2
Perkins, SD	67	11.7	54	NA	43	5	5 496	6.7	34.7	58.6	4 463	5 579	59.8
Potter, SD	48	12.1	54	NA	18	2	3 748	6.0	23.2	70.8	3 120	5 342	68.1
Roberts, SD	191	12.9	124	NA	144	7	10 540	17.3	33.7	49.0	9 913	5 012	61.9
Sanborn, SD	49	13.4	51	NA	31	4	3 098	9.4	40.9	49.7	2 771	4 205	59.3
Shannon, SD	272	13.1	65	NA	355	47	8 953	50.6	41.9	7.5	8 614	8 537	57.0
Spink, SD	128	12.9	91	NA	113	9	8 735	6.8	28.6	64.7	8 108	5 058	64.1
Stanley, SD	37	16.3	43	NA	23	2	2 688	10.6	15.4	73.9	2 679	4 458	59.1
Sully, SD	43	9.9	33	NA	22	3	3 198	4.6	10.0	85.4	2 671	6 344	63.9
Todd, SD	210	13.5	117	NA	283	24	11 962	56.3	32.8	10.9	11 517	5 438	58.0
Tripp, SD	102	13.8	80	NA	60	5	6 212	10.5	26.8	62.7	5 670	4 160	66.3
Turner, SD	120	13.6	110	NA	86	7	7 243	6.2	25.8	68.0	6 847	4 227	62.2
Union, SD	171	15.0	171	NA	147	12	13 706	5.3	24.8	69.9	11 256	4 385	61.7
Walworth, SD	72	15.5	68	NA	45	5	5 825	9.3	38.1	52.6	5 148	4 706	60.9
Yankton, SD	203	18.4	249	NA	157	5	16 897	4.9	20.0	75.1	13 710	3 700	63.4
Ziebach, SD	55	11.5	23	NA	29	3	1 988	43.0	34.4	22.6	1 819	5 793	65.4

Table D-2.   School and Student Characteristics by County

State/County code	County	County type[1]	Population, 1996		Number of school districts, 1995-1996	Level of schools, 1995-1996				Level of students, 1995-1996				Characteristics of students, 1995-1996		
			Total persons	Percent age 5-17		Number of schools	Percent Primary	Middle	High	Number of students	Percent Primary	Middle	High	Percent with IEP[2]	Percent free-lunch eligible	Percent minority
			1	2	3	4	5	6	7	8	9	10	11	12	13	14
47000	**TENNESSEE**															
47001	Anderson, TN	2	71 587	17.4	3	26	65.4	23.1	11.5	13 095	47.1	24.1	28.8	18.1	NA	8.0
47003	Bedford, TN	6	33 856	18.4	1	9	44.4	22.2	11.1	5 889	28.3	22.2	18.7	15.5	NA	14.3
47005	Benton, TN	7	16 014	16.9	1	5	40.0	20.0	20.0	2 572	29.8	29.1	22.7	15.1	NA	3.1
47007	Bledsoe, TN	8	10 386	18.1	1	4	75.0	—	25.0	1 738	71.3	—	28.7	22.1	NA	2.3
47009	Blount, TN	2	99 010	16.5	3	24	70.8	12.5	16.7	15 497	61.0	9.9	29.1	17.4	NA	5.5
47011	Bradley, TN	4	80 133	18.1	2	25	72.0	12.0	8.0	13 623	52.5	19.5	23.8	13.8	NA	7.3
47013	Campbell, TN	6	37 340	18.9	1	17	70.6	11.8	11.8	6 609	51.8	18.4	28.7	14.5	NA	0.7
47015	Cannon, TN	8	11 722	18.5	1	7	85.7	—	14.3	1 999	71.1	—	28.9	13.8	NA	2.6
47017	Carroll, TN	6	28 836	17.2	5	13	46.2	15.4	30.8	5 166	52.6	12.9	26.1	15.8	NA	14.4
47019	Carter, TN	2	53 193	16.1	2	21	61.9	9.5	23.8	8 573	57.4	11.5	30.9	17.7	NA	1.8
47021	Cheatham, TN	2	33 175	20.0	1	11	63.6	18.2	18.2	6 347	44.0	22.9	33.2	12.5	NA	2.3
47023	Chester, TN	6	14 099	17.1	1	6	50.0	33.3	16.7	2 366	45.4	23.3	31.2	12.5	NA	17.8
47025	Claiborne, TN	6	28 828	19.1	1	11	54.5	18.2	18.2	4 640	49.8	18.0	24.9	15.8	NA	1.1
47027	Clay, TN	9	7 323	17.3	1	4	50.0	—	25.0	1 227	51.3	—	23.6	13.6	NA	1.7
47029	Cocke, TN	7	31 495	17.9	2	11	81.8	—	9.1	5 254	60.9	—	22.2	16.7	NA	4.1
47031	Coffee, TN	5	44 780	18.5	3	18	66.7	22.2	11.1	8 625	48.2	23.5	28.3	15.2	NA	5.9
47033	Crockett, TN	8	13 686	17.9	3	7	71.4	14.3	14.3	2 619	49.4	24.2	26.3	15.7	NA	25.1
47035	Cumberland, TN	7	42 048	17.1	1	9	88.9	—	11.1	6 375	74.2	—	25.8	12.6	NA	0.5
47037	Davidson, TN	2	535 036	15.9	1	119	68.1	16.8	10.9	70 455	57.5	14.9	25.9	12.5	NA	47.1
47039	Decatur, TN	9	10 731	17.3	1	5	40.0	20.0	20.0	1 880	37.6	22.1	27.9	18.6	NA	5.2
47041	De Kalb, TN	6	15 474	17.7	1	4	50.0	25.0	25.0	2 698	45.7	24.5	29.9	14.6	NA	2.8
47043	Dickson, TN	2	39 666	19.6	1	11	63.6	27.3	9.1	7 487	55.8	23.1	21.1	15.9	NA	7.2
47045	Dyer, TN	7	36 193	18.7	2	12	66.7	16.7	16.7	6 857	54.3	17.3	28.5	13.8	NA	16.4
47047	Fayette, TN	1	28 309	22.2	1	8	87.5	—	12.5	4 166	73.5	—	26.5	16.5	NA	68.9
47049	Fentress, TN	9	15 714	19.4	1	6	83.3	—	16.7	2 302	83.1	—	16.9	15.3	NA	0.1
47051	Franklin, TN	7	36 850	18.0	1	12	66.7	16.7	8.3	5 939	50.3	20.7	18.5	15.8	NA	7.9
47053	Gibson, TN	4	47 657	17.5	5	19	52.6	21.1	21.1	8 648	46.9	19.1	26.7	14.0	NA	27.3
47055	Giles, TN	6	28 430	18.0	1	8	62.5	12.5	25.0	4 894	62.3	9.4	28.3	16.1	NA	15.6
47057	Grainger, TN	8	19 107	17.9	1	5	60.0	—	20.0	3 186	56.3	—	24.2	15.4	NA	0.4
47059	Greene, TN	6	58 613	16.8	2	21	71.4	4.8	23.8	9 180	63.5	5.9	30.6	15.2	NA	4.7
47061	Grundy, TN	6	13 859	21.0	1	7	85.7	—	14.3	2 504	65.9	—	34.1	24.8	NA	0.4
47063	Hamblen, TN	5	53 321	17.4	1	20	60.0	20.0	10.0	8 826	47.6	22.9	28.9	18.2	NA	7.4
47065	Hamilton, TN	2	295 373	17.4	2	80	58.8	20.0	16.3	44 400	46.3	22.5	26.5	12.9	NA	32.1
47067	Hancock, TN	9	6 879	18.8	1	6	83.3	—	16.7	1 247	61.3	—	38.7	14.9	NA	0.3
47069	Hardeman, TN	6	24 228	20.9	1	9	66.7	11.1	22.2	4 858	58.1	11.6	30.3	14.7	NA	53.1
47071	Hardin, TN	6	24 566	18.2	1	10	80.0	10.0	10.0	4 146	49.2	20.7	30.1	13.2	NA	6.3
47073	Hawkins, TN	2	48 388	17.4	2	17	64.7	17.6	11.8	7 218	48.8	20.6	28.4	15.7	NA	1.6
47075	Haywood, TN	6	19 764	22.2	1	6	50.0	33.3	16.7	4 275	42.6	28.5	28.9	12.0	NA	65.0
47077	Henderson, TN	6	23 451	18.4	2	9	77.8	—	11.1	4 360	64.5	—	26.1	15.7	NA	10.4
47079	Henry, TN	7	29 736	16.8	2	10	70.0	20.0	10.0	4 890	59.7	10.9	29.4	15.4	NA	13.7
47081	Hickman, TN	6	19 430	17.1	1	5	40.0	40.0	20.0	3 320	40.9	31.2	27.9	20.1	NA	3.1
47083	Houston, TN	8	7 782	18.1	1	3	66.7	—	33.3	1 381	71.3	—	28.7	12.8	NA	6.0
47085	Humphreys, TN	6	16 675	18.5	1	5	40.0	20.0	20.0	3 007	27.9	19.4	23.8	12.4	NA	5.0
47087	Jackson, TN	9	9 409	16.7	1	4	75.0	—	25.0	1 511	71.5	—	28.5	15.2	NA	—
47089	Jefferson, TN	6	40 268	16.3	1	10	70.0	20.0	10.0	5 989	54.6	16.7	28.7	14.3	NA	3.5
47091	Johnson, TN	8	16 485	15.7	1	8	75.0	12.5	12.5	2 405	57.8	15.0	27.2	15.7	NA	1.3
47093	Knox, TN	2	364 566	16.0	1	82	65.9	15.9	15.9	53 081	49.1	22.7	27.9	17.3	NA	15.4
47095	Lake, TN	9	8 331	13.6	1	3	66.7	—	33.3	1 075	71.9	—	28.1	15.5	NA	27.1
47097	Lauderdale, TN	6	23 972	20.1	1	6	33.3	33.3	33.3	5 088	37.4	32.4	30.1	17.1	NA	40.5
47099	Lawrence, TN	6	38 785	18.6	1	13	69.2	7.7	23.1	6 882	61.2	6.9	31.8	14.1	NA	2.7
47101	Lewis, TN	7	10 548	20.0	1	3	33.3	33.3	33.3	1 921	38.5	32.1	29.4	12.8	NA	2.2
47103	Lincoln, TN	6	28 756	18.0	2	11	45.5	27.3	9.1	5 392	43.3	20.0	20.0	14.0	NA	10.9
47105	Loudon, TN	2	37 240	16.9	2	12	50.0	25.0	16.7	6 343	44.3	18.9	25.8	11.8	NA	2.5
47107	McMinn, TN	7	45 706	18.1	3	15	73.3	13.3	13.3	8 067	62.6	9.0	28.3	18.2	NA	8.4
47109	McNairy, TN	7	23 679	18.1	1	8	62.5	12.5	25.0	3 999	52.8	11.6	35.6	11.2	NA	10.1
47111	Macon, TN	6	17 373	18.2	1	6	50.0	16.7	16.7	3 275	38.0	17.9	22.1	12.7	NA	0.5
47113	Madison, TN	3	84 390	19.1	1	23	60.9	21.7	17.4	13 565	48.3	23.4	28.3	16.5	NA	48.9
47115	Marion, TN	2	26 533	19.3	2	11	45.5	18.2	27.3	4 754	40.8	23.4	29.5	13.5	NA	5.1
47117	Marshall, TN	6	25 173	18.7	1	6	33.3	16.7	16.7	4 568	28.9	14.6	18.4	15.7	NA	10.2
47119	Maury, TN	4	66 683	18.9	1	15	53.3	6.7	13.3	11 879	41.6	11.2	20.7	14.2	NA	23.1
47121	Meigs, TN	8	9 289	18.9	1	6	83.3	—	—	1 628	67.8	—	22.1	NA	NA	1.8
47123	Monroe, TN	6	33 289	18.5	2	14	57.1	21.4	21.4	6 088	52.7	17.3	30.0	13.3	NA	3.8
47125	Montgomery, TN	3	120 923	18.3	1	24	58.3	25.0	16.7	21 609	49.3	25.0	25.7	10.8	NA	29.4
47127	Moore, TN	9	5 241	19.1	1	2	50.0	—	50.0	1 016	50.9	—	49.1	10.9	NA	4.0
47129	Morgan, TN	8	18 280	19.1	1	7	28.6	—	14.3	3 319	35.0	—	13.3	15.4	NA	0.3
47131	Obion, TN	7	32 053	18.7	2	12	50.0	16.7	33.3	5 799	53.3	10.2	36.5	14.5	NA	15.6

1. County type code is from the Economic Research Service of the USDA. See notes and definitions at the end of this section.   2. IEP = Individual Education Program. See notes and definitions at the end of this section.

Table D-2. School and Student Characteristics by County — Continued

County	Staff and students, 1995–1996						Revenues, fiscal 1995					Current expenditures, fiscal 1995		
	Number of teachers	Pupil/ teacher ratio	Number of graduates	Dropouts grades 9–12 (percent)	Local school non-teaching staff	Central admin. staff	Total revenue ($1000)	Percent of Revenue from			Amount	Amount per pupil	Percent for instruction
								Federal Gov't	State Gov't	Local Gov't			
	15	16	17	18	19	20	21	22	23	24	25	26	27
TENNESSEE													
Anderson, TN	874	15.0	762	NA	777	18	71 092	10.5	45.3	44.2	61 937	4 832	63.9
Bedford, TN	333	17.7	327	NA	320	6	22 721	8.2	56.4	35.4	19 869	3 372	65.1
Benton, TN	153	16.8	132	NA	132	3	11 002	10.0	54.1	35.9	9 528	3 747	66.2
Bledsoe, TN	72	24.1	90	NA	125	1	7 122	14.7	64.6	20.7	6 018	3 643	63.8
Blount, TN	913	17.0	824	NA	618	13	69 706	6.4	47.1	46.5	64 065	4 200	66.0
Bradley, TN	744	18.3	751	NA	559	11	54 948	8.0	51.3	40.6	50 292	3 775	69.2
Campbell, TN	401	16.5	346	NA	344	7	27 206	14.0	57.9	28.1	24 041	3 711	66.7
Cannon, TN	112	17.8	110	NA	94	2	7 347	10.2	62.3	27.5	6 505	3 404	60.7
Carroll, TN	314	16.5	348	NA	198	11	22 973	9.2	56.3	34.5	18 865	3 685	64.2
Carter, TN	529	16.2	482	NA	522	11	37 706	12.1	55.4	32.5	33 882	4 030	65.0
Cheatham, TN	367	17.3	354	NA	338	7	22 298	6.4	59.6	34.1	19 777	3 229	63.5
Chester, TN	130	18.2	120	NA	118	1	8 958	10.7	65.1	24.2	7 215	3 049	68.0
Claiborne, TN	310	15.0	232	NA	320	4	21 222	14.4	56.3	29.2	17 394	3 774	64.6
Clay, TN	89	13.8	100	NA	93	2	6 353	13.1	63.7	23.2	5 818	4 625	65.1
Cocke, TN	289	18.2	330	NA	310	7	21 870	13.9	56.1	29.9	18 915	3 616	65.9
Coffee, TN	568	15.2	481	NA	421	16	40 662	7.5	45.2	47.3	35 215	4 204	66.4
Crockett, TN	152	17.2	120	NA	120	4	10 208	11.7	59.4	28.9	9 007	3 571	59.2
Cumberland, TN	377	16.9	265	NA	355	6	24 440	11.2	54.3	34.4	21 531	3 437	65.9
Davidson, TN	3 165	22.3	2 840	NA	3 305	32	361 966	7.6	36.2	56.1	342 535	4 786	63.2
Decatur, TN	108	17.4	117	NA	127	2	7 476	10.4	64.4	25.2	6 205	3 325	65.5
De Kalb, TN	151	17.9	137	NA	140	4	9 596	11.9	60.8	27.2	7 918	2 996	67.8
Dickson, TN	422	17.7	242	NA	402	5	30 490	8.6	54.0	37.4	25 748	3 453	64.7
Dyer, TN	387	17.7	379	NA	373	8	29 856	9.5	49.4	41.2	28 235	4 186	64.4
Fayette, TN	250	16.1	215	NA	204	6	18 467	10.8	68.3	21.0	15 793	3 529	58.3
Fentress, TN	157	14.7	45	NA	142	2	10 400	14.6	59.6	25.8	9 108	4 035	65.8
Franklin, TN	372	16.0	349	NA	434	4	24 295	8.1	58.2	33.7	21 787	3 692	71.8
Gibson, TN	505	17.1	557	NA	411	11	35 763	10.0	55.8	34.2	30 655	3 565	65.2
Giles, TN	290	16.9	274	NA	240	4	19 422	8.9	55.5	35.7	17 807	3 737	61.9
Grainger, TN	212	15.0	205	NA	136	2	12 954	13.2	64.8	22.0	10 505	3 357	67.8
Greene, TN	538	17.1	533	NA	510	11	41 096	9.0	50.8	40.1	36 535	4 039	67.4
Grundy, TN	178	14.1	144	NA	151	2	10 680	14.3	64.5	21.1	9 507	3 827	66.3
Hamblen, TN	541	16.3	486	NA	435	7	41 033	8.9	45.3	45.8	35 793	4 030	70.4
Hamilton, TN	2 571	17.3	2 212	NA	1 958	39	208 486	8.1	40.1	51.8	188 595	4 251	65.0
Hancock, TN	94	13.3	71	NA	127	6	6 374	24.6	60.2	15.2	5 195	4 153	61.6
Hardeman, TN	313	15.5	285	NA	323	5	19 805	13.2	61.1	25.7	16 714	3 446	67.3
Hardin, TN	267	15.5	240	NA	244	6	17 021	13.9	57.7	28.4	14 020	3 439	64.7
Hawkins, TN	457	15.8	384	NA	490	7	30 258	9.9	55.4	34.7	27 684	3 871	65.6
Haywood, TN	263	16.3	216	NA	585	3	17 487	17.8	55.4	26.9	15 355	3 865	65.1
Henderson, TN	254	17.2	245	NA	167	7	16 401	9.0	63.6	27.3	14 022	3 316	66.8
Henry, TN	296	16.5	289	NA	323	6	21 798	9.4	55.2	35.4	18 077	3 710	64.2
Hickman, TN	207	16.0	165	NA	189	1	12 501	9.7	62.1	28.2	11 839	3 739	60.9
Houston, TN	82	16.8	80	NA	93	1	5 363	10.4	65.0	24.6	4 572	3 384	59.0
Humphreys, TN	163	18.4	212	NA	384	4	11 880	10.2	55.5	34.3	10 893	3 630	65.5
Jackson, TN	101	15.0	93	NA	89	3	6 530	13.8	59.7	26.5	5 427	3 637	60.9
Jefferson, TN	335	17.9	341	NA	306	4	22 293	9.6	59.9	30.5	20 143	3 551	64.1
Johnson, TN	168	14.3	127	NA	198	3	11 001	15.7	56.0	28.3	9 455	4 054	62.1
Knox, TN	2 926	18.1	2 774	NA	2 525	187	243 518	4.2	40.0	55.8	208 616	3 990	66.6
Lake, TN	82	13.1	67	NA	60	2	4 784	15.6	60.7	23.7	4 271	3 915	65.7
Lauderdale, TN	305	16.7	249	NA	278	5	18 728	14.0	63.1	22.9	16 373	3 207	64.3
Lawrence, TN	409	16.8	390	NA	376	2	25 898	9.7	58.1	32.2	23 509	3 472	65.9
Lewis, TN	112	17.2	129	NA	96	5	6 588	11.0	67.8	21.1	5 768	2 937	63.1
Lincoln, TN	326	16.5	277	NA	293	5	20 356	8.5	59.4	32.1	17 935	3 390	67.8
Loudon, TN	330	19.2	348	NA	294	3	26 996	7.1	54.5	38.4	22 959	3 754	65.6
McMinn, TN	454	17.8	420	NA	326	13	33 533	9.1	51.5	39.4	29 949	3 826	66.2
McNairy, TN	250	16.0	277	NA	252	5	16 194	10.6	59.1	30.3	13 968	3 479	65.6
Macon, TN	164	20.0	143	NA	200	1	11 538	9.9	60.5	29.6	9 916	3 140	65.4
Madison, TN	888	15.3	784	NA	744	7	69 194	10.1	40.7	49.2	65 188	4 801	69.1
Marion, TN	284	16.7	294	NA	216	3	19 447	10.1	59.9	30.0	17 032	3 504	67.2
Marshall, TN	252	18.1	279	NA	278	3	18 271	7.2	53.5	39.4	16 671	3 715	62.0
Maury, TN	693	17.1	642	NA	584	6	45 342	6.7	54.3	38.9	39 475	3 375	69.4
Meigs, TN	97	16.8	103	NA	92	4	7 044	12.4	60.3	27.4	6 097	3 727	64.2
Monroe, TN	356	17.1	406	NA	268	7	24 724	11.8	55.8	32.4	21 189	3 585	62.9
Montgomery, TN	1 230	17.6	974	NA	955	10	78 536	8.7	52.9	38.5	70 824	3 445	64.3
Moore, TN	56	18.1	74	NA	29	1	4 350	6.5	54.8	38.7	3 688	3 677	61.2
Morgan, TN	214	15.5	216	NA	160	4	13 093	12.4	64.7	22.9	11 715	3 567	65.1
Obion, TN	387	15.0	371	NA	413	8	25 612	8.4	52.0	39.6	23 253	4 200	66.1

Table D-2.   School and Student Characteristics by County

State/County code	County	County type[1]	Population, 1996		Number of school districts, 1995–1996	Level of schools, 1995–1996				Level of students, 1995–1996				Characteristics of students, 1995–1996		
			Total persons	Percent age 5–17		Number of schools	Percent			Number of students	Percent			Percent with IEP[2]	Percent free-lunch eligible	Percent minority
							Primary	Middle	High		Primary	Middle	High			
			1	2	3	4	5	6	7	8	9	10	11	12	13	14
	TENNESSEE—Con.															
47133	Overton, TN	7	18 654	17.9	1	8	62.5	12.5	12.5	3 023	55.7	14.8	28.6	17.4	NA	0.2
47135	Perry, TN	9	7 217	17.8	1	3	66.7	—	33.3	1 172	69.5	—	30.5	18.9	NA	3.0
47137	Pickett, TN	9	4 633	17.8	1	2	50.0	—	50.0	822	53.4	—	46.6	15.9	NA	—
47139	Polk, TN	9	14 421	18.0	1	6	66.7	—	33.3	2 246	64.3	—	35.7	15.2	NA	0.3
47141	Putnam, TN	5	57 928	16.0	1	14	57.1	7.1	28.6	9 239	50.9	16.1	26.6	15.1	NA	3.1
47143	Rhea, TN	6	27 214	18.7	2	6	83.3	—	16.7	4 759	71.1	—	28.9	11.2	NA	5.3
47145	Roane, TN	4	49 859	17.5	2	19	42.1	21.1	31.6	7 768	45.6	19.8	33.9	17.9	NA	4.6
47147	Robertson, TN	2	49 672	19.6	1	16	56.3	18.8	18.8	9 538	50.7	16.0	24.3	17.6	NA	12.1
47149	Rutherford, TN	2	154 333	19.4	2	35	71.4	8.6	14.3	27 288	60.2	11.7	26.0	11.5	NA	14.1
47151	Scott, TN	6	19 575	21.6	2	10	60.0	20.0	20.0	4 173	55.9	13.4	30.7	12.6	NA	0.1
47153	Sequatchie, TN	6	9 994	19.0	1	3	33.3	33.3	33.3	1 697	37.2	30.4	32.4	26.1	NA	0.2
47155	Sevier, TN	2	61 335	17.5	1	19	63.2	15.8	21.1	11 050	53.1	18.4	28.5	13.6	NA	1.2
47157	Shelby, TN	0	867 409	19.5	2	199	63.8	15.1	17.6	156 812	54.5	15.4	28.3	12.3	NA	66.3
47159	Smith, TN	8	15 663	17.8	1	8	75.0	—	12.5	3 031	49.0	—	27.2	10.2	NA	3.2
47161	Stewart, TN	8	11 009	16.8	1	3	66.7	—	33.3	1 805	70.6	—	29.4	16.2	NA	1.3
47163	Sullivan, TN	2	149 844	16.3	3	49	63.3	22.4	12.2	23 380	48.6	21.7	29.5	14.7	NA	3.0
47165	Sumner, TN	2	119 675	20.1	1	34	52.9	26.5	20.6	21 769	42.7	25.7	31.6	15.6	NA	8.1
47167	Tipton, TN	1	45 006	22.0	2	11	45.5	27.3	18.2	10 916	43.0	24.3	32.5	18.5	NA	28.9
47169	Trousdale, TN	6	6 588	18.1	1	2	50.0	—	50.0	1 224	54.7	—	45.3	12.7	NA	14.5
47171	Unicoi, TN	2	17 135	16.0	1	6	66.7	16.7	16.7	2 651	45.0	24.3	30.8	20.6	NA	3.7
47173	Union, TN	2	15 539	19.4	1	5	80.0	—	20.0	2 831	67.1	—	32.9	17.3	NA	0.3
47175	Van Buren, TN	9	5 046	19.2	1	2	50.0	—	50.0	805	45.5	—	—	11.2	NA	—
47177	Warren, TN	7	35 556	18.4	1	11	72.7	9.1	18.2	6 354	54.0	15.3	30.7	14.4	NA	7.8
47179	Washington, TN	2	100 265	15.9	2	23	69.6	13.0	13.0	14 474	52.5	17.5	26.2	12.0	NA	6.6
47181	Wayne, TN	8	16 308	17.1	1	7	28.6	28.6	28.6	2 675	34.1	26.7	27.5	16.6	NA	1.3
47183	Weakley, TN	7	32 568	16.0	1	11	27.3	18.2	18.2	5 119	28.9	14.2	18.3	10.8	NA	9.2
47185	White, TN	7	21 872	17.4	1	8	75.0	12.5	12.5	3 777	55.8	16.4	27.8	15.0	NA	2.5
47187	Williamson, TN	2	106 119	21.1	2	30	63.3	23.3	13.3	19 280	48.2	25.0	26.9	12.7	NA	9.9
47189	Wilson, TN	2	79 502	19.8	2	19	68.4	10.5	15.8	13 794	56.6	13.6	29.7	12.2	NA	8.2
48000	**TEXAS**															
48001	Anderson, TX	6	52 174	17.1	7	25	48.0	20.0	32.0	8 766	50.8	17.4	31.8	13.4	33.4	30.2
48003	Andrews, TX	6	14 087	25.1	1	7	71.4	14.3	14.3	3 638	48.5	25.0	26.6	18.9	36.2	49.3
48005	Angelina, TX	5	76 069	21.3	6	36	41.7	27.8	16.7	15 614	44.4	28.7	20.4	13.3	39.2	36.7
48007	Aransas, TX	6	21 803	18.4	1	6	50.0	33.3	16.7	3 320	39.0	34.2	26.8	14.6	44.9	38.9
48009	Archer, TX	3	8 247	20.7	4	9	44.4	11.1	33.3	1 976	48.3	11.9	23.8	11.8	15.4	5.2
48011	Armstrong, TX	8	2 162	21.0	1	2	50.0	—	—	418	42.3	—	—	12.2	19.9	4.3
48013	Atascosa, TX	6	35 044	24.0	5	21	38.1	28.6	28.6	7 937	46.5	24.5	28.9	14.9	50.4	64.5
48015	Austin, TX	6	22 768	19.7	3	13	38.5	38.5	23.1	5 117	35.4	36.3	28.3	11.1	26.6	34.1
48017	Bailey, TX	7	6 789	23.3	2	5	40.0	20.0	20.0	1 611	46.9	23.1	23.0	13.5	54.5	59.0
48019	Bandera, TX	8	14 287	17.2	2	5	40.0	20.0	20.0	2 462	42.6	21.0	21.7	12.6	27.8	16.0
48021	Bastrop, TX	2	46 819	20.8	4	21	28.6	28.6	28.6	9 651	34.3	30.7	26.4	13.3	37.0	39.4
48023	Baylor, TX	7	4 153	15.8	1	2	50.0	—	50.0	806	57.1	—	42.9	17.9	43.9	23.8
48025	Bee, TX	6	27 833	19.8	4	14	50.0	21.4	28.6	5 601	40.8	28.4	30.8	13.7	52.5	67.4
48027	Bell, TX	2	222 450	19.9	9	86	55.8	25.6	14.0	47 680	51.6	28.1	20.1	11.0	30.8	48.5
48029	Bexar, TX	0	1 318 322	20.3	15	364	59.3	17.3	15.1	245 947	51.6	22.1	25.7	13.9	50.7	71.1
48031	Blanco, TX	8	7 774	18.2	2	6	33.3	33.3	33.3	1 454	50.2	20.8	29.0	16.5	28.1	24.5
48033	Borden, TX	9	807	20.4	1	1	—	—	—	201	—	—	—	16.9	21.9	22.9
48035	Bosque, TX	6	16 756	17.4	8	12	25.0	8.3	25.0	3 178	34.5	9.4	25.9	16.4	38.3	20.8
48037	Bowie, TX	3	84 969	20.4	13	40	47.5	20.0	22.5	16 539	44.4	24.0	27.5	13.4	37.2	32.9
48039	Brazoria, TX	1	220 854	21.6	8	69	47.8	31.9	13.0	45 228	42.3	28.1	26.6	12.4	25.8	35.2
48041	Brazos, TX	3	131 904	15.5	2	30	60.0	20.0	13.3	19 514	48.3	25.6	20.7	12.4	31.0	44.6
48043	Brewster, TX	7	9 221	16.4	4	6	50.0	16.7	16.7	1 530	48.4	18.4	25.3	9.0	45.1	58.8
48045	Briscoe, TX	9	1 917	20.6	1	1	—	—	—	285	—	—	—	13.3	48.1	30.9
48047	Brooks, TX	7	8 493	22.3	1	5	40.0	20.0	20.0	1 984	22.0	24.9	26.2	9.7	73.4	93.3
48049	Brown, TX	7	36 746	19.7	7	33	48.5	15.2	27.3	7 162	46.1	24.9	28.9	14.0	33.9	24.4
48051	Burleson, TX	6	15 288	19.9	3	8	25.0	25.0	25.0	3 272	31.4	15.3	22.1	15.8	42.5	40.8
48053	Burnet, TX	6	29 753	17.8	2	11	36.4	27.3	27.3	5 667	43.3	28.8	27.2	12.8	32.9	22.2
48055	Caldwell, TX	2	30 514	21.6	3	16	37.5	18.8	18.8	5 736	42.9	28.7	24.8	15.2	45.7	54.5
48057	Calhoun, TX	6	20 711	21.4	1	9	55.6	22.2	11.1	4 269	49.7	22.4	27.3	11.4	38.2	54.8
48059	Callahan, TX	6	12 580	20.6	4	12	41.7	25.0	33.3	3 037	42.0	22.8	35.2	14.2	28.6	7.6
48061	Cameron, TX	2	315 015	24.9	10	110	57.3	19.1	17.3	80 592	50.2	20.7	28.6	11.0	49.7	93.1
48063	Camp, TX	6	10 913	19.7	1	4	50.0	25.0	25.0	2 093	48.0	21.2	30.8	15.1	39.8	38.9
48065	Carson, TX	8	6 714	22.8	3	8	37.5	12.5	37.5	1 426	47.1	10.7	27.6	15.0	16.0	7.6
48067	Cass, TX	6	30 621	20.6	8	21	42.9	23.8	33.3	6 313	44.2	25.3	32.3	17.3	39.3	27.1
48069	Castro, TX	7	8 535	26.0	3	6	33.3	16.7	33.3	2 306	33.4	26.0	29.3	8.8	60.5	68.1

1. County type code is from the Economic Research Service of the USDA. See notes and definitions at the end of this section.   2. IEP = Individual Education Program. See notes and definitions at the end of this section.

Table D-2. School and Student Characteristics by County — Continued

County	Staff and students, 1995–1996						Revenues, fiscal 1995				Current expenditures, fiscal 1995		
	Number of teachers	Pupil/ teacher ratio	Number of graduates	Dropouts grades 9–12 (percent)	Local school non-teaching staff	Central admin. staff	Total revenue ($1000)	Percent of Revenue from			Amount	Amount per pupil	Percent for instruction
								Federal Gov't	State Gov't	Local Gov't			
	15	16	17	18	19	20	21	22	23	24	25	26	27
TENNESSEE—Con.													
Overton, TN	190	15.9	193	NA	166	2	12 449	12.9	61.0	26.2	10 766	3 582	64.5
Perry, TN	84	14.0	60	NA	81	2	4 769	10.9	63.2	25.9	4 314	3 697	63.4
Pickett, TN	57	14.4	48	NA	50	2	3 853	16.1	64.5	19.4	3 254	3 888	60.4
Polk, TN	140	16.0	133	NA	142	2	9 650	10.7	58.4	30.9	8 308	3 716	65.6
Putnam, TN	537	17.2	510	NA	483	7	35 031	8.0	52.7	39.3	30 709	3 401	65.9
Rhea, TN	266	17.9	234	NA	174	5	17 336	11.2	60.3	28.5	15 223	3 279	69.0
Roane, TN	480	16.2	461	NA	414	7	35 242	9.0	53.4	37.6	31 575	4 126	65.4
Robertson, TN	561	17.0	468	NA	416	3	35 536	6.3	58.4	35.3	31 107	3 371	70.3
Rutherford, TN	1 443	18.9	1 299	NA	1 022	19	111 550	5.1	49.1	45.8	101 216	3 890	67.1
Scott, TN	268	15.6	256	NA	279	7	17 670	13.4	58.4	28.2	15 752	3 809	64.3
Sequatchie, TN	108	15.7	88	NA	106	2	7 740	11.9	56.1	31.9	6 343	3 923	60.4
Sevier, TN	602	18.4	558	NA	650	4	45 801	7.6	42.3	50.1	39 768	3 794	62.6
Shelby, TN	8 148	19.2	6 977	NA	6 635	141	702 316	9.6	43.3	47.1	631 678	4 143	63.3
Smith, TN	160	18.9	149	NA	136	3	10 440	8.6	57.6	33.9	9 204	3 161	65.0
Stewart, TN	94	19.2	107	NA	125	5	7 784	8.4	68.9	22.7	6 258	3 649	58.4
Sullivan, TN	1 457	16.0	1 474	NA	1 468	21	129 530	6.0	39.8	54.2	117 821	5 054	64.2
Sumner, TN	1 315	16.6	1 270	NA	1 075	8	84 743	5.7	52.6	41.7	77 428	3 682	65.0
Tipton, TN	550	19.8	473	NA	545	8	35 544	10.9	60.9	28.2	30 423	3 141	68.0
Trousdale, TN	72	17.0	67	NA	61	2	4 290	7.6	65.2	27.3	3 560	3 080	67.3
Unicoi, TN	157	16.9	148	NA	137	4	10 523	11.1	59.2	29.7	9 529	3 691	65.4
Union, TN	154	18.4	152	NA	92	1	10 322	11.9	64.1	24.0	8 333	3 003	65.0
Van Buren, TN	55	14.6	36	NA	49	2	3 633	11.9	60.4	27.7	2 996	3 876	57.0
Warren, TN	450	14.1	311	NA	350	5	25 014	8.7	54.3	37.0	22 321	3 552	65.0
Washington, TN	834	17.4	756	NA	841	12	68 044	6.8	42.1	51.1	58 681	4 008	66.6
Wayne, TN	172	15.6	154	NA	155	2	11 137	11.6	65.0	23.4	9 453	3 552	64.2
Weakley, TN	298	17.2	323	NA	263	4	20 137	7.7	57.3	35.0	17 650	3 429	65.4
White, TN	215	17.6	219	NA	220	5	13 452	10.6	62.1	27.4	11 893	3 239	65.9
Williamson, TN	1 203	16.0	969	NA	858	12	82 172	3.5	45.0	51.5	77 014	4 174	64.8
Wilson, TN	744	18.5	778	NA	663	14	52 184	5.4	51.5	43.1	45 005	3 378	65.5
TEXAS													
Anderson, TX	642	13.7	437	2.0	531	38	46 593	7.2	55.2	37.5	41 601	4 784	63.3
Andrews, TX	249	14.6	135	2.6	233	6	30 787	4.2	12.5	83.4	19 906	5 479	59.7
Angelina, TX	1 025	15.2	769	5.0	901	23	80 983	8.2	54.0	37.8	65 455	4 267	62.0
Aransas, TX	237	14.0	162	0.9	247	7	18 520	8.8	31.0	60.2	16 206	4 953	59.4
Archer, TX	154	12.8	115	0.7	101	12	10 251	4.5	57.4	38.1	9 658	5 102	65.4
Armstrong, TX	36	11.6	23	0.8	23	2	2 614	3.2	56.3	40.5	2 070	4 964	64.9
Atascosa, TX	561	14.2	392	1.8	486	28	43 431	9.9	56.4	33.7	35 968	4 635	61.2
Austin, TX	337	15.2	266	2.3	277	9	26 501	5.2	47.5	47.4	23 053	4 574	61.4
Bailey, TX	132	12.2	62	3.5	115	6	10 524	10.0	49.8	40.3	9 132	5 585	60.4
Bandera, TX	175	14.1	101	0.3	154	7	12 890	4.3	37.5	58.2	9 819	4 385	60.6
Bastrop, TX	694	13.9	427	3.9	596	15	50 382	7.0	58.5	34.5	41 546	4 572	61.0
Baylor, TX	64	12.5	36	1.4	36	2	4 994	5.4	61.3	33.3	4 173	5 177	65.9
Bee, TX	368	15.2	261	1.2	435	11	30 568	10.6	63.7	25.6	25 902	4 659	61.9
Bell, TX	3 048	15.6	1 888	1.3	3 082	47	237 451	12.8	58.7	28.6	204 408	4 371	60.2
Bexar, TX	15 625	15.7	10 763	3.2	15 324	327	1 403 783	8.7	53.7	37.6	1 202 388	4 970	62.1
Blanco, TX	119	12.2	74	0.5	79	4	8 642	3.8	54.2	41.9	6 811	4 900	66.2
Borden, TX	20	10.2	15	NA	20	1	4 001	1.2	9.1	89.7	2 046	10 656	53.4
Bosque, TX	247	12.9	184	1.1	202	18	18 171	6.0	58.8	35.2	15 363	4 951	63.7
Bowie, TX	1 200	13.8	933	2.6	922	35	85 232	9.3	56.4	34.3	72 838	4 408	64.4
Brazoria, TX	2 676	16.9	1 958	2.9	2 507	81	235 253	4.9	35.8	59.3	199 504	4 479	60.1
Brazos, TX	1 295	15.1	840	3.0	1 268	22	106 498	5.1	39.5	55.4	89 892	4 669	61.8
Brewster, TX	127	12.0	84	1.7	84	10	9 031	6.3	56.6	37.1	7 768	5 111	63.2
Briscoe, TX	27	10.7	15	NA	20	2	1 864	8.8	60.9	30.3	1 538	5 359	62.0
Brooks, TX	145	13.7	101	3.5	127	4	11 119	11.3	44.5	44.2	10 621	5 367	61.0
Brown, TX	520	13.8	395	3.0	472	13	38 761	6.9	57.8	35.3	33 950	4 778	64.6
Burleson, TX	251	13.0	157	2.7	196	23	17 520	8.5	40.6	51.0	16 200	5 104	59.9
Burnet, TX	401	14.1	245	2.4	375	7	30 377	7.1	40.4	52.5	26 006	4 877	61.8
Caldwell, TX	354	16.2	198	1.5	371	7	28 655	11.3	65.0	23.7	25 990	4 702	61.2
Calhoun, TX	262	16.3	199	3.2	273	6	29 286	5.3	14.7	80.0	19 564	4 535	57.9
Callahan, TX	246	12.3	160	2.0	193	5	17 194	5.1	65.2	29.7	14 452	4 763	64.2
Cameron, TX	5 183	15.5	3 898	2.4	6 236	87	456 650	13.0	68.6	18.3	400 147	4 986	63.1
Camp, TX	144	14.5	130	3.3	137	3	9 613	9.9	47.4	42.8	9 296	4 459	68.3
Carson, TX	124	11.5	123	1.9	89	6	10 180	3.6	22.1	74.3	8 729	6 173	62.9
Cass, TX	484	13.1	382	1.9	416	20	34 991	8.1	53.7	38.2	29 855	4 783	64.2
Castro, TX	192	12.0	118	3.1	150	8	13 706	11.9	58.2	29.8	12 381	5 376	62.5

Table D-2.   School and Student Characteristics by County

State/ County code	County	County type[1]	Population, 1996 Total persons	Population, 1996 Percent age 5–17	Number of school districts, 1995–1996	Level of schools, 1995–1996 Number of schools	Percent Primary	Percent Middle	Percent High	Level of students, 1995–1996 Number of students	Percent Primary	Percent Middle	Percent High	Characteristics of students, 1995–1996 Percent with IEP[2]	Percent free-lunch eligible	Percent minority
			1	2	3	4	5	6	7	8	9	10	11	12	13	14
	TEXAS—Con.															
48071	Chambers, TX	1	22 789	22.8	3	10	40.0	30.0	30.0	4 675	46.7	24.1	29.3	13.0	27.1	23.9
48073	Cherokee, TX	6	42 484	18.7	5	16	43.8	18.8	31.3	7 574	39.5	27.7	28.6	10.8	42.5	36.9
48075	Childress, TX	7	7 580	17.1	1	3	33.3	33.3	33.3	1 297	46.0	23.7	30.3	21.0	34.2	36.5
48077	Clay, TX	6	10 450	19.7	5	7	14.3	14.3	14.3	2 013	23.3	13.2	15.8	15.1	20.2	6.0
48079	Cochran, TX	7	4 083	24.2	3	7	42.9	14.3	42.9	1 260	46.7	13.2	40.1	11.0	58.4	60.2
48081	Coke, TX	8	3 437	17.4	2	13	23.1	7.7	30.8	766	18.8	0.1	32.6	14.6	27.2	28.1
48083	Coleman, TX	6	9 700	16.9	4	13	23.1	15.4	23.1	1 869	45.9	14.2	27.0	15.4	43.0	24.2
48085	Collin, TX	0	372 445	20.7	14	102	56.9	23.5	12.7	66 713	51.0	23.5	16.4	11.0	10.9	19.9
48087	Collingsworth, TX	9	3 269	19.8	2	4	25.0	25.0	25.0	824	40.5	19.9	25.8	14.9	48.3	42.2
48089	Colorado, TX	7	18 757	19.7	3	12	41.7	25.0	25.0	3 720	47.3	20.9	31.2	17.0	38.9	46.3
48091	Comal, TX	1	67 687	18.4	2	22	54.5	22.7	18.2	14 284	47.5	23.7	28.6	13.1	24.9	30.5
48093	Comanche, TX	7	13 645	16.7	4	10	30.0	20.0	30.0	2 403	43.1	19.6	22.1	14.6	41.7	31.9
48095	Concho, TX	8	3 186	17.2	2	9	33.3	11.1	22.2	571	34.9	0.2	34.0	16.3	39.1	46.1
48097	Cooke, TX	6	32 254	20.9	8	20	55.0	10.0	15.0	5 774	44.8	14.4	19.3	14.3	29.3	16.1
48099	Coryell, TX	2	74 446	19.0	5	19	52.6	21.1	15.8	10 667	42.3	27.5	26.9	11.1	21.0	32.3
48101	Cottle, TX	9	1 975	19.9	1	2	50.0	—	50.0	401	68.8	—	31.2	10.0	57.9	40.9
48103	Crane, TX	6	4 514	26.1	1	3	33.3	33.3	33.3	1 191	45.6	25.8	28.6	20.7	31.2	52.1
48105	Crockett, TX	7	4 372	21.6	1	4	50.0	25.0	25.0	965	46.7	24.7	28.6	8.9	42.3	60.8
48107	Crosby, TX	8	7 349	22.6	3	11	27.3	18.2	36.4	1 776	49.2	18.4	31.4	15.9	65.3	68.0
48109	Culberson, TX	7	3 210	23.4	1	3	33.3	33.3	33.3	794	58.7	16.9	24.4	9.8	73.8	80.0
48111	Dallam, TX	7	6 269	21.7	2	5	20.0	40.0	20.0	1 748	32.2	31.6	25.7	17.7	37.0	30.4
48113	Dallas, TX	0	2 000 192	18.5	15	507	65.3	18.7	13.4	362 478	55.5	20.2	23.9	10.2	40.7	61.0
48115	Dawson, TX	7	15 172	21.5	4	13	38.5	23.1	15.4	3 284	34.7	32.3	22.3	11.8	50.7	63.0
48117	Deaf Smith, TX	6	19 519	25.4	2	10	60.0	20.0	10.0	4 595	42.1	23.2	27.7	11.7	55.3	72.9
48119	Delta, TX	8	4 923	17.9	2	5	40.0	20.0	40.0	1 119	50.9	17.4	31.6	18.1	38.9	21.1
48121	Denton, TX	0	348 453	18.9	11	89	58.4	20.2	13.5	53 714	53.0	21.0	22.7	13.4	14.0	17.8
48123	De Witt, TX	6	19 657	18.2	6	16	50.0	18.8	18.8	4 675	45.8	22.8	29.0	13.7	44.7	45.7
48125	Dickens, TX	9	2 317	18.3	2	3	33.3	—	33.3	512	37.9	—	37.1	9.8	37.7	39.5
48127	Dimmit, TX	7	10 475	25.6	2	8	50.0	25.0	25.0	2 679	40.2	27.8	32.0	13.7	72.3	89.6
48129	Donley, TX	9	3 863	16.1	2	4	25.0	25.0	25.0	674	34.4	16.9	24.6	13.1	33.8	18.7
48131	Duval, TX	7	13 383	21.3	4	11	45.5	27.3	27.3	3 324	48.7	23.9	27.4	11.7	68.6	92.8
48133	Eastland, TX	7	18 064	17.5	5	14	35.7	14.3	35.7	3 519	49.6	15.5	27.0	17.8	40.2	16.4
48135	Ector, TX	3	123 398	22.6	1	44	65.9	11.4	15.9	28 528	57.6	20.1	17.3	10.6	56.2	54.9
48137	Edwards, TX	9	3 374	23.7	2	4	50.0	—	50.0	856	70.9	—	29.1	13.4	61.1	52.7
48139	Ellis, TX	1	97 054	22.5	10	41	48.8	24.4	22.0	20 789	45.8	25.1	27.1	14.0	27.6	32.6
48141	El Paso, TX	2	684 446	22.7	9	195	57.4	16.9	21.5	149 211	53.6	19.0	25.4	8.2	61.9	86.3
48143	Erath, TX	6	30 815	17.1	7	15	40.0	20.0	13.3	5 437	38.4	29.8	23.0	12.7	29.4	21.9
48145	Falls, TX	6	17 727	17.8	4	12	41.7	33.3	16.7	3 270	40.6	25.2	22.7	17.4	49.1	55.0
48147	Fannin, TX	6	27 614	17.2	8	19	42.1	15.8	21.1	4 928	44.5	17.2	23.2	18.9	33.3	12.2
48149	Fayette, TX	7	21 185	18.0	5	13	38.5	23.1	30.8	3 674	38.9	25.0	32.5	12.5	26.5	27.4
48151	Fisher, TX	9	4 449	19.9	2	7	28.6	14.3	42.9	777	50.1	19.2	30.6	18.3	39.1	36.6
48153	Floyd, TX	7	8 334	22.4	2	8	25.0	37.5	37.5	2 086	42.0	31.8	26.2	13.6	54.7	65.0
48155	Foard, TX	9	1 719	18.3	1	2	50.0	—	50.0	397	62.7	—	37.3	33.5	54.2	33.5
48157	Fort Bend, TX	0	306 832	23.5	5	72	59.7	16.7	16.7	58 629	50.5	18.1	29.9	9.2	12.0	56.3
48159	Franklin, TX	9	9 320	18.6	1	4	25.0	50.0	25.0	1 433	32.6	39.0	28.4	16.2	26.2	18.4
48161	Freestone, TX	7	17 476	18.9	4	11	45.5	27.3	27.3	3 203	38.1	30.6	31.3	13.3	31.0	28.5
48163	Frio, TX	7	15 824	22.5	2	9	44.4	22.2	22.2	3 324	49.1	23.2	27.3	13.2	55.9	85.6
48165	Gaines, TX	7	14 719	25.9	3	9	33.3	33.3	22.2	3 281	35.1	36.1	24.0	11.6	52.3	50.1
48167	Galveston, TX	0	240 653	19.9	9	82	56.1	25.6	15.9	63 022	47.0	24.9	27.9	10.0	21.3	37.2
48169	Garza, TX	6	4 729	23.0	2	5	40.0	20.0	20.0	1 194	47.9	19.1	24.2	13.4	54.9	52.0
48171	Gillespie, TX	7	19 635	17.5	3	10	50.0	20.0	30.0	3 144	47.2	22.7	30.2	14.5	28.8	29.3
48173	Glasscock, TX	8	1 407	25.0	1	2	50.0	—	50.0	406	57.9	—	42.1	10.3	39.9	34.5
48175	Goliad, TX	8	6 586	19.8	1	3	33.3	33.3	33.3	1 437	43.4	26.6	30.1	17.4	36.5	45.6
48177	Gonzales, TX	6	17 608	20.6	3	12	41.7	25.0	25.0	3 902	48.9	22.6	25.3	14.2	53.6	61.3
48179	Gray, TX	7	23 335	19.3	4	12	58.3	8.3	16.7	4 365	44.1	20.6	27.4	12.9	29.6	21.8
48181	Grayson, TX	3	100 589	18.8	13	51	49.0	23.5	25.5	18 992	45.4	27.0	27.6	14.4	29.8	15.9
48183	Gregg, TX	3	112 138	20.0	7	49	46.9	30.6	16.3	23 362	43.0	31.0	25.5	12.3	33.9	33.2
48185	Grimes, TX	6	22 192	19.3	4	11	45.5	18.2	36.4	4 128	43.5	24.5	32.0	10.6	42.9	45.9
48187	Guadalupe, TX	1	75 235	20.4	4	29	41.4	31.0	24.1	13 892	37.8	33.7	28.4	14.2	33.1	46.0
48189	Hale, TX	4	36 548	22.4	5	22	40.9	27.3	18.2	8 526	44.1	27.6	24.9	13.7	49.3	66.1
48191	Hall, TX	9	3 750	17.8	3	6	16.7	33.3	16.7	905	20.2	22.9	17.0	19.2	48.5	55.4
48193	Hamilton, TX	6	7 570	16.1	2	4	50.0	—	50.0	1 530	66.7	—	33.3	16.1	30.5	10.5
48195	Hansford, TX	7	5 372	22.9	3	7	42.9	28.6	28.6	1 356	46.4	25.1	28.5	13.6	25.7	36.7
48197	Hardeman, TX	7	4 808	18.9	2	5	40.0	20.0	40.0	1 085	55.1	11.0	33.9	21.4	34.3	30.6
48199	Hardin, TX	2	47 574	22.4	5	22	40.9	31.8	22.7	11 147	40.8	29.0	30.2	15.1	24.8	13.5
48201	Harris, TX	0	3 126 966	20.0	20	706	62.6	19.8	13.7	594 862	52.0	22.0	24.4	10.1	41.3	64.0

1. County type code is from the Economic Research Service of the USDA. See notes and definitions at the end of this section.   2. IEP = Individual Education Program. See notes and definitions at the end of this section.

Table D-2. School and Student Characteristics by County — Continued

County	Staff and students, 1995–1996						Revenues, fiscal 1995					Current expenditures, fiscal 1995		
	Number of teachers	Pupil/ teacher ratio	Number of graduates	Dropouts grades 9–12 (percent)	Local school non-teaching staff	Central admin. staff	Total revenue ($1000)	Percent of Revenue from			Amount	Amount per pupil	Percent for instruction
								Federal Gov't	State Gov't	Local Gov't			
	15	16	17	18	19	20	21	22	23	24	25	26	27
TEXAS—Con.													
Chambers, TX	310	15.1	233	1.8	284	8	40 295	2.8	21.5	75.7	25 183	5 586	59.4
Cherokee, TX	552	13.7	362	2.5	445	19	40 345	9.6	59.5	31.0	35 205	4 659	62.1
Childress, TX	93	13.9	67	4.8	114	3	6 963	10.2	67.4	22.4	6 386	4 947	67.6
Clay, TX	165	12.2	120	1.6	121	13	11 691	4.8	61.4	33.8	10 080	5 030	63.0
Cochran, TX	115	10.9	63	6.3	92	5	13 925	6.0	24.7	69.3	9 468	7 255	59.5
Coke, TX	66	11.6	45	NA	43	1	5 284	3.3	45.2	51.5	4 247	6 007	62.3
Coleman, TX	168	11.1	119	1.2	140	7	12 152	7.0	66.9	26.1	10 857	5 837	59.9
Collin, TX	4 214	15.8	3 232	1.8	2 895	129	384 550	2.6	21.0	76.4	300 963	4 821	62.2
Collingsworth, TX	74	11.2	48	0.4	60	3	4 757	6.4	70.1	23.4	4 737	5 619	67.0
Colorado, TX	270	13.8	220	2.5	233	15	21 435	8.3	43.5	48.2	17 795	4 828	60.9
Comal, TX	907	15.8	726	0.7	819	18	71 722	5.2	35.4	59.4	59 129	4 362	63.3
Comanche, TX	183	13.1	126	2.3	128	10	12 254	8.0	57.5	34.5	10 676	4 529	64.6
Concho, TX	54	10.6	32	1.0	42	3	4 015	6.5	35.5	58.0	3 377	6 162	61.9
Cooke, TX	424	13.6	257	3.8	307	11	32 574	7.3	55.9	36.9	26 741	4 664	63.6
Coryell, TX	700	15.2	565	2.0	676	16	52 680	13.6	61.2	25.2	47 378	4 495	64.3
Cottle, TX	35	11.5	29	0.8	35	1	3 084	7.0	57.1	35.9	2 829	6 951	67.6
Crane, TX	92	13.0	65	3.5	74	2	16 333	2.2	10.2	87.6	8 032	6 589	65.2
Crockett, TX	79	12.2	49	3.6	66	3	9 767	4.3	13.8	81.9	6 281	6 598	57.9
Crosby, TX	144	12.3	95	5.7	165	10	11 978	12.4	58.5	29.2	11 282	5 907	59.6
Culberson, TX	69	11.5	52	NA	51	3	5 003	9.7	34.7	55.6	4 232	5 398	59.9
Dallam, TX	127	13.7	86	1.0	112	7	9 136	9.3	46.5	44.3	7 848	4 797	62.8
Dallas, TX	21 617	16.8	14 457	2.0	17 326	463	1 940 944	6.0	27.6	66.4	1 651 483	4 670	60.4
Dawson, TX	245	13.4	190	2.6	255	9	18 897	11.3	27.5	61.2	17 840	5 197	61.5
Deaf Smith, TX	334	13.8	210	4.2	297	12	22 805	13.6	57.9	28.4	21 562	4 780	64.2
Delta, TX	100	11.2	82	1.3	76	2	6 557	6.4	71.0	22.6	5 972	5 144	64.2
Denton, TX	3 622	14.8	2 339	1.7	2 584	99	273 501	3.1	38.0	58.9	224 503	4 403	63.0
De Witt, TX	357	13.1	290	1.9	351	10	25 734	9.5	52.9	37.6	24 032	5 111	65.1
Dickens, TX	52	9.8	29	1.7	48	3	3 732	7.0	37.9	55.0	4 014	7 631	64.7
Dimmit, TX	206	13.0	126	3.3	264	13	17 191	14.0	62.7	23.2	15 934	5 796	59.4
Donley, TX	65	10.4	44	2.9	36	3	4 251	5.7	58.3	35.9	3 749	5 741	64.5
Duval, TX	270	12.3	176	2.2	231	12	22 563	14.6	45.5	39.8	21 971	6 462	56.8
Eastland, TX	262	13.4	191	1.2	221	26	19 135	7.9	63.6	28.6	17 244	5 000	64.0
Ector, TX	1 676	17.0	1 101	4.3	1 501	42	133 712	9.3	43.7	47.0	117 614	4 176	59.8
Edwards, TX	74	11.6	30	0.4	78	3	5 712	8.9	47.7	43.4	5 004	6 058	64.1
Ellis, TX	1 351	15.4	980	2.4	1 012	56	107 029	3.9	51.2	44.9	87 193	4 340	62.7
El Paso, TX	9 330	16.0	6 931	3.5	8 202	170	776 739	10.2	60.5	29.3	694 029	4 688	61.6
Erath, TX	344	15.8	279	2.3	270	16	26 320	6.5	52.8	40.7	21 659	4 048	63.6
Falls, TX	264	12.4	160	2.1	246	15	18 694	10.4	68.5	21.1	16 190	4 918	62.2
Fannin, TX	377	13.1	257	2.3	326	12	27 265	8.8	60.4	30.8	23 323	4 957	64.2
Fayette, TX	277	13.3	216	1.2	230	9	23 163	4.7	26.8	68.5	18 035	4 885	61.5
Fisher, TX	72	10.8	63	1.7	54	2	5 946	7.7	63.5	28.8	4 711	5 859	61.9
Floyd, TX	165	12.7	100	4.0	166	5	12 222	11.2	58.7	30.1	11 552	5 660	62.6
Foard, TX	39	10.1	17	2.1	34	1	2 493	6.3	59.1	34.6	2 290	5 979	64.1
Fort Bend, TX	3 166	18.5	3 124	1.9	3 071	54	328 771	3.8	40.8	55.3	267 215	4 374	60.0
Franklin, TX	97	14.8	77	1.7	70	2	7 269	5.2	33.3	61.4	5 924	4 244	64.7
Freestone, TX	224	14.3	194	0.6	188	18	18 537	6.4	24.9	68.7	15 673	4 761	61.9
Frio, TX	257	12.9	182	2.8	254	6	18 176	16.2	57.3	26.5	17 484	5 185	62.1
Gaines, TX	248	13.2	161	1.7	221	5	43 279	4.4	8.9	86.8	19 466	5 917	60.8
Galveston, TX	3 881	16.2	3 074	2.8	3 359	79	364 104	4.9	23.5	71.6	298 244	4 822	59.7
Garza, TX	94	12.7	75	0.8	72	2	7 554	6.2	21.7	72.1	6 724	5 613	64.8
Gillespie, TX	208	15.1	173	2.3	181	10	17 403	6.4	34.4	59.2	14 244	4 650	61.9
Glasscock, TX	36	11.3	30	1.8	25	1	5 672	2.7	11.6	85.7	2 909	6 943	63.7
Goliad, TX	102	14.0	49	NA	94	13	7 585	9.6	24.2	66.2	7 304	5 451	55.3
Gonzales, TX	280	13.9	178	3.5	256	10	20 126	10.5	62.5	27.0	17 881	4 642	63.6
Gray, TX	322	13.6	228	2.8	237	9	23 744	6.4	29.9	63.7	20 918	4 822	62.1
Grayson, TX	1 285	14.8	979	1.2	1 025	31	100 011	5.7	49.6	44.8	84 648	4 539	63.2
Gregg, TX	1 583	14.8	1 266	3.0	1 387	43	120 724	6.9	33.6	59.5	106 319	4 552	61.5
Grimes, TX	288	14.3	182	4.0	255	12	23 702	7.9	49.1	43.0	18 656	4 608	62.3
Guadalupe, TX	965	14.4	655	3.6	932	23	76 385	7.4	56.8	35.9	65 656	4 868	62.5
Hale, TX	597	14.3	377	4.0	480	22	44 795	10.4	58.0	31.6	39 956	4 694	63.0
Hall, TX	89	10.2	61	1.8	84	3	5 650	8.5	63.3	28.2	5 482	6 044	64.7
Hamilton, TX	110	13.9	81	2.5	84	12	8 360	7.2	63.3	29.5	7 711	5 355	64.4
Hansford, TX	124	10.9	80	0.8	72	7	9 907	4.0	19.2	76.8	8 282	6 218	61.2
Hardeman, TX	91	12.0	77	1.5	83	11	7 616	8.6	42.6	48.8	6 479	5 890	63.6
Hardin, TX	725	15.4	586	2.4	692	26	56 586	5.9	58.4	35.7	48 508	4 411	61.9
Harris, TX	35 714	16.7	25 047	3.1	31 874	618	3 153 394	6.6	32.3	61.1	2 763 306	4 772	59.6

Table D-2. School and Student Characteristics by County

State/ County code	County	County type[1]	Population, 1996		Number of school districts, 1995–1996	Level of schools, 1995–1996				Level of students, 1995–1996				Characteristics of students, 1995–1996		
			Total persons	Percent age 5–17		Number of schools	Percent Primary	Percent Middle	Percent High	Number of students	Percent Primary	Percent Middle	Percent High	Percent with IEP[2]	Percent free-lunch eligible	Percent minority
			1	2	3	4	5	6	7	8	9	10	11	12	13	14
	TEXAS—Con.															
48203	Harrison, TX	3	59 685	21.8	6	29	44.8	31.0	24.1	12 652	38.7	31.3	30.0	10.0	36.9	35.6
48205	Hartley, TX	7	5 210	16.4	2	2	—	—	—	296	—	—	—	13.5	38.2	12.8
48207	Haskell, TX	7	6 247	18.3	4	5	20.0	—	20.0	1 235	33.7	—	27.0	18.9	46.1	36.0
48209	Hays, TX	2	81 744	18.0	4	26	34.6	34.6	19.2	15 926	31.8	35.4	28.7	14.5	30.9	44.2
48211	Hemphill, TX	9	3 648	23.2	1	6	16.7	33.3	16.7	878	24.5	38.0	28.0	16.7	29.3	27.6
48213	Henderson, TX	1	65 664	18.0	8	28	32.1	25.0	32.1	9 691	36.3	28.1	28.2	15.7	32.9	20.1
48215	Hidalgo, TX	2	495 594	25.6	15	176	58.5	24.4	15.3	129 484	49.4	25.8	24.7	8.5	71.2	95.4
48217	Hill, TX	6	29 698	18.4	12	24	37.5	16.7	20.8	5 505	38.4	19.7	22.4	14.9	41.8	27.1
48219	Hockley, TX	6	23 931	23.6	6	20	45.0	10.0	25.0	5 507	44.2	13.3	22.0	11.6	42.2	51.7
48221	Hood, TX	1	34 976	18.7	3	13	38.5	30.8	23.1	6 550	32.1	35.6	27.6	13.0	23.3	9.1
48223	Hopkins, TX	6	30 455	19.6	7	16	43.8	6.3	18.8	5 908	33.4	15.1	23.3	13.4	30.9	19.1
48225	Houston, TX	7	21 962	18.8	5	14	42.9	21.4	35.7	4 093	47.2	20.1	32.7	16.5	47.2	44.2
48227	Howard, TX	5	32 836	19.7	3	17	52.9	17.6	17.6	6 140	50.6	21.0	22.5	10.3	38.7	43.0
48229	Hudspeth, TX	8	3 265	23.0	3	4	—	—	25.0	825	—	—	1.8	10.8	73.1	81.2
48231	Hunt, TX	1	67 906	19.1	10	37	43.2	27.0	29.7	13 329	41.8	29.6	28.6	15.9	34.3	23.0
48233	Hutchinson, TX	6	24 425	21.7	4	15	40.0	20.0	40.0	5 498	39.7	29.0	31.3	12.3	24.2	20.4
48235	Irion, TX	8	1 718	19.5	1	2	50.0	—	—	390	51.0	—	—	16.7	35.1	29.0
48237	Jack, TX	6	7 285	19.6	3	7	28.6	14.3	42.9	1 798	41.9	14.8	29.5	17.1	32.4	10.1
48239	Jackson, TX	6	13 687	21.2	3	13	53.8	15.4	30.8	3 354	47.6	20.8	31.5	13.4	34.8	35.5
48241	Jasper, TX	6	32 954	21.6	5	14	42.9	21.4	35.7	7 553	49.1	22.3	28.7	14.9	37.5	28.1
48243	Jeff Davis, TX	9	2 155	20.0	2	4	25.0	—	25.0	408	32.1	—	35.5	29.7	18.9	43.6
48245	Jefferson, TX	2	243 733	19.4	6	73	53.4	24.7	11.0	44 706	45.1	27.2	22.2	11.6	44.3	56.3
48247	Jim Hogg, TX	6	5 036	21.1	1	3	33.3	33.3	33.3	1 300	47.8	24.2	27.9	13.1	28.0	95.2
48249	Jim Wells, TX	4	39 725	22.5	5	23	52.2	26.1	17.4	8 925	42.7	30.6	21.9	10.1	53.9	80.8
48251	Johnson, TX	1	110 344	21.5	9	48	50.0	22.9	20.8	22 162	49.9	22.7	26.4	13.8	28.4	15.1
48253	Jones, TX	6	18 692	17.9	5	15	33.3	20.0	46.7	3 278	46.7	16.7	36.6	17.8	44.4	29.7
48255	Karnes, TX	6	12 567	21.8	4	11	36.4	18.2	45.5	2 927	50.1	18.8	31.1	14.1	53.3	64.1
48257	Kaufman, TX	1	62 116	21.9	7	34	35.3	32.4	23.5	15 302	41.3	28.3	26.6	14.5	30.8	23.1
48259	Kendall, TX	6	19 639	18.8	2	8	50.0	25.0	25.0	4 863	52.8	19.8	27.4	13.5	19.2	22.9
48261	Kenedy, TX	9	438	20.8	1	1	100.0	—	—	50	100.0	—	—	10.0	18.0	94.0
48263	Kent, TX	9	864	19.3	1	2	50.0	—	50.0	195	52.8	—	47.2	16.4	33.3	19.5
48265	Kerr, TX	7	41 406	16.9	5	16	43.8	18.8	25.0	6 669	44.7	26.9	28.0	14.7	35.4	31.8
48267	Kimble, TX	7	4 215	18.8	1	3	33.3	33.3	33.3	774	43.5	30.5	26.0	14.9	38.1	30.9
48269	King, TX	9	336	25.0	1	1	—	—	—	81	—	—	—	7.4	32.1	14.8
48271	Kinney, TX	9	3 402	17.4	1	4	25.0	25.0	50.0	615	48.3	25.4	26.3	18.9	61.6	64.9
48273	Kleberg, TX	4	30 325	20.0	4	19	47.4	21.1	15.8	6 626	45.2	28.1	25.1	9.5	49.3	77.3
48275	Knox, TX	9	4 425	20.0	4	7	28.6	14.3	28.6	1 040	41.0	13.3	28.1	16.3	47.3	48.3
48277	Lamar, TX	5	45 255	19.0	5	20	45.0	25.0	25.0	8 804	47.7	19.6	26.4	13.0	35.1	23.7
48279	Lamb, TX	6	14 989	21.8	6	16	31.3	18.8	37.5	3 681	44.4	21.0	26.1	11.2	52.3	62.0
48281	Lampasas, TX	6	17 163	20.1	2	8	37.5	—	25.0	3 484	42.5	—	26.1	13.4	37.7	22.4
48283	La Salle, TX	6	6 063	20.8	1	8	37.5	25.0	25.0	1 388	41.9	29.0	26.4	11.1	70.7	86.2
48285	Lavaca, TX	6	18 872	18.8	6	10	50.0	10.0	30.0	2 249	33.6	15.4	33.7	12.2	29.8	19.8
48287	Lee, TX	6	14 442	22.7	3	10	40.0	20.0	30.0	2 897	41.9	21.2	28.6	11.7	33.2	38.3
48289	Leon, TX	8	14 190	19.0	5	12	41.7	16.7	41.7	2 947	50.0	12.4	37.6	13.1	33.4	21.9
48291	Liberty, TX	1	63 294	20.8	7	27	40.7	29.6	25.9	12 979	44.9	26.8	27.8	10.6	34.3	23.8
48293	Limestone, TX	6	20 829	19.4	3	14	35.7	28.6	21.4	4 148	43.5	27.3	28.4	16.5	45.1	39.6
48295	Lipscomb, TX	9	3 081	21.7	4	6	33.3	16.7	16.7	747	28.4	17.4	16.6	11.9	34.4	25.8
48297	Live Oak, TX	6	10 195	20.0	2	7	28.6	42.9	28.6	2 180	35.6	33.6	30.8	12.6	38.4	48.2
48299	Llano, TX	7	12 861	11.7	1	3	33.3	33.3	33.3	1 457	48.7	23.9	27.4	17.2	28.5	9.5
48301	Loving, TX	9	141	22.7	NA	NA	NA	NA	NA	NA	NA	NA	NA	NA	NA	NA
48303	Lubbock, TX	3	232 035	19.1	8	91	58.2	23.1	15.4	43 047	51.1	25.6	21.4	13.7	40.5	48.9
48305	Lynn, TX	6	6 588	21.5	4	9	33.3	22.2	33.3	1 655	47.6	13.8	26.0	12.0	50.3	59.3
48307	McCulloch, TX	7	8 694	19.5	3	7	14.3	28.6	14.3	1 828	9.5	29.8	21.2	17.6	50.6	36.2
48309	McLennan, TX	3	201 775	19.1	18	96	42.7	21.9	22.9	38 419	43.8	24.7	25.0	13.2	40.0	43.1
48311	McMullen, TX	9	799	17.3	1	1	—	—	—	191	—	—	—	19.4	37.7	42.4
48313	Madison, TX	6	11 984	16.2	2	6	50.0	16.7	33.3	2 216	51.4	20.6	28.0	11.5	44.5	36.0
48315	Marion, TX	8	10 430	18.6	1	3	33.3	33.3	33.3	1 670	32.9	37.9	29.2	15.9	48.5	46.5
48317	Martin, TX	6	4 957	24.7	2	4	25.0	25.0	25.0	1 093	39.2	19.3	20.8	11.3	49.1	55.2
48319	Mason, TX	9	3 598	17.0	1	5	40.0	20.0	20.0	689	32.5	37.7	29.6	14.2	36.0	31.1
48321	Matagorda, TX	4	38 192	22.5	5	20	50.0	30.0	20.0	8 775	46.5	24.8	28.8	13.2	45.4	53.2
48323	Maverick, TX	5	46 563	26.5	1	17	70.6	11.8	17.6	11 585	56.6	23.0	20.4	5.6	79.6	98.2
48325	Medina, TX	5	35 363	22.1	5	19	31.6	26.3	26.3	7 671	40.9	28.9	26.3	10.5	39.6	53.8
48327	Menard, TX	8	2 361	17.4	1	4	25.0	25.0	50.0	445	46.1	27.6	26.3	17.8	54.4	53.9
48329	Midland, TX	3	116 016	22.0	2	37	67.6	16.2	13.5	24 702	54.5	22.7	20.6	8.2	35.3	45.2
48331	Milam, TX	6	23 972	21.1	6	13	46.2	15.4	30.8	4 726	47.2	19.0	30.8	13.7	40.9	39.0
48333	Mills, TX	9	4 767	17.9	4	6	16.7	—	16.7	984	31.2	—	26.7	23.3	38.3	18.1

1. County type code is from the Economic Research Service of the USDA. See notes and definitions at the end of this section.   2. IEP = Individual Education Program. See notes and definitions at the end of this section.

Table D-2. School and Student Characteristics by County — Continued

County	Staff and students, 1995–1996						Revenues, fiscal 1995				Current expenditures, fiscal 1995		
	Number of teachers	Pupil/ teacher ratio	Number of graduates	Dropouts grades 9–12 (percent)	Local school non-teaching staff	Central admin. staff	Total revenue ($1000)	Percent of Revenue from			Amount	Amount per pupil	Percent for instruction
								Federal Gov't	State Gov't	Local Gov't			
	15	16	17	18	19	20	21	22	23	24	25	26	27
TEXAS—Con.													
Harrison, TX	824	15.4	663	3.2	749	30	65 410	8.3	34.4	57.3	55 346	4 379	61.1
Hartley, TX	33	9.0	18	1.2	19	2	2 638	4.4	29.2	66.4	2 263	8 351	57.2
Haskell, TX	119	10.4	78	NA	92	4	8 970	7.0	45.0	48.0	7 239	5 638	64.3
Hays, TX	1 086	14.7	698	1.7	1 027	35	90 382	6.1	50.6	43.3	73 676	4 826	60.3
Hemphill, TX	72	12.3	53	1.3	51	1	8 596	2.6	14.4	83.0	5 402	6 588	63.3
Henderson, TX	655	14.8	525	2.4	596	36	52 658	7.1	45.2	47.7	42 866	4 527	62.9
Hidalgo, TX	8 109	16.0	5 779	2.6	10 726	188	761 381	13.3	69.0	17.6	646 508	5 074	60.9
Hill, TX	422	13.1	312	1.3	376	36	31 917	7.5	61.9	30.6	27 307	4 879	61.3
Hockley, TX	420	13.1	316	2.5	349	20	41 025	6.4	20.7	72.9	31 799	5 626	61.7
Hood, TX	425	15.4	321	2.6	302	9	32 576	4.2	42.4	53.4	25 222	3 983	64.0
Hopkins, TX	422	14.0	331	4.1	333	13	32 041	8.2	48.1	43.7	26 726	4 502	64.5
Houston, TX	326	12.5	193	2.0	282	11	22 019	10.2	55.5	34.2	21 098	5 104	62.7
Howard, TX	416	14.8	281	2.1	368	8	33 429	7.9	43.4	48.8	29 450	4 737	61.9
Hudspeth, TX	71	11.6	45	1.6	62	4	7 001	7.7	56.3	36.0	5 229	6 369	57.8
Hunt, TX	930	14.3	704	2.1	737	50	69 453	6.6	58.7	34.7	58 723	4 473	61.8
Hutchinson, TX	392	14.0	343	1.8	320	8	31 139	6.4	35.2	58.3	26 527	4 744	65.1
Irion, TX	36	10.9	22	NA	28	1	3 975	3.3	14.8	81.9	2 753	8 097	58.3
Jack, TX	153	11.8	97	1.5	98	3	10 269	4.4	48.9	46.7	9 276	5 431	64.3
Jackson, TX	251	13.4	153	0.9	221	20	19 233	5.5	54.9	39.6	16 541	4 939	62.6
Jasper, TX	511	14.8	409	1.6	496	21	44 517	6.8	54.6	38.7	36 550	4 856	59.7
Jeff Davis, TX	49	8.3	25	NA	25	3	3 077	2.1	61.1	36.8	2 862	6 564	69.1
Jefferson, TX	2 821	15.8	2 088	3.9	2 649	60	242 253	9.2	27.5	63.2	226 735	5 003	59.0
Jim Hogg, TX	92	14.2	74	1.1	83	3	8 765	7.4	45.2	47.4	6 997	5 198	63.6
Jim Wells, TX	594	15.0	446	2.3	599	17	47 898	9.9	64.6	25.5	43 464	4 918	60.9
Johnson, TX	1 430	15.5	1 043	3.0	1 159	50	117 058	5.5	58.5	35.9	94 664	4 360	63.7
Jones, TX	275	11.9	183	2.0	218	20	18 892	8.7	63.1	28.1	17 895	5 434	64.1
Karnes, TX	241	12.1	162	1.2	210	8	17 241	9.1	62.2	28.7	15 032	5 267	63.3
Kaufman, TX	1 003	15.3	720	1.7	869	41	77 287	7.4	56.1	36.4	63 891	4 272	61.8
Kendall, TX	324	15.0	235	3.1	291	8	23 745	5.3	40.9	53.8	19 751	4 331	63.2
Kenedy, TX	7	7.0	—	NA	7	1	2 624	—	2.4	97.6	716	16 651	47.8
Kent, TX	22	8.9	13	NA	19	2	9 666	0.6	3.7	95.7	1 892	9 906	54.1
Kerr, TX	454	14.7	345	3.3	470	18	36 648	6.9	42.1	51.0	30 771	4 822	61.6
Kimble, TX	65	11.9	48	2.0	58	2	4 961	4.6	66.3	29.1	4 093	5 188	64.3
King, TX	17	4.7	14	NA	8	2	3 493	0.4	6.5	93.1	1 343	15 988	60.7
Kinney, TX	54	11.4	31	4.3	42	2	4 346	8.9	60.4	30.7	3 729	6 385	68.3
Kleberg, TX	468	14.2	333	2.2	463	18	38 310	10.9	52.1	37.0	34 017	5 188	60.2
Knox, TX	99	10.5	61	0.7	83	10	7 194	9.6	64.0	26.3	6 763	6 159	60.4
Lamar, TX	620	14.2	412	3.2	554	18	45 952	7.3	47.9	44.8	41 176	4 730	63.5
Lamb, TX	285	12.9	199	2.5	258	18	27 205	7.8	39.3	52.9	19 968	5 401	62.0
Lampasas, TX	225	15.5	186	0.8	219	6	17 499	7.9	60.1	32.0	13 634	4 192	63.0
La Salle, TX	99	14.1	62	1.0	80	3	7 287	12.3	46.6	41.1	6 579	4 947	59.4
Lavaca, TX	163	13.8	143	1.1	138	6	12 523	5.0	46.5	48.5	10 658	4 773	63.2
Lee, TX	217	13.4	155	2.4	206	7	16 802	9.6	46.6	43.9	13 925	4 859	63.5
Leon, TX	232	12.7	168	2.1	196	13	19 158	4.5	33.2	62.3	14 471	4 946	59.8
Liberty, TX	839	15.5	579	2.4	756	25	64 676	6.6	55.6	37.8	57 951	4 506	60.7
Limestone, TX	305	13.6	202	3.2	290	9	38 553	5.2	13.3	81.4	21 420	5 166	63.0
Lipscomb, TX	81	9.2	49	1.8	54	4	7 431	3.7	19.5	76.8	5 147	7 060	61.2
Live Oak, TX	158	13.8	117	1.3	152	5	12 966	6.0	30.7	63.4	11 071	5 058	64.5
Llano, TX	107	13.7	70	2.8	97	3	11 731	4.0	15.9	80.1	7 115	5 126	59.9
Loving, TX	NA	NA	NA	NA	NA	NA	NA	NA	NA	NA	NA	NA	NA
Lubbock, TX	2 922	14.7	2 166	2.7	1 883	78	235 588	7.8	49.1	43.2	205 384	4 787	62.1
Lynn, TX	144	11.5	87	1.3	122	5	10 311	10.2	58.8	31.0	9 591	5 855	61.2
McCulloch, TX	139	13.1	114	1.2	156	11	11 056	10.3	62.3	27.4	10 007	5 715	58.9
McLennan, TX	2 529	15.2	1 620	2.3	2 093	177	194 939	6.1	57.3	36.6	179 743	4 778	61.0
McMullen, TX	19	9.8	11	NA	19	1	4 154	0.9	11.5	87.6	1 664	8 320	55.3
Madison, TX	154	14.4	109	6.1	116	5	11 294	8.2	53.0	38.8	10 193	4 676	60.5
Marion, TX	127	13.1	88	3.9	135	5	9 507	10.6	49.0	40.4	7 909	4 716	64.0
Martin, TX	93	11.8	55	1.7	67	10	8 652	7.1	38.8	54.2	7 202	6 577	59.8
Mason, TX	60	11.6	46	5.9	50	1	4 511	6.9	56.2	36.9	4 074	5 787	64.0
Matagorda, TX	561	15.6	457	2.3	560	24	78 916	4.8	22.9	72.3	43 111	4 960	61.1
Maverick, TX	653	17.7	537	3.4	756	10	58 151	16.7	68.7	14.7	51 110	4 375	61.8
Medina, TX	492	15.6	386	1.7	467	17	36 929	8.0	63.2	28.8	31 484	4 330	63.2
Menard, TX	39	11.4	30	1.7	36	7	3 559	10.8	52.9	36.2	3 247	7 280	58.3
Midland, TX	1 427	17.3	1 054	4.7	1 381	22	119 158	8.4	45.7	45.9	106 696	4 345	61.3
Milam, TX	329	14.4	266	2.6	295	12	25 216	7.2	46.4	46.4	21 658	5 096	65.3
Mills, TX	100	9.8	66	0.6	67	4	6 433	7.2	64.3	28.6	5 684	6 021	63.2

Table D-2. School and Student Characteristics by County

State/County code	County	County type[1]	Population, 1996 Total persons	Population, 1996 Percent age 5–17	Number of school districts, 1995–1996	Level of schools, 1995–1996 Number of schools	Level of schools, 1995–1996 Percent Primary	Percent Middle	Percent High	Level of students, 1995–1996 Number of students	Level of students, 1995–1996 Percent Primary	Percent Middle	Percent High	Characteristics of students, 1995–1996 Percent with IEP[2]	Percent free-lunch eligible	Percent minority
			1	2	3	4	5	6	7	8	9	10	11	12	13	14
	TEXAS—Con.															
48335	Mitchell, TX	7	9 002	17.7	3	8	25.0	12.5	25.0	1 619	34.6	18.1	22.3	16.7	41.9	44.6
48337	Montague, TX	6	18 030	18.0	7	15	46.7	13.3	26.7	3 323	47.0	17.3	29.0	16.2	33.5	8.5
48339	Montgomery, TX	1	245 845	21.8	6	63	49.2	25.4	20.6	47 641	43.6	28.5	27.8	14.6	24.9	17.8
48341	Moore, TX	6	19 427	23.8	2	10	50.0	10.0	30.0	4 549	51.9	13.5	25.3	9.9	36.9	53.3
48343	Morris, TX	6	13 262	20.6	2	8	50.0	25.0	25.0	2 901	45.5	23.9	30.7	17.5	43.3	37.1
48345	Motley, TX	9	1 330	17.7	1	1	—	—	—	261	—	—	—	12.6	50.6	27.2
48347	Nacogdoches, TX	5	56 533	17.5	9	24	41.7	12.5	20.8	9 793	40.3	21.5	22.8	13.7	39.8	36.8
48349	Navarro, TX	4	41 290	19.4	7	21	52.4	14.3	23.8	8 047	44.1	20.0	25.8	13.6	41.4	37.3
48351	Newton, TX	8	14 259	22.4	3	9	44.4	22.2	33.3	2 750	48.4	21.1	30.5	17.8	48.0	30.9
48353	Nolan, TX	6	16 370	20.3	4	13	30.8	15.4	30.8	3 677	31.7	29.7	27.0	20.1	42.1	44.8
48355	Nueces, TX	2	315 722	21.7	12	106	56.6	21.7	17.0	64 657	45.9	25.4	27.5	12.2	45.2	68.4
48357	Ochiltree, TX	7	8 791	22.5	1	4	50.0	25.0	25.0	2 053	49.9	23.9	26.2	13.9	32.1	32.3
48359	Oldham, TX	8	2 270	34.8	4	7	42.9	14.3	28.6	874	28.4	11.8	48.2	18.8	18.4	20.3
48361	Orange, TX	2	84 488	21.5	5	27	48.1	29.6	22.2	17 492	42.8	28.2	28.9	15.4	29.7	14.9
48363	Palo Pinto, TX	6	25 463	18.9	6	12	41.7	16.7	25.0	4 748	36.2	28.5	27.0	14.9	38.4	20.1
48365	Panola, TX	6	22 899	21.0	3	9	33.3	33.3	22.2	4 097	28.2	36.1	29.0	16.3	29.6	27.8
48367	Parker, TX	1	76 073	20.7	8	28	42.9	25.0	21.4	13 402	37.9	31.2	25.9	13.3	21.0	8.1
48369	Parmer, TX	7	10 403	23.7	4	11	36.4	27.3	27.3	2 621	45.1	21.7	23.8	13.9	51.9	60.9
48371	Pecos, TX	7	16 349	22.2	3	12	33.3	25.0	25.0	3 712	32.4	34.0	28.5	18.7	47.5	68.8
48373	Polk, TX	6	44 906	17.2	6	16	43.8	25.0	25.0	6 451	43.6	24.2	26.4	14.4	42.0	28.7
48375	Potter, TX	3	108 636	19.6	4	57	66.7	17.5	12.3	32 466	51.0	22.2	26.1	12.0	14.7	38.4
48377	Presidio, TX	7	7 966	23.1	2	7	57.1	14.3	28.6	1 690	54.9	18.3	26.8	7.2	80.0	94.7
48379	Rains, TX	8	7 869	18.9	1	5	20.0	20.0	60.0	1 332	42.6	27.0	30.4	15.4	31.8	9.6
48381	Randall, TX	3	97 379	20.6	1	13	53.8	23.1	15.4	6 874	44.6	30.1	24.5	12.2	12.9	12.2
48383	Reagan, TX	6	4 254	27.5	1	3	33.3	33.3	33.3	1 121	46.7	24.8	28.5	21.4	41.7	59.3
48385	Real, TX	9	2 724	18.0	1	1	—	—	—	268	—	—	—	23.5	49.3	24.3
48387	Red River, TX	6	13 959	18.1	4	12	41.7	25.0	33.3	2 848	54.1	18.1	27.8	14.9	47.1	33.2
48389	Reeves, TX	7	14 993	23.6	2	11	36.4	36.4	9.1	3 426	31.8	37.4	24.1	11.3	55.7	86.4
48391	Refugio, TX	6	7 903	20.2	3	8	37.5	25.0	37.5	1 661	37.6	29.8	32.6	13.8	40.9	59.3
48393	Roberts, TX	9	988	23.4	1	1	—	—	—	186	—	—	—	17.7	15.6	5.9
48395	Robertson, TX	6	15 522	20.6	5	13	46.2	23.1	30.8	3 230	52.8	18.4	28.8	13.7	54.1	55.5
48397	Rockwall, TX	0	34 153	21.9	2	13	53.8	23.1	23.1	7 533	50.8	21.9	27.3	12.0	14.5	15.1
48399	Runnels, TX	6	11 410	20.1	4	16	43.8	12.5	37.5	2 675	52.5	16.8	30.5	13.7	40.9	38.5
48401	Rusk, TX	6	45 596	20.6	8	23	39.1	21.7	21.7	7 722	31.9	27.8	27.6	13.7	40.0	33.5
48403	Sabine, TX	9	10 443	15.5	2	4	50.0	—	50.0	1 621	57.3	—	42.7	13.9	38.7	18.8
48405	San Augustine, TX	9	8 051	18.0	2	6	33.3	16.7	50.0	1 590	46.7	21.6	31.7	14.6	51.8	45.8
48407	San Jacinto, TX	8	19 957	19.8	2	7	42.9	28.6	28.6	3 426	45.4	27.7	26.9	9.7	44.1	27.7
48409	San Patricio, TX	2	68 334	23.3	7	34	38.2	35.3	20.6	15 382	39.9	33.2	26.6	9.8	46.4	60.9
48411	San Saba, TX	7	6 024	19.5	3	8	37.5	12.5	25.0	1 182	47.5	9.0	27.4	15.0	47.0	29.4
48413	Schleicher, TX	8	3 088	24.0	1	3	33.3	33.3	33.3	769	40.6	32.5	26.9	15.0	40.2	54.4
48415	Scurry, TX	7	18 248	20.6	3	10	50.0	10.0	20.0	3 743	49.1	14.9	26.9	17.1	35.3	40.0
48417	Shackelford, TX	8	3 296	20.2	2	3	33.3	—	33.3	676	47.6	—	38.0	16.6	29.9	13.8
48419	Shelby, TX	7	22 677	19.2	6	14	42.9	14.3	28.6	4 850	43.9	14.3	25.8	15.6	36.5	34.6
48421	Sherman, TX	9	2 818	21.8	2	4	25.0	25.0	25.0	837	22.6	22.1	18.5	12.7	32.7	28.2
48423	Smith, TX	3	165 002	19.4	8	56	46.4	26.8	17.9	29 737	44.4	26.6	26.6	8.7	32.6	40.3
48425	Somervell, TX	8	5 986	23.8	1	4	25.0	50.0	25.0	1 492	32.3	38.1	29.6	16.6	31.2	17.6
48427	Starr, TX	6	53 974	27.2	3	21	47.6	19.0	19.0	14 194	43.0	25.2	25.5	10.7	82.3	99.6
48429	Stephens, TX	7	9 798	20.3	1	6	33.3	33.3	16.7	2 024	33.3	40.2	26.1	16.4	32.7	23.1
48431	Sterling, TX	8	1 411	24.3	1	3	—	—	33.3	373	—	—	0.3	18.8	24.4	34.3
48433	Stonewall, TX	9	1 813	18.8	1	3	33.3	33.3	33.3	376	55.3	17.8	26.9	21.0	38.6	26.1
48435	Sutton, TX	7	4 449	22.5	1	3	33.3	33.3	33.3	1 095	45.6	23.7	30.7	10.6	31.0	53.9
48437	Swisher, TX	6	8 495	19.9	3	9	44.4	22.2	33.3	2 086	52.0	19.2	28.8	19.3	53.1	53.1
48439	Tarrant, TX	0	1 305 185	18.9	17	358	57.3	21.5	14.8	236 170	53.2	23.6	22.0	11.3	29.4	40.4
48441	Taylor, TX	3	122 130	19.4	5	57	50.9	19.3	17.5	24 672	50.6	23.4	25.0	16.6	34.8	32.4
48443	Terrell, TX	9	1 237	21.3	1	3	33.3	33.3	33.3	246	40.2	24.0	35.8	15.4	44.3	61.4
48445	Terry, TX	6	13 093	23.5	4	10	30.0	20.0	20.0	3 105	26.8	30.7	22.6	12.5	48.4	62.3
48447	Throckmorton, TX	9	1 797	17.0	2	3	33.3	—	33.3	385	44.9	—	17.7	23.4	39.2	10.1
48449	Titus, TX	7	24 909	20.2	4	12	66.7	8.3	16.7	5 315	59.1	16.5	23.0	11.4	41.2	43.7
48451	Tom Green, TX	3	102 580	19.5	6	52	59.6	19.2	15.4	19 997	55.1	23.0	21.8	14.5	30.4	45.5
48453	Travis, TX	2	683 967	17.0	7	145	60.0	19.3	15.9	101 279	52.9	22.6	23.9	11.5	35.1	53.9
48455	Trinity, TX	7	12 454	17.2	4	12	33.3	16.7	25.0	2 361	48.4	14.6	31.2	17.5	43.7	25.8
48457	Tyler, TX	6	20 283	16.9	5	16	43.8	25.0	31.3	3 867	47.2	21.9	30.9	16.2	37.6	20.0
48459	Upshur, TX	3	34 909	20.6	7	20	40.0	25.0	30.0	6 681	47.5	20.8	28.1	13.9	28.2	16.9
48461	Upton, TX	8	3 816	26.1	2	5	40.0	20.0	40.0	1 089	43.1	21.4	35.5	16.3	46.0	52.1
48463	Uvalde, TX	7	25 343	22.5	4	15	40.0	26.7	20.0	6 300	40.3	26.6	26.2	9.6	61.3	74.6
48465	Val Verde, TX	5	43 131	23.0	2	16	62.5	12.5	12.5	10 333	50.2	14.7	28.3	9.7	63.6	85.5

1. County type code is from the Economic Research Service of the USDA. See notes and definitions at the end of this section.   2. IEP = Individual Education Program. See notes and definitions at the end of this section.

Table D-2. School and Student Characteristics by County — Continued

County	Staff and students, 1995–1996						Revenues, fiscal 1995				Current expenditures, fiscal 1995		
	Number of teachers	Pupil/ teacher ratio	Number of graduates	Dropouts grades 9–12 (percent)	Local school non-teaching staff	Central admin. staff	Total revenue ($1000)	Percent of Revenue from			Amount	Amount per pupil	Percent for instruction
								Federal Gov't	State Gov't	Local Gov't			
	15	16	17	18	19	20	21	22	23	24	25	26	27
TEXAS—Con.													
Mitchell, TX	148	10.9	102	3.8	119	4	12 508	7.1	34.6	58.3	10 040	6 096	60.9
Montague, TX	257	12.9	165	1.3	205	19	19 664	6.5	58.0	35.5	16 196	4 766	63.4
Montgomery, TX	3 170	15.0	2 087	2.3	3 024	49	259 793	3.6	44.8	51.6	232 136	5 079	57.3
Moore, TX	316	14.4	225	2.3	244	9	24 313	6.1	17.2	76.7	20 989	4 655	62.6
Morris, TX	219	13.3	187	1.6	199	5	18 637	8.7	34.5	56.8	14 663	5 013	62.4
Motley, TX	26	10.1	16	1.1	24	4	1 901	12.8	34.6	52.6	1 955	7 109	58.2
Nacogdoches, TX	688	14.2	413	3.9	582	42	51 863	7.7	55.6	36.7	46 672	4 834	60.0
Navarro, TX	590	13.6	360	3.0	462	21	46 287	6.5	52.5	41.0	36 317	4 609	64.7
Newton, TX	222	12.4	154	3.6	193	8	17 927	8.2	61.1	30.7	14 631	5 220	62.9
Nolan, TX	296	12.4	222	3.3	258	9	22 092	9.1	50.1	40.8	19 759	5 356	63.2
Nueces, TX	3 990	16.2	3 016	1.5	3 772	117	358 844	8.7	47.0	44.3	307 333	4 749	60.9
Ochiltree, TX	141	14.6	109	1.3	116	4	10 586	7.1	32.0	60.9	9 347	4 674	59.7
Oldham, TX	115	7.6	84	1.0	63	7	8 155	5.9	59.4	34.7	7 186	7 393	68.0
Orange, TX	1 139	15.4	1 013	2.7	1 060	27	102 979	6.3	43.9	49.8	84 181	4 782	59.9
Palo Pinto, TX	360	13.2	265	3.2	299	11	26 198	7.5	51.1	41.4	22 584	4 717	62.9
Panola, TX	305	13.4	222	2.8	318	8	29 017	5.5	18.0	76.6	21 712	5 316	61.6
Parker, TX	859	15.6	618	1.8	636	36	66 314	3.6	55.9	40.5	55 863	4 303	63.8
Parmer, TX	215	12.2	136	3.0	189	7	14 951	8.0	50.7	41.3	13 505	5 202	62.9
Pecos, TX	292	12.7	213	0.7	260	10	48 202	4.4	10.7	84.9	22 503	6 025	60.1
Polk, TX	418	15.4	283	1.5	389	19	38 042	9.3	47.1	43.6	29 099	4 572	60.4
Potter, TX	2 036	15.9	1 309	3.1	1 676	36	161 792	7.2	47.3	45.5	139 105	4 339	62.6
Presidio, TX	140	12.1	67	6.8	123	5	9 929	17.8	64.4	17.8	8 984	5 445	65.7
Rains, TX	88	15.2	69	4.0	76	2	7 685	4.3	46.0	49.7	5 537	4 169	59.8
Randall, TX	407	16.9	356	1.1	390	8	29 980	5.1	51.2	43.7	24 981	3 788	65.1
Reagan, TX	83	13.5	77	1.3	69	2	7 414	5.6	23.0	71.4	6 542	5 679	63.8
Real, TX	25	10.7	15	2.4	19	3	1 910	10.1	38.3	51.7	1 599	5 793	64.9
Red River, TX	226	12.6	186	2.8	221	16	16 861	11.9	62.0	26.1	14 824	5 209	62.9
Reeves, TX	254	13.5	170	4.9	273	9	20 209	9.6	54.5	35.9	17 270	4 865	60.9
Refugio, TX	141	11.7	97	3.0	120	6	12 580	5.5	26.9	67.5	10 450	6 349	59.6
Roberts, TX	21	9.0	24	NA	15	1	3 186	1.0	9.0	90.0	1 483	7 452	58.7
Robertson, TX	264	12.2	162	1.4	214	12	25 216	6.8	39.5	53.7	17 911	5 545	60.7
Rockwall, TX	466	16.2	329	2.2	403	12	34 460	2.5	37.4	60.1	29 691	4 094	59.9
Runnels, TX	207	13.0	129	2.1	164	5	14 909	5.9	64.6	29.6	13 252	5 075	65.7
Rusk, TX	602	12.8	395	2.7	525	35	49 962	7.6	41.4	51.0	40 860	5 293	61.6
Sabine, TX	114	14.2	82	0.7	93	7	9 576	7.0	53.7	39.3	7 452	4 722	63.9
San Augustine, TX	130	12.2	101	0.7	138	5	9 292	9.9	64.1	26.0	8 262	5 213	62.7
San Jacinto, TX	226	15.1	150	1.0	218	11	18 800	8.6	47.7	43.7	15 596	4 735	58.7
San Patricio, TX	1 012	15.2	768	1.9	866	37	81 406	8.7	53.5	37.8	70 043	4 546	61.9
San Saba, TX	104	11.4	58	0.6	91	4	7 958	7.7	64.7	27.5	6 701	5 837	63.3
Schleicher, TX	60	12.9	57	1.4	57	2	5 280	5.0	40.4	54.6	4 196	5 311	63.0
Scurry, TX	268	14.0	239	1.9	182	7	21 117	7.4	40.4	52.2	20 353	5 313	62.7
Shackelford, TX	57	11.9	42	1.0	42	2	4 374	5.8	55.1	39.1	3 836	5 786	62.2
Shelby, TX	391	12.4	245	4.4	307	15	28 158	8.8	66.4	24.8	23 797	4 919	63.2
Sherman, TX	55	15.2	37	0.8	38	2	4 976	3.5	19.1	77.4	3 584	5 671	59.7
Smith, TX	1 976	15.0	1 509	3.4	1 751	54	144 590	7.1	43.9	49.0	131 426	4 454	61.8
Somervell, TX	127	11.7	82	2.9	120	4	91 631	0.4	2.0	97.6	9 564	6 628	59.8
Starr, TX	954	14.9	553	3.3	1 496	30	80 668	16.4	67.9	15.7	80 224	5 802	57.0
Stephens, TX	117	17.2	90	4.1	100	3	9 806	6.2	34.5	59.3	7 734	3 902	61.8
Sterling, TX	35	10.8	28	NA	20	1	6 065	1.5	10.1	88.3	2 463	6 639	63.7
Stonewall, TX	37	10.2	21	NA	30	1	2 880	5.6	26.3	68.1	2 415	6 406	64.8
Sutton, TX	84	13.0	59	2.4	70	2	7 623	3.6	18.3	78.1	6 310	5 859	64.4
Swisher, TX	172	12.1	116	2.4	149	7	12 885	9.9	62.8	27.3	11 181	5 473	61.7
Tarrant, TX	13 922	17.0	9 771	2.5	11 987	221	1 161 671	5.4	35.7	58.9	988 820	4 318	61.3
Taylor, TX	1 771	13.9	1 107	2.5	1 471	36	134 143	6.9	60.2	32.9	115 303	4 684	66.4
Terrell, TX	26	9.4	27	NA	26	2	3 328	3.8	16.4	79.8	2 390	8 415	56.8
Terry, TX	229	13.5	157	2.4	211	13	16 260	12.6	26.2	61.2	16 836	5 348	62.8
Throckmorton, TX	39	9.8	31	1.8	24	2	2 658	4.7	43.5	51.8	2 426	6 189	63.8
Titus, TX	385	13.8	225	2.4	324	11	27 745	10.5	38.2	51.4	23 066	4 466	66.0
Tom Green, TX	1 253	16.0	932	3.3	1 087	73	90 746	12.0	48.2	39.8	87 542	4 433	63.3
Travis, TX	6 323	16.0	4 061	3.8	5 035	95	566 350	5.9	22.6	71.5	477 597	4 872	60.7
Trinity, TX	191	12.4	123	4.1	171	20	14 144	9.8	56.2	34.0	12 279	5 142	64.1
Tyler, TX	296	13.1	223	2.5	272	11	21 472	7.0	57.4	35.6	19 341	5 008	59.3
Upshur, TX	482	13.9	326	2.0	398	16	35 973	6.0	59.7	34.3	30 427	4 657	63.8
Upton, TX	99	11.1	79	NA	74	9	13 235	3.7	13.3	82.9	8 253	7 090	58.7
Uvalde, TX	452	13.9	293	5.8	480	8	32 611	13.5	61.2	25.2	30 013	4 817	61.4
Val Verde, TX	627	16.5	466	3.7	697	15	52 721	15.3	66.9	17.8	49 388	4 762	59.4

Table D-2. School and Student Characteristics by County

State/County code	County	County type[1]	Population, 1996		Number of school districts, 1995–1996	Level of schools, 1995–1996				Level of students, 1995–1996				Characteristics of students, 1995–1996		
			Total persons	Percent age 5–17		Number of schools	Percent			Number of students	Percent			Percent with IEP[2]	Percent free-lunch eligible	Percent minority
							Primary	Middle	High		Primary	Middle	High			
			1	2	3	4	5	6	7	8	9	10	11	12	13	14
	TEXAS—Con.															
48467	Van Zandt, TX	6	42 579	19.1	7	24	41.7	20.8	29.2	8 789	48.4	22.2	27.6	12.4	29.8	11.6
48469	Victoria, TX	3	81 541	22.6	3	27	59.3	14.8	18.5	15 699	48.0	23.2	28.6	12.8	40.5	57.3
48471	Walker, TX	4	54 417	14.2	2	14	50.0	28.6	14.3	7 685	42.3	30.9	25.2	9.9	37.1	43.5
48473	Waller, TX	1	26 195	19.1	3	14	42.9	35.7	14.3	6 118	44.4	28.9	11.3	9.9	42.7	52.8
48475	Ward, TX	6	11 994	25.0	2	10	50.0	30.0	20.0	2 706	39.4	32.8	27.8	11.2	41.3	51.6
48477	Washington, TX	6	28 610	18.5	2	9	33.3	22.2	44.4	5 219	33.1	35.8	31.2	12.1	32.4	40.0
48479	Webb, TX	3	176 792	24.7	4	59	66.1	20.3	13.6	43 659	53.5	20.6	25.9	9.7	70.7	96.6
48481	Wharton, TX	6	40 224	21.6	5	18	44.4	22.2	27.8	8 760	41.7	22.2	32.9	10.2	39.5	56.2
48483	Wheeler, TX	9	5 344	20.5	5	5	20.0	—	—	1 016	4.0	—	—	14.5	32.3	19.9
48485	Wichita, TX	3	128 064	18.7	5	41	63.4	17.1	17.1	23 176	55.8	17.4	26.1	15.4	30.3	28.5
48487	Wilbarger, TX	6	14 308	19.3	3	8	25.0	12.5	12.5	2 939	27.7	22.9	22.5	15.0	38.8	37.4
48489	Willacy, TX	6	19 419	25.8	4	11	54.5	18.2	18.2	5 136	47.9	21.2	25.8	9.4	73.0	93.8
48491	Williamson, TX	2	198 286	22.5	11	72	50.0	20.8	15.3	47 194	46.9	24.9	26.0	12.1	16.2	24.7
48493	Wilson, TX	1	28 867	22.5	4	14	35.7	28.6	35.7	6 186	41.5	29.3	29.1	12.1	31.2	41.4
48495	Winkler, TX	6	8 043	24.7	2	6	50.0	16.7	33.3	1 968	47.2	19.9	32.9	18.5	44.9	52.3
48497	Wise, TX	6	40 451	20.5	7	23	26.1	39.1	30.4	7 093	36.9	32.5	26.9	12.2	26.0	15.9
48499	Wood, TX	6	33 321	18.1	6	21	28.6	19.0	28.6	6 089	44.1	20.5	28.6	13.4	29.0	14.7
48501	Yoakum, TX	7	8 325	25.9	2	7	28.6	42.9	28.6	2 334	32.6	39.7	27.7	8.7	42.8	53.5
48503	Young, TX	7	17 528	19.2	3	11	36.4	27.3	36.4	3 702	38.1	32.7	29.2	12.5	29.8	16.2
48505	Zapata, TX	6	11 100	23.7	1	6	50.0	33.3	16.7	2 894	44.0	30.1	26.0	10.1	68.9	93.9
48507	Zavala, TX	7	12 322	24.3	2	8	25.0	37.5	37.5	2 489	40.6	34.1	25.3	9.5	74.8	96.8
49000	**UTAH**															
49001	Beaver, UT	9	5 591	25.9	1	5	60.0	—	40.0	1 480	53.1	—	46.9	10.1	21.0	5.9
49003	Box Elder, UT	6	39 177	27.9	1	25	68.0	12.0	12.0	11 239	47.6	23.3	28.3	12.2	18.0	7.1
49005	Cache, UT	4	83 710	23.6	2	30	56.7	23.3	20.0	18 887	45.1	29.5	25.4	9.5	17.4	5.4
49007	Carbon, UT	7	20 437	24.6	1	12	41.7	25.0	25.0	5 069	42.2	27.8	28.9	14.7	30.8	12.4
49009	Daggett, UT	9	752	23.9	1	3	66.7	—	33.3	209	54.1	—	45.9	12.0	19.6	—
49011	Davis, UT	0	214 990	27.3	1	75	64.0	17.3	13.3	58 782	51.7	24.1	22.1	10.3	12.3	5.5
49013	Duchesne, UT	7	13 778	30.1	1	15	40.0	13.3	33.3	4 557	36.3	22.0	40.5	12.5	33.6	11.0
49015	Emery, UT	9	10 402	30.8	1	10	60.0	20.0	20.0	3 364	48.3	24.1	27.6	12.5	22.4	3.6
49017	Garfield, UT	9	4 076	24.4	1	9	55.6	11.1	33.3	1 167	50.7	9.5	39.8	13.0	24.1	5.6
49019	Grand, UT	7	7 826	22.5	1	5	20.0	40.0	40.0	1 580	29.3	41.1	29.6	15.7	32.9	7.9
49021	Iron, UT	7	26 875	24.2	1	13	53.8	15.4	30.8	6 238	46.2	28.4	25.4	11.0	26.3	7.0
49023	Juab, UT	6	6 845	27.9	2	9	55.6	11.1	33.3	2 134	45.6	21.2	33.2	14.4	24.1	2.2
49025	Kane, UT	7	5 751	25.7	1	7	28.6	14.3	28.6	1 491	39.9	15.8	34.3	14.0	28.3	3.7
49027	Millard, UT	7	12 019	29.8	1	9	44.4	22.2	33.3	3 816	39.2	27.7	33.2	16.2	27.3	6.5
49029	Morgan, UT	8	6 660	29.5	1	3	33.3	33.3	33.3	2 032	33.6	34.3	32.2	7.9	8.2	2.2
49031	Piute, UT	9	1 404	24.2	1	3	66.7	—	33.3	404	45.5	—	54.5	21.8	56.9	4.2
49033	Rich, UT	9	1 799	28.8	1	4	50.0	25.0	25.0	535	41.9	24.9	33.3	10.5	42.6	1.7
49035	Salt Lake, UT	0	827 818	23.2	4	220	65.9	16.4	13.6	181 361	53.1	22.9	23.1	10.4	19.7	12.7
49037	San Juan, UT	7	13 221	29.9	1	12	58.3	8.3	33.3	3 395	49.3	10.6	40.1	17.3	52.0	53.4
49039	Sanpete, UT	6	19 883	26.9	2	13	61.5	15.4	23.1	5 475	48.3	15.1	36.6	15.0	31.3	7.5
49041	Sevier, UT	7	17 156	28.0	1	12	33.3	33.3	33.3	4 909	36.0	29.0	35.0	11.9	29.2	5.5
49043	Summit, UT	6	23 988	22.6	3	11	45.5	27.3	27.3	5 387	45.9	26.7	27.5	8.9	6.3	2.9
49045	Tooele, UT	6	29 558	25.5	1	18	55.6	11.1	27.8	7 495	50.6	16.0	33.2	11.7	24.1	13.7
49047	Uintah, UT	7	24 472	28.9	1	13	46.2	30.8	15.4	6 699	38.6	38.3	22.5	14.4	30.7	11.8
49049	Utah, UT	2	319 694	25.0	3	98	61.2	15.3	17.3	75 051	50.4	23.9	25.2	10.4	17.7	6.2
49051	Wasatch, UT	6	12 046	27.4	1	7	57.1	14.3	28.6	3 389	44.9	23.4	31.7	10.7	12.6	2.9
49053	Washington, UT	4	73 161	24.9	1	26	53.8	19.2	26.9	17 418	46.7	29.3	24.0	10.2	14.7	5.5
49055	Wayne, UT	9	2 371	27.1	1	4	50.0	25.0	25.0	602	43.7	22.9	33.4	7.8	33.7	4.5
49057	Weber, UT	0	175 034	22.8	4	64	62.5	18.8	12.5	41 356	49.8	23.8	23.1	13.7	22.6	13.4
50000	**VERMONT**															
50001	Addison, VT	6	35 079	18.7	21	22	77.3	4.5	13.6	5 688	56.4	6.1	37.1	10.3	14.5	1.1
50003	Bennington, VT	6	36 357	18.5	18	23	73.9	4.3	21.7	7 819	49.2	8.6	42.2	9.3	16.1	2.6
50005	Caledonia, VT	7	28 800	21.0	19	20	80.0	5.0	5.0	4 810	69.6	7.6	8.6	11.3	27.7	1.5
50007	Chittenden, VT	3	141 115	16.9	22	51	60.8	17.6	15.7	22 578	51.1	18.6	28.2	8.4	12.6	4.2
50009	Essex, VT	9	6 511	20.5	9	9	66.7	—	11.1	1 281	34.0	—	23.7	8.0	16.2	1.0
50011	Franklin, VT	3	43 465	22.4	19	23	60.9	8.7	17.4	9 000	51.1	7.0	31.6	10.1	21.5	6.5
50013	Grand Isle, VT	3	5 968	19.7	6	6	100.0	—	—	844	100.0	—	—	11.0	25.6	0.7
50015	Lamoille, VT	8	21 373	19.1	12	14	71.4	—	14.3	3 922	56.1	—	34.3	10.1	20.1	1.4
50017	Orange, VT	9	27 562	20.7	24	26	73.1	—	7.7	6 183	56.6	—	19.0	10.9	23.7	1.1
50019	Orleans, VT	7	25 117	22.5	22	22	81.8	4.5	9.1	4 817	59.3	7.0	31.3	11.7	34.7	2.1
50021	Rutland, VT	7	62 757	17.9	31	36	69.4	2.8	16.7	10 530	58.1	3.2	33.7	9.0	20.9	1.5
50023	Washington, VT	6	56 437	18.8	23	28	60.7	7.1	17.9	10 298	51.7	6.5	33.7	9.5	15.9	1.8

1. County type code is from the Economic Research Service of the USDA. See notes and definitions at the end of this section.   2. IEP = Individual Education Program. See notes and definitions at the end of this section.

Table D-2. School and Student Characteristics by County — Continued

County	Staff and students, 1995–1996						Revenues, fiscal 1995				Current expenditures, fiscal 1995		
	Number of teachers	Pupil/ teacher ratio	Number of graduates	Dropouts grades 9–12 (percent)	Local school non-teaching staff	Central admin. staff	Total revenue ($1000)	Percent of Revenue from			Amount	Amount per pupil	Percent for instruction
								Federal Gov't	State Gov't	Local Gov't			
	15	16	17	18	19	20	21	22	23	24	25	26	27
TEXAS—Con.													
Van Zandt, TX	563	15.6	484	3.1	470	32	42 110	7.0	57.6	35.5	34 702	4 077	62.5
Victoria, TX	966	16.3	795	3.0	1 059	24	81 153	7.9	41.2	51.0	75 512	4 835	61.8
Walker, TX	515	14.9	375	3.2	519	12	40 685	6.5	58.8	34.7	35 021	4 502	59.5
Waller, TX	411	14.9	245	3.0	363	8	32 767	6.5	51.1	42.4	27 421	4 687	56.6
Ward, TX	190	14.2	180	1.5	174	5	16 246	6.8	18.2	75.0	14 649	5 275	61.4
Washington, TX	342	15.3	286	2.7	289	9	28 277	6.1	41.6	52.4	23 091	4 443	62.8
Webb, TX	2 659	16.4	2 019	2.0	3 727	58	224 214	9.3	54.9	35.8	211 809	4 968	58.9
Wharton, TX	586	15.0	493	2.4	602	18	45 725	8.3	46.2	45.5	41 623	4 792	63.6
Wheeler, TX	117	8.7	81	1.6	80	19	12 765	4.3	22.6	73.1	8 334	7 745	62.8
Wichita, TX	1 552	14.9	1 205	2.1	1 125	21	115 864	7.5	49.1	43.3	104 276	4 487	63.7
Wilbarger, TX	206	14.3	153	2.7	125	8	14 063	5.1	30.0	64.9	12 450	4 265	65.0
Willacy, TX	358	14.3	264	4.3	427	16	30 656	17.1	64.9	18.1	27 948	5 378	60.8
Williamson, TX	3 202	14.7	2 329	1.1	2 461	66	259 429	3.9	44.9	51.2	211 408	4 743	63.7
Wilson, TX	409	15.1	311	1.7	325	11	29 150	7.2	63.2	29.6	24 539	4 173	64.6
Winkler, TX	151	13.0	130	NA	143	7	17 350	5.2	27.7	67.1	11 719	5 776	60.1
Wise, TX	500	14.2	332	2.0	371	23	37 714	5.1	52.3	42.6	31 936	4 719	60.7
Wood, TX	425	14.3	341	1.3	346	22	32 563	6.0	43.6	50.4	28 978	4 810	62.6
Yoakum, TX	178	13.1	132	1.7	134	5	30 931	3.2	8.9	87.9	15 413	6 427	61.9
Young, TX	257	14.4	198	4.4	175	12	18 268	7.4	54.4	38.2	16 464	4 408	64.3
Zapata, TX	195	14.9	154	1.1	206	8	17 437	10.9	19.3	69.7	14 629	5 076	58.9
Zavala, TX	180	13.9	129	3.3	259	10	15 937	14.4	65.6	20.0	15 154	6 002	59.3
UTAH													
Beaver, UT	76	19.6	108	0.8	40	5	6 469	4.9	50.8	44.3	5 013	3 515	65.3
Box Elder, UT	517	21.7	721	2.4	411	17	44 296	5.5	56.4	38.1	36 748	3 255	64.0
Cache, UT	890	21.2	1 269	0.9	609	30	73 768	5.3	60.3	34.4	64 194	3 403	68.8
Carbon, UT	243	20.9	361	2.8	215	20	21 802	8.7	54.5	36.8	19 125	3 706	60.6
Daggett, UT	18	11.7	12	1.7	15	3	2 215	6.8	38.3	54.9	1 640	7 736	51.9
Davis, UT	2 558	23.0	3 738	4.9	1 893	269	213 123	8.1	62.0	29.9	183 113	3 150	63.4
Duchesne, UT	239	19.0	324	4.8	225	9	19 192	8.2	62.5	29.3	16 865	3 628	57.9
Emery, UT	178	18.9	225	1.9	169	9	23 113	4.0	17.4	78.6	14 376	4 295	68.6
Garfield, UT	70	16.8	81	NA	56	6	6 394	5.4	63.2	31.4	5 316	4 709	65.6
Grand, UT	90	17.5	104	9.6	85	9	7 127	7.1	49.5	43.4	6 417	3 949	60.9
Iron, UT	284	22.0	423	5.0	230	16	28 692	5.4	50.0	44.5	21 088	3 430	61.2
Juab, UT	105	20.3	108	3.8	89	8	9 732	5.9	59.3	34.7	7 785	3 826	61.3
Kane, UT	79	18.9	123	5.2	65	5	7 159	6.0	61.4	32.5	6 062	4 099	66.6
Millard, UT	210	18.1	321	1.5	224	8	23 554	6.0	21.4	72.6	16 221	4 201	61.2
Morgan, UT	104	19.6	161	1.7	69	5	7 836	5.2	62.6	32.2	7 226	3 521	63.0
Piute, UT	27	15.0	34	NA	30	6	2 893	7.5	76.6	15.8	2 346	5 586	56.2
Rich, UT	37	14.4	54	0.6	34	3	3 613	5.2	50.6	44.2	2 864	4 990	59.6
Salt Lake, UT	8 259	22.0	10 588	5.1	6 406	408	756 132	6.5	50.8	42.8	641 318	3 524	65.4
San Juan, UT	233	14.6	199	8.3	209	26	23 225	30.2	47.6	22.3	20 525	5 946	56.0
Sanpete, UT	273	20.1	396	1.0	258	15	24 343	9.9	67.2	22.9	20 361	3 730	62.9
Sevier, UT	227	21.6	363	5.4	194	13	21 057	8.4	60.5	31.1	18 400	3 701	66.8
Summit, UT	295	18.3	318	1.6	192	23	31 147	2.2	21.6	76.2	21 406	4 138	61.1
Tooele, UT	387	19.4	495	2.3	286	13	31 556	9.5	52.8	37.7	27 399	3 659	69.0
Uintah, UT	342	19.6	350	2.9	238	16	29 446	10.7	45.3	44.0	25 006	3 661	64.4
Utah, UT	3 390	22.1	4 811	1.1	1 701	165	302 747	5.5	57.7	30.8	250 323	3 382	67.0
Wasatch, UT	163	20.8	248	2.2	136	6	11 689	4.3	58.3	37.4	10 442	3 176	71.8
Washington, UT	751	23.2	1 080	2.4	515	19	59 880	5.4	57.7	36.8	49 903	3 015	65.3
Wayne, UT	41	14.5	35	NA	27	5	3 534	6.9	69.6	23.5	3 145	5 224	61.8
Weber, UT	2 038	20.3	2 522	1.6	1 374	153	158 099	7.7	61.5	30.8	142 885	3 541	63.2
VERMONT													
Addison, VT	434	13.1	327	NA	461	48	59 895	2.9	18.3	78.8	37 266	6 698	63.9
Bennington, VT	575	13.6	721	NA	568	60	58 679	3.6	21.3	75.1	37 205	6 304	64.6
Caledonia, VT	332	14.5	116	NA	350	25	43 113	5.4	40.2	54.4	26 895	5 824	63.7
Chittenden, VT	1 520	14.9	1 295	NA	1 512	62	195 664	2.8	16.9	80.4	147 174	6 611	65.5
Essex, VT	101	12.7	84	NA	91	7	8 503	4.2	34.5	61.3	5 587	5 808	61.2
Franklin, VT	663	13.6	534	NA	509	45	63 906	4.5	40.7	54.8	43 682	5 529	64.8
Grand Isle, VT	59	14.2	—	NA	57	4	8 469	4.2	13.3	82.5	5 597	6 944	58.5
Lamoille, VT	293	13.4	217	NA	259	10	34 042	3.5	25.4	71.1	25 218	6 689	63.4
Orange, VT	450	13.7	316	NA	407	27	55 808	4.0	30.8	65.2	38 337	6 333	60.1
Orleans, VT	372	13.0	318	NA	320	39	45 165	5.0	38.6	56.4	28 583	6 001	62.3
Rutland, VT	753	14.0	619	NA	621	66	93 672	3.5	26.1	70.4	63 967	6 272	67.3
Washington, VT	757	13.6	511	NA	693	53	93 025	3.0	27.6	69.4	66 625	6 638	64.0

Table D-2. School and Student Characteristics by County

State/County code	County	County type [1]	Population, 1996		Number of school districts, 1995–1996	Level of schools, 1995–1996				Level of students, 1995–1996				Characteristics of students, 1995–1996		
			Total persons	Percent age 5–17		Number of schools	Percent Primary	Middle	High	Number of students	Percent Primary	Middle	High	Percent with IEP [2]	Percent free-lunch eligible	Percent minority
			1	2	3	4	5	6	7	8	9	10	11	12	13	14
	VERMONT—Con.															
50025	Windham, VT	7	42 923	19.1	29	36	75.0	5.6	8.3	7 458	55.9	11.6	24.0	10.7	15.1	2.5
50027	Windsor, VT	7	55 190	18.6	33	46	65.2	8.7	15.2	10 337	54.3	12.4	30.2	9.8	15.6	1.6
51000	**VIRGINIA**															
51001	Accomack, VA	7	32 065	17.5	1	12	41.7	25.0	16.7	5 538	47.3	19.3	25.1	9.5	51.7	55.5
51003	Albemarle, VA	3	74 189	15.7	1	23	65.2	21.7	13.0	11 123	48.7	23.5	27.8	16.4	12.3	15.9
51005	Alleghany, VA	6	12 586	18.2	(3)1	(3)8	(3)75.0	(3)12.5	(3)12.5	(3)3 070	(3)59.8	(3)9.4	(3)30.8	(3)14.7	(3)24.3	(3)7.9
51007	Amelia, VA	8	9 912	19.2	1	3	33.3	33.3	33.3	1 743	45.6	25.4	29.0	15.7	29.6	39.1
51009	Amherst, VA	3	30 065	17.5	1	10	70.0	20.0	10.0	4 723	47.0	23.7	29.4	12.3	22.3	25.1
51011	Appomattox, VA	8	12 879	18.5	1	4	50.0	25.0	25.0	2 331	55.6	15.7	28.8	11.0	26.3	28.1
51013	Arlington, VA	0	175 334	10.3	1	29	69.0	17.2	6.9	17 178	51.1	20.6	18.2	16.7	35.6	57.6
51015	Augusta, VA	4	59 515	18.3	1	19	57.9	15.8	26.3	10 673	46.1	23.9	30.0	12.5	15.0	3.6
51017	Bath, VA	9	4 959	15.6	1	3	66.7	—	33.3	870	60.5	—	39.5	12.0	22.6	4.7
51019	Bedford, VA	3	52 768	17.3	(4)1	(4)19	(4)68.4	(4)15.8	(4)15.8	(4)9 956	(4)47.4	(4)21.8	(4)30.8	(4)10.5	(4)18.5	(4)12.4
51021	Bland, VA	9	6 834	16.9	1	4	50.0	—	50.0	1 004	59.3	—	40.7	17.8	20.4	1.1
51023	Botetourt, VA	3	27 813	17.4	1	9	66.7	11.1	22.2	4 514	54.9	15.0	30.1	17.8	8.6	4.5
51025	Brunswick, VA	8	16 458	17.9	1	6	66.7	16.7	16.7	2 570	54.6	23.2	22.2	10.4	61.5	75.6
51027	Buchanan, VA	9	30 033	21.6	1	17	58.8	11.8	29.4	5 210	49.1	16.5	34.4	14.0	46.4	—
51029	Buckingham, VA	8	14 388	15.7	1	6	50.0	33.3	16.7	2 210	37.6	34.8	27.7	15.1	43.6	50.2
51031	Campbell, VA	3	48 946	17.9	1	14	57.1	14.3	14.3	8 386	43.1	20.7	19.9	11.4	21.4	19.5
51033	Caroline, VA	8	21 399	18.9	1	6	66.7	16.7	16.7	3 667	47.8	25.0	27.2	13.4	29.1	46.1
51035	Carroll, VA	7	27 703	16.6	1	10	80.0	10.0	10.0	3 987	61.7	16.1	22.2	17.4	28.7	2.2
51036	Charles City County, VA	2	6 887	17.9	1	3	33.3	33.3	33.3	1 029	42.1	24.4	33.5	14.5	29.9	84.6
51037	Charlotte, VA	8	12 218	18.3	1	6	66.7	16.7	16.7	2 183	48.7	22.4	28.9	14.6	31.8	42.3
51041	Chesterfield, VA	2	242 686	21.5	1	55	63.6	20.0	16.4	49 057	48.4	23.4	28.2	14.3	8.6	22.7
51043	Clarke, VA	1	12 543	16.3	1	5	60.0	20.0	20.0	1 853	46.1	24.4	29.5	11.6	14.6	9.6
51045	Craig, VA	8	4 839	16.7	1	2	50.0	—	—	706	48.0	—	—	13.3	21.4	0.6
51047	Culpeper, VA	1	31 981	18.4	1	7	57.1	28.6	14.3	5 166	45.0	36.2	18.8	13.8	22.5	25.1
51049	Cumberland, VA	8	7 845	19.1	1	3	33.3	33.3	33.3	1 177	49.3	22.3	28.5	13.1	30.0	59.0
51051	Dickenson, VA	9	17 381	21.5	1	8	62.5	—	37.5	3 181	54.9	—	45.1	13.4	47.8	0.5
51053	Dinwiddie, VA	2	22 961	17.1	1	7	71.4	14.3	14.3	3 900	49.7	21.2	29.1	12.6	29.6	40.8
51057	Essex, VA	8	9 373	17.5	1	3	33.3	33.3	33.3	1 578	39.2	23.1	37.7	18.9	39.2	52.7
51059	Fairfax, VA	0	902 492	17.5	(5)1	(5)203	(5)65.5	(5)10.8	(5)13.8	(5)140 820	(5)52.5	(5)13.9	(5)32.8	(5)13.2	(5)12.6	(5)34.4
51061	Fauquier, VA	1	51 765	19.0	1	17	58.8	23.5	11.8	8 919	48.4	23.0	28.4	15.5	12.0	13.1
51063	Floyd, VA	8	12 832	17.1	1	5	80.0	—	20.0	1 852	59.7	—	40.3	16.7	19.9	3.2
51065	Fluvanna, VA	3	16 887	18.1	1	6	66.7	16.7	16.7	2 605	47.5	22.7	29.8	14.2	20.1	28.3
51067	Franklin, VA	6	43 574	16.9	1	14	78.6	14.3	7.1	6 758	47.6	23.0	29.4	14.6	25.0	14.4
51069	Frederick, VA	4	52 459	19.3	1	14	64.3	21.4	14.3	9 605	47.6	24.5	27.9	11.5	11.7	4.2
51071	Giles, VA	9	16 349	16.4	1	5	60.0	—	40.0	2 575	60.6	—	39.4	11.9	22.5	1.7
51073	Gloucester, VA	1	33 659	19.8	1	8	62.5	25.0	12.5	6 553	47.8	23.7	28.5	11.6	14.4	13.7
51075	Goochland, VA	2	16 586	15.0	1	5	60.0	20.0	20.0	1 860	51.3	22.6	26.0	21.0	17.0	37.3
51077	Grayson, VA	9	16 420	16.7	1	11	63.6	18.2	9.1	2 258	47.5	21.3	28.0	14.3	32.8	3.6
51079	Greene, VA	3	12 972	19.0	1	4	50.0	25.0	25.0	2 299	49.5	23.6	26.9	20.3	19.0	10.3
51081	Greensville, VA	6	10 954	15.9	(6)1	(6)6	(6)50.0	(6)33.3	(6)16.7	(6)2 772	(6)40.7	(6)29.0	(6)30.2	(6)12.7	(6)50.4	(6)71.0
51083	Halifax, VA	6	(7)37 581	(7)18.4	(7)1	(7)18	(7)66.7	(7)22.2	(7)11.1	(7)6 453	(7)46.6	(7)23.0	(7)30.5	(7)17.5	(7)34.8	(7)48.1
51085	Hanover, VA	2	76 781	18.2	1	17	64.7	17.6	17.6	14 014	48.3	23.9	27.8	11.5	7.2	12.0
51087	Henrico, VA	2	232 810	16.4	1	54	68.5	14.8	13.0	37 112	48.8	23.2	26.9	11.5	13.7	35.3
51089	Henry, VA	4	56 326	17.1	1	20	60.0	20.0	20.0	9 167	48.3	22.9	28.8	14.9	26.6	34.3
51091	Highland, VA	9	2 543	15.6	1	2	50.0	—	50.0	378	54.0	—	46.0	14.8	25.1	1.1
51093	Isle of Wight, VA	1	28 391	18.7	1	8	50.0	25.0	25.0	4 669	50.1	23.2	26.8	11.5	28.1	38.0
51095	James City County, VA	0	41 370	17.7	(8)1	(8)10	(8)60.0	(8)30.0	(8)10.0	(8)7 385	(8)50.6	(8)23.0	(8)26.4	(8)10.0	(8)16.3	(8)28.7
51097	King and Queen, VA	8	6 390	18.3	1	3	66.7	—	33.3	867	66.6	—	33.4	17.8	53.3	61.2
51099	King George, VA	1	16 379	20.1	1	4	50.0	25.0	25.0	2 833	48.0	23.2	28.7	16.4	22.4	28.5
51101	King William, VA	6	12 333	19.4	2	5	40.0	20.0	40.0	2 345	54.4	16.9	28.7	18.0	18.6	31.5
51103	Lancaster, VA	9	11 418	15.3	1	3	33.3	33.3	33.3	1 634	28.0	42.4	29.7	13.0	41.7	52.5
51105	Lee, VA	9	24 257	19.7	1	13	69.2	15.4	15.4	4 283	46.1	19.9	33.9	13.7	54.8	0.6
51107	Loudoun, VA	1	123 333	18.5	1	35	74.3	14.3	11.4	19 827	52.3	22.1	25.5	11.4	6.3	16.4
51109	Louisa, VA	8	23 321	18.6	1	5	60.0	20.0	20.0	3 897	56.8	15.9	27.3	12.3	29.9	29.6
51111	Lunenburg, VA	8	11 104	19.4	1	4	50.0	25.0	25.0	2 102	46.4	22.7	30.9	16.2	49.6	47.1
51113	Madison, VA	8	12 405	18.6	1	5	40.0	40.0	20.0	1 951	30.4	38.2	31.4	13.9	18.3	18.1
51115	Mathews, VA	1	8 967	15.4	1	3	66.7	—	33.3	1 269	69.3	—	30.7	14.6	21.5	16.6
51117	Mecklenburg, VA	7	30 946	17.5	1	11	63.6	18.2	18.2	5 047	46.3	24.0	29.7	11.4	37.8	49.8
51119	Middlesex, VA	8	9 396	14.8	1	3	33.3	33.3	33.3	1 349	48.6	22.5	28.9	13.6	21.5	30.4
51121	Montgomery, VA	4	75 443	13.1	1	19	68.4	10.5	10.5	8 959	48.8	18.0	20.9	13.9	23.1	7.9
51125	Nelson, VA	8	13 529	17.7	1	5	60.0	20.0	20.0	2 092	50.7	16.6	32.7	10.9	28.3	25.9
51127	New Kent, VA	2	12 047	18.4	1	4	50.0	25.0	25.0	2 109	48.6	23.9	27.5	18.2	12.7	21.6

1. County type code is from the Economic Research Service of the USDA. See notes and definitions at the end of this section. 2. IEP = Individual Education Program. See notes and definitions at the end of this section. 3. Clifton Forge City included with Alleghany County. 4. Bedford City included with Bedford County. 5. Fairfax City included with Fairfax County. 6. Emporia City included with Greensville County. 7. South Boston is now part of Halifax County. 8. Williamsburg City included with James City County.

Table D-2. School and Student Characteristics by County — Continued

County	Staff and students, 1995–1996						Revenues, fiscal 1995				Current expenditures, fiscal 1995		
	Number of teachers	Pupil/ teacher ratio	Number of graduates	Dropouts grades 9–12 (percent)	Local school non-teaching staff	Central admin. staff	Total revenue ($1000)	Percent of Revenue from			Amount	Amount per pupil	Percent for instruction
								Federal Gov't	State Gov't	Local Gov't			
	15	16	17	18	19	20	21	22	23	24	25	26	27
VERMONT—Con.													
Windham, VT................	568	13.1	407	NA	539	59	78 860	5.0	13.5	81.5	51 487	7 065	64.9
Windsor, VT................	770	13.4	524	NA	777	68	95 841	3.1	17.7	79.2	68 271	6 699	63.6
VIRGINIA													
Accomack, VA................	NA	NA	291	NA	368	21	27 606	9.4	48.3	42.3	26 604	4 837	61.9
Albemarle, VA................	NA	NA	599	NA	722	69	78 799	3.6	21.2	75.2	64 249	5 900	62.1
Alleghany, VA................	[1]NA	[1]NA	[1]225	[1]NA	[1]201	[1]13	[1]18 560	[1]5.6	[1]42.6	[1]51.8	[1]16 414	[1]5 034	[1]56.5
Amelia, VA................	NA	NA	82	NA	104	10	8 833	5.8	46.7	47.5	7 333	4 321	58.8
Amherst, VA................	NA	NA	249	NA	244	20	22 026	5.7	51.2	43.1	19 439	4 223	61.1
Appomattox, VA................	NA	NA	157	NA	125	15	10 894	8.1	53.2	38.8	9 758	4 184	64.7
Arlington, VA................	NA	NA	795	NA	805	322	166 942	3.5	7.3	89.2	144 609	8 580	54.4
Augusta, VA................	NA	NA	590	NA	508	36	59 828	5.3	38.6	56.1	49 587	4 737	65.1
Bath, VA................	NA	NA	39	NA	173	9	7 543	5.6	9.1	85.3	6 988	7 896	52.3
Bedford, VA................	[2]NA	[2]NA	[2]522	[2]NA	[2]419	[2]19	[2]42 232	[2]5.8	[2]45.0	[2]49.2	[2]36 730	[2]3 871	[2]63.9
Bland, VA................	NA	NA	87	NA	70	9	5 900	6.4	62.5	31.2	5 617	5 375	56.1
Botetourt, VA................	NA	NA	268	NA	234	12	21 826	4.4	43.8	51.9	19 037	4 374	63.3
Brunswick, VA................	NA	NA	168	NA	190	17	13 909	13.5	52.8	33.7	12 996	5 045	56.1
Buchanan, VA................	NA	NA	428	NA	279	28	29 144	10.5	48.1	41.4	28 370	5 228	59.4
Buckingham, VA................	NA	NA	100	NA	141	16	11 249	9.3	51.2	39.6	10 625	4 935	61.1
Campbell, VA................	NA	NA	451	NA	418	36	47 659	5.0	38.8	56.3	35 245	4 297	59.0
Caroline, VA................	NA	NA	161	NA	296	11	19 879	7.1	41.4	51.5	17 445	4 791	60.2
Carroll, VA................	NA	NA	251	NA	240	19	19 522	8.7	57.5	33.8	18 357	4 690	62.0
Charles City County, VA ...	NA	NA	40	NA	90	24	8 666	6.6	31.8	61.6	6 770	6 361	63.9
Charlotte, VA................	NA	NA	111	NA	159	11	11 095	10.0	54.4	35.6	10 664	4 988	56.0
Chesterfield, VA................	NA	NA	2 652	NA	2 226	102	257 367	3.3	34.3	62.3	216 974	4 516	63.0
Clarke, VA................	NA	NA	88	NA	103	18	10 685	4.2	24.9	71.0	9 232	5 228	58.2
Craig, VA................	NA	NA	48	NA	33	7	3 387	7.4	54.2	38.3	3 124	4 375	63.2
Culpeper, VA................	NA	NA	252	NA	318	23	31 877	5.0	30.8	64.2	26 026	5 136	63.6
Cumberland, VA................	NA	NA	64	NA	78	7	5 900	11.5	47.4	41.1	5 939	5 205	54.3
Dickenson, VA................	NA	NA	241	NA	173	18	19 178	9.8	47.0	43.1	17 949	5 452	56.0
Dinwiddie, VA................	NA	NA	194	NA	307	15	20 708	7.1	48.8	44.1	16 495	4 333	60.4
Essex, VA................	NA	NA	92	NA	125	11	8 461	8.9	38.2	52.9	8 163	5 219	56.8
Fairfax, VA................	[3]NA	[3]NA	[3]8 850	[3]NA	[3]8 145	[3]569	[3]1 004 892	[3]2.9	[3]11.1	[3]86.0	[3]923 668	[3]6 708	[3]61.2
Fauquier, VA................	NA	NA	467	NA	576	44	58 587	3.0	18.1	79.0	50 509	5 816	61.0
Floyd, VA................	NA	NA	140	NA	128	8	9 200	6.4	52.4	41.3	8 561	4 585	60.5
Fluvanna, VA................	NA	NA	129	NA	148	14	13 010	5.6	43.4	51.0	11 491	4 686	63.7
Franklin, VA................	NA	NA	369	NA	405	23	33 661	6.0	43.8	50.2	28 883	4 381	57.9
Frederick, VA................	NA	NA	460	NA	479	33	56 066	3.5	30.6	65.9	44 687	4 832	58.3
Giles, VA................	NA	NA	173	NA	166	10	14 419	6.8	45.4	47.8	12 905	5 041	64.4
Gloucester, VA................	NA	NA	356	NA	362	21	33 399	4.9	41.5	53.5	28 319	4 446	60.9
Goochland, VA................	NA	NA	91	NA	121	16	10 691	5.7	20.9	73.4	10 162	5 810	58.5
Grayson, VA................	NA	NA	146	NA	154	15	11 321	6.8	56.1	37.1	11 084	4 993	59.6
Greene, VA................	NA	NA	102	NA	190	16	13 353	5.5	45.5	48.9	10 426	4 728	66.6
Greensville, VA................	[4]NA	[4]NA	[4]158	[4]NA	[4]148	[4]19	[4]15 937	[4]9.7	[4]53.8	[4]36.5	[4]15 240	[4]5 500	[4]64.4
Halifax, VA................	[5]NA	[5]NA	[5]403	[5]NA	[5]389	[5]118	[5]35 866	[5]8.3	[5]46.3	[5]45.4	[5]20 191	[5]4 510	[5]50.1
Hanover, VA................	NA	NA	779	NA	581	49	69 309	3.6	32.3	64.1	57 912	4 318	62.7
Henrico, VA................	NA	NA	2 013	NA	1 519	127	209 069	3.5	26.9	69.6	182 093	5 067	61.6
Henry, VA................	NA	NA	618	NA	459	27	44 937	5.9	46.9	47.2	42 321	4 670	63.0
Highland, VA................	NA	NA	21	NA	41	5	2 341	7.9	38.7	53.4	2 353	6 033	53.7
Isle of Wight, VA................	NA	NA	232	NA	195	17	26 708	6.1	35.3	58.6	22 721	4 986	62.1
James City County, VA.....	[6]NA	[6]NA	[6]373	[6]NA	[6]450	[6]30	[6]53 684	[6]2.5	[6]16.4	[6]81.1	[6]38 952	[6]5 554	[6]59.3
King and Queen, VA.........	NA	NA	51	NA	73	11	6 536	11.2	35.8	53.0	5 546	6 260	55.5
King George, VA................	NA	NA	169	NA	158	15	14 998	5.6	38.0	56.4	13 550	4 958	59.4
King William, VA................	NA	NA	150	NA	130	22	13 370	4.4	39.3	56.3	12 089	5 368	61.1
Lancaster, VA................	NA	NA	102	NA	92	13	8 862	6.3	22.0	71.7	7 491	4 633	55.1
Lee, VA................	NA	NA	269	NA	255	33	24 633	17.1	53.5	29.4	22 141	5 145	65.1
Loudoun, VA................	NA	NA	1 007	NA	936	51	122 914	2.5	10.0	87.5	105 335	5 810	61.0
Louisa, VA................	NA	NA	180	NA	211	28	22 415	5.6	19.5	74.9	17 961	4 677	57.7
Lunenburg, VA................	NA	NA	153	NA	131	174	10 859	9.9	56.5	33.6	10 001	4 556	58.0
Madison, VA................	NA	NA	129	NA	137	12	10 514	6.1	41.3	52.7	9 188	4 813	54.7
Mathews, VA................	NA	NA	81	NA	88	9	6 277	6.1	36.7	57.2	5 886	4 591	62.2
Mecklenburg, VA................	NA	NA	274	NA	329	24	23 610	8.9	52.6	38.5	22 695	4 447	62.2
Middlesex, VA................	NA	NA	74	NA	88	8	7 794	8.4	27.4	64.2	6 365	4 750	60.9
Montgomery, VA................	NA	NA	509	NA	589	43	48 296	5.6	40.0	54.4	45 406	5 125	60.9
Nelson, VA................	NA	NA	132	NA	152	13	13 127	6.1	30.1	63.8	10 890	5 132	55.7
New Kent, VA................	NA	NA	120	NA	161	11	11 304	4.9	36.1	59.0	9 778	4 786	61.1

1. Clifton Forge City included with Alleghany County.   2. Bedford City included with Bedford County.   3. Fairfax City included with Fairfax County.   4. Emporia City included with Greensville County.   5. South Boston is now part of Halifax County.   6. Williamsburg City included with James City County.

Table D-2. School and Student Characteristics by County

State/County code	County	County type[1]	Population, 1996		Number of school districts, 1995–1996	Level of schools, 1995–1996				Level of students, 1995–1996				Characteristics of students, 1995–1996		
			Total persons	Percent age 5–17		Number of schools	Percent Primary	Middle	High	Number of students	Percent Primary	Middle	High	Percent with IEP[2]	Percent free-lunch eligible	Percent minority
			1	2	3	4	5	6	7	8	9	10	11	12	13	14
	VIRGINIA—Con.															
51131	Northampton, VA	9	12 908	19.1	1	4	50.0	25.0	25.0	2 514	44.9	23.6	31.5	8.5	54.0	60.9
51133	Northumberland, VA	9	11 226	14.8	1	4	50.0	25.0	25.0	1 551	43.2	27.7	29.1	13.5	38.6	49.4
51135	Nottoway, VA	6	15 230	16.7	1	6	50.0	33.3	16.7	2 477	39.3	32.4	28.3	18.9	41.9	48.8
51137	Orange, VA	6	24 512	17.9	1	7	57.1	28.6	14.3	3 823	46.4	24.5	29.1	12.5	22.9	20.8
51139	Page, VA	6	22 891	17.2	1	7	71.4	—	28.6	3 507	62.2	—	37.8	12.5	25.4	3.5
51141	Patrick, VA	9	18 075	16.7	1	7	71.4	14.3	14.3	2 601	53.7	9.7	36.6	13.6	26.4	11.6
51143	Pittsylvania, VA	3	55 774	18.4	1	20	55.0	25.0	20.0	9 378	40.8	24.2	35.1	10.2	26.9	33.5
51145	Powhatan, VA	2	19 794	17.4	1	3	33.3	33.3	33.3	2 764	34.4	32.5	33.1	13.2	12.7	13.4
51147	Prince Edward, VA	7	18 751	15.5	1	3	33.3	33.3	33.3	2 634	43.4	29.6	27.0	14.2	47.6	60.1
51149	Prince George, VA	2	28 401	19.6	1	10	70.0	20.0	10.0	5 521	47.8	24.3	27.9	10.4	13.8	40.3
51153	Prince William, VA	0	249 278	21.8	1	66	62.1	16.7	13.6	47 072	47.7	22.6	27.3	13.4	14.6	30.9
51155	Pulaski, VA	7	34 290	16.5	1	11	72.7	18.2	9.1	5 146	46.9	22.6	30.5	13.1	26.2	7.9
51157	Rappahannock, VA	8	7 206	15.9	1	2	50.0	—	50.0	1 051	62.4	—	37.6	15.6	15.3	11.0
51159	Richmond, VA	9	8 496	14.9	1	3	33.3	33.3	33.3	1 315	44.9	26.0	29.0	8.8	28.9	35.6
51161	Roanoke, VA	3	81 585	17.0	1	26	65.4	15.4	15.4	13 753	45.9	25.1	28.2	17.0	5.9	5.3
51163	Rockbridge, VA	6	19 006	17.0	1	8	62.5	25.0	12.5	3 187	42.9	23.5	33.6	13.1	20.5	4.8
51165	Rockingham, VA	5	62 432	17.8	1	19	63.2	21.1	15.8	10 228	47.7	22.8	29.5	11.5	15.9	4.8
51167	Russell, VA	6	29 134	19.5	1	13	69.2	7.7	23.1	4 713	48.4	8.7	43.0	15.6	34.8	0.9
51169	Scott, VA	2	22 949	16.9	1	13	53.8	23.1	23.1	3 863	47.2	21.4	31.4	14.1	35.9	1.0
51171	Shenandoah, VA	6	33 612	15.9	1	9	33.3	33.3	33.3	5 302	39.4	30.4	30.2	12.5	15.8	4.0
51173	Smyth, VA	6	33 076	17.3	1	11	54.5	18.2	27.3	5 267	47.9	17.3	34.8	14.7	25.5	2.7
51175	Southampton, VA	6	17 682	17.4	1	7	71.4	14.3	14.3	2 857	50.1	21.8	28.1	12.6	39.6	54.3
51177	Spotsylvania, VA	0	74 106	22.0	1	22	59.1	22.7	13.6	15 279	47.6	23.0	28.9	12.4	11.2	16.3
51179	Stafford, VA	1	82 488	21.6	1	19	57.9	26.3	15.8	16 520	47.8	24.1	28.1	11.2	11.0	14.5
51181	Surry, VA	8	6 406	19.4	1	3	33.3	33.3	33.3	1 283	37.8	33.4	28.8	10.6	40.9	68.9
51183	Sussex, VA	8	10 088	17.9	1	5	60.0	20.0	20.0	1 520	50.6	21.3	28.2	13.3	59.2	80.5
51185	Tazewell, VA	7	47 070	19.7	1	17	58.8	17.6	23.5	8 033	42.5	23.2	34.3	12.6	32.7	3.9
51187	Warren, VA	1	29 879	17.1	1	6	66.7	16.7	16.7	4 606	49.8	22.8	27.4	13.0	16.0	7.4
51191	Washington, VA	2	48 498	16.8	1	15	46.7	26.7	26.7	7 539	43.5	24.6	31.8	12.4	25.5	2.3
51193	Westmoreland, VA	6	16 549	16.7	2	6	50.0	16.7	16.7	2 736	36.9	19.4	18.7	10.3	42.9	48.2
51195	Wise, VA	7	39 494	20.5	1	15	40.0	20.0	40.0	7 853	36.6	22.6	40.8	11.7	34.2	2.2
51197	Wythe, VA	7	26 357	17.5	1	10	60.0	10.0	30.0	4 356	53.0	8.4	38.6	12.8	24.3	4.3
51199	York, VA	0	55 010	22.5	1	16	62.5	18.8	18.8	10 729	46.4	24.3	29.2	7.3	8.6	23.3
51510	Alexandria City, VA	NA	117 586	10.4	1	18	66.7	16.7	16.7	10 044	52.2	28.3	19.4	16.6	41.9	74.4
51515	Bedford City, VA	NA	6 530	14.9	[3]NA	[3]NA	[3]NA	[3]NA	[3]NA	[3]NA	[3]NA	[3]NA	[3]NA	[3]NA	[3]NA	[3]NA
51520	Bristol City, VA	NA	17 957	15.7	1	6	66.7	16.7	16.7	2 533	53.1	15.1	31.8	15.4	33.1	9.8
51530	Buena Vista City, VA	NA	6 368	16.6	1	4	50.0	25.0	25.0	1 062	46.1	22.8	31.1	13.2	28.6	7.8
51540	Charlottesville City, VA	NA	40 767	12.6	1	9	66.7	22.2	11.1	4 440	43.9	30.7	25.4	18.4	41.9	50.7
51550	Chesapeake City, VA	0	192 342	20.8	1	38	60.5	26.3	13.2	34 980	43.2	30.7	26.1	12.4	20.6	36.3
51560	Clifton Forge City, VA	NA	4 457	15.3	[4]NA	[4]NA	[4]NA	[4]NA	[4]NA	[4]NA	[4]NA	[4]NA	[4]NA	[4]NA	[4]NA	[4]NA
51570	Colonial Heights City, VA	NA	17 154	16.3	1	5	60.0	20.0	20.0	2 752	45.9	23.7	30.4	13.0	9.7	8.6
51580	Covington City, VA	NA	6 781	14.3	1	3	33.3	33.3	33.3	960	30.7	30.1	39.2	19.3	28.1	21.0
51590	Danville City, VA	NA	53 472	16.5	1	15	53.3	40.0	6.7	8 273	40.3	39.2	20.5	9.9	43.7	60.4
51595	Emporia City, VA	NA	5 831	17.2	[5]NA	[5]NA	[5]NA	[5]NA	[5]NA	[5]NA	[5]NA	[5]NA	[5]NA	[5]NA	[5]NA	[5]NA
51600	Fairfax City, VA	NA	20 990	13.9	[6]NA	[6]NA	[6]NA	[6]NA	[6]NA	[6]NA	[6]NA	[6]NA	[6]NA	[6]NA	[6]NA	[6]NA
51610	Falls Church City, VA	NA	9 781	13.8	1	4	50.0	25.0	25.0	1 462	46.3	23.4	30.3	14.4	4.1	21.1
51620	Franklin City, VA	NA	8 586	19.5	1	3	33.3	33.3	33.3	1 796	31.2	31.7	37.1	15.4	43.1	60.3
51630	Fredericksburg City, VA	NA	22 586	12.7	1	3	33.3	33.3	33.3	2 217	36.9	30.3	32.7	14.1	40.4	47.7
51640	Galax City, VA	NA	6 649	14.5	1	3	33.3	33.3	33.3	1 235	50.7	22.4	26.9	8.3	31.3	15.1
51650	Hampton City, VA	NA	138 757	17.7	1	34	70.6	14.7	11.8	23 611	48.6	23.7	27.5	8.9	32.0	56.5
51660	Harrisonburg City, VA	NA	33 446	11.5	1	6	66.7	16.7	16.7	3 529	48.8	24.8	26.4	15.9	34.5	19.5
51670	Hopewell City, VA	NA	22 566	18.6	1	5	60.0	20.0	20.0	4 060	50.0	23.3	26.7	15.8	37.9	46.6
51678	Lexington City, VA	NA	7 164	9.4	1	2	50.0	50.0	—	486	66.5	33.5	—	20.0	16.7	19.5
51680	Lynchburg City, VA	NA	67 250	16.0	1	19	63.2	21.1	15.8	9 476	48.5	22.4	29.1	13.8	35.3	47.6
51683	Manassas City, VA	NA	33 200	19.5	1	8	62.5	12.5	25.0	5 685	59.7	21.9	18.4	12.9	12.4	29.1
51685	Manassas Park City, VA	NA	7 541	22.2	1	5	40.0	40.0	20.0	1 561	36.3	41.3	22.4	18.4	21.8	23.2
51690	Martinsville City, VA	NA	15 850	16.2	1	6	50.0	33.3	16.7	2 836	33.1	40.3	26.6	15.2	38.0	54.1
51700	Newport News City, VA	NA	176 122	19.1	1	40	65.0	17.5	12.5	32 574	53.2	22.4	24.0	10.5	36.6	57.0
51710	Norfolk City, VA	NA	233 430	15.9	1	51	72.5	15.7	9.8	36 771	53.8	22.7	23.3	12.2	54.3	68.0
51720	Norton City, VA	NA	4 288	20.0	1	2	50.0	—	50.0	793	50.3	—	49.7	15.1	35.9	12.0
51730	Petersburg City, VA	NA	38 234	16.9	1	9	66.7	22.2	11.1	6 167	54.4	21.7	23.9	10.9	62.5	96.6
51735	Poquoson City, VA	NA	11 922	21.4	1	4	50.0	25.0	25.0	2 436	43.2	23.8	33.0	9.1	3.6	3.5
51740	Portsmouth City, VA	NA	101 308	19.0	1	27	70.4	14.8	11.1	17 891	50.6	23.2	25.8	15.2	47.2	69.3
51750	Radford City, VA	NA	16 145	10.3	1	4	25.0	50.0	25.0	1 506	32.2	38.4	29.4	16.1	13.7	14.3
51760	Richmond City, VA	NA	198 267	14.4	1	56	53.6	16.1	17.9	27 708	54.9	22.0	22.3	12.0	65.0	91.6
51770	Roanoke City, VA	NA	95 548	15.2	1	29	72.4	17.2	10.3	13 219	54.1	21.4	24.6	17.0	44.2	43.0

1. County type code is from the Economic Research Service of the USDA. See notes and definitions at the end of this section. 2. IEP = Individual Education Program. See notes and definitions at the end of this section. 3. Bedford City included with Bedford County. 4. Clifton Forge City included with Alleghany County. 5. Emporia City included with Greensville County. 6. Fairfax City included with Fairfax County.

Table D-2. School and Student Characteristics by County — Continued

County	Staff and students, 1995–1996						Revenues, fiscal 1995					Current expenditures, fiscal 1995		
	Number of teachers	Pupil/ teacher ratio	Number of graduates	Dropouts grades 9–12 (percent)	Local school non-teaching staff	Central admin. staff	Total revenue ($1000)	Percent of Revenue from			Amount	Amount per pupil	Percent for instruction
								Federal Gov't	State Gov't	Local Gov't			
	15	16	17	18	19	20	21	22	23	24	25	26	27
VIRGINIA—Con.													
Northampton, VA.............	NA	NA	145	NA	187	11	13 157	11.7	46.9	41.4	11 913	4 767	62.1
Northumberland, VA..........	NA	NA	66	NA	92	10	9 176	8.8	22.4	68.7	7 698	4 983	59.1
Nottoway, VA...................	NA	NA	142	NA	140	12	13 583	12.6	49.7	37.7	12 087	4 911	61.4
Orange, VA......................	NA	NA	211	NA	257	19	22 105	7.3	34.1	58.6	18 877	4 893	60.2
Page, VA........................	NA	NA	193	NA	191	16	17 581	6.8	48.3	44.9	15 832	4 517	66.5
Patrick, VA......................	NA	NA	192	NA	166	14	12 856	6.6	51.0	42.4	12 179	4 670	63.9
Pittsylvania, VA...............	NA	NA	519	NA	494	27	41 468	9.5	56.2	34.3	40 357	4 334	65.8
Powhatan, VA..................	NA	NA	138	NA	183	10	14 086	4.1	39.2	56.7	12 409	4 670	59.1
Prince Edward, VA............	NA	NA	148	NA	134	16	17 255	7.9	36.6	55.5	12 297	4 690	63.9
Prince George, VA............	NA	NA	261	NA	296	22	28 444	10.8	44.9	44.2	25 460	4 786	58.3
Prince William, VA............	NA	NA	2 591	NA	2 402	184	288 000	3.3	30.4	66.3	257 956	5 648	59.8
Pulaski, VA.....................	NA	NA	367	NA	289	15	26 119	7.2	47.5	45.3	24 706	4 757	62.9
Rappahannock, VA	NA	NA	61	NA	60	14	5 974	5.5	22.1	72.4	5 197	5 156	55.5
Richmond, VA	NA	NA	66	NA	67	10	7 208	6.5	42.8	50.8	6 302	4 893	62.1
Roanoke, VA	NA	NA	943	NA	742	21	83 056	3.1	32.4	64.5	75 427	5 509	64.8
Rockbridge, VA	NA	NA	216	NA	201	9	16 455	5.6	41.5	52.9	14 814	4 676	64.3
Rockingham, VA...............	NA	NA	579	NA	539	20	66 365	3.9	32.0	64.1	49 577	4 959	61.1
Russell, VA.....................	NA	NA	351	NA	229	14	22 877	9.8	55.4	34.8	21 596	4 559	60.8
Scott, VA........................	NA	NA	270	NA	234	10	19 850	9.2	57.8	33.0	18 561	4 780	62.0
Shenandoah, VA..............	NA	NA	292	NA	315	18	31 294	3.8	33.2	62.9	26 648	5 133	62.8
Smyth, VA.......................	NA	NA	346	NA	195	26	25 714	8.4	53.3	38.2	24 521	4 601	66.9
Southampton, VA..............	NA	NA	142	NA	170	25	18 981	8.1	35.6	56.3	14 057	5 035	58.3
Spotsylvania, VA..............	NA	NA	827	NA	908	31	71 285	4.2	41.5	54.3	66 965	4 548	62.7
Stafford, VA....................	NA	NA	928	NA	700	47	88 814	3.0	34.2	62.0	70 710	4 700	62.1
Surry, VA	NA	NA	63	NA	96	14	9 989	5.7	9.5	84.8	8 379	6 785	62.6
Sussex, VA.....................	NA	NA	94	NA	113	14	9 194	10.1	40.5	49.3	8 536	5 668	54.4
Tazewell, VA	NA	NA	636	NA	337	21	39 272	8.3	50.5	41.2	36 476	4 401	61.8
Warren, VA......................	NA	NA	229	NA	327	41	20 966	5.3	39.9	54.8	19 741	4 292	60.2
Washington, VA...............	NA	NA	503	NA	343	28	36 675	8.6	46.5	45.0	34 559	4 621	62.4
Westmoreland, VA	NA	NA	125	NA	133	19	13 474	8.7	44.3	47.0	11 547	4 333	59.2
Wise, VA	NA	NA	539	NA	350	27	41 726	10.3	51.3	38.4	38 062	4 731	65.1
Wythe, VA.......................	NA	NA	307	NA	224	19	22 068	8.3	50.1	41.6	21 121	4 801	66.7
York, VA	NA	NA	743	NA	505	28	56 604	10.5	35.9	53.6	48 006	4 482	61.5
Alexandria City, VA	NA	NA	498	NA	654	61	88 388	4.8	8.8	86.4	84 304	8 609	60.1
Bedford City, VA..............	[1]NA	[1]NA	[1]NA	[1]NA	[1]NA	[1]NA	[1]NA	[1]NA	[1]NA	[1]NA	[1]NA	[1]NA	[1]NA
Bristol City, VA	NA	NA	158	NA	127	11	18 410	6.4	34.1	59.6	14 272	5 646	65.2
Buena Vista City, VA.........	NA	NA	76	NA	53	3	5 515	6.9	54.0	39.1	5 366	4 978	63.4
Charlottesville City, VA......	NA	NA	202	NA	446	603	35 690	5.6	25.1	69.2	33 878	7 565	57.8
Chesapeake City, VA........	NA	NA	1 902	NA	1 964	113	171 727	5.2	40.4	54.5	162 340	4 757	63.3
Clifton Forge City, VA........	[2]NA	[2]NA	[2]NA	[2]NA	[2]NA	[2]NA	[2]NA	[2]NA	[2]NA	[2]NA	[2]NA	[2]NA	[2]NA
Colonial Heights City, VA..	NA	NA	146	NA	132	14	16 305	2.9	27.5	69.7	15 230	5 653	67.4
Covington City, VA...........	NA	NA	55	NA	57	8	6 056	6.5	36.7	56.8	5 705	5 869	64.9
Danville City, VA..............	NA	NA	457	NA	851	422	42 756	8.6	41.7	49.7	38 003	4 579	66.1
Emporia City, VA..............	[3]NA	[3]NA	[3]NA	[3]NA	[3]NA	[3]NA	[3]NA	[3]NA	[3]NA	[3]NA	[3]NA	[3]NA	[3]NA
Fairfax City, VA	[4]NA	[4]NA	[4]NA	[4]NA	[4]NA	[4]NA	[4]17 717	[4]0.1	[4]8.5	[4]91.4	[4]NA	[4]NA	[4]NA
Falls Church City, VA........	NA	NA	81	NA	113	31	14 587	1.5	6.5	92.0	12 282	9 058	53.9
Franklin City, VA	NA	NA	102	NA	84	11	9 977	9.0	44.8	46.2	8 917	5 069	62.6
Fredericksburg City, VA	NA	NA	105	NA	117	17	14 574	11.0	19.4	69.6	13 289	6 144	62.2
Galax City, VA.................	NA	NA	72	NA	48	11	6 197	7.7	46.9	45.3	5 659	4 487	60.8
Hampton City, VA.............	NA	NA	1 278	NA	1 139	74	122 634	7.1	39.7	53.1	112 485	4 800	63.6
Harrisonburg City, VA	NA	NA	178	NA	147	15	24 693	4.6	20.4	75.0	18 926	5 394	60.8
Hopewell City, VA	NA	NA	185	NA	206	18	24 936	10.4	38.0	51.6	21 828	5 325	61.6
Lexington City, VA............	NA	NA	—	NA	14	10	3 565	5.2	35.8	59.0	2 284	4 798	57.0
Lynchburg City, VA	NA	NA	512	NA	599	30	61 630	8.4	31.7	59.9	50 994	5 423	59.1
Manassas City, VA	NA	NA	261	NA	257	25	34 806	2.5	24.3	73.3	28 775	5 292	60.5
Manassas Park City, VA ...	NA	NA	49	NA	53	11	7 820	4.6	51.2	44.2	7 088	4 757	59.8
Martinsville City, VA	NA	NA	166	NA	214	13	14 883	7.2	39.1	53.7	14 774	5 220	68.7
Newport News City, VA.....	NA	NA	1 411	NA	1 703	113	168 127	8.9	40.5	50.6	148 126	4 583	60.6
Norfolk City, VA...............	NA	NA	1 111	NA	1 767	196	227 936	10.2	36.4	53.4	200 885	5 507	59.7
Norton City, VA	NA	NA	54	NA	45	4	4 331	9.1	44.4	46.5	3 929	4 739	65.2
Petersburg City, VA..........	NA	NA	229	NA	287	33	33 032	12.1	44.6	43.3	30 196	4 856	58.9
Poquoson City, VA	NA	NA	182	NA	100	18	10 555	3.7	46.5	49.7	10 338	4 216	65.4
Portsmouth City, VA	NA	NA	784	NA	982	78	100 670	11.4	46.4	42.2	90 729	5 103	57.7
Radford City, VA	NA	NA	85	NA	93	12	8 262	4.2	39.0	56.8	7 822	5 225	62.3
Richmond City, VA............	NA	NA	1 024	NA	1 172	202	201 324	9.1	25.9	65.0	189 515	6 833	56.7
Roanoke City, VA.............	NA	NA	536	NA	902	51	84 366	12.0	31.8	56.2	73 261	5 668	60.7

1. Bedford City included with Bedford County.   2. Clifton Forge City included with Alleghany County.   3. Emporia City included with Greensville County.   4. Fairfax City included with Fairfax County.

Table D-2. School and Student Characteristics by County

State/County code	County	County type[1]	Population, 1996		Number of school districts, 1995–1996	Level of schools, 1995–1996				Level of students, 1995–1996				Characteristics of students, 1995–1996		
			Total persons	Percent age 5–17		Number of schools	Percent			Number of students	Percent			Percent with IEP[2]	Percent free-lunch eligible	Percent minority
							Primary	Middle	High		Primary	Middle	High			
			1	2	3	4	5	6	7	8	9	10	11	12	13	14
	VIRGINIA—Con.															
51775	Salem City, VA	NA	24 159	14.6	1	6	66.7	16.7	16.7	3 841	45.7	23.5	30.8	12.9	12.4	8.0
51780	South Boston City, VA	NA	[3]NA	[3]NA	[3]NA	[3]NA	[3]NA	[3]NA	[3]NA	[3]NA	[3]NA	[3]NA	[3]NA	[3]NA	[3]NA	[3]NA
51790	Staunton City, VA	NA	24 800	15.0	1	6	66.7	16.7	16.7	2 923	57.4	15.5	27.1	15.7	25.4	23.5
51800	Suffolk City, VA	0	58 901	19.8	1	16	62.5	18.8	12.5	10 024	49.0	22.8	27.8	13.3	43.4	58.7
51810	Virginia Beach City, VA	0	430 385	19.9	1	79	65.8	17.7	15.2	76 508	49.2	23.7	27.0	12.7	16.6	31.0
51820	Waynesboro City, VA	NA	18 928	16.4	1	6	66.7	16.7	16.7	3 019	50.6	23.9	25.5	9.3	18.8	18.5
51830	Williamsburg City, VA	NA	12 922	7.4	[4]NA	[4]NA	[4]NA	[4]NA	[4]NA	[4]NA	[4]NA	[4]NA	[4]NA	[4]NA	[4]NA	[4]NA
51840	Winchester City, VA	NA	23 649	14.8	1	7	57.1	14.3	14.3	3 297	49.4	21.6	28.1	18.7	30.6	21.6
53000	**WASHINGTON**															
53001	Adams, WA	6	15 254	25.3	5	11	54.5	9.1	27.3	3 685	57.6	12.5	26.7	NA	NA	54.1
53003	Asotin, WA	7	20 761	20.7	2	10	50.0	10.0	30.0	3 713	50.9	14.0	34.8	NA	NA	4.7
53005	Benton, WA	3	134 359	22.3	6	45	57.8	22.2	15.6	27 078	45.1	23.0	25.5	NA	NA	16.5
53007	Chelan, WA	5	59 532	19.6	7	31	51.6	19.4	25.8	12 562	45.8	23.9	30.2	NA	NA	26.0
53009	Clallam, WA	5	63 419	18.2	5	22	45.5	18.2	22.7	10 631	41.8	21.6	29.8	NA	NA	14.5
53011	Clark, WA	1	305 171	21.2	9	95	58.9	20.0	14.7	57 550	48.6	23.7	26.3	NA	NA	10.6
53013	Columbia, WA	9	4 265	19.8	2	3	66.7	—	—	843	28.9	—	—	NA	NA	14.6
53015	Cowlitz, WA	4	89 984	20.3	6	39	53.8	17.9	15.4	17 473	48.2	22.5	19.8	NA	NA	8.8
53017	Douglas, WA	7	32 689	21.4	6	17	52.9	17.6	23.5	6 189	44.8	27.9	22.2	NA	NA	26.2
53019	Ferry, WA	9	7 195	24.2	5	6	50.0	—	16.7	1 398	36.0	—	20.2	NA	NA	25.4
53021	Franklin, WA	3	45 590	25.7	4	20	65.0	10.0	15.0	9 860	49.2	11.7	26.7	NA	NA	57.8
53023	Garfield, WA	9	2 306	21.1	1	2	50.0	—	50.0	454	50.2	—	49.8	NA	NA	2.9
53025	Grant, WA	5	67 597	23.3	9	41	46.3	26.8	24.4	14 683	48.4	27.6	23.6	NA	NA	35.3
53027	Grays Harbor, WA	4	67 923	20.1	13	38	55.3	10.5	21.1	14 021	50.8	12.2	29.7	NA	NA	13.8
53029	Island, WA	1	69 194	18.4	3	21	57.1	9.5	28.6	9 857	63.3	9.0	27.6	NA	NA	18.3
53031	Jefferson, WA	6	25 477	16.9	5	11	45.5	18.2	27.3	3 837	42.1	20.8	29.4	NA	NA	8.2
53033	King, WA	0	1 619 411	16.1	19	446	62.3	15.7	17.3	239 404	52.4	20.9	25.2	NA	NA	28.1
53035	Kitsap, WA	3	231 741	20.2	5	65	63.1	16.9	16.9	41 149	53.5	24.1	21.7	NA	NA	18.0
53037	Kittitas, WA	6	30 846	16.3	6	14	42.9	14.3	21.4	4 778	42.8	20.3	24.0	NA	NA	9.1
53039	Klickitat, WA	7	18 526	22.1	10	15	33.3	13.3	20.0	3 927	33.4	22.4	27.6	NA	NA	17.1
53041	Lewis, WA	6	66 848	21.7	14	38	52.6	15.8	23.7	13 309	43.1	17.9	31.4	NA	NA	8.0
53043	Lincoln, WA	8	9 594	20.7	8	16	50.0	—	50.0	2 313	59.2	—	40.8	NA	NA	7.1
53045	Mason, WA	6	48 577	19.2	7	18	55.6	16.7	27.8	8 549	46.8	22.4	30.8	NA	NA	13.9
53047	Okanogan, WA	7	38 005	21.3	9	29	37.9	27.6	34.5	9 147	48.7	17.7	33.6	NA	NA	34.1
53049	Pacific, WA	7	21 067	18.0	6	18	44.4	11.1	33.3	3 789	48.1	5.0	41.9	NA	NA	17.9
53051	Pend Oreille, WA	8	11 141	22.6	3	9	44.4	22.2	33.3	2 385	42.7	21.4	35.9	NA	NA	6.3
53053	Pierce, WA	2	657 272	19.6	15	228	59.6	20.2	15.8	117 550	52.0	23.2	24.0	NA	NA	24.7
53055	San Juan, WA	8	12 061	15.0	4	11	72.7	—	9.1	1 825	52.2	—	14.4	NA	NA	6.8
53057	Skagit, WA	4	95 543	19.6	7	41	63.4	14.6	19.5	17 382	56.7	15.3	27.9	NA	NA	18.2
53059	Skamania, WA	8	9 371	22.2	4	7	71.4	14.3	14.3	1 486	57.4	13.2	29.4	NA	NA	10.0
53061	Snohomish, WA	0	546 102	19.7	14	162	59.3	17.9	18.5	93 107	52.2	21.3	24.6	NA	NA	13.2
53063	Spokane, WA	2	404 920	19.6	14	144	59.0	14.6	20.1	72 301	51.8	18.6	27.5	NA	NA	9.5
53065	Stevens, WA	6	38 624	24.5	12	24	45.8	20.8	25.0	6 738	38.1	24.0	29.4	NA	NA	12.3
53067	Thurston, WA	3	197 109	20.3	8	69	58.0	18.8	23.2	37 159	48.1	19.3	32.5	NA	NA	17.3
53069	Wahkiakum, WA	9	3 775	19.2	1	2	50.0	—	50.0	576	69.1	—	30.9	NA	NA	11.1
53071	Walla Walla, WA	4	53 488	18.5	7	23	52.2	21.7	21.7	9 750	48.2	22.2	27.1	NA	NA	25.2
53073	Whatcom, WA	3	152 512	18.8	7	51	62.7	17.6	17.6	24 270	45.6	19.3	32.3	NA	NA	14.5
53075	Whitman, WA	5	39 456	13.5	13	24	45.8	12.5	29.2	5 035	46.6	13.2	27.2	NA	NA	9.2
53077	Yakima, WA	3	216 234	22.4	15	83	51.8	16.9	26.5	46 809	50.8	19.9	25.7	NA	NA	50.4
54000	**WEST VIRGINIA**															
54001	Barbour, WV	7	16 360	17.6	1	9	66.7	22.2	11.1	2 842	48.8	20.5	30.7	13.8	52.8	2.0
54003	Berkeley, WV	3	68 197	17.2	1	25	60.0	20.0	12.0	11 666	47.8	24.0	27.9	12.8	27.7	6.9
54005	Boone, WV	6	26 403	19.7	1	18	66.7	16.7	16.7	4 880	47.3	19.5	33.2	16.5	43.9	1.3
54007	Braxton, WV	9	13 449	17.7	1	8	75.0	12.5	12.5	2 672	44.2	28.0	27.8	18.3	50.0	0.8
54009	Brooke, WV	3	26 573	16.3	1	12	75.0	16.7	—	4 050	34.1	29.8	—	15.3	27.4	1.9
54011	Cabell, WV	1	96 178	15.0	1	32	71.9	18.8	9.4	14 065	44.8	23.7	31.5	16.1	37.1	7.3
54013	Calhoun, WV	9	7 982	19.0	1	5	80.0	—	20.0	1 597	61.7	—	38.3	19.5	60.4	0.3
54015	Clay, WV	8	10 412	21.0	1	7	71.4	14.3	14.3	2 123	44.0	24.2	31.7	15.4	62.0	0.1
54017	Doddridge, WV	9	7 235	19.0	1	6	66.7	16.7	16.7	1 366	32.7	35.1	32.2	18.1	49.0	0.3
54019	Fayette, WV	6	48 908	18.3	1	33	57.6	21.2	21.2	8 544	38.9	25.4	35.7	14.5	47.7	8.0
54021	Gilmer, WV	9	7 184	15.9	1	5	80.0	—	20.0	1 276	56.0	—	44.0	19.4	57.4	0.5
54023	Grant, WV	8	11 172	17.5	1	5	60.0	—	20.0	1 875	47.6	—	38.2	15.6	36.0	1.8
54025	Greenbrier, WV	7	35 734	16.7	1	13	46.2	7.7	—	6 045	38.6	18.3	—	13.3	39.3	4.2
54027	Hampshire, WV	8	18 808	17.8	2	11	63.6	18.2	9.1	3 698	49.8	21.9	19.8	21.0	36.2	1.7
54029	Hancock, WV	3	34 705	16.4	1	12	66.7	16.7	16.7	4 866	47.7	20.0	32.3	13.3	27.0	3.5

1. County type code is from the Economic Research Service of the USDA. See notes and definitions at the end of this section. 2. IEP = Individual Education Program. See notes and definitions at the end of this section. 3. South Boston is now part of Halifax County. 4. Williamsburg City included with James City County.

Table D-2. School and Student Characteristics by County — Continued

County	Staff and students, 1995–1996						Revenues, fiscal 1995				Current expenditures, fiscal 1995		
	Number of teachers	Pupil/ teacher ratio	Number of graduates	Dropouts grades 9–12 (percent)	Local school non-teaching staff	Central admin. staff	Total revenue ($1000)	Percent of Revenue from			Amount	Amount per pupil	Percent for instruction
								Federal Gov't	State Gov't	Local Gov't			
	15	16	17	18	19	20	21	22	23	24	25	26	27
VIRGINIA—Con.													
Salem City, VA	NA	NA	202	NA	171	19	21 334	3.5	33.2	63.2	19 481	5 184	67.0
South Boston City, VA	[1]NA	[1]NA	[1]NA	[1]NA	[1]NA	[1]NA	[1]NA	[1]NA	[1]NA	[1]NA	[1]NA	[1]NA	[1]NA
Staunton City, VA	NA	NA	129	NA	109	14	16 184	5.1	44.5	50.4	13 812	4 668	65.8
Suffolk City, VA	NA	NA	465	NA	504	43	52 691	9.0	40.1	50.9	45 979	4 779	63.4
Virginia Beach City, VA	NA	NA	3 613	NA	3 723	214	386 470	7.1	39.5	53.5	350 790	4 620	64.5
Waynesboro City, VA	NA	NA	141	NA	115	13	14 863	5.1	34.3	60.6	13 509	4 715	61.7
Williamsburg City, VA	[2]NA	[2]NA	[2]NA	[2]NA	[2]NA	[2]NA	[2]NA	[2]NA	[2]NA	[2]NA	[2]NA	[2]NA	[2]NA
Winchester City, VA	NA	NA	145	NA	199	12	24 049	4.6	20.5	74.9	20 049	6 219	60.7
WASHINGTON													
Adams, WA	207	17.8	177	NA	157	14	23 833	8.1	74.7	17.2	21 951	5 852	62.3
Asotin, WA	182	20.4	223	NA	131	15	20 790	7.6	78.4	14.0	19 131	5 224	63.8
Benton, WA	1 301	20.8	1 598	NA	1 037	89	158 441	5.1	73.3	21.6	142 158	5 230	61.2
Chelan, WA	610	20.6	669	NA	470	51	82 032	8.3	68.0	23.6	69 803	5 826	56.8
Clallam, WA	547	19.4	569	NA	369	41	61 890	8.2	72.6	19.1	55 772	5 275	61.3
Clark, WA	2 648	21.7	2 992	NA	1 988	231	357 653	3.9	72.3	23.8	310 428	5 617	57.7
Columbia, WA	44	19.2	49	NA	37	5	5 528	9.1	70.4	20.5	5 227	6 320	59.8
Cowlitz, WA	850	20.6	908	NA	731	64	104 840	5.4	71.1	23.5	93 299	5 403	58.8
Douglas, WA	311	19.9	304	NA	238	23	35 640	5.3	75.7	19.0	31 612	5 347	63.2
Ferry, WA	79	17.7	83	NA	58	12	9 238	16.1	70.7	13.2	8 351	5 923	59.3
Franklin, WA	527	18.7	465	NA	432	45	63 636	9.5	73.3	17.2	53 726	5 462	58.4
Garfield, WA	28	16.3	30	NA	18	3	3 137	5.5	71.8	22.7	2 767	6 081	62.1
Grant, WA	740	19.8	711	NA	593	59	87 785	7.0	74.5	18.5	72 952	5 154	62.6
Grays Harbor, WA	686	20.4	743	NA	550	59	94 191	7.3	74.3	18.4	75 519	5 404	61.8
Island, WA	428	23.0	507	NA	320	34	51 132	5.8	77.6	16.6	45 242	4 721	62.9
Jefferson, WA	195	19.7	204	NA	141	19	27 114	9.5	65.0	25.5	20 063	5 329	59.9
King, WA	11 147	21.5	13 258	NA	9 300	868	1 565 920	4.6	62.6	32.8	1 331 059	5 660	58.6
Kitsap, WA	1 851	22.2	2 164	NA	1 498	145	248 010	5.7	72.2	22.1	209 668	5 172	59.5
Kittitas, WA	250	19.1	270	NA	190	22	31 345	5.5	74.4	20.1	26 146	5 496	61.9
Klickitat, WA	203	19.3	256	NA	150	21	23 890	6.0	78.1	15.8	21 223	5 478	61.4
Lewis, WA	659	20.2	745	NA	511	58	81 895	7.4	71.1	21.5	73 500	5 657	62.0
Lincoln, WA	150	15.4	155	NA	117	19	19 201	3.9	72.9	23.2	17 000	7 315	57.3
Mason, WA	408	20.9	393	NA	332	33	47 882	6.8	73.2	20.0	42 707	5 134	58.2
Okanogan, WA	468	19.5	453	NA	364	42	58 630	10.9	73.5	15.6	48 850	5 410	61.8
Pacific, WA	207	18.3	199	NA	151	20	25 165	5.9	74.4	19.7	22 872	6 111	61.5
Pend Oreille, WA	87	27.3	125	NA	103	12	18 897	8.4	80.6	11.0	13 832	5 856	60.2
Pierce, WA	5 643	20.8	5 414	NA	4 353	438	734 718	6.2	66.8	27.0	638 161	5 497	59.5
San Juan, WA	101	18.0	94	NA	65	12	13 395	3.9	64.3	31.8	10 586	5 763	61.8
Skagit, WA	821	21.2	882	NA	658	64	109 179	5.7	67.0	27.3	93 598	5 489	60.4
Skamania, WA	80	18.6	76	NA	67	8	10 411	39.4	46.8	13.9	8 465	5 794	60.4
Snohomish, WA	4 310	21.6	4 167	NA	3 407	326	576 370	3.5	68.7	27.8	472 609	5 213	60.9
Spokane, WA	3 419	21.1	4 181	NA	2 811	219	445 905	6.2	69.3	24.5	395 339	5 549	59.8
Stevens, WA	336	20.1	385	NA	272	34	41 920	8.5	79.1	12.4	35 254	5 256	60.4
Thurston, WA	1 814	20.5	2 205	NA	1 433	120	229 178	5.4	69.6	25.0	203 133	5 589	59.4
Wahkiakum, WA	28	20.7	34	NA	20	3	3 009	3.2	75.2	21.6	2 639	4 851	59.5
Walla Walla, WA	491	19.9	457	NA	360	39	62 806	7.7	69.2	23.2	53 869	5 869	62.1
Whatcom, WA	1 129	21.5	1 321	NA	899	83	140 812	5.1	68.5	26.4	120 172	5 098	60.8
Whitman, WA	295	17.1	344	NA	226	33	38 794	4.0	72.5	23.6	33 525	6 629	58.3
Yakima, WA	2 211	21.2	2 134	NA	1 822	184	281 213	11.6	72.6	16.0	251 045	5 497	61.0
WEST VIRGINIA													
Barbour, WV	196	14.5	183	3.8	130	23	15 891	10.4	77.4	12.2	15 734	5 645	61.8
Berkeley, WV	687	17.0	589	5.2	575	91	69 623	9.0	59.2	31.8	64 063	5 649	60.6
Boone, WV	348	14.0	369	6.2	236	49	34 173	6.6	60.7	32.7	29 847	5 926	60.2
Braxton, WV	185	14.5	178	3.4	131	22	15 178	12.7	73.9	13.3	14 852	5 565	64.5
Brooke, WV	280	14.5	325	4.3	179	39	26 646	5.1	58.9	36.0	24 407	5 995	63.3
Cabell, WV	963	14.6	888	7.0	679	135	101 549	8.5	56.4	35.1	85 594	5 990	61.6
Calhoun, WV	103	15.5	95	3.2	78	16	10 294	11.2	76.8	11.9	9 720	5 927	62.3
Clay, WV	146	14.5	149	2.7	126	15	12 480	13.5	72.6	13.8	12 449	5 774	60.2
Doddridge, WV	93	14.8	75	2.9	82	12	9 000	7.8	66.1	26.1	8 513	6 085	57.6
Fayette, WV	548	15.6	670	3.0	397	71	49 616	10.0	67.7	22.3	47 754	5 398	66.2
Gilmer, WV	77	16.6	80	3.7	67	13	7 685	13.3	61.9	24.8	7 208	5 631	60.6
Grant, WV	119	15.7	139	3.2	91	17	11 202	8.4	57.9	33.7	10 726	5 648	62.8
Greenbrier, WV	370	16.4	381	3.5	290	47	31 207	9.6	66.8	23.6	29 754	4 585	66.6
Hampshire, WV	274	13.5	200	5.4	303	27	17 903	7.8	68.9	23.3	16 574	4 971	62.2
Hancock, WV	312	15.6	392	3.6	238	30	30 819	3.7	57.9	38.3	28 865	5 792	65.7

1. South Boston is now part of Halifax County.   2. Williamsburg City included with James City County.

Table D-2. School and Student Characteristics by County

State/ County code	County	County type[1]	Population, 1996		Number of school districts, 1995–1996	Level of schools, 1995–1996				Level of students, 1995–1996				Characteristics of students, 1995–1996		
			Total persons	Percent age 5–17		Number of schools	Percent			Number of students	Percent			Percent with IEP[2]	Percent free-lunch eligible	Percent minority
							Primary	Middle	High		Primary	Middle	High			
			1	2	3	4	5	6	7	8	9	10	11	12	13	14
	WEST VIRGINIA—Con.															
54031	Hardy, WV	9	11 723	15.9	1	4	50.0	—	50.0	2 046	60.1	—	39.9	16.4	33.1	1.9
54033	Harrison, WV	5	71 143	17.1	1	27	51.9	18.5	18.5	12 266	45.6	21.2	33.0	15.2	36.5	2.5
54035	Jackson, WV	6	27 399	17.9	1	12	66.7	16.7	16.7	5 118	46.8	23.5	29.6	16.5	35.4	0.4
54037	Jefferson, WV	1	39 979	17.1	1	13	61.5	30.8	7.7	6 668	50.2	30.9	18.9	14.8	26.7	10.6
54039	Kanawha, WV	2	204 968	16.0	2	93	64.5	14.0	8.6	32 372	49.2	22.3	20.5	13.8	30.5	10.9
54041	Lewis, WV	7	17 642	16.9	1	9	77.8	11.1	11.1	2 880	42.9	24.4	32.7	19.0	49.1	0.7
54043	Lincoln, WV	8	22 150	20.1	1	16	75.0	—	25.0	4 249	50.2	—	49.8	21.1	61.0	—
54045	Logan, WV	7	41 839	20.6	1	27	55.6	22.2	11.1	7 464	38.6	29.8	25.9	14.5	45.0	3.9
54047	McDowell, WV	7	31 524	21.2	1	20	65.0	15.0	20.0	6 307	59.4	9.4	31.2	19.4	69.7	15.4
54049	Marion, WV	5	57 571	15.9	1	21	57.1	28.6	14.3	9 109	44.7	21.9	33.4	11.9	35.0	5.9
54051	Marshall, WV	3	36 284	17.1	1	16	68.8	18.8	12.5	5 897	52.6	19.9	27.4	16.0	32.2	0.9
54053	Mason, WV	6	25 838	18.4	1	15	66.7	6.7	20.0	4 645	50.6	11.2	38.1	20.3	39.2	1.1
54055	Mercer, WV	7	64 521	17.1	1	29	75.9	10.3	13.8	10 252	55.2	16.1	28.7	15.4	42.8	9.8
54057	Mineral, WV	3	27 563	17.2	1	13	69.2	7.7	15.4	4 841	52.7	11.7	29.7	16.8	35.3	4.1
54059	Mingo, WV	7	32 986	22.1	1	24	54.2	25.0	20.8	6 551	42.6	25.1	32.3	14.8	50.6	3.1
54061	Monongalia, WV	5	78 234	13.4	1	28	75.0	14.3	10.7	10 280	48.8	22.1	29.1	11.1	28.1	5.9
54063	Monroe, WV	9	13 015	16.9	1	5	60.0	20.0	20.0	2 000	54.3	16.7	29.1	14.3	38.8	1.2
54065	Morgan, WV	8	13 520	15.6	1	8	75.0	—	25.0	2 287	53.8	—	46.2	11.8	29.2	1.0
54067	Nicholas, WV	7	27 604	19.4	1	16	75.0	12.5	12.5	5 091	52.8	23.1	24.0	16.2	45.8	0.4
54069	Ohio, WV	3	49 502	14.7	1	15	66.7	26.7	6.7	6 393	46.1	22.8	31.1	12.1	30.3	7.8
54071	Pendleton, WV	9	8 112	15.8	1	6	66.7	—	—	1 463	47.6	—	—	15.4	32.4	4.4
54073	Pleasants, WV	8	7 484	18.6	1	4	50.0	25.0	25.0	1 478	38.1	30.1	31.8	19.0	30.0	0.4
54075	Pocahontas, WV	9	9 086	15.6	1	5	80.0	—	20.0	1 539	68.1	—	31.9	16.2	47.0	0.6
54077	Preston, WV	7	29 903	19.0	1	13	46.2	23.1	7.7	5 397	35.8	16.3	22.1	17.8	47.5	0.8
54079	Putnam, WV	2	49 607	18.4	1	21	61.9	19.0	19.0	8 625	46.1	24.1	29.9	16.2	25.0	0.8
54081	Raleigh, WV	5	78 963	18.9	1	36	63.9	16.7	16.7	13 422	49.5	22.1	28.3	14.0	40.4	10.8
54083	Randolph, WV	7	28 999	16.7	1	15	60.0	6.7	13.3	4 956	46.9	16.6	30.2	16.6	45.9	1.2
54085	Ritchie, WV	8	10 286	17.2	1	7	71.4	14.3	14.3	1 816	43.0	23.6	33.4	19.1	44.3	0.5
54087	Roane, WV	8	15 400	19.3	1	7	57.1	28.6	14.3	2 964	41.1	26.7	32.2	19.0	56.0	0.8
54089	Summers, WV	7	13 909	16.6	1	5	60.0	20.0	20.0	1 913	40.6	25.2	34.1	15.6	49.4	3.5
54091	Taylor, WV	7	15 387	17.2	1	6	66.7	16.7	16.7	2 746	39.2	31.4	29.4	16.4	43.9	0.8
54093	Tucker, WV	9	7 787	16.9	1	3	66.7	—	33.3	1 358	64.4	—	35.6	15.3	43.7	0.5
54095	Tyler, WV	9	9 995	17.7	1	4	50.0	25.0	25.0	1 706	44.7	24.2	31.1	18.5	44.3	0.3
54097	Upshur, WV	7	23 640	17.4	1	13	76.9	15.4	7.7	4 266	40.0	28.6	31.4	13.4	44.2	0.7
54099	Wayne, WV	2	42 431	18.2	1	23	52.2	26.1	21.7	7 863	44.1	24.2	31.7	15.6	37.3	0.4
54101	Webster, WV	9	10 420	19.3	1	5	80.0	—	20.0	1 966	68.6	—	31.4	16.4	63.0	0.4
54103	Wetzel, WV	6	18 688	17.9	1	8	50.0	—	50.0	3 798	68.0	—	32.0	15.4	37.1	0.6
54105	Wirt, WV	8	5 589	18.7	1	3	33.3	33.3	33.3	1 208	37.3	33.7	29.0	15.6	49.3	0.4
54107	Wood, WV	3	87 770	16.7	1	28	71.4	17.9	10.7	14 885	54.1	21.6	24.3	12.9	29.6	2.2
54109	Wyoming, WV	9	27 993	21.0	1	18	50.0	22.2	22.2	5 446	46.1	20.1	33.3	15.0	49.9	1.5
55000	**WISCONSIN**															
55001	Adams, WI	9	17 836	16.0	1	8	75.0	12.5	12.5	1 993	53.6	15.7	30.7	15.4	36.6	6.0
55003	Ashland, WI	7	16 569	20.2	4	12	50.0	16.7	33.3	3 480	47.0	17.9	35.1	11.6	27.0	13.1
55005	Barron, WI	7	43 451	21.0	7	28	53.6	17.9	25.0	8 705	45.0	20.1	34.5	10.2	19.3	3.5
55007	Bayfield, WI	8	15 059	20.2	4	13	46.2	23.1	30.8	2 298	43.3	20.8	35.8	14.1	27.9	19.6
55009	Brown, WI	3	213 072	19.9	8	66	63.6	16.7	16.7	35 866	46.5	21.2	30.6	13.7	16.4	11.5
55011	Buffalo, WI	8	14 215	20.2	4	11	45.5	18.2	36.4	2 525	48.4	12.9	38.8	10.1	18.5	2.6
55013	Burnett, WI	8	14 383	19.1	3	9	44.4	22.2	33.3	2 304	56.1	13.5	30.4	13.8	29.0	11.9
55015	Calumet, WI	2	37 762	22.8	5	14	50.0	14.3	35.7	4 449	45.7	14.0	40.3	13.0	6.8	1.9
55017	Chippewa, WI	3	54 348	21.3	7	25	52.0	12.0	32.0	9 347	48.6	6.9	29.8	11.8	21.0	1.6
55019	Clark, WI	6	32 866	22.9	8	22	45.5	18.2	36.4	6 354	48.7	11.2	40.1	11.8	20.5	1.7
55021	Columbia, WI	6	49 914	19.6	9	33	54.5	18.2	21.2	9 485	46.6	22.3	25.8	11.3	10.0	3.5
55023	Crawford, WI	7	16 479	21.9	4	13	46.2	23.1	30.8	2 851	45.5	15.0	39.6	13.6	21.3	1.5
55025	Dane, WI	2	395 366	16.2	16	126	60.3	20.6	18.3	60 347	49.5	21.7	28.7	12.5	12.3	14.7
55027	Dodge, WI	4	81 750	19.9	9	30	60.0	16.7	23.3	8 836	46.2	20.3	33.5	13.5	8.0	3.5
55029	Door, WI	7	26 934	19.4	5	16	50.0	18.8	31.3	4 441	47.0	16.7	36.2	12.2	11.8	3.2
55031	Douglas, WI	3	43 051	19.3	3	20	65.0	15.0	20.0	7 460	49.7	16.3	34.0	11.1	28.6	6.9
55033	Dunn, WI	6	38 494	18.9	4	16	62.5	12.5	25.0	6 069	53.0	12.3	34.7	10.9	22.8	7.8
55035	Eau Claire, WI	3	88 897	18.3	4	30	66.7	13.3	16.7	14 578	46.5	21.6	30.7	11.6	20.1	9.6
55037	Florence, WI	9	5 230	20.7	1	4	50.0	25.0	25.0	1 000	61.5	10.2	28.3	8.2	23.5	3.5
55039	Fond du Lac, WI	4	94 400	20.6	7	41	61.0	17.1	19.5	16 472	51.4	14.3	31.7	12.5	10.5	4.6
55041	Forest, WI	9	9 588	20.2	3	7	42.9	14.3	42.9	2 044	51.4	12.2	36.4	14.4	29.2	19.1
55043	Grant, WI	6	49 531	20.5	10	34	47.1	23.5	29.4	9 291	45.6	18.9	35.5	13.8	16.9	1.4
55045	Green, WI	6	32 755	20.5	6	18	44.4	22.2	27.8	5 797	51.5	16.2	26.6	14.6	10.0	1.8
55047	Green Lake, WI	6	19 414	19.9	4	12	50.0	16.7	33.3	3 926	38.8	24.2	37.0	11.7	13.2	5.3

1. County type code is from the Economic Research Service of the USDA. See notes and definitions at the end of this section.   2. IEP = Individual Education Program. See notes and definitions at the end of this section.

Table D-2.   School and Student Characteristics by County — Continued

County	Staff and students, 1995–1996						Revenues, fiscal 1995				Current expenditures, fiscal 1995		
	Number of teachers	Pupil/ teacher ratio	Number of graduates	Dropouts grades 9–12 (percent)	Local school non-teaching staff	Central admin. staff	Total revenue ($1000)	Percent of Revenue from			Amount	Amount per pupil	Percent for instruction
								Federal Gov't	State Gov't	Local Gov't			
	15	16	17	18	19	20	21	22	23	24	25	26	27
WEST VIRGINIA—Con.													
Hardy, WV	129	15.8	116	3.4	86	15	10 725	7.9	68.6	23.5	10 218	5 171	60.8
Harrison, WV	763	16.1	770	2.7	577	90	78 160	6.5	60.0	33.5	71 498	5 830	62.4
Jackson, WV	328	15.6	359	4.4	255	44	32 492	6.5	64.2	29.2	30 596	5 983	61.1
Jefferson, WV	422	15.8	322	8.3	279	53	38 877	5.0	56.2	38.8	34 865	5 299	64.4
Kanawha, WV	2 098	15.4	2 185	6.1	1 535	277	198 611	7.7	56.0	36.3	180 103	5 444	64.2
Lewis, WV	202	14.3	220	6.8	150	22	21 843	8.0	73.2	18.8	17 586	6 008	63.5
Lincoln, WV	294	14.5	300	3.8	237	36	26 992	11.4	71.7	16.8	25 917	5 914	62.8
Logan, WV	530	14.1	676	5.2	386	60	49 898	9.8	66.4	23.8	47 057	5 969	63.8
McDowell, WV	431	14.7	448	5.2	392	52	41 859	12.6	71.3	16.2	40 949	6 225	67.2
Marion, WV	576	15.8	658	1.7	426	89	58 011	8.2	62.2	29.6	52 649	5 813	62.4
Marshall, WV	399	14.8	445	3.5	289	35	38 621	5.7	55.3	39.0	37 183	6 204	64.3
Mason, WV	331	14.1	269	5.6	210	37	29 706	8.2	59.7	32.2	28 186	6 081	66.6
Mercer, WV	668	15.3	706	4.0	512	71	65 825	8.3	69.0	22.8	58 616	5 593	64.7
Mineral, WV	305	15.9	338	2.0	233	36	29 221	9.0	70.0	21.0	27 552	5 751	61.6
Mingo, WV	454	14.4	435	3.4	342	44	42 603	10.4	54.6	35.0	42 202	6 240	67.9
Monongalia, WV	618	16.6	671	4.3	515	63	66 859	5.8	50.7	43.5	57 246	5 636	60.6
Monroe, WV	122	16.5	117	5.7	105	16	16 141	8.8	84.0	7.1	11 180	5 678	62.3
Morgan, WV	144	15.9	121	8.6	98	20	12 843	4.8	61.4	33.8	11 675	5 375	62.4
Nicholas, WV	339	15.0	367	2.9	252	41	32 883	10.3	70.1	19.6	29 653	5 841	61.1
Ohio, WV	396	16.2	388	3.9	287	78	39 790	7.4	57.7	34.9	35 409	5 605	63.6
Pendleton, WV	94	15.5	90	2.3	71	11	8 352	9.2	74.5	16.2	7 901	5 479	63.6
Pleasants, WV	98	15.1	101	3.4	80	18	10 756	5.2	43.2	51.5	10 532	7 234	61.9
Pocahontas, WV	110	14.0	107	3.5	81	13	9 272	11.1	70.0	18.9	8 827	5 754	64.9
Preston, WV	350	15.4	364	3.8	262	39	31 789	7.9	69.9	22.2	28 619	5 317	65.2
Putnam, WV	541	15.9	549	2.5	377	61	47 333	4.7	60.2	35.1	44 547	5 199	64.2
Raleigh, WV	839	16.0	964	4.1	697	109	81 232	8.1	65.4	26.6	73 444	5 358	61.3
Randolph, WV	330	15.0	320	2.8	221	46	28 588	9.3	74.1	16.5	27 334	5 481	65.0
Ritchie, WV	126	14.5	134	7.1	110	15	11 934	9.7	68.0	22.3	11 362	6 089	62.2
Roane, WV	206	14.4	194	3.0	145	24	17 459	10.8	74.7	14.5	16 256	5 299	61.3
Summers, WV	117	16.4	131	5.7	110	16	14 313	8.4	83.0	8.7	11 491	5 920	62.8
Taylor, WV	168	16.3	160	3.2	134	27	17 071	9.4	70.1	20.6	15 334	5 582	57.5
Tucker, WV	84	16.2	132	1.2	70	11	12 091	6.6	78.7	14.7	7 896	5 676	62.5
Tyler, WV	121	14.1	132	3.8	84	16	11 839	6.6	59.1	34.3	10 486	6 058	62.0
Upshur, WV	252	17.0	277	3.7	197	38	24 229	10.0	76.2	13.8	23 186	5 346	64.3
Wayne, WV	500	15.7	537	4.2	420	62	47 645	8.6	65.4	26.1	42 923	5 407	65.0
Webster, WV	135	14.6	123	4.9	97	20	11 902	13.5	71.8	14.7	11 549	5 631	66.2
Wetzel, WV	250	15.2	242	4.0	167	24	22 787	6.3	68.6	25.1	21 283	5 613	62.3
Wirt, WV	76	16.0	78	3.1	54	10	6 858	6.9	75.1	18.0	6 277	5 306	62.2
Wood, WV	952	15.6	911	2.7	658	126	88 967	6.5	60.0	33.5	82 597	5 532	64.2
Wyoming, WV	369	14.8	493	5.0	272	36	36 962	9.8	67.8	22.4	34 465	5 990	66.7
WISCONSIN													
Adams, WI	129	15.4	96	NA	115	12	13 282	6.3	40.1	53.6	12 184	6 095	63.3
Ashland, WI	210	16.5	214	NA	144	30	24 650	5.7	64.3	30.0	21 816	6 342	59.9
Barron, WI	527	16.5	591	NA	348	37	55 789	3.5	56.1	40.4	48 032	5 515	62.4
Bayfield, WI	159	14.4	146	NA	103	13	17 962	8.0	40.9	51.1	14 869	6 556	61.2
Brown, WI	2 164	16.6	2 309	NA	1 387	174	232 277	4.0	43.5	52.5	208 619	5 926	65.1
Buffalo, WI	164	15.4	205	NA	137	17	17 609	3.9	57.5	38.6	15 100	6 004	61.6
Burnett, WI	145	15.9	139	NA	100	17	15 552	5.0	43.4	51.5	13 277	5 919	62.9
Calumet, WI	300	14.8	372	NA	209	20	27 419	1.9	51.5	46.6	23 648	5 394	62.9
Chippewa, WI	590	15.9	622	NA	369	44	62 255	3.7	54.8	41.5	53 890	5 768	64.6
Clark, WI	431	14.7	448	NA	291	39	44 108	4.6	60.1	35.2	36 932	5 794	62.2
Columbia, WI	604	15.7	532	NA	442	43	60 187	2.5	48.1	49.4	52 014	5 615	62.6
Crawford, WI	199	14.4	217	NA	137	13	18 742	4.9	56.7	38.3	16 755	5 925	64.9
Dane, WI	4 066	14.8	3 454	NA	3 060	328	447 464	2.5	28.6	68.9	395 474	6 677	65.0
Dodge, WI	558	15.8	564	NA	382	40	59 726	2.3	49.3	48.4	48 918	5 598	63.9
Door, WI	311	14.3	344	NA	222	24	32 629	3.6	28.7	67.6	29 025	6 499	64.8
Douglas, WI	426	17.5	466	NA	329	35	47 582	5.6	58.3	36.1	43 904	5 951	63.4
Dunn, WI	351	17.3	401	NA	231	29	40 840	3.6	58.8	37.6	35 118	5 920	62.6
Eau Claire, WI	884	16.5	863	NA	633	71	101 612	4.1	50.5	45.4	88 085	6 218	62.9
Florence, WI	59	17.0	62	NA	52	9	5 898	5.1	49.0	45.9	5 313	5 652	62.9
Fond du Lac, WI	972	16.9	986	NA	671	66	101 912	2.9	50.4	46.6	89 733	5 465	63.7
Forest, WI	123	16.6	120	NA	101	15	14 102	9.0	44.9	46.1	11 748	5 930	61.4
Grant, WI	635	14.6	724	NA	424	48	63 697	3.8	58.2	38.0	57 110	6 224	62.9
Green, WI	402	14.4	357	NA	315	30	39 950	2.9	49.4	47.7	36 347	6 289	66.0
Green Lake, WI	241	16.3	264	NA	137	21	24 758	3.0	40.6	56.3	20 031	5 134	62.3

Items 15–27

WV (Hardy, WV)–WI (Green Lake, WI)

Table D-2.　School and Student Characteristics by County

State/ County code	County	County type[1]	Population, 1996		Number of school districts, 1995–1996	Level of schools, 1995–1996				Level of students, 1995–1996				Characteristics of students, 1995–1996		
			Total persons	Percent age 5–17		Number of schools	Percent			Number of students	Percent			Percent with IEP[2]	Percent free-lunch eligible	Percent minority
							Primary	Middle	High		Primary	Middle	High			
			1	2	3	4	5	6	7	8	9	10	11	12	13	14
	WISCONSIN—Con.															
55049	Iowa, WI	6	21 862	21.2	5	13	46.2	15.4	38.5	3 866	56.3	11.6	32.0	13.2	13.0	0.6
55051	Iron, WI	9	6 520	16.5	2	4	50.0	—	50.0	1 073	57.3	—	42.7	13.7	26.4	1.3
55053	Jackson, WI	6	17 325	20.5	3	13	61.5	15.4	23.1	3 333	52.6	16.0	31.4	12.1	21.0	9.6
55055	Jefferson, WI	4	73 042	19.5	7	29	58.6	17.2	24.1	11 997	45.6	18.3	36.1	13.1	10.4	5.4
55057	Juneau, WI	7	23 753	20.5	5	16	56.3	12.5	31.3	4 705	53.4	13.1	33.5	10.9	23.2	3.2
55059	Kenosha, WI	1	141 646	19.4	13	45	75.6	11.1	13.3	24 984	61.3	16.2	22.5	11.3	19.8	18.0
55061	Kewaunee, WI	6	19 661	21.4	3	8	37.5	25.0	37.5	3 633	39.8	22.7	37.5	13.9	7.7	1.5
55063	La Crosse, WI	3	102 318	18.2	5	32	62.5	18.8	18.8	15 533	43.8	25.0	31.1	11.2	21.3	11.6
55065	Lafayette, WI	9	16 568	22.1	7	19	52.6	10.5	36.8	3 818	52.9	9.1	38.0	13.0	11.4	0.2
55067	Langlade, WI	6	20 535	20.3	3	17	76.5	5.9	17.6	3 901	48.1	15.5	36.3	13.5	26.3	4.1
55069	Lincoln, WI	6	29 395	20.6	2	14	71.4	14.3	14.3	5 154	46.7	25.2	28.1	10.9	14.3	1.7
55071	Manitowoc, WI	4	82 588	20.0	6	27	51.9	22.2	22.2	12 281	42.9	21.9	30.7	10.6	5.8	7.2
55073	Marathon, WI	3	121 791	21.2	8	43	65.1	11.6	20.9	19 564	46.5	16.8	32.0	11.0	17.6	11.8
55075	Marinette, WI	7	42 751	20.2	8	24	50.0	12.5	29.2	8 010	44.5	13.7	33.6	12.1	18.0	1.2
55077	Marquette, WI	9	14 566	18.8	2	7	71.4	—	28.6	2 314	60.9	—	39.1	11.4	19.2	4.8
55078	Menominee, WI	NA	4 609	30.4	1	4	25.0	50.0	25.0	1 088	43.4	30.6	26.0	25.3	60.8	99.5
55079	Milwaukee, WI	0	922 243	18.6	18	253	68.8	15.4	13.4	150 171	54.1	18.0	25.4	12.6	46.4	55.4
55081	Monroe, WI	6	39 044	21.8	4	21	66.7	14.3	19.0	6 997	47.4	17.2	35.5	10.5	19.4	4.3
55083	Oconto, WI	6	32 795	20.5	5	19	52.6	21.1	26.3	5 293	48.7	19.7	31.6	16.1	16.8	2.8
55085	Oneida, WI	7	35 516	17.5	5	17	70.6	11.8	17.6	6 348	51.0	13.9	35.1	11.1	16.4	4.6
55087	Outagamie, WI	2	153 099	20.8	8	50	62.0	18.0	20.0	28 158	52.9	15.5	31.6	11.9	8.3	7.5
55089	Ozaukee, WI	0	80 257	19.8	5	25	56.0	24.0	20.0	12 437	41.3	24.5	34.2	10.1	2.5	5.3
55091	Pepin, WI	8	7 130	21.9	2	5	40.0	20.0	40.0	1 702	37.0	24.4	38.5	13.9	21.3	0.9
55093	Pierce, WI	1	34 994	20.3	6	24	50.0	25.0	20.8	7 458	43.7	25.1	28.3	12.0	10.0	2.7
55095	Polk, WI	6	37 761	21.5	8	25	40.0	28.0	28.0	8 166	41.7	24.7	28.7	11.2	19.5	3.4
55097	Portage, WI	4	65 146	19.5	4	22	63.6	18.2	18.2	10 836	52.2	21.2	26.6	11.0	16.2	9.6
55099	Price, WI	7	15 910	20.2	3	12	41.7	33.3	25.0	2 931	40.4	26.0	33.6	10.1	17.3	2.9
55101	Racine, WI	3	185 003	20.5	12	57	64.9	19.3	15.8	30 290	47.7	22.2	30.1	12.6	21.4	27.5
55103	Richland, WI	7	17 958	20.4	2	11	63.6	18.2	18.2	2 209	50.9	16.0	33.1	17.2	16.2	2.0
55105	Rock, WI	3	150 584	19.9	9	58	62.1	19.0	15.5	27 419	46.2	21.5	29.6	14.4	14.6	13.1
55107	Rusk, WI	7	15 433	20.9	4	13	53.8	15.4	30.8	2 929	51.1	12.4	36.5	13.1	37.6	4.3
55109	St. Croix, WI	1	56 137	22.2	6	22	50.0	22.7	27.3	10 210	46.9	21.3	31.8	11.9	7.4	1.9
55111	Sauk, WI	6	52 164	20.1	6	35	68.6	14.3	17.1	11 648	50.1	20.3	29.6	13.6	13.2	3.9
55113	Sawyer, WI	9	15 985	20.0	2	8	50.0	25.0	25.0	2 512	38.9	30.1	30.9	13.3	31.7	23.8
55115	Shawano, WI	6	38 487	20.2	5	20	60.0	10.0	30.0	6 238	53.1	10.6	36.3	11.6	18.0	12.4
55117	Sheboygan, WI	3	109 705	20.0	9	46	58.7	19.6	21.7	19 548	45.2	21.5	33.3	12.2	11.1	11.5
55119	Taylor, WI	6	19 264	22.8	3	10	50.0	20.0	30.0	3 933	38.9	23.9	27.0	10.8	16.7	1.1
55121	Trempealeau, WI	8	26 191	19.5	7	24	50.0	20.8	29.2	5 853	52.3	13.7	34.0	12.9	17.4	1.6
55123	Vernon, WI	6	27 279	20.4	6	19	52.6	15.8	31.6	4 807	47.9	14.7	37.4	12.1	21.5	1.3
55125	Vilas, WI	9	20 769	16.4	4	10	70.0	10.0	20.0	2 530	61.5	15.3	23.2	11.9	29.4	18.7
55127	Walworth, WI	4	83 355	17.8	16	36	61.1	16.7	19.4	13 687	48.3	19.7	30.7	9.8	10.8	9.0
55129	Washburn, WI	9	15 132	19.8	4	12	41.7	25.0	33.3	3 115	41.3	24.9	33.8	15.2	27.6	3.8
55131	Washington, WI	1	111 358	21.1	9	36	63.9	16.7	16.7	19 002	45.0	20.2	34.8	11.0	5.1	3.0
55133	Waukesha, WI	0	343 791	20.4	19	101	66.3	16.8	15.8	57 368	50.4	18.6	30.9	11.2	4.4	6.2
55135	Waupaca, WI	6	49 811	20.2	7	29	58.6	17.2	20.7	10 634	45.9	20.5	29.7	11.1	12.3	3.2
55137	Waushara, WI	8	21 272	18.7	3	10	40.0	20.0	30.0	3 347	32.4	26.7	32.4	10.3	29.0	10.2
55139	Winnebago, WI	2	149 703	17.5	5	52	71.2	15.4	11.5	23 025	47.1	19.1	29.8	12.0	11.7	7.0
55141	Wood, WI	4	76 219	20.8	6	32	65.6	15.6	18.8	14 202	49.2	20.2	30.6	11.3	13.1	6.3
56000	**WYOMING**															
56001	Albany, WY	5	30 831	14.3	1	18	72.2	16.7	11.1	4 196	53.2	23.9	22.9	12.9	29.5	14.6
56003	Big Horn, WY	9	11 276	21.5	4	19	47.4	26.3	26.3	2 595	44.7	23.2	32.1	13.1	26.6	8.7
56005	Campbell, WY	7	32 012	26.1	1	23	65.2	21.7	13.0	7 975	52.5	25.3	22.2	8.5	14.1	3.7
56007	Carbon, WY	7	15 855	21.5	2	23	52.2	21.7	26.1	3 297	45.3	22.5	32.2	11.9	16.6	18.0
56009	Converse, WY	6	11 989	24.1	2	15	66.7	20.0	13.3	2 740	42.1	26.4	31.5	11.8	17.0	6.9
56011	Crook, WY	9	5 763	22.8	1	11	36.4	27.3	36.4	1 315	49.1	16.8	34.1	10.1	18.0	2.4
56013	Fremont, WY	7	35 940	22.8	9	33	51.5	27.3	21.2	7 686	48.3	22.0	29.7	13.0	30.5	29.8
56015	Goshen, WY	7	12 731	19.9	1	12	50.0	25.0	25.0	2 300	45.2	22.8	32.0	13.6	29.6	14.3
56017	Hot Springs, WY	7	4 627	19.7	1	4	25.0	50.0	25.0	860	29.7	40.0	30.3	13.0	25.0	5.2
56019	Johnson, WY	7	6 690	19.2	1	9	44.4	33.3	22.2	1 331	34.9	31.7	33.4	13.3	15.2	4.4
56021	Laramie, WY	3	79 175	18.7	2	42	71.4	14.3	14.3	14 898	55.1	22.9	22.0	11.3	21.0	18.6
56023	Lincoln, WY	7	13 971	28.0	2	13	53.8	23.1	23.1	3 745	46.7	19.4	34.0	8.8	10.6	2.5
56025	Natrona, WY	3	63 875	20.4	1	40	77.5	12.5	10.0	12 936	53.4	23.5	23.1	10.9	21.7	6.4
56027	Niobrara, WY	9	2 637	17.5	1	4	50.0	25.0	25.0	505	44.2	26.9	28.9	10.5	26.7	4.0
56029	Park, WY	7	25 373	19.6	3	16	62.5	18.8	18.8	4 829	44.7	24.9	30.4	8.1	12.8	5.0
56031	Platte, WY	7	8 425	20.2	2	13	38.5	30.8	30.8	1 746	51.4	15.6	33.0	11.5	17.0	7.6

1. County type code is from the Economic Research Service of the USDA. See notes and definitions at the end of this section.　2. IEP = Individual Education Program. See notes and definitions at the end of this section.

Table D-2.   School and Student Characteristics by County — Continued

County	Staff and students, 1995–1996						Revenues, fiscal 1995					Current expenditures, fiscal 1995		
	Number of teachers	Pupil/ teacher ratio	Number of graduates	Dropouts grades 9–12 (percent)	Local school non-teaching staff	Central admin. staff	Total revenue ($1000)	Percent of Revenue from			Amount	Amount per pupil	Percent for instruction
								Federal Gov't	State Gov't	Local Gov't			
	15	16	17	18	19	20	21	22	23	24	25	26	27
WISCONSIN—Con.													
Iowa, WI	279	13.9	249	NA	195	20	28 949	3.0	46.5	50.6	24 971	6 554	61.9
Iron, WI	73	14.6	78	NA	44	6	8 608	4.1	44.5	51.4	6 797	6 323	59.5
Jackson, WI	220	15.1	195	NA	210	15	20 905	5.8	58.5	35.7	18 577	5 643	60.8
Jefferson, WI	780	15.4	852	NA	596	72	86 431	2.7	45.6	51.7	77 049	6 535	62.0
Juneau, WI	310	15.2	213	NA	235	18	29 909	4.1	53.8	42.0	25 514	5 539	62.7
Kenosha, WI	1 430	17.5	1 150	NA	970	130	160 057	4.4	40.7	54.9	142 107	5 962	63.0
Kewaunee, WI	220	16.5	321	NA	160	9	22 284	3.0	50.7	46.3	19 796	5 412	62.9
La Crosse, WI	1 006	15.4	904	NA	782	76	111 808	3.8	45.9	50.3	96 804	6 352	64.3
Lafayette, WI	269	14.2	277	NA	174	17	26 214	2.8	54.2	43.0	22 522	5 965	62.2
Langlade, WI	261	15.0	271	NA	203	22	28 085	5.2	52.5	42.3	25 287	6 438	61.9
Lincoln, WI	304	17.0	364	NA	182	20	33 737	4.7	52.1	43.2	30 004	5 895	62.4
Manitowoc, WI	722	17.0	810	NA	521	55	76 025	3.1	40.6	56.3	65 516	5 462	64.4
Marathon, WI	1 242	15.8	1 458	NA	880	98	131 510	3.2	50.5	46.3	114 874	5 941	65.3
Marinette, WI	478	16.8	492	NA	310	45	51 926	3.5	52.9	43.7	46 520	5 807	64.9
Marquette, WI	143	16.2	151	NA	130	10	14 843	3.6	35.0	61.5	11 852	5 144	64.6
Menominee, WI	85	12.8	39	NA	79	14	10 461	32.4	55.7	11.9	9 035	9 053	57.3
Milwaukee, WI	8 721	17.2	6 253	NA	3 712	448	1 125 865	7.4	47.3	45.3	1 056 121	6 801	62.8
Monroe, WI	450	15.5	437	NA	334	39	41 947	6.0	55.5	38.6	36 566	5 392	64.0
Oconto, WI	335	15.8	325	NA	221	25	32 954	4.2	54.7	41.1	28 138	5 369	62.7
Oneida, WI	383	16.6	452	NA	279	27	44 248	4.0	31.5	64.5	39 027	6 263	62.2
Outagamie, WI	1 644	17.1	1 818	NA	1 031	113	174 672	2.8	44.3	52.9	154 530	5 583	66.0
Ozaukee, WI	774	16.1	904	NA	482	71	92 789	1.4	24.1	74.6	83 894	6 723	63.7
Pepin, WI	116	14.7	147	NA	94	10	13 588	3.9	60.1	36.0	12 604	7 256	61.4
Pierce, WI	476	15.7	484	NA	392	35	50 724	2.9	54.0	43.1	45 822	6 131	66.1
Polk, WI	499	16.4	519	NA	401	35	55 348	3.3	53.7	43.0	46 271	5 720	63.5
Portage, WI	671	16.2	773	NA	519	56	70 295	3.7	47.2	49.2	61 386	5 621	66.6
Price, WI	181	16.2	235	NA	149	14	18 263	4.2	52.7	43.2	15 972	5 401	61.3
Racine, WI	1 854	16.3	1 592	NA	1 260	123	202 523	3.9	46.2	49.9	189 169	6 159	65.0
Richland, WI	162	13.6	156	NA	122	11	16 744	3.5	57.4	39.1	15 010	6 848	64.0
Rock, WI	1 754	15.6	1 449	NA	1 211	150	182 367	3.5	54.8	41.7	165 095	6 208	66.1
Rusk, WI	211	13.9	208	NA	166	19	24 635	5.4	61.5	33.1	21 098	7 056	62.9
St. Croix, WI	603	16.9	681	NA	414	40	67 829	2.3	50.2	47.5	58 247	5 799	63.6
Sauk, WI	739	15.8	716	NA	612	61	74 151	3.6	42.1	54.4	65 708	5 766	62.2
Sawyer, WI	163	15.4	142	NA	131	10	17 355	10.1	30.0	59.9	15 558	6 047	60.1
Shawano, WI	390	16.0	391	NA	294	28	38 162	5.5	52.4	42.1	34 452	5 588	63.5
Sheboygan, WI	1 192	16.4	1 297	NA	832	97	134 946	2.7	46.0	51.3	118 484	6 120	64.6
Taylor, WI	240	16.4	256	NA	148	19	22 709	4.3	63.2	32.5	20 613	5 326	61.7
Trempealeau, WI	395	14.8	376	NA	336	33	40 693	4.1	56.0	39.9	35 498	6 232	61.9
Vernon, WI	331	14.5	339	NA	294	29	33 227	5.1	56.1	38.8	30 098	6 192	62.7
Vilas, WI	177	14.3	134	NA	146	21	21 671	11.7	13.8	74.5	18 085	7 199	59.3
Walworth, WI	898	15.2	812	NA	592	79	92 285	2.4	22.9	74.7	81 660	6 190	64.3
Washburn, WI	202	15.5	201	NA	128	25	22 472	4.2	38.7	57.1	18 757	6 126	62.7
Washington, WI	1 127	16.9	1 301	NA	709	80	128 163	2.3	31.8	65.9	113 149	6 043	63.7
Waukesha, WI	3 615	15.9	3 744	NA	2 268	232	426 353	1.5	23.4	75.1	382 897	6 767	63.9
Waupaca, WI	645	16.5	751	NA	525	50	65 999	3.0	50.3	46.6	56 737	5 441	63.3
Waushara, WI	196	17.1	201	NA	145	13	19 753	6.3	36.6	57.2	16 844	5 175	64.3
Winnebago, WI	1 330	17.3	1 327	NA	932	88	142 721	2.9	38.4	58.7	130 362	5 754	66.4
Wood, WI	869	16.3	994	NA	583	54	91 709	3.3	49.1	47.7	83 178	5 853	65.3
WYOMING													
Albany, WY	292	14.4	236	7.2	252	11	24 310	6.3	64.2	29.5	22 904	5 493	62.0
Big Horn, WY	192	13.6	165	3.1	182	16	18 243	6.3	67.0	26.6	16 617	6 456	61.1
Campbell, WY	527	15.1	510	2.7	586	24	53 266	4.3	10.4	85.4	47 614	5 930	59.4
Carbon, WY	252	13.1	202	10.2	212	12	24 060	3.5	39.4	57.2	21 069	6 282	58.3
Converse, WY	202	13.5	153	2.7	188	10	17 994	5.1	32.1	62.7	17 057	6 283	59.8
Crook, WY	103	12.8	91	1.6	89	7	9 754	4.2	55.5	40.3	8 860	6 895	57.8
Fremont, WY	542	14.2	420	10.2	587	36	59 248	20.9	56.5	22.6	51 918	6 780	60.6
Goshen, WY	184	12.5	151	1.2	147	6	14 496	8.9	67.2	24.0	14 590	6 450	63.3
Hot Springs, WY	62	13.9	68	9.2	62	5	6 251	3.5	35.2	61.3	5 997	6 738	60.4
Johnson, WY	103	13.0	85	1.8	89	5	8 558	4.7	54.1	41.2	8 091	6 200	59.3
Laramie, WY	917	16.3	860	5.6	850	42	83 450	6.7	69.2	24.1	80 571	5 421	63.3
Lincoln, WY	240	15.6	273	2.9	185	10	24 741	3.7	42.4	53.9	21 805	5 738	61.3
Natrona, WY	765	16.9	759	9.7	624	31	71 833	6.3	69.1	24.6	68 125	5 200	63.7
Niobrara, WY	41	12.4	30	1.4	37	4	3 947	5.0	54.6	40.4	3 275	6 767	58.4
Park, WY	279	17.3	273	4.2	228	21	28 212	3.8	51.3	44.9	23 584	4 879	62.4
Platte, WY	154	11.3	122	4.3	118	9	11 268	7.8	50.8	41.4	11 137	6 106	64.2

Table D-2.   School and Student Characteristics by County

State/County code	County	County type[1]	Population, 1996		Number of school districts, 1995–1996	Level of schools, 1995–1996				Level of students, 1995–1996				Characteristics of students, 1995–1996		
			Total persons	Percent age 5–17		Number of schools	Percent			Number of students	Percent			Percent with IEP[2]	Percent free-lunch eligible	Percent minority
							Primary	Middle	High		Primary	Middle	High			
			1	2	3	4	5	6	7	8	9	10	11	12	13	14
	WYOMING—Con.															
56033	Sheridan, WY	7	25 318	19.5	3	22	59.1	22.7	18.2	4 593	41.5	31.4	27.2	13.2	20.1	4.7
56035	Sublette, WY	9	5 577	19.5	2	8	50.0	25.0	25.0	1 358	45.7	23.1	31.1	10.3	13.1	3.9
56037	Sweetwater, WY	5	40 322	24.8	2	35	65.7	22.9	11.4	9 599	46.6	26.2	27.2	12.5	12.4	10.0
56039	Teton, WY	7	13 587	15.7	1	10	70.0	10.0	20.0	2 226	50.2	22.3	27.5	9.7	2.8	3.0
56041	Uinta, WY	7	20 255	29.3	3	15	40.0	40.0	20.0	5 750	38.4	31.5	30.1	10.9	17.8	5.4
56043	Washakie, WY	7	8 617	22.0	2	8	50.0	25.0	25.0	1 900	45.1	22.4	32.5	15.3	21.6	12.7
56045	Weston, WY	7	6 554	21.9	2	8	50.0	25.0	25.0	1 479	42.5	25.8	31.6	12.4	14.1	3.6

1. County type code is from the Economic Research Service of the USDA. See notes and definitions at the end of this section.   2. IEP = Individual Education Program. See notes and definitions at the end of this section.

Table D-2.   School and Student Characteristics by County — Continued

County	Staff and students, 1995–1996						Revenues, fiscal 1995				Current expenditures, fiscal 1995		
	Number of teachers	Pupil/ teacher ratio	Number of graduates	Dropouts grades 9–12 (percent)	Local school non-teaching staff	Central admin. staff	Total revenue ($1000)	Percent of Revenue from			Amount	Amount per pupil	Percent for instruction
								Federal Gov't	State Gov't	Local Gov't			
	15	16	17	18	19	20	21	22	23	24	25	26	27
WYOMING—Con.													
Sheridan, WY	303	15.2	276	8.8	294	16	27 889	5.3	72.4	22.3	25 809	5 552	63.1
Sublette, WY	94	14.4	84	2.4	104	9	12 103	3.1	7.4	89.5	8 606	6 245	55.7
Sweetwater, WY	581	16.5	558	10.9	597	35	61 108	4.9	19.2	75.9	55 674	5 697	60.6
Teton, WY	135	16.5	117	3.1	115	6	14 121	3.0	10.3	86.7	11 877	5 511	64.1
Uinta, WY	362	15.9	329	6.8	336	26	38 351	4.3	32.3	63.5	31 457	5 433	67.2
Washakie, WY	120	15.9	122	3.6	104	5	11 246	4.9	60.9	34.2	10 463	5 472	65.4
Weston, WY	118	12.5	112	3.6	96	6	9 788	4.2	62.1	33.7	8 941	5 913	63.5

Notes and Definitions: State- and County-level Education Statistics

Section D presents 27 data items for the United States as a whole, each state, and the District of Columbia, and each county, county equivalent, or independent city. Table D-1 includes the 50 states and the District of Columbia, as well as a United States total. Table D-2 includes the counties, county equivalents, and independent cities. The counties are presented in alphabetical order within states, which are also in alphabetical order. Independent cities, which are found in Maryland, Missouri, Nevada, and Virginia, are placed in alphabetical order at the end of the list of counties for those states. The District of Columbia is included as both a county and a state.

Common core of data. Most of the data in this section are from the Common Core of Data from the National Center for Education Statistics (NCES), U.S. Department of Education. NCES uses the Common Core of Data (CCD) system to acquire and maintain statistical data from each of the 50 states, the District of Columbia, and the outlying areas. Information about staff and students is collected annually at the school, LEA (local education agency, or school district), and state levels. Information about revenues and expenditures is also collected at the state level. In addition, information about revenues and expenditures at the school district level is assembled from the annual surveys of government finances conducted by the Bureau of the Census.

Data are collected for a particular school year (July 1 through June 30) via survey instruments sent to the state education agencies during the subsequent school year. States have one year in which to modify the data originally submitted. This volume uses the data from the school year 1995–1996, except for the revenue and expenditure data for counties, which is for school year 1994–1995.

Since the CCD is a universe survey, the CCD information is not subject to sampling error. However, nonsampling errors could come from two sources— nonreturn and inaccurate reporting. Almost all of the states submit the six CCD survey instruments each year, but submissions are sometimes incomplete or too late for publication.

Understandably, when 57 education agencies compile and submit data for approximately 85,000 public schools and 15,000 local school districts, misreporting can occur. Typically, this results from varying interpretation of NCES definitions and differing recordkeeping systems. NCES attempts to minimize these errors by working closely with the Council of Chief State School Officers (CCSSO) and its Committee on Evaluation and Information Systems (CEIS).

The state education agencies report data to NCES from data collected and edited in their regular reporting cycles. NCES encourages the agencies to incorporate into their own survey systems the NCES items they do not already collect so that those items will also be available for the subsequent CCD survey. Over time, this has meant fewer missing data cells in each state's response, reducing the need to impute data.

NCES subjects data from the education agencies to a comprehensive edit. Where data are determined to be inconsistent, missing, or out of range, NCES contacts the education agencies for verification. NCES-prepared state summary forms are returned to the state education agencies for verification. States are also given an opportunity to revise their state-level aggregates from the previous survey cycle.

The CCD data are collected at three levels: the school, the school district, and the state. Table D-1 presents data from the CCD state-level file. In table D-2, selected school and school district data items have been aggregated to the county level because the county is a widely used statistical area. School districts, and even some schools, can serve populations in different counties. In this volume, schools and school districts are assigned to the county where the school district office is located, as coded by NCES in its files. Consequently, the numbers do not necessarily represent the population of a given county. The structure of school districts ranges from that in states such as West Virginia and Nevada, where most counties have a single school district, to that in Cook County, Illinois, which includes 151 separate school districts. Some counties have no school districts. Hawaii has a single statewide school district whose offices are located in Honolulu County. New York City's school system headquarters are in Brooklyn, so Kings County includes information for all five boroughs (counties) in New York City. A few other counties report no school districts; usually these are counties with very small populations or independent cities in Virginia whose school systems are run by the neighboring or surrounding county.

Geographic identification. Data are presented for 3,140 counties and county equivalents, 50 states, and the District of Columbia. In table D-1, a two-digit state code is included. In table D-2, a five-digit state and county code is given for each entity. The first two digits indicate the state;

the remaining three identify the county. Within each state, the counties are numbered in alphabetical order, beginning with 001, with even numbers usually omitted. Independent cities follow the counties and begin with the number 510.

These codes have been established by the U.S. government as Federal Information Processing Standards and are often referred to as "FIPS codes." They are used by U.S. government agencies and many other organizations for data presentation. They are provided in this volume for use in matching the data given here with other data sources in which counties may be identified by FIPS code.

Independent cities. Independent cities are not included in any county; data are presented separately in this volume where available.

Maryland
    Baltimore (separate from Baltimore County)
Missouri
    St. Louis (separate from St. Louis County)
Nevada
    Carson City
Virginia
    Alexandria
    Bedford
    Bristol
    Buena Vista
    Charlottesville
    Chesapeake
    Clifton Forge
    Colonial Heights
    Covington
    Danville
    Emporia
    Fairfax
    Falls Church
    Franklin
    Fredericksburg
    Galax
    Hampton
    Harrisonburg
    Hopewell
    Lexington
    Lynchburg
    Manassas
    Manassas Park
    Martinsville
    Newport News
    Norfolk
    Norton
    Petersburg
    Poquoson
    Portsmouth
    Radford
    Richmond
    Roanoke
    Salem
    South Boston*
    Staunton
    Suffolk
    Virginia Beach
    Waynesboro
    Williamsburg
    Winchester

*In 1995, South Boston City became a town within Halifax County.

County type. Table D-2 (Counties) provides, in the third column, a "county type" code that identifies each county by its metropolitan/nonmetropolitan status and its size. These codes were developed by the Economic Research Service of the U.S. Department of Agriculture and are commonly referred to as "Beale" codes after their originator, Calvin Beale. The ERS county typology scheme goes beyond the Beale codes to a detailed typology of economic and land use classifications. In this volume, the basic Beale codes are used as follows.

Metropolitan counties

(0) Central county of a metropolitan area of 1 million population or more.

(1) Fringe county of a metropolitan area of 1 million population or more.

(2) County in a metropolitan area of 250,000 to 1,000,000 population.

(3) County in a metropolitan area of less than 250,000 population.

Nonmetropolitan counties

(4) Urban population of 20,000 or more, adjacent to a metropolitan area.

(5) Urban population of 20,000 or more, not adjacent to a metropolitan area.

(6) Urban population of 2,500–19,999, adjacent to a metropolitan area.

(7) Urban population of 2,500–19,999, not adjacent to a metropolitan area.

(8) Completely rural (no places with a population of 2,500 or more), adjacent to a metropolitan area.

(9)   Completely rural (no places with a population of 2,500 or more), not adjacent to a metropolitan area.

Data sources and explanations. The column numbers and data items in both tables are the same. This section describes table D-1 and table D-2 separately because there are slight differences in definitions. The CCD state data that are presented in table D-1 are compiled by NCES in cooperation with state education agencies. Table D-2 has been developed by Bernan from the individual school and school district data from the CCD. Some data items in table D-1, such as revenues and expenditures, include statewide numbers that are inappropriate at the local level.

Table D-1 (States)
Population (Items 1–2)
Source: U.S. Bureau of the Census

The population data for 1996 are U.S. Bureau of the Census estimates for the resident population as of July 1, 1996.

School districts (Item 3)
Source: U.S. Department of Education, National Center for Education Statistics, Common Core of Data, 1995–1996.

A school district or local education agency (LEA) is an education agency at the local level that exists primarily to operate public schools or to contract for public school services.

The state numbers are from the CCD state universe and include 14,367 regular school districts with students in membership. Not included are special districts that typically offer research, administrative, or other support services to client agencies.

Number of schools and students (Items 4–11)
Source: U.S. Department of Education, National Center for Education Statistics, Common Core of Data, 1995–1996.

The state data are from the CCD state universe as published in NCES's *Overview of Public Elementary and Secondary Schools and Districts: School Year 1995–1996*. There are 85,102 schools represented. Primary schools are those with a low grade of prekindergarten through grade 3 and a high grade of up to 8. Middle schools are those with a low grade of 4 through 7 and a high grade ranging from 4 to 9. High schools have a low grade of 7 to 12 and must extend through grade 12. All other grade configurations, including schools that are completely ungraded, are included only in the totals, not in the percent distributions.

Students with individual education programs (Item 12)
Source: U.S. Department of Education, National Center for Education Statistics, Common Core of Data, 1995–1996.

An individualized education program (IEP) is a written instructional plan for students with disabilities designated as special education students under IDEA (Individuals with Disabilities Education Act). This includes a statement of present levels of educational performance of a child; a statement of annual goals, including short-term instructional objectives; a statement of specific educational services to be provided and the extent to which the child will be able to participate in regular educational programs; a projected date for initiation and anticipated duration of services; appropriate objectives, criteria, and evaluation procedures; and schedules for determining, on at least an annual basis, whether instructional objectives are being achieved.

IEP counts for the states are from the NCES *Overview of Public Elementary and Secondary Schools and Districts: School Year 1995–1996*. Three states did not report this information. When information is missing for one or more states, NCES does not calculate national totals.

Students who are eligible for free lunch (Item 13)
Source: U.S. Department of Education, National Center for Education Statistics, Common Core of Data, 1995–1996.

The Free Lunch Program is a program under the National School Lunch Act that provides cash subsidies for free lunches to students based on family size and income criteria. Because participation in the Free Lunch Program depends on income, eligibility is often used to estimate student needs.

The state counts of free lunch–eligible students are from the NCES *Overview of Public Elementary and Secondary Schools and Districts: School Year 1995–1996*. A state is considered to have missing data if free lunch eligibility is reported by fewer than 70 percent of the schools in the state. Because 13 states had missing data on free lunch eligibility, NCES does not calculate a national total.

Minority students (Item 14)
Source: U.S. Department of Education, National Center for Education Statistics, Common Core of Data, 1995–1996.

The percentage of a state's students who were members of a minority includes those who were American Indian/Alaskan Native, Asian/Pacific Islander, Hispanic, and Black non-Hispanic. The state data are from the NCES *Overview of Public Elementary and Secondary Schools and Districts: School Year 1995–1996*.

Teachers (Items 15–16)

Source: U.S. Department of Education, National Center for Education Statistics, Common Core of Data, 1995–1996.

The state numbers are from the CCD state universe. Unlike the county numbers, these include teachers who are employed by agencies and not assigned to specific schools. The pupil-teacher ratio for the states is calculated by dividing the number of students in all schools by the number of full-time equivalent teachers employed by all schools and agencies.

Graduates (Item 17)

Source: U.S. Department of Education, National Center for Education Statistics, Common Core of Data, 1995–1996.

The state data are from the CCD state universe. The number of graduates includes individuals who received a regular diploma, individuals who received a diploma from other than the regular school program, and individuals who received a certificate of attendance or other certificate of completion in lieu of a diploma during the previous school year and subsequent summer school. Recipients of high school equivalency certificates are not included.

Dropouts (Item 18)

Source: U.S. Department of Education, National Center for Education Statistics, Common Core of Data, 1995–1996.

A dropout is a student who was enrolled in school at some time during the previous school year; was not enrolled at the beginning of the current school year; has not graduated from high school or completed a state or district-approved educational program; and does not meet any of the following exclusionary conditions: has transferred to another public school district, private school, or state- or district-approved educational program; is temporarily absent due to suspension or school-approved illness; or has died.

The state data are from the NCES *Overview of Public Elementary and Secondary Schools and Districts: School Year 1995–1996.*

Staff (Items 19–20)

Source: U.S. Department of Education, National Center for Education Statistics, Common Core of Data, 1995–1996.

The state data are from the CCD state universe. Staff in local schools who are not classroom teachers include teacher aides; guidance counselors; librarians and library/media support staff; principals and their assistants and support staff; and all noninstructional staff such as health services workers, bus drivers, social workers, and all others employed in the schools. Central administration staff and support include the local education agency superintendents, deputies, assistant superintendents, all persons with districtwide responsibilities, and their support staffs, as well as all staff supervising instructional programs at the district or subdistrict level, such as curriculum coordinators.

Revenues (Items 21–24)

Source: U.S. Department of Education, National Center for Education Statistics, Common Core of Data, fiscal year 1996.

The state data are from the National Public Education Financial Survey data file for fiscal year 1996 (school year 1995–1996.) The state data include adjustments made by NCES. Values that were missing and not reported elsewhere in the survey were imputed based on proportions in reporting states. Other adjustments were made when a single value was reported that included two or more categories. NCES distributed portions of the single reported value to the missing items.

Revenues from federal sources include direct grants-in-aid from the federal government; federal grants-in-aid through the state or an intermediate agency; and other revenue that, in lieu of taxes, had the tax base been subject to taxation.

Revenues from state government sources include those that can be used without restriction, those for categorical purposes; and revenues in lieu of taxation. Included are revenues from payments made by a state for the benefit of the LEA or contributions of equipment or supplies. Such revenues include the payment of a pension fund by the state on behalf of an LEA employee for services rendered to the LEA and contributions of fixed assets (property, plant, and equipment) such as school buses and textbooks.

Revenues from local sources include revenues from a local education agency, including local property and nonproperty tax revenues; local government; tuition; transportation; food services; student activities; textbook sales; donations; and property rentals. Revenues from local sources include taxes levied or assessed by an LEA, revenues from a local government to the LEA, tuition received, transportation fees, earnings on investments from LEA holdings, net revenues from food services (gross receipts less gross expenditures), net revenues from student activities (gross receipts less gross expenditures), and other revenues (textbook sales, donations, property rentals).

A fourth category, intermediate revenues, is not included in this volume but can be derived by subtracting the federal, state, and local revenues from the total revenue. Intermediate revenues come from sources that are not local or state education agencies, but operate at an intermediate level between local and state education agencies and possess an independent fund-raising capability.

Expenditures (Items 25–27)
Source: U.S. Department of Education, National Center for Education Statistics, Common Core of Data, fiscal year 1996.

The state data are from the National Public Education Financial Survey data file for fiscal year 1996 (school year 1995–96.) The state data include adjustments made by NCES. Values that were missing and not reported elsewhere in the survey were imputed based on proportions in reporting states. Other adjustments were made when a single value was reported that included two or more categories. NCES distributed portions of the single reported value to the missing items.

Current expenditures are defined as expenditures for the categories of instruction, support services, and noninstructional services for salaries, employee benefits, purchased services and supplies; and payments by the state made for or on behalf of school systems. This does not include expenditures for debt service and capital outlay, property (i.e., equipment), or direct costs (e.g., Head Start, adult education, community colleges, etc.), and community services expenditures.

Current expenditures per pupil for states were derived for this volume by dividing total current expenditures by the student membership count from the CCD State Nonfiscal Survey. NCES recommends student membership as a more comparable student count than average daily attendance. Student membership is the count of students enrolled on or about October 1 and is comparable across all states.

In some other sources, per-pupil expenditures are calculated by dividing net current expenditures by average daily attendance. This alternate definition of per-pupil expenditures meets the requirements of Title 1 of the Elementary and Secondary Education Act of 1965 as amended by the Improving America's Schools Act of 1994 (Title I). Net current expenditures are defined by the Hawkins-Stafford Education Amendments of 1988 (P.L. 100–297) as total current expenditures minus the following exclusions: tuition and transportation fees paid by individuals; Chapter 1 and Chapter 2 revenues and carryover funds; and revenues

from food service, textbooks, student activities, and summer school.

Average daily attendance figures are collected as required under Title 1 of the Elementary and Secondary Education Act of 1965 as amended by the Improving America's Schools Act of 1994 (Title I). Under this law, states are to provide average daily attendance in accordance with state law; however, NCES provides a definition for states to use in the absence of state law. Per-pupil expenditures (calculated by dividing net current expenditures by average daily attendance) are used in the formula to allocate Title I and other program funds to states and school districts. Because some states use their own definitions and others use the NCES definition, the data on average daily attendance are not comparable across states and are not used in this volume.

Current expenditures for instruction are expenditures for activities dealing directly with the interaction between students and teachers (salaries, including sabbatical leave, employee benefits, and purchased instructional services).

Table D-2 (Counties)
Population (Items 1–2)
Source: U.S. Bureau of the Census

The population data for 1996 are U.S. Bureau of the Census estimates for the resident population as of July 1, 1996.

School districts (Item 3)
Source: U.S. Department of Education, National Center for Education Statistics, Common Core of Data, 1995–1996.

A school district or local education agency (LEA) is an education agency at the local level that exists primarily to operate public schools or to contract for public school services.

The agency universe of the Common Core of Data includes information for 16,427 agencies. The county totals in this volume include 14,887 regular and special school districts. Special districts typically offer research, administrative, or other support services to client agencies. Excluded are all regular and special districts that reported no students in membership.

Number of schools and students (Items 4–11)
Source: U.S. Department of Education, National Center for Education Statistics, Common Core of Data, 1995–1996.

The county data were aggregated from 85,102 individual schools in the CCD school universe. Primary schools are those with a low grade of prekindergarten through grade 3 and a high grade of up to 8. Middle schools are those with a low grade above grade 3 and a high grade ranging from 4 to 9. High schools have a low grade of 7 to 12 and must extend through grade 12. All other grade configurations, including schools that are completely ungraded, are included only in the totals.

Students with individual education programs (Item 12)
Source: U.S. Department of Education, National Center for Education Statistics, Common Core of Data, 1995–1996.

An individualized education program (IEP) is a written instructional plan for students with disabilities designated as special education students under IDEA (Individuals with Disabilities Education Act). This includes a statement of present levels of educational performance of a child; a statement of annual goals, including short-term instructional objectives; a statement of specific educational services to be provided and the extent to which the child will be able to participate in regular educational programs; a projected date for initiation and anticipated duration of services; appropriate objectives, criteria, and evaluation procedures; and schedules for determining, on at least an annual basis, whether instructional objectives are being achieved.

IEP counts for the counties are from the agency universe. Some agencies did not report this information. If 20 percent or more of a county's student membership were represented by agencies with missing data, the county was considered "missing." Students with IEPs were counted as a percentage of students in agencies who reported this information, not as a percentage of all students in the county.

Students who are eligible for free lunch (Item 13)
Source: U.S. Department of Education, National Center for Education Statistics, Common Core of Data, 1995–1996.

The Free Lunch Program is a program under the National School Lunch Act that provides cash subsidies for free lunches to students based on family size and income criteria. Because participation in the Free Lunch Program depends on income, eligibility is often used to estimate student needs.

The number of students who apply for and are eligible to receive free lunches is included in the CCD school universe, from which the county totals in this volume were derived. If 20 percent or more of a county's student membership were in schools with missing data, the county was considered "missing." Free lunch–eligible students were counted as a percentage of students in schools who re-

ported this information, not as a percentage of all students in the county.

Minority students (Item 14)
Source: U.S. Department of Education, National Center for Education Statistics, Common Core of Data, 1995–1996.

The percentage of a county's students who were members of a minority was tallied from the CCD school universe. Individual schools reported the number of students who were American Indian/Alaskan Native, Asian/Pacific Islander, Hispanic, Black non-Hispanic, and White non-Hispanic. "Minority" includes all categories except White non-Hispanic.

Teachers (Items 15–16)
Source: U.S. Department of Education, National Center for Education Statistics, Common Core of Data, 1995–1996.

The number of teachers in each county is aggregated from the full-time equivalent numbers in the CCD school universe. The pupil-teacher ratio is calculated from this school-based number and the number of students reported by individual schools in the county.

Graduates (Item 17)
Source: U.S. Department of Education, National Center for Education Statistics, Common Core of Data, 1995–1996.

The county data are from the CCD agency universe. The number of graduates includes individuals who received a regular diploma, individuals who received a diploma from other than the regular school program, and individuals who received a certificate of attendance or other certificate of completion in lieu of a diploma during the previous school year and subsequent summer school. Recipients of high school equivalency certificates are not included.

Dropouts (Item 18)
Source: U.S. Department of Education, National Center for Education Statistics, Common Core of Data, 1995–1996.

The county data are from the CCD agency universe (number of dropouts in grades 9 through 12) and the CCD school universe (number of students in grades 9 through 12).

A dropout is a student who was enrolled in school at some time during the previous school year; was not enrolled at the beginning of the current school year; has not graduated from high school or completed a state- or district-approved educational program; and does not meet any of the following exclusionary conditions: has transferred to another public school district, private school, or state- or district-approved educational program; is temporarily absent due to suspension or school-approved illness; or has died.

Staff (Items 19–20)

Source: U.S. Department of Education, National Center for Education Statistics, Common Core of Data, 1995–1996.

The county data are aggregated from the CCD agency universe. Staff in local schools who are not classroom teachers include teacher aides; guidance counselors; librarians and library/media support staff; principals and their assistants and support staff; and all noninstructional staff such as health services workers, bus drivers, social workers, and all others employed in the schools. Central administration staff and support include the local education agency superintendents, deputies, assistant superintendents, all persons with districtwide responsibilities, and their support staffs, as well as all staff supervising instructional programs at the district or subdistrict level, such as curriculum coordinators.

Revenues (Items 21–24)

Source: U.S. Department of Education, National Center for Education Statistics, Common Core of Data, fiscal year 1995.

The county data are aggregated from the 15,553 agencies in the Public School District Financial Survey data file for fiscal year 1995 (school year 1994–1995.) Some of these school districts have no students in membership but they have revenues and expenditures, usually because of financial arrangements with neighboring counties or regional agencies. These revenue and expenditure data are obtained by the U.S. Bureau of the Census through its annual surveys of government finances and are supplied by the Bureau of the Census to the National Center for Education Statistics.

Revenues from federal sources include direct grants-in-aid from the federal government; federal grants-in-aid through the state or an intermediate agency; and other revenue that, in lieu of taxes, had the tax base been subject to taxation.

Revenues from state government sources include those that can be used without restriction, those for categorical purposes, and revenues in lieu of taxation. Included are revenues from payments made by a state for the benefit of the LEA or contributions of equipment or supplies. Such revenues include the payment of a pension fund by the state on behalf of an LEA employee for services rendered to the LEA and contributions of fixed assets (property, plant, and equipment) such as school buses and textbooks.

Revenues from local sources include revenues from a local education agency, including local property and non-property tax revenues; local government; tuition; transportation; food services; student activities; textbook sales; donations; and property rentals. Revenues from local sources include taxes levied or assessed by an LEA, revenues from a local government to the LEA, tuition received, transportation fees, earnings on investments from LEA holdings, net revenues from food services (gross receipts less gross expenditures), net revenues from student activities (gross receipts less gross expenditures), and other revenues (textbook sales, donations, property rentals).

A fourth category, intermediate revenues, is not included in this volume but can be derived by subtracting the federal, state, and local revenues from the total revenue. Intermediate revenues come from sources that are not local or state education agencies, but operate at an intermediate level between local and state education agencies and possess an independent fund-raising capability.

Expenditures (Items 25–27)

Source: U.S. Department of Education, National Center for Education Statistics, Common Core of Data, fiscal year 1995.

The county data are aggregated from the 15,553 agencies in the Public School District Financial Survey data file for fiscal year 1995 (school year 1994–1995.) Some of these school districts have no students in membership but they have revenues and expenditures, usually because of financial arrangements with neighboring counties or regional agencies. These revenue and expenditure data are obtained by the U.S. Bureau of the Census through its annual surveys of government finances and are supplied by the Bureau of the Census to the National Center for Education Statistics.

Current expenditures are defined as expenditures for the categories of instruction, support services, and noninstructional services for salaries, employee benefits, purchased services and supplies; and payments by the state made for or on behalf of school systems. This does not include expenditures for debt service and capital outlay, property (i.e., equipment); or direct costs (e.g., Head Start, adult education, community colleges, etc.), and community services expenditures.

Current expenditures per pupil for counties are calculated by dividing current expenditures by the number of students in fall membership. Student membership is the count of students enrolled on or about October 1 and is comparable across all counties. However, comparisons should be made with caution because counties vary greatly in type of school districts as well as contractual arrangements with regional administrative school agencies or neighboring counties. For example, a county with a small population may have a school district that operates an elementary school and pays an intergovernmental fee to a neighboring county's school district for educational services to children in middle and high school. This hypothetical county would have artificially high per-pupil expenditures because only the elementary school children would be included in the membership count.

Current expenditures for instruction are expenditures for activities dealing directly with the interaction between students and teachers (salaries, including sabbatical leave, employee benefits, and purchased instructional services).

INDEX